E. **Comparability:** Enables users to identify and explain similarities and differences between two (or more) items of information. Includes *Consistency:* Conformity of information from period to period.

F. **Constraints:** Limits to help identify useful accounting information. Includes (1) *Benefits Greater Than Costs:* Benefits obtained by users of information must be greater than costs of providing information, and (2) *Materiality:* Monetary impact of the information must be large enough to make a difference in decision making *(quantitative constraint.)*

## V. ACCOUNTING ASSUMPTIONS AND CONVENTIONS

A. **Entity:** Information is recorded and reported about each separate economic entity (company).

B. **Continuity (Going Concern):** Company is assumed to continue future operations, unless substantial contrary evidence exists.

C. **Period of Time:** Information is reported in a company's financial statements at least on an annual basis.

D. **Historical Cost:** Generally, exchange price is retained in the accounting records as the value of an item until it is consumed, sold, or liquidated and removed from records.

E. **Monetary Unit:** National currency of company is used as stable unit of measure in preparing financial reports.

F. **Realization:** Process of converting noncash resources into cash or rights to cash.

G. **Recognition:** Process of formally recording and reporting an item in a company's financial statements.

H. **Accrual Accounting:** Process of relating financial effects of transactions, events, and circumstances having cash consequences to the period in which they occur rather than when the cash receipt or payment occurs.

I. **Prudence (Conservatism):** Process of ensuring, to extent possible, that uncertainties and risks related to a company are reflected in its accounting information.

## VI. GENERALLY ACCEPTED ACCOUNTING PRINCIPLES (GAAP)

A. **Definition:** Guidelines, procedures, and practices that a company is required to use in recording and reporting the accounting information in its audited financial statements.

B. **Sources:** (in descending order of importance)
  1. Pronouncements of authoritative bodies (FASB, APB, CAP, SEC); e.g., FASB *Statements of Financial Accounting Standards and Interpretations,* APB *Opinions,* and CAP (AICPA) *Accounting Research Bulletins* (and SEC *Regulation S-X* and *Financial Reporting Releases*).
  2. Pronouncements of bodies of expert accountants that have been exposed for public comment; e.g., FASB *Technical Bulletins,* AICPA *Industry Audit and Accounting Guides,* and AICPA *Statements of Position.*
  3. Pronouncements of bodies of expert accountants that have not been exposed for public comment; e.g., FASB EITF *Consensus Positions* and AICPA *Practice Bulletins.*
  4. Widely accepted practices and pronouncements representing prevalent practice in a particular industry or applications to specific circumstances; e.g., AICPA *Accounting Interpretations,* FASB *Q's and A's,* and AICPA *Accounting Trends and Techniques.*
  5. Other accounting literature; e.g., FASB *Statements of Financial Accounting Concepts,* APB *Statements,* AICPA *Issue Papers,* AICPA *Technical Practice Aids,* and accounting texts and articles.

*(Continued on inside back cover.)*

# INTERMEDIATE ACCOUNTING

*6th Edition*

**LOREN A. NIKOLAI, Ph.D., CPA**

Ernst & Young Professor

School of Accountancy

University of Missouri – Columbia

**JOHN D. BAZLEY, Ph.D., CPA**

Professor

School of Accountancy

University of Denver

COLLEGE DIVISION South-Western Publishing Co.

Cincinnati Ohio

| Vice President/Publisher: | Mark Hubble |
| Developmental Editor: | Sara E. Bates |
| Associate Editor: | Holly Terry |
| Interior Designer: | Tom Hubbard |
| Cover Designer: | David Betz/D. Betz Design |
| Cover Photographer: | Alan Brown/Photonics |
| Compositor: | Beacon Graphics |
| Director of Marketing: | Martin Lewis |

AC65FA

ISBN: 0-538-82531-6

2 3 4 5 K 7 6 5 4

Printed in the United States of America.

Material from the Uniform CPA Examination, Questions and Unofficial Answers, Copyright © 1948, 1952, 1954, 1957, 1960, 1961, 1962, 1963, 1964, 1965, 1966, 1967, 1968, 1969, 1970, 1971, 1972, 1973, 1974, 1975, 1976, 1977, 1978, 1979, 1980, 1981, 1982, 1983, 1984, 1985, 1986, 1987, 1988 and 1989 by American Institute of Certified Public Accountants, Inc., is adapted with permission.

Material from the Certified Management Accountant Examination, Copyright © 1975, 1981, 1982, 1983, 1986 and 1987.

Sections of various FASB documents, copyright by Financial Accounting Standards Board, 401 Merritt 7, P.O. Box 5116, Norwalk, Connecticut 06856-5116, U.S.A., are reprinted with permission. Copies of the complete documents are available from the FASB.

Library of Congress Cataloging-in-Publication Data:

Nikolai, Loren A.
    Intermediate accounting / Loren A. Nikolai, John D. Bazley. -- 6th ed.
        p. cm.
    Includes index.
    ISBN 0-538-82531-6
    1. Accounting. I. Bazley, John D. II. Title.
    HF5635.N6924 1994
    657'.044--dc20
                                                            93-28986
                                                                 CIP

 South-Western Publishing Co. is an ITP Company.
The ITP trademark is used under license.

# ABOUT THE AUTHORS

## LOREN A. NIKOLAI

Loren Nikolai is the Ernst & Young Professor in the School of Accountancy at the University of Missouri-Columbia (MU). He received his B.A. and M.B.A. from St. Cloud State University, and his Ph.D. from the University of Minnesota. Professor Nikolai has taught at the University of Wisconsin at Platteville and at the University of North Carolina at Chapel Hill. Professor Nikolai is the recipient of the Missouri Society of CPAs 1993 Outstanding Accounting Educator of the Year Award, the MU 1992 Kemper Fellowship for Teaching Excellence, the MU College of Business and Public Administration 1991 Faculty Member of the Year Award, the St. Cloud State University 1990 Distinguished Alumni Award, and the Federation of Schools of Accountancy 1989 Faculty Award of Merit. He holds a CPA certificate in the state of Missouri and previously worked for the 3M Company. Professor Nikolai is the coauthor of *Financial Accounting: Concepts and Uses*, Second Edition textbook (South-Western Publishing Co.).

Professor Nikolai has published numerous articles in *The Accounting Review, Journal of Accounting Research, The Accounting Educator's Journal, The CPA Journal, Management Accounting, Policy Analysis, Academy of Management Journal, Journal of Business Research*, and other professional journals. He was also lead author of a monograph published by the National Association of Accountants. Professor Nikolai is the Faculty Vice President of the Beta Alpha Psi chapter at MU. He is a member of the American Accounting Association, the American Institute of Certified Public Accountants (AICPA), and the Missouri Society of CPAs (MSCPA). He has served on the AICPA's Accounting and Auditing Practice Analysis Task Force Panel and the Accounting Careers Subcommittee; he has also served on the MSCPA's Relations with Educators, Accounting Careers, and Accounting and Auditing Committees. Professor Nikolai has chaired or served on numerous Federation of Schools of Accountancy (FSA) and American Accounting Association (AAA) committees, was AAA Director of Education for 1985–1987, and is President of the FSA for 1994.

## JOHN D. BAZLEY

John D. Bazley, Ph.D., CPA, is Professor of Accountancy in the School of Accountancy at the University of Denver where he has received the University 1990 Distinguished Teaching Award, the Vernon Loomis Award for Excellence in Advising, the Alumni Award for Faculty Excellence, and the Jerome Kesselman Endowment Award for Excellence in Research. Professor Bazley earned a B.A. from the University of Bristol in England and an M.S. and Ph.D. from the University of Minnesota. He has taught at the University of North Carolina at Chapel Hill and holds a CPA certificate in the state of Colorado. He has taught national professional development classes for a major CPA firm and was consultant for another CPA firm. Professor Bazley is the lead author of *Financial Accounting: Concepts and Uses*, Second Edition textbook (South-Western Publishing Co.).

Professor Bazley has published articles in professional journals, including *The Accounting Review, Management Accounting, Accounting Horizons, Practical Accountant, Academy of Management Journal, The Journal of Managerial Issues*, and *The International Journal of Accounting*, and is a member of the Editorial Boards of *Issues in Accounting Education* and the *Journal of Managerial Issues*. He is also a coauthor of a monograph on environmental accounting published by the National Association of Accountants. Professor Bazley has served on numerous committees of the Federation of Schools of Accountancy, including chair of the Student Lyceum Committee; the American Accounting Association; and the Colorado Society of CPAs, including the Continuing Professional Education Board. He is a member of the American Institute of Certified Public Accountants, the Colorado Society of CPA, and the American Accounting Association.

# PREFACE

## OVERVIEW

Accountancy is a growing and dynamic discipline requiring ever-increasing knowledge in many areas. Intermediate accounting is one of those areas. Although the subject material of intermediate accounting is expanding and becoming both more conceptual and more technical, it can be made relevant and readily understandable by a textbook that contains (1) conceptual overviews, (2) the frequent use of examples, (3) clear, direct discussion that anticipates the student's learning process, (4) up-to-date and authoritative treatment of current accounting theory and practice, (5) illustrations taken from the financial statements of real corporations, and (6) plentiful and varied assignment materials. We feel that we have incorporated these teaching and learning tools into this textbook.

**Intermediate Accounting**, Sixth Edition, is a comprehensive yet readable text. Our goal has been to achieve the most educationally effective blend of concepts and practice relating to the current intermediate accounting body of knowledge presented in a pedagogically sound format. Generally accepted accounting principles are clearly identified and the related concepts discussed, in conjunction with a thorough explanation of the corresponding practices and procedures. Key terms, concepts, definitions, and official statements are **boldfaced**; italics are used for *emphasis*. Illustrations of journal entries, supporting schedules, and financial statement disclosures are frequently used to clarify concepts or procedures. Margin notes help students cross-reference information with discussions in other chapters. Where there is a conceptual disagreement on an accounting principle, we present a succinct and objective discussion of the alternative views. Numerous excerpts from actual annual reports illustrate the proper disclosure for many topics and help students to appreciate the immediate relevance of classroom work to real-world accountancy practice. The financial reporting section of the 1992 annual report of The Coca-Cola Company is also included in Appendix A at the end of the book.

We have included an abundance of end-of-chapter assignment materials, divided into questions, cases, multiple choice items, exercises, and problems. The questions primarily address key concepts and terms in the chapter. The cases focus on the various conceptual and reporting issues within the chapters. The multiple choice items are based on past Uniform CPA Examination questions. Each exercise reinforces a chapter topic at a relatively elementary level. The problems either consolidate a number of chapter topics or else focus on a comprehensive analysis of a single topic. A variety of problems and cases have also been selected from past Uniform CPA Examinations, and are so designated. A boldfaced title is included beside each case, exercise, and problem number to indicate the subject content.

## SPECIFIC FEATURES

The text is organized primarily in a balance-sheet format and consists of 5 parts containing 24 chapters, as follows:

Part I   Financial Reporting: Concepts and Financial Statements (Chapters 1-4)
Part II  Financial Reporting: Asset Measurement and Income Determination (Chapters 5-10)
Part III Financial Reporting: Valuation of Liabilities and Investments (Chapters 11-13)
Part IV  Financial Reporting: Stockholders' Equity (Chapters 14-15)
Part V   Financial Reporting: Special Topics (Chapters 16-24)

Some of the major features of the chapters are summarized as follows:

1. *Environment of accounting.* Students are introduced to the environment of financial reporting in Chapter 1. The discussion includes an explanation of capital markets (Exhibit 1-1), external users' decision making, and the hierarchy of generally accepted accounting principles (Exhibit 1-4). It also includes a discussion of the various organizations that influence GAAP and their interrelationship (Exhibit 1-8).

2. *FASB conceptual framework.* Students are introduced to the "conceptual framework" in Chapter 2. This discussion involves an identification and explanation of the objectives of financial reporting (Exhibit 2-3) and the qualitative characteristics of useful accounting information (Exhibit 2-5). It also includes an explanation of the interrelationship between financial reports, types of useful information, and external decision making (Exhibit 2-4), as well as a framework of financial accounting theory and practice (Exhibit 2-6).

3. *Asset and liability concepts, definitions, and measurement.* Because the FASB defines revenues and expenses in terms of changes in assets and liabilities, a clear understanding of asset and liability concepts and definitions as well as alternative measurement approaches (i.e., current cost, current exit value) is necessary. These topics are introduced in Chapter 3. The concept and definition of liabilities is reinforced and expanded later in Chapter 11, which is the first of two chapters on liabilities.

4. *Revenue and expense recognition.* Because of the importance of the income statement, a thorough understanding of the related conceptual and practical issues is vital. In Chapter 4, the concept of capital maintenance is introduced and contrasted to the transactional approach to measuring income, including the concept of *comprehensive income.* Conceptual reporting guidelines are identified, followed by a discussion of revenue and expense recognition criteria. A brief exposure to the alternative revenue recognition methods is given in Chapter 4; a complete discussion is presented in Chapter 16.

5. *Conceptual discussion.* Based on the FASB conceptual framework introduced in Chapter 2, later chapters relate the discussion of specific topics to the objectives of financial reporting, qualitative characteristics of accounting information, and conceptual reporting guidelines, and to the concepts of liquidity, financial flexibility, risk, operating capability, and return on investment. This integrated discussion of accounting theory is not at the expense of sound, procedural pedagogy; we emphasize a balanced presentation of concepts and practice.

6. *Flowcharts and diagrams.* Numerous flowcharts and diagrams helpful in the students' learning process are provided. For instance, Chapter 8 includes a flowchart for similar productive asset exchanges (Exhibit 8-3), Chapter 19 includes a diagram for classifying leases (Exhibit 19-3), and Chapter 21 includes a flowchart for earnings per share (Exhibit 21-8).

7. *Computational steps.* Many complex computational procedures have been reduced to a series of "steps" outlined in a list format. For instance, a series of steps for dollar-value LIFO calculations is included in Exhibit 6-14 of Chapter 6. Similar lists of steps are included in Chapter 7 for the gross profit inventory method, retail inventory method, and dollar-value LIFO retail method. Other computational steps are included where appropriate throughout the rest of the book.

8. *Summary exhibits.* Helpful summary exhibits are included at appropriate points in the text. For instance, Exhibit 4-13 summarizes corporate earnings and cash flows topics, Exhibit 19-2 summarizes the criteria and classifications for leases, and Exhibit 22-8 summarizes the impacts on financial statements of the methods used for accounting changes and errors.

9. *Back-to-back coverage of long-term liabilities and investments.* Due to the reciprocal nature of accounting for certain liabilities and assets (i.e., bonds payable and investments in bonds held to maturity, notes payable and notes receivable), these topics are presented in back-to-back coverage in Chapters 12 and 13. This facilitates the students' understanding of these complex issues.

10. *Flexibility in coverage.* Certain chapters have been written, to the extent possible, to allow flexibility in reading assignments. Coverage of Chapter 16 on revenue recognition may be accelerated to correspond with the discussion of the income statement in Chapter 4. Some may prefer an earlier assignment of Chapter 20 (statement of cash flows) because of the increased emphasis on the financial statement. Others may prefer earlier assignment of Chapter 22 (accounting changes) due to occasional references to different types of changes throughout the text.

## MAJOR CHANGES

To improve the pedagogy and to reflect several significant changes in accounting principles, numerous changes have been made in this Sixth Edition. The major changes are summarized as follows:

1. *Expansion of conceptual discussion.* The conceptual discussion in several chapters has been expanded, added, or clarified in regard to various topics. For instance, the text includes revised conceptual discussion of the types of useful information, limitations of the financial statements, valuation of receivables and inventories, intangibles, contingencies, investments, income taxes, and pensions.

2. *Clarification of technical discussion.* The discussion and examples of technical procedures have been thoroughly reviewed and modified where necessary to clarify the explanations.

3. *Rearrangement of topical coverage.* Based on reviewers' comments, the topics in several chapters have been rearranged. The environment of financial reporting and the conceptual framework of financial reporting are now discussed

in two separate chapters (1 and 2). The statement of changes in owners' equity now is discussed with the balance sheet in Chapter 3. The introduction to the statement of cash flows now is discussed with the income statement in Chapter 4.

4. *Improvement of readability.* To improve the "user-friendliness" of the book, the entire text has been reviewed and modified, where appropriate, to simplify the sentence structure and terminology. These changes have not altered the content or meaning of any discussion.

5. *Realignment of coverage of present value and review of accounting process.* Based on reviewers' comments, the coverage of present value and future value previously discussed in Chapter 5 has been moved to Appendix D at the end of the book. Similarly, the review of the accounting process previously discussed in Chapter 2 has been moved to Appendix C. The discussions of both of these topics have *not* been shortened, but are placed in these Appendices to allow for more flexibility in coverage.

6. *Addition of ethics coverage.* In response to the need for students to be more aware of ethical issues in the accounting environment, a new section has been added to Chapter 1. Cases dealing with ethical dilemmas are also included.

7. *Addition of creative and critical thinking coverage.* Due to the increased emphasis on enhancing students' abilities to think creatively and critically in the accounting environment, a new section has been added to Chapter 1. Existing and newly added cases at the ends of most chapters are identified by a logo as relating to the creative and/or critical thinking process.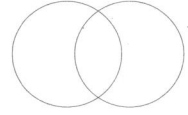

8. *Addition of cases requiring the researching of GAAP.* In response to the need for students to become more familiar with how to find generally accepted accounting principles applicable to a particular topic, new "researching GAAP" cases have been added to most chapters. These cases generally are designed to be used with the FASB *Current Text* or *Original Pronouncements*.

9. *Addition of international coverage.* Due to the increased "globalization" of business, a section has been added to most chapters that briefly discusses the differences between U.S. GAAP and international accounting principles for the chapter topics. Where applicable, the section also discusses the accounting principles for specific foreign countries. International topic discussion is designated by the use of a logo.

10. *Expanded use of chapter appendices.* In response to users' suggestions, coverage of several topics has been moved to chapter appendices. For example, appendices are included for serial bonds (Chapter 12), the incorporation of an entity (Chapter 14), quasi-reorganizations (Chapter 15), specialized lease issues (Chapter 19), the direct method for operating cash flows (Chapter 20), and financial analyses (Chapter 23). Discussion of these and other topics in chapter appendices allows for more flexibility in topical coverage.

11. *Addition of exhibits.* Several exhibits have been added to clarify issues. These include, for instance, Exhibit 1-1 on capital markets, Exhibit 5-5 on financing agreements, Exhibit 14-5 on treasury stock transactions, and Exhibit 18-1 on pension relationships.

12. *Revision of accounting for income taxes.* Chapter 17 has been revised to reflect the new generally accepted accounting principles for income taxes established in *FASB Statement No. 109*. The conceptual and procedural portions of the chapter also have been rearranged to improve the flow of discussion.

13. *Revision of accounting for investments.* The text and homework in Chapter 13 have been completely revised to reflect the new generally accepted accounting principles for investments established in *FASB Statement No. 115*. Included is a discussion of accounting for investments in trading securities, securities available for sale, and debt securities held to maturity.

14. *Clarification of accounting for pensions and OPEBs.* In Chapter 18, the discussion of accounting for pensions has been clarified in regard to the components of pension expense. The conceptual and procedural discussion has been rearranged for better pedagogy. The discussion of accounting for OPEBs in the Fifth Edition that was based on the *Exposure Draft* has been slightly modified to reflect the provisions of *FASB Statement No. 106*.

15. *Modification of accounting for troubled-debt restructuring.* In accordance with *FASB Statement No. 114*, the discussion of accounting by a creditor for a troubled-debt restructuring involving a modification of terms has been modified in Chapter 12. A related discussion of accounting for impairments of loans also has been added.

16. *Clarification of LCM for inventories.* A section has been added to Chapter 7 that further explains the conceptual and practical issues involving the application of the lower of cost or market method to inventories.

17. *Clarification of issues involving property, plant, and equipment.* In Chapter 8, the discussion of similar asset exchanges has been modified to consider the types of companies (dealers or nondealers) involved in an exchange, and the amount of "boot" that distinguishes a monetary from a nonmonetary exchange. The discussion of interest capitalization also has been modified to better explain the treatment of interest from previous periods.

18. *Modification of discussion of stock option plans.* In Chapter 15, the discussion of accounting for compensatory stock option plans has been clarified. Diagrams have been added to help explain the allocation of compensation cost across the service period.

19. *Reorganization of discussion of statement of cash flows.* The material in Chapter 20 on the preparation of the statement of cash flows has been reorganized to shorten and simplify the discussion. The steps used in the visual inspection method and the worksheet method have been placed in separate exhibits to enhance understanding.

20. *Revision of accounting for changing prices.* The text and homework in Chapter 24 has been significantly rearranged and revised to reflect the growing importance of fair values in financial accounting. The coverage of *FASB Statement Nos. 33* and *89* has been substantially reduced.

21. *Revision of homework assignments.* In addition to the new cases, exercises, and problems, the numbers and solutions have been changed in over 70 percent of the previous homework.

## SUPPLEMENTARY MATERIALS

In addition to the textbook, several supplementary aids are available. For the student, these include:

1. A **Study Guide** prepared by Natalie Krawitz, Stephens College, and Theodora Arthur and Loren A. Nikolai, University of Missouri. The **Study Guide** includes a list of objectives, a synopsis of each chapter, self-evaluation exercises, and a set of post-tests with accompanying answers.

2. **Working Papers** for the problems; a two-volume set in which selected problems are partially completed.

3. **Check Figures** of key answers to all exercises and problems.

For the instructor, the supplementary aids include:

1. A **Solutions Manual** for all homework materials. This two-volume manual, which was prepared by the authors, includes a suggested solution for each question, case, multiple choice item, exercise, and problem, all supporting calculations, and helpful notes to the instructor concerning any difficult areas within each problem. It also includes a content analysis of the exercises and problems in each chapter.

2. An **Instructor's Manual** containing, for each chapter, a list of objectives, synopsis, lecture outline, instructional notes, and content analysis of exercises and problems by topic. Appendix D provides compound interest tables for convenient reference.

3. A **Test Bank** of examination materials for each chapter prepared by Jerry Kreuze, Western Michigan University; Alan Falcon, Loyola Marymount University; and Dick Wasson, Southwestern College. The **Test Bank** comes in two volumes and includes approximately 2,000 multiple choice, essay and short-answer problems and solutions.

4. A **Computerized Test Bank** ("MicroExam") containing the same questions as the printed **Test Bank**. It is available on 3-1/2″ and 5-1/4″ disks for the IBM PC or compatible. An Apple Macintosh version is also available on 3-1/2″ disk.

5. A two-volume set of acetate **Transparencies** (set in large type) for all problems and exercises. Several "teaching visuals" showing complex exhibits from the text are included.

## ACKNOWLEDGEMENTS

We wish to express our sincere appreciation to Richard D. Schroeder and Isaac N. Reynolds, our former coauthors, for their valuable contributions to the earlier editions of this textbook. These contributions served as the groundwork for several of the chapters of this Sixth Edition.

We also wish to express appreciation to users of the earlier editions who provided meaningful comments and constructive criticism. We are grateful to Professors Norman A. Sunderman, Angelo State University; Peggy Dwyer, Florida International University; Tom W. Schmidt, University of Tennessee at Martin; Billie Cunningham, University of North Texas; Robin Roberts, Iowa State University; Kenneth R. Lambert, Memphis State University; Emil J. Hensler, Jr., Seton Hall University;

James P. Dunigan, University of Wisconsin-Stevens Point; Sandra D. Byrd, Southwest Missouri State University; Rita J. Hopewell; Ben Hsien Bao, University of Colorado at Denver; Judy Wenzel, Mankato State University; and Raymond C. Dockweiler, John Sweeney, Inder Khurana, Earl Wilson, and Joe Silvoso, University of Missouri-Columbia; for their reactions to selected topics. Special thanks go to Donald Geren, Northeastern Illinois University; Scott I. Jerris, University of West Virginia; Paula Koch, University of Illinois at Chicago; Walter Parker, Central Connecticut State University; Norma Powell, University of Massachusetts at Lowell; and Daryl G. Krause, CPA for their contributions of homework. We also wish to thank our graduate and undergraduate students, including Jenny Reed, Verna Hazelrigg, Beth Adair, JoAnne Lueders, Stephen Underhill, Devra Niemann, Teresa Hickam, Cherie Wadlin, Trish Nikolai, Lori Thompson, Lisa Klempert, Lori Hamilton, and Terry Phillips. We are sincerely indebted to our typists, Anita Blanchar, Karen Staggs, and Mary Meyer, whose quality work and perseverance enabled us to complete the manuscript in a timely and orderly fashion. Appreciation is also extended to our editorial and production staffs, including Mark Hubble, Mary Draper, Sara Bates, Leslie Kauffman, Tonya Sutton, and Holly Terry.

We are grateful to our respective Schools of Accountancy and to the American Institute of Certified Public Accountants, the Financial Accounting Standards Board, and the Institute of Certified Management Accountants of the Institute of Management Accountants for granting us permission to quote from their respective pronouncements and use their examination questions and unofficial answers. We are also grateful to our wives, children, and friends who provided us with considerable moral support and understanding during the entire manuscript production process.

**Loren A. Nikolai**
**John D. Bazley**

The authors wish to express their appreciation to those who served as reviewers and who provided insightful comments and valuable suggestions in the planning and writing of this textbook:

**James W. Bannister**
*University of Illinois at Chicago*

**J. Lawrence Bergin**
*Winona State University*

**Barney R. Cargile**
*University of Alabama*

**Philip Drake**
*Southern Methodist University*

**Lawrence J. Eaton**
*Gateway Technical College*

**Richard G. Elmendorf**
*University of Wyoming*

**Richard G. Files**
*University of Nebraska at Omaha*

**Harriette Griffin**
*North Carolina State University*

**Abo-El-Yazeed T. Habib**
*Mankato State University*

**Susan S. Hamlen**
*State University of New York at Buffalo*

**Gary W. Heesacker**
*Central Washington University*

**Lee Higgins**
*Southeast Community College*

**James P. Jennings**
*St. Louis University*

**Fred R. Jex**
*Macomb County Community College*

**Robert S. Johnson**
*Jefferson College*

**Mark E. Kaiser**
*State University of New York
at Plattsburgh*

**Sara York Kenny**
*University of Utah*

**William Kross**
*Purdue University*

**Stan Locknar**
*McHenry County College*

**R. David Mautz, Jr.**
*University of North Carolina
at Greensboro*

**Steven Paskin**
*Western Washington University*

**Bhanu Raghunathan**
*University of Toledo*

**William J. Read**
*Bentley College*

**James P. Reburn**
*University of Missouri at St. Louis*

**Mary Rolfes**
*Mankato State University*

**Michael R. Ruble**
*Western Washington University*

**Paul H. Schwinghammer**
*Mankato State University*

**Daniel T. Simon**
*University of Notre Dame*

**Barbara R. Stewart**
*Towson State University*

**Donald Tang**
*Portland State University*

**Eamonn Walsh**
*New York University*

**Ralph E. Welton, Jr.**
*Clemson University*

**Loren Wenzel**
*Mankato State University*

# BRIEF CONTENTS

# CONTENTS

Other Assets. Long-Term Liabilities. Other Liabilities. Conceptual Guidelines for Reporting Assets and Liabilities. Stockholders' Equity. Contributed Capital. Capital Stock and Additional Paid-In Capital. Unrealized Capital. Retained Earnings. STATEMENT OF CHANGES IN STOCKHOLDERS' EQUITY. OTHER DISCLOSURE ISSUES. Summary of Accounting Policies. Fair Value and Risk of Financial Instruments. Contingent Liabilities and Assets. Subsequent Events. Segment Reporting. Related Party Transactions. Comparative and Interim Financial Statements. Auditor's Report. SEC Integrated Disclosures. Miscellaneous Disclosures. International Accounting Differences. REPORTING TECHNIQUES. Statement Format (Balance Sheet). Combined Amounts. Rounding. Notes, Supporting Schedules, and Parenthetical Notations. ILLUSTRATIVE STATEMENTS.

CONCEPTS OF INCOME. Capital Maintenance Concept. Transactional Approach. CONCEPTUAL REPORTING GUIDELINES. General Conceptual Guidelines. Specific Conceptual Guidelines. ELEMENTS OF THE INCOME STATEMENT. Revenues. Expenses. Gains and Losses. INCOME STATEMENT CONTENT. All-Inclusive Versus Current Operating. Condensed Income Statements. Income from Continuing Operations. Results from Discontinued Operations. Extraordinary Items. Cumulative Effects of Accounting Changes. Earnings Per Share. Limitations of the Income Statement. International Accounting Differences. STATEMENT OF RETAINED EARNINGS. Prior Period Adjustments. Net Income and Dividends. Combined Statements. STATEMENT OF CASH FLOWS. Conceptual Overview and Uses of Statements. Reporting Guidelines and Practices. SUMMARY OF DISCLOSURES.

CASH. Cash and Cash Equivalents. Cash Management. Petty Cash. BANK RECONCILIATION. Causes of the Difference. Procedures for Preparing a Bank Reconciliation. Illustration. Proof of Cash (Four-Column Reconciliation). SPECIAL TOPICS INVOLVING CASH. Electronic Funds Transfer Systems. Compensating Balances. RECEIVABLES. REVENUE RECOGNITION AND VALUATION OF TRADE RECEIVABLES. Right of Return. Valuation Issues. ACCOUNTS RECEIVABLE. Trade Discounts. Cash (Sales) Discounts. Sales Returns and Allowances. Freight Charges. VALUATION OF ACCOUNTS RECEIVABLE FOR UNCOLLECTIBLE ACCOUNTS. Estimated Bad Debts Method. Percentage of Sales. Percentage of Outstanding Accounts Receivable. Aging of Accounts Receivable. Writing Off Uncollectible Accounts. Collection of an Account Previously Written Off. Direct Write-Off Method. GENERATING IMMEDIATE CASH FROM ACCOUNTS RECEIVABLE. Pledging of Accounts Receivable. Assignment of Accounts Receivable. Factoring (Sale) of Accounts Receivable. Disclosure of Financing Agreements of Accounts Receivable. NOTES RECEIVABLE. Short-Term Interest-Bearing Notes Receivable. Short-Term Non-Interest-Bearing Notes Receivable. Notes Receivable Discounted. FINANCIAL STATEMENT DISCLOSURES OF RECEIVABLES.

CLASSIFICATIONS OF INVENTORY. Raw Materials Inventory. Goods in Process Inventory. Finished Goods Inventory. ALTERNATIVE INVENTORY SYSTEMS.

Perpetual Inventory System. Periodic Inventory System. ITEMS TO BE INCLUDED IN INVENTORY QUANTITIES. Goods in Transit. Consigned Goods and Installment Sales. DETERMINATION OF INVENTORY COSTS. Manufacturing Overhead Costs. Standard Costs. Variable Costing. Purchases Discounts. COST FLOW ASSUMPTIONS. Specific Identification. First-In, First-Out (FIFO). Average Cost. Last-In, Last-Out (LIFO). Comparison of Inventory Cost Flow Assumptions. CONCEPTUAL EVALUATION OF INVENTORY COST FLOW ASSUMPTIONS. Income Measurement. Income Tax Effects. Liquidation of LIFO Layers. Income Manipulation. Inventory Valuation. Average Cost. Management's Selection of an Inventory Cost Flow Assumption. DOLLAR-VALUE LIFO. Determination of Cost Index. Inventory Pools. ADDITIONAL LIFO CONSIDERATIONS. LIFO Valuation Adjustment. Interim Statements Using LIFO. Change to or from LIFO. International Accounting Differences. DISCLOSURE OF INVENTORY VALUES AND METHODS. APPENDIX: FOREIGN CURRENCY TRANSACTIONS INVOLVING INVENTORY.

Depreciation. Composite Depreciation. Retirement and Replacement Methods. Inventory Systems. DEPRECIATION FOR PARTIAL PERIODS. Compute Depreciation to the Nearest Whole Month. Compute Depreciation to the Nearest Whole Year. Compute One-Half Year's Depreciation on All Assets Purchased or Sold During the Year. IMPAIRMENT OF NONCURRENT ASSETS. International Accounting Differences. DEPRECIATION AND INCOME TAX. MACRS Principles. Illustration of MACRS. CHANGES AND CORRECTIONS OF DEPRECIATION. DEPLETION.

## PART 3
### Financial Reporting: Valuation of Liabilities and Investments

ment of Debt. Defeasance of Debt. BONDS WITH EQUITY CHARACTERISTICS. Bonds Issued with Detachable Stock Warrants. Convertible Bonds. LONG-TERM NOTES PAYABLE. Notes Payable Issued for Cash. Notes Payable Exchanged for Cash and Rights or Privileges. Notes Payable Exchanged for Property, Goods, or Services. Disclosure of Long-Term Liabilities. LONG-TERM NOTES RECEIVABLE. Loan Fees. Impairment of a Loan. APPENDIX 1: TROUBLED DEBT RESTRUCTURINGS. TYPES OF TROUBLED DEBT RESTRUCTURINGS. MODIFICATION OF TERMS. No Gain Recognized by the Debtor. Gain Recognized by the Debtor. EQUITY OR ASSET EXCHANGE. Equity Exchange. Asset Exchange. EQUITY OR ASSET EXCHANGE COMBINED WITH A MODIFICATION OF TERMS. DISCLOSURE OF RESTRUCTURING AGREEMENTS. ACCOUNTING BY THE CREDITOR. Equity or Asset Exchange. Modification of Terms. Equity or Asset Exchange Combined with Modification of Terms. CONCEPTUAL EVALUATION OF ACCOUNTING FOR TROUBLED DEBT RESTRUCTURINGS. APPENDIX 2: SERIAL BONDS. RECORDING THE ISSUANCE AND INTEREST EXPENSE OF SERIAL BONDS. EARLY REDEMPTION OF SERIAL BONDS.

INVESTMENTS: CLASSIFICATION AND VALUATION. INVESTMENTS IN DEBT AND EQUITY TRADING SECURITIES. INVESTMENTS IN DEBT AND EQUITY SECURITIES AVAILABLE FOR SALE. Recording Initial Cost. Recording Interest and Dividend Revenue. Recognition of Unrealized Holding Gains and Losses. Realized Gains and Losses on Sales of Securities Available for Sale. INVESTMENTS IN DEBT SECURITIES HELD TO MATURITY. Recording Initial Cost. Recognition and Amortization of Bond Premiums and Discounts. Amortization for Bonds Acquired Between Interest Dates. Sale of Investment in Bonds Before Maturity. TRANSFERS AND IMPAIRMENTS. Transfers of Investments Between Categories. Impairments. DISCLOSURES. Financial Statement Classification. EFFECTIVE DATE AND TRANSITION. FASB STATEMENT NO. 115: AN EVALUATION. Fair Value Is Required for Certain Investments. Fair Value Is Not Required for Certain Liabilities. Reporting of Unrealized Gains and Losses. Classification of Securities Is Based on Management Intent. EQUITY METHOD. Accounting Procedures. Financial Statement Disclosures. Special Issues. ADDITIONAL ISSUES. Nonmarketable Securities. Stock Dividends and Splits. Stock Warrants. Convertible Bonds. Cash Surrender Value of Life Insurance. Investments in funds.

# PART 4
## Financial Reporting: Stockholders' Equity

CORPORATE FORM OF ORGANIZATION. Types of Corporations. Formation of a Corporation. CORPORATE CAPITAL STRUCTURE. Capital Stock and Stockholders' Rights. Basic Terminology. Legal Capital. Additional Paid-in Capital. Stockholders' Equity. ISSUANCE OF CAPITAL STOCK. Authorization. Issuance for Cash. Stock Issuance Costs. Stock Subscriptions. Subscription Defaults. Combined Sales of Stock. Nonmonetary Issuance of Stock. Stock Splits. Stock Rights to Current Stockholders. PREFERRED STOCK CHARACTERISTICS. Preference as to Dividends. Cumulative Preferred Stock. Participating Preferred Stock. Convertible Preferred Stock. Preferred Stock with Stock Warrants (Rights). Callable Preferred Stock. Redeemable Preferred Stock. Preference in Liquidation. Voting Rights. Disclosures. CONTRIBUTED CAPITAL SECTION. TREASURY STOCK (CAPITAL STOCK REACQUISITION). Cost Method. Par Value Method. Balance Sheet

Presentation. Acquisition at Greater Than Market Value. Donated Treasury Stock. Retirement of Treasury Stock. Overview of Treasury Stock. APPENDIX: INCORPORATION OF A GOING CONCERN. PARTNERSHIP ACCOUNTING RECORDS RETAINED. NEW CORPORATE ACCOUNTING RECORDS OPENED.

STOCK OPTION PLANS. NONCOMPENSATORY STOCK OPTION PLANS. COMPENSATORY STOCK OPTION PLANS. Compensation Cost. Applicable Accounting Periods. Accounting for Compensatory Stock Option Plans: Date of Measurement Is Date of Grant. Accounting for Compensatory Stock Option Plans: Date of Measurement Later Than Date of Grant. Stock Appreciation Rights. Junior Stock Plans. Illustration of Disclosure. Conceptual Issues. CONTENT OF RETAINED EARNINGS. DIVIDENDS. Cash Dividends. Property Dividends. Scrip Dividends. Stock Dividends. Liquidating Dividends. PRIOR PERIOD ADJUSTMENTS (RESTATEMENTS). APPROPRIATIONS OF RETAINED EARNINGS. Legal Requirements. Contractual Agreements. Discretionary Actions. Alternative Accounting for Appropriations. STATEMENT OF RETAINED EARNINGS. Illustration of Retained Earnings Statement. OTHER CHANGES IN STOCKHOLDERS' EQUITY. STATEMENT OF CHANGES IN STOCKHOLDERS' EQUITY. International Accounting Differences. APPENDIX: QUASI-REORGANIZATION.

## PART 5
### Financial Reporting: Special Topics

OVERVIEW OF REVENUE RECOGNITION ALTERNATIVES. EXAMPLES OF REVENUE RECOGNITION ALTERNATIVES. Example 1: Revenue Recognition at Time of Sale. Example 2: Revenue Recognition During Production. Example 3: Revenue Recognition at Time of Cash Receipt. Summary of Revenue Recognition Alternatives. CONCEPTUAL ISSUES. ALTERNATIVE REVENUE RECOGNITION METHODS. REVENUE RECOGNITION PRIOR TO THE PERIOD OF SALE. Long-Term Construction Contracts. Percentage-of-Completion Method. Completed-Contract Method. Illustration of the Two Methods. Losses on Long-Term Construction Contracts. Additional Considerations in Accounting for Long-Term Construction Contracts. Long-Term Service Contracts. Proportional Performance Method. REVENUE RECOGNITION AFTER THE PERIOD OF SALE. Installment Method. Example of the Installment Method. Additional Considerations for the Installment Method. Cost Recovery Method. Comparison of the Installment and Cost Recovery Methods. REVENUE RECOGNITION DELAYED UNTIL A FUTURE EVENT OCCURS. Deposit Method. ADDITIONAL REVENUE RECOGNITION ISSUES. Consignment Sales. Franchises. Real Estate Sales. Retail Land Sales. International Accounting Differences. SUMMARY OF ALTERNATIVE REVENUE RECOGNITION METHODS.

OVERVIEW AND DEFINITIONS. Causes of Differences. Definitions. INTERPERIOD INCOME TAX ALLOCATION: BASIC ISSUES. Permanent Differences. Temporary Differences. Conceptual Issues. Recording and Reporting of Current and Deferred Taxes. OPERATING LOSS CARRYBACKS AND CARRYFORWARDS. Conceptual Issues. Generally Accepted Accounting Principles. COMPREHENSIVE ILLUSTRATION. INTRAPERIOD INCOME TAX ALLOCATION. FINANCIAL

STATEMENT PRESENTATION AND DISCLOSURES. Balance Sheet Presentation. Financial Statement Disclosures. MISCELLANEOUS ISSUES. Change in Income Tax Laws or Rates. Investment Tax Credit. Alternative Minimum Tax and Other Tax Credits. International Accounting Differences. ILLUSTRATIVE DISCLOSURES. APPENDIX: ADDITIONAL CONCEPTUAL ISSUES CONCERNING INTERPERIOD INCOME TAX ALLOCATION. ALLOCATION VERSUS NONALLOCATION. COMPREHENSIVE VERSUS PARTIAL ALLOCATION. ALTERNATIVE ALLOCATION METHODS. Asset/Liability Method. Deferred Method. Net-of-Tax Method. CONTROVERSIAL CONCLUSIONS.

CHARACTERISTICS OF PENSION PLANS. HISTORICAL PERSPECTIVE OF PENSION PLANS. ACCOUNTING PRINCIPLES FOR DEFINED BENEFIT PENSION PLANS. Key Terms Related to Pension Plans. Pension Expense. Pension Liabilities and Assets. Measurement Methods. Disclosures. EXAMPLES OF ACCOUNTING FOR PENSIONS. Example 1: Pension Expense Equal to Pension Funding. Example 2: Pension Expense Greater Than Pension Funding. Example 3: Pension Expense Less Than Pension Funding, and Actual Return on Plan Assets Different From Discount Rate. Example 4: Pension Expense Including Amortization of Unrecognized Prior Service Cost. Example 5: Calculation of Amortization of Unrecognized Prior Service Cost. Example 6: Pension Expense Including Net Gain or Loss (to Extent Recognized). Example 7: Recognition of Additional Pension Liability. Example 8: Disclosures. Summary of Issues Related to Pensions. CONCEPTUAL ISSUES RELATED TO DEFINED BENEFIT PENSION PLANS. Pension Expense. Pension Liabilities. Balance Sheet Presentation of Pension Plan Assets. Disclosures. ADDITIONAL ASPECTS OF PENSION ACCOUNTING. Transition Requirements. Vested Benefits. Accounting for Defined Contribution Plans. Disclosures by Funding Agencies. Employee Retirement Income Security Act of 1974. Pension Plan Settlements and Curtailments. Termination Benefits Paid to Employees. Multi-Employer Plans. International Accounting Differences. OTHER POSTEMPLOYMENT BENEFITS. Similarities to and Differences from Pensions. Accounting Principles. OPEB Expense. OPEB Liability or Asset. Transition. Disclosures. Settlements and Curtailments. Differences from Accounting for Pensions. ILLUSTRATION OF ACCOUNTING FOR OPEBs. ACCOUNTING FOR OPEBs: AN EVALUATION. Relevance and Reliability. Differences in Funding. Transition Liability. Attribution Period. Interaction with Deferred Income Taxes. Minimum Liability. Impacts of the Adoption of FASB Statement No. 106. APPENDIX: ILLUSTRATION OF PRESENT VALUE CALCULATIONS FOR DEFINED BENEFIT PENSION PLANS. Service Cost. Interest on Projected Benefit Obligation. Actual Return on Plan Assets. Amortization of Unrecognized Prior Service Cost. Pension Expense and Liability.

ADVANTAGES OF LEASING AND AN HISTORICAL PERSPECTIVE. Advantages of Leasing from Lessee's Viewpoint. Historical Perspective of Leasing. Advantages of Leasing from Lessor's Viewpoint. KEY TERMS RELATED TO LEASING. CLASSIFICATION OF PERSONAL PROPERTY LEASES. ACCOUNTING AND REPORTING BY LESSEES. Operating Lease (Lessee). Capital Lease (Lessee). Illustration of Lessee's Capital Lease Method. Other Lessee Capitalization Issues. Disclosure Requirements of the Lessee. ACCOUNTING AND REPORTING BY LESSORS. Operating Lease (Lessor). Direct Financing Leases (Lessor). Initial Direct Costs Involved in a Direct Financing Lease. Sales-Type Leases (Lessor). Initial Direct Costs Involved in a Sales-Type Lease. Unguaranteed and Guaranteed Residual Values. Disclosure Requirements for the Lessor. SUMMARY OF ACCOUNTING

BY LESSEE AND LESSOR. ADDITIONAL LEASE ISSUES. Evaluation of Accounting for Leases. International Accounting Differences. APPENDIX: SPECIALIZED LEASE ISSUES AND CHANGES IN LEASE PROVISIONS. LEASE ISSUES RELATED TO REAL ESTATE. Lease of Land Only. CHANGES IN LEASE PROVISIONS. Review of Estimated Unguaranteed Residual Value. Impact of Renewal of Lease on Guarantee of Residual Value. Changes to Sales-Type or Direct Financing Lease Prior to Lease Term Expiration That Result in an Operating Lease. Renewal or Extension of Sales-Type Lease or Direct Financing Lease Resulting in a New Lease That Qualifies as a Sales-Type Lease.

MARKET EFFICIENCY. AUDITOR'S REPORT (OPINION). AUDIT COMMITTEE AND MANAGEMENT'S REPORT. MANAGEMENT'S DISCUSSION AND ANALYSIS. SEGMENT REPORTING. Reporting on Industry Operations. Reporting on Foreign Operations and Export Sales. Information About Major Customers. INTERIM FINANCIAL REPORTS. Revenues. Expenses. Income Taxes. Extraordinary Items, Discontinued Operations, and Cumulative Effects. Earnings Per Share. Preparation and Disclosure of Summarized Interim Financial Data. SEC REPORTS. APPENDIX: FINANCIAL ANALYSIS COMPARISONS. INTRACOMPANY COMPARISONS. INTERCOMPANY COMPARISONS. PERCENTAGE ANALYSES. Horizontal Analysis. Vertical Analysis. RATIO ANALYSIS. Stockholder Profitability Ratios. Company Profitability Ratios. Liquidity Ratios. Activity Ratios. Stability Ratios.

CURRENT VALUE AND THE GENERAL PRICE LEVEL. Current Value. General Price Level. Four Alternative Concepts. THREE ALTERNATIVES TO HISTORICAL COST. Current Cost Financial Statements. Historical Cost/Constant Purchasing Power Financial Statements. Current Cost/Constant Purchasing Power Financial Statements. ADDITIONAL MEASUREMENT ISSUES. Constant Purchasing Power Adjustments. MEASUREMENT OF CURRENT COST. THE CONSTANT PURCHASING POWER ADJUSTMENT PROCESS. Income Statement Adjustments (First Year). Comparative Balance Sheets (First Year). Financial Statement Adjustments (Second Year). Comparative Financial Statements (Second Year). THE CURRENT COST ADJUSTMENT PROCESS. Inventory and Cost of Goods Sold. Building and Equipment and Depreciation. Other Income Statement Items. Holding Gains and Losses. Other Balance Sheet Items. Alternative Reporting in Current Cost Financial Statements. CONCEPTUAL ISSUES RELATING TO ALTERNATIVES TO HISTORICAL COST. Capital Maintenance Concept (Income Statement). Balance Sheet. Reliability. Understandability. Costs and Benefits. Alternative Concepts of Current Cost. Current Cost and Operating Savings. Current Cost Versus Partial Adjustments. Current Exit Values. DISCLOSURES CONSIDERED BY THE APB, FASB, AND SEC. FASB DISCLOSURE GUIDELINES. Impacts of *FASB Statement No. 33.* Evaluation of the Elimination of the Disclosures of the Effects of Changing Prices. International Accounting Differences.

THE ACCOUNTING SYSTEM. Accounting Equation. Transactions, Events, and Supporting Documents. Accounts. Financial Statements. THE ACCOUNTING CYCLE. Recording in the General Journal (Step 1). Posting to the Ledger (Step 2).

## APPENDIX D
### Compound Interest                                                      D1

## INDEX                                                                   I1

# FINANCIAL REPORTING

## Concepts and Financial Statements

## PART

# 1

# 1

# THE ENVIRONMENT OF FINANCIAL REPORTING

**Chapter Topics**

*Primary and Secondary Markets*

*Investment and Credit Decisions Made by External Users*

*Generally Accepted Accounting Principles*

*Development of Accounting Standards*

*Operation of the FASB*

*Organizations Affecting GAAP*

*Ethics in the Accounting Environment*

Accounting has been described as the process of identifying, measuring, recording, and communicating economic information to permit informed judgments and decisions by users of information.[1] It has also been called the "language of business." In the United States economy, most published accounting information is about different types of companies (primarily corporations). Companies engage in many transactions and generate large amounts of data. Since people can absorb only limited amounts of information,[2] accounting systems are designed to report that data in a concise, understandable format. In this sense, accounting can be viewed as the link between a company's economic activities and decision makers.

In this chapter, we review the uses and users of accounting information, the development of principles for the accumulation and communication of accounting information, and the ethical frameworks within which these accounting principles are applied.

---

1.  Committee to Prepare a Statement of Basic Accounting Theory, *A Statement of Basic Accounting Theory* (Evanston, Ill.: AAA, 1966), p. 1.
2.  See, for example, Robert Libby, *Accounting and Human Information Processing: Theory and Applications* (Englewood Cliffs, N.J.: Prentice-Hall, 1981).

## ACCOUNTING INFORMATION: USERS, USES, AND GAAP

The U.S. economy is a free-market economy in which the decisions of many buyers and sellers influence the demand for and supply of products and services offered by companies. Individuals acting within this economy have limited resources to consume or to invest, whereas companies *typically* need large amounts of capital for their operations. These companies may obtain this capital from the issuance of capital stock and bonds, from other borrowings, or from resources generated by their operations. The exchange of capital by investors for the stocks and bonds of companies occurs in **capital markets** as shown in Exhibit 1-1. There are organized capital markets, such as the New York Stock Exchange and the American Stock Exchange, in which the capital stock and bonds of many corporations are purchased and sold daily. These markets sometimes are referred to as *secondary markets* because the exchanges are among the investors themselves. That is, the corporation that initially issued the capital stock or bonds is not involved in the exchange.

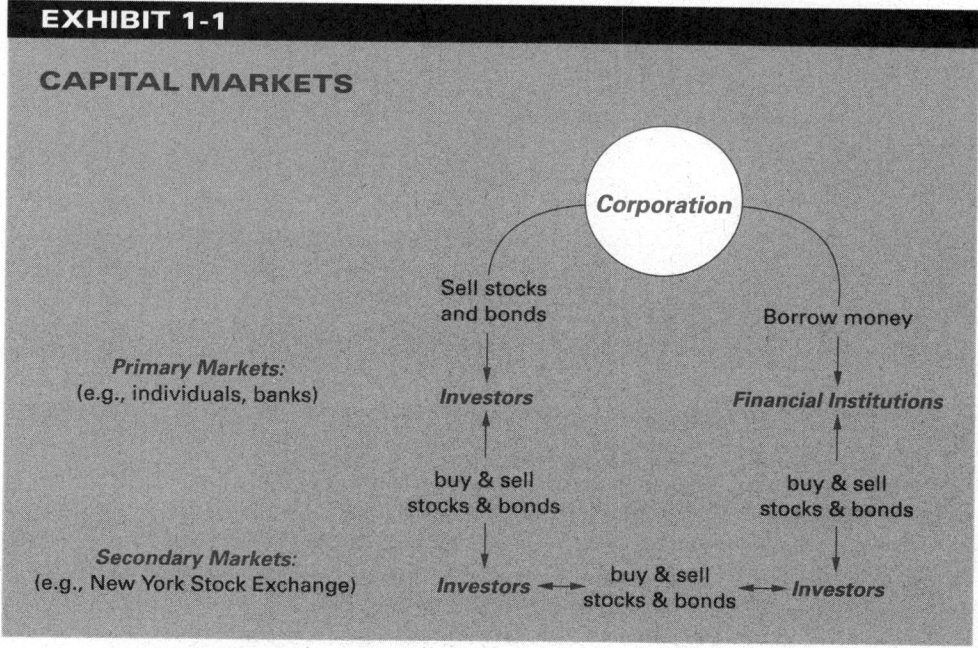

**EXHIBIT 1-1**

**CAPITAL MARKETS**

There also are more loosely organized capital markets in which fewer exchanges occur. For instance, companies may borrow from lending institutions, or corporations initially may issue capital stock or bonds either through "public offerings" or through "private placements." Public offerings involve the advertising and sale to many investors (i.e., the general public). Private placements involve the advertising and sale to a few private institutions such as insurance companies and pension funds, as well as to employees. These markets are sometimes called *primary markets* because the exchange is directly between a corporation and the investors. Whether an investor or lending institution is involved in a primary or secondary market, they are interested in earning dividends and interest with a safe return of their resources. Investors in publicly-traded securities participate in the increase in the market price of the capital stock and bonds. These investors are concerned with the efficient allocation of their scarce resources to achieve these objectives. Accounting information is useful in the decision making for this allocation process within these capital markets. It is useful for other purposes as well.

### External and Internal Users

As already mentioned, accounting information is the link between a company's economic activities and decision makers. The decision makers, or users of accounting information, can be divided into two major categories, external users and internal users, as shown in Exhibit 1-2. These two user groups have somewhat dissimilar information needs because of their different relationships to the company providing the economic information. **External users are actual or potential investors (stockholders and bondholders), creditors such as suppliers and lending institutions, and other users** such as employees, financial analysts, advisers, brokers, underwriters, stock exchanges, taxing and regulatory authorities, labor unions, and the general public. (Note that bondholders are "creditors" by contract and legal definition, but are included as "investors" as this term is commonly used.) Investors have a direct relationship with the company, and their capital market information needs revolve around three basic decisions:

1. *Buy.* A potential investor decides to purchase a particular security (e.g., stock or bond) on the basis of communicated accounting information.

2. *Hold.* An actual investor decides to retain a particular security on the basis of communicated accounting information.

3. *Sell.* An actual investor decides to dispose of a particular security on the basis of communicated accounting information.

Creditors, such as suppliers and lending institutions, also have a direct relationship with companies. While creditors do not purchase securities, they make similar decisions requiring accounting information. The decisions in this case are to extend credit, to maintain the credit relationship, or not to extend credit. Other users employ

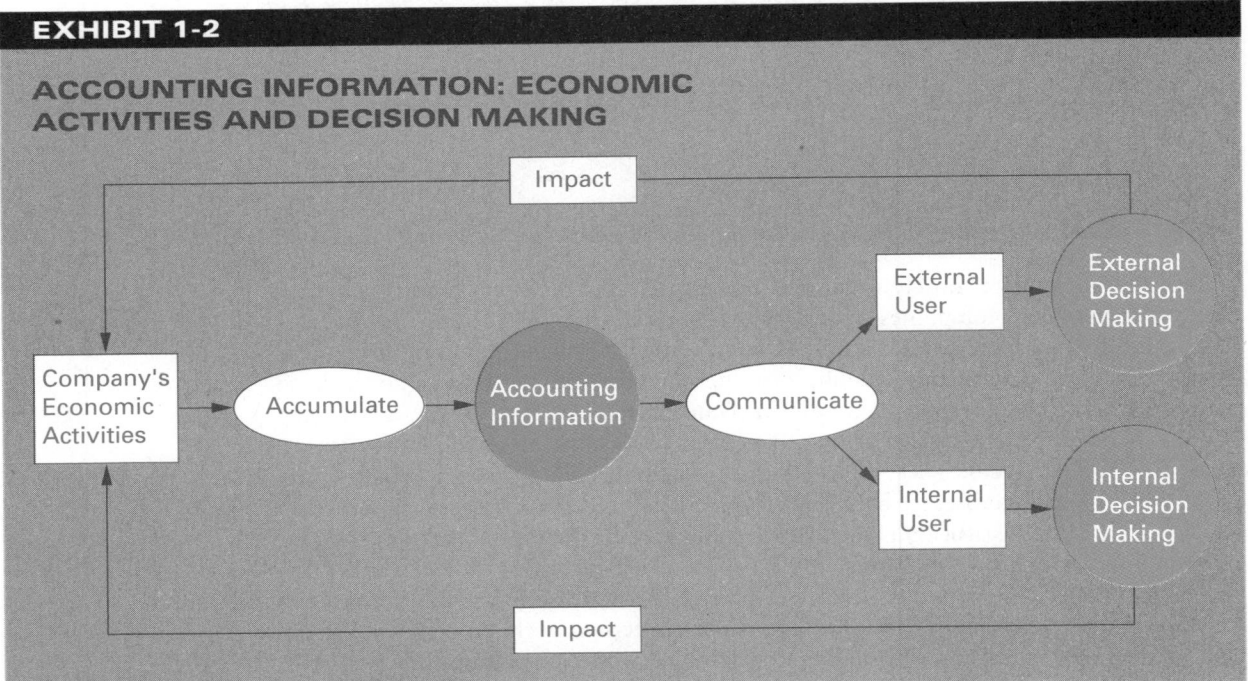

**EXHIBIT 1-2**

**ACCOUNTING INFORMATION: ECONOMIC ACTIVITIES AND DECISION MAKING**

accounting information in their decision making. For instance, stock exchanges use accounting information for listings, cancellations, and rule-making decisions. Labor unions use accounting information in negotiating wage agreements. Financial analysts use accounting information for making investment and credit recommendations.

Investment and credit decisions should be continuously reevaluated. A timely communication of information to external decision makers is very important. The publication of financial statements is a primary method by which relevant information is communicated. Studies have shown, however, that decision makers also use other reporting sources to satisfy their information needs.[3]

**Internal users are the company managers who are responsible for the planning and control of operations on a day-by-day and a long-term basis.** In contrast to external users, who mainly use financial statement information in their decision processes, internal users may request any type of information that the accounting system is capable of providing to assist them in making decisions on internal operations. For example, internal users may request information relating specifically to the purchase of new facilities or the addition of a new product.

*This area of study, known as efficient capital markets research, is discussed in Chapter 23.*

## Financial and Managerial Accounting Information Systems

Two major branches of accounting have evolved to meet the specialized needs of external and internal users. **Financial accounting is the information accumulation, processing, and communication system designed to satisfy the investment and credit decision-making information needs of external users.** Financial accounting information is communicated (reported) through published financial statements and must follow the pronouncements of several policy-making groups. **Managerial accounting is the information accumulation, processing, and communication system designed to meet the decision-making information needs of internal users.** Managerial accounting information is communicated via internal company reports and is not subject to the policy standards applied to externally transmitted information. It is restricted by the usefulness of the information provided for a specific decision and the cost of providing that information. Financial and managerial accounting thus have somewhat different objectives, as they provide information with which to make different decisions. Exhibit 1-3 summarizes some of their more important differences.

The company's accountants prepare both the financial accounting and the managerial accounting reports, and the information comes from the same information system. The differences lie in the selection and presentation of the communicated information. This book focuses on financial accounting and its usefulness in investor, creditor, and other users' decision making. The selection of managerial accounting information generally is not discussed. On the other hand, it has been said that the rules of a game influence how the game is played. The management of a company often is evaluated based on "performance criteria" (i.e., net income, rate of return) that are a function of accounting measures used in financial accounting reports. Thus, the financial accounting system may influence the managerial accounting

---

3.  In addition to the use of published financial statements, accounting information may be communicated to external users by other methods, such as reports filed with the Securities and Exchange Commission (discussed later), news releases, and management forecasts. Evidence from capital markets research studies shows that security prices fully reflect all *publicly* available information. For a more detailed discussion, see T. R. Dyckman and D. Morse, *Efficient Capital Markets and Accounting: A Critical Analysis,* 2nd ed. (Englewood Cliffs, N.J.: Prentice-Hall, 1986), R. L. Watts and J. R. Zimmerman, *Positive Accounting Theory* (Englewood Cliffs, N.J.: Prentice Hall, 1986), or W. H. Beaver, *Financial Reporting: An Accounting Revolution* (Englewood Cliffs, N.J.: Prentice Hall, 1981).

## EXHIBIT 1-3

## COMPARISON OF FINANCIAL AND MANAGERIAL ACCOUNTING

|  | Financial Accounting | Managerial Accounting |
|---|---|---|
| 1. Source of authority | Generally accepted accounting principles (GAAP) | Internal needs |
| 2. Time frame of reported information | Primarily historical | Present and future |
| 3. Scope | Mainly total company | Individual departments, divisions, and total company |
| 4. Type of information | Primarily quantitative | Qualitative as well as quantitative |
| 5. Statement format | Prescribed by GAAP, oriented toward investment and credit decisions | Determined by company, focused upon specific decisions being made |
| 6. Decision focus | External | Internal |

system, or vice versa. That is, the amounts reported or methods used for financial accounting may influence management decisions, or the management of a company (perhaps in its own self-interest) may use the managerial accounting system to influence financial reporting. Where these interrelationships have occurred or are likely to occur, we discuss the effects on financial reporting.

### Financial Reporting

**Financial reporting is the process of communicating financial accounting information about a company to external users.** A company's financial accounting information may be reported in several ways, but the primary way is in the company's *annual report.* The financial reporting section of a company's annual report includes the company's financial statements and the notes to the financial statements. There are three major financial statements of a company: (1) the *balance sheet* (or statement of financial position), which summarizes the company's financial position at a given data, (2) the *income statement,* which summarizes the results of the company's income-producing activities for a period of time, and (3) the *statement of cash flows,* which summarizes the cash inflows and cash outflows for a period of time. There are numerous supporting schedules (e.g., statement of changes in stockholders' equity) as well as *notes* that further explain information that is included in the financial statements. This information is essential to understanding the company's activities. Most financial statements and accompanying notes presented to external users are *audited* by an independent certified public accountant (CPA). As discussed in Chapters 3 and 23, after completion of the audit, the CPA expresses an opinion as to the fairness, in accordance with *generally accepted accounting principles,* of the financial statements and accompanying notes. These financial statements, supporting schedules, and notes to the financial statements as they relate to financial reporting are the subject of this book.

*The Coca-Cola Company's annual report is included in Appendix A at the end of this book.*

## Generally Accepted Accounting Principles

The information communicated to external users in financial reporting is based on accounting standards that establish generally accepted accounting principles (GAAP). **Generally accepted accounting principles are the guidelines, procedures, and practices that a company is required to use in recording and reporting the accounting information in its audited financial statements.** GAAP define accepted accounting practices at a particular time and provide a standard by which to report financial results. They are like laws and are the rules that must be followed in financial reporting.

The evolution of GAAP took place over many years and involved several accounting policy-making bodies, including the Financial Accounting Standards Board (FASB), Accounting Principles Board (APB), American Institute of Certified Public Accountants (AICPA), and Securities and Exchange Commission (SEC). Unfortunately, there is no single document that includes all the accounting standards. Nonetheless, an accountant must be able to determine if a particular procedure for handling a business transaction is acceptable under GAAP. Accountants therefore must know the sources of generally accepted accounting principles and must know how to find authoritative sources to aid in recording and reporting a particular transaction. Throughout this text we discuss GAAP for various transactions, events, and circumstances. However, to aid in researching the sources of generally accepted accounting principles, Exhibit 1-4 provides a "hierarchy" of five categories of GAAP and the authoritative sources applicable to each category for companies.[4]

These categories are listed in descending order of importance, with Category A as the most important. Accountants must follow the GAAP established by the pronouncements applicable to this category unless, in unusual circumstances, they result in misleading financial statements. In these circumstances or in situations where the accounting for a transaction or event is not specified by a pronouncement in Category A, then pronouncements in Categories B through D may be used to identify GAAP. Generally, pronouncements in Category B take precedence over those in Category C which, in turn, take precedence over those in Category D. When none of the pronouncements in Categories A through D are applicable, then the accountant may consider other accounting literature (Category E). Each of the policy-making bodies and related pronouncements is discussed in the sections that follow.

## THE ESTABLISHMENT OF ACCOUNTING STANDARDS

Even though accounting records dating back thousands of years have been discovered in various parts of the world,[5] there was little organized effort to develop accounting standards in the United States prior to the 1930s. One of the most important initial attempts to develop standards began shortly after the onset of the Great Depression in 1929 with a series of meetings in the early 1930s between representatives of the New York Stock Exchange and the American Institute of Accountants (later to become the American Institute of Certified Public Accountants). The goal was to discuss accounting and reporting issues involving the interests of investors, the New York Stock Exchange, and accountants.

---

4. See *Codification of Statements on Auditing Standards* (New York: AICPA, 1992), sec. 411.05–.07, for more discussion. Note: A hierarchy of GAAP for state and local governments also exists.
5. Michael Chatfield, *A History of Accounting Thought*, rev. ed. (Huntington, N.Y.: Robert E. Krieger, 1977).

## EXHIBIT 1-4

### HIERARCHY OF SOURCES OF GAAP

| Categories | Authoritative Sources (Pronouncements) |
|---|---|
| A. Pronouncements of authoritative bodies (FASB, APB, CAP, SEC) | FASB *Statements of Financial Accounting Standards and Interpretations,* APB *Opinions,* and CAP (AICPA) *Accounting Research Bulletins* (as well as SEC *Regulation S-X* and *Financial Reporting Releases*) |
| B. Pronouncements of bodies of expert accountants that have been exposed for public comment* | FASB *Technical Bulletins,* AICPA *Industry Audit and Accounting Guides,* and AICPA *Statements of Position* |
| C. Pronouncements of bodies of expert accountants that have not been exposed for public comment* | FASB Emerging Issues Task Force *Consensus Positions* and AICPA *Practice Bulletins* |
| D. Widely accepted practices and pronouncements representing prevalent practice in a particular industry or applications to specific circumstances | AICPA *Accounting Interpretations,* FASB *Q's and A's,* and AICPA *Accounting Trends and Techniques* |
| E. Other accounting literature | For instance, FASB *Statements of Financial Accounting Concepts,* APB *Statements,* AICPA *Issue Papers,* AICPA *Technical Practice Aids,* and accounting texts and articles |

*"Exposed for public comment" means that accountants and external users (the "public") have an opportunity to make suggestions (comment) on proposed pronouncements. Pronouncements in Categories B and C must also be "cleared" by an authoritative body from Category A, which means that the authoritative body does not object to the pronouncement.

*These concepts are discussed in Chapters 3 and 23.*

The result of these meetings was a form of the auditor's opinion similar to the one used today. Specifically, the concepts of *fairness* and *consistency,* in the application of accounting principles were introduced into the auditor's opinion. Fairness, in this regard, means that the accounting methods and procedures adopted by a company comply with traditional and conventional practice and that they adequately portray the economic reality of the company. Since these meetings several groups have been influential in the establishment of generally accepted accounting principles in the private sector of the United States. A "time-line" of the establishment of GAAP (Category A of Exhibit 1-4) in the private sector is shown in Exhibit 1-5.

### Committee on Accounting Procedure (CAP)

In 1938, the AICPA formed the **Committee on Accounting Procedure (CAP).** This group was responsible for issuing pronouncements to narrow the differences in accounting procedures and practice. Its conclusions were published as **Accounting Research Bulletins (ARB's).** However, because at that time the AICPA did not have the authority to require compliance, the CAP could not enforce its pronouncements, and

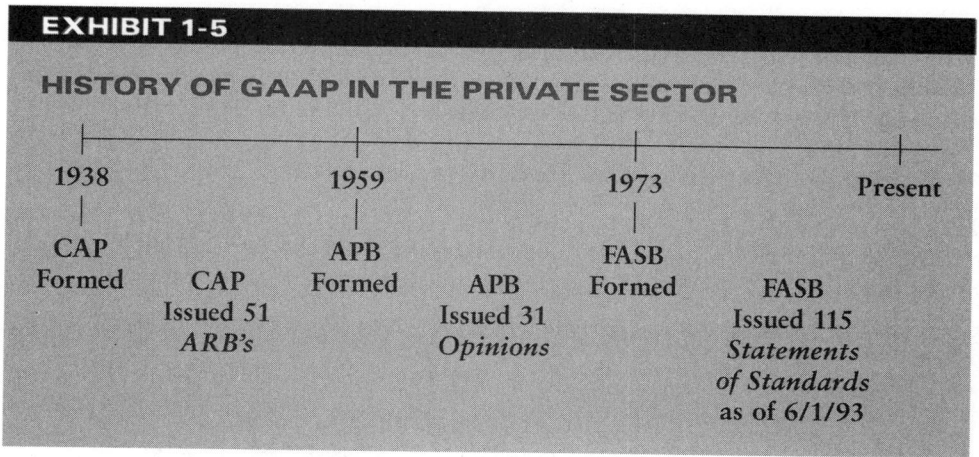

**EXHIBIT 1-5**

## HISTORY OF GAAP IN THE PRIVATE SECTOR

| 1938 | 1959 | 1973 | Present |
|---|---|---|---|
| CAP Formed | APB Formed | FASB Formed | |
| | CAP Issued 51 *ARB's* | APB Issued 31 *Opinions* | FASB Issued 115 *Statements of Standards* as of 6/1/93 |

their application was optional. By 1953 the CAP had issued 42 *Accounting Research Bulletins,* and these pronouncements were then reviewed and codified into **Accounting Research Bulletin No. 43.** The CAP subsequently issued eight more *Accounting Research Bulletins,* ending with No. 51 before it was replaced by the Accounting Principles Board in 1959. All *Accounting Research Bulletins* now constitute generally accepted accounting principles unless specifically superseded or amended by other authoritative bodies.

## Accounting Principles Board (APB)

After World War II the process of formulating accounting principles was increasingly criticized, and wider representation in rule making was sought. In 1959 the **Accounting Principles Board (APB)** was formed by the AICPA as an attempt to (1) alleviate this criticism and (2) create a policy-making body whose rules would be binding rather than optional. The APB comprised 17 to 21 members, selected primarily from the accounting profession. Representatives from industry, the government, and academia also served on the Board. The pronouncements of the APB were termed **Opinions of the Accounting Principles Board,** and 31 of these Opinions were issued. All *APB Opinions* also still constitute generally accepted accounting principles unless specifically amended or rescinded. Many of these Opinions were based upon *Accounting Research Studies.* However, the conclusions drawn in these studies were solely the opinion of the individuals commissioned by the APB to write them. In several cases the APB either did not act upon the recommendations or came to different conclusions.

The members of the APB were volunteers whose employers allowed them time to serve on the Board. But by the late 1960s, criticism again arose concerning the development of accounting principles. This criticism centered on three factors:

1. *Independence.* The members of the APB were part-time volunteers whose major responsibilities were to the business, governmental, or academic organizations employing them.

2. *Representation.* The public accounting firms and the AICPA were too closely associated with the development of accounting standards.

3. *Response time.* Emerging problems were not solved quickly enough by the part-time members of the APB.

The AICPA reacted to those criticisms by appointing a committee to evaluate the method of formulating accounting principles. This committee, termed the Wheat Committee after its chairman Francis Wheat, recommended that the APB be abolished and that a new full-time body be established with even wider representation.

## Financial Accounting Standards Board (FASB)

The AICPA adopted the recommendations of the Wheat Committee. The APB was phased out and replaced in 1973 by a new body, the **Financial Accounting Standards Board (FASB)**. Exhibit 1-6 illustrates the current structure of the FASB.

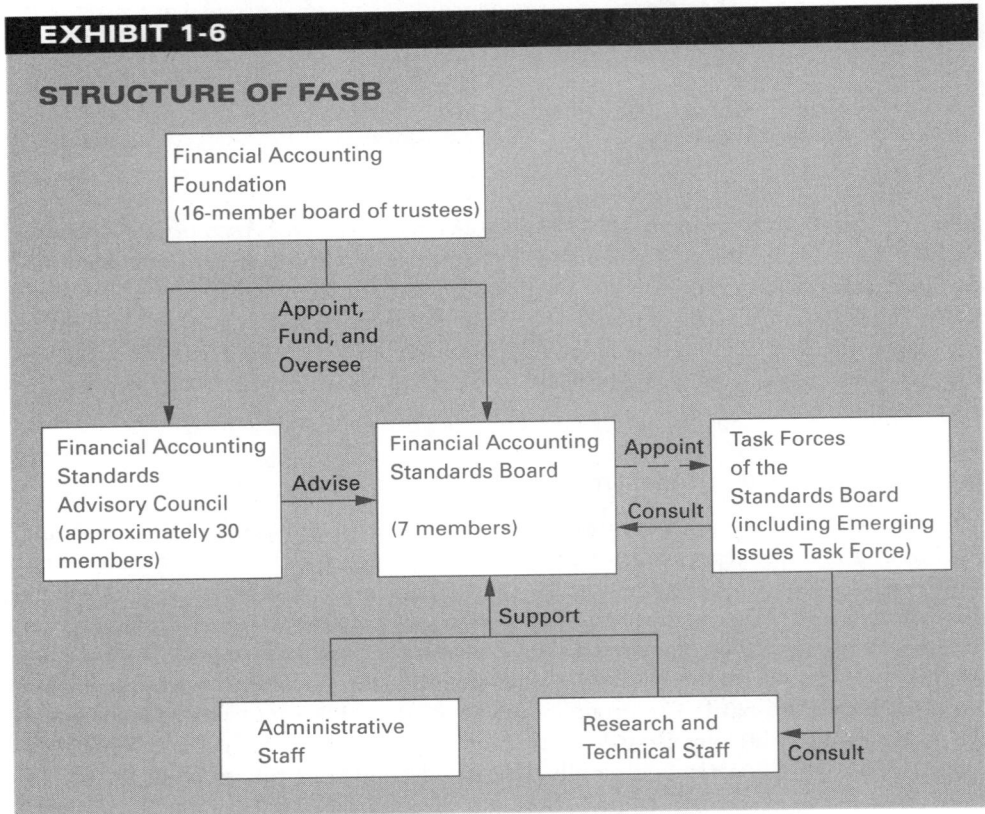

### EXHIBIT 1-6

### STRUCTURE OF FASB

*Source:* "Report of the Study on Establishment of Accounting Principles," American Institute of Certified Public Accountants (New York, 1972) as modified.

### *Organization*

The FASB is organized as follows. The Financial Accounting Foundation is the parent organization. It is governed by a 16-member Board of Trustees appointed from the memberships of eight organizations (the AICPA, Financial Executives Institute, Institute of Management Accountants, Financial Analysts Federation, American Accounting Association, Securities Industry Association, Government Finance Officers Association, and National Association of State Auditors) interested in the formulation of accounting principles.[6] The primary responsibilities of the Financial Account-

---

6. The Financial Accounting Foundation also is the parent organization of the *Governmental Accounting Standards Board* (GASB), which establishes accounting principles for state and local governmental entities. The GASB is briefly discussed later in the chapter.

ing Foundation are to raise funds for the operations of the organization, provide general oversight to its operations, and appoint the members of the Financial Accounting Standards Advisory Council (FASAC) and the FASB. The FASAC consists of about 30 influential members. It is responsible for advising the FASB about major policy issues, the priority of topics, the selection of task forces, the suitability of tentative decisions, and other matters.

There are seven members of the FASB. Appointees to the FASB are full-time, fully paid members with no other organizational ties and are selected to represent a wide cross-section of interests. Each Board member is required to have a knowledge of accounting, finance, and business; high intelligence, integrity, and discipline; and a concern for the public interest regarding financial reporting. Currently, the FASB includes (1) three members who are CPAs and who have been in public practice, and (2) four members from other areas related to accounting (e.g., academia, government, and industry). The FASB is responsible for identifying financial accounting issues, conducting research to address these issues, and resolving them. The FASB is supported by a research and technical staff that performs numerous functions such as researching issues, communicating with constituents, and drafting preliminary findings. The administrative staff assists the FASB by handling library, publications, personnel, and other activities.[7]

The FASB issues several types of pronouncements:

1. *Statements of Financial Accounting Standards.* These Statements establish generally accepted accounting principles. They are releases indicating the methods and procedures required on specific accounting issues and are included in Category A of Exhibit 1-4.

2. *Interpretations.* These pronouncements provide clarification of conflicting or unclear issues relating to previously issued *FASB Statements of Standards, APB Opinions,* or *Accounting Research Bulletins.* Interpretations also establish or clarify generally accepted accounting principles. They are also included in Category A of Exhibit 1-4.

3. *Technical Bulletins.* These are issued by the staff of the FASB to provide guidance on accounting and reporting problems related to *Statements of Standards* or *Interpretations.* The guidance may clarify, explain, or elaborate upon an underlying standard. These pronouncements are included in Category B of Exhibit 1-4.

4. *Statements of Financial Accounting Concepts.* These Statements establish a theoretical foundation upon which to base financial accounting and reporting standards. These Statements are the output of the FASB's "Conceptual Framework" project (discussed in Chapter 2).[8] They are included in Category E of Exhibit 1-4.

5. *Other Pronouncements.* On a major topic, the FASB staff may also issue a *Guide for Implementation,* which is in the form of questions and answers (referred to as *FASB Q's and A's.* These are included in Category D of Exhibit 1-4.

---

7. For a more detailed look at the FASB's operations, see P. B. Miller and R. J. Redding, *The FASB: The People, the Process, and the Politics,* 2nd ed. (Homewood, Ill.: Richard D. Irwin, Inc., 1988).

8. The similarity in the titles *Statement of Financial Accounting Concepts* and *Statement of Financial Accounting Standards* makes an abbreviated reference to each potentially ambiguous. To avoid confusion, throughout this book a reference to **FASB Statement No. __** in the body of the text will always refer to a statement of *standards* while a full reference will be presented for each statement of *concepts.*

These documents may be purchased individually from the FASB. As a service to its constituency, the FASB also offers other publications. Two of these, published each year as part of the FASB's Accounting Standards series, are useful references for accountants. One two-volume set entitled *Original Pronouncements* includes all of the first four types of pronouncements as of its date of publication. Another two-volume set entitled *Current Text* (*General Standards* and *Industry Standards*) is a topical integration of currently effective accounting and reporting standards as of its date of publication.

### Operating Procedures

Before issuing a statement of concepts or standards, the FASB generally completes a multistage process as outlined in Exhibit 1-7, although the sequence and number of steps may vary. Initially, a topic or project is identified and placed on the FASB's agenda. This topic may be the result of suggestions from the FASAC, the accounting profession, industry, or other interested parties. On major issues a Task Force may be appointed to advise and consult with the FASB's Research and Technical Staff on such matters as the scope of the project and the nature and extent of additional research. The Staff then conducts any research specifically related to the project.

A Discussion Memorandum or Invitation to Comment, which outlines the research related to the issues, then usually is published and a public comment period is set. During this period, public hearings, similar to those conducted by Congress, may be held. The intent is to receive information from and views of interested individuals and organizations on the issues. Many parties submit written comments ("position papers") or make oral presentations. These parties include representatives of CPA firms and interested corporations, security analysts, members of professional accounting associations, and academicians. After deliberating on the views expressed and information collected, the FASB issues an Exposure Draft of the proposed Statement. Interested parties generally have 30-90 days to provide written comments of reaction. On major issues, more public hearings may be held. A modified draft is prepared, if necessary, and brought to the FASB for a final vote. After a *super majority* (i.e., at least 5 to 2) vote is attained, the *Statement* is issued.

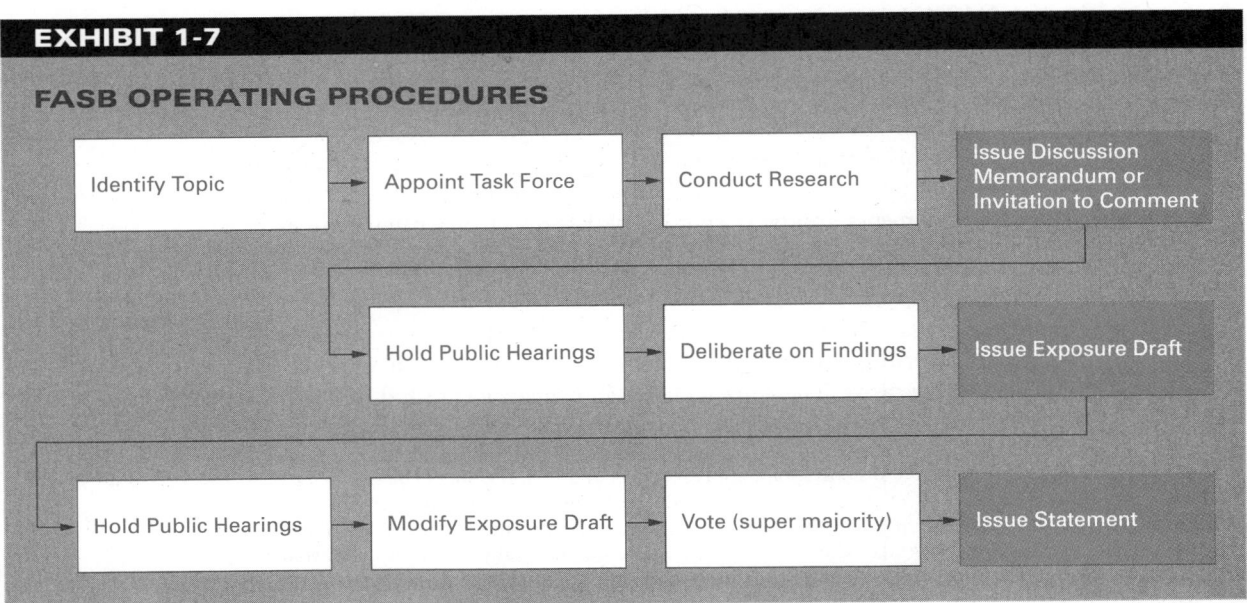

**EXHIBIT 1-7**

**FASB OPERATING PROCEDURES**

Identify Topic → Appoint Task Force → Conduct Research → Issue Discussion Memorandum or Invitation to Comment

Hold Public Hearings → Deliberate on Findings → Issue Exposure Draft

Hold Public Hearings → Modify Exposure Draft → Vote (super majority) → Issue Statement

The time involved to complete each of the steps varies depending on the complexity of the topic. For some complex topics the time frame involves several years; for other less-complex topics only a few months are needed. For instance, the FASB deliberated on basic conceptual and practical issues involving the statement of cash flows for more than 10 years. The Board issued a Discussion Memorandum in 1980, but then deferred consideration of cash flows reporting until it dealt with related theoretical issues in its Conceptual Framework project. In 1985, the FASB reactivated the topic. It held public hearings and received over 450 comment letters in response to its Exposure Draft. Eventually, *FASB Statement No. 95* entitled "Statement of Cash Flows" was issued in November, 1987, as shown in the following summary.

| Step in Procedures | FASB Statement No. 95 | FASB Statement No. 102 |
|---|---|---|
| Issue *Discussion Memorandum* | Dec., 1980 | None |
| Receive public comments | May, 1981 | None |
| Appoint Task Force | May, 1985 | None |
| Issue *Exposure Draft* | July, 1986 | Nov., 1988 |
| Receive public comments | Through Mar., 1987 | Through Jan., 1989 |
| Issue *Statement* | Nov., 1987 | Feb., 1989 |

On the other hand, *FASB Statement No. 102*, which amended *FASB Statement No. 95* for banks, brokers and dealers in securities, and other similar companies, was issued within three months after the related Exposure Draft was issued. In this case the FASB concluded that it could reach an informed decision without a public hearing. During the public comment period it did receive 69 comment letters which were used in the deliberation process.

*Socio-Political Environment*

As can be seen from Exhibit 1-7 and the related discussion, the operating procedures of the FASB are designed so that accounting standards are developed in an efficient manner, with due process, and in a public forum. The intent is to consider all related research on a particular topic, as well as the views of all interested parties, before coming to a logical conclusion concerning the appropriate accounting standard for the topic.

An inexperienced viewer of the FASB operating procedures might think that accounting standards are always "ideal" because they are the result of "rational policy making," where there are clearly defined objectives, an integrated body of theory, and known consequences of the actions. Yet this may not always be the case because accounting is part of a broader social system. Often, objectives are not clear, research results are conflicting, and only "best guesses" can be made of the future consequences of current standards because "...in no instance involving complex social [e.g., accounting] issues has anyone demonstrated...that a particular [accounting] policy decision was 'right' in the sense of coming closer than another decision to specified objectives."[9]

Furthermore, a former member of the Accounting Principles Board argues that "the setting of accounting standards is as much a product of political action as of flawless logic...."[10] He feels that since accounting standard setting is a social

---

9. D. L. Gerboth, "'Muddling Through' with the APB," *Journal of Accountancy* (May, 1972), p. 43.
10. C. T. Horngren, "The Marketing of Accounting Standards," *Journal of Accountancy* (October, 1973), p. 61.

decision that places restrictions on behavior, these decisions must be accepted by the affected parties. To achieve "acceptable decisions," it is only natural for the affected parties to attempt to influence the decisions. Since the FASB holds public hearings and open meetings, it is relatively easy for various external user groups (e.g., investors and creditors) and other interested groups (e.g., affected corporations and CPA firms), often with conflicting views, to attempt to influence the FASB to develop new standards or change old standards in their own best interests. Because the FASB has such a wide constituency and focuses on general purpose financial reporting, it often must establish accounting standards that are the result of *compromise*.

For a given topic, each FASB member will have certain issues of high priority and others of lower priority. In the FASB's deliberation process each Board member will attempt to persuade the other members to accept the important issues and to drop the less important ones. This negotiation is necessary to reach a consensus so that a majority vote may be attained on the topic.[11] Whenever a compromise is reached, some of the FASB's constituency are unhappy because they perceive that the new GAAP is somehow "unfair" to them. This dissatisfaction was especially true in cases where, prior to January 1, 1991, only a simple majority (4 to 3 vote) was necessary to issue a standard. In such a situation, many of the constituency found fault with the conclusions reached by the FASB. They have criticized the FASB for failing to listen to constituents, moving too quickly on topics, not giving sufficient consideration to cost/benefit issues, creating logically inconsistent rules, and establishing complex standards that are too difficult to implement. The Financial Accounting Foundation, in its general oversight role of the FASB, has implemented procedures to overcome these criticisms. These procedures include use of an oversight committee to monitor the FASB's standard-setting process, periodic Financial Accounting Foundation and FASB discussions, stronger input by the FASAC on agenda determination and task force use, additional publication of preliminary views, and field testing of preliminary views. Furthermore, effective January 1, 1991, at least a 5 to 2 vote is required to issue new standards as a way to minimize compromise. Compromise, however, is not necessarily bad; in fact, it can be beneficial. In a democratic society, "...only politically responsible institutions have the right to command others to obey their rules."[12] Accounting standards are not unchangeable. The FASB fulfills its responsibility by (1) establishing standards that are the most acceptable, given the various affected constituencies, and (2) continually monitoring the consequences of its actions so that revised standards can be issued where appropriate. As Dennis Beresford (Chairman of the FASB) points out, the FASB carries out its public responsibility in an environment characterized by subtlety, complexity, and an absence of clear-cut answers. The FASB works hard to develop accounting standards that can be defended in terms of facts and circumstances, logic, and the fairness of the process that produces them.[13]

## Other Organizations Currently Influencing Generally Accepted Accounting Principles

In addition to the policy-making bodies discussed in the previous section, several other organizations have had an impact on the development of generally accepted accounting principles during the past several decades.

---

11. For additional discussion of the FASB's political process, see Miller and Redding, *op. cit.,* chap. 1.
12. D. L. Gerboth, "Research, Intuition, and Politics in Accounting Inquiry," *The Accounting Review,* (July, 1973), p. 481.
13. D.R. Beresford and R.V. Riper, "The Not-So-Mysterious Ways of the FASB," *Journal of Accountancy* (February, 1992), p. 83.

## Securities and Exchange Commission (SEC)

The SEC was created to administer various securities acts under powers provided by Congress in the Securities Act of 1933 and the Securities Exchange Act of 1934. Under these Acts, **the SEC has the legal authority to prescribe accounting principles and reporting practices for all companies issuing publicly-traded securities.** While this authority has seldom been used, from time to time the SEC has exerted pressure on the CAP, the APB, and the FASB. It has been especially interested in narrowing areas of difference in accounting practice and in increasing disclosures.

The 1933 Act requires each company offering securities for sale to the public in the primary and secondary markets to file a registration statement and to provide each investor with a proxy statement prior to each stockholders' meeting. The 1934 Act established extensive reporting requirements to aid in full disclosure. Among the most commonly required reports are:

*Form S-1.* A registration statement.

*Form 10-K.* An annual report.

*Form 10-Q.* A quarterly report of operations.

*Form 8-K.* A report used to describe any significant events that may affect the company.

*Proxy Statement.* A report used when management requests the right to vote through proxies for shareholders at stockholders' meetings.

The SEC establishes accounting principles with respect to the information contained within the preceding reports and issues reporting guidelines in the form of its *Regulation S-X* and its *Financial Reporting Releases*. In some instances the SEC has required the disclosure of information not typically found in published financial reports.

*These disclosures are further discussed in Chapters 3 and 23.*

Generally speaking, the impact of the SEC has been through its informal approval of *APB Opinions* and *FASB Statements* before their issuance. While the SEC has the authority to decide what constitutes "generally accepted accounting principles," in many cases this authority has been exercised through persuasion rather than edict. Evidence of the SEC's position can be found where it endorsed the concept of "substantial authoritative support" by asserting that "principles, standards, and practices promulgated by the FASB in its *Statements* and *Interpretations* will be considered by the Commission as having substantial authoritative support, and those contrary to such FASB promulgations will be considered to have no such support."[14] The result of this position has been to *allow accounting principles to be formulated in the private sector* rather than by the government. However, the SEC has been criticized for not exercising its responsibility, and there is no assurance that the position will remain in effect. In fact, during 1978 the SEC refused to support **FASB Statement No. 19** requiring the use of the successful-efforts method in the oil and gas industry, and the FASB reacted by suspending the effective date of this release. Furthermore, in the late 1980s the House Energy and Commerce Committee's Oversight and Investigations Subcommittee, chaired by Congressman John Dingell, was critical of the SEC for its alleged failure to monitor the detection of fraud and to establish an "early warning"

---

14. "Codification of Financial Reporting Policies," *SEC Accounting Rules* (Chicago: Commerce Clearing House, August, 1989), sec. 101. This Codification contains the accounting principles and reporting guidelines issued prior to 1982 in the SEC's *Accounting Series Releases*. In 1982 the name was changed to *Financial Reporting Releases* to better reflect the nature of the documents.

system for identifying potential business failures. Although these hearings did not result in changes involving the establishment of generally accepted accounting principles, they did have an impact on *auditing* standards. Recently, the SEC pressured the FASB to adopt a standard requiring the use of market values by companies for reporting certain types of investments, and the Board issued **FASB Statement No. 115** in response to this pressure.

### American Institute of Certified Public Accountants (AICPA)

The AICPA dates back to 1887 and is the professional organization for all certified public accountants in the United States. To be a member of the AICPA, an individual must have passed the Uniform CPA Examination, possess a CPA certificate, and agree to abide by its bylaws and Code of Professional Ethics. The primary purpose of the AICPA is to provide the necessary technical support to assure that CPAs serve the public interest in performing quality professional services.

To fulfill this purpose, the AICPA publishes numerous documents that, in certain circumstances, may be considered as sources of generally accepted accounting principles as listed in Exhibit 1-4. *Industry Audit Guides* and *Industry Accounting Guides* (Category B of Exhibit 1-4) are publications designed to assist independent auditors in examining and reporting on financial statements of various types of entities in specialized industries (e.g., banking). *Statements of Position* (Category B of Exhibit 1-4) are publications intended to influence the development of financial accounting principles that best serve the public interest. *Practice Bulletins* (Category C of Exhibit 1-4) are publications that provide guidance on specific technical issues.

During the tenure of the Accounting Principles Board, the AICPA issued numerous *AICPA Accounting Interpretations* to provide timely guidance on accounting issues without the formal procedures necessary for an APB Opinion. These Interpretations (Category D of Exhibit 1-4) are still sources of generally accepted accounting principles unless specifically rescinded or amended. The AICPA also annually publishes *Accounting Trends and Techniques* (Category D of Exhibit 1-4), which provides a study of the latest accounting practices and trends, as identified from a survey of 600 published annual reports. Reference may be made to this publication to identify a consensus about generally accepted accounting principles for a particular issue. In this book we often cite disclosure information from *Accounting Trends and Techniques* that applies to a specific accounting practice. Finally, the AICPA also develops *Issue Papers* (Category E of Exhibit 1-4) to help the FASB identify accounting areas that need to be addressed and clarified.

### FASB Emerging Issues Task Force (EITF)

The EITF was established in 1984. It was a response by the FASB to criticisms that the Board did not always provide timely guidance on new accounting issues. Members of the EITF meet every six weeks, and include technical experts from all the major CPA firms and representatives from smaller CPA firms and from industry. These individuals are knowledgeable in accounting and financial reporting and are in positions to be aware of emerging problems. The Chief Accountant of the SEC also participates in EITF meetings. The primary objectives of the EITF are (1) to identify significant emerging accounting issues (i.e., unique transactions and accounting problems) that it feels the FASB should address and (2) to develop *consensus positions* on the implementation issues involving the application of standards. As shown in Category C of Exhibit 1-4, in some cases these consensus positions may be viewed as the "best available guidance" on generally accepted accounting principles, particularly as they relate to new accounting issues. The FASB publishes a summary of the proceedings of the EITF in a loose-leaf service and in an annual bound version entitled *EITF Abstracts*.

## Cost Accounting Standards Board (CASB)

The CASB was established in 1970 as an agency of the Congress of the United States. It ceased to exist in 1980 when Congress failed to vote funds for its existence, but was reinstated in 1988. The CASB is responsible only for negotiated federal contracts and subcontracts exceeding $500,000 and has issued several *Cost Accounting Standards* in this regard. Since internal cost accounting procedures often impact on externally reported financial information, these cost accounting standards occasionally influence external reporting. In the past, consideration has been given to replacing the FASB with a governmental board like the CASB. Although this change has not been implemented, the possibility of additional governmental involvement in the formulation of accounting principles should not be discounted.

## Internal Revenue Service (IRS)

The IRS administers the provisions of the Internal Revenue Code enacted by Congress. Federal income tax laws have had a significant impact upon financial reporting practices since they were first enacted in 1913. Although the Internal Revenue Code generally does not affect financial accounting practice directly, managers often prefer to lessen its impact upon the accounting systems within their companies. The result in many cases has been the adoption of those accounting methods and procedures that result in the lowest taxable income, without regard for what is proper from the standpoint of financial accounting theory and practice.

*The impact of the Internal Revenue Code on financial accounting for income taxes is discussed in Chapter 17.*

It should be understood that accounting for income tax purposes and for financial reporting purposes *is* and *should be* different. The goal of financial accounting is to provide information to financial statement users so that they may make decisions. The goal of income tax accounting is to legally minimize or postpone the payment of income taxes. Frequently the goals of financial reporting and income tax reporting come in conflict. For this reason, in this book we are concerned with determining the proper *financial* accounting recording and reporting procedures. What is, or should be, proper under the Internal Revenue Code is an entirely different question, which in general will not be discussed.

## American Accounting Association (AAA)

The AAA is an organization composed primarily of academicians and practicing accountants. The goals of this organization are to (1) advance accounting knowledge, (2) encourage accounting research, (3) improve accounting practice, and (4) promote the development of accounting standards. These goals are primarily implemented in various meetings; the AAA's journals—*The Accounting Review, Issues in Accounting Education,* and *Accounting Horizons;* and the work of various committees such as the AAA Committee on Financial Accounting Standards (FAS). The FAS responds to the FASB's exposure drafts relating to proposed statements of concepts and standards. The AAA has no official stature in the development of financial accounting practice, so its impact is through education and persuasion rather than through formal pronouncements. However, its members have served on the APB, FAF, and the FASB, and have appeared before the FASB in its hearings on particular issues.

## International Accounting Standards Committee (IASC)

Companies are becoming increasingly international in scope by selling and buying products and services as well as establishing operations in other countries. This "globalization" of business activity has lead to increased information in a company's financial statements about its international operations. Investors and creditors in international markets, in turn, prefer that the information they are using for investment and credit decisions is consistently prepared within countries and is internationally comparable from company to company across countries. The IASC was formed in 1973; currently the professional accountancy groups of about

50 countries are members. The role of the IASC is to contribute to the establishment of sound, internationally comparable accounting principles, especially in developing countries. The operating structure of the IASC consists of: (1) a *Board*, which issues *Standards* and includes representatives from 13 countries, (2) a *Consultative Group*, which provides input to the Board on practical and conceptual issues and includes various organizations such as The World Bank, and (3) *Steering Committees*, which are formed to consider issues about a particular accounting topic and include members from four participating countries. The operating procedure of the IASC is somewhat similar to that of the FASB and includes study of the topic, issuance of an Exposure Draft, evaluation of comments, and consideration of a revised draft. If approved by at least three-fourths of the Board, the revised draft becomes an *International Accounting Standard*. To date, the IASC has issued 31 Standards.

There are, however, important differences between the environment within which the FASB operates, as compared to the IASC. The FASB operates as a private standard-setting organization, and the emphasis for establishing accounting standards in the U.S. is on the usefulness of accounting information to investors and creditors. On the other hand, in many other countries, the emphasis in financial reporting is on meeting legal (e.g., tax) requirements so that standard setting has evolved as a governmental rather than private function. A role of the IASC, then, is to consolidate many countries' accounting regulations into international standards. This consolidation often requires compromise and the acceptance of alternative accounting methods for certain transactions. Although there are areas of difference, financial statements prepared according to U.S. generally accepted accounting principles usually will comply with international accounting standards. In later chapters, where significant U.S. accounting practices differ from those of other major countries, we will discuss briefly those differences as they relate to the topics being covered.

### Governmental Accounting Standards Board (GASB)

The GASB was established in 1984 and operates under the auspices of the Financial Accounting Foundation. The GASB operates in a manner similar to the FASB. It consists of a full-time chair and four other members, with a supporting staff. The GASB's responsibility is to establish accounting standards for certain state and local governmental entities. Its impact on accounting principles for the private sector is minimal.

### Professional Associations

There are also several professional organizations that play an important role in the accounting standard-setting process. The **Financial Executives Institute (FEI)** consists primarily of high-level financial executives (such as financial vice-presidents, treasurers, and controllers) of major corporations. The FEI publishes a monthly journal called the *Financial Executive* and has sponsored research projects dealing with financial reporting issues. Membership in the **Institute of Management Accountants (IMA)**, formerly the National Association of Accountants, is open to all accountants although its primary focus is on managerial and cost accounting issues. The IMA publishes a monthly journal called *Management Accounting,* which includes articles on the relationship between managerial and financial reporting issues. In contrast to the FEI and IMA whose members tend to be preparers of accounting information, members of the **Financial Analysts Federation (FAF)** are financial analysts who use the accounting information in various investment decisions. The FAF publishes the *Financial Analysts Journal,* and its members participate in FASB research studies dealing with the impact of proposed accounting standards on users of financial accounting information. As noted earlier, each of these organizations is also a member of the Financial Accounting Foundation and provides input to the FASB through its operations, as well as through position papers and oral presentations in the public hearings process.

### Relationship of Organizations in Current Standard-Setting Environment

As discussed earlier, accounting standards are set in a socio-political environment. Currently there are three major organizations in the private and public sector that develop GAAP for companies: the FASB, the AICPA, and the SEC. To a lesser extent, the other organizations discussed in this section also are influential in the standard-setting process. The relationship of the various participants in this process is shown in Exhibit 1-8.

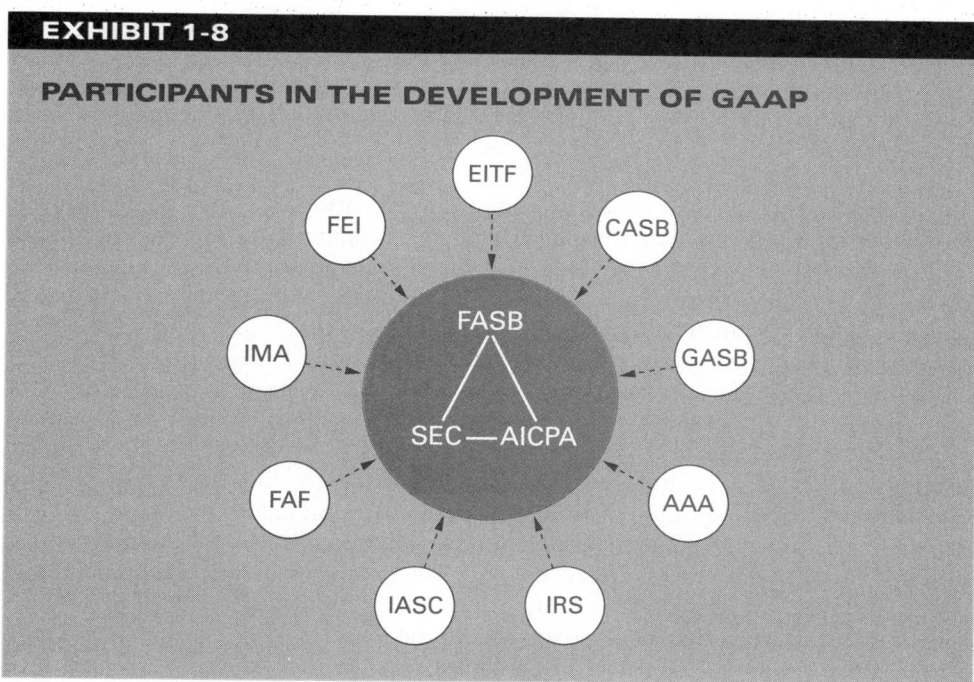

**EXHIBIT 1-8**

**PARTICIPANTS IN THE DEVELOPMENT OF GAAP**

## ETHICS IN THE ACCOUNTING ENVIRONMENT

In recent years there have been an increasing number of news reports about unethical behavior on the part of companies or individuals acting in their own self-interests without regard to the impact on society. These unethical actions include, for instance, polluting of lakes and streams, illegal shipments of weapons to foreign countries, savings and loan scandals, selling products that are hazardous to the user's health, overcharging on government contracts, false advertising, and "insider trading" activities. All of these unethical behaviors have a common theme: increased profits at the expense of some aspect of society. While these unethical actions often are sensational and capture the national headlines, there are many situations of a smaller scale in which accountants face ethical dilemmas.

Earlier we mentioned that accountants who record and report financial information must follow generally accepted accounting principles, and that auditors must express an opinion as to the fairness (in accordance with GAAP) of the financial statements. Among other things, the financial statements of a company communicate how well the employees of the company at the department, division, and top levels have done in operating the company. The results reported in the audited financial statements are likely to have an impact on the company's ability to sell stock or borrow money, as well as on employees' raises and promotion opportunities. Consequently, these employees have a vested interest in portraying their performances in the best light and may pressure accountants to do so. We also mentioned that in the FASB's public hearings and open meetings various parties attempt to influence the Board in their own self-interests. These are but a few examples of situations in which accountants may be faced with *ethical dilemmas* (*ethical conflicts*), situations where an accountant must make a decision about what is the "right" (ethical) action to take in a given set of circumstances. With the realization that accounting is a service activity that plays an important role in society, professional accounting organizations have established "codes of ethics" for their members. One of these applies to members of the AICPA.[15]

Members of the AICPA recognize that they assume an obligation of self-discipline above and beyond the requirements of laws and regulations. To help guide members in public practice, industry, government, and education in performing their responsibilities, the AICPA adopted the **Code of Professional Conduct (CPC)**. The CPC includes six *Principles* that express the basic tenets of ethical and professional conduct and which call for an unswerving commitment to honorable behavior, even at the sacrifice of personal advantage. These Principles are summarized in Exhibit 1-9.[16]

While this code of ethics establishes guidelines for accountants in performing their responsibilities, it does not provide a structured approach for "moral reasoning" in ethical dilemmas. Ethical behavior goes beyond what is legally acceptable behavior; what is legal may still be unethical in certain circumstances. Ethicists have developed alternative "models" to help individuals make sound moral judgments and guide their behavior when faced with ethical dilemmas involving various stakeholders. In the business environment of a company, the *stakeholders* may include past, current, and potential investors, creditors, employees, suppliers, competing companies, local, state, and federal governments, and citizens in the local, regional, national, and even international communities. According to Velasquez, a noted ethicist, there are three basic approaches to moral reasoning. Each of these approaches uses a different set of moral standards in distinguishing between right and wrong. These approaches include: (1) the *utilitarian* model, which evaluates actions based on the extent to which they result in the "greatest good for the greatest number," (2) the *rights* model, which embraces actions that protect individual moral rights, and (3) the *justice* model, which emphasizes a fair distribution of benefits and burdens. In determining whether an action is ethical or in determining which of several alternative behaviors is the most ethical, Velasquez suggests that no single set of moral standards is sufficient. Instead, he proposes a several step process which combines all three types of moral standards. This process includes: (1) gathering the facts (e.g., who are the "stakeholders," what are my responsibilities); (2) asking whether the action is

---

15. For the code of ethics of the IMA, another professional accounting organization, see "Standards of Ethical Conduct for Management Accountants," *Management Accounting* (February, 1992), p. 11.
16. *Code of Professional Conduct* as amended May 20, 1991 (New York: AICPA, 1991), p. 3–8.

---

**EXHIBIT 1-9**

## PRINCIPLES OF THE AICPA CODE OF PROFESSIONAL CONDUCT

I. *Responsibilities:* In carrying out their responsibilities as professionals, members should exercise sensitive professional and moral judgments in all their activities.

II. *The Public Interest:* Members should accept the obligation to act in a way that will serve the public interest, honor the public trust, and demonstrate commitment to professionalism.

III. *Integrity:* To maintain and broaden public confidence, members should perform all professional responsibilities with the highest sense of integrity.

IV. *Objectivity and Independence:* A member should maintain objectivity and be free from conflicts of interest in discharging professional responsibilities. A member in public practice should be independent in fact and appearance.

V. *Due Care:* A member should observe the profession's technical and ethical standards, strive continually to improve competence and the quality of services, and discharge professional responsibility to the best of the member's ability.

VI. *Scope and Nature of Services:* A member in public practice should observe the Principles of the CPC in determining the scope and nature of services to be provided.

---

acceptable according to three ethical criteria, (a) utility: does the action optimize the satisfactions of all stakeholders? (b) rights: does the action respect the rights of all individuals?, and (c) justice: is the action fair and just?; (3) considering whether there are any "overwhelming factors" such as conflicts between criteria that may justify disregarding one or more of the ethical criteria; and (4) deciding whether the action is ethical (or what ethical action to take) based on an evaluation of the applicable ethical criteria.[17]

Accountants are noted to have high ethical standards.[18] Acting in an ethically appropriate manner is not always easy; sometimes it is very difficult. However, because of the important role of accounting in society, every accountant must have high moral standards and strive to behave at the highest ethical level.

## CREATIVE AND CRITICAL THINKING IN THE ACCOUNTING ENVIRONMENT

The business environment in which accountants work is constantly changing and becoming more complex. New products and services are continually introduced and existing products are modified. Production techniques are changing, as are the channels of distribution and the approaches to promoting these products. There is an explosion of information technology as computers are networked, satellites allow global audio/visual communication, fax machines and electronic-mail enable

---

17. M. Velasquez, *Business Ethics: Concepts and Cases,* 2nd ed. (Englewood Cliffs, N.J.: Prentice Hall, 1988), pp. 65–118.
18. "Ethics Survey Ranks Accountants First," *Journal of Accountancy* (October, 1989), p. 110.

nearly instantaneous information transmittal, and cellular phones link customers and suppliers during commuting time. Globalization is occurring, with more and more companies becoming international in their operating activities, buying, producing, and selling products in foreign countries. Government regulations are also increasing, as more concern is given to such issues as worker safety and control of pollution.

In response to these changes, companies are becoming more innovative in the ways they manage their businesses, how they finance their activities, what they invest in to expand their operating capabilities, and what approaches they use in their credit and collection processes. They are restructuring their organizations and operations to increase efficiency, and are more sensitive to changing technology and product obsolescence. They are also more creative in the ways they structure their executive and employee compensation packages. Accounting systems that are designed to accumulate, process, and communicate information for decision making in this changing environment must change to satisfy the needs of users. Accounting principles must evolve to reflect this changing environment. Accountants responsible for establishing, modifying, operating, monitoring, and evaluating these systems, as well as for establishing and applying accounting principles, must be both *creative* thinkers and *critical* thinkers.

Research in psychology has found that each side of the brain deals with a different type of thinking. The right side focuses on creative thinking, involving visualizing and developing ideas. The left side focuses on critical thinking, involving analyzing and evaluating ideas. All individuals think creatively and critically, but the degrees to which each side of the brain is used differs among individuals. However, through practice, it is possible to increase an individual's ability to think creatively and critically.

Different aspects of creative thinking and critical thinking have been studied and discussed for many years and in numerous areas. We will discuss briefly what role these concepts play in financial accounting. There are many ways creative thinking and critical thinking have been defined, in part because they are not mutually exclusive and the differences between the two types of thinking are not clear-cut. For our purposes, **creative thinking is the process of finding new relationships (ideas) among items of information that potentially solve a problem.** Creative thinking involves constructively using imagination and insight to see issues in a different light. Terms that have been used to describe a creative thinker include insightful, intuitive, imaginative, sensitive, flexible, original, adaptable, and tolerant of ambiguity.[19] In contrast, **critical thinking is the process of testing these new relationships (ideas) to determine how well they will work.** Critical thinking involves using inductive or deductive reasoning to analyze an issue logically. Terms that have been used to describe a critical thinker include objective, independent, analytical, logical, rational, able to synthesize, consistent, and organized.[20]

In financial accounting, accountants tend to be "problem solvers." When an accounting issue or problem arises, the accountant is responsible for its resolution. Several steps have been identified in the problem-solving process, as shown in Exhibit 1-10. These steps include: (1) recognizing a problem, (2) identifying alternative solutions, (3) evaluating the alternatives, (4) selecting a solution from among the alternatives, and (5) implementing the solution. Creative thinking and critical thinking

---

19. For a more extensive discussion of creative thinking, see J.R. Evans, *Creative Thinking in the Decision and Management Sciences* (Cincinnati: South-Western Publishing Company, 1991).
20. For a more extensive discussion of critical thinking, see J. Chaffee, *Thinking Critically*, 3rd ed. (New York: Houghton Mifflin Company, 1990).

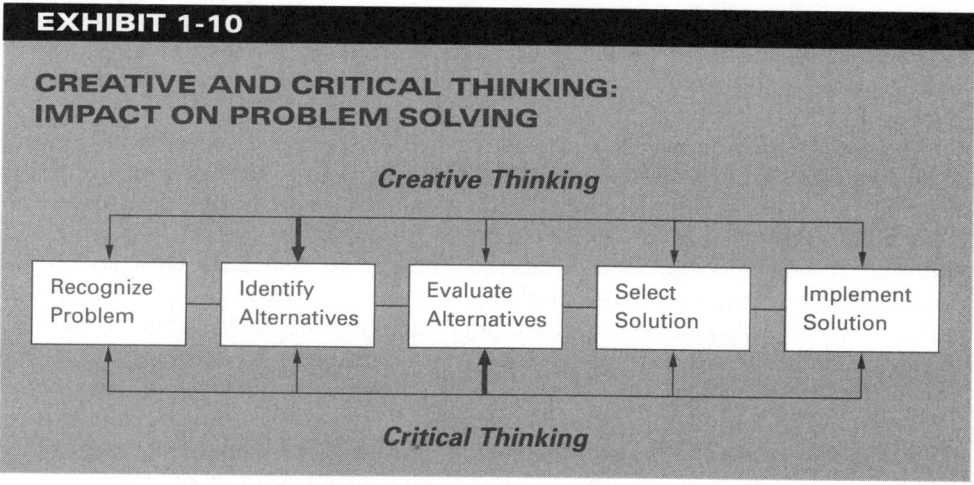

EXHIBIT 1-10

CREATIVE AND CRITICAL THINKING:
IMPACT ON PROBLEM SOLVING

*Creative Thinking*

| Recognize Problem | Identify Alternatives | Evaluate Alternatives | Select Solution | Implement Solution |

*Critical Thinking*

both play a role in each step of the problem-solving process. However, creative thinking is probably most critical in the *identification* of alternative solutions, while critical thinking is most critical in the *evaluation* of the alternative solutions.

The degree of complexity may differ from one problem to another. Problems can range from structured problems to unstructured problems. For *structured* problems, virtually complete information is known about the alternatives (in fact, there may be only one alternative) so that identifying, evaluating, selecting, and implementing an alternative is straightforward. At the other extreme are *unstructured* problems where even the basic issue may not be readily apparent, the alternative solutions are unclear once the problem is identified, and there is a lack of information about the alternatives, so that the identification, evaluation, selection, and implementation process is much more complex. Between these extremes is the *partially-structured* problem, where either the alternative solutions are unclear or there is a lack of information about the alternative solutions.

At the policy-making level, the FASB deals with complex unstructured problems. The Board members engage in higher-order creative thinking and critical thinking in their problem-solving processes involving the *establishment* of generally accepted accounting principles. In this book, we discuss the major issues faced by the FASB in setting standards. However, our primary focus is to discuss the *application* of generally accepted accounting principles in the recording and reporting of various topics. These topics may be general (e.g., the income statement) or specific (e.g., inventory). For each topic, we identify GAAP, discuss the related conceptual issues, and explain the recording and reporting procedures. In the exercises and problems at the end of each chapter, we primarily focus on assignments intended to help you reinforce your understanding of the topical material. We do so by requiring you to prepare solutions to issues involving the chapter topics. These assignments generally involve structured problems for which there are only one or two correct alternative solutions so that the steps of identification, evaluation, and selection of alternatives in the problem-solving process are reduced or omitted. This approach does not mean that your creative thinking and critical thinking processes are not at work, however. In solving these assignments, you are practicing both creative and critical thinking, but at a lower level. It is important to master the understanding of basic recording and reporting issues in financial accounting before moving to more complex accounting issues that involve less structured problems and entail higher-level creative and critical thinking.

As a step in helping you develop your higher-level creative and critical thinking skills, there are also cases at the end of each chapter. These cases may require you to explain your understanding of interrelated concepts and practices. They may also require you to determine solutions to issues for which specific generally accepted accounting principles do not apply directly. These cases may deal with accounting issues that are emerging because of changes in the business environment discussed earlier. They may also focus on topics that are too "industry specific" to be included in the chapter material. In these latter situations, the cases will require you to "research GAAP" in a document like the FASB's *Current Text* or *Original Pronouncements* and, in so doing, stimulate your higher-level creative thinking and critical thinking as you complete the problem-solving process. If your instructor does not assign these cases, you may still want to solve them yourself as a way of practicing your creative and critical thinking. Your ability to think creatively and critically will be very important in your future accounting and business (as well as personal) activities.

*These cases are identified by a ⓒ in the margin.*

## QUESTIONS

*Q1-1*  Distinguish between the categories of users of financial statements. Why might their decision-making needs be different?

*Q1-2*  Compare and contrast financial and managerial accounting.

*Q1-3*  What is financial reporting and what is the primary way a company's financial information is reported?

*Q1-4*  What are the three major financial statements of a company and what do they summarize?

*Q1-5*  What are generally accepted accounting principles? List the four accounting bodies that have established generally accepted accounting principles.

*Q1-6*  How many "categories" are in the hierarchy of generally accepted accounting principles? List the pronouncements that are included in Category A.

*Q1-7*  What are (were) the CAP, APB, and FASB? What documents that constitute generally accepted accounting principles have been issued by each of these organizations?

*Q1-8*  Briefly discuss the procedures followed by the FASB for issuing a statement of concepts or standards.

*Q1-9*  List and briefly discuss the types of pronouncements issued by the FASB.

*Q1-10*  List several organizations other than the FASB that have had an impact on the development of generally accepted accounting principles.

*Q1-11*  What is the IASC and what is its role?

*Q1-12*  List several professional organizations that play an important role in the accounting standard-setting process.

*Q1-13*  What is the *Code of Professional Conduct* and what are the six areas covered in the Principles of this code?

*Q1-14*  List the steps a person should follow to determine whether an action is ethical?

*Q1-15*  What is creative thinking? How would you describe a creative thinker?

*Q1-16*  What is critical thinking? How would you describe a critical thinker?

# CASES

## C1-1 Pronouncements

Various pronouncements establishing or related to generally accepted accounting principles have been issued by several accounting groups. The following is a list of six pronouncements, as well as a list of statements describing each pronouncement.

A. Statements of Financial Accounting Standards
B. Opinions
C. Technical Bulletins
D. Statements of Financial Accounting Concepts
E. Interpretations
F. Accounting Research Bulletins

_____ 1. Pronouncements that provide clarification of conflicting or unclear issues relating to previously issued *FASB Statements of Standards, APB Opinions,* or *Accounting Research Bulletins.*

_____ 2. Issued by the FASB to provide guidance on accounting and reporting problems related to *Statements of Standards* or *Interpretations.*

_____ 3. Pronouncements of the APB that constitute generally accepted accounting principles unless specifically amended or rescinded, many of which were based on *Accounting Research Studies.*

_____ 4. Issued by the FASB as a series establishing a theoretical foundation upon which to base financial accounting and reporting standards.

_____ 5. Pronouncements of the Committee on Accounting Procedure (CAP) that constitute generally accepted accounting principles unless superseded or amended by other authoritative bodies.

_____ 6. Pronouncements issued by the FASB that establish generally accepted accounting principles and indicate the methods and procedures required on specific accounting issues.

**Required**
Place the appropriate letter identifying each pronouncement on the line in front of the statement describing the pronouncement.

## C1-2 Organizations

Certain organizations have been influential in the establishment of accounting principles. The following is a list of abbreviations for several of these organizations, as well as a list of statements describing the organizations.

A. IRS        G. CASB
B. APB        H. FASB
C. CAP        I. AAA
D. IASC       J. GASB
E. SEC        K. AICPA
F. FASAC      L. EITF

_____ 1. First organization in United States to be given authority to issue pronouncements on accounting procedures and practice. Issued *Accounting Research Bulletins.*

_____ 2. Establishes cost accounting standards for United States government contracts.

_____ 3. Administers the provisions of the Internal Revenue Code.

_____ 4. Helps establish internationally comparable accounting principles.

_____ 5. Establishes accounting standards for state and local governmental entities.

_____ 6. Establishes generally accepted accounting principles in the private sector of the United States.

_____ 7. Organization of academicians and practicing accountants.

_____ 8. Responsible for advising the FASB about technical areas, task forces, and other matters.

_____ 9. Established 31 *Opinions,* many of which still constitute generally accepted accounting principles.

_____ 10. Has legal authority to prescribe accounting principles and reporting practices for all companies issuing publicly-traded securities.

_____ 11. Professional organization for all CPAs in the United States.

_____ 12. Develops consensus positions on the implementation issues involving the application of standards.

**Required**
Place the appropriate letter (A-L) for each organization in front of the statement describing the organization. In addition, write out the full name of the organization.

## C1-3 Establishment of GAAP

Since the later 1930s, three organizations have been primarily responsible for the establishment of generally accepted accounting principles in the private sector of the United States.

**Required**
Identify the three organizations and provide a brief chronological history of each, including the pronouncements issued that still constitute generally accepted accounting principles.

### C1-4   Accounting Principles
At the completion of the Darby Department Store audit, the president asks about the meaning of the phrase "in conformity with generally accepted accounting principles" that appears in your audit report on the management's financial statements. He observes that the meaning of the phrase must include more than what he thinks of as "principles."

**Required**
1. Explain the meaning of the term "accounting principles" as used in the audit report. (Do not discuss in this part the significance of "generally accepted.")
2. The president wants to know how you determine whether or not an accounting principle is generally accepted. Discuss the sources of evidence for determining whether an accounting principle has substantial authoritative support. Do not merely list the titles of publications. *(AICPA adapted)*

### C1-5   Standard Setting
When the Accounting Principles Board was founded in 1959, it planned to establish financial accounting standards using empirical research and logical reasoning only; the role of political action was little recognized at this time. Today, there is wide acceptance of the view that political action is as much an ingredient of the standard-setting process as is research evidence. Considerable political and social influence is wielded by user groups, those parties who are most interested in or affected by accounting standards.

Two basic premises of the Financial Accounting Standards Board (FASB) are that (1) it should be responsive to the needs and viewpoints of the entire economic community and (2) it should operate in full view of the public, affording interested parties ample opportunity to make their views known. The extensive procedural steps employed by the FASB in the standard-setting process support these premises.

**Required**
Describe why financial accounting standards inspire or encourage political action and social involvement during the standard-setting process. *(CMA adapted)*

### C1-6   GAAP Hierarchy
A friend of yours says, "I understand there are 'rules' for financial reporting. But what are these rules, where can a person find them, and which ones are more important?"

**Required**
Prepare an answer for your friend.

### C1-7   Organization of the FASB
The FASB is organized to establish generally accepted accounting principles. The Board is assisted by various groups and operates under a set of procedures.

**Required**
Prepare a short written report that summarizes the structure, types of pronouncements, and operating procedures of the FASB.

### C1-8   GAAP and the AICPA
The American Institute of Certified Public Accountants (AICPA) has been in existence for many years to help CPAs provide high-quality professional services. Among other activities, in certain circumstances, the AICPA establishes or provides guidance on generally accepted accounting principles (GAAP).

**Required**
Summarize the GAAP-related documents that the AICPA publishes.

### C1-9   Code of Professional Conduct
In a few years, you may become a member of the AICPA and be subject to its Code of Professional Conduct (CPC).

**Required**
Identify and briefly discuss the first five principles of the CPC. Provide examples that illustrate each principle.

### C1-10   Ethical Responsibilities
Each person in one of your accounting classes is required to write a report on an accounting topic. Included in the report must be a discussion from a specific library book. When you go to the library, you find that the only copy of the book is "missing." While sitting at a study desk, you overhear one of your classmates say that he has "misfiled" the book in the library so he can use it again later without having to wait for other students to finish using it.

**Required**
Discuss the steps you would take to address this ethical dilemma. It is not necessary to state what ethical action you would take, but be prepared to discuss your findings for each step.

### C1-11   Ethical Responsibilities
You and a friend are in the same accounting class. During the first test, you observe that your friend cheated by copying one of her answers from another student (who was unaware of the copying). When the exams are returned, your grade is a B, while your friend's grade is an A.

**Required**
Discuss the steps you would take to address this ethical dilemma. It is not necessary to state what ethical action you would take, but be prepared to discuss your findings for each step.

# FINANCIAL REPORTING: ITS CONCEPTUAL FRAMEWORK

As we saw in Chapter 1, accounting standards were developed in the United States by the Committee on Accounting Procedure (CAP) and the Accounting Principles Board (APB) prior to the inception of the Financial Accounting Standards Board (FASB). Neither the CAP nor the APB attempted to develop a broad, normative conceptual framework of accounting theory. In 1970, the APB did issue APB Statement No. 4, "Basic Concepts and Accounting Principles Underlying Financial Statements of Business Enterprises." However, this document described current practice at that time rather than what *should* be appropriate accounting. Although the CAP and APB gave some consideration to theoretical accounting concepts in the establishment of accounting standards, generally this was limited to the concepts related to the particular accounting issue at hand. This led, at times, to the development of accounting principles that were inconsistently applied from one issue to another. In this chapter, we discuss a conceptual framework of accounting theory. This framework includes the objectives of financial reporting, the types of useful accounting information, the qualitative characteristics of accounting information, and accounting assumptions and conventions, as well as a brief review of generally accepted accounting principles and financial statements.

## FASB CONCEPTUAL FRAMEWORK

Since its establishment, the FASB has been given two charges. First, it is to develop a conceptual framework of accounting theory. Second, it is to establish standards (generally accepted accounting principles) for financial accounting practice. The intent is to develop **a theoretical foundation of interrelated objectives and concepts that leads to the establishment of consistent financial accounting standards.** In other words, the conceptual framework should provide a logical structure and direction to financial accounting and reporting. This conceptual framework is expected to: (1) guide the FASB in establishing accounting standards, (2) provide a frame of reference for resolving accounting questions in situations where a standard does not exist, (3) determine the bounds for judgment in the preparation of financial statements, (4) increase users' understanding of and confidence in financial reporting, and (5) enhance comparability (discussed later). It is expected that the conceptual framework will serve the public by encouraging companies to provide financial (and related) information that is useful in efficiently allocating scarce economic resources in capital and other markets.[1]

The relationship among the objectives, concepts, and standards, their purposes, and the documents issued by the FASB is shown in Exhibit 2-1. The outputs of the conceptual framework are *Statements of Financial Accounting Concepts.* The conceptual

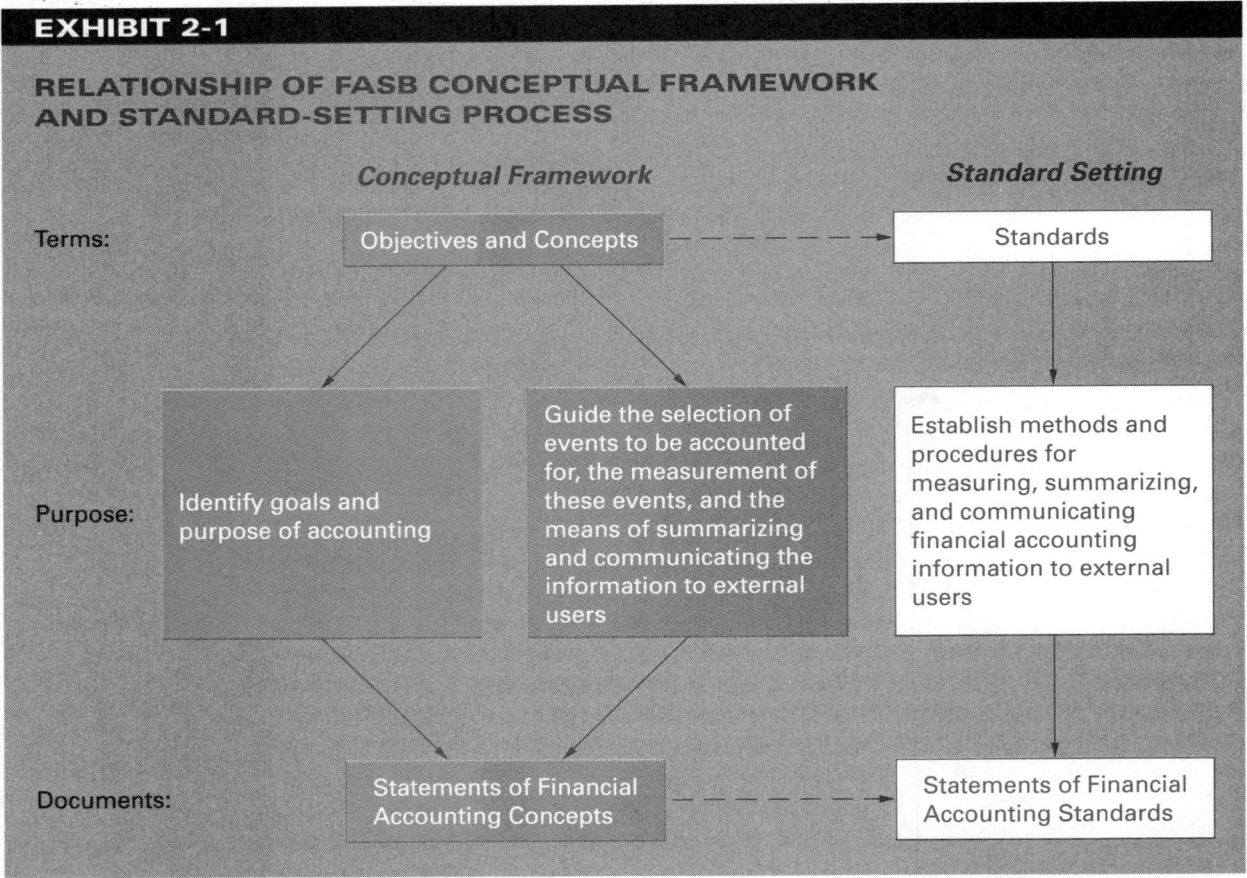

**EXHIBIT 2-1**

**RELATIONSHIP OF FASB CONCEPTUAL FRAMEWORK AND STANDARD-SETTING PROCESS**

|  | *Conceptual Framework* | *Standard Setting* |
|---|---|---|
| Terms: | Objectives and Concepts | Standards |
| Purpose: | Identify goals and purpose of accounting — Guide the selection of events to be accounted for, the measurement of these events, and the means of summarizing and communicating the information to external users | Establish methods and procedures for measuring, summarizing, and communicating financial accounting information to external users |
| Documents: | Statements of Financial Accounting Concepts | Statements of Financial Accounting Standards |

---

1. This discussion is based on a background paper, "The Conceptual Framework Project," Financial Accounting Standards Board (Stamford, Conn., 1980).

framework essentially is complete and 6 Statements of Concepts have been issued. The outputs of the standard-setting process are *Statements of Financial Accounting Standards*: to date 115 have been issued. The numerous "statements of standards" have been required in order to identify the preferable accounting practice from among the various alternatives that arise in response to the constantly changing, dynamic business environment. As much as possible, the FASB gives due consideration to the output of its conceptual framework in establishing these standards.

Because of the enormity of the task, the FASB divided its conceptual framework activities into several projects. These projects are shown in Exhibit 2-2. The first project dealt with identifying the objectives of financial reporting. This project resulted in the issuance of **FASB Statement of Financial Accounting Concepts No. 1,** entitled "Objectives of Financial Reporting by Business Enterprises." This document established the focus of the remaining projects, which are divided into two groups (accounting and reporting). The Qualitative Characteristics Project linked together the accounting and reporting projects, as illustrated by the dashed lines in Exhibit 2-2. It also resulted in the issuance of **FASB Statement of Financial Accounting Concepts No. 2,** entitled "Qualitative Characteristics of Accounting Information."

The accounting projects are concerned with defining the accounting elements (e.g., assets, liabilities, revenues, expenses) and identifying which elements should be

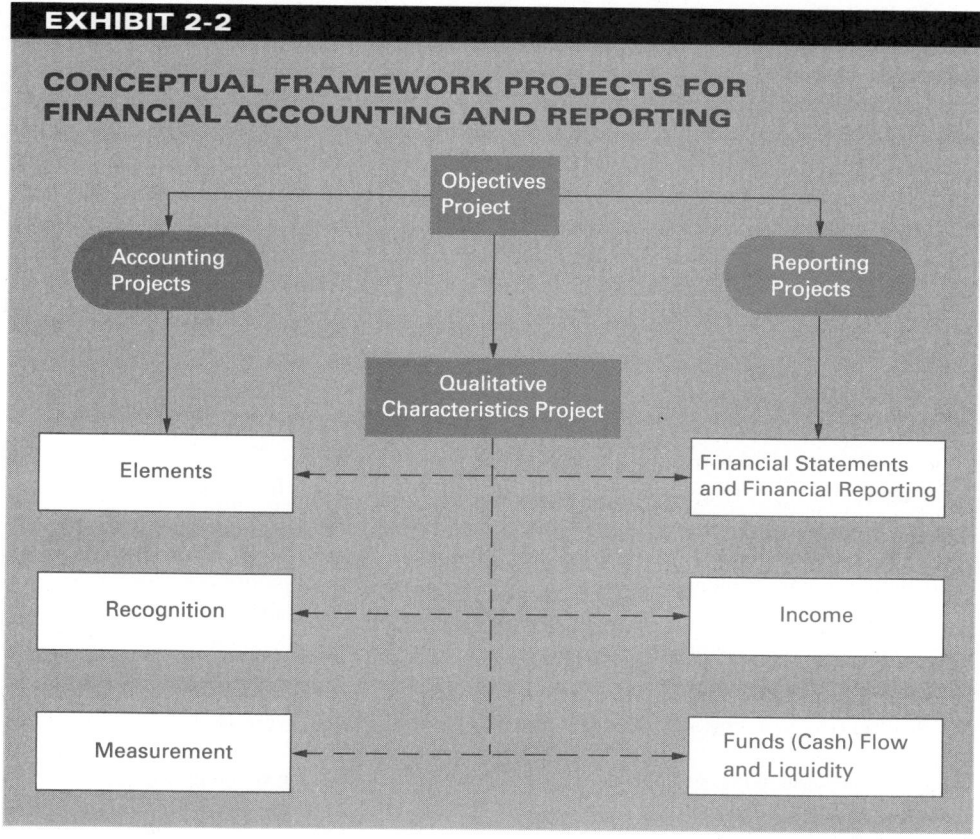

**EXHIBIT 2-2**

**CONCEPTUAL FRAMEWORK PROJECTS FOR FINANCIAL ACCOUNTING AND REPORTING**

Objectives Project

Accounting Projects

Reporting Projects

Qualitative Characteristics Project

Elements

Financial Statements and Financial Reporting

Recognition

Income

Measurement

Funds (Cash) Flow and Liquidity

Adapted from Figure 1 in "The Conceptual Framework Project," Financial Accounting Standards Board (Stamford, Conn., 1980).

reported, when they should be reported (recognized), and how they should be measured.[2] The reporting projects are concerned with the "display" of the elements of financial reports. Issues of concern include general questions such as what information should be provided, who should be required to provide the information, and where the information should be presented. Also included are more specific questions about income and its components as well as cash (funds) flow and its components.

*The Statements of Concepts dealing with the elements, recognition and measurement, and reporting income and cash flows are discussed in Chapters 3 and 4.*

Several Statements of Concepts have been issued that deal with one or more of these accounting and reporting projects. **FASB Statement of Financial Accounting Concepts No. 3** was issued in 1980. However, this Statement of Concepts was replaced in 1986 by **FASB Statement of Financial Accounting Concepts No. 6,** entitled "Elements of Financial Statements." **FASB Statement of Financial Accounting Concepts No. 5,** entitled "Recognition and Measurement in Financial Statements of Business Enterprises," was issued in 1984.[3] An Exposure Draft, *FASB Proposed Statement of Financial Accounting Concepts,* entitled "Reporting Income, Cash Flows, and Financial Position of Business Enterprises," has been issued regarding these two reporting projects. In addition, several working documents dealing with both accounting and reporting issues have been published that may eventually lead to the issuance of other statements of financial accounting concepts.

The first two Statements of Concepts dealing with the objectives of financial reporting and the qualitative characteristics of accounting information, as well as parts of the Exposure Draft dealing with types of useful information, are discussed in this chapter.

## OBJECTIVES OF FINANCIAL REPORTING

In its first concepts statement, the FASB observed that the objectives of financial reporting are those of *general-purpose* external reporting by companies. That is, the objectives relate to a *variety* of *external* users (as opposed to specific internal users, such as management) who do not have the authority to prescribe the financial information they desire from a particular company and therefore must use the information that the management of the company communicates to them.[4]

The FASB identified several objectives of financial reporting. These objectives proceed from the more general to the more specific. They are shown in Exhibit 2-3 and are discussed in the following sections.[5]

### Information Useful in Decision Making

The most general objective is shown at the top of Exhibit 2-3. This objective states that **financial reporting should provide useful information for present and potential investors, creditors, and other external users in making their investment, credit, and similar decisions.** Investors include both equity security holders (stockholders) and debt security holders (bondholders). Creditors include suppliers, customers and employees with claims, individual lenders, and lending institutions. Other external

---

2. For a discussion of these and other issues, see L. T. Johnson and R. K. Storey, "Recognition in Financial Statements: Underlying Concepts and Practical Conventions," *Research Report* (Stamford, Conn.: FASB, 1982).

3. **FASB Statement of Financial Accounting Concepts No. 4,** entitled "Objectives of Financial Reporting by Nonbusiness Organizations," has also been issued but is not discussed in this book.

4. "Objectives of Financial Reporting by Business Enterprises," *FASB Statement of Financial Accounting Concepts No. 1* (Stamford, Conn.: FASB, 1978), par. 28.

5. The discussion in this section primarily is a summary of that presented by the FASB in its "Objectives of Financial Reporting by Business Enterprises."

users include brokers, lawyers, security analysts, and regulatory agencies. These external users are expected to have a reasonable understanding of business and economic activities and be willing to study the information with reasonable diligence in order to comprehend the financial information.

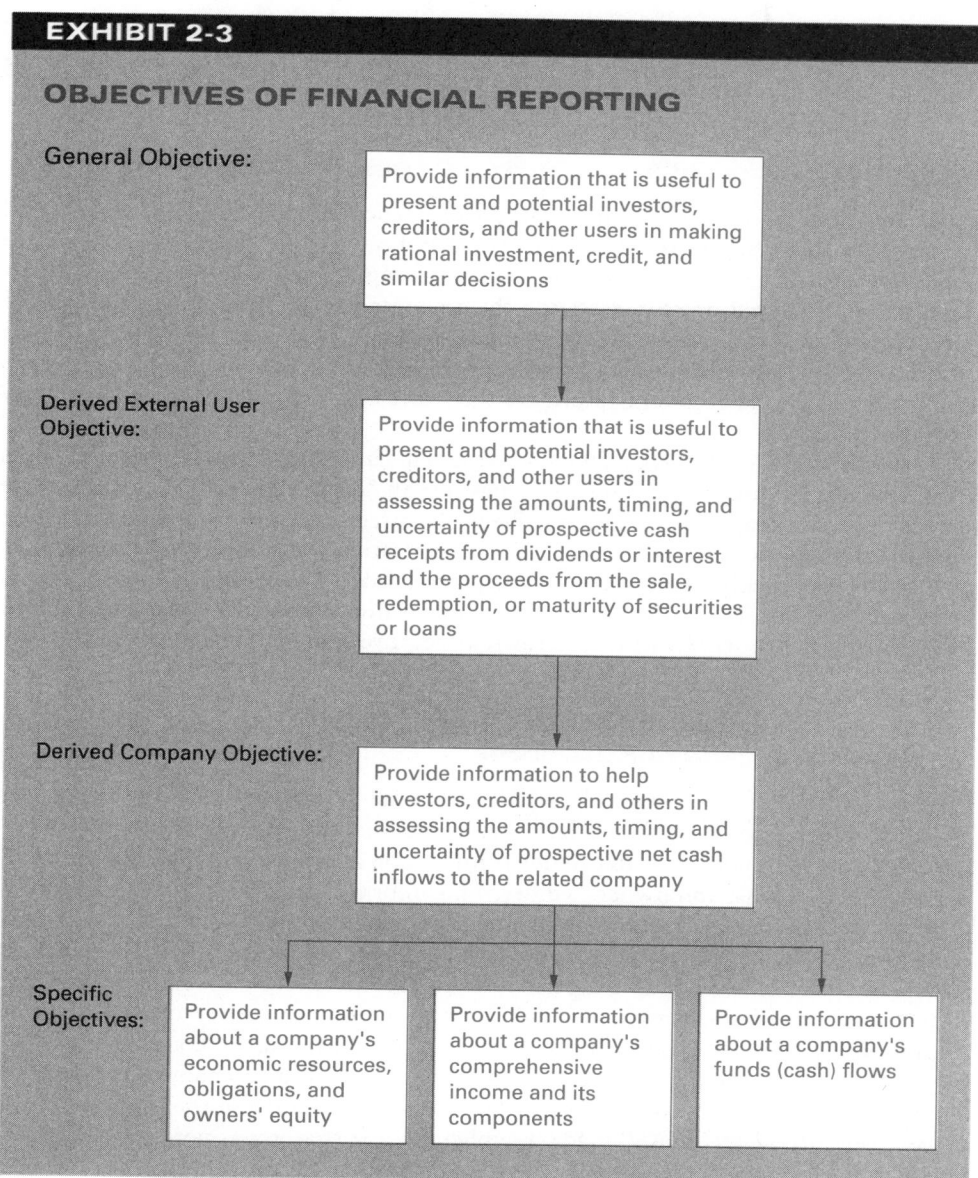

**EXHIBIT 2-3**

## OBJECTIVES OF FINANCIAL REPORTING

**General Objective:**

> Provide information that is useful to present and potential investors, creditors, and other users in making rational investment, credit, and similar decisions

**Derived External User Objective:**

> Provide information that is useful to present and potential investors, creditors, and other users in assessing the amounts, timing, and uncertainty of prospective cash receipts from dividends or interest and the proceeds from the sale, redemption, or maturity of securities or loans

**Derived Company Objective:**

> Provide information to help investors, creditors, and others in assessing the amounts, timing, and uncertainty of prospective net cash inflows to the related company

**Specific Objectives:**

> Provide information about a company's economic resources, obligations, and owners' equity

> Provide information about a company's comprehensive income and its components

> Provide information about a company's funds (cash) flows

## Information Useful in Assessing External Users' Cash Receipts

The second objective shown in Exhibit 2-3 relates to external users' needs. It states that **financial reporting should provide information that is useful to external users in assessing the amounts, timing, and uncertainty of prospective cash receipts.** This objective is important because individuals and institutions make cash outflows for investing and lending activities primarily to increase their cash inflows. Whether or not they are successful depends on the extent to which they receive a return of cash, goods, or services greater than their investment or loan. That is, they must receive not only a return *of* investment, but also a return *on* investment relative to the risk involved. Investment and credit decisions involve choices between present and prospective future cash flows. Financial information is needed to help establish expectations about the timing and amount of prospective cash receipts (e.g., dividends, interest, proceeds from resale or repayment) and assess the risk involved.

### Information Useful in Assessing Company Cash Flows

Since investors invest in and creditors lend to a particular company, their current and prospective cash receipts are affected by the cash flows of the company. Thus, a third objective shown in Exhibit 2-3 is that **financial reporting should provide information to help external users in assessing the amounts, timing, and uncertainty of the prospective net cash inflows to the related company.** This objective logically flows from the second objective because companies also invest cash in noncash resources to earn more cash and receive a return *on* their investment in addition to a return *of* their investment.

A company's activities regarding its investments are more complex, however, than those of external users. The company completes an "operating cycle" or cycles where goods or services are acquired, their value is increased, the goods or services are sold, and the selling price is collected. Within this operating cycle numerous cash receipts and payments are collected and paid, in no precise order. The company's ability to generate net cash inflows affects both its ability to pay dividends and interest and the market prices of its securities, which, in turn, affect investors' and creditors' cash flows.

### Information About Economic Resources and Claims to These Resources

The bottom tier of objectives in Exhibit 2-3 are the most specific. They indicate the types of information that should be provided in financial reports. **A specific objective of financial reporting is to provide information about a company's economic resources, obligations, and owners' equity.** This information is useful to external users for four reasons: (a) to identify the company's financial strengths and weaknesses and to assess its liquidity, (b) to provide a basis to evaluate information about the company's performance during a period, (c) to provide direct indications of the cash flow potentials of some resources and the cash needed to satisfy obligations, and (d) to indicate the potential cash flows that are the joint result of combining various resources in the company's operations. Information about a company's economic resources, obligations, and owners' equity is currently presented in the company's balance sheet, although the FASB made it explicitly clear that it was not advocating any particular type, form, or content of financial statements in this document.

*Balance sheets are discussed in Chapter 3.*

### Information About Comprehensive Income and Its Components

**Another specific objective of financial reporting is to provide information about a company's financial performance during a period** in order to help external users form expectations about its future performance. **The *primary* focus of financial reporting about a company's performance is information concerning the company's *comprehensive income* and its components. Information about comprehensive income is useful to external users in (a) evaluating management's performance, (b) estimating the "earning power" or other amounts perceived as representative of long-term income-producing ability, (c) predicting future income, and (d) assessing the risk of investing in or lending to the company.

In order to better reflect a company's financial performance during a period, the measurement of comprehensive income should relate (i.e., match) the costs (sacrifices) of operations to the benefits from operations. The measurement should also include the benefits and costs of other nonoperating transactions, events, and circumstances. This is accomplished through the use of **accrual accounting,** where the financial effects of transactions, events, and circumstances having cash consequences are related to the period in which they occur rather than when the cash receipt or cash payment takes place.[6] Information about a company's comprehensive income and its components currently is reported in the income statement and retained earnings statement.

*Comprehensive income and net income are discussed in Chapter 4.*

### Information About Funds (Cash) Flows

Although information about comprehensive income is a significant concern of external users, **another specific objective of financial reporting is to provide information about a company's cash flows.** Cash flow information shows how a company obtains and spends cash in regard to operations, investments, borrowings, and capital transactions, including cash dividends and other distributions of company resources to owners. External users use cash (or cash and cash equivalents) flow information about a company (a) to help understand its operations, (b) to evaluate its financing and investing activities, (c) to assess its liquidity, and (d) to interpret the comprehensive income information provided. Information about a company's funds flows is currently reported in the company's statement of cash flows.

*The statement of cash flows is discussed in Chapters 4 and 20.*

### Other Issues

Several other important issues were raised in this *Statement of Concepts.* First, **financial reporting should provide information about how the management of a company has discharged its stewardship responsibility** to owners (stockholders) for use of the company resources entrusted to it. The management is responsible to the owners for the custody and safekeeping of the resources, their efficient and profitable use, and their protection against unfavorable economic impacts, technological developments, and social changes.

Second, **financial statements and other means of financial reporting should include explanations and interpretations by management to help external users understand the financial information provided.** This often is referred to as **full disclosure.** Since management knows more about a company's activities than "outsiders," the usefulness of financial information can be enhanced by, for instance, (a) explanations of certain transactions, events, and circumstances, (b) interpretations of the effects on the financial results of dividing continuous operations into accounting periods, and (c) explanations of underlying assumptions or methods used and any related significant uncertainties.

*Management's discussion and analysis is discussed in Chapter 23.*

---

6. *FASB Statement of Concepts No. 1* originally used the term "earnings" instead of "comprehensive income." This latter term was substituted in *FASB Statement of Concepts No. 5* because comprehensive income encompasses more components. This issue is discussed more fully in Chapter 4.

Third, no decision was made concerning the qualitative characteristics (e.g., relevance, reliability) that accounting information should possess in order to be included in financial reports. These concepts are discussed in *FASB Statement of Concepts No. 2* and are included in the next section of this chapter. Finally, no definitions of the elements (e.g., assets, liabilities, revenues, and expenses) of financial statements were included in the discussion. These are discussed in *FASB Statement of Concepts No. 6* and are included later in this chapter.

*Financial statement elements are discussed in Chapters 3 and 4.*

The establishment of the objectives of financial reporting was the FASB's first step in developing its conceptual framework for financial accounting and reporting. The FASB intends that the objectives within this framework will act as guidelines for providing financial information for investment and credit decisions, thus facilitating the efficient operation of the capital markets and promoting the efficient allocation of scarce resources.

### Objectives in Other Countries

Many countries have objectives for financial reporting that are very different than those of the United States. To illustrate, we will briefly discuss those of Germany, Sweden, and France. German accounting principles are affected by legal and income tax requirements. In Germany, banks often provide the majority of both equity and debt capital to companies. These factors have led German accounting to emphasize information for creditors and to have a conservative balance sheet orientation. If published financial statements misrepresent the status of the company, it is considered unimportant because the stockholders (in their capacity as management) and the banks (represented on the Board of Directors) have separate access to information about the company.

In Sweden, maintenance of full employment is an important objective. Swedish companies use "income smoothing" in their financial statements to make profits seem uniform from year to year. "Secret reserves" are created (by overestimating depreciation, by establishing reserves for future losses, and by undervaluing assets) in good years and are drawn down in bad years. Such income smoothing is considered by some to contribute to the economic stability of the country.

In France, accounting rules essentially are controlled by law and are also influenced by income tax rules. These factors have created extreme conservatism in French accounting rules and the dominance of legal form over economic substance.[7] The French legal system makes the officers of a company personally responsible, to a great extent, for the consequences of business bankruptcy. This personal accountability has influenced the directors of French companies to create secret reserves in a manner similar to the practice in Sweden. Furthermore, since 1978 all French companies employing more than 750 people have been required to produce an annual "social" report that details such matters as pay, conditions of health and safety, absenteeism, training, industrial relations, and hours worked. Thus, it can be seen that in countries other than the United States different types of reports are prepared based on different financial reporting objectives.[8]

---

7. In the United States, accounting principles emphasize reporting the economic substance of a transaction instead of its legal form, as discussed in Chapter 4.

8. For additional information, see "International Financial Reporting," *DRT International* Vol. 1, No. 1 (New York, December 1991) and M.M. McClure, "Internationalization of the Introductory Financial Accounting Course," *Journal of Accounting Education* Vol. 6 (1988), pp. 159–181.

## TYPES OF USEFUL INFORMATION

The general objective of financial reporting is to provide information that is useful in investment and credit decision making. On a more specific level, a company's financial reports should provide information to help external users assess the amounts, timing, and uncertainty of the future net cash inflows of the company. Five types of information, explained in this section, have been identified by the FASB as being useful in meeting this specific objective. The interrelationship of this useful information with financial reports and external decision making is shown in Exhibit 2-4.

### EXHIBIT 2-4

#### INTERRELATIONSHIP OF FINANCIAL REPORTS, USEFUL INFORMATION, AND DECISION MAKING

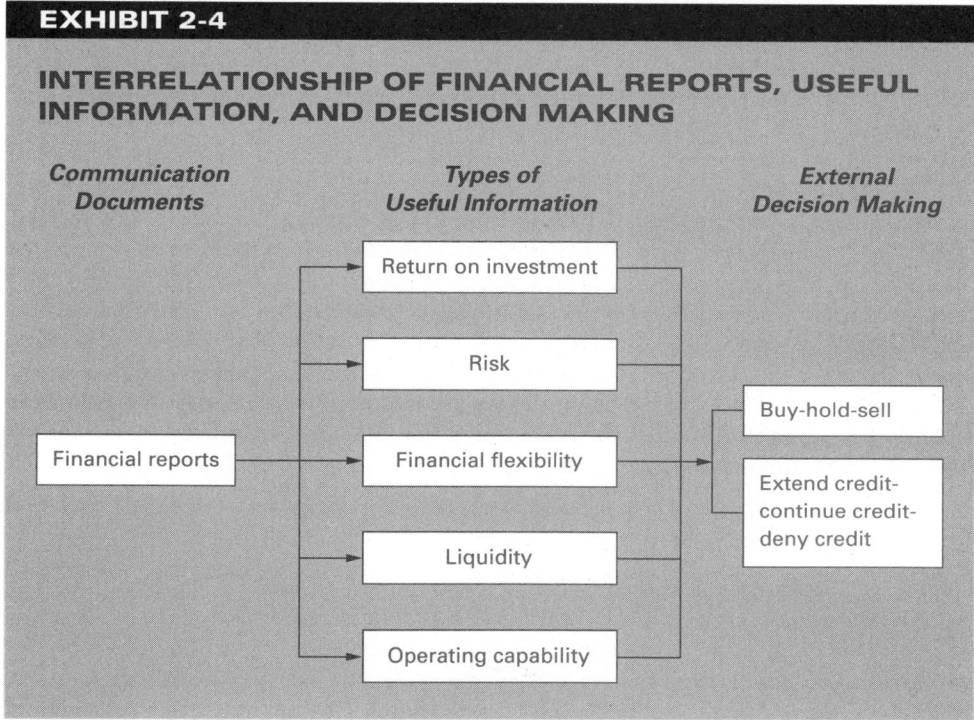

### Return on Investment

**Return on investment provides a measure of overall company performance.** Shareholders (stockholders) invest capital for a share of the equity (stockholders' equity) of a company. These investors are concerned with a return *on* capital. Before a company can provide a return on capital, its capital must be maintained or recovered (i.e., there must first be a return *of* capital to the company). Once a company's capital is maintained, the return *on* capital (i.e., comprehensive income) may be distributed to investors or may be retained by the company for reinvestment.

### Risk

**Risk is the uncertainty or unpredictability of the future results of a company.** The greater the range within which future results are likely to fall, the greater the risk associated with an investment in or extension of credit to the company. Risk is caused by numerous factors including, for example, high rates of technological change, uncertainty about demand, exposure to the effects of price changes, and political changes in the United States and other countries. In general, the greater the risk associated with an investment in a particular company, the higher the rate of return expected by investors (or the higher the rate of interest charged by creditors).

### Financial Flexibility

**Financial flexibility is the ability of a company to take effective actions to change the amounts and timing of cash flows.** Financial flexibility is important because it enables a company to respond to unexpected needs and opportunities. Financial flexibility comes from the ability of a company to: (a) adapt operations to increase net operating cash inflows, (b) raise new capital through, for instance, the sale of debt or stock securities at short notice, and (c) obtain cash by selling assets without disrupting ongoing operations. Financial flexibility affects risk as well as cash flows. It reduces the risk of failure in the event of a shortage in net cash flows from operations.

### Liquidity

**Liquidity is the term used to describe the amount of time until an asset is converted into cash or a liability is paid.** For operating assets, liquidity relates to the timing of cash flows in the normal course of business. For nonoperating assets, liquidity refers to marketability. The liquidity of a company is an indication of its ability to meet its obligations when they come due. Liquidity is positively related to financial flexibility but negatively related to both risk and return on investment. A more liquid company is likely to have a superior ability to adapt to unexpected needs and opportunities and a lower risk of failure. On the other hand, liquid assets often offer lower rates of return than nonliquid assets.

### Operating Capability

**Operating capability refers to the ability of a company to maintain a given physical level of operations.** This level of operations may be indicated by the quantity of goods or services (e.g., inventory) of a specified quality produced in a given period or by the physical capacity of the fixed assets (e.g., property, plant, and equipment). Information about operating capability is helpful in understanding a company's past performance and in predicting future changes in its volume of activities. Operating capability may be affected by changes in methods of operations, changes in product lines, and by the timing of the replacement of the service potential used up in operations.[9]

## QUALITATIVE CHARACTERISTICS OF USEFUL ACCOUNTING INFORMATION

The previous sections discussed the types of information that are helpful in investment and credit decision making. But what are the characteristics of useful information? The purpose of *FASB Statement of Financial Accounting Concepts No. 2* was to specify the qualitative characteristics or "ingredients" that accounting information should possess in order to be most useful.[10] These characteristics should be consid-

---

9. "Reporting Income, Cash Flows, and Financial Position of Business Enterprises," *FASB Proposed Statement of Financial Accounting Concepts* (Stamford, Conn.: FASB, 1981), par. 7–33.

10. The discussion in this section primarily is a summary of that presented by the FASB in its "Qualitative Characteristics of Accounting Information," *FASB Statement of Financial Accounting Concepts No. 2* (Stamford, Conn.: FASB, 1980).

ered when choosing among accounting alternatives, because these qualities distinguish more useful from less useful information.

Each accounting alternative, however, may possess more of one quality and less of another. Although considerable agreement exists about the qualitative characteristics that "good" accounting information should possess, no mathematical "model" or "equation" can determine which information has the "best" combination of qualitative characteristics for decision-making purposes. Furthermore, the FASB strives to meet the needs of all users through *general-purpose* financial statements. This does not reduce the importance of using the qualitative characteristics to establish common accounting standards. The qualitative criteria are helpful to the FASB in establishing "minimum" and "maximum" limits of useful accounting information so that it can develop logical accounting standards consistent with these "limits."

## Hierarchy of Qualitative Characteristics

A hierarchy of the qualitative characteristics of accounting information is shown in Exhibit 2-5. This section presents an overview of the hierarchy, after which the components are defined and discussed in detail. The hierarchy is bounded by *two constraints:* (1) in order to justify providing the accounting information, **the benefits must be greater than the costs;** and (2) **the dollar amount of the information must be material** (i.e., large enough to make a difference in decision making). The hierarchy is not designed to assign priorities among the qualitative characteristics in all circumstances. To be useful, **accounting information must have each of the qualitative characteristics to a minimum degree.** However, different situations may require tradeoffs whereby the level of one quality is sacrificed for an increase in that of another quality.

## Understandability

Accounting information should be **understandable to users who have a reasonable knowledge of business and economic activities and who are willing to study the information with reasonable diligence.** *Understandability* serves as a "link" between the decision makers and the accounting information. Since the FASB establishes standards for general-purpose financial statements, it is concerned with the understandability of accounting information to *broad classes* of decision makers.

## Decision Usefulness

**Decision usefulness is the *overall* qualitative characteristic to be used in judging the quality of accounting information.** Whether or not information is useful depends on the decision to be made, the way in which it is made, the information already available, and the decision maker's ability to process the information. Since the FASB establishes standards for broad classes of users, however, it must consider the quality of decision usefulness in a broad context. For purposes of evaluation, this overall quality can be separated into the primary qualities of relevance and reliability.

## Relevance

**Relevant accounting information is information that can make a difference in a decision by helping users to form predictions about the outcomes of past, present, and future events or to confirm or correct prior expectations.** In this context, "event" is a happening that is significant to a company (e.g., purchase of a building), while

**EXHIBIT 2-5**

**A HIERARCHY OF QUALITATIVE CHARACTERISTICS OF ACCOUNTING INFORMATION**

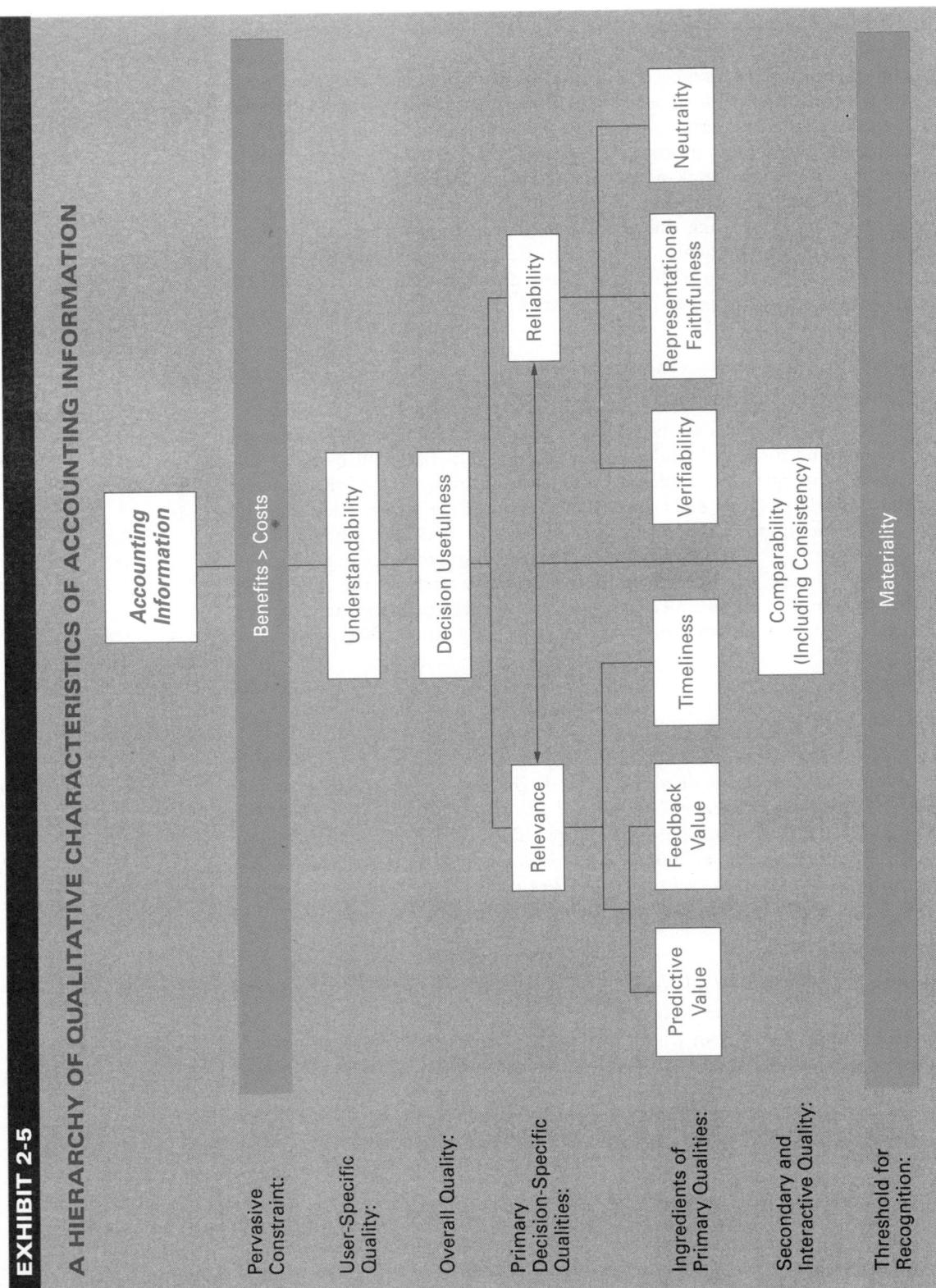

Pervasive Constraint:    Benefits > Costs

User-Specific Quality:    Understandability

Overall Quality:    Decision Usefulness

Primary Decision-Specific Qualities:    Relevance    Reliability

Ingredients of Primary Qualities:    Predictive Value    Feedback Value    Timeliness    Verifiability    Representational Faithfulness    Neutrality

Secondary and Interactive Quality:    Comparability (Including Consistency)

Threshold for Recognition:    Materiality

Accounting Information

Adapted from Figure 1 in "Qualitative Characteristics of Accounting Information," *FASB Statement of Financial Accounting Concepts No. 2* (Stamford, Conn.: FASB, 1980), p. 15.

"outcome" is the effect or result of an event or series of events (e.g., cash flows generated by use of the building). To be relevant, accounting information need not be expressed as a prediction. Information about the current status of a company's resources or obligations or about its past performance is commonly useful as a basis for expectations. To be relevant, accounting information should have either predictive or feedback value, or both. In addition, it should be timely.

### Predictive Value and Feedback Value

Accounting information has **predictive value** when it helps decision makers to forecast more accurately the outcome of past or present events. Accounting information has **feedback value** when it enables decision makers to confirm or correct prior expectations. Often, information has both predictive value and feedback value because knowledge about the previous actions of a company (i.e., feedback) will generally improve a decision maker's ability to predict the results of similar future actions. An example is an interim income statement, which provides feedback about past income to date and serves as a basis for forecasting the annual income.

### Timeliness

Accounting information is **timely** when it is available to decision makers before it loses its ability to influence decisions. Timeliness is an ingredient of relevance. If information is not available when it is needed, it lacks relevance and is of little or no use. Timeliness alone cannot make information relevant, but a lack of timeliness reduces its potential relevance. However, a gain in relevance resulting from increased timeliness may involve a sacrifice of other desirable qualitative characteristics (e.g., reliability). Timeliness has been defined by the SEC. The SEC requires that each company under its jurisdiction file a Form 10-K annual report within 90 days of its fiscal year-end and a Form 10-Q quarterly report within 45 days of the end of each quarter.

## Reliability

To be useful, accounting information must be reliable as well as relevant. **Reliable information is reasonably free from error and bias and faithfully represents what it is intended to represent.** That is, to be reliable, information must be verifiable, neutral, and possess representational faithfulness. Reliability does not necessarily imply certainty or precision. For instance, estimates may be reliable. Reliability has different degrees, and what is an acceptable degree of reliability will depend on the circumstances.

### Verifiability

Accounting information is **verifiable** (sometimes called **objective**) when measurers (i.e., accountants) can form a consensus (agree) that the selected method has been used without error or bias—that is, the measurement results can be duplicated. Verification is useful in reducing *measurer bias,* because by repeated measurements using the same method both unintentional and intentional errors are reduced.

Verification is a primary concern of auditing. The **Certified Public Accountant (CPA)** is an independent professional who reviews (audits) the published financial statements of a company. The performance of this duty is termed the **attest function.** It involves a review of the recording and reporting of a sample of the transactions for the company during the reporting period in order to provide assurance that the financial information shown can be substantially duplicated by an independent measurer. As a result of the review, the CPA issues an auditor's report. Verification does not, however, ensure the appropriateness of the accounting methods used. That quality of accounting information is representational faithfulness.

*Audit reports are discussed in Chapters 3 and 23.*

### *Representational Faithfulness*

Accounting information has **representational faithfulness** when there is a relationship between the reported accounting measurements or descriptions and the economic resources, obligations, and the transactions and events causing changes in these items. Social scientists define this concept as "validity." For instance, a company may record an item leased from another firm on a long-term basis as an economic resource even though it does not own the item. This recording increases the representational faithfulness of the reported economic resources available to the company. Having a high degree of representational faithfulness is useful in reducing *measurement bias*. Having representational faithfulness in one decision-making context, however, does not mean that accounting information will have validity for other decisions. For instance, the current cost would be important for an economic resource that a company expected to replace in the near future, but it might not be valid if there were no intention of replacing it.

### *Neutrality*

Accounting information is **neutral** when there is an absence of bias intended to attain a predetermined result or to influence behavior in a *particular* direction. Neutrality does not mean that accounting information has no purpose or does not influence human behavior. The purpose of providing accounting information is to serve a variety of different users with diverse interests. Furthermore, accounting information is intended to be useful in decision making, thereby influencing the decision makers' behavior but not in a predetermined direction. Neutrality also implies a *completeness* of information. An omission of information can lead to bias if it is intended to induce or inhibit a particular behavior.

## Comparability and Consistency

A secondary qualitative characteristic of accounting information is comparability (including consistency). Information about a company is more useful if it can be compared with similar information from other companies (this is referred to as *intercompany* comparison) or with similar information from past periods within the company (*intracompany* comparison). Comparability is not considered a primary quality of useful information like relevance and reliability because it must involve more than one item of information. It is an *interactive quality* of the relationship between two or more items of information. **Comparability of accounting information enables users to identify and explain similarities and differences between two (or more) sets of economic facts.**

Closely linked to comparability is consistency. **Consistency means conformity from period to period, with accounting policies and procedures remaining unchanged.** Consistency, like comparability, is a quality of the relationship between numbers rather than a quality of the numbers themselves. Consistency is an important condition to enhance comparability across periods. Without consistency, it would be difficult to determine whether differences in results were caused by economic differences or simply by differences in accounting methods. On the other hand, a change in accounting method is sometimes desirable. Economic situations may change, or new, more preferable accounting methods may evolve. Some sacrifice in consistency must be made at certain times in order to improve the usefulness of accounting information.

## Constraints to the Hierarchy

Two constraints to the hierarchy of qualitative characteristics help to identify further what accounting information should be disclosed in financial reports. The first is a benefit/cost constraint; the second is a threshold-for-recognition, or materiality, constraint.

### Benefits Greater Than Costs

Accounting information is a commodity. Unless the benefits expected to be received from a commodity exceed its costs, the commodity will not be sought after. The costs of providing financial information fall initially on the preparer and are then passed on to consumers. These costs include the cost of collecting, processing, auditing, and communicating the information as well as those associated with losing a competitive advantage by disclosing the information. The benefits are enjoyed by a diverse group of investors and creditors, by consumers (because they are assured a steady supply of goods and services), and by the preparer itself (for use in internal decision making). To be reported, accounting information must not only be relevant and reliable but it must also satisfy the benefit/cost constraint. That is, the FASB must have reasonable assurance that the costs of implementing a standard will not exceed the benefits.

### Materiality

The second constraint, that of materiality, is really a *quantitative* "threshold" constraint linked very closely to the qualitative characteristic of relevance. **Materiality refers to the magnitude of an omission or misstatement of accounting information that, considering the circumstances, makes it likely that the judgment of a reasonable person relying on the information would have been influenced by the omission or misstatement.** Materiality and relevance are both defined in terms of the influences that affect a decision maker, but the two terms can be distinguished. A decision to disclose certain information may be made because users have a need for that information (it is relevant) *and* because the amount is large enough to make a difference (it is material). Alternatively, a decision not to disclose certain information may be made because the user has no need for the information (it is not relevant) *or* because the amount is too small to make a difference (it is not material).

The FASB did not set overall quantitative guidelines for materiality in the *Statements of Concepts.* It felt that materiality involves judgment, and that no general standards could be set that took into account all the elements of sound human judgment. Materiality judgments should be concerned with thresholds of recognition. Is an item large enough to pass over the threshold that separates material from immaterial items? To answer that question, the FASB suggested that consideration should be given to (1) the *nature* of the item (i.e., items considered too small to be significant when they result from routine transactions might be material if they arose from abnormal circumstances) and (2) the *relative size* rather than absolute size of an item (i.e., a $10,000 error in inventory of a large company may be insignificant while a similar $10,000 error by a small company may be material). The FASB observed that quantitative guidelines have been and will continue to be set for specific accounting issues where appropriate.[11]

---

11. The Auditing Standards Board has addressed the issue of materiality, but has not set general quantitative guidelines. See "Audit Risk and Materiality in Conducting an Audit," *Codification of Statements on Auditing Standards* (New York: AICPA, 1992), sec. 312.

## ACCOUNTING ASSUMPTIONS AND CONVENTIONS

To this point we have identified the objectives of financial reporting, the types of useful information for investment and credit decision making, and the qualitative characteristics of useful accounting information. Consideration of these factors is necessary for the establishment of accounting standards. In addition, certain accounting assumptions and conventions have had an important impact upon the development of generally accepted accounting principles. Exhibit 2-6 is useful in understanding the relationship among the objectives, types of useful information, qualitative characteristics, accounting assumptions and conventions, generally accepted accounting principles, financial reports, and elements of financial statements. The accounting assumptions and conventions listed in Exhibit 2-6 are discussed in this section. Others will be discussed later in the book as they apply to specific accounting standards.

### Entity

The majority of the economic activity in the United States can be directly or indirectly attributed to business enterprises termed **economic entities.** These entities vary in size from small, one-owner companies such as hair salons or restaurants, to partnerships such as law or accounting firms, and to large multinational corporations such as the Exxon Corporation. Financial accounting is concerned with the economic activity of each of these entities, regardless of its size, and involves recording and reporting its transactions and events. A transaction involves the transfer of something of value between the entity and another party. In certain instances the financial records of related but separate legal entities may be *consolidated* (combined) to report more realistically the resources, obligations, and operating results of the overall economic entity.

Because the entity assumption distinguishes each organization from its owners, financial records and reports are prepared for each separate entity. The personal transactions of the owners are kept separate from those of the business enterprise. Throughout this book we refer to a business enterprise as a *company* (and when the discussion applies to a type of company, we use the specific type of entity, e.g., *corporation*).

### Continuity

The **continuity assumption** is also known as the **going-concern assumption.** This assumption is that the company will continue to operate in the near future, unless substantial evidence to the contrary exists. Obviously not all companies are successful, and failures do occur. However, the continuity assumption is valid in the majority of cases and is necessary for many of the accounting procedures used. For example, if the company is not regarded as a going concern, fixed assets should not be depreciated over their expected useful lives or inventory should not be recorded at its cost, because the receipt of future economic benefits from these items is uncertain.

Nevertheless, the continuity assumption does not imply permanence. It simply indicates that the economic entity will operate long enough to carry out its existing commitments. If a company appears to be on the verge of going bankrupt, the continuity assumption must be discarded. The company's financial statements should be reported on a liquidation basis with all assets and liabilities valued at the amounts estimated to be collected or paid when they are sold or liquidated.

## EXHIBIT 2-6

# FRAMEWORK OF FINANCIAL ACCOUNTING THEORY AND PRACTICE

| Framework | Content |
|---|---|
| Objectives | 1. Provide information useful to external users in assessing amounts, timing, and uncertainty of a company's cash flows.<br>2. Provide information about a company's economic resources, obligations, and owners' equity.<br>3. Provide information about a company's earnings and its components.<br>4. Provide information about a company's cash flows.<br>5. Provide information about the stewardship responsibility of a company's management.<br>6. Provide full disclosure to help external users understand the preceding information. |
| Types of Useful Information | 1. Return on investment.<br>2. Risk.<br>3. Financial flexibility.<br>4. Liquidity.<br>5. Operating capability. |
| Qualitative Characteristics of Useful Accounting Information | 1. Decision usefulness.<br>2. Relevance (predictive value, feedback value, timeliness).<br>3. Reliability (verifiability, neutrality, and representational faithfulness).<br>4. Comparability (including consistency).<br>5. Benefits greater than costs, materiality. |
| Accounting Assumptions and Conventions | 1. Entity.<br>2. Continuity (going concern).<br>3. Period of time.<br>4. Historical cost.<br>5. Monetary unit.<br>6. Realization and recognition.<br>7. Matching and accrual.<br>8. Conservatism (prudence). |
| Generally Accepted Accounting Principles | 1. Guidelines, procedures, and practices required by a company to record and report its accounting information in audited financial statements.<br>2. Sources of GAAP are financial accounting standards established in pronouncements of FASB, APB, AICPA, and SEC, and other accounting literature (see Exhibit 1-4). |
| Financial Reports | 1. Balance sheet.<br>2. Income statement.<br>3. Statement of cash flows.<br>4. Supplementary schedules (e.g., statement of changes in stockholders' equity).<br>5. Notes to financial statements.<br>6. Supplementary and other information. |
| Elements of Financial Statements | 1. Assets, liabilities, and equity.<br>2. Revenues, expenses, gains, and losses.<br>3. Operating, investing, and financing cash flows.<br>4. Investments by and distributions to owners. |

## Period of Time

The profit or loss earned by a company cannot be determined accurately, unless it ceases to function. At that time the total lifetime profit or loss may be determined by comparing the cash on hand after liquidating the business plus any cash distributions to the owners during the period of operations with the amount invested by the owners during the company's lifetime. Obviously, financial statement users need more current information to evaluate a company's profitability. Accountants have primarily adopted the year as the reporting period. In accordance with the **period-of-time assumption**, financial statements are prepared at the end of each year and disclosed in a company's annual report. Furthermore the annual reporting period (called the **accounting period** or **fiscal year**) is used for reports issued to government regulators such as the Internal Revenue Service (IRS) and the Securities and Exchange Commission (SEC).

The period-of-time assumption is the basis for the adjusting entry process in accounting (reviewed in Appendix C at the end of this book), because if financial statements were not prepared on a yearly (or shorter time) basis, there would be no reason to determine the time frame affected by particular business transactions. Historically the calendar year was adopted as the accounting period for most companies. However, many companies are now choosing a fiscal year that more closely approximates the company's annual *business cycle*. (The yearly period from lowest sales through highest sales and back to lowest sales is known as a business cycle.) For example, consider Exhibit 2-7, which illustrates the annual sales pattern for Company G. Notice that peak sales occur each year in January, while the lowest sales volume occurs in June. Such a sales pattern might be representative of a company that sells ski equipment. If Company G were to report on a calendar-year basis, the financial reports would be prepared at about the time of peak yearly sales (i.e., the midpoint of the

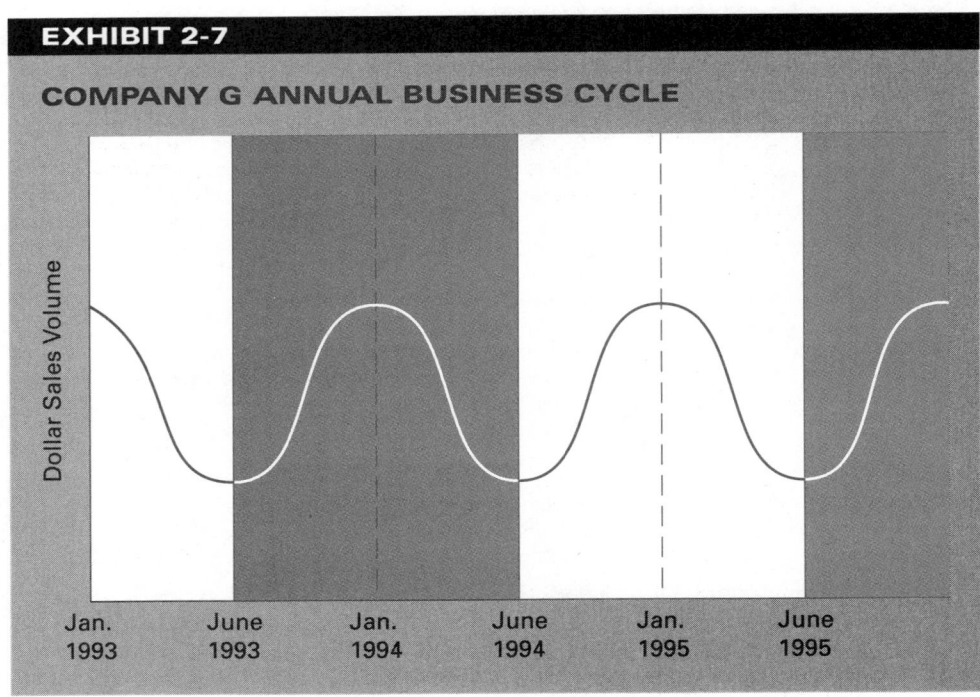

**EXHIBIT 2-7**

**COMPANY G ANNUAL BUSINESS CYCLE**

Dollar Sales Volume

| Jan. 1993 | June 1993 | Jan. 1994 | June 1994 | Jan. 1995 | June 1995 |

business cycle). Alternatively, a fiscal year that ended on June 30 would incorporate a single complete annual business cycle. Fiscal-year reports incorporating an annual business cycle contain information that is more easily comparable to past and future periods because annual sales patterns are not broken by the reporting period.

In addition to annual reports, publicly-traded companies issue financial statements for interim periods. These interim reports are considered integral parts of the annual periods, but they essentially disclose summary information to provide investors with more timely information.

## Historical Cost

The economic activities and resources of a company initially are measured by the exchange price of a transaction at the time the transaction occurs. Usually the exchange price (the **historical cost**) is retained in the accounting records as the value of an item until the item is consumed, sold, or liquidated and removed from the records. That is, recognition of gains and losses resulting from value changes of assets (or liabilities) usually are delayed until another exchange has taken place. The rationale behind the use of historical cost (as opposed to other valuation methods such as current market value or appraisal value) is that it is reliable, and that source documents usually are available to substantiate the recorded amount. Also, historical cost provides evidence that an independent buyer and seller were in agreement on the value of an exchanged good or service at the time of the transaction and thus has the qualities of representational faithfulness, neutrality, and verifiability.

One of the most frequently heard criticisms of accounting comes from those who would prefer alternative valuation methods that they believe would disclose information more relevant for user decisions. Accountants do recognize that historical cost information may not always be completely *relevant* for all decisions, but it does have a significant degree of *reliability*. In certain cases accountants use valuation methods other than historical cost in the financial statements, when these methods provide more relevant information which possesses an acceptable degree of reliability. Generally, however, it is felt that the measurement problems inherent in alternative valuation methods are greater than those of historical cost. That is, when in doubt, reliability generally takes precedence over relevance. The FASB, however, has recognized the significance of this relevance/reliability tradeoff by encouraging companies to disclose *supplemental* current value information in their annual reports.

*Supplemental current value information is discussed in Chapter 24.*

## Monetary Unit

Since the time when gold and other precious metals were accepted in exchange for goods and services, thereby replacing the barter system, there has been a unit of exchange. This unit of exchange is different for almost every nation, but accountants generally have adopted the national currency of the reporting company as the unit of measure in preparing financial reports.

In using the dollar or any other currency as the unit of measure, accountants have traditionally assumed that it is a stable measuring unit. Prior to the FASB, accounting policy-making bodies had taken the position that fluctuations in the value of the dollar were not a serious enough problem to have an adverse effect upon the comparability of accounting information and thus did not warrant any adjustment in the monetary unit assumption.

In today's world the assumption that the dollar or any other national currency is a stable measure over time is not necessarily valid. Consider the building you are now in. If you were to measure its width in feet and inches today, next year, and five years from now, an accurate physical measurement would undoubtedly yield the same results each time. In contrast, consider the monetary value of the same building. Real estate prices have changed (increased or decreased) during the past several years and will undoubtedly continue to vary, thereby reflecting changing monetary measures of value even though the physical capacity remains the same.

There are two primary reasons for the changes in reported values over time:

1. The real value of the item in question may change in relation to the real value of all other goods and services in the economy.

2. The purchasing power of the measuring unit (in this case the dollar) may change.

Although currently the dollar is considered to be a stable monetary unit for preparing a company's financial statements, as mentioned earlier, to enhance comparability the FASB now encourages companies to make supplemental disclosures relating to the impacts of changing prices.

## Realization and Recognition

*Recognition criteria are discussed in Chapters 3 and 4.*

**Realization** means the process of converting noncash resources and rights into cash or rights to cash. **Recognition** means the process of formally recording and reporting an item in the financial statements of a company. A recognized item is depicted in both words and numbers, with the amount included in the financial statement totals. The FASB has identified four fundamental recognition criteria. To be recognized, an item must: (1) meet the definition of an element, (2) be measurable, (3) be relevant, and (4) be reliable. In regard to revenues, two other factors provide guidance for revenue recognition. Revenues should be recognized when: (1) realization has taken place, and (2) they have been earned. These factors provide an acceptable level of assurance of the existence and amounts of revenues. It is an accounting convention to recognize revenue at the time of sale because this is usually when realization occurs (i.e., cash or receivables are obtained) and the earning process is substantially complete. Actually, revenue is earned by a company throughout the *earning process* as economic utility is added to goods. This process includes acquisition, production and/or distribution, sales, and the collection and payment of cash. Revenue could be recognized at one or more points in this process. In this regard, the FASB suggests that revenues are considered to be earned when a company has substantially completed what it must do to be entitled to the benefits (e.g., assets) generated by the revenues. Usually, this is the point of sale.[12]

*Revenue recognition is discussed in Chapters 4 and 16.*

Occasionally the recognition of revenue may be advanced (accrued) or delayed (deferred) in the earning process in order to reflect more accurately the nature of a company's operations. Thus, revenue may not be recognized (recorded) at the same time as realization. Revenue might be recognized (1) during production, (2) at the end of production, or (3) after the sale. In the case of certain long-term construction contracts extending over more than one accounting period, revenue might be recognized

---

12. "Recognition and Measurement in Financial Statements of Business Enterprises," *FASB Statement of Financial Accounting Concepts No. 5* (Stamford, Conn.: FASB, 1984), par. 63 and 83.

during production to better depict economic reality by the use of the **percentage-of-completion** method. Similarly, revenue might be recognized for certain long-term service contracts by use of the **proportional performance** method. These methods allocate the revenues of each contract to each period based on an estimate of the percentage completed during the period. Revenue might be recognized at the completion of production when a fixed selling price has been established and there is no limit on the amount that can be sold. This situation might be the case for certain valuable minerals or for farm products sold on the futures market. Finally, revenue might be recognized after the sale because the ultimate collectibility of the revenue is highly uncertain. This situation might arise, for instance, in the case of real estate land sales where a very small down payment is required and the payment terms extend over many years. In situations of high uncertainty about collections, either the installment or the cost-recovery method might be used to recognize revenue. Under the **installment** method, a portion of each receipt is recognized as revenue. Under the **cost-recovery** method, no revenue is recognized until the cost of the product has been recovered.

## Matching and Accrual Accounting

Earlier, **accrual accounting** was defined as the process of relating the financial effects of transactions, events, and circumstances having cash consequences to the period in which they occur rather than when the cash receipt or payment occurs. The **matching** principle is closely linked to accrual accounting and to revenue recognition. The matching principle states that to determine the income of a company for an accounting period, the total expenses involved in obtaining the revenues of the period must be computed and related to (matched against) the revenues recorded in the period. Thus, expenses may be advanced (accrued) or delayed (deferred) in a manner similar to revenues. The intent is to match the sacrifices against the benefits (i.e., the efforts against the accomplishments) in the appropriate accounting period.

Expenses are recognized and matched against revenues on the basis of three principles: (1) association of cause and effect, (2) systematic and rational allocation, and (3) immediate recognition. Expenses recorded as a result of associating cause and effect include sales commissions and the **product costs** included in cost of goods sold. Expenses recorded on the basis of systematic and rational allocation include depreciation of property and equipment and amortization of intangibles. Immediate recognition is appropriate for **period costs**—those expenses related to a period of time, such as administrative salaries.[13]

*Expense and loss recognition are discussed in Chapter 4.*

Some companies, particularly smaller companies, do not use accrual accounting and matching. Instead they use **cash basis** accounting for simplicity. In cash basis accounting, the income of a company for an accounting period is computed by subtracting the cash payments from the cash receipts for operations. While this method may be convenient to use, it may also lead to incorrect evaluations of a company's operating results because the receipt and payment of cash may occur much earlier or later than the sale of goods or the providing of services to customers (benefits) and the related costs (sacrifices). Because cash basis accounting does not attempt to match expenses against revenues, it is not in conformity with generally accepted accounting principles.

---

13. "Elements of Financial Statements," *FASB Statement of Financial Accounting Concepts No. 6* (Stamford, Conn.: FASB, 1985), par. 146–149.

## Conservatism

The convention of **conservatism** states, in effect, that when alternative accounting valuations are equally possible, the accountant should select the one that is least likely to overstate assets and income. Over the years conservatism gained prominence because of the optimism of management and the tendency, during the first three decades of the twentieth century, to overstate assets and net income on financial statements. Recently, conservatism has been criticized for being "anticonservative" in the years following the conservative act. That is, a deliberate understatement of an asset with a corresponding loss and understatement of income in one year will result in an overstatement of income in a later year when the asset is sold because of the greater difference between the selling price and recorded value of the asset. Furthermore, conservatism can conflict with the qualitative characteristics such as neutrality. For instance, conservative financial statements may be unfair to present stockholders and biased in favor of prospective stockholders because the net valuation of the company does not include all future expectations. This factor may be reflected in a relatively lower current market price of the company's common stock. These criticisms notwithstanding, conservatism has played an important role in the establishment of certain generally accepted accounting principles.

The FASB has attempted to modify the convention of conservatism so that it is more synonymous with **prudence.** That is, conservatism should be a prudent reaction to uncertainty so as to ensure, to the extent possible, that the uncertainties and risks inherent in business situations are adequately considered. These uncertainties and risks should be reflected in accounting information so as to improve its predictive value and neutrality. Prudent reporting based on a healthy skepticism promotes integrity and best serves the various users of financial reports.[14]

## GAAP AND FINANCIAL STATEMENTS

As we noted in Chapter 1, generally accepted accounting principles (GAAP) are the guidelines, procedures, and practices that a company is required to use in recording and reporting its accounting information in its audited financial statements. In its *Conceptual Framework,* the FASB has identified various "financial reports" from which investors, creditors, and other users might obtain information useful in decision making. These sources of information are shown in Exhibit 2-8.

Although conceptually the FASB identified the four specific financial statements listed in Exhibit 2-8, in practice most companies prepare three primary financial statements: (1) the balance sheet (statement of financial position), (2) the income statement, and (3) the statement of cash flows. They also prepare a schedule (statement) of changes in equity. This schedule may be included as a separate financial statement or in a note to the financial statements. This section discusses briefly these financial statements and the elements of the financial statements. **The elements of each financial statement are the broad classes of items comprising it.** In other words, they are the "building blocks" with which each financial statement is prepared.[15] The financial statements and their elements are discussed in more depth in later chapters.

---

14. *FASB Statement of Financial Accounting Concepts No. 2, op. cit.,* par. 95–97.
15. The discussion in this section primarily is a summary of that presented by the FASB in its "Elements of Financial Statements of Business Enterprises," *FASB Statement of Financial Accounting Concept No. 6* (Stamford, Conn.: FASB, 1985) and "Statement of Cash Flows," *FASB Statement of Financial Accounting Standards No. 95* (Stamford, Conn.: FASB, 1987).

**EXHIBIT 2-8**

## SOURCES OF INFORMATION USED IN EXTERNAL DECISION MAKING

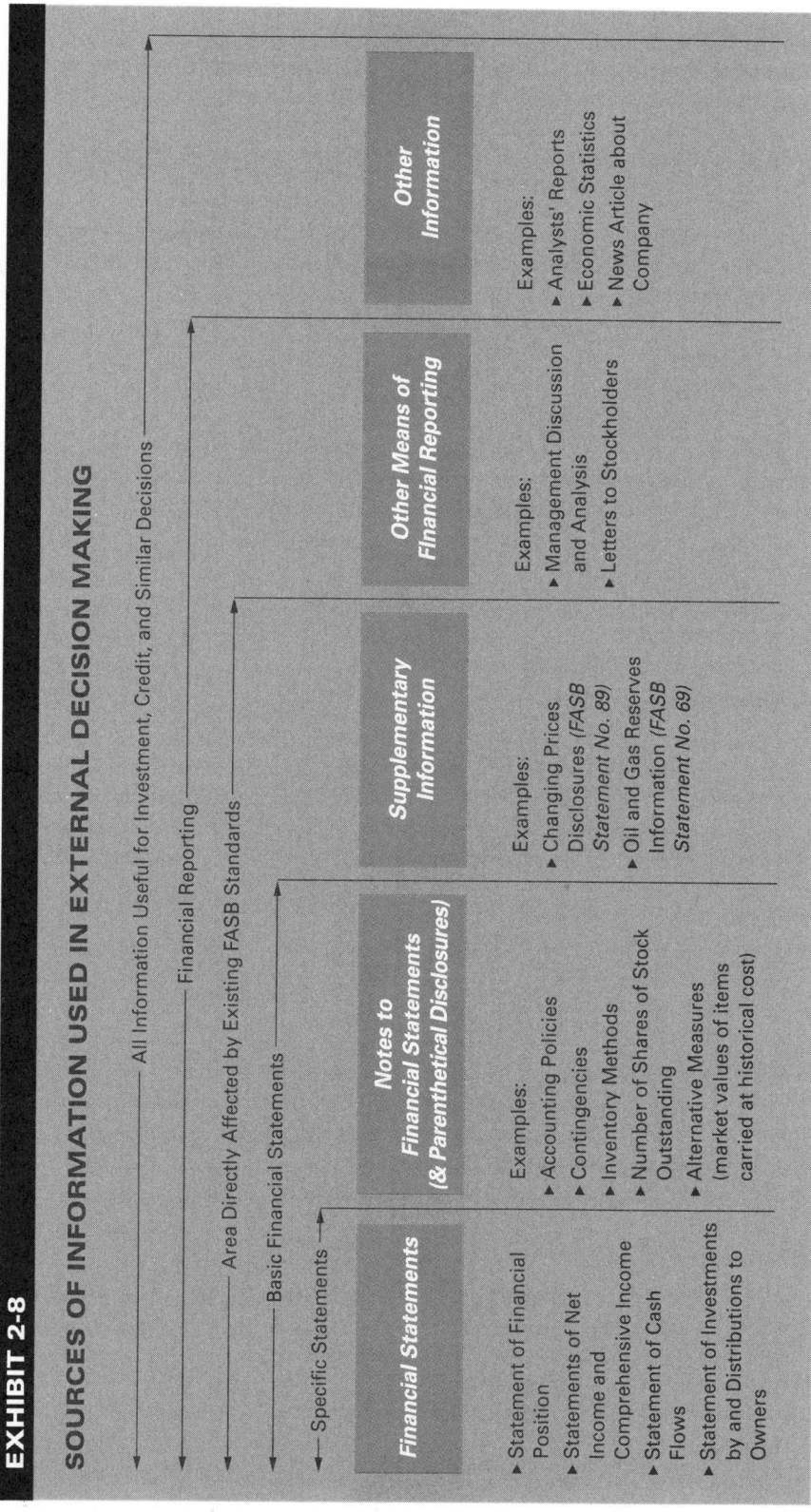

Adapted from diagram in "Recognition and Measurement in Financial Statements of Business Enterprises," *FASB Statement of Financial Accounting Concepts No. 5* (Stamford, Conn.: FASB, 1985), p. 5.

## Balance Sheet

A **balance sheet** (or statement of financial position) is a financial statement that summarizes the financial position of a company on a particular date (usually the end of the accounting period). The financial position of a company includes its economic resources, economic obligations, equity, and their relationships to each other. There are three elements of a balance sheet:

1. **Assets:**      Assets are the probable future economic benefits obtained and controlled by a company as a result of past transactions or events.

2. **Liabilities:**      Liabilities are the probable future sacrifices of economic benefits arising from present obligations of a company to transfer assets or provide services in the future as a result of past transactions or events.

3. **Equity:**      Equity is the owners' residual interest in the assets of a company that remains after deducting its obligations.

In other words, the assets of a company are its economic resources and the liabilities are its economic obligations. The equity of a corporation is referred to as stockholders' equity because the owners are the stockholders.

## Income Statement

An **income statement** is a financial statement that summarizes the results of a company's operations (i.e., net income) for a period of time (generally a one-year accounting period). A company's operations (sometimes called the earning process) include its purchasing, producing, selling, delivering, servicing, and administrating activities. There are four elements of an income statement:

1. **Revenues:**      Revenues are inflows or other enhancements of assets of a company or settlement of its liabilities (or a combination of both) during a period from delivering or producing goods, rendering services, or other activities that constitute the company's ongoing major or central operations.

2. **Expenses:**      Expenses are outflows or other using up of assets of a company or incurrences of liabilities (or a combination of both) during a period from delivering or producing goods, rendering services, or carrying out other activities that constitute the company's ongoing major or central operations.

3. **Gains:**      Gains are increases in equity from peripheral or incidental transactions of a company and from all other transactions and other events and circumstances affecting the company during a period except those that result from revenues or investments by owners.

4. **Losses:**      Losses are decreases in equity from peripheral or incidental transactions of a company and from all other transactions and other events and circumstances affecting the company during a period except those that result from expenses or distributions to owners.

Revenues may be thought of as measures of the accomplishments of a company during its accounting period, while expenses are measures of the efforts to achieve the revenues. Gains are similar to revenues and losses are similar to expenses, except that revenues and expenses relate to a company's primary operations while gains and losses relate to its secondary activities.

## Statement of Cash Flows

A **statement of cash flows** is a financial statement that summarizes the cash inflows and outflows of a company for a period of time (generally one year). There are three elements of a statement of cash flows:

1. **Operating Cash Flows:** Operating cash flows are the inflows and outflows of cash from transactions involving acquiring, selling, and delivering goods for sale, as well as providing services.

2. **Investing Cash Flows:** Investing cash flows are the inflows and outflows of cash from transactions involving lending money and collecting on loans, and acquiring and selling assets.

3. **Financing Cash Flows:** Financing cash flows are the inflows and outflows of cash from transactions involving obtaining resources from owners and providing them with a return on, and of, their investment, as well as obtaining and repaying resources from creditors.

In addition to these three elements, the statement of cash flows also reconciles the amount of cash a company reports on its balance sheets at the beginning and end of the accounting period.

## Statement of Changes in Equity

A **statement of changes in equity** summarizes the changes in a company's equity for a period of time (generally one year). For a corporation, the statement is called the statement of changes in stockholders' equity. There are two elements in a statement of changes in equity:

1. **Investments by Owners:** Investments by owners are increases in equity of a company resulting from transfers of something valuable to the company from other companies in order to obtain or increase ownership interests.

2. **Distributions to Owners:** Distributions to owners are decreases in equity of a company caused by transferring assets, rendering services, or incurring liabilities to owners.

In addition to these elements, the statement of changes in equity also reconciles the amounts of the equity items a company reports on its beginning and ending balance sheets for such items as net income and dividends.

## Overview

The financial statements and their elements are discussed in depth in the later chapters of this book. In addition, supplementary schedules and notes to the financial statements are discussed, along with various recognition and measurement issues. As you read the discussions, it may be helpful for you to place them in the context of the *FASB Conceptual Framework* as summarized in Exhibit 2-6. If you feel that it would be helpful to review the recording and reporting procedures that comprise an accounting system, please refer to Appendix C at the end of this book.

## QUESTIONS

*Q2-1* What is the "conceptual framework" of the FASB? What are the titles of the "Statements of Concepts" issued by the FASB?

*Q2-2* What is the most general objective of financial reporting? Who are investors and creditors?

*Q2-3* What is the "derived external user objective" and why is it important?

*Q2-4* What is the "derived company objective" and what are the types of information about a company that should be reported to satisfy this objective?

*Q2-5* List the reasons why external users use information about a company's (a) economic resources and claims to these resources, (b) comprehensive income and its components, and (c) funds (cash) flows.

*Q2-6* Define (a) return on investment, (b) risk, (c) financial flexibility, (d) liquidity, and (e) operating capability.

*Q2-7* What is the overall qualitative characteristic of useful accounting information and what are its two primary qualities?

*Q2-8* What is relevant accounting information? Identify and define the ingredients of relevant accounting information.

*Q2-9* What is reliable accounting information? Identify and define the ingredients of reliable accounting information.

*Q2-10* Identify the secondary quality of useful accounting information. Why is this important and how does it relate to consistency?

*Q2-11* What is materiality and how does it relate to relevance?

*Q2-12* What is the continuity assumption and why is it important in financial accounting?

*Q2-13* What is the period-of-time assumption and why is it important in financial accounting?

*Q2-14* Discuss the relationship between historical cost and reliability.

*Q2-15* What is realization? What is recognition? What two factors provide guidance for revenue recognition? Why is revenue usually recognized at the time of sale?

*Q2-16* What is accrual accounting and how does it relate to the matching principle?

*Q2-17* List the three principles for matching expenses against revenues.

*Q2-18* What is conservatism and how might it conflict with neutrality?

*Q2-19* Define a balance sheet and list its three elements.

*Q2-20* Define an income statement and list its four elements.

*Q2-21* Define a statement of cash flows and list its three elements.

*Q2-22* Define a statement of changes in equity and list its two elements.

# CASES

## C2-1 Qualitative Characteristics

In *FASB Statement of Concepts No. 2,* several qualitative characteristics of useful accounting information were identified. The following is a list of these qualities as well as a list of statements describing the qualities.

A. Comparability    H. Verifiability
B. Decision usefulness    I. Neutrality
C. Relevance    J. Representational
D. Reliability          faithfulness
E. Predictive value    K. Consistency
F. Feedback value    L. Materiality
G. Timeliness

_____ 1. Ability of measurers to form a consensus that the selected accounting method has been used without error or bias.

_____ 2. Having information available to decision makers before it loses its capacity to influence decisions.

_____ 3. Capacity to make a difference in a decision.

_____ 4. Overall qualitative characteristic.

_____ 5. Absence of bias intended to influence behavior in a particular direction.

_____ 6. Reasonably free from error and bias.

_____ 7. Helps decision makers to correctly forecast.

_____ 8. Validity.

_____ 9. Interactive quality; helps identify and explain similarities and differences.

_____ 10. Quantitative "threshold" constraint.

_____ 11. Conformity from period to period.

_____ 12. Helps decision makers to confirm or correct prior expectations.

**Required**
Place the appropriate letter identifying each quality on the line in front of the statement describing the quality.

## C2-2 Accounting Assumptions and Conventions

Certain accounting assumptions and conventions have had an important impact on the development of generally accepted accounting principles. The following is a list of these assumptions and conventions as well as a list of statements describing certain accounting practices.

A. Entity          E. Monetary unit
B. Continuity       F. Realization
C. Period of time    G. Matching
D. Historical cost    H. Conservatism

_____ 1. The business, rather than its owners, is the reporting unit.

_____ 2. Depreciation costs are expensed in the periods of use rather than at the time of the acquisition of the asset.

_____ 3. Accounting measurements are reported in dollars.

_____ 4. The year is the normal reporting unit.

_____ 5. In the absence of evidence to the contrary, the business will operate long enough to carry out its existing commitments.

_____ 6. Revenue is usually recognized at the time of sale.

_____ 7. Exchange price is retained in the accounting records.

_____ 8. An accounting alternative is selected that is least likely to overstate assets and income.

**Required**
Select the accounting assumption or convention that justifies each accounting practice and place the appropriate letter on the line preceding the statement.

## C2-3 Objectives of Financial Reporting

The FASB has identified several objectives of financial reporting. These objectives proceed from the more general to the more specific and are intended to act as guidelines for providing accounting information in financial reports.

**Required**
Starting with the most general objective, identify and briefly discuss the objectives of financial reporting.

## C2-4 Qualities of Useful Accounting Information

A friend of yours, who is not an accounting major, is concerned about the "usefulness" of accounting information. She states: "I have watched you prepare many financial statements in completing your homework assignments. But how do you determine whether the information in these financial statements is useful? What are the characteristics or qualities of useful accounting information?"

**Required**
Prepare a written response for your friend that identifies and discusses the qualitative characteristics of useful accounting information.

## C2-5 Relevance Versus Reliability

You are listening to two accounting majors, both of whom are seniors. They are debating the merits of having relevant versus reliable accounting information for external decision making. One student states: "In my decision making, if given a choice between relevant and reliable accounting information, I would prefer to have relevant information." The other student replies: "Nonsense! If you cannot rely on the information, then of what use is it?"

**Required**
Based on your knowledge of the FASB's conceptual framework, define the qualitative characteristics of relevance

and reliability. Include definitions of the ingredients of each. Which do you think is more important?

## C2-6  Inconsistent Statements on Accounting Principles

The following two statements have been taken directly or with some modification from the accounting literature. Each of them is either taken out of context, involves circular reasoning, and/or contains one of more fallacies, half-truths, erroneous comments, conclusions, or inconsistencies (internally or with generally accepted principles or practices).

### Statement 1

Accounting is a service activity. Its function is to provide quantitative financial information that is intended to be useful in making economic decisions about and for economic entities. Thus the accounting function might be viewed primarily as being a tool or device for providing quantitative financial information to management to facilitate decision making.

### Statement 2

Financial statements that were developed in accordance with generally accepted accounting principles, which apply the conservatism convention, can be free from bias (or can give a presentation that is fair with respect to continuing and prospective stockholders as well as to retiring stockholders).

### Required

Evaluate each of the preceding numbered statements as follows:

1. List the fallacies, half-truths, circular reasoning, erroneous comments or conclusions, and/or inconsistencies.
2. Explain by what authority and/or on what basis each item listed in (1) can be considered to be fallacious, circular, inconsistent, a half-truth, or an erroneous comment or conclusion. If the statement or a portion of it is merely out of context, indicate the context(s) in which the statement would be correct. *(AICPA adapted)*

## C2-7  Accounting Entity

The concept of the accounting entity often is considered to be the most fundamental of accounting concepts, one that pervades all of accounting.

### Required

1. a. What is an accounting entity? Explain.
   b. Explain why the accounting entity concept is so fundamental that it pervades all of accounting.
2. For each of the following indicate whether the accounting concept of entity is applicable; discuss and give illustrations.
   a. A unit created by or under law
   b. The product-line segment of an enterprise

c. A combination of legal units and/or product-line segments
d. All of the activities of an owner or a group of owners
e. An industry
f. The economy of the United States *(AICPA adapted)*

## C2-8  Timing of Revenue Recognition

Revenue is usually recognized at the point of sale. Under special circumstances, however, bases other than the point of sale are used for the timing of revenue recognition.

### Required

1. Why is the point of sale usually used as the basis for the timing of revenue recognition?
2. Disregarding the special circumstances when bases other than the point of sale are used, discuss the merits of each of the following objections to the sales basis of revenue recognition:
   a. It is too conservative because revenue is earned throughout the entire process of production.
   b. It is not conservative enough because accounts receivable do not represent disposable funds; sales returns and allowances may be made; and collection and bad debt expenses may be incurred in a later period.
3. Revenue may also be recognized (a) during production and (b) when cash is received. For each of these two bases of timing revenue recognition, give an example of the circumstances in which it is properly used and discuss the accounting merits of its use in lieu of the sales basis. *(AICPA adapted)*

## C2-9  Cost and Expense Recognition

An accountant must be familiar with the concepts involved in determining earnings of a company. The amount of earnings reported for a company is dependent on the proper recognition, in general, of revenue and expense for a given time period. In some situations costs are recognized as expenses at the time of product sale; in other situations guidelines have been developed for recognizing costs as expenses or losses by other criteria.

### Required

1. Explain the rationale for recognizing costs as expenses at the time of product sale.
2. What is the rationale underlying the appropriateness of treating costs as expenses of a period instead of assigning the costs to an asset? Explain.
3. Some expenses are assigned to specific accounting periods on the basis of systematic and rational allocation of asset cost. Explain the underlying rationale for recognizing expenses on this basis. *(AICPA adapted)*

## C2-10  Accruals and Deferrals

Generally accepted accounting principles require the use of accruals and deferrals in the determination of income.

**Required**

1. How does accrual accounting affect the determination of income? Include in your discussion what constitutes an accrual and a deferral, and give appropriate examples of each.
2. Contrast accrual accounting with cash accounting. (AICPA adapted)

## C2-11 Revenue Recognition

The following are brief descriptions of several companies in different lines of business.

A. Company A is a construction company. It has recently signed a contract to build a highway over a 3-year period. A down payment was collected; the remaining collections will occur periodically over the construction period based upon the degree of completion.
B. Company B is a retailer. It makes sales for cash and on credit cards on a daily basis.
C. Company C is a health spa. It has recently signed contracts with numerous individuals to use its facilities over a 2-year period. The contract price was collected in advance.
D. Company D is a land development company. It has recently begun developing a "retirement community" and has sold lots to senior citizens. The sales contract required a small down payment and periodic payments until completion of the roads and a clubhouse, after which the remainder of the purchase price is due. Prior to this point, a purchaser may cancel the contract and receive a refund of all payments.

**Required**

Describe when revenue should be recognized by each company. If revenue should not be recognized at the time of sale, indicate what method should be used to recognize the revenue. Justify your decision.

## C2-12 Violations of Assumptions and Conventions

The following are accounting procedures and practices used by several companies.

A. As soon as it purchases inventory, Sokolich Company records the purchase price as cost of goods sold to simplify its accounting procedures.
B. At the end of each year Sloan Company records and reports its economic resources based on appraisal values.
C. Ebert Company prepares financial statements only every two years to reduce its costs of preparing the statements.
D. Guthrie Company sells on account and records revenue at that time, even though it knows that collection is highly uncertain and very significant efforts have to be made to collect the accounts.
E. Because of inflation, Cross Company adjusts its financial statements each year to show the current purchasing power for all items.

F. David Thomas combines his personal transactions and business transactions when he prepares his company's financial statements so that he can tell how well he is doing on an "overall" basis.
G. At the end of each year Vann Company reports its economic resources on a liquidation basis even though it is likely to operate in the future.

**Required**

Identify what accounting assumption, principle, or convention each procedure or practice violates, and indicate what should be done to rectify the violation.

## C2-13 Characteristics of Useful Information

Financial accounting and reporting provide information that is used in decision making regarding the allocation of resources. In **Statement of Financial Accounting Concepts No. 1,** "Objectives of Financial Reporting by Business Enterprises," the Financial Accounting Standards Board (FASB) defined the following basic objectives of financial reporting.

Financial reporting should provide understandable information to present and potential users:

> That is useful in making rational decisions.
> That facilitates assessing the amounts, timing, and uncertainty related to the company's cash flows.
> About the company's economic resources, its claims to those resources, and the changes in its resources and obligations occurring from earnings and other operating activities.

The qualitative characteristics of useful accounting information were identified in the FASB's **Statement of Financial Accounting Concepts No. 2,** "Qualitative Characteristics of Accounting Information." These characteristics distinguish better information (more useful) from inferior information (less useful).

**Required**

1. For the primary quality relevance,
   a. define relevance
   b. explain the meaning and importance of each of the three ingredients of relevance
2. For the primary quality reliability,
   a. define reliability
   b. explain the meaning and importance of each of the three ingredients of reliability
3. Explain the concepts of
   a. comparability
   b. consistency
   c. materiality (CMA adapted)

## C2-14 Conceptual Framework

The Financial Accounting Standards Board (FASB) has been working on a conceptual framework for financial accounting and reporting. The FASB has issued 6 **Statements** of **Financial Accounting Concepts.** These statements are intended to set forth objectives and fundamentals that will be the basis for developing financial accounting and reporting standards. The objectives identify the goals and purposes of financial reporting. The fundamentals are the underlying concepts of financial accounting—concepts that guide the selection of transactions, events, and circumstances to be accounted for; their recognition and measurement; and the means of summarizing and communicating them to interested parties.

The purpose of **Statement of Financial Accounting Concepts No. 2,** "Qualitative Characteristics of Accounting Information," is to examine the characteristics that make accounting information useful. The characteristics or qualities of information discussed in *Concepts No. 2* are the ingredients that make information useful and are the qualities to be sought when accounting choices are made.

**Required**
1. Identify and discuss the benefits which can be expected to be derived from the FASB's conceptual framework study.
2. What is the most important quality for accounting information as identified in **Statement of Financial Accounting Concepts No. 2?** Explain why it is the most important.

3. **Statement of Financial Accounting Concepts No. 2** describes a number of key characteristics or qualities for accounting information. Briefly discuss the importance of understandability, relevance, and reliability for financial reporting purposes. *(CMA adapted)*

*C2-15 Objectives, Users, and Stewardship*
The owners of CSC Inc., a privately-held company, are considering a public offering of the company's common stock as a means of acquiring additional funding. Prior to making a decision about a public offering, the owners had a lengthy conversation with John Duncan, CSC's Chief Financial Officer. Duncan informed the owners of the reporting requirements of the Securities and Exchange Commission, including the necessity for audited financial statements. At the request of the owners, Duncan also discussed the objectives of financial reporting, the sophistication of users of financial information, and the stewardship responsibilities of management, all of which are addressed in **Statement of Financial Accounting Concepts No. 1,** "Objectives of Financial Reporting by Business Enterprises."

**Required**
1. Discuss the primary objectives of financial reporting.
2. Describe the level of sophistication that can be expected of the users of financial information.
3. Explain the stewardship responsibilities of management. *(CMA adapted)*

## MULTIPLE CHOICE

*Select the best answer for each of the following.*

M2-1   Accruing net losses on noncancelable purchase commitments for inventory is an example of the accounting concept of
  a. Conservatism
  b. Realization
  c. Consistency
  d. Materiality

M2-2   The information provided by financial reporting pertains to
  a. Individual companies, rather than to industries or an economy as a whole or to members of society as consumers.
  b. Individual companies and industries, rather than to an economy as a whole or to members of society as consumers.
  c. Individual companies and an economy as a whole, rather than to industries or to members of society as consumers.
  d. Individual companies, industries, and an economy as a whole, rather than to members of society as consumers.

M2-3   According to Statement of Financial Accounting Concepts No. 2, an interim earnings report is expected to have which of the following?

|    | Predictive value | Feedback value |
|----|------------------|----------------|
| a. | No               | No             |
| b. | Yes              | Yes            |
| c. | Yes              | No             |
| d. | No               | Yes            |

M2-4   A patent, purchased in 1992 and being amortized over a ten-year life, was determined to be worthless in 1995. The write-off of the asset in 1995 is an example of which of the following principles?

   a. Associating cause and effect
   b. Immediate recognition
   c. Systematic and rational allocation
   d. Objectivity

M2-5   An accrued expense is an expense

   a. Incurred but not paid
   b. Incurred and paid
   c. Paid but not incurred
   d. Not reasonably estimable

M2-6   Which of the following accounting concepts states that an accounting transaction should be supported by sufficient evidence to allow two or more qualified individuals to arrive at essentially similar measures and conclusions?

   a. Matching
   b. Verifiability
   c. Periodicity
   d. Stable monetary unit

M2-7   Which of the following is considered a pervasive constraint by Statement of Financial Accounting Concepts No. 2?

   a. Benefits/costs
   b. Conservatism
   c. Timeliness
   d. Verifiability

M2-8   The valuation of a promise to receive cash in the future at present value on the financial statements of a company is valid because of the accounting concept of

   a. Entity
   b. Materiality
   c. Going concern
   d. Neutrality

M2-9   Under Statements of Financial Accounting Concepts, which of the following relates to both relevance and reliability?

   a. Timeliness
   b. Neutrality
   c. Feedback value
   d. Consistency

M2-10  Under Statement of Financial Accounting Concepts No. 6, which of the following, in the most precise sense, means the process of converting noncash resources and rights into cash or claims to cash?

   a. Allocation
   b. Recordation
   c. Recognition
   d. Realization

*(AICPA adapted)*

# 3

# THE BALANCE SHEET AND STATEMENT OF CHANGES IN STOCKHOLDERS' EQUITY

*FASB Statement of Concepts No. 5* recommends that a full set of financial statements for an accounting period should show a company's (1) financial position at the end of the period, (2) net income for the period, (3) comprehensive income for the period, (4) cash flows during the period, and (5) investments by and distributions to owners during the period.[1] Currently, companies must present three major financial statements and numerous supporting schedules as the "full set" of financial statements in their *annual reports.* The three major financial statements are: (1) the balance sheet or statement of financial position, which summarizes the company's financial position at one point in time in the accounting period, (2) the income statement, which summarizes the results of the company's income-producing activities for the accounting period, and (3) the statement of cash flows, which summarizes the cash inflows and cash outflows of the company during the accounting period. Several supporting schedules and explanatory notes are usually included in a company's annual report to supplement these financial statements. The supporting schedules may include (1) the statement of changes in stockholders' equity, which itemizes the changes in the various components of stockholders' equity on the balance sheet, (2) the retained earnings statement, which reports the impact of the net income and the dividends of the period on retained earnings, and (3) the schedule of investing and financing activities not involving cash receipts or cash payments, which may supplement the statement of cash flows.

---

1.  "Recognition and Measurement in Financial Statements of Business Enterprises," *FASB Statement of Financial Accounting Concepts No. 5* (Stamford, Conn.: FASB, 1984), par. 13.

The focus of this chapter is primarily on the balance sheet, its supporting schedules, and the accompanying notes. The balance sheet is the first financial statement discussed because the FASB has defined revenues and expenses in terms of changes in assets and liabilities. Thus, a thorough understanding of the nature and measurement of assets and liabilities is needed to understand net income and its components. Furthermore, the chapters of this book primarily follow a balance sheet framework. Consequently an understanding of its purpose, content, format, and preparation is helpful if the more complex issues discussed later are to be understood. The discussion focuses on the corporation, the major business entity in the United States.

*The income statement and statement of cash flows are discussed in Chapter 4.*

## INTERRELATIONSHIP OF FINANCIAL STATEMENTS

The interrelationship of the information contained in the major financial statements is illustrated in Exhibit 3-1. The solid lines indicate the major flow of interrelated financial accounting information among the financial statements as a result of transactions and events during the period. For instance, assets from the beginning balance sheet (i.e., the ending balance sheet from the previous period) may be consumed in an income-producing activity or may be sold as a source of cash. The related financial accounting information will affect the income statement and the statement of cash flows, respectively. The information relating to the income-producing activities in the income statement and the information pertaining to the cash inflows and cash outflows reported in the statement of cash flows will both affect the accounting information reported in the ending balance sheet. The dashed line indicates a secondary flow of the interrelated information; that is, the income-producing activities reported on the income statement also provide a net source of cash from operating activities. The relationships between the balance sheet, income statement, and statement of cash flows are further explored in the remaining sections of this chapter and in the subsequent chapters of this book.

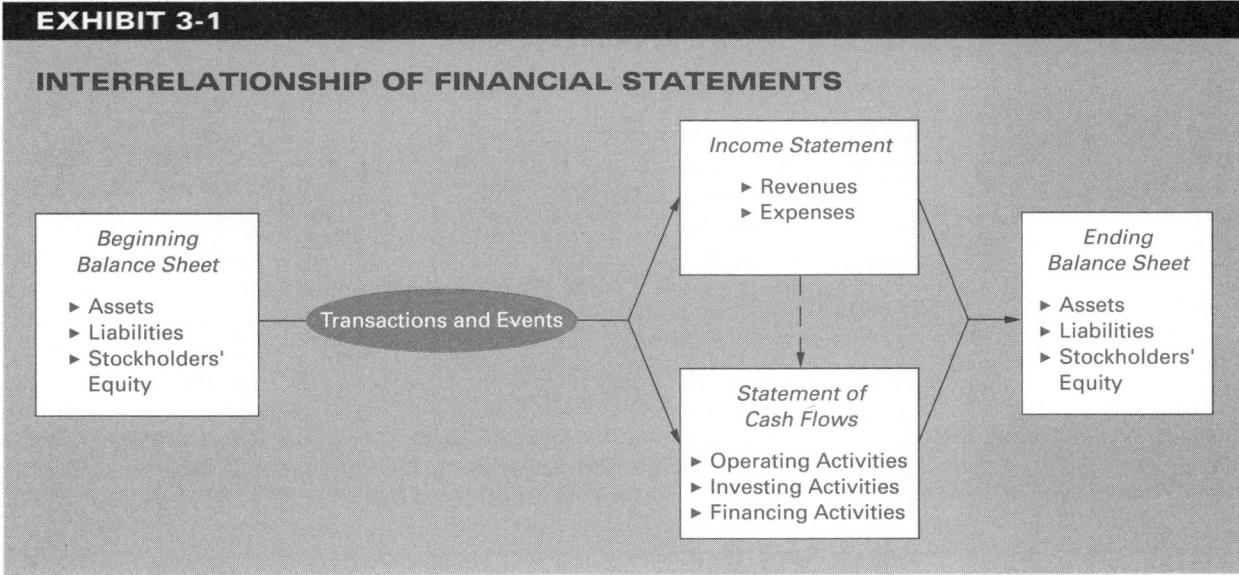

**EXHIBIT 3-1**

**INTERRELATIONSHIP OF FINANCIAL STATEMENTS**

## PURPOSES OF THE BALANCE SHEET

One objective of financial reporting for a company is to help investors, creditors, and others in assessing the amounts, timing, and uncertainty of the prospective net cash inflows of the company. To meet this objective, it was suggested that certain types of accounting information should be provided in a company's financial statements. A specific objective of a company's financial statements is to provide information about its economic resources, obligations, and owners' equity. This information is reported on a balance sheet. **A balance sheet summarizes the *financial position* of a company at a particular date.** A balance sheet may also be called a **statement of financial position.** The financial position of a company includes its economic resources (i.e., assets), economic obligations (i.e., liabilities), and equity and their relationships to each other at a moment in time. A corporate balance sheet, then, discloses the assets, liabilities, stockholders' equity, and related information of the corporation on a specific date. The statement reports a corporation's *resource structure* (i.e., major classes and amounts of assets) and its *financial structure* (i.e., major classes and amounts of liabilities and equity). Its name evolved because the balance sheet is a detailed summary of the basic accounting equation (which must always remain in balance):

**Assets = Liabilities + Stockholders' Equity**

The balance sheet does not attempt to show the value of a company. Together with other financial statements and other information, however, it should provide information that is useful to external users who desire to make their own estimates of the company's value.[2] More specifically, the balance sheet is intended to help external users to (1) assess the company's liquidity, financial flexibility, and operating capability and (2) evaluate information about its income-producing performance during the period.

### Liquidity, Financial Flexibility, and Operating Capability

*Liquidity, financial flexibility, and operating capability are discussed in Chapter 2.*

**The term *liquidity* is used to describe the amount of time until an asset is converted into cash or a liability is paid.** That is, liquidity refers to the "nearness to cash" of a company's economic resources and obligations. Information about liquidity is important in evaluating the *timing* of cash flows in the near future. Information about short-term cash inflows is useful because these cash inflows are part of total cash inflows. Furthermore, short-term cash inflows are necessary for a company to take advantage of new investment opportunities and to meet short-term obligations. Liquidity is also one aspect of a company's financial flexibility.

**Financial flexibility refers to the ability of a company to use its financial resources to adapt to change.** Adaptation may be thought of as being "offensive" or "defensive." Offensive adaptation is necessary to take advantage of an unexpected new investment opportunity, while defensive adaptation is required to survive a crisis caused by a change in operating activities. Financial flexibility comes from a quick access to the cash generated from more "liquid" economic resources. But liquidity is only part of financial flexibility. Financial flexibility stems from the ability to generate sufficient net cash inflows from operations, from additional capital contributed by investors or long-term creditors, or from liquidation of long-term economic resources without disrupting continuing operations. Information about a company's

---

2.  *Ibid.*, par. 26 and 27.

financial flexibility is important to external users in assessing the uncertainty of the company's future cash flows.

**Operating capability refers to the ability of a company to maintain a given physical level of operations.** This level may be indicated by the quantity of goods or services produced in a given period (i.e., inventory) or by the physical capacity of the operating assets (i.e., property, plant, and equipment) used to produce the goods or services. Information about operating capability may be helpful to external users in understanding a company's performance and predicting future changes in its volume of activity and related cash flows.[3]

## Capital and Capital Maintenance

The balance sheet provides a basis for evaluating a company's income-producing performance during a period. In this regard, a company's capital is important. **The capital (or *net assets*) of a company is the economic resources (assets) less economic obligations (liabilities), or owners' equity.** For a corporation, the stockholders' equity is the capital. This capital is used by the management of the corporation in fulfilling its responsibilities to the corporate stockholders. When a stockholder invests in a corporation, the stockholder is interested in a return *of* investment as well as a return *on* investment. To provide for a return of investment, the stockholders' equity (capital) of the corporation must be maintained; this is referred to as **capital maintenance.** Once this capital is maintained, any income of the corporation is an increase in stockholders' equity and is the basis for providing a return on investment to stockholders. Dividends are a return on investment, but so is the market price appreciation on the stock. Some investors prefer market price appreciation to dividends. Information about a corporation's capital is important in assessing the adequacy of a corporation's profitability and its ability to provide a return on investment.

Another way of looking at Exhibit 3-1 is to think in terms of capital and capital maintenance. The beginning balance sheet can be thought of as presenting the capital of the corporation at the beginning of the accounting period. The income statement and the statement of cash flows disclose the results of management's activities to use, maintain, and increase the capital during the accounting period. The ending balance sheet reports the capital at the end of the accounting period. But before it can be determined whether capital is maintained or a corporation has earned income, the initial (beginning) and subsequent (ending) capital must be determined.

Capital can be thought of in terms of (1) financial capital or (2) physical capital. **Financial capital is the monetary value of the net assets** contributed by stockholders and the value of the increase in net assets resulting from earnings retained by the corporation (cumulative income in excess of cumulative dividends). **Physical capital is a quantitative measure of the physical productive capacity** of the corporation to provide goods or services and is related to the concept of operating capability discussed in the previous section.[4] The difference between financial capital and physical capital is important in considering whether and when capital is maintained and income is earned (Chapter 4). The difference is not as important for reporting the capital at a

*Capital maintenance and income are discussed in Chapter 4.*

---

3.  *Ibid.*, par. 24, and "Reporting Income, Cash Flows, and Financial Position of Business Enterprises," *FASB Proposed Statement of Financial Accounting Concepts* (Stamford, Conn.: FASB, 1981), par. 25–32.

4.  For a further discussion, see "Conceptual Framework for Financial Accounting and Reporting: Elements of Financial Statements and Their Measurement," *FASB Discussion Memorandum* (Stamford, Conn.: FASB, 1976), ch. 6.

point in time because accounting information is primarily expressed in dollars. Thus, a dollar value must be attached to the physical capital before it is reported on a balance sheet. The alternative ways of measuring the net assets (capital) of a corporation are discussed later in the chapter.

## RECOGNITION IN THE BALANCE SHEET

An item of information related to the balance sheet may be disclosed in the balance sheet, in a supporting schedule, or as part of the notes accompanying the financial statements. Recall from Chapter 2 that **recognition is the process of formally recording and reporting an element in the financial statements.** It includes depiction of an element in both words and numbers, with the amount included in the totals. Generally, the most useful (i.e., the best combination of relevance and reliability) information about assets, liabilities, and equity should be recognized and included in the main body of the balance sheet. There are four fundamental recognition criteria. To be recognized, an item (and information about it) must meet the definition of an element and be measurable, relevant, and reliable.[5] Thus, to meet the objectives of a company's balance sheet—to provide relevant and reliable information to assess its liquidity, financial flexibility, and operating capability and to evaluate its income-producing performance during the period—the company must determine what, how, and where to disclose the "elements" of the balance sheet. That is, the company must complete a three-stage process:

1. Identification of what items meet the definitions of the elements

2. Measurement (valuation) of the elements

3. Reporting (classification) of the elements

## ELEMENTS OF THE BALANCE SHEET

In order for an item of information to be reported in a balance sheet, it must meet the definition of an element. **The elements of the balance sheet are the broad classes of items comprising it.** They are the building blocks with which the balance sheet is prepared. The elements of financial statements are defined in **FASB Statement of Concepts No. 6.** Each of the elements of a corporate balance sheet—assets, liabilities, and stockholders' equity—is defined and discussed in the following sections.[6]

### Assets

> **Assets are probable future economic benefits obtained or controlled by a company as a result of past transactions or events.**

Assets are the economic resources used to carry out a company's economic activities of consumption, production, and exchange. The primary attribute of all assets is *service potential,* the capacity to provide services or benefits to the company

---

5. "Recognition and Measurement in Financial Statements of Business Enterprises," *FASB Statement of Financial Accounting Concepts No. 5, op. cit.,* par. 58–64.

6. The discussion of the elements in the following sections is a summary of that presented in "Elements of Financial Statements of Business Enterprises," *FASB Statement of Financial Accounting Concepts No. 6* (Stamford, Conn.: FASB, 1985).

that uses them. To be considered an asset, an economic resource must have three characteristics.

1.  The resource must be able to contribute directly or indirectly to the company's future net cash inflows. This service potential may exist because the asset is expected to be exchanged for something else of value to the company (e.g., accounts receivable), to be used in producing goods (e.g., factory) or services, to increase the value of other assets (e.g., patent), or to be used to settle its liabilities (e.g., cash).

2.  The company must be able to obtain the future benefit and control others' access to it. Control means that the company can deny or regulate the ability of others to use the asset.

3.  The transaction or event giving rise to the company's right to or control over the benefit must have occurred. That is, a company has no asset for a particular future benefit if the transaction or event giving it access to or control over the benefit has yet to occur. As a corollary, once an asset is acquired by a company, it continues to be an asset until it is exchanged or used up or until some other event destroys the future benefit or removes the company's ability to obtain or control it.

Assets may be natural or man-made, tangible or intangible, and either exchangeable or useful only in the company's activities. Furthermore, they may be acquired by purchase, production, stockholder investments, discovery, or other nonreciprocal (one-way) transfers.

## Liabilities

> **Liabilities are probable future sacrifices of economic benefits arising from present obligations of a company to transfer assets or provide services to other entities in the future as a result of past transactions or events.**

An obligation of a company must have three characteristics to be considered a liability.

1.  It must involve a responsibility to another entity or entities that will be settled by a sacrifice involving the transfer of assets, provision of services, or other use of assets at a specified or determinable date, on occurrence of a specified event, or on demand. The specific identity of the "creditor" need not be known with certainty for a liability to exist as long as a future transfer or use of assets to settle the liability is *probable.*

2.  The responsibility must obligate the company in such a way that it has little or no discretion to avoid the future sacrifice. Although most liabilities involve legal rights and duties, some are the result of equitable (ethical or moral) obligations or constructive (inferred from the facts) obligations. Thus, the company must be bound by a legal, equitable, or constructive responsibility to transfer assets or provide services to one or more other entities.

3.  The transaction or other event obligating the company must already have occurred. Once a liability has been incurred, it continues to be a liability until the company settles it or another event discharges it or removes it from the company's responsibility.

Liabilities arise primarily from deferring payment for goods or services received and from borrowing funds. Other liabilities result from collecting economic resources in advance of providing goods or services to customers. Liabilities also arise from selling products subject to warranties, from regulations imposed by governmental units, and from nonreciprocal transfers to owners or other entities.

### Stockholders' Equity

**Equity is the residual interest in the assets of a company that remains after deducting its liabilities.**

The equity of a company is equal to its net assets (assets minus liabilities). Equity stems from ownership rights and therefore it is the ownership interest. Since a company is generally not obligated to transfer assets to its owners, owners' equity ranks after liabilities as a claim to or interest in the assets and thus is a residual interest. For a corporation, stockholders' equity represents the interest of the stockholders who bear the ultimate risks and uncertainties involved in the company's operations and activities and who obtain the resulting rewards. It is created by stockholders' investments of economic resources and subsequently is modified by additional investments, net income, distributions to owners, and other changes in assets and liabilities. Stockholders' equity may not exist apart from the corporate assets and liabilities, since it is a residual interest.

## MEASUREMENT OF THE ELEMENTS OF THE BALANCE SHEET

In order for an element to be reported on the balance sheet of a company, it must be reliably measured (valued) in monetary terms. The FASB has identified five alternatives for measuring elements. These alternative valuation methods are shown in Exhibit 3-2 and are discussed in the following sections. Stockholders' equity is not included in Exhibit 3-2 because it may not exist apart from assets or liabilities. That is, the measurement of assets and liabilities (i.e., net assets) will determine the dollar amount of stockholders' equity. To conserve space, the discussion proceeds in terms of the measurement of assets, but the comments generally are equally applicable to liabilities.

### Historical Cost

**The historical cost of an asset is the exchange price in the transaction in which the asset was acquired.** The historical cost is measured by the cash paid for the asset or, in the case of a noncash exchange, by the estimated cash equivalent of the noncash asset or liability exchanged. After acquisition, the historical cost of an asset may be reduced due to the recognition of depreciation, amortization, or other adjustments. In today's financial statements the measurement most often used is historical cost.

### Current Cost

**The current cost of an asset is the amount of cash (or equivalent) that would be required on the date of the balance sheet to obtain the same asset.** The "same asset"

### EXHIBIT 3-2

## MEASUREMENT OF ASSETS AND LIABILITIES

| Alternative | Assets | Liabilities |
|---|---|---|
| 1. Historical cost/historical proceeds | Initially, the amount of cash (or its equivalent) paid to acquire an asset (historical cost); subsequent to acquisition, the historical amount may be adjusted for depreciation, amortization, or other adjustments. | Initially, the amount of cash (or its equivalent) received when an obligation was incurred (historical proceeds); subsequent to incurrence, the historical amount may be adjusted for amortization. |
| 2. Current cost/current proceeds | Amount of cash (or its equivalent) that would have to be paid if the same asset were acquired currently. | Amount of proceeds (or its equivalent) that would be obtained if the same obligation were incurred currently. |
| 3. Current exit value | Amount of cash (or its equivalent) that could be obtained currently by selling the asset in orderly liquidation. | Cash outlay (or its equivalent) that would be required currently to eliminate the liability. |
| 4. Net realizable value | Amount of cash (or its equivalent) into which the asset is expected to be converted in due course of business less direct costs necessary to make that conversion. | Amount of cash (or its equivalent) expected to be paid to eliminate the liability in due course of business including direct costs necessary to make those payments (nondiscounted amount of expected cash outlays). |
| 5. Present value | Present value of future cash inflows into which the asset is expected to be converted in due course of business less present value of cash outflows necessary to obtain those inflows. | Present value of future cash outflows to eliminate the liability in due course of business including cash outflows necessary to make those payments. |

Source: Adapted from "Conceptual Framework for Financial Accounting and Reporting: Elements of Financial Statements and Their Measurement," *FASB Discussion Memorandum* (Stamford, Conn.: FASB, 1976), p. 193.

may be an identical asset or one with equivalent productive capacity. Alternative methods for obtaining the current cost include quoted market prices, the use of specific price indexes, and appraisals. Current cost is an *input value* and is sometimes referred to as *current replacement cost*.

*Current cost methods are discussed in Chapter 24.*

### Current Exit Value

**The current exit value of an asset is the amount of cash (or equivalent) that could be obtained on the date of the balance sheet by selling the asset, in its present condition, in an orderly liquidation.** An orderly liquidation means the asset is disposed of in a systematic and organized fashion. A current exit value would be determined by obtaining a quoted market price for the sale of an asset of similar kind and condition. Current exit value is sometimes referred to as *current market value*. This is potentially misleading because current cost and current exit value are both "market values."

### Net Realizable Value

**The net realizable value of an asset is the amount of cash (or equivalent) into which the asset is expected to be converted in the ordinary operations of the company, less any expected conversion costs** (e.g., completion, disposal, or collection costs). Net realizable value differs from current exit value by being based upon expected *future* sales proceeds of the asset (perhaps in a different form) rather than upon the *current* disposal value of an asset in its existing form. Net realizable value is sometimes referred to as *expected exit value*.

### Present Value

*Discounting and the computation of present value are discussed in Appendix D.*

**The present value of an asset is the net amount of discounted expected cash inflows less the discounted expected cash outflows relating to the asset.** The expected cash flows used to determine present value are similar to those used to determine net realizable value; the difference between the two alternatives is that under the present value approach consideration is given to the time value of money (i.e., interest).[7]

### Valuations on Today's Balance Sheet

As indicated earlier, the valuation method primarily used in balance sheets is historical cost. In general, each asset and liability of a company is recorded at the exchange price of the transaction in which the asset is obtained or the liability is incurred. Usually this exchange price is then reported in the company's balance sheet until another exchange has taken place. Certain assets such as property, plant, and equipment are measured and reported at their exchange price (historical cost) adjusted for depreciation. Historical cost is used extensively as a valuation method because it is based on transactions and provides information that has a high degree of *reliability*. It has been criticized, however, because some users of financial statements argue that historical cost is not as *relevant* as the amounts reported under some alternative valuation methods. That is, historical cost does not represent the amount of future cash inflows (or outflows) that the company is likely to obtain (or pay) for the asset (or liability).

---

7.  *FASB Statement of Financial Accounting Concepts No. 5, op. cit.,* par. 67, and "Conceptual Framework for Financial Accounting and Reporting: Elements of Financial Statements and Their Measurement," *FASB Discussion Memorandum, op. cit.,* pp. 196–206.

The alternative valuation methods of current cost, current exit value, net realizable value, and present value are used in certain circumstances for selected elements of the balance sheet. For instance, current cost might be used for valuing "inventories," current exit value for "marketable securities," net realizable value for "receivables," and present value for "bonds payable." The valuation method used for each type of asset and liability is identified in the next section and discussed more fully in later chapters. As increased emphasis is placed upon reporting information concerning a company's liquidity, financial flexibility, and operating capability, it may be more likely that there will be an increased use of valuation methods other than historical cost on balance sheets (or related notes). The extent of the use of other valuation methods will depend, among other considerations, on the tradeoff between relevance and reliability.

## Limitations of the Balance Sheet

In addition to the criticism that the use of historical costs for valuing assets and liabilities does not help users assess the likely amounts of future cash flows relating to these items, there are other limitations of the balance sheet. First, the balance sheet does not include all of a company's economic resources and economic obligations. For instance, "human resources" such as high-quality management or highly motivated employees are not included as assets, primarily because of the difficulty of reliably measuring their values. Or, possible legal obligations for air or water pollution may not be reported as liabilities, again due to measurement problems. Second, many of the amounts reported are based on estimates, which are subject to change. As discussed in the next section, estimates are involved in the determination of amounts for items such as uncollectible accounts and depreciation, as well as warranty and pension liabilities. Finally, in periods of inflation the amounts listed on a company's balance sheet do not show the "purchasing power" of its assets and liabilities. The FASB is aware of these limitations and in certain instances, as discussed later in the chapter, requires companies to disclose additional information in the notes to the financial statements to help users in their decision making.

## REPORTING CLASSIFICATIONS ON THE BALANCE SHEET

Accounting systems process vast amounts of data. The preparation of financial statements includes the simplification, condensation, and aggregation of that data. Classifications in financial statements involve aggregations designed to facilitate analysis by grouping items with essentially similar characteristics. The intent is to improve the predictive value, and hence the usefulness, of the financial information in regard to assessing the amounts, timing, and uncertainty of future cash flows.[8] **The arrangement of each company's balance sheet items and subtotals should be designed in a manner to be useful to its various external user groups.** Flexibility in classifications is necessary to ensure such usefulness, due to differences in companies, industries, and economic conditions. Nonetheless a general classification scheme may be presented that captures the majority of items disclosed by most companies.

---

8.  *Ibid., FASB Statement of Financial Accounting Concepts No. 5,* par. 20–22.

The balance sheet of a corporation is usually divided into three sections, with the items reported within each usually grouped in some informative manner. A representative classification would be:

1. *Assets*
   a. Current assets
   b. Long-term investments
   c. Property, plant, and equipment
   d. Intangible assets
   e. Other assets

2. *Liabilities*
   a. Current liabilities
   b. Long-term liabilities
   c. Other liabilities

3. *Stockholders' equity*
   a. Contributed capital
      (1) Capital stock
      (2) Additional paid-in capital
   b. Unrealized capital
   c. Retained earnings

Each of these groupings is discussed in the following sections. A comprehensive illustration of a balance sheet at December 31, 1995, for the Caron Manufacturing Company is shown in Exhibit 3-4 on pages 70 and 71. For selected items, illustrations of disclosures of actual companies are shown in related exhibits. The Coca-Cola Company's balance sheet at December 31, 1992 is shown in Appendix A.

## Current Assets

**Current assets are cash and other assets that are reasonably expected to be converted into cash, sold, or consumed within one year or the normal operating cycle, whichever is longer.** An *operating cycle* is the average time taken by a company to expend cash for inventory, process and sell the inventory, and collect the receivables, converting them back into cash. An example of a company's operating cycle is shown in Exhibit 3-3. Note the relationship between current assets, current liabilities (discussed in the next section), and operating cash flows. Most companies have operating cycles of a year or less. A few, such as construction, lumber, distillery, and tobacco companies, have operating cycles that are longer than one year. In that case the longer time period should be used to determine the current assets.[9]

*Operating cash flows are discussed in Chapters 2 and 4.*

Current assets may include five items: (1) cash (and cash equivalents), (2) temporary investments in marketable securities, (3) receivables, (4) inventories, and (5) prepaid items. These items usually are presented in the current asset section in the order of their liquidity, as shown in Exhibit 3-4.

**Cash** includes cash on hand and readily available in checking and savings accounts. It is listed at its monetary value. Many companies also include "cash equivalents" with cash. *Cash equivalents* are securities held such as money market funds

9. "Restatement and Revision of Accounting Research Bulletins," *Accounting Research and Terminology Bulletins, Final Edition, No. 43* (New York: AICPA, 1961), ch. 3, sec. A, par. 4 and 5.

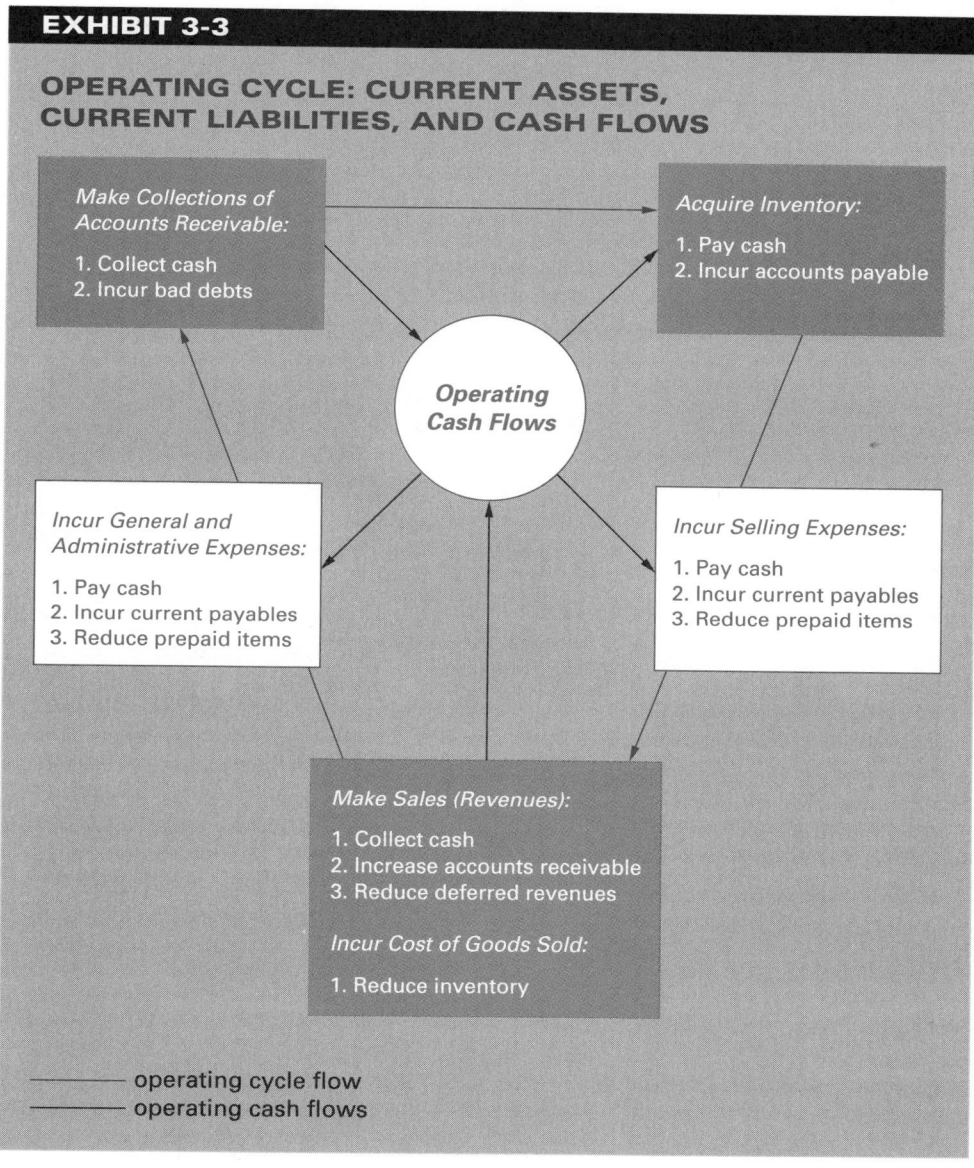

**EXHIBIT 3-3**

**OPERATING CYCLE: CURRENT ASSETS, CURRENT LIABILITIES, AND CASH FLOWS**

*Make Collections of Accounts Receivable:*

1. Collect cash
2. Incur bad debts

*Acquire Inventory:*

1. Pay cash
2. Incur accounts payable

*Operating Cash Flows*

*Incur General and Administrative Expenses:*

1. Pay cash
2. Incur current payables
3. Reduce prepaid items

*Incur Selling Expenses:*

1. Pay cash
2. Incur current payables
3. Reduce prepaid items

*Make Sales (Revenues):*

1. Collect cash
2. Increase accounts receivable
3. Reduce deferred revenues

*Incur Cost of Goods Sold:*

1. Reduce inventory

—— operating cycle flow
—— operating cash flows

and treasury bills with maturity dates of three months or less. **Temporary investments in marketable securities** include debt and equity securities that are classified as "trading securities" (as discussed in Chapter 13) and "securities available for sale" that management intends to convert into cash within the longer of one year or the normal operating cycle. Also included are "financial instruments" such as options to buy stock. Alternative captions are *short-term marketable securities* and *short-term investments*. They are listed at their market (fair) value (current exit value). **Receivables** include accounts receivable and notes receivable with short-term maturity dates. They are listed at their estimated collectible amounts (net realizable values). Any pledged or discounted accounts or notes receivable should be disclosed parenthetically or in the notes to the financial statements. **Inventories** include goods held

**EXHIBIT 3-4**

## CARON MANUFACTURING COMPANY

Balance Sheet
December 31, 1995

*Assets*

| | | | |
|---|---|---:|---:|
| Current Assets | | | |
| Cash | | | $ 14,300 |
| Temporary investments in securities available for sale | | | 19,700 |
| Accounts receivable | | $ 68,200 | |
| Less: Allowance for doubtful accounts | | (3,200) | 65,000 |
| Inventories | | | |
| Raw materials | | $ 32,000 | |
| Goods in process | | 49,500 | |
| Finished goods | | 66,100 | 147,600 |
| Prepaid items: | | | |
| Insurance | | $ 4,800 | |
| Office supplies | | 2,200 | 7,000 |
| Total current assets | | | $253,600 |
| Long-Term Investments | | | |
| Investment in bonds held to maturity | | $ 17,000 | |
| Fund to retire long-term bonds payable | | 17,400 | |
| Total long-term investments | | | 34,400 |

Property, Plant, and Equipment

| | Cost | Accumulated Depreciation | Book Value | |
|---|---:|---:|---:|---:|
| Land | $ 36,000 | — | $ 36,000 | |
| Buildings | 428,000 | $207,000 | 221,000 | |
| Equipment | 192,000 | 63,700 | 128,300 | |
| Totals | $656,000 | $270,700 | $385,300 | |
| Total property, plant, and equipment | | | | 385,300 |

| | | | |
|---|---|---:|---:|
| Intangible Assets | | | |
| Trademarks (net) | | $ 12,600 | |
| Patents (net) | | 16,900 | |
| Total intangible assets | | | 29,500 |
| Total Assets | | | $702,800 |

for resale in the normal course of business plus, in the case of a manufacturing company, raw materials (items to be converted into finished goods) and goods in process (partially completed goods) inventories. They are listed at their cost or market value (current cost), whichever is lower. The inventory costing method (LIFO, FIFO, average cost) is disclosed parenthetically or in the related notes. To reduce the detail on

## EXHIBIT 3-4, Continued

### Liabilities

| | | |
|---|---:|---:|
| **Current Liabilities** | | |
| Accounts payable | | $ 87,100 |
| Salaries payable | | 3,300 |
| Income taxes payable | | 27,400 |
| Advances from customers | | 19,600 |
| Current portion of mortgage payable | | 8,400 |
| Total current liabilities | | $145,800 |
| **Long-Term Liabilities** | | |
| Bonds payable (10%, due 2008) | $90,000 | |
| Less: Unamortized bond discount | (8,200) | |
| | | $ 81,800 |
| Mortgage payable (12%, due 1996–2000) | | 52,600 |
| Accrued pension cost | | 34,700 |
| Total long-term liabilities | | 169,100 |
| **Other Liabilities** | | |
| Deferred income taxes | | 14,300 |
| Total Liabilities | | $329,200 |

### Stockholders' Equity

| | | |
|---|---:|---:|
| **Contributed Capital (see Exhibit 3-8)** | | |
| Common stock, $5 par (20,000 shares authorized, 14,300 shares issued and outstanding) | | $ 71,500 |
| Additional paid-in capital on common stock | | 173,900 |
| Total contributed capital | | $245,400 |
| **Unrealized Capital** | | |
| Unrealized increase in value of securities available for sale (see Exhibit 3-8) | | 12,000 |
| Retained Earnings (see Exhibit 3-8) | | 116,200 |
| Total Stockholders' Equity | | $373,600 |
| Total Liabilities and Stockholders' Equity | | $702,800 |

its balance sheet, a company might show a total inventory amount in current assets and include a breakdown in the notes to the financial statements. This procedure is used by Apple Computer, Inc., as shown in Exhibit 3-5. **Prepaid items** such as insurance, rent, office supplies, and taxes will not be converted into cash but will be consumed. Conceptually, prepaid items should not be classified as current assets in the

**EXHIBIT 3-5**
**Inventory Disclosures**

**APPLE COMPUTER, INC.**

|                                | September 25, 1992 | September 27, 1991 |
| ------------------------------ | -----------------: | -----------------: |
| (in thousands)                 |                    |                    |
| Current assets (in part):      |                    |                    |
|   Inventories        |          $580,097  |          $671,655  |

NOTES TO CONSOLIDATED FINANCIAL STATEMENTS (in part):

*Inventories*

Inventories consist of the following:

|                  |      1992 |      1991 |
| ---------------- | --------: | --------: |
| Purchased parts  | $150,147  | $154,812  |
| Work in process  |   94,790  |   72,301  |
| Finished goods   |  335,160  |  444,542  |
|                  | $580,097  | $671,655  |

sense that they do not directly enter into the operating cycle. However, they are included as current assets because had they not been paid in advance, cash would have been paid out within the cycle. Furthermore, even though a 2-year prepayment of insurance would extend over more than an annual operating cycle, the payment is usually classified as a current asset on the basis of a lack of materiality. Prepaid items are listed at their historical cost, less any amortized amount.

### Current Liabilities

Current liabilities are discussed next because of their close relation to current assets. **Current liabilities are those obligations whose liquidation is reasonably expected to require the use of existing resources properly classified as current assets, or the creation of other current liabilities within one year or the normal operating cycle, whichever is longer.** Several types of liabilities should be included as current liabilities:

1. Obligations for items (goods or services) that have entered the operating cycle. These include, for instance, accounts payable, salaries payable, and taxes payable.

2. Advance collections for the future delivery of goods or performance of service—for instance, obligations under short-term financial instruments (such as options to sell stock) as well as unearned rent and unearned ticket sales. These latter items sometimes are referred to as short-term deferred (unearned) revenues.

3. Other obligations that will be paid within one year or the operating cycle, such as short-term notes payable, dividends payable, the estimated liability for

short-term product warranties, and the portions of long-term liabilities that mature during this period.[10]

These obligations are listed on the balance sheet at the amount owed (historical proceeds) or estimated to be owed, as shown in Exhibit 3-4.

Certain obligations, even though they become due and will be satisfied within the next accounting period, are not classified as current liabilities. These include obligations that will be refinanced by issuing new long-term liabilities and obligations that will be paid out of a fund accumulated for that purpose and classified as a long-term investment. These obligations are not current liabilities because they will not require the use of current assets to satisfy the debt.

## Working Capital

The working capital of a company relates primarily to the financial resources utilized in its operating cycle. **Working capital is the excess of current assets over current liabilities.** Although working capital is seldom computed on the balance sheet, it is an indicator of the short-run liquidity of the company and often is used by creditors and others for such an evaluation. Often a slightly different computation, the current ratio (current assets divided by current liabilities), is used for the same purpose. Care must be taken in the use of working capital information in the current ratio because the liquidity *composition* of the working capital components (particularly current assets) is of critical importance. In this regard, the FASB has suggested several general guidelines for more homogeneous classifications of assets that should help external users assess the nature, amounts, and liquidity of available resources. One classification alternative might be to separate the current assets into two groups. The first group would include the *liquid* assets of cash and temporary investments in marketable securities that are immediately convertible into cash. The second group would be comprised of *separable assets,* those assets that can be separated from the company and converted into cash but with some time lag and conversion costs. These would include such items as receivables and inventories.[11] Users can develop alternative groupings of current assets and current liabilities, as well as other ratios for assessing liquidity and financial flexibility.

## Long-Term Investments

Companies make investments for a variety of reasons. They may be interested in appreciation of the investment (the company expects the market value of the investment to increase), in income in the form of interest or dividends, in exercising control over certain other companies as in the case of a subsidiary or a major supplier, and in the use of the investment for specific future purposes such as the payment of pensions. Whether or not the investment is readily marketable, **if management expects to hold the item for more than one year or the operating cycle, whichever is longer, it is properly classified as a long-term (noncurrent) investment.**

Long-term investments include holdings of debt and equity securities available for sale that management does not intend to convert into cash within the longer of one year or the normal operating cycle. Long-term investments also include investments

---

10. *Ibid.*, par. 7.
11. For a further discussion, see "Reporting Funds Flows, Liquidity, and Financial Flexibility," *FASB Discussion Memorandum* (Stamford, Conn.: FASB, 1980), ch. 8 and 9.

in debt securities (e.g., bonds) held to maturity, noncurrent notes receivable from unaffiliated companies, long-term advances to unconsolidated affiliated companies, and financial instruments (such as options to buy stock) that are noncurrent. Investments in property and equipment being held for future operations, such as land being held for a future building site, are also included. Special funds established to retire bonds payable or preferred stock (often called sinking funds) or to acquire future facilities are included as long-term investments. Finally, miscellaneous investments, including the cash surrender value of life insurance policies, should be listed in this section of the balance sheet. Investments are listed at their market (fair) value, historical cost, book value, or present value, depending on the type of investment. The method of valuation for each long-term investment should be disclosed either parenthetically or in the notes to the financial statements. The long-term investments section is illustrated in Exhibit 3-4.

## Property, Plant, and Equipment

**The property, plant, and equipment section of the balance sheet includes the tangible assets used in the operations of the company.** Often these are referred to as the *fixed assets* because of their relative permanency in the company's operations. A merchandising company sometimes will title this section as Property and Equipment because it does not have manufacturing (plant) facilities. Listed in this category are assets that have a physical existence, such as land, buildings, equipment, machinery, furniture, and natural resources. Except for land, all the fixed assets are depreciable or depletable (in the case of natural resources). Land is listed at its historical cost, while the remaining fixed assets are listed at their book values (historical cost less accumulated depreciation or depletion). A *contra-asset* account, such as accumulated depreciation, usually is used to reduce the fixed assets (except natural resources) to their book values while the historical cost is still disclosed. The method of depreciating the fixed assets is disclosed in the notes to the financial statements. The property, plant, and equipment section of Caron Manufacturing Company is illustrated in Exhibit 3-4. Some companies show a total amount of property, plant, and equipment on their balance sheets and a breakdown in the related notes. This procedure is used by Campbell Soup Company for its plant assets, as shown in Exhibit 3-6.

*Accounting for leases is discussed in Chapter 19.*    Certain long-term lease contracts relating to leased property, plant, and equipment are also included in this section. Long-term leases of assets have become a popular way by which a lessee may acquire the rights to the use of the assets without the initial capital outlay to finance the acquisitions. In the case of a *capital lease*, one that contains many of the characteristics of a purchase, both the assets and the liabilities sections of the lessee's balance sheet are affected. Since the lease allows the lessee company relatively unrestricted rights to the use of the asset for an extended period, the rights represent economic resources to the company, even though the asset is not legally owned. A capital lease initially is recorded by the lessee as an asset, Leased Equipment Under Capital Lease, at the present value of the future lease payments. It is amortized in a manner similar to other legally owned assets of the company. The book value of the leased asset is disclosed in the property, plant, and equipment section. Similarly, since the capital lease payments usually are noncancelable over an extended number of years, these payments represent a long-term liability of the lessee company. The obligation in regard to a capital lease also is recorded initially at the present value of the future lease payments and subsequently reduced by the amount of each lease payment (after adjustment for interest). As discussed later, the capital lease liability is disclosed in the long-term liabilities section of the balance sheet.

---

**EXHIBIT 3-6**
**Plant Assets**

---

## CAMPBELL SOUP COMPANY

|  | August 2, 1992 | July 28, 1991 |
|---|---|---|
| (in millions) | | |
| Assets (in part): | | |
| Plant assets, net of depreciation (Note 16) | $1,965.8 | $1,790.4 |

NOTES TO CONSOLIDATED FINANCIAL STATEMENTS (in part):

*16 Plant Assets (in part):*

|  | 1992 | 1991 |
|---|---|---|
| Land | $ 66.7 | $ 56.3 |
| Buildings | 909.0 | 758.7 |
| Machinery and equipment | 2,010.0 | 1,779.3 |
| Projects in progress | 223.3 | 327.6 |
|  | 3,209.0 | 2,921.9 |
| Accumulated depreciation | (1,243.2) | (1,131.5) |
|  | $1,965.8 | $1,790.4 |

## Intangible Assets

**Intangible assets are those economic resources that are used in the operations of the business but have no physical existence.** They generally derive their value from the rights held by the company for their use. They include such items as patents, copyrights, franchises, trademarks, computer software costs, goodwill, and organization costs. Intangibles are recorded initially at the historical cost incurred in an external transaction and are listed on the balance sheet at their book values (historical cost less accumulated amortization). A contra account is seldom used. The method of amortizing the intangibles is disclosed in the notes to the financial statements. Many companies have valuable "intangible assets," such as the human resources of their employees, but these resources are not reported on the balance sheet because of the difficulty in reliably measuring their value. The intangibles section is illustrated in Exhibit 3-4.

## Other Assets

Finally an "other assets" section occasionally is used to report miscellaneous assets that may not be readily classified within one of the previous sections. This section is sometimes referred to as *deferred charges*. Examples of items that have been classified in this section include long-term prepayments (such as for rent, insurance), deferred tax assets, prepaid pension costs, bond issue costs, organization costs, assets of a segment of the company that is being discontinued, advances to officers, idle fixed assets, cash from security deposits of customers on returnable containers, assets leased to others, and assets temporarily restricted by foreign countries. Classification within this section should be made judiciously. Many items that have been listed in this section could be classified correctly in one of the previous sections.

## Long-Term Liabilities

**Long-term liabilities are those obligations that are *not* expected to require the use of current assets or creation of current liabilities within the next year or operating cycle (if longer than a year). Long-term liabilities may be called noncurrent liabilities.** It is usual for these obligations to be outstanding for several years. Included in this category are such items as long-term notes payable, obligations under capital lease contracts, mortgages payable, obligations under noncurrent financial instruments (e.g., options to sell stock), estimated liabilities from long-term warranties, accrued pension cost (i.e., obligation for future pension payments), and bonds payable.

As a means of financing its activities, a corporation may issue long-term bonds. A bond entails a written promise to repay a specific amount (its *face value*) at some future maturity date. Nearly all bonds also pay a specified interest rate (either semiannually or annually) that may vary from company to company. Many bonds sell in a bond market similar to that of a stock market. Frequently a corporation may issue a bond at more or less than its face value. This occurs when the bond pays a stated interest rate greater or less than the yield rate investors can earn elsewhere on a similar security, consequently making it more or less valuable.

When a bond is issued for more than its face value, it is said to have been sold at a *premium*; when it is issued for less, it is sold at a *discount*. At the time of sale the Bonds Payable account is recorded at the face value of the bond and an account called Premium on Bonds Payable (or Discount on Bonds Payable) is recorded for the amount by which the selling price is greater than (less than) the face value. Subsequently this premium (or discount) is amortized as an adjustment to periodic interest expense (generally by use of a present value approach), and at the maturity date only the bonds payable face value remains. Whenever a balance sheet is prepared, the remaining premium is added to (or the discount is subtracted from) the face value of the bonds payable to determine the book value. Other long-term liabilities are listed at the present values of the amounts owed. Any applicable interest rates, maturity values, and other provisions are disclosed parenthetically on the balance sheet or in the notes to the financial statements. The long-term liabilities section of Caron Manufacturing Company is illustrated in Exhibit 3-4. Some companies show a total amount of long-term liabilities on their balance sheets and a breakdown in the related notes. This procedure is used by Centex Corporation for its long-term debt, as shown in Exhibit 3-7.

## Other Liabilities

A final section is sometimes used to disclose miscellaneous liabilities not meeting the definition of either a current or a long-term liability. This section might include such items as deferred tax liabilities, obligations of a segment of the company that is being discontinued, and long-term advances from customers. As in the case of other assets, this category should be used judiciously.

## Conceptual Guidelines for Reporting Assets and Liabilities

The previous sections discussed the typical classifications of assets and liabilities in a balance sheet. A company, however, should classify its assets and liabilities in the most informative manner for its external user groups. In this regard, in addition to the "liquid" and "separable" subclassifications of current assets discussed earlier, the

## EXHIBIT 3-7
## Long-Term Debt

### CENTEX CORPORATION

Liabilities and Stockholders' Equity (in part):

|                | March 31, 1992 | March 31, 1991 |
|----------------|----------------|----------------|
| (in thousands) |                |                |
| Long-term Debt | $232,294       | $137,235       |

NOTES TO CONSOLIDATED FINANCIAL STATEMENTS (in part):

*Long-term Debt*

Balances of long-term debt were:

|                                              | March 31, 1992 | March 31, 1991 |
|----------------------------------------------|----------------|----------------|
| Senior Notes, 9.05% Due in May, 1996         | $100,000       | $ —            |
| Subordinated Debentures, 8.75% to 8.8% Due in 2007 | 119,229  | 119,205        |
| Other Indebtedness, 4.5% to 10% Due Through 2009 | 13,065     | 18,030         |
|                                              | $232,294       | $137,235       |

*Maturities of long-term debt during the next five fiscal years are: 1993, $6,384; 1994, $3,905; 1995, $2,731; 1996, $2; 1997, $100,002.*

Included in other long-term debt is a $2.1 million convertible subordinated debenture sold in August 1985 to a corporate officer at par. The indebtedness bears interest at prime and is convertible into shares of the company's common stock at the rate of one share per $21 of principal. In connection with this transaction, the company has guaranteed the payment of a $2.1 million note payable to a bank by the officer.

FASB has suggested several guidelines for developing *homogeneous classes* of assets and liabilities. These guidelines include:

1. Reporting assets according to their type or expected function in the central operations or other activities of the company. For example, assets held for resale (inventory) should be reported separately from assets held for use in production (property, plant, and equipment).

2. Reporting, as separate items, assets and liabilities with different implications for the financial flexibility of the company; for example, assets used in operations, assets held for investment, and assets subject to restrictions (such as leased equipment).

3. Reporting assets and liabilities according to the measurement method used to value the items; for example, assets and liabilities measured at net realizable value versus those measured at current cost.

These general guidelines are intended to result in asset and liability classifications that help users to assess the nature, amounts, and liquidity of available resources, including the intentions of management regarding their functional use, and the amounts and timing of obligations that require liquid resources for settlement.[12]

## Stockholders' Equity

**Stockholders' equity is the residual interest of the ownership group in the assets of the corporation; that is, the equity of the owners is the assets less the liabilities.** A company may be organized in three different ways: as a sole proprietorship, a partnership, or a corporation.

A sole proprietorship is a single-owner company. Because this is typically a small company where the owner acts as manager and has direct access to the accounting records, separate accounts typically are not maintained for the owner's investment and retained earnings. Normally the total owner's equity is summarized in a single *capital* account.

A partnership involves two or more persons who have agreed to combine their capital and efforts in the operations of a company. The partnership is usually evidenced by a *partnership agreement,* a legal document that includes the investment requirements, allocation of income, and withdrawal provisions for each partner. Separate capital accounts are used for each partner to summarize the partner's equity.

The corporate form of business organization is the most complex. *Absentee* ownership, where the stockholders are external to the corporate management activities, is common. To protect these absentee owners, numerous state laws have been established, many of which relate to the accounting for the stockholders' equity. Stockholders' equity consists of three components: (1) contributed capital, (2) unrealized capital, and (3) retained earnings.

## Contributed Capital

*Protection of the interests of stockholders and creditors is discussed in Chapter 14.*

Ownership in a corporation is evidenced by holding the corporation's shares of stock. A stockholder may acquire shares directly from the corporation or by purchase on the stock market from another investor. Only in the first instance does the acquisition affect the corporation's balance sheet. Most state laws protecting stockholders and creditors entail the establishment of a certain amount of legal capital. **Legal capital is the minimum amount that the corporation may not pay out in dividends,** and is one element of the total amount of contributed capital. The accounting for contributed capital relates as much to the satisfaction of these legal requirements as it does to the provision of significant financial information. Contributed capital frequently is separated into two components, capital stock (relating to the legal capital) and additional paid-in capital.

## Capital Stock and Additional Paid-In Capital

Corporations may issue two types of capital stock, preferred stock and common stock. **Preferred stock** has different ownership features (which some investors consider

---

12. "Reporting Income, Cash Flows, and Financial Position of Business Enterprises," *FASB Proposed Statement of Financial Accounting Concepts, op. cit.,* par. 50, 51, and 170.

more attractive) from common stock, including preference to a specified dividend, if one is paid. **Common stock** carries the right to vote at the annual stockholders' meeting and to share in residual profits. The number of shares that a corporation is legally authorized to issue as well as the types and characteristics of its capital stock are included in the corporate charter. Common stock is the most prevalent type of capital stock. Each of these types of stock typically sells on a stock market, which establishes its *market value* per share.

Based upon state laws, a corporation may issue (1) par value, (2) stated value, or (3) no-par (no stated value) capital stock. Capital stock by law may be required to carry a par value or a stated value. Par value or stated value refers to a specific dollar amount per share that is printed on the stock certificate.[13] Often this par value is a very small amount, say $1 or $5 per share, because states generally do not allow the issuance of stock at less than par. The par value of a share of stock has no direct relationship to the share's market value. Nonetheless, the legal (par) value must be separately accounted for.

When a corporation issues par value capital stock (common or preferred), the proceeds (market price) must be allocated between a capital stock account for the par value and another contributed capital account for the difference between the par and the market value. This latter account has a title such as Additional Paid-in Capital, Paid-in Capital in Excess of Par, or Premium on Common (or Preferred) Stock. For instance, if a corporation sold 100 shares of its $5 par common stock for $30 per share, the journal entry to record the transaction is as follows (the number of shares issued in the transaction would also be recorded):

| | | |
|---|---|---|
| Cash | 3,000 | |
| Common Stock, $5 par | | 500 |
| Additional Paid-in Capital on Common Stock | | 2,500 |

Many states also allow corporations to issue no-par capital stock. When no-par capital stock is issued, the total proceeds from the sale usually constitute the legal capital, and the entire amount is recorded in the capital stock account. Due to various other stock transactions, it is possible for a corporation issuing no-par stock to also have certain additional paid-in capital accounts.

A corporation sometimes will repurchase its own capital stock. This reacquisition reduces the number of shares outstanding. The *cost* of the reacquisition usually is recorded in a contra stockholders' equity account entitled Treasury Stock. This account has a debit balance and is deducted from the total of contributed capital, unrealized capital, and retained earnings to determine total stockholders' equity.

Regardless of whether the corporation issues par or no-par stock, the balances in the Preferred Stock, Common Stock, and Additional Paid-in Capital accounts are listed separately on the balance sheet and summed to determine the total amount of contributed capital. The par value or stated value per share as well as the number of shares authorized, issued, and outstanding should be disclosed either parenthetically in the contributed capital section or in the notes to the financial statements. The contributed capital section is illustrated in Exhibit 3-4.

---

13. There are certain legal differences between par value and stated value. These are discussed in Chapter 14. Since the accounting for stated value stock is virtually identical to that for par value stock, the remaining discussion focuses on par value stock.

## Unrealized Capital

In certain instances a corporation may increase its assets without a corresponding outflow of assets, increase in liabilities, recognition of income, or issuance of capital stock. For instance, a company may receive donated assets or it may discover previously unrecorded assets. In either case, recognition of the asset fair market value is accompanied by an increase in stockholders' equity. In other instances, (1) certain unrealized increases or decreases in the market (fair) value of securities available for sale and (2) any excess of additional pension liability over unrecognized prior service cost must be listed as *negative* components of stockholders' equity. These items may be important in assessing a company's operations, and should be listed in an **unrealized capital** section of stockholders' equity, as illustrated in Exhibit 3-4.

*Items 1 and 2 are discussed in Chapters 13 and 18, respectively.*

## Retained Earnings

**Retained earnings is the total amount of corporate earnings that has not been distributed to stockholders in the form of dividends.** A corporation may retain the assets generated from these earnings for use in its daily operations, to maintain its productive facilities, or for growth. In any event the existence of a retained earnings balance has no relationship to the funds that are available for cash dividends. The resources generated by earnings are invested in all assets. The Retained Earnings account balance is added to the contributed capital and the unrealized capital to determine the total stockholders' equity. A negative (debit) retained earnings balance (due to cumulative losses and dividends exceeding cumulative earnings), properly entitled a *deficit,* would be subtracted from contributed capital and unrealized capital.

Sometimes a portion of retained earnings is *restricted* or *appropriated* to indicate that it cannot be reduced by the distribution of dividends. This may occur as a result of a legal or contractual requirement. When a separate account, such as Retained Earnings Restricted Due to Bond Requirements, is established, its balance is added to the Unrestricted Retained Earnings account balance to determine the total retained earnings on the balance sheet.

## STATEMENT OF CHANGES IN STOCKHOLDERS' EQUITY

When financial statements are issued, a disclosure of the changes in the separate stockholders' equity accounts is required. This disclosure may be in the form of a financial statement, a supporting schedule, or a note to the financial statements.[14] This reporting is consistent with the FASB's suggestion that a full set of financial statements should show, among other information, investments by and distributions to owners during the period. The intent is to help report on the changes in a company's financial structure to aid in assessing its financial flexibility.

In this regard, **FASB Statement of Concepts No. 6** has defined the two elements, investments by owners and distributions to owners, as follows:

> **Investments by owners are increases in equity of a company resulting from transfers of something valuable to the company from other entities in order to obtain or increase ownership interests.**

> **Distributions to owners are decreases in equity of a company caused by transferring assets, rendering services, or incurring liabilities to owners.**

---

14. "Omnibus Opinion—1967," *APB Opinion No. 12* (New York: AICPA, 1967), par. 10.

Assets are the valuable items most commonly received from investments by owners, but the items received may include services or the conversion of liabilities of the company. Through investments by owners, a company obtains resources it needs to begin or expand operations, to retire liabilities, or for other business purposes. Distributions by a company to its owners decrease its net assets and decrease or terminate ownership interests of those who receive them.[15]

To disclose investments by owners and distributions to owners, many companies will combine the retained earnings changes normally contained in a retained earnings statement with the other capital account changes in a single schedule entitled Statement of Changes in Stockholders' Equity. This schedule is illustrated in Exhibit 3-8. Note that the totals of the columns in this exhibit are the same as those shown in the stockholders' equity section of Exhibit 3-4.

*The statement of changes in stockholders' equity is discussed in Chapter 15.*

## OTHER DISCLOSURE ISSUES

All the relevant financial information pertaining to a company's activities cannot be disclosed directly in the body of the financial statements because certain items do not meet the recognition criteria discussed earlier in the chapter. As indicated throughout the balance sheet discussion, many disclosures may be made in the notes accompanying the financial statements. Other significant disclosure issues are discussed here.

### Summary of Accounting Policies

A knowledge of the accounting policies, practices, and methods used in the accounting process is necessary in order to understand the content of the financial statements. For this reason, generally accepted accounting principles require the disclosure of certain information in the annual report presented to external users.

---

**EXHIBIT 3-8**

**SCHEDULE A**
**CARON MANUFACTURING COMPANY**

Statement of Changes in Stockholders' Equity
For Year Ended December 31, 1995

| | Common Stock, $5 par | Additional Paid-in Capital | Unrealized Capital | Retained Earnings | Total |
|---|---|---|---|---|---|
| Balance, January 1, 1995 | $65,000 | $143,400 | $10,000 | $ 64,900 | $283,300 |
| Increase in value of securities available for sale | | | 2,000 | | 2,000 |
| Net income | | | | 62,500 | 62,500 |
| Cash dividends paid | | | | (11,200) | (11,200) |
| Common stock issued | 6,500 | 30,500 | | | 37,000 |
| Balance, December 31, 1995 | $71,500 | $173,900 | $12,000 | $116,200 | $373,600 |

---

15. *FASB Statement of Financial Accounting Concepts No. 6, op. cit.,* par. 66–69.

APB Opinion No. 22 requires that a description of all significant accounting policies of a company be included as an integral part of its financial statements. The *Opinion* also states that the disclosure should encompass principles relating to revenue recognition and asset allocation, particularly when these principles and methods involve (1) a selection from existing acceptable alternatives, (2) principles and methods peculiar to the industry in which the company operates, and (3) unusual or innovative applications of generally accepted accounting principles. Examples cited include, among others, those policies related to the basis for consolidation, depreciation methods, amortization of intangibles, inventory pricing, recognition of profits on long-term contracts, and revenue recognition from franchise and leasing operations. Although allowing for flexibility, it is suggested that the disclosure is particularly useful when made in a separate *Summary of Significant Accounting Policies* preceding the notes to the financial statements or as the initial note.[16] This summary (in part) for the Black & Decker Corporation is illustrated in Exhibit 3-9. A complete summary is included in the Coca-Cola Company financial statements in Appendix A.

### EXHIBIT 3-9
### Summary of Accounting Policies

**BLACK & DECKER CORPORATION**
Notes to Consolidated Financial Statements (in part)

*Note 1: Summary of Accounting Policies (in part):*
   *Principles of Consolidation:*   The consolidated financial statements include the accounts of the Corporation and its subsidiaries. Intercompany transactions have been eliminated.
   *Inventories:*   Inventories are stated at the lower of cost or market. The cost of United States inventories is based on the last-in, first-out (LIFO) method; all other inventories are based on the first-in, first-out (FIFO) method.
   *Property and Depreciation:*   Property, plant and equipment is stated at cost. Costs assigned to property, plant and equipment of acquired businesses are based on estimated fair value as of the date of acquisition. Depreciation is computed generally on the straight-line method for financial reporting purposes and on accelerated and straight-line methods for tax reporting purposes.

### Fair Value and Risk of Financial Instruments

Some companies, such as banks and brokerage firms, deal in financial instruments. These *financial instruments* include such items as notes payable and receivable, contracts for loan commitments, collateralized mortgages, interest rate swaps, and put and call options on stocks. In recent years, both the types and use of financial instruments have increased to the point where the FASB has become concerned about the disclosure of their fair values and risk. **FASB Statement No. 107** requires the disclosure of the fair value of all financial instruments (both assets and liabilities),

*Disclosures about fair values and risks of financial instruments are discussed in Chapter 11.*

---

16. "Disclosure of Accounting Policies," *APB Opinion No. 22* (New York: AICPA, 1972), par. 8, 12, 13, and 15.

whether recognized or not on the balance sheet. The fair value is the amount at which the instrument could be exchanged in a current transaction between willing parties (i.e., current exit value). The intent is to improve the reporting of a company's liquidity and financial flexibility. **FASB Statement No. 105** requires the disclosure of the credit, market, and liquidity risk associated with certain debt financial instruments. These disclosures include such items as the contract amount, the nature and terms, the amount of loss the company would incur if the counterparty failed to perform, the company's policy regarding collateral, and any significant concentrations of credit risk. The disclosures about the fair values and risk of financial instruments may be made either in the body of the financial statements or in the notes to the financial statements.[17]

## Contingent Liabilities and Assets

Certain conditions, situations, or circumstances exist on the balance sheet date that involve uncertainty as to possible losses or gains that a company may incur should some future event(s) occur. These are known as **loss contingencies** or **gain contingencies** and may need to be included directly in the financial statements by establishing related accounts through a journal entry, or disclosed in a note accompanying the financial statements.[18]

*Loss and gain contingencies are discussed in Chapter 11.*

An estimated loss from a loss contingency is accrued (reported as a loss and a liability or a reduction of an asset) if (1) it is *probable* that a liability has been incurred (or an asset impaired) and (2) the amount of the loss can be *reasonably estimated*. Examples of this type of loss contingency include product warranties and uncollectible accounts receivable. If either of these conditions is *not* met—that is, if there is only a reasonable possibility that the loss may have been incurred or if the amount of the loss cannot be reasonably estimated—disclosure is made, but in the form of a note. Examples of the latter type of loss contingency include guarantees of the debts of others and pending litigation against the company, where either the outcome of the litigation or the amount of possible loss is uncertain. An illustration of this type of contingency for Ashland Oil is shown in Exhibit 3-10. Gain contingencies are not reported in the financial statements and, if disclosed in a note, should be carefully explained to avoid misleading implications as to the likelihood of future revenues or gains.[19]

## Subsequent Events

An annual report usually is not issued for several weeks or months after the end of the accounting period, due to the time necessary for adjusting and closing the books and auditing the financial statements. During this time it is possible for significant business events and transactions to occur, which if not disclosed in the annual report would cause this report to be misleading. Subsequent events are discussed more fully in an auditing book; they are briefly summarized here.

---

17. "Disclosures about Fair Value of Financial Instruments," *FASB Statement of Financial Accounting Standards No. 107* (Norwalk, Conn.: FASB, 1991) and "Disclosure of Information about Financial Instruments with Off-Balance Sheet Risk and Financial Instruments with Concentrations of Credit Risk," *FASB Statement of Financial Accounting Standards No. 105* (Norwalk, Conn.: FASB, 1990).
18. "Accounting for Contingencies," *FASB Statement of Financial Accounting Standards No. 5* (Stamford, Conn.: FASB, 1975), par. 1.
19. *Ibid.*, par. 8–17.

### EXHIBIT 3-10
### Contingency

**ASHLAND OIL**
Notes to Consolidated Financial Statements (in part)

*Note I—Litigation, Claims and Contingencies (in part)*
  Four actions are pending against Ashland representing almost a thousand individual plaintiffs seeking damages in excess of $3.1 billion for Ashland's alleged introduction of pollutants into the air near its refinery in Catlettsburg, Ky. In 1990, a jury awarded four randomly selected plaintiffs in one of these actions a total of $10,320,000 in compensatory and punitive damages. On December 20, 1991, the West Virginia Supreme Court unanimously reversed the $10,320,000 verdict and remanded the case for retrial. In addition, Ashland and its subsidiaries are parties to numerous other claims and lawsuits (some of which are also for substantial amounts) with respect to product liability and commercial and other matters. While these claims and actions are being contested, the outcome of individual matters is not predictable with assurance.

**A subsequent event is one that occurs between the balance sheet date and the date of issuance of the annual report**, as illustrated in the following time diagram:

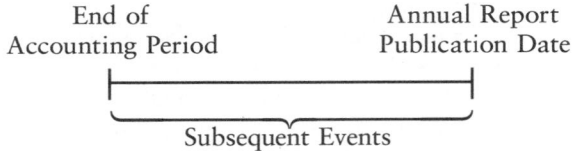

If a subsequent event occurs that (1) provides additional evidence concerning conditions that *existed* on the balance sheet date and (2) significantly affects the estimate(s) used in the preparation of the financial statements, an adjustment is made to the financial statements. For instance, if additional information is obtained indicating that a major customer's account receivable is unlikely to be collected, an adjustment to allowance for doubtful accounts and a recognition of a loss are appropriate.

  When a subsequent event occurs that provides evidence concerning conditions that did *not* exist on the balance sheet date, but instead occurred after that date, adjustment to the financial statements is *not* made. Instead, the information is disclosed in a note, pro forma ("as if") statements, or an explanatory paragraph in the audit report, depending upon the materiality of the financial impact. Examples of these events include a fire or flood loss, a litigation settlement, and the sale of a bond or stock issue after the balance sheet date.[20]

### Segment Reporting

*Segment reporting is discussed in Chapter 23.*

**FASB Statement No. 14** requires companies that do business in more than one industry to report on revenue, income, and asset data about each *significant industry segment*. Companies also are required to report on their foreign operations, major

---

20. *Codification of Statements on Auditing Standards* (New York: AICPA, 1993), sec. 560.03–560.09.

customers, and export sales. Information on a segment must be reported if the segment contributes 10% or more of a company's total revenue, operating profit or loss, or identifiable assets. The required disclosures for each significant segment include such items as (1) **revenues** (*excluding* general corporate revenues such as interest revenue), (2) **pretax operating profit or loss**, which is defined as revenues less all direct and allocable operating expenses (*excluding* general corporate expenses such as interest expense, extraordinary items, and income taxes), and (3) **identifiable assets** (*excluding* general corporate assets).[21] The revenues, pretax operating profits, and identifiable assets are combined and reported, respectively, for any insignificant industry segments. These segment totals must be *reconciled* to the total revenues, pretax income from continuing operations, and assets of the entire company.

Although the segment information may be reported directly on the face of the financial statements, most companies make the disclosure in the notes to the financial statements or in separate schedules. The Coca-Cola Company, whose financial statements are presented in Appendix A, discloses its segment information in schedules in Notes 18 and 19. The Caron Manufacturing Company, in the chapter example, operates in only one industry.

## Related Party Transactions

Transactions between related parties frequently occur in the normal course of business. Related parties of a company include affiliated entities such as subsidiaries, trusts for the benefit of employees, its management, and its principal owners or immediate families. Relationships between related parties may enable one of the parties to exercise influence over the other so that it is given preferential treatment. To provide sufficient information for external users to understand a company's financial statements, **FASB Statement No. 57** requires certain disclosures by the company. For each related party these include (1) the nature of the relationship involved, (2) a description of the transactions, (3) the dollar amounts of the transactions, and (4) any amounts due to or from the related party on the balance sheet date.[22] Centex Corporation discloses a related party transaction in Exhibit 3-7.

## Comparative and Interim Financial Statements

The illustrations in Exhibits 3-4 and 3-8 presented the ending balance sheet and the statement of changes in stockholders' equity of the Caron Manufacturing Company for a single year. Many external users are interested in comparing the current financial statements with those of the previous year. Furthermore many times *trend* information will reveal useful insights as to a company's past performance and future success. For this reason nearly all companies present **comparative financial statements** for the current and preceding accounting periods. Additionally in a supplemental schedule most companies will present a summary of critical accounting information for, say, the past 10 years. The Coca-Cola Company presents comparative financial statements as well as a supplemental schedule, as may be seen in Appendix A.

---

21. "Financial Reporting for Segments of a Business Enterprise," *FASB Statement of Financial Accounting Standards No. 14* (Stamford, Conn.: FASB, 1976), par. 23–27.
22. "Related Party Transactions," *FASB Statement of Financial Accounting Standards No. 57* (Stamford, Conn.: FASB, 1982), par. 2.

Companies whose stock is publicly traded are required by the SEC, as well as by the stock exchange on which their stock is traded, to issue quarterly financial statements. These **interim financial statements** rarely are as comprehensive as those contained in the annual report. In fact, in many instances only a condensed income statement is presented, although selected asset and liability information frequently is reported. Interim reports are prepared according to the generally accepted accounting principles established in **APB Opinion No. 28**, entitled "Interim Financial Reporting." This *Opinion* focuses primarily on the resolution of issues arising from revenue and cost allocations *within* the annual accounting period and upon the minimum necessary disclosures for a fair presentation of the company's activities.

*Interim financial reporting (APB Opinion No. 28) is discussed in Chapter 23.*

## Auditor's Report

*The auditor's report is discussed in Chapter 23.*

Many major financial decisions by investors, bankers, other creditors, and other users are based upon the financial information presented within a company's financial statements and related notes. These financial statements are the responsibility of the company's management. In order to help ensure a fair presentation of corporate financial resources, obligations, and activities, most financial statements and accompanying notes presented to external users are audited by an independent certified public accountant. In an audit the certified public accountant is responsible for making an examination of the accounting system, records, and reports *in accordance with generally accepted auditing standards*. Based on this examination, the auditor expresses an *opinion* as to the *fairness in accordance with generally accepted accounting principles* of the financial statements and accompanying notes. Although this opinion is *not* itself part of the financial statements, it is an extremely important item of information, upon which external users place much significance.

The auditor's report may take several forms, depending upon the results of the audit examination. These reports are discussed in detail in any auditing book. The most favorable report is an unqualified opinion, as illustrated in Exhibit 3-11 for Eli Lilly and Company.

## SEC Integrated Disclosures

*The contents of a Form 10-K annual report are discussed in Chapter 23.*

As noted in Chapter 1, the Securities and Exchange Commission has the legal authority to prescribe accounting principles and reporting practices for all regulated companies. Each year, within 90 days of its fiscal year-end, a regulated company must file a *Form 10-K* annual report with the SEC. Of significance to the present discussion is that the SEC has developed an "integrated" set of disclosure requirements that enable a company to satisfy certain Form 10-K disclosure requirements by referring to its stockholders' annual report, provided the latter report includes certain items. Since many regulated companies now include these items in their annual reports, the items are briefly summarized as follows. For a more detailed discussion, see *Regulation S-X* of the SEC.

### Comparative Financial Statements

As discussed in the previous section, most companies present comparative financial statements for at least two years. The SEC requires comparative balance sheets for *two* years and comparative income statements and statements of cash flows for *three* years.

**EXHIBIT 3-11**
**Unqualified Opinion**

**REPORT OF INDEPENDENT AUDITORS**
Board of Directors and Shareholders
Eli Lilly and Company

We have audited the accompanying consolidated balance sheets of Eli Lilly and Company and subsidiaries as of December 31, 1992 and 1991, and the related consolidated statements of income and cash flows for each of the three years in the period ended December 31, 1992. These financial statements are the responsibility of the company's management. Our responsibility is to express an opinion on these financial statements based on our audits.

We conducted our audits in accordance with generally accepted auditing standards. Those standards require that we plan and perform the audit to obtain reasonable assurance about whether the financial statements are free of material misstatement. An audit includes examining, on a test basis, evidence supporting the amounts and disclosures in the financial statements. An audit also includes assessing the accounting principles used and significant estimates made by management, as well as evaluating the overall financial statement presentation. We believe that our audits provide a reasonable basis for our opinion.

In our opinion, the financial statements referred to above present fairly, in all material respects, the consolidated financial position of Eli Lilly and Company and subsidiaries at December 31, 1992 and 1991, and the consolidated results of their operations and their cash flows for each of the three years in the period ended December 31, 1992, in conformity with generally accepted accounting principles.

As discussed in Note 3 to the financial statements, in 1992 the company changed its methods of accounting for income taxes and postretirement health benefits.

*Ernst & Young*
Indianapolis, Indiana
January 30, 1993

*Selected Financial Data*
As discussed in the previous section, most companies present a summary of important accounting information for several years. The SEC requires *specific* disclosures for a *five-year period*. These include net sales or operating revenues, income (loss) from continuing operations and related earnings per share, total assets, long-term obligations and redeemable stock, and cash dividends declared per share. The SEC encourages the inclusion of other information that will help users understand and highlight trends.

*Management's Discussion and Analysis*
Management must include a discussion and analysis (MD&A) of the company's financial condition, changes in financial condition, and results of operations. The intent is to give investors the opportunity to look at the company from management's perspective. Management is asked to discuss the dynamics of the company's business and to analyze the financial statements. The discussion is intended to provide information that does not clearly appear in the financial statements but is useful in evaluating cash flows from operations and from outside sources. The major features should include, for instance, specific information about short-term and long-term liquidity and capital resources, a narrative discussion of the impact of inflation on

sales and on income from continuing operations, explanations of material changes in financial statement items between years, and known events and uncertainties expected to impact future operations. Other kinds of "forward-looking" information (e.g., trends) are required as well.

*Common Stock Market Prices and Dividends*

Several disclosures must be made. These include the principal trading markets for the company's common stock, the high and low market prices for each quarter in the last two years, the approximate number of stockholders, the dividends paid in the last two years, and any dividend restrictions.

## Miscellaneous Disclosures

In addition to the disclosures discussed throughout this chapter, numerous other disclosures are necessary in order to provide adequate information concerning a company's activities. These include information about such items as the company's stock option, pension, and insurance plans, long-term lease and purchase commitments, bond indenture provisions, notes receivable, and notes payable provisions. Specific disclosure requirements are discussed as we address each topic in the remaining chapters.

## International Accounting Differences

One of the objectives of the IASC is to ensure, to the extent possible, that published financial statements comply with international accounting standards. The financial statements required by the IASC are similar to those in the U.S. They include a balance sheet, income statement, and statement of cash flows, as well as related notes and other explanatory materials. However, International Accounting Standards do not *require* a particular format; the appropriate format depends on the type of company.

Companies may classify their assets on the balance sheet into long-term assets and current assets, with long-term assets presented first. Long-term assets include property, plant, and equipment, as well as other items (investments, long-term receivables, intangibles). These classifications are similar to those in the U.S., although companies are allowed to include "preliminary costs" and "reorganization costs" as other long-term assets. Current assets are similar to those under U.S. GAAP. Liabilities may be classified into three groups: long-term, current, and other, with long-term liabilities presented first. Long-term liabilities include secured and unsecured loans, intercompany loans, and loans from associated companies. Current liabilities are similar to those under U.S. GAAP. Other liabilities include such items as deferred taxes, deferred income, and provisions for pensions. Deferred income may include government grants, which are forms of financial assistance to a company by its government for compliance with certain conditions. On the other hand, some government grants for the construction of assets are treated as a reduction in the book value of the asset. A company is not *required* to separately classify current assets and current liabilities; it decides on the disclosures based on their usefulness. No offsetting of current assets and current liabilities is allowed.

The final section of the balance sheet is entitled *shareholders' interests*. Included in this section are (a) share capital and (b) other equity. Share capital includes items similar to those in the U.S. (e.g., par value, preferences, reacquired shares), as well as "capital not yet paid in." The other equity includes capital in excess of par value, revaluation surplus, reserves, and retained earnings. Although International Accounting Standards are based on historical cost, a revaluation surplus may arise because some countries allow companies to revalue (upward and downward) their property, plant, and equipment. Reserves may arise because of foreign statutes or tax laws.

Companies are also required to disclose their various accounting policies, as well as such items as restrictions on the title to assets, security given for liabilities, contingent assets and liabilities, and amounts committed for future capital expenditures. Furthermore, companies in "hyperinflationary" economies (e.g., the cumulative inflation rate over 3 years exceeds 100 percent) are required to prepare general price-level adjusted financial statements. In the following chapters, we briefly discuss the major differences between international and U.S. accounting standards as they apply to specific assets, liabilities, and income.

*Restatement of a company's nonmonetary assets, liabilities, and owners' equity items is discussed in Chapter 24.*

## REPORTING TECHNIQUES

Numerous reporting techniques are used in the presentation of the annual report. The major ones relating to the financial statement presentations are discussed next.

### Statement Format (Balance Sheet)

The format of a balance sheet for a particular company depends upon its size, the industry in which it operates, certain regulatory requirements, and tradition. However, three basic formats are generally used: the report form, the account form, and the financial position form.

The **report form** is used by most companies. Here the balance sheet takes a vertical format. The asset accounts are listed first, and the liability and stockholders' equity accounts are listed in sequential order directly below the assets. In contrast, the **account form** of the balance sheet is organized in a horizontal fashion, with the asset accounts listed on the left-hand side and liabilities and stockholder's equity accounts listed on the right-hand side. This is the format used in Exhibit 3-4. In the seldom used **financial position form**, current assets and current liabilities are vertically listed first to derive the working capital. The remaining assets are added and the remaining liabilities deducted to derive the residual stockholders' equity. Of 600 companies surveyed, the report form, account form, and financial position form are used by 412, 187, and 1 companies, respectively.[23]

### Combined Amounts

To reduce the size of the financial statements, certain related amounts are often combined. For instance, a company may list a single amount for property and equipment on the face of its balance sheet and then itemize the amounts applicable to land, buildings, and equipment in a note to the financial statements. Frequently the amounts for inventories are similarly combined and itemized, as illustrated in Exhibit 3-5. Generally, it is *not* proper to offset asset and liability accounts. For instance, the amount in a special Bond Sinking Fund account to retire long-term bonds would not be offset against the Bonds Payable account balance. In a few circumstances, a *right of offset* exists whereby a debtor (Company A) has a legal right to discharge all or some of the liability owed to another party (Company B) by applying an amount that the other party (Company B) owes to the debtor (i.e., a receivable of Company A)

*Right of offset is discussed in Chapter 5.*

---

23. *Accounting Trends and Techniques,* (New York: AICPA, 1992), p. 125.

against the liability.[24] For instance, when a bank loans money to a company in exchange for the company's accounts receivable that are assigned to the bank, the company would offset the assigned accounts receivable on its balance sheet against the liability owed to the bank. The Coca-Cola Company has combined its inventories and itemized the related amount in a separate note, as shown in its financial statements presented in Appendix A.

### Rounding

In Exhibits 3-3 and 3-8 the amounts presented for each account, subtotal and total, were rounded to the nearest hundred dollars. Rounding is usually undertaken to increase readability and to reduce the likelihood that readers will attach more precision to the numbers than is warranted. In fact, many major companies round to the nearest million dollars. In the Coca-Cola Company financial statements the amounts have been rounded as indicated.

### Notes, Supporting Schedules, and Parenthetical Notations

Additional information not included in the accounts on the financial statements is disclosed by means of a note, supporting schedule, or parenthetical notation.

The **notes** (sometimes called *footnotes*) accompanying the financial statements are extremely useful ways of presenting additional information. Generally accepted accounting principles *require* that certain information (for instance, contingent liabilities) be disclosed in the notes to the financial statements, while sound accounting practice mandates additional note disclosures when they add to the completeness of the annual report. Notes usually contain narrative discussion, additional monetary amounts, and sometimes supplemental schedules.

Several notes of actual companies were illustrated earlier in this chapter. Required and suggested disclosures in notes are also discussed throughout this text as they apply to specific topics. Because notes must communicate technical accounting information in a narrative format, several suggestions have been made to improve their clarity and readability. In the preparation and writing of financial reporting notes, the accountant should (1) specify what data are to be disclosed, (2) outline the desired format of the note, (3) construct and use short sentences in the note, (4) use terminology understandable to the external user, and (5) be concise but complete.[25]

**Supporting schedules** may be freestanding or part of the notes. A supporting schedule may complement an entire financial statement (such as the statement of changes in stockholders' equity) or may explain a summary amount on a specific financial statement (such as an itemization of inventories). Supporting schedules are discussed and illustrated throughout the text.

**Parenthetical notations** following specific accounts are used to explain such items as the method of valuation (for example, cost, lower of cost or market) or of determining the ending inventory (for example, average cost), or to cross-reference certain related asset and liability accounts (for example, bond sinking fund and bonds payable).

---

24. For the criteria to be met for a right of offset to exist, see "Offsetting of Amounts Related to Certain Contracts," *FASB Interpretation No. 39* (Norwalk, Conn.: FASB, 1992), par. 5.
25. For a further discussion of notes to the financial statements, see J. S. Worthington, "Footnotes: Readability or Liability," *The CPA Journal,* May, 1978, pp. 27–32.

## ILLUSTRATIVE STATEMENTS

The actual financial statements and accompanying notes of the Coca-Cola Company for the year ended December 31, 1992 are shown in Appendix A. Although you may not understand all of these items at this point, pay particular attention to each statement's format and content and, in particular, to the notes accompanying the reports. Your understanding will increase as you study this book.

## QUESTIONS

*Q3-1* What are the major financial statements of a company and what do they disclose?

*Q3-2* What are the supporting schedules for the financial statements and what do these schedules disclose?

*Q3-3* What does a company's financial position include?

*Q3-4* What are two purposes of the balance sheet?

*Q3-5* Define liquidity, financial flexibility, and operating capability.

*Q3-6* What is financial capital? Why is capital maintenance important?

*Q3-7* Define an asset. What are the three characteristics of an asset?

*Q3-8* Define a liability. What are the three characteristics of a liability?

*Q3-9* What is stockholders' equity?

*Q3-10* Identify the five alternatives for measuring (valuing) assets. Which is the valuation method primarily used in a company's balance sheet?

*Q3-11* List the major sections (and the components of each section) of a balance sheet.

*Q3-12* a. How are current assets defined and what are the major items that may be included in current assets?
b. How are current liabilities defined? Give three examples of such liabilities.

*Q3-13* a. Define a company's operating cycle.
b. How does working capital relate to this cycle?
c. How is working capital computed?

*Q3-14* What items are properly classified as (a) long-term investments, (b) property, plant, and equipment, and (c) intangible assets?

*Q3-15* What items are properly classified as (a) long-term liabilities and (b) other liabilities?

*Q3-16* What is a bond? Give an illustration of how bonds payable would be disclosed on the balance sheet.

*Q3-17* Define (a) capital stock, (b) additional paid-in capital in excess of par, (c) retained earnings, (d) treasury stock, and (e) deficit.

*Q3-18* What are investments by owners? Distributions to owners? In what statement do many companies disclose these items?

*Q3-19* What accounting policies are disclosed in the notes accompanying a company's financial statements? Why is this disclosure important?

*Q3-20* Give several examples of financial instruments and identify the required disclosures for financial instruments.

*Q3-21* What is a loss contingency? What criteria have to be met to accrue a contingent liability? If these criteria are not met, how is a contingent liability disclosed?

*Q3-22* Why is it necessary to disclose subsequent events? What subsequent events are disclosed by an adjustment to the financial statements and what are disclosed in a note?

*Q3-23* What items of information must be disclosed in the financial statements for each significant industry segment of a company?

*Q3-24* What is an audit and why is the auditor's report an important item of information?

*Q3-25* Why are comparative financial statements important?

*Q3-26* Briefly describe the SEC "integrated" disclosures that most regulated companies include in their annual reports.

*Q3-27* Briefly list the format of a company's balance sheet under international accounting standards.

*Q3-28* What is the difference between the report form and the account form of the balance sheet?

*Q3-29* What alternative methods are used to disclose additional information on the financial statements? Give examples of the types of information disclosed by each method.

*Q3-30* What factors should be considered when an accountant prepares and writes financial reporting notes?

# CASES

### C3-1   *Valuation of Assets and Stock*

A friend has come to you for advice. He states that he owns several shares of stock in a corporation. He has examined the most recent balance sheet of the corporation and has found that the common stock issued and outstanding totals 40,000 shares, and the market price per share is $25 on the balance sheet date. He is sure that the balance sheet must be in error because in his words "the total assets are $1,100,000 and this current value should be the same as the $1,000,000 total value of the outstanding common stock."

**Required**

Explain to your friend how the "values" of the various assets of the corporation typically are measured and reported on its balance sheet, and how the "value" of the $1,100,000 total assets is determined. Continue the discussion by explaining to your friend why the "values" of the assets and the stock are not the same.

### C3-2   *Alternative Valuation Methods*

A friend of yours who had a bookkeeping course in high school and who is currently a business major says, "I thought that assets were always reported at their historical cost amount on a company's balance sheet. Recently, however, I heard several accounting majors discussing 'alternative valuation methods' for measuring the value of assets. I know that historical cost is the exchange price paid for an asset, so I cannot understand how there can be any other 'value' for the asset."

**Required**

Identify and briefly discuss the valuation methods (other than historical cost) that could be used to measure the value of an asset. For each valuation method, include in your discussion examples of assets whose values are often reported based on the use of that method.

### C3-3   *Valuation of Assets*

Valuation of assets is an important topic in accounting theory. Suggested valuation methods include the following:

   Historical cost (past purchase prices)
   Historical cost adjusted to reflect general price-level changes
   Discounted cash flow (future exchange prices)
   Market price (current selling prices)
   Replacement cost (current purchase prices)

**Required**

1. Why is the valuation of assets a significant issue?
2. Explain the basic theory underlying each of the valuation methods cited. Do not discuss advantages and disadvantages of each method. (*AICPA adapted*)

### C3-4   *Accounting Policies*

A company must include a summary of its accounting policies in the notes to its financial statements. The Coca-Cola Company includes this summary as the first note in its notes to the consolidated financial statements shown in Appendix A.

**Required**

1. Describe what is required to be disclosed about the accounting policies of a company.
2. Review the Coca-Cola Company's note on its accounting policies and answer the following questions:
   a. What accounts do the consolidated financial statements include?
   b. What items are classified as cash equivalents?
   c. How are inventories valued, and generally what inventory costing method(s) is used?
   d. How are property, plant and equipment stated, and what depreciation method is used?
   e. How are goodwill and other intangible assets stated, and what was the accumulated amortization at December 31, 1992?

### C3-5   *Contingencies and Subsequent Events*

The bookkeeper of a company you are auditing states, "Our balance sheet is dated December 31, the end of our accounting period. I don't understand contingent liabilities and subsequent events. Furthermore, I see no reason for disclosing these items on the balance sheet because they deal with events that might occur or have occurred *after* the balance sheet date."

**Required**

Explain contingent liabilities and subsequent events to the bookkeeper and discuss the importance of their disclosure on the balance sheet.

### C3-6   *Securities and Exchange Commission Disclosures*

The Securities and Exchange Commission (SEC) has encouraged managements of public companies to disclose more information in the shareholders' annual report. As a consequence, a significant amount of the information required in the SEC's Form 10-K now appears in published annual reports.

At the same time, the SEC has attempted to make the annual financial reporting process simpler and more efficient by approving an integrated disclosure system.

**Required**

1. Identify the major classes of information that must be included in both the annual report to shareholders and Form 10-K filed with the SEC.

2. The integrated disclosure system is intended to simplify the annual reporting process with the SEC by expanding the ability to incorporate by reference.

a. Define what is meant by *incorporating by reference* and identify the documents that are involved when incorporating by reference.

b. Explain how the integrated disclosure system should reduce managements' efforts in filing annual reports with the SEC.

c. Explain the SEC's principal reasons for making the changes in the annual reporting process.

d. Identify and explain potential problems the integrated disclosure system could have on the annual reporting process from the aspect of users of financial information. (*CMA adapted*)

*C3-7    Researching GAAP*    ⦾

You are the accountant for Tarwater Corporation, a diversified manufacturing company. The president says to you, "Our company has a good managerial accounting system. For financial accounting, I know we must report the revenues, profits, and assets of our significant industry segments. However, what is a logical starting point and what factors should we consider in determining which are our industry segments? Can you find out for me?"

**Required**

Research the related generally accepted accounting principles and prepare a short memo to the president that answers his question. Cite your reference and applicable paragraph numbers.

*C3-8    Asset Valuation*

It is the end of 1995 and you are an accountant for the Stone Company. During 1995, sales of the company's products slumped so that the company's earnings are expected to be much less than those of 1994. The president comes to you with an idea. He says, "Our company's property, plant, and equipment cost $300,000, and that is the amount we usually report on our balance sheet. However, I just had these assets appraised by an independent appraiser, and she says they are worth $400,000. I think that the company should report the property, plant, and equipment at this amount on its December 31, 1995 balance sheet, and should report the $100,000 increase in value as a gain on the 1995 income statement. If we use this approach, it will show how much our company is really worth and increase our earnings. This will make our stockholders happy. What do you think?"

**Required**

Prepare a written response to the president.

## MULTIPLE CHOICE

*Select the best answer for each of the following.*

M3-1    *APB Opinion No. 22*, "Disclosure of Accounting Policies,"

a. Requires a description of every accounting policy followed by a reporting entity

b. Provides a specific listing of all types of accounting policies that must be disclosed

c. Requires disclosure of the format for the statement of cash flows

d. Requires a description of all significant accounting policies to be included as an integral part of the financial statements

M3-2    Which of the following contingencies should generally be accrued on the balance sheet when the occurrence of the contingent event is reasonably possible and its amount can be reasonably estimated?

|  | Gain contingency | Loss contingency |
|---|---|---|
| a. | Yes | Yes |
| b. | Yes | No |
| c. | No | Yes |
| d. | No | No |

M3-3    A donated fixed asset for which the fair value has been determined should be recorded as a debit to fixed assets and a credit to

a. Unrealized capital

b. Retained earnings

c. Deferred income

d. Other income

M3-4     On October 2, 1995, a company borrowed cash and signed a 3-year interest-bearing note on which both the principal and interest are payable on October 2, 1998. At December 31, 1997 the accrued interest should

   a.  Be reported on the balance sheet as a current liability
   b.  Be reported on the balance sheet as a noncurrent liability
   c.  Be reported on the balance sheet as part of long-term notes payable
   d.  Not be reported on the balance sheet as a liability

M3-5     Financial statements that are expressed assuming a stable monetary unit are

   a.  General price-level financial statements
   b.  Historical-dollar financial statements
   c.  Current-value financial statements
   d.  Fair-value financial statements

M3-6     Rent revenue collected one month in advance should be accounted for as

   a.  Revenue in the month collected
   b.  A current liability
   c.  A separate item in stockholders' equity
   d.  An accrued liability

M3-7     Which of the following should be disclosed in the Summary of Significant Accounting Policies?

   a.  Rent expense amount
   b.  Maturity dates of long-term debt
   c.  Methods of amortizing intangibles
   d.  Composition of plant assets

M3-8     A company receives an advance payment for special order goods to be manufactured and delivered within six months. The advance payment should be reported on the company's balance sheet as a

   a.  Deferred charge
   b.  Contra-asset account
   c.  Current liability
   d.  Noncurrent liability

M3-9     The FASB has identified five alternatives for measuring balance sheet elements. Which of the following alternatives may be used?

|     | Net realizable value | Present value |
|-----|----------------------|---------------|
| a.  | No                   | No            |
| b.  | No                   | Yes           |
| c.  | Yes                  | No            |
| d.  | Yes                  | Yes           |

M3-10     The balance sheet provides information about each of the following items, except

   a.  Operating capability of entity
   b.  Results of entity's operations
   c.  Entity's liquidity
   d.  Financial flexibility of entity

*(AICPA adapted)*

## EXERCISES

E3-1     *Current Assets*     Listed here are certain accounts of the Jenkins Company at the end of 1995:

| Account | Debit (Credit) |
|---------|----------------|
| Land | $12,000 |
| Prepaid insurance | 1,530 |
| Cash on hand | 840 |
| Notes receivable (due 1998) | 4,300 |
| Cash in bank | 5,400 |
| Allowance for doubtful accounts | (1,100) |
| Marketable securities (short-term) | 3,380 |
| Accumulated depreciation | (8,700) |
| Accounts receivable | 15,600 |
| Office supplies | 970 |
| Buildings | 27,200 |
| Inventory | 17,800 |

**Required**
Prepare the current asset section of the balance sheet.

E3-2    *Plant and Equipment*  Your analysis of the fixed asset accounts at the end of 1995 for the Moen Corporation reveals the following information:

1. The company owns two tracts of land. The first, which cost $18,000, is being held as a future building site. It has a current market value of $20,000. The second, which cost $19,000, was purchased 10 years ago. On this site were built the current office and factory buildings. It has a current market value of $56,000.
2. The company owns two buildings. The office building and the factory building were both built 10 years ago at a cost of $50,000 and $120,000, respectively. At that time each was expected to have a life of 30 years and a residual value of 10% of its original cost. They are being depreciated on a straight-line basis.
3. The company owns factory machinery with a total cost of $51,000 and accumulated depreciation of $35,300. Included in factory machinery is one machine that cost $7,000 and has accumulated depreciation of $4,200. This machine is being held for resale and is not being used in operations.
4. The company owns office equipment that cost $14,500 and has a book value of $6,300. It owns office furniture that cost $17,900 and has a book value of $11,400.

**Required**
Prepare the property, plant, and equipment section of the 1995 ending balance sheet.

E3-3    *Stockholders' Equity*  The following are several accounts of the Graf Corporation at the end of 1995:

| Account | Credit Balance |
| --- | --- |
| Common stock, $10 par | $  47,100 |
| Bonds payable (due 2002) | 126,000 |
| Premium on preferred stock | 37,500 |
| Retained earnings (unrestricted) | 146,000 |
| Premium on bonds payable | 12,300 |
| Unearned rent | 4,800 |
| Preferred stock, $100 par | 65,400 |
| Premium on common stock | 53,900 |
| Unfunded accrued pension cost | 18,400 |
| Treasury stock (cost) | (7,800) debit |
| Retained earnings restricted due to bond contract | 63,000 |
| Donated capital from land | 9,300 |

**Required**
Prepare the stockholders' equity section of the 1995 ending balance sheet.

E3-4    *Classifications on Balance Sheet*  A balance sheet may contain the following major sections:

A. Current assets
B. Long-term investments
C. Property, plant, and equipment
D. Intangible assets
E. Other assets
F. Current liabilities
G. Long-term liabilities
H. Other liabilities
I. Contributed capital
J. Unrealized capital
K. Retained earnings

The following is a list of fifteen accounts. Using the letters A through K, indicate in which section of the balance sheet each account would most likely be classified. Place a check mark (√) beside each item that is a contra account. If an account cannot be classified in any of the preceding sections, indicate with an X and explain.

_____  1. Temporary investments in marketable securities
_____  2. Discount on bonds payable (bonds due in 5 years)
_____  3. Additional paid-in capital on common stock
_____  4. Accounts receivable
_____  5. Notes payable (due in 5 years)
_____  6. Patents (net)
_____  7. Unrealized decrease in value of securities available for sale
_____  8. Preferred stock
_____  9. Unearned rent (to be earned within next 6 months)
_____  10. Accrued pension cost
_____  11. Trademarks (net)
_____  12. Deficit
_____  13. Salaries payable
_____  14. Land
_____  15. Investment in Ace Company preferred stock

E3-5   *Classifications on Balance Sheet*   The balance sheet contains the following major sections:

A. Current assets        G. Long-term liabilities
B. Long-term investments     H. Other liabilities
C. Property, plant, and equipment     I. Contributed capital
D. Intangible assets        J. Unrealized capital
E. Other assets          K. Retained earnings
F. Current liabilities

The following is a list of several accounts. Using the letters A through K, indicate in which section of the balance sheet each of the accounts would be classified. Place a check mark (√) beside each item that is a contra account. If an account cannot be classified in any of the preceding sections, indicate with an X and explain.

| | | |
|---|---|---|
| _____ 1. Cash | _____ 12. Allowance for doubtful accounts |
| _____ 2. Bonds payable (due 2004) | _____ 13. Notes receivable (due in 3 years) |
| _____ 3. Machinery | _____ 14. Property taxes payable |
| _____ 4. Deficit | _____ 15. Deferred taxes payable |
| _____ 5. Unexpired insurance | _____ 16. Premium on preferred stock |
| _____ 6. Franchise (net) | _____ 17. Premium on bonds payable (due 2004) |
| _____ 7. Fund to retire preferred stock | _____ 18. Goods in process |
| _____ 8. Current portion of mortgage payable | _____ 19. Common stock, $1 par |
| _____ 9. Accumulated depreciation | _____ 20. Land |
| _____ 10. Copyrights (net) | _____ 21. Treasury stock (at cost) |
| _____ 11. Investment in bonds held to maturity | _____ 22. Donated capital |

E3-6   *Balance Sheet*   The balance sheet accounts and amounts of the Baggett Company as of December 31, 1995 are shown in random order as follows:

| Account | Debit (Credit) | Account | Debit (Credit) |
|---|---|---|---|
| Income taxes payable | $ (3,800) | Premium on preferred stock | $ (7,900) |
| Prepaid items | 1,800 | Allowance for doubtful accounts | (1,600) |
| Premium on common stock | (9,300) | Bonds payable (due 2005) | (23,000) |
| Land | 12,200 | Buildings | 57,400 |
| Notes payable (due 1998) | (6,000) | Sinking fund to retire bonds payable | 5,000 |
| Notes receivable (due 1997) | 16,400 | Advances from customers (long-term) | (2,600) |
| Accounts receivable | 12,600 | Cash | 3,500 |
| Premium on bonds payable | (1,400) | Accumulated depreciation: equipment | (9,700) |
| Accounts payable | (12,900) | Retained earnings | (18,300) |
| Inventory | 7,400 | Preferred stock, $100 par | (18,000) |
| Accumulated depreciation: buildings | (21,000) | Wages payable | (1,400) |
| Patents (net) | 4,600 | Common stock, $10 par | (12,700) |
| Equipment | 28,700 | | |

**Required**
Prepare a December 31, 1995 balance sheet for the Baggett Company.

E3-7   *Balance Sheet*   The December 31, 1995 balance sheet accounts of the Hitt Company are shown here in alphabetical order:

| Account | Amount | Account | Amount |
|---|---|---|---|
| Accounts payable | $ 22,400 | Current taxes payable | $10,400 |
| Accounts receivable | 21,500 | Discount on bonds payable | 6,900 |
| Accumulated depreciation: buildings | 53,000 | Equipment | 72,400 |
| Accumulated depreciation: equipment | 35,100 | Inventory | 37,200 |
| Additional paid-in capital on common stock | 24,000 | Land | 30,000 |
| | | Marketable securities (short-term) | 6,100 |
| Additional paid-in capital on preferred stock | 11,500 | Patents (net) | 9,800 |
| | | Preferred stock, $100 par | 21,000 |
| Allowance for doubtful accounts | 800 | Retained earnings | 46,200 |
| Bonds payable (due 2009) | 77,000 | Salaries payable | 2,000 |
| Buildings | 144,000 | Trademarks (net) | 3,700 |
| Cash | 2,900 | Unrealized increase in value of marketable securities | 1,100 |
| Common stock, $10 par | 30,000 | | |

**Required**
Prepare the December 31, 1995 balance sheet of the Hitt Company.

E3-8    *Balance Sheet Calculations*  The balance sheet information at the end of 1995 and 1996 for the Dawson Company is as follows:

|  | 1995 | 1996 |
|---|---|---|
| Current assets | $   (a) | $25,000 |
| Long-term liabilities | (b) | 34,900 |
| Total contributed capital | (c) | (g) |
| Long-term investments | 19,200 | (h) |
| Retained earnings | 50,000 | 60,000 |
| Total liabilities | (d) | (i) |
| Intangible assets | 10,400 | 9,200 |
| Current liabilities | 14,500 | 12,300 |
| Capital stock, $5 par | (e) | 20,000 |
| Total assets | 142,600 | (j) |
| Additional paid-in capital | 15,400 | (k) |
| Property, plant, and equipment (net) | 85,700 | 92,800 |
| Unrealized capital | 6,900 | 6,900 |
| Total stockholders' equity | (f) | (l) |

*Additional information*: The company did not issue any common stock during 1996.

**Required**
Fill in the blanks labeled (a) through (l). All the necessary information is provided. (*Hint*: It is not necessary to calculate your answers in alphabetical order.)

E3-9    *Balance Sheet Calculations*  The balance sheet information of the Fermer Company at the end of 1995 and 1996 is as follows:

|  | 1995 | 1996 |
|---|---|---|
| Total stockholders' equity | $   (1) | $100,700 |
| Unrealized capital | 4,800 | 4,800 |
| Current liabilities | (2) | 9,800 |
| Intangible assets | 12,600 | 12,000 |
| Property, plant, and equipment (net) | (3) | 87,500 |
| Current assets | 18,500 | (8) |
| Total contributed capital | 51,000 | (9) |
| Long-term liabilities | (4) | 30,200 |
| Retained earnings | 40,300 | (10) |
| Total assets | (5) | (11) |
| Common stock, $10 par | (6) | (12) |
| Working capital | 9,300 | 10,200 |
| Additional paid-in capital | (7) | 36,000 |
| Long-term investments | 23,700 | (13) |
| Total liabilities | 38,100 | (14) |

*Additional information*: At the end of 1995, additional paid-in capital is twice the amount of capital stock. In 1996, the company issued (sold) 100 shares of common stock.

**Required**
Fill in the blanks numbered (1) through (14). All the necessary information is provided. (*Hint*: It is not necessary to calculate your answers in numerical order.)

E3-10    *Correction of Balance Sheet*    On December 31, 1995, the Stevens Company bookkeeper prepared the following erroneously classified balance sheet:

**STEVENS COMPANY**
**Balance Sheet**
**For Year Ended December 31, 1995**

| Current Assets | | Current Liabilities | |
|---|---|---|---|
| Inventory | $ 6,000 | Accounts payable | $10,200 |
| Accounts receivable | 5,900 | Allowance for doubtful accounts | 800 |
| Cash | 1,900 | Salaries payable | 1,500 |
| Treasury stock (at cost) | 3,300 | Taxes payable | 2,500 |
| Long-Term Investments | | Long-Term Liabilities | |
| Temporary investments in marketable | | Bonds payable (due 2001) | 11,000 |
| securities | 2,800 | Unearned rent (for 3 months) | 900 |
| Investment in X Company stock | 10,300 | | |
| Plant and Equipment | | | |
| Land | 8,100 | | |
| Office supplies | 800 | Owners' Equity | |
| Buildings and equipment | 35,600 | Retained earnings | 24,200 |
| Intangibles | | Accumulated depreciation on buildings | |
| Patents (net) | 4,700 | and equipment | 9,200 |
| Prepaid insurance (for 6 months) | 1,200 | Premium on common stock | 9,300 |
| Discount on bonds payable | 1,000 | Common stock, $10 par | 12,000 |
| Total Assets | $81,600 | Total Credits | $81,600 |

**Required**
You determine that the account balances listed on the balance sheet are correct but, in certain cases, incorrectly classified. Prepare a properly classified balance sheet as of December 31, 1995.

E3-11    *Changes in Stockholders' Equity*    On January 1, 1995 the Powder Company listed the following stockholders' equity section of its balance sheet:

| Contributed capital | |
|---|---|
| Preferred stock, $100 par | $ 92,800 |
| Common stock, $5 par | 37,400 |
| Additional paid-in capital on preferred stock | 21,500 |
| Additional paid-in capital on common stock | 58,700 |
| Total contributed capital | $210,400 |
| Retained earnings | 185,700 |
| Total stockholders' equity | $396,100 |

During 1995 the following transactions and events occurred and were properly recorded:
1. The company issued 1,700 shares of common stock at $13 per share.
2. The company issued 340 shares of preferred stock at $130 per share.
3. The company earned net income of $38,950.
4. The company paid a $7 per share dividend on the preferred stock and a $1 per share dividend on the common stock outstanding at the end of 1995.

**Required**
Prepare a statement of changes in stockholders' equity for 1995. (Include retained earnings.)

E3-12  *Changes in Stockholders' Equity*  On January 1, 1995 the Osborne Company reported the following alphabetical list of stockholders' equity items:

| | |
|---|---|
| Additional paid-in capital on common stock | $170,000 |
| Additional paid-in capital on preferred stock | 12,000 |
| Common stock, $2 par | 80,000 |
| Preferred stock, $100 par | 60,000 |
| Retained earnings | 209,000 |

During 1995, the company sold 3,000 shares of common stock for $10 per share and 500 shares of preferred stock for $125 per share. It also earned income of $99,000 and paid dividends of $8 per share on the preferred stock and $1.50 per share on the common stock outstanding at the end of 1995.

**Required**
Prepare a statement of changes in stockholders' equity for 1995. (Include retained earnings.)

## PROBLEMS

P3-1  *Classifications on Balance Sheet*  The current balance sheet of Day Company contains the following major sections:

A. Current assets
B. Long-term investments
C. Property, plant, and equipment
D. Intangible assets
E. Other assets
F. Current liabilities
G. Long-term liabilities
H. Other liabilities
I. Contributed capital
J. Unrealized capital
K. Retained earnings

The following is a list of 37 accounts. Using the letters A through K, indicate in which section each account would most likely be classified. Place a check mark (√) beside each item that is a contra account. If an account cannot be classified in any of the preceding sections, indicate with an X and explain.

1. Organization costs
2. Income taxes payable
3. Notes receivable (due in 5 months)
4. Unearned rent (for 10 months)
5. Discount on bonds payable (long-term bonds)
6. Data processing center
7. Furniture
8. Land held for future expansion
9. Timberland (net)
10. Treasury stock, at cost
11. Advances to sales personnel
12. Idle machinery
13. Deferred taxes payable
14. Raw materials
15. Retained earnings restricted due to bond provisions
16. Pollution control facilities
17. Cash from security deposits of customers on returnable containers
18. Donated capital from industrial park building site
19. Trademarks (net)
20. Finished goods
21. Cash dividends payable
22. Bond sinking fund
23. Temporary investments
24. Retained earnings, unrestricted
25. Advances to affiliated company (long-term)
26. Cash surrender value of life insurance
27. Leased equipment under capital lease
28. Additional paid-in capital on preferred stock
29. Interest receivable (due in 5 months)
30. Office supplies
31. Accrued pension cost
32. Obligation under capital lease contract
33. Investment in 8-year certificates of deposit
34. Unearned ticket sales
35. Estimated warranty (6-months) obligations
36. Unrealized decrease in value of securities held for sale
37. Cash

P3-2     *Balance Sheet Without Amounts*  The following is an alphabetical list of the accounts of the Oliver Manufacturing Company as of December 31, 1995:

| | |
|---|---|
| Accounts payable | Interest payable |
| Accounts receivable | Interest receivable |
| Accrued pension cost | Interest revenue |
| Accumulated depreciation: buildings | Investment in stock available for sale |
| Accumulated depreciation: equipment | Land |
| Accumulated depreciation: machinery | Land for future plant site |
| Additional paid-in capital on common stock | Loss on sale of equipment |
| Additional paid-in capital on preferred stock | Machinery |
| Administrative expenses | Mortgage payable (20 equal annual payments) |
| Allowance for doubtful accounts | Notes payable (short-term) |
| Bond sinking fund | Notes receivable (short-term) |
| Bonds payable (due 2007) | Office supplies |
| Buildings | Patents (net) |
| Cash in bank | Preferred stock |
| Cash on hand | Premium on bonds payable |
| Cash surrender value of life insurance | Prepaid insurance |
| Common stock | Raw materials |
| Cost of goods sold | Retained earnings |
| Deferred taxes payable | Salaries payable |
| Dividends payable | Sales |
| Equipment | Sales discounts taken |
| Estimated warranty (1-year) obligations | Sales returns |
| Finished goods | Selling expenses |
| General expenses | Temporary investments in marketable securities |
| Goods in process | Trademarks (net) |
| Income tax expense | Treasury stock, at cost |
| Income taxes payable | Unearned rent |
| Interest expense | Unrealized increase in value of securities available for sale |

**Required**
Prepare a balance sheet (without amounts) in proper format for the Oliver Manufacturing Company.

P3-3     *Balance Sheet*  The following is an alphabetical list of the December 31, 1995 balance sheet accounts and
amounts for the Green Manufacturing Company:

| | | | |
|---|---|---|---|
| Accounts payable | $20,900 | Interest payable | $ 500 |
| Accounts receivable | 15,300 | Investment in stock available for | |
| Accrued pension cost | 13,300 |  sale | 16,400 |
| Accumulated depreciation: buildings | 32,400 | Land | 17,000 |
| Accumulated depreciation: machinery | | Machinery and equipment | 57,800 |
|  and equipment | 30,000 | Marketable securities (short-term) | 8,400 |
| Allowance for doubtful accounts | 1,000 | Notes payable (short-term) | 4,900 |
| Bond sinking fund | 7,700 | Patents (net) | 8,600 |
| Bonds payable (due 2009) | 28,000 | Preferred stock, $100 par | 30,000 |
| Buildings | 92,500 | Premium on common stock | 16,300 |
| Cash | 6,100 | Premium on preferred stock | 7,000 |
| Common stock, $10 par | 44,100 | Prepaid insurance | 2,600 |
| Deferred taxes payable | 2,800 | Raw materials | 10,100 |
| Discount on bonds payable | 2,500 | Retained earnings | 28,100 |
| Dividends payable | 5,600 | Unearned rent | 5,000 |
| Finished goods | 23,800 | Unrealized increase in value of stock | |
| Goods in process | 14,700 |  available for sale | 2,000 |
| Income taxes payable | 8,900 | Wages payable | 2,700 |

**Required**
Prepare a properly classified balance sheet for the Green Manufacturing Company on December 31, 1995. List
the additional parenthetical or note disclosures (if any) that should be made for each item.

P3-4    *Balance Sheet*   The following is a list (in random order) of the December 31, 1995 balance sheet accounts of the Midwest Company:

| | | | |
|---|---|---|---|
| Additional paid-in capital on preferred stock | $ 1,600 | Accounts payable | $16,500 |
| Accounts receivable | 13,800 | Prepaid insurance | 900 |
| Dividends payable | 1,800 | Discount on bonds payable | 2,000 |
| Buildings | 50,000 | Common stock, $10 par | 15,000 |
| Bonds payable (due 2001) | 29,000 | Equipment | 29,000 |
| Retained earnings | 25,800 | Allowance for doubtful accounts | 700 |
| Office supplies | 1,900 | Preferred stock, $50 par | 10,000 |
| Current income taxes payable | 4,200 | Accumulated depreciation: buildings | 12,400 |
| Accumulated depreciation: equipment | 8,300 | Current interest payable | 2,900 |
| Organization costs | 2,400 | Investment in bonds held to maturity | 9,000 |
| Notes payable (due January 1, 1998) | 17,000 | Cash | 8,200 |
| Inventory | 24,400 | Treasury stock (at cost) | 1,500 |
| Additional paid-in capital on common stock | 7,700 | Accrued wages | 3,700 |
| Sinking fund for bond retirement | 4,000 | Land | 9,500 |

**Required**
Prepare a properly classified balance sheet for the Midwest Company on December 31, 1995.

P3-5    *Balance Sheet From Adjusted Trial Balance*   The following is the alphabetical adjusted trial balance of the Meadows Company on December 31, 1995:

| | Debits | Credits |
|---|---|---|
| Accounts receivable | $ 18,000 | |
| Accounts payable | | $ 11,100 |
| Accrued payables | | 6,500 |
| Accumulated depreciation | | 44,000 |
| Additional paid-in capital | | 44,200 |
| Cash | 4,700 | |
| Common stock, $5 par | | 29,600 |
| Cost of goods sold | 175,500 | |
| Current portion of long-term debt | | 6,200 |
| Deferred taxes payable | | 12,500 |
| Dividends distributed | 7,000 | |
| General expenses | 27,560 | |
| Income tax expense | 12,340 | |
| Income taxes payable | | 7,500 |
| Interest expense | 4,300 | |
| Inventories | 32,000 | |
| Investment in bonds held to maturity | 36,000 | |
| Long-term debt | | 56,300 |
| Long-term receivables | 37,500 | |
| Marketable securities (short-term) | 9,300 | |
| Patents (net) | 13,000 | |
| Prepaid insurance | 5,000 | |
| Property, plant, and equipment | 148,000 | |
| Retained earnings, 1/1/95 | | 64,800 |
| Sales | | 278,000 |
| Sales returns | 8,000 | |
| Selling expenses | 21,500 | |
| Unrealized decrease in value of securities available for sale | 1,000 | |
| | $560,700 | $560,700 |

**Required**
Prepare the December 31, 1995 balance sheet of the Meadows Company.

**P3-6**     *Balance Sheet and Notes*   Listed here in random order are the balance sheet accounts and related ending balances of the Eubanks Company as of December 31, 1995:

| | | | |
|---|---|---|---|
| Income taxes payable | $ 24,700 | Allowance for doubtful accounts | $ 1,500 |
| Prepaid items | 3,100 | Temporary investments | 16,000 |
| Cash surrender value of life insurance | 8,900 | Bonds payable | 80,000 |
| Preferred stock | 40,000 | Additional paid-in capital on common stock | 30,300 |
| Premium on bonds payable | 4,800 | Inventories | 98,500 |
| Cash | 12,700 | Accounts receivable | 32,300 |
| Property, plant, and equipment (net) | 229,300 | Patents | 18,200 |
| Accounts payable | 59,100 | Investment in bonds | 25,000 |
| Common stock | 62,800 | Additional paid-in capital on preferred stock | 23,400 |
| Retained earnings | 123,400 | Miscellaneous current payables | 6,200 |
| Land held for building site | 19,500 | Estimated liability for product warranties | 7,300 |

Additional information:
1. The company uses control accounts for inventories and property, plant, and equipment and lists the latter at its book value.
2. The straight-line method is used to depreciate buildings, machinery, and equipment based upon their cost and estimated residual values and lives. A breakdown of property, plant, and equipment shows the following: land at a cost of $32,000, buildings at a cost of $182,400 and a book value of $120,200, machinery at a cost of $63,900 and related accumulated depreciation of $18,600, and equipment (40% depreciated) at a cost of $53,000.
3. Patents are amortized on a straight-line basis directly to the patent account.
4. Inventories are listed at the lower of cost or market value using an average cost. The inventories include raw materials $22,200, goods in process $34,700, and finished goods $41,600.
5. Common stock has a $10 par value per share, 12,000 shares are authorized, 6,280 shares have been issued.
6. Preferred stock has a $100 par value per share, 1,000 shares are authorized, 400 shares have been issued.
7. The investment in bonds is carried at the original cost, which is the face value, and is being held to maturity.
8. Temporary investments in marketable securities were purchased at year-end.
9. The bonds payable mature on December 31, 2000.
10. The company attaches a one-year warranty on all the products it sells.

**Required**
1. Prepare the December 31, 1995 balance sheet of the Eubanks Company (including appropriate parenthetical notations).
2. Prepare notes to accompany the balance sheet that itemize company accounting policies, inventories, and property, plant, and equipment.

**P3-7**     *Comprehensive: Balance Sheet, Schedules, and Notes*   The following is an alphabetical listing of the balance sheet accounts and account balances of the Trale Company on December 31, 1995:

| | | | |
|---|---|---|---|
| Accounts payable | $ 44,200 | Income taxes payable | $ 19,700 |
| Accounts receivable | 37,100 | Inventory | 85,300 |
| Accumulated depreciation | 109,300 | Investment in affiliate | 30,000 |
| Additional paid-in capital on common stock | 20,000 | Long-term liabilities (book value) | 91,000 |
| Additional paid-in capital on preferred stock | 3,200 | Miscellaneous current payables | 6,800 |
| Allowance for doubtful accounts | 1,600 | Notes receivable | 17,000 |
| Bond sinking fund | 12,500 | Preferred stock | 32,000 |
| Cash | 13,800 | Property and equipment | 296,700 |
| Common stock | 80,000 | Retained earnings | 84,600 |

Additional information:
1. The company uses a control account for property and equipment, accumulated depreciation, and for long-term liabilities. The latter account is listed at its book value.
2. The straight-line method is used to depreciate property and equipment based upon cost, estimated residual value, and estimated life. The costs of the assets in this account are: land $29,500, buildings $164,600, store fixtures $72,600, and office equipment $30,000.
3. The accumulated depreciation breakdown is as follows: buildings $54,600, store fixtures $37,400, and office equipment $17,300.

4. The long-term debt includes 12%, $36,000 face value bonds that mature on December 31, 2000 and have unamortized bond discount of $1,000; 11%, $48,000 face value bonds that mature on December 31, 2004, have a premium on bonds payable of $1,800, and whose retirement is being funded by a bond sinking fund; and a 13% note payable that has a face value of $6,200 and matures on January 1, 1998.
5. The noninterest-bearing note receivable matures on June 1, 1996.
6. Inventory is listed at lower of cost or market; cost is determined on the basis of average cost.
7. The investment in affiliate is carried at cost. The company has guaranteed the interest on 12%, $50,000, 15-year bonds issued by this affiliate, the Jay Company.
8. Common stock has a $10 par value per share, 10,000 shares are authorized, and 1,000 shares were issued during 1995 at a price of $13 per share, resulting in 8,000 shares issued at year-end.
9. Preferred stock has a $50 par value per share, 2,000 shares are authorized, and 140 shares were issued during 1995 at a price of $55 per share resulting in 640 shares issued at year-end.
10. On January 15, 1996, before the December 31, 1995 balance sheet was issued, a building with a cost of $20,000 and a book value of $7,000 was totally destroyed. Insurance proceeds will amount to only $5,000.
11. Net income and dividends paid during the year were $50,500 and $21,000, respectively.

**Required**

1. Prepare the December 31, 1995 balance sheet (including appropriate parenthetical notations) of the Trale Company.
2. Prepare a statement of changes in stockholders' equity for 1995. (*Hint*: Work back from the *ending* account balances.)
3. Prepare notes that itemize the balance sheet control accounts and those necessary to disclose any company accounting policies, contingent liabilities, and subsequent events.

P3-8    *Corrections to Balance Sheet*   The Cable Company prepared the following balance sheet:

**CABLE COMPANY**
**Balance Sheet For Year Ended December 31, 1995**

| | | | |
|---|---|---|---|
| Working capital | $ 21,500 | Noncurrent liabilities | $ 62,000 |
| Other assets | 153,300 | Stockholders' equity | 112,800 |
| Total | $174,800 | Total | $174,800 |

Your analysis of these accounts reveals the following information:

1. Working capital consists of:

| | |
|---|---|
| Land | $ 12,000 |
| Accounts due from customers | 18,000 |
| Accounts due to suppliers | (24,000) |
| Inventories, including office supplies of $3,500 | 35,500 |
| Income taxes owed to government | (16,400) |
| Wages owed to employees | (3,600) |
| Note owed to bank (due December 31, 1997) | (17,000) |
| Securities held as a temporary investment | 17,000 |
| | $ 21,500 |

2. Other assets include:

| | |
|---|---|
| Cash | $ 14,000 |
| Prepaid insurance | 2,400 |
| Buildings and equipment | 100,000 |
| Discount on bonds payable | 3,000 |
| Investment in stock available for sale | 29,000 |
| Treasury stock (at cost) | 4,900 |
| | $153,300 |

3. Noncurrent liabilities consist of:

| | |
|---|---|
| Bonds payable (due 2005) | $ 33,000 |
| Allowance for doubtful accounts | 1,400 |
| Premium on preferred stock | 2,600 |
| Common stock, $5 par | 25,000 |
| | $ 62,000 |

4. Stockholders' equity includes:

| | |
|---|---|
| Accumulated depreciation: buildings and equipment | $ 40,000 |
| Preferred stock, $100 par | 12,000 |
| Premium on common stock | 16,900 |
| Retained earnings | 38,700 |
| Accrued pension cost | 6,500 |
| Unrealized decrease in value of securities available for sale | (1,300) |
| | $112,800 |

**Required**

Based on your analysis, prepare a properly classified December 31, 1995 balance sheet for the Cable Company.

P3-9     *Corrections to Balance Sheet*   The Brandt Company presents the following December 31, 1995 balance sheet:

### BRANDT COMPANY
### Sheet of Balances
### For Year Ended December 31, 1995

| | | | |
|---|---|---|---|
| Current assets | $ 44,300 | Current liabilities | $ 66,600 |
| Long-term investments | 13,600 | Long-term liabilities | 24,100 |
| Property and equipment | 123,500 | Contributed capital | 17,000 |
| Intangible assets | 7,700 | Unrealized capital | 22,500 |
| Other assets | 13,600 | Retained earnings | 72,500 |
| Total assets | $202,700 | Total equities | $202,700 |

The following information is also available:

1. Current assets include cash $4,700, accounts receivable $18,500, notes receivable (maturity date July 1, 1997) $10,000, and land $14,000.
2. Long-term investments include a $4,600 investment in stock available for sale that is expected to be sold in 1996 and a $9,000 investment in Dray Company bonds that are expected to be held until their December 31, 2004 maturity date.
3. Property and equipment include buildings costing $63,400, inventory costing $30,500, and equipment costing $29,600.
4. Intangible assets include patents that cost $8,200 and on which $2,300 amortization has accumulated and treasury stock that cost $1,800.
5. Other assets include prepaid insurance (which expires on November 30, 1996) $2,900, sinking fund for bond retirement $7,000, and trademarks that cost $5,200 and on which $1,500 amortization has accumulated.
6. Current liabilities include accounts payable $18,300, bonds payable (maturity date December 31, 2006) $40,000, and accrued income taxes payable $7,200.
7. Long-term liabilities include accrued wages $4,100 and mortgage payable (which is due in 5 equal annual payments starting December 31, 1996) $20,000.
8. Contributed capital includes common stock ($5 par) $11,000 and preferred stock ($100 par) $10,000.
9. Unrealized capital includes premium on bonds payable $4,300, premium on preferred stock $2,400, premium on common stock $14,700, and unrealized increase in value of securities available for sale, $1,100.
10. Retained earnings includes unrestricted retained earnings, $37,800, allowance for doubtful accounts $700, and accumulated depreciation on buildings and equipment of $21,000 and $13,000, respectively.

**Required**
Based on the preceding information, prepare a properly classified December 31, 1995 balance sheet for the Brandt Company.

P3-10     *Balance Sheet Calculations*   The balance sheet information of the John Company at the end of 1994 and 1995 is as follows:

| | 1994 | 1995 |
|---|---|---|
| Long-term liabilities | $  (a) | $ 33,100 |
| Unrealized capital | 8,000 | 8,000 |
| Working capital | 17,900 | 19,800 |
| Intangible assets | 19,400 | 18,000 |
| Common stock, $10 par | (b) | (i) |
| Total stockholders' equity | (c) | 178,400 |
| Accumulated depreciation | (37,500) | (48,600) |
| Total liabilities | 51,900 | (j) |
| Current assets | (d) | 39,800 |
| Retained earnings | 83,600 | (k) |
| Total contributed capital | 66,700 | (l) |

|  | 1994 | 1995 |
|---|---|---|
| Total assets | (e) | (m) |
| Additional paid-in capital | (f) | (n) |
| Long-term investments | 40,100 | (o) |
| Current liabilities | (g) | (p) |
| Property, plant, and equipment | (h) | 180,000 |

*Additional information*: At the end of 1994, (a) the amount of long-term liabilities is twice the amount of current liabilities, and (b) there are 2,900 shares of common stock outstanding. During 1995, the company (a) issued 100 shares of common stock for $25 per share, (b) earned net income of $20,600, and (c) paid dividends of $1 per share on the common stock outstanding at year-end.

**Required**

Fill in the blanks lettered (a) through (p). All of the necessary information is provided. (*Hint*: It is not necessary to calculate your answers in alphabetical order.)

P3-11 *Erroneous Balance Sheet* The Cutler Corporation prepared the following balance sheet:

**CUTLER CORPORATION**
**Balance Report For Year Ended December 31, 1995**

| Current Assets | | | Current Liabilities | | |
|---|---|---|---|---|---|
| Cash | | $ 7,100 | Accounts payable | | $ 13,800 |
| Accounts receivable | | 15,900 | Accumulated depreciation: | | |
| Inventory, at higher of cost or market | | | buildings | | 17,100 |
| (cost $27,200) | | 28,000 | Wages payable | | 3,000 |
| Long-Term Investments | | | Additional paid-in capital | | |
| Treasury stock (at cost) | | 1,400 | on common stock | | 23,200 |
| Investment in D Company bonds | | | Long-Term Liabilities | | |
| (at book value) | | 7,300 | Bonds payable | $46,000 | |
| Marketable securities, | | | Less: Sinking fund to retire | | |
| short-term at market value | | 10,000 | bonds | (6,000) | 40,000 |
| Property, Plant, and Equipment | | | Preferred stock, $50 par | | 15,000 |
| Land | | 11,300 | Premium on preferred stock | | 5,100 |
| Patents | $8,000 | | Accumulated depreciation: | | |
| Less: Accumulated amortization | (2,800) | 5,200 | equipment | | 7,000 |
| Buildings | | 40,800 | Current taxes payable | | 9,600 |
| Equipment | | 19,000 | Owners' Equity: | | |
| Intangibles | | | Common stock, $2 par | | 8,000 |
| Trademarks (net) | | 3,400 | Unrealized gain on write-up | | |
| Other Assets | | | of marketable securities | | |
| Cash surrender value of life insurance | | 5,000 | to market value | | 1,300 |
| Organization costs | | 2,300 | Unrealized gain on write-up | | |
| Discount on bonds payable | | 3,900 | of inventory to market value | | 800 |
| Total Assets | | $160,600 | Retained earnings | | 16,000 |
| | | | Allowance for doubtful accounts | | 700 |
| | | | Total Equities | | $160,600 |

**Required**

1. Identify the errors made in the Cutler balance sheet.
2. Prepare a corrected, properly classified balance sheet.

*P3-12*     *Complex Balance Sheet*     Presented below is the unaudited balance sheet as of December 31, 1995, prepared by the bookkeeper of Zues Manufacturing Corporation.

**ZUES MANUFACTURING CORPORATION**
**Balance Sheet**
**For the Year Ended December 31, 1995**

| Assets | | Liabilities & Stockholders' Equity | |
|---|---:|---|---:|
| Cash | $ 225,000 | Accounts payable | $ 133,800 |
| Accounts receivable (net) | 345,700 | Mortgage payable | 900,000 |
| Inventories | 560,000 | Notes payable | 500,000 |
| Prepaid income taxes | 40,000 | Lawsuit liability | 80,000 |
| Investments | 57,700 | Income taxes payable | 61,200 |
| Land | 450,000 | Deferred tax liability | 28,000 |
| Building | 1,750,000 | Accumulated depreciation | 420,000 |
| Machinery and equipment | 1,964,000 | Total Liabilities | $2,123,000 |
| Goodwill | 37,000 | Common stock, $50 par; 40,000 | |
| Total Assets | $5,429,400 | shares issued | 2,231,000 |
| | | Retained earnings | 1,075,400 |
| | | Total Stockholders' Equity | $3,306,400 |
| | | Total Liabilities and Stockholders' Equity | $5,429,400 |

Your firm has been engaged to perform an audit, during which the following data are found:

1. Checks totaling $14,000 in payment of accounts payable were mailed on December 30, 1995 but were not recorded until 1996. Late in December 1995, the bank returned a customer's $2,000 check, marked "NSF," but no entry was made. Cash includes $100,000 restricted for building purposes.
2. Included in accounts receivable is a $30,000 note due on December 31, 1998 from Zues' president.
3. During 1995, Zues purchased 500 shares of common stock of a major corporation that supplies Zues with raw materials. Total cost of this stock was $51,300, and market value on December 31, 1995 was $47,000. The decline in market value is considered temporary. Zues plans to hold these shares indefinitely.
4. Treasury stock was recorded at cost when Zues purchased 200 of its own shares for $32 per share in May 1995. This amount is included in investments.
5. On December 30, 1995, Zues borrowed $500,000 from a bank in exchange for a 10% note payable, maturing December 30, 2000. Equal principal payments are due December 30 of each year, beginning in 1996. This note is collateralized by a $250,000 tract of land acquired as a potential future building site, which is included in land.
6. The mortgage payable requires $50,000 principal payments, plus interest, at the end of each month. Payments were made on January 31 and February 28, 1996. The balance of this mortgage was due June 30, 1996. On March 1, 1996, prior to issuance of the audited financial statements, Zues consummated a noncancelable agreement with the lender to refinance this mortgage. The new terms require $100,000 annual principal payments, plus interest, on February 28 of each year, beginning in 1997. The final payment is due February 28, 2004.
7. The lawsuit liability will be paid in 1996.
8. Of the total deferred tax liability, $5,000 is considered a current liability.
9. The current income tax expense reported in Zues' 1995 income statement was $61,200.
10. The company was authorized to issue 100,000 shares of $50 par value common stock.

**Required**
Prepare a corrected classified balance sheet as of December 31, 1995. This financial statement should include a proper heading, format, and necessary descriptions. (*AICPA adapted*)

P3-13    *Changes in Stockholders' Equity*   On January 1, 1995 the Knox Company showed the following alphabetical list of stockholders' equity balances:

| | |
|---|---:|
| Additional paid-in capital on common stock | $130,000 |
| Additional paid-in capital on preferred stock | 6,000 |
| Common stock, $10 par | 100,000 |
| Preferred stock, $100 par | 50,000 |
| Retained earnings | 224,000 |

During 1995 the following events occurred and were properly recorded by the company:

1. The city of Greenville donated a factory site to the company for locating its factory in the Greenville industrial park. The factory site was recorded at its fair market value of $20,000.
2. The company issued 2,000 shares of common stock for $24 per share.
3. The company issued 110 shares of preferred stock for $115 per share.
4. The company reacquired 400 shares of its common stock as treasury stock at a cost of $26 per share. (*Hint*: Record the reacquisition cost in a Treasury Stock account.)
5. The company earned net income of $57,000.
6. The company paid a $7 per share dividend on the preferred stock and a $1.25 per share dividend on the common stock outstanding at the end of 1995 (treasury stock is not entitled to dividends).

**Required**
Prepare a statement of changes in stockholders' equity for 1995. (Include retained earnings.)

P3-14    *The Coca-Cola Company*   Review the financial statements and related notes of the Coca-Cola Company in Appendix A.

**Required**
Answer the following questions. (*Note*: You do not need to make any calculations. All answers may be found in the financial report.) Indicate on what page of the financial report you located the answer.

1. What was the amount of the current assets on December 31, 1992?
2. What was the amount in the allowance for doubtful accounts on December 31, 1992?
3. What is the par value of the company's common stock? How many shares had been issued at the end of 1992?
4. What was the total amount of inventories on December 31, 1992? What were the principal categories of inventory and related amounts on this date?
5. What was the long-term debt on December 31, 1992? Of this total, how much was for the 6 5/8% U.S. dollar notes due 2002?
6. What amount of accrued taxes on December 31, 1992 was for income taxes?
7. What was the amount of accounts payable and accrued expenses on December 31, 1992?
8. What inventory costing (valuation) method(s) was used for most inventories in 1992?
9. What was the reinvested (retained) earnings on December 31, 1992?
10. What was the total property, plant, and equipment before and after allowances for depreciation on December 31, 1992?
11. What were the total assets on December 31, 1992?
12. What were the current liabilities on December 31, 1992?
13. What were the number of shares and cost of the treasury stock held by the company on December 31, 1992?
14. What were the major lines of business of the company in 1992? What was the international operating income for soft drinks in 1992?
15. What were the net operating revenues in Latin America for 1992? What were the identifiable operating assets in Latin America at the end of 1992?

# 4

# THE INCOME STATEMENT AND STATEMENT OF CASH FLOWS

**Chapter Topics**

The income statement summarizes the results of a company's operations for the accounting period. This statement is alternatively referred to as a *statement of income*, *statement of earnings*, or *statement of operations*. It often is considered to be the most important financial statement in the annual report. Supporting the balance sheet and income statement is a schedule entitled the *statement of retained earnings* (or simply the *retained earnings statement*), which serves as the link between the two statements. The operations of a company may encompass routine ongoing activities as well as activities that are infrequent or unusual. In addition, a company may divest itself of a major segment of operations, report extraordinary items, make changes in accounting principles, and make adjustments to prior periods' financial statements. The proper disclosure of each of these items is discussed in this chapter as it relates to the income statement or retained earnings statement presentation. The statement of cash flows is also introduced in this chapter because of the relationship of operating, investing, and financing cash flows to different sections of the income statement and balance sheet.

# CONCEPTS OF INCOME

The income statement is an important financial statement for several reasons. The growth of large-scale corporations has resulted in absentee ownership, in which management operates the corporation while the ownership rests with a diverse set of stockholders. Accounting fulfills a **stewardship** function. The capital invested in the corporation by stockholders and the corporate income are both reported so that stockholders may evaluate management's operating effectiveness in maintaining and increasing capital. The *past* income of a corporation has been considered to be a useful indicator in **predicting cash flows** for *current* and *future* dividend payments by the corporation as well as its stock prices—important considerations on the part of current and potential investors. Similarly, short-and long-term creditors have found that an analysis of corporate income data provides useful information concerning the corporation's ability to generate cash from operations for use in the payment of interest charges and operating obligations.

While corporate income information has been recognized as being useful to a variety of user groups, accountants and economists have long debated what constitutes "income" and how it should be measured. One concept of income is that of capital maintenance, while a useful way to measure income is by means of the transactional approach.

## Capital Maintenance Concept

The capital maintenance concept focuses upon the capital, or net assets (assets minus liabilities) of the corporation. Under this concept, corporate income for a period of time is the amount that may be paid to stockholders during that period and still enable the corporation to be as well off at the end of the period as it was at the beginning.[1] In other words, **capital must be maintained before a corporation earns income on that capital.** Although capital may be thought of as financial capital or physical capital, the FASB subscribes to a financial capital maintenance concept. Application of this concept requires a comparison of the beginning and ending capital (that is, the net assets) after adjusting for any additional investments or disinvestments during the period. The resulting difference represents the corporate income. Given this definition, accountants and economists probably would agree upon the total income that a corporation earned over its entire lifetime. This lifetime income would be computed by comparing the total proceeds received from the liquidation of the net assets at the end of the life with the capital invested at the beginning of the life, adjusted for any additional investments or withdrawals. Here a condition of certainty exists regarding the value of the net assets at the two points in time.

*The capital maintenance concept is discussed in Chapter 3.*

However, **income information is needed on a more timely basis** (for example, on an annual basis) and, correspondingly, more uncertainty exists as to the value of the net assets that have not been liquidated at the end of such a shorter time period. For a shorter time period the values of a company's assets and liabilities at the beginning and end of the period may be measured in a variety of different ways. For a particular corporation these might include use of (1) the historical cost, (2) the current cost, (3) the current exit value in orderly liquidation, (4) the net realizable value in the due course of business, or (5) the present value of expected cash flows. Once the values of the assets and liabilities at the two points in time are measured using one of these

---

1. S. S. Alexander, "Income Measurement in a Dynamic Economy," *Five Monographs on Business Income* (New York: Study Group on Business Income, AICPA, 1950), p. 15.

methods, corporate income can be computed as the difference between the beginning and ending net assets (after any adjustments for additional investments or disinvestments). Many accountants and economists have advocated a particular valuation concept and methodology.[2] (A thorough discussion of the conceptual merits of these alternatives is an appropriate topic in an accounting theory book.)

A brief example of the capital maintenance approach to determining corporate income is presented here, using the historical cost method of valuing net assets. Assume that a corporation has net assets of $50,000 at the beginning and $90,000 at the end of the year and that no additional investments or withdrawals were made. Based upon a comparison of the ending and the beginning net assets, the corporation could pay out $40,000 to stockholders and still be as well off at year-end. This $40,000 is the corporate income for the year, using the capital maintenance concept *based on historical costs*. To illustrate further, assume that a corporation has beginning net assets of $45,000 and ending net assets of $80,000. An additional capital investment of $10,000 was made by stockholders during the year. The total income of the corporation for the year is $25,000 computed as follows:

| | |
|---|---:|
| Ending net assets | $80,000 |
| Less: Additional investment | (10,000) |
| Ending net assets excluding additional investments | $70,000 |
| Less: Beginning net assets | (45,000) |
| Total income for the year | $25,000 |

Unfortunately, in either of the two examples, **the aggregate income information is not very useful to various interested user groups.** The total income includes all amounts affecting net assets, whether they relate to usual or unusual, to extraordinary or ordinary events. Furthermore **no breakdown is presented that identifies the causal relationships and operating activities** that account for the various items included in this aggregated income amount and that may be of particular interest to a specific user group. Such specific information is available under the transactional approach to income measurement.

## Transactional Approach

As noted in Chapter 2, an objective of financial reporting is to provide information that is useful to investors, creditors, and other external user groups to evaluate the amounts, timing, and uncertainty of the future net cash inflows for a particular company. A derived specific objective is to **provide information about a company's comprehensive income and its components.** That is, the user groups are interested not only in an aggregate income figure, but also in the resources obtained from and the resources given up for ongoing operations, discontinued operations, and unusual and infrequent activities. Accountants are also concerned with developing reliable (verifiable) evidence of the income-producing and other business activities reported in the financial statements. As a result, a transactional approach to income measurement has evolved. Generally, **in the transactional approach, net assets are carried at historical cost, and changes in the assets and liabilities are not recorded unless a**

---

2.   See, for instance, E. O. Edwards and P. W. Bell, *The Theory and Measurement of Business Income* (Berkeley: University of California Press, 1970).

transaction, event, or circumstance has occurred that provides verifiable evidence of a change in value. The transactional approach is applied using the accrual basis of accounting. **In accrual accounting the financial impacts of transactions and other events and circumstances are recorded in the periods in which they occur rather than only in the periods in which cash is received or paid by the company.** In the transactional approach certain changes in values of the specific assets or liabilities are associated with the earning activities and included the company's income.

The transactional approach to income measurement is used in accounting today. It is consistent with the traditional capital maintenance concept since the income represents the difference between the beginning and ending adjusted net assets on an historical cost basis. However, **the accrual-based transactional approach to income measurement** is considered more informative because it **relates (matches) the accomplishments and the efforts** so that the reported income measures the performance of a company's earnings activities.[3] In this regard, the FASB has developed the concept of "comprehensive income" as follows:

> **Comprehensive income is the change in equity of a company during a period from transactions, other events, and circumstances relating to nonowner sources. It includes all changes in equity during a period except those resulting from investments by owners and distributions to owners.**[4]

The intent of the FASB is: (1) to develop a concept of income broad enough to include changes in value not traditionally reported in net income under the transactional approach and (2) to allow for flexibility as to where certain components of income are reported in the financial statements. Thus, comprehensive income might include various items not currently included in net income such as donated capital, discovery capital, corrections of errors, foreign currency translation adjustments, increases or decreases in value of certain investments, and the excess of additional pension liability over unrecognized prior service cost (discussed in later chapters). Furthermore, net income might be more narrowly defined to include only amounts related to usual and ordinary events; net income could then be combined with other items of earnings to determine comprehensive income. In any event, comprehensive income includes the same broad components as net income, namely revenues, expenses, gains, and losses. Since comprehensive income is an evolutionary concept, the focus here is primarily on the concept of net income used in today's financial reporting environment.

In the accrual-based transactional approach, a corporation's net income for an accounting period currently is measured as follows:

**Net Income = Revenues − Expenses + Gains − Losses**

The FASB has defined the various elements (revenues, expenses, gains, and losses) comprising net income. These definitions and their relationships are discussed later in the chapter. Additional discussions are presented throughout the book as they relate to specific situations. The definitions are intended to distinguish between the elements of net income but not to draw a fine line between them. The identification of what elements to include in the determination of net income, when these should be included (recognized), and the measurement of each element depends on the definitions. Accounting rules and conventions (generally accepted accounting principles)

---

3. "Objectives of Financial Reporting by Business Enterprises," *FASB Statement of Financial Accounting Concepts No. 1* (Stamford, Conn.: FASB, 1978), par. 45.
4. "Elements of Financial Statements," *FASB Statement of Financial Accounting Concepts No. 6* (Stamford, Conn.: FASB, 1985), par. 70.

also play a role in determining net income. Before we look at the definitions and generally accepted accounting principles, it is important to have an understanding of the concepts underlying the reporting of net income.

## CONCEPTUAL REPORTING GUIDELINES

By following the transactional approach to income measurement, the FASB is concerned with how a company reports net income and its components. In particular, the FASB is interested in improving the reporting of income statement information relating to return on investment, risk, financial flexibility, and operating capability. **Return on investment is a measure of overall company performance.** Stockholders (investors) invest capital to obtain a return *on* capital. Before a company can provide a return on investment, its capital must be maintained. **Risk is the uncertainty or unpredictability of the future results of a company.** The greater the range and time frame within which future results are likely to fall, the greater the risk associated with an investment in or extension of credit to the company. Generally, the greater the risk, the higher the rate of return expected. **Financial flexibility is the ability of a company to adapt to unexpected needs and opportunities.** Financial flexibility stems from, among other qualities, the ability to adapt operations to increase net operating cash flows and the ability to sell assets without disrupting operations. **Operating capability refers to a company's ability to maintain a given physical level of operations.** This level of operations may be indicated by the quantity of goods or services (e.g., inventory) produced in a given period or by the physical capacity of the fixed assets (e.g., property, plant, and equipment).[5]

*Return on investment, risk, financial flexibility, and operating capability are discussed in Chapter 2.*

### General Conceptual Guidelines

The FASB suggests that the contribution of a company's income statement to the preceding purposes of financial reporting can be improved by:

1. Providing information about its operating performance separately from other aspects of its performance.

2. Presenting the results of particular activities or events that are significant for predicting the amounts, timing, and uncertainty of its future income and cash flows.

3. Providing information useful for assessing the return on investment.

4. Providing feedback to users to assess their previous predictions of income and its components.

5. Providing information to help assess the cost of maintaining its operating capability.

6. Presenting information about how effectively management has discharged its stewardship responsibility regarding the company's resources.

5. "Reporting Income, Cash Flows, and Financial Position of Business Enterprises," *FASB Proposed Statement of Financial Accounting Concepts* (Stamford, Conn.: FASB, 1981), par. 7–33.

To accomplish these goals, the FASB has established general concepts to guide decisions about reporting information on (or related to) the income statement. It suggests that **the components of net income may be more important than the total amount.** A component of net income should be shown separately if it is important for the assessment of some aspect of future income. This guide implies the separate reporting of income from ongoing central operations, discontinued operations, and one or more components relating to peripheral activities, unusual activities, and other events and circumstances affecting the company. The guide also indicates that it is desirable to report information about industrial and geographic segments.

## Specific Conceptual Guidelines

More specific guidelines have been provided to aid in decisions concerning the presentation of revenues, expenses, gains, and losses. These guidelines are summarized as follows:

1. Those items that are judged to be unusual in amount based on past experience should be reported separately.

2. Revenues, expenses, gains, and losses that are affected in different ways by changes in economic conditions should be distinguished from one another. For instance, changes in revenues are the joint result of changes in sales volume and selling prices. Information about both types of changes is helpful in assessing future operating results.

3. Sufficient detail should be given to aid in understanding the primary relationships among revenues, expenses, gains, and losses. In particular, it is helpful to report separately: (a) expenses that vary with volume of activity or with various components of income, (b) expenses that are discretionary, and (c) expenses that are stable over time or depend upon other factors, such as the level of interest rates or the rate of taxation.

4. When the measurements of revenues, expenses, gains, or losses are subject to different levels of reliability, they should be reported separately.

5. Items whose amounts must be known for the calculation of summary indicators (e.g., rate of return) should be reported separately.[6]

These guidelines are intended to provide assistance for decisions concerning the grouping of items to show the components of net income and the elements that should be reported separately. The benefits of any additional information should, of course, be weighed against the costs of providing the information.

## ELEMENTS OF THE INCOME STATEMENT

The elements of the income statement are the broad classes of items comprising the statement. They are the "building blocks" with which the income statement is prepared. Each of the four elements—revenues, expenses, gains, and losses—is defined in **FASB Statement of Concepts No. 6.**

---

6. *Ibid.*, par. 34 and 46–48.

## Revenues

**Revenues are inflows or other enhancements of assets of a company or settlement of its liabilities (or a combination of both) during a period from delivering or producing goods, rendering services, or other activities that constitute the company's ongoing major or central operations.**

Revenues represent actual or expected cash inflows (or the equivalent) that occur as a result of the company's ongoing primary operating activities. Revenues are a measurement of the *accomplishments* of the operating activities during the accounting period. It is important to remember that revenues are a component of equity. The transactions that result in revenues are of various types, depending on the kinds of operations involved and the way revenues are recognized.[7]

*Revenue Recognition*
Recognition is the process of formally recording and reporting an item in the financial statements. To be recognized, an item must meet the definition of an element and be reliably measured in monetary terms. Recognition involves the depiction of an item in both words and numbers with the amount included in the totals of the financial statements. Most revenues are the joint result of many operating activities of a company and are "earned" gradually and continually as a result of this entire set of activities. These activities may be described as the earning process. **The earning process includes purchasing, producing, selling, delivering, administering, and cash collecting and paying.** Although revenues are defined in conjunction with this entire earnings (operating) process, **revenues are generally recognized when two criteria have been met: (1) realization has taken place and (2) they have been earned.** These criteria provide an acceptable level of assurance (i.e., reliability) of the existence and amounts of revenues. Sometimes one and sometimes the other criterion is the more important, but both must be satisfied to a reasonable degree for revenue to be recognized.

In regard to the first criterion, *realization* **means the process of converting noncash resources into cash or rights to cash.** Realization encompasses two terms: (1) realized and (2) realizable. *Realized* refers to the actual exchange of noncash resources into cash or near cash (e.g., receivables). *Realizable* refers to the situation where noncash resources are readily convertible into known amounts of cash or claims to cash. "Readily convertible" noncash resources have interchangeable units and can be sold at quoted prices on an active market. In regard to the second criterion, **revenues have been** *earned* **when the earning process is complete or essentially complete.** This occurs when the company has accomplished what it must do in order to be entitled to the benefits (e.g., assets) represented by the revenues.

**Revenue recognition usually takes place at the time goods are sold or services are rendered.** At this point, generally realization has occurred and the earning process is

---

7. The discussion in this section primarily is a summary of that presented by the FASB in *FASB Statement of Financial Accounting Concepts No. 6, op. cit.* and "Recognition and Measurement in Financial Statements of Business Enterprises," *FASB Statement of Financial Accounting Concepts No. 5* (Stamford, Conn.: FASB, 1984).

complete, or essentially complete. Although the general rule in accounting is to recognize revenue at the time of sale, in exceptional cases revenue is recognized in a period before or after the sale. This is done to reflect more accurately the nature of a company's operations (i.e., to increase the predictive value and representational faithfulness of the accounting information). These *exceptional* cases arise because:

1. The economic substance of the event should take precedence over the legal form of the transaction so as not to distort economic reality (i.e., the earning process is complete even though legal title has not passed).

2. There is great uncertainty about the collectibility of the receivable involved in a sale (i.e., realization has not occurred).

3. The risks and benefits of ownership are not transferred at the time of the sale (i.e., the earning process is not complete).

The alternative methods to recognize revenue in a period other than the period of sale include (1) the **percentage-of-completion method,** used for certain long-term construction contracts, (2) the **proportional performance method,** used for certain long-term service contracts, (3) the **installment method,** used when the collectibility of the receivable is very uncertain, and (4) the **cost recovery method,** used when the collectibility of the receivable is extremely uncertain. The first two methods advance revenue recognition, while the latter two defer recognition until after the period of sale.[8]

*Revenue recognition methods are discussed in Chapter 16.*

## Expenses

**Expenses are outflows or other using up of assets of a company or incurrences of liabilities (or a combination of both) during a period from delivering or producing goods, rendering services, or carrying out other activities that constitute the company's ongoing major or central operations.**

Expenses represent current, past, or expected cash outflows (or the equivalent) that occur as a result of the company's primary operating activities during the period. Expenses are a measurement of the *efforts* or *sacrifices* made in the operating activities. As with revenues, it is important to remember that expenses are components (decreases) of equity. The transactions and events that cause expenses are of many types, depending on the kinds of operations involved and the way expenses are recognized.

### Expense Recognition
To determine the income related to a company's primary operations during the accounting period, **the expenses (efforts) are matched against the revenues (benefits).**

---

8. See also L. T. Johnson and R. K. Storey, "Recognition in Financial Statements: Underlying Concepts and Practical Conventions," *Research Report* (Stamford, Conn.: FASB, 1982), and H. J. Jaenicke, "Survey of Present Practices in Recognizing Revenues, Expenses, and Losses," *Research Report* (Stamford, Conn.: FASB, 1981).

Three pervasive expense recognition principles have been identified by the FASB in order to properly match expenses against revenues:

1. **Association of Cause and Effect.** Certain costs are recognized as expenses on the basis of a presumed direct association with specific revenues.

Some transactions result simultaneously in both a revenue and an expense. The revenue and expense are directly related to each other, so that the expense is recognized at the same time as the revenue. Examples include costs of products sold, transportation costs for delivery of goods to customers, and sales commissions.

2. **Systematic and Rational Allocation.** Some costs are recognized as expenses in a particular accounting period on the basis of a systematic and rational allocation among the periods in which benefits are provided.

Many assets provide benefits for several periods. In the absence of a direct cause-and-effect relationship, a portion of the cost of each of these assets is rationally expensed each period. The allocation system should be based upon the pattern of benefits anticipated and should appear reasonable to an unbiased observer. Examples include depreciation of fixed assets, amortization of intangible assets, and the allocation of insurance costs.

3. **Immediate Recognition.** Some costs are recorded as expenses in the current accounting period because (1) the costs incurred during the period provide no discernible future benefits or (2) the allocation of costs among accounting periods or due to cause-and-effect relationships does not serve a useful purpose.

Examples of costs that are recognized immediately as expenses in the current period include items such as management's salaries and most selling and administrative costs. Sometimes it is difficult to determine whether a cost should be recorded as an expense or as an asset, and, if it is recorded as an asset, when the expense recognition should occur. Exhibit 4-1 is helpful in understanding the relationships among the terms cost, asset, and expense.

**EXHIBIT 4-1**

**COST: ASSET OR EXPENSE**

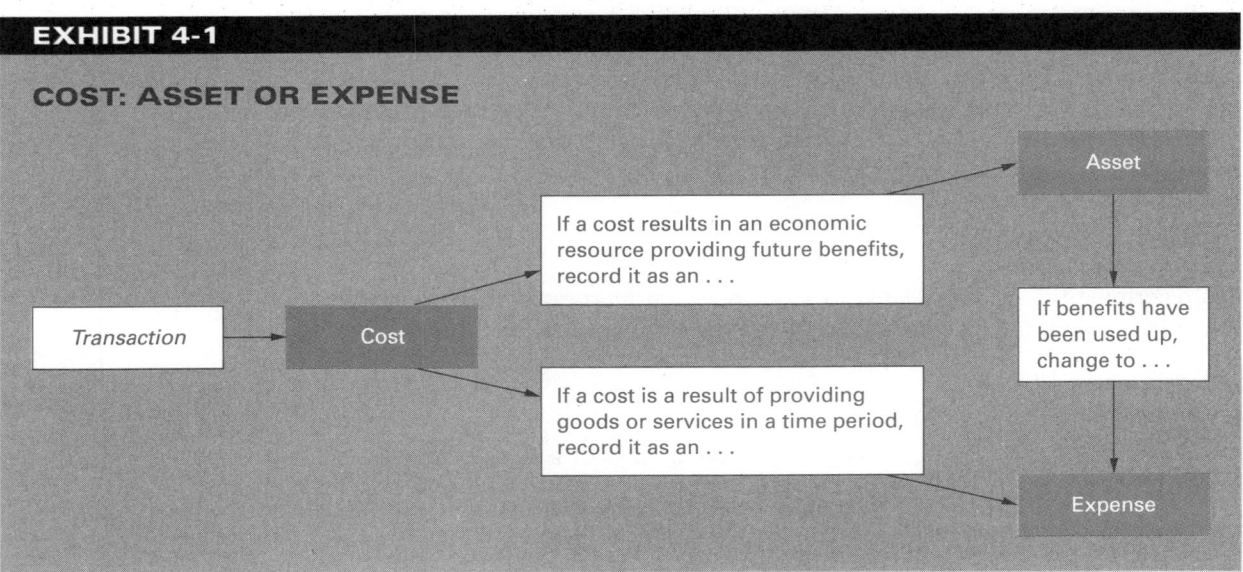

## Gains and Losses

**Gains are increases in equity of a company from peripheral or incidental transactions, and all other events and circumstances during a period except those that result from revenues or investments by owners.**

**Losses are decreases in equity of a company from peripheral or incidental transactions, and all other events and circumstances during a period except those that result from expenses or distributions to owners.**

Gains and losses, like revenues and expenses, are components of equity. Revenues and gains are similar, and expenses and losses are similar, but several differences are important in communicating information about a company's performance. First, while revenues and expenses are associated with a company's major operating activities, **gains and losses are identified with peripheral activities or with the effects of other events and circumstances,** many of which are beyond its control. Second, revenues and expenses are reported at "gross" amounts, which are matched against each other to determine earnings. **Gains and losses are reported "net"** —either because two or more measures are offset against each other or because they involve only a single increase or decrease in an asset or liability without an offsetting or related decrease or increase in some other asset or liability. A third difference between revenues and gains relates to the terms "realized" and "realizable," discussed earlier. In the case of revenues, these are generally recognized when *realized;* that is, when noncash goods or services are exchanged for cash or near cash. Whereas many gains are recognized when realized, some gains may be recognized when *realizable;* that is, when recorded assets are readily convertible into known amounts of cash based on interchangeable units and quoted prices in an active market.

Although the definitions of revenues, expenses, gains, and losses give broad guidance, they do not distinguish precisely between revenues and gains and between expenses and losses. The distinction depends to a significant degree upon the nature of the company, its operations, and its other activities. Items that are revenues (expenses) for one may be gains (losses) for another. In general, **gains and losses may be classified in three categories** as being derived from:

1. Exchange transactions

2. The holding of resources or obligations while their values change

3. Nonreciprocal (i.e., "one-way") transfers between a company and nonowners

An item falling in the first category, such as a gain or loss on the sale of used equipment, is the net result of comparing the proceeds to the sacrifice involved in the exchange transaction. Examples of gains or losses resulting from value changes include those from the writing down of inventory from cost to market, from the change in the market price of trading securities held by financial institutions, and from the change in a foreign exchange rate. Finally, gains or losses from nonreciprocal transfers include those due to lawsuits, assessments of fines or damages by a court, or natural catastrophes such as an earthquake or fire.

The revenues, expenses, gains, and losses as defined here are classified and measured in accordance with generally accepted accounting principles. The results of the major operating activities as well as peripheral activities are reported on the income statement.

## INCOME STATEMENT CONTENT

Although the *form* of the income statement may differ from company to company, its *content* has become relatively standard. The major components and items within each component of the income statement are:

1. Income from continuing operations
   a. Sales revenue (net)
   b. Cost of goods sold
   c. Operating expenses
   d. Other items
   e. Income tax expense related to continuing operations

2. Results from discontinued operations
   a. Income (loss) from operations of discontinued segments (net of income taxes)
   b. Gain (loss) from disposals of discontinued segments (net of income taxes)

3. Extraordinary items (net of income taxes)

4. Cumulative effects of changes in accounting principles (net of income taxes)

5. Net income

6. Earnings per share

Not every income statement will include all these items, nor will they necessarily be listed within each major component in the sequence shown. Each is discussed in the following sections of this chapter. A comprehensive illustration of the Banner Corporation income statement is shown in Exhibit 4-2. Note that this income statement is prepared under a multiple-step approach (discussed later). Supporting schedules for this income statement are illustrated in related exhibits. The Coca-Cola Company's 1992 income statement is shown in Appendix A at the end of this book.

### All-Inclusive Versus Current Operating

For many years accountants have debated about which items should be included in net income to make the income statement most informative. Some advocated the **current operating performance** concept. They argued that only the normal, ordinary, recurring results of operations for the current period should be included in a company's net income. Any unusual and nonrecurring items of income or loss should be disclosed in the statement of retained earnings. The reasoning was that investors are interested primarily in continuing operating income and that the disclosure of additional information would unnecessarily "clutter" the income statement. Others advocated the **all-inclusive** concept. Under this viewpoint all items increasing or decreasing stockholders' equity during the current period, with the exception of dividends and capital transactions, should be included in net income. Here it was argued that unusual and nonrecurring income or loss items are part of the earnings history of a company, and their omission from the income statement might cause them to be overlooked. With the issuance of **APB Opinion No. 9** the all-inclusive concept gained prominence. In this *Opinion* it was concluded that net income should include all items of profit or loss during the period, with the exception of certain material prior period adjustments that should be reflected as adjustments of the opening retained earnings balance. **APB Opinions No. 15, 20, and 30** require disclosure of the

## EXHIBIT 4-2
## Multiple-Step Income Statement

### BANNER CORPORATION

Income Statement
For Year Ended December 31, 1995

| | | |
|---|---:|---:|
| Sales revenue | | $150,000 |
| Less: Sales returns and allowances | $ 4,000 | |
| Sales discounts taken | 2,300 | (6,300) |
| Net sales | | $143,700 |
| Cost of goods sold (Exhibit 4-3) | | (86,000) |
| Gross profit | | $ 57,700 |
| Operating expenses | | |
| Selling expenses (Exhibit 4-5) | $10,200 | |
| General and administrative expenses (Exhibit 4-5) | 16,000 | |
| Depreciation expense (Exhibit 4-5) | 7,800 | |
| Total operating expenses | | (34,000) |
| Operating income | | $ 23,700 |
| Other items | | |
| Interest revenue | $ 1,800 | |
| Dividend revenue | 600 | |
| Loss on sale of equipment | (4,000) | |
| Interest expense | (2,100) | (3,700) |
| Pretax income from continuing operations | | $ 20,000 |
| Income tax expense | | (6,000) |
| Income from continuing operations | | $ 14,000 |
| Results from discontinued operations | | |
| Income from operations of discontinued segment A (net of $1,950 income taxes) | $ 4,550 | |
| Loss on disposal of segment A (net of $3,150 income tax credit) | (7,350) | (2,800) |
| Income before extraordinary items | | $ 11,200 |
| Extraordinary loss from explosion (net of $750 income tax credit) | | (1,750) |
| Cumulative effect on prior years' income of change in depreciation method (net of $600 income taxes) | | 1,400 |
| Net income | | $ 10,850 |

| Components of Income | Earnings Per Share (5,000 shares) |
|---|---:|
| Income from continuing operations | $2.80 |
| Results from discontinued operations | (0.56) |
| Extraordinary loss from explosion | (0.35) |
| Cumulative effect on prior years' income of change in depreciation method | 0.28 |
| Net income | $2.17 |

earnings per share, cumulative effects of changes in accounting principles, extraordinary items, and results from discontinued operations on the income statement. With the issuance of these opinions, application of the all-inclusive concept became even more prominent. Finally **FASB Statement No. 16** narrowed the interpretation of prior period adjustments so that the all-inclusive content of the income statement currently is as shown in the preceding outline.

Although the FASB subscribes to the all-inclusive concept of income, it has suggested that, theoretically, a company might use more than one income statement to report all the components of income in the most effective presentation. As noted earlier, in *FASB Statement of Concepts No. 5,* the Board suggested that a full set of financial statements should show, among other items, (1) net income for the period and (2) comprehensive income for the period.[9] The FASB sees the potential of net income evolving to be a measure of performance for the current period. In this case net income would be concerned with the extent to which net asset inflows associated with completed and substantially completed operating cycles during a period are greater (or less) than net asset outflows associated with the same cycles. The FASB views **comprehensive income** as a broad measure of the effects of transactions and other events and circumstances on a company. That is, it includes all recognized changes in net assets during a period (including net income) except those resulting from investments by and distribution to owners. The FASB acknowledges that some companies might choose to combine both of these items (net income and comprehensive income) in a single statement, and that changes in the form and content of the income statement will be an orderly, evolutionary process. To date, companies continue to use a single income statement for reporting their net income.

## Condensed Income Statements

In the interest of full disclosure the financial statements should disclose all information of sufficient importance to influence the judgment of informed external users. However, disclosures may be made in a variety of ways. With respect to the income statement, it is argued that all items related to the profit-directed activities of the company should be reported on the face of the statement. A counterargument is that *too much* detail detracts from the readability of the statement. Most companies take a compromise position and present a condensed income statement. Here only the major items of significance are disclosed directly on the income statement, frequently in an aggregated form, while supporting schedules and note disclosures supplement this information. In our discussions that follow, we identify those items that are likely to be aggregated on the income statement and give illustrations of the related supporting schedules.

## Income from Continuing Operations

This section summarizes the income from usual and recurring operating activities. It includes sales revenue, the various expenses related to these sales, any other items, and the associated income taxes.

### Sales Revenue (Net)

Sales revenue includes the gross charges to customers for the goods and services provided during the period. To determine the *net* sales revenue (or simply "net sales"), any sales returns or allowances given to customers (or reasonably estimated) and any

---

9. *FASB Statement of Financial Accounting Concepts No. 5, op. cit.,* par. 13.

sales discounts taken by credit customers (or reasonably estimated) are subtracted from sales revenue. As mentioned earlier, in order to increase the predictive value of the sales revenue information, the FASB advocates presenting sales volume and sales price information. To date, very few companies present this information.

*Cost of Goods Sold*

The cost of goods sold is the cost of the inventory items sold to customers during the period. In the case of a perpetual inventory system, this amount is recorded at the time of the sale and is reflected in the Cost of Goods Sold account. When a periodic inventory system is used, no reduction in inventory is made at the time of the sale. Consequently the amount must be calculated on the basis of a physical inventory taken at the end of the period. Usually the computation of the cost of goods sold is not shown on the face of the income statement, but instead in a supporting schedule. The form of the schedule will depend upon whether the company is a merchandising company or a manufacturing company. In the case of a merchandising company, net purchases are added to its beginning inventory. Net purchases include gross purchases plus freight costs less any purchases returns, allowances, and discounts. Theoretically such costs as receiving, storing, and insurance during transport should also be included in purchases. However, as a practical matter, these latter costs are usually treated as periodic expenses. From the resulting **Cost of Goods Available for Sale** amount the ending inventory is subtracted to determine the **Cost of Goods Sold.** The cost of goods sold schedule for the Banner Corporation is shown in Exhibit 4-3.

In the case of a company that manufactures instead of purchases its inventory, a **Cost of Goods Manufactured** amount replaces net purchases. To determine the cost of goods manufactured, the current factory cost is computed by adding (1) the cost of **raw materials** used in the production process, (2) the cost of **direct labor** used to convert raw materials into partially or fully completed inventory, and (3) the cost of the other factory items (referred to as **factory overhead**), such as factory utilities and depreciation, supervision, maintenance, and supplies. This total current factory cost is added to the beginning goods in process inventory (partially completed inventory from the previous period), from which the ending goods in process inventory is subtracted to determine the cost of goods manufactured. The cost of goods sold

---

**EXHIBIT 4-3**
**Cost of Goods Sold: Merchandising Company**

**BANNER CORPORATION**

Schedule 1: Cost of Goods Sold
For Year Ended December 31, 1995

| | | |
|---|---:|---:|
| Inventory, January 1, 1995 | | $ 41,000 |
| Purchases | $80,300 | |
| Freight-in | 5,500 | |
| Delivered cost of purchases | $85,800 | |
| Less: Purchases returns | (2,800) | |
| Net purchases | | 83,000 |
| Cost of goods available for sale | | $124,000 |
| Less: Inventory, December 31, 1995 | | (38,000) |
| Cost of goods sold | | $ 86,000 |

is computed by adding the cost of goods manufactured to the beginning finished goods inventory and subtracting the ending finished goods inventory. The cost of goods sold schedule, assuming that the Banner Corporation is a manufacturing concern, is shown in Exhibit 4-4. The cost of goods sold is subtracted from net sales to determine gross profit, as shown in Exhibit 4-2.

**EXHIBIT 4-4**
**Cost of Goods Sold: Manufacturing Company**

**BANNER MANUFACTURING COMPANY**

Schedule 1: Cost of Goods Sold
For Year Ended December 31, 1995

| | | |
|---|---|---|
| Raw materials used | | $ 35,000 |
| Direct labor | | 29,000 |
| Factory overhead: | | |
| Depreciation of factory items | $5,100 | |
| Heat, light, and power | 4,000 | |
| Indirect factory labor | 7,300 | |
| Repairs and maintenance | 3,400 | |
| Miscellaneous factory expense | 1,200 | 21,000 |
| Current manufacturing costs | | $ 85,000 |
| Add: Goods in process, January 1, 1995 | | 27,000 |
| Less: Goods in process, December 31, 1995 | | (29,000) |
| Cost of goods manufactured | | $ 83,000 |
| Add: Finished goods inventory, January 1, 1995 | | 41,000 |
| Cost of goods available for sale | | $124,000 |
| Less: Finished goods inventory, December 31, 1995 | | (38,000) |
| Cost of goods sold | | $ 86,000 |

### *Operating Expenses*

Operating expenses are those primary recurring costs (other than cost of goods sold) incurred in order to generate sales revenues. These expenses are typically classified according to *functional categories.* A common classification scheme is to separate (1) **selling expenses,** those expenses directly related to sales efforts, from (2) **general and administrative expenses.** Because of its significance, depreciation expense (excluding that included in cost of goods manufactured) may be shown as a separate classification. Research and development expense[10] may also be shown as a separate classification. Frequently single aggregate amounts are listed on the income statement for the selling, general and administrative, and depreciation expense classifications. When this occurs, a supporting schedule may be included that identifies the amounts of the individual expenses contained in each major classification. This supporting schedule for Banner is shown in Exhibit 4-5.

*Research and development costs are discussed in Chapter 10.*

10. Research and development expense is the cost incurred in the planned search for new knowledge and the translation of that knowledge into a plan or design for a new product or process or for a significant improvement to an existing product or process.

**EXHIBIT 4-5**
**Operating Expenses**

**BANNER CORPORATION**

Schedule 2: Operating Expenses
For Year Ended December 31, 1995

*Selling Expenses*

| | |
|---|---|
| Delivery expense | $ 1,800 |
| Advertising expense | 3,300 |
| Sales salaries expense | 4,100 |
| Sales supplies expense | 700 |
| Miscellaneous selling expenses | 300 |
| Total selling expenses | $10,200 |

*General and Administrative Expenses*

| | |
|---|---|
| Administrative salaries | $ 6,900 |
| Office salaries | 3,700 |
| Taxes and insurance expenses | 2,200 |
| Bad debts expense | 1,500 |
| Office supplies expense | 700 |
| Miscellaneous expenses | 1,000 |
| Total general and administrative expenses | $16,000 |

*Depreciation Expense*

| | |
|---|---|
| Office equipment | $ 3,300 |
| Store equipment | 4,500 |
| Total depreciation expense | $ 7,800 |

An alternative to classifying expenses by functions is to classify them according to how they vary with the volume of the main activities of the company. Under this scheme, expenses would be categorized as **variable** if they varied in direct proportion to changes in volume. Expenses would be categorized as **fixed** if their amount was not affected by changes in volume during the accounting period. As discussed earlier, the FASB suggests that this classification scheme would improve the predictive value of the expense information. Although many companies classify their costs as fixed and variable for internal (management) reports, virtually all continue to classify them by functions on their external financial statements. The total of the operating expenses is subtracted from the gross profit to determine the operating income, as shown in Exhibit 4-2.

*Other Items*

Included here are those significant recurring items of revenue and expense that are not directly related to the primary operations of the company. Examples include dividend revenue, interest revenue and expense, and items such as rent, storage, and service revenues (for a manufacturing or merchandising company). Also included in this section are (1) material gains and losses from the disposals of facilities that are *not* considered to be "segments" (as discussed in the results of discontinued operations section of this chapter), and (2) material but "nonextraordinary" gains and losses that result from events that are *either* unusual in nature *or* infrequent in occurrence, such as the write-down of obsolete inventories or the disposal of property (as discussed in the extraordinary items section of this chapter). As shown in Exhibit 4-2, a loss on the sale of equipment is included in this section of the Banner Corporation income statement because the sale is considered to be an infrequent but not unusual event. The total of the other items is added to or subtracted from the operating income to determine the pretax income from continuing operations, as shown in Exhibit 4-2.

### Income Tax Expense Related to Continuing Operations

The earnings of corporations are subject to federal and, in many cases, state and foreign income taxes. The amount of income taxes paid is determined according to the provisions of the Internal Revenue Code as well as state and foreign tax regulations. Income taxes are a significant expense on a corporation's income statement presented in its annual report. The tax regulations used for determining *taxable income* reported on a corporation's income tax return frequently are different from the accounting principles used to determine *pretax financial income* reported in the corporation's income statement. Additionally, pretax financial income consists of several major components. Because of these differences, two types of tax allocation are necessary.

*Interperiod and intraperiod tax allocation are discussed in Chapter 17.*

**Interperiod tax allocation involves allocating a corporation's income tax obligation as an expense to various accounting periods** because of temporary (timing) differences between its taxable income and pretax financial income. Generally, interperiod tax allocation requires that the annual income tax *expense* for financial reporting be based on pretax *financial* income and prior period adjustments, that the *current* income tax *liability* be based on *taxable* income, and that the *deferred* income tax *liability* (or asset) be based on the *temporary* differences.[11] Once the total income tax expense for the period is determined, intraperiod (or *within*-the-period) tax allocation is necessary.

**Intraperiod tax allocation involves allocating a corporation's total income tax expense of a period to the various components of its net income and retained earnings.** That is, a portion of the income tax expense is *matched* against (1) the income from continuing operations, (2) the income (loss) from the operations of a discontinued segment, (3) the gain (loss) from the disposal of a discontinued segment, (4) the extraordinary items, (5) the cumulative effect of any change in accounting principle, and (6) any prior period adjustments. The rationale behind intraperiod tax allocation is to give a fair presentation of the after-tax impact of the major components upon net income. The portion of the total income tax expense applicable to each segment of the Banner Corporation's income statement and statement of retained earnings is calculated in Exhibit 4-6. (For the sake of simplicity a constant 30% tax rate is applied on all taxable items in this chapter.) As shown in Exhibit 4-2, the portion of the income tax expense applicable to continuing operations is listed as a separate "line item" and subtracted from pretax income from continuing operations to determine income from continuing operations. However, the results from discontinued operations, each extraordinary item, the cumulative effect of a change in accounting principle, and any prior period adjustments are shown *net* of the income tax effect.

---

11. "Accounting for Income Taxes," *FASB Statement of Financial Accounting Standards No. 109* (Norwalk, Conn.: FASB, 1992), par. 8.

## EXHIBIT 4-6
## Intraperiod Tax Allocation

**BANNER CORPORATION**

Schedule of Income Tax Expense (Intraperiod Allocation)
For Year Ended December 31, 1995

| Component (Pretax) | Pretax Amount | × | Income Tax Rate | = | Income Tax Expense (Credit) |
|---|---|---|---|---|---|
| Income from continuing operations | $20,000 | × | 0.30 | = | $6,000 |
| Income from operations of discontinued segment A | 6,500 | × | 0.30 | = | 1,950 |
| Loss on disposal of segment A | (10,500) | × | 0.30 | = | (3,150) |
| Extraordinary loss from explosion | (2,500) | × | 0.30 | = | (750) |
| Cumulative effect of change in accounting principle on prior years' income | 2,000 | × | 0.30 | = | 600 |
| Prior period adjustment | 5,000 | × | 0.30 | = | 1,500 |
| Total income tax expense | | | | | $6,150 |

That is, for the latter items, the income tax expense (or tax *credit* in the case of a loss) is deducted directly from each item and only the after-tax amount is shown. However, it is sound accounting practice to disclose the amount of the tax impact on these items either parenthetically or in a note to the financial statements.

*Single-Step and Multiple-Step Formats*
The *form* in which the *income from continuing operations* is disclosed may vary from company to company. Many variations of two basic forms, the *single-step* and the *multiple-step* formats, are found in actual practice. **Under the pure single-step format, items are classified into two groups, revenues and expenses.** Income from continuing operations is computed in a single step as the difference between the totals of the two groups; hence the term single-step format. A variation in this format involves the income tax expense applicable to continuing operations. Because of the magnitude of the income tax expense, this amount is frequently listed as a separate item of income from continuing operations. In this case a subtotal entitled pretax income from continuing operations is computed, from which the associated income tax expense is deducted to determine income from continuing operations. The single-step format has been advocated because of its simplicity and flexibility and because the limited number of subclassifications does not impart more importance to certain items of revenue and expense than may be warranted. Although it is still a fairly common form of income statement, the number of companies using it is decreasing. Currently about 36% of surveyed companies use some variation of the single-step format.[12] This format is illustrated in Exhibit 4-7. Note that the lower portion (after

12. *Accounting Trends and Techniques* (New York: AICPA, 1992), p. 251.

income from continuing operations) of Exhibit 4-7 is the same as the lower portion of Exhibit 4-2, which illustrated the multiple-step format.

Some accountants argue that the simplicity of the single-step format detracts from the usefulness of the income statement to external users. The FASB suggests that components of a financial statement often reflect more homogeneous classes of items than the whole statement. Furthermore, the individual items, subtotals, or other parts of a financial statement may be more useful than the aggregate for external decision making. This supports the contention that **additional subclassifications on the multiple-step income statement are more informative.** The multiple-step format has a number of variations, but typically at least three subtotals are derived. Initially the cost of goods sold amount is deducted from net sales to determine the **gross profit** or **gross margin on sales.** The operating expenses are then deducted from (that is, matched against) gross profit to derive **operating income,** the major portion of income from continuing operations. The other revenues, expenses, gains, and losses, those important but nonoperating items that do not relate to the primary activities of the company, are then summarized in a subsequent section often entitled "Other Items." The net total of this section is added to (or deducted from) operating income to determine pretax income from continuing operations, which is reduced by the related income tax expense to determine **income from continuing operations.**

Two criticisms may be raised against the multiple-step format. First, this format may give the misleading inference that there is a priority in the recovery of expenses. However, *all* expenses must be recovered in order to earn income. Second, disagreement, particularly across different industries, as to what items of revenue and expense should be classified as operating (or primary) and nonoperating can lead to different classification schemes and result in noncomparable income statement formats. Nonetheless the multiple-step format is becoming more popular and is currently being used by about 64% of surveyed firms. The multiple-step format is the one used in Exhibit 4-2.

### Alternative Income Captions

In the preceding discussion of both single-step and multiple-step formats, the total of the initial section on the income statement has been referred to as Income from Continuing Operations. This caption presumes that the company is disclosing results from discontinued operations, extraordinary items, and cumulative effects of changes in accounting principles. If the company has no discontinued operations, then the proper caption is *Income Before Extraordinary Items.* If no extraordinary items exist, then a caption *Income Before the Cumulative Effects of Changes in Accounting Principles* should be used. Finally, if none of these latter three items appears on the income statement, then the total of the initial section should be labeled *Net Income.* At this point it may be useful to go back and review the upper portion of Exhibit 4-2 through Income from Continuing Operations.

## Results from Discontinued Operations

**APB Opinion No. 30** addresses a number of issues on reporting the operating results of a company. One issue deals with reporting the results of the discontinued operations of a "segment" of a business. **Discontinued operations are the operations of a segment that has been sold, abandoned, spun off, or otherwise disposed of. A segment is a component of a company whose activities represent a separate *major* line of business or class of customer.** This segment might be a subsidiary, division, or department provided that its assets, results of operations, and activities can be clearly

**EXHIBIT 4-7**
**Single-Step Income Statement**

BANNER CORPORATION

**Income Statement**
**For Year Ended December 31, 1995**

| | | |
|---|---:|---:|
| Revenues | | |
| Sales revenue (net of $2,300 discounts and $4,000 returns | | |
| and allowances) | $143,700 | |
| Interest revenue | 1,800 | |
| Dividend revenue | 600 | |
| Total revenues | | $146,100 |
| Expenses | | |
| Cost of goods sold (Exhibit 4-3) | $ 86,000 | |
| Selling expenses (Exhibit 4-5) | 10,200 | |
| General and administrative expenses (Exhibit 4-5) | 16,000 | |
| Depreciation expense (Exhibit 4-5) | 7,800 | |
| Loss on sale of equipment | 4,000 | |
| Interest expense | 2,100 | |
| Income tax expense | 6,000 | |
| Total expenses | | (132,100) |
| Income from continuing operations | | $ 14,000 |
| Results from discontinued operations | | |
| Income from operations of discontinued segment A | | |
| (net of $1,950 income taxes) | $ 4,550 | |
| Loss on disposal of segment A (net of $3,150 | | |
| income tax credit) | (7,350) | (2,800) |
| Income before extraordinary items | | $ 11,200 |
| Extraordinary loss from explosion (net of $750 income | | |
| tax credit) | | (1,750) |
| Cumulative effect on prior years' income of change in | | |
| depreciation method (net of $600 income taxes) | | 1,400 |
| Net Income | | $ 10,850 |

| Components of Income | Earnings Per Share (5,000 shares) |
|---|---:|
| Income from continuing operations | $2.80 |
| Results from discontinued operations | (0.56) |
| Extraordinary loss from explosion | (0.35) |
| Cumulative effect on prior years' income of change in depreciation method | 0.28 |
| Net income | $2.17 |

distinguished physically, operationally, and for financial reporting purposes, from the remainder of the company.[13]

The disposal of a segment is distinguished from the disposal of assets related to part of a line of business, the shifting of a particular line of business from one location to another, or the phasing out of a product line or class of service. The APB realized that it is sometimes difficult to determine what is a disposal of a segment and what is not. It provided several examples of transactions involving the disposal of a segment, which include (1) the sale by a diversified company of a major division that represents the company's only activities in the electronics industry, (2) the sale by a meat packing company of its 20% interest in a professional football team, (3) the sale by a communications company of its radio stations, but none of its television stations, and (4) the disposal by a food distributor of its wholesale supermarket division while maintaining its wholesale fast-food restaurants division. Transactions that should *not* be considered as a disposal of a segment include (1) the sale by a diversified company of one of its two furniture manufacturing subsidiaries, (2) the disposal by a manufacturer of children's wear of its foreign children's wear designing, selling, and manufacturing division, and (3) the sale by an apparel manufacturer of a woolen suit manufacturing plant in order to concentrate on the manufacture of suits from synthetic products.[14] While these examples are helpful, an accountant must use good judgment in determining when a company should report information concerning the disposal of a segment.

To enhance the usefulness of the income statement information for predicting the amounts, timing, and uncertainty of a company's earnings, the APB concluded that it is important to (1) disclose separately the results of ongoing, routine, and typical operations of a company, and also to (2) highlight the material results from the disposal of a business segment. **The results of discontinued operations are reported on a company's income statement after the income from continuing operations, but before extraordinary items,** as follows:

| | | |
|---|---:|---:|
| Income from continuing operations | | $XXXX |
| Results from discontinued operations (Note ___ ): | | |
|    Income (loss) from operations of discontinued | | |
|       Division X (less applicable income taxes of $___ ) | $XXXX | |
|    Loss (gain) on disposal of Division X (less | | |
|       applicable income tax credit of $___ ) | (XXXX) | XXXX |
| Income before extraordinary items | | $XXXX |

Note that the income or loss from discontinued operations and the loss or gain from the disposal of the segment are reported *net* of income tax. That is, the related income taxes are deducted directly from each item, and only the after-tax amount is included in the computation of net income. The amount of the related tax may be disclosed on the face of the income statement or in the accompanying notes. Listing these items net of income taxes requires intraperiod tax allocation, as discussed in an earlier section. The revenues applicable to the discontinued operations are separately

---

13. "Reporting the Results of Operations," *APB Opinion No. 30* (New York: AICPA, 1973), par. 8 and 13.
14. These examples were taken from *Accounting Interpretations of APB Opinion No. 30* (New York: AICPA, 1973).

disclosed in the related notes to the financial statements. When comparative income statements are presented, for each prior income statement the income from the discontinued segment is shown separately from the income from continuing operations of that period. Exhibit 4-2 illustrates the results from discontinued operations of the Banner Corporation (the tax amounts are taken from Exhibit 4-6). Exhibit 4-8 shows the disclosure by Westinghouse of the results of its discontinued segments. Observe in Note 2 that the discontinued segments involved its financial services and other non-strategic businesses. It is interesting to note that *Accounting Trends and Techniques* indicates that only 9% of surveyed companies reported results of discontinued operations.[15]

Any material gain or loss resulting from a transaction identified earlier as *not* being a disposal of a segment is disclosed as a separate component of income from continuing operations. As suggested earlier, this disclosure may be reported in the Other Items section. This gain or loss is *not* shown net of income taxes.

### Components

As may be seen in the preceding disclosure format, there are two components of the results from discontinued operations section: (1) **the operating income (loss)** and (2) **the gain (loss) on the disposal.** A business segment might be disposed of in the middle of an accounting period. Furthermore, the actual disposal date may take place later than the date when the management of the company decides to proceed with the disposal. That is, there may be a **"phase-out" period.** This phase-out period may be necessary to find a buyer, to reorganize the company's ongoing operations, or to help the acquiring company plan the integration of the segment into its business. During these periods of time, the segment to be disposed of may continue to operate and to earn an operating income or incur an operating loss. It would be inappropriate to include this income or loss as part of income from continuing operations, since the segment is being discontinued. Consequently, the APB identified two relevant dates, the measurement date and the disposal date. **The measurement date is the date when the management of a company commits itself to a formal plan to dispose of the segment. The disposal date is the date of actual sale or abandonment.**

### Operating Income (or Loss)

A segment usually operates for part of a year before it is discontinued. In this case the operating income (or operating loss) of the discontinued segment for the period from the beginning of the year up to the *measurement date* is reported separately from the income from continuing operations of the rest of the company. The calculation of the operating income (or loss) of the discontinued segment for the period of time up to the measurement date is relatively straightforward. The revenues and expenses from operating the discontinued segment are segregated from those related to continuing operations. The expenses of the discontinued segment are subtracted from the related revenues to determine the pretax operating income or loss. The related income taxes are deducted to determine the after-tax operating income or loss.

### Gain or Loss on Disposal

Any gain or loss from the disposal of the segment is reported in conjunction with the income (or loss) from discontinued operations. When the disposal date is the *same* as the measurement date, calculation of the related gain or loss is also relatively

---

15. *Accounting Trends and Techniques, op. cit.,* p. 331.

## EXHIBIT 4-8
## Discontinued Operations

**WESTINGHOUSE**

CONSOLIDATED STATEMENT OF INCOME (in part):

| | Year Ended December 31 | | |
| | 1992 | 1991 | 1990 |
|---|---|---|---|
| (in millions) | | | |
| Income from Continuing Operations | $ 348 | $ 265 | $ 746 |
| Discontinued Operations, net of income taxes (note 2): | | | |
|   Loss from operations | $ (21) | $(1,351) | $(478) |
|   Estimated loss on disposal of Discontinued Operations | (1,280) | — | — |
| Loss from Discontinued Operations | $(1,301) | $(1,351) | $(478) |

NOTES TO THE FINANCIAL STATEMENTS (in part):

*Note 2: Discontinued Operations (in part):*

In November 1992, the Board of Directors adopted a strategy that entails exiting the financial services business, over a three year-period, through the disposition of assets, the divestiture of other non-strategic businesses and the use of the net proceeds primarily to reduce debt. These businesses will be accounted for in accordance with APB 30.

As a result of this action, the Corporation recorded during the fourth quarter a pre-tax charge of $1,914 million. This pre-tax charge consists of $2,350 million for an addition to the valuation allowance for Financial Services portfolios, $300 million for estimated losses from operations for Financial Services during the phase-out period and $180 million for restructuring charges related to the change in corporate strategy. These charges were partially offset by an estimated $400 million gain from the disposition of other non-strategic businesses and an estimated $516 million of earnings from those operations during the phase-out period. Income tax benefits totalling $634 million were recorded in connection with this plan. The after-tax estimated loss on disposal of Discontinued Operations was $1,280 million.

   ⋮

In accordance with APB 30, the consolidated financial statements reflect the operating results of Discontinued Operations separately from Continuing Operations. Prior periods have been restated. In segregating the income statement components, corporate interest expense of $28 million for the eleven months ended November 30, 1992, and $26 million and $15 million for the years ended December 31, 1991 and 1990, respectively, has been allocated to WCI. The assets and activities of this operation, like WFSI, are atypical of the other non-strategic operations to be sold. The allocation of interest expense to WCI reflects the higher degree of leverage typically associated with the real estate development business. Summarized operating results of Discontinued Operations follow.

Operating Results of Discontinued Operations
(in millions)
*Eleven Months ended November 30, 1992*

| | Financial Services | Other Operations | Total |
|---|---|---|---|
| Sales and operating revenues | $ 699 | $2,926 | $3,625 |
| Income (loss) before income taxes | (181) | 123 | (58) |
| Income taxes (benefit) | (71) | 20 | (51) |
| Minority interest in income | 10 | 4 | 14 |
| Income (loss) from operations | (120) | 99 | (21) |

   ⋮

straightforward. Essentially, the proceeds received (if any) are compared to the book value of the net assets of the segment plus any costs of disposal to determine the pretax gain or loss. This is similar to the accounting treatment for the disposal of a single asset. The related income taxes are then deducted to determine the after-tax gain or loss. When the disposal date is *later* than the measurement date, the calculation becomes more complex because the segment may continue to operate during the phase-out period.

The phase-out period may fall within the same accounting period or it may extend beyond the end of the company's fiscal year. Each of these two situations requires different calculations.

**1. Phase-Out Within Accounting Period.** When the disposal date is later than the measurement date but falls within the same accounting period, the pretax gain or loss on the disposal of the discontinued segment is the *sum* of: (1) pretax operating income (or loss) of the discontinued segment from the measurement date to the disposal date, and (2) the pretax gain (or loss) on the disposal of the net assets. To illustrate, assume that on July 1, 1995 Timmons Company commits to a formal plan to dispose of Segment X, and sells it to another company on December 1, 1995. Thus, the measurement date is July 1, 1995 and the disposal date is December 1, 1995. Timmons Company's year-end is December 31. Segment X had operating income (pretax) during 1995 as follows:

January 1, 1995 to July 1, 1995:     $8,000
July 1, 1995 to December 1, 1995:     2,000

On December 1, 1995 Segment X was sold for $80,000. At that time the net assets of Segment X had a book value of $92,000. No disposal costs were incurred, and the company is subject to a 30% income tax rate.

The computations of Timmons Company's pretax operating income and loss on disposal of Segment X are shown in the following diagram:

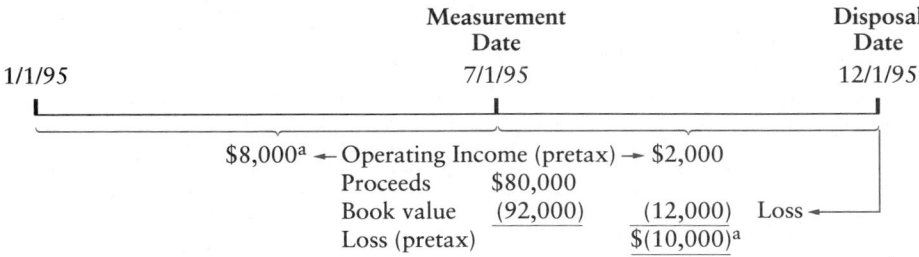

|  | Measurement<br>Date |  | Disposal<br>Date |
|---|---|---|---|
| 1/1/95 | 7/1/95 |  | 12/1/95 |

$8,000[a] ← Operating Income (pretax) → $2,000
Proceeds     $80,000
Book value   (92,000)    (12,000)   Loss ←
Loss (pretax)         $(10,000)[a]

[a]Recognized on the *measurement* date

Based on these computations, Timmons Company reports $5,600 ($8,000 x 0.70) income from the operations of discontinued Segment X (net of $2,400 income taxes) and a $7,000 ($10,000 × 0.70) loss[16] on the disposal of Segment X (net of $3,000

---

16. If Timmons Company prepared interim (quarterly) financial statements (discussed later), the company would have to estimate the gain or loss on the disposal at the measurement date, as illustrated in Example 2.

income tax credit) in the results from discontinued operations section of its 1995 income statement, as follows:

Results from discontinued operations
Income from operations of discontinued Segment X
   (net of $2,400 income taxes)            $5,600
Loss on disposal of Segment X (net of $3,000 income
   tax credit)                       (7,000)    $(1,400)

**2. Phase-Out After Fiscal Year-End.** When the phase-out extends beyond a company's year-end, additional complexities arise. In such a case, an *estimate* of the pretax gain or loss on the disposal of the discontinued segment must be made *on the measurement date*. The pretax gain or loss on the disposal is the *sum* of: (1) the estimated pretax operating income (or loss) from the measurement date to the disposal date, and (2) the estimated pretax gain (or loss) on the disposal of the net assets. The estimated pretax operating income (or loss) is separated into two components: (1) the estimated amount expected to be realized between the measurement date and the fiscal year-end, and (2) the estimated amount for the period from the beginning of the next fiscal year until the disposal date. The estimated pretax gain (or loss) is computed by comparing the estimated proceeds (if any) to the estimated book value of the net assets (plus any actual and estimated costs of disposal). If the two components result in an estimated *loss*, it is recognized on the measurement date in accordance with the *conservatism* convention. If the two components result in an estimated *gain*, however, it is deferred and recognized when realized, which is ordinarily the disposal date.

To illustrate the recognition of a loss, assume that on August 1, 1995 Crandall Company agreed to sell Segment Y to Dock Company, the sale to be consummated on May 1, 1996. Crandall Company is subject to a 30% income tax rate. The following information regarding Segment Y is available on the measurement date:

Actual pretax operating income, 1/1/95–8/1/95     $14,000
Estimated pretax operating income, 8/1/95–12/31/95     11,000
Estimated pretax operating loss, 1/1/96–5/1/96     (8,000)
Estimated pretax loss on disposal, 5/1/96     (22,000)

The computations of Crandall Company's pretax operating income and loss on the *measurement date* for the disposal of Segment Y are shown in the following diagram:

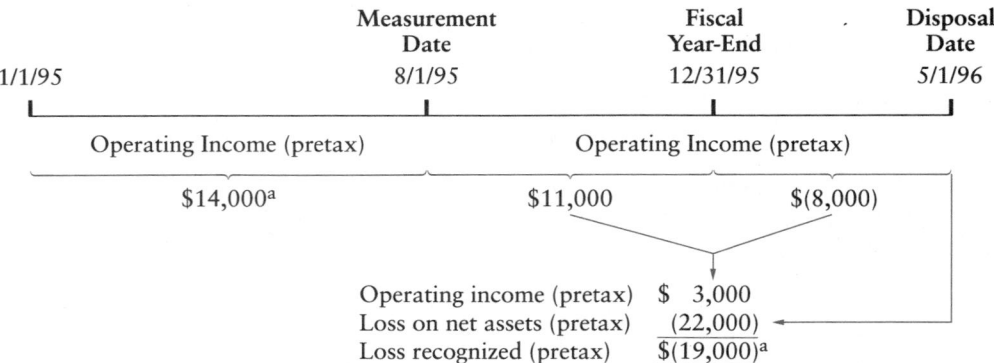

[a]Recognized on the *measurement* date

Based on these computations (and assuming actual and estimated pretax operating income is the same for 8/1/95–12/31/95), Crandall Company reports $9,800 ($14,000 × 0.70) income from operations of discontinued Segment Y (net of $4,200 income taxes) and a $13,300 ($19,000 × 0.70) loss on the disposal of Segment Y (net of $5,700 income tax credit) in the results from discontinued operations sections of its *1995* income statement, in the same manner as illustrated earlier. If actual operating results differ from estimated between the measurement date and the fiscal year-end, the reported loss is adjusted as a change in estimate.

*A change in estimate is discussed in Chapter 22.*

To illustrate the deferral of a gain, assume the same information for the Crandall Company, except for the following:

| | |
|---|---|
| Actual pretax operating loss, 1/1/95–8/1/95: | $(13,000) |
| Estimated pretax operating loss, 8/1/95–12/31/95: | (4,000) |
| Estimated pretax operating income, 1/1/96–5/1/96: | 5,000 |
| Estimated pretax gain on disposal, 5/1/96: | 15,000 |

The computations of Crandall Company's pretax operating income and deferred gain on the measurement date for the disposal of Segment Y are shown in the following diagram:

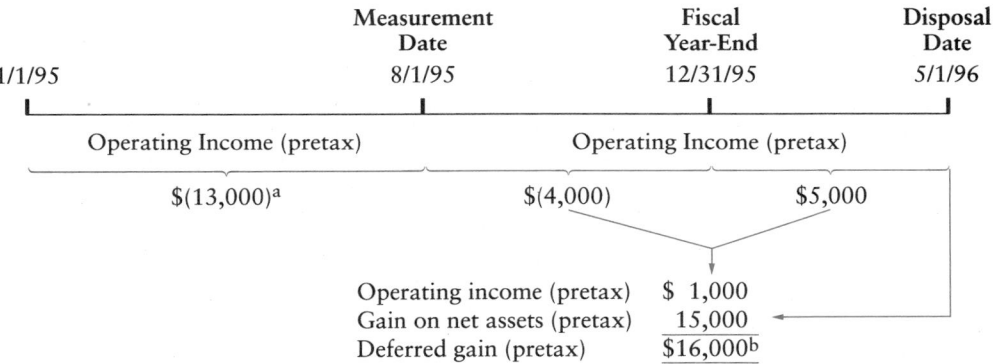

| | | | |
|---|---|---|---|
| **1/1/95** | **Measurement Date** **8/1/95** | **Fiscal Year-End** **12/31/95** | **Disposal Date** **5/1/96** |

Operating Income (pretax)      Operating Income (pretax)

$(13,000)ᵃ      $(4,000)      $5,000

| | |
|---|---|
| Operating income (pretax) | $ 1,000 |
| Gain on net assets (pretax) | 15,000 |
| Deferred gain (pretax) | $16,000ᵇ |

ᵃRecognized on the *measurement* date
ᵇRecognized on the *disposal* date

Based on these computations (assuming actual results are as estimated), Crandall Company reports a $9,100 ($13,000 × 0.70) loss from operations of discontinued Segment Y (net of $3,900 income tax credit) in the results from discontinued operations section of its *1995* income statement. The $16,000 gain, however, would be deferred and recognized in 1996 on the disposal date and reported (net of tax) in the results from discontinued operations section of its *1996* income statement.

Other combinations of actual and estimated operating income or loss and gains or losses on disposals of net assets are possible, and therefore the accountant should analyze each situation carefully. Also, as discussed in Chapter 3, when a segment is being discontinued by a company, the assets and liabilities of the discontinued segment are reported separately on the company's year-end balance sheet. Any difference between the actual and estimated gain or loss on the disposal of a discontinued segment is treated as a change in accounting estimate on the disposal date.

## Extraordinary Items

For some companies **extraordinary items** may occur that result in material gains or losses. **APB Opinion No. 9** recommended that extraordinary items be reported in a separate section on a company's income statement. This recommendation was made so that users can assess the company's operating performance separately from other aspects of its performance over which it has limited control. Unfortunately the criteria to be used in identifying an extraordinary item were not well defined, resulting in considerable variations in judgment. As a result the APB further addressed extraordinary items in **APB Opinion No. 30.** It established very narrow criteria that must be met before an event may be classified as extraordinary. **An extraordinary item is an event or a transaction that is unusual in nature *and* infrequent in occurrence.** *Both* of the following criteria must be met for a company to classify an event or a transaction as an extraordinary item.[17]

a. **Unusual nature—the underlying event or transaction possesses a high degree of abnormality and is of a type clearly unrelated to, or only incidentally related to, the ordinary and typical activities of the company, taking into account the environment in which the company operates.**

b. **Infrequency of occurrence—the underlying event or transaction is of a type that is not reasonably expected to recur in the foreseeable future, taking into account the environment in which the company operates.**

In discussing the **unusual nature** criterion, the APB suggested that **the environment in which a company operates is a primary consideration.** This environment includes such factors as the characteristics of the industry in which the company operates, its geographical location(s), and the nature and extent of government regulation. An event may be unusual in nature for one company but not for another because of differences in their respective environments. Similarly, the determination of whether an event is **infrequent** in occurrence should consider the operating environment of the company. An event might be considered infrequent for one company and frequent for another because of different probabilities of recurrence within each respective operating environment.

To illustrate, a loss from an explosion in an office building of a company may be classified as extraordinary, while a loss from an explosion in a munitions factory may *not* be considered extraordinary because the nature of the event is not unusual. Other examples of events that may give rise to extraordinary gains or losses include earthquakes, tornadoes, floods, expropriation of assets by a foreign country, and a prohibition under a newly enacted law or regulation, provided each event is *both* unusual and infrequent. Furthermore, as prescribed in **FASB Statement No. 4,** material gains or losses from the extinguishment of debt are always reported as extraordinary items. In this situation the two criteria are not always met, but disclosure as an extraordinary item is required to avoid misunderstandings of the nature of these items by users of financial statements, as discussed in Chapter 12.

The APB considered several events or transactions to be either usual in nature or expected to recur as a consequence of customary and continuing business activities. These are *not* extraordinary items and include (1) the write-down or write-off of receivables, inventories, equipment leased to others, or intangible assets, (2) gains or losses from exchanges or translation of foreign currencies, (3) gains or losses from

---

17. *APB Opinion No. 30, op. cit.,* par. 20.

the disposal of a business segment, (4) other gains or losses from the sale or abandonment of property, plant, or equipment, (5) the effects of a strike, and (6) the adjustment of accruals on long-term contracts.[18]

In order to clarify further the distinction between extraordinary and nonextraordinary items, the following illustrations were presented in a separate pronouncement. **Events or transactions that are reported as extraordinary items** because they meet both criteria include the following cases:

1. A large portion of a tobacco manufacturer's crops is destroyed by a hailstorm. Severe damage from hailstorms in the locality where the manufacturer grows tobacco is rare.

2. A steel-fabricating company sells the only land it owns. The land was acquired 10 years ago for future expansion, but shortly thereafter the company abandoned all plans for expansion and held the land for appreciation.

3. A company sells an investment in a block of common stock of a publicly traded firm. The block of shares, which represents less than 10% of the publicly held firm, is the only security investment the company has ever owned.

4. An earthquake destroys one of the oil refineries owned by a large multinational oil company.

**Events or transactions that are *not* reported as extraordinary items** because they do not meet both criteria include these examples:

1. A citrus grower's Florida crop is damaged by frost. Frost damage is normally experienced every 3 to 4 years. The criterion of infrequency of occurrence taking into account the environment in which the company operates would not be met since the history of losses caused by frost damage provides evidence that such damage may reasonably be expected to recur in the foreseeable future.

2. A company that operates a chain of warehouses sells the excess land surrounding one of its warehouses. When the company buys property to establish a new warehouse, it usually buys more land than it expects to use for the warehouse with the expectation that the land will appreciate in value. In the past 5 years there have been two instances in which the company sold such excess land. The criterion of infrequency of occurrence has not been met since past experience indicates that such sales may reasonably be expected to recur in the foreseeable future.

3. A large diversified company sells a block of shares from its portfolio of securities that it has acquired for investment purposes. This is the first sale from its portfolio of securities. Since the company owns several securities for investment purposes, it should be concluded that sales of such securities are related to its ordinary and typical activities in the environment in which it operates, and thus the criterion of unusual nature would not be met.

4. A textile manufacturer with only one plant moves to another location. It has not relocated a plant in 20 years and has no plans to do so in the foreseeable future. Notwithstanding the infrequency of occurrence of the event as it relates to this particular company, moving from one location to another is an

18. *Ibid.*, par. 23.

occurrence that is a consequence of customary and continuing business activities. Therefore the criterion of unusual nature has not been met.[19]

As in the case of discontinued operations, good judgment must be exercised in determining when to report extraordinary items.

**Material extraordinary gains or losses are reported (net of income taxes) in a separate section, below the section summarizing the results from discontinued operations (if such a section exists).** Materiality of the gain or loss should be assessed in relation to income before extraordinary items, to trends in this income, or by other appropriate criteria. Assuming no cumulative effects of a change in accounting principle (discussed in the next section), the suggested format is as follows:

| | |
|---|---|
| Income before extraordinary items | $XXX |
| Extraordinary items (less applicable income taxes of $___ ) (Note ___ ) | XXX |
| Net income | $XXX |

Within the extraordinary item section, *individual* extraordinary events should be described and disclosed when practical. Otherwise disclosure in the notes to the financial statements is acceptable. The income taxes applicable to the extraordinary items should be disclosed on the face of the income statement, although disclosure in the notes is acceptable. Either of these disclosure techniques requires intraperiod tax allocation. The extraordinary item section of the Banner Corporation income statement is shown in Exhibit 4-2 (the related income taxes were taken from Exhibit 4-6). Phillips Petroleum Company reported extraordinary items in both 1991 and 1990, as shown in Exhibit 4-9.

The APB also addressed the disclosure of material gains and losses from events that are *either* unusual in nature *or* infrequent in occurrence *but not both*. The examples cited earlier as events that are not extraordinary in nature would generally fall into this category. The APB required that material unusual or infrequent gains or losses be reported as a separate component of income from continuing operations. The authors suggest including these items in the Other Items section, as illustrated earlier. Because these items are a component of income from continuing operations for which a related income tax expense is computed, unusual or infrequent gains or losses are *not* shown net of income taxes. While the interpretation of what is unusual and infrequent still requires professional judgment, it was the intent of the APB to reduce the number of extraordinary items, and the issuance of *APB Opinion No. 30* has, in fact, reduced the incidence of such reporting. According to *Accounting Trends and Techniques,* only about 9% of surveyed companies reported extraordinary items.[20]

### Cumulative Effects of Accounting Changes

*Accounting changes are discussed in Chapter 22.*

Occasionally a company makes an accounting change. Accounting changes may be classified into four categories: (1) a change in an accounting principle, (2) a change in an accounting estimate, (3) a correction of an error, and (4) a change in the reporting entity. A change in an accounting principle is briefly discussed here because it has an impact upon the income statement.

---

19. *Accounting Interpretations of APB Opinion No. 30* (New York: AICPA, 1973).
20. *Accounting Trends and Techniques, op. cit.,* p. 338.

## EXHIBIT 4-9
### Extraordinary Items

**PHILLIPS PETROLEUM COMPANY**

|  | Years Ended December 31, | | |
|---|---|---|---|
|  | 1991 | 1990 | 1989 |
| (in millions) | | | |
| Income before Extraordinary Items and Cumulative Effect of Changes in Accounting Principles | $ 98 | $541 | $219 |
| Extraordinary items | 213 | 101 | — |
| Cumulative effect of changes in accounting principles | (53) | 137 | — |
| Net Income | $258 | $779 | $219 |

NOTES TO FINANCIAL STATEMENTS (in part):

*Note 1—Extraordinary Items and Accounting Changes (in part)*

During 1991, the company incurred before-tax extraordinary losses of $65 million on the early retirement of high-interest-rate debt. The company repurchased the debt on the open market, using internally generated funds and the proceeds from recent debt issues. The after-tax losses were $43 million ($.16 per share).

During fourth quarter 1991, the company recognized a before-tax extraordinary gain of $388 million from a settlement that concludes all claims under the company's replacement cost property insurance related to an accident which destroyed polyethylene facilities at the Houston Chemical Complex (HCC) in October 1989. The after-tax gain was $256 million ($.98 per share).

In January 1990, the company recognized a $101 million extraordinary gain ($.40 per share) from the settlement of litigation with the Government of Iran and the National Iranian Oil Company, which concludes all claims and counterclaims. The dispute was over the 1979 expropriation of Phillips' interest in two producing offshore Iranian oil fields.

*Change in Accounting Principle*

In **APB Opinion No. 20** the APB defined **a change in accounting principle as occurring when a company adopts a generally accepted accounting principle different from the one that it has previously been using in its financial reporting.** Here the term "accounting principle" includes not only principles, but also accounting practices and the methods of application.[21] It was suggested in Chapter 2 that the consistent use of accounting principles from period to period improves intracompany comparability. Consequently there is a presumption that once an accounting principle is adopted, it continues to be used for similar transactions. However, consistent use of an accounting principle does not preclude a change in that principle when this change results in more informative financial statements. The burden of justifying a voluntary change in accounting principle rests with the company. Examples of changes in principles include

---

21. "Accounting Changes," *APB Opinion No. 20* (New York: AICPA, 1971), par. 7.

a change in the method of inventory pricing, such as from first-in, first-out (FIFO) to average cost, and a change in the depreciation *method* for previously recorded assets (such as a switch from double-declining-balance to straight-line depreciation).

**In most instances, to report a material change in accounting principle, the cumulative effect of the change upon *prior* periods income is included in the net income for the *period of the change*.** That is, the related existing asset or liability account balance at the *beginning* of the current period is recalculated. The *new* balance is determined under the assumption that the new accounting principle had been applied during prior periods. The account is debited or credited to bring its balance to the required amount, and the offsetting credit or debit is the cumulative effect of the change in accounting principle on *prior* periods' earnings and is included in net income. **This cumulative effect (net of the related income tax effect) is reported directly after the extraordinary items section and directly preceding net income.** For instance, suppose a company acquired certain equipment in 1991 and has been depreciating it using the double-declining-balance method. At the beginning of 1995, it decides to change to the straight-line method for this equipment. The company would calculate its total depreciation to date under the straight-line method. The difference in total depreciation between the two methods would be recorded as a decrease in the Accumulated Depreciation account balance at the beginning of 1995 because of the lesser depreciation charges in prior years, had the straight-line method been applied during those years. These lesser depreciation charges in prior years would have resulted in increased earnings in those years. The cumulative increase in the prior earnings (net of income taxes) would be disclosed on the income statement. This disclosure is illustrated in Exhibit 4-2 for the Banner Corporation.

The new accounting principle then would be applied during the current year in the normal fashion. The effect of adopting the new principle on income before extraordinary items, net income, and earnings per share for the *current* period would be disclosed in a note to the financial statements.[22] This note would include an explanation and justification for the adoption of the new accounting principle. In our example the effect on net income due to the difference in depreciation expense for 1995 from using the straight-line method, instead of the double-declining-balance method, would be disclosed in such a note. Changes in accounting principles that have a material effect on income are relatively rare. Some changes in accounting principles are accounted for differently, as explained in Chapter 22.

## Earnings Per Share

Net income frequently is referred to as the "bottom line" on the income statement because it is the result of combining income from continuing operations with the results from discontinued operations, extraordinary items, and the cumulative effects of a change in accounting principle. Actually the term "bottom line" is a misnomer because **earnings per share information must be disclosed on the face of the income statement, and this disclosure usually is shown directly below the net income figure.**

Earnings per share is a ratio of considerable importance in financial analysis. It is often used in predicting future earnings and dividends, and in comparison to the market price at which a stock currently is selling, to determine the attractiveness of

---

22. In addition, the pro forma effects of the retroactive application of the accounting principle are disclosed on the face of the income statement. This is beyond the scope of the current discussion and is discussed in Chapter 22.

that stock. **In its simplest form, earnings per share is computed by dividing the net income by the number of common shares outstanding throughout the entire year.** However, many companies have preferred stock outstanding, which has first priority to dividends. They also have shares of common stock outstanding for only a portion of the year. Other companies have complex capital structures that include securities such as convertible preferred stock, convertible bonds, and stock options that may be converted into shares of common stock. The conversion of these securities to common stock would have an impact on the denominator (and in certain cases the numerator) of the earnings per share ratio. To improve the comparability of the earnings per share amounts listed by different companies, *APB Opinion No. 15* was issued. This *Opinion* includes a complicated set of rules designed to encourage consistent treatment of complex corporate capital transactions such as those discussed previously. Only the income statement disclosures are discussed here.

*Earnings per share is discussed in Chapter 21.*

    **APB Opinion No. 15** requires disclosure on the face of the income statement of the earnings per share amounts relating to income before extraordinary items and net income. It suggests that it may also be desirable to present earnings per share amounts for extraordinary items, if any. **APB Opinions No. 20 and 30** either require or suggest that the earnings per share information disclosed on the income statement include the per share amounts related to income from continuing operations, the results from discontinued operations, and the cumulative effect of any change in accounting principle.[23] As a result the authors suggest the presentation of an earnings per share schedule that shows the per share amounts (after tax) associated with each of the major components of net income and culminates in the per share amount related to net income. The schedule also should disclose the number of common shares used in the calculations. The format of this schedule is shown here:

Net Income          $XXXX

| **Components of Income** | **Earnings Per Share (No. of Common Shares)** |
| --- | --- |
| Income from continuing operations | $X |
| Results from discontinued operations | X |
| Extraordinary items | X |
| Cumulative effect of change in accounting principle | X |
| Net income | $X |

A similar schedule is shown on the Banner Corporation income statement in Exhibit 4-2. The earnings per share disclosure of General Mills is shown in Exhibit 4-10.

## Limitations of the Income Statement

The income statement has several limitations. First, many of the expenses that are matched against revenues are based on an allocation process of historical cost amounts (e.g., depreciation expense) instead of "current value" amounts. It is argued that the amount of net income under this approach does not adequately distinguish between a return *of* capital and a return *on* capital. Second, many of the expenses

---

23. "Earnings per Share," *APB Opinion No. 15* (New York: AICPA, 1969), par. 13, *APB Opinion No. 20, op. cit.*, par. 20, and *APB Opinion No. 30, op. cit.*, par. 9.

---

**EXHIBIT 4-10**
**Earnings Per Share**

**GENERAL MILLS**

| | Fiscal Year Ended | | |
| | May 31, 1992 | May 26, 1991 | May 27, 1990 |
| --- | --- | --- | --- |
| (in millions except per share data) | | | |
| Net Earnings | $495.6 | $472.7 | $381.4 |
| | | | |
| Earnings per Share: | | | |
|   Continuing operations | $ 3.05 | $ 2.82 | $ 2.27 |
|   Discontinued operations | (.06) | .05 | .05 |
| Net Earnings per Share | $ 2.99 | $ 2.87 | $ 2.32 |

---

(e.g., bad debts, warranties) are based on estimates that are subject to change and are less reliable. Third, in some cases companies may have too much leeway in selecting an accounting method (e.g., LIFO, FIFO for cost of goods sold), which leads to a lack of comparability across companies. Fourth, adherence to rigid accounting rules (e.g., recognizing revenue at the point of sale, expensing research and development costs when incurred) may lead to a distorted picture of a company's earnings activities. Fifth, the use of different formats (e.g., single-step versus multiple-step) by companies in the same industry may hide differences in operating results. Finally, the use of "functional" classifications (e.g., selling and administration) for operating expenses instead of "activity" classifications (fixed, variable) may not provide sufficient information for predicting future cash outflows. The FASB is aware of these limitations and either requires or encourages companies to disclose additional information in the notes or supplemental schedules to their financial statements to help users in their decision making.

### International Accounting Differences

International Accounting Standards require companies to use accrual accounting under the historical cost framework, considering economic substance instead of legal form. U.S. and international accounting standards related to income are very similar. In addition, much of the income statement content is similar in that international accounting standards require disclosure of sales (or other operating revenues), depreciation, interest revenue and expense, income from investments, taxes on income, unusual items, significant intercompany transactions, and net income. However, since it is difficult to obtain agreement on uniform international accounting standards, many of these standards allow a choice of alternative accounting treatments leading to a lack of comparability. The IASC recently implemented a program to eliminate these alternative treatments by issuing an *Exposure Draft* (ED) entitled "Comparability of Financial Statements," from which several related ED's were spun-off. If adopted, these ED's will lead to significant changes in several International Accounting Standards, which will probably bring them closer to U.S. standards.

In the meantime, several differences exist between U.S. and international accounting standards. Selected differences are discussed in later chapters as they relate to specific topics; a few are briefly identified here. For instance, under international accounting standards, either the percentage-of-completion or completed-contract method for long-term contracts may be used, while U.S. standards specify the conditions for use of each method. Under international standards, adjustments may be made to depreciation and cost of goods sold to reflect the effects of changing prices. Furthermore, as discussed in Chapter 3, companies in hyperinflationary economies are required to restate all revenues and expenses to reflect the general purchasing power and to include any purchasing power gain or loss on net monetary items in net income. The classification of research and development expense may also differ between U.S. and international accounting standards. As noted in Chapter 3, some foreign countries provide government grants to companies for compliance with certain conditions. When these grants are reported as deferred income on the balance sheet, they are recognized in later periods on a systematic and rational basis and are included as other income on the income statement. When they are treated as a reduction in the book value of an asset, they are recognized in later periods on the income statement as a reduction in depreciation expense. In addition to these differences related to operating income, there are also differences in reporting nonoperating income. For instance there are no specific international accounting standards for disclosing the results of discontinued operations. Although international accounting standards allow for the reporting of "unusual" items, they do not specify a separate category for "extraordinary" items. Finally, there is no international accounting standard for reporting earnings per share.

## STATEMENT OF RETAINED EARNINGS

Retained earnings is the link between the balance sheet and the income statement. It represents the total amount of corporate earnings that have not been returned to stockholders as dividends and is a major component of stockholders' equity. Although *not* a required financial statement, usually whenever an income statement and a balance sheet are issued, a schedule is included that reconciles the beginning retained earnings balance with the ending retained earnings balance. This schedule is referred to as the **statement of retained earnings.** Because the all-inclusive concept of net income is used in the income statement presentation, the content of the retained earnings statement is generally limited to the addition of net income to and the deduction of dividends from the beginning retained earnings balance. Any prior period adjustments are the primary other component. The suggested format for the statement is as follows:

| | |
|---|---:|
| Beginning retained earnings | $XXXX |
| Plus (minus): Prior period adjustments (net of income taxes) | XX |
| Adjusted beginning retained earnings | $XXXX |
| Plus (minus): Net income (loss) | XX |
| | $XXXX |
| Minus: Dividends (specifically identified, including per share amounts) | (XX) |
| Ending retained earnings | $XXXX |

### Prior Period Adjustments

**FASB Statement No. 16** addressed the issue of prior period adjustments to the Retained Earnings account. Before its issuance, a lack of agreement existed on how to report certain items that are in some way related to previous operations. In the *Statement* the FASB concluded that the correction of a material error in the financial statements of a prior period should be accounted for and reported as a prior period adjustment.[24]

A company occasionally may make an error in the financial statements of one accounting period that is not discovered until a subsequent period. The error may be due to such items as mathematical mistakes, the incorrect use of existing facts, oversights, the use of an accounting principle that is not generally accepted, or fraud. The correction of a material error is accounted for as a prior period adjustment to the beginning Retained Earnings account balance in the period of correction. The asset or liability account balance in error at the beginning of the period is corrected, and the offsetting debit or credit amount is made directly to retained earnings. For instance, suppose that during 1995 a company found it had inadvertently not recorded depreciation expense on a building in 1994. Thus, in 1994, depreciation expense was too low, accumulated depreciation was too low, and net income (which was closed to retained earnings) was too high. The correction in 1995 would include a debit to retained earnings and a credit to accumulated depreciation for the amount of the misstated depreciation. Any related impact upon income taxes would be similarly recorded. The prior period adjustment (net of income taxes) is appropriately described and reported as an adjustment (increase or decrease) to the beginning retained earnings on the statement of retained earnings. As a result, the adjusted beginning retained earnings balance is the amount of retained earnings that *would have been* in the account if the error had not been made. Corrections of material errors are relatively rare. The prior period adjustment for the Banner Corporation due to an error in counting the 1994 ending inventory is shown in Exhibit 4-11.

### EXHIBIT 4-11
### Statement of Retained Earnings

**BANNER CORPORATION**

Statement of Retained Earnings
For Year Ended December 31, 1995

| | |
|---|---|
| Retained earnings, January 1, 1995 | $68,150 |
| Add: Prior period adjustment, correction of understatement of 1994 ending inventory (net of $1,500 income taxes) | 3,500 |
| Adjusted retained earnings, January 1, 1995 | $71,650 |
| Add: Net income | 10,850 |
| | $82,500 |
| Less: Cash dividends, $0.50 per share | (2,500) |
| Retained earnings, December 31, 1995 | $80,000 |

24. "Prior Period Adjustments," *FASB Statement of Financial Accounting Standards No. 16* (Stamford, Conn.: FASB, 1977), par. 11, as amended by "Accounting for Income Taxes," *FASB Statement of Financial Accounting Standards No. 109* (Norwalk, Conn.: FASB, 1992), par. 288(n). This *Statement* did not affect the reporting of a few other rare items as prior period adjustments in accordance with the requirements set out in previous *Opinions* and *Statements*. These are discussed in Chapter 22.

## Net Income and Dividends

The two more common components of the statement of retained earnings are net income and dividends. The net income figure from the income statement is added to the adjusted beginning retained earnings. In the case of a net loss, this amount would be subtracted. All dividends declared during the accounting period, including cash dividends on preferred stock and common stock as well as any stock dividends (dividends in the form of the company's own stock), are subtracted to determine the ending retained earnings balance. Typically the per share amounts of the cash dividends are disclosed parenthetically on the statement. The net income and dividend components for the Banner Corporation are shown in Exhibit 4-11.

## Combined Statements

The statement of retained earnings may be issued as a separate schedule, or included either in a schedule that summarizes the changes in stockholders' equity or as a supporting schedule on the income statement directly below the net income. Companies are required to disclose the changes in all the separate stockholders' equity accounts. When these disclosures are made in the statement of changes in stockholders' equity, the statement of retained earnings usually is included as part of this statement. Either a separate retained earnings statement or inclusion of the reconciliation in the statement of changes in stockholders' equity is recommended. The authors do not recommend the reconciliation of the beginning and ending balances of the retained earnings account directly on the income statement, because this would add unnecessary additional data to an already complex financial statement.

# STATEMENT OF CASH FLOWS

Traditionally every company prepared an income statement and a balance sheet at the end of its accounting period. The income statement reported the results of its operating activities while the balance sheet reported its ending financial position. Certain external users asked questions about a company's "funds" flows, such as how were funds from operations generated, how was expansion financed, how was long-term debt retired, and what happened to the proceeds from the issuance of capital stock? These questions could not always be answered directly from the income statement or the balance sheet information. It was realized that a gap existed in the accounting summary of corporate financial activities, and *APB Opinion No. 19* was issued. This *Opinion* required that a statement of changes in financial position be prepared along with the balance sheet and income statement. The *Opinion* permitted companies flexibility in their choice of the definition of funds, classifications, and formats of the statement. Since that time, however, external users have recognized the importance of information about a company's *cash* flows. Furthermore, concern has been expressed that diversity in the focus of the statement, differences in the definitions of funds from operating activities, variations in classifications of funds flows, and differences in formats of the statement have led to a lack of comparability across companies.

As a result, **FASB Statement No. 95,** entitled "Statement of Cash Flows," was issued. This *Statement* requires that **a company present a statement of cash flows for the accounting period along with its income statement and balance sheet.** The primary purpose of a statement of cash flows is to provide relevant information about a company's cash receipts and cash payments during an accounting period. Therefore,

*The preparation of the statement of cash flows is discussed in Chapter 20.*

the statement of cash flows should provide information about the cash effects of a company's operating, investing, and financing activities during an accounting period. Because this statement is interrelated to the other financial statements and is an integral part of a company's annual report, it is briefly discussed next.

## Conceptual Overview and Uses of Statement

In Chapter 2 we noted that one of the specific objectives of financial reporting is to provide information about a company's funds flows. The statement of cash flows is useful in meeting this objective. Furthermore, external users are interested in information to assess a company's **liquidity** (the nearness to cash of its assets and liabilities), **financial flexibility** (its ability to take effective actions to alter the amount and timing of future cash flows so the company can respond to unexpected needs and opportunities), and **operating capability** (its ability to maintain a given physical level of operations). The statement of cash flows also is useful in meeting these information needs. In this regard, when used with other financial statements, **the statement of cash flows helps external users to assess:**

1. A company's ability to generate positive future cash flows

2. A company's ability to meet its obligations and pay dividends

3. A company's need for external financing

4. The reasons for differences between a company's net income and associated cash receipts and payments

5. Both the cash and noncash aspects of a company's investing and financing transactions during the accounting period[25]

## Reporting Guidelines and Practices

To aid external users in making the preceding assessments, *FASB Statement No. 95* requires that **a statement of cash flows must report on a company's cash inflows, cash outflows, and net change in cash from its operating, investing, and financing activities during the accounting period, in a manner that reconciles the beginning and ending cash balances.** This reconciliation causes the statement of cash flows to **articulate** with the balance sheet.

*Operating activities* include all transactions and other events related to the earning process. These include transactions involving acquiring, producing, selling, and delivering goods for sale, as well as providing services. *Investing activities* include, transactions involving lending money and collecting on the loans, and acquiring and selling long-term investments and property, plant, and equipment. *Financing activities* include transactions involving obtaining resources from owners and providing them with a return on, and of, their investment, as well as obtaining resources from creditors and repaying the amounts borrowed.

The statement of cash flows of a company includes three major sections: (1) net cash flow from operating activities, (2) cash flows from investing activities, and (3) cash flows from financing activities.[26] The **Net Cash Flow From Operating**

25. "Statement of Cash Flows," *FASB Statement of Financial Accounting Standards* No. 95 (Stamford, Conn.: FASB, 1987), par. 3–6.

**Activities** section reports on the cash flows from the operating activities of the company. The most common way of preparing this section is called the *indirect method*.[27] Under the indirect method, net income is listed first and then adjustments (additions or subtractions) are made to net income:

1.  To eliminate certain amounts (such as depreciation expense) that were included in net income but that did not involve a cash inflow or cash outflow for operating activities

2.  To include any changes in the current assets (other than cash) and current liabilities involved in the company's operating cycle that affected cash flows differently than net income

The intent is to convert net income to the net cash provided by (or used in) operating activities. The indirect method has the advantage of showing the "quality" of income by providing information about differences between income flows and operating cash flows. The **Cash Flows From Investing Activities** section includes all the cash inflows and cash outflows involved in the investing activities transactions of the company. The most common cash inflows from and cash outflows for investing activities can be classified as follows:

1.  Receipts from selling investments in stocks and debt securities (e.g., bonds)

2.  Receipts from selling property, plant, and equipment

3.  Payments for investments in stocks and debt securities

4.  Payments for purchases of property, plant, and equipment

Similarly, the **Cash Flows From Financing Activities** section includes all the cash inflows and cash outflows involved in the financing activities transactions of the company. The most common cash inflows from and cash outflows for financing activities can be classified as follows:

1.  Receipts from the issuance of debt securities (e.g., bonds, mortgages, notes)

2.  Receipts from the issuance of stocks

3.  Payments of dividends

4.  Payments to retire debt securities

5.  Payments to reacquire stock (i.e., treasury stock)

To complete the statement of cash flows, the cash inflows and outflows within each section are subtotaled, the subtotals are summed to determine the net increase (or decrease) in cash of the company during the accounting period, and the net change in cash is added to or subtracted from the beginning cash balance to reconcile to the ending cash balance reported on the company's year-end balance sheet.[28]

---

26. Transactions involving investing and financing activities *not* affecting cash receipts or cash payments might also be included in a separate schedule to accompany the statement of cash flows. This schedule is discussed in Chapter 20.

27. According to *Accounting Trends and Techniques* (New York: AICPA, 1992, p. 392), over 97% of surveyed companies use the indirect method.

28. As noted in Chapter 3, a company may report cash and cash equivalents on its balance sheet. When this is done, the reconciliation on the statement of cash flows is to the ending cash and cash equivalents.

The statement of cash flows of the Trevor Corporation for 1995 (using the *indirect* method for operating activities) is shown in Exhibit 4-12. The statement of cash flows of the Coca-Cola Company presented in its 1992 annual report is shown in Appendix A. Note in Exhibit 4-12 that the Trevor Corporation provided a net cash inflow of $70,400 from its *operating activities* in 1995. This amount was determined by adjusting the $59,600 net income for several differences between income flows and cash flows. For instance, depreciation expense of $16,500 was "added back" to net income because it had been deducted as an expense on the income statement but there was no cash outflow. On the other hand, the $7,300 increase in accounts receivable was subtracted because this increase resulted from credit sales, which increased sales revenue (and net income) on the income statement, but there was no cash inflow. The other adjustments to net income were made for similar reasons, as discussed more fully in Chapter 20.

## EXHIBIT 4-12

### TREVOR CORPORATION

Statement of Cash Flows
For Year Ended December 31, 1995

**Net Cash Flow From Operating Activities**

| | | |
|---|---:|---:|
| Net income | $ 59,600 | |
| Adjustments for differences between income flows and cash flows from operating activities: | | |
| Add: Depreciation expense | 16,500 | |
| Amortization expense | 2,000 | |
| Bond discount amortization | 1,100 | |
| Decrease in prepaid items | 400 | |
| Increase in salaries payable | 700 | |
| Increase in income taxes payable | 2,200 | |
| Increase in deferred income taxes | 900 | |
| Less: Increase in accounts receivable (net) | (1,800) | |
| Increase in inventories | (7,300) | |
| Decrease in accounts payable | (2,600) | |
| Decrease in advances from customers | (1,300) | |
| Net cash provided by operating activities | | $ 70,400 |
| **Cash Flows From Investing Activities** | | |
| Payment for purchase of building | $(73,900) | |
| Payment for investment in bonds | (10,000) | |
| Proceeds from sale of land | 5,000 | |
| Net cash used for investing activities | | (78,900) |
| **Cash Flows From Financing Activities** | | |
| Payment of dividends | $(12,400) | |
| Payment of mortgage | (14,000) | |
| Proceeds from issuance of common stock | 43,000 | |
| Net cash provided by financing activities | | 16,600 |
| Net Increase in Cash | | $  8,100 |
| Cash, January 1, 1995 | | 17,200 |
| Cash, December 31, 1995 | | $ 25,300 |

The net cash used for *investing activities* amounted to $78,900. The cash out-flows for investing activities were for the purchase of a building and for an invest-ment in bonds. The cash inflow was from the sale of land. The net cash provided by *financing activities* amounted to $16,600. The cash outflows for financing activities were for the payment of dividends and a mortgage. The cash inflow was from the is-suance of common stock.

The $8,100 net increase in cash was determined by adding the $70,400 net cash provided by operating activities and the $16,600 net cash provided by financing ac-tivities, and subtracting the $78,900 net cash used for investing activities. The $8,100 net increase in cash was added to the $17,200 cash balance on January 1, 1995 to reconcile to the $25,300 cash balance on December 31, 1995.

The other way to report cash flows from operating activities is the *direct method.* In *FASB Statement No. 95,* the FASB encourages use of the direct method. This method has the advantage of separating operating cash inflows from operating cash outflows, which may be useful in estimating future cash flows. Under the direct method, a company's operating cash inflows are listed first. The operating cash out-flows are then deducted from the operating cash inflows to determine the net cash provided by (or used in) operating activities. The most common cash inflows from and cash outflows for operating activities can be classified as follows:

*The direct and indirect methods are discussed in Chapter 20.*

**Operating Cash Inflows**
1. Collections from customers

2. Interest and dividends collected

**Operating Cash Outflows**
1. Payments to suppliers and employees

2. Payments of interest

3. Payments of income taxes

If the Trevor Corporation had used the direct method *instead* of the indirect method, the operating cash flows section of Exhibit 4-12 would have appeared as follows:

Cash Flows From Operating Activities
    Cash Inflows:

| | | |
|---|---:|---:|
|     Collections from customers | $ 248,100 | |
|     Interest and dividends collected | 3,800 | |
|     Cash inflows from operating activities | | $ 251,900 |
|   Cash Outflows: | | |
|     Payments to suppliers and employees | $(143,600) | |
|     Payments of interest | (17,200) | |
|     Payments of income taxes | (20,700) | |
|     Cash outflows for operating activities | | (181,500) |
|   Net cash provided by operating activities | | $ 70,400 |

Note that the $70,400 reported as the net cash provided by operating activities is the same under the direct and indirect methods, only the approach to determining the amount is different. The remainder of the statement of cash flows is the same under either method. You should use the *indirect* method for all homework, unless indicated otherwise.

## SUMMARY OF DISCLOSURES

In this chapter we have discussed the conceptual issues and disclosure requirements of numerous complex items concerning corporate earnings and cash flows. Exhibit 4-13 presents a brief summary of the related pronouncements, the conceptual criteria, and the disclosure requirements for material items. A review of the specific related pronouncements is recommended for a complete technical discussion of each topic.

**EXHIBIT 4-13**

### SUMMARY OF GAAP FOR CORPORATE EARNINGS AND CASH FLOWS

| Item | Pronouncement | Criteria | Disclosure |
|---|---|---|---|
| Income from continuing operations | APB Opinion No. 30 | Revenues and expenses related to usual and recurring operating activities | Upper portion of income statement. Multiple- or single-step format. |
| Nonextraordinary gains or losses | APB Opinion No. 30 | Either unusual in nature or infrequent in occurrence but not both | In income from continuing operations (other items) on income statement. |
| Results from discontinued operations | APB Opinion No. 30 | Disposal of a segment (major line of business or class of customer) of a firm | On income statement, directly below income from continuing operations. Include (a) gain or loss on disposal and (b) income or loss from operations of discontinued segment. Show both net of income taxes. |
| Extraordinary gains or losses | APB Opinions No. 9, 11, and 30; FASB Statement No. 4 | Unusual in nature *and* infrequent in occurrence | On income statement, directly below results from discontinued operations. Show net of income taxes. |
| Cumulative effect of change in accounting principle | APB Opinion No. 20 | Adoption of a generally accepted accounting principle different from one previously used | On income statement, directly below extraordinary items. Show net of income taxes. |

## EXHIBIT 4-13, Continued

| Item | Pronouncement | Criteria | Disclosure |
|---|---|---|---|
| Earnings per share | APB Opinions No. 15, 20, and 30 | Net income and components divided by number of common shares outstanding | On income statement, directly below net income. Show earnings per share related to net income and each major component of net income. |
| Prior period adjustments | APB Opinions No. 9 and 20; FASB Statements No. 16 and 109 | Correction of a material error in financial statements of a prior period | On statement of retained earnings as adjustment to beginning retained earnings. Show net of income taxes. |
| Operating cash flows | FASB Statement No. 95 | Cash flows related to earning process. | First section on statement of cash flows. |
| Investing cash flows | FASB Statement No. 95 | Cash flows from lending activities, and from buying and selling noncurrent assets. | Second section on statement of cash flows. |
| Financing cash flows | FASB Statement No. 95 | Cash flows from issuing and reacquiring debt and equity securities, and for paying dividends. | Third section on statement of cash flows. |

## QUESTIONS

*Q4-1* Define income under the "capital maintenance" concept. Identify the alternative ways of measuring capital under this concept.

*Q4-2* Briefly discuss the transactional approach to income measurement. Explain its relationship (if any) to the capital maintenance concept of income.

*Q4-3* Define comprehensive income. What was the intent of the FASB in developing this conceptual definition?

*Q4-4* Discuss (a) return on investment, (b) risk, (c) financial flexibility, and (d) operating capability.

*Q4-5* List the specific conceptual guidelines for reporting (presenting) revenues, expenses, gains, and losses.

*Q4-6* Define revenues. What operating activities are likely to result in revenues?

*Q4-7* What two criteria must ordinarily be met for revenues to be recognized? When is revenue usually recognized?

*Q4-8* Why might revenue be recognized at a time other than the sale? What are the alternative revenue recognition methods and for what might they be used?

*Q4-9* Define expenses. Of what are expenses a measurement?

*Q4-10* What are three principles for recognizing the expenses to be matched against revenues? Give examples of expenses that would be recognized under each principle.

*Q4-11* Define gains and losses. Give examples of three different types of gains and losses.

*Q4-12* What items are included in the "income from continuing operations?" How are these categorized if a company uses (a) a single-step format or (b) a multiple-step format?

*Q4-13* Discuss the difference between the "current operating performance" and the "all-inclusive" concepts of net income. Which concept is currently used?

*Q4-14* Why do companies prepare condensed income statements? What items are likely to be aggregated on the income statement?

*Q4-15* What items are included in the cost of goods manufactured, and how is the cost of goods manufactured computed?

*Q4-16* What elements are listed as other items on the income statement?

*Q4-17* What is intraperiod tax allocation, and why is it necessary? How is the income tax expense related to each major component of income disclosed on the income statement?

*Q4-18* What items are included in results from discontinued operations? For this purpose, how are a "segment" and "discontinued operations" defined?

*Q4-19* How is an extraordinary item defined? Explain the two criteria that must be met to classify an event as extraordinary. Give two examples of gains or losses from extraordinary items.

*Q4-20* How are gains or losses that are either unusual or infrequent reported on the income statement?

*Q4-21* What is a change in accounting principle, and how is it reported on the income statement?

*Q4-22* Where is earnings per share disclosed in the financial statements? What components of earnings per share should be disclosed?

*Q4-23* Briefly list several differences between international and U.S. accounting standards in regard to a company's income statement.

*Q4-24* What items are included in the statement of retained earnings?

*Q4-25* What are the possible causes of an error in the financial statements? How is the correction of a material error accounted for and how is the correction reported on the financial statements?

*Q4-26* What is a statement of cash flows? What are the three major sections of the statement?

*Q4-27* When used with other financial statements, what does the statement of cash flows help external users assess?

*Q4-28* What are the three types of activities that a statement of cash flows reports on for a company? Provide examples of transactions for each type of activity.

*Q4-29* Under the indirect method, how is the net cash provided by operating activities determined in the statement of cash flows?

*Q4-30* Under the direct method, what are the most common cash inflows from and most common cash outflows for operating activities in the statement of cash flows?

## CASES

*C4-1 Capital Maintenance*
At the beginning of 1983 the Hill family organized the Hill Corporation and issued 8,000 shares of stock to family members for $20 per share. During 1986 it issued an additional 1,600 shares of stock for $25 per share to family members. The 9,600 shares were held by the family until the liquidation of the corporation at the end of 1995. At that time the corporate assets were sold for $600,000, and the $50,000 of corporate liabilities were paid off. The remainder was returned to stockholders. During the 13 years of operation the corporation had a volatile operating life. It started out slowly but then increased its activities in later years. It had operated in several industry segments, being quite successful in some, not so successful in others. It had survived a major earthquake, but not without incurring significant losses. The corporation paid out dividends of $100,000 during its lifetime.

You are a member of the Hill family who has just inherited a sizable fortune from one of your relatives. Although you were quite young during the operating life of the Hill Corporation, you are considering establishing and investing in a new corporation operating in some of the same lines of business, providing the corporation would be profitable. You have just received your undergraduate accounting degree and find upon investigation that, with the exception of the preceding information, all the corporate accounting records were destroyed in a recent fire. You have been told that these records were sketchy at best, but that a capital maintenance approach to income measurement might yield some useful information.

**Required**
Compute the lifetime income of the Hill Corporation and comment upon what additional information you would desire before making your investment decision.

## C4-2 Revenue Recognition

A friend of yours who is not an accounting major states: "I always thought that revenues are recognized at the time of sale. Recently, however, I heard that there are specific criteria for revenue recognition and that included in the criteria is something about realization (whatever that means). Furthermore, I also heard that revenue may be recognized before or after the sale. Please explain revenue recognition to me."

### Required

Prepare a written response for your friend. Include a discussion of the revenue recognition criteria and realization. Also include a discussion of the reasons for, and alternative methods of, recognizing revenue in a period other than the period of sale.

## C4-3 Expense Recognition

The FASB states that expenses are recognized according to three pervasive principles in order to properly match expenses against revenues.

### Required

Identify the three principles, briefly discuss each principle, and provide examples of expenses that would be recognized under each principle.

## C4-4 Cost, Expense, and Loss

You were requested to personally deliver your auditor's report to the board of directors of Sebal Manufacturing Corporation and answer questions posed about the financial statements. While reading the statements, one director asked, "What are the precise meanings of the terms 'cost,' 'expense,' and 'loss'? These terms seem sometimes to identify similar items and other times dissimilar items."

### Required

1. Explain the meanings of the terms (a) "cost," (b) "expense," and (c) "loss" as used for financial reporting in conformity with generally accepted accounting principles. In your explanation discuss the distinguishing characteristics of the terms and their similarities and interrelationships.
2. Classify each of the following items as a cost, expense, loss, or other category, and explain how the classification of each item may change:
   a. Cost of goods sold
   b. Bad debts expense
   c. Depreciation expense for plant machinery
   d. Organization costs
   e. Spoiled goods
3. The terms "period cost" and "product cost" are sometimes used to describe certain items in financial statements. Define these terms and distinguish between them. To what types of items do each apply? (*AICPA adapted*)

## C4-5 Results of Discontinued Operations

*APB Opinion No. 30* dealt with, among other issues, reporting the results of discontinued operations. In the *Opinion*, a new section of the income statement was created and several terms were defined, including "discontinued operations," "segment," "measurement date," and "disposal date."

### Required

Identify the components of the results of discontinued operations section of the income statement. Define the previously listed terms and discuss how the components of the section are computed.

## C4-6 Extraordinary Items

*APB Opinion No. 30* establishes two narrow criteria that must be met in order for an event or transaction to be classified as an extraordinary item.

### Required

1. Identify and discuss each criterion.
2. Develop examples of events that might be extraordinary to one company but not extraordinary to another, such as
   a. An earthquake
   b. A flood
   c. A tornado
   d. A severe frost
   Justify your reasoning.
3. Discuss how the following are disclosed on the income statement:
   a. An extraordinary item
   b. An event or transaction that does not meet both criteria

## C4-7 Extraordinary Items

Morgan Company grows various crops and then processes them for sale to retailers. In the latter part of this year, Morgan had a large portion of its crops destroyed by a hail storm. Morgan has incurred substantial costs in raising the crops destroyed by the hail storm. Severe damage from hail storms in the locality where the crops are grown is rare.

### Required

1. Where should Morgan report the effects of the hail storm in its income statement? Why?
2. How does the classification in the income statement of an extraordinary item differ from that of an operating item? Why? Do not discuss earnings per share requirements. (*AICPA adapted*)

## C4-8 Accrual Accounting

Generally accepted accounting principles require the use of accruals and deferrals in the determination of income.

**Required**
1. How does accrual accounting affect the determination of income? Include in your discussion what constitutes an accrual and a deferral, and give appropriate examples of each.
2. Contrast accrual accounting with cash accounting. (*AICPA adapted*)

## C4-9   *Nonrecurring Items*

Lynn Company discontinued operations of a segment of its business in the middle of the year. The segment was operating at a loss from the beginning of the year. At the measurement date, a loss is expected from the proposed sale of the segment. This expected loss includes operating losses during the phase-out period, which will extend into next year.

In addition, Lynn had one of its manufacturing plants destroyed by an earthquake during the year. The loss is properly reported as an extraordinary item.

**Required**
1. How should Lynn report discontinued operations of a segment of its business on its income statement for this year? Do not discuss earnings per share requirements.
2. What are the criteria for classification as an extraordinary item?
3. How should Lynn report the extraordinary loss from the earthquake on its income statement for this year? Do not discuss earnings per share requirements. (*AICPA adapted*)

## C4-10   *Nonrecurring Items*

Hillside Company had a loss during the year ended December 31, 1995 that is properly reported as an extraordinary item.

On July 1, 1995, Hillside committed itself to a formal plan for sale of a business segment. A loss is expected from the proposed sale. Segment operating losses were incurred continuously throughout 1995 and were expected to continue until final disposition in 1996. Costs were incurred in 1995 to relocate segment employees.

**Required**
1. How should Hillside report the extraordinary item in its income statement? Why?
2. How should Hillside report the effect of the discontinued operations in its 1995 income statement?
3. How should Hillside report the costs that were incurred to relocate employees of the discontinued segment? Why?

Do not discuss earnings per share requirements. (*AICPA adapted*)

## C4-11   *Discontinued Activities*    ⓓ

XYZ Company is a general contractor in the commercial construction industry with several subsidiaries. On October 31, 1995, XYZ entered into an agreement to dispose of the assets and certain liabilities of its ABC subsidiary. Prior to that date, management had intended to try to improve the operations of the subsidiary. ABC has operated as a general contractor for commercial construction primarily in New England. It is the only subsidiary of XYZ that operates in the New England market. The disposal of ABC will be effected by discontinuing the subsidiary's operations, selling its assets and related liabilities, and dissolving the subsidiary corporation.

ABC's operations had resulted in an operating loss of $250,000 during the ten months ended October 31, 1995. Losses to wrap up outstanding contracts and phase out operations of ABC were $75,000 for the last two months of 1995. The company projects with reasonable accuracy that ABC will incur an additional $50,000 operating loss to complete the phase-out during the month of January 1996.

The company estimates the net book value of the assets and liabilities to be sold will be $700,000 as of January 31, 1996. The agreement entered into on October 31, 1995 provides for a sales price of $1,000,000. The transfer of title of the assets sold will occur on January 31, 1996 as called for in the agreement. All of the preceding amounts are pretax; the company's effective income tax rate is 40 percent.

**Required**
Describe how the preceding information should be reflected in the XYZ Company's income statement for the year ended December 31, 1995, and explain why. Ignore any disclosures in the notes to the financial statements. (*Contributed by Daryl G. Krause*)

## C4-12   *Statement of Cash Flows*

The president of a company, which is being audited for the first time, is concerned about all the unnecessary financial information the company is being required to disclose. He states, "We have always prepared only a balance sheet and an income statement. Surely these are enough. The only information anyone is interested in is how much we earned and what we have left. Now I am told we must prepare a statement of cash flows. What is this statement, what information does it provide, what are the major sections of the statement, and what is included in each section (under the direct method)?"

**Required**
Prepare a response that answers the president's questions.

## C4-13   *Researching GAAP*    ⓓ

During 1995, one of the customers of Klote Company declared bankruptcy. This customer had been a major purchaser of Klote's products and had owed $40,000 on account to Klote (a material portion of its receivables) at the time of bankruptcy. As a result of the bankruptcy, Klote had to write off the entire $40,000 account receivable of the customer as a loss. The president of Klote is concerned about how to report this loss on the company's 1995 income statement. He states to you, "Since this company that went bankrupt was a major customer, surely that is an unusual and infrequent event, and the $40,000 should be reported as an extraordinary loss. What do you think?"

**Required**

Research the related generally accepted accounting principles and prepare a short memo to the president that summarizes how to report the $40,000 loss on Klote's income statement. Cite your reference and applicable paragraph numbers.

### C4-14  Researching GAAP

The Kelly Company, a small corporation, is preparing its 1995 financial statements. At the end of 1995, the company purchased a building for $100,000, paying $20,000 as a down payment and signing an $80,000 mortgage. The president of Kelly is concerned about how to report this transaction on the company's statement of cash flows and has asked you to "research this issue for me."

**Required**

Research the related generally accepted accounting principles and prepare a short memo to the president that summarizes how to report this transaction on the statement of cash flows. Cite your reference and applicable paragraph numbers.

## MULTIPLE CHOICE

*Select the best answer for each of the following.*

**M4-1** The following information is available for Cooke Company for the current year:

| | |
|---|---|
| Net sales | $1,800,000 |
| Freight-in | 45,000 |
| Purchases discounts | 25,000 |
| Ending inventory | 120,000 |

The gross margin is 40% of net sales. What is the cost of goods available for sale?
a. $840,000
b. $960,000
c. $1,200,000
d. $1,220,000

**M4-2** A transaction that is material in amount, unusual in nature, and infrequent in occurrence should be presented in the income statement separately as a component of income
a. Net of applicable income taxes
b. As a prior period adjustment
c. From continuing operations
d. From discontinued operations

**M4-3** Effective January 1, 1995, Younger Company adopted the accounting principle of expensing as incurred advertising and promotion costs. Previously, advertising and promotion costs applicable to future periods were recorded in prepaid expenses. Younger can justify the change, which was made for both financial statement and income tax reporting purposes. Younger's prepaid advertising and promotion costs totaled $500,000 at December 31, 1994. Assume that the income tax rate is 30% for 1994 and 1995. The adjustment for the effect of this change in accounting principle should result in a net charge against income in the 1995 income statement of
a. $0
b. $150,000
c. $350,000
d. $500,000

**M4-4** A company changes from the double-declining-balance method of depreciation for previously recorded assets to the straight-line method. The cumulative effect of the change on the amount of retained earnings at the beginning of the period in which the change is made should be reported separately as a (an)
a. Extraordinary item
b. Component of income after extraordinary items
c. Component of income from continuing operations
d. Prior period adjustment

**M4-5** Palo Corporation incurred the following losses, net of applicable income taxes, for the year ended December 31, 1995:

| | |
|---|---|
| Loss on disposal of a segment of Palo's business | $400,000 |
| Loss on translation of foreign currency due to devaluation | 500,000 |

How much should Palo report as extraordinary losses on its 1995 income statement?

a.  $0
b.  $400,000

c.  $500,000
d.  $900,000

M4-6    Which of the following is expensed under the principle of systematic and rational allocation?

a.  Salespeople's monthly salaries
b.  Insurance premiums

c.  Transportation to customers
d.  Electricity to light office building

M4-7    The following information is available for Wagner Corporation for the current year:

| | | | |
|---|---|---|---|
| Sales | $500,000 | Freight-out | $ 45,000 |
| Beginning inventory | 180,000 | Purchases | 215,000 |
| Ending inventory | 95,000 | | |

How much is the cost of goods sold?

a.  $200,000
b.  $300,000

c.  $345,000
d.  $440,000

M4-8    Dobbin Corporation, a manufacturer of household paints, is preparing annual financial statements at December 31, 1995. Because of a recently proven health hazard in one of its paints, the government has clearly indicated its intention of having Dobbin recall all cans of this paint sold in the last six months. The management of Dobbin estimates that this recall would cost $1,000,000. What accounting recognition, if any, should be accorded this situation?

a.  No recognition
b.  Footnote disclosure

c.  Operating expense of $1,000,000
d.  Extraordinary loss of $1,000,000

M4-9    A loss from the disposal of a segment of a business enterprise should be reported separately as a component of income

a.  After cumulative effect of accounting changes and before extraordinary items
b.  Before cumulative effect of accounting changes and after extraordinary items

c.  After extraordinary items and cumulative effect of accounting changes
d.  Before extraordinary items and cumulative effect of accounting changes

M4-10   In a statement of cash flows, receipts from sales of property, plant, and equipment generally should be classified as

a.  Investing activities
b.  Selling activities

c.  Operating activities
d.  Financing activities

*(AICPA adapted)*

## EXERCISES

E4-1    *Simple Income Statement*   The following are selected account balances of the Albertson Company as of December 31, 1995:

| | | | |
|---|---|---|---|
| Purchases (net) | $ 63,000 | Sales (net) | $110,000 |
| Merchandise inventory, January 1, 1995 | 20,000 | Operating expenses | 22,000 |
| Gain on sale of equipment | 5,000 | Extraordinary loss (pretax) | 8,000 |

The merchandise inventory on December 31, 1995 is $31,000. Ten thousand shares of common stock have been outstanding the entire year.

**Required**
Assuming a 30% income tax rate on all items of income, prepare an income statement using (1) a multiple-step format and (2) a single-step format.

**E4-2** *Simple Income Statement, Manufacturing* The following are selected accounts taken from the adjusted trial balance of the Dibb Manufacturing Company on December 31, 1995:

| | | | |
|---|---|---|---|
| Finished goods inventory, January 1, 1995 | $ 70,000 | Sales (net) | $203,000 |
| Loss on sale of land | 5,000 | Operating expenses | 45,000 |
| Cost of goods manufactured | 120,000 | Extraordinary gain (pretax) | 6,000 |

The finished goods inventory on December 31, 1995, is $60,000. Twelve thousand shares of common stock were outstanding the entire year.

**Required**

Assuming a 30% income tax rate on all items of income, prepare an income statement using (1) a multiple-step format and (2) a single-step format.

**E4-3** *Classifications* Where would each of the following fifteen items most likely be reported in the financial statements? Assume the monetary amount of each item is material.

1. Purchases returns and allowances
2. Sales discounts taken
3. Depreciation expense on sales equipment
4. Loss from operations of discontinued segment B
5. Earnings per share
6. Gain on sale of land
7. Administrative salaries
8. Cash dividends on common stock
9. Correction of an error made in a prior period
10. Gain from disposal of discontinued segment B
11. Cumulative effect on prior years' income of change in accounting principle
12. Advertising expense
13. Merchandise inventory (ending)
14. Loss from write-off of obsolete inventory
15. Net income

**E4-4** *Classifications* Where would each of the following fifteen items most likely be reported in the financial statements? Assume the monetary amount of each item is material.

1. Loss on sale of equipment
2. Office supplies used
3. Correction of miscount of last year's ending finished goods inventory
4. Raw materials used
5. Delivery expense
6. Dividend revenue
7. Gain from retirement of debt
8. Change in the estimated useful life of office equipment
9. Summary of accounting policies
10. Sales returns and allowances
11. Income tax expense on continuing income
12. Stock dividend
13. Loss resulting from tornado damage
14. Goods in process inventory (ending)
15. Gain from foreign currency transactions

**E4-5** *Cost of Goods Sold and Income Statement* The Fanta Company presents you with the following account balances taken from its December 31, 1995, adjusted trial balance:

| | | | |
|---|---|---|---|
| Inventory, January 1, 1995 | $ 43,000 | Purchases returns | $3,500 |
| Selling expenses | 35,000 | Interest expense | 4,000 |
| Extraordinary gain (pretax) | 23,000 | Sales discounts taken | 2,000 |
| Purchases | 100,000 | Gain on sale of property (pretax) | 7,000 |
| Sales | 220,000 | Freight-in | 5,000 |
| General and administrative expenses | 22,000 | | |

Additional data:

1. A physical count reveals an ending inventory of $22,500 on December 31, 1995.
2. Twenty-five thousand shares of common stock have been outstanding the entire year.
3. The income tax rate is 30% on all items of income.

**Required**

1. As a supporting document for Requirements 2 and 3, prepare a separate schedule for cost of goods sold.
2. Prepare a 1995 multiple-step income statement.
3. Prepare, instead, a single-step income statement.

E4-6   *Cost of Goods Sold and Income Statement* The Engle Company lists the following accounts on its adjusted trial balance as of December 31, 1995.

| | | | |
|---|---|---|---|
| Sales | $147,100 | Purchases discounts taken | $ 2,700 |
| Purchases returns | 5,200 | Inventory, January 1, 1995 | 12,100 |
| Gain on sale of equipment (pretax) | 3,800 | Sales returns | 8,100 |
| Freight-in | 3,400 | Purchases | 89,700 |
| Selling expenses | 15,600 | Administrative expenses | 24,200 |
| Interest revenue | 3,300 | Extraordinary loss (pretax) | 6,500 |

The following additional information is also available. The December 31, 1995 ending inventory is $14,700. During 1995, 4,200 shares of common stock were outstanding the entire year. The income tax rate is 30% on all items of income.

**Required**

1. As a supporting document for Requirements 2 and 3, prepare a separate schedule for the cost of goods sold.
2. Prepare a 1995 single-step income statement.
3. Prepare, instead, a multiple-step income statement.

E4-7   *Cost of Goods Manufactured and Income Statement* Included in the December 31, 1995 adjusted trial balance of the Gold Company are the following accounts:

| | | | |
|---|---|---|---|
| Goods in process, January 1, 1995 | $ 24,000 | Finished goods inventory, January 1, 1995 | $34,000 |
| Sales | 190,000 | Selling expenses | 28,000 |
| General and administrative expenses | 20,000 | Sales returns and allowances | 5,000 |
| Raw materials used | 42,000 | Interest revenue | 4,000 |
| Loss from strike (pretax) | 9,000 | Extraordinary loss (pretax) | 17,000 |
| Direct labor | 30,000 | Factory overhead | 31,000 |

Additional data:

1. The December 31, 1995 ending inventories are (a) goods in process, $28,000, and (b) finished goods, $32,000.
2. Seven thousand shares of common stock have been outstanding the entire year.
3. The income tax rate is 30% on all items of income.

**Required**

1. As a supporting document for Requirements 2 and 3, prepare a separate schedule for the cost of goods sold.
2. Prepare a 1995 single-step income statement.
3. Prepare, instead, a multiple-step income statement.

E4-8   *Cost of Goods Manufactured and Income Statement* On December 31, 1995 the Adant Company listed the following items in its adjusted trial balance:

| | | | |
|---|---|---|---|
| Factory overhead | $ 28,000 | Direct labor | $ 32,000 |
| Extraordinary loss (pretax) | 8,000 | Loss on sale of equipment (pretax) | 2,000 |
| Interest revenue | 2,500 | Raw materials used | 39,000 |
| Sales returns and allowances | 3,000 | General and administrative expenses | 17,000 |
| Selling expenses | 14,000 | Sales | 163,000 |
| Finished goods inventory, January 1, 1995 | 35,000 | Goods in process inventory, January 1, 1995 | 21,000 |

Additional data:

1. The December 31, 1995 ending inventories are (a) goods in process, $18,000, and (b) finished goods, $42,000.
2. Seven thousand shares of common stock have been outstanding the entire year.
3. The income tax rate is 30% on all items of income.

**Required**

1. As a supporting document for Requirements 2 and 3, prepare a separate schedule for the cost of goods sold.
2. Prepare a 1995 multiple-step income statement.
3. Prepare, instead, a single-step income statement.

E4-9   *Income Statement and Retained Earnings*   The Senger Company presents the following partial list of account balances taken from its December 31, 1995 adjusted trial balance:

| | | | |
|---|---|---|---|
| Retained earnings, January 1, 1995 | $ 95,800 | Operating expenses | $30,400 |
| Sales (net) | 118,000 | Inventory, January 1, 1995 | 18,400 |
| Interest expense | 3,700 | Common stock, $5 par | 22,000 |
| Purchases (net) | 67,000 | | |

The following information is also available for 1995 and is not reflected in the preceding accounts:

1. The ending inventory is $19,200.
2. The common stock has been outstanding all year. A cash dividend of $1.28 per share was declared and paid.
3. Land was sold at a pretax gain of $6,200.
4. Division X was sold at a pretax gain of $4,700. It had incurred a $9,500 pretax operating loss during 1995.
5. A tornado, which is an unusual and infrequent event in the area, caused a $5,400 pretax loss.
6. The income tax rate on all items of income is 30%.

**Required**

1. Prepare a 1995 multiple-step income statement.
2. Prepare a retained earnings statement.

E4-10   *Income Statement and Retained Earnings*   The Cobler Manufacturing Company presents the following partial list of account balances taken from its December 31, 1995 adjusted trial balance:

| | | | |
|---|---|---|---|
| Operating expenses | $ 35,800 | Common stock, $15 par | $45,000 |
| Dividend revenue | 1,000 | Finished goods inventory, January 1, 1995 | 24,000 |
| Retained earnings, January 1, 1995 | 68,700 | Cost of goods manufactured | 79,200 |
| Sales (net) | 139,600 | | |

The following information is also available for 1995 and is not reflected in the preceding accounts:

1. The common stock has been outstanding the entire year. A cash dividend of $0.84 per share was declared and paid.
2. The income tax rate on all items of income is 30%.
3. The ending finished goods inventory is $27,300.
4. A pretax $4,000 loss was recognized on the sale of Division X. This division had earned a pretax operating income of $1,900 during 1995.
5. Obsolete raw materials were written off at a pretax loss of $6,600.
6. An earthquake, which is an unusual and infrequent event in the area, caused a $3,700 pretax loss.

**Required**

1. Prepare a cost of goods sold schedule.
2. Prepare a 1995 single-step income statement.
3. Prepare a retained earnings statement.

E4-11    *Income Statement Calculations*    The income statement information for 1995 and 1996 of the Clawson Company (a sole proprietorship) is as follows:

|  | 1995 | 1996 |
|---|---|---|
| Beginning inventory | $ (a) | $ (d) |
| Sales | 210,000 | (e) |
| Purchases | 130,000 | 140,000 |
| Purchases returns and allowances | 7,000 | 6,000 |
| Ending inventory | 62,000 | (f) |
| Sales returns and allowances | 4,000 | 15,000 |
| Gross profit | (b) | 100,000 |
| Cost of goods sold | 110,000 | 120,000 |
| Selling expenses | 35,000 | 36,000 |
| Transportation-in | 2,000 | 5,000 |
| General and administrative expenses | 20,000 | (g) |
| Net income | (c) | 43,000 |

**Required**
Fill in the blanks labeled *a.* through *g.* All the necessary information is listed. (*Hint:* It is not necessary to calculate your answers in alphabetical order.)

E4-12    *Income Statement Calculations*    The income statement information for 1995 and 1996 of the Thompson Company (a sole proprietorship) is as follows:

|  | 1995 | 1996 |
|---|---|---|
| Cost of goods manufactured | $68,000 | $ 59,000 |
| Raw materials used | 20,000 | 18,000 |
| Sales | (1) | 130,000 |
| Beginning finished goods inventory | 42,000 | 26,000 |
| Direct labor | 30,000 | (5) |
| Sales returns and allowances | 5,000 | 4,000 |
| Operating expenses | 30,000 | (6) |
| Factory overhead | (2) | 13,000 |
| Gross profit | 58,000 | (7) |
| Beginning goods in process inventory | 24,000 | (8) |
| Cost of goods sold | 84,000 | (9) |
| Ending finished goods inventory | (3) | 20,000 |
| Ending goods in process inventory | 21,000 | 18,000 |
| Sales discounts taken | 3,000 | 2,600 |
| Net income | (4) | 30,000 |

**Required**
Fill in the blanks numbered 1 through 9. All the necessary information is listed. (*Hint:* It is not necessary to calculate your answers in numerical order.)

E4-13    *Results of Discontinued Operations*    On April 1, 1995 Smythe Company decided to dispose of segment M. The disposal process was not completed until November 10, 1995, at which time segment M was sold for $430,000. From January 1, 1995 until November 10, 1995, segment M earned pretax operating income of $130,000 of which 35% was attributable to the first quarter. Segment M had a book value of $673,000 on November 10, 1995. Smythe Company is subject to a 30% income tax rate.

**Required**

Prepare the results from discontinued operations section of Smythe Company's income statement for 1995. Show supporting computations.

**E4-14** **Results of Discontinued Operations** On August 1, 1995 Feiner Company announced its plans to discontinue the operations of segment P by selling segment P to the Bassett Company on February 1, 1996 for $860,000. During 1995 segment P incurred a pretax operating loss of $222,500, of which 60% was incurred prior to August 1. During January 1996, segment P is expected to earn pretax operating income of $2,000; at the end of this time it is expected to have a book value of $900,000. Feiner Company is subject to a 30% income tax rate.

**Required**

Prepare the results from discontinued operations section of Feiner Company's income statement for 1995. Show supporting calculations.

**E4-15** **Income Statement Deficiencies** David Company's Statements of Income for the year ended December 31, 1996 and December 31, 1995 are presented here:

| | Year Ended December 31, 1996 | 1995 |
|---|---|---|
| Net sales | $900,000 | $750,000 |
| Costs and expenses: | | |
| Cost of goods sold | $720,000 | $600,000 |
| Selling, general and administrative expenses | 112,000 | 90,000 |
| Other, net | 11,000 | 9,000 |
| Total costs and expenses | $843,000 | $699,000 |
| Income from continuing operations before income taxes | $ 57,000 | $ 51,000 |
| Income taxes | 23,000 | 24,000 |
| Income from continuing operations | $ 34,000 | $ 27,000 |
| Loss on disposal of Dex Division, including provision of $1,500 for operating losses during phase-out period, less applicable income taxes of $8,000 | 8,000 | — |
| Cumulative effect on prior years of change in depreciation method, less applicable income taxes of $1,500 | — | 3,000 |
| Net income | $ 26,000 | $ 30,000 |
| Earnings per share of common stock: | | |
| Income before cumulative effect of change in depreciation method | $2.60 | $2.70 |
| Cumulative effect on prior years of change in depreciation method, less applicable income taxes | — | .30 |
| Net income | $2.60 | $3.00 |

Additional facts are as follows:

a. On January 1, 1995, David Company changed its depreciation method for previously recorded plant machinery from the double-declining-balance method to the straight-line method. The effect of applying the straight-line method for the year of and the year after the change is included in David Company's Statements of Income for the year ended December 31, 1996 and December 31, 1995 in "cost of goods sold."

b. The loss from operations of the discontinued Dex Division from January 1, 1996 to September 30, 1996 (the portion of the year prior to the measurement date) and from January 1, 1995 to December 31, 1995 is included in David Company's Statements of Income for the year ended December 31, 1996 and December 31, 1995, respectively, in "other, net."

c. David Company has a simple capital structure with only common stock outstanding, and the net income per share of common stock was based on the weighted average number of common shares outstanding during each year.

d. David Company common stock is listed on the New York Stock Exchange and closed at $13 per share on December 31, 1996 and $15 per share on December 31, 1995.

**Required**

Determine from the additional facts listed whether the presentation of those facts in David Company's Statements of Income is appropriate. If the presentation is appropriate, discuss the theoretical rationale for the presentation. If the presentation is not appropriate, specify the appropriate presentation and discuss its theoretical rationale. Do *not* discuss disclosure requirements for the Notes to the Financial Statements. (*AICPA adapted*)

*E4-16    Net Cash Flow From Operating Activities*    The following are accounting items taken from the records of the Wilson Company for 1995:

a. Net income, $21,300
b. Payment for purchase of land, $4,000
c. Payment for retirement of bonds, $6,000
d. Depreciation expense, $7,500
e. Proceeds from issuance of common stock, $7,000

f. Patent amortization expense, $2,700
g. Bond discount amortization, $1,000
h. Increase in accounts receivable, $3,400
i. Payment of dividends, $5,000
j. Decrease in accounts payable, $2,600

**Required**

Prepare the net cash flow from operating activities section of the Wilson Company's 1995 statement of cash flows.

*E4-17    Operating Cash Flows: Direct Method*    The following are various cash flows and other information of the Billings Company for 1995:

a. Payments of interest, $8,200
b. Proceeds from sale of land, $7,900
c. Interest collected, $10,000
d. Payment of dividends, $12,100
e. Depreciation expense, $24,700

f. Collections from customers, $101,600
g. Payments of income taxes, $15,400
h. Proceeds from issuance of stock, $18,900
i. Payments to suppliers and employees, $67,500
j. Increase in inventories, $4,600

**Required**

Using the direct method, prepare the cash flows from operating activities section of the Billings Company's 1995 statement of cash flows.

*E4-18    Statement of Cash Flows*    The following are several items involving the cash flow activities of the Rocky Company for 1995:

a. Net income, $39,000
b. Payment of dividends, $12,000
c. Ten-year, $28,000 bonds payable were issued at face value
d. Depreciation expense, $11,000
e. Building was acquired at a cost of $43,000

f. Accounts receivable decreased by $2,000
g. Accounts payable decreased by $4,000
h. Equipment was acquired at a cost of $8,000
i. Inventories increased by $7,000
j. Beginning cash balance, $13,000

**Required**

Prepare the statement of cash flows of the Rocky Company for 1995.

E4-19 *Statement of Cash Flows* The following are several items involving the cash flow activities of the Jones Company for 1995:

a. Net income, $59,700
b. Proceeds from issuance of common stock, $32,000
c. Payment for purchase of equipment, $41,500
d. Payment for purchase of land, $19,600
e. Depreciation expense, $20,500
f. Patent amortization expense, $1,200
g. Payment of dividends, $21,000
h. Decrease in salaries payable, $2,600
i. Increase in accounts receivable, $10,300
j. Beginning cash balance, $33,400

**Required**
Prepare the statement of cash flows of the Jones Company for 1995.

## PROBLEMS

P4-1 *Framework of Income Statement* The following is an alphabetical list of accounts for the Mack Company:

Accounts payable
Accounts receivable
Accumulated depreciation: buildings and office equipment
Accumulated depreciation: store and delivery equipment
Administrative salaries
Advertising expense
Allowance for doubtful accounts
Bad debts expense
Bonds payable
Buildings
Cash
Cash dividends declared
Common stock, $10 par
Correction of previous years' error
Cumulative effect on prior years' income of change in accounting principle
Delivery expense
Depreciation expense: buildings and office equipment
Depreciation expense: store and delivery equipment
Dividend revenue
Dividends payable
Freight on purchases
Fund to retire long-term bonds
Gain on retirement of debt
Gain on sale of equipment
Gain on sale of segment T
Income tax expense
Insurance expense
Interest expense
Interest payable
Interest revenue

Investment in securities (long-term)
Loss from expropriation
Loss from operations of discontinued segment T
Loss on sale of office equipment
Merchandise inventory, January 1, 1995
Merchandise inventory, December 31, 1995
Miscellaneous office expenses
Miscellaneous sales expenses
Mortgage payable
Office salaries
Office supplies used
Paid-in capital on common stock
Prepaid office supplies
Property tax expense
Purchases
Purchases discounts taken
Purchases returns and allowances
Rent revenue
Retained earnings, January 1, 1995
Salaries payable
Sales
Sales commissions
Sales discounts taken
Sales returns and allowances
Sales salaries
Service revenues
Stock dividends declared
Unearned rent
Unexpired insurance
Utilities expense
Unrealized decrease in value of securities available for sale

**Required**

Ignoring amounts, select the appropriate accounts and prepare:

1. A multiple-step income statement with proper subheadings
2. A retained earnings statement

P4-2    *Account Classifications*    Given the following code letters and components of financial statements, indicate where each item would most likely be reported in the financial statements by inserting the corresponding code letters. Assume the monetary amount of each item is material.

| Code Letter | Component |
|---|---|
| A | Sales revenues (net) |
| B | Cost of goods sold |
| C | Selling expenses |
| D | General and administrative expenses |
| E | Other items |
| F | Results from discontinued operations |
| G | Extraordinary items |
| H | Prior period adjustments |
| I | Additions to retained earnings (other than H) |
| J | Deductions from retained earnings (other than H) |
| K | Notes to financial statements |
| L | Ending balance sheet |

1. Purchases
2. Loss on sale of equipment
3. Utilities expense
4. Cash dividends declared on common stock
5. Bad debts expense
6. Sales salaries
7. Sales discounts taken
8. Transportation-in
9. Net income
10. Gain on retirement of long-term debt
11. Purchases returns and allowances
12. Premium on bonds payable
13. Gain on sale of land
14. Interest expense
15. Delivery expense
16. Expenses incurred as a result of a strike
17. Summary of accounting policies
18. Gain on disposal of division J
19. Interest revenue

20. Additional paid-in capital on common stock
21. Loss from write-down of obsolete inventory
22. Administrative salaries
23. Stock dividends declared on common stock
24. Correction of erroneous understatement of last years' ending inventory
25. Operating loss related to discontinued division J
26. Additional depreciation on office equipment resulting from decrease in estimated useful life
27. Gain from foreign currency transactions
28. Loss from frost in southern Arizona
29. Sales returns
30. Depreciation expense for office equipment
31. Sales commissions
32. Promotion expense
33. Merchandise inventory (beginning)

P4-3    *Income Statement, Lower Portion*    At the beginning of 1995 the retained earnings of the Bise Company was $212,000. For 1995 the company has calculated its pretax income from continuing operations to be $110,000. During 1995 the following events also occurred:

1. During July the company disposed of segment M. It has determined that the pretax income from the operations of segment M during 1995 totals $39,000 and that a pretax loss of $40,500 was incurred on the sale of segment M.

2. The company had 21,000 shares of common stock outstanding during all of 1995. It declared and paid a $1-per-share cash dividend on this stock.
3. The company retired ("extinguished") some long-term debt. It recognized a material pretax gain of $25,000 on the retirement.
4. The company found and corrected a pretax $18,000 understatement of the 1994 ending inventory due to a mathematical error.
5. With the agreement of its auditors the company switched from straight-line to double-declining-balance depreciation on certain assets at the beginning of 1995. Had double-declining-balance depreciation been used prior to 1995, the cumulative effect would have been a pretax increase in depreciation expense for prior years of $11,000.

**Required**
Assuming that all the "pretax" items are subject to a 30% income tax rate:
1. Complete the lower portion of Bise Company's 1995 income statement, beginning with "pretax income from continuing operations."
2. Prepare an accompanying retained earnings statement.

P4-4    *Income Statement, Lower Portion*    Baker Company reports a retained earnings balance of $365,200 at the beginning of 1995. For the year ended December 31, 1995, the company reports pretax income from continuing operations of $150,500. The following information is also available pertaining to 1995:

1. The company declared and paid a $0.72 cash dividend per share on the 30,000 shares of common stock that were outstanding the entire year.
2. The company found and corrected a pretax $48,000 understatement of 1994 depreciation expense due to a mathematical error.
3. The company incurred a pretax $21,000 loss as a result of an earthquake, which is unusual and infrequent for the area.
4. The company sold division P in May. From January through May, division P had incurred a pretax loss from operations of $33,000. A pretax gain of $15,000 was recognized on the sale of division P.
5. Because of additional information, the company determined that its estimated useful life of certain depreciable assets had decreased. As a result, the current depreciation expense included in the 1995 pretax income from continuing operations is $7,000 higher than it would have been had the original estimated useful life been used in the calculations.

**Required**
Assuming that all the "pretax" items are subject to a 30% income tax rate:
1. Complete the lower portion of Baker Company's 1995 income statement beginning with "pretax income from continuing operations."
2. Prepare an accompanying retained earnings statement.

P4-5    *Comprehensive: Income Statement and Supporting Schedules*    The following selected accounts are taken from the Crandle Corporation's December 31, 1995 adjusted trial balance:

| | | | |
|---|---|---|---|
| Retained earnings, January 1, 1995 | $428,900 | Transportation-out (deliveries) | $ 6,000 |
| Interest expense | 4,900 | Purchases | 187,700 |
| Depreciation expense: sales fixtures | 8,500 | Sales discounts taken | 5,200 |
| Purchases discounts taken | 3,000 | Transportation-in | 14,300 |
| Sales returns and allowances | 11,300 | Bad debt expense | 1,900 |
| Advertising expense | 14,100 | Purchases returns and allowances | 8,000 |
| Common stock, $10 par | 110,000 | Sales supplies expense | 4,600 |
| Administrative and office salaries expense | 28,500 | Inventory, January 1, 1995 | 42,200 |
| Dividend revenue | 900 | Sales salaries expense | 16,500 |
| Sales | 373,000 | Depreciation expense: buildings and | |
| Property tax expense | 7,700 |    office equipment | 10,000 |
| Gain on sale of sales fixtures (pretax) | 5,000 | Income tax expense | 19,590 |
| Office supplies used | 1,800 | | |

In addition to the preceding account balances, you have available the following information:

1. The December 31, 1995 ending inventory is $45,000, as determined by a physical count.
2. In the middle of December 1995 the company incurred a material $5,500 pretax loss as a result of a freak flood of a river that had never flooded before.
3. While making its December 31, 1995 adjusting entries, the company discovered the following:
   a. In recording its December 31, 1994 adjusting entries, it had inadvertently recorded depreciation expense twice for the same asset. The amount of the error was $4,000 pretax and is considered material. The error did not have any effect upon the depreciation recorded for 1995.
   b. Based on an analysis of the company's recent favorable experience with uncollectible accounts receivable, the company decided to reduce the percentage used in computing bad debt expense. The use of the new percentage resulted in the $1,900 bad debt expense being $500 less than the amount that would have been calculated using the old percentage.
4. On April 1, 1995 the company sold segment M, which had been unprofitable for several years. For the first 3 months of 1995, segment M had incurred a pretax operating loss of $8,800. Segment M was sold at a pretax loss of $7,500.
5. When the company retired (extinguished) bonds on July 1, 1995 it recognized a pretax gain of $13,400 on the retirement.
6. The company paid cash dividends of $0.90 per share on its common stock. All the stock was outstanding the entire year.
7. The $19,590 income tax expense account balance consists of $20,910 tax on continuing income, $1,200 tax on the depreciation correction, $4,020 tax on the gain from bond retirement, and tax credits of $2,640 on the operating loss of segment M, $2,250 on the loss from disposal of segment M, and $1,650 on the loss due to the flood.

**Required**

1. As supporting documents for Requirement 2, prepare separate schedules for cost of goods sold, selling expenses, and general and administrative expenses (include each depreciation expense where applicable in these schedules).
2. Prepare a 1995 single-step income statement for the Crandle Corporation.
3. Prepare a retained earnings statement.

P4-6   *Comprehensive: Income Statement and Supporting Schedules*   The following is a partial list of the account balances, after adjustments, of the Vance Company on December 31, 1995:

| | | | |
|---|---|---|---|
| Depreciation expense: buildings and | | Office supplies expense | $ 1,400 |
|    office equipment | $ 14,500 | Common stock, $10 par | 80,000 |
| Sales commissions and salaries | 18,200 | Loss on sale of office equipment (pretax) | 5,000 |
| Inventory, January 1, 1995 | 37,800 | Insurance and property tax expense | 8,500 |
| Sales supplies used | 5,600 | Sales | 340,700 |
| Retained earnings, January 1, 1995 | 183,700 | Rent revenue | 6,900 |
| Purchases returns and allowances | 6,200 | Office and administrative salaries expense | 32,000 |
| Bad debts expense | 2,700 | Promotion and advertising expense | 17,000 |
| Transportation-in | 13,500 | Sales returns and allowances | 12,100 |
| Sales discounts taken | 4,900 | Purchases discounts taken | 4,100 |
| Purchases | 173,000 | Depreciation expense: sales equipment | 9,600 |
| Delivery expense | 7,700 | Interest expense | 3,700 |

The following information is also available:

1. The company declared and paid a $0.60 per share cash dividend on its common stock. The stock was outstanding the entire year.
2. A physical count determined that the December 31, 1995 ending inventory is $34,100.
3. A tornado destroyed a warehouse, resulting in a pretax loss of $12,000. The last tornado in this area had occurred 20 years earlier.
4. While making its December 31, 1995 adjusting entries, the company determined that:
   a. In 1994 it had inadvertently omitted $11,000 depreciation expense on its buildings and office equipment. The error did not have any effect upon the depreciation recorded in 1995.
   b. Due to recently increased obsolescence, its sales equipment should be depreciated over a shorter useful life. The resulting $2,500 additional depreciation has been included in the 1995 depreciation expense.

5. On May 1, 1995, the company disposed of an unprofitable segment (R). From January through April, segment R had incurred a pretax operating loss of $8,700. Segment R was sold at a pretax gain of $10,000.

6. The income tax expense for 1995 totals $930. The breakdown is as follows:

| Income Tax Expense (Credit) Related to | Amount |
|---|---|
| Continuing income | $ 7,440 |
| Operating loss of segment R | (2,610) |
| Gain on sale of segment R | 3,000 |
| Loss from tornado | (3,600) |
| Error in recording 1994 depreciation expense | (3,300) |
| | $    930 |

### Required

1. As supporting documents for Requirement 2, prepare separate supporting schedules for cost of goods sold, selling expenses, general and administrative expenses, and depreciation expense.
2. Prepare a 1995 multiple-step income statement for the Vance Company.
3. Prepare a retained earnings statement.

P4-7   *Comprehensive: Manufacturing Income Statement*   The Houston Manufacturing Company presents the following partial list of account balances, after adjustments, as of December 31, 1995:

| | | | |
|---|---|---|---|
| Sales salaries expense | $ 27,400 | Factory maintenance expense | $  7,000 |
| Miscellaneous administrative expenses | 3,000 | Sales personnel travel expenses | 8,300 |
| Raw materials used | 70,200 | Property taxes and insurance expense | 9,000 |
| Sales returns | 5,000 | Retained earnings, January 1, 1995 | 197,800 |
| Factory superintendent's salaries expense | 25,000 | Factory utilities expense | 21,000 |
| Finished goods inventory, January 1, 1995 | 32,000 | Depreciation expense: sales equipment | 9,000 |
| Sales | 472,100 | Factory indirect labor expense | 23,000 |
| Direct labor | 81,000 | Advertising expense | 15,700 |
| Interest revenue | 3,200 | Depreciation expense: factory | 18,000 |
| Office and administrative salaries | 30,000 | Miscellaneous rent revenue | 5,900 |
| Delivery expenses | 11,700 | Common stock, $10 par | 200,000 |
| Goods in process inventory, January 1, 1995 | 19,900 | Depreciation expense: buildings and | |
| Loss on sale of factory equipment (pretax) | 4,100 | office equipment | 14,400 |

The following information is also available but is not reflected in the preceding accounts:

1. The company sold segment E on August 1, 1995. During 1995 segment E had incurred a pretax loss from operations of $16,000. However, because the acquiring company could vertically integrate segment E into its facilities, the Houston Manufacturing Company was able to recognize a $42,000 pretax gain on the sale.
2. On January 2, 1995, without warning, a foreign country expropriated a factory of Houston Manufacturing Company, which had been operating in that country. As a result of that expropriation, the company has incurred a pretax loss of $27,000.
3. In preparing its 1995 adjusting entries at year-end, the company discovered that it had not recorded $10,100 of depreciation on its office building during 1994. This error did not affect the 1995 depreciation expense.
4. A December 31, 1995 physical inventory yielded the following ending inventories: goods in process, $22,000; finished goods, $36,000.
5. The common stock was outstanding the entire year. A cash dividend of $1.20 per share was declared and paid in 1995.
6. The 1995 income tax expense totals $28,020 and consists of the following:

| | |
|---|---|
| Tax expense on income from continuing operations | $31,350 |
| Tax credit on segment E operating loss | (4,800) |
| Tax expense on gain from sale of segment E | 12,600 |
| Tax credit on loss from expropriation | (8,100) |
| Tax credit on 1994 depreciation error | (3,030) |
| | $28,020 |

**Required**

1. As supporting documents for Requirement 2, prepare separate supporting schedules for cost of goods sold, selling expenses, and general and administrative expenses (include depreciation expense where applicable in these schedules).
2. Prepare a 1995 multiple-step income statement for the Houston Manufacturing Company.
3. Prepare a retained earnings statement.

P4-8    *Misclassifications*   The Rox Corporation's multiple-step income statement and retained earnings statement for the year ended December 31, 1995, as developed by its bookkeeper, are shown here:

**ROX CORPORATION**
**Revenue Statement**
**December 31, 1995**

| | | |
|---|---:|---:|
| Sales (net) | | $179,000 |
| Plus: Income from operations of discontinued segment P (net of $960 income taxes) | | 2,240 |
| Less: Dividends declared ($1.50 per common share) | | (7,500) |
| Net revenues | | $173,740 |
| Less: Selling expenses | | (19,000) |
| Gross profit | | $154,740 |
| Less: Operating expenses | | |
|     Interest expense | $ 4,100 | |
|     Loss on sale of segment P (net of $1,200 income tax credit) | 2,800 | |
|     Cost of goods sold | 110,700 | |
|     Income tax expense on income from continuing operations | 5,370 | |
|       Total operating expenses | | (122,970) |
|     Operating income | | $ 31,770 |
| Miscellaneous Items | | |
|     Dividend revenue | $ 1,800 | |
|     General and administrative expenses | (24,300) | |
|     Gain on retirement of bonds (net of $1,650 income taxes) | 3,850 | (18,650) |
| Income before extraordinary items | | $ 13,120 |
| Extraordinary Items | | |
|     Loss on sale of land | $ (4,800) | |
|     Correction of error in last year's income (net of $1,500 income taxes) | 3,500 | (1,300) |
| Net income | | $ 11,820 |

**ROX CORPORATION**
**Retained Earnings Statement**
**December 31, 1995**

| | |
|---|---:|
| Beginning retained earnings | $59,000 |
| Add: Net income | 11,820 |
| Adjusted retained earnings | $70,820 |
| Less: Loss from expropriation (net of $2,760 income tax credit) | (6,440) |
| Ending retained earnings | $64,380 |

You determine that the account *balances* listed in the statements are correct but, in certain cases, incorrectly classified. No shares of common stock were issued or retired during 1995.

**Required**
1. Review both statements and indicate where each incorrectly classified item should be classified.
2. Prepare a correct multiple-step income statement.
3. Prepare a correct retained earnings statement.

P4-9    *Misclassifications*   The bookkeeper for the Olson Company prepared the following income statement and retained earnings statement for the year ended December 31, 1995:

**OLSON COMPANY**
**December 31, 1995**
**Expense and Profits Statement**

| | | |
|---|---:|---:|
| Sales (net) | | $211,000 |
| Less: Selling expenses | | (19,600) |
| Net sales | | $191,400 |
| Add: Interest revenue | | 2,300 |
| Add: Gain on sale of equipment | | 3,200 |
| Gross sales revenues | | $196,900 |
| Less: Costs of operations | | |
| Cost of goods sold | $120,100 | |
| Correction of overstatement in last year's income due to error (net of $1,650 income tax credit) | 3,850 | |
| Dividend costs ($0.50 per share for 8,000 common shares) | 4,000 | |
| Extraordinary loss due to earthquake (net of $1,800 income tax credit) | 4,200 | (132,150) |
| Taxable revenues | | $ 64,750 |
| Less: Income tax on income from continuing operations | | (13,980) |
| Net income | | $ 50,770 |
| Miscellaneous deductions: | | |
| Loss from operations of discontinued segment L (net of $900 income tax credit) | $ 2,100 | |
| Administrative expenses | 26,800 | (28,900) |
| Net revenues | | $ 21,870 |

**OLSON COMPANY**
**Retained Revenues Statement**
**For Year Ended December 31, 1995**

| | |
|---|---:|
| Beginning retained earnings | $60,300 |
| Add: Gain on sale of segment L (net of $1,350 income taxes) | 3,150 |
| Recalculated retained earnings | $63,450 |
| Add: Net revenues | 21,870 |
| | $85,320 |
| Less: Interest expense | (3,400) |
| Ending retained earnings | $81,920 |

The preceding account *balances* are correct but, in certain instances, have been incorrectly classified.

**Required**

Prepare a corrected multiple-step income statement and a retained earnings statement.

*P4-10*    *Classification of Unusual and/or Infrequent Items*    The following are a number of unusual and/or infrequent gains or losses that might be disclosed on the income statement or retained earnings statement. All items are considered to be material in amount.

1. A loss from an earthquake that destroyed a chemical plant of a major chemical company. The region where the plant was destroyed had not had an earthquake in 15 years.
2. A gain resulting from the retirement of bonds payable. The bonds payable had been classified as current liabilities on the ending balance sheet of last year because of their expected retirement during the current year.
3. A reduction in the current depletion expense as a result of the discovery of additional mineral deposits.
4. A gain from the sale of land. The land had been purchased for the construction of a new factory. The company has built several new factories over the past several years and in each instance has acquired more land than necessary for the factory site. After completion of the factory, the excess land is sold at its appreciated value.
5. A loss incurred by a corporation on the sale of an investment in bonds of a publicly-held company. The bonds constitute 5% of the net assets of the publicly-held company. The corporation has been holding these bonds as an investment for several years. This is the only investment in securities the corporation has ever made.
6. A loss incurred as a result of an earthquake that destroyed a 2-year-old storage facility of a large retail chain. The storage facility is located in California. A major earthquake occurred in the same region 2 years ago, just prior to the construction of the facility.
7. A decrease in previous years' earnings as a result of a change from straight-line to sum-of-the-years'-digits depreciation on factory equipment at the beginning of the current year.
8. An increase in current depreciation expense as a result of the change in depreciation methods discussed in item 7.
9. A loss incurred in the spring by a retail store in a shopping center as a result of a flood of a nearby stream. Although the stream has overflowed several times in the past 6 years, only 3 stores (out of 38) in the shopping center had previously incurred a significant flood loss.
10. A gain recognized as the result of the sale by a food processing company of a 15% interest in a professional baseball team.
11. A reduction in last year's income as a result of the discovery in the current year of a miscount (overstatement) of last year's ending inventory.
12. A loss incurred by a diversified citrus grower due to frost damage in southern California. No frost damage has occurred in the region for 7 years, although last year the citrus grower had incurred a loss due to frost damage to its Florida operations.

**Required**
For each item, indicate in which section of the income statement or retained earnings statement it should be disclosed. Justify your disclosure.

*P4-11*    *Results of Discontinued Operations*    The following are three independent situations in which separate companies decided to discontinue the operations of a segment. Each company is subject to a 30% income tax rate.

1. On June 1, 1995 Company X decided to sell segment A; the sale was made on November 2, 1995 for $800,000. Financial data for segment A: Pretax operating income, 1/1/95–5/31/95: $87,000; 6/1/95–10/31/95, $70,000; Book value, 11/2/95: $900,000.
2. On May 1, 1995 Company Y decided to sell segment B. The sale is to be made on March 1, 1996 for $326,000; at that time segment B is expected to have a book value of $320,000. Actual and expected pretax operating results for segment B are as follows:

|  | 1/1/95–4/30/95 | 5/1/95–12/31/95 | 1/1/96–2/28/96 |
|---|---|---|---|
| Operating income (loss) | $12,000 | $(2,000) | $(23,000) |

3. On July 1, 1995 Company Z decided to sell segment C. The sale is to be made on April 1, 1996 for $980,000; at that time segment C is expected to have a book value of $900,000. Actual and estimated pretax operating information for segment C is as follows:

|  | 1/1/95–6/30/95 | 7/1/95–12/31/95 | 1/1/96–3/31/96 |
|---|---|---|---|
| Sales | $125,000 | $100,000 | $19,000 |
| Operating expenses | 183,000 | 108,000 | 22,000 |

**Required**

Prepare the results from discontinued operations section of each company's income statement for 1995. Show supporting calculations.

P4-12 *The Coca-Cola Company* Review the financial statements and related notes of the Coca-Cola Company in Appendix A.

**Required**

Answer the following questions. (*Note:* You do not need to make any calculations. All information may be found in the financial report.) Indicate on what page of the financial report you located the answer.

1. What was the net income for 1992? What was the net income (earnings) per common share for 1992?
2. What was the gross profit for 1992?
3. Does the company use a multiple-step or a single-step format on its income statement? Explain.
4. How much interest expense was incurred in 1992?
5. What were the income taxes related to pretax income from continuing operations for 1992?
6. What was the amount of the change in accounting principle for postretirement benefits other than pensions in regard to consolidated operations in 1992?
7. By what percent and why did revenues from the soft drink business increase in 1992? Approximately what percentage of soft drink gallon shipments were made outside the United States in 1992?
8. What were the amounts of selling expenses in 1991 and 1992? What was the reason for the increase?
9. What amount of dividends on common stock were paid per share and in total in 1992?
10. What were the net operating revenues and gross profit, respectively, for the fourth quarter of 1992?
11. What was the net cash provided by operating activities in 1992?
12. What was the net cash used in investing activities in 1992?
13. What was the cash provided by the issuances of debt in 1992?

P4-13 *Complex Income Statement* The following is the adjusted trial balance for the Woodbine Circle Corporation on December 31, 1995:

|  | Debit | Credit |
|---|---|---|
| Cash | $ 500,000 | |
| Accounts receivable, net | 1,500,000 | |
| Inventory | 2,500,000 | |
| Property, plant, and equipment | 15,100,000 | |
| Accumulated depreciation | | $ 4,900,000 |
| Accounts payable | | 1,400,000 |
| Income taxes payable | | 100,000 |
| Notes payable | | 1,000,000 |
| Common stock ($1 par value) | | 1,000,000 |
| Additional paid-in capital | | 6,200,000 |
| Retained earnings, Jan. 1, 1995 | | 3,000,000 |
| Sales—regular | | 10,100,000 |
| Sales—AL Division | | 2,000,000 |
| Cost of sales—regular | 6,200,000 | |
| Cost of sales—AL Division | 900,000 | |
| Administrative expenses—regular | 2,000,000 | |
| Administrative expenses—AL Division | 300,000 | |
| Interest expense—regular | 210,000 | |
| Interest expense—AL Division | 140,000 | |
| Loss on disposal of AL Division | 250,000 | |
| Gain on repurchase of bonds payable | | 300,000 |
| Income tax expense | 400,000 | |
| | $30,000,000 | $30,000,000 |

Other financial data for the year ended December 31, 1995:

### Federal Income Taxes

| | |
|---|---:|
| Paid on Federal Tax Deposit Form | $300,000 |
| Accrued | 100,000 |
| Total charged to income tax expense (estimated) | $400,000 |
| Tax rate on all types of taxable income | 40% |

### Discontinued Operations

On September 30, 1995 Woodbine sold its Auto Leasing (AL) Division for $4,000,000. Book value of this business segment was $4,250,000 at that date. For financial statement purposes, this sale was considered as discontinued operations of a segment of a business. Since there was no phase-out period, the measurement date was September 30, 1995.

### Liabilities

On June 30, 1995 Woodbine repurchased $1,000,000 carrying value of its long-term bonds for $700,000. All other liabilities mature in 1996.

### Capital Structure

Common stock, par value $1 per share, traded on the New York Stock Exchange:

| | |
|---|---:|
| Number of shares outstanding during all of 1995 | 1,000,000 |

**Required**
Using the multiple-step format, prepare a formal income statement for Woodbine for the year ended December 31, 1995 together with the appropriate supporting schedules. All income taxes should be appropriately shown. (*AICPA adapted*)

P4-14     *Complex Income Statement*  The following trial balance of Garr Corporation at December 31, 1995 has been adjusted except for income tax expense:

| | Debit | Credit |
|---|---:|---:|
| Cash | $ 675,000 | |
| Accounts receivable (net) | 1,695,000 | |
| Inventory | 2,185,000 | |
| Property, plant, and equipment (net) | 8,660,000 | |
| Accounts payable and accrued liabilities | | $ 1,895,000 |
| Income tax payable | | 360,000 |
| Deferred income tax | | 285,000 |
| Common stock | | 2,300,000 |
| Additional paid-in capital | | 3,675,000 |
| Retained earnings, 1/1/95 | | 3,350,000 |
| Net sales—Regular | | 10,750,000 |
| —Plastics Division | | 2,200,000 |
| Cost of sales—Regular | 5,920,000 | |
| —Plastics Division | 1,650,000 | |
| Selling and administrative expenses—Regular | 2,600,000 | |
| —Plastics Division | 660,000 | |
| Interest income—Regular | | 65,000 |
| Gain on litigation settlement—Regular | | 200,000 |
| Depreciation adjustment from accounting change—Regular | 350,000 | |
| Gain on disposal of Plastics Division | | 150,000 |
| Income tax expense | 835,000 | |
| | $25,230,000 | $25,230,000 |

Other financial data for the year ended December 31, 1995:

### Income Tax Expense

| | |
|---|---:|
| Estimated tax payments | $475,000 |
| Accrued | 360,000 |
| Total charged to income tax expense (estimated) | $835,000 |
| Tax rate on all types of income | 40% |

Gain from litigation settlement is a taxable gain and is not considered infrequent.

### Discontinued Operations

On October 31, 1995 Garr sold its Plastics Division for $2,950,000 when the carrying amount was $2,800,000. For financial statement reporting, this sale was considered a disposal of a segment of a business. Since there was no phase-out period, the measurement date was October 31, 1995.

### Change in Depreciation Method

On January 1, 1995 Garr changed to the 150% declining-balance method from the straight-line method of depreciation for certain of its plant assets. The pretax cumulative effect of this accounting change was determined to be a charge of $350,000.

### Capital Structure

Common stock, $10 par, traded on a national exchange: 230,000 shares outstanding during 1995.

**Required**

Using the multiple-step format, prepare a formal income statement for Garr for the year ended December 31, 1995. All components of income tax expense should be appropriately shown. (*AICPA adapted*)

P4-15 *Comparative Income Statements* The Century Company, a diversified manufacturing company, had four separate operating divisions engaged in the manufacture of products in each of the following areas: food products, health aids, textiles, and office equipment. Financial data for the 2 years ended December 31, 1995 and 1994 are presented here:

### Net Sales

| | 1995 | 1994 |
|---|---:|---:|
| Food products | $3,500,000 | $3,000,000 |
| Health aids | 2,000,000 | 1,270,000 |
| Textiles | 1,580,000 | 1,400,000 |
| Office equipment | 920,000 | 1,330,000 |
| | $8,000,000 | $7,000,000 |

### Cost of Sales

| | 1995 | 1994 |
|---|---:|---:|
| Food products | $2,400,000 | $1,800,000 |
| Health aids | 1,100,000 | 700,000 |
| Textiles | 500,000 | 900,000 |
| Office equipment | 800,000 | 1,000,000 |
| | $4,800,000 | $4,400,000 |

### Operating Expenses

| | 1995 | 1994 |
|---|---:|---:|
| Food products | $ 550,000 | $ 275,000 |
| Health aids | 300,000 | 125,000 |
| Textiles | 200,000 | 150,000 |
| Office equipment | 650,000 | 750,000 |
| | $1,700,000 | $1,300,000 |

On January 1, 1995 Century adopted a plan to sell the assets and product line of the office equipment division and expected to realize a gain on this disposal. On September 1, 1995 the division's assets and product line were sold for $2,100,000 cash, resulting in a gain of $640,000 (exclusive of operations during the phase-out period).

The company's textiles division had six manufacturing plants that produced a variety of textile products. In April 1995 the company sold one of these plants and realized a gain of $130,000. After the sale the operations at the plant that was sold were transferred to the remaining five textile plants, which the company continued to operate.

In August 1995 the main warehouse of the food products division, located on the banks of the Bayer River, was flooded when the river overflowed. The resulting damage of $420,000 is not included in the financial data given previously. Historical records indicate that the Bayer River normally overflows every 4 to 5 years, causing flood damage to adjacent property.

For the 2 years ended December 31, 1995 and 1994 the company had interest revenue earned on investments of $70,000 and $40,000, respectively.

For the 2 years ended December 31, 1995 and 1994 the company's net income was $960,000 and $670,000, respectively.

The provision for income tax expense for each of the 2 years should be computed at a rate of 40%.

**Required**
Prepare in proper form a multiple-step comparative statement of income of the Century Company for the 2 years ended December 31, 1995 and December 31, 1994. Footnotes are not required. (*AICPA adapted*)

P4-16     *Financial Statement Deficiencies*   The following is the complete set of financial statements prepared by Oberlin Corporation:

### OBERLIN CORPORATION
### Statement of Earnings and Retained Earnings
### For the Fiscal Year Ended August 31, 1995

| | | |
|---|---:|---:|
| Sales | | $3,500,000 |
| Less returns and allowances | | (35,000) |
| Net sales | | $3,465,000 |
| Less cost of goods sold | | (1,039,000) |
| Gross margin | | $2,426,000 |
| Less: | | |
|   Selling expenses | $1,000,000 | |
|   General and administrative expenses (Note 1) | 1,079,000 | (2,079,000) |
| Operating earnings | | $ 347,000 |
| Add other revenues | | |
|   Purchase discounts | $ 10,000 | |
|   Gain on increased value of investments in | | |
|     real estate | 100,000 | |
|   Gain on sale of treasury stock | 200,000 | |
|   Correction of error in last year's statement | 90,000 | 400,000 |
| Ordinary earnings | | $ 747,000 |
| Add extraordinary item—gain on sale of fixed asset | | 53,000 |
| Earnings before income tax | | $ 800,000 |
| Less income tax expense | | (320,000) |
| Net earnings | | $ 480,000 |
| Add beginning retained earnings | | 2,690,000 |
| | | $3,170,000 |
| Less: | | |
|   Dividends (12% stock dividend declared but not yet issued) | | (120,000) |
|   Contingent liability (Note 3) | | (300,000) |
| Ending unappropriated retained earnings | | $2,750,000 |

## Statement of Financial Position
### August 31, 1995

*Assets*

| | | |
|---|---:|---:|
| Current Assets | | |
| Cash | $ 80,000 | |
| Accounts receivable, net | 110,000 | |
| Inventory | 130,000 | |
| Total current assets | | $ 320,000 |
| Other Assets | | |
| Land and building, net | $4,000,000 | |
| Investments in real estate (current value) | 1,668,000 | |
| Goodwill (Note 2) | 250,000 | |
| Discount on bonds payable | 42,000 | |
| Total other assets | | 5,960,000 |
| Total assets | | $6,280,000 |

*Liabilities and Stockholders' Equity*

| | | |
|---|---:|---:|
| Current Liabilities | | |
| Accounts payable | $ 160,000 | |
| Income taxes payable | 300,000 | |
| Stock dividend payable | 120,000 | |
| Total current liabilities | | $ 580,000 |
| Other Liabilities | | |
| Due to Grant, Inc. (Note 3) | $ 300,000 | |
| Unfunded accrued pension cost | 450,000 | |
| Bonds payable (including portion due within one year) | 1,000,000 | |
| Deferred taxes | 58,000 | |
| Total other liabilities | | 1,808,000 |
| Total liabilities | | $2,388,000 |
| Stockholders' Equity | | |
| Common stock | $1,000,000 | |
| Paid-in capital in excess of par | 142,000 | |
| Unappropriated retained earnings | 2,750,000 | |
| Total stockholders' equity | | 3,892,000 |
| Total liabilities and stockholders' equity | | $6,280,000 |

*Notes to Financial Statements:*

1. Depreciation expense is included in general and administrative expenses. During the fiscal year the Company changed from the straight-line method of depreciation to the sum-of-the-years'-digits method.
2. As per federal income tax laws, goodwill is not amortized. The goodwill was "acquired" in 1995.
3. The amount due to Grant, Inc., is contingent upon the outcome of a lawsuit, which is currently pending. The amount of loss, if any, is not expected to exceed $300,000.

**Required**

Identify and explain the deficiencies in the presentation of Oberlin's financial statements. There are no arithmetical errors in the statements. Organize your answer as follows:

1. Deficiencies in the statement of earnings and retained earnings
2. Deficiencies in the statement of financial position
3. General comments

If an item appears on both statements, identify the deficiencies for each statement separately. (*AICPA adapted*)

P4-17 *Financial Statement Violations of GAAP* The following are the financial statements issued by Allen Corporation for its fiscal year ended October 31, 1995:

## ALLEN CORPORATION
### Statement of Financial Position
### October 31, 1995

*Assets*

| | |
|---|---|
| Cash | $ 15,000 |
| Accounts receivable, net | 150,000 |
| Inventory | 120,000 |
| Total current assets | $285,000 |
| Trademark (Note 3) | 250,000 |
| Land | 125,000 |
| Total assets | $660,000 |

*Liabilities*

| | |
|---|---|
| Accounts payable | $ 80,000 |
| Accrued expenses | 20,000 |
| Total current liabilities | $100,000 |
| Deferred income tax payable (Note 4) | 80,000 |
| Total liabilities | $180,000 |

*Stockholders' Equity*

| | | |
|---|---|---|
| Common stock, par $1 (Note 5) | $100,000 | |
| Additional paid-in capital | 180,000 | |
| Retained earnings | 200,000 | 480,000 |
| Total liabilities and stockholders' equity | | $660,000 |

### Earnings Statement
### For the Fiscal Year Ended October 31, 1995

| | | |
|---|---|---|
| Sales | | $1,000,000 |
| Cost of goods sold | | (750,000) |
| Gross margin | | $ 250,000 |
| Expenses: | | |
| Bad debt expense | $ 7,000 | |
| Insurance | 13,000 | |
| Lease expenses (Note 1) | 40,000 | |
| Repairs and maintenance | 30,000 | |
| Pensions (Note 2) | 12,000 | |
| Salaries | 60,000 | (162,000) |
| Earnings before provision for income tax | | $ 88,000 |
| Provision for income tax | | (28,740) |
| Net earnings | | $ 59,260 |
| Earnings per common share outstanding | | $ 0.5926 |

### Statement of Retained Earnings
### For the Fiscal Year Ended October 31, 1995

| | |
|---|---|
| Retained earnings, November 1, 1994 | $150,000 |
| Extraordinary gain, net of income tax | 25,000 |
| Net earnings for the fiscal year ended October 31, 1995 | 59,260 |
| | $234,260 |
| Dividends ($0.3426 per share) | (34,260) |
| Retained earnings, October 31, 1995 | $200,000 |

*Notes to Financial Statements:*

1. *Long-Term Lease.* Under the terms of a 5-year noncancellable lease for buildings and equipment, the Company is obligated to make annual rental payments of $40,000 in each of the next four fiscal years. At the conclusion of the lease period, the Company has the option of purchasing the leased assets for $20,000 (a bargain purchase option) or entering into another 5-year lease of the same property at an annual rental of $5,000.

2. *Pension Plan.* Substantially all employees are covered by the Company's pension plan. Pension expense is equal to the total of pension benefits paid to retired employees during the year.

3. *Trademark.* The Company's trademark was purchased from Apex Corporation on January 1, 1993 for $250,000.

4. *Deferred Income Tax Payable.* The entire balance in the deferred income tax payable account arose from tax-exempt municipal bonds that were held during the previous fiscal year, giving rise to a difference between taxable income and reported net earnings for the fiscal year ended October 31, 1995. The deferred liability amount was calculated on the basis of past tax rates.

5. *Warrants.* On January 1, 1994, one common stock warrant was issued to stockholders of record for each common share owned. An additional share of common stock is to be issued upon exercise of ten stock warrants and receipt of an amount equal to par value. For the six months ended October 31, 1995, the average market value for the Company's common stock was $5 per share and no warrants had yet been exercised.

6. *Contingent Liability.* On October 31, 1995, the Company was contingently liable for product warranties in an amount estimated to aggregate $75,000.

**Required**

Review the preceding financial statements and related notes. Identify any inclusions or exclusions from them that would be in violation of generally accepted accounting principles, and indicate corrective action to be taken. Do *not* comment as to format or style. Respond in the following order:

1. Statement of Financial Position
2. Notes
3. Earnings Statement
4. Statement of Retained Earnings
5. General (*AICPA adapted*)

P4-18 *Comprehensive: Comparative Income Statements* The accountant for the Tiger Company prepared comparative income statements for 1994 and 1995 as follows:

**TIGER COMPANY**
**Comparative Statements of Income**
**For Years Ended December 31**

| | 1995 | 1994 |
|---|---|---|
| Sales | $3,500,000 | $4,600,000 |
| Cost of goods sold | (1,600,000) | (2,600,000) |
| Gross profit | $1,900,000 | $2,000,000 |
| Operating expenses | (1,300,000) | (1,500,000) |
| Operating income | $ 600,000 | $ 500,000 |
| Other items | (200,000) | 100,000 |
| Income before income taxes | $ 400,000 | $ 600,000 |
| Income tax expense (30%) | (120,000) | (180,000) |
| Net income | $ 280,000 | $ 420,000 |

The auditor of Tiger Company reviewed the accounting records and income statements and discovered the facts described in items 1 and 2. All amounts incurred during 1994 and 1995 are included in the preceding statements, but no estimated amounts are included.

1. Included in the category "Other revenues and expenses" (along with other smaller miscellaneous items) were the following:

   a. A casualty loss of $60,000 in 1994 that was considered to be both unusual and infrequent
   b. A $150,000 loss in 1995 from an unusually large write-down of inventory due to obsolescence
   c. A $250,000 gain in 1994 on the early retirement of bonds

2. On July 1, 1995 Tiger has announced its intention to sell its backscratcher business. This business is considered a segment according to the criteria of *APB Opinion No. 30*. Operating results for this business segment are included in the company's overall operating results for 1994 and 1995 as shown previously and are as follows:

| | 1995 (7/1–12/31) | 1995 (1/1–6/30) | 1994 |
|---|---|---|---|
| Sales | $200,000 | $400,000 | $700,000 |
| Cost of goods sold | 300,000 | 320,000 | 290,000 |
| Operating expenses | 100,000 | 180,000 | 110,000 |

The business segment had not been sold by the end of 1995. The company had hired an investment banker to help find a buyer. The company had paid $50,000 in the second half of 1995 and estimated paying another $30,000 before the anticipated sale date of March 31, 1996. The segment consisted of the following properties with anticipated book values and selling prices on March 31, 1996:

| Item | Cost | Accumulated Depreciation | Expected Selling Price |
|---|---|---|---|
| Land | $40,000 | — | $90,000 |
| Buildings | 80,000 | $60,000 | 30,000 |

Between January 1, 1996 and March 31, 1996, the company estimated the following amounts related to the business segment: sales, $50,000; cost of goods sold, $120,000; and operating expenses, $40,000.

**Required**

Prepare corrected comparative statements of income for 1995 and 1994 for the Tiger Company.

P4-19  *Statement of Cash Flows*  A list of selected items involving the cash flow activities of the Topps Company for 1995 is presented here:

a. Patent amortization expense, $3,500
b. Machinery was purchased for $44,500
c. At year-end, bonds payable with a face value of $20,000 were issued for $17,000
d. Net income, $51,200
e. Dividends paid, $16,000
f. Depreciation expense, $12,900

g. Preferred stock was issued for $13,600
h. Investments were acquired for $21,000
i. Accounts receivable increased by $4,300
j. Land was sold at cost, $11,000
k. Inventories increased by $15,400
l. Accounts payable increased by $2,700
m. Beginning cash balance, $20,600

**Required**

Prepare the statement of cash flows of the Topps Company for 1995.

P4-20  *Statement of Cash Flows*  The following are several items involving the cash flow activities of the Mueller Company for 1995:

a. Net income, $72,000
b. Increase in accounts receivable, $4,400
c. Proceeds from sale of common stock, $12,300
d. Depreciation expense, $11,300
e. Dividends paid, $24,500
f. Payment for purchase of building, $65,000
g. Bond discount amortization, $2,700
h. Proceeds from sale of long-term investments at cost, $10,600

i. Payment for purchase of equipment, $5,000
j. Proceeds from sale of preferred stock, $20,000
k. Increase in income taxes payable, $3,500
l. Payment for purchase of land, $9,700
m. Decrease in accounts payable, $2,900
n. Increase in inventories, $10,300
o. Beginning cash balance, $38,000

**Required**

Prepare the statement of cash flows of the Mueller Company for 1995.

P4-21  *Statement of Cash Flows: Direct Method*  The following are various cash flows and other information of the Trainer Company for 1995:

a. Payments of interest, $5,000
b. Depreciation expense, $22,700
c. Proceeds from sale of land, $3,100
d. Payments of income taxes, $6,200
e. Beginning cash balance, $16,500
f. Decrease in receivables, $7,400
g. Interest and dividends collected, $6,300

h. Payments of dividends, $5,200
i. Decrease in accounts payable, $8,600
j. Payments to suppliers and employees, $50,300
k. Proceeds from issuance of common stock, $11,000
l. Collections from customers, $61,700
m. Payment for purchase of investments, $17,800
n. Net income, $73,400

**Required**

Using the direct method for operating cash flows, prepare the Trainer Company's 1995 statement of cash flows.

P4-22   *Comprehensive: Balance Sheet from Statement of Cash Flows*   Gibb Company prepared the following balance sheet at the *beginning* of 1995:

**GIBB COMPANY**
**Balance Sheet**
**January 1, 1995**

| Assets | | Liabilities and Stockholders' Equity | |
|---|---|---|---|
| Cash | $ 1,000 | Accounts payable | $ 4,000 |
| Accounts receivable (net) | 3,900 | Salaries payable | 1,100 |
| Inventory | 4,700 | | $ 5,100 |
| Land | 9,800 | | |
| Buildings and equipment | 68,900 | Common stock, $10 par | 13,500 |
| Less: Accumulated depreciation | (14,100) | Additional paid-in capital | 11,200 |
| | | Retained earnings | 44,400 |
| Total Assets | $74,200 | | |
| | | Total Liabilities and Stockholders' Equity | $74,200 |

At the *end* of 1995 it prepared the following statement of cash flows:

**GIBB COMPANY**
**Statement of Cash Flows For Year Ended December 31, 1995**

**Net Cash Flow From Operating Activities**

| | | |
|---|---|---|
| Net Income | $ 5,000 | |
| Adjustments for differences between income flows and cash flows from operating activities: | | |
| Add: Depreciation expense | 1,900 | |
| Decrease in inventory | 500 | |
| Increase in salaries payable | 400 | |
| Less: Increase in accounts receivable (net) | (1,100) | |
| Decrease in accounts payable | (1,000) | |
| Net cash provided by operating activities | | $ 5,700 |

**Cash Flows From Investing Activities**

| | | |
|---|---|---|
| Payment for purchase of building | $(13,900) | |
| Proceeds from sale of land | 3,000 | |
| Net cash used for investing activities | | (10,900) |

**Cash Flows From Financing Activities**

| | | |
|---|---|---|
| Payment of dividends | $ (3,100) | |
| Proceeds from issuance of bonds | 5,700 | |
| Proceeds from issuance of common stock | 4,500 | |
| Net cash provided by financing activities | | 7,100 |
| Net Increase in Cash | | $ 1,900 |
| Cash, January 1, 1995 | | 1,000 |
| Cash, December 31, 1995 | | $ 2,900 |

Additional information related to the statement of cash flows:

1. The long-term bonds have a face value of $6,000 and were issued on December 31, 1995.
2. The building was purchased on December 29, 1995.
3. The land was sold at its original cost.
4. The common stock which was sold totaled 300 shares and had a par value of $10 per share.

**Required**

Prepare a classified balance sheet for the Gibb Company as of December 31, 1995. (*Hint:* Review the information on the statement of cash flows and the balances in the beginning balance sheet accounts to determine the impact on the ending balance sheet accounts.)

# FINANCIAL REPORTING

## Asset Measurement and Income Determination

PART

2

# 5

# CASH AND RECEIVABLES

**Chapter Topics**

*Internal Control over Cash
(and Petty Cash)*

*Bank Reconciliations (and
Proof of Cash)*

*Valuation of Trade
Receivables (and Revenue
Recognition)*

*Initial Recording of Accounts
Receivable*

*Sales Returns and Allowances*

*Estimating the Probability of
Uncollectible Receivables*

*Generating Cash from
Accounts Receivable
(Factoring, Assigning, and
Pledging)*

*Notes Receivable*

Financial statement users focus upon a variety of information in making credit and investment decisions. Investors, long-term creditors, and short-term creditors are interested in a company's *financial flexibility,* the ability to use its financial resources to adapt to change. One part of a company's financial flexibility external users are concerned about is *liquidity.* Liquidity is the availability of liquid assets (cash or assets that may be quickly converted into cash) to pay operating costs, dividends, and interest and to repay short-term debts. The most common types of liquid assets are cash, temporary investments, accounts receivable, and notes receivable. In this chapter we discuss the measurement and valuation procedures associated with cash, accounts receivable, and notes receivable. Because the accounting principles for temporary investments are similar to those for long-term investments, we defer discussion of temporary investments to Chapter 13.

# CASH

Cash represents the resources on hand to meet planned expenditures and emergency situations. **The amount reported as cash in the current assets section on the balance sheet must be available to pay current obligations.** It may not be subject to any contractual restrictions that prevent this money from being used to pay current debts. For example, many companies establish sinking funds into which they deposit cash over an extended period. At the end of the period, the cash (plus accumulated interest) is to be used for a specific purpose (e.g., to retire long-term bonds). Amounts in sinking funds should not be classified under the cash heading on the balance sheet; they normally are reported in the long-term investments category.

The measurement of **cash classified as a current asset includes coins, currency, unrestricted funds on deposit with a bank** (either checking accounts or savings accounts[1]), **negotiable checks,** and **bank drafts.** On the other hand, some items may be confused with cash but normally are listed under other balance sheet captions. Among these items are certificates of deposit, bank overdrafts, postdated checks, travel advances, and postage stamps. *Certificates of deposit (CDs)* are short-term investments issued by banks that allow a company to invest idle cash for short periods of time. CDs are normally classified as temporary investments. *Bank overdrafts* are overdrawn checking accounts. They are disclosed as current liabilities and should *not* be offset against positive balances in other bank accounts. *Postdated checks* are checks dated in the future so they become payable on a date later than the issue date. Postdated checks are included as receivables until the date they become negotiable. *Travel advances* are funds or checks given to company employees to cover out-of-pocket expenses while traveling on company business. Since travel advances normally are satisfied when the employee submits receipts for business expenses, they are generally classified as prepaid items. *Postage stamps* on hand are classified as prepaid items because they will be used rather than exchanged for cash.

In summary, to be classified under the current asset—Cash—caption on the balance sheet, amounts must be available immediately to pay current debts and may not be bound by any contractual or legal restrictions. Items that do not meet these criteria are reported elsewhere within the assets (or liabilities) section on the balance sheet.

## Cash and Cash Equivalents

Many companies use the title Cash on their balance sheets. An increasing number (approximately 71 percent)[2], however, are using a title such as *Cash and Cash Equivalents.* In addition to cash, these companies include in this category items that are considered to be "cash equivalents" because of their liquidity and low risk. **Cash equivalents** are short-term, highly liquid investments that are readily convertible into known amounts of cash and so near their maturity that there is little risk of changes in value because of changes in interest rates. Generally, only investments with maturity dates of three months or less are considered to be cash equivalents.[3] Securities such as commercial paper, treasury bills, and money market fund securities are examples of cash equivalents. A clear understanding of what items a company includes in Cash

---

1. Although some banks place restrictions on the withdrawal of funds from savings accounts, they generally are included as a component of cash.
2. *Accounting Trends and Techniques* (New York: AICPA, 1992), p. 125.
3. "Statements of Cash Flows," *FASB Statement of Financial Accounting Standards No. 95* (Stamford, Conn.: FASB, 1987), par. 8.

*The statement of cash flows is discussed in Chapter 20.*

and Cash Equivalents is important because when the company prepares its statement of cash flows, it must reconcile its cash inflows and outflows to the change in cash and cash equivalents. In this chapter for simplicity we focus our discussion on Cash.

## Cash Management

Efficient management of cash is of primary importance to every company. Care must be taken to ensure that adequate cash resources are available to meet current obligations. However, the fact that idle cash is a nonproductive resource also must be recognized.

After the Great Depression many companies wished to protect themselves against business failure. Consequently these companies amassed large amounts of cash to keep themselves liquid. Subsequently business managers realized that such monies were simply idle resources, and that company performance could be improved by investing them and earning interest. Proper cash management requires the investment of idle funds and the estimation of the timing of cash inflows and outflows to ensure the availability of cash to meet the company's needs. However, too many liquid resources may make a company the target of a takeover attempt.

Information on cash management is important in financial accounting because one objective of financial reporting is to communicate how well the managers of a company have discharged their stewardship responsibility to stockholders for the use of the company assets. In regard to these duties, cash management can be subdivided into planning and control aspects. **Cash planning** systems consist of those methods and procedures adopted to ensure that adequate cash is available to meet maturing obligations and that any unused or excess cash is invested. **Cash control** systems are the methods and procedures adopted to ensure the safeguarding of the company's funds.

The major component of a cash planning system is the cash budget. **The cash budget is a plan of cash activity that forecasts cash inflows and outflows and identifies the timing of potential cash surpluses and shortages.** The cash budget is primarily a managerial accounting technique and as such is outside the scope of this book.

Cash control systems are effected through adequate internal control measures. **Internal control** consists of the policies and procedures used in a company to safeguard its assets, check the accuracy and reliability of its accounting data, promote operational efficiency, and encourage adherence to prescribed managerial policies.[4] Internal control measures are designed to reduce the possibility of errors or omissions throughout the organization. The importance of such control is emphasized by the Securities and Exchange Commission's requirement that all publicly-traded companies maintain adequate internal control systems. Since cash cannot be traced easily, internal control over cash is enhanced by routine reviews of the accuracy of the recording of cash transactions and by the separation of employee duties. These procedures will help to ensure that theft can occur only if there is collusion among employees. However, whenever internal control measures are adopted, the cost associated with the use of the measures should not exceed the value of the derived benefits. Any measure that costs more than its benefits ultimately will result in lower profits for the company.

---

4. For auditing purposes, a company's internal control structure consists of the control environment, the accounting system, and control procedures. For more detail, see *Codification of Statements on Auditing Standards* (New York: AICPA, 1992), sec. 319.

Cash control systems can be subdivided into two main functions: (1) control over receipts and (2) control over disbursements. The control procedures adopted for receipts should be designed to safeguard all cash inflows from the time they arrive at the company until they are deposited in its bank account. Among the key elements in a cash receipts internal control system are: (1) an immediate counting of receipts by the person opening the mail or the salesperson using the cash register, (2) a daily recording of all cash receipts in the accounting records, and (3) the daily deposit of all receipts intact in the company's bank account.

The control procedures for disbursements should ensure that only authorized payments for actual company expenditures are approved and made. The key elements in a cash disbursements internal control system include: (1) making all disbursements by check so that a record exists for every company expenditure (for some payments a petty cash system may be used, as discussed next), (2) authorizing and signing checks only after an expenditure is verified and approved, and (3) periodically reconciling the cash balance in the bank statement with that in the company's accounting records.

Two important elements of the internal control over cash are a petty cash system and a bank reconciliation. Each of these elements is discussed in more detail in the following sections.

## Petty Cash

**A petty cash system involves a cash fund established under the control of an employee to allow a company to make small expenditures that might be impractical or impossible by check.** For example, a company requiring employees to work overtime may have a policy of sending late working employees home by taxi. Since taxi drivers do not usually accept checks, the company may provide these employees with cash to pay the taxi fare. Small amounts of cash may also be needed to pay for postage, collect deliveries, the purchase of limited amounts of office supplies, and other reasons. A petty cash system (sometimes called an *imprest system*) may be used for these purposes. The design and operation of a petty cash system includes the following steps:

1. An employee is appointed petty cash custodian. The petty cash fund is established at an amount estimated to be adequate to cover expenditures over a short period of time, and the fund is turned over to the employee for control and disbursement. The journal entry to record the establishment of the fund (assuming the amount is $500) is a debit to Petty Cash and a credit to Cash for $500.

2. Petty cash vouchers are printed, prenumbered, and given to the custodian of the fund. The vouchers are used as evidence of expenditures and to record the expenses incurred in the accounting records. Therefore at all times the total of the cash in the fund plus the amounts of expenditure vouchers should be equal to the original amount of the fund, in this case $500. A petty cash voucher is completed each time a disbursement from the fund is made, but journal entries are *not* recorded when disbursements are made.

3. When the amount of cash in the petty cash fund becomes low and/or at the end of an accounting period, the vouchers are sorted into expense categories and the remaining cash is counted. The expenses are recorded and the fund is replenished. At this time, a Cash Short and Over account may have to be established. This account is used to record any "shortage" or "overage" between

the original petty cash fund balance and the remaining cash in the fund plus the amounts of the petty cash vouchers. It helps to highlight errors and improve internal control over the petty cash system. To illustrate, assume that a count at the end of the month shows $67.54 remaining in the petty cash fund, and the sorting of vouchers indicates the following costs had been incurred during the month:

| | |
|---|---:|
| Office supplies | $ 34.16 |
| Postage | 178.00 |
| Transportation | 132.14 |
| Miscellaneous | 83.76 |
| Total expenses | $428.06 |

Since these expenses total $428.06 and the amount needed to replenish the fund is $432.46 ($500 − $67.54), the fund is "short" by $4.40. The actual expenses (along with Cash Short and Over), rather than petty cash, are recorded (debited) when the fund is replenished in the following journal entry:

| | | |
|---|---:|---:|
| **Office Supplies Expense** | 34.16 | |
| **Postage Expense** | 178.00 | |
| **Transportation Expense** | 132.14 | |
| **Miscellaneous Expense** | 83.76 | |
| **Cash Short and Over** | 4.40 | |
| Cash | | 432.46 |

The $432.46 is given to the fund custodian, and the actual amount of cash in the petty cash fund is now equal to the original fund balance of $500. The expenses are reported on the income statement. A debit balance in the Cash Short and Over account at the end of the accounting period would be reported as a miscellaneous expense; a credit balance would be reported as a miscellaneous revenue. The balance of the petty cash fund is included as part of the Cash amount reported on the balance sheet when financial statements are issued.

## BANK RECONCILIATION

The Cash account is a company's only account that also is kept by an independent party, the company's bank. Therefore it is possible, and desirable, to use one as a verification of the other. **A bank reconciliation is a schedule prepared to analyze the difference between the ending cash balance in the company's accounting records and the ending cash balance reported by its bank in a bank statement in order to adjust for timing differences in the recorded cash receipts and cash payments and to discover errors.**

Banks send a monthly statement to each depositor summarizing the activities that have taken place in the depositor's account. These activities include deposits, checks cleared, miscellaneous items, and the ending balance in the checking account. Also included with the bank statement may be the depositor's canceled checks. Each company has a checking account and maintains its own accounting records for its deposits and checks. The bank statement and the company's accounting records usually will not be in complete agreement. When the bank statement is received each month, the company prepares a bank reconciliation to compare the bank statement balance and the company's cash balance so that they may be reconciled.

## Causes of the Difference

The causes of the difference between the cash balance listed on a company's bank statement and the balance shown in the company's cash account include the following factors:

1. *Outstanding Checks.* **An outstanding check is a check that has been written by the company and deducted from the company's cash balance but has not yet been deducted from the balance reported in the bank statement.** On the date a company issues a check, it reduces its Cash account. A period of time is necessary for the check to be received by the payee (the recipient of the check), deposited in the payee's bank, and forwarded to the company's bank to be subtracted from the company's bank balance. Therefore a company has a certain number of outstanding checks at the end of each month that causes its cash account balance to be less than the balance on the bank statement.

2. *Deposits in Transit.* **A deposit in transit is a cash receipt that has been added to the company's cash balance but has not yet been added to the balance reported on the bank statement.** When a company receives a check, it increases its Cash account. A period of time may pass before the check is deposited by the company and recorded by the bank. At the end of each month there may be deposits in transit (either cash or checks) that cause the company's cash balance to be greater than the balance on the bank statement.

3. *Charges Made Directly by the Bank.* A bank frequently imposes a service charge for a depositor's checking account and deducts this charge directly from the account. Banks also charge for the cost of printing checks and for stopping payment on checks. These charges are reported on the bank statement.

    When a customer's check is received by the company it is deposited in the company's bank as a cash receipt even though the cash has not been transferred from the customer's bank account to the company's bank account. The company's bank is occasionally unable to collect the amount of the customer's check. That is, the customer's check has "bounced." **NSF (not sufficient funds) is the term used for a customer's check that has been deposited in a company's bank account but has not been paid by the customer's bank because there are insufficient funds in the customer's account.** Because the bank has not received payment from the customer, it deducts this amount from the company's bank account. Consequently, there may be some NSF checks included in the bank statement that have not been recorded by the company.

    At the end of the month all of the previously mentioned charges made directly by the bank are listed as deductions from the company's cash balance on the bank statement even though they may not have been deducted from the company's cash balance in its accounting records. Therefore the bank statement balance is less than the balance in the company's cash account.

4. *Deposits Made Directly by the Bank.* A bank often acts as a collecting agency for its customers on items such as notes receivable. In addition, most checking accounts now earn interest. When a note is collected the bank records the principal and interest as an increase in the company's bank account. Consequently, the bank statement may include notes received by the bank that have not yet been recorded in the company's accounting records. The amount of interest earned by a company on its checking account is typically not known by the

company until it receives the bank statement. In both these situations the bank statement balance is greater than the balance in the company's cash account.

5. *Errors*. Despite the internal control procedures established by the bank and the company, errors may arise in either the bank's records or the company's records, and they may not be discovered until the bank reconciliation is performed. For example, a bank may include a deposit or a check in the wrong customer's account or make an error in recording an amount. A company may similarly make an error in recording an amount. For example, a common error is to transpose two numbers so that the correct amount of $426 is recorded as $462.

## Procedures for Preparing a Bank Reconciliation

Given the items that might cause a difference between the ending balance in the company's cash account and the ending cash balance from the bank statement, a list of procedures can be developed and followed in preparing a bank reconciliation:

1. **Compare the deposits listed on the company's records with the deposits shown on the bank statement.** Determine that the deposits in transit included in the *last* month's bank reconciliation are listed in this month's bank statement. These deposits do not need any adjustment in the bank reconciliation. If they are *not* shown on the bank statement, an immediate investigation should be made to determine if an error or theft has occurred. Identify any deposits for the current month that are not listed on the bank statement. The amounts of all the deposits in transit are added to the ending cash balance of the bank statement in the reconciliation.

2. **Compare the checks listed on the company's records with the checks shown on the bank statement.** Determine that the outstanding checks included in last month's bank reconciliation are listed in this month's bank statement. These checks do not need any adjustment in the bank reconciliation. If they are *not* shown on the bank statement, an investigation should be made to determine if the checks were received by the creditors so that the company's "credit rating" is not affected. Identify any checks for the current month not deducted in the bank statement. The amounts of all the outstanding checks are subtracted from the ending cash balance of the bank statement in the reconciliation.

3. **Identify any deposits or charges made directly by the bank that are not included on the company's records.** These items include collections of notes receivable, interest earned on the checking account, service charges, NSF checks, and so on, which are listed on the bank statement. The collections or charges are added to or subtracted from the company's ending cash balance in the bank reconciliation.

4. **Determine the effect of any errors.** If an error is found, the nature of the error determines whether the error is added to or subtracted from the company's ending cash balance or from the ending cash balance of the bank statement.

5. **Complete the bank reconciliation.**

Generally accepted accounting principles require the reporting on the balance sheet of the amount of cash over which the company has control at the end of an accounting period. Our discussion focuses upon the form of reconciliation that arrives at an *adjusted*, or *corrected*, cash balance, indicating the amount of cash available for current operations. This form of bank reconciliation is illustrated as follows:

| | | |
|---|---|---:|
| Balance per bank statement | | $XXX |
| Add: | Receipts recorded on the company records but not reported on the bank statement. *Examples*: deposit in transit and cash received and recorded but not yet deposited | XXX |
| | | $XXX |
| Deduct: | Disbursements recorded on the company records but not reported on the bank statement. *Example*: outstanding checks | (XXX) |
| Adjusted Cash Balance | | $XXX |
| Balance per company records | | $XXX |
| Add: | Receipts reported on the bank statement but not recorded on the company records. *Examples*: notes receivable and interest collected by the bank or interest earned on the funds on deposit | XXX |
| | | $XXX |
| Deduct: | Disbursements reported on the bank statement but not recorded on the company records. *Examples*: bank service charge and customers' checks returned for lack of funds (NSF checks) | (XXX) |
| Adjusted Cash Balance | | $XXX |

**Upon completion of the bank reconciliation, journal entries are made by the company to bring its records up to date.** These entries are required because the adjustments to the company records on the reconciliation have not been previously recorded by the company. The adjustments made to the bank statement balance on the reconciliation were necessary to bring the bank statement balance into agreement with the company's adjusted cash balance, which is reported on the balance sheet. The company does *not* record these adjustments in its records, because they will be recorded by the bank at the appropriate time.

## Illustration

The following example illustrates the preparation of a bank reconciliation and the required adjusting entries for the Craig Corporation for the month ended June 30, 1995. The unadjusted cash balances are as follows:

| | |
|---|---|
| Cash balance per bank statement, June 30 | $12,461.15 |
| Cash balance per company records, June 30 | 12,437.94 |

The bank statement disclosed the following information:

1. A customer note for $1,200 plus $12 interest was collected on June 29.

2. A customer check for $138.14 was returned because of insufficient funds (NSF check).

3. The monthly service charge was $15.

A review of the company records disclosed the following:

1. A deposit for $1,142.87 mailed to the bank on June 29 did not appear on the bank statement.

2. Customer checks totaling $327.40 were on hand at the end of June awaiting deposit.

3. The following company checks were outstanding at the end of June:
   #862   $ 96.19
   #864    147.18
   #865    263.25

4. Check #843 written for $91.20 in payment of a creditor account and included with the canceled checks in the bank statement has been erroneously recorded as $19.20 on the company records.

Exhibit 5-1 illustrates the preparation of a bank reconciliation based on these data.

**EXHIBIT 5-1**

**CRAIG CORPORATION**

**Bank Reconciliation**
**June 30, 1995**

| | | |
|---|---:|---:|
| Balance per bank statement | | $12,461.15 |
| Add:   Deposit in transit | $1,142.87 | |
|        Checks on hand | 327.40 | 1,470.27 |
| | | $13,931.42 |
| Deduct: Outstanding checks: | | |
|        #862 | $  96.19 | |
|        #864 | 147.18 | |
|        #865 | 263.25 | (506.62) |
| Adjusted Cash Balance | | $13,424.80 |
| | | |
| Balance per company records | | $12,437.94 |
| Add:   Note collected by bank | $1,200.00 | |
|        Interest on note | 12.00 | 1,212.00 |
| | | $13,649.94 |
| Deduct: Bank service charge | $  15.00 | |
|        NSF check returned | 138.14 | |
|        Error in recording check #843 | 72.00 | (225.14) |
| Adjusted Cash Balance | | $13,424.80 |

Upon completion of the reconciliation, adjusting entries are prepared to record those items not previously included in the company records. The following adjusting entries are prepared by the Craig Corporation:

| | | |
|---|---|---|
| Cash | 1,212.00 | |
|     Notes Receivable (note collected) | | 1,200.00 |
|     Interest Revenue (interest collected) | | 12.00 |
| | | |
| Miscellaneous Expense (bank service charge) | 15.00 | |
| Accounts Receivable (NSF check) | 138.14 | |
| Accounts Payable (error) | 72.00 | |
|     Cash | | 225.14 |

These entries adjust the cash account to $13,424.80, the amount that would appear as the Cash balance (along with any petty cash) on the June 30, 1995 balance sheet.

## Proof of Cash (Four-Column Reconciliation)

The independent CPA responsible for auditing the company records normally will prepare a more comprehensive bank reconciliation. This type of reconciliation, termed a **proof of cash, incorporates the monthly cash receipts and payments to test the internal control over cash and provides additional evidence of the accuracy of the cash balance.** Therefore the proof of cash identifies the sources of differences between the company records and the bank statement (such as receipts and disbursements). There are several forms of a proof of cash (sometimes called a **four-column reconciliation**); again, our discussion focuses on the form that arrives at adjusted balances. This form of the proof of cash begins with the reconciliation made the previous month and accounts, in summary form, for all of the receipts and payments that have occurred during the current month. In essence, the proof of cash provides four separate reconciliations:

1. The reconciliation of the bank and book balance for the previous month

2. The reconciliation of the receipts recorded by the bank for the current month with the receipts recorded on the books

3. The reconciliation of the payments recorded by the bank for the current month with the payments recorded on the books

4. The reconciliation of the bank and book balances for the current month

The proof of cash for the Craig Corporation is shown in Exhibit 5-2. Note the far right column contains the June 30, 1995 bank reconciliation that was presented in Exhibit 5-1. The May 31, 1995 reconciliation, shown in the far left numerical column, would have been prepared the previous month using the same procedures as those for Exhibit 5-1. The June receipts and payments for the bank and company are obtained from the June 30, 1995 bank statement and company records, respectively.

---

## EXHIBIT 5-2

## CRAIG CORPORATION

Proof of Cash
June 30, 1995

| | Reconciliation May 31, 1995 | June Receipts | June Payments | Reconciliation June 30, 1995 |
|---|---|---|---|---|
| Balance per bank | $13,617.42 | $26,421.17 | $27,577.44 | $12,461.15 |
| Deposit in transit: | | | | |
| May 31 | 1,240.15  (1a) | (1,240.15)  (1a) | | |
| June 30 | | 1,142.87  (1b) | | 1,142.87  (1b) |
| Undeposited cash | | 327.40  (1c) | | 327.40  (1c) |
| Outstanding checks: | | | | |
| May 31 | | | | |
| #781 | (163.15) (2a) | | (163.15) (2a) | |
| #782 | (212.90) (2a) | | (212.90) (2a) | |
| June 30 | | | | |
| #862 | | | 96.19  (2b) | (96.19) (2b) |
| #864 | | | 147.18  (2b) | (147.18) (2b) |
| #865 | | | 263.25  (2b) | (263.25) (2b) |
| Adjusted Balance | $14,481.52 | $26,651.29 | $27,708.01 | $13,424.80 |
| | | | | |
| Balance per books | $14,481.52 | $25,439.29 | $27,482.87 | $12,437.94 |
| Note and interest collected | | 1,212.00  (1d) | | 1,212.00  (1d) |
| June service charge | | | 15.00  (2c) | (15.00)  (2c) |
| NSF check | | | 138.14  (2d) | (138.14)  (2d) |
| Error in recording check #843 | | | 72.00  (2e) | (72.00)  (2e) |
| Adjusted Balance | $14,481.52 | $26,651.29 | $27,708.01 | $13,424.80 |

The reconciliation of the receipts and payments for the month of June is explained below. The numbers and letters in parentheses after the amounts in Exhibit 5-2 reference the items in the following discussion.

1. *Reconciliation of June receipts.*
   a. The May 31 deposit in transit of $1,240.15 was received and recorded by the bank on June 1. This amount was recorded as a May receipt by the company and was added to the bank balance on the May 31 reconciliation. Since it is a May receipt, it is deducted from the June receipts listed by the bank.
   b. The June 30 deposit in transit of $1,142.87 has been properly recorded by the company as a June receipt and is added to the June receipts listed by the bank.
   c. Checks on hand (undeposited cash) of $327.40 are June receipts of the company and have been recorded by Craig. They are added to the June receipts listed by the bank.

d. The $1,212.00 note and interest collected by the bank has been included in the June receipts listed by the bank and is properly a part of the month's receipts for the company. The amount is added to June receipts of the company.

2. *Reconciliation of June payments.*
   a. The outstanding checks of $163.15 and $212.90 at the end of May were deducted from the bank balance to determine the adjusted cash balance on May 31. The actual payments of these checks by the bank have been included in the bank's June payments, but they must be excluded because they were May payments by the company. Therefore they are deducted from the June payments listed by the bank.
   b. The June 30 outstanding checks of $96.19, $147.18, and $263.25 have been deducted from the company's records and must be included in the bank's June payments. Therefore they are added to the June payments listed by the bank.
   c. The service charge ($15.00) has been included in the June payments by the bank and is a proper charge. This amount is added to the June payments by the company.
   d. The NSF check of $138.14 returned by the bank originally was included in the June receipts by the bank and by the company. When payment was refused, the bank recorded the NSF check as a June payment from the company's account. Consequently, the NSF check is added to the June payments by the company.
   e. The June payments listed by the bank reflect the correct $91.20 amount of check #843, erroneously recorded by the company at $19.20. The $72.00 difference is added to the June payments by the company.

Note that by adding the adjusted June receipts ($26,651.29) and deducting the adjusted June payments ($27,708.01) to the ending adjusted cash balance for May ($14,481.52) results in the ending adjusted cash balance for June ($13,424.80).

## SPECIAL TOPICS INVOLVING CASH

Two additional topics relate to the recording and reporting of cash. These items are electronic funds transfers and compensating balances.

### Electronic Funds Transfer Systems

In the previous example of a bank reconciliation, for simplicity we dealt with a few outstanding checks. In reality, a large company prepares and processes hundreds or even thousands of checks each month to pay its suppliers and employees. Furthermore, it receives and processes an equally large number of checks from its customers. Whether for payments or receipts, processing the paperwork for checks is becoming increasingly expensive. In conjunction with the increased sophistication of computer networks, banks offer **electronic funds transfers** (EFT) to their customers. Under EFT, funds may be transferred between parties electronically without the need of a check. EFT systems are becoming more compatible, and their "networking" capabilities are increasing. As more and more parties begin using EFT systems, fewer physical documents (e.g., checks) will be processed. The need for a bank reconciliation is not reduced, however. In fact, even greater emphasis should be placed on internal control systems as they apply to computer technology because fewer physical source documents are available to substantiate cash inflows and outflows.

## Compensating Balances

It is a common practice for banks to require a portion of any amount loaned to a company to remain on deposit in the bank for the duration of the loan period. These required deposits are termed **compensating balances.** For example, a bank loaning a company $100,000 may require that the company maintain a $10,000 deposit with the bank until the loan is repaid. Such arrangements have two main effects. First, they reduce the amount of cash available to the borrower, and second, they increase the effective interest rate the borrower pays for the use of the funds. For example, if the stated interest rate for the $100,000 loan is 12%, the effective rate for the actual funds used for a year is 13.33% ($12,000 ÷ $90,000), assuming the $10,000 compensating balance does not earn any interest.

The SEC undertook a study of funds subject to such withdrawal or usage restrictions. This study was partially in response to *liquidity* problems that were being reported by corporations with apparently adequate cash balances. The SEC detected many cases in which a portion of the reported cash balance was legally restricted, and consequently required that compensating balances against short-term borrowings be separately stated in the current assets section of the balance sheet. Compensating balances for long-term borrowings are separately stated as noncurrent assets (as either investments or other assets). Compensating balance agreements that do not legally restrict the amount of funds shown on the balance sheet are described in the notes to the financial statements. Since the SEC has the ultimate authority to issue accounting pronouncements, these procedures are generally accepted accounting principles for public companies.

# RECEIVABLES

**Receivables** consist of a variety of claims against customers and other parties arising from the operations of the company. Most receivables are satisfied through the receipt of cash, although others may be canceled through the receipt of other assets or services. Receivables are reported on the balance sheet as either **current** or **noncurrent** items. **Those receivables expected to be collected or satisfied within one year or the current operating cycle, whichever is longer, are classified as current assets; the remainder are classified as noncurrent.** Furthermore, receivables often are grouped within classified balance sheets as trade receivables and nontrade receivables.

**Trade receivables** arise from the sale of the company's products or services to customers and generally will comprise the majority of the total receivables balance. Trade receivables may be subclassified into **accounts receivable** (nonwritten promises by customers to pay for goods or services) and **notes receivable** (unconditional written agreements to receive a certain sum of money on a specific date). These subclassifications are discussed later in the chapter.

**Nontrade receivables** arise from transactions that are not directly related to the sale of goods and services. Nontrade receivables are recorded in separate accounts and disclosed on the balance sheet in individual groups as current or noncurrent assets, depending upon the length of their collection period. Examples of nontrade receivables include deposits with utilities, advances to subsidiary companies, deposits made to guarantee performance, and declared dividends and accrued interest on investments.

Deposits with utility companies often are required to guarantee utility expense payments. These deposits normally are classified as noncurrent receivables because the timing of repayment by the utility company is indeterminate. Advances to subsidiaries are typically classified as long-term because repayment may be postponed indefinitely. Deposits made to guarantee contract performance are classified as either current or noncurrent, depending upon the expected completion date of the project guaranteed. Declared dividends and accrued interest on investments are disclosed as current assets. In this chapter we focus upon the valuation issues associated with current trade receivables. Nontrade receivables and noncurrent receivables are discussed in other chapters throughout this book.

## REVENUE RECOGNITION AND VALUATION OF TRADE RECEIVABLES

The sales of goods and services usually are made on "open accounts" that result in short-term extensions of credit by the seller. **The recognition of revenue from credit sales is based on the revenue recognition criteria.** Revenue is recognized when **realization has occurred** (i.e., a noncash resource is exchanged for cash or a near cash resource) and the **revenue is earned** (i.e., the earning process is complete or virtually complete). Typically, the sale of goods and services on credit results in the creation of an asset termed a receivable (account receivable or note receivable) and the recognition of revenue at the time of sale. This approach is used because the asset (receivable) is expected to be collected and very few activities remain in the earning process. However, in some cases revenue recognition may be deferred because the collectibility of the receivable is *not* reasonably assured. In this case, a receivable is recorded, but a deferred gross profit account is deducted from the receivable until the revenue is recognized. In other cases, revenue also may be deferred because a right of return exists.

*Revenue recognition criteria are discussed in Chapter 4.*

*Two methods of recognizing revenue on a deferred basis, the installment method and the cost recovery method, are discussed in Chapter 16.*

### Right of Return

In most industries sales returns and allowances are not material, so that companies typically record them at the time of the return or allowance even if they occur in a period later than the period of sale (as discussed later in the chapter). In some industries, such as book publishing, the right of return is quite common and the amounts are quite large. In these cases, credit "sales" in one period may be followed by substantial returns in another. These factors create a revenue recognition issue because sometimes (1) reliable estimates cannot be made of the collectibility of the receivable and (2) the risks and benefits of ownership have not been transferred (the earning process is not complete). As a result, **FASB Statement No. 48** has established criteria for recording sales revenue when the right of return exists. **Each of the following criteria must be satisfied in such cases in order to recognize revenue at the time of sale**; if they are not, then revenue recognition must be deferred:

1. The sales price is fixed or determinable at the date of sale.

2. The buyer has paid or will pay the seller, and the obligation is not contingent upon resale of the product.

3. The buyer's obligation to the seller would not be changed by theft or damage to the merchandise.

4. The buyer has an economic substance apart from the seller. (The buyer has its own physical facilities and employees.)

5. The seller does not have sufficient obligations for future performance to directly bring about resale of the product by the buyer.

6. The amount of future returns can reasonably be estimated.[5]

In the event that the recognition of sales revenue and cost of goods sold is deferred because one or more of the preceding conditions have not been met, both should be recorded either when the return privilege has expired or when the conditions have been met, whichever occurs first.

### Valuation Issues

When the conditions in the previous section do *not* exist so that a receivable and revenue *are* recorded at the time of sale, there still is an issue of valuing the trade receivable. As discussed in Chapter 3, one purpose of reporting current assets is to disclose the **liquidity** of a company; that is, the "nearness to cash" of its economic resources. In this regard, the accounting issues associated with the valuation of current trade receivables are (1) the initial recording of the receivables based on the total future cash flows and (2) the estimation of the probability of collection. Since a time value is associated with money, a difference exists between the maturity value of a receivable and its present value. The longer the time period until maturity, the greater the difference. **APB Opinion No. 21** (discussed in Chapter 13) provides specific guidelines for recording and reporting receivables at their present values. However, the provisions do not apply to "receivables...arising from transactions with customers...in the normal course of business which are due in customary trade terms not exceeding approximately one year."[6] Consequently **most trade receivables are recorded initially at their maturity values** and not at their present values. Furthermore, since the collection period for most trade receivables is 60 days or less, the difference between their present value and maturity value is not considered material under normal circumstances.

The uncertainty of collection also affects the value of trade receivables. Whenever credit is extended, the likelihood exists that a few receivables will not be collected, and this factor should be recognized in the valuation of receivables on the balance sheet so as to report on their liquidity. The accounting procedures used to deal with the uncertainty of collection of receivables are discussed later in this chapter.

## ACCOUNTS RECEIVABLE

As discussed earlier, trade accounts receivable result from credit sales. Companies sell on credit in order to increase sales, but credit sales create the need for a credit department to investigate credit ratings, approve the extension of credit, and attempt to collect delinquent accounts. Credit sales result in a certain amount of bad debts due to nonpayment by customers. When a company is considering whether or not to sell on credit, it must evaluate the trade-off between the additional gross profit received from the expected credit sales and the additional expenses incurred due to these credit sales. In this regard, most companies establish a credit policy. A credit policy reflects the degree of risk a company is willing to accept in order to increase

---

5. "Revenue Recognition When Right of Return Exists," *FASB Statement of Financial Accounting Standards No. 48* (Stamford, Conn.: FASB, 1981), par. 6.
6. "Interest on Receivables and Payables," *APB Opinion No. 21* (New York: AICPA, 1971), par. 3.

sales. Credit policies are closely associated with customers' credit ratings. High credit ratings indicate low risk, whereas low credit ratings indicate high risk. A company should adopt a credit policy that results in the maximum increased profit consistent with the maintenance of customer satisfaction—that is, the combination of increased sales revenue and bad debt losses which results in the highest incremental profit and cash inflows. However, other factors such as the cost of additional sales and credit personnel necessary to handle these increased sales should also be considered. A few companies have decided that this trade-off is negative. These companies apparently feel that they can lower costs and increase profits by selling exclusively for cash. Most companies, however, sell on credit (although retail "credit card" sales often are treated as cash sales, as discussed later in the chapter).

If a company decides to sell on credit and establishes a credit department, it must install an effective internal control system for processing sales on account and cash collections. The internal control procedures used for cash collections were discussed earlier in the chapter, but it is also necessary to establish internal control procedures for the processing of accounts receivable. These control features include (1) prenumbered sales invoices so that all invoices are accounted for and (2) the separation of the sales function from the cash collection responsibilities so that collusion is required for theft to take place.

Once management is satisfied that a reasonable trade-off exists between the incremental revenues and expenses associated with credit sales, and an adequate system of internal control for credit sales has been established, several other issues may arise in recording accounts receivable. These issues include trade discounts, cash discounts, sales returns and allowances, and freight charges. Bad debts are discussed in a later section.

## Trade Discounts

The list prices quoted in catalogs often are subject to discounts for purchases in excess of a certain quantity. Discounts may also be used when merchandise is reduced for rapid sale or as a means of determining the price when the purchaser is a wholesaler or middleman between the producer and the ultimate consumer.

**Trade discounts** (also known as *volume* or *quantity* discounts) usually are quoted as a percentage of the list price. They may appear in a catalog as follows:

Item F — $80 less 20%, 10%, 5%

This quoted price indicates that the list price of $80 is subject to discounts of 20%, 10%, and 5% under certain circumstances. Each discount applies to the net price computed *after* deducting the previous discount. For example, if a purchaser is allowed all these discounts, the invoice price for 100 items would be calculated as follows:

| | |
|---|---:|
| List price (100 × $80) | $8,000 |
| Less 20% discount (0.20 × $8,000) | (1,600) |
| | $6,400 |
| Less 10% discount (0.10 × $6,400) | (640) |
| | $5,760 |
| Less 5% discount (0.05 × $5,760) | (288) |
| Invoice price | $5,472 |

Trade discounts are *not* recorded for financial reporting purposes, because they are used to establish a pricing policy. The sale of goods subject to trade discounts is recorded at the invoice price—in our example, $5,472.

### Cash (Sales) Discounts

Companies may offer another type of discount to induce prompt payment. These discounts are termed **cash discounts** (or **sales discounts**) and frequently are expressed as 2/10, n/30 or perhaps 2/10, n/EOM (end of month). In both cases **the first component refers to the discount rate and period and the second to the invoice due date.** These terms are read in the first case as: A 2% discount may be subtracted from the invoice price if payment is made by the purchaser within 10 days, and the total invoice price is due within 30 days. In the second example full payment must be made by the end of the month. To illustrate, assume that Company S sells $5,000 of merchandise to Company B with expressed terms of 2/10, n/30. If Company B pays for the merchandise within 10 days, it may remit $4,900 in payment of the invoice. This $100 cash discount is a strong inducement to pay within the discount period because it represents a relatively high effective annual interest rate to Company B. By paying within the discount period, Company B is giving up the use of funds for 20 days (that is, the invoice is due 20 days after the discount period expires) to earn an expressed discount of 2%. This is approximately equal to an annual effective interest rate of 36% ($0.02 \times 360/20$).

Cash discounts are an important consideration in the financial management of companies. Their potential effects should be carefully analyzed by both sellers and purchasers. As noted, the theory behind cash discounts is that they will induce prompt payment. A purchasing company should take advantage of any cash discounts that have a higher effective annual interest rate than the rate it must pay to borrow money. For a selling company, a cash discount has two main positive effects: (1) it stimulates a more rapid collection of cash for use in current operations, and (2) it tends to reduce the likelihood of losses resulting from uncollectible accounts. However, the negative effect to the seller of the reduced total cash inflow because of the discount should not be overlooked. Sellers should attempt to set the cash discount rate at a level so that its positive effects exceed any negative effects.

If the seller extends cash discounts to customers, two methods (a "gross" method or a "net" method) may be used to account for the discounts:[7]

1. *Accounts Receivable and Sales Recorded at Gross Price.* In using the gross price method the total invoice price is recorded in both the Accounts Receivable and Sales accounts at the time of sale as if no cash discount were involved. When the customer pays, if the allowable cash discount is taken, the difference between the cash received and the original amount of Accounts Receivable is recorded as a debit to Sales Discounts Taken. If the cash discount is not taken, the amount of cash paid by the customer will be equal to the original balance in the Accounts Receivable account, and no further adjustment is necessary. Sales discounts taken are deducted from sales on the income statement to determine net sales.

---

7. In a third method, accounts receivable are recorded at the gross price, sales are recorded at the net price, and the difference is recorded in an allowance account (a contra account to accounts receivable). The allowance account then is reduced by the difference between the cash collected from the customer and the accounts receivable balance. It also is adjusted for sales discounts not taken.

2. *Accounts Receivable and Sales Recorded at Net Price.* Under the net price method, the net invoice price (after deducting the cash discount) is recorded in both the Accounts Receivable and Sales accounts at the time of sale. When the customer pays, if the allowable cash discount is taken by the customer, no adjustment is necessary because the amount of cash received is equal to the recorded amount of the receivable. However, if the customer does *not* take advantage of the cash discount, the amount of cash received is greater than the recorded Accounts Receivable balance. This excess is credited to an account entitled Sales Discounts Not Taken. At the end of the accounting period, an adjusting entry may be made for any cash discounts no longer available on the outstanding accounts receivable. This entry involves a debit to Accounts Receivable and a credit to Sales Discounts Not Taken. A reversing entry is usually made so that when these sales are ultimately collected, the collections may be recorded in the usual manner for when no discount is taken. Sales discounts that are not taken are viewed as interest revenue and are reported in the Other Items section of the income statement.

To illustrate the application of these methods, assume the following: The Howe Corporation sold $8,000 of merchandise to various customers on December 4, 1995 with terms of 2/10, n/EOM. On December 14 Howe had received payment on goods originally billed at $5,500. Payment on goods billed at $1,500 was received on December 30. The remaining $1,000 had not been collected by the end of the year. The journal entries to record these transactions and the year-end adjustments are illustrated in Exhibit 5-3.

## Conceptual Evaluation

The use of the net price method is theoretically sound because it values the accounts receivable at the net realizable value and also properly states the amount of sales revenue and financial revenue. The gross price method has the advantage over the net price method of stating receivable accounts at gross amounts, which simplifies communications with customers. The gross price method also has the advantage of

---

### EXHIBIT 5-3

## ALTERNATIVE METHODS OF ACCOUNTING FOR SALES DISCOUNTS

| | Gross Price Method | | | Net Price Method | | |
|---|---|---|---|---|---|---|
| To record sale on December 4, 1995 | Accounts Receivable | 8,000 | | Accounts Receivable | | |
| | Sales | | 8,000 | [$8,000 − (0.02 × $8,000)] | 7,840 | |
| | | | | Sales | | 7,840 |
| To record payment received on December 14, 1995 | Cash | | | Cash | 5,390 | |
| | [$5,500 − ($5,500 × 0.02)] | 5,390 | | Accounts Receivable | | 5,390 |
| | Sales Discounts Taken | 110 | | | | |
| | Accounts Receivable | | 5,500 | | | |
| To record payment received on December 30, 1995 | Cash | 1,500 | | Cash | 1,500 | |
| | Accounts Receivable | | 1,500 | Accounts Receivable | | |
| | | | | [$1,500 − ($1,500 × 0.02)] | | 1,470 |
| | | | | Sales Discounts Not Taken | | 30 |
| To adjust the accounts at the end of the period | No entry required | | | Accounts Receivable | 20 | |
| | | | | Sales Discounts Not Taken | | 20 |

enabling sales returns and allowances (discussed later) to be recorded at gross instead of net amounts. But since most customers are expected to take advantage of the cash discount, the gross price method overstates the current sales and the accounts receivable at the end of the period. However, because the gross price method requires less record keeping, most companies use this method. Furthermore, when the timing of collections does not vary significantly from period to period, no material difference is likely to result from using either method.

In recent years many companies have established a cash discount policy that is in effect an interest charge; that is, the quoted cash selling price is in fact the net price (after deducting the cash discount). The merchandise is then quoted to credit customers at a higher price that includes the cash discount. Thus credit customers who pay within the discount period are in effect purchasing at the cash price, and those who defer payment are charged the cash price plus interest on the outstanding receivable. If the gross price method is used in these circumstances, Accounts Receivable and Sales initially are overstated by the amount of the computed interest charge. Furthermore, should the customers pay the account after the discount period has expired, the Sales account would include the amount of interest revenue. The use of the net price method overcomes these problems. Both sales at the cash sales price and any amount of interest revenue arising from payment by customers after the discount period would be recorded separately.

### Sales Returns and Allowances

When merchandise is sold, a few defective items may be returned by customers. In other cases existing practice or contractual agreements also may allow products that are not defective to be returned. **When goods are sold that are found to be defective, the customer may retain the goods and be allowed a reduction in the purchase price. This reduction is termed a** *sales allowance.* **When goods are returned to the seller, the exchange is termed a sales** *return.* Sometimes a sales return or allowance will occur in an accounting period after the sale. If reliable estimates can be made, from a theoretical standpoint **the estimated amount of future returns and allowances should be recorded in the period of sale so as to properly report net sales revenue and correctly value ending accounts receivable.**

To illustrate the accounting for sales returns and allowances, assume that the Barclay Corporation sells $500,000 of goods during 1995 and the company estimates that returns and allowances will be 5% of sales. To anticipate the returns and allowances, the following adjusting entry is made at the end of the period of sale (assuming the gross price method of recording sales is used):

| | | |
|---|---|---|
| Sales Returns and Allowances ($500,000 × 0.05) | 25,000 | |
|     Allowance for Sales Returns and Allowances | | 25,000 |

Consequently, when sales returns and allowances of $6,000 actually occur for goods sold on account, this transaction is recorded as follows:

| | | |
|---|---|---|
| Allowance for Sales Returns and Allowances | 6,000 | |
|     Accounts Receivable | | 6,000 |

If the net price method had been used to record sales, the preceding entries would have been based on the net price after deducting the cash discounts.

When sales returns and allowances are estimated in the period of sale, any balance in the Allowance for Sales Returns and Allowances account is included on the balance sheet as a valuation account offset against Accounts Receivable. In cases where returns and allowances are usually not material, most companies do not estimate these items. Instead they record the returns and allowances on account when they actually occur by debiting Sales Returns and Allowances and crediting Accounts Receivable (at the gross price or net price depending on which method is being used). Whether estimated or actual, sales returns and allowances should be disclosed on the income statement as a deduction from sales revenue.

### Freight Charges

Freight charges are a significant cost to many companies. The term *Free-on-Board (FOB)* refers to the point at which legal title passes to the purchaser, after which the purchaser must incur all further shipping charges for goods acquired. For example, if the terms of shipment are **FOB shipping point, title passes to the purchaser at the seller's shipping point (warehouse), and the purchaser is responsible for all freight or shipping charges from this shipping point.** Alternatively, if the terms of shipment are **FOB destination, title does not pass until the goods reach their destination, and the seller is responsible for all freight or shipping charges to the purchaser's place of business.** Large national corporations also frequently establish a number of FOB points throughout the country when they have multiple warehouses. In these cases freight on goods sent FOB shipping point is charged from the nearest warehouse.

Although one party is ultimately responsible for payment of the freight charges, to facilitate shipment and delivery of the goods the other party may make initial payment to the freight carrier. Consequently in recording accounts receivable involving freight charges, it is important to (1) determine whether the seller or purchaser is responsible for the freight charges and (2) review the sale and collection transactions to determine how the freight charges are actually paid. Consider the following two examples:

1. Carlson Company sells goods at an invoice price of $5,000 on credit to the Harris Company, terms FOB destination, and records the sale. Upon receipt of the goods, the Harris Company pays the freight charges of $175 to the trucking company but is allowed to deduct the amount from the invoice price. Upon receipt of Harris Company's check for $4,825, Carlson Company makes the following journal entry:

| | | |
|---|---|---|
| Cash | 4,825 | |
| Freight-Out | 175 | |
|    Accounts Receivable | | 5,000 |

Freight-Out is a selling expense on the Carlson Company income statement.

2. The Conlin Company sells $4,300 of merchandise to Larson, Inc., terms FOB shipping point. The trucking company requires that all shipments be paid in advance, so Conlin Company prepays the shipping charges of $138. The following journal entry is made by Conlin Company at the time of the sale:

| | | |
|---|---|---|
| **Accounts Receivable** | 4,438 | |
|    Cash | | 138 |
|    Sales | | 4,300 |

A $138 debit memorandum for the freight bill is then sent along with the $4,300 invoice to Larson, Inc.

## VALUATION OF ACCOUNTS RECEIVABLE FOR UNCOLLECTIBLE ACCOUNTS

The preceding discussion focused on the issues involved in the initial recording of trade accounts receivable. Not all accounts receivable will be collected, however. Some will become bad debts. A company might record uncollectible accounts (bad debts) by either of two procedures:

1. In the year of sale based upon an estimate of the amount of uncollectible accounts, or

2. As the actual loss is determined.

**FASB Statement No. 5** requires that estimated losses from loss contingencies be accrued against income and recorded as reductions in assets (or as liabilities) when both of the following conditions are met:

1. Information available prior to the issuance of the financial statements indicates that it is probable that an asset has been impaired or a liability has been incurred at the date of the financial statements.

2. The amount of the loss can be reasonably estimated.[8]

Since both conditions normally are met in regard to uncollectible accounts, most companies estimate bad debts. For instance, of the 600 companies surveyed in the 1992 edition of *Accounting Trends and Techniques*, 521 reported estimates of bad debts on their financial statements. This approach enables these companies to **properly value their receivables and match current expenses against current revenues.**

### Estimated Bad Debts Method

Under the **estimated bad debts method** the actual amount of bad debts incurred as a result of a particular credit policy is evidenced by historical data. These historical data are then compared to current sales or accounts receivable to determine certain relationships upon which to base estimates of current uncollectible accounts. **These relationships provide the information needed to prepare the adjusting entry to record the estimated bad debt expense for the year.**

When the estimate of bad debts is recorded, the journal entry involves a debit to Bad Debt Expense and a credit to Allowance for Doubtful Accounts (or, for instance, Allowance for Bad Debts or Allowance for Uncollectible Accounts). Bad debt expense is normally reported on the income statement as an operating expense. However, some companies offset the account against gross sales, or disclose it as a financial expense in the Other Revenues and Expenses section. The authors advocate reporting bad debt expense as an operating expense because its characteristics are similar to those of other operating expenses. This disclosure has gained the most acceptance among accountants, and financial statement users normally expect companies to report bad debt expense in this manner.

The account Allowance for Doubtful Accounts is a valuation (contra) account that is offset against Accounts Receivable in the current assets section of the balance sheet. Although current credit sales create a likelihood of losses from bad debts, the

---

8. "Accounting for Contingencies," *FASB Statement of Financial Accounting Standards No. 5* (Stamford, Conn.: FASB, 1975), par. 8.

actual customer accounts that will ultimately be defaulted are not known at the time of sale (if they were known, the company would not have extended credit to these customers). **Offsetting Allowance for Doubtful Accounts against Accounts Receivable informs financial statement users of the net realizable value (the amount of cash expected to be collected) of the receivables.**[9]

It is possible to base the estimation of bad debt expense upon historical relationships between the actual bad debts incurred and (1) sales or (2) accounts receivable. These relationships may be classified as follows:

1. Relationship to sales (income statement approach):
   a. Percentage of sales
   b. Percentage of net credit sales

2. Relationship to accounts receivable (balance sheet approach):
   a. Percentage of outstanding accounts receivable
   b. Aging of accounts receivable

## Percentage of Sales

Estimating bad debts on the basis of the historical relationship to sales matches current expenses against current revenues. This method is income statement oriented because it is based upon the matching principle and results in recording bad debt expense in the period during which credit sales occur. A percentage of total sales may be used as the basis for the estimate when there is a stable relationship between cash and credit sales. However, if the proportion of credit to total sales varies from period to period, the use of a percentage of total sales in any one period may not be appropriate. For this reason most accountants favor the estimation of bad debts on the basis of the historical relationship between bad debts and net *credit* sales. For example, if net credit sales during the year were $350,000 and bad debts have historically amounted to 3% of net credit sales, the following year-end adjusting entry is made:

| | | |
|---|---|---|
| Bad Debt Expense ($350,000 × 0.03) | 10,500 | |
|     Allowance for Doubtful Accounts | | 10,500 |

**Since this method focuses upon an expense account, any existing balance in the allowance account is ignored when determining the amount of the adjusting entry.** Also, if a company sells many products in different locations, it may choose to extend this analysis and estimate bad debts on the basis of historical credit sales of particular products or in specific locations. Although basing bad debt expense upon sales is a relatively straightforward income statement approach and adheres to the matching concept, it may not provide the best estimate of the net realizable value of accounts receivable because the balance in the allowance account is ignored when making the adjusting entry. Also if deviations from the expected net realizable value of the accounts receivable balance are material, a change in the accounting estimate may be necessary. Furthermore it provides only limited information for the credit department to use in its collection activities. These disadvantages may be offset by the use of a balance sheet approach.

---

9. If a company has other accounts such as Allowance for Sales Returns and Allowances, Allowance for Sales Discounts, and Deferred Gross Profit, these accounts would also be deducted from Accounts Receivable to determine the net realizable value.

## Percentage of Outstanding Accounts Receivable

Bad debts may be estimated on the basis of the historical relationship between actual losses and accounts receivable. This approach is balance sheet oriented because the resulting accounts receivable net balance is reported on the balance sheet at its estimated net realizable value. A relatively simple balance sheet approach is to base the estimated expense on the historical relationship between the actual bad debts and the outstanding accounts receivable balance at the end of the year. However, use of this approach may not appropriately match current expenses against current revenues.

**In using this method the focus of attention is on determining the ending balance in Allowance for Doubtful Accounts.** To determine the amount of the adjusting entry, it is necessary to consider the existing balance (prior to adjustment) in the allowance account. Bad Debt Expense then is recorded as the amount necessary to adjust the existing allowance account balance to the required ending balance. For example, assume that a company has determined that historically there has been a 4% relationship between actual bad debts and the year-end accounts receivable balance. The company records at the end of the year (prior to adjustment) disclose the following:

| | |
|---|---|
| Accounts Receivable | $475,000 |
| Allowance for Doubtful Accounts | 4,500 (credit balance) |

The expected net realizable value of Accounts Receivable is $456,000 [$475,000 − ($475,000 × 0.04)], and the required balance in Allowance for Doubtful Accounts is therefore $19,000 ($475,000 − $456,000, or simply $475,000 × 0.04). However, since the current balance in the allowance account is $4,500, only the amount necessary to increase the account to its required ending balance is recorded as Bad Debt Expense. In this example the amount is $14,500 ($19,000 − $4,500), and the following year-end adjusting entry is recorded:

| | | |
|---|---|---|
| **Bad Debt Expense** | 14,500 | |
| **Allowance for Doubtful Accounts** | | 14,500 |

A potential weakness of basing bad debts on a percentage of total outstanding accounts receivable is its failure to consider the due date of the many individual accounts comprising the total balance. This deficiency is resolved by the aging of accounts receivable.

## Aging of Accounts Receivable

The length of time an account is outstanding is an important factor in estimating the probability of its future collection. A company is much more likely to collect an open account that is 30 days old than one that is 360 days old. For this reason a more sophisticated method of estimating bad debts as a percentage of accounts receivable is used. **Aging accounts receivable categorizes individual accounts based upon the length of time they have been outstanding, and then applies the historically developed bad debts percentage to each age category.** The information in Exhibit 5-4 is taken from the records of the Rhorke Corporation and illustrates how bad debts can be estimated with the use of an *aging schedule* (or aging analysis).[10]

---

10. A company with few accounts receivable would probably not find an aging analysis to be a useful procedure, because each customer could be evaluated individually. Aging is appropriate when there are large numbers of customers who cannot reasonably be evaluated individually at the end of the period. In this example, for simplicity, only a few customers are used.

**EXHIBIT 5-4**

## RHORKE CORPORATION

December 31, 1995

### (a) Aging Schedule of Accounts Receivable

| Customer | Balance 12/31/95 | Under 60 Days | 60–120 Days | 121–240 Days | 241–360 Days | Over 1 Year |
|---|---|---|---|---|---|---|
| Goodwin Co. | $ 33,100 | $21,000 | $12,100 | | | |
| Hobson Inc. | 14,500 | | | | | $14,500 |
| Lomas Manufacturing | 20,600 | 15,000 | 5,600 | | | |
| McClendon Co. | 15,700 | | | | $15,700 | |
| Schauer Corporation | 37,900 | 17,500 | 16,800 | $3,600 | | |
| | $121,800 | $53,500 | $34,500 | $3,600 | $15,700 | $14,500 |

### (b) Estimated Uncollectibles

| Age | Amount | Estimated Percentage Uncollectible | Estimated Amounts Uncollectible |
|---|---|---|---|
| Under 60 days | $ 53,500 | 2% | $ 1,070 |
| 60–120 days | 34,500 | 8 | 2,760 |
| 121–240 days | 3,600 | 15 | 540 |
| 241–360 days | 15,700 | 30 | 4,710 |
| Over 1 year | 14,500 | 50 | 7,250 |
| | $121,800 | | $16,330 |

In developing the aging schedule, the unpaid invoices in each customer's account are reviewed, and the invoice amounts are classified into columns according to the length of time the invoice has been outstanding. The amounts in each column are then totaled. The total amount in each age group is subsequently multiplied by the applicable estimated uncollectible percentage to determine the estimated amount uncollectible for that age group. The total estimated uncollectible amount is derived by summing the estimated uncollectible amounts related to each age group.

This analysis indicates that the ending balance of Allowance for Doubtful Accounts should be $16,330 on December 31, 1995. **Since the objective in an aging analysis is to determine the ending allowance account balance, the previous balance of the allowance account must also be considered in recording the amount of bad debt expense at the end of the period.** If a review of Rhorke's accounting records indicated a current $1,350 *debit* balance in the allowance account, the amount of recorded expense necessary to bring the allowance account up to its required balance would be $17,680 ($16,330 + $1,350). Note that in this case the current *debit* balance in the allowance account was added. A credit balance would be *subtracted* to determine the necessary adjustment amount. The events that might cause the allowance account to have a debit balance are discussed in the next section. Based upon the preceding calculations, the following year-end adjusting entry is recorded:

| | | |
|---|---|---|
| **Bad Debt Expense** | 17,680 | |
| **Allowance for Doubtful Accounts** | | 17,680 |

Application of the aging method, particularly when prepared in conjunction with interim financial reports, is very useful to the credit department. As each new aging schedule is prepared, it focuses attention on any accounts that have not been collected and have shifted to an older age category. While the aging method has the advantage of properly reflecting the net realizable value of accounts receivable on the balance sheet and of providing useful information to the credit department, it may not precisely match bad debt expense against revenue in the year of sale.

### Conceptual Evaluation

In summary, companies should estimate bad debts rather than record them as they are actually incurred. Two main approaches to the estimation of bad debts are available. **The income statement approach, in which a percentage of sales (or credit sales) is used, results in a matching of current expenses with current sales.** However, this approach does not necessarily result in reporting accounts receivable at their net realizable value, since it does not consider the characteristics of the individual accounts that comprise the total receivables balance. **The balance sheet approach, which uses a percentage of outstanding accounts receivable or an aging analysis as the basis for estimating bad debts, results in reporting accounts receivable at their expected net realizable value on the balance sheet.** Furthermore, the aging analysis provides useful credit information. However, the balance sheet approach may result in matching past expenses against current revenues if a portion of the receivables balance has been outstanding for over a year. With the FASB's increased concern for reporting on a company's *liquidity* and *future expected cash flows*, the balance sheet method may be more appropriate. Currently, both methods are used in practice, and both are appropriate under generally accepted accounting principles.

## Writing Off Uncollectible Accounts

If bad debt expense is recorded based upon an estimate, an individual account that is actually determined to be uncollectible is written off the records, regardless of the period in which this determination is made. The journal entry is a debit to Allowance for Doubtful Accounts and a credit to Accounts Receivable. This write-off is simply an adjustment required because a previously estimated expense has now occurred. It does not affect the carrying value of the accounts receivable on the balance sheet. Consider the following information for Ellis, Inc.:

| | |
|---|---|
| Accounts Receivable | $175,000 |
| Allowance for Doubtful Accounts | 8,750 (credit balance) |
| Customer account deemed uncollectible | 850 |

At the time of the write-off, the following journal entry is made:

| | | |
|---|---|---|
| **Allowance for Doubtful Accounts** | 850 | |
| **Accounts Receivable** | | 850 |

This write-off has *no effect* on the net realizable value of the accounts receivable because the allowance account and the accounts receivable balance are reduced by the same amount. As shown in the following schedule, before the write-off, the net realizable accounts receivable was $166,250 ($175,000 − $8,750). After the write-off, the net carrying value of the accounts receivable is still $166,250, but it now consists of a $174,150 accounts receivable balance and a $7,900 allowance account balance. Similarly, there is no impact on the income statement as a result of this write-off because it did not involve a revenue or expense account.

|  | Before Write-off | Write-off | After Write-off |
|---|---|---|---|
| Accounts receivable | $175,000 | $(850) | $174,150 |
| Less: Allowance for doubtful accounts | (8,750) | 850 | (7,900) |
| Net realizable value | $166,250 |  | $166,250 |

Write-offs of accounts receivable are recorded as the individual accounts are determined to be uncollectible. In some cases write-offs occur during the period of sale *prior to* recording the estimated bad debts at the end of the period. In these cases the journal entry for the write-off is the same as shown previously: a debit to Allowance for Doubtful Accounts and a credit to Accounts Receivable. The result may be a *debit* balance in Allowance for Doubtful Accounts prior to the year-end adjustment. When the company is using a balance sheet approach, the debit balance is considered in determining the amount of the adjusting entry. When the income statement approach is used, debit (and credit) balances are disregarded. Additionally, estimates always involve future uncertainties, and the actual losses incurred from bad debts will not be the same as the amount of estimated expense. As new information becomes available, it may be necessary to change the estimated percentage of bad debts. If the balance sheet approach is used, the balance of the allowance account is modified each year to reflect the most current information. When either the estimated percentage of bad debts or the method of estimating bad debts is changed, these changes are simply treated as adjustments of bad debt expense in current and future periods. Such changes are considered to be changes in estimates as defined by *APB Opinion No. 20*.

*Changes in estimates are discussed in Chapter 20.*

## Collection of an Account Previously Written Off

Occasionally payment will be received from a customer whose account has been previously written off. Most accountants favor reestablishing the customer's account receivable on the books and then recording the payment. This procedure has the advantage of providing a complete credit history for each customer account and has the impact of eliminating the previous write-off entry. For example, if a $300 payment is received from the Burgois Corporation whose account has previously been written off, the following journal entries are made by a company using an estimated bad debts method:

| | | |
|---|---|---|
| Accounts Receivable | 300 | |
|     Allowance for Doubtful Accounts | | 300 |
| | | |
| Cash | 300 | |
|     Accounts Receivable | | 300 |

Note that the first entry "reverses" the initial write-off and the second entry records the cash collection in the usual manner.

### Direct Write-Off Method

The second method of recording uncollectible accounts is referred to as the direct write-off method. This method has the advantages of simplicity and of reporting actual losses rather than estimates. **When the direct write-off method is used, bad debt expense is recorded when a specific customer account has been determined to be uncollectible.** At that time the account is written off by debiting Bad Debt Expense and crediting Accounts Receivable. However, this determination and write-off may not occur until a period later than the period of sale. The use of the direct write-off method has the disadvantage of matching the bad debt expenses associated with previous sales against revenues of the current period and of overstating accounts receivable associated with previous sales. Furthermore, it allows the manipulation of income because management selects the period of write-off (and expense). For these reasons the direct write-off method is not allowed under generally accepted accounting principles. However, some companies use it because the results do not differ materially from those obtained under the estimated methods discussed earlier.

## GENERATING IMMEDIATE CASH FROM ACCOUNTS RECEIVABLE

The net realizable value of the accounts receivable disclosed on the balance sheet is usually indicative of the amount of cash the company expects to collect in its normal operating cycle. However, in certain circumstances a company may find it necessary or desirable to accelerate the cash inflows from its accounts receivable.

In today's business environment, there are many companies that specialize in "financing" other companies' accounts receivable. These finance companies include General Motors Acceptance Corporation (GMAC), General Electric Financial Services (GEFS), and Sears Roebuck Acceptance Corporation (SRAC), as well as credit card companies such as VISA, MasterCard, American Express, and Diner's Club. There are many variations in financing arrangements, including which receivables are involved, which company collects the receivables, who has title, and who incurs bad debts.

In this section, we are concerned about the accounting issues faced by a company that "transfers" its accounts receivable to a financing company in exchange for cash. From a financial reporting standpoint, these issues involve revenue recognition, asset valuation, liquidity, and financial flexibility. For **revenue recognition**, consideration is given to whether the risks of ownership of the receivables have been transferred (so revenue should be recognized). For **asset valuation**, consideration is given to who has control over the future benefits from the receivables (to determine who "owns" the asset). In addition, reporting on these types of arrangements is important in providing information about a company's **liquidity**, the nearness to cash of its receivables, and **financial flexibility**, its ability to use its receivables to adapt to changing financial conditions.

There are three basic forms of financing agreements to obtain cash from accounts receivable: (1) **pledging**, (2) **assigning**, and (3) **factoring (sale)**. There may be variations in the conditions of each agreement such that the distinctions are not always clear-cut. These agreements are evaluated on a "continuum" based on the transfer of risks of ownership and control over the benefits of the receivables, as shown in Exhibit 5-5.

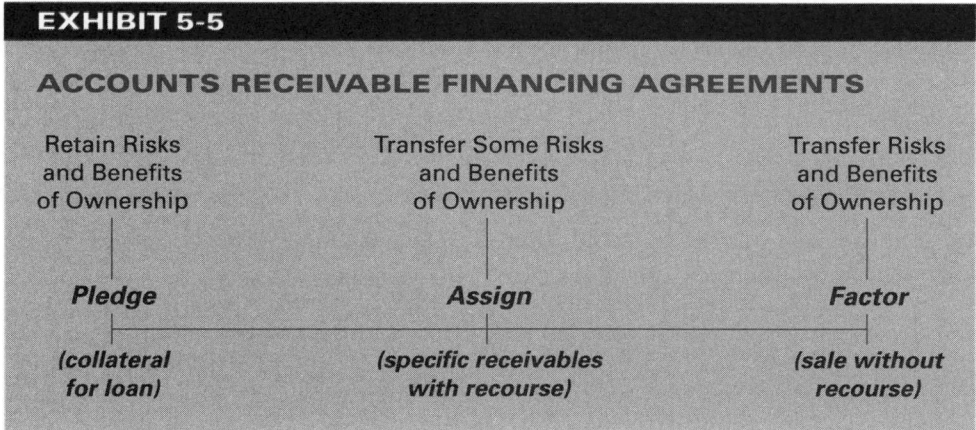

**EXHIBIT 5-5**

**ACCOUNTS RECEIVABLE FINANCING AGREEMENTS**

| Retain Risks and Benefits of Ownership | Transfer Some Risks and Benefits of Ownership | Transfer Risks and Benefits of Ownership |
|---|---|---|
| *Pledge* | *Assign* | *Factor* |
| *(collateral for loan)* | *(specific receivables with recourse)* | *(sale without recourse)* |

The FASB addressed some of these issues when it concluded in **FASB Statement No. 77** that a transfer of receivables with recourse (defined later in this section) is recorded as a sale when *all* of the following conditions are met:

1. The transferor surrenders its control of the future economic benefits embodied in the receivables. Control has not been surrendered if the transferor has an option to repurchase the receivables at a later date.

2. The transferor can reasonably estimate its remaining obligations to the transferee.

3. The transferee cannot require the transferor to repurchase the receivables except according to the recourse provisions (i.e., for failure of the debtor to pay when due). Otherwise, the amount of the proceeds from the transfer of receivables with recourse is recorded as a liability.[11]

In the 1992 edition of *Accounting Trends and Techniques*, 124 of the 600 surveyed companies reported the pledging, assigning, or factoring of their accounts receivable. These three arrangements are discussed in the following sections.

## Pledging of Accounts Receivable

When a company *pledges* its accounts receivable, it is using these accounts only as collateral for a loan, and the servicing activities remain the responsibility of the borrower. (*Servicing activities* are the routine collection and administration functions.) The borrower records the loan in the usual manner and then uses the cash collected from the receivables to repay the loan plus any interest charges. Upon full payment the pledge is canceled. In the event that the borrower defaults, the lender has the legal right to take title to the pledged receivables and sell them to recover the amount of the loan. Pledge agreements are usually not formally entered in the company's accounting records because there is no transfer of risks, and the company retains

---

11. "Reporting by Transferors for Transfers of Receivables with Recourse," *FASB Statement of Financial Accounting Standards No. 77* (Stamford, Conn.: FASB, 1983), par. 5–8.

control over the receivables. These agreements generally are disclosed parenthetically or in the notes to the financial statements to indicate that a portion of the accounts receivable balance may not be available to general creditors.

### Assignment of Accounts Receivable

**When a company *assigns* its accounts receivable, a financial institution enters into a lending agreement with the company to advance cash on specific customer accounts.** Frequently, these agreements are long-term in nature. Under an assignment agreement, usually the borrowing company (assignor) retains ownership of the assigned accounts, incurs bad debts, collects the amounts due from customers, and uses these funds to repay the loan. Occasionally, the finance company will require the assigned accounts to remit their payments directly to it (this procedure is called *notification*). The finance company (assignee) may impose collection guidelines on the assigned accounts or may agree to share in the risks of non-payment. In these cases, some of the risks and control of ownership have been transferred to the assignee; this is the major difference between assigning and pledging accounts receivable. Since the assignor (borrowing company) usually retains the risks of ownership, accounts are assigned *with recourse*. "With recourse" means that if the cash collected from the accounts is insufficient to repay the amount owed by the assignor, the assignee still can demand payment from (has recourse against) the assignor. This is the major difference between assignment agreements and factoring agreements, where the receivables are sold without recourse and the buyer assumes all the risks of ownership.

In assignment agreements, the company's relationship with the purchasers of its goods and services is not disrupted because the purchaser usually makes remittances directly to the company (*non-notification*) and is unaware of the financing arrangement. Usually, the amount of receivables assigned is somewhat greater than the amount of the advance; the excess amount serves to protect the finance company from sales returns and allowances. Under assignment arrangements the borrower pays a service charge and interest on the loan and is required to absorb any reductions due to sales returns and allowances or losses from uncollectible accounts. On the balance sheet, assigned accounts are presented separately from unassigned accounts receivable because cash receipts from these assigned receivables must be used for a specific purpose. That is, some of the benefits of ownership of the asset have been transferred to the finance company. The amount of the outstanding liability the company has incurred in borrowing against these assigned accounts is offset against the Assigned Accounts Receivable balance. This is one of the few times where generally accepted accounting principles allow a liability to be offset against an asset.[12] It is an acceptable procedure because the finance company has a specific claim against the accounts receivable. The difference between assigned accounts receivable and the outstanding liability is entitled Equity in Assigned Accounts Receivable.

To illustrate, assume that on December 1, 1995 the Trussel Company assigns $60,000 of its accounts to a finance company. The finance company advances 80% of the accounts receivable assigned less a service charge of $500. It also charges an

---

12. See "Offsetting of Amounts Related to Certain Contracts," *FASB Interpretation No. 39* (Norwalk, Conn.: FASB, 1992).

annual interest rate of 12% on any outstanding loan balance. The journal entries to record this assignment are:

| | | |
|---|---|---|
| Cash [($60,000 × 0.80) − $500] | 47,500 | |
| Assignment Service Charge Expense | 500 | |
| Note Payable ($60,000 × 0.80) | | 48,000 |
| | | |
| Accounts Receivable Assigned | 60,000 | |
| Accounts Receivable | | 60,000 |

The first journal entry records the receipt of cash. The Assignment Service Charge Expense account is a cost of borrowed funds and usually is recorded as an expense by most companies at the time of the advance due to the lack of materiality. The second journal entry is necessary to reclassify the receivables as assigned accounts receivable.

On December 31, 1995 Trussel collects $10,000 on assigned accounts. This amount along with the 12% interest for 1 month is remitted to the finance company. These transactions are recorded as follows:

| | | |
|---|---|---|
| Cash | 10,000 | |
| Accounts Receivable Assigned | | 10,000 |
| | | |
| Note Payable | 10,000 | |
| Interest Expense ($48,000 × 0.12 × 1/12) | 480 | |
| Cash | | 10,480 |

The interest expense on any future remittances is based upon the *remaining* note payable balance at that time (for example, the interest expense for the next payment in our example would be based on the $38,000 note payable balance). During the period the note is outstanding, any bad debt losses and sales returns and allowances related to the assigned accounts receivable are credited against the Accounts Receivable Assigned account. Upon full payment of the note, any remaining balance in Accounts Receivable Assigned is reclassified as Accounts Receivable.

On the December 31, 1995 balance sheet of the Trussel Company, the assigned accounts and the remaining liability (including any accrued interest payable) are disclosed as follows:

| | |
|---|---|
| Current Assets: | |
| Accounts receivable assigned | $50,000 |
| Less: Note payable | (38,000) |
| Equity in assigned accounts receivable | $12,000 |

The receivable and payable are netted because a right of offset exists. A description of the financing agreement should also be included in the notes to the financial statements.

## Factoring (Sale) of Accounts Receivable

When a company factors its accounts receivable, it sells individual accounts to a financial institution (called a factor). Since the receivables are *sold*, title is transferred to the factor who assumes all the risks of ownership. That is, the accounts receivable are sold *without recourse*, which means that if the receivables are not collectible, the factor cannot demand payment from the company that sold them. Consequently, factoring agreements focus on control of the receivables and usually require (1) notification of the credit customers to remit the amounts owed directly to the factor, and

(2) assumption by the factor of all collection activities, setting of credit policies, and losses from uncollectible accounts.

At the time of sale, the factor (finance company) charges the selling company a commission. The commission usually is based on the amount of receivables transferred and is relatively high, although it varies depending on the perceived risk of noncollection. The way in which the selling company records the commission depends on its normal operating activities. A selling company would record the commission as an *expense* if it normally factors its accounts receivable, or as a *loss* if it usually does not sell its accounts receivable. In addition to a commission, as a protection against sales returns and allowances, the factor will usually only pay 80% to 90% of the value of the accounts receivable transferred. The selling company records this amount in a separate Receivable from Factor account to indicate the amount that may be returned by the factor. Since title is transferred, the selling company reduces (credits) accounts receivable for the amount of the receivables sold.

To illustrate, assume that the Farber Corporation sells $80,000 of accounts receivable to a factor, receives 90% of the value of the factored accounts, and is charged a 15% commission based on the gross amount of factored accounts receivable. The following journal entry is recorded by Farber (assuming that it normally factors its accounts receivable):

| | | |
|---|---:|---:|
| **Cash** [($80,000 × 0.90) − $12,000] | 60,000 | |
| **Receivable from Factor** ($80,000 × 0.10) | 8,000 | |
| **Factoring Expense** ($80,000 × 0.15) | 12,000 | |
| **Accounts Receivable** | | 80,000 |

If sales returns or allowances are encountered on factored accounts, Sales Returns and Allowances is debited and Receivable from Factor is credited. At the conclusion of the factoring agreement for a particular group of receivables, any balance remaining in the Receivable from Factor account is collected from the factor and recorded by a debit to Cash and a credit to Receivable from Factor. When a factoring agreement exists, it should be disclosed in a note to the financial statements. Separate disclosure of the factored accounts in the body of the financial statements is not necessary because the receivables are no longer on the company's books. Although factoring agreements are common in the furniture and textile industries, many companies are reluctant to use factoring agreements because their customers may dislike being required to make payments to a bank or finance company rather than the seller.

### Credit Card Sales

Many retail companies make agreements with national credit card companies, which operate either independently or in affiliation with banks. Among the most popular are VISA, MasterCard, American Express, and Diner's Club. Under these arrangements, card holders establish a **line of credit** which may be used for retail purchases of goods and services. Once purchases are made by a customer, the bank or credit card company pays the retailer and the customer repays the bank or credit card company. These types of agreements are in essence factoring agreements.

The retail establishments accepting these credit cards charge customers the selling price for goods and services, but the retailer is then assessed a service charge on credit card sales by the bank or credit card company. This charge is usually a percentage of each sale, and in essence it is a fee for the use of a credit and collection department. Thus, the retailer usually records the charge as an operating expense. The individual retailer assumes little or no risk in accepting national credit cards, because most risk is borne by the bank or credit card company (except where fraud or negligence by the retailer is in evidence) since it originally granted the line of credit. The service charge assessed on credit card sales usually varies between 1 and 5% and is partially determined by the annual amount of sales or by exclusive arrangements. In an **exclusive arrangement** a retailer will only accept one national credit card, and in return the credit card company charges the retailer a lower service charge. For example, Sam's Club accepts only Discover cards in its stores.

To illustrate, assume that Kerns Shoes sold $1,500 of merchandise which was billed to an independent national credit card company during the month of July. If the collection fee charged by the credit card company is 5%, the following journal entry is made by Kerns when these credit card sales receipts are forwarded for collection (assuming the gross price method of recording sales is being used):

| | | |
|---|---:|---:|
| **Accounts Receivable** | 1,425 | |
| **Credit Card Expense ($1,500 × 0.05)** | 75 | |
|     **Sales** | | 1,500 |

Any sales returns or allowances are recorded in a similar (but opposite) manner. Upon receipt of cash from the credit card company, the receivable is eliminated. For credit cards affiliated with banks, any credit card sales receipts of a retail company may be deposited directly in its checking account. In this case the credit card sales are treated as cash sales so the journal entry to record the sales involves a debit to Cash (instead of Accounts Receivable).

## Disclosure of Financing Agreements of Accounts Receivable

As noted in the previous discussion, the existence of pledge, assignment, or factor (sale) agreements must be disclosed parenthetically or in the notes to the financial statements under generally accepted accounting principles. An example of this type of disclosure for a factoring agreement can be seen in the first note of the UNIFI, Inc., 1992 financial statements shown in Exhibit 5-6.

**EXHIBIT 5-6**
**Disclosure of Factoring Agreement**

**UNIFI, INC.**
**Notes to Consolidated Financial Statements (in part)**

Accounting Policies and Financial Statement Information (in part)
   *Accounts Receivable.* Certain customer accounts receivable are factored. An allowance for losses is provided for accounts not factored based on a periodic review of the accounts. Reserve for such losses was $4.7 million in 1992 and $2.4 million in 1991.

## NOTES RECEIVABLE

**A note receivable is an unconditional written agreement to collect a certain sum of money on a specific date.** Notes receivable generally have two attributes that are not found in accounts receivable:

1. They are negotiable instruments, which means that they are legally and readily transferable among parties and may be used to satisfy debts by the holders of these instruments.

2. They usually involve interest, necessitating the separation of the receivable into its principal and interest components.

Notes receivable frequently are required when customers wish to extend the repayment period on an outstanding account receivable. Sometimes they are required in the normal course of extending credit to new customers, and in some cases they may be required for all credit sales. Notes receivable also may result from long-term contracts.

*Recording long-term notes at their fair (present) value is discussed in Chapter 12.*

Two types of short-term notes may be received: (1) those bearing interest on the face amount of the note and (2) non-interest-bearing notes. These notes are discussed in the following sections.

### Short-Term Interest-Bearing Notes Receivable

When an interest-bearing note is issued, the amount borrowed (the principal) is listed as the face value, and the interest charged is expressed as a specific rate applied to this face value. At issuance the Note Receivable account is debited for the face value. After issuance, interest revenue on the note is recorded in the usual fashion, including any necessary year-end adjustments for interest receivable. To illustrate, assume that on October 1, 1995 Trent Company made a $5,000 credit sale to Jaynik Company and required the company to sign a $5,000, 60-day, 12% note. The journal entries on October 1, 1995 for the Trent Company to record the receipt of the interest-bearing note, and on December 1, 1995 to record the receipt of the principal and interest (assuming, for simplicity, a 360-day business year), are shown in the middle column of Exhibit 5-7. If the note had extended past the end of the year, a year-end adjusting entry would have been necessary to record the interest receivable and recognize the interest revenue.

### EXHIBIT 5-7

## ACCOUNTING FOR SHORT-TERM NOTES RECEIVABLE

|  | Interest-Bearing | | | Non-interest-Bearing | | |
|---|---|---|---|---|---|---|
| To record receipt of note on October 1, 1995 | Notes Receivable<br>  Sales | 5,000 | 5,000 | Notes Receivable<br>  Interest Revenue<br>  Sales | 5,100 | 100<br>5,000 |
| To record receipt of maturity value on December 1, 1995 | Cash<br>  Notes Receivable<br>  Interest Revenue* | 5,100 | 5,000<br>100 | Cash<br>  Notes Receivable | 5,100 | 5,100 |

*$5,000 × 0.12 × 60/360

Bad debt losses may occur on transactions evidenced by short-term notes receivable, particularly when it is common practice to require customers to sign notes for all credit sales. In these cases the accountant should assess the likelihood of these losses and establish an allowance for doubtful notes when it is appropriate. This procedure is the same as that discussed earlier for accounts receivable, and results in an increase in expenses and a decrease in the net realizable value of notes receivable.

## Short-Term Non-Interest-Bearing Notes Receivable

In the case of a non-interest-bearing note, the maturity value (the amount to be collected, which includes both principal and implicit interest) is listed as the face value. Actually the term non-interest-bearing is a misnomer because all notes implicitly contain interest. It is simply a case of the interest being included in the face value rather than being stated as a separate rate. A better term would be a note with no stated interest *rate. APB Opinion No. 21* does not require current trade receivables to be recorded at their present values because the difference between the present value and the maturity value is not likely to be significant. Consequently, many companies record short-term non-interest-bearing trade notes receivable at their maturity values. This approach, however, overstates sales revenue and understates interest revenue.

A conceptually better approach is to record the note receivable at its present value and to recognize interest revenue as it is earned. To illustrate, assume the same facts as in the earlier example except that Jaynik Company signs a $5,100 non-interest-bearing note, due on December 1, 1995. The journal entry on October 1, 1995 for the Trent Company to record the receipt of the non-interest-bearing note is shown at the top of the right column in Exhibit 5-7. Observe in this entry that interest revenue is credited[13] for $100. Although technically the interest is not yet earned, it will be before the end of the accounting period. This procedure simplifies the accounting process. The journal entry on December 1, 1995 to record the receipt of the face value is shown at the bottom of the right column of Exhibit 5-7. If the note had extended past the end of the year, a year-end adjusting entry would have been necessary to *reduce* (debit) the interest revenue for the interest not yet earned and to adjust (credit) an account entitled Discount on Notes Receivable. This Discount account is a contra account and is deducted from the Notes Receivable account to report the net realizable value on the balance sheet.

## Notes Receivable Discounted

Occasionally a company may find that current conditions dictate the need for additional cash on a short-term basis, but the company does not wish to incur additional debt or sell or assign its accounts receivable. In these cases customer notes receivable may be **discounted** at a bank in return for cash. **A company that discounts a customer note receivable at the bank is in essence transferring the note to the bank with recourse.** That is, the customer is notified to pay the bank directly at the maturity date, and the company guarantees payment of the note if the customer defaults. During the interim period between the discount date and the maturity date, the note represents a contingent liability to the company. Under the provisions of **FASB Statement**

---

13. Alternatively, Discount on Notes Receivable could be credited (instead of Interest Revenue) at the time of issuance. Then when the face value is collected (or at the end of the year if an adjustment is required), a journal entry must be made to reduce the discount account and increase interest revenue for the amount of interest earned.

**No. 5,** this type of *contingent liability* must be disclosed in the financial statements, even if the possibility of default by the customer is remote.[14] To make this disclosure, when the note is transferred to the bank, it is common practice to record the discounted note in a separate contra account entitled Notes Receivable Discounted. This account is then offset against Notes Receivable on any balance sheet prepared prior to the note's maturity date. If the customer pays the note at maturity, Notes Receivable and Notes Receivable Discounted are removed from the accounting records, and the contingent liability is canceled.

**When a customer's note is discounted, the proceeds (cash received) are determined by applying the discount percentage to the maturity value of the note (face value of the note plus total interest) for the discount period, and deducting the resulting discount from the maturity value.** The *discount percentage* is the interest rate charged by the bank. It has no relationship to the interest rate charged the customer on the note receivable. The *discount period* is the length of time from the date of discount to the maturity date. Accounting for a discounted note receivable involves the following computational steps:

1. Determine the face value of the note.

2. Compute the interest to maturity (face value of the note times the interest rate times the entire interest period).

3. Compute the maturity value of the note (face value of the note plus interest to maturity).

4. Compute the discount (maturity value of the note times the bank discount percentage times the discount period).

5. Compute the proceeds (maturity value less the discount).

6. Compute the accrued interest revenue on the note (face value of the note times the interest rate times the length of time the note has been outstanding to the date of discount).

7. Compute the book value of the note (face value of the note plus accrued interest).

8. Compute the gain or loss (proceeds less the book value of the note).

Once these computations are completed, journal entries are made on the date of the discount to accrue the interest revenue and to record the proceeds received, any gain or loss on the transfer of the note, and the contingent liability. To illustrate, assume that on August 1, 1995 the Kasper Corporation receives a $5,000, 12%, 90-day note from a credit customer wishing to extend its repayment period. On August 31, 1995, after 30 days, Kasper discounts the note at a bank at 14%. The customer pays

---

14. *FASB Statement No. 5, op. cit.,* par. 12.

the note to the bank as promised on October 30, 1995. The following journal entries are made to record these transactions (assuming a 360-day business year):

**August 1, 1995**

| | | |
|---|---|---|
| Notes Receivable | 5,000.00 | |
| Accounts Receivable | | 5,000.00 |

**August 31, 1995**

| | | |
|---|---|---|
| Interest Receivable | 50.00 | |
| Interest Revenue | | 50.00 |
| Cash | 5,029.83 | |
| Loss from Discounting of Note | 20.17 | |
| Notes Receivable Discounted | | 5,000.00 |
| Interest Receivable | | 50.00 |

**October 30, 1995**

| | | |
|---|---|---|
| Notes Receivable Discounted | 5,000.00 | |
| Notes Receivable | | 5,000.00 |

The calculation of the amounts for the August 31, 1995, journal entries is as follows:

| | |
|---|---|
| 1. Face value of note | $5,000.00 |
| 2. Interest to maturity ($5,000 $\times$ 0.12 $\times$ 90/360) | 150.00 |
| 3. Maturity value of note | $5,150.00 |
| 4. Discount ($5,150 $\times$ 0.14 $\times$ 60/360) | (120.17) |
| 5. Proceeds | $5,029.83 |
| 6. Accrued interest revenue: $50 ($5,000 $\times$ 0.12 $\times$ 30/360) | |
| 7. Book value of note ($5,000 + $50) | (5,050.00) |
| 8. Loss from discounting of note | $ 20.17 |

The elements included in the first five items of the discounting calculation may be illustrated as follows:

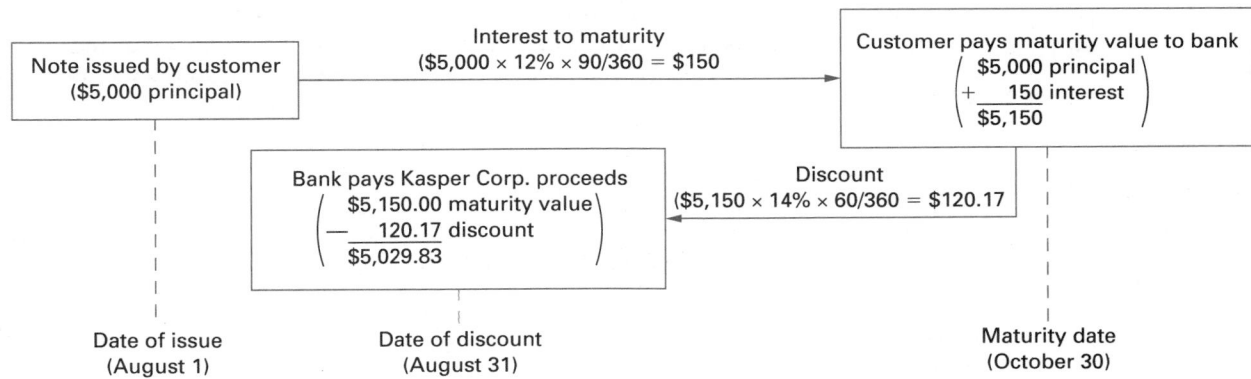

When a note is discounted, the difference between the book value of the note and its proceeds is recorded as a gain or loss if a company usually does not discount its notes. Alternatively, if a company normally discounts its notes, the difference would be reported as interest revenue or interest expense.

If the Kasper Corporation prepared an interim balance sheet on September 30, 1995 and on that date it had a $43,000 balance in notes receivable, it discloses the discounted note as follows:

Current Assets:
Notes receivable                                $43,000
Less: Notes receivable discounted       (5,000)      $38,000

An alternative method of recording and disclosing discounted notes is to reduce the Notes Receivable account directly at the time of the transfer to the bank. The contingent liability is then disclosed either by a footnote or parenthetically until the note is paid at maturity. If this alternative method had been used to record the contingent liability, on August 31 the journal entry would have been the same except that the $5,000 credit would have been to Notes Receivable instead of Notes Receivable Discounted. A parenthetical explanation or a footnote describing the contingent liability would then be included with the September 30, 1995 interim balance sheet. This footnote might read as follows: "The company is contingently liable for a note receivable discounted in the amount of $5,000. The company does not anticipate that this note will be defaulted on its maturity date."

In this illustration the contingent liability was eliminated on the maturity date when the customer paid the note. In some cases the company may not be notified by the bank of the customer's payment on the maturity date. Consequently any discounted notes that have passed the maturity date by a reasonable amount of time without notification of default by the bank can be assumed to have been paid (or the bank can be contacted for verification of payment), and the contingent liability may be eliminated from the accounting records.

In the event that this note was not paid at maturity, the bank would require Kasper to pay the maturity value of the note plus a service charge on the dishonored note. Kasper's only recourse then is to attempt to collect these amounts from the customer. Consequently upon default the Notes Receivable and Notes Receivable Discounted accounts are canceled and an account Notes Receivable Dishonored is established. For example, assume instead that on November 3, 1995 the bank notified Kasper that the note had not been paid and also charged Kasper a $10 fee. At that time Kasper would record the following journal entry:

| | | |
|---|---|---|
| Notes Receivable Dishonored | 5,160 | |
| Notes Receivable Discounted | 5,000 | |
|     Notes Receivable | | 5,000 |
|     Cash [$5,000 + ($5,000 × 0.12 × 90/360) + $10] | | 5,160 |

If Kasper does not collect the dishonored note in the future, a loss on the default is recognized.

# FINANCIAL STATEMENT DISCLOSURES OF RECEIVABLES

Companies are required to disclose any accounting policies related to their receivables that might be helpful to external users. **FASB Statement No. 105** also requires companies to disclose information about the credit risk related to their financial instruments (e.g., receivables). This information includes, for instance, the company's policy of requiring collateral, its access to the collateral, any concentrations of credit risk, and the potential loss the company would incur if the debtor failed to perform.[15] Exhibit 5-8 shows an excerpt from the Quaker Oats Company's 1992 balance sheet and related Note 3 illustrating the presentation of receivables on corporate financial statements. Observe that Quaker Oats provides for doubtful accounts as well as discounts and allowances in determining the net realizable value of its trade accounts receivable.

---

**EXHIBIT 5-8**
**Disclosure of Accounts Receivable**

## QUAKER OATS COMPANY

|  | June 30 | | |
| --- | --- | --- | --- |
|  | 1992 | 1991 | 1990 |
| (in millions) | | | |
| Current Assets: (in part) | | | |
|    Trade accounts receivable—net of allowances | $575.3 | $655.6 | $575.6 |

Notes to the Consolidated Financial Statements (in part)
*Note 3*
*Trade Accounts Receivable Allowances*

|  | 1992 | 1991 | 1990 |
| --- | --- | --- | --- |
| Balance at beginning of year | $ 18.7 | $ 16.5 | $ 16.5 |
| Provision for doubtful accounts | 7.2 | 5.8 | 3.8 |
| Provision for discounts and allowances | 13.5 | 15.8 | 6.7 |
| Write-offs of doubtful accounts, net of recoveries | (5.4) | (4.6) | (2.0) |
| Discounts and allowances taken | (17.4) | (14.8) | (8.5) |
| Balance at end of year | $ 16.6 | $ 18.7 | $ 16.5 |

---

15. "Disclosure of Information about Financial Instruments with Off-Balance Sheet Risk and Financial Instruments with Concentrations of Credit Risk," *FASB Statement of Financial Accounting Standards No. 105* (Stamford, Conn.: FASB, 1990), par. 18–20.

## QUESTIONS

**Q5-1** What are the components of cash? What items may be confused with cash, but normally are categorized under other balance sheet captions? What are "cash equivalents?"

**Q5-2** What does internal control consist of? What are two important elements of internal control over cash?

**Q5-3** What is the purpose of a petty cash system?

**Q5-4** Why are actual expenses, rather than the account Petty Cash, debited when the fund is replenished?

**Q5-5** What is a bank reconciliation? List the causes of the difference between the cash balance listed on a company's bank statement and the balance shown in the company's cash account.

**Q5-6** Why are adjusting entries required upon completion of the bank reconciliation? Give an example of an item on a bank reconciliation which would require an adjusting entry.

**Q5-7** What four separate reconciliations are provided by the proof of cash?

**Q5-8** What are the two revenue recognition criteria and how do they relate to receivables in some industries?

**Q5-9** Briefly discuss the two methods of recording accounts receivable when cash discounts are involved.

**Q5-10** What is a sales return? Allowance? Conceptually, when should sales returns and allowances be recorded?

**Q5-11** Explain the term *Free-on-Board (FOB)*. Discuss the difference between the terms *FOB shipping point* and *FOB destination*.

**Q5-12** Discuss the differences between the estimation methods of recording bad debts and the direct write-off method.

**Q5-13** Explain the estimation of bad debts using (a) the sales or income statement approach; and (b) the accounts receivable or balance sheet approach.

**Q5-14** Define *net realizable value* of accounts receivable. How is the net realizable value of accounts receivable disclosed on the balance sheet?

**Q5-15** What method of bad debt estimation categorizes individual accounts receivable based on the length of time outstanding? Why is this length of time an important factor?

**Q5-16** Why does the write-off of uncollectible accounts not have an effect on the net realizable accounts receivable on the balance sheet if bad debts are estimated? What is the effect of this write-off on the income statement?

**Q5-17** Define pledging, assigning, and factoring of accounts receivable.

**Q5-18** When is the transfer of receivables reported as a sale? As a liability?

**Q5-19** What are notes receivable? How do they differ from accounts receivable?

**Q5-20** What is a non-interest-bearing note? How does the accounting treatment for a short-term non-interest-bearing note differ from a short-term interest-bearing note?

**Q5-21** What are notes receivable discounted? How are discounted notes disclosed on the financial statements during the period between the discount date and maturity date?

**Q5-22** How are the cash proceeds determined when a note receivable is discounted?

## CASES

*C5-1   Components of Cash*
1. What are the normal components of cash?
2. Under what circumstances, if any, do valuation problems arise in connection with cash? (*AICPA adapted*)

*C5-2   Cash Management*
The president of Poor Corporation, who likes to have large balances of cash on hand, has recently been reading articles in highly respected financial magazines about very successful businesses. The president noticed that each company stressed the importance of cash management and internal control in making it a success. The president of Poor Corporation comes to you, the accountant, and asks you to explain the concept of cash management.

**Required**
Discuss the concept of cash management, including the two major subdivisions and their components.

*C5-3   Bank Reconciliations*
A discrepancy will usually exist between the bank statement balance and the cash records due to a time lag associated with the use of a checking account. The time lag results in many transactions being recorded on the company's records prior to their appearance on the bank statement. The bank statement balance and the cash records must be brought into agreement to determine their accuracy. This result can be achieved by using a two-column or a four-column reconciliation.

**Required**

Compare and contrast the two-column and four-column reconciliations.

## C5-4  Estimated Bad Debts

On December 31, 1995 Carme Company had significant amounts of accounts receivable as a result of credit sales to its customers. Carme Company uses the allowance method based on credit sales to estimate bad debts. Based on past experience, 1% of credit sales normally will not be collected. This pattern is expected to continue.

**Required**

1. Discuss the rationale of using the allowance method based on credit sales to estimate bad debts. Contrast this method with the allowance method based on the balance in the trade receivables accounts.
2. How should Carme Company report the allowance for bad debts account on its balance sheet at December 31, 1995? Also, describe the alternatives, if any, for presentation of bad debt expense in Carme Company's 1995 income statement. (*AICPA adapted*)

## C5-5  Bad Debt Expense

When a company has a policy of making sales for which credit is extended, it is reasonable to expect a portion of those sales to be uncollectible. As a result of this, a company must recognize bad debt expense. There are basically two methods of recognizing bad debt expense: (1) direct write-off method, and (2) allowance method.

**Required**

1. Describe fully both the direct write-off method and the allowance method of recognizing bad debt expense.
2. Discuss the reasons why one of these methods is preferable to the other and the reasons why the other method is not usually in accordance with generally accepted accounting principles. (*AICPA adapted*)

## C5-6  Cash Discounts

In order to induce prompt payment, the Swope Company offers a cash discount of 2% to customers who make payment on their account within 10 days of the invoice date. The company's bookkeeper is not sure how these discounts should be recorded.

**Required**

1. Discuss the methods of recording accounts receivable with cash discounts.
2. Discuss the theoretical soundness of each method.

## C5-7  Accounts Receivable

The Moore Company is undergoing a time of financial stress due to the depressed oil economy. The company is in desperate need of cash, which it is temporarily short of. The only liquid asset that the company holds is $500,000 of accounts receivable.

**Required**

1. Discuss the various types of arrangements that may be used to secure cash from outstanding accounts receivable.
2. Indicate how each method should be disclosed in the financial statements.
3. If Moore Company decides to sell its accounts receivable, should it account for the transfer as a pledge or a factoring agreement?

## C5-8  Assignment and Factoring

Marie Company has significant amounts of trade accounts receivable as a result of credit sales to its customers. On October 2, 1995 some trade accounts receivable were assigned to Daniel Finance Company on a with recourse, nonnotification basis for an advance of 75% of their amount at an interest charge of 20% on the balance outstanding.

On November 3, 1995 other trade accounts receivable were factored on a without recourse basis. The factor withheld 5% of the trade accounts receivable factored as protection against sales returns and allowances and charged a finance charge of 3%.

**Required**

1. How should Marie account for subsequent collections on the trade accounts receivable assigned on October 2, 1995 and the payments to Daniel Finance? Why?
2. How should Marie account for the trade accounts receivable factored on November 3, 1995? Why? (*AICPA adapted*)

## C5-9  Receivables Issues

Hogan Company uses the net method of accounting for sales discounts. Hogan also offers trade discounts to various groups of buyers. On August 1, 1995 Hogan factored some accounts receivable on a without recourse basis. Hogan incurred a finance charge.

Hogan also has some notes receivable bearing an appropriate rate of interest. The principal and total interest are due at maturity. The notes were received on October 2, 1995 and mature on October 1, 1996. Hogan's operating cycle is less than one year.

**Required**

1. Using the net method, how should Hogan account for the sales discounts at the date of sale? What is the rationale for the amount recorded as sales under the net method?
2. a. Using the net method, what is the effect on Hogan's sales revenues and net income when customers do not take the sales discounts?
   b. What is the effect of trade discounts on sales revenues and accounts receivable? Why?
   c. How should Hogan account for the accounts receivable factored on August 1, 1995? Why?

d. How should Hogan report the effects of the interest-bearing notes receivable on its December 31, 1995 balance sheet and its income statement for the year ended December 31, 1995? Why? (*AICPA adapted*)

## C5-10   Receivables Issues

Magrath Company has an operating cycle of less than one year and provides credit terms for all of its customers. On April 3, 1995, the company factored, without recourse, some of its accounts receivable.

On August 1, 1995, Magrath sold special order merchandise and received an interest-bearing note due April 30, 1996.

Magrath uses the allowance method to account for uncollectible accounts. During 1995, some accounts were written off as uncollectible, and other accounts previously written off as uncollectible were collected.

**Required**

1. How should Magrath account for and report the accounts receivable factored on April 3, 1995? Why is this accounting treatment appropriate?
2. How should Magrath report the effects of the interest-bearing note on its income statement for the year ended December 31, 1995, and its December 31, 1995 balance sheet?
3. How should Magrath account for the collection of the accounts previously written off as uncollectible?
4. What are the two basic approaches to estimating uncollectible accounts under the allowance method? What is the rationale for each approach? (*AICPA adapted*)

## C5-11   Assignment and Discounting

Tidal Company has significant amounts of trade accounts receivable. In March of this year, Tidal assigned specific trade accounts receivable to Herb Finance Company on a with recourse, nonnotification basis as collateral for a loan. Tidal signed a note and received 70% of the amount assigned. Tidal was charged a 5% finance fee and agreed to pay interest at 12% on the unpaid balance. Some specific accounts of the assigned receivables were written off as uncollectible. The remainder of the trade accounts receivable assigned were collected by Tidal in March and April of this year. Tidal paid Herb Finance in full at the end of April of this year.

Tidal also sold some special order merchandise and received a 90-day, 15%, interest-bearing note receivable on July 1 of this year. After 30 days, the note receivable was discounted with recourse at 18% at a bank.

**Required**

1. How should Tidal account for the transactions described here for the assignment of trade accounts receivable?

2. a. How should Tidal determine the amount of the discount for the note receivable?
   b. How should the discounting transaction be accounted for? (*AICPA adapted*)

## C5-12   Lockbox Account Bank Reconciliation

DGK Company maintains a lockbox account to facilitate the collection of its accounts receivable. All of the company's cash receipts from credit sales are sent directly to a post office box held in the company's name, which is accessed directly by bank personnel. Each day the bank processes the receipts, credits DGK's account, and provides the company with a hard copy package, which includes a detail and summary listing of all checks deposited, copies of actual checks, invoices, enclosures, and envelopes. The company usually receives its hard copy packages a day after the bank has processed the receipts.

In addition, DGK Company has authorized the bank to apply "collected balances" (balances for which the holding period allowed for collection and return of deposited items has elapsed) directly against the company's outstanding line of credit with the bank, unless instructed otherwise by the company. The company receives hard copy notices of amounts applied, generally within two business days.

The accounting records for DGK Company contain the following details for December, 1995:

1. Balance per bank for the lockbox account, 12/31/95                           $55,000
2. Balance per books, 12/31/95                        50,050
3. Deposit in transit from cash sales             5,000
4. Lockbox receipts, 12/31/95                       30,000
5. Collected balances applied to line of credit on 12/31/95                           20,000
6. Bank service charge for December               50
7. No checks are drawn on the lockbox account

**Required**

1. Explain how a lockbox account might benefit a company.
2. Prepare a December 31, 1995 bank reconciliation of DGK Company's lockbox bank account.
3. Prepare any journal entries necessary to adjust DGK Company's books to reflect the results of the reconciliation performed in Requirement 2. (*Contributed by Daryl G. Krause.*)

## C5-13   Researching GAAP   ⊕

Hamilton Company is experiencing a shortage of cash and decides to obtain money from a large bank by using some of its receivables as collateral. Hamilton pledges $100,000 of its receivables, is charged a 12% fee on this amount, and notifies these credit customers to make their payments directly to the bank. The bank assumes the servicing activities, but Hamilton is responsible for all bad debts, which it reasonably estimates to be 2% of the receivables amount. When the balance of the receivables pledged is reduced to $3,000, Hamilton is required to "repurchase" the receivables, notify the remaining credit customers to make payments to it, and reassume the servicing activities. Hamilton's president has asked you how to account for (and record) this transaction.

**Required**
Research the related generally accepted accounting principles and prepare a short memo to the president that answers his question. Cite your reference and applicable paragraph numbers.

## MULTIPLE CHOICE

*Select the best answer for each of the following.*

M5-1   Which of the following items should be classified under the heading of cash on the balance sheet?

|  | Postdated checks | Certificates of deposit |
|---|---|---|
| a. | Yes | Yes |
| b. | Yes | No |
| c. | No | No |
| d. | No | Yes |

M5-2   The following bank reconciliation is presented for the Kingston Company for the month of November 1995:

| Balance per bank statement, 11/30/95 | | $18,040 |
|---|---|---|
| Add: Deposit in transit | | 4,150 |
| | | $22,190 |
| Less: Outstanding checks | $ 6,300 | |
| Bank credit recorded in error | 20 | (6,320) |
| Balance per books, 11/30/95 | | $15,870 |

Data for the month of December 1995 follow:

**Per bank**

| December deposits | $26,100 |
|---|---|
| December disbursements | 22,420 |
| Balance, 12/31/95 | 21,720 |

All items that were outstanding as of November 30 cleared through the bank in December, including the bank credit. In addition, $2,500 in checks were outstanding as of December 31, 1995. What is the balance of cash per books at December 31, 1995?
a. $19,220
b. $19,240
c. $21,720
d. $24,220

M5-3   Greenfield Company had the following cash balances at December 31, 1995:

| Cash in banks | $1,500,000 |
|---|---|
| Petty cash funds (all funds were reimbursed on December 31, 1995) | 20,000 |
| Cash legally restricted for additions to plant (expected to be disbursed in 1997) | 2,000,000 |

Cash in banks includes $500,000 of compensating balances against short-term borrowing arrangements at December 31, 1995. The compensating balances are not legally restricted as to withdrawal by Greenfield. In the current assets section of Greenfield's December 31, 1995 balance sheet, what total amount should be reported as cash?

a. $1,020,000

b. $1,520,000

c. $3,020,000

d. $3,520,000

M5-4   On January 1, 1995 King Company's Allowance for Doubtful Accounts had a credit balance of $15,000. During 1995 King: (1) charged $32,000 to bad debt expense, (2) wrote off $23,000 of uncollectible accounts receivable, and (3) unexpectedly recovered $6,000 of bad debts written off in the prior year. The Allowance for Doubtful Accounts balance at December 31, 1995 should be

a. $47,000

b. $32,000

c. $30,000

d. $24,000

M5-5   A company is in its first year of operations and has never written off any accounts receivable as uncollectible. When the allowance method of recognizing bad debt expense is used, the entry to recognize that expense

a. Increases net income

b. Decreases current assets

c. Has no effect on current assets

d. Has no effect on net income

M5-6   Tallent Company received a $30,000, 6-month, 10% interest-bearing note from a customer. After holding the note for two months, Tallent was in need of cash and discounted the note at the United National Bank at a 12% discount rate. The amount of cash received by Tallent from the bank was

a. $31,260

b. $30,870

c. $30,300

d. $30,240

M5-7   When the accounts receivable of a company are sold outright to a company that normally buys accounts receivable of other companies without recourse, the accounts receivable have been

a. Factored

b. Assigned

c. Pledged

d. Collateralized

M5-8   A method of estimating bad debts that focuses on the income statement rather than the balance sheet is the allowance method based on

a. Direct write-off

b. Aging the trade receivable accounts

c. Credit sales

d. The balance in the trade receivable accounts

M5-9   Prior to adjustments, Barrett Company's account balances at December 31, 1995 for Accounts Receivable and the related Allowance for Doubtful Accounts were $1,200,000 and $60,000, respectively. An aging of accounts receivable indicated that $106,000 of the December 31, 1995 receivables may be uncollectible. The net realizable value of accounts receivable was

a. $1,034,000

b. $1,094,000

c. $1,140,000

d. $1,154,000

M5-10  Marmol Corporation uses the allowance method for bad debts. During 1995 Marmol charged $30,000 to bad debt expense and wrote off $25,200 of uncollectible accounts receivable. These transactions resulted in a decrease in working capital of

a. $0

b. $4,800

c. $25,200

d. $30,000

*(AICPA adapted)*

## EXERCISES

**E5-1**  *Computing the Cash Balance*  Indicate whether or not each of the following ten items should be included in the cash balance presented on the balance sheet. Also indicate the normal balance sheet treatment for those items not included as cash.

| Item | Include in Cash Balance | Classification of Items Excluded |
|---|---|---|
| 1. NSF checks | | |
| 2. Savings account | | |
| 3. Postage stamps | | |
| 4. Postdated checks | | |
| 5. IOUs | | |
| 6. Cash on hand | | |
| 7. Cash in sinking fund | | |
| 8. Travel advance | | |
| 9. Bank draft | | |
| 10. Traveler's checks | | |

**E5-2**  *Reporting Cash on the Balance Sheet*  Your audit of the Watt Corporation discovers the following information:

| | |
|---|---|
| 1. Reconciled balance in First National Bank checking account | $ 1,960.75 |
| 2. Reconciled balance in City National Bank checking account | (40.20) |
| 3. Balance in First Federal savings account | 28,750.00 |
| 4. Certificate of deposit | 30,000.00 |
| 5. Petty cash fund | 500.00 |
| 6. Postage stamps | 100.00 |
| 7. Employee's IOU | 125.00 |
| 8. Employees' travel advances | 1,640.00 |
| 9. Cash on hand (undeposited sales receipts) | 3,109.40 |
| 10. Traveler's checks | 600.00 |
| 11. Customer's postdated check | 290.40 |

**Required**
1. What amount should be reported as cash on Watt's balance sheet?
2. Describe the balance sheet treatment of the items not included in the cash balance.

**E5-3**  *Petty Cash Transactions*  The Crown Company established a petty cash fund of $600 for incidental expenditures on January 2, 1995. At the end of the month the count of cash on hand indicated that $57.35 remained in the fund. A sorting of petty cash vouchers disclosed that the following expenses had been incurred during the month, and the fund was replenished.

| | |
|---|---|
| Postage expense | $250.40 |
| Office supplies expense | 165.90 |
| Miscellaneous expense | 119.05 |

**Required**

Prepare the journal entries necessary to record the Crown Company's petty cash transactions during the month of January 1995.

*E5-4*     *Adjusting an Unknown Cash Balance*   The information that follows is available from the general ledger and bank statement of the Gentry Corporation for the month of August 1995:

| | |
|---|---:|
| 1. Bank statement balance, August 31 | $1,342.50 |
| 2. Note collected by the bank not previously recorded by Gentry | 600.00 |
| 3. Interest on the preceding note (not previously recorded) | 25.00 |
| 4. NSF check returned with the bank statement (not previously recorded) | 212.60 |
| 5. Outstanding checks at the end of August | 684.70 |
| 6. Bank service charge for August | 12.85 |
| 7. Deposit in transit, August 31 | 329.42 |

**Required**

1. Starting with the bank statement balance, prepare a schedule to determine Gentry's cash balance on August 31, 1995, prior to any required adjustments.
2. Prepare a bank reconciliation to determine Gentry's adjusted cash balance on August 31, 1995.
3. Prepare the journal entries necessary to bring Gentry's cash account balance up to date.

*E5-5*     *Bank Reconciliation*   The following information is extracted from the bank statement and accounting records of the Wilson Corporation for the month of July 1995:

| | |
|---|---:|
| 1. Balance per books, July 31 | $2,041.85 |
| 2. Balance per bank, July 31 | 2,055.40 |
| 3. NSF check returned by bank with bank statement | 81.00 |
| 4. Note collected by bank on July 31 | 190.00 |
| 5. Interest on preceding note | 6.20 |
| 6. Bank service charge for July | 4.40 |
| 7. Outstanding checks at end of July | 150.00 |
| 8. Deposit in transit at end of July | 247.25 |

**Required**

1. Prepare a bank reconciliation for the Wilson Corporation for July 31, 1995.
2. Prepare the journal entries necessary to adjust Wilson's books on July 31, 1995.

*E5-6*     *Bank Reconciliation and Adjusting Entries*   The Fowler Corporation's cash account showed a balance of $17,310.80 on March 31, 1995. The bank statement balance for the same date indicated a balance of $18,112.35. The following additional information is available concerning Fowler's cash balance on March 31, 1995.

1. Undeposited cash on hand on March 31 amounted to $724.50.
2. A customer's NSF check for $173.80 was returned with the bank statement.
3. A note for $2,000 plus interest of $100 was collected for Fowler by the bank during March. The bank notified Fowler of this collection on the bank statement.
4. The bank service charge for March was $15.
5. A deposit of $951.75 mailed to the bank on March 31 did not appear on the bank statement.
6. The following checks mailed to creditors had not been processed by the bank on March 31:

    | | |
    |---|---|
    | #429 | $ 57.40 |
    | #432 | $147.50 |
    | #433 | $214.80 |
    | #434 | $191.90 |

7. A customer check in payment of his account for $149.50 and listed correctly for that amount on the bank statement had been incorrectly recorded on the accounting records as $194.50.

**Required**

1. Prepare a bank reconciliation for the Fowler Corporation for March 31, 1995.
2. Prepare any adjusting journal entries necessary to record the information from Requirement 1.

E5-7  *Computing the Bank Statement Balance*   Your cashier I. Amakrook has notified you that he has misplaced all the bank statements for the past year. You decide to review selected accounting records during the year and discover that the following journal entry was made to reconcile the June 30, 1995 bank statement and the accounting records:

| | | |
|---|---|---|
| Accounts Receivable | 1,520.24 | |
| Miscellaneous Expense | 12.50 | |
| Notes Receivable | | 200.00 |
| Interest Revenue | | 10.00 |
| Cash | | 1,322.74 |

**Required**

1. What events might have caused each of the preceding reconciling items to occur?
2. Compute the amount that would have appeared as the balance per bank statement on a bank reconciliation if the preadjustment cash balance in the accounting records was $7,683.70, outstanding checks were $207.50, and no other adjustments were required.
3. Assume that you contact the bank and are informed that a balance of $5,542.90 had been reported on the June 30, 1995 bank statement. What does this discrepancy indicate? How would you begin investigating your suspicions?

E5-8  *Journal Entry to Separate Receivables*   An examination of the accounting records for the Hutton Corporation indicates that all receivables are being recorded in a single account entitled **Receivables.** An analysis of the account reveals the following:

| | |
|---|---|
| Accounts receivable (trade) | $16,200 |
| Accounts receivable (officers) | 3,600 |
| Common stock subscriptions receivable (current) | 12,000 |
| Advances to employees | 1,800 |
| Notes receivable (trade), due in 3 years | 6,000 |
| Deposit to guarantee contract performance | 5,000 |
| Utility deposit | 500 |
| Total | $45,100 |

**Required**

1. Prepare a journal entry to separate the preceding items into their proper accounts.
2. How would each of the preceding items normally be reflected on Hutton's balance sheet?

E5-9  *Trade Discounts*   The Dillon Corporation sells merchandise for a list price of $30,000 that is subject to trade discounts of 20%, 10%, and 5%.

**Required**

1. Prepare the journal entry to record the sale if the first two discounts are allowed to a particular customer.
2. Prepare the journal entry to record the sale if all three discounts are allowed.

E5-10  *Accounting for Sales Discounts*   On December 11, 1995 Lynch Incorporated sold $9,000 of merchandise with terms 2/10, n/EOM. On December 21, 1995 collections were made on sales originally billed for $4,000, and on December 31, 1995 additional collections on sales originally billed for $3,000 were received.

**Required**

Prepare the journal entries to record the sale, collections, and any required year-end adjustments under:
1. The gross price method
2. The net price method

E5-11    *Comparison of Discount Methods*    The Eastman Corporation sells merchandise with a list price of $14,000 on February 1, 1995, with terms of 1/10, n/30. On February 10, 1995, payment was received on merchandise originally billed for $7,500, and the balance due was received on February 28, 1995.

**Required**
Prepare journal entries to record the preceding information using:
1.  The gross price method
2.  The net price method

E5-12    *Returns and Allowances*    Towbin Products sells merchandise on credit for $7,000 on December 1, 1995. The company estimates that returns and allowances will amount to 4% of sales. On December 22, 1995 a customer returns for credit merchandise originally sold on December 1 for $200.

**Required**
1.  Prepare journal entries to record the preceding sale and the return of merchandise if returns are recorded as they occur.
2.  Prepare journal entries to record the preceding sale, the estimation of returns and allowances, and the actual return of goods, if returns and allowances are estimated at the end of the period of sale.
3.  How would the preceding information be reflected on Towbin's December 31, 1995 financial statements if:
    a.  Returns are recorded as they occur.
    b.  Returns are estimated in the period of sale.

E5-13    *Recording Freight Charges*    The Rhoades Corporation sells $3,500 of merchandise to the Paine Company on November 6, 1995 terms 2/10, n/30. On November 7, 1995 Rhoades pays the freight charges of $150 and ships the merchandise to Paine. On December 1, 1995 Paine's payment is received by Rhoades. Rhoades uses the gross price method to record discounts.

**Required**
Prepare the journal entries necessary for Rhoades to record the preceding information, assuming that the freight terms are:
1.  FOB shipping point
2.  FOB destination

E5-14    *Estimation vs. Direct Write-Off of Bad Debts*    The Blunt Company sells products for $18,000 during the month of February 1995. During 1995 collections are received on February sales of $17,500, accounts representing $500 of these sales are written off as uncollectible, and a $100 account previously written off is collected.

**Required**
Prepare the journal entries necessary to record the preceding information if:
1.  Bad debts are estimated as 3% of sales at the time of sale.
2.  The bad debts are recorded as they actually occur.

E5-15    *Estimating Bad Debts from Receivable Balances*    The following information is extracted from the accounting records of the Shelton Corporation at the beginning of 1995:

Accounts Receivable                  $63,000
Allowance for Doubtful Accounts        1,200 (credit)

During 1995 sales on account amounted to $575,000, $557,400 was collected on outstanding receivables, and $2,600 of receivables were written off as uncollectible. On December 31, 1995 Shelton estimates its bad debts to be 4% of the outstanding gross accounts receivable balance.

**Required**
1.  Prepare the journal entry necessary to record Shelton's estimate of bad debt expense for 1995.
2.  Prepare the accounts receivable section of Shelton's December 31, 1995 balance sheet.

E5-16    *Aging Analysis of Accounts Receivable*    Cowen's, a large department store located in a metropolitan area, has been experiencing difficulty in estimating its bad debts. The company has decided to prepare an aging schedule for its outstanding accounts receivable and estimate bad debts by the due dates of its receivables. This analysis discloses the following information:

| Balance | Age of Receivable | Estimated Percentage Uncollectible |
|---|---|---|
| $193,000 | Under 30 days | 0.8% |
| 114,000 | 30–60 days | 2.0% |
| 73,000 | 61–120 days | 5.0% |
| 41,000 | 121–240 days | 20.0% |
| 27,000 | 241–360 days | 35.0% |
| 19,000 | Over 360 days | 60.0% |
| $467,000 | | |

**Required**

1. Use the preceding analysis to compute the estimated amount of uncollectible receivables.
2. Prepare the journal entry to record Cowen's estimated uncollectibles assuming the balance in the Allowance for Doubtful Accounts prior to adjustment is:
   a. 0
   b. $13,000 (debit)
   c. $5,800 (credit)

E5-17 *Comparison of Bad Debt Estimation Methods* The following information (prior to adjustment) is available from the accounting records of the Bradford Company on December 31, 1995:

| | | |
|---|---|---|
| Cash sales | $ 92,600 | |
| Net credit sales | 262,900 | |
| Total sales (net) | | $355,500 |
| Accounts receivable | | 126,300 |
| Allowance for doubtful accounts | | 3,150 (credit) |

**Required**

Prepare journal entries to record the estimate of Bradford's bad debt expense for 1995 assuming:

1. Bad debts are estimated to be 1.5% of total sales (net).
2. Bad debts are estimated to be 2% of net credit sales.
3. Bad debts are estimated to be 6% of gross accounts receivable.

E5-18 *Receivables—Bad Debts* At January 1, 1995 the credit balance in the Allowance for Doubtful Accounts of the Master Company was $400,000. For 1995 the provision for doubtful accounts is based on a percentage of net sales. Net sales for 1995 were $50,000,000. Based on the latest available facts, the 1995 provision for doubtful accounts is estimated to be 0.7% of net sales. During 1995 uncollectible receivables amounting to $410,000 were written off against the allowance for doubtful accounts.

**Required**

Prepare a schedule computing the balance in Master's Allowance for Doubtful Accounts at December 31, 1995. Show supporting computations in good form. (*AICPA adapted*)

E5-19 *Assigning Accounts Receivable* White Corporation has entered into a long-term assignment agreement with a finance company. Under the terms of this agreement, White receives 80% of the value of all accounts assigned and is charged a 1% service charge which is based upon the actual dollar amount of cash received. Additionally, the finance company charges White 12% annual interest on the outstanding loan. The following selected transactions relate to this agreement:

| | |
|---|---|
| December 1, 1995 | Accounts receivable of $175,000 are assigned. |
| December 11, 1995 | A sales return of $1,000 on an assigned account is allowed by White. |
| December 31, 1995 | Collections are made on $86,000 of assigned accounts. This amount and 1 month's interest on the outstanding loan are remitted to the finance company. (For simplicity, compute interest to the nearest month.) |
| January 29, 1996 | $60,000 of assigned accounts are collected and the remainder of the loan is repaid. |

**Required**

1. Prepare journal entries on White's books to record the preceding transactions.
2. How would this assignment agreement be disclosed on White's December 31, 1995 balance sheet?

E5-20    *Factoring Accounts Receivable*    The Weil Corporation is experiencing a temporary cash shortage and decides to factor a group of its accounts receivable. The factor accepts $80,000 of Weil's accounts receivable, remits 90% of the accounts receivable factored, and charges a 16% commission on the gross amount of the factored receivables. During the period, sales returns and allowances on factored accounts amounted to $1,500.

**Required**

Prepare all the journal entries necessary by Weil to record the preceding information.

E5-21    *Receivables from Credit Card Sales*    Dillon Shoes sold $2,400 of merchandise during the month of September 1995 which was charged to a national credit card. On September 15, 1995 Dillon bills the independent national credit card company for these sales and is assessed a 5% service charge. On September 21, 1995, a customer returns merchandise originally sold for $200 and Dillon notifies the credit card company of the return. On September 29, 1995, the credit card company remitted the amount owed to Dillon.

**Required**

Prepare the journal entries necessary to record this information on Dillon's books.

E5-22    *Generating Cash from Receivables*    The Guide Company requires additional cash for its business. Guide has decided to use its accounts receivable to raise the additional cash as follows:

On July 1, 1995 Guide assigned $200,000 of accounts receivable to the Cell Finance Company. Guide received an advance from Cell of 85% of the assigned accounts receivable less a commission on the advance of 3%. Prior to December 31, 1995 Guide collected $150,000 on the assigned accounts receivable and remitted $160,000 to Cell, $10,000 of which represented interest on the advance from Cell.

On December 1, 1995 Guide sold $300,000 of net accounts receivable to the Factoring Company for $260,000. The receivables were sold outright on a nonrecourse basis.

On December 29, 1995 Guide received an advance of $100,000 from the Domestic Bank by pledging $120,000 of Guide's accounts receivable. Guide's first payment to Domestic is due on January 29, 1996.

**Required**

Prepare a schedule showing the income statement effect for the year ended December 31, 1995, as a result of the preceding facts. Show supporting computations in good form. (*AICPA adapted*)

E5-23    *Interest-Bearing and Non-Interest-Bearing Notes*    On December 11, 1995, the Hooper Bank loans a customer $6,000 on a 60-day, 12% note.

**Required**

Prepare the journal entries necessary by Hooper to record the receipt of the note, the accrual of interest on December 31, 1995, and the customer's repayment on February 9, 1996, assuming:

1. Interest was assessed in addition to the face value of the note.
2. The note was issued as a $6,000 non-interest-bearing note.

E5-24    *Computing the Proceeds from Discounted Notes*    Determine the proceeds from each of the following discounted customer notes:

1. An $8,000, 60-day, non-interest-bearing note discounted after 15 days at 12%.
2. A $12,000, 12%, 60-day note discounted after 30 days at 14%.
3. A $6,000, 10%, 90-day note discounted after 30 days at 12%.
4. A $10,000, 12%, 120-day note discounted after 45 days at 15%.

E5-25    *Recording Notes Receivable Discounted*    The following are events of the Singer Corporation for the current year:

June 30    Barney Manufacturing gives Singer a $5,000, 11%, 90-day note for merchandise purchased.

July 15    Dillon Construction Co. gives Singer a $6,000, 10%, 60-day note for merchandise originally purchased on April 20 of the current year.

July 30    The Barney and Dillon notes are discounted by Singer at its bank at 12%.
Sept. 15   The bank notifies Singer that the Dillon note was paid.
Sept. 30   The bank notifies Singer that Barney defaulted on the note and charges the amount of principal, interest, and a fee of $10 against Singer's bank account.

**Required**

Prepare journal entries to record the preceding information on Singer's accounting records. (Assume that the company does not normally discount its notes and uses a Notes Receivable Discounted account.)

## PROBLEMS

P5-1    *Cash and Other Items*   The following information has been extracted from the accounting records of the Drexel Corporation:

| | |
|---|---|
| 1. Cash on hand (undeposited sales receipts) | $ 1,020 |
| 2. Certificates of deposit | 25,000 |
| 3. Customer's note receivable | 1,000 |
| 4. Reconciled balance in University National Bank checking account | (350) |
| 5. Reconciled balance in Second National Bank checking account | 9,350 |
| 6. Balance in City Federal savings account | 8,560 |
| 7. Customer's postdated check | 1,350 |
| 8. Employee travel advances | 1,600 |
| 9. Cash in bond sinking fund | 1,200 |
| 10. Bond sinking fund investments | 8,090 |
| 11. Postage stamps | 430 |

**Required**

Determine the balance in Drexel's Cash account, and discuss the balance sheet treatment of any items not included as cash.

P5-2    *Reconciliation of Bank and Company Cash Amounts*   The December 31, 1995 bank statement for Miller Corporation showed a $1,978.40 balance. On this date the company's Cash account reflected a $325.60 overdraft. In reconciling these amounts, the following information is discovered:

1. Cash on hand for undeposited sales receipts, December 31, 1995, $130.25.
2. Customer NSF check returned with bank statement, $420.40.
3. Cash sales of $640.25 for the week ended December 22, 1995 were recorded on the books. The cashier reports this amount missing, and it was not deposited in the bank.
4. Note receivable of $2,500 and interest of $25 collected by the bank and not recorded on the books.
5. Deposit in transit December 31, 1995, $350.00.
6. A customer check for $290.40 in payment of its account was recorded on the books at $940.20.
7. Outstanding checks, $1,969.70. Includes a duplicate check of $70.85 to C. Brown, who notified Miller that the original was lost. Miller stopped payment on the original check and has already adjusted the cash account in the accounting records for this amount.

**Required**

1. Prepare a December 31, 1995 bank reconciliation for Miller.
2. Prepare any journal entries necessary by Miller to record the information from Requirement 1.

**P5-3**   *Unknown Book Balance*   The following information pertains to the Cash account of the Hanford Corporation for the month of July 1995:

| Bank statement: | |
|---|---|
| Balance July 31 | $22,639.54 |
| Service charge for July | 15.00 |
| NSF check returned with July bank statement | 184.50 |
| Note receivable collected by bank (not previously recorded on the books) | 2,000.00 |
| Interest on note collected by bank (not previously recorded on the books) | 60.00 |
| Books: | |
| Balance July 31 | ? |
| Cash on hand awaiting deposit | 1,824.42 |
| Outstanding checks: | |
| #257      $42.17 | |
| #271      $19.19 | |
| #272      $80.82 | |
| Deposit in transit | 2,420.98 |

**Required**

1. Prepare a bank reconciliation to determine Hanford's adjusted cash balance on July 31, 1995.
2. Determine Hanford's unadjusted cash balance (per books) on July 31, 1995.
3. Prepare the adjusting entries necessary to bring Hanford's cash account balance up to date on July 31, 1995.

**P5-4**   *Bank Reconciliation*   The Daisy Company received a bank statement for February 1995, as follows:

**Daisy Company**
1313 Williams St.
Denver, Co. 80218

**Central Bank**
Denver, Co. 80222

| Date | Checks | Deposits | Balance |
|---|---|---|---|
| Feb.  1 | | | $4,524.80 |
| 7 | $2,700.33 | $8,642.61 | |
| 10 | 3,484.81 | | |
| 13 | 6.00 SC | 460.00 CM | |
| 17 | 274.09 | | |
| 21 | 4,133.60 | 3,385.49 | |
| 24 | 69.69 NSF | | |
| 28 | | | $6,344.38 |

SC = Service Charge          NSF = Check Returned
CM = Credit Memo             DM = Debit Memo

The receipt of $460 on February 13 was for a note of $445 collected by the bank, plus $20 current interest, less a $5 service charge. The company's accounting records contained the following information:

Cash Balance on February 28 from the books: $2,610.42

| Cash Disbursements | | Cash Receipts | |
|---|---|---|---|
| Check No. 155 | $2,700.33 | Feb.  6 | $8,624.61 |
| 156 | 3,484.81 | 20 | 3,385.49 |
| 157 | 274.09 | All receipts are verified and correct. | |
| 158 | 589.02 | | |
| 159 | 4,133.60 | | |
| 160 | 2,742.63 | | |

**Required**

1. Prepare a bank reconciliation on February 28, 1995 for the Daisy Company.
2. Prepare the journal entries that the Daisy Company should record as a result of the reconciliation.

P5-5      *Comprehensive Reconciliation*    In auditing the Wye Company, you obtain directly from the bank Wye's bank statement, canceled checks, and other memoranda which relate to the company's bank account, for December 1995. In reconciling the bank balance on December 31, 1995 with that shown on the company's books, you observe the following facts:

| | | |
|---|---:|---:|
| 1. Balance per bank statement | | $91,174.63 |
| 2. Balance per books | | 59,088.46 |
| 3. Outstanding checks 12/31/95 | | 33,378.82 |
| 4. Receipts of 12/30/95 deposited on 1/1/96 | | 5,317.20 |
| 5. Service charge for December | | 22.50 |
| 6. Proceeds of bank loan, 12/15/95 omitted from company records (discounted for 3 months at 12% per year) | | 11,640.00 |
| 7. Deposit of 12/20/95 omitted from the bank statement | | 2,892.41 |
| 8. Check of Rome Products Co. charged back on 12/21/95 for lack of counter-signature. Redeposited 1/5/96. No entry was made for the chargeback or the redeposit. | | 873.74 |
| 9. Error on bank statement in entering deposit of 12/18/95: | | |
|      Correct amount | $3,182.40 | |
|      Entered in statement | 3,181.40 | 1.00 |
| 10. Check no. 3917 of Wyeth Manufacturing Co. charged in error to company's account | | 2,690.00 |
| 11. Proceeds of note of J. Somers & Co. collected by bank 12/11/95 not entered on books: | | |
|      Principal | $2,000.00 | |
|      Interest | 40.00 | |
| | $2,040.00 | |
|      Less: collection charge | 5.00 | 2,035.00 |
| 12. Erroneous debit memo of 12/22/95 to charge company's account with settlement of bank loan, which was paid by check no. 8714 on same date | | 5,000.00 |
| 13. Error on bank statement in entering deposit of 12/4/95 | | |
|      Entered as | $4,817.10 | |
|      Correct amount | 4,807.10 | 10.00 |
| 14. Deposit of Wyeth Manufacturing Co. of 12/7/95 credited in error to the company | | 1,819.20 |

**Required**

1. Prepare a reconciliation of the Wye Company's bank account.
2. Prepare journal entries to adjust the Wye company's books to reflect the correct bank balance on December 31, 1995. (*AICPA adapted*)

P5-6      *Proof of Cash*    The following information is available concerning the cash balance of the Smith Corporation on July 31, 1995:

| | |
|---|---:|
| 1. Cash balance per bank statement June 30 | $13,031.78 |
| 2. Cash balance per bank statement July 31 | 18,056.43 |
| 3. Cash balance per company records June 30 (adjusted) | 12,057.16 |
| 4. Cash balance per company records July 31 | 18,714.92 |
| 5. Deposit made by Smith on July 31 received by the bank August 1 | 1,098.51 |
| 6. NSF check returned by bank with the July bank statement | 113.15 |

7. July 31 outstanding checks:
   #1345      $27.00
   #1353      $13.23
   #1354      $14.24
8. A check written by Smith during July for $162.50 was erroneously recorded on the books as $126.50.

| | |
|---|---:|
| 9. Note collected by the bank on July 31 (not previously recorded by Smith) | 1,000.00 |
| 10. Interest on the preceding note (not previously recorded) | 15.00 |
| 11. July bank service charge | 7.80 |
| 12. June deposit in transit received by the bank July 3 | 146.73 |
| 13. Total receipts recorded by the bank during July | 10,051.17 |
| 14. Total payments recorded by the bank during July | 5,026.52 |
| 15. July 31 cash on hand (undeposited customers checks) | 472.50 |

16. June outstanding checks:
   #1082      $372.15 received by bank July 1
   #1086      $552.40 received by bank July 3
   #1087      $196.80 received by bank July 5

| | |
|---|---:|
| 17. Total July receipts per books | 10,460.45 |
| 18. Total July payments per books | 3,802.69 |

**Required**
Prepare a four-column proof of cash for the Smith Corporation for the month ended July 31, 1995.

*P5-7    Proof of Cash*   The following information is available concerning the cash balance of the Jones Corporation on August 31, 1995:

| | |
|---|---:|
| 1. Cash balance per bank statement July 31 | $ 9,852.46 |
| per bank statement August 31 | 11,679.25 |
| per company records July 31 (adjusted) | 10,206.76 |
| per company records August 31 | 11,306.74 |
| 2. Total receipts recorded by the bank during August | 16,755.64 |
| Total August receipts per books | 15,913.93 |
| 3. Total payments recorded by the bank during August | 14,928.85 |
| Total August payments per books | 14,813.95 |
| 4. Deposit made by Jones on August 31; received by the bank September 1 | 1,235.32 |
| July 31 deposit in transit received by the bank August 1 | 953.71 |

5. July 31 outstanding checks:
   #2150      $345.26 received by bank August 3
   #2151      $156.72 received by bank August 4
   #2152       $97.43 received by bank August 5
   August 31 outstanding checks:
   #2265       $56.89
   #2269      $341.72
   #2270      $185.75

| | |
|---|---:|
| 6. NSF check returned by bank with the August bank statement | 96.75 |

7. A check written by Jones during August for $112.51 was erroneously recorded on the books as $121.51.

| | |
|---|---:|
| 8. Note collected by the bank on August 31 (not previously recorded by Jones) | 1,500.00 |
| Interest on the preceding note (not previously recorded) | 45.00 |
| 9. August bank service charge | 12.10 |
| 10. August 31 cash on hand (undeposited customer's checks) | 421.68 |

**Required**
Prepare a four-column proof of cash for the Jones Corporation for the month ended August 31, 1995.

P5-8    *Analyzing Bad Debt Expense*  In 1995, 3 years after it began operations, the Pearce Corporation decided to change from the direct write-off method of recording bad debts to estimating bad debts. The following information is available to you:

| | Year | | | |
|---|---|---|---|---|
| | **1992** | **1993** | **1994** | **1995** |
| Sales | $125,000 | $180,000 | $250,000 | $280,000 |
| Credit sales | 90,000 | 158,000 | 210,000 | 235,000 |
| Collections on accounts receivable | | | | |
| 1992 sales | 78,000 | 8,500 | 200 | |
| 1993 sales | | 137,000 | 15,000 | 300 |
| 1994 sales | | | 178,800 | 19,500 |
| 1995 sales | | | | 200,000 |
| Accounts receivable written off | | | | |
| 1992 accounts | 2,500 | 500 | 300 | 0 |
| 1993 accounts | | 4,600 | 700 | 400 |
| 1994 accounts | | | 6,200 | 1,000 |
| 1995 accounts | | | | 6,800 |

**Required**

1.  Prepare an analysis to determine Pearce's estimated bad debt expense percentage based upon the average relationship of actual bad debts to credit sales.
2.  Prepare an analysis to determine Pearce's estimated percentage of allowance for doubtful accounts based on year-end accounts receivable.
3.  What amount should Pearce record as bad debts expense for 1995 if:
    a.  Bad debts are estimated as a percentage of credit sales?
    b.  Allowance for doubtful accounts is estimated as a percentage of outstanding year-end accounts receivable?

P5-9    *Analyzing Accounts Receivable*  The June 30, 1994 balance sheet of the Upham Company included the following information:

| | | |
|---|---|---|
| Notes receivable | $ 59,800 | |
| Less: Notes receivable discounted | (38,000) | $ 21,800 |
| | | |
| Accounts receivable | $224,000 | |
| Less: Allowance for doubtful accounts | (14,100) | 209,900 |
| Total receivables | | $231,700 |

During the company's fiscal year ending June 30, 1995 the following transactions occurred:

| | |
|---|---|
| 1. Sales on account | $881,200 |
| 2. Collections on account | 841,000 |
| 3. Accounts receivable written off as uncollectible | 13,800 |
| 4. Notes receivable collected | 29,000 |
| 5. Customer notes received in payment of accounts receivable | 74,000 |
| 6. Notes receivable discounted paid at maturity | 36,000 |
| 7. Notes receivable discounted defaulted including interest of $20 and a $5 fee. This amount is expected to be collected during the 1996 fiscal year | 2,025 |
| 8. Proceeds from customer notes discounted (face value $45,000, accrued interest revenue $200) | 45,075 |
| 9. Collections on accounts previously written off | 500 |
| 10. Sales returns and allowances (on credit sales) | 2,000 |
| 11. Bad debts were estimated to be 1.5% of credit sales | |

**Required**

1. Prepare journal entries necessary for Upham to record the preceding transactions.
2. Prepare an analysis that shows the amount of the notes receivable, notes receivable discounted, accounts receivable, and allowance for doubtful accounts balance that will be disclosed on Uphams June 30, 1995 balance sheet.

P5-10    *Recording Note Transactions*   The following information is extracted from the accounting records of the Tara Corporation:

| | |
|---|---|
| May 1 | Received a $7,000, 12%, 90-day note from V. Leigh, a customer. |
| May 6 | Received a $9,000, 10%, 120-day note from C. Gable, a customer. |
| May 11 | Discounted the Leigh and Gable notes at the bank at 13%. In addition, borrowed $10,000 from the bank for 90 days at 12%. The bank remits the face value less the interest. |
| July 31 | The July bank statement indicated that the Leigh note had been paid. |
| Sept. 4 | Received notice that Gable had defaulted on the May 6 note. The bank charged a fee of $10. Paid the amount due on the Gable note to the bank. Informed Gable to pay Tara the entire amount due plus 11% interest on the total of the face amount of the note, the accrued interest, and the fee from the maturity date until Gable remits the amount owed. |
| Sept. 23 | Received the amount due from Gable. |

**Required**

Prepare journal entries to record the preceding information, assuming that Tara usually does not discount its notes.

P5-11    *Reconstructing Accounts Receivable and Expense Journal Entries*   The 1995 audit of the accounting records of the Webber Company discloses the following information:

| | 1994 | 1995 |
|---|---|---|
| Accounts receivable (ending) | $186,000 | $187,100 |
| Allowance for doubtful accounts (ending) | 7,400 | 7,000 |
| Allowance for sales returns and allowances (ending) | 4,700 | 3,916 |
| Gross sales returns and allowances (estimated for the year) | 4,900 | 5,200 |
| Accounts receivable written off during the year | 6,800 | 7,900 |
| Estimated bad debts for the year | 7,200 | 7,500 |
| Actual gross sales returns and allowances for the year | 4,700 | 6,000 |
| Sales discounts not taken at end of year | 0 | 400 |
| Credit sales during the year (terms, 2/10, n/60) | 375,000 | 380,000 |
| Cash collected on accounts receivable during the year (net of discounts taken) | 352,000 | 367,500 |

**Required**

1. Reconstruct the journal entries that were made by Webber during 1995 to record changes in the following accounts, assuming sales returns and allowances are estimated in the period of sale and the net price method is used to account for sales discounts.
   a. Allowance for doubtful accounts
   b. Allowance for sales returns and allowances
   c. Accounts receivable
2. What is the 1995 ending balance in each of the accounts in (1) and how will it be disclosed on Webber's 1995 financial statements?

P5-12    *Cash Discounts*   The Lambert Corporation sells merchandise at a list price of $60,000 with accompanying terms of 2/10, n/30 on December 8, 1995. By December 18, 1995 Lambert had collected from customers for merchandise originally billed at $34,000. By December 31, 1995 additional collections had been received on sales originally billed for $18,000, and sales returns and allowances of $1,500 had been granted by Lambert. By January 15, 1996 all the remaining balances due had been collected.

**Required**

1. Prepare the journal entries using (a) the gross price method and (b) the net price method to record each of the following items:
   a. The sale of the merchandise
   b. Collections received by December 18, 1995
   c. Collections received by December 31, 1995
   d. Sales returns and allowances (*not* estimated in the period of sale)
   e. Any required year-end adjustments
   f. Any January 1, 1996 reversing entries
   g. The collections received by January 15, 1996
2. Calculate the accounts receivable balance that would be reported under (a) the gross price method, and (b) the net price method on the Lambert Corporation's December 31, 1995 balance sheet.

P5-13 *Aging Accounts Receivable* On September 30, 1994 (the end of its fiscal year), the Lufkin Corporation reported accounts receivable of $331,800 and an allowance for doubtful accounts of $16,700. During fiscal 1995 the following transactions occurred:

| | |
|---|---|
| Credit sales | $1,017,800 |
| Collections on accounts receivable | 956,000 |
| Accounts receivable written off | 16,200 |

On September 30, 1995 an aging of the accounts receivable balance indicated the following:

| Age | Amount | Estimated Percentage Uncollectible |
|---|---|---|
| Under 30 days | $169,200 | 0.8% |
| 30–90 days | 100,100 | 1.6 |
| 91–180 days | 55,900 | 5.0 |
| 181–360 days | 38,200 | 15.0 |
| Over 360 days | 14,000 | 40.0 |
| | $377,400 | |

**Required**

1. Prepare the journal entries necessary to record the credit sales, collections on account, write-off of accounts receivable, and the bad debts expense for Lufkin for fiscal 1995.
2. What are Lufkin's September 30, 1995 balances in Accounts Receivable and Allowance for Doubtful Accounts and how will they be disclosed on the September 30, 1995 balance sheet?

P5-14 *Estimating Bad Debts* An examination of the accounting records of the Keegan Corporation disclosed the following information for 1995:

| | |
|---|---|
| Cash sales | $680,000 |
| Net credit sales | 500,000 |
| Accounts receivable (12/31/95) | 200,000 |
| Allowance for doubtful accounts (12/31/95, prior to adjustment) | 1,500 (debit) |

Keegan wishes to examine the effect of various alternative bad debt estimation policies.

**Required**

1. Prepare the adjusting entry that would be required under each of the following methods:
   a. Bad debts are estimated at 1.5% of total sales (net).
   b. Bad debts are estimated at 3% of net credit sales.
   c. Bad debts are estimated at 7.5% of gross accounts receivable.
   d. An aging of accounts receivable indicates that half of the outstanding accounts will incur a 3% loss, a quarter will incur a 6% loss, the remaining quarter will incur a 20% loss.
2. Discuss the difference between the income statement and balance sheet approaches to estimating bad debts.

*P5-15*   *Notes Receivable and Notes Receivable Discounted*   The following notes receivable transactions occurred for the Harris Company during the last three months of the current year. (Assume all notes are dated the day the transaction occurred.)

Oct.   9     Received a $5,000, 12%, 60-day note from K. Weedon, a customer.
Oct. 12     Received a $4,000, 10%, 90-day note from M. Black, a customer.
Oct. 15     Discounted the Weedon note at the bank at 14%.
Nov. 11     Discounted the Black note at the bank at 15%.
Nov. 16     Received an $8,000, 12%, 60-day note from B. Butcher, a customer.
Nov. 20     Received a $6,000, 11%, 120-day note from D. Goldman, a customer.
Dec.   1     Received a $9,000, 13%, 60-day note from S. Lambert, a customer.
Dec.   8     Received notice that the Weedon note was paid at maturity.
Dec. 10     Discounted the Goldman note at the bank at 13%.

**Required**
1. Prepare journal entries to record the preceding note transactions and the necessary adjusting entries on December 31. (Assume that Harris does not normally discount its notes.)
2. Show how Harris Company's notes receivable would be disclosed on the December 31 balance sheet. (Assume these are the only note transactions encountered by Harris during the year.)

*P5-16*   *Assigning Accounts Receivable*   The Furman Corporation entered into an assignment agreement with a finance company whereby Furman would be advanced 80% of all accounts assigned less a $2,000 service charge. During the year, $400,000 of accounts receivable were assigned, $250,000 collections were made on outstanding assigned accounts, and $230,000 was remitted to the finance company. This remittance included interest charges of $2,300. Sales returns and allowances on assigned accounts amounted to $5,000.

**Required**
1. Prepare the journal entries necessary to record the preceding information.
2. Show how the preceding information would be reported on Furman's year-end balance sheet.

*P5-17*   *Factoring Accounts Receivable*   Faeber Textile Company frequently factors its accounts receivable. During 1995 Faeber made credit sales of $120,000 to customers, under terms of 2/10, n/30. Faeber records its credit sales using the gross price method. From the past experience, sales returns and allowances are expected to be minimal. In 1995 Faeber sold $80,000 of these receivables to a factor. The factor remitted 90% of the accounts receivable factored and charged a 12% commission on the gross amount of the factored receivables. The factoring agreement also requires that Faeber is responsible for any cash discounts taken by customers upon payment of the factored receivables. Faeber is charged for these cash discounts upon reimbursement by the factor. During 1995 sales returns and allowances were $3,000 on the factored accounts receivable and $1,300 on the unfactored accounts receivable. The factor collected the remaining amount of the factored receivables, less the 2% discount on 94% of the collected receivables, and returned the balance owed to Faeber. Faeber collected the remaining amount of the unfactored accounts receivable, less the 2% discount on 96% of the collected receivables.

**Required**
Prepare all the journal entries necessary for Faeber to record the preceding information.

*P5-18*   *Factoring and Assignment of Accounts Receivable*   The Lazard Corporation has experienced cash flow problems and decides to improve its current cash position by factoring 30% of its receivables and assigning the remainder with the same finance company. The agreement with the finance company stipulates that a 10% commission will be assessed on factored accounts and 15% annual interest will be charged on the outstanding note payable balance related to the assigned accounts. Additionally, the finance company will advance only 80% of the factored and assigned accounts, and Lazard must continue the collection responsibilities on the assigned accounts. At the beginning of the last month of the company's fiscal year the accounts receivable transferred to the finance company amounted to $187,000. During the month, collections on factored accounts were $46,000, and collections on assigned accounts amounted to $84,000. All collections on assigned accounts plus accrued interest were remitted to the finance company at the end of the month.

**Required**

1. Prepare all journal entries to record the preceding information on Lazard's books.
2. How would the accounts related to Lazard's factoring and assignment agreements be reported on Lazard's year-end financial statements?

P5-19    *Examination of Accounts Receivable*    You are engaged in the annual examination of Faulane Company, a wholesale office supply business, for the year ended June 30, 1995. You have been assigned to examine the accounts receivable. The following information is available at June 30, 1995.

1. Your review of accounts receivable and discussions with the client disclose that the following items are included in the accounts receivable (of both the control and the subsidiary ledgers):
   a. Accounts with credit balances total $1,746.
   b. Receivables from officers total $8,500.
   c. Advances to employees total $1,411.
   d. Accounts that are definitely uncollectible total $1,187.
2. Uncollectible accounts are estimated to be 0.50% of the year's net credit sales of $15,750,000.

**Required**

Prepare any journal entry (entries) required

1. to reclassify items that are not trade accounts receivable,
2. to write off uncollectible accounts, and
3. to adjust the allowance for doubtful accounts. (*AICPA adapted*)

P5-20    *Allowance for Bad Accounts*    The Installment Jewelry Company has been in business for 5 years but has never had an audit made of its financial statements. Engaged to make an audit for 1995, you find that the company's balance sheet carries no allowance for bad accounts, bad accounts having been expensed as written off and recoveries credited to income as collected. The company's policy is to write off at December 31 of each year those accounts on which no collections have been received for 3 months. The installment contracts generally are for 2 years.

Upon your recommendation the company agrees to revise its accounts for 1995 to give effect to bad account treatment on the allowance basis. The allowance is to be based on a percentage of sales that is derived from the experience of prior years. Statistics for the past 5 years are shown in the following table:

|      | Charge Sales | Accounts Written Off and Year of Sale | | | Recoveries and Year of Sale |
|------|--------------|------------|--------|--------|----------|
| 1991 | $100,000 | (1991) $ 550 | | | |
| 1992 | 250,000 | (1991) 1,500 | (1992) $1,000 | | (1991) $100 |
| 1993 | 300,000 | (1991) 500 | (1992) 4,000 | (1993) $1,300 | (1992) 400 |
| 1994 | 325,000 | (1992) 1,200 | (1993) 4,500 | (1994) 1,500 | (1993) 500 |
| 1995 | 275,000 | (1993) 2,700 | (1994) 5,000 | (1995) 1,400 | (1994) 600 |

Accounts receivable at December 31, 1995 were as follows:

| | |
|---|---|
| 1994 Sales | $ 15,000 |
| 1995 Sales | 135,000 |
| | $150,000 |

**Required**

Prepare the adjusting journal entry or entries with appropriate explanations to set up the Allowance for Bad Accounts. (Support each item with organized computations; income tax implications should be ignored.) (*AICPA adapted*)

P5-21    *Allowance for Doubtful Accounts*   From inception of operations to December 31, 1994 Harris Corporation provided for uncollectible accounts receivable under the allowance method: Provisions were made monthly at 2% of credit sales; bad debts written off were charged to the allowance account; recoveries of bad debts previously written off were credited to the allowance account; and no year-end adjustments to the allowance account were made. Harris's usual credit terms are net 30 days.

The balance in the Allowance for Doubtful Accounts was $130,000 at January 1, 1995. During 1995 credit sales totaled $9,000,000, interim provisions for doubtful accounts were made at 2% of credit sales, $90,000 of bad debts were written off, and recoveries of accounts previously written off amounted to $15,000. Harris installed a computer facility in November 1995 and an aging of accounts receivable was prepared for the first time as of December 31, 1995. A summary of the aging is as follows:

| Classification by Month of Sale | Balance in Each Category | Estimated % Uncollectible |
|---|---|---|
| Nov.–Dec. 1995 | $1,140,000 | 2% |
| July–Oct. | 600,000 | 10 |
| Jan.–June | 400,000 | 25 |
| Prior to 1/1/95 | 130,000 | 75 |
| | $2,270,000 | |

Based on the review of collectibility of the account balances in the "prior to 1/1/95" aging category, additional receivables totaling $60,000 were written off as of December 31, 1995. Effective with the year ended December 31, 1995 Harris adopted a new accounting method for estimating the allowance for doubtful accounts at the amount indicated by the year-end aging analysis of accounts receivable.

**Required**
1. Prepare a schedule analyzing the changes in the allowance for doubtful accounts for the year ended December 31, 1995. Show supporting computations in good form.
2. Prepare the journal entry for the year-end adjustment to the Allowance for Doubtful Accounts balance as of December 31, 1995. (*AICPA adapted*)

P5-22    *Correction of Allowance Account*   From inception of operations in 1991 Summit carried no allowance for doubtful accounts. Uncollectible receivables were expensed as written off, and recoveries were credited to income as collected. On March 1, 1995 (after the 1994 financial statements were issued), management recognized that Summit's accounting policy with respect to doubtful accounts was not correct, and determined that an allowance for doubtful accounts was necessary. A policy was established to maintain an allowance for doubtful accounts based on Summit's historical bad debt loss percentage applied to year-end accounts receivable. The historical bad debt loss percentage is to be recomputed each year based on the relationship of net write-offs to credit sales for all available past years up to a maximum of five years.

Information from Summit's records for five years is as follows:

| Year | Credit Sales | Accounts Written Off | Recoveries |
|---|---|---|---|
| 1991 | $1,500,000 | $15,000 | $0 |
| 1992 | 2,250,000 | 38,000 | 2,700 |
| 1993 | 2,950,000 | 52,000 | 2,500 |
| 1994 | 3,300,000 | 65,000 | 4,800 |
| 1995 | 4,000,000 | 83,000 | 5,000 |

Accounts receivable balances were $1,250,000 and $1,460,000 at December 31, 1994 and December 31, 1995, respectively.

**Required**
1. Prepare the journal entry, with appropriate explanation, to set up the allowance for doubtful accounts as of January 1, 1995. Disregard income taxes. Show supporting computations in good form.
2. Prepare a schedule analyzing the changes in the Allowance for Doubtful Accounts account for the year ended December 31, 1995. Show supporting computations in good form. (*AICPA adapted*)

P5-23  *Comprehensive Receivables Problem*  The December 31, 1994 balance sheet of the Blackmon Corporation disclosed the following information relating to its receivables:

| | | |
|---|---:|---:|
| Accounts receivable | $245,000 | |
| Less: Allowance for doubtful accounts | (15,000) | |
| | | $230,000 |
| Notes receivable | $ 60,000 | |
| Less: Notes receivable discounted | (10,000) | |
| | | 50,000 |
| Total receivables | | $280,000 |

During 1995, credit sales totaled $1,200,000 and collections on accounts receivable (unassigned) amounted to $900,000. Uncollectible accounts totaling $18,000 from several customers were written off, and a $1,350 accounts receivable previously written off was collected. Additionally, the following transactions relating to Blackmon's receivables occurred during the year:

| | |
|---|---|
| Mar.  6 | Received payment of $12,460 on a note from the Renko Company. The payment included interest revenue of $460. |
| Mar. 31 | The March bank statement indicated that the discounted note had been paid at maturity. |
| May   1 | Accepted a 120-day, 13% note from the Licata Company in exchange for its account receivable of $4,800. |
| May  18 | Received a $6,900, 90-day, 12% note from the Eagle Manufacturing Corporation for a credit sale. |
| June   2 | Discounted both the Licata and Eagle notes at the bank at 14% (assume that Blackmon normally does not discount its notes). |
| July   1 | Assigned $140,000 of accounts receivable to a finance company. Under the terms of the agreement, Blackmon receives 85% of the value of the accounts assigned less a service charge of $5,000, and is charged 1.5% per month on the outstanding loan balance. |
| July   6 | A sales allowance of $2,500 on an assigned account is allowed by Blackmon. |
| July  13 | A sales return of $800 on an assigned account is granted by Blackmon. |
| July  31 | Collections of $50,000 are made on assigned accounts. This amount and 1 month's interest are remitted to the finance company. |
| Aug. 31 | Assigned accounts of $60,000 are collected, and the remainder of the loan is repaid, including interest. |
| Aug. 31 | The August bank statement indicated the Eagle note had been paid. |
| Sept.  1 | The bank notifies Blackmon that Licata defaulted on its note and charges a fee of $25. |
| Sept.  4 | Collected the amount due from the Licata Company. |
| Dec. 31 | Collected interest of $5,000 on the outstanding notes receivable. |

On December 31, 1995 an aging of the accounts receivable balance indicated the following:

| Age | Amount | Estimated Percentage Uncollectible |
|---|---:|:---:|
| Under 30 days | $240,487 | 0.5% |
| 31–60 days | 113,421 | 1.5 |
| 61–90 days | 30,933 | 8.0 |
| 91–240 days | 17,185 | 35.0 |
| Over 240 days | 6,874 | 70.0 |
| | $408,900 | |

**Required**

1. Prepare the journal entries to record the preceding receivable transactions during 1995 and the necessary adjusting entry on December 31, 1995.
2. Prepare the receivables portion of Blackmon's December 31, 1995 balance sheet.

# 6

# INVENTORIES: COST MEASUREMENT AND FLOW ASSUMPTIONS

**Chapter Topics**

*Inventory Classifications*

*Perpetual and Periodic Inventory Systems*

*Determination of Inventory Quantities and Costs*

*Alternative Cost Flow Assumptions*

*Advantages and Disadvantages of Alternative Cost Flow Assumptions*

*Dollar-Value LIFO*

*Foreign Currency Transactions (Appendix)*

*Inventories are the assets of a company that are (1) held for sale in the ordinary course of business, (2) in the process of production for sale, or (3) held for use in the production of goods or services to be made available for sale.* The category of inventory specifically excludes any assets that are not sold in the normal course of business, such as marketable securities, or property, plant, and equipment which the company intends to sell.

Accounting for inventories is especially significant because of the importance of the acquisition, manufacture, and sale of products to the profitability of companies. The cost (carrying value) of the inventory usually has a material impact on a company's balance sheet. Since the ending inventory of one period is the beginning inventory of the next period, the cost of the inventory on the balance sheet will have an impact on the next period's cost of goods sold and net income. In addition, various accounting practices, such as alternative cost flow assumptions and valuation principles, are in widespread use and may have a significant impact on asset valuation and income determination. In this chapter, we discuss the classifications of inventory, the perpetual and periodic inventory systems, the determination of inventory quantities and costs, and alternative inventory cost flow assumptions.

## CLASSIFICATIONS OF INVENTORY

Inventory may be classified in several alternative accounts, depending on the type of business. A merchandising company, whether wholesale or retail, acquires goods for resale and does not alter their physical form. Consequently it needs only one type of inventory account, usually entitled **merchandise inventory.** A manufacturing company *does* change the physical form of the goods and typically uses three inventory accounts in the financial statements (although more may be used internally), usually called **raw materials inventory, goods in process inventory,** and **finished goods inventory.** The flow of inventory costs through these two types of companies is illustrated in Exhibit 6-1. The three categories of inventory accounts used by a manufacturing company are discussed in the following sections.

**EXHIBIT 6-1**

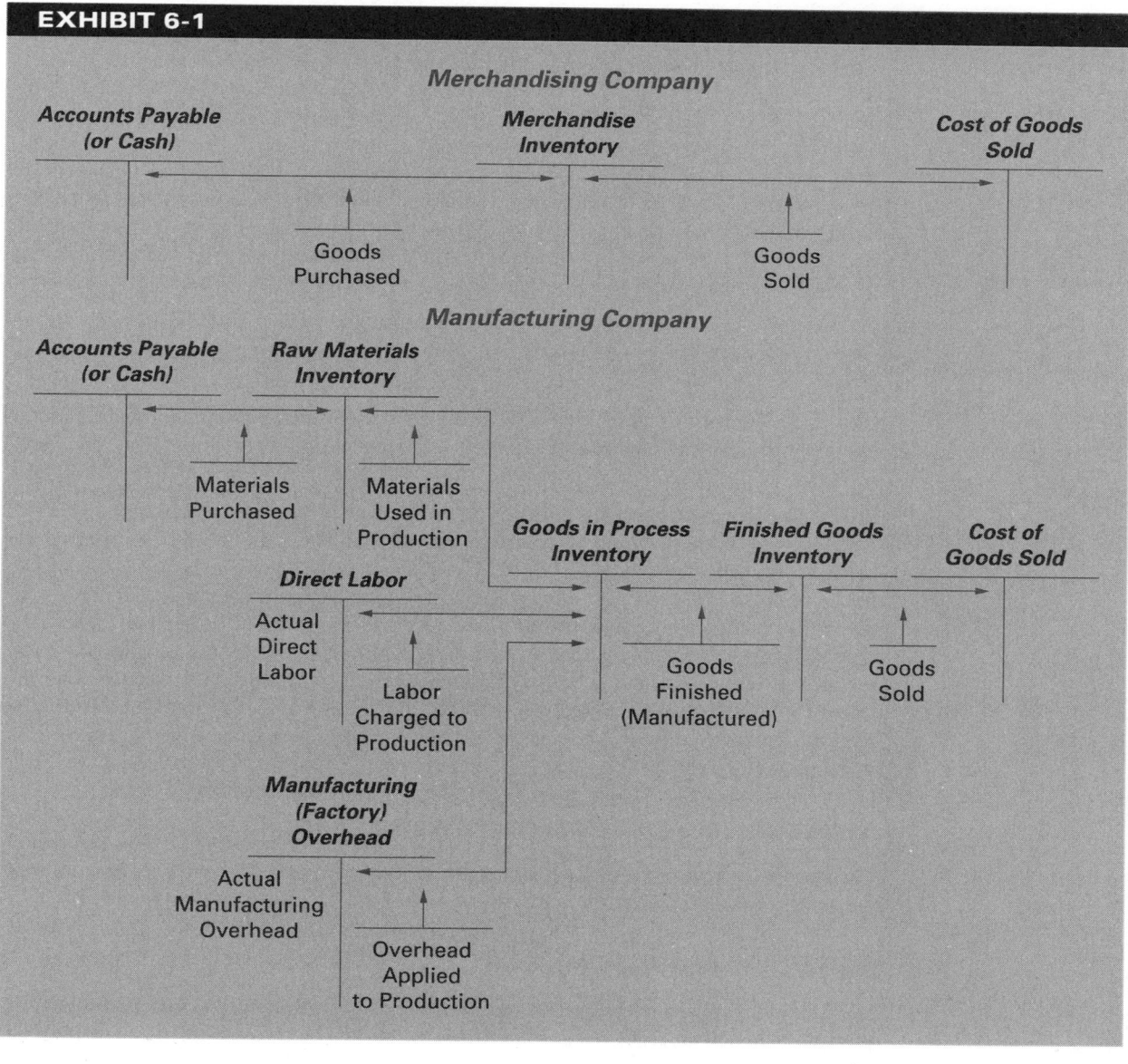

### Raw Materials Inventory

**Raw materials inventory includes the tangible goods acquired for direct use in the production process.** This inventory includes materials acquired from natural sources, such as the iron ore used by a steel mill. Raw materials may also include some products purchased from other companies, such as the steel or subassemblies used in the manufacture of appliances. Raw materials should be contrasted with **parts inventory,** which is the term often used for the inventory of replacement parts.

Materials that are not directly part of the manufacturing process, but are necessary for its successful operation, sometimes are included in raw materials inventory. However, they are more normally separated in an account called **factory supplies, manufacturing supplies,** or **indirect materials.** Examples of materials in this category include lubricating oil and cleaning supplies.

### Goods in Process Inventory

**Goods in process** (sometimes called **work in process**) **inventory includes the products that have been started in the manufacturing process but have not yet been completed.** This partially completed inventory includes three cost components: (1) raw materials, (2) direct labor, which is the cost of the labor used directly in the manufacture of the product, and (3) manufacturing (or factory) overhead, which includes the costs other than raw materials and direct labor that are associated with the manufacturing process. These latter costs include **variable manufacturing overhead,** such as supplies and some indirect labor, and **fixed manufacturing overhead,** such as insurance, utilities, and depreciation on the assets used in the production activities.

### Finished Goods Inventory

**Finished goods inventory includes the completed manufactured products awaiting sale.** The inventory includes the same three cost components as the goods in process inventory, but all the costs are combined into a single cost per unit for all the completed units.

The inventory cost included in the balance sheet is the final amount that results from a series of steps. First the company must decide what items to properly include in the inventory and count the physical inventory quantities. Then the costs of the units purchased or produced during the accounting period must be determined, taking into consideration the costs for freight-in and the reductions for purchases discounts, returns, and allowances. A cost flow assumption is used to allocate the costs of the beginning inventory and the units purchased or produced between ending inventory and cost of goods sold. A manufacturing company may determine the cost per unit produced in conjunction with the cost flow assumption rather than as a separate step. Each of these steps is discussed in the following sections.

## ALTERNATIVE INVENTORY SYSTEMS

Inventory quantities and costs may be accounted for using either the **perpetual system** or the **periodic system.**

### Perpetual Inventory System

**A company using the perpetual system maintains a continuous record of the physical quantities in its inventory.** The purchase, or production, and use of each item of inventory is recorded in detailed subsidiary records, although often only in units without including costs. Such a perpetual physical system is essential if adequate management planning and control over inventory are to be maintained and stockouts avoided. Many perpetual systems also include costs so that management control and the preparation of periodic financial statements are facilitated. Such systems are becoming much more common with the increased sophistication and lower cost of computer-based accounting systems. For example, most retail stores are using "point of sale" cash register systems in which each product has a unique code, such as the UPC code on groceries, that is entered into the system as each unit is sold. This enables the retailer to immediately update its Inventory and Cost of Goods Sold accounts as each sale is made. These accounts are maintained as summary accounts, thereby making it possible for the inventory and the cost of goods sold to be continually known. Purchases returns and allowances, purchases discounts taken, and freight-in usually are recorded in separate accounts that are closed to Income Summary at the end of the period.

When the perpetual system is used, a physical count should be made at least once a year to confirm the balance in the inventory account. Variation between the physical count and the account balance results from errors in recording, shrinkage, waste, breakage, theft, and other causes. The accounts are adjusted for the cost of the difference in the two quantities so that the perpetual records are in agreement with the physical count. The size of the difference provides useful information for management control purposes and is another advantage of the perpetual system.

## Periodic Inventory System

**A company using the periodic system does *not* maintain a continuous record of the physical quantities (or costs) of inventory on hand.** Physical counts are taken periodically, which should be at least once a year. This is the only time(s) when physical quantities on hand, and therefore the quantities used or sold during the period, are known accurately. The cost of the ending inventory is determined by attaching costs to the physical quantities on hand based on the cost flow assumption used. Then the cost of goods sold is calculated by subtracting the ending inventory from the cost of goods available for sale. The cost of goods available for sale is the sum of the beginning inventory and either the net purchases for a merchandising company or the costs of the units produced for the period for a manufacturing company. This system is adequate for relatively low cost inventory items, particularly when the costs of a perpetual inventory system are likely to outweigh its benefits.

In the periodic system the costs of acquisitions of inventory typically are not recorded (debited) in an inventory account. Such a procedure would lead to an overstatement of the permanent Inventory account, because the account is not reduced (credited) during the period for the cost of the inventory sold. Therefore in a periodic system the costs of acquisitions of inventory usually are recorded (debited) in a temporary account, Purchases, while the beginning inventory cost remains in the Inventory account. As with the perpetual system, purchases returns and allowances, purchases discounts taken, and freight-in usually are recorded in separate accounts. Each of these amounts is used in the computation of net purchases as follows:

$$\text{Net Purchases} = \text{Purchases} + \text{Freight-in} - \begin{array}{c}\text{Purchases Returns}\\\text{and Allowances}\end{array} - \begin{array}{c}\text{Purchases}\\\text{Discounts}\\\text{Taken}\end{array}$$

All the accounts are closed to the Income Summary account at the end of the period.

*Closing entries are discussed in Appendix C.*

In summary, the difference between the perpetual and the periodic inventory systems can be illustrated by the following equations:

Perpetual Inventory System

Beginning Inventory + Purchases (net) − Goods Sold = Ending Inventory

Periodic Inventory System

Beginning Inventory + Purchases (net) − Ending Inventory = Goods Sold

Note that each equation can be thought of in terms of *units* or *costs*.

## ITEMS TO BE INCLUDED IN INVENTORY QUANTITIES

The basic criterion for including items in inventory is *economic control* rather than physical possession. For inventory, economic control is usually consistent with legal ownership, but when there is a difference, economic substance should always take precedence over legal form. Thus when control transfers to a company that is purchasing inventory, the item should be included in its inventory, even if it does not have physical possession. Before transfer of control, the item should be included in the inventory of the seller, even though the seller may not have physical possession. Likewise, when control passes to a customer because of a sale, the item should be excluded from the seller's inventory and included in the purchaser's inventory, even though physical possession has not been transferred. Normally control is easy to determine. Control may be affected by product financing arrangements (discussed in Chapter 7) and sales made when there is a right of return (discussed in Chapter 5). Also, goods in transit and consigned goods require special consideration.

### Goods in Transit

Goods are often shipped under one of two alternatives: **FOB** (Free-on-Board) **shipping point** or **FOB destination.** When goods are in transit at the end of the accounting period, the terms of shipment determine whether the seller or the purchaser includes them in its inventory. **If the goods are shipped FOB shipping point, control of (and legal title to) the goods is transferred at the shipping point when the seller delivers them to the common carrier,** which is acting as an agent for the buyer. The purchaser includes those goods in its inventory and the seller excludes them. **If goods are shipped FOB destination, control of (and legal title to) the goods is not transferred until the goods are delivered to the buyer's destination.** The seller includes those goods in its inventory, and the purchaser excludes them. These situations may be illustrated as follows:

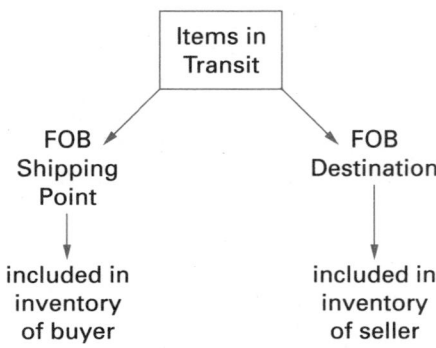

Physical receipt of the goods by the buyer usually determines when it records the inventory in its accounting system. Since control and legal ownership occur at the same time as the receipt, no particular issues arise for the purchaser. However, the seller must review the records of sales and shipments so that goods in transit shipped to a customer FOB destination are included in its own ending inventory.

It is possible that economic control may be transferred before shipment occurs. For example, if the sales contract specifies that the buyer will pick up the goods at the seller's place of business and the goods are segregated from the other inventory, control has passed; the seller should exclude the goods from inventory and the purchaser should include them.

Frequently companies establish a consistent policy for including or excluding goods in transit from inventory, ignoring the distinction between shipping point and destination. Although adjustments should be made when financial statements are prepared, they may be ignored if they are not material.

### Consigned Goods and Installment Sales

Goods may be transferred on **consignment** from one party to another for purposes of sale without the ownership and ultimate economic control changing hands. The company delivering the goods, the **consignor,** retains control (and ownership), while the company receiving the goods, the **consignee,** attempts to sell them. If the goods are sold, the consignee retains a commission and returns the net amount to the consignor. Unsold goods are returned to the consignor.

*Accounting for consignments and installment sales is discussed in Chapter 16.*

Since the consignor still retains control (and ownership) of the goods, they must be included in its inventory at cost, plus the handling and shipping costs incurred in the delivery to the consignee. The consignee, acting as an agent of the consignor, excludes them from its inventory. However, the consignee should include a note to its financial statements, summarizing the activity and disclosing any legal liability.

When goods are sold on an **installment** plan, the seller usually retains legal title to the goods until full payment has been received. However, since control has been transferred to the purchaser, the goods are recorded as sold when delivered and are excluded from the inventory of the seller. This is an acceptable accounting procedure when it is expected that the purchaser will make payment in the normal course of business. In exceptional cases, recognition of gross profit on installment sales is deferred until the cash is collected.

## DETERMINATION OF INVENTORY COSTS

There are two issues in the determination of inventory costs. The costs attached to each unit *available for sale* are discussed in this section. The costs attached to the *ending inventory* and *cost of goods sold* (the inventory cost flow assumption) are discussed later in this chapter.

The cost principle is applied as follows:

**The primary basis of accounting for inventories is cost, which has been defined generally as the price paid or consideration given to acquire an asset.**[1]

---

1. "Restatement and Revision of Accounting Research Bulletins," *Accounting Research and Terminology Bulletins, Final Edition, No. 43* (New York: AICPA, 1961), ch. 4, par. 4.

Thus, **inventory cost includes applicable expenditures and charges directly or indirectly incurred in bringing an item to its existing condition and location** (which includes maintaining it until it is sold). For each item of inventory, whether purchased or manufactured, a decision must be made as to whether each cost meets this definition and is included in the cost of the inventory or whether it does not and, therefore, is immediately recognized as an expense. The cost of purchased inventory should include the purchase price (net of purchases discounts, as discussed later) plus payments directly associated with the inventory, such as freight, receiving, unpacking, inspecting, storage, insurance, personal property, sales and other applicable taxes, and similar costs. When more than one type of inventory is purchased for a single sum and the costs of each type are not identifiable, the relative fair market value method should be used to apportion the cost.

*The relative fair market value method is discussed in Chapter 8.*

Some costs that should be attached to inventory normally are excluded on the grounds of the cost/benefit relationship. For example, the costs of the purchasing department are necessary to bring the item to its existing condition and location, but the practical difficulties involved in allocating such costs to the separate inventories often outweigh the significance of the differences (i.e., benefits) that result from not making an allocation.

Another cost that *could* be considered for inclusion in the cost of inventory is the interest cost associated with amounts borrowed to finance the purchase of the inventory. It can be argued that such an interest cost is incurred indirectly in order to bring an item to its existing condition and location and, therefore, should be added to the inventory cost. Alternatively, it can be argued that borrowing costs are period costs associated with the general activities of the company, and none is related specifically to the acquisition of a particular inventory item. According to *FASB Statement No. 34,* interest costs are not to be included in the cost of inventory that is *routinely manufactured* (discussed in Chapter 9).

Additional issues in the determination of inventory costs are manufacturing overhead costs, standard costs, variable costs, and purchases discounts.

### Manufacturing Overhead Costs

When inventory is manufactured, costs directly and indirectly incurred in the production activity are included in the cost of inventory. **Accounting Research Bulletin No. 43** clarified which manufacturing overhead costs should be considered as being "directly or indirectly incurred" by stating that inventory costs include acquisition and production costs (including manufacturing overhead), whereas

> general and administrative expenses should be included as period charges, except for the portion of such expenses that may be clearly related to production and thus constitute a part of inventory costs. Selling expenses constitute no part of inventory costs. It should also be recognized that the exclusion of all overhead from inventory costs does not constitute an accepted accounting practice.[2]

Manufacturing costs that are related directly to the production of inventory and are included in the cost of that inventory may be either variable or fixed manufacturing overhead. Variable overhead costs should always be included in the cost of inventory. The allocation of fixed overhead costs is a difficult issue and the final allocation of costs usually involves somewhat arbitrary procedures. A discussion of these issues is beyond the scope of this book but may be found in a cost accounting

---

2. *Ibid.*

book. An interpretation of "related directly" presents some practical problems. One way in which this criterion can be applied is to ask whether the economic benefit to be derived from the asset in the future (i.e., sales revenue) has been directly increased by the expenditure in question. In other words, **the relationship between the costs incurred and the benefits produced has to be traceable.**

For example, a supervisor's salary may increase directly the economic benefit associated with the asset if without the supervisor the item would not have been produced or would not have been of the same quality. That is, there is a traceable relationship. Therefore the supervisor's salary should be included in the cost of the inventory. In contrast, the company president's salary does not lead directly to an increase in the economic benefits to be derived from a particular unit of inventory. In this case there is no traceable relationship and the salary should be a period expense. Similarly, the cost of *normal* spoilage is considered an inventory cost, since some spoilage is a part of the production process. However, the cost of *abnormal* spoilage is an expense of the period, because it has not increased the economic benefits to be derived from the inventory.

In addition to traceability, **materiality is relevant to the decision to include overhead costs in the cost of inventory.** If the inclusion or exclusion of the cost will not have a material effect on the financial statements, for simplicity the costs typically will be expensed in the period incurred.

Some costs should never be considered for inclusion in the cost of inventory because they are not associated with bringing the item to its existing condition and location. For example, selling costs are a cost of the period and not an inventory cost because they apply to the units sold during the period and not to the units held in inventory.

## Standard Costs

For internal reporting purposes, most manufacturing companies use a standard-cost system in which unit costs are based on budgeted standards for the period. However, standard costs are acceptable for financial reporting only

> **if adjusted at reasonable intervals to reflect current conditions so that at the balance sheet date standard costs reasonably approximate costs computed under one of the recognized bases.**[3]

In other words, the standard costs must be adjusted for the cost variances (direct materials, direct labor, and manufacturing overhead) that occur during the period. The usual practice is to close all the variances to cost of goods sold, although the preferred practice would be to allocate the variances, if material, between cost of goods sold and ending inventory on the basis of relative total costs.

## Variable Costing

Under variable (or direct) costing, the cost of the inventory includes only the variable costs incurred in production, such as direct materials, direct labor, and variable manufacturing overhead. Fixed costs are treated as period expenses. In contrast, under absorption (or full) costing, the cost of the inventory includes allocated fixed manufacturing overhead in addition to the variable costs. A discussion of the relative merits of variable and absorption costing is not the concern of this book, but if a

---

3.  *Ibid.*

company uses variable costing for internal purposes, it must adjust to absorption costing for financial reporting purposes. Thus a portion of the fixed manufacturing overhead must be allocated to the units produced to convert to an absorption costing basis.

### Purchases Discounts

Many sellers offer discounts to buyers in order to encourage prompt payment. These discounts, called purchases discounts, may be accounted for by the gross price method or the net price method. These methods raise questions about whether purchases discounts should directly affect income or be treated as adjustments to inventory cost, and how management efficiency can best be highlighted.

**In the gross price method, the purchase is recorded at the gross price, and the amount of the discount is recorded in the accounting system only if the discount is *taken*.** This discount should be deducted from the acquisition cost of the inventory. **In the net price method, the purchase is recorded at its net price, and the amount of the discount appears in the accounting system only if the discount is *not taken*.** This discount lost should be treated as a period expense.[4] These two alternatives are illustrated by an example in which a company purchases $1,000 of goods under terms of 1/10, n/30 (a 1% discount is allowed if payment is made within 10 days; otherwise, full payment is due within 30 days). The journal entries are shown in Exhibit 6-2.

### EXHIBIT 6-2

#### ALTERNATIVE METHODS OF ACCOUNTING FOR PURCHASES DISCOUNTS

|  | Gross Price Method | | | Net Price Method | | |
|---|---|---|---|---|---|---|
| To record the purchase | Purchases (or Inventory) | 1,000 | | Purchases (or Inventory) | 990 | |
|  | Accounts Payable | | 1,000 | Accounts Payable | | 990 |
| To record payment within the discount period | Accounts Payable | 1,000 | | Accounts Payable | 990 | |
|  | Purchases Discounts Taken | | 10 | Cash | | 990 |
|  | Cash | | 990 | | | |
| To record payment outside the discount period | Accounts Payable | 1,000 | | Accounts Payable | 990 | |
|  | Cash | | 1,000 | Purchases Discounts Lost | 10 | |
|  | | | | Cash | | 1,000 |
| Adjusting entry at end of period if discount has expired and invoice is unpaid | No entry required | | | Purchases Discounts Lost | 10 | |
|  | | | | Accounts Payable | | 10 |

---

4. In a third method, the allowance method, the purchase is recorded at the net price, the accounts payable at the gross price, and the difference is debited to an allowance account. The allowance account is reduced by the difference between the cash paid to the supplier and the accounts payable balance. It is also adjusted for purchases discounts not taken.

*Conceptual Evaluation of the Two Methods*

The purchases discounts lost under the net price method should be treated as a financing expense for the period and should not be included in inventory cost, because **losing the discount does not increase the economic benefit to be derived from the inventory.** Therefore the net price method produces the correct inventory cost, which is the invoice price less all available discounts. To be consistent, the purchases discounts taken under the gross price method should be treated as a reduction in inventory cost. However, the gross price method does not necessarily produce the correct inventory cost, because if some discounts are not taken, the inventory cost will include those discounts lost, even though they do not increase the economic benefits to be derived from the inventory. If material, an adjustment should be made to remove the discounts lost from the cost of the inventory and record the cost as a financing expense.

Sometimes it is argued that the discounts taken under the gross method should be treated as an increase in income. This is not correct because the matching principle would be violated, since the discounts may relate to goods that have not yet been sold. Furthermore a company does not earn income by buying goods and paying bills. **The revenue recognition principle requires that a sale of goods occur before income is recognized.** However, for practical reasons, purchases discounts taken sometimes are included in income; this is acceptable provided that the amount is not material. This procedure often is followed by retailing companies.

Another advantage of the net price method is that it isolates the purchases discounts lost, thereby highlighting inefficiencies, which assists the management control process. For example, if a company purchases goods on terms of 2/10, n/30 and does not take the discount, it is paying 2% to delay payment by 20 days (the 30-day maximum less the 10 days allowed to take the discount), which is an approximate annual rate of 36% (2% $\times$ 360/20).

The net price method can be criticized, though, because Accounts Payable does not represent the maximum amount of the liability that the company may be required to pay out, although it does reflect the most likely amount if the company generally takes the discounts. However, an adjusting entry will ensure that the correct liability appears on the financial statements. The adjustment increases the Purchases Discounts Lost (debit) and the Accounts Payable (credit) accounts. After this adjustment, the Accounts Payable account reports the gross price, which is the amount that the company is obligated to pay. Despite the advantages of the net price method, the gross price method is more widely used in practice because it is simpler to use and the results produced are not often materially different from the net price method.

Purchases discounts should be distinguished from trade discounts. **Trade discounts are discounts deducted prior to arriving at the invoice price** and do not enter into the accounting system.

*Trade discounts are discussed in Chapter 5.*

## COST FLOW ASSUMPTIONS

A company typically starts an accounting period with some units in the beginning inventory and then purchases or produces additional units during the period. Together these constitute the *goods available for sale,* which are then either sold or remain in the ending inventory.

For financial statement purposes, *costs* must be attached to these units. The cost of the beginning inventory (the cost of the ending inventory of the preceding period) is the beginning balance in the Inventory account. The beginning balance in Inventory plus the cost of purchases or production (discussed earlier) constitute the *cost of the goods available for sale.* This total cost is allocated between the cost of goods sold and ending inventory by means of a *cost flow assumption*. The major cost flow assumptions currently used are specific identification, first-in, first-out (FIFO), average cost, and last-in, first-out (LIFO). Both the unit relationship and the cost flow relationship are illustrated in Exhibit 6-3.

Cost flow assumptions are important for two reasons. First, a company has inventories at each year-end. If there were none, all the cost of goods available for sale would be transferred to cost of goods sold. Second, the costs of purchases and production change. If these costs did not change, all units would have the same cost; therefore alternative cost flow assumptions would not affect the cost of goods sold or the ending inventory. Note that we are discussing *cost* flow assumptions here, which have no particular relationship to the *physical* flow (except for the specific identification method).

Each cost flow assumption is discussed in the following sections. They are applied to both the perpetual and the periodic inventory systems, using the information for the Dalton Company given in Exhibit 6-4. Recall that under the periodic system, the ending inventory is computed before the cost of goods sold, whereas under the perpetual system, the cost of goods sold is calculated first. This reflects the differences between the two systems. To make the illustration less complicated, a merchandising company is used, although the cost flow assumptions are applied to manufacturing companies by following the same principles.

### Specific Identification

**Use of the specific identification inventory cost flow assumption requires that each unit sold and each unit remaining in the ending inventory be identified and that the actual costs of those units be included in cost of goods sold and ending inventory, respectively.** For example, each unit sold on April 27 must be specifically identified. If they are all from the units that were in the beginning inventory, cost of goods sold is increased $10 for each unit, whereas if they were from the units purchased on April 10 or April 20, cost of goods sold would be increased $11 or $12 for each unit, respectively. Similarly, each unit in the ending inventory has to be identified and the appropriate cost of $10, $11, or $12 attached to each.

**EXHIBIT 6-3**

## ILLUSTRATION OF UNIT AND COST FLOW RELATIONSHIPS

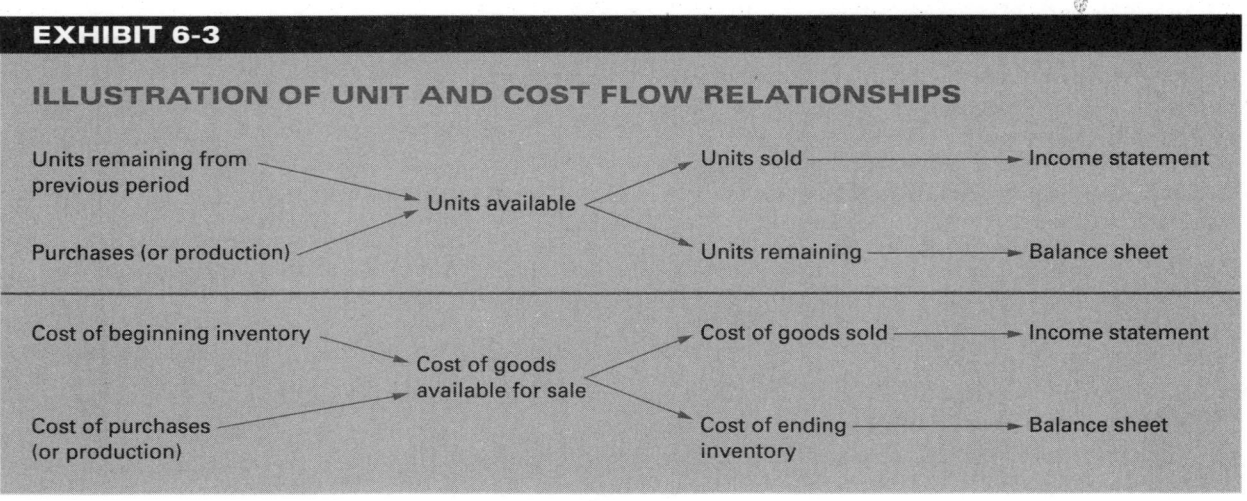

**EXHIBIT 6-4**

**DALTON COMPANY**

Inventory Inflows and Outflows

| | | | |
|---|---|---|---|
| Inventory, April 1 | 100 | units @ $10 per unit | $1,000 |
| Purchases, April 10 | 80 | units @ $11 per unit | 880 |
| Purchases, April 20 | 70 | units @ $12 per unit | 840 |
| Goods Available for Sale | 250 | units | $2,720 |
| | | | |
| Sales, April 18 | (90) units ⎫ | 140 units | |
| Sales, April 27 | (50) units ⎭ | | |
| Inventory, April 30 | 110 | units | |

*Notes:* (1) It is assumed that the beginning inventory is valued at $10 per unit for all the flow assumptions although if costs are changing this value would be different for different flow assumptions, because the beginning inventory for the current period is the ending inventory of the preceding period. (2) The company uses a monthly accounting period.

The specific identification method can be applied in either a perpetual or a periodic inventory system, but it is more reasonable to use it with a perpetual system in which each unit sold is identified and the appropriate cost attached. While it appears that the specific identification method is desirable because of its apparent simplicity and its success at matching costs as expenses against revenues, there are significant practical and theoretical objections to its use. It may be practical in a few situations in which units are costly and can be easily distinguished (for example, a car dealership), but in many complex manufacturing and retailing situations, it is impossible to apply the specific identification method because the cost of each individual unit is not identifiable (for example, a single can of soup), and it is not known which specific units are sold. In addition, as volume increases, so does the cost of record keeping, and the method may become too expensive to use. Another argument against the method is that it allows manipulation of profits when the units of inventory are identical. Continuing the preceding example, if the units were sold on April 27 for $30, then the selection by management of a $10 unit or a $12 unit for sale would make the gross profit either $20 per unit or $18 per unit, respectively. In summary, the specific identification method can produce ending inventory and cost of goods sold figures at the two extremes of FIFO and LIFO, or at values in between. This ability of management to select, or "manipulate," profits is considered undesirable. However, the method is appropriate if each item is unique. No conclusive figures are presented in this section because they are so dependent on the assumptions regarding the particular units selected for sale.

### First-In, First-Out (FIFO)

**Under the FIFO cost flow assumption, the earliest costs incurred are included in the cost of goods sold, and the most recent costs are included in the ending inventory.** In other words, the first costs incurred are the first transferred to cost of goods sold (in a merchandising company) or to goods in process and then to finished goods and cost of goods sold (in a manufacturing company). Consequently the ending inventory consists of the most recent costs incurred. Therefore, in periods of rising costs, FIFO produces a lower cost of goods sold figure based on older costs, whereas ending inventory is based on the most recent and higher costs, as further discussed in the evaluation section later in this chapter.

If the periodic method is being used by the Dalton Company, the ending inventory of $1,280 is computed first, as shown in Exhibit 6-5. The ending inventory of 110 units is based on the latest costs incurred. It includes 40 units from the purchase on April 10 for $11 each and 70 units purchased on April 20 for $12 each. The cost of goods sold of $1,440 is calculated by subtracting the ending inventory from the cost of goods available for sale as shown in Exhibit 6-5. Therefore, it is based on the earliest costs incurred and includes the beginning inventory of 100 units at $10 each and 40 units from the April 10 purchase at $11 each.

**EXHIBIT 6-5**

**DALTON COMPANY**

**First-In, First-Out Inventory Cost Flow Assumption (Periodic Inventory System)**

Ending Inventory (110 units):
| | |
|---|---|
| 40 units @ $11 | $ 440 |
| 70 units @ $12 | 840 |
| | $1,280 |

Cost of Goods Sold (140 units):
Beginning Inventory + Purchases − Ending Inventory = Cost of Goods Sold
$1,000 + $1,720 − $1,280 = $1,440

If the Dalton Company is using a perpetual inventory system (for costs as well as physical quantities), the cost of goods sold of $1,440 and the ending inventory of $1,280 are calculated as shown in Exhibit 6-6. The $1,440 cost of goods sold for 140 units is based on the earliest costs incurred. For the April 18 sale, the 90 units have a cost of $10 per unit (from the beginning inventory). For the April 27 sale of 50 units, 10 units have a cost of $10 per unit from the beginning inventory and 40 units have a cost of $11 per unit (from the April 10 purchase). The $1,280 ending inventory is determined by deducting the $1,440 cost of goods sold from the $2,720 cost of goods available for sale. It consists of 110 units and includes the latest costs: the cost of the remaining 40 units from the first purchase on April 10 and the 70 units purchased on April 20.

Note that the ending inventory and the cost of goods sold under both the perpetual and the periodic systems are identical; this always will be true for the FIFO cost flow assumption because the latest costs incurred always are included in the ending inventory.

### Average Cost

The average cost flow assumption considers all the costs and units to be commingled so that no individual units or costs can be identified. When the periodic inven-

**EXHIBIT 6-6**

**DALTON COMPANY**

**First-In, First-Out Inventory Cost Flow Assumption**
**(Perpetual Inventory System)**

Cost of Goods Sold (140 units):

| | | |
|---|---|---|
| April 18 | 90 units @ $10 | $ 900 |
| April 27 | 50 units: 10 units @ $10 | 100 |
| | 40 units @ $11 | 440 |
| Total | | $1,440 |

Ending Inventory (110 units):

Beginning Inventory + Purchases − Cost of Goods Sold = Ending Inventory
$1,000        +   $1,720   −        $1,440         =      $1,280*

| | | |
|---|---|---|
| *40 units @ $11 = | $ | 440 |
| 70 units @ $12 = | | 840 |
| | | $1,280 |

tory system is used, the average cost method is known as the **weighted average method**. The cost of the units for the period is calculated on the basis of the cost of the beginning inventory and the average cost of the units purchased or manufactured, weighted according to the number of units at each cost. In other words, **under the weighted average method, the average cost per unit for the period is the cost of goods available for sale divided by the number of units available for sale.** This average cost is used for both the ending inventory and the cost of goods sold.

The weighted average unit cost for the Dalton Company in April is $10.88 (the cost of goods available for sale of $2,720 ÷ the number of units available for sale of 250), as shown in Exhibit 6-7. The ending inventory is recorded at this $10.88 cost per unit, resulting in a total cost of $1,197. The $1,523 cost of goods sold is determined by deducting the ending inventory from the cost of goods available for sale of $2,720. It is also equal to the 140 units sold multiplied by the $10.88 weighted average cost.

**EXHIBIT 6-7**

**DALTON COMPANY**

**Weighted Average Inventory Cost Flow Assumption**
**(Periodic Inventory System)**

| | |
|---|---|
| Cost of goods available for sale ($1,000 + $1,720) | $2,720 |
| Units available for sale | 250 |
| Average cost (Cost ÷ Number of units) | $10.88 |
| Ending inventory (110 units @ $10.88) | $1,197 |

Beginning Inventory + Purchases − Ending Inventory = Cost of Goods Sold
$1,000        +   $1,720   −      $1,197       =      $1,523

When the average cost method is used under a perpetual inventory system (for costs as well as physical quantities), the same principles are applied, but it is known as a **moving average** method because a new weighted average cost must be calculated after *each* purchase as shown in Exhibit 6-8. The new weighted average is computed in the same way as in the weighted average method. That is, **under the moving average method, the average cost per unit is the cost of the units available for sale after the purchase divided by the number of units available for sale at that time.** This average cost is used to determine the cost of each sale made until the next purchase when a new average cost must be calculated. The average cost after the April 10 purchase is $10.44 (cost of goods available for sale of $1,880 ÷ the number of units available for sale of 180). Therefore the sales on April 18 have a cost of $10.44 per unit for a total cost of goods sold of $940. The purchase on April 20 increases the average cost to $11.125 per unit, and therefore the 50 units sold on April 27 have a total cost of $556. The total cost of goods sold for April is $1,496 ($940 + $556). The ending inventory is recorded at the final average cost for the period, which is calculated after the last purchase. The cost of $11.125 per unit for the 110 units results in a total ending inventory of $1,224 (see Exhibit 6-8).

---

### EXHIBIT 6-8

**DALTON COMPANY**

Moving Average Inventory Cost Flow Assumption
(Perpetual Inventory System)

| | | |
|---|---|---|
| April  1, Beginning Inventory | 100  units @ $10 | $1,000 |
| April 10, Purchases | 80  units @ $11 | 880 |
| April 10, Balance | 180  units @ $10.44 | $1,880 |
| April 18, Sales | (90) units @ $10.44 | (940) |
| April 18, Balance | 90  units @ $10.44 | $  940 |
| April 20, Purchases | 70  units @ $12 | 840 |
| April 20, Balance | 160  units @ $11.125 | $1,780 |
| April 27, Sales | (50) units @ $11.125 | (556) |
| April 30, Balance | 110  units @ $11.125 | $1,224 |
| Cost of Goods Sold (140 units) | $940 + $556 | $1,496 |
| Ending Inventory (110 units @ $11.125) | | $1,224 |

---

### Last-In, First-Out (LIFO)

**Under the LIFO cost flow assumption, the most recent costs incurred are included in the cost of goods sold, and the earliest costs (part or all of which are costs incurred in previous periods) are included in the ending inventory.** Therefore, in periods of rising costs, LIFO produces a high cost of goods sold figure based on the most recent costs, whereas inventory is based on the oldest, and lowest, costs. The logic behind this procedure is discussed later in this chapter.

If the Dalton Company is using a periodic inventory system, no consideration is given to the timing of the individual sales. The ending inventory of $1,110 and the cost of goods sold of $1,610 are calculated as shown in Exhibit 6-9. The ending inventory includes the earliest costs, which consist of the beginning inventory and the cost of the 10 units from the first purchase on April 10. The cost of goods sold is computed by subtracting the ending inventory from the cost of goods available for sale and implicitly includes the cost of the 70 units purchased on April 20 ($840) and the cost of 70 units purchased on April 10 ($770).

---

**EXHIBIT 6-9**

**DALTON COMPANY**

**Last-In, First-Out Inventory Cost Flow Assumption (Periodic Inventory System)**

Ending Inventory (110 units):

| | |
|---|---:|
| 100 units @ $10 | $1,000 |
| 10 units @ $11 | 110 |
| | $1,110 |

Cost of Goods Sold (140 units):

| Beginning Inventory | + | Purchases | − | Ending Inventory | = | Cost of Goods Sold |
|---|---|---|---|---|---|---|
| $1,000 | + | $1,720 | − | $1,110 | = | $1,610 |

---

If the Dalton Company is using a perpetual inventory system (for costs as well as physical quantities), the cost of goods sold is calculated for each sale at the cost(s) of the most recent purchase(s). The $1,580 cost of goods sold for 140 units includes the sale of 90 units on April 18 and 50 units on April 27, as shown in Exhibit 6-10. For the April 18 sale, 80 of the 90 units have a cost of $11 each from the April 10 purchase and 10 units have a cost of $10 each from the beginning inventory. The 50 units on April 27 have a cost of $12 from the April 20 purchase. The $1,140 ending inventory is determined by deducting the $1,580 cost of goods sold from the $2,720 cost of goods available for sale. It consists of 110 units and includes the earliest costs: the cost of the 90 units left from the beginning inventory and the remaining 20 units from the April 20 purchase.

Note that the cost of goods sold and the ending inventory are different between the LIFO perpetual method and the LIFO periodic method due to the differing assumptions about the timing of the sales. Under the periodic method, the whole accounting period (a month in this example) is treated as a single time period, and all the sales are assumed to take place after all the units have been purchased during the period. Therefore the cost of goods sold includes the costs of the *most recent purchases of the period*. Under the perpetual method, each event is recorded as it occurs. Therefore, the cost of goods sold is calculated when each sale is made and includes the costs of the *most recent purchase(s) at that time*.

In the Dalton Company example, unit sales are less than unit purchases for the period. Therefore, under the *periodic* inventory system, costs from the beginning inventory are *not* included in cost of goods sold. However, the first sale in the month is

---

**EXHIBIT 6-10**

**DALTON COMPANY**

Last-In, First-Out Inventory Cost Flow Assumption
(Perpetual Inventory System)

Cost of Goods Sold (140 units):

| | | | |
|---|---|---|---|
| April 18 | 90 units: 80 units @ $11 | | $ 880 |
| | 10 units @ $10 | | 100 |
| April 27 | 50 units @ $12 | | 600 |
| | | | $1,580 |

Ending Inventory (110 units):

Beginning Inventory + Purchases − Cost of Goods Sold = Ending Inventory
    $1,000    +   $1,720  −      $1,580    =     $1,140*

---

*90 units @ $10 = $ 900
 20 units @ $12 =   240
              $1,140

---

larger than the first purchase. Therefore, under the *perpetual* inventory system, the costs of 10 units of the beginning inventory are included in cost of goods sold. Furthermore, under the perpetual system, the second sale of 50 units has a cost of $12 per unit from the second purchase, leaving 20 units of that purchase in inventory. However, under the periodic system, the entire purchase of units at $12 each is included in the cost of goods sold, leaving none in inventory. These factors explain the difference of $30 in the cost of goods sold and the ending inventory between the two methods.

In each case the LIFO ending inventory of the Dalton Company consists of two layers. Each period in which the number of units in inventory *increases,* a layer of costs is added to the LIFO inventory. When the number of units in inventory *decreases,* the costs are removed from the beginning inventory of the period in the reverse order in which they were added—that is, the most recent layers added are removed first.

## Comparison of Inventory Cost Flow Assumptions

The cost of goods sold and the inventory amounts for the Dalton Company calculated in the preceding examples are summarized in Exhibit 6-11. However, the specific identification method is excluded because, as discussed previously, the results are dependent on the assumptions regarding the particular units selected for sale.

In this example, costs rose throughout the period. As a result the FIFO method produces the lowest cost of goods sold because it includes the oldest, and lowest, costs. Since the cost of goods sold is lowest, the income is highest. Correspondingly, the ending inventory using FIFO has the highest cost because it includes the most recent, and highest, costs. In contrast, the LIFO method produces the highest cost of goods sold (and the lowest income) because it includes the most recent, and highest, costs. The LIFO ending inventory is lowest because it includes the earliest, and lowest, costs. The average cost amounts are between the FIFO and LIFO extremes because

**EXHIBIT 6-11**

## DALTON COMPANY

Effects of Inventory Cost Flow Assumptions

| Cost Flow Assumption | Cost of Goods Available for Sale | Cost of Goods Sold | Ending Inventory |
|---|---|---|---|
| FIFO, periodic | $2,720 | $1,440 | $1,280 |
| FIFO, perpetual | 2,720 | 1,440 | 1,280 |
| Weighted average, periodic | 2,720 | 1,523 | 1,197 |
| Moving average, perpetual | 2,720 | 1,496 | 1,224 |
| LIFO, periodic | 2,720 | 1,610 | 1,110 |
| LIFO, perpetual | 2,720 | 1,580 | 1,140 |

the ending inventory and the cost of goods sold include an average of both the lower and higher costs of the period. Note that this example is simplified because the beginning inventory was assumed to be $10 per unit for FIFO, average, and LIFO. When an inventory cost flow assumption is used in consecutive periods, the beginning inventory in each period is not the same under the alternative cost flow assumptions.

The Dalton Company was experiencing rising costs, but if costs were falling consistently, the opposite relationships would occur. The use of LIFO would produce a higher ending inventory, a lower cost of goods sold, and a higher income than FIFO. When costs fluctuate, no general relationships can be described.

The differences between the amounts under the periodic and the perpetual inventory systems for each flow assumption result from the different calculations and not from any differences in the logic underlying the flow assumptions. As noted earlier, the LIFO cost of goods sold under the periodic system is the highest because the costs of all sales are assumed to be from the most recent purchases (regardless of when the sale occurs). When LIFO is used with a perpetual system, the cost of each sale is assumed to be from the most recent purchase at that point in time. Under the average cost flow assumption, the differences occur because the moving average method computes a new average cost after each purchase, whereas the weighted average method computes a single average cost for the period. There are no differences between the amounts under the periodic and perpetual methods for the FIFO system.

## CONCEPTUAL EVALUATION OF INVENTORY COST FLOW ASSUMPTIONS

Many arguments can be made in favor of each of the alternative cost flow assumptions. These arguments focus on a comparison of LIFO and FIFO, although they also apply to the average cost method, which usually represents a middle ground. The advantages of LIFO are that it provides a better measure of income in times of rising costs, and it results in the payment of less income taxes. The disadvantages of LIFO are the impact of the liquidation of LIFO layers, the possibility of income manipulation, the inventory valuation on the balance sheet, and the lack of comparability between companies using LIFO. There also are several issues involved in management's selection of a method. Each of these is discussed and evaluated in the following sections. In addition, specific arguments that relate solely to the average cost method are discussed. The arguments for and against the specific identification method were discussed earlier in the chapter.

### Income Measurement

*Income measurement in situations of changing prices is discussed in Chapter 24.*

For financial reporting, the basic criterion to be used in the choice of a cost flow method is to achieve a "proper determination of income through the process of matching appropriate costs and revenues."[5] **There is no requirement that the assumed flow of costs be related to the actual physical flow of goods.** Most companies would be expected to use a FIFO method for the physical management of inventory so as to reduce the likelihood of obsolescence. Such companies may use any of the alternative cost flow assumptions in their financial statements.

But what are "appropriate" costs? Unfortunately there is no simple answer as to whether income is better measured under LIFO or FIFO. Both methods match historical costs with revenues, but **the major argument in favor of LIFO is that it matches the most recent costs with revenue.** The most recent costs are closer to replacement costs. Therefore LIFO excludes from net income some (but not all) of the holding gains, so that net income reflects the earnings after capital has been maintained. **A holding gain (or inventory profit) is the difference between the historical cost and the replacement cost of units sold.** In contrast, FIFO matches the earliest costs with revenue and *includes* all the holding gains in income.

In the Dalton Company example, when the company sells a unit on April 27 for $30, if the unit cost of the goods sold is considered to be $10 (FIFO) and the most recent acquisition cost has been $12 per unit, the gross profit of $20 per unit (the selling price of $30 minus the cost of $10) includes a holding gain of $2 per unit (the most recent cost to replace the inventory of $12 less the cost of $10). The LIFO method records in cost of goods sold the cost of $12 per unit, resulting in a gross profit of $18 per unit, thereby *excluding* the holding gain of $2 from income. These two alternatives are illustrated in Exhibit 6-12. To continue this example, suppose that the company started with $10 cash, which it used to purchase a unit of inventory. When that unit is sold for $30, the profit (under FIFO) is recognized as $20. If the $20 income is distributed as a dividend, the company is left with $10 cash, which is not enough to purchase a unit of inventory at its higher price of $12. Thus the

---

### EXHIBIT 6-12

#### ALTERNATIVE COST FLOW ASSUMPTIONS AND HOLDING GAINS (PER UNIT)

|  | FIFO | LIFO ($12) | LIFO ($11) |
|---|---|---|---|
| Revenue | $30 | $30 | $30 |
| Cost of goods sold | (10) | (12) | (11) |
| Gross profit | $20 | $18 | $19 |
| Holding gains (excluded from income) |  | 2 | 1 |
|  |  | $20 | $20 |

---

5.  *Accounting Research and Terminology Bulletins, Final Edition, op. cit.*

income of $20 includes a holding gain of $2, which is not real income since it cannot be distributed to the owners without leaving the company worse off in terms of its ability to maintain the same level of inventory.

In this example, the LIFO method excluded all the holding gains. However, in other situations, it may not exclude them all. Under LIFO the Dalton Company included units at $11 per unit in the cost of goods sold (for the periodic method), whereas the most recent purchase price was $12 per unit. This alternative also is illustrated in Exhibit 6-12. Therefore the gross profit included holding gains of $1 on each of these units.

Also note that if the replacement cost of the inventory was $13 at the end of the month, the Dalton Company has not achieved the matching of current costs with revenue, even on the $12 units, and would include even more holding gains in income. In summary, it can be seen that "matching appropriate costs and revenues" is interpreted very widely. FIFO, LIFO, average cost, and specific identification all match historical cost with revenue, and are generally accepted accounting principles.

## Income Tax Effects

As has been seen, LIFO produces the lowest income under conditions of rising costs. Although it might be thought that management would consider it undesirable to report low *accounting* income, it must be remembered that lower *taxable* income results in payment of lower income taxes. For example, three long-time LIFO users— Amoco, General Motors, and Ford—have together saved more than $2 billion in taxes compared to what they would have paid using FIFO.

The use of LIFO for the computation of federal income taxes presents a special situation. The Internal Revenue Code permits the use of LIFO for income tax purposes only if it is also used in the company's financial statements. This requirement is known as the LIFO conformity rule. The management of a company might prefer to report the highest income for accounting purposes when costs are rising by using FIFO even though, as discussed before, the income is overstated because holding gains are included. The LIFO conformity rule prevents management from having "the best of both worlds" by using FIFO for financial reporting and LIFO for income taxes, in contrast to many situations in which different methods can be used (for example, when straight-line depreciation is used for financial reporting and accelerated depreciation for income tax reporting). Management must decide whether it is willing to report a lower accounting income in order to achieve the advantages of the real economic benefits of reduced cash payments for income taxes. Because of rulings by the Internal Revenue Service that allow a company using LIFO more latitude in the supplementary reporting of cost of goods sold and income, on a FIFO basis, the Securities and Exchange Commission issued a ruling indicating how such disclosures should be made.[6] Also, since there was a lack of authoritative literature on the specifics of applying LIFO in complex situations, the tendency was to follow the income tax rules, which were much more specific. Since this did not always lead to appropriate financial reporting, the AICPA published an *Issues Paper* that was endorsed by the SEC, thereby giving it authoritative status.[7] The specific topics included in these two publications are beyond the scope of this book.

6. "Codification of Financial Reporting Policies," *SEC Accounting Rules* (Chicago: Commerce Clearing House, August, 1988), sec. 205.

7. "Identification and Discussion of Certain Financial Accounting and Reporting Issues Concerning LIFO Inventories," *Issues Paper* (New York: AICPA, 1984), and "LIFO Inventory Accounting Practices for Financial Statement Purposes," *Staff Accounting Bulletin 58* (Washington, D.C.: SEC, 1985).

The Tax Reform Act of 1986 established "uniform capitalization rules" that require companies to include in inventory certain costs that previously had been expensed as incurred for tax purposes. These costs include such items as purchasing, warehousing, and distribution costs, including related officer salaries and administrative costs. Because a cost must be capitalized for income tax purposes does not mean that capitalizing it for financial reporting is preferable, or even appropriate. Each situation would have to be analyzed based on the particular circumstances. The likely result in many situations is that inventory cost will be different between financial reporting and income tax reporting.

## Liquidation of LIFO Layers

A company using the LIFO method may liquidate inventory during a period. This occurs when the number of units in ending inventory is less than the number in beginning inventory because unit sales have exceeded units acquired during the period (that is, all purchased units plus some units from the beginning inventory are sold). Some of the beginning inventory costs are included in cost of goods sold. In other words, the layers of LIFO inventory costs added in previous periods are removed in reverse order; the last costs added are the first expensed. Assuming rising costs, these units have lower costs attached to them; thus cost of goods sold is lower and income is higher than if the liquidation did not occur. This increased amount of gross profit is referred to as a **LIFO liquidation profit.** Many companies adopted LIFO when, in 1939, the method was first allowed to be used by all companies for income tax purposes and also in the higher inflation period between 1975 and 1985. An extreme example of LIFO liquidation profits arises if there is a liquidation of inventory down to the base (the beginning inventory in the year LIFO was adopted). In summary, liquidations bring units with a cost from previous years into cost of goods sold and produce an unrealistically high income figure.

To illustrate the concept of a LIFO liquidation profit, assume that a company was formed in 1991. Its 1995 beginning inventory of $644,000 is made up of four layers as follows:

| | | |
|---|---|---|
| 1991: | 10,000 units at $20 per unit = | $200,000 |
| 1992: | 6,000 units at $22 per unit = | 132,000 |
| 1993: | 8,000 units at $24 per unit = | 192,000 |
| 1994: | 4,000 units at $30 per unit = | 120,000 |
| Inventory, January 1, 1995 | | $644,000 |

In 1995 the company purchases (or manufactures) 50,000 units at $35 per unit but sells 60,000 units. The company has experienced an inventory liquidation of 10,000 units. These 10,000 units are included in cost of goods sold at the most recent beginning inventory costs; that is, the most recently added layers. Therefore, the company's cost of goods sold for 1995 includes costs from 1995, 1994, and 1993, as follows:

| | |
|---|---|
| 50,000 units at $35 per unit = $1,750,000 | (1995 costs) |
| 4,000 units at $30 per unit = 120,000 | (1994 costs) |
| 6,000 units at $24 per unit = 144,000 | (1993 costs) |
| 60,000 | $2,014,000 |

If, instead, the company had purchased (or produced) 60,000 units at $35 each (thus avoiding the LIFO liquidation), the company would have had a cost of goods sold in 1995 of $2,100,000 (60,000 units × $35 per unit) consisting entirely of 1995 costs. The difference of $86,000 ($2,100,000 − $2,014,000) is the LIFO liquidation profit (before income taxes). If we assume an income tax rate of 30%, the effect of the LIFO liquidation is to increase net income by $60,200 ($86,000 × 70%) and income tax expense by $25,800 ($86,000 × 30%). Note that the company's income is higher (because cost of goods sold includes older, and lower, costs) even though there is **no economic substance to the higher income and the company would pay the additional income taxes** (because of the higher taxable income reported under the LIFO conformity rule). Companies that report to the SEC are required to disclose the amount of the LIFO liquidation profit so that users of the financial statements may obtain a better understanding of the profit earned by the company.

## Income Manipulation

As we have seen, the liquidation of inventory under LIFO, whether intentional or not, results in higher income (assuming rising costs). Such a liquidation may be caused by economic factors beyond the control of the company, such as a strike or a scarcity of raw materials, or as a result of a management decision, such as the adoption of a "just-in-time" inventory system, which results in a permanent reduction in the size of the inventory. Also a liquidation may be deliberately created by delaying purchases. Intentional liquidation to increase income artificially is a significant concern. If a company is facing a period of lower profits, management can increase profits intentionally by liquidating inventory. This can be achieved by delaying purchases until after the end of the fiscal year.

Also a company may influence (manipulate) its income by increasing its purchases. To illustrate, refer back to the Dalton Company periodic LIFO example and assume that the company purchased an additional 40 units on April 29 at $12 per unit. Total purchases then would be $2,200 ($1,720 + $480). The ending inventory would then consist of 150 units (110 + 40) and have a cost of $1,550 (100 units at $10 each from the beginning inventory + 50 units at $11 each from the April 10 purchase). The cost of goods sold would be computed as follows:

$$\textbf{Beginning Inventory} + \textbf{Purchases} - \textbf{Ending Inventory} = \textbf{Cost of Goods Sold}$$
$$\$1,000 \quad\quad + \quad \$2,200 \quad - \quad\quad \$1,550 \quad\quad = \quad\quad \underline{\$1,650}$$

Thus purchasing additional units has increased cost of goods sold by $40 ($1,650 − $1,610) even though unit sales remain unchanged. **It is inconsistent with the revenue recognition principle for income to be affected by the purchasing activities of a company,** but it is an inevitable result of the LIFO method. The FIFO and average cost methods do not produce unusual results when inventory liquidation occurs, nor are they as susceptible to profit manipulation by management.

Management should make decisions about purchasing or manufacturing inventory on the basis of economic and operational factors. The use of LIFO, however, does allow management to influence the company's income through the acceleration of, or delay in, acquiring inventory.

## Inventory Valuation

The LIFO method produces a lower ending (and beginning) inventory value on the balance sheet (again assuming rising costs) because the oldest costs remain in this inventory. The recorded amount of this inventory often bears little or no relationship to the costs of the current period or the costs that will be incurred to replace the inventory, and therefore is *not relevant*. This low valuation affects the computation and evaluation of current assets, working capital, and any financial ratios that include inventory, thereby *reducing comparability* between companies using LIFO and those using FIFO. Furthermore, comparability between two or more companies using LIFO is impaired, because the inventory valuation depends on the year in which LIFO was adopted by each company. For example, if companies in the same industry adopted LIFO in different years, the LIFO base will include costs of different years. (The year of adoption is *not* a required disclosure.) In addition, if the companies increase their inventories by different amounts in subsequent years, the additional LIFO layers will have been added at different costs.

The FIFO method produces a higher ending inventory value on the balance sheet (assuming rising costs) because it includes the most recent costs. This value tends to approximate the costs that will be incurred to replace the inventory, but how closely depends on when the purchases included in the ending inventory were made and how fast costs are rising. Therefore, the FIFO inventory value is more *relevant*.

## Average Cost

The average cost method is based on the assumption that during the period all the costs are commingled so that those included in cost of goods sold cannot be distinguished from those remaining in inventory. Thus the method produces the same cost in a particular period for identical units that have the same utility. The weighted average method treats the accounting period as a single time period and produces the same unit cost for cost of goods sold and ending inventory. The general principle underlying the moving average method is the same, except that the period used is the time between the respective purchases. The same unit cost is used for the sales made in that time period and for the inventory at the end of that period. However, over the total accounting period, the unit costs used for the cost of goods sold vary as each purchase is made, and the unit cost for the ending inventory is the average cost calculated after the last purchase of the period.

The disadvantage of the average cost method is that the average is continually affected by the costs incurred in previous periods. Although the influence from these past periods becomes minimal as time passes, it still means that the average cost does not reflect the actual costs paid either for the units sold or for those held in inventory in the current period.

## Management's Selection of an Inventory Cost Flow Assumption

The previous discussion has shown that there are many financial accounting and tax issues involved in the selection of an inventory cost flow assumption. In most cases, however, the decision should focus on the expectation of future cost changes.

If the management of a company expects that costs will *rise* for several years into the future, LIFO should be selected because, as discussed earlier, it is a better measure of income. Also the LIFO conformity rule will allow the use of LIFO for income tax reporting and the company will save income taxes. Therefore the financial reporting rules and the income tax rules are consistent.

The additional cash that results from the tax savings is reduced because the LIFO method is more costly to use than the FIFO method. These costs result from the additional costs of record keeping and financial statement preparation such as keeping track of the LIFO layers for each type of inventory and the requirements imposed by the Internal Revenue Service. For a small company, these additional costs may be greater than the income tax savings that would result from the adoption of LIFO. For larger companies, however, the income tax savings are likely to exceed the additional costs (assuming rising prices), as is evidenced by the number of companies that use LIFO (see Exhibit 6-18).

Alternatively, if the expectation is that costs will *fall* for several years in the future, the decision is not as simple. For financial reporting purposes, it can be argued that LIFO is still preferable because the latest (and lowest) costs should be included in cost of goods sold because the inventory can be replaced at those lower costs. However, for income tax purposes, the use of FIFO is preferable because the company pays less income taxes. Although a company could use LIFO internally and FIFO for income taxes, it is unlikely to do so because of the additional record keeping costs it would incur. Therefore, if falling costs are expected, FIFO will be used. Unfortunately, this means that income tax considerations are determining the accounting principle used for financial reporting.

Arguments are made that LIFO should not be adopted even when costs are expected to rise because of the lower income that will result and a possible perception that the company is less successful and that the stock price will be lower. However, efficient capital markets research, discussed in Chapter 1, has indicated that stock market prices are *not* affected by the selection of an inventory cost flow assumption.

In most situations the FIFO and weighted average *cost* flow assumptions approximate the *physical* flow of the items in inventory, whereas LIFO does not. For example, a retail store will try to impose a FIFO physical flow on its customers by selling the oldest items first, but the customers may impose more of an average flow on the store by the way they select items from the shelves. However, accounting principles do *not* require that the selected cost flow method approximate the physical flow of goods but only that the method be systematic, based on cost, and match costs and revenues appropriately, as discussed earlier. Therefore selection of a particular cost flow assumption should not depend on the perceived physical flow of goods.

Management also may be reluctant to adopt LIFO if bonuses are paid on the basis of accounting income. This tends to discourage management from using LIFO in periods of rising costs, since the lower reported income produces lower bonuses. In addition, a higher income results in higher earnings per share and a higher rate of return, factors that are considered important by many users of financial statements. It must be remembered, however, that using a method other than LIFO in periods of rising costs causes the company to pay additional taxes.

There are several additional miscellaneous disadvantages of LIFO that a company should consider before adopting LIFO. First, the adoption of LIFO could increase income taxes initially because the income tax rules require that the opening inventory in the year that LIFO is adopted must be stated at cost. Therefore, if the inventory previously had been written down to a market value lower than cost for income tax purposes (as discussed in Chapter 7), it would be necessary to write the inventory back up and pay additional taxes on that amount. Second, the use of LIFO might also cause a company to be limited in its financial flexibility because of covenants included in its bond indentures or other borrowing agreements. For example, the company might be required to maintain a certain current ratio or debt-to-equity ratio.

Finally, the use of LIFO might cause a company to be less concerned about controlling the level of its inventories because of the company's lower *apparent* investment in those inventories.

Although our discussion focuses on FIFO and LIFO, many manufacturing companies that expect falling costs use the average cost flow assumption in their financial statements. This method is used because (1) the company operates a standard cost system (discussed in a cost accounting book) for its budgeting and control and (2) it is unlikely to result in significantly more income taxes than FIFO.

## DOLLAR-VALUE LIFO

The dollar-value LIFO method follows the same cost flow assumption as the LIFO method, but it overcomes three difficulties involved in the application of the simple LIFO approach.

First, the LIFO method requires a great deal of detailed record keeping. As with other methods, it is necessary to record the physical quantities of each item in inventory from either a physical count or the perpetual inventory records. Then, in addition, unit costs must be applied from the years since LIFO was adopted, in the LIFO order. Finally the liquidations in LIFO inventory that may have occurred over the years must be accounted for correctly.

Second, fluctuations in the physical quantities of similar inventory items may occur. For example, the quantity of one inventory item may significantly decline during a period causing a partial liquidation of its LIFO layers, whereas the quantity of a very similar inventory item may increase. As these fluctuations occur over time, the LIFO layers for each individual item would be reduced, thereby removing many of the advantages of LIFO.

Third, as technological changes take place, inventory made with one material is replaced by inventory made with substitute materials or an outdated design is replaced by a newer design. Strict application of the LIFO method requires a new LIFO base be started for the new inventory item and as the old item is phased out, its inventory would be reduced to zero. This would eliminate the advantages of LIFO built up in previous periods. With the rate of technological change in many industries, the advantages of LIFO would be lost.

Dollar-value LIFO overcomes part of the first problem by the use of current costs and cost indexes, and the second and third problems by the use of *inventory pools*. Under the dollar-value LIFO method, the inventory may be grouped into pools that are similar as to types of material or use. It would be possible for some companies to consider their entire inventory as one pool, but usually several pools are used. Cost indexes and inventory pools are discussed in more detail later in the chapter.

The general principle underlying the dollar-value LIFO method is that the ending inventory is initially valued at current cost and this cost is "rolled back" to the cost at the beginning of the base year (the year in which LIFO was adopted) to *eliminate the change in costs* from the physical quantity of the ending inventory. A comparison of the year's beginning and ending inventory at base-year costs indicates whether there has been a real increase (or decrease) in the physical quantity of the inventory. The increase (or decrease) is "rolled forward" to the appropriate current cost level, and this layer of current cost is added to (or subtracted from) the beginning inventory to determine the ending inventory. The application of the dollar-value LIFO method requires the steps shown in Exhibit 6-13.

> ### EXHIBIT 6-13
>
> ## DOLLAR-VALUE LIFO CALCULATION STEPS
>
> 1. Value the total ending inventory at current-year costs.
>
> 2. Convert (roll back) the ending inventory cost to base-year costs by applying the base-year conversion index:
>
> $$\text{Ending Inventory at Base-Year Costs} = \frac{\text{Base-Year Cost Index}}{\text{Current Cost Index}} \times \text{Ending Inventory at Current-Year Costs}$$
>
> 3. Compute the change in the inventory level (physical quantity) for the year at base-year costs by comparing the ending inventory at base-year costs with the beginning inventory at base-year costs.
>
> 4. a. If there is an increase in the inventory level at base-year costs, there has been a real *increase* in the physical quantity of the inventory over the year. Convert (roll forward) this increase to current-year costs by applying the current-year conversion index:
>
> $$\text{Layer Increase at Current-Year Costs} = \text{Increase at Base-Year Costs} \times \frac{\text{Current Cost Index}}{\text{Base-Year Cost Index}}$$
>
> The ending inventory is the dollar-value LIFO inventory cost at the beginning of the year *plus* the layer increase at current-year costs.
>
> b. If there is a decrease in the inventory level at base-year costs, there has been a real *decrease* in the physical quantity of the inventory over the period. This decrease reduces the inventory on a LIFO layer basis, and therefore it must be converted to the costs of the most recently added layer, or layers:
>
> $$\begin{array}{l}\text{Decrease at Costs of} \\ \text{Most Recently Added Layer}\end{array} = \text{Decrease at Base-Year Costs} \times \frac{\text{Cost Index of Most Recently Added Layer}}{\text{Base-Year Cost Index}}$$
>
> The ending inventory is the dollar-value LIFO cost at the beginning of the year *minus* the decrease at the costs of the most recently added layer. Note that the decrease may eliminate more than one layer of LIFO inventory, and therefore the decrease at base-year costs has to be converted to the costs of as many layers as is necessary to eliminate the total decrease.

It is necessary to convert the inventory to base-year costs in order to isolate the *quantity* increase from the *cost* increase. To illustrate that a comparison of base-year *costs* reflects changes in *quantity,* consider the following two simplified examples. First, assume a company has a beginning inventory of 100 units at $20 each, or $2,000, when it adopts dollar-value LIFO. At the end of the year, it has an ending inventory of 100 units at a current cost of $21 each, or $2,100. It might appear from a simple comparison of the two costs ($2,100 versus $2,000) that the *physical quantity* of the inventory has increased. However, this is not the case. The quantity has remained unchanged, and the cost change (from $20 to $21 per unit, or an increase of 5%) has accounted for the entire change in the cost of the inventory. Reducing the inventory of $2,100 to the base-year costs gives an amount of $2,000 [$2,100 × (100 ÷ 105) = $2,000]. Since the beginning and ending inventory amounts are $2,000 when they are both measured in terms of the same costs (base year), there has been no increase in quantity. The increase from $2,000 to $2,100 has resulted solely from the increase in costs.

In the second example, we can isolate the quantity increase from the cost increase without knowing the number and costs of the units. To illustrate, assume a beginning inventory of $1,000 and a cost index (discussed later) of 100 when dollar-value LIFO was adopted. Assume further that the ending inventory at current cost is $1,430 and costs have increased 10%; that is, the cost index is 110 (100 × 1.10 = 110). The quantity increase in the inventory is not 43% ($1,430 ÷ $1,000 = 1.43). Rather, the ending inventory at base-year costs is $1,300 [$1,430 × (100 ÷ 110) = $1,300], and therefore inventory has increased in quantity by 30% ($1,300 ÷ $1,000 = 1.30). The total increase of 43% in the value of the inventory is made up of an increase in the quantity of 30% and a cost increase of 10% (1.30 × 1.10 = 1.43). To complete the example, the increase in inventory of $300 at base-year costs is converted to ending costs of $330 [$300 × (110 ÷ 100)], and therefore the LIFO ending inventory is valued at $1,330 ($1,000 + $330).

The application of the four steps discussed in Exhibit 6-13 is illustrated for the Wagner Company. The basic data are provided in Exhibit 6-14. The Wagner Company adopted LIFO at the beginning of 1994 and has taken an ending inventory at the *current costs* for each year as indicated. In addition, the company has experienced yearly changes in the level of its costs as indicated by its cost index for each year (the determination of a cost index is discussed later).

## EXHIBIT 6-14

### WAGNER COMPANY

| Date | Ending Inventory at Current Costs | Cost Index |
|---|---|---|
| January 1, 1994 | $10,000 | 100 |
| December 31, 1994 | 12,100 | 110 |
| December 31, 1995 | 13,125 | 125 |
| December 31, 1996 | 16,800 | 140 |
| December 31, 1997 | 12,360 | 120 |

The calculation of the dollar-value LIFO ending inventory is shown in Exhibit 6-15. The base year is 1994 and therefore the beginning inventory (i.e., the 1993 ending inventory) needs no adjustment. The 1994 ending inventory at the current cost of $12,100 is reduced to $11,000 at base-year costs. Therefore the real (quantity) increase in inventory is $1,000 ($11,000 − $10,000 at base-year costs), which is $1,100 [$1,000 × (110 ÷ 100)] in 1994 costs. The ending LIFO inventory cost for 1994 is $11,100, which is made up of two layers, the base layer of $10,000 plus the layer added in 1994 of $1,100.

In 1995 the ending inventory at the current cost of $13,125 is reduced to $10,500 at base-year costs. This indicates a real (quantity) *decrease* in inventory of $500 (the $10,500 1995 ending inventory less the $11,000 1994 ending inventory, *both* at base-year costs). The decrease must be subtracted from the most recently added layer, which is that layer added in 1994. Therefore the decrease of $500 in base-year costs is converted to 1994 costs and *not* to 1995 costs. Consequently the 110 cost index is applied to the $500 decrease, resulting in a decrease of $550 in terms of 1994 costs and an ending inventory of $10,550.

## EXHIBIT 6-15

### WAGNER COMPANY

Dollar-Value LIFO Inventory Calculations

| Date | Ending Inventory at Current Costs | × | Base-Year Cost Index / Current Cost Index | = | Inventory at Base-Year Costs | Increase (Decrease) at Base-Year Costs | × | Relevant Cost Index = Base-Year Cost Index / Base-Year Cost Index | = | Increase (Decrease) at Relevant Current Costs | Ending Inventory at LIFO | Layers in LIFO Ending Inventory |
|---|---|---|---|---|---|---|---|---|---|---|---|---|
| 1/1/94 | | | | | $10,000 | — | | — | | — | $10,000 | $10,000 |
| 12/31/94 | $12,100 | × | $\frac{100}{110}$ | = | 11,000 | $1,000 | × | $\frac{110}{100}$ | = | $1,100 | 11,100 | 10,000 ($10,000 @ 100) 1,100 ($1,000 @ 110) |
| 12/31/95 | 13,125 | × | $\frac{100}{125}$ | = | 10,500 | (500) | × | $\frac{110}{100}$ | = | (550) | 10,550 | 10,000 ($10,000 @ 100) 550 ($500 @ 110) |
| 12/31/96 | 16,800 | × | $\frac{100}{140}$ | = | 12,000 | 1,500 | × | $\frac{140}{100}$ | = | 2,100 | 12,650 | 10,000 ($10,000 @ 100) 550 ($500 @110) 2,100 ($1,500 @ 140) |
| 12/31/97 | 12,360 | × | $\frac{100}{120}$ | = | 10,300 | (1,500) (200) | × | $\frac{140}{100}$ $\frac{110}{100}$ | = | (2,100) (220) | 10,330 | 10,000 ($10,000 @ 100) 330 ($300 @ 110) |

In 1995 there is an increase in inventory at base-year costs, and therefore another layer is added, so that the ending LIFO inventory of $12,650 consists of three layers.

In 1997 there is a decrease in the cost index. The ending inventory at base-year costs is calculated in exactly the same manner as discussed previously. In this case the $10,300 ending inventory at base-year costs is $1,700 lower than the $12,000 beginning inventory at base-year costs. This completely eliminates the layer of $1,500 (at base-year costs) added in 1996, and so it is necessary to go back into the 1994 layer to account for the remaining decrease of $200 at base-year costs (no layer was added in 1995). The ending LIFO inventory of $10,330 consists of the base inventory plus the remainder of the layer added in 1994.

## Determination of Cost Index

The preceding discussion has referred to the use of a cost index rather than a price index. A **cost index** refers to an internally generated index that is specific to the company's particular inventory, whereas a **price index** is a more general index prepared by an external organization, such as a government or trade association. Although the concepts underlying the two are identical, the term *cost index* was used because IRS regulations required that in most situations an internally developed index specific to the company's particular industry be used. However, the IRS has simplified the LIFO method by allowing the use of published price indexes.

If the company uses an internally developed cost index, it must compute an index based on the particular cost per unit it has experienced in the current year as compared to the base year. Typically, the index is prepared using a sample of the total inventory. Two methods to compute the cost index are used in practice, the double-extension method and the link-chain method.

Under the **double-extension** method, a sample of the ending inventory is priced at current-year costs and at base-year costs, and the cost index is computed as follows:

$$\text{Cost Index} = \frac{\text{Sample of Ending Inventory at Current-Year Costs}}{\text{Sample of Ending Inventory at Base-Year Costs}} \times 100$$

This is known as the double-extension method because the ending inventory is priced and extended twice—once at current costs and once at base-year costs. The double-extension method is appropriate for companies that have little change in the characteristics of their inventory items. When changes are frequent, determination of base-year costs for new items is difficult. For example, if a company adopted LIFO in 1980 and develops a new product in 1995, the double-extension method would require the computation of the cost in 1980 of the new product. Since the product, perhaps including the technology, did not exist in 1980, the difficulties of such a calculation are obvious. In such situations, the link-chain method should be used.

Under the **link-chain** method, a sample of the ending inventory is priced at current cost at the end of the current year and at the end of the previous year. The ratio of the current-year current cost to the previous-year current cost is used to compute a cost index for the *year*. This index is multiplied by the cost index carried forward from the previous year to determine the current year cumulative index as follows:

$$\text{Cost Index} = \frac{\begin{array}{c}\text{Sample of Ending Inventory}\\ \text{at Ending Current Costs}\end{array}}{\begin{array}{c}\text{Sample of Ending Inventory}\\ \text{at Previous-Year Current Costs}\end{array}} \times \begin{array}{c}\text{Previous Year}\\ \text{Cost Index}\end{array}$$

## Inventory Pools

As discussed earlier in the chapter, companies may use inventory pools in conjunction with dollar-value LIFO. The purpose of the pools is to maintain the benefits from using LIFO when fluctuations in the physical quantities of similar inventory items occur and when technological change takes place.

To illustrate the concept of an inventory pool, consider the Herrmann Soup Company, which adopts dollar-value LIFO on January 1, 1995, using a single pool. The pool includes three types of soup that the company manufactures, and the calculation of the total cost of the beginning inventory is shown in Exhibit 6-16. A cost index of 100 is assigned to the beginning inventory by the company and will be used as the base for the calculation of the cost index in subsequent years.

### EXHIBIT 6-16

**HERRMANN SOUP COMPANY**

Inventory, January 1, 1995

| Type | Quantity | Cost per Unit | Total Cost |
|---|---|---|---|
| Mushroom | 10,000 | $0.25 | $2,500 |
| Vegetable | 8,000 | 0.20 | 1,600 |
| Tomato | 22,000 | 0.16 | 3,520 |
| | 40,000 | | $7,620 |

During 1995, the transactions shown in Exhibit 6-17 occurred. The company purchased a total of 150,000 cans of soup and sold 139,000 cans, leaving 51,000 cans in ending inventory, including the quantities of each type as illustrated. Using the double-extension method, the company calculates the cost index of 107 for the ending inventory by dividing the ending inventory at current-year costs by the ending inventory at base-year costs. Completing the remaining steps in the dollar-value LIFO calculations results in an ending inventory at LIFO cost of $10,167, as shown in Exhibit 6-17.

The preceding discussion assumed that the entire ending inventory cost was considered to be a single inventory "pool." When a company is using the dollar-value LIFO method, however, the inventory may be included in one or several "inventory pools." IRS regulations do not specify what types of items are to be included in the same pool other than to say they should be "substantially similar." If a company uses more than one pool, a separate cost index must be computed for each (or a representative sample of the pool). In general, the more items included in a pool, the more likely it is that increases in some items will offset decreases in other items in the pool, thereby avoiding the liquidation of LIFO layers and the loss of the tax benefits of LIFO. In other words, a company would typically prefer to have the fewest number of pools. In a surprising decision in 1982, Stauffer Chemical Company increased its LIFO pools from 8 to 280 which increased its income by $16.5 million (and resulted in additional taxes being paid).

**EXHIBIT 6-17**

## HERRMANN SOUP COMPANY

Purchases and Sales During 1995

| Type | Beginning Quantity | Quantity Purchased | Cost per Unit | Quantity Sold | Inventory Quantity December 31, 1995 |
|------|------|------|------|------|------|
| Mushroom | 10,000 | 60,000 | $0.30 | 54,000 | 16,000 |
| Vegetable | 8,000 | 40,000 | 0.24 | 38,000 | 10,000 |
| Tomato | 22,000 | 50,000 | 0.14 | 47,000 | 25,000 |
|  | 40,000 | 150,000 |  | 139,000 | 51,000 |

$$\text{Cost Index} = \frac{\text{Ending Inventory at Current-Year Costs}}{\text{Ending Inventory at Base-Year Costs}} \times 100$$

$$= \frac{(16,000 \times \$0.30) + (10,000 \times \$0.24) + (25,000 \times \$0.14)}{(16,000 \times \$0.25) + (10,000 \times \$0.20) + (25,000 \times \$0.16)} \times 100$$

$$= \frac{\$10,700}{\$10,000} \times 100$$

$$= 107$$

LIFO Cost of Ending Inventory

$$\text{Ending Inventory at Base-Year Costs} = \frac{\text{Base-Year Cost Index}}{\text{Current Cost Index}} \times \begin{array}{c}\text{Ending Inventory} \\ \text{at Current-Year Costs}\end{array}$$

$$= \frac{100}{107} \times \$10,700$$

$$= \$10,000$$

$$\text{Increase in Inventory at Base-Year Costs} = \begin{array}{c}\text{Ending Inventory at} \\ \text{Base-Year Costs}\end{array} - \begin{array}{c}\text{Beginning Inventory} \\ \text{at Base-Year Costs}\end{array}$$

$$= \$10,000 - \$7,620$$

$$= \$2,380$$

$$\text{Layer Increase at Current-Year Costs} = \begin{array}{c}\text{Increase at} \\ \text{Base-Year Costs}\end{array} \times \frac{\text{Current Cost Index}}{\text{Base-Year Cost Index}}$$

$$= \$2,380 \times \frac{107}{100}$$

$$= \$2,547 \text{ (rounded)}$$

$$\text{Total LIFO Ending Inventory Cost} = \$7,620 + \$2,547$$

$$= \underline{\$10,167}$$

Note also that the current cost used in the dollar-value LIFO calculations can be the cost of the first acquisitions in a year, the last acquisitions in a year, or the average cost of all acquisitions during the year as assumed in the preceding example. Once a choice is made, however, it must be applied consistently.

## ADDITIONAL LIFO CONSIDERATIONS

Several other items concerning LIFO are important, including the LIFO valuation adjustment, interim statements using LIFO, a change to or from LIFO and international accounting differences. These topics are discussed in the following sections.

### LIFO Valuation Adjustment

Frequently, a company uses LIFO for external financial reporting and income tax purposes but uses another method for internal reporting. In this case, a valuation adjustment is made to convert the company's internally reported ending inventory to LIFO for external reporting. This adjustment increases (decreases) cost of goods sold for the period and decreases (increases) the ending inventory by the amount of the *change* in the difference between the beginning and ending inventories under the two methods. The inventory account, however, is not adjusted directly. Instead, a valuation account is used. This account has a variety of names including *Valuation Allowance* or (inappropriately) *LIFO Reserve*. Typically, this account is not part of the formal accounting system, but it often does appear in the balance sheet or the notes, because the SEC requires its disclosure. When this occurs, the *cumulative* balance in the account is treated as an adjustment to report the ending inventory at LIFO. This situation is illustrated by the disclosures of Wal-Mart and Harsco in Exhibit 6-19.

It should also be noted that the *change* in the LIFO reserve for the year is the difference between the LIFO cost of goods sold and what the cost of goods sold would have been under the method used internally. The *total* amount of the LIFO reserve is the cumulative difference between the two cost of goods sold amounts since LIFO was adopted. Multiplying this amount by the income tax rate gives the cumulative savings in income tax expense, while multiplying the amount by the after-tax rate gives the cumulative effect on income.

### Interim Statements Using LIFO

If a company uses LIFO for annual reporting purposes, it must, of course, use LIFO for interim (e.g., quarterly) reporting purposes. **APB Opinion No. 28** states that if a company using LIFO has an inventory liquidation at an interim date that is expected to be replaced by the end of the annual period, the inventory does not include the LIFO liquidation, and cost of sales includes the expected cost of replacement of the liquidated LIFO inventory.[8]

*Interim financial reporting is discussed in Chapter 23.*

Consequently, when a company has an inventory liquidation at the end of a quarter, it must make a forecast of its year-end physical quantities. If the forecast indicates that there will be no liquidation at the end of the year, the impact of the LIFO liquidation is removed from the interim financial statements. The inventory value is decreased, and the cost of goods sold increased, by the difference between the replacement cost and the LIFO cost of the number of units that have been liquidated. If the forecast indicates that the liquidation will still exist at the end of the year, the impact of the LIFO liquidation is included in the interim financial statements.

### Change to or from LIFO

*Accounting changes are discussed in Chapter 22.*

Although the adoption of an inventory cost flow assumption is a long-term decision, a company may occasionally change its method. When the change is *to* LIFO from

---

8. "Interim Financial Reporting," *APB Opinion No. 28* (New York: AICPA, 1973), par. 14(b).

another method, usually the effect on the results of prior periods is not determinable. Thus, as prescribed by **APB Opinion No. 20,** only the effect of the change on the results of current operations is disclosed. If the effect on prior periods is determinable, then it is disclosed by a cumulative effect change. A change to another method *from* LIFO is applied by retroactively restating the results of prior periods.[9]

### International Accounting Differences

There is one significant difference among international accounting principles for inventory costing. LIFO is not allowed for financial reporting in many foreign countries, such as Australia, Sweden, and the United Kingdom. This prohibition may exist because LIFO is not permitted to be used for income tax purposes in those countries and therefore there has been no incentive to allow its use for financial reporting. It also may be prohibited because it is clearly inconsistent with any presumed physical flow of the inventory, an issue that has not been considered relevant for U.S. accounting principles.

## DISCLOSURE OF INVENTORY VALUES AND METHODS

It has been seen that there are many alternative inventory methods. The relative use of the different methods by 600 surveyed companies and the proportion of the inventory cost determined by LIFO are shown in Exhibit 6-18. The trend to the use of LIFO between 1975 and 1985 is clearly indicated, although the trend has reversed with the lower inflation since then. There were more than 600 responses to the methods used, since many companies apply more than one method, as indicated by the categories listed in the second section.

### EXHIBIT 6-18

#### INVENTORY COST DETERMINATION

| | Number of Companies | | | | | | | | |
|---|---|---|---|---|---|---|---|---|---|
| | 1991 | 1989 | 1987 | 1985 | 1983 | 1981 | 1979 | 1977 | 1975 |
| **Methods** | | | | | | | | | |
| First-in, first-out (FIFO) | 421 | 401 | 392 | 381 | 366 | 371 | 390 | 392 | 376 |
| Last-in, first-out (LIFO) | 361 | 366 | 393 | 402 | 408 | 408 | 374 | 332 | 315 |
| Average cost | 200 | 200 | 216 | 223 | 235 | 241 | 241 | 227 | 235 |
| Other | 50 | 48 | 49 | 48 | 52 | 52 | 56 | 47 | 34 |
| | 1,032 | 1,015 | 1,050 | 1,054 | 1,061 | 1,072 | 1,061 | 998 | 960 |
| **Use of LIFO** | | | | | | | | | |
| All inventories | 23 | 26 | 18 | 26 | 31 | 26 | 20 | 10 | 11 |
| 50% or more inventories | 186 | 191 | 221 | 231 | 204 | 210 | 194 | 194 | 125 |
| Less than 50% of inventories | 95 | 99 | 86 | 83 | 93 | 89 | 94 | 93 | 86 |
| Not determinable | 57 | 50 | 68 | 62 | 80 | 83 | 66 | 35 | 93 |
| Not used | 239 | 234 | 207 | 198 | 192 | 192 | 226 | 268 | 285 |
| | 600 | 600 | 600 | 600 | 600 | 600 | 600 | 600 | 600 |

Source: *Accounting Trends and Techniques* (New York: AICPA, 1976, 1978, 1980, 1982, 1984, 1986, 1988, 1990, and 1992).

9. "Accounting Changes," *APB Opinion No. 20* (New York: AICPA, 1971), par. 26.

Examples of the way in which four companies disclose the methods used for inventory are shown in Exhibit 6-19. Companies are required to disclose the inventory method, or methods, used. Masco Corporation and Royal Dutch/Shell each report a single inventory figure in the balance sheet and show the breakdown in the notes to the financial statements. Masco categorizes its inventory by the traditional groups of raw materials, goods in process, and finished goods, while Royal Dutch/Shell categorizes its inventory by type and product. Masco uses FIFO, while Royal Dutch/Shell uses LIFO in the United States and FIFO elsewhere. Wal-Mart Stores discloses the "LIFO reserve" directly in the balance sheet and discloses that it uses the retail method. Harsco Corporation has inventories on long-term contracts and uses FIFO, Average, and LIFO for its remaining inventories. It also discloses the difference between LIFO costs and current costs and the effects of LIFO liquidations.

*The retail method is discussed in Chapter 7.*

*Inventories on long-term contracts are discussed in Chapter 16.*

---

### EXHIBIT 6-19
### Examples of Disclosure of Inventory Values and Methods

**MASCO CORPORATION**

**Balance Sheet**

| Assets (in part) | December 31, 1991 | December 31, 1990 |
|---|---|---|
| Inventories | $738,940,000 | $753,420,000 |

*Notes to Consolidated Financial Statements (in part)*

Inventories (in thousands)

| | At December 31 | |
|---|---|---|
| | 1991 | 1990 |
| Finished goods | $272,130 | $323,160 |
| Raw material | 269,100 | 252,380 |
| Work in process | 197,710 | 177,880 |
| | $738,940 | $753,420 |

Inventories are stated at the lower of cost or net realizable value, with cost determined principally by use of the first-in, first-out method.

**ROYAL DUTCH/SHELL GROUP OF COMPANIES**

**Statement of Assets and Liabilities (in part)**

**(in £ million)**

| | 1991 | 1990 |
|---|---|---|
| Inventories (Note 14) | 4,491 | 5,222 |

*Note 14 Inventories*

(in £ million)

| | 1991 | 1990 |
|---|---|---|
| Inventories of oil, chemicals, coal and metals | 3,794 | 4,576 |
| Inventories of materials | 697 | 646 |
| | 4,491 | 5,222 |

**EXHIBIT 6-19, Continued**
**Examples of Disclosure of Inventory Values and Methods**

Of the total inventories, approximately £399 million in 1991 and £366 in 1990 wholly in the United States are valued by the LIFO method. The excess of FIFO cost over the carrying value of such LIFO inventories was approximately £618 million in 1991 and £914 million in 1990.

**WAL-MART STORES, INC. AND SUBSIDIARIES**

**Balance Sheets**

**(Amounts in thousands)**

|  | January 31, | |
|---|---|---|
|  | **1991** | **1990** |
| *Assets* | | |
| Current assets: | | |
| Cash and cash equivalents | $    13,014 | $    12,790 |
| Receivables | 305,070 | 155,811 |
| Recoverable costs from sale/leaseback | 239,867 | 78,727 |
| Inventories: | | |
| At replacement cost | 6,207,852 | 4,750,619 |
| Less LIFO reserve | 399,436 | 322,546 |
| LIFO | 5,808,416 | 4,428,073 |
| Prepaid expenses | 48,408 | 37,215 |
| Total Current Assets | $6,414,775 | $4,712,616 |

*Notes to Consolidated Financial Statements (in part)*
**Note 1 Summary of significant accounting policies (in part)**

**Inventories**—Inventories are stated principally at cost (last-in, first-out), which is not in excess of market, using the retail method for inventories in stores.

**HARSCO CORPORATION**

**Notes to Consolidated Financial Statements (in part)**

*Note 2 Inventories:*
Inventories are summarized as follows:

(in thousands)

|  | 1991 | 1990 |
|---|---|---|
| Classification: | | |
| Long-term contract costs (including general and administrative costs of $6,057 and $8,315) | $212,484 | $297,031 |
| Contract loss reserves | (6,068) | (6,987) |
| Progress payments—U.S. Government | (82,995) | (68,336) |
|  | 123,421 | 221,708 |
| Finished goods | 31,108 | 32,987 |
| Work in process | 25,661 | 25,457 |
| Raw materials and purchased parts | 38,884 | 46,083 |
| Stores and supplies | 6,056 | 6,275 |
|  | $225,130 | $332,510 |

> ### EXHIBIT 6-19, Continued
> ### Examples of Disclosure of Inventory Values and Methods
>
> |  | 1991 | 1990 |
> |---|---|---|
> | Valued at lower of cost or market: | | |
> | LIFO basis | $ 82,019 | $ 91,515 |
> | FIFO basis | 9,329 | 10,337 |
> | Average cost basis | 133,782 | 230,658 |
> |  | $225,130 | $332,510 |
>
> The Company has incurred costs that are assignable to units not yet produced. The aggregate amount incurred, exclusive of raw materials and purchased parts included in long-term contract costs, was $21,299,000 and $30,760,000 as of December 31, 1991 and 1990, respectively. These costs relate primarily to U.S. Government contracts for certain tracked vehicles and five-ton trucks.
>
> Inventories valued on the LIFO basis at December 31, 1991 and 1990 were approximately $40,762,000 and $41,256,000, respectively, less than the amounts of such inventories valued at current costs.
>
> As a result of reducing certain inventory quantities valued on the LIFO basis, profits from liquidation of inventories were recorded which increased net income by $877,000, $687,000 and $252,000 in 1991, 1990 and 1989, respectively.

## APPENDIX

## FOREIGN CURRENCY TRANSACTIONS INVOLVING INVENTORY

Many U.S. companies conduct inventory transactions with customers and suppliers in foreign countries. Sometimes the transaction is expressed in U.S. dollars. For example, most purchases and sales of crude oil are expressed in terms of the U.S. dollar. In these situations, there is no accounting issue. For example, if a U.S. oil company purchases 10,000 barrels of crude oil from Saudi Arabia, the price would be quoted in dollars and not in the equivalent amount of riyals. If the price is $20 per barrel, the company would record a purchase of inventory and the related payment of $200,000 ($20 × 10,000).

In many situations, however, the transaction is expressed in terms of the foreign currency. In these cases the transaction must be recorded by the company in U.S. dollars. Therefore, the foreign currency amount must be converted into dollars at the exchange rate on the day of the transaction. Selected foreign exchange rates are shown in Exhibit 6-20. For example, suppose a U.S. company purchases inventory of electronic components from a Japanese company for 50 million yen (Y) when the exchange rate is $0.007 (1 yen = $0.007). If the U.S. company pays cash of $350,000 (Y50,000,000 × $0.007) on the same day to purchase yen to settle the transaction, it is recorded by the U.S. company as follows:

| | | |
|---|---|---|
| **Inventory** | 350,000 | |
| **Cash** | | 350,000 |

## EXHIBIT 6-20

### SELECTED FOREIGN EXCHANGE RATES

| Country (currency) | Price in U.S. dollars* |
|---|---|
| Britain (pound) | $1.42 |
| Canada (dollar) | 0.80 |
| France (franc) | 0.18 |
| Israel (shekel) | 0.36 |
| Japan (yen) | 0.0083 |
| Mexico (peso) | 0.322 |
| Saudi Arabia (riyal) | 0.27 |
| Switzerland (franc) | 0.65 |
| West Germany (mark) | 0.60 |

\* Note that the exchange rates are stated in terms of $ per unit of foreign currency. Exchange rates are often stated in terms of units of foreign currency per $.
*Source:* The *Wall Street Journal* (February 12, 1993).

More often, transactions between companies in different countries involve credit terms, if only to allow time for the processing of the orders and payment across international borders. In addition, currency exchange rates change continuously. As a result, the exchange rate is likely to have changed between the date the U.S. company records a purchase transaction and the date it makes the payment. On the date of the payment, the company must record an exchange gain or loss to account for the difference between the purchase price of the inventory and the amount of the payment. **An exchange gain or loss is caused by a change in the exchange rate between the date of a purchase or sale on account and the date of the payment or receipt.** More specifically, when exchange rates are stated in terms of $ per unit of foreign currency, exchange gains and losses occur for purchases or sales on account as follows:

1. An exchange *gain* occurs when the exchange rate *declines* between the date a *payable* is incurred for the purchase of inventory and the date of the cash *payment*.

2. An exchange *gain* occurs when the exchange rate *increases* between the date a *receivable* is acquired from the sale of inventory and the date of the cash *receipt*.

3. An exchange *loss* occurs when the exchange rate *increases* between the date a *payable* is incurred for the purchase of inventory and the date of the cash *payment*.

4. An exchange *loss* occurs when the exchange rate *declines* between the date a *receivable* is acquired from the sale of inventory and the date of the cash *receipt*.

To illustrate an exchange gain that occurs when the exchange rate declines between the date a credit purchase of inventory is recorded and the date of the cash payment, suppose that in the preceding example the U.S. company made the purchase of the electronic components on account. Because the inventory was purchased when the exchange rate was $0.007, the acquisition is recorded as follows:

| | | |
|---|---|---|
| Inventory | 350,000 | |
|     Accounts Payable | | 350,000 |

The Japanese company has a right to receive 50 million yen, and the U.S. company is obligated to pay sufficient dollars that will convert to 50 million yen on the date that the payment is made. Now assume that the exchange rate on the date of payment is $0.0068 (1 yen = $0.0068). In this case, since only $0.0068 now buys 1 yen, the U.S. company will have to pay fewer dollars to buy 50 million yen. That is, the yen has become less expensive. More specifically, the U.S. company has to pay only $340,000 (Y50,000,000 × $0.0068). Therefore, the company has incurred an exchange *gain* of $10,000 ($350,000 − $340,000), which it records at the time of payment for the inventory as follows:

| | | |
|---|---|---|
| Accounts Payable | 350,000 | |
| Cash | | 340,000 |
| Exchange Gain | | 10,000 |

The exchange gain occurs because the U.S. company has to pay only $340,000 to settle its credit purchase of inventory originally recorded at $350,000. The gain can also be computed by multiplying the amount owed by the change in the exchange rate [Y50,000,000 × ($0.007 − $0.0068) = $10,000]. Remember that the Japanese company still receives 50 million yen; it is the U.S. company that has the exchange gain.

To illustrate an exchange loss that occurs when the exchange rate declines between the date a credit sale of inventory is recorded and the date of the cash receipt, suppose that a U.S. company sells computer equipment to a West German company on account and agrees to a price of 300,000 marks (DM) rather than a price in dollars. On the date of the sale, the exchange rate is $0.61 (1 mark = $0.61), and therefore the U.S. company records the sale of $183,000 (DM300,000 × $0.61) as follows (assuming the inventory has a cost of $100,000):

| | | |
|---|---|---|
| Accounts Receivable | 183,000 | |
| Sales Revenue | | 183,000 |
| | | |
| Cost of Goods Sold | 100,000 | |
| Inventory | | 100,000 |

The West German company has an obligation to pay 300,000 marks regardless of the exchange rate on the date of payment. If the exchange rate is $0.59 when its pays the amount owed, the U.S. company can convert those marks into only $177,000 (DM300,000 × $0.59). As a result, it has incurred an exchange *loss* of $6,000 ($177,000 − $183,000), which it records at the time of the cash collection as follows:

| | | |
|---|---|---|
| Cash | 177,000 | |
| Exchange Loss | 6,000 | |
| Accounts Receivable | | 183,000 |

The exchange loss can also be computed by multiplying the amount receivable by the change in the exchange rate [DM300,000 × ($0.61 − $0.59) = $6,000]. For financial reporting purposes, the net amount of the Exchange Gains and Losses is reported in the Other Items section of the income statement. This amount is included in the income statement because the exchange gains and losses were caused by fluctuations in the exchange rates that resulted in increased or decreased dollar cash flows during the accounting period.

Note that the U.S. company experienced exchange gains and losses in the preceding situations because it agreed to transactions expressed in terms of foreign currencies. In such situations, the U.S. company accepts the risks associated with exchange rate changes. When the transactions are expressed in U.S. dollars, the foreign company accepts, and the U.S. company avoids, the risks associated with exchange rate changes.

## QUESTIONS

*Q6-1*    Distinguish between the types of inventory accounts used for merchandising and manufacturing companies.

*Q6-2*    What are the cost components of each of the three inventory accounts of a manufacturing company?

*Q6-3*    Explain the differences between the perpetual and periodic inventory systems in terms of inventory quantity and cost. Does the use of the perpetual system eliminate the need for taking a physical inventory count?

*Q6-4*    What is the general rule used to determine if an item is included in inventory? Apply the concept to the accounting for goods in transit and goods on consignment.

*Q6-5*    Which of the following items are included in the inventory account of a manufacturing concern?
a.   Goods in transit purchased FOB shipping point, invoice received
b.   Raw materials
c.   Goods out on consignment
d.   Goods in transit sold to Breyer, Inc., shipped FOB destination
e.   Manufacturing supplies

*Q6-6*    Which of these costs are included in the determination of inventory cost?
a.   Sales commissions
b.   Supervisor's salary
c.   Freight charges
d.   Indirect factory production labor
e.   Storage costs
f.   Corporate executive salaries

*Q6-7*    Discuss the advantages and disadvantages of the two methods of accounting for purchases discounts taken in regard to management's needs, inventory cost, and the valuation of accounts payable.

*Q6-8*    What criteria should be used to decide between alternative inventory cost flow assumptions? Evaluate the relevance of the LIFO cost flow assumption. Why is LIFO not allowed in most foreign countries?

*Q6-9*    During a period of rising costs, indicate whether the LIFO cost flow assumption results in a larger or a smaller net income as compared to the FIFO cost flow assumption and explain why. Explain how net income would compare during a period of falling costs.

*Q6-10*    Discuss the cost flow assumptions of the LIFO inventory method. Under what conditions would the ending inventory differ under a perpetual and a periodic LIFO system?

*Q6-11*    Explain the issue of inventory liquidation when the LIFO cost flow assumption is used. Why is this an issue exclusive to LIFO?

*Q6-12*    Discuss the LIFO and FIFO cost flow assumptions relative to the issue of holding gains (inventory profits).

*Q6-13*    Explain the dollar-value LIFO method of inventory valuation. What are the advantages of dollar-value LIFO as compared to simple LIFO?

*Q6-14*    Describe the double-extension and link-chain methods used in dollar-value LIFO and when each should be used.

*Q6-15*    What is the difference between variable costing and absorption costing? Which of these two methods is considered acceptable for financial reporting?

*Q6-16*    Are standard costs of inventory acceptable for financial reporting? Describe two alternative methods of accounting for the standard cost variances and discuss the advantages of each.

*Q6-17*    When a company changes from FIFO to LIFO, what effect does the change have on the current period's net income and working capital?

*Q6-18*    What is the impact of LIFO inventory liquidation on interim financial statements?

## CASES

*C6-1    Cash Discounts*
The Atgar Corporation records all purchases and the corresponding liabilities net of cash discounts. Whenever payment is made after the discount period, cash is credited for the full amount of the invoice, and debits are made to accounts payable for the net amount and to an expense account for the discount lost.

**Required**
Give the arguments for and against this treatment of cash discounts. (*AICPA adapted*)

*C6-2    Purchases Discounts*
The Auge Company annually purchases 1,000 tons of raw material at a cost of $100,000 with terms of 2/10, n/30. Freight costs amount to $10,000 and storage and handling costs to $7,500.

**Required**
1.  What is the correct inventory cost?
2.  Would your answer to Requirement 1 change if the discount were not taken?

3. Would your answer to Requirement 1 change if the storage and handling costs were fixed costs and therefore not dependent on the volume of material stored?

## C6-3  Cost Flow Assumptions

Cost for inventory purposes should be determined by the inventory cost flow method most clearly reflecting periodic income.

### Required

1. Describe the fundamental cost flow assumptions of the average cost, FIFO, and LIFO inventory cost flow methods.
2. Discuss the reasons for using LIFO in an inflationary economy.
3. Where there is evidence that the utility of goods, in their disposal in the ordinary course of business, will be less than cost, what is the proper accounting treatment and under what concept is that treatment justified? (*AICPA adapted*)

## C6-4  LIFO

The 1976 financial statements of the Ford Motor Company included the following note:

*Note 1 (in part)*: Inventory valuation. Inventories are stated at the lower of cost or market. In 1976 the company changed its method of accounting from first-in, first-out (FIFO) to last-in, first-out (LIFO) for most of its U.S. inventories.

The change to LIFO reduced net income in 1976 by $81 million or $0.86 a share. There is no effect on prior years' earnings resulting from the change to LIFO in 1976 and, accordingly, prior years' earnings have not been restated. If the FIFO method of inventory accounting had been used by the company, inventories on December 31, 1976, would have been $166 million higher than reported.

### Required

1. What arguments must have been used in favor of LIFO for the management of Ford to accept a reduction in net income of $81 million?
2. What disadvantages are likely to result from the adoption of LIFO?
3. Why were prior years' earnings not adjusted?
4. Why is the effect on earnings $81 million when the effect on the inventory valuation is $166 million?
5. Would your answers to Requirements 1 and 2 change if you were discussing a change to LIFO for a Ford dealer?

## C6-5  Dollar-Value LIFO

In January 1995 Broome, Inc., requested and secured permission from the Commissioner of Internal Revenue to compute inventories under the last-in, first-out (LIFO) method and elected to determine inventory cost under the dollar-value method. Broome, Inc., satisfied the Commis-

sioner that cost could be accurately determined by use of an index number computed from a representative sample selected from the Company's single inventory pool.

### Required

1. Why should inventories be included in (a) a statement of financial position and (b) the computation of net income?
2. The Internal Revenue Code allows some accountable events to be considered differently for income tax reporting purposes and financial accounting purposes, while other accountable events must be reported the same for both purposes. Discuss why it might be desirable to report some accountable events differently for financial accounting purposes than for income tax reporting purposes.
3. Discuss the ways and conditions under which the FIFO and LIFO inventory costing methods produce different inventory valuations. Do not discuss procedures for computing inventory cost.
4. Discuss the specific advantages and disadvantages of using the dollar-value LIFO application as compared to traditional LIFO methods. Ignore income tax considerations. (*AICPA adapted*)

## C6-6  FIFO and LIFO

*Part a.* Inventory may be computed under one of various cost flow assumptions. Among these assumptions are first-in, first-out (FIFO) and last-in, first-out (LIFO). In the past, some companies have changed from FIFO to LIFO for computing portions or all of their inventory.

### Required

1. Ignoring income tax, what effect does a change from FIFO to LIFO have on net earnings and working capital? Explain.
2. Explain the difference between the FIFO assumption of earnings and operating cycle and the LIFO assumption of earnings and operating cycle.

*Part b.* Companies using LIFO inventory sometimes establish a "Reserve for the Replacement of LIFO Inventory" account.

### Required

Explain why and how this "reserve" account is established and where it should be shown on the statement of financial position. (*AICPA adapted*)

## C6-7  Cash Discounts, FIFO, and LIFO

Taylor Company, a household appliances dealer, purchases its inventories from various suppliers. Taylor has consistently stated its inventories at the lower of cost (FIFO) or market.

### Required

1. Taylor is considering alternate methods of accounting for the cash discounts it takes when paying its

suppliers promptly. From a theoretical standpoint, discuss the acceptability of each of the following methods:

a. Financial income when payments are made.

b. Reduction of cost of goods sold for period when payments are made.

c. Direct reduction of purchase cost.

2. Identify the effects on both the balance sheet and the income statement of using the LIFO inventory method instead of the FIFO method over a substantial time period when purchase prices of household appliances are rising. State why these effects take place. (*AICPA adapted*)

### C6-8    *Specific Identification*

Happlia Co. imports expensive household appliances. Each model has many variations and each unit has an identification number. Happlia pays all costs for getting the goods from the port to its central warehouse in Des Moines. After repackaging, the goods are consigned to retailers. A retailer makes a sale, simultaneously buys the appliance from Happlia, and pays the balance due within one week.

To alleviate the overstocking of refrigerators at a Minneapolis retailer, some were reshipped to a Kansas City retailer where they were still held in inventory at December 31, 1995. Happlia paid the costs of this reshipment.

Happlia uses the specific identification inventory costing method.

#### Required

1. In regard to the specific identification inventory costing method

a. Describe its key elements.

b. Discuss why it is appropriate for Happlia to use this method.

2. a. What general criteria should Happlia use to determine inventory carrying amounts at December 31, 1995? Ignore lower of cost or market considerations.

b. Give four examples of costs included in these inventory carrying amounts.

3. What costs should be reported in Happlia's 1995 income statement? Ignore lower of cost or market considerations. (*AICPA adapted*)

### C6-9    *Researching GAAP*    ⊙⊙

To pump up sales of all brands, Philip Morris is moving aggressively to ship extra cases of cigarettes into distribu-

tors' warehouses and record them as sales, a practice generally known as "trade loading." (Adapted from *Fortune*, April 6, 1992). Philip Morris' president has asked you whether these shipments may be recognized as revenue.

#### Required

Research the related generally accepted accounting principles and prepare a short memo to the president. Cite your references and applicable paragraph numbers.

### C6-10    *Researching GAAP*    ⊙⊙

The Fenimore Manufacturing Company uses the average cost method. It has followed a policy of expensing all its manufacturing cost variances. It is considering a change in its policy that will involve allocating them between cost of goods sold and inventory. Fenimore's president has asked you which of these alternative policies is consistent with GAAP.

#### Required

Research the related generally accepted accounting principles and prepare a short memo to the president. Cite your references and applicable paragraph numbers.

### C6-11    *Selection of an Inventory Method and*    ⊙⊙
### *Ethical Issues*

The Kelly Company is using FIFO. It has experienced rising costs for the last 5 years and expects that trend to continue. The King Company increased the number of LIFO pools it uses to account for its inventory.

#### Required

1. Why do you think each company follows its policy?

2. Does either practice create ethical issues?

### C6-12    *Interpretation of GAAP*

Robin Smith is considering buying shares in the Mah Company. The company has reported an increase in net income this year. On careful reading of the notes to the financial statements, Robin learns that the company had a LIFO liquidation this year. Robin understands what caused the liquidation but has asked you for advice about how to interpret it.

#### Required

Prepare a short memo to Robin to answer the question.

## MULTIPLE CHOICE

*Select the best answer for each of the following.*

M6-1    The moving average inventory cost flow method is applicable to which of the following inventory systems?

|     | Periodic | Perpetual |
| --- | --- | --- |
| a. | Yes | Yes |
| b. | Yes | No |
| c. | No | No |
| d. | No | Yes |

Items 2 and 3 are based on the following data: City Stationers, Inc., had 200 calculators on hand at January 1, 1995, costing $18 each. Purchases and sales of calculators during the month of January were as follows:

| Date | Purchases | Sales |
|------|-----------|-------|
| Jan. 11 | | 150 @ $28 |
| 14 | 100 @ $20 | |
| 27 | 100 @ $22 | |
| 30 | | 100 @ $32 |

City does not maintain perpetual inventory records. According to a physical count, 150 calculators were on hand at January 31, 1995.

M6-2   The cost of the inventory at January 31, 1995 under the FIFO method is
a. $400
b. $2,700
c. $3,100
d. $3,200

M6-3   The cost of the inventory at January 31, 1995 under the LIFO method is
a. $400
b. $2,700
c. $3,100
d. $3,200

M6-4   Goods on consignment should be included in the inventory of
a. The consignor but not the consignee
b. Both the consignor and the consignee
c. The consignee but not the consignor
d. Neither the consignor nor the consignee

M6-5   On December 31, 1994 Kern Company adopted the dollar-value LIFO inventory method. All of Kern's inventories constitute a single pool. The inventory on December 31, 1994 using the dollar-value LIFO inventory method was $600,000. Inventory data for 1995 are as follows:

| | |
|---|---|
| Dec. 31, 1995 inventory at year-end prices | $780,000 |
| Relevant price index at year-end (base year 1994) | 120 |

Under the dollar-value LIFO inventory method, Kern's inventory method, Kern's inventory at December 31, 1995 would be
a. $650,000
b. $655,000
c. $660,000
d. $720,000

M6-6   Assuming no beginning inventory, what can be said about the trend of inventory prices if cost of goods sold computed when inventory is valued using the FIFO method exceeds cost of goods sold when inventory is valued using the LIFO method?
a. Prices decreased.
b. Prices remained unchanged.
c. Prices increased.
d. Price trend *cannot* be determined from information given.

M6-7   Dixon Menswear Shop regularly buys shirts from Colt Company and is allowed trade discounts of 20% and 10% from the list price. Dixon purchased shirts from Colt on May 27, 1995, and received an invoice with a list price amount of $5,000, and payment terms of 2/10, n/30. Dixon uses the net method to record purchases. Dixon should record the purchase at
a. $3,600
b. $3,528
c. $3,500
d. $3,430

M6-8   The following items were included in Venicio Corporation's inventory account at December 31, 1995:

| | |
|---|---|
| Merchandise out on consignment, at sales price, including 40% markup on selling price | $14,000 |
| Goods purchased, in transit, shipped F.O.B. shipping point | 12,000 |
| Goods held on consignment by Venicio | 9,000 |

Venicio's inventory account at December 31, 1995 should be reduced by

a.  $14,600                    c.  $23,000
b.  $17,400                    d.  $35,000

M6-9    When the double-extension approach to the dollar-value LIFO inventory cost flow method is used, the inventory layer added in the current year is multiplied by an index number. How would the following be used in the calculation of this index number?

|     | Ending inventory at current year cost | Ending inventory at base year cost |
|-----|------------------------|------------------------|
| a.  | Numerator              | Denominator            |
| b.  | Numerator              | Not Used               |
| c.  | Denominator            | Numerator              |
| d.  | Not Used               | Denominator            |

M6-10   The LIFO inventory cost flow method may be applied to which of the following inventory systems?

|     | Periodic | Perpetual |
|-----|----------|-----------|
| a.  | No       | No        |
| b.  | No       | Yes       |
| c.  | Yes      | Yes       |
| d.  | Yes      | No        |

*(AICPA adapted)*

## EXERCISES

E6-1    *Inventory Accounts for a Manufacturing Company*    The Fujita Company produces a single product. Costs accumulated at the end of the period are as follows:

| | | | |
|---|---|---|---|
| Raw material purchases | $ 54,000 | Production supervisor's salary | $ 20,000 |
| Depreciation on manufacturing equipment | 3,000 | Shipping costs on units sold | 43,500 |
| Sales commissions | 20,000 | Materials used in production | 81,400 |
| Factory labor | 36,000 | Goods completed | 130,000 |
| Property tax on manufacturing equipment | 3,500 | Costs of units sold | 140,000 |

Assume the beginning raw material inventory to be $67,400, the beginning finished goods inventory to be $123,500, and no beginning goods in process inventory.

**Required**
Compute the closing account balances of each of the three inventory accounts: Raw Materials, Goods in Process, and Finished Goods.

E6-2    *Goods in Transit*    The Gervais Company made two purchases on December 30, 1995. One purchase for $1,000 was shipped FOB destination, and the second for $2,000 was shipped FOB shipping point. Neither purchase had been received on December 31, 1995.

**Required**
Which of these purchases, if either, are included in the Gervais Company inventory on December 31, 1995? What cost is assigned?

E6-3   *Items to Be Included in Inventory*   The following are several items that the controller of the Golosow Company has questioned regarding their inclusion in Inventory:

1. An invoice has been received for goods ordered. The goods were shipped FOB destination but have not been received.
2. Purchases have been ordered and received, but no invoice has arrived.
3. Product was shipped to customer today FOB destination and the invoice mailed.
4. Purchases are in the receiving department, but they are damaged and will be returned.
5. Product is in the shipping department, and the invoice has not been mailed to the customer.
6. Product is in the receiving department. It was returned by a customer without notification.

**Required**
For each of the preceding items indicate whether they are included in Inventory.

E6-4   *Inventory Valuation*   A retailer of washing machines receives a rebate of $20 per machine purchased if total purchases exceed 1,000 units. On reviewing the inventory records in December, it is discovered that 1,100 units have been purchased during the year. The rebate is claimed immediately but not received until January.

**Required**
Prepare journal entries to record the claiming of the rebate and its receipt. What effect do these events have on the inventory valuation on December 31?

E6-5   *Discounts*   The Hirsch Company buys inventory for $20,000 on terms of 2/10, n/30. Payment was made within the discount period.

**Required**
Prepare the journal entries to record the purchase and the payment under both the (1) gross price and (2) net price methods.

E6-6   *Discounts*   The Nelson Company bought inventory for $40,000 on terms of 2/15, n/60. Payment for the first $30,000 of inventory purchased was made within the discount period, the remaining $10,000 being paid two months later.

**Required**
Prepare the journal entries to record the purchase and the payment under both the (1) gross price and (2) net price methods.

E6-7   *Alternative Inventory Methods*   The Nevens Company uses a periodic inventory system. During November the following transactions occurred:

| Date | | Transaction | Units | Cost/Unit |
|---|---|---|---|---|
| November | 1 | Balance | 500 | $3.00 |
| | 8 | Sale | 350 | |
| | 13 | Purchase | 300 | 4.00 |
| | 21 | Purchase | 200 | 5.00 |
| | 28 | Sale | 150 | |

**Required**
Compute the cost of goods sold for November and the inventory at the end of November for each of the following cost flow assumptions:
1. FIFO
2. LIFO
3. Average cost

E6-8     *Alternative Inventory Methods*     The perpetual inventory records of the Park Company indicate the following transactions in the month of June:

|                    | Units | Cost/Unit |
|--------------------|-------|-----------|
| Inventory, June 1  | 200   | $3.20     |
| Purchases          |       |           |
| June 3             | 200   | 3.50      |
| June 17            | 250   | 3.60      |
| June 24            | 300   | 3.65      |
| Sales              |       |           |
| June 6             | 300   |           |
| June 21            | 200   |           |
| June 27            | 150   |           |

**Required**

Compute the cost of goods sold for June and the inventory at the end of June, using each of the following cost flow assumptions:

1. FIFO
2. LIFO
3. Average cost (round unit costs to 2 decimal places)

E6-9     *Alternative Inventory Methods*     The Frate Company was formed on December 1, 1994. The following information is available from Frate's inventory records for Product Ply:

|                                        | Units | Unit Cost |
|----------------------------------------|-------|-----------|
| January 1, 1995 (beginning inventory)  | 800   | $ 9.00    |
| Purchases:                             |       |           |
| January 6, 1995                        | 1,500 | 10.00     |
| January 24, 1995                       | 1,200 | 10.50     |
| February 17, 1995                      | 600   | 11.00     |
| March 27, 1995                         | 900   | 11.50     |

A physical inventory on March 31, 1995 shows 1,600 units on hand.

**Required**

Prepare schedules to compute the ending inventory at March 31, 1995 under each of the following inventory methods:

1. FIFO
2. LIFO
3. Weighted average

Show supporting computations in good form. (*AICPA adapted*)

E6-10     *LIFO, Perpetual and Periodic*     The inventory records of the Riedel Company showed the following transactions for the fiscal period ended June 30:

|                          | Units | Cost/Unit |
|--------------------------|-------|-----------|
| June 1 Inventory         | 700   | $6.20     |
| June 3 Purchases         | 400   | 6.40      |
| June 15 Sales @ $12.00   | 300   |           |
| June 22 Sales @ $12.50   | 500   |           |
| June 30 Purchases        | 600   | 6.70      |

**Required**

Compute the ending inventory and the cost of goods sold under the LIFO cost flow assumption, assuming both a perpetual and a periodic inventory system. Explain any difference in the final inventory valuations.

**E6-11** *Dollar-Value LIFO* A company adopted the LIFO method when its inventory was $1,800. One year later its ending inventory was $2,100 and costs had increased 5% during the year.

**Required**

What is the ending inventory using dollar-value LIFO?

**E6-12** *Dollar-Value LIFO* On January 1, 1994 the Sato Company adopted the dollar-value LIFO method of inventory costing. The company's ending inventory records appear as follows:

| Year | Current Cost | Index |
|------|------------|-------|
| 1993 | $40,000 | 100 |
| 1994 | 56,100 | 120 |
| 1995 | 58,300 | 130 |
| 1996 | 70,000 | 140 |

**Required**

Compute the ending inventory for the years 1993, 1994, 1995, and 1996, using the dollar-value LIFO method (round to the nearest dollar).

**E6-13** *Dollar-Value LIFO* The Belstock Company manufactures one product. On December 31, 1993 Belstock adopted the dollar-value LIFO inventory method. The inventory on that date, using the dollar-value LIFO inventory method, was $200,000. Inventory data are as follows:

| Year | Inventory at Respective Year-End Prices | Price Index (Base Year 1993) |
|------|------------------------------------------|-------------------------------|
| 1994 | $231,000 | 1.05 |
| 1995 | 299,000 | 1.15 |
| 1996 | 300,000 | 1.20 |

**Required**

Compute the inventory for the following dates using the dollar-value LIFO method for each year.
1. December 31, 1994,
2. December 31, 1995, and
3. December 31, 1996. (*AICPA adapted*)

**E6-14** *Dollar-Value LIFO* The Acute Company manufactures a single product. On December 31, 1993 Acute adopted the dollar-value LIFO inventory method. The inventory on that date using the dollar-value LIFO inventory method was determined to be $300,000. Inventory data for succeeding years are as follows:

| Year Ended December 31, | Inventory at Respective Year-End Prices | Relevant Price Index (Base Year 1993) |
|-------------------------|------------------------------------------|----------------------------------------|
| 1994 | $363,000 | 1.10 |
| 1995 | 420,000 | 1.20 |
| 1996 | 430,000 | 1.25 |

**Required**

Compute the inventory amounts at December 31, 1994, 1995, and 1996, using the dollar-value LIFO inventory method for each year. (*AICPA adapted*)

E6-15   *Inventory Pools*   The Stone Shoe Company adopted dollar-value LIFO on January 1, 1995. The company produces four products and uses a single inventory pool. The company's beginning inventory consists of the following:

| Type | Quantity | Cost per Unit | Total Cost |
|---|---|---|---|
| Running | 80,000 | $16 | $1,280,000 |
| Tennis | 30,000 | 15 | 450,000 |
| Basketball | 60,000 | 14 | 840,000 |
| Soccer | 40,000 | 17 | 680,000 |
| | 210,000 | | $3,250,000 |

During 1995 the company has the following purchases and sales:

| Type | Quantity Purchased | Cost per Unit | Quantity Sold | Selling Price per Unit |
|---|---|---|---|---|
| Running | 150,000 | $19 | 140,000 | $40 |
| Tennis | 130,000 | 16 | 100,000 | 38 |
| Basketball | 100,000 | 14 | 90,000 | 37 |
| Soccer | 120,000 | 18 | 140,000 | 42 |
| | 500,000 | | 470,000 | |

**Required**
1. Compute the LIFO cost of the ending inventory. (Round the cost index to 4 decimal places.)
2. By how much would the company's gross profit be different if it had used four pools instead of a single pool?

E6-16   *FIFO Used Internally, LIFO Used Externally*   The Grimstad Company uses FIFO for internal reporting purposes and LIFO for financial reporting and income tax purposes. At the end of 1995 the following information was obtained from the inventory records:

| | 1994 | 1995 |
|---|---|---|
| Ending inventory, FIFO | $100,000 | $140,000 |
| Ending inventory, LIFO | 80,000 | 110,000 |

**Required**
1. Prepare the necessary adjusting journal entry, assuming that the accounts are converted to LIFO at the end of 1995.
2. Indicate how the inventory value would be disclosed on the comparative balance sheets prepared at the end of 1995.

E6-17   *LIFO and Interim Financial Reports*   The following values were obtained from the inventory records of the Harris Company, which has a fiscal year ending on December 31:

| | |
|---|---|
| Inventory, January 1, 1995, LIFO | $80,000 |
| Inventory, March 31, 1995, LIFO | 70,000 |

**Required**
1. Under what conditions is the inventory liquidation not reflected in the first quarter interim financial statements?

2. Assuming that the liquidation is not to be reflected, what adjusting worksheet entry would be necessary and how would you determine the amount?

E6-18    *Appendix: Exchange Gains and Losses*   On January 15, 1995, the Searle Company, a U.S. company, acquired machinery on account from a British company for £12,000. The company paid for the machine on January 30, 1995. The exchange rates on January 15 and 30 were $1.85 and $1.80, respectively.

**Required**

Record the journal entries for the acquisition and payment by the Searle Company.

E6-19    *Appendix: Exchange Gains and Losses*   On June 20, 1995, the Livingston Company, a U.S. company, sold merchandise on account to a Swiss company for 25,000 francs. The company received payment for the merchandise on July 10, 1995. The exchange rates on June 20 and July 10 were $0.69 and $0.68, respectively.

**Required**

Record the journal entries for the sale and collection by the Livingston Company.

## PROBLEMS

P6-1    *Items to Be Included in Inventory*   As the auditor of the Hayes Company for the year ended December 31, 1995 you found the following transactions occurred near its closing date:

1. Merchandise received on January 8, 1996 costing $800, was recorded on January 6, 1996. An invoice on hand showed the shipment was made FOB supplier's warehouse on December 31, 1995. Since the merchandise was not on hand at December 31, 1995, it was not included in the inventory.
2. A product costing $600 was in Hayes' shipping room when the physical inventory was taken. It was not included in the inventory because it was marked "Hold for customer's shipping instructions." Investigation revealed that the customer's order was dated December 18, 1995, but that the case was shipped and the customer billed on January 10, 1996.
3. A machine, made to order for a customer, was finished on December 31, 1995. The customer had inspected it and was satisfied with it. The customer was billed in full for $2,000 on that date. The machine was excluded from inventory, although it was shipped on January 2, 1996.
4. Merchandise costing $800 was received on December 28, 1995, and a purchase was not recorded. The goods were "on consignment from Milliken Company."
5. Merchandise costing $4,000 was received on January 3, 1996, and the related purchase invoice recorded January 5. The invoice showed that the shipment was made on December 29, 1995, FOB destination.

**Required**

For each situation, state whether the merchandise should be included in Hayes Company's inventory. Give your reason for the decision on each item.

P6-2    *Valuation of Inventory*   The inventory on hand at the end of 1995 for the Reddall Company is valued at a cost of $87,450. The following items were *not* included in this inventory:

1. Purchased goods in transit, under terms FOB shipping point, invoice price $3,300, freight costs $170.
2. Goods out on consignment to Marlman Company, sales price $2,800, shipping costs of $210.
3. Goods sold to Grina Co. under terms FOB destination, invoiced for $1,700, including $251 freight charges to deliver the goods. Goods are in transit.
4. Goods held on consignment by the Reddall Company at a sales price of $3,700, including sales commission of 20% of sales price.
5. Purchased goods in transit shipped FOB destination, invoice price $2,100 including freight charges of $190.

**Required**

Determine the cost of the ending inventory to be reported on the December 31, 1995 balance sheet of the Reddall Company, assuming that the company's selling price is 140% of the cost of the inventory.

P6-3    *Cost of Sales*  As an accountant for the Lee Company, your supervisor has given you the following calculations of the gross profit for the first quarter:

| Alternative | Sales ($50 per unit) | Cost of Goods Sold | Gross Profit |
|---|---|---|---|
| A | $500,000 | $200,000 | $300,000 |
| B | 500,000 | 228,000 | 272,000 |
| C | 500,000 | 213,333 | 286,667 |

The three alternative cost flow assumptions are FIFO, Average, and LIFO (the alternatives are not necessarily presented in this sequence). The company uses the periodic inventory system.

The computation of the cost of goods sold under each alternative is based on the following data:

| | Units | Cost/Unit |
|---|---|---|
| Inventory, January 1 | 12,000 | $20 |
| Purchase, January 10 | 4,000 | 21 |
| Purchase, February 15 | 6,000 | 22 |
| Purchase, March 10 | 8,000 | 23 |

**Required**
Prepare schedules computing the ending inventory (in units and dollars) and proving the cost of goods sold shown here under each of the three alternatives.

P6-4    *Discounts*  On April 11, Edwards Construction Company purchased inventory for $18,000 on terms of 2/10, n/30. Payment of the account balance was made on April 21.

**Required**
1. Prepare the journal entries to record the purchase and payment using each of the following methods:
   a. Gross price
   b. Net price
2. If half the inventory was sold during April for $20,000, how much income would be recognized under each method?
3. Assume that the invoice was misfiled, and as a result payment was not made until April 30. Prepare the journal entries to record the purchase and payment under each of the methods. If half the inventory was sold during April for $20,000, how much income would be recognized under each method?

P6-5    *Alternative Inventory Methods*  The Garrett Company has the following transactions during the months of April and May:

| Date | Transaction | Units | Cost/Unit |
|---|---|---|---|
| April 1 | Balance | 400 | |
| 17 | Purchase | 200 | $5.50 |
| 25 | Sale | 150 | |
| 28 | Purchase | 100 | 5.75 |
| May 5 | Purchase | 250 | 5.50 |
| 18 | Sale | 300 | |
| 22 | Sale | 50 | |

The cost of the inventory on April 1 is $5, $4, and $2 per unit, respectively, under the FIFO, average, and LIFO cost flow assumptions.

**Required**
1. Compute the costs of goods sold for each month and the inventories at the end of each month for the following alternatives:
   a. FIFO periodic
   b. FIFO perpetual

c. LIFO periodic
d. LIFO perpetual
e. Weighted average (round unit costs to 2 decimal places)
f. Moving average (round unit costs to 2 decimal places)
2. Reconcile the difference between the LIFO periodic and the LIFO perpetual results.

**P6-6**    *Alternative Inventory Methods*    The Totman Company has the following transactions during the months of January and February:

| Date | Transaction | Units | Cost/Unit |
|------|-------------|-------|-----------|
| January 1 | Balance | 200 | |
| 10 | Purchase | 50 | $25 |
| 22 | Sale | 40 | |
| 28 | Purchase | 60 | $27 |
| February 4 | Purchase | 30 | $28 |
| 14 | Sale | 40 | |
| 23 | Sale | 20 | |

The cost of the inventory at January 1 is $24, $23, and $15 per unit, respectively, under the FIFO, average, and LIFO cost flow assumptions.

**Required**

1. Compute the cost of goods sold for each month and the inventories at the end of each month for the following alternatives:
   a. FIFO periodic
   b. FIFO perpetual
   c. LIFO periodic
   d. LIFO perpetual
   e. Weighted average (round unit costs to 2 decimal places)
   f. Moving average (round unit costs to 2 decimal places)
2. Reconcile the difference between the LIFO periodic and the LIFO perpetual results.
3. If the company had purchased an additional 25 units for $30 each on February 27, compute the cost of goods sold for February under FIFO periodic and LIFO periodic.

**P6-7**    *Alternative Inventory Methods*    The Habicht Company was formed in 1993 to produce a single product. The production and sales for the next four years were as follows:

| | Production | | Sales | | |
|------|--------|-------------|--------|---------------|-------------------------|
| | Units | Total Costs | Units | Sales Revenue | Units in Ending Inventory |
| 1993 | 100,000 | $200,000 | 80,000 | $400,000 | 20,000 |
| 1994 | 120,000 | 234,000 | 110,000 | 550,000 | 30,000 |
| 1995 | 130,000 | 247,000 | 150,000 | 750,000 | 10,000 |
| 1996 | 130,000 | 240,500 | 120,000 | 600,000 | 20,000 |

**Required**

Determine the gross profit for each year under each of the following periodic inventory methods:
1. FIFO
2. LIFO
3. Average cost (round unit costs to 3 decimal places)

**P6-8**    *LIFO and Inventory Pools*    On January 1, 1992 Grover Company changed its inventory cost flow method to the LIFO cost method from the FIFO cost method for its raw materials inventory. The change was made for both financial statement and income tax reporting purposes. Grover uses the multiple-pools approach under which substantially identical raw materials are grouped into LIFO inventory pools; weighted average costs are used in valuing annual incremental layers. The composition of the December 31, 1994 inventory for the Class F inventory pool is as follows:

| | Units | Weighted Average Unit Cost | Total Cost |
|---|---|---|---|
| Base year inventory—1992 | 9,000 | $10.00 | $ 90,000 |
| Incremental layer—1993 | 3,000 | 11.00 | 33,000 |
| Incremental layer—1994 | 2,000 | 12.50 | 25,000 |
| Inventory, December 31, 1994 | 14,000 | | $148,000 |

Inventory transactions for the Class F inventory pool during 1995 were as follows:
- On March 2, 1995, 4,800 units were purchased at a unit cost of $13.50 for $64,800.
- On September 1, 1995, 7,200 units were purchased at a unit cost of $14.00 for $100,800.
- A total of 15,000 units were used for production during 1995.

The following transactions for the Class F inventory pool took place during 1996:
- On January 11, 1996, 7,500 units were purchased at a unit cost of $14.50 for $108,750.
- On May 14, 1996, 5,500 units were purchased at a unit cost of $15.50 for $85,250.
- On December 29, 1996, 7,000 units were purchased at a unit cost of $16.00 for $112,000.
- A total of 16,000 units were used for production during 1996.

**Required**
1. Prepare a schedule to compute the inventory (units and dollar amounts) of the Class F inventory pool at December 31, 1995. Show supporting computations in good form.
2. Prepare a schedule to compute the cost of Class F raw materials used in production for the year ended December 31, 1995.
3. Prepare a schedule to compute the inventory (units and dollar amounts) of the Class F inventory pool at December 31, 1996. Show supporting computations in good form. (*AICPA adapted*)

*P6-9*    *Dollar-Value LIFO*    The Olson Company adopted the dollar-value LIFO method for inventory valuation at the beginning of 1994. The following information about the inventory at the end of each year is available from the company records:

| Year | Current Costs | Index |
|---|---|---|
| 1993 | $50,000 | 100 |
| 1994 | 60,000 | 108 |
| 1995 | 70,000 | 115 |
| 1996 | 72,000 | 125 |
| 1997 | 75,000 | 135 |

**Required**
Calculate the dollar-value LIFO inventory at the end of each year.

*P6-10*    *Dollar-Value LIFO*    The Kwestel Company adopted the dollar-value LIFO method for inventory valuation at the beginning of 1994. The following information about the inventory at the end of each year is available from the company records:

| Year | Cost | Index |
|---|---|---|
| 1993 | $ 8,000 | 100 |
| 1994 | 10,800 | 120 |
| 1995 | 11,500 | 130 |
| 1996 | 14,000 | 145 |
| 1997 | 11,000 | 125 |

**Required**
Calculate the dollar-value LIFO inventory at the end of each year.

P6-11    *Dollar-Value LIFO and Inventory Pools*   The Webster Company adopted dollar-value LIFO on January 1, 1995. The company produces three products: X, Y, and Z. The company's beginning inventory consisted of the following:

| Type | Quantity | Cost per Unit | Total Cost |
|---|---|---|---|
| X | 30,000 | $4.25 | $127,500 |
| Y | 10,000 | 3.50 | 35,000 |
| Z | 25,000 | 2.00 | 50,000 |
|  | 65,000 |  | $212,500 |

During 1995, the company had the following purchases and sales:

| Type | Quantity Purchased | Cost per Unit | Quantity Sold | Selling Price per Unit |
|---|---|---|---|---|
| X | 110,000 | $4.75 | 90,000 | $10.00 |
| Y | 100,000 | 3.75 | 85,000 | 7.50 |
| Z | 75,000 | 2.10 | 70,000 | 5.00 |
|  | 285,000 |  | 245,000 |  |

**Required**
1. Compute the LIFO cost of the ending inventory assuming Webster Company uses a single inventory pool. (Round cost index to 4 decimal places.)
2. Compute the LIFO cost of the ending inventory assuming Webster Company uses 3 inventory pools. (Round cost indexes to 4 decimal places.)

P6-12    *Comprehensive*   The Kelly Company adopted dollar-value LIFO on January 1, 1993 using two inventory pools, each of which includes two types of inventory items. The following information about the inventory at the end of each year is available:

| | Pool 1 | | | Pool 2 | | |
|---|---|---|---|---|---|---|
| Year | Number of Units | Type | Average Cost per Unit | Number of Units | Type | Average Cost per Unit |
| 1993 | 20,000 | A | $10 | 40,000 | C | $5 |
|  | 10,000 | B | 20 | 20,000 | D | 8 |
| 1994 | 30,000 | A | 11 | 50,000 | C | 7 |
|  | 12,000 | B | 24 | 22,000 | D | 9 |
| 1995 | 40,000 | A | 12 | 46,000 | C | 6 |
|  | 14,000 | B | 22 | 20,000 | D | 8 |
| 1996 | 45,000 | A | 12 | 60,000 | C | 7 |
|  | 13,000 | B | 25 | 25,000 | D | 8 |

**Required**
1. Compute the cost index for each year for each pool using a base of 100 for each index. (Round each cost index to 4 decimal places.)
2. Compute the dollar-value LIFO inventory at the end of each year.

P6-13    *Double-Extension: Dollar-Value LIFO*   On January 1, 1995 Lucas Distributors, Inc., adopted the dollar-value LIFO inventory method for income tax and external financial reporting. However, Lucas continued to use the FIFO inventory method for internal accounting and management purposes. In applying the LIFO method,

Lucas uses internal conversion cost indexes and the multiple-pools approach under which substantially identical inventory items are grouped into LIFO inventory pools. The following data were available for Inventory Pool No. 1, which is comprised of products A and B, for the 2 years following the adoption of LIFO:

|  | FIFO Basis per Records | | |
|---|---|---|---|
|  | Units | Unit Cost | Total Cost |
| Inventory, 1/1/95 | | | |
| Product A | 12,000 | $30 | $360,000 |
| Product B | 8,000 | 25 | 200,000 |
|  | | | $560,000 |
| Inventory, 12/31/95 | | | |
| Product A | 17,000 | $35 | $595,000 |
| Product B | 9,000 | 28 | 252,000 |
|  | | | $847,000 |
| Inventory, 12/31/96 | | | |
| Product A | 13,000 | $40 | $520,000 |
| Product B | 10,000 | 32 | 320,000 |
|  | | | $840,000 |

**Required**

1. Prepare a schedule to compute the internal conversion cost indexes for 1995 and 1996. Round indexes to two decimal places.
2. Prepare a schedule to compute the inventory amounts at December 31, 1995 and 1996, using the dollar-value LIFO inventory method. (*AICPA adapted*)

P6-14   *LIFO Liquidation Profit*   The Hammond Company adopted LIFO when it was formed on January 1, 1993. Since then, the company has had the following purchases and sales of its single inventory item:

| Year | Units Purchased | Cost per Unit | Units Sold | Price per Unit |
|---|---|---|---|---|
| 1993 | 10,000 | $5 | 8,000 | $12 |
| 1994 | 12,000 | 6 | 9,000 | 13 |
| 1995 | 15,000 | 8 | 14,000 | 16 |

In December 1996 the controller realized that because of an unexpected increase in demand the company had sold 22,000 units, but had only purchased 18,000 units during the year. In 1996 each unit had been sold for $19, and each unit purchased had cost $10. The income tax rate is 30%.

**Required**

1. If the company makes no additional purchases in 1996, how much LIFO liquidation profit will it report?
2. If the company purchases an additional 7,000 units in December 1996, how much income tax will the company save?
3. If the company purchases the additional 7,000 units, how much income tax has the company saved over the 4-year period by using LIFO instead of the FIFO cost flow assumption?

P6-15   *Comprehensive*   The following information for 1994 is available for the Marino Company:

1. The beginning inventory is $100,000.
2. Purchases of $300,000 were made on terms of 2/10, n/30. Eighty percent of the discounts were taken.
3. Purchases returns of $4,000 were made.

4. At December 31, purchases of $20,000 were in transit, FOB destination, on terms of 2/10, n/30.
5. The company made sales of $620,000. The gross selling price per unit is twice the net cost of each unit sold.
6. Sales allowances of $6,000 were made.
7. The company uses the LIFO periodic method and the gross method for purchases discounts.

**Required**

1. Compute the cost of the ending inventory before the physical inventory is taken.
2. Compute the amount of the cost of goods sold that came from the purchases of the period and the amount that came from the beginning inventory.

P6-16    *Inventory Valuation*   You are engaged in an audit of the Roche Mfg. Company for the year ended December 31, 1995. To reduce the workload at year-end, the company took its annual physical inventory under your observation on November 30, 1995. The company's inventory account, which includes raw materials and work in process, is on a perpetual basis and the first-in, first-out method of pricing is used. There is no finished goods inventory. The company's physical inventory revealed that the book inventory of $60,570 was understated by $3,000. To avoid distorting the interim financial statements, the company decided not to adjust the book inventory until year-end except for obsolete inventory items. Your audit revealed this information about the November 30th inventory:

a. Pricing tests showed that the physical inventory was overpriced by $2,200.
b. Footing and extension errors resulted in a $150 understatement of the physical inventory.
c. Direct labor included in the physical inventory amounted to $10,000. Overhead was included at the rate of 200% of direct labor. You determined that the amount of direct labor was correct and the overhead rate was proper.
d. The physical inventory included obsolete materials recorded at $250. During December, these materials were removed from the inventory account by a charge to cost of sales. Your audit also disclosed the following information about the December 31, 1995 inventory.
e. Total debits to certain accounts during December are:

|  | December |
|---|---|
| Purchases | $24,700 |
| Direct labor | 12,100 |
| Manufacturing overhead expense | 25,200 |
| Cost of sales | 68,600 |

f. The cost of sales of $68,600 included direct labor of $13,800.
g. Normal scrap loss on established product lines is negligible. However, a special order started and completed during December had excessive scrap loss of $800, which was charged to Manufacturing Overhead Expense.

**Required**

1. Compute the correct amount of the physical inventory at November 30, 1995.
2. Without prejudice to your solution to Requirement 1, assume that the correct amount of the inventory at November 30, 1995 was $57,700. Compute the amount of the inventory at December 31, 1995. (*AICPA adapted*)

P6-17    *Comprehensive*   The Allen Company is a wholesale distributor of automotive replacement parts. Initial amounts taken from Allen's accounting records are as follows:

| | |
|---|---|
| Inventory at December 31, 1995 (based on physical count of goods in Allen's warehouse on December 31, 1995) | $1,250,000 |
| Sales in 1995 | $9,000,000 |

Accounts payable at December 31, 1995:

| Vendor | Terms | Amount |
|---|---|---|
| Baker Company | 2% 10 days, net 30 | $   265,000 |
| Charlie Company | Net 30 | 210,000 |
| Dolly Company | Net 30 | 300,000 |
| Eager Company | Net 30 | 225,000 |
| Full Company | Net 30 | — |
| Greg Company | Net 30 | — |
| | | $1,000,000 |

Additional information is as follows:

1. Parts held on consignment from Charlie to Allen, the consignee, amounting to $155,000, were included in the physical count of goods in Allen's warehouse on December 31, 1995 and in accounts payable at December 31, 1995.
2. $22,000 of parts which were purchased from Full and paid for in December 1995 were sold in the last week of 1995 and appropriately recorded as sales of $28,000. The parts were included in the physical count of goods in Allen's warehouse on December 31, 1995 because the parts were on the loading dock waiting to be picked up by customers.
3. Parts in transit on December 31, 1995 to customers, shipped F.O.B. shipping point, on December 28, 1995 amounted to $34,000. The customers received the parts on January 7, 1996. Sales of $40,000 to the customers for the parts were recorded by Allen on January 2, 1996.
4. Retailers were holding $210,000 at cost ($250,000 at retail), of goods on consignment from Allen, the consignor, at their stores on December 31, 1995.
5. Goods were in transit from Greg to Allen on December 31, 1995. The cost of the goods was $25,000, and they were shipped F.O.B. shipping point on December 29, 1995.
6. A quarterly freight bill in the amount of $2,000 specifically relating to merchandise purchases in December 1995, all of which was still in the inventory at December 31, 1995, was received on January 4, 1996. The freight bill was not included in either the inventory or in accounts payable at December 31, 1995.
7. All of the purchases from Baker occurred during the last seven days of the year. These items have been recorded in accounts payable and accounted for in the physical inventory at cost before discount. Allen's policy is to pay invoices in time to take advantage of all cash discounts, adjust inventory accordingly, and record accounts payable, net of cash discounts.

### Required

Prepare a schedule of adjustments to the initial amounts of inventory, accounts payable, and sales. Show the effect, if any, of each of the transactions separately and indicate if the transactions would have no effect on the amount. (*AICPA adapted*)

# 7

# INVENTORIES: SPECIAL VALUATION ISSUES

In the preceding chapter the various methods of determining the historical cost of inventory were described. In certain situations inventory is not reported at its historical cost. The alternatives to historical cost are the valuation at the lower of cost or market, valuation above cost, and estimation of cost by the gross profit or retail inventory methods, including the dollar-value LIFO retail inventory method. Each of these topics is discussed in this chapter, as well as purchase obligations, product financing arrangements, and the effects of errors in inventory on the financial statements.

**Chapter Topics**

*Lower of Cost or Market Rule*

*Purchase Obligations and Product Financing Arrangements*

*The Gross Profit Method*

*The Retail Inventory Method*

*The Dollar-Value LIFO Retail Method*

*The Effects of Inventory Errors*

## LOWER OF COST OR MARKET

The generally accepted accounting principle of valuation at historical cost, as determined by the cost flow assumption used, is modified in those situations where the market value of the inventory has declined below its historical cost. The decline might occur for reasons such as declining costs, obsolescence, or physical deterioration. In these situations the lower of cost or market rule is applied. **The lower of cost or market rule requires that the inventory be written down to its market value when its utility has declined.** The write-down of the inventory is appropriate because the utility of the asset has declined, and to leave the inventory at its historical cost would overstate both its value and the expected future cash inflows. The lower of cost or market rule is consistent with the conservatism convention. Since the asset is written down, it is necessary to record a loss (or expense) in the income statement because the decline is an economic event of the period.

**Accounting Research Bulletin No. 43** states:

> **A departure from the cost basis of pricing the inventory is required when the utility of the goods is no longer as great as its cost. Where there is evidence that the utility of goods, in their disposal in the ordinary course of business, will be less than cost, whether due to physical deterioration, obsolescence, changes in price levels or other causes, the difference should be recognized as a loss of the current period. This is generally accomplished by stating such goods at a lower level commonly designated as market.**[1]

Since utility is difficult to measure except through a changed market value, the measurement of the decline in utility is, in practice, always accomplished by valuation at the lower of cost or market (LCM). *Accounting Research Bulletin No. 43* defines the **market value as the current replacement cost** (either by purchase or manufacture) and *not* as the selling price.

### Application of Lower of Cost or Market Method

To apply the lower of cost or market method, the cost is compared to the market value. The current replacement cost is not always used as the market value, however. An upper (*ceiling*) and a lower (*floor*) constraint on the market value are imposed as follows:

1.  **The upper constraint is that the market value should not exceed the net realizable value** (the estimated selling price in the ordinary course of business less reasonably predictable costs of completion and disposal).

2.  **The lower constraint is that the market value should not be below the net realizable value reduced by an allowance for a normal profit margin (normal markup).**

These two constraints are used to determine which "market value" (current replacement cost, ceiling, or floor) is to be compared to cost. Note that the appropriate market value is determined before the comparison with the cost is made. **The purpose of the ceiling is to ensure that the write-down of the inventory is sufficient to cover all expected losses and therefore prevent the recognition of further losses in the future.**

---

1.  "Restatement and Revision of Accounting Research Bulletins," *Accounting Research Bulletins, Final Edition, No. 43* (New York: AICPA, 1961), ch. 4, par. 7.

In contrast, **the purpose of the floor is to prevent an excessive loss from being recognized and therefore prevent the recognition of excessive profits in the future.**

Thus, three steps are needed to apply the lower of cost or market method: (1) selection of the market value, (2) comparison of the market value to cost, and (3) reporting the results in the financial statements, as illustrated in the following diagram:

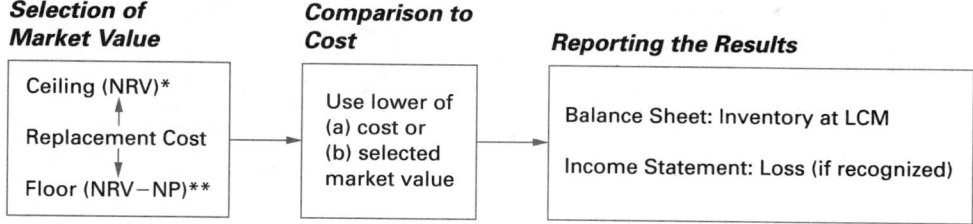

*Net realizable value
**Normal profit

In the first step, the current replacement cost, ceiling, and floor are calculated. Whichever is the middle value of the three is selected. Then, the lower of the selected market value or the historical cost is chosen. Finally, the lower value is reported on the balance sheet, and if a loss is recognized, it is reported on the income statement, perhaps by being included in cost of goods sold.

To illustrate the first step in the application of the lower of cost or market method, suppose that a unit of inventory has the following characteristics:

| | |
|---|---|
| Selling price | $165 |
| Packaging cost | 10 |
| Transportation cost | 15 |
| Profit margin | 40 |

The computation of the ceiling and floor is as follows:

| | |
|---|---|
| Selling price | $165 |
| Less: Costs of completion (i.e., packaging) | (10) |
| Costs of disposal (i.e., transportation) | (15) |
| Ceiling (net realizable value) | $140 |
| Less: Normal profit margin | (40) |
| Floor (net realizable value less normal profit) | $100 |

If the current replacement cost is between $100 and $140, it would be used as the market value. Otherwise, the ceiling would be used if the replacement cost is above $140, or the floor would be used if the replacement cost is below $100.

All three steps in the application of the lower of cost or market method are illustrated in Exhibit 7-1 for a single unit of inventory. The logic behind the ceiling and floor can be explained by reference to Cases 5 and 6. If the ceiling constraint was ignored in Case 5 and the current replacement cost was used as market, the inventory would be written down to only $105 and a loss of $5 recognized. However, in a later period when the unit was sold for $90, there would be an additional loss of $15. Therefore the inventory would not have been written down to its expected utility, and the total loss associated with the decline in utility would not have been recognized in the period in which it occurred. Imposing an upper limit of net realizable

## EXHIBIT 7-1

## APPLICATION OF THE LOWER OF COST OR MARKET RULE

| Case | Current Replacement Cost | Net Realizable Value (Ceiling) | Net Realizable Value Less a Normal Markup (Floor) | Market (Constrained by Ceiling and Floor) | Cost | Lower of Cost or Market Inventory Value* | Loss |
|------|------|------|------|------|------|------|------|
| 1 | $120 | $140 | $100 | $120 | $110 | $110 | $ 0 |
| 2 | 150 | 140 | 100 | 140 | 110 | 110 | 0 |
| 3 | 75 | 140 | 120 | 120 | 110 | 110 | 0 |
| 4 | 105 | 140 | 100 | 105 | 110 | 105 | 5 |
| 5 | 105 | 90 | 80 | 90 | 110 | 90 | 20 |
| 6 | 80 | 140 | 100 | 100 | 110 | 100 | 10 |

*Cases 1, 2 and 3: Cost is used because it is lower than market.
Case 4: Replacement cost is used because it is between floor and ceiling and is less than cost.
Case 5: Net realizable value (ceiling) is used because replacement cost is higher than ceiling and net realizable value is less than cost.
Case 6: Net realizable value less a normal markup (floor) is used because replacement cost is less than floor and net realizable value less a normal markup is less than cost.

value ensures that the full decline in utility is recognized in the period in which it occurred. At first it might be considered unusual that the net realizable value is below the replacement cost (of a new asset), but this can happen when there has been physical deterioration to the inventory. If the volume of such items becomes significant, they should be transferred to a separate account.

If the floor constraint was ignored in Case 6 and the current replacement cost was used as market, the inventory would be written down to $80 and a loss of $30 recognized. However, in a later period when the unit was sold for $140, there would be a profit of $60, which is higher than the normal profit of $40. Therefore the inventory would have been written down below its expected utility, and an excessive loss followed by an excessive profit would have been recognized. Imposing a lower limit of net realizable value less normal profit prevents a write-down below the expected utility of the inventory and the arbitrary transfer of profit from one accounting period to another.

### Conceptual Evaluation of the Ceiling and Floor

The implicit assumption underlying the lower of cost or market method is that selling (exit) prices move in parallel to replacement costs (entry prices) within the constraints of ceiling and floor. While the general trends of the two prices are likely to move together, there will be exceptions. Also, the lower of cost or market method may be criticized because it uses three different concepts for the loss recognized in the period. This loss recognition also affects the amount of profit recognized in future periods. These differences create conceptual inconsistencies both within the lower of cost or market method and between the method and other applications of conservatism.

To illustrate these issues, assume the following facts for 1 unit of inventory of the Sahara Company, a retailer:

Cost:      $19
Ceiling:   14 (Net realizable value)
Floor:     10 (Net realizable value − Normal profit)

### Situation 1

If we also assume that the replacement cost is $15, the ceiling of $14 is used as the market value. Why would the Sahara Company sell an item for $14 when the replacement cost is $15? One explanation would be that the supplier of the inventory has introduced a lower price on a new product so that the inventory held by the Sahara Company has become obsolete.

The loss in the period of the *writedown* is equal to the historical cost less the net realizable value (ceiling). The expected profit in the period of *sale* is equal to the net realizable value less the ceiling (the new carrying value of the inventory). The loss and expected profit are:

$$\text{Loss in period of writedown} = \$14 - \$19$$
$$= \underline{\underline{\$(5)}}$$

$$\text{Expected profit in period of sale} = \$14 - \$14$$
$$= \underline{\underline{\$\ 0}}$$

The loss of $5 is a measure of the expected loss that *would* have been recognized at the time of sale if the lower of cost or market rule had *not* been used. The loss is recognized in the current period instead of a future period and, therefore, the expected profit at the time of the sale is zero. This loss concept is the same concept applied in other areas where the conservatism principle is used (such as contingencies and construction contracts, discussed in Chapters 11 and 16, respectively) because no provision is made for the recognition of a profit when the sale occurs in a future period.

### Situation 2

Assume now that the replacement cost is $12. In this situation the replacement cost is used as the market value. Why would the Sahara Company sell an item for $14 when the replacement cost is $12 and its normal profit (the difference between the ceiling and floor) is $4? One explanation would be that the supplier has reduced its price on the product so that the Sahara Company has to reduce its selling price to remain competitive with other retailers that have reduced their prices.

The loss in the period of the *writedown* is equal to the historical cost less the replacement cost. The expected profit in the period of *sale* is the net realizable value less the replacement cost (the new carrying value of the inventory). The loss and expected profit are:

$$\text{Loss in period of writedown} = \$12 - \$19$$
$$= \underline{\underline{\$(7)}}$$

$$\text{Expected profit in period of sale} = \$14 - \$12$$
$$= \underline{\underline{\$\ 2}}$$

The loss of $7 is the measure of the cost saving that was missed because the inventory was purchased before the price decline. This alternative does allow the company to recognize a profit of $2 at the time of sale, although it is less than the normal profit of $4.

*Situation 3*

Assume now that the replacement cost is $9. In this situation the floor of $10 is used as the market value. Why would the Sahara Company be able to sell an item for $14 when the replacement cost is $9 and its normal profit is $4? One explanation would be that the supplier has reduced the price on the product and stimulated demand so that the retail price has not fallen as much.

The loss in the period of the *writedown* is equal to the historical cost less the net receivable value minus the normal profit (floor). The expected profit in the period of *sale* is equal to the net realizable value less the floor (the new carrying value of the inventory). The loss and expected profit are:

$$\text{Loss in period of writedown} = \$10 - \$19$$
$$= \underline{\underline{\$ (9)}}$$

$$\text{Expected profit in period of sale} = \$14 - \$10$$
$$= \underline{\underline{\$ 4}}$$

The loss of $9 is measured as the amount needed to provide a normal profit in the future. The expected profit at the time of sale is the normal profit of $4.

The loss concept in Situations 2 and 3 is *not* consistent with the conservatism principle applied in other situations because it allows for the recognition of profits in future periods when the sale is made. Note also that the total loss in all three situations is $5 [$(5) + $0; $(7) + $2; $(9) + $4]. At issue is the inconsistent application of accounting principles which results in varied amounts of loss and profit that may be recognized in the period of writedown and the period of sale.[2]

## Approaches to Implementing Lower of Cost or Market Rule

The lower of cost or market rule may be applied:

> to each item or to the total of the inventory (or, in some cases, to the total of the components of each major category). The method should be that which most clearly reflects periodic income.[3]

The implementation of the rule to each individual item in inventory results in an inventory value less than (or equal to) the values obtained by the other two alternatives. Under these alternatives the price declines of some of the units in inventory are offset by price rises in some other items. This can be seen in Exhibit 7-2, which illustrates the three alternative methods of implementing the lower of cost or market rule for a company in the first year of its operations. Exhibit 7-2 is simplified because it assumes that there was no beginning inventory. Similar results would be obtained if the cost of the beginning inventory was less than or equal to the market value. If the lower of cost or market rule is applied to individual items, the inventory valuation is $6,100 and a loss of $600 ($6,100 market − $6,700 cost) is recognized. This method is the most conservative alternative. If the rule is applied to each category, the inventory valuation is $6,500 and a loss of $200 is recognized. If it is applied to the total inventory, the valuation is $6,600 and a loss of $100 is recognized. As discussed in

---

2. For additional discussion of these issues, see S.E. Warner and F.D. Whitehurst, "An Illustration of Inventory Loss Measurements Under the LCM Rule," *The Accounting Educators' Journal* (Fall, 1988), pp. 32−7.

3. *Accounting Research Bulletin No. 43, op. cit.*, par. 10.

the next section, the amount of the loss recognized in a given year is a function of the relationship between cost and market value of both the beginning and ending inventory.

---

**EXHIBIT 7-2**

**APPROACHES TO IMPLEMENTING LOWER OF COST OR MARKET**

| Inventory | Cost | Market | Individual Items | Category | Total |
|---|---|---|---|---|---|
| Category A: | | | | | |
| Item 1 | $1,000 | $ 700 | $ 700 | | |
| Item 2 | 1,200 | 1,300 | 1,200 | | |
| | $2,200 | $2,000 | | $2,000 | |
| Category B: | | | | | |
| Item 3 | $2,000 | $2,400 | 2,000 | | |
| Item 4 | 2,500 | 2,200 | 2,200 | | |
| | $4,500 | $4,600 | | 4,500 | |
| Total | $6,700 | $6,600 | | | $6,600 |
| Inventory valuation | | | $6,100 | $6,500 | $6,600 |
| Loss recognition | | | $ 600 | $ 200 | $ 100 |

---

The use of three alternative methods to account for the *same economic events* is inappropriate, since the qualitative characteristic of *comparability* among companies is enhanced when only one method is allowed. However, it can be expected that in many situations no material differences will result from the use of the alternative methods. The most common practice is to apply the lower of cost or market rule to each individual item, since it is required for income tax purposes and is the most conservative alternative. Of course the method chosen should be applied consistently each period.

Once the inventory has been reduced to market, it is *not* written back up to cost even if the market value subsequently rises above cost. Effectively, the written-down value becomes the new "cost" for subsequent valuation purposes and, if the company is using the FIFO or average cost flow assumptions, affects the cost of goods sold in the next period. Therefore, recoveries of losses may be *implicitly* recognized, as shown in the next section.

## Recording the Reduction of Inventory to Market

Although it is acceptable to record the write-down of inventory cost to market value directly in the inventory and cost of goods sold accounts (*direct* method), it is more desirable to use a separate inventory valuation account and a loss account (*allowance* method) so that the effects of the write-down can be clearly identified. The journal entries for both methods are illustrated in Exhibit 7-3 for a company using FIFO and the periodic inventory system that has the following inventory values:

|  | Cost | Market |
|---|---|---|
| December 31, 1994 | $20,000 | $20,000 |
| December 31, 1995 | 25,000 | 22,000 |
| December 31, 1996 | 30,000 | 28,000 |

In the *direct* method, the $3,000 decline in the value of the inventory at the end of 1995 is included in the year-end closing entry by recording the ending inventory at its lower *market* value of $22,000. Consequently the Inventory account balance is $3,000 *lower* and Cost of Goods Sold is $3,000 *higher* than they otherwise would be. This lower inventory value of $22,000 is the beginning inventory for 1996. At the end of 1996 the market value is $2,000 below the cost of $30,000, and so the market value of $28,000 is included in the closing entry. The effect of the value of the beginning and ending inventory on cost of goods sold in 1996 should be considered carefully. The market value of the beginning inventory is $3,000 below cost, and this causes the cost of goods sold to be $3,000 *lower* than it otherwise would be. The

---

**EXHIBIT 7-3**

## RECORDING THE REDUCTION OF INVENTORY TO MARKET

|  | Periodic Inventory System | | | |
|---|---|---|---|---|
|  | Direct Method | | Allowance Method | |
| **December 31, 1995** | | | | |
| 1. To close beginning inventory: | | | | |
| Income Summary | 20,000 | | 20,000 | |
| Inventory | | 20,000 | | 20,000 |
| 2. To record ending inventory: | | | | |
| Inventory | 22,000 | | 25,000 | |
| Income Summary | | 22,000 | | 25,000 |
| 3. To record inventory at market: | | | | |
| Loss Due to Market Valuation | Not required | | 3,000 | |
| Allowance to Reduce Inventory to Market | | | | 3,000 |
| **December 31, 1996** | | | | |
| 1. To close beginning inventory: | | | | |
| Income Summary | 22,000 | | 25,000 | |
| Inventory | | 22,000 | | 25,000 |
| 2. To record ending inventory: | | | | |
| Inventory | 28,000 | | 30,000 | |
| Income Summary | | 28,000 | | 30,000 |
| 3. To record inventory at market: | | | | |
| Allowance to Reduce Inventory to Market | Not required | | 1,000 | |
| Loss Recovery Due to Market Valuation | | | | 1,000 |

market value of the ending inventory is $2,000 below cost, and this causes the cost of goods sold to be $2,000 *higher* than it otherwise would be. Therefore the net effect is that the cost of goods sold is $1,000 lower and income $1,000 higher in 1996, because the lower of cost or market value method is used.

The same net results are obtained when the *allowance* method is used. However, more information about the impact of the lower of cost or market method on a company's cost of goods sold is revealed. In the allowance method, the amount by which the market value is below cost is recorded in an Allowance account and the effect on the cost of goods sold is shown explicitly in a Loss (or Loss Recovery) account. In the closing entry at the end of 1995, the inventory is recorded at its cost of $25,000, and the decline in value of $3,000 is recorded separately in the Loss account and the Allowance account. At the end of 1996 the inventory is recorded in the closing entry at its cost of $30,000. As discussed later, the net effect of recording the beginning inventory at a book value of $3,000 below cost and the ending inventory at a book value of $2,000 below cost is to cause cost of goods sold to be $1,000 lower than it otherwise would be. Therefore the Allowance account is reduced by $1,000 and a Loss Recovery of $1,000 is recognized. These losses and recoveries are shown as adjustments to cost of goods sold (as in the example in Exhibit 7-4) and therefore disclose more information than the direct method. However, many companies may combine the two amounts in their published financial statements.

If the company were using the perpetual inventory system instead of the periodic system, the net results would again be the same. The journal entries to record the reductions to market would be as follows:

| | Direct Method | | Allowance Method | |
| --- | --- | --- | --- | --- |
| | **1995** | **1996** | **1995** | **1996** |
| Cost of Goods Sold | 3,000 | 2,000 | | |
| Inventory | 3,000 | 2,000 | | |
| Loss (Loss Recovery) due to Market Valuation | | | 3,000 | 1,000 |
| Allowance to Reduce Inventory to Market | | | 3,000 | 1,000 |

If the **direct** method is used, the reduction of $3,000 in the 1995 ending inventory is recognized by increasing cost of goods sold and reducing inventory. In 1996 the reduction of $2,000 in the ending inventory is recognized in exactly the same way. Again note that the net effect of the reduction of the beginning and ending inventory ($3,000 and $2,000, respectively) on cost of goods sold in 1996 is that it is $1,000 lower than it would otherwise be. If the **allowance** method is used, the amount recorded in the Allowance and the Loss (or Loss Recovery) accounts is the same as for the periodic method.

The financial statement reporting of the direct and allowance methods for the periodic inventory method is shown in Exhibit 7-4, assuming purchases in each year are $100,000. The advantage of the allowance method is that it clearly discloses the loss and loss recovery in the income statements (but not as extraordinary items) and the valuation adjustment in the respective balance sheets. Although this method is recommended and is used for many companies' internal financial statements, published financial statements generally do not disclose the size of the loss and the valuation allowance (unless one, or both, is material) but merely indicate that the lower of cost or market method is being used.

## EXHIBIT 7-4

### FINANCIAL STATEMENT REPORTING OF THE LOWER OF COST OR MARKET (LCM) METHOD

|  | Direct Method | Allowance Method |
|---|---|---|
| *Income Statement 1995* | | |
| Beginning inventory | $ 20,000 (cost) | $ 20,000 (cost) |
| Purchases | 100,000 | 100,000 |
| Cost of goods available | $120,000 | $120,000 |
| Less: Ending inventory | (22,000) (LCM) | (25,000) (cost) |
|  | | $ 95,000 |
| Loss due to market decline | | 3,000 |
| Cost of goods sold | $ 98,000 | $ 98,000 |
| | | |
| *Balance Sheet 12/31/1995* | | |
| Inventory at cost | | $ 25,000 |
| Less: Allowance to reduce inventory to market | | (3,000) |
| Inventory at lower of cost or market | $ 22,000 | $ 22,000 |
| | | |
| *Income Statement 1996* | | |
| Beginning inventory | $ 22,000 (LCM) | $ 25,000 (cost) |
| Purchases | 100,000 | 100,000 |
| Cost of goods available | $122,000 | $125,000 |
| Less: Ending inventory | (28,000) (LCM) | (30,000) (cost) |
|  | | $ 95,000 |
| Loss recovery due to market recovery | | (1,000) |
| Cost of goods sold | $ 94,000 | $ 94,000 |
| | | |
| *Balance Sheet 12/31/1996* | | |
| Inventory at cost | | $ 30,000 |
| Less: Allowance to reduce inventory to market | | (2,000) |
| Inventory at lower of cost or market | $ 28,000 | $ 28,000 |

### Lower of Cost or Market and Interim Financial Statements

APB Opinion No. 28 specifies that for interim financial statements if a market decline occurs in an interim period and it is considered temporary, it should be ignored. If the decline is unlikely to be recovered, it should be recognized. If a decline is recognized and subsequently reverses in a later *interim* period, a loss recovery should be recognized and the inventory value increased by the amount of the recovery, but only up to the original cost.[4]

---

4. "Interim Financial Reporting," *APB Opinion No. 28* (New York: AICPA, 1973), par. 14(c).

# CONCEPTUAL EVALUATION OF LOWER OF COST OR MARKET

The reduction of the value of the inventory to market and the recognition of a loss are appropriate for both the balance sheet and income statement. As discussed in Chapter 3, *FASB Statement of Concepts No. 6* defines *assets* as "probable future economic benefits." When the cost of the inventory exceeds the expected benefits, it is appropriate to reduce the asset value to its market value, which is a better measure of the expected benefits. In other words, an unrecoverable cost is not an asset. As discussed in Chapter 4, the *Statement* also defines *losses* as "decreases in net assets from peripheral or incidental transactions. . . and other events. . . except those that result from expenses or distributions to owners." Thus the decline in value of the inventory should be recognized as a reduction in the income of the period in which the loss occurs.

Although the lower of cost or market method is used with all cost flow assumptions, it is unlikely that it will be applied to LIFO because the replacement cost should not be less than the LIFO cost. Such a situation would be very unusual, especially since LIFO is used when there is an expectation of rising costs.

The major criticism of the lower of cost or market rule is that it is applied only in one direction. Declines and (holding) losses are recognized but increases and (holding) gains are not. Obviously this is inconsistent but it is justified by the conservatism (prudence) convention. Conservatism requires the recognition of all losses that can reasonably be expected and no anticipation of possible gains, which is exactly what the lower of cost or market rule achieves. Some accountants argue that the market value of inventory should be recognized when the replacement cost is *higher* than the historical cost. They argue that the replacement cost of the inventory is *reliable* regardless of its relationship to historical cost. Furthermore, it is argued that valuation of inventory at replacement cost (when higher than historical cost) is *relevant* because it better reflects the **cash flow potential** of the inventory and enhances the predictive value of the information. This valuation, however, is not allowed under generally accepted accounting principles, because it would be a violation of the historical cost principle.

It could be argued that another principle, the *revenue recognition* principle, is violated by the lower of cost or market method, since a loss is recognized before the earning process is complete and before an exchange transaction has occurred. Modification of the revenue recognition principle is justified in these circumstances because the decline in the value of the inventory is an **economic event of the period** that has caused a reduction in the stockholders' equity. Therefore it should be included in the determination of income. However, the revenue recognition principle may be used to support the nonrecognition of increases in value, because the total difference between selling price and cost is usually recognized in the period of the sale.

Since a loss is recognized in the period of the market decline, income will be *higher* in the subsequent period when the inventory is sold than it would otherwise have been. In other words, the loss is transferred from the future period of the sale to the current period of the decline in market value. Total income over the two periods will be the same whether or not the lower of cost or market rule is used. This is shown by the earlier example in which recording the inventory at the lower of cost or market caused income to be lower by $3,000 in 1995 and higher by $1,000 in 1996. If the inventory is recorded at cost in a subsequent year(s), income will be higher by the $2,000 remaining in the Allowance account in that year(s). Therefore total income over the years in which inventory was recorded at lower of cost or market will

*The valuation of assets at market value is discussed in Chapter 24.*

be the same as if the inventory had been recorded at cost for those years (because the beginning and ending inventory for the several years are both at cost).

### International Accounting Differences

The lower of cost or market method is widely used throughout the world with many countries, including Japan, defining market as replacement cost. However, market is defined as net realizable value in some countries such as Australia and the United Kingdom. Other countries, including Canada, Brazil, and Germany, allow either replacement cost or net realizable value.[5]

## PURCHASE OBLIGATIONS AND PRODUCT FINANCING ARRANGEMENTS

Accounting principles generally require that purchase obligations not be recorded in the accounts (except in governmental accounting), because neither an asset nor a liability is created by placing an order. **If unconditional purchase obligations have been made at a definite price, these commitments should be disclosed in a note to the financial statements.**[6] This requirement is imposed because these commitments are important for the prediction of the cash outflows that the company will make in the future.

**If a company has an unconditional (noncancelable) purchase obligation to acquire inventory and the current market price (i.e., replacement cost) is less than the fixed purchase price, the company must recognize the loss in the period in which the decline occurs just as if it already owned the inventory.** This procedure is consistent with the conservatism convention and also provides the users of the financial statements with information about the decision-making ability of the management. For example, if a company entered into a noncancelable commitment to purchase inventory at a fixed price of $500,000 and the market price (replacement cost) at the end of the year is $450,000, the following year-end adjusting entry would be made:

| | | |
|---|---|---|
| Loss on Purchase Commitments | 50,000 | |
|     Accrued Loss on Purchase Commitments | | 50,000 |

The accrued loss is shown as a liability on the balance sheet and is written off when the goods are purchased as follows:

| | | |
|---|---|---|
| Purchases (or Inventory) | 450,000 | |
| Accrued Loss on Purchase Commitments | 50,000 | |
|     Accounts Payable | | 500,000 |

If the market price rises by the time the purchase is made, the accrued loss is reduced and a loss recovery is recognized. The purchases are then recorded at the market price on the date of acquisition.

---

5.  For additional discussion, see Coopers & Lybrand, *1991 International Accounting Summaries: A Guide for Interpretation and Comparison* (New York: John Wiley and Son, Inc., 1991).

6.  "Disclosure of Long-Term Obligations," *FASB Statement of Financial Accounting Standards No. 47* (Stamford, Conn.: FASB, 1981), par. 7.

An accrual of the loss is made only when there is a loss on a *noncancelable* purchase commitment. Such a loss satisfies the criterion of a contingent loss contained in **FASB Statement No. 5,** namely, that the existence of the loss is probable and can be reasonably estimated. Losses on *cancelable* purchase commitments would not be accrued because it can be assumed that the purchase commitment would be canceled and the loss avoided.

Some companies have engaged in product financing arrangements as a way of financing the cost of inventory before the sale to the ultimate purchaser occurs. **In a product financing arrangement the company "sells" the inventory to another company and, in a related transaction, agrees to purchase the inventory (or a substantially identical item) back from the other company at specified prices over specified periods.** Typically the inventory is not delivered to the "buyer" and is repurchased at a higher price, the difference being an interest charge. When the "sale" under the product financing arrangement occurs, the transaction is similar to borrowing cash with the inventory being used as collateral, sometimes referred to as a "parking" transaction. Thus, according to **FASB Statement No. 49,** the company does *not* record sales revenue but instead records the proceeds received as a liability.[7] This procedure avoids the overstatement of revenues and stockholders' equity and the understatement of liabilities. As a result of not recording a sale, the inventory also remains in the accounts at cost. Note, however, that this *Statement* does *not* apply to agreements to repurchase at prices that are not specified.

*Accounting for contingencies is discussed in Chapters 3 and 11.*

## VALUATION ABOVE COST

It has been stated earlier in this chapter that the lower of cost or market method does not result in a valuation of inventory above cost. However, generally accepted accounting principles do allow valuation above cost in certain circumstances. **Accounting Research Bulletin No. 43** states:

> Only in exceptional cases may inventories properly be stated above cost. For example, precious metals having a fixed monetary value with no substantial cost of marketing may be stated at such monetary value; any other exceptions must be justifiable by inability to determine appropriate approximate costs, immediate marketability at quoted market price, and the characteristic of unit interchangeability. Where goods are stated above cost this fact should be fully disclosed.
>
> A similar treatment is not uncommon for inventories representing agricultural, mineral and other products, units of which are interchangeable and have an immediate marketability at quoted prices and for which appropriate costs may be difficult to obtain.[8]

An example of valuation at replacement market prices is provided in Exhibit 7-5 for the International Multifoods Corporation. Justification for this method exists when it is highly certain that the inventory can be sold at the market price. Such a situation indicates that the income is earned by production rather than by sale. Therefore valuation at market, above cost, is considered to be appropriate. However, this practice violates the conservatism convention and the usual application of the revenue recognition principle and is acceptable only in selected industries.

*Revenue recognition is discussed in Chapter 16.*

---

7. "Accounting for Product Financing Arrangements," *FASB Statement of Financial Accounting Standards No. 49* (Stamford, Conn.: FASB, 1981).
8. *Accounting Research Bulletin No. 43, op. cit.,* ch. 4, par. 15 and 16.

**EXHIBIT 7-5**
**Inventory Valuation Above Cost**

**INTERNATIONAL MULTIFOODS CORPORATION**
NOTES (in part):

*Inventories*   Inventories, excluding grain in the United States and Canada, are valued principally at the lower of cost (first-in, first-out) or market (replacement or net realizable value).

In the United States and Canada, inventories of grain are valued on the basis of replacement market prices prevailing at fiscal year-end. The Company generally minimizes risks associated with market price fluctuations by hedging those inventories with futures contracts. Therefore, included in inventories is the amount of gain or loss on open grain contracts, including futures contracts, which generally has the effect of adjusting those inventories to cost.

## GROSS PROFIT METHOD

Two commonly used methods of estimating inventory costs are the gross profit method and the retail inventory method. The retail inventory method is used by companies in retail industries and is discussed later in this chapter.

**The gross profit method is used to estimate the cost of the inventory by applying a gross profit rate based on the income statements of previous periods to the net sales of the current period.** It may be used in the following situations:

1.  To determine the cost of the inventory at the end of an interim period without taking a physical count. Because of the cost of taking a physical inventory, a company using a periodic inventory system may use the gross profit method for its internal financial statements. It is also an acceptable method for published interim financial statements, provided that the company "disclose the method used at the interim date and any significant adjustments that result from reconciliations with the annual physical inventory."[9]

2.  For the internal or external auditor to check the reasonableness of an inventory value developed from a physical inventory or a perpetual inventory system.

3.  To estimate the cost of the inventory destroyed by a casualty such as a fire.

4.  To estimate the cost of the inventory from incomplete records. For example, if the inventory records are destroyed, the inventory can be estimated provided the cost of goods available for sale and the sales are known or can be reconstructed.

5.  To develop a budget of cost of goods sold and ending inventory from a sales budget.

The application of the gross profit method assumes that the gross profit rate (the rate of gross profit on net sales) in the current period is not materially different from

---

9.   *APB Opinion No. 28, op. cit.,* par. 14(a).

that of the previous period(s). If there are any identifiable differences, adjustments should be made, as discussed later. The steps involved in the gross profit method include:

1. The historical gross profit rate is estimated by dividing the gross profit of the prior period(s) by the net sales of the prior period(s).

2. The gross profit for the current period is estimated by multiplying the historical gross profit rate by the actual net sales for the period.

3. The estimated gross profit is subtracted from the actual net sales to determine the estimated cost of goods sold for the period.

4. The estimated cost of goods sold is subtracted from the actual cost of goods available for sale (the beginning inventory plus the net purchases) for the period to determine the estimated cost of the ending inventory.

The application of this method is illustrated in Exhibit 7-6 and each of the preceding steps is listed in parentheses. The historical gross profit rate of 40% is used because it is believed to represent the best estimate of conditions in the current year; that is, no material changes in conditions from previous years have occurred.

One step may be removed from the calculation shown in Exhibit 7-6, thereby reducing the amount of computation. Since the gross profit is 40% of net sales, the cost of goods sold is 60% of net sales. Therefore the cost of goods sold could be calculated directly as $78,000 (60% × $130,000).

---

**EXHIBIT 7-6**

**ESTIMATION OF THE COST OF THE ENDING INVENTORY BY THE GROSS PROFIT METHOD**

*Given Information*

| | |
|---|---|
| Beginning inventory, at cost | $ 10,000 |
| Net purchases for the period | 90,000 |
| Net sales for the period | 130,000 |
| Estimated historical gross profit rate (on net sales) | 40%  (1) |

*Estimation of Ending Inventory*

| | | |
|---|---|---|
| Beginning inventory, at cost | | $ 10,000 |
| Net purchases | | 90,000 |
| Cost of goods available for sale | | $100,000 |
| Less: Estimated cost of goods sold: | | |
|     Net sales | $130,000 | |
|     Gross profit rate | 0.40 | |
|     Estimated gross profit | $ 52,000 (2) | |
|     Cost of goods sold ($130,000 − $52,000) | | (78,000) (3) |
| Estimated cost of ending inventory | | $ 22,000  (4) |

## Gross Profit Stated as a Percentage of Cost of Goods Sold

Sometimes a company will express the gross profit as a percentage of the cost of goods sold instead of as a percentage of net sales. In this case the gross profit percentage must be converted to a percentage of net sales before the gross profit method can be applied. The method of conversion is illustrated in Exhibit 7-7, where a gross profit of 25% of the cost of goods sold is assumed.

---

**EXHIBIT 7-7**

**GROSS PROFIT AS A PERCENTAGE OF COST OF GOODS SOLD CONVERTED INTO GROSS PROFIT AS A PERCENTAGE OF NET SALES**

$$\text{If } \frac{\text{Gross Profit}}{\text{Cost of Goods Sold}} = 0.25$$

then the relationship is:

| | |
|---|---|
| Net sales | 1.25 |
| Cost of goods sold | (1.00) |
| Gross profit | 0.25 |

$$\text{and } \frac{\text{Gross Profit}}{\text{Net Sales}} = \frac{0.25}{1.25}$$

$$= 0.20 \text{ or } \underline{20\%}$$

---

The gross profit is determined to be 20% of net sales. The gross profit method can then be applied as shown in Exhibit 7-6. The general relationship between the two measures of gross profit rates can be stated as follows:

$$\frac{\text{Gross Profit to Net}}{\text{Sales Ratio}} = \frac{\text{Gross Profit to Cost of Goods Sold Ratio}}{1 + \text{Gross Profit to Cost of Goods Sold Ratio}}$$

Using the data from Exhibit 7-7,

$$\text{Gross Profit to Net Sales Ratio} = 0.25 \div (1 + 0.25)$$
$$= \underline{0.20}$$

Alternatively, if the gross profit to net sales ratio is known, and calculation of the gross profit to cost of goods sold ratio (often called the markup percentage) is required, the following formula may be used:

$$\frac{\text{Gross Profit to Cost of}}{\text{Goods Sold Ratio}} = \frac{\text{Gross Profit to Net Sales Ratio}}{1 - \text{Gross Profit to Net Sales Ratio}}$$

or, continuing the preceding example,

$$\text{Gross Profit to Cost of Goods Sold Ratio} = \frac{0.20}{1 - 0.20}$$
$$= \underline{\underline{0.25}}$$

### Conceptual Evaluation of the Gross Profit Method

The gross profit method is useful in the situations outlined at the beginning of this section, but the accuracy of the results depends on the accuracy of the gross profit percentage. Three modifications to the procedure outlined previously may enhance its accuracy.

First, the gross profit rate should be adjusted for known changes in the relationship between gross profit and net sales. For example, if costs of purchases have increased, but the increases have not been passed along through increased sales prices, the gross profit percentage should be reduced accordingly. The gross profit rate may also need to be adjusted if a change in productivity has occurred, or if there has been a change in the amount of sales (and purchases) returns and allowances.

Second, a separate gross profit rate may be used for each department or type of inventory that has a different markup percentage. Each rate would then be applied to each department's net sales, with the resulting amounts summed to compute the total inventory. Use of a single overall gross profit rate assumes that all types of inventory are sold or held in inventory in equal proportions at all times. Since this is unlikely, use of separate gross profit rates enhances the accuracy of the cost of the ending inventory and the cost of goods sold.

Third, an average gross profit rate based on several past periods may be used to average out period-to-period fluctuations. However, use of an average rate assumes that no significant changes have taken place over the periods selected for the calculation of the average rate and that no adjustments have been made to account for such changes. The use of an average rate is particularly appropriate when there is an environment of relatively stable costs, selling prices, and operating methods.

The ending inventory estimated by the gross profit method is consistent with the cost flow assumption previously (and currently) used by the company. This occurs because the gross profit rate is based on the past results developed from using the particular cost flow assumption. However, if there has been a special situation in the past, such as the reduction of the inventory to market, or a liquidation of LIFO inventory, appropriate adjustments to the gross profit rate will be required.

## RETAIL INVENTORY METHOD

The retail inventory method is used widely to estimate the cost of inventory when there is a consistently observable pattern between the cost of a company's purchases and selling prices (either for the whole company or for identifiable departments within the company). The method is particularly appropriate for retail stores where prices often are set on the basis of a consistent markup above cost and their accounting systems are based on retail values rather than costs. The retail inventory method can be applied on the basis of the average, FIFO, and LIFO cost flow assumptions, and the lower of cost or market method can be used in conjunction with each. The retail inventory method has gained wide acceptance because it is allowed under generally accepted accounting principles and for income tax purposes.

The retail inventory method requires the use of the following information:

1. Beginning inventory at cost and retail.

2. Goods purchased at cost and retail.

3. Changes in selling price resulting from additional markups and markdowns.

4. Sales.

Assuming that the retail inventory method is being used in conjunction with the average cost flow assumption, the following steps are necessary:

1. The total goods available for sale (beginning inventory plus purchases) is computed at both cost and retail value (selling price).

2. A cost-to-retail ratio is computed by dividing the cost of the goods available for sale by the retail value of the goods available for sale.

3. The ending inventory at retail is computed by subtracting the sales for the period from the retail value of the goods available for sale.

4. The ending inventory at cost is computed by multiplying the ending inventory at retail by the cost-to-retail ratio.

The application of this method is illustrated using the following simplified data:

|  | Cost | Retail |
|---|---|---|
| Beginning inventory | $10,000 | $17,000 |
| Purchases | 50,000 | 83,000 |
| Sales |  | 80,000 |

The ending inventory at cost is computed as follows (each of the preceding steps is referenced in the calculation):

|  | Cost | Retail |  |
|---|---|---|---|
| Beginning inventory | $10,000 | $ 17,000 |  |
| Purchases | 50,000 | 83,000 |  |
| Goods available for sale | $60,000 | $100,000 | (1) |
| Cost-to-retail ratio: $\dfrac{\$60,000}{\$100,000} = 0.60$ |  |  | (2) |
| Less: Sales |  | (80,000) |  |
| Ending inventory at retail |  | $ 20,000 | (3) |
| Ending inventory at cost (0.60 × $20,000) | $12,000 |  | (4) |

The retail inventory method is similar to the gross profit method because it estimates inventory based on a profit percentage. It differs, however, and is more sensitive to price changes because it uses a current period estimate of the profit percentage, whereas the gross profit method uses an estimate based on past periods. This similarity is summarized as follows:

| Gross Profit Method | Retail Inventory Method |
|---|---|
| Cost of goods available | Retail value of goods available |
| Less: Cost of goods sold (sales × gross profit rate) | Less: Retail value of goods sold (sales) |
| | Ending inventory at retail × cost-to-retail ratio |
| Ending inventory at cost | Ending inventory at cost |

The major advantages of the retail inventory method are:

1.  It permits interim reports to be prepared without a physical inventory being taken, but as with any inventory system, a physical count should be taken at least annually.

2.  It simplifies the record-keeping procedures because the costs of *individual* purchases do not need to be maintained and do not have to be related to the particular units in inventory. In addition, merchandise in retail stores is typically priced and displayed immediately, and the record keeping is based on retail prices.

3.  It expedites the verification of the ending inventory by physical count because the inventory in the retail store is recorded at retail values and can therefore be compared directly with the accounting records, which are also based on retail prices. Thus, it is not necessary to refer to the individual purchase invoices to determine the cost of each item.

## Retail Inventory Method Terminology

In the preceding illustration the retail value of the goods available for sale is the original sales price, and it is assumed that no subsequent changes in retail prices were made. However, the typical retail store does make many changes in selling prices after setting the original price. (For the average retail food store the changes are likely to be over a hundred each week.) The following seven terms are used to describe these changes:

1.  *Markup.* The original markup from cost to the first selling price (also known as *mark-on*).

2.  *Additional Markup.* An increase above the original sales price.

3.  *Markup Cancellation.* A reduction in the selling price after there has been an additional markup. The markup cancellation cannot be greater than the additional markup.

4.  *Net Markup.* The total additional markups less the total markup cancellations.

5. *Markdown.* A decrease below the original sales price.

6. *Markdown Cancellation.* An increase in the selling price after there has been a markdown. The markdown cancellation cannot be greater than the markdown.

7. *Net Markdown.* The total markdowns less the total markdown cancellations.

To illustrate the meaning of these terms, suppose that an item is purchased for $6 and is initially priced to sell for $10. The markup is $4. If the selling price is subsequently increased to $12, there is an additional markup of $2. If the selling price is then lowered to $7, there is a markup cancellation of $2 and a markdown of $3. If the selling price is then raised to $8, there is a markdown cancellation of $1. The net markup is zero ($2 − $2), and the net markdown is $2 ($3 − $1).

## Application of the Retail Inventory Method

In the simplified example shown earlier, the average cost flow assumption was used. However, the retail inventory method may be used to develop inventory valuations under four alternatives (the lower of cost or market used with FIFO and LIFO is not illustrated):

1. *FIFO.* The cost and the retail value of the beginning inventory are excluded from the computation of the cost-to-retail ratio for the period. The ratio includes both net markups and net markdowns.

2. *Average Cost.* The cost and the retail value of the beginning inventory and net markups and markdowns are included in the cost-to-retail ratio.

3. *LIFO.* Separate ratios are computed for each layer in the beginning inventory and for the purchases of the current period; both net markups and net markdowns are included in the cost-to-retail ratio for the current period.

4. *Lower of Average Cost or Market.* The cost and retail value of the beginning inventory and net markups are included in the cost-to-retail ratio. Thus, the net markdowns are excluded from the computation of the cost-to-retail ratio. This method is also known as the *conventional retail* method.

The calculation of the cost-to-retail ratio of the current period for each of the alternative methods may be summarized as follows:

|  | FIFO | Average Cost | LIFO* | Lower of Average Cost or Market |
|---|---|---|---|---|
| Beginning inventory | Exclude | Include | Exclude | Include |
| Purchases | Include | Include | Include | Include |
| Markups (net) | Include | Include | Include | Include |
| Markdowns (net) | Include | Include | Include | Exclude |

*A separate cost-to-retail ratio is also computed for each layer in the beginning inventory.

Note that these alternative methods differ in the calculation of the cost-to-retail ratio, but that the net markups and markdowns *always* are added and subtracted in order to compute the retail value of the ending inventory. Also note that markups and markdowns are recorded only at *retail*. Each of these methods is illustrated in the following sections, using the data for the Thompson Company given in Exhibit 7-8.

---

**EXHIBIT 7-8**

**THOMPSON COMPANY**
Cost and Retail Value

| | Cost | Retail |
|---|---|---|
| Beginning inventory | $20 | $ 35 |
| Purchases | 40 | 80 |
| Net markups | — | 5 |
| Net markdowns | — | (10) |
| Goods available for sale | — | $110 |
| Sales | — | (66) |
| Ending inventory at retail | — | $ 44 |

---

*Note*: It is assumed that the beginning inventory is valued at a cost of $20 for all flow assumptions, although this value would be different for different cost flow assumptions because the beginning inventory for the current period is the ending inventory of the previous period.

## FIFO

Under the FIFO cost flow assumption the beginning inventory is excluded from the computation of the cost-to-retail ratio for the period. The Thompson Company would compute the cost of its ending inventory at $23.45, as shown in Exhibit 7-9.

---

**EXHIBIT 7-9**

**THOMPSON COMPANY**
Retail Inventory Method—FIFO

| | Cost | Retail |
|---|---|---|
| Purchases | $40 | $ 80 |
| Net markups | | 5 |
| Net markdowns | | (10) |
| | $40 | $ 75 |
| Cost-to-retail ratio: $\frac{\$40}{\$75} = 0.533$ | | |
| Beginning inventory | 20 | 35 |
| Goods available for sale | $60 | $110 |
| Less: Sales | | (66) |
| Ending inventory at retail | | $ 44 |
| Ending inventory at FIFO cost (0.533 × $44) | $23.45 | |

Excluding the beginning inventory from the computation of the cost-to-retail ratio produces the layering effect of FIFO for cost of goods sold. Since the ending inventory cost is based only on the activities of the current period, the entire beginning inventory is included in the cost of goods sold. Therefore the *cost of goods sold* is made up of two layers as follows:

|  | Cost | Retail |
|---|---|---|
| Beginning inventory | $20.00 | $35 |
| Purchases at retail |  | 31 |
| Purchases at cost ($31 × 0.533) | 16.52 |  |
|  | $36.52 | $66 |

Thus the cost of goods available of $60 is allocated (amounts rounded) between cost of goods sold ($36.52) and ending inventory ($23.45). Note that in this example it has been assumed that the units sold during the period exceed the units in the beginning inventory, and therefore under FIFO the cost of the entire beginning inventory is included in cost of goods sold during the current period. If at the end of the period some of the beginning inventory still remained, the ending inventory would be comprised of two layers, each with its own cost-to-retail ratio.

*Average Cost*

Under the average cost flow assumption the beginning inventory and the net markups and markdowns are included in the cost-to-retail ratio. The Thompson Company would estimate the cost of its ending inventory at $24, as shown in Exhibit 7-10.

**EXHIBIT 7-10**

**THOMPSON COMPANY**
Retail Inventory Method—Average Cost

|  | Cost | Retail |
|---|---|---|
| Beginning inventory | $20 | $ 35 |
| Purchases | 40 | 80 |
| Net markups |  | 5 |
| Net markdowns |  | (10) |
| Goods available for sale | $60 | $110 |

Cost-to-retail ratio: $\dfrac{\$60}{\$110} = 0.545$

|  |  |  |
|---|---|---|
| Less: Sales |  | (66) |
| Ending inventory at retail |  | $ 44 |
| Ending inventory at average cost (0.545 × $44) | $24 |  |

The similarities between this application of the average cost flow assumption and the more general average cost method discussed in the preceding chapter should be apparent. The beginning inventory and the purchases are commingled. Since the company sold at retail 60% ($66 ÷ $110) of the goods available for sale, 40% of the goods are left in ending inventory. The cost of the inventory is $24, which is 40% of the cost of the goods available for sale (40% × $60 = $24).

*LIFO*

Separate cost-to-retail ratios for the beginning inventory and the purchases have to be calculated when the LIFO cost flow assumption is applied to the retail inventory method. The ratio for the purchases includes both markups and markdowns if the cost basis is used. (Remember that LIFO may be used for income tax purposes only if it is also used for financial reporting.) The layers of inventory are accounted for by using the same principles as those discussed in the preceding chapter. The Thompson Company would compute the cost of its ending inventory at $24.80, as shown in Exhibit 7-11.

---

**EXHIBIT 7-11**

**THOMPSON COMPANY**
Retail Inventory Method—LIFO

|  | Cost | Retail |
|---|---|---|
| Beginning inventory | $20 | $ 35 |
| Cost-to-retail ratio: $\frac{\$20}{\$35} = 0.57$ |  |  |
| (for beginning inventory) |  |  |
| Purchases | 40 | 80 |
| Net markups |  | 5 |
| Net markdowns |  | (10) |
|  |  | $ 75 |
| Cost-to-retail ratio: $\frac{\$40}{\$75} = 0.533$ |  |  |
| (for purchases) |  |  |
| Goods available for sale | $60 | $110 |
| Less: Sales |  | (66) |
| Ending inventory at retail |  | $ 44 |
| Ending inventory at LIFO cost: |  |  |
| $35 × 0.57 (beginning inventory layer) | $20.00 |  |
| $9 × 0.533 (added layer) | 4.80 |  |
|  | $24.80 |  |

---

The company had sales of $66, which left an inventory at retail of $44. This inventory consists of two layers, which are the base inventory at retail of $35, and an addition at retail of $9. Each layer is converted to cost at its own cost-to-retail ratio. Another way of looking at this example is to see that the Thompson Company sold 88% ($66 ÷ $75) of the goods purchased during the period. Therefore at cost the company sold $35.20 (88% × $40) of the purchases, leaving $4.80 ($40 − $35.20) as an added layer in inventory.

Note that in the Thompson Company example, the LIFO method does not produce the lowest ending inventory cost compared to FIFO or average. The reason is that the cost-to-retail ratio for the purchases is less than the cost-to-retail ratio for the beginning inventory. This situation was caused by the large markdowns during the period, indicating the existence of falling costs (which may be caused by a decline in the prices charged by the supplier or by obsolescence due to a change in tastes or the season of the year). When costs are rising, the retail method using LIFO will produce a lower inventory cost.

If there had been a decrease in inventory over the period, the ending inventory would be composed only of a portion of the beginning inventory, and there would be no need to compute a cost-to-retail ratio for the purchases of the current period. In more complex situations the beginning inventory would be comprised of LIFO layers, and the decrease would have to be removed according to the general LIFO principles discussed in the preceding chapter.

*Lower of Average Cost or Market*
The retail inventory method can be used in conjunction with lower of cost or market under either the average, FIFO, or LIFO cost flow assumptions. In all three cases, net markdowns are excluded from the cost-to-retail ratio for the period to achieve the effects of the lower of cost or market method, and the appropriate flow assumption is used. Because the lower of average cost or market is commonly used, we will illustrate this alternative. The calculations follow the average cost example earlier, except that the net markdowns are *excluded* from the computation of the cost-to-retail ratio. The Thompson Company would compute the value of its ending inventory at $22, as shown in Exhibit 7-12.

Since the net markdowns are excluded from the computation of the cost-to-retail ratio, the denominator of the ratio is higher ($120 in Exhibit 7-12 as compared to $110 in Exhibit 7-10). Therefore, the ratio is lower (0.50 versus 0.545) and the cost of

---

### EXHIBIT 7-12

**THOMPSON COMPANY**
Retail Inventory Method—Lower of Average Cost or Market

|  | Cost | Retail |
|---|---|---|
| Beginning inventory | $20 | $ 35 |
| Purchases | 40 | 80 |
| Net markups |  | 5 |
|  | $60 | $120 |

Cost-to-retail ratio: $\dfrac{\$60}{\$120} = 0.50$

|  | Cost | Retail |
|---|---|---|
| Net markdowns |  | (10) |
| Goods available for sale | $60 | $110 |
| Less: Sales |  | (66) |
| Ending inventory at retail |  | $ 44 |
| Ending inventory at lower of cost or market (0.50 × $44) | $22 |  |

the ending inventory is lower ($22 versus $24). The assumptions underlying this calculation are discussed later in the chapter.

### Additional Cost and Retail Adjustments

Additional costs and activities frequently occur when the retail inventory method is applied. The cost of purchases includes the costs directly or indirectly incurred in bringing the items to their existing condition and location (as discussed in Chapter 6). Two items that affect net purchases are freight charges, which are added to the cost of purchases, and purchases discounts taken under the gross price method, which are subtracted from the cost of purchases. These two items affect only the *cost* of purchases and not the retail amount of purchases, because it is assumed that the original markup applied to the invoice cost by the retailer covers such incidental items. A third item that affects net purchases is purchases returns and allowances. Once the purchases have been recorded by a company at retail, any subsequent purchases returns and allowances are subtracted from *both the cost and retail value* of the purchases so as not to distort the computation of the cost-to-retail ratio.

Several items also affect the estimate of the ending inventory at retail. Sales returns and allowances are subtracted from sales at retail to determine net sales, which in turn are subtracted from goods available for sale at retail to compute ending inventory at retail. Sales discounts taken are *not* deducted to determine the ending inventory at retail, because they are considered to be financing items and not part of the original markup. Since inventory shrinkage, especially that due to breakage and theft, is a common problem in retail stores, whenever the retail inventory method is used for interim financial statements, an estimate should be made of normal shrinkage (such as 1% of sales) based on past experience. This estimate is then subtracted, in addition to the usual items, to determine the ending inventory at retail. An estimate is not necessary at year-end because a physical inventory is taken. Employee discounts—discounts from the normal sales price that are made available to employees—also are subtracted to compute ending inventory at retail (in the same way as sales). Both inventory shrinkage and employee discounts are subtracted because they are normal costs incurred by the company and therefore were reflected in the retail selling price determined by the original markup. Abnormal inventory spoilage would be subtracted at both cost and retail in the determination of goods available for sale so as not to distort the cost-to-retail ratio.

## CONCEPTUAL EVALUATION OF THE RETAIL INVENTORY METHOD

Two general assumptions underlie the use of the retail inventory method. The first is that the items in inventory are sufficiently homogeneous so that all have the same markup, or, if they have different markups, that the proportion of the different items in the ending inventory is the same as that in the goods available for sale. The limitations imposed by this assumption can be reduced by using a separate cost-to-retail ratio for each category of inventory or for each department. The second general assumption is that the cost-to-retail ratio remains constant over the accounting period or that changes in the prices of the retail market parallel the price changes of the wholesale market. The limitations imposed by this assumption can also be reduced by weighting the different cost-to-retail ratios used during the period according to the volume of activity that occurred for inventory items under each ratio.

Since the lower of average cost or market method is the most widely used version of the retail inventory method, it is important to consider whether this method actually does produce an inventory at lower of cost or market, or just a value that is lower than cost. This is evaluated in the three examples of Exhibit 7-13, which use the same basic data for the Thompson Company.

In all three examples it is assumed that 60% of the goods available for sale are sold, but different assumptions regarding the markups and markdowns are used in each example. In the first example it is assumed that there are only markups and no markdowns. Thus the cost-to-retail ratio is $60 ÷ $120 and the ending inventory $24. This cost is the same as the average cost figure computed in Exhibit 7-10. Since there were no markdowns, it can be assumed that the market value has not declined below cost, and therefore the inventory value is the lower of cost or market.

In the second example it is assumed that there are no markups but that there are markdowns. This produces a cost-to-retail ratio of $60 ÷ $115 and an ending inventory of $21.91. Since there are markdowns of $10, it can be assumed that prices have declined by a factor of 10 ÷ 115. To reflect this change, the ending inventory is valued at the lower of cost or market, which is $21.91 [$24 − ($24 × 10 ÷ 115)]. Therefore in this situation the method again has produced an inventory amount equal to the lower of cost or market.

Now refer back to the original computation of the lower of cost or market in Exhibit 7-12. Since $22 is greater than $21.91, the $22 value is *not* the true lower of

---

**EXHIBIT 7-13**

**THOMPSON COMPANY**
**Assumptions Underlying the Use of the Retail**
**Inventory Method: Lower of Average Cost or Market**

|  | Example 1 (no markdowns) | | Example 2 (no markups) | | Example 3 (all markdowns sold) | |
|---|---|---|---|---|---|---|
|  | Cost | Retail | Cost | Retail | Cost | Retail |
| Beginning inventory | $20 | $ 35 | $20 | $ 35 | $20 | $ 35 |
| Purchases | 40 | 80 | 40 | 80 | 40 | 80 |
| Net markups |  | 5 |  | — |  | 5 |
|  | $60 | $120 | $60 | $115 | $60 | $120 |
| Cost-to-retail ratio: | 0.50[1] | | 0.52[2] | | 0.50[3] | |
| Net markdowns |  | — |  | (10) |  | (10) |
| Goods available for sale | $60 | $120 | $60 | $105 | $60 | $110 |
| Less: Sales |  | (72)[4] |  | (63)[5] |  | (62)[6] |
| Ending inventory at retail |  | $ 48 |  | $ 42 |  | $ 48 |
| Ending inventory at lower of cost or market | $24[7] |  | $21.91[8] |  | $24[9] |  |

1. $\dfrac{\$60}{\$120} = 0.50$    2. $\dfrac{\$60}{\$115} = 0.52$    3. $\dfrac{\$60}{\$120} = 0.50$    4. ($120 × 60%)    5. ($105 × 60%)

6. ($120 × 60% − $10)    7. $\dfrac{\$60}{\$120} \times \$48$    8. $\dfrac{\$60}{\$115} \times \$42$    9. $\dfrac{\$60}{\$120} \times \$48$

cost or market of the inventory, but simply a value that is lower than cost. This indicates that the lower of cost or market method is accurate only if the goods in the inventory are perfectly homogeneous. In other words, markups and markdowns for separate items within inventory cannot exist at the same time.

In the third example, again, there are both markups and markdowns. The cost-to-retail ratio is $60 ÷ $120. But now it is assumed that all the goods that are marked down are sold. Since it is assumed also that 60% of the goods available for sale are sold, sales would be equal to 60% of the goods available for sale less the $10 markdowns [(60% × $120) − $10 = $62]. The ending inventory is $24, which is again the lower of cost or market, because all goods marked down are assumed to have been sold and thus the ending inventory contains items that have a retail value that is higher than their cost. Therefore for the lower of cost or market method to be accurate, the goods in inventory do not have to be perfectly homogeneous if it can be assumed that all the units that have been marked down have been sold. To summarize, the lower of average cost or market method is completely accurate only if either markups and markdowns do not exist at the same time or all the marked-down items have been sold. Under other conditions the method produces an inventory value that is less than cost but only approximates the lower of cost or market.

## DOLLAR-VALUE LIFO RETAIL METHOD

The advantages of the dollar-value LIFO method were discussed in the previous chapter, and the advantages of the retail method were discussed earlier in this chapter. Many retail companies take advantage of both these methods by using the dollar-value LIFO retail method, which combines the principles of the retail LIFO method with the dollar-value LIFO method. Although no new principles are involved, an illustration of the dollar-value retail LIFO inventory method is provided for the Weston Company because of the complexity involved. The basic information is presented in Exhibit 7-14, while the calculation of the cost of the ending inventory is shown in Exhibit 7-15.

### EXHIBIT 7-14

**WESTON COMPANY**
Cost and Retail Values and Price Indexes

|  | 1994 Cost | 1994 Retail | 1995 Cost | 1995 Retail | 1996 Cost | 1996 Retail |
|---|---|---|---|---|---|---|
| Jan. 1, inventory | $ 8,000 | $12,000 | | | | |
| Purchases | 20,400 | 32,000 | $25,600 | $41,000 | $26,040 | $45,000 |
| Net markups | | 3,000 | | 2,000 | | 1,000 |
| Net markdowns | | (1,000) | | (3,000) | | (4,000) |
| Sales | | (29,800) | | (32,240) | | (42,990) |
| Price Index: | | | | | | |
| Jan. 1, 1994 | 100 | | | | | |
| Dec. 31, 1994 | 108 | | | | | |
| Dec. 31, 1995 | 115 | | | | | |
| Dec. 31, 1996 | 120 | | | | | |

*Note*: It is assumed that LIFO is adopted on January 1, 1994.

**EXHIBIT 7-15**

## WESTON COMPANY
Dollar-Value LIFO Retail Inventory Method

| | 1994 Cost | 1994 Retail | 1995 Cost | 1995 Retail | 1996 Cost | 1996 Retail |
|---|---|---|---|---|---|---|
| Beginning inventory* | $ 8,000 | $12,000 | $ 9,944 | $16,200 | $14,238 | $23,960 |
| Purchases | 20,400 | $32,000 | 25,600 | $41,000 | 26,040 | $45,000 |
| Net markups | | 3,000 | | 2,000 | | 1,000 |
| Net markdowns | | (1,000) | | (3,000) | | (4,000) |
| | | 34,000 | | 40,000 | | 42,000 |
| Goods available for sale | $28,400 | $46,000 | $35,544 | $56,200 | $40,278 | $65,960 |
| Sales | | (29,800) | | (32,240) | | (42,990) |
| Ending inventory at retail | | $16,200 (1) | | $23,960 | | $22,970 |
| Ending inventory at retail at base-year prices: | | | | | | |
| $16,200 × (100 ÷ 108) | | $15,000 (2) | | | | |
| $23,960 × (100 ÷ 115) | | | | $20,835 | | |
| $22,970 × (100 ÷ 120) | | | | | | $19,142 |
| Inventory change at retail base-year prices: | | | | | | |
| $15,000 − $12,000 | | $ 3,000 (3) | | | | |
| $20,835 − $15,000 | | | | $ 5,835 | | |
| $19,142 − $20,835 | | | | | | $ (1,693) |
| Change at retail at relevant current prices: | | | | | | |
| $3,000 × (108 ÷ 100) | | $ 3,240 (4) | | | | |
| $5,835 × (115 ÷ 100) | | | | $ 6,710 | | |
| ($1,693) × (115 ÷ 100) | | | | | | $ (1,947) |
| Change at relevant current costs:* | | | | | | |
| $3,240 × 0.60 | $ 1,944 (5) | | | | | |
| $6,710 × 0.64 | | | $ 4,294 | | | |
| ($1,947) × 0.64 | | | | | $ (1,246) | |
| Year-end LIFO inventory: | | | | | | |
| Base-year layer | $ 8,000 | | $ 8,000 | | $ 8,000 | |
| Layer added in 1994 | 1,944 | | 1,944 | | 1,944 | |
| Layer added in 1995 | | | 4,294 | | 4,294 | |
| Layer subtracted in 1996 at 1995 costs | | | | | (1,246) | |
| Ending inventory | $ 9,944 (6) | | $14,238 | | $12,992 | |

*1994 cost-to-retail ratio for beginning inventory: $8,000 ÷ $12,000 = 0.667; 1994 cost-to-retail ratio for purchases: $20,400 ÷ $34,000 = 0.60; 1995 cost-to-retail ratio for purchases: $25,600 ÷ $40,000 = 0.64

The cost-to-retail ratio is computed in the same manner as described earlier for the LIFO retail method; that is, the ratio includes both net markups and net markdowns but excludes the beginning inventory. The dollar-value LIFO concepts are applied to the retail values as follows (the numbers in parentheses are from Exhibit 7-15 for 1994):

1.  The ending inventory at retail ($16,200) is computed by adding the beginning inventory, purchases, and the markups, and subtracting the markdowns and sales, or at year-end by taking a physical inventory in which the number of units in ending inventory is multiplied by the current-year retail prices.

2.  The ending inventory at retail ($16,200) is converted to base-year retail prices ($15,000) by applying the base-year conversion index:

$$\text{Ending Inventory at Base-Year Retail Prices} = \frac{\text{Base-Year Retail Price Index}}{\text{Current-Year Price Index}} \times \text{Ending Inventory at Retail}$$

Note that the conversion index used here is based on a *price* index, while the conversion index used in Chapter 6 was based on a *cost* index. A price index is computed in the same way as a cost index except that retail prices are used.

3.  The increase (decrease) in the inventory at retail in base-year prices is computed by comparing the ending inventory with the beginning inventory when both are measured at retail in base-year prices (an increase of $3,000).

4.  The increase (decrease) in the inventory at retail in base-year prices ($3,000) is converted to current-year retail prices ($3,240) by multiplying times the appropriate conversion index. If there is an *increase,* the current year conversion index is used as follows:

$$\text{Layer Increase at Current-Year Retail Prices} = \text{Increase at Base-Year Retail Prices} \times \frac{\text{Current-Year Price Index}}{\text{Base-Year Price Index}}$$

Alternatively, if there is a *decrease,* the conversion index for the appropriate LIFO layer is used as follows:

$$\text{Decrease at Retail Prices of Most Recently Added Layer} = \text{Decrease at Base-Year Retail Prices} \times \frac{\text{Price Index of Most Recently Added Layer}}{\text{Base-Year Price Index}}$$

Note that for large decreases that affect more than one layer of inventory, the price index applicable to each layer must be used in the conversion index.

5.  The increase (decrease) at current-year retail prices is converted to cost ($1,944) by multiplying times the cost-to-retail ratio for the appropriate year. If there is an increase, the cost-to-retail ratio for the current year is used (0.60). If there is a decrease, the cost-to-retail ratio(s) for the LIFO layer(s) being removed is used.

6.  The ending inventory at cost ($9,944) is computed by adding (subtracting) the increase (decrease) at cost to the beginning inventory at cost ($1,944 + $8,000).

Continuing the example, in 1995 the ending inventory at retail of $23,960 is converted to base-year retail prices of $20,835 by multiplying times the base-year conversion index (100 ÷ 115). Comparing the $20,835 to the ending inventory at retail base-year prices in 1994 of $15,000 results in an increase in inventory at base-year retail prices of $5,835. This increase is multiplied by the current-year conversion index of 115 ÷ 100 to compute the increase at current retail prices of $6,710. The $6,710 is multiplied times the cost-to-retail ratio of 0.64 to compute the $4,294 increase at current-year costs, which is added to the $9,944 ending inventory cost from 1994 to determine the $14,238 cost of the ending inventory for 1995.

In 1996 there is a *decrease* in the inventory of $1,693 at base-year retail prices. This is converted into a $1,947 decrease by applying the conversion index for 1995, since part of the layer added in 1995 is being removed. This decrease of $1,947 at retail is converted to cost by applying the cost-to-retail ratio for 1995 of 0.64, resulting in a decrease at cost of $1,246. Note that the conversion index of 115 ÷ 100 and the cost ratio of 0.64 would only be used for a reduction in inventory at base-year retail prices of $5,835, because this is the amount of the increase from 1995. The next $3,000 reduction at base-year retail prices would be at the conversion index of 108 ÷ 100 and the cost ratio of 0.60 (for the layer added in 1994) and the remaining $12,000 at a conversion index of 100 ÷ 100 and the cost ratio of 0.667 (for the beginning inventory from 1994).

## EFFECTS OF INVENTORY ERRORS

In addition to the special methods described earlier in the chapter, the ending inventory valuation may be affected by errors. Errors in the valuation of inventory and the recording of purchases can result in inaccurate values on the balance sheet and income statement. The effects of some common errors (assuming a periodic inventory system and disregarding income taxes) are summarized next:

I. A purchase on credit is omitted from both the Purchases account and ending inventory and is *not* recorded in the succeeding year.
   A. **Current year:**
      1. *Income Statement.* Income is correct because the errors in the purchases and ending inventory offset each other.
      2. *Balance Sheet.* Ending inventory and accounts payable are understated.
   B. **Succeeding year:**
      1. *Income Statement.* Income is overstated because beginning inventory is understated and therefore cost of goods sold is understated.
      2. *Balance Sheet.* Accounts payable is understated and retained earnings is overstated. Note that if the purchase omitted from the current year was included in the succeeding year, the income would be correct in the second year because the errors would again offset each other. Accounts payable and retained earnings would also be correct.

II. A purchase on credit is omitted from the Purchases account but ending inventory is correct.
   A. **Current year:**
      1. *Income Statement.* Income is overstated because purchases are understated and therefore cost of goods sold is understated.
      2. *Balance Sheet.* Accounts payable are understated because a purchase has been omitted. Retained earnings is overstated because income is overstated.
   B. **Succeeding year:**
      1. *Income Statement.* No effect because the beginning inventory, purchases, and ending inventory are correct.

2. *Balance Sheet.* Accounts payable is understated and retained earnings is overstated, due to the error in the previous period.

III. Ending inventory is over(under)stated due to quantity and/or costing errors, but purchases are correct.
   A. **Current year:**
      1. *Income Statement.* Income is over(under)stated because cost of goods sold is under(over)stated.
      2. *Balance Sheet.* Ending inventory and retained earnings are over(under)-stated.
   B. **Succeeding year:**
      1. *Income Statement.* Income is under(over)stated because beginning inventory is over(under)stated, and therefore cost of goods sold is over(under)stated.
      2. *Balance Sheet.* Correct because the errors in inventory and retained earnings in the previous year were counterbalanced in this year.

Note that in this third situation the total income for the two years combined is correct, as is the ending inventory for the succeeding year. To illustrate, assume that the periodic inventory at December 31, 1995 is overstated by $5,000 but purchases are correct. The following errors occur (ignoring income taxes):

1995: *Income Statement:* Cost of goods sold is understated by $5,000 and income is overstated by $5,000.
       *Balance Sheet:* Ending inventory and retained earnings are overstated by $5,000.
1996: *Income Statement:* Cost of goods sold is overstated by $5,000 and income is understated by $5,000.
       *Balance Sheet:* Ending inventory and retained earnings are correct because the errors have counterbalanced each other.

These errors are illustrated by the following equations:

| | Beginning Inventory | + Purchases | = Cost of Goods Sold | + Ending Inventory |
|---|---|---|---|---|
| **1995:** | Correct | Correct | −$5,000 | +$5,000 |
| **1996:** | +$5,000 | Correct | +$5,000 | Correct |

Note that if income taxes had been considered, the effect of the error on income would be reduced. For example, if the company had an income tax rate of 30%, the inventory would still be overstated by $5,000, but net income in 1995 would be overstated by only $3,500 [$5,000 × (1 − 0.30)] and income taxes payable would be increased by $1,500 ($5,000 × 0.30). Thus the errors affect more items on the balance sheet, but the balance sheet still balances because assets are overstated by $5,000, liabilities by $1,500, and stockholders' equity by $3,500.

The discovery of inventory errors requires careful analysis and the preparation of adjusting entries to correct the accounts. If a material error is discovered after the books have been closed, the correction is treated as a prior period adjustment. In this case permanent (real) accounts are corrected, but corrections that would have been made to temporary (nominal) accounts have to be made instead to Retained Earnings.

*Accounting for errors is discussed in Chapter 22.*

## QUESTIONS

*Q7-1*   Define the terms *cost* and *market* as used in the lower of cost or market inventory valuation rule.

*Q7-2*   Define the *upper* and *lower* constraints used in the lower of cost or market rule. What is the purpose of each constraint?

*Q7-3*   How may the lower of cost or market method be applied to inventory?

*Q7-4*   What arguments may be used against the lower of cost or market rule?

*Q7-5*   Under what conditions are anticipated price declines recognized?

*Q7-6*   How, and under what conditions, are a purchase obligation and a product financing arrangement each recognized in the financial statements?

*Q7-7*   What are the exceptions to historical cost valuation of inventory allowed under generally accepted accounting principles? Under what conditions is each allowed?

*Q7-8*   Name four situations in which the gross profit method of estimating inventory would be useful.

*Q7-9*   What is the basic assumption underlying the gross profit method? How may the gross profit percentage for the prior year be modified to provide a better estimate of the inventory value?

*Q7-10*   What are the necessary conditions for the retail inventory method to provide valid results?

*Q7-11* Explain the meaning of the following terms: *markup, additional markup, markup cancellation, net markup, markdown, markdown cancellation, net markdown.*

*Q7-12*   Describe how the cost-to-retail ratio is computed for the following cost flow assumptions: FIFO, average cost, LIFO, lower of average cost or market. Why do the different methods approximate each cost flow assumption?

*Q7-13*   What assumptions are necessary for the lower of cost or market retail inventory method to actually produce an inventory value equal to the lower of average cost or market?

*Q7-14*   The retail inventory method indicated an inventory value of $80,000. A physical inventory indicated a value of $70,000. Suggest possible causes of this discrepancy.

*Q7-15*   Indicate the effect of each of the following errors on the balance sheet and income statement of the current and succeeding years:

a. The ending inventory is overstated.

b. Merchandise received was not recorded in the Purchases account until the succeeding year although the item was included in inventory of the current year.

c. Merchandise purchases shipped FOB shipping point were not recorded in either the Purchases account or the ending inventory.

d. The ending inventory was understated as a result of the exclusion of goods sent out on consignment.

## CASES

*C7-1   Retail Inventory Method*
The Sandberg Paint Company, your client, manufactures paint. The company's president, Ms. Sandberg, has decided to open a retail store to sell Sandberg paint as well as wallpaper and other supplies that would be purchased from other suppliers. She has asked you for information about the retail method of pricing inventories at the retail store.

**Required**
Prepare a report to the president explaining the retail method of pricing inventories. Your report should include these four points:
1. Description and accounting features of the method.
2. The conditions that may distort the results under the method.

3. A comparison of the advantages of using the retail method with those of using cost methods of inventory pricing.
4. The accounting theory underlying the treatment of net markdowns and net markups under the method. (*AICPA adapted*)

*C7-2   Gross Profit*
The Shelly Corporation is an importer and wholesaler. Its merchandise is purchased from several suppliers and is warehoused by Shelly Corporation until sold to consumers.

In conducting her audit for the year ended June 30, 1995 the corporation's CPA determined that the system of internal control was good. Accordingly, she observed the physical inventory at an interim date, May 31, 1995, instead of at year-end.

The following information was obtained from the general ledger:

| | |
|---|---|
| Inventory, July 1, 1994 | $ 87,500 |
| Physical inventory, May 31, 1995 | 95,000 |
| Sales for 11 months ended May 31, 1995 | 840,000 |
| Sales for year ended June 30, 1995 | 960,000 |
| Purchases for 11 months ended May 31, 1995 (before audit adjustments) | 675,000 |
| Purchases for year ended June 30, 1995 (before audit adjustments) | 800,000 |

The CPA's audit disclosed the following information:

| | |
|---|---|
| Shipments received in May and included in the physical inventory but recorded as June purchases | $7,500 |
| Shipments received in unsalable condition and excluded from physical inventory; credit memos had not been received nor had chargebacks to vendors been recorded: | |
| Total at May 31, 1995 | $1,000 |
| Total at June 30, 1995 (including the May unrecorded chargebacks) | $1,500 |
| Deposit made with vendor and charged to purchases in April 1995. Product was shipped in July 1995. | $2,000 |
| Deposit made with vendor and charged to purchases in May 1995. Product was shipped, FOB destination, on May 29, 1995, and was included in May 31, 1995 physical inventory as goods in transit. | $5,500 |
| Through the carelessness of the receiving department, a June shipment was damaged by rain. This shipment was later sold in June at its cost of $10,000. | |

**Required**

In audit engagements in which interim physical inventories are observed, a frequently used auditing procedure is to test the reasonableness of the year-end inventory by the application of gross profit ratios. Prepare in good form the following schedules:

1. Computation of the gross profit ratio for 11 months ended May 31, 1995.
2. Computation by the gross profit ratio method of cost of goods sold during June 1995.
3. Computation by the gross profit ratio method of June 30, 1995 inventory. (*AICPA adapted*)

*C7-3  Retail Inventory Method*
Retail, Inc., sells normal brand-name household products both from its own store and on consignment through The Mall Space Company.

**Required**

1. Should Retail, Inc., include in its inventory normal brand-name goods purchased from its suppliers but not yet received if the terms of purchase are FOB shipping point (manufacturer's plant)? Why?
2. Should Retail, Inc., include freight-in expenditures as an inventoriable cost? Why?
3. Retail, Inc., purchased cooking utensils for sale in the ordinary course of business three times during the current year, each time at a higher price than the previous purchase. What would be the effect on ending inventory and cost of goods sold if Retail, Inc., used the weighted-average cost method instead of the FIFO method?
4. How and why will Retail, Inc., treat net markdowns when it calculates the estimated cost of ending inventory using the conventional (lower of cost or market) retail inventory method?
5. What are products on consignment and how are they presented on the balance sheets of Retail, Inc., and The Mall Space Company? (*AICPA adapted*)

*C7-4  Various Inventory Issues*
Diane Company, a retailer and wholesaler of national brand-name household lighting fixtures, purchases its inventories from various suppliers.

**Required**

1. a. What criteria are used to determine which of Diane's costs are inventoriable?
   b. Are Diane's administrative costs inventoriable? Defend your answer.
2. a. Diane uses the lower of cost or market rule for its wholesale inventories. What are the theoretical arguments for that rule?
   b. The replacement cost of the inventories is below the net realizable value less a normal profit margin, which, in turn, is below the original cost. What amount is used to value the inventories? Why?
3. Diane calculates the estimated cost of its ending inventories held for sale at retail using the conventional (lower of average cost or market) retail inventory method. How would Diane treat the beginning inventories and net markdowns in calculating the cost ratio used to determine its ending inventories? Why? (*AICPA adapted*)

*C7-5  LCM, Dollar-Value LIFO, and Consignments*
Caddell Company, a wholesaler, purchases its inventories from various suppliers FOB destination; it incurs substantial warehousing costs. Caddell uses the dollar-value LIFO inventory cost flow method. Caddell also consigns some of its inventories to Reed Company.

Reed also has items for sale that it purchases from other wholesalers. Reed uses the lower of FIFO cost or market inventory method.

**Required**

1. When are the purchases from various suppliers generally included in Caddell's inventory? Why?
2. Theoretically, how should Caddell account for the warehousing costs? Why?
3. a. What are the advantages of using the dollar-value LIFO inventory cost flow method as opposed to the conventional quantity of goods LIFO method?
   b. How does the calculation of dollar-value LIFO differ from the conventional quantity of goods method?
4. How should Caddell account for the inventories consigned to Reed Company? Why?
5. When Reed applies the lower of cost or market method, what are the ceiling and floor limits? (*AICPA adapted*)

### C7-6     Inventory Valuation Issues

Hanlon Company purchased a significant amount of raw materials inventory for a new product that it is manufacturing. Hanlon purchased insurance on these raw materials while they were in transit from the supplier.

Hanlon uses the lower of cost or market rule for these raw materials. The replacement cost of the raw materials is above the net realizable value and both are below the original cost.

Hanlon uses the average cost inventory method for these raw materials. In the last two years, each purchase has been at a lower price than the previous purchase, and the ending inventory quantity for each period has been higher than the beginning inventory quantity for that period.

**Required**

1. What is the theoretically appropriate method that Hanlon should use to account for the insurance costs on the raw materials while they were in transit from the supplier? Why?
2. a. At which amount should Hanlon's raw materials inventory be reported on the balance sheet? Why?
   b. In general, why is the lower of cost or market rule used to report inventory?
3. What would have been the effect on ending inventory and cost of goods sold had Hanlon used the LIFO inventory method instead of the average cost inventory method for the raw materials? Why? (*AICPA adapted*)

### C7-7     Various Inventory Issues

Hudson Company, which is both a wholesaler and a retailer, purchases its inventories from various suppliers. Additional facts for Hudson's wholesale operations are as follows:

- Hudson incurs substantial warehousing costs.
- Hudson uses the lower of cost or market method.
- The replacement cost of the inventories is below the net realizable value and above the net realizable value less the normal profit margin. The original cost of the inventories is above the replacement cost and below the net realizable value.

Additional facts for Hudson's retail operations are as follows:

- Hudson determines the estimated cost of its ending inventories held for sale at retail using the conventional retail inventory method, which approximates lower of average cost or market.
- Hudson incurs substantial freight-in costs.
- Hudson has net markups and net markdowns.

**Required**

1. Theoretically, how should Hudson account for the warehousing costs related to its wholesale inventories? Why?
2. a. In general, why is the lower of cost or market method used to report inventory?
   b. At which amount should Hudson's wholesale inventories be reported on the balance sheet? Explain the application of the lower of cost or market method in this situation.
3. In the calculation of the cost-to-retail percentage used to determine the estimated cost of its ending retail inventories, how should Hudson treat
   a. Freight-in costs?
   b. Net markups?
   c. Net markdowns?
4. Why does Hudson's retail inventory method approximate lower of average cost or market? (*AICPA adapted*)

## MULTIPLE CHOICE

*Select the best answer for each of the following.*

M7-1   Moore Company carries product A in inventory on December 31, 1994 at its unit cost of $7.50. Because of a sharp decline in demand for the product, the selling price was reduced to $8.00 per unit. Moore's normal profit margin on product A is $1.60, disposal costs are $1.00 per unit, and the replacement cost is $5.30. Under the rule of cost or market, whichever is lower, Moore's December 31, 1994 inventory of product A should be valued at a unit cost of

a. $5.30                         c. $7.00
b. $5.40                         d. $7.50

M7-2    Under the retail inventory method, freight-in would be included in the calculation of the goods available for sale for which of the following?

| | Cost | Retail |
|---|---|---|
| a. | No | No |
| b. | No | Yes |
| c. | Yes | No |
| d. | Yes | Yes |

M7-3    The following information is available for the Silver Company for the three months ended March 31, 1995:

| Merchandise inventory, January 1, 1995 | $ 900,000 | Freight-in | $ 200,000 |
|---|---|---|---|
| Purchases | 3,400,000 | Sales | 4,800,000 |

The gross margin recorded was 25% of sales. What should be the merchandise inventory at March 31, 1995?
a. $700,000        c. $1,125,000
b. $900,000        d. $1,200,000

M7-4    The retail inventory method would include which of the following in the calculation of the goods available for sale at both cost and retail?
a. Freight-in        c. Markups
b. Purchases returns        d. Markdowns

M7-5    During 1995 R Corp., a manufacturer of chocolate candies, contracted to purchase 100,000 pounds of cocoa beans at $1.00 per pound, delivery to be made in the spring of 1996. Because a record harvest is predicted for 1996, the price per pound for cocoa beans had fallen to $.80 by December 31, 1995.
     Of the following journal entries, the one that would properly reflect in 1995 the effect of the commitment of R Corp. to purchase the 100,000 pounds of cocoa is

| | Debit | Credit |
|---|---|---|
| a.   Cocoa Inventory | 100,000 | |
|      Accounts Payable | | 100,000 |
| b.   Cocoa Inventory | 80,000 | |
|     Loss on Purchase Commitments (an expense account) | 20,000 | |
|      Accounts payable | | 100,000 |
| c.   Loss on Purchase Commitments (an expense account) | 20,000 | |
|      Accrued Loss on Purchase Commitments (a liability | | |
|      account) | | 20,000 |
| d.   No entry would be necessary in 1995 | | |

M7-6    The replacement cost of an inventory item is below the net realizable value and above the net realizable value less the normal profit margin. The original cost of the inventory item is above the replacement cost and below the net realizable value. As a result, under the lower of cost or market method, the inventory item should be valued at the
a. Net realizable value        c. Replacement cost
b. Original cost        d. Net realizable value less the
                              normal profit margin

M7-7    At December 31, 1995 the following information was available from Crisford Company's books:

| | Cost | Retail |
|---|---|---|
| Inventory, 1/1/95 | $14,700 | $ 20,300 |
| Purchases | 83,300 | 115,500 |
| Additional markups | — | 4,200 |
| Available for sale | $98,000 | $140,000 |

Sales for the year totaled $110,600; markdowns amounted to $1,400. Under the approximate lower of average cost or market retail method, Crisford's inventory at December 31, 1995 was

a.  $30,800
b.  $28,000

c.  $21,560
d.  $19,600

M7-8    Hestor Company's records indicate the following information:

| | |
|---|---|
| Merchandise inventory, January 1, 1995 | $ 550,000 |
| Purchases, January 1 through December 31, 1995 | 2,250,000 |
| Sales, January 1 through December 31, 1995 | 3,000,000 |

On December 31, 1995 a physical inventory determined that ending inventory of $600,000 was in the warehouse. Hestors gross profit on sales has remained constant at 30%. Hestor suspects some of the inventory may have been taken by some new employees. At December 31, 1995 what is the estimated cost of missing inventory?

a.  $100,000
b.  $200,000

c.  $300,000
d.  $700,000

M7-9    Estimates of price-level changes for specific inventories are required for which of the following inventory methods?

a.  Conventional retail
b.  Weighted average cost

c.  FIFO
d.  Dollar-value retail LIFO

M7-10   A company forgets to record a purchase on credit in the Purchases account, but ending inventory is correct. The effect of this mistake in the current year is:

| Income | Cost of goods sold | Accounts payable | Retained earnings |
|---|---|---|---|
| a.  Overstated | Understated | Understated | Overstated |
| b.  Understated | Overstated | Overstated | Understated |
| c.  Overstated | Understated | Overstated | Understated |
| d.  Understated | Overstated | Understated | Overstated |

*(AICPA adapted)*

## EXERCISES

E7-1    *Lower of Cost or Market*   The Stiles Corporation uses the lower of cost or market method for each of two products in its ending inventory. A profit margin of 30% on the selling price is considered normal for each product. Specific data for each product are as follows:

| | Product A | Product B |
|---|---|---|
| Historical cost | $ 68 | $ 91 |
| Replacement cost | 60 | 93 |
| Estimated cost of disposal | 22 | 52 |
| Estimated selling price | 120 | 200 |

**Required**
What is the correct inventory value for each product?

E7-2    *Lower of Cost or Market*   The following information for the Tuell Company is available:

|  | Case | | | | |
|---|---|---|---|---|---|
|  | 1 | 2 | 3 | 4 | 5 |
| Cost | $5.00 | $5.00 | $5.00 | $5.00 | $5.00 |
| Net realizable value | 5.10 | 5.50 | 4.80 | 4.20 | 4.70 |
| Net realizable value less normal profit | 4.80 | 5.30 | 4.70 | 4.00 | 4.60 |
| Replacement cost | 5.30 | 5.20 | 4.60 | 4.10 | 4.80 |

**Required**
What is the correct inventory value in each of the preceding situations?

E7-3    *Lower of Cost or Market*   The following information is taken from the records of the Aden Company:

| Product | Group | Units | Cost/Unit | Market/Unit |
|---|---|---|---|---|
| A | 1 | 400 | $ 1.00 | $ 0.80 |
| B | 1 | 250 | 1.50 | 1.55 |
| C | 2 | 150 | 5.00 | 5.25 |
| D | 2 | 100 | 6.50 | 6.40 |
| E | 3 | 80 | 25.00 | 24.60 |

**Required**
What is the correct inventory value if the lower of cost or market is applied to each of the following?
1.  Individual items
2.  Groups of items
3.  The inventory as a whole

E7-4    *Lower of Cost or Market*   The inventories of the Berry Company for the years 1995 and 1996 are as follows:

|  | Cost | Market |
|---|---|---|
| January 1, 1995 | $10,000 | $10,000 |
| December 31, 1995 | 13,000 | 11,000 |
| December 31, 1996 | 15,000 | 14,000 |

**Required**
Prepare the necessary journal entries at the end of each year to record the correct inventory valuation. Use the allowance method and assume that a periodic inventory system is used.

E7-5    *Loss on Purchase Commitment*   During 1995 the Boge Corporation signed a noncancelable contract to purchase 10,000 bushels of soybeans at $4 per bushel with delivery to be made in 1996. On December 31, 1995, the price of soybeans had fallen to $3.60 per bushel. On May 1, 1996, the Boge Corporation takes delivery of the soybeans when the price is $3.75 per bushel.

**Required**
Prepare the journal entries required on December 31, 1995 and May 1, 1996.

E7-6    *Estimation of Fire Loss*   On September 28, 1995 a fire destroyed the entire merchandise inventory of the Carroll Corporation. The following information is available:

| | |
|---|---|
| Sales, January 1—September 28, 1995 | $540,000 |
| Inventory, January 1, 1995 | $120,000 |
| Merchandise purchases, January 1—September 28, 1995 (including $60,000 of goods in transit on September 28, 1995, shipped FOB shipping point) | $495,000 |
| Markup percentage on cost | 20% |

**Required**

What is the estimated inventory on September 28, 1995 immediately prior to the fire?

E7-7     *Gross Profit Method*    On November 21, 1995 a fire at Hodge Company's warehouse caused severe damage to its entire inventory of Product Tex. Hodge estimates that all usable damaged goods can be sold for $10,000. The following information was available from Hodge's accounting records for Product Tex:

| | |
|---|---|
| Inventory at November 1, 1995 | $100,000 |
| Purchases from November 1, 1995 to date of fire | 140,000 |
| Net sales from November 1, 1995 to date of fire | 220,000 |

Based on recent history, Hodge had a gross margin (profit) on Product Tex of 30% of net sales.

**Required**

Prepare a schedule to calculate the estimated loss on the inventory in the fire, using the gross margin (profit) method. Show supporting computations in good form. (*AICPA adapted*)

E7-8     *Gross Profit*    The following gross profit data are taken from the financial records of the Eckhardt Company:

| | 1994 | 1995 |
|---|---|---|
| Sales | $300,000 | $296,000 |
| Cost of goods sold | (200,000) | (203,300) |
| Gross profit | $100,000 | $ 92,700 |

**Required**

1. If it is known that volume declined 5% from 1994 to 1995, by how much did selling prices change?
2. If it is known that volume declined 5% from 1994 to 1995, by how much did costs change?
3. If selling prices increased 4% from 1994 to 1995, what effect would this factor alone have on gross profit?
4. If costs increased by 7% from 1994 to 1995, what effect would this factor have on gross profit?

E7-9     *Gross Profit Percentage*    An accountant sometimes must convert gross profit percentages.

**Required**

1. Convert the following gross profit percentages based on net sales to gross profit as a percentage of the cost of goods sold: 20%, 25%, and 40%.
2. Convert the following gross profit percentages based on the cost of goods sold to gross profit as a percentage of net sales: 20%, 25%, and 40%.

E7-10     *Retail Inventory Method*    The Harmes Company is a clothing store that uses the retail inventory method. The following information relates to its operations during 1995:

| | Cost | Retail |
|---|---|---|
| Inventory, January 1 | $28,400 | $ 40,200 |
| Purchases | 65,200 | 100,000 |
| Markups (net) | — | 1,900 |
| Markdowns (net) | — | 400 |
| Sales | — | 70,000 |

**Required**

Compute the ending inventory by the retail inventory method for the following cost flow assumptions:

1. FIFO
2. Average cost
3. LIFO
4. Lower of cost or market (based on average cost)

E7-11  *Retail Inventory Method*  The following data were available from the records of the Hegge Department Store for the year ended December 31, 1996:

|  | At Cost | At Retail |
|---|---|---|
| Merchandise inventory, January 1, 1996: | $ 90,000 | $130,000 |
| Purchases | 330,000 | 460,000 |
| Markups | — | 10,000 |
| Markdowns | — | 40,000 |
| Sales | — | 480,000 |

**Required**

Using the retail method, what is the estimate of the merchandise inventory at December 31, 1996 valued at the lower of cost or market? (*AICPA adapted*)

E7-12  *Retail Inventory Method*  The following information relates to the retail inventory method used by the Jeffress Company:

|  | Cost | Retail |
|---|---|---|
| Beginning inventory | $11,160 | $18,000 |
| Purchases | 54,600 | 92,400 |
| Freight-in | 840 | — |
| Net markups | — | 600 |
| Net markdowns | — | 1,144 |
| Sales | — | 94,056 |

**Required**

Compute the ending inventory by the retail inventory method, using the following cost flow assumptions:
1. FIFO
2. Average cost
3. LIFO
4. Lower of cost or market (based on average cost)

E7-13  *Dollar-Value LIFO Retail*  The Johns Company adopts the dollar-value LIFO retail inventory method on January 1, 1995. The following information for 1995 is obtained from the company's records:

|  | Cost | Retail |
|---|---|---|
| Inventory, January 1, 1995 | $20,000 | $29,000 |
| Purchases | 60,000 | 92,000 |
| Net markups | — | 1,000 |
| Net markdowns | — | 3,000 |
| Sales | — | 75,000 |

The price index on January 1, 1995 was 100 and on December 31, 1995 it was 110.

**Required**

Compute the cost of the inventory on December 31, 1995.

E7-14  *Dollar-Value LIFO Retail*  The Wyatt Company adopts the dollar-value LIFO retail inventory method on January 1, 1995. The company's records reveal that the inventory on January 1, 1995 had a cost of $75,000 and a retail value of $120,000. During 1995 the cost of purchases made was $110,000, and the retail value was $165,000. In addition, net markdowns were $6,000, net markups were $8,000, and sales were $140,000. The price index on January 1, 1995 was 100 and the index for 1995 was 110.

**Required**

Compute the cost of inventory on December 31, 1995. (Round the cost-to-retail index to 3 decimal places.)

**E7-15**   *Dollar-Value LIFO Retail*   On December 31, 1995 Davison Company adopted the dollar-value LIFO retail inventory method. Inventory data for 1996 are as follows:

|  | LIFO Cost | Retail |
|---|---|---|
| Inventory, 12/31/95 | $360,000 | $500,000 |
| Inventory, 12/31/96 | ? | 660,000 |
| Increase in price level for 1996 |  | 10% |
| Cost-to-retail ratio for 1996 |  | 70% |

**Required**

Compute the cost of Davison Company's inventory at December 31, 1996. (*AICPA adapted*)

**E7-16**   *Errors*   The following errors are made by a company that uses the periodic inventory system:

1. A purchase on account is omitted from the Purchases account and the ending inventory.
2. A purchase on account is omitted from the Purchases account, but the ending inventory is correct.
3. The ending inventory is overstated, but purchases are correct.

**Required**

Indicate the effect of the preceding errors on the income statement and the balance sheet of the current and succeeding years.

**E7-17**   *Errors*   During the course of your examination of the financial statements of Burnett Co., a new client, for the year ended December 31, 1995, you discover the following:

Inventory at January 1, 1995 was understated by $6,000.
Inventory at December 31, 1995 was overstated by $5,000.

During 1995 the company received a $1,000 cash advance from a customer for merchandise to be manufactured and shipped during 1996. The $1,000 had been credited to sales revenue. The company's gross profit on sales is 50%. Net income reported on the 1995 income statement (before reflecting any adjustments for the above items) is $20,000.

**Required**

What is the correct net income for 1995? (*AICPA adapted*)

## PROBLEMS

**P7-1**   *Lower of Cost or Market*   The Palmquist Company has five different inventory items that are being valued by the lower of cost or market method. The normal markup on all items is 20% of cost. The following information is obtained from the company's records:

| Item | Units | Cost | Replacement Cost | Net Realizable Value |
|---|---|---|---|---|
| 1 | 500 | $10.00 | $ 9.30 | $ 9.20 |
| 2 | 400 | 8.00 | 8.10 | 7.80 |
| 3 | 300 | 15.00 | 13.50 | 14.00 |
| 4 | 200 | 18.00 | 12.00 | 17.00 |
| 5 | 100 | 25.00 | 25.50 | 25.30 |

**Required**

1. Compute the lower of cost or market value for each item.
2. Compute the total inventory value if the lower of cost or market is applied to (a) each individual item and (b) the inventory as a whole. Explain the reason for the difference between the two values.

P7-2    *Lower of Cost or Market*  The following are the inventories for the years 1994, 1995, and 1996 for the Parry Company:

|  | Cost | Market |
|---|---|---|
| January 1, 1994 | $50,000 | $50,000 |
| December 31, 1994 | 65,000 | 60,000 |
| December 31, 1995 | 72,000 | 70,000 |
| December 31, 1996 | 75,000 | 78,000 |

**Required**
Prepare journal entries to record the lower of cost or market for each of the following alternatives:
1. Allowance method, periodic inventory system
2. Allowance method, perpetual inventory system
3. Direct method, periodic inventory system
4. Direct method, perpetual inventory system

P7-3    *Lower of Cost or Market and Interim Financial Statements*  The following values were obtained from the inventory records of the Robb Company, which has a fiscal year ending on December 31:

|  | Cost | Market |
|---|---|---|
| Inventory, January 1, 1995 | $10,000 | $10,500 |
| Inventory, March 31, 1995 | 12,000 | 11,500 |

**Required**
1. Under what conditions is the decline in inventory value below cost ignored in the interim financial statements?
2. Assuming that the market value is to be recorded, what is the necessary journal entry to record the decline if a perpetual inventory system and the allowance method are used?

P7-4    *Lower of Cost or Market*  The inventory records of the Frost Company for the years 1995 and 1996 reveal the cost and market of the January 1, 1995 inventory to be $125,000. On December 31, 1995 the cost of inventory was $130,000, while the market value was only $128,000. The December 31, 1996 market value of inventory was $140,000, and the cost was only $135,000. The Frost Company uses a periodic inventory system. Purchases for 1995 were $100,000 and for 1996 were $110,000.

**Required**
1. Prepare the journal entries at the end of 1995 and 1996 to record the lower of cost or market under the (a) allowance method, and (b) direct method.
2. Prepare the cost of goods sold section of the income statement and show how the inventory would be recorded on the balance sheet for 1995 and 1996 under the (a) allowance method, and (b) direct method.

P7-5    *Gross Profit*  The following information relates to the activities of the Skeen Corporation for 1995:

| | | | |
|---|---|---|---|
| Goods in process, January 1 | $ 25,000 | Finished goods, December 31 | $ 30,000 |
| Goods in process, December 31 | 40,000 | Cost of production | 70,000 |
| Finished goods, January 1 | 37,000 | Sales (net) | 100,000 |

**Required**
What is the gross profit as a percentage of net sales?

P7-6    *Estimation of Theft Loss*  You are requested by a client on September 28 to prepare an insurance claim for a theft loss which occurred on that day. An inventory is immediately taken and the following data are available:

| | | | |
|---|---|---|---|
| Inventory, September 1 | $38,000 | Sales, September 1—September 28 | $52,000 |
| Purchases received, September 1—September 28 | 19,000 | Sales returns | 1,000 |

The inventory on September 28 indicates that an inventory of $15,000 remains after the theft. During the past year, net sales have been made at 50% above the cost of goods sold.

**Required**

Compute the inventory lost during the theft.

P7-7     *Estimation of Fire Loss*     On January 19, 1995 the records of the Stewart Company revealed the following information:

| | | | |
|---|---|---|---|
| Inventory, July 1, 1994 | $ 51,600 | Purchases discounts taken | $5,800 |
| Purchases, July 1, 1994—January 20, 1995 | 368,000 | Freight-in | 3,800 |
| Sales, July 1, 1994—January 20, 1995 | 583,000 | Sales returns | 8,600 |
| Purchases returns | 11,200 | | |

A fire destroyed the entire inventory on January 20, 1995 except for purchases in transit, FOB shipping point, of $2,000 and goods having a selling price of $4,700 that were salvaged from the fire. The salvaged goods had an estimated salvage value of $2,900. The average gross profit on net sales in previous periods had been 40%.

**Required**

Compute the cost of the inventory lost in the fire.

P7-8     *Estimation of Loss*     On February 17, 1995 a flood destroyed the goods in process inventory and half the raw materials inventory of the LRT Company. There was no damage to the finished goods inventory. A physical inventory taken after the flood indicated the following values:

| | | | |
|---|---|---|---|
| Raw materials | $35,000 | Finished goods | 75,000 |

A review of the accounting records indicated the following:

| | | | |
|---|---|---|---|
| Inventories, December 31, 1994: | | | |
| Raw materials | $65,000 | Raw materials purchases | $20,000 |
| Goods in process | 80,000 | Direct labor cost | 30,000 |
| Finished goods | 72,000 | Manufacturing overhead cost | 15,000 |
| Sales (to February 17) | 40,000 | Gross profit rate (on sales) | 40% |

**Required**

Compute the value of the inventory destroyed by the flood.

P7-9     *Estimation of Flood Loss*     On June 30, 1995 a flash flood damaged the warehouse and factory of Padway Corporation, completely destroying the work-in-process inventory. There was no damage to either the raw materials or finished goods inventories. A physical inventory taken after the flood revealed the following valuations:

| | |
|---|---|
| Raw materials | $ 62,000 |
| Work in process | -0- |
| Finished goods | 119,000 |

The inventory on January 1, 1995 consisted of the following:

| | |
|---|---|
| Raw materials | $ 30,000 |
| Work in process | 100,000 |
| Finished goods | 140,000 |
| | $270,000 |

A review of the books and records disclosed that the gross profit margin historically approximated 25% of sales. The sales for the first six months of 1995 were $340,000. Raw material purchases were $115,000. Direct labor costs for this period were $80,000, and manufacturing overhead has historically been applied at 50% of direct labor.

**Required**

Compute the value of the work-in-process inventory lost at June 30, 1995. Show supporting computations in good form. (*AICPA adapted*)

**P7-10** *Retail Inventory Method* The Turner Corporation uses the retail inventory method. The following information relates to 1995:

|  | Cost | Retail |  | Cost | Retail |
|---|---|---|---|---|---|
| Inventory, January 1 | $ 29,000 | $ 45,000 | Additional markups | — | $ 50,000 |
| Purchases (gross price) | 140,000 | 190,000 | Markup cancellations | — | 10,000 |
| Purchases discounts taken | 3,000 | — | Markdowns | — | 15,000 |
| Purchases returns | 5,000 | 8,000 | Markdown cancellations | — | 3,000 |
| Freight-in | 20,000 | — | Sales | — | 190,000 |
| Employee discounts | — | 3,000 |  |  |  |

**Required**

Compute the cost of the ending inventory under each of the following cost flow assumptions:
1. FIFO
2. Average cost
3. LIFO
4. Lower of cost or market (based on average cost)

**P7-11** *Comprehensive* The EKC Company uses the retail inventory method. The following information for 1994 is available:

|  | Cost | Retail |  | Cost | Retail |
|---|---|---|---|---|---|
| Inventory, January 1 | $100,000 | $180,000 | Markdowns | — | $ 15,000 |
| Purchases (gross price) | 320,000 | 600,000 | Markdown cancellations | — | 4,000 |
| Purchases discounts taken | 6,000 | — | Sales | — | 630,000 |
| Freight-in | 16,000 | — | Sales returns | — | 30,000 |
| Additional markups | — | 60,000 | Sales discounts | — | 10,000 |
| Markup cancellations | — | 12,000 |  |  |  |

**Required**

Compute the cost of the ending inventory under each of the following cost flow assumptions:
1. FIFO
2. Average cost
3. LIFO
4. Lower of cost or market (based on average cost)

**P7-12** *Retail Inventory Method* The Red Department Store uses the retail inventory method. Information relating to the computation of the inventory at December 31, 1995 is as follows:

|  | Cost | Retail |  | Cost | Retail |
|---|---|---|---|---|---|
| Inventory at January 1, 1995 | $ 32,000 | $ 80,000 | Markups | — | $60,000 |
| Sales | — | 600,000 | Markup cancellations | — | 10,000 |
| Purchases | 270,000 | 590,000 | Markdowns | — | 25,000 |
| Freight-in | 7,600 | — | Markdown cancellations | — | 5,000 |

Estimated normal shrinkage is 2% of sales.

**Required**

Prepare a schedule to calculate the estimated ending inventory at the lower of average cost or market at December 31, 1995, using the retail inventory method. Show supporting computations in good form. (*AICPA adapted*)

**P7-13**   *Retail Inventory Method*   The Weber Corporation uses the retail inventory method to estimate its inventory balances. The following information is available on June 30:

|  | Cost | Retail |  | Cost | Retail |
|---|---|---|---|---|---|
| Inventory, January 1 | $25,000 | $ 60,000 | Markdowns | — | $7,000 |
| Purchases | 75,000 | 180,000 | Additional markups | — | 3,000 |
| Sales | — | 200,000 | Markdown cancellations | — | 2,000 |
| Purchases returns | 2,000 | 5,000 | Markup cancellations | — | 1,000 |
| Sales returns | — | 5,000 |  |  |  |

**Required**

1. Compute the inventory on June 30 using the "normal" retail inventory method (lower of average cost or market).
2. Independent of Requirement 1, assume that the June 30 inventory was $80,000 at retail and that the cost-to-retail ratio is 50%. If the price level of the inventory has risen by 5% during the period, compute the cost of the June 30 inventory under the dollar-value retail LIFO method, assuming that the company adopted the method at the beginning of the year.

**P7-14**   *Dollar-Value LIFO Retail*   The following information is obtained from the records of the Burger Company, which uses the dollar-value LIFO retail method:

|  | 1994 | | 1995 | | 1996 | |
|---|---|---|---|---|---|---|
|  | Cost | Retail | Cost | Retail | Cost | Retail |
| Purchases | $200,000 | $420,000 | $250,000 | $550,000 | $240,000 | $500,000 |
| Net markups | — | 20,000 | — | 30,000 | — | 10,000 |
| Net markdowns | — | 10,000 | — | 40,000 | — | 20,000 |
| Sales | — | 400,000 | — | 600,000 | — | 450,000 |

The company adopted LIFO on January 1, 1994, when the cost and retail values of the inventory were $50,000 and $100,000, respectively. The following price indexes were experienced by the Burger Company:

| January 1, 1994 | 100 | December 31, 1995 | 115 |
|---|---|---|---|
| December 31, 1994 | 108 | December 31, 1996 | 120 |

**Required**

Compute the cost of the ending inventory for 1994, 1995, and 1996.

**P7-15**   *Dollar-Value LIFO Retail*   Intella, Inc., adopted the dollar-value retail LIFO method on January 1, 1993. The following data apply to the 4 subsequent years:

|  |  | Cost | Retail |  |  | Cost | Retail |
|---|---|---|---|---|---|---|---|
| 1993 | Inventory, January 1 | $ 40,000 | $ 80,000 | 1995 | Purchases | $117,600 | $280,000 |
|  | Purchases | 85,500 | 190,000 |  | Sales | — | 260,000 |
|  | Sales | — | 200,000 | 1996 | Purchases | 147,200 | 320,000 |
| 1994 | Purchases | 92,000 | 230,000 |  | Sales | — | 300,000 |
|  | Sales | — | 210,000 |  |  |  |  |

In addition the following price indexes are available:

| January 1, 1993 | 100 | December 31, 1995 | 120 |
| December 31, 1993 | 105 | December 31, 1996 | 125 |
| December 31, 1994 | 110 | | |

### Required
Compute the inventory at the end of each of the 4 years.

P7-16    *Dollar-Value LIFO Retail and Fire Loss*   The Golden Company adopted the dollar-value retail LIFO method on January 1, 1994. The following information relates to the following 2 years:

| | 1994 | | | 1995 (through September 7) | | |
|---|---|---|---|---|---|---|
| | Cost | Retail | | | Cost | Retail |
| Inventory, January 1 | $ 40,000 | $ 90,000 | Purchases | | $150,000 | $330,000 |
| Purchases | 100,000 | 210,000 | Sales | | — | 280,000 |
| Sales | — | 200,000 | Net markups | | — | 40,000 |
| Net markups | — | 20,000 | Net markdowns | | — | 70,000 |
| Net markdowns | — | 40,000 | | | | |

In addition the following price indexes are available:

January 1994    100      December 1994    106      September 1995    110

On September 8, 1995 a fire destroyed the inventory except for goods in transit (properly recorded), FOB shipping point, at a cost of $8,000, and undamaged goods salvaged from the fire, which had a retail value of $10,000.

### Required
Compute the cost of the inventory destroyed in the fire.

P7-17    *Errors*   As controller of the Lerner Company, which uses a periodic inventory system, you discover the following errors in the current year:
1. Merchandise with a cost of $17,500 was properly included in the final inventory, but the purchase was not recorded until the following year.
2. Merchandise purchases are in transit under terms of FOB shipping point. They have been excluded from the inventory, but the purchase was recorded in the current year on the receipt of the invoice of $4,300.
3. Goods out on consignment have been excluded from inventory.
4. Merchandise purchases under terms FOB shipping point have been omitted from the Purchases account and the ending inventory. The purchases were recorded in the following year.
5. Goods held on consignment from Talbert Supply Co. were included in the inventory.

### Required
For each error indicate the effect on the ending inventory and the net income for the current year and on the net income for the following year.

P7-18    *Comprehensive*   Layne Corporation, a manufacturer of small tools, provided the following information from its accounting records for the year ended December 31, 1995:

| | |
|---|---|
| Inventory at December 31, 1995 (based on physical count of goods in Layne's plant at cost on December 31, 1995) | $1,750,000 |
| Accounts payable at December 31, 1995 | 1,200,000 |
| Net sales (sales less sales returns) | 8,500,000 |

Additional information is as follows:

1. Included in the physical count were tools billed to a customer FOB shipping point on December 31, 1995. These tools had a cost of $28,000 and had been billed at $35,000. The shipment was on Layne's loading dock waiting to be picked up by the common carrier.

2. Goods were in transit from a vendor to Layne on December 31, 1995. The invoice cost was $50,000, and the goods were shipped FOB shipping point on December 29, 1995.

3. Work-in-process inventory costing $20,000 was sent to an outside processor for plating on December 30, 1995.

4. Tools returned by customers and held pending inspection in the returned goods area on December 31, 1995 were not included in the physical count. On January 8, 1996 the tools costing $26,000 were inspected and returned to inventory. Credit memos totaling $40,000 were issued to the customers on the same date.

5. Tools shipped to a customer FOB destination on December 26, 1995 were in transit at December 31, 1995 and had a cost of $25,000. Upon notification of receipt by the customer on January 2, 1996 Layne issued a sales invoice for $42,000.

6. Goods, with an invoice cost of $30,000, received from a vendor at 5:00 p.m. on December 31, 1995, were recorded on a receiving report dated January 2, 1996. The goods were not included in the physical count, but the invoice was included in accounts payable at December 31, 1995.

7. Goods received from a vendor on December 26, 1995 were included in the physical count. However, the related $60,000 vendor invoice was not included in accounts payable at December 31, 1995 because the accounts payable copy of the receiving report was lost.

8. On January 4, 1996, a monthly freight bill in the amount of $4,000 was received. The bill specifically related to merchandise purchased in December 1995, one-half of which was still in the inventory at December 31, 1995. The freight charges were not included in either the inventory or in accounts payable at December 31, 1995.

**Required**
Prepare a schedule of adjustments as of December 31, 1995 to the initial amounts in inventory, accounts payable, and sales. Show separately the effect, if any, of each of the eight transactions on the December 31, 1995 amounts. Indicate if the transactions would have no effect on the initial amount shown. (*AICPA adapted*)

# PROPERTY, PLANT, AND EQUIPMENT: ACQUISITION AND DISPOSAL

## Chapter Topics

*Characteristics of Property, Plant, and Equipment*

*Determination of the Cost of Property, Plant, and Equipment*

*Acquisition by Lump-Sum Purchase, Deferred Payments, Issuance of Securities, Donation, Exchange of Assets, and Self-Construction*

*Costs Subsequent to Acquisition*

*Disposal of Property, Plant, and Equipment*

*Oil and Gas Properties (Appendix 1)*

*Casualty Insurance (Appendix 2)*

Property, plant, and equipment are very important components of a company's assets. They include assets that are necessary for a company to conduct its business, such as land, office buildings, factories, machinery, equipment, warehouses, retail stores, and delivery vehicles. They usually are a major portion of the total assets of a company. This chapter includes a discussion of the costs of acquisition, costs subsequent to acquisition, and disposal of property, plant, and equipment. Additional issues related to oil and gas properties and casualty insurance are included in appendices to the chapter.

## CHARACTERISTICS OF PROPERTY, PLANT, AND EQUIPMENT

Property, plant, and equipment is the title used for the classification of tangible noncurrent assets that are used by a company in the normal operations of its business. Alternative terms are **plant assets, fixed assets, and operational assets.** To be included in this category, an asset must have three characteristics:

1. *The Asset Must Be Held for Use and Not for Investment.* Only assets used in the normal course of business should be included. However, the asset does not have to be used continuously; therefore machinery owned for standby purposes in case of breakdowns would be included. In contrast, idle land or buildings should not be included but should be categorized separately as an investment. It is possible that a particular type of asset may be categorized as property, plant, and equipment by one company and as inventory by another. For example, trucks owned by a dealer are categorized as inventory.

2. *The Asset Must Have an Expected Life of More Than One Year* (or will not be converted into cash within the operating cycle). The asset represents a bundle of future services that will be received by the company over the life of the asset. To be included in property, plant, and equipment, the benefits must extend for one year or the operating cycle, whichever is longer; therefore the asset is distinguished from other assets, such as supplies, that are expected to be consumed within the current year.

3. *The Asset Must Be Tangible in Nature.* There must be a physical substance that can be seen and touched. In contrast, intangible assets such as goodwill or patents do not have a physical substance. Unlike raw materials, generally, property, plant, and equipment do not change their physical characteristics and are not incorporated into the product. Wasting assets are natural resources, such as minerals, oil and gas, and timber, that are used up by extraction. They usually are included under the category of property, plant, and equipment, even though they may be incorporated into the product. For example, an iron mine owned by a steel company produces iron ore which changes its characteristics as it is used in the manufacture of steel.

*Intangible assets are discussed in Chapter 10.*

An asset included in the property, plant, and equipment category is valued initially at its acquisition cost. Since the asset provides benefits to the company over a period of more than one year, the matching principle requires that the cost of the asset be allocated as an expense to each period in which the asset is consumed and benefits are received. This process of depreciation is discussed in the next chapter.

### Evaluation of Use of Historical Cost

The use of acquisition (historical) cost as the basis for valuation of property, plant, and equipment is consistent with the valuation of other assets, liabilities, and stockholders' equity items. The advantages are that (1) the cost is equal to the fair market value at the date of acquisition, (2) the cost is a very *reliable* valuation, and (3) gains and losses from holding the asset are recognized only when realized through a sale transaction. However, the use of historical cost for reporting property, plant, and equipment on the financial statements raises more issues than for other assets because usually the time since acquisition is greater. For example, many accountants question the continued use of historical cost for recording an asset such as land. How *relevant* is the cost of land purchased in the past, perhaps as much as 50 years ago? Similar issues arise with depreciable assets such as machinery and buildings. Although depreciation is a process of cost allocation rather than of valuation, the book value of the assets (cost less accumulated depreciation) may become less relevant as it becomes very different from their current value. In addition, as discussed in the next chapter, property, plant, and equipment occasionally may be written down to its fair market value as a result of a major event, but the lower of cost or market rule is not routinely used as a valuation method for this category of asset.

Another factor to be considered is the manner in which the asset is used. The process of allocating the historical cost may be more relevant if the asset is to be held for use in the productive operations of the company, because there is an appropriate matching of the cost of the asset against the revenues it produces. Alternatively, the current value may be more relevant if the company intends to sell the asset, or the entire company is for sale.

Since generally accepted accounting principles require that property, plant, and equipment be valued at their historical costs, their current cost generally is not available to users of financial statements. However, supplementary disclosure of the current cost of property, plant, and equipment is encouraged.

*Supplementary disclosures and the arguments for and against the use of current value are discussed in Chapter 24.*

## ACQUISITION OF PROPERTY, PLANT, AND EQUIPMENT

The major types of assets included in the general category of property, plant, and equipment are land, buildings, equipment, machinery, furniture and fixtures, leasehold improvements, and wasting assets. The acquisition of an item of property, plant, and equipment raises many issues. These include the determination of the cost of an asset acquired singly or by a lump-sum purchase, with deferred payments, through the issuance of securities, or by donation. Furthermore, in more complex situations, assets may be acquired in exchange for other assets or by self-construction. Each of these issues is discussed in the following sections.

### Determination of Cost

The cost of property, plant, and equipment is the cash outlay (not the "list" price) or its equivalent that is necessary to acquire the asset and put it in operating condition. In other words, **the acquisition costs that are necessary to obtain the benefits to be derived from the asset are capitalized** (recorded as an asset). These costs include the contract price, less discounts available, plus freight, assembly, installation, and testing costs. As in the case of inventory, discounts *available* should be subtracted from the cost of the asset rather than discounts *taken,* because the benefits to be received from the asset are not increased by a discount not taken. To illustrate the acquisition of an asset, assume that the Devon Company purchases a machine with a contract price of $100,000 on terms of 2/10, n/30. The cash discount of $2,000 is not taken and the company incurs transportation costs of $2,500, as well as installation and testing costs of $3,000. Sales tax is 5% of the invoice price, or $5,000. During the installation of the machine, uninsured damages of $500 were incurred and paid by the company. The following summary journal entry is made to record these costs:

| | | |
|---|---|---|
| Machine | | |
| ($100,000 − $2,000 + $2,500 + $3,000 + $5,000) | 108,500 | |
| Repair Expense | 500 | |
| Discounts Lost | 2,000 | |
| Cash | | 111,000 |

The $500 damage cost is not included in the cost of the asset because it was not a "necessary" cost. The issues associated with the determination of the cost of various types of property, plant, and equipment are discussed in the following sections.

### Land

**The recorded cost of land includes (1) the contract price, (2) the costs of closing the transaction and obtaining title, including commissions, options, legal fees, title search, insurance, and past due taxes, (3) the costs of surveys, and (4) the costs of preparing the land for its particular use such as clearing, grading, and razing old buildings (net of any proceeds from salvage) when such improvements have an indefinite life.** The costs of improvements having a limited economic life, such as landscaping, streets, sidewalks, and sewers, should be recorded in a Land Improvements account and depreciated over their economic lives. Alternatively, if the local government authority is responsible for the continued upkeep of the improvements, then effectively the improvements have an indefinite economic life to the company and should be added to the cost of the land. Since land is considered not to have a limited economic life and its residual value is unlikely to be less than its acquisition cost, land generally is not depreciated.

Land purchased for future use or as an investment should not be considered part of property, plant, and equipment. Questions arise about accounting for interest and property taxes on such land. **FASB Statement No. 34** (discussed later in the chapter) requires that interest be capitalized only when an asset is undergoing the activities necessary to get it ready for its intended use. Therefore, if any planning activity is being undertaken, such as architectural design or the obtaining of permits, interest should be capitalized. The *Statement* does not address the issue of property taxes (or other costs such as insurance). **FASB Statement No. 67** applies to real estate held for sale or rental and requires costs incurred for property taxes and insurance to be capitalized only during periods in which activities necessary to get the property ready for its intended use are in progress. Costs incurred for such items after the property is substantially complete and ready for its intended use are expensed as incurred.[1] Thus the rules for interest, property taxes, and insurance are the same for real estate projects developed for sale or lease to others. However, the *Statement* does not apply to real estate developed by a company for use in its own operations and, therefore, property taxes and insurance could be capitalized or expensed during the development period. Arguments in favor of capitalizing property taxes are (1) the matching principle does not require expensing the costs since the asset is not being used in a revenue-producing activity, and (2) if the advance purchase of the land were made at a lower price, capitalizing the costs would result in a cost nearer to that which the company would have paid later. Arguments in favor of expensing the property taxes are (1) property taxes are a maintenance cost that do not add value to the property, and (2) it is consistent with the conservatism convention. Once the land is used in the operating activities, both interest and property taxes must be expensed.

### Buildings

**The recorded cost of buildings includes (1) the contract price, (2) the costs of remodeling and reconditioning, (3) the costs of excavation for the specific building, (4) architectural costs and the costs of building permits, (5) capitalized interest costs in**

---

1. "Accounting for Costs and Initial Rental Operations of Real Estate Projects," *FASB Statement of Financial Accounting Standards No. 67* (Stamford, Conn.: FASB, 1982), par. 6.

the particular circumstances discussed later in the chapter, and (6) unanticipated costs resulting from the condition of the land (such as blasting rock or channeling an underground stream). However, unanticipated costs associated with the construction of the building, such as a strike or a fire, should be expensed. The different treatment of such unanticipated events is justified because the avoidable costs of the fire or strike were not necessary to obtain the economic benefits of the building. The costs of property taxes and insurance during construction may be capitalized or expensed, as discussed for land.

## Leasehold Improvements

Improvements made by the lessee to leased property, unless specifically exempted in the lease agreement, revert to the lessor at the end of the lease. Therefore **the cost of a leasehold improvement,** such as the interior design of a retail store, **is capitalized and amortized over its economic life or the life of the lease, whichever is shorter.**

The preceding discussion has indicated the general rules to be followed but is not intended to provide solutions for all possible situations. The decision to expense a cost immediately, to capitalize it as an asset that is subsequently depreciated, such as a building, or to capitalize the cost to a nondepreciable asset, such as land, has an impact on both the income statement and the balance sheet values. **The general procedure is to determine whether incurring the cost has generated economic benefits beyond the current period, and which asset is associated with the increase in benefits.** For example, the cost of razing an old building when land is purchased is properly capitalized to the land, because the benefits to be derived from the land are increased since the old building is no longer there. Also if the seller had razed the old building, the selling price would presumably have been higher. When an old building is razed on land already owned so that a new building can be erected, the cost of razing is associated with the benefits previously realized from the old building and therefore is included in the calculation of the gain or loss on disposal. The new building does not have greater benefits because the old building is obsolete. Similarly if an old building is purchased with the expectation of incurring some costs of renovation, but the actual costs exceed the planned costs because of unforeseen difficulties, the added cost should not be capitalized, since it resulted from an error of judgment and did not increase the economic benefits of the building above those benefits originally expected. However, given the difficulties of accurate budgeting, the total costs often are capitalized whether or not those total costs exceed the budgeted amount.

## Lump-Sum Purchase

Companies often acquire several dissimilar assets for a single lump-sum purchase price. The purchase price in such situations is allocated to the individual assets purchased, because some of the assets may be depreciable and some not, and the depreciable assets may have different economic lives and be depreciated by different methods. **The basis for the allocation of the acquisition price in a lump-sum purchase is the relative fair market values of the individual assets.**

For example, suppose a company pays $120,000 for land and a building. If there is no evidence in the contract of separate prices agreed upon for the land and the building, the $120,000 is allocated between the two assets based on their relative fair market values. Evidence of such values can be obtained from several sources, such as an appraisal or the assessed values for property taxes, if those values are considered to be reasonably accurate indications of relative market values. Suppose that an appraisal of the land and building indicates values of $50,000 and $75,000, respectively. The cost of each is determined as follows:

| | Appraisal Value | Relative Fair Market Value | × Total Cost | = Allocated Cost |
|---|---|---|---|---|
| Land | $ 50,000 | $50,000/$125,000 × | $120,000 = | $ 48,000 |
| Building | 75,000 | 75,000/ 125,000 × | 120,000 = | 72,000 |
| Total | $125,000 | | | $120,000 |

In the journal entry for the acquisition, land is recorded at a cost of $48,000 and the building at a cost of $72,000. If the cost of obtaining an appraisal is material, it should be added to the purchase price to be allocated to the respective assets. In some situations, it may be possible to determine only one of the market values. Then the remaining portion of the total cost is assigned to the other asset.

## Deferred Payments

When property, plant, and equipment is acquired on a deferred payment basis, such as by issuing notes or bonds or assuming a mortgage, the asset is recorded at its fair value or the fair value of the liability on the date of the transaction, whichever is more reliable. If neither is determinable, the asset should be recorded at the present value of the deferred payments at the stated interest rate, unless the stated rate is materially different from the market rate, in which case the market rate should be used.[2] For example, suppose that a company purchases equipment by issuing a $10,000 non-interest-bearing 5-year note, when the market rate for obligations of this type is 12%. The note is to be paid off at the rate of $2,000 at the end of each year. Neither the fair value of the equipment nor the note is determinable directly. In this case both the equipment and the note are valued at the present value of the payments, which is $7,210 ($2,000 × 3.604776, the factor from Table 4 of Appendix D for a 5-year life and a 12% rate). The acquisition of the equipment is recorded as follows:

| | | |
|---|---|---|
| Equipment | 7,210 | |
| Discount on Notes Payable | 2,790 | |
|     Notes Payable | | 10,000 |

If the equipment was purchased by issuing a $7,500 5-year note with a stated interest rate of 12%, the present value of the note is $7,500 (assuming that 12% is a fair rate), and the acquisition would be recorded as follows:

| | | |
|---|---|---|
| Equipment | 7,500 | |
|     Notes Payable | | 7,500 |

*Accounting for notes and bonds is discussed in Chapter 12.*

Property, plant, and equipment may be purchased by issuing bonds. The same principles are followed, and the asset is recorded at the present value of the future payments.

## Issuance of Securities

When assets are acquired by issuing securities such as common stock or preferred stock, the company must determine the fair value of the transaction. In many cases

---

2. "Interest on Receivables and Payables," *APB Opinion No. 21* (New York: AICPA, 1971), par. 11.

two measures of fair value are available: the fair value of the asset acquired and the fair value of the securities issued. **The general rule is to record the exchange at the fair value of the asset acquired or of the stock issued, whichever is more reliable.** Normally the two values would be very similar, but if they are materially different, it is necessary to select one. In some situations, one of the values may be considered more reliable because it is quoted in an active market. For example, if the security is actively traded on a stock exchange and the asset being acquired is very specialized, the security value would be the preferred choice. Alternatively, if the security is not actively traded, but the asset is one that is commonly traded, the asset value would be the better choice. But what if neither of the two values can be readily determined?

For example, suppose that a company whose stock is not traded publicly issues stock to acquire a mining claim. Conceptually the value of the asset would be preferred to the value of the stock, because the value of the asset acquired is independent of the value of the stock. The value of the stock is not independent of the asset being acquired, because the more valuable the asset is, the more valuable is the stock. The more reasonable solution in such a situation may be to obtain an appraisal of either the value of the asset or the value of the stock. In the absence of any other valuation approach, a final alternative is to allow the directors of the company to place a value on the transaction. State laws generally allow this procedure, provided the value is established in good faith.

*Exchanges of stock for assets are discussed in Chapter 14.*

### Assets Acquired by Donation

When property, plant, and equipment is acquired through donation (usually by a governmental unit or an individual), a strict interpretation of the cost concept would require that the asset be valued at zero. However, such transactions are defined by **APB Opinion No. 29** as nonreciprocal transfers of nonmonetary assets. A **nonreciprocal transfer** is a transfer of assets or services in one direction. Assets received in such an exchange are required to be recorded at their fair market values. The justification is that when assets are donated, cost provides an inadequate method of accounting for the asset and for subsequent income measurement. Therefore the cost principle is modified to produce more relevant asset and income values.

To illustrate, suppose the City of Julesberg donates land worth $20,000 to the Klemme Company to encourage the company to relocate its production facilities to Julesberg. The journal entry by the company to record this event is:

| | | |
|---|---|---|
| Land | 20,000 | |
|     Donated Capital | | 20,000 |

Donations of this type often are accompanied by conditions. For example, the Klemme Company might be required to employ 100 people for 10 years. Such a condition is reported in the notes to the financial statements, if material, but it is not recorded as a liability. The Donated Capital account is included in Unrealized Capital in the Stockholders' Equity section of the balance sheet, as discussed in Chapters 3 and 15.

## ASSETS ACQUIRED BY EXCHANGE OF OTHER ASSETS

Accounting for assets acquired by the exchange of other assets (e.g., trade-in, swap) is covered by **APB Opinion No. 29.** This *Opinion* defines a **nonmonetary exchange** as a reciprocal transfer between a company and another entity, resulting in the company acquiring nonmonetary assets or services or satisfying liabilities by surrendering other nonmonetary assets or services or incurring other obligations. The general principle is that the cost of a nonmonetary asset acquired in exchange for another nonmonetary asset is the fair value of the asset surrendered. A gain or loss is recognized on the exchange as the difference between the fair market value of the asset surrendered and its book value.[3] When **boot**[4] (monetary consideration) is given or received, the cost of the asset acquired and the gain or loss in a nonmonetary exchange generally is determined by these equations:

$$\text{Cost of Asset Acquired} = \frac{\text{Fair Value of}}{\text{Asset Surrendered}} + \text{Boot Paid or} - \text{Boot Received}$$

and

$$\text{Gain (Loss)} = \frac{\text{Fair Value of}}{\text{Asset Surrendered}} - \text{Book Value of Asset Surrendered}$$

If the fair value of the asset received is more reliable than the fair value of the asset surrendered, it should be used to measure the cost of the asset acquired. Of course, the recorded cost of the asset acquired cannot be greater than its fair market value. Exchanges may involve similar or dissimilar assets and each type of exchange may involve a gain or loss.

### Exchanges of Dissimilar Productive Assets

**Productive assets** are held for or used in the production of goods and services. *Dissimilar productive assets* are assets that are not of the same general type, do not perform the same function, *or* are not employed in the same line of business. Concerned about a lack of comparability, in 1986 the FASB Emerging Issues Task Force (EITF) tightened the definition.[5] The EITF concluded that dissimilar productive assets are both dissimilar *and* are not employed in the same line of business. Accounting for dissimilar productive assets follows the principles in the equations just cited, and all gains and losses are recognized in full.

An exchange of dissimilar productive assets between Company A and Company B is illustrated, both with and without boot, in Exhibit 8-1. Company A exchanges a building for Company B's equipment. Before studying the exhibit, it is helpful to refer back to the equations for nonmonetary asset exchanges.

In example (a), boot is not involved . Each company is giving up and receiving an asset with a fair value of $40,000, which is, therefore, the fair value of the transaction. Since Company A is giving up a building with a fair value of $40,000 and a book value of $46,000 (the cost of $100,000 less the accumulated depreciation of

3. "Accounting for Nonmonetary Transactions," *APB Opinion No. 29* (New York: AICPA, 1973), par. 18.
4. *APB Opinion No. 29* refers to a *small* amount of boot. However, the intent was that the rules would apply no matter how much boot was involved. See James B. Hobbs and D. R. Bainbridge, "Nonmonetary Exchange Transactions: Clarification of APB Opinion No. 29," *The Accounting Review* (January, 1982), p. 171. This interpretation has been modified by the Emerging Issues Task Force as discussed later.
5. "Accounting for Certain Nonmonetary Transactions," *FASB Emerging Issues Task Force Issue Summary 86–29* (FASB, Stamford, Conn., 1986). For an additional discussion, see D. Marcinko and E. Petri, "A Clarification of Certain Issues Arising out of Nonmonetary Exchanges," *Journal of Accounting Education* (Fall, 1991), pp. 365–372.

---

**EXHIBIT 8-1**

## EXCHANGE OF DISSIMILAR PRODUCTIVE ASSETS

### (a) No Boot

|  | Company A (Building) | Company B (Equipment) |
|---|---|---|
| Cost of asset surrendered | $100,000 | $60,000 |
| Accumulated depreciation | 54,000 | 32,000 |
| Fair value of asset surrendered | 40,000 | 40,000 |

| Company A |  |  | Company B |  |  |
|---|---|---|---|---|---|
| Equipment | 40,000 |  | Building | 40,000 |  |
| Accumulated Depreciation | 54,000 |  | Accumulated Depreciation | 32,000 |  |
| Loss [$40,000 − |  |  | Equipment |  | 60,000 |
|   ($100,000 − $54,000)] | 6,000 |  | Gain [$40,000 − |  |  |
|   Building |  | 100,000 |   ($60,000 − $32,000)] |  | 12,000 |

### (b) With Boot

|  | Company A (Building) | Company B (Equipment) |
|---|---|---|
| Cost of asset surrendered | $100,000 | $60,000 |
| Accumulated depreciation | 54,000 | 32,000 |
| Fair value of asset surrendered | 40,000 | 35,000 |
| Cash received (paid) | 5,000 | (5,000) |

| Company A |  |  | Company B |  |  |
|---|---|---|---|---|---|
| Equipment |  |  | Building |  |  |
|   ($40,000 − $5,000) | 35,000 |  |   ($35,000 + $5,000) | 40,000 |  |
| Accumulated Depreciation | 54,000 |  | Accumulated Depreciation | 32,000 |  |
| Cash | 5,000 |  | Equipment |  | 60,000 |
| Loss [$40,000 − |  |  | Cash |  | 5,000 |
|   ($100,000 − $54,000)] | 6,000 |  | Gain [$35,000 − |  |  |
|   Building |  | 100,000 |   ($60,000 − $32,000)] |  | 7,000 |

---

$54,000), it recognizes a loss of $6,000 ($40,000 − $46,000) and records the cost of the acquired equipment at the fair value of $40,000. Company B is giving up equipment with a fair value of $40,000 and a book value of $28,000 ($60,000 − $32,000); therefore it recognizes a gain of $12,000 ($40,000 − $28,000) and records the cost of the building acquired at the fair value of $40,000.

In example (b), Company A receives boot of $5,000. Since Company A is giving up a building with a fair value of $40,000 and a book value of $46,000, it recognizes a loss of $6,000. It records the acquired equipment at a cost of $35,000 (the $40,000 fair value of the building surrendered minus the $5,000 boot received). Company B gives up equipment with a fair value of $35,000 and a book value of $28,000. Therefore it records a gain of $7,000 and the acquired building at a cost of $40,000 (the $35,000 fair value of the equipment surrendered plus the $5,000 boot paid).

## Exchanges of Similar Productive Assets

*Similar productive assets* are of the same general type, perform the same function, *and* are used in the same line of business. The intent of the APB was to have special rules for exchanges of similar productive assets only when the earning process is not complete for either party. Thus, an exchange must be between companies that are using the asset in the same line of business for the special rules of similar productive asset exchanges to be applied. These rules are discussed below. An exchange between two dealers or between two nondealers qualifies because they are both using the assets in the same line of business. However, an exchange between a dealer and a nondealer does not qualify because the dealer has completed its earning process in the normal course of business. Therefore, all gains and losses are recognized in full by both the dealer and nondealer. When similar productive assets are exchanged, two modifications to the general rule are necessary. First, revenue (gain) is not recognized, because the asset that originally was acquired has been exchanged for an asset with a similar purpose and the exchange is "not essentially the culmination of the earning process." Thus, the total revenue expected from the original asset has not yet been earned but will be continued by the newly acquired asset. For example, suppose that two construction companies each purchase land for development. Before development occurs, but after the values of the two parcels of land have increased, the two companies agree to an exchange of the parcels. Considering that the purpose of the original acquisitions was development and that the revenue was to be generated by the sale of developed land, the earning process is not complete when the land is exchanged. Therefore the gain on the exchange transaction is deferred. In contrast, if one of the companies exchanges the land for machinery (dissimilar assets), the revenue (gain) is recognized. The earning process is complete because the original purpose of the land purchase has been superseded. Similarly, if two manufacturing companies (nondealers) or two truck dealers exchange delivery trucks, then any gain is deferred. However, if a truck dealer and a manufacturing company exchange delivery trucks, the gain is recognized.

There is an opposing view that argues that the gain on the exchange of similar productive assets should be recognized because a transaction has taken place. The transaction clearly has established a market value for the asset disposed of, and this value should be recognized in the financial statements. The newly acquired asset would be valued on a basis similar to that for dissimilar productive assets or assets acquired by means other than an exchange. However, this view is not supported by generally accepted accounting principles as defined in *APB Opinion No. 29.*

In situations in which no gain is recognized on the disposal of the original asset, the newly acquired asset is recorded at the book value of the asset surrendered. However, the conservatism convention also is considered. If there is a *loss* on the disposal of the original asset, the loss is recognized.

The second modification arises when boot is involved in the exchange. When boot is *received* in the exchange of similar productive assets, it is considered that the earning process is complete *to the extent that boot is received.* Therefore a gain is recognized in proportion to the boot received. As before, a loss is recognized in full, irrespective of whether boot is involved.

The EITF established that the exchange is *monetary* if the boot is equal to or exceeds 25% of the total value of the exchange. Then the special rules discussed here do *not* apply and the exchange is recorded at fair value by both the recipient and payer of boot. That is, deferral or partial recognition of a gain only occurs when the exchange is nonmonetary, which means that the boot must be less than 25% of the total value of the exchange.

The general principle modified by these two factors leads to six alternative situations for nonmonetary exchanges of *similar* productive assets. Each of these alternatives is discussed in examples in the chapter, and they are summarized in Exhibit 8-3. When boot is neither received nor paid by a company, a loss is recognized in full (alternative 1) and a gain is ignored (alternative 2). When boot is *received,* a loss is recognized in full (alternative 5), while a gain is recognized in proportion to the boot received (alternative 6). When the boot is *paid,* a gain is not recognized (alternative 4) and a loss is again recognized in full (alternative 3). Note that these same rules apply to exchanges of products or property held for sale in the ordinary course of business (primarily inventory). However, the discussion in this chapter concentrates on exchanges of productive assets.

Two general equations were given earlier for computing the cost of the asset acquired when boot was paid or received. These equations apply to dissimilar productive asset exchanges. The modifications that have been discussed provide alternative equations that can be used to determine the cost of the asset acquired in a nonmonetary exchange of similar productive assets. When the fair market value of the asset being surrendered is *less* than the book value, the following equation applies:

$$\text{Cost of Asset Acquired} = \begin{array}{c}\text{Fair Value of}\\ \text{Asset Surrendered}\end{array} + \text{Boot Paid or} - \text{Boot Received}$$

When the fair market value of the asset being surrendered is *greater* than the book value, the following equations apply:

$$\text{Cost of Asset Acquired} = \text{Book Value of Asset Surrendered} + \text{Boot Paid}$$

or

$$\text{Cost of Asset Acquired} = \begin{array}{c}\text{Book Value of}\\ \text{Asset Surrendered}\end{array} - \text{Boot Received} + \text{Gain Recognized}$$

Note that the difference between the two sets of equations is the use of fair value when a loss is recognized and the use of book value when the gain is not recognized or recognized partially. Each of these situations is illustrated in Exhibit 8-2.

(a) *No Boot.* The exchange of two similar productive assets (equipment) without boot is illustrated in Exhibit 8-2 (a). Since no boot is involved, Company B does not recognize the gain that is apparent in the transaction and records the cost of the acquired equipment at $28,000 ($60,000 − $32,000), which is the book value of the equipment surrendered. The reason for deferring the gain when similar productive assets are exchanged is that the earning process is not complete, so revenue (i.e., a gain) should not be recognized. Company A recognizes a loss of $6,000, which is the difference between the fair value of the equipment surrendered ($40,000) and the book value of the equipment surrendered ($100,000 − $54,000 = $46,000). Since Company A recognizes a loss, it records the acquired equipment at the fair value of $40,000. The treatment of Company A and Company B follows the conservatism convention and is consistent with alternatives 1 and 2 in Exhibit 8-3. It also results in the asset being valued at the lower of cost (or book value when the equipment has been depreciated) or market.

(b) *Boot Received by Company Incurring a Loss.* When similar productive assets are exchanged for a loss and boot is involved, the company *receiving* the boot recognizes the loss in full. This situation is illustrated for Company A in Exhibit 8-2 (b). Company A incurs a loss of $6,000 ($40,000 − $46,000), recognizes it in full, and records the cost of the acquired equipment at its fair value of $35,000. This treatment is consistent with alternative 5 in Exhibit 8-3.

**EXHIBIT 8-2**

## EXCHANGE OF SIMILAR PRODUCTIVE ASSETS

*(a) No Boot*

|                                      | Company A  | Company B |
|--------------------------------------|------------|-----------|
| Cost of equipment surrendered        | $100,000   | $60,000   |
| Accumulated depreciation             | 54,000     | 32,000    |
| Fair value of equipment surrendered  | 40,000     | 40,000    |

| Company A                        |         |         | Company B                       |        |        |
|----------------------------------|---------|---------|---------------------------------|--------|--------|
| Equipment                        | 40,000  |         | Equipment                       | 28,000 |        |
| Accumulated Depreciation         | 54,000  |         | Accumulated Depreciation        | 32,000 |        |
| Loss ($40,000 − $46,000)         | 6,000   |         | Equipment                       |        | 60,000 |
| Equipment                        |         | 100,000 |                                 |        |        |

*With Boot:*
*(b) Boot Received by Company A Incurring a Loss; (c) Boot Paid by Company B Incurring a Gain*

|                                      | Company A  | Company B |
|--------------------------------------|------------|-----------|
| Cost of equipment surrendered        | $100,000   | $60,000   |
| Accumulated depreciation             | 54,000     | 32,000    |
| Fair value of equipment surrendered  | 40,000     | 35,000    |
| Cash received (paid)                 | 5,000      | (5,000)   |

| Company A                        |         |         | Company B                       |        |        |
|----------------------------------|---------|---------|---------------------------------|--------|--------|
| Equipment                        |         |         | Equipment                       |        |        |
| ($40,000 − $5,000)               | 35,000  |         | ($28,000 + $5,000)              | 33,000 |        |
| Accumulated Depreciation         | 54,000  |         | Accumulated Depreciation        | 32,000 |        |
| Loss [$40,000 −                  |         |         | Equipment                       |        | 60,000 |
| ($100,000 − $54,000)]            | 6,000   |         | Cash                            |        | 5,000  |
| Cash                             | 5,000   |         |                                 |        |        |
| Equipment                        |         | 100,000 |                                 |        |        |

*With Boot:*
*(d) Boot Received by Company A Incurring a Gain; (e) Boot Paid by Company B Incurring a Loss*

|                                      | Company A  | Company B |
|--------------------------------------|------------|-----------|
| Cost of equipment surrendered        | $100,000   | $60,000   |
| Accumulated depreciation             | 80,000     | 32,000    |
| Fair value of equipment surrendered  | 30,000     | 27,000    |
| Cash received (paid)                 | 3,000      | (3,000)   |

| Company A                        |         |         | Company B                       |        |        |
|----------------------------------|---------|---------|---------------------------------|--------|--------|
| Equipment ($20,000 −             |         |         | Equipment                       |        |        |
| $3,000 + $1,000)                 | 18,000  |         | ($27,000 + $3,000)              | 30,000 |        |
| Accumulated Depreciation         | 80,000  |         | Accumulated Depreciation        | 32,000 |        |
| Cash                             | 3,000   |         | Loss [$27,000 −                 |        |        |
| Equipment                        |         | 100,000 | ($60,000 − $32,000)]            | 1,000  |        |
| Gain*                            |         | 1,000   | Equipment                       |        | 60,000 |
|                                  |         |         | Cash                            |        | 3,000  |

$$* \text{ Gain} = \frac{\text{Boot}}{\text{Boot} + \text{Fair Value of Asset Acquired}} \times \left( \begin{array}{c} \text{Fair Value of} \\ \text{Asset Surrendered} \end{array} - \begin{array}{c} \text{Book Value of} \\ \text{Asset Surrendered} \end{array} \right)$$

$$= \frac{\$3,000}{\$3,000 + \$27,000} \times (\$30,000 - \$20,000) = \$1,000$$

(c) *Boot Paid by Company Incurring a Gain.* When similar productive assets are exchanged for a gain and boot is involved, the company *paying* the boot does not recognize the gain if the boot is less than 25% of the value exchanged. This situation is illustrated for Company B in Exhibit 8-2 (c). Company B records the equipment acquired at $33,000, which is the book value of the equipment surrendered ($28,000) plus the boot paid ($5,000, which is less than 25% of the value exchanged). This treatment is consistent with alternative 4 in Exhibit 8-3.

(d) *Boot Received by Company Incurring a Gain.* When similar productive assets are exchanged for a gain and boot is involved, the company *receiving* the boot recognizes the gain in proportion to the boot received if the boot is less than 25% of the value exchanged. This proportion of the gain has been realized through cash receipt, and therefore the earning process is complete for this portion. In this situation, the APB indicated that the proportion should be based on the ratio of the boot received to the total consideration received (i.e., boot plus the fair value of the asset *acquired*).[6] The gain is computed as follows:

$$\text{Gain} = \frac{\text{Boot}}{\text{Boot} + \text{Fair Value of Asset Acquired}} \times \text{Gain on Asset Surrendered}$$

$$= \frac{\text{Boot}}{\text{Boot} + \begin{array}{c}\text{Fair Value}\\ \text{of Asset Acquired}\end{array}} \times \left( \begin{array}{c}\text{Fair Value of}\\ \text{Asset Surrendered}\end{array} - \begin{array}{c}\text{Book Value of}\\ \text{Asset Surrendered}\end{array} \right)$$

Typically the sum of the boot plus the fair value of the asset acquired is equal to the fair value of the asset surrendered. Since this may not be true when an advantageous exchange takes place, the gain should always be computed by the method indicated.

This situation is illustrated for Company A in Exhibit 8-2 (d). Company A has received boot of $3,000, which is less than 25% of the value exchanged. The sum of the boot plus the fair value of the equipment acquired is $30,000. So the company is receiving 1/10 ($3,000 ÷ $30,000) of the value of the transaction in the form of boot, and recognizes 1/10 of the gain on the equipment surrendered. Since the total gain on the equipment surrendered is $10,000 (the fair value of $30,000 less the book value of $20,000), Company A recognizes a gain of $1,000. Following the formula developed previously, the gain is computed as follows:

$$\text{Gain} = \frac{\$3,000}{\$3,000 + \$27,000} (\$30,000 - \$20,000) = \$1,000$$

The equipment acquired by Company A is recorded at $18,000, the book value of the equipment surrendered less the cash received plus the gain recognized ($20,000 − $3,000 + $1,000). This treatment is consistent with alternative 6 in Exhibit 8-3.

(e) *Boot Paid by Company Incurring a Loss.* When similar productive assets are exchanged for a loss and boot is involved, the company *paying* the boot recognizes the loss in full. This situation is illustrated for Company B in Exhibit 8-2 (e). Company B incurs a loss of $1,000 ($27,000 fair value − $28,000 book value), recognizes it in full, and records the acquired equipment at $30,000 ($27,000 + $3,000). This treatment is consistent with alternative 3 in Exhibit 8-3.

Although these illustrations have used examples where one company incurs a loss and the other a gain, it should be noted that it is possible for both companies to have a loss, or for both companies to have a gain, depending on the relationship between each company's book value and market value.

---

6. James B. Hobbs and D.R. Bainbridge, *op. cit.*, par. 22.

**EXHIBIT 8-3**

## NONMONETARY PRODUCTIVE ASSET EXCHANGES

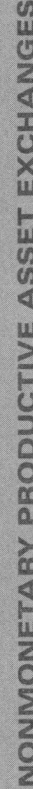

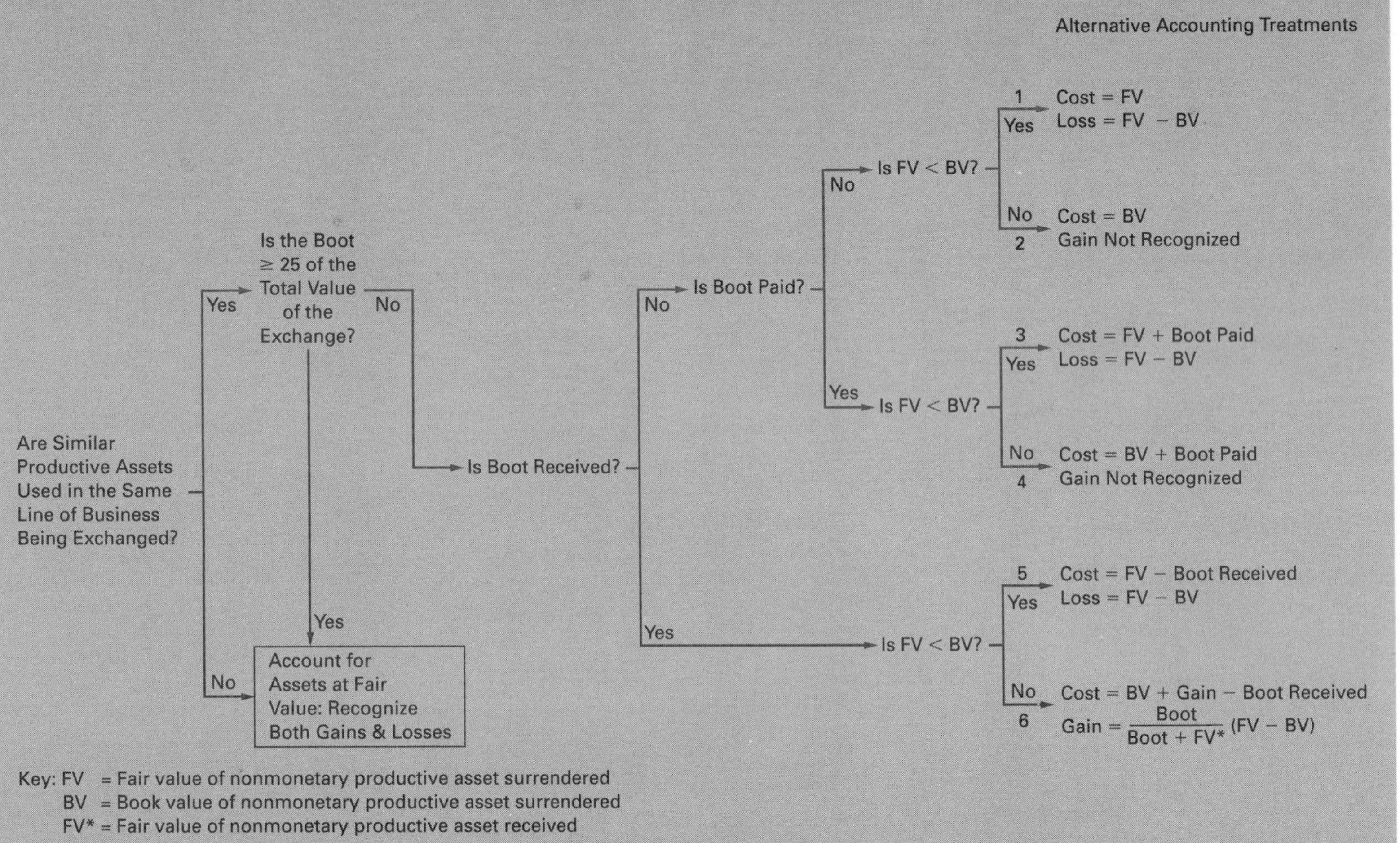

Alternative Accounting Treatments

Are Similar Productive Assets Used in the Same Line of Business Being Exchanged?

Yes → Is the Boot ≥ 25 of the Total Value of the Exchange?

No → Account for Assets at Fair Value: Recognize Both Gains & Losses

Is the Boot ≥ 25 of the Total Value of the Exchange?

No → Is Boot Received?

Yes → Account for Assets at Fair Value: Recognize Both Gains & Losses

Is Boot Received?

No → Is Boot Paid?

Yes → Is FV < BV?

Is Boot Paid?

No → Is FV < BV?

Yes → Is FV < BV?

Is FV < BV? (first)

Yes → 1  Cost = FV
Loss = FV − BV

No → 2  Cost = BV
Gain Not Recognized

Is FV < BV? (second)

Yes → 3  Cost = FV + Boot Paid
Loss = FV − BV

No → 4  Cost = BV + Boot Paid
Gain Not Recognized

Is FV < BV? (third)

Yes → 5  Cost = FV − Boot Received
Loss = FV − BV

No → 6  Cost = BV + Gain − Boot Received

$$Gain = \frac{Boot}{Boot + FV^*}(FV - BV)$$

Key: FV  = Fair value of nonmonetary productive asset surrendered
BV  = Book value of nonmonetary productive asset surrendered
FV* = Fair value of nonmonetary productive asset received

*Source:* Adapted from L. A. Nikolai, "Simplifying Nonmonetary Exchanges," *The CPA Journal,* January 1977, pp. 64–71.

## Summary of Productive Asset Exchanges

There are four issues involved in productive asset exchanges.

1. **Are similar or dissimilar productive assets used in the same line of business exchanged?** Gains and losses on dissimilar asset exchanges are recognized in full because the earning process is complete.

2. **Does the boot equal or exceed 25% of the total value of the exchange?** If the boot equals or exceeds 25%, the exchange is recorded at fair value by both the recipient and the payer of boot.

3. **For exchanges of similar productive assets is there a loss?** A loss is recognized in full, following the conservatism principle.

4. **For exchanges of similar productive assets between two dealers or between two nondealers in which there is a gain, is cash received or paid?** If cash is paid, the "gain" is not recognized because the earning process is considered not to be complete. If cash is received, a partial gain is recognized because part of the earning process has been realized (completed).

To summarize, no gain (or a partial gain) is recognized when the exchange involves similar productive assets used in the same line of business (i.e., an exchange between two dealers or between two nondealers), the boot is less than 25% of the fair market value of the transaction, and cash is received. In other situations the total gain is recognized. A loss is recognized in all situations.

## SELF-CONSTRUCTION

Sometimes an item of property, plant, and equipment is constructed by the company that intends to use it in its production process. The costs directly related to the construction are added to the cost of the asset, including materials, labor, engineering, and variable manufacturing overhead. Three other components of the asset cost need additional consideration: (1) interest costs, (2) fixed manufacturing overhead costs, and (3) profit on the construction. Each of these is discussed in the following sections.

### Interest During Construction

There has been a great deal of controversy as to whether interest on the funds borrowed to finance construction of an asset should be capitalized as part of the acquisition cost or expensed directly. Furthermore, if internally generated funds are used to finance the acquisition, should imputed interest be added to the cost of the asset? Regulating authorities for public utilities usually allow the inclusion of both actual and imputed interest in the cost of the asset because the impact of the interest on the utility rates is deferred until the new plant is in operation. Therefore, the cost of the plant is assigned (through depreciation expense) to the periods of use and to the customers who use the product. In the early 1970s the capitalization of interest by nonutility companies gained wider acceptance, but the SEC stopped this trend by preventing companies from adopting a policy of capitalization of interest cost. In 1979 FASB Statement No. 34 was issued requiring the capitalization of interest in certain instances as discussed later in this chapter.[7]

---

7. "Capitalization of Interest Cost," *FASB Statement of Financial Accounting Standards No. 34* (Stamford, Conn.: FASB, 1979).

*Conceptual Alternatives*

The *Statement* outlines the three alternatives that were considered for the treatment of interest during construction.

(a) *No Interest Is Capitalized During Construction.* This alternative would treat interest as a cost of borrowing funds, and the interest would be recorded as an expense during the period incurred. This treatment would be consistent with all other interest costs, such as interest on funds borrowed to purchase inventory, or to purchase property, plant, and equipment. The principal argument in favor of this alternative is that interest is the price paid in exchange for receiving funds for a period of time, and the benefit received is the availability of the funds. Therefore, matching requires that the cost be charged against revenues in the period in which the funds are made available. Another argument is that expensing interest as incurred results in income flows that are more similar to cash flows.

(b) *Capitalize an Amount of Interest for All Funds Used for Construction.* This alternative would require that an interest cost be assigned to all funds used in construction, whether borrowed or not. Therefore, an interest cost for the equity funds (common stock) used in construction would have to be imputed and capitalized in addition to the cost of borrowed funds. While it often is argued that this alternative provides the fairest economic cost of the asset, two major problems have prevented its adoption. First, there is considerable disagreement about how to measure the interest rate to be used for the imputed cost of the equity funds, and this amount would lack *reliability*. Second, since the computed interest cost of the equity funds would be debited to the asset, it is necessary to record a credit. The credit could be to a revenue account, but that would violate the revenue recognition principle, since revenue should not be recognized as a result of acquiring assets. Another alternative would be to credit stockholders' equity directly, but there has been no contribution of capital by the owners, and the net worth of the company has not increased.

(c) *Capitalize the Interest on Funds Borrowed for the Construction.* This alternative treats the cost of borrowed funds as part of the cost of acquiring an asset and therefore as equivalent to the other costs of construction, such as materials and labor. The advantages are: (1) the cost of the borrowed funds is necessary to obtain the benefits to be derived from the asset, and (2) since the asset is not yet generating revenue, matching requires that the cost of interest (and depreciation) not be expensed. The disadvantage is that the cost of the asset will differ depending on the type of financing (debt or equity) used for construction. There are two ways of interpreting this third alternative. The cost to be capitalized could be either the cost of funds *specifically* borrowed to finance the project or the *average* cost of all borrowed funds. Elements of both approaches are required by *FASB Statement No. 34.*

Three major factors must be considered in the application of the *Statement*: (1) which assets qualify for interest capitalization; (2) what amount of interest must be capitalized; and (3) over what period is the interest capitalized?

*Assets Qualifying for Interest Capitalization*

**Interest is *required* to be capitalized on assets that are either constructed for a company's own use or constructed as discrete projects for sale or lease to others** (for example, long-term construction projects such as ships or real estate developments, as discussed in Chapter 16). Interest *cannot* be capitalized for the following types of assets:

1. Inventories that are routinely manufactured or otherwise produced in large quantities on a repetitive basis. Inventories are not qualifying assets because,

in the view of the FASB, "the informational benefit does not justify the cost"[8] of capitalization.

2. Assets that are in use or ready for their intended use.

3. Assets that are not being used in the earning activities of the company.

### *Amount of Interest to Be Capitalized*

The amount of interest to be capitalized for a qualifying asset is based on the actual amounts borrowed and the cost of those borrowings. The amount is "intended to be that portion of the interest cost incurred during the asset's acquisition periods that theoretically could have been avoided."[9] **The amount capitalized is determined by applying an interest rate to the average cumulative invested costs (expenditures) for the qualifying asset during the capitalization period.**

If a company incurs a specific borrowing for a qualifying asset, the interest rate on that borrowing is used on the expenditures for the asset. If the expenditures on the asset exceed the cost of the specific borrowing or if no specific borrowing is made, the weighted average interest rate on all other borrowings is used. Because no imputed interest is allowed to be capitalized, **the total amount of interest cost that is capitalized each period may not exceed the interest cost incurred during the period.**

The expenditures to which this rate is applied are the cumulative capitalized expenditures and include any capitalized interest on the qualifying asset from previous years. Typically, it is assumed for simplicity that the expenditures are incurred evenly throughout the year. Therefore, the average cumulative capitalized expenditures for a given year are computed as follows: [(beginning cumulative costs + ending cumulative costs) ÷ 2]. If expenditures are not incurred evenly throughout the year, a weighted average calculation would be used. If the company receives any progress payments from the eventual purchaser of the asset, these amounts are deducted from the expenditures, so that interest is capitalized on the net expenditures made by the company.

### *Period of Interest Capitalization*

**The capitalization period begins when (a) expenditures for the asset have been made, (b) activities that are necessary to get the asset ready for its intended use are in progress, and (c) interest cost is being incurred.** Interest capitalization continues as long as the three conditions are present. The term *activities* is to be construed broadly and should include all the steps necessary to prepare the asset for its intended use. For example, it includes administrative and technical activities during the preconstruction stage and activities undertaken to overcome technical difficulties after construction has begun, such as labor disputes or litigation. If a company suspends substantially *all* the activities related to the construction of the asset, however, interest capitalization is suspended until activities are resumed.

**The capitalization period ends when the asset is (a) substantially complete and (b) ready for its intended use.** If the asset is completed in parts and each part is capable of being used independently, interest capitalization stops for each part when that part satisfies the two criteria. In this case the interest to be capitalized is based on the average cost for that part. If the asset must be completed in its entirety before any part of the asset may be used, however, interest capitalization continues until the entire asset satisfies the two criteria.

8. *Ibid.*, par. 10.
9. *Ibid.*, par. 12.

*Illustration*

To illustrate these provisions of *FASB Statement No. 34*, consider the Cia Company, which started a building project on January 1, 1995 and completed it on December 31, 1996. The relevant facts are as follows:

Capitalization period: January 1, 1995 through December 31, 1996
Annual expenditures on the project (excluding capitalized interest):
    1995   $1 million
    1996   $2.9 million
Amounts borrowed and outstanding:
    $1.5 million at 10% borrowed specifically for the project
    $4 million at 12%
    $6 million at 13%

It is assumed that the costs (expenditures) are incurred evenly during each year. The average cumulative capitalized costs in the project to date for each year are computed using the equations discussed earlier as follows:

Average cumulative costs: 1995, $500,000 [($0 + $1,000,000) ÷ 2]
Average cumulative costs: 1996, $2,500,000 [($1,000,000 + $50,000[a])
                               + ($1,050,000 + $2,900,000) ÷ 2]

[a]Capitalized interest for 1995 as calculated below.

Since $1.5 million was borrowed specifically for the project, the 10% interest rate on this borrowing is used for each of the two years on the first $1.5 million of costs. Interest each year on costs greater than $1.5 million is based on the weighted average of the remaining borrowings of the company. The amount of interest to be capitalized in each of the two years is calculated as follows:

Capitalized interest, 1995 = Average cumulative cost × Interest rate
                           = $500,000 × 10%
                           = <u>$50,000</u>

Capitalized interest, 1996 = Average cumulative cost × Interest rate
                           = ($1,500,000 × 10%) + ($1,000,000[b] × 12.6%[c])
                           = $150,000 + $126,000
                           = <u>$276,000</u>

[b] $2,500,000 average cumulative cost for 1996 − $1,500,000 specific borrowing

[c] Weighted average interest rate $= \left( 12\% \times \dfrac{\$4,000,000}{\$10,000,000} \right) + \left( 13\% \times \dfrac{\$6,000,000}{\$10,000,000} \right)$
                                   = 4.8% + 7.8%
                                   = 12.6%

The $50,000 interest capitalized in 1995 is calculated by multiplying the $500,000 average cumulative cost times the 10% interest rate on the specific borrowing for the project. The interest capitalized in 1996 requires two calculations, since the $2,500,000 average cumulative cost exceeds the $1,500,000 specific borrowing for the project. First, the $150,000 ($1,500,000 × 10%) annual interest on the specific borrowing is calculated. Next, the $1,000,000 excess of average cost over specific borrowing ($2,500,000 − $1,500,000) is multiplied times the 12.6% weighted average interest rate to determine the $126,000 additional interest to be capitalized. Thus a total of $276,000 ($150,000 + $126,000) interest is capitalized in 1996.

As mentioned earlier, the total amount of interest that is capitalized each period may not exceed the interest cost incurred during the period. Each year the company incurs interest costs of $1.41 million [($1.5 million × 10%) + ($4 million × 12%) + ($6 million × 13%)]. This amount is clearly more than the capitalized interest in either year. If it were less, however, it would be the maximum amount that the company could capitalize in any given year. Assuming interest expense has been recorded for the $1.41 million interest cost each year, the journal entries at the end of 1995 and 1996 respectively to record the capitalized interest are:

| | | |
|---|---|---|
| Building | 50,000 | |
|     Interest Expense | | 50,000 |
| Building | 276,000 | |
|     Interest Expense | | 276,000 |

Note that these journal entries *reduce* the interest expense each year and *increase* the cost of the building because of the capitalized interest. The interest expense of $1,360,000 and $1,134,000 are reported on the company's 1995 and 1996 income statements, respectively. In addition, the capitalized interest amounts of $50,000 and $276,000 are disclosed in the notes to the financial statements. (Note that the total interest paid each year is also disclosed, as discussed in Chapter 20.)

The total interest capitalized over the two years is $326,000 ($50,000 + $276,000). Therefore the cost of the asset is increased by this amount, which will reduce the gross profit on the sale if the asset is sold when completed, or increase the depreciation expense each year if the asset is held by the company. Of course, in the two years that the interest is capitalized, interest expense is reduced and therefore pretax income is increased by $326,000.

In certain cases, some companies borrow larger amounts than required for their immediate construction needs. A question arises concerning whether the interest revenue earned by investing the excess funds should be offset against the interest cost in determining the amount of interest to be capitalized. Since *FASB Statement No. 34* states that the amount of interest to be capitalized is the portion of the interest that theoretically could have been avoided, the interest revenue should *not* be offset against the interest cost. The decision of a company to borrow greater amounts than needed and to invest the excess does not affect the avoidable interest and therefore does not affect the amount of interest to be capitalized.[10] Consequently, the interest earned is recognized as interest revenue in the normal way.

## International Accounting Differences

While interest capitalization is allowed in most countries, it is optional in many countries including Australia, Germany, and the United Kingdom. In a few countries, including Brazil and Japan, capitalization of interest costs is prohibited.

10. "Offsetting Interest Cost to Be Capitalized with Interest Income," *FASB Technical Bulletin No. 81–5* (Stamford, Conn.: FASB, 1981).

## Fixed Overhead Costs

There are three alternatives for including fixed overhead costs in the cost of a self-constructed asset. These alternatives are (1) to allocate a portion of the total fixed overhead, (2) to include only the incremental fixed overhead, and (3) not to include any fixed overhead in the cost of the asset. Each alternative should be considered in the context of two production situations. First, the company may be operating at full capacity, so that the construction activity reduces normal production activity. Second, the company may be operating at below-normal capacity, so that the construction activity does not affect normal production activity.

1. *Allocate a Portion of Total Fixed Overhead to the Self-Constructed Asset.* Under this alternative, fixed overhead is allocated to the construction in the same manner as to units of inventory produced. This is a "full costing" concept, because the total overhead costs of the period are allocated to the production of inventory and the construction of the asset. Arguments in favor of this alternative are (1) the construction should be accounted for in the same way as regular products, even though this means that the regular products will be allocated less of the overhead, and (2) the cost of the constructed asset will tend to approximate more closely the cost of an equivalent purchased asset, since the seller normally would include fixed overhead in its selling price. The first argument is especially relevant if the company was operating at full capacity prior to the construction, so that the construction causes less regular production to take place. Then the lower total overhead allocated to production coupled with lower productive output results in more consistent unit costs. When the company is operating at below-normal capacity prior to construction, allocation of some fixed overhead to self-constructed assets reduces the costs allocated to regular production and therefore increases the income reported for these products when they are sold. Thus there is a transfer of overhead costs from regular production to the self-constructed asset.

2. *Include Only Incremental Fixed Overhead in the Cost of the Self-Constructed Asset.* Under this alternative, only the fixed overhead that increases as a result of the construction (but no allocated overhead) is included in the cost of the self-constructed asset. Arguments in favor of this alternative are: (1) the cost of an asset is the additional cost incurred to produce it, (2) the normal operations should not receive different treatment by reducing the cost of the regular product and increasing income because of the construction, (3) the overhead would be incurred whether or not the construction takes place, and (4) the decision to construct the asset should be based on the total incremental cost and not include allocated fixed overhead. This method is particularly appropriate when there is excess capacity available so that regular production and profits are not affected by the construction. If this method is used in a full-capacity situation, the unit cost of the regular production will be increased because the same total fixed overhead would be allocated to the reduced production.

3. *Include No Fixed Overhead in the Cost of the Self-Constructed Asset.* The primary argument in favor of this alternative is that the fixed overhead does not change as a result of the construction. Therefore, to include some overhead would result in less overhead being expensed in the current period (or included in the cost of inventory) and an increase in income. Of course, this alternative is reasonable only if the fixed overhead does not increase as a result of the construction.

In summary, **the allocation of fixed overhead to a self-constructed asset is most appropriate when the company is operating at full capacity, the inclusion of only incremental fixed overhead is most appropriate in excess-capacity situations, and**

**no allocation is appropriate if the overhead does not change.** Otherwise the self-construction activity affects income, an effect that many accountants consider undesirable. Income should be a measure of the success of selling goods and services, and it should not depend on the amount of construction undertaken.

However, the first alternative of allocating a portion of the total fixed overhead to the self-constructed asset is supported for both situations by the Cost Accounting Standards Board as follows:

> Tangible capital assets constructed for a contractor's own use must be capitalized at amounts which include general and administrative expenses when such expenses are identifiable with the constructed asset and are material in amount. When the constructed assets are identical with or similar to the contractor's regular product, such assets must be capitalized at amounts which include a full share of indirect costs.[11]

This method is the most commonly used and does tend to produce an asset cost that is closer to the cost of a purchased asset, because an independent contractor would include an allowance to cover its overhead and profit. However, it will tend to result in increased income during construction.

## Profit on Self-Construction

If a company constructs an asset for less than it would cost to purchase, should it recognize a profit of the difference between the two costs? An argument can be made in favor of recognizing a profit, since it would tend to produce an asset cost similar to the purchase price of the asset. However, generally accepted accounting principles do not allow recognition of a profit in this case. To do so would violate the revenue recognition principle that requires that profits be recognized through asset use and disposal and not through acquisition. In addition, accounting is based on actions taken, not on what might have been. The saving through self-construction will be realized through reduced depreciation charges in the future. However, the conservatism convention requires that, if the construction cost materially exceeds the fair market value of the asset, the capitalized construction costs of the asset be written down to the fair market value and a loss recognized.

## Development Stage Companies

Development stage companies are companies that devote substantially all their efforts to establishing a new business, and planned principal operations have not yet commenced or no significant revenue has been generated. Some accountants argue that the costs of interest, taxes, and general overhead should be capitalized during the development stage of a new company—that is, before significant sales are made. They argue that the costs incurred in the development stage will benefit future periods, and consequently losses should not be reported before sales are made. In **FASB Statement No. 7**, this argument was rejected. Instead normal capitalization criteria are applied to development stage companies. Therefore such costs as interest (except for the provisions of *FASB Statement No. 34*), taxes, and general overhead are expensed in the period incurred. *FASB Statement No. 7* does impose some special disclosure requirements on development stage companies, but these are beyond the scope of the book.

---

11. "Capitalization of Tangible Assets," *CASB Standard 404* (Washington, D.C.: CASB, 1973).

## COSTS SUBSEQUENT TO ACQUISITION

Costs are incurred over the life of property, plant, and equipment for purposes ranging from routine repairs to major overhauls and improvements. The related accounting decision is whether these costs should be recorded (capitalized) to an asset account (a **capital expenditure**) or expensed (an **operating** or **revenue expenditure**). **A cost that increases the future economic benefits of the asset above those that originally were expected is a capital expenditure.** The future economic benefits can be increased by (1) extending the life of the asset, (2) improving productivity, (3) producing the same product at lower cost, or (4) increasing the quality of the product. **A cost that does not increase the economic benefits but is incurred to maintain the existing benefits is an operating expenditure.** Special consideration is given to additions, improvements and replacements, rearrangement and moving, and repairs and maintenance in the following sections.

### Additions

The cost of an **addition** represents a new asset and therefore is capitalized. A new wing to a building and the installation of a pollution-control device are examples of additions. When the addition involves removing an old asset, an issue arises as to how to account for the cost of the removal. For example, when a new wing is added to a building, alterations are frequently made to the old building. If these alterations increase the economic benefits originally anticipated for the old building, then the cost of alteration is capitalized. If the alterations do not increase the original benefits of the old building, the cost is expensed. In addition, the cost of any part of the asset that is demolished (for example, a connecting wall) should be removed from the accounts as the disposal of an asset, although this is rarely done because of immateriality or the difficulty of measurement.

### Improvements and Replacements

**Improvements** (sometimes called **betterments**) and **replacements** (sometimes called **renewals**) involve the substitution of new parts for old ones and increase the economic benefits to be derived from the asset. An improvement is the substitution of a better asset for the one currently used, such as the installation of a solar heating system in a building. A replacement is the substitution of an equivalent asset, such as a new engine in a truck. The related costs of improvements and replacements are capitalized. There are three alternative ways to account for such capitalized expenditures, and the choice depends on the particular circumstances.

1. *Substitution Method.* When the book value of the old asset is known, it is removed from the accounts and the new asset recorded. For example, suppose that a company decides to replace its oil furnace with a gas furnace. The oil furnace is carried on the books at a cost of $50,000 with accumulated depreciation of $30,000. The scrap value of the old furnace is $5,000, and the new furnace costs $70,000. The journal entry to record these transactions is:

| | | |
|---|---:|---:|
| Furnace | 70,000 | |
| Accumulated Depreciation: Furnace | 30,000 | |
| Loss on Disposal of Furnace ($20,000 − $5,000) | 15,000 | |
|     Furnace | | 50,000 |
|     Cash ($70,000 − $5,000) | | 65,000 |

Although this is the ideal method, it often is not practical because the book value of the asset being replaced is not known. For example, when the engine on a truck is replaced, the book value of the engine may not be known. In these situations, one of the two alternative methods should be used.

2. *Reduce Accumulated Depreciation.* The costs of improvements and replacements are often debited to Accumulated Depreciation on the grounds that some of the service potential that previously was written off has been restored. Therefore, it is appropriate to use this method for replacements when the service life of the asset has been extended. If the same depreciation rate is used, the reduction of (debit to) Accumulated Depreciation will extend the depreciable life of the asset. The depreciable life should be extended by the same amount as the economic life is increased. For example, suppose that a capital expenditure of $50,000 is incurred in replacing a roof on a factory. The company had not planned to replace the roof, but it has extended the life of the factory. The cost is recorded as follows:

| | | |
|---|---|---|
| Accumulated Depreciation | 50,000 | |
| Cash | | 50,000 |

3. *Increase the Asset Account.* The costs of improvements and replacements may be capitalized directly to the asset account on the grounds that an addition to the service potential of the asset has been made. This method is particularly appropriate for improvements when the benefits are increased above those originally expected. For example, a capital expenditure of $50,000 to enlarge a factory that increases its usefulness is recorded as follows:

| | | |
|---|---|---|
| Factory | 50,000 | |
| Cash | | 50,000 |

Note that alternatives 2 and 3 have exactly the same effect on the book value of the asset, although the gross amounts in the two accounts would be different.

## Rearrangement and Moving

The costs of rearranging the facilities within a building or moving them to a new location are capitalized and expensed over the period expected to benefit. (This period is shorter than the economic life of the assets being moved if it is expected that the assets will be moved again before the end of their service lives.) However, many companies expense such costs immediately, which is an acceptable procedure if the difference is immaterial.

## Repairs and Maintenance

Routine repair and maintenance costs, which are incurred to maintain the asset in its operating condition and do not increase the economic benefits over those originally intended, are expensed in the period incurred. However, the classification of an expenditure as a repair may depend on how the company accounts for its assets. For example, if landscaping costs are included in a Land Improvements account, replacement of some trees would be accounted for as repairs and maintenance. If the landscaping costs were included in a separate account, then the replacement of these trees more likely would be accounted for as an improvement or replacement.

Since repair and maintenance costs may be incurred unevenly during the year (for example, repairs may be scheduled for slack production periods), interim financial statements (such as quarterly reports) will absorb different amounts of repair costs that, in turn, may give a misleading picture of the income flows. The amount of repair costs recorded as an expense in each interim period may be equalized by using an allowance account. For example, suppose a company anticipates spending $60,000 on repair and maintenance during the year, but $45,000 will be spent in the third quarter, with the remainder spread equally over the remaining three quarters. The journal entries to record these events are:

**First Quarter**

| | | |
|---|---|---|
| Repair Expense ($60,000 ÷ 4) | 15,000 | |
|     Allowance for Repairs | | 10,000 |
|     Cash, Accounts Payable, Inventory, etc. | | 5,000 |

**Second Quarter**

| | | |
|---|---|---|
| Repair Expense | 15,000 | |
|     Allowance for Repairs | | 10,000 |
|     Cash, Accounts Payable, Inventory, etc. | | 5,000 |

**Third Quarter**

| | | |
|---|---|---|
| Repair Expense | 15,000 | |
| Allowance for Repairs | 30,000 | |
|     Cash, Accounts Payable, Inventory, etc. | | 45,000 |

**Fourth Quarter**

| | | |
|---|---|---|
| Repair Expense | 15,000 | |
|     Allowance for Repairs | | 10,000 |
|     Cash, Accounts Payable, Inventory, etc. | | 5,000 |

The repair expense is $15,000 each quarter (one fourth of the annual cost of $60,000), and Allowance for Repairs has a zero balance at the end of the year. This procedure is acceptable for interim reporting because it allows equal expenses to be recorded each interim period. The balance in Allowance for Repairs is reported as an addition to or offset from the property, plant, and equipment and not as a liability because nothing is owed. However, a balance in Allowance for Repairs is not carried over from one annual fiscal period to another, because such smoothing of income is not allowed under generally accepted accounting principles. If a balance does remain in the Allowance for Repairs account at the end of the year, it is closed to the Repairs Expense account.

## DISPOSAL OF PROPERTY, PLANT, AND EQUIPMENT

Property, plant, and equipment may be disposed of by sale, involuntary conversion, abandonment, or exchange (which was discussed earlier in the chapter). Ideally the depreciation, which is accumulated up to the time of disposal, will have reduced the book value down to the disposal value. Usually, however, this does not occur, and a gain or a loss on the disposal must be recognized. The gain or loss results from a transaction of the period and may also be considered a correction of the income that has been recorded in the years the asset has been owned, since it is an indication that the depreciation was not correct. The gain or loss usually is included in ordinary income, but it could also be reported as an extraordinary item or a disposal of a segment of a business if it meets the appropriate criteria established in **APB Opinion No. 30**, discussed in Chapter 4.

Accounting for the disposal of property, plant, and equipment is not difficult. The depreciation is recorded up to the date of the disposal, using the practice adopted by the company for recognizing depreciation. This is discussed in the next chapter. The cost of the asset and the related amount of accumulated depreciation are then removed from the respective accounts. For example, assume that a company has a machine that originally cost $10,000, has accumulated depreciation of $8,000 at the beginning of the current year, and is being depreciated at $1,000 per year. If the company sells the machine for $600 on December 30, it must first bring the depreciation up to date as follows:

| | | |
|---|---|---|
| Depreciation Expense | 1,000 | |
|     Accumulated Depreciation | | 1,000 |

Once the book value is up to date, it is compared to the proceeds to determine the gain or loss. Comparing the $1,000 [$10,000 − ($8,000 + $1,000)] book value of the asset on December 30 to the $600 proceeds yields a loss of $400, which is recorded as follows:

| | | |
|---|---|---|
| Cash | 600 | |
| Accumulated Depreciation | 9,000 | |
| Loss on Disposal | 400 | |
|     Machine | | 10,000 |

An involuntary disposal such as condemnation of land by a governmental unit is accounted for in the same manner.[12] An abandonment is handled in a similar way, except that there is no receipt of cash, so the loss is equal to the remaining book value.

## DISCLOSURE OF PROPERTY, PLANT, AND EQUIPMENT

**APB Opinion No. 12** requires disclosure of the balances of major classes of depreciable assets by nature or function.[13] An example of each of these methods is given in Exhibit 8-4. AMP Corporation illustrates disclosure by the nature of the assets, such as land, buildings, and machinery. Norfolk Southern discloses by function, such as road and equipment.

---

12. "Accounting for Involuntary Conversions of Nonmonetary Assets to Monetary Assets," *FASB Interpretation No. 30* (Stamford, Conn.: FASB, 1979), requires that a gain or loss be recognized when a nonmonetary asset is involuntarily converted to monetary assets even though a company reinvests or is obligated to reinvest the monetary assets in replacement nonmonetary assets.

13. "Omnibus Opinion—1967," *APB Opinion No. 12* (New York: AICPA, 1967), par. 5.

## EXHIBIT 8-4
## ALTERNATIVE METHODS OF DISCLOSURE
## OF DEPRECIABLE ASSETS

### AMP CORPORATION
Notes to Combined Financial Statements

*1. Summary of Accounting Principles (in part)*
**Property, Plant and Equipment and Depreciation**—Property, plant and equipment is stated at cost, adjusted to current exchange rates where applicable. Depreciation is computed by applying principally the straight-line method to individual items. Depreciation rate ranges are substantially as follows:

| | |
|---|---|
| Buildings | 5% |
| Leasehold improvements | Life of lease |
| Machinery and equipment | 7 1/2% to 33 1/3% |
| Machines and tools with customers | 20% to 33 1/3% |

Where different depreciation methods of lives are used for tax purposes, deferred income taxes are recorded.

Maintenance and repairs are charged to expense as incurred. Major repairs and improvements are capitalized and depreciated at applicable straight-line rates.

The cost and accumulated depreciation of items of plant and equipment retired or otherwise disposed of are removed from the related accounts, and any residual values are charged or credited to operating income.

*5. Property, Plant and Equipment*
At December 31, property, plant and equipment was comprised of the following:

| (dollars in thousands) | 1991 | 1990 |
|---|---|---|
| Land | $    50,582 | $    48,766 |
| Buildings and leasehold improvements | 512,546 | 479,243 |
| Machinery and equipment | 1,643,934 | 1,451,566 |
| Machines and tools with customers | 343,344 | 323,753 |
| | $2,550,406 | $2,303,328 |

### NORFOLK SOUTHERN CORPORATION AND SUBSIDIARIES
Notes to Consolidated Financial Statements

*1. Summary of Significant Accounting Policies (in part)*
*Properties*: Properties are stated principally at cost. Rail is primarily depreciated on the basis of use measured by gross ton miles. The effect of this method is to write off these costs over 41 years on average. Other properties are depreciated generally using the straight-line method over estimated service lives at annual rates that range from approximately 1.0% to 18.0% and average approximately 2.6% for roadway and 3.7% for equipment. NS capitalizes interest on major capital projects during the period of their construction. Maintenance expense is recognized when repairs are performed. When properties other than land are sold or retired, the cost of the assets less the sale proceeds or salvage is charged to accumulated depreciation rather than recognized through income. Gains and losses on disposal of land are included in other income.

**EXHIBIT 8-4, Continued**
**ALTERNATIVE METHODS OF DISCLOSURE**
**OF DEPRECIABLE ASSETS**

*7. Properties*

| (in millions of dollars) | December 31, 1991 | December 31, 1990 |
|---|---|---|
| Transportation property: | | |
|   Road | $ 7,273.4 | $ 7,058.3 |
|   Equipment | 4,594.9 | 4,557.3 |
| Other property | 466.3 | 385.5 |
| | 12,334.6 | 12,001.1 |
| Less: Accumulated depreciation | 3,962.4 | 3,873.1 |
| Net properties | $ 8,372.2 | $ 8,128.0 |

Other property in 1991 includes $66.6 million for assets acquired from a real estate partnership in which an NS subsidiary owns an equity interest. Of this transaction, $54.0 million was noncash and relates to amounts invested in or advanced to that partnership which previously has been classified in Investments. In 1990, properties include a noncash addition of $27.2 million relating to assumption of notes in connection with the acquisition of a coal terminal facility.

Total interest cost incurred on debt for 1991, 1990 and 1989 was $117.3 million, $93.1 million and $66.7 million, respectively, of which $17.6 million, $15.1 million and $16.0 million was capitalized.

## APPENDIX 1: OIL AND GAS PROPERTIES

Companies face special issues when accounting for oil and gas properties that are included in property, plant, and equipment. Two alternative methods of accounting for the cost of oil and gas properties are widely used. The principal difference between the two methods concerns costs that cannot be directly related to the discovery of specific oil and gas reserves—the cost of dry wells. Under the **successful-efforts** method, those costs are charged to expense; under the **full-cost** method, they are capitalized, carried forward to future periods as the cost of oil and gas reserves, and subsequently amortized.

Proponents of the successful-efforts method argue that a direct relationship between costs incurred and specific reserves discovered is required before costs are recorded as assets. Costs of acquisition and development activities that are known not to have resulted in the discovery of reserves are charged to expense. In contrast, the full-cost method regards the costs of unsuccessful acquisition and exploration activities as necessary for the discovery of reserves. Thus all costs incurred in oil and gas drilling are regarded as integral to the development of whatever reserves ultimately result from the efforts as a whole, and are thus associated with the company's reserves. Establishing a direct cause-and-effect relationship between drilling costs incurred and specific reserves discovered is not relevant to full costing. The basic difference between the two methods focuses on the nature of an asset. If the asset is viewed as an individual well, it is appropriate to expense the costs incurred if no oil or gas is found, because no future cash flows will result. Alternatively, if the asset is viewed as the oil or gas that lies underground, it is appropriate to capitalize the costs of drilling even if no oil or gas is found from a particular well, because the activity was necessary in the general activity of searching for oil or gas. It is the oil or gas that is discovered that will contribute to the future cash flows rather than the costs incurred to drill any particular well. Companies that use the full-cost method are required (by the SEC, as discussed later) to use a country as a cost center. Thus if costs are incurred in a new country and no oil or gas results, the costs are expensed.

Because both methods are widely used, difficulties are created for users of financial statements when making comparisons between companies that are each using different methods. Large oil and gas companies generally use the successful-efforts method, whereas small independent producers prefer the full-cost method because it enables them to defer more costs, thereby reducing current expenses and increasing current income.

In 1977 **FASB Statement No. 19** was issued, which required the use of the successful-efforts method. Two primary reasons justified the adoption of the successful-efforts method by the FASB. First, an asset is an economic resource that is expected to provide future benefits, so costs that are known not to have resulted in identifiable future benefits should be expensed. Second, financial statements should reflect risk and unsuccessful results, and the successful-efforts method highlights the cost of failures and the risks involved in the search for oil and gas reserves. The SEC decided not to support the FASB's position in a politically motivated decision. Many of the owners and managers of oil and gas companies that were using full-cost accounting objected to its elimination and lobbied Congress. They argued that the use of successful efforts would cause reported income and assets to be lower, and would impair the ability of their companies to raise capital and search for oil and gas. This argument is inconsistent with efficient markets research, which indicates that users of financial statements would not be "fooled" by the different reporting of the same underlying economic facts. However, Congress accepted the argument and directed that the SEC must accept the use of the full-cost method in reports filed with it, thereby allowing both methods to continue in use. Consequently, the FASB suspended *FASB Statement No. 19.*

It can be argued that neither method satisfies the needs of users of the financial statements because they do not reflect the economic substance of oil and gas exploration; that is, neither one includes the current values of the oil and gas reserves in the financial statements. Thus the SEC proposed a completely new method of accounting, Reserve Recognition Accounting (RRA), which would allow the current values of reserves to be recognized in the balance sheet and changes in the values of those reserves to be included in the income statement. Effective in 1979 companies were required to present a supplementary income statement on the basis of RRA, while continuing to use successful-efforts accounting or full-cost accounting. Subsequently the SEC rescinded the requirement to use RRA, and therefore oil companies now either use the full-cost or the successful-efforts method. Once a company has selected one of the two alternative methods, it must follow specific SEC accounting rules.[14] If the successful-efforts method is chosen, the SEC requires that the rules of *FASB Statement No. 19* must be followed. In addition, *FASB Statement No. 69* requires

14. "Codification of Financial Reporting Policies," *SEC Accounting Rules* (Chicago: Commerce Clearing House, October, 1988), sec. 406.

that oil companies disclose the physical and dollar amounts of reserves at year-end and changes in these amounts. Since these accounting problems relate to a specific industry, they are not discussed in greater detail.

*Current value accounting is discussed in Chapter 24.*

## APPENDIX 2: CASUALTY INSURANCE

Most companies insure their property, plant, and equipment against casualty losses such as fire, theft, or accident. The alternative is for the company to carry the risk itself, which is known as self-insurance. When insurance is carried, the premium is paid to the insurance company in advance. Since a discount is often given for a multi-year policy, the insurance premium may be paid in advance for a period of several years and recorded in an account titled Prepaid Insurance.

*Self-insurance is discussed in Chapter 15.*

A coinsurance clause often is written into the insurance contract to discourage a company from taking out only minimum insurance. **A coinsurance clause requires that an asset be insured for a certain minimum amount** (usually 80% of fair market value) **if a loss is to be fully covered by the insurance company.** For example, suppose that the Anderson Company has assets with a fair market value of $1,250,000. The company may believe that it would not lose more than one fourth of the assets in a single casualty loss and therefore would limit its insurance coverage to $312,500. However, from the insurance company's point of view, it is insuring the $1,250,000 of assets against all casualty losses over a period of time and therefore is not concerned only with the size of a single loss. With an 80% coinsurance clause, the Anderson Company is required to have insurance to cover 80% of the fair market value of the assets at the time of the loss if it is to recover the full amount of the loss on any casualty, up to the face amount of the policy. If the Anderson Company has a policy for less than 80% of the fair value of the assets, then it shares the risk with the insurance company.

To continue, suppose that the Anderson Company only insured the assets for one fourth of their value, or $312,500, under a policy with an 80% coinsurance clause. The amount recoverable if an asset that has a fair market value of $100,000 is destroyed is:

$$\frac{\text{Amount}}{\text{Recoverable}} = \frac{\text{Face Value of Policy}}{\text{Coinsurance \% × Fair Market Value of Assets Covered by Insurance Policy}} \times \frac{\text{Fair Market Value of Asset Destroyed}}{\text{(Amount of the Loss)}}$$

$$= \frac{\$312,500}{80\% \times \$1,250,000} \times \$100,000 = \underline{\underline{\$31,250}}$$

In other words, the insurance company covers only 31.25% of the loss—that is, the ratio of the face value of the policy ($312,500) to the coinsurance value (80% × $1,250,000)—and the Anderson Company assumes the remaining 68.75% of the risk. The amount recoverable is calculated in this manner up to a maximum of the face value of the policy.

Only if the loss exceeded $1 million would the amount recoverable be limited by the face value of the policy. With a loss of $1 million, the amount recoverable is $312,500 [($312,500 ÷ (0.80 × $1,250,000)) × $1,000,000], which is the face value of the policy and therefore the maximum the insurance company will pay. When the insurance coverage is greater than or equal to the coinsurance requirement, the formula need not be applied because the loss is covered in full by the insurance company up to the face value of the policy.

Insurance policies normally also carry a **contribution clause,** which provides that when more than one policy is carried, recovery of a loss is limited to the ratio of the face value of the policy to the total insurance carried. However, if the policies have different coinsurance requirements, the amount recovered is calculated as follows:

$$\text{Amount Recovered} = \begin{array}{c}\text{Fair Market Value of}\\ \text{Asset Destroyed}\\ \text{(Amount of the Loss)}\end{array} \times \dfrac{\text{Face Value of Individual Policy}}{\begin{array}{c}\text{Higher of Total Face Value of}\\ \text{All Policies or Coinsurance}\\ \text{Requirement of Individual Policy}\end{array}}$$

For example, suppose that the Anderson Company insures its $1,250,000 assets with three insurance policies having face values of $400,000, $400,000, and $100,000 and with coinsurance requirements of 80%, 70%, and 70%, respectively. If the fair market value of the asset destroyed is $100,000, the amount recoverable under each policy is as follows:

| Policy | Face Value | Coinsurance* Requirement | Fraction† | Fair Market Value of Asset Destroyed | Amount Collectible |
|---|---|---|---|---|---|
| A | $400,000 | $1,000,000 | 40/100 | $100,000 | $40,000 |
| B | 400,000 | 875,000 | 40/90 | 100,000 | 44,444 |
| C | 100,000 | 875,000 | 10/90 | 100,000 | 11,111 |
| | $900,000 | | | | $95,555 |

\* Coinsurance Percentage × Fair Market Value
†The fractions are computed as follows:
A: $400,000 ÷ $1,000,000 (coinsurance requirement)
B: $400,000 ÷ $ 900,000 (face value of all policies)
C: $100,000 ÷ $ 900,000

Accounting for a casualty loss requires procedures similar to those for any other disposal. The depreciation account is brought up to date, and the cost of the asset and the related amount of accumulated depreciation for the destroyed asset are removed from the respective accounts (as discussed previously), and a receivable account is established for the amount due from the insurance company. A gain or loss is recorded for the difference between the amount receivable and the book value of the asset destroyed. The total amount receivable from the insurance company is classified as a current asset, unless a delay in collection of more than one year or the operating cycle, whichever is longer, is anticipated.

## QUESTIONS

**Q8-1**  What characteristics are necessary for an asset to be included in the category of property, plant, and equipment?

**Q8-2**  What is the general criterion used to decide whether an expenditure should be included in the cost of property, plant, and equipment rather than being expensed?

**Q8-3**  How is land held for investment categorized on the balance sheet?

**Q8-4**  What is the book value of an asset?

**Q8-5**  What is the relationship between the book value and the market value of an asset during the life of the asset?

Q8-6 When several assets are purchased for a single lump sum, what is the principle used for cost apportionment? Why is it necessary to apportion the cost?

Q8-7 How is the acquisition cost of an asset determined when the asset is acquired in exchange for securities?

Q8-8 What is the distinction between similar and dissimilar productive assets made by *APB Opinion No. 29*? What is the reason for the distinction?

Q8-9 Under what situations is a gain or loss recognized when similar productive assets are exchanged? When dissimilar productive assets are exchanged?

Q8-10 What is meant by the term *boot*? How is it relevant to accounting for a similar productive asset exchange?

Q8-11 What is the general principle underlying the accounting for dissimilar productive assets? For similar productive assets?

Q8-12 Under what conditions is the interest incurred during self-construction of an asset capitalized? Contrast your answer with accounting for interest on a note payable that is not associated with the construction of an asset.

Q8-13 Explain how the amount of interest to be capitalized is determined when a company constructs an asset.

Q8-14 A company borrows some money, which it uses to acquire a parcel of land for a real estate development project. Before construction begins, a period of time passes while the company obtains the necessary planning permission. May the company capitalize interest during this period? If so, should the interest be capitalized to the land or the building account?

Q8-15 What are the three common alternative treatments of overhead costs during self-construction of an asset? What are the arguments in favor of each?

Q8-16 May profit be recognized during self-construction of an asset under generally accepted accounting principles? May a loss be recognized?

Q8-17 What is the distinction between a capital and an operating expenditure? Give two examples of each.

Q8-18 Distinguish between additions and improvements/replacements. How should each be accounted for?

Q8-19 Distinguish between ordinary repairs and maintenance, and extraordinary repairs. How should each be accounted for?

Q8-20 What are leasehold improvements? How should they be accounted for?

Q8-21 Under what conditions would you expect to see "allowance for repairs" in a balance sheet?

Q8-22 How is the disposal of an asset accounted for? How are gains and losses shown on the financial statements?

Q8-23 (*Appendix 1*). Distinguish between successful-efforts and full-cost accounting for oil and gas properties.

Q8-24 (*Appendix 2*). What is a coinsurance clause? What is a contribution clause? How do they affect casualty insurance?

## CASES

### C8-1   *Acquisition and Retirement*
Among the principal topics related to the accounting for the property, plant, and equipment of a company are acquisition and retirement.

**Required**
1. What expenditures are capitalized when equipment is acquired for cash?
2. Assume that the market value of equipment acquired is not determinable by reference to a similar purchase for cash. Describe how the acquiring company determines the capitalizable cost of equipment purchased by exchanging it for each of the following three items:
   a. Bonds having an established market price.
   b. Common stock not having an established market price.
   c. Similar equipment having a determinable market value.
3. Describe the factors that determine whether expenditures relating to property, plant, and equipment already in use are capitalized.
4. Describe how to account for the gain or loss on the sale of property, plant, and equipment for cash. (*AICPA adapted*)

### C8-2   *Lump-Sum Acquisition*
In 1975 a trial was held to settle a tax dispute between the owners of the Atlanta Falcons, a National Football League franchise, and the Internal Revenue Service. In 1966 the owners had paid $8.5 million to purchase the franchise. They considered $50,000 to be the cost of the franchise (which is not depreciable for income tax reporting), $727,000 was deferred interest, and the remaining $7.7 million was claimed to be the cost of the players'

contracts and options. The dispute centered on several variables:

1. How much of the purchase price was assignable to television rights?
2. Is the value assignable to television rights depreciable? If so, what is the expected life?
3. How much of the purchase price was assignable to player contracts and options?
4. Over what life should the value assigned to the players be depreciated?
5. What is the value of the franchise?

**Required**

As an independent accountant, discuss the approach you would take and the information you would need to provide advice to the court for the resolution of the points in dispute.

### C8-3   Capitalization Issues

George Company purchased land for use as its corporate headquarters. A small factory that was on the land when it was purchased was torn down before construction of the office building began. Furthermore, a substantial amount of rock blasting and removal had to be done to the site before construction of the building foundation began. Because the office building was set back on the land far from the public road, George Company had the contractor construct a paved road that led from the public road to the parking lot of the office building.

Three years after the office building was occupied, George Company added four stories to the office building. The four stories had an estimated useful life of 5 years more than the remaining estimated useful life of the original office building.

Ten years later the land and building were sold at an amount more than their book value, and George Company had a new office building constructed in another state for use as its new corporate headquarters.

**Required**

1. Which of the preceding expenditures are capitalized? How is each depreciated or amortized? Discuss the rationale for your answers.
2. How is the sale of the land and building accounted for? Include in your answer how to determine the book value at the date of sale. Discuss the rationale for your answer. (*AICPA adapted*)

### C8-4   Interest Capitalization

The Gold Creek Company has borrowed large amounts of money to purchase 5,000 acres of land, which are to be developed as a new ski area over the next 10 years. Development is currently under way on the first 2,000 acres, with trails being cut and ski lifts being built. When this initial development is completed after 4 years, the remaining acreage will be developed at the rate of approximately 500 acres per year. The company also used some of the

money it borrowed to purchase adjacent land, which will be used to expand the ski area if it is successful.

Since this is the first year of the company's existence, it has not developed a policy about interest capitalization. Specifically, it is uncertain whether it is entitled to capitalize interest on the amounts borrowed to acquire the first 2,000 acres, the 5,000 acres, the 5,000 acres plus the adjacent land, or the land and the development.

**Required**

Explain the interest capitalization that is appropriate under these circumstances.

### C8-5   Purchase Options

The Morgan Company was planning to expand its production facilities. Therefore it acquired 1-year options to purchase two alternative sites. Each option cost $5,000 and could not be applied against the contract. One of the sites was bought for $100,000. The company was unsure whether to capitalize the land at $100,000, or $105,000, or $110,000.

**Required**

Present arguments in favor of each alternative.

### C8-6   Donated Asset and Its Modification

The Birkby Company acquires a building as a donation from the City of Avalon. The controller argues that since there was no payment by the company, it is not necessary to record the asset and therefore no depreciation should be recorded.

The company has to spend $15,000 altering the building to suit its unique needs. The controller argues that the $15,000 should be expensed because if the building is sold or returned to the city, the $15,000 cannot be recovered. In addition, excluding the $15,000 results in a closer approximation of the apparent market value of the asset and reduces income taxes immediately if the $15,000 is expensed.

**Required**

Evaluate each of the arguments made by the controller.

### C8-7   Natural Resource Assets

You have been engaged to examine the financial statements of Brahe Corporation for the year ending December 31, 1995. Brahe Corporation was organized in January 1995 by Messrs. Moses and Price, original owners of options to acquire oil leases on 5,000 acres of land for $350,000. They expected that first the oil leases would be acquired by the corporation and subsequently 180,000 shares of the corporation's common stock would be sold to the public at $6 per share. In February 1995 they exchanged their options, $150,000 cash, and $50,000 of other assets for 75,000 shares of common stock of the corporation. The corporation's board of directors appraised the leases at $600,000, basing its appraisal on the price of other acreage recently leased in the same area. The options were therefore recorded at $250,000 ($600,000 − $350,000 option price).

The options were exercised by the corporation in March 1995 prior to the sale of common stock to the public in April 1995. Leases on approximately 500 acres of land were abandoned as worthless during the year.

### Required

1. Why is the valuation of assets acquired by a corporation in exchange for its own common stock sometimes difficult?
2. a. What reasoning might Brahe Corporation use to support valuing the leases at $600,000, the amount of the appraisal by the board of directors?
   b. Assuming the board's appraisal was sincere, what steps might Brahe Corporation have taken to strengthen its position to use the $600,000 value and to provide additional information if questions were raised about possible overvaluation of the leases?
3. Discuss the propriety of charging one-tenth of the recorded value of the leases against income at December 31, 1995 because leases on 500 acres of land were abandoned during the year. (*AICPA adapted*)

### C8-8 Cost Issues

Deskin Company purchased a new machine to be used in its operations. The new machine was delivered by the supplier, installed by Deskin, and placed into operation. It was purchased under a long-term payment plan for which the interest charges approximated the prevailing market rates. The estimated useful life of the new machine is ten years, and its estimated residual (salvage) value is significant. Normal maintenance was performed to keep the new machine in usable condition.

Deskin also added a wing to the manufacturing building that it owns. The addition is an integral part of the building. Furthermore, Deskin made significant leasehold improvements to office space used as corporate headquarters.

### Required

1. What costs should Deskin capitalize for the new machine?
2. How should Deskin account for the normal maintenance performed on the new machine? Why?
3. How should Deskin account for the wing added to the manufacturing building? Where should the added wing be reported on Deskin's financial statements?
4. How should Deskin account for the leasehold improvements made to its office space? Where should the leasehold improvements be reported on Deskin's financial statements? (*AICPA adapted*)

### C8-9 Acquisition Costs

A company may acquire plant assets (among other ways) for cash, on a deferred-payment plan, by exchanging other assets, or by a combination of these ways.

### Required

1. Identify six costs that should be capitalized as the cost of land. For your answer, assume that land with an existing building is acquired for cash and that the existing building is to be removed in the immediate future in order that a new building can be constructed on that site.
2. At what amount should a company record a plant asset acquired on a deferred-payment plan?
3. In general, at what amount should plant assets received in exchange for other nonmonetary assets be recorded? Specifically, at what amount should a company record a new machine acquired by exchanging an older, similar machine and paying cash? (*AICPA adapted*)

### C8-10 Capital and Revenue Expenditures

Bristol Company purchased land as a site for construction of a factory. Outside contractors were engaged to:

1. Construct the factory
2. Grade and pave a parking lot adjacent to the factory for the exclusive use of the factory workers.

Operations at the new location began during the year and normal factory maintenance costs were incurred after production began.

### Required

1. Distinguish between capital and revenue (operating) expenditures.
2. Indicate how expenditures for each of the following should be accounted for and reported by Bristol at the time incurred and in subsequent accounting periods.
   a. Purchase of land.
   b. Construction of factory.
   c. Grading and paving parking lot.
   d. Payment of normal factory maintenance costs.

Do not discuss capitalization of interest during construction in your response. (*AICPA adapted*)

### C8-11 Researching GAAP ⓞ

The Tenth National Bank had taken possession of a shopping mall in foreclosure of a mortgage. When the mall was inspected prior to being sold by the bank to a real estate company, it was discovered that it had extensive asbestos problems. An estimate indicated that it would cost $1 million to remove the asbestos. The bank has also purchased an office building for its headquarters. The building was inspected before the purchase and a similar asbestos problem was discovered. An estimate indicated that it would cost $2 million to remove the asbestos, and the bank completed the purchase. The bank's president has asked you how to account for these transactions.

### Required

Research the related generally accepted accounting principles and prepare a short memo to the president that answers her question. Cite your references and applicable paragraph numbers.

### C8-12 Researching GAAP    ∞
The Perry Park Company was searching for a way to expand its operating capacity even though it was short of cash. The president of the company was playing golf and mentioned his concern to his playing partner, who owned some land and a building and was interested in disposing of them. After some negotiation, the two agreed to swap the land and building for shares in the company. The president of the company has asked you how to account for this transaction, including whether the transaction qualifies as a nonmonetary exchange and the value to place on the transaction and its components.

**Required**
Research the related generally accepted accounting principles and prepare a short memo to the president. Cite your references and applicable paragraph numbers.

## MULTIPLE CHOICE

*Select the best answer for each of the following.*

M8-1    The Hickory Company made a lump-sum purchase of three pieces of machinery for $115,000 from an unaffiliated company. At the time of acquisition, Hickory paid $5,000 to determine the appraised value of the machinery. The appraisal disclosed the following values:

Machine A    $70,000
Machine B    42,000
Machine C    28,000

What cost should be assigned to machines A, B, and C, respectively?

|    | A | B | C |
|----|------|------|------|
| a. | $40,000 | $40,000 | $40,000 |
| b. | $57,500 | $34,500 | $23,000 |
| c. | $60,000 | $36,000 | $24,000 |
| d. | $70,000 | $42,000 | $28,000 |

M8-2    A donated plant asset for which the fair value has been determined, and for which incidental costs were incurred in acceptance of the asset, should be recorded at an amount equal to its
a.  Incidental costs incurred
b.  Fair value and incidental costs incurred
c.  Book value on books of donor and incidental costs incurred
d.  Book value on books of donor

M8-3    The following expenditures were among those incurred by Jensen Corporation during the year ended December 31, 1995:

| | |
|---|---:|
| Replacement of tiles on portion of roof that had been leaking | $4,000 |
| Overhaul of machinery that is expected to extend its useful life for another two years | 6,000 |

How much should be charged to repairs and maintenance in 1995?
a.  $0
b.  $4,000
c.  $6,000
d.  $10,000

M8-4    The sale of a depreciable asset resulting in a loss indicates that the proceeds from the sale were
a.  Less than current market value
b.  Greater than cost
c.  Greater than book value
d.  Less than book value

M8-5  Electro Corporation bought a new machine and agreed to pay for it in equal annual installments of $5,000 at the end of each of the next 5 years. Assume a prevailing interest rate of 15%. The present value of an ordinary annuity of $1 at 15% for 5 periods is 3.35. The future amount of an ordinary annuity of $1 at 15% for 5 periods is 6.74. The present value of $1 at 15% for 5 periods is 0.5. How much should Electro record as the cost of the machine?

    a.  $12,500                                 c.  $25,000

    b.  $16,750                                 d.  $33,700

M8-6  When a company purchases land with a building on it and immediately tears down the building so that the land can be used for the construction of a plant, the costs incurred to tear down the building should be

    a.  Expensed as incurred                   c.  Added to the cost of the land

    b.  Added to the cost of the plant           d.  Amortized over the estimated time period between the tearing down of the building and the completion of the plant

M8-7  When a company replaces an old asphalt roof on its plant with a new fiberglass insulated roof, which of the following types of expenditure occurs?

    a.  Ordinary repair and maintenance           c.  Rearrangement

    b.  Addition                                d.  Betterment

M8-8  On January 2, 1995 Yuki Yogurt Company decided to replace its obsolete refrigeration system with a more efficient one. The old system had a book value of $9,000 and a fair market value of $1,000. Yuki's new refrigeration system has a fair market value of $190,000, for which Yuki paid $189,000 after permitting the contractor to keep the old refrigeration equipment. How much should Yuki capitalize as the cost of the new refrigeration system?

    a.  $189,000                            c.  $197,000

    b.  $190,000                            d.  $198,000

M8-9  During 1995 Belardo Corporation constructed and manufactured certain assets, and incurred the following interest costs in connection with those activities:

| | Interest Costs Incurred |
| --- | --- |
| Warehouse constructed for Belardo's own use | $20,000 |
| Special-order machine for sale to unrelated customer, produced according to customer's specifications | 9,000 |
| Inventories routinely manufactured, produced on a repetitive basis | 7,000 |

All of these assets required an extended period of time for completion. Assuming the effect of interest capitalization is material, what is the total amount of interest costs to be capitalized?

    a.  $0                                   c.  $29,000

    b.  $20,000                             d.  $36,000

M8-10  Lyle, Inc., purchased certain plant assets under a deferred payment contract on December 31, 1994. The agreement was to pay $20,000 at the time of purchase and $20,000 at the end of each of the next 5 years. The plant assets should be valued at

    a.  The present value of a $20,000           c.  $120,000 less imputed interest
        ordinary annuity for five years          d.  $120,000 plus imputed interest

    b.  $120,000

*(AICPA adapted)*

# EXERCISES

**E8-1**    *Determination of Cost*   Which of the following twenty-two items are included in the cost of property, plant, and equipment?

1. Contract price
2. List price
3. Freight costs
4. Discounts taken
5. Discounts not taken
6. Installation costs
7. Testing costs
8. Cost of overhaul before initial use
9. Costs of grading land prior to construction
10. Tax assessment for street improvements
11. Delinquent property taxes on acquired property
12. Cost of tearing down an old building (already owned) in preparation for new construction
13. Cost of insurance during construction
14. Excess of costs over revenues during the development stage of the company
15. Interest costs during construction
16. Landscaping costs
17. Severance pay for employees dismissed because of the acquisition of a new machine
18. Cost of tearing down a building on newly acquired land
19. Replacement of an electric motor in a machine
20. Expansion of the heating/cooling system to accommodate an expansion of a building and certain expected future needs
21. Service contract for 2 years on the acquired asset
22. Cost of training new employees

**E8-2**    *Inclusion in Property, Plant, and Equipment*   Which of the following are included in property, plant, and equipment on the balance sheet?

1. Idle equipment awaiting sale
2. Land held for future use as a plant site
3. Land held for investment
4. Deposits on machinery not yet received
5. Progress payments on building being constructed by a contractor
6. Fully depreciated assets still being used
7. Leasehold improvements
8. Assets leased to others

**E8-3**    *Acquisition Costs*   The Voiture Company manufactures compact, energy efficient cars. On April 1, it purchased a machine for its assembly line at a contract price of $200,000 with terms of 2/10, n/30. The company paid the contract price on April 8 and also incurred installation and transportation costs of $5,000, sales tax of $10,000, and testing costs of $2,000. During testing the machine was accidentally damaged, so the company had to pay $1,000 to repair it.

**Required**
Prepare the journal entry to record the acquisition of the machine.

**E8-4**    *Determination of Acquisition Cost*   In January 1995 Cordova Company entered into a contract to acquire a new machine for its factory. The machine, which has a cash price of $210,000, was paid for as follows:

| | |
|---|---:|
| Down payment | $ 50,000 |
| Note payable in four equal annual payments starting in January 1996 | 120,000 |
| 600 shares of Cordova preferred stock with an agreed value of $100 per share (par value $100) | 60,000 |
| Fair rate of interest on the non-interest-bearing note | 10% |

**Required**

1. Prepare the journal entry to record the acquisition of the machine.
2. How would your answer change, if at all, if the $210,000 cash price were not available?

E8-5   *Determination of Acquisition Cost*   On August 1, 1995 Darmow Corporation purchased a new machine on a deferred payment basis. A down payment of $1,000 was made and four monthly installments of $2,500 each are to be made beginning on September 1, 1995. The cash equivalent price of the machine was $9,500. Darmow incurred and paid installation cost amounting to $300.

**Required**

Prepare the journal entry to record the acquisition of the machine. (*AICPA adapted*)

E8-6   *Acquisition of Land and Building*   On February 1, 1995 Edwards Corporation purchased a parcel of land as a factory site for $50,000. An old building on the property was demolished, and construction began on a new building that was completed on October 2, 1995. Costs incurred during this period are listed next:

| | |
|---|---|
| Demolition of old building | $  4,000 |
| Architect's fees | 20,000 |
| Legal fees for title investigation and purchase contract | 2,000 |
| Construction costs | 500,000 |

Salvaged materials resulting from demolition were sold for $3,000.

**Required**

At what amount should Edwards record the cost of the land and the new building, respectively? (*AICPA adapted*)

E8-7   *Lump-Sum Purchase*   The Garrett Corporation paid $200,000 to acquire land, buildings, and equipment. At the time of acquisition, the company paid $20,000 for an appraisal, which revealed the following values: land, $100,000; buildings, $125,000; and equipment, $25,000.

**Required**

What cost is assigned to the land, buildings, and equipment, respectively?

E8-8   *Exchange of Assets*   Two independent companies, Denver and Bristol, each own a warehouse, and they have agreed to an exchange in which no cash changes hands. Neither company is a dealer. The following information for the two warehouses is available:

| | Denver | Bristol |
|---|---|---|
| Cost | $90,000 | $35,000 |
| Accumulated depreciation | 50,000 | 10,000 |
| Fair value | 30,000 | 30,000 |

**Required**

Prepare journal entries for the Denver Company and the Bristol Company to record the exchange.

E8-9   *Exchange of Assets*   Use the same information as in E8-8, except that the warehouse owned by Denver Company has a fair value of $28,000, and therefore Denver agrees to pay Bristol $2,000 to complete the exchange.

**Required**

Prepare journal entries for the Denver Company and the Bristol Company to record the exchange.

E8-10   *Exchange of Assets*   Use the same information as in E8-8, except that the warehouse owned by Denver Company has a fair value of $33,000, and therefore the Bristol Company agrees to pay the Denver Company $3,000 to complete the exchange.

**Required**

Prepare journal entries for the Denver Company and the Bristol Company to record the exchange.

E8-11   *Exchange of Assets*   The Goodman Company acquired a truck from the Harmes Company in exchange for a machine. The machine cost $30,000, has a book value of $6,000, and has a market value of $9,000. The truck has a cost of $12,000 and a book value of $8,000 on Harmes' books. Neither company is a dealer.

**Required**

Prepare journal entries for the Goodman Company and the Harmes Company to record the exchange.

E8-12   *Exchange of Assets*   Use the same information as in E8-11, except that the machine has a market value of $8,500, and therefore the Goodman Company agrees to pay $500 to complete the exchange.

**Required**

Prepare journal entries for the Goodman Company and the Harmes Company to record the exchange.

E8-13   *Exchange of Assets*   Minor Baseball Company had a player contract with Doe that was recorded in its accounting records at $145,000. Better Baseball Company had a player contract with Smith that was recorded in its accounting records at $140,000. Minor traded Doe to Better for Smith by exchanging each player's contract. The fair value of each contract was $150,000.

**Required**

What amount should be shown in the accounting records of each company after the exchange of player contracts? (*AICPA adapted*)

E8-14   *Self-Construction*   The Harshman Company constructed a building for its own use. The company incurred costs of $20,000 for materials and supplies, $45,000 for direct labor, and $5,000 for a supervisor's overtime that was caused by the construction. The company uses a factory overhead rate of 50% of direct labor cost. Before construction, the company had received a bid of $100,000 from an outside contractor.

**Required**

1.  At what value should the company capitalize the building? Justify your answer.
2.  Would your answer change if the bid from the outside contractor had been $80,000? $60,000?

E8-15   *Asset Acquired by Donation*   The City of Littleton donated a building and land to the Hetting Co. without charge. The agreement provided that the company employ 350 people for 10 years. The land was appraised at $60,000 and the building at $40,000.

**Required**

1.  Prepare the journal entry to record the acquisition of the land and building.
2.  How should the 10-year agreement be reported in the financial statements?
3.  If the title were not to pass until after 10 years, would your answer change?

E8-16   *Interest During Construction*   The Snowbird Company is constructing a building that qualifies for interest capitalization. It is built between January 1 and December 31, 1995. Expenditures, which occur evenly throughout the year, are $700,000. The company borrowed $500,000 at 12% to help finance the project. In addition, the Snowbird Company had outstanding borrowings of $2 million at 8%.

**Required**

1.  Compute the amount of interest capitalized on the building.
2.  What effect does the interest capitalization have on the financial statements after the building is completed?

E8-17   *Calculating Capitalized Interest*   The Kit Company borrows $8 million at 12% on January 1, 1995 specifically for the purpose of financing a construction project. The total amount is invested at 11% until payments are made for the construction project. During the first year of construction, the company incurs construction costs of $6 million evenly over the year.

**Required**

Compute the amount of interest that would be capitalized and the amount of interest revenue the company would recognize.

E8-18   *Capital and Operating Expenditures*   Which of the following ten items are recorded as a capital expenditure and which as an operating expenditure?

1. Cost of installing machinery
2. Cost of moving machinery
3. Repairs as a result of an accident
4. Cost of major overhaul
5. Installation of safety device as a result of an OSHA inspection
6. Property taxes on land and buildings
7. Property taxes on land and buildings held for investment
8. Cost of rearranging offices
9. Cost of repainting offices
10. Ordinary repairs

E8-19  *Appendix 1: Oil and Gas Accounting*  The Lawrence Company spends $2 million in 1995 drilling oil wells. Sixty percent of the drilling is successful and results in commercial quantities of oil being found.

### Required

1. How much drilling expense does the company recognize under
   a. The successful-efforts method?
   b. The full-cost method?
2. At what value does the asset Oil and Gas Properties appear in the balance sheet under
   a. The successful-efforts method?
   b. The full-cost method?

E8-20  *Appendix 2: Casualty Insurance*  The information for three independent casualty losses is presented next:

|  | Loss 1 | Loss 2 | Loss 3 |
|---|---|---|---|
| Fair market value of total assets covered by insurance policy | $20,000 | $20,000 | $20,000 |
| Book value of asset | 15,000 | 18,000 | 22,000 |
| Amount of loss | 10,000 | 16,000 | 12,000 |
| Face value of policy | 12,000 | 12,000 | 18,000 |
| Coinsurance requirement | 80% | 70% | 75% |

### Required

Compute the amount recoverable in each situation.

## PROBLEMS

P8-1  *Acquisition Costs*  The Mawn Company bought land and built a warehouse during 1995. The following related costs were debited to an account titled Land and Buildings:

| | |
|---|---|
| Land purchase | $20,000 |
| Demolition of old building | 3,000 |
| Legal fees for land acquisition | 1,500 |
| Interest on loan for construction (based on average costs incurred) | 2,700 |
| Building construction | 50,000 |
| Assessment by city for sewer connection | 1,200 |
| Landscaping | 3,500 |
| Equipment purchased for excavation | 18,000 |
| Fixed overhead charged to building | 15,000 |
| Insurance on building during construction | 1,000 |
| Profit on construction | 12,000 |
| Compensation for injury to construction worker | 3,000 |
| Modifications to building ordered by building inspectors | 7,500 |
| Property taxes on land paid in 1995 | 2,500 |

The following credits were made to the account:

| | |
|---|---|
| Salvage from demolished old building | $   700 |
| Sale of excavation equipment | 14,000 |

In addition you discover that compensation for the worker's injury was necessary because it was not covered by the particular insurance policy purchased by the company. Accident insurance that would have covered the injury would have cost an additional $350. The modifications ordered by the building inspectors resulted from poor planning by the company.

**Required**

Prepare adjusting entries on December 31, 1995 to properly reclassify the preceding items.

P8-2    *Costs Subsequent to Acquisition*    As the first auditor of the Newberg Company, you discover that the following entries have been made in the property, plant, and equipment account:

**Property, Plant, and Equipment**

| 1994 | | | 1994 | | |
|---|---|---|---|---|---|
| Plant purchased | 60,000 | | Depreciation | 6,310 | |
| Legal fees | 700 | | 1995 | | |
| Insurance | 2,400 | | Depreciation | 6,879 | |
| 1995 | | | 1996 | | |
| Repairs | 2,000 | | Machine sold | 500 | |
| Addition to building | 10,000 | | Depreciation | 7,421 | |
| 1996 | | | | | |
| Repairs | 3,000 | | | | |
| Insurance | 2,800 | | | | |
| Machine purchased | 7,000 | | | | |

Additional information is discovered as follows:

1. The purchase of the plant included a building and machinery. When the plant was purchased, an appraisal showed that the building was valued at $39,000 and the machinery at $26,000.
2. Depreciation has been recorded each year at 10% of the balance in the account. The 10% was chosen because the property is being depreciated over 10 years for tax purposes. Subsequent investigation indicates that the expected lives at the time of acquisition were: building 20 years, machinery 8 years.
3. Each insurance payment was made on January 1 and was for a 2-year policy.
4. The machine that was sold in 1996 had an original cost of $800.
5. All purchases and sales of property, plant, and equipment items occurred at the beginning of the year indicated.

**Required**

Prepare adjusting entries at December 31, 1996 to correct the books assuming they have not been closed for the year.

P8-3    *Classification of Costs Associated with Assets*    The following account balances were included in the balance sheet of the Bromley Company on December 31, 1994:

| Land | $100,000 |
|---|---|
| Land improvements | 20,000 |
| Buildings | 300,000 |
| Machinery and equipment | 500,000 |

During 1995 the following transactions occurred:

1. Land was acquired for $70,000 for a future building site. Commissions of $4,000 were paid to a real estate agent.
2. A factory and land were acquired from the Kent Development Company by issuing 20,000 shares of $3 par common stock. At that time, the stock was selling for $10 per share on the New York Stock Exchange. The appraised values of the land and the factory were $60,000 and $180,000, respectively.
3. Machinery and equipment was acquired at a cost of $120,000. In addition, sales tax, freight costs, and installation costs were $7,000, $10,000, and $16,000, respectively. During installation, the machinery was damaged, and $2,000 was spent in repairs.

4. A new parking lot was installed at a cost of $30,000.
5. A machine that had cost $20,000 on January 1, 1991 and had a book value on December 31, 1995 of $4,000 was sold on that date for $6,000.
6. Half the land purchased in item 1 was prepared as a building site. Costs of $26,000 were incurred to clear the land, and the timber recovered was sold for $3,000. A new building was built for $60,000 plus architect's fees and imputed interest on equity funds used during construction of $18,000 and $15,000, respectively. No debt is outstanding.
7. Costs of $20,000 were incurred to improve some leased office space. The lease will terminate in 1997 and is not expected to be renewed.
8. A group of new machines was purchased under a royalty agreement that provides for payment of annual royalties based on units produced. The invoice price of the machines was $30,000, freight costs were $2,000, and royalty payments for 1995 were $12,000.

**Required**

Prepare journal entries to record all the preceding events. Unless otherwise indicated, assume all payments are made in cash.

P8-4    *Self-Construction*   The Olson Machine Company manufactures small and large milling machines. Selling prices of these machines range from $35,000 to $200,000. During the 5-month period of August 1, 1995 through December 31, 1995, the company manufactured a milling machine for its own use. This machine was built as part of the regular production activities. The project required a large amount of time from planning and supervisory personnel, as well as that of some of the company's officers, because it was a more sophisticated type of machine than their regular production models.

Throughout the 5-month period, all costs directly associated with the construction of the machine were charged to a special account entitled "Asset Construction Account." An analysis of the charges to this account as of December 31, 1995 follows:

ASSET CONSTRUCTION ACCOUNT

| Item Description | Cost | |
|---|---:|---:|
| *Raw Materials* | | |
| Iron castings: | | |
|    Main housing, 3 sections | $37,480 | |
|    Movable heads, 2 heads @ $3,900 | 7,800 | |
|    Machine bed | 4,760 | |
| Table, 2 sections @ $5,500 | 11,000 | $ 61,040 |
| Other raw materials: | | |
|    Electrical components and wiring | $28,000 | |
|    Worm screws and housing | 8,600 | |
|    Cutter housings | 2,700 | |
|    Conveyor system | 8,400 | |
|    Other parts | 2,500 | 50,200 |
| *Direct Labor Costs* | | |
| Layout    90 hr. @ $5.00 | $    450 | |
| Electricians  380 hr. @ 9.00 | 3,420 | |
| Machining  1,100 hr. @ 8.00 | 8,800 | |
| Heat treatment  100 hr. @ 7.50 | 750 | |
| Assembly   450 hr. @ 7.00 | 3,150 | |
| Testing   180 hr. @ 8.00 | 1,440 | 18,010 |
| *Other Direct Charges* | | |
| Repairs and maintenance during testing period | $ 1,340 | |
| Interest expense from 8/1/95 to 12/31/95 on funds borrowed for construction purposes | 4,260 | |
| Additional labor to assist during machine testing period, 180 hr. @ $5.00 | 900 | 6,500 |
| Balance, December 31, 1995 | | $135,750 |

Factory overhead is allocated to normal production as a percent of direct labor dollars as follows:

| Departments | Factory Overhead Rates (applied as a percent of direct labor dollars) | | |
| --- | --- | --- | --- |
| | Variable | Fixed | Total |
| Layout and electricians | 50% | 20% | 70% |
| Machining,* heat treatment, and assembly | 50% | 50% | 100% |

*All testing is conducted by employees in the machining department.

A flat rate of 40% of direct labor dollars is used to allocate general and administrative overhead.

During the machine testing period, a cutter head malfunctioned and did extensive damage to the machine table and one cutter housing. This damage was not anticipated and was the result of an error in the assembly operation. Although no additional raw materials were needed to make the machine operational after the accident, the following labor for rework was required:

| | Direct Labor Hours |
| --- | --- |
| Electric | 80 |
| Machining | 200 |
| Assembly | 100 |
| Testing (conducted by machining department) | 20 |

All these labor charges have been included in the Asset Construction account. In addition, the repairs and maintenance charges of $1,340 included in the account were incurred as a result of the malfunction.

**Required**

1. Compute in accordance with generally accepted accounting principles the amount that should be capitalized on the books of Olson Machine Company for the milling machine as of December 31, 1995 when the machine was declared operational.
2. Identify the costs you included in Requirement 1 for which there are acceptable alternative procedures. Describe the alternative procedure(s) in each case. (*CMA adapted*)

P8-5    *Acquisition Cost*    The following transactions of the Weber Company occurred during 1995:
1. The company acquired a tract of land in exchange for 1,000 shares of $10 par value common stock. The stock was traded on the New York Stock Exchange at $25 on the date of exchange. The land had a book value on the selling company's records of $5,000, and it was believed to be worth "anything up to $30,000."
2. An engine on a truck was replaced. The truck originally cost $10,000 three years ago and was being depreciated at $2,000 per year. The engine cost $1,000 to replace.
3. The company acquired a tract of land that was believed to have mineral deposits by issuing 500 shares of preferred stock of $50 par value. The preferred stock was rarely traded. The last transaction was 2 months earlier, when 50 shares were sold at $75 per share. The owner of the land was willing to accept cash of $45,000, and an appraisal had shown a value of $50,000.
4. The company purchased a machine with a list price of $8,500 by issuing a 2-year $10,000 non-interest-bearing note when the market rate of interest was 10%.

**Required**
Prepare journal entries to record the preceding events.

P8-6    *Comprehensive*    At December 31, 1994 certain accounts included in the property, plant, and equipment section of the Townsand Company's balance sheet had the following balances:

| | |
| --- | --- |
| Land | $100,000 |
| Buildings | 800,000 |
| Leasehold improvements | 500,000 |
| Machinery and equipment | 700,000 |

During 1995 the following transactions occurred:

1. Land site number 621 was acquired for $1,000,000. Additionally, to acquire the land Townsand paid a $60,000 commission to a real estate agent. Costs of $15,000 were incurred to clear the land. During the course of clearing the land, timber and gravel were recovered and sold for $5,000.

2. A second tract of land (site number 622) with a building was acquired for $300,000. The closing statement indicated that the land value was $200,000 and the building value was $100,000. Shortly after acquisition, the building was demolished at a cost of $30,000. A new building was constructed for $150,000 plus the following costs:

| | |
|---|---|
| Excavation fees | $11,000 |
| Architectural design fees | 8,000 |
| Building permit fee | 1,000 |

The building was completed and occupied on September 30, 1995.

3. A third tract of land (site number 623) was acquired for $600,000 and was put on the market for resale.

4. Extensive work was done to a building occupied by Townsand under a lease agreement that expires on December 31, 2004. The total cost of the work was $125,000, which consisted of the following:

| | |
|---|---|
| Painting of ceilings | $ 10,000 (estimated useful life is one year) |
| Electrical work | 35,000 (estimated useful life is ten years) |
| Construction of extension to current working area | 80,000 (estimated useful life is thirty years) |
| | $125,000 |

The lessor paid one-half of the costs incurred in connection with the extension to the current working area.

5. During December 1995 costs of $65,000 were incurred to improve leased office space. The related lease will terminate on December 31, 1997, and is not expected to be renewed.

6. A group of new machines was purchased under a royalty agreement which provides for payment of royalties based on units of production for the machines. The invoice price of the machines was $75,000, freight costs were $2,000, unloading charges were $1,500, and royalty payments for 1995 were $13,000.

**Required**

1. Prepare a detailed analysis of the changes in each of the following balance sheet accounts for 1995:
    Land
    Buildings
    Leasehold improvements
    Machinery and equipment
   Disregard the related accumulated depreciation accounts.

2. List the items in the fact situation which were not used to determine the answer to Requirement 1, and indicate where, or if, these items should be included in Townsand's financial statements. (*AICPA adapted*)

**P8-7** *Assets Acquired by Exchange* The Bremer Company made the following exchanges of assets during 1995:

1. Acquired a machine worth $10,000 by paying $2,000 cash and giving a similar machine that had originally cost $40,000 and has a book value of $15,000.

2. Acquired a building worth $55,000 by paying $5,000 cash and giving a piece of land that had originally cost $30,000.

3. Acquired a machine worth $20,000 by paying $2,000 cash and giving a similar machine that had originally cost $13,000 and has a book value of $11,000.

4. Acquired an automobile with a list price of $6,000. The company traded in an old automobile that had originally cost $7,000, has a book value of $5,000, and has a "blue book" value of $6,800. In addition the company received $800 cash.

**Required**

Prepare journal entries for the Bremer Company and for the other company involved in each exchange. Assume in each case that the other company is giving up a new undepreciated asset and that both Bremer Company and the other company are nondealers.

*P8-8*    *Assets Acquired by Exchange*    The Bussell Company exchanged the following assets during 1995:

1. Acquired a machine worth $34,000 by paying $4,000 cash and giving a similar machine that originally cost $40,000, has a book value of $25,000, and is worth $30,000.
2. Same facts as in item 1, except that the asset being surrendered has a book value of $33,000.
3. Acquired a machine worth $27,000 by giving a similar machine that originally cost $45,000, has a book value of $20,000, and is worth $32,000. In addition $5,000 cash was received.
4. Same facts as in item 3, except that the asset being surrendered has a book value of $36,000.
5. Acquired a machine worth $90,000 by giving up a similar machine of equal value. The machine surrendered had originally cost $150,000 and has a book value of $80,000.
6. Same facts as in item 5, except that the asset being surrendered has a book value of $97,000.
7. Acquired a building worth $200,000 in exchange for land that had originally cost $120,000 and is now worth $200,000.
8. Same facts as in item 7, except that $30,000 was paid, because the land is worth $170,000.
9. Same facts as in item 7, except that $20,000 was received and the land is worth $220,000.

**Required**
Prepare journal entries to record each acquisition of the Bussell Company. Assume that neither the Bussel Company nor the other company is a dealer.

*P8-9*    *Interest During Construction*    The Alta Company is constructing a production complex which qualifies for interest capitalization. The following information is available:

Capitalization period: January 1, 1995 to June 30, 1997
Expenditures on project (incurred evenly during each period and excluding capitalized interest from previous years):

| | |
|---|---|
| 1995 | $2,000,000 |
| 1996 | $3,760,000 |
| 1997 | $4,324,000 |

Amounts borrowed and outstanding:
$3 million borrowed at 12%, specifically for the project
$6 million borrowed on July 1, 1991, at 14%
$14 million borrowed on January 1, 1987, at 8%

**Required**
1. Compute the amount of interest costs capitalized each year.
2. If it is assumed that the production complex has an estimated life of 20 years and a residual value of zero, compute the straight-line depreciation in 1998.

*P8-10*    *Comprehensive*    The Foothills Power Company begins a 2-year construction project on a power plant on January 1, 1995. The following information is available:

1. The company borrows $10 million on January 1, 1995 at 12% specifically for use on the project.
2. The company's other borrowings are:
     $20 million at 10%
     $60 million at 8%
3. The expenditures for the project incurred evenly each year (excluding capitalized interest from previous years) are as follows:
     $6,000,000 in 1995
     $11,460,000 in 1996
     $1,800,000 in 1997
4. The project is completed on March 31, 1997. It took longer than originally planned because the company suspended construction for the last 3 months of 1995 because of a concern about the salability of the electricity produced by the plant.
5. Because of reduced demand for electricity, the plant does not begin operations until October 1, 1997.
6. The company invests at 11% the unused amounts of the $10 million borrowed in item 1.
7. Assume all transactions are in cash unless otherwise indicated.

**Required**

1. Prepare all the necessary journal entries for each of the 3 years. Record all construction costs in a Construction in Progress inventory account.
2. How would your answer to Requirement 1 change if the 3-month suspension in the construction activity was due to an environmental dispute with the federal government?

P8-11    *Events Subsequent to Acquisition*    The following selected events occurred during 1995:

Jan. 10    A motor breaks on a machine and is replaced for $800. This replacement was expected when the machine was purchased.

Jan. 24    A machine that was purchased for $10,000 and has a book value of $1,000 is sold for $400.

Feb. 3    A fully depreciated building that originally cost $25,000 is demolished so that a new building may be constructed. The demolition cost $2,200 and resulted in $500 of salvageable materials.

Feb. 14    A machine breaks down unexpectedly and requires repairs of $700.

Mar. 10    An accident damages some equipment. Repairs cost $2,000.

Mar. 18    A motor breaks on a machine and is replaced for $900. The new motor is of an improved design that increases the capacity of the machine.

Mar. 27    Office layout is rearranged at a cost of $700. At the same time, the walls are repainted for $300.

**Required**

Prepare journal entries for the preceding transactions.

P8-12    *Comprehensive*    You are engaged in the examination of financial statements of the Dewoskin Company and are auditing the Machinery and Equipment account and the related depreciation accounts for the year ended December 31, 1995. Your permanent file contains the following schedules:

| | Balance 12/31/93 | 1994 Retirements | 1994 Addition | Balance 12/31/94 |
|---|---|---|---|---|
| | *Machinery and Equipment* | | | |
| 1984 | $ 8,000 | $2,100 | — | $ 5,900 |
| 1985 | 400 | — | — | 400 |
| 1986 | — | — | — | — |
| 1987 | — | — | — | — |
| 1988 | 3,900 | — | — | 3,900 |
| 1989 | — | — | — | — |
| 1990 | 5,300 | — | — | 5,300 |
| 1991 | — | — | — | — |
| 1992 | 4,200 | — | — | 4,200 |
| 1993 | — | — | — | — |
| 1994 | — | — | $5,700 | 5,700 |
| | $21,800 | $2,100 | $5,700 | $25,400 |
| | *Accumulated Depreciation* | | | |
| 1984 | $ 7,840 | $2,100 | $ 160 | $ 5,900 |
| 1985 | 340 | — | 40 | 380 |
| 1986 | — | — | — | — |
| 1987 | — | — | — | — |
| 1988 | 2,145 | — | 390 | 2,535 |
| 1989 | — | — | — | — |
| 1990 | 1,855 | — | 530 | 2,385 |
| 1991 | — | — | — | — |
| 1992 | 630 | — | 420 | 1,050 |
| 1993 | — | — | — | — |
| 1994 | — | — | 285 | 285 |
| | $12,810 | $2,100 | $1,825 | $12,535 |

Here is a transcript of the Machinery and Equipment for 1995:

| 1995 | Machinery and Equipment | Ref. | Debit | Credit |
|---|---|---|---|---|
| Jan. 1 | Balance forward | | $25,400 | |
| Mar. 1 | Burnham grinder | VR | 1,200 | |
| May 1 | Air compressor | VR | 4,500 | |
| June 1 | Power lawnmower | VR | 600 | |
| June 1 | Lift-truck battery | VR | 320 | |
| Aug. 1 | Rockwood saw | CR | | $ 150 |
| Nov. 1 | Electric spot welder | VR | 4,500 | |
| Nov. 1 | Baking oven | VR | 2,800 | |
| Dec. 1 | Baking oven | VR | 236 | |
| | | | $39,556 | 150 |
| Dec. 31 | Balance | | | $39,406 |
| | | | $39,556 | $39,556 |

Your examination reveals the following eight items:

1. The company uses a 10-year life for all machinery and equipment for depreciation purposes. Depreciation is computed by the straight-line method. Six months' depreciation is recorded in the year of acquisition or retirement. For 1995 the company recorded depreciation of $2,800 on machinery and equipment.
2. The Burnham grinder was purchased for cash from a firm in financial distress. The chief engineer and a used machinery dealer agreed that the machine, which was practically new, was worth $2,100 in the open market.
3. For production reasons, the new air compressor was installed in a small building that was erected in 1995 to house the machine. The building will also be used for general storage. The cost of the building, which has a 25-year life, was $2,000 and is included in the $4,500 voucher for the air compressor.
4. The power lawnmower was delivered to the home of the company president for personal use.
5. On June 1, the battery in a battery-powered lift truck was accidentally damaged beyond repair. The damaged battery was included at a price of $600 in the $4,200 cost of the lift truck purchased on July 1, 1992. The company decided to rent a replacement battery instead of buying a new battery. The $320 expenditure is the annual rental for the battery paid in advance, net of a $40 allowance for the scrap value of the damaged battery that was returned to the battery company.
6. The Rockwood saw sold on August 1 had been purchased on August 1, 1982, for $1,500. The saw was in use until it was sold.
7. On September 1, the company determined that a production casting machine was no longer needed and advertised it for sale for $1,800 after having determined from a used machinery dealer that this was its market value. The casting machine had been purchased for $5,000 on September 1, 1990.
8. On November 1 a baking oven was purchased for $10,000. A $2,800 down payment was made, and the balance will be paid in monthly installments over a 3-year period. The December 1 payment includes interest charges of $36. Legal title to the oven will not pass to the company until the payments are completed.

### Required

1. Prepare the auditor's adjusting journal entries required on December 31, 1995, for machinery and equipment and the related depreciation.
2. Prepare schedules for detailing the effect of additions and retirements on the assets and related accumulated depreciation balances. (*AICPA adapted*)

P8-13   *Adjusting Entries*   In your examination of the financial statements of Ericson Corporation at December 31, 1995 you observe the contents of certain accounts and other pertinent information as follows:

| | *Building* | | | | |
|---|---|---|---|---|---|
| Date | Explanation | Post REF | Debit | Credit | Balance |
|---|---|---|---|---|---|
| 12/31/94 | Balance | X | $100,000 | — | $100,000 |
| 7/1/95 | New boiler | CD | 16,480 | $1,480 | 115,000 |
| 9/1/95 | Insurance recovery | CR | — | 2,000 | 113,000 |

### Accumulated Depreciation—Building

| Date | Explanation | LF | Debit | Credit | Balance |
|---|---|---|---|---|---|
| 12/31/94 | Balance: 15 years @ 4% | | | | |
| | of $100,000 (no salvage value) | X | | $60,000 | $60,000 |
| 12/31/95 | Annual depreciation | GJ | | 4,440 | 64,440 |

You learn that on June 15 the company's old high-pressure boiler exploded and was partially damaged. Damage to the building was insignificant, but the boiler was replaced by a more efficient oil-burning boiler. The company received $2,000 as an insurance adjustment under terms of its policy for damage to the boiler. The disbursement voucher charged to the building account on July 1, 1995 is reproduced here:

To: Leetsdale Heating Company

| | |
|---|---:|
| Fair market value—new oil-burning boiler (including fuel oil tank and 1,000 gallons fuel oil) | $16,000 |
| Sales tax—3% of $16,000 | 480 |
| Total | $16,480 |
| Less: | |
| Allowance (fair market value) for old coal-burning boiler in building—to be removed at the expense of the Leetsdale Heating Company | 1,480 |
| Total price | $15,000 |

In vouching the expenditure, you determine that the terms included a 2% cash discount that was properly computed and taken. Neither the sales tax nor the trade-in allowance on the old boiler is subject to discount. Your audit discloses that a voucher for $1,000 was paid to Monaco Company on July 3, 1995 and charged to the repair expense account. The voucher is adequately supported and is marked "installation costs for new oil-burning boiler."

The company's fuel oil supplier advises that fuel oil had a market price of 80¢ per gallon on July 1 and 85¢ per gallon on December 31. The fuel oil inventory at December 31 was 100 gallons.

A review of subsidiary property records discloses that the replaced coal-burning boiler was installed when the building was constructed and was recorded at a cost of $10,000. According to its manufacturers, the new boiler should be serviceable for the estimated useful life of the building.

In computing depreciation for retirements, Ericson Corporation consistently treats a fraction of a month as a full month.

### Required

Prepare the adjusting journal entries that you would suggest for entry on the books of the Ericson Corporation. The books have not been closed. Support your entries with computations in good form. Assume that the building has no salvage value. (*AICPA adapted*)

P8-14 *Appendix 1: Oil and Gas Accounting Methods*  The Iwata Oil Company incurred costs of $5 million during 1995 drilling for oil. Half the costs resulted in oil being found and half resulted in dry wells. The oil wells are expected to produce 10% of their capacity each year from 1996 to 2005.

### Required

1. What amounts appear in the financial statements for 1996 under
   a. The successful-efforts method?
   b. The full-cost method?
2. Why do small oil companies generally prefer the full-cost method?

P8-15 *Appendix 2: Fire Loss*  The Henry Corporation is a small manufacturing company producing a highly flammable cleaning fluid. On May 31, 1995 the company had a fire that completely destroyed the processing building and the in-process inventory. Some of the equipment was saved. The cost of the fixed assets destroyed and their related accumulated depreciation accounts on May 31, 1995 were as follows:

| | Cost | Accumulated Depreciation |
|---|---|---|
| Building | $40,000 | $24,667 |
| Equipment | 15,000 | 4,375 |

At present prices, the cost to replace the destroyed property would be: building, $80,000; equipment, $37,500. At the time of the fire, it was determined that the destroyed building was 62 1/2% depreciated, and the destroyed equipment was 33 1/3% depreciated. The insurable value of the building and equipment was determined to be $75,000.

After the fire, a physical inventory was taken. The raw materials were valued at $30,000, the finished goods at $60,000, and supplies at $5,000. The inventories on January 1, 1995 consisted of:

| | |
|---|---|
| Raw materials | $ 15,000 |
| Goods in process | 50,000 |
| Finished goods | 70,000 |
| Supplies | 2,000 |
| Total | $137,000 |

A review of the accounts showed that the sales and gross profit for the last 5 years were:

| | Sales | Gross Profit |
|---|---|---|
| 1990 | $300,000 | $ 86,200 |
| 1991 | 320,000 | 102,400 |
| 1992 | 330,000 | 108,900 |
| 1993 | 250,000 | 62,500 |
| 1994 | 280,000 | 84,000 |

The sales for the first 5 months of 1995 were $150,000. Raw materials purchases were $50,000. Freight on purchases was $5,000. Direct labor for the 5 months was $40,000. For the past 5 years, manufacturing overhead was 50% of direct labor. Insurance on the property and inventory was carried with three companies. Each policy included an 80% coinsurance clause. The amount of insurance carried with the various companies was:

| | Buildings and Equipment | Inventories |
|---|---|---|
| Company A | $30,000 | $38,000 |
| Company B | 20,000 | 35,000 |
| Company C | 15,000 | 35,000 |

The cost of cleaning up the debris was $7,000. The value of the scrap salvaged from the fire was $600.

**Required**
1. Compute the value of inventory lost.
2. Compute the expected recovery from each insurance company. (*AICPA adapted*)

P8-16  *Appendix 2: Casualty Insurance*  The Asil Company has two fire insurance policies. Policy A covers the factory for $100,000 and the equipment for $200,000. Policy B covers the equipment for an additional amount of $120,000. The fair market values of the factory and the equipment were $180,000 and $400,000, respectively. After a fire, the fair market values were $100,000 and $50,000, respectively. Each policy has a coinsurance requirement of 80%; Policy A applies this requirement separately to the factory and to the equipment. There is no contribution clause in either policy.

**Required**
Compute the amount due from each insurance company for the loss on each asset.

# 9

# DEPRECIATION AND DEPLETION

In the preceding chapter, property, plant, and equipment was described as a group of assets held for use for a period of more than one year; that is, the assets are acquired for their long-term revenue-generating ability. Since these assets are being used to produce revenue, the matching principle requires that all expenses connected with their use be matched against the revenue. What is the expense? Over the life of the asset, the expense is the difference between the purchase price of the asset and its eventual residual value. *Depreciation is the process of allocating in a systematic and rational manner this total expense to each period benefited by the asset.* Land is not depreciated because it generally does not have a limited life and its expected residual value (that is, future selling price) usually is higher than its cost. Thus, there is no expense to be recognized over the life of the asset and, therefore, no periodic cost allocation.

Different terms are used to describe this allocation process, depending on the type of asset:

1. *Depreciation* describes the allocation of the cost of *tangible* assets, such as property, plant, and equipment.

2. *Depletion* describes the allocation of the cost of *natural resource* assets, such as oil, gas, minerals, and timber.

3. *Amortization* describes the allocation of the cost of *intangible* assets, such as patents and copyrights. It may be used as a general term to describe the periodic allocation of costs and in that case is synonymous with depreciation and depletion.

The three terms all describe the same principle of cost allocation to match expenses with revenue, but differ in their application to different types of assets. It is important to note that depreciation, depletion, and amortization are *not* recorded in an attempt to reflect a market value of the asset. Depreciation and depletion are discussed in this chapter, and the amortization of intangible assets is included in the next chapter.

## Chapter Topics

*Factors Affecting Depreciation Amounts*

*Alternative Depreciation Methods*

*Special Depreciation Methods Such as Group, Composite, Retirement, and Replacement Methods*

*Depreciation for Partial Periods*

*Depreciation and Income Tax*

*Changes and Corrections to Depreciation*

*Depletion of Natural Resources*

# FACTORS INVOLVED IN DEPRECIATION

Four factors are involved in the computation of the depreciation for the period: (1) asset cost, (2) service life, (3) residual value, and (4) method of cost allocation.[1]

## Asset Cost

*The recording and reporting of asset cost is discussed in Chapter 8.*

**The cost of an asset includes all the acquisition costs necessary to obtain the benefits to be derived from the asset.** These costs include the contract price plus freight, assembly, installation, and testing costs.

## Service Life

**The service life of an asset is the measure of the number of units of service expected from the asset before its disposal.** Service life may be measured in *units of time*, such as years and months, or *units of activity or output*, such as hours of operation of a machine, tons produced for a steel mill, or miles driven for a truck.

The factors that limit the service life of an asset can be divided into the two general categories of (1) physical causes and (2) functional causes. **Physical causes include wear and tear due to operational *use*, deterioration and decay that is independent of use but is a function of *time* (such as rust), and damage and destruction. Functional causes limit the service life of the asset, even though the physical life is not exhausted, through obsolescence and inadequacy.** *Obsolescence* is a common occurrence in a technologically advanced economy when an asset is rendered obsolete by the introduction of new technology. *Inadequacy* refers to the situation in which an asset is no longer suitable for the size of the company's operations. For example, a warehouse may be physically sound and useful, but too small for the company's operations.

All these factors should be taken into consideration when the service life is estimated, because in many situations it is affected by a combination of factors. For example, the service life of an automobile is likely to be affected by the passage of time (deterioration, decay, and possibly obsolescence) as well as by the amount of use. In addition, the company may be able to influence the service life by the amount it plans to spend on repairs and maintenance and on improvements and replacements. The accountant will have to rely on others, such as engineers, for advice about such estimates, but does have to agree to their reasonableness.

## Residual Value

**The residual (salvage) value is the net amount that can be expected to be obtained from the disposition of an asset at the end of its service life.** It is the difference between the expected value of the asset at the end of its service life and the costs of disposal, such as dismantling, removing, and selling the asset. The service life and the residual value are determined by company policy. If a company plans to hold an asset until it is physically exhausted or functionally obsolete and not useful to anyone else, the expected residual value is the expected scrap value, which is probably very low. Alternatively, if the company plans to dispose of the asset when it still has considerable economic usefulness to others (the service life to the company is less than the

---

1. The service life, residual value, and method of cost allocation are different for income tax purposes under the Modified Accelerated Cost Recovery System (MACRS), as discussed later in the chapter.

physical life), the expected residual value is the estimated net market value of the asset (the selling price less the disposal costs) at the time of the disposal, which may be relatively high. For example, many airlines sell their planes long before the end of their physical lives, in order to replace them with technologically more advanced planes and to avoid passenger resistance to flying in old planes. In certain situations, such as a nuclear power plant, the cost to dismantle and remove an asset may be more than the selling price or scrap value, in which case there is a negative residual value. This negative value is added to the cost to determine the amount to be depreciated.

In practice, because the residual value is difficult to estimate, it often is ignored in the computation of the depreciation charge, or else a standard rate, such as 10% of original cost, is used. This practice is acceptable if it does not have a material effect on the measurement of income and the book value of the asset.

## METHODS OF COST ALLOCATION

Accounting principles require that the method of cost allocation be "systematic and rational."[2] *Systematic* means that the calculation should follow a formula and not be determined in an arbitrary manner. *Rational* means that the amount of the depreciation should relate to the benefits that the asset produces in each period. Although these criteria may appear to be very general and to allow numerous methods, only the following methods are used frequently in practice:

1. Activity (or use) methods

2. Time-based methods
   a. Straight line
   b. Accelerated (declining charge)
      (1) Sum of the years' digits
      (2) Declining balance

Each of these methods is discussed in the following sections, using the data for the Troup Company shown in Exhibit 9-1. **The depreciation base (depreciable cost) of the asset is the cost less the estimated residual value,** or $100,000. The different depreciation methods all allocate the total of $100,000 over the expected service life of the asset, but differ in the pattern in which the cost is allocated to each year or each unit produced. Additional special depreciation methods are discussed later in the chapter.

---

### EXHIBIT 9-1

#### TROUP COMPANY

| | |
|---|---|
| Asset cost | $120,000 |
| Date of purchase | January 1, 1994 |
| Estimated residual value | $20,000 |
| Estimated service life | 5 years; 10,000 hours; 20,000 units |

---

2. *Accounting Terminology Bulletin No. 1* (New York: AICPA, 1953), par. 56.

## Activity Methods

Activity methods should be used when it is assumed that the service life of the asset is affected primarily by the amount the asset is used and not by the passage of time. The activity usually is measured in terms of the number of hours worked or the output produced (such as miles driven or tons produced). In the case of the Troup Company, one measure of the life of the asset is estimated to be 10,000 hours of activity. The calculation of the depreciation per hour is shown in Exhibit 9-2.

### EXHIBIT 9-2

### TROUP COMPANY

**Depreciation Based on Activity**

$$\text{Depreciation Rate} = \frac{\text{Cost} - \text{Residual Value}}{\text{Total Lifetime Activity Level}}$$

$$= \frac{\$120,000 - \$20,000}{10,000 \text{ hours}}$$

$$= \underline{\underline{\$10 \text{ per hour}}}$$

The depreciation base of $100,000 is divided by the life of 10,000 hours to derive a depreciation rate of $10 per hour. The total depreciation for the period is determined by multiplying the depreciation rate by the number of hours the asset is used in the period. For example, if the Troup Company asset is used for 2,100 hours during 1994, the depreciation for the year will be $21,000 ($10 × 2,100).

It is important to note that this application of the activity method has produced a constant depreciation rate per *hour,* but one that varies per *unit* of production as the output per hour changes. For example, if the company produces 2 units per hour, the depreciation cost per unit is $5. If productivity increases so that the company produces 2.5 units per hour, the depreciation cost per unit is $4, although the depreciation per hour remains at $10. In contrast, if the activity method is based on the number of *units* expected to be produced over the life of the asset, then a depreciation rate is developed that is constant per *unit* produced but would vary per *hour* as productivity changes. For example, if the depreciation is based on the expected lifetime production of 20,000 units, the depreciation rate is $5 per unit produced ($100,000 ÷ 20,000). If productivity increases so that the company produces 2.5 units per hour, the depreciation cost per unit remains at $5, but the depreciation per hour increases to $12.50.

Although an activity method is appropriate for many assets because their lives are limited by physical causes, it often is not used because of the difficulty of estimating the lifetime units of activity. It would be a costly method to implement because of the need to measure the activity level of each asset each period.

## Time-Based Methods

Time-based methods should be used when it is assumed that the service life of the asset is affected primarily by the passage of time and not by the usage of the asset.

This situation includes the physical causes of deterioration and decay and the functional causes of obsolescence and inadequacy. Two general categories of time-based methods are the straight-line method and the accelerated methods. **The straight-line method is appropriate when it is estimated that the benefits to be derived from the asset will be approximately constant each period of its life.** Since straight-line depreciation is the same each period, the matching principle is satisfied because an equal cost each period is matched against benefits that are approximately the same each period. Support for the straight-line method is enhanced further if maintenance costs are expected to be the same each period. Then the total costs of depreciation and maintenance each period are equal and matched against benefits that are approximately the same each period. It might be thought that the activity method based on hours is a time-based method, but the logic underlying that method is to compute depreciation from the activity of the asset.

The **accelerated (or declining-charge) methods are appropriate when it is estimated that the benefits to be derived from the asset will decline each period.** Thus, the accelerated methods match a depreciation cost that declines each period against revenues that also are declining each period. However, the benefits to be derived from the asset may be measured in physical terms or in dollars of revenue, as discussed later. The choice of a particular accelerated method basically is arbitrary, because in most situations, the particular declining depreciation amount of each method cannot be matched against the expected pattern of declining revenue. The estimates required cannot be that accurate. Instead, the general principle is that if declining benefits are expected, then an accelerated (declining-charge) method is selected.

### Straight Line

The straight-line method allocates an equal cost to each period. For the Troup Company, the calculation is shown in Exhibit 9-3. The depreciation base of $100,000 is allocated equally to the estimated life of 5 years at the rate of $20,000 per year. The straight-line depreciation sometimes is expressed as a percentage of original cost ($20,000 $\div$ $120,000 = 16.67\%$) or of depreciable cost ($20,000 $\div$ $100,000 = 20\%$). Although widely adopted, the use of the straight-line method may be criticized because it often is used for convenience when an activity method would be more appropriate.

---

**EXHIBIT 9-3**

**TROUP COMPANY**

Straight-Line Depreciation

$$\text{Depreciation} = \frac{\text{Cost} - \text{Residual Value}}{\text{Service Life}}$$

$$= \frac{\$120,000 - \$20,000}{5}$$

$$= \$20,000 \text{ per year}$$

---

### Sum of the Years' Digits

The sum-of-the-years'-digits method produces declining depreciation each period by applying a declining fraction each year to the depreciation base. The denominator of

$\dfrac{n(n+1)}{2}$

the fraction is the sum of the years' digits. So, for an asset with a 5-year life, the sum is $5 + 4 + 3 + 2 + 1 = 15$.[3] The numerator of the fraction is the years' digits taken in reverse order — that is, 5 the first year, 4 the second year, etc. An alternative way of looking at the numerator is that it is the number of years remaining in the asset's life as of the *beginning* of the year. The fractions for the 5 years of the asset's life are 5/15, 4/15, 3/15, 2/15, and 1/15. The calculation of the depreciation for the Troup Company is shown in Exhibit 9-4. Each year, the depreciation declines, and at the end of the fifth year, the book value of the asset is equal to the estimated residual value of $20,000. Note that in this method, the depreciation base remains constant, while the fraction decreases each year.

### EXHIBIT 9-4

## TROUP COMPANY

Sum-of-the-Years'-Digits Depreciation

| Year | Depreciation Base | Fraction | Depreciation | Book Value at Year-End* |
|------|------|------|------|------|
| 1994 | $100,000 | 5/15 | $ 33,333 | $86,667 |
| 1995 | 100,000 | 4/15 | 26,667 | 60,000 |
| 1996 | 100,000 | 3/15 | 20,000 | 40,000 |
| 1997 | 100,000 | 2/15 | 13,333 | 26,667 |
| 1998 | 100,000 | 1/15 | 6,667 | 20,000 |
|  |  |  | $100,000 |  |

*Cost minus accumulated depreciation.

### Declining Balance

The declining-balance methods produce a declining depreciation amount each period by applying a *constant* rate to the book value of the asset at the beginning of the period. Note that the periodic depreciation declines because the book value is used and *not* the depreciation base. Also, the residual value is ignored in the calculation of the depreciation each period, although the asset must not be depreciated below the estimated residual value. The constant rate is a function of the straight-line rate. The highest rate that can be used is double the straight-line rate. This rate was established as the highest rate by the income tax regulations and was also adopted as the highest rate for financial reporting. An asset that has a 5-year life is depreciated on a straight-line basis at the rate of 20% per year, so the double-declining rate is 40%. However, an alternative rate could be chosen, such as a 150% declining rate, which is 1-1/2 times the straight-line rate or, in this example, 30% per year. The application of both alternatives is illustrated for the Troup Company in Exhibit 9-5.

---

3. The general formula to compute the sum of the years' digits is $n(n + 1)/2$. So, for an asset with a 50-year life, the sum is $50(50 + 1)/2 = 1,275$.

---

**EXHIBIT 9-5**

## TROUP COMPANY

Declining-Balance Depreciation Methods

### (a) Double-Declining Balance

| Year | Book Value of Asset at Beginning of Year | Rate | Depreciation | Book Value at End of Year |
|------|------------------------------------------|------|--------------|---------------------------|
| 1994 | $120,000 | 40% | $ 48,000 | $72,000 |
| 1995 | 72,000 | 40% | 28,800 | 43,200 |
| 1996 | 43,200 | 40% | 17,280 | 25,920 |
| 1997 | 25,920 | — | 5,920 | 20,000 |
| 1998 | 20,000 | — | — | 20,000 |
|      |        |     | $100,000 |        |

### (b) 150% Declining Balance

| Year | Book Value of Asset at Beginning of Year | Rate | Depreciation | Book Value at End of Year |
|------|------------------------------------------|------|--------------|---------------------------|
| 1994 | $120,000 | 30% | $ 36,000 | $84,000 |
| 1995 | 84,000 | 30% | 25,200 | 58,800 |
| 1996 | 58,800 | 30% | 17,640 | 41,160 |
| 1997 | 41,160 | 30% | 12,348 | 28,812 |
| 1998 | 28,812 | — | 8,812 | 20,000 |
|      |        |     | $100,000 |        |

Note the special situations that arise toward the end of the asset's life. Under the double-declining-balance method, the book value at the beginning of 1997 is $25,920. A strict application of the 40% rate would result in depreciation of $10,368. However, this would reduce the book value below the estimated residual value. Therefore, the 1997 depreciation is only $5,920, which reduces the book value to the residual value, and there is no depreciation in 1998. A similar issue arises under the 150%-declining-balance method. Applying the 30% rate in 1998 would result in depreciation of $8,643.60, which would not be sufficient to reduce the book value down to the residual value. Consequently, the depreciation in 1998 is $8,812, which reduces the book value to the expected residual value of $20,000.

Many companies avoid these problems by switching from the declining-balance method to the straight-line method during the life of the asset. The change in the depreciation method might be made at the midpoint of the life of the asset or when the depreciation under the straight-line method exceeds the declining-balance depreciation. Either method is consistent with the requirement of being systematic and rational if the policy is decided upon at the time of purchase and is applied to all assets. In addition, this practice avoids the possible distortion in the depreciation in the last years of the asset's life. The procedure probably will not produce depreciation that is materially different from the continued application of the accelerated method.[4]

## RECORDING DEPRECIATION

It is important to note that not all depreciation is expensed in the period. **Depreciation on manufacturing assets is included as a cost of the inventory produced and is recorded as an increase (debit) to the Goods in Process Inventory account.** In other words, the depreciation is capitalized to inventory rather than being expensed directly. Costs incurred during the period either remain in the inventory accounts, Goods in Process and Finished Goods Inventory, or they are included in Cost of Goods Sold. Only the portion of the total depreciation included in the units sold appears in the income statement as part of the cost of goods sold (and not separately as depreciation expense). Consequently, depreciation included in the cost of the units produced but not sold is part of the two asset accounts on the balance sheet. Also note, when units produced in previous periods are sold in the current period, the cost of goods sold includes an element of depreciation from previous periods.

Depreciation on assets owned by a manufacturing company that are used for the selling, general, and administrative functions is expensed in the period, and the total Depreciation Expense each period is included on the income statement. Similarly, depreciation on all the assets owned by a merchandising company is expensed each period.

The credit entry to record depreciation is to a contra-asset account usually called Accumulated Depreciation, or Allowance for Depreciation. In the past, the credit sometimes was made to an account entitled Reserve for Depreciation, but such terminology now is considered undesirable because of the uncertain meaning of the term *reserve*. A separate contra-asset account is maintained for each class of assets and should be deducted on the balance sheet directly from the cost of that class. Alternatively, the book value may be reported on the balance sheet and the cost and book value disclosed in the notes to the financial statements. However, many companies combine all the accumulated depreciation amounts and report only the total.

## CONCEPTUAL EVALUATION OF DEPRECIATION METHODS

The use of any one of the previously discussed depreciation methods is acceptable, provided the method relates the allocation of the depreciable cost of the asset to the

---

4. Another depreciation method also solves the issue of computing the correct amount of depreciation in the last year of an asset's life. It is the **fixed-percentage-of-declining-balance method,** in which a percentage depreciation rate is calculated that is multiplied times the book value to reduce it to the residual value at the end of the service life. The depreciation rate is calculated as follows:

$$\text{Depreciation Rate} = 1 - n\sqrt{\frac{\text{Residual Value}}{\text{Cost}}}$$

where $n$ is the life of the asset. (The residual value cannot be zero because that makes the fraction zero and the depreciation rate 100%.) The Troup Company would compute the rate as follows:

$$\text{Depreciation Rate} = 1 - 5\sqrt{\frac{\$20,000}{\$120,000}} = 0.3012$$

This method is rarely used in practice because of its complexity.

expected pattern of benefits to be derived from the asset. The choice of a particular method can have a significant impact on income and assets, as may be seen by comparing the various depreciation amounts and the book value of the asset computed for the Troup Company. These differences are illustrated in Exhibit 9-6. Use of an inappropriate method has an adverse impact on the measurement of income each year, although total income over the life of the asset is unaffected because the same total depreciable cost is expensed. For example, if an asset produces equal (or increasing) benefits each year, but an accelerated depreciation method is used, income will increase each year of the asset's life (if other factors remain the same each period) even though there has been no change in the activity each period. The rising income may be misleading to readers of the financial statements.

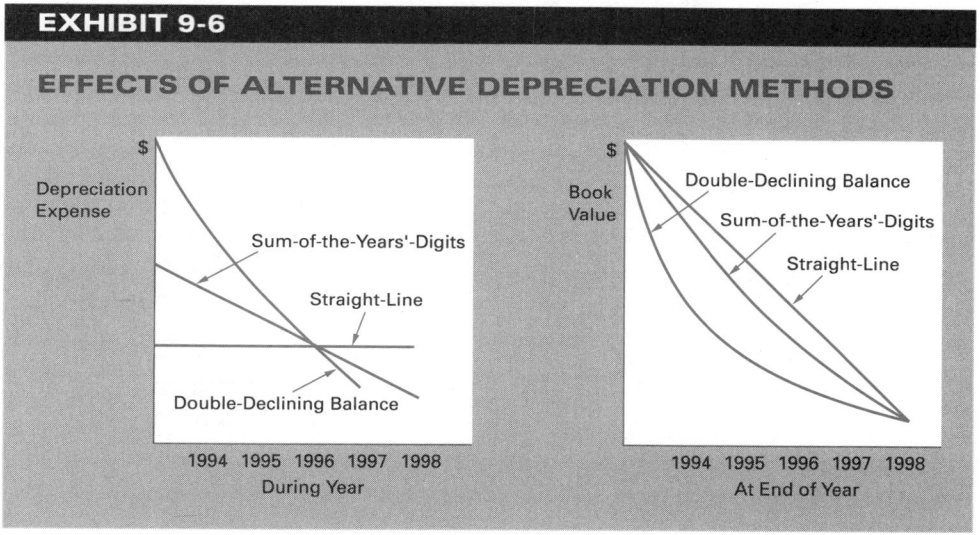

**EXHIBIT 9-6**

**EFFECTS OF ALTERNATIVE DEPRECIATION METHODS**

Three additional factors that should be considered when selecting a depreciation method are repair and maintenance costs, changing prices, and the risk associated with the cash flows from the asset. Unfortunately, none have been addressed by generally accepted accounting principles. The selection of the depreciation method should be considered together with the expected repair and maintenance costs, so that it is the matching of the *total* costs associated with the asset and the benefits derived from the asset that is evaluated. For example, if it is expected that repair and maintenance costs and the total economic benefits of the asset all remain similar each period, a similar total cost each period can be achieved through straight-line depreciation and the similar repair and maintenance costs. Alternatively, if increasing repair and maintenance costs are expected, accelerated (declining-charge) depreciation and the increasing repair and maintenance costs each period will produce similar total costs each period. These two situations are illustrated in Exhibit 9-7. Alternatively, if it is expected that benefits will decline each year for the life of the asset, and that repair and maintenance costs that are constant each period or are not rising as fast as the depreciation is declining, a declining total cost will be achieved by using accelerated (declining-charge) depreciation along with the expected repair and maintenance costs.

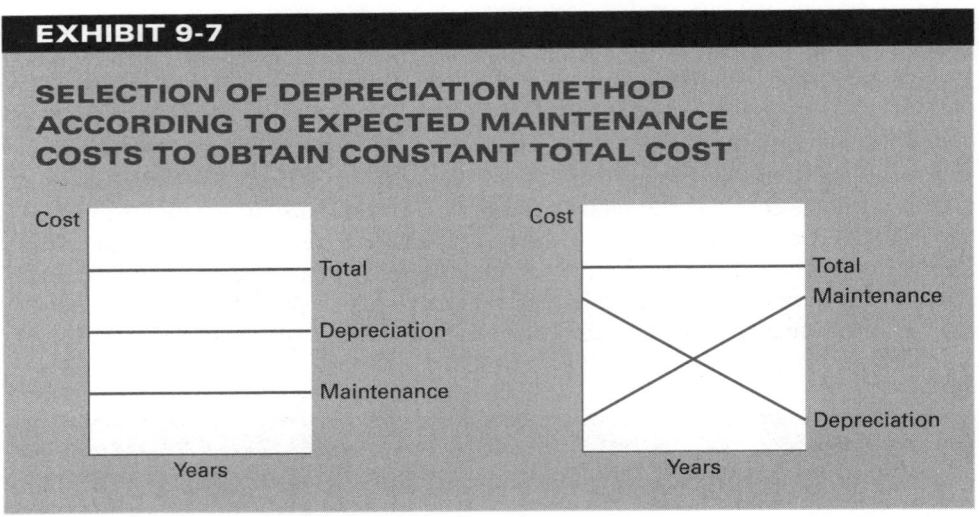

**EXHIBIT 9-7**

**SELECTION OF DEPRECIATION METHOD ACCORDING TO EXPECTED MAINTENANCE COSTS TO OBTAIN CONSTANT TOTAL COST**

*Accounting under conditions of changing prices is discussed in Chapter 24.*

Inflation is likely to have a significant effect on the measurement of the benefits, or revenue, over the life of the asset. In selecting a depreciation method, consideration should be given to whether benefits are to be measured in terms of constant dollars or dollars realized in future periods. Since GAAP is silent on this issue, either alternative is acceptable.

In these periods of technological change, an asset may become obsolete before the end of its originally estimated useful life. Therefore, there is a greater risk associated with the estimated operating cash flows near the end of the life of the asset than for those at the beginning. Use of accelerated depreciation may be appropriate in such situations because the lower depreciation recorded late in the life of the asset reduces the amount of revenues that have to be earned for the asset to be profitable.

A ratio commonly used in financial analysis is the rate of return on total assets, which is defined as (net) income divided by the assets. An unfortunate impact of recording depreciation is that the rate of return on assets increases over time. Refer back to the Troup Company example using straight-line depreciation in Exhibit 9-3. Suppose, in addition, that net income after depreciation and income taxes is $12,000 per year and that the company owns only this one asset. The rate of return earned by the company increases each year as shown in Exhibit 9-8. (The calculation of the rate of return could also be based on the average of the beginning and ending book values of the asset.) The increase in the rate of return over the life of the asset would be even more dramatic if an accelerated depreciation method were used. As a result of this relationship, caution should always be exercised when the rate of return is calculated during financial statement analysis. Comparison between two companies can be distorted if one company has a newer asset base and hence a lower rate of return. Alternatively, if one company is analyzed over time, its rate of return will increase as its asset base gets older, other things being equal.

Depreciation is intended only to allocate cost in a systematic and rational manner. It is *not* an attempt to measure the *value* of the asset, and it is *not* recorded in an attempt to provide funds for the replacement of the asset. Over the life of the asset, the total depreciation expense is equal to the depreciable cost. Since depreciation is a tax-deductible expense, there is an income tax savings over the life of the asset, but it is equal only to the tax rate multiplied by the total amount of tax depreciation.

---

**EXHIBIT 9-8**

**TROUP COMPANY**

Effect of Depreciation on Rate of Return

| Year | Net Income | Book Value of Asset at Beginning of Year | Rate of Return |
|------|-----------|------------------------------------------|----------------|
| 1994 | $12,000 | $120,000 | 10% |
| 1995 | 12,000 | 100,000 | 12 |
| 1996 | 12,000 | 80,000 | 15 |
| 1997 | 12,000 | 60,000 | 20 |
| 1998 | 12,000 | 40,000 | 30 |

---

Therefore, there can be no expectation that there will be sufficient cash saved over the life of the asset. Also, the purchase of an asset requires that cash be available at the time of the purchase, or that the company be able to obtain the necessary funds by borrowing or selling stock. However, the cash saved in income taxes may have been used to finance the operations of the company and be unavailable for asset acquisitions. Furthermore, in times of rising prices, the cost of replacing the asset will be higher than the original cost, so that additional funds will be required for the replacement.

*Depreciation based on the current value of assets is discussed in Chapter 24.*

## DISCLOSURE OF DEPRECIATION

The following disclosure requirements for depreciation were established by **APB Opinion No. 12**:

a. Depreciation expense for the period,

b. Balances of major classes of depreciable assets, by nature or function, at the balance sheet date,

c. Accumulated depreciation, either by major classes of depreciable assets or in total, at the balance sheet date, and

d. A general description of the method or methods used in computing depreciation with respect to major classes of depreciable assets.[5]

The disclosure of these items for Anheuser-Busch is shown in Exhibit 9-9.

The relative use of alternative depreciation methods for 600 surveyed companies is shown in Exhibit 9-10. There are more than 600 responses because many companies use more than one method of depreciation. Even with the current disclosure requirements, the reader of a company's financial statements is not able to evaluate whether the chosen depreciation method(s) is appropriate for the particular assets, but must accept that management and the company's auditors consider the method(s) to be systematic and rational. Nor is the reader able to estimate accurately the effect

---

5. "Omnibus Opinion—1967," *APB Opinion No. 12* (New York: AICPA, 1971), par. 5.

**EXHIBIT 9-9**
**Consolidated Balance Sheet**

**ANHEUSER-BUSCH COMPANIES, INC. AND SUBSIDIARIES**

Assets (in millions) (in part)

|  | December 31 | |
|---|---|---|
|  | **1991** | **1990** |
| Plant and Equipment: | | |
| Land | $ 308.9 | $ 307.7 |
| Buildings | 3,027.8 | 2,825.2 |
| Machinery and equipment | 6,583.9 | 6,080.3 |
| Construction in progress | 669.0 | 803.5 |
|  | 10,589.6 | 10,016.7 |
| Accumulated depreciation | (3,393.1) | (2,952.9) |
|  | 7,196.5 | 7,063.8 |

NOTES TO CONSOLIDATED FINANCIAL STATEMENTS

*Note 1. Summary of Significant Accounting Principles and Policies (in part):*

PLANT AND EQUIPMENT

Plant and equipment is carried at cost and includes expenditures for new facilities and those which substantially increase the useful lives of existing plant and equipment. Maintenance, repairs and minor renewals are expensed as incurred. When properties are retired or otherwise disposed, the related cost and accumulated depreciation are eliminated from the respective accounts and any profit or loss on disposition is reflected in income.

Depreciation is provided principally on the straight-line method over the estimated useful lives of the assets, resulting in depreciation rates on buildings ranging from 2% to 10% and on machinery and equipment from 4% to 25%.

on income and assets of the use of an alternative depreciation method, which might be useful when comparing the financial activities of two companies using different depreciation methods.

**EXHIBIT 9-10**

**USE OF ALTERNATIVE DEPRECIATION METHODS**

|  | Number of Companies | | |
|---|---|---|---|
|  | **1991** | **1990** | **1989** |
| Straight line | 558 | 560 | 562 |
| Declining balance | 28 | 38 | 40 |
| Sum of the years' digits | 8 | 11 | 16 |
| Accelerated method, not specified | 70 | 69 | 69 |
| Units of production | 50 | 50 | 50 |

Source: *Accounting Trends and Techniques* (New York: AICPA, 1992).

## International Accounting Differences

The basic principles of depreciation generally are followed worldwide, although most countries allow any appropriate systematic method. A few countries are more restrictive than the United States. For example, Spain allows only the straight-line and declining-balance methods, and Italy allows only the straight-line method.[6]

There are also differences in disclosures. For example, International Accounting Standards require, for each major class of asset, the disclosure of total depreciation allocated for the period and accumulated depreciation. U.S. accounting principles require similar disclosures in total, but not for each major class of assets. Also International Accounting Standards require disclosure of the useful lives or the depreciation rates used for each major class of asset. No equivalent disclosure is required by U.S. accounting principles.

## ADDITIONAL DEPRECIATION METHODS

Some additional depreciation methods are **group-rate** and **composite-rate** methods that are used frequently in conjunction with the straight-line or accelerated methods, and **retirement** and **replacement** methods that are used in special industries.[7]

Group and composite depreciation are conceptually similar methods of applying depreciation to more than one asset. Group depreciation is applied to *homogeneous* assets that are expected to have similar service lives and residual values. Composite depreciation is applied to *heterogeneous* assets having some similar characteristics that are expected to have varying service lives and residual values. Thus, group depreciation would be used for assets such as typewriters, whereas composite depreciation would be applied to assets such as office machines.

### Group Depreciation

Group depreciation is used when a group of homogeneous (similar) assets is owned by a company, the assets are capitalized in a single asset account, and the group is treated as a single "asset" for purposes of depreciation. The group depreciation rate is based on the average life of the assets in the group, and the depreciation is accumulated in a single contra-asset account. Depreciation each period is calculated by multiplying this rate by the balance in the asset account. When an item in the group is retired, no gain or loss is recognized on that item because the entire "asset" is not retired. The individual retirement is recorded by a credit to the asset account for the original cost, and a debit to the accumulated depreciation account for the difference between the cost and the proceeds received. A total net gain or loss on the group as a whole is recognized when the final unit in the group is retired.

For example, suppose that a company purchases ten cars for $20,000 each, and the average expected service life is 3 years with a residual value of $5,000 each. Of those cars, three are sold after 2 years for $8,000 each, five after 3 years for $6,000

---

6. For additional discussion, see Coopers & Lybrand, *1991 International Accounting Summaries: A Guide for Interpretation and Comparison* (New York: John Wiley and Son, Inc., 1991).

7. Two other methods, the **compound-interest** and **sinking-fund** methods, are based on present value concepts. They result in an *increasing* depreciation amount and a constant rate of return on the asset each period. They are very rarely used because increasing depreciation each period generally is not considered to satisfy the matching principle.

each, and two after 4 years for $4,800 each. The depreciation rate is computed as follows:

$$\text{Depreciation} = \frac{\text{Cost} - \text{Residual Value}}{\text{Life}}$$

$$= \frac{\$200,000 - \$50,000}{3}$$

$$= \$50,000 \text{ (or 25\% of the cost of the assets)}$$

The journal entries used to record these events are shown in Exhibit 9-11. Depreciation expense is based on the original estimates, and the rate is not changed by the particular experience of the early retirement of 3 cars after the second year. No gain or loss is recognized on the retirement at the end of the second and third years. The journal entries in the fourth year (the year of the final retirement) need further explanation. First, although the usual procedure in group depreciation is to multiply the asset cost times the group depreciation rate to determine the annual depreciation expense, it is a general rule that assets should not be depreciated below their residual value. Since the book value of the group asset is $11,000 ($40,000 Cars − $29,000 Accumulated Depreciation) at the beginning of the year and the residual value of the two remaining cars is $10,000 (2 × $5,000), the depreciation expense must be $1,000 in this year. Second, the $400 loss on the *entire* group is determined by comparing the $9,600 (2 × $4,800) proceeds to the $10,000 book value at the end of the fourth year.

If a new asset (i.e., more cars) had been purchased before the group was retired, a new depreciation rate would be computed by dividing the new depreciation base (book value at the beginning of the period plus the additional cost less the estimated residual value of the group) by the new weighted average of the remaining lives of the assets in the group.

### Composite Depreciation

Composite depreciation may be applied to heterogeneous (dissimilar) assets that have somewhat similar characteristics or purposes. As with group depreciation, the assets are combined in a single asset account and depreciated accordingly. One accumulated depreciation account is used, no gain or loss is recognized on each item retired, and a net gain or loss is recognized when the final asset is retired.

For example, suppose that a company purchases three assets with the following characteristics:

| Asset | Cost | Residual Value | Life | Annual Depreciation |
|-------|------|----------------|------|---------------------|
| A | $25,000 | $5,000 | 10 years | $2,000 |
| B | 13,000 | 1,000 | 6 | 2,000 |
| C | 12,000 | — | 4 | 3,000 |
| | $50,000 | $6,000 | | $7,000 |

Assuming that straight-line depreciation is used, the composite depreciation rate is computed as follows:

$$\text{Depreciation Rate} = \frac{\$7,000}{\$50,000} = 14\%$$

---

**EXHIBIT 9-11**

## JOURNAL ENTRIES FOR GROUP DEPRECIATION

1. To record the purchase:

| | | |
|---|--:|--:|
| Cars | 200,000 | |
| Cash | | 200,000 |

2. To record the first year's depreciation expense:

| | | |
|---|--:|--:|
| Depreciation Expense | 50,000 | |
| Accumulated Depreciation | | 50,000 |

3. To record the second year's depreciation expense:

| | | |
|---|--:|--:|
| Depreciation Expense | 50,000 | |
| Accumulated Depreciation | | 50,000 |

4. To record the disposal of three cars at the end of the second year for $8,000 each:

| | | |
|---|--:|--:|
| Cash | 24,000 | |
| Accumulated Depreciation | 36,000 | |
| Cars | | 60,000 |

5. To record the third year's depreciation expense:

| | | |
|---|--:|--:|
| Depreciation Expense [25% × ($200,000 − $60,000)] | 35,000 | |
| Accumulated Depreciation | | 35,000 |

6. To record the disposal of five cars at the end of the third year for $6,000 each:

| | | |
|---|--:|--:|
| Cash | 30,000 | |
| Accumulated Depreciation | 70,000 | |
| Cars | | 100,000 |

7. To record the depreciation expense for the fourth year, the disposal of two cars at the end of the fourth year for $4,800 each, and the *net* gain or loss of the *entire* group:

| | | |
|---|--:|--:|
| Depreciation Expense | 1,000[a] | |
| Accumulated Depreciation | | 1,000 |
| | | |
| Cash | 9,600 | |
| Accumulated Depreciation | 30,000 | |
| Loss on Disposal | 400[b] | |
| Cars | | 40,000 |

---

a. The depreciation expense is the amount needed to reduce the $11,000 book value ($40,000 remaining cost minus $29,000 remaining accumulated depreciation) of the group to the estimated residual value (2 × $5,000).

b. The loss is equal to the proceeds of $9,600 (2 × $4,800) minus the remaining book value of $10,000 ($40,000 − $30,000).

The depreciation is computed as 14% of the cost of the assets remaining in service until the book value equals the estimated residual value of $6,000. If another asset is purchased, it may be included in the group by adding the cost to the asset account. Then a new composite depreciation rate is calculated.

The advantage of both the group and the composite methods is that they simplify the record keeping required, especially when a large number of low-cost items are acquired. The methods also recognize that depreciation estimates are based on averages and that gains or losses on disposals of single assets are often immaterial. The major disadvantage of the two methods is that faulty estimates might be concealed for long periods and gains and losses deferred beyond the period in which they actually occurred. This is particularly true when heterogeneous assets are combined for the composite depreciation method and the average life is the result of combining varying individual lives.

### Retirement and Replacement Methods

The retirement and replacement methods of expense recognition, instead of the depreciation methods discussed in the chapter, have been used by public utilities and railroads for such items as poles and tracks. In using these methods, an expense is recognized only when an asset is retired or replaced. Under the *retirement* method, the cost of the *old* asset (less its residual value) is expensed when it is retired. Under the *replacement* method, the cost of the *new* asset (less the residual value of the old asset) is expensed when it is acquired. Basically, the retirement method is a FIFO approach, whereas the replacement method is a LIFO approach. Neither method is desirable because neither matches expenses with revenues in each period of the asset's life. If no retirement or replacement occurs, no expense is recognized. However, these methods did gain acceptance as special industry practices, particularly when there are large numbers of low-cost interrelated items for which it is difficult to estimate the economic life and to distinguish between maintenance and replacement. Although it would be difficult to argue that these methods satisfy the criteria of being "systematic and rational," they are sometimes used in the railroad and utility industries.[8] Furthermore, if a company has a policy of regular replacement so that the amount expensed remains fairly stable, the difference in expense from straight-line depreciation is probably immaterial.

### Inventory Systems

The inventory (or appraisal) system typically is used in situations where there are large numbers of similar low-cost items, such as tools for a manufacturing company or dishes for a restaurant. The method is similar to a periodic inventory system, in that a cost is assigned to an expense by a physical count at the end of the year. That is, the cost assigned to depreciation is determined by multiplying the physical number of units at the end of the year by the replacement cost. A key difference, however, is that the account debited is depreciation expense rather than cost of goods sold. Also, the ending inventory usually is computed as the value (not the cost) of the assets, so that the depreciation becomes a measure of the change in the value of the assets. The method is criticized because it does not result in a systematic and rational allocation of cost, but rather is a measure of the value of the assets. Also, the value assigned to the inventory tends to lack reliability.

## DEPRECIATION FOR PARTIAL PERIODS

The discussion so far has assumed that assets have been purchased on the first day of the fiscal year and disposed of on the last day. Of course, transactions occur throughout the fiscal year and depreciation could be computed to the nearest day, but such precision is unnecessary, considering the estimates involved in the calculation of

8. In 1983, the Interstate Commerce Commission required the use of depreciation accounting in ICC filings. As a result, many railroads adopted depreciation accounting for financial reporting.

depreciation. There are three common alternative policies that companies use to handle depreciation for partial periods.

## Compute Depreciation to the Nearest Whole Month

Under this method, assets purchased on or before the 15th of the month are considered owned for the whole month; assets purchased after the 15th are considered *not* to be owned during the month. Similarly, assets sold on or before the 15th are considered not to be owned for the month; assets sold after the 15th are considered owned for the whole month. Depreciation is based on the fraction of the year the asset is used. For example, suppose a $6,000 asset with a 3-year life and no residual value is purchased on August 18; thus 4 months remain in the year. The sum-of-the-years'-digits depreciation extends over 4 fiscal years and is computed as follows:

| Fiscal Year | Annual Depreciation by Sum-of-the-Years'-Digits Method | Months | Computation | Annual Depreciation |
|---|---|---|---|---|
| 1 | $3,000 | 4 | 4/12 × $3,000 | $1,000 |
| 2 | 2,000 | 12 | 8/12 × $3,000 + 4/12 × $2,000 | 2,667 |
| 3 | 1,000 | 12 | 8/12 × $2,000 + 4/12 × $1,000 | 1,667 |
| 4 | — | 8 | 8/12 × $1,000 | 666* |
| | $6,000 | | | $6,000 |

*Adjusted for $1 rounding error.

When double-declining depreciation is used for partial periods, two alternatives are available. In the first alternative, the double-declining-balance method can be used in the same manner as described previously for the sum-of-the-years'-digits method. That is, the depreciation on an annual basis is allocated to each fiscal year on the basis of the number of months. In the second alternative, after the computation of the depreciation for the first year as described for the first alternative, the double-declining-balance method can be applied by multiplying the book value by the appropriate percentage (66.7%) for the asset described previously. The two alternatives give the following depreciation amounts:

| Fiscal Year | Annual Depreciation by the Double-Declining-Balance | Months | Computation | Reported Annual Depreciation |
|---|---|---|---|---|
| *Alternative 1* | | | | |
| 1 | $4,000 | 4 | 4/12 × $4,000 | $1,333 |
| 2 | 1,333 | 12 | 8/12 × $4,000 + 4/12 × $1,333 | 3,111 |
| 3 | 667 | 12 | 8/12 × $1,333 + 4/12 × $667 | 1,111 |
| 4 | — | 8 | 8/12 × $667 | 445 |
| | $6,000 | | | $6,000 |

| *Alternative 2* | | |
|---|---|---|
| Depreciation Year 1 | 4/12 × $4,000 | $1,333 |
| Depreciation Year 2 | 0.667* × ($6,000 − $1,333) | 3,113 |
| Depreciation Year 3 | 0.667 × ($4,667 − $3,113) | 1,037 |
| Depreciation Year 4 | remaining balance | 517 |
| | | $6,000 |

*Two times straight-line rate = 2 × 1/3.

When straight-line depreciation is used and it is necessary to calculate depreciation for months instead of years, the denominator of the depreciation calculation frequently is expressed in terms of the total months in the estimated service life, resulting in readily determinable depreciation per month.

### Compute Depreciation to the Nearest Whole Year

For this partial depreciation method, exactly the same procedure is used as for the monthly situation, except that 6 months is used as the cutoff instead of the 15th of the month. That is, assets purchased during the first six months of the year are considered to be owned for the entire year, and assets purchased during the second six months are not depreciated for that year. Using the same example, there is no depreciation in the first fiscal year, since the asset was purchased in the second half of the year, but a full year's depreciation is recorded in the last year. Depreciation in the next 3 fiscal years is $3,000, $2,000, and $1,000, respectively, under the sum-of-the-years'-digits method.

### Compute One-Half Year's Depreciation on All Assets Purchased or Sold During the Year

Under this method, all assets purchased or sold during the fiscal year are considered to have been purchased or sold at the midpoint of the year, so that one-half year's depreciation is recorded in all such situations. Using the same example, the depreciation for each fiscal year is computed as follows:

| Fiscal Year | Annual Depreciation by Sum-of-the-Years'-Digits Method | Computation | Reported Annual Depreciation |
|---|---|---|---|
| 1 | $3,000 | 1/2 × $3,000 | $1,500 |
| 2 | 2,000 | 1/2 × $3,000 + 1/2 × $2,000 | 2,500 |
| 3 | 1,000 | 1/2 × $2,000 + 1/2 × $1,000 | 1,500 |
| 4 | — | 1/2 × $1,000 | 500 |
| | $6,000 | | $6,000 |

## IMPAIRMENT OF NONCURRENT ASSETS

Under generally accepted accounting principles, an asset initially is recorded at its acquisition cost and then depreciated over its life to its expected residual value by use of a systematic and rational method. There is no provision for use of the lower of cost or market method. In recent years, however, many companies have written down the carrying value of their noncurrent assets such as property, plant and equipment even though they have no intention of disposing of them. In effect, the companies are applying the lower of cost or market method to these assets. Usually, this write-down occurs at the time of a major restructuring of the operating activities and/or the financial structure of the company. Although the write-down of assets in a formal quasi-reorganization is addressed in *Accounting Research Bulletin No. 43* (and discussed in Chapter 15), write-downs in other situations are not addressed by GAAP even though the actions of companies indicate that write-downs have been found acceptable in certain circumstances. However, the criteria that should be used in these situations are uncertain. The general concept that often is suggested is that if the book value of the asset cannot be recovered through use (or sale), then it may be written down to its net realizable value. A wide variety of recognition criteria, measurement methods, terminology, and disclosure have been used, resulting in a lack of *comparability*. The absence of rules contrasts with accounting for inventories, where the lower of cost or market method must be used.

To reduce the level of diversity in practice, the FASB added a project on impairment of assets to its agenda and subsequently issued a *Discussion Memorandum*.[9] Among the issues to be resolved are:

1. Which types of assets should be written down?

2. When should impairment be recognized? Does the write-down have to be part of a general restructuring? Does the impairment have to be "permanent" or just "probable"?

3. How should impairment be measured? Should present value or net realizable value be used?

4. If impairment occurs, can it be recovered if conditions change?

5. Should individual assets, or groups of assets, be revalued?

6. How should an impairment be reported and disclosed?

The FASB has addressed the issue of the impairment of noncurrent assets in one specialized industry situation. According to **FASB Statement No. 90** entitled "Regulated Enterprises—Accounting for Abandonment and Disallowances of Plant Costs," a company computes the present value of the future revenue that is expected to result from the inclusion by a regulator (e.g., a state regulatory commission) of the cost of an abandoned plant in allowable costs for rate-making purposes. This present value is recorded as a separate asset, and if the book value of the abandoned plant exceeds that present value, a loss is recognized. Also, any costs of a recently completed plant that are disallowed by a regulator are recognized as a loss. Thus, it can be seen that the FASB decided to use a present value approach, but the measurement of revenues in a regulated environment is more reliable than for a company operating in a free market. Also, the FASB decided that the cost of a plant should not exceed the value of the asset that can be recovered through use. It remains to be seen whether these principles will be applied in the FASB's more general project.

## International Accounting Differences

U.S. accounting principles do not allow the write-up of property, plant, and equipment to their market values, and the possibility of such a principle seems remote. Some other countries, including Canada, Germany, and Japan, also prohibit revaluation. However, in many other countries, including Denmark, Mexico, and the United Kingdom, such write-ups (and write-downs) do occur, with the credit usually recorded as an increase in stockholders' equity. Such write-ups create significant differences that reduce international comparability among companies.

---

9. "Accounting for the Impairment of Long-Lived Assets and Identifiable Intangibles," *FASB Discussion Memorandum* (Norwalk, Conn.: FASB, December 7, 1990).

## DEPRECIATION AND INCOME TAX

Companies follow different depreciation rules for computing taxable income than for computing income for financial reporting purposes. The use of different methods is acceptable because the purpose of the depreciation methods required by the income tax laws is to stimulate capital investment through the rapid recovery of capital costs, whereas accounting income should present fairly the activities of the company over a particular period.

For assets acquired before 1981, depreciation for income tax purposes is based on use of the straight-line, sum-of-the-years'-digits, and declining-balance methods discussed earlier. The asset may not be depreciated below the estimated residual value, and the IRS publishes tables that give a range of the estimated lives to use. For assets purchased in the years 1981 through 1986, the Accelerated Cost Recovery System (ACRS) is used. For assets purchased in 1987 and later, ACRS was modified and is known as MACRS.[10] The following discussion is based on these latest rules.

### MACRS Principles

For assets purchased in 1987 and later, computation of depreciation for federal income tax purposes and financial reporting purposes differ in three major respects: (1) a mandated tax life, which is usually shorter than the economic life, (2) acceleration of the cost recovery (except for buildings), and (3) elimination of the residual value. Each of these differences tends to cause depreciation early in the life of the asset to be higher for income tax purposes than for financial statement reporting, thereby lowering income taxes payable in those years. Over the life of the asset, the sum of the total depreciation and the gain or loss on disposal for both income tax reporting and financial reporting usually will be the same for both methods. Therefore, the total effect on taxable income over the asset's life usually will be equal to the total effect on income before income taxes reported in the financial statements. However, the transfer of income tax payments from early in the life of the asset to later in the life is desirable when present value concepts are taken into consideration. Since MACRS depreciation is so different from the depreciation used in the financial statements, it is briefly discussed. It should also be noted that for income tax reporting the straight-line method over the mandated tax life may be used instead of MACRS. Refer to the Internal Revenue Code, or an income tax book, for a more detailed and technical discussion.

*Shorter Life*
The MACRS establishes lives (recovery periods) of 3, 5, 7, 10, 15, 20, 27½ (residential buildings), and 31½ (nonresidential buildings) years. Each asset is defined to be in one of the categories, and that life is used no matter what economic life is used for financial reporting purposes.

---

10. An asset other than a building had an ACRS life of 3, 5, 10, or 15 years. A building had an ACRS life of 18 or 19 years, depending on the year it was purchased. The depreciation was computed by multiplying the cost of the asset by a defined percentage. For example, an asset with a 3-year ACRS life was depreciated using 25% in the first year, 38% in the second year, and 37% in the third year. An asset with a 5-year ACRS life was depreciated using 15%, 22%, 21%, 21%, and 21% over the respective 5 years.

## Acceleration of Cost Recovery

The depreciation is computed based on the *cost* of the asset. The method used depends on the life of the asset mandated by MACRS, as follows:

| Method | MACRS Life (in Years) |
|---|---|
| Double-declining balance | 3, 5, 7, 10 |
| 150% declining balance | 15, 20 |
| Straight line | 27 ½, 31 ½ |

All the depreciation calculations for income tax purposes are based on the half-year convention; that is, depreciation for half a year is recorded in the year of acquisition and in the last year of the MACRS life. Therefore, the depreciation for tax purposes is spread over one more tax year than the number of calendar years listed previously. Also, when one of the accelerated methods is used, a change is made to the straight-line method in the period in which the straight-line depreciation exceeds the amount calculated under the accelerated method. The IRS has published tables to simplify the application of these methods, as illustrated in Exhibit 9-12.

## EXHIBIT 9-12

### MACRS DEPRECIATION AS A PERCENTAGE OF THE COST OF THE ASSET

| Year of Life | Tax Life of Asset in Years | | | | | |
|---|---|---|---|---|---|---|
| | 3 | 5 | 7 | 10 | 15 | 20 |
| 1 | 33.33% | 20.00% | 14.29% | 10.00% | 5.00% | 3.750% |
| 2 | 44.45 | 32.00 | 24.49 | 18.00 | 9.50 | 7.219 |
| 3 | 14.81 | 19.20 | 17.49 | 14.40 | 8.55 | 6.677 |
| 4 | 7.41 | 11.52 | 12.49 | 11.52 | 7.70 | 6.177 |
| 5 | | 11.52 | 8.93 | 9.22 | 6.93 | 5.713 |
| 6 | | 5.76 | 8.92 | 7.37 | 6.23 | 5.285 |
| 7 | | | 8.93 | 6.55 | 5.90 | 4.888 |
| 8 | | | 4.46 | 6.55 | 5.90 | 4.522 |
| 9 | | | | 6.56 | 5.91 | 4.462 |
| 10 | | | | 6.55 | 5.90 | 4.461 |
| 11 | | | | 3.28 | 5.91 | 4.462 |
| 12 | | | | | 5.90 | 4.461 |
| 13 | | | | | 5.91 | 4.462 |
| 14 | | | | | 5.90 | 4.461 |
| 15 | | | | | 5.91 | 4.462 |
| 16 | | | | | 2.95 | 4.461 |
| 17 | | | | | | 4.462 |
| 18 | | | | | | 4.461 |
| 19 | | | | | | 4.462 |
| 20 | | | | | | 4.461 |
| 21 | | | | | | 2.231 |

*Residual Value*

The residual value is *not* considered when the MACRS system is used, and so the asset is depreciated to a zero value at the end of its MACRS life. However, the entire proceeds from the disposal of the asset will be taxable since the entire value received will represent a gain.

## Illustration of MACRS

To illustrate the use of the MACRS system and the differences from the calculation of depreciation for financial reporting, consider the following facts for an asset (a light-duty truck) purchased by the Melville Company on January 1, 1995:

| | |
|---|---|
| Cost | $200,000 |
| Estimated economic life | 8 years |
| Estimated residual value | $20,000 |
| Depreciation method for financial statements | Straight-line |
| MACRS life | 5 years |
| MACRS method | 200% declining balance |
| Disposal | $15,000 on January 3, 2003 |

The MACRS depreciation is computed using the rates from Exhibit 9-12 as follows:

| | | | |
|---|---|---|---|
| 1995 | $200,000 × 20% | = | $ 40,000 |
| 1996 | $200,000 × 32% | = | $ 64,000 |
| 1997 | $200,000 × 19.20% | = | $ 38,400 |
| 1998 | $200,000 × 11.52% | = | $ 23,040 |
| 1999 | $200,000 × 11.52% | = | $ 23,040 |
| 2000 | $200,000 × 5.76% | = | $ 11,520 |
| | | | $200,000 |

Note that the total depreciation deductions on the income tax returns for 1995 through 2000 are $200,000. Thus, the MACRS depreciation recovers the total cost of the asset on an accelerated basis and ignores any residual value. The taxable gain in 2000 when the truck is sold is $15,000, since the asset has been depreciated to a zero residual value. Therefore, the total effect on taxable income for the years 1995 through 2003 is $185,000 ($200,000 − $15,000).

The depreciation for financial reporting purposes is $22,500 [($200,000 − $20,000) ÷ 8] for each of the 8 years of the asset's economic life from 1995 through 2002. The loss on disposal in 2003 is $5,000 ($20,000 book value − $15,000 proceeds). The total effect on income before income taxes for the years 1995 through 2003 in the income statement is $185,000 ($180,000 + $5,000), which is the same as the total effect on taxable income. The different amounts of depreciation for income tax reporting and financial reporting in each year result in temporary differences, which require interperiod tax allocation.

*Interperiod tax allocation is discussed in Chapter 17.*

## CHANGES AND CORRECTIONS OF DEPRECIATION

**APB Opinion No. 20,** discussed more fully in Chapter 22, describes how each of the various changes in and corrections of depreciation may be made for the following situations:

1. A change in the depreciation method for currently owned assets (change in accounting principle) is accounted for by a cumulative-effect change. The accumulated depreciation at the beginning of the year of the change is

computed based on the old and the new methods, and the difference is reported on the income statement (net of income taxes) in the year of the change as a cumulative effect on prior years' income of a change in accounting principle (as illustrated in Chapter 4).

2. Adoption of a new depreciation method for newly acquired assets does not require any adjustment to the accounts, but it does require disclosure in the notes to the financial statements of the nature of the change, its effects on income from continuing operations, and on net income, together with related earnings per share amounts.

3. A change in an estimate of the residual value or the service life of a currently owned asset is handled prospectively; that is, the undepreciated cost of the asset at the beginning of the year of the change is allocated over the new remaining life, giving consideration to the new residual value. An illustration (using depletion) is included in the next section of the chapter.

4. Correction of an error in depreciation is treated as a prior period adjustment; that is, the previous financial statements are corrected (restated). The effect on the current period's financial statements involves a correction to the amount in the accumulated depreciation account and an increase or decrease in retained earnings (net of income taxes) for the amount of the error in previously reported net income. This reporting is illustrated in Chapters 4 and 15 and is consistent with the requirements of **FASB Statement No. 16.**

## DEPLETION

**Depletion is the allocation of the depletable cost for the consumption of a natural resource (wasting asset) to the periods in which benefits are received.** It is the same concept as depreciation, but the different term is used for natural resources. Examples of such resources are oil, gas, minerals, timber, and gravel.

The recorded cost of natural resources is determined by the same principles used for property, plant, and equipment. It is possible that if there are extensive reclamation costs, the net residual value might be negative because the reclamation costs exceed the expected selling price of the land. In this case, the net amount would have to be *added* to the cost to determine the depletion base.

Depletion normally is recorded on the basis of an activity method. The activity measure is the number of units of the resource that are expected to be extracted over the life of the asset. A unit depletion rate is calculated as follows:

$$\text{Unit Depletion Rate} = \frac{\text{Cost} - \text{Residual Value}}{\text{Units}}$$

To determine the actual depletion for a period, the unit depletion rate is multiplied by the actual production for that period. Suppose that a company purchases land for $3,000,000 from which it expects to extract 1,000,000 tons of coal, and the estimated residual value is $200,000. It is assumed that 80,000 tons of coal are mined in the first year. The depletion for that year is calculated as follows:

$$\text{Unit Depletion Rate} = \frac{\$3,000,000 - \$200,000}{1,000,000 \text{ tons}}$$

$$= \$2.80 \text{ per ton}$$

$$\text{Depletion for Year} = \$2.80 \times 80,000 \text{ tons}$$

$$= \$224,000$$

The journal entry to record the depletion typically is made directly to an inventory account (so that the cost is included in Cost of Goods Sold for the units that are sold and in ending inventory for the units on hand at the end of the period). The credit is made either to Accumulated Depletion or directly to the asset account.

The nature of natural resources is such that additional capital expenditures may be made in future periods. In addition, the estimation of the remaining number of units is often uncertain and therefore subject to revision based on new geological information. When additional capital expenditures have been incurred or estimates are revised, a new depletion rate has to be calculated. The new depletion rate is based on the current book value of the asset (including the additional capital expenditures), the new estimate of the residual value, and the new estimate of the remaining units as of the beginning of the year. Continuing the preceding example, suppose that at the beginning of the second year of operation of the coal mine, a new estimate indicates that the mine has a capacity to produce another 1,600,000 tons (for a lifetime production of 1,680,000 tons). A new unit depletion rate is computed as follows:

$$\text{Unit Depletion Rate} = \frac{\text{Book Value} - \text{Residual Value}}{\text{Remaining Units}}$$

$$= \frac{(\$3,000,000 - \$224,000) - \$200,000}{1,600,000}$$

$$= \underline{\$1.61 \text{ per ton}}$$

The new unit depletion rate is used to compute each year's depletion until new estimates are made and another depletion rate is calculated.

The cost of a natural resource asset may include certain tangible assets, such as buildings and roads on the site of a mine. Since the useful life of the tangible assets is limited by the life of the mine, their cost is depreciated on the basis of the same activity method as used for the mine. Of course, if other improvements have a life shorter than the expected life of the mine, they are depreciated over their expected economic lives.

Depletion for income tax purposes involves a different concept than for financial reporting. The taxpayer can deduct as depletion expense either the **cost depletion** just illustrated (based on the units sold) or **percentage depletion.** Under percentage (or **statutory**) depletion, a stated percentage of gross income may be deducted as depletion expense. This percentage varies, depending on the type of natural resource, from a minimum of 5% to a maximum of 22%. Furthermore, the total depletion over the life of the asset for income tax purposes may exceed the cost of the asset less the expected residual value. Consequently, most companies use percentage depletion for income tax purposes and cost depletion for financial reporting. This results in a permanent tax difference.

*Permanent tax differences are discussed in Chapter 17.*

## QUESTIONS

*Q9-1* Distinguish among the use of the terms *depreciation, depletion,* and *amortization.*

*Q9-2* Briefly explain the meaning of the four factors that are involved in the computation of the periodic charge for depreciation.

*Q9-3* What is the *depreciation base*?

*Q9-4* What is the objective of accounting for depreciation?

*Q9-5* Explain how recording depreciation affects (a) the income statement, (b) the balance sheet, and (c) the statement of cash flows.

*Q9-6* Does recording depreciation generate funds for the replacement of the asset? Explain.

**Q9-7** Under what circumstances is depreciation a fixed cost or a variable cost?

**Q9-8** What are the primary causes of depreciation? For each cause, indicate which depreciation method may be most appropriate. Would it be desirable to require all companies to use the same method?

**Q9-9** Under what circumstances are accelerated methods of depreciation most appropriate?

**Q9-10** Compare the group and composite methods of depreciation.

**Q9-11** Compare the retirement and replacement methods of expense recognition.

**Q9-12** Under what circumstances is an asset's depreciation amount not included in total in the current income statement?

**Q9-13** In a year in which the cost of replacing an asset rises, should depreciation be recorded for that asset? Why?

**Q9-14** An accelerated depreciation method should be used because of the large decline in the value of an asset early in its life. Evaluate this statement.

**Q9-15** The manager of a utility stated that since its transmission lines are kept in good condition by regular repairs and maintenance and their efficiency remains constant, the lines do not depreciate. Do you agree with this statement?

**Q9-16** What disclosures of depreciation are required in financial statements and the accompanying notes?

**Q9-17** Why may depreciation on the financial statements be different from depreciation computed for income tax purposes?

**Q9-18** How does depletion for income tax purposes vary from depletion for financial reporting purposes?

## CASES

### C9-1 Depreciation Concepts

Depreciation continues to be one of the most controversial, difficult, and important problem areas in accounting.

**Required**

1. a. Explain the conventional accounting concept of depreciation accounting, and
   b. Discuss its conceptual merit with respect to (1) the value of the asset, (2) the amount(s) expensed, and (3) the discretion of management in selecting the method.
2. a. Explain the factors that should be considered when applying the conventional concept of depreciation to the determination of how the value of a newly acquired computer system should be assigned to expense for financial reporting purposes. (Income tax considerations should be ignored for this case.)
   b. What depreciation methods might be used for the computer system? (*AICPA adapted*)

### C9-2 Depreciation Concepts ∞

Evaluate each of the following statements separately:

1. "Since our plant was shut down for part of the year, we will not depreciate it. Depreciating it for the full year would increase our costs and overstate the inventory."
2. "I think we should have increasing depreciation each period because it will increase the funds recovered near the end of the asset's life when maintenance costs are high and we will need to replace the asset. Also, I think tax rates will be higher toward the end of the asset's life, so we will be better off to have larger depreciation then."

### C9-3 Depreciation

May Manufacturing Company was organized January 2, 1995. During 1995, it has used in its reports to management the straight-line method of depreciating its plant assets.

On November 9, you are having a conference with May's officers to discuss the depreciation method to be used for income tax and stockholder reporting. The president of May has suggested the use of a new method, which he feels is more suitable than the straight-line method for the needs of the company during the period of rapid expansion of production and capacity that he foresees. The following is a schedule in which the proposed method is applied to a fixed asset with an original cost of $32,000, an estimated useful life of 5 years, and a scrap value of approximately $2,000.

| Year | Years of Life Used | Fraction Rate | Depreciation Expense | Accumulated Depreciation, Year-End | Book Value at Year-End |
|------|------|------|------|------|------|
| 1 | 1 | 1/15 | $ 2,000 | $ 2,000 | $30,000 |
| 2 | 2 | 2/15 | 4,000 | 6,000 | 26,000 |
| 3 | 3 | 3/15 | 6,000 | 12,000 | 20,000 |
| 4 | 4 | 4/15 | 8,000 | 20,000 | 12,000 |
| 5 | 5 | 5/15 | 10,000 | 30,000 | 2,000 |

The president favors the new method because he has heard that:

1. It will increase the funds recovered during the years near the end of the asset's useful life when maintenance and replacement disbursements are high.
2. It will result in increased write-offs in later years, thereby reducing taxes.

**Required**

1. What is the purpose and, hence, the nature of accounting for depreciation?
2. Is the president's proposal within the scope of generally accepted accounting principles? In making your decision, discuss the circumstances, if any, under which the method would be reasonable and those, if any, under which it would not be reasonable.
3. The president wants your advice.
   a. Does depreciation recover or create funds? Explain.
   b. Assume that the Internal Revenue Service accepts the proposed depreciation method in this particular case. If the proposed method were used for stockholder and tax reporting purposes, how would it affect the availability of funds generated by operations? (*AICPA adapted*)

### C9-4   Depreciation

The certified public accountant is frequently called upon by management for advice regarding methods of computing depreciation. Although the question arises less frequently, of comparable importance is whether the depreciation method should be based on the consideration of the assets as units, a group, or as having a composite life.

**Required**

1. Briefly describe the depreciation methods based on treating assets as:
   a. Units
   b. A group or as having a composite life
2. Present the arguments for and against the use of each of the two methods.
3. Describe how retirements are recorded under each of the two methods. (*AICPA adapted*)

### C9-5   Capitalization and Depreciation

Gehl Company purchased significant amounts of new equipment this year to be used in its operations. The equipment was delivered by the suppliers, installed by Gehl, and placed into operation. Some of it was purchased for cash with discounts available for prompt payments. Some of it was purchased under long-term payment plans, for which the interest charges approximate prevailing rates. As a result, Gehl is studying its capitalization and depreciation policies.

**Required**

1. What costs should Gehl capitalize for the new equipment purchased this year?
2. What factors cause the equipment to lose its future economic benefit?
3. What factors should be considered in computing the equipment's depreciation expense?
4. What theoretical justifications are there for the use of accelerated depreciation methods? (*AICPA adapted*)

### C9-6   Capitalization and Depreciation

At the beginning of the year, Patrick Company acquired a computer to be used in its operations. The computer was delivered by the supplier, installed by Patrick, and placed into operation. The estimated useful life of the computer is five years, and its estimated residual (salvage) value is significant.

During the year, Patrick received cash in exchange for an automobile that was purchased in a prior year.

**Required**

1. a. What costs should Patrick capitalize for the computer?
   b. What is the objective of depreciation accounting? (Do not discuss specific methods of depreciation.)
2. What is the rationale for using accelerated depreciation methods?
3. How should Patrick account for and report the disposal of the automobile? (*AICPA adapted*)

### C9-7   Straight-Line and Composite Depreciation

Portland Co. uses the straight-line depreciation method for depreciable assets. All assets are depreciated individually except manufacturing machinery, which is depreciated by the composite method.

During the year, Portland exchanged a delivery truck with Maine Co. for a larger delivery truck. It paid cash equal to 10% of the larger truck's value.

**Required**

1. What factors should have influenced Portland's selection of the straight-line depreciation method?
2. How should Portland account for and report the truck exchange transaction?
3. a. What benefits should Portland derive from using the composite method rather than the individual basis for manufacturing machinery?
   b. How should Portland have calculated the manufacturing machinery's annual depreciation expense in its first year of operation? (*AICPA adapted*)

### C9-8   Operating and Capital Expenditures

Property, plant, and equipment (plant assets) generally represent a material portion of the total assets of most companies. Accounting for the acquisition and usage of such assets is, therefore, an important part of the financial reporting process.

**Required**

1. Distinguish between operating (revenue) and capital expenditures and explain why this distinction is important.
2. Briefly define depreciation as used in accounting.
3. Identify the factors that are relevant in determining the annual depreciation and explain whether these factors are determined objectively or whether they are based on judgment.

4. Explain why depreciation is usually shown in the net cash flow from operating activities section of the statement of cash flows. (*AICPA adapted*)

### C9-9    Researching GAAP    ⓪

The Magic Movie Company has been formed to produce films for showing in movie theaters. The president knows that there are some unusual accounting issues regarding asset valuation and income recognition and has asked for your advice.

**Required**

Research the related generally accepted accounting principles and prepare a short memo to the president. Cite your references and applicable paragraph numbers.

### C9-10   Asset Writedowns    ⓪

NBC paid $401 million for the rights to televise the 1992 Summer Olympic Games, and it was widely reported that it had a loss of over $60 million. CBS purchased the rights to the 1992 and 1994 Winter Olympic Games for a combined $543 million. CBS reported a $322 million pretax loss on its baseball and football contracts in 1991.

**Required**

Under what conditions, if any, should NBC and CBS have written-down the value of their assets?

### C9-11   Researching GAAP    ⓪

Scientific Software sells software to the oil industry. Its policy is to recognize revenue when it signs a licensing agreement for the software. It uses a 13-year amortization period for the software products it capitalizes. (Adapted from *The Wall Street Journal*, 11/6/90.) The president has asked you to evaluate these revenue recognition and amortization policies.

**Required**

Research the related generally accepted accounting principles and prepare a short memo to the president. Cite your references and applicable paragraph numbers.

## MULTIPLE CHOICE

*Select the best answer for each of the following.*

**M9-1**    A method that excludes residual value from the base for the depreciation calculation is

    a. Straight-line
    b. Sum-of-the-years'-digits
    c. Double-declining-balance
    d. Productive-output

Items 2 through 4 are based on the following information:
    Vorst Corporation's schedule of depreciable assets at December 31, 1995 was as follows:

| Asset | Cost | Accumulated Depreciation | Acquisition Date | Residual Value |
|---|---|---|---|---|
| A | $100,000 | $ 64,000 | 1994 | $20,000 |
| B | 55,000 | 36,000 | 1993 | 10,000 |
| C | 70,000 | 33,600 | 1993 | 14,000 |
|  | $225,000 | $133,600 |  | $44,000 |

Vorst takes a full year's depreciation expense in the year of an asset's acquisition, and no depreciation expense in the year of an asset's disposition. The estimated useful life of each depreciable asset is 5 years.

**M9-2**    Vorst depreciates asset A on the double-declining-balance method. How much depreciation expense should Vorst record in 1996 for asset A?

    a. $32,000
    b. $25,600
    c. $14,400
    d. $6,400

**M9-3**    Using the same depreciation method as used in 1993, 1994, and 1995, how much depreciation expense should Vorst record in 1996 for asset B?

    a. $6,000
    b. $9,000
    c. $11,000
    d. $12,000

M9-4    Vorst depreciates asset C by the straight-line method. On June 30, 1996, Vorst sold asset C for $28,000 cash. How much gain (loss) should Vorst record in 1996 on the disposal of asset C?

    a. $2,800                   c. ($5,600)

    b. ($2,800)               d. ($8,400)

M9-5    The composite depreciation method

    a. Is applied to a group of homogeneous assets

    b. Is an accelerated method of depreciation

    c. Does not recognize gain or loss on the retirement of single assets in the group

    d. Excludes residual value from the base of the depreciation calculation

M9-6    On July 1, 1994, Mundo Corporation purchased factory equipment for $50,000. Residual value was estimated at $2,000. The equipment will be depreciated over 10 years using the double-declining-balance method. Counting the year of acquisition as one-half year, Mundo should record 1995 depreciation expense of

    a. $7,680                   c. $9,600

    b. $9,000                 d. $10,000

M9-7    A fixed asset with a 5-year estimated useful life is sold during the second year. How would the use of the straight-line method of depreciation instead of the double-declining-balance method of depreciation affect the amount of gain or loss on the sale of the fixed asset?

|   | Gain | Loss |
|---|------|------|
| a. | No effect | No effect |
| b. | No effect | Increase |
| c. | Decrease | Increase |
| d. | Increase | Decrease |

M9-8    Crowder Company acquired a tract of land containing an extractable natural resource. Crowder is required by the purchase contract to restore the land to a condition suitable for recreational use after it has extracted the natural resource. Geological surveys estimate that the recoverable reserves will be 5,000,000 tons and that the land will have a value of $1,000,000 after restoration. Relevant cost information follows:

| Land | $9,000,000 |
|------|------------|
| Estimated restoration costs | 1,500,000 |

If Crowder maintains no inventories of extracted material, what should be the depletion expense per ton of extracted material?

    a. $2.10                   c. $1.80

    b. $1.90                 d. $1.60

M9-9    A machine with a 4-year estimated useful life and an estimated 15% residual value was acquired on January 1. Would depreciation expense using the sum-of-the-years'-digits method be higher or lower than depreciation expense using the double-declining-balance method in the first and second years?

|   | First year | Second year |
|---|-----------|-------------|
| a. | Higher | Higher |
| b. | Higher | Lower |
| c. | Lower | Higher |
| d. | Lower | Lower |

M9-10    At the end of the expected useful life of a depreciable asset with an estimated 15% residual value, the accumulated depreciation would equal the original cost of the asset under which of the following depreciation methods?

|   | Straight-line | Sum-of-the-years'-digits |
|---|---------------|--------------------------|
| a. | Yes | Yes |
| b. | No | No |
| c. | Yes | No |
| d. | No | Yes |

*(AICPA adapted)*

## EXERCISES

**E9-1** *Depreciation Methods*  The Gruman Company purchased a machine for $220,000 on January 2, 1995. The following estimates are made:

| | |
|---|---|
| Service life | 5 years or 10,000 hours |
| Production | 200,000 units |
| Residual value | $20,000 |

In 1995, the company uses the machine for 1,800 hours and produces 44,000 units.

**Required**

Compute the depreciation for 1995 under each of the following methods:

1. Straight-line
2. Hours worked
3. Units of output

**E9-2** *Depreciation Methods*  The Sorter Company purchased equipment for $100,000 on January 2, 1995. The equipment has an estimated service life of 8 years and an estimated residual value of $10,000.

**Required**

Compute the depreciation for 1995 under each of the following methods:

1. Straight-line
2. Sum-of-the-years'-digits
3. Double-declining-balance

**E9-3** *Acquisition Cost and Depreciation*  Reveille, Inc. purchased Machine #204 on April 1, 1995 and placed the machine into production on April 3, 1995. The following information is relevant to Machine #204:

| | |
|---|---|
| Price | $60,000 |
| Freight-in costs | 2,500 |
| Preparation and installation costs | 3,900 |
| Labor costs during regular production operation | 10,200 |
| Credit terms | 2/10, n/30 |
| Total productive output | 138,500 units |

It was expected that the machine could be used for 10 years, after which the salvage value would be zero. However, Reveille, Inc. intends to use the machine only 8 years, after which it expects to be able to sell it for $9,800. The invoice for Machine #204 was paid April 10, 1995. The number of units produced in 1995 and 1996 were 23,200 and 29,000, respectively. Reveille computes depreciation to the nearest whole month.

**Required**

Compute the depreciation for the years indicated using the following methods (round your answer to the nearest dollar):

1. 1995: Units of production.
2. 1996: Sum-of-the-years'-digits method. *(Contributed by Norma C. Powell)*

**E9-4**   *Depreciation Methods*   The Nickle Company purchased an asset for $17,000 on January 2, 1995. The asset has an expected residual value of $1,000. The depreciation expense for 1995 and 1996 is shown next for three alternative depreciation methods:

| Year | Method A | Method B | Method C |
|---|---|---|---|
| 1995 | $4,000 | $6,400 | $6,375 |
| 1996 | 4,000 | 4,800 | 3,984 |

**Required**
1. Which depreciation method is being used in each example?
2. Compute the depreciation expense for 1997 and 1998 under each method.

**E9-5**   *Depreciation and Rate of Return*   The Burrell Company purchased a machine for $20,000 on January 2, 1995. The machine has an estimated service life of 5 years and a zero estimated residual value. The asset earns income before depreciation and income taxes of $10,000 each year. The tax rate is 30%.

**Required**

Compute the rate of return earned (on the average net asset value) by the company each year of the asset's life under the straight-line and the double-declining-balance depreciation methods. Assume that the machine is the company's only asset.

**E9-6**   *Determination of Acquisition Cost*   On January 1, 1994, the Emming Corporation purchased some machinery. The machinery has an estimated life of 10 years and an estimated residual value of $5,000. The depreciation on this machinery was $24,000 in 1996.

**Required**

Compute the acquisition cost of the equipment under the following depreciation methods:

1. Straight-line
2. Sum-of-the-years'-digits
3. Double-declining-balance

**E9-7**   *Group Depreciation*   The Loban Company purchased four cars for $9,000 each. It was expected that they would be sold in 3 years for $1,500 each. Group depreciation on a straight-line basis is used.

**Required**
1. Prepare journal entries to record the acquisition and the first year's depreciation.
2. If one of the cars is sold at the beginning of the second year for $7,000, what journal entry is required?

**E9-8**   *Composite Depreciation*   The Wilcox Company acquires four machines that have the following characteristics:

| Machine | Cost | Estimated Residual Value | Estimated Service Life |
|---|---|---|---|
| A | $20,000 | $2,000 | 9 years |
| B | 25,000 | 1,000 | 6 |
| C | 30,000 | 5,000 | 5 |
| D | 28,000 | — | 7 |

**Required**
1. Prepare journal entries to record the acquisition and the first year's depreciation, assuming that the composite method is used on a straight-line basis.
2. If machine B is sold after 4 years for $5,000, what journal entry is required?
3. What arguments may be used to support the composite depreciation method?

**E9-9**   *Retirement and Replacement Methods*   The Rifkin Company replaced 100 tools at a cost of $30 each. The old tools originally cost $20 each and have no residual value.

**Required**

1. Prepare the journal entries to record the replacement under the retirement method.
2. Prepare the journal entries to record the replacement under the replacement method.

E9-10   *Depreciation*   On January 2, 1995, Lapar Corporation purchased a machine for $50,000. Lapar paid shipping expenses of $500, as well as installation costs of $1,200. The machine was estimated to have a useful life of 10 years and an estimated salvage value of $3,000. In January 1996, additions costing $3,600 were made to the machine in order to comply with pollution-control ordinances. These additions neither prolonged the life of the machine nor increased the salvage value.

**Required**

If Lapar records depreciation under the straight-line method, how much is depreciation expense for 1996? (*AICPA adapted*)

E9-11   *Partial Periods*   On May 10, 1995, the Horan Company purchased equipment for $20,000. The equipment has an estimated service life of 5 years and zero residual value. Assume that straight-line depreciation is used.

**Required**

Compute the depreciation for 1995 for each of the following four alternatives:

1. Depreciation is computed to the nearest day. (Use 12 months of 30 days each.)
2. Depreciation is computed to the nearest month. Assets purchased in the first half of the month are considered owned for the whole month.
3. Depreciation is computed to the nearest whole year. Assets purchased in the first half of the year are considered owned for the whole year.
4. One-half year's depreciation is taken on all asset's purchased during the year.

E9-12   *Depreciation for Financial Statements and Income Tax Purposes*   The Dinkle Company purchased equipment for $50,000. It has an estimated residual value of $2,000 and an expected useful life of 10 years. The company uses straight-line depreciation for its financial statements.

**Required**

What is the difference between the company's income before income taxes reported on its financial statements and the taxable income reported on its tax return in each of the first two years of the asset's life if the asset was purchased on January 2, 1995 and its tax life is 5 years?

E9-13   *Changes and Corrections of Depreciation*   The Bailand Company purchased a building for $110,000 that had an estimated residual value of $10,000 and an estimated service life of 10 years. The building was purchased 4 years ago, and straight-line depreciation has been used. At the beginning of the fifth year (before depreciation is recorded for the year), the following *independent* situations occur:

1. The company changes to the sum-of-the-years'-digits method.
2. It is estimated that the asset has 8 years' life remaining (for a total of 12 years).
3. It is discovered that the estimated residual value has been ignored in the computation of the depreciation.

**Required**

For each of the independent situations, prepare all the journal entries relating to the building for the fifth year. Ignore income taxes.

E9-14   *Change in Depreciation Method*   The Wing Company purchased a machine on January 1, 1992 for $240,000. At the date of acquisition, the machine had an estimated useful life of 10 years with an estimated salvage value of $20,000. The machine is being depreciated on a straight-line basis. On January 1, 1995, Wing appropriately adopted the sum-of-the-years'-digits method of depreciation for this machine.

**Required**

1. Prepare a schedule computing the book value of this machine, net of accumulated depreciation, that would be included in Wing's balance sheet at December 31, 1995. Show supporting computations in good form.
2. Prepare a schedule computing the cumulative effect on prior years of changing to a different depreciation method for the year ended December 31, 1995. Assume that the income tax rate was 50% in all years. Show supporting computations in good form. (*AICPA adapted*)

**E9-15**  *Depletion*  The Feller Company purchased a site for a limestone quarry for $100,000 on January 2, 1995. It is estimated that the quarry will yield 400,000 tons of limestone. Restoration costs are expected to be $20,000, after which the land could be sold for $10,000. In 1995, 80,000 tons were quarried and 60,000 tons sold. Costs of production (excluding depletion) are $5 per ton.

**Required**

1. Compute the depletion cost per ton.
2. Compute the total cost of the inventory at December 31, 1995.
3. Compute the total cost of goods sold for 1995.

**E9-16**  *Depletion*  The Lorton Company acquired land containing coal. Lorton will restore the land to a condition suitable for recreational use after it has extracted the coal. Geological surveys estimate that the recoverable reserves will be 4,000,000 tons and that the land will have a value of $1 million after restoration. Relevant cost information follows:

| | |
|---|---|
| Land | $12,000,000 |
| Estimated restoration costs | 1,200,000 |

**Required**

If Lorton maintains no inventories of coal, what is the depletion expense per ton of coal? (*AICPA adapted*)

## PROBLEMS

**P9-1**  *Depreciation Methods*  The Winsey Company purchased equipment on January 2, 1995 for $700,000. The equipment has the following characteristics:

| | |
|---|---|
| Estimated service life | 20 years |
| | 100,000 hours |
| | 950,000 units of output |
| Estimated residual value | $50,000 |

During 1995 and 1996, the company used the machine for 4,500 and 5,500 hours, respectively, and produced 40,000 and 60,000 units, respectively.

**Required**
Compute the depreciation for 1995 and 1996 under each of the following methods:

1. Straight-line
2. Hours worked
3. Units of output
4. Sum-of-the-years'-digits
5. Double-declining-balance
6. 150%-declining-balance

**P9-2**  *Depreciation Methods*  The Lord Company purchased a machine on January 2, 1995 for $70,000. The machine had an expected residual value of $10,000, an expected life of 8 years or 24,000 hours, and a capacity to produce 100,000 units. During 1995, the company produced 12,000 units in 2,500 hours. In 1996, the company produced 15,000 units in 3,000 hours.

**Required**
Prepare a schedule showing the depreciation for 1995 and 1996 and the book value of the asset at the end of 1995 and 1996 for each of the following methods:

1. Straight-line
2. Hours worked
3. Units of output

**P9-3** *Depreciation Methods*  The Sayers Company purchased a building for $200,000 on January 2, 1995. The building has an expected residual value of $20,000 at the end of its expected life of 20 years.

**Required**

Prepare a schedule showing the depreciation for 1995 and 1996 and the book value on December 31, 1995 and December 31, 1996 for each of the following methods:

1. Straight-line
2. Sum-of-the-years'-digits
3. Double-declining-balance
4. 150%-declining-balance

**P9-4** *Fixed Percentage of Declining Balance*  The Tubbs Company purchased a machine for $8,000 that has an estimated residual value of $1,000 and a life of 3 years.

**Required**

1. Compute the depreciation rate under the fixed-percentage-of-the-declining-balance method.
2. Compute the depreciation for each year of the asset's life.

**P9-5** *Changing Depreciation*  The Kam Company purchased a machine on January 2, 1995 for $20,000. The machine had an expected life of 8 years and a residual value of $300. The double-declining-balance method of depreciation is used.

**Required**

1. Compute the depreciation for each year of the asset's life.
2. Assuming that the company has a policy of always changing to the straight-line method at the midpoint of the asset's life, compute the depreciation for each year of the asset's life.
3. Assuming that the company always changes to the straight-line method at the beginning of the year when the annual straight-line amount exceeds the double-declining-balance amount, compute the depreciation for each year of the asset's life.

**P9-6** *Cost of Asset and Depreciation Methods*  The Heist Company purchased a machine on January 2, 1995 and uses the 150% declining-balance depreciation method. The machine has an expected life of 10 years and an expected residual value of $5,000. The following costs relate to the acquisition and use of the machine during the first year of its operations:

| | | | |
|---|---|---|---|
| Invoice price | $50,000 | Testing | $ 1,000 |
| Discounts available and taken | 1,000 | Normal spoilage of materials during the year | 750 |
| Freight | 1,250 | Abnormal spoilage of materials during the year | 250 |
| Installation | 1,150 | Wages of machine operator | 15,000 |

**Required**

Compute the depreciation expense for 1995 and 1996.

**P9-7** *Depreciation and Partial Periods*  The following assets are owned by the Dinnell Company:

| | Asset | | |
|---|---|---|---|
| | A | B | C |
| Year purchased | 1993 | 1994 | 1995 |
| Cost | $20,000 | $40,000 | $100,000 |
| Expected life | 5 years | 8 years | 10 years |
| Residual value | $2,000 | — | $10,000 |
| Depreciation method | Straight-line | Sum-of-the-years'-digits | Double-declining-balance |

In the year of acquisition and retirement of an asset, depreciation for one-half year is recorded. During 1996, asset A was sold for $7,000.

**Required**

Prepare the journal entries to record depreciation on each asset for 1993 through 1996 and the sale of asset A.

**P9-8**   *Group and Composite Depreciation*   The Cheadle Company purchased a fleet of 20 delivery trucks for $8,000 each on January 2, 1995. It was decided to use composite depreciation on a straight-line basis, and the depreciation was calculated from the following schedule:

| Year | Number of Trucks to Be Retired at Year-End | Estimated Residual Value per Truck |
|------|------|------|
| 1996 | 2 | $4,000 |
| 1997 | 6 | 4,000 |
| 1998 | 8 | 2,000 |
| 1999 | 4 | — |

The trucks were actually retired according to the following schedule (assume each truck was retired at the beginning of the year):

| Year | Number of Trucks Retired | Total Proceeds from Retirements |
|------|------|------|
| 1996 | 1 | $ 4,000 |
| 1997 | 3 | 11,000 |
| 1998 | 6 | 19,000 |
| 1999 | 5 | 6,000 |
| 2000 | 3 | 4,000 |
| 2001 | 2 | 1,000 |

**Required**

1. Prepare the journal entries necessary to record the preceding events.
2. Assume that all the trucks were expected to last 4 years and be retired for $1,600 each. Using group depreciation, prepare journal entries for all 6 years, assuming the trucks were retired as shown by the latter schedule.

**P9-9**   *Composite Depreciation*   The Borrell Company purchased four delivery trucks on January 2, 1995 for $20,000 each. Two of the trucks were expected to last 5 years and have a residual value of $2,500 each. The other two trucks had an expected life of 8 years and no residual value. Straight-line depreciation is used on a composite basis.

**Required**
Prepare journal entries to record the following events:

1. January 1, 1997. One of the two trucks expected to last 5 years is destroyed in an accident. The truck was not insured and the scrap value is $400.
2. January 5, 1997. A new truck is acquired for $24,000. It has an expected life of 4 years and a residual value of $4,240.
3. Depreciation expense for 1997.

**P9-10**   *Depreciation for Financial Statements and Income Tax Purposes*   The Hunter Company purchased a light truck on January 2, 1995 for $18,000. The truck, which will be used for deliveries, has the following characteristics:

Estimated life: 5 years
Estimated residual value: $3,000
Depreciation for financial statements: straight-line
Depreciation for income tax purposes: MACRS (3-year-life)

From 1995 through 1999, each year, the company had sales of $100,000, cost of goods sold of $60,000, and operating expenses (excluding depreciation) of $15,000. The truck was disposed of on December 31, 1999 for $2,000.

**Required**

1.  Prepare an income statement for financial reporting through pretax accounting income for each of the 5 years, 1995 through 1999.
2.  Prepare, instead, an income statement for income tax purposes through taxable income for each of the 5 years, 1995 through 1999.
3.  Compare the total income for all 5 years under Requirement 1 and Requirement 2.

**P9-11**  *Depletion*  On January 2, 1995, the Whistler Company purchased land for $450,000, from which it is estimated that 400,000 tons of ore could be extracted. It is estimated that it will cost $80,000 to restore the land, after which it could be sold for $30,000.

During 1995, the company mined 80,000 tons and sold 50,000 tons. During 1996, the company mined 100,000 tons and sold 120,000 tons. At the beginning of 1997, the company spent an additional $100,000, which increased the reserves by 60,000 tons. In 1997, the company mined 140,000 tons and sold 130,000 tons. The company uses a FIFO cost flow assumption.

**Required**

1.  Calculate the depletion included in the income statement and ending inventory for 1995, 1996, and 1997.
2.  Prepare the natural resources section of the balance sheet on December 31, 1995, 1996, and 1997, assuming that an accumulated depletion account is used.

**P9-12**  *Depletion*  On July 1, 1995, the Amplex Company purchased a coal mine for $2 million. The estimated capacity of the mine was 700,000 tons. During 1995, the company mines 10,000 tons of coal per month and sells 9,000 tons per month. The selling price is $30 per ton and production costs (excluding depletion and depreciation) are $8 per ton. At the end of the mine's life, it is expected that it will cost $200,000 to restore the land, after which it can be sold for $100,000. The company also purchased some temporary housing for the miners at a cost of $150,000. The housing has an expected life of 10 years but is expected to be sold for $10,000 at the end of the mine's life. The company uses the FIFO cost flow assumption.

**Required**

1.  Compute the company's expenses included on the 1995 income statement.
2.  Compute the cost of the company's inventory at December 31, 1995.
3.  In January 1996, a new estimate indicated that the capacity of the mine was only 500,000 tons at that time. Compute the company's expenses included on the 1996 income statement if the company mines and sells 10,000 tons per month.

**P9-13**  *Changes and Corrections of Depreciation*  During 1995, the controller of the Ryel Company asked you to prepare correcting journal entries for the following three situations:

1.  Machine A was purchased for $30,000 on January 1, 1993. It had an estimated residual value of $5,000 and an estimated service life of 10 years. It has been depreciated under the double-declining-balance method for 2 years. Now, at the beginning of the third year, Ryel has decided to change to the straight-line method.
2.  Machine B was purchased for $50,000 on January 1, 1990. Straight-line depreciation has been recorded for 5 years, and the Accumulated Depreciation account has a balance of $25,000. The estimated residual value remains at $5,000, but the service life is now estimated to be 2 years longer than estimated originally.
3.  Machine C was purchased for $20,000 on January 1, 1994. Double-declining-balance depreciation has been recorded for 1 year. The estimated residual value of the machine is $2,000 and the estimated service life is 5 years. The computation of the depreciation erroneously included the estimated residual value.

**Required**

Prepare any necessary correcting journal entries for each situation. Also prepare the journal entry necessary for each situation to record the depreciation for 1995. (Assume that the debit is to Depreciation Expense.)

**P9-14**  *Adjusting Entries*  You are engaged in the examination of the financial statements of the Madle Corporation for the year ended December 31, 1995. The schedules for the property, plant, and equipment and the related accumulated depreciation accounts which follow have been prepared by the client. You have checked the opening balances to your prior year's audit workpapers. Your examination reveals the following information:

1.  All equipment is depreciated on the straight-line basis (no salvage value taken into consideration) using the following estimated lives: buildings 25 years, all other items 10 years. The company's policy is to take one-half year's depreciation on all asset acquisitions and disposals during the year.

2. The company completed the construction of a wing on the plant building on June 30. The useful life of the building was not extended by this addition. The lowest construction bid received was $17,500, the amount recorded in the Buildings account. Company personnel were used to construct the addition at a cost of $16,000 (materials $7,500, labor $5,500, and overhead $3,000).
3. On August 18, $5,000 was paid for paving and fencing a portion of land owned by the company and used as a parking lot for employees. The expenditure was capitalized to the Land account.
4. The amount shown in the Machinery and Equipment asset retirement column represents cash received on September 4 upon disposal of a machine purchased 4 years ago in July for $48,000. The bookkeeper recorded depreciation expense of $3,500 on this machine in 1995.
5. Sydney City donated land and building appraised at $10,000 and $40,000, respectively, to the Madle Corporation for a plant. On September 1, the company began operating the plant. Because no costs were involved, the bookkeeper made no entry to record the transaction.

**MADLE CORP.**
**Analysis of Property, Plant, and Equipment, and of**
**Related Accumulated Depreciation Accounts**
**Year Ended December 31, 1995**

| Description | Final 12/31/94 | Additions | Retirements | Per Books 12/31/95 |
|---|---|---|---|---|
| Assets: | | | | |
| Land | $ 22,500 | $ 5,000 | — | $ 27,500 |
| Buildings | 120,000 | 17,500 | — | 137,500 |
| Machinery and Equipment | 385,000 | 40,400 | $26,000 | 399,400 |
| | $527,500 | $62,900 | $26,000 | $564,400 |
| | | | | |
| Accumulated Depreciation: | | | | |
| Buildings | $ 60,000 | $ 5,150* | | $ 65,150 |
| Machinery and Equipment | 173,250 | 39,220* | | 212,470 |
| | $233,250 | $44,370 | | $277,620 |

*Depreciation expenses for the year.

**Required**
Prepare the formal journal entries that you would suggest at December 31, 1995 to adjust the accounts for the transactions noted previously. Disregard income tax implications. The books have not been closed. Computations should be rounded off to the nearest dollar. (*AICPA adapted*)

P9-15    *Comprehensive*    On December 31, 1995, the Vail Company owned the following assets:

| Asset | Date of Purchase | Cost | Accumulated Depreciation | Life in Years | Residual Value |
|---|---|---|---|---|---|
| Building | 1/1/1993 | $100,000 | $ 7,500[a] | 40 | $ 0 |
| Office machinery | 1/1/1993 | 20,000 | 9,760[b] | 10 | 2,000 |
| Office fixtures | 1/1/1993 | 30,000 | 20,000[c] | 5 | 5,000 |

a. Straight-line depreciation.
b. Double-declining-balance depreciation.
c. Sum-of-the-years'-digits depreciation.

The company computes depreciation and amortization expense to the nearest whole year. During 1996, the company engaged in the following transactions:

Jan. 2    Extended the building at a cost of $30,000. The extension provided an addition to the service potential of the building.

| | |
|---|---|
| Mar. 6 | Sold a piece of office machinery that had originally cost $4,000 and that had accumulated depreciation of $1,952 on December 31, 1995. The machine was sold for $3,000. |
| Apr. 28 | Obtained a patent on an invention by paying $7,000. It was expected that the patent would provide protection against competition for 10 years. |
| May 15 | Purchased office fixtures and office machinery for $9,200. The supplier reduced the price because of the joint purchase. If purchased separately, the office fixtures would have cost $6,000 and the office machinery $4,000. Delivery costs paid by Vail were $200. The machinery was accidentally damaged during installation and cost $230 to repair. The office fixtures have an estimated life of 5 years and a residual value of $250. The office machinery has an estimated life of 10 years and a residual value of $500. |
| Aug. 10 | Exchanged the president's desk (classified as office fixtures) for another desk. The desk had cost $600 and had accumulated depreciation on December 31, 1995 of $400 and an estimated residual value of $100. The new desk had a list price of $900 and $700 cash was paid. |
| Oct. 20 | Serviced and adjusted the office machinery at a cost of $125. |

**Required**

1. Check the accuracy of the accumulated depreciation balances at December 31, 1995. (Round to the nearest whole dollar in all requirements.)
2. Prepare journal entries to record the preceding events in 1996, as well as the year-end recording of depreciation expense.
3. Prepare an accumulated depreciation account for each category of assets, enter the beginning balance, post the journal entries from Requirement 2, and compute the ending balance.

P9-16    *Comprehensive*    On January 2, 1995, Brock Corporation purchased a tract of land (site number 101) with a building for $600,000. Additionally, Brock paid a real estate broker's commission of $36,000, legal fees of $6,000, and title guarantee insurance of $18,000. The closing statement indicated that the land value was $500,000 and the building value was $100,000. Shortly after acquisition, the building was razed at a cost of $75,000.

Brock entered into a $3,000,000 fixed-price contract with Barnett Builders, Inc. on March 2, 1995 for the construction of an office building on land site number 101. The building was completed and occupied on September 30, 1996. Additional construction costs were incurred as follows:

| | |
|---|---|
| Plans, specifications, and blueprints | $12,000 |
| Architects' fees for design and supervision | 95,000 |

The building is estimated to have a 40-year life from date of completion and will be depreciated using the 150%-declining-balance method.

To finance the construction cost, Brock borrowed $3,000,000 on March 2, 1995. The loan is payable in 10 annual installments of $300,000 plus interest at the rate of 14%. Brock's average amounts of accumulated building construction expenditures were as follows:

| | |
|---|---|
| For the period March 2 to December 31, 1995 | $ 900,000 |
| For the period January 1 to September 30, 1996 | 2,300,000 |

**Required**

1. Prepare a schedule that discloses the individual costs making up the balance in the land account with respect to land site number 101 as of September 30, 1996.
2. Prepare a schedule that discloses the individual costs that should be capitalized in the office building account as of September 30, 1996. Show supporting computations in good form.
3. Prepare a schedule showing the depreciation expense computation of the office building for the year ended December 31, 1996. (*AICPA adapted*)

**P9-17**  *Comprehensive*  Logan Corporation, a manufacturer of steel products, began operations on October 1, 1994. The accounting department of Logan has started the fixed asset and depreciation schedule shown below:

| Assets | Acquisition Date | Cost | Salvage | Depreciation Method | Estimated Life in Years | Depreciation Expense Year Ended September 30 1995 | 1996 |
|---|---|---|---|---|---|---|---|
| Land A | October 1, 1994 | (1) ___ | N/A* | N/A | N/A | N/A | N/A |
| Building A | October 1, 1994 | (2) ___ | $47,500 | Straight line | (3) ___ | $14,000 | (4) ___ |
| Land B | October 3, 1994 | (5) ___ | N/A | N/A | N/A | N/A | N/A |
| Building B | Under construction | $210,000 to date | — | Straight line | 30 | — | (6) ___ |
| Donated equipment | October 3, 1994 | (7) ___ | 2,000 | 150% declining balance | 10 | (8) ___ | (9) ___ |
| Machinery A | October 3, 1994 | (10) ___ | 5,500 | Sum of the years' digits | 10 | (11) ___ | (12) ___ |
| Machinery B | October 2, 1995 | (13) ___ | — | Straight line | 15 | — | (14) ___ |

\* "N/A" means "not applicable."

You have been asked to assist in completing this schedule. In addition to ascertaining that the data already on the schedule are correct, you have obtained the following information from the company's records and personnel:

1. Depreciation is computed from the first of the month of acquisition to the first of the month of disposition.
2. Land A and building A were acquired from a predecessor corporation. Logan paid $812,500 for the land and building together. At the time of acquisition, the land had an appraised value of $72,000 and the building had an appraised value of $828,000.
3. Land B was acquired on October 3, 1994 in exchange for 3,000 newly issued shares of Logan's common stock. At the date of acquisition, the stock had a par value of $5 per share and a fair value of $25 per share. During October 1994, Logan paid $10,400 to demolish an existing building on this land so that it could construct a new building.
4. Construction of building B on the newly acquired land began on October 2, 1995. By September 30, 1996 Logan had paid $210,000 of the estimated total construction costs of $300,000. Estimated completion and occupancy are July 1997.
5. Certain equipment was donated to the corporation by a local university. An independent appraisal of the equipment when donated placed the fair value at $16,000 and the salvage at $2,000.
6. Machinery A's total cost of $110,000 includes installation expense of $550 and normal repairs and maintenance of $11,000. Salvage value is estimated at $5,500. Machinery A was sold on February 1, 1996.
7. On October 2, 1995, machinery B was acquired with a down payment of $4,000 and the remaining payments to be made in ten annual installments of $4,000 each beginning October 2, 1996. The prevailing interest rate was 10%. The data that follow were abstracted from present value tables:

| Present Value of $1.00 at 10% | | Present Value of Annuity of $1.00 in Arrears at 10% | |
|---|---|---|---|
| 10 years | 0.386 | 10 years | 6.145 |
| 11 years | 0.350 | 11 years | 6.495 |
| 15 years | 0.239 | 15 years | 7.606 |

**Required**

For each numbered item in the schedule, supply the correct amount next to the corresponding number. Round each answer to the nearest dollar. Show supporting computations in good form. (*AICPA adapted*)

**P9-18**  *Errors*  A depreciation schedule for trucks of the Jarrett Company was requested by the auditor soon after December 31, 1995, showing the additions, retirements, depreciation, and other data affecting the income of the company in the 4-year period 1992 to 1995, inclusive. The following data were in the truck account as of January 1, 1992:

| | |
|---|---|
| Truck no. 1 purchased January 1, 1989 | $12,000 |
| Truck no. 2 purchased July 1, 1989 | 10,400 |
| Truck no. 3 purchased January 1, 1991 | 12,800 |
| Truck no. 4 purchased July 1, 1991 | 15,000 |
| Balance January 1, 1992 | $50,200 |

The Accumulated Depreciation—Trucks account, previously adjusted to January 1, 1992 and duly entered in the ledger, had a balance on that date of $16,460. This amount represented the straight-line depreciation on the four trucks from the respective dates of purchase, based on a 5-year life and no residual value. No debits had been made to this account prior to January 1, 1992.

Transactions between January 1, 1992 and December 31, 1995 and their record in the ledger were as follows:

1. July 1, 1992: Truck no. 1 was sold for $2,000 cash. The entry was a debit to Cash and a credit to Trucks, $2,000.
2. January 1, 1993: Truck no. 3 was traded for a larger one (no. 5) with a 5-year life. The agreed purchase price was $12,000. The Jarrett Company paid the automobile dealer $1,780 cash on the transaction. The entry was a debit to Trucks, $1,780, and a credit to Cash, $1,780.
3. July 1, 1994: Truck no. 4 was damaged in a wreck to such an extent that it was sold as junk for $50 cash. Jarrett Company received $950 from the insurance company. The entry made by the bookkeeper was a debit to Cash, $1,000, and credits to Miscellaneous Revenue, $50, and Trucks, $950.
4. July 1, 1994: A new truck (no. 6) was acquired for $12,500 cash and debited at that amount to the Trucks account. The truck has a 5-year life.

Entries for depreciation had been made at the close of each year as follows: 1992, $8,840; 1993, $5,436; 1994, $4,146; 1995, $2,856.

**Required**

1. For each of the 4 years, calculate separately the increase or decrease in earnings arising from the company's errors in determining or entering depreciation or in recording transactions affecting trucks.
2. Prove your work by one compound journal entry as of December 31, 1995; the adjustment of the Trucks account is to reflect the correct balances, assuming that the books have not been closed for 1995.

P9-19 *Comprehensive* Information pertaining to Blake Corporation's property, plant, and equipment for 1995 is presented next:

### Account Balances at January 1, 1995

| | Debit | Credit |
|---|---|---|
| Land | $ 150,000 | |
| Building | 1,200,000 | |
| Accumulated depreciation | | $263,100 |
| Machinery and equipment | 900,000 | |
| Accumulated depreciation | | 250,000 |
| Automotive equipment | 115,000 | |
| Accumulated depreciation | | 84,600 |

### Depreciation Method and Useful Life

Building: 150%-declining-balance; 25 years.
Machinery and equipment: Straight-line; 10 years.
Automotive equipment: Sum-of-the-years'-digits; 4 years.
Leasehold improvements: Straight-line.
The residual value of the depreciable assets is immaterial.
Depreciation is computed to the nearest month.

Transactions during 1995 and other information were as follows:

1. On January 2, 1995, Blake purchased a new car for $10,000 cash and a trade-in of a 2-year-old car with a cost of $9,000 and a book value of $2,700. The new car has a cash price of $12,000; the market value of the trade-in is not known.
2. On April 1, 1995, a machine purchased for $23,000 on April 1, 1990 was destroyed by fire. Blake recovered $15,500 from its insurance company.

3. On May 1, 1995, costs of $168,000 were incurred to improve leased office premises. The leasehold improvements have a useful life of 8 years. The related lease, which terminates on December 31, 2001 is renewable for an additional 6-year term. The decision to renew will be made in 2001 based on office space needs at that time.
4. On July 1, 1995, machinery and equipment were purchased at a total invoice cost of $280,000; additional costs of $5,000 for freight and $25,000 for installation were incurred.
5. Blake determined that the automotive equipment comprising the $115,000 balance at January 1, 1995 would have been depreciated at a total amount of $18,000 for the year ended December 31, 1995.

**Required**

1. For each asset classification, prepare schedules showing depreciation and amortization expense, and accumulated depreciation and amortization that would appear on Blake's income statement for the year ended December 31, 1995 and balance sheet at December 31, 1995, respectively.
2. Prepare a schedule showing the gain or loss from disposal of assets that would appear in Blake's income statement for the year ended December 31, 1995.
3. Prepare the property, plant, and equipment section of Blake's December 31, 1995 balance sheet. (*AICPA adapted*)

P9-20    *Comprehensive*    The plant asset and accumulated depreciation accounts of Pell Corporation had the following balances at December 31, 1994:

|  | Plant Asset | Accumulated Depreciation |
|---|---|---|
| Land | $ 350,000 | $ — |
| Land improvements | 180,000 | 45,000 |
| Building | 1,500,000 | 350,000 |
| Machinery and equipment | 1,158,000 | 405,000 |
| Automobiles | 150,000 | 112,000 |

Depreciation method and useful lives:

- Land improvements: Straight-line; 15 years.
- Building: 150% declining balance; 20 years.
- Machinery and equipment: Straight-line; 10 years.
- Automobiles: 150% declining balance; 3 years.
- Depreciation is computed to the nearest month. No salvage values are recognized.

Transactions during 1995:

1. On January 2, 1995, machinery and equipment were purchased at a total invoice cost of $260,000, which included a $5,500 charge for freight. Installation costs of $27,000 were incurred.
2. On March 31, 1995, a machine purchased for $58,000 on January 2, 1991 was sold for $36,500.
3. On May 1, 1995, expenditures of $50,000 were made to repave parking lots at Pell's plant location. The work was necessitated by damage caused by severe winter weather.
4. On November 2, 1995, Pell acquired a tract of land with an existing building in exchange for 10,000 shares of Pell's $20 par common stock, that had a market price of $38 a share on this date. Pell paid legal fees and title insurance totaling $23,000. The last property tax bill indicated assessed values of $240,000 for land and $60,000 for building. Shortly after acquisition, the building was razed at a cost of $35,000 in anticipation of new building construction in 1996.
5. On December 31, 1995, Pell purchased a new automobile for $15,250 cash and trade-in of an automobile purchased for $18,000 on January 1, 1994. The new automobile has a cash value of $19,000.

**Required**

1. Prepare a schedule analyzing the changes in each of the plant assets during 1995, with detailed supporting computations. Disregard the related accumulated depreciation accounts.
2. For each asset classification, prepare a schedule showing depreciation expense for the year ended December 31, 1995.
3. Prepare a schedule showing the gain or loss from each asset disposal that would be recognized in Pell's income statement for the year ended December 31, 1995. (*AICPA adapted*)

P9-21   *Comprehensive*   The Lurch Company's December 31, 1994 balance sheet follows:

### Assets

| | | |
|---|---|---|
| Cash | | $ 540,000 |
| Inventory | | 450,000 |
| Prepaid rent | | 60,000 |
| Machine | $500,000 | |
| Less: Accumulated depreciation | (135,000) | 365,000 |
| | | $1,415,000 |

### Liabilities and Equities

| | |
|---|---|
| Accounts payable | $ 400,000 |
| Common stock, $10 par | 300,000 |
| Additional paid-in capital | 515,000 |
| Retained earnings | 200,000 |
| | $1,415,000 |

During 1995, the following transactions occurred:

1. To avoid paying monthly rent of $5,000 on existing plant facilities, the company decided to buy a tract of land and construct a building of its own on it. On January 2, 1995, Lurch exchanged 7,000 shares of its common stock to acquire the land; the stock was selling for $25 per share. Construction of the building also began on January 2, 1995. At the time, Lurch borrowed funds by issuing a one-year, $500,000 note at 12% to help finance the project. The principal and interest on the note is due January 2, 1996. Construction costs (paid in cash) that occurred evenly throughout the year totaled $700,000. The building was completed on December 30, 1995 and the move-in to the new building was to occur during the next week.
2. On January 2, 1995, Lurch exchanged its one existing machine plus $60,000 for a new and improved, similar machine with a fair-market value of $430,000. The new machine is to be depreciated using straight-line depreciation based on an economic life of 5 years and a residual value of $55,000.
3. Lurch uses a FIFO perpetual inventory system. Lurch sold $350,000 of its inventory for $800,000 cash, paid for its beginning accounts payable, and purchased $480,000 of inventory on account during the year.
4. On July 31, 1995, Lurch declared and paid a $2.50 per share cash dividend to its shareholders.
5. Lurch is subject to a 30% income tax rate, and income taxes are accrued at year-end.

### Required

Prepare Lurch's income statement and statement of retained earnings for the fiscal year ended December 31, 1995 and a balance sheet as of December 31, 1995. Show all supporting journal entries and computations made during 1995. (*Contributed by Scott I. Jerris*)

# 10

# INTANGIBLES

## Chapter Topics

*The Nature of and
Accounting for Intangibles*

*Research and Development
Costs*

*Identifiable Intangible Assets,
Including Patents,
Copyrights, Trademarks
and Tradenames, Franchises,
Organization Costs,
Computer Software Costs,
and Leasehold Improvements*

*Unidentifiable Intangible
Assets (Goodwill)*

*Estimating the Value of
Goodwill (Appendix)*

As discussed in Chapter 8, tangible noncurrent assets are characterized by a physical substance that can be seen and touched. In
contrast, *intangible assets which generally result from legal
or contractual rights do not have a physical substance.* Intangible and tangible noncurrent assets do have characteristics in
common, since both are (1) held for use and not for investment
(although they are "used" in very different ways), (2) have an expected life of more than one year, (3) derive their value from their
ability to generate revenue for their owners, and (4) are expensed
in the periods in which their benefits are received.

Intangible assets have four additional characteristics that distinguish them from tangible assets:

1.  There is generally a higher degree of uncertainty regarding the
    future benefits that can be expected to be derived.

2.  Their value is subject to wider fluctuations because it may de-
    pend to a considerable extent on competitive conditions.

3.  They may have value only to a particular company.

4.  They may have indeterminate (but not necessarily indefinite)
    lives.

Accounting terminology includes only noncurrent assets in intangible assets, whereas legal terminology includes as intangibles
all assets without physical substance and therefore includes such
current assets as accounts and notes receivable, and investments
in securities. Accounting practice restricts the use of the term *intangible* to such items as patents, licenses, copyrights, trademarks
and tradenames, franchises, organization costs, computer software costs, and goodwill. Each of these items is discussed later in
the chapter.

## ACCOUNTING FOR INTANGIBLE ASSETS

The accounting for intangible assets follows the same general principles as those used for tangible assets. They are both disclosed on the balance sheet at the **book value,** which is the cost less the accumulated amortization. The accumulated amortization results from a periodic allocation of the cost as an expense on the income statement. As discussed in Chapter 9, amortization follows the same principle as depreciation but is the term used for intangible assets. The specific issues related to the measurement of the expense on the income statement and the book value of the asset on the balance sheet are discussed in the following sections. The other accounting principles that have been discussed in the previous two chapters also apply to intangible assets. Thus the principles used for the determination of acquisition cost, capital and operating expenditures, disposal, etc., apply to both tangible and intangible assets.

### Cost of Intangibles

Intangibles may be classified according to whether they are *purchased* from others (externally acquired) or *internally developed*. In addition they may be classified according to whether they are *identifiable* or *unidentifiable*. **APB Opinion No. 17** makes a distinction between identifiable and unidentifiable intangibles.[1] Although these two terms are not clearly defined by the *Opinion*, **identifiable intangible assets** include such items as patents, franchises, and trademarks, whereas the primary **unidentifiable intangible asset** is goodwill. The *Opinion* does specify that an unidentifiable asset cannot be acquired in isolation and cannot be separated from the other assets. These classifications lead to the four alternatives shown in Exhibit 10-1 and the proper method of accounting for each.

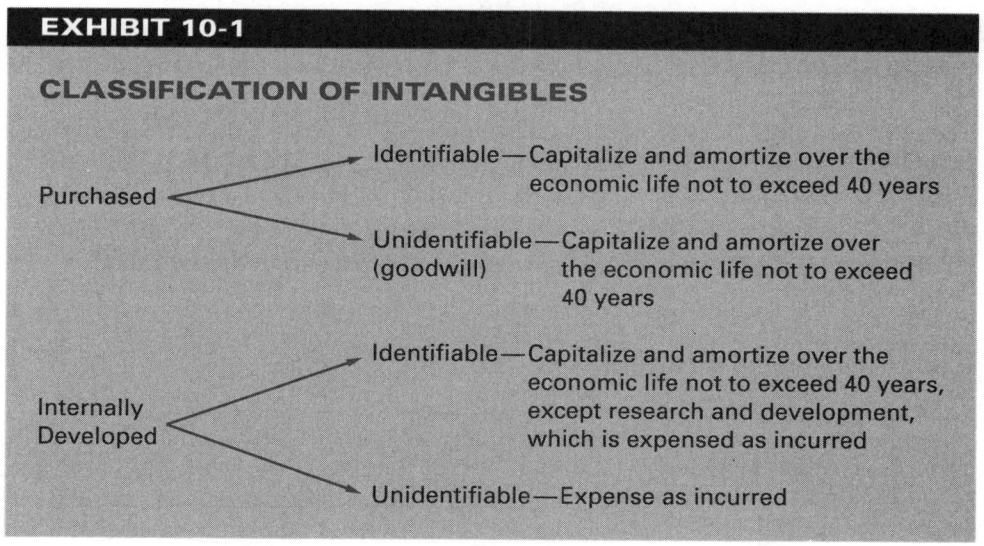

**EXHIBIT 10-1**

**CLASSIFICATION OF INTANGIBLES**

Purchased
- Identifiable—Capitalize and amortize over the economic life not to exceed 40 years
- Unidentifiable (goodwill)—Capitalize and amortize over the economic life not to exceed 40 years

Internally Developed
- Identifiable—Capitalize and amortize over the economic life not to exceed 40 years, except research and development, which is expensed as incurred
- Unidentifiable—Expense as incurred

---

1. "Accounting for Intangible Assets," *APB Opinion No. 17* (New York: AICPA, 1970).

Accounting for the cost of intangibles is discussed in *APB Opinion No. 17* as follows:

1. *Purchased Identifiable Intangibles.* A company may purchase an intangible asset, such as a patent, from another company. The initial accounting for the acquisition of a purchased intangible presents no special issues and is handled in the same manner as a purchased tangible asset as discussed in Chapter 8 for the acquisition of a single asset, in a group of assets, or in an exchange of similar or dissimilar assets.

2. *Purchased Unidentifiable Intangibles.* The cost of a purchased unidentifiable intangible asset is capitalized. The principal example of an unidentifiable intangible is goodwill, which can be acquired only through the purchase of another company or segment of a company. The nature of and accounting for goodwill are discussed in more detail later in this chapter.

3. *Internally Developed Identifiable Intangibles.* When a company internally develops an intangible asset, such as a patent, only certain costs can be capitalized. The costs of a patent include the legal and related costs of establishing the *rights* associated with a patent but *not* the costs of developing the product or process that is being patented. Those latter costs are included in research and development costs and are required to be expensed as incurred according to FASB Statement No. 2. Thus the expensing of research and development costs represents an *exception* to the general rule of capitalization of internally developed identifiable intangibles. (This topic is discussed later in the chapter.)

4. *Internally Developed Unidentifiable Intangibles.* The costs of internally developed unidentifiable intangibles, such as employee training and design of quality products, are expensed as incurred even though they may be expected to have benefits extending beyond the current period. This procedure is justified because either the measurement of the costs incurred or the determination of the expected life of the benefits is difficult to measure reliably. These measurement problems are discussed more fully in the section on research and development costs in this chapter.

## Amortization of Intangibles

Prior to the issuance of *APB Opinion No. 17*, the cost of some intangible assets was amortized *only* when there was evidence of a decline in value or limited economic life. However, *APB Opinion No. 17* disallowed this practice and stated that

> The value of intangible assets at any one date eventually disappears and...the recorded costs of intangible assets should be amortized by systematic charges to income over the periods estimated to be benefited.[2]

Unfortunately, the APB did not change the previous rule; therefore intangibles acquired before November 1, 1970 (the effective date of *APB Opinion No. 17*), which were not considered to have a decline in value or limited economic life, still need not be amortized. Therefore, current practice requires that intangible assets acquired on or after November 1, 1970 must be amortized, whereas intangible assets acquired

---

2. *Ibid.*, par. 27.

before November 1, 1970 are amortized only if there is evidence of a decline in value or limited economic life.

Factors that should be considered in estimating the useful lives of intangible assets include:

1. Legal, regulatory, or contractual provisions that place a limit on the maximum economic life.

2. Provisions for renewal or extension of rights or privileges covered by specific intangible assets.

3. Effects of obsolescence, customer demand, competition, rate of technological change, and other economic factors.

4. Possibility that the economic lives of intangibles may be related to life expectancies of certain groups of employees.

5. Expected actions of competitors, regulatory bodies, and others.

6. An apparently unlimited economic life may in fact be only indefinite and benefits cannot be reasonably projected.

7. An intangible asset may be a composite of many individual factors with varying estimated economic lives.[3]

The estimation of the economic life of an intangible asset should be made after considering all relevant factors, but in no case may it exceed *40 years*.[4] Obviously the 40-year limitation is arbitrary, but it is required to prevent management from setting unrealistically long lives for intangibles and thereby reducing amortization expense and increasing income. This limitation is particularly appropriate given the rapid rate of change in modern society, because in such circumstances it is unlikely that many intangibles would have a life of more than 40 years or that a life of more than 40 years could be reliably predicted. For example, it is unlikely that a copyright for a book will have a significant value for more than a few years. However, it may be argued that some intangibles, such as licenses to operate radio and television stations, do not decline in value through the passage of time. This argument suggests that the requirement that all intangibles be amortized is incorrect, rather than the 40-year limitation being inappropriate. Nonetheless, current generally accepted accounting principles require that **an intangible asset (acquired on or after November 1, 1970) must be amortized over its economic life, but not to exceed 40 years.** The rule is an attempt to reduce the diversity of accounting practices, though occasionally it does appear inconsistent with economic reality.

The calculation of the amortization for intangibles follows the same principles as the depreciation of tangible assets, except that **the straight-line method is required unless there is convincing evidence that an alternative method provides a better matching of expenses against revenues.**[5] The straight-line method is used because the expiration of the benefits provided by an intangible usually is caused by the passage of time and a particular pattern of benefits or relationship to units of a product difficult to estimate *reliably*. As for tangible assets, the amortization (debit entry) may be

3. *Ibid.*
4. *Ibid.*, par. 29.
5. *Ibid.*, par. 30.

either a production cost and included in Goods in Process through fixed overhead (such as a patent on a manufacturing process) or an operating expense (such as a trademark). The credit entry may be made either to a contra account, Accumulated Amortization: Intangibles, or directly to the asset account. This latter alternative is used frequently because disclosure of the accumulated amortization on intangible assets is not required by generally accepted accounting principles, although it may be included in the notes to the financial statements. In contrast, disclosure of accumulated depreciation on tangible assets is required.

For example, suppose that a patent was purchased for $85,000 and was to be amortized over 10 years (the estimated economic life) with no expected residual value. The journal entries to record the acquisition and the amortization for the first year are as follows:

| | | |
|---|---|---|
| Patent | 85,000 | |
|   Cash | | 85,000 |
| | | |
| Amortization Expense (or Factory Overhead) | 8,500 | |
|   Patent (or Accumulated Amortization: Patent) | | 8,500 |

*APB Opinion No. 17* requires that a company periodically evaluate the estimated economic life to determine whether a revised estimate is warranted.[6] Such a change in estimate is accounted for by using the method discussed in Chapter 9—that is, by computing a new periodic amortization amount based on the current book value and the new estimated remaining economic life.

If there is evidence that the market value of an intangible asset has decreased below its book value, the asset should be written down to its market value. For example, years ago motor carriers recorded the cost of acquiring interstate operating rights as an intangible asset. One of the effects of the Motor Carriers Act of 1980 was to allow easier entry into the motor carrier industry by removing most restrictions, thereby eliminating any value associated with interstate operating rights. Therefore, the unamortized cost of this intangible asset had to be written off and an extraordinary loss recognized.[7]

The remaining sections of this chapter discuss specific intangibles, starting with research and development costs. Although research and development costs are not capitalized, they are discussed first because of the impact they have on the capitalization of many other intangibles. Identifiable intangible assets and goodwill are discussed in the remaining two sections.

## RESEARCH AND DEVELOPMENT COSTS

Many companies spend large sums each year on research and development (R&D). Prior to 1974 some companies expensed their R&D costs, whereas other companies (even in the same industry) capitalized them. To prevent the use of alternative accounting principles in similar economic circumstances, **FASB Statement No. 2** requires that **all research and development costs be expensed as incurred.**[8] Even though R&D costs often benefit future periods, the decision to require expensing in all circumstances was made primarily in the belief that uniformity would enhance

---

6. *Ibid.*, par. 31.
7. "Accounting for Intangible Assets of Motor Carriers," *FASB Statement of Financial Accounting Standards No. 44* (Stamford, Conn.: FASB, 1980).
8. "Accounting for Research and Development Costs," *FASB Statement of Financial Accounting Standards No. 2* (Stamford, Conn.: FASB, 1974), par. 8.

<br>

comparability and would eliminate the possibility of income manipulation. It also avoids the reliability problems of how much to capitalize and over what period to amortize such capitalized costs. An evaluation of the FASB's decision to require expensing of R&D costs is presented at the end of this section.

At issue in the expensing of R&D are what activities and what costs to include in each category. Research and development activities are defined by the FASB as follows:

(a) **Research** is the planned search or critical investigation aimed at discovery of new knowledge with the hope that such knowledge will be useful in developing a new product or service ("product") or a new process or technique ("process") or in bringing about a significant improvement to an existing product or process.

(b) **Development** is the translation of research findings or other knowledge into a plan or design for a new product or process or for a significant improvement to an existing product or process whether intended for sale or use. It includes the conceptual formulation, design, and testing of product alternatives, construction of prototypes, and operation of pilot plants. It does not include routine or periodic alterations to existing products, production lines, manufacturing processes, and other ongoing operations, even though those alterations may represent improvements, and it does not include market research or market testing activities.[9]

To assist in the implementation of these general definitions, examples of activities that would be included as R&D and those that would be excluded are presented in Exhibit 10-2.

Costs associated with activities *excluded* from R&D are either expensed or capitalized according to the normal capitalization criteria. Once it has been determined that an activity is included in R&D, the costs have to be identified so that the correct amount of R&D expense may be recorded. Expenditures for the following elements of R&D activities are *included* in R&D costs and, thus, expensed as incurred:

*Capitalization criteria are discussed in Chapter 8.*

1. Materials, equipment, and facilities

2. Personnel

3. Intangibles purchased from others

4. Contract services—the costs of services performed by others in connection with the R&D activities of an enterprise

5. Indirect costs—R&D includes a reasonable allocation of indirect costs. However, general and administrative costs that are not clearly related to R&D activities are not included as R&D costs.[10]

The inclusion of the cost of materials, equipment, facilities, and intangibles purchased from others in R&D expense needs further explanation. If the items have *alternative future uses*, then normal accrual procedures are followed. For example, costs of personnel are expensed as payments are made and accrued at year-end, whereas costs of materials are recorded in inventory and included as R&D expense when the materials are used. Also, the cost of a machine that has alternative future uses (even if only in other R&D projects) is capitalized and *depreciated* over its estimated useful life. The depreciation is included in the R&D expense shown on the

9. *Ibid.*
10. *Ibid.*, par. 9–10.

## EXHIBIT 10-2

### EXAMPLES OF ACTIVITIES INCLUDED IN AND EXCLUDED FROM R&D

#### Included in R&D

(a) Laboratory research aimed at discovery of new knowledge.
(b) Searching for applications of new research findings or other knowledge.
(c) Conceptual formulation and design of possible product or process alternatives.
(d) Testing in search for or evaluation of product or process alternatives.
(e) Modification of the formulation or design of a product or process.
(f) Design, construction, and testing of preproduction prototypes and models.
(g) Design of tools, jigs, molds, and dies involving new technology.
(h) Design, construction, and operation of a pilot plant that is not of a scale economically feasible to the company for commercial production.
(i) Engineering activity required to advance the design of a product to the point that it meets specific functional and economic requirements and is ready for manufacture.

#### Excluded from R&D

(a) Engineering follow-through in an early phase of commercial production.
(b) Quality control during commercial production, including routine testing of products.
(c) Trouble-shooting in connection with breakdowns during commercial production.
(d) Routine, ongoing efforts to refine, enrich, or otherwise improve upon the qualities of an existing product.
(e) Adaptation of an existing capability to a particular requirement or customer's need as part of a continuing commercial activity.
(f) Seasonal or other periodic design changes to existing products.
(g) Routine design of tools, jigs, molds, and dies.
(h) Activity, including design and construction engineering, related to the construction, relocation, rearrangement, or start-up of facilities or equipment other than (1) pilot plants and (2) facilities or equipment whose sole use is for a particular research and development project.
(i) Legal work in connection with patent applications or litigation, and the sale or licensing of patents.

Source: *FASB Statement No. 2*, par. 9 and 10.

income statement. However, the costs of any materials, equipment, facilities, and intangibles purchased from others that have *no alternative future uses* in research and development or other activities are included in R&D expense as incurred. For example, if inventory or a machine can be used only for one R&D project and so has no alternative future uses, the total acquisition costs are included in R&D expense in the period the cost is incurred.

To illustrate the accounting for R&D, assume that the Kent Company incurred the following costs for R&D activities:

| | |
|---|---|
| Material used from inventory | $50,000 |
| Wages and salaries | 90,000 |
| Allocation of general and administrative costs | 20,000 |
| Depreciation on building housing R&D activities | 25,000 |
| Machine purchased for R&D project that has no alternative future uses | 30,000 |

All these costs are included in R&D expense, and therefore the journal entry is:

| | | |
|---|---|---|
| **Research and Development Expense** | 215,000 | |
| Cash, Payables, etc. | | 140,000 |
| Inventory | | 50,000 |
| Accumulated Depreciation: Building | | 25,000 |

*FASB Statement No. 2* does not cover costs of R&D activities conducted for others (including the government) under a contractual arrangement. These costs may be expensed as incurred or capitalized and expensed when the revenue from the contract is recognized. The *Statement* also does not cover research and development costs incurred by a company for a product or process that is used in its selling or administrative activities. Such costs may be expensed or capitalized, as explained in the discussion of computer software costs later in the chapter.

## Conceptual Evaluation of Accounting for Research and Development Costs

The FASB considered four methods of accounting for R&D costs when *FASB Statement No. 2* was being prepared: (1) expense all costs when incurred, (2) capitalize all costs when incurred and amortize them over the periods benefited, (3) capitalize costs when incurred if specified conditions are fulfilled and record all other costs as expenses, and (4) accumulate all costs in a special category until the existence of future benefits can be determined.

The first alternative is supported and the second alternative countered by the argument that there is a high degree of uncertainty about the future benefits of individual R&D projects. The majority of projects do not result in any identifiable future benefits; therefore it is desirable to expense all costs in the periods incurred. In addition, since it is difficult to demonstrate a direct relationship between R&D costs and specific future revenue generated, it is not possible to estimate *reliably* the expected life and the pattern of the benefits received so that the appropriate amortization can be determined. Furthermore, if R&D costs are approximately the same each period, the amount of the expense each period will be similar, regardless of whether the cost was capitalized and then expensed by the straight-line method or simply expensed immediately. However, immediate expensing does mean that no asset is recorded on the balance sheet. This omission may lead to a very significant understatement of assets for some companies, if it is agreed that the costs incurred on R&D projects do generate benefits for future periods.

The second alternative, capitalize all costs as incurred, is supported by the argument that companies undertake R&D projects only to develop future benefits. Therefore an asset is created and should be recognized by capitalizing the entire costs of R&D without regard to the certainty of future benefits from individual projects. However, such an approach is inconsistent with other areas of accounting where the cost of each asset is recorded and expensed over its individual life. In addition, capitalization of the entire costs of R&D would make it difficult to develop a meaningful amortization period.

The third alternative, selective capitalization, has desirable conceptual features. The costs of each individual project would be accumulated and then capitalized and expensed over the life of the benefits to be received. If no such benefits were expected, the costs would be expensed immediately. Thus R&D costs would be capitalized and expensed on the same basis as other costs. However, this alternative would be difficult to implement. What criteria for capitalization would be used? The FASB considered a number of criteria such as definition of the product or process, technological feasibility, marketability and usefulness, economic feasibility, management action, and distortion of net income comparisons. Any set of criteria would have been very difficult to define and implement reliably, and in all likelihood, would have led to a lack of comparability when implemented. In addition, it might be several periods after the costs have been incurred before the likelihood of benefits being received could be reasonably evaluated.

The fourth alternative is to classify the costs in a special category on the balance sheet. The two alternative categories suggested were below the assets or as a reduction of stockholders' equity. Such a procedure is not appealing because it violates the basic concepts underlying the fundamental accounting equation. It was suggested as an alternative to draw attention to the basic uncertainty surrounding the nature of R&D costs, and to allow a decision regarding capitalizing or expensing to be delayed until sufficient information for a reliable decision becomes available.

The choice basically was between an alternative that has desirable conceptual features but significant implementation difficulties (capitalization) and an alternative that is less desirable conceptually but is much easier to implement and is likely to lead to greater uniformity between companies (immediate expensing). As in so many situations, the choice was between *relevance* and *reliability*. It is not surprising that the FASB decided on the latter alternative. In addition, income tax regulations allow immediate expensing of R&D costs, so a major difference between financial and tax reporting was eliminated.

### International Accounting Differences

Under International Accounting Standards, the costs of items that are acquired for a particular research project and have no alternative future uses are expensed as the items are used in the project. In contrast, such costs are expensed when incurred under U.S. GAAP. A few countries, including Germany and Mexico, also require expensing of all R&D. Capitalization of R&D occurs in several countries, including Brazil and Japan. Some other countries, including Canada and the United Kingdom, require that research costs be expensed while development costs are capitalized.

## IDENTIFIABLE INTANGIBLE ASSETS

Identifiable intangible assets are those intangibles that can be purchased or sold separately from the other assets of the company. Costs of identifiable intangibles are capitalized under generally accepted accounting principles according to the provisions of *APB Opinion No. 17* discussed earlier (except for R&D costs). It should be remembered that since R&D and operating costs are expensed, only certain costs of the *internally developed* identifiable intangibles are capitalized, and not the total costs that might be related to the item. For example, only the direct legal costs of applying for and registering a tradename are capitalized, while all indirect costs, such as advertising to promote the tradename, are expensed as incurred. It also should be remembered that if the identifiable intangible asset is *purchased*, the cost is capitalized on the same basis as for a tangible asset by including all necessary costs. Exhibit 10-3 illustrates the differences between the expensing of intangible assets and the expensing of R&D costs in the period incurred. Each of these identifiable intangible assets is discussed in the following sections.

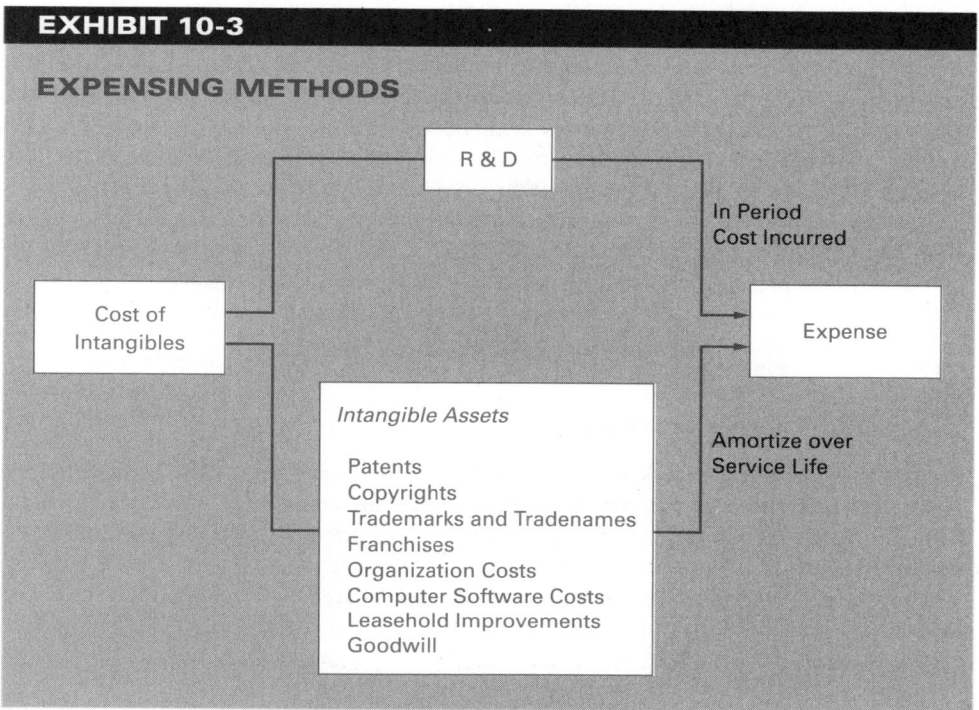

**EXHIBIT 10-3**

**EXPENSING METHODS**

## Patents

**A patent is an exclusive right granted by the federal government giving the owner control of the manufacture, sale, or other use of an invention for 17 years.** Patents cannot be renewed, but their effective life often is extended by obtaining new patents on modifications and improvements to the original invention.

A patent has value if it enables the company to obtain higher profits through selling products at a higher price, producing products at a lower cost, or producing a product for which there is lessened competition. In many situations, the value of a patent is eliminated before the end of its legal life by the actions of other companies that produce a competing product without violating the patent, or through technological change or a change in demand for the product. Therefore the patent is amortized over its expected *economic* life if that life is shorter than 17 years.

Licenses often are granted to others to use the invention covered by a patent. Amounts received under such agreements are accounted for under the normal revenue recognition criteria by including them in income when earned and realizable rather than when received. License agreements are disclosed in the notes to the financial statements if their effect on income is material.

It may be necessary for the owner of a patent to defend it against infringement by others. The costs of successfully defending the legal validity of a patent are capitalized because the benefits of the patent are maintained for its remaining economic life. However, given the length of time it may take to resolve a patent infringement suit, some companies may expense the legal costs when incurred because of the uncertainty of eventual success in the suit. If the suit is lost, all legal costs not previously expensed and the remaining book value of the patent are expensed immediately because there is no remaining economic value.

## Copyrights

**A copyright is a grant by the federal government covering the right to publish, sell, or otherwise control literary or artistic products for the life of the author plus 50 years.** Copyrights cover such items as books, music, and films. Accounting for copyrights follows the same principles as used for patents. The cost is amortized over the economic life (not to exceed 40 years) either on a straight-line or on an activity basis.

It is possible that a fully amortized copyright may develop a significant value, such as in the case of some old films or music. Under current generally accepted accounting principles, which require that assets be recorded at cost, such an increase in value is not recognized in the financial statements but should be disclosed in the notes to the financial statements, if material.

## Trademarks and Tradenames

**Registration of a trademark or tradename with the U.S. Patent Office establishes a right to exclusive use of a name, symbol, or other device used for product identification** (for example, Coke™ or Scotch™ Tape). The right lasts for 20 years and is renewable indefinitely as long as the trademark or tradename is used continuously. Therefore from a legal standpoint, it may be considered to have an indefinite life. However, for accounting purposes, the cost must be amortized over the expected economic life, not to exceed 40 years.

## Franchises

**Franchises are agreements entered into by two parties in which, for a fee, one party (the franchisor) gives the other party (the franchisee) rights to perform certain functions or sell certain products or services.** In addition the franchisor may agree to provide certain services to the franchisee. Many franchises exist between governments and companies, such as a franchise to provide a monopoly service (for example, utilities) or to use public property to provide a service (for example, a ferry). A common example of a franchise between two companies is in the restaurant business where many units of national chains, such as McDonald's, are locally owned and operated under the terms of a franchise agreement. Another example is the selling of name-brand items in the automotive parts market, such as Midas Muffler. The initial franchise cost paid by the franchisee is capitalized, whereas continuing franchise fees that are paid for services provided by the franchisor in subsequent years are expensed according to the normal matching criteria. Although some franchises are granted in perpetuity, the related initial franchise cost must be amortized over the useful economic life, not to exceed 40 years.

*Accounting for franchises by the franchisor is discussed in Chapter 16.*

## Organization Costs

**When a corporation is formed, organization costs are incurred such as legal fees, stock certificate costs, underwriting fees, accounting fees, and promotional fees.** Since these costs are essential to the formation of a corporation and since the life of the company is indefinite, it can be argued that these organization costs are an intangible asset with an indefinite life (which would have to be amortized over a life not to exceed 40 years).

It may be argued that organization costs primarily benefit the early years of a company's existence and should be amortized over a fairly short period. (Income tax regulations allow organization costs to be written off over a period as short as 60 months.) Certainly, if the company meets with reasonable success, the organization costs quickly become immaterial. A third alternative would be to expense the organization costs immediately. This is supported by the argument that once the costs have been incurred and the company is formed, all the benefits associated with those costs have been realized. However, since no revenue has been earned, the company would commence operations in a deficit position. Furthermore, the matching principle would be violated because the expense of forming the company has not been matched against the revenue generated by the newly formed company.

The normal practice is to capitalize the intangible costs and amortize them over the first few years of the company's existence. This procedure is acceptable because organization costs are relatively small, and many companies follow income tax guidelines in their financial accounting if there is no conflict with generally accepted accounting principles.

## Computer Software Costs

Until the early 1980s, most companies expensed the cost of software development. At that time, however, many companies started to adopt a policy of capitalizing software costs. In 1983 the SEC imposed a moratorium on such changes until the FASB adopted appropriate accounting principles. In 1985, the FASB issued **FASB Statement No. 86,** entitled "Accounting for the Costs of Computer Software to Be Sold, Leased, or Otherwise Marketed."[11]

There are three categories of costs associated with software that is to be sold, leased, or otherwise marketed directly or indirectly as part of a product, process, or service. First, **software production costs** are the costs of design, coding, testing, documentation, and preparation of training materials. These costs are included in research and development expense until technological feasibility of the product is established. Since companies use different development methods, **technological feasibility is established either on the date of the completion of a detail program design or, in its absence, on completion of a working model of the product.** After this date, all software production costs are capitalized until the product is available for **general release** to customers. No software production costs may be capitalized after the product is ready for general release; they are expensed as incurred. The accounting for software production costs may be summarized as follows:

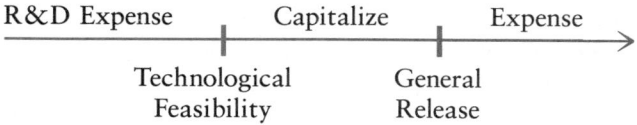

The capitalized software production costs incurred during the period between technological feasibility and general release are amortized over the expected life of the product, which typically will be a relatively short period, such as 5 years. The amount of the amortization expense is the greater of (1) the ratio of current gross revenues to the total amount of current and anticipated future gross revenues or (2) the

11. "Accounting for the Costs of Computer Software to Be Sold, Leased, or Otherwise Marketed," *FASB Statement of Financial Accounting Standards No. 86* (Stamford, Conn.: FASB, 1985). For additional discussion, see Naomi Erickson and David Herskovits, "Accounting for Software Costs: Cracking the Code," *Journal of Accountancy*, November 1985, pp. 81–96.

straight-line method. If the net realizable value of the software product is lower than the asset's book value, the asset is written down to this value and a loss recognized. The lower value is then recognized as the new cost and the write-down may not be recovered. Note that two new concepts are involved. First, a new concept of amortization that is based on estimated revenues is introduced. Second, the lower of cost or market method is applied to this one intangible asset.

The second category of costs is the **unit cost of producing the software,** such as costs of the disks and duplication of the software, packaging, documentation, and training materials. These unit costs are recorded as inventory and expensed as cost of goods sold when the related revenue is recognized. The third category of costs is the **maintenance and customer support costs** incurred after the software is released. These costs are expensed as incurred.

Note that these rules do *not* apply to the costs of software that is developed for internal use. If such an activity is considered to be research and development, it is covered by the rules of *FASB Statement No. 2* and therefore the costs are expensed until it can be concluded that the software project no longer constitutes research or development. Also, *FASB Interpretation No. 6,* "Applicability of FASB Statement No. 2 to Computer Software," specifies that the costs of developing or improving software used in a company's selling or administrative activities, such as an airline's computer reservation system or a company's management information system, are not included as research and development.[12] Therefore, such costs may be capitalized or expensed, although most companies do follow the practice of expensing them.[13]

*FASB Statement No. 86* was adopted by a 5 to 2 majority with the dissents being based on three factors. First, the *Statement* is likely to result in most computer software costs being expensed because, for many companies, the detail program design occurs after the detailed logic of the program is complete and after coding has already begun. For many companies, software may be a significant, or perhaps the only, revenue-generating asset. As the U.S. economy moves towards intangible outputs and creative processes, it may be argued that accounting should accommodate this transition by allowing the results of creative processes to be recorded as assets when they are likely to result in probable future cash flows. Second, many costs incurred before the completion of the detail program design are not part of research and development but are incurred to perform an activity, just like other production processes. Therefore, the dissenters argued that the *Statement* expands the definitions of research and development established in *FASB Statement No. 2.* Third, the amount of the costs that may be capitalized is dependent on the organization of the programming process and, in particular, the date on which technological feasibility is established. Because the capitalization criterion is based on a point in time rather than a function, the costs capitalized may vary significantly depending on whether the coding and testing parallels, or follows, the detail program design.

### Leases and Leasehold Improvements

*Leases are discussed in Chapter 19.*

*Leasehold improvements are discussed in Chapter 8.*

**Leases (or leaseholds) are intangible assets because a right to use the property is held by the lessee, but the property itself is still owned by the lessor.** However, capital leases are normally included on the balance sheet within property, plant, and equipment rather than under intangible assets. Leasehold improvements are also intangible assets but normally are included as a separate item in property, plant, and equipment.

12. "Applicability of FASB Statement No. 2 to Computer Software," *FASB Interpretation No. 6* (Stamford, Conn.: FASB, 1975).
13. *FASB Statement of Financial Accounting Standards No. 86, op. cit.,* par. 26.

## Deferred Charges

Deferred charges (or other "noncurrent assets") is a category that often is used on the balance sheet as a catch-all category in which several individually immaterial items are accumulated. Examples of items included are intangibles from any of the categories previously discussed if the company does not include intangibles as a separate category in the balance sheet. In addition, long-term prepayments such as for insurance, rent, taxes, or moving and plant rearrangement costs may be included in deferred charges. All deferred charges are amortized over their expected economic lives, which are likely to be much less than the maximum allowable 40 years. As discussed in Chapter 3, most of these deferred charges can, and should, be included in other asset categories on the balance sheet.

## UNIDENTIFIABLE INTANGIBLES

Identifiable intangible assets have been discussed in previous sections of this chapter. However, many additional intangibles of a company also contribute to its earning power. These unidentifiable intangibles are often called "goodwill." Accounting for such goodwill depends on whether it is internally developed or purchased through a transaction.

### Internally Developed Goodwill

All companies develop unidentifiable intangibles. For example, employees at all levels are an integral part of a company. They are an essential component in the utilization of the assets that are included in the balance sheet and that produce the products and services of the company. Superior employees may produce products with a higher quality and enable a company to earn a higher income. Another example is a company that has an advantageous geographical location. Perhaps it is closer to its raw materials or suppliers or to its major customers. Such a geographical advantage may enable the company to earn a higher income. Yet the balance sheet does not include assets relating to such internally developed intangibles as quality, human resources, or geographical location.[14]

Two characteristics distinguish intangibles of this type. First, they are considered to be unidentifiable because they are not separable from the identified and recorded assets. For example, the employees of the company cannot be sold to another company, and the geographical location cannot be sold without selling the other assets of the company. Second, measuring the value of these unidentifiable intangibles would be very difficult and less *reliable* than measuring the value of identifiable intangibles. Because of these two characteristics, the costs associated with such *internally developed* intangibles (internally developed goodwill) are expensed as incurred.

### Purchased Goodwill

**Purchased goodwill arises when a company is acquired and is the difference between the purchase price (market value) of a company as a whole and the fair market value of the identifiable net assets.** Goodwill is recorded *only* when a transaction

---

14. A few attempts have been made to value human resources and record them on the balance sheet. See, for instance, E. H. Caplan and S. Landekich, *Human Resource Accounting* (New York: National Association of Accountants, 1974).

*Methods to value goodwill and set the purchase price are discussed in the chapter's Appendix.*

occurs—that is, when a company (or a significant part of a company) is acquired by another company. The purchased goodwill is the price paid for the unidentifiable intangibles that were internally developed by the acquired company. It is recorded as an asset because a transaction has occurred that establishes a *reliable* valuation. From this perspective, goodwill can be considered a residual valuation account for the additional value associated with the unidentifiable intangible assets. In other words, it is the amount paid for the acquisition in excess of the cost of the identifiable net assets acquired.

The capitalization of purchased goodwill is required by **APB Opinion No. 16:**

> **The excess of the cost of the acquired company over the sum of the amounts assigned to identifiable assets less liabilities assumed [is] recorded as goodwill.**[15]

Inconsistencies may appear to develop because only purchased goodwill is recorded as an asset, while internally developed goodwill is expensed. Suppose Company A internally develops goodwill, while Company B has purchased a company identical to A and records goodwill as an asset. Company A, without recorded goodwill, expenses the costs of internally developed goodwill (such as the costs of hiring and training employees), while Company B not only amortizes its purchased goodwill (over a period not to exceed 40 years), but also expenses the continuing costs of developing internal goodwill. The latter situation is sometimes referred to as double charging because there are two charges related to "goodwill" in the income statement. However, the dual charges relate to two different elements. One is the amortizing of goodwill that was developed in the *past* and was purchased; the other is the expensing of the costs of internally generated goodwill in the *current period*.

Two major arguments can be used to justify the expensing of internally generated goodwill and the capitalization and subsequent amortization of purchased goodwill. First, the capitalization of internally generated goodwill would tend to obscure the relationship between a company's earnings and the stockholders' actual investment (the rate of return earned on the net assets of the company). Including internally generated goodwill would increase the recorded value of the net assets and the value would then be based on the expectation of future earnings rather than on the net assets purchased by the company. The investment of the current stockholders is the book value of the recorded net assets, and the earnings should be related to the book value. However, after a purchase of a company, the investment of the stockholders in the combined company is the purchase price of the company including the goodwill purchased. Thus for these stockholders, the earning of higher income represents a return on their purchased investment (goodwill) rather than income generated by the ongoing activities of the company. The second major argument is that it would be very difficult to measure the value of internally generated goodwill with a reasonable degree of *reliability*. The techniques and issues involved in estimating the value of *purchased* goodwill are discussed in the Appendix to provide a better understanding of the process management goes through when considering the purchase of another company. However, this process does *not* result in the value of the goodwill included on the acquiring company's balance sheet. That value results from the actual price paid by the acquiring company, the recording of which is discussed in depth in an advanced accounting book. While the estimation of goodwill is a valid component of the process, the agreed purchase price for a company is the result of negotiation. It is

15. "Business Combinations," *APB Opinion No. 16* (New York: AICPA, 1970), par. 87.

influenced by many other factors such as the market price of any securities being exchanged and the synergy that is expected to result from the acquisition.

### Recording the Acquisition

The acquisition of a company can be a very complex matter. To illustrate a simple alternative, suppose that after negotiation the Sara Company purchases all the assets of the Trevor Company for $790,000 cash and the Trevor Company is dissolved. If the Trevor Company has identifiable assets with a fair value of $920,000 and liabilities with a fair value of $200,000, the condensed journal entry to record the acquisition is:

| | | |
|---|---:|---:|
| Assets | 920,000 | |
| Goodwill | 70,000 | |
|     Liabilities | | 200,000 |
|     Cash | | 790,000 |

To record an actual acquisition, instead of debiting Assets and crediting Liabilities as was shown, each of the individual asset and liability accounts would be debited or credited based on their current market values. Alternatively, if the Trevor Company is not dissolved, the entire acquisition cost would be recorded by Sara Company in an Investments account. Subsequently, either the equity method (discussed in Chapter 13) or consolidated financial statements (discussed in an advanced accounting book) would be used to account for the investment.

### Amortization of Goodwill

When purchased goodwill is recorded as an asset, the question arises as to whether it should be amortized. It is difficult to visualize a situation in which goodwill has an indefinite life. The forces of competition and technological change will eventually eliminate the benefits of the goodwill. *APB Opinion No. 17* supports this view by requiring that **goodwill be expensed, like other intangibles, over a period not to exceed 40 years** (except those acquired before November 1, 1970 for which there is no evidence of a limited life or a decline in value).

Another alternative, which was supported by **Accounting Research Study No. 10,** is to write off the goodwill immediately to stockholders' equity.[16] Several major arguments can be made in favor of this position. First, purchased goodwill is different in nature from other assets and cannot be sold or used independently of the other assets. Therefore it is inappropriate to include it with the other assets on the balance sheet. Second, since internally developed goodwill is expensed immediately, this alternative creates a degree of consistency between internally developed and purchased goodwill. Third, since it is so difficult to estimate the life of the benefits, any choice of periods over which to amortize the goodwill is arbitrary, so immediate write-off is justifiable. However, this alternative ignores the fact that the purchaser believes that an asset does exist and that the value of the asset has been established by a transaction. Consequently this alternative is not allowed under generally accepted accounting principles.

---

16. G. R. Catlett and N. O. Olson, "Accounting for Goodwill," *Accounting Research Study No. 10* (New York: AICPA, 1968).

To illustrate the amortization of goodwill, suppose that the $70,000 goodwill resulting from the acquisition of Trevor Company assets is amortized over 20 years. The journal entry on Sara Company's books to record the amortization is:

| | | |
|---|---|---|
| Goodwill Amortization Expense | 3,500 | |
|     Goodwill (or Accumulated Amortization: Goodwill) | | 3,500 |

Amortization of goodwill is not a tax-deductible expense, thus creating a permanent difference between financial income and taxable income, as discussed in Chapter 17.

### Negative Goodwill

The discussion and examples in this chapter have assumed that purchased goodwill is positive. That is, the price paid for the company is greater than the fair market value of the net assets acquired. However, it is possible that the cash paid is less than the fair market value of the net assets acquired. In such cases, goodwill is a negative amount. This situation tends to raise questions about the rational behavior of the parties involved. The best course of action for the current owners of the company would be to liquidate rather than sell it. An exception is when the acquisition is made by buying common stock that is trading at less than the value of the net assets.

If such a purchase transaction does occur, *APB Opinion No. 16* requires that negative goodwill *not* be recorded. Instead, the negative amount is allocated proportionately to reduce the cost assigned to the noncurrent assets acquired (except long-term investments in marketable securities) on the basis of their relative market values.[17] If these assets are reduced to zero, the remaining negative goodwill is recorded as a deferred credit and amortized over a period not to exceed 40 years. A complete discussion of this topic is beyond the scope of this book and is covered more fully in an advanced accounting book.

## DISCLOSURE OF INTANGIBLES

*FASB Statement No. 2* requires that the total R&D expense be disclosed. This may be accomplished either through a line item on the income statement or more usually by disclosure in the notes to the financial statements. There is considerably less uniformity regarding the disclosure of intangible assets on the balance sheet. Intangible assets usually are distinguished from tangible assets in the financial statements, but sometimes they are all included under one heading such as property, plant, and equipment. Two examples are given in Exhibit 10-4. International Multifoods has goodwill and other intangibles that are being amortized over not more than 40 years. Monsanto includes intangibles on its balance sheet, and then shows a breakdown in the notes to the financial statements. Note also that goodwill is often called **costs in excess of net assets acquired** (or a similar term such as that used by International Multifoods).

In addition to the disclosure on the balance sheet, *APB Opinion No. 17* requires that the method and period of amortization be disclosed. These are disclosed in the notes to the financial statements of International Multifoods and Monsanto as illustrated in Exhibit 10-4. Often accumulated amortization on the intangibles is not shown, although it must be disclosed on reports filed with the SEC.

---

17. *APB Opinion No. 16, op. cit.,* par. 87.

> ## EXHIBIT 10-4
> ## Disclosure of Intangible Assets
>
> ### INTERNATIONAL MULTIFOODS
>
> ### NOTES TO CONSOLIDATED FINANCIAL STATEMENTS
>
> Note 1: Summary of Significant Accounting Policies (in part):
> *Goodwill and other intangibles.* Goodwill represents the excess of cost of businesses acquired over the fair market value of net tangible and identifiable intangible assets. Goodwill and other intangibles are amortized on a straight-line basis over not more than a 40-year period. Other intangibles are included in other assets on the consolidated balance sheets. Accumulated amortization of goodwill and other intangibles amounted to $26,106,000 in fiscal 1992 and $32,707,000 in fiscal 1991.
>
> ### MONSANTO
>
> | | At December 31 | |
> | --- | --- | --- |
> | | 1991 | 1990 |
> | (in millions) | | |
> | Assets (in part): | | |
> | *Intangible Assets*, net of accumulated amortization of $1,480 in 1991 and $1,259 in 1990 | $1,290 | $1,425 |
>
> NOTES TO FINANCIAL STATEMENTS (in part):
>
> Depreciation and Amortization (in part):
> *Intangible assets are recorded at cost less accumulated amortization.* The components of intangible assets and their estimated remaining useful lives were:
>
> | | Estimated Remaining Life* | 1991 | 1990 |
> | --- | --- | --- | --- |
> | Goodwill | 31 | $ 279 | $ 482 |
> | Patents | 3 | $ 733 | $ 679 |
> | Other intangible assets | 17 | 278 | 264 |
> | Total | | $1,290 | $1,425 |

*Weighted average, in years, at December 31, 1991.

## CONCEPTUAL EVALUATION OF ACCOUNTING FOR INTANGIBLES

Earlier in the chapter, the arguments for and against expensing R&D and amortizing goodwill were discussed. While GAAP require that R&D be expensed and purchased goodwill be capitalized, it is helpful to consider whether these two rules are consistent. For example, one of the arguments for expensing R&D is that capitalization would require amortization and it is very difficult to identify the revenues generated against which the amortization should be matched. But it is probably even more difficult to identify the revenues generated by goodwill. Therefore, goodwill should, perhaps, be written off immediately against stockholders' equity.

Alternatively, if capitalizing purchased goodwill is supported, it can be argued that it would be more consistent to also capitalize R&D. The *relevance* associated with consistent principles may outweigh the lesser *reliability* from capitalizing R&D. Furthermore, it is very difficult to defend the APB's decision to allow different principles depending on whether the intangible was acquired before or after November 1, 1970. This difference is not consistent with *comparability*.

The 40-year constraint on the amortization period is also a questionable principle. On one hand, it can be argued that the expected benefits of an intangible will rarely last 40 years. Since many companies automatically use the maximum period, they are being allowed to artificially increase income early in the life of the intangible and reduce income in later periods. On the other hand, it can be argued that some intangibles, such as tradenames and some franchises, have an indeterminate life that may be greater than 40 years and the mandatory maximum period is inappropriate. However, it is unlikely that extending the amortization period for the few such intangibles would have a *material* effect on any company's financial statements.

### International Accounting Differences

Accounting principles for intangibles vary across countries. In several European countries, including Germany and the United Kingdom, goodwill may be written off immediately against stockholders' equity. Furthermore, when goodwill is recorded as an asset, most foreign countries have an amortization period of 5 to 20 years. Thus, U.S. accounting principles are not consistent with those around the world because they require the recognition of an asset and allow a longer amortization period. Also, in many countries, intangibles may be revalued upwards and not amortized. For example, in the U.K., brand names such as Schweppes are accounted for this way.[18]

### APPENDIX: ESTIMATING THE VALUE OF GOODWILL

Purchased goodwill was discussed in the chapter, and a purchase price was assumed so that the goodwill was the difference between that price and the fair value of the identifiable net assets. Methods of estimating the value of goodwill for negotiations or other reasons are discussed in this Appendix.

Goodwill can also be considered from an income perspective. In the chapter discussion, it was suggested that higher quality products, superior employees, and an advantageous geographical location would result in a higher income. But higher than what? A higher income than the company would earn otherwise, or more generally a higher income than is normal for companies in that industry. In this context, the rate of return earned by the company is more meaningful than the absolute value of the income. Therefore goodwill can also be defined as the **value attached to the ability of a company to earn a higher than normal rate of return (an excess rate of return) on the market value of its identifiable net assets.**

### Estimating the Value of Goodwill

When one company is negotiating to buy another company, the price offered is typically much greater than the book value of the net assets to be acquired. Three factors can account for the difference between the value of the company as a whole and the

---

18. For an additional discussion, see Arthur Andersen, et. al., *Survey of International Accounting Principles* (New York, AICPA, 1991).

*book* value of the net assets (assets less liabilities). First, **identifiable net assets are generally listed on the balance sheet at their historical costs.** While some current assets and liabilities are listed at amounts that typically approximate their market values, others (such as land and buildings) may have current market values that are very different from the recorded historical costs. Second, **identifiable intangible assets may be unrecorded** (or undervalued). As has been discussed in the chapter, R&D costs are expensed as incurred. Therefore internally developed intangibles either are not recorded or are recorded at only the costs directly associated with the intangible after all R&D costs have been expensed. Third, **unidentifiable intangibles may exist that are categorized as goodwill.** In the following sections, several methods are discussed that might be used to value the goodwill of a purchased company. However, it should be remembered that these methods are only guidelines. The price must be agreed upon by both the purchaser and seller. Therefore the amount paid for goodwill in any transaction is determined solely by the parties involved and is not defined by generally accepted accounting principles.

To provide additional meaning to the previously mentioned concepts, consider the Kasper Company, which has a condensed balance sheet as shown in Exhibit 10-5. The book value of the company's net assets is $200,000 ($400,000 − $50,000 − $150,000). Since goodwill has been defined to include all the assets that cannot be identified, how is the value of goodwill to be determined? Goodwill has been discussed in terms of the ability to earn an above-normal return, and this approach can be used to develop a value for goodwill. To continue the example of the Kasper Company, it is necessary to make two assumptions. First, suppose that the Kasper Company can be expected to earn $50,000 per year in perpetuity and that the normal return earned by companies in the industry is 10% of the identifiable net assets. In other words, 10% is the normal return required by investors (the acquiring company) for investments of this riskiness.

## EXHIBIT 10-5

### KASPER COMPANY

Balance Sheet, December 31, 1995

| | | | |
|---|---|---|---|
| Current assets | $125,000 | Current liabilities | $ 50,000 |
| Noncurrent assets | 275,000 | Noncurrent liabilities | 150,000 |
| | | Stockholders' equity | 200,000 |
| | $400,000 | | $400,000 |

What is the value of the whole company? It is the amount that must be invested to earn $50,000 per year, when $50,000 is a return of 10% on the investment. Therefore it is the present value of $50,000 in perpetuity discounted at 10%, which is calculated as follows:

$$\text{Value of Company} = \frac{\text{Earnings}}{\text{Discount Rate}}$$
$$= \frac{\$50,000}{0.10}$$
$$= \$500,000$$

This valuation means that the Kasper Company is worth $300,000 more than the $200,000 book value of its identifiable net assets. Discounting expected cash flows would result in a more meaningful measure of value, but net income is used in this example as an approximation of net cash flows.

As discussed previously, the difference of $300,000 may result from three causes. First, individual assets may be recorded at less than their market values (or liabilities may be overvalued). Suppose that the $200,000 of recorded net assets are estimated to have a market value of $320,000. For example, land may be worth more than was originally paid. Also since depreciation on plant and equipment is not related to market value, it can be expected that the market values of these assets will be different from their book values. Second, identifiable intangible assets may be unrecorded. Suppose that the Kasper Company owns an internally developed patent that has a market value of $50,000. This provides a total market value of identifiable net assets of $370,000. Third, the remaining difference between the value of the company as a whole and the value of its identifiable net assets is goodwill. For the Kasper Company, this is $130,000 ($500,000 − $370,000). The determination of the value of goodwill can be summarized as follows:

| | | |
|---|---:|---:|
| Value of estimated annual earnings of $50,000 in perpetuity discounted at 10% ($50,000 ÷ 0.10) | | $500,000 |
| Less: Book value of recorded net assets | $200,000 | |
| Excess of market value over book value of recorded net assets ($320,000 − $200,000) | 120,000 | |
| Market value of unrecorded identifiable intangible asset | 50,000 | |
| Value of identifiable net assets | | (370,000) |
| Value of goodwill | | $130,000 |

Goodwill has also been discussed in terms of an excess return, and it may be instructive to look at the example of the Kasper Company in this way. The company earns a return of 25% per year on the book value of its identifiable net assets ($50,000 net income ÷ $200,000 net assets), which is above the normal return of 10%. The excess of 15% (25% − 10%) or $30,000 per year can be analyzed in the following way:

$$\text{Income} \div \frac{\text{Book Value of}}{\text{Net Recorded Assets}} = \$50,000 \div \$200,000 = 25.0\%$$

$$\text{Income} \div \frac{\text{Market Value of}}{\text{Net Recorded Assets}} = \$50,000 \div \$320,000 = 15.6\%$$

$$\text{Income} \div \frac{\text{Market Value of}}{\text{Net Identifiable Assets}} = \$50,000 \div \$370,000 = 13.5\%$$

$$\text{Income} \div \frac{\text{Market Value of}}{\substack{\text{Net Assets} \\ \text{Including Goodwill}}} = \$50,000 \div \$500,000 = 10.0\%$$

In summary, the ability to earn an excess return of 15% results from the existence of unidentifiable intangible assets (goodwill) of $130,000, identifiable unrecorded intangible assets of $50,000, and an excess of the market value over the book value of the recorded assets of $120,000.

## Steps Used in Estimating the Value of Goodwill

Now that the relationship between excess earnings and the valuation of goodwill has been established, a series of six steps may be used to compute a particular value:

1. Estimate the average future annual earnings from the identifiable net assets.

2. Estimate the rate (or rates) of return that should be earned by the company on its identifiable net assets.

3. Estimate the current market value of the identifiable net assets.

4. Compute the estimated excess annual earnings.

5. Estimate the expected life of the excess annual earnings.

6. Compute the present value of the estimated excess annual earnings.

Two additional steps may follow the calculation of the value of the goodwill:

7. Compute the total value of the acquired company.

8. Apply sensitivity analysis.

Each of these steps is discussed in the following sections, although they may not actually be carried out in the sequence outlined. For example, the estimation in Step 1 may be a function of the values in Step 3. In addition it should be recognized that access to the records of the company being considered for acquisition makes the estimation process easier.

### Step 1: Estimate the Average Future Earnings

It is very difficult to develop an estimate of the average future annual earnings from a company's existing net assets. Many internal variables, such as management decisions and employee productivity, affect future earnings. There are also numerous external variables, such as the general state of the economy and the actions of competitors. Companies find it difficult enough to develop accurate budgets of earnings for a short time in the future, and it is usually impractical to consider using normal budgeting techniques to estimate annual earnings for sufficient years into the future that would be useful for the valuation of goodwill.

The alternative approach is to base estimated future annual earnings on the earnings of recent years. A single year is not likely to be reliable, and extending too many years into the past may be misleading because of changed conditions. The goal is to select a period that is relevant to the prediction of expected future earnings. The trend of earnings (or a simple average) over, say, the last 5 years may be extrapolated into the future to provide the estimate of future annual earnings. Such estimates should be adjusted for any nonrecurring items and for changes in operating and competitive conditions that can be reliably predicted. Examples of adjustments are:

1. Eliminating extraordinary items, the results of discontinued operations, and the effects of changes in accounting principles included in the income statement of the company being considered for purchase because they are not expected to recur in the future.

2. Adjusting for differences in accounting principles. For example, the company being considered for purchase may use FIFO and accelerated depreciation, whereas other companies in the same industry may use LIFO and straight-line depreciation. To permit better comparisons, the accounting principles (and related account balances) should be adjusted to conform to those of the other companies in the industry.

A more sophisticated variation of the extrapolation of earnings is to separate income into its revenue and expense components and to project each separately based on the past figures. It is also desirable to adjust these past figures so that they are based on the current values that are used to value the identifiable assets being purchased (as calculated in Step 3).

The Baley Company, which is considering acquiring the Greenfield Company, uses the data presented in Exhibit 10-6 for an analysis. This example is simplified because it calculates an average of past earnings rather than considering trends in each component. Three adjustments are made to the past income figures. First, expected increases in wages that will *not* be recovered by future price increases cause a reduction in future income. Second, depreciation is adjusted so that it is based on the fair value of the assets. Third, intangible assets not previously recorded are amortized. The amounts of the depreciation ($12,000) and amortization ($10,000) are based on the additional values ($120,000 and $150,000, respectively) recorded in Step 3. These amounts are based on an assumed 10-year economic life for the property and plant and a 15-year life for the intangible asset. The Greenfield Company had an extraordinary loss in one of the past 5 years that has been excluded from the analysis because it is not expected to recur in the future.

### Step 2: Estimate the Rate of Return

The rate of return that should be earned by the acquired company on its identifiable net assets is based on the risk of the investment and the alternatives that are available. It is the rate necessary to attract investment capital to this kind of business under current conditions. Data on average rates of return are available in publications of the government and various financial services. Such rates are based on the book value of the net assets of the company, and it may be necessary to adjust this rate to reflect the use of the market value of the assets in the calculation. Care should be taken to consider the effects of particular accounting methods used by the company. For example, if the acquired company uses FIFO but most comparable companies use LIFO, appropriate adjustments should be made. In the Greenfield Company example, it is assumed that the appropriate rate of return is 10% after income taxes.

---

### EXHIBIT 10-6

### GREENFIELD COMPANY

Estimate of the Average Future Annual Earnings

| | | |
|---|---:|---:|
| Average annual revenue for the past 5 years | | $628,000 |
| Average annual cost of goods sold for the past 5 years | $266,000 | |
| Average annual operating expenses for the past 5 years | 180,000 | |
| Expected annual increase in wages not to be recovered by increased revenues | 40,000 | |
| Increase in annual depreciation on the current fair value of the assets | 12,000 | |
| Annual amortization of intangible assets not previously recorded | 10,000 | |
| Expected expenses | | (508,000) |
| Expected average annual earnings before income taxes | | $120,000 |
| Estimated income taxes (30%) | | (36,000) |
| Expected average annual earnings | | $ 84,000 |

### Step 3: Estimate the Current Market Value of the Identifiable Net Assets

Since accounting records are based on the historical cost principle, it is unlikely that the book value of the net assets of the company being purchased approximates the current market value of its identifiable net assets.

The book value of the current assets and liabilities is usually a reasonable approximation of the fair value of these items. One major exception occurs when the LIFO inventory method is used, because the inventory book value will be less than the fair value if prices have risen since the adoption of LIFO. Other minor adjustments may be necessary, such as to reflect the current market value of all investments and to update the allowance for uncollectible accounts. Property, plant, and equipment book values are likely to need significant adjustments and an appraisal may be required. Identifiable intangible assets must be adjusted to their market values. Noncurrent liabilities may present some valuation problems. If interest rates have changed since bonds or notes were issued, these liabilities should be revalued using present value analysis based on current market rates. Also there may be unrecorded liabilities in the form of future pension payments or contingencies.

The assets may be worth more to the Baley Company than to the Greenfield Company because a combination of the assets of the two companies may result in total profits greater than the sum of the profits of the two separate companies. Furthermore, since the Baley Company records the purchased assets at their current market values, higher depreciation will result if the current values are greater than the book values.

Revaluation of the Greenfield Company's identifiable net assets is as follows:

| | |
|---|---:|
| Book value of identifiable net assets | $570,000 |
| Revaluation of LIFO inventory to market value | 90,000 |
| Increase in allowance for uncollectible accounts | (10,000) |
| Revaluation of property, plant, and equipment to market value | 120,000 |
| Market value of fully amortized tradename | 150,000 |
| Revaluation of bonds payable due to decline in interest rates | (60,000) |
| Unfunded projected benefit obligation of the pension plan | (140,000) |
| Current market value of identifiable net assets | $720,000 |

### Step 4: Compute the Estimated Excess Annual Earnings

The estimated excess annual earnings is the difference between the estimated average future annual earnings and the normal rate of return multiplied by the market value of the net identifiable assets. For the Greenfield Company, this amount is computed as follows:

| | |
|---|---:|
| Average expected annual earnings (from Step 1) | $84,000 |
| 10% return on market value of identifiable net assets | (72,000) |
| Estimated excess annual earnings | $12,000 |

Annual earnings of $72,000 are necessary for a normal return of 10% on identifiable net assets having a value of $720,000. Since the company expects to earn $84,000 annually, there must be additional unidentifiable assets in the form of goodwill. It should be noted that the 10% return was the normal rate based on the historical cost of the assets, but in this example it has been used as the normal return on the market value of the net identifiable assets. In ordinary circumstances, this is an acceptable approximation, but if there is a significant difference between the book value and the market value, a downward adjustment of the normal rate may be appropriate.

*Step 5: Estimate the Expected Life of Excess Annual Earnings*
It is sometimes argued that the excess annual earnings have an infinite life. This is not a realistic assumption, because the forces of competition or technological change can eventually be expected to eliminate the advantages that exist at the time of purchase. This does *not* mean that the company cannot earn a higher-than-normal return in the future, but it means that if the company does, it will be increasingly a result of the activities that occur *after* the purchase. In other words, it will be the result of continuing expenditures on such things as training employees, R&D, advertising, and production of high-quality products. If such continuing efforts are not made, the goodwill that existed at the time of purchase cannot be expected to continue. Therefore it seems clear that the excess annual earnings have a limited life. For the Greenfield Company, it will be assumed that the excess annual earnings are expected to last for 10 years.

*Step 6: Compute the Present Value of the Estimated Excess Annual Earnings*
The usual approach to computing the present value of the estimated excess annual earnings (goodwill) is to discount these earnings at the normal rate of return for their estimated life. For the Greenfield Company, the excess annual earnings of $12,000 are discounted at 10% for 10 years as follows:

| | |
|---|---:|
| Estimated excess annual earnings | $12,000 |
| Present value factor for an annuity of 10 periods at 10% (from Table 4 of Appendix D) | × 6.144567 |
| Present value of estimated excess annual earnings (goodwill) | $73,735 |

An alternative is to use a discount rate higher than the normal rate of return. This has been suggested because the risk associated with higher-than-normal earnings is greater than the risk associated with normal earnings. For example, if a discount rate of 20% is used to capitalize the 10-year excess annual earnings of the Greenfield Company, goodwill is computed at $50,310 ($12,000 × 4.192472).

*Step 7: Compute the Total Value of the Company*
The ultimate purpose of estimating the value of goodwill is to determine the total value of the company being considered for purchase. In our example, the total *estimated* value of the Greenfield Company is $793,735, which consists of the $720,000 current market value of the identifiable net assets on which a 10% return is anticipated and the $73,735 goodwill on which a 10% return is also anticipated.

*Step 8: Apply Sensitivity Analysis*
Estimates of the future earnings, the rate of return, the current market value of the assets, and the expected life of the excess annual earnings are used in the calculation of goodwill. A great deal of uncertainty and subjectivity is involved in these estimates. It cannot be emphasized too strongly that the calculation of goodwill does not produce a definitive valuation and is certainly not a final indication of the value of the company being considered for purchase. One additional step to improve the information management has when it is involved in the negotiation process to acquire a company is to perform sensitivity analysis on the estimates used in the goodwill calculation. **Sensitivity analysis involves calculating the change in the estimated value of the acquired company as a result of changing the values of the items used in the calculation.** For example, a change in the discount rate used to value the excess earnings from 10% to 20% reduced the goodwill to $50,310. By performing sensitivity analysis, management has both a value based on its best estimates and a range of values if those estimates are in error.

The valuation of the goodwill is an initial step toward the valuation of the company being considered for acquisition, but the actual purchase price is the result of the negotiation process. Bargaining strength and skill are probably at least as important in determining the final price. Nevertheless, knowledge of the value of goodwill is an important element in improving this bargaining strength.

## Other Methods of Estimating Goodwill

Because of the uncertainties involved in the estimation of goodwill, it is sometimes suggested that even simpler rules be used for its valuation. These include valuing goodwill by such arbitrary amounts as (1) 10 times annual earnings, (2) 4 times excess annual earnings (of course, numbers other than 10 and 4 could be used), and (3) determining the value of the company by capitalizing annual earnings at a normal rate (as used in an illustration earlier in this chapter). Although these might be useful rules of thumb, it is difficult to argue that because of the difficulties of measurement it is better to attempt only a simple measurement. However, these alternative valuation methods might be used as a form of sensitivity analysis to complement the value of goodwill computed under the preferred method discussed earlier, even though they ignore the time value of money.

Another more rational way of reducing the uncertainties is to negotiate a price that involves contingent payments based on future excess income actually earned. It has also been suggested that the market value of the shares outstanding of a company may be a useful basis for estimating the value of that company. However, the price established by the stock market is based on the trading of a small number of the outstanding shares and probably does not give a valid indication of the value of all the shares. In addition, the prices of stocks tend to fluctuate as a result of many factors, some of which may not reflect changes in the underlying value of the company.

## QUESTIONS

*Q10-1* How are intangible assets distinguished from tangible assets? What do they have in common?

*Q10-2* How are identifiable intangibles distinguished from unidentifiable intangibles?

*Q10-3* Explain how identifiable and unidentifiable intangibles are accounted for.

*Q10-4* Are all intangible assets amortized? If not, which ones are not? Why?

*Q10-5* Which amortization method is required for intangibles? Are there any exceptions?

*Q10-6* What factors should be considered in estimating the economic life of an intangible?

*Q10-7* What is meant by the terms *research* and *development*?

*Q10-8* What activities are included in R&D? Excluded?

*Q10-9* What expenditures for R&D are included in R&D costs?

*Q10-10* What alternative methods of accounting for R&D were considered in *FASB Statement No. 2*? List an argument in favor and one against each alternative.

*Q10-11* Over how many years are patents amortized? Copyrights? Organization costs? Goodwill?

*Q10-12* How is a patent worth $100,000 recorded if: (a) It has just been purchased for $90,000? (b) It has been developed by the company?

*Q10-13* A controller suggested writing off organization costs against the amount contributed by shareholders in excess of par. Evaluate this proposal.

*Q10-14* List four possible causes of goodwill.

*Q10-15* What is the definition of *goodwill* from an asset valuation perspective? From an income perspective?

*Q10-16* What are the three factors that may account for the difference between the value of the company as a whole and the book value of the net assets?

**Q10-17** Under what conditions is goodwill capitalized at acquisition? Expensed at acquisition? Explain the arguments used to justify this accounting.

**Q10-18** Distinguish between internal and external goodwill. In which situations is each capitalized or expensed?

**Q10-19** Under what conditions is purchased goodwill amortized? Discuss the major arguments in favor of and against amortization.

**Q10-20** It has been proposed that purchased goodwill should be written off immediately to stockholders' equity.

Evaluate the arguments in favor of and against this proposal.

**Q10-21** What is meant by the term *negative goodwill*? How is it recorded?

**Q10-22** *(Appendix)* What are the eight steps in the valuation of goodwill?

**Q10-23** *(Appendix)* What is meant by the following terms: *average future annual earnings; normal rate of return; excess annual earnings; expected life of excess annual earnings; current market value of identifiable net assets?*

---

## CASES

### C10-1    Nature of Intangibles

The Johnson Company operates several plants at which limestone is processed into quicklime and hydrated lime. The Bland Plant, where most of the equipment was installed many years ago, continually deposits a dusty white substance over the surrounding countryside. Citing the unsanitary condition of the neighboring community of Adeltown, the pollution of the Adel River, and the high incidence of lung disease among workers at Bland, the state's Pollution Control Agency has ordered the installation of air pollution control equipment. Also, the Agency has assessed a substantial penalty, which will be used to clean up Adeltown. After considering the costs involved (which could not have been reasonably estimated prior to the Agency's action), Johnson decides to comply with the Agency's orders, the alternative being to cease operations at Bland at the end of the current fiscal year. The officers of Johnson agree that the air pollution control equipment should be capitalized and depreciated over its useful life, but they disagree over the period(s) to which the penalty should be expensed.

**Required**
Discuss the conceptual merits and reporting requirements of accounting for the penalty as a
1. Charge to the current period
2. Correction of prior periods
3. Capitalizable item to be amortized over future periods
   (*AICPA adapted*)

### C10-2    Patents

In examining the books of Samson Manufacturing Company, you find on the December 31, 1995 balance sheet the item, "Costs of patents, $308,440." Referring to the ledger accounts, you note the following items regarding one patent acquired in 1992:

| | | |
|---|---|---|
| 1992 | Legal costs incurred in defending the validity of the patent | $3,500 |

| | | |
|---|---|---|
| 1994 | Legal costs in prosecuting an infringement suit | 7,900 |
| 1994 | Legal costs (additional expenses) in the infringement suit | 1,500 |
| 1994 | Cost of improvements (unpatented) on the patented device | 4,800 |

There are no credits in the account, and no allowance for amortization has been set up on the books for any of the patents. There are three other patents issued in 1989, 1991, and 1992; all were developed by the staff of the client. The patented articles are presently very marketable, but are estimated to be in demand only for the next few years.

**Required**
Discuss the items included in the Patent account from an accounting standpoint. (*AICPA adapted*)

### C10-3    Patents

On June 30, 1995 your client, Sprauge Corporation, was granted two patents covering plastic cartons that it has been producing and marketing profitably for the past 3 years. One patent covers the manufacturing process and the other covers the related products.

Sprauge executives tell you that these patents represent the most significant breakthrough in the industry in the past 30 years. The products have been marketed under the registered trademarks Safetainer, Duratainer, and Sealrite. Licenses under the patents have already been granted by your client to other manufacturers in the United States and abroad and are producing substantial royalties.

On July 1 Sprauge commenced patent infringement actions against several companies whose names you recognize as those of substantial and prominent competitors. Sprauge management is optimistic that these suits will result in a permanent injunction against the manufacture and sale of the infringing products and collection of damages for loss of profits caused by the alleged infringement. The financial vice-president has suggested that the patents be recorded at the discounted value of expected royalty receipts.

**Required**

1. What is the meaning of "discounted value of expected net receipts"? Explain.
2. How would such a value be calculated for net royalty receipts?
3. What basis of valuation of Sprauge's patents would be generally accepted in accounting? Give supporting reasons for this basis.
4. Assuming no practical problems of implementation and ignoring generally accepted accounting principles, what is the preferable basis of evaluation for patents? Explain.
5. What would be the preferable theoretical basis of amortization? Explain.
6. What recognition, if any, should be made of the infringement litigation in the financial statements for the year ending September 30, 1995? Discuss. (*AICPA adapted*)

### C10-4  Patent and R&D

Clonal, Inc., a biotechnology company, developed and patented a diagnostic product called Trouver. Clonal purchased some research equipment to be used exclusively for Trouver and other research equipment to be used on Trouver and subsequent research projects. Clonal defeated a legal challenge to its Trouver patent, and began production and marketing operations for the product.

Corporate headquarters' costs were allocated to Clonal's research division as a percentage of the division's salaries.

**Required**

1. How should the equipment purchased for Trouver be reported in Clonal's income statements and balance sheets?
2. a. Describe the matching principle.
   b. Describe the accounting treatment of research and development costs and consider whether this is consistent with the matching principle. What is the justification for the accounting treatment of research and development costs?
3. How should corporate headquarters' costs allocated to the research division be classified in Clonal's income statement? Why?
4. How should the legal costs incurred in defending Trouver's patent be reported in Clonal's statement of cash flows? (*AICPA adapted*).

### C10-5  Cost of Intangibles

After securing lease commitments from several major stores, Silver Springs Shopping Center, Inc., was organized and built a shopping center in a growing suburb. The shopping center would have opened on schedule on January 2, 1995 if it had not been struck by a severe tornado in December; it opened for business on October 2, 1995. All the additional construction costs that were incurred as a result of the tornado were covered by insurance.

In July 1994 in anticipation of the scheduled January opening, a permanent staff was hired to promote the shopping center, obtain tenants for the uncommitted space, and manage the property. A summary of some of the costs incurred in 1994 and the first 9 months of 1995 follows:

|  | 1994 | Jan. 1, to Sept. 30, 1995 |
|---|---|---|
| Interest on mortgage bonds | $60,000 | $90,000 |
| Cost of obtaining tenants | 28,000 | 58,000 |
| Promotional advertising | 34,000 | 34,000 |

The promotional advertising campaign was designed to familiarize shoppers with the center. Had it been known in time that the center would not open until October 1995, the 1994 expenditure for promotional advertising would not have been made. The advertising had to be repeated in 1995.

All the tenants who had leased space in the shopping center at the time of the tornado accepted the October occupancy date on condition that the monthly rental charges for the first 9 months of 1995 be canceled.

**Required**

Explain how each of the costs for 1994 and the first 9 months of 1995 should be treated in the accounts of the shopping center corporation. Give the reasons for each treatment. (*AICPA adapted*)

### C10-6  Research and Development Costs

The Gratwick Company is in the process of developing a revolutionary new product. A new division of the company was formed to develop, manufacture, and market this new product. As of year-end (December 31, 1994), the new product has not been manufactured for resale; however, a prototype unit was built and is in operation.

Throughout 1995 the new division incurred certain costs. These costs include design and engineering studies, prototype manufacturing costs, administrative expenses (including salaries of administrative personnel), and market research costs. In addition, approximately $500,000 in equipment (estimated useful life, 10 years) was purchased for use in developing and manufacturing the new product. Approximately $200,000 of this equipment was built specifically for the design and development of the new product; the remaining $300,000 of equipment was used to manufacture the preproduction prototype and will be used to manufacture the new product once it is in commercial production.

**Required**

1. What is the definition of *research* and of *development* as defined in *FASB Statement No. 2*?
2. Briefly indicate the practical and conceptual reasons for the conclusion reached by the FASB on accounting practices for research and development costs.
3. In accordance with *FASB Statement No. 2*, how should the various costs of Gratwick be recorded in the

financial statements for the year ended December 31, 1995? (*AICPA adapted*)

## C10-7   Goodwill

After extended negotiations, Rothman Corporation bought from Felzar Company most of the latter's assets on June 30, 1995. At the time of the sale, Felzar's accounts (adjusted to June 30, 1995) reflected the following descriptions and amounts for the assets transferred:

|  | Cost | Contra (Valuation) Account | Book Value |
|---|---|---|---|
| Receivables | $ 83,600 | $ 3,000 | $ 80,600 |
| Inventory | 107,000 | 5,200 | 101,800 |
| Land | 20,000 | — | 20,000 |
| Buildings | 207,500 | 73,000 | 134,500 |
| Fixtures and equipment | 205,000 | 41,700 | 163,300 |
| Goodwill | 50,000 | — | 50,000 |
|  | $673,100 | $122,900 | $550,200 |

You ascertain that the contra (valuation) accounts were allowance for doubtful accounts, allowance to reduce inventory to market, and accumulated depreciation. During the extended negotiations, Felzar held out for a consideration of approximately $600,000 (depending on the level of the receivables and inventory). As of June 30, 1995, however, Felzar agreed to accept Rothman's offer of $450,000 cash plus 1% of the net sales (as defined in the contract) of the next 5 years with payments at the end of each year. Felzar expects that Rothman's total net sales during this period will exceed $15 million.

### Required

1. How should Rothman Corporation record this transaction? Explain.
2. Discuss the propriety of recording goodwill in the accounts of Rothman Corporation for this transaction. (*AICPA adapted*)

## C10-8   Interpreting GAAP   ⓪⓪

Consider the following three statements:

1. In accordance with *APB Opinion No. 17*, Capital Cities/ABC amortizes substantially all purchased goodwill over 40 years. This practice is arbitrarily mandated without regard to whether these assets have or have not declined in value. All the company's goodwill has resulted from the acquisition of broadcasting and publishing properties. Historically, such intangible assets have substantially increased in value and have long and productive lives. We believe that the requirements of *APB Opinion No. 17* when applied to such publishing and broadcasting assets understate net income and stockholders' equity. (Adapted from Capital Cities/ABC annual report, 1991.)
2. The purchase price of Hughes Aircraft Company exceeded the book value of the net assets by $4,244.7 million, which included $500 million for patents and related technology and $3,619.7 million for other intangible assets including goodwill. These amounts are being amortized on a straight-line basis: patents and related technology over 15 years and other intangible assets over 40 years. The purchase price of EDS exceeded the book value of the net assets by $2,179.5 million, which included $1,069.9 million for existing customer contracts, $646.2 million for computer software programs, and $290.2 million for other intangible assets including goodwill. These amounts are being amortized on a straight-line basis: existing customer contracts over 7 years, computer software programs over 5 years, and goodwill over 10 years. (Adapted from General Motors' annual report, 1991.)
3. Though some investors put AnnTaylor's pro forma earnings for this fiscal year at around 80 cents per share, per-share profit would be $1.30 if one ignored a yearly 50 cent-a-share charge to write off goodwill. Based on the latter figure, AnnTaylor could one day be a very big stock, concluded the analyst. (Adapted from *The Wall Street Journal*, May 2, 1991.)

### Required

1. Do Capital Cities/ABC and General Motors appear to be consistent in their application of generally accepted accounting principles?
2. Do you agree with the argument made by Capital Cities/ABC?
3. Do you agree with the analyst's argument about AnnTaylor?

## C10-9   Appendix: Goodwill

Elson Corporation, a retail fuel oil distributor, has increased its annual sales volume to a level three times greater than the annual sales of a dealer it purchased in 1991 in order to begin operations.

The board of directors recently received an offer to negotiate the sale of Elson Corporation to a large competitor. As a result, the majority of the board wants to increase the stated value of goodwill on the balance sheet to reflect the larger sales volume developed through intensive promotion and the current market price of sales gallonage. A few of the board members, however, would prefer to eliminate goodwill altogether from the balance sheet in order to prevent "possible misinterpretations." Goodwill was recorded properly in 1991.

### Required

1. Discuss the meaning of the term *goodwill*.
2. List the techniques used to calculate the tentative value of goodwill in negotiations to purchase a going concern.
3. Why are the book and market values of the goodwill of Elson Corporation different?
4. Discuss the propriety of (a) increasing the stated value of goodwill prior to the negotiations and (b) eliminating goodwill completely from the balance sheet prior to negotiations. (*AICPA adapted*)

# MULTIPLE CHOICE

*Select the best answer for each of the following.*

M10-1  The Plaza Company originated late in 1995 and began operations on January 2, 1996. Plaza is engaged in conducting market research studies on behalf of manufacturers. Prior to the start of operations, the following costs were incurred:

| | |
|---|---:|
| Attorney's fees in connection with organization of Plaza | $ 4,000 |
| Improvements to leased offices prior to occupancy | 7,000 |
| Meetings of incorporators, state filing fees and other organization expenses | 5,000 |
| | $16,000 |

Plaza has elected to record amortization of organization costs over the maximum period allowable under generally accepted accounting principles. What is the amount of organization costs amortized for 1996?

a. $225
b. $400
c. $1,800
d. $3,200

M10-2  A purchased patent has a remaining legal life of 15 years. It should be

a. Expensed in the year of acquisition
b. Amortized over 15 years regardless of its useful life
c. Amortized over 40 years
d. Amortized over its useful life if less than 15 years

M10-3  Frye Company incurred research and development costs in 1995 as follows:

| | | | |
|---|---:|---|---:|
| Equipment acquired for use in research and development projects | $1,000,000 | Compensation costs of personnel | $500,000 |
| | | Outside consulting fees | 100,000 |
| Depreciation on the equipment | 150,000 | Indirect costs appropriately | |
| Materials used | 200,000 | allocated | 250,000 |

The total research and development costs charged in Frye's 1995 income statement should be

a. $650,000
b. $900,000
c. $1,200,000
d. $1,800,000

M10-4  Which of the following assets acquired in 1995 are amortizable?

| | Goodwill | Trademarks |
|---|---|---|
| a. | No | No |
| b. | Yes | Yes |
| c. | No | Yes |
| d. | Yes | No |

M10-5  What is the proper time or time period over which to match the cost of an intangible asset with revenues if it is likely that the benefit of the asset will last for an indeterminate but very long period of time?

a. Forty years
b. Fifty years
c. Immediately
d. At such time as diminution in value can be quantitatively determined

M10-6  The general ledger of the Flint Corporation as of December 31, 1995 includes the following accounts:

| | |
|---|---:|
| Organization costs | $ 5,000 |
| Deposits with advertising agency (will be used to promote goodwill) | 8,000 |
| Discounts on bonds payable | 15,000 |
| Excess of cost over book value of net assets of acquired subsidiary | 70,000 |
| Trademarks | 12,000 |

In the preparation of Flint's balance sheet as of December 31, 1995, what should be reported as total intangible assets?

a. $87,000
b. $92,000

c. $95,000
d. $110,000

M10-7   Goodwill represents the excess of the cost of an acquired company over the

a. Sum of the fair values assigned to tangible assets acquired less liabilities assumed
b. Sum of the fair values assigned to identifiable assets acquired less liabilities assumed
c. Sum of the fair values assigned to intangible assets acquired less liabilities assumed
d. Book value of an acquired company

M10-8   During 1991 Traco Machine Company spent $176,000 on research and development costs for an invention. This invention was patented on January 2, 1992 at a nominal cost that was expensed in 1992. The patent had a legal life of 17 years and an estimated useful life of 8 years. In January 1996 Traco paid $16,000 for legal fees in a successful defense of the patent. Amortization for 1996 should be

a. $0
b. $1,231

c. $4,000
d. $26,000

M10-9   Which of the following amounts incurred in connection with a trademark should be capitalized?

|   | Cost of a successful defense | Registration fees |
|---|---|---|
| a. | Yes | No |
| b. | Yes | Yes |
| c. | No | Yes |
| d. | No | No |

M10-10  Sherwood Corporation incurred $68,000 of research and development costs in its laboratory to develop a patent that was granted on January 2, 1995. Legal fees and other costs associated with registration of the patent totaled $13,600. Sherwood estimates that the economic life of the patent will be 8 years. What amount should Sherwood charge to patent amortization expense for the year ended December 31, 1995?

a. $0
b. $800

c. $1,700
d. $10,200

*(AICPA adapted)*

## EXERCISES

E10-1   *Cost of a Patent*   The Befort Company received a patent on a new type of machine. The legal and patent application costs totaled $12,000. R&D costs incurred to create the machine were $75,000. In the year in which the company received the patent, $20,000 was spent in the successful defense of a patent infringement suit.

**Required**
1. At what amount should the patent be capitalized?
2. How would you determine the economic life of the patent?

E10-2   *Cost of a Patent*   On January 5, 1994 the Franc Company purchased for $30,000 a patent that had been granted 5 years earlier. The patent covers a manufacturing process that the company plans to use for 15 years. On January 2, 1995 the company paid its lawyers $10,000 for successfully defending the patent in a lawsuit.

**Required**
Prepare all the journal entries associated with the patent in 1994 and 1995.

E10-3   *Cost of a Tradename*   On January 10, 1994 the Hughes Company applied for a tradename. Legal costs associated with the application were $10,000. In January 1995 the company incurred $8,000 of legal fees in a successful defense of its tradename.

**Required**

Compute the amortization and ending book value of the tradename for 1994 and 1995 if the company amortizes the tradename over the maximum allowable life.

E10-4  *Organization Costs*  Kling Company was organized in late 1994 and began operations on January 2, 1995. The company is engaged in conducting market research studies on behalf of manufacturers. Prior to the start of operations, the following costs were incurred:

| | |
|---|---|
| Attorney's fees in connection with the organization of the company | $12,000 |
| Improvements to leased offices prior to occupancy | 6,000 |
| Meetings of incorporators and state filing fees | 5,000 |

The company has decided to amortize organization costs over the maximum period allowable.

**Required**

What is the amount of the organization costs amortized in 1995?

E10-5  *Research and Development Costs*  The KLK Clothing Company manufactures professional clothing for women. In order to keep costs low while still producing quality clothes, KLK conducts many research and development projects. On a current project, KLK researchers used $35,000 of cotton and $27,000 of wool from its inventory. KLK paid its researchers $30,000 in wages and purchased a special weaving machine for $60,000 cash. The machine was not suitable for use in production activities and was not expected to be used in other research projects. In addition, depreciation of the project's research lab amounted to $20,000.

**Required**

Prepare the journal entry to record KLK's research and development costs.

E10-6  *Research and Development Costs*  In 1995 Lalli Corporation incurred R&D costs as follows:

| | |
|---|---|
| Materials and equipment | $100,000 |
| Personnel | 100,000 |
| Indirect costs | 50,000 |
| | $250,000 |

These costs relate to a product that will be marketed in 1996. It is estimated that these costs will be recouped by December 31, 1999.

**Required**

What is the amount of R&D costs expensed in 1995? (*AICPA adapted*)

E10-7  *Research and Development Activities*  Which of the following activities are considered R&D? Justify your reasons for each answer.
1. Building an oil shale plant to test the feasibility of large-scale exploitation
2. Testing a new type of machine to evaluate its potential usefulness in production
3. Modifying a machine to make it suitable for filling a customer's order
4. Designing a new plant to produce the same products more efficiently
5. Testing in an attempt to find a more efficient production method

E10-8  *Research and Development Costs*  Which of the following are included in R&D costs of the current period? Justify each answer.
1. Current-period depreciation on the building housing the R&D activities
2. Cost of a market research study
3. Current-period depreciation on a machine used in R&D activities
4. Salary of the director of R&D
5. Salary of the vice-president who spends one-third of her time overseeing the R&D activities
6. Pension costs for the salaries in items 4 and 5

E10-9    *Goodwill*    The Marino Company had the following balance sheet on January 1, 1995:

| Current assets | $ 50,000 | Current liabilities | $ 30,000 |
| Property, plant, and equipment | 200,000 | Noncurrent liabilities | 100,000 |
| Intangible assets | 20,000 | Stockholders' equity | 140,000 |
| | $270,000 | | $270,000 |

On January 2, 1995 the Paul Company purchased the Marino Company by acquiring all its outstanding shares for $300,000 cash. On that date, the market value of the current assets was $40,000, and the property, plant, and equipment was valued at $240,000. In addition, a previously unrecorded intangible asset was valued at $25,000.

**Required**

Compute the goodwill associated with the purchase of the Marino Company.

E10-10    *Appendix: Normal Earnings and Goodwill*    The total earnings of the Jaeger Company for 1995 were $100,000 and included the following items:

| Extraordinary gain | $10,000 | Depreciation on building (straight-line) | $20,000 |
| Liquidation of LIFO layer | 7,000 | Profit sharing payments to employees | 25,000 |
| Amortization of intangibles | 12,000 | | |

The profit sharing is based on a constant percent of total earnings *before* deducting the profit sharing amount. The building is worth 50% more than its recorded cost, and its economic life is double the current estimate.

**Required**

Compute normal earnings for the year.

E10-11    *Appendix: Goodwill*    For the past 5 years, the Satin Company has had average assets of $120,000, average liabilities of $40,000, and average annual earnings of $12,000. In the past 5 years, the company has had an extraordinary loss of $10,000 and a nonrecurring gain of $15,000. A 12% return on investment is considered normal for the industry. The expected life of any excess earnings is 10 years.

**Required**

1. Compute the implied goodwill of the Satin Company.
2. If excess annual earnings are capitalized at 14%, compute the implied goodwill.

E10-12    *Appendix: Goodwill*    The Hayes Company is considering acquiring the Ryan Company. The balance sheet of the Ryan Company is as follows:

| Current assets | $ 50,000 | Current liabilities | $ 30,000 |
| Noncurrent assets | 150,000 | Noncurrent liabilities | 50,000 |
| | | Stockholders' equity | 120,000 |
| | $200,000 | | $200,000 |

The Hayes Company believes that goodwill should be based on the book value of the assets and that excess earnings last only 5 years and should be capitalized at 12%. The Ryan Company believes that the assets are undervalued by 25%, that excess annual earnings will last forever, and that they should be capitalized at the normal rate of return. Both companies agree that the expected future annual earnings are $25,000 per year and the normal rate of return is 10%.

**Required**

1. Compute the implied goodwill under the proposal of each company.
2. Which of the two companies has the more reasonable approach to computing goodwill?

E10-13  *Appendix: Goodwill*  The owners of the Urwill Clothing Store are contemplating selling the business to new interests. The cumulative earnings for the past 5 years amounted to $550,000 including extraordinary gains of $40,000. The annual earnings based on an average rate of return on investment for this industry would have been $76,000. Excess earnings are to be capitalized at 10%.

**Required**

Compute the value of the implied goodwill. (*AICPA adapted*)

E10-14  *Appendix: Goodwill*  The net assets of the Wiese Company were appraised at $100,000. Estimated future annual earnings are $15,000.

**Required**

Compute the value of the goodwill under each of the following assumptions:

1. The future annual earnings will continue in perpetuity and are capitalized at 15%. The normal rate of return is 15%.
2. The excess annual earnings are expected to have a life of 5 years. The normal rate of return (and capitalization rate) is 10%.
3. The excess annual earnings are expected to have a life of 10 years. The normal rate of return is 10%, and excess annual earnings are capitalized at 12%.

E10-15  *Appendix: Estimated Future Annual Earnings*  The Stegman Company acquired the Band Company for $150,000. Excess annual earnings were capitalized at 20% in perpetuity. The normal rate of return is 11%. The goodwill was computed as $20,000.

**Required**

What are the estimated future annual earnings of the Band Company?

## PROBLEMS

P10-1  *Cost of Intangibles*  The Brush Company engaged in the following transactions at the beginning of 1995:

1. Purchased a patent for $70,000 that had originally been issued in January 1989. The purchase was made to protect another patent that the company had received in January 1992.
2. Purchased the rights to a novel by a best-selling novelist in exchange for 10,000 shares of $10 par value common stock selling for $60 per share. The book sells 1 million copies in 1995 and is expected to sell a total of 500,000 copies in future years.
3. Purchased the franchise to operate a ferry service from the state government for $10,000. A bridge has been planned to replace the ferry, and it is expected that it will be completed in 5 years. Brush hopes that the ferry will continue as a tourist attraction, but profits are expected to be only 20% of those earned before the bridge is opened.
4. Paid $18,000 of legal costs to successfully defend the patent acquired in transaction 1.
5. Paid a race car driver $50,000 to have the Brush Company name prominently displayed on his car for 2 years.

**Required**

Prepare journal entries to record the preceding transactions, including the first year's amortization of intangible assets where appropriate. Amortize over the legal life unless a better alternative is indicated.

P10-2  *Cost of Intangibles*  The Byrd Corporation engaged in the following transactions at the beginning of 1995:

1. Purchased a Hogburger Franchise for a 5-year, $60,000, 10%-interest-bearing note. The franchise has an unlimited life providing the terms of the franchise are not violated.
2. Sold a tradename for $50,000. The tradename had a book value of $1,000.
3. Paid an advertising agency $80,000 to develop a 2-year advertising campaign to promote a new tradename.
4. Incurred legal fees of $3,000 to register a new tradename.
5. Purchased the copyright to a new movie for $500,000. The movie is made during 1995 at a cost of $15 million. It will begin showing in 1996 and is expected to gross $10 million during 1996, $20 million during 1997, and $10 million during 1998.

**Required**

Prepare journal entries to record the preceding transactions, including the amortization of intangible assets for 1995. Amortize over the legal life unless a better alternative is indicated.

P10-3   *Correct Classification of Intangibles*   During the current year, the accountant for the Cartwright Corporation recorded numerous transactions in an account labeled Intangibles as follows:

| | | |
|---|---|---:|
| Jan. 2 | Incorporation fees | $17,500 |
| Jan. 10 | Legal fees for the organization of the company | 7,500 |
| Jan. 25 | Paid for large-scale advertising campaign for the year | 15,000 |
| Apr. 1 | Acquired land for $15,000 and a building for $20,000 to house the R&D activities. The building has a 20-year life. | 35,000 |
| May 15 | Purchased materials exclusively for use in R&D activities. Of these materials, 20% are left at the end of the year and will be used in the same project next year. (They have no alternative use.) | 15,000 |
| June 30 | Purchased a patent | 10,000 |
| July 1 | Operating loss for first 6 months of the year | 12,000 |
| Dec. 11 | Purchased an experimental machine from an inventor. The machine is expected to be used for a particular R&D activity for 2 years, after which it will have no residual value. | 12,000 |
| Dec. 31 | Paid employees involved in R&D | 30,000 |

**Required**

Prepare adjusting journal entries to eliminate the Intangibles account and correctly record all the items. Organization costs are amortized over 5 years and any other intangibles are amortized over their legal lives.

P10-4   *Correcting Entries for Patents*   During the year-end audit of the Cressman Corporation's financial statements for 1995, the following items are discovered:

1. The company had capitalized $57,000 to the Patent account at the beginning of 1994, for the cost of a patent. This amount included $50,000 of R&D costs. The patent has been amortized over a 17-year life in 1994 and 1995.
2. At the beginning of 1994, the company had paid its lawyers $5,000 to successfully defend a patent infringement suit regarding the patent in Item 1. This cost had been debited to legal fees expense.
3. At the beginning of 1995, the company purchased a patent for $20,000 from the Baylor Company to prevent potential competition. It recorded the cost in the Patent account and amortized this cost over the remaining legal life of the patent obtained in Item 1. However, the company agreed to a suggestion by the auditors that the life of the company patent obtained in Item 1 was protected for only 7 more years as of the beginning of 1995.

**Required**

Prepare adjusting journal entries on December 31, 1995.

P10-5   *Cost of Patents*   The Davis Research Company engaged in the following six transactions during 1995:

1. Purchased a patent for $35,000. Legal costs of $5,000 were also incurred.
2. Costs of improving patent:

| | |
|---|---:|
| Engineering costs | $20,000 |
| Assembling and testing prototypes | 10,000 |
| Other R&D costs | 25,000 |

3. Sold a prototype machine for $7,000. The research and development was performed in previous years.
4. Licensed a manufacturing process to another company and received $80,000 as an advance payment.
5. Successfully defended a patent infringement suit at a cost of $12,000.
6. Earned $5,000 of the advance payment on the licensed manufacturing process in Item 4.

**Required**

Prepare journal entries to record the preceding transactions.

**P10-6** *Research and Development Costs* Cressman Company incurred research and development costs in 1995 as follows:

| | |
|---|---:|
| Materials used in research and development projects | $ 400,000 |
| Equipment acquired that will have alternate future uses in future research and development projects for 4 years | 2,000,000 |
| Personnel costs of employees involved in research and development projects | 1,000,000 |
| Consulting fees paid to outsiders for research and development projects | 100,000 |
| Indirect costs reasonably allocable to research and development projects | 200,000 |

**Required**

What is the amount of research and development costs charged to Cressman's 1995 income? (*AICPA adapted*)

**P10-7** *Intangibles* The Jolis Company has provided information on the following items:

1. A patent was purchased from the Totley Company for $500,000 on January 1, 1994. At that time, Jolis estimated the remaining useful life to be 10 years. The patent was carried on Totley's books at $20,000 when it sold the patent.
2. On March 2, 1995 a franchise was purchased from the Unal Company for $220,000. In addition, 8% of the revenue from the franchise must be paid to Unal. Revenue earned during 1995 was $640,000. Jolis believes that the life of the franchise is indeterminate.
3. Research and development costs were incurred as follows: (a) materials and equipment: $50,000; (b) personnel: 80,000; and (c) indirect costs: 40,000. The costs were incurred to develop a product that will go on sale in 1996 and will have an expected life of 5 years.
4. A tradename had been purchased for a sugar substitute at the beginning of 1991 for $70,000. In January 1995 it was suspected that the product caused cancer and so the tradename was abandoned.
5. The company purchased the net assets of Lansing Company on September 1, 1995 for $950,000 and the Lansing Company was liquidated. The Lansing Company had the following book (market) values: current assets: $200,000 ($210,000); property, plant, equipment: $750,000 ($900,000); liabilities: $250,000 ($250,000).

**Required**

Prepare journal entries for the Jolis Company for 1995. The company uses the straight-line method of amortization computed to the nearest month over the maximum allowable life. Assume that all costs are paid in cash, unless otherwise indicated.

**P10-8** *Cost of a Copyright* The Gansac Publishing Company signed a contract with an author to publish her book. The signing took place on January 1, 1995 and a payment of $10,000 was made. The agreement was that the author would receive 10% of the selling price of $10 per book. Sales of the book were expected to be 100,000 copies in 1995, 60,000 in 1996, and 40,000 in 1997. Production costs of $800,000 for 200,000 copies were incurred during 1995.

**Required**

1. Prepare journal entries to record the preceding events during 1995 and 1996, assuming that sales were as projected.
2. How would your answer change if the projected sales were considered to be "probable"?

**P10-9** *R&D Costs* The controller of the Halpern Company prepared the following income statement and balance sheet at the end of the first year of the company's existence:

**Income Statement**

| | |
|---|---:|
| Sales revenue | $20,000 |
| Cost of sales | (10,000) |
| Operating expenses | (8,000) |
| Net income | $ 2,000 |

**Balance Sheet**

| | | | |
|---|---:|---|---:|
| Cash | $ 33,000 | Accounts payable | $ 5,000 |
| Inventory | 24,000 | Notes payable | 40,000 |
| R&D costs | 30,000 | Common stock | 60,000 |
| Property, plant, and equipment (net) | 20,000 | Retained earnings | 2,000 |
| | $107,000 | | $107,000 |

Investigation shows that R&D costs include, among others, half the year's operating costs because "the company is not yet operating at capacity." In addition R&D costs include $5,000 of materials that were wasted during early production because "our employees made some unnecessary mistakes."

**Required**

Prepare the financial statements according to generally accepted accounting principles.

P10-10    *Goodwill*    The Hamilton Company balance sheet on January 1, 1995 was as follows:

| | | | |
|---|---|---|---|
| Cash | $ 30,000 | Current liabilities | $ 20,000 |
| Accounts receivable | 80,000 | Bonds payable | 120,000 |
| Marketable securities (short-term) | 40,000 | Pension liability | 50,000 |
| Inventory | 100,000 | Common stock | 200,000 |
| Property, plant, and equipment (net) | 200,000 | Retained earnings | 60,000 |
| | $450,000 | | $450,000 |

The Korbel Company is considering purchasing the Hamilton Company (a privately-held company) and discovers the following about the Hamilton Company:

1. No allowance for uncollectibles has been established. A $10,000 allowance is considered appropriate.
2. Marketable securities are valued at cost. The current market value is $60,000.
3. The LIFO inventory method is used. The FIFO inventory of $140,000 would be used if the company is acquired.
4. Land, included in property, plant, and equipment, which is recorded at its cost of $50,000, is worth $120,000. The remaining property, plant, and equipment is worth 10% more than its depreciated cost.
5. The company has an unrecorded trademark that is worth $70,000.
6. The company's bonds are currently trading for $130,000 and the common stock for $300,000.
7. The pension liability is understated by $40,000.

**Required**

1. Compute the value of the implied goodwill if the Korbel Company agrees to pay $500,000 cash for the Hamilton Company.
2. Prepare the journal entry to record the acquisition on the books of the Korbel Company, assuming the Hamilton Company is liquidated.
3. Prepare the journal entry to record the first year's amortization of goodwill (over the maximum life) on the books of the Korbel Company.
4. If the Korbel Company agrees to pay only $400,000 cash, how much is the implied goodwill?
5. If the Korbel Company pays only $400,000 cash, prepare the journal entry to record the acquisition on its books assuming the Hamilton Company is liquidated.

P10-11    *Intangibles: Expense and Disclosure*    Munn, Inc., had the following intangible account balances at December 31, 1994:

| | |
|---|---|
| Patent | $192,000 |
| Accumulated amortization | (24,000) |

Transactions during 1995 and other information relating to Munn's intangible assets were as follows:

1. The patent was purchased from Grey Company for $192,000 on January 1, 1993, at which date the remaining legal life was 16 years. On January 1, 1995 Munn determined that the useful life of the patent was only 8 years from the date of acquisition.
2. On January 3, 1995, in connection with the purchase of a trademark from Cody Corporation, the parties entered into a noncompetition agreement and a consulting contract. Munn paid Cody $800,000, of which three-quarters was for the trademark and one-quarter was for Cody's agreement not to compete for a 5-year period in the line of business covered by the trademark. Munn considers the life of the trademark to be indefinite. Under the consulting contract, Munn agreed to pay Cody $50,000 annually on January 3 for 5 years. The first payment was made on January 3, 1995.

**Required**

1. Prepare a schedule of the expenses for 1995 relating to Munn's intangible asset balances at December 31, 1994 and transactions during 1995.
2. Prepare the intangible assets section of Munn's balance sheet at December 31, 1995. (*AICPA adapted*)

P10-12  *Intangibles: Assets and Expenses*  The Barb Company has provided information on intangible assets as follows:

1. A patent was purchased from the Lou Company for $1,500,000 on January 1, 1994. Barb estimated the remaining useful life of the patent to be ten years. The patent was carried in Lou's accounting records at a net book value of $1,250,000 when Lou sold it to Barb.
2. During 1995 a franchise was purchased from the Rink Company for $500,000. In addition, 5% of revenue from the franchise must be paid to Rink. Revenue from the franchise for 1995 was $2,000,000. Barb estimates the useful life of the franchise to be ten years and takes a full year's amortization in the year of purchase.
3. Barb incurred research and development costs in 1995 as follows:

| | |
|---|---|
| Materials and equipment | $120,000 |
| Personnel | 140,000 |
| Indirect costs | 60,000 |
| | $320,000 |

Barb estimates that these costs will be recouped by December 31, 1996.

4. On January 1, 1995 Barb, based on new events that have occurred in the field, estimates that the remaining life of the patent purchased on January 1, 1994 is only five years from January 1, 1995.

**Required**

1. Prepare a schedule showing the intangibles section of Barb's balance sheet at December 31, 1995. Show supporting computations in good form.
2. Prepare a schedule showing the income statement effect for the year ended December 31, 1995 as a result of the previously mentioned facts. Show supporting computations in good form. (*AICPA adapted*)

P10-13  *Comprehensive*  Lee Manufacturing Corporation was incorporated on January 3, 1994. The corporation's financial statements for its first year's operations were not examined by a CPA. You have been engaged to examine the financial statements for the year ended December 31, 1995, and your examination is substantially completed. The corporation's trial balance at December 31, 1995 appears here:

| | Debit | Credit |
|---|---|---|
| Cash | $ 11,000 | |
| Accounts receivable | 42,500 | |
| Allowance for doubtful accounts | | $ 500 |
| Inventories | 38,500 | |
| Machinery | 75,000 | |
| Equipment | 29,000 | |
| Accumulated depreciation | | 10,000 |
| Patents | 85,000 | |
| Leasehold improvements | 26,000 | |
| Prepaid expenses | 10,500 | |
| Organization costs | 29,000 | |
| Goodwill | 24,000 | |
| Licensing agreement No. 1 | 50,000 | |
| Licensing agreement No. 2 | 49,000 | |
| Accounts payable | | 147,500 |
| Unearned revenue | | 12,500 |
| Capital stock | | 300,000 |
| Retained earnings, January 1, 1995 | 27,000 | |
| Sales | | 668,500 |
| Cost of goods sold | 454,000 | |
| Selling and general expenses | 173,000 | |
| Interest expense | 3,500 | |
| Extraordinary losses | 12,000 | |
| Total | $1,139,000 | $1,139,000 |

The following information relates to accounts that may yet require adjustment:

1. Patents for Lee's manufacturing process were acquired January 2, 1995 at a cost of $68,000. An additional $17,000 was spent in December 1995 to improve machinery covered by the patents and charged to the Patents account. Depreciation on fixed assets has been properly recorded for 1995 in accordance with Lee's practice, which provides a full year's depreciation for property on hand June 30 and no depreciation otherwise. Lee uses the straight-line method for all depreciation and amortization and amortizes its patents over their legal life.
2. On January 3, 1994 Lee purchased Licensing Agreement No. 1, which was believed to have an unlimited useful life. The balance in the Licensing Agreement No. 1 account includes its purchase price of $48,000 and expenses of $2,000 related to the acquisition. On January 1, 1995 Lee purchased Licensing Agreement No. 2, which has a life expectancy of 10 years. The balance in the Licensing Agreement No. 2 account includes its $48,000 purchase price and $2,000 in acquisition expenses, but it has been reduced by a credit of $1,000 for the advance collection of 1996 revenue from the agreement. In late December 1994 an explosion caused a permanent 60% reduction in the expected revenue-producing value of Licensing Agreement No. 1, and in January 1996 a flood caused additional damage that rendered the agreement worthless.
3. The balance in the Goodwill account includes (a) $8,000 paid December 30, 1994 for an advertising program it is estimated will assist in increasing Lee's sales over a period of 4 years following the disbursement, and (b) legal expenses of $16,000 incurred for Lee's incorporation on January 3, 1994.
4. The Leasehold Improvements account includes (a) the $15,000 cost of improvements with a total estimated useful life of 12 years, which Lee, as tenant, made to leased premises in January 1994, (b) movable assembly line equipment costing $8,500 that was installed in the leased premises in December 1995, and (c) real estate taxes of $2,500 paid by Lee in 1995, which under the terms of the lease should have been paid by the landlord. Lee paid its rent in full during 1995. A 10-year nonrenewable lease was signed January 3, 1994 for the leased building that Lee used in manufacturing operations.
5. The balance in the Organization Costs account properly includes costs incurred during the organizational period. The corporation has exercised its option to amortize organization costs over a 60-month period for federal income tax purposes and wishes to amortize these for accounting purposes on the same basis.

**Required**
Prepare a worksheet to adjust accounts that require adjustment and prepare financial statements. A separate account should be used for the accumulation of each type of amortization and for each prior period adjustment. Formal adjusting journal entries and financial statements are not required. (*Hint*: Make sure that Licensing Agreement No. 1 is amortized over the maximum life required in *APB Opinion No. 17* before the explosion damage loss is determined.) (*AICPA adapted*)

P10-14 *Comprehensive* Information concerning Tully Corporation's intangible assets is as follows:

a. On January 1, 1995 Tully signed an agreement to operate as a franchisee of Rapid Copy Service, Inc., for an initial franchise fee of $85,000. Of this amount, $25,000 was paid when the agreement was signed, and the balance is payable in four annual payments of $15,000 each beginning January 1, 1996. The agreement provides that the down payment is not refundable and no future services are required of the franchisor. The present value at January 2, 1995 of the four annual payments discounted at 14% (the implicit rate for a loan of this type) is $43,700. The agreement also provides that 5% of the revenue from the franchise must be paid to the franchisor annually. Tully's revenue from the franchise for 1995 was $900,000. Tully estimates the useful life of the franchise to be 10 years.
b. Tully incurred $78,000 of experimental and development costs in its laboratory to develop a patent, which was granted on January 2, 1995. Legal fees and other costs associated with registration of the patent totaled $16,400. Tully estimates that the useful life of the patent will be 8 years.
c. A trademark was purchased from Walton Company for $40,000 on July 1, 1992. Expenditures for successful litigation in defense of the trademark totaling $10,000 were paid on July 1, 1995. Tully estimates that the useful life of the trademark will be 20 years from the date of acquisition.

**Required**
1. Prepare a schedule showing the intangibles section of Tully's balance sheet at December 31, 1995. Show supporting computations in good form.
2. Prepare a schedule showing all expenses resulting from the transactions that would appear on Tully's income statement for the year ended December 31, 1995. Show supporting computations in good form. (*AICPA adapted*)

Problems

**469**

*P10-15  Comprehensive*  Bryant Corporation was incorporated on December 1, 1994 and began operations 1 week later. Before closing the books for the fiscal year ended November 30, 1995, Bryant's controller prepared the following financial statements:

### Balance Sheet
### November 30, 1995

| Assets | | Liabilities and Stockholders' Equity | |
|---|---:|---|---:|
| Current assets | | Current liabilities | |
| Cash | $ 180,000 | Accounts payable and accrued expenses | $ 592,000 |
| Accounts receivable | 480,000 | Income taxes payable | 168,000 |
| Less: Allowance for doubtful accounts | (59,000) | Total current liabilities | $ 760,000 |
| Inventories | 430,000 | | |
| Prepaid insurance | 15,000 | Stockholders' equity | |
| Total current assets | $1,046,000 | Common stock, $10 par value | $ 400,000 |
| Property, plant, and equipment | 426,000 | Retained earnings | 392,000 |
| Less: Accumulated depreciation | (40,000) | Total stockholders' equity | $ 792,000 |
| Research and development costs | 120,000 | Total Liabilities and Stockholders' Equity | $1,552,000 |
| Total Assets | $1,552,000 | | |

### Statement of Income
### For Year Ended November 30, 1995

| | |
|---|---:|
| Net sales | $2,950,000 |
| Operating expenses: | |
| Cost of sales | $1,670,000 |
| Selling and administrative | 650,000 |
| Depreciation | 40,000 |
| Research and development | 30,000 |
| Total expenses | $2,390,000 |
| Income before income taxes | $ 560,000 |
| Income tax expense | 168,000 |
| Net Income | $ 392,000 |

Bryant Corporation is in the process of negotiating a loan for expansion purposes, and the bank has requested audited financial statements. During the course of the audit, the following additional information was obtained:

1. Included in selling and administrative expenses were $5,000 of costs incurred on software being developed for sale to others. The technological feasibility of the software has been established.
2. Based on an aging of the accounts receivable as of November 30, 1995 it was estimated that $36,000 of the receivables will be uncollectible.
3. Inventories at November 30, 1995 did not include work-in-process inventory costing $12,000 sent to an outside processor on November 27, 1995.
4. A $3,000 insurance premium paid on November 30, 1995 on a policy expiring 1 year later was charged to insurance expense.
5. Bryant adopted a pension plan on June 1, 1995 for eligible employees to be administered by a trustee. Based upon actuarial computations, the first 12 month's accrued pension plan expense was estimated at $45,000.
6. On June 1, 1995 a production machine purchased for $24,000 was charged to repairs and maintenance. Bryant depreciates machines of this type on the straight-line method over a 5-year life, with no salvage value, for financial and tax purposes.
7. Research and development costs of $150,000 were incurred in the development of a patent that Bryant expects to be granted during the fiscal year ending November 30, 1996. Bryant initiated a 5-year amortization of the $150,000 total cost during the fiscal year ended November 30, 1995.
8. During December 1995 a competitor company filed suit against Bryant for patent infringement claiming $200,000 in damages. Bryant's legal counsel believes that an unfavorable outcome is probable. A reasonable accrual based on an estimate of the court's award to the plaintiff is $50,000.
9. The 30% effective tax rate was determined to be appropriate for calculating the provision for income taxes for the fiscal year ended November 30, 1995. Ignore computation of deferred portion of income taxes.

**Required**

1. Prepare the necessary correcting entries.
2. Prepare a corrected balance sheet of Bryant Corporation as of November 30, 1995 and a corrected statement of income for the year ended November 30, 1995. (*AICPA adapted*)

P10-16 *Appendix: Goodwill* The Humphries Company has earned the following net income for the last 5 years:

| | |
|---|---|
| 1991 | $100,000 |
| 1992 | 120,000 |
| 1993 | 140,000 (including an extraordinary loss of $4,000) |
| 1994 | 150,000 (including an extraordinary loss of $22,800) |
| 1995 | 215,000 (including an extraordinary gain of $7,640) |

The market value of the identifiable net assets is $1.4 million. The normal rate of return earned by a company in this industry is 10%. The excess annual earnings are expected to last 5 years and are to be capitalized at 12%.

**Required**

1. Compute the value of the implied goodwill if estimated future annual earnings are based on the average of the excess annual earnings for the past 5 years.
2. Compute the value of the implied goodwill if estimated future annual earnings are based on the trend apparent in the normal earnings of the past 5 years.

P10-17 *Appendix: Goodwill* The Elm Company is considering purchasing the EKC Company. The balance sheet of the EKC Company at December 31, 1995 is as follows:

| | | | |
|---|---|---|---|
| Cash | $ 50,000 | Current liabilities | $ 60,000 |
| Accounts receivable | 70,000 | Bonds payable | 200,000 |
| Inventory | 120,000 | Common stock | 300,000 |
| Property, plant, and equipment (net) | 600,000 | Retained earnings | 280,000 |
| | $840,000 | | $840,000 |

The EKC Company has earned the following net income for the last 5 years:

| | |
|---|---|
| 1991 | $150,000 |
| 1992 | 162,000 |
| 1993 | 182,960 (including an extraordinary gain of $8,000) |
| 1994 | 188,957 |
| 1995 | 200,073 (including an extraordinary loss of $4,000) |

At December 31, 1995 the Elm Company discovered the following about the EKC Company:

1. No allowance for uncollectible accounts has been established. An allowance of $5,000 is considered appropriate.
2. The LIFO inventory method has been used. The FIFO inventory method would be used if EKC were purchased by Elm. The FIFO inventory valuation of the December 31, 1995 ending inventory would be $180,000.
3. The market value of the property, plant, and equipment (net) is $730,000.
4. The company has an unrecorded patent that is worth $120,000.
5. The book values of the current liabilities and bonds payable are the same as their market values. The normal rate of return earned by a company in EKC's industry is 12%. Excess annual earnings are expected to last 7 years and should be capitalized at 14%.

**Required**

1. Compute the value of the implied goodwill if the Elm Company pays $1,350,000 for EKC.
2. Compute the value of the implied goodwill if estimated future annual earnings are based on the average of the excess annual earnings for the last 5 years.
3. Compute the value of the implied goodwill if estimated future annual earnings are based on the trend apparent in the normal annual earnings of the past 5 years.

# FINANCIAL REPORTING

## Valuation of Liabilities and Investments

PART

# 3

# 11

# CURRENT LIABILITIES AND CONTINGENCIES

**Chapter Topics**

*Concept and Definition of Liabilities*

*Nature and Definition of Current Liabilities*

*Measuring Known Liabilities of a Definite Amount*

*Measuring Liabilities, the Amount of Which Depends on Operations*

*Measuring Estimated Liabilities*

*Accounting for Contingencies*

*Short-Term Debt Expected to Be Refinanced*

*Current Liability Disclosures*

This is the first of two chapters on liabilities. Chapter 11 focuses on current liabilities (including contingencies), while Chapter 12 addresses long-term (noncurrent) liabilities. In the past, accountants have paid only limited attention to identifying and measuring the liabilities that arise in the operating process. More attention is now being given to the concept of liabilities and their measurement. This is a natural evolution stemming from an increased use of special financing and sales agreements, lease arrangements, new labor contracts including pension plans, and more complex tax laws. Emphasis on liability measurement has made the liability section of the balance sheet more meaningful. It has tended to eliminate the practice of using this section as a "catchall" for various credit items.

Since the topics in both chapters hinge on an understanding of the term *liabilities*, the initial discussion expands on the concept and definition of a liability presented in the review of the balance sheet in Chapter 3. The nature, definition, and valuation of current liabilities are addressed and the items comprising three major groups of current liabilities are explained. Then the broad issue of contingencies is examined, followed by a discussion of short-term debt expected to be refinanced and obligations that are callable by the creditor. Last, specific methods of reporting current liabilities on the balance sheet and in the notes to the financial statements are discussed, and examples of disclosures by actual companies are presented.

## CONCEPTUAL OVERVIEW OF LIABILITIES

As part of its *Conceptual Framework,* the FASB defined liabilities in **FASB Statement of Financial Accounting Concepts No. 6** as follows:

> Liabilities are probable future sacrifices of economic benefits arising from present obligations of a company to transfer assets or provide services to other entities in the future as a result of past transactions or events.[1]

The FASB also explained two of the terms. The word **probable refers to what can reasonably be expected or believed based on available evidence or logic but is neither certain nor proved.** The word **obligations refers to duties imposed legally or socially which one is bound to do by contract, promise, moral responsibility, and so forth.**[2] In other words, liabilities include both legal and nonlegal (but not illegal) obligations. **Legal liabilities are incurred in exchange transactions that are contractual in nature—based on written or oral agreements to pay cash or to provide goods or services to specified or determinable entities on demand at specified or determinable dates on occurrence of specified events.** Legal liabilities include such items as notes payable and sales tax payable. **The nonlegal group (also called accounting liabilities) includes those obligations where there is no *legal* requirement for assets to be transferred, yet a transfer of assets typically occurs as a part of the normal operations of a business.**[3] Nonlegal liabilities include equitable and constructive obligations, such as the liability to employees for vacation pay or year-end bonuses, that a company chooses to create by paying them every year even though it is not contractually bound to do so and has not announced a policy to do so. The accounting for both types of liabilities is discussed later in this chapter.

As introduced in Chapter 3, for a company there are **three essential characteristics of a liability:**

1. It involves a present duty or responsibility of the company to one or more other entities that will be settled by the probable *future transfer* or *use of assets* at a specified or determinable date, on occurrence of a specific event, or on demand.

2. The duty or responsibility obligates the company, *leaving it little or no discretion to avoid* the future sacrifice.

3. The transaction or other event obligating the company *has already happened.*

The main features of these three essential characteristics are highlighted by italics: the requirement that a company transfer or use assets, the requirement that the obligation must be settled, and the fact that the liability transaction has already occurred.

There are two additional factors involving a liability. First, as long as payment or other transfer of assets to settle an existing obligation is probable, the identity of the recipient need not be known to the obligated company before the time of settlement. Second, as implied in the definition, the existence of a legally enforceable claim is not a prerequisite for an obligation to qualify as a liability if for other reasons the company has a duty or responsibility to pay cash, transfer other assets, or provide

---

1.  "Elements of Financial Reporting of Business Enterprises," *FASB Statement of Financial Accounting Concepts No. 6* (Stamford, Conn.: FASB, December 1985), par. 28.
2.  *Ibid.,* fn. 21 and 22.
3.  *Ibid.,* par. 38.

services to another company.[4] It should be noted that in reality, however, some liabilities are "liquidated" by conversion into common or preferred stock or by refinancing into other liabilities, as discussed in Chapter 12.

The financial accounting issues related to liabilities are important in both income and financial position measurement. The primary issues discussed in the remainder of this chapter are:

1. The *identification* of liabilities—the detection of a company's debts

2. The *measurement* or *valuation* of the liabilities and the related expense—the determination of an amount to attach to each debt and to match as an expense against revenues

3. The *reporting* on the financial statements—the specific disclosures in both the company's financial statements and the related notes

*Long-term liabilities are discussed in Chapter 12 and in other chapters.*

Liabilities generally are classified as either (1) current or (2) long-term. The preceding issues are discussed in this chapter as they relate to the obligations classified as current liabilities.

## NATURE AND DEFINITION OF CURRENT LIABILITIES

The specific meaning, nature, and classification of current liabilities, which are considered in the following sections, are very important to users of financial statements.

### Classification and the Operating Cycle or Year

Recall that current liabilities are obligations whose liquidation is reasonably expected to require the use of existing current assets or the creation of other current liabilities within one year or an operating cycle, whichever is longer. The usual criterion is one year. For certain companies, however, where the **operating cycle—from cash to inventory to receivables and back to cash**—extends beyond the year, the length of the operating cycle becomes the determinant of the classification of the liability. An example of a company's operating cycle is shown in Exhibit 11-1. Many current liabilities, such as accounts payable, wages payable, warranty obligations, and notes payable, are incurred (and paid) in the process. For example, a current liability—Accounts Payable—is created when an inventory item is acquired. Also, a current liability, Salaries Payable, often arises as a result of accrued salaries for selling as well as general and administrative personnel.

Some accountants question the inconsistency of using different time periods for classifying liabilities as current—that is, the use of a year or an operating cycle, whichever is longer. They prefer to use the length of the operating cycle as the period for determining the classification of liabilities regardless of whether it is longer or shorter than a year. Since this issue deals primarily with the question of liquidity, it and the related issue of financial flexibility are introduced next.

### Liquidity, Financial Flexibility, and Current Liabilities

One attribute of a liability (and also an asset) is its liquidity. **Liquidity refers to a liability's nearness to cash.** The FASB has become increasingly concerned about

4.  *Ibid.*, par. 36.

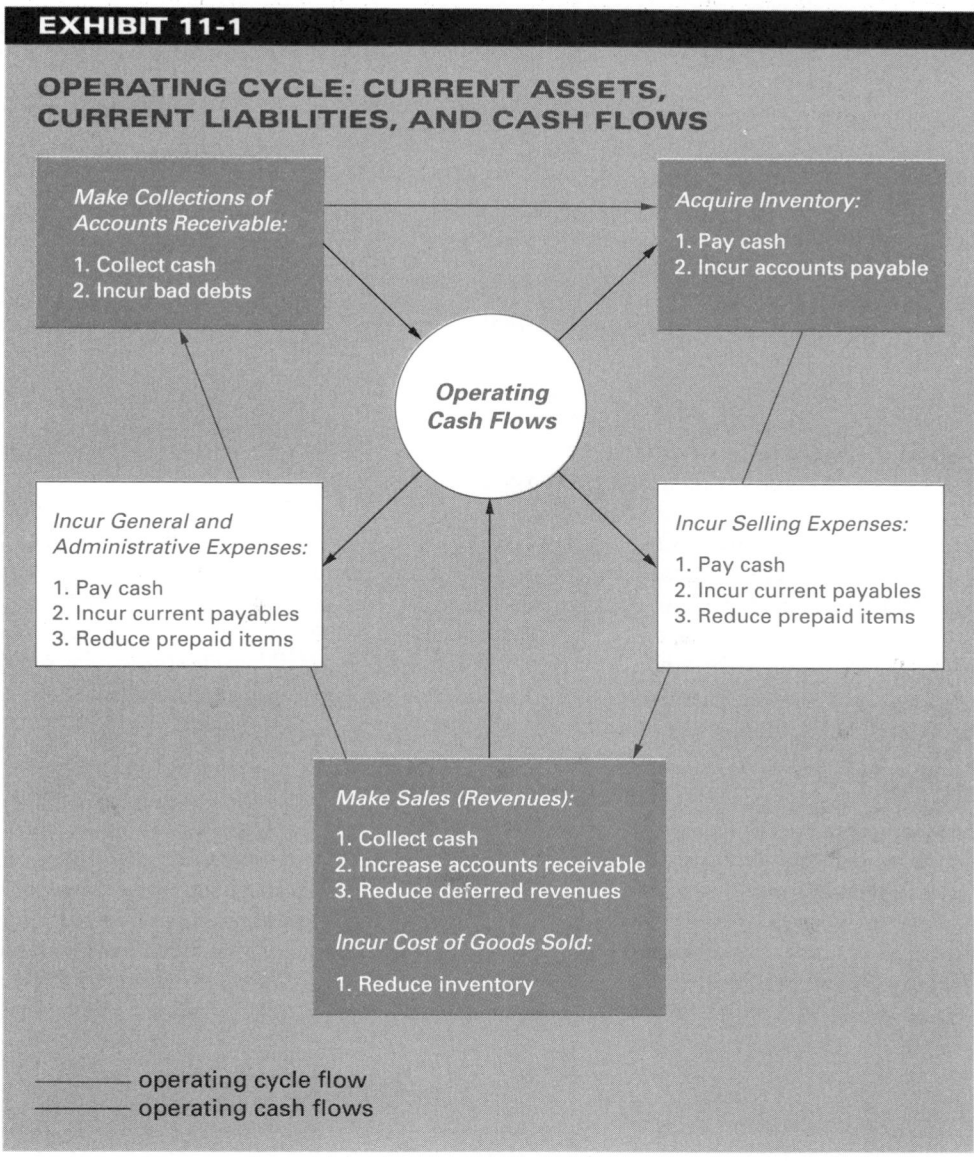

**EXHIBIT 11-1**

**OPERATING CYCLE: CURRENT ASSETS, CURRENT LIABILITIES, AND CASH FLOWS**

*Make Collections of Accounts Receivable:*

1. Collect cash
2. Incur bad debts

*Acquire Inventory:*

1. Pay cash
2. Incur accounts payable

*Operating Cash Flows*

*Incur General and Administrative Expenses:*

1. Pay cash
2. Incur current payables
3. Reduce prepaid items

*Incur Selling Expenses:*

1. Pay cash
2. Incur current payables
3. Reduce prepaid items

*Make Sales (Revenues):*

1. Collect cash
2. Increase accounts receivable
3. Reduce deferred revenues

*Incur Cost of Goods Sold:*

1. Reduce inventory

————— operating cycle flow
————— operating cash flows

reporting the liquidity of liabilities and assets because users evaluate future cash flows in their decision-making processes. In part, these *future cash flows are predicted based on the nearness to cash of liabilities and assets.* Therefore, the liquidity of liabilities and assets is important in these decision-making processes.

The FASB has discussed various ways of reporting the liquidity of both liabilities and assets, including (1) continuing the current practice for classifying current liabilities and assets (mixture of operating-cycle and maturity-date approach), (2) classifying current liabilities and assets using the "pure" operating-cycle approach, (3) classifying current liabilities and assets under the maturity approach only, (4) adopting a different classification scheme, possibly using more classes, and

(5) leaving the balance sheet unclassified but arranging in order of liquidity.[5] Each method has certain advantages and disadvantages in terms of revealing liquidity, but they are beyond the scope of this book.

The FASB has also observed that the principal objective of financial reporting—that of providing information useful in assessing the amount, timing, and uncertainty of future cash flows—depends on a knowledge of the liquidity of liabilities and assets.[6] The Board, in examining the classification of liabilities and assets, studied ways of relating these items to each other and of relating them to other financial statement data to obtain information about liquidity and to determine what relationships might be the best predictors of failure. Five "liquidity" ratios were listed as providing information to lending institutions, creditors, and other external users of financial information: (1) cash flows to total debt, (2) net income to total assets, (3) total debt to total assets, (4) current assets to current liabilities, and (5) cash to current liabilities. Four of the five require information about liabilities; two require information about current liabilities. Since ratio analysis is discussed in detail in Chapter 23, these ratios are not discussed here.

Related to liquidity is a company's financial flexibility. **Financial flexibility refers to a company's ability to use its financial resources to adapt to change.** This ability primarily involves the management of cash and other resources to achieve certain financial advantages from both an offensive and defensive point of view. In part, it also involves the potential to create new current and long-term liabilities, to restructure existing debt, and to manage debt in other ways. These features relating to financial flexibility are covered later in this chapter and in other chapters.

## Classification of Current Liabilities

Many current liabilities are easily identifiable and of a definite amount. Others, though identifiable, have amounts that depend upon operations, while still others require the amounts to be estimated. Many current liabilities arise out of operations of the current period. Others, such as dividends payable and the current portion of long-term debt, do not relate to operations but are still current liabilities. The primary types of current liabilities discussed in this chapter are classified in the following three groups:

1. *Current liabilities having a definite amount*, which include trade accounts payable, short-term notes payable, currently maturing portion of long-term debt, dividends payable, advances and refundable deposits, liabilities from product financing agreements, accrued liabilities (including those for compensated absences, off-balance sheet financing obligations, and product financing arrangements), and unearned (deferred) items (revenues collected in advance).

2. *Current liabilities whose amounts depend on operations*, which include sales and use taxes, various liabilities relating to payrolls, income taxes payable, and bonus obligations.

3. *Current liabilities requiring amounts to be estimated*, which include property taxes, warranty obligations, and premium and coupon obligations.

---

5.  "An Analysis of Issues Related to Reporting Funds Flows, Liquidity, and Financial Flexibility," *FASB Discussion Memorandum* (Stamford, Conn.: FASB, December 15, 1980), p. 87.
6.  "Reporting Income, Cash Flows, and Financial Flexibility of Business Enterprises," *FASB Proposed Statement of Financial Accounting Concepts* (Stamford, Conn.: FASB, November 16, 1981), par. 28.

## VALUATION OF CURRENT LIABILITIES

Conceptually, all liabilities should be recorded by a company (and reported on its balance sheet) at the present value of the future outlays they require and should be disclosed in a manner that will provide useful information about their liquidity. Most current liabilities in practice, however, are measured, recorded, and reported at their maturity or face amount. The difference between the maturity amount and the present value of the maturity amount is usually not material because of the short time period involved (usually one year or less). While a slight overstatement of liabilities will result from the recording of these liabilities at their maturity amount, this overstatement is justified on the basis of cost/benefit and materiality constraints. It can be alleviated partially, however, by making certain that any applicable recorded discount items are shown as offsets (contra accounts) to the appropriate current liabilities on the balance sheet. This procedure will reduce the related current liabilities to their current cash equivalent amount; and this amount, in most cases, is not materially different from their discounted present value.

## CURRENT LIABILITIES HAVING A DEFINITE AMOUNT

The short-term liabilities in this group result from the provisions of contracts or from the existence of laws. In these cases, the debt and its maturity are known with reasonable certainty. The accounting issues discussed in this section with each current liability are (1) identifying the item, (2) measuring it, and (3) recording it in the accounts.

### Trade Accounts Payable

**Trade accounts payable arise from the purchase of inventory, supplies, or services on an open charge-account basis.** The credit time period generally varies from 30 to 120 days without any interest being charged on the deferred payment. The amount of the liability usually is recorded in the accounting system when the invoice is received from the supplier. The accounting system is standardized so that efficient processing and payment are made.

Issues often arise when purchases of inventory are made near the end of the accounting period. Goods may be shipped by the supplier and still be in transit at year-end as discussed in Chapter 6. The purchaser should record both the purchase and the liability in the accounting period in which the control of the goods passes. For goods shipped FOB shipping point, control of (and legal title to) the goods passes to the purchaser at the supplier's shipping point. For goods shipped FOB destination, control of (and legal title to) the goods is transferred to the purchaser when it receives the merchandise. The owner of the merchandise in transit bears the cost of the freight.

The amount of the trade accounts payable usually is readily determinable, based on an inspection of the source document, the invoice. An accounting issue arises when cash discount terms (for example, 2/10, n/30; 3/10 EOM) are offered. A company should take advantage of all cash discounts because of the high effective interest rate involved. Theoretically, then, inventory (purchases) and the associated liability (accounts payable) should be shown less the cash discount. As discussed in Chapter 6, however, the accounts payable is, in practice, recorded in two different ways: (1) *gross price method:* at the invoice price—the liability is stated at the maximum amount required to be paid, or (2) *net price method:* at the invoice price less the cash discount—the liability is stated at its current cash equivalent amount. Assuming a policy of taking cash discounts, use of the gross price method overstates accounts payable at the end of the accounting period because the company expects to pay less than the gross amount due to taking the cash discount. Use of the net price method more accurately measures accounts payable (and liquidity) because it reflects the most likely amount that the company will pay. (However, under the net price method, an adjusting entry debiting Purchases Discounts Lost and crediting Accounts Payable is required at the end of the year to record all purchases discounts that have been lost on the year-end trade accounts payable.) Furthermore, the net price method highlights management inefficiency because purchases discounts lost are recorded whenever an invoice is paid after the cash discount period has expired. The gross price method is more widely used, however, because of its simplicity and the lack of materiality of the differences between the two methods.

## Notes Payable

**A note payable is an unconditional written agreement to pay a sum of money to the bearer on a specific date.** Notes payable may be either short term (discussed here) or long term (discussed in Chapter 12). Notes arise out of either a trade situation—the purchase of goods or services on credit—or the borrowing of money from a bank. The promissory note itself is the source document for determining the initial amount of the liability. However, interest plays an important part in determining the subsequent value of the liability. The interest inherent in notes payable may be stated or implied in different ways. One note may be *interest-bearing* with the principal listed as the face value and the interest rate stated on the note, with the interest payable at maturity. Another note may be *non-interest-bearing* (that is, a note stated at its maturity value, that includes both the principal and interest to maturity), the note being discounted and the borrower receiving less than the face value. The interest in this latter case is the amount of the discount.

*Issuance of an Interest-Bearing Trade Note for Merchandise*
For an interest-bearing note, the principal amount (face value) is the present value of the liability and is used to record the current liability. Interest expense then is recorded over the life of the note by applying the stated interest rate to the face value. To illustrate, assume that Trishan Corporation uses a perpetual inventory system and purchases merchandise for $7,000 on September 1, 1995 by issuing a $7,000, 12%, 30-day note to the supplier. The journal entries on September 1, 1995 and October 1, 1995 to record the issuance of the note and the payment of the principal and interest (assuming, for simplicity, a 360-day business year), respectively, are as follows:

**September 1, 1995**

| | | |
|---|---|---|
| Inventory | 7,000 | |
| Notes Payable | | 7,000 |

**October 1, 1995**

| | | |
|---|---|---|
| Interest Expense ($7,000 × 0.12 × 30/360) | 70 | |
| Notes Payable | 7,000 | |
| Cash | | 7,070 |

If the note spans two fiscal periods, an adjusting entry is made at the end of the first fiscal period to accrue the interest expense and to record another current liability, Interest Payable.

*Issue of Non-interest-Bearing Note to Borrow Money*

For a non-interest-bearing note, the face value (which includes the interest to maturity) and the discount (the interest to maturity) of the note are used to record the current liability. Interest expense is then recorded over the life of the note as an adjustment of this discounted amount. To illustrate, assume that on December 1, 1995, the Trollingwood Corporation borrows money at First National Bank of Orange City by the issuance of a $10,000, 90-day, non-interest-bearing note that is discounted on a 12% basis. Trollingwood receives only $9,700 [$10,000 − ($10,000 × 0.12 × 3/12)]. Four journal entries are made to record the events related to this note. First, the proceeds of the note are recorded on December 1, 1995 as follows:

| | | |
|---|---|---|
| Cash | 9,700 | |
| Discount on Notes Payable | 300 | |
| Notes Payable | | 10,000 |

Observe that $10,000 is the maturity (face) value, but the liability is recorded at its present value. The $300 amount of the discount (the interest expense applicable to the entire term of the note) is debited to Discount on Notes Payable, and this account is shown on the balance sheet as a contra account to Notes Payable in order to report the net amount of the current liquidation value (that is, the present value).[7] Since the life of this note extends into 1996, a second journal entry is made on December 31, 1995 to record a portion of the discount (1/3 × $300) as interest expense[8] for 1995 as follows:

| | | |
|---|---|---|
| Interest Expense | 100 | |
| Discount on Notes Payable | | 100 |

Observe in the preceding entry that the reduction in the Discount on Notes Payable account correspondingly increases the current liability amount shown on the balance sheet. The last two journal entries are recorded at maturity on March 1, 1996 as follows:

| | | |
|---|---|---|
| Interest Expense | 200 | |
| Discount on Notes Payable | | 200 |
| | | |
| Notes Payable | 10,000 | |
| Cash | | 10,000 |

After the entry adjusting Interest Expense is made, Discount on Notes Payable has a zero balance so that the carrying value of the current liability equals the maturity value of the note. The second journal entry records the payment of the maturity value, that is, the payment of the amount borrowed, $9,700, plus the $300 total interest recognized (i.e., the amount of the discount).

---

7. Alternatively, Notes Payable could be recorded at the current value ($9,700), in which case the maturity value would be shown parenthetically on the balance sheet. Subsequently the interest expense adjusting entry credit would be made directly to Notes Payable to increase it gradually to maturity value.

8. In this situation, for simplicity the "straight line" method is used to allocate the interest expense. In Chapter 14, for long-term notes the more conceptually correct "effective interest" method is used to calculate interest expense.

An alternative approach involves debiting the original discount amount first to Interest Expense. Then, at the end of the period, an adjusting entry would be necessary to transfer the *unexpired* portion from the expense to the Discount on Notes Payable account. The Discount on Notes Payable account would be disclosed as a contra account to Notes Payable, as discussed earlier.

In borrowing money, a manager must be aware of the effective interest rate, referred to in practice as the annual percentage rate (or APR), for each source of credit. In the preceding case, the approximate annual effective interest on the cash actually borrowed is higher than the discount rate of 12%. It is 12.37% [($300 ÷ $9,700) × 4 quarters]. Federal laws require lenders to disclose the APR to borrowers.

Alternatively, a company may specify that a given interest rate apply to the *cash proceeds*. To determine the cash proceeds, it is necessary to make a present value calculation (see Appendix D). This calculation is the present value of a single sum of $10,000 to be paid at the end of a single period of 90 days at 3% (1/4 × 12%). The journal entries to record a note with the discount calculated as indicated previously are identical to the preceding ones for the Trollingwood Corporation, except for a difference in the cash proceeds and interest amounts.

### Currently Maturing Portion of Long-Term Debt

As a general rule, although not directly related to the operating cycle, the currently maturing portion of long-term debt is classified as a current liability. Two different situations are involved here. First, any long-term debt requiring the use of current assets for its retirement will become a current liability on the balance sheet prepared immediately before the year of retirement. If a company has issued 20-year bonds and these are scheduled to become due on July 1, 1996, they are shown as current liabilities on the balance sheet prepared as of December 31, 1995. The second situation involves the issuance of serial bonds—that is, bonds payable that are retired in periodic installments. For example, assume that on July 1, 1994, Rexlow Corporation issues 13% serial bonds with a face value of $1 million. These bonds are to be retired in serial installments of $100,000 beginning on July 1, 1996 and each year thereafter until all bonds are retired. A balance sheet prepared as of December 31, 1995, would show as a current liability the currently maturing installment of $100,000 and a long-term liability item of $900,000 (the remaining installments due after December 31, 1996). Other long-term debt is treated in the same manner. These items, however, are not included in current liabilities if it is expected that they will be refinanced on a long-term basis, as discussed later in this chapter.

*Serial bonds are discussed in Chapter 12.*

### Dividends Payable

*Dividends are discussed in Chapter 15.*

The declaration (at the dividend declaration date by the board of directors) of a cash dividend, a property dividend (a dividend payable in property other than cash), or a scrip dividend (a dividend that creates a promissory note) results in the reduction of retained earnings and recognition of a current liability if there is an intention to distribute the dividend in the coming year or operating cycle. These dividends are recorded at the amount to be paid. The liability is entitled Dividends Payable, Property Dividends Payable, or Dividends Payable in Scrip. Observe that in each of the dividend cases, accounting for the declaration results in a shift of a stockholders' equity element, retained earnings, to a current liability element. The liability is eliminated when liquidated on the date of payment.

There are two exceptions to the creation of current liabilities arising from dividend situations. First, a stock dividend to be issued is *not* reported as a current liability. Since it is liquidated by the issuance of the corporation's own stock, it is reported as an element of stockholders' equity. Second, undeclared dividends in arrears on cumulative preferred stock (discussed in Chapter 14) are *not* reported as liabilities until they are formally declared by the corporation's board of directors, but they are disclosed in the notes to the financial statements.

## Advances and Refundable Deposits

Many utility and other companies require customers and employees to make deposits as guarantees to cover equipment or keys used by the customer, to cover payments that may arise in the future, or to guarantee performance of a contract or service. Since these deposits either are refundable or are subject to be offset against a trade accounts receivable, they are a special type of liability. The accounting for these deposits involves an increase in a liability account appropriately describing the nature of the refundable deposit. For example, the liability for a refundable deposit received by a utility company may be called Refundable Deposits Received from Customers. The law frequently requires that interest be paid on these deposits; therefore most utility companies refund the deposits as soon as good credit standing is established by customers. Any related interest must be accounted for by the utility company on a regular accrual basis. Thus the current liability, Interest Payable, would arise.

## Accrued Liabilities

Accrued liabilities represent those obligations that *accumulate* in a systematic way over time. Often companies wait until the end of the accounting period to record these liabilities and the accompanying expenses as adjusting entries, because it is more convenient to do so. Most accrued liabilities are current liabilities. Many accrued liabilities are definite in amount, while the amount of others is based on operations or estimates. Because of special characteristics, several major accrued liabilities, such as those arising from property taxes and payrolls, are discussed in separate sections of this chapter. Two additional issues need special consideration: (1) the liability for compensated absences and (2) the disclosure of "off-balance sheet" financing obligations.

### Accrued Liability for Compensated Absences
The accounting for compensated absences is discussed in **FASB Statement No. 43. Compensated absences include vacation, holiday, illness, or other personal activities for which the employee is paid.** They do not include such items as severance pay, stock options, or long-term fringe benefits. An expense is recognized and a liability for employees' compensation for future absences is accrued by a company if *all* the following conditions are met:

1.  The company's obligation relating to the employee's rights to receive compensation for future absences is attributable to the employee's services already rendered;

2.  The obligation relates to rights that vest or accumulate;

3.  Payment of the compensation is probable; and

4.  The amount can be reasonably estimated.[9]

---

9.  "Accounting for Compensated Absences," *FASB Statement of Financial Accounting Standards No. 43* (Stamford, Conn.: FASB, November, 1980), par. 6. These criteria also apply to postemployment benefits under *FASB Statement of Financial Accounting Standards No. 112.*

If the company meets conditions (1), (2), and (3) and does not accrue a liability because the last condition is not met, the known facts about compensated absences are disclosed in the notes to the financial statements.

Two of the terms used in the preceding paragraph require additional explanation. A **vested right** exists when an employer has an obligation to make payment to an employee that is not contingent upon employees' future services. **Accumulated rights** are those that can be carried forward by the employee to future periods if not taken in the period in which they are earned. The most common type of this right is vacation time that is allowed to accumulate and for which payment is probable. Even if these rights are not vested, they do accumulate and, therefore, the employer must recognize an expense and accrue a liability, allowing for those rights not expected to be exercised.

The second most frequent compensated absence is sick pay, which is treated by *FASB Statement No. 43* differently from vacation pay. If sick pay benefits *vest* and have not been used by the end of the period, then an expense is recognized and an accrued liability is recorded. If sick pay benefits *accumulate* but do *not* vest, recognition and accrual is optional. The reason for this exception to the general rule of recognition is that employers administer sick pay in at least two different ways. Some companies permit employees to accumulate unused sick pay and take compensated time off from work even though they are not ill. A current liability must be accrued for this type of sick pay because it is probable that it will be paid in the future regardless of whether or not the employees are ill. Other companies require that employees receive accumulated sick pay only if they are absent from work because of illness. In this case, accrual is optional because payment is less likely and measurement of the amount is less reliable. It can also be argued that there is a **conceptual difference** between vacation pay and sick pay. *Vacation pay is earned as a result of employment* (the services rendered by the employee), whereas *sick pay is earned only when the future event* (sickness) *occurs.* In the latter case, the criteria for a liability have not been fulfilled during employment because the transaction or event obligating the company has not yet occurred.

When an accrual is made, the expense and related current liability are recorded in the period in which the sick pay benefits are earned by the employees. In measuring the amount of the accrual, the rate of pay that may be used to record the liability is: (1) the rate applicable to the current period, or (2) the rate applicable to the estimated time of absence. Since the current period's rate is more reliable than the future period's rate, and the difference is unlikely to be material, most companies use the current period's rate for the accrual. If the amount paid in the future for the compensated absence is larger than the amount of the previous accrual (because of a pay raise or promotion), the difference is recorded as an adjustment to the expense recorded in the period of the payment. In other words, the difference is treated as a change in estimate that is accounted for in the current (and future) period, as discussed in Chapter 22.

### Compensated Absence Example

To illustrate a compensated absence for vacations, assume that the Milton Corporation has 100 employees, who are each paid an average of $100 per day, and has a policy (which meets the *FASB Statement No. 43* conditions) of allowing each employee 12 days paid vacation per year. The total annual cost of the paid vacations—a form of compensated absence—is $120,000 (100 × 12 × $100). The company records the related liability on a quarterly basis for interim reporting purposes. Employees are paid monthly; half of the employees are in the sales force and the remaining half are in the office staff. Assuming no vacation days were taken in the first quarter of 1995, the journal entry to record the expense and accrued liability on March 31, 1995 is as follows:

| | | |
|---|---|---|
| **Sales Salaries Expense: Compensated Absences** | 15,000 | |
| **Office Salaries Expense: Compensated Absences** | 15,000 | |
|     **Liability for Employees' Compensation for Future** | | |
|         **Absences (3/12 × $120,000)** | | 30,000 |

Some companies prefer to record the debit entry as Vacation Pay Expense. Generally, no payroll taxes are recorded at this time because companies wait until payment of the payroll to do so. Note that, as a result of this journal entry, **the salaries expense is recognized in the period during which the employee works and earns the vacation time and *not* during the vacation period,** thus adhering to the matching principle. The first quarter interim financial statements, then, would include the expense and liability for compensated absences.

The liability for compensated absences will be satisfied at the time the employees take their vacations. The elimination of the liability will be recorded, however, when the regular payroll is paid after the employees take their vacations. To illustrate, assume that the $200,000 April 30, 1995 payroll, including paid vacation time taken by the sales and office staff, is as follows:

| | Payroll for | |
|---|---|---|
| | **Time Worked** | **Vacation Taken** |
| Sales Staff | $97,000 | $3,000 |
| Office Staff | 96,500 | 3,500 |

The journal entry on April 30, 1995 to record the payment of this payroll (ignoring payroll taxes) is:

| | | |
|---|---|---|
| **Sales Salaries Expense** | 97,000 | |
| **Office Salaries Expense** | 96,500 | |
| **Liability for Employees' Compensation** | | |
|     **for Future Absences** | 6,500 | |
|     **Cash** | | 200,000 |

As discussed earlier, if the $6,500 payroll for vacation time were larger than the respective amount accrued earlier (because of a pay raise or promotion), the liability would be reduced by the accrued amount, and the difference would be added to the two expense accounts. In addition, payroll taxes would normally be recorded at this time. However, since payroll taxes are discussed later in the chapter, for simplicity, we have not illustrated them here. If payroll taxes had been recorded, the withheld payroll taxes of the employees would apply to the entire $200,000 as of April 30, 1995 (the date of payment of the salaries and the vacation time) because the taxes are legally assessable. Furthermore, the payroll taxes applicable to the employer also would be recorded at this time.

Similar journal entries would be made to record the expense for compensated absences and accrue (and eliminate) the liability during the remaining quarters for interim reporting purposes. At year-end, any remaining balance in the liability account would be reported as a current liability on the Milton Corporation's ending balance sheet.[10]

---

10. *FASB Statement No. 43* does not specifically address the allocation of the costs of compensated absences to interim periods. If a company did not make quarterly accruals for compensated absences because they were not material, it would need to determine its remaining liability for compensated absences at year-end and make the related accrual journal entry at that time.

### Disclosure of Off-Balance Sheet Financing Obligations

**FASB Statement No. 47,** though entitled "Disclosure of Long-Term Obligations," deals with issues relating to *off-balance sheet financing*. This topic was discussed in Chapter 7 as it related to inventories; it is also discussed in Chapter 19 as it applies to leasing arrangements. Here it is discussed briefly as it relates to liabilities. This *Statement* focuses on accounting for an unconditional purchase obligation, which is one requiring transfer of funds in the future for fixed or minimum amounts or quantities of goods or services at fixed or minimum prices. The obligation or contingent obligation created may be in part short term and in part long term. If a company enters into an unconditional purchase obligation that: (1) is noncancellable, (2) is negotiated as part of arranging financing for facilities to provide the contracted items, and (3) contains a term in excess of one year, the company is required to make certain disclosures in the notes to its financial statements regardless of whether the obligation and related asset are reported on the balance sheet. These disclosures include, for example, information about required payments over the next five years.[11] The intent is to enhance the *prediction of future cash outflows.* Because of the complex nature of these disclosures, they are not discussed further, but any part of the required payment falling within the year or operating cycle is similar to a current liability and is disclosed in the note.

The FASB continues to be concerned with off-balance sheet financing because innovations in financial instruments involving such items as interest rate swaps, collateralized mortgages, and put and call options have arisen in recent years. Critics argue that these items have resulted in inadequate disclosures of potential liabilities, unjustifiable deferrals of losses, and premature recognitions of gains. In response, the FASB has issued **FASB Statements No. 105 and 107.** *FASB Statement No. 105* requires the reporting of selected information about debt financial instruments having a risk of loss to the company that exceeds the amount recognized, and about financial instruments with concentrations of credit risk. These disclosures are complex, but include the contract amount, the nature and terms, the amount of loss that the company would incur if the counterparty failed to perform, the company's policy regarding collateral, and any significant concentrations of credit risk. *FASB Statement No. 107* requires the disclosure of the fair value of all financial instruments (both *assets* and *liabilities*), whether recognized or not on the balance sheet. The disclosures may be made either in the body of the financial statements or in the notes accompanying the financial statements.[12]

### Liabilities from Product Financing Arrangements

In **FASB Statement No. 49,** "Accounting for Product Financing Arrangements," the FASB also deals with off-balance sheet financing transactions in which a company "sells" inventory and agrees to repurchase it (perhaps additionally processed) at a specified price. As discussed in Chapter 7, the company does not record the transaction as a sale or remove the inventory from its balance sheet. Instead, the company records a liability for any additional amount in excess of the original inventory price

---

11. "Disclosure of Long-Term Obligations," *FASB Statement of Financial Accounting Standards No. 47* (Stamford, Conn.: FASB, June, 1981), par. 10.

12. "Disclosure of Information about Financial Instruments with Off-Balance Sheet Risk and Financial Instruments with Concentrations of Credit Risk," *FASB Statement of Financial Accounting Standards No. 105* (Norwalk, Conn.: FASB, 1990), par. 17–20 and "Disclosures about Fair Value of Financial Instruments," *FASB Statement of Financial Accounting Standards No. 107* (Norwalk, Conn.: FASB, 1991), par. 7.

due to the buying, processing, and reselling of the product by the other company. *FASB Statement No. 49* covers transactions where a company has another entity purchase a product on its behalf. In this case, the company records the asset (often an inventory item) and related liability when the product is purchased by the other entity.[13] A part or all of both of the preceding liabilities are likely to be current and are reported as such on the company's balance sheet.

### Unearned Items

Unearned items (sometimes called deferred revenues) include amounts collected in advance that have not yet been earned and recorded as revenues (i.e., the product or service has not yet been provided). Although often erroneously classified under the balance sheet caption Deferred Credits, these unearned items should receive more appropriate classifications: some should be classified as current liabilities and some as long-term liabilities, while others should be shown as contra accounts to certain assets or as part of stockholders' equity. In this chapter, only the unearned items properly classified as current liabilities are considered.

Examples of unearned items that could be classified as either current or long-term liabilities are revenues collected in advance such as interest, rent, magazine subscriptions, royalties, tickets, tokens, gift certificates, and service contracts. Most of these items are current liabilities; a few, however, may be long-term liabilities. If more than one year (or one operating cycle, if longer) is required in the earning process and if noncurrent assets are primarily used to earn the revenue, then the unearned item is classified as a long-term liability. On the other hand, unearned interest included in the face value of notes receivable should be classified as a contra (Discount) account to Notes Receivable on the balance sheet.

The accounting for these unearned items involves an increase in a liability account (or possibly a revenue account). An adjusting entry is made at the end of the accounting period to correctly state the amount of revenue earned to be reported on the income statement and the ending liability to be reported on the balance sheet.

## CURRENT LIABILITIES WHOSE AMOUNTS DEPEND ON OPERATIONS

Several kinds of current liabilities arise out of operations, and their amounts depend on these operations. Included are liabilities related to sales and use taxes, payrolls, the corporation's own income taxes, and bonus agreements.

### Sales and Use Taxes

**A sales tax is a tax levied on the transfer of tangible personal property and on certain services.** It must be collected from the customer by the seller and remitted— usually on a monthly basis—to the proper governmental authority. **A use tax is a tax levied by a state or local governmental unit on goods bought from a nonsales-tax area or sector.** It is levied on the buyer of merchandise purchased for the buyer's own use or consumption. To illustrate, suppose that a company goes out of state to buy trucks because of an advantageous price. Upon registering the vehicles in its own

13. "Accounting for Product Financing Arrangements," *FASB Statement of Financial Accounting Standards No. 49* (Stamford, Conn.: FASB, June, 1981), par. 8.

state, the company would have to file a use tax return and remit the tax. The sales taxes and use taxes are essentially the same, except for collection and remittance. In the following discussion, only the sales tax is considered, since it involves a sales outlet that collects and remits the tax.

Two accounting situations are discussed. The first is a typical recording of the sale when the sales tax is added to the invoice price. For example, assume that Selleroy Company sells merchandise for cash with a retail sales price of $50,000 on which a sales tax of 6% is levied. The company collects $53,000 from its customers and records the collection as follows:

| | | |
|---|---|---|
| **Cash** | **53,000** | |
| Sales | | **50,000** |
| Sales Taxes Payable | | **3,000** |

The $3,000 sales taxes collected by the Selleroy Company are owed to the state or local government levying the tax; hence the amount is *not* part of the revenue and is recorded in a current liability account. Later, when the sales tax return is filed and the tax paid to the governmental agency, the current liability is eliminated.

The second situation arises when some small businesses include the amount of the sales taxes directly in the price charged for merchandise, therefore crediting the Sales account for the sum of the sales taxes payable and the sales amount. When this procedure is followed, since sales taxes generally must be remitted monthly, an adjusting entry is necessary at the end of each month to reduce the Sales account and to create the current liability, Sales Taxes Payable. To illustrate, suppose that the Smally Corporation collects sales taxes but records the amount of both the sales and the sales taxes in the Sales account. To calculate the sales, the amount in the Sales account must be divided by 1 plus the tax rate. The sales taxes owed are determined by subtracting the calculated sales from the amount in the Sales account. For instance, suppose that at the end of January, the Sales account shows a credit balance of $169,600. Assuming a 6% sales tax on all goods, an adjusting entry for $9,600 [$169,600 − ($169,600 ÷ 1.06)] must be made at the end of January as follows:

| | | |
|---|---|---|
| **Sales** | **9,600** | |
| Sales Taxes Payable | | **9,600** |

In some cases, the sales taxes payable computed by the company may differ slightly from the amount calculated as owed by the governmental authority (e.g., because of the use of graduated sales tax tables). In these cases, an adjustment is made to sales taxes payable and a gain or loss on sales tax collections is recorded.

## Liabilities Related to Payrolls

Companies are required by law to withhold from the pay of each employee a legal amount representing anticipated federal and state (and sometimes local governmental unit) taxes payable by employees. They also may voluntarily withhold amounts for union dues, group insurance, and various other amounts payable by the employees to third parties. In addition to these withheld items, federal and state (and sometimes local) laws levy on employers other taxes that are based on the payroll amount. These include social security taxes and unemployment insurance taxes. Since these taxes and voluntary withholdings must be remitted within a year, they are classified as current liabilities.

Exhibit 11-2 presents an overview of the withheld groups of items and related voluntary payroll deductions. Each item indicated there is discussed briefly in the following sections.

## EXHIBIT 11-2

### PAYROLL TAXES AND RELATED VOLUNTARY PAYROLL DEDUCTIONS

| Payroll Tax Group | 1993 Rate on | | 1993 Annual Salary per Employee Subject to Tax |
|---|---|---|---|
| | Employee | Employer | |
| Federal income tax | Graduated rates | — | 100% |
| State income tax | Graduated rates | — | 100% |
| F.I.C.A. taxes | | | |
| OASDI | 6.20% | 6.20% | $ 57,600 |
| Medicare | 1.45% | 1.45% | $135,000 |
| Federal unemployment tax | — | 0.8% | $ 7,000 |
| State unemployment tax | — | 5.4% | $ 7,000 |

*Voluntary Payroll Deductions Group*

Union dues
Government bonds  } Amount withheld is stated in contract
Group insurance
Others

*Payroll Tax Group*

The federal income tax law, most state income tax laws, and some local governmental unit laws require employers to withhold from the pay of each employee an amount representing anticipated income taxes payable by the employee to the respective governmental units. (Since only a few local governmental units levy taxes based on the payroll, these taxes are ignored in the discussion that follows.) The amount withheld depends upon the number of exemptions claimed and the amount of income earned by the employee. Employers determine the amount to be withheld from wages by using applicable legal rates or by referring to withholding tax tables. The withheld amounts must be remitted to the respective governmental unit at specified times and through specified channels. For example, the withheld federal income taxes must be paid to the Internal Revenue Service through local depositories (e.g., banks).

Social security legislation requires that employers withhold taxes, entitled Federal Insurance Contribution Act taxes (F.I.C.A.), from the wages of each employee under certain conditions. Also, employers must match the taxes of the employee and pay the sum of both taxes to the Internal Revenue Service along with the income taxes withheld. FICA taxes consist of two items. The first tax is used for paying federal old-age, survivor, and disability insurance (O.A.S.D.I.) benefits. The second is used for paying federal hospital insurance (Medicare) benefits. Together, these taxes are referred to as *social security taxes*. As indicated in Exhibit 11-2, the 1993 F.I.C.A. taxes are 15.30% (6.20% + 1.45% + 6.20% + 1.45%) on the first $57,600 earned by each employee. One half of these taxes—7.65% (6.20% + 1.45%)—is paid by the employee; the other half is paid by the employer. On income between $57,601 and $135,000 earned by the employee, F.I.C.A. taxes of 1.45% are paid by both the employee and employer. The actual tax rates and wage base for future years will be determined by Congress. Because Congress has changed these items virtually on an annual basis, in the following examples and homework, for simplicity, an assumed rate of 16%—8% on the employee and 8% on the employer—and a taxable wage base of $60,000 on *both* F.I.C.A. taxes will be used.

The fifth and sixth taxes indicated in Exhibit 11-2 are unemployment insurance taxes, another type of social security tax. These taxes are used by governmental units to make payments for a limited period of time to individuals who become unemployed. The Federal Unemployment Tax Act (F.U.T.A.) requires a tax with a maximum rate of 6.2% to be levied wholly on employers of one or more persons, but the rate applies to only the first $7,000 paid to each employee. The law provides, however, that 5.4% of the 6.2% be payable to the state, assuming that the state levies an approved unemployment insurance tax. Thus, in these cases, the net effective federal unemployment tax rate is 0.8%. Most state laws allow for a reduction of the typical 5.4% tax through merit-rating plans for those employers who maintain steady employment because the steady employment minimizes the amount of funds drawn from the fund.

### Voluntary Payroll Deduction Group

Through a contractual arrangement between individual employees and their employer many kinds of payroll deductions can be authorized. Typical examples of these voluntary contractual deductions are for payment of group hospital insurance, accident insurance, life insurance, union dues, government bonds, tax-sheltered retirement annuities, and any other purchase of goods or services. These payroll deductions are made for the convenience of and service to the employees of a company.

### Accounting for Payroll Taxes and Deductions

To illustrate the accounting for payroll taxes and voluntary payroll deductions, assume that the Wager Corporation summarizes the following weekly payroll from its payroll register during early February 1995:

| Type of Salary | Gross Pay | F.I.C.A. Tax* | Federal Income Tax | State Income Tax | Union Dues | Net Pay |
|---|---|---|---|---|---|---|
| | | | Withheld Amounts | | | |
| Sales staff | $10,000 | $ 800 | $730 | $300 | $100 | $ 8,070 |
| Office staff | 4,000 | 320 | 260 | 200 | 80 | 3,140 |
| | $14,000 | $1,120 | $990 | $500 | $180 | $11,210 |

* Assumed 8% rate.

Further assume that the effective federal and state unemployment tax rates are 0.8% and 5.4%, respectively, and *that all wages are subject to all payroll taxes.* The following two journal entries are made to record the payment of the payroll and to record the payroll taxes imposed on the employer:

1. To record salaries and employee withholding items:

| | | |
|---|---|---|
| Sales Salaries Expense | 10,000 | |
| Office Salaries Expense | 4,000 | |
|    F.I.C.A. Taxes Payable | | 1,120 |
|    Employee Federal Income Taxes Withholding Payable | | 990 |
|    Employee State Income Taxes Withholding Payable | | 500 |
|    Employee Union Dues Withholding Payable | | 180 |
|    Cash | | 11,210 |

2. To record employer payroll taxes:

| | | |
|---|---:|---:|
| Payroll Taxes Expense | 1,988 | |
|     F.I.C.A. Taxes Payable (8% × $14,000) | | 1,120 |
|     Federal Unemployment Taxes Payable | | |
|       (0.8% × $14,000) | | 112 |
|     State Unemployment Taxes Payable | | |
|       (5.4% × $14,000) | | 756 |

Instead of recording Payroll Taxes Expense in the second entry, it is theoretically sound to increase the respective salaries expense accounts for the appropriate amounts that, in essence, represent the additional cost of employing the sales and office staff. Regardless of approach, when Wager Corporation remits the payroll deductions, the applicable current liability accounts from the preceding entries are eliminated.

## Income Taxes Payable

The income of corporations is subject to a federal income tax separate from that of individuals. In addition, corporations may be subject to state and foreign income taxes. The separate federal corporate income tax imposes a rate schedule for 1993 that is a five-step progressive structure, as shown here:

| Taxable Income | Tax Rate |
|---|---|
| $0 − $50,000 | 15% |
| $50,001 − $75,000 | 25% |
| $75,001 − $100,000 | 34% |
| $100,001 − $335,000 | 39% |
| Over $335,000 | 34% |

The three lower steps in the structure are, in effect, phased out by the imposition of an additional 5% tax on taxable income over $100,000 and up to $335,000. As a result, corporations with a taxable income greater than $335,000 are taxed at an effective rate of 34%. To illustrate, assume a corporation has taxable income of $400,000. The corporation could calculate its federal income tax as follows:

| | | |
|---|---|---:|
| $ 50,000 × 0.15 | = $ | 7,500 |
| 25,000 ($75,000 − $50,000) × 0.25 | = | 6,250 |
| 25,000 ($100,000 − $75,000) × 0.34 | = | 8,500 |
| 235,000 ($335,000 − $100,000) × 0.39 | = | 91,650 |
| 65,000 ($400,000 − $335,000) × 0.34 | = | 22,100 |
| Federal income tax | | $136,000 |

Alternatively, the corporation simply could have multiplied the $400,000 taxable income times the single flat rate of 34% to arrive at the $136,000 federal income tax. Because Congress may change the income tax rates and the actual income tax computations are complex, for simplicity we generally assume an effective income tax rate of 30% in our discussions and homework.

The Corporate Income Tax Return, Form 1120, must be filed 2 1/2 months after the end of the taxable fiscal year. Most corporations must pay estimated taxes

*Income taxes for financial reporting is discussed in Chapter 17.*

throughout the fiscal year. Guidelines for the calculation of both estimated and actual income taxes are provided by the Internal Revenue Service. Since these guidelines are subject to change, they are not presented in this book.

Accounting for the current liability for income taxes is briefly considered here. In accruing the applicable income taxes for either interim or end-of-period statement purposes, the journal entry is a debit to Income Tax Expense and a credit to a current liability, Income Taxes Payable. If a prepayment of income taxes is required to be made, a debit to Prepaid Income Taxes is appropriate. Later, when the actual liability for taxes is determined, a journal entry is made to appropriately report the Income Tax Expense item, to reduce the Prepaid Income Taxes, and to record a current liability for any excess of actual income taxes owed over the prepaid amount.

## Bonus Obligations

As incentives to certain employees—particularly officers and managers—to increase company earnings, many companies establish an earnings-based bonus agreement. The bonus is usually payable shortly after the end of the year. The bonus, which is additional salary, is an operating expense of the company. It is recorded as an expense and as a current liability when it has been earned by the employees. As additional salaries, bonus payments are deductible in computing taxable income. Legal documents for bonus agreements may be written in a number of different ways. Two typical plans provide for the calculation of the bonus as follows:[14]

1.  The bonus is based on the net income after deducting income taxes, but before deducting the bonus.

2.  The bonus is based on net income after deducting both the bonus and the income taxes.

In either of these two approaches, the income tax cannot be determined until the bonus is calculated. Thus the computation requires the solving of two simple simultaneous equations. The computation of the bonus and income tax for each of these approaches is shown in Exhibit 11-3.

The journal entries to record the bonus and income taxes in Example 2 of Exhibit 11-3 are as follows:

1.  To record the bonus:

| | | |
|---|---|---|
| Salaries Expense (Officer's Bonus) | 17,009 | |
| Officer's Bonus Payable | | 17,009 |

2.  To record income tax expense:

| | | |
|---|---|---|
| Income Tax Expense | 72,897 | |
| Income Taxes Payable | | 72,897 |

3.  To record the payment of the officer's bonus:

| | | |
|---|---|---|
| Officer's Bonus Payable | 17,009 | |
| Cash | | 17,009 |

If a balance sheet were prepared before entry 3 had been made, both Officer's Bonus Payable and Income Taxes Payable would be disclosed as current liabilities.

---

14. Two other approaches are: (1) the bonus could be based on income before income taxes and before bonus, or (2) the bonus could be based on income before income taxes and after the bonus is deducted. The computations involved in these two approaches are similar to (but simpler than) the methods discussed and are not presented here.

**EXHIBIT 11-3**

## COMPUTATION OF BONUS AND INCOME TAX

*Basic Information*
In the two examples, let:

$B$ = Bonus

$T$ = Income Tax

The two examples involve these assumptions: the Bonex Corporation reported income for the current year of $260,000 before deducting income taxes and before a bonus to the president; the effective tax rate is 30%, and the bonus rate is 10%.

*Example 1*
**Bonus computed on income after deducting income taxes but before deducting the bonus**
The two equations for calculating the bonus are:

$B = 0.10\ (\$260,000 - T)$      (1)

$T = 0.30\ (\$260,000 - B)$      (2)

To solve the simultaneous equations, the value of $T$ is substituted in Equation (2) for the element $T$ in Equation (1) as follows:

$B = 0.10\ [\$260,000 - 0.30\ (\$260,000 - B)]$      (3)

Now Equation (3) has only one unknown and is solved as follows:

$$B = 0.10\ [\$260,000 - \$78,000 + 0.30B]$$
$$B = \$26,000 - \$7,800 + 0.03B$$
$$B - 0.03B = \$18,200$$
$$0.97B = \$18,200$$
$$B = \$18,200 \div 0.97$$
$$B = \underline{\$18,763}\ \text{(rounded to nearest dollar)}$$

To calculate the amount of the income tax, the amount of the bonus is substituted into Equation (2) as follows:

$T = 0.30\ (\$260,000 - \$18,763)$

$T = \underline{\$72,371}$ (rounded to nearest dollar)

*Example 2*
**Bonus computed on net income after deducting both income taxes and the bonus**
The two equations for calculating the bonus are:

$B = 0.10\ (\$260,000 - B - T)$      (4)

$T = 0.30\ (\$260,000 - B)$      (5)

To solve the simultaneous equations, the value of $T$ in Equation (5) is substituted for the element $T$ in Equation (4) as follows:

$$B = 0.10\ [\$260,000 - B - 0.30\ (\$260,000 - B)]\quad (6)$$
$$B = 0.10\ [\$260,000 - B - \$78,000 + 0.30B]$$
$$B = \$26,000 - 0.10B - \$7,800 + 0.03B$$
$$B + 0.10B - 0.03B = \$18,200$$
$$1.07B = \$18,200$$
$$B = \$18,200 \div 1.07$$
$$B = \underline{\$17,009}\ \text{(rounded to nearest dollar)}$$

To calculate the amount of the income tax, the amount of the bonus is substituted into Equation (5) as follows:

$T = 0.30\ (\$260,000 - \$17,009)$

$T = \underline{\$72,897}$ (rounded to nearest dollar)

# CURRENT LIABILITIES REQUIRING AMOUNTS TO BE ESTIMATED

A number of liabilities have amounts that must be estimated as of the balance sheet date. The obligations that typically are current liabilities, namely property taxes, warranties, and premium obligations, and their related issues are discussed in this section. Because these items are specific types of "contingent liabilities," a discussion of the general issue of contingencies follows this section.

### Property Taxes

The accrual of property taxes is an example of an estimated liability. These taxes are assessed by municipal, county, and some state governments on the value of certain property as of a given date and become a lien against the property at a date specified by law. Legally a liability arises on this lien date. The lien date may precede the billing date by several months. For example, in Columbia, Missouri, the property tax is assessed on the value of the property as of January 1 of each year. The date that the tax becomes a lien against the property is July 1. The fiscal year of the city is July 1 to June 30. Property tax statements are mailed to property owners during November. Thus if the property taxes are recorded before the tax statement is received, they must be estimated. Also, when the accounting year of the company is different from the fiscal year of the municipality, another accounting issue arises. Therefore three accounting questions arise regarding property taxes:

1.  When should the company record the property tax liability?
2.  To which accounting period should the property tax expense be charged?
3.  How should the tax be estimated and how should any variation of actual from estimated tax be accounted for?

The Committee on Accounting Procedure of the AICPA, in considering the various periods that should be charged for property taxes, concluded that generally, the most acceptable method of recording property taxes is equal monthly accrual on the taxpayer's books during the fiscal periods of the taxing authority for which the taxes are levied. The accounting records then will show, at any closing date, the appropriate accruals or prepayment.[15] This method is preferred because it recognizes the property tax expense in the same period that services are received by the company from the governmental unit(s).

It is not difficult to estimate the amount of property taxes applicable to the fiscal year of the taxing authority. By law the tax rate cannot vary too much from past rates; and the value of the property being taxed is generally determined by the municipality with a notification to the owner. Thus the company can determine the total valuation subject to the tax. The estimated property tax is calculated by applying the estimated rate to the assessed valuation amount. If a variation between the actual property taxes and the estimated property taxes occurs, *APB Opinion No. 20* requires that it be accounted for prospectively.

To illustrate, assume that the Ezzell Corporation closes its books annually each December 31. The fiscal year for the town and county in which the Ezzell Corporation is located begins on July 1 and ends on the following June 30. The tax becomes

---

15. "Restatement and Revision of Accounting Research Bulletins," *Accounting Research Bulletin No. 43* (New York: AICPA, 1961), par. 14.

a lien against the property on July 1 of each year. The estimated property taxes for the period July 1, 1995 to June 30, 1996 are $7,200. The tax bill is mailed in October with a requirement that the tax be paid before December 31, 1995. The tax bill for the Ezzell Corporation reported an actual tax of $7,290, and the corporation pays this amount on October 31, 1995. The company elects to record monthly property tax adjustments for interim statements required by its management.

Assuming that the full property tax liability is not recognized at the lien date of July 1 and the Ezzell Corporation records the property tax on a monthly accrual basis (the preferred approach), the following series of journal entries may be made:

### July 1, 1995, Lien Date

**No entry**

### Three Monthly Entries: July 31–September 30, 1995

| | | |
|---|---|---|
| Property Tax Expense | 600 | |
|     Property Taxes Payable | | 600 |

### October 31, 1995: Payment of Property Taxes

| | | |
|---|---|---|
| Property Taxes Payable | 1,800 | |
| Prepaid Property Taxes | 5,490 | |
|     Cash | | 7,290 |

### Three Monthly Entries: October 31–December 31, 1995

| | | |
|---|---|---|
| Property Tax Expense | 610 | |
|     Prepaid Property Taxes | | 610 |

Note that the $610 amount in the last entry is the result of the allocation of the $90 difference ($7,290 − $7,200) between the actual and estimated property taxes to the remaining 9-month period ending June 30, 1996. That is, the $610 is computed by subtracting the previously estimated property tax expense to date ($600 × 3) from the total actual property tax ($7,290) and dividing the difference ($5,490) by the remaining months (9) in the year.

Assuming that Ezzell had recorded $598 each month from January 31 to June 30, 1995 (the portion of the tax authority's *previous* fiscal year occurring during the company's *current* accounting year), its Property Tax Expense for 1995 would be $7,218 [($598 × 6) + ($600 × 3) + ($610 × 3)].

## Warranty Obligations

Another estimated liability arises out of product warranties. These agreements, whether oral or in writing, require the seller, over a specified period of time after the sale, to correct any deficiency in quality, quantity, or performance of the merchandise sold, to replace the item, or to refund the selling price. These promises are made by manufacturers and other merchants as a sales promotion technique.

The period of the warranty may span two or more accounting periods. Adherence to **the matching principle requires that the warranty expense be recognized in the period during which the sale is made,** because the flaws in the merchandise are assumed to be present at the time of the sale. The actual use of cash and other resources to correct the defects in the merchandise, however, may occur partly in the period of sale and partly in a later period. Consequently, recognition of the warranty expense in the period of sale and the corresponding current liability requires an estimate of all costs that will be incurred after the sale to correct any defects and deficiencies. These issues are considered for three methods of accounting for warranty costs:

1.  Expense warranty accrual method

2.  Sales warranty accrual method

3.  Modified cash basis

*Expense Warranty Accrual Method*

As indicated previously, adherence to the matching principle requires that a liability for warranty costs be recorded during the period of the sale of the product under warranty. At the time of sale, there is a definite liability, but one whose amount must be estimated. **The expense warranty accrual method recognizes in the period of sale the estimated warranty expense and a liability for future performance under the warranty provision.** This method assumes that the warranty offer is made to increase sales; hence, the estimated warranty expense is matched against these sales. The estimated portion of the warranty liability applicable to the next accounting period (or operating cycle, if longer) is classified as a current liability; the remainder is classified as a long-term liability. During the period when cash and other resources are used in fulfilling the warranty agreement, the liability is debited and the respective assets are credited.

To illustrate, assume that Anglee Machinery Corporation begins production on a new machine in April 1995 and sells 200 of these machines at $6,000 each by December 31, 1995. Each machine carries a warranty for 1 year. Experience from the sale of similar machinery in the past has shown that the warranty costs will average approximately $150 per unit or a total of $30,000 (200 × $150). The corporation spent $5,000 in 1995 and $25,150 in 1996 to fulfill the warranty agreement for the 200 machines sold in 1995. The series of journal entries to record this information under the expense warranty accrual method for the year 1995 are:

**Sale of 200 Machines during April–December, 1995**

| | | |
|---|---|---|
| Cash or Accounts Receivable ($6,000 × 200) | 1,200,000 | |
|     Sales | | 1,200,000 |

**Recognition of Warranty Expense for Period, April–December, 1995**

| | | |
|---|---|---|
| Warranty Expense | 30,000 | |
|     Estimated Liability under Warranties | | 30,000 |

**Payment or Incurrence of Warranty Costs for Period, April–December, 1995**

| | | |
|---|---|---|
| Estimated Liability under Warranties | 5,000 | |
|     Cash (or other assets) | | 5,000 |

Warranty Expense is an operating expense of the Anglee Machinery Corporation. On a balance sheet prepared for December 31, 1995, the remaining $25,000 ($30,000 accrued − $5,000 paid) unpaid Estimated Liability under Warranties is a current liability since the warranty period for this corporation was a year in length.

The transactions in 1996 affecting only the 200 machines sold in 1995 are recorded as follows:

### Payment or Incurrence of Warranty Costs during 1996

| | | |
|---|---|---|
| Estimated Liability under Warranties | 25,000 | |
| Warranty Expense | 150 | |
| Cash (or other assets) | | 25,150 |

In the preceding journal entry, the actual warranty costs are $150 more than were estimated. This amount was debited to Warranty Expense for 1996 because it resulted from a change in accounting estimate.

*Accounting for changes in estimates is discussed in Chapter 22.*

### Sales Warranty Accrual Method

Many companies encourage customers to buy a "service contract" when they buy merchandise. Service contracts require customers to make fixed payments for future services.

Even though there is no explicit separate service contract, the sales price of each product may in fact include the sale of two items: the product and an implied warranty contract. Use of the **sales warranty accrual method** separates the accounting for these two items *even when no separate service contract is involved*. Under this method, revenue from the implied warranty contract is assumed to be equal to the estimated warranty costs, and is deferred and recognized in an amount equal to the warranty costs incurred. In essence, this is a *cost recovery approach to warranty revenue recognition*. To illustrate, in the case of the Anglee Machinery Corporation, the selling price of each machine, $6,000, may be assumed to be an implied service contract (sale of the warranty) of $150 and a sale of a machine with a selling price of $5,850 ($6,000 − $150). Under the sales warranty accrual method, the journal entries to reflect the transactions of the Anglee Machinery Corporation for 1995 typically are recorded as follows:

*The proportional performance method for separate service contracts is introduced in Chapter 4 and also discussed in Chapter 16.*

### Sale of 200 Machines during April–December, 1995

| | | |
|---|---|---|
| Cash or Accounts Receivable ($6,000 × 200) | 1,200,000 | |
| Sales ($5,850 × 200) | | 1,170,000 |
| Unearned Warranty Revenue ($150 × 200) | | 30,000 |

### Recognition of Warranty Expense for Period, April–December, 1995

| | | |
|---|---|---|
| Warranty Expense | 5,000 | |
| Cash (or other assets) | | 5,000 |

### Recognition of Earning of Warranty Revenue for Period, April–December, 1995

| | | |
|---|---|---|
| Unearned Warranty Revenue | 5,000 | |
| Warranty Revenue | | 5,000 |

On the balance sheet prepared for December 31, 1995, the $25,000 balance in Unearned Warranty Revenue is shown as a current liability. Note that on the 1995 income statement the Sales amount is $30,000 smaller than under the expense warranty accrual method. It lists another revenue item, Warranty Revenue, of $5,000 and also Warranty Expense for $5,000 (as compared to $30,000 under the expense warranty accrual approach). Thus the net income for 1995 is the same under each method, but the amounts of revenue and expense and the classifications of revenues are different, reflecting the different nature of revenue earned.

The transactions for 1996 affecting the 200 machines sold in 1995 are recorded as follows:

**Recognition of Warranty Expense during 1996**

| | | |
|---|---|---|
| Warranty Expense | 25,150 | |
|     Cash (or other assets) | | 25,150 |

**Recognition of Earning of Warranty Revenue during 1996**

| | | |
|---|---|---|
| Unearned Warranty Revenue | 25,000 | |
|     Warranty Revenue | | 25,000 |

Observe that these entries are related to the sale of the 200 machines. Other sales and other warranty costs would be mingled with these revenues and costs on the 1996 income statement. Also, note that it is assumed that, in general, no profit will be realized from the sale of the implied warranty service contract. As a matter of fact, in the Anglee Machinery Corporation example, there is a loss of $150; this loss results from the actual warranty costs exceeding the estimated costs by that amount. Thus, this method assumed the most conservative possible recognition of that part of the revenue applicable to the warranty.

*Modified Cash Basis*
The modified cash basis is the only method accepted for federal income tax purposes, and for this reason, it is often used for financial reporting. **Under the modified cash basis, the warranty costs are recorded as an expense during the period in which the repairs are made to merchandise under warranty.** Thus the expense is recognized in the period of the *repair,* and this period may be later than the period of the sale. A current liability is recorded only if an obligation is incurred for the repair that is not paid at the time of the repair. Since the full warranty costs are not estimated and recognized during the period of sale, no liability for these future warranty costs is recorded. This method is inappropriate for financial reporting because it violates the matching principle. In general, since an expenditure of cash or other resources in the future is expected to be made, a liability *does* in fact exist from the date of sale to the end of the warranty period. Therefore, despite its popularity, the modified cash basis is theoretically unsound. It is justified for accounting under two conditions:

1. From a cost/benefit standpoint, when the warranty costs are immaterial or when the warranty period is relatively short.

2. When it is not possible to make a reliable estimate of the amount of the warranty obligation at the time of sale.

## Premium and Coupon Obligations

Many companies offer premiums such as toys, dishes, and small appliances in exchange for labels, coupons, box tops, and wrappers from their products. Other companies offer coupons printed in newspapers and magazines that can be used to reduce the purchase price of their products. Still others offer a cash rebate upon the return of a cash register receipt for the purchase of their products. Many of these offers expire after a specified time, but some do not have an expiration date. All of these offers are intended to increase the companies' sales. Accordingly, **their related costs are matched as expenses against the revenues in the period of sale.** Furthermore, at the end of the accounting period, any outstanding offers that are expected to be redeemed or claimed within the next year (or operating cycle, if longer) are reported as current liabilities.

For example, assume that on October 1, 1995, the American Meatball Corporation began offering to customers a serving dish in return for 30 meatball can labels. This offer expires on April 1, 1996. The cost of each premium serving dish is $2. Based on past experience, the company estimates that only 60% of the labels will be redeemed. During 1995, the company purchased 12,000 serving dishes. In 1995, it sold 300,000 cans of meatballs at $1.80 per can. From these sales 105,000 labels were returned for redemption in 1995. The following series of journal entries is necessary in 1995 to properly match expenses against revenues and to record current liabilities:

**Purchase of 12,000 Serving Dishes**

| | | |
|---|---|---|
| Inventory of Premium Serving Dishes | 24,000 | |
|     Cash (or Accounts Payable) | | 24,000 |

**Sale of 300,000 Cans of Meatballs**

| | | |
|---|---|---|
| Cash (or Accounts Receivable) | 540,000 | |
|     Sales | | 540,000 |

**Redemption of 105,000 Labels**

| | | |
|---|---|---|
| Premium Expense [(105,000 ÷ 30) × $2] | 7,000 | |
|     Inventory of Premium Serving Dishes | | 7,000 |

**End-of-Year Recording of Estimated Liability for Outstanding Premium Offers**

| | | |
|---|---|---|
| Premium Expense | 5,000 | |
|     Estimated Premium Claims Outstanding | | 5,000 |

The year-end adjustment to premium expense is computed as follows:

| | |
|---|---|
| Total meatball cans (with labels) sold in 1995 | $300,000 |
| Total labels estimated for redemption (60% × 300,000) | 180,000 |
| Deduct labels redeemed during 1995 | (105,000) |
| Estimated number of labels for future redemption | 75,000 |
| Premium expense for estimated future redemptions [(75,000 ÷ 30) × $2] | $ 5,000 |

The Premium Expense is included as a selling expense on the income statement, the Inventory of Premium Serving Dishes is reported as a current asset, and the Estimated Premium Claims Outstanding is reported as a current liability on the balance sheet since the offer expires in less than a year.

The future redemptions of these labels in 1996 will require a debit to the Estimated Premium Claims Outstanding liability account and a credit to Inventory of Premium Serving Dishes. Any corrections necessary because actual redemptions differ from estimated redemptions are treated as changes in accounting estimates and are recognized as an adjustment to Premium Expense in the period of change.

Some companies prefer to record an estimate of the premium expense and liability at the time of sale and reduce the liability each time a premium is claimed. Others prefer to record an estimate of the entire liability at the end of the accounting period, but reduce the liability as premiums are claimed during the period. In either case, the effects on the financial statements are the same as those illustrated.

### Advertising Costs

Most advertising costs are either expensed as incurred or the first time the advertising takes place because it is uncertain whether there are future economic benefits. In the case of "direct-response" advertising, however, the AICPA has issued an Exposure Draft for a *Statement of Position* that, if adopted, would require certain costs initially to be recorded as assets. **Direct-response advertising** is advertising that is expected to result in a customer's decision to buy the company's product based on a specific response to the advertising. The specific response must be documented through, for instance, a coded coupon turned in by the customer or a coded order form included with an advertisement. In such a situation, specific costs would be capitalized if the company provides evidence (e.g., historical patterns) that they will result in future revenues in excess of future costs.

The costs of direct-response advertising that would be capitalized include: (1) incremental direct costs incurred in transactions with independent third parties (e.g., costs of artwork, magazine space, mailing) and (2) payroll costs for activities (e.g., idea development, writing advertising copy) of employees directly related to the advertising. As discussed in the previous section, also included as assets are premiums, contest prizes, gifts, and similar promotions directly related to the direct-response advertising activities. Costs for administration and occupancy (e.g., depreciation) would *not* be included as assets. The costs of direct-response advertising that are reported as assets would be amortized as advertising expense over the period during which the future benefits are expected to be received (e.g., up to the date a coupon expires).[16]

## CONTINGENCIES

External users are interested in information that helps them assess the amounts, timing, and uncertainty of the net cash inflows of a company. They need accounting information that has predictive value that helps them forecast more accurately the future outcome of past or present events. The financial information reported in a company's financial statements is based primarily on transactions that have affected the company. However, there may be some information available about a company at year-end that has not yet been recorded in the company's accounting system, but may be useful to external users in predicting what might happen to the company. These items commonly are referred to as "contingencies."

Specifically, **FASB Statement No. 5** defines the term **contingency** as:

an *existing condition,* situation, or set of circumstances involving *uncertainty* as to possible gain (hereafter a "gain contingency") or loss (hereafter a "loss contingency") to [a company] that will ultimately be resolved when one or more future events occur or fail to occur. *Resolution* of the uncertainty may confirm the acquisition of an asset or the reduction of a liability or the loss or impairment of an asset or the incurrence of a liability.[17]

---

16. "Reporting on Advertising Costs," *AICPA Proposed Statement of Position* (New York: AICPA, 1992), par. 25–40.
17. "Accounting for Contingencies," *FASB Statement of Financial Accounting Standards No. 5* (Stamford, Conn.: FASB, 1975), par. 1. (Emphasis added.)

This definition includes three primary characteristics of a contingency: **(1) an existing condition, (2) uncertainty as to the ultimate effect of this condition, and (3) resolution of the uncertainty based on one or more future events.** *FASB Statement No. 5* focuses primarily on *loss* contingencies and lists a number of examples. Some of these are familiar, such as the noncollectibility of receivables (accounting for bad debts) and the obligations relating to product warranties and premium offers discussed earlier in this chapter. Less familiar loss contingencies include the risk of loss or damage of a company's property by fire, explosion, or other hazards, threat of expropriation of assets, pending or threatened litigation, actual or possible claims and assessments, guarantees of indebtedness of others, and agreement to repurchase receivables (or to repurchase the related property) that have been sold.

When a loss contingency exists, the likelihood that the future event or events will confirm the loss and the impairment of an asset or the incurrence of a liability can vary over a wide range. *FASB Statement No. 5* uses the terms *probable, reasonably possible,* and *remote* to identify three areas within this range. These terms are defined as follows:

1. **Probable.** The future event or events are *likely* to occur.

2. **Reasonably possible.** The chance of the future event or events occurring is *more* than remote but *less* than likely.

3. **Remote.** The chance of the future event occurring is *slight*.[18]

The **accounting for loss contingencies** depends upon the likelihood of occurrence of the future event(s). Two separate methods of accounting are prescribed by *FASB Statement No. 5.*

1. *Accrual in Accounts.* An estimated loss from a loss contingency *is accrued* in the accounts and reported in financial statements as a reduction of income and as a liability (or a reduction in an asset) if *both* of the following two conditions are met:
   a. Information available prior to issuance of the financial statements indicates that it is *probable* that an asset has been impaired or a liability has been incurred at the date of the financial statements. It is implicit in this condition that it must be *probable* that one or more future events will occur confirming the occurrence of the loss.
   b. The amount of loss can be *reasonably estimated*. In certain situations, a company's reasonable estimate of the loss may be a *range* of amounts. When some amount within the range is a better estimate than any other amount in the range, it is the amount accrued. When no amount within the range is a better estimate, the minimum amount in the range is accrued because it is not likely that the loss will be less than this minimum.[19]

2. *Disclosure in Notes to Financial Statements.* If no loss accrual is made because one or both of the preceding conditions are not met and when there is at least a reasonable possibility that a loss may have been incurred, then the loss contingency is disclosed in the notes to the financial statements. (Some remote loss contingencies are also disclosed in the notes, as discussed later.)

---

18. *Ibid.,* par. 3. (Emphasis added.)
19. "Reasonable Estimation of the Amount of a Loss," *FASB Interpretation No. 14* (Stamford, Conn.: FASB, 1976), par. 3.

To summarize, **a loss contingency is recognized if the future event is** *probable* **and if its amount can be** *reasonably estimated.* If a liability is recorded in this process, it is not necessary to know the exact payee or the exact date that it is to be paid. Disclosure in the notes to the financial statements is required if one of these criteria is not met and if there is a reasonable possibility that a loss may have been incurred.

The discussion that follows is concerned with the accounting for the accrual of loss contingencies, disclosure of loss contingencies in the notes to the financial statements, and disclosure of gain contingencies in the notes to the financial statements.

## Accrual of Loss Contingencies

Certain loss contingencies *usually* are accrued because they meet both conditions stated in the preceding section. They include the noncollectibility of receivables and sales returns and allowances (discussed in Chapter 5), as well as obligations related to property taxes, product warranties, and premium offers discussed earlier in this chapter. Several other loss contingencies *may be* accrued provided that they meet the two stated conditions. These include the threat of expropriation of assets, pending or threatened litigation, actual or possible claims and assessments, guarantees of indebtedness of others, and agreements to repurchase receivables (or the related property) that have been sold. On the other hand, at least three contingencies are *usually not* accrued in accounts. These include the uninsured risk of loss or damage of company property by fire, explosion, or other hazards, general or unspecified business risks, and risk of loss from catastrophes assumed by property and casualty insurance companies including reinsurance companies. For this latter group of items, the mere exposure to risk does not mean that an asset is impaired or that a liability has been incurred.

When a loss contingency is recognized, there is a debit to an *expense* (or *loss*) account and a credit to a *liability* account, *asset* account, or *contra-asset* account. To illustrate, assume a company estimates that its bad debt expense is $12,000 for 1995. The journal entry at the end of the year to record this loss contingency is:

| | | |
|---|---|---|
| **Bad Debt Expense** | 12,000 | |
| **Allowance for Doubtful Accounts** | | 12,000 |

Note the debit made to an expense account and the credit made to a contra-asset account to accrue the loss contingency.

The accounting for damage lawsuits presents a very difficult problem. These pending lawsuits must be analyzed as possible loss contingencies. Consideration should be given to the opinion of legal counsel, the nature of the litigation, precedent experience of the company and other companies in similar cases, and management reaction to the lawsuit. If the cause for litigation has occurred before the date of issuance of the financial statements, if the loss of the lawsuit is *probable,* and if the loss amount can be *estimated,* the loss should be recognized. Management may decide that disclosure of the pending lawsuit only should be made in the notes to the financial statements because the loss is not probable or it is not possible to reliably estimate the loss. However, this decision may be based as much on management's desire to maintain higher reported earnings and to minimize the amount of reported liabilities.

In regard to potential unfiled lawsuits and other possible assessments and unasserted claims, a company must determine the likelihood that the suit may be filed or, in the case of a claim or assessment, the likelihood that it may be asserted, and the probability of an unfavorable outcome. For example, if Patterson Corporation is being investigated for a possible patent infringement suit, it must determine the probability that the suit will be filed and that the suit will be lost. If these future events are probable, the loss is reasonably estimable, and the cause for action has occurred on or before the date of the issuance of the financial statements, the loss and the liability are accrued in its accounts.

## Disclosure of Loss Contingencies in the Notes to the Financial Statements

If no loss accrual is made for a loss contingency because one or both of the conditions listed are not met, or if an exposure to loss exists in excess of the amount that actually is accrued, disclosure of the contingency must be made when there is at least a reasonable possibility that a loss or an additional loss may have been incurred. Recall that a loss contingency is reasonably possible when the chance is more than remote but less than likely that the future event or events will confirm the loss or impairment of an asset or the incurrence of a liability. Most of the examples of loss contingencies listed earlier could fall into this category, particularly the threat of expropriation of assets, pending or threatened litigation, and actual or possible claims and assessments. For this type of loss contingency, the disclosure is made in the notes to the financial statements. The disclosure must indicate the nature of the contingency and give an estimate of the possible loss, or range of loss or state that such an estimate cannot be made.

Certain loss contingencies where the possibility of loss is only remote are also disclosed in the notes to the financial statements. Examples of these loss contingencies include direct and indirect guarantees of indebtedness of others, obligations of commercial banks under "standby letters of credit," and guarantees to repurchase receivables that have been sold or otherwise assigned. **Indirect guarantees as those arising out of an agreement requiring one company to transfer funds to another entity upon the occurrence of specified events, under conditions whereby (1) the funds are legally available to creditors of the other entity, and (2) those creditors may enforce that entity's claims against the company under the agreement.**[20] A common characteristic of these remote contingencies is a guarantee, normally with a right to proceed against an outside party in the event that the guarantor is called upon to satisfy the guarantee.[21] The disclosure of this group of guarantees must include the nature and amount of the guarantee and, if estimable, the value of any recovery that could be expected to result. This latter requirement would result from the guarantor's right to proceed against an outside party.

## Disclosure of Gain Contingencies in the Notes to the Financial Statements

Provided that the three characteristics are present (as stated in the definition of a contingency), a gain contingency may exist. This kind of contingency results in a potential increase in assets or a potential decrease in liabilities. Adhering to the convention of conservatism and to the revenue recognition criteria, these gains are *not*

---

20. "Disclosure of Indirect Guarantees of Indebtedness of Others," *FASB Interpretation No. 34* (Stamford, Conn.: FASB, 1981), par. 2.
21. *FASB Statement No. 5, op. cit.,* par. 10 and 12.

accrued, but are disclosed in the notes to the financial statements. **FASB Statement No. 5** states:

(a) Contingencies that might result in gains usually are not reflected in the accounts since to do so might be to recognize revenue prior to its realization.
(b) Adequate disclosure shall be made of contingencies that might result in gains, but care shall be exercised to avoid misleading implications as to the likelihood of realization.[22]

An example of a gain contingency is the case where one company is suing another company for patent infringement, and the probability of winning the suit is excellent. A second example is the case of a probable expropriation of property by a foreign government where probable reimbursement will exceed the book value of the property expected to be taken over by the foreign government.

### Executory Contracts

An **executory contract** is a contract in which two parties agree to a future exchange of resources or services, but neither party has performed any of its responsibilities. Examples of executory contracts include unused lines of credit, purchase commitments, agreements to pay future compensation, and commitments for plant expansion. Since in an executory contract (sometimes called an *unexecuted* contract) no exchange of resources or services has occurred, no liability (or asset reduction) or contingent liability exists. However, when an executory contract has a likely material impact on the future cash flows of a company, to enhance the predictive value of the information, disclosure in the notes to the financial statements is made.

### Illustrations of Contingency Disclosures

Exhibit 11-4 illustrates the loss contingency disclosures in the notes to the 1992 financial statements of several companies. These disclosures involve prior litigation against Westinghouse for which an accrual had previously been made, litigation against Quaker Oats regarding its *Gatorade* advertising, and litigation against Exxon regarding the Valdez oil spill.

---

**EXHIBIT 11-4**
**Disclosure of Contingencies**

**WESTINGHOUSE**

**NOTES TO THE FINANCIAL STATEMENTS (in part):**
*Note 17. Contingent Liabilities and Commitments (in part):*
*Uranium Settlements:*
The Corporation had previously provided for all estimated future costs associated with the resolution of all uranium supply contract suits and related litigation. The remaining balance at December 31, 1992, is deemed adequate considering all facts and circumstances known to management. The future obligations require providing specific quantities of uranium and products and services over a period extending beyond the year 2010. Variances from estimates which may occur will be considered in determining if an adjustment of the liability is necessary.

---

22. *Ibid.*, par. 17.

## EXHIBIT 11-4, Continued
## Disclosure of Contingencies

### QUAKER OATS

**NOTES TO THE CONSOLIDATED FINANCIAL STATEMENTS (in part):**
*Note 19.*
*Litigation (in part):*
On December 19, 1990, Judge Prentice H. Marshall of the United States District Court for the Northern District of Illinois issued a memorandum opinion stating that the Court would enter judgment against the Company in favor of Sands, Taylor & Wood Co. The Court found that the use of the words "thirst aid" in advertising *Gatorade* thirst quencher infringed the Plaintiff's rights in the trademark THIRST-AID. On July 9, 1991, Judge Marshall entered a judgment of $42.6 million, composed of $31.4 million in principal, plus prejudgment interest of $10.6 million and fees, expenses and costs of $0.6 million. The order enjoined use of the phrase "THIRST-AID" in connection with the advertising or sale of *Gatorade* thirst quencher in the United States. The Company and its subsidiary, Stokely-Van Camp, Inc., ceased use of the words "thirst aid" in December 1990. The Company subsequently appealed the judgment. On September 2, 1992, the Court of Appeals for the Seventh Circuit vacated the District Court's judgment. The appellate court affirmed the finding of the infringement, but found that the monetary award was an inequitable "windfall" to the Plaintiff. The case was remanded to the District Court for further proceedings. Further appeal or request for rehearing is possible and the Company is reviewing its options. The amount of any liability which might finally exist cannot reasonably be estimated and no provision for loss has been made in the accompanying financial statements.

### EXXON

**NOTES TO CONSOLIDATED FINANCIAL STATEMENTS (in part):**
*Note 14. Litigation and Other Contingencies (in part):*
More than 350 lawsuits, including class actions, have been brought in various courts against Exxon Corporation and certain of its subsidiaries relating to the release of crude oil from the tanker Exxon Valdez in 1989. Most of these lawsuits seek unspecified compensatory and punitive damages; several lawsuits seek damages in varying specific amounts. Certain of the lawsuits seek injunctive relief. Of these lawsuits, more than 81 have been dismissed or settled. The cost to the corporation from these lawsuits is not possible to predict; however, it is believed that the final outcome will not have a materially adverse effect upon the corporation's operations or financial condition.

## OTHER LIABILITY CLASSIFICATION ISSUES

Two additional liability classification issues addressed by the FASB are discussed in this section: (1) short-term debt expected to be refinanced and (2) classification of obligations that are callable by the creditor.

### Short-Term Debt Expected to Be Refinanced

Generally, debt that is maturing within one year or the operating cycle, whichever is longer, is classified as a current liability. This classification affects liquidity ratios such as the current and acid test ratios. In certain situations, short-term debt that is expected to be refinanced on a long-term basis is not classified as a current liability.

**FASB Statement No. 6** states that short-term obligations are *excluded* from current liabilities if two conditions are met: (1) there is an intention to refinance on a *long-term basis* and (2) there is an ability to refinance.

**Refinancing on a long-term basis** refers to replacing the short-term debt with long-term debt (such as bonds payable) or with ownership securities (such as common stock); or, instead, extending, renewing, or replacing the short-term debt with other short-term obligations that in turn will be renewed or extended beyond one year or the operating cycle, whichever is longer. The **intent to refinance** on a long-term basis means that the company intends to refinance the short-term obligations so that working capital will not be required to be used during the subsequent year or operating cycle, whichever is longer. The **ability to refinance** on a long-term basis must be demonstrated by the fact that the company: (1) has issued long-term obligations or equity securities after the date of its balance sheet but before that balance sheet is issued, or (2) has entered into a bona fide long-term financing agreement before the balance sheet is issued that clearly permits the company to refinance the short-term obligations on a long-term basis on terms that are readily determinable, non-cancellable, and capable of being honored by the lender.

If a company actually has refinanced short-term debt after the end of the year but before the statements are issued, it excludes from current liabilities shown on the year-end balance sheet only the portion of the short-term obligation that is equal to the proceeds from the new long-term obligations or equity securities issued to retire the short-term obligation. For example, assume that Rayvon Datrix Corporation, with $2,000,000 of short-term debt on December 31, 1995, issued 75,000 shares of common stock for $20 per share on January 10, 1996. The proceeds of $1,500,000 were scheduled to be used to retire the short-term obligation when it matured. On the December 31, 1995 balance sheet (issued on February 28, 1996), the short-term debt of $1,500,000 expected to be refinanced is shown as a noncurrent liability item. Note that the refinanced portion continues to be shown as a liability and not as stockholders' equity since as of year-end the item was debt and not equity. The other $500,000 is shown as a current liability item.

When a company relies on a **financing agreement** to demonstrate the ability to refinance, the amount of the short-term debt excluded from current liabilities is reduced to an amount that is the *lesser* of

1. The amount available for refinancing under the agreement, or

2. The amount obtainable under the agreement after consideration is given to the restrictions included in other agreements or of transferability of funds, or

3. A reasonable estimate of the minimum amount expected to be available for future refinancing if the amount that could be obtained fluctuates (for example, in relation to the company's needs, in proportion to the value of the collateral, or in accordance with other terms of the agreement).[23]

If no reasonable estimate can be made, the entire outstanding short-term obligation must be included as a current liability.

When a short-term obligation to be refinanced is excluded from current liabilities, the notes to the financial statements include a general description of the financing

23. "Classification of Short-Term Obligations Expected to Be Refinanced," *FASB Statement of Financial Accounting Standards No. 6* (Stamford, Conn.: FASB, 1975), par. 9–12.

agreement and the terms of any new obligations incurred or expected to be incurred, or equity securities issued or expected to be issued as a result of a refinancing. These obligations may also be shown in captions distinct from both the current liabilities and long-term debt, such as "Interim Debt," "Short-Term Debt Expected to Be Refinanced," and "Intermediate Debt."

### Repayment and Replacement

After the issuance of *FASB Statement No. 6,* a controversy arose as to whether a short-term debt should be excluded from current liabilities if it were repaid by the use of current assets after the balance sheet date and then later replaced by long-term debt (or common stock) before the balance sheet actually was issued. This action would constitute a reimbursement of the working capital used to liquidate the short-term debt. **FASB Interpretation No. 8** concluded that such short-term debt is *not* excluded from current liabilities at the balance sheet date.[24] Thus since the repayment of a short-term debt required the use of existing actual current assets (even though they are later replaced), the short-term debt is reported on the preceding year-end balance sheet as a current liability.

## Classification of Obligations That Are Callable by the Creditor

As noted earlier in the chapter, the *currently maturing portion* of long-term debt generally is classified as a current liability. Regarding this general principle, **FASB Statement No. 78** concluded that the *entire amount* of a long-term obligation is classified as a current liability if: (1) the debtor is in violation of a provision of a long-term debt agreement (a requirement in the debt indenture or contract) at the balance sheet date, and the violation makes the liability callable by the creditor within one year from the balance sheet date, or (2) the violation, if not resolved within a specified grace period, *will make* the liability callable within one year from the balance sheet date (or operating cycle, if longer, in both of the preceding situations). An exception to this requirement is a callable obligation that meets the following conditions: (1) the creditor has waived or lost the right to request repayment for more than one year (or operating cycle, if longer) from the balance sheet date, or (2) it is probable that the violation of a debt agreement for a long-term obligation containing a grace period will be resolved within that grace period, thus preventing it from becoming callable. In this case, the obligation is reported as long-term debt; furthermore, the circumstances involving an obligation under item (2) are disclosed in the notes to the financial statements.[25]

The preceding GAAP indicate the FASB concluded that the current liability classification is intended to include obligations that, by their terms, are due on demand or will be due on demand within one year (or the operating cycle, if longer) from the balance sheet date, *even though liquidation may not be expected within that period.* As indicated by the italicized phrase, this concept does not conform to the requirement that a current liability be "reasonably expected to require either the use of existing current assets or the creation of other current liabilities within one year or the

---

24. "Classification of a Short-Term Obligation Repaid Prior to Being Replaced by a Long-Term Security," *FASB Interpretation No. 8* (Stamford, Conn.: FASB, 1976), par. 3.
25. "Classification of Obligations That Are Callable by the Creditor," *FASB Statement of Financial Accounting Standards No. 78* (Stamford, Conn.: FASB, 1983), par. 5.

operating cycle, whichever is longer." Rather, it substitutes a notion that obligations should be classified as current when they are legally callable within one year, whether or not they are likely to be called. In dissenting to *FASB Statement No. 78*, three Board members stated that:

> It is asserted that this amendment will improve comparability. It will, in fact, cause situations to appear the same even when underlying facts and circumstances are sufficiently different to justify different reasonable expectations. This is not comparability; it is substituting an arbitrary rule for judgment.[26]

## FINANCIAL STATEMENT PRESENTATION OF CURRENT LIABILITIES

Conceptually, the three main balance sheet elements—assets, liabilities, and equity—should be reported in homogeneous classes because this disclosure along with accompanying subtotals is helpful to users in making decisions. One factor for deciding the number of classes and content of each is that the result should help users to assess the nature, amount, and liquidity of available resources, including management's intentions regarding their function in use. Another factor is the amount and timing of obligations that require liquid resources for settlement. Liabilities and assets can be reported as items in the balance sheet in various ways. In this regard, the FASB has suggested broad guidelines as follows:

1. Assets and liabilities with different implications for the *financial flexibility* of the enterprise should be reported as separate items.

2. Assets and liabilities with different general *liquidity* characteristics should be reported as separate items.

3. Assets and liabilities that differ regarding the attribute that is measured should be reported in separate categories.[27]

These broad (but not specific) guidelines suggest that companies should arrange the disclosure of their current liabilities in a manner that will **highlight their liquidity characteristics and their implications for financial flexibility.**

Currently, most companies present current liabilities at the top of the first classification under Liabilities. Items within the current liability section typically are listed in the order of average length of the maturities, according to amount (largest to smallest), or in the order of liquidation preference—that is, in the order of their legal claims against assets: those liabilities having legal priority would be shown first, secured obligations second, and unsecured third. A popular way of presenting these items is by groupings:

- Notes payable
- Accounts payable
- Accrued liability items
- Unearned revenue items
- Other current liabilities

---

26. *Ibid.*, page 4.
27. "Reporting Income, Cash Flows, and Financial Flexibility of Business Enterprises," *FASB Proposed Statement of Financial Accounting Concepts, op. cit.*, par. 50 and 51. (Emphasis added.)

Since a description of all significant accounting policies is included as an integral part of the financial statements, any major issue affecting the measurement or disclosure of current liabilities is presented in the notes to the financial statements. The purpose is that notes and other supplemental information concerning current liabilities are sufficient to meet the requirement of full disclosure. For example, secured liabilities are identified clearly, and the related assets pledged as collateral are disclosed. If the due date of any liability can be extended, that fact and any related details are disclosed. Current liabilities are not offset against the assets that are scheduled to be used for their liquidation, and currently maturing long-term debt is classified as current liabilities (unless refinanced). Existing lines of credit and material commitments requiring obligations in subsequent periods are also disclosed.

Exhibit 11-5 is an excerpt of the Gerber balance sheets showing how it discloses its current liabilities, along with the applicable note to the financial statements. This method of disclosure is representative of the reporting techniques used by most large companies.

## EXHIBIT 11-5
## Disclosure of Current Liabilities

### GERBER

|  | March 31 | |
| --- | --- | --- |
|  | 1992 | 1991 |
| (thousands of dollars) | | |
| *Liabilities and Stockholders' Equity (in part):* | | |
| **Current Liabilities** | | |
| Short-term borrowings — Note H | $ 10,287 | $ 475 |
| Trade accounts payable | 65,311 | 56,770 |
| Salaries, wages and other compensation | 43,815 | 43,992 |
| Local taxes, interest and other expenses | 62,221 | 58,302 |
| Income taxes | 18,387 | 20,567 |
| Policy claims and reserves | 14,239 | 10,884 |
| Current maturities of long-term debt | 1,176 | 1,117 |
| Total Current Liabilities | $215,436 | $192,107 |

### NOTES TO CONSOLIDATED FINANCIAL STATEMENTS (in part):

*Note H.*
*Short-Term Borrowings:*
Short-term borrowings consist of borrowings under bank lines of credit.

At March 31, 1992, the company had committed lines of credit of $62,393,000, for which the company pays nominal fees. These committed lines of credit support the issuance of commercial paper and are subject to annual renewal. Unused credit under such lines totaled $52,106,000 at March 31, 1992.

Under the terms of other short-term credit facilities, the company may borrow up to $195,000,000 on such terms as may be mutually agreed upon. These arrangements do not have termination dates and are reviewed periodically. No commitment fees or compensating balances are required for the short-term credit facilities. No borrowings were outstanding under these arrangements at March 31, 1992.

## QUESTIONS

*Q11-1* Define *liabilities*. Explain the meanings of *probable* and *obligations* in the context of a liability.

*Q11-2* Distinguish between a legal and a nonlegal (accounting) liability. Give an example of each.

*Q11-3* List the three essential characteristics of a liability identified in *FASB Statement of Financial Accounting Concepts No. 6*. Discuss briefly.

*Q11-4* Before a liability can be reported, the identity of the recipient must be known. True or false? Justify your answer.

*Q11-5* What are the primary issues in accounting for current liabilities?

*Q11-6* Define a company's operating cycle.

*Q11-7* Why is the liquidity of liabilities important in the accounting for liabilities?

*Q11-8* How does the constraint of materiality affect the accounting for current liabilities?

*Q11-9* Define a non-interest-bearing note that is discounted at a bank at a specific rate. How are the proceeds computed for a non-interest-bearing note?

*Q11-10* What are compensated absences? How are these accounted for?

*Q11-11* *FASB Statement No. 49* requires that a company selling inventory and agreeing to repurchase it later neither record the transaction as a sale nor remove the inventory from the balance sheet. If so, does a new current liability arise? How is its amount measured?

*Q11-12* Identify how to account for warranty costs under the expense warranty accrual method, sales warranty accrual method, and modified cash basis.

*Q11-13* Define *contingency*. What exactly is the company uncertain about—whether a future event will take place giving rise to a liability, or whether a future event will take place that will confirm that a liability exists from an event that has already taken place?

*Q11-14* How do the matching principle and the conservatism convention enter into the accounting for contingencies?

*Q11-15* What two criteria must be met before a loss contingency is accrued in the accounts?

*Q11-16* With regard to a loss contingency, by what date must the event have occurred giving rise to a probable loss before accrual is required? By what date must information be available to assess the probability that a loss has been incurred?

*Q11-17* What conditions would have to be met in order to accrue the loss from an unfiled lawsuit?

*Q11-18* Define *gain contingency*. Describe the accounting requirements for a gain contingency.

*Q11-19* What two criteria must be met before a short-term debt expected to be refinanced can be classified as a noncurrent liability?

*Q11-20* How does a company demonstrate the ability to refinance currently maturing short-term debt?

*Q11-21* *FASB Statement No. 78* requires that certain obligations due on demand within one year (or operating cycle, if longer) be classified as current liabilities. Do you agree with this statement? Explain.

## CASES

*C11-1   Short-Term Debt Expected to Be Refinanced*
The following is the current liability section of Hollo Hardware Company on December 31, 1995:

| | |
|---|---:|
| Accounts payable, trade | $ 50,000 |
| Notes payable, 12%, due February 19, 1996 | 70,000 |
| Unearned interest and revenue | 12,000 |
| Total current liabilities | $132,000 |

On January 15, 1996 Hollo enters into an agreement with the local bank to receive a line of credit for $60,000 available for the next 2 years with payment due 2 years after the date of the loan. Interest at 1% above the prime rate will be charged quarterly. On February 15, 1996 Hollo borrows the money to refinance the short-term note due in 4 days.

**Required**

1. Does the preceding agreement allow Hollo to exclude any of the short-term note from current liabilities on the December 31, 1995 balance sheet? If so, how much? Discuss.

2. Would the result be the same if Hollo borrowed the money on February 26, 1996?

*C11-2   Various Liability Issues*
Angela Company is a manufacturer of toys. During the year, the following situations arose:

a. A safety hazard related to one of its toy products was discovered. It is considered probable that liabilities have been incurred. Based on past experience, a reasonable estimate of the amount of loss can be made.

b. One of its small warehouses is located on the bank of a river and could no longer be insured against flood losses. No flood losses have occurred after the date that the insurance became unavailable.

c. This year, Angela began promoting a new toy by including a coupon, redeemable for a movie ticket, in each toy's carton. The movie ticket, which cost Angela $2, is purchased in advance and then mailed to the customer when the coupon is received by Angela. Angela estimated, based on past experience, that 60% of the coupons would be redeemed. Forty percent of the coupons were actually redeemed this year, and the remaining 20% of the coupons are expected to be redeemed next year.

**Required**

1. How should Angela report the safety hazard? Why? Do not discuss deferred income tax implications.
2. How should Angela report the noninsurable flood risk? Why?
3. How should Angela account for the toy promotion campaign in this year? *(AICPA adapted)*

### C11-3    *Pending Damage Suit Disclosure*

On January 15, 1996 a truck driver for Cork Transfer Company negligently rounded a curve that was also a bridge covering several local merchant shops. The truck jumped the guardrail and fell 30 feet onto one of the shops, causing highly flammable chemicals in the truck to explode. Although by February 22, 1996 (the date Cork's financial statements for 1995 are issued), no claims had been filed against Cork, it fully expected some to be filed in the future.

**Required**

Discuss the accounting treatment, if any, Cork should give the contingent loss occurring from the wreck in the December 31, 1995 financial statements.

### C11-4    *Estimate Liability Arising from Loss Contingency*

Worldwide Motors has produced "Stallions" for 10 years as of December 31, 1995. In a civil judgment against it on July 20, 1995, it was found that for the period of January 1, 1992 until the present, Worldwide was negligent in the design of the cars because the gasoline tank was positioned in the rear in such a way that it would explode upon impact with another car. On December 30, 1995 Worldwide estimated that its ultimate liability on the Stallions would total $6 million.

**Required**

Discuss fully the accounting treatment Worldwide should give to the contingency on its financial statements as of December 31, 1995.

### C11-5    *Short-Term Debt Expected to Be Refinanced*

While auditing the 1995 financial statements of Warder Corporation, you found evidence that the following were not included in their current liabilities on the December 31, 1995 balance sheet:

1. Convertible bonds maturing in 60 days that were never converted.
2. Note payable due 2 months after balance sheet date, with refinancing agreement entered into 4 weeks after balance sheet date.
3. Notes payable of Warder's completely owned subsidiary due its stockholders and payable upon demand.
4. Deposits from customers on equipment ordered by them from Warder.

**Required**

Discuss the assumptions needed for Warder to correctly exclude the previously mentioned items from the December 31, 1995 current liabilities. The balance sheet was issued on March 1, 1996.

### C11-6    *Loss Contingencies*

*Part a.* The two basic requirements for the accrual of a loss contingency are supported by several basic concepts of accounting. Three of these concepts are: periodicity (time periods), measurement, and objectivity.

**Required**

Discuss how the two basic requirements for the accrual of a loss contingency relate to the three concepts listed previously.

*Part b.* The following three **independent** sets of facts relate to (1) the possible accrual or (2) the possible disclosure by other means of a loss contingency.

**Situation I**

A company offers a one-year warranty for the product that it manufactures. A history of warranty claims has been compiled and the probable amount of claims related to sales for a given period can be determined.

**Situation II**

Subsequent to the date of a set of financial statements, but prior to the issuance of the financial statements, a company enters into a contract that will probably result in a significant loss to the company. The amount of the loss can be reasonably estimated.

**Situation III**

A company has adopted a policy of recording self-insurance for any possible losses resulting from injury to others by the company's vehicles. The premium for an insurance policy for the same risk from an independent insurance company would have an annual cost of $2,000. During the period covered by the financial statements, there were no accidents involving the company's vehicles that resulted in injury to others.

**Required**

Discuss the accrual and/or type of disclosure necessary (if any) and the reason(s) why such disclosure is appropriate for each of the three independent sets of facts in the situations described here. Complete your response to each situation before proceeding to the next situation. *(AICPA adapted)*

### C11-7    *Various Contingency Issues*

Skinner Company has the following contingencies:

1. Potential costs due to the discovery of a possible defect related to one of its products. These costs are probable and can be reasonably estimated.
2. A potential claim for damages to be received from a lawsuit filed this year against another company. It is probable that proceeds from the claim will be received by Skinner next year.
3. Potential costs due to a promotion campaign whereby a cash refund is sent to customers when coupons are redeemed. Skinner estimated, based on past experience, that 70 percent of the coupons would be redeemed. Forty percent of the coupons were actually redeemed and the cash refunds sent this year. The remaining 30 percent of the coupons are expected to be redeemed next year.

**Required**

1. How should Skinner report the potential costs due to the discovery of a possible product defect? Why?
2. How should Skinner report this year the potential claim for damages that may be received next year? Why?
3. This year, how should Skinner account for the potential costs and obligations due to the promotion campaign? *(AICPA adapted)*

### C11-8    *Contingency Conditions and Disclosure*

Loss contingencies may exist for companies.

**Required**

1. What conditions should be met for an estimated loss from a loss contingency to be accrued by a charge to income?
2. When is disclosure required, and what disclosure should be made for an estimated loss from a loss contingency that need not be accrued by a charge to income? *(AICPA adapted)*

### C11-9    *Product and Lawsuit Contingencies*

Reese Company sells two types of merchandise, Type A and Type B. Each carries a one-year warranty.

Type A merchandise: Product warranty costs, based on past experience, will normally be 1% of sales.

Type B merchandise: Product warranty costs cannot be reasonably estimated because this is a new product line. However, the chief engineer believes that product warranty costs are likely to be incurred.

Reese Company is also being sued for $2,000,000 for an injury caused to a child as a result of alleged negligence while the child was visiting the Reese Company plant in March 1995. The suit was filed in July 1995. Reese's lawyer states that it is probable that Reese will lose the suit and be found liable for a judgment costing anywhere from $200,000 to $900,000. However, the lawyer states that the most probable judgment is $400,000.

**Required**

1. How should Reese report the estimated product warranty costs for each of the two types of merchandise mentioned earlier? Discuss the rationale for your answer. Do not discuss deferred income tax implications, or disclosures that should be made in Reese's 1995 financial statements or notes.
2. How should Reese report the suit in its 1995 financial statements? Discuss the rationale for your answer. Include in your answer disclosures, if any, that should be made in Reese's financial statements or notes. *(AICPA adapted)*

### C11-10    *Contingency and Commitment*

Supey Chemical Co. encountered the following two situations in 1995:

Supey must pay an indeterminate amount for toxic waste cleanup on its land. An adjoining land owner, Gap Toothpaste, sold its property because of possible toxic contamination by Supey of the water supply and resulting potential adverse public reaction towards its product. Gap sued Supey for damages. There is a reasonable possibility that Gap will prevail in the suit.

At December 31, 1995, Supey had a noncancellable purchase contract for 10,000 pounds of Chemical XZ, for delivery in June 1996. Supey does not hedge its contracts. Supey uses this chemical to make Product 2-Y. In December 1995, the U.S. Food and Drug Administration banned the sale of Product 2-Y in concentrated form. Supey will be allowed to sell Product 2-Y in a diluted form; however, it will take at least five years to use the 10,000 pounds of Chemical XZ. Supey believes the sales price of the diluted product will not be sufficient to recover the contract price of Chemical XZ.

**Required**

1. (a) In its 1995 financial statements, how should Supey report the toxic waste cleanup? Why is this reporting appropriate?
   (b) In its 1995 financial statements, how should Supey report Gap's claim against it? Why is this reporting appropriate?
2. In its 1995 financial statements, how should Supey report the effects of the contract to purchase Chemical XZ? Why is this reporting appropriate? *(AICPA adapted)*

## C11-11  Researching GAAP

Bogan Company is in need of cash to finance its operations. The company creates a new company, Hall Company, which is wholly owned by Bogan. On November 1, 1995 Bogan sells $50,000 of inventory on credit to Hall Company, which in turn immediately uses the inventory for a $40,000, 12% loan (guaranteed by Bogan) from 8th National Bank. Hall then uses the proceeds from the loan to repay $40,000 of the $50,000 owed to Bogan. Bogan agrees to continue to extend credit for 9 months to Hall for the remaining $10,000. The inventory is Hall's only asset and is stored in a public warehouse. Bogan agrees to pay Hall the $200 monthly storage fee and $400 per month for a financing fee at the end of each month. Bogan also agrees to repurchase the inventory from Hall for $50,000 at the end of July, 1996. Bogan uses a perpetual inventory system; the cost of the inventory sold to Hall is $42,000. The president of Bogan has asked you how to account for this series of transactions in 1995.

### Required

Research the related generally accepted accounting principles and prepare a short memo to the president that explains how Bogan Company should record the sale of the inventory on November 1, 1995 and the payment of the fees at the end of November and December. Also explain how Bogan should report the recorded items in its 1995 financial statements. Cite your reference and applicable paragraph numbers.

## C11-12  Researching GAAP

Gilmatt Company developed a new product that it planned to sell directly to customers and to promote heavily because of "stiff" competition in the market place. Its marketing department did extensive market surveys and developed a marketing plan for this product. The plan called for a series of television commercials and magazine advertisements. The television commercials aired for two months (September and October) in 1994 to (a) advertise the product and (b) indicate to viewers that "$5 off" coupons would be appearing in forthcoming magazine advertisements. The magazine advertisements appeared evenly over a 3-month period from November 1994 through January 1995 and further promoted the product, as well as included the coded $5-off coupons (which expired at the end of February, 1995.) Gilmatt expected 20,000 coupons to be redeemed. During November and December 1994, Gilmatt sold 2,000 units of the new product at the $50 regular price and 8,000 units at the $45 coded-coupon price. In January 1995, the company sold another 3,000 units at $50 each and 7,000 units at $45 each. It expects customers to redeem another 5,000 coupons before the coupons expire. It is now late January, 1995 and the company is preparing its 1994 annual report.

The marketing department has prepared the following schedule of its 1994 costs related to the advertising and promotion of the new product: supervisor's salary, $10,000; payroll of employees working on magazine advertising copy, $40,000; depreciation, $7,500; cost of television commercials (independently produced), $180,000; cost of magazine space for advertisements, $100,000; cost of television airtime, $300,000.

### Required

Research the related generally accepted accounting principles and indicate how Gilmatt Company should report the costs of marketing the new product and the related sales revenues on its 1994 financial statements. Cite your reference and applicable paragraph numbers.

---

## MULTIPLE CHOICE

*Select the best answer for each of the following.*

**M11-1**  Which of the following is classified as an accrued payroll liability?

| | Federal income tax withheld | Employee's share of F.I.C.A. taxes |
|---|---|---|
| a. | No | Yes |
| b. | No | No |
| c. | Yes | No |
| d. | Yes | Yes |

**M11-2**  During 1994 Lawton Company introduced a new line of machines that carry a 3-year warranty against manufacturer's defects. Based on industry experience, warranty costs are estimated at 2% of sales in the year of sale,

4% in the year after sale, and 6% in the second year after sale. Sales and actual warranty expenditures for the first 3-year period were as follows:

| | Sales | Actual Warranty Expenditures |
|---|---|---|
| 1994 | $ 200,000 | $ 3,000 |
| 1995 | 500,000 | 15,000 |
| 1996 | 700,000 | 45,000 |
| | $1,400,000 | $63,000 |

What amount should Lawton report as a liability at December 31, 1996?

a. $0

b. $5,000

c. $68,000

d. $105,000

M11-3   How should a loss contingency that is reasonably possible and for which the amount can be reasonably estimated be reported?

| | Accrued | Disclosed |
|---|---|---|
| a. | Yes | No |
| b. | No | Yes |
| c. | Yes | Yes |
| d. | No | No |

M11-4   All of Rolf Co.'s employees are entitled to 2 weeks of paid vacation for each full year in Rolf's employ. Unused vacation time can be accumulated and carried forward to succeeding years and will be compensated at the salary in effect when the vacation is taken. Mary Beal started her employment with Rolf on January 1, 1988. As of December 31, 1994 when Beal's salary was $500 per week, Beal had used 10 weeks of her accumulated vacation time. In December 1994 Beal notified Rolf of her intention to use her accumulated vacation weeks in June 1995. Rolf regularly scheduled salary adjustments in July of each year. Rolf properly did not deduct compensation for unused vacations in Rolf's 1994 income tax return. How much should Rolf report as a liability at December 31, 1994 for Beal's accumulated vacation time?

a. $0

b. $500

c. $1,000

d. $2,000

M11-5   Bronson Apparel, Inc., operates a retail store and must determine the proper December 31, 1995 year-end accrual for the following expenses:

The store lease calls for fixed rent of $1,000 per month, payable at the beginning of the month, and additional rent equal to 6% of net sales over $200,000 per calendar year, payable on January 31 of the following year. Net sales for 1995 are $800,000.

Bronson has personal property subject to a city property tax. The city's fiscal year runs from July 1 to June 30 and the tax, assessed at 3% of personal property on hand at April 30, is payable on June 30. Bronson estimates that its personal property tax will amount to $6,000 for the city's fiscal year ending June 30, 1996.

In its December 31, 1995 balance sheet, Bronson should report accrued expenses of

a. $39,000

b. $39,600

c. $51,000

d. $51,600

M11-6   When a company receives a deposit from a customer to protect itself against nonpayment for future services, the deposit should be classified by the company as

a. Revenue

b. A liability

c. Part of the allowance for doubtful accounts

d. A deferred credit deducted from accounts receivable

M11-7   The balance in Ashwood Company's accounts payable account at December 31, 1995 was $900,000 before any necessary year-end adjustment relating to the following:

Goods were in transit from a vendor to Ashwood on December 31, 1995. The invoice cost was $50,000, and the goods were shipped F.O.B. shipping point on December 29, 1995. The goods were received on January 4, 1996.

Goods shipped F.O.B. shipping point on December 20, 1995 from a vendor to Ashwood were lost in transit. The invoice cost was $25,000. On January 5, 1996 Ashwood filed a $25,000 claim against the common carrier.

Goods shipped F.O.B. destination on December 21, 1995 from a vendor to Ashwood were received on January 6, 1996. The invoice cost was $15,000.

What amount should Ashwood report as accounts payable on its December 31, 1995 balance sheet?

a. $925,000          c. $950,000
b. $940,000          d. $975,000

M11-8  On September 1, 1995 a company borrowed cash and signed a 1-year, interest-bearing note on which both the principal and interest are payable on September 1, 1996. How will the note payable and the related interest be classified in the December 31, 1995 balance sheet?

|   | Note payable | Accrued interest |
|---|---|---|
| a. | Current liability | Noncurrent liability |
| b. | Noncurrent liability | Current liability |
| c. | Current liability | Current liability |
| d. | Noncurrent liability | No entry |

M11-9  Morgan Company determined that: (1) it has a material obligation relating to employees' rights to receive compensation for future absences attributable to employees' services already rendered, (2) the obligation relates to rights that vest, and (3) payment of the compensation is probable. The amount of Morgan's obligation as of December 31, 1995 is reasonably estimated for the following employee benefits:

Vacation pay     $100,000
Holiday pay        25,000

What total amount should Morgan report as its liability for compensated absences in its December 31, 1995 balance sheet?

a. $0                c. $100,000
b. $25,000           d. $125,000

M11-10  Gain contingencies are usually recognized in the income statement when

a. Realized
b. Occurrence is reasonably possible and the amount can be reasonably estimated
c. Occurrence is probable and the amount can be reasonably estimated
d. The amount can be reasonably estimated

*(AICPA adapted)*

## EXERCISES

E11-1  *Accounts Payable and Cash Discounts*  On January 2, 1995 Dunbar Company purchased, on account, 2,000 television sets at $500 each. Terms of the purchase were 2/10, n/30. Dunbar paid for one-fifth of these sets within 10 days and the remaining four-fifths by January 31.

**Required**
Prepare the journal entries on Dunbar Company's books, assuming that it uses the net price method to record its merchandise. (Dunbar uses a perpetual inventory system.)

E11-2  *Notes Payable*  On November 1, 1995 Insto Photo Company purchased merchandise, invoice price $30,000, and issued a 12%, 120-day note to Ringo Chemicals Company. Insto uses the calendar year as its fiscal year and uses the periodic inventory system.

**Required**
Prepare journal entries on Insto Photo's books to record the preceding information, including the adjusting entry at the end of the year and payment of the note at maturity.

*E11-3*    *Non-interest-Bearing Notes Payable*   On November 16, 1995 the Rice Glass Company borrowed $26,000 from First American Bank by issuing a 90-day, non-interest-bearing note. The bank discounted this note at 14% and remitted to Rice Glass Company the difference.

**Required**

1. Prepare the journal entries of Rice Glass to record the preceding information, related calendar year-end adjusting entry, and payment of the note at maturity.
2. Show how the preceding items would be reported on the December 31, 1995 balance sheet.
3. What is Rice Glass Company's effective interest rate?

*E11-4*    *Discounting of Notes Payable*   On October 30, 1995 the Curtiss Wright Company acquired a piece of machinery and signed a 12-month note for $24,000. The face value of the note includes the price of the machinery and interest. The note is to be paid in four $6,000 quarterly installments. The value of the machinery is the present value of the four quarterly payments discounted at an annual interest rate of 16%.

**Required**

1. Prepare all the journal entries required to record the preceding information including the year-end adjusting entry and the installment payments. Present value techniques should be used.
2. Show how the preceding items would be reported on the December 31, 1995 balance sheet.

*E11-5*    *Compensated Absences*   The Champion Corporation began business on January 2, 1995 with 5 employees. It created a sick leave and vacation policy stated as follows: Each employee is allowed 8 days of paid sick leave each year and 1 day of paid vacation leave for each month worked. The accrued vacation leave cannot be taken until the employee has been with the company 1 year. The sick leave, if not used, accumulates to an 18-day maximum. The vacation leave accumulates for 5 years, but the employee may request at any time additional compensation in lieu of taking paid vacation leave. The company considers that the requirements of *FASB Statement No. 43* have been met and desires to record the liability for both compensated absences on a quarterly basis. The daily gross wages for each employee are $80.

**Required**

1. Prepare journal entries to record the liability for compensated absences for the first quarter of 1995. Assume no sick leave had been taken by the employees.
2. Prepare a partial interim balance sheet showing how the liability created in Requirement 1 would be disclosed on March 31, 1995.

*E11-6*    *Sales Taxes*   During August 1995 the Hill Sales Company had these summary transactions:

1. Cash sales of $210,000, excluding sales taxes of 6%
2. Sales on account of $260,000, excluding sales taxes of 6%
3. Paid the sales taxes to the state

**Required**

Prepare journal entries to record the preceding transactions.

*E11-7*    *Payroll and Payroll Taxes*   The payroll of the Rand Company on December 31, 1995 is as follows:

1. Total payroll, $500,000
2. Payroll in excess of $60,000 to each employee, $350,000
3. Payroll in excess of $7,000 to each employee, $400,000
4. Income taxes withheld, $85,000
5. Union dues withheld, $10,000
6. Tax rates: State unemployment tax, 5.4%; F.I.C.A. tax, 8% for both employees and employers; federal unemployment tax, 0.8%; 1% merit-rating reduction of state unemployment tax from normal rate of 5.4%

**Required**

Prepare the journal entries for Rand's payroll and payroll taxes.

*E11-8*    *Bonus Obligation*   Raymond Moss, vice-president of Moss Auto Parts, gets an annual bonus of 15% of net income after bonus and income taxes. Income before bonus and income taxes is $250,000. The effective income tax rate is 30%.

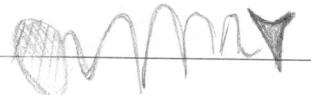

**Required**

1. Compute the amount of Raymond Moss's bonus.
2. Compute the income tax expense.

**E11-9** *Property Taxes* Family Practice Associates has an estimated property tax liability of $6,000 assessed as of January 1, 1995 for the year May 1, 1995 to April 30, 1996. The property tax is paid on September 1, 1995. The property tax becomes a lien against the property on May 1.

**Required**

Prepare the necessary monthly journal entries to record the preceding information for the period of May 1 to September 30, 1995 (assuming actual taxes are the same as estimated). What would be the amount of the liability on December 31, 1995?

**E11-10** *Property Taxes* The Ames Company is located in a city and county that issue property tax statements in May of each year. The fiscal year for the two local governmental units is May 1 to April 30. Property taxes of $48,000 are assessed against the Ames Company property held on January 1, 1995. The taxes become a lien against Ames Company property on May 1, 1995. The actual amount of the property taxes of $48,000 is determinable on May 1, 1995; therefore no estimate of taxes is required. The tax bills are payable in two equal installments on July 15 and September 15.

**Required**

Assuming that monthly accruals are recorded, prepare all property tax journal entries for the period May 1 to September 30, 1995.

**E11-11** *Expense Warranty Accrual Method* On September 1, 1995 Carolina Calculator Company has ready for sale 1,000 calculators. On October 2, 1995, 900 are sold at $40 each with a 1-year warranty. Carolina estimates that the warranty cost on each calculator sold will probably average $4 per unit. During the final three months of 1995, Carolina incurred warranty costs of $1,600, and in 1996 warranty costs were $2,000.

**Required**

1. Prepare the journal entries for the preceding transactions, using the expense warranty accrual method.
2. Show how the preceding items would be reported on the December 31, 1995 balance sheet.

**E11-12** *Sales Warranty Accrual Method* On August 1, 1995 Firstun Corporation has ready for sale 2,000 Wiglow instruments. During the next 5 months, 1,600 Wiglows are sold at $460 each with a 1-year warranty. Firstun estimates that the warranty cost on each Wiglow will probably average $10 per unit. In this period, Firstun incurred warranty costs of $9,200. Costs for 1996 were $7,000.

**Required**

1. Prepare the journal entries for the preceding transactions, using the sales warranty accrual method.
2. Show how the items would be reported on the December 31, 1995 balance sheet.

**E11-13** *Premium Obligation* The Sweet Dates Company offers to its customers a premium—a glass bowl (cost to Sweet Dates, $0.90) upon return of 50 coupons. Two coupons are placed in each box of dates sold. The company estimates, on the basis of past experience, that only 60% of the coupons will ever be redeemed. During 1995, 10 million boxes of dates are sold at $0.30 each. Eight million coupons are redeemed during 1995. Sweet Dates purchased 250,000 glass bowls for the plan in 1995.

**Required**

1. Prepare the journal entries related to the sales of dates and the premium plan in 1995.
2. Show how the preceding items would be disclosed on the December 31, 1995 balance sheet.

**E11-14** *Premium Obligation* On the back of its cereal boxes, the Tiger Cereal Company offers a premium to its customers. The premium, a toy truck, may be claimed by sending in $1 plus 10 coupons; one coupon is included in each box of cereal sold. The company estimates, based on past experience, that 60% of the coupons will be redeemed. During 1995, the company purchased 310,000 toy trucks at $1.25 each for the premium promotion and sold 5,000,000 boxes of cereal at $1.50 per box. In 1995, 2,200,000 coupons were redeemed.

**Required**
1. Prepare the journal entries related to the previous promotion (including sales) for 1995.
2. Show how the items related to the premium plan would be disclosed on the December 31, 1995 balance sheet.

**E11-15    *Gift Certificates***    On December 5, 1995 Super Circuit Store sold gift certificates totaling $3,000. By December 31, 1995 all but $700 worth of these certificates had been redeemed for merchandise. Outstanding certificates were then redeemed by January 15, 1996.

**Required**
1. Prepare journal entries on Super Circuit Store's books to reflect the preceding transactions.
2. How would the gift certificates be shown on Super Circuit's balance sheet on December 31, 1995?

**E11-16    *Loss Contingency***    On December 4, 1995 Dan Johnson, delivery truck driver for Farmers Products, Inc., ran a stop sign and collided with another vehicle. On January 8, 1996 the driver of the other vehicle filed suit against Farmers Products for damages to the vehicle. Estimated damages to this vehicle were $4,500. The dairy issued its 1995 financial statements on March 1, 1996.

**Required**
Prepare the disclosures and/or journal entries Farmers Products should make in preparation of its December 31, 1995 financial statements.

**E11-17    *Gain Contingency***    On December 31, 1995 Braino Tech., Inc. learned that its competitor had introduced a product making use of an accessory over which Braino Tech. has exclusive patent rights. Braino Tech. planned to file suit and in all likelihood, its attorneys felt, Braino should recover at least $100,000. Braino Tech.'s December 31, 1995 year-end financial statements were issued March 1, 1996 and Braino Tech. still planned to file suit, even though it had not yet done so.

**Required**
Discuss the accounting treatment in regard to the 1995 financial statements of Braino Tech. called for by *FASB Statement No. 5* concerning the circumstances described previously.

**E11-18    *Disclosure of Serial Bonds Payable***    On April 1, 1995 the Ramden Company issues 13% serial bonds with a face value of $2 million. The bond contract calls for retirement of the bonds in periodic installments of $200,000 starting on April 1, 1996 and continuing on each April 1 thereafter until all bonds are retired.

**Required**
How would the preceding information appear in the Ramden Company's balance sheets on December 31, 1995 and 1996?

**E11-19    *Short-Term Debt Expected to Be Refinanced***    On December 31, 1995 Excello Electric Company had $1 million of short-term notes payable due February 8, 1996. On January 15, 1996 the company issued bonds with a face value of $900,000 at 96; brokerage fees and other costs of issuance were $3,450. On January 22, 1996 the proceeds from the bond issue plus additional cash held by the company on December 31, 1995 were used to liquidate the $1 million of short-term notes. The December 31, 1995 balance sheet is issued on February 12, 1996.

**Required**
Prepare a partial balance sheet as of December 31, 1995, showing how the $1 million of short-term notes payable should be disclosed. Include an appropriate footnote for proper disclosure.

**E11-20    *Short-Term Debt Expected to Be Refinanced***    On December 31, 1995 Carrboro Textile Company had short-term debt in the form of notes payable totaling $500,000. These notes were due on June 1, 1996. On February 2, 1996 Carrboro entered into an agreement with Worldwide Life Insurance Company whereby Worldwide will lend Carrboro $400,000, payable in 5 years at 14%. The money will be available to Carrboro on May 20, 1996. Carrboro issues its December 31, 1995 year-end financial statements on March 1, 1996.

**Required**
Show how the $600,000 notes payable will be classified on Carrboro Textile Company's balance sheet on December 31, 1995.

## PROBLEMS

**P11-1**   *Accounts Payable and Cash Discounts*   The Byrd Company had the following transactions during 1995 and 1996:

1. On December 23, 1995 a small minicomputer was purchased from Minicomputers International, on account, for $60,000. Terms of the sale were 2/10, n/30.
2. Byrd calculated that to forgo the discount for the minicomputer would be the equivalent of paying 36% interest annually for the $58,800 left in the company for the extra 20 days. Therefore Byrd went to First Local Bank and signed a $60,000, 30-day note at 12% in order to take advantage of the discount terms. This transaction took place on December 29, 1995. (The account payable was paid on January 2, 1996 and the note was paid at maturity.)
3. On December 30, 1995, Byrd declared a $2.00 cash dividend to the common stockholders. Ten thousand shares were outstanding on this date. The dividend is to be paid on January 5, 1996.

**Required**

1. Prepare the journal entries for the Byrd Company for both 1995 and 1996. Assume that the net price method is used to account for the credit terms.
2. Show how the preceding items would be disclosed in the current liabilities section of Byrd's December 31, 1995 balance sheet.

**P11-2**   *Notes Payable and Effective Interest*   On October 1, 1995 Edwin, Inc., borrowed cash and signed a $60,000, one-year note payable.

**Required**

1. Compute the following items assuming (i) an interest-bearing note at 12%, (ii) a non-interest-bearing note discounted at 12%:
   a. Cash received
   b. Effective interest rate
   c. Interest expense for 1995
2. Prepare the necessary journal entries under each case for 1995 and 1996.

**P11-3**   *Trade Note Transactions*   The Adjusto Corporation engaged in the following transactions during 1994 and 1995:

**1994**

| | |
|---|---|
| Oct. 1 | Issued a 120-day, 10% note, face value of $15,000, to Johnson Company to settle an open account of that amount. |
| Nov. 1 | Issued a 90-day, 10% note, face value of $27,000, to Winslow Corporation for the purchase of merchandise (the periodic inventory method is used). |
| Dec. 31 | Fiscal year ended and adjusting entries were recorded. |

**1995**

| | |
|---|---|
| Feb. 1 | Paid the principal and interest on both the Johnson and the Winslow notes. |

**Required**

Prepare journal entries to record the preceding transactions on Adjusto's books, including the adjusting entries at the end of 1994.

**P11-4**   *Compensated Absences*   The Rexallo Company begins business on January 2, 1995 with 18 employees. Its company policy is to permit each employee to take 6 days of paid sick leave each year and 1 1/2 days of paid vacation leave for each month worked. The accrued vacation leave cannot be taken until the employee has been with the company 9 months. The sick leave, if not used, accumulates to a 24-day maximum. The vacation leave accumulates for 2 years, but the employee may request at any time after a 1-year period additional compensation in lieu of taking paid vacation leave. The company desires to record the liability for compensated absences on a quarterly basis. Assume that the gross wages for each employee are $100 per day.

The following selected events take place during the first two quarters of 1995:
1. On March 31, 1995 the quarterly liability for compensated absences is to be recorded.
2. On April 30, 1995 the following $36,000 monthly payroll, including paid vacation and sick leave, is summarized from the records of Rexallo:

|  | Payroll for | | |
|---|---|---|---|
|  | Time Worked | Vacation Taken | Sick Leave Taken |
| Salaries | $33,000 | $1,800 | $1,200 |

3. On June 30, 1995 the quarterly liability for compensated absences is to be recorded.

**Required**
1. Prepare journal entries to record the preceding events, ignoring payroll taxes and assuming that both sick leave and vacation time meet the requirements of *FASB Statement No. 43* for accrual.
2. Prepare a partial interim balance sheet as of March 31, 1995 to disclose the liability created in Requirement 1.

P11-5   *Sales Taxes*   The Durham Tobacco Company makes sales on which a 5% sales tax is assessed. The following summary transactions were made during 1995:
1. Sales for cash of $1,665,400, excluding sales taxes
2. Sales on open charge account of $2,820,500, excluding sales taxes
3. Sales taxes of $168,220 were paid to the state government during 1995

**Required**
1. Prepare journal entries to record the preceding transactions.
2. Show how the unpaid sales taxes would be disclosed on the December 31, 1995 balance sheet.

P11-6   *Payroll and Payroll Taxes*   Bailey Dry Cleaners has six employees who were paid the following wages during 1995:

| Frank Johnson | $ 27,000 |
|---|---|
| Bill Long | 18,000 |
| Duff Morse | 65,000 |
| Laura Stewart | 28,000 |
| Cindy Sharpe | 16,000 |
| Melissa Ledbetter | 30,000 |
| Total | $184,000 |

The state allows the company a 1% unemployment compensation merit-rating reduction from the normal rate of 5.4%. The federal unemployment rate is 0.8%. The maximum unemployment wages per employee are $7,000 for both the state and the federal government. Income tax withholdings of 18% are applied to all employees. An 8% F.I.C.A. tax for both employees and employers is applied to the first $50,000 of each employee's wages.

**Required**
1. Calculate the amount of payroll taxes to be paid by Bailey.
2. Prepare the journal entries to record the payment of payroll and the payroll tax expense.

P11-7   *Bonus Obligation and Income Tax Expense*   James Kimberley, president of National Motors, receives a bonus of 10% of National's profits after his bonus and the corporation's income taxes are deducted. National's effective income tax rate is 30%. Profits before income taxes and his bonus are $4,500,000 for 1995.

**Required**
1. Compute the amount of Kimberley's bonus for 1995.
2. Compute National Motors' income tax expense for 1995.
3. Prepare journal entries at the end of 1995 to record the bonus and income taxes.
4. Show how the bonus and income taxes would be disclosed on the December 31, 1995 balance sheet.

P11-8   *Property Taxes*   The Orange Corporation was formed on December 12, 1994. It plans to close its books annually each December 31. The corporation is located in Lanmark City and Apple County. The fiscal period of these two governmental units runs from July 1 to June 30. The property tax that they assess on the property held on January 1 of each year becomes a lien against the property on July 1. The estimated property taxes for Orange Corporation for the period July 1, 1995 to June 30, 1996 are $15,300. The tax bill is mailed in October with a requirement that the tax be paid before December 31. The tax bill received on October 30, 1995 for the Orange Corporation revealed an actual tax of $15,680, and the corporation paid this amount on November 30, 1995. The corporation elects to record monthly property tax adjustments for interim statements required by management.

**Required**

1. Prepare all property-tax related entries for Orange for the period July 1, 1995 to June 30, 1996.
2. Show how the preceding information would be disclosed on the December 31, 1995 balance sheet of Orange Corporation.

P11-9   *Expense Warranty Accrual Method*   Clean-All, Inc., sells washing machines with a 3-year warranty. In the past Clean-All has found that in the year after sale, warranty costs have been 3% of sales; in the second year after sale, 5% of sales; and in the third year after sale, 7% of sales. The following data are also available:

| Year | Sales | Warranty Expenditures |
|------|-------|-----------------------|
| 1995 | $550,000 | $63,000 |
| 1996 | 680,000 | 72,000 |
| 1997 | 700,000 | 85,000 |

**Required**

1. Prepare the journal entries for the preceding transactions for 1995–1997, using the expense warranty accrual method. Closing entries are not required.
2. What amount would Clean-All report as a liability on its December 31, 1997 balance sheet, assuming the liability had a balance of $88,200 on December 31, 1994?

P11-10   *Sales Warranty Accrual Method*   Wright Machinery Corporation manufactures automobile engines for major automobile producers. These engines have a warranty against any defects for a period of 5 years. Even though Wright Machinery does not have a separate warranty contract, it assumes that the $853 selling price of each engine includes an implied service contract of $33 per engine. During 1995 Wright Machinery sold 6,000 engines to National Motors. During 1995 Wright Machinery repaired defective motors at a cost of $34,400.

**Required**

Prepare the journal entries for the preceding transactions, assuming that Wright Machinery uses the sales warranty accrual method to account for warranties.

P11-11   *Premium Obligation*   Goodwin Cereal Company is offering one toy shovel set for 15 box tops of its cereal. Year-to-date sales have been off, and it is hoped that this offer will stimulate demand. Each shovel set costs the company $3. The following data are available for the last three months of 1995:

| Month | Boxes of Cereal Sold | Shovel Sets Purchased by the Company | Box Tops Redeemed by Customers |
|-------|----------------------|--------------------------------------|--------------------------------|
| October | 21,000 | 880 | 12,000 |
| November | 24,000 | 1,083 | 16,005 |
| December | 33,000 | 1,697 | 20,745 |

It is estimated that only 70% of the box tops will be redeemed. The cereal sells for $1 per box.

**Required**

1. Prepare journal entries for each month to record sales, shovel set purchases, redemptions, and closing entries, assuming that the books are closed at the end of each month.
2. Assuming Goodwin prepares monthly financial statements, indicate how the premiums and the estimated liability would be disclosed on Goodwin's ending balance sheets for October, November, and December.

**P11-12** *Contingencies*  Fallon Company, a toy manufacturer that also operates several retail outlets, is preparing its December 31, 1995 financial statements. It has identified the following legal situations that may qualify as contingencies:

1. A customer is suing the company for $800,000 in damages because her child was injured in November, 1995 while riding an escalator that suddenly stopped in one of its stores. The child was hurt when he tripped and fell while walking "down" an escalator that was going "up." Legal counsel feels that the child is partially at fault, but that it is probable that the lawsuit will be settled for between $50,000 and $100,000, with $75,000 being the most likely amount.

2. The company has discovered that a skateboard it began manufacturing and selling in 1995 has defective bearings, sometimes causing a wheel to fall off. The company has issued a "recall" notice in newspapers and magazines in which it offers to replace the bearings. It estimates a cost of $200,000 for these repairs. No lawsuits have been filed for injury claims, although the company feels that there is a reasonable possibility that claims may total as high as $2 million.

3. The company has an incinerator behind one of its retail outlets which is used to burn cardboard boxes received in shipments of inventory from suppliers. The state environmental protection agency filed suit against the company in August 1995 for air pollution. The company expects to stop using the incinerator and begin recycling. However, its lawyers believe that it is probable that a fine of between $40,000 and $60,000 will be levied against the company, although they cannot predict the exact amount.

4. In early 1995, the company signed a contract with a computer vendor to install "state of the art" cash registers in all of its retail outlets. Due to the vendor's inability to acquire sufficient cash registers, the vendor canceled the contract. The company has filed a breach of contract suit against the vendor, claiming $300,000 in damages. The company's lawyers expect that it will settle the suit "out-of-court" for $150,000.

**Required**

For each situation, prepare the journal entry (if any) on December 31, 1995 to record the information for Fallon Company, and explain your reasoning. If no journal entry is recorded, explain how the information would be reported in Fallon Company's 1995 annual report.

**P11-13** *Contingencies*  Greenlaw, Inc., a publishing company, is preparing its December 31, 1995 financial statements and must determine the proper accounting treatment for each of the following situations:

1. Greenlaw sells subscriptions to several magazines for a one-year, two-year, or three-year period. Cash receipts from subscribers are credited to magazine subscriptions collected in advance, and this account had a balance of $2,500,000 at December 31, 1995. Outstanding subscriptions at December 31, 1995 expire as follows:

   During 1996 — $600,000
   During 1997 —  900,000
   During 1998 —  400,000

2. On January 2, 1995 Greenlaw discontinued collision, fire, and theft coverage on its delivery vehicles and became self-insured for these risks. Actual losses of $45,000 during 1995 were charged to delivery expense. The 1994 premium for the discontinued coverage amounted to $100,000, and the controller wants to set up a reserve for self-insurance by a debit to delivery expense of $55,000 and a credit to the reserve for self-insurance of $55,000.

3. A suit for breach of contract seeking damages of $1,000,000 was filed by an author against Greenlaw on July 3, 1995. The company's legal counsel believes that an unfavorable outcome is probable. A reasonable estimate of the court's award to the plaintiff is in the range between $100,000 and $500,000. No amount within this range is a better estimate of potential damages than any other amount.

4. During December 1995 a competitor company filed suit against Greenlaw for industrial espionage claiming $2,000,000 in damages. In the opinion of management and company counsel, it is reasonably possible that damages will be awarded to the plaintiff. However, the amount of potential damages awarded to the plaintiff cannot be reasonably estimated.

**Required**

For each of the preceding situations, prepare the journal entry that should be recorded as of December 31, 1995, or explain why an entry should not be recorded. Show supporting computations in good form. *(AICPA adapted)*

*P11-14*   *Short-Term Debt Expected to Be Refinanced*   Several times during 1995, Palmer Company issued short-term commercial paper totaling $7 million. On December 31, 1995, the company's year-end, Palmer intends to refinance the commercial paper by issuing long-term debt. However, because of the temporary existence of excess cash, $3 million of the liability is liquidated in February 1996, as the commercial paper matures. On March 1, 1996 Palmer issues $9 million of long-term bonds, with $3 million of the proceeds going to replenish the working capital used to liquidate the $3 million of commercial paper, $4 million to pay the remaining balance of the commercial paper due after April, and the remaining $2 million to finance an equipment modernization program at Palmer's plant. Palmer's December 31, 1995 year-end financial statements are issued on March 15, 1996.

**Required**

1. How will the $3 million of commercial paper liquidated prior to the refinancing be classified on Palmer's December 31, 1995 balance sheet? Explain your reasoning.
2. How will the remaining $4 million of commercial paper be classified on Palmer's December 31, 1995 balance sheet? Explain your reasoning.

*P11-15*   *Short-Term Debt Expected to Be Refinanced*   On December 31, 1995 Atlantic Tobacco Company has $8 million in the form of short-term notes payable to City National Bank. On February 2, 1996 Atlantic negotiates a revolving credit agreement providing for unrestricted borrowings up to $5 million. Borrowings will bear interest at 1% over the prevailing prime rate, will have stated maturities of 120 days, and will be continuously renewable for 120-day periods for 4 years. Atlantic plans to refinance as much as possible of the notes outstanding with the proceeds available from this agreement. Assume that Atlantic's December 31, 1995 year-end financial statements are issued on March 30, 1996.

**Required**

Prepare a partial December 31, 1995 balance sheet showing how the $8 million short-term debt should be reported.

*P11-16*   *Non-interest-Bearing Note Payable: Present Value*   On January 1, 1995 Northern Manufacturing Company bought a piece of equipment by signing a non-interest-bearing $80,000, one-year note. The face value of the note includes the price of the equipment and the interest. The effective interest rate is an annual rate of 16%, and the note is to be paid in four $20,000 quarterly installments. The price of the equipment is the present value of the four payments discounted at the effective interest rate.

**Required**

1. Prepare all journal entries to record the preceding information. Present value techniques should be used.
2. If financial statements were issued on June 30, 1995, what amount would Northern report as notes payable?

*P11-17*   *Comprehensive*   Described as follows are selected transactions of the Lizard Lick Corporation during 1995:

| | | |
|---|---|---|
| Jan. | 6 | Purchased merchandise from Boston Company for $40,000; terms, 2/10, n/30. Purchases and accounts payable are recorded by Lizard Lick using the net price method. |
| Jan. | 26 | Paid the January 6 invoice. |
| Mar. | 31 | Purchased a van for $17,950 from the Hill Sales Company, paying $7,950 in cash and issuing a 12%, one-year note for the balance of the purchase price. |
| Apr. | 1 | Borrowed money from the Mebane National Bank by discounting its own 1-year, non-interest-bearing note made out for the maturity value of $50,000 at an interest rate of 13%. |
| Nov. | 2 | Received $500 from the Carr Mill Playhouse as a deposit to be refunded after certain rental furniture to be used in a play is returned on January 6, 1996. |
| Nov. | 3 | Made sales on account to Jones Company for $15,000. Sales taxes of 5 1/2% were added to the $15,000 price. |
| Nov. | 6 | Purchased another van at a cost of $17,000 from a company located in a state that does not levy a sales tax. The entire purchase price was paid in cash. Lizard Lick is located in a state that assesses a use tax of 5 1/2% on nonsalable equipment bought outside its sales tax authority. The van and the liability for the use tax are to be recorded. |
| Dec. | 1 | Estimated property taxes for the year December 1, 1995 to November 30, 1996, are $36,000 (ignore previous property taxes). The corporation follows the practice of recording its property tax by a monthly accrual starting 1 month following the lien date. The tax becomes a lien on December 1 and is payable in two installments on May 1 and October 1. |
| Dec. | 31 | Estimated quarterly income taxes for the last quarter of the year are $120,000. |

**Required**
Prepare journal entries to record the preceding transactions for 1995. Include year-end interest accruals. Assume the use of the periodic inventory system.

P11-18     *Comprehensive*     Described as follows are selected transactions of the Shadrach Corporation during November and December of 1995:

Nov.  1     Borrowed money from the bank by issuing a non-interest-bearing, $40,000, 90-day note. The note is discounted on a 12% basis.

        10     Sold 100 computers with a 1-year warranty for $5,000 each. Past experience indicates that warranty costs average $125 per computer. The corporation uses the expense warranty accrual method for record keeping.

        16     Sold 100 software packages at $300 each. With each software package the corporation offered a premium in the form of a package of disks for the return of one proof of purchase. The offer expires June 30, 1996. The cost of each package of disks is $5, and the company estimates that 80% of the premiums will be redeemed so that 80 packages of disks were purchased.

        20     Paid $2,900 in fulfillment of the warranty agreement on several of the computers sold on November 10.

        30     Accrued monthly vacation pay. Shadrach Corporation has 90 employees, who are each paid an average of $80 per day. The corporation has a policy of allowing each employee 12 days' paid vacation per year; the related liability is recorded on a monthly basis. Employees are paid monthly; two-thirds of the employees work in the sales force and one-third work in the office.

        30     Paid monthly payroll. Gross salaries for the sales force were $96,000 and for the office staff were $48,000. No vacations were taken during November. Income tax withholdings of 15% are applicable to the salaries of all employees. An 8% F.I.C.A. tax for both employees and employers is also applicable. These rates apply to all salaries, because no employee's salary has exceeded the maximum wage limit. The state allows the corporation a 1% unemployment compensation merit-rating reduction from the normal rate of 5.4%. The federal unemployment rate is 0.8%. Prior to October, each individual employee had accumulated a gross salary in excess of $7,000 for 1995.

Dec. 15     Twenty proofs of purchase were returned from the November 16 sale.

        29     An individual filed suit against Shadrach Corporation for damages caused in a November 5 accident that resulted when a member of the sales force hit the individual's car while on personal business. The amount of the suit filed was $1,500. Because the employee was on personal business, the company's insurance company will not pay the claim. In the opinion of the company's attorney, the amount of the suit is reasonable; furthermore, the company believes it is likely to lose the suit.

        31     Accrued monthly vacation pay.

        31     Paid monthly payroll. Gross salaries for the sales force were $97,200 and for the office staff were $48,600. The salaries included $3,400 of vacation pay in the sales force and $1,600 of vacation pay in the office staff. The F.I.C.A. tax rate still applies to all wages, because no employee's salary exceeded the maximum wage limit.

        31     Recorded president's bonus. The president receives a 10% bonus computed on income after deducting income taxes but before deducting the bonus. The corporation's effective income tax rate is 30%, and income before income taxes and bonus for 1995 was $560,000. The bonus will be paid in January 1996.

**Required**
Prepare journal entries to record the preceding transactions of the Shadrach Corporation for 1995. Include year-end accruals. Round all calculations to the nearest dollar.

# LONG-TERM LIABILITIES AND RECEIVABLES

An item is classified as a long-term liability if it is not expected to be repaid within one year or the current operating cycle, whichever is longer. The most common examples of long-term liabilities are bonds payable, long-term notes payable, lease obligations, pension obligations, deferred income taxes and other long-term deferrals, and, occasionally, contingent liabilities. In this chapter, we examine the recording and reporting requirements for bonds payable and long-term notes payable. The other items of long-term liabilities listed are covered elsewhere in this book. Long-term notes receivable are also discussed in this chapter, including accounting for an impairment in such notes.

## REASONS FOR ISSUANCE OF LONG-TERM LIABILITIES

Long-term liabilities are one of the choices available to corporations to obtain financial resources. There are four basic reasons that a company might issue such debt rather than other types of securities.

1. *Debt may be the only available source of funds.* Many small- and medium-sized companies may appear too risky to attract equity (i.e., capital stock) investments. Debt issued by a company may be a less risky investment because interest is required by law to be paid on each interest payment date, and also some types of debt are secured by a lien against specific company assets.

2. *Debt financing may have a lower cost.* Historically, since debt has a lower investment risk than stock, it usually has offered a relatively lower rate of return. In general, investors in equity securities have earned a higher return. However, in recent years market conditions have changed, and the cost of debt financing has varied, so that this advantage is not always as distinct as it once was.

3. *Debt financing offers an income tax advantage.* Interest payments to debt holders are deductible as interest expense for income tax purposes, whereas dividend payments on equity securities are not.

4. *The voting privilege is not shared.* Corporate stockholders may not wish to share ownership. Thus, by issuing debt which does not provide voting rights, ownership interests are not diluted.

The term **leverage** (or **trading on the equity**) refers to a company's use of borrowed funds. By investing these funds, the company expects to **earn a return greater than the interest to be paid for their use** and thereby to benefit the stockholders. Earnings in excess of interest charges (net of the applicable income tax reduction) increase earnings per share, but if the return falls below the effective interest rate, earnings per share will decline. Expectations of current and future earnings, inflation, and the debt/equity relationship influence the rate of interest needed to issue debt.

## BONDS PAYABLE

One common method of creating long-term liabilities is by issuing bonds. **A bond is a type of note in which a company agrees to pay the holder the face value at the maturity date and usually to pay interest periodically at a specified rate on the face value.** Thus the company that issues the bonds (the *issuer*) is borrowing money from the holder of the bonds (the *lender*). **The face (or par) value is the amount of money that the issuer agrees to pay at maturity.** It is the same concept as the principal of a note. **The maturity date is the date on which the issuer of the bond agrees to pay the face value to the holder.** The issuer also agrees to pay interest each period. **The contract rate is the rate at which the issuer of the bond agrees to pay interest each period until maturity.** The contract rate is also called the *stated, face,* or *nominal* rate. This information is printed on a bond certificate, which is the document that indicates ownership of the bond. **A bond certificate is a serially numbered legal document that specifies the face value, the annual interest rate, the maturity date, and other characteristics of the bond issue.** Each bond usually has a bond indenture. **A bond indenture is a document (contract) that defines the rights of the bondholders.** Since bonds usually are issued as a means of borrowing large amounts of money, corporations (and government entities) are the most common issuers of bonds. Corporate bonds nearly always are issued so that each bond has a face value of $1,000. The entire bond issue may be sold to one purchaser or to numerous individual purchasers. Thus a $1 million bond issue includes 1,000 bonds, each with a $1,000 face value. In addition, interest usually is paid twice each year (semiannually) on dates stated on the bond certificate. Therefore the stated annual interest rate must be halved to obtain the interest rate per semiannual period. For example, a 10%, $1,000 bond will pay the annual interest of $100 (10% × $1,000) in two semiannual installments of $50 (10% × 1/2 × $1,000).

## Characteristics of Bonds

Companies issue bonds that may have different characteristics, as summarized in Exhibit 12-1. While some of these characteristics are mutually exclusive, several can be combined for a bond issue. The characteristics of a particular bond issue are listed on the bond certificates for that issue and spelled out in detail in the bond indenture. In addition to establishing these characteristics, to protect the bondholders and improve the marketability of a bond issue, a company may include in the bond indenture certain restrictions on its financial operations. These restrictions may include limitations on dividends, adherence to certain minimum working capital amounts, or the maintenance of a certain debt/equity relationship. In this chapter, we focus primarily on the accounting for debenture bonds. We also discuss the accounting principles that apply when a callable, convertible, or serial (Appendix 2) feature is included in the bond issue.

---

### EXHIBIT 12-1

### CHARACTERISTICS OF BONDS

1. *Debenture bonds.* Debenture bonds are bonds that are not secured by specific property. Their marketability is based on the general credit rating of the company. Generally, a company must have a long period of earnings and continued favorable predictions of future earnings and liquidity to sell debenture bonds. Debenture bondholders are considered as general creditors with the same rights as other creditors if the issuer fails to pay the interest or principal and declares bankruptcy.

2. *Mortgage bonds.* Mortgage bonds are bonds that are secured by a lien against specific property of the company. If the company becomes bankrupt and is liquidated, the holders of these bonds have first claim against the proceeds of the sale of the assets that secured their debt. If the proceeds from the sale of pledged assets are not sufficient to repay the debt, mortgage bondholders become general creditors for the balance of the unpaid debt.

3. *Registered bonds.* Registered bonds are bonds whose ownership is registered with the company. That is, the company maintains a record of the holder of each bond. Therefore, on each interest payment date, interest is paid to the individuals listed on the corporate records as owners of the bonds. When an owner sells registered bonds, the issuer or transfer agent must be notified so that interest will be paid to the proper person.

4. *Coupon bonds.* Coupon bonds are unregistered bonds on which interest is claimed by the holder presenting a coupon to the company. These bonds can be transferred between individuals without the company or its agent being notified. Currently, coupon bonds are rarely issued because bonds issued after December 31, 1982 must be registered for the related interest expense to be deductible for income tax purposes.

5. *Zero-coupon bonds.* Zero-coupon bonds (also called *deep-discount* bonds) are bonds on which the interest is not paid until the maturity date. That is, the bonds are sold at a price considerably below their face value, interest accrues until maturity, and then the bondholders are paid the interest along with the principal at maturity.

6. *Callable bonds.* Callable bonds are bonds that are callable by the company at a predetermined price for a specified period. That is, the company has the right to require the bondholders to return the bonds before the maturity date, with the company paying the predetermined price and interest to date.

7. *Convertible bonds.* Convertible bonds are bonds that are convertible into a predetermined number of shares. That is, the owner of each bond has the right to exchange it for a predetermined number of shares of the company. Thus, upon conversion, the bondholder becomes a stockholder of the company.

8. *Serial bonds.* Serial bonds are bonds issued at one time, but portions of the total face value mature in periodic installments at different future dates. For example, a serial bond issued in 1995 may have a face value of $50,000, and bonds with a face value of $10,000 mature each year for five years from 2001 through 2005.

## Bond Selling Prices

When a company issues bonds, it may offer them to the public or privately to an institution, such as an insurance company or a pension fund. When the bonds are offered to the public, the company usually deals with a stockbrokerage firm (or an investment banker). The stockbroker, or a group of brokers, agrees on a price for the bonds, pays the company for them and then sells the bonds to its clients. Because the issuing company avoids having to find the purchasers and being involved in cash transactions with each purchaser, it pays the brokers a fee for this service.

There are certain steps a company must follow when it issues bonds. The company must (1) receive approval from the regulatory authorities such as the Securities and Exchange Commission, (2) set the terms of the bond issue such as the contract rate and the maturity date, and (3) make a public announcement of its intent to sell the bonds on a particular date and print the bond certificates. At the time of the sale, the stockbroker negotiates with the company to determine an appropriate selling price. The selling price is based on the terms of the bond issue and such factors as the general bond market conditions, the relative risk of the bonds, and the expected state of the economy. The stockbroker determines the rate (yield) that it believes best reflects the current market conditions for the particular bond issue. The yield (effective rate) is the market rate at which the bonds are issued.[1] The yield on the bonds may be different from the contract (stated) rate set by the company and printed on the bond certificates. Such a difference may result from a difference of opinion between the stockbroker and the company about the correct yield, or a change of economic conditions between the date the company announced the bond issue, set the contract rate and had the rate printed on the bond certificates, and the date it was issued.

Once the terms of the bond issue have been set and the yield determined, the selling price of the bonds is determined. The calculation is illustrated later in the chapter. Three alternatives are possible.

1. If the yield is *equal* to the contract rate, the purchasers of the bonds pay the face value of the bonds—the bonds are sold at *par*.

2. If the yield is *more* than the contract rate, the purchasers of the bonds pay *less* than the face value of the bonds—the bonds are sold at a *discount*.

3. If the yield is *less* than the contract rate, the purchasers of the bonds pay *more* than the face value of the bonds—the bonds are sold at a *premium*.

The issuance price of bonds sold at a premium or discount is often quoted as a percentage of the face value. For example, bonds with a face value of $100,000 that are quoted at 103 (meaning 103% of the face value) are sold for $103,000—that is, at a premium of $3,000. Alternatively, bonds with a $200,000 face value quoted at 98 are sold for $196,000 (i.e., $200,000 × 0.98), a $4,000 discount.

It is important to understand why bonds sell at a price different from the face value when the yield is different from the contract rate. The difference between the price paid and the face value enables the purchaser to earn a return on the bonds equal to the yield at the time the bonds are purchased. For instance, bonds are sold at a discount because the yield is higher than the contract rate. The "savings" (i.e., the discount) between the lower selling price that the purchaser pays at acquisition and

---

1. After bonds have been issued, their yield will fluctuate in the bond market as changes occur in the risk premium and expected inflation rate. It is the yield at the time of *issuance*, however, that is relevant to a company in accounting for the bonds.

the face value that the purchaser collects at maturity, coupled with the contract interest received by the purchaser each interest period, results in a return equal to the higher yield. Alternatively, bonds are sold at a premium because the yield is lower than the contract rate. The "excess" (i.e., the premium) between the higher selling price and the face value, coupled with the contract interest received by the purchaser each interest period, results in a return equal to the lower yield. These relationships may be summarized as follows:

| Bonds Sold at | Yield Compared to Contract Rate | Interest Over the Life of the Bonds |
|---|---|---|
| Premium | Yield < Contract Rate | Interest Expense < Interest Paid |
| ↑ Par | Yield = Contract Rate | Interest Expense = Interest Paid |
| ↓ Discount | Yield > Contract Rate | Interest Expense > Interest Paid |

When the bonds are yielding a rate either lower (for bonds sold at a premium) or higher (for bonds sold at a discount) than the contract rate, the interest *expense* recorded by the issuing company each period is different from the interest *paid*. When bonds are sold at a *premium,* the interest expense is *less* than the interest paid. When bonds are sold at a *discount,* the interest expense is *more* than the interest paid. The difference between the interest expense and the interest payment is the amount of the premium or discount amortized in the period (discussed later).

## RECORDING THE BOND ISSUANCE

At the time of sale, the face value of bonds is recorded in a Bonds Payable account, and any premium or discount is recorded in a separate account entitled Premium on Bonds Payable or Discount on Bonds Payable. For example, assume bonds with a face value of $400,000 are sold on the authorization date at 102. The following journal entry is made to record the sale:

| | | |
|---|---|---|
| Cash ($400,000 × 1.02) | 408,000 | |
|     Bonds Payable | | 400,000 |
|     Premium on Bonds Payable | | 8,000 |

A Premium account is an *adjunct* account and is shown as an addition to the Bonds Payable account in the long-term liability section of the balance sheet. A Discount account is a *contra* account and is shown as a deduction from the Bonds Payable account. **The book value (carrying value) of the bond issue at any time is the face value plus any unamortized premium or minus any unamortized discount.** In the preceding example, the book value on the issuance date is $408,000.

### Bonds Issued Between Interest Payment Dates

Recall that the interest on bonds usually is paid semiannually on the dates indicated on the bond certificates. Bonds often are sold after their authorization date and between interest payment dates. In such cases, the issuer is obligated to pay interest only for the period of time the bonds are outstanding—that is, from the sale date to the next interest payment date. When the sale of bonds occurs between interest dates, to reduce the record keeping for the first interest payment, the company issuing the bonds normally will collect from the investors, in addition to the selling price, the interest accrued on the bonds from the interest payment date prior to the date of sale. This interest amount collected typically is *credited* to Interest Expense and is computed by multiplying the face value by the stated interest rate for the fraction of the year from the interest payment date prior to the sale date. On the next interest payment date, each bondholder is paid 6 months of interest and Interest Expense is recorded as usual.

To illustrate, assume that on March 1, 1995, Grimes Corporation issues $800,000 of 10-year bonds dated January 1, 1995 at par. The bonds have a contract (stated) interest rate of 12% and pay interest semiannually on January 1 and July 1. On March 1, because two months have elapsed since the interest payment date prior to the sale, the company collects $16,000 ($800,000 × 0.12 × 2/12) accrued interest in addition to the face value. The journal entry on March 1, 1995 to record the issue of the bonds is as follows:

| Cash | 816,000 | |
| Interest Expense | | 16,000 |
| Bonds Payable | | 800,000 |

On July 1, 1995, the following journal entry is made to record the semiannual interest payment:

| Interest Expense ($800,000 × 0.12 × 6/12) | 48,000 | |
| Cash | | 48,000 |

As a result of the preceding journal entries, the Interest Expense account on July 1, 1995 has a debit balance of $32,000 ($48,000 − $16,000) representing the interest cost ($800,000 × 0.12 × 4/12) since the bonds were issued.

Alternatively, it is possible to record the previous transaction by using a liability account that reflects the fact that part of the proceeds (i.e., the accrued interest) will be repaid in the future. Using this approach, the original transaction would be recorded as follows:

| Cash | 816,000 | |
| Interest Payable | | 16,000 |
| Bonds Payable | | 800,000 |

On July 1, 1995, the date of the first interest payment, the journal entry would be recorded as follows:

| Interest Expense ($800,000 × 0.12 × 4/12) | 32,000 | |
| Interest Payable | 16,000 | |
| Cash | | 48,000 |

Most companies use the first method because it has less potential for errors in subsequent transactions. Also, this method enables companies to develop a single routine in their computerized accounting systems for recording and distributing all interest payments.

## AMORTIZING DISCOUNTS AND PREMIUMS

Recall that when a company sells bonds at a discount, or premium, it is incurring an effective interest (yield) rate that is more, or less, than the stated rate of interest. When a company pays the interest on the bonds, this *payment* reflects an amount based upon the *stated* rate. However, in order to properly disclose the interest cost on the bonds, the Interest *Expense* on the income statement must reflect an amount based on the *effective* interest rate. This amount is computed by multiplying the effective interest rate (yield) times the book value of the bonds. Consequently, a portion of the bond discount or premium is amortized, and this amortization is determined by finding the difference between the amount of interest expense and the actual cash payment. This process is known as the effective interest method (sometimes called the *interest method*) of amortization. Another approach is the **straight-line method** of amortization. APB Opinion No. 21 requires the use of the effective interest method unless the results produced by the straight-line method are *not materially different* from those obtained by using the effective interest method.[2] However, we discuss the straight-line method first because it is simple and thus easier to understand and use.

### Straight-Line Method

When using the straight-line method, the premium or discount is amortized to interest expense in *equal amounts* each period during the life of the bonds. Therefore, the straight-line method amortizes bond premium or discount so that the interest expense is an average cost for the period. For instance, assume that the Jet Company sells bonds for $92,976.39 on January 1, 1995. The bonds have a face value of $100,000 and a 12% stated annual interest rate. Interest is paid semiannually on June 30 and December 31, and the bonds mature on December 31, 1999. Thus, the bonds have a 5-year life, with 10 semiannual interest periods. The journal entry on January 1, 1995 to record the sale is as follows:

| | | |
|---|---:|---:|
| Cash | 92,976.39 | |
| Discount on Bonds Payable | 7,023.61 | |
| Bonds Payable | | 100,000.00 |

On the first interest payment date, both the cash payment and discount amortization are recorded. The discount amortization per semiannual period of $702.36 is computed by dividing the total discount ($7,023.61) by the number of semiannual periods (10) *until maturity*[3] (monthly or yearly amortization periods may also be used, whichever is more convenient). The interest expense is the sum of the cash payment and the discount amortization. The journal entry to record the first interest payment on June 30, 1995 is as follows:

| | | |
|---|---:|---:|
| Interest Expense ($6,000 + $702.36) | 6,702.36 | |
| Discount on Bonds Payable ($7,023.61 ÷ 10) | | 702.36 |
| Cash ($100,000 × 0.12 × 1/2) | | 6,000.00 |

In this case, the interest expense is higher than the cash paid, indicating that the effective rate is higher than the stated rate. A similar journal entry to record the second interest payment is made by Jet on December 31, 1995 and every 6 months after that. After this second entry, the long-term liabilities section of Jet's December 31, 1995 balance sheet includes the following:

| | |
|---|---:|
| Bonds Payable | $100,000.00 |
| Less: Discount on Bonds Payable | (5,618.89) |
| | $ 94,381.11 |

---

2.  "Interest on Receivables and Payables," *APB Opinion No. 21* (New York: AICPA, 1971), par. 15.
3.  It is important to note that the maturity date of bonds is established on the date they are authorized. When bonds are issued subsequent to the authorization date, any discount or premium is amortized over the *remaining* life until the maturity date.

Note that the $5,618.89 ($7,023.61 − $702.36 − $702.36) unamortized discount is subtracted from the $100,000 face value of the bonds to determine the $94,381.11 book value.

The straight-line amortization of a bond premium follows the same principles. Suppose the Jet Company bonds were sold on January 1, 1995 for $107,721.71. In this case, the premium amortization per semiannual period is $772.17 ($7,721.71 ÷ 10) and the interest expense is the cash payment less the premium amortization. The journal entries to record the sale and first interest payment are as follows:

**January 1, 1995**

| | | |
|---|---|---|
| Cash | 107,721.71 | |
|   Bonds Payable | | 100,000.00 |
|   Premium on Bonds Payable | | 7,721.71 |

**June 30, 1995**

| | | |
|---|---|---|
| Interest Expense ($6,000 − $772.17) | 5,227.83 | |
| Premium on Bonds Payable ($7,721.71 ÷ 10) | 772.17 | |
|   Cash ($100,000 × 0.12 × 1/2) | | 6,000.00 |

Here the interest expense is lower than the cash paid, indicating an effective rate lower than the stated rate. After a similar journal entry to record the second interest payment, Jet's December 31, 1995 balance sheet includes the following:

| | |
|---|---|
| Bonds Payable | $100,000.00 |
| Add: Premium on Bonds Payable | 6,177.37 |
| | $106,177.37 |

Note that the $6,177.37 ($7,721.71 − $772.17 − $772.17) unamortized premium is added to the $100,000 face value of the bonds to determine the $106,177.37 book value. By the maturity date, the entire premium will have been amortized, so that the book value equals the maturity value. Thus, throughout the life of the bonds, the investor is repaid a portion of the initial investment in the form of higher interest payments.

In summary, for both premiums and discounts, **the straight-line method results in a constant amount of interest expense each semiannual period** even though the book value of the liability changes each period. A schedule may be developed that summarizes the interest expense, discount or premium amortization, and book value of the bonds each period. Exhibit 12-2 shows a partial schedule for the Jet Company bonds sold at a discount. Exhibit 12-3 presents a partial schedule for the same bonds sold at a premium. Again, the reader is reminded that the straight-line method is acceptable only when it results in amounts of interest expense and book value that are not materially different from that computed by using the effective interest method.

## Effective Interest Method

The assumption inherent in the use of the straight-line method of a stable interest *expense* per year is not realistic when a premium or discount is involved. Instead, the use of a stable interest *rate* per year (the *yield*) is appropriate. The yield is used in the calculation of the proceeds received when bonds are issued. The selling price of a bond issue is calculated by summing the present value of the principal and interest

## EXHIBIT 12-2

### JET COMPANY

Bond Interest Expense and *Discount* Amortization Schedule
*Straight-Line Method*

| Date | Cash Credit[a] | Unamortized Discount Credit[b] | Interest Expense Debit[c] | Book Value of Bonds[d] |
|---|---|---|---|---|
| 1/01/95 | | | | $ 92,976.39 |
| 6/30/95 | $6,000.00 | $702.36 | $6,702.36 | 93,678.75 |
| 12/31/95 | 6,000.00 | 702.36 | 6,702.36 | 94,381.11 |
| 6/30/96 | 6,000.00 | 702.36 | 6,702.36 | 95,083.47 |
| ⋮ | ⋮ | ⋮ | ⋮ | ⋮ |
| 12/31/98 | 6,000.00 | 702.36 | 6,702.36 | 98,595.27 |
| 6/30/99 | 6,000.00 | 702.36 | 6,702.36 | 99,297.63 |
| 12/31/99 | 6,000.00 | 702.37[e] | 6,702.37 | 100,000.00 |

a. $100,000 (face value) × 0.12 (stated annual interest rate) × 1/2 (year).
b. [$100,000 − $92,976.39 (issue price)] ÷ 10 (semiannual periods until maturity).
c. $6,000.00 + $702.36.
d. Previous book value + amount from footnote *b*.
e. Difference due to $0.01 rounding error.

## EXHIBIT 12-3

### JET COMPANY

Bond Interest Expense and *Premium* Amortization Schedule
*Straight-Line Method*

| Date | Cash Credit[a] | Unamortized Premium Debit[b] | Interest Expense Debit[c] | Book Value of Bonds[d] |
|---|---|---|---|---|
| 1/01/95 | | | | $107,721.71 |
| 6/30/95 | $6,000.00 | $772.17 | $5,227.83 | 106,949.54 |
| 12/31/95 | 6,000.00 | 772.17 | 5,227.83 | 106,177.37 |
| 6/30/96 | 6,000.00 | 772.17 | 5,227.83 | 105,405.20 |
| ⋮ | ⋮ | ⋮ | ⋮ | ⋮ |
| 12/31/98 | 6,000.00 | 772.17 | 5,227.83 | 101,544.35 |
| 6/30/99 | 6,000.00 | 772.17 | 5,227.83 | 100,772.18 |
| 12/31/99 | 6,000.00 | 772.18[e] | 5,227.82 | 100,000.00 |

a. $100,000 (face value) × 0.12 (stated annual interest rate) × 1/2 (year).
b. [$107,721.71 (issue price) − $100,000] ÷ 10 (semiannual periods until maturity).
c. $6,000.00 − $772.17.
d. Previous book value − amount from footnote *b*.
e. Difference due to $0.01 rounding error.

payments discounted at the effective interest (yield) rate. Recall the Jet Company discount example of $100,000 of 5-year bonds paying semiannual interest with a stated rate of 12%. These bonds sold for $92,976.39, a price that yields an effective interest rate of 14%. **To determine this selling price and the related discount, the effective rate is applied to both the future principal and periodic interest payments,** as shown in the computations that follow. As pointed out in Appendix D, in present value analyses when interest is paid semiannually, the effective rate (14%) is divided by the interest periods per year (two) to determine the effective rate (7%) per semiannual period. Similarly, the time to maturity is expressed in semiannual periods (10). The discount of $7,023.61 is computed[4] as follows:

| | |
|---|---:|
| Present value of principal: $100,000 × 0.508349[a] | $ 50,834.90 |
| Present value of interest: $6,000[b] × 7.023582[c] | 42,141.49 |
| Selling price | $ 92,976.39 |
| Face value | $100,000.00 |
| Selling price | (92,976.39) |
| Discount | $   7,023.61 |

a. From Present Value of 1 Table in Appendix D (*n* = 10; *i* = 0.07).
b. $100,000 × 0.12 × 1/2.
c. From Present Value of an Ordinary Annuity of 1 Table in Appendix D (*n* = 10; *i* = 0.07).

Similarly, in the second example, in which the Jet Company bonds were sold at a premium, they yielded 10%. The premium of $7,721.71 is computed as follows:

| | |
|---|---:|
| Present value of principal: $100,000 × 0.613913[a] | $ 61,391.30 |
| Present value of interest: $6,000 × 7.721735[b] | 46,330.41 |
| Selling price | $107,721.71 |
| Selling price | $107,721.71 |
| Face value | (100,000.00) |
| Premium | $   7,721.71 |

a. From Present Value of 1 Table in Appendix D (*n* = 10; *i* = 0.05).
b. From Present Value of an Ordinary Annuity of 1 Table in Appendix D (*n* = 10; *i* = 0.05).

Again, to compute the present value, the effective rate is expressed on a semiannual basis, and the time to maturity is expressed in semiannual periods.

---

4.  The discount (or premium) and the selling price to yield a given interest rate can also be calculated by a shortcut method. The amount of the discount is the present value of the *deficiency* produced by the difference between the yield rate multiplied by the face value of the bonds and the stated rate multiplied by the face value of the bonds, discounted at the yield rate. The shortcut calculations of the discount and selling price for the Jet Company bonds are shown below:

| | | |
|---|---:|---:|
| Face value | | $100,000.00 |
| Less: Discount on bonds payable | | |
| Yield amount: 7% × $100,000 | $7,000 | |
| Stated amount: 6% × $100,000 | (6,000) | |
| Deficiency | $1,000 | |
| Discount ($1,000 × 7.023582; Present Value | | |
| of an Ordinary Annuity Table in Appendix D) | | (7,023.58)* |
| Selling price | | $ 92,976.42 |

* The difference between the $7,023.61 calculated in the text and the $7,023.58 calculated by the shortcut method is due to a rounding error.

As noted earlier, the book (carrying) value of the bond issue at any time is its face value plus any unamortized premium or minus any unamortized discount. Thus, this book value will change with each successive premium or discount amortization and reflect **the present value of the remaining cash payments.** (Under the straight-line method, the book value is *not* equal to the present value of the remaining cash payments.) Since the bonds were issued to yield a particular interest rate and the issue price is computed by determining the discounted value of the future principal and interest payments, this interest rate should be reflected over the life of the bond issue. Also, as noted earlier, *APB Opinion No. 21* requires the use of the effective interest method for amortizing premiums or discounts, unless the use of another method produces results that are *not materially* different from those obtained by the effective interest method. The effective interest method applies the actual semiannual yield to the book value of the bonds in each successive semiannual period to determine the interest expense. In this procedure, the premium or discount amortization is computed by finding the difference between the actual cash payment and the interest expense under the effective interest method. This method is based on the compound interest techniques discussed in Appendix D.

To illustrate, for the Jet Company bonds sold for $92,976.39 (and yielding an effective annual interest rate of 14%), the first two interest payments under the effective interest method are recorded as follows:

**June 30, 1995**

| | | |
|---|---:|---:|
| Interest Expense ($92,976.39 × 0.14 × 1/2) | 6,508.35 | |
| Discount on Bonds Payable | | |
| ($6,508.35 − $6,000.00) | | 508.35 |
| Cash ($100,000 × 0.12 × 1/2) | | 6,000.00 |

**December 31, 1995**

| | | |
|---|---:|---:|
| Interest Expense | | |
| [($92,976.39 + $508.35) × 0.14 × 1/2] | 6,543.93 | |
| Discount on Bonds Payable | | |
| ($6,543.93 − $6,000.00) | | 543.93 |
| Cash | | 6,000.00 |

On the other hand, if the Jet Company bonds originally sold for $107,721.71 (equivalent to an annual yield rate of 10%), the first two interest payments would be recorded as follows, using the effective interest method:

**June 30, 1995**

| | | |
|---|---:|---:|
| Interest Expense ($107,721.71 × 0.10 × 1/2) | 5,386.09 | |
| Premium on Bonds Payable | | |
| ($6,000.00 − $5,386.09) | 613.91 | |
| Cash ($100,000 × 0.12 × 1/2) | | 6,000.00 |

**December 31, 1995**

| | | |
|---|---:|---:|
| Interest Expense | | |
| [($107,721.71 − $613.91) × 0.10 × 1/2] | 5,355.39 | |
| Premium on Bonds Payable | | |
| ($6,000.00 − $5,355.39) | 644.61 | |
| Cash | | 6,000.00 |

Schedules may also be developed that show the interest expense, amortization of discounts and premiums, and book values using the effective interest method. Exhibit 12-4 illustrates a schedule for the Jet Company bonds issued at a discount. Exhibit 12-5 illustrates a schedule for these bonds issued at a premium. Note that **the amount of interest expense using the effective interest method reflects a constant** *rate* **based upon the remaining book value of the bonds.** (In contrast, in Exhibits 12-2 and 12-3 for the straight-line method, the *amount* of interest expense was constant.)

---

### EXHIBIT 12-4

#### JET COMPANY

Bond Interest Expense and *Discount* Amortization Schedule
*Effective Interest Method: 12% Bonds Sold to Yield 14%*

| Date | Cash Credit[a] | Interest Expense Debit[b] | Unamortized Discount Credit[c] | Book Value of Bonds[d] |
|------|------|------|------|------|
| 1/01/95 | | | | $ 92,976.39 |
| 6/30/95 | $6,000.00 | $6,508.35 | $508.35 | 93,484.74 |
| 12/31/95 | 6,000.00 | 6,543.93 | 543.93 | 94,028.67 |
| 6/30/96 | 6,000.00 | 6,582.01 | 582.01 | 94,610.68 |
| 12/31/96 | 6,000.00 | 6,622.75 | 622.75 | 95,233.43 |
| 6/30/97 | 6,000.00 | 6,666.34 | 666.34 | 95,899.77 |
| 12/31/97 | 6,000.00 | 6,712.98 | 712.98 | 96,612.75 |
| 6/30/98 | 6,000.00 | 6,762.89 | 762.89 | 97,375.64 |
| 12/31/98 | 6,000.00 | 6,816.29 | 816.29 | 98,191.93 |
| 6/30/99 | 6,000.00 | 6,873.44 | 873.44 | 99,065.37 |
| 12/31/99 | 6,000.00 | 6,934.63[e] | 934.63 | 100,000.00 |

a. $100,000 (face value) × 0.12 (stated annual interest rate) × 1/2 (year).
b. Previous book value × 0.14 (effective interest rate) × 1/2 (year).
c. Amount from footnote *b* − $6,000.00.
d. Previous book value + amount from footnote *c*.
e. Difference due to $0.05 rounding error.

### Bond Issue Costs

In addition to the separate recording of premiums and discounts, *APB Opinion No. 21* requires that any expenditures connected with a bond issue (such as legal and accounting fees, printing costs, or registration fees) be deferred. Conceptually a company with deferred bond issue costs should compute a new yield. However, because of a lack of materiality, generally these deferred bond issue costs are amortized over the life of the bond issue by the *straight-line* method. For example, assume that on January 1, 1995 Bergen Company issues 10-year bonds with a face value of $500,000 at 104. Expenditures connected with the issue totaled $8,000. The journal entry to record this issue is as follows:

| | | |
|------|------|------|
| Cash ($520,000 − $8,000) | 512,000 | |
| Deferred Bond Issue Costs | 8,000 | |
|     Premium on Bonds Payable (0.04 × $500,000) | | 20,000 |
|     Bonds Payable | | 500,000 |

---

**EXHIBIT 12-5**

**JET COMPANY**

Bond Interest Expense and *Premium* Amortization Schedule
*Effective Interest Method: 12% Bonds Sold to Yield 10%*

| Date | Cash Credit[a] | Interest Expense Debit[b] | Unamortized Premium Debit[c] | Book Value of Bonds[d] |
|------|------|------|------|------|
| 1/01/95 | | | | $107,721.71 |
| 6/30/95 | $6,000.00 | $5,386.09 | $613.91 | 107,107.80 |
| 12/31/95 | 6,000.00 | 5,355.39 | 644.61 | 106,463.19 |
| 6/30/96 | 6,000.00 | 5,323.16 | 676.84 | 105,786.35 |
| 12/31/96 | 6,000.00 | 5,289.32 | 710.68 | 105,075.67 |
| 6/30/97 | 6,000.00 | 5,253.78 | 746.22 | 104,329.45 |
| 12/31/97 | 6,000.00 | 5,216.47 | 783.53 | 103,545.92 |
| 6/30/98 | 6,000.00 | 5,177.30 | 822.70 | 102,723.22 |
| 12/31/98 | 6,000.00 | 5,136.16 | 863.84 | 101,859.38 |
| 6/30/99 | 6,000.00 | 5,092.97 | 907.03 | 100,952.35 |
| 12/31/99 | 6,000.00 | 5,047.65[e] | 952.35 | 100,000.00 |

a. $100,000 (face value) × 0.12 (stated annual interest rate) × 1/2 (year).
b. Previous book value × 0.10 (effective interest rate) × 1/2 (year).
c. $6,000.00 − amount from footnote *b*.
d. Previous book value − amount from footnote *c*.
e. Difference due to $0.03 rounding error.

Deferred bond issue costs of $800 are amortized to bond interest expense (i.e., debit Bond Interest Expense and credit Deferred Bond Issue Costs) each year over the 10-year life of the bonds. The unamortized deferred bond issue costs typically are disclosed as deferred charges or other assets on any subsequent balance sheet.

## Accruing Bond Interest

In the previous examples, the semiannual interest payments coincided with the company's fiscal year. However, frequently bonds are issued with interest payment dates that differ from the fiscal year. In such cases, the matching concept dictates that an accrual of interest and a partial premium or discount amortization be made at the end of the fiscal year. For example, assume that McAdams Company issues $200,000 of 10%, 5-year bonds on October 1, 1995 for $185,279.87. Interest on these bonds is payable each October 1 and April 1. The journal entry to record this issue is as follows:

| | | |
|---|---|---|
| Cash | 185,279.87 | |
| Discount on Bonds Payable | 14,720.13 | |
|     Bonds Payable | | 200,000.00 |

At the end of the fiscal year, December 31, 1995, it is necessary to accrue interest and amortize the discount for the months of October, November, and December. Thus, the company must compute the amount of interest to record as interest expense in 1995 for these 3 months. This adjusting entry (assuming straight-line amortization) is recorded as follows:

| | | |
|---|---|---|
| Interest Expense | 5,736.01 | |
|     Discount on Bonds Payable | | |
|       [($14,720.13 ÷ 5) × 3/12] | | 736.01 |
|     Interest Payable ($200,000 × 0.10 × 3/12) | | 5,000.00 |

Typically, a reversing entry will be recorded on January 1, 1996 so that the April 1, 1996 entry to record interest expense can be made as usual. If a reversing entry is not made, when the company records interest expense it eliminates the Interest Payable account and records the 3 months of interest expense incurred in 1996.

If the effective interest method is being used to amortize a premium or discount, the amount of interest expense to be accrued on December 31, 1995 is determined by computing the semiannual effective interest cost for the next interest and amortization period, and using the straight-line approach to allocate this amount over the number of months of interest accrual. For example, the effective annual interest rate on the McAdams bonds is 12%; therefore, the amount of semiannual interest for the six-month period ending April 1, 1996 is computed as follows:

$$\$185,279.87 \times 0.12 \times 1/2 = \$11,116.79$$

There are 6 months in the interest period and the elapsed time since the date of issue (October 1) is 3 months; therefore $5,558.40, or 3/6 of the $11,116.79 semiannual interest charge is expensed. The amount of discount amortization is computed as the difference between the effective interest expense, $5,558.40, and the $5,000.00 ($200,000 × 0.10 × 3/12) amount of interest owed, or $558.40. The December 31, 1995 adjusting entry necessary to record the accrued interest on the McAdams bonds using the effective interest method of discount amortization is as follows:

| | | |
|---|---|---|
| Interest Expense | 5,558.40 | |
|     Discount on Bonds Payable | | 558.40 |
|     Interest Payable | | 5,000.00 |

### Zero Coupon Bonds

As explained earlier in the chapter, zero coupon bonds are sometimes issued by companies. As the name implies, zero coupon bonds *pay* no interest each period. The only cash outflow associated with the bonds is the payment of the principal amount on the maturity date. The calculation of the selling price follows the principles discussed earlier; that is, it is the present value (based on the yield) of the face value. The issuance of zero coupon bonds is recorded in the usual way; that is, the discount account is debited for the difference between the selling price and the face value.

Even though the bonds *pay* no interest, the company must still recognize an interest *expense* because it has incurred a cost each period on the amount borrowed. The interest expense is computed, as discussed earlier, by multiplying the yield times the book value of the bonds at the beginning of the period. (Alternatively, the straight-line method may be used.) Since there is no cash payment for interest, the total interest expense is recognized as a decrease (credit) in the discount account (and therefore raises the book value of the bonds).

## International Accounting Differences

Most countries require that debt be recorded at its present value. However, some countries including Canada and Japan, require that a discount be recorded as a deferred charge (asset).

## EXTINGUISHMENT AND DEFEASANCE

The agreement between the bondholders and the company always includes a specified retirement date. On this date the company agrees to repay the face value of the bonds to the investors. At this time, any premium or discount associated with the issuance of the bonds will have been completely amortized so that the book value of the bonds is equal to the face value. Occasionally, under certain circumstances, bonds may be retired (extinguished) prior to their scheduled maturity date.

Over the past three decades, both the APB and the FASB have considered the various circumstances under which debt should be considered to be extinguished and what, if any, gain or loss should be recognized on that extinguishment. Under **FASB Statement No. 76,** debt with a specific maturity date and fixed interest payments is considered extinguished for financial reporting purposes when any of the following occur:

1. *Extinguishment of debt.* The debtor pays the creditor and is relieved of all its obligations regarding the debt. This payment may take place at maturity, or prior to maturity by recall or by reacquisition of the debt securities in the bond securities market.

2. *Defeasance of debt.* The debtor is released legally from being the primary obligor for the debt, either by law or by the creditor. Furthermore, it must be probable (as defined in *FASB Statement No. 5* on contingencies) that the debtor will not be required to make future payments for the debt under any guarantees.

3. *In-substance defeasance of debt.* The debtor irrevocably places cash or other assets in a trust to be used solely for satisfying the payments of both interest and principal on a specific debt obligation. Furthermore, the possibility that the debtor will be required to make future payments for the debt must be remote, even though the debtor is not legally released from being the primary obligor for the debt.[5]

*FASB Statement No. 76* does not address debt conversions or troubled debt restructurings. These are discussed later in the chapter.

## Extinguishment of Debt

Bonds may be extinguished by retirement at maturity or prior to maturity. The accounting issues related to these retirements are discussed in the following sections.

### Bonds Retired at Maturity

On the balance sheet issued immediately prior to the maturity date, the face value (and any related premium or discount) of the bonds to be retired is reclassified from

---

5. "Extinguishment of Debt," *FASB Statement of Financial Accounting Standards No. 76* (Stamford, Conn.: FASB, 1983), par 3.

a noncurrent (long-term) to a current liability if current assets are to be used to repay the obligation. On the maturity date, after the last interest payment is recorded, any premium or discount on bonds payable is fully amortized. Therefore, the book value of the bonds is equal to the maturity value. The retirement of bonds on the maturity date is recorded by a debit to Bonds Payable to eliminate the liability and a credit to Cash.

*Bonds Retired Prior to Maturity*

In order to be able to reduce their level of debt, eliminate any restrictions on operations included in the bond contract, or protect themselves from the inability to take advantage of future favorable changes in market conditions, many companies will include a **call provision** on long-term debt. **This provision allows the company to recall the debt issue at a prestated percentage of the face value prior to the maturity date.** Since the call price generally is above the issue price (if not, it is unlikely that the company would be able to sell the debt issue), a loss or, in unusual circumstances, a gain occurs when the debt is recalled. An alternative method of retiring bonds prior to their maturity is for the company to purchase them on the open market. Then a loss or gain arises depending on the relationship between the book value and the market value of the bonds. This type of extinguishment of debt may take two forms: (1) the borrowed funds may no longer be needed, and the debt is not replaced (**debt retirement**) or (2) the existing debt may be replaced with another debt issue (**debt refunding**).

Conceptually, gains or losses from refundings could be recognized either (1) over the remaining life of the old issue, (2) over the life of the new bond issue, or (3) in the current period. Recognizing the gain or loss over the remaining life of the old issue is favored by some accountants because they view this as the period affected by the refunding. That is, a different interest cost would have been incurred if the old issue had not been refunded. Those who favor recognizing the gain or loss over the life of the new issue base their arguments on the matching concept. That is, the different interest cost obtained for the life of the new issue should be adjusted to reflect any refunding gain or loss. Finally, those who favor an immediate write-off argue that this method is the most logical because the value of the debt has changed in prior periods and paying the call price recognizes this change in value through a transaction of the current period.

When **APB Opinion No. 26** was issued, the Board took the position that all extinguishments of debt prior to maturity were basically alike (whether retirements or refundings) and should be accounted for in the same way. Since gains or losses on retirements of debts are reported in the period of recall, it was decided that current income should reflect any gains or losses from refunding.[6] Thus, the gain or loss reported in a refunding transaction is computed in exactly the same way as a retirement.

After *APB Opinion No. 26* was issued, the FASB conducted a study of the reporting requirements for gains and losses from the extinguishment of debt. This review was partly in response to pressure from the SEC. The SEC was concerned because prevailing market conditions (i.e., high inflation and high interest rates) in 1973 and 1974 enabled many companies to reacquire their long-term debt at market prices well below face value, resulting in gains that were reported as ordinary income. For example, in 1973, United Brands recorded a $37.5 million gain by exchanging $12.5 million in cash and $75 million in 9 1/8% debentures for $125 million of 5 1/2% convertible subordinated debentures. The total gain was reported as ordinary income.

---

6.  "Early Extinguishment of Debt," *APB Opinion No. 26* (New York: AICPA, 1972).

After completing the study, the Board issued **FASB Statement No. 4,** which requires that **all material gains and losses from debt extinguishments (both retirements and refundings) are classified as extraordinary items**[7] without regard to the criteria of "unusual nature" or "infrequency of occurrence," established in *APB Opinion No. 30*.

In summary, whether debt is recalled, retired, or refunded prior to maturity, **any difference between the book value of the bonds (plus any unamortized bond issue costs) and the call price (or market price) is treated as an extraordinary gain or loss in the year the cancellation occurs.** As an example of debt retirement prior to maturity, assume that Channing Corporation originally issued $100,000 of 12% bonds at 97 on January 1, 1990. The bonds have a 10-year life, pay interest on January 1 and July 1, and are callable at 105 plus accrued interest. Assume, for simplicity, that the discount is being amortized by the straight-line method. On June 30, 1995 the bonds are recalled. First, it is necessary to record the current interest expense and liability, including the amortization of the discount that has expired since the last interest payment, as follows:

| | | |
|---|---:|---:|
| Interest Expense | 6,150 | |
|     Discount on Bonds Payable [($3,000 ÷ 10) × 1/2] | | 150 |
|     Interest Payable ($100,000 × 0.12 × 1/2) | | 6,000 |

The journal entry to record the reacquisition of the bonds is as follows:

| | | |
|---|---:|---:|
| Bonds Payable | 100,000 | |
| Interest Payable | 6,000 | |
| Extraordinary Loss on Bond Redemption | 6,350[b] | |
|     Discount on Bonds Payable | | 1,350[a] |
|     Cash [($100,000 × 1.05) + $6,000] | | 111,000 |

| | | |
|---|---:|---:|
| a. Original discount | | $ 3,000 |
|   Amortization on straight-line basis for | | |
|     5 1/2 years = 5.5 × $300 | | (1,650) |
|   Unamortized discount 6/30/95 | | $ 1,350 |
| | | |
| b. Call price (excluding interest) | | $105,000 |
|   Less: Face value | $100,000 | |
|     Unamortized discount | (1,350) | (98,650) |
|   Loss on bond redemption (extraordinary) | | $ 6,350 |

The extraordinary loss of $6,350 is disclosed on the income statement as an extraordinary item (net of income taxes), as illustrated in Chapter 4.

It is important to understand the FASB's reason behind requiring the extraordinary classification. The intent was to discourage a company from manipulating (increasing) its ordinary income by purchasing its own securities at a gain. By highlighting the gain as an extraordinary item, it was felt that users of financial statements would not be misled about the future earnings and cash flow potential of the company.

## Defeasance of Debt

Earlier we noted that the FASB has concluded that, in addition to retirement at maturity or prior to maturity, debt can be extinguished in two other ways: (1) the debtor can be legally released from being the primary obligor of the debt either by law or by

---

7. "Reporting Gains and Losses from Extinguishment of Debt," *FASB Statement of Financial Accounting Standards No. 4* (Stamford, Conn.: FASB, 1975), par. 8.

the creditor or (2) the debtor can irrevocably place cash or other assets in a trust to be used solely for satisfying a specific debt obligation. In these cases, for defeasance to occur it must be *probable* that the debtor will not be required to make future payments on the debt.

The first case might arise when an affiliate agrees to become the primary obligor for the debt. The Board argued that being legally released from being the primary obligor of a debt is a "transaction or other event" affecting the company, so that the liability is satisfied. Thus, the company removes the liability (e.g., bonds payable) from its balance sheet and reports an extraordinary gain consistent with *FASB Statement No. 4* (or perhaps a reduction in an investment in affiliate account). The company may still be required to disclose a contingent liability. This situation would arise if the debtor has been released from being the primary obligor because a third party has assumed the debt, but the creditor requires the debtor to be a guarantor of the third party's debt.

*Contingent liabilities
are discussed in
Chapter 11.*

The second case might arise for several reasons. First, a debtor may be in a refunding situation where it has issued new debt and received the proceeds, but is waiting for more favorable market conditions to retire the old debt. Second, the debtor may desire to recall certain debt and has the cash available to do so, but the recall date has not been reached. Third, the debtor may have sufficient cash available to retire the debt, but the recall price is too high. The FASB argued that placement of assets in an irrevocable trust also results in a transaction or event that satisfies the company's obligation because no future sacrifices of economic benefits are likely to occur. Thus, both the assets placed in trust and the liability are removed from the company's balance sheet. An extraordinary gain or loss is recorded when the cost of the assets placed in trust is less than or greater than the book value of the liability. Additionally, the FASB established specific requirements about the nature of the assets held in trust to help ensure against any future sacrifice of economic benefits. These requirements include:

1.  The trust must be restricted to owning only monetary assets that are essentially risk free as to the amount, timing, and collection of interest and principal. These monetary assets generally are limited to investments in direct obligations of the U.S. government or obligations guaranteed by the U.S. government.

2.  The monetary assets must provide cash flows (from interest and principal) that are similar, as to timing and amount, to the scheduled interest and principal payments on the debt being extinguished.

To determine the amount of debt considered to be extinguished when assets are placed in an irrevocable trust, only the expected cash inflows (i.e., interest and principal) from assets initially held by the trust (net of any trust costs) are considered. For reporting purposes, as long as the debt remains outstanding, the notes to the company's financial statements at the end of each period must include a general description of the transaction and disclose the amount of the debt considered to be extinguished.[8]

To illustrate in-substance defeasance of debt, assume that on January 1, 1993 Holmes Company issued $200,000 of 5-year, 12% bonds to yield 10%. On December 31, 1995, these bonds have a book value of $207,092. At this time, Holmes invests $193,225 in $200,000, 12% U.S. government bonds currently yielding 14% and

---

8.  *FASB Statement of Financial Accounting Standards No. 76*, op. cit., par. 46.

maturing on December 31, 1997 and places them in an irrevocable trust to be used to satisfy its debt obligations. The journal entry to record this extinguishment is as follows:

### December 31, 1995

| | | |
|---|---|---|
| Bonds Payable | 200,000 | |
| Premium on Bonds Payable | 7,092 | |
|     Cash | | 193,225 |
|     Extraordinary Gain on Bond Extinguishment | | 13,867 |

Note that the cash of $24,000 per year ($200,000 $\times$ 0.12) received from the trust is equal to the cash paid on the bonds.

*Conceptual Evaluation*

*FASB Statement No. 76* was approved by only a 4 to 3 vote of the Board, reflecting less than full agreement about the proper accounting principles for in-substance defeasance of debt. From a practical standpoint, some accountants argue that these principles allow a debtor to artificially increase income (i.e., by an extraordinary gain) in the year of defeasance in a situation where it extinguishes debt with a lower interest cost by placing higher interest-earning government securities in trust. From a conceptual standpoint, it also may be argued that placing the asset in an irrevocable trust simply ensures that the debt will be serviced; it does not satisfy, eliminate, or extinguish the obligation. Following this line of reasoning, the creditor should be fully satisfied before the liability is removed from the company's balance sheet.

Other accountants, however, argue that the accounting principles applicable to in-substance defeasance of debt are appropriate because placing the assets in an irrevocable trust is similar to a cash settlement, and any future payments on the debt are *remote*. These accountants argue that the liability should be removed from the company's balance sheet and that this procedure is generally consistent with accounting for contingencies (discussed in Chapter 11). It is interesting to note that, shortly after the issuance of the *Statement*, Standard and Poor's stated that it would ignore any gain that results from an in-substance defeasance of debt transaction in any financial analysis, such as return on investment.[9]

## BONDS WITH EQUITY CHARACTERISTICS

Companies may issue bonds that allow creditors to ultimately become stockholders by either attaching **stock warrants** to the bonds or including a **conversion feature** in the bond indenture. In either case, the investor has acquired a dual set of rights: (1) the right to receive interest on the bonds and (2) the right to acquire common stock and to participate in the potential appreciation of the market value of the company's common stock. Conceptually, it can be argued that the economic substance of the issue of bonds with either detachable warrants or a conversion feature is similar, and, for consistency, a portion of the proceeds of a bond issue carrying either of these features could be assigned to stockholders' equity. However, generally accepted accounting principles differ in their treatment of these securities.

---

9. Standard and Poor's, *Credit Week* (New York: Standard and Poor's, November 28, 1983), p. 550.

## Bonds Issued with Detachable Stock Warrants

When bonds are issued with detachable stock warrants, these **warrants represent rights that enable the security holder to acquire a specified number of common shares at a given price within a certain time period.** Stock warrants are attached to bonds to increase their marketability and generally will result in either a relatively lower interest rate or greater proceeds when compared with other bond issues with similar risk but without such rights. (The terms stock *warrants* and stock *rights* often are used interchangeably.) Because these warrants are detachable, they usually will sell separately from the bonds on the open market within a short time of issue.

*APB Opinion No. 14* requires that a portion of the proceeds of bonds issued with detachable warrants be allocated to the stock warrants and accounted for as additional paid-in capital. This allocation is based on the relative fair market values of the bonds and warrants as soon as both elements sell separately on the open market. The allocation is made as follows:

$$\text{Amount Assigned to Bonds} = \frac{\text{Market Value of Bonds Without Warrants}}{\text{Market Value of Bonds Without Warrants} + \text{Market Value of Warrants}} \times \text{Issuance Price}$$

$$\text{Amount Assigned to Warrants} = \frac{\text{Market Value of Warrants}}{\text{Market Value of Bonds Without Warrants} + \text{Market Value of Warrants}} \times \text{Issuance Price}$$

For example, assume Paul Company sold $800,000 of 12% bonds at 101, or $808,000. Each $1,000 bond carried 10 warrants, and each warrant allowed the holder to acquire one share of $5 par common stock for $25 per share. After issuance, the bonds were quoted at *99 ex rights* (without the rights attached), and the warrants (rights) were quoted at $3 each. The values assigned to each security are calculated as follows:

$$\text{Value Assigned to Bonds} = \frac{\$990 \times 800}{(\$990 \times 800) + (\$3 \times 800 \times 10)} \times \$808,000$$

$$= \frac{\$792,000}{\$792,000 + \$24,000} \times \$808,000 = \underline{\underline{\$784,235.29}}$$

$$\text{Value Assigned to Warrants} = \frac{\$3 \times 800 \times 10}{(\$990 \times 800) + \$3 \times 800 \times 10} \times \$808,000$$

$$= \frac{\$24,000}{\$792,000 + \$24,000} \times \$808,000 = \underline{\underline{\$23,764.71}}$$

In the denominator of each equation, note that the $792,000 market value of the bonds without warrants is computed by multiplying the $990 (99 ex rights) quoted price times the 800 bonds. The market value of the warrants is determined by multiplying the $3 quoted price times the 8,000 warrants (800 × 10). The following journal entry is made to record this transaction:

| | | |
|---|---|---|
| Cash | 808,000.00 | |
| Discount on Bonds Payable | | |
| ($800,000 − $784,235.29) | 15,764.71 | |
| Bonds Payable | | 800,000.00 |
| Common Stock Warrants | | 23,764.71 |

Each warrant is assigned a value of $2.971 ($23,764.71 ÷ 8,000), and if 500 of the warrants were later exercised at the $25 per share exercise price, the following journal entry is made:

| | | |
|---|---|---|
| Cash ($25 × 500) | 12,500.00 | |
| Common Stock Warrants ($2.971 × 500) | 1,485.50 | |
|    Common Stock ($5 × 500) | | 2,500.00 |
|    Additional Paid-in Capital on Common Stock | | 11,485.50 |

If the remaining warrants expire, the following journal entry would be made:

| | | |
|---|---|---|
| Common Stock Warrants | | |
|    ($23,764.71 − $1,485.50) | 22,279.21 | |
|    Additional Paid-in Capital from Expired | | |
|    Warrants | | 22,279.21 |

This journal entry transfers the value assigned to the warrants to the existing stockholders.

### Convertible Bonds

Bonds may be convertible into common stock. **At conversion, the bondholder (creditor) exchanges the bonds for a specified number of common shares (and becomes a stockholder).** Debt securities that are convertible into common stock often have played a role in corporate financing, and this role appears to be growing. The use of such instruments gives rise to two questions. Why do companies issue such securities? Are such securities really bonds or are they a form of common stock?

Most financial analysts agree that a company sells convertible bonds for one of two primary reasons. Either the company eventually wants to increase its equity capital at a later date and decides that the issuance of convertible bonds is the best way to do so, or it wants to increase its debt and finds the conversion feature necessary to make the security sufficiently marketable at a reasonable interest rate.

Several other factors have motivated companies to issue convertible bonds rather than common stock. For example, a company may wish to:

1.  Avoid the downward price pressures on its stock that placing a large new issue of common stock on the market would cause

2.  Avoid the direct sale of common stock when it believes its stock currently is undervalued in the market

3.  Penetrate that segment of the capital market that is unwilling or unable to participate in a direct common stock issue

4.  Minimize the costs associated with selling securities

For similar reasons, companies may issue convertible preferred stock (discussed in Chapter 15). In this chapter, we focus only on accounting for convertible bonds.

*Recording the Issuance*

When a company issues convertible debt, the proper valuation of these securities and their balance sheet presentation must be determined. Two methods for recording the issuance of convertible debt have been discussed in the accounting literature. The company could either (1) attribute part of the proceeds from the sale of the security to the conversion privilege and allocate this to additional paid-in capital as part of stockholders' equity, or (2) treat the issue solely as debt. Conceptually, both the conversion feature and the right to receive interest on the debt are valuable to an investor. Additionally, advocates of the first position argue that a lower interest rate or a higher selling price (or both) than might otherwise have been available usually accompanies the conversion feature. This indicates that investors are paying for the right to acquire common stock. Thus, an amount equal to the difference between the price at which the bonds might have been sold without the conversion privilege and the actual issue price should be allocated to additional paid-in capital. This position was taken in *APB Opinion No. 10* but soon was suspended in *APB Opinion No. 12*.[10] Companies had expressed widespread opposition to the convertible debt provisions of the earlier *Opinion*, and this viewpoint may have influenced the APB's suspension decision.

The decision was reversed in **APB Opinion No. 14**[11] and the proceeds from the issuance of convertible debt are treated solely as debt. The APB based its position on the inseparability of the debt and the conversion option, and on the lack of sufficiently reliable market-place valuations. That is, the difficulty in assigning a reliable valuation to the conversion feature outweighed the arguments cited for the first method. Thus treating the issue solely as debt is now the only generally accepted accounting principle. The issuance of convertible debt is recorded in the same manner as the issuance of nonconvertible debt, without attaching a value to the conversion feature.

*Recording the Conversion*

When bonds are converted into common stock, the amount to record as stockholders' equity must be determined. If the conversion takes place between interest dates, it is first necessary to record interest expense and any discount or premium amortization to bring the book value of the bonds up to date. There are two methods for recording the conversion:

1. *Book Value Method.* The stockholders' equity (common stock and additional paid-in capital) is recorded at the book value of the convertible bonds on the date of conversion, and no gain or loss is recorded upon conversion. (If the par value of the common stock is greater than the book value of the bonds, the difference is recorded as a reduction of retained earnings.)

2. *Market Value Method.* The stockholders' equity (common stock and additional paid-in capital) is recorded at the market value of the shares issued on the date of conversion, and a gain or loss is recorded. The gain or loss is computed by comparing the market value of the shares with the book value of the bonds at the time of conversion. This gain or loss is included in ordinary income on the income statement. It is *not* considered to be extraordinary because the conversion is not unusual, since the option was included in the original debt issuance and was likely to be exercised.

To illustrate, assume that Shannon Corporation has outstanding convertible bonds with a face value of $10,000, interest has just been paid on these bonds, and the bonds have a book value of $10,500. Each $1,000 bond is convertible into 40 shares of common stock (par value $20 per share). If all the bonds are converted into

---

10. "Omnibus Opinion—1966," *APB Opinion No. 10* (New York: AICPA, 1966), par. 8 and "Omnibus Opinion 1967," *APB Opinion No. 12* (New York: AICPA, 1967), par. 11.
11. "Accounting for Convertible Debt and Debt Issued with Stock Purchase Warrants," *APB Opinion No. 14* (New York: AICPA, 1969), par. 12.

common stock when the market value of Shannon's common stock is $26.50 per share, the following alternative journal entries may be made:

**Book Value Method**

| | | |
|---|---|---|
| Bonds Payable | 10,000 | |
| Premium on Bonds Payable | 500 | |
|     Common Stock (40 × 10 × $20) | | 8,000 |
|     Additional Paid-in Capital from Bond Conversion | | |
|       ($10,500 − $8,000) | | 2,500 |

**Market Value Method**

| | | |
|---|---|---|
| Bonds Payable | 10,000 | |
| Premium on Bonds Payable | 500 | |
| Loss on Conversion ($10,600 − $10,500) | 100 | |
|     Common Stock (40 × 10 × $20) | | 8,000 |
|     Additional Paid-in Capital from Bond Conversion | | |
|       (40 × 10 × $6.50) | | 2,600 |

Some accountants favor the market value method because they view the conversion as an economic event that should be recorded at fair value. Other accountants criticize the market value method because it allows a company to manipulate its income by recording a gain or loss on transactions involving its own securities. They also argue that the book value method should be used because the conversion is not a new economic event, but rather a continuation of the contract terms established when the bonds were issued initially. For these reasons, most companies use the book value method, although both methods are acceptable under generally accepted accounting principles.

*Induced Conversions*

A company that has issued convertible bonds may desire to induce conversion of these bonds to common stock in order to reduce interest costs, improve its debt/equity ratio, or for other reasons. To induce conversion, the company may add a "sweetener" to the convertible bond issue so that the conversion privileges are changed or additional consideration is paid to the bondholder. A question arises about accounting for this circumstance.

*FASB Statement No. 84* applies in situations where the conversion privileges are changed after the initial issuance, are effective for a limited period of time, involve additional consideration, and are made to induce conversion. The changed terms (privileges) may involve a reduction of the original conversion price resulting in the issuance of additional shares of common stock, the issuance of warrants or other securities not included in the original conversion terms, or the payment of cash to those bondholders who convert during the specified time period.

When convertible bonds are converted to common stock in such a situation, the debtor company recognizes an expense equal to the excess of the fair value of the common stock (and any other consideration) transferred in the transaction over the fair value of the common stock issuable under the original conversion terms. The expense is *not* reported as an extraordinary item. The fair values are measured on the date the inducement offer is accepted by the convertible bondholders.[12]

---

12. "Induced Conversions of Convertible Debt," *FASB Statement of Financial Accounting Standards No. 84* (Stamford, Conn.: FASB, 1985), par. 3 and 4.

To illustrate, assume that the Harmon Company previously had issued convertible bonds with a face value of $10,000 at par. At the time of issuance, the conversion terms allowed each $1,000 bond to be converted into 40 shares of no-par common stock. To induce conversion, the company later changed the conversion terms so that each bond is convertible into 50 shares of no-par common stock if conversion is made in 60 days. All the bonds are converted within the time limit when the market price of the common stock is $30 per share. The bond conversion expense is $3,000 because the $15,000 (10 × 50 × $30) fair market value of the no-par common stock issued in the transaction is in excess of the $12,000 (10 × 40 × $30) fair market value of the shares that would have been issued under the original terms. Under the *book value method,* the bond conversion expense is recorded at $3,000, the $10,000 par value of the bonds payable is eliminated, and the no-par common stock is recorded at $13,000 as follows:

| | | |
|---|---|---|
| Bond Payable | 10,000 | |
| Bond Conversion Expense | 3,000 | |
| Common Stock, no par | | 13,000 |

The bond conversion expense is reported in the Other Items section of the company's income statement and not as an extraordinary item.

## LONG-TERM NOTES PAYABLE

A long-term note is similar to a debenture bond because it represents a future obligation of the borrower to repay debt, and in many cases no collateral backs the note. Similarly, a long-term note generally includes a provision for interest on the borrowed funds, and the rate of interest charged will depend on such factors as the credit standing of the borrower, the amount of current debt, and usual business customs.

The APB reviewed procedures used by various companies to account for notes receivable and payable and found that some note transactions were conducted without an accompanying interest charge (i.e., these transactions involved *non-interest-bearing notes*). These transactions apparently were carried out to maintain favorable customer or supplier relations or to ensure future services. *APB Opinion No. 21* was issued to provide guidelines for cases in which a note does not stipulate a rate of interest or the stated interest rate is clearly inappropriate. The basic principle is that, regardless of how a note is structured legally, **the note is recorded at its present value and the effective interest method is used to record the subsequent interest.**[13] In essence, accounting for a note is based on its economic substance and not its legal form. The variety of transactions discussed in the *Opinion* did not allow the use of the same interest rate in all situations. In some situations, the present value is known so that the interest rate implicit in the transaction is calculated and used to apply the effective interest method. In other situations where the present value is not known, the incremental interest rate of the borrower is used to determine the present value and to apply the effective interest method. **The incremental interest rate is the rate that the borrower would be required to pay to obtain similar financing in the credit market at the time the note is issued.** Three major categories of notes were addressed:

---

13. The straight-line method may be used if the results obtained are not materially different from the effective interest method.

(1) notes exchanged for cash, (2) notes exchanged for cash and rights or privileges, and (3) notes exchanged for property, goods, or services.

Although *APB Opinion No. 21* addressed the accounting for most notes receivable and payable, it specifically exempted the following items: (1) normal trade transactions not exceeding one year, (2) amounts that will not be repaid but will be applied against the purchase of property, goods, or services, (3) security deposits, (4) customary activities of financial institutions, (5) transactions where the rate is affected by the regulations of government agencies, and (6) transactions between parent and subsidiary companies (and subsidiaries of a common parent).[14]

## Notes Payable Issued for Cash

When a long-term note payable bearing a stated (and fair) interest rate is issued for cash, the note is recorded initially at its face value (because it is equal to the present value). Subsequently, interest payments and accruals are recorded as debits to Interest Expense and credits to Cash or Interest Payable. Upon payment at maturity, the Notes Payable account is eliminated.

A more complex situation involves the receipt of cash in exchange for a long-term non-interest-bearing note. **When a long-term, non-interest-bearing note is exchanged solely for cash, the note is assumed to have a present value equal to the cash proceeds. The difference between the cash proceeds and the face value of the note is recorded as a discount and amortized over the life of the note by the effective interest method.** To apply the effective interest method, the implicit (effective) interest rate of the note must be determined. Since the cash received is the present value of the note and the face value is the future value of the note at maturity, **the effective (implicit) interest rate is the rate that equates the future value on the maturity date to the present value.** To illustrate, assume that on January of the current year Johnson Company issues a 3-year, non-interest-bearing note with a face value of $8,000 and receives $5,694.24 in exchange. The journal entry to record the issuance of the note is as follows:

| | | |
|---|---|---|
| Cash | 5,694.24 | |
| Discount on Notes Payable | 2,305.76 | |
| Notes Payable | | 8,000.00 |

The discount account is a contra account and is offset against the Notes Payable account on the balance sheet to report the carrying (book) value of the note.[15] From the Present Value of 1 Table (Appendix D), we find that the effective (implicit) interest rate that equates the present value of $5,694.24 to $8,000 at the end of 3 years is 12%.[16] The interest expense each year is computed by multiplying the 12% effective interest rate times the carrying value at the beginning of the year. This amount also

---

14. *APB Opinion No. 21, op. cit.*, par. 1, 3, and 15.
15. An alternative method is to record the Notes Payable account at its present value without the use of a Discount account. In this case, the subsequent adjusting entries for interest would involve a debit to Interest Expense and a credit directly to the Notes Payable account. When this method is used, the difference between the maturity value and the carrying value would be disclosed parenthetically on the balance sheet as the amount of the discount.
16. Present value = Future value × Factor
    $$\$5,694.24 = \$8,000 \times \text{Factor}$$
    $$\text{Factor}_{n=3, i=?} = \$5,694.24 \div \$8,000 = 0.711780$$
    $$i = 12\%$$

increases the carrying value of the note by reducing the discount. The interest each year is computed as follows:

|  | Year 1 | Year 2 | Year 3 |
|---|---|---|---|
| Note payable | $8,000.00 | $8,000.00 | $8,000.00 |
| Less: Unamortized discount | (2,305.76) | (1,622.45)[a] | (857.14)[b] |
| Carrying value at beginning of year | $5,694.24 | $6,377.55 | $7,142.86 |
| × Effective interest rate | 0.12 | 0.12 | 0.12 |
| Interest expense and discount amortization | $ 683.31 | $ 765.31 | $ 857.14 |

a. $2,305.76 − $683.31
b. $1,622.45 − $765.31

The $683.31 interest expense for the first year is recorded as follows:

| Interest Expense ($5,694.24 × 0.12) | 683.31 | |
|---|---|---|
| Discount on Notes Payable | | 683.31 |

Interest expense for the next two years is recorded in the same way so that the Discount account has a zero balance at the end of the third year. Therefore, the carrying value at the end of the third year is $8,000 (the face value of the note) so that the repayment involves a debit to Notes Payable and credit to Cash for the $8,000 face value of the note.

## Notes Payable Exchanged for Cash and Rights or Privileges

Long-term notes exchanged for cash may include special rights or privileges. These rights or privileges are considered when accounting for such long-term notes. For instance, a company might sign a contract with a customer in which the company borrows cash from the customer on a non-interest-bearing basis, with the understanding that the customer has the right to purchase certain goods from the company at less than prevailing prices over the period of the contract. In this situation, the consideration received from the customer for the note is, in essence, a prepayment for future purchases. In such a case for the company issuing the note, **the note is recorded at its present value at the time of issuance by discounting the maturity value using the incremental interest rate of the borrower, and interest expense is recorded over the life of the note using the effective interest method.** In addition, **the difference between the cash proceeds and the present value of the note is recorded as unearned revenue, and revenue is recognized over the life of the contract using appropriate revenue recognition criteria.** For instance, revenue might be recognized on a per unit basis as goods are sold, or evenly throughout the contract on a straight-line basis.

To illustrate, assume that the Verna Company borrows $100,000 by issuing a 3-year, non-interest-bearing note to a customer. In addition, Verna Company agrees to sell inventory to the customer at reduced prices over a 5-year period. Verna's incremental borrowing rate is 12% so that the present value of $100,000 to be repaid at the end of 3 years is $71,178 ($100,000 × 0.711780, from the Present Value of 1 Table in Appendix D). The customer agrees to purchase an equal amount of inventory each year over the 5-year period so that a straight-line method of revenue recognition is appropriate. In this situation, the following journal entries are recorded by Verna Company during the first two years:

### Issuing the Note

| | | |
|---|---:|---:|
| Cash | 100,000.00 | |
| Discount on Notes Payable | | |
| ($100,000 − $71,178) | 28,822.00 | |
| Notes Payable | | 100,000.00 |
| Unearned Revenue | | 28,822.00 |

### End of First Year

| | | |
|---|---:|---:|
| Interest Expense ($71,178 × 0.12) | 8,541.36 | |
| Discount on Notes Payable | | 8,541.36 |
| | | |
| Unearned Revenue ($28,822 ÷ 5 years) | 5,764.40 | |
| Sales Revenue | | 5,764.40 |

### End of Second Year

| | | |
|---|---:|---:|
| Interest Expense [($71,178 + $8,541.36) × 0.12] | 9,566.32 | |
| Discount on Notes Payable | | 9,566.32 |
| | | |
| Unearned Revenue | 5,764.40 | |
| Sales Revenue | | 5,764.40 |

Recording the transaction according to these procedures results in the proper recognition of both the revenue and expense components. The revenue is recognized as it is earned and the expense is recognized as the proceeds from the loan are being used.

## Notes Payable Exchanged for Property, Goods, or Services

When a note is exchanged solely for property, goods, or services in an external transaction, *APB Opinion No. 21* states that the stipulated rate of interest should be presumed fair. This presumption can be overcome only if:

1. No interest is stated, or

2. The stated rate of interest is clearly unreasonable, or

3. The face value of the note is materially different from the cash sales price of the property, goods, or services, or the market value of the note at the date of the transaction.[17]

In any of these cases, **the note is recorded at the fair market value of the property, goods, or services, or the fair market value of the note, whichever is more reliable.** That is, the fair market value is considered to be the present value of the note. The interest rate implicit in the transaction then is calculated and used to calculate the

---

17. *APB Opinion No. 21, op. cit.*, par. 12.

subsequent interest expense using the effective interest method. **If neither of these fair market values is determinable, the note is recorded at its present value by discounting the future cash flow(s) using the incremental interest rate of the borrower.** The incremental interest rate then is used to apply the effective interest method to determine the subsequent interest expense.

In either situation, the carrying value of the note and the cost of the assets or services acquired are recorded at an amount that is less than the face value of the note. If the liability and asset had been erroneously recorded at the face value of the note, both would be overstated in the current period. Additionally, this would result in an overstatement of depreciation expense (or cost of goods sold) and an understatement of interest expense over the life of the asset and note, respectively. Recording the note at its fair (present) value results in correct asset and liability valuations and in the proper timing of expense recognition.

To illustrate, assume that on January 1, 1995 the Marsden Company purchases used equipment from the Joyce Company, issuing a non-interest-bearing $10,000, 5-year note in exchange. Neither the fair market value of the equipment nor that of the note is determinable, so the incremental interest rate of Marsden Company must be used to compute the present value. If Marsden's incremental borrowing rate is 12%, the present value of $10,000 to be repaid at the end of 5 years at 12% is $5,674.27 ($10,000 × 0.567427, from Present Value of 1 Table in Appendix D). Assume the remaining asset life is 10 years (no residual value). The journal entries to record the issuance of the note, the first two interest payments, and annual straight-line depreciation are as follows:

**January 1, 1995**

| | | |
|---|---|---|
| Equipment | 5,674.27 | |
| Discount on Notes Payable | 4,325.73 | |
|     Notes Payable | | 10,000.00 |

**December 31, 1995**

| | | |
|---|---|---|
| Interest Expense [($10,000 − $4,325.73) × 0.12] | 680.91 | |
|     Discount on Notes Payable | | 680.91 |
| Depreciation Expense | 567.43 | |
|     Accumulated Depreciation ($5,674.27 ÷ 10) | | 567.43 |

**December 31, 1996**

| | | |
|---|---|---|
| Interest Expense | | |
|     {[$10,000 − ($4,325.73 − $680.91)] × 0.12} | 762.62 | |
|     Discount on Notes Payable | | 762.62 |
| Depreciation Expense | 567.43 | |
|     Accumulated Depreciation | | 567.43 |

This example assumes that a 12% interest rate is appropriate for the transaction, but an attempt should be made to determine the fair market values of the property and of the note before applying the borrower's incremental interest rate. If either the fair market value of the property or of the note is used, the note payable is recorded at the market value, and it is necessary to find the implicit interest rate that equates the recorded (market) value to the face value over the term of the loan. For example, assume in the previous example that the fair market value of the equipment was determined to be $6,209.21. From the Present Value of 1 Table (Appendix D), we find that the rate that equates $6,209.21 to $10,000 at the end of 5 years is 10%.[18] The note payable would be recorded initially at $6,209.21, and interest expense of 10% on the carrying value of the note would be recorded each year over the life of the note.

This example also assumes the issuance of a non-interest-bearing note. As discussed earlier, the same principles apply in the case where a note carries a stated interest rate that is unreasonable. For example, assume that on January 1, 1995 Fox Company issues a $30,000, 3-year note bearing interest of 6% for equipment when Fox's incremental borrowing rate is 10%. If the fair market value of the equipment or the note is not determinable, the present value of the future cash flows using the 10% rate for the 3-year life is used to record the transaction. In this case, the equipment and note are recorded at $27,015.78 [($30,000 face value × 0.751315) + ($1,800 annual interest × 2.486852)]. The effective interest method using the 10% rate is then applied at the end of each year to determine the interest expense. For instance, at the end of 1995 the Interest Expense is debited for $2,701.58 ($27,015.78 × 0.10), Cash is credited for $1,800 ($30,000 × 0.06), and the book value of the note is increased by $901.58.

### Disclosure of Long-Term Liabilities

The disclosure by Martin Marietta Corporation of its long-term (and short-term) debt is shown in Exhibit 12-6. Also included are disclosures about interest payments, capitalized interest, a revolving credit agreement, and the existence of restrictive covenants.

## LONG-TERM NOTES RECEIVABLE

Although this is a chapter on long-term liabilities, because the same generally accepted accounting principles apply to notes receivable and notes payable, accounting for long-term notes receivable is discussed briefly here. Companies may acquire long-term notes receivable as a result of lending cash to another entity or in return for the extension of certain rights or privileges. However, long-term notes receivable are acquired primarily as a result of an exchange for property, goods, or services. This type of exchange is the focus of this section.

As discussed in the previous section, when a note is received in exchange for property, goods, or services, the stipulated interest rate should be presumed fair unless no interest rate is stated, the stated interest rate is clearly unreasonable, or the face value of the note is materially different from the cash sales price of the property, goods, or services, or the market value of the note on the transaction date. In any of these situations, **the note receivable is recorded at the fair market value of the property, goods, or services or the fair market value of the note, whichever is more reliable. If neither of these values is reliable, the note is recorded at its present value by using the *borrower's* incremental interest rate.** The effective interest method is used to record the subsequent interest revenue. Recording the note at its fair market value (present value) and using the effective interest method results in the correct asset valuation and in the proper timing of revenue recognition.

---

18. $6,209.21 ÷ $10,000 = 0.620921. In the *n* = 5 row, we find 0.620921 in the 10% column.

**EXHIBIT 12-6**
**Long-Term Liabilities**

## MARTIN MARIETTA CORPORATION AND CONSOLIDATED SUBSIDIARIES

Balance Sheets (Partial)
*Liabilities and Shareowners' Equity*

|  | December 31 | |
|---|---|---|
|  | 1991 | 1990 |
| (add 000) | | |
| Long-term debt | $595,942 | $463,288 |

*Note F: Debt*

|  | December 31 | |
|---|---|---|
|  | 1991 | 1990 |
| Short-term borrowing | $    — | $ 25,000 |
| Long-term debt: | | |
| 8-1/2% Notes due 1996 | $100,000 | $    — |
| 9% Notes due 2003 | 100,000 | — |
| 9-1/2% Notes due 1995 | 125,000 | 125,000 |
| 9-1/4% Notes due 1997 | 125,000 | 125,000 |
| 7% Debentures due 2011 | 99,478 | 98,632 |
| Adjustable Rate Notes due 1994 | 68,465 | 68,465 |
| 8-5/8% Real Estate Mortgage due 2012 | 18,057 | 18,367 |
| Industrial Development Revenue Bonds | 17,800 | 17,800 |
| Other notes and capital lease obligations | 17,050 | 15,215 |
| Total | 670,850 | 468,479 |
| Less current maturities | 74,908 | 5,191 |
| Long-term debt | $595,942 | $463,288 |

The short-term borrowing outstanding at December 31, 1990 was retired on January 4, 1991.

The 8-1/2% Notes and 9% Notes were sold in a public offering in March 1991. The notes are not redeemable prior to maturity.

The 9-1/2% Notes are not redeemable prior to maturity.

The 9-1/4% Notes are callable at the Corporation's option at par in 1992.

The 7% Debentures were sold at 53.835% of their principal amount of $175,000,000 in 1981. These debentures are carried net of original issue discount, which is being amortized by the interest method over the life of the issue. The effective interest rate is 13-1/4% The debentures are redeemable in whole or in part at the Corporation's option at any time at 100% of their principal amount.

The interest rate on the Adjustable Rate Notes has been 9.35% since May 1, 1990. The rate is adjustable biennially based on a percentage of the prevailing two-year U.S. Treasury rate. The notes are redeemable at par by either the Corporation or the holders on May 1, 1992. Consequently, these notes have been classified with current maturities at December 31, 1991.

The 8-5/8% Real Estate Mortgage is secured by property in Maryland having a net book value of $18,600,000 at December 31, 1991.

Industrial Development Revenue Bonds, issued to finance various construction projects throughout the Corporation for environmental and industrial development purposes, mature after the year 2000 and have an average interest rate of 7.75%.

Maturities of long-term debt during the five-year period ending December 31, 1996 are $74,908,000 in 1992, $2,746,000 in 1993, $2,771,000 in 1994, $127,806,000 in 1995 and $103,551,000 in 1996.

---

> **EXHIBIT 12-6, Continued**
> **Long-Term Liabilities**
>
> Interest payments were $55,320,000 in 1991, $47,180,000 in 1990 and $47,710,000 in 1989. Interest expense on debt was net of capitalized interest of $5,757,000 in 1991, $7,771,000 in 1990 and $6,668,000 in 1989 and included commitment fees of approximately $750,000 in 1991 and 1990 and $830,000 in 1989.
>
> A $500,000,000 Revolving Credit Agreement with a group of banks may be used for general corporate purposes, including working capital and back-up for commercial paper. This agreement provides for a revolving line of credit through May 1994. Loans may be paid and re-borrowed during the revolving credit period. Under this agreement, options are available to borrow at variable rates based on spreads over the banks' cost of funds. Additionally, under the Revolving Credit Agreement, Martin Marietta is subject to limitations on its financial leverage as defined by the Agreement.
>
> The financing agreements of Martin Marietta Corporation contain certain restrictive covenants, including requirements for limitations on encumbrances and on sale and lease-back transactions.

---

To illustrate, consider the previous example in which the Joyce Company accepted a $10,000, non-interest-bearing, 5-year note on January 1, 1995 in exchange for used equipment it sold to Marsden Company. Since a reliable fair market value for the equipment or the note was not available, Marsden's 12% incremental borrowing rate was used to determine a present value of $5,674.27 for the note. Assume further that the equipment had originally cost the Joyce Company $8,000 and had a book value of $5,000 on the date of sale. The following journal entries are made by the Joyce Company to record the exchange and the first two interest receipts:

**January 1, 1995**

| | | |
|---|---|---|
| Notes Receivable | 10,000.00 | |
| Accumulated Depreciation | 3,000.00 | |
| Discount on Notes Receivable | | |
| ($10,000 − $5,674.27) | | 4,325.73 |
| Equipment | | 8,000.00 |
| Gain on Sale of Equipment | | 674.27 |

**December 31, 1995**

| | | |
|---|---|---|
| Discount on Notes Receivable | 680.91 | |
| Interest Revenue | | |
| [($10,000 − $4,325.73) × 0.12] | | 680.91 |

**December 31, 1996**

| | | |
|---|---|---|
| Discount on Notes Receivable | 762.62 | |
| Interest Revenue | | |
| {[$10,000 − ($4,325.73 − $680.91)] × 0.12} | | 762.62 |

At the date of exchange, the difference between the present value and face value of the note is recorded in a Discount on Notes Receivable account.[19] This account is a

---

19. An alternative method is to record the Notes Receivable account at its present value without the use of a Discount account. The Notes Receivable account would then be increased for each subsequent entry to record interest revenue and would eventually increase to the maturity value on the due date.

contra account and is offset against the Notes Receivable account to report the carrying (book) value of the note on the balance sheet. The $674.27 gain is computed by comparing the book value ($5,000) of the equipment with the present value ($5,674.27) of the note. If the exchange had taken place in the middle of the year, a depreciation adjusting entry would have been necessary to bring the book value of the equipment up to date. Had cash been received in addition to the note, the gain would have been computed by comparing the book value of the equipment with the sum of the cash received plus the present value of the note.

At the end of each year, interest revenue is recorded by use of the effective interest method. By the maturity date, the entire discount will have been amortized to interest revenue so that the carrying value will equal the face value of the note. If a reliable value for the equipment or the note had been available, the note would have been recorded at this fair market value and the implicit interest rate would have to be computed as discussed in the previous section. This interest rate would then be used to recognize periodic interest revenue under the effective interest method.

### Loan Fees

The proper matching of revenues and expenses associated with the lending activities of financial services companies is defined by **FASB Statement No. 91.** Lending activities precede the disbursement of funds and generally include efforts to identify and attract potential borrowers and to originate a loan or loan commitment. The nonrefundable fees charged to borrowers for these activities are called *loan origination fees* and *commitment fees*. Generally, any loan origination fees or commitment fees are deferred and recognized over the life of the loan as an increase in the interest revenue related to the note receivable. Likewise, the direct loan origination costs are deferred and recognized over the life of the loan as a decrease in the interest revenue. In either case, a new effective interest rate (yield) is computed. In other words, the revenues and expenses for these lending activities are matched over the life of the loan rather than recognized in the period the loan is originated.[20]

### Impairment of a Loan

Since loans typically are made by financial institutions such as banks, it is helpful to understand how they estimate bad debts as compared to retailers or manufacturers which make sales on credit. The retailer or manufacturer estimates bad debts in the period of the sales because it is probable that a portion of the asset (accounts receivable) has been impaired and the amount of the loss can be reasonably estimated based on historical information (as discussed in Chapter 5). Thus, the bad debt expense is matched against the revenues in the period of sale, and the receivables are reported at their net realizable value at the end of the period. In a later period, a specific account receivable is written off when it is determined that the amount is not collectible.

There are several differences between the receivables of a financial institution and those of a retailer or manufacturer: (1) the notes receivable result primarily from loans made to customers; (2) the loans are made to more heterogeneous customers; (3) the repayment periods for the loans are frequently longer (i.e., several years); (4) there are fewer receivables because fewer loans are made; and (5) more thorough credit analyses are made before extending loans. These differences affect when and how bad debt expense is recognized by a financial institution.

---

20. "Accounting for Nonrefundable Fees and Costs Associated with Originating or Acquiring Loans and Initial Direct Costs of Leases," *FASB Statement of Financial Accounting Standards No. 91* (Stamford, Conn.: FASB, 1986), par. 5–9.

A financial institution is likely to make a more thorough credit analysis in the period of the loan and to analyze the noncollectibility of each individual loan. Therefore, it is likely to recognize bad debts in a later period than a retailer or manufacturer, both of which are likely to use historical percentages. In a later period, however, a financial institution will recognize bad debt expense when, for instance, there is evidence that a loan may not be collectible (e.g., when the customer misses a payment on a loan). Then, in an even later period, a specific note receivable is written off when it is determined that the amount is not collectible, perhaps after taking possession of, and selling, the collateral provided by the borrower. The difference between bad debt recognition for a retailer or manufacturer and a financial institution is illustrated in the following diagram of events occurring during several (perhaps nonconsecutive) accounting periods.

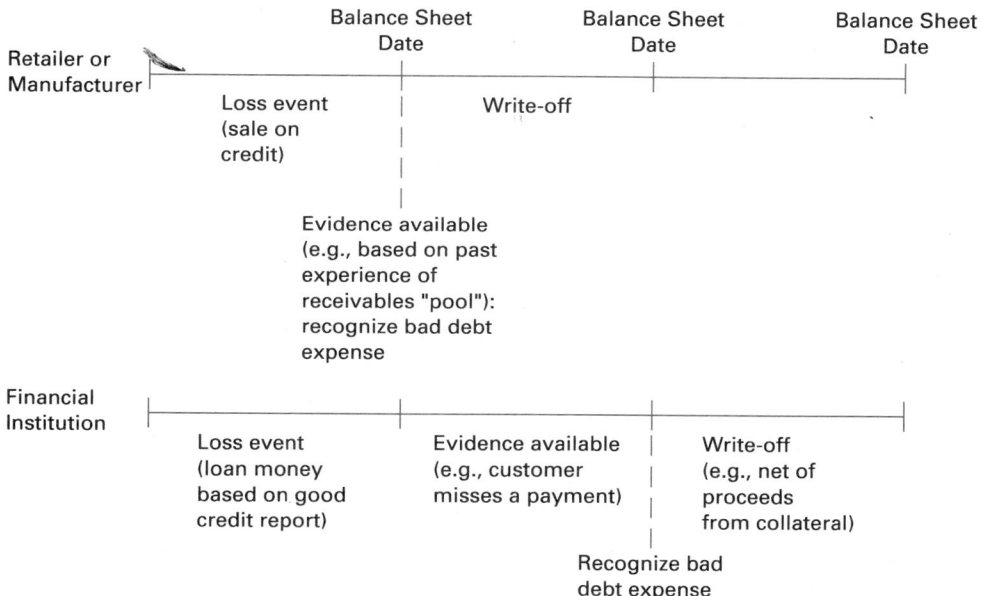

Note that as a result of the delay in the recognition of bad debts by a financial institution, it does not match expenses against revenues in the period in which the loan originates, and it does not report its receivables at their net realizable value at the end of that period. However, *relevant* expense recognition and receivables valuation does occur when *reliable* information becomes available that a loan is impaired.

**A loan (note receivable) is impaired if it is *probable* that the creditor will be unable to collect all amounts due according to the contractual terms of the loan agreement.**[21] Impairment occurs when there is a delay in the payment, or a shortfall in the amount, of the principal or interest. The creditor company, often a financial institution, applies its normal loan review procedures in making this determination. A loan is *not* impaired if there is a delay in making interest or principal payments and the creditor expects to collect all amounts due, including interest accrued during the period of delay. When a loan is found to be impaired, the company computes the

---

21. "Accounting by Creditors for Impairment of a Loan," *FASB Statement No. 114* (Norwalk, Conn.: FASB, 1993). The *Statement* is effective for fiscal years beginning after December 15, 1994. This *Statement* also applies to the impairment of accounts receivable of more than one year (which are not discussed here). It does *not* apply to investments in debt securities, as defined in *FASB Statement No. 115* (which are discussed in Chapter 13).

present value of the expected future cash flows of the impaired loan using the effective interest rate on the loan. **The effective interest rate is the original (contractual) interest rate on the loan** (adjusted for any loan fees, discount, or premium). The amount by which the present value is less than the recorded investment in the loan is recognized as Bad Debt Expense and an Allowance for Doubtful Notes. Alternatively, the creditor may measure the impairment based on the loan's market price, or the fair value of the collateral if the repayment of the loan is expected to be provided solely by the underlying collateral (net of the costs of selling the loan or the collateral).

Once the loan is written down, interest revenue is computed each period by multiplying the carrying value of the loan by the effective interest rate. The interest revenue is recognized as a reduction of the allowance account.[22] If there are additional changes in the amount or timing of an impaired loan's expected cash flows, or if actual cash flows are different than expected cash flows, the amount of the impairment is recalculated. The difference, whether an increase or decrease, is recognized as an adjustment to Bad Debt Expense and the Allowance account.

To illustrate the impairment of a loan using present value calculations, assume that the Snook Company has a note receivable of $100,000 from the Ullman Company that is being carried at face value. The original loan agreement specifies that interest of 8% is payable each December 31 and the principal is to be paid on December 31, 2000. The Ullman Company paid the interest due on December 31, 1995, but informed the Snook Company at that time that it probably would have to miss the next two year's interest payments because of its financial difficulties.[23] After that, it expected to resume the $8,000 annual interest payments, but the principal payment would be made one year late with interest paid for that additional year. On December 31, 1995, the Snook Company computes the present value of the impaired loan as follows:

$$\text{Present value of principal} = \$100,000 \times \text{present value of a single sum for 6 years at 8\% (from Appendix D)}$$
$$= \$100,000 \times 0.630170$$
$$= \$63,017.00$$

$$\text{Present value of interest} = \$8,000 \times \text{present value of an annuity for 4 years at 8\% deferred 2 years (from Appendix D)}$$
$$= \$8,000 \times 3.312127 \times 0.857339$$
$$= \$22,716.93$$

$$\text{Value of the impaired loan} = \$63,017.00 + \$22,716.93$$
$$= \$85,733.93$$

At December 31, 1995, the Snook Company recognizes the impairment of $14,266.07 ($100,000 carrying value − $85,733.93 present value) as follows:

| | | |
|---|---|---|
| **Bad Debt Expense** | 14,266.07 | |
| **Allowance for Doubtful Notes** | | 14,266.07 |

---

22. Alternatively, each year the entire change in the present value (the bad debt expense *and* the interest revenue) may be recognized as a single amount and reported as an increase or decrease in bad debt expense.

23. In more complex situations, knowledge of the loan impairment would occur when a payment is missed. If the company has accrued interest revenue for the period, the bad debt expense would be the difference between the carrying value (including the accrued interest) and the present value of the expected cash flows (including any late interest payments).

At December 31, 1996, the Snook Company recognizes interest revenue of $6,858.71 (8% × $85,733.93) as follows:

| | | |
|---|---|---|
| **Allowance for Doubtful Notes** | 6,858.71 | |
| Interest Revenue | | 6,858.71 |

At December 31, 1997, the Snook Company recognizes interest revenue of $7,407.41 [8% × ($85,733.93 + $6,858.71)]. This eliminates the balance in the Allowance for Doubtful Notes account (adjusted for a $0.04 rounding error), and the carrying value of the receivable is now $100,000. Interest revenue of $8,000 will be recognized each year for 1998 through 2001 as the cash payment is received. The $100,000 carrying value will be eliminated on December 31, 2001 when the principal payment is received. If the company's expectations of future cash flows decreased (increased) before December 31, 1997, the company would debit (credit) Bad Debt Expense and credit (debit) the Allowance account for the decrease (increase) in the present value. In either situation, the company would recognize interest revenue each year, as discussed earlier.

### Conceptual Evaluation

*FASB Statement No. 114* was issued because companies were using a variety of practices when a loan was impaired. Some would make no adjustment to the value of the loan, some would value the loan based on undiscounted cash flows, and some would use discounted cash flows. Thus, one objective of issuing the *Statement* was to establish a consistent method for valuing impaired loans. Another objective was to require the measurement of the economic losses on impaired loans and their inclusion in income.

Perhaps the only controversial issue in the required principles is the use of the original (contractual) interest rate rather than a current market rate that would reflect the risk involved in the loan (which is now higher than at the origination of the loan). The FASB concluded that the loan impairment measurement should reflect only the deterioration in the borrower's credit quality (which is evidenced by the reduced future cash inflows), and should not reflect changes in interest rates.

The *Statement* was adopted by a 5-to-2 vote, however, with the two dissenters arguing that the *fair value* of the loan should be recognized. Such a fair value would be the market value of the loan or the present value of the expected cash flows discounted at the *market* rate of interest. The market rate reflects current economic events and conditions, and is commensurate with the risk involved. The dissenters argued that the fair value provides the most *relevant* information about the amount and riskiness of the expected future cash flows. The historical effective interest rate reflects the risk characteristics of the loan at the time it was originated or acquired, but not at the time it was impaired. Also they note that bad debt expense would be *overstated* if the historical rate is *higher* than the current market rate.

At first sight, it may seem surprising that interest revenue (based on the new carrying value) is recognized even though a loan is impaired. For example, the Snook Company recognizes interest revenue in 1996 when no cash is received. However, it must be remembered that in 1995, the economic loss of $14,266.07 associated with the receivable is recognized and the loan is valued at the present value of the future cash flows. Interest revenue is then recognized on that reduced value. As always, one of the major issues of income recognition is the period in which income (and losses) should be recognized. These principles for the impairment of a loan do recognize the true economic situation appropriately because a loss is recognized in the period of impairment and interest revenue is recognized in subsequent periods.

## APPENDIX 1:  TROUBLED DEBT RESTRUCTURINGS

Some companies that have experienced difficulty in repaying long-term debt obligations have entered into financial arrangements with their creditors to allow them to avoid bankruptcy. Accounting for these financial arrangements raises three issues for the debtor:

1. Do certain kinds of troubled debt restructurings require reductions in the carrying amounts of debt?

2. If a reduction is required, should its effect be reported as current income, deferred to a future period, or reported as contributed capital?

3. Should contingently payable interest on the restructured debt be recognized before it becomes payable?

The underlying issues in each of these questions relate to the valuation of liabilities and the recognition of holding gains. A liability *should* be recorded at the amount of probable future sacrifice of economic benefits arising from present obligations. A holding gain *should* be recognized when the value of a liability decreases.

### TYPES OF TROUBLED DEBT RESTRUCTURINGS

The three issues were addressed by *FASB Statement No. 15,* which states that **a troubled debt restructuring occurs when a creditor for economic or legal reasons related to a debtor's financial difficulties grants a concession to the debtor that it would not otherwise consider.** A troubled debt restructuring may include, but is not limited to, one or any combination of the following:

1. **Modification of terms** of a debt such as one or a combination of:
   a. Reduction of the stated interest rate for the remaining original life of the debt.
   b. Extension of the maturity date at a stated interest rate lower than the current market rate for new debt with similar risk.
   c. Reduction of the face amount or maturity amount of the debt.
   d. Reduction of accrued interest.

2. **Issuance or other granting of an equity interest** to the creditor by the debtor to satisfy a debt unless the equity interest is granted under existing terms for converting the debt into an equity interest.

3. **Transfer of receivables, real estate, or other assets** from the debtor to the creditor to satisfy a debt.[24]

### MODIFICATION OF TERMS

When a restructuring agreement involves only a modification of terms, the carrying value of the *liability* (face value of the debt plus any unpaid accrued interest) is compared to the *undiscounted* future cash payments (principal plus interest) specified by the new terms. Then, two different situations may arise:

1. If the undiscounted total future cash payments are *greater* than (or equal to) the carrying value of the liability, the debtor does *not* recognize a gain, the carrying value of the liability is *not* reduced, and interest expense is recognized in future periods using an imputed interest rate.

---

24. "Accounting by Debtors and Creditors for Troubled Debt Restructurings," *FASB Statement of Financial Accounting Standards No. 15* (Stamford, Conn.: FASB, 1977), par. 2 and 5.

2. If the future cash payments are *less* than the carrying value of the liability, the debtor recognizes a gain, the carrying value of the liability is reduced, and interest expense is *not* recognized in future periods.

## No Gain Recognized by the Debtor

When there is a modification of terms and the total cash to be repaid over the remaining life of the loan is greater than (or equal to) the carrying value of the liability, no adjustment is made to the carrying value. Subsequently, annual interest expense is recognized by the effective interest method. **The imputed interest rate used is the rate that equates the total amount of cash to be paid with the current carrying value of the debt.** In this situation, a portion of each cash payment is recorded as interest expense and the remainder is recorded as a reduction in the carrying value of the liability.

For example, assume that on December 31, 1994 Chapin Company restructures a $1,178,073 debt with its bank (a note payable of $1,100,000 plus accrued interest of $78,073). The bank (1) forgives the $78,073 of accrued interest and $100,000 of principal; (2) extends the maturity date from December 31, 1994 to December 31, 1999; and (3) reduces the interest rate from 10% to 8%. The total future cash payments under the new terms are $1,400,000 (principal of $1,000,000 at the end of 5 years and interest of $80,000 at the end of each year for 5 years). Since the *undiscounted* amount of the principal and interest to be paid ($1,400,000) exceeds the carrying value of the liability ($1,178,073), no gain is recognized. The difference of $221,927 is recorded as interest expense over the next 5 years by using the effective interest method. The interest expense each period is determined by multiplying the effective interest rate times the carrying value at the beginning of the period.

The effective interest rate is that rate which discounts the principal of $1,000,000 and the interest payments of $80,000 to the $1,178,073 carrying value of the note. This discounting procedure involves two present value calculations, as summarized in the following diagram:

| | 12/31/1994 | 12/31/1995 | 12/31/1996 | 12/31/1997 | 12/31/1998 | 12/31/1999 |
|---|---|---|---|---|---|---|
| PV of principal | ← | | | | | $1,000,000 |
| + PV of interest | ← | $80,000 | $80,000 | $80,000 | $80,000 | $80,000 |
| = Carrying value of debt on 12/31/1994 ($1,178,073) | | | | | | |

This rate is found by trial and error (or calculation) to be 4%, as proven below:

Present Value of Interest Payments:
(Present Value of an Ordinary Annuity Table
   in Appendix D, $n = 5$, $i = 0.04$)       $80,000 × 4.451822 = \$ \ 356,146$
Present Value of Principal:
(Present Value of 1 Table in Appendix D,
   $n = 5$, $i = 0.04$       $1,000,000 × 0.821927 = \underline{\ \ \ 821,927}$
Carrying Value of the Debt on 12/31/1994       $\underline{\underline{\$1,178,073}}$

On December 31, 1994, a journal entry is made transferring the accrued interest payable balance to the Notes Payable account as follows:

**Interest Payable**                             78,073
    **Notes Payable**                                              78,073

The Notes Payable account now contains the entire $1,178,073 carrying value of the note. The interest expense to be recorded in each period is then determined by applying the effective interest rate of 4% to the carrying value of the note each year. Exhibit 12-7 illustrates the computation of the interest expense and principal reduction for each year of the Chapin Company's restructuring agreement.

---

**EXHIBIT 12-7**

### CHAPIN COMPANY

**Debt Restructuring Agreement**
Schedule to Compute Interest Expense

| Date | Cash Credit[a] | Interest Expense Debit[b] | Notes Payable Debit[c] | Carrying Value of Note[d] |
|------|------|------|------|------|
| 12/31/94 | | | | $1,178,073.00 |
| 12/31/95 | $   80,000 | $47,122.92 | $   32,877.08 | 1,145,195.92 |
| 12/31/96 | 80,000 | 45,807.84 | 34,192.16 | 1,111,003.76 |
| 12/31/97 | 80,000 | 44,440.15 | 35,559.85 | 1,075,443.91 |
| 12/31/98 | 80,000 | 43,017.76 | 36,982.24 | 1,038,461.67 |
| 12/31/99 | 1,080,000 | 41,538.33[e] | 1,038,461.67 | -0- |

a. From terms of restructuring agreement.
b. Previous carrying value × 0.04.
c. Amount from footnote *a* − amount from footnote *b*.
d. Previous carrying value − amount from footnote *c*.
e. Difference due to $0.14 rounding error.

---

In reviewing Exhibit 12-7, note that each cash payment is separated into its principal and interest components by multiplying the carrying value of the note in each year times the imputed interest rate in the agreement (4% in this case). Chapin Company records the difference between the interest expense and each cash payment as a reduction in the carrying value of the note payable. For example, Chapin Company records the following journal entry at the end of 1995:

**December 31, 1995**

|  |  |  |
|---|---|---|
| **Interest Expense** | 47,122.92 | |
| **Notes Payable** | 32,877.08 | |
| Cash | | 80,000.00 |

### Gain Recognized by the Debtor

An adjustment to the carrying value of the liability is required if the total cash to be repaid over the remaining life of the loan is less than that value. In this case, the debtor recognizes an *extraordinary* gain (because it arises from an extinguishment of debt) equal to the excess of the carrying value (face value plus accrued interest) over the sum of the future payments.

For example, assume that the Chapin Company was allowed the terms stated previously (reduction of principal by $100,000, forgiving of $78,073 of accrued interest, and extension of repayment period by 5 years), except that the stated interest rate was reduced to 3%. The aggregate future cash payments in this case total $1,150,000 ($1,000,000 principal and $30,000 interest per year for 5 years). This amount is $28,073 less than the carrying value of $1,178,073 ($1,100,000 face value + $78,073 accrued interest). Chapin Company reports this amount as an extraordinary gain in 1994. The accrued interest is eliminated, and the difference between the gain and the accrued interest is credited to the Notes Payable account so that the balance is now $1,150,000. The journal entry to record the restructuring on December 31, 1994 is as follows:

| | | |
|---|---|---|
| Interest Payable | 78,073 | |
| Notes Payable | | 50,000 |
| Extraordinary Gain on Debt Restructure | | 28,073 |

Subsequently, each future cash payment reduces the carrying value of the payable and no interest expense is recognized, since the effective interest rate is 0%. That is, since the amount to be repaid is less than the original carrying value of the liability, the creditor is, in effect, accepting repayment without an accompanying interest charge. The journal entry to recognize the first cash payment on December 31, 1995 is as follows:

| | | |
|---|---|---|
| Notes Payable | 30,000 | |
| Cash | | 30,000 |

The reduction of the Notes Payable account by $30,000 each year for five years will reduce this account to $1,000,000. This amount will then be eliminated at the time of the lump-sum principal payment at the end of the fifth year.

## EQUITY OR ASSET EXCHANGE

When a debtor satisfies a liability by exchanging an equity interest or an asset of lesser value, the transfer is recorded on the basis of the fair market value of the equity interest or asset transferred and an *extraordinary* gain is recognized. Furthermore, when an *asset* is exchanged, if the fair value is greater or less than its carrying value, an *ordinary* gain or loss also is recorded.

### Equity Exchange

To illustrate an equity exchange, assume that on December 31, 1994 the Chapin Company satisfies the note payable and the accrued interest totaling $1,178,073 by issuing 35,000 shares of its own common stock to the bank. The shares have a par value of $10 per share and are selling currently for $25 per share on the open market. The stock is recorded at the total market value of $875,000, the liability is reduced by $1,178,073, and an extraordinary gain of $303,073 is recognized. Chapin Company prepares the following journal entry to record the debt restructuring:

| | | |
|---|---|---|
| Notes Payable | 1,100,000 | |
| Interest Payable | 78,073 | |
| Common Stock (35,000 × $10) | | 350,000 |
| Additional Paid-in Capital on Common Stock | | 525,000 |
| Extraordinary Gain on Debt Restructure | | 303,073 |

### Asset Exchange

To illustrate an asset exchange, assume the same information as the equity exchange except that the Chapin Company satisfies the liability by transferring land it owns to the bank. The land has a current market value of $800,000 and had cost the Chapin Company $600,000 five years ago. The Chapin Company recognizes an extraordinary gain of $378,073 ($1,178,073 − $800,000) on the restructuring and an ordinary gain of $200,000 ($800,000 − $600,000) on the disposal of the land. Chapin Company records the debt restructuring as follows:

| | | |
|---|---|---|
| Notes Payable | 1,100,000 | |
| Interest Payable | 78,073 | |
| Extraordinary Gain on Debt Restructure | | 378,073 |
| Gain on Disposal of Land | | 200,000 |
| Land | | 600,000 |

## EQUITY OR ASSET EXCHANGE COMBINED WITH A MODIFICATION OF TERMS

In some situations, a troubled debt restructuring includes an equity or asset exchange as well as a modification of terms. In this case, the equity or asset transfer is recorded first at the fair market value as discussed previously. The *remaining* carrying value of the liability after deducting the fair market value of the equity or assets transferred then is compared to the total undiscounted future cash payments specified under the new terms. If the remaining carrying value is less than the total payments, a gain is not recognized, the carrying value of the liability is not reduced, and interest expense is recognized in future periods using an imputed interest rate. If the remaining carrying value is greater than the total payments, an extraordinary gain is recognized, the carrying value of the liability is reduced, and interest expense is not recorded in future periods. The accounting procedures to be followed in these two situations are the same as discussed earlier.

## DISCLOSURE OF RESTRUCTURING AGREEMENTS

The following disclosures are required for debtors that have entered into restructuring agreements:

1. A description of the principal changes in terms and/or the major features of settlement for each restructuring agreement
2. The aggregate gain on debt restructures and the related income tax effect
3. The per share amount of the aggregate gain on restructuring net of the related income tax effect
4. The aggregate gain or loss recognized during the period on transfers of assets
5. Information on any contingent payments[25]

The following is an example of the disclosure required for the Chapin Company's exchange of equity securities discussed previously:

During the year, Chapin Company exchanged common stock with a fair market value of $875,000 to the bank in full settlement of a 10% note in the amount of $1,100,000 and

---

25. *Ibid.*, par. 25 and 26.

accrued interest of $78,073. As a result of this exchange, the company recognized a gain of $303,073. This gain was classified as an extraordinary item (net of $90,922 related income taxes) and increased earnings per share by $0.08.

## ACCOUNTING BY THE CREDITOR

The accounting principles to be followed by the creditor are defined by *FASB Statement No. 15* and *FASB Statement No. 114*. Some of the principles are "mirror images" of those for the debtor, while others are not.

### Equity or Asset Exchange

The accounting by the creditor (e.g., the bank) for a troubled debt restructuring that involves an equity or asset exchange is a "mirror image" of the accounting by the debtor, except that any losses recognized by the creditor are reported as *ordinary* losses on its income statement (because such losses are not considered to be unusual or infrequent). These principles are defined by *FASB Statement No. 15*.

Thus, when an equity interest or asset is received to satisfy the receivable, **the equity or asset investment is recorded at fair value, the carrying value of the receivable is eliminated, and an ordinary loss is recognized.**

Exhibit 12-8 illustrates the journal entries for the Tenth National Bank to record the equity and asset exchanges for the troubled debt restructuring of the Chapin Company discussed earlier. It is helpful to observe the mirror image by contrasting the bank's journal entries with those of the Chapin Company shown earlier.

---

### EXHIBIT 12-8

#### CREDITOR JOURNAL ENTRIES FOR TROUBLED DEBT RESTRUCTURING

Equity Exchange

| | | | |
|---|---|---|---|
| 12/31/94 | Investment in Chapin | 875,000 | |
| | Loss on Restructured Loan | 303,073 | |
| | Notes Receivable | | 1,100,000 |
| | Interest Receivable | | 78,073 |

Asset Exchange

| | | | |
|---|---|---|---|
| 12/31/94 | Land | 800,000 | |
| | Loss on Restructured Loan | 378,073 | |
| | Notes Receivable | | 1,100,000 |
| | Interest Receivable | | 78,073 |

---

### Modification of Terms

The accounting principles for a modification of terms are *not* a mirror image because the creditor is always required to recognize a new value for the loan. **The investment in the restructured loan is valued by discounting the total future cash flows specified**

**by the new contractual terms to their present value.** An ordinary loss is recognized as the difference between the present value of the future cash flows and the carrying value of the receivable. **The effective interest rate used in the present value calculation is the original (contractual) interest rate on the loan** (i.e., the same interest rate used for a loan impairment), and *not* the rate specified in the restructuring agreement.[26]

A loan whose terms are modified in a troubled debt restructuring usually will have been identified as impaired in a previous period. The accounting principles for an impaired loan were discussed earlier in the chapter.

To illustrate the accounting for a modification of terms in a troubled debt restructuring, consider the first Chapin Company example that was discussed earlier. Assume that the loan was from the Tenth National Bank and that the bank has *not* recognized a previous impairment. The bank's note receivable is $1,100,000 and the accrued interest is $78,073. On December 31, 1994, the bank restructures the note so that the new principal is $1,000,000, payable in 5 years, with an interest rate of 8% (i.e., the annual interest payment is $80,000). Since 10% is the original interest rate on the loan to the Chapin Company, the loan is valued as follows:

$$\text{Present value of principal} = \$1,000,000 \times \text{present value of a single sum for}$$
$$\text{5 years at 10\% (from Appendix D)}$$
$$= \$1,000,000 \times 0.620921$$
$$= \$620,921.00$$

$$\text{Present value of interest} = \$80,000 \times \text{present value of an annuity for}$$
$$\text{5 years at 10\% (from Appendix D)}$$
$$= \$80,000 \times 3.790787$$
$$= \$303,262.96$$

$$\text{Value of the restructured loan} = \$620,921.00 + \$303,262.96$$
$$= \$924,183.96$$

On December 31, 1994, the bank records an *ordinary* loss of $253,889.04 ($1,178,073 − $924,183.96) on the restructuring as follows:

| | | |
|---|---|---|
| Loss on Restructured Loan | 253,889.04 | |
|    Interest Receivable | | 78,073.00 |
|    Notes Receivable | | 175,816.04 |

The carrying value of the Notes Receivable is now $924,183.96 ($1,100,000 − $175,816.04).

In subsequent periods, the bank earns interest at the original rate of 10% applied to the current carrying value. The 1995 interest revenue of $92,418.40 (10% × $924,183.96) is recognized on December 31, 1995 as follows:

| | | |
|---|---|---|
| Cash | 80,000.00 | |
| Notes Receivable | 12,418.40 | |
|    Interest Revenue | | 92,418.40 |

After five years of recording interest under the effective interest method, the Notes Receivable will have grown to the principal amount of $1,000,000.

---

26. "Accounting by Creditors for Impairment of a Loan," *FASB Statement No. 114, op. cit.*

For another illustration, consider the second Chapin Company example, where the stated interest rate was reduced to 3% (i.e., the annual interest payment is $30,000) by the Tenth National Bank. Since the original interest rate for the loan is 10%, the bank computes the value of the loan as follows:

Present value of principal = $1,000,000 × present value of a single sum for 5 years at 10% (from Appendix D)

= $1,000,000 × 0.620921

= $620,921.00

Present value of interest = $30,000 × present value of an annuity for 5 years at 10% (from Appendix D)

= $30,000 × 3.790787

= $113,723.61

Value of the restructured loan = $620,921.00 + $113,723.61

= $734,644.61

On December 31, 1994, the bank records an *ordinary* loss of $443,428.39 ($1,178,073 − $734,644.61) on the restructuring as follows:

| | | |
|---|---|---|
| Loss on Restructured Loan | 443,428.39 | |
| Interest Receivable | | 78,073.00 |
| Notes Receivable | | 365,355.39 |

The carrying value of the Notes Receivable is now $734,644.61 ($1,100,000 − $365,355.39).

Since the bank earns interest at the original rate of 10%, the 1995 interest revenue of $73,464.46 (10% × $734,644.61) is recognized on December 31, 1995 as follows:

| | | |
|---|---|---|
| Cash | 30,000.00 | |
| Notes Receivable | 43,464.46 | |
| Interest Revenue | | 73,464.46 |

After five years of recording interest under the effective interest method, the Notes Receivable will have grown to the principal amount of $1,000,000.

It is important to note the difference between the accounting by the debtor and creditor for a modification of terms. As discussed earlier, the debtor does *not* record the liability at a present value and, therefore, either recognizes no interest expense at all or recognizes an interest expense that is based on a below-market rate that was never part of the contractual agreement. In contrast, the creditor records the receivable at a present value and, therefore, recognizes interest revenue at the original contractual rate. The FASB may eventually require that the debtor also use a present value.

## Equity or Asset Exchange Combined with Modification of Terms

When an equity interest or asset is received and a modification of terms is made, the equity or asset is recorded first at its fair value. Then, the future cash receipts are discounted to their present value at the effective (contractual) rate of interest. An ordinary loss is recognized as the difference between the carrying value of the receivable and the sum of the fair value of the equity interest or asset and the present value of the future cash flows.

## CONCEPTUAL EVALUATION OF ACCOUNTING FOR TROUBLED DEBT RESTRUCTURINGS

When *FASB Statement No. 15* was issued, many accountants and financial statement users criticized the accounting principles due to the modification of terms for troubled debt restructuring. With the issuance of *FASB Statement No. 114,* these criticisms only apply to the accounting by the debtor because there is no longer a mirror image between the debtor and creditor, as discussed earlier. The critics argue that the procedures for the debtor (i.e., a limited or no gain) lead to inconsistencies in recording events that have similar economic substance (i.e., a modification of terms and an asset or equity exchange). They view a modification of terms as an economic event that should be recorded at a present value. In other words, they argue that the debtor should follow the procedures that are now required for the creditor. However, as discussed earlier in the chapter for loan impairment, the *Statement* was adopted by a 5-to-2 vote with the two dissenters arguing that the fair value of the loan should be recognized.

At the time that *FASB Statement No. 15* was issued, it was widely believed that the rules to be followed by the creditor in a modification of terms were the result of lobbying by financial institutions. These institutions argued that the recognition of large losses under the fair value approach would undermine the public's confidence in the banking system and have an adverse effect on the economy. A counter-argument was that the nonrecognition of losses enabled banks to continue in business longer than they should have, resulting in larger payments by taxpayers to "bail out" failing banks.

Since these original rules for the creditor have now been superseded, there seems to be little reason why the rules for the debtor should not also be modified. However, some supporters of the original rules point out that the FASB was just being conservative in its approach so as to minimize the gain recognized in a restructuring by a financially distressed debtor. Therefore, the choice of the accounting principle for debtors is based on whether a person believes that conservatism or the recognition of fair value is more important to external decision makers.

## APPENDIX 2: SERIAL BONDS

In the main part of this chapter, we focused on accounting for bonds in which the entire face value was due on one maturity date. Bonds also may contain provisions that require **repayment of the face value in periodic installments over a number of years;** these bonds are termed **serial bonds.** Serial bonds may be especially attractive in cases where the bond issue is used to finance a particular project, because the yearly cash flow from that project can be used to retire the bond issue.

## RECORDING THE ISSUANCE AND INTEREST EXPENSE OF SERIAL BONDS

Serial bonds may sell at a premium or discount because of differences between the prevailing market rate and the stated rate of interest. Since the bonds mature over a number of periods and interest rates depend partly on the terms of the issue, some accountants have questioned the use of a single interest rate to record the initial issue of serial bonds. There are, however, no generally accepted principles for determining the different interest rates to assign to each individual installment, so it is assumed that they all yield the same rate of interest. Thus, the initial issuance of serial bonds is recorded in the same manner as other bonds. That is, the entire face value is recorded in a Bonds Payable account and any discount or premium is recorded in a separate contra or adjunct account. After issuance, interest expense and any premium or discount amortization on serial bonds are computed by the **effective interest method.** Alternatively, a method similar to the straight-line method, known as the **bonds outstanding method,** may be used. It results in recording an amount of discount or premium amortization proportionate to the face value of the bonds outstanding. Under this method, if \$400,000 of 13% serial bonds are to be repaid in four \$100,000 installments, a proportionate (fractional) share of any premium or discount is amortized over the number of periods each installment is outstanding. The denominator of this fraction is derived by summing the face values of the bonds outstanding at the *beginning* of each period over the life of the entire issue. The numerator of this fraction is the face value of bonds outstanding at the *beginning* of each period.

To illustrate these two methods, assume that the Wallace Corporation issues \$400,000 of serial bonds with a 13% stated rate of interest for \$410,460.92 on January 1, 1993. The bonds are to be repaid in four semiannual \$100,000 installments beginning June 30, 1995 and interest is paid semiannually. The \$410,460.92 selling price of this serial bond issue reflects a yield of 12%, as shown in the following calculations using factors from Appendix D:

Present Value of Principal
   Installment due 6/30/95
      Present value of \$100,000 ($n = 5$, $i = 0.06$) $\times$ 0.747258       \$74,725.80
   Installment due 12/31/95
      Present value of \$100,000 ($n = 6$, $i = 0.06$) $\times$ 0.704961       70,496.10
   Installment due 6/30/96
      Present value of \$100,000 ($n = 7$, $i = 0.06$) $\times$ 0.665057       66,505.70
   Installment due 12/31/96
      Present value of \$100,000 ($n = 8$, $i = 0.06$) $\times$ 0.627412       <u>62,741.20</u>
      Present Value of Principal       \$274,468.80

Present Value of Interest Payments
   Installment due 6/30/95
      Present Value of an annuity of \$6,500 ($n = 5$, $i = 0.06$) $\times$ 4.212364   \$27,380.37
   Installment due 12/31/95
      Present value of an annuity of \$6,500 ($n = 6$, $i = 0.06$) $\times$ 4.917324   31,962.61
   Installment due 6/30/96
      Present value of an annuity of \$6,500 ($n = 7$, $i = 0.06$) $\times$ 5.582381   36,285.48
   Installment due 12/31/96
      Present value of an annuity of \$6,500 ($n = 8$, $i = 0.06$) $\times$ 6.209794   <u>40,363.66</u>
   Present value of interest       135,992.12
   Selling Price of Serial Bonds       <u>\$410,460.92</u>

The journal entry to record the issuance is as follows:

| | | |
|---|---|---|
| **Cash** | 410,460.92 | |
|    **Bonds Payable** | | 400,000.00 |
|    **Premium on Bonds Payable** | | 10,460.92 |

## EXHIBIT 12-9

### WALLACE CORPORATION

Interest Expense and Premium Amortization Schedule for Serial Bonds
*Straight-Line (Bonds Outstanding) Method*

| Date | Fraction of Premium Amortized[a] | Cash Credit[b] | Premium Amortization Debit[c] | Interest Expense Debit[d] | Unamortized Premium[e] | Bonds Payable Debit[f] | Bonds Outstanding[g] | Book Value of Bonds[h] |
|---|---|---|---|---|---|---|---|---|
| 1/01/93 | | | | | $10,460.92 | | $ 400,000 | $410,460.92 |
| 6/30/93 | 4/26 | $ 26,000 | $1,609.37 | $24,390.63 | 8,851.55 | | 400,000 | 408,851.55 |
| 12/31/93 | 4/26 | 26,000 | 1,609.37 | 24,390.63 | 7,242.18 | | 400,000 | 407,242.18 |
| 6/30/94 | 4/26 | 26,000 | 1,609.37 | 24,390.63 | 5,632.81 | | 400,000 | 405,632.81 |
| 12/31/94 | 4/26 | 26,000 | 1,609.37 | 24,390.63 | 4,023.44 | | 400,000 | 404,023.44 |
| 6/30/95 | 4/26 | 126,000 | 1,609.37 | 24,390.63 | 2,414.07 | $100,000 | 300,000 | 302,414.07 |
| 12/31/95 | 3/26 | 119,500 | 1,207.03 | 18,292.97 | 1,207.04 | 100,000 | 200,000 | 201,207.04 |
| 6/30/96 | 2/26 | 113,000 | 804.69 | 12,195.31 | 402.35 | 100,000 | 100,000 | 100,402.35 |
| 12/31/96 | 1/26 | 106,500 | 402.35[i] | 6,097.65 | -0- | 100,000 | -0- | -0- |
| | 26/26 | | | | | | $2,600,000 | |

a. Bonds outstanding at beginning of each period ÷ sum of bonds outstanding, or
   $400,000 ÷ $2,600,000 in the first period.
b. Bonds outstanding ($400,000 in first period) × interest rate (0.13) × 6/12 + installment payment
   (amount from footnote *f*).
c. $10,460.92 × fraction from footnote *a*.
d. Amount from footnote *b* − amount from footnote *c* − installment payment.
e. Previous balance − amount from footnote *c*.
f. Installment payment.
g. Face value − amount from footnote *f*.
h. Amount from footnote *e* + amount from footnote *g*.
i. Difference due to $0.01 rounding error.

Exhibit 12-9 shows the use of the bonds outstanding (straight-line) method of amortization for these serial bonds. Exhibit 12-10 illustrates the use of the effective interest method for the same bonds.

In both Exhibits 12-9 and 12-10, the interest expense debit column reflects the interest that Wallace records for each period. The decreasing amounts of interest expense for the semiannual periods in 1995 and 1996 are attributable to the fact that partial repayments are made during these periods. The cash credit column during these periods also reflects these repayments. For example, on December 31, 1995 the following journal entry is made to record the interest expense and partial retirement of the bonds (using straight-line amortization):

| | | |
|---|---|---|
| Bonds Payable | 100,000.00 | |
| Premium on Bonds Payable | 1,207.03 | |
| Interest Expense | 18,292.97 | |
| Cash | | 119,500.00 |

### EARLY REDEMPTION OF SERIAL BONDS

If bonds from any individual series are redeemed prior to their maturity date, the amount of unamortized discount or premium associated with these bonds is eliminated. When

## EXHIBIT 12-10

### WALLACE CORPORATION

Interest Expense and Premium Amortization Schedule for Serial Bonds
*Effective Interest Method: 13% Bonds Sold to Yield 12%*

| Date | Cash Credit[a] | Interest Expense Debit[b] | Premium Amortization Debit[c] | Unamortized Premium[d] | Bonds Payable Debit[e] | Book Value of Bonds[f] |
|------|------|------|------|------|------|------|
| 1/01/93 | | | | $10,460.92 | | $410,460.92 |
| 6/30/93 | $ 26,000 | $24,627.66 | $1,372.34 | 9,088.58 | | 409,088.58 |
| 12/31/93 | 26,000 | 24,545.31 | 1,454.69 | 7,633.89 | | 407,633.89 |
| 6/30/94 | 26,000 | 24,458.03 | 1,541.97 | 6,091.92 | | 406,091.92 |
| 12/31/94 | 26,000 | 24,365.52 | 1,634.48 | 4,457.44 | | 404,457.44 |
| 6/30/95 | 126,000 | 24,267.45 | 1,732.55 | 2,724.89 | $100,000 | 302,724.89 |
| 12/31/95 | 119,500 | 18,163.49 | 1,336.51 | 1,388.38 | 100,000 | 201,388.38 |
| 6/30/96 | 113,000 | 12,083.30 | 916.70 | 471.68 | 100,000 | 100,471.68 |
| 12/31/96 | 106,500 | 6,028.32[g] | 471.68 | -0- | 100,000 | -0- |

a. Bonds outstanding ($400,000 in first period) × interest rate
   (0.13 × 6/12) + installment payment (amount from footnote *e*).
b. Previous balance of footnote *f* × 0.12 × 6/12.
c. Amount from footnote *a* − amount from footnote *b* − installment payment.
d. Previous balance − amount from footnote *c*.
e. Installment payment.
f. Previous balance − amount from footnote *c* − amount from footnote *e*.
g. Difference due to $0.02 rounding error.

the bonds outstanding method is used, this amount can be determined from the amortization table by applying the following formula:

$$\frac{\text{Number of Periods Before Maturity of Issue}}{\text{Total of Bonds Outstanding Column}} \times \text{Par Value of Bonds Redeemed} \times \text{Total Premium or Discount}$$

To illustrate, assume that on January 1, 1995 the $100,000 of the Wallace Corporation bonds due December 31, 1996 are redeemed. The unamortized premium associated with this redemption is calculated as:

$$\frac{4 \text{ periods} \times \$100,000}{\$2,600,000} \times \$10,460.92 = \$1,609.37$$

When the redemption is recorded, the Unamortized Premium account is debited for $1,609.37, and an extraordinary gain or loss on the transaction is calculated by comparing the book value of the bonds redeemed with the redemption price. In addition, the amount of premium amortization shown in Exhibit 12-9 is reduced by $402.34 ($1,609.37 ÷ 4) for each semiannual period in 1995 and 1996.

When the effective interest method is used, the book value of the bonds being retired is the present value of the future cash payments required (principal and interest) on the bonds being retired at that time. The book value is calculated by discounting the future principal and interest payments to the retirement date, using the effective interest rate. The extraordinary gain or loss is computed and reported as discussed in the preceding paragraph, and the book value of the retired bonds is eliminated.

## QUESTIONS

**Q12-1** Why may a company that requires additional funds choose to issue long-term liabilities rather than equity securities?

**Q12-2** What is a *bond*? Define *face value, maturity date, contract rate, bond certificate,* and *bond indenture*.

**Q12-3** Distinguish between mortgage and debenture bonds.

**Q12-4** Distinguish between registered and coupon bonds.

**Q12-5** What are callable bonds? Convertible bonds?

**Q12-6** Why does the stated (contract) rate and the effective rate (yield) of interest on bonds frequently differ?

**Q12-7** Why do bond discounts and bond premiums arise at the time of sale?

**Q12-8** Distinguish between bond premiums or discounts and bond issue costs.

**Q12-9** Why does the recorded amount of interest expense for the first interest payment differ from the expense recorded for other interest payments when bonds are issued between interest payment dates?

**Q12-10** What two methods may be used to allocate a premium or discount over the life of a bond issue? Briefly describe each method.

**Q12-11** How is the amount of interest expense recorded each period affected by the amortization of a bond discount using the straight-line method?

**Q12-12** How is the amount of interest expense recorded each period affected by the amortization of a bond premium using the straight-line method?

**Q12-13** How is the amount of proceeds from a bond issue determined once the market (yield) rate of interest is specified?

**Q12-14** What is a call provision? Why do companies often include call provisions on bond issues?

**Q12-15** Distinguish between bond retirements and bond refundings.

**Q12-16** What are the three alternatives that could be used to account for gains or losses on bond refundings? What reasons support each of these methods? Which method did the APB finally favor? Why?

**Q12-17** According to *FASB Statement No. 76*, what is "in-substance defeasance of debt" and how is it accounted for?

**Q12-18** Why is a bond issued with detachable warrants (rights)? At what value is each of these securities recorded at the time of the bond issuance?

**Q12-19** What are convertible bonds? Why would a company issue convertible debt?

**Q12-20** What two alternative methods are available to account for the issuance of convertible debt? What method did the APB finally require? Why?

**Q12-21** When a long-term, non-interest-bearing note is exchanged for cash and no interest rate is stated, how is the effective interest rate determined?

**Q12-22** Describe the steps necessary to determine the value at which to record a non-interest-bearing note payable exchanged for property, goods, or services.

**Q12-23** What is the incremental interest rate of a borrower? When and for what calculations is this rate used if a note is exchanged for property, goods, or services?

**Q12-24** (*Appendix 1*) When does a troubled debt restructuring occur? What are three conditions a troubled debt restructuring may involve?

## CASES

*C12-1*   *Amortization of Bond Premium or Discount*
The appropriate method of amortizing a premium or discount on issuance of bonds is the effective interest method.

**Required**

1. What is the effective interest method of amortization and how is it different from and similar to the straight-line method of amortization?

2. How is amortization computed using the effective interest method, and why and how do amounts obtained using the effective interest method differ from amounts computed under the straight-line method? (*AICPA adapted*)

*C12-2*   *Recording Convertible Debt*
Zakin Co. recently issued $1,000,000 face value, 10%, 30-year subordinated debentures at 97. The debentures are redeemable at 103 upon demand by the issuer at any date upon 30 days notice 10 years after the issue. The debentures are convertible into $10 par value common stock of the Company at the conversion price of $12.50 per share for each $500 or multiple thereof of the principal amount of the debentures.

**Required**

1. Explain how the conversion feature of convertible debt has a value to the:
   a. Issuer
   b. Purchaser

2. Management of Zakin Co. has suggested that in recording the issuance of the debentures a portion of the proceeds should be assigned to the conversion feature.
   a. What are the arguments for according separate accounting recognition to the conversion feature of the debentures?
   b. What are the arguments supporting accounting for the convertible debentures as a single element?
3. Assume that no value is assigned to the conversion feature upon issue of the debentures. Assume further that 5 years after issue, debentures with a face value of $100,000 and book value of $97,500 are tendered for conversion on an interest payment date when the market price of the debentures is 104 and the common stock is selling at $14 per share and that the Company records the conversion as follows:

| | | |
|---|---|---|
| Bonds Payable | 100,000 | |
| Bond Discount | | 2,500 |
| Common Stock | | 80,000 |
| Premium on | | |
| Common Stock | | 17,500 |

Discuss the propriety of the preceding accounting treatment. (*AICPA adapted*)

### C12-3   Debt with Detachable Stock Warrants

Incurring long-term debt with an arrangement whereby lenders receive an option to buy common stock during all or a portion of the time the debt is outstanding is a frequently used corporate financing practice. In some situations, the result is achieved through the issuance of convertible bonds; in others, the debt instruments and the warrants to buy stock are separate.

**Required**

1. a. Describe the differences that exist in current accounting for original proceeds of the issuance of convertible bonds and of debt instruments with separate warrants to purchase common stock.
   b. Discuss the underlying rationale for the differences described in Requirement 1a.
   c. Summarize the arguments that have been presented for the alternative accounting treatment.
2. At the start of the year, AB Company issued $6 million of 7% notes along with warrants to buy 400,000 shares of its $10 par value common stock at $18 per share. The notes mature over the next 10 years, starting one year from date of issuance, with annual maturities of $600,000. At the time, AB had 3,200,000 shares of common stock outstanding and the market price was $23 per share. The company received $6,680,000 for the notes and the warrants. For AB Company, 7% was a relatively low borrowing rate. If offered alone, at this time, the notes would have been

issued at a 20 to 24% discount. Prepare journal entries for the issuance of the notes and warrants for the cash consideration received. (*AICPA adapted*)

### C12-4   Long-Term Notes Payable

Business transactions often involve the exchange of property, goods, or services for notes or similar instruments that may stipulate no interest rate or an interest rate that varies from prevailing rates.

**Required**

1. When a note is exchanged for property, goods, or services, what value is placed on the note:
   a. If it bears interest at a reasonable rate and is issued in a bargained transaction entered into at arm's length? Explain.
   b. If it bears no interest and/or is not issued in a bargained transaction entered into at arm's length? Explain.
2. If the recorded value of a note differs from the face value:
   a. How should the difference be accounted for? Explain.
   b. How should this difference be presented in the financial statements? Explain. (*AICPA adapted*)

### C12-5   Various Bond Characteristics

One way for a corporation to accomplish long-term financing is through the issuance of long-term debt instruments in the form of bonds.

**Required**

1. Describe how to account for the proceeds from bonds issued with detachable stock purchase warrants.
2. Contrast a serial bond with a term (straight) bond.
3. For a 5-year term bond issued at a premium, why is the amortization in the first year of the life of the bond different using the interest method of amortization instead of the straight-line method? Include in your discussion whether the amount of amortization in the first year of the life of the bond is higher or lower using the interest method instead of the straight-line method.
4. When a bond issue is sold between interest dates at a discount, what journal entry is made and how is the subsequent amortization of bond discount affected? Include in your discussion an explanation of how the amounts of each debit and credit are determined.
5. Describe how to account for and classify the gain or loss from the reacquisition of a long-term bond prior to its maturity. (*AICPA adapted*)

### C12-6   Convertible and Nonconvertible Bonds

On February 1, 1992 Aubrey Company sold its 5-year, $1,000 par value, 9% bonds, which were convertible at the option of the investor into Aubrey Company common stock at a ratio of 10 shares of common stock for each bond. The convertible bonds were sold by Aubrey Company at a discount. Interest is payable annually each February 1. On February 1, 1995 Mel Company, an investor in the Aubrey Company convertible bonds, tendered 1,000 bonds for conversion into 10,000 shares of Aubrey Company common stock, which had a market value of $110 per share at the date of the conversion.

On May 1, 1995 Aubrey Company sold its 10-year, $1,000 par value, 10% nonconvertible term bonds dated April 1, 1995. Interest is payable semiannually, and the first interest payment date is October 1, 1995. Due to market conditions, the bonds were sold at an effective interest rate (yield) of 12%.

**Required**

1. How does Aubrey Company account for the conversion of the convertible bonds into common stock under both the book value and market value methods? Discuss the rationale for each method.
2. Were the nonconvertible term bonds sold at par, at a discount, or at a premium? Discuss the rationale for your answer.
3. Identify and discuss the effects on Aubrey Company's 1995 income statement associated with the nonconvertible term bonds. (*AICPA adapted*)

### C12-7     Bonds: Sale, Interest, and Recall
On March 2, 1995 Wesley Company sold its 5-year, $1,000 face value, 8% bonds dated March 2, 1995 at an effective annual interest rate (yield) of 10%. Interest is payable semiannually and the first interest payment date is September 2, 1995. Wesley uses the interest method of amortization. Bond issue costs were incurred in preparing and selling the bond issue. The bonds can be called by Wesley at 101 at any time on or after March 2, 1996.

**Required**

1. a. How is the selling price of the bonds determined?
   b. Specify how all items related to the bonds are presented in a balance sheet prepared immediately after the bond issue is sold.
2. What items related to the bond issue are included in Wesley's 1995 income statement, and how is each determined?
3. Will the amount of bond discount amortization using the interest method of amortization be lower in the second or third year of the life of the bond issue? Why?
4. Assuming that the bonds are called in and retired on March 2, 1996, how does Wesley report the retirement of the bonds on the 1996 income statement? (*AICPA adapted*)

### C12-8     Bonds: Issuance, Expense, and Conversion
On January 1, 1994 Brewster Company issued 2,000 of its 5-year, $1,000 face value, 11% bonds dated January 1

at an effective annual interest rate (yield) of 9%. Brewster uses the effective interest method of amortization. On December 31, 1995 the 2,000 bonds were extinguished early through acquisition in the open market by Brewster for $1,980,000.

On July 1, 1994 Brewster issued 5,000 of its 6-year, $1,000 face value, 10% convertible bonds dated July 1 at an effective annual interest rate (yield) of 12%. The convertible bonds are convertible at the option of the investor into Brewster's common stock at a ratio of 10 shares of common stock for each bond. Brewster uses the effective interest method of amortization. On July 1, 1995 an investor in Brewster's convertible bonds tendered 1,500 bonds for conversion into 15,000 shares of Brewster's common stock, which had a market value of $105 per share at the date of the conversion.

**Required**

1. a. Were the 11% bonds issued at par, at a discount, or at a premium? Why?
   b. Is the amount of interest expense for the 11% bonds using the effective interest method of amortization higher in the first or second year of the life of the bond issue? Why?
2. a. How is a gain or loss on early extinguishment of debt determined? Does the early extinguishment of the 11% bonds result in a gain or loss? Why?
   b. How does Brewster report the early extinguishment of the 11% bonds on the 1995 income statement?
3. a. Does recording the conversion of the 10% convertible bonds into common stock under the book value method affect net income? What is the rationale for the book value method?
   b. Does recording the conversion of the 10% convertible bonds into common stock under the market value method affect net income? What is the rationale for the market value method? (*AICPA adapted*)

### C12-9     Bond Refunding
Gains or losses from the early extinguishment of debt that is refunded theoretically can be accounted for in three ways:

(a) Amortized over remaining life of old debt.
(b) Amortized over the life of the new debt issue.
(c) Recognized in the period of extinguishment.

**Required**

1. Discuss the supporting arguments for each of the three theoretic methods of accounting for gains and losses from the early extinguishment of debt.
2. Which of the preceding methods is generally accepted and how should the appropriate amount of gain or loss be shown in a company's financial statements? (*AICPA adapted*)

### C12-10 Serial Bonds

On November 1, 1994 Janine Company sold directly to underwriters at a lump-sum price, $1,000 face value, 9% serial bonds dated November 1, 1994 at an effective annual interest rate (yield) of 11%. A total of 25% of these serial bonds are due on November 1, 1996, a total of 35% on November 1, 1997, and a total of 40% on November 1, 1997. Interest is payable semiannually and the first interest payment date is May 1, 1995. Janine uses the interest method of amortization. Bond issue costs were incurred in preparing and selling the bond issue.

**Required**

1. How is the market price of the serial bonds determined?
2. How are all items related to the serial bonds, except for bond issue costs, presented in a balance sheet prepared immediately after the serial bond issue was sold?
3. How is the amount of interest expense for the serial bonds determined for 1994? (*AICPA adapted*)

### C12-11 Researching GAAP

You are auditing the York Company when you come across a note receivable signed by the president of a company that is a major supplier. The note has a face value of $100,000, is payable to the York Company, is dated January 1, 1995, and is payable January 1, 1999. The interest rate on the note is 1%. You ask the president of the York Company about the note and she responds "That is fine. We lent him some money to help him through a difficult divorce. We wanted him to pay interest, but he couldn't afford the going rate of 8%. So how do you think we should account for the note?"

**Required**

1. Research the related generally accepted accounting principles and prepare a short memo to the president that answers her question. Cite your references and applicable paragraph numbers.
2. How would your answer change if the interest rate on the note is 16%?

### C12-12 Researching GAAP

The Wales Company has a $90,000, non-interest-bearing 4-year note receivable from the Spenser Company that was received on July 1, 1995 when a used machine was sold to it. The machine was custom made five years ago, cost the Wales Company $100,000, and was being depreciated over a 10-year life by the straight-line method to a zero residual value. As the accountant for the Wales Company you know that *APB Opinion No. 21* requires that the note be discounted using the borrower's interest rate. You phone the accountant for the Spenser Company and ask her what that company's incremental borrowing rate is. She responds cheerfully "Sorry, I have no idea. We never borrow money because the owner provides all the capital we need." The president asks you to resolve this issue.

**Required**

Research the related generally accepted accounting principles and prepare a short memo to the president that answers her question. Cite your references and applicable paragraph numbers.

## MULTIPLE CHOICE

*Select the best answer for each of the following.*

**M12-1**  Should the following bond issue costs be expensed as incurred?

|  | Legal fees | Underwriting costs |
|---|---|---|
| a. | No | No |
| b. | No | Yes |
| c. | Yes | No |
| d. | Yes | Yes |

**M12-2**  On December 31, 1994 Dumont Corporation had outstanding 8%, $2,000,000 face value convertible bonds maturing on December 31, 1998. Interest is payable annually on December 31. Each $1,000 bond is convertible into 60 shares of Dumont's $10 par value common stock. The unamortized balance on December 31, 1995 in the premium on bonds payable account was $45,000. On December 31, 1995 an individual holding 200 of the bonds exercised the conversion privilege when the market value of Dumont's common stock was $18 per share. Using the book value method, Dumont's entry to record the conversion should include a credit to additional paid-in capital of

a. $80,000
b. $84,500

c. $96,000
d. $125,000

M12-3   On January 1, 1995 when the market rate for bond interest was 14%, Luba Corporation issued bonds in the face amount of $500,000, with interest at 12% payable semiannually. The bonds mature on December 31, 2005, and were issued at a discount of $53,180. How much of the discount should be amortized by the effective interest method at July 1, 1995?

    a.  $1,277                      c.  $3,191
    b.  $2,659                      d.  $3,723

M12-4   When the cash proceeds from a bond issued with detachable stock purchase warrants exceed the sum of the par value of the bonds and the fair value of the warrants, the excess should be credited to

    a.  Additional paid-in capital            c.  Premium on bonds payable
    b.  Retained earnings                   d.  Detachable stock warrants outstanding

M12-5   When the issuer of bonds exercises the call provision to retire the bonds, the excess of the cash paid over the carrying amount of the bonds should be recognized separately as a (an)

    a.  Extraordinary loss                c.  Loss from continuing operations
    b.  Extraordinary gain               d.  Loss from discontinued operations

M12-6   Peterson Company has a $500,000, 15%, 3-year note dated January 1, 1994, payable to Forest National Bank. On December 31, 1995 the bank agreed to settle the note and unpaid interest of $75,000 for 1995 for $50,000 cash and marketable securities having a current market value of $375,000. Peterson's acquisition cost of the securities is $385,000. Ignoring income taxes, what amount should Peterson report as a gain from the debt restructuring in its 1995 income statement?

    a.  $65,000                     c.  $140,000
    b.  $75,000                     d.  $150,000

M12-7   When the interest payment dates of a bond are May 1 and November 1, and a bond issue is sold on June 1, the amount of cash received by the issuer will be

    a.  Increased by accrued interest           c.  Decreased by accrued interest
         from June 1 to November 1             from June 1 to November 1
    b.  Increased by accrued interest           d.  Decreased by accrued interest
         from May 1 to June 1                  from May 1 to June 1

M12-8   On January 1, 1995 Parke Company borrowed $360,000 from a major customer evidenced by a non-interest-bearing note due in 3 years. Parke agreed to supply the customer's inventory needs for the loan period at lower than market price. At the 12% imputed interest rate for this type of loan, the present value of the note is $255,000 at January 1, 1995. What amount of interest expense should be included in Parke's 1995 income statement?

    a.  $43,200                     c.  $30,600
    b.  $35,000                     d.  $0

M12-9   For the issuer of a 10-year term bond, the amount of amortization using the effective interest method would increase each year if the bond was sold at a

|     | Discount | Premium |
| --- | --- | --- |
| a.  | No  | No  |
| b.  | Yes | Yes |
| c.  | No  | Yes |
| d.  | Yes | No  |

M12-10  On April 1, 1995 Girard Corporation issued at 98 plus accrued interest, 200 of its 10%, $1,000 bonds. The bonds are dated January 1, 1995, and mature on January 1, 2005. Interest is payable semiannually on January 1 and July 1. From the bond issuance Girard would realize net cash receipts of

    a.  $191,000                   c.  $198,500
    b.  $196,000                   d.  $201,000

*(AICPA adapted)*

## EXERCISES

**E12-1**  *Recording Bond Issue and Interest Payments*  The Kurten Corporation is authorized to issue $500,000 of 8% bonds. Interest on the bonds is payable semiannually; the bonds are dated January 1, 1995, and are due December 31, 2000.

**Required**

Prepare the journal entries necessary to record the following:

| | |
|---|---|
| April 1, 1995 | Sold the bonds at par plus accrued interest |
| June 30, 1995 | First interest payment |
| Dec. 31, 1995 | Second interest payment |

**E12-2**  *Straight-Line Premium Amortization*  On April 29, 1995 Hackman Corporation issued $1 million face value 9% bonds dated January 1, 1995, for $1,028,600 plus accrued interest. The bonds pay interest semiannually on June 30 and December 31 and are due December 31, 2002. The company uses the straight-line amortization method.

**Required**

Record the issuance of the bonds and the first two interest payments.

**E12-3**  *Straight-Line Discount Amortization*  The Bryan Company issued $500,000 of 10% face value bonds on January 1, 1995, for $478,000. The bonds are due December 31, 1997, and pay interest semiannually on June 30 and December 31. The company uses the straight-line amortization method.

**Required**

Prepare the journal entries necessary to record the issuance of the bonds and the first two interest payments.

**E12-4**  *Effective Interest Discount Amortization*  The Cotton Corporation issued $100,000 of 10% bonds dated January 1, 1995 for $97,158.54 on July 1, 1995. The bonds are due December 31, 1998, were issued to yield 11%, and pay interest semiannually on June 30 and December 31. The company uses the effective interest method of amortization.

**Required**

Record (1) the issuance of the bonds and (2) the payment of interest and the discount amortization on December 31, 1995; June 30, 1996; and December 31, 1996.

**E12-5**  *Effective Interest Premium Amortization*  Caldwell Incorporated issued $400,000 of 13% bonds on July 1, 1995, for $413,603.19. The bonds were dated January 1, 1995, pay interest on each June 30 and December 31, are due December 31, 1999, and were issued to yield 12%. The company uses the effective interest method of amortization.

**Required**

Prepare the journal entries necessary to record the issue of the bonds on July 1, 1995, and the interest payments on December 31, 1995, and June 30, 1996.

**E12-6**  *Determining the Proceeds from Bond Issues*  The Madison Corporation is authorized to issue $800,000 of 5-year bonds dated June 30, 1995, with a face rate of interest of 10%. Interest on the bonds is payable semiannually and the bonds are sold on June 30, 1995.

**Required**

Determine the proceeds that will be received if (1) the bonds are sold to yield 9% and (2) the bonds are sold to yield 11%.

**E12-7**  *Effective Interest Amortization of Premium or Discount*  The Taylor Company issued $100,000 of 13% bonds on January 1, 1995. The bonds pay interest semiannually on June 30 and December 31 and are due December 31, 1997.

**Required**

1. Assume the bonds are sold for $102,458.71 to yield 12%. Prepare the journal entries necessary to record:
   a. The sale of the bonds.
   b. Each 1995 semiannual interest payment and premium amortization, using the effective interest method.
2. Assume the bonds are sold for $97,616.71 to yield 14%. Prepare the journal entries necessary to record:
   a. The sale of the bonds.
   b. Each 1995 semiannual interest payment and discount amortization, using the effective interest method.

E12-8 *Bond Amortization Tables* On January 1, 1995 the Calvert Company issues 12%, $100,000 face value bonds for $103,545.91, a price to yield 10%. The bonds mature on January 1, 1997. Interest is paid semiannually on June 30 and December 31.

**Required**

1. Prepare a bond interest expense and premium amortization schedule, using the straight-line method.
2. Prepare a bond interest expense and premium amortization schedule, using the effective interest method.
3. Prepare the journal entries to record the interest payments on June 30, 1995, and December 31, 1995, using both methods.

E12-9 *Premium Amortization and Partial Retirement* Rockwood Company issued $100,000 of 10% bonds on November 1, 1994, at 102. Interest on the bonds is payable on November 1 and May 1 of each year, and the maturity date is November 1, 2004. Rockwood Company retired bonds with a face value of $30,000 on February 1, 1996, at 98 plus accrued interest. The company uses straight-line amortization and reverses any calendar year-end adjusting entries.

**Required**

1. Prepare the journal entry to record the issuance of the bonds on November 1, 1994.
2. Prepare all the journal entries to record the interest expense during 1995.
3. Prepare the journal entries to record the retirement of $20,000 of the bonds on February 1, 1996.

E12-10 *Effective Interest vs. Straight-Line Discount Amortization* Burr Motor Company, a manufacturer of small- to medium-sized electric motors, needs additional funds to market a revolutionary new motor. Burr has arranged for private placement of a $50,000, 5-year, 11% bond issue. Interest on these bonds is paid annually each year on August 31. The issue was dated and sold on September 1, 1994, for proceeds of $48,197.62 to yield 12%. The company reverses any year-end adjusting entries.

**Required**

1. Prepare a bond interest expense and discount amortization schedule showing interest expense for each year, using the effective interest method.
2. Prepare journal entries to record the issuance of the bonds and the interest payments for 1995 and 1996, using (a) the effective interest method and (b) the straight-line method.

E12-11 *Redemption of Bonds Prior to Maturity* The Hill Corporation issued $1,500,000 of 11% bonds at 98 on January 2, 1992. Interest is paid semiannually on June 30 and December 31. The bonds had a 10-year life from the date of issue, and the discount is being amortized by use of the straight-line method. On March 31, 1995, the bonds are recalled at the call price of 105 plus accrued interest.

**Required**

Prepare the journal entries necessary to record the reacquisition (recall) of the Hill Corporation bonds.

E12-12 *Extinguishment of Bonds Prior to Maturity* On December 1, 1992 the Cone Company issued its 10%, $2 million face value bonds for $2.3 million, plus accrued interest. Interest is payable on November 1 and May 1. On December 31, 1994 the book value of the bonds, inclusive of the unamortized premium, was $2.1 million. On July 1, 1995 Cone reacquired the bonds at 98, plus accrued interest. Cone appropriately uses the straight-line method for the amortization of bond premium because the results do not materially differ from those of the interest method.

**Required**

Prepare a schedule to compute the gain or loss on this extinguishment of debt. Show supporting computations in good form. (*AICPA adapted*)

**E12-13** *In-Substance Defeasance of Debt* On December 31, 1991 Webster Company issued $200,000 of 10-year, 13% bonds at a premium. On December 31, 1995 the remaining unamortized premium on these bonds amounts to $8,384. At this time, Webster purchases, for $192,058, U.S. government bonds with a face value of $100,000 and a 13% stated interest rate. These bonds are placed in an irrevocable trust to be used to satisfy the Webster Company's bond obligations. The U.S. government bonds mature on December 31, 2001, and pay interest on the same dates as do the Webster Company bonds.

**Required**

1. Prepare the journal entry for Webster to record the December 31, 1995 transaction.
2. Prepare the note to accompany Webster's 1995 financial statements.

**E12-14** *Convertible Bond Entries* On July 2, 1993, the McGraw Corporation issued $800,000 of convertible bonds. Each $1,000 bond could be converted into 20 shares of the company's $5 par value stock. On July 3, 1995, when the bonds had an unamortized discount of $7,400, and the market value of the McGraw shares was $52 per share, all the bonds were converted into common stock.

**Required**

Prepare the journal entry necessary to record the conversion of the bonds under:
1. The book value method
2. The market value method

**E12-15** *Convertible Bonds* On January 1, 1994, when its $30 par value common stock was selling for $80 per share, a corporation issued $10 million of 10% convertible debentures due in 10 years. The conversion option allowed the holder of each $1,000 bond to convert it into six shares of the corporation's $30 par value common stock. The debentures were issued for $11 million. The present value of the bond payments at the time of issuance was $8.5 million, and the corporation believes the difference between the present value and the amount paid is attributable to the conversion feature. On January 1, 1995 the corporation's $30 par value common stock was split 3 for 1. On January 1, 1996, when the corporation's $10 par value common stock was selling for $90 per share, holders of 40% of the convertible debentures exercised their conversion options. The corporation uses the straight-line method for amortizing any bond discounts or premiums.

**Required**

1. Prepare in general journal format the entry to record the original issuance of the convertible debentures.
2. Prepare in general journal format the entry to record the exercise of the conversion option, using the book value method. Show supporting computations in good form. (*AICPA adapted*)

**E12-16** *Induced Conversion* On July 1, 1995 the Tuttle Company had bonds payable outstanding with a face value of $200,000 and a book value of $194,000. The interest on these bonds was paid on June 30. When these bonds were issued, each $1,000 bond was convertible into 20 shares of $10 par common stock. To induce conversion, on June 15, 1995 the terms were changed so that each bond was convertible into 22 shares of common stock if the conversion was made within 30 days. All the bonds were converted on July 1, 1995 when the market price of the common stock was $50 per share.

**Required**

Using the book value method, record the conversion of the bonds on July 1, 1995.

**E12-17** *Detachable Stock Warrants* Conroe Corporation sold $500,000 of 13% bonds at 106. Each $1,000 bond carried 20 warrants, and each warrant allowed the holder to acquire one share of $10 par value common stock for $20 per share. Subsequent to the issuance of the securities, the bonds were quoted at 102 ex rights, and the warrants were quoted at $4 each.

**Required**

1. Determine the value to be assigned to the bonds and the warrants, and prepare the journal entry to record the issuance of the convertible bonds.
2. Assume that 4,000 warrants are subsequently exercised. Prepare the journal entry for the issuance of the common stock.

*E12-18*   *Bonds with Detachable Warrants*   On July 1, 1995 Salem Corporation issued $3 million of 12% bonds payable in 10 years. The bonds pay interest semiannually. The bonds include detachable warrants giving the bondholder the right to purchase for $30, one share of $1 par value common stock at any time during the next 10 years. The bonds were sold for $3 million. The value of the warrants at the time of issuance was $200,000.

**Required**

Prepare in general journal format the entry to record the issuance of the bonds. (*AICPA adapted*)

*E12-19*   *Long-Term Notes Payable*   On January 1, 1994 the Johnson Corporation issued a 2-year note due December 31, 1995, with a face value of $10,000, receiving $8,264.46 in exchange.

**Required**

Prepare the journal entries necessary to account for the note:

1. On the date the note is issued
2. At the end of 1994
3. At the end of 1995

*E12-20*   *Note Payable Exchanged for Cash and Rights*   The Spath Company borrows $75,000 by issuing a 4-year, non-interest-bearing note to a customer on January 1, 1995. In addition, Spath Company agrees to sell inventory to the customer at reduced prices over a 5-year period. Spath's incremental borrowing rate is 12%. The customer agrees to purchase an equal amount of inventory each year over the 5-year period so that a straight-line method of revenue recognition is appropriate.

**Required**

Prepare the journal entries necessary on Spath Company's books for 1995 and 1996. (Round answers to two decimal places.)

*E12-21*   *Exchange of a Note Payable for an Asset*   The Webb Corporation purchased an asset from the Shaw Corporation on January 1, 1995. Shaw accepted a 3-year, non-interest-bearing note of $20,000 due December 31, 1997 in exchange for the asset. Neither the fair market value of the asset nor that of the note is available. Webbs incremental borrowing rate is 12%.

**Required**

Prepare the journal entries necessary to record the issuance of the note, retirement, and any interest expense on the books of Webb on each of the following dates:

1. January 1, 1995               3. December 31, 1996
2. December 31, 1995             4. December 31, 1997

*E12-22*   *Note Payable Issued in Exchange for an Asset*   On January 1, 1995 the Sanders Corporation purchased equipment having a fair market value of $68,301.30 by issuing a non-interest-bearing, $100,000, 4-year note due December 31, 1998.

**Required**

Prepare the journal entries necessary to record (1) the purchase of the equipment, (2) the annual interest charges over the life of the note, and (3) the repayment of the note.

*E12-23*   *Note Payable in Installments*   On January 1, 1995 the Billips Corporation purchased equipment having a fair market value of $72,054.94 by issuing a $90,000 note, payable in three $30,000 annual installments beginning December 31, 1995.

**Required**

Prepare (1) the journal entry to record the purchase of the equipment, (2) a schedule to compute the annual interest expense, and (3) the journal entries to record yearly interest expense and note repayments over the life of the note.

*E12-24*   *Notes Receivable*   On January 1, 1995 Crouser Company sold land to Chad Company, accepting a 2-year, $150,000 non-interest-bearing note due January 1, 1997. The fair market value of the land was $123,966.90 on the date of sale. The land had been purchased at a cost of $120,000 on January 1, 1989.

**Required**
Prepare all the journal entries on Crouser Company's books for January 1, 1995 through January 1, 1997, in regard to the Chad Company note.

**E12-25 *Notes Receivable***   On January 1, 1995 Worthylake Company sold used machinery to Brown Company, accepting a $20,000 non-interest-bearing note maturing on January 1, 1997. Worthylake Company carried the machinery on its books at a cost of $22,000 and a current book value of $15,000. Neither the fair market value of the machinery nor the note was determinable at the time of sale; however, Brown's incremental borrowing rate was 12%.

**Required**
Prepare the journal entries on Worthylake Company's books to record:
1.  The sale of the machinery
2.  The related adjusting entries on December 31, 1995 and 1996
3.  The payment of the note by Brown Company on January 1, 1997

**E12-26 *Note Receivable in Installments***   On January 1, 1995 Tabor Company sold land with a book value of $25,000 to Wilson Company, accepting a $30,000 note, payable in three $10,000 annual installments beginning December 31, 1995. The note carried no stated interest rate and the fair market values of the land and the note were not determinable. An appropriate interest rate for this note is 12%.

**Required**
Prepare the journal entries on Tabor Company's books to record:
1.  The sale
2.  The annual interest revenue and receipt of each $10,000 installment

**E12-27 *Notes Receivable Discounted***   On January 1, 1995 Boiler Company received two notes for merchandise sold:

*Note 1:*   A $10,000, 10%, 60-day note from Wildcat, Inc.
*Note 2:*   A $20,000, 8%, 3-year interest-bearing note from Gopher, Inc.

On January 1, 1995 the fair market rate of interest was 10%. Needing cash to meet the upcoming payroll, Boiler Company discounted the Wildcat, Inc. note at the local bank at 14% on January 11, 1995. On March 2, 1995 Wildcat, Inc. remitted the full amount owed to the bank.

**Required**
Prepare journal entries on the books of Boiler Company to record the receipt of the two notes on January 1, 1995, the discounting of the Wildcat note on January 11, 1995, the payment by Wildcat to the bank on March 2, 1995, and the interest on the Gopher note on December 31, 1995. Round all calculations to the nearest dollar and use a 360-day year. (*Contributed by Scott I. Jerris*)

**E12-28 *Notes Receivable and Income***   On January 1, 1995 the Pitt Company sold a patent to Chatham, Inc., which had a carrying value on Pitt's books of $10,000. Chatham gave Pitt a $60,000 non-interest-bearing note payable in five equal annual installments of $12,000, with the first payment due and paid on January 1, 1996. There was no established price for the patent, and the note has no ready market value. The prevailing rate of interest for a note of this type at January 1, 1995 was 12%. Information on present value and future amount factors is as follows:

|  | Period | | | | |
|---|---|---|---|---|---|
|  | 1 | 2 | 3 | 4 | 5 |
| Present value of $1 at 12% | 0.89 | 0.80 | 0.71 | 0.64 | 0.57 |
| Present value of an annuity of $1 at 12% | 0.89 | 1.69 | 2.40 | 3.04 | 3.60 |
| Future amount of $1 at 12% | 1.12 | 1.25 | 1.40 | 1.57 | 1.76 |
| Future amount of an annuity of $1 at 12% | 1.00 | 2.12 | 3.37 | 4.78 | 6.35 |

**Required**

Prepare a schedule showing the income or loss before income taxes (rounded to the nearest dollar) that Pitt should record for the years ended December 31, 1995 and 1996, as a result of the preceding facts. Show supporting computations in good form. (*AICPA adapted*)

E12-29    *Loan Impairment*    The Perry National Bank has a note receivable of $200,000 from the Mogren Company that is being carried at face value and is due on December 31, 1999. Interest on the note is payable at 9% each December 31. The Mogren Company paid the interest due on December 31, 1995, but informed the bank that it would probably miss the next two years' interest payments because of its financial difficulties. After that, it expected to resume its annual interest payments, but the principal payment would be made one year late, with interest paid for that additional year at the time of the principal payment.

**Required**

1. Compute the value of the impaired loan on December 31, 1995.
2. Prepare the journal entries from 1995 to 2000 for the bank to record the above events.

E12-30    *Loan Impairment*    The Oaks National Bank has a note receivable of $500,000 from the Haldane Company that is being carried at face value and is due on December 31, 2001. Interest on the note is payable at 6% each December 31. The Haldane Company paid the interest due on December 31, 1995, but informed the bank that it would probably miss the next three years' interest payments because of its financial difficulties. After that, it expected to resume its annual interest payments, but the principal payment would be made two years late, with interest paid for the additional years. On January 1, 1998, the bank received new information and now expected the Haldane Company to pay the interest for 1998 through 2003 on December 31st of each year.

**Required**

1. Compute the value of the impaired loan on December 31, 1995.
2. Prepare the journal entries from 1995 to 2003 for the bank to record the above loan impairment events.

E12-31    *Appendix 1: Troubled Debt Restructuring (Debtor)—Modification of Terms*    On January 1, 1995 Northfield Corporation becomes delinquent on a $100,000, 14% note to the First National Bank on which $16,651 of interest has accrued. On January 2, 1995 the bank agrees to restructure the note. It forgives the accrued interest, extends the repayment date to December 31, 1997, and reduces the interest rate to 10%.

**Required**

Prepare a schedule for Northfield Corporation to compute the annual interest expense in regard to the preceding note for each year of the restructuring agreement.

E12-32    *Appendix 1: Troubled Debt Restructuring (Debtor)—Equity and Asset Exchange*    On January 1, 1995 the Boonville Corporation is delinquent on a $300,000 note to the Great National Bank on which $72,000 of interest has accrued. On January 2, 1995 Boonville enters into a debt restructuring agreement with the bank.

**Required**

Prepare the journal entries for Boonville to record the restructuring agreement assuming:

1. The bank accepts 10,000 shares of Boonville's $10 par common stock that is currently selling for $35 per share in full settlement of the debt.
2. The bank accepts land with a fair market value of $342,000 in full settlement of the debt. The land is being carried on Boonville's books at a cost of $324,000.

E12-33    *Appendix 1: Troubled Debt Restructuring (Creditor)—Modification of Terms*    On December 31, 1994 Central Bank agrees to a restructuring of a 12% note with a $200,000 face value and $60,000 of accrued interest owed to the bank by Carter Company. The bank agrees to forgive the accrued interest, extend the maturity date to December 31, 1997, and reduce the annual interest rate to 6%. Carter Company paid the interest due on December 31, 1995.

**Required**

1. Prepare the journal entry for Central Bank to record the restructuring of the note on December 31, 1994.
2. Prepare the journal entry for Central Bank to record the receipt of the interest on December 31, 1995.

**E12-34** *Appendix 1: Troubled Debt Restructuring (Creditor)—Equity and Asset Exchange*    Refer to the debt restructuring information in E12-32.

### Required

Prepare the journal entries for Great National Bank to record the restructuring agreement assuming:
1. The bank accepts the 10,000 shares of Boonville's stock.
2. The bank accepts the land.

**E12-35** *Appendix 2: Serial Bonds Entries*    On July 1, 1994 the Nicholsen Corporation issued $300,000 of bonds with a 13% face rate of interest for $318,000. The bonds pay interest semiannually on each January 1 and July 1 and are to be repaid in three equal semiannual installments beginning July 1, 1996. Assume the company's fiscal year ends May 31 and reversing entries are made for year-end accruals.

### Required

Prepare the journal entries necessary to account for this serial bond issue on each of the following dates using the bonds outstanding method of amortization:
1. July 1, 1994
2. January 1, 1995
3. July 1, 1995
4. January 1, 1996
5. July 1, 1996
6. January 1, 1997
7. July 1, 1997

**E12-36** *Appendix 2: Serial Bond Issue Using the Effective Interest Method*    The Lewis Company sells $200,000 of 13% bonds dated January 1, 1994, on that date for $204,650.74 to yield 12%. The bonds pay interest *annually* on December 31, and bonds of $40,000 mature on each December 31 for the next 5 years. The company uses the effective interest method of amortization.

### Required

1. Prepare a serial bond premium amortization schedule for these bonds.
2. Prepare the journal entries necessary to record the yearly interest payments, premium amortization, and serial bond redemption.

**E12-37** *Appendix 2: Serial Bonds*    On January 1, 1994 Mykoo Corporation issued $1 million in 5-year, 10% serial bonds to be repaid in the amount of $200,000 on January 1, 1995, 1996, 1997, 1998, and 1999. Interest is payable at the end of each year. The bonds were sold to yield a rate of 12%. Information on present value and future amount factors is as follows:

| Present Value of an Ordinary Annuity of $1 for 5 Years | | Future Amount of an Ordinary Annuity of $1 for 5 Years | |
|---|---|---|---|
| 10% | 12% | 10% | 12% |
| 3.7908 | 3.6048 | 6.1051 | 6.3528 |

| Number of Years | Present Value of $1 | | Future Amount of $1 | |
|---|---|---|---|---|
| | 10% | 12% | 10% | 12% |
| 1 | .9091 | .8929 | 1.1000 | 1.1200 |
| 2 | .8264 | .7972 | 1.2100 | 1.2544 |
| 3 | .7513 | .7118 | 1.3310 | 1.4049 |
| 4 | .6830 | .6355 | 1.4641 | 1.5735 |
| 5 | .6209 | .5674 | 1.6105 | 1.7623 |

### Required

1. Prepare a schedule showing the computation of the total amount received from the issuance of the serial bonds. Show supporting computations in good form.
2. Assume the bonds were originally sold at a discount of $46,498. Prepare a schedule of amortization of the bond discount for the first two years after issuance, using the interest (effective rate) method. Show supporting computations in good form. (*AICPA adapted*)

## PROBLEMS

**P12-1**    *Amortizing Bond Issue Costs and Bond Premiums*    On January 1, 1994 the Baker Corporation issued $100,000 of 5-year bonds due December 31, 1998, for $99,854.79 net of bond issue costs of $3,000. The bonds carry a face rate of interest of 13% payable annually on December 31 and were issued to yield 12%. The company uses the effective interest method of amortization.

**Required**

Prepare the journal entries necessary to record the issuance of the bonds, all the interest payments, premium amortizations, bond issue cost amortizations, and the repayment of the bonds.

**P12-2**    *Computation of Effective Interest Rate*    On June 30, 1995 the Watson Corporation sold $800,000 of 9% face value bonds for $758,481.29. On December 31, 1995 the Watson Corporation sold $700,000 of this same bond issue for $736,970.87. The bonds were dated January 1, 1995, pay interest semiannually on each December 31 and June 30, and are due December 31, 2002.

**Required**

Compute the effective yield rate on each issuance of the Watson Corporation 9% bonds.

**P12-3**    *Premium Amortization Schedule with Retirement Before Maturity*    The Dorsett Corporation issued $600,000 of 13% bonds on January 1, 1994 for $614,752.24. The bonds are due December 31, 1996, were issued to yield 12%, and pay interest semiannually on June 30 and December 31. The company uses the effective interest method.

**Required**

1. Prepare a bond interest expense and premium amortization schedule.
2. Assume the bonds were retired on September 29, 1996 for $630,000, which includes accrued interest. Prepare the journal entry to record the bond retirement.

**P12-4**    *Comprehensive*    The Batson Corporation issued $800,000 of 12% face value bonds for $851,705.70. The bonds are dated and issued on April 1, 1995, are due March 31, 1999, and pay interest semiannually on September 30 and March 31. The bonds were sold to yield 10%.

**Required**

1. Prepare a bond interest expense and premium amortization schedule using the straight-line method.
2. Prepare a bond interest expense and premium amortization schedule using the effective interest method.
3. Prepare any necessary adjusting entries for the end of the fiscal year, December 31, 1995, using:
    a. The straight-line method of amortization
    b. The effective interest method of amortization
4. Assume the bonds are retired on June 30, 1996, at 102 plus accrued interest. Prepare the journal entries necessary to record the bond retirement using:
    a. The straight-line method of amortization
    b. The effective interest method of amortization

**P12-5**    *Discount Amortization Schedule and Retirement Before Maturity*    Donaldson Incorporated sold $500,000 of 12% bonds on January 1, 1994 for $470,143.47, a price that yields a 14% interest rate. The bonds pay interest semiannually on June 30 and December 31 and are due December 31, 1997. The company uses the effective interest method.

**Required**

1. Prepare an interest expense and discount amortization schedule.
2. Assume the bonds were reacquired on July 1, 1996, at 104. Prepare whatever journal entries are necessary to record the bond retirement.

**P12-6**    *Comprehensive*    The Wilkerson Corporation issued $1 million of 13.5% bonds for $985,071.68. The bonds are dated and issued October 1, 1995, are due September 30, 1999, and pay interest semiannually on March 31 and September 30. Assume an effective yield rate of 14%.

**Required**

1. Prepare a bond interest expense and discount amortization schedule using the straight-line method.
2. Prepare a bond interest expense and discount amortization schedule using the effective interest method.
3. Prepare any necessary adjusting entries for the end of the fiscal year December 31, 1995 using:
    a. The straight-line method of amortization
    b. The effective interest method of amortization
4. Assume the bonds are retired on June 30, 1996 at 98 plus accrued interest. Prepare the journal entries necessary to record the bond retirement using:
    a. The straight-line method of amortization
    b. The effective interest method of amortization

**P12-7** *Bond Refunding* The Baxter Corporation issued $400,000 of 11% bonds for $385,279.91 on January 1, 1994. The bonds pay interest semiannually on June 30 and December 31, were issued to yield 12%, and are due on December 31, 1998. Interest is amortized using the effective interest method, and the bonds are callable at 105. In 1996, Baxter wishes to take advantage of more favorable market interest rate conditions and issues $450,000 of 11% 10-year bonds at 102 on June 1. Interest on these bonds is payable each May 31 and November 30. Sufficient proceeds from this issue are used to recall the original issue on July 1, 1996.

**Required**
Prepare the journal entries necessary to record:

1. The original issue
2. The new issue
3. The recall of the old issue

**P12-8** *Convertible Bonds* The Shank Corporation issued $1,500,000 of 10% convertible bonds for $1,620,000 on March 1, 1994. The bonds are dated March 1, 1994, pay interest semiannually on August 31 and February 28, and the premium is being amortized by use of the straight-line method. The bonds are due on February 28, 2004, and each $1,000 bond is convertible into 25 shares of Shank Corporation $10 par common stock. On March 1, 1996, when the shares were selling for $28 per share, $300,000 of bonds were converted. On September 1, 1998, when the shares were selling for $30 per share, the remainder of the bonds were converted.

**Required**
Prepare the journal entries necessary to record each bond conversion using:

1. The book value method
2. The market value method

**P12-9** *Bonds with Detachable Warrants* On January 1, 1995 the London Corporation issued $500,000 of 11.5% bonds due January 1, 2005, at 103. The bonds pay interest semiannually on June 30 and December 31. Each $1,000 bond carried 30 warrants, and the exchange of three warrants allowed the holder to acquire one share of $10 par common stock for $50. Shortly after the time of issue, the bonds were quoted at 98 ex rights and each individual warrant was quoted at $5. Subsequently, on March 31, 1995, 9,000 rights were exercised.

**Required**

1. Prepare the journal entry necessary to record the bond issue.
2. Prepare the journal entries on March 31, 1995 necessary to record the exchange of the warrants for common shares.

**P12-10** *Notes Payable* The Houston Corporation acquires machinery from the South Company in exchange for a $20,000 non-interest-bearing, 5-year note on June 30, 1994. The note is due on June 30, 1999. The machinery has a market value of $12,418.42, is subject to straight-line depreciation, and has an estimated life of 10 years (no residual value). Houston's fiscal year ends June 30.

**Required**
Prepare the journal entries necessary on each of the following dates to record the preceding information for Houston Corporation:

1. June 30, 1994
2. June 30, 1995
3. June 30, 1996
4. June 30, 1997
5. June 30, 1998
6. June 30, 1999

*P12-11   Notes Payable in Installments*   Hamlet Corporation purchases computer equipment at a price of $100,000 on January 1, 1995, paying $40,000 down and agreeing to pay the balance in three $20,000 annual installments beginning December 31, 1995. It is not possible to value either the equipment or the $60,000 note directly; however, Hamlet's incremental borrowing rate is determined to be 12%.

**Required**

1.  Prepare a schedule to compute the interest expense and discount amortization on the note.
2.  Prepare all the journal entries necessary for Hamlet to record the issuance of the note, each annual interest expense, and the three annual installment payments.

*P12-12   Notes Receivable*   On January 1, 1995 the Somerville Corporation sold a used truck to the Cornelius Company and accepted a $28,000 non-interest-bearing note due January 1, 1998. Somerville carried the truck on its books at a cost of $30,000 and a current book value of $23,000. Neither the fair market value of the truck nor the note was available at the time of the sale; however, Cornelius's incremental borrowing rate was 12%.

**Required**

1.  Prepare the journal entries on Somerville's books to record:
    a.  The sale of the truck
    b.  The related adjusting entries on December 31, 1995, 1996, and 1997
    c.  The collection of the note on January 1, 1998
2.  Prepare the notes receivable portion of Somerville's December 31, 1995, 1996, and 1997 balance sheets.

*P12-13   Notes Receivable*   On January 1, 1995 Lisa Company sold machinery with a book value of $120,000 to Mark Company. Mark Company signed a $180,000 non-interest-bearing note, payable in three $60,000 annual installments on December 31, 1995, 1996, and 1997. The fair market value of the machinery was $149,211.12 on the date of sale. The machinery had been purchased by Lisa Company at a cost of $160,000.

**Required**

1.  Prepare all the journal entries on Lisa Company's books for January 1, 1995 through December 31, 1997.
2.  Prepare the notes receivable portion of the Lisa Company's balance sheet on December 31, 1995 and 1996.

*P12-14   Comprehensive*   On January 1, 1994 Seaver Company sold land with a book value of $25,000 to Bench Company. Bench Company paid $15,000 down and signed a $15,000 non-interest-bearing note, payable in two $7,500 annual installments on December 31, 1994 and 1995. Neither the fair market value of the land nor of the note is determinable. Bench Company's incremental borrowing rate is 12%. Later in the year, on July 1, 1994, Seaver Company sold a building to Hane Company, accepting a 2-year, $100,000 non-interest-bearing note due July 1, 1996. The fair market value of the building was $82,644.60 on the date of the sale. The building had been purchased at a cost of $90,000 on January 1, 1989, and had a book value of $67,500 on December 31, 1993. It was being depreciated on a straight-line basis (no residual value) over a 20-year life.

**Required**

1.  Prepare all the journal entries on Seaver Company's books for January 1, 1994 through December 31, 1995 in regard to the Bench Company note.
2.  Prepare all the journal entries on Seaver Company's books for July 1, 1994 through July 1, 1996 in regard to the Hane Company note.
3.  Prepare the notes receivable portion of the Seaver Company's balance sheet on December 31, 1994 and 1995.

*P12-15   Comprehensive*   Linden, Inc., had the following long-term receivable account balances at December 31, 1994:

| | |
|---|---|
| Note receivable from sale of division | $1,500,000 |
| Note receivable from officer | 400,000 |

Transactions during 1995 and other information relating to Linden's long-term receivables were as follows:

1.  The $1,500,000 note receivable is dated May 1, 1994, bears interest at 9%, and represents the balance of the consideration received from the sale of Linden's electronics division to Pitt Company. Principal payments of $500,000 plus appropriate interest are due on May 1, 1995, 1996, and 1997. The first principal and interest payment was made on May 1, 1995. Collection of the note installments is reasonably assured.

2. The $400,000 note receivable is dated December 31, 1992, bears interest at 8%, and is due on December 31, 1997. The note is due from Robert Finley, president of Linden, Inc., and is collateralized by 10,000 shares of Linden's common stock. Interest is payable annually on December 31 and all interest payments were paid on their due dates through December 31, 1995. The quoted market price of Linden's common stock was $45 per share on December 31, 1995.

3. On April 1, 1995 Linden sold a patent to Bell Company in exchange for a $100,000 non-interest-bearing note due on April 1, 1997. There was no established exchange price for the patent, and the note had no ready market. The prevailing rate of interest for a note of this type at April 1, 1995, was 15%. The present value of $1 for two periods at 15% is 0.756. The patent had a carrying value of $40,000 at January 1, 1995, and the amortization for the year ended December 31, 1995 would have been $8,000. The collection of the note receivable from Bell is reasonably assured.

4. On July 1, 1995 Linden sold a parcel of land to Carr Company for $200,000 under an installment sale contract. Carr made a $60,000 cash down payment on July 1, 1995 and signed a 4-year 16% note for the $140,000 balance. The equal annual payments of principal and interest on the note will be $50,000 payable on July 1, 1996 through July 1, 1999. The land could have been sold at an established cash price of $200,000. The cost of the land to Linden was $150,000. Circumstances are such that the collection of the installments on the note is reasonably assured.

### Required

1. Prepare the long-term receivables section of Linden's balance sheet at December 31, 1995.
2. Prepare a schedule showing the current portion of the long-term receivables and accrued interest receivable that would appear in Linden's balance sheet at December 31, 1995.
3. Prepare a schedule showing interest income from the long-term receivables and gains recognized on sale of assets that would appear on Linden's income statement for the year ended December 31, 1995. (*AICPA adapted*)

**P12-16** *Comprehensive* An examination of the accounting records of the Durham Corporation on January 1, 1996 (after reversing entries had been made for all accrued interest at the end of 1995) disclosed the following information regarding the company's long-term debt:

| | |
|---|---:|
| 12.5% bonds dated January 1, 1992, paying interest semiannually on June 30 and December 31, and due December 31, 1998. | $1,300,000 |
| 11% convertible bonds dated April 1, 1994, paying interest semiannually on March 31 and September 30, and due March 31, 1999. | $ 500,000 |
| Discount on convertible bonds payable | (17,500) |
| | $ 482,500 |
| 9% bonds dated March 1, 1995, paying interest annually on February 28, and due February 28, 2000. | $ 100,000 |
| Discount on bonds payable | (3,960) |
| | $ 96,040 |
| 4-year, non-interest-bearing note issued January 1, 1995. (Durham's incremental borrowing rate on the date the note was issued was 10%.) | $ 80,000 |
| Discount on note payable | (19,895) |
| | $ 60,105 |

Additional information disclosed in the notes to Durham Corporation's 1995 financial statements:

1. The conversion option allows the holder of each $1,000 bond to exchange it for 30 shares of $10 par common stock. Durham uses the book value method to record conversions of bonds to common stock.
2. Each $1,000 bond of the 9% bonds dated March 1, 1995 carries 15 detachable warrants. The company had recorded the 1,500 warrants on the bonds at $4,800 in a Common Stock Warrants account. The exchange of three warrants allows the holder to acquire one share of $10 par common stock for $27.
3. The discount on the convertible bonds and the discount on the 9% bonds with detachable warrants are being amortized using the straight-line method.
4. The discount on the note payable is being amortized annually using the effective interest method.

During 1996, the Durham Corporation engaged in the following long-term debt transactions:

Jan.  1     Issued 11%, $800,000 face value bonds for $820,302, a price to yield 10%. Interest on these bonds is payable semiannually on June 30 and December 31, and they are due December 31, 1998. The effective interest method is to be used to amortize the premium. The bonds are callable at 105.

May  1     Six hundred warrants from the 9% bonds were exercised when the common stock was selling for $42 per share.

Sept. 29     Convertible bonds of $100,000 were exchanged when the common stock was selling for $45 per share.

Nov.  1     Retired $200,000 of the bonds issued on January 1, 1996, at the call price plus accrued interest.

**Required**

1. Prepare the journal entries necessary for Durham Corporation to record all the transactions that occurred during 1996 relating to the preceding information.
2. Prepare the long-term debt section of the Durham Corporation's balance sheet on December 31, 1996.

*P12-17*    *Appendix 1: Troubled Debt Restructuring (Debtor)*    The Oakwood Corporation is delinquent on a $2,400,000, 10% note to the Second National Bank that was due January 1, 1995. At that time Oakwood owed the principal amount plus $34,031.82 of accrued interest. Oakwood enters into a debt restructuring agreement with the bank on January 2, 1995.

**Required**

Prepare the journal entries necessary for Oakwood to record the debt restructuring agreement and all subsequent interest payments assuming:

1. The bank extends the repayment date to December 31, 1998, forgives the accrued interest owed, reduces the principal by $200,000, and reduces the interest rate to 8%.
2. The bank extends the repayment date to December 31, 1998, forgives the accrued interest owed, reduces the principal by $200,000, and reduces the interest rate to 1%.
3. The bank accepts 160,000 shares of Oakwood's $5 par value common stock that is currently selling for $14.50 per share in full settlement of the debt.
4. The bank accepts land with a fair market value of $2,300,000 in full settlement of the debt. The land is being carried on Oakwood's books at a cost of $2,200,000.

*P12-18*    *Appendix 1: Troubled Debt Restructuring (Creditor)*    Refer to the debt restructuring information listed in P12-17.

**Required**

For each of the alternatives listed in Requirements 1 through 4 of P12-17, prepare the journal entries necessary for Second National Bank to record the debt restructuring agreement and all subsequent interest receipts.

*P12-19*    *Comprehensive: Loan Impairment and Troubled Debt Restructuring*    The 10th National Bank has a $200,000 12% note receivable from the Priday Company that is due on December 31, 1998. On December 31, 1995, the company misses the interest payment due on that date. The bank expects that the company will also miss the next payment, but will pay the principal on the maturity date. On December 31, 1996, the company misses the interest payment due on that date. On December 31, 1997, the company pays half the interest payment due on that date and is not expected to pay the other half.

In early January 1998, the bank and the company agree to a loan restructuring because of the financial condition of the company. The bank forgives the unpaid interest, extends the loan to December 31, 2000, and reduces the interest rate to 6%. The market rate for the loan is estimated to be 10% at this time.

**Required**

1. Compute the value of the impaired loan on December 31, 1995.
2. Prepare the journal entries from 1995 to 2000 for the bank to record the above events.

P12-20 *Appendix 2: Serial Bond Amortization and Repayment Schedule*  On July 1, 1995 the Hubbard Corporation issued $600,000 of bonds with an 8% face rate of interest. The bonds were issued for $589,381.93, pay interest semiannually on June 30 and December 31, carry an effective yield rate of 9%, and are payable in three annual installments of $200,000 each, beginning June 30, 1996.

**Required**

1. Prepare a serial bond discount amortization schedule using the bonds outstanding method.
2. Prepare a serial bond discount amortization schedule using the effective interest method.
3. Prepare the journal entries necessary to record the payment of interest and the bond retirements on June 30, 1996, June 30, 1997, and June 30, 1998 using (a) the bonds outstanding method and (b) the effective interest method.

P12-21 *Appendix 2: Call Provision of Serial Bonds*  The Case Corporation issued $600,000 of 13% bonds on January 1, 1994, for $636,000. The bonds are payable in three annual $200,000 installments beginning December 31, 1995, pay interest semiannually on June 30 and December 31, and are callable at 106. On January 1, 1996, the bonds due December 31, 1997, are recalled at the call price. The corporation uses the bonds outstanding method of amortization.

**Required**

Prepare a serial bond premium amortization schedule and the journal entries to record the bond issue, payment of interest, and bond retirement on each of the following dates:

1. January 1, 1994
2. December 31, 1994
3. December 31, 1995
4. January 1, 1996
5. December 31, 1996

# 13

# INVESTMENTS

## Chapter Topics

*Debt and Equity Trading Securities*

*Debt and Equity Securities Available for Sale*

*Debt Securities Held to Maturity*

*Equity Method*

*Cash Surrender Value of Life Insurance*

*Sinking Funds*

Securities of other corporations are acquired for many reasons. One reason is to obtain additional income. In Chapter 5, it was emphasized that proper cash management requires the temporary investment of excess cash. Many companies have excess cash because the period of highest cash inflows does not coincide with the period of highest cash needs. Seasonal fluctuations in sales patterns frequently result in the period of greatest cash needs preceding the peak production or purchasing period when inventories are increasing. On the other hand, peak cash inflows follow the highest levels of sales activity. For efficient cash management, excess cash must be invested from the time of peak inflows until the next period of cash outflows. For example, a department store must purchase large amounts of inventory for its peak selling season around Christmas. Cash inflows from any credit sales do not occur until later when the receivables are collected. The company may have excess cash until purchases are made for the next Christmas season. Companies may also have excess cash available to invest for longer periods of time.

Thus companies may invest in common stock, preferred stock, or bonds of other corporations as well as municipal, state, or federal bonds. All these securities are classified as investments and each group of securities is often referred to as a *portfolio* of *marketable securities*. Another reason that securities of other corporations are acquired is to create long-term relationships with suppliers or to obtain significant influence or control over related companies. It is also common practice to include the cash surrender value of life insurance policies and sinking funds under the investments category on the balance sheet. The recording and reporting issues associated with these types of investments are discussed in this chapter.

## INVESTMENTS: CLASSIFICATION AND VALUATION

**FASB Statement No. 115** establishes generally accepted accounting principles for investments in debt securities and investments in equity securities that have readily determinable fair values.[1] A fair value is readily determinable if a sales price is currently available on a securities exchange registered with the SEC (e.g., the New York Stock Exchange) or in an over-the-counter market whose prices are publicly reported. A foreign market must be of a breadth and scope comparable to one of the U.S. markets. At acquisition, each investment in debt and equity "marketable" securities is classified into one of three categories. At each reporting date, the company must assess the appropriateness of the classifications. The three categories are:

1. *Trading Securities*. Investments in debt and equity securities that are purchased and held principally for the purpose of selling them in the near term are classified as trading securities. Trading generally reflects active and frequent buying and selling, and the securities are used to profit on short-term differences in price. For example, a stockbroker that holds an "inventory" of securities for sale to its customers classifies them as trading securities. A bank that holds securities for active and frequent buying and selling to generate profits on short-term differences in price also classifies them as trading securities.

2. *Securities Available for Sale*. Investments in securities available for sale are (a) debt securities that are not classified as held to maturity (see below), and (b) debt and equity securities that are not classified as trading securities.

3. *Debt Securities Held to Maturity*. Investments in debt securities held to maturity are debt securities for which the company has the "positive intent and ability to hold those securities to maturity."[2] Any sales of these securities prior to their maturity should be rare. A company does not classify a security as held to maturity if it has the intent to hold the security only for an indefinite period. So the classification is *not* appropriate if the security will be sold for such reasons as a change in market interest rates or a need for liquid funds. However, sales of these securities are considered to be at maturity if (a) the security is sold near enough to its maturity (or its call date if exercise of the call is probable) that interest rate risk is substantially eliminated (e.g., within three months of maturity or the call date), or (b) the sale occurs after the company has collected a substantial portion (e.g., 85%) of the principal. The sale of a debt security is *not* inconsistent with the original classification if there is a change of circumstances such as a deterioration in the issuer's creditworthiness or a major acquisition or disposal that requires a restructuring of securities to maintain its existing credit risk policy; or a change in statutory or regulatory requirements, such as a change in a tax exempt status; or other events that are isolated, nonrecurring, and unusual for the company.

Each category of securities is initially recorded at cost, and dividend revenue, interest revenue, and realized gains or losses on sales are included in the income statement.

---

1. "Accounting for Certain Investments in Debt and Equity Securities," *FASB Statement of Financial Accounting Standards No. 115* (Norwalk, Conn.: FASB, 1993), par. 3–13. This *Statement* applies, in the case of equity securities, to investments in equity securities for which the investor does *not* have "significant influence." *Significant influence* generally occurs when the ownership percentage is more than 20%, as discussed later in the chapter.
2. *Ibid.*, par. 7.

However, the subsequent valuation of the securities on the balance sheet and the reporting of unrealized holding gains and losses (the changes in the fair value of the securities during the period) vary as follows:

1. *Trading Securities.* Investments in trading securities are reported at their fair values on the balance sheet date, and unrealized holding gains and losses are included in income of the current period.

2. *Securities Available for Sale.* Investments in securities available for sale are reported at their fair values on the balance sheet date, and unrealized holding gains and losses are included as a separate component of stockholders' equity until realized. Therefore, the unrealized holding gains and losses are *not* included in income.

3. *Debt Securities Held to Maturity.* Investments in debt securities held to maturity are reported at their amortized cost[3] on the balance sheet date. Therefore, they are *not* valued at fair value.

Some definitions are important for the application of these principles for investments in debt and equity securities:

1. **A debt security represents a creditor relationship with another company.** Thus, *investments* in debt securities include U.S. treasury securities, municipal securities, corporate bonds, convertible debt, and commercial paper. Also included are investments in preferred stock that have a mandatory redemption feature or are redeemable at the option of the holder (discussed in Chapter 14). Trade accounts receivable are *not* investments in debt securities.

2. **An equity security represents an ownership interest in another company.** Thus, *investments* in equity securities include common stocks, preferred stocks, preferred stocks that are redeemable at the option of the company that issued the stock, stock warrants, stock rights, and put and call options. Investments in convertible debt or preferred stock with a mandatory redemption feature or that is redeemable at the option of the holder are *not* investments in equity securities.

3. **Fair value is the amount at which a security could be exchanged in a current transaction between willing parties.** Thus, the fair value is the number of units of the security times the quoted market price on a stock exchange. Note that there is no adjustment for any estimated change in the market price that might result from the attempted sale of a large number of a particular security.

There are two additional methods of accounting for investments. However, these methods are *not* alternatives but are applied depending on the level of ownership that the investor has in the investee. The **equity method** is used for investments in equity securities when the investor has *significant influence* over the investee. Significant influence generally occurs when the investor owns between 20% and 50% of the voting common stock of the investee, as discussed later in the chapter. **Consolidation**

---

3. "Amortized cost" is the term used by the FASB. It is the remaining amount (i.e., carrying value) of the cost (face value plus any premium or less any discount at acquisition) after any premium or discount has been amortized each period as interest revenue is recognized.

occurs when the investor *controls* the investee through an investment in equity securities. Control generally occurs when the investor owns over 50% of the voting common stock of the investee. The investor issues consolidated financial statements which are the combined financial statements of both companies. The preparation of consolidated financial statements is discussed in an advanced accounting book and is beyond the scope of this chapter, although the underlying concepts of consolidation accounting are discussed briefly in a later section.

The various categories and methods for recording and reporting investments in securities are summarized in Exhibit 13-1.

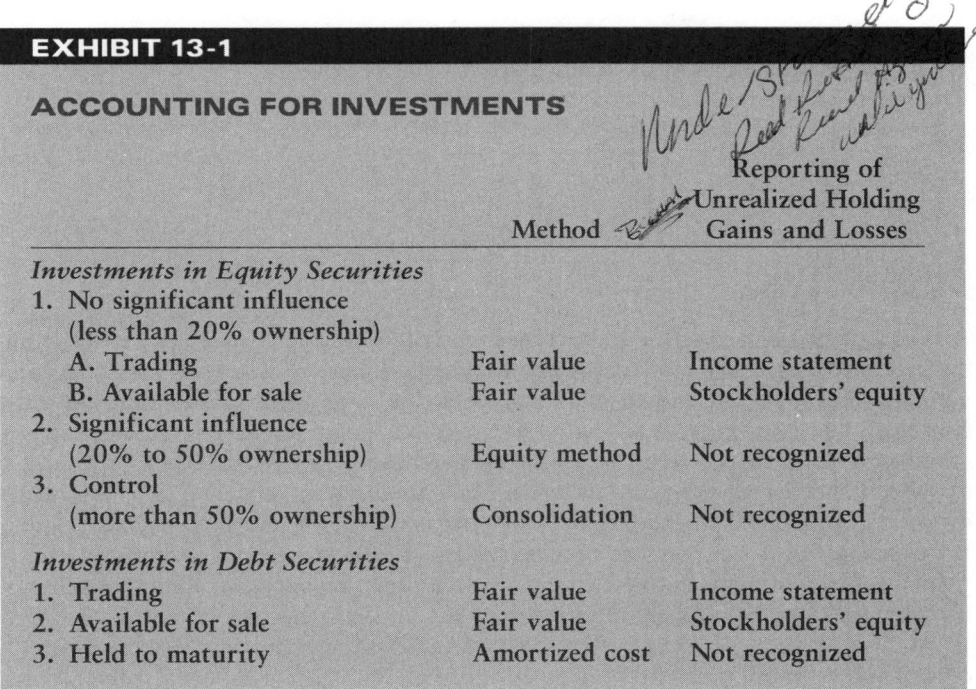

## EXHIBIT 13-1

### ACCOUNTING FOR INVESTMENTS

| | Method | Reporting of Unrealized Holding Gains and Losses |
|---|---|---|
| *Investments in Equity Securities* | | |
| 1. No significant influence (less than 20% ownership) | | |
|    A. Trading | Fair value | Income statement |
|    B. Available for sale | Fair value | Stockholders' equity |
| 2. Significant influence (20% to 50% ownership) | Equity method | Not recognized |
| 3. Control (more than 50% ownership) | Consolidation | Not recognized |
| *Investments in Debt Securities* | | |
| 1. Trading | Fair value | Income statement |
| 2. Available for sale | Fair value | Stockholders' equity |
| 3. Held to maturity | Amortized cost | Not recognized |

## INVESTMENTS IN DEBT AND EQUITY TRADING SECURITIES

The generally accepted accounting principles for investments in debt and equity securities classified as trading securities are: (1) the investment is initially recorded at cost, (2) it is subsequently reported at fair value, (3) unrealized holding gains and losses are included in income of the current period, and (4) interest and dividend revenue, as well as realized gains and losses on sales, are included in income of the current period. As noted earlier, investments in debt and equity trading securities are held primarily by such institutions as banks and stockbrokers. Since the accounting principles on trading securities tend to apply to "specialized industries," they are not illustrated here. However, they are the same as those discussed in the next section on securities available for sale *except* that (1) unrealized holding gains and losses on changes in value are included in the income statement for the current period and (2) any realized gains or losses on sales are computed by comparing the selling price to the *fair value* recorded on the most recent balance sheet date.

## INVESTMENTS IN DEBT AND EQUITY SECURITIES AVAILABLE FOR SALE

The accounting principles for investments in debt and equity securities classified as available for sale are: (1) the investment is initially recorded at cost, (2) it is subsequently reported at fair value, (3) unrealized holding gains and losses are reported as a separate component of stockholders' equity, and (4) interest and dividend revenue, as well as realized gains and losses on sales, are included in income for the current period. To illustrate each of these issues, assume that the Kent Company acquires the following securities on May 1, 1995 as an investment in securities available for sale:

A Company common stock       100 shares at $50 per share
B Company common stock       300 shares at $80 per share
C Company preferred stock     200 shares at $120 per share
D Company 10% bonds with a face value of $15,000 at par plus accrued interest.

Interest on the bonds is payable on May 31 and November 30 each year.

### Recording Initial Cost

**All investments in securities are recorded initially at the acquisition price of the securities plus any other costs necessary for the transaction.** Thus the cost of equity securities is simply the quoted market price at the time of the transaction plus any brokerage fees and taxes. A special issue arises with debt securities because any accrued interest must be separated from the purchase price. Recall from Chapter 12 that bondholders receive 6 months' interest on each interest payment date. Since interest accrues over time, whenever bonds are purchased between interest payment dates, the purchaser pays the previous bondholder for the interest earned to date.

The accrued interest on the D Company bonds purchased by the Kent Company is the interest from November 30, 1994 to May 1, 1995, or 5 months, and is $625 ($15,000 × 0.10 × 5/12). Therefore, the payment for the bonds includes the $15,000 cost of the bonds plus the $625 accrued interest. Thus, the total cost of the securities purchased by the Kent Company is $68,000 [(100 × $50) + (300 × $80) + (200 × $120) + $15,000].[4] The total payment is $68,625 ($68,000 cost + $625 accrued interest) and is recorded as follows:

| | | |
|---|---|---|
| Investment in Securities Available for Sale | 68,000 | |
| Interest Revenue | 625 | |
| Cash | | 68,625 |

Note that Kent debited Interest Revenue for the accrued interest. This procedure reduces the possibility of error in recording the next interest revenue transaction.[5]

---

4. Any costs necessary for the acquisition, such as brokerage fees and taxes, would be included in the cost of the securities. However, those amounts then would have to be allocated among each security purchased to determine its cost. This procedure is not discussed in this chapter because the amounts would not be material.

5. Alternatively, Kent Company could have debited Interest Receivable for $625. In this case, the Interest Receivable account is eliminated when the interest is received on May 31, 1995.

If securities are obtained in a nonmonetary transaction, the valuation is based on the fair value of the consideration given or the fair value of the stock acquired, whichever is more reliable.

## Recording Interest and Dividend Revenue

Interest revenue is recorded as it is earned during the period. On May 31, 1995, the semiannual interest on the D Company bonds is received and recorded as follows:

| | | |
|---|---|---|
| Cash | 750 | |
| Interest Revenue ($15,000 × 0.10 × 6/12) | | 750 |

Because the Kent Company initially debited interest revenue for 5 months of accrued interest on the date of acquisition, it credits interest revenue for the full 6 months of interest received. Therefore, by May 31 it has earned one month's interest and has that amount recorded in its accounting system. If the D Company bonds were purchased at a premium or discount, the interest revenue would be computed using the effective interest (or straight-line) method and a portion of the premium or discount would be amortized, as discussed later in the chapter.

On November 30, 1995, the next interest payment is received and recorded with the same journal entry. Finally, on December 31, 1995, one month's interest is accrued as follows: *only for December 31, 1995*

| | | |
|---|---|---|
| Interest Receivable | 125 | |
| Interest Revenue ($15,000 × 0.10 × 1/12) | | 125 |

For the year, the Kent Company has earned interest revenue for 8 months, or $1,000 ($750 − $625 + $750 + $125, or $15,000 × 0.10 × 8/12).

Dividend revenue is recorded as it is received. So if the Kent Company receives dividends during 1995 of $3,000 on its investments in the stock of A, B, and C companies, it records the following:

| | | |
|---|---|---|
| Cash | 3,000 | |
| Dividend Revenue | | 3,000 |

It is technically more correct to record the Dividend Revenue when the dividends are declared by the investee company because that is the date on which the investor has the right to receive them. However, the receipt of the dividends is usually used for convenience. If dividends have been declared at year-end but not received, then the investor should recognize Dividends Receivable and Dividend Revenue (1) so as to recognize the appropriate asset values and income and (2) because the dividends receivable affect the calculation of any unrealized holding gain or loss, as discussed later.

Note the different recognition of interest revenue and dividend revenue. Interest revenue accrues continuously over time, whereas dividend revenue is only recognized when dividends are received (or declared).

## Recognition of Unrealized Holding Gains and Losses

At the balance sheet date the securities available for sale are reported at fair value and the unrealized holding gains and losses are included directly in stockholders' equity. Also, the fair values are determined by the year-end market prices on a securities exchange. To illustrate, assume that the total fair value of the securities held by the Kent Company is $71,000 on December 31, 1995 as follows:

| Security | Cost | 12/31/95 Fair Value | Cumulative Change in Fair Value |
|---|---|---|---|
| 100 shares of A Company common stock | $ 5,000 | $ 6,000 | $1,000 |
| 300 shares of B Company common stock | 24,000 | 23,500 | (500) |
| 200 shares of C Company preferred stock | 24,000 | 26,000 | 2,000 |
| $15,000 D Company 10% bonds | 15,000 | 15,500 | 500 |
| Totals | $68,000 | $71,000 | $3,000 |

The fair value of the securities was determined based on the December 31, 1995 ending quoted market prices, with one adjustment. The quoted market price of the 10% D Company bonds was $15,625, but this included the $125 of accrued interest previously recorded by the Kent Company. To avoid double-counting, this interest is eliminated to determine the $15,500 ($15,625 − $125) fair value of the bonds. (If dividends had been declared but not paid on the equity securities, a similar adjustment would be made.) Furthermore, if the bonds had been purchased at a premium or discount, the amortized cost (i.e., carrying value) would have been used in the "cost" column.

The $3,000 increase in the value of the securities is recorded as follows:

| | | |
|---|---|---|
| **Allowance for Change in Value of Investment** | 3,000 | |
| Unrealized Increase/Decrease in Value of Securities Available for Sale | | 3,000 |

The Allowance account is an adjunct/contra account to the Investment in Securities Available for Sale account and the Unrealized Increase/Decrease account is an adjunct/contra stockholders' equity account. We are assuming that the Kent Company uses an Allowance account to record the changes in the fair values of the securities so that information about the original cost of each security is retained in the accounts to facilitate the computation of the realized gain or loss on the sale of a security, as discussed later.[6] Also, note that the fair value method is *not* allowed for federal income tax purposes so cost information also has to be retained for computing taxable income.[7]

The company reports the investment as an asset at the $71,000 fair value of the securities ($68,000 cost *plus* the $3,000 increase in fair value recorded in the Allowance account) and the $3,000 unrealized holding gain (recorded in the Unrealized Increase/Decrease account) in the unrealized capital section of stockholders' equity on its December 31, 1995 balance sheet (as discussed in Chapter 3). If some investments

---

6. Alternatively, a company may choose to record any changes in fair value directly in the Investment account. For example, companies investing in *trading securities* generally do *not* use an Allowance account because these securities "turn over" quickly. When this "direct" method is used for investments in securities available for sale, however, it is more difficult to determine information needed for transactions in subsequent periods and therefore is not used in this book for these securities.

7. Since unrealized holding gains and losses on investments in *trading securities* are included in income for the current period but are not taxable income, the difference is a temporary difference on which the company recognizes deferred income taxes, as discussed in Chapter 17.

are current and some noncurrent, the asset account is separated between the current and noncurrent components, as discussed later.

*FASB Statement No. 115* uses the phrase "unrealized holding gains and losses" to describe the change in the value of investment securities. This may be confusing since gains and losses are income statement items, whereas the unrealized holding gains and losses on investments in securities available for sale are included in stock-holders' equity (and *not* in the income statement). We use the term "unrealized holding gains and losses" in the text but prefer a more appropriate title for the account, Unrealized Increase/Decrease in Value of Securities Available for Sale, in recording journal entries and reporting on the balance sheet. Note that this account is a permanent account whose value carries over to the next period.[8] A credit balance (unrealized holding gain) in the account is reported as an increase in stockholders' equity, whereas a debit balance (unrealized holding loss) is reported as a decrease.

Any subsequent increases or decreases in fair value are recognized in a similar way. Suppose that on December 31, 1996, the fair value of the securities is $66,000 as follows:

| Security | Cost | 12/31/96 Fair Value | Cumulative Change in Fair Value |
|---|---|---|---|
| 100 shares of A Company common stock | $ 5,000 | $ 6,100 | $ 1,100 |
| 300 shares of B Company common stock | 24,000 | 22,700 | (1,300) |
| 200 shares of C Company preferred stock | 24,000 | 23,200 | (800) |
| $15,000 D Company 10% bonds | 15,000 | 14,000 | (1,000) |
| Totals | $68,000 | $66,000 | $(2,000) |

Once the Allowance account has been established, the amount of the adjustment of the Unrealized Increase/Decrease in Value in a subsequent period is determined by comparing the required carrying value of the Allowance account with the previous balance in the account. At December 31, 1996, the required carrying value of the Allowance account is a $2,000 *credit* balance, but the previous balance at December 31, 1995 was a $3,000 *debit* balance. Therefore, the Allowance account is credited for $5,000 to record the decline in value (unrealized holding loss) as follows:

| | | |
|---|---|---|
| **Unrealized Increase/Decrease in Value of** | | |
| **Securities Available for Sale** | 5,000 | |
| **Allowance for Change in Value of Investment** | | 5,000 |

On its December 31, 1996 balance sheet, the Kent Company reports the investment as an asset at the $66,000 fair value of the securities ($68,000 cost − $2,000 allowance) and the $2,000 *cumulative* unrealized decrease in value ($3,000 unrealized holding gain at 12/31/95 − $5,000 unrealized holding loss at 12/31/96) as a reduction in stockholders' equity.[9]

---

8. The term "unrealized holding gains and losses" for investments in trading securities is appropriate because the amounts are included in income for the current period. Also the account is a temporary account which is closed to Income Summary each year.

9. A company preparing interim (quarterly) financial statements would use the same accounting procedures, applied each quarter.

### Realized Gains and Losses on Sales of Securities Available for Sale

Realized gains and losses on sales of securities are reported in the income statement. They are measured as the difference between the selling price and the *cost* (of an equity security) or the *amortized cost* (of a debt security). Furthermore, since the security is no longer in the portfolio of securities available for sale, the cumulative balance in the allowance account and the cumulative unrealized increase/decrease in the value of the security reported at the previous balance sheet date must be "reversed" out of the accounts.

To illustrate, suppose that in 1997 the Kent Company sold the 100 shares of A Company common stock for $6,000. The cost of the securities was $5,000 and the fair value at the previous balance sheet was $6,100 as follows:

| Security | Cost | 12/31/96 Fair Value | Cumulative Change in Fair Value |
|---|---|---|---|
| 100 shares of A Company common stock | $5,000 | $6,100 | $1,100 |

The company recognizes a gain of $1,000 ($6,000 selling price − $5,000 cost) and eliminates the $1,100 cumulative unrealized increase (and allowance) on the A company stock. The company records the sale as follows:

| | | |
|---|---|---|
| Cash | 6,000 | |
| Unrealized Increase/Decrease in Value of | | |
| Securities Available for Sale | 1,100 | |
| Investment in Securities Available for Sale | | 5,000 |
| Allowance for Change in Value of Investment | | 1,100 |
| Gain on Sale of Securities Available for Sale | | 1,000 |

*[handwritten margin notes: "Cost Recorded is Recorded", "Adjusted", "Closed out", "Into Income Statement"]*

To illustrate a loss on a sale, suppose that in 1997 the Kent Company also sold the 300 shares of B Company common stock for $22,000. The cost of the securities was $24,000 and the fair value at the previous balance sheet was $22,700 as follows:

| Security | Cost | 12/31/96 Fair Value | Cumulative Change in Fair Value |
|---|---|---|---|
| 300 shares of B Company common stock | $24,000 | $22,700 | $(1,300) |

In this case, the company recognizes a loss of $2,000 ($22,000 selling price − $24,000 cost) and eliminates the $1,300 cumulative unrealized decrease (and allowance) on the B company stock. The company records the sale as follows:

| | | |
|---|---|---|
| Cash | 22,000 | |
| Allowance for Change in Value of Investment | 1,300 | |
| Loss on Sale of Securities Available for Sale | 2,000 | |
| Unrealized Increase/Decrease in Value of | | |
| Securities Available for Sale | | 1,300 |
| Investment in Securities Available for Sale | | 24,000 |

*[handwritten margin note: "Securities held for Resale hit the Income Statement Only After"]*

In each case, the gain or loss is reported in the income statement because it is realized. As a result of these two sales, a net debit adjustment of $200 ($1,300 − $1,100) is made to the Allowance account and a net credit adjustment of $200 is made to the Unrealized Increase/Decrease account. However, the balances in the accounts will be adjusted at the end of the year when the remaining securities are valued at fair value. Only the ending balances are reported on the balance sheet (although the disclosures are more detailed, as discussed later).

## INVESTMENTS IN DEBT SECURITIES HELD TO MATURITY

The generally accepted accounting principles for investments in debt securities held to maturity are: (1) the investment is initially recorded at cost, (2) it is subsequently reported at amortized cost, (3) unrealized holding gains and losses are not recorded, and (4) interest revenue and realized gains and losses on sales (if any) are all included in income. In Chapter 12, it was pointed out that bonds carrying a stated interest rate above the prevailing yield for securities with a similar amount of risk will sell at a premium. This premium lowers the stated interest rate to the market (yield) rate. Bonds carrying a stated interest below the prevailing market rate for securities with a similar amount of risk will sell at a discount. The discount effectively increases the stated interest rate to the market rate. In contrast to accounting for premiums and discounts by debtor companies, investor companies generally have *not* used a separate valuation account to account for the premiums and discounts on investments in bonds. Instead, the acquisition price is recorded in the investment account, which is directly adjusted for any premium and discount amortization even though *APB Opinion No. 21* recommended separate disclosure. The effect of not separately disclosing premiums or discounts is to report the Investment in Bonds Held to Maturity account directly at its carrying value (amortized cost) on each balance sheet date.

*The theoretical and practical issues related to the recording and reporting of bonds by the debtor are discussed in Chapter 12.*

### Recording Initial Cost

Investments in debt securities held to maturity are recorded in the same way as discussed earlier. To illustrate, assume that 9% bonds with a face value of $100,000 are purchased on August 1, 1995 at 99 plus accrued interest. Interest on these bonds is paid semiannually on May 31 and November 30. The journal entry on August 1, 1995 to record this acquisition is:

| | | |
|---|---|---|
| Investment in Debt Securities Held to Maturity ($100,000 × 0.99) | 99,000 | |
| Interest Revenue ($100,000 × 0.09 × 2/12) | 1,500 | |
| Cash | | 100,500 |

Note that the Investment account is debited for $99,000. Therefore the $1,000 discount is included directly in the Investment account and is amortized as an adjustment to interest revenue, as discussed later. Note also that, as illustrated for investments in securities available for sale, the Interest Revenue account is debited for the two months of accrued interest. The Interest Revenue account will be credited for $4,500 when the November 30, 1995 semiannual interest is received, resulting in the recognition of $3,000 interest earned for the period August 1 through November 30, 1995.

## Recognition and Amortization of Bond Premiums and Discounts

Investments in debt securities held to maturity that are purchased at a premium or discount result in an effective interest rate that is different than the stated rate. Consequently, for these investments in bonds, **the amount of interest revenue recognized each accounting period is based on the effective interest rate (yield) at the time of acquisition.** Therefore, **any premium or discount is amortized over the remaining life of the bonds in order to assign the proper amount of interest revenue to each accounting period.** The effective interest and straight-line methods are the alternative procedures that are used to record interest revenue and account for premiums and discounts. However, *APB Opinion No. 21* requires use of the effective interest method, unless the use of the straight-line method does not result in a material difference in the amount of interest revenue recognized in any year. Premium amortizations result in an effective interest rate lower than the stated rate, whereas discount amortizations result in an effective interest rate higher than the stated rate.

*The effective interest and straight-line methods are explained in Chapter 12.*

### Accounting for Premiums

Assume that the Colburn Company acquires an investment in bonds that will be held to maturity with a face value of $100,000 for $102,458.71 on January 1, 1995. These bonds carry a stated interest rate of 13% that is payable semiannually on June 30 and December 31, mature on December 31, 1997, and yield an effective interest rate of 12%. The journal entry on January 1, 1995 to record the acquisition is as follows:

| | | |
|---|---|---|
| Investment in Debt Securities Held to Maturity | 102,458.71 | |
| Cash | | 102,458.71 |

Exhibits 13-2 and 13-3 show the schedules for computing interest revenue, the premium amortization, and the carrying value under the straight-line and effective interest methods for these bonds. The preparation of similar schedules for bonds payable was explained in Chapter 12, so discussion here is limited. The first interest receipt on June 30, 1995 using the effective interest method for the bonds purchased at a premium is recorded as follows:

| | | |
|---|---|---|
| Cash | 6,500.00 | |
| Investment in Debt Securities Held to Maturity | | 352.48 |
| Interest Revenue | | 6,147.52 |

Note that the premium amortization is credited directly to the Investment account. If the straight-line method is used, a similar entry is made using the amounts from Exhibit 13-2.

### Accounting for Discounts

Now, assume that the bonds were acquired by Colburn at a discount for $97,616.71. This discount indicates that the rate of interest desired by investors is greater than the stated rate of 13%. These bonds yield an effective interest rate of 14%. Exhibits 13-4 and 13-5 illustrate the schedules for computing interest revenue, the discount amortization, and the carrying value under the straight-line and effective interest methods for these bonds. The journal entry on January 1, 1995 to record the acquisition is as follows:

| | | |
|---|---|---|
| Investment in Debt Securities Held to Maturity | 97,616.71 | |
| Cash | | 97,616.71 |

---

**EXHIBIT 13-2**

**COLBURN COMPANY**

Bond Investment Interest Revenue and Premium Amortization Schedule
*Straight-Line Method*

| Date | Cash Debit[a] | Investment in Debt Securities Credit[b] | Interest Revenue Credit[c] | Carrying Value of Investment in Debt Securities[d] |
|---|---|---|---|---|
| 1/1/95 | | | | $102,458.71 |
| 6/30/95 | $6,500.00 | $409.79 | $6,090.21 | 102,048.92 |
| 12/31/95 | 6,500.00 | 409.79 | 6,090.21 | 101,639.13 |
| 6/30/96 | 6,500.00 | 409.79 | 6,090.21 | 101,229.34 |
| 12/31/96 | 6,500.00 | 409.79 | 6,090.21 | 100,819.55 |
| 6/30/97 | 6,500.00 | 409.79 | 6,090.21 | 100,409.76 |
| 12/31/97 | 6,500.00 | 409.76[e] | 6,090.24 | 100,000.00 |

a. $100,000 (face value) × 0.13 (stated rate of interest) × 1/2 (year)
b. ($102,458.71 − $100,000) = $2,458.71 ÷ 6 (remaining semiannual periods of bond life)
c. $6,500 − $409.79
d. Previous investment carrying value − amount from footnote *b*
e. Difference due to $0.03 rounding error

---

**EXHIBIT 13-3**

**COLBURN COMPANY**

Bond Investment Interest Revenue and Premium Amortization Schedule
*Effective Interest Method*

| Date | Cash Debit[a] | Interest Revenue Credit[b] | Investment in Debt Securities Credit[c] | Carrying Value of Investment in Debt Securities[d] |
|---|---|---|---|---|
| 1/1/95 | | | | $102,458.71 |
| 6/30/95 | $6,500.00 | $6,147.52 | $352.48 | 102,106.23 |
| 12/31/95 | 6,500.00 | 6,126.37 | 373.63 | 101,732.60 |
| 6/30/96 | 6,500.00 | 6,103.96 | 396.04 | 101,336.56 |
| 12/31/96 | 6,500.00 | 6,080.19 | 419.81 | 100,916.75 |
| 6/30/97 | 6,500.00 | 6,055.01 | 444.99 | 100,471.76 |
| 12/31/97 | 6,500.00 | 6,028.24[e] | 471.76 | 100,000.00 |

a. $100,000 (face value) × 0.13 (stated rate of interest) × 1/2 (year)
b. Previous investment carrying value × 0.12 (effective interest rate) × 1/2 (year)
c. Amount from footnote *a* − amount from footnote *b*
d. Previous investment carrying value − amount from footnote *c*
e. Difference due to $0.07 rounding error

**EXHIBIT 13-4**

## COLBURN COMPANY

Bond Investment Interest Revenue and Discount Amortization Schedule
*Straight-Line Method*

| Date | Cash Debit[a] | Investment in Debt Securities Debit[b] | Interest Revenue Credit[c] | Carrying Value of Investment in Debt Securities[d] |
|------|------|------|------|------|
| 1/1/95 | | | | $ 97,616.71 |
| 6/30/95 | $6,500.00 | $397.22 | $6,897.22 | 98,013.93 |
| 12/31/95 | 6,500.00 | 397.22 | 6,897.22 | 98,411.15 |
| 6/30/96 | 6,500.00 | 397.22 | 6,897.22 | 98,808.37 |
| 12/31/96 | 6,500.00 | 397.22 | 6,897.22 | 99,205.59 |
| 6/30/97 | 6,500.00 | 397.22 | 6,897.22 | 99,602.81 |
| 12/31/97 | 6,500.00 | 397.19[e] | 6,897.19 | 100,000.00 |

a. $100,000 (face value) $\times$ 0.13 (stated rate of interest) $\times$ 1/2 (year)
b. ($100,000 $-$ $97,616.71) = $2,383.29 $\div$ 6 (remaining semiannual periods of bond life)
c. $6,500 + $397.22
d. Previous investment carrying value + amount from footnote *b*
e. Difference due to $0.03 rounding error

**EXHIBIT 13-5**

## COLBURN COMPANY

Bond Investment Interest Revenue and Discount Amortization Schedule
*Effective Interest Method*

| Date | Cash Debit[a] | Interest Revenue Credit[b] | Investment in Debt Securities Debit[c] | Carrying Value of Investment in Debt Securities[d] |
|------|------|------|------|------|
| 1/1/95 | | | | $ 97,616.71 |
| 6/30/95 | $6,500.00 | $6,833.17 | $333.17 | 97,949.88 |
| 12/31/95 | 6,500.00 | 6,856.49 | 356.49 | 98,306.37 |
| 6/30/96 | 6,500.00 | 6,881.45 | 381.45 | 98,687.82 |
| 12/31/96 | 6,500.00 | 6,908.15 | 408.15 | 99,095.97 |
| 6/30/97 | 6,500.00 | 6,936.72 | 436.72 | 99,532.69 |
| 12/31/97 | 6,500.00 | 6,967.31[e] | 467.31 | 100,000.00 |

a. $100,000 (face value) $\times$ 0.13 (stated rate of interest) $\times$ 1/2 (year)
b. Previous investment carrying value $\times$ 0.14 (effective interest rate) $\times$ 1/2 (year)
c. Amount from footnote *b* $-$ amount from footnote *a*
d. Previous investment carrying value + amount from footnote *c*
e. Difference due to $0.02 rounding error

The first interest receipt on June 30, 1995 using the effective interest method for the bonds purchased at a discount is recorded as follows:

| | | |
|---|---|---|
| **Cash** | 6,500.00 | |
| **Investment in Debt Securities Held to Maturity** | 333.17 | |
| **Interest Revenue** | | 6,833.17 |

Note that the discount amortization is debited directly to the Investment account. If the straight-line method is used, a similar entry is made using the amounts from Exhibit 13-4.

### Amortization for Bonds Acquired Between Interest Dates

As we illustrated earlier, bonds held to maturity may be acquired between interest dates. When these bonds are purchased at a premium or discount, the premium or discount is amortized over the remaining life of the bonds. To illustrate, assume that 13% bonds with a face value of $200,000 are purchased by the Tallen Company for $204,575.07 on April 3, 1995. Interest on these bonds is payable June 30 and December 31, and the bonds mature December 31, 1997 (33 months after the date of purchase). The journal entry on April 3, 1995 to record the acquisition is as follows:

| | | |
|---|---|---|
| **Investment in Debt Securities Held to Maturity** | 204,575.07 | |
| **Interest Revenue ($200,000 × 0.13 × 3/12)** | 6,500.00 | |
| **Cash** | | 211,075.07 |

The $4,575.07 premium ($204,575.07 − $200,000) is amortized over the remaining 33-month life of the bond issue. If straight-line amortization is used, $138.64 ($4,575.07 ÷ 33) of the premium is amortized to reduce interest revenue for each month the bonds are held.

When the effective interest method is used, the actual yield[10] is computed and then used to amortize the premium over the length of time the investment is to be held. The purchase of a $200,000 investment due in 33 months with a stated 13% interest rate, payable semiannually, for $204,575.07 results in an effective interest rate of 12%. Use of the effective interest method of amortization to record the first two interest receipts is shown here:

**June 30, 1995**

| | | |
|---|---|---|
| **Cash** | 13,000.00 | |
| **Interest Revenue** [($204,575.07 × 0.12 × 1/4) + $6,500*] | | 12,637.25 |
| **Investment in Debt Securities Held to Maturity ($13,000 − $12,637.25)** | | 362.75 |

* Amount debited to interest revenue on the date the bonds were acquired.

**December 31, 1995**

| | | |
|---|---|---|
| **Cash** | 13,000.00 | |
| **Interest Revenue** [($204,575.07 − $362.75) × 0.12 × 1/2] | | 12,252.74 |
| **Investment in Debt Securities Held to Maturity ($13,000 − $12,252.74)** | | 747.26 |

10. See Chapter 12 for an illustration of the calculation of yields.

In calculating the premium amortization for the first interest payment, note that the actual amount of interest revenue is only $6,137.25 ($204,575.07 × 0.12 × 1/4)[11] even though the interest revenue account was credited for $12,637.25. The additional $6,500 credit reflects the interest payment to the former owner. Subsequently, the amount of interest revenue is determined by multiplying the carrying value of the investment (acquisition price less amortized premium) by the 6% semiannual yield (0.12 × 1/2). The difference between the amount of cash received and the amount of interest revenue is recorded as premium amortization in each successive period.

## Sale of Investment in Bonds Before Maturity

A sale before the maturity date of an investment in bonds being held to maturity should be rare because the sale may violate the original intent behind the acquisition and the valuation procedures underlying that intent. Alternatively, as discussed earlier in the chapter, certain changes in circumstances are *not* inconsistent with the original intent. When such a sale occurs, it is necessary to record any gain or loss from the transaction. Also, the Investment account is eliminated, and any interest earned since the last interest date is collected from the purchaser.

Before computing the gain or loss on the sale of an investment, any premium or discount on the bonds is amortized from the last interest date to the sale date. This procedure is necessary to ensure that the correct amount of interest revenue has been recorded, and to determine the carrying value of the investment on the date of the sale. The carrying value of the bonds is then compared with the sales price (*excluding* any accrued interest) to determine the gain or loss. To illustrate, assume that the $100,000 of 13% bonds purchased for $97,616.71 discussed earlier were sold on March 31, 1996 for $102,000 plus accrued interest. The following journal entries are made on March 31, 1996 (assuming the bond discount is being amortized by the straight-line method illustrated in Exhibit 13-4):

| | | |
|---|---|---|
| **Investment in Debt Securities Held to Maturity** | | |
| [($2,383.29 ÷ 6) × 1/2] | 198.61 | |
| **Interest Revenue** | | 198.61 |
| | | |
| Cash ($102,000 + $3,250) | 105,250.00 | |
| Interest Revenue ($100,000 × 0.13 × 1/4) | | 3,250.00 |
| **Investment in Debt Securities Held to** | | |
| Maturity ($98,411.15 from Exhibit 13-4 | | |
| + $198.61) | | 98,609.76 |
| **Gain on Sale of Debt Securities** | | 3,390.24 |

The first journal entry brings the investment carrying value up to date. In the second journal entry, the debit to Cash records the sales price plus the $3,250 interest earned in the 3 months since the last interest payment date, and the credit to the Investment account eliminates the current carrying value of the investment on the sale date. The gain is computed by comparing the $98,609.76 current carrying value of the Investment account on the sale date with the $102,000 selling price of the investment. This gain is reported as ordinary income, unless considered unusual and infrequent, in which case it is reported as an extraordinary item.

---

11. This calculation assumes that the purchase price yields 12% interest for 33 months. Normally, it is necessary to find the present value of the bonds at the last interest payment date (December 31, 1994 in this case), subtract the present value of the bonds on the next interest payment date (June 30, 1995), and apply the straight-line method to amortize the premium for the interim period. See Chapter 12 (p. 536) for an illustration of this procedure.

## TRANSFERS AND IMPAIRMENTS

Two additional issues arise in accounting for investments. The first involves transfers between categories, while the second involves impairments of investments.

### Transfers of Investments Between Categories

The transfer of a security between categories is accounted for at the fair value at the time of the transfer. However, transfers into or out of the trading category should be rare, as should transfers *from* the held to maturity category. In the journal entry to record the transfer, the fair value is used as the "new" investment carrying value, and the "old" investment carrying value is eliminated. However, the accounting for any related unrealized gain or loss varies depending on the type of transfer as follows:

1. A transfer *from the trading* category. No accounting for the unrealized holding gain or loss is necessary because it has already been recognized in income.

2. A transfer *into the trading* category. The previous unrealized holding gain or loss is eliminated and a gain or loss is included in income.

3. A transfer *into the available for sale* category *from the held to maturity* category. An unrealized holding gain or loss is established and included in stockholders' equity.

4. A transfer of a debt security *into the held to maturity* category *from the available for sale* category. The unrealized holding gain or loss on the security available for sale is eliminated and an unrealized holding gain or loss on the security held to maturity is created for the same amount and included in stockholders' equity. The amount is amortized over the remaining life of the security as an adjustment of interest revenue by computing a new yield to maturity for that security.

We will use three examples to illustrate transfers (a transfer *from* the trading category is not discussed). To illustrate a transfer *into* the trading category *from* the available for sale category, assume the same facts as earlier for the Kent Company at December 31, 1996. Assume also that in 1997 the Company A securities are transferred into the trading category when their fair value is $6,300. Because an Allowance account generally is not used for investments in trading securities, the asset account is debited directly for the fair value of the securities. Since the securities available for sale had a cost of $5,000, a $1,300 realized holding gain is recorded. Furthermore, the Unrealized Increase/Decrease account and the Allowance account related to the securities available for sale are debited and credited for $1,100, respectively, to eliminate the December 31, 1996 adjustment ($6,100 fair value − $5,000 cost) recorded on that date. The transfer is recorded as follows:

| | | |
|---|---|---|
| Investment in Trading Securities | 6,300 | |
| Unrealized Increase/Decrease in Value of Securities Available for Sale | 1,100 | |
|     Investment in Securities Available for Sale | | 5,000 |
|     Allowance for Change in Value of Investment | | 1,100 |
|     Gain on Transfer of Securities | | 1,300 |

The gain is included in the income statement for 1997.

To illustrate the transfer *into* the available for sale category *from* the held to maturity category, assume that the Devon Company has bonds included in the category of investments held to maturity. The bonds have a face value of $10,000 and were purchased at par. When the fair value of the bonds is $9,500, the company transfers the bond into the available for sale category. Since an Investment in Securities Available for Sale is recorded at cost and an Allowance account is used to adjust the carrying value to fair value (with a corresponding adjustment to the Unrealized Increase/Decrease account), the company records the transfer as follows:

| | | |
|---|---|---|
| Investment in Securities Available for Sale | 10,000 | |
| Unrealized Increase/Decrease in Value of | | |
|     Securities Available for Sale | 500 | |
|         Allowance for Change in Value of Investment | | 500 |
|         Investment in Debt Securities Held to Maturity | | 10,000 |

If the bonds being held to maturity had been purchased at a premium or discount, the investment in securities available for sale would be recorded at amortized cost, and the adjustment to the Allowance and Unrealized Increase/Decrease accounts would be computed by comparing the fair value to the amortized cost.

To illustrate the transfer *into* the held to maturity category *from* the available for sale category, assume the same facts for the Devon Company except that the bonds are currently classified as available for sale and are transferred into the held to maturity category. Assume further that the bonds available for sale had a fair value of $9,700 on the previous balance sheet date. In this case, the investment in debt securities is recorded at the current fair value of $9,500, and the previous $300 ($9,700 − $10,000) amounts in the Allowance and Unrealized Increase/Decrease accounts are eliminated. A new stockholders' equity account, Unrealized Increase/Decrease in Value of Debt Securities Held to Maturity is created for the $500 difference between the current fair value and the original cost. The transfer is recorded as follows:

| | | |
|---|---|---|
| Investment in Debt Securities Held to Maturity | 9,500 | |
| Allowance for Change in Value of Investment | 300 | |
| Unrealized Increase/Decrease from Transfer | | |
|     of Securities | 500 | |
|         Investment in Securities Available for Sale | | 10,000 |
|         Unrealized Increase/Decrease in Value of | | |
|         Securities Available for Sale | | 300 |

In subsequent periods, the $500 discount in the Investment account ($10,000 face value − $9,500 carrying value) is amortized using the effective interest method over the remaining life of the bonds. This requires the computation of a new effective interest rate. The new rate is computed by equating, on a present value basis, the future cash flows and the new "carrying value."[12] Interest revenue is then computed by multiplying the carrying value each period by the effective interest rate. This procedure was discussed in Chapter 12 in the section on troubled debt restructuring. The $500 unrealized amount is also amortized as an adjustment to interest revenue using the effective interest method over the remaining life of the debt security (bonds), and this amount offsets the amortization of the discount.

---

12. This procedure is used for investments in marketable debt securities. Accounting for the impairment of a loan (which does not have a fair value available on a stock exchange) was discussed in Chapter 12.

## Impairments

There may be an "other than temporary" decline below its amortized cost of an investment in a debt security classified as available for sale or held to maturity. Such factors as the reason for the decline, the duration of the decline, the future potential of the investee, and the current state of the economy are used to determine whether a particular decrease in the value of a security should be considered other than temporary. Impairment occurs when it is probable that the company will be unable to collect all the amounts due. The amortized cost of the security is written down to the fair value and the amount of the writedown is included in income as a realized loss. The fair value becomes the new "cost" and is not changed for subsequent recoveries in fair value, although increases and decreases in fair value of securities available for sale are included in stockholders' equity as discussed earlier.

To illustrate this situation, suppose that the Tracy Company has a bond investment categorized as held to maturity which has a carrying value (amortized cost) of $21,500, and has a fair value of $6,500. If the decline in value is considered to be other than temporary, the company records the decline of $15,000 ($21,500 − $6,500) as follows:

| | | |
|---|---|---|
| Realized Loss on Decline in Value | 15,000 | |
| Investment in Debt Securities Held to Maturity | | 15,000 |

The $6,500 becomes the new "cost" of the security. Interest revenue is computed using the effective interest method based on the new effective interest rate computed as discussed earlier for bonds transferred into the held to maturity category.

A similar procedure is followed for an investment in a security classified as available for sale which experiences a decline in value that is considered to be other than temporary. Since the security is already being reported at fair value by use of an allowance account, a new cost basis is established at the fair value. The allowance and unrealized increase/decrease accounts are eliminated, and the loss from the writedown is recorded as a realized loss. Subsequent changes in value (that are considered to be temporary) are included as unrealized holding gains and losses in the separate component of stockholders' equity. The realized gain or loss on the eventual sale of the security is the difference between the selling price and the new "cost."

## DISCLOSURES

The following disclosures for investments in securities are required by *FASB Statement No. 115:*

1. *Trading securities.* Companies must disclose the change in the net unrealized holding gain or loss that is included in each income statement.

2. *Securities available for sale.* For each balance sheet date, companies must disclose the aggregate fair value, gross unrealized holding gains and gross unrealized holding losses, and (amortized) cost by major security types. Also the contractual maturities of debt securities must be disclosed. For each income statement period, companies must disclose (a) the proceeds from sales and the gross realized gains and gross realized losses on those sales, (b) the basis on which cost was determined (e.g., the average cost method), (c) the gross gains and gross losses included in income from transfers of securities from this category into the trading category, and (d) the change in the net unrealized holding gain or loss included as a separate component of stockholders' equity.

*bonds*

3. *Debt securities held to maturity*. For each balance sheet date, companies must disclose the aggregate fair value, gross unrealized holding gains, gross unrealized holding losses, and amortized cost by major security types. Also the contractual maturities of these securities must be disclosed. For any sales or transfers from this category, the disclosures must include the amortized cost, the related realized or unrealized gain or loss, and the circumstances leading to the decision to sell or transfer the security.

Financial institutions must make additional disclosures which are not discussed here.

## Financial Statement Classification

Investments in trading securities are always classified as current assets (if the company presents a classified balance sheet). Investments in securities available for sale are classified as current or noncurrent assets depending on whether or not they will be sold within one year or the operating cycle, whichever is longer.[13] For example, if the Kent Company investments in A and B are current and in C and D are noncurrent at December 31, 1995, the $71,000 fair value would be reported as follows:

| Assets | |
|---|---:|
| *Current assets* | |
| Temporary investment in securities available for sale (at cost) | $29,000 |
| Plus: Allowance for change in value of investment | 500 |
| Temporary investment in securities available for sale (at fair value) | $29,500 |
| | |
| *Noncurrent assets* | |
| Investment in securities available for sale (at cost) | $39,000 |
| Plus: Allowance for change in value of investment | 2,500 |
| Investment in securities available for sale (at fair value) | $41,500 |

Investments in debt securities held to maturity are classified as noncurrent assets unless they mature within the next year.

Cash flows from purchases, sales, and maturities of securities available for sale and held to maturity are classified as cash flows from investing activities. The gross amounts of inflows and outflows are reported for each category. Cash flows from purchases, sales, and maturities of trading securities are classified as cash flows from operating activities.

## EFFECTIVE DATE AND TRANSITION

*FASB Statement No. 115* is effective for fiscal years beginning after December 15, 1993. The effect of applying the *Statement* is reported as the effect of a change in accounting principle, except that the unrealized holding gain or loss (net of tax effects) for securities available for sale at the beginning of the year of adoption of the *Statement* is an adjustment to the Unrealized Increase/Decrease account.

---

13. *FASB Statement No. 115, op. cit.,* par. 17.

# FASB STATEMENT NO. 115: AN EVALUATION

Prior to the issuance of *FASB Statement No. 115,* investments in marketable equity securities were accounted for by the lower of cost or market (LCM) method. There were no defined general principles for investments in debt securities. Most companies used the cost method but financial institutions followed regulatory accounting principles which did require some securities to be accounted for by the fair value method.

The use of the LCM method was widely criticized for two primary reasons. First, it was argued that it was not a *relevant* value because it did not reflect the *liquidity* of the securities when the fair value exceeded the cost. In that situation, more funds could be obtained through a sale in the current market than was indicated by the balance sheet. Secondly, the method allowed companies to engage in what was often referred to as "gains trading." Gains trading meant that companies would sell those securities that had a fair value above cost so that the realized gain on the sale would be included in income.

The major controversies involved in the new principles focus on four issues: (1) fair value is required in the balance sheet for trading securities and securities available for sale, whereas amortized cost is required for securities held to maturity; (2) fair value is *not* required for certain liabilities; (3) unrealized holding gains and losses are reported in the income statement for trading securities but directly in stockholders' equity for securities available for sale; and (4) the classification of securities is based on management intent. The *Statement* was adopted by a 5-to-2 majority and the dissenters raised some of the issues. They argued that all three categories should be reported at fair value with all unrealized holding gains and losses included in income.

## Fair Value is Required for Certain Investments

It may be argued that the fair value of trading securities and securities available for sale is more *relevant* than the LCM value. In particular, reporting the fair value may assist users in evaluating the performance of a company's investment strategies and increase the *comparability* of balance sheets. Fair value is the market's estimate of the present value of the net future cash flows of those securities discounted to reflect both the current interest rate and the market's estimate of the *risk* associated with those cash flows.

The fair value of investments also may provide a better indication of the *financial flexibility,* or *solvency,* of companies, particularly financial institutions for which a large portion of their assets are such securities. In a *liquidity* shortage, the fair value of investments is the amount available to cover a company's obligations.

It also may be argued that the fair value of debt securities held to maturity is *not* relevant. Amortized cost may provide relevant information because it focuses on the decision to acquire the asset, the earnings effects of that decision that will be realized over time, and the ultimate future recoverable value of the asset. Fair value ignores those concepts and focuses instead on the effects of transactions and events that do not directly involve the company. If a debt security is held to maturity, the maturity value will be realized and any interim unrealized holding gains and losses will reverse. In summary, if a company has no intent to sell a security and has no need to, then the fair value may *not* be relevant because that cash flow will not occur. However, the two dissenters argued that fair value would be preferable for these securities also.

The FASB made the held-to-maturity category restrictive so that the use of the amortized cost method must be justified by management for each investment in a debt security. At each acquisition, the company must establish the positive intent and ability to hold the security to maturity, which is *not* the same as the absence of an intent to sell. Thus the amortized cost method is appropriate if the security is actually held to maturity, but is not appropriate if management merely has no intent to sell it. Of course, the classification does involve judgment by management and that judgment may prove to be incorrect. Also, the judgment may be changed by unforeseen circumstances such as changes in tax laws or in the security's credit risk.

Note that the arguments in favor of reporting fair value for some securities do not necessarily apply to the reporting of inventories. Therefore the arguments do not invalidate the use of the LCM method for inventories.

### Fair Value Is Not Required for Certain Liabilities

The FASB also considered the desirability of requiring certain liabilities to be reported at fair value because they are "mirror images" of the assets. This was supported particularly by financial institutions which manage their interest rate risk by coordinating their holdings of financial assets and liabilities. Therefore they argued that financial statements would provide a more *relevant* view of a company's exposure to *risk* if some liabilities were also reported at fair value. In other words, they felt that recognizing fair value on only one side of their portfolio introduces an inappropriate bias into their financial statements.

The FASB rejected the fair value reporting of liabilities because of the difficulty of (a) determining which liabilities should be reported at fair value and (b) obtaining a *reliable* value because many of the liabilities do not trade in an established market. Also nonfinancial companies do not manage risk in the same way, and use the proceeds from borrowing to invest in physical and intangible assets that are not reported at fair value. Since liabilities are not reported at fair value, the FASB concluded that it would not require all investments (i.e., those held to maturity) to be valued at fair value. The FASB admitted that this conclusion represents a compromise, and one of the dissenters voted against adoption partly for this reason.

### Reporting of Unrealized Gains and Losses

Since trading securities are actively managed, the FASB concluded that income measurement for those securities is more relevant if it includes the results of changes in fair value—the unrealized holding gains and losses. Therefore income includes the results of economic events that occur in the period and provides a better measure of the company's *return on investment.*

Partly in response to the issue of not reporting liabilities at fair value, the FASB concluded that including unrealized holding gains and losses in income for securities available for sale would create an unnecessary volatility into reported income. Such volatility does not represent the way that companies manage their business and the impact of economic events of the period. In addition, when the intent is to hold securities for a long period, it is more likely that any unrealized holding gains and losses will offset before the sale occurs. Therefore including those gains and losses in income would also create an unnecessary volatility in income. For these reasons, the FASB concluded that unrealized holding gains and losses on securities available for sale should not be included in income but instead be reported as a component of stockholders' equity.

This reporting of unrealized holding gains and losses, however, does not eliminate the possibility of "gains trading" because the realized gain on a sale is the difference between the selling price and the cost of the security, and is included in income. Note also that a company may tend to avoid selling a security classified as available for sale when its fair value is less than its cost. The sale would result in the recognition of a realized loss in the income statement, whereas if the company continues to hold the security, the decline in value is included in stockholders' equity. Therefore the decision not to sell avoids any income recognition of the decline in value. Thus companies are able to "manage" the amount of income that they report by selecting which securities to sell. The two dissenters were concerned that the *Statement* does not prevent this practice.

### Classification of Securities is Based on Management Intent

Classifying securities into three categories, each of which has different accounting principles, and using management intent as a criterion to distinguish among the categories may result in an inconsistent application of the principles. Companies with three identical securities could account for those securities using three different accounting methods. Both issues may create a lack of *comparability*.

In addition, transfers between categories, which are also based partly on management intent and judgment, allow for management of earnings because the gain (or loss) is included in income. Combined with the opportunities for gains trading, the new principles may not produce sufficient *relevance*.

## EQUITY METHOD

When an investor corporation owns a sufficiently large percentage of common stock, it is able to exert significant influence over the operating and financial policies of the investee corporation. In particular, the investor may be able to influence the investee's dividend policy. The dividends paid may be affected by the investor's cash needs, desire to raise its income, or by tax considerations. The fair value methods recognize income as dividends are received (declared) and are therefore inappropriate when significant influence exists. The equity method of accounting is used to account for these investments.

The equity method (1) acknowledges the existence of a material economic relationship between the investor and the investee, (2) is based upon the requirements of accrual accounting, and (3) reflects the change in stockholders' equity of the investee company.

**APB Opinion No. 18 requires the use of the equity method by an investor who is able to exercise significant influence over the operating and financial policies of an investee.** "Significant influence" is determined by such factors as representation on the board of directors, participation in policy-making processes, material intercompany transactions, interchange of managerial personnel, and technological dependency. In the absence of evidence to the contrary, however, an investment of *20% or more* in the outstanding common stock of the investee leads to the *presumption* of significant influence and the use of the equity method of accounting.[14] The equity method is also used when significant influence exists even though the investor holds less than a 20% investment in the common stock of the investee. On the other hand, there are situations in which an investor holds 20% or more of the outstanding common stock of an investee and does not have the ability to exercise significant influence over the investee. In these cases, the equity method is not used to account for the

---

14. "The Equity Method of Accounting for Investments in Common Stock," *APB Opinion No. 18* (New York: AICPA, 1971), par. 17.

investment. **FASB Interpretation No. 35** suggests that the following facts and circumstances indicate that an investor holding an investment of 20% or more in the investee should *not* use the equity method:

1. Opposition by the investee, such as litigation or complaints to governmental regulatory authorities, challenges the investor's ability to exercise significant influence.

2. The investor and investee sign an agreement under which the investor surrenders significant rights as a shareholder.

3. Majority ownership of the investee is concentrated among a small group of shareholders who operate the investee without regard to the views of the investor.

4. The investor needs or wants more financial information to apply the equity method than is available to the investee's other shareholders, tries to obtain that information, and fails. (The application of the equity method requires information not typically included in published financial statements.)

5. The investor tries and fails to obtain representation on the investee's board of directors.[15]

## Accounting Procedures

When the equity method is used, an investment in common stock is recorded initially at its acquisition cost; however, in contrast to the fair value method, income is recorded by the investor when it is *reported* by the investee. The investor records income and an increase in the carrying value of the investment account at an amount that is based on the investor's percentage of ownership in the investee. Dividends received (or receivable) are recorded as reductions in the carrying value of the investment account whenever they are paid (or declared) by the investee. Furthermore, (1) since a material relationship is presumed, the effects of all intercompany items of revenue and expense are removed from the investor's accounts to avoid "double counting," and (2) if the acquisition cost is greater than the proportionate book value of the investee, additional depreciation and/or goodwill amortization is recognized. Therefore, it is necessary to make certain adjustments to the investment income. The most frequent are to:

1. Eliminate intercompany transactions in the determination of investor net income (e.g., a sale from the investor to the investee that results in revenue to the investor and an expense to the investee.)

2. Depreciate the proportionate share of any difference between the fair market values and book values of investee depreciable assets implied by the acquisition price of the investee shares. [In the event the investor cannot determine the fair market value of the specific investee assets, the entire excess of cost (i.e., acquisition price) over the proportionate book value is treated as goodwill and amortized.]

---

15. "Criteria for Applying the Equity Method of Accounting for Investments in Common Stock," *FASB Interpretation No. 35* (Stamford, Conn.: FASB, 1981), par. 4.

3. Amortize any purchased goodwill.

4. Treat the proportionate share of investee extraordinary items as investor extraordinary items. The proportionate share of investee results of discontinued operations and cumulative effects of changes in accounting principles are treated similarly.[16]

In summary, the investor accounts for the investment and income under the equity method as follows:

$$\text{Investment} = \text{Acquisition Cost} + \frac{\text{Investor's Share of}}{\text{Investee Income}} - \text{Dividends Received}$$

*where*:

$$\frac{\text{Investor's Share of}}{\text{Investee Income}} = (\text{Investee's Net Income} \times \text{Ownership \%}) - \text{Adjustments}$$

*and*:

$$\text{Dividends Received} = \text{Total Dividends Paid by Investee} \times \text{Ownership \%}$$

The use of the equity method more closely fits the requirements of accrual accounting because the investor's share in investee income is reported by the investor during the period in which it is earned rather than as cash is received. The equity method, therefore, supplies more relevant information for decision makers who rely on financial statements.

To illustrate, assume Cliborn Company purchases 4,200 shares of the S Company's outstanding common stock on January 1, 1995. (On that date, S Company had 16,800 shares outstanding, so Cliborn's investment is 25% and significant influence is presumed to exist.) The shares were acquired for $125,000, and on the date of acquisition the following information concerning S Company is available:

|  | Balance Sheet Book Value | Fair Market Value |
|---|---|---|
| Depreciable assets (remaining life, 10 years) | $400,000 | $450,000 |
| Other nondepreciable assets (e.g., land) | 190,000 | 226,000 |
| Total | $590,000 | $676,000 |
|  |  |  |
| Liabilities | $200,000 | $200,000 |
| Common stock | 250,000 |  |
| Retained earnings | 140,000 |  |
| Total | $590,000 |  |

There were no intercompany transactions during the year, S Company paid a $20,000 dividend on August 28, 1995, and reported net income for 1995 of $81,000 consisting of ordinary income of $75,000 and an extraordinary gain of $6,000.

---

16. In addition, deferred income taxes are recognized for any difference between income reported under the equity method for financial reporting purposes and dividend income reported for income tax purposes. Deferred income taxes are not considered further in this chapter; they are discussed in Chapter 17.

The journal entries necessary to record these events on Cliborn Company's books are as follows:

1.  To record the original investment on January 1, 1995:

| | | |
|---|---|---|
| Investment in Stock: S Company | 125,000 | |
|     Cash | | 125,000 |

2.  To record the receipt of dividends on August 28, 1995:

| | | |
|---|---|---|
| Cash | 5,000 | |
|     Investment in Stock: S Company | | |
|         (0.25 × $20,000) | | 5,000 |

The effect of this transaction is simply to exchange one asset (Investment in Stock: S Company) for another (Cash).

3.  To record Cliborn Company's 25% share in the year's net income on December 31, 1995:

| | | |
|---|---|---|
| Investment in Stock: S Company | | |
|     (0.25 × $81,000) | 20,250 | |
|     Investment Income: Ordinary | | |
|         (0.25 × $75,000) | | 18,750 |
|     Investment Income: Extraordinary | | |
|         (0.25 × $6,000) | | 1,500 |

Note that the investment account is increased by Cliborn's share of the total net income, and that the investment income is separated into Cliborn's share of the ordinary and extraordinary income.

4.  To depreciate the increase in the recorded value of depreciable assets acquired:

| | | |
|---|---|---|
| Investment Income: Ordinary | 1,250 | |
|     Investment in Stock: S Company | | |
|         ($12,500 ÷ 10) | | 1,250 |

Recall that the depreciable assets acquired have a fair market value that exceeds book value by $50,000 ($450,000 − $400,000) and that the remaining useful life of the assets is 10 years. Cliborn acquired 25% of this increase in asset value, so $12,500 (0.25 × $50,000) of the additional depreciable asset value is depreciated over the remaining useful life of the assets according to the matching principle. This $12,500 divided by the 10-year life results in $1,250 additional depreciation, which is recorded directly as a deduction from the ordinary investment income and the investment on December 31, 1995.

5.  To amortize goodwill:

| | | |
|---|---|---|
| Investment Income: Ordinary | 300 | |
|     Investment in Stock: S Company ($6,000 ÷ 20) | | 300 |

The proportionate excess of the cost of the investment over the underlying market value of the assets acquired is goodwill (see Chapter 10). This intangible is amortized over its useful life. An amortization period for goodwill of 20 years is chosen. The $6,000 of goodwill is calculated as follows:

| | | |
|---|---:|---:|
| Purchase price | | $125,000 |
| Book value of net asset acquired | | |
|   [0.25 × ($590,000 − $200,000)] | $97,500 | |
| Adjustments: Increase in depreciable assets acquired | | |
|         [($450,000 − $400,000) × 0.25] | 12,500 | |
|       Increases in other nondepreciable | | |
|       assets acquired | | |
|         [($226,000 − $190,000) × 0.25] | 9,000 | |
| Fair market value of identifiable net assets acquired | | (119,000) |
| Purchased goodwill | | $ 6,000 |

This $6,000 divided by the 20-year life results in $300 amortization that is recorded directly as a deduction from the ordinary investment income and the investment on December 31, 1995.

## Financial Statement Disclosures

The carrying value of the Investment in Stock: S Company account is determined by adding the reported income for the year and deducting the dividends, depreciation, and goodwill amortization. The Investment in Stock: S Company account is disclosed in the long-term investment section of the December 31, 1995 balance sheet of Cliborn Company. This account has a carrying value of $138,700, which is computed as follows:

**Investment in S Company**

| | | |
|---|---:|---:|
| Acquisition price January 1, 1995 | | $125,000 |
| Add: Share of 1995 reported ordinary income | $18,750 | |
|      Share of 1995 reported extraordinary income | 1,500 | 20,250 |
| | | $145,250 |
| Less: Dividends received August 28, 1995 | $ 5,000 | |
|      Depreciation on excess market value of | | |
|        acquired assets | | |
|        ($12,500 ÷ 10; see earlier computation) | 1,250 | |
|      Amortization of goodwill ($6,000 ÷ 20; | | |
|        see earlier computation) | 300 | (6,550) |
| Carrying value | | $138,700 |

The total amount of investee income disclosed on Cliborn's income statement for 1995 is $18,700. This amount consists of $17,200 that is reported as income from continuing operations and $1,500 that is reported as an extraordinary item. The accompanying notes to the financial statements include a supporting schedule reconciling these amounts. This schedule appears as follows:

### Income from Investment

| | | |
|---|---:|---:|
| Share of 1995 ordinary income | | $18,750 |
| Less: Depreciation on excess market value of acquired assets | $1,250 | |
| Amortization of goodwill | 300 | (1,550) |
| Ordinary investment income | | $17,200 |
| Plus: Share of investee extraordinary income | | 1,500 |
| Net investment income | | $18,700 |

## Special Issues

Sometimes an investor acquires enough additional common shares during a year to justify a change from the fair value method to the equity method, or an investor may dispose of a portion of its investment so that a change from the equity method to the fair value method is necessary. Additionally, an investment carried under the equity method may be acquired for a cost that is less than the fair market value of the assets. Or investments carried under the equity method may suffer declines in value that are not temporary. Finally, a company may acquire enough of an investee's outstanding common stock to issue consolidated financial statements.

### Change to Equity Method

*Prior period adjustments are discussed in Chapter 22.*

When an investor currently using the fair value method acquires enough additional common shares during a year to exercise significant influence over the investee, the investor is required to adopt the equity method of accounting. It is most likely (and assumed in this discussion) that the shares were included in the category of securities available for sale. When the equity method is adopted, the investor restates its investment in the investee by debiting the Investment account and crediting Retained Earnings for its *previous* percentage of investee income (less dividends) for the period from the original date of acquisition to the date that significant influence was obtained. This is a prior period (retroactive) adjustment. The company also eliminates any amounts included in the allowance and unrealized increase/decrease accounts that recorded these shares at fair value. Thereafter, the equity method is applied in the usual manner based on the *current* percentage ownership.

For example, assume that on January 2, 1994, Short Company purchased as its only investment 15% of the outstanding common stock of J Corporation for $150,000 (when the book value of its net assets was $1,000,000). At the end of 1994, the J Corporation reported net income of $300,000 and paid dividends of $60,000; at this time, the market value of the shares was $186,000 so the company wrote up the carrying value of the investment (using an allowance account) to fair value. On January 2, 1995, to exert significant influence on J Corporation, Short Company purchased an additional 25% of the outstanding common stock of the J Corporation for $310,000.

The journal entries that Short Company recorded in 1994 and 1995 related to this information are shown in the upper portion of Exhibit 13-6. In 1994, Short Company used the fair value method to account for its investment. It recorded the dividends received as dividend revenue and made an adjustment to the allowance and increase/decrease accounts to record the increase in the investment's carrying value to fair value. In 1995, the Short Company recorded the $31,000 additional investment that increased its ownership to 40%. The company also made two journal entries to account for its *previous* 15% ownership under the equity method. First, it recognized $45,000 ($300,000 × 0.15) of the 1994 net income of J Corporation as an increase in its Investment account and in Retained Earnings. Second, it reduced its Investment account and Retained Earnings by $9,000, its share of the 1994 dividends of J Corporation. (Note that Retained Earnings was adjusted directly for the share of net income and dividends because these are from the *prior* year.) Thus, an increase in value of $36,000 ($45,000 − $9,000) was recognized in the Investment and Retained Earnings accounts. The company also "reversed" its December 31, 1994 adjustment to increase the carrying value of the investment. Because the purchase price (fair value) of the shares was equal to their underlying book value, no additional depreciation or goodwill amortization was recorded. Had these adjustments been necessary, they would have been recorded (based on the 15% ownership) as reductions in the Investment and Retained Earnings accounts.

The lower portion of Exhibit 13-6 explains the rationale behind the adjustments. Note that the book value of the net assets of J Corporation was $1,240,000 on January 2, 1995. By increasing the $150,000 initial investment for the $45,000 share of 1994 net income and decreasing it for the $9,000 share of 1994 dividends, the book

---

### EXHIBIT 13-6

## Journal Entries to Illustrate a Change to the Equity Method

*Fair Value Method*

| | | | *Change to Equity Method* | | |
|---|---|---|---|---|---|
| 1/2/94 Investment in J | 150,000 | | 1/2/95 Investment in J | 310,000 | |
| Cash | | 150,000 | Cash | | 310,000 |
| | | | | | |
| 12/31/94 Cash | 9,000[a] | | 1/2/95 Investment in J | 45,000[c] | |
| Dividend Revenue[b] | | 9,000 | Retained Earnings | | 45,000 |
| | | | | | |
| 12/31/94 Allowance for Change in | | | 1/2/95 Retained Earnings | 9,000 | |
| Value of Investment | 36,000 | | Investment in J | | 9,000 |
| Unrealized Increase/Decrease in | | | | | |
| Value of Securities Available | | | 1/2/95 Unrealized Increase/Decrease | | |
| for Sale | | 36,000 | in Value of Securities | | |
| | | | Available for Sale | 36,000 | |
| | | | Allowance for Change in | | |
| | | | Value of Investment | | 36,000 |

*Comparison of Book Values*

| | J Corporation Net Assets | Investment in J |
|---|---|---|
| Book value, 1/2/94 | $1,000,000 | $150,000 |
| + Net income for 1994 | 300,000 | 45,000 |
| − Dividends for 1994 | (60,000) | (9,000) |
| Book value, 1/2/95 | $1,240,000 | $186,000 (15%[d]) |
| Additional investment (25%) | | 310,000 (25%) |
| Book value, 1/2/95 (40%) | | $496,000 |

a. $60,000 × 0.15
b. Closed to Retained Earnings
c. $300,000 × 0.15
d. $186,000 ÷ $1,240,000

value of the Investment account is $186,000 (prior to the additional investment), or 15% of the $1,240,000 net assets of J Corporation on January 2, 1995. Increasing the $186,000 for the $310,000 (25%) additional investment results in an Investment account balance of $496,000, or 40% of the net assets. From this point on, Short Company will apply the equity method using the 40% ownership interest.

### Change from Equity Method

Sometimes an investor using the equity method sells a portion of the investment so that its portion of ownership falls below 20%, or the investor may lose significant influence over the investee. Under these conditions, the use of the equity method is no longer appropriate and the investor no longer accrues its share of investee income. However, previously recorded income remains as a part of the book value of the Investment account. The investment is then accounted for under the fair value method. Any dividends received in later periods that exceed the investor's share of income for those periods are deducted from the book value of the Investment account.

### Acquisition at Less Than Fair Market Value

When the purchase price of an investment in common stock accounted for by the equity method is less than the proportionate fair market value of the net assets acquired, the investment initially is recorded at cost. However, the difference between the cost and proportionate fair market values of the net assets acquired (i.e., "negative goodwill") is allocated to reduce the increase in values assigned to noncurrent assets (except noncurrent investments in marketable securities).

### Declines Other Than Temporary

The investor must recognize "other than temporary" declines in the value of investments accounted for under the equity method. These declines may be evidenced by the bankruptcy of the investee, by lengthy declines in the market value of the stock, or by a number of years of operating losses, which bring into question the ability of the investee to sustain income sufficient to justify the carrying value of the investment. When a decline occurs that is considered to be other than temporary, the investor debits a Loss account and credits the Investment account for the difference between the carrying value of the investment and the fair market value. If the market value of the investment later increases, no recovery is recognized by the investor.

### Consolidated Financial Statements

When an investor using the equity method acquires more than 50% of the outstanding common stock of an investee, it exercises *control* over the investee's operations. In this situation, the entity concept is enhanced by preparing financial statements for the combined set of companies; however, the two (or more) companies continue to maintain separate accounting records. During the year, the investor accounts for its investment in the investee by the equity method, as previously discussed. At the end of the year, the accounting results of the investor and investee are combined (and the Investment account is eliminated) and reported in consolidated financial statements.

The underlying philosophy of consolidation accounting is the presentation of financial statements for a single economic entity even though there are separate legal entities. Two major principles provide the guidelines for the preparation of consolidated financial statements. These principles are:

1. The entity cannot make a profit by selling to itself. That is, intercompany sales and profits must be eliminated from the consolidated financial statements.

2. The entity cannot own or owe itself. That is, intercompany receivables and payables are not disclosed in consolidated financial reports.

Discussion of the preparation of consolidated financial statements is included in an advanced accounting book.

## ADDITIONAL ISSUES

Additional issues for investments include accounting for investments in nonmarketable securities, stock dividends and stock splits, stock warrants, convertible bonds, the cash surrender value of life insurance, and investments in funds. Each of these is discussed in the following sections.

### Nonmarketable Securities

Nonmarketable securities are those that are not traded in a "qualifying" market (e.g., New York Stock Exchange), as discussed earlier in the chapter. For example, shares or bonds issued by a privately-held company are considered nonmarketable (even though they may be traded between individual investors). Investments in nonmarketable securities are outside the scope of *FASB Statement No. 115*. Therefore there is no requirement to report them at fair value. It can be expected that they typically are reported at their historical cost so that any unrealized holding gains and losses are ignored.

### Stock Dividends and Splits

Corporations occasionally distribute additional shares of stock to current shareholders (as discussed in Chapters 14 and 15). In such cases, the investor retains the same relative percentage of ownership in the investee because no additional percentage of outstanding shares is acquired. Consequently, no income from the distribution is recorded by the investor when the new shares are received. The fair value of each share typically falls. The fair value at year-end, however, is simply the new number of shares multiplied by the year-end fair value.

A formal journal entry is not made in the investor's accounts to record the receipt of shares of stock from either a stock dividend or a stock split. However, the cost is now spread over a larger number of shares, thereby lowering the average unit cost of the shares. A memorandum entry is necessary to assign the average unit cost to the old and new shares. This average cost is then used when there is a sale transaction involving the shares.

To illustrate, assume that 2,000 shares of Kell Company common stock were originally purchased for $30 per share, or a total of $60,000, by the Smith Corporation. Two months later, Kell issued a 50% stock dividend and Smith Corporation received another 1,000 shares. The memo entry to record the receipt of the stock dividend is as follows:

**Memo: Received 1,000 shares of Kell Company common stock as a stock dividend. The cost of the shares is now $20 per share, computed as follows: $60,000 ÷ 3,000 (2,000 + 1,000) shares.**

Subsequently, 500 of the shares were sold for $25 per share, and the fair value at the most recent balance sheet data was $23 per share. The journal entry to record the *sale* of the 500 shares is:

| | | |
|---|---:|---:|
| Cash (500 × $25) | 12,500 | |
| Unrealized Increase/Decrease in Value of Securities Available for Sale [500 × ($23 − $20)] | 1,500 | |
| Investment in Securities Available for Sale (500 × $20) | | 10,000 |
| Allowance for Change in Value of Investment | | 1,500 |
| Gain on Sale of Investment [500 × ($25 − $20)] | | 2,500 |

Note that the reduction of the Investment account and calculation of the Gain are based on the $20 per share cost and not the $30 original purchase price. A total of 2,500 shares are still owned and will be valued at fair value at year-end.

### Stock Warrants

As discussed in Chapter 12, stock warrants are certificates that enable their holders to purchase a specified number of shares of common stock at a predetermined price. They generally are issued to existing stockholders as evidence of preemptive rights (discussed in Chapter 14) or for other reasons. Each shareholder usually receives a warrant for each share owned, though it may take more than one warrant to purchase a share. Warrants are defined as equity securities under *FASB Statement No. 115.*

Stock warrants have value because they usually allow the holder the right to purchase additional shares below the existing market price. Thus, the warrants representing these rights will trade on the stock market soon after they are issued. Eventually, the right to purchase additional shares will expire, so the shareholder (the investor corporation) who receives these warrants has three alternatives:

1. Purchase additional shares by exercising the warrants.

2. Sell the warrants.

3. Do nothing and allow the warrants to expire.

Option 3 obviously is not a suitable choice in most circumstances, because by selling the warrants the shareholder can convert them to cash and still retain the original number of shares held. The shareholder thus should choose either alternative 1 or 2, although either the exercise or the sale of the warrants creates a valuation issue. To determine the cost of the new investment shares, or the gain or loss on the sale of the warrants, some cost must be assigned to the warrants. Since no additional cost is incurred when the warrants are received by the corporation holding the investment in common stock, it is necessary to assign a portion of the cost of the stock to the warrants upon their receipt. This amount is determined by use of a weighted average based on the market value of the stock *ex rights* (without the rights attached) and the market value of the warrants (rights) as discussed in Chapter 12.[17] The accounting for any subsequent purchase of additional shares by exercising the warrants (or the sale of the warrants) would use the amount assigned to the warrants.

### Convertible Bonds

As discussed in Chapter 12, some bonds (and preferred stock) carry a conversion privilege that allows investors to exchange them for common stock. Investments in convertible bonds generally would *not* be included in the held to maturity category because it is probable that conversion would occur before the bonds mature. Since these investments in convertible bonds would be included in the available for sale (or trading) category and valued at fair value, conversion only requires a memorandum entry which specifies the number of shares that are now owned instead of the bonds. Also, the cost per share would be calculated to facilitate the accounting for future transactions, such as the sale of the shares.

---

17. If the market value is not available on receipt of the warrants, this process must be delayed until the market value becomes known.

## Cash Surrender Value of Life Insurance

Since a company is dependent upon the skill and expertise of its officers, frequently it will purchase insurance policies on their lives. The rationale for this practice is that the company will be at least partly compensated for the loss of executive skill in the event of an unexpected death.

Many insurance policies allow a portion of accumulated premiums to build up as a savings plan; if the policy is canceled, this savings plan or **cash surrender value** of the policy is returned to the company buying the life insurance policy. When a company is guaranteed a return equal to the amount of the cash surrender value of the policy, part of each annual premium represents an investment. The portion of the yearly premium that does not increase the cash surrender value of the policy is recorded as insurance expense. The amount of cash surrender value of life insurance policies is included as a long-term investment on the balance sheet. It increases from year to year and is stated in the policy. Typically, the yearly increase in this investment is recorded at the end of the year. Additionally, some life insurance policies pay dividends. Any dividends received by a corporation holding such a policy is treated as a reduction of insurance expense.

For example, suppose at the beginning of the year, the Mele Corporation pays an annual insurance premium of $5,500 to cover the lives of its officers. The following journal entry is made at this time:

| | | |
|---|---|---|
| Prepaid Insurance | 5,500 | |
| Cash | | 5,500 |

According to the terms of the insurance contract, the cash surrender value of the policies increases from $7,200 to $8,300 during that year. The adjusting entry at the end of the year to record the Insurance Expense and the increase in the Cash Surrender Value of Life Insurance is as follows:

| | | |
|---|---|---|
| Insurance Expense | 4,400 | |
| Cash Surrender Value of Life Insurance | | |
| ($8,300 − $7,200) | 1,100 | |
| Prepaid Insurance | | 5,500 |

Upon the death of any of the insured officers, Mele would collect the face amount of the insurance policy and credit the cash surrender value account to close out the balance in the account related to this policy. The difference between the proceeds and the cash surrender value is reported as an ordinary gain because the insuring of officers' lives is a usual operating procedure. For income tax purposes, the premiums are not tax deductible, and the gain is not taxable.

## Investments in Funds

Companies may place assets in special funds for specific purposes, and some of these assets then become unavailable for normal operations because of indenture or other contractual arrangements. Funds may be current, such as petty cash funds, or they may be long-term. The most common long-term funds are those to be used to accumulate cash to retire long-term liabilities (**sinking funds**), those to retire preferred stock (**stock redemption funds**), and those to be used to purchase long-term assets (**plant expansion funds**). Long-term funds are reported as investments on the balance sheet. It is important to understand the distinction between a fund and an appropriation of retained earnings. A fund actually sets aside cash and other assets to accomplish specific objectives, whereas an appropriation of retained earnings discloses managerial policy or legal or contractual restrictions (as discussed in Chapter 15). An appropriation does not provide any cash.

Accounting for long-term funds requires separate accounts. In essence, the fund is accounted for as an individual set of books. For example, the accounts that might be used in connection with a bond sinking fund are Sinking Fund Cash, Sinking Fund Securities, Sinking Fund Revenues, Sinking Fund Expenses, Allowance for Change in Value of Sinking Fund Securities, Unrealized Increase/Decrease in Value of Sinking Fund Securities, Gain on Sale of Sinking Fund Securities, and Loss on Sale of Sinking Fund Securities. Journal entries are made to these accounts to record the company's: (1) initial and/or periodic cash contributions to the sinking fund, (2) investments in various securities to earn dividends and interest, (3) expenses to administer the fund, (4) unrealized increases and decreases in value, and (5) sale of the securities to acquire cash to retire the bonds. Any revenues, expenses, gains, and losses are reported in the usual manner on the income statement.

## QUESTIONS

Q13-1   Why do companies purchase securities of other corporations?

Q13-2   What are the three categories of investments in debt and equity securities when there is no significant influence?

Q13-3   Provide brief definitions for the following terms: (a) *debt security*, (b) *equity security*, and (c) *fair value*.

Q13-4   Identify the accounting methods to be used for investments of 20 percent or more in the voting common stock of the investee.

Q13-5   Briefly summarize the accounting for an investment in trading securities.

Q13-6   Briefly summarize the accounting for an investment in securities available for sale.

Q13-7   Briefly summarize the accounting for an investment in debt securities held to maturity.

Q13-8   Briefly describe how to determine and record any subsequent increases or decreases in the fair value of an investment in securities available for sale.

Q13-9   Briefly describe how to determine and record the gain or loss on the sale of an investment in securities available for sale.

Q13-10   When are investments in bonds held to maturity purchased at a premium? How does the amortization of a premium under the effective interest method affect interest revenue?

Q13-11   When are investments in bonds held to maturity purchased at a discount? How does the amortization of a discount under the effective interest method affect interest revenue?

Q13-12   Briefly describe the two methods available to determine interest revenue and account for premiums and discounts on investments in bonds held to maturity.

Q13-13   Briefly describe how to record the transfer of an investment in a debt security (a) from the "held to maturity" category to the "available for sale" category and (b) from the "available for sale" category to the "held to maturity" category.

Q13-14   Show the balance sheet disclosures of an investment in securities available for sale that is classified as current and has a fair value in excess of cost.

Q13-15   Discuss the rationale behind the use of the equity method for an investment in common stock.

Q13-16   Briefly describe the accounting for an investment in common stock under the equity method.

Q13-17   Identify the facts and circumstances that would preclude an investor from using the equity method, even if it owns more than a 20% investment in an investee.

Q13-18   Discuss the appropriate accounting treatment to use when (a) an investor acquires enough additional common stock during a year to change from using the fair value method to using the equity method and (b) an investor using the equity method sells enough common stock so that its portion of ownership falls below 20%.

Q13-19   Why is the cash surrender value of a life insurance policy on which the corporation is the beneficiary carried as an investment? How is the increase in this amount and the amount of insurance expense determined each year?

Q13-20   What is a fund? Distinguish between a fund and an appropriation of retained earnings.

# CASES

## C13-1 Realized and Unrealized Losses: Temporary Investments

The FASB issued *FASB Statement No. 115* to change accounting principles with respect to certain marketable securities. An important part of this *Statement* is the distinction between investments categorized as trading, available for sale, or held to maturity.

**Required**

1. What types of securities are covered by this *Statement?*
2. How is the distinction between the three categories made?
3. Discuss the distinction between realized and holding gains and losses on investments in debt and equity securities.
4. How are realized and holding gains and losses on investments in equity securities disclosed on financial statements?

## C13-2 Investments in Securities

Cane Company has two portfolios of investments in marketable equity securities. One is classified as trading securities, and the other is classified as securities available for sale. Cane does not have the ability to exercise significant influence over any of the companies in either portfolio. Some securities from each portfolio were sold during the year. One of the securities in the available for sale category was reclassified to the trading category when its fair value was less than cost. At the beginning and end of the year, the aggregate cost of each portfolio exceeded its aggregate market value by different amounts.

**Required**

1. How does Cane measure and report the income statement effects of the securities sold during the year from each portfolio?
2. How does Cane account for the security which was reclassified?
3. How does Cane report the effects of investments in each portfolio in its balance sheet as of the end of the year and its income statement for the year? Why? Do not discuss the securities sold.

## C13-3 Investments in Securities

The Financial Accounting Standards Board issued its *FASB Statement No. 115* to change accounting methods and procedures with respect to investments in debt and equity securities. An important part of the *Statement* concerns the distinction between trading securities, securities available for sale, and securities held to maturity.

**Required**

1. Why does a company invest in debt and equity securities?

2. What factors should be considered in determining whether investments should be classified in each of the three categories, and how do these factors affect the accounting treatment for unrealized gains and losses?

## C13-4 Securities Available for Sale

The following are four *unrelated* situations involving investments in securities available for sale:

**Situation I**

A portfolio of securities available for sale with an aggregate fair value in excess of cost includes one particular security whose fair value has declined to less than one-half of the original cost. The decline in value is considered to be other than temporary.

**Situation II**

The statement of financial position of a company does not classify assets and liabilities as current and noncurrent. The portfolio of securities available for sale includes securities normally considered current that have a net cost in excess of fair value of $2,000. The remainder of the portfolio has a net fair value in excess of cost of $5,000.

**Situation III**

A security available for sale, whose fair value is currently less than cost, is reclassified as a trading security.

**Situation IV**

A company's portfolio of securities available for sale consists of the common stock of one company. At the end of the prior year, the fair value of the security was 50% of original cost, and the effect was properly reflected in an allowance account. However, at the end of the current year, the fair value of the security had appreciated to twice the original cost.

**Required**

What is the effect upon classification, carrying value, and earnings for each of the preceding situations? (*AICPA adapted*)

## C13-5 Equity Method

The most common method of accounting for unconsolidated subsidiaries is the equity method.

**Required**

Answer the following questions with respect to the *equity* method.

1. Under what circumstances is the equity method applied?
2. At what amount is the initial investment recorded and what events subsequent to the initial investment (if any) change this amount?
3. How are investment earnings recognized under the equity method, and how is the amount determined? (*AICPA adapted*)

## C13-6   Change in Percent Ownership

For the past five years, Herbert has maintained an investment (properly accounted for and reported upon) in Broome amounting to a 10% interest in the voting common stock of Broome. The purchase price was $700,000 and the underlying net equity in Broome at the date of purchase was $620,000. On January 2 of the current year, Herbert purchased an additional 15% of the voting common stock of Broome for $1,200,000; the underlying net equity of additional investment at January 2 was $1,000,000. Broome has been profitable and has paid dividends annually since Herbert's initial acquisition.

### Required

Discuss how this increase in ownership affects the accounting for and reporting upon the investment in Broome. Include in your discussion adjustments, if any, to the amount shown prior to the increase in investment to bring the amount into conformity with generally accepted accounting principles. Also include how current and subsequent periods would be reported upon. (*AICPA adapted*)

## C13-7   Investments in Stocks and Bonds

Victoria Company has investments in equity securities classified as trading and available for sale. At the beginning of the year, the aggregate market value of each portfolio exceeded its cost. During the year, Victoria sold some securities from each portfolio. At the end of the year, the aggregate cost of each portfolio exceeded its market value.

Victoria also has investments in bonds classified as held to maturity, all of which were purchased for face value. During the year, some of these bonds held by Victoria were called prior to the maturity by the bond issuer. Three months before the end of the year, additional similar bonds were purchased for face value plus two months' accrued interest.

### Required

1. a.  How does Victoria account for the sale of securities from each portfolio? Why?
   b.  How does Victoria account for each equity securities portfolio at year-end? Why?
2. How does Victoria account for the disposition prior to their maturity of the long-term bonds called by their issuer? Why?
3. How does Victoria report the purchase of the additional similar bonds at the date of the acquisition? Why? (*AICPA adapted*)

## C13-8   Investments in Equity Securities

Walker Company has an investment portfolio of equity securities available for sale. Walker does not own more than 5% of the outstanding voting stock for any of the securities in the portfolio. At the beginning of the year, the ag-

gregate market value of the portfolio exceeded its cost. Cash dividends on these securities were received during the year. None of the securities in the portfolio were sold during the year. At the end of the year, the aggregate cost of the portfolio exceeded its market value. The decline in the market price of the securities in the portfolio is attributable to general market decline.

During this year, Walker purchased for cash 35% of the outstanding voting stock of Sipe Company. Cash dividends on this investment were received from Sipe during the year, and the earnings of Sipe after the acquisition date were reported by Sipe to Walker.

### Required

1. How does Walker report on its balance sheet and income statement the effects of its investment in the securities available for sale portfolio for the year? Why?
2. How does Walker report on its balance sheet and income statement the effects of its investment in Sipe for the year? Why? (*AICPA adapted*)

## C13-9   Various Investments

Houston Company has a portfolio of investments in securities available for sale that it classifies as a noncurrent asset. Houston owns less than 5% of the outstanding voting stock of each company's securities in the portfolio. At the beginning of the year, the aggregate market value of the portfolio exceeded its aggregate cost. Cash dividends on these securities were received during the year. All cash dividends received represent distribution of earnings subsequent to Houston's acquisition of these securities. Some of the securities in the portfolio were sold during the year. At the end of the year, the aggregate cost of the portfolio exceeded its aggregate market value.

Houston also owns 40% of the outstanding voting stock of Joy Company. The remainder of Joy's outstanding voting stock is widely dispersed among unrelated investors.

### Required

1. a.  How does Houston report the income statement effects of the cash dividends received during the year on the securities in the available for sale portfolio?
   b.  How does Houston report the income statement effects of the securities sold during the year?
2. How does Houston report the effect of ownership of the portfolio of securities available for sale in its balance sheet as of the end of the year and income statement for the year? Why? Do *not* discuss the cash dividends or the securities sold.
3. Identify the method of accounting that Houston uses for its 40% investment in the outstanding voting stock of Joy. Why is this method appropriate? (*AICPA adapted*)

## MULTIPLE CHOICE

*Select the best answer for each of the following.*

M13-1  On its December 31, 1995 balance sheet, Fay Company appropriately reported a $2,000 credit balance in its Allowance for Change in Value of Investment. There was no change during 1996 in the composition of Fay's portfolio of marketable equity securities held as available for sale. Pertinent data are as follows:

| Security | Cost | Market Value at 12/31/96 |
|---|---|---|
| A | $ 60,000 | $ 63,000 |
| B | 45,000 | 40,000 |
| C | 80,000 | 78,500 |
|  | $185,000 | $181,500 |

What amount of loss on these securities should be included in Fay's income statement for the year ended December 31, 1996?

a.  $0
b.  $1,500

c.  $3,500
d.  $5,500

M13-2  A security in a portfolio of securities available for sale is transferred to the trading category. The security should be transferred between the corresponding portfolios at

a.  The book value at date of transfer if higher than the fair value at date of transfer
b.  The fair value at date of transfer, regardless of its cost
c.  Its cost, regardless of the fair value at date of transfer
d.  The lower of its cost or fair value at date of transfer

M13-3  On April 1, 1995, Aldrich Company purchased as a security available for sale $200,000 face value, 9% U.S. Treasury notes for $198,500, which included accrued interest of $4,500. The notes mature July 1, 1996, and pay interest semiannually on January 1 and July 1. The notes were sold on December 1, 1995 for $206,500, which included accrued interest of $7,500. In its income statement for the year ended December 31, 1995, what amount should Aldrich report as a gain on sale of security available for sale?

a.  $1,800
b.  $5,000

c.  $6,500
d.  $8,000

M13-4  When the market value of a company's portfolio of securities available for sale is lower than its cost, the difference should be

a.  Accounted for as a liability
b.  Disclosed and described in a note to the financial statements but not accounted for
c.  Accounted for as a valuation allowance deducted from the asset to which it relates
d.  Accounted for as an addition in the shareholders' equity section of the balance sheet

M13-5  On January 2, 1995, Portela, Inc. bought 30% of the outstanding common stock of Bracero Corporation for $258,000 cash. Portela accounts for this investment by the equity method. At the date of acquisition of the stock, Bracero's net assets had a book and fair value of $620,000. The excess of Portela's cost of the investment over its share of Bracero's net assets has an estimated life of 40 years. Bracero's net income for the year ended December 31, 1995 was $180,000. During 1995, Bracero declared and paid cash dividends of $20,000. On December 31, 1995, Portela should have carried its investment in Bracero in the amount of

a.  $234,000
b.  $258,000

c.  $304,200
d.  $306,000

M13-6    Cash dividends declared out of current earnings were distributed to an investor. How will the investor's investment account be affected by those dividends under each of the following accounting methods?

|   | Fair value method | Equity method |
|---|---|---|
| a. | Decrease | No effect |
| b. | No effect | Decrease |
| c. | Decrease | Decrease |
| d. | No effect | No effect |

M13-7    During 1995, Anthony Company purchased securities as a long-term investment and classified them as available for sale. Pertinent data are as follows:

| Security | Cost | Market Value at 12/31/95 |
|---|---|---|
| A | $ 20,000 | $ 18,000 |
| B | 40,000 | 30,000 |
| C | 90,000 | 93,000 |
|   | $150,000 | $141,000 |

The amount of the holding gain or loss included in Anthony's year-end balance sheet should be

a. $0

b. $3,000

c. $9,000

d. $12,000

M13-8    For a securities available for sale portfolio included in noncurrent assets, which of the following should be included in net income of the period?

a. Realized gains during the period

b. Unrealized losses during the period

c. Accumulated changes in the valuation allowance

d. Increases in the valuation allowance during the period

M13-9    In 1994, Cromwell Corporation bought 30,000 shares of Fleming Corporation's listed stock for $300,000 and classified the investment as available for sale. In 1995, the market value declined to $200,000. In 1996, the market value of the Fleming stock rose to $230,000 and the stock was sold. How much should Cromwell record as a realized gain or loss in its determination of net income for 1996?

a. $0

b. $30,000 gain

c. $70,000 loss

d. $100,000 loss

M13-10   On January 1, 1995, Weaver Company purchased as debt securities held to maturity $500,000 face value of Park Corporation's 8% bonds for $456,200. The bonds were purchased to yield 10% interest and pay interest annually. The bonds mature on January 1, 2000. Weaver uses the effective interest method of amortization. What amount should Weaver report on its December 31, 1995 balance sheet as an investment in debt securities held to maturity?

a. $450,580

b. $456,200

c. $461,820

d. $466,200

(*AICPA adapted*)

# EXERCISES

E13-1    *Trading Securities*    Midwest Bank invests in trading securities. At the beginning of December 1995, the bank held no trading securities. During December of 1995, it entered into the following trading securities transactions:

Dec. 12 Purchased 500 shares of C Company common stock for $71 per share

Dec. 21 Purchased 800 shares of D Company common stock for $29 per share

At the end of December, the C Company common stock had a quoted market price of $74 per share and the D Company common stock had a quoted market price of $28 per share.

**Required**

1. Prepare journal entries to record the preceding information.
2. What is the unrealized holding gain or loss and where is it reported in the 1995 financial statements?
3. Show how the bank reports the trading securities on its December 31, 1995 balance sheet.

*Trading Securities*  Southeast Bank invests in trading securities and prepares quarterly financial statements. At the beginning of the fourth quarter of 1995, the bank held as trading securities 200 shares of Company E common stock which cost $5,500. At that time, these securities had a fair value of $5,200. During the fourth quarter, the bank engaged in the following trading securities transactions:

Oct. 26    Purchased 300 shares of Company F common stock for $35 per share
Nov. 28    Sold 200 shares of Company E common stock for $25 per share
Dec. 12    Purchased 400 shares of Company G common stock for $41 per share

On December 31, 1995, the quoted market prices of the shares were as follows: E, $52 per share; F, $38 per share; and G, $40 per share.

**Required**

1. Prepare journal entries to record the preceding information.
2. Show what the bank reports on its fourth quarter 1995 income statement for these trading securities.
3. Show how the bank reports these trading securities on its balance sheet at the end of the fourth quarter of 1995.

*Long-Term Investments*  On December 31, 1994, Marsh Company held 1,000 shares of X Company common stock in its portfolio of long-term investments in securities available for sale. The stock had cost $15 per share and has a current market value of $13 per share. The December 31, 1994 balance sheet showed the following:

*Assets*

| | |
|---|---|
| Long-term investment in securities available for sale | $15,000 |
| Less: Allowance for change in value of investment | (2,000) |
| | $13,000 |

*Stockholders' Equity*

| | |
|---|---|
| Unrealized decrease in value of securities available for sale | $ (2,000) |

During 1995, as long-term investments, the company acquired 900 shares of Y Company common stock for $18 per share and 800 shares of Z Company common stock for $22 per share. At the end of 1995, the respective market values per share were: X—$14, Y—$17, and Z—$20.

**Required**

Record the purchase of the investments in 1995 and the adjusting entry on December 31, 1995, and show the respective December 31, 1995 balance sheet accounts.

E13-4    *Securities Available for Sale*  At the beginning of 1995, Ace Company had the following portfolio of investments in securities (common stock) available for sale:

| Security | Cost | 12/31/94 Fair Value |
|---|---|---|
| A | $20,000 | $25,000 |
| B | 30,000 | 29,000 |
| | $50,000 | $54,000 |

During 1995, the following transactions occurred:

May  1     Purchased C securities (common stock) for $15,000.
July 18    Sold all of the A securities for $23,000.
Dec. 31    Received dividends of $800 on the B and C securities, for which the following information was available:

| Security | 12/31/95<br>Fair Value |
|----------|-----------|
| B | $32,000 |
| C | 15,500 |

**Required**

1. Prepare journal entries to record the preceding information.
2. What is the balance in the Unrealized Increase/Decrease account on December 31, 1995?

E13-5    *Securities Available for Sale*    At the end of 1994, Terry Company prepared the following schedule of investments in securities (common stock) available for sale:

| Security | Cost | 12/31/94<br>Fair Value | Cumulative<br>Change in<br>Fair Value |
|----------|------|-----------|-----------|
| M | $37,000 | $34,200 | $(2,800) |
| N | 42,000 | 43,100 | 1,100 |
| Totals | $79,000 | $77,300 | $(1,700) |

During 1995, the following transactions occurred:

June  8     Purchased O securities (common stock) for $50,000.
Oct. 10     Sold all of the M securities for $35,400.
Dec. 31     Received dividends of $900 on the N and O securities, and the following year-end total market values were available: N common stock, $43,900; O common stock, $49,600.

**Required**

1. Prepare journal entries to record the preceding information.
2. Show the December 31, 1995 balance sheet disclosures of the Terry Company. Assume all investments are noncurrent.

E13-6    *Purchase of Bonds Between Interest Dates*    On March 31, 1995, the Brodie Corporation acquired bonds with a par value of $400,000 for $425,800. The bonds are due December 31, 2000, carry a 12% annual interest rate, pay interest on June 30 and December 31, and are being held to maturity. The accrued interest is included in the acquisition price of the bonds. The company uses straight-line amortization.

**Required**

Prepare journal entries for Brodie to record the purchase of the bonds and the first two interest receipts.

E13-7    *Amortizing a Discount on a Bond Investment*    On January 1, 1995 the Kelly Corporation acquired bonds with a face value of $500,000 for $483,841.79, a price that yields a 10% effective annual interest rate. The bonds carry a 9% stated rate of interest, pay interest semiannually on June 30 and December 31, are due December 31, 1998, and are being held to maturity.

**Required**

Prepare journal entries to record the purchase of the bonds and the first two interest receipts using:

1. The straight-line method of amortization.
2. The effective interest method of amortization.

E13-8   *Purchase, Discount Amortization, and Sale of Bond Investment*   On November 1, 1994 the Reid Corporation acquired bonds with a face value of $800,000 for $769,849.84. The bonds carry a stated rate of interest of 10%, were purchased to yield 11%, pay interest semiannually on April 30 and October 31, were purchased to be held to maturity, and are due October 31, 1999. On November 1, 1995, in contemplation of a major acquisition, the bonds were sold for $780,000. Reid Corporation is on a fiscal year accounting period ending October 31. The company uses the effective interest method.

**Required**

Prepare journal entries to record the purchase of the bonds, the interest receipts on April 30, 1995 and October 31, 1995, and the sale of the bonds.

E13-9   *Investment Discount Amortization Schedule*   On January 1, 1995, Rodgers Company purchased $200,000, 10%, 3-year bonds for $190,163.35, a price that yields a 12% effective annual interest rate. The bonds pay interest semiannually on June 30 and December 31.

**Required**

1. Record the purchase of the bonds.
2. Prepare an investment interest revenue and discount amortization schedule, using the effective interest method.
3. Record the receipts of interest on June 30, 1995 and June 30, 1997.

E13-10   *Investment Premium Amortization Schedule*   On January 1, 1995, Lynch Company acquired 13% bonds with a face value of $50,000. The bonds pay interest on June 30 and December 31 and mature on December 31, 1997. Lynch Company paid $51,229.35, a price that yields a 12% effective annual interest rate.

**Required**

1. Record the purchase of the bonds.
2. Prepare an investment interest revenue and premium amortization schedule using the effective interest method.
3. Record the receipts of interest on June 30, 1995 and December 31, 1997.

E13-11   *Purchase, Premium Amortization, and Sale of Bond Investment*   The Glover Corporation purchased bonds with a face value of $300,000 for $307,493.34 on January 1, 1995. The bonds carry a face rate of interest of 12%, pay interest semiannually on June 30 and December 31, were purchased to be held to maturity, are due December 31, 1997, and were purchased to yield 11%. On January 1, 1996, in contemplation of a major acquisition, the bonds were sold for $300,000. The company uses the effective interest method.

**Required**

Prepare journal entries to record the purchase of the bonds, the first two interest receipts, and the sale of the bonds.

E13-12   *Transfer Between Categories*   On December 31, 1994, the Leslie Company held an investment in bonds of Kaufmann Company which it categorized as being held to maturity. At that time, the 8%, $100,000 face value bonds had a carrying value of $107,023.56 and were being amortized using the effective interest method based on a yield of 7%. Interest on these bonds is paid annually each December 31.

On December 31, 1995, after recording the interest earned, the Leslie Company decided to reclassify the Kaufmann bonds to its securities available for sale category in anticipation of a major restructuring. At that time, the ending quoted market price for the bonds was 105.

**Required**

Prepare the journal entries on December 31, 1995 to record the interest earned and the reclassification.

E13-13   *Equity Method*   The Miller Corporation acquired 30% of the outstanding common stock of the Crowell Corporation for $180,000 on January 1, 1995 and obtained significant influence. The purchase price of the shares was equal to their book value. During 1995, the following information is available for Crowell:

| | |
|---|---|
| Mar. 31 | Declared and paid a cash dividend of $40,000. |
| June 30 | Reported semiannual earnings of $100,000 for the first half of 1995. |
| Sept. 30 | Declared and paid a cash dividend of $40,000. |
| Dec. 31 | Reported semiannual earnings of $120,000 for the second half of 1995. |

**Required**

1. Prepare journal entries for Miller to reflect the preceding information.
2. What is the balance in Miller's investment account on December 31, 1995? (Show your computations.)

E13-14  *Equity Method*   On January 1, 1995, the Field Company acquired 40% of the North Company by purchasing 8,000 shares for $144,000 and obtained significant influence. On the date of acquisition, Field calculated that its share of the excess of the fair value over the book value of North's depreciable assets was $15,000, and that the purchased goodwill was $12,000. At the end of 1995, North reported net income of $45,000 and paid dividends of $0.70 per share. Field Company depreciates its depreciable assets over a 12-year remaining life and amortizes its goodwill over a 20-year life.

**Required**

Prepare all the journal entries of Field Company to record the preceding information for 1995.

E13-15  *Equity Method*   On January 1, 1995, Jones acquires a 30% interest in Fink Company by purchasing 3,000 of its 10,000 common shares for $15 per share and obtains significant influence. On the date of acquisition, the net assets of Fink Company were as shown here:

|  | Book Value | Fair Value |
|---|---|---|
| Nondepreciable assets (for example, land) | $ 15,000 | $ 25,000 |
| Depreciable assets (10-year remaining life) | 90,000 | 110,000 |
|  | $105,000 | $135,000 |
| Liabilities | $ 10,000 | $ 10,000 |

During 1995, Fink Company earned income of $18,000 and paid dividends of $6,000. Jones Company amortizes goodwill over a 40-year life.

**Required**

Prepare all journal entries on Jones Company's books to record the acquisition, dividends, and income from the investment in Fink Company. Show supporting calculations.

E13-16  *Convertible Bonds*   On January 1, 1994, the Taylor Corporation purchased $10,000 of the Kalanda Corporation's 12% convertible bonds for $9,880. The bonds pay interest semiannually each December 31 and June 30 and are due December 31, 1998. Each $1,000 bond is convertible into 15 shares of the Kalanda Corporation's $10 par common stock. Taylor uses the straight-line method of discount amortization. At the end of 1994 and 1995, the quoted market price of the bonds was not materially different than the amortized cost. On July 2, 1996, Taylor exchanged all of the bonds for Kalanda common stock. At that time, the market value of the common stock was $72 per share.

**Required**

Prepare whatever entries are necessary to record the acquisition and conversion of the Kalanda bonds.

E13-17  *Receipt of Stock Dividends*   On March 2, 1995, the Dawson Corporation acquired 5,000 common shares, representing a 1% interest in the Foreman Corporation, for $60,000. On May 1, 1995, Foreman issued a 20% stock dividend, and on December 31, 1995, the market value was $10 per share. On February 1, 1996, Dawson sold 1,500 shares for $12 per share.

**Required**

Prepare journal entries for Dawson to record the acquisition, stock dividend, and sale of the shares.

E13-18  *Cash Surrender Value of Life Insurance*   The Westford Corporation purchases life insurance policies on its officers, and these policies all carry a cash surrender value clause. At the beginning of 1995, Westford paid $13,300 in life insurance premiums for one year. During 1995, the cash surrender value of the policies increased from $98,450 to $103,900. At the beginning of 1996, the corporation's vice president lost his life in an automobile accident. The policy carried on this officer paid $50,000, and the cash surrender value of the policy was $6,480.

**Required**

Prepare journal entries to record the preceding information on the Westford Corporation's books.

E13-19  *Sinking Funds Entries*  The following information is available concerning the Nunan Corporation's sinking fund:

| | |
|---|---|
| Jan.  1, 1995 | Established a sinking fund to retire an outstanding bond issue by contributing $425,000. |
| Feb.  3, 1995 | Purchased securities for $400,000. |
| July 30, 1995 | Sold securities originally costing $48,000 for $45,000. |
| Dec. 31, 1995 | Collected dividends and interest on the remaining securities in the amount of $49,000. These securities had a market value of $355,000 at this time. |
| Dec. 31, 1996 | Collected dividends and interest on the remaining securities in the amount of $40,000. |
| Dec. 31, 1996 | Paid sinking fund expenses of $4,500. |
| Dec. 31, 1996 | Sold the remaining securities in the fund for $360,000. |
| Dec. 31, 1996 | Retired an outstanding bond issue of $500,000 with the cash from the fund and transferred the remaining fund balance back to the cash account. |

**Required**

Prepare journal entries to record the preceding transactions for the Nunan Corporation.

## PROBLEMS

P13-1  *Trading Securities*  The investment manager of 4th National Bank invests some of the bank's financial resources in trading securities. During the last quarter of 1995, the following transactions occurred in regard to these trading securities:

| | |
|---|---|
| Nov.  6 | Purchased 200 shares of M Company common stock at $82 per share. |
| Nov. 20 | Purchased 300 shares of P Company preferred stock at $66 per share. |
| Nov. 28 | Sold 100 shares of M Company common stock at $85 per share. |
| Dec. 15 | Purchased 400 shares of T Company common stock at $37 per share. |
| Dec. 18 | Sold 100 shares of P Company preferred stock at $65 per share. |

On December 31, 1995, the market values of the shares were as follows: M, $83 per share; P, $64 per share; and T, $37.25 per share. The bank held no trading securities at the beginning of the last quarter of 1995.

**Required**

1. Prepare journal entries to record the preceding information.
2. Show what the bank reports on its fourth quarter 1995 income statement for these trading securities.
3. Show how the bank reports these trading securities on its December 31, 1995 balance sheet.

P13-2  *Trading Securities*  The 8th State Bank prepares interim financial statements and follows an investment strategy of investing in trading securities. At the beginning of the third quarter of 1995, the bank held the following portfolio of trading securities:

| Security | Cost | June 30, 1995 Fair Value |
|---|---|---|
| 100 shares of G Company common stock | $ 2,900 | $ 2,800 |
| 600 shares of O Company common stock | 12,000 | 12,600 |
| Totals | $14,900 | $15,400 |

During the third quarter of 1995, the bank entered into the following trading securities transactions:

| | |
|---|---|
| July  3 | Received dividends of $1.50 per share on the G Company common stock. |
| July 14 | Sold 600 shares of O Company common stock for $20 per share. |
| Aug.  8 | Purchased 300 shares of P Company common stock for $36 per share. |
| Aug. 24 | Sold 100 shares of G Company common stock for $30 per share. |
| Sept. 18 | Purchased 500 shares of U Company common stock for $22 per share. |

On September 30, 1995, the P Company common stock had a quoted market price of $36.50 per share and the U Company common stock had a quoted market price of $21 per share.

**Required**

1. Prepare journal entries to record the preceding information.
2. Show what the bank reports on its third quarter 1995 income statement for these trading securities.
3. Show how the bank reports these trading securities on its September 30, 1995 balance sheet.

P13-3   *Securities Available for Sale*   Holly Company invests its excess cash in marketable securities. At the beginning of 1995, it had the following portfolio of investments in securities available for sale:

| Security | Cost | 12/31/94 Fair Value |
|---|---|---|
| 400 shares of I Company common stock | $ 8,400 | $ 9,400 |
| 700 shares of O Company common stock | 23,100 | 21,700 |
| Totals | $31,500 | $31,100 |

During 1995, the following transactions occurred:

| | |
|---|---|
| Mar. 31 | Purchased U Company 8% bonds with a face value of $10,000 for $10,000 plus accrued interest. Interest is payable on the bonds each June 30 and December 31. |
| May 17 | Sold 200 shares of O Company common stock for $30 per share. |
| June 30 | Received the semiannual interest on the U Company bonds. |
| Oct. 12 | Sold 100 shares of I Company common stock for $24 per share. |
| Dec. 31 | Received the semiannual interest on the U Company bonds and dividends of $1 per share and $1.50 per share on the I and O Company common stock, respectively. |

The December 31 closing market prices were as follows: I Company common stock, $25 per share; O Company common stock, $31 per share; U Company 8% bonds, 101.

**Required**

1. Prepare journal entries to record the preceding information.
2. Show what is reported on the Holly Company's 1995 income statement.
3. Assuming the investment in I Company stock is considered to be a current asset and the remaining investments are noncurrent, show the December 31, 1995 balance sheet disclosures of the Holly Company.

P13-4   *Investments in Equity Securities*   The Noonan Corporation prepares quarterly financial statements and invests its excess funds in marketable securities. At the end of 1994, Noonan's portfolio of investments available for sale consisted of the following equity securities:

| Security | Number of Shares | Cost Per Share | Fair Value Per Share |
|---|---|---|---|
| Keene Company | 500 | $60 | $60 |
| Sachs, Inc. | 800 | 40 | 41 |
| Bacon Company | 400 | 70 | 72 |

During the first half of 1995, Noonan engaged in the following investment transactions:

| | |
|---|---|
| Jan. 6 | Sold one-half of the Sachs shares for $42 per share. |
| Feb. 3 | Purchased 700 shares of Jackson Corporation common stock for $45 per share. |
| Mar. 31 | Dividends of $2,500 were received on the investments, and the following information is available on market prices: |

| Security | Fair Value Per Share |
|---|---|
| Keene Company | $59 |
| Sachs, Inc. | 42 |
| Bacon Company | 70 |
| Jackson Corporation | 43 |

Apr. 14    Purchased 300 shares of Quinn Company preferred stock for $52 per share.
May 11     Sold the remainder of the Sachs shares for $39 per share.
June 30    Dividends of $2,800 were received on investments, and the following information is available:

| Security | Fair Value Per Share |
|---|---|
| Keene Company | $62 |
| Bacon Company | 69 |
| Jackson Corporation | 46 |
| Quinn Company | 50 |

**Required**

1. Record Noonan's investment transactions for January 6 through June 30, 1995.
2. Show the items of income or loss from investment transactions that Noonan reports for each of the first and second quarters of 1995.
3. Show the first and second quarter 1995 ending balance sheet disclosures, assuming that management expects to dispose of the Keene and Sachs securities within the next year.

P13-5    *Temporary Investments Available for Sale*    Manson Incorporated reported the following current asset in its December 31, 1994 balance sheet:

| | |
|---|---|
| Temporary investment in securities available for sale (at cost) | $63,475 |
| Less: Allowance for change in value of investment | (2,980) |
| Temporary investment in securities available for sale (at fair value) | $60,495 |

An analysis of Manson's temporary investments on December 31, 1994 reveals the following:

| Equity Security | Cost | Fair Value |
|---|---|---|
| 400 shares of Turben Company, common | $14,275 | $13,590 |
| 500 shares of Cook Corp., common | 12,650 | 13,175 |
| 700 shares of Hill Corp., common | 17,450 | 18,180 |
| 200 shares of Web Engines, preferred | 19,100 | 15,550 |
| Totals | $63,475 | $60,495 |

During 1995, the following transactions related to Manson's temporary investments occurred:

Jan.  6    Received a $265 dividend on the Turben Company common.
Mar. 31   Received the semiannual dividend of $500 on the Web Engines preferred.

On March 31, 1995, the following information is available concerning Manson's temporary investments:

| Equity Security | Fair Value |
|---|---|
| Turben Company | $13,470 |
| Cook Corp. | 13,765 |
| Hill Corp. | 18,940 |
| Web Engines | 15,500 |

June 30    Received a $375 dividend on the Cook Corp. common and a $700 dividend on the Hill Corp. common.

On June 30, 1995, the following information is available concerning Manson's temporary investments:

| Equity Security | Fair Value |
|---|---|
| Turben Company | $13,300 |
| Cook Corp. | 14,125 |
| Hill Corp. | 19,300 |
| Web Engines | 15,400 |

July   6     Sold the Turben Company common for $13,750.

Sept. 29    Received the semiannual dividend of $500 on the Web Engines preferred.

On September 30, 1995, the following information is available concerning Manson's temporary investments:

| Equity Security | Fair Value |
|---|---|
| Cook Corp. | $14,230 |
| Hill Corp. | 19,500 |
| Web Engines | 15,900 |

Nov.  2    Sold the Hill Corp. common for $19,780.

Dec. 30    Received a $375 dividend on the Cook Corp. common.

On December 31, 1995, the following information is available:

| Equity Security | Fair Value |
|---|---|
| Cook Investment Corp. | $14,280 |
| Web Engines | 16,400 |

### Required

1. Assuming Manson prepares quarterly financial statements, prepare journal entries to record the preceding information.
2. Show the items of income or loss from temporary investment transactions that Manson reports for each quarter of 1995?
3. Show how Manson's temporary investments are disclosed on the balance sheet on March 31, 1995; June 30, 1995; September 30, 1995; and December 31, 1995.

P13-6   *Investment in Bonds Available for Sale*   The following information relates to the Starr Company's Investment in Bonds Available for Sale account for 1995:

Jan.  1     Purchased $30,000 face value of Bradford Company 8% bonds at 97 to yield 10%. Interest on the bonds is payable each June 30 and December 31.

Jan.  1     Purchased $40,000 face value of Morris Company 10% bonds at 101 to yield 9.8%. Interest on the bonds is payable each June 30 and December 31.

On June 30, the interest is collected and the following information is available:

| Security | Fair Value |
|---|---|
| Bradford Company 8% | 97.2 |
| Morris Company 10% | 102.0 |

July  1     Purchased $25,000 face value of Whipple Corporation 11% bonds at 92 to yield 12%. Interest on the bonds is payable each June 30 and December 31.

Nov. 30    Sold the Whipple bonds at 91 plus accrued interest.

On December 31, the interest is collected, the Morris bonds are sold at 102, and the following information is also available:

| Security | Fair Value |
|---|---|
| Bradford Company 8% | 96 |

### Required

1. Prepare journal entries to record the previous information for 1995. Use the effective interest method and round all amounts to the nearest *dollar*. Assume that Starr prepares semiannual financial statements.

2. Show the items of income or loss from investment transactions that Starr reports for each 1995 semiannual income statement.
3. Show each of the 1995 semiannual balance sheet disclosures for the investments, assuming that management expects to dispose of all investments within one year of purchase.

P13-7   *Temporary Investments in Bonds and Equity Securities Available for Sale*   During 1995, the Dana Company decided to begin investing its idle cash in marketable securities. The information contained below relates to Dana's 1995 marketable security transactions:

Feb. 3     Purchased 3,000 shares of Blair Company common stock for $12 per share.

Apr. 1     Purchased $20,000 face value of Solomon Inc. 10% bonds at par plus accrued interest. Interest on the bonds is payable each June 30 and December 31.

June 30    Received the semiannual interest on the Solomon bonds and a $0.25 per share dividend on the Blair common.

Sept. 1    Purchased 4,000 shares of Woodman Corporation common for $22 per share.

Nov. 1     Purchased $30,000 face value of Edwards Company 12% bonds at par plus accrued interest. Interest on the bonds is payable each June 1 and December 1.

Dec. 1     Received the interest on the Edwards bonds and sold the bonds at 101.

Dec. 30    Received a $0.20 dividend per share on the Blair common and sold all the shares for $35,300.

Dec. 31    Received the interest on the Solomon bonds.

On December 31, the following information is available concerning the year-end market prices:

| Security | Quoted Market |
|---|---|
| Solomon 10% bonds | 101 |
| Woodman common | $23 |

**Required**

1. Record Dana's transactions in temporary investments for 1995.
2. Show the items of income or loss on temporary investments Dana reports on its 1995 income statement.
3. Show the carrying value of Dana's Temporary Investment on its December 31, 1995 balance sheet.

P13-8   *Investments, Petty Cash, Bank Reconciliation*   During the first quarter of 1995, the Payne Corporation entered into the following transactions:

Jan. 1     Acquired 150 shares of Block Corporation common stock for $20 per share, 200 shares of Bridle Corporation common stock for $30 per share, and 100 shares of Alpha Corporation common stock for $25 per share. These are the only shares the company owns and are classified as securities available for sale.

Feb. 1     Purchased 12% A Company bonds with a face value of $20,000 at par plus accrued interest. Interest on the bonds is payable February 28 and August 31 each year, and the bonds are due August 31, 1998. Also purchased 10% B Company bonds with a face value of $12,000 at par plus accrued interest. Interest on the bonds is payable March 31 and September 30, and the bonds are due September 30, 2001. These are the only bonds the company owns and are classified as securities available for sale.

Feb. 1     Established a petty cash fund for incidental expenditures at $500.

Feb. 28    Received the semiannual interest on the A Company bonds.

Feb. 28    A count of cash on hand indicated that $125.50 remained in the petty cash fund. A sorting of petty cash vouchers disclosed that $110.00 was spent for postage, $170.65 was spent for office supplies, $45.00 was spent for transportation, and $43.50 was spent for miscellaneous items. The fund was replenished.

Mar. 31    Received first quarter dividends of $1,500 and the semiannual interest on the B Company bonds. On this date, the aggregate fair value of Payne's securities available for sale is $42,600.

Mar. 31    A count of cash on hand indicated that $230.50 remained in the petty cash fund. A sorting of petty cash vouchers disclosed that $140.00 was spent for postage, $75.30 was spent for office supplies, and $54.20 was spent for miscellaneous items. The fund was replenished.

The bank statement and the accounting records of the Payne Corporation for the month of March 1995 indicated that the cash collected from the dividends and from the B Company bond interest was deposited on March 31, but did not appear on the March bank statement. There were no other deposits in transit. The bank statement showed a balance on March 31 of $13,459.75, which included a $1,500 note and $100 of interest collected by the bank for the Payne Corporation. Also listed was a $20 bank service charge and a $75.60 NSF check returned by the bank. The cash balance per the accounting records on March 31 was $11,689.95, which included checks totaling $2,365.40 that had not yet cleared the bank.

### Required

1. Prepare journal entries to record the preceding transactions of the Payne Corporation for the first quarter of 1995.
2. Prepare a bank reconciliation for Payne for March 31, 1995.
3. Prepare any journal entries necessary to adjust Payne's books on March 31, 1995.

**P13-9**    *Premium Amortization on Bond Investment and Partial Sale of the Investment Using the Effective Interest Method*    On January 1, 1995, the Hyde Corporation purchased bonds with a face value of $300,000 for $308,373.53. The bonds are due June 30, 1998, carry a 13% stated interest rate, and were purchased to yield 12%. Interest is payable semiannually on June 30 and December 31. On March 31, 1996, in contemplation of a major acquisition, one-half the bonds were sold for $159,500 including accrued interest; the remainder were held until maturity.

### Required

Prepare the journal entries necessary to record the purchase of the bonds, each interest payment, the partial sale of the investment on March 31, 1996, and the retirement of the bond issue on June 30, 1998.

**P13-10**    *Bond Investment Discount Amortization Schedule*    The Tudor Company acquired $500,000 of Carr Corporation bonds for $487,706.69 on January 1, 1995. The bonds carry an 11% stated interest rate, pay interest semiannually on January 1 and July 1, were issued to yield 12%, and are due January 1, 1998.

### Required

1. Prepare an investment interest revenue and discount amortization schedule using:
   a. The straight-line method
   b. The effective interest method
2. Prepare the July 1, 1997 journal entries to record the interest revenue under both methods.

**P13-11**    *Discount Amortization on Bonds Purchased Between Interest Dates*    On October 1, 1994, the Jenkins Corporation bought bonds with a face value of $200,000 for $199,472, including accrued interest. The bonds are due December 31, 1996 and carry a face rate of interest of 10.5%. Interest on the bonds is payable semiannually on June 30 and December 31. The company uses the straight-line method to amortize the discount.

### Required

Prepare journal entries to record the purchase of the bonds, each interest receipt, and the retirement of the issue on December 31, 1996.

**P13-12**    *Bond Investment Premium Amortization Schedule*    The Mercer Corporation acquired $400,000 of the Park Company's bonds on June 30, 1994 for $409,991.12. The bonds carry a 12% stated interest rate, pay interest semiannually on June 30 and December 31, were issued to yield 11%, and are due June 30, 1997.

### Required

1. Prepare an investment interest revenue and premium amortization schedule, using
   a. The straight-line method
   b. The effective interest method
2. Prepare journal entries to record the December 31, 1994 and December 31, 1996 interest receipts using both methods.

**P13-13**    *Discount Amortization on Bond Investment and Partial Sale of Investment Using Effective Interest Method*    On January 1, 1995, the Mark Corporation purchased bonds with a face value of $500,000 for $475,413.60. The bonds are due December 31, 1997, carry a 10% stated rate, and were purchased to yield 12%. Interest is payable semiannually on June 30 and December 31. On January 1, 1997, in contemplation of a major acquisition, one-fourth of the bonds were sold for $127,000. The remainder were held until maturity.

**Required**

Prepare journal entries to record the purchase of the bonds, each interest payment, the partial sale of the investment on December 31, 1996, and the retirement of the bond issue on December 31, 1997.

P13-14 *Comparison of Fair Value and Equity Methods*  On January 1, 1994, Snow Corporation purchased 20% of the 200,000 outstanding shares of common stock of Garvey Company for $3.75 per share as a long-term investment. The purchase price of the shares was equal to their book value. The following information is available about Garvey Company for 1994 and 1995:

| End of 1994 | Reported net income | $80,000 |
|---|---|---|
| | Cash dividends declared and paid | $30,000 |
| | Market value of shares | $3.50 per share |
| End of 1995 | Reported net income | $90,000 |
| | Cash dividends declared and paid | $30,000 |
| | Market value of shares | $4.25 per share |

**Required**

1. Prepare journal entries to record this information, assuming
   a. The fair value method is used by Snow
   b. The equity method is used by Snow
2. Assume 10,000 of the Garvey shares are sold on January 4, 1996 by Snow for $4.20 per share. Prepare the journal entry for this sale, assuming
   a. Snow is using the fair value method
   b. Snow is using the equity method

P13-15 *Application of Equity Method*  On January 1, 1995, Doe Company purchased 3,000 of the 10,000 common shares outstanding of the Ray Company for $14 per share and obtained significant influence. Doe amortizes its intangibles over the maximum life. The December 31, 1994 condensed balance sheet of the Ray Company is shown here:

*Balance Sheet (12/31/94)*

| Current assets | $ 10,000 | Liabilities | $ 50,000 |
|---|---|---|---|
| Fixed assets (net) | 100,000 | Common stock, no par | 30,000 |
| Intangible assets (net) | 40,000 | Retained earnings | 70,000 |
| | $150,000 | | $150,000 |

Doe Company was unable to determine the fair market value of the Ray Company's identifiable net assets shown on the preceding balance sheet. It did, however, determine that Ray Company uses the straight-line method (no residual value) to depreciate its fixed assets and to amortize its identifiable intangible assets over 20 years and 10 years, respectively. At the end of 1995, Ray Company disclosed the following condensed income statement and retained earnings statement for 1995:

*Income Statement (1995)*

| Revenues | $100,000 |
|---|---|
| Expenses | (60,000) |
| Operating income | $ 40,000 |
| Extraordinary loss | (10,000) |
| Net income | $ 30,000 |

*Retained Earnings Statement (1995)*

| Beginning retained earnings | $ 70,000 |
|---|---|
| Add: Net income | 30,000 |
| | $100,000 |
| Less: Cash dividends | (20,000) |
| Ending retained earnings | $ 80,000 |

**Required**

Prepare all the 1995 journal entries that Doe should have made related to this investment. Show and label all supporting calculations.

**P13-16**   *Recording Investments Under the Equity Method*   The Harper Corporation acquired 80,000 of the 200,000 outstanding shares of the Moore Corporation on April 1, 1995 for $400,000 and obtained significant influence. The following information concerning the Moore Corporation is available on the date of acquisition:

|  | Book Value | Fair Value |
|---|---|---|
| Depreciable assets (remaining life, 15 years) | $ 600,000 | $ 700,000 |
| Other assets | 500,000 | 450,000 |
| Total | $1,100,000 | $1,150,000 |
| Liabilities | $ 300,000 | $ 300,000 |
| Common stock | 250,000 | |
| Retained earnings | 550,000 | |
| Total | $1,100,000 | |

Subsequently, Moore Corporation paid a cash dividend of $40,000 on August 31, 1995 and reported annual income from operations of $125,000 and extraordinary income (earned in the third quarter) of $30,000 on December 31, 1995.

**Required**

1.  Prepare journal entries for Harper to record the preceding information. (Amortize goodwill over 40 years.)
2.  What is the balance in Harper's investment account on December 31, 1995? (Show all computations.)

**P13-17**   *Equity Method and Subsequent Sale*   On January 1, 1995, the Easton Corporation acquired 30% of the outstanding common shares of Feeley Corporation for $140,000, and 25% of the outstanding common shares of Holmes Company for $82,500 and obtained significant influence in both situations. On this date, the financial statements of Feeley and Holmes disclosed the following information:

|  | Feeley | Holmes |
|---|---|---|
| Current assets | $190,000 | $140,000 |
| Long-term assets | 370,000 | 180,000 |
|  | $560,000 | $320,000 |
| Liabilities | $120,000 | $ 90,000 |
| Common stock (no par) | 200,000 | 150,000 |
| Retained earnings | 240,000 | 80,000 |
|  | $560,000 | $320,000 |

During 1995, Feeley reported income of $70,000 and paid dividends of $40,000; Holmes reported income of $45,000 and paid dividends of $28,000. On January 1, 1996, all the Holmes shares were sold for $90,000. Assume both investments are recorded under the equity method and that any difference between each purchase price and the respective book value of the net assets acquired is considered to be goodwill and amortized over 10 years.

**Required**

Prepare journal entries to record: (1) the purchase of the Feeley and Holmes shares, (2) the recognition of investment income, (3) the receipt of investee dividends, and (4) the sale of the Holmes shares.

**P13-18**   *Change to Equity Method*   On January 1, 1995, Lion Company paid $600,000 for 10,000 shares of Wolf Company's voting common stock, which was a 10% interest in Wolf. At that date, the net assets of Wolf totaled $6,000,000. The fair values of all of Wolf's assets and liabilities were equal to their book values. Lion does not have the ability to exercise significant influence over the operating and financial policies of Wolf. Lion received dividends of $1.00 per share from Wolf on October 2, 1995. Wolf reported net income of $400,000 for the year ended December 31, 1995 and the ending market price was $63 per share.

On July 2, 1996, Lion paid $1,950,000 for 30,000 additional shares of Wolf Company's voting common stock, which represents a 30% investment in Wolf. The fair values of all of Wolf's assets net of liabilities were equal to their book values of $6,500,000. As a result of this transaction, Lion has the ability to exercise significant influence over the operating and financial policies of Wolf. Lion received dividends of $1.00 per share from Wolf on April 2, 1996 and $1.35 per share on October 1, 1996. Wolf reported net income of $500,000 for the year ended December 31, 1996, and $200,000 for the 6 months ended December 31, 1996.

**Required**

1. For the Lion Company, show the dividend revenue for 1995, as well as the December 31, 1995 unrealized increase in value of securities available for sale and carrying value of the investment account.
2. Assuming that at the beginning of 1997 the Lion Company issues comparative financial statements for 1995 and 1996, show the investment income for 1995 and 1996, as well as the December 31, 1995 and 1996 carrying value of the investment account.

P13-19 *Cash Surrender Value of Life Insurance* On January 1, 1994, Kehoe Corporation insured its president, vice-president, controller, and treasurer for $100,000 each. The annual premium on each policy is $4,200 payable on January 1 of each year and the cash surrender values for the policies increase by 4% of the annual premiums paid. Premium payments were made on the scheduled date by the Kehoe Corporation through 1996, and the following dividends were received at the end of the year on each policy: 1994—$450, 1995—$575, 1996—$550. On February 1, 1997, the treasurer died and Kehoe Corporation collected the face value of his policy plus eleven months' premium.

**Required**

Prepare journal entries to record the preceding information for the years 1994 through 1997. (Round calculation to the nearest dollar.)

# FINANCIAL REPORTING

## Stockholders' Equity

PART

# 4

# 14

# CONTRIBUTED CAPITAL

## Chapter Topics

*Corporate Form of Organization*

*Corporate Capital Structure*

*Issuance of Capital Stock*

*Preferred Stock Characteristics*

*Contributed Capital*

*Reacquisition of Capital Stock (Treasury Stock)*

*Incorporation of a Going Concern (Appendix)*

This chapter is the first of two on stockholders' equity. *FASB Statement of Concepts No. 6* defines *equity* as *the residual interest in the assets of a company that remains after deducting its liabilities.*[1] That is, the equity in a company is the ownership interest. Equity, which arises because of ownership rights, is created originally by owners' investments in the company. It may change because of several transactions or events including cash dividends or other distributions of assets, which are summarized in Exhibit 14-1.[2]

In the previous chapters, the discussion primarily focused on changes in assets and liabilities and their impact on net income (and equity). The main focus of Chapters 14 and 15, however, is on investments by owners, distributions to owners, and changes in equity not affecting assets or liabilities, as they apply to corporations.

Chapter 14 primarily addresses topics involving contributed capital. These issues include the formation of a corporation, the terminology relating to capital stock, the issuance of capital stock, the contributed capital section of stockholders' equity, the reacquisition of capital (treasury) stock, and the incorporation of a going concern (Appendix). Chapter 15 primarily addresses issues involving retained earnings.

---

1. "Elements of Financial Statements of Business Enterprises," *FASB Statement of Concepts No. 6* (Stamford, Conn.: FASB, 1985), par. 49.
2. *Ibid.*, par. 60–63.

**EXHIBIT 14-1**

## CHANGES IN EQUITY*

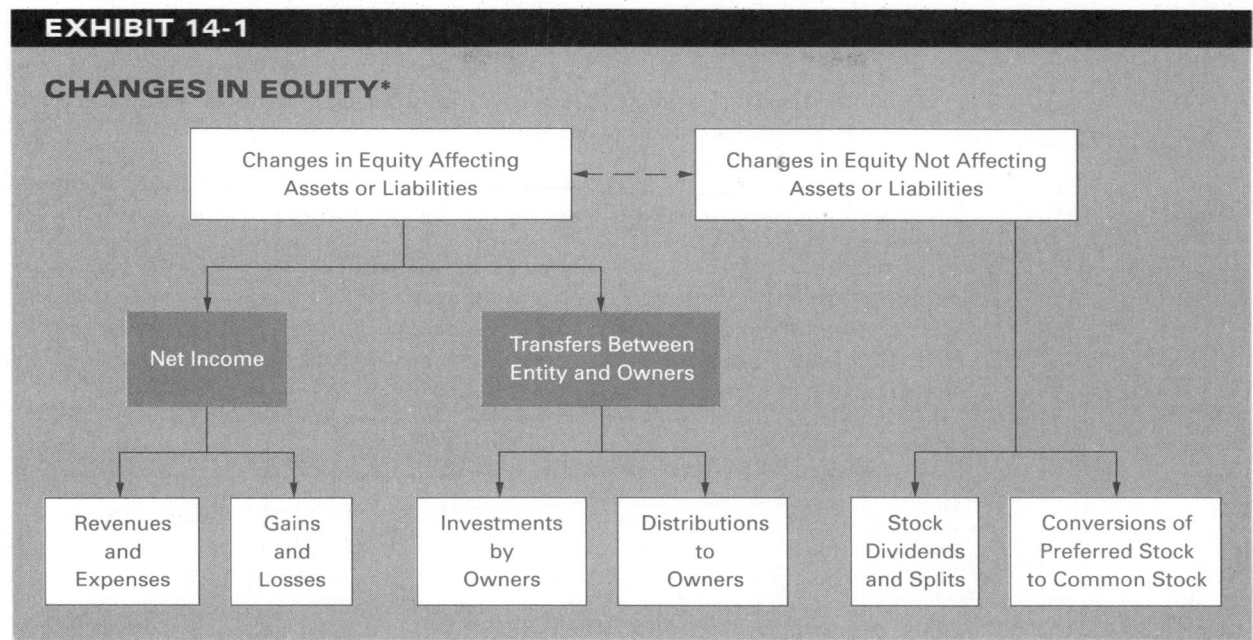

*Adapted from diagram in "Elements of Financial Statements of Business Enterprises," *FASB*
*Statement of Concepts No. 6* (Stamford, Conn.: FASB, 1985), p. 23.

## CORPORATE FORM OF ORGANIZATION

The corporation is the dominant form of company in the U.S. economy today. The number of sole proprietorships and partnerships is much greater than the number of corporations, but corporations produce and sell many more goods and services. For example, according to recent government statistics, corporations comprised only 19% of the number of companies in the U.S., but provided 90% of the total revenues of all companies.

### Types of Corporations

Corporations may be classified in several different ways. These classifications include private versus public, open versus closed, and domestic versus foreign corporations. Each of these classifications is summarized briefly as follows:

1. **Private** corporations are privately owned. They include *nonstock* companies that do not issue stock and do not operate for profit (e.g., universities, hospitals, and churches), and *stock* companies that issue shares of stock to stockholders and operate for profit. Stock companies include open and closed corporations.
   A. **Open** corporations are those whose stock is available for purchase by the public, on a stock exchange or over-the-counter, and so is widely held. Open corporations sometimes are called *publicly-traded* corporations.
   B. **Closed** corporations do not allow the sale of stock to the general public; such stock usually is held by a few stockholders. Closed corporations sometimes are called *privately-held* corporations.

2. **Public** corporations are owned or operated by governmental units, such as the Federal Deposit Insurance Corporation.

3. **Domestic** corporations, as viewed by an individual state, are those companies that are incorporated in that state.

4. **Foreign** corporations, as viewed by an individual state, are those companies that are operating in the state but are incorporated in another state.

The federal government applies a more global definition to domestic and foreign corporations. To the federal government a domestic corporation is one incorporated in the United States; a foreign corporation is one incorporated in another country.

In this book, we are concerned primarily with private corporations that issue shares of stock.

## Formation of a Corporation

Although a corporation actually is a collection of individual owners, legally it is treated as an artificial entity, separate from and independent of these individuals. Thus, ownership is readily transferable. Owners (**stockholders**) have a limited liability. The stockholders ordinarily have no personal liability for the corporation's debts and risk only their capital investment. Furthermore, they frequently play no active part in its management. As a result, the success of the corporation rests on its ability to attract significant amounts of capital (from a diverse set of stockholders, each with limited liability), which is controlled by a professional management group for an indefinite period.

In the United States, a corporation is a legal entity of a particular state. Each state has its own laws of incorporation; many are uniform throughout the country, others are not. Normally, one or more individuals may apply for approval to form a corporation. The application includes the names of the individual incorporators; the corporate name, address, and nature of business; the types, par value (if any), and number of shares of capital stock to be issued; and any other information required by the state's law. The application may also include the names and addresses of the initial subscribers to the capital stock, the number of subscribed shares, the subscription price, and the down payment (if any). If approved, the application is referred to as the **articles of incorporation** (or corporate *charter*). A stockholders' meeting may then be held at which the initial issuance of capital stock is made to the incorporators, a board of directors is elected, a set of rules (bylaws) regulating the corporate operations is established, and the board appoints the executive officers ("top management") of the corporation.

In order for a corporation to perform its functions, the state gives it various rights and powers, including the right to enter into contracts, to hold, buy, and sell property, to sue and be sued, and to continue in perpetuity. In conjunction with these rights and powers, a corporation has a number of responsibilities. A corporation may engage only in the activities for which it was established, it must adhere to state laws concerning the distribution of income, and it must pay state and federal taxes. Because management has the responsibility to abide by state and federal laws and to safeguard and ensure the proper use of capital contributed by a diverse set of owners, accounting for corporate capital has become a significant activity in itself.

This chapter focuses on capital stock transactions and their impact upon the corporate capital structure. It should be noted that any statements made about the characteristics of corporations, capital stock, and a corporation's capital structure are general statements. In any particular state, or for any particular corporation, these generalities may not hold.

## CORPORATE CAPITAL STRUCTURE

Ownership in a corporation is evidenced by a **stock certificate,** a serially numbered document that indicates the number of shares owned and the par value (if any). Exhibit 14-2 shows a stock certificate for General Motors Corporation. Because stock certificates may be freely transferred from one individual to another, state laws require that each corporation maintain appropriate records of its stockholders. The **stockholders' ledger** contains an account for each stockholder that shows the number of shares held. Whenever new shares are issued or shares are exchanged between stockholders, the ledger must be updated. Exchanges of stock are recorded initially in a **stock transfer journal.** This journal contains the names and addresses of the new and former stockholders involved in each stock transfer, the date of exchange, the stock certificate numbers, and the number of shares exchanged. Many corporations employ an independent **transfer agent** to handle the issuance of stock certificates as well as a **registrar** to maintain the stockholder records.

### EXHIBIT 14-2
### Illustration of Stock Certificate

## Capital Stock and Stockholders' Rights

The term **capital stock refers to the shares of stock issued by the corporation and owned by its stockholders.** Each stockholder has various rights. Generally, these include:

1. The right to share in the profits when a dividend is declared.

2. The right to vote in the election of directors and to establish corporate policies.

3. The right (called a **preemptive right**) to maintain a proportionate interest in the ownership of the corporation by purchasing a proportionate (pro rata) share of additional capital stock, if the stock is issued.

4. The right to share in the distribution of the assets of the corporation if it is liquidated.

These rights may be modified or waived for some types of capital stock or in specific circumstances. For instance, stockholders who own a certain class of stock may only be entitled to vote on particular issues. Another example is the case where the preemptive right is eliminated in order to allow a corporation to raise significant capital or acquire another company by issuing a large number of additional shares of stock.

A corporation may issue capital stock for cash, in installment sales, for nonmonetary assets, and in other types of transactions. It may issue two basic classes of stock, generally designated as **common stock** and **preferred stock.** In exchange for certain other privileges, the preferred class of stock usually is not granted all of the previously mentioned rights. The various stock transactions, as well as the characteristics and privileges of preferred stock, are discussed later in this chapter.

## Basic Terminology

Several terms often are used in the discussion of capital stock and related transactions, as follows:

- **Authorized capital stock.** The number of shares of capital stock (both preferred and common) that the corporation may issue as stated in its corporate charter.

- **Issued capital stock.** The number of shares of capital stock that a corporation has issued to its stockholders as of a specific date.

- **Outstanding capital stock.** The number of shares of capital stock that have been issued to stockholders and that are still being held by them as of a specific date.

- **Treasury stock.** The number of shares of capital stock that have been issued to stockholders and have been reacquired by the corporation but not retired. Treasury shares represent the difference between issued shares and outstanding shares.

- **Subscribed capital stock.** The number of shares of capital stock that will be issued upon the completion of an installment purchase contract with an investor.

## Legal Capital

As indicated earlier, stockholders have a *limited liability*. That is, generally they cannot be held legally responsible for the debts of the corporation unless it is determined that the corporation has been operated for the personal benefit of particular stockholders. In order to protect the corporation's creditors, state laws have established the concept of **legal capital as the amount of stockholders' equity that cannot be distributed to stockholders.** A corporation may not pay dividends or reacquire capital stock if such a transaction would impair legal capital. The definition of legal capital varies among states. Reference to the corporate laws of each state is necessary to determine the corporate legal capital in that state. However, in most states the par value or stated value of the issued capital stock is some or all of the legal capital.

### *Par Value Stock*

Historically, the primary way to establish legal capital has been by issuing par value stock. **The par value of capital stock (either common or preferred) is a designated dollar amount per share that is established in the articles of incorporation and is printed on each stock certificate.** When par value stock is issued, most states designate that the par value of all issued stock is the legal capital. The legal capital of a corporation thus is determined by multiplying the par value per share by the number of shares issued. The par value of a share often is set very low—perhaps $5, $1, or even less per share. Note that the par value of the common stock listed on the stock certificate of General Motors in Exhibit 14-2 is $1\frac{2}{3}$ per share. Since capital stock normally will sell at a price far in excess of the par value (e.g., General Motors' common stock was recently selling for $40 per share), the legal capital is usually only a small proportion of the total proceeds received. Stock rarely sells initially for less than its par value, because it is illegal to do so in most states. If such a sale occurs, the stock is said to have been sold at a *discount,* in which case the stockholder is contingently responsible to contribute sufficient additional capital to meet the legal capital requirements. In any event, par value has no direct relationship to the **market value**, the price at which the stock is issued. Generally, state regulations require only that a separate accounting be made of the legal capital.

### *No-Par Stock*

In order to avoid the contingent liability that would arise if stock were issued at less than par value, and to alert investors that the par and market value of stock are not directly related, most states now allow the issuance of no-par capital stock. As the term implies, such stock does not carry a par value. When no-par stock is issued, some states require that the entire proceeds received by the corporation be designated as legal capital. Many states, however, allow the corporate board of directors to establish a **stated value** per share of no-par stock. This stated value, when multiplied by the number of shares issued, generally determines the amount of legal capital. The accounting for stated-value, no-par stock parallels that of the accounting for par value stock.

The concept of legal capital has had a significant impact upon corporate reporting practices, particularly as they apply to the accounting for stockholders' equity. Capital Stock accounts (for either common stock or preferred stock) are established to accumulate at least a part of the legal capital, and Additional Paid-in Capital accounts are used for the remainder of the total amount of capital contributed by stockholders (part of which also may be legal capital).

## Additional Paid-in Capital

As indicated earlier, a corporation may issue capital stock in a variety of transactions. Each of these transactions is likely to involve an exchange price (i.e., market value) significantly higher than the par or stated value of the stock. Adherence to state law requires recording of the par or stated value. Sound accounting practice (as well as state laws in certain states) also requires identification, measurement, and recording of the excess value received (the difference between the market value and the par value) in each type of stock transaction. This excess is recorded in a specific **Additional Paid-in Capital** account. This account alternatively is entitled *Paid-in Capital in Excess of Par* (or *Stated*) *Value*, *Premium on Capital Stock*, or *Contributed Capital in Excess of Par* (or *Stated*) *Value*, or by an outdated term, *Capital Surplus*. Because this additional paid-in capital is likely to arise from a variety of transactions, a corporation may establish a single Additional Paid-in Capital *control* account and then have a subsidiary ledger containing separate additional paid-in capital accounts for each different source. When this occurs, only the control account balance is reported on the balance sheet. In this chapter, we assume a control account is *not* used.

## Stockholders' Equity

As discussed earlier, total stockholders' equity is the residual interest of the owners in the net assets of the corporation—the equity or *capital* of the owners is the assets less the liabilities. In Chapter 3 we noted that the values of the assets and liabilities could be measured by several methods, although historical cost continues to be the most common. The way in which assets and liabilities are measured will determine the measurement of total stockholders' equity, since the accounting equation: Assets = Liabilities + Stockholders' Equity must remain in balance. Total stockholders' equity, however, may be made up of several components.

The various components of a corporation's capital structure are disclosed in the stockholders' equity section of its balance sheet. We noted earlier that the results of all corporate stock transactions are recorded in capital stock accounts and additional paid-in capital accounts. To disclose the total amount invested by stockholders, these accounts are listed and added together in the **Contributed Capital** (or **Paid-in Capital**) section of stockholders' equity.

In addition to disclosing total investments by stockholders, state laws and sound accounting practice require disclosure of any corporate income that has been reinvested in the corporation and not paid out to stockholders in the form of dividends. This element of the corporate capital structure is disclosed in the **Retained Earnings** section of stockholders' equity. Also, in rare instances, stockholders' equity may increase or decrease as a result of events not related to the issuance of stock or to retained earnings. These elements of the capital structure may be disclosed in an **Unrealized Capital** section of stockholders' equity.

*Unrealized capital and retained earnings are discussed in Chapter 15.*

The basic framework of the stockholders' equity is as follows:

**Stockholders' Equity**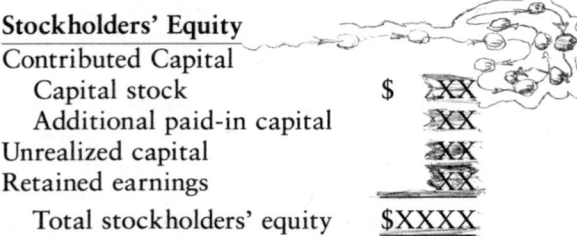

| | |
|---|---|
| Contributed Capital | |
| Capital stock | $  XX |
| Additional paid-in capital | XX |
| Unrealized capital | XX |
| Retained earnings | XX |
| Total stockholders' equity | $XXXX |

The transactions that affect contributed capital are covered in this chapter.

## ISSUANCE OF CAPITAL STOCK

**When only one class of capital stock is issued, it is referred to as common stock.** Common stockholders are the claimants to the residual interest in the corporation. Unless waived or modified, all the rights discussed earlier in the chapter generally accrue to common stockholders. As pointed out previously, corporations may engage in a variety of transactions related to the issuance of capital stock. The proper accounting for each of these transactions is described next. Because most capital stock is common stock, the examples are in terms of common stock. However, the illustrated journal entries apply equally to preferred stock, with appropriate terminology changes.

### Authorization

The corporate charter contains the authorization to issue capital stock. This authorization usually is recorded in a memorandum journal entry. The entry identifies the number of authorized shares, the par or stated value per share, and, in the case of preferred stock, any preference provisions. Generally, a separate account is established for each class of capital stock, and a similar memorandum entry is also made in each account.

### Issuance for Cash

Capital stock may be issued with a par value, as no-par stock with a stated value, or as true no-par stock. In the case of par value stock issued for cash, the difference between the proceeds and the total par value is recorded in an additional paid-in capital account. To illustrate, assume a corporation issues 500 shares of its $10 par common stock for $18 per share. The following journal entry is made to record the transaction:

| | | |
|---|---:|---:|
| **Cash ($18 × 500)** | 9,000 | |
|     **Common Stock, $10 par ($10 × 500)** | | 5,000 |
|     **Additional Paid-in Capital on Common Stock** | | 4,000 |

If, instead, the stock were no-par stock with a stated value of $10 per share, the preceding transaction would be recorded as follows:

| | | |
|---|---:|---:|
| **Cash** | 9,000 | |
|     **Common Stock, $10 stated value** | | 5,000 |
|     **Additional Paid-in Capital on Common Stock** | | 4,000 |

Note that, with the exception of the terminology change, the accounting for the issuance of no-par stock with a stated value is identical to that of par value stock.

Alternatively, the company may be authorized to issue no-par stock without a stated value. In this case, unless otherwise stipulated, the entire amount of the proceeds is the legal capital and is recorded in the capital stock account. If the preceding transaction had involved no-par, no-stated-value stock, the following journal entry would have been made:

| | | |
|---|---:|---:|
| **Cash** | 9,000 | |
|     **Common Stock, no-par (500 shares)** | | 9,000 |

Note that in this journal entry the number of *shares* issued was included. This was necessary because the number of shares issued in this transaction cannot be determined by dividing the total increase in the Common Stock account by the par value per share. The remaining examples of stock issuances assume a par value for the stock.

Although most states prohibit such transactions, it is theoretically possible to issue capital stock initially at a price below its par or stated value. In such cases, the stock sells at a discount, and the original stockholder may be required to pay into the corporation the amount of the discount if the corporation is unable to meet its financial obligations. The difference between the proceeds and the par value is *debited* to an account entitled Discount on Common Stock. This account is listed as a contra (negative) account in the Contributed Capital section of stockholders' equity.

## Stock Issuance Costs

Miscellaneous costs may be incurred that are related directly to the issuance of capital stock. They include such items as legal fees, accounting fees, stock certificate costs, underwriter's fees, promotional costs, and postage. When related to the initial issuance of stock at incorporation, such costs are recorded as an intangible asset, Organization Costs, because they are essential to the formation of the corporation. On the other hand, the costs related to subsequent issuances of stock are considered to be normal financing expenditures and, as such, reduce the proceeds from the issuances. When these costs are incurred, additional paid-in capital is reduced for the amount of the costs.

*Organization costs are discussed in Chapter 10.*

## Stock Subscriptions

Investors sometimes agree to purchase capital stock on an "installment" basis. This means the corporation and the future stockholder enter into a legally binding subscription contract, which provides that the subscriber (investor) will buy a certain number of shares at an agreed-upon price, with payment spread over a specified time period. The contract often requires a down payment and may contain provisions for the handling of any defaults (nonpayments) by the subscriber. Usually, shares of capital stock are not issued until the subscriber has completed full payment of the subscription price.

To illustrate the accounting for a stock subscription, assume that a corporation enters into a subscription contract with several subscribers that calls for the purchase of 1,000 shares of $6 par common stock at a price of $13 per share. The contract further requires a down payment of $3 per share, with the remaining $10 per share collectible at the end of 1 month. The stock will be issued to each subscriber upon full payment. The journal entry to record the subscription is as follows:

| | | |
|---|---:|---:|
| Cash ($3 × 1,000) | 3,000 | |
| Subscriptions Receivable: Common Stock ($10 × 1,000) | 10,000 | |
| Common Stock Subscribed ($6 × 1,000) | | 6,000 |
| Additional Paid-in Capital on Common Stock | | 7,000 |

Note that the balance to be received is recorded in a Subscriptions Receivable account. There is disagreement among accountants as to how to report the subscriptions receivable on the balance sheet. Some accountants have argued that Subscriptions Receivable should be listed as a contra-stockholders' equity account because collection is uncertain and therefore the company is not assured of obtaining a future benefit. Consequently, they claim the receivable does not meet the definition of an asset established in *FASB Statement of Concepts No. 6*. They also claim that receivables from subscriptions are different from normal trade receivables in that no goods or services have been provided. The Securities and Exchange Commission supports this view by requiring companies to report subscriptions receivable as a contra-stockholders' equity account in financial statements filed with it. The only exception is when the receivable is collected after the balance sheet date but before the financial statements are issued.

Other accountants argue that since the subscription contract is legally binding and most subscriptions actually are collected in full, reporting subscriptions receivable as an asset on the balance sheet is more appropriate. In this case, the account would be listed as a current asset when the subscription contract calls for its collection within one year or the operating cycle, whichever is longer. Regardless of which disclosure method is used, when the subscription contract involves a number of different subscribers, Subscriptions Receivable is a control account. A *stock subscribers* subsidiary ledger is used to record the shares subscribed by each individual subscriber and the payments to date.

The Common Stock Subscribed account is credited for the par value of the shares subscribed. This account is used because the shares have not yet been issued. Since completion of the contract is anticipated, the Common Stock Subscribed account is listed in the Contributed Capital section of stockholders' equity. It indicates that the corporation has contracted to issue additional stock. Additional Paid-in Capital is credited for the entire difference between the subscription price (the proceeds) and the par value of the subscribed stock under the assumption that the contract will be completed and the stock fully paid for.

If no-par, no-stated-value common stock is used in a stock subscription, the entire subscription price is credited to the Common Stock Subscribed account. No-par stock with a stated value and preferred stock are accounted for as in the example, with suitable changes in terminology.

Subscribers may make their payments in the form of any assets stipulated in the contract and acceptable to the corporation. Usually, cash is paid. When received, the asset account (for example, Cash) is debited and the Subscriptions Receivable account is credited. At the final payment by a subscriber, a journal entry is made to transfer the balance in the Common Stock Subscribed account to the Common Stock account, and stock certificates are issued for the number of subscribed shares fully paid for by that subscriber. To illustrate, assume in the previous example that the $10 per share final payment was received from subscribers to 950 shares at the end of the month. The following journal entries are made to record the final payment and the issuance of the 950 shares of stock:

| | | |
|---|---|---|
| Cash (950 × $10) | 9,500 | |
|     Subscriptions Receivable: Common Stock | | 9,500 |
| Common Stock Subscribed (950 × $6) | 5,700 | |
|     Common Stock, $6 par | | 5,700 |

## Subscription Defaults

Occasionally, a subscriber will not make the entire payment as required by the subscription contract. When a default occurs, the accounting is determined by the relevant contract provisions, such as:

1. Return to the subscriber the entire amount paid in.

2. Return to the subscriber the amount paid in, less any costs incurred by the corporation to reissue the stock.

3. Issue to the subscriber a lesser number of shares based upon the total amount of payment received.

4. Require the forfeiture of all amounts paid in.

For example, assume the subscriber to the 50 remaining shares in the previous example defaults on the contract. If the contract requires a forfeiture of the entire amount paid in, the following journal entry is made:

| | | |
|---|---|---|
| Common Stock Subscribed (50 × $6) | 300 | |
| Additional Paid-in Capital on Common Stock (50 × $7) | 350 | |
| Subscriptions Receivable: Common Stock (50 × $10) | | 500 |
| Additional Paid-in Capital from Subscription Default (50 × $3) | | 150 |

If the subscription contract does not include a provision for subscription defaults, the laws of the state in which the corporation is incorporated usually will have provided for one of the preceding alternatives.

## Combined Sales of Stock

Instead of issuing different classes of securities separately, a corporation may combine two or more classes and issue them in a single "package" transaction. When the securities are widely traded, to make the package attractive to investors the selling price of each package usually will be somewhat less than what would have been received if each class of securities had been sold separately. These transactions may include combinations of common stock, preferred stock, and long-term bonds. When different classes of securities are issued in a combined sale, to account for the different equity contributed by each type of security holder the proceeds are allocated between the two (or more) securities. This allocation is based upon the **individual relative market values of the separate securities.** If a market value is not known, the securities with the known market values are assigned a portion of the proceeds equal to their market values and the remaining proceeds are assigned to the security with the unknown market value.

Suppose, for example, that a corporation issues 100 "packages" of securities for $82.80 per package, or a total of $8,280. Each package consists of two shares of $10 par common stock and one share of $50 par preferred stock. If the separate market values of $16 per share for the common stock and $60 per share for the preferred stock are both known, the journal entry and supporting computations are as follows:

| | | |
|---|---|---|
| Cash | 8,280 | |
| Common Stock, $10 par (200 shares) | | 2,000 |
| Additional Paid-in Capital on Common Stock | | 880 |
| Preferred Stock, $50 par (100 shares) | | 5,000 |
| Additional Paid-in Capital on Preferred Stock | | 400 |

Computations:

**Aggregate fair market value:**

Common Stock: $16 × 2 Shares × 100 Packages = $3,200
Preferred Stock: $60 × 1 Share × 100 Packages = 6,000
$9,200

**Allocation:**

Common Stock: $\frac{\$3,200}{\$9,200} \times \$8,280 = \$2,880$

Preferred Stock: $\frac{\$6,000}{\$9,200} \times \$8,280 = \underline{5,400}$
$\underline{\$8,280}$

Note that the market value assigned to each class of stock is separated into the par value and additional paid-in capital in the journal entry.

If only the separate market value of $16 per share for the common stock were known, $3,200 ($16 × 2 shares × 100 packages) of the proceeds would be assigned to the common stock, and the remainder of $5,080 allocated to the preferred stock, as follows:

| | | |
|---|---|---|
| Cash | 8,280 | |
| Common Stock, $10 par | | 2,000 |
| Additional Paid-in Capital on Common Stock | | 1,200 |
| Preferred Stock, $50 par | | 5,000 |
| Additional Paid-in Capital on Preferred Stock | | 80 |

In the rare case when the separate market values of all the securities are indeterminable, the allocation must be made on an arbitrary basis. Care must be exercised so that a reasonable allocation is made to the various elements of equity. If a market value is established for one (or all) of the securities in the near future that makes this allocation unreasonable, an adjustment of the allocation is made. If in the preceding examples the stock had been issued in combination with bonds, then the bonds would be recorded at a premium or discount based upon their relative market value as discussed.

## Nonmonetary Issuance of Stock

In certain instances, capital stock may be issued for assets other than cash, or for services performed. This type of transaction is called a *nonmonetary exchange*. An appropriate value must be assigned to the transaction so that the exchange can be recorded properly. This valuation is a particularly troublesome issue when it involves intangible assets such as patents, copyrights, or organization costs. The general rule is to record the exchange at the fair market value of the stock issued or the asset received, whichever is more reliable. For instance, at the time of the exchange the stock may be selling on the stock market at a specified price but a verifiable value of the asset may be difficult to ascertain. In this case, the stock market price is used as the fair market value at which to record the exchange transaction.

To illustrate, suppose a corporation issues 200 shares of $10 par common stock in exchange for a patent. The stock currently is selling for $22 per share on the open market, and no significant impact on the market price by the issuance of the additional shares is expected. A value of $4,400 is assigned to the exchange, and the transaction is recorded as follows:

| | | |
|---|---|---|
| Patent ($22 × 200) | 4,400 | |
| Common Stock, $10 par | | 2,000 |
| Additional Paid-in Capital on Common Stock | | 2,400 |

The issuance of a large number of additional shares may significantly reduce the market price, however. In such a case, the transaction is not recorded until the reduced market price is known, and the asset is recorded at that price.

Alternatively, the stock may be closely held and not actively traded. Here, the fair market value of the assets received may be more reliable to use in recording the exchange transaction. This determination may be based on a review of recent transactions involving similar assets or on an appraisal by an independent appraiser. To illustrate, assume a corporation issues 500 shares of $8 par common stock that is not widely traded in exchange for an acre of land. An independent appraiser indicates the land has a value of $20,000. The appraisal value of the land is used as the fair market value and the journal entry is recorded as follows:

| | | |
|---|---:|---:|
| Land | 20,000 | |
|     Common Stock, $8 par | | 4,000 |
|     Additional Paid-in Capital on Common Stock | | 16,000 |

When two or more securities are issued for an asset, the combination of the most reliable fair market values is used to determine the total value at which to record the transaction. In the absence of reliable fair market values for both the stock and the asset exchanged, the corporate board of directors is responsible for assigning the value used in recording the exchange. Such an assignment should be carefully made on the basis of available supporting evidence. Incorrect valuation of the exchange would lead either to an overstatement of assets with a corresponding overstatement in stockholders' equity (referred to as **watered stock**) or to an understatement of assets and stockholders' equity (referred to as **secret reserves**). Furthermore, errors would arise in later financial statements if the asset is depreciated or amortized against future revenues.

## Stock Splits

The market price of a corporation's common stock may increase to the point where it limits investments by some stockholders. Many corporations believe a wide distribution of ownership improves their public image and increases the likelihood of product sales to these stockholders. In order to reduce the market price so that it falls within the "trading range" of most investors, the board of directors—upon meeting state legal requirements—may authorize a stock split. **A stock split (or *stock split-up*) results in a decrease in the par value per share of stock accompanied by a proportional increase in the number of shares issued.** Generally, a stock split also results in a proportional increase in the number of shares authorized through an amendment to the articles of incorporation. For example, assume that a corporation has 250,000 authorized shares and has issued 60,000 shares of $10 par common stock. If the corporation declares a two-for-one stock split with a reduction to a $5 par value, after the split 500,000 shares will be authorized and a total of 120,000 shares of $5 common stock will be issued. Generally, the additional number of shares participating in the same amount of earnings will cause a corresponding decrease in the market price per share.

When a stock split occurs, the existing shares generally are not recalled. Instead, each stockholder is informed of the new par value per share and issued an additional number of shares to compensate for the split. From an accounting standpoint, a stock split has no dollar impact upon any element of stockholders' equity; consequently, it has no effect on total stockholders' equity. In the previous example, the total par value of the common stock is $600,000 prior to and after the stock split.

A stock split ordinarily is recorded by a memorandum entry in the general journal that indicates the new par value, the total number of shares issued, and the impact (if any) on the number of authorized shares. For instance, in the previous example the memorandum entry might read as follows:

> The board of directors split the common stock two for one, increasing the issued stock from 60,000 to 120,000 shares. The par value of the stock has been reduced from $10 per share to $5 per share and the authorized shares have been increased to 500,000 shares.

Occasionally, a corporation will issue a **disproportionate stock split in which the reduction in par value is not proportionate to the increase in the number of shares.**

A journal entry is necessary to adjust the legal capital and additional paid-in capital. In the previous example, suppose instead that the par value was reduced to $4 per share. The journal entry would be as follows:

| | | |
|---|---|---|
| Common Stock, $10 par (60,000 × $10) | 600,000 | |
| Common Stock, $4 par (60,000 × 2 × $4) | | 480,000 |
| Additional Paid-in Capital from Stock Split | | 120,000 |

Although a disproportionate stock split does not affect total stockholders' equity, it does have an impact on the components of Contributed Capital. Occasionally, a company may declare a reverse stock split to increase the market value of its stock. **A reverse stock split decreases the number of shares and increases the par value per share,** and is recorded in a manner opposite to that of a stock split.

Some companies issue *stock dividends* in lieu of or in conjunction with cash dividends. Certain large stock dividends are similar to stock splits.

*Stock dividends are discussed in Chapter 15.*

### Stock Rights to Current Stockholders

As discussed earlier, the preemptive right allows current stockholders the opportunity to maintain their proportionate share in the ownership of the corporation if additional shares of the same class of stock are issued. Thus, if the board of directors authorizes the issuance of additional shares, this preemptive right must be extended to the present stockholders, unless that right has been waived. The right is fulfilled by the issuing of stock **warrants** to each present stockholder; these may then be exchanged for additional shares of stock. Although one stock warrant (right) usually attaches to each share outstanding, usually more than one warrant must be exchanged to acquire each additional share. Even if the corporation has satisfied the preemptive right (or the right has been waived), stock rights still may be issued to stockholders for a new issue of stock to encourage rapid sale of the stock. In either case, the rights usually allow purchase of the additional shares at a price slightly less than the current market price. The rights thus acquire a value themselves, and because the warrants are certificates that are readily transferable, they trade on the stock market in a manner similar to stocks. These stock warrants (rights) generally expire within a short period of time, usually a few weeks.

At the time the warrants are issued, no formal journal entry is required. However, a memorandum entry listing the number of additional shares that may be acquired through the exercise of the stock rights is made in the general journal so that a sufficient number of unissued shares may be held by the corporation for this purpose. This entry also provides information for disclosure of the outstanding warrants in the notes to the financial statements. If the rights are exercised, the usual journal entry is made to record the issuance of the stock. If the rights expire, another memorandum entry is made to this effect.

## PREFERRED STOCK CHARACTERISTICS

Some investors consider certain stockholder rights to be more important than others and are willing to forgo the latter in exchange for preferences regarding these rights. To attract these investors, a class of capital stock called **preferred stock** may be issued. The preferred stock contract will identify the stockholders' rights as well as the rights of the corporation. Various preferred stock characteristics may be specified in the contract, including: (1) preference as to dividends, (2) accumulation of dividends, (3) participation in excess dividends, (4) convertibility into common stock, (5) attachment of stock warrants (rights), (6) callability by the corporation, (7) redemption at a future maturity date, (8) preference as to assets upon liquidation of the corporation, and (9) lack of voting rights.

### Preference as to Dividends

**Holders of preferred stock have a preference to dividends** because a corporation must first pay any applicable dividends to preferred stockholders before a dividend may be paid to common stockholders. Since most preferred stock is issued with a par value, the annual dividends may be expressed as a percentage of this par value. If no-par stock is issued, the preferred dividend is expressed as a dollar amount per share. For instance, assume a corporation has outstanding 2,000 shares of 8%, $100 par preferred stock. Each stockholder is entitled to an $8 ($100 × 0.08) annual dividend per share. The corporation must pay $16,000 of dividends (8% × $100 × 2,000 shares) to preferred stockholders before it may pay any dividends to common stockholders.

A preference to dividends does not guarantee that a preferred dividend will be paid in any given year because dividend payments are at the discretion of the board of directors. To protect preferred stockholders further, a provision may be written into the preferred stock contract that calls for the accumulation of dividends. The preferred stock then is said to be cumulative.

### Cumulative Preferred Stock

Stockholders are not legally entitled to share in dividends unless these dividends have been declared by the board of directors of the corporation. If dividends are "passed" (that is, *not* declared) in a particular year, a holder of **noncumulative** preferred stock will never be paid that dividend. For this reason, noncumulative preferred stock is seldom issued because investors perceive this feature as a distinct disadvantage.

*Dividend declarations are discussed in Chapter 15.*

Most preferred stock is **cumulative.** If a corporation fails to declare a dividend on cumulative preferred stock at the stated rate on the usual dividend date, the amount of passed dividends becomes **dividends in arrears.** Dividends in arrears accumulate from period to period. Common stockholders cannot be paid any dividends until the preferred dividends in arrears have been satisfied. The dividends in arrears are *not* a liability to the corporation, because no liability exists until the dividend declaration. Nonetheless, such information is very important to investors and other interested parties in predicting future cash flows, and is disclosed in a note to the financial statements.

To illustrate dividends in arrears, assume a corporation has outstanding 1,000 shares of 10%, $100 par cumulative preferred stock. Each share of stock is entitled to a $10 annual dividend (computed by multiplying the 10% times the $100 par value). If dividends are not distributed in 1994 and 1995, preferred stockholders would be entitled to dividends in arrears of $10,000 at the end of 1994 and $20,000 at the end of 1995. At the end of 1996, $30,000 (for 3 years) would have to be paid to preferred stockholders before any payments could be made to common stockholders.

### Participating Preferred Stock

When preferred stock is **participating,** preferred stockholders share with the common stockholders in any "extra" dividends. Extra dividends are paid only after preferred stockholders have been paid their stated dividend *amount* and common stockholders have been paid at a *rate* equal to that paid on the preferred stock. For example, if a corporation has 9%, $100 par participating preferred stock and $10 par common stock outstanding, it must pay preferred stockholders $9 per share (9% of the $100 par) and common stockholders 90 cents per share (9% of the $10 par). Then, if the total dividend to be paid is greater than the amount needed to meet these dividend requirements, an extra dividend arises.

Participating preferred stock may be either fully or partially participating. **Fully participating preferred stockholders share equally with the common stockholders in any extra dividends.** When extra dividends are paid, they are distributed to the fully participating preferred stockholders and common stockholders on a proportionate basis relative to the respective total par values of each class of stock. **Partially participating preferred stockholders share in extra dividends, but this participation is limited to a fixed rate or amount per share.** In the preceding example, if the 9% preferred stockholders participated up to a maximum of 12% of the preferred stock par value, their share in any extra dividends would be limited to 3% of this par value. A numerical example of participating preferred stock dividends is presented in Chapter 15 in the section dealing with cash dividends. Participating preferred stock, whether fully or partially participating, is rare. Corporations generally agree that preferred stockholders receive too much preference when they are given first preferences as to dividends and also are allowed to share in all dividends.

### Convertible Preferred Stock

**Convertible preferred stock allows stockholders, at their option, under specified conditions to convert the shares of preferred stock into another security of the corporation.** Usually this security is common stock, and the conversion provisions stipulate the conditions and a specific exchange ratio. This exchange ratio will be modified, however, if there is a stock split. Since most preferred stock is not participating, the conversion feature allows the holder to exchange the dividend preferences attached to preferred stock for the unlimited rights to corporate income held by common stockholders. This feature is attractive to investors because the exchange ratio tends to tie the preferred stock market price to the common stock market price when the latter is rising, thereby increasing the value of the preferred stock. Conversely, the preferred stock dividend rate tends to stabilize the preferred stock market value when common stock values are falling.

Theoretically, both the preferred features and the potential for common stock equity are valuable to an investor in convertible preferred stock. Conceptually, then, the proceeds received upon issuance should be separated into preferred and common stockholders' equity. However, APB Opinion No. 14 requires that when convertible preferred stock is issued, no consideration is given to the conversion provision and any difference between par and market value is recorded as additional paid-in capital on preferred stock.[3] Thus, the accounting for the *issuance* of convertible preferred stock is identical to that for the issuance of nonconvertible stock. This method of accounting is required because of the inseparability of the stock and conversion option, and the difficulty in reliably determining the fair value to attach to the conversion provision. Unfortunately, use of this method places more importance on the legal form of the security than the economic substance of the transaction.

---

3. "Accounting for Convertible Debt and Debt Issued with Stock Purchase Warrants," *APB Opinion No. 14* (New York: AICPA, 1969), par. 12.

*The book value method is discussed in Chapter 12.*

Accounting for the *conversion* of preferred to common stock is very straight-forward because the *book value* method is used. The book value method is used (and the market value method is *not* allowed) because it does not result in a recorded gain or loss on a transaction involving the company's own capital stock. Under the book value method, the contributed capital (that is, the par value and additional paid-in capital) associated with the preferred stock is eliminated and replaced with the par (or stated) value of the common stock. If the total contributed capital eliminated in regard to the preferred stock is more than the common stock par value, the excess is recorded as an increase in additional paid-in capital related to the conversion. If less, the deficit reduces retained earnings because it is considered to be a dividend distri-bution to the preferred stockholders.

To illustrate the accounting at conversion, assume that a corporation originally issued 500 shares of $100 par convertible preferred stock at $120 per share. If each preferred share may be converted into four shares of $20 par common stock, the fol-lowing journal entry is made at conversion:

| | | |
|---|---|---|
| Preferred Stock, $100 par | 50,000 | |
| Additional Paid-in Capital on Preferred Stock | 10,000 | |
| Common Stock, $20 par (4 × 500 × $20) | | 40,000 |
| Additional Paid-in Capital from Preferred Stock Conversion ($60,000 − $40,000) | | 20,000 |

Alternatively, if each preferred share may be converted into seven shares of common stock, upon conversion the following entry is made:

| | | |
|---|---|---|
| Preferred Stock, $100 par | 50,000 | |
| Additional Paid-in Capital on Preferred Stock | 10,000 | |
| Retained Earnings ($70,000 − $60,000) | 10,000 | |
| Common Stock, $20 par (7 × 500 × $20) | | 70,000 |

The conversion of preferred to common stock changes the components of, but does not affect the total, stockholders' equity.

### Preferred Stock with Stock Warrants (Rights)

Corporations may also attach warrants to preferred stock to enhance their attrac-tiveness. As discussed earlier in the chapter and in Chapter 12 with regard to bonds payable, these **warrants** represent **rights** that allow the holder to purchase additional shares of common stock at a specified price over some future period. This period fre-quently involves a number of years, and in some cases no time limit is set. The longer the time period, the greater the attractiveness of such warrants, since stock prices over the long run have tended to increase. Because these warrants are separable (*de-tachable*) from the preferred stock, they usually begin trading on the stock market at some market price regardless of whether the specified purchase price of the common stock is greater than, less than, or the same as the current market price.

Theoretically, an investor in preferred stock with attached (detachable) warrants is investing in "dual" rights, each of which has a value. These rights include the right to dividends that will be paid on the preferred stock as well as the right to the market value appreciation of the common stock that may be purchased as a result of the warrants. Accounting theory suggests that, in recording the issuance of these securi-ties, the economic substance of the event should take precedence over the legal form of the security. In accordance with this theory, *APB Opinion No. 14* states that **the proceeds from the issuance of preferred stock with attached warrants is allocated to** preferred stockholders' equity and to common stockholders' equity, based on the relative fair values of the two securities at the time of issuance.[4]

*The relative fair market value method is discussed in Chapter 12.*

To illustrate, assume a corporation issues 1,000 shares of $100 par value preferred stock at a price of $121 per share. To each share of stock a warrant is attached that allows the holder to purchase one share of $10 par common stock at $40 per share. Immediately after the issuance, the preferred stock begins selling ex rights (without rights attached) on the market for $119 per share. The warrants begin selling for $6 each. On the basis of the $119,000 ($119 × 1,000) and $6,000 ($6 × 1,000) relative market values of the preferred stock (ex rights) and the warrants, respectively, the following journal entry is made to allocate the $121,000 ($121 × 1,000) issuance price:

| | | |
|---|---:|---:|
| Cash ($121 × 1,000) | 121,000 | |
|     Preferred Stock, $100 par | | 100,000 |
|     Additional Paid-in Capital on Preferred Stock | | 15,192 |
|     Common Stock Warrants | | 5,808 |

Computations:

$$\text{Preferred Stock:} \quad \frac{\$119,000}{\$119,000 + \$6,000} \times \$121,000 = \$115,192$$

$$\text{Common Stock Warrants:} \quad \frac{\$6,000}{\$119,000 + \$6,000} \times \$121,000 = \underline{\quad 5,808\quad}$$

$$\underline{\$121,000}$$

If, for some reason, the warrants did not begin trading at some market price, the allocation must be made based on an estimate of the value paid for the stock acquisition privilege.

Prior to exercise or expiration, the Common Stock Warrants account is listed as an element of contributed capital in stockholders' equity. Assuming all warrants are exercised, the following journal entry is made to record the issuance of the 1,000 shares of common stock in exchange for the warrants and $40 per share.

| | | |
|---|---:|---:|
| Cash ($40 × 1,000) | 40,000 | |
| Common Stock Warrants | 5,808 | |
|     Common Stock, $10 par | | 10,000 |
|     Additional Paid-in Capital on Common Stock | | 35,808 |

If any warrants are not exercised, a journal entry is made debiting Common Stock Warrants and crediting Additional Paid-in Capital from Expired Warrants to transfer the value assigned to the warrants to the existing common stockholders.

Conceptually, it might be preferable that the accounting principles related to convertible preferred stock and preferred stock with detachable warrants be consistent with the two securities' similar economic substance. One suggestion is to determine the economic value to attach to the conversion feature at the issuance of convertible preferred stock. A way of measuring this value is to estimate the proceeds that would be received if the convertible preferred stock had, instead, been issued as nonconvertible preferred stock. Then the difference between these estimated proceeds and the actual issuance price would be attributed to the value of the conversion feature. In

---

4. *Ibid.*, par. 16.

this manner, consistency would be promoted because economic value would be assigned to common stockholders' equity upon the issuance of either convertible preferred stock or preferred stock with detachable warrants.

### Callable Preferred Stock *option of issuer*

Preferred stock frequently will have a *call* provision. **Callable preferred stock may be retired (recalled) under specified conditions by the corporation at *its* option.** The specified conditions and call price are stipulated in the stock contract. The call price is usually several points (dollars) higher than the issuance price and usually establishes a ceiling on the market value of the stock. Typically, the stock contract requires the payment of dividends in arrears before the call is executed. Occasionally, callable preferred stock also will be convertible. In this case, the call price may be lower than the issuance price but will usually be higher than the par value. Upon recall of convertible preferred stock, the corporation will ordinarily allow the stockholder the choice of conversion or recall.

When callable preferred stock is *issued*, no special accounting is required. The difference between the market and par value is credited to Additional Paid-in Capital. Upon *recall*, the difference between the call price and the original issuance price is *not* treated as a gain or loss. This restriction has been applied so that a company cannot influence its earnings by recognizing a gain (or incurring a loss) in transactions involving its own equity securities. Instead, the original contributed capital—that is, the par value in the preferred stock account and the additional paid-in capital associated with the recalled preferred stock—is eliminated. If the call price exceeds the total of these amounts, the "loss" is debited to retained earnings because it is treated like a dividend distribution. In the case in which the call price is less than the total of these amounts, the "gain" is recorded as a credit to Additional Paid-in Capital because it is considered to be an additional contribution by the stockholder.

Assume, for example, that a corporation has outstanding 1,000 shares of $100 par callable preferred stock that were issued at $110 per share and that no dividends are in arrears. If the call price is $112 per share, the following journal entry is made to record the recall of these shares:

| | | |
|---|---:|---:|
| Preferred Stock, $100 par | 100,000 | |
| Additional Paid-in Capital on Preferred Stock | 10,000 | |
| Retained Earnings ($112,000 − $110,000) | 2,000 | |
|     Cash ($112 × 1,000) | | 112,000 |

Although unlikely, if the call price had been $105 per share, the following journal entry would have been made:

| | | |
|---|---:|---:|
| Preferred Stock, $100 par | 100,000 | |
| Additional Paid-in Capital on Preferred Stock | 10,000 | |
|     Cash ($105 × 1,000) | | 105,000 |
|     Additional Paid-in Capital from Recall of | | |
|     Preferred Stock ($110,000 − $105,000) | | 5,000 |

The recall and retirement of preferred stock causes a permanent reduction in stockholders' equity. (This is not to be confused with *treasury stock*, which is reacquired but not retired, as discussed in Chapter 15.)

### Redeemable Preferred Stock *option of holder*

In contrast to convertible preferred stock and callable preferred stock, some preferred stock is redeemable. **Redeemable preferred stock either may be subject to mandatory** redemption at a specified future maturity date for a specified price or redeemable at the option of the holder (instead of being callable at the option of the issuer). The Securities and Exchange Commission, for its reporting purposes, considers redeemable preferred stock to have some of the characteristics of a liability because of the likelihood of a cash outflow in the future that the company has no ability to prevent. In reports filed by companies with the SEC, it requires this stock to be reported as a separate component of the balance sheet (for instance, directly before stockholders' equity). Furthermore, it requires separate disclosure of the redemption features, shares issued and redeemed, and other related issues in the notes to the financial statements.[5] Although not requiring separate reporting, the FASB requires a similar disclosure.[6]

## Preference in Liquidation

If a corporation is liquidated, the preferred stock contract usually allows the preferred stockholders **preference** over the common stockholders (but secondary to the creditors) with respect to the corporate assets. The preference is typically expressed as a percentage of (or equal to) the par value and frequently requires the payment of dividends in arrears. This liquidation preference is important to external users and should be disclosed either parenthetically in the stockholders' equity section or in the notes accompanying the financial statements.[7]

## Voting Rights

Often in exchange for the previously discussed provisions the preferred stock contract will state that the holder has **no voting rights.** If there is no such statement, the preferred stockholder has full voting rights.

## Disclosures

It is possible for preferred stock to have various combinations of the previously discussed provisions. For instance, a preferred stock may be cumulative, nonparticipating, nonconvertible, and callable, with no voting rights. Some accountants have argued that this stock has more of the characteristics of long-term debt than it does of capital stock, and that it should be classified as a long-term liability or in a separate section between long-term liabilities and stockholders' equity. This view has not gained acceptance (except for redeemable preferred stock covered by the SEC rules), and preferred stock continues to be listed in the stockholders' equity section of the balance sheet. As discussed in the next section, the preferred stock characteristics are disclosed either parenthetically or in a note to the financial statements.

## CONTRIBUTED CAPITAL SECTION

The results of the various transactions involving the issuance of capital stock by a corporation are listed in the Contributed Capital (frequently called Paid-in Capital) section of stockholders' equity on its balance sheet. Contributed capital is usually separated into the par (or stated) value of the outstanding capital stock (or, in the

---

5. "Codification of Financial Reporting Policies," *SEC Accounting Rules* (Chicago: Commerce Clearing House, August, 1992), sec. 211.01 and 211.04.
6. "Disclosure of Long-Term Obligations," *FASB Statement of Financial Accounting Standards No. 47* (Stamford, Conn.: FASB, 1981).
7. "Omnibus Opinion—1966," *APB Opinion No. 10* (New York: AICPA, 1966), par. 10.

case of no-par stock, the total proceeds received from the stock issue) and the additional paid-in capital arising from the different transactions. The two segments of the contributed capital section include:

1. Capital stock
   a. Par value of preferred stock
   b. Par value of common stock
   c. Common (or preferred) stock subscribed
   d. Stock warrants and stock options (discussed in Chapter 15)
   e. Stock dividends to be distributed (discussed in Chapter 15)

2. Additional paid-in capital
   a. On preferred stock
   b. On common stock
   c. From other sources (e.g., stock splits, preferred stock conversions, treasury stock)

In addition to listing the specific amounts for the capital stock and additional paid-in capital accounts, certain other information is necessary for adequate disclosure. For each class of stock this disclosure includes the par value and the number of shares authorized, issued, and outstanding. It also includes the preferred stock dividend rate, preferred stock characteristics, any dividends in arrears, and any relevant details relating to the common stock. The information may be presented parenthetically adjacent to each capital stock account or in a note to the financial statements. As discussed in the next chapter, a schedule summarizing the changes in these various components of contributed capital is also an integral part of the financial statements.

To illustrate the preceding contributed capital framework, Exhibit 14-3 presents the Contributed Capital section of a hypothetical company, Newsom Corporation. Exhibit 14-4 shows the contributed capital of GTE on its comparative balance sheets

## EXHIBIT 14-3

### NEWSOM CORPORATION

Contributed Capital
December 31, 1995

*Stockholders' Equity*
Contributed Capital:

| | |
|---|---:|
| Preferred stock, $100 par (9%, cumulative, convertible, 10,000 shares authorized, 4,300 shares issued and outstanding) | $ 430,000 |
| Common stock, $5 par (80,000 shares authorized, 32,800 shares issued and outstanding) | 164,000 |
| Common stock subscribed, $5 par (3,600 shares at a subscription price of $34 per share) | 18,000 |
| Additional paid-in capital on preferred stock | 107,500 |
| Additional paid-in capital on common stock | 590,400 |
| Additional paid-in capital from conversion of preferred stock into common stock | 10,100 |
| Total contributed capital | $1,320,000 |

## EXHIBIT 14-4
## Contributed Capital

### GTE CORPORATION AND SUBSIDIARIES

|  | December 31 | |
|  | 1992 | 1991 |
| --- | --- | --- |
| (millions of dollars) | | |
| *Shareholders' Equity (in part):* | | |
| Preferred stock | $ 112 | $ 459 |
| Common stock—shares issued 945,147,187 and 911,311,077 | 47 | 46 |
| Amounts paid in, in excess of par value | 7,134 | $6,232 |

*Note 6. Shareholders' Equity (in part)*

*Common Stock*

In September 1992, GTE sold 33 million shares of its common stock in a public offering at a price of $32.875 per share. The net proceeds of $1.1 billion were used to reduce short-term obligations, including obligations that as of December 31, 1991 were expected to be refinanced on a long-term basis and were therefore classified as long-term debt.

In April 1990, the shareholders approved an increase in the number of authorized shares of common stock from 750 million to 2 billion shares and a reduction in the par value of each share from $.10 per share to $.05 per share in order to effect a 2-for-1 stock split, which became effective on May 23, 1990. All share and per share data in the accompanying financial statements have been restated to give effect to the 2-for-1 stock split.

The following table represents the actual number of shares before and after the 2-for-1 stock split issued in the last three years (in thousands):

|  | 1992 | 1991 | 1990 |
| --- | --- | --- | --- |
| Public offering | 33,000 | — | — |
| Contel merger | — | 203,900 | — |
| Two-for-one stock split | — | — | 329,520 |
| Employee stock purchase plan | 9,050 | 7,370 | 7,303 |
| Other employee and shareholder plans | 7,737 | 6,901 | 5,815 |
| Conversion of Contel stock options | 448 | 1,063 | — |
| Other | 388 | 282 | 222 |
| Total | 50,623 | 219,516 | 342,860 |

During 1990, GTE purchased 3.8 million common shares primarily to satisfy various share requirements of its employee benefit and shareholder stock purchase plans. As of December 31, 1992, 43 million shares were reserved for issuance under the various plans.

*Preferred Stock*

Preferred stock has voting rights generally on an equal basis with common stock except for the $2.475 series, which are entitled to half of a vote for each share. Dividends are cumulative on all preferred stock.

As of December 31, 1992, each share of $50 convertible preferred stock is convertible into 2.64 common shares, except for the 5.00%, 4.00%, 4.36% and 5.28% series which are convertible into 2.68, 3.60, 6.94 and 9.06 common shares, respectively. In addition, at December 31, 1992, each share of $2.00 convertible preferred stock is convertible into 1.56 common shares. During the years 1992–1990, preferred shares totaling 63,128; 112,666 and 215,390 were converted into 105,696; 243,289 and 352,849 common shares, respectively. During 1992, GTE redeemed at par value all of its outstanding auction rate preferred stock.

dated December 31, 1992 and 1991, and the accompanying Note 6 (in part), which describes the capital stock. Observe from Note 6 that the common stock was split 2-for-1 in 1990 and that the preferred stock is both cumulative and convertible.

This concludes the discussion of the major items affecting contributed capital. We now turn to a discussion of accounting for the reacquisition of capital (treasury) stock, which may or may not affect contributed capital.

## TREASURY STOCK (CAPITAL STOCK REACQUISITION)

In most states, a corporation may reacquire its own previously issued capital stock, after which the stock may be formally retired (canceled) or held in the corporate treasury. **Treasury stock is a corporation's own capital stock that (1) has been fully paid for by stockholders, (2) has been legally issued, (3) is reacquired by the corporation, and (4) is being held by the corporation for future reissuance.** The reacquisition of previously issued shares may result from the exchange of corporate cash or other assets, the satisfaction of a debt owed *to* the corporation, or the donation of the treasury stock by the corporate stockholders.

A corporation may acquire treasury stock for various reasons:

1. To use for stock option, bonus, and employee purchase plans.

2. To use in the conversion of convertible preferred stock or bonds.

3. To use excess cash and help maintain the market price of its stock.

4. To use in the acquisition of other companies.

5. To reduce the number of shares outstanding and thereby increase the earnings per share.

6. To reduce the number of shares held by outside shareholders and thereby reduce the likelihood of being acquired by another company.

7. To use for the issuance of a stock dividend.

Each of these is subject to legal, governmental, and stock exchange regulations.

Treasury stock is clearly *not* an asset; a corporation cannot own itself. A corporation cannot recognize a gain or loss when reacquiring its own stock; this restricts a corporation from influencing its net income by buying and selling its own stock. Consequently, treasury stock is treated as a reduction of stockholders' equity as we will discuss. To ensure that treasury stock is handled in the best interests of the stockholders, states have passed laws regulating corporate activities in this respect. Generally, treasury stock must be acquired for some legitimate corporate purpose. Treasury stock carries no voting or preemptive rights, ordinarily cannot participate in any type of dividends, and has no rights at liquidation. However, it does participate in stock splits, since the par value must be reduced accordingly (a memorandum entry is made showing the increase in the number of treasury shares and the decrease in the par value). Although the acquisition of treasury stock does not formally reduce legal capital, the amount that may be paid to acquire the stock is usually limited to the balance in retained earnings (and perhaps additional paid-in capital) so that legal capital is not impaired. Furthermore, the amount of retained earnings available for dividends must ordinarily be restricted by the cost of the treasury stock held so that the payment of dividends does not reduce contributed capital.

Just as the original issuance of capital stock causes an increase in stockholders' equity and the number of shares outstanding, its reacquisition has an opposite effect. Stockholders' equity (and the number of shares outstanding) is reduced. Reacquired capital stock may be formally retired, generally by filing the required documents in the state of incorporation. The shares then revert to authorized but unissued shares and legal capital is appropriately reduced. If the shares are *not* retired, the treasury stock may be reissued at a price above or below par value. Ordinarily, the board of directors need not consider the par value at reissuance because the legal capital requirements were met when the stock was originally issued. Upon reissuance, stockholders' equity and the number of shares outstanding are again increased.

Treasury stock transactions may be accounted for by either (1) the par (or stated) value method or (2) the cost method. Both are generally accepted accounting principles, although they affect the various components of stockholders' equity differently. Furthermore, the application of each method may differ according to the legal requirements of different states, and also may involve variations in accounting. Only the basic aspects of each method are presented here. Since the cost method is more widely used,[8] it is discussed first.

## Cost Method

When the cost method is used, the treasury stock "event" is treated as though it consists of two elements: (1) the purchase (reacquisition) that initiates the event and (2) the reissuance that completes the event. Under this method, it is assumed that the corporation reacquires its capital stock with the intent of reissuing rather than retiring it. When the stock is reacquired, a temporary account entitled Treasury Stock is debited (and Cash, or other appropriate asset account, credited) for the *cost* of the shares. A separate Treasury Stock account should be established for each class of stock (common and preferred). During the period between reacquisition and reissuance, the Treasury Stock account is treated as a contra-stockholders' equity account representing a temporary reduction in stockholders' equity. If a balance sheet is prepared during this period, the cost of the treasury stock is deducted from the total of contributed capital, unrealized capital (if any), and retained earnings (this is illustrated later in the chapter).

When the treasury shares are reissued, the Treasury Stock account is reduced (credited for the *cost* of the shares reissued) and the difference between the proceeds received and this cost is treated as an adjustment of stockholders' equity. If the proceeds exceed the cost of the reissued treasury stock, the excess is treated as an increase in additional paid-in capital from the treasury stock transaction. If the proceeds are less than the cost, the deficit is treated as a reduction of additional paid-in capital related to previous issuances or retirements of treasury stock of the same class. Should this additional paid-in capital be insufficient to absorb the deficit, the remainder is recorded as a reduction in retained earnings.[9] Since treasury stock may be acquired at different dates and at different costs, companies may maintain records to use the specific identification method when the stock is reissued. If such records are not kept, either FIFO or average costing may be used to record the reduction in the Treasury Stock account.

---

8. *Accounting Trends and Techniques* (New York: AICPA, 1992, p. 240) reports that of the companies disclosing treasury stock holdings in common stock, 355 used the cost method and only 28 used the par or stated value method.
9. "Status of Accounting Research Bulletins", *APB Opinion No. 6* (New York: AICPA, 1965), par. 12.

To illustrate the cost method, assume that Ball Corporation is authorized to issue 20,000 shares of $10 par common stock and enters into several treasury stock transactions. These transactions (1 through 5) are listed in the left column of Exhibit 14-5, followed by the journal entries to record the transactions under the *cost method*. In journal entry 4, note that although the treasury stock was reissued at less than par, no consideration was given to this because the legal capital requirements were met in journal entry 1. Only the *cost* of the treasury stock is used to determine the impact on additional paid-in capital.[10]

Finally, it is possible that, when shares are reissued at a price below cost, any additional paid-in capital from the same class of treasury stock is insufficient to cover the deficit between the reissuance price and cost. In this case, the deficit is debited to retained earnings. For example, after journal entry 4 the additional paid-in capital related to common treasury stock transactions amounts to $200. Suppose, in transaction 5, that the company reissues 100 shares of treasury stock at $10 per share. When this transaction is recorded, the Additional Paid-in Capital from Treasury Stock account is reduced to zero and the remaining deficit is recorded as a reduction of Retained Earnings (as a kind of dividend). The accounting for no-par treasury stock follows the same procedures as just discussed.

### Par Value Method

If the par value method is used to account for treasury stock, the *reacquisition* of capital stock is treated as an event entirely separate from the stock's *reissuance*. That is, when capital stock is reacquired from a stockholder, it is assumed that the corporate financial relationship with that stockholder is ended. Contributed capital must be reduced in a manner that is essentially the reverse of the recording made when the stock was originally issued.

A corporation may issue shares of capital stock at many different times during its life. At each issuance, the Capital Stock account is credited for the par value and the excess of the proceeds over the par is credited to an Additional Paid-in Capital account. Consequently, when capital stock is reacquired the Treasury Stock (either common or preferred) account is debited for the *par* value of the stock and the original Additional Paid-in Capital (on common or preferred) account is debited for a pro rata amount based on the average price received from all the *original* issuances of the stock. If the reacquisition price is less than the original average issuance price, the excess is credited to a new Additional Paid-in Capital from Treasury Stock account. If the reacquisition price is more than the original average issuance price, the deficit is recorded first as a reduction of Additional Paid-in Capital from Treasury Stock (if

---

10. Some corporations will prepare a slightly different journal entry from that shown in transaction 4 when treasury stock is reissued at substantially less than cost. This involves reducing the additional paid-in capital from all the *original* issuances of the same class of stock by an average pro rata amount per share. Any further deficit below the average original issuance price is then debited to retained earnings. To illustrate, recall from transaction 1 that the original issuance price of $12 per share resulted in a $2 per share increase in additional paid-in capital (because this is the only issuance, the $2 excess per share is also the *average* excess per share). Since the reissuance price for $8 per share in transaction 4 is $5 below the per share cost of the treasury stock, a corporation might record transaction 4 as follows:

| | | |
|---|---|---|
| Cash | 1,600 | |
| Additional Paid-in Capital on Common Stock ($2 per share) | 400 | |
| Retained Earnings ($3 per share) | 600 | |
| Treasury Stock (200 shares at $13) | | 2,600 |

## EXHIBIT 14-5

## COMPARISON OF JOURNAL ENTRIES FOR TREASURY STOCK

### Cost Method

1. *Issuance of 6,000 shares of $10 par common stock for $12 per share:*

| | | |
|---|---:|---:|
| Cash | 72,000 | |
|   Common Stock, $10 par | | 60,000 |
|   Additional Paid-in Capital on Common Stock | | 12,000 |

2. *Reacquisition of 1,000 shares of common stock at $13 per share:*

| | | |
|---|---:|---:|
| Treasury Stock | 13,000 | |
|   Cash | | 13,000 |

3. *Reissuance of 600 shares of treasury stock at $15 per share:*

| | | |
|---|---:|---:|
| Cash | 9,000 | |
|   Treasury Stock (600 shares at $13 per share) | | 7,800 |
|   Additional Paid-in Capital from Treasury Stock | | 1,200 |

4. *Reissuance of another 200 shares of treasury stock at $8 per share:*

| | | |
|---|---:|---:|
| Cash | 1,600 | |
| Additional Paid-in Capital from Treasury Stock | 1,000 | |
|   Treasury Stock (200 shares at $13 per share) | | 2,600 |

5. *Reissuance of another 100 shares of treasury stock at $10 per share:*

| | | |
|---|---:|---:|
| Cash | 1,000 | |
| Additional Paid-in Capital from Treasury Stock | 200 | |
| Retained Earnings | 100 | |
|   Treasury Stock (100 shares at $13 per share) | | 1,300 |

### Par Value Method

1. *Issuance of 6,000 shares of $10 par common stock for $12 per share:*

| | | |
|---|---:|---:|
| Cash | 72,000 | |
|   Common Stock, $10 par | | 60,000 |
|   Additional Paid-in Capital on Common Stock | | 12,000 |

2. *Reacquisition of 1,000 shares of common stock at $13 per share:*

| | | |
|---|---:|---:|
| Treasury Stock (1,000 shares at $10 par) | 10,000 | |
| Additional Paid-in Capital on Common Stock | 2,000 | |
|   ($2 average excess × 1,000 shares) | | |
| Retained Earnings | 1,000 | |
|   Cash | | 13,000 |

3. *Reissuance of 600 shares of treasury stock at $15 per share:*

| | | |
|---|---:|---:|
| Cash | 9,000 | |
|   Treasury Stock (600 shares at $10 par) | | 6,000 |
|   Additional Paid-In Capital on Common Stock | | 3,000 |

4. *Reissuance of another 200 shares of treasury stock at $8 per share:*

| | | |
|---|---:|---:|
| Cash | 1,600 | |
| Additional Paid-in Capital on Common Stock | 400 | |
|   Treasury Stock (200 shares at $10 par) | | 2,000 |

5. *Reissuance of another 100 shares of treasury stock at $10 per share:*

| | | |
|---|---:|---:|
| Cash | 1,000 | |
|   Treasury Stock (100 shares at $10 par) | | 1,000 |

any) and then as a reduction of Retained Earnings (as a kind of dividend paid upon reacquisition).

During the period between reacquisition and reissuance, the Treasury Stock account is treated as a contra-capital stock account. Since fewer shares are outstanding, it is deducted from the Capital Stock (common or preferred) account to reduce the total par value (this is illustrated later in the chapter).

When the treasury stock is reissued, the proceeds are accounted for as an investment by a new stockholder. Contributed capital (and the number of outstanding shares) is increased by crediting the Treasury Stock account at *par* and crediting the existing Additional Paid-in Capital (on common or preferred) account for the excess of the proceeds over the par value. If the proceeds are less than par, the Additional Paid-in Capital account is reduced. If no additional paid-in capital exists related to this class of stock, the debit is made to Retained Earnings. Note that a Discount on Capital Stock account is *not* debited because no contingent liability exists on the part of the new stockholders. The accounting for treasury stock with a stated value follows the same procedures as just discussed for par value stock.

To illustrate the par (stated) value method, the same transactions for the Ball Corporation as shown in the cost method example are listed in the right column of Exhibit 14-5, followed by the journal entries to record the transactions. Note that because there was only one issuance of common stock in transaction 1, the average price received is the same as the original issuance price. Consequently in the journal entry to record transaction 2, the $2 original excess per share is used to determine the total reduction in additional paid-in capital. Typically, the average additional paid-in capital originally received per share is computed by dividing the total additional paid-in capital from the various original issuances of common stock by the number of common shares issued.

## Balance Sheet Presentation

If treasury stock is held on the balance sheet date, the stockholders' equity presentation will differ slightly depending upon the method used to account for the stock. Under the cost method, the Treasury Stock account is deducted from the total of contributed capital, unrealized capital (if any), and retained earnings. When the par value method is used, it is deducted from the appropriate Capital Stock account (preferred stock or common stock). For example, assume that the stockholders' equity section for the Ball Corporation is prepared immediately after recording transactions 1-5 of the preceding example (assume further that retained earnings is $40,000 *prior to* recording any treasury stock transactions). The stockholders' equity, based on use of the two methods, is shown in Exhibits 14-6 and 14-7.

*Restrictions of retained earnings are discussed in Chapter 15.*

Note that total stockholders' equity is the *same* regardless of the method used; only the subtotals of the component parts are different. State laws generally require retained earnings to be restricted in the amount of the *cost* of the treasury stock, regardless of which accounting method is used.

## Acquisition at Greater Than Market Value

Recently, there have been numerous "takeover" attempts by stockholders in which their goal is to acquire a sufficient number of shares of a company's common stock to

## EXHIBIT 14-6

### COST METHOD

**Stockholders' Equity**

| | |
|---|---|
| Contributed capital: | |
| Common stock, $10 par (20,000 shares authorized, 6,000 shares issued, of which 100 are being held as treasury stock) | $ 60,000 |
| Additional paid-in capital on common stock | 12,000 |
| Total contributed capital | $ 72,000 |
| Retained earnings (see note) | 39,900 |
| Total contributed capital and retained earnings | $111,900 |
| Less: Treasury stock (100 shares at cost) | (1,300) |
| Total stockholders' equity | $110,600 |

*Note*: Retained earnings are restricted regarding dividends in the amount of $1,300, the cost of the treasury stock.

## EXHIBIT 14-7

### PAR VALUE METHOD

**Stockholders' Equity**

| | |
|---|---|
| Contributed capital: | |
| Common stock, $10 par (20,000 shares authorized, 6,000 shares issued) | $ 60,000 |
| Less: Treasury stock (100 shares at par) | (1,000) |
| Common stock outstanding (5,900 shares) | $ 59,000 |
| Additional paid-in capital on common stock | 12,600 |
| Total contributed capital | $ 71,600 |
| Retained earnings (see note) | 39,000 |
| Total stockholders' equity | $110,600 |

*Note*: Retained earnings are restricted regarding dividends in the amount of $1,300, the cost of the treasury stock.

exercise control over its activities. To thwart these attempts, some companies have reacquired their common stock from these stockholders at prices in excess of the fair market value of the stock. This excess is often referred to as "greenmail." In return for this greenmail, the selling stockholders may agree to abandon certain acquisition plans, to restrict purchases of additional shares, or to other limitations. When this occurs, an accounting question arises as to how to account for the acquisition of this treasury stock and the related greenmail.

In such a situation, when a company pays more than the fair market value to acquire treasury stock, *FASB Technical Bulletin 85-6* requires that the treasury stock is recorded at its fair market value. The difference between the price paid to acquire the treasury stock and the fair market value is recorded as an expense. This expense is *not* reported as an extraordinary item on the company's income statement.[11] After the acquisition of the treasury stock is recorded at its fair market value, any subsequent reissuances are recorded in the usual manner under either the cost or par value method.

### Donated Treasury Stock

Stockholders may donate treasury stock to the corporation, which may then be reissued. This relatively rare procedure usually occurs when the corporation needs to attract more working capital without increasing the number of outstanding shares. If the cost method is used to account for treasury stock, at reacquisition a memorandum entry is made indicating the number of reacquired shares. When the stock is reissued, the entire proceeds are credited to Donated Capital. If the par value method is used, at reacquisition Treasury Stock is debited and Donated Capital from Treasury Stock (discussed in a later section of the chapter) is credited for the par value of the stock. Reissuance requires a credit to Treasury Stock for the par value of the reissued shares and a credit (or debit) to Donated Capital from Treasury Stock for the difference between the proceeds and the par value.

A corporation must adhere to state laws regarding donated treasury stock. Many of these laws were established to discourage what is referred to as *treasury stock subterfuge,* an activity that occurred in times of high par values and resulted in *watered stock* (discussed earlier). An excess number of shares of par value stock would be issued in exchange for a nonmonetary asset. A limited number of shares then would be donated back to the corporation and reissued at a price less than par, thereby avoiding the contingent liability on the part of the stockholder. However, such subterfuges are unlikely in today's financial world with its legal restrictions.

### Retirement of Treasury Stock

Occasionally, the board of directors may decide to retire treasury stock. As a result, legal capital is reduced. Thus, a corporation must adhere to all legal requirements, because the reduction in legal capital can affect both creditor and stockholder financial security. After retirement, the shares are accounted for as authorized but unissued stock.

The journal entry made to record the retirement of treasury stock will depend upon which method the corporation uses for its treasury stock transactions. Under the *cost* method, the cost of the retired shares in the Treasury Stock account is offset against both the par value in the Capital Stock account and a pro rata share from the Additional Paid-in Capital (on common or preferred) account. Any difference between these latter amounts and the cost of the treasury stock either is debited to Retained Earnings or credited to an Additional Paid-in Capital from Treasury Stock account. Under the *par value* method, the par value of the retired shares in the Treasury Stock account is simply offset against the Capital Stock account. To illustrate,

11. *FASB Technical Bulletin No. 85–6* (Stamford, Conn.: FASB, 1985), par. 3–7.

assume the Ball Corporation retires the remaining 100 shares of treasury stock from the previous example. The alternative journal entries are as follows:

1.  Cost Method Retirement:

| | | |
|---|---:|---:|
| Common Stock, $10 par | 1,000 | |
| Additional Paid-in Capital on Common Stock | 200* | |
| Retained Earnings | 100 | |
|     Treasury Stock (100 shares at $13 per share) | | 1,300 |

$$* \frac{\$12,000}{6,000} \times 100 \text{ shares} = \$200$$

Note that the pro rata reduction per share in additional paid-in capital on common stock was computed on the basis of the current balance in additional paid-in capital on common stock ($12,000) divided by the number of shares *issued* (6,000).

2.  Par Value Method Retirement:

| | | |
|---|---:|---:|
| Common Stock, $10 par | 1,000 | |
|     Treasury Stock (100 shares at $10 par) | | 1,000 |

Regardless of which method is used, when the stock is retired the restriction of retained earnings regarding dividends is lifted and the related note is eliminated from the balance sheet.

## Overview of Treasury Stock

The cost method of accounting for treasury stock is widely used because of its relative simplicity, but it is difficult to justify theoretically. Its use results in a mingling of the various components of corporate capital. Moreover, the application of this method falsely assumes that the same corporate body of stockholders exists after the reissuance as existed prior to the reacquisition. Although the par value method requires more analysis and record keeping, it is theoretically preferable because it properly identifies the separate sources and amounts of corporate capital. It is also more logical than the cost method in the sense that when a particular stockholder "disinvests" in the corporation, the associated contributed capital is eliminated and replaced by the contributed capital of the new stockholder.

Regardless of whether the cost or the par value method is used, the following items are important:

1.  Treasury stock is not an asset; it is treated as a reduction in stockholders' equity.

2.  Treasury stock does not vote, has no preemptive right, ordinarily does not share in dividends, and does not participate in assets at liquidation, but does participate in stock splits.

3.  Treasury stock transactions do not result in gains or losses on the income statement, so that a corporation cannot influence its net income by buying and selling its own stock.

4.  Treasury stock transactions may reduce retained earnings but may never increase retained earnings.

5.  Retained earnings usually must be restricted regarding dividends when treasury stock is held.

6.  The total amount of stockholders' equity is not affected by whether the cost or par value method is used, but the subtotals of the component elements (retained earnings, treasury stock, and additional paid-in capital) are likely to differ.

## APPENDIX: INCORPORATION OF A GOING CONCERN

To increase their capital-raising potential, limit their liability, attract top-level management, reduce their taxes, or for other reasons, the owners of a partnership (or the owner of a sole proprietorship) may decide to incorporate. From an accounting standpoint, one company is then terminated and a new company created. When such an incorporation takes place, the net assets (that is, assets less liabilities) of the partnership are "exchanged" for shares of stock in the corporation, and several accounting procedures are undertaken. The accounting procedures involved are based on an extension of the concept introduced earlier that the amount at which to record the noncash exchange of stock is the fair value of the stock issued or the asset received, whichever is more reliable. The procedures include: (1) revaluation and exchange of the net assets, (2) adjustment of the partnership capital accounts, and (3) closing out of the partnership capital accounts and issuance of the capital stock. Because these procedures affect the contributed capital of the new corporation, they are discussed in this Appendix.

The net assets of the partnership are revalued to their fair market value in order to recognize the gain or loss accruing to the owners upon termination of the partnership and to record the value of the net assets transferred to the corporation. The capital accounts are adjusted according to the partners' profit and loss sharing ratio in order to reflect each partner's share in the gain or loss resulting from the revaluation. Furthermore, since an exchange takes place, it is possible for an intangible asset, Goodwill, to be recognized. This occurs when the fair market value of the corporate stock issued to the partners exceeds the fair market value of the partnership's identifiable net assets exchanged. The recognition of goodwill as an asset increases the partners' capital accounts correspondingly. Finally, each capital account is eliminated and capital stock is issued in proportion to the values in each capital account.

The specific accounting procedures for the incorporation depend upon whether the accounting records of the partnership will continue to be used or an entirely new set of records will be established. To illustrate the alternative accounting procedures related to an incorporation, assume that partners X and Y decide to form the ABC Corporation. The partners share profits in a 70%/30% ratio. The balance sheet of the partnership on January 1, 1995, the date of incorporation, is shown in Exhibit 14-8.

### EXHIBIT 14-8

**X AND Y PARTNERSHIP**

**Balance Sheet**
**January 1, 1995**

| *Assets* | | | *Liabilities* | | |
|---|---|---|---|---|---|
| Cash | $ 4,000 | | Accounts payable | | $15,000 |
| Accounts receivable | 13,300 | | | | |
| Less: Allowance for doubtful accounts | (800) | | | | |
| Inventory | 17,500 | | *Owners' Equity* | | |
| Property and equipment | 32,000 | | X, Capital | $27,000 | |
| Less: Accumulated depreciation | (14,000) | | Y, Capital | 10,000 | 37,000 |
| Total assets | $52,000 | | Total liabilities and owners' equity | | $52,000 |

The ABC Corporation is authorized to issue 12,000 shares of $5 par common stock. It agrees to acquire all the assets (*except* cash) and assume all the liabilities of the X and Y partnership in exchange for shares of stock of equivalent fair value. In determining a fair market value for the net assets, the following information is assembled from an analysis of the partnership's accounting records and current economic conditions.

1. Allowance for doubtful accounts should be $1,500.

2. Inventory has a current replacement cost of $20,200.

3. Property and equipment have a combined appraised value of $30,000.

4. Unrecorded accrued liabilities are $1,000.

The partners agree to accept 7,000 shares of stock to be distributed as 5,000 shares to X and 2,000 shares to Y. The partners withdraw the $4,000 partnership cash balance according to their remaining adjusted partnership capital balances, and the corporation sells 2,000 shares of stock to other investors at $8 per share.

## PARTNERSHIP ACCOUNTING RECORDS RETAINED

If the partnership accounting records are used in the new corporation, the following journal entries are made to reflect the incorporation.

1. To revalue the identifiable net assets and recognize the gain:

| | | |
|---|---|---|
| Inventory ($20,200 − $17,500) | 2,700 | |
| Accumulated Depreciation | | |
| [$30,000 − ($32,000 − $14,000)] | 12,000 | |
|     Allowance for Doubtful Accounts ($1,500 − $800) | | 700 |
|     Accrued Liabilities | | 1,000 |
|     X, Capital (70% of $13,000 gain from revaluation) | | 9,100 |
|     Y, Capital (30% of $13,000 gain from revaluation) | | 3,900 |

Typically, Accumulated Depreciation is reduced (credited) in the revaluation journal entry to bring the carrying value up to the fair market value. If it is necessary to reduce Accumulated Depreciation to zero, any further adjustment to increase the asset to fair market value is made directly to the asset account.

2. To record the intangible asset:

| | | |
|---|---|---|
| Goodwill | 10,000 | |
|     X, Capital (70%) | | 7,000 |
|     Y, Capital (30%) | | 3,000 |

Computations:

| | |
|---|---|
| Value of shares issued to partners (7,000 × $8) | $56,000 |
| Fair value of identifiable net assets (*except* cash)[a] | (46,000) |
| Goodwill | $10,000 |

---

a.  $37,000 unadjusted identifiable net assets + $13,000 ($2,700 + $12,000 − $700 − $1,000) net asset write-up − $4,000 cash.

Note in the computation of goodwill that the value of the shares received by the partners is based on the $8 per share selling price to other investors. Note also that the fair market value of the net identifiable assets exchanged, *in this case*, does not include the cash because the cash is withdrawn by the partners.[12]

3.  To issue stock to X and Y:

| | | |
|---|---|---|
| X, Capital (5,000 × $8) | 40,000 | |
| Y, Capital (2,000 × $8) | 16,000 | |
|     Common Stock, $5 par | | 35,000 |
|     Additional Paid-in Capital on Common Stock | | 21,000 |

4.  To withdraw cash and close the partners' accounts:

| | | |
|---|---|---|
| X, Capital | 3,100 | |
| Y, Capital | 900 | |
|     Cash | | 4,000 |

Computations:

| | X | Y |
|---|---|---|
| Unadjusted capital (from partnership balance sheet) | $27,000 | $10,000 |
| Gain from revaluation (from journal entry #1) | 9,100 | 3,900 |
| Goodwill adjustment (from journal entry #2) | 7,000 | 3,000 |
| Adjusted capital | $43,100 | $16,900 |
| Value of shares (from journal entry #3) | (40,000) | (16,000) |
| Cash distribution | $ 3,100 | $ 900 |

5.  To record the sale of 2,000 shares of stock at $8 per share to investors:

| | | |
|---|---|---|
| Cash | 16,000 | |
|     Common Stock, $5 par | | 10,000 |
|     Additional Paid-in Capital on Common Stock | | 6,000 |

## NEW CORPORATE ACCOUNTING RECORDS OPENED

If new corporate accounts are established, the net assets (including goodwill) are revalued and the resulting gain or loss is recorded in the partnership accounts. The partnership accounts are then closed out (often in a several-step process) upon the receipt and distribution of the stock. The new corporate accounts are opened based on the fair market value of the assets, liabilities, and capital stock. The journal entries for the X and Y Partnership and the ABC Corporation are shown in Exhibit 14-9.

Regardless of whether the partnership accounting records are retained or new corporate accounts are established, the beginning balance sheet for the ABC Corporation as of January 1, 1995 is as shown in Exhibit 14-10.

---

12. Had the cash been transferred to the corporation, it would have been included in the fair value of the net assets exchanged, and goodwill would have been correspondingly less. In such a situation, journal entry 3 would close out the partners' accounts.

## EXHIBIT 14-9

## NEW CORPORATE ACCOUNTING RECORDS OPENED UPON PARTNERSHIP INCORPORATION

### To Close Partnership Accounts

1. To revalue net assets and recognize gain:

| | | |
|---|---|---|
| Goodwill* | 10,000 | |
| Inventory | 2,700 | |
| Accumulated Depreciation | 12,000 | |
| Allowance for Doubtful Accounts | | 700 |
| Accrued Liabilities | | 1,000 |
| X, Capital (70%) | | 16,100 |
| Y, Capital (30%) | | 6,900 |

2. To record receipt of stock and to close out other asset and liability account balances (except cash):

| | | |
|---|---|---|
| Investment in ABC Stock ($8 × 7,000) | 56,000 | |
| Allowance for Doubtful Accounts | 1,500 | |
| Accumulated Depreciation | 2,000 | |
| Accounts Payable | 15,000 | |
| Accrued Liabilities | 1,000 | |
| Goodwill | | 10,000 |
| Accounts Receivable | | 13,300 |
| Inventory | | 20,200 |
| Property and Equipment | | 32,000 |

3. To distribute stock to partners:

| | | |
|---|---|---|
| X, Capital | 40,000 | |
| Y, Capital | 16,000 | |
| Investment in ABC Stock | | 56,000 |

4. To distribute cash and close partners' capital accounts:

| | | |
|---|---|---|
| X, Capital | 3,100 | |
| Y, Capital | 900 | |
| Cash | | 4,000 |

### To Open Corporate Accounts

1. To record exchange of stock for net assets:

| | | |
|---|---|---|
| Goodwill* | 10,000 | |
| Accounts Receivable | 13,300 | |
| Inventory | 20,200 | |
| Property and Equipment | 32,000 | |
| Allowance for Doubtful Accounts | | 1,500 |
| Accumulated Depreciation | | 2,000 |
| Accounts Payable | | 15,000 |
| Accrued Liabilities | | 1,000 |
| Common Stock, $5 par | | 35,000 |
| Additional Paid-in Capital on Common Stock | | 21,000 |

2. To record sale of stock to investors:

| | | |
|---|---|---|
| Cash | 16,000 | |
| Common Stock, $5 par | | 10,000 |
| Additional Paid-in Capital on Common Stock | | 6,000 |

*See computation on p. 671.

## EXHIBIT 14-10

### ABC CORPORATION

**Balance Sheet**
**January 1, 1995**

| *Assets* | | | *Liabilities* | |
|---|---|---|---|---|
| Cash | | $16,000 | Accounts payable | $15,000 |
| Accounts receivable | 13,300 | | Accrued liabilities | 1,000 |
| Less: Allowance for doubtful accounts | (1,500) | | | $16,000 |
| Inventory | | 20,200 | | |
| Property and equipment | 32,000 | | *Stockholders' Equity* | |
| Less: Accumulated depreciation | (2,000) | | Common stock, $5 par | $45,000 |
| Goodwill | | 10,000 | Additional paid-in capital | 27,000 |
| Total assets | | $88,000 | Total liabilities and stockholders' equity | $88,000 |

## QUESTIONS

*Q14-1* What information is contained in a corporation's articles of incorporation?

*Q14-2* What is the difference between (a) a public and private corporation, (b) an open and closed corporation, and (c) a domestic and foreign corporation (as viewed by a particular state)?

*Q14-3* What is (a) a *stock certificate,* (b) a *stockholders' ledger,* (c) a *stock transfer journal,* and (d) a *transfer agent*?

*Q14-4* List the basic rights of a stockholder. Which do you consider to be the most important?

*Q14-5* What is the meaning of the following terms: (a) *authorized capital stock,* (b) *issued capital stock,* (c) *outstanding capital stock,* and (d) *treasury stock*? What is the difference between the issued and outstanding capital stock?

*Q14-6* What is *legal capital* and why is it important?

*Q14-7* How is legal capital determined, assuming capital stock has a par value, a stated value, or no-par value?

*Q14-8* What are the three components and the basic framework of stockholders' equity?

*Q14-9* How does preferred stock differ from common stock?

*Q14-10* What amount of the proceeds from the issuance of no-par, no-stated-value stock is recorded in the Capital Stock account?

*Q14-11* What is a *stock subscription*? How are the accounts Subscriptions Receivable and Preferred Stock Subscribed classified on the balance sheet? Why are they so classified?

*Q14-12* What alternatives are possible if a subscriber defaults on a stock subscription? How would you determine which alternative to use?

*Q14-13* How would you record the proceeds received from the combined issuance by a corporation of shares of common stock with shares of preferred stock?

*Q14-14* If capital stock is issued for an asset other than cash, what amount would you use to record the transaction?

*Q14-15* When do (a) watered stock or (b) secret reserves result from the recording of a nonmonetary issuance of stock? What impact does each have on the balance sheet?

*Q14-16* What is a *stock split* and a *disproportionate stock split*? How do they affect each element of stockholders' equity?

*Q14-17* Define the following terms regarding preferred stock: (a) *dividend preference;* (b) *cumulative;* (c) *participating;* (d) *convertible;* (e) *warrants;* (f) *callable;* and (g) *redeemable.*

*Q14-18* Why is a preferred stock similar to a long-term bond? Why is it similar to common stock?

*Q14-19* What are the two segments of contributed capital and what might be included in each segment?

*Q14-20* (a) What is *treasury stock?* (b) Why might a corporation wish to acquire treasury stock?

*Q14-21* If the cost method is used to account for treasury stock, the treasury stock "event" is treated as though it consists of two elements; if the par value method is used, the reacquisition and reissuance transactions are viewed as separate events. Explain the accounting differences resulting from these concepts.

*Q14-22* What is the proper balance sheet treatment of the Treasury Stock account under the cost method of accounting for treasury stock? Under the par value method?

*Q14-23* How should the reacquisition and reissuance of donated treasury stock be accounted for under (a) the cost method and (b) the par value method?

*Q14-24* What accounting procedures are involved under (a) the cost method and (b) the par value method when a company retires treasury stock?

*Q14-25* (*Appendix*) What accounting procedures must be undertaken when a partnership incorporates?

*Q14-26* (*Appendix*) When would the intangible asset, Goodwill, be recorded in the incorporation of a partnership? How would the amount be computed?

# CASES

## C14-1  Stockholder Rights and Preferences
A stockholder has several rights as an "owner" of a corporation. Furthermore, the rights of preferred stockholders are sometimes modified upon the issuance of preferred stock.

### Required
1. List and briefly discuss stockholders' rights as they pertain to common stockholders. Indicate the relative importance of each.
2. List and briefly discuss what characteristics might be attached to preferred stock. Indicate the set of characteristics that makes preferred stock more like a long-term bond than a common stock.

## C14-2  Exchange of Stock for Asset
As a general rule, when capital stock is issued for assets other than cash, it is said that the exchange should be valued at the fair market value of the stock or the asset, whichever is more reliable.

### Required
Discuss the reasoning behind this rule, including the concepts of *watered stock* and *secret reserves*. Give an example of a situation where the fair market value of (1) the stock and, alternatively, (2) the asset is used to record an exchange.

## C14-3  Issuance of Security Packages
Occasionally, a corporation will combine securities into a "package" (for example, common stocks, preferred stocks, bonds) and issue these securities as a single unit.

### Required
Assuming that two securities (common stock and preferred stock) are issued as a unit, discuss the alternative ways of valuing the separate stocks of the unit in an exchange for (1) cash or (2) an asset(s) other than cash.

## C14-4  Subscriptions
Corporations may enter into subscription contracts for the purchase of their stock.

### Required
What is a subscription contract and how does it work? What provisions are usually included in the contract? What are the arguments for reporting the Subscriptions Receivable account as a contra-stockholders' equity item and for reporting it as a current asset? Why is the Capital Stock account not credited at the time of the subscription instead of the Capital Stock Subscribed account? How is this latter account listed on the balance sheet? What are the alternative methods of handling subscription defaults?

## C14-5  Convertible Preferred Stock and Warrants
The stockholders' equity of a corporation may include both preferred stock and common stock. Preferred stock may (1) be convertible into common stock or (2) be issued with warrants attached enabling the acquisition of common stock.

### Required
Discuss the following three items:
1. The similarities and differences between these types of preferred stock.
2. Theoretically, the appropriate accounting treatment for the proceeds from the issuance of both types of preferred stock.
3. Which accounting treatment is generally acceptable for each type and why?

## C14-6  Capital Stock
Capital stock is an important area of a corporation's equity section. Generally the term "capital stock" embraces common and preferred stock issued by a corporation.

**Required**

1. What are the basic rights inherent in ownership of common stock, and how are they exercised?
2. What is preferred stock? Discuss the various preferences afforded preferred stock. (*AICPA adapted*)

## C14-7    *Treasury Stock*

For numerous reasons a corporation may reacquire shares of its own capital stock. When a company purchases treasury stock, it has two options as to how to account for the shares: (1) cost method, and (2) par value method.

**Required**

Compare and contrast the cost method with the par value method for each of the following:

1. Purchase of shares at a price less than par value.
2. Purchase of shares at a price greater than par value.
3. Subsequent resale of treasury shares at a price less than purchase price, but more than par value.
4. Subsequent resale of treasury shares at a price greater than both purchase price and par value.
5. Effect on net income. (*AICPA adapted*)

## C14-8    *Treasury Stock*

Corporations sometimes engage in "treasury stock" transactions.

**Required**

1. Define *treasury stock*.
2. Why would a corporation acquire treasury stock?
3. Briefly discuss the two alternative methods of accounting for the reacquisition and reissuance of treasury stock. Assume the treasury stock is common stock and has a par value.
4. Briefly discuss the balance sheet presentation of treasury stock for each of the alternative methods.

## C14-9    *Definitions*

In dealing with the various equity securities of a corporate entity, it is important to understand certain related terminology.

**Required**

Define the following terms: (1) treasury stock; (2) legal capital; (3) stock right; and (4) stock warrant. (*AICPA adapted*)

## C14-10    *Changes in Equity*

*FASB Statement of Concepts No. 6* defines equity and discusses the various changes in equity.

**Required**

Define and discuss the term *equity*. Identify the various changes in equity in regard to their impact on assets and liabilities.

## C14-11    *Researching GAAP*

Russell International, a publicly-traded company, reacquired 500,000 shares of its common stock during July of 1995 at a cost of $25 per share. The current market price of the stock was $20 per share when the 500,000 shares were reacquired.

The shares that were reacquired had been owned by a group of minority shareholders who had been dissatisfied with Russell International's earnings trend, stock price, and dividends paid. In fact these minority shareholders had been so disgruntled that they had filed a suit against Russell's directors during 1994. The minority shareholders' suit claimed damages of $3.0 million because of the board's failure to fulfill its fiduciary responsibility to maximize shareholders' value.

In August of 1995, the minority shareholders' suit was dropped with neither Russell International nor its directors having to offer or pay a settlement. Russell International accounts for its treasury stock transactions using the cost method.

**Required**

Research the related generally accepted accounting principles and explain how Russell International should account for the treasury stock transaction. Cite your reference and applicable paragraph numbers. (*Contributed by Daryl G. Krause*)

## C14-12    *Researching GAAP*

Bowsher Company had 10% bonds payable outstanding with a total face value of $185,000. Each bond had an individual face value of $1,000 and paid interest semiannually on June 30 and December 31. On July 1, 1995 the 10% bonds had a total book value of $210,000. At that time, because of a financial restructuring the company executed an "exchange agreement" in which all of these 10% bonds were extinguished. In exchange for their 10% bonds, the bondholders were given cash of $125 per 10% bond, 6 shares of 7%, $100 preferred stock per 10% bond, and 50 warrants per 10% bond allowing the holder to acquire 50 shares of $5 par common stock for $25 per share. On July 1, 1995 the 7% preferred stock was selling at $106 per share and the warrants were selling at $5 each on the open market. You are the assistant accountant for Bowsher Company and have been asked by the head accountant to recommend how to record this transaction.

**Required**

Research the related generally accepted accounting principles and prepare a short memo that explains and justifies your recommended journal entry to record the transaction. Cite your reference and applicable paragraph numbers.

## MULTIPLE CHOICE

*Select the best answer for each of the following.*

**M14-1** On July 14, JX Corporation exchanged 1,000 shares of its $8 par value common stock for a plot of land. JX's common stock is listed on the NYSE and traded at an average price of $21 per share on July 14. The land was appraised by independent real estate appraisers on July 14 at $23,000. As a result of this exchange, JX's additional paid-in capital will increase by

a. $0
b. $8,000
c. $13,000
d. $15,000

**M14-2** When treasury stock is purchased for cash at <u>more than its par value</u>, what is the effect <u>on total stockholders'</u> equity under each of the following methods?

|     | Cost method | Par value method |
| --- | --- | --- |
| a. | Increase | Increase |
| b. | Decrease | Decrease |
| c. | No effect | Decrease |
| d. | No effect | No effect |

**M14-3** On July 5, 1995 Metaro Corporation purchased for $108,000, 2,000 shares of Jean Corporation's newly issued 6% cumulative $20 par value preferred stock. Each share also had <u>one stock warrant attached</u>, which entitled the holder to acquire, <u>at $19</u>, <u>one share of Jean $10 par value common stock for each two warrants held</u>. On July 6, 1995 the market price of the preferred stock (without warrants) was $50 per share and the market price of the stock warrants was $10 per warrant. On September 1, 1995 Metaro sold all the stock warrants for $19,800. What should be the gain on the sale of the stock warrants?

a. $0
b. $800
c. $1,800
d. $9,800

**M14-4** What is the most likely effect of a stock split on the par value per share and the number of shares outstanding?

|     | Par value per share | Number of shares outstanding |
| --- | --- | --- |
| a. | Decrease | Increase |
| b. | Decrease | No effect |
| c. | Increase | Increase |
| d. | No effect | No effect |

**M14-5** Landy Corporation was organized on January 2, 1995 with authorized capital of 100,000 shares of $10 par value common stock. During 1995 Landy had the following transactions:

Jan. 13    Issued 20,000 shares at $12 per share.
Apr 23    Issued 1,000 shares for legal services when the market price was $14 per share.

What should be the amount of additional paid-in capital at December 31, 1995?

a. $4,000
b. $14,000
c. $40,000
d. $44,000

**M14-6** During 1994 Bradley Corporation issued for $110 per share, 5,000 shares of $100 par value convertible preferred stock. One share of preferred stock can be converted into three shares of Bradley's $25 par value common stock at the option of the preferred shareholder. On December 31, 1995 all of the preferred stock was converted into common stock. The market value of the common stock at the conversion date was $40 per share. What amount should be credited to the common stock account on December 31, 1995?

a. $375,000
b. $500,000
c. $550,000
d. $600,000

*M14-7*  The Amlin Corporation was incorporated on January 1, 1995, with the following authorized capitalization:

20,000 shares of common stock, no par value, stated value $40 per share
5,000 shares of 5% cumulative preferred stock, par value $10 per share

During 1995 Amlin issued 12,000 shares of common stock for a total of $600,000 and 3,000 shares of pre-
ferred stock at $16 per share. In addition, on December 21, 1995 subscriptions for 1,000 shares of preferred
stock were taken at a purchase price of $17. These subscribed shares were paid for on January 4, 1996. What
should Amlin report as total contributed capital on its December 31, 1995 balance sheet issued on February 1,
1996?

| | |
|---|---|
| a. $520,000 | c. $665,000 |
| b. $648,000 | d. $850,000 |

*M14-8*  The stockholders' equity account balances of Rice Corporation as of December 31, 1995 are as follows:

| | |
|---|---|
| Common stock, $10 par; 50,000 shares authorized; 25,000 shares issued | $250,000 |
| Paid-in capital in excess of par | 50,000 |
| Retained earnings | 100,000 |
| Less treasury stock, 2,000 shares at cost | (32,000) |
| Total stockholders' equity | $368,000 |

On January 4, 1996 Rice sold the treasury shares on the open market at $20 per share. The entry to record this
sale on Rice's books should include a credit to

| | |
|---|---|
| a. Paid-in capital from treasury stock of $8,000 | c. Retained earnings of $8,000 |
| b. Paid-in capital from treasury stock of $20,000 | d. Gain from sale of treasury stock of $8,000 |

*M14-9*  When treasury stock accounted for by the cost method is subsequently sold for more than its purchase price, the
excess of the cash proceeds over the carrying value of the treasury stock should be recognized as

| | |
|---|---|
| a. Extraordinary gain | c. Income from continuing operations |
| b. Increase in additional paid-in capital | d. Increase in retained earnings |

*M14-10*  Preferred stock that may be retired by the corporation at its option is known as

| | |
|---|---|
| a. Convertible | c. Cumulative |
| b. Redeemable | d. Callable |

*(AICPA adapted)*

## EXERCISES

*E14-1*  *Par Value and No-Par Stock Issuance*  Cutler Corporation is authorized to issue 10,000 shares of common
stock. It sells 6,000 shares at $14 per share.

**Required**
Record the sale of the common stock, given the following independent assumptions:
1. The stock has a par value of $10 per share.
2. The stock is no-par stock, but the board of directors has assigned a stated value of $8 per share.
3. The stock has no par and no stated value.

*E14-2*  *Combined Sale of Stock*  Estes Company issues 300 shares of $50 par preferred stock and 1,000 shares of
$10 par common stock in a "package" sale. Total proceeds received amount to $39,000.

**Required**

Record the transaction for each independent assumption shown:

1. The common stock has a current market value of $19 per share; the current market value of preferred stock is not known.
2. The common stock and the preferred stock have a current market value per share of $22 and $60 respectively.

E14-3  *Sale of Stock with Bonds*  Kelly Company issues 12% bonds with a face value of $10,000 and 600 shares of $10 par common stock in a combined sale, receiving total proceeds of $24,000.

**Required**

Record the transaction for each independent assumption shown:

1. The common stock has a current market value of $22 per share; the market value of the bonds is not known.
2. The common stock has a current market value of $24.50 per share; the bonds are selling at 98.

E14-4  *Issuance of Stock for Land*  The Putt Company issues 500 shares of $100 preferred stock for land. This land was carried on the seller's books for $40,000.

**Required**

Prepare the journal entry to record the acquisition of the land for each of the following independent situations:

1. The preferred stock is currently selling for $120 per share. No appraisal is available on the land.
2. The land is appraised at $65,000. There have been no recent sales of the preferred stock.
3. The preferred stock is currently selling for $125 per share. The land is appraised at $64,000.

E14-5  *Stock Subscription*  On February 3, 1995 the Teel Corporation enters into a subscription contract with several subscribers for 5,000 shares of $10 par common stock at a price of $16 per share. The contract requires a down payment of 25%, with the remaining balance to be paid on May 3, 1995. The stock will be issued to each subscriber upon full payment.

**Required**

Prepare journal entries to record the following:

1. The February 3 receipt of the down payment and signing of the contract.
2. The May 3 receipt of the remaining balance from subscribers to 4,000 shares. The market price is currently $17 per share.
3. The default of a subscriber to 1,000 shares. These shares are sold on the open market for $17 per share on May 4, and the down payment is returned to the subscriber.

E14-6  *Stock Split*  Holton Company currently has 8,000 shares of $12 par common stock outstanding that had been issued at an average price of $60 per share. It declares a three-for-one stock split.

**Required**

Prepare whatever entry is necessary to record the stock split, assuming the following independent alternatives:

1. The par value is reduced to $4 per share.
2. The par value is reduced to $6 per share.
3. The par value is reduced to $3 per share.

E14-7  *Convertible Preferred Stock*  On January 2, 1994 the Bray Corporation issues 900 shares of $100 par convertible preferred stock for $117 per share. On January 6, 1995, all the preferred stockholders convert their shares to common stock.

**Required**

1. Prepare the January 2, 1994 journal entry to record the issuance of the preferred stock.
2. Prepare the January 6, 1995 journal entry to record the conversion, assuming the preferred stock contract states that
   a. Each share of preferred stock is convertible into seven shares of $10 par common stock.
   b. Each share of preferred stock is convertible into twelve shares of $10 par common stock.

E14-8  *Callable Preferred Stock*  On March 2, 1995 the Hein Corporation issues 1,000 shares of $100 par preferred stock for $120 per share. The stock is not callable by the corporation until 3 years have expired. On April 7, 1998, all the stock is called by the corporation.

**Required**

1. Prepare the journal entry to record the issuance of the stock.
2. Prepare the journal entry to record the recall
   a. At a price of $130 per share.
   b. At a price of $114 per share.

E14-9   *Stock Rights with Preferred Stock*   The Nelson Corporation issues 6,000 shares of $100 par preferred stock at a price of $113 per share. A stock warrant is attached to each share of preferred stock that enables the holder to purchase one share of $10 par common stock for $25. Immediately after issuance, the preferred stock begins selling ex rights for $110 per share. The warrants (which expire in 30 days) also begin trading for $4 per warrant.

**Required**

1. Prepare the journal entry to record the sale of the preferred stock.
2. Prepare the journal entry to record the issuance of 5,000 shares of common stock in exchange for 5,000 warrants and $25 per share.
3. Prepare the journal entry to record the expiration of 1,000 warrants.

E14-10   *Various Journal Entries*   Sapp Company is authorized to issue 20,000 shares of no-par, $5 stated-value common stock and 5,000 shares of 9%, $100 par preferred stock. It enters into the following transactions:

1. Accepts a subscription contract to 7,000 shares of common stock at $42 per share and receives a 30% down payment.
2. Collects the remaining balance of the subscription contract and issues the common stock.
3. Acquires a building by paying $23,000 cash and issuing 2,000 shares of common stock and 600 shares of preferred stock. Common stock is currently selling at $46 per share; preferred stock has no current market value. The building is appraised at $180,000.
4. Sells 1,000 shares of common stock at $45 per share.
5. Sells 900 shares of preferred stock at $112 per share.
6. Declares a two-for-one stock split on the common stock, reducing the stated value to $2.50 per share.

**Required**

Prepare journal entries to record the preceding transactions.

E14-11   *Contributed Capital*   The following is a list of selected accounts and ending account balances taken from the books of the Adams Company on December 31, 1995:

| Account Title | Amount |
|---|---|
| Premium on preferred stock | $ 19,000 |
| Common stock | 60,000 |
| Premium on bonds payable | 4,000 |
| Preferred stock | 80,000 |
| Bonds payable | 100,000 |
| Preferred stock subscribed | 20,000 |
| Retained earnings | 121,000 |
| Premium on common stock | 84,000 |

Additional information:

1. Common stock has a $5 par value, 50,000 shares are authorized, 12,000 shares have been issued and are outstanding.
2. Preferred stock has a $100 par value, 3,000 shares are authorized, 800 shares have been issued and are outstanding. Two hundred shares have been subscribed at $120 per share. The stock pays an 8% dividend, is cumulative and callable at $130 per share.
3. Bonds payable mature on January 1, 1999. They carry a 12% annual interest rate, payable semiannually.

**Required**

Prepare the contributed capital section of the December 31, 1995 balance sheet for the Adams Company. Include appropriate parenthetical notes.

E14-12 *Treasury Stock, Cost Method*   On January 1, 1995 the Sanders Corporation had 1,000 shares of $10 par common stock authorized and outstanding. These shares were originally issued at a price of $25 per share. In addition, 500 shares of $50 par preferred stock were outstanding. These were issued at a price of $75 per share. During 1995 the following stock transactions occurred:

1. March 3: Sanders Corporation reacquired 100 shares of its own common stock at a cost of $23 per share.
2. April 27: It sold 25 shares of the stock acquired on March 3 for $29 per share.
3. July 10: It sold 25 shares of the stock acquired on March 3 for $21 per share.
4. October 12: It retired the remaining shares acquired on March 3.

**Required**

Prepare journal entries to record the treasury stock transactions assuming the cost method is used.

E14-13 *Treasury Stock, Par Value Method*   The records of TMP Incorporated provide the following information on January 1, 1995:

| | |
|---|---:|
| Preferred stock, $50 par (5,000 shares authorized, issued, and outstanding) | $250,000 |
| Common stock, $10 par (20,000 shares authorized, 10,000 shares issued and outstanding) | 100,000 |
| Additional paid-in capital on preferred stock | 50,000 |
| Additional paid-in capital on common stock | 80,000 |
| Retained earnings | 95,000 |

During 1995 the following transactions were recorded by TMP:

1. Reacquired 250 shares of preferred stock for $53 per share.
2. Reacquired 500 shares of common stock for $20 per share.
3. Sold 200 shares of the common stock acquired in (2) for $27 per share.
4. Sold 250 shares of preferred stock acquired in (1) for $59 per share.
5. Sold 100 shares of the common stock acquired in (2) for $18 per share.

**Required**

1. Prepare journal entries to record the stock transactions of TMP Incorporated, assuming the par value method of accounting for treasury stock is used.
2. Prepare the stockholders' equity section of the TMP balance sheet at December 31, 1995 (assume 1995 net income was $30,000 and dividends distributed were $10,000).

E14-14 *Treasury Stock, Cost and Par Value Methods*   On January 1, 1995 the West Company had outstanding 10,000 shares of $10 par common stock, which had been originally issued at an average price of $30 per share. During 1995 the company engaged in the following treasury stock transactions:

1. Reacquired 1,000 shares of its common stock for $28 per share.
2. Reissued 600 shares of the treasury stock for $30 per share.
3. Reissued 300 shares of the treasury stock for $27 per share.
4. Retired the remaining 100 shares of treasury stock.

**Required**

Prepare journal entries to record the preceding treasury stock transactions assuming use of (1) the cost method and (2) the par value method.

E14-15 *Treasury Stock, No Par*   The following information is taken from the accounting records of the Propst-Steele Production Corporation:

1. Issued 5,000 shares of no-par common stock at $15 per share.
2. Issued an additional 5,000 shares of no-par common stock at $17 per share.
3. Reacquired 500 shares of its no-par common stock at a cost of $12.50 per share.
4. Reissued 200 of its treasury shares at $14 per share.
5. Reissued the remaining treasury shares at $11 per share.

**Required**

Prepare journal entries to account for the preceding stock transactions on the books of the Propst-Steele Production Corporation using the cost method for treasury stock.

*E14-16* *Appendix: Incorporation*   D and B partnership decides to incorporate as the Debo Corporation. The partners' profit and loss ratio is 60%, 40%, respectively. The current balance sheet for the partnership is as follows:

| | | | |
|---|---|---|---|
| Cash | $ 2,000 | Accounts payable | $ 8,000 |
| Accounts receivable (net) | 6,000 | | |
| Inventory | 10,000 | | |
| Fixed assets | 24,000 | D, Capital | 13,000 |
| Less: Accumulated depreciation | (13,000) | B, Capital | 8,000 |
| | $29,000 | | $29,000 |

At the incorporation date, inventory is to be valued at $12,000 and fixed assets at their appraisal value of $18,000. Debo Corporation is authorized to issue 10,000 shares of no-par, no-stated-value common stock. The partners agree to accept 3,800 and 2,400 shares, respectively, and to withdraw the $2,000 cash from the partnership according to their remaining capital balances. The corporation acquires the net assets (except cash) of the partnership and sells 3,000 shares of stock to investors at $5 per share.

**Required**

Assuming the partnership accounting records will be retained, prepare whatever journal entries are necessary to record the incorporation.

*E14-17* *Appendix: Incorporation*   On January 1, 1995, F, a sole proprietor, decides to incorporate as the Fox Corporation. The 1994 ending trial balance of the sole proprietorship is as follows:

| | Debit | Credit |
|---|---|---|
| Cash | $ 2,000 | |
| Accounts receivable (net) | 10,000 | |
| Inventory | 17,000 | |
| Property and equipment | 66,000 | |
| Accumulated depreciation | | $15,000 |
| Accounts payable | | 11,000 |
| Note payable (due 7/1/95) | | 18,000 |
| F, Capital | | 51,000 |
| | $95,000 | $95,000 |

Fox Corporation is authorized to issue 20,000 shares of $5 par common stock. The corporation sells 4,000 shares of stock to investors at $7 per share. At the incorporation date, inventory is to be increased by $1,900 and accumulated depreciation is to be decreased by $6,000. In addition, one-half year of interest at a 10% annual rate is to be accrued on the note payable. F agrees to accept 8,600 shares of corporate stock in exchange for all the sole proprietorship net assets. His shares of stock are initially recorded as an investment on the sole proprietorship books when its net assets are transferred to the corporation. The investment account is then offset against his capital account to close out the sole proprietorship accounts.

**Required**

Assuming new books will be opened by the corporation:

1. On the sole proprietorship books, prepare whatever journal entries are necessary to adjust and close the books.
2. On the corporation's books, prepare journal entries to record the incorporation.

## PROBLEMS

*P14-1* *Issuances of Stock*   The Cada Corporation is authorized to issue 10,000 shares of $100 par, convertible, callable preferred stock and 80,000 shares of no-par, no-stated-value common stock. There are currently 7,000 shares of preferred and 30,000 shares of common stock outstanding. The following are several *alternative* transactions:

1.  Purchased land by issuing 600 shares of preferred stock and 1,000 shares of common stock. Preferred and common are currently selling at $113 and $38 per share, respectively. No reliable appraisal of the land is available.
2.  Same as transaction 1 except land is appraised at $104,000 and the preferred stock has no current market value.
3.  Issued, for $99,000 cash, a combination of 400 shares of preferred stock and bonds payable with a face value of $50,000. Currently, the preferred stock is selling for $120 per share and the bonds at 104.
4.  Same as transaction 3 except the bonds do not have a current market value.
5.  Same as transaction 3 except the preferred stock does not have a current market value.
6.  Preferred stockholders (who had originally paid the corporation $110 per share for their stock) convert 6,500 preferred shares into 19,500 shares of common stock. The current market price of the preferred stock and the common stock is $120 and $41 per share, respectively.
7.  The corporation calls the 7,000 shares of preferred stock (originally issued at $110 per share) at $122 per share. Common stock is currently selling for $42 per share. Stockholders elect *not* to convert into common stock.
8.  Same as transaction 7 except stockholders owning 2,000 shares of preferred stock elect to convert each share into three shares of common stock. The remaining 5,000 preferred shares are retired.

**Required**
Prepare the journal entry necessary to record each transaction. Justify the amounts used.

P14-2   *Issuances of Stock*   The Epple Corporation is authorized to issue 20,000 shares of $100 par, convertible, callable preferred stock and 100,000 shares of $10 stated value common stock. Currently, the company has outstanding 6,000 shares of preferred stock and 40,000 shares of common stock. The following are several *alternative* transactions:

1.  Acquired a patent by issuing 2,500 shares of common stock and bonds with the face value of $100,000. The stock is currently selling for $27 per share and the bonds are selling at 98.
2.  Sold, for $96,000 cash, a "package" consisting of 500 shares of preferred stock and 2,000 shares of common stock. Currently, the preferred and common stock are independently selling for $112 and $22 per share, respectively.
3.  Purchased land by issuing 300 shares of preferred stock and 1,000 shares of common stock. The common stock is selling for $25 per share, but the preferred stock is not being actively traded. The value of the land is appraised at $57,000.
4.  The corporation calls the 6,000 shares of preferred stock (originally issued at $108 per share) at a call price of $112 per share. Common stock is currently selling for $23 per share. The stockholders elect *not* to convert into common stock.
5.  Same as transaction 4 except stockholders owning 4,000 shares of preferred stock elect to convert each share into five shares of common stock. The remaining 2,000 shares of preferred stock are retired.
6.  Upon approval by the state, the board of directors decides to split the common stock two for one, reducing the stated value to $5 per share and increasing the authorization to 200,000 shares (remember, only 40,000 shares are issued and outstanding).
7.  Same as transaction 6 except the stated value is reduced to $4 per share.

**Required**
Prepare the journal entry necessary to record each transaction. Justify the amounts used.

P14-3   *Subscriptions*   On August 3, 1995, the date of incorporation, the Quinn Company accepts separate subscriptions for 1,000 shares of $100 par preferred stock at $102 per share and 9,000 shares of no-par, no-stated-value common stock for $22 per share. The subscription contracts require a 10% down payment, with the balance due by November 2, 1995. Shares are issued to each subscriber upon full payment. Any defaulted shares will be sold on November 3, 1995, and the down payment returned to the defaulting subscribers.

   On November 2, the company received the remaining balances for 920 shares of preferred stock and 8,900 shares of common stock. The defaulted preferred shares and common shares were sold for $103 and $22.50 per share, respectively, on November 3, and the down payment was returned to the defaulting subscribers.

**Required**

Prepare journal entries to record all the transactions related to

1. The preferred stock
2. The common stock

P14-4   *Subscriptions*   On July 3, 1995 the Wallace Company enters into a subscription contract with various investors. Terms of the contract are as follows:

1. Number of shares: 10,000 shares of no-par, $6 stated-value common stock.
2. Price and payment schedule: Subscription price is $13 per share. A $3 per share down payment is required with a $5 per share payment due on both August 3 and October 3. Shares are issued to each subscriber upon full payment.
3. Default provisions: Defaulted shares are to be sold on October 4 at the then current market price. If the proceeds from this sale are less than the total subscription price of the defaulted shares, an amount necessary to bring the proceeds up to the total subscription price is to be withheld from defaulted subscribers. Any remaining payments received from defaulted subscribers are to be returned to them.

**Required**

Record the July 3, August 3, and the October 3 and 4 journal entries, assuming that a subscriber to 500 shares of stock defaulted after making the down payment. The 500 shares were sold on October 4 for $11 per share.

P14-5   *Comprehensive*   The Young Corporation has been operating successfully for several years. It is authorized to issue 24,000 shares of no-par common stock and 6,000 shares of 8%, $100 par preferred stock. The Contributed Capital section of its January 1, 1995 balance sheet is as follows:

| | |
|---|---:|
| 8% preferred stock, $100 par | $210,000 |
| Common stock, no par | 207,000 |
| Premium on preferred stock | 18,900 |
| | $435,900 |

*Part a.* A stockholder has raised the following questions:

1. What is the legal capital of the corporation?
2. At what average price per share has the preferred stock been issued?
3. How many shares of common stock have been issued (the common stock has been issued at an average price of $23 per share)?

*Part b.* The company engaged in the following transactions in 1995:

| | |
|---|---|
| Mar. 2 | Received a subscription to 400 shares of the 8% preferred stock. The total subscription price is $122 per share and the contract requires a $10 per share down payment. The remaining balance must be paid within 60 days or the stock subscription is defaulted. In the case of default, 20% of the down payment on the defaulted shares is forfeited, and the remainder is returned to the defaulting subscribers. |
| Apr. 3 | Sold 900 shares of common stock for $33 per share. |
| Apr. 11 | Issued 400 shares of common stock in exchange for land. The stock is currently selling at $34 per share. |
| May 1 | Received remaining subscription balance (from March 2) owed on 350 shares of preferred stock and issued the stock. |
| May 5 | Returned 80% of their down payment to defaulting subscribers and canceled the related account balances. |
| June 2 | Reacquired 500 shares of common stock at $37 per share. The company uses the cost method to account for treasury stock. |
| Oct. 19 | Issued for $27,000 a combination of 500 shares of common stock and 100 shares of preferred stock. The common and preferred stock are currently selling for $35 and $125 per share, respectively. |
| Nov. 17 | Reissued the 500 shares of treasury stock at $39 per share. |
| Dec. 31 | Distributed an $8 per share dividend on all preferred stock outstanding and a $2 per share dividend on all common stock outstanding on this date (debit Retained Earnings and credit Cash for each dividend). |

**Required**

1. Answer the questions in part *a*.
2. Prepare journal entries to record the transactions in part *b*.
3. Prepare the contributed capital section of the December 31, 1995 balance sheet.

**P14-6**  *Comprehensive*  The Byrd Company's Contributed Capital section of its January 1, 1995 balance sheet is as follows:

| | |
|---|---:|
| Preferred stock (6%, $50 par, 8,000 shares authorized, 3,400 shares issued and outstanding) | $170,000 |
| Common stock ($10 stated value, 30,000 shares authorized, 12,000 shares issued and outstanding) | 120,000 |
| Preferred stock subscribed (800 shares subscribed at $54 per share) | 40,000 |
| Additional paid-in capital on preferred stock | 12,800 |
| Additional paid-in capital on common stock | 72,000 |
| Total contributed capital | $414,800 |

During 1995 the company entered into the following transactions:

Mar. 6    Received the remaining $40 per share on the subscribed preferred stock and issued the shares.

Apr. 24    Sold 300 shares of preferred stock at $55 per share.

May 3    Received a subscription down payment of $6 per share on 1,000 shares of common stock. The remaining $11 per share balance is due in 60 days.

June 6    Sold 600 shares of common stock at $17 per share.

July 3    Received the remaining balance on subscribed common stock and issued the shares.

Sept. 21    Purchased building by paying $9,000 cash and issuing 800 shares of common stock and 450 shares of preferred stock. Common and preferred stock are currently selling for $19 and $57 per share, respectively.

Oct. 13    Reacquired 900 shares of common stock at $19.50 per share. The company uses the cost method to account for treasury stock.

Nov. 14    Issued for $32,000 a combination of 700 shares of common stock and 12% bonds payable with a face value of $20,000. The common stock is currently selling for $18 per share. No market value exists for the bonds.

Dec. 15    Reissued the 900 shares of treasury stock at $20.50 per share.

Dec. 29    Distributed a $3.00 per share dividend to all outstanding preferred stock and a $1.50 per share dividend to all common stock outstanding on this date (debit Retained Earnings and credit Cash for each dividend).

Dec. 31    Declared a two-for-one stock split on the common stock, reducing the stated value to $4 per share and increasing the authorized shares to 60,000.

**Required**

1. Prepare journal entries to record the preceding transactions.
2. Prepare the contributed capital section of the December 31, 1995 balance sheet.

**P14-7**  *Stock Rights to Stockholders*  The Nichols Electronics Corporation has been experiencing a steadily growing demand for its products. In order to meet this demand, a major expansion of production facilities is necessary. The company plans to raise the money for this proposed expansion by issuing 10,000 shares of $50 par preferred stock and 50,000 shares of $10 par common stock. These shares were previously authorized but have not yet been issued.

There are presently 200,000 shares of $10 par common stock issued and outstanding. In order that the preemptive right of the current stockholders be maintained, the board of directors authorizes the issuance of stock rights to the current common stockholders on March 3, 1995. The current market price of the common stock at this date is $22 per share. Each common stockholder is to receive one stock warrant for each share of common stock owned. One additional share of common stock may be purchased at any time prior to April 5, 1995 for $21 and four of the stock warrants.

There are presently 20,000 shares of the $50 par preferred stock issued and outstanding. They were selling for $77 per share on March 6, 1995. No preemptive right applies to the preferred stock. In order to assure the sale of the additional 10,000 shares of the preferred stock, the board of directors also authorizes one stock warrant to be attached to each share of preferred stock in the new issue. One of these stock warrants allows the preferred stockholder to purchase one share of $10 par common stock for $17 per share at any time prior to April 6, 1995. The preferred shares with warrants attached are issued on March 7, 1995 at a price of $81 per share. The warrants begin trading in the market at $5 each.

**Required**

1. Prepare the journal entry to record the issuance of the common stock warrants on March 3, 1995.
2. Prepare journal entries to record the following transactions:
   a. The sale of the 10,000 shares of $50 par preferred stock with detachable warrants on March 7, 1995.
   b. The exercise on March 20, 1995 of 6,000 of the stock warrants that had been attached to the preferred stock (the common stock price is currently $23 per share and the preferred stock is selling ex rights for $78 per share).
   c. The exercise on April 3, 1995 of 120,000 stock warrants issued in conjunction with the preemptive right (the common stock is currently selling at $22.50 per share).
   d. 4,000 stock warrants related to the preferred stock and 80,000 stock warrants related to the preemptive right expire on April 5, 1995.

 **P14-8** *Contributed Capital* A partial list of the accounts and ending account balances taken from the post-closing trial balance of the Jordan Corporation on December 31, 1995 is shown as follows:

| Account Title | Amount |
| --- | --- |
| Retained earnings | $410,000 |
| Bonds payable | 220,000 |
| Common stock subscribed | 50,000 |
| Long-term investments in stock | 210,000 |
| Additional paid-in capital on common stock | 460,000 |
| Organization costs *Intangible asset.* | 12,000 |
| Premium on bonds payable | 30,000 |
| Common stock | 400,000 |
| Preferred stock subscribed | 45,000 |
| Additional paid-in capital on preferred stock | 112,000 |
| Preferred stock | 300,000 |
| Additional paid-in capital from treasury stock | 4,000 |
| Unrealized increase in value of securities available for sale | 3,000 |

Additional information:

1. Common stock is no-par, with a stated value of $10 per share, 90,000 shares are authorized, 40,000 shares are issued and outstanding, 5,000 shares have been subscribed at a price of $28 per share.
2. Preferred stock has a $50 par value, 8,000 shares are authorized, 6,000 shares are issued and outstanding, 900 shares have been subscribed at a price of $70 per share. Each share is cumulative, convertible into five shares of common stock, and pays a 7% annual dividend. Dividends are not in arrears.
3. Bonds payable mature on July 1, 2007. They carry a 12% annual interest rate, payable semiannually. The premium is being amortized using the straight-line method.

**Required**

Prepare the contributed capital section of the December 31, 1995 balance sheet for the Jordan Corporation. Include appropriate parenthetical notes for the common and preferred stock.

**P14-9** *Contributed Capital* The following is a partial list of the accounts and ending account balances taken from the post-closing trial balance of the Runyan Corporation on December 31, 1995:

| | | | |
| --- | --- | --- | --- |
| Common stock subscribed | $ 10,000 | Long-term investments in preferred stock | $ 90,000 |
| Premium on bonds payable | 50,000 | Preferred stock subscribed | 100,000 |
| Preferred stock | 400,000 | Retained earnings | 610,000 |
| Temporary investments in common stock | 110,000 | Premium on common stock | 542,000 |
| Bonds payable | 500,000 | Unrealized decrease in value of securities available for sale | 6,000 |
| Common stock | 150,000 | | |
| Premium on preferred stock | 76,000 | | |

Additional information:

1. Bonds payable mature on December 31, 2010. They carry a 12% interest rate, payable semiannually. The premium is being amortized using the straight-line method.
2. The 7.5% preferred stock is cumulative and convertible into 3 shares of common stock. It has a par value of $100 per share, 20,000 shares are authorized, 4,000 shares are issued and outstanding, 1,000 shares have been subscribed at $125 per share.
3. Common stock has a par value of $5 per share, 100,000 shares are authorized, 30,000 shares are issued and outstanding, 2,000 shares have been subscribed at $41 per share.

**Required**

Prepare the contributed capital section of the December 31, 1995 balance sheet for the Runyan Corporation. Include appropriate parenthetical notes for the common and preferred stock.

P14-10 **Reconstruct Journal Entries**  At the end of its first year of operations, the Martin Company lists the following accounts and ending account balances related to stock transactions and dividends:

| | Balance | |
|---|---|---|
| Account | Debit | Credit |
| Cash (from stock and for dividends paid) | $250,000 | |
| Subscriptions receivable: common stock | 14,000 | |
| Subscriptions receivable: preferred stock | 33,600 | |
| Equipment | 69,000 | |
| Preferred stock subscribed (for 300 shares) | | $ 30,000 |
| 8% preferred stock, $100 par (2,300 shares) | | 230,000 |
| Additional paid-in capital on preferred stock | | 33,000 |
| Common stock subscribed (2,000 shares) | | 10,000 |
| Common stock, $5 stated value (9,000 shares) | | 45,000 |
| Additional paid-in capital on common stock | | 46,000 |
| Retained earnings | | 2,600 |

During the first year the following events occurred:

1. Subscription contracts were entered into for common stock at $9 per share and preferred stock at $112 per share. Common stock subscriptions required a $2-per-share down payment. Preferred stock subscriptions required no down payment. Shares (either common or preferred) were issued to subscribers upon full payment.
2. One thousand shares of common stock were sold for $11 per share, and the stock was issued to stockholders.
3. Equipment with an appraised value of $69,000 was acquired by issuing 600 shares of preferred stock. The appraised value of the equipment was used to record the transaction.
4. Net income of $30,000 was closed to Retained Earnings from Income Summary at the end of the year.
5. Dividends of $8 per share on all the preferred stock outstanding and $1 per share on all the common stock outstanding were distributed at the end of the year (the company debited Retained Earnings and credited Cash for each dividend).

**Required**

On the basis of the preceding information, reconstruct all the journal entries that the company made to record the stock transactions, net income, and dividends.

P14-11 **Treasury Stock, Alternative Methods**  Bush-Caine Company reported the following data on its December 31, 1994 balance sheet:

| Preferred stock, $50 par | $ 50,000 | Common stock, $10 par | $100,000 |
|---|---|---|---|
| Additional paid-in capital on | | Additional paid-in capital on common stock | 80,000 |
| preferred stock | 4,000 | Retained earnings | 95,000 |

The following transactions were reported by the company during 1995:

1. Reacquired 200 shares of its own preferred stock at $56 per share.
2. Reacquired 500 shares of its own common stock at $15 per share.
3. Sold 100 shares of preferred treasury stock at $57 per share.
4. Sold 200 shares of common treasury stock at $16 per share.
5. Sold 100 shares of common treasury stock at $9 per share.
6. Retired the shares of common stock remaining in the treasury.

The company maintains separate treasury stock accounts and related additional paid-in capital accounts for each class of stock.

**Required**

1. Prepare the journal entries required to record the treasury stock transactions using (a) the cost method, and (b) the par value method.
2. Assuming the company earned a net income in 1995 of $30,000 and declared and paid dividends of $10,000, prepare the stockholders' equity section of the balance sheet at December 31, 1995 (a) using the cost method to account for treasury stock, and (b) using the par value method to account for treasury stock.

**P14-12** *Treasury Stock Analysis*   The Ray Holt Company has retained you as a consultant on accounting policies and procedure. During 1995 the company engaged in a number of treasury stock transactions, having foreseen an opportunity to realize a profit in trading its own stock. The transactions were as follows:

1. Reacquired 100 shares of its $10 par common stock at $20 per share. The shares had originally been issued at $23 per share.
2. Reacquired 150 shares of its $10 par common stock at $24 per share. The shares had originally been issued at $23 per share.
3. Reacquired 50 shares of its $100 par preferred stock at $140 per share. The shares had originally been issued at $170 per share.
4. Sold all common treasury shares held at $25 per share.
5. Reacquired 150 shares of its $100 par preferred stock at $130 per share. The shares had originally been issued at $170 per share.
6. Retired all preferred shares held in the treasury.

**Required**

1. Is the company correct in assuming a profit or gain is to be realized from treasury stock transactions? Explain.
2. Prepare an analysis of treasury stock accounting for Mr. Robert Richter, the controller. This analysis should contain proper journal entries for each of the treasury stock transactions occurring during 1995, prepared using (a) the cost method and (b) the par value method discussed in the chapter.
3. Conclude the analysis with your assessment of the strengths and weaknesses of each method of accounting for treasury stock.

**P14-13** *Comprehensive*   Chee Corporation's post-closing trial balance at December 31, 1994 was as follows:

| | Debit | Credit |
|---|---|---|
| Accounts payable | | $ 290,000 |
| Accounts receivable | $ 550,000 | |
| Accumulated depreciation—building and equipment | | 200,000 |
| Additional paid-in capital—common | | |
| In excess of par value | | 1,560,000 |
| From sale of treasury stock | | 250,000 |
| Allowance for doubtful accounts | | 30,000 |
| Bonds payable | | 400,000 |
| Building and equipment | 1,100,000 | |
| Cash | 220,000 | |
| Common stock ($1 par value) | | 150,000 |
| Dividends payable on preferred stock—cash | | 4,000 |
| Inventories | 620,000 | |
| Land | 380,000 | |
| Long-term equity securities (at market) | 285,000 | |
| Marketable equity securities (at market) | 215,000 | |
| Preferred stock ($50 par value) | | 500,000 |
| Prepaid expenses | 40,000 | |
| Retained earnings | | 231,000 |
| Treasury stock—common (at cost) | 180,000 | |
| Unrealized decrease in value of securities available for sale | 25,000 | |
| Totals | $3,615,000 | $3,615,000 |

At December 31, 1994 Chee had the following number of common and preferred shares:

| | Common | Preferred |
|---|---|---|
| Authorized | 500,000 | 50,000 |
| Issued | 150,000 | 10,000 |
| Outstanding | 140,000 | 10,000 |

The dividends on preferred stock are $4 cumulative. In addition, the preferred stock has a preference in liquidation of $50 per share.

**Required**

Prepare the stockholders' equity section of Chee's balance sheet at December 31, 1994. (*AICPA adapted*)

P14-14  *Appendix: Incorporation*   On January 1, 1995 Partners B, A, and Y (whose profit and loss ratio is 50%, 40%, and 10%, respectively) agree to transfer the net assets (except cash) and liabilities of their partnership to the newly incorporated BAY Company. The December 31, 1994 partnership post-closing trial balance is shown as follows:

| | | |
|---|---|---|
| Cash | $ 8,000 | |
| Accounts receivable | 14,000 | |
| Allowance for doubtful accounts | | $ 200 |
| Inventory | 18,000 | |
| Investment in bonds (long-term) | 10,000 | |
| Equipment | 37,000 | |
| Accumulated depreciation | | 11,000 |
| Accounts payable | | 16,000 |
| Note payable (due 12/31/97) | | 7,000 |
| B, Capital | | 25,000 |
| A, Capital | | 18,400 |
| Y, Capital | | 9,400 |
| | $87,000 | $87,000 |

The BAY Company is authorized to issue 500 shares of $100 par preferred stock and 10,000 shares of $10 par common stock. Adjustments to the accounts are to be made as follows: Allowance for Doubtful Accounts increased to $1,400, Inventory increased to $22,900, Investment in Bonds (long-term) increased to $11,500, Equipment increased to its fair market value of $32,000, and Accrued Liabilities recognized in the amount of $3,000. Furthermore, an $1,800 advance payment was made by the partnership at the end of 1994 for 1995 rent on the building it occupies. This payment was recorded at that time on the partnership books as rent expense.

Partners are to be given shares of stock as follows: B to receive 30 shares of preferred and 2,000 shares of common stock; A to receive 120 shares of preferred and 700 shares of common stock; and Y to receive 10 shares of preferred and 700 shares of common stock. The $8,000 cash is to be distributed according to the remaining adjusted capital balances.

The corporation sells 100 shares of preferred stock and 800 shares of common stock to investors at $110 and $13 per share, respectively.

**Required**

1. Assuming the partnership accounting records will continue to be used by the corporation, prepare journal entries to reflect the incorporation.
2. Prepare a beginning balance sheet for the BAY Company.

P14-15  *Appendix: Incorporation*   On July 1, 1995 Green Company is incorporated to assume the assets (including cash) and liabilities and take over the business operations of the C and D partnership. An unclassified balance sheet of the partnership as of June 30, 1995 is as follows:

| | | | |
|---|---|---|---|
| Cash | $ 6,000 | Accounts payable | $10,000 |
| Inventory | 10,000 | Note payable (due 7/1/99) | 5,000 |
| Prepaid rent | 3,000 | | |
| Store fixtures | 33,000 | C, Capital | 20,000 |
| Less: Accumulated depreciation | (11,000) | D, Capital | 6,000 |
| | $41,000 | | $41,000 |

C and D Partnership has operated a "cash and carry" variety store for many years and maintains a favorable relationship with its customers and community. It is incorporating to attract sufficient capital to significantly expand its operations.

At incorporation, the appraised values of the assets are as follows: Inventory $16,400, Store fixtures $29,000; all other listed assets and liabilities are valued at their book value. It is determined that accrued salaries total $400, interest for one year at 10% (which will be paid on the maturity date) has accrued on the note payable, and a few "responsible customers" have purchased $4,500 of goods on credit (no journal entries were made to record these sales). It is expected that the entire amount will be collectible. Goodwill is to be recognized in the amount of $3,000.

Partners share in profits and losses as follows: 80% to C, 20% to D. At incorporation, the corporation is authorized to issue 10,000 shares of $3 par common stock. The partners each agree to accept shares of common stock equal in value to their respective adjusted partnership capital account balances. The partners' shares of stock are initially turned over to the partnership in exchange for the partnership net assets; the stock is then distributed to each partner.

At incorporation, 1,000 shares of common stock are sold by the Green Company to investors for $8 per share.

**Required**

Assuming new books will be opened by the corporation:

1. On the partnership books, prepare journal entries to adjust and close the accounts (include a schedule determining the number of shares distributed to each partner).
2. On the corporation's books, prepare journal entries to record the transactions.
3. Prepare a balance sheet for the corporation as of July 1, 1995.

P14-16   *Appendix: Incorporation*   The following is information pertaining to Cox Stationery Supply, a calendar-year sole proprietorship owned by John Cox. The business maintains its books on the cash basis except that, at year-end, the closing inventory and depreciation are recorded. On December 31, 1994 after recording inventory and depreciation, and closing the nominal accounts, Cox had the following general ledger trial balance:

|  | Debit | Credit |
|---|---|---|
| Cash | $ 16,500 |  |
| Merchandise inventory | 39,000 |  |
| Equipment | 52,500 |  |
| Accumulated depreciation |  | $ 20,500 |
| Note payable, bank |  | 10,000 |
| Payroll taxes withheld |  | 1,300 |
| Cox, capital |  | 76,200 |
|  | $108,000 | $108,000 |

During the last quarter of 1994 John Cox and Mary Rice, an outside investor, agreed to incorporate the business under the name of Cox Stationers, Inc. Cox will receive 1,000 shares for his business, and Rice will pay $86,000 cash for her 1,000 shares. On January 1, 1995 they received the certificate of incorporation for Cox Stationers, Inc., and the corporation issued 1,000 shares of common stock each to Cox and Rice for the preceding consideration. The agreement between Cox and Rice requires that the December 31, 1994 balance sheet of the proprietorship should be converted to the accrual basis, with all assets and liabilities stated at current fair values, including Cox's goodwill implicit in the terms of the common stock issuance.

Additional information:

1. Amounts due from customers totaled $23,500 at December 31, 1994. A review of collectibility disclosed that an allowance for doubtful accounts of $3,300 is required.
2. The $39,000 merchandise inventory is based on a physical count of goods priced at cost. Unsalable damaged goods costing $2,500 are included in the count. The current fair value of the total merchandise inventory is $45,000.

3. On July 1, 1994 Cox paid $3,800 to renew the comprehensive insurance coverage for one year.
4. The $10,000 note payable is dated July 1, 1994, bears interest at 12%, and is due July 1, 1995.
5. Unpaid vendors' invoices totaled $30,500 at December 31, 1994.
6. During January 1995 final payroll tax returns filed for Cox Stationery Supply required remittances totaling $2,100.
7. Not included in the trial balance is the $3,500 principal balance at December 31, 1994, of the three-year loan to purchase a delivery van on December 31, 1992. The debt was assumed by the corporation on January 1, 1995. The current fair value of the used equipment is $40,000, including the delivery van.
8. Cox Stationers, Inc., has 7,500 authorized shares of $50 par common stock.

**Required**

1. Prepare a schedule to compute Cox's goodwill implicit in the issuance to him of 1,000 shares of common stock for his business.
2. Prepare a formal balance sheet of Cox Stationers, Inc., at January 1, 1995, immediately after the issuance of common stock to Cox and Rice. Journal entries and trial balance worksheet are *not* required. (*AICPA adapted*)

# 15

# RETAINED EARNINGS AND OTHER EQUITY ISSUES

**Chapter Topics**

*Stock Option Plans*

*Types of Dividends*

*Prior Period Adjustments*

*Appropriations of Retained Earnings*

*Statement of Retained Earnings*

*Statement of Changes in Stockholders' Equity*

*Quasi-Reorganizations (Appendix)*

The previous chapter introduced stockholders' equity by discussing the contributed capital that arises from the issuance of capital stock in a variety of exchange transactions. It also discussed the impact of the reacquisition of a corporation's capital stock (treasury stock) on stockholders' equity. This chapter continues the discussion of stockholders' equity by focusing primarily on retained earnings. The chapter begins, however, with a discussion of stock option plans, because the accounting for these plans affects both contributed capital and retained earnings (through net income). The chapter then moves to a discussion of items affecting retained earnings, such as dividends, prior period adjustments, and appropriations. The main part of the chapter concludes with a discussion of the statement of retained earnings, other changes in stockholders' equity, and the statement of changes in stockholders' equity. A discussion of quasi-reorganizations is included in an Appendix at the end of the chapter.

## STOCK OPTION PLANS

Corporations frequently have programs that enable employees to acquire ownership by purchasing shares of stock, often at a price less than the current market price. These programs involve the issuance of warrants (rights) to the employees and are commonly referred to as **stock option plans.** The degree of allowed participation in a stock option plan does vary. At one extreme, the plan is available only to one, or a few, key officers and managers within the company; at the other extreme, all employees are eligible to participate. Such plans are established for various reasons: (1) the need to attract more equity capital, (2) the belief that employee ownership will lead to a greater commitment to corporate activities, and (3) the desire to provide further compensation for certain employees.

APB Opinion No. 25 governs the accounting for the warrants involved in employee stock option plans. It is a complex *Opinion,* of which only the primary elements are summarized here. The *Opinion* differentiates between noncompensatory and compensatory stock option plans.

## NONCOMPENSATORY STOCK OPTION PLANS

A noncompensatory stock option plan (sometimes called an *employee stock purchase plan*) is one that is designed to raise capital or to obtain more widespread employee ownership of the corporate stock rather than to provide additional compensation for certain employees. Four characteristics are identified as essential in a plan of this type:

1. Substantially all full-time employees who meet limited employment qualifications are able to participate in the plan.

2. Stock is offered to eligible employees on an equal basis or on a basis related to a uniform percentage of salaries.

3. The time permitted for exercise of the option by the employees is limited to a reasonable period.

4. The discount from the market price is not greater than what would be reasonable in an offer of stock to stockholders or others.[1]

If **all** these characteristics are met, the plan is defined as **noncompensatory** and the accounting is very straightforward. No compensation is considered to be paid to employees under such a plan; consequently, no formal journal entry is necessary when the stock warrants are issued. A memorandum entry is made indicating the number of additional shares that may be acquired upon exercise of the stock warrants. If the warrants are exercised, the usual journal entry is made to record the stock issuance. If not exercised, a memorandum entry to this effect is made upon expiration.

In some cases, employees of a company (with its assistance) will set up an employee stock ownership plan (called an ESOP) for investment purposes. The complexity of ESOPs varies from company to company. In one type of ESOP, a trustee borrows money from a financial institution and uses the funds to purchase shares in the company for the employees. Usually, the company guarantees the liability of the ESOP. It also may agree to make contributions to the ESOP to pay the interest on the

---

1. "Accounting for Stock Issued to Employees," *APB Opinion No. 25* (New York: AICPA, 1972), par. 7.

liability and to help the ESOP acquire more of the company's stock. If the company only assists in the initial financing of the ESOP, at the time of borrowing, the company records a liability and a decrease in stockholders' equity. The liability then is reduced (and stockholders' equity increased) as the ESOP makes payments on the debt that was guaranteed by the company. In this situation, the ESOP has some of the characteristics of a noncompensatory stock option plan. If the company also makes contributions to the ESOP, these contributions are treated as interest expense and "deferred compensation" (a "negative" component of stockholders' equity), which is allocated to compensation expense by the company. In this situation, accounting for the ESOP is similar to a compensatory stock option plan, as discussed in the next section.

## COMPENSATORY STOCK OPTION PLANS

Any stock option plan that does *not* possess *all* the four characteristics listed in the previous section is defined as a compensatory plan. **A compensatory stock option plan is intended to provide additional compensation to selected key officers or managers within the corporation.** The terms of a compensatory plan are often complex and relate to such items as the number of shares to which each employee is entitled and the option price (both of which may depend on some future event), whether "special" shares (sometimes called "restricted stock") will be received, whether cash may be received instead of shares, the period of service the employee must complete before becoming eligible, the date the option can first be exercised, and the date of expiration (if any).

Since a compensatory stock option plan may affect both the income statement and balance sheet, several accounting issues must be addressed regarding compensatory plans. These include determination of: (1) the compensation cost (if any), (2) the accounting period(s) to which the compensation cost applies as an expense, and (3) the proper accounting for and disclosure of the compensatory stock option plan.

### Compensation Cost

Compensation cost is a function of the fair value of the stock option plan. There are various methods of determining the plan's fair value (and compensation cost). A reliable method is to consider that the compensation cost incurred consists of the difference between the amount of proceeds the corporation will receive from the issuance of the shares related to the stock option plan and the amount of proceeds that it could receive if the stock were issued on the open market. The difference represents the proceeds (or fair value) forgone by the corporation in lieu of paying higher cash salaries. The question arises, however, as to when this difference should be measured. It could be measured at any number of dates, including (1) the date of the adoption of the plan, (2) the date on which an option is granted to a particular employee, (3) the date on which the employee has satisfied any conditions related to the option, (4) the date when the employee may first exercise the option, (5) the date on which the option is exercised, or (6) the date on which the employee disposes of the acquired stock.

Furthermore, in order to make a precise measurement of the compensation cost, the option price and the number of shares offered in the stock option plan must be known. Sometimes these factors are based on successful future operations. For instance, they may depend upon divisional performance, upon maintenance of the previous year's net income, or upon a percentage increase in net income.

The various theoretical and practical issues are discussed in the Appendices to *APB Opinion No. 25.* In order to provide reliable evidence upon which to base the accounting for compensatory stock option plans, the total compensation cost related to a stock option plan is defined as the excess of the quoted market price over the option price for the specified number of shares on the measurement date. The quoted market price of the same class of stock trading freely in an established market is used to measure the market price of the shares. The measurement date is the first date on which *both* (1) the number of shares an individual employee is entitled to receive, and (2) the option or purchase price, if any are known.[2] For many plans, both the number of shares and the option price are known on the date that the option is *granted* to the employee. Thus, in these situations, the date of grant is the same as the measurement date. For those plans with terms dependent upon future events, a later measurement date is used.

Note that in cases where the option price is *equal to or higher than* the market price on the measurement date, *no* compensation cost is incurred. Prior to 1976, in many stock option plans, the option price was set at the market price because it provided the employee with significant federal income tax advantages (for example, the tax was generally deferred until the recipient *sold* the stock, at which time any gain was taxed at the lower long-term capital gains rate). These plans were referred to as *qualified (incentive) stock option plans*. While qualified stock option plans were advantageous to the employee, they were a disadvantage to the corporation because under the federal income tax regulations the corporation could not deduct any related cost as compensation expense. However, the Tax Reform Act of 1976 repealed most of these tax incentives for recipients. This action made *nonqualified stock option plans* (where the option price is less than the market price on the date of measurement) more attractive to corporations. Under these plans, a corporation is entitled to a tax deduction based on the difference between the market price and the option price on the date the option is exercised. Under this type of plan, however, the employee is taxed on the difference between the option price and the market price when the option is exercised. Then, in the 1981 Economic Recovery Tax Act, Congress reinstated qualified stock option plans in a new, more liberal form to provide an incentive device for corporations to attract and retain key executives. However, in the Tax Reform Act of 1986, Congress changed the tax provisions so that capital gains are currently taxed at ordinary income rates. Whether or not these actions by Congress result in an option price equal to the market price, accountants must be familiar with the generally accepted accounting principles for compensatory stock option plans.

## Applicable Accounting Periods

The total compensation cost of a stock option plan is recognized as an expense over the service period. The service period is the years in which the company receives the benefit of the employee's services. This approach adheres to the *matching principle,* where expenses are recognized in the years benefitted. The provisions of the stock option plan may specify this period, or it may be inferred from the terms or pattern of previous stock option plans. If the compensation cost cannot be determined immediately (because, for instance, the measurement date occurs *later* than the grant date), compensation expense is still recognized from the date of grant to the later measurement date by using estimates based on the quoted market price at the end of each intervening period.[3]

---

2. *Ibid.*, par. 10.
3. *Ibid.*, par. 12 and 13.

## Accounting for Compensatory Stock Option Plans: Date of Measurement Is Date of Grant

If the option price is *equal to or higher than* the market price on the date of measurement, there is *no* compensation cost and therefore *no* expense is recognized. On the date of exercise, the issuance of the stock is recorded in the usual manner.

When the option price is *less* than the market price on the date of measurement, and the date of measurement is also the date of grant, journal entries are made to record (1) the total actual compensation cost, (2) the annual compensation expense related to the plan, and (3) the issuance of the stock when the option is exercised. On the date of grant, a journal entry is made debiting an account entitled Deferred Compensation and crediting Common Stock Option Warrants for the total actual compensation cost. The Deferred Compensation account is treated as a negative (contra) stockholders' equity account on the balance sheet, and its balance is subtracted from the Common Stock Option Warrants account balance in the contributed capital section.

The total deferred compensation cost is allocated as compensation expense to each year in the service period by use of the straight-line approach, as illustrated in the following diagram:

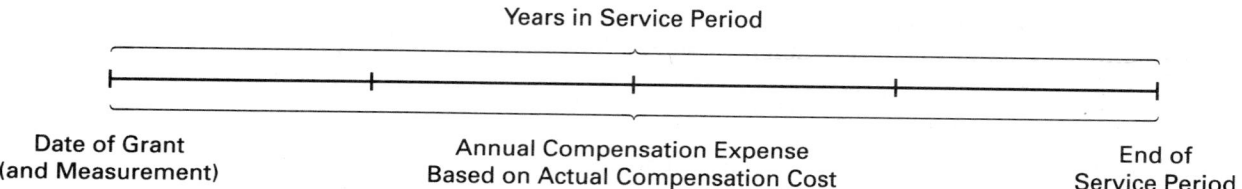

Years in Service Period

Date of Grant (and Measurement)      Annual Compensation Expense Based on Actual Compensation Cost      End of Service Period

The journal entry at the end of each year involves a debit to Compensation Expense and a credit to Deferred Compensation. At the end of the service period, the entire amount of Deferred Compensation has been allocated to Compensation Expense, but the Common Stock Option Warrants account still has a balance. If an executive fails to fulfill the conditions of the stock option plan during the service period (because, for instance, the executive leaves the company), the Common Stock Option Warrants account is debited for its related balance, the Deferred Compensation account is credited for its related balance, and the difference is credited to Compensation Expense to adjust the amount of expense previously recognized for the executive.

When the option is exercised, Cash (for the proceeds, if any) and the Common Stock Option Warrants accounts are debited, and the credit is allocated between the Common Stock account and the Additional Paid-in Capital on Common Stock account. That is, the exercise is recorded at the market price on the date of measurement. If an option is not exercised before its expiration date, this does not negate the previous recognition of compensation expense related to the plan. At the time of expiration, the related balance in the Common Stock Option Warrants account is transferred to the Additional Paid-in Capital from Expired Stock Options account because the executive has chosen to leave this amount in the corporation.

To illustrate, assume that on December 31, 1994, a corporation grants to a key executive, Anthony Paul, the nontransferable right to acquire 1,000 shares of $10 par common stock for $27 per share. Since both the number of shares and the option price are known on December 31, 1994, the date of grant is also the measurement date. The market price on that date is $29 per share, and the service period is 4 years. The stock option may not be exercised until the service period has expired, and the rights terminate at the end of 7 years or if the executive leaves the corporation. The total compensation cost is $2,000 [($29 market price − $27 option price) × 1,000 shares] and is recorded as follows:

**December 31, 1994**

| | | |
|---|---|---|
| Deferred Compensation | 2,000 | |
|     Common Stock Option Warrants | | 2,000 |

The annual compensation expense ($500) is computed by dividing the total compensation cost ($2,000) by the number of years of required service (4 years). The journal entry made at the end of *each* year to record the compensation expense is as follows:

**December 31, 1995, 96, 97, and 98**

| | | |
|---|---|---|
| Compensation Expense | 500 | |
|     Deferred Compensation | | 500 |

When the option is exercised on March 6, 2000, the following journal entry is made:

**March 6, 2000**

| | | |
|---|---|---|
| Cash ($27 × 1,000 shares) | 27,000 | |
| Common Stock Option Warrants | 2,000 | |
|     Common Stock, $10 par | | 10,000 |
|     Additional Paid-in Capital on Common Stock | | 19,000 |

Note that the exercise is recorded at $29,000 ($29 × 1,000 shares), the market price on the date of measurement.

*Disclosure*

Each year, the Compensation Expense is included in the operating expenses on the income statement. The Common Stock Option Warrants account balance offset by the Deferred Compensation account balance is listed on the balance sheet as an element of contributed capital. To illustrate the balance sheet disclosure, the following items (among others) would appear in contributed capital on December 31, 1995:

| | | |
|---|---|---|
| Common stock option warrants | $2,000 | |
| Less: Deferred compensation | (1,500) | $500 |

The terms of the stock option plan, including the number of shares under option, the option price, the shares exercisable, and any shares exercised (along with the exercise price) are disclosed in the notes to the financial statements.[4] For illustrative purposes, the preceding example involved only one executive. In reality, it is likely that many executives of a company would be involved in its compensatory stock option plan, and the accounting would follow the same principles as discussed for this one executive.

## Accounting for Compensatory Stock Option Plans: Date of Measurement Later Than Date of Grant

As indicated earlier, some stock option plans have terms whereby the number of shares or the option price cannot be determined until a date later than the date of grant. These plans are sometimes referred to as **variable-term** plans. Since the total actual compensation cost cannot be determined on the date of grant, only a memorandum entry is made on this date to indicate the terms of the stock option plan. The annual compensation expense is recorded in each year of the service period on the

---

4. "Restatement and Revision of Accounting Research Bulletins," *Accounting Research Bulletin No. 43* (New York: AICPA, 1961), ch. 13, sec. B, par. 15.

basis of estimates until the date of measurement is reached, as illustrated in the following diagram:

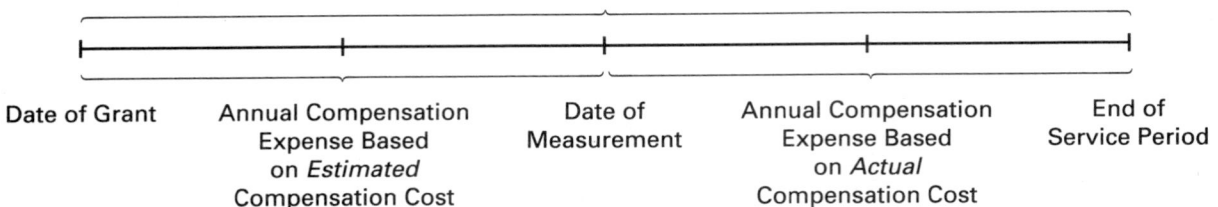

The journal entry involves a debit to Compensation Expense and a credit to Common Stock Option Warrants. The estimated annual compensation expense is based on the excess of the market price at the end of each year over the estimated option price for the estimated number of shares, allocated over the applicable service period. Any measurement error resulting from the use of these estimates, as well as any change necessary because a stock option is not exercised due to an employee failing to fulfill the conditions of the stock option plan, is treated as an adjustment to compensation expense in the current period. After the measurement date, the compensation expense is based upon the actual compensation cost, as illustrated in the preceding diagram. If an executive has fulfilled the obligations of the plan but the option is not exercised before its expiration date, the related balance in the Common Stock Option Warrants account is transferred to Additional Paid-in Capital from Expired Stock Options as discussed earlier.

To illustrate, assume the same information as in the previous example except that the option price is to be 90% of the market price on December 31, 1997 (3 years after grant). Assume further that the market price per share at the end of 1995, 1996, and 1997 is $30.00, $31.50, and $32.60, respectively. The memorandum entry in the general journal on the date of grant is as follows:

### December 31, 1994

Memorandum entry: One thousand shares of $10 par common stock may be acquired by Anthony Paul in accordance with the company stock option plan. The option price is 90% of the quoted market price on December 31, 1997. The service period is 4 years, after which the option may be exercised. The rights terminate at the end of 7 years or if Mr. Paul leaves the corporation.

The 1995 compensation expense is $750, computed by multiplying the $3,000 total estimated compensation cost times the percentage of the service period expired (25%; $1 \div 4$ years). The journal entry to record this compensation expense is as follows:

### December 31, 1995

| | | |
|---|---|---|
| **Compensation Expense** | 750 | |
|    **Common Stock Option Warrants** | | 750 |

Computations:

| | |
|---|---|
| $30,000 | Market price ($30 × 1,000 shares) |
| (27,000) | Option price (90%) |
| $ 3,000 | Estimated total compensation cost |
| × 0.25 | Percentage of service period expired ($1 \div 4$ years) |
| $ 750 | Current compensation expense |

The 1996 compensation expense is $825 based on the $3,150 estimated total compensation cost. Since 50% (2 ÷ 4 years) of the service period has expired, $1,575 ($3,150 × 0.50) of the cost is the compensation expense to date. Because $750 compensation expense was recorded in 1995, this means that $825 ($1,575 − $750) is recognized as compensation expense in 1996. Use of this approach includes a "catch-up" adjustment (correction) in the current period for the previous measurement error resulting from the use of an estimate. The journal entry is as follows:

### December 31, 1996

| | | |
|---|---|---|
| **Compensation Expense** | 825 | |
| **Common Stock Option Warrants** | | 825 |

Computations:

| | |
|---|---|
| $31,500 | Market price ($31.50 × 1,000 shares) |
| (28,350) | Option price (90%) |
| $ 3,150 | Estimated total compensation cost |
| × 0.50 | Percentage of service period expired (2 ÷ 4 years) |
| $ 1,575 | Estimated compensation expense to date |
| (750) | Previously recognized compensation expense |
| $ 825 | Current compensation expense |

December 31, 1997 is the measurement date. The 1997 compensation expense of $870 is computed by multiplying the $3,260 *actual* total compensation cost times 75% (3 years of the 4-year service period have expired) to determine the $2,445 actual compensation expense to date, and subtracting the $1,575 ($750 + $825) previously recognized compensation expense. Again, this adjusts for the previous measurement error. The journal entry is as follows:[5]

### December 31, 1997

| | | |
|---|---|---|
| **Compensation Expense** | 870 | |
| **Common Stock Option Warrants** | | 870 |

Computations:

| | |
|---|---|
| $32,600 | Market price ($32.60 × 1,000 shares) |
| (29,340) | Option price (90%) |
| $ 3,260 | Actual total compensation cost |
| × 0.75 | Percentage of service period expired (3 ÷ 4 years) |
| $ 2,445 | Actual compensation expense to date |
| (1,575) | Previously recognized compensation expense ($750 + $825) |
| $ 870 | Current compensation expense |

The last year of the service period is 1998. The 1998 compensation expense is $815, computed by deducting the previously recognized compensation expense of $2,445 ($750 + $825 + $870) from the $3,260 actual total compensation cost. The December 31, 1998 journal entry is the same as shown earlier (except for the amount) and is not repeated here. After this journal entry, the entire $3,260 compensation cost has been recorded over the 4-year service period. When the stock option is exercised,

---

5. At this point, some companies prefer to establish a Deferred Compensation account for the $815 ($3,260 − $2,445) remaining unrecognized compensation expense. For consistency with the journal entries made in previous years, we do not use this procedure.

the issuance of the stock is recorded at the market price on the measurement date as illustrated earlier.[6]

*Disclosure*

As in the previous illustration, each year the compensation expense is included on the income statement. However, when the date of measurement is later than the date of grant, a Deferred Compensation account normally is not used. Consequently, on the balance sheet the only related item shown is the balance in the Common Stock Option Warrants account, as a segment of contributed capital. A note outlining the stock option plan is also included with the financial statements.

### Stock Appreciation Rights

Although nonqualifying compensatory stock option plans provide key executives with the opportunity to acquire shares of stock with a market value in excess of the option price, these plans have some disadvantages. At the time of exercise, the executive must have sufficient cash to pay both the option price and the income taxes on the excess of the market price over the option price. In certain situations, this places a significant cash flow burden on the executive. To remedy at least part of this problem, companies have developed compensation plans involving stock appreciation rights. **Stock appreciation rights (SARs)** are rights granted to key employees that enable them to receive cash, stock, or a combination of both equal to the *excess* of the market value over a stated price of the company's stock on the date of exercise. SARs are advantageous to an executive because the market appreciation of the company's stock can be received in cash on the date of exercise, thereby avoiding the cash outflow to actually acquire the stock. Furthermore, although the executive is taxed on this appreciation, the executive may use the cash received from the SAR to pay the income taxes. In **FASB Interpretation No. 28,** the FASB concluded that plans involving stock appreciation rights are similar to other variable-term stock option plans and are accounted for in accordance with *APB Opinion No. 25.*[7]

For SAR plans, the measurement date is deferred until the date the rights are *exercised.* Since the exercise date normally falls after the service period, (1) an estimate of the total compensation cost is made at the end of each year, (2) compensation expense is recorded over the service period on the basis of these estimates (and any corrections of previous estimation errors), and (3) because corrections of estimates are not made retroactively, additional adjustments to compensation expense are made at the end of each year *after* the service period has expired, up to the date of exercise, as illustrated in the following diagram:

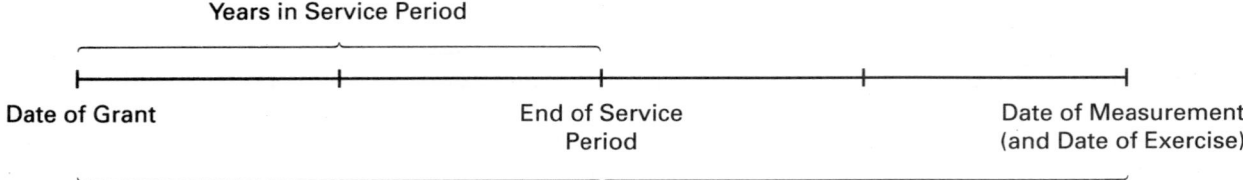

Years in Service Period

Date of Grant

End of Service Period

Date of Measurement (and Date of Exercise)

Annual Compensation Expense Based on *Estimated* Compensation Cost (until date of exercise)

---

6. In the case in which the stock is issued *before* all the services are performed, part of the consideration recorded for the stock issued would be deferred compensation and would be shown as a separate reduction of stockholders' equity, as illustrated in the earlier example.
7. "Accounting for Stock Appreciation Rights and Other Variable Stock Option or Award Plans," *FASB Interpretation No. 28* (Stamford, Conn.: FASB, 1978), par. 2.

Use of this approach follows the *matching principle.*

Accounting for SAR plans is similar to accounting for compensatory stock option plans where the measurement date is later than the date of grant. There are two key differences, however. First, the adjustments (increases or decreases) that are made at the end of each year to compensation expense *after* the service period has expired (until the date of exercise) are based on the difference between 100% of the estimated total compensation cost and the accrued compensation expense recognized to date. Second, the credit entry to recognize the accrued compensation is made to either a liability or a stockholders' equity account depending on whether it is expected that the executive will elect to receive cash or stock on the date of exercise.

To illustrate, assume that on January 1, 1994, when the market price is $10 per share, a corporation grants stock appreciation rights to a key executive, Cynthia Talbert. Under the SAR plan, Talbert is entitled to receive cash or stock for the difference between the quoted market price and a $10 option price for 1,000 shares of the company's stock on the date of exercise. The service period is 4 years and the rights must be exercised within 6 years. The year-end market prices per share of the company's stock are as shown in Exhibit 15-1. Talbert exercises the rights on December 31, 1998. The calculations of the annual compensation expense are shown in Exhibit 15-1. In each year, the corporation records the SAR compensation by debiting Compensation Expense and crediting SAR Compensation Payable (since it is assumed that Talbert will elect to receive cash upon exercise) for the amount calculated in the last column of Exhibit 15-1. For instance, on December 31, 1995, the following journal entry is made:

| | | |
|---|---|---|
| Compensation Expense | 1,000 | |
|     SAR Compensation Payable | | 1,000 |

An exception to this procedure occurs in 1996. Because the market price at the end of 1996 decreased below that of 1994, an adjusting entry is made *debiting* SAR Compensation Payable and *crediting* Compensation Expense for $150 to reduce the total

## EXHIBIT 15-1

### SAR ANNUAL COMPENSATION EXPENSE

| Date | Market Price | Option Price | Estimated Total Compensation Cost[a] | Percent Accrued[b] | Total Compensation Expense to Date[c] | Accrued Compensation Expense to Date[d] | Yearly Compensation Expense[e] |
|---|---|---|---|---|---|---|---|
| 12/31/94 | $12.00 | $10 | $2,000 | 25% | $ 500 | — | $ 500 |
| 12/31/95 | 13.00 | 10 | 3,000 | 50 | 1,500 | $ 500 | 1,000 |
| 12/31/96 | 11.80 | 10 | 1,800 | 75 | 1,350 | 1,500 | (150) |
| 12/31/97[f] | 12.60 | 10 | 2,600 | 100 | 2,600 | 1,350 | 1,250 |
| 12/31/98[g] | 13.40 | 10 | 3,400 | 100 | 3,400 | 2,600 | 800 |
| | | | | | | | $3,400 |

a. (Market price − Option price) × 1,000 shares; in 1994, ($12 − $10) × 1,000
b. Service years to date ÷ Total service period; in 1994, 1 ÷ 4 = 25%
c. Amount from footnote *a* × Percent from footnote *b*; in 1994, $2,000 × 0.25
d. Amount for previous year from footnote *c*
e. Amount from footnote *c* − Amount from footnote *d*
f. End of service period
g. Date of exercise (date of measurement)

accrued liability. Although such entries are rare, they are possible in today's volatile stock market. Of course, the SAR Compensation Payable account can never have a debit *balance* because the cumulative compensation expense can never be negative. On December 31, 1998, the following journal entry is made to recognize the SAR compensation expense for 1998 and to record the exercise of the rights:

| | | |
|---|---|---|
| Compensation Expense | 800 | |
| SAR Compensation Payable | 2,600 | |
|    Cash | | 3,400 |

Note that by the end of 1998, total compensation expense of $3,400 had been recognized for this SAR plan, the amount paid to the executive on the date of exercise.

### Junior Stock Plans

Some companies have established "junior stock plans" for their key employees. **Junior stock** is stock of a corporation that generally does not have voting, liquidation, or dividend rights and is convertible in the future into the corporation's regular common stock if certain corporate performance goals are achieved. Junior stock is usually not transferable and has a lower value than the regular corporate common stock because of the restrictions of stockholders' rights and the uncertainty of conversion. Under a **junior stock plan,** key employees are allowed to purchase a certain number of shares of junior stock at the lower value with the expectation that they will convert at some future conversion ratio to regular common stock (with a higher market value) when the performance goals are met.

In **FASB Interpretation No. 38,** the FASB concluded that junior stock plans are similar to other variable-term stock option plans and are accounted for in accordance with *APB Opinion No. 25* and *FASB Interpretation No. 28.*[8] That is, for purposes of measuring the total compensation cost, the measurement date is the first date on which both the number of shares of regular common stock that an employee is entitled to receive in exchange for the junior stock and the option price, if any, are known. Prior to the measurement date, compensation cost is estimated and allocated to expense over the service period when it becomes probable that the performance goals will be achieved. If the junior stock becomes convertible to regular common stock after the measurement date, compensation expense is recognized each period until the date the junior stock becomes convertible, if this is later than the end of the service period, as discussed for SAR plans.

### Illustration of Disclosure

Exhibit 15-2 shows Note 11 of the 1992 annual report of the Johnson & Johnson Corporation relating to its common stock, stock option plans, and stock compensation agreements. It is interesting to note that the price of the options exercised in 1992 ranged from $7.39 to $35.66, while the year-end market price was $50.50.

### Conceptual Issues

From a conceptual standpoint, many accountants believe that for stock option plans (including stock appreciation rights and junior stock plans), establishing the

---

8. "Determining the Measurement Date for Stock Option, Purchase, and Award Plans Involving Junior Stock," *FASB Interpretation No. 38* (Stamford, Conn.: FASB, 1984), par. 2–6.

## EXHIBIT 15-2
## Disclosure of Stock Option Plan

### JOHNSON & JOHNSON CORPORATION

*11. Common Stock, Stock Option Plans and Stock Compensation Agreements*

On April 23, 1992, the Board of Directors approved an increase in the authorized shares of common stock from 540 million to 1.08 billion, enabling the Company to complete a two-for-one split of its common stock. Par value remained at $1.00 per common share. All references to common stock, retained earnings, treasury stock and per share amounts appearing in this report have been adjusted to reflect the split.

The Company has stock option plans which provide for the granting of options to certain officers and employees to purchase shares of its common stock within prescribed periods at prices equal to the fair market value on the date of grant. Share activity during 1992 and 1991 under the Company's stock option plans is summarized below:

| (Shares in Thousands, Price Per Share) | 1992 | 1991 |
|---|---|---|
| Held at beginning of year by 2,810 employees (1991 – 2,851) | 28,912 | 30,165 |
| Granted to 1,056 employees (1991 – 1,274) | 2,737 | 3,812 |
| | 31,649 | 33,977 |
| Exercised (1990 – 5,868) | (3,928) | (4,318) |
| Cancelled or expired | (735) | (747) |
| Held at end of year by 3,002 employees (1991 – 2,810) | 26,986 | 28,912 |
| Shares exercisable, end of year (1990 – 11,885) | 11,947 | 11,768 |
| Shares available for future grants, end of year (1990 – 9,106) | 19,693 | 22,324 |
| Price range of options exercised (1990 – $1.26 to $22.60) | $7.39 to $35.66 | $1.76 to $28.94 |
| Price range of options held, end of year | $8.85 to $57.75 | $7.39 to $50.28 |

At year-end, the Company was obligated to deliver, over a period of not more than two years, 699 thousand shares of common stock (1991 – 759) in performance of outstanding stock compensation agreements with 7,508 employees (1991 – 6,833).

compensation cost as the excess of the market price over the option price on the measurement date is inappropriate. They feel that use of this technique understates—in many cases, significantly—the fair value of the stock option and the corresponding compensation expense. Many views are held concerning what the proper compensation expense related to a stock option plan should be. There is consensus that the value of a stock option is a significant portion of the total compensation package of each executive. However, both the *date* on which to measure and the appropriate *measurement* of this value are the subject of controversy.

In regard to the **date**, arguments have been raised for measuring the value on the date of grant, the end of the service period, and the date of exercise. For instance, there are several arguments for using the date of grant as the measurement date. First, this is the date that an arm's-length transaction with a fair value was entered into by both the corporation and the executive, and accounting is transaction based. Second, events occurring after a "liability" is incurred (grant date) do not pertain to the liability.

Finally, use of the grant date is considered to be practical and avoids the use of unreliable estimates. The primary argument for using the end of the service period as the date of measurement is that this is the date on which the obligation of the executive is complete. There are also several arguments for using the date of exercise as the measurement date. First, the commitment to transfer stock or cash is only a contingency until the exercise date. Second, the fair value can only be known with certainty on the exercise date. Finally, use of estimates in compensation plans is consistent with, and as reliable as, estimates used in other accounting areas.

In regard to the **measurement** of the value of the compensation, there are two primary alternatives. One alternative favored by some accountants is that the measurement of the compensation should be based upon the value of the benefit *received* (that is, the value of the executive's services) by the corporation at the time of grant. These accountants advocate an estimation of the cash salary forgone in lieu of the stock option, perhaps adjusted to a present value basis, as a measurement of the stock option value. The second alternative is that the value of the option should be based on the costs *sacrificed* (the value of the stock given up) by the corporation. Several measurement approaches have been suggested regarding these positions, including use of a minimum value method and both conceptual and empirical "option pricing models." A minimum value approach would base the measurement on the difference between the market price (or fair value) and the discounted amount of the exercise price on the grant date. A conceptual option pricing model is a statistical model that estimates an option's value as a function of several factors including the market price, exercise price, risk-free rate of return, variance of the market price, and life of the option. An empirical option pricing model estimates an option's value by, for instance, analyzing the relationship between an option price and the market price as well as considering other factors (e.g., time to maturity) to develop a valuation formula.[9]

Because of this controversy, the FASB is reexamining the issue of accounting for stock options and has issued an *Exposure Draft*. In regard to the measurement date, although not currently GAAP, the FASB has tentatively concluded that the compensation cost for stock option plans should be measured at the date of grant. The Board has also tentatively concluded that "fair value" should be used as the measurement value. Under this approach, fair value would be measured using an option pricing model that takes into account the variables discussed in the previous paragraph. The compensation cost would be allocated as compensation expense over the service period during which the award is earned, usually from the grant date to the vesting date. These tentative conclusions continue to be controversial and are opposed by many business groups, institutional investors, compensation consultants, and major accounting firms. If enacted as GAAP, the tentative conclusions would not become effective until the 1997 financial statements at the earliest. Thus, the generally accepted accounting principles for the measurement date, measurement method, and service period established in *APB Opinion 25* and *FASB Interpretations No. 28* and *38* remain in effect.

## CONTENT OF RETAINED EARNINGS

Retained earnings is the primary link between the balance sheet and the income statement. Assets are financed by liabilities and stockholders' equity. The stockholders'

---

9.  For more discussion of option pricing models, minimum value, and related issues, see "Accounting for Compensation Plans Involving Certain Rights Granted to Employees," *Invitation to Comment* (Stamford, Conn.: FASB, 1984).

share of assets results primarily from their investments and from net income (earnings) not distributed as dividends. The Retained Earnings account is used to summarize this latter component of stockholders' equity.

Most corporations (over 80%) prefer the account title **Retained Earnings,** with the terms *Earnings* or *Income* (with additional words) used by about 8%. A few companies (about 12%) have *negative* retained earnings and use the terms *Retained Earnings (Deficit)* or *Accumulated Deficit* (a **deficit**, or a negative retained earnings balance, is the result of accumulated prior net losses or dividends in excess of earnings).[10]

In addition to net income (or net loss), the primary factors that affect Retained Earnings include (1) dividends, (2) prior period adjustments, (3) appropriations, and (4) quasi-reorganizations.

## DIVIDENDS

Whereas net income increases the assets of the corporation and this increase is recorded in retained earnings, the distribution of dividends has the opposite effect. That is, the distribution of cash or property dividends reduces the assets and is recorded as a reduction in retained earnings. Thus, the phrase "retained earnings paid out in dividends," or some similar phrase, often found in summaries of corporate financial activities is somewhat misleading. Cash or property dividends are paid out of *cash* or some other asset, and retained earnings are reduced because the payment is a return *of* capital to the stockholders.

In order for a corporation to pay cash or property dividends, it must meet legal requirements and have assets available for distribution. The board of directors is responsible for the establishment of a dividend policy and determines the amount, timing, and type of dividends to be declared. In so doing, it must consider the articles of incorporation, applicable state regulations for dividends, the impact upon legal capital (established to protect corporate creditors), and compliance with contractual agreements, as well as the financial well-being of the corporation.

Legal requirements for dividends vary from state to state, but most states require a positive (credit) retained earnings balance before dividends may be declared. Furthermore, the amount of dividends declared generally cannot exceed this retained earnings balance. It is usually required that the amount of retained earnings available for dividends be restricted by the cost of treasury shares held. However, a few states allow the declaration of a dividend equal to the amount of current income even though the company may have a prior deficit. In certain instances, some states allow dividends that reduce contributed capital, as long as legal capital is not impaired. Other states may allow a dividend from donated capital but not from other unrealized items in stockholders' equity. Furthermore, contractual agreements (such as long-term bond provisions) may restrict a corporation from declaring dividends. Corporate legal counsel is responsible for reviewing applicable state laws and corporate contracts to determine the legality of dividends. Nonetheless, accountants also should be aware of state regulations and contractual obligations, particularly as they affect restrictions of dividends.

In addition to meeting legal requirements, the board of directors must evaluate the financial desirability of a particular dividend. In this regard, the board may consult with the corporate accountants. Consideration should be given to the corporation's financial flexibility and operating capability, including such factors as the impact of

---

10. *Accounting Trends and Techniques* (New York: AICPA, 1992), p. 234.

a dividend upon the current assets and working capital, the ability to finance capital expansion projects, the effect upon the stock market price per share, and the maintenance of a liquidity "cushion" against possible future deteriorating economic conditions. The declaration of a dividend must be in the financial long- and short-term best interests of the stockholders. Several types of dividends may be considered, including: (1) cash, (2) property, (3) scrip, (4) stock, and (5) liquidating dividends.

The impact of each type of dividend upon the corporate capital structure is as follows: (1) cash, property, and scrip dividends decrease retained earnings (and stockholders' equity); (2) liquidating dividends decrease contributed capital (and stockholders' equity); (3) stock dividends decrease retained earnings and increase contributed capital by the same amount (so there is no change in total stockholders' equity; and (4) stock splits do not affect any element of stockholders' equity.

## Cash Dividends

The most common type of dividend is the cash dividend—the distribution of cash by the corporation to its stockholders. When used without a qualifying adjective, the term *dividends* refers to cash dividends.

Four dates are significant in regard to a cash dividend (or any type of dividend): (1) the date of declaration, (2) the ex-dividend date, (3) the date of record, and (4) the date of payment. **On the date of declaration, the board of directors formally declares that a dividend will be paid to** *stockholders of record* **on a specific future date**, typically 4 to 6 weeks later. At this declaration date, the corporation becomes legally liable to pay the dividend. Prior to this date, stockholders ordinarily have no power to require that a dividend be paid; dividend policy has been legally entrusted to the board of directors. Since a liability has been incurred on the date of declaration, a journal entry is made to reduce retained earnings and establish the current liability. After the date of declaration, the outstanding stock of the corporation trading in the open market normally sells "with dividends attached" (that is, at a higher market price that includes the amount of the future dividend payment). The **ex-dividend date** occurs several days before the date of record to enable the corporation to update its *stockholders' ledger* by the date of record. The ex-dividend date is important to investors because **on the ex-dividend date the stock stops selling with dividends attached.** Any purchaser of the stock on or after this date will not receive the current dividend. No accounting entry is required on the ex-dividend date. Normally, it takes a corporation some time to process the dividend checks. Thus, a "cut-off" date is needed—the date of record. **Only investors listed in the stockholders' ledger on the date of record can receive the dividend.** The date of record usually occurs several weeks after the declaration date and several weeks before the payment date, as specified in the dividend provisions. On the date of record, the corporation makes a memorandum entry indicating that the date of record has been reached and showing the future dividend payment date. **On the date of payment, the corporation distributes the dividend checks, and a journal entry is made to eliminate the liability and reduce the cash.**

On the date of declaration, the total amount of the dividend liability, as well as the portions applicable to preferred stock (if any) and to common stock, are determined and recorded. Retained Earnings is usually reduced (debited) directly. However, some companies prefer to use a contra-retained earnings account entitled Dividends Declared for the dividends related to each class of stock. A current liability, Dividends Payable, is also established. Separate liability accounts for the amounts owed to each class of stockholder also may be created.

To illustrate, assume that on November 3, 1995, the board of directors of a corporation declares preferred dividends totaling $10,000 and common dividends totaling $20,000. These dividends are payable on December 15, 1995 to stockholders of record on November 24, 1995. The journal entries to record the dividend are as follows:

**November 3, 1995**

| | | |
|---|---|---|
| Retained Earnings | 30,000 | |
|     Dividends Payable: Preferred Stock | | 10,000 |
|     Dividends Payable: Common Stock | | 20,000 |

**November 24, 1995**

Memorandum entry: The company will pay dividends on December 15, 1995, to preferred and common stockholders of record as of today, the date of record.

**December 15, 1995**

| | | |
|---|---|---|
| Dividends Payable: Preferred Stock | 10,000 | |
| Dividends Payable: Common Stock | 20,000 | |
|     Cash | | 30,000 |

If the accounting period ends before the dividend payment, the Dividends Payable account(s) is reported as a current liability on the balance sheet. If a company uses the contra account, Dividends Declared, this account is closed directly to Retained Earnings as part of the year-end closing process.

*Participating Preferred Stock*

Usually the amounts of dividends payable to each class of stock are readily determinable. In certain cases, however, preferred stock may be either fully or partially participating. In these cases, computations must be made to determine the dividends payable to preferred and common stockholders. Recall from Chapter 14 that *fully participating* preferred stock shares equally with the common stock in any extra dividends. These extra dividends are distributed proportionally, based on the respective *total* par values of each class of stock. *Partially participating* preferred stock is limited in its participation to a fixed rate (based on the respective par value) or amount per share.

To illustrate, assume that a company has issued 10% participating cumulative preferred stock with a total par value of $20,000 and common stock with a total par value of $30,000. Therefore, preferred stock constitutes 40% and common stock 60% of the total par value. The company intends to distribute cash dividends of $9,000, and there are no dividends in arrears. The dividend distribution is shown in Exhibit 15-3, assuming (a) the preferred stock is fully participating, and (b) the preferred stock participates up to 12% of its par value. If any preferred stock dividends had been in arrears, these would have been distributed *before* any participation calculations. In the participation calculations, common stock initially receives a rate equal to preferred *for the current year*. Common stock does *not* share in any dividends in arrears.

**EXHIBIT 15-3**

## DIVIDEND DISTRIBUTION

|  | | Preferred | Common |
|---|---|---|---|
| **(a) Preferred Stock Is Fully Participating** | | | |
| 10% dividend to Preferred (on $20,000 par) | | $2,000 | |
| Common dividend (equal to 10% of $30,000 par) | | | $3,000 |
| Extra dividend proportionate to par values: | | | |
|    Total to allocate | $9,000 | | |
|    Allocated ($2,000 + $3,000) | (5,000) | | |
|    Remainder (40% to preferred, 60% to common) | $4,000 | 1,600 | 2,400 |
|    Dividends to each class of stock | | $3,600 | $5,400 |
| | | | |
| **(b) Preferred Stock Participates up to 12%** | | | |
| 10% dividend to Preferred | | $2,000 | |
| Common dividend (equal to 10% of par) | | | $3,000 |
| 2% dividend on par of Preferred (2% × $20,000) | | 400 | |
| 2% dividend on par of Common (2% × $30,000) | | | 600 |
| Remainder to common ($9,000 − $6,000 allocated) | | | 3,000 |
|    Dividends to each class of stock | | $2,400 | $6,600 |

### Property Dividends

Occasionally, a corporation will declare a **property dividend that is payable in assets other than cash.** Marketable securities of other companies held by the corporation are typically used for a property dividend because they are more easily distributable to the stockholders. However, the dividend may be paid with any assets designated by the board of directors.

A property dividend is classified as a *nonreciprocal nonmonetary transfer to owners.* That is, the corporation enters into an exchange in which it gives up something of value (the asset) but for which it receives no asset or service in return. Furthermore, because no cash is involved, the exchange is a nonmonetary transfer. In accordance with **APB Opinion No. 29,** a property dividend is recorded at the fair market value of the asset transferred, and a gain or a loss is recognized.[11]

The logic behind the use of fair market value for a property dividend is that the assets distributed in the dividend could have been sold for cash and the proceeds (fair market value) used to pay a cash dividend. The fair market value is determined *on the date of declaration* (because this is the date the dividend becomes a legal liability) by referring to existing stock or bond market prices, recent cash exchanges of similar assets, or objective independent appraisals.

To illustrate, assume the board of directors of Corporation A declares a property dividend, payable in bonds of Company B being held to maturity. The bonds are carried on Corporation A's books at a book value of $40,000 but their current market

---

11. "Accounting for Nonmonetary Transactions," *APB Opinion No. 29* (New York: AICPA, 1973), par. 18.

*Investments are discussed in Chapter 13.*

value is $48,000. On the date of declaration, the investment account is revalued to its fair market value and the dividend obligation is recorded at this value so that the amounts of both the gain and the dividend liability are properly reported. The journal entries to record this property dividend are as follows:

### Date of Declaration

| | | |
|---|---|---|
| Investment in Company B Bonds ($48,000 − $40,000) | 8,000 | |
|   Gain on Disposal of Investments | | 8,000 |
| Retained Earnings | 48,000 | |
|   Property Dividends Payable | | 48,000 |

### Date of Payment

| | | |
|---|---|---|
| Property Dividends Payable | 48,000 | |
|   Investment in Company B Bonds | | 48,000 |

On the date of payment, no adjustment of the gain or loss is made, even though the market value may have changed since the date of declaration. The gain or loss is reported in the Other Items section of the income statement. If payment of the dividend will not be made until next year, the dividend liability is reported as a current liability on the balance sheet.

In the case where marketable debt or equity securities "available for sale" are distributed in a property dividend, the computation of the gain or loss is more complex. This is because it involves consideration of any previously recorded unrealized increase or decrease in value. The marketable securities asset account (whether current or noncurrent) is being carried at the fair value (by use of an Allowance account) of the securities *on the last balance sheet date*, along with an "unrealized increase (or decrease) in value" stockholders' equity account whose balance is the difference between the cost and the fair value. However, the realized gain or loss on this type of property dividend is computed as the difference between the fair value of the securities *on the date of declaration* and the original *cost* of the securities. The journal entry on the date of declaration to revalue the Investment account (by adjusting the Allowance account) and to record the realized gain or loss must also eliminate the unrealized increase (decrease) in value for these securities.

To illustrate, assume Corporation C declares a property dividend on March 15, 1995, payable in Company D stock. The Company D stock had been purchased early in 1994 for $24,000 and was reported as an asset at a fair value of $29,000 (i.e., at a cost of $24,000 plus an allowance for an increase in value of $5,000, along with an unrealized increase in value of $5,000 reported in stockholders' equity) on the December 31, 1994 balance sheet. If the market value is $31,000 on March 15, 1995, the gain is $7,000, computed by comparing the current fair value ($31,000) to the original cost ($24,000). The following journal entries are made on the date of declaration to record this property dividend:

| | | |
|---|---|---|
| Allowance for Change in Value of Investment in Securities Available for Sale | 2,000 | |
| Unrealized Increase in Value of Securities Available for Sale | 5,000 | |
|   Gain on Disposal of Investments | | 7,000 |
| Retained Earnings | 31,000 | |
|   Property Dividends Payable | | 31,000 |

The journal entry to record the distribution of the securities to stockholders on the date of payment is as follows:

| | | |
|---|---|---|
| Property Dividends Payable | 31,000 | |
| Investment in Securities Available for Sale | | 24,000 |
| Allowance for Change in Value of Investment in Securities Available for Sale | | 7,000 |

## Scrip Dividends

As discussed earlier, in establishing dividend policy, the board of directors must consider both the legal requirements and the corporate financial well-being. In certain instances, a corporation with adequate retained earnings to meet the legal dividend requirements but insufficient funds to justify a current cash dividend may declare a **scrip dividend.** Here, the corporation issues promissory notes (called "scrip") requiring it to pay dividends at some future date. The usual journal entries are made at the date of declaration (although some companies may credit notes payable instead of dividends payable) and date of payment, except when the notes carry an interest rate. In this case, interest expense is also recorded on the date of payment. If the scrip payment will not be made until next year, a year-end adjusting entry is necessary to record accrued interest expense. A review of the maturity date is necessary to determine the proper classification of the dividend liability on the balance sheet. Scrip dividends are rare, however. If a corporation is having liquidity problems, it is usually unwise for the board of directors to commit it to cash outflows, even if these would be made in the future.

## Stock Dividends

Another type of dividend that a corporation may declare and distribute is a stock dividend. **A stock dividend is a pro rata (proportional) distribution of additional shares of a corporation's own stock to its stockholders.** A stock dividend usually consists of the same class of shares; that is, a common stock dividend is declared on common stock outstanding. This type of distribution is referred to as an *ordinary* stock dividend. The distribution of a different class of stock (common on preferred or preferred on common) sometimes is referred to as a *special* stock dividend. Stock dividends are usually issued out of authorized but unissued shares, although treasury stock shares may be used. Unlike other dividends, the declaration of a stock dividend usually may be legally rescinded. A stock dividend also differs from other dividends in that *no corporate assets are distributed.* Each stockholder maintains the same percentage ownership in the corporation as was held prior to the distribution.

Stock dividends are often viewed favorably by stockholders even though: (1) they receive no corporate assets; (2) their percentage ownership does not change; (3) theoretically, the total market value of their investment will not increase because the increased number of shares will be offset by a decrease in the stock market price per share because a larger total number of shares participate in the same corporate earnings; and (4) future cash dividends may be limited because retained earnings is decreased by the amount of the stock dividend, and most states set legal dividend restrictions based on positive retained earnings. However, the following factors may enhance the perceived attractiveness of stock dividends:

1. The stockholders may see the stock dividend as evidence of corporate growth.

2. The stockholders may see the stock dividend as evidence of sound financial policy.

3. Other investors may see the stock dividend in a similar light, and by trading in the stock may cause the market price *not* to decrease proportionally.

4. The corporation may state that it will pay the same fixed cash dividend per share, in which case individual stockholders will receive higher total future cash dividends.

5. The stockholders may see the market price decreasing to a lower trading range, making the stock more attractive to additional investors so that the market price may eventually rise.

## Conceptual Issues

The **economic substance** of a stock dividend is that it is not really a "dividend" but instead is similar to a stock split. In both cases even though the number of shares increases, no assets are distributed to the stockholders and each stockholder's percentage ownership stays the same, so that total assets and stockholders' equity remain unchanged. To depict the similar economic substance, then, in theory a stock dividend should be recorded in a manner similar to a stock split. Recall from Chapter 14 that although a stock split usually is proportional and requires only a memorandum entry, in the case of a disproportionate stock split, the capital stock and additional paid-in capital accounts must be adjusted by a formal journal entry. A similar entry could be made for a stock dividend. The capital stock account could be increased (credited) for the par value (legal capital) of the additional shares issued. It would be logical, then, to decrease (debit) additional paid-in capital for the same amount, since the excess of the original issuance price over the current legal capital has now been reduced.

From an accounting standpoint, however, a stock dividend is *not* accounted for like a stock split, but instead is recorded in a manner similar to other dividends. When a stock dividend is recorded, total stockholders' equity is not changed. Retained earnings is decreased by the amount of the "dividend," and contributed capital is increased by the same amount because of the additional shares issued. This treatment is based on an **"opportunity cost"** argument. That is, the "dividend" should be recorded at the fair value of the stock because this is the value forgone by the corporation to issue the stock dividend.

Under this method, the fair market value may be determined by assuming the stock is sold for cash at the current market price and the proceeds used to pay a cash dividend. In determining the "current market price," consideration should be given to the impact on this price of the additional shares outstanding as a result of the stock dividend. The appropriate fair market value at which to record the stock dividend is the market price *after* the declaration of the dividend. The issuance of a very small number of shares in a stock dividend would cause only a small decrease in the market price, whereas larger stock dividends would cause greater decreases in the market price. To implement this fair market value approach, an estimation technique for determining the decrease in market value would need to be developed. However, no such technique has been implemented. Instead, a distinction is made between "small" and "large" stock dividends, and generally accepted accounting principles in accordance with state legal requirements have been developed for each.

## GAAP

In the case of a **small stock dividend** (presumably having no apparent effect upon the market price per share), the Committee on Accounting Procedure suggested that many recipients of the dividend consider it a distribution of corporate earnings in an amount equal to the fair market value of the additional shares received. Even though no corporate assets are distributed in a stock dividend (regardless of stockholder "perceptions"), the Committee apparently accepted the view that a stock dividend is a simultaneous sale of stock and payment of a dividend. **Therefore, a *small* stock dividend is accounted for by transferring from retained earnings to contributed capital an amount equal to the fair market value of the additional shares issued.**

In distinguishing between a small and a large stock dividend, the Committee accepted the representations of a corporation as to the nature of the stock dividend as one of the principal considerations. However, it did say that **fair market value is ordinarily the appropriate value to capitalize whenever the stock dividend (that is, small dividend) is less than 20% or 25% of the previously outstanding shares.**

State legal requirements govern the *minimum* amount to be capitalized (transferred from retained earnings to contributed capital as part of legal capital) in conjunction with stock dividends. Generally, this amount is the par or stated value of the additional shares distributed. In the case of no-par stock, the amount may be based on the average price at which all similar stock was previously issued, or it may be determined by the board of directors. The accounting for a **large stock dividend** relates to this legal capital. The Committee said that **a large stock dividend is similar in nature to a stock split so that there is no need to capitalize more than the amount necessary to satisfy legal requirements (that is, the par value).** In such cases, it was also suggested that the use of the term dividend be avoided or, when this is not possible because of legal restrictions, the transaction should be described in terminology such as *split-up effected in the form of a dividend.*[12]

Given the Committee's acceptance of the argument that a stock dividend is a distribution of earnings and should be based upon fair market value, use of par value to record a large stock dividend seems inappropriate. Par value has no direct relationship to market value. Furthermore, use of par value for large stock dividends and fair market value for small stock dividends can lead to illogical accounting results. For instance, if a corporation with 2,000 shares of $10 par common stock outstanding were to issue a 15% (300 shares) small stock dividend when the market price per share is $40, it would reduce retained earnings and increase contributed capital by $12,000. When issuing a 50% (1,000 shares) large stock dividend, the same corporation would reduce retained earnings and increase contributed capital by only $10,000. In this example, a small stock dividend has a greater effect on the components of stockholders' equity than a large stock dividend! Nonetheless, use of market value to record a small stock dividend and use of par value to record a large dividend are generally accepted accounting principles. The following diagram shows the effects on the various elements of stockholders' equity of a small and large stock dividend, respectively.

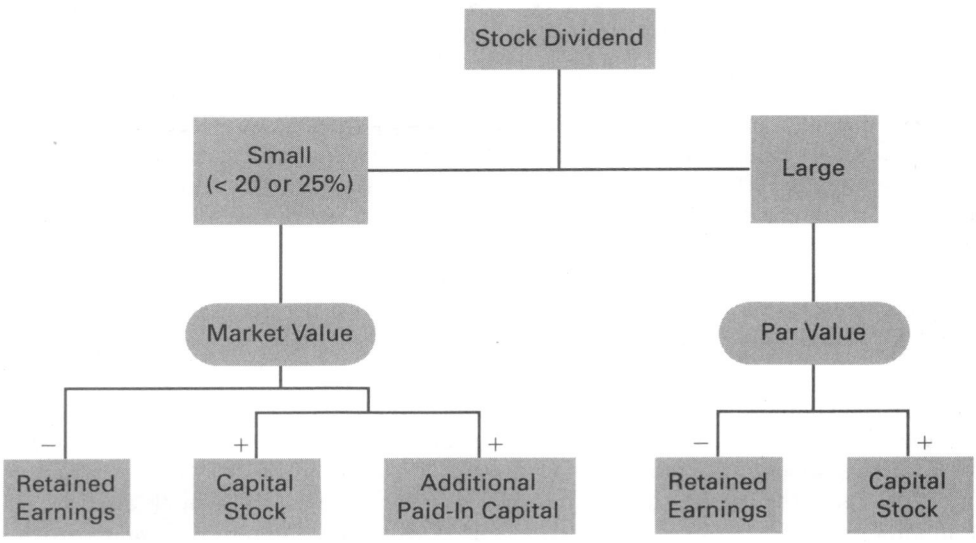

---

12. *Accounting Research Bulletin No. 43, op. cit.*, ch. 7, sec. B, par. 10 and 11.

To illustrate the accounting for the two sizes of stock dividend, assume a corporation has the following stockholders' equity prior to the stock dividend:

| | |
|---|---:|
| Common stock, $10 par (20,000 shares issued and outstanding) | $200,000 |
| Additional paid-in capital | 180,000 |
| Retained earnings | 320,000 |
| Total stockholders' equity | $700,000 |

Note, in this example there are 20,000 shares issued and outstanding; therefore, there is no treasury stock. Treasury stock normally does not participate in a small stock dividend because the dividend is based on the outstanding shares of stock. However, treasury stock may participate in a large stock dividend because the dividend is considered to be similar to a stock split.

*Example 1: Small Stock Dividend*

Assume that the corporation declares and issues a 10% stock dividend. On the date of declaration, the stock sells for $23 per share. The 2,000-share stock dividend is recorded at the fair value of $46,000, as shown in the following journal entries:

**Date of Declaration**

| | | |
|---|---:|---:|
| **Retained Earnings** | 46,000 | |
|     **Common Stock To Be Distributed** | | 20,000 |
|     **Additional Paid-in Capital From Stock Dividend** | | 26,000 |

**Date of Issuance**

| | | |
|---|---:|---:|
| **Common Stock To Be Distributed** | 20,000 | |
|     **Common Stock, $10 par** | | 20,000 |

The resulting stockholders' equity is as follows:

| | |
|---|---:|
| Common stock, $10 par (22,000 shares issued and outstanding) | $220,000 |
| Additional paid-in capital | 206,000 |
| Retained earnings | 274,000 |
| Total stockholders' equity | $700,000 |

Note that the amounts of the components of stockholders' equity have changed, but the total stockholders' equity ($700,000) remains the same as before the small stock dividend.

If a balance sheet is prepared after the declaration but before the issuance of the stock dividend, the Common Stock To Be Distributed account is listed as a component of Contributed Capital. The account is *not* a liability like the dividend payable accounts related to other types of dividends because it will not be satisfied by the distribution of assets. Instead, it is a temporary stockholders' equity item representing the legal capital related to the stock to be issued. As illustrated, it is eliminated when the stock is issued.

*Example 2: Large Stock Dividend*

Assume, *instead*, that the corporation declares and issues a 40% stock dividend when the stock is selling for $23 per share. In this case, the par value of $80,000 for the 8,000 shares is used to record the stock dividend as follows:

**Date of Declaration**

| | | |
|---|---|---|
| Retained Earnings | 80,000 | |
|     Common Stock To Be Distributed | | 80,000 |

**Date of Issuance**

| | | |
|---|---|---|
| Common Stock To Be Distributed | 80,000 | |
|     Common Stock, $10 par | | 80,000 |

The resulting stockholders' equity is as follows:

| | |
|---|---|
| Common stock, $10 par (28,000 shares issued and outstanding) | $280,000 |
| Additional paid-in capital | 180,000 |
| Retained earnings | 240,000 |
|     Total stockholders' equity | $700,000 |

Note again that the total stockholders' equity ($700,000) remains the same as before the large stock dividend.

*Fractional Shares*

In the case of a stock dividend, the number of shares that many stockholders own will not entitle them to receive additional whole shares from the dividend. For example, if a 10% stock dividend were declared, a stockholder owning 43 shares would be entitled to $4\frac{3}{10}$ additional shares. Some corporations have a policy of not issuing fractional shares. These corporations usually offer stockholders two alternatives: (1) to receive cash equal to the market price of the fractional share, or (2) to pay in sufficient cash to receive a full share. In the first case, the cash paid by the corporation is accounted for as a cash dividend and fewer shares are issued. In the second case, the stock dividend is recorded in the usual manner and an adjustment of contributed capital is made for the cash received by the corporation.

## Liquidating Dividends

**Liquidating dividends** represent a return of contributed capital rather than a distribution of retained earnings. These dividends usually are declared when a corporation is ceasing or reducing operations. A liquidating dividend also may arise when a natural resources corporation pays a dividend based on earnings before depletion. That portion of the dividends equal to the amount of depletion is considered the liquidating dividend.

When a dividend is paid that is in part (or in total) a liquidating dividend, the corporation must adhere to state legal requirements in recording the dividend. The *normal* portion of the dividend is recorded as a reduction of retained earnings and the *liquidating* portion as a reduction of contributed capital. The latter may be recorded as a debit either to an additional paid-in capital account or to a special contra-contributed capital account entitled, for instance, Contributed Capital Distributed as a Liquidating Dividend. Full disclosure of the liquidating dividend in a note to the financial statements is essential to notify stockholders that a portion of contributed capital is being returned.

## PRIOR PERIOD ADJUSTMENTS (RESTATEMENTS)

A few items are reported as **prior period adjustments (restatements)** of retained earnings. These include certain changes in accounting principles, a change in accounting entity, and corrections of errors of prior periods. All other profit and loss items are included in the determination of net income of the current period.[13] The specific accounting treatment of these items is discussed in Chapter 22; the emphasis here is on the impact on retained earnings. To illustrate, the following discussion focuses on corrections of errors.

A company may make an error in the financial statements of one accounting period that is not discovered until a later period. These errors may be attributable to oversights, the incorrect use of existing facts, or mistakes in mathematics or in the application of accounting principles. Usually these errors affect an asset or liability and a revenue or expense of a prior year. Corrections of all material errors are treated as prior period adjustments (restatements) of retained earnings. That is, in the year of correction, the asset or liability account balance is corrected and the offsetting debit or credit (which involved a revenue or expense previously closed to retained earnings) is made directly to the Retained Earnings account or to an account such as Correction of Prior Years' Income Due to Material Error in.... If the latter account is used, it is closed directly to Retained Earnings in the year-end closing entries. Any related impact on income taxes is similarly recorded. For instance, assume that in 1995 Fox Company discovers that it inadvertently did not accrue $10,000 of interest expense for 1994. This material error overstated 1994 income before income taxes by a similar amount. Assuming a related income tax effect of $3,000, the correcting entries in 1995 are as follows:

| | | |
|---|---|---|
| Retained Earnings (or Correction of Prior...) | 10,000 | |
|     Interest Payable | | 10,000 |
| Income Tax Refund Receivable | 3,000 | |
|     Retained Earnings (or Correction of Prior...) | | 3,000 |

When a prior period adjustment is made, the item (net of the applicable income taxes) is reported as an adjustment of the beginning balance of retained earnings on the statement of retained earnings. If the January 1, 1995 retained earnings balance of the Fox Company was $102,400, the correction is disclosed on its December 31, 1995 statement of retained earnings as a prior period adjustment as follows:

| | |
|---|---|
| Retained earnings, as previously reported January 1, 1995 | $102,400 |
| Less: Correction of overstatement in 1994 net income due to | |
|     interest expense understatement (net of $3,000 income taxes) | (7,000) |
| Adjusted retained earnings, January 1, 1995 | $ 95,400 |

---

13. "Accounting Changes," *APB Opinion No. 20* (New York: AICPA, 1971), par. 27 and 34, and "Prior Period Adjustments," *FASB Statement of Financial Accounting Standards No. 16* (Stamford, Conn.: FASB, 1977), par. 10–12, as amended by "Accounting for Income Taxes," *FASB Statement of Financial Accounting Standards No. 109* (Norwalk, Conn.: FASB, 1992), par. 288(n).

The remaining portion of the statement is then completed as illustrated in Exhibit 15-4 later in the chapter. The effect of the error on the prior year's net income and earnings per share is disclosed in the period in which the correction is made. If comparative financial statements are presented, corresponding adjustments are made to the net income (and components thereof), retained earnings, asset, or liability account balances for all the periods reported.[14]

## APPROPRIATIONS OF RETAINED EARNINGS

The board of directors is responsible for establishing dividend policy, while following legal requirements and sound financial practice. Stockholders sometimes consider only the legal requirements. As the Retained Earnings account balance increases, they may expect to be paid higher dividends. However, the *assets* represented by retained earnings must be used for a variety of corporate activities, including financing ongoing operations and long-term expansion projects, meeting principal and interest payments on debt securities, as well as making dividend payments.

To indicate that a certain portion of retained earnings is not available for dividends, a corporation may appropriate (restrict) retained earnings. An **appropriation** (or **restriction**) of retained earnings means that the board of directors establishes a formal policy that a portion of retained earnings is "earmarked" for a designated purpose and is unavailable for dividends. It is important to note that such a policy does *not* directly earmark or restrict the use of any assets; it merely requires that the corporation not distribute any assets that would correspondingly reduce this restricted retained earnings.

A board of directors may appropriate retained earnings for the following reasons: (1) to meet *legal* requirements, (2) to meet *contractual* restrictions, or (3) because of *discretionary* actions.

### Legal Requirements

Corporations must adhere to the laws of the state in which they are incorporated. Certain states require restrictions of retained earnings when a corporation reacquires its own stock as treasury stock. Usually, the appropriation of retained earnings is in an amount equal to the cost of the treasury shares. The argument for this appropriation is that the acquisition of treasury stock reduces the amount of invested (permanent) capital, and by restricting retained earnings for an equal amount, permanent capital is not impaired.

### Contractual Agreements

Retained earnings also may be restricted as a result of a contractual agreement. This type of agreement often is made when a corporation issues long-term bonds. In order to provide some assurance that sufficient assets will be maintained in the corporation to satisfy bondholders' claims, the bond provisions (sometimes called "debt covenants") may require the periodic appropriation of a certain amount of retained earnings.

---

14. "Reporting the Results of Operations," *APB Opinion No. 9* (New York: AICPA, 1966), par. 18 and 26.

## Discretionary Actions

Retained earnings also may be appropriated as a result of management discretion. This type of restriction may be related to planning for future expansion or in anticipation of potential future losses. In the first case, a company may be planning to build a new plant or to add to existing facilities. It may be desirable to finance this activity through internally generated funds (those funds that the corporation already holds or will soon receive from operations) rather than seek external funding from creditors or through the issuance of more stock. To indicate that these internal funds are being held within the corporation for this purpose and are not available for dividends, the board of directors may appropriate a portion of retained earnings.

Corporations may also restrict retained earnings when future losses are anticipated. For instance, a company may establish a policy of *self-insurance*. That is, it may elect to accept the risk of a future hazard (for example, an earthquake, flood, or fire) and its accompanying losses rather than transfer this risk to an insurance company through the payment of insurance premiums. A company may self-insure because insurance companies will not insure the risk, insurance premiums are too high, or it is widely dispersed geographically and large enough that the probability of a significant loss is relatively low. Actually, self-insurance is *no* insurance.

When a company decides to self-insure, it has no expense but may restrict retained earnings each year in an amount equal to the insurance premiums that would have been paid. When a hazard results in a loss, that loss must be listed as a component on the income statement. Under *no* circumstances should the amount be closed directly to Retained Earnings. **FASB Statement No. 5** clearly states that "Costs or losses shall not be charged to an appropriation of retained earnings, and no part of the appropriation shall be transferred to income."[15] The corporation discloses the loss as usual on the income statement and simply cancels a portion (or all) of the appropriated retained earnings. This type of retained earnings restriction should be discouraged because it may mislead stockholders into thinking that the corporation has somehow "protected" itself against future losses, when, in fact, it carries no related insurance.

## Alternative Accounting for Appropriations

Appropriations of retained earnings may be accounted for by (1) making journal entries or (2) reporting the restrictions in a note accompanying the financial statements or a parenthetical note in stockholders' equity.

### Journal Entries

If an appropriation of retained earnings is accounted for by a journal entry, an **Appropriated Retained Earnings**[16] account is established and the Retained Earnings account is reduced. When the appropriation is no longer needed, the initial journal entry is reversed, thereby eliminating the appropriated retained earnings balance and increasing unappropriated retained earnings. To illustrate, suppose a corporation has a $300,000 retained earnings balance when it acquires treasury stock at a cost of $20,000. The journal entry to record a restriction of retained earnings is as follows:

| | | |
|---|---|---|
| **Retained Earnings** | 20,000 | |
| **Retained Earnings Appropriated for Treasury Stock** | | 20,000 |

---

15. "Accounting for Contingencies," *FASB Statement of Financial Accounting Standards No. 5* (Stamford, Conn.: FASB, 1975), par. 15.
16. As discussed elsewhere in this book, use of the term *reserve* in financial statements, including appropriations of retained earnings, is misleading and should be avoided.

Note that the journal entry involves no assets; only retained earnings accounts are affected. Furthermore, when journal entries are used for appropriations, *total* retained earnings does not change. It is merely separated into two elements. On the balance sheet, retained earnings is shown as follows:

| | |
|---|---:|
| Retained earnings, unappropriated | $280,000 |
| Retained earnings appropriated for treasury stock | 20,000 |
| Total retained earnings | $300,000 |

When the treasury stock is reissued and the board of directors cancels the appropriation, the following journal entry is made:

| | | |
|---|---|---|
| **Retained Earnings Appropriated for Treasury Stock** | **20,000** | |
| **Retained Earnings** | | **20,000** |

Again, no change occurs in *total* retained earnings. The Appropriated Retained Earnings account balance is canceled and the amount transferred back to unappropriated Retained Earnings. The same journal entries (with slightly different titles) would be made for appropriations related to contractual agreements or management discretion.

*Note to the Financial Statements*
A major disadvantage of using journal entries to disclose appropriations of retained earnings is that stockholders still may be confused about the availability of dividends. When, in the last example, stockholders see "Retained Earnings, Unappropriated" in the amount of $280,000 on the balance sheet, they may expect dividends to be paid in that amount. In order to improve the reporting of retained earnings appropriations, most companies disclose this information in a note (or sometimes by parenthetical notations) to the financial statements.

Disclosure of restrictions (appropriations) of retained earnings in this manner is the practice recommended by the authors. When a note is used, a clear description of the legal, contractual, or discretionary provisions and the amount of the appropriation is required. To illustrate, the $300,000 retained earnings balance and the note for the treasury stock would appear as follows:

Retained earnings (see *Note A*)     $300,000

*Note A*: Retained earnings are restricted regarding dividends in the amount of $20,000, the cost of the treasury stock.

When the appropriation is canceled, the note is no longer included in the financial statements.

## STATEMENT OF RETAINED EARNINGS

Although not a required separate statement, corporations sometimes include a statement of retained earnings in their financial statements. To disclose the earnings, dividends, prior period adjustments, and other reductions, the format shown in

Exhibit 15-4 is suggested. This format is used by a corporation that discloses its appropriations of retained earnings in a note to the financial statements.

---

**EXHIBIT 15-4**

**STATEMENT OF RETAINED EARNINGS**

For Year Ended December 31, 1995

Retained earnings, as previously reported, January 1, 1995
Plus (minus): Prior period adjustments (net of income tax effect)
Adjusted retained earnings, January 1, 1995
Plus (minus): Net income (loss)
Minus: Dividends (specifically identified, including per share amounts)
         Reductions due to retirement or reacquisition of capital stock
         Reductions due to conversion of bonds or preferred stock
Minus (plus): Adjustments due to quasi-reorganizations
Retained earnings, December 31, 1995

---

The retained earnings statement may be prepared as a separate statement within the financial statements, as a supporting schedule directly beneath the income statement, or, as is common, included in the required statement of changes in stockholders' equity discussed later in the chapter. Although the format in Exhibit 15-4 includes all items affecting retained earnings, items such as prior period adjustments, reductions due to conversions or to the retirement of capital stock, and adjustments due to quasi-reorganizations are relatively rare. Consequently, a retained earnings statement usually includes only adjustments to retained earnings for net income and dividends. Any restrictions (appropriations) of retained earnings would be disclosed by means of a note to the financial statements.

If a corporation appropriates retained earnings by using journal entries, two sections of the statement of retained earnings are necessary. The first includes all of the changes in *unappropriated* retained earnings. This section is similar to that shown in Exhibit 15-4, except that it also lists any increases in appropriations as deductions from unappropriated retained earnings and any decreases in appropriations as increases in unappropriated retained earnings. The second section starts with the beginning balances (if any) of all appropriated retained earnings items, to which any increases in appropriations are added and from which any decreases in appropriations are deducted to determine the ending appropriated retained earnings balances. The ending unappropriated retained earnings balance from the first section is added to the ending total appropriated retained earnings balance from the second section to determine the total retained earnings.

## Illustration of Retained Earnings Statement

The 1992, 1991, and 1990 consolidated statements of retained earnings for Colgate-Palmolive Company are shown in Exhibit 15-5. Notice that the company identifies the amount of dividends declared for each type of stock.

**EXHIBIT 15-5**
**Retained Earnings Statement**

## COLGATE-PALMOLIVE COMPANY

Consolidated Statement of Retained Earnings

| | Years Ended December 31 | | |
| (Dollars in Millions) | 1992 | 1991 | 1990 |
|---|---|---|---|
| Balance, January 1 | $1,928.6 | $1,960.8 | $1,778.1 |
| Add: | | | |
| Net income | 477.0 | 124.9 | 321.0 |
| | 2,405.6 | 2,085.7 | 2,099.1 |
| Deduct: | | | |
| Dividends declared: | | | |
| Series B Convertible Preference | | | |
| Stock, net of income taxes | 20.2 | 20.3 | 19.1 |
| Preferred stock | .5 | .5 | .5 |
| Common stock | 180.0 | 136.3 | 118.7 |
| | 200.7 | 157.1 | 138.3 |
| Balance, December 31 | $2,204.9 | $1,928.6 | $1,960.8 |

## OTHER CHANGES IN STOCKHOLDERS' EQUITY

*Donated treasury stock is discussed in Chapter 14.*

In certain instances, a corporation may increase stockholders' equity for events not related to the issuance of stock or to retained earnings. For example, as discussed in Chapter 8, it is possible for a corporation to receive donated assets, such as a plant site, to induce it to locate in a particular community. As discussed earlier in the chapter, since this is a nonreciprocal, nonmonetary transfer, the asset is recorded at its fair market value. The resulting credit is recorded in a *donated capital* account. Donated capital may also arise because of donated treasury stock. The *discovery value* of natural resources is another example. Here, an increase in assets and stockholders' equity might be recorded as a result of the discovery of previously unknown valuable natural resources. A final example relates to the accounting principles for current or noncurrent investments in debt and equity securities "available for sale." As discussed in Chapter 13, these investments are reported as assets at their fair values on the balance sheet date. The corresponding *unrealized increase* (or *decrease*) in value of these securities available for sale is reported in stockholders' equity.

Although some corporations list the preceding items as a component of contributed capital, it is the authors' opinion these are so important that they should be disclosed in a separate section of stockholders' equity entitled Unrealized Capital and listed directly below the Contributed Capital section and prior to Retained Earnings. Furthermore, as discussed in Chapter 18, any excess of additional pension liability over unrecognized prior service cost is required to be listed as a *negative* component of stockholders' equity[17], and also should be disclosed in this separate section.

---

17. "Employers' Accounting for Pensions," *FASB Statement of Financial Accounting Standards No. 87* (Stamford, Conn.: FASB, 1985), par. 37.

# STATEMENT OF CHANGES IN STOCKHOLDERS' EQUITY

As you learned from the discussion in this and the previous chapter, a corporation may engage in a variety of transactions that affect some component of stockholders' equity. Conceptually, as discussed in Chapter 3, **FASB Statement of Concepts No. 5** suggests that a full set of financial statements should show investments by and distributions to owners during the period. In order to inform external users of financial statements about corporate capital activities, **APB Opinion No. 12** states:

> ...disclosure of changes in the separate accounts comprising stockholders' equity (in addition to retained earnings) and of the changes in the number of shares of equity securities during at least the most recent annual fiscal period...is required to make the financial statements sufficiently informative.[18]

Thus, the changes in the different classes of common stock, additional paid-in capital, unrealized capital, retained earnings, and treasury stock are disclosed in the annual report. The intent is to help report on the changes in a corporation's financial structure as an aid in assessing its **financial flexibility, profitability,** and **risk.** Although this disclosure may be made parenthetically or in a note to the financial statements, many corporations prepare a statement of changes in stockholders' equity that includes an analysis of the changes in these items as well as a schedule of the changes in retained earnings. The ending amounts in this statement then tie to the stockholders' equity section of the year-end balance sheet. To illustrate, Exhibits 15-6 and 15-7 present a comprehensive statement of changes in stockholders' equity and the ending stockholders' equity for the hypothetical Bardwell Corporation. An example of more condensed disclosures are Hasbro, Inc.'s 1992 and 1991 consolidated ending shareholders' equity and statements of shareholders' equity shown in Exhibits 15-8 and 15-9. Notice the horizontal versus vertical formats of Exhibits 15-6 and 15-9. Both are acceptable presentations.

## International Accounting Differences

Under *International Accounting Standards,* shareholders' interests (the term used for stockholders' equity) consists of two sections: (a) share capital, and (b) other equity. Many of the disclosures required under *share capital* are the same as those required under U.S. GAAP; for example, the number of shares authorized, issued, and outstanding, par value, reacquired shares, and rights, preferences, and restriction regarding dividends. The differences from those required by U.S. GAAP include disclosure of any capital not yet paid in, any restrictions on the repayment of capital, and the shares reserved for future issuance under sales contracts.

Share premium (additional paid-in capital) is disclosed in the *other equity* section, along with revaluation surplus, reserves, and retained earnings. Revaluation surplus and reserves are different equity items from those allowed under U.S. GAAP. Although International Accounting Standards are based on historical cost, some countries allow companies to revalue (upward and downward) their property, plant, and equipment based on professionally qualified appraisals. When a company increases its asset values due to a revaluation, the related "credit" is made to a revaluation surplus account. (A decrease due to revaluation would reduce this revaluation account.)

---

18. "Omnibus Opinion—1967," *APB Opinion No. 12* (New York: AICPA, 1967), par. 10.

**EXHIBIT 15-6**

## BARDWELL CORPORATION

Statement of Changes in Stockholders' Equity
For Year Ended December 31, 1995

| Explanation | Common Stock Shares Issued | Par Value | Additional Paid-in Capital Common Stock | Treasury Stock | Common Stock Option Warrants | Deferred Compensation | Unrealized Capital | Retained Earnings | Treasury Stock (Cost) |
|---|---|---|---|---|---|---|---|---|---|
| Balances, 1/1/1995 | 10,000 | $50,000 | $170,000 | $2,300 | $12,200 | $ (8,400) | | $322,000 | $(7,500) |
| Issued for cash | 1,100 | 5,500 | 22,000 | | | | | | |
| Reissued treasury stock | | | | 2,700 | | | | | 4,500 |
| Issued for exercise of stock options | 300 | 1,500 | 5,400 | | (900) | | | | |
| Compensation expense for stock options | | | | | | 700 | | | |
| Compensation cost for new stock options | | | | | 3,300 | (3,300) | | | |
| Accepted donated land for plant site | | | | | | | $40,000 | | |
| Net income | | | | | | | | 97,000 | |
| Cash dividends | | | | | | | | (32,800) | |
| Balances, 12/31/1995 | 11,400 | $57,000 | $197,400 | $5,000 | $14,600 | $(11,000) | $40,000 | $386,200 | $(3,000) |

**EXHIBIT 15-7**

## BARDWELL CORPORATION

Stockholders' Equity
December 31, 1995

| | | | |
|---|---|---:|---:|
| Contributed capital: | | | |
| Common stock, $5 par (30,000 shares authorized, 11,400 shares issued, of which 100 shares are being held as treasury stock) | | | $ 57,000 |
| Additional paid-in capital on common stock | | | 197,400 |
| Additional paid-in capital from treasury stock | | | 5,000 |
| Common stock option warrants | | $14,600 | |
| Less: Deferred compensation | | (11,000) | 3,600 |
| Total contributed capital | | | $263,000 |
| Unrealized capital: | | | |
| Donated land for plant site | | | 40,000 |
| Retained earnings (see note) | | | 386,200 |
| Total contributed capital, unrealized capital, and retained earnings | | | $689,200 |
| Less: Treasury stock (at cost) | | | (3,000) |
| Total stockholders' equity | | | $686,200 |

*Note:* Retained earnings are restricted regarding dividends in the amount of $3,000, the cost of the treasury stock.

**EXHIBIT 15-8**
**Shareholders' Equity**

## HASBRO, INC.

| (thousands of dollars) | Dec. 27, 1992 | Dec. 29, 1991 |
|---|---:|---:|
| Shareholders' equity | | |
| Preference stock of $2.50 par value. | | |
| Authorized 5,000,000 shares; none issued | — | — |
| Common stock of $.50 par value. Authorized 150,000,00 shares; issued 87,176,079 shares in 1992 and 86,793,061 shares in 1991 | $ 43,588 | $ 43,397 |
| Additional paid-in capital | 287,478 | 276,725 |
| Retained earnings | 741,987 | 580,211 |
| Cumulative translation adjustments | 32,568 | 60,297 |
| Treasury stock, at cost, no shares in 1992 and 608,784 shares in 1991 | — | (5,361) |
| Total shareholders' equity | $1,105,621 | $955,269 |

**EXHIBIT 15-9**
**Consolidated Statements of Shareholders' Equity**

## HASBRO, INC.

| Fiscal Years Ended in December (Thousands of Dollars) | 1992 | 1991 | 1990 |
|---|---|---|---|
| **Common stock** | | | |
| Balance at beginning of year | $ 43,397 | $ 28,931 | $ 29,355 |
| Three-for-two stock split | — | 14,466 | — |
| Stock option and warrant transactions | 191 | — | 46 |
| Purchased and retired | — | — | (470) |
| Balance at end of year | 43,588 | 43,397 | 28,931 |
| **Additional paid-in-capital** | | | |
| Balance at beginning of year | 276,725 | 286,433 | 302,770 |
| Stock optioin and warrant transactions | 10,753 | 4,758 | 912 |
| Three-for-two common stock split | — | (14,466) | — |
| Retirement of purchased common stock | — | — | (17,249) |
| Balance at end of year | 287,478 | 276,725 | 286,433 |
| **Retained earnings** | | | |
| Balance at beginning of year | 580,211 | 512,291 | 434,556 |
| Net earnings | 179,164 | 81,654 | 89,182 |
| Dividends declared | (17,388) | (13,734) | (11,447) |
| Balance at end of year | 741,987 | 580,211 | 512,291 |
| **Cumulative translation adjustments** | | | |
| Balance at beginning of year | 60,297 | 58,233 | 35,643 |
| Equity adjustments from foreign currency translation | (27,729) | 2,064 | 22,590 |
| Balance at end of year | 32,568 | 60,297 | 58,233 |
| **Treasury stock** | | | |
| Balance at beginning of year | (5,361) | (18,061) | — |
| Purchases | — | — | (18,111) |
| Stock option and warrant transactions | 5,361 | 12,700 | 50 |
| Balance at end of year | — | (5,361) | (18,061) |
| Total shareholders' equity | $1,105,621 | $955,269 | $867,827 |

In some respects, reserves under international accounting standards are similar to appropriations of retained earnings under U.S. GAAP. They may differ, however, in that reserves may be required by foreign statutes or tax laws, whereas there are no such requirements in the U.S.

A company must disclose the "movement" in share capital accounts and in other equity for the period. In effect, these international disclosure requirements result in reporting the changes in shareholders' interests and are similar to those of U.S. GAAP requiring a statement of changes in stockholders' equity, although the format of the disclosures may be different.

# APPENDIX: QUASI-REORGANIZATION

A corporation that incurs net losses over an extended period may find itself in serious financial difficulty. Its assets may be overvalued and its liquidity position may be such that the corporation is, or shortly will be, unable to meet creditor claims. The long period of losses may have reduced retained earnings to a very low amount or to a deficit (negative) figure, in which case most states restrict the payment of dividends. When this occurs, investors and creditors may feel that the current corporate management is unable to operate the company successfully. Nonetheless, the corporation may be entering different markets or developing new products that could lead to future profitability.

Rather than enter into formal bankruptcy or other legal proceedings, it may be more beneficial for the corporation to establish a new management group capable of improving operating efficiency and effectiveness. At the same time, the corporation may engage in a process termed a quasi-reorganization. **A quasi-reorganization is primarily an accounting procedure, sanctioned by the applicable state laws, that involves a revaluation of corporate assets and liabilities, and a realignment of the corporate capital structure to enable the corporation to have a "fresh start" toward financial solvency and profitability.** Typically, the individual corporate net assets are written down (or occasionally up) to their fair market value and the retained earnings deficit is offset against existing additional paid-in capital. In so doing, the corporation must adhere to the state laws and to generally accepted accounting principles. The suggested readjustment procedures include the following steps:

1. The corporation makes a clear report to the stockholders of the restatements proposed and obtains the stockholders' formal consent.

2. The corporation presents a balance sheet as of the date of readjustment in which the assets and liabilities are reported at their fair market values.

3. Any amounts written off are first charged (debited) against retained earnings and then against additional paid-in capital.

4. The corporation begins its "fresh start" with a zero retained earnings balance.

After the quasi-reorganization, several additional accounting procedures are suggested:

5. If losses or readjustments are identified that are determined to have occurred *before* the readjustment date, they are recorded as a reduction of additional paid-in capital and not current income or retained earnings.

6. Additional paid-in capital is *not* reduced for losses occurring *after* the readjustment.

7. Retained earnings is *dated* as of the readjustment date, and this dating is disclosed in a note to the financial statements until such dating loses its significance (usually 5 to 10 years).[19]

The specific accounting procedures involved in a quasi-reorganization generally include: (1) a write-down of the assets to their fair market value, with the loss being

---

19. *ARB No. 43, op. cit.,* ch. 7, sec. A, par. 3–11.

debited directly to retained earnings; (2) an increase in additional paid-in capital accomplished by a decrease in the par value of the capital stock; and (3) the elimination of the retained earnings deficit by a reduction of the additional paid-in capital.

Assume, for example, that the Blue Corporation reports the condensed balance sheet shown in Exhibit 15-10 prior to a quasi-reorganization. In the quasi-reorganization process, the following information is relevant:

1. Property and equipment are determined to have a combined fair market value of $92,000.

2. Contained within current assets are inventories that are overvalued by $8,000, and $4,000 of uncollectible accounts receivable.

3. The board of directors, with stockholder and state approval, has authorized a reduction in par value to $4 per share.

The journal entries necessary to accomplish the reorganization are as follows:

1. To write down the fixed assets to fair market value (typically accumulated depreciation is increased so that the new carrying value reflects the fair market value):

| | | |
|---|---|---|
| **Retained Earnings** (200,000 - 60,000 - 92,000) to be written off | 48,000 | |
| **Accumulated Depreciation** | | 48,000 |

2. To write down the current assets:

| | | |
|---|---|---|
| **Retained Earnings** | 12,000 | |
| **Current Assets (inventories, $8,000, and accounts receivable, $4,000)** | | 12,000 |

3. To reduce the par value of the common stock and increase additional paid-in capital:

| | | |
|---|---|---|
| **Common Stock, $10 par** | 150,000 | |
| **Common Stock, $4 par** | | 60,000 |
| **Additional Paid-in Capital** | | 90,000 |

4. To eliminate the retained earnings deficit:

| | | |
|---|---|---|
| **Additional Paid-in Capital** | 110,000 | |
| **Retained Earnings** ($50,000 + $48,000 + $12,000) | | 110,000 |

The Blue Corporation balance sheet immediately following its quasi-reorganization is shown in Exhibit 15-11, and reflects the preceding adjustments.

## EXHIBIT 15-10

### BLUE CORPORATION

**Balance Sheet**
**December 31, 1995**

| | | | |
|---|---|---|---|
| Current assets | $ 30,000 | Liabilities | $ 40,000 |
| Property and equipment | 200,000 | Common stock, $10 par | 150,000 |
| Less: Accumulated depreciation | (60,000) | Additional paid-in capital | 30,000 |
| | | Retained earnings (deficit) | (50,000) |
| Total assets | $170,000 | Total liabilities and stockholders' equity | $170,000 |

---

**EXHIBIT 15-11**

**BLUE CORPORATION**

Balance Sheet
December 31, 1995

| | | | |
|---|---|---|---|
| Current assets | $ 18,000 | Liabilities | $ 40,000 |
| Property and equipment | 200,000 | Common stock, $4 par | 60,000 |
| Less: Accumulated depreciation | (108,000) | Additional paid-in capital | 10,000 |
| | | Retained earnings (see note) | 0 |
| Total assets | $110,000 | Total liabilities and stockholders' equity | $110,000 |

*Note:* Retained earnings as of December 31, 1995 has a zero balance due to a quasi-reorganization on that date in which net assets were revalued, a deficit of $110,000 was charged against additional paid-in capital, and the par value of common stock was reduced from $10 to $4 per share.

---

## QUESTIONS

*Q15-1* (a) What are the characteristics of a noncompensatory stock option plan? (b) How does a compensatory plan differ from a noncompensatory plan? (c) What is the intent of a noncompensatory plan? A compensatory plan?

*Q15-2* How is the amount of total compensation cost in a compensatory stock option plan measured?

*Q15-3* (a) What is the measurement date of a compensatory stock option plan? (b) Why might the measurement date occur after the date of grant of the stock option?

*Q15-4* How is the annual compensation expense determined when (a) the measurement date is the date of grant, and (b) the measurement date is later than the date of grant?

*Q15-5* What are stock appreciation rights? Why are they advantageous to an executive?

*Q15-6* What are the two key differences between accounting for stock appreciation rights plans and compensatory stock option plans?

*Q15-7* What are the primary factors affecting retained earnings?

*Q15-8* What are the four dates of importance in regard to a cash dividend? What journal entry is made on each date?

*Q15-9* What is fully participating preferred stock? Partially participating preferred stock?

*Q15-10* Discuss the recording of a property dividend declaration.

*Q15-11* Distinguish between an ordinary and special stock dividend.

*Q15-12* Distinguish between a small and large stock dividend. What amounts are used to record the declaration of each dividend?

*Q15-13* Distinguish between a stock split and a large stock dividend. How does each affect stockholders' equity?

*Q15-14* How does the accounting for a liquidating dividend differ from that for a normal cash dividend?

*Q15-15* How are corrections of material errors made in previous years recorded and reported in the current year's financial statements?

*Q15-16* For what reasons would retained earnings be appropriated? What alternative accounting methods might be used for an appropriation?

*Q15-17* What is the suggested format for the statement of retained earnings? What are the two most common elements in this statement?

*Q15-18* What items might be included in the unrealized capital section of stockholders' equity?

*Q15-19* What changes would be included in the statement of changes in stockholders' equity?

*Q15-20 (Appendix)* (a) What is a quasi-reorganization? (b) Under what circumstances might it be advantageous for a corporation to engage in quasi-reorganization procedures?

*Q15-21 (Appendix)* What accounting procedures are generally included in a quasi-reorganization?

# CASES

## C15-1 Stock Options
Stock options are often used as a form of compensation for corporate executives.

**Required**

In regard to a compensatory stock option:
1. How is the "measurement date" defined?
2. Briefly discuss the accounting for a stock option if the measurement date is the date of grant.
3. How would your answer in Requirement 2 differ if the measurement date were later than the date of grant?
4. What information should be disclosed in the annual report?

## C15-2 Stock Options
A corporation has a noncompensatory stock purchase plan for all its employees and a compensatory stock option plan for some of its corporate officers.

**Required**

1. Compare and contrast the accounting at the date the stock is issued for the noncompensatory stock purchase plan and the compensatory stock option plan.
2. What entry should be made for the compensatory stock option plan at the date of the grant? (*AICPA adapted*)

## C15-3 Stock Options
On November 5, 1993, Gunpowder Corp.'s board of directors approved a stock option plan for key executives. On January 2, 1994, a specific number of stock options were granted. These options were exercisable between January 2, 1996 and December 31, 1998 at 90% of the quoted market price on January 2, 1994. The service period is for 1994 and 1995. Some options were forfeited when an executive resigned in 1995. All other options were exercised during 1996.

**Required**

1. When is Gunpowder's stock option measurement date? Why?
2. How should Gunpowder determine the compensation expense, if any, for the stock option plan in 1994?
3. What is the effect of forfeiture of the stock options on Gunpowder's financial statements for 1995? Why?
4. What is the effect of the stock option plan on the balance sheet at December 31, 1996? Be specific as to the changes in balance sheet accounts between November 5, 1993 and December 31, 1996. (*AICPA adapted*)

## C15-4 Stock Appreciation Rights
Instead of a compensatory stock option plan, Wright Company is considering providing its key executives with a stock appreciation rights (SAR) plan.

**Required**

1. Explain an SAR plan.
2. Identify the key differences between accounting for an SAR plan and a compensatory stock option plan.
3. Briefly summarize the steps in accounting for an SAR plan (assume that the executive is expected to receive cash on the date of exercise).

## C15-5 Categories of Capital
A corporation's capital (stockholders' equity) is a very important part of its statement of financial position.

**Required**

Identify and discuss the general categories of capital (stockholders' equity) for a corporation. Be sure to enumerate specific sources included in each general category. (*AICPA adapted*)

## C15-6 Dividends and Journal Entries
Problems may be encountered in accounting for transactions involving the stockholders' equity section of the balance sheet.

**Required**

1. Explain the significance of the three dates that are important in accounting for cash dividends to stockholders. State the journal entry, if any, needed at each date.
2. Assume retained earnings can be used for stock dividends distributable in shares. What is the effect of an ordinary 10% common stock dividend on retained earnings and total stockholders' equity? (*AICPA adapted*)

## C15-7 Stock Dividends and Splits
Stock splits and stock dividends may be used by a corporation to change the number of shares of its stock outstanding.

**Required**

1. What is meant by a stock split effected in the form of a dividend?
2. From an accounting viewpoint, explain how the stock split effected in the form of a dividend differs from an ordinary stock dividend.
3. How should a stock dividend that has been declared but not yet issued be classified in a statement of financial position? Why? (*AICPA adapted*)

## C15-8 Dividends and Treasury Stock
Brady Company has 30,000 shares of $10 par value common stock authorized and 20,000 shares issued and outstanding. On August 14, 1995, Brady purchased 1,000 shares of treasury stock for $12 per share. Brady uses the cost method to account for treasury stock. On September 14, 1995, Brady sold 500 shares of the treasury stock for $14 per share.

In October 1995, Brady declared and distributed 2,000 shares as a stock dividend from unissued shares when the market value of the common stock was $16 per share.

On December 21, 1995, Brady declared a $1 per share cash dividend, payable on January 12, 1996 to shareholders of record on December 31, 1995.

**Required**
1. How should Brady account for the cash dividend, and how would it affect Brady's balance sheet at December 31, 1995? Why?
2. How should Brady account for the stock dividend, and how would it affect Brady's stockholders' equity at December 31, 1995? Why?
3. How should Brady account for the purchase and sale of the treasury stock, and how should the treasury stock be presented in Brady's balance sheet at December 31, 1995? (*AICPA adapted*)

*C15-9   Quasi-Reorganization*
A corporation may engage in a quasi-reorganization.

**Required**
What is a corporate quasi-reorganization? Why is it undertaken? What accounting-related steps and procedures do you suggest during and after the quasi-reorganization process?

*C15-10   Researching GAAP*   ⊙
On January 1, 1994, the Schmidt Company granted a stock option to Ms. Caren Wolke, a top executive. The stock option allowed her to acquire 2,000 shares of $10 par common stock for $35 per share after completing a 3-year service period. The market price of the stock was $50 per share on January 1, 1994. Assume that the option price was set at 70% of this market price to comply with federal tax guidelines so that the plan was "qualified" and Ms. Wolke was not subject to income tax until she sold the stock.

Schmidt Company appropriately recorded compensation expense on Wolke's stock option for each of the years 1994 and 1995. Assume that early in 1996, the federal tax law was changed so that in order to qualify for tax deferral, the option price in a stock option plan must be 82% of the market price on the date of measurement. This law was made retroactive for 5 years. On January 1, 1996, the Schmidt Company stock had a market value of $55 per share.

The board of directors of Schmidt Company wanted the stock option plan for Ms. Wolke to continue to qualify for tax deferral. Therefore, on December 31, 1996, the plan was modified so that Wolke must pay 82% of the market price on the date of grant to exercise her option. The other aspects of the plan were not changed. The board is unsure how to account for the change in the option percentage on December 31, 1996 and has asked for your recommendation.

**Required**
Research the related generally accepted accounting principles and prepare a short memo to the board that explains how Schmidt Company should account for the change in the option percentage on December 31, 1996. Cite your reference and applicable paragraph numbers.

## MULTIPLE CHOICE

*Select the best answer for each of the following.*

*M15-1*  On January 1, 1995, Stoner Corporation granted stock options to key employees for the purchase of 10,000 shares of the company's common stock at $25 per share. The options are intended to compensate employees for the next 2 years. The options are exercisable within a 4-year period beginning January 1, 1995 by grantees still in the employ of the company. The market price of Stoner's common stock was $32 per share at the date of grant. Stoner plans to distribute up to 10,000 shares of treasury stock when options are exercised. The treasury stock was acquired by Stoner during 1994 at a cost of $28 per share and was recorded under the cost method. Assume that no stock options were terminated during the year. How much should Stoner charge to compensation expense for the year ended December 31, 1995?
a. $70,000
b. $35,000
c. $30,000
d. $15,000

*M15-2*  A prior period adjustment should be reflected, net of applicable income taxes, in the financial statements of a business entity in the
a. Retained earnings statement after net income but before dividends
b. Retained earnings statement as an adjustment of the opening balance
c. Income statement after income from continuing operations
d. Income statement as part of income from continuing operations

**M15-3**   Cash dividends on the $10 par value common stock of Ray Company were as follows:

| | |
|---|---|
| 1st quarter of 1995 | $ 800,000 |
| 2nd quarter of 1995 | 900,000 |
| 3rd quarter of 1995 | 1,000,000 |
| 4th quarter of 1995 | 1,100,000 |

The 4th quarter cash dividend was declared on December 21, 1995 to stockholders of record on December 31, 1995. Payment of the 4th quarter cash dividend was made on January 12, 1996.

In addition, Ray declared a 5% stock dividend on its $10 par value common stock on December 1, 1995 when there were 300,000 shares issued and outstanding and the market value of the common stock was $20 per share. The shares were issued on December 21, 1995.

What was the effect on Ray's stockholders' equity accounts as a result of the preceding transactions?

| | Common stock | Additional paid-in capital | Retained earnings |
|---|---|---|---|
| a. | $ 0 | $ 0 | $3,800,000 debit |
| b. | $150,000 credit | $ 0 | $3,950,000 debit |
| c. | $150,000 credit | $150,000 credit | $4,100,000 debit |
| d. | $300,000 credit | $300,000 debit | $3,800,000 debit |

**M15-4**   An example of an item that should be reported as a prior period adjustment is the

a. Collection of previously written-off accounts receivable

b. Payment of taxes resulting from examination of prior year income tax returns

c. Correction of error in financial statements of a prior year

d. Receipt of insurance proceeds for damage to building sustained in a prior year

**M15-5**   The following information was abstracted from the accounts of the Oar Corporation at December 31, 1995:

| | |
|---|---|
| Total income since incorporation | $840,000 |
| Total cash dividends paid | 260,000 |
| Proceeds from sale of donated stock | 90,000 |
| Total value of stock dividends distributed | 60,000 |
| Excess of proceeds over cost of treasury stock sold | 140,000 |

What should be the current balance of retained earnings?

a. $520,000

b. $580,000

c. $610,000

d. $670,000

**M15-6**   A property dividend should be debited to retained earnings at the property's

a. Book value at date of issuance (payment)

b. Market value at date of issuance (payment)

c. Book value at date of declaration

d. Market value at date of declaration

**M15-7**   Effective April 27, 1995, the stockholders of Bennett Corporation approved a two-for-one split of the company's common stock, and an increase in authorized common shares from 100,000 shares (par value $20 per share) to 200,000 shares (par value $10 per share). Bennett's stockholders' equity accounts immediately before issuance of the stock split shares were as follows:

| | |
|---|---|
| Common stock, par value $20; 100,000 shares authorized; 50,000 shares outstanding | $1,000,000 |
| Additional paid-in capital (premium of $3 per share on issuance of common stock) | 150,000 |
| Retained earnings | 1,350,000 |

What should be the balances in Bennett's additional paid-in capital and retained earnings accounts immediately after the stock split is effected?

|    | Additional paid-in capital | Retained earnings |
|----|----------------------------|-------------------|
| a. | $        0                 | $    500,000      |
| b. | $  150,000                 | $    350,000      |
| c. | $  150,000                 | $1,350,000        |
| d. | $1,150,000                 | $    350,000      |

M15-8   A company with a substantial deficit undertakes a quasi-reorganization. Certain assets will be written down to their present fair market value. Liabilities will remain the same. How would the entries to record the quasi-reorganization affect each of the following?

|    | Contributed capital | Retained earnings |
|----|---------------------|-------------------|
| a. | Increase            | Decrease          |
| b. | Decrease            | No effect         |
| c. | No effect           | Increase          |
| d. | Decrease            | Increase          |

M15-9   The Gaston Company has sustained heavy losses over a period of time and conditions warrant that Gaston undergo a quasi-reorganization at December 31, 1995.

Selected balance sheet items prior to the quasi-reorganization are as follows:

Inventory was recorded in the accounting records at December 31, 1995 at its market value of $6,000,000. Cost was $6,500,000.

Property, plant, and equipment was recorded in the accounting records at December 31, 1995 at $12,000,000, net of accumulated depreciation. The appraised value was $8,000,000.

Stockholders' equity on December 31, 1995 was as follows:

| | |
|---|---:|
| Common stock, par value $10 per share; authorized, issued and outstanding, 700,000 shares | $7,000,000 |
| Capital in excess of par | 1,600,000 |
| Retained earnings (deficit) | (900,000) |
| | $7,700,000 |

Under the terms of the quasi-reorganization, the par value of the common stock is to be reduced from $10 per share to $5 per share.

Immediately after the quasi-reorganization has been accomplished, the total of stockholders' equity should be
a. $3,700,000          c. $3,300,000
b. $3,500,000          d. $4,200,000

M15-10  Newton Corporation was organized on January 1, 1993. On that date it issued 200,000 shares of its $10 par value common stock at $15 per share (400,000 shares were authorized). During the period January 1, 1993 through December 31, 1995, Newton reported net income of $750,000 and paid cash dividends of $380,000. On January 6, 1995, Newton purchased 12,000 shares of its common stock at $12 per share. On December 29, 1995, 8,000 treasury shares were sold at $8 per share. Newton used the cost method of accounting for treasury shares. What is the total stockholders' equity of Newton as of December 31, 1995?
a. $3,290,000          c. $3,338,000
b. $3,306,000          d. $3,370,000

*(AICPA adapted)*

## EXERCISES

*E15-1*  *Compensatory Stock Option Issues*   Corporations may grant stock option plans to their key executives as partial compensation. The following are three such plans:

1.  On December 31, 1995, a corporation grants to a key executive the nontransferable right to acquire 500 shares of $5 par common stock for $11 per share. The current market price of the stock is $16 per share, but the option may not be exercised until 3 years of service have been performed.
2.  On December 31, 1995, a corporation grants to a key executive the right to acquire 1,000 shares of $10 par common stock for $20 per share. The current market price of the stock is $27 per share, but the option may not be exercised until 4 years of continuous service from the date of grant have been performed.
3.  On December 31, 1995, a corporation grants to a key executive the right to obtain 2,000 shares of $10 par common stock for $25 per share. The current market price of the stock is $24 per share, but the option may not be exercised until 2 years of service have been performed.

**Required**

For each of the preceding independent compensatory stock option plans, determine the compensation cost involved, the accounting periods to which this cost would be charged as expense, and the measurement date of the compensation cost.

*E15-2*  *Compensatory Stock Options*   On December 31, 1994, Remley Research Corporation grants to Mr. Thaddeus Basham, a key executive, the nontransferable right to acquire 1,000 shares of $10 par common stock for $44 per share. At that date, the market price of the stock is $50 per share. The grant is contingent upon Mr. Basham's completing 3 years of continuous service to Remley subsequent to December 31, 1994. The corporation is on a calendar year accounting period.

**Required**

Prepare journal entries to record the grant, the 1995, 1996, and 1997 annual compensation expense, and the issuance of the stock, assuming Basham exercises his option on May 15, 1998. Show how the stock option would be disclosed on the December 31, 1995 balance sheet.

*E15-3*  *Stock Options, One Executive*   Ms. Ellen Hugmann, a top executive, was granted a stock option by her company on December 31, 1994 when the market price of the company's common stock was $60 per share. The stock option allows her to acquire 3,000 shares of $10 par common stock for $56 per share, after completing a 2-year service period. The option expires on December 31, 1997. On April 15, 1997, Ms. Hugmann exercises her option to acquire 2,500 shares. No other transactions involving this stock option occurred during 1994 through 1997. The company's fiscal year ends December 31.

**Required**

Prepare the journal entries of the company for 1994 through 1997 in regard to this stock option.

*E15-4*  *Compensatory Stock Options, Estimates*   On December 31, 1994, Tye Corporation grants a nontransferable stock option to Ms. Lois Turner, a key executive. The option is for 2,000 shares of $5 par common stock at 90% of the quoted market price on December 31, 1997. The service period is 4 years, after which the option may be exercised. The market prices per share of the Tye Corporation stock on December 31, 1994, 1995, 1996, 1997, and 1998 are $19, $20, $21.50, $21, and $23, respectively.

**Required**

Prepare journal entries to record the grant and the 1995, 1996, 1997, and 1998 compensation expense related to this stock option. The corporation's fiscal year ends December 31.

*E15-5*  *Compensatory Stock Options, Estimates*   On December 31, 1994, the Welch Corporation grants a nontransferable stock option to each of 10 key executives. Each executive may acquire 600 shares of $10 par common stock for 80% of the market price on December 31, 1996. The rights are not exercisable until 3 years of continuous service have been completed beginning December 31, 1994. Market prices per share of Welch stock on December 31, 1994, 1995, 1996, and 1997, respectively, are $42, $45, $48, and $51. Mr. Scott Morgan, one of the executives, exercises his entire option on January 10, 1998. The corporate accounting period ends December 31.

**Required**

Prepare appropriate related journal entries for the following dates: (1) date of grant; (2) end of 1995, 1996, and 1997; and (3) exercise date.

E15-6  *Stock Appreciation Rights*  On January 1, 1994, as a form of executive compensation, Wadlin Corporation granted stock appreciation rights to Robert Brandt. These rights entitle Brandt to receive cash equal to the excess of the quoted market price over a $20 option price for 4,000 shares of the company's common stock on the exercise date. The service period is 3 years and the rights must be exercised within 5 years. Brandt exercises his rights on December 31, 1997. The quoted market price per share of common stock was $20 on January 1, 1994, $23 on December 31, 1994, $24.20 on December 31, 1995, $24 on December 31, 1996, and $25 on December 31, 1997.

**Required**

1. Prepare a schedule to compute the compensation expense related to this SAR plan for 1994 through 1997.
2. Prepare the December 31, 1997 journal entry related to this SAR plan.

E15-7  *Dividends*  Uhler Company has $80,000 available to pay dividends. It has 2,000 shares of 10%, $100 par preferred stock and 30,000 shares of $10 par common stock outstanding.

**Required**

Determine the amount of dividends to be paid to each class of stockholder for each of the following independent assumptions:

1. Preferred stock is nonparticipating and noncumulative.
2. Preferred stock is nonparticipating and cumulative. Preferred dividends are 2 years in arrears at the beginning of the year.
3. Preferred stock is fully participating and cumulative. Preferred dividends are 1 year in arrears at the beginning of the year.
4. Preferred stock is participating up to a maximum of 15% of its par value and is noncumulative.

E15-8  *Various Dividends*  The Goodson Company listed the following account balances on December 31, 1994:

| | | | |
|---|---:|---|---:|
| Investment in Xurk Company bond | $ 25,000 | Common stock, $10 par | $400,000 |
| Dividends payable: preferred | 4,000 | Additional paid-in capital on preferred stock | 20,000 |
| Dividends payable: common | 40,000 | Additional paid-in capital on common stock | 210,000 |
| Preferred stock, 8%, $100 par | 100,000 | Retained earnings | 270,000 |

During 1995, the following transactions occurred:

| | |
|---|---|
| Feb. 3 | Paid the semiannual dividends declared on December 16, 1994. |
| Mar. 2 | Declared a property dividend, payable to common stockholders on April 3 in Xurk Company bonds being held to maturity. The bonds (which have a book value of $25,000) have a current market value of $30,000. |
| April 3 | Paid the property dividend. |
| July 5 | Declared a $4 per share semiannual cash dividend on preferred stock and a $1.15 per share semiannual dividend on common stock, to be paid on August 18. |
| Aug. 18 | Paid the cash dividends. |
| Oct. 16 | Declared a 2% stock dividend on common stock to be issued on December 1. The current market price is $22 per share. |
| Dec. 1 | Issued the stock dividend. |
| Dec. 28 | Declared a $4 and $1.20 per share semiannual cash dividend on preferred and common stock, respectively, to be paid on February 15, 1996. |

**Required**

Prepare journal entries to record the preceding transactions.

E15-9   *Various Dividends*   Mills Company lists the following condensed balance sheet as of the beginning of 1995:

| | | | |
|---|---|---|---|
| Current assets | $ 60,000 | Current liabilities | $ 30,000 |
| Investment in M bonds | 9,000 | Common stock, no par | 150,000 |
| Fixed assets (net) | 200,000 | Retained earnings | 89,000 |
| | $269,000 | | $269,000 |

It is considering the impact of various types of dividends upon this balance sheet. Each dividend would be de-clared and paid in 1995. These include:

1. Cash dividend of $1.00 per share on the 10,000 shares outstanding.
2. Stock dividend of 5% on the 10,000 shares outstanding when the market price is $17 per share.
3. Property dividend consisting of the $9,000 (book value) investment in M bonds being held to maturity. This investment has a current market value of $13,000. (For Requirement 2 below, assume any gain or loss is to be reflected in retained earnings. Disregard income taxes.)
4. Scrip dividend of $0.80 per share on the 10,000 shares outstanding. The scrip earns interest at a 12% an-nual rate and is to be declared on January 31 and paid on December 30, 1995. (For Requirement 2 below, assume any interest expense is to be reflected in retained earnings. Disregard income taxes.)
5. Cash dividend consisting of a $0.70 per share normal dividend and a $0.30 per share liquidating dividend.

**Required**

For each preceding *independent* dividend:

1. Prepare the appropriate journal entries for the declaration and payment of the dividend.
2. Prepare a condensed balance sheet after the dividend has been *paid*.

E15-10   *Stock Dividend*   The stockholders' equity of the Sadler Company is as shown:

| | |
|---|---|
| Common stock, $10 par | $250,000 |
| Additional paid-in capital on common stock | 150,000 |
| Retained earnings | 200,000 |
| | $600,000 |

The company is considering the declaration and issuance of a stock dividend at a time when the market price is $30 per share.

**Required**

1. Assuming the board of directors recommends a 5% stock dividend, prepare
   a. the journal entry at the date of declaration,
   b. the journal entry at the date of issuance, and
   c. the stockholders' equity after the issuance.
2. Assuming, instead, that a 40% stock dividend is recommended, repeat (a), (b), and (c) of Requirement 1.

E15-11   *Stock Dividend Comparison*   Although the Weaver Company has sufficient retained earnings legally to de-clare a dividend, its working capital is low. The board of directors is considering a stock dividend instead of a cash dividend. The following is its current stockholders' equity:

| | |
|---|---|
| Common stock, $10 par | $ 400,000 |
| Premium on common stock | 800,000 |
| Total contributed capital | $1,200,000 |
| Retained earnings | 1,300,000 |
| Total stockholders' equity | $2,500,000 |

The common stock is currently selling at $34 per share.

**Required**

1. Assuming a 15% stock dividend is declared and issued, prepare the stockholders' equity section immediately after the date of issuance.
2. Assuming, instead, that a 30% stock dividend is declared and issued, prepare the stockholders' equity section immediately after the date of issuance.
3. What unusual result do you notice when you compare your answers from (1) with (2)? From a theoretical standpoint, how might this have been avoided?

**E15-12** *Prior Period Adjustments*   Miles Company began 1995 with a retained earnings balance of $142,400. During an examination of its accounting records on December 31, 1995, the company found it had made the following material errors, for both financial reporting and income tax reporting, during 1994.

1. Depreciation expense of $14,000 had been inadvertently recorded twice for the same machine.
2. No accrual had been made at year-end for interest, so that interest expense had been understated by $5,000.

The Miles Company's net income during 1995 was $60,000. The company has been subject to a 30% income tax rate for the past several years. It declared and paid dividends of $13,000 during 1995.

**Required**

1. Prepare whatever journal entries are necessary to correct the Miles Company books for its previous errors. Make your corrections directly to the retained earnings account.
2. Prepare the statement of retained earnings for 1995.

**E15-13** *Appropriations*   Perry Company has an unappropriated retained earnings balance of $400,000 at the end of 1995, before preparation of its financial statements. During 1995, it had issued 5-year, 12%, $100,000 long-term bonds. The bond provisions require that each year over the 5-year period an additional $20,000 of retained earnings be unavailable for dividends. This restriction is in addition to any other retained earnings restrictions that the company might make. Also during 1995, the company decided to "self-insure" against fire losses, because of its previous safety record and high insurance premiums. The board of directors decided to restrict retained earnings at the end of *each* year in an amount equal to the $8,000 annual premium that would have been paid.

During 2000, the Perry Company retired its bonds, and on July 1, 2000, a building with a cost of $90,000 and a current book value of $60,000 was completely destroyed by fire. After this loss, the company reassessed its policy of self-insurance and acquired a comprehensive fire insurance policy.

**Required**

1. a. If the company decides to make formal journal entries to recognize each appropriation, prepare whatever entries would be necessary at the end of 1995.
   b. If the company decides, instead, to disclose each restriction by means of a note to accompany the financial statements, prepare a note at the end of 1995 fully describing the appropriations.
2. a. Assuming the company had made formal journal entries to record its appropriations, prepare whatever journal entries are necessary to record the fire loss and to eliminate the appropriations at the end of 2000.
   b. Assuming, instead, the company had disclosed the appropriations by means of a note, prepare whatever journal entries are necessary to record the fire loss and indicate how the appropriations would be eliminated at the end of 2000.

**E15-14** *Retained Earnings Statement*   Taggart Company began 1995 with a $120,000 balance in retained earnings. During the year, the following events occurred:

1. The company earned net income of $80,000.
2. A material error in net income from a previous period was corrected. This error correction increased retained earnings by $9,800 after related income taxes of $4,200.
3. Cash dividends totaling $13,000 and stock dividends totaling $17,000 were declared.
4. One thousand shares of callable preferred stock that originally had been issued at $110 per share were recalled and retired at the beginning of 1995 for the call price of $120 per share.
5. Treasury stock (common) was acquired at a cost of $20,000. State law requires an appropriation of retained earnings in an equal amount. The company makes journal entries to record appropriations.

**Required**
Prepare a statement of retained earnings for the year ended December 31, 1995.

E15-15  *Retained Earnings Statement*  On January 1, 1995, Sloan Company had a retained earnings balance of $206,000. During 1995 the following events occurred:

1. Treasury stock (common) was acquired at a cost of $14,000. State law requires a restriction of retained earnings in an equal amount. The company reports its retained earnings restrictions by means of a note to the financial statements.
2. Cash dividends totaling $9,000 and stock dividends totaling $6,000 were declared and distributed.
3. Net income was $58,000.
4. Two thousand shares of callable preferred stock were recalled and retired at a price of $150 per share. This stock had originally been issued at $130 per share.
5. A material error in net income of a previous period was corrected. This error correction decreased retained earnings by $12,600 after a related income tax credit of $5,400.

**Required**
1. Prepare a statement of retained earnings for the year ended December 31, 1995.
2. Prepare the note to disclose the restriction of retained earnings.

E15-16  *Stockholders' Equity*  Wake Manufacturing Corporation completed the following transactions during its first year of operation, 1995:

1. The state authorized the issuance of 30,000 shares of $5 par common stock. 15,000 shares were issued at $22 per share.
2. The state authorized the issuance of 5,000 shares of $50 par preferred stock. All 5,000 shares were issued at $70 per share.
3. The Clear Valley Regional Development Authority donated land with a fair market value of $20,000, in the Clear Valley Industrial Park, to Wake as inducement for, and contingent upon, Wake's building a plant on the land and beginning operations in Clear Valley. These contingencies have been met.
4. Wake reacquired 1,000 shares of its own outstanding common stock at $18 per share. The cost method is used to account for treasury stock.
5. Wake invested $50,000 of excess cash, not needed to finance operations, in long-term equity securities available for sale. At year-end, the market value of these securities was $47,500.
6. Wake sold 500 shares of treasury stock for $23 per share.
7. Net income for the first year of operations was $16,000. No dividends were declared.

**Required**
Prepare the stockholders' equity section of the Wake Manufacturing Corporation balance sheet as of December 31, 1995.

E15-17  *Changes in Stockholders' Equity*  The stockholders' equity section of Winslow Design Company's December 31, 1994 balance sheet appeared as follows:

| | |
|---|---:|
| Contributed Capital | |
| Preferred stock, $100 par (10,000 shares authorized, 1,250 shares issued) | $125,000 |
| Additional paid-in capital on preferred stock | 55,000 |
| Common stock, $10 par (60,000 shares authorized, 15,000 shares issued) | 150,000 |
| Additional paid-in capital on common stock | 105,000 |
| Total contributed capital | $435,000 |
| Retained earnings | 78,000 |
| Contributed capital and retained earnings | $513,000 |
| Less: Treasury stock (300 shares of common at $14 per share) | (4,200) |
| Total stockholders' equity | $508,800 |

During 1995, the company entered into the following transactions affecting stockholders' equity:

1. Issued 250 shares of preferred stock at $164 per share.
2. Issued 3,000 shares of common stock at $17 per share.
3. Reacquired 200 of its own common shares as treasury stock for $15 per share.
4. Reissued 250 shares of treasury stock at $17 per share (FIFO basis).
5. Net income for 1995 was $42,500. Dividends of $25,000 were distributed.

**Required**

Prepare a statement of changes in stockholders' equity for the year ended December 31, 1995.

**E15-18** **Appendix: Quasi-Reorganization** HCI Corporation has experienced a net loss for a number of years. On the advice of the board of directors, a new management team was appointed. Furthermore, the corporation has agreed to a quasi-reorganization and to the revaluation of certain balance sheet account balances, subject to stockholder approval. The HCI balance sheet on December 31, 1995 contained the following information prior to the reorganization:

| | | | |
|---|---|---|---|
| Current assets | $ 20,000 | Liabilities | $ 30,000 |
| Property and equipment | 110,000 | Common stock, $10 par | 100,000 |
| Less: Accumulated depreciation | (30,000) | Additional paid-in capital on common stock | 40,000 |
| Total assets | $100,000 | Retained earnings (deficit) | (70,000) |
| | | Total liabilities and stockholders' equity | $100,000 |

The following information is relevant to the quasi-reorganization as approved by the stockholders:

1. Property and equipment is determined to have a fair market value of $45,000.
2. Current assets contain inventories overstated by $6,000.
3. Current assets contain uncollectible accounts receivable of $3,000.
4. Par value of common stock is to be reduced to $1 per share as approved by the state of incorporation.

**Required**

1. Prepare journal entries to record the quasi-reorganization.
2. Prepare the balance sheet of HCI Corporation immediately following the quasi-reorganization. Include a note to accompany retained earnings.

**E15-19** **Appendix: Quasi-Reorganization** Current conditions warrant that the Austin Company have a quasi-reorganization (corporate readjustment) at December 31, 1995. Selected balance sheet items prior to the quasi-reorganization (corporate readjustment) are as follows:

Inventory was recorded in the accounting records at December 31, 1995 at its market value of $3 million.

Property, plant, and equipment was recorded in the accounting records at December 31, 1995 at $6 million net of accumulated depreciation.

Stockholders' equity consisted of:

| | |
|---|---|
| Common stock, par value $10 per share; authorized, issued, and outstanding 350,000 shares | $3,500,000 |
| Additional paid-in capital | 800,000 |
| Retained earnings (deficit) | (450,000) |
| Total stockholders' equity | $3,850,000 |

Additional information is as follows:

Inventory cost at December 31, 1995 was $3,250,000.
Property, plant, and equipment had a fair market value of $4 million.
The par value of the common stock is to be reduced from $10 per share to $5 per share.

**Required**

Prepare the stockholders' equity section of the Austin Company's balance sheet at December 31, 1995 as it should appear after the quasi-reorganization (corporate readjustment) has been accomplished. Show supporting computations in good form. Ignore income tax and deferred tax considerations. (*AICPA adapted*)

## PROBLEMS

**P15-1**   *Compensatory Stock Options, Several Executives*   On January 1, 1994, the Goldman Tool Company institutes a stock option plan for selected upper-echelon managers. A nontransferable stock option is granted to each executive as soon as the executive qualifies for the plan. The plan allows each qualified executive to purchase 1,000 shares of $10 par common stock at a specified option price. No option is exercisable until 3 years of employment have been completed subsequent to the date of grant. Exercise of an option is contingent upon continued employment with the company.

On January 1, 1994, five executives qualify for the stock option plan at an option price of $46 per share. On January 1, 1995, three more executives qualify for the plan at an option price of $47 per share. On February 20, 1995, one of the executives who had qualified for the plan at the beginning of 1994 leaves the company. On January 1, 1996, four more executives qualify for the plan at an option price of $49 per share. No additional executives qualify for the plan on January 1, 1997. On March 4, 1997, one executive exercises his entire option (granted January 1, 1994). On April 8, 1997, another executive exercises part of her option (granted January 1, 1994) and acquires 400 shares.

Selected quoted market prices per share of common stock are as follows: January 1, 1994, $48.40; January 1, 1995, $50.30; February 20, 1995, $52; January 1, 1996, $52.90; March 4, 1997, $53; April 8, 1997, $53.40.

**Required**

1.  Prepare all the journal entries related to the preceding stock option plan for the period January 1, 1994 through April 8, 1997.
2.  Show how the stock options would be disclosed on the year-end December 31, 1994, 1995, and 1996 balance sheets.
3.  Draft a note describing the terms of the stock option plan to accompany the December 31, 1995 balance sheet.

**P15-2**   *Compensatory Stock Options, Estimates*   Maltby Corporation institutes a stock option plan for its top executives on January 1, 1994. A nontransferable stock option is granted to each executive as soon as the executive qualifies for the plan. Each qualified executive may purchase 600 shares of $5 par common stock at an option price that is 80% of the quoted market price on the December 31 that is 3 years subsequent to the date of grant. No option may be exercised until a 4-year continuous service period has been completed subsequent to the date of grant.

On January 1, 1994, four executives qualify for the stock option plan. Five more executives qualify for the plan on January 1, 1995, and three more executives qualify on January 1, 1996. One executive who was granted an option on January 1, 1994 leaves the company on January 4, 1996.

The quoted market price per share on December 31 of each year is as follows: 1994, $37.50; 1995, $40; 1996, $39; 1997, $41.

**Required**

1.  Prepare all the journal entries related to the preceding stock option plan for the period January 1, 1994 through December 31, 1997.
2.  Prepare the note describing the stock option plan to accompany the year-end December 31, 1997 balance sheet.

**P15-3**   *Compensatory Stock Options, Multiple Estimates*   White Company has a nontransferable stock option plan for its divisional managers. This plan was initiated on January 1, 1992 and calls for a stock option to be granted to each divisional manager as soon as the manager qualifies for the plan. However, both the option price and the number of $10 par common shares under option are contingent upon future events. The option price is set at 90% of the quoted market price 3 years after the date of grant. The number of shares under option is dependent upon the level of divisional "earnings" reported for the third year after the date of grant. The number of shares is determined by dividing the divisional earnings by the par value of the shares of stock. No option may be exercised until a 4-year continuous service period has been completed subsequent to the date of grant.

On December 31, 1993, Ms. Linda Fargerson, manager of Division A, qualifies for the stock option plan. During 1994, Division A reported earnings of $8,200 and the year-end market price was $38 per share. During 1995 through 1997, the following divisional earnings and ending market prices were reported:

| Year | Division A Earnings | Ending Quoted Market Price |
|------|---------------------|----------------------------|
| 1995 | $8,500 | $40.00 per share |
| 1996 | 8,800 | 39.50 per share |
| 1997 | 9,000 | 41.00 per share |

On February 14, 1998, Ms. Fargerson exercises her option when the quoted market price is $42 per share.

**Required**

Prepare journal entries to record the grant, the 1994, 1995, 1996, and 1997 compensation expense, and the exercise. The company is on a calendar-year accounting period.

P15-4  *Stock Options, Issuance, Expense, Termination, Exercise*  On January 1, 1994, Holt, Inc., granted stock options to officers and key employees for the purchase of 20,000 shares of the company's $10 par common stock at $25 per share. The options were exercisable within a 4-year period beginning January 1, 1996 by grantees still in the employ of the company, and expiring December 31, 1999. The market price of Holt's common stock was $33 per share at the date of grant. Holt prepared a formal journal entry to record this award.

On April 3, 1995, 2,000 option shares were terminated when the employees resigned from the company. The market value of the common stock was $35 per share on this date.

On March 30, 1996, 12,000 option shares were exercised when the market value of the common stock was $40 per share.

**Required**

Prepare journal entries to record the issuance of the stock options, termination of the stock options, exercise of the stock options, and charges to compensation expense, for the years ended December 31, 1994, 1995, and 1996. Show supporting computations in good form. (*AICPA adapted*)

P15-5  *Stock Appreciation Rights*  Smythe Company has a stock appreciation rights plan for its key executives. This SAR plan allows each qualifying executive to receive cash, stock, or a combination of both equal to the excess of the quoted market price over the option price of the company's $10 par common stock on the date of exercise. The key characteristics and requirements of this SAR plan are as follows:

Option price: Market price on date of grant
Service period: 4 years
Exercise limit: Within 6 years

On January 1, 1994, Sarah Mendelson was granted SARs to 3,000 shares of the company's common stock under the requirements of the SAR plan. On January 1, 1995, Donald Freeman was granted SARs to 4,000 shares under the requirements of the plan. Both executives are expected to receive cash on the date of exercise. On December 31, 1998, Mendelson exercised her rights to receive cash, while Freeman exercised his rights to receive $1,400 cash and the remainder in common stock. The quoted market prices per share of the company's common stock are as follows:

| | |
|---|---|
| 12/31/93 | $16.00 |
| 12/31/94 | 20.00 |
| 12/31/95 | 21.00 |
| 12/31/96 | 20.80 |
| 12/31/97 | 21.50 |
| 12/31/98 | 22.00 |

**Required**

1. Prepare a schedule to compute the compensation expense related to this SAR plan for 1994 through 1998.
2. Prepare the journal entries related to the SAR plan on December 31, 1994 through December 31, 1998.

*P15-6*   *Dividends*   The Keener Company has had 1,000 shares of 7%, $100 par-value preferred stock and 40,000 shares of $5 stated-value common stock outstanding for the last 3 years. During that period, dividends paid totaled $6,000, $28,000, and $30,000 for each year, respectively.

**Required**

Compute the amount of dividends that must have been paid to preferred stockholders and common stockholders in each of the 3 years, given the following four independent assumptions:

1. Preferred stock is nonparticipating and noncumulative.
2. Preferred stock is nonparticipating and cumulative.
3. Preferred stock is fully participating and cumulative.
4. Preferred stock participates up to a maximum of 9% of its par value and is cumulative.

*P15-7*   *Dividends*   Tomasco, Inc., began operations in January 1991 and had the following reported net income or loss for each of its 5 years of operations:

| | |
|---|---|
| 1991 | $  150,000 loss |
| 1992 | 130,000 loss |
| 1993 | 120,000 loss |
| 1994 | 250,000 income |
| 1995 | 1,000,000 income |

At December 31, 1995, the Tomasco capital accounts were as follows:

| | |
|---|---:|
| Common stock, par value $10 per share; authorized 100,000 shares; issued and outstanding 50,000 shares | $  500,000 |
| 4% nonparticipating noncumulative preferred stock, par value $100 per share; authorized, issued, and outstanding 1,000 shares | 100,000 |
| 8% fully participating cumulative preferred stock, par value $100 per share; authorized, issued, and outstanding 10,000 shares | 1,000,000 |

Tomasco has never paid a cash or stock dividend. There has been no change in the capital accounts since Tomasco began operations. The appropriate state law permits dividends only from retained earnings.

**Required**

Prepare a work sheet showing the maximum amount available for cash dividends on December 31, 1995 and how it would be distributable to the holders of the common shares and each of the preferred shares. Show supporting computations in good form. (*AICPA adapted*)

*P15-8*   *Comprehensive*   The Gray Company lists the following stockholders' equity items on December 31, 1994:

| | |
|---|---:|
| Preferred stock (8%), $100 par | $120,000 |
| Common stock, $10 par | 180,000 |
| Additional paid-in capital on preferred stock | 21,600 |
| Additional paid-in capital on common stock | 90,000 |
| Total contributed capital | $411,600 |
| Unrealized increase in value of securities available for sale | 6,000 |
| Retained earnings | 230,000 |
| Contributed capital, unrealized capital, and retained earnings | $647,600 |
| Less: Treasury stock (2,000 shares of common at $21 per share, acquired on March 1, 1994) | (42,000) |
| Total stockholders' equity | $605,600 |

The following stock transactions occurred during 1995:

Jan.   2    Issued 3,000 shares of common stock at $24 per share.

Jan.   30    Paid the annual 1994 per share dividend on preferred stock and the $2 per share dividend on common stock. These dividends had been declared on December 31, 1994.

| Mar. 3 | Issued 400 shares of preferred stock at $125 per share. |
|---|---|
| May 8 | Reissued 600 shares of treasury stock at $22 per share. |
| June 15 | Split the common stock two for one, reducing the par value to $6 per share. |
| July 3 | Declared a 5% stock dividend on the outstanding common stock, to be issued on August 3. The stock is selling for $13 per share. |
| Aug. 3 | Issued the stock dividend. |
| Oct. 2 | Declared a property dividend payable to common stockholders on November 2. The dividend consists of 2,000 shares of an investment in Lamb Company common stock available for sale, which had been acquired at a cost of $12 per share and which have a carrying value of $15 per share. The stock is currently selling for $16 per share. |
| Nov. 2 | Issued the property dividend to common stockholders. |
| Dec. 30 | Declared the annual per share dividend on the outstanding preferred stock and a $1 per share dividend on the outstanding common stock, to be paid on January 29, 1996. |

**Required**

1. Prepare journal entries to record the preceding transactions.
2. Prepare the December 31, 1995 stockholders' equity section (assume that 1995 net income was $225,000).

P15-9    *Comprehensive*    Included in the December 31, 1994 Keaton Company balance sheet was the following stockholders' equity section:

| | | |
|---|---:|---:|
| Preferred stock (6%), $100 par | $200,000 | |
| Premium on preferred stock | 12,000 | $ 212,000 |
| Common stock, $5 par | $150,000 | |
| Premium on common stock | 240,000 | 390,000 |
|    Total contributed capital | | $ 602,000 |
| Unrealized capital | | |
|    Unrealized decrease in value of securities available for sale | | (41,000) |
| Retained earnings | | 627,000 |
|    Contributed capital, unrealized capital, and retained earnings | | $1,188,000 |
| Less: Treasury stock (1,000 shares of common stock at cost, acquired on 2/1/1994) | | (20,000) |
|    Total stockholders' equity | | $1,168,000 |

The company engaged in the following stock transactions during 1995:

| Jan. 2 | Paid the semiannual dividend on the outstanding preferred stock and a $1.60 per share annual dividend on the outstanding common stock. These dividends had been declared on December 1 of 1994. |
|---|---|
| Jan. 3 | Issued 500 shares of preferred stock at $110 per share. |
| Jan. 20 | Issued 4,000 shares of common stock at $23 per share. |
| Apr. 3 | Reissued 700 shares of treasury stock at $24 per share. |
| May 15 | Declared a 10% stock dividend on the outstanding common stock, payable on June 30. The common stock is currently selling for $25 per share. |
| June 1 | Declared the semiannual cash dividend on the outstanding preferred stock, payable on July 3. |
| June 30 | Issued the stock dividend declared on May 15. |
| July 3 | Paid the cash dividend declared on June 1. |
| July 20 | Split the common stock two for one and reduced the par value to $2.50 per share. |
| Aug. 3 | Declared a property dividend, payable to common stockholders on September 15. The dividend consists of an investment in 5,000 shares of Drot Company common stock available for sale. The stock had been acquired at $9 per share, but has a carrying value of $6 per share. The stock is currently selling for $4 per share. |
| Sept. 15 | Paid the property dividend declared on August 3. |
| Dec. 1 | Declared the semiannual cash dividend on the outstanding preferred stock and a $0.90 per share annual dividend on the outstanding common stock. |

**Required**

1. Prepare journal entries to record the preceding transactions.
2. Prepare the December 31, 1995 stockholders' equity section (assume that 1995 net income was $270,000).

**P15-10** *Stock Dividends, Splits*    The stockholders' equity of the Nance Company prior to any of the following events is as follows:

| | |
|---|---:|
| Preferred stock (8%), $100 par | $100,000 |
| Common stock, $10 par | 150,000 |
| Premium on preferred stock | 16,000 |
| Premium on common stock | 220,000 |
| Retained earnings | 264,000 |
| | $750,000 |

The company is considering the following *alternative* items:

1. An 8% stock dividend on the common stock when it is selling for $30 per share.
2. A 30% stock dividend on the common stock when it is selling for $32 per share.
3. A *special* stock dividend to common stockholders consisting of one share of preferred stock for every 100 shares of common stock. The preferred stock and common stock are selling for $123 and $31 per share, respectively.
4. A two-for-one stock split on the common stock, reducing the par value to $4 per share (assume the same date for declaration and issuance). The market price is $30 per share on the common stock.
5. A property dividend to common stockholders consisting of 1,000 shares of West Company common stock. This stock is being carried on the Nance Company books at a cost of $48 per share; it has a current value of $54 per share.
6. A cash dividend, consisting of a normal dividend and a liquidating dividend, on both the preferred and the common stock. The 10% preferred dividend includes a 2% liquidating dividend and the $2.30 per share common dividend includes a $0.30 per share liquidating dividend (separate liquidating dividend contra accounts should be used).

**Required**

For each of the preceding *alternative* items:

1. Record (a) the journal entry at the date of declaration, and (b) the journal entry at the date of issuance.
2. Compute the balances in the stockholders' equity accounts immediately after the issuance (any gains or losses are to be reflected in the retained earnings balance; ignore income taxes).

**P15-11** *Retained Earnings Statement*    The Tate Company began 1995 with a Retained Earnings account balance of $182,000. During 1995, the following eight events occurred and were properly recorded by the company:

1. Bonds payable with a face value of $100,000 were issued on January 1 at 98. The bonds mature in 10 years. The bond provisions require the restriction of retained earnings (by means of a note to the financial statements) equal to one-half the face value of the bonds during the period the bonds are outstanding.
2. On April 14, the company reissued 2,400 shares of treasury stock for $25 per share. The company had reacquired these shares in 1993 at a cost of $20 per share. At that time, it had appropriated retained earnings (by means of a note to the financial statements) in an amount equal to the cost of the treasury shares.
3. On January 3, the company recalled and retired 800 shares of $100 par preferred stock at the call price of $120 per share. The stock had originally been issued for $108 per share.
4. During June, the company declared and issued a two-for-one stock split on its common stock, reducing the par value from $10 to $5 per share. Immediately prior to the split, 10,000 shares of common stock were outstanding. The stock market price on the date of the split was $25 per share.
5. In August, the company declared and issued a 15% stock dividend when the common stock was selling at $13 per share.

6. During December, the company declared and paid its annual $1.30 per share cash dividend on the outstanding common stock.
7. Net income amounted to $72,000.
8. During the year-end audit, it was found that in 1994 the company had recorded depreciation on a particular machine twice. The error resulted in a $12,000 overstatement of depreciation during 1994. It was also found that, due to an oversight, a $9,000 loss on the sale of land was omitted from the 1994 income statement. Both items are material. The company has been subject to a 30% income tax rate for several years.

**Required**

Prepare a statement of retained earnings and any related notes for the year ended December 31, 1995.

P15-12 *Corrections, Dividends, Retained Earnings Statement* On January 1, 1995, the Fastor Company had a retained earnings balance of $218,600. It is subject to a 30% corporate income tax rate. During 1995, the company earned net income of $67,000, and the following events occurred:

1. Cash dividends of $2 per share on 4,000 shares of common stock were declared and paid.
2. A small stock dividend was declared and issued. The dividend consisted of 600 shares of $10 par common stock. On the date of declaration, the market price of the company's common stock was $26 per share.
3. The company recalled and retired 500 shares of $100 par preferred stock. The call price was $125 per share; the stock had originally been issued for $110 per share.
4. The company discovered that it had erroneously recorded depreciation expense of $44,000 in 1994 for both financial reporting and income tax reporting. The correct depreciation for 1994 should have been $20,000. This is considered a material error.

**Required**

1. Prepare journal entries to record items 1 through 4.
2. Prepare a statement of retained earnings for the year ended December 31, 1995.

P15-13 *Comprehensive* The stockholders' equity of the Reed Company on January 1, 1995 is as follows:

| | |
|---|---|
| Preferred stock (8%), $100 par, callable at $116 | $100,000 |
| Preferred stock (7%), $100 par | 150,000 |
| Common stock, $10 par | 220,000 |
| Premium on capital stock | 160,000 |
| Retained earnings | 182,200 |
| | $812,200 |

In January 1995, the company recalled and retired the 8% preferred stock. This stock had originally been issued for $105 per share. In April, it declared and issued a 10% stock dividend on the common stock when the stock was selling for $16 per share. This was the only issuance of common or preferred stock during the year. During November, the company reacquired as treasury stock 1,000 shares of its common stock at $18 per share (it uses the cost method for treasury stock). State law requires an appropriation of retained earnings equal to the cost of all treasury shares held. The company discloses this appropriation by means of a note to the financial statements. In December, the annual cash dividends on the outstanding preferred stock and a $1 per share cash dividend on the outstanding common stock were declared and paid. At the end of December, net income of $87,000 was closed from Income Summary to Retained Earnings. During the year-end audit, it was found that two errors had been made during 1994 for both financial reporting and income tax reporting. First, depreciation on certain machinery in the amount of $10,000 was inadvertently omitted. Second, a mathematical mistake was made in the calculation of the accumulated depreciation related to the sale of equipment. Consequently, the reduction in accumulated depreciation and the amount of the gain recognized were both understated by $8,000. Both errors are considered material. The company has been subject to a 30% income tax rate for the past several years.

**Required**

1. Prepare journal entries to record the preceding transactions.
2. Prepare a statement of retained earnings and any related notes for the year ended December 31, 1995.

P15-14   *Corrections*   You are engaged to perform the first audit of the Marble Company for the year ended December 31, 1995. You find the following account balances related to stockholders' equity:

| | |
|---|---:|
| Preferred stock, $100 par | $ 30,000 |
| Common stock, $10 par | 65,000 |
| Capital surplus | (16,400) |
| Retained earnings | 150,000 |

Due to the antiquated terminology and negative balance, you first examine the Capital Surplus account and find in it the following entries:

| | Credit (Debit) |
|---|---:|
| Premium on common stock | $ 27,100 |
| Capital from donated land | 16,000 |
| Treasury stock (500 common shares at cost) | (7,500) |
| Premium on preferred stock | 3,000 |
| Appropriation for self-insurance | 25,000 |
| Stock dividend (50%) | (20,000) |
| Prior period adjustment (net of income taxes) | (12,000) |
| Loss from fire (uninsured), 1994 | (18,000) |
| Property dividend declared | (6,000) |
| Cash dividends declared | (24,000) |
| Balance | $(16,400) |

Your examination of the Preferred Stock and Common Stock accounts reveals that the amounts shown correctly state the total par value of the issued capital stock. The Retained Earnings account contains the accumulated earnings of the company with the exception of any items of retained earnings that were inappropriately debited or credited to the Capital Surplus account.

**Required**
1. Prepare whatever journal entries are necessary to eliminate the Capital Surplus account and to correct the Marble Company's stockholders' equity accounts.
2. Prepare a corrected stockholders' equity section of the December 31, 1995 balance sheet.

P15-15   *Comprehensive*   Ashwood, Inc. is a public enterprise whose shares are traded in the over-the-counter market. At December 31, 1994, Ashwood had 6,000,000 authorized shares of $10 par value common stock, of which 2,000,000 shares were issued and outstanding. The stockholders' equity accounts at December 31, 1994 had the following balances:

| | |
|---|---:|
| Common stock | $20,000,000 |
| Additional paid-in capital | 7,500,000 |
| Retained earnings | 6,470,000 |

Transactions during 1995 and other information relating to the stockholders' equity accounts were as follows:
1. On January 6, 1995, Ashwood issued at $54 per share, 100,000 shares of $50 par value, 9% cumulative convertible preferred stock. Each share of preferred stock is convertible, at the option of the holder, into two shares of common stock. Ashwood had 600,000 authorized shares of preferred stock.
2. On February 3, 1995, Ashwood reacquired 20,000 shares of its common stock for $16 per share. Ashwood uses the cost method to account for treasury stock.
3. On April 28, 1995, Ashwood sold 500,000 shares (previously unissued) of $10 par value common stock to the public at $17 per share.
4. On June 19, 1995, Ashwood declared a cash dividend of $1 per share of common stock, payable on July 14, 1995 to stockholders of record on July 3, 1995.

5. On November 10, 1995, Ashwood sold 10,000 shares of treasury stock for $21 per share.
6. On December 15, 1995, Ashwood declared the yearly cash dividend on preferred stock, payable on January 15, 1996 to stockholders of record on December 31, 1995.
7. On January 19, 1996, before the books were closed for 1995, Ashwood became aware that the ending inventories at December 31, 1994 were understated by $300,000 (the after-tax effect on 1994 net income was $210,000). The appropriate correcting entry was recorded the same day.
8. After correcting the beginning inventory, net income for 1995 was $4,500,000.

**Required**

1. Prepare a statement of retained earnings for Ashwood for the year ended December 31, 1995. Assume that only single-period financial statements for 1995 are presented.
2. Prepare the stockholders' equity section of Ashwood's balance sheet at December 31, 1995. (*AICPA adapted*)

P15-16 *Comprehensive* Carr Corporation had the following stockholders' equity account balances at December 31, 1994:

| | |
|---|---|
| Preferred stock | $1,800,000 |
| Additional paid-in capital from preferred stock | 90,000 |
| Common stock | 5,150,000 |
| Additional paid-in capital from common stock | 3,500,000 |
| Retained earnings | 4,000,000 |
| Unrealized decrease in value of marketable equity securities | 245,000 |
| Treasury common stock | 270,000 |

Transactions during 1995 and other information relating to the stockholders' equity accounts were as follows:

1. Carr's preferred and common shares are traded on the over-the-counter market. At December 31, 1994, Carr had 100,000 authorized shares of $100 par, 10% cumulative preferred stock; and 3,000,000 authorized shares of no-par common stock with a stated value of $5 per share.
2. On January 10, 1995, Carr formally retired all 30,000 shares of its treasury common stock and had them revert to an unissued basis. The treasury stock had been acquired on January 21, 1994. The shares were originally issued at $10 per share.
3. Carr owned 10,000 shares of Bush, Inc., common stock purchased in 1992 for $750,000. The Bush stock was included in Carr's short-term marketable securities portfolio at the end of 1994 at a value of $650,000. On February 14, 1995, Carr declared a dividend in kind of one share of Bush for every hundred shares of Carr common stock held by a stockholder of record on February 28, 1995. The market price of Bush common stock was $63 per share on February 14, 1995. The dividend in kind was distributed on March 13, 1995.
4. On April 3, 1995, 250,000 stock rights were issued to the common stockholders permitting the purchase of one new share of common stock in exchange for one right and $11 cash. On April 24, 1995, 210,000 stock rights were exercised when the market price of Carr's common stock was $13 per share. Carr issued new shares to settle the transaction. The remaining 40,000 rights were not exercised and expired.
5. On January 1, 1992, Carr granted stock options to employees for the purchase of 100,000 shares of the company's common stock at $8 per share, which was also the market price. The options are exercisable within a three-year period beginning January 1, 1994. The measurement date is the same as the grant date. On July 3, 1995, employees exercised 80,000 options for $8 per share. On July 3, 1995, the market price of Carr's common stock was $15 per share. Carr used new shares to settle the transaction.
6. On December 11, 1995, Carr declared the yearly cash dividend on preferred stock, payable on January 15, 1996 to stockholders of record on December 31, 1995.
7. After year-end adjustment, the Unrealized Decrease in Value of Marketable Equity Securities account had a debit balance of $135,000 at December 31, 1995.
8. On January 16, 1996, before the accounting records were closed for 1995, Carr became aware that rent income for the year ended December 31, 1994 was overstated by $500,000. The after-tax effect on 1994 net income was $275,000. The appropriate correcting entry was recorded the same day.
9. After correcting the rent income, net income for 1995 was $2,600,000.

**Required**

1. Prepare Carr's statement of retained earnings for the year ended December 31, 1995. Assume that only single-period financial statements for 1995 are presented.
2. Prepare the stockholders' equity section of Carr's balance sheet at December 31, 1995. (*AICPA adapted*)

P15-17    *Comprehensive*   CRP Company reported the following amounts in the stockholders' equity section of the December 31, 1994 balance sheet:

| | |
|---|---:|
| Preferred stock, 9%, $100 par (10,000 shares authorized, 1,000 shares issued) | $100,000 |
| Common stock, $10 par (20,000 shares authorized, 9,000 shares issued) | 90,000 |
| Additional paid-in capital on preferred stock | 20,000 |
| Additional paid-in capital on common stock | 99,000 |
| Retained earnings | 330,000 |

During 1995, the following chronological transactions affecting stockholders' equity were completed by CRP:

1. Purchased 750 shares of its own outstanding common stock as treasury stock for $22 per share.
2. Instituted a stock option plan for the company's five top executives on January 2, 1995. Each executive was granted the option to purchase 1,000 shares of common stock at $20 per share, contingent upon completing 4 years of continuous service from the date of grant. The market price was $26 per share on this date.
3. Sold 500 shares of treasury stock at $27 per share.
4. Accepted land for a plant site valued at $60,000 from the Richardson Run Industrial Authority.
5. Retired 200 of the common shares held in the treasury.
6. The aggregate market value of the company's long-term investments in equity securities available for sale dropped below the carrying value of these securities at year-end. The difference between the carrying value and the year-end market value totals $10,000.
7. Issued 100 shares of preferred stock for $125 per share.
8. Net income for 1995 was $83,000; dividends on preferred and common were $9,900 and $17,600, respectively.

**Required**

1. Prepare journal entries to record the preceding 1995 transactions for CRP Company. Assume the company uses the cost method to account for treasury stock.
2. Prepare the statement of changes in stockholders' equity for 1995. (*Hint*: This statement will include more than 11 numerical columns.)
3. Prepare the stockholders' equity section of the balance sheet as of December 31, 1995. Include appropriate notes to accompany this section.

P15-18    *Comprehensive*   The stockholders' equity section of Gaines Industries' balance sheet appeared as follows at December 31, 1994:

| | | |
|---|---:|---:|
| Contributed capital | | |
|    Preferred stock, 8%, $100 par (5,000 shares authorized, 3,000 shares issued) | | $ 300,000 |
|    Common stock, $10 par (25,000 shares authorized, 20,000 shares issued) | $200,000 | |
|    Less: Treasury stock (500 shares at $10 par) | (5,000) | 195,000 |
|    Premium on preferred stock | | 120,000 |
|    Premium on common stock | | 280,000 |
|    Common stock option warrants | $ 30,000 | |
|    Less: Deferred compensation | (18,000) | 12,000 |
|      Total contributed capital | | $ 907,000 |
| Retained earnings | | 260,000 |
|      Total stockholders' equity | | $1,167,000 |

During 1995, the following chronological transactions were recorded:

1. The company issued 1,000 shares of common stock for $40 per share.
2. The company has a stock option plan for key executives. In accordance with the plan, the shares under option and the option price per share for each executive are known on the date of grant. During 1995 no new

options were granted, and compensation expense of $3,000 was recorded in regard to the existing stock options.

3. Stock options to 500 common shares were exercised in 1995 at an option price of $30 per share. The compensation cost originally recorded in the Common Stock Option Warrants account in regard to these shares amounted to $3 per share.
4. The company reissued 200 shares of its treasury stock for $41 per share.
5. The company accepted land in an industrial park for a factory building site from the Columbus Development Association. The fair value of the land is estimated by an independent appraiser to be $50,000.
6. The law firm of Crook, Rezich, and Romero agreed to accept 100 shares of preferred stock in lieu of legal fees. At the time, the preferred stock was selling for $142 per share.
7. Net income for 1995 of $182,000 was transferred from Income Summary to Retained Earnings. Dividends on preferred and common were $24,800 and $43,000, respectively (debit Retained Earnings and credit Cash).

### Required

1. Prepare journal entries to record the preceding 1995 transactions for Gaines Industries.
2. Prepare the statement of changes in stockholders' equity for 1995. (*Hint*: This statement will require more than 10 numerical columns.)
3. Prepare the stockholders' equity section of the December 31, 1995 balance sheet. Include appropriate notes to the financial statements (assume the treasury stock has a cost of $10,500 at year-end).

*P15-19* *Stockholders' Equity* Raun Company had the following account titles on its December 31, 1995 trial balance:

9% cumulative convertible preferred stock, $100 par value
Premium on preferred stock
Common stock, $1 stated value
Premium on common stock
Retained earnings

The following additional information about the Raun Company was available for the year ended December 31, 1995:

1. There were 2 million shares of preferred stock authorized, of which 1 million were outstanding. All 1 million shares outstanding were issued on January 2, 1992 for $120 a share. The preferred stock is convertible into common stock on a one-for-one basis until December 31, 2001; thereafter, the preferred stock ceases to be convertible and is callable at par value by the company. No preferred stock has been converted into common stock, and there were no dividends in arrears at December 31, 1995.
2. The common stock has been issued at amounts above stated value per share since incorporation in 1977. Of the 5 million shares authorized, 3,580,000 were outstanding at January 1, 1995. The market price of the outstanding common stock has increased slowly, but consistently, for the last 5 years.
3. The company has an employee stock option plan where certain key employees and officers may purchase shares of common stock at 100% of the market price at the date of the option grant. All options are exercisable in installments of one-third each year, commencing one year after the date of the grant, and expire if not exercised within 4 years of the grant date. On January 1, 1995, options for 70,000 shares were outstanding at prices ranging from $47 to $83 a share. Options for 20,000 shares were exercised at $47 to $79 a share during 1995. During 1995, no options expired and additional options for 15,000 shares were granted at $86 a share. The 65,000 options outstanding at December 31, 1995 were exercisable at $54 to $86 a share; of these, 30,000 were exercisable at that date at prices ranging from $54 to $79 a share.
4. The company also has an employee stock purchase plan whereby the company pays one-half and the employee pays one-half of the market price of the stock at the date of the subscription. During 1995, employees subscribed to 60,000 shares at an average price of $87 a share. All 60,000 shares were paid for and issued late in September 1995.
5. On December 31, 1995, there was a total of 355,000 shares of common stock set aside for the granting of future stock options and for future purchases under the employee stock purchase plan. The only changes in the stockholders' equity for 1995 were those described previously, 1995 net income, and cash dividends paid.

### Required

Prepare the stockholders' equity section of the balance sheet of Raun Company at December 31, 1995. Substitute, where appropriate, X's for unknown dollar amounts. Use good form and provide full disclosure. Write appropriate notes as they should appear in the published financial statements. (*AICPA adapted*)

*P15-20  Comprehensive*  Fay, Inc. finances its capital needs approximately one-third from long-term debt and two-thirds from equity. At December 31, 1994, Fay had the following liability and equity account balances:

| | | | |
|---|---|---|---|
| 11% Debenture bonds payable, face amount | $5,000,000 | Additional paid-in capital | $2,295,000 |
| Premium on bonds payable | 352,400 | Retained earnings | 2,465,000 |
| Common stock | 8,000,000 | Treasury stock, at cost | 325,000 |

Transactions during 1995 and other information relating to Fay's liabilities and equity accounts were as follows:

1. The debenture bonds were issued on December 31, 1992 for $5,378,000 to yield 10%. The bonds mature on December 31, 2007. Interest is payable annually on December 31. Fay uses the interest method to amortize bond premium.
2. Fay's common stock shares are traded on the over-the-counter market. At December 31, 1994 Fay had 2,000,000 authorized shares of $10 par common stock.
3. On January 16, 1995, Fay reissued 15,000 of its 25,000 shares of treasury stock for $225,000. The treasury stock had been acquired on February 26, 1994.
4. On March 2, 1995, Fay issued a 5% stock dividend on all issued shares. The market price of Fay's common stock at time of issuance was $14 per share.
5. On November 2, 1995, Fay borrowed $4,000,000 at 9%, evidenced by an unsecured note payable to United Bank. The note is payable in five equal annual principal installments of $800,000. The first principal and interest payment is due on November 2, 1996.
6. On December 31, 1995, Fay owned 10,000 shares of Ryan Corp.'s common stock, which represented a 1% ownership interest. Fay treats this marketable equity investment as a long-term investment in securities available for sale. The stock was purchased on November 3, 1995 at $20 per share. The market price was $18 per share on December 31, 1995.
7. Fay's net income for 1995 was $2,860,000.

**Required**
1. Prepare the long-term liabilities section of Fay's December 31, 1995 balance sheet, including all disclosures applicable to each obligation.
2. Prepare the stockholders' equity section of Fay's December 31, 1995 balance sheet.
3. Prepare a schedule showing interest expense for the year ended December 31, 1995. (*AICPA adapted*)

*P15-21  Appendix: Quasi-Reorganization*  The Moore Corporation experienced several years of operating losses and encountered serious financial difficulty, resulting in liquidity problems and a deficit in retained earnings. However, recent entry into several new markets has been encouraging. The board of directors, with its stockholders' consent, decides to complete a quasi-reorganization on December 31, 1995. The balance sheet, prior to any adjustments, is shown below:

| | | | |
|---|---|---|---|
| Cash | $ 6,000 | Accounts payable | $ 51,000 |
| Accounts receivable | 18,000 | Accrued liabilities | 7,000 |
| Inventories | 42,000 | Bonds payable (due 1/1/99) | 84,000 |
| Investments in M Company bonds | 66,000 | Common stock, $10 par | 100,000 |
| Property and equipment | 193,000 | Additional paid-in capital | 82,000 |
| Less: Accumulated depreciation | (71,000) | Retained earnings | (41,000) |
| Patents (net) | 29,000 | | |
| Total assets | $283,000 | Total liabilities and stockholders' equity | $283,000 |

On December 31, 1995, an examination of the company accounts discloses the following information:

1. Some $3,000 of the current accounts receivable are estimated to be uncollectible.
2. The inventories consist of several obsolete items. An analysis places the fair market value of the inventory at $30,000.
3. The M Company bonds had been purchased in November 1995. They are being held to maturity and have a current market value of $60,000.
4. The appraisal value of the property and equipment is $100,000.
5. Several obsolete patents are being carried on the books at a carrying value of $8,000.

In addition, on December 31, 1995, approval is received to reduce the par value of the common stock to $5 per share.

During 1996, the company discovers additional obsolete inventory with no resale value. This inventory had been carried on the books since 1992 at a cost of $4,000. It is determined that the inventory had become obsolete during 1995.

### Required

1. Prepare the journal entries to complete the quasi-reorganization.
2. Prepare the revised balance sheet on December 31, 1995, including an appropriate note to the financial statements.
3. Prepare the journal entry in 1996 to account for the obsolete inventory.

**P15-22** *Appendix: Quasi-Reorganization* FAHRS Corporation has experienced losses in each of the last 3 years. A reorganization of top management has taken place and the new chief executive officer is confident the company can be saved from bankruptcy. A quasi-reorganization has been proposed contingent upon stockholder approval. Prior to the reorganization, the December 31, 1995 balance sheet reflects the following amounts:

| | | | |
|---|---|---|---|
| Cash | $ 10,000 | Accounts payable | $ 90,000 |
| Accounts receivable | 70,000 | Notes payable, long-term | 43,000 |
| Inventory | 100,000 | Preferred stock, $100 par | 100,000 |
| Fixed assets | 220,000 | Premium on preferred stock | 20,000 |
| Less: Accumulated depreciation | (80,000) | Common stock, $20 par | 200,000 |
| Other assets | 15,000 | Premium on common stock | 60,000 |
| | | Retained earnings (deficit) | (178,000) |
| Total assets | $335,000 | Total liabilities and stockholders' equity | $335,000 |

The following information relates to the quasi-reorganization as approved by the FAHRS Corporation stockholders:

1. Accounts receivable of $10,000 are estimated to be uncollectible.
2. Inventories have increased for several years but now have a fair market value of only $80,000.
3. Fixed assets have a fair market value of $100,000.
4. Other assets are composed of accumulated store fixtures that were replaced several years ago. It is estimated that proceeds from the sale of these fixtures will just cover the disposal costs involved.
5. Short-term creditors have agreed to a 10% reduction in the obligations owed to them.
6. The board of directors, with stockholder and state approval, has authorized:
   a. A reduction in par value of the common stock to $5 per share.
   b. A reduction in par value of the preferred stock to $50 per share.
   c. The retained earnings deficit to be charged against the premiums on preferred and common stock in proportion to their respective account balances.

### Required

1. Prepare journal entries to record the quasi-reorganization.
2. Prepare the FAHRS Corporation balance sheet immediately after the reorganization. Include a retained earnings note to the financial statements.

# FINANCIAL REPORTING

## Special Topics

## PART

# 5

# 16

# INCOME RECOGNITION AND MEASUREMENT OF NET ASSETS

## Chapter Topics

*Revenue Recognition Alternatives*

*Conceptual Issues Related to Revenue Recognition*

*Revenue Recognition Prior to the Period of Sale: Percentage-of-Completion Method, Completed-Contract Method, and Proportional Performance Method*

*Revenue Recognition After the Period of Sale: Installment Method and Cost Recovery Method*

*Revenue Recognition Delayed Until a Future Event Occurs: Deposit Method*

*Additional Revenue Recognition Issues: Consignment Sales, Franchises, and Real Estate Sales*

In Chapters 3 and 4, we discussed issues of importance to external users in evaluating the performance of a company. *Return on investment* is a measure of a company's overall performance, *risk* is the uncertainty or unpredictability of the future results of a company, *financial flexibility* is the ability of a company to use its financial resources to adapt to unexpected needs and opportunities, *operating capability* is a measure of a company's ability to maintain a given physical level of operations, and *liquidity* is a measure of the amount of time until an asset is converted into cash or a liability is paid. We also discussed that revenues and expenses are defined in terms of changes in assets and liabilities, and that revenues are typically *recognized* in the period of sale even though they are *earned* gradually and continuously during a company's earning process. This recognition of revenue occurs if at the time of sale (1) realization has taken place and (2) the revenues have been earned. We also noted that expenses are matched against revenues. In the discussion, we observed the difference between recognition and realization. *Recognition* is the process of formally recording and reporting an item in the financial statements, whereas *realization* means the process of converting noncash resources into cash or rights to cash.

In today's business world, some transactions are very complex so that in certain situations, revenues (and expenses) may be advanced and recognized prior to the period of sale. In other situations, revenues (and expenses) may be deferred and recognized after the period of the sale. The purpose of advancing or deferring recognition is to increase the *usefulness* of the financial statements by a more relevant portrayal of the nature of the company's operations without a significant decrease in the reliability of the information. Note that in this discussion, we are referring to the "sale" as the transaction in which the product is transferred or the service is performed. It is also usually, but not necessarily, the point at which legal title is transferred. It is helpful to understand that the "sale," the transfer of legal title, and the recognition of revenue are three separate, but related, events. In this chapter, we discuss the conceptual and practical issues of revenue recognition, the matching of expenses against the revenue, and the related issue of the measurement of the net assets (assets minus liabilities). The discussion proceeds from an overview of revenue recognition alternatives, through a consideration of the conceptual issues, to an examination of the revenue recognition alternatives, and concludes with a discussion of consignment sales, franchises, and real estate sales.

## OVERVIEW OF REVENUE RECOGNITION ALTERNATIVES

The alternatives for recognizing revenue at various points in the earning process are illustrated in Exhibit 16-1. In this example of a simple situation, a manufacturer purchases raw materials, converts them to finished goods in the production process, sells the finished goods on account, and later collects the cash. The usual point of revenue recognition at the time of sale is shown in the middle, preceded by the alternative of advancing revenue recognition by recording revenue during production, and followed by the alternative of deferring revenue recognition until the receipt of cash. (Note also that the cash receipt may be spread out over several time periods.)

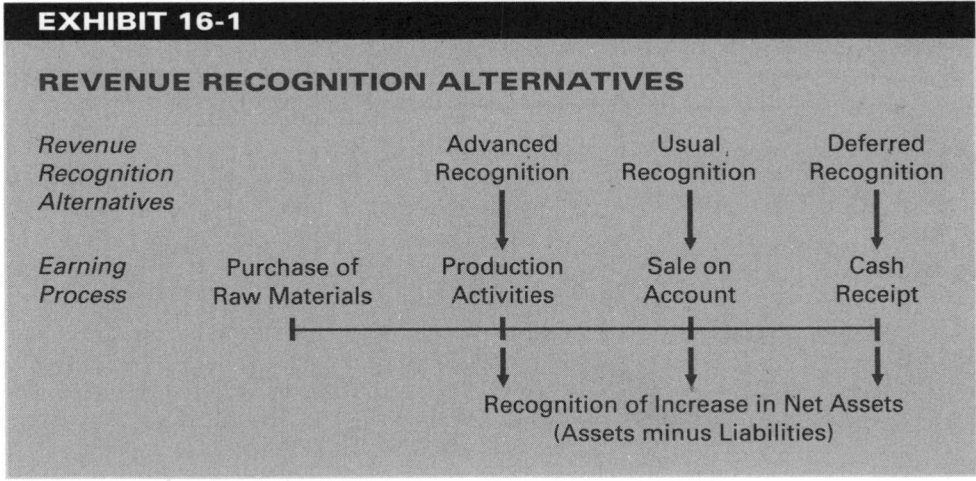

**EXHIBIT 16-1**

**REVENUE RECOGNITION ALTERNATIVES**

| Revenue Recognition Alternatives | | Advanced Recognition | Usual Recognition | Deferred Recognition |

| Earning Process | Purchase of Raw Materials | Production Activities | Sale on Account | Cash Receipt |

Recognition of Increase in Net Assets
(Assets minus Liabilities)

As alternative revenue recognition methods are evaluated, consideration must be given to the related asset and liability recognition. The period in which the revenue and expenses are recognized is also the period in which the accompanying increase in the value of the (net) assets is recognized. This relationship is illustrated in the next section.

## EXAMPLES OF REVENUE RECOGNITION ALTERNATIVES

The discussion of revenue recognition alternatives tends to focus on the income statement through the recognition of revenue and the matching of expenses. However, it is very important to understand the relationship between income (revenue and expense) recognition on the income statement and the measurement of the net assets (assets minus liabilities) on the balance sheet. In this section, we illustrate the effects on the financial statements of the three basic revenue recognition alternatives using the following facts for the Ringwood Company, a small manufacturer of special order items in its first year of operations that uses the perpetual inventory system:

1. The company begins the year with cash and contributed capital of $100.

2. The company contracts with a customer to produce and sell an item of inventory for $150. It costs $100 cash to manufacture the item.

3. The company sells the item on account.

4. The company collects $60 cash from the customer in partial payment.

### Example 1: Revenue Recognition at Time of Sale

Assuming the company recognizes the revenue, expense, and increase in net assets at the time of sale, it records the preceding events as follows:

1. The company manufactures the inventory:

| | | |
|---|---|---|
| Inventory | 100 | |
|     Cash | | 100 |

2. The company sells the inventory, recognizes revenue of $150, the related expense of $100, and the increase in net assets of $50 ($150 − $100):

| | | |
|---|---|---|
| Accounts Receivable | 150 | |
|     Revenue | | 150 |
| Cost of Goods Sold | 100 | |
|     Inventory | | 100 |

3. The company collects cash of $60:

| | | |
|---|---|---|
| Cash | 60 | |
|     Accounts Receivable | | 60 |

Following these events, the company prepares the financial statements shown in the first section of Exhibit 16-2. The income statement shows the revenue of $150, the cost of goods sold of $100, and the resulting gross profit of $50. In the balance sheet, the accounts receivable is reported at $90, which is the billing of $150 less the partial payment of $60. The contributed capital is unchanged at $100, and the retained earnings is the gross profit for the period of $50.

## EXHIBIT 16-2

## RINGWOOD COMPANY

### 1. Revenue Recognition at Time of Sale

#### Income Statement

| | |
|---|---|
| Revenue | $150 |
| Cost of goods sold | (100) |
| Gross profit | $ 50 |

#### Balance Sheet

| Assets | | Stockholders' Equity | |
|---|---|---|---|
| Cash | $ 60 | Contributed capital | $100 |
| Accounts receivable (150−60) = | 90 | Retained earnings | 50 |
| Total assets | $150 | Total stockholders' equity | $150 |

### 2. Revenue Recognition During Production

#### Income Statement

| | |
|---|---|
| Revenue | $150 |
| Cost of goods sold | (100) |
| Gross profit | $ 50 |

#### Balance Sheet

| Assets | | | Stockholders' Equity | |
|---|---|---|---|---|
| Cash | | $ 60 | Contributed capital | $100 |
| Accounts receivable (130−60) | | 70 | Retained earnings | 50 |
| Inventory | $150 | | | |
| Less: Partial billings | (130) | 20 | | |
| Total assets | | $150 | Total stockholders' equity | $150 |

### 3. Revenue Recognition at Time of Cash Receipt

#### Income Statement

| | |
|---|---|
| Revenue | $ 60 |
| Cost of goods sold | (40) |
| Gross profit | $ 20 |

#### Balance Sheet

| Assets | | | Stockholders' Equity | |
|---|---|---|---|---|
| Cash | | $ 60 | Contributed capital | $100 |
| Accounts receivable | $ 90 | | Retained earnings | 20 |
| Less: Deferred gross profit | (30) | 60 | | |
| Total assets | | $120 | Total stockholders' equity | $120 |

## Example 2: Revenue Recognition During Production

Now assume the same facts for the Ringwood Company, except that the company advances the recognition of revenue to the period of production. During production, the company recognizes a gross profit of $50 (revenue of $150 minus the related expense of $100) and bills the customer for $130. The company now records the preceding events as follows:

1. The company manufactures the inventory:

   | | | |
   |---|---|---|
   | Inventory | 100 | |
   |     Cash | | 100 |

2. The company recognizes revenue of $150, the related expense of $100, and the increase in the value of the inventory during production of $50:

   | | | |
   |---|---|---|
   | Cost of Goods Sold | 100 | |
   | Inventory | 50 | |
   |     Revenue | | 150 |

   In this situation, the company is recognizing revenue of $150 and expense of $100 during production even though the inventory has not been transferred to the customer. Since the company does not yet have a receivable, the value of the inventory is increased from its cost of $100 to its selling price of $150. In other words, since a gross profit has been recognized, the value of the net assets (inventory) must be increased.

3. The company bills the customer for $130:

   | | | |
   |---|---|---|
   | Accounts Receivable | 130 | |
   |     Partial Billings | | 130 |

   When the company bills the customer, the credit is made to Partial Billings, which is a contra account to the inventory. Thus, the net value of the inventory is reduced to the selling price less the amount billed, or $20 ($150 − $130). In other words, the $20 represents the net investment of the Ringwood Company in the inventory.

4. The company collects cash of $60:

   | | | |
   |---|---|---|
   | Cash | 60 | |
   |     Accounts Receivable | | 60 |

Following these events, the company prepares the financial statements in the second section of Exhibit 16-2. The income statement shows the revenue of $150, the cost of goods sold of $100, and the resulting gross profit of $50. In the balance sheet, the accounts receivable is reported at $70 ($130 − $60), and the inventory is reported at its net value of $20.

After the remaining $20 is billed to the customer, the inventory and partial billings accounts have equal balances (of $150) and are credited and debited, respectively, to eliminate their balances. Since all the gross profit (revenue and expense) was recognized during production, no further income is recognized.

## Example 3: Revenue Recognition at Time of Cash Receipt

Now assume the same facts for the Ringwood Company, except that the company defers the recognition of revenue to the period when the cash is received. The company now records the preceding events as follows:

1. The company manufactures the inventory:

   | | | |
   |---|---|---|
   | Inventory | 100 | |
   |    Cash | | 100 |

2. The company "sells" (i.e., delivers) the inventory and defers the recognition of revenue:

   | | | |
   |---|---|---|
   | Accounts Receivable | 150 | |
   |    Inventory | | 100 |
   |    Deferred Gross Profit | | 50 |

   Since the company has transferred the item, it records the receivable of $150, removes the inventory of $100, and records the difference as Deferred Gross Profit, which is a contra account to accounts receivable. Thus, the net value of the accounts receivable is the *cost* of the item of $100 ($150 − $50).

3. The company collects cash of $60:

   | | | |
   |---|---|---|
   | Cash | 60 | |
   |    Accounts Receivable | | 60 |

4. The company recognizes revenue on the basis of the cash received:

   | | | |
   |---|---|---|
   | Cost of Goods Sold | 40 | |
   | Deferred Gross Profit | 20 | |
   |    Revenue | | 60 |

   Since the company collects $60, it recognizes revenue of $60. This collection is 40% ($60 ÷ $150) of the total sale price of $150. Therefore, it recognizes 40% of the cost of the item as cost of goods sold of $40 (40% × $100). The deferred gross profit is reduced by $20 ($60 − $40), thereby increasing the value of the net receivable.

Following these events, the company prepares the financial statements shown in the third section of Exhibit 16-2. The income statement shows the revenue of $60, the cost of goods sold of $40, and the resulting gross profit of $20. In the balance sheet, the accounts receivable is reported at a net value of $60, which represents the remaining $90 ($150 − $60) balance of the receivable, less the remaining $30 ($50 − $20) balance of the deferred gross profit. In other words, the $60 represents the *cost* of the receivable (60% of the cost of $100) to the Ringwood Company since revenue has not yet been recognized on that portion.

As the remaining $90 (60% of the total sale price of $150) is collected, 60% of the total revenue (60% × $150 = $90) and cost of goods sold (60% × $100 = $60) is recognized. This recognition eliminates the balance in the deferred gross profit account of $30, thereby increasing the value of the net assets.

## Summary of Revenue Recognition Alternatives

As discussed in later sections of the chapter, revenue recognition is advanced or deferred in certain situations because realization and the completion of the earning process occur in periods other than the period of sale. These alternative methods increase the relevance of the financial statements. For all three examples, note that when revenue is recognized, expenses are also recognized, and (net) assets are increased from cost to selling price. In Example 1, revenue and expense are recognized at the time of sale, and accounts receivable is recorded at the selling price and inventory cost is reduced. At this point, realization has occurred, revenue and expense have been recognized, and (net) assets are increased by the amount of the gross profit.

In Example 2, revenue and expense are recognized during production and the inventory is increased from cost to selling price. Therefore, the increase in (net) assets is recorded when revenue and expense are recognized. Even though the sale has not occurred, realization has occurred and the earning process is complete. This situation is discussed later in the chapter as it relates to the percentage-of-completion method.

Alternatively, if revenue is not recognized at the time of sale the (net) assets remain at cost. In Example 3, revenue is recognized at the time of cash receipt, so that even though an account receivable is recorded at the selling price at the time of sale, it is reduced to cost through the subtraction of deferred gross profit. The increase to selling price only occurs as cash is received, revenue and expense are recognized, and deferred gross profit is reduced. In this situation, realization occurs only as cash is received, as discussed later in the chapter for the installment method.

Note also that the company starts the period with assets of $100. In Examples 1 and 2, gross profit of $50 is recognized and the (net) assets increase to $150. In Example 3, gross profit of $20 is recognized and the (net) assets increase to $120.

In the last two examples, the expenses are matched against the revenues so that they are either advanced or deferred in a consistent manner. It should be noted that this matching occurs only for certain expenses, usually those for which there is a direct "association of cause and effect" (as discussed in Chapter 4). Other expenses that are recognized on the basis of "systematic and rational allocation" or "immediate recognition" are usually recognized in the normal manner, unless they can be directly associated with the product. For example, depreciation on a machine used to make a product is included in the inventory cost, and recognition of the expense is advanced or deferred in a manner consistent with revenue recognition. Depreciation on an office building used by selling and administrative personnel is expensed in the normal manner, and therefore the recognition of that expense is *not* related to the revenue recognition alternative used by the company.

The selection of a revenue recognition alternative depends on the particular circumstances faced by each company. The conceptual issues that influence the decision are discussed in the next section.

## CONCEPTUAL ISSUES

The decision as to when to recognize revenue focuses on three factors:

1. **The economic substance of the event takes precedence over the legal form of the transaction.** Usually an exchange (sale) is considered to have taken place at the time of the legal transaction at which title to the property is transferred. However, if economic "reality" is substantially different from the legalities of a transaction, the recognition of revenues may be advanced to a period prior to

the sale or deferred to a period after the sale; that is, the period in which the revenues are earned and realizable. For example, as discussed in Chapter 19, the gross profit on a sales-type lease is recognized by the lessor even though it retains legal title. As discussed later in this chapter, gross profit may be recognized on long-term construction contracts each year during the contract instead of when the construction is completed, even though title has not passed. Also, as discussed in Chapter 7, no revenue is recognized on a product financing arrangement even though title has passed because the exchange is, in an economic sense, a loan and not a sale.

2. **The collectibility of the receivable from the sale.** If the collectibility is *"not reasonably assured,"*[1] then realization has not taken place and the earning process is not complete, so the recognition of revenue is deferred. This occurs when there is an inability to predict whether customers will pay their accounts or when significant collection efforts may be required, as for certain real estate situations and franchises discussed later in this chapter. Deferral of revenue recognition may also be appropriate when future refunds or returns cannot be reasonably estimated, as discussed in Chapter 5.

3. **The risks and benefits of ownership have been transferred to the buyer.** For revenue to be earned (and recognized), the risks and benefits of ownership must have been substantially transferred from the seller to the buyer. The benefits are the expected net cash flows, while the risks are the likelihood of larger or smaller net cash flows actually being received. For example, revenue may be recognized during a long-term construction contract because the risks and benefits are transferred to the buyer, as discussed later in this chapter. Alternatively, if the seller of a franchise has not substantially completed its obligations related to the exchange, then the benefits of ownership have not been transferred to the buyer, the earning process is not complete, and revenue recognition is deferred as discussed later in this chapter. Also, if the seller of receivables can reacquire the benefits under the recourse provision, the exchange of benefits may not have occurred and revenue is not recognized, as discussed in Chapter 5. If the seller of real estate has substantial exposure to risk after the sale, a "full exchange" has not taken place and revenue recognition is deferred, as discussed later in this chapter. Finally, sales-type leases require the recognition of revenue by the lessor because the transfer of the risks and benefits of ownership has occurred, even though a legal sale has not taken place, as discussed in Chapter 19.

In this chapter, several revenue recognition methods are discussed. In many specialized situations, the FASB has not issued *Statements of Standards*. In these situations, generally accepted accounting principles are defined by alternative sources, such as *Statements of Position, Industry Accounting Guides,* and *Industry Audit Guides,* which cover particular industries and are issued by the AICPA, as discussed in Chapter 1.

---

1. "Omnibus Opinion—1966," *APB Opinion No. 10* (New York: AICPA, 1966), par. 12. In "Recognition and Measurement in Financial Statements of Business Enterprises," *FASB Statement of Concepts No. 5* (Stamford, Conn.: FASB, 1984), par. 84(g), the term "doubtful" is used. It is assumed that these two terms have the same meaning.

## ALTERNATIVE REVENUE RECOGNITION METHODS

Once it has been decided when to recognize revenues (during, before, or after the period of sale), then a particular accounting method is selected. The revenue recognition alternatives and the methods used are briefly summarized here:

1. **Revenue Recognition in the Period of Sale.** This method is generally used because realization has taken place and revenues have been earned at the time of sale. The *accrual method* of accounting is used in which revenues (accomplishments) are recognized at the time of the sales transaction and expenses (sacrifices) are matched against the revenues in the period of sale. The inventory is recorded at cost and the resulting accounts receivable are recorded at net realizable value.

2. **Revenue Recognition Prior to the Period of Sale.** This method is used to reflect economic substance instead of legal form so that economic reality is not distorted. The *percentage-of-completion method* may be used for long-term construction contracts (or some real estate sales) or the *proportional performance method* may be used for long-term service contracts to advance revenue recognition. These methods recognize revenues (and certain expenses) based on the percentage completed during the period. The inventory for a long-term construction project, for example, is recorded at cost until revenue is recognized, at which time it is raised to net realizable value.

3. **Revenue Recognition at the Completion of Production.** This method has been advocated for certain precious metals and farm products with immediate marketability at quoted prices, unit interchangeability, and an inability of the producer to determine unit acquisition costs. This method has become less appropriate over time as markets with fixed prices become less common. Also, since mining and agricultural companies generally recognize revenue in the period of the sale, this method is not discussed further in this chapter.[2] The inventory would be recorded at replacement cost or net realizable value, and a brief example was presented in Chapter 7.

4. **Revenue Recognition After the Period of the Sale.** This method is appropriate when the collectibility of the receivable is not reasonably assured or there is no reliable basis for estimating the collectibility so that revenue recognition is deferred. In the *installment method,* a portion of the total gross profit on the sale is recognized in proportion to the cash received. In the *cost recovery method,* no gross profit is recognized until the cost of the product has been recovered; after the cost recovery, gross profit is recognized as an amount equal to the subsequent cash receipts. The accounts receivable, less the deferred gross profit, are recorded at their cost until the revenue is recognized.

5. **Revenue Recognition Delayed Until a Future Event Occurs.** This method is appropriate when there has been an insignificant transfer of the risks and benefits of ownership, so that revenue is not recognized either at the time of the sale or as cash is received. The *deposit method* is used and all cash receipts are recorded as deposits until an event occurs that transfers sufficient risks and benefits to the buyer so that revenue may be recognized. Related assets are recorded at their cost or book value until the revenue recognition occurs.

---

2.  H. J. Jaenicke, "Survey of Present Practices in Recognizing Revenues, Expenses, Gains, and Losses," *Research Report* (Stamford, Conn.: FASB, 1981), p. 75.

The accounting issues involved in the recognition of revenue (and expenses) in the period of sale have been discussed in numerous places throughout this book and will not be discussed further in this chapter. In the next section, we discuss revenue recognition prior to sale as it applies to construction contracts and service contracts. Following this section, revenue recognition after the period of sale is discussed.

## REVENUE RECOGNITION PRIOR TO THE PERIOD OF SALE

Three methods of revenue recognition are discussed in this section. Each applies to long-term contracts where the production of a product or the provision of a service extends over several accounting periods. The percentage-of-completion method is widely used by construction companies for long-term contracts and is discussed in considerable detail. The completed-contract method also may be used by construction companies for long-term contracts. Even though this method does *not* advance the recognition of revenue, it is presented here for contrast with the percentage-of-completion method. The proportional performance method is used for long-term service contracts and is discussed in less detail.

### Long-Term Construction Contracts

Some companies engage in long-term construction contracts in which they agree to construct an asset for another entity (e.g., company or governmental agency) over an extended period. Long-term construction contracts may involve such items as buildings, ships, roads, bridges, and dams, which may take several years to complete. Such a contract may involve advance payments by the buyer to help the seller finance the construction and to reflect the buyer's ownership interest in the asset under construction. The contract also may include specific responsibilities of the seller involving the use of certain materials and the completion of production on a specific timetable. At completion, the buyer typically inspects and approves the finished asset before the legal "sale" takes place.

The construction process may extend over more than one period, and so the question arises as to how revenue should be recognized by the construction company. The **percentage-of-completion method** is generally used. Under this method, profit is recognized each period during the life of the contract in proportion to the amount of the contract that has been completed during the period. As the profit is recognized, the value of the inventory is also increased, so that the inventory is valued at the costs incurred plus the profit recognized to date (less any partial billings). In certain situations, the **completed-contract method** is used. Under this method, profit is *not* recognized during the life of the contract but is recognized only when the contract is complete. During the life of the contract, therefore, the inventory is recorded at cost (less any partial billings).

Most long-term contracts are accounted for by the percentage-of-completion method, because it produces a more relevant measure of periodic income. When this method is used, **economic substance takes precedence over legal form;** i.e., the legal sale occurs at the completion of the contract, but to depict economic reality better, revenue recognition is advanced.

The earning process is virtually complete because a "continuous sale" takes place. The arguments to support a continuous sale are:

1. The buyer and the seller obtain enforceable rights including the right of the buyer to enforce specific performance.

2. The buyer usually makes progress payments to support its ownership investment and therefore realization is occurring.

3. The buyer has the right to take over the work in progress.[3]

Thus, in accordance with the continuous sale concept, revenue should be recognized continuously by using the percentage-of-completion method. The method also has the following advantages:

1. It achieves the goal of accrual accounting to report the effects of transactions and other events in the periods in which they occur.

2. It is consistent with the argument that revenue is earned continuously over the entire earning process.

3. It results in a more relevant measure of periodic income because income includes the results of the activities that occurred during the period.

Generally accepted accounting principles have supported the use of the percentage-of-completion method. **Accounting Research Bulletin No. 45** recommended its use when total gross profit on the contract could be estimated with reasonable accuracy and ultimate realization is reasonably assured.[4] However *ARB No. 45* allowed the use of both the percentage-of-completion and completed-contract methods in all circumstances and did not specify the situations under which each method would be preferable. To clarify the use of the two methods, **AICPA Statement of Position No. 81-1** requires that the percentage-of-completion method be used for long-term contracts when *all* the following conditions are met:

1. Reasonably dependable estimates can be made of the extent of progress toward completion, contract revenues, and contract costs.

2. The contract clearly specifies the enforceable rights regarding goods or services to be provided and received by the parties, the consideration to be exchanged, and the manner and terms of settlement.

3. The buyer can be expected to satisfy its obligations under the contract.

4. The contractor can be expected to perform its contractual obligations.[5]

The *Statement* also requires that the completed-contract method is used only when at least one of the preceding conditions are *not* met, for short-term contracts, and when there are inherent hazards in the contract beyond the normal business risks for which

---

3. "Accounting for Performance of Construction-Type and Certain Production-Type Contracts," *AICPA Statement of Position No. 81–1* (New York: AICPA, 1981), par. 22.

4. "Long-Term Construction-Type Contracts," *Accounting Research Bulletin No. 45* (New York: AICPA, 1955), par. 4.

5. "Accounting for Performance of Construction-Type and Certain Production-Type Contracts," *op. cit.*, par. 23.

reasonably dependable estimates cannot be made. As a result of *SOP No. 81-1,* there has been a considerable, and desirable, narrowing of generally accepted accounting principles. Instead of the two methods being allowed in all circumstances, each is acceptable only under specific and separate circumstances.

## Percentage-of-Completion Method

When the percentage-of-completion method is used, the percentage completed can be determined by the use of either "input" or "output" measures.

### Input Measures

An input to the production activity may be used to measure the percentage of completion if a relationship is assumed to exist between the input and the production activity. Two input measures are the cost-to-cost method and the efforts-expended method. In the **cost-to-cost** method, the percentage of completion is measured by comparing the costs incurred to date with the expected total costs for the contract. This percentage is multiplied by the total revenue on the contract to compute the total revenue to be recognized to date. This revenue to date minus the revenue recognized in previous years is the revenue to be recognized in the current year. The expense to be recognized is determined in the same way.

In the **efforts-expended** method, the percentage of completion is measured by the work performed to date, such as labor hours, labor dollars, machine hours, or material quantities compared to the expected total work to be performed in the contract. The revenue and expense recognized in the current year are computed by following the same procedures as for the cost-to-cost method.

### Output Measures

Output measures use the results achieved to date compared to the total expected results of the contract to measure the percentage of completion. Theoretically, output measures may be considered preferable to input measures, since they measure the results achieved (that is, the actual production completed). However, output measures often cannot be reliably measured. For example, it is difficult to measure output for a contract that involves research, engineering, and physical construction. Examples of output measures are units produced, units delivered, contract milestones, value added, or units of work completed (such as cubic yards of pavement laid on a highway contract). Once the output percentage of completion has been determined, the revenue and expense recognized each period are computed in the same way as for input measures.

### Accounting Procedures

In accounting for a long-term contract under the percentage-of-completion method, an inventory account entitled Construction in Progress is used to record all costs incurred on the project. In addition, the gross profit that is recognized on the project is added to the account, so that at the end of the period the account is valued at cost plus gross profit recognized (i.e., net realizable value). Most long-term projects are financed by receipts from partial billings paid by the purchaser, which are specified by the contract provisions and are usually less than the amount of revenue recognized. When these partial billings are made, a receivable account is debited and a Partial Billings account is credited. The balance in the Partial Billings account is reported on the balance sheet as an offset (contra account) to the Construction in Progress account. Therefore the net balance sheet amount is either an asset if Construction in Progress (which includes incurred costs plus gross profit recognized) exceeds Partial Billings, or a liability if Partial Billings exceeds Construction in Progress.

If the project's total estimated cost exceeds the contract price, then a loss is expected on the project. The conservatism convention requires that the total expected loss is recognized in the current year and the Construction in Progress account is credited. The recognition of losses is discussed later in this chapter.

### Completed-Contract Method

The completed-contract method requires that no revenue is recognized until the project is completed or substantially so (although anticipated losses are recognized immediately). In effect, this method is just like the production and sale of any unit of inventory. The recording and reporting of inventory costs and partial billings are handled in the same way as the percentage-of-completion method. The principal advantage of the completed-contract method is that the revenue recognized is *more reliable* because it is based on final results rather than on estimates. The principal disadvantage is that it is *less relevant* because net income does not reflect current performance but rather is a function of the date the contract is completed. Indeed, net income may be negative if no contracts are completed in a period and selling and administrative costs are expensed.

### Illustration of the Two Methods

To illustrate the two methods, assume that the Calder Company is engaged in the construction of a dam that takes 3 years to complete. The contract price, costs incurred, estimated costs to complete, partial billings, and collections are as shown in Exhibit 16-3. The company estimates the percent complete by the cost-to-cost method.

*Computations for the Percentage-of-Completion Method*
The gross profit recognized each year under the percentage-of-completion method is shown in Exhibit 16-4. In 1994, the Calder Company incurred $100,000 of construction costs and estimates that it will incur another $400,000 to complete the contract. Therefore the total cost of the contract is expected to be $500,000. Since the contract price is $700,000, a gross profit of $200,000 is projected. The contract is 20% complete ($100,000 ÷ $500,000), and therefore 20% of the total revenue on the contract is recognized. This amounts to $140,000 (20% × $700,000). Since total estimated construction costs are $500,000, the construction expense recognized for 1994 is

---

**EXHIBIT 16-3**

**CALDER COMPANY**

|  | 1994 | 1995 | 1996 |
|---|---|---|---|
| Construction costs incurred during the year | $100,000 | $186,000 | $314,000 |
| Estimated costs to complete the contract | 400,000 | 264,000 | — |
| Partial billings to customer | 80,000 | 350,000 | 270,000 |
| Collections from customer | 50,000 | 330,000 | 320,000 |
| Total contract price: $700,000 | | | |

## EXHIBIT 16-4

### CALDER COMPANY

Gross Profit Recognition: Percentage-of-Completion Method

|  | 1994 | 1995 | 1996 |
|---|---|---|---|
| Construction costs incurred to date | $100,000 | $286,000 | $600,000 |
| Estimated costs to complete | 400,000 | 264,000 | — |
| Total estimated costs | $500,000 | $550,000 | $600,000 |
| Percent complete (construction cost incurred to date ÷ total estimated costs) | 20% | 52% | 100% |
| Revenue to date (% complete × $700,000 contract price) | $140,000 | $364,000 | $700,000 |
| Revenue to be recognized for the year (revenue to date − revenue previously recognized) | $140,000 | $224,000 | $336,000 |
| Construction cost (expense) incurred for the year | (100,000) | (186,000) | (314,000) |
| Gross profit to be recognized | $ 40,000 | $ 38,000 | $ 22,000 |

$100,000 (20% × $500,000)[6] and the gross profit is $40,000. Note that the contract is 20% complete, and the company has recognized 20% of the $200,000 projected gross profit.

In 1995, the same procedure is followed. The costs incurred *to date* are $286,000 (the sum of the costs incurred in 1994 and 1995). Since estimated costs to complete the project are $264,000, the contract is 52% complete. Therefore the revenue to be recognized *to date* is $364,000 (52% × $700,000), and the revenue recognized for *the year* is $224,000 (the revenue to date of $364,000 less the revenue previously recognized of $140,000). Since total estimated construction costs are $550,000, the construction expense recognized for 1995 is $186,000 [(52% × $550,000) − $100,000], and there is a gross profit of $38,000. Note that the contract is 52% complete, the total profit expected on the contract is now $150,000 ($700,000 − $550,000), and therefore the total profit recognized to date is $78,000 (52% × $150,000). This is consistent with the $40,000 and $38,000 gross profit recognized in the 2 years.

In 1996, the contract is completed at a total cost of $600,000. The revenue for *the year* is $336,000, which is the total revenue of $700,000 less the revenue *to date* of $364,000. Since construction costs for *the year* are $314,000, the gross profit for the year is $22,000. Note that the total gross profit for the 3 years is $100,000 ($40,000 + $38,000 + $22,000), which is consistent with the total revenue less the total actual costs ($700,000 − $600,000).

---

6. Under the cost-to-cost method, construction expenses recognized for the year are equal to the construction costs incurred during the year (unless a loss is expected on the contract, as discussed later), so that the construction expense computations may be simplified as shown in Exhibit 16-4. If this method is not used, construction expenses recognized in a given year may differ from the actual yearly construction costs incurred.

### Computations for the Completed-Contract Method

Under the completed-contract method, no gross profit is recognized until the contract is complete. In the case of the Calder Company, the entire gross profit on the contract is recognized at the end of 1996. The total construction costs incurred over the three years (and recorded in Construction in Progress) are $600,000 ($100,000 + $186,000 + $314,000). The revenue recognized is the total contract price of $700,000, and therefore a gross profit of $100,000 ($700,000 − $600,000) is recognized in 1996.

### Journal Entries for the Two Methods

The journal entries to record the activities of the Calder Company for both the percentage-of-completion and the completed-contract methods are shown in Exhibit 16-5. Under both methods, in 1994 through 1996 the construction costs (from Exhibit 16-3) are debited to the inventory account Construction in Progress. The accompanying credits are to various accounts such as Accounts Payable, Raw Materials Inventory, Cash, Prepaid Expenses, Accumulated Depreciation, etc. The billings to the customer are debited to Accounts Receivable and credited to Partial Billings, which is a contra account to Construction in Progress. The collection of cash from the customer is recorded in the normal manner. Under the percentage-of-completion method, the gross profit (calculated in Exhibit 16-4) is recognized each year by a journal entry to a revenue and an expense account. The difference between these two amounts, the gross profit, is debited to Construction in Progress, thereby raising the asset value from cost to net realizable value and eventually to the contract selling price. The increase in stockholders' equity (the gross profit) has been accompanied by a corresponding increase in an asset value. Under the completed-contract method, no profit is recognized in 1994 or 1995, so no journal entry is required.

In 1996 when the contract is completed, closing entries for the contract are required. Under the percentage-of-completion method, Partial Billings is closed against Construction in Progress. Note that both accounts include the selling price. Under the completed-contract method, the total gross profit on the contract is recognized at the completion date. This is accomplished by closing Partial Billings against Construction Revenue because both accounts include the selling price, and Construction in Progress against Construction Expense because both accounts include the cost. At the end of the period, the revenue and expense accounts are closed to Income Summary.

The Calder Company reports its activities for this contract under each method, as shown in Exhibit 16-6. To complete the income statement under each method, the company's operating expenses are deducted from the gross profit to determine income. On the balance sheet under each method, Partial Billings is offset against Construction in Progress. At the end of 1994, Construction in Progress exceeds Partial Billings, so the net amount is reported as an inventory in the current asset section of the balance sheet. At the end of 1995, Partial Billings exceeds Construction in Progress, so the net amount is shown as a current liability in the balance sheet. Note that the difference in the book values under the two methods is equal to the gross profit to date on the contract. Thus, at December 31, 1994, the book value under the percentage-of-completion method is $60,000 and under the completed-contract method is $20,000; the difference of $40,000 is the gross profit for 1994 (which is recognized under the percentage-of-completion but not under the completed-contract method).

## EXHIBIT 16-5

### CALDER COMPANY

Journal Entries to Record Dam Construction for the Percentage-of-Completion and Completed-Contract Methods

| | Percentage-of-Completion | | Completed-Contract | |
|---|---|---|---|---|
| **1994** | | | | |
| 1. *To record construction costs:* | | | | |
| Construction in Progress | 100,000 | | 100,000 | |
| Accounts Payable, Raw Materials Inventory, Cash, etc. | | 100,000 | | 100,000 |
| 2. *To record partial billings:* | | | | |
| Accounts Receivable | 80,000 | | 80,000 | |
| Partial Billings | | 80,000 | | 80,000 |
| 3. *To record collections:* | | | | |
| Cash | 50,000 | | 50,000 | |
| Accounts Receivable | | 50,000 | | 50,000 |
| 4. *To record gross profit:* | | | | |
| Construction Expense | 100,000 | | No Entry | |
| Construction in Progress | 40,000 | | | |
| Construction Revenue | | 140,000 | | |
| **1995** | | | | |
| 1. *To record construction costs:* | | | | |
| Construction in Progress | 186,000 | | 186,000 | |
| Accounts Payable, Raw Materials Inventory, Cash, etc. | | 186,000 | | 186,000 |
| 2. *To record partial billings:* | | | | |
| Accounts Receivable | 350,000 | | 350,000 | |
| Partial Billings | | 350,000 | | 350,000 |
| 3. *To record collections:* | | | | |
| Cash | 330,000 | | 330,000 | |
| Accounts Receivable | | 330,000 | | 330,000 |
| 4. *To record gross profit:* | | | | |
| Construction Expense | 186,000 | | No Entry | |
| Construction in Progress | 38,000 | | | |
| Construction Revenue | | 224,000 | | |
| **1996** | | | | |
| 1. *To record construction costs:* | | | | |
| Construction in Progress | 314,000 | | 314,000 | |
| Accounts Payable, Raw Materials Inventory, Cash, etc. | | 314,000 | | 314,000 |
| 2. *To record partial billings:* | | | | |
| Accounts Receivable | 270,000 | | 270,000 | |
| Partial Billings | | 270,000 | | 270,000 |
| 3. *To record collections:* | | | | |
| Cash | 320,000 | | 320,000 | |
| Accounts Receivable | | 320,000 | | 320,000 |
| 4. *To record gross profit and to close out Construction in Progress and Partial Billings:* | | | | |
| Construction Expense | 314,000 | | No Entry | |
| Construction in Progress | 22,000 | | | |
| Construction Revenue | | 336,000 | | |
| Partial Billings | 700,000 | | No Entry | |
| Construction in Progress | | 700,000 | | |
| Partial Billings | No Entry | | 700,000 | |
| Construction Revenue | | | | 700,000 |
| Construction Expense | No Entry | | 600,000 | |
| Construction in Progress | | | | 600,000 |

## EXHIBIT 16-6

## CALDER COMPANY

Financial Statement Reporting

| (a) Percentage-of-Completion Method | 1994 | 1995 | 1996 |
|---|---|---|---|
| Income Statement (partial): | | | |
| Construction revenue | $140,000 | $224,000 | $336,000 |
| Construction expense | (100,000) | (186,000) | (314,000) |
| Gross profit | $ 40,000 | $ 38,000 | $ 22,000 |
| Balance Sheet (partial; end of year): | | | |
| Current Assets: | | | |
| Accounts receivable | $ 30,000 | $ 50,000 | |
| Inventories | | | |
| Construction in progress | 140,000 | | |
| Less: Partial billings | (80,000) | | |
| Costs and recognized profit not yet billed | $ 60,000 | | |
| Current Liabilities: | | | |
| Partial billings | | $430,000 | |
| Less: Construction in progress | | (364,000) | |
| Billings in excess of costs and recognized profit | | $ 66,000 | |

Notes to Financial Statements: Summary of Significant Accounting Policies (in part). The Company reports profits from long-term construction contracts in progress using the percentage-of-completion method of accounting. Profits are accrued based on the ratio of cost incurred to total estimated costs. Costs include direct material, direct labor, and job-related overhead. General and administrative expenses are charged to operations as incurred and are not allocated to contract costs.

| (b) Completed-Contract Method | 1994 | 1995 | 1996 |
|---|---|---|---|
| Income Statement (partial): | | | |
| Construction revenue | — | — | $700,000 |
| Construction expense | — | — | (600,000) |
| Gross profit | | | $100,000 |
| Balance Sheet (partial; end of year): | | | |
| Current Assets: | | | |
| Accounts receivable | $ 30,000 | $ 50,000 | |
| Inventories | | | |
| Construction in progress | 100,000 | | |
| Less: Partial billings | (80,000) | | |
| Excess of costs over related billings | $ 20,000 | | |
| Current Liabilities: | | | |
| Partial billings | | $430,000 | |
| Less: Construction in progress | | (286,000) | |
| Excess of billings over related costs | | $144,000 | |

Notes to Financial Statements: Summary of Significant Accounting Policies (in part). The Company reports profit from long-term construction contracts using the completed-contract method of accounting. Under this method, billings and costs are accumulated during the period of construction, but no profits are recorded before the contract is either completed or substantially completed. A contract is considered substantially completed if the costs to complete are not significant in amount. Costs include direct labor, direct materials, and job-related overhead. General and administrative expenses are charged to operations as incurred and are not allocated to contract costs.

## Losses on Long-Term Construction Contracts

When the estimate of future costs indicates that a loss is expected, both *ARB No. 45* and *SOP 81-1* require that the total estimated loss on the entire contract be recognized under both the percentage-of-completion and the completed-contract methods. This procedure is consistent with the *conservatism* convention of anticipating all foreseeable losses.

A loss can be of two types. First, the estimate of future costs may indicate that there is a **loss in the current period,** but that there will still be a profit on the total contract. Second, the estimate may indicate that an **overall loss on the contract** is expected.

### Loss in Current Period

As an illustration of the computation of a loss for a period under the percentage-of-completion method, suppose that in 1995 the Calder Company estimates that the costs to complete are $364,000 *instead of* $264,000. Assuming that the data for 1994 are the same as in Exhibit 16-3, an $18,000 loss is recognized in 1995, which is calculated as follows:

|  | 1995 |
|---|---|
| Construction costs incurred to date | $286,000 |
| Estimated costs to complete | 364,000 |
| Total estimated costs | $650,000 |
| Percent complete ($286,000 ÷ $650,000) | 44% |
| Revenue to date (44% × $700,000) | $308,000 |
| Revenue to be recognized for year ($308,000 − $140,000) | $168,000 |
| Construction costs incurred for year | (186,000) |
| Loss to be recognized | $(18,000) |

If the costs in 1996 are $364,000 as expected, the Calder Company recognizes the remaining 56% of the revenue, or $392,000. Therefore the company reports a gross profit of $28,000 in 1996, with a total profit over the 3 years of the contract of $50,000 ($40,000 − $18,000 + $28,000). This is equal to the total revenue of $700,000 less the total cost of $650,000. No adjustment is needed in 1995 under the completed-contract method, because an overall profit on the contract is expected.

### Overall Loss on Contract

A more complicated situation arises if the estimated total costs exceed the contract price, so that an overall loss on the contract is anticipated. To illustrate this situation for the percentage-of-completion method, suppose that at the end of 1995 the estimated costs to complete are $429,000. Therefore total costs are expected to be $715,000 ($286,000 + $429,000), indicating an overall loss of $15,000 by the end of the contract. Therefore, the gross profit to date has to be removed and the loss of $15,000 recognized in 1995. The revenue for 1995 is recognized in the normal way, as shown in Exhibit 16-7. The project is 40% complete ($286,000 ÷ $715,000) and therefore the revenue to date is $280,000 (40% × $700,000). The revenue recognized in 1995 is $140,000 ($280,000 − $140,000). The total expense recognized includes two components: (1) the amount needed to create a cumulative profit of zero and (2) the amount of the overall loss recognized. Since the revenue to date is $280,000 and the expense recognized in 1994 was $100,000, an expense of $180,000 is recognized in 1995 to make the cumulative profit equal to zero.[7] In addition, the overall loss of $15,000 is recognized so the total expense for 1995 is $195,000. The journal entry to record the revenue and expense is as follows:

| | | |
|---|---|---|
| Construction Expense | 195,000 | |
|     Construction in Progress | | 40,000 |
|     Construction Revenue | | 140,000 |
|     Provision for Loss on Contract | | 15,000 |

---

**EXHIBIT 16-7**

### CALDER COMPANY

Calculation of Revenues and Expenses When
There Is an Expected Loss on the Contract

| | Current Year | Total to Date |
|---|---|---|
| **1994** | | |
| Construction revenue | $140,000[a] | $140,000 |
| Construction expense | (100,000)[b] | (100,000) |
| Gross profit | $ 40,000 | $ 40,000 |
| | | |
| **1995** | | |
| Construction revenue | $140,000 | $280,000 |
| Construction expense | (195,000)[d] | (295,000)[c] |
| Gross profit | $(55,000) | $(15,000) |
| | | |
| **1996** | | |
| Construction revenue | $420,000 | $700,000 |
| Construction expense | (420,000) | (715,000) |
| Gross profit | $    0 | $(15,000) |

---

a. (20% × $700,000)
b. (20% × $500,000)

c.
| | |
|---|---|
| Contract price | $700,000 |
| Percent complete | 40% |
| Cost of earned revenue before loss provision | $280,000 |
| Estimated total loss | 15,000 |
| Construction expense to date | $295,000 |

d.
| | |
|---|---|
| Cumulative construction expense | $295,000 |
| Less: Construction expense in previous year | (100,000) |
| Current construction expense | $195,000 |

---

7. "Accounting for Performance of Construction-Type and Certain Production-Type Contracts," *op. cit.*, par. 88, requires that the amount of the loss be added to the contract cost unless the amount is material, unusual, or infrequent, in which case the amount is reported separately.

The credit to the Construction in Progress account removes the increase in value resulting from the gross profit recognized in 1994, and therefore the account includes only the costs incurred on the project to date. The provision for the loss is a contra-account to Construction in Progress (less Partial Billings), or it may be recorded as a liability.

If costs in 1996 are $429,000 as projected, the company recognizes a zero gross profit in 1996. The revenue recognized is the remaining amount of $420,000 ($700,000 − $140,000 − $140,000) left to be recognized on the contract, and the expense is also $420,000. Thus the total loss incurred on the contract has been recognized in the year in which it was first estimated (1995).

The costs incurred on the contract in 1996 are debited to the Construction in Progress account in the normal way up to a total of $700,000 ($414,000 in 1996). The balance in the account should not exceed the contract price, since the asset value cannot be greater than the total proceeds to be received on the contract. The additional costs incurred over $700,000 are debited to the Provision for Loss on Contract account. Since the total costs incurred are $715,000, the excess of $15,000 eliminates the balance established in the account at the end of 1995.

The calculations just discussed are summarized in Exhibit 16-7. The journal entries in 1996 to record the construction costs and the revenue and expense are as follows:

| | | |
|---|---|---|
| Construction in Progress | 414,000 | |
| Provision for Loss on Contract | 15,000 | |
|     Cash, Accounts Payable, etc. | | 429,000 |
| | | |
| Construction Expense | 420,000 | |
|     Construction Revenue | | 420,000 |

Note that the amounts ($429,000 and $420,000) in these two journal entries are not equal. This difference occurs because the percentage complete each year is computed on the basis of different expected total costs. In 1994, the percentage complete of 20% is based on the expected total costs of $500,000, whereas in 1995, the 40% completion is based on the expected total cost of $715,000.

Under the completed-contract method, the loss in 1995 is recognized because there is an overall loss on the contract. This loss is recorded as follows:

| | | |
|---|---|---|
| Construction Expense | 15,000 | |
|     Provision for Loss on Contract | | 15,000 |

An expense account is debited to recognize the "loss" because it is assumed that the construction activity is *not* an incidental or peripheral activity. Revenue is not adjusted because the contract is not complete and the company is using the completed-contract method. Note also that there is no credit to the Construction in Progress account because under the completed-contract method no profit has been added to the account in previous years.

If the actual costs incurred in 1996 were less than or greater than the estimated amount, a gross profit or loss would be recognized. This procedure is consistent with accounting for a change in estimate under *APB Opinion No. 20*.

## Additional Considerations in Accounting for Long-Term Construction Contracts

Several additional factors that affect the accounting for long-term construction contracts are discussed in this section.

### Overhead Costs

Contract costs include all direct costs, such as materials and direct labor, and indirect costs (overhead) identifiable with or allocable to the contract. This is consistent with generally accepted accounting principles for inventory and production costs. Therefore general and administrative costs are usually expensed as incurred but may be accounted for as contract costs under the completed-contract method. Accounting for such costs theoretically provides a better matching of costs as expenses against revenues than would result from treating such costs as period expenses, particularly in years when no contracts were completed, and it is less likely to be misleading to users of financial statements.

### Operating Cycle

*Accounting Research Bulletin No. 45* requires that the net amounts of Construction in Progress and Partial Billings are included as current assets or current liabilities. The operating-cycle concept is used to justify this classification. When a contractor specializes in a certain type of project, the operating cycle is likely to be easy to discern, but when the business is diverse, a typical operating cycle may be difficult to identify and, therefore, the classification of the asset as current or noncurrent may become somewhat unreliable.

### Offsetting Amounts

It is a basic principle of accounting that the offsetting, or netting, of assets and liabilities is not acceptable, except when a right of offset exists. However, *Accounting Research Bulletin No. 45* does allow offsetting when contracts are closely related—for example, when separate contracts are parts of the same project. Therefore in these circumstances a contract that has a net liability (Partial Billings exceeds Construction in Progress) may be offset against one that has a net asset balance. The decision as to whether offsetting is appropriate in any situation should be based on economic substance rather than legal form. For example, if separate legal contracts are economically one contract, then the right to offset exists in spite of the legal form of the separate contracts.

### Capitalized Interest

*The capitalization of interest is discussed in Chapter 8.*

When a company constructs an asset, it is required to include in the cost of the asset the interest cost associated with the funds used in the construction. Thus, if interest costs are incurred that are related to a long-term construction contract, these costs are included in the Construction in Progress account rather than as interest expense.

### Disclosure

Disclosure of the method used to account for long-term construction contracts is illustrated in Exhibit 16-6. Note that disclosure of the use of an "accrual basis" is not sufficient because both the percentage-of-completion and the completed-contract methods are accrual methods. The SEC requires additional long-term contract disclosures for financial statements filed with it. The overall effect is to require more detailed disclosure of accounts receivable and inventory components and the accounting policies and assumptions on which the amounts are based.

## Long-Term Service Contracts

The percentage-of-completion method is used when a company has a long-term contract for the construction and sale of a *product.* Other companies are in the business of providing a *service* instead of a product. **APB Statement No. 4** indicated that revenues from services rendered are recognized when these services have been performed and are billable.[8] Many service transactions involve a single service "act." In these cases, revenues (and expenses) are recognized under the accrual method of accounting in the period when the service is performed. Some companies, however, have long-term contracts in which they agree to provide a service over an extended period. Generally, at the inception of the agreement, a service contract is signed at an agreed-on price and the seller agrees to perform certain service "acts" at a later date. The service contract may require performance of (a) a specified number of similar acts, (b) a specified number of defined but not similar acts, or (c) an unspecified number of similar acts. In these cases, revenue should be based on performance, but when has the "performance" been completed and how should revenue be recognized? This is a difficult question to answer because long-term service contracts can be complex, sometimes service contracts are sold in conjunction with products, and performance activities can vary depending on the service industry involved.

There are many service companies in numerous service industries—to name a few, advertising agencies, cable television companies, computer service firms, and companies engaged in research and development for the government. The accounting principles in these industries are sometimes underdeveloped and at other times very specialized. In 1978, an *FASB Invitation to Comment* entitled "Accounting for Certain Service Transactions" was issued as a prelude to the FASB's deliberations on setting general accounting standards of revenue (and expense) recognition for service transactions. The FASB has not completed these deliberations because it decided to focus first on more conceptual revenue and expense recognition issues. However, the content of this *FASB Invitation to Comment* does provide a good overview of revenue and expense recognition for long-term service contracts and forms the basis for the following general discussion.[9]

## Proportional Performance Method

Revenue for service transactions is recognized on the basis of performance because performance determines the extent to which the earnings process is complete. **When a long-term service contract requires services to be performed in more than one act, revenue is recognized by the proportional performance method—that is, based on the proportionate performance of each act.** In this regard, revenue recognition depends on the type and number of service acts as follows:

1. *Specified number of similar acts.* Recognize an equal amount of revenue for each act.

2. *Specified number of defined but not similar acts.* Recognize revenue for each act based on the ratio of the direct costs (defined next) incurred to perform each act to the total estimated direct costs for the long-term contract.

3. *Unspecified number of similar acts.* Recognize revenue on a straight-line method over the performance period.

Several types of service costs are involved in a long-term service contract. These include (a) **initial direct costs**, those costs that are directly associated with negotiating and signing a service contract (e.g., legal fees); (b) **direct costs**, those costs that

---

8. "Basic Concepts and Accounting Principles Underlying Financial Statements of Business Enterprises," *APB Statement No. 4* (New York: AICPA, 1970), par. 151.

9. The following discussion summarizes par. 10–19 of "Accounting for Certain Service Transactions," *FASB Invitation to Comment* (Stamford, Conn.: FASB, 1978), par. 5.

have a clear causal relationship to the services performed (e.g., labor costs); and (c) **indirect costs**, those costs other than initial direct costs and direct costs (e.g., advertising and depreciation). Under the proportional performance method, these costs are recognized as expenses as follows:

1. *Initial direct costs.* Defer and allocate over the performance period in proportion to the recognition of service revenues, because initial direct costs are expensed when revenue is recognized.

2. *Direct costs.* Expense as incurred, because there is a close relationship between the direct costs incurred and the extent of performance achieved.

3. *Indirect costs.* Expense as incurred, because indirect costs provide no discernible future benefits.

To illustrate revenue recognition under the proportional performance method, assume the Health Spa Company sells memberships to use its facilities. For $500 in advance, a person signs a two-year contract which allows use of area X (exercise room) 50 times and area Y (whirlpool and sauna) 100 times during the two-year period. At the beginning of 1995, 120 people sign the service contract and the company collects $60,000 (120 × $500). Thus, the company is obligated to perform a total of 6,000 (120 × 50) and 12,000 (120 × 100) service acts in 1995 and 1996 involving areas X and Y, respectively. This service contract involves a specified number of defined but not similar acts so revenue is recognized based on a ratio of direct costs per act to total estimated direct costs.

During 1995, members used area X 3,600 times and area Y 4,800 times. In 1996, members used area X 2,400 times and area Y 7,200 times.[10] The following is a summary of the relevant cost information regarding the 120 membership contracts:

| | |
|---|---|
| Initial direct costs | $ 1,000 |
| Annual indirect costs | 2,000 |
| Estimated (and actual) total direct costs (for two-year period) | 24,000 |
| Direct cost per service act: | |
| Area X | $1.00   3600 |
| Area Y | 1.50   7200 |

The condensed income statements of the Health Spa Company for 1995 and 1996 are shown in Exhibit 16-8. The direct costs incurred in 1995 and 1996 are $10,800 and $13,200, or 45% and 55% of the total estimated (and actual) direct costs. Thus, revenues of $27,000 (45% × $60,000) and $33,000 (55% × $60,000) are recognized in each year. The $1,000 initial direct costs are allocated $450 to 1995 and $550 to 1996 based upon the 45% and 55% recognition of revenues. Use of the proportional performance method is appropriate in this case because it recognizes revenues neither too early (at the time of the signing) before the earning process is complete nor too late (at the completion of the contract) and, therefore, the method helps to ensure that economic reality is not distorted.

---

10. In this example, all members used the health spa facilities their entire allotted number of times. In reality this usage would probably not occur. In such a situation, estimates would have to be made of the expected usage and adjustments made for the differences between actual and estimated usage. This topic is beyond the scope of this chapter. Also, in this example, it is assumed for simplicity that no new memberships are sold in 1996.

**EXHIBIT 16-8**

## HEALTH SPA COMPANY

Condensed Income Statements (Proportional Performance Method)

| | For Year Ended December 31 | | | |
|---|---|---|---|---|
| | **1995** | | **1996** | |
| Revenues | | $27,000[b] | | $33,000[e] |
| Expenses: | | | | |
|   Initial direct costs | $ 450[c] | | $ 550[f] | |
|   Direct costs | 10,800[a] | | $13,200[d] | |
|   Indirect costs | 2,000 | | 2,000 | |
|     Total expenses | | (13,250) | | (15,750) |
| Net Income | | $13,750 | | $17,250 |

a. $(\$1 \times 3,600) + (\$1.50 \times 4,800) = \$10,800$

b. $\dfrac{(\$1 \times 3,600) + (\$1.50 \times 4,800)}{\$24,000 \text{ total direct costs}} = 45\%; \$60,000 \text{ receipts} \times 45\% = \$27,000$

c. $45\% \times \$1,000 = \$450$

d. $(\$1 \times 2,400) + (\$1.50 \times 7,200) = \$13,200$

e. $\dfrac{(\$1 \times 2,400) + (\$1.50 \times 7,200)}{\$24,000} = 55\%; \$60,000 \text{ receipts} \times 55\% = \$33,000$

f. $55\% \times \$1,000 = \$550$

## REVENUE RECOGNITION AFTER THE PERIOD OF SALE

As discussed earlier in the chapter, the installment and cost recovery methods are the two principal ways of recognizing revenue after the sale. Each method is discussed in this section.

### Installment Method

Retail companies have engaged in installment sales for many years. Installment sales involve a financing agreement whereby the customer signs a contract, makes a small down payment, and agrees to make periodic payments for the merchandise over an extended period, often several years. Installment sales are common for such items as large appliances, furniture, and cars. Typically, the customer accepts possession of the merchandise when the contract is signed (thereby enjoying its use during the payment period), while the seller retains legal title to the merchandise until the payments are complete. Before the establishment of "credit bureaus" and improved techniques for establishing, evaluating, and maintaining records of individuals' "credit ratings," installment sales contracts were often used because the collection of the installment payments was highly uncertain. Today, installment sales contracts may still be used because of a customer's lower credit rating.

In the past, revenue was not recognized at the time of an installment sale. Instead, by use of the installment method, revenue (and the cost of goods sold for the merchandise) was deferred for recognition until a later date. Due, in part, to improved credit procedures (whereby most of the credit effort is now completed in the earning process *before* the sale) that increase the likelihood of collection, **APB Opinion No. 10** found the installment method of recognizing revenue generally to be unacceptable. The Board, however, did recognize that there are *exceptional* cases where

receivables are collected over an extended period and the probability of collection is not reasonably assured. In these exceptional cases, the installment method is used.[11] In addition, the installment method is still acceptable for income tax purposes under certain circumstances.

It is important to distinguish between an "installment sale" as a legal contract involving a buyer and a seller, and the "installment method" of revenue recognition. For example, on an installment *sale,* a company may recognize revenue in full at the time of the sale if collectibility is not an issue. In such a case, care must be taken to estimate the costs to be incurred in the future, such as costs of collection and bad debts, so that appropriate matching occurs. Alternatively, a company may use the installment *method* of revenue recognition for a sales transaction that is *not* an installment *sale.* In summary, the installment method of revenue recognition is selected because the collectibility of the receivable from the sale is not reasonably assured, and this decision is independent of the legal form of the contract. Therefore, we discuss the installment method of revenue recognition in this chapter irrespective of the legal form of the contract.

The steps involved in the installment method are as follows:

1.  Total sales, cost of goods sold, and collections are recorded in the normal manner during the year.

2.  At the end of the year, sales for which the installment method is to be used are identified. The revenue and the related cost of goods sold that had been recorded during the year are "reversed," and the deferred gross profit is recognized.

3.  At the end of the year, the gross profit rate on the sales recognized under the installment method for that year is computed. The rate is calculated by dividing the deferred gross profit recognized in step 2 by these installment sales for the year.

4.  A portion of the deferred gross profit is recognized as gross profit for the year by multiplying the cash collected on the sales recognized under the installment method during the year times the gross profit rate calculated in step 3.

5.  In future years, the remaining deferred gross profit is reduced and the gross profit is recognized based on the cash collected during each year from the previous sales recognized under the installment method times the gross profit rate for the year in which those sales were made.

## Example of the Installment Method

To illustrate the installment method, consider the following information for the Lee Company in the first two years of its operations:

|  | 1995 | 1996 |
| --- | --- | --- |
| Total credit sales | $500,000 | $600,000 |
| Total cost of goods sold | 390,000 | 430,000 |
| Installment method sales* | 100,000 | 150,000 |
| Installment method cost of goods sold* | 75,000 | 105,000 |
| Gross profit rate on installment method sales | 25% | 30% |
| Cash receipts on installment method sales |  |  |
| 1995 sales | 20,000 | 30,000 |
| 1996 sales |  | 40,000 |
| Cash receipts on other credit sales | 300,000 | 480,000 |

* Included in total credit sales and total cost of goods sold, respectively.

11. "Omnibus Opinion—1966," *op. cit.,* par. 12 and fn. 8.

Assume that the company uses the perpetual inventory method and that, for simplicity, interest on the installment receivables is ignored. The Lee Company records the preceding events with the following journal entries:

**During 1995**

| | | |
|---|---|---|
| Accounts Receivable | 500,000 | |
| Sales | | 500,000 |
| Cost of Goods Sold | 390,000 | |
| Inventory | | 390,000 |

The total sales and cost of goods sold for the year are recorded in the normal manner. No differentiation is made for the sales recognized under the installment method.

**During 1995**

| | | |
|---|---|---|
| Cash | 320,000 | |
| Accounts Receivable | | 320,000 |

Cash collections are recognized in the normal manner. Of these collections, $20,000 is for installment sales and $300,000 for other credit sales.

**December 31, 1995**

| | | |
|---|---|---|
| Sales | 100,000 | |
| Cost of Goods Sold | | 75,000 |
| Deferred Gross Profit, 1995 | | 25,000 |

The sales recognized under the installment method and the related cost of goods sold are identified from the accounting records and "reversed," and the deferred gross profit is recognized. The gross profit rate for 1995 is computed to be 25% by dividing the deferred gross profit of $25,000 by the sales of $100,000.

**December 31, 1995**

| | | |
|---|---|---|
| Deferred Gross Profit, 1995 | 5,000 | |
| Gross Profit Realized on Installment Method Sales | | 5,000 |

The gross profit rate of 25% is used to recognize the gross profit on the cash collected. Since the company collected $20,000 on these sales for 1995, deferred gross profit is reduced and a gross profit of $5,000 ($20,000 × 25%) is recognized. The gross profit account is closed to income summary along with the other sales, cost of goods sold, and expense accounts (not illustrated). The company reports the preceding events in its financial statements as shown in Exhibit 16-9.

Three aspects of the financial statements should be understood. First, in the income statement, the gross profit on the sales recognized under the installment method is shown separately from the gross profit on the other sales. Some companies, however, might combine the two amounts and disclose the gross profit on these sales in the notes to the financial statements. Second, installment accounts receivable are usually included in current assets on the balance sheet under the operating cycle concept.

**EXHIBIT 16-9**

**LEE COMPANY**

**Partial Income Statement**
**For Year Ended December 31, 1995**

| | |
|---|---:|
| Sales | $400,000[a] |
| Cost of goods sold | (315,000)[b] |
| Gross profit | $ 85,000 |
| Gross profit realized on installment method sales | 5,000 |
| Total gross profit | $ 90,000 |

**Partial Balance Sheet**
**December 31, 1995**

| Current Assets | | |
|---|---:|---:|
| Accounts receivable | | $100,000[c] |
| Installment accounts receivable | $ 80,000[d] | |
| Less: Deferred gross profit | (20,000)[e] | 60,000 |

a. $500,000 − $100,000.
b. $390,000 − $75,000.
c. $500,000 − $320,000 − $80,000 (from footnote *d*).
d. $100,000 − $20,000.
e. $25,000 − $5,000.

Finally, note that the deferred gross profit is deducted from the installment accounts receivable on the balance sheet. Some companies, however, include the deferred gross profit as a current liability rather than as a contra asset. Such reporting is inconsistent with the concept of a liability because no future cash outflow will occur. The authors advocate the presentation as a contra asset because, as discussed earlier in the chapter, the accounts receivable is reduced from selling price to cost.

In 1996, the Lee Company records the following journal entries:

**During 1996**

| | | |
|---|---:|---:|
| Accounts Receivable | 600,000 | |
|    Sales | | 600,000 |
| Cost of Goods Sold | 430,000 | |
|    Inventory | | 430,000 |
| Cash | 550,000 | |
|    Accounts Receivable | | 550,000 |

Of these collections, $70,000 is for installment sales and $480,000 for other credit sales. Note that the cash collections on the installment sales in 1996 include amounts from sales made in 1995 ($30,000) and 1996 ($40,000).

**December 31, 1996**

| | | |
|---|---:|---:|
| Sales | 150,000 | |
|    Cost of Goods Sold | | 105,000 |
|    Deferred Gross Profit, 1996 | | 45,000 |

The sales recognized under the installment method and the related cost of goods sold for 1996 are "reversed" and the deferred gross profit for 1996 is recognized. The gross profit rate in 1996 is 30% ($45,000 ÷ $150,000).

### December 31, 1996

| | | |
|---|---|---|
| Deferred Gross Profit, 1995 | 7,500 | |
| Deferred Gross Profit, 1996 | 12,000 | |
|    Gross Profit Realized on Installment Method Sales | | 19,500 |

During 1996, the company collected $30,000 on its 1995 installment method sales for which its gross profit is 25%. Therefore, the company reduces the deferred gross profit from 1995 and recognizes a gross profit of $7,500 ($30,000 × 25%). The company also collected $40,000 on its 1996 installment method sales for which its gross profit is 30%. Therefore, the company reduces the deferred gross profit for 1996 and recognizes a gross profit of $12,000 ($40,000 × 30%) on those collections. The combined gross profit for 1996 is $19,500, which is closed to Income Summary.

The Lee Company includes the realized gross profit of $19,500 in its 1996 income statement in addition to the sales and the cost of goods sold from those sales on which revenue is recognized at the time of sale. The installment accounts receivable of $160,000 ($100,000 − $20,000 + $150,000 − $30,000 − $40,000) and a deferred gross profit of $45,500 ($25,000 − $5,000 + $45,000 − $7,500 − $12,000) are included on its December 31, 1996 balance sheet.

## Additional Considerations for the Installment Method

Several additional factors that affect the accounting under the installment method are discussed in this section.

### Alternative Accounting and Reporting

In the preceding example, it has been assumed that it is acceptable to report only the gross profit amount in the income statement because the installment sales are not material. If the installment sales were considered to be material, then it would be necessary to report both the installment sales and cost of goods sold separately (a procedure that was used in the discussion of long-term construction contracts earlier in the chapter). In this situation, the Lee Company would prepare an alternative journal entry as follows (using the amounts for 1995):

| | | |
|---|---|---|
| Deferred Gross Profit, 1995 | 5,000 | |
| Installment Cost of Goods Sold | 15,000 | |
|    Installment Sales | | 20,000 |

Under this alternative, when cash is received the deferred gross profit is reduced as before. However, an amount equal to the cash collected is recorded as the sales revenue and an appropriate amount of cost of goods sold is recognized; in this case, 75% of the sales amount. Then the company would disclose the installment sales of $20,000 and deduct the installment cost of goods sold of $15,000 to report its gross profit of $5,000 for 1995.

### Operating Expenses

As we have seen, the cost of goods sold is matched against the installment sales and recognized in the same period as the sales. Operating expenses are *not* deferred and recognized in the same manner. Instead, they are recognized in the normal way on an accrual basis. That is, they are either recognized in the period incurred, such as general and administrative salaries, or by systematic and rational allocation, such as depreciation on an office building.

### Interest Charges

The company making an installment sale typically charges the buyer interest because of the extended collection period. The interest charge is usually included as a component of the periodic payment specified in the sales contract. The normal practice is to make the payment an equal amount each period so that each succeeding payment includes a lower interest component and a larger principal payment. In other words, the interest is treated in the same way as a loan.

When interest is included in an installment sale, the interest revenue is accounted for separately. Each payment received is separated into interest revenue and a reduction in the installment accounts receivable. Also, the interest revenue is recorded on an accrual basis in the normal manner (the period earned), whereas the gross profit is recognized as cash is received, as discussed earlier.

### Uncollectible Accounts

Installment sales contracts usually provide for repossession of the item if the buyer defaults. If the experience of the company indicates that the price at which the repossessed merchandise can be sold is usually sufficient to cover the remaining payments on the original installment sale, then a provision for bad debts is not necessary. However, if past experience indicates that the expected resale price is usually insufficient to cover the payments, the recognition of bad debt expense and an allowance for doubtful installment accounts receivable is appropriate.

### Defaults and Repossessions

When merchandise is repossessed, the inventory is recorded and the related receivable and deferred gross profit written off. To illustrate, assume that the Lee Company repossesses an item it sold in 1995 with a gross profit of 25%, and the fair market value of the repossessed item is $600. If $1,000 remained unpaid, the repossession is recorded as follows:

| | | |
|---|---|---|
| Repossessed Inventory | 600 | |
| Deferred Gross Profit | 250 | |
| Allowance for Doubtful Installment Accounts Receivable | 150 | |
| Accounts Receivable | | 1,000 |

The deferred gross profit ($1,000 × 25%) related to the remaining cash payments is eliminated and the $150 "lost" on the recovery is debited to the Allowance for Doubtful Installment Accounts Receivable, which was established when the bad debt expense was recognized.

## Cost Recovery Method

If a company makes a sale in which there is a very high degree of uncertainty about the collectibility of the sales price, it is appropriate to defer the recognition of any profit until the cost of the entire sale has been recovered. As with the installment method, **APB Opinion No. 10** found the **cost recovery method** of recognizing revenue generally to be unacceptable. The Board, however, did recognize that there are exceptional cases where receivables are collected over an extended period and where the terms of the transaction provide no reasonable basis for estimating the degree of collectibility. In such exceptional situations, the cost recovery method may be used. For example, a company may sell a distressed division, thereby transferring the risks and benefits of ownership, but agree that the purchaser will pay with the net operating cash inflows generated by the division.

Under the cost recovery method, sales, cost of goods sold, and collections are recorded during the year in the usual manner (as with the installment method). In contrast to the installment method, however, no gross profit is recognized under the cost recovery method until all the cost of the item sold has been recovered. Once the cost has been recovered, gross profit is recorded at an amount equal to the cash received in the period. To illustrate the cost recovery method, consider the following information for the Patken Company:

| | |
|---|---|
| Sale of property under cost recovery method | $20,000 |
| Cost of property sold (net) | 12,000 |
| Cash collections | |
| 1995 | 5,000 |
| 1996 | 9,000 |
| 1997 | 6,000 |

It is assumed that the Patken Company has made no sales in previous periods for which it has used the cost recovery method. The company records the preceding events using the cost recovery method as follows:

**During 1995**

| | | |
|---|---|---|
| Accounts Receivable | 20,000 | |
| Deferred Gross Profit | | 8,000 |
| Property (net) | | 12,000 |
| Cash | 5,000 | |
| Accounts Receivable | | 5,000 |

The transaction is recorded and the profit is deferred. No gross profit is recognized when the cash is collected because the cost of the property sold of $12,000 has not yet been fully recovered.

**During 1996**

| | | |
|---|---|---|
| Cash | 9,000 | |
| Accounts Receivable | | 9,000 |

**December 31, 1996**

| | | |
|---|---|---|
| Deferred Gross Profit | 2,000 | |
| Gross Profit Realized on Cost Recovery Transactions | | 2,000 |

In 1995, $5,000 of the $12,000 cost of the property sold was recovered. Therefore, the first $7,000 collected in 1996 completes the recovery of the cost, and the remaining $2,000 collected results in the recognition of a gross profit of $2,000.

**During 1997**

| | | |
|---|---|---|
| Cash | 6,000 | |
| Accounts Receivable | | 6,000 |

**December 31, 1997**

| | | |
|---|---|---|
| Deferred Gross Profit | 6,000 | |
| Gross Profit Realized on Cost Recovery Transactions | | 6,000 |

Since the total cost was recovered in 1996, the $6,000 cash collected in 1997 results in an equal amount of gross profit being recognized. The Patken Company includes the gross profit in its income statement each year. The accounts receivable less the balance in the Deferred Gross Profit account is included on the company's balance sheet.

### Comparison of the Installment and Cost Recovery Methods

As discussed earlier, *APB Opinion No. 10* allows the use of either the installment or cost recovery methods in certain exceptional circumstances and makes no distinction between the situations in which each should be applied. If collectibility is not reasonably assured, revenue should *not* be recognized at the time of sale. Instead, the installment method should be used. (Also, income tax rules allow the installment method to be used in certain situations for the computation of taxable income.) Since the cost recovery method is a more conservative revenue recognition method, it should be used only when such conservatism is appropriate. For example, **if the collectibility is *extremely* uncertain or there is *no* reliable basis for estimating the collectibility, then the cost recovery method is appropriate.** In addition, the method may be used if there is significant uncertainty about the profitability of a new venture or product. It may also be used for certain real estate transactions, as discussed later in the chapter.

## REVENUE RECOGNITION DELAYED UNTIL A FUTURE EVENT OCCURS

In certain situations, **there may not be a sufficient transfer of the risks and benefits of ownership for a sale to be recognized.** For example, a company may "sell" a subsidiary and accept a long-term interest-bearing note receivable but maintain a continuing involvement in its management through representation on the board of directors, perhaps because the buyer made a very small down payment. In such situations, neither the receivable nor a deferred gross profit should be recognized. Instead, the deposit method is used.

### Deposit Method

To illustrate the deposit method, assume that the Oscar Company sells a subsidiary to the Pet Company and accepts a $500,000 down payment and a 10% note for the balance of the sale price of $7 million. The net assets (i.e., book value) of the subsidiary are $5 million and the deposit method is used because the Pet Company has the right to cancel the agreement for the next year. **The deposit method postpones the recognition of a sale until a determination can be made as to whether a sale has occurred for accounting purposes.** Until the sale can be recognized (by any of the revenue recognition methods), the Oscar Company does not record a note receivable, and continues to report the property and any related debt (even if assumed by the Pet Company) on its balance sheet. However, the assets and liabilities are separately classified under such headings as "assets of business transferred under contract" and "liabilities of business transferred." Furthermore, for depreciable assets, the Oscar Company continues to record depreciation expense on the property. The down payment and all payments of principal and interest received from Pet Company are recorded as a deposit and reported as a liability on the balance sheet if the interest will be returned should the terms of the contract not be fulfilled. For example, the Oscar Company records the receipt of the down payment as follows:

| | | |
|---|---|---|
| Cash | 500,000 | |
|     Deposit from Purchaser | | 500,000 |

When the liability for the deposit is eliminated because the circumstances have changed, the revenue is recognized. To illustrate, suppose that the Pet Company recognizes revenue 1 year after the original transaction. The note receivable and a gain are recorded, the net assets of the subsidiary and the deposit are eliminated, and the interest revenue is recognized by the Oscar Company as follows:

| | | |
|---|---|---|
| Interest Receivable (10% × $6,500,000) | 650,000 | |
| Note Receivable | 6,500,000 | |
| Deposit from Purchaser | 500,000 | |
|     Interest Revenue | | 650,000 |
|     Gain ($7,000,000 − $5,000,000) | | 2,000,000 |
|     Net Assets of Subsidiary | | 5,000,000 |

Alternatively, any interest that is *not* subject to refund is recognized as earned in the normal manner with only the principal portion of any payments being recorded as a deposit. If, instead, the contract is canceled without a refund, the deposits forfeited by Pet Company are recognized as income.

## ADDITIONAL REVENUE RECOGNITION ISSUES

In certain industries, consignment sales are used frequently and the recognition of revenue on such sales is an important issue. The specific accounting principles used for sales of franchises, real estate sales, and retail land sales are also important because of the significance of the industries and the relevance of their rules to a general understanding of revenue recognition. International accounting differences are also discussed in this section.

### Consignment Sales

In certain situations, a manufacturer or wholesaler transfers goods to a dealer for purposes of sale but retains the risks and benefits of ownership (as well as legal title). In these situations, the dealer is acting as an *agent* for the manufacturer or wholesaler in the sale of the goods to a third party. The transfer of goods is known as a **consignment.** In a consignment, the manufacturer or wholesaler is known as the **consignor** and the dealer as the **consignee.** The consignor is usually responsible for all costs associated with the goods and the consignee must exercise due care in storing and selling the goods. When the sale to the third party takes place, legal title passes directly to the third party from the consignor.

Accounting for consignments may be summarized as follows:

1. Since title remains with the consignor, when the goods are transferred from the consignor to the consignee, the consignor does *not* record the sale of inventory, and the consignee does *not* record the acquisition of inventory.

2. The consignor only recognizes revenue when the sale to the third party occurs because that is when the revenue is earned. The consignee must notify the consignor of the sale and must maintain detailed records of items held on consignment and various costs incurred.

3.  The consignee uses a **Consignment-in** account. The account is credited for the proceeds received from the sale of the consigned goods and is debited for costs that will be reimbursed by the consignor and for commissions earned by the consignee.

4.  The consignor uses a **Consignment-out** account, which is a special inventory account. When goods are shipped on consignment, the account is debited for the cost of the inventory shipped (and the normal inventory account is credited). In addition, any consignment costs (e.g., transportation charges) incurred by the consignor are debited to the account. On notification by the consignee, the account is credited for the costs incurred for the sale of consigned goods and these costs are debited to the respective expense accounts. Any balance in the Consignment-out account is reported as consignment inventory on the ending balance sheet of the consignor.

To illustrate the accounting by the *consignee*, consider the following sequence of events:

1.  To record the receipt of consigned goods:

    **A memorandum entry is prepared recording the name of the consignor and the quantity and type of the goods received.**

2.  To record advertising costs incurred of $100 to be reimbursed by the consignor:

    | | | |
    |---|---:|---:|
    | Consignment-in | 100 | |
    |     Cash | | 100 |

3.  To record the sale of consigned goods for $700:

    | | | |
    |---|---:|---:|
    | Cash | 700 | |
    |     Consignment-in | | 700 |

4.  To record the commission of $140 earned on the sales:

    | | | |
    |---|---:|---:|
    | Consignment-in | 140 | |
    |     Commissions Earned | | 140 |

5.  To record the payment of $460 ($700 − $100 − $140) to the consignor:

    | | | |
    |---|---:|---:|
    | Consignment-in | 460 | |
    |     Cash | | 460 |

Following these events, the Consignment-in account has a zero balance. If the account has a debit balance, the consignor has an obligation for that amount to the consignee; that is, it represents a receivable of the consignee. Generally, this receivable is entitled Consignment Receivable and is reported as a current asset on the consignee's balance sheet. Alternatively, if the account has a credit balance, the consignee has an obligation to the consignor; that is, it represents a liability of the consignee. Generally, this liability is entitled Consignment Obligation and is reported as a current liability on the consignee's balance sheet. The Commissions Earned account is reported as an operating revenue on the consignee's income statement.

To illustrate the accounting by the *consignor*, consider the same events as described previously for the consignee.

1.  To record the delivery of consigned goods costing $450, for which transportation charges of $60 are paid by the consignor:

    | | | |
    |---|---:|---:|
    | Consignment-out | 510 | |
    |     Inventory | | 450 |
    |     Cash | | 60 |

2.  To record the sale of consigned goods for $700, consignee's reimbursable costs of $100, consignee's commission of $140, and the receipt of $460 from the consignee:

| | | |
|---|---|---|
| **Cash** | 460 | |
| **Advertising Expense** | 100 | |
| **Sales Commissions Expense** | 140 | |
| Sales | | 700 |

3.  To record the costs of consigned goods sold:

| | | |
|---|---|---|
| **Cost of Goods Sold** | 450 | |
| **Delivery Expense** | 60 | |
| Consignment-out | | 510 |

Following these events, the Consignment-out account has a zero balance. If the account has a debit balance, it is reported as an inventory item in the current asset section of the consignor's balance sheet. The sales are reported as an operating revenue and the various expenses are reported as operating expenses on the consignor's income statement.

## Franchises

A **franchise agreement** involves the granting of business rights by the **franchisor** to a **franchisee** who will operate the franchised business. Franchises are common in several industries such as fast foods (McDonald's), motels (Holiday Inn), and auto rentals (Hertz). Franchise agreements vary in complexity but usually involve an initial payment (called an **initial franchise fee**) by the franchisee and ongoing payments of **continuing franchise fees.** In return for the initial franchise fee, the franchisor may provide assistance in site selection and construction, equipment acquisitions, projections of franchisee's revenues and expenses, and other matters. For the continuing franchise fees, the franchisor may provide advertising, quality control, training of personnel, and budgeting and other accounting services.

Sometimes the initial franchise fee is collected by the franchisor far in advance of the performance of its services. At other times collection of part of the initial franchise fee is deferred until the franchise is operating successfully. Occasionally the continuing franchise fee is not large enough to cover the franchisor's cost of the ongoing services provided, but the initial franchise fee is unusually large (so, in effect, it involves a prepayment by the franchisee for the continuing services). Or the franchise agreement may involve the potential refund of the initial franchise fee if certain conditions or obligations are not met by the franchisor.

All these revenue recognition issues of the franchisor are addressed by **FASB Statement No. 45.**[12] Initial franchise fees are recognized as revenue when all material services have been substantially performed by the franchisor. **Substantial performance** means that there is no obligation or intent to refund any cash received or forgive any unpaid notes receivable, and substantially all the initial services required by the franchise agreement have been performed. The commencement of operations by the franchisee is presumed to be the earliest point at which substantial performance has occurred, unless earlier performance can be demonstrated. At this point, revenue may be recognized under the accrual method. Installment or cost recovery methods

---

12. "Accounting for Franchise Fee Revenue," *FASB Statement of Financial Accounting Standards No. 45* (Stamford, Conn.: FASB, 1981), par. 3–7.

are used for revenue recognition only in those exceptional cases when revenue is collectible over an extended period and no reasonable basis exists for estimating collectibility.

Continuing franchise fees are recognized as revenue by the franchisor as the fees are earned and receivable from the franchisee. The continuing fee may not cover the cost of continuing services provided by the franchisor because there is a large initial fee that is, in effect, a prepayment for continuing services. In such cases, a portion of the initial fee is recorded as a liability and amortized as franchise revenue over the life of the franchise.

### Illustration of Accounting for Initial Franchise Fees

To illustrate the accounting for an initial franchise fee, assume that the Castle Company sells a franchise that requires an initial franchise fee of $70,000. A down payment of $20,000 cash is required with the balance covered by the issuance of a $50,000, 10% note, payable by the franchisee in 5 equal annual installments. The following alternatives exist for accounting for this fee by the Castle Company (the franchisor):

1. If all material services have been substantially performed by the franchisor, the refund period has expired, and the collectibility of the note is reasonably assured, revenue is recognized as follows:

| | | |
|---|---|---|
| **Cash** | 20,000 | |
| **Notes Receivable** | 50,000 | |
| **Franchise Revenue** | | **70,000** |

2. If the refund period has expired and the collectibility of the note is reasonably assured, but all material services have not been substantially performed by the franchisor, revenue is not recognized. Instead, a liability is recognized as follows:

| | | |
|---|---|---|
| **Cash** | 20,000 | |
| **Notes Receivable** | 50,000 | |
| **Unearned Franchise Fees** | | **70,000** |

The unearned franchise fees are recognized as revenue when all material services have been performed by the franchisor.

3. If all material services have been substantially performed by the franchisor and the collectibility of the note is reasonably assured, but the refund period has not expired, revenue is not recognized. Instead, a liability is recognized as follows:

| | | |
|---|---|---|
| **Cash** | 20,000 | |
| **Notes Receivable** | 50,000 | |
| **Unearned Franchise Fees** | | **70,000** |

The unearned franchise fees are recognized as revenue when the refund period expires.

4. If all material services have been substantially performed by the franchisor and the refund period has expired, but the collectibility of the note is not reasonably

assured, revenue is recognized by the installment or cost recovery method. If we assume that the installment method is used, revenue of $20,000 is recognized as follows:

| | | |
|---|---|---|
| Cash | 20,000 | |
| Notes Receivable | 50,000 | |
|     Unearned Franchise Fees | | 50,000 |
|     Franchise Revenue | | 20,000 |

Since the installment method is being used, the unearned franchise fees are recognized as revenue in the amount of $10,000 each year as cash is received.

5. If the refund period has expired, but all material services have not been substantially performed by the franchisor and there is no basis for estimating the collectibility of the note, then the note is *not* recognized as an asset. Instead, a form of the deposit method is used. For example, suppose the franchisor has developed an entirely new product whose success is uncertain and payment of the note will be made from the cash flows from the sale of the product, if any. The journal entry to record the initial transaction is as follows:

| | | |
|---|---|---|
| Cash | 20,000 | |
|     Unearned Franchise Fees | | 20,000 |

The unearned franchise fees are recognized as revenue either under the accrual method in the normal manner at the completion of the services to be performed by the franchisor (if collectibility is reasonably assured) or under the installment method if there is no basis for estimating the collectibility of the note. Alternatively, if the franchise fees had been earned through the substantial performance of all material services, franchise revenue of $20,000 would be recognized instead of the liability.

6. Now assume that only $30,000 has been earned from providing initial services with the balance being a down payment for continuing services. If the refund period has expired and the collectibility of the note is reasonably assured, revenue of $30,000 is recognized as follows:

| | | |
|---|---|---|
| Cash | 20,000 | |
| Notes Receivable | 50,000 | |
|     Franchise Revenue | | 30,000 |
|     Unearned Franchise Fees | | 40,000 |

The unearned franchise fees of $40,000 are recognized as revenue when the continuing services are performed.

In all these cases except the fifth, the franchisor accounts for the collection of interest and principal on the note receivable in the usual manner. In the fifth situation, the note is not recognized until a future event occurs and revenue is recognized. In addition, the franchisor accounts for its costs in a manner consistent with its revenue recognition. That is, if revenue is deferred, then the related cost of goods sold is deferred. Then, when revenue is recognized, the cost of goods sold is matched against the revenues. The franchisee accounts for its payments as an intangible asset.

*Intangible assets are discussed in Chapter 10.*

*Illustration of Accounting for Continuing Franchise Fees*

To illustrate the accounting for continuing franchise fees, assume that the Castle Company also charges the franchisee a continuing franchise fee of $9,000 per year. The following alternatives exist for accounting for this fee by the Castle Company (the franchisor):

1. If the fee is earned for providing continuing services:

| | | |
|---|---:|---:|
| Cash | 9,000 | |
|     Continuing Franchise Fee Revenue | | 9,000 |

2. If $1,000 of the fee is for national advertising:

| | | |
|---|---:|---:|
| Cash | 9,000 | |
|     Continuing Franchise Fee Revenue | | 8,000 |
|     Unearned Franchise Fees | | 1,000 |

The earned franchise fees are recognized as revenue when the advertising services are performed and recorded as expenses.

In addition to providing services as part of the continuing franchise fee, a franchisor often sells many supplies to the franchisee. These sales occur because the franchisor may be able to obtain quantity discounts from manufacturers or wholesalers, or to maintain uniform quality of the supplies. These sales and related expenses are recorded by the franchisor in the normal manner.

*Option to Purchase*

In some franchise situations, the franchise agreement will include a provision so that the franchisor has an option to purchase the franchisee's business. If at the time the franchise agreement is signed and the option is granted, an understanding exists that the option will be exercised (or it is probable that the franchisor ultimately will acquire the franchise), the initial franchise fee is not recognized as revenue. Instead the initial franchise fee is recorded as a liability. When the option is exercised and the franchisor acquires the franchise, the liability is then recorded as a reduction in the franchisor's investment.

## Real Estate Sales

In real estate sales, a company may sell either land or a building or both. The land may be developed or undeveloped and the seller may be responsible for making improvements. The building may be completed or in the process of construction and may be for commercial use such as a factory or office building, or residential use, such as a house or apartment building. Accounting for real estate sales is a complex area of accounting that is defined by **FASB Statement No. 66,** "Accounting for Sales of Real Estate." Only the basic rules are discussed here because of their relevance to an understanding of revenue recognition alternatives.[13]

For real estate sales, **revenue and related expenses are recognized on the accrual basis in the normal manner in the period of the sale if *all* of the following conditions are met:**

1. A sale is consummated.

2. The buyer's initial and continuing investments are adequate to demonstrate a commitment to pay for the property.

---

13. "Accounting for Sales of Real Estate," *FASB Statement of Financial Accounting Standards No. 66* (Stamford, Conn.: FASB, 1982), par. 5–43.

3.  The seller's receivable is not subject to future subordination (reduced in its liquidation rights).

4.  The seller has transferred to the buyer the usual risks and rewards of ownership in a transaction that is in substance a sale and does not have a continuing involvement with the property.

The evidence necessary to meet these criteria is discussed in the *Statement* but is beyond the scope of the text. It is important to understand that these criteria address the conceptual issues discussed earlier in the chapter, namely the economic substance of the transaction, the collectibility (realizability) of the receivable, and the transfer of the risks and benefits of ownership. **When any of the criteria are *not* met, the revenue is recognized under an alternative method as follows:**

1.  If the sale is not consummated, the *deposit method* is used.

2.  If the buyer's initial and continuing investment is not adequate, the *installment method* is used if the recovery of the cost of the property is reasonably assured, and the *cost recovery method* is used if recovery of the cost is not reasonably assured.

3.  If the seller's receivable is subject to future subordination, the *cost recovery method* is used.

4.  If the seller has continuing involvement with the property and does not transfer substantially all the risks and benefits of ownership, generally revenue and related expenses are recognized at the time of sale with a deduction for the maximum exposure to loss. Other methods may be appropriate depending on the circumstances.

Thus, various revenue recognition methods are appropriate depending on the circumstances. When revenue is earned and the related receivable is realized or realizable, the revenue is recognized in full using the accrual method. When the earning process is not complete or realization has not occurred, an alternative method is appropriate.

## Retail Land Sales

In retail land sales, a company may acquire a large tract of unimproved land which it divides into lots. These lots then are "sold" to widely dispersed retail customers (individuals) through intensive marketing programs. Generally, part of the marketing program involves an agreement by the company to improve the lots by installing roads, utilities, and related amenities such as golf courses, lakes, and recreational centers. These improvements will require large future capital outlays on the part of the company. The company may agree to be continually involved in the operations of the recreational centers and to provide ongoing maintenance. The "sales contract" often has a low down payment, no (or limited) credit investigation of the buyer, periodic payments by the buyer that extend over several years, and the ability of the buyer to cancel the contract and obtain a refund within a specified period.

Several factors involved in retail land sales have a potential impact on the timing of revenue recognition by the company. These include the collectibility of the receivables, the financial ability of the company to fulfill its obligations, the length of the refund period, the accumulation of collections, and the ongoing completion of the project. For retail land sales, **revenue and the related expenses are recognized in the period of the sale on the accrual basis if** *all* **of the following conditions are met:**

1. The buyer has made the down payment and each required subsequent payment until the period of cancellation with refund has expired.

2. The cumulative payments of principal and interest equal or exceed 10% of the contract sales price.

3. Collection experience for the project indicates that at least 90% of the contracts will be collected in full. A down payment of 20% is an acceptable indication of collectibility.

4. The receivable from the sale is not subject to subordination to new loans on the property.

5. The seller is not obligated to complete improvements of lots sold or to construct amenities or other facilities applicable to lots sold.

As with real estate sales, the intent of these rules is to be consistent with the conceptual issues related to revenue recognition. **When at least one of the preceding criteria is** *not* **met, the revenue is recognized under an alternative method as follows:**

1. The *percentage-of-completion method* is used if the first four criteria are met, there has been progress on the improvements, there are indications that the work will be completed according to plan, there is no indication of significant delaying factors, and development is practical.

2. The *installment method* of accounting is used if only the first two criteria are met and the seller is financially capable of honoring its obligations.

3. The *deposit method* is used if the first two criteria are not met.

Again, it may be seen that revenue is recognized in full using the accrual method if it is earned and the receivable is realized or realizable; an alternative method is used if either criterion is not met.[14]

 ### International Accounting Differences

There is general consistency worldwide about the basic criteria used for revenue recognition, even though there are variations in terminology. For example, while the U.S. uses the "earned" and "realizable" criteria, International Accounting Standards require the transfer of "the significant risks and rewards of ownership." The application of these two alternatives should result in virtually the same decisions about when to recognize revenue.

There are more significant differences for specialized revenue recognition issues. For example, International Accounting Standards do not require the use of the percentage-of-completion method when specified criteria are met, whereas in the U.S. it must be used when the four criteria are met. Differences also exist among countries. For example, in Japan while revenue is generally recognized at the time of sale, the percentage-of-completion method is *allowed* on long-term contracts, and the installment method is commonly used when the collection period exceeds two years, independent of the likelihood of collection.

14. *Ibid.*, par. 45–49.

## SUMMARY OF ALTERNATIVE REVENUE RECOGNITION METHODS

The various alternative revenue recognition methods are summarized in Exhibit 16-10. The reasons for the use of each method and primary impacts on the financial statements are listed.

### EXHIBIT 16-10

### SUMMARY OF ALTERNATIVE REVENUE RECOGNITION METHODS

| Method | Reasons for Use | Impact on Financial Statements |
|---|---|---|
| Accrual | Revenue is earned and receivable is realized or realizable in the period of sale. | Revenue and expenses are recognized in the period of sale, and net assets are increased. |
| Percentage-of-completion | Revenue is recognized during production because all 4 criteria are met (see p. 762). | Revenue and expenses are recognized in the period of production and inventory (net assets) is increased. |
| Completed-contract | Revenue is recognized at the completion of the contract because at least 1 of the 4 criteria is not met. | Revenue and expenses are recognized at the completion of production (sale) and net assets are increased. |
| Proportional performance | Same principles as percentage-of-completion, but applied to service contracts. | |
| Completion-of-production | Revenue is recognized at the completion of production because it is earned and the selling price is realizable due to the immediate marketability at quoted prices and unit interchangeability. | Revenue and expenses are recognized at the completion of production and inventory (net assets) is increased. |
| Installment | Revenue is recognized as cash is received because it is earned in the period of sale but the receivable is not realizable until the period of collection. | Gross profit is deferred in the period of sale and recognized as cash is received, at which time net assets are increased (deferred gross profit is reduced). |
| Cost recovery | Revenue is recognized after the cost has been recovered because it is earned in the period of sale but the receivable is not realizable due to the extreme uncertainty of collection. | Gross profit is deferred in the period of sale and recognized after the cost has been recovered, at which time net assets are increased (deferred gross profit is reduced). |
| Deposit | Revenue is not recognized until a future event occurs because it has not been earned since the risks and benefits of ownership have not been transferred. | All cash receipts are recorded as liabilities until a future event occurs, at which time revenue is recognized using one of the alternative methods. |

## QUESTIONS

**Q16-1** Why is revenue sometimes recognized at a time other than the sale?

**Q16-2** Distinguish between the terms *recognition* and *realization*.

**Q16-3** Describe the effects on the financial statements of recognizing revenue at the time of sale, during production, and at the time of cash receipt.

**Q16-4** What three factors affect the decision as to when to recognize revenue?

**Q16-5** What are the five revenue recognition alternatives?

**Q16-6** Under what circumstances is revenue recognized prior to the period of sale? What two methods are used?

**Q16-7** What are the differences between the two methods of accounting for long-term construction contracts?

**Q16-8** Under what circumstances is the percentage-of-completion method used for long-term contracts?

**Q16-9** How may the departure from the principle of only recognizing revenue at the time of the sale be justified when the percentage-of-completion method is used?

**Q16-10** Describe input and output measures used in the percentage-of-completion method. Give an example of each.

**Q16-11** How are losses accounted for under the two methods of accounting for long-term construction contracts?

**Q16-12** How are the following accounts classified in the financial statements: Construction in Progress, Partial Billings, Construction Revenue, and Construction Expense?

**Q16-13** How are initial direct costs, direct costs, and indirect costs recognized as expenses under the proportional performance method? Explain the reason for each method.

**Q16-14** Under what circumstances is revenue recognized after the period of the sale? What two methods are used?

**Q16-15** Describe the steps involved in the installment method.

**Q16-16** Describe the differences between the cost recovery method and the installment method.

**Q16-17** Describe the basic characteristics of the deposit method.

**Q16-18** In a consignment, does the consignee or consignor retain title to the property? When is revenue recognized by the consignor? The consignee?

**Q16-19** Distinguish between the initial franchise fee and continuing franchise fee. When is each recognized as revenue?

**Q16-20** How is revenue recognized for real estate sales?

**Q16-21** How is revenue recognized for retail land sales?

## CASES

*C16-1    Revenue Recognition Methods*  ⓓ
The following situations are independent.

1. Carlson Company is an international consulting firm that has received a 2-year engagement from a client for a fee of $2 million. The company will assign differing numbers of personnel to the project depending on the needs of the project and the availability of personnel. The company requires a down payment of 10% and makes periodic billings based on the hours worked by the personnel plus 20% profit. At the end of the engagement, the company and the client will negotiate whether an adjustment to the fee is appropriate.
2. The Fast Loss Health Club has three types of memberships: 1 year, 3 year, and 10 year. Each type of membership requires an initial fee as well as monthly fees. To encourage memberships, the company offers numerous incentives such as free dues for the first two months and drawings for free vacation trips. In addition, the company advertises heavily at certain times

of the year, such as during the Christmas period. The company also offers special programs to its members for a fee and allows nonmembers to participate for a higher fee.
3. The New Encyclopedia Company ships 5 complete sets of its 12-volume encyclopedia to each of its new distributors. Each distributor has 6 months to sell all the encyclopedias and pay the company the selling price, less a 40% commission, within 5 days of each sale. During this period, the distributor may return the encyclopedias without obligation and at the company's expense. At the end of 6 months, the distributor must pay the selling price of the unsold encyclopedias, less a 60% commission.

**Required**
Discuss the revenue recognition issues that exist in each independent situation. Discuss any issues that exist in matching the expenses against the revenues.

## C16-2  *Criteria for Revenue Recognition*

The earning of revenue by a company is recognized for accounting purposes when the transaction is recorded. In some situations, revenue is recognized approximately as it is earned in the economic sense; in others, accountants have developed guidelines for recognizing revenue by other criteria, for example, at the point of sale.

**Required** (*ignore income taxes*)

1. Explain and justify why revenue is often recognized as earned at the time of sale.
2. Explain in what situations it would be appropriate to recognize revenue as the productive activity takes place.
3. At what times, other than those included in items (1) and (2), may it be appropriate to recognize revenue? Explain. (*AICPA adapted*)

## C16-3  *Revenue Recognition*

Bonanza Trading Stamps, Inc. was formed early this year to sell trading stamps throughout the Southwest to retailers who distribute them free to their customers. Books for accumulating the stamps and catalogs illustrating the merchandise for which the stamps may be exchanged are given free to retailers for distribution to stamp recipients. Centers with inventories of merchandise premiums have been established for redemption of the stamps. Retailers may not return unused stamps to Bonanza.

The following schedule expresses Bonanza's expectations of the percentages of a normal month's activity that will be attained. For this purpose, a normal month's activity is defined as the level of operations expected when expansion of activities ceases or tapers off to a stable rate. The company expects that this level will be attained in the third year, and that sales of stamps will average $2,000,000 per month throughout the third year.

| Month | Actual Stamp Sales Percentage | Merchandise Premium Purchases Percentage | Stamp Redemptions Percentage |
|---|---|---|---|
| 6 | 30% | 40% | 10% |
| 12 | 60 | 60 | 45 |
| 18 | 80 | 80 | 70 |
| 24 | 90 | 90 | 80 |
| 30 | 100 | 100 | 95 |

**Required**

1. Discuss the factors to be considered in determining when revenue should be recognized in measuring the income of a business enterprise.
2. Discuss the accounting alternatives that should be considered by Bonanza Trading Stamps, Inc. for the recognition of its revenues and related expenses.
3. For each accounting alternative discussed in (2), give balance sheet accounts that should be used and indicate how each should be classified. (*AICPA adapted*)

## C16-4  *Revenue Recognition Methods*

In exceptional cases, revenue is recognized by the use of several methods, including (a) percentage-of-completion method, (b) proportional performance method, and (c) installment method.

**Required**

Briefly describe each of the methods and indicate the situations in which each is used.

## C16-5  *Exchanges and Revenue Recognition Issues*

Certain business "exchanges" are very complex and may qualify as exceptional cases in which the related revenues and expenses are advanced or deferred. The following are four such cases:

1. Franchisor grants a franchise to a franchisee; it collects part of the initial franchise fee and agrees to perform related initial services over an extended period.
2. Land development company acquires land for future development into a "sports retirement community," subdivides the land into lots, and sells the lots on "credit" with payment to be made on a long-term basis.
3. Lessor leases equipment to a lessee on a long-term noncancelable lease; the fair value of the leased item is greater than the cost, and the ownership of the leased item is transferred to the lessee by the end of the lease life.
4. A construction company builds bridges; it enters into a contract to construct a bridge for Rice County over a two-year period.

**Required**

For each of the preceding exchanges, (a) indicate the revenue recognition issues involved, and (b) discuss when the revenue is recognized and by what method.

## C16-6  *Construction Contracts*

Village Company is accounting for a long-term construction contract using the percentage-of-completion method. It is a 3-year, fixed-fee contract that is presently in its first year. The latest reasonable estimates of total contract costs indicate that the contract will be completed at a profit. Village will submit progress billings to the customer and has reasonable assurance that collections on these billings will be received in each year of the contract.

**Required**

1.  a. What is the justification for the percentage-of-completion method for long-term construction contracts?
    b. What facts in the preceding situation indicate that Village should account for this long-term construction contract using the percentage-of-completion method?
2. How would the income recognized in each year of this long-term construction contract be determined using the cost-to-cost method of determining percentage of completion?

3. What is the effect on income, if any, of the progress billings and the collections on these billings? (*AICPA adapted*)

## C16-7    Long-Term Contracts

In accounting for long-term contracts (those taking longer than one year to complete), the two methods commonly followed are the percentage-of-completion method and the completed-contract method.

### Required

1. Discuss how earnings on long-term contracts are recognized and computed under these two methods.
2. Under what circumstances is it preferable to use one method over the other?
3. Why is earnings recognition as measured by interim billings not generally accepted for long-term contracts?
4. How are job costs and interim billings reflected on the balance sheet under the percentage-of-completion method and the completed-contract method? (*AICPA adapted*)

## C16-8    Construction Contracts

At December 31, 1995, Roko Co. has two fixed price construction contracts in progress. Both contracts have monthly billings supported by certified surveys of work completed. The contracts are:

(a) The Ski Park contract, begun in 1994, is 80% complete, is progressing according to bid estimates, and is expected to be profitable.
(b) The Nassu Village contract, a project to construct 100 condominium units, was begun in 1995. Thirty-five units have been completed. Work on the remaining units is delayed by conflicting recommendations on how to overcome unexpected subsoil problems. While the total cost of the project is uncertain, a loss is not anticipated.

### Required

1. Identify the alternatives available to account for long-term construction contracts, and specify the criteria used to determine which method is applicable to a given contract.
2. Identify the appropriate accounting method for each of Roko's two contracts, and describe each contract's effect on net income for 1995.
3. Indicate how the accounts related to the Ski Park contract should be reported on the balance sheet at December 31, 1995. (*AICPA adapted*)

## C16-9    Franchise and Revenue Recognition

Southern Fried Shrimp sells franchises to independent operators throughout the southeastern part of the United States. The contract with the franchisee includes the following provisions:

1. The franchisee is charged an initial fee of $25,000. Of this amount, $5,000 is payable when the agreement is

signed and a $4,000 non-interest-bearing note is payable at the end of each of the 5 subsequent years.
2. All of the initial franchise fee collected by Southern Fried Shrimp is to be refunded and the remaining obligation canceled if, for any reason, the franchisee fails to open his franchise.
3. In return for the initial franchise fee, Southern Fried Shrimp agrees to (1) assist the franchisee in selecting the location for his business, (2) negotiate the lease for the land, (3) obtain financing and assist with building design, (4) supervise construction, (5) establish accounting and tax records, and (6) provide expert advice over a 5-year period relating to such matters as employee and management training, quality control and promotion.
4. In addition to the initial franchise fee, the franchisee is required to pay to Southern Fried Shrimp a monthly fee of 2% of sales for menu planning, recipe innovations and the privilege of purchasing ingredients from Southern Fried Shrimp at or below prevailing market prices.

Management of Southern Fried Shrimp estimates that the value of the services rendered to the franchisee at the time the contract is signed amounts to at least $5,000. All franchisees to date have opened their locations at the scheduled time and none has defaulted on any of the notes receivable.

The credit ratings of all franchisees would entitle them to borrow at the current interest rate of 10%. The present value of an ordinary annuity of five annual receipts of $4,000 each discounted at 10% is $15,163.

### Required

1. Discuss the alternatives that Southern Fried Shrimp might use to account for the initial franchise fee, evaluate each by applying generally accepted accounting principles to this situation, and give illustrative entries for each alternative.
2. Given the nature of Southern Fried Shrimp's agreement with its franchisees, when should revenue be recognized? Discuss the question of revenue recognition for both the initial franchise fee and the additional monthly fee of 2% of sales and give illustrative entries for both types of revenue.
3. Assume that (a) Southern Fried Shrimp sells some franchises for $35,000 (which includes a charge of $10,000 for the rental of equipment for its useful life of ten years); (b) $15,000 of the fee is payable immediately and the balance on non-interest-bearing notes at $4,000 per year; (c) no portion of the $10,000 rental payment is refundable in case the franchisee goes out of business; and (d) title to the equipment remains with the franchisor. What would be the preferable method of accounting for the rental portion of the initial franchise fee? Explain. (*AICPA adapted*)

## C16-10 Publishing and Revenue Recognition

After the presentation of your report on the examination of the financial statements to the board of directors of the Savage Publishing Company, one of the new directors says he is surprised the income statement assumes that an equal proportion of the revenue is earned with the publication of every issue of the company's magazine. He feels that the "crucial event" in the process of earning revenue in the magazine business is the cash sale of the subscription. He says that he does not understand why—other than for the smoothing of income—most of the revenue cannot be "recognized" in the period of the sale.

### Required

Discuss the propriety of timing the recognition of revenue in the Savage Publishing Company's accounts with

1. The cash sale of the magazine subscription.
2. The publication of the magazine every month.
3. Both events, by recognizing a portion of the revenue with cash sale of the magazine subscription and a portion of the revenue with the publication of the magazine every month. (*AICPA adapted*)

## C16-11 Recognition of Revenues and Expenses

On May 6, 1994, Sterling Corporation signed a contract with Stony Associates under which Stony agreed (1) to construct an office building on land owned by Sterling, (2) to accept responsibility for procuring financing for the project and finding tenants, and (3) to manage the property for 50 years. The annual profit from the project, after debt service, is to be divided equally between Sterling Corporation and Stony Associates. Stony is to accept its share of future profits as full payment for its services in construction, obtaining finances and tenants, and management of the project.

By April 30, 1995, the project was nearly completed and tenants had signed leases to occupy 90% of the available space at annual rentals aggregating $2,600,000. It is estimated that, after operating expenses and debt service, the annual profit will amount to $850,000. The management of Stony Associates believed that the economic benefit derived from the contract with Sterling should be reflected on its financial statements for the fiscal year ended April 30, 1995 and directed that revenue be accrued in an amount equal to the commercial value of the services Stony had rendered during the year, that this amount be carried in contracts receivable, and that all related expenditures be charged against the revenue.

### Required

Is the belief of Stony's management in accord with generally accepted accounting principles for the measurement of revenue and expense for the year ended April 30, 1995? Support your opinion by discussing the application to this case of the factors to be considered for asset measurement and revenue and expense recognition. (*AICPA adapted*)

## C16-12 Recognition of Expenses

Kwik-Bild Corporation sells and erects shell houses. These are frame structures that are completely finished on the outside but are unfinished on the inside except for flooring, partition studding and ceiling joists. Shell houses are sold chiefly to customers who are handy with tools and who have time to do the interior wiring, plumbing, wall completion and finishing and other work necessary to make the shell houses livable dwellings.

Kwik-Bild buys shell houses from a manufacturer in unassembled packages consisting of all lumber, roofing, doors, windows and similar materials necessary to complete a shell house. Upon commencing operations in a new area, Kwik-Bild buys or leases land as a site for its local warehouse, field office and display houses. Sample display houses are erected at a total cost of from $10,000 to $30,000 including the cost of the unassembled packages. The chief element of cost of the display houses is the unassembled packages, since erection is a short low-cost operation. Old sample models are torn down or altered into new models every three to seven years. Sample display houses have little salvage value because dismantling and moving costs amount to nearly as much as the cost of an unassembled package.

### Required

1. A choice must be made between (1) expensing the costs of sample display houses in the period in which the expenditure is made and (2) spreading the costs over more than one period. Discuss the advantages of each method.
2. Is it preferable to amortize the cost of display houses on the basis of (1) the passage of time or (2) the number of shell houses sold? Explain. (*AICPA adapted*)

## C16-13 Installment Method Sales

Installment sales usually are accounted for by one of the following methods: (1) the profit may be recognized as earned in the period of sale; (2) the profit may be recognized on a proportionate basis in the periods of collection (commonly called the "installment method").

### Required

1. Discuss the propriety of the two methods, including in your discussion a list of the circumstances under which recognition of profit in the period of sale would be preferable to recognition of profit on the installment method.
2. The collection period of an installment sale contract is frequently 24 months or longer. Discuss in terms of both methods the presentation of the installment contracts receivable on the balance sheet.
3. Deferred gross profit arising from installment sales has been reported on the balance sheet variously as a contra or valuation account to installments receivable, an estimated liability, a part of stockholders' equity, or a deferred credit.

Discuss the nature and, hence, the appropriate balance sheet classification(s) of "deferred gross profit" for an accrual-basis business that uses the installment sales method for financial reporting and income tax purposes. (*AICPA adapted*)

### C16-14   Installment Method Sales

On October 2, 1995, the Television Company sold a set costing $400 to Jones for $600. Jones made a down payment of $150 and agreed to pay $25 the first of each month for 18 months thereafter.

The first two installments due on November 1 and December 1, 1995 were paid. In 1996, five payments were made by Jones, who then defaulted on the balance of his payments. The set was repossessed on November 1, 1996. The company closes its books as of December 31.

**Required**

1. Give three different amounts that might be shown as realized income for 1995 and indicate the circumstances under which each of these amounts would be acceptable.
2. Assuming that the repossessed television set has a wholesale value of $50 and a retail value of $75, prepare a journal entry to record the repossession under the "installment method" of accounting. Explain fully the reasoning applicable to your entry. (*AICPA adapted*)

### C16-15   Researching GAAP      ⓒⓒ

When asked about a $518 million "prepaid expense and deferred charge" on its balance sheet for 1990, Sears says that about $100 million of the figure—mainly for the catalog—consists of advertising costs whose impact on profit has been deferred. "These costs are paid but aren't charged against profits" yet, says a spokesman.

Procter and Gamble generally allocates advertising costs based on the number of cases of products it ships.

A spokesman for McDonald's says that a "small portion" of the $108 million in prepaid expenses and other current assets on its balance sheet for 1990 is deferred production costs for certain commercials and creative development.

Nike says that it deducts all advertising costs immediately, and calls advertising-cost deferral "a bogus exercise."

Philip Morris accrued $1.4 billion in marketing costs on the liability side of its balance sheet for 1990. This means that Philip Morris is deducting advertising costs it has not yet paid to help smooth out profits from year to year. An analyst says, "I call such amounts 'hidden earnings' for future years when financial results aren't as good as Philip Morris would like. Then, it could lower its advertising-cost deductions with this accrual." (Adapted from *The Wall Street Journal*, 1/8/92).

**Required**

1. Research the generally accepted accounting principles and prepare a short memo that summarizes how to report advertising costs. Cite your reference and applicable paragraph numbers.
2. Are each of the companies complying with the policy? Assume that all the companies recognize revenue at the time of sale.

### C16-16   Researching GAAP      ⓒⓒ

Amre Inc. capitalized its marketing costs, such as the cost of purchasing mailing lists, instead of treating the costs as expenses.

Inspeech capitalized estimated selling, general, and administrative costs of various acquired companies' accounting and billing activities for a period of three months following the acquisition. Similarly, the company capitalized search costs to hire new management employees and salaries of individuals involved with the integration of newly-acquired companies and fees for studies by outside consultants. Management justified capitalizing these expenses because they were required to implement the company's expansion strategy and would benefit future periods.

Among the costs Chambers deferred were portions of executives' salaries for time spent on developing projects such as new landfills. In addition, the company delayed recognizing some public relations and legal costs as well as executive travel expenses.

**Required**

Research the generally accepted accounting principles and prepare a short memo that summarizes how to report advertising costs. Cite your reference and applicable paragraph numbers.

---

## MULTIPLE CHOICE

*Select the best answer for each of the following.*

M16-1   Real estate sales are recognized by the accrual method if all of the conditions defined by *FASB Statement No. 66* are met. Which of the following is *not* one of the conditions defined by the *Statement*?

  a. The seller has transferred to the buyer the usual risks and rewards of ownership in a transaction that is in substance a sale and does not have a continuing involvement with property.
  b. A sale is consummated.

    c. The buyer's initial and continuing investments are adequate to demonstrate a commitment to pay for the property.

    d. The seller's receivable is subject to future subordination.

M16-2   Green Company, which began operations on January 1, 1995, appropriately uses the installment method of accounting. The following information is available for 1995:

| | |
|---|---|
| Gross profit on sales | 40% |
| Deferred gross profit at 12/31/95 | $240,000 |
| Cash collected on installment sales | 450,000 |

What is the total amount of Green's installment sales for 1995?

    a. $600,000               c. $850,000

    b. $690,000               d. $1,050,000

M16-3   When should an indicated loss on a long-term contract be recognized under the completed-contract method and the percentage-of-completion method, respectively?

| | Completed-contract | Percentage-of-completion |
|---|---|---|
| a. | Immediately | Over life of project |
| b. | Immediately | Immediately |
| c. | Contract complete | Over life of project |
| d. | Contract complete | Immediately |

M16-4   In accounting for a long-term construction contract for which there is a projected profit, the balance in the construction-in-progress asset account at the end of the first year of work using the completed-contract method would be

    a. Zero

    b. The same as the percentage-of-completion method

    c. Lower than the percentage-of-completion method

    d. Higher than the percentage-of-completion method

M16-5   Warren Construction Company has consistently used the percentage-of-completion method of recognizing income. In 1995, Warren started work on a $6,000,000 construction contract, which was completed in 1996. The accounting records disclosed the following data:

| | 1995 | 1996 |
|---|---|---|
| Progress billings | $2,200,000 | $3,800,000 |
| Costs incurred | 1,800,000 | 3,600,000 |
| Collections | 1,400,000 | 4,600,000 |
| Estimated cost to complete | 3,600,000 | — |

How much income should Warren have recognized in 1995?

    a. $200,000               c. $300,000

    b. $220,000               d. $400,000

M16-6   Kramer Manufacturing Company ships goods to Sikes Company on consignment. When the consigned goods are delivered to Sikes, Kramer should record

| | Sale of inventory | Revenue |
|---|---|---|
| a. | No | Yes |
| b. | No | No |
| c. | Yes | No |
| d. | Yes | Yes |

M16-7    During 1995, Morgan Company recognized $30,000 of sales under the cost recovery method. This is the first time the Morgan Company has used the cost recovery method in recognizing sales. The cost of goods sold related to these sales was $21,000. Cash collections in 1995 were $15,000, in 1996 were $10,000, and in 1997 were $5,000. What amount of gross profit should be recognized in 1995, 1996, and 1997?

|     | 1995 | 1996 | 1997 |
|-----|------|------|------|
| a.  | $9,000 | $ -0- | $-0- |
| b.  | $4,500 | $3,000 | $1,500 |
| c.  | $ -0- | $ -0- | $9,000 |
| d.  | $ -0- | $4,000 | $5,000 |

M16-8    On January 1, 1995, Bartell Company sold its idle plant facility to Cooper, Inc., for $1,050,000. On this date, the plant had a depreciated cost of $735,000. Cooper paid $150,000 cash on January 1, 1995, and signed a $900,000 note bearing interest at 10%. The note was payable in three annual installments of $300,000 beginning January 1, 1996. Bartell appropriately accounted for the sale under the installment method. Cooper made a timely payment of the first installment on January 1, 1996 of $390,000, which included interest of $90,000 to date of payment. At December 31, 1996, Bartell has deferred gross profit of

a. $153,000
b. $180,000

c. $225,000
d. $270,000

M16-9    The Schmidt Company sells a franchise that requires an initial franchise fee of $50,000. A $10,000 down payment is required with the balance covered by the issuance of a 12% note, payable in 4 equal installments. All material services have been substantially performed by the Schmidt Company, the refund period has expired, and the collectibility of the note is reasonably assured. The journal entry recorded by Schmidt Company should be

a.  Cash                          10,000
    Notes Receivable               40,000
        Franchise Revenue                        10,000
        Unearned Franchise Fees                  40,000
b.  Cash                          10,000
    Notes Receivable               40,000
        Franchise Revenue                        50,000
c.  Cash                          10,000
    Notes Receivable               40,000
        Unearned Franchise Fees                  50,000
d.  Cash                          10,000
        Franchise Revenue                        10,000

M16-10   On April 1, 1995, Pine Construction Company entered into a fixed-price contract to construct an apartment building for $6,000,000. Pine appropriately accounts for this contract under the percentage-of-completion method. Information relating to the contract is as follows:

|                               | At December 31, 1995 | At December 31, 1996 |
|-------------------------------|---------------------|---------------------|
| Percentage of completion      | 20%                 | 60%                 |
| Estimated costs at completion | $4,500,000          | $4,800,000          |
| Income recognized (cumulative)| $ 300,000           | $ 720,000           |

What is the amount of contract costs incurred during the year ended December 31, 1996?

a. $1,200,000
b. $1,920,000

c. $1,980,000
d. $2,880,000

*(AICPA adapted)*

# EXERCISES

**E16-1** *Revenue Recognition Alternatives*  The Smith Construction Company received a contract on September 30, 1995 to build a warehouse over a period of 18 months. The contract price was $600,000 and the estimated cost to build was $400,000. The actual (and estimated) costs incurred and the payments made by the purchaser are as follows:

|  | Costs | Payments |
|---|---|---|
| September 30–December 31, 1995 | $120,000 | $ 90,000 |
| January 1–December 31, 1996 | 240,000 | 210,000 |
| January 1–March 31, 1997 | 40,000 | 300,000 |

**Required**

1. Compute the amount of revenue, expense, and gross profit each year for each of the following methods:
   a. Revenue recognition at the time of sale (completion)
   b. Revenue recognition during production
   c. Revenue recognition at the time of cash receipt
   d. Cost recovery (only compute the gross profit)
2. Which method provides the most useful information to users? Under what circumstances would the other methods provide more useful information?

**E16-2** *Percentage-of-Completion Method*  In 1995, Tarlo Company agrees to construct a highway for Brice County over a 3-year period (1995 through 1997). The contract price is $1,200,000 and the construction costs (both actual and estimated) total $705,000 for the 3 years. The percentage completed at the end of each year is as follows: 1995, 20%; 1996, 70%; 1997, 100%.

**Required**

1. Prepare a schedule showing the amount of gross profit that Tarlo Company recognizes each year using the percentage-of-completion method.
2. Prepare a schedule showing the amount of gross profit that Tarlo Company recognizes each year using the completed-contract method.

**E16-3** *Percentage of Completion*  The King Construction Company began work on a contract in 1995. The contract price is $4,000,000, and the company uses the percentage-of-completion method. Other information relating to the contract is as follows:

|  | 1995 |
|---|---|
| Costs incurred during the year | $ 900,000 |
| Estimated costs to complete, December 31 | 2,100,000 |
| Billings during the year | 700,000 |
| Collections during the year | 500,000 |

**Required**

1. How much is the gross profit or loss recognized in 1995?
2. Prepare the appropriate sections of the 1995 income statement and ending balance sheet.

**E16-4** *Percentage of Completion*  The Koolman Construction Company began work on a contract in 1995. The contract price is $3,000,000, and the company uses the percentage-of-completion method. Other information relating to the contract is as follows:

|  | 1995 | 1996 |
|---|---|---|
| Costs incurred during the year | $ 600,000 | $ 700,000 |
| Estimated costs to complete, December 31 | 1,400,000 | 1,200,000 |
| Billings during the year | 500,000 | 850,000 |
| Collections during the year | 400,000 | 800,000 |

**Required**
1. Compute the gross profit or loss to be recognized in 1995 and 1996.
2. Prepare the appropriate sections of the income statement and ending balance sheet for each year.

E16-5  *Percentage of Completion*   Newberg Construction Corporation contracted to construct a building for $400,000. Construction began in 1995 and was completed in 1996. Data relating to the contract are as follows:

|                           | Year Ended December 31, | |
| --- | --- | --- |
|                           | **1995** | **1996** |
| Costs incurred            | $200,000 | $110,000 |
| Estimated costs to complete | 100,000 | — |

**Required**
Newberg uses the percentage-of-completion method as the basis for income recognition. For the years ended December 31, 1995 and 1996, respectively, how much income should Newberg report? (*AICPA adapted*)

E16-6  *Long-Term Construction Contract*   The Osborn Construction Company began operations January 2, 1995. During the year, Osborn entered into a contract with Redbeard Razor Corporation to construct a manufacturing facility. At that time, Osborn estimated that it would take 5 years to complete the facility at a total cost of $4,800,000. The total contract price for construction of the facility is $6,000,000. During the year, Osborn incurred $1,250,000 in construction costs related to the construction project. The estimated cost to complete the contract is $3,750,000. Redbeard was billed and paid 30% of the contract price.

**Required**
Prepare schedules to compute the amount of gross profit to be recognized for the year ended December 31, 1995 and the amount to be shown as "cost of uncompleted contract in excess of related billings" or "billings on uncompleted contract in excess of related costs" on December 31, 1995, under each of the following methods:
1. Completed-contract method
2. Percentage-of-completion method

Show supporting computations in good form. (*AICPA adapted*)

E16-7  *Proportional Performance Method*   The New Recreational Company sells 2-year memberships to its recreational facilities. For $2,000 in advance, each member receives the right to 30 nights at the company's campgrounds, 20 rounds on its golf courses, and 50 hours on its bowling lanes. In 1995, the company sold 400 memberships.

In 1995, members used the campgrounds for 4,100 nights, played 3,000 rounds of golf, and bowled for 10,000 hours. The relevant cost information for the 400 contracts is as follows:

| | |
| --- | --- |
| Initial direct costs | $ 40,000 |
| Annual indirect costs | 100,000 |
| Estimated (and actual) total direct costs for two-year period | 340,000 |
| Direct cost per: | |
|     Night at campground | 10 |
|     Round of golf | 15 |
|     Hour of bowling | 5 |

**Required**
Prepare the income statement for 1995.

E16-8  *Revenue Recognition at Completion of Production*   In 1995, the Sterling Farm Company produced 100,000 bushels of wheat at a cost of $2.00 per bushel. The company has a contract to deliver 80,000 bushels at $2.10 per bushel in 1996. Delivery costs are estimated to be $0.02 per bushel. For guaranteed price contracts, the company recognizes revenue at the completion of production; otherwise, it recognizes revenue at the time of delivery.

**Required**

1. Prepare summary journal entries for 1995 and 1996:
2. At what value is the inventory of the company carried after the delivery of the 80,000 bushels? Why?

*Sales Under the Installment Method*  Anibonita Company began operations in 1995. It sells goods on installment sales contracts; these transactions are considered to be exceptional, so it uses the installment method to recognize gross profit. The following is a summary of the installment sales, costs of installment sales, operating expenses, and collections for 1995 and 1996:

|  | 1995 | 1996 |
|---|---|---|
| Installment method sales | $80,000 | $90,000 |
| Costs of installment method sales | 52,000 | 59,400 |
| Operating expenses | 13,000 | 15,000 |
| Cash collections from: | | |
| 1995 installment method sales | 42,000 | 21,000 |
| 1996 installment method sales |  | 41,000 |

**Required**

Using the installment method to recognize gross profits, prepare 1995 and 1996 condensed income statements for the Anibonita Company.

E16-10  *Sales Under the Installment Method*  The following information is available for the Butler Company in 1995, the first year of its operations:

| | |
|---|---|
| Total credit sales (including installment method sales) | $200,000 |
| Total cost of goods sold (including installment method cost of goods sold) | 125,000 |
| Installment method sales | 60,000 |
| Installment method cost of goods sold | 36,000 |
| Cash receipts on credit sales (including installment method sales of $20,000) | 120,000 |

**Required**

1. Prepare the journal entries for 1995.
2. If the company collected $40,000 in 1996 on its 1995 installment method sales, prepare the appropriate journal entries in 1996.

E16-11  *Sales Under the Installment Method*  The following information is available for the Butler Company, which began its operations in 1995:

|  | 1995 | 1996 |
|---|---|---|
| Total credit sales (including installment method sales) | $100,000 | $160,000 |
| Total cost of goods sold (including installment method cost of goods sold) | 72,000 | 105,000 |
| Installment method sales | 60,000 | 80,000 |
| Installment method cost of goods sold | 42,000 | 52,000 |
| Cash receipts on installment method sales | | |
| 1995 sales | 25,000 | 26,000 |
| 1996 sales | | 30,000 |
| Cash receipts on other credit sales | 28,000 | 85,000 |

**Required**

1. Prepare the journal entries for 1995 and 1996.
2. Prepare a partial income statement and a partial balance sheet for 1995.

E16-12   *Analysis of Installment Sales*   The following partial information is available for the Cupp Company:

| | | |
|---|---|---|
| Installment method sales | $120,000 | (3) |
| Installment method cost of goods sold | (1) | $63,000 |
| Gross profit percentage | (2) | 30% |
| Cash receipts on installment method sales | | |
|    1995 sales | 25,000 | (4) |
|    1996 sales | | (5) |
| Realized gross profit on installment method sales | | |
|    1995 sales | 5,000 | 7,000 |
|    1996 sales | | 9,000 |

**Required**
Compute the unknown amounts. (Note: It is not necessary to compute the amounts in the numerical sequence.)

E16-13   *Adjusting Entries for Installment Sales*   The Smookler Company uses the installment method for certain sales and experiences a constant gross profit rate of 20%. The following are the account balances at December 31, 1995 and 1996:

| | Installment Receivables | Deferred Gross Profit | Installment Method Sales |
|---|---|---|---|
| 1995 | $50,000 | $30,000 | $100,000 |
| 1996 | 80,000 | 35,000 | 120,000 |

**Required**
Prepare the journal entries for 1996.

E16-14   *Cost Recovery*   In 1995, the Huxley Company, a real estate company, purchased some raw land for $60,000 and resold it on credit for $90,000. Because of the speculative nature of the usefulness of the land, the company used the cost recovery method for the sale of the land. The cash collections in 1995, 1996, and 1997 were $25,000, $45,000, and $20,000, respectively.

**Required**
Prepare the journal entries for each year.

E16-15   *Deposit Method*   On January 1, 1995, the Fritz Company sold a building in a depressed area for $200,000. The building had originally cost $500,000 and had a book value of $100,000. The sale agreement required the purchaser to pay $5,000 down and sign an 8% note for the balance. Interest on the note is payable at the end of each year; the interest is refundable if the following contingency is not met. The sale agreement was contingent on the commitment by the city government to support redevelopment of the area in which the building was located. Therefore, the company used the deposit method to record the sale.

**Required**
1. Prepare the journal entries for 1995.
2. On January 1, 1996, the city government made the necessary commitments. Prepare the appropriate journal entry.

E16-16   *Consignee*   On April 17, 1995, the Winger Company shipped 10 tractors to the Yuma Farm Supply Company on consignment. Each tractor cost $30,000 and the Winger Company incurred cash shipment costs of $100 per tractor. The consignment agreement required payment to Winger 30 days after the sale was made to a third party. On December 31, 1995, the consignee reported that 6 tractors had been sold for $36,000 each, of which two were sold after December 5. The consignee paid the Winger Company the amount required under the agreement, after deducting the commission of 5% and advertising costs of $2,000 incurred by the consignee.

**Required**
1. Prepare the 1995 journal entries for the Yuma Farm Supply Company.
2. What amount related to the consignment activities, and in what category, would the company report on its balance sheet on December 31, 1995?

E16-17 *Consignor*  Refer to the information in E16-16.

**Required**

1. Prepare the 1995 journal entries for the Winger Company.
2. What amount related to the consignment activities, and in what category, would the company report on its balance sheet on December 31, 1995?

E16-18 *Franchise*  The Chocomalt Company sells franchises. For each franchise, the company charges an initial franchise fee of $28,000. The franchise agreement requires a down payment of $8,000, with the balance covered by the issuance of a $20,000 12% note, payable by the franchisee in 2 equal annual installments.

**Required**

Prepare the journal entry required by the Chocomalt Company to record each initial franchise fee under each of the following independent situations:

1. All material services have been substantially performed, the refund period has expired, and the collectibility of the note is reasonably assured.
2. All material services have been substantially performed, the refund period has expired, and the collectibility of the note is not reasonably assured.
3. All material services have been substantially performed, the refund period has not expired, and the collectibility of the note is reasonably assured.
4. All material services have not been substantially performed, the refund period has expired, and there is no basis for estimating the collectibility of the note.
5. The refund period has expired and the collectibility of the note is reasonably assured, but all material services have not been substantially performed.

## PROBLEMS

P16-1 *Revenue Recognition Alternatives*  Each of the following independent situations relates to the recognition of revenue:

a. Interest on loans made by a bank
b. Interest on loans made by a bank when the loans are in default
c. Collection of fares by an airline when the passengers make the reservations
d. Shipment of freight and mail by an airline before it receives payment
e. Imposition of a penalty (service charge) by a retailer on overdue accounts
f. Building a submarine for a foreign government
g. Growing and harvesting soybeans
h. Selling lots for vacation homes on long-term contracts with small down payments
i. Building houses in a subdivision
j. Growing timber over a 10-year period
k. Payments received by a producer for films that are licensed to movie theaters for 2 years, after which the rights are licensed to television networks for 1 year, and finally the rights revert to the producer
l. Rental of a building to another company for 5 years, with no payment of rent in the first year
m. "One cent" sale in which the first item is sold at full price and the second identical item is sold for one cent
n. Sale of a season pass by a ski resort

**Required**

For each situation, indicate when revenue should be recognized.

P16-2 *Revenue Recognition Alternatives*  The Slattery Company was formed on January 1, 1995 to build a single product. The company issued no-par common stock on that date for $300,000 cash. The product costs $20 to make, all of which is paid in cash at the time of production. The company sells each unit of the product for $35 on account and incurs sales commissions per unit of $5 cash. In 1995, the company produced 10,000 units, shipped 8,000 units, and received payment for 7,000 units.

**Required**

1. Prepare the 1995 income statement and ending balance sheet under each of the following methods:
   a. Revenue recognition at the time of sale (shipment)
   b. Revenue recognition during production
   c. Revenue recognition at the time of cash receipt
2. Which method provides the most useful information to users? Under what circumstances would the other methods provide more useful information?
3. In 1996, the company produced 15,000 units, shipped 17,000 units, and received payment for 18,000 units. What conclusion can be made about the balance in retained earnings on December 31, 1996 for each method of revenue recognition?

P16-3  *Percentage of Completion*  In 1995, Dreyer Corporation began construction work under a 3-year contract. The contract price is $800,000. Dreyer uses the percentage-of-completion method. The financial statement presentations relating to this contract on December 31, 1995 follow:

| Balance Sheet | | |
|---|---|---|
| Accounts receivable | | $15,000 |
| Construction in progress | $50,000 | |
| Less contract billings | (47,000) | |
| Cost of uncompleted contract in excess of billings | | 3,000 |

| Income Statement | |
|---|---|
| Gross profit (before tax) on the contract | $10,000 |

**Required**

1. How much cash was collected during 1995?
2. What was the initial estimated total income before tax on this contract? (*AICPA adapted*)

P16-4  *Long-Term Construction Contracts*  The Fender Construction Company receives a contract to build a building over a period of 3 years for a price of $700,000. Information relating to the performance of the contract is summarized as follows:

| | 1994 | 1995 | 1996 |
|---|---|---|---|
| Construction costs incurred during the year | $150,000 | $242,000 | $168,000 |
| Estimated costs to complete | 350,000 | 168,000 | — |
| Billings during the year | 120,000 | 260,000 | 320,000 |
| Collections during the year | 100,000 | 270,000 | 330,000 |

**Required**

Prepare journal entries for all 3 years under (1) the percentage-of-completion method and (2) the completed-contract method.

P16-5  *Long-Term Construction Contracts*  The Forman Company has contracted to build a dam over a period of 4 years for $3,000,000. Information relating to the performance of the contract is summarized as follows:

| | 1993 | 1994 | 1995 | 1996 |
|---|---|---|---|---|
| Construction costs incurred during the year | $ 300,000 | $1,100,000 | $ 863,000 | $837,000 |
| Estimated costs to complete | 2,200,000 | 1,400,000 | 837,000 | — |
| Billings during the year | 280,000 | 870,000 | 1,030,000 | 820,000 |
| Collections during the year | 270,000 | 875,000 | 1,010,000 | 845,000 |

**Required**

1. Compute the profit or loss for each year of the contract under (a) the percentage-of-completion method and (b) the completed-contract method.
2. Prepare the relevant sections of the income statement and ending balance sheet for each year under (a) the percentage-of-completion method and (b) the completed-contract method.

**P16-6**     *Long-Term Construction Contracts*   The Rice Company signed a contract to build a dam over a period of 3 years for a price of $10,000,000. Information relating to the performance of the contract is summarized as follows:

|  | 1994 | 1995 | 1996 |
|---|---|---|---|
| Construction costs incurred during the year | $2,000,000 | $4,000,000 | $6,000,000 |
| Estimated costs to complete | 6,000,000 | 6,000,000 | — |
| Billings during the year | 1,500,000 | 3,500,000 | 5,000,000 |
| Collections during the year | 1,300,000 | 3,600,000 | 5,100,000 |

**Required**

Prepare journal entries for all 3 years under (1) the percentage-of-completion method and (2) the completed-contract method.

**P16-7**     *Proportional Performance Method*   The Hilt Company, a public relations company, signs 2-year contracts with its clients. For $75,000 in advance, the company agrees to ensure that the client's name is mentioned 5 times on a network national news program, 10 times in a national news magazine, and 15 times on a local news program. In 1995, the company signed 8 contracts, and no additional contracts were signed in 1996.

    In 1995, the company's clients were mentioned 10 times on network national news programs, 40 times in national news magazines, and 22 times on local news programs. In 1996, the company's clients were mentioned 30 times on national news programs, 40 times in national news magazines, and 98 times on local news programs. The relevant cost information for the 8 contracts is as follows:

| | |
|---|---|
| Initial direct costs | $ 20,000 |
| Annual indirect costs | 80,000 |
| Estimated (and actual) total direct costs for two-year period | 260,000 |
| Direct cost per: | |
|     National news program | 2,000 |
|     National news magazine | 1,500 |
|     Local news program | 500 |

**Required**

1. Prepare the income statements for 1995 and 1996.
2. From a theoretical viewpoint, how should the company compute the depreciation of its office building and office equipment that would be included in the preceding costs? Why?

**P16-8**     *Sales Under the Installment Method*   The following information is available for the Dassler Company, which began its operations in 1995:

1. Installment method sales
   - 1995     $500,000
   - 1996     600,000
2. Gross profit percentage
   - 1995     20%
   - 1996     24%
3. Cash collections on installment method sales
   - 1995     25% of 1995 sales
   - 1996     50% of 1995 sales
   -           30% of 1996 sales
4. Bad debt policy
   - The company estimates its bad debts to be 2% of installment method sales.
5. Defaults and repossessions
   - 1995     $10,000 of 1995 installment method sales, of which $1,000 had been collected
   - 1996     $20,000 of 1995 installment method sales, of which $4,000 had been collected
   -           $15,000 of 1996 installment method sales, of which $2,000 had been collected

The policy of the company is to value repossessed items at 40% of their original selling price.

**Required**

Prepare the journal entries for 1995 and 1996.

**P16-9** *Sales Under the Installment Method*   The Dyson Company sells computer games to teenagers. Selected accounts included in the trial balance at December 31, 1994 and 1995 are as follows:

|  | 1994 | 1995 |
|---|---|---|
| Installment accounts receivable, 1994 | $80,000 | $ 20,000 |
| Installment accounts receivable, 1995 |  | 112,500 |
| Allowance for doubtful installment accounts receivable, 1994 | (5,000) | (3,700) |
| Allowance for doubtful installment accounts receivable, 1995 |  | (7,000) |
| Deferred gross profit, 1994 | (16,000) | (3,500) |
| Deferred gross profit, 1995 |  | (22,500) |

During 1995, installment method sales and cost of goods sold were $200,000 and $160,000, respectively. In 1995, the company repossessed games that had been sold in 1994 for $6,000, on which $2,500 had been collected. The games were believed to be worth $1,000. No repossessions occurred on 1995 sales.

**Required**

Prepare summary journal entries for 1995.

**P16-10** *Cost Recovery Method*   After a two-year search for a buyer, Hobson, Inc. sold its idle plant facility to Jackson Company for $700,000 on January 1, 1993. On this date, the plant had a depreciated cost on Hobson's books of $500,000. Under the agreement, Jackson paid $100,000 cash on January 1, 1993, and signed a $600,000 note bearing interest at 10%. The note was payable in installments of $100,000, $200,000, and $300,000 on January 1, 1994, 1995, and 1996, respectively. The note was secured by a mortgage on the property sold. Hobson appropriately accounted for the sale under the cost recovery method since there was no reasonable basis for estimating the degree of collectibility of the note receivable. Jackson repaid the note with three late installment payments, which were accepted by Hobson, as follows:

| Date of Payment | Principal | Interest |
|---|---|---|
| July 1, 1994 | $100,000 | $90,000 |
| December 31, 1995 | 200,000 | 75,000 |
| February 1, 1997 | 300,000 | 32,500 |

**Required**

Prepare a schedule (using the following format) to record the initial transaction for the sale of the idle plant facility, the application of subsequent cash collections on the note, and the necessary journal entry on the date the transaction is complete. (*AICPA adapted*)

| Date | Cash Received Debit | Note Receivable Dr.   (Cr.) | Idle Plant (Net) (Credit) | Deferred Income Dr. (Cr.) | Income Recognized (Credit) |
|---|---|---|---|---|---|
| Jan. 1, 1993 | $100,000 |  |  |  |  |
| July 1, 1994 | 190,000 |  |  |  |  |
| Dec. 31, 1995 | 275,000 |  |  |  |  |
| Feb. 1, 1997 | 332,500 |  |  |  |  |
| Feb. 1, 1997 |  |  |  |  |  |

**P16-11** *Consignments*   On January 1, 1995, the Hadad Company entered into a consignment agreement with the Trinidad Company. The agreement specifies that the consignee (Trinidad) is to sell the merchandise at a price of 30% above cost. Trinidad is required to pay Hadad the net sales price within 15 days of each sale to a third party. The net sales price is defined as the sales price, less any advertising costs incurred by Trinidad, and less a commission of 10% deducted from the sales price less the advertising costs. Hadad pays any costs incurred in shipping the merchandise to Trinidad.

In 1995, Hadad shipped merchandise costing $300,000 to Trinidad, and incurred delivery costs of $8,000. During the year (through December 15), Trinidad made sales of $195,000 and incurred advertising costs of

$15,000, and paid the required amount to Hadad. On December 31, 1995, Hadad phoned Trinidad and was told that additional sales of $39,000 had been made, and advertising costs of $3,000 incurred, since December 15. (Record this information in separate journal entries.)

**Required**

1. Prepare the journal entries for the Hadad Company.
2. What amount, and in what category, would Hadad Company report on its balance sheet on December 31, 1995?
3. Prepare the journal entries for the Trinidad Company.
4. What amount related to the consignment activities, and in what category, would the Trinidad Company report on its balance sheet on December 31, 1995?

**P16-12** *Franchise*  Year-Round Golf sells franchises for indoor golf driving ranges and putting greens. For each franchise, the company charges a nonrefundable initial franchise fee of $40,000. The franchise agreement requires a down payment of $10,000, with the balance covered by the issuance of a $30,000, 10% note, payable by the franchisee at the end of 5 years. Interest does not begin to accrue until the franchise opens, and the first interest payment is required 12 months after the franchise opens. The company only sells to qualified buyers so the collectibility of the note is always reasonably assured. The services required for the initial franchise fee are completed 6 months after the agreement is signed.

The franchisee is also required to pay a continuing fee of $6,000 per year, plus 10% of its gross sales. Half the $6,000 is applied against purchases of supplies from the franchisor, which are paid for in cash at the time of purchase. The franchisor charges a sale price of 50% above its cost on these supplies.

In the first six months of 1995, the company sold 4 franchises, which began operating at the end of December. These franchisees had sales of $160,000 in 1996, and purchased the allowable amount of supplies. In the second six months of 1995, the company sold one franchise, which began operating on April 1, 1996. The franchisee had sales of $25,000 in 1996 and purchased $1,500 of supplies.

**Required**

Prepare the journal entries required by Year-Round Golf in 1995 and 1996 to record the preceding events.

**P16-13** *Real Estate*  On January 1, 1995, the Hogback Company sold the Red Rocks Ranch, which constituted 20,000 acres of undeveloped land, to a limited partnership for $50 million. The land had originally cost Hogback $5 million. The terms of the sale included a cash payment of $9 million and a 10% note for $41 million to be paid in equal annual installments for 30 years. The note is secured by the land. Hogback paid a commission of 5% on the selling price to a real estate company.

**Required**

1. Should Hogback record the transaction as a sale? If so, prepare all the journal entries for 1995.
2. Assume instead that the company uses the installment method. Prepare all the journal entries for 1995.
3. Assume instead that the payments made to the Hogback Company were returnable at the option of the purchaser until June 30, 1996. Prepare all the journal entries for 1995. Ignore the sales commission.
4. Assume instead that the Hogback Company is obligated to make improvements costing $4 million over the next three years. In 1995, it made improvements costing $1 million. Prepare all the journal entries for 1995.
5. If the Hogback Company was the general partner of the limited partnership, would your answer to Requirement 1 change? A limited partner?

**P16-14** *Revenue Recognition Alternatives*  The following are the operating activities of three different companies:

*Company A:*  Engages in long-term construction contracts. Uses the percentage-of-completion method to recognize gross profits. Started contract X in 1994, contract Y in 1995, and contract Z in 1996. The total gross profit (estimated and actual) and the percentage completed for each contract during 1995 through 1997 are:

|  | Contract X | Contract Y | Contract Z |
|---|---|---|---|
| Gross profit | $600,000 | $400,000 | $500,000 |
| % completed during: |  |  |  |
| 1995 | 60% | 40% | — |
| 1996 | 25% | 35% | 30% |
| 1997 | — | 25% | 50% |

*Company B:*    Engages in long-term service contracts involving a specific number of defined but not similar service acts. Uses proportional performance method to recognize revenues. Sells two-year service contracts for $400 in advance. Each service contract requires Company B to perform service act 1 a total of 50 times and service act 2 a total of 20 times during the two-year period. At the beginning of 1995, 100 service contracts were sold. The following is a summary of the related cost information for the 100 service contracts:

| | |
|---|---:|
| Initial direct costs | $ 3,500 |
| Annual indirect costs | 4,500 |
| Estimated (and actual) total direct costs (for 2-year period) | 10,000 |
| Direct cost per service act: | |
|    Service act 1 | $1.20 |
|    Service act 2 | 2.00 |

During 1995, service act 1 was performed 2,700 times and service act 2 was performed 800 times. During 1996, service acts 1 and 2 were performed 2,300 and 1,200 times, respectively.

*Company C:*    Sells goods on the installment basis. Uses the installment method (because these are exceptional cases) to recognize gross profits. The following is a summary of the installment sales, costs of installment sales, operating expenses, and collections for 1995 and 1996:

| | 1995 | 1996 |
|---|---:|---:|
| Installment method sales | $80,000 | $100,000 |
| Costs of installment method sales | 48,000 | 62,000 |
| Operating expenses | 17,000 | 20,000 |
| Cash collections from: | | |
|    1994 installment method sales (1994 gross profit is 39%) | 58,000 | — |
|    1995 installment method sales | 56,000 | 24,000 |
|    1996 installment method sales | — | 68,000 |

**Required**

1. Prepare a schedule that shows Company A's gross profit for 1995, 1996, and 1997.
2. Prepare 1995 and 1996 condensed income statements for Company B.
3. Prepare 1995 and 1996 condensed income statements for Company C.

P16-15   *Revenue Recognition Alternatives*    The following are the operating activities of three different companies.

*Company X:*    Engages in long-term service contracts involving a specific number of defined but not similar service acts. Uses proportional performance method to recognize revenues. Sells two-year service contracts for $500 in advance. Each service contract requires Company X to perform service act 1 a total of 30 times and service act 2 a total of 50 times during the two-year period. At the beginning of 1995, 200 service contracts were sold. The following is a summary of the related cost information for the 200 service contracts:

| | |
|---|---:|
| Initial direct costs | $ 8,500 |
| Annual indirect costs | 9,300 |
| Estimated (and actual) total direct costs (for two-year period) | 20,000 |
| Direct cost per service act: | |
|    Service act 1 | $1.60 |
|    Service act 2 | 1.04 |

During 1995, service act 1 was performed 5,000 times and service act 2 was performed 4,000 times. During 1996, service acts 1 and 2 were performed 1,000 and 6,000 times, respectively.

*Company Y:*    Sells goods on the installment basis. Uses the installment method (because these are exceptional cases) to recognize gross profits. The following is a summary of the installment sales, gross profit, operating expenses, and collections for 1995 and 1996:

|  | 1995 | 1996 |
|---|---|---|
| Installment method sales | $90,000 | $110,000 |
| Gross profit | 35,100 | 45,100 |
| Operating expenses | 18,000 | 21,000 |
| Cash collections from: |  |  |
|    1994 installment method sales (1994 gross profit is 40%) | 35,000 | — |
|    1995 installment method sales | 67,000 | 23,000 |
|    1996 installment method sales | — | 80,000 |

*Company Z:*    Engages in long-term construction contracts. Uses the percentage-of-completion method to recognize gross profits. Started contract 1 in 1994, contract 2 in 1995, and contract 3 in 1996. The total gross profit (estimated and actual) and the percentage complete for each contract at the end of 1995 through 1997 are:

|  | Contract 1* | Contract 2 | Contract 3 |
|---|---|---|---|
| Gross profit | $800,000 | $350,000 | $600,000 |
| % complete at the end of: |  |  |  |
|   1995 | 75% | 50% | — |
|   1996 | 100% | 70% | 35% |
|   1997 | — | 100% | 90% |

\* 30% was complete at the end of 1994.

### Required

1. Prepare 1995 and 1996 condensed income statements for Company X.
2. Prepare 1995 and 1996 condensed income statements for Company Y.
3. Prepare a schedule that shows Company Z's gross profit for 1995, 1996, and 1997.

# 17

# ACCOUNTING FOR INCOME TAXES

The objectives of financial reporting and the Internal Revenue Code are quite different. The objective of generally accepted accounting principles for financial reporting is to provide useful information to decision makers about companies—information that will enable external users to make the investment and credit decisions discussed in Chapter 1. The overall objective of the Internal Revenue Code, on the other hand, is to obtain funds, in an equitable manner, to operate the federal government. Additionally, tax laws frequently have been used to stimulate and regulate the economy (for example, the percentage depletion deduction attempts to stimulate new investment in natural resource productive capacity). In view of these different goals, most accountants favor the conformity of financial accounting and income tax reporting procedures *only* when the goals are equally applicable. For instance, when an expense represents both an expired cost and a tax deduction, it should be deducted from revenue to arrive at both pretax financial income and taxable income.

Some people have maintained that the accounting procedures adopted for financial reporting and income tax reporting should be the same. However, this conformity would result in the use of procedures that are chosen for their acceptability under the Internal Revenue Code, because reports filed for income taxation purposes must comply with the statutory provisions of the tax code. Moreover, since corporations try to legally avoid or postpone taxes, the conformity of financial accounting and income taxation reporting procedures would result in a tendency to select practices that minimize or delay income taxes (and income) without considering the usefulness of the practices for financial reporting.

Financial accounting practices may be influenced by the procedures adopted for income tax reporting. For example, under the provisions of the Internal Revenue Code, a corporation only may use the LIFO method of inventory costing for income tax reporting if it also uses LIFO for financial reporting. Because of such influences, and in an effort to save costs, some corporations attempt to minimize the effect of the Code on their accounting systems by using similar practices for both financial accounting and income tax purposes.

As a result of their differing objectives, financial accounting is governed by generally accepted accounting principles and income tax reporting is governed by the Internal Revenue Code.[1] If items of revenue and expense for a corporation are coincidentally reported simultaneously, there is no issue. If they are not, it is necessary to determine: (1) the current and noncurrent income tax liabilities and/or assets to be reported on its balance sheet and (2) the income tax expense to be reported in regard to the pretax financial income[2] on its income statement. The procedures used to determine and report these items are discussed in the following sections.

## OVERVIEW AND DEFINITIONS

Consider the condensed income statements and income tax returns for the Freese Corporation for 1995 and 1996 shown in Exhibit 17-1.

### EXHIBIT 17-1

### FREESE CORPORATION

Income Statement and Income Tax Return
Years Ended December 31, 1995 and 1996

|  | Income Statement | | Income Tax Return | |
|---|---|---|---|---|
|  | 1995 | 1996 | 1995 | 1996 |
| Revenue | $180,000 | $200,000 | $170,000 | $210,000 |
| Cost of goods sold | (75,000) | (85,000) | (70,000) | (90,000) |
| Gross profit | $105,000 | $115,000 | $100,000 | $120,000 |
| Other expenses | (60,000) | (50,000) | (60,000) | (60,000) |
| Pretax income from continuing operations | $ 45,000 | $ 65,000 | $ 40,000 | $ 60,000 |
| Income taxes | (11,000) | (16,000) | (9,200) | (15,300) |
| Income from continuing operations | $ 34,000 | $ 49,000 | $ 30,800 | $ 44,700 |
| Extraordinary item (net of income tax effect) | — | (10,000) | — | — |
| Net income | $ 34,000 | $ 39,000 | $ 30,800 | $ 44,700 |

---

1. Corporations may be subject to federal, state, and foreign income taxes. In this chapter, we limit the discussion to the impact of federal income taxes on financial reporting.
2. The terms *financial income, financial accounting income, book income,* and *accounting income* are synonymous and are used interchangeably. Because the FASB uses the term *financial income* in its discussion of accounting for income taxes, that term is used throughout this chapter.

## Causes of Differences

Several differences between the Freese Corporation's income statements and income tax returns in Exhibit 17-1 should be noted: (1) the amounts of revenue recognized in 1995 and 1996 are different; (2) the expenses deductible as cost of goods sold differ in 1995 and 1996; (3) other expenses differ in 1996; and (4) an extraordinary item was separately reported on the income statement in 1996 but did not appear on the income tax return for that year. The causes of differences between pretax financial income and taxable income (and potentially between income tax expense and income taxes payable) can be categorized into five groups:

1. *Permanent Differences.* Some items of revenue and expense reported for financial accounting purposes are never reported for income tax purposes under the provisions of the Internal Revenue Code. Moreover, other items classified as allowable deductions for income tax reporting do not qualify as expenses under generally accepted accounting principles. These items result in permanent differences between pretax financial income and taxable income.

2. *Temporary Differences.* Some items of revenue and expense are reported in one period for financial accounting purposes, but are reported in an earlier or later period for income tax purposes. These items result in temporary differences between pretax financial income and taxable income.

3. *Operating Loss Carrybacks and Carryforwards.* When an operating loss is reported in a given year, the Internal Revenue Code allows the loss to be carried back or carried forward to offset previous or future reported taxable income on the corporation's income tax income. Pretax financial income or loss is reported in the year of occurrence on the corporation's income statement.

4. *Tax Credits.* To stimulate certain investments, or to provide tax relief in special circumstances, the Internal Revenue Code provides specific tax credits that may be deducted from income taxes owed by qualifying corporations to determine current income taxes payable. Although use of a tax credit does not cause a difference between pretax financial income and taxable income, it may cause a difference between income tax expense and income taxes payable.

5. *Intraperiod Tax Allocation.* Income tax is apportioned for financial accounting purposes to: (a) income from continuing operations, (b) results from discontinued operations, (c) extraordinary items, (d) the cumulative effects of changes in accounting principles, and (e) prior period adjustments. No similar apportionment is made on the income tax return.

## Definitions

The impact of using different accounting procedures for financial accounting and income tax reporting was studied by the FASB and resulted in the issuance of **FASB Statement No. 109**, entitled "Accounting for Income Taxes." The following sections include a discussion of the provisions of the *Statement* as they apply to the areas of difference between income reported for financial accounting purposes and income reported for taxation purposes. The discussion includes a number of terms related to income taxes, which are defined[3] in Exhibit 17-2.

---

3. These definitions are adapted from "Accounting for Income Taxes," *FASB Statement of Financial Accounting Standards No. 109* (Stamford, Conn.: FASB, 1992), par. 289.

## EXHIBIT 17-2

### KEY TERMS RELATED TO INCOME TAXES

**Deductible temporary difference.** Temporary difference that results in deductible amounts in future years when the related asset or liability is recovered or settled, respectively.

**Deferred tax asset.** The deferred tax consequences attributable to deductible temporary differences and operating loss carryforwards. A deferred tax asset is measured using the applicable enacted tax rate and provisions of the enacted tax law. A deferred tax asset is reduced by a valuation allowance if, based on the weight of evidence available, it is more likely than not that some portion or all of a deferred tax asset will not be realized.

**Deferred tax consequences.** The future effects on income taxes, as measured by the applicable enacted tax rate and provisions of the enacted tax law, resulting from temporary differences and operating loss carryforwards at the end of the current year.

**Deferred tax expense (or benefit).** The change during the year in a corporation's deferred tax liabilities and assets.

**Deferred tax liability.** The deferred tax consequences attributable to taxable temporary differences. A deferred tax liability is measured using the applicable enacted tax rate and provisions of the enacted tax law.

**Income tax expense (or benefit).** The sum of income tax obligation and deferred tax expense (or benefit).

**Income tax obligation (or refund).** The amount of income taxes paid or payable (or refundable) for a year as determined by applying the provisions of the enacted tax law to the taxable income or operating loss for that year. Sometimes called *current tax expense (or benefit)*.

**Operating loss carryback.** An excess of tax deductible expenses over taxable revenues in a year that may be carried back to reduce taxable income in a prior year.

**Operating loss carryforward.** An excess of tax deductible expenses over taxable revenues in a year that may be carried forward to reduce taxable income in a future year.

**Permanent difference.** A difference between pretax financial income and taxable income in an accounting period that will never reverse in a later accounting period.

**Taxable income.** The excess of taxable revenues over tax deductible expenses and exemptions for the year as defined by the governmental taxing authority.

**Taxable temporary difference.** Temporary difference that results in taxable amounts in future years when the related asset or liability is recovered or settled, respectively.

**Temporary difference.** A difference between the tax basis of an asset or liability and its reported amount in the financial statements that will result in taxable or deductible amounts in future years when the reported amount of the asset is recovered or liability is settled.

**Valuation allowance.** The portion of a deferred tax asset for which it is more likely than not that a tax benefit will not be realized.

## INTERPERIOD INCOME TAX ALLOCATION: BASIC ISSUES

**Interperiod income tax allocation involves the allocation of a corporation's income tax obligation as an expense to various accounting periods.** Differences between pretax financial income and taxable income arise from both temporary and permanent differences. Temporary differences ultimately reverse and require interperiod tax allocation. Although permanent differences are not subject to interperiod tax allocation, they are discussed first in this section because an accountant must be able to classify differences as permanent or temporary for interperiod tax allocation purposes.

### Permanent Differences

As the definition in Exhibit 17-2 indicates, a difference between pretax financial income and taxable income in an accounting period that will *never* reverse in a later accounting period is called a **permanent difference**. These differences arise as the

U.S. Congress sets economic policy or partially offsets a provision of the tax code that may impose too heavy a tax burden on a particular segment of the economy. There are three types of permanent differences between pretax financial income and taxable income; they are shown in Exhibit 17-3.

Permanent differences affect *either* reported pretax financial income *or* taxable income, *but not both*. In other words, permanent differences do *not* have deferred tax consequences. They do not require interperiod income tax allocation because later events will not alter the fact that generally accepted accounting principles and the tax code differ on the items of revenue and expense to be recognized. A corporation that has nontaxable revenue or additional deductions for income tax reporting purposes will report a relatively lower taxable income (as compared to pretax financial income) than it would have if these items were not present, whereas a corporation with expenses that are not tax deductible will report a relatively higher taxable income.

### Temporary Differences

As the definition in Exhibit 17-2 indicates, a difference between the tax basis (i.e., book value) of an asset (or liability) for income tax purposes and the reported amount (i.e., book value) of the asset (or liability) in the financial statements that will result in taxable or deductible amounts in future years when the reported amount of the

---

### EXHIBIT 17-3

### PERMANENT DIFFERENCES

1. *Revenues that are recognized for financial reporting purposes, but are never taxable.* For example:
   a. Interest on municipal bonds. For income tax purposes, the Internal Revenue Code provides that receipt of interest on municipal bonds by an investor corporation generally is never recognized as revenue. The provision enables municipalities to offer bonds that pay a relatively lower rate of interest than corporate bonds of a similar quality, thus reducing the cost of borrowing for these municipalities.
   b. Life insurance proceeds payable to a corporation upon the death of an insured employee. For income tax purposes, the proceeds received are not considered revenue to the corporation, but rather, as partial compensation for the loss of the employee.
2. *Expenses that are recognized for financial reporting purposes but are never deductible for income tax purposes.* For example:
   a. Life insurance premiums on officers. For income tax purposes, the periodic premiums for life insurance policies on officers are not deductible as expenses. This procedure is consistent with the treatment of the insurance proceeds discussed earlier.
   b. Amortization of goodwill. For income tax purposes, the undeterminability of the estimated future period of benefit has resulted in the legislative decision not to allow a deduction of the amortization of goodwill (unless there is evidence of a decline in value or limited life).
3. *Deductions that are allowed for income tax purposes but do not qualify as expenses under generally accepted accounting principles.* For example:
   a. Percentage depletion in excess of cost depletion. Certain corporations that own wasting assets are allowed to deduct a percentage depletion in excess of the cost depletion on a wasting asset from their revenues for income tax purposes. This provision of the tax code was designed to encourage exploration for natural resources.
   b. Special dividend deduction. For income tax purposes, a special deduction (usually 70%) for certain dividends from investments in equity securities is allowed.

**EXHIBIT 17-4**

## TEMPORARY DIFFERENCES

### Future Taxable Income Will Exceed Future Pretax Financial Income

1. *Revenues or gains are included in pretax financial income prior to the time they are included in taxable income.* For example, gross profit on installment sales normally is recognized at the point of sale for financial reporting purposes, but for income tax purposes, in certain situations, it is recognized as cash is collected. Or gross profit on long-term construction contracts may be recognized for financial reporting purposes under the percentage-of-completion method and for income tax purposes for certain companies under the percentage-of-completion capitalized cost method. Also, investment income may be recognized under the equity method for financial reporting purposes but in a subsequent period as dividends are received for income tax purposes.

2. *Expenses or losses are deducted to compute taxable income prior to the time they are deducted to compute pretax financial income.* For example, a depreciable asset purchased before 1981 may be depreciated by an accelerated method for income tax purposes and the straight-line method for financial accounting purposes. Or a depreciable asset purchased between 1981 and 1986 may be depreciated by the Accelerated Cost Recovery System (ACRS) or, after 1986, by the Modified Accelerated Cost Recovery System (MACRS) over the prescribed tax life (discussed in Chapter 9) for income tax purposes. For financial reporting purposes, however, it may be depreciated by a financial accounting (often straight-line) method over a longer period. Also, interest and taxes on certain self-construction projects may be deducted as incurred in arriving at taxable income, but may be capitalized in certain instances as a part of the cost of the self-constructed assets for financial reporting.

### Future Taxable Income Will Be Less Than Future Pretax Financial Income

3. *Revenues or gains are included in taxable income prior to the time they are included in pretax financial income.* For example, such items as rent, interest, and royalties received in advance are taxable when received but are not reported for financial reporting purposes until the service actually has been provided. Additionally, gains on "sales and leasebacks" are taxed at the date of sale, but reported over the life of the lease contract for financial reporting purposes.

4. *Expenses or losses are deducted to compute pretax financial income prior to the time they are deducted to compute taxable income.* For example, product warranty costs, bad debts, and losses on inventories may be estimated and recorded as expenses in the current year for financial reporting purposes but deducted as actually incurred in a later year for the determination of taxable income. Or indirect costs of producing inventory may be recorded as expenses in the current year for financial reporting purposes, but capitalized in the cost of inventory and therefore deducted as part of cost of goods sold in a later year to determine taxable income. Also, a contingent liability may be expensed for financial reporting purposes if a loss is probable and is measurable, but is deducted in arriving at taxable income as it is actually paid.

asset is recovered (or the liability is settled) is called a **temporary difference**.[4] In other words, a temporary difference causes a difference between pretax financial income and taxable income that "originates" in one or more years and "reverses" in later years. Temporary differences sometimes are called *timing* differences because of the different time periods in which they affect pretax financial income and taxable income. Temporary differences generally relate to individual assets and liabilities and may be classified into four groups[5], which are shown in Exhibit 17-4.

---

4. Temporary differences also include items that cannot be identified with a particular asset or liability for financial reporting but which: (a) result from events that have been recognized in the financial statements, and (b) will result in taxable or deductible amounts in future years based on provisions in the tax law.

5. *FASB Statement No. 109* identifies four other temporary differences: (1) a reduction in the tax basis of depreciable assets because of an investment tax credit accounted for by the deferred method, (2) a reduction in the tax basis of depreciable assets because of other tax credits, (3) an increase in the tax basis of assets because of indexing whenever the local currency is the functional currency, and (4) business combinations accounted for by the purchase method. These temporary differences are not discussed in this chapter.

Temporary differences between pretax financial income and taxable income raise numerous conceptual issues regarding the measurement and reporting of the income tax liability (asset) and the income tax expense (benefit) in the accounting periods affected.

## Conceptual Issues

In 1992, after much debate over a 25-year period, the FASB issued *FASB Statement No. 109* which defines the generally accepted accounting principles for income taxes. The accounting principles for income taxes initially were defined in *APB Opinion No. 11*, issued in 1967. This *Opinion* required the use of comprehensive income tax allocation applied under the deferred method. This approach meant that the annual income tax expense was based on all transactions and events included in pretax income on the income statement (i.e., comprehensive allocation), and the deferred tax amount reported on the ending balance sheet was based on the income tax rates in existence when the temporary differences originated (i.e., deferred method). During its life, *APB Opinion No. 11* was the subject of much controversy because of significant disagreements concerning its conclusions. Furthermore, the *FASB Statements of Concepts* issued after the *Opinion* contradicted these conclusions. Consequently, *FASB Statement No. 96* was issued in 1987, requiring the use of comprehensive income tax allocation applied under the asset/liability method. Under this approach, the deferred tax asset or liability reported on the ending balance sheet was based on the enacted future income tax rates when the temporary differences were scheduled to reverse. The conclusions of the FASB in this *Statement* also were controversial because of scheduling complexities and restrictions imposed for recognizing deferred tax assets. It eventually was superseded by *FASB Statement No. 109*. In its deliberations, the FASB reexamined several conceptual questions (identified in Exhibit 17-5) summarized as follows:

*Many arguments in favor of and against each of these approaches and the controversial conclusions of* FASB Statement No. 96 *are discussed in the Appendix to this chapter.*

1. Should corporations be required to make interperiod income tax allocations for temporary differences, or should there be no interperiod tax allocation?

2. If interperiod tax allocation is required:
   a. Should it be based on a comprehensive approach for all temporary differences or on a partial approach for certain temporary differences?
   b. Should it be applied using the asset/liability method (based on enacted future tax rates), the deferred method (based on originating tax rates), or the net-of-tax method?

After considering the criticisms raised regarding *FASB Statement No. 96*, the FASB issued an *Exposure Draft* on accounting for income taxes in 1991. Based on responses from constituents and a limited-scope "field test" by participating corporations, the Board (in a unanimous vote) issued *FASB Statement No. 109*, in which it identified two objectives of accounting for income taxes. The first is to recognize the amount of income tax obligation or refund of a corporation for the current year. The second is to recognize deferred tax liabilities and assets for the future tax consequences of all events that have been recognized in the corporation's financial statements or income tax returns. Based on these objectives, the FASB concluded that:

1. Interperiod income tax allocation of temporary differences is appropriate.

2. The comprehensive allocation approach should be applied.

3. The asset/liability method of income tax allocation should be used.

Thus, nonallocation, partial allocation, and the deferred and net-of-tax methods listed in Exhibit 17-5 (and discussed in the Appendix) were rejected and are *not* gen-

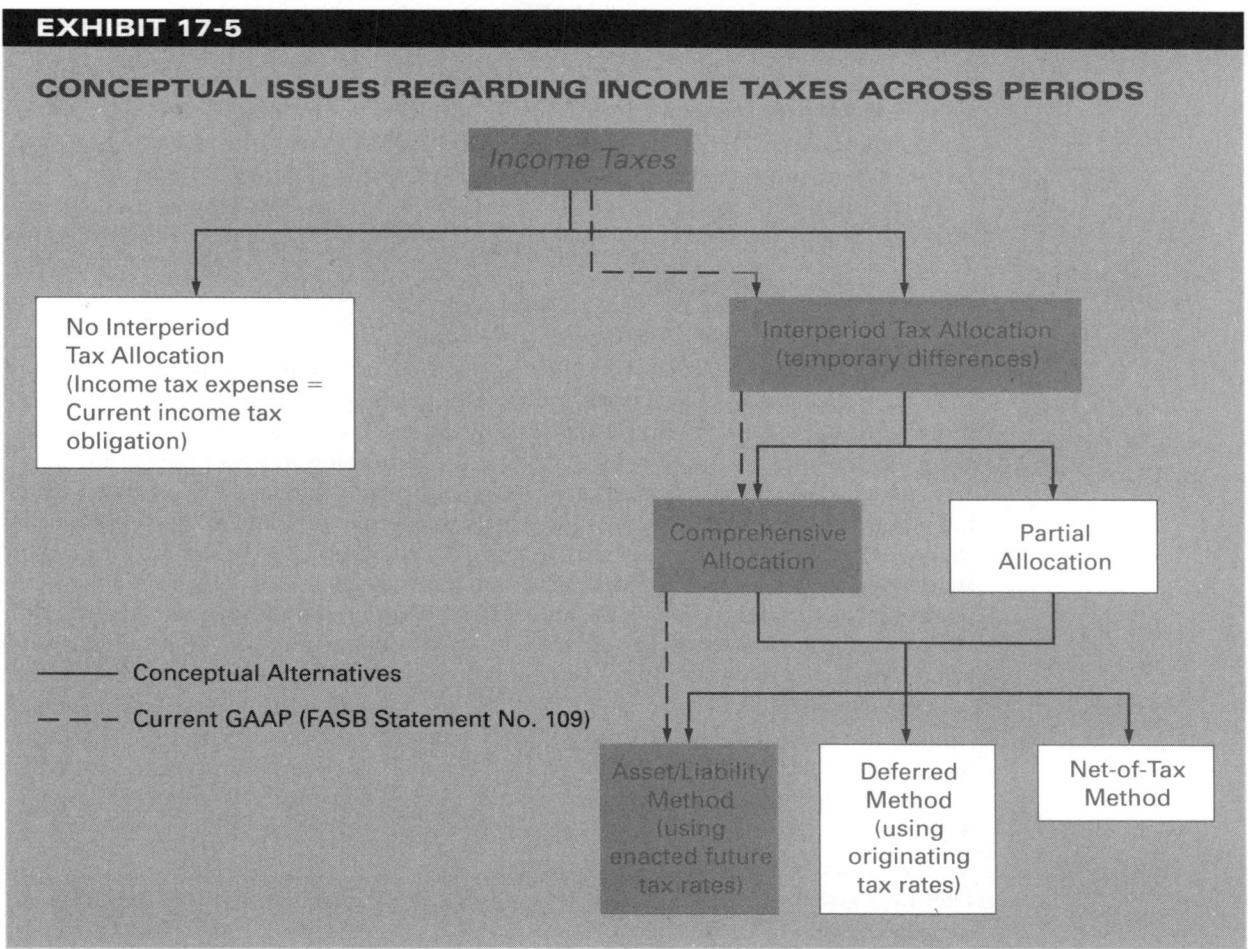

**EXHIBIT 17-5**

**CONCEPTUAL ISSUES REGARDING INCOME TAXES ACROSS PERIODS**

erally accepted accounting principles. Furthermore, reporting of deferred taxes using a present value approach was not considered by the FASB and is *not* acceptable.

To implement the objectives, the FASB established four basic principles to be applied in accounting for income taxes at the date of a corporation's financial statements:

1. A current tax liability or asset is recognized for the estimated income tax obligation or refund on its income tax return for the current year.

2. A deferred tax liability or asset is recognized for the estimated future tax effects of each temporary difference.

3. The measurement of deferred tax liabilities and assets is based on provisions of the enacted tax law; the effects of future changes in tax laws or rates are not anticipated.

4. The measurement of deferred tax assets is reduced, if necessary, by the amount of any tax benefits that, based on available evidence, are not expected to be realized.[6]

---

6. *FASB Statement No. 109, op. cit.,* par. 6 and 8. *FASB Statement No. 109* also addressed the accounting for operating loss carrybacks and carryforwards. For simplicity, these items are discussed in a later section.

Thus, under generally accepted accounting principles, **interperiod income tax allocation is used to determine the deferred tax assets and liabilities for all temporary differences, based on the currently enacted income tax rates and laws that will be in existence when the temporary differences result in future taxable amounts or deductible amounts. The deferred tax assets and liabilities are adjusted when changes in the income tax rates are enacted.**

In regard to interperiod income tax allocation, the FASB discussed deferred tax liabilities, deferred tax assets, and the measurement of these items in the context of the *FASB Conceptual Framework.*

### Deferred Tax Liability

The three essential characteristics of a liability established in *FASB Statement of Concepts No. 6* are: (1) it must embody a present responsibility to another entity that involves settlement by probable future transfer or use of assets at a specified or determinable date, on occurrence of a specified event, or on demand, (2) the responsibility obligates the corporation, leaving it little or no discretion to avoid the future sacrifice, and (3) the transaction or other event obligating the corporation has already happened. The deferred tax consequences of temporary differences of a corporation that will result in taxable amounts in future years meet these characteristics. The first characteristic is met by a deferred tax liability because: (a) the deferred tax consequences stem from the requirements of tax law and, hence, are a responsibility to the government, (b) settlement will involve a probable future transfer or use of assets when the taxes are paid, and (c) settlement will result from events specified by the tax law. The second characteristic is met because, based on the government rules and regulations, income taxes definitely will be payable when the temporary differences result in taxable amounts in future years. The third characteristic is met because the past events that created the taxable temporary differences are the same events that result in the deferred tax liability.

### Deferred Tax Asset

The three essential characteristics of an asset are: (1) it must embody a probable future benefit that involves a capacity to contribute to the corporation's future net cash inflows, (2) the corporation must be able to obtain the benefit and control other entities' access to it, and (3) the transaction or other event resulting in the corporation's right to or control of the benefit must already have occurred.[7] The deferred tax consequences of temporary differences of a corporation that will result in deductible amounts in future years meet these characteristics. The first characteristic is met because the deductible amounts in future years will result in reduced taxable income, therefore contributing to future net cash inflows through reduced taxes paid. The second characteristic is met because the corporation will have an exclusive right to the reduced taxes paid. Finally, the third characteristic is met because the past events that created the deductible temporary differences are the same events that result in the deferred tax asset.

### Measurement

Once a taxable or deductible temporary difference has been identified, it is "measured" before being recorded and reported as a deferred tax liability or deferred tax asset in a corporation's financial statements. The FASB addressed two issues regarding the measurement of deferred tax liabilities and assets: (1) the applicable income

---

7.  "Elements of Financial Statements of Business Enterprises," *FASB Statement of Financial Accounting Concepts No. 6* (Stamford, Conn.: FASB, 1985), par. 26 and 36.

tax rates, and (2) whether a valuation allowance should be established for deferred tax assets.

The U.S. federal corporate income taxes are assessed based on a "several step" rate schedule. However, if a corporation's taxable income exceeds a specified amount, its entire taxable income essentially is taxed at a "single flat rate," as discussed in Chapter 11. In regard to deferred taxes, the question arose as to what rate to use in measuring deferred tax liabilities and assets. For simplicity, the FASB decided to require a corporation to use the enacted income tax rate expected to apply to its *last* dollars of taxable income (i.e., its *marginal tax rate*) in the periods when the deferred tax liability or asset is expected to be settled or realized. In other words, most corporations are required to use the single flat rate in their deferred tax calculations.[8]

The second issue—the possible use of a valuation allowance for deferred tax assets—was more controversial. The tax benefits from a deferred tax asset will be realized only if there is enough future taxable income from which to subtract the deductible temporary difference. If there is sufficient uncertainty about a corporation's future taxable income, the FASB decided that a valuation allowance should be established to reduce the corporation's deferred tax asset(s) to its realizable amount. (This approach is similar to reporting accounts receivable at a gross amount and then reducing the amount by an allowance for doubtful accounts.) But how much uncertainty is "sufficient" and how does a corporation make a judgment about the realizable amount? In regard to sufficiency, the FASB considered the use of "probable" as it was applied in *FASB Statement No. 5* to define contingencies, and "beyond a reasonable doubt" as it was used in *APB Opinion No. 11* for recognizing operating loss carryforwards. The Board rejected the use of "probable" for deferred taxes because of confusion as to its meaning in that context. It also rejected the use of "beyond a reasonable doubt" because of its implementation complexities. Instead, the Board decided to apply a "more likely than not" (a likelihood of more than 50 percent) criterion to measure uncertainty. In other words, the FASB concluded that a valuation allowance is needed if, based on available evidence, it is *more likely than not* that the deferred asset will *not* be realized.

In regard to making a judgment about the realizable amount, the FASB considered various "quantitative" and "qualitative" approaches. The Board stated that all available evidence, both positive and negative, should be considered to determine whether a valuation allowance is required. Four possible sources of taxable income (positive evidence) that might be used to realize the tax benefits from a deferred tax asset were identified. These sources include:

1. Future reversals of existing taxable temporary differences.

2. Future taxable income exclusive of reversing temporary differences.

3. Taxable income in prior carryback year(s) if carryback is permitted under the tax law.

4. Prudent and feasible tax-planning strategies.[9]

---

8. Corporations for which graduated rates are a significant factor must use an "average graduated tax rate" approach for measuring their deferred tax liabilities and assets. This approach is not discussed further in this book.

9. A tax planning strategy is an action a corporation ordinarily would not take except to ensure that a deductible temporary difference could be realized (e.g., acceleration of taxable income).

The FASB concluded that if *at least one* of these sources is sufficient to conclude that a valuation allowance is not necessary, then other sources do not have to be considered.

The Board stated that it would be difficult for a corporation to conclude that a valuation allowance is *not* needed when there is negative evidence, such as cumulative losses in recent years. It also provided other examples of negative evidence, such as: (1) a history of unused operating loss carryforwards, (2) losses expected in the near future years, and (3) unsettled circumstances that are potentially unfavorable. The Board noted, however, that other positive evidence may overcome negative evidence so that a valuation allowance may not be needed. Examples of positive evidence cited include: (1) existing contracts or sales backlogs that will produce sufficient taxable income, (2) an excess of fair market value over the tax basis (book value) sufficient enough to realize the deferred tax asset, and (3) a strong earnings history exclusive of the loss that created the future deductible amount, coupled with evidence that the loss was an aberration. A corporation must use good judgment in weighing the verifiable positive and negative evidence to determine whether a valuation allowance is not needed for some or all of a deferred tax asset.

If a valuation allowance is established, there may be a change in circumstances at a later date that may cause a change in judgment about the realizability of the related deferred tax asset. There also may be a change in tax laws or rates that would affect the amount of previously recorded deferred tax assets and liabilities. In each case, the effect of the change is included as an adjustment to income tax expense related to income from continuing operations in the year of the change.[10]

### Recording and Reporting of Current and Deferred Taxes

Recall that *FASB Statement No. 109* has as its objectives to recognize (record and report) the amount of a corporation's income tax obligation (refund), as well as the amount of its deferred tax liabilities and deferred tax assets. To measure and record the amount of a corporation's current and deferred income taxes, the following steps are completed:

*Step 1.*    Identify the temporary differences and classify each as either "taxable" or "deductible."

*Step 2.*    Measure the deferred tax liability for each taxable temporary difference using the applicable tax rate.

*Step 3.*    Measure the deferred tax asset for each deductible temporary difference using the applicable tax rate.

*Step 4.*    Reduce deferred tax assets by a valuation allowance if, based on available evidence, it is *more likely than not* that some or all of the deferred tax assets will not be realized.

*Step 5.*    Measure the income tax obligation by applying the applicable tax rate to the current taxable income.

*Step 6.*    Record the income tax expense [including the deferred tax expense (or benefit)], income tax obligation, change in deferred tax liabilities and/or deferred tax assets, and change in valuation allowance (if any).

---

10. *FASB Statement No. 109, op. cit.,* par. 18–27.

*Basic Entries*

A corporation's deferred tax expense or benefit is the change in its deferred tax liabilities or assets during the year. The amount of this change, then, coupled with the amount of income tax obligation (or refund) is the amount of income tax expense (or benefit) for the year. Thus, in the case of a corporation that has one deferred tax liability at the beginning of the year, earns pretax income for the year, and incurs an increase in the liability, the following journal entry is made:

| | | |
|---|---|---|
| Income Tax Expense | XX | |
| Deferred Tax Liability | | XX |
| Income Taxes Payable | | XX |

For a similar situation involving one deferred tax asset (and *no* valuation allowance) instead of a deferred tax liability, the following journal entry is made:

| | | |
|---|---|---|
| Income Tax Expense | XX | |
| Deferred Tax Asset | | XX |
| Income Taxes Payable | | XX |

The amount of income tax expense is allocated to the various components of comprehensive income, as discussed in a later section. The amount of income tax obligation is determined by applying the current tax rate(s) to the taxable income for the year. It is assumed here (and in the later examples and homework) that the corporation does *not* make estimated income tax payments during the year; therefore, the entire obligation for the year is recorded as income taxes payable. The amount of the adjustment to the deferred tax liability (asset) in the journal entry is calculated by determining the amount [based on the currently enacted future tax rate(s)] of the year-end deferred tax liability (asset) and then comparing this amount to the amount of the beginning deferred tax liability (asset). The amount of the year-end deferred tax liability (asset) is reported on the corporation's ending balance sheet, classified as "current" or "noncurrent," as discussed in a later section.

If, in the last example, the corporation previously had no valuation allowance but determined that one was necessary, the following additional journal entry is made:

| | | |
|---|---|---|
| Income Tax Expense | XX | |
| Allowance to Reduced Deferred Tax | | |
| Asset to Realizable Value | | XX |

The debit to Income Tax Expense is combined with the amount from the journal entry in the last example to determine the total income tax expense. The allowance account is subtracted from the deferred tax asset account on the corporation's ending balance sheet to report the expected net realizable value of the deferred tax asset.

When a corporation has such items as more than one taxable or deductible temporary difference, permanent differences, and changes in enacted future tax rates, completion of the steps listed earlier becomes more complex.

*Example 1: Deferred Tax Liability—Single Temporary Difference*

Assume that in 1995, Track Company purchased an asset at a cost of $6,000. For financial reporting purposes, the asset has a 4-year life, no residual value, and is depreciated by the units-of-output method over 6,000 units (1995: 1,600 units, 1996: 2,800 units, 1997: 1,100 units, 1998: 500 units). For income tax purposes, the asset is depreciated under MACRS using the 200% declining balance method over a 3-year life (no residual value), as discussed in Chapter 9. Prior to 1995, the company had no deferred tax liability or asset. The difference between depreciation for financial reporting purposes and income tax purposes is the only temporary difference between pretax financial income and taxable income.[11] In 1995, the company has taxable income of $7,500. The income tax rate for 1995 is 30% and no change in the tax rate has been enacted for future years.

Based on the preceding information, the depreciation expense for 1995 is $1,600 [1,600 × ($6,000 ÷ 6,000)] for financial reporting purposes and $2,000 [$6,000 × 33.33% (from Exhibit 9-12)] for income tax purposes. At the end of 1995, the asset has a book value of $4,400 ($6,000 − $1,600) for financial reporting purposes and a book value of $4,000 ($6,000 − $2,000) for income tax purposes. This $400 ($4,400 − $4,000) difference in book values is a result of a temporary difference in depreciation that originated in 1995 (and that caused taxable income to be lower than pretax financial income in that year). This difference will reverse in future years because tax depreciation will be *lower* than financial depreciation by $400 (to depreciate each book value to zero). Thus, the $400 is a *taxable temporary difference* because future taxable income will be *higher* than future pretax financial income.

In applying the steps to determine the Track Company's current and deferred income taxes, the depreciation difference is identified as the only taxable temporary difference (Step 1). In Step 2, the $120 total deferred tax liability is calculated (measured) by multiplying the total taxable temporary difference ($400) times the enacted future tax rate (30%). Steps 3 and 4 are not necessary because the company has no deferred tax asset. The $2,250 income tax obligation for 1995 (Step 5) is calculated by multiplying the taxable income ($7,500) times the current tax rate (30%). In Step 6, the following journal entry is made at the end of 1995:

| | | |
|---|---|---|
| **Income Tax Expense ($120 + $2,250)** | 2,370 | |
| Deferred Tax Liability | | 120 |
| Income Taxes Payable | | 2,250 |

The income tax expense includes the deferred tax expense and the current income taxes payable. Note that since the company has no deferred tax liability at the beginning of 1995, the deferred tax expense for 1995 is $120 and this is the amount of the credit to the deferred tax liability. (If a deferred tax liability had existed at the beginning of 1995, the change necessary to bring the balance up (or down) to the ending deferred tax liability would be recorded in the journal entry.) The income tax expense of $2,370 is reported on the company's 1995 income statement, subject to intraperiod tax allocation (discussed in a later section of the chapter). The income taxes payable are reported as a current liability on the company's 1995 ending balance sheet. As discussed in a later section, the deferred tax liability also is reported on the ending balance sheet.

*Example 2: Deferred Tax Liability—Single
Temporary Difference and Multiple Rates*
Now assume the same information as in Example 1, except that the income tax rate for 1995 is 40%, but Congress has enacted tax rates of 35% for 1996, 33% for 1997, and 30% for 1998 and beyond. In Example 1, the calculation of the deferred tax liability was straightforward because a 30% tax rate was applicable to all the future years when the depreciation temporary difference reversed and resulted in higher taxable income. However, when different enacted tax rates apply to taxable income in

---

11. In reality, a company would have several depreciable assets of different ages and with varying lives, perhaps resulting in both originating (and deductible) and reversing (and taxable) depreciation differences in a given year. For simplicity in the text and homework, when dealing with depreciable assets, we generally focus on a single depreciable asset, with depreciation that results in a reversing (and taxable) difference in the future. The computations are best understood in this context.

different future years, the calculation of the amount of the ending deferred tax liability is more complicated. The calculation requires a company to prepare a schedule to determine the reversing difference (i.e., taxable amount) for each future year, multiply each yearly taxable amount times the applicable tax rate to determine the additional income taxes payable (deferred taxes) for that year, and sum the yearly deferred taxes to determine the total deferred tax liability.

In Example 2, before the Track Company can prepare a deferred tax liability schedule, it must first prepare a schedule to compute the 1996 through 1998 depreciation expense for financial reporting and income tax purposes. This schedule is shown in the upper portion of Exhibit 17-6. Based on the differences in depreciation for financial reporting and income tax purposes, the company prepares a schedule to calculate its deferred tax liability. This schedule is shown in the lower portion of Exhibit 17-6.

## EXHIBIT 17-6

### TRACK COMPANY

*Depreciation Expense*

| Year | Financial Depreciation | Income Tax Depreciation |
|------|------------------------|-------------------------|
| 1996 | $2,800[a] | $2,667[b] |
| 1997 | 1,100 | 889[c] |
| 1998 | 500 | 444[d] |

*Deferred Tax Liability*

| | 1996 | 1997 | 1998 |
|------|------|------|------|
| Financial depreciation | $2,800 | $1,100 | $500 |
| Income tax depreciation | (2,667) | (889) | (444) |
| Taxable amount[e] | $ 133 | $ 211 | $ 56 |
| Income tax rate | 0.35 | 0.33 | 0.30 |
| Deferred tax liability[f] | $ 47 + | $ 70 + | $ 17 = $134 |

a. Units produced × $1/unit.
b. $6,000 × 44.45% from Exhibit 9-12.
c. $6,000 × 14.81% from Exhibit 9-12.
d. $6,000 × 7.41% from Exhibit 9-12; $1 rounding error.
e. Lower income tax depreciation results in higher taxable income.
f. Amounts rounded to nearest dollar.

In Exhibit 17-6, for each year, the income tax depreciation is deducted from the financial reporting depreciation to determine the taxable amount. Given the enacted tax rates for the respective years, the income taxes payable on the taxable amounts are $47 in 1996, $70 in 1997, and $17 in 1998. Thus, the total deferred tax liability is $134 at the end of 1995. Since the taxable income for 1995 is $7,500, the income tax obligation is $3,000 ($7,500 × 0.40) based on the 40% tax rate for 1995. The journal entry at the end of 1995 is recorded as follows:

| | | |
|---|---:|---:|
| Income Tax Expense ($134 + $3,000) | 3,134 | |
|     Deferred Tax Liability | | 134 |
|     Income Taxes Payable | | 3,000 |

The expense and liabilities are reported in the financial statements as discussed in Example 1.

### Example 3: Deferred Tax Asset—Single Temporary Difference

Assume that Klemper Company has been operating profitably for several years selling a product on which it provides a 3-year warranty. For financial reporting purposes, the company estimates its future warranty costs and records a warranty expense and liability at year-end. For income tax purposes, the company deducts its warranty costs when paid. This difference in reporting warranty costs is the only temporary difference between pretax financial income and taxable income. It is a *deductible temporary difference* (deferred tax asset) because, in future years, the warranty costs deducted for income tax purposes will exceed the warranty expense deducted for financial reporting purposes, causing future taxable income to be *lower* than future pretax financial income. At the beginning of 1995, the company had a deferred tax asset in the amount of $330 related to the warranty liability on its balance sheet. At the end of 1995, the company estimates that its ending warranty liability is $1,400. In 1995, the company has taxable income of $5,000. The income tax rate for 1995 is 30% and no change in the tax rate has been enacted for future years.

In determining the Klemper Company's current and deferred income taxes, its 1995 year-end deferred tax asset is calculated to be $420 ($1,400 deductible temporary difference × 0.30). The $1,400 deductible difference arises because the book value of the ending warranty liability is $1,400 for financial reporting purposes, but $0 for income tax purposes. The company's 1995 income tax obligation is $1,500 ($5,000 × 0.30). The change in the deferred tax asset is $90, computed by deducting the beginning deferred tax asset ($330) from the required ending deferred tax asset ($420). This $90 is also the 1995 deferred tax benefit; it is subtracted from the $1,500 income taxes payable to determine the $1,410 income tax expense for 1995. The journal entry at the end of 1995 is recorded as follows:

| | | |
|---|---:|---:|
| Income Tax Expense ($1,500 − $90) | 1,410 | |
| Deferred Tax Asset | 90 | |
|     Income Taxes Payable | | 1,500 |

The deferred tax asset is reported on the company's balance sheet, as discussed in a later section. Since the company has a successful earnings history and expects to be profitable in the future, no valuation allowance is required.

### Example 4: Deferred Tax Asset and Valuation Allowance

Now assume the same information as in Example 3, except that during the past few years, the Klemper Company's sales (and profits) have been declining. At the end of 1995, due to uncertain future economic conditions, the company decides that it is more likely than not that $600 of the deductible temporary difference will not be realized. Therefore, in addition to the income tax entry made in Example 3, the company also records a valuation allowance of $180 ($600 × 0.30) at the end of 1995 as follows:

| | | |
|---|---:|---:|
| Income Tax Expense | 180 | |
|     Allowance to Reduce Deferred Tax | | |
|         Asset to Realizable Value | | 180 |

The $180 allowance account ending balance is subtracted from the $420 deferred tax asset ending balance to report the realizable value of $240 on the company's ending balance sheet as follows:

| | |
|---|---|
| Deferred tax asset | $420 |
| Less: Allowance to reduce deferred tax asset to realizable value | (180) |
| | $240 |

In 1996 and future years, the company must reexamine the available evidence to determine whether an adjustment (increase or decrease) in the valuation allowance is necessary.

### Example 5: Permanent and Temporary Differences

Assume that the Sand Company has been in operation for several years and has earned income in each of those years. At the end of 1995, the company reports pretax income of $75,000 for financial reporting purposes. Included in the calculation of this income are the following items:

1. Interest revenue of $1,000 on investments in municipal bonds.

2. Gross profit of $10,000 on installment sales recognized under the accrual method.

3. Rent revenue of $3,000 for the first year of a 3-year, $9,000 rental contract collected in advance.

For income tax purposes, the company reports gross profit on installment sales under the installment sales method as cash is collected. It also reports rent revenue for tax purposes as cash is collected. During 1995, the company reports gross profit of $2,000 on installment sales. The company had a deferred tax liability of $300 related to the installment sales temporary difference at the beginning of 1995. The income tax rate is 30% for 1995 and no change in the tax rate has been enacted for future years.

To determine the Sand Company's current and deferred income taxes, the company must first compute its 1995 taxable income. This computation is shown in Exhibit 17-7; it is similar to the schedule required to reconcile a corporation's pretax income to its taxable income on Form 1120, the federal corporate income tax return. In preparing the schedule in Exhibit 17-7, one permanent difference and two temporary differences are identified. The permanent difference ($1,000 tax-exempt interest revenue) is deducted from pretax financial income to determine taxable income because it was included in pretax financial income but is not taxable. It is ignored for deferred tax calculations because it will *never* reverse and never be taxable.

The $8,000 excess of the gross profit on installment sales included in pretax financial income over the gross profit reported for taxes is subtracted to determine taxable income because less cash is collected (and taxed). This difference is a *taxable temporary difference* because it will be included in future taxable income when the cash is collected. On the other hand, the $6,000 excess of rent collected in advance is added to pretax financial income to determine taxable income because more cash is collected (and taxed) than reported as rent revenue in pretax financial income. This difference is a *deductible temporary difference* because future taxable income will be less than future pretax financial income when the rent is recognized as rent revenue for financial reporting purposes.

**EXHIBIT 17-7**

**SAND COMPANY**

Computation of 1995 Taxable Income

| | |
|---|---:|
| Pretax financial income | $75,000 |
| Less: Tax-exempt interest revenue on municipal bonds (permanent difference) | (1,000) |
| Excess of gross profit on installment sales over gross profit for taxes (temporary difference) | (8,000)[a] |
| Add: Excess of rent collected in advance over rent revenue (temporary difference) | 6,000[b] |
| Taxable income | $72,000 |

a. $10,000 gross profit on installment sales recognized under accrual method for financial reporting − $2,000 gross profit recognized under installment sales method for income taxes.
b. $9,000 collected in advance and reported for income taxes − $3,000 rent revenue recognized for financial reporting.

The Sand Company's 1995 year-end deferred tax liability (for the installment sales temporary difference) is calculated to be $2,400 ($8,000 × 0.30). The $8,000 taxable temporary difference is the difference between the book value of the installment accounts receivable reported under the accrual method for financial reporting purposes and the book value of the receivable reported under the installment sales method for income tax purposes. Since the company had a $300 beginning deferred tax liability, it is increased by $2,100 ($2,400 − $300). The company's 1995 year-end deferred tax asset (for the rent revenue temporary difference) is $1,800 ($6,000 × 0.30). The $6,000 deductible temporary difference is the difference between the book value of the $6,000 unearned rent reported for financial reporting purposes and the $0 book value reported for income tax purposes. The company's 1995 income taxes payable are $21,600 ($72,000 taxable income from Exhibit 17-7 × 0.30). The journal entry at the end of 1995 is recorded as follows:

| | | |
|---|---:|---:|
| Income Tax Expense ($21,600 + $2,100 − $1,800) | 21,900 | |
| Deferred Tax Asset | 1,800 | |
| Deferred Tax Liability | | 2,100 |
| Income Taxes Payable | | 21,600 |

Because the company's taxable temporary difference is greater than its deductible temporary difference, a valuation allowance for the deferred tax asset is not necessary.

## OPERATING LOSS CARRYBACKS AND CARRYFORWARDS

The previous section and examples dealt with the recognition of a deferred tax liability (or asset) when a corporation had taxable *income* in the current year. This section deals with the situation where a corporation has a taxable *loss* (and a pretax financial loss) in the current year, resulting in an operating loss carryback or carryforward for income tax purposes.

The Internal Revenue Code allows a corporation reporting an operating loss for income tax purposes in the current year to carry this loss back or carry it forward to offset previous or future taxable income. The corporation may first carry a reported operating loss back 3 years (in sequential order, starting with the *earliest* of the 3 years). This procedure is called an **operating loss carryback.** In such a case, the corporation files amended income tax returns showing lower taxable income for those years and receives a refund of income taxes previously paid. If the taxable income for the past 3 years is not enough to offset the amount of the currently reported operating loss, the loss is then sequentially carried forward 15 years and offset against future taxable income, if there is any. This procedure is called an **operating loss carryforward.** The corporation then pays lower income taxes in the future based on lower future taxable income. A diagram of the operating loss carryback and carryforward sequence is shown in Exhibit 17-8. A corporation also may elect to forgo the carryback and, instead, only carry forward an operating loss. Unless higher future income tax rates have been enacted, most corporations do not make this election because an operating loss carryback will result in a definite and immediate income tax refund, whereas a carryforward will reduce income taxes payable in future years only to the extent that taxable income is earned.

## Conceptual Issues

When a corporation reports an operating loss for financial reporting purposes in a given year, several important accounting questions arise concerning the valuation of assets, the recognition of income tax expense, and the reporting of net income. These issues primarily involve operating loss carryforwards, but also relate to operating loss carrybacks.

*Operating Loss Carrybacks*
Two conceptual questions are important in accounting for an operating loss carryback of a company.

1.  Should the tax benefit of the carryback be treated as a prior period adjustment, or should it be reported as a reduction of the operating loss in the year of the loss?

In the case of an operating loss carryback, a tax benefit is obtained in the year of the operating loss. This benefit is a refund of prior income taxes paid (and reported as income tax expense in those prior periods). An argument in favor of reporting the

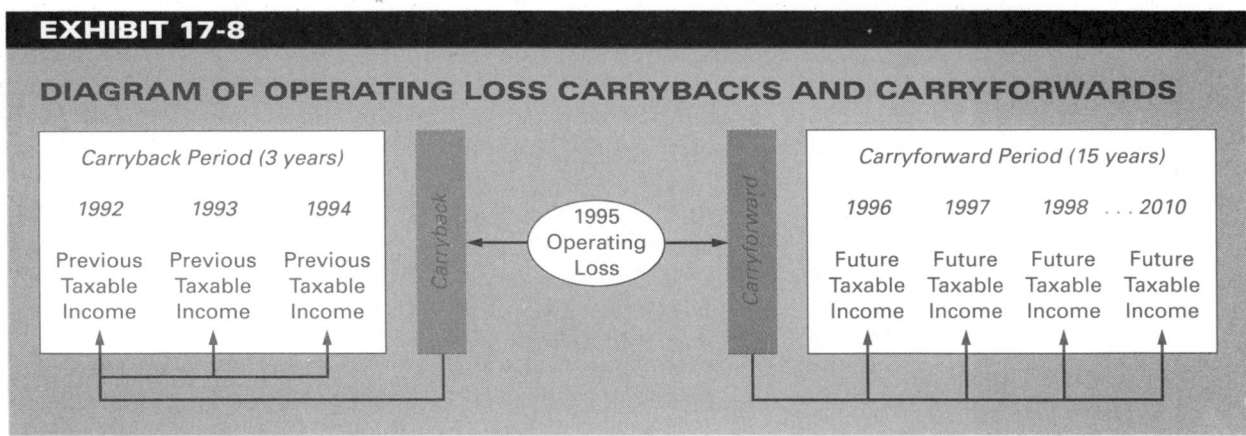

**EXHIBIT 17-8**

**DIAGRAM OF OPERATING LOSS CARRYBACKS AND CARRYFORWARDS**

| *Carryback Period (3 years)* | | |
|---|---|---|
| *1992* | *1993* | *1994* |
| Previous Taxable Income | Previous Taxable Income | Previous Taxable Income |

1995 Operating Loss

| *Carryforward Period (15 years)* | | | |
|---|---|---|---|
| *1996* | *1997* | *1998 . . . 2010* | |
| Future Taxable Income | Future Taxable Income | Future Taxable Income | Future Taxable Income |

tax benefit of a carryback as a prior period adjustment is that the prior income is what makes possible the realization of the benefit. Therefore, the income of that prior period(s) should be adjusted for the tax benefit of the carryback by reporting a prior period adjustment (i.e., decrease in prior income tax expense) on the retained earnings statement in the year of the loss. The counter-argument is that the prior income that enables use of the carryback only gives value to the carryback. It is the operating loss that creates the tax benefit. Thus, under the all-inclusive concept of income, the tax benefit should be deducted from the operating loss on the income statement in the year of the loss.

     2.   Should the corporation incurring the operating loss recognize a current receivable in regard to the tax benefit of the carryback?

The recognition of a receivable by a corporation in regard to the tax benefit of an operating loss carryback appears conceptually sound. The tax benefit will be realized as an income tax refund when the refund is issued by the federal government. Thus, it represents an economic benefit obtained and controlled by the corporation as a result of a past transaction or event.

### Operating Loss Carryforwards

Two conceptual questions are important in accounting for an operating loss carryforward of a corporation that arises because it either has no prior taxable income or its prior taxable income is insufficient to absorb the entire operating loss carryback.

     1.   When should the tax effect of an operating loss carryforward be recognized?

In the case of an operating loss carryforward, the tax effect is the result of an operating loss in the *current* year that will be realized in a *future* year(s) if sufficient future taxable income is earned. One alternative accounting treatment is to recognize the tax effect (i.e., future tax savings) in the year of the operating loss. This approach is consistent with the concepts of interperiod tax allocation and matching. If this approach were taken, a deferred tax asset would be recognized on the ending balance sheet and the tax effect would be deducted from the operating loss on the income statement in the year of the loss, in a manner similar to that discussed for an operating loss carryback. Arguments in favor of recognizing the tax effects of an operating loss carryforward in the year of the loss are: (1) the tax effects represent an economic resource that qualifies as an asset because the corporation has a right to and control over the future tax benefit, (2) there is better matching because the tax benefit is offset against the operating loss in the year the loss generated the benefit, (3) it enables better comparisons because a corporation with an available operating loss carryforward is better off than one without it, and (4) it is consistent with the going-concern assumption; if it is assumed that there will not be sufficient taxable income in the future to realize the tax benefit, then the entire corporation should be valued on a liquidation basis.

     Another alternative is to defer recognition of an operating loss carryforward until it is realized. If this approach were taken, no asset would be recognized in the loss year. If and when realization occurs, the tax benefit would be recognized as a reduction in the income taxes payable for that future period. Arguments in favor of recognizing the tax effects of an operating loss carryforward in the year of realization are: (1) an operating loss carryforward is not a current economic resource because it will provide a future tax benefit only if there is sufficient future taxable income, (2) this approach is consistent with the consensus that the realization principle should take precedence over matching (that is, when collectibility is not reasonably assured, recognition should be deferred), and (3) the operating loss is the past event that created a right to the future benefit; however, it is the future event of earning taxable income that gives value to the carryforward.

2. How should the tax effect of an operating loss carryforward be reported on the income statement?

If an operating loss carryforward is recognized in the year of the loss, it is generally agreed that the tax benefit should be deducted from the operating loss. The second question becomes significant only if recognition of the tax effect of the carryforward is deferred until realized. If recognized in the year of realization, the tax effect could be: (1) deducted from the current income tax expense, (2) reported as a prior period adjustment of the year in which the operating loss occurred, or (3) reported in a separate category on the income statement. An argument in favor of the first approach is that the earning of taxable income in that year enables the corporation to reduce its income taxes, so income tax expense should be decreased accordingly. An argument in favor of reporting the tax benefit as a prior period adjustment is that the tax benefit arose in the year of the operating loss; it was just a matter of confirming the amount at the time of realization. An argument in favor of reporting the tax benefit in a separate section of the income statement is that, although it relates to the current period, the tax benefit is so significant that it warrants separate disclosure.[12]

## Generally Accepted Accounting Principles

The FASB addressed the preceding issues in its deliberations concerning *FASB Statement No. 109* and accepted parts of both alternatives. It concluded that the generally accepted accounting principles for the financial reporting of operating loss carrybacks and carryforwards are as follows:

1. The tax benefit of an operating loss **carryback** is recognized in the period of the loss as an asset (current receivable) on the balance sheet and as a reduction of the operating loss on the income statement.

2. The tax benefit of an operating loss **carryforward** is recognized in the period of the loss as a deferred tax asset. However, the deferred tax asset is reduced by a valuation allowance if, based on the available evidence, it is *more likely than not* that some or all of the deferred tax asset will *not* be realized.[13]

In other words, operating loss carryforwards are handled in the same manner as the deductible temporary differences discussed earlier in the chapter. That is, at year-end, a deferred tax asset for an operating loss carryforward is measured using the enacted future tax rate. If necessary, a valuation allowance is measured and deducted from the deferred tax asset to determine its net realizable value. In the year-end journal entry to record a corporation's current and deferred taxes, any increase (decrease)

---

12. For a further discussion, see "Accounting for Income Taxes" *FASB Discussion Memorandum* (Stamford, Conn.: 1983) and D. Beresford, L. Best, P. Craig, and J. Weber, "Accounting for Income Taxes: A Review of Alternatives," *FASB Research Report* (Stamford, Conn.: FASB, 1983), par. 150–164 and pp. 95–106.
13. *FASB Statement No. 109, op. cit.*, par. 17.

in the deferred tax asset and valuation allowance is treated as an adjustment of income tax expense (benefit). It is more likely that a corporation will need a valuation allowance for a deferred tax asset related to an operating loss carryforward, because the operating loss itself provides negative evidence as to the likelihood of having sufficient future taxable income to realize the tax benefits.

*Example 1: Operating Loss Carryback*

Assume that Monk Company reports a pretax operating loss of $90,000 in 1995 for both financial reporting and income tax purposes, and that reported pretax financial income and taxable income for the previous 3 years had been: 1992 − $20,000 (tax rate 20%); 1993 − $40,000 (tax rate 25%); and 1994 − $50,000 (tax rate 30%). Thus, the $110,000 total pretax income in the previous 3 years is more than sufficient to offset the $90,000 pretax operating loss. When the company carries back its 1995 operating loss, it is entitled to a tax refund of $23,000, calculated as shown in Exhibit 17-9.

## EXHIBIT 17-9

### MONK COMPANY

Refund From Operating Loss Carryback

| Year | Pretax Financial Income and Taxable Income Offset by Carryback | Income Tax Rate | Income Tax Refund |
|---|---|---|---|
| 1992 | $20,000 | 0.20 | $ 4,000 |
| 1993 | 40,000 | 0.25 | 10,000 |
| 1994 | 30,000 | 0.30 | 9,000 |
| | $90,000 | | $23,000 |

Note in Exhibit 17-9 that all of the 1992 and 1993 income is offset by the operating loss carryback, but only $30,000 of the $50,000 income in 1994 is offset because the carryback is first applied to the earlier years. (Therefore, the remaining $20,000 of the 1994 income is available to offset any operating losses that might occur in 1996 or 1997.) At the end of 1995, the following journal entry is made:

| | | |
|---|---|---|
| Income Tax Refund Receivable | 23,000 | |
|   Income Tax Benefit From Operating | | |
|     Loss Carryback | | 23,000 |

The receivable is reported on the company's balance sheet as a current asset until it is collected. The operating loss carryback tax benefit is reported on the company's 1995 income statement as follows:

| | |
|---|---|
| Pretax operating loss | $(90,000) |
| Less: Income tax benefit from operating loss carryback | 23,000 |
| Net loss | $(67,000) |

*Example 2: Operating Loss Carryforward and Valuation Allowance*

Assume that Lake Company reports a pretax operating loss of $60,000 in 1994 (its first year of operations) for both financial reporting and income tax purposes. The income tax rate is 30% and no change in the tax rate has been enacted for future years. Because the company has no income prior to 1994, no carryback of the operating loss in 1994 is allowed. Since the operating loss is to be carried forward, the company reports a deferred tax asset at the end of 1994 for the deferred tax consequences (future tax benefit) of the carryforward. It calculates the deferred tax asset to be $18,000 ($60,000 × 0.30) and makes the following journal entry at the end of 1994:

| | | |
|---|---|---|
| Deferred Tax Asset | 18,000 | |
|   Income Tax Benefit From Operating | | |
|     Loss Carryforward | | 18,000 |

Because the company has no history of taxable income and has insufficient positive evidence of future taxable income, it must also reduce the deferred tax asset by a valuation allowance. If we assume the company establishes a valuation allowance for the entire amount of the deferred tax asset, the following journal entry also is made at the end of 1994:

| | | |
|---|---|---|
| Income Tax Benefit From Operating | | |
|   Loss Carryforward | 18,000 | |
|   Allowance to Reduce Deferred Tax | | |
|     Asset to Realizable Value | | 18,000 |

The operating loss is shown as $60,000 on the Lake Company's 1994 income statement because no tax benefit from the operating loss carryforward was considered realizable in 1994. The deferred tax asset, offset by the valuation allowance, normally is reported on a company's balance sheet, but the net amount is zero in this example. The operating loss carryforward is disclosed in a note accompanying the company's 1994 financial statements as follows: "The company has a $60,000 operating loss carryforward that can be used within 15 years to offset future taxable income and reduce income taxes."

Now assume that in 1995, Lake Company operates successfully and earns pretax operating income of $100,000 for both financial reporting and income tax purposes. The tax benefit of the operating loss carryforward is realized in 1995 as a reduction of the company's income tax obligation. The $60,000 carryforward from 1994 is offset against the $100,000 pretax income in 1995, resulting in taxable income of $40,000. Based on the 30% income tax rate, income taxes payable (and income tax expense) are $12,000 ($40,000 × 0.30). Since the tax benefit of the operating loss carryforward has been used up, the deferred asset and related valuation allowance are eliminated. The following journal entry is made at the end of 1995:

| | | |
|---|---|---|
| Income Tax Expense | 12,000 | |
| Allowance to Reduce Deferred Tax Asset | | |
|   to Realizable Value | 18,000 | |
|     Income Taxes Payable | | 12,000 |
|     Deferred Tax Asset | | 18,000 |

The lower portion of the company's 1995 income statement is as follows:

| | |
|---|---|
| Pretax operating income | $100,000 |
| Less: Income tax expense | (12,000) |
| Net income | $ 88,000 |

The effect of the operating loss carryforward is to reduce the income tax expense for 1995 from $30,000 ($100,000 × 0.30)—the amount without the tax benefit of the carryforward—to $12,000, so that the 1995 net income (after-tax) is increased by $18,000.

*Example 3: Operating Loss Carryforward and No Valuation Allowance*
Now assume the same information as in Example 2, except that the Lake Company has signed a substantial number of contracts for the sales of its products in 1995. Based on this verifiable positive evidence, the company decides that the tax benefit of its operating loss carryforward will be realized in 1995, so that a valuation allowance is not necessary at the end of 1994.

In this case, the journal entry to record the $18,000 deferred tax asset is the same as in Example 2. However, since no valuation allowance is recorded, the lower portion of the company's 1994 income statement is as follows:

| | |
|---|---|
| Pretax operating loss | $(60,000) |
| Less: Income tax benefit from operating loss carryforward | 18,000 |
| Net loss | $(42,000) |

The realizable tax benefit has reduced the $60,000 pretax operating loss to a $42,000 net loss. This is in contrast to Example 2, where a $60,000 net loss was reported on the company's 1994 income statement.

Continuing with the same assumptions as Example 2, Lake Company earns pretax operating income of $100,000 in 1995. The $60,000 operating loss carryforward reduces the taxable income to $40,000 so that the company's income tax obligation is $12,000, as in Example 2. The deferred tax asset is eliminated, but since there is no valuation allowance, the 1995 income tax expense is $30,000, as shown in the following 1995 year-end journal entry:

| | | |
|---|---|---|
| **Income Tax Expense** | 30,000 | |
| **Income Taxes Payable** | | 12,000 |
| **Deferred Tax Asset** | | 18,000 |

The lower portion of the company's 1995 income statement is as follows:

| | |
|---|---|
| Pretax operating income | $100,000 |
| Income tax expense | (30,000) |
| Net income | $ 70,000 |

Note that the total net income for 1994 and 1995 is $28,000 in both Examples 2 and 3. The income is accelerated in Example 3, however (through a lower net loss in 1994), because the company had sufficient positive verifiable evidence in 1991 that the tax benefit from its operating loss carryforward was realizable in 1992.

In some cases, the pretax operating income of a given year is not sufficient to offset the entire amount of an operating loss carryforward. In this situation, a portion of the operating loss is offset against the income and the remainder continues to be carried forward as a deferred tax asset (and disclosed in a note). For instance, if in the previous example, Lake Company had earned only $50,000 pretax operating (and taxable) income in 1995, then $50,000 of the $60,000 operating loss carryforward would be offset against this income and the company would pay no income taxes for 1995. The company would report income tax expense of $15,000 ($50,000 × 0.30) and would reduce its deferred tax asset by $15,000. The $3,000 ($18,000 − $15,000) deferred tax asset (30% of the $10,000 remaining operating loss carryforward) would be eliminated in a future year(s) when the tax benefit is realized.

## COMPREHENSIVE ILLUSTRATION

The examples in the previous sections were straightforward because they illustrated the accounting for temporary differences separately from operating losses. In this comprehensive example, we illustrate a temporary difference, as well as both an operating loss carryback and an operating loss carryforward. Assume that Branton Company begins operations in 1991 and is profitable through 1994. In 1995, the company reports a pretax financial loss of $8,000 and a taxable loss of $8,800. In 1996 through 1997, the company is again profitable, although at the end of 1995 the company was uncertain as to future profits. The income tax rate is 30%. The company's pretax financial income (loss) and taxable income (loss) for the years 1991 through 1997, as well as its income taxes payable (receivable), are shown in Exhibit 17-10. It is assumed that the only difference between pretax financial income (loss) and taxable income (loss) in any year results from additional (MACRS) depreciation reported for income tax purposes.

As shown in Exhibit 17-10, the company pays $360 of income taxes in 1991 and $840 in 1992 through 1994. In 1995, $2,800 of the $8,800 operating loss is carried back to offset the 1992–1994 taxable income, resulting in a tax refund of $840. Note that the 1995 operating loss is *not* carried back to 1991 because of the 3-year carryback limitation. In 1996 and 1997, the $6,000 remaining operating loss is carried forward and (1) offsets the $1,500 taxable income in 1996 so that no income taxes are paid, and (2) offsets $4,500 of the $6,400 taxable income in 1997 so that $570 of income taxes are paid.

### EXHIBIT 17-10

**BRANTON COMPANY**

Income Taxes Payable or Receivable

| Year | Pretax Financial Income (Loss) | Depreciation Difference | Taxable Income (Loss) | Income Taxes Payable (Receivable) |
|------|-------------------------------|------------------------|----------------------|-----------------------------------|
| 1991 | $ 2,000 | $ 800 | $ 1,200 | $360[a] |
| 1992–94 | 5,000 | 2,200 | 2,800 | 840[a] |
| 1995 | (8,000) | 800 | (8,800) | (840)[b] |
| 1996 | 2,200 | 700 | 1,500 | 0[c] |
| 1997 | 7,000 | 600 | 6,400 | 570[d] |

a. Taxable income × 0.30 income tax rate.
b. $2,800 carryback to years 1992–1994, resulting in tax refund of $840; remaining carryforward of $6,000 ($8,800 − $2,800).
c. $1,500 taxable income offset by carryforward, therefore no income taxes owed; remaining carryforward of $4,500 ($6,000 − $1,500).
d. $6,400 taxable income offset by $4,500 carryforward; $1,900 × 0.30.

For financial reporting purposes, the company must determine its deferred tax liability (or asset) and income tax expense (or refund) for each year. Both the depreciation taxable temporary difference and the operating loss carryforward for each year affect the company's deferred taxes; their calculations are shown in Exhibit 17-11. Note in Exhibit 17-11 that the depreciation taxable temporary difference increases each year by the difference in depreciation for financial reporting purposes and income tax purposes shown in Exhibit 17-10. The operating loss carryforward of $6,000 at the end of 1995 is the $8,800 operating loss in 1995 less the $2,800 operating loss carryback, as discussed earlier. The operating loss carryforward at the end of 1996 is only $4,500 because $1,500 was used to offset the taxable income in 1996. The following "timeline" diagram further explains the relationships between the taxable incomes and the operating loss carrybacks and carryforwards for the various years:

|  | 1991 | 1992 | 1993 | 1994 | 1995 | 1996 | 1997 |
|---|---|---|---|---|---|---|---|
| Taxable income before adjustments | $1,200 | | $2,800 | | $(8,800) | $1,500 | $6,400 |
| Loss carrybacks | | | (2,800) ← | | 2,800 | | |
| | | | | | $(6,000) | | |
| Loss carryforward (to 1996) | | | | | 1,500 → | (1,500) | |
| Loss carryforward (to 1997) | | | | | 4,500 | → | (4,500) |
| Taxable income | | | | | $ 0 | $ 0 | $1,900 |

**EXHIBIT 17-11**

**BRANTON COMPANY**

Deferred Tax Information

| Year | Depreciation Temporary Difference Beginning | Addition | Ending[a] | Operating Loss Carryforward |
|---|---|---|---|---|
| 1991 | $ 0 | $ 800 | $ 800 | — |
| 1992–94 | 800 | 2,200 | 3,000 | — |
| 1995 | 3,000 | 800 | 3,800 | (6,000)[b] |
| 1996 | 3,800 | 700 | 4,500 | (4,500)[c] |
| 1997 | 4,500 | 600 | 5,100 | — |

a. Beginning depreciation temporary difference + additional difference for current year.
b. $8,800 taxable loss − $2,800 operating loss carryback (see Exhibit 17-10).
c. $6,000 operating loss carryforward from 1995 − $1,500 taxable income in 1996 (see Exhibit 17-10).

The computations of the company's deferred tax liability and asset (and valuation allowance) for each year are shown in Exhibit 17-12, based on the information in

Exhibit 17-11. As shown in Exhibit 17-11, the company has $800 additional depreciation for tax purposes at the end of 1991, which will result in taxable income of the same amount in future years. As shown in Exhibit 17-12, applying the 30% tax rate to the future taxable amount results in a deferred tax liability of $240 at the end of 1991. Since there was a $0 deferred tax liability at the beginning of 1991, a $240 adjustment (credit) to the deferred tax liability is made. Similar computations are made for 1992 through 1997.

At the end of 1995, the $6,000 operating loss carryforward results in an ending deferred tax asset of $1,800 ($6,000 × 0.30). Since there was a $0 deferred tax asset at the beginning of 1995, an $1,800 adjustment (debit) is made to the deferred tax asset. A valuation allowance is required at the end of 1995 because the company does not expect to be profitable in future years. However, the valuation allowance does not have to be for the full amount of the deferred tax asset resulting from the operating loss carryforward. This is because the company has an existing depreciation temporary difference that will result in additional future taxable income against which to offset the operating loss carryforward. Since the operating loss carryforward is $6,000, but the total ending depreciation taxable temporary difference is $3,800 at the end of 1995 (see Exhibit 17-11), a valuation allowance of only $660 [($6,000 − $3,800) × 0.30] is required and an adjustment (credit) is made for that amount.

At the end of 1996, the company has a $1,350 deferred tax asset ($4,500 operating loss carryforward × 0.30), which requires a $450 adjustment (credit) to that account. Since the $4,500 total ending depreciation taxable temporary difference is the same as the $4,500 remaining operating loss carryforward, no valuation allowance is needed. This requires an adjustment (debit) of $660 to the valuation allowance account. In 1997, the $4,500 remaining operating loss carryforward is used to offset an equal amount of taxable income, so the $1,350 related deferred tax asset is eliminated (credited).

---

## EXHIBIT 17-12

### BRANTON COMPANY

Annual Deferred Taxes

| Year | Deferred Tax Liability | | | Deferred Tax Asset | | | Valuation Allowance | | |
|---|---|---|---|---|---|---|---|---|---|
| | Beginning | Ending[a] | Adjustment | Beginning | Ending | Adjustment | Beginning | Ending | Adjustment |
| 1991 | $ 0 | $ 240 | $240 | — | — | — | — | — | — |
| 1992–94 | 240 | 900 | 660 | — | — | — | — | — | — |
| 1995 | 900 | 1,140 | 240 | — | $1,800[b] | $1,800 | — | $660[c] | $660 |
| 1996 | 1,140 | 1,350 | 210 | $1,800 | 1,350[d] | (450) | $660 | 0[e] | (660) |
| 1997 | 1,350 | 1,530 | 180 | 1,350 | 0 | (1,350) | — | — | — |

a. Ending depreciation taxable temporary difference (from Exhibit 17-11) × 0.30.
b. $6,000 operating loss carryforward (from Exhibit 17-11) × 0.30.
c. [$6,000 carryforward − $3,800 ending depreciation temporary difference (from Exhibit 17-11)] × 0.30.
d. $4,500 operating loss carryforward × 0.30.
e. ($4,500 carryforward − $4,500 ending depreciation temporary difference) × 0.30.

At the end of each year, the company prepares a journal entry to record its income taxes, based on the information in Exhibits 17-10 and 17-12. For instance, at the end of 1995, the following journal entry is made:

| | | |
|---|---|---|
| Income Tax Refund Receivable | 840 | |
| Deferred Tax Asset | 1,800 | |
| Deferred Tax Liability | | 240 |
| Allowance to Reduce Deferred Tax Asset to | | |
| Realizable Value | | 660 |
| Income Tax Benefit From Operating Loss Carryback | | 840 |
| Income Tax Benefit From Operating Loss Carryforward | | 900 |

The $840 income tax benefit from the operating loss carryback relates to the income tax refund receivable. The $900 income tax benefit from the operating loss carryforward is the net amount that will be realized in future years and that is related to the deferred tax asset, valuation allowance, and deferred tax liability.

The operating loss carryback and carryforward tax benefits are disclosed on the company's 1995 income statement as follows:

| | | |
|---|---|---|
| Pretax operating loss | | $(8,000) |
| Less: Income tax benefit from operating loss carryback | $840 | |
| Income tax benefit from operating loss carryforward | 900 | 1,740 |
| Net loss | | $(6,260) |

The remaining operating loss carryforwards in 1995 and 1996 are disclosed in a note accompanying the respective year's financial statements.

## INTRAPERIOD INCOME TAX ALLOCATION

**Intraperiod income tax allocation is the apportionment of a company's total income tax expense for a period to the various components of its income statement (and occasionally the statement of retained earnings or statement of changes in stockholders' equity).** Income tax allocation within a period has become mandatory under the provisions of several *APB Opinions*. For example, *APB Opinion No. 9* requires an allocation of the income tax effects to extraordinary items and to prior period adjustments, *APB Opinion No. 20* requires an allocation of the income tax consequences of the cumulative effects of changes in accounting principles, and *APB Opinion No. 30* requires an allocation of the income tax effects to a disposal of a segment of a business. *FASB Statement No. 109* continues these required disclosures and extends the disclosures to the income tax effects of gains and losses included in comprehensive income but excluded from net income, and to capital transactions that have tax effects.[14] When a corporation has these types of income, income taxes are apportioned between them and income from continuing operations. The rationale behind intraperiod tax allocation is based on the matching concept. Income tax expense is *matched* against the major components of pretax income in order to give a fair presentation of the after-tax impact of each of these items on net income.

For intraperiod income tax allocation purposes, on the income statement the income tax expense applicable to pretax income from continuing operations is listed

---

14. These may include, for instance, the increase or decrease in the value of investments in securities available for sale, or a translation adjustment recorded in accordance with *FASB Statement No. 52*, "Foreign Currency Translation." These items are not considered further in this chapter.

separately. The disclosure of the tax effect on income from continuing operations is important because business activities that are expected to continue are of the greatest interest to external users. The amount is based on the normal income tax rates applied to this income. However, extraordinary items, cumulative effects of changes in accounting principles, the income or loss from the operations of a discontinued segment, the gain or loss from the disposal of a discontinued segment, and prior period adjustments (shown on the statement of retained earnings) are all disclosed *net* of the related income tax effects (with each related income tax effect disclosed in parentheses). Because these items are considered to be "incremental," the amount of income tax expense or tax credit applicable to each of these items is determined by applying the marginal (incremental) tax rate to each item.

To illustrate, assume the Kalloway Company reports the following items of *pretax* financial (and taxable) "income" for 1995:

| | |
|---|---:|
| Income from continuing operations (revenues of $270,000 less expenses of $190,000) | $80,000 |
| Gain on disposal of discontinued Segment X | 18,000 |
| Loss from operations of discontinued Segment X | (5,000) |
| Extraordinary loss on bond redemption | (10,000) |
| Cumulative effect of change in accounting principle (accelerated depreciation to straight-line) | 15,000 |
| Prior period adjustment (error in calculating bad debt expense for 1994) | (8,000) |
| Amount subject to income taxes | $90,000 |

The company is subject to income tax rates of 20% on the first $50,000 of income and 30% on all income in excess of $50,000. Exhibit 17-13 illustrates the schedule to allocate the total income tax expense, and Exhibit 17-14 illustrates Kalloway Company's 1995 income statement and statement of retained earnings as a result of applying intraperiod income tax allocation.

## EXHIBIT 17-13

### KALLOWAY COMPANY

Schedule of Income Tax Expense
For Year Ended December 31, 1995

| Component (Pretax) | Pretax Amount | × | Income Tax Rate | = | Income Tax Expense (Credit) |
|---|---:|:---:|:---:|:---:|---:|
| Income from continuing operations | $50,000 | × | 0.20 | = | $10,000 |
| | 30,000 | × | 0.30 | = | 9,000 |
| Gain on disposal of discontinued Segment X | 18,000 | × | 0.30 | = | 5,400 |
| Loss from operations of discontinued Segment X | (5,000) | × | 0.30 | = | (1,500) |
| Extraordinary loss on bond redemption | (10,000) | × | 0.30 | = | (3,000) |
| Cumulative effect of change in accounting principle on prior years' income | 15,000 | × | 0.30 | = | 4,500 |
| Prior period adjustment | (8,000) | × | 0.30 | = | (2,400) |
| Total income tax expense | | | | | $22,000 |

**EXHIBIT 17-14**

## KALLOWAY COMPANY

**Income Statement**
**For Year Ended December 31, 1995**

| | | | |
|---|---|---|---|
| Revenues (listed separately) | | | $270,000 |
| Expenses (listed separately) | | | (190,000) |
| Pretax income from continuing operations | | | $ 80,000 |
| Income tax expense | | | (19,000) |
| Income from continuing operations | | | $ 61,000 |
| Results of discontinued operations: | | | |
|   Gain on disposal of discontinued Segment X | | | |
|     (net of $5,400 income taxes) | | $12,600 | |
|   Loss from operations of discontinued Segment X | | | |
|     (net of $1,500 income tax credit) | | (3,500) | 9,100 |
| Income before extraordinary loss | | | $ 70,100 |
| Extraordinary loss on bond redemption (net of $3,000 income tax credit) | | | (7,000) |
| Cumulative effect of change in accounting principle | | | |
|   (net of $4,500 income taxes) | | | 10,500 |
| Net income | | | $ 73,600 |

**Statement of Retained Earnings**
**For Year Ended December 31, 1995**

| | |
|---|---|
| Retained earnings, January 1, 1995 | $435,000 |
| Less: Prior period adjustment, understatement of 1994 bad debt expense | |
|   (net of $2,400 income tax credit) | (5,600) |
| Adjusted retained earnings, January 1, 1995 | $429,400 |
| Add: Net income | 73,600 |
| | $503,000 |
| Less: Cash dividends | (23,500) |
| Retained earnings, December 31, 1995 | $479,500 |

As shown in Exhibit 17-13, the total income taxes for the Kalloway Company on the $90,000 subject to income taxes in 1995 are $22,000. The income tax expense applicable to pretax income from continuing operations is computed by multiplying this $80,000 income by the normal income tax rates. This provision for income tax does *not* consider the tax consequences of any items not included in pretax income from continuing operations. It amounts to $19,000 [(0.20 × $50,000) + (0.30 × $30,000)], is shown in Exhibit 17-14 on a separate line directly below pretax income from continuing operations, and is deducted to determine income from continuing operations. The gain on the disposal of the discontinued Segment X, the loss from the operations of the discontinued Segment X, the extraordinary loss, and the cumulative effect of the change in accounting principle are all shown net of income tax on the income statement in Exhibit 17-14, with each related income tax effect disclosed in parentheses. The prior period adjustment is disclosed net of its income tax effect on the statement of retained earnings in Exhibit 17-14. Each of the related income tax effects was computed in Exhibit 17-13 by multiplying the marginal tax rate (30%) by the pretax gain or loss.[15] The journal entry to record the 1995 intraperiod income tax allocation of the Kalloway Company, based on the preceding information, is as follows:

| | | |
|---|---|---|
| Income Tax Expense | 19,000 | |
| Gain on Disposal of Segment X | 5,400 | |
| Cumulative Effect of Change in Accounting Principle | 4,500 | |
| Loss from Operations of Discontinued Segment X | | 1,500 |
| Extraordinary Loss on Bond Redemption | | 3,000 |
| Retained Earnings (prior period adjustment) | | 2,400 |
| Income Taxes Payable | | 22,000 |

Note that the debit to Income Tax Expense of $19,000 relates only to the income taxes applicable to income from continuing operations. Since results of discontinued operations, extraordinary items, cumulative effects of changes in accounting principles, and prior period adjustments are shown on the financial statements *net* of their respective income tax effects, the income tax expense or credit related to each of these items is debited or credited directly to the applicable account (as shown in the journal entry) to reduce the account balance to its after-tax amount, as reported in Exhibit 17-14. Note also that, in this example, taxable income and pretax financial income are assumed to be the same. If taxable income is not the same as pretax financial income because of temporary differences, the total income tax expense is the sum of the income tax obligation and the adjustments to the deferred tax liabilities and assets. In this situation, the impact of the adjustments on each component of pretax financial income must be determined before the income tax expense can be properly allocated. In the case of adjustments of: (1) a valuation allowance because of changes in circumstances and (2) deferred tax liabilities and assets because of changes in tax rates or laws, the amounts of the adjustments are included in income tax expense related to continuing operations.[16]

## FINANCIAL STATEMENT PRESENTATION AND DISCLOSURES

In addition to the intraperiod allocation of income taxes on a corporation's income statement (and statement of retained earnings or statement of changes in stockholders' equity), *FASB Statement No. 109* specifies the required: (1) presentation of deferred tax liabilities and assets on the corporation's balance sheet, and (2) disclosures in the notes to the corporation's financial statements.

### Balance Sheet Presentation

A corporation must report its deferred tax liabilities and assets in two classifications: a *net* current amount and a *net* noncurrent amount. These classifications are based

---

15. In our example, only two tax rates were in effect, and the income from continuing operations was sufficiently large that the gain and losses were taxed at a single marginal rate. It is possible for several tax rates to be in effect at the same time, and for the total income to be increased or decreased by the other gains and losses, so that more than one marginal tax rate may be applicable. In these cases, a weighted averaging process is completed to determine the appropriate tax effects on the gains and losses. This process is beyond the scope of this book.
16. *FASB Statement No. 109, op. cit.,* par. 35.

on the classifications of the related assets or liabilities for financial reporting. For instance, a deferred tax liability related to the excess of tax depreciation over financial depreciation is reported as a noncurrent liability because the depreciable assets are noncurrent assets. A deferred tax liability or asset not directly related to an asset or liability (e.g., related to an operating loss carryforward) is classified according to the expected reversal date of the temporary difference. A valuation allowance is allocated between current and noncurrent deferred assets on a proportional basis.[17]

In other words, a corporation must: (1) separate its deferred tax liabilities into current and noncurrent groups, (2) separate its deferred tax assets into current and noncurrent groups, (3) combine (*net*) the amounts in the current groups, and (4) combine (*net*) the amounts in the noncurrent groups.[18] If the net amount of the current groups is a debit balance, the company reports the amount as a current asset, whereas a net credit amount is reported as a current liability. A net debit balance for the noncurrent groups is reported as a noncurrent asset, while a net credit balance is reported as a noncurrent liability. This procedure is one of the few situations in which "offsetting" of assets and liabilities is allowed in financial reporting. The FASB requires this approach because of the close relationship between deferred tax assets and liabilities, and to avoid the detailed analyses necessary for more refined classification methods.

To illustrate, assume that the Anicar Company has four deferred tax items shown in Exhibit 17-15. In this situation, the company combines the $6,000 credit balance of the current deferred tax liability (Item 1) with the $3,400 debit balance of the current deferred tax asset (Item 3), and reports a $2,600 net deferred tax liability as a *current liability* on its year-end balance sheet. Likewise, the company combines the $12,000 credit balance of the noncurrent deferred tax liability (Item 2) with the $2,500 debit balance of the noncurrent deferred tax asset (Item 4), and reports a $9,500 net deferred tax liability as a *noncurrent liability* on its year-end balance sheet.

## EXHIBIT 17-15

### ANICAR COMPANY

Schedule of Deferred Assets and Liabilities

| Deferred Tax Accounts | Account Balance | Related Balance Sheet Account | Deferred Income Tax Reporting Classification |
|---|---|---|---|
| *Deferred Tax Liabilities* | | | |
| 1. Installment sales | $ 6,000 credit | Accounts receivable | Current |
| 2. Depreciation | 12,000 credit | Property, plant, and equipment | Noncurrent |
| *Deferred Tax Assets* | | | |
| 3. Warranty costs | 3,400 debit | Warranty liability | Current |
| 4. Rent revenue (long-term) | 2,500 debit | Unearned rent | Noncurrent |

17. *Ibid.*, par. 41.
18. A corporation may have some assets and liabilities (e.g., warranty liability) for which the portion due to be collected or paid in the next year is classified as current and the remainder is classified as noncurrent. In such a case, the related deferred tax liability or asset must also be proportionately classified into current and noncurrent amounts. This classification is beyond the scope of this book.

## Financial Statement Disclosures

*FASB Statement No. 109* also requires extensive income tax disclosures in the notes to a corporation's financial statements (or directly on the statements themselves). In regard to the net deferred tax liability or asset reported on a corporation's balance sheet, the total of all deferred tax liabilities, total of all deferred tax assets, total valuation allowance, and net change in the valuation allowance are disclosed. In conjunction with a corporation's income statement (and statement of retained earnings or statement of changes in stockholders' equity), disclosure of the components of income tax expense is required. This disclosure includes the amount of income tax expense or benefit allocated to continuing operations, discontinued operations, extraordinary items, the cumulative effect of accounting changes, prior period adjustments, gains and losses included in comprehensive income but excluded from net income, and capital transactions. Furthermore, the significant components of income tax expense related to continuing operations for each year are disclosed. These components include, for instance, (a) current tax expense or benefit (i.e., income tax obligation or refund), (b) deferred tax expense or benefit, (c) tax credits, (d) benefits of operating loss carryforwards, (e) adjustments of a deferred tax liability or asset for enacted changes in tax laws or rates, and (f) adjustments of the valuation allowance for changes in circumstances.

Other income statement related disclosures are also required. These include: (1) a reconciliation of the income tax expense related to continuing operations to the income tax expense that would result from applying federal tax rates to pretax income from continuing operations, (2) identification of the nature and amount of each significant item in the previous reconciliation, and (3) the amounts and expiration dates of any operating loss and tax credit carryforwards for income tax purposes.[19]

The intraperiod allocation of income taxes on the face of the income statement (and statement of retained earnings or statement of changes in stockholders' equity), as previously illustrated, partially satisfies the preceding disclosure requirements. The remaining information typically is included in a note with the financial statements. These disclosures are illustrated in Exhibit 17-16 later in the chapter for Campbell Soup Company.

## MISCELLANEOUS ISSUES

The previous discussion and examples focused on the common issues involved in accounting for income taxes. For simplicity, a number of miscellaneous topics were omitted.

## Change in Income Tax Laws or Rates

As discussed earlier, the balances of a corporation's deferred tax liabilities (or assets) at the end of a given year are determined by applying the currently enacted income tax rate(s) and laws to its taxable (or deductible) temporary differences. Occasionally, Congress may change the income tax laws or rates so that they differ from those laws or rates previously used to calculate the corporation's deferred tax liabilities (or assets). Disclosure of the financial impact of this congressional action is required because such a change is an event that has economic consequences to a corporation.

---

19. *Ibid.*, par. 43–48.

That is, a corporation's financial condition improves if it owes a smaller amount of future taxes (or would receive a larger refund) and its condition weakens if the corporation owes more future taxes (or would receive a smaller refund). When a change in the income tax laws or rates occurs, the deferred tax liabilities (and assets) are adjusted for the effect of the change. The adjustment is made to the balance of each deferred tax liability (and asset) as of the beginning of the year in which the change is made, and the resulting tax effect is included in the income tax expense related to income from continuing operations.[20] The amount of the adjustment is the difference between the deferred tax liability (or asset) balance at the beginning of the year, based on the newly enacted laws or rates, and the balance that had been computed under the old law or rates.

For instance, refer back to Example 1 (Page 821) for a deferred tax liability. If, in May 1996, Congress increases the income tax rate from 30% to 35%, then the deferred tax liability at the end of 1995 should be $140 ($400 × 0.35) instead of $120, as previously computed. Therefore, the deferred tax liability is increased and a tax effect recognized in the amount of $20 ($140 − $120). The journal entry in May 1996 to record the increase and recognize the loss is:

| | | |
|---|---|---|
| Income Tax Expense | 20 | |
| Deferred Tax Liability | | 20 |

The income tax expense related to income from continuing operations is increased by $20 on the 1996 income statement, and the deferred tax liability has a credit balance of $140. At the end of 1996, deferred taxes are computed in the usual manner, except that the newly enacted 35% income tax rate is used. A change in the balance of a valuation allowance—because of changes in circumstances concerning the future realization of a deferred tax asset—is recorded and reported in a similar fashion.

## Investment Tax Credit

To encourage investment in productive facilities, corporations have been permitted to deduct a specified percentage of the cost of certain depreciable assets directly from their income taxes payable in the year when the assets were acquired. This deduction is known as the **investment tax credit**. It was first introduced in 1962 and has been suspended and reenacted at various times. Most recently, the Tax Reform Act of 1986 suspended this credit, although there has been some discussion about its possible renewal on a permanent basis for small companies and a temporary basis for large companies.

For financial reporting purposes, the investment tax credit could be accounted for by either the deferred method or the flow-through method. **APB Opinion No. 2,** issued in 1962, required use of the deferred method. Under the **deferred method,** the investment tax credit was considered to be a reduction in the effective cost of the asset, and the tax benefit was recognized as a reduction of depreciation expense over the life of the asset. In response to political pressure, **APB Opinion No. 4** was issued in 1964, allowing use of the flow-through method. Under the **flow-through method,** the total tax benefit was recognized in the year of acquisition by a reduction in the income tax expense for the amount of the investment tax credit.

Although the flow-through method violated the matching principle, most corporations used this method because it resulted in an immediate increase in earnings.

20. *Ibid.,* par. 27.

Those corporations that used the deferred method continue to have a reduced cost of their assets for financial reporting purposes, resulting in a temporary difference in regard to depreciation. This temporary difference is accounted for in the same manner as the other temporary differences discussed earlier in the chapter.[21] Because, at the time of this writing, few corporations have investment tax credits, they are not considered further in this chapter.

## Alternative Minimum Tax and Other Tax Credits

The Tax Reform Act of 1986 imposed an *alternative minimum tax* (AMT) on corporations, designed to help ensure equity in income tax payments. A corporation pays the higher of its AMT (as computed according to the income tax laws) or its regular income tax liability. Thus, the AMT may affect the corporation's income tax obligation in a given year. The AMT also may affect the corporation's deferred tax liability or asset because calculation of the AMT depends, in part, on "adjusted current earnings (ACE) adjustments" related to certain temporary differences. Furthermore, if a corporation pays the AMT, generally the amount paid can be credited against future income taxes. This credit is used in a given future year when the regular tax liability exceeds the AMT. The minimum tax credit may not be carried back, but may be carried forward indefinitely.

The federal tax law also allows certain other "tax credits" that are deductible by a corporation from its computed income taxes to determine the corporation's income taxes owed. Among the tax credits that are, or have been, in the tax law are credits for certain research and experimental activities, for foreign taxes paid, for hiring certain employees, and for using certain fuels. Specific restrictions apply to tax credits, and sometimes a corporation cannot use all of its tax credits in a given year. In certain circumstances, these tax credits may be carried forward and applied against future taxes owed in a manner similar to operating loss carryforwards. When this arises, the steps outlined earlier in the chapter for computing a corporation's deferred taxes must be modified to include measurement of a deferred tax asset for each type of tax credit. Because the AMT and tax credits are complex and vary across companies, they are not considered further in this chapter.

## International Accounting Differences

The international accounting principles for deferred income taxes differ considerably from those in the U.S. Recall that *FASB Statement No. 109* requires comprehensive income tax allocation of temporary differences using the asset/liability method. The International Accounting Standards are more flexible and allow either comprehensive or partial allocation of timing differences (which are not as broad as temporary differences). Furthermore, use of either the deferred method or asset/liability method is acceptable, and the basis for recognizing a deferred tax asset is a reasonable expectation of realization. International accounting standards do not address the balance sheet classification of deferred taxes.

From the standpoint of individual foreign countries, accounting for deferred taxes also varies. For instance, Australia is similar to the U.S. in that deferred taxes are determined under comprehensive allocation using the asset/liability method based on future enacted tax rates. On the other hand, in Canada, deferred taxes are determined

---

21. *Ibid.*, par. 117.

under comprehensive allocation using the deferred method based on current tax rates. In the United Kingdom and Italy, partial allocation is used, while in the Netherlands, discounting is permitted in certain circumstances. In France and Japan, deferred taxes are not recognized in separate financial statements of individual corporations, but accounting principles in France require recognition of deferred taxes in consolidated financial statements. Although accounting principles in Japan permit recognition of deferred taxes in consolidated financial statements, many Japanese companies do not report deferred taxes.[22]

## ILLUSTRATIVE DISCLOSURES

The 1992 income tax disclosures of Campbell Soup Company are shown in Exhibit 17-16. These disclosures are representative of the type necessary under the generally accepted accounting principles of *FASB Statement No. 109*.

### APPENDIX: ADDITIONAL CONCEPTUAL ISSUES CONCERNING INTERPERIOD INCOME TAX ALLOCATION

As noted earlier in the chapter, there has been much debate about interperiod income tax allocation. This debate has centered on whether or not there should be interperiod income tax allocation and, if so, whether it should be based on a comprehensive approach or a partial allocation approach. Furthermore, regardless of which approach is selected, the debate also involves whether the asset/liability, deferred, or net-of-tax method should be used. This Appendix discusses the arguments for and against each issue. It also briefly discusses the controversial conclusions of *FASB Statement No. 96*, which was superseded by *FASB Statement No. 109*.

### EXHIBIT 17-16
### Income Tax Disclosures

**CAMPBELL SOUP COMPANY**

*Income Statement (in part):*

|  | 1992 (53 weeks) | 1991 (52 weeks) | 1990 (52 weeks) |
|---|---|---|---|
| (in millions) |  |  |  |
| Earnings before taxes | $799.3 | $667.4 | $179.4 |
| Taxes on earnings (Note 9) | 308.8 | 265.9 | 175.0 |
| Net earnings | $490.5 | $401.5 | $ 4.4 |

---

22. *Survey of International Accounting Practices,* compiled by Big Six accounting firms, (New York: AICPA, 1992), pp. 13–15, 52–56.

**EXHIBIT 17-16, Continued**
**Income Tax Disclosures**

*Balance Sheet (in part):*

|  | August 2, 1992 | July 28, 1991 |
|---|---|---|
| Other liabilities, principally deferred income taxes (Note 20) | 333.2 | 305.0 |

NOTES TO CONSOLIDATED FINANCIAL STATEMENTS (in part):

*9. Taxes on Earnings (in part)*

The provision for income taxes consists of the following:

|  | 1992 | 1991 | 1990 |
|---|---|---|---|
| **Currently payable** |  |  |  |
| Federal | $225.0 | $185.8 | $132.4 |
| State | 27.5 | 23.4 | 20.8 |
| Non-U.S. | 21.9 | 21.2 | 17.9 |
|  | 274.4 | 230.4 | 171.1 |
| **Deferred** |  |  |  |
| Federal | 20.5 | 21.9 | 1.2 |
| State | 10.5 | 7.5 | 2.6 |
| Non-U.S. | 3.4 | 6.1 | .1 |
|  | 34.4 | 35.5 | 3.9 |
|  | $308.8 | $265.9 | $175.0 |

The deferred income taxes result from temporary differences between financial statement earnings and taxable earnings as follows:

|  | 1992 | 1991 | 1990 |
|---|---|---|---|
| Depreciation | $ 7.0 | $ 5.9 | $ 18.6 |
| Pensions | 21.5 | 13.6 | 11.7 |
| Prefunded employee benefits | (.6) | (3.3) | (4.8) |
| Accruals not currently deductible for tax purposes | (12.2) | (11.4) | (5.8) |
| Divestitures, restructuring and unusual charges | 16.1 | 29.3 | (11.1) |
| Other | 2.6 | 1.4 | (4.7) |
|  | $ 34.4 | $ 35.5 | $ 3.9 |

...The provision for income taxes was reduced by $4.4 in 1992, $3.2 in 1991 and $5.2 in 1990 due to the utilization of loss carryforwards by certain non-U.S. subsidiaries.

## ALLOCATION VERSUS NONALLOCATION

Some people argue that the amount of income tax expense reported on a corporation's income statement should be the same as the income tax obligation for the accounting period (as determined on the corporation's income tax return). Under this approach, there would be *no* interperiod allocation of income tax expense. Advocates of this nonallocation approach raise many arguments in favor of their position. Some of the more significant arguments[23] are:

1. Income taxes result only from taxable income. Thus, the income tax expense should be related to (matched against) taxable income and not pretax financial income.

2. Income taxes are different from other expenses and, therefore, matching is not relevant. Other expenses are usually incurred to generate revenues, whereas income taxes arise as a result of taxable income.

3. Income taxes are levied on the total taxable income, not on individual taxable and deductible items of revenue and expense. Therefore, there can be no temporary differences related to these individual items.

4. Interperiod tax allocation hides an economic difference between a corporation that reduces current tax payments (and is economically better off) and one that does not.

5. Reporting a corporation's income tax expense at the amount paid or currently payable is a better predictor of the future cash outflows of the corporation, because many of the deferred taxes will never be paid or will only be paid in the distant future.

6. The accounting record keeping and procedures involving interperiod tax allocation are too costly for the perceived benefits.

On the other hand, many people favor interperiod allocation of income tax expense, as required by *FASB Statement No. 109,* for the following reasons:

1. Income taxes are the result of a given transaction or event. As a result, income tax expense should be based on the results of the transactions or events that are included in pretax financial income and should not be related to taxable income.

2. Income taxes are an expense of doing business and should involve the same accrual, deferral, and estimation concepts that are applied to other expenses.

3. Interperiod tax allocation makes a corporation's net income a more relevant measure of its long-term earning power and avoids periodic income distortions resulting from income tax regulations.

4. Nonallocation of a corporation's income tax expense hinders the prediction of its future cash flows. For instance, a corporation's future cash outflows for

---

23. The discussion in this and the following sections is primarily a summary of the discussion presented in "Accounting for Income Taxes," *FASB Discussion Memorandum* (Stamford, Conn.: FASB, 1983), and D. Beresford, L. Best, P. Craig, and J. Weber, "Accounting for Income Taxes: A Review of Alternatives," *FASB Research Report* (Stamford, Conn.: FASB, 1983). The footnote at the end of each section identifies the paragraphs of the *Discussion Memorandum* and pages of the *Research Report* from which the discussion was taken.

warranty payments would usually be offset by reduced outflows for income taxes.

5. A corporation is a going concern, and income taxes that are currently deferred will eventually have to be paid.[24]

## COMPREHENSIVE VERSUS PARTIAL ALLOCATION

If the arguments raised in favor of the interperiod allocation of income tax expense are accepted, the next issue involves whether this allocation should be applied on a comprehensive or partial allocation basis. **Under comprehensive allocation, the income tax expense reported in an accounting period is affected by all transactions and events entering into the determination of pretax financial income for that period.** This approach is required by *FASB Statement No. 109* and results in consideration of the impact on income tax expense for *all* temporary differences, regardless of how significant or recurrent, during the period in which they may affect income taxes payable. The tax effect is recognized for *each individual* temporary difference and is deferred and allocated to the period or periods when the difference reverses. Under the comprehensive approach, income taxes on all transactions and events that create temporary differences are viewed as affecting cash flows in the period of origination *and* the period of reversal. An originating temporary difference is analogous to an unpaid accounts receivable or accounts payable invoice; when the difference reverses, it is collected or paid.

In contrast, **under partial allocation, the income tax expense reported in an accounting period would be affected only by those temporary differences that are expected to reverse in the foreseeable future.** That is, in certain cases under partial allocation, groups of similar, recurring transactions or events continually may create originating differences in the future that will offset any reversing differences, resulting in an indefinite postponement of deferred tax payments. In effect, these types of temporary differences are more like permanent differences. Examples of these temporary differences include depreciation for manufacturing companies with large amounts of depreciable assets, and bad debts for merchandising companies.

For instance, consider depreciation. On a particular piece of equipment, assume a corporation uses MACRS depreciation for income tax purposes and straight-line depreciation for financial reporting purposes. In the early life of the equipment, MACRS depreciation is higher than straight-line, resulting in lower current income taxes payable and a deferral of income taxes. In the equipment's later life, the difference in depreciation reverses and, *everything else held constant,* the company pays the income taxes deferred earlier. The point is that seldom is "everything else held constant." Most manufacturing companies have numerous pieces of equipment that they are continually replacing (generally at a higher price); most companies are expanding, requiring additional investments in depreciable assets. In these situations, the originating depreciation differences (that is, MACRS depreciation in excess of straight-line) on these newer assets offset the reversing depreciation differences for the older assets. Thus, when a corporation is maintaining or increasing its investment in depreciable assets, and these assets are *viewed as a group,* there will never be a payment of taxes deferred from earlier periods in regard to this group.

---

24. *Ibid.,* par. 41–47 and pp. 19–22.

Advocates of comprehensive income tax allocation raise the following arguments:

1. Individual temporary differences do reverse. By definition, a temporary difference cannot be permanent; the offsetting effect of future events should not be assumed. It is inappropriate to look at the effect of a group of temporary differences on income taxes. Instead, the focus should be on the *individual* items comprising the group. Temporary differences should be viewed in the same manner as accounts payable. That is, although the total balance of accounts payable may not change, many individual credit and payment transactions affect the total.

2. Accounting is primarily historical. It is inappropriate to offset the income tax effects of possible future transactions against the tax effects of transactions that have already occurred.

3. The income tax effects of temporary differences should be reported in the same period that the related transactions and events are included in pretax financial income.

4. Accounting results should not be subject to manipulation by management. That is, a corporation's management should not be able to alter the corporation's results of operations and ending financial position by arbitrarily deciding what temporary differences will and will not reverse in the future.

In contrast, advocates of partial income tax allocation disagree with the preceding points and argue that:

1. All groups of income tax temporary differences are not similar to certain other groups of accounting items, such as accounts payable. Accounts payable "roll over" as a result of actual individual credit and payment transactions. Income taxes, however, are based on total taxable income and not on the individual items comprising that income. Therefore, consideration of the impact of the *group* of temporary differences on income taxes is the appropriate viewpoint.

2. Comprehensive income tax allocation distorts economic reality. The income tax regulations that cause the temporary differences will continue to exist in the future. For instance, Congress is not likely to eliminate investment incentives with respect to depreciation. Consequently, future investments are virtually certain to result in originating depreciation temporary differences of an amount to at least offset reversing differences. Thus, consideration should be given to the impact of future, as well as historical, transactions.

3. Assessment of a corporation's future cash flows is enhanced by using the partial allocation approach. That is, the deferred income taxes (if any) reported on a corporation's balance sheet under partial allocation would be more reflective of the future cash flows.

4. Accounting results should not be distorted by the use of a rigid, mechanical approach, such as comprehensive tax allocation. Furthermore, an objective of the audit function is to identify and deter any management manipulation.[25]

---

25. *Ibid.*, par. 115–149 and pp. 35–40.

# ALTERNATIVE ALLOCATION METHODS

Three methods of interperiod income tax allocation, which may be used in conjunction with either the comprehensive or partial allocation approach, have been advocated. These are: (1) the asset/liability method, (2) the deferred method, and (3) the net-of-tax method. They are closely linked to the income tax rates used to report deferred taxes.

## Asset/Liability Method

The asset/liability method is balance sheet-oriented and is required by *FASB Statement No. 109*. The intent is to accrue and report the total tax that actually will be assessed on temporary differences when they reverse. A temporary difference is viewed as giving rise to either a tax liability that will be paid in the future or a tax asset that will result in a decrease in future tax payments at the then current tax rates. **Under the asset/liability method, the deferred tax amount reported on the balance sheet is the effect of temporary differences that will reverse in the future and that are measured using the currently enacted income tax rates and laws that will be in existence when the temporary differences reverse.** Adjustments, however, are made to the deferred tax amount for any changes in the income tax rates or laws when these changes are enacted. When using the asset/liability method, income tax expense is the sum of (or difference between) the change in deferred taxes for the period and the income taxes currently payable. In general, deferred taxes under the asset/liability method more closely meet the conceptual definitions of assets and liabilities established in *FASB Statement of Concepts No. 6*. For instance, the deferred tax liability of a corporation can be viewed as the probable future sacrifices (i.e., tax payments based on future tax rates) arising from present obligations as a result of past transactions (originating differences).

Arguments in favor of the asset/liability method of interperiod tax allocation include:

1. The balance sheet is an important financial statement. Reporting deferred taxes based upon the enacted future tax rates when the temporary differences reverse increases the predictive value of a corporation's future cash flows, liquidity, and financial flexibility.

2. As discussed earlier, reporting deferred taxes based on the enacted future tax rates is conceptually more sound because the amount represents either the likely future economic sacrifice (future tax payments) or economic benefit (future reduction in taxes).

3. Deferred taxes may be the result of historical transactions but, by definition, they are taxes that are postponed and will be paid (or reduce taxes) in the future at the enacted future tax rates.

4. Estimates are used extensively in accounting. The use of enacted future tax rates for deferred taxes creates information that is, perhaps, more reliable than depreciation based on estimated lives and residual values.

### Discounting
As a corollary, a further refinement of reporting deferred taxes under the asset/liability method is to use a present value approach. That is, deferred taxes would be reported at their discounted amounts. Proponents of this approach argue that the corporation

that reduces tax payments is economically better off. It is their belief that by discounting deferred taxes, a corporation best reflects the operational advantages in its financial statements. Furthermore, they argue that discounted amounts are considered to be the most appropriate indicators of future cash flows. Proponents feel that discounting deferred taxes is consistent with the accounting principles established for such items as notes receivable and notes payable, pension costs, and leases.

On the other hand, critics of discounting argue that discounting deferred taxes mismatches taxable transactions and the related tax effects. That is, the taxable transaction would be reported in one period and the related tax effects over several periods. They also argue that discounting would conceal a corporation's actual tax burden by reporting as interest expense the discount factor that would otherwise be reported as part of income tax expense. Furthermore, deferred taxes may be considered as interest-free loans from the government and, as such, they do not require discounting because the effective interest rate is zero.

## Deferred Method

The deferred method is income statement-oriented and was the method used under *APB Opinion No. 11.* The intent is to match expenses against revenues in the determination of net income, and to spread the tax benefit (or cost) of originating temporary differences over the periods in which the differences reverse. In applying the deferred method, income tax expense in a period includes the income tax effects of all revenues and expenses recognized in pretax financial income. The tax effect of a temporary difference is the difference between income taxes computed with and without inclusion of the temporary difference; this difference is called a deferred tax credit or deferred tax charge and is reported on the balance sheet. **Under the deferred method, the deferred tax amount reported on the balance sheet is the effect of temporary differences that will reverse in the future and that are measured using the income tax rates and laws in effect when the differences originated.** No adjustments are made to deferred taxes for changes in the income tax rates or tax laws that occur after the period of origination. When the deferrals reverse, they are recorded at the rates in existence *when the temporary differences originated.* Thus, under the deferred method, deferred taxes are not receivables or payables in a theoretical sense. They do not meet the conceptual definitions of assets or liabilities established in *FASB Statement of Concepts No. 6* because they are not measurements of probable future economic benefits or sacrifices. Deferred taxes simply represent the cumulative effects of temporary differences waiting to be adjusted in the matching process of some future accounting period.

Arguments in favor of the deferred method of interperiod tax allocation include:

1. The income statement is the most important financial statement, and matching is a critical aspect of the accounting process. Consequently, it is of limited concern that deferred taxes on the balance sheet are not true assets or liabilities in the conceptual sense.

2. Deferred taxes are the result of historical transactions or events that created the temporary differences. Since accounting reports most economic events on an historical cost basis, deferred taxes should be reported in a similar manner.

3. Historical income tax rates are verifiable. Reporting deferred taxes based on historical rates increases the reliability of accounting information.

## Net-of-Tax Method

The net-of-tax method is more a method of disclosure than a different method of calculating deferred taxes. Under this method, the income tax effect of any temporary difference is computed using either the enacted future tax rate for the period when the temporary difference reverses (asset/liability method) or the tax rate in effect when the temporary difference originated (deferred method). The resulting deferred taxes, however, are not separately disclosed on the balance sheet. Instead, **under the net-of-tax method the deferred tax assets (charges) or deferred tax liabilities (credits) are treated as adjustments to the accounts to which the temporary differences relate.** Generally, the accounts are adjusted through the use of valuation allowances rather than directly. For instance, if a temporary difference results from additional tax depreciation, the related tax effect would be subtracted (by means of a valuation account) from the cost of the asset (along with accumulated depreciation) to determine the carrying value of the depreciable asset. Or the carrying value of a warranty liability would be reduced for the expected decrease in income taxes when the warranty is paid (and is a tax deduction). Reversals of temporary differences would reduce the valuation allowance accounts.

Two alternatives exist for disclosing the periodic income tax expense on the income statement under the net-of-tax method. Under the first alternative, the tax effects of temporary differences are included in the total income tax expense. Thus, income tax expense is reported in a manner similar to the deferred method or asset/liability method. Under the second alternative, income tax expense is reported at the same amount as current income taxes payable. The tax effects of temporary differences, then, are combined with the revenue or expense items to which they relate. For instance, the tax effect of additional tax depreciation would be an adjustment to depreciation expense.

The basic argument in favor of the net-of-tax method of interperiod tax allocation is that all revenue and expense transactions involve changes in specific asset and liability accounts and are recorded accordingly. Therefore, accounting for the tax effects of temporary differences should be no different. Because temporary differences are the result of events that affect the future taxability and tax deductibility of specific assets and liabilities, they have future economic consequences that should be reflected in the value of the assets and liabilities. For instance, when tax depreciation exceeds financial accounting depreciation, income tax expense is higher than the income tax obligation because an excess amount of the cost of the depreciable asset has been deducted from taxable income. Thus, the excess temporary difference has reduced the future tax deductibility of the depreciable asset cost, and the carrying value of the asset should be reduced accordingly.[26]

There are several arguments against the net-of-tax method. The primary argument is that there are many factors that affect the value of assets and liabilities but are not recorded in the accounts. To single out one factor (impact on future taxes) as affecting value is inappropriate. Furthermore, it is argued that the net-of-tax method is too complex to use and that it distorts traditional concepts for measuring assets and liabilities.

## CONTROVERSIAL CONCLUSIONS

After weighing the various arguments in favor of and against the alternative approaches, the FASB concluded in *FASB Statement No. 96* that comprehensive interperiod income tax allocation applied under the asset/liability method should be used.

---

26. *Ibid.*, par. 50–90 and pp. 53–62.

Although most accountants agreed with its general conclusions, a number disagreed with two specific issues: (1) the restrictions imposed on the recognition of certain deferred tax assets, and (2) the required scheduling of future reversals of temporary differences, along with consideration of hypothetical tax-planning strategies.

One of the characteristics of an asset is that the transaction or other event resulting in a corporation's right to or control over the benefit must already have occurred. In regard to deferred tax assets, the FASB took the position that to obtain the tax benefit of a deductible amount for a temporary difference that must be *carried forward,* the corporation must earn future income against which to offset the carryforward. Since earning income in future years has not yet occurred and has never been assumed in preparing externally-reported financial statements, the Board felt that this "critical event" characteristic was *not* met. Hence, it concluded in *FASB Statement No. 96* that the deferred tax consequences of temporary differences that result in net deductible amounts in future years and that must be carried forward should *not* be recorded as an asset. Many people disagreed with this conclusion. They felt that the FASB's recognition requirements for a deferred tax asset were more stringent than for other assets (such as receivables), and that the Board was taking more of a "liquidation" approach rather than a "going-concern" approach to accounting for income taxes. They argued that the critical event for recognition of a deferred tax asset is the past event that resulted in the deductible temporary difference. This past event gives the corporation a right to or control over the future tax benefits; therefore, a deferred tax asset should be recorded.

*FASB Statement No. 96* required that a corporation estimate the particular future years in which its temporary differences would result in taxable or deductible amounts. The corporation was then required to prepare a "schedule" to offset ("net") the taxable and deductible amounts applicable to future years. In the case of depreciable assets, for example, this schedule might involve some 20 to 30 years. Furthermore, the corporation was to consider "hypothetical" tax-planning strategies in the scheduling of its future taxable or deductible amounts. While generally agreeing that the scheduling approach was conceptually correct, many accountants raised practical implementation concerns. They argued that the scheduling was so complex and time-consuming that its required use violated the *benefit/cost* constraint of the *FASB Conceptual Framework.* That is, the *usefulness* of the resulting information was less than the cost of preparing the information. They also argued that the hypothetical tax-planning strategies were confusing to users and reduced the *understandability* of the information. As a result of these criticisms, the FASB reexamined the accounting principles for reporting income taxes in corporations' financial statements and eventually issued *FASB Statement No. 109* (discussed earlier in the chapter). It remains to be seen whether this *Statement* will end the long-standing debate on the interperiod allocation of income taxes.

## QUESTIONS

*Q17-1*  Distinguish between the objectives of financial reporting and the Internal Revenue Code.

*Q17-2*  Identify the five groups of possible differences between pretax financial income and taxable income (or between income tax expense and income taxes payable).

*Q17-3*  What is a permanent difference? Give two examples.

*Q17-4*  What is a temporary difference? Give two examples.

*Q17-5*  What did the FASB conclude in *FASB Statement No. 109* regarding interperiod income tax allocation?

*Q17-6*  What are the two objectives of accounting for income taxes identified in *FASB Statement No. 109?*

Q17-7 How are deferred taxes determined under generally accepted accounting principles?

Q17-8 What are the three essential characteristics of a liability and why does a deferred tax liability of a corporation meet these characteristics?

Q17-9 What are the three essential characteristics of an asset and why does a deferred tax asset of a corporation meet these characteristics?

Q17-10 When is a valuation allowance needed? List the four sources of taxable income that might be used to justify that a valuation allowance is not needed.

Q17-11 List the steps necessary to measure and record a corporation's current and deferred income taxes.

Q17-12 Describe an operating loss carryback. List the two conceptual questions concerning accounting for a carryback.

Q17-13 Describe an operating loss carryforward. List the two conceptual questions concerning accounting for a carryforward.

Q17-14 Briefly summarize the generally accepted accounting principles for the financial reporting of operating loss carrybacks and carryforwards.

Q17-15 What is intraperiod income tax allocation? How is income tax expense reported on a corporation's income statement and retained earnings statement?

Q17-16 How are deferred tax liabilities and assets reported on a corporation's balance sheet?

Q17-17 Briefly describe the adjustment of a deferred tax liability (or asset) and the related income statement disclosure for a change in the income tax rate.

Q17-18 (Appendix). What are the arguments in favor of the nonallocation of income tax expense across accounting periods?

Q17-19 (Appendix). What is interperiod income tax allocation? List the arguments in favor of interperiod income tax allocation.

Q17-20 (Appendix). What is comprehensive interperiod tax allocation? List the arguments in favor of this allocation.

Q17-21 (Appendix). What is partial interperiod tax allocation? List the arguments in favor of this allocation.

Q17-22 (Appendix). What are the three methods of interperiod tax allocation? *Briefly* describe each method.

# CASES

### C17-1 Asset/Liability Method and Temporary Differences

Interperiod tax allocation is necessary because there are differences in the timing of revenues and expenses between financial statements and federal income tax returns.

**Required**

1. Identify the two goals and four basic principles of accounting for income taxes.
2. Briefly describe interperiod income tax allocation under generally accepted accounting principles.
3. List the four groups of items that result in temporary differences and give examples for each group.

### C17-2 Permanent and Temporary Differences

To implement interperiod income tax allocation, an accountant must be able to distinguish between permanent and temporary differences. The following is a list of three differences between a corporation's pretax financial income and taxable income:

a. Estimated warranty costs (covering a 3-year warranty) are expensed for financial reporting purposes at the time of sale but are deducted for tax purposes when incurred.
b. MACRS depreciation for income tax purposes exceeds straight-line depreciation for financial reporting purposes.

c. Percentage depletion for tax purposes exceeds cost depletion for financial reporting purposes.

**Required**

1. Define (a) *permanent difference* and (b) *temporary difference*.
2. Define *interperiod income tax allocation* and briefly describe its application under generally accepted accounting principles.
3. Indicate and explain whether each of the three differences listed in this case should be treated as a temporary or permanent difference.

### C17-3 Deferred Tax Assets and Liabilities

A friend says to you, "I don't understand how taxable temporary differences can be 'liabilities' and how deductible temporary differences can be 'assets.' It seems to me that these temporary differences only relate to the future, and accounting is based on 'historical cost.' Furthermore, the government frequently changes the tax laws, so no one knows what the future tax laws will be."

**Required**

Prepare a written response for your friend that explains why deferred tax assets and deferred tax liabilities are recognized and reported on a corporation's balance sheet. Include a discussion of a valuation allowance.

### C17-4    Operating Losses

The Internal Revenue Code allows a corporation to carry back or carry forward an "operating loss" for a given year.

**Required**

1. Describe an operating loss carryback and a carryforward.
2. For a carryback, identify and briefly discuss the two important conceptual questions.
3. For a carryforward, identify and briefly discuss the two important conceptual questions.
4. Briefly summarize the generally accepted accounting principles for the financial reporting of an: (a) operating loss carryback and (b) operating loss carryforward.

### C17-5    Intraperiod Tax Allocation

Income tax allocation is an integral part of generally accepted accounting principles. Income tax allocation consists of both intraperiod and interperiod tax allocation.

**Required**

1. Explain the difference between interperiod and intraperiod income tax allocation.
2. Discuss how to disclose the income tax expense (or credit) for the year under intraperiod allocation.
3. Provide an example of intraperiod tax allocation on a corporation's income statement that includes income from continuing operations, a loss from the sale of a discontinued segment, a gain from the operations of the discontinued segment, and an extraordinary gain. Assume a 30% tax rate.

### C17-6    Appendix: Interperiod Tax Allocation

A friend in a business policy class says, "I always thought the income taxes reported on a corporation's income statement were the same as the income taxes paid during that period. Now I am not so sure because some other students mentioned interperiod income tax allocation. Furthermore, I have heard about comprehensive and partial allocation. I am confused. Please explain this to me."

**Required**

Prepare a written response for your friend. In your discussion, be sure to compare interperiod income tax allocation with nonallocation, and comprehensive allocation with partial allocation. Include the arguments cited for each.

### C17-7    Appendix: Methods of Interperiod Tax Allocation

Three methods of interperiod income tax allocation have been advocated. These include (1) the asset/liability method, (2) the deferred method, and (3) the net-of-tax method.

**Required**

Define *interperiod income tax allocation* and briefly describe the three methods, including the arguments cited for each. Conclude by summarizing the generally accepted accounting principles for interperiod income tax allocation.

---

## MULTIPLE CHOICE

*Select the best answer for each of the following.*

M17-1    A permanent difference is a difference between pretax financial income and taxable income in an accounting period that will never reverse in a later period. Which of the following is *not* an example of a permanent difference?

    a. Amortization of goodwill      c. Interest on municipal bonds
    b. Percentage depletion in excess of      d. Rent received in advance
       cost depletion on a wasting asset

M17-2    Prior to and during 1995, the Shadrach Company reported tax depreciation at an amount higher than the amount of financial depreciation, resulting in a book value of the depreciable assets of $24,500 for financial reporting purposes and of $20,000 for tax purposes at the end of 1995. In addition, the company recognized a $3,500 estimated liability for legal expenses in the financial statements during 1995; it expects to pay this liability (and deduct it for tax purposes) in 1999. The current tax rate is 30%, no change in the tax rate has been enacted, and the company expects to be profitable in future years. What is the amount of the net noncurrent deferred tax liability at the end of 1995?

    a. $300      c. $1,050
    b. $450      d. $1,350

M17-3    Which of the following is an argument in favor of the asset/liability method of interperiod income tax allocation?

    a. Deferred taxes are the result of historical transactions and should be reported in a similar manner.

b. Tax effects should be recorded in the same manner as all other revenue and expense transactions that involve changes in specific asset and liability accounts.

c. The predictive value of future cash flows, liquidity, and financial flexibility are increased when deferred taxes are reported based upon tax rates enacted that will be in effect when the temporary differences reverse.

d. Historical tax rates are more verifiable and, therefore, the deferred tax amount is more reliable.

M17-4    At the beginning of 1995, Conley Company purchased an asset at a cost of $10,000. For financial reporting purposes, the asset has a 4-year life with no residual value, and is depreciated by the straight-line method beginning in 1995. For tax purposes, the asset is depreciated under MACRS using a 5-year recovery period. Prior to 1995, the company had no deferred tax liability or asset. The difference between depreciation for financial reporting purposes and income tax purposes is the only temporary difference between pretax financial income and taxable income. The current income tax rate is 30% and no change in the tax rate has been enacted for future years. In 1995 and 1996, taxable income will be higher or lower than financial income by what amount?

| | 1995 | 1996 |
|---|---|---|
| a. | Higher by $150 | Lower by $210 |
| b. | Higher by $500 | Lower by $700 |
| c. | Lower by $500 | Higher by $700 |
| d. | Lower by $1,500 | Higher by $100 |

M17-5    Brooks Company reported a prior period adjustment of $12,000 in pretax financial "income" and taxable income for 1995. The prior period adjustment was the result of an error in calculating bad debt expense for 1994. The current tax rate is 30% and no change in the tax rate has been enacted for future years. When the company applies intraperiod income tax allocation, the prior period adjustment will be

a. Shown on the income statement at $12,000

b. Shown on the income statement at $8,400 (net of $3,600 income taxes)

c. Shown on the retained earnings statement at $12,000

d. Shown on the retained earnings statement at $8,400 (net of $3,600 income taxes)

M17-6    In 1995, Swope Company reports a pretax operating loss of $70,000 for both financial reporting and income tax purposes. Pretax financial income and taxable income for the previous 3 years had been: 1992—$15,000 (tax rate 20%); 1993—$24,000 (tax rate 25%); and 1994—$39,000 (tax rate 30%). The current tax rate is 30% and no change in the tax rate has been enacted for future years. At the end of 1995, the journal entry recorded would contain an income tax benefit from an operating loss carryback of

a. $0                              c. $20,700

b. $18,300                         d. $21,000

M17-7    *FASB Statement No. 109* came to which of the following conclusions regarding interperiod income tax allocation?

a. The partial allocation approach should be applied.

b. The net-of-tax method of income tax allocation should be used.

c. Nonallocation of income tax expense is appropriate.

d. The asset/liability method of income tax allocation should be used.

M17-8    Which of the following is *not* a cause of difference between pretax financial income and taxable income in a given period?

a. Operating loss carrybacks and carryforwards          c. Applicable tax rates

b. Permanent differences                                d. Temporary differences

M17-9    Which component of current income is not disclosed on the income statement net of tax effects?

a. Extraordinary loss on bond redemption          c. Cumulative effect of change in accounting principle

b. Gain on disposal of milling machine             d. Loss from operations of discontinued segment

*M17-10* The Oliver Company earned taxable income of $7,500 during 1995, its first year of operations. A reconciliation of pretax financial income and taxable income indicated that an additional $2,500 of accelerated depreciation was deducted for tax purposes and that an estimated expense of $5,800 was deducted for financial reporting purposes. The estimated expense is not expected to be deductible for tax purposes until 1998, when the liability is paid. The current tax rate is 30% and no change in the tax rate has been enacted for future years. The resulting journal entry for 1995 would be:

a.  Income Tax Expense            1,260
    Deferred Tax Asset            1,740
        Deferred Tax Liability                  750
        Income Taxes Payable                  2,250
b.  Income Tax Expense            1,260
    Deferred Tax Asset             990
        Income Taxes Payable                  2,250
c.  Income Tax Expense            3,240
        Deferred Tax Liability                  990
        Income Taxes Payable                  2,250
d.  Income Tax Expense            3,000
        Deferred Tax Liability                  750
        Income Taxes Payable                  2,250

## EXERCISES

*E17-1*  **Single Temporary Difference**  The Durn Company began operations at the beginning of 1995. At the end of 1995, the company reported taxable income of $9,800 and pretax financial income of $12,200, due to a single temporary difference. The income tax rate for the current year is 30%, but Congress has enacted a 40% tax rate for 1996 and beyond.

**Required**
Prepare the income tax journal entry of the Durn Company at the end of 1995.

*E17-2*  **Temporary Difference**  At the end of 1995, its first year of operations, Slater Company reported a book value for its depreciable assets of $40,000 for financial reporting purposes and $34,000 for income tax purposes. The company earned taxable income of $97,000 during 1995. The company is subject to a 30% income tax rate and no change has been enacted for future years. The depreciation was the only temporary difference between taxable income and pretax financial income.

**Required**
1.  Prepare the income tax journal entry of the Slater Company at the end of 1995.
2.  Show how the deferred taxes would be reported on the Slater Company's December 31, 1995 balance sheet.

*E17-3*  **Single Temporary Difference: Multiple Rates**  At the end of 1995, Holden Company reported taxable income of $9,000 and pretax financial income of $10,600. The difference is due to depreciation for tax purposes in excess of depreciation for financial reporting purposes. The income tax rate for the current year is 40%, but Congress has enacted tax rates of 35% for 1996 and 30% for 1997 and beyond.

Holden Company has calculated the excess of its financial depreciation over its tax depreciation for future years as follows: 1996, $600; 1997, $700; and 1998, $300. Prior to 1995, the company had no deferred tax liability or asset.

**Required**
Prepare the income tax journal entry of the Holden Company at the end of 1995.

*E17-4*  **Single Temporary Difference**  Crat Company has been in operation for several years. During those years the company has been profitable, and it expects to continue to be profitable in the foreseeable future. At the beginning of 1995, the company has a deferred tax asset of $400 pertaining to one deductible temporary difference. During 1995, the company earned taxable income of $50,000, which was taxed at a rate of 30% (no change in the tax rate has been enacted for future years). At the end of 1995, the book value of the current liability to which the deferred tax asset relates for financial reporting purposes exceeded the book value for income tax purposes by $6,000.

**Required**

1. Prepare the income tax journal entry of the Crat Company at the end of 1995.
2. Show how the deferred tax asset is reported on the Crat Company's December 31, 1995 balance sheet.

E17-5 *Valuation Account*  At the end of 1995, its first year of operations, the Hansen Company reported taxable income of $38,000 and pretax financial income of $34,400. The difference is due to the way the company handles its warranty costs. For tax purposes, the company deducts the warranty costs as they are paid. For financial reporting purposes, the company provides for a year-end estimated warranty liability based on future expected costs. The company is subject to a 30% tax rate for 1995 and no change in the tax rate has been enacted for future years. Based on verifiable evidence, the company decides it should establish a valuation allowance of 60% of its ending deferred tax asset.

**Required**

1. Prepare the income tax journal entry of the Hansen Company at the end of 1995.
2. Prepare the lower portion of the Hansen Company's 1995 income statement.

E17-6 *Income Taxes*  Thun Company has been in operation for several years. It has both a deductible and a taxable temporary difference. At the beginning of 1995, its deferred tax asset was $690 and its deferred tax liability was $750. The company expects its deductible temporary difference to be "deductible" in 1996 and its taxable temporary difference to be "taxable" in 1997. In 1994 Congress enacted income tax rates for future years as follows: 1995, 30%; 1996, 34%; and 1997, 35%. At the end of 1995, the company reported income taxes payable of $15,600, an increase in its deferred tax liability of $230, and an ending balance in its deferred tax asset of $860. The company has prepared the following schedule of items related to its income taxes for 1995.

| Item | Amount |
|---|---|
| Taxable income for 1995 | _____ |
| Taxable temporary difference, 12/31/95 | _____ |
| Increase in deductible temporary difference during 1995 | _____ |
| Income tax expense for 1995 | _____ |

**Required**

Fill in the blanks in the preceding schedule. Show your calculations.

E17-7 *Originating and Reversing Difference*  The Tanner Corporation begins operations in 1995 and reports the following amounts of pretax financial income and taxable income for the years 1995 through 1999. The company has only one temporary difference, and only one originating or reversing difference occurs in any single year. The company is subject to a tax rate of 30% for all the years.

| Year | Pretax Financial Income | Taxable Income |
|---|---|---|
| 1995 | $70,000 | $ 50,000 |
| 1996 | 85,000 | 75,000 |
| 1997 | 90,000 | 90,000 |
| 1998 | 82,000 | 92,000 |
| 1999 | 93,000 | 113,000 |

**Required**

1. Prepare the income tax journal entry for each year.
2. What do you notice about the balance in the deferred taxes over the 5 years?

E17-8 *Multiple Temporary Differences*  Vickers Company reports taxable income of $5,500 for 1995. The company has two temporary differences between pretax financial income and taxable income at the end of 1995. The first difference is expected to result in taxable amounts totaling $2,470 in future years. The second difference is expected to result in deductible amounts totaling $1,360 in future years. The company has a deferred tax asset of $372 and a deferred tax liability of $660 at the beginning of 1995. The current tax rate is 30% and no change in the tax rate has been enacted for future years. The company has positive, verifiable evidence of future taxable income.

**Required**

Prepare the income tax journal entry of the Vickers Company at the end of 1995.

**E17-9    *Operating Loss***    At the end of 1995, Keil Company reports a pretax operating loss of $80,000 for both financial reporting and income tax purposes. Prior to 1995 the company had been successful and had reported and paid taxes on the following pretax financial income and taxable income: 1991, $22,000; 1992, $27,000; 1993, $30,000; and 1994, $34,000. The company had been subject to tax rates of 20% in 1991, 25% in 1992, and 30% in 1993 and 1994.

**Required**

1. Prepare the income tax journal entry of the Keil Company at the end of 1995.
2. Prepare the lower portion of Keil's 1995 income statement.

**E17-10    *Operating Loss***    At the end of 1994, its first year of operations, the Swelland Company reported a pretax operating loss of $34,000 for both financial reporting and income tax purposes. At that time, the company had no positive verifiable evidence that it would earn future taxable income. However, due to successful management, the company reported pretax operating income (and taxable income) of $60,000 in 1995. During both years, the income tax rate was 30% and no change had been enacted for future years.

**Required**

1. Prepare the income tax journal entries of the Swelland Company at the end of 1994.
2. Prepare the income tax journal entry of the Swelland Company at the end of 1995.
3. Prepare the lower portion of Swelland's 1995 income statement.

**E17-11    *Operating Loss***    Baxter Company began operations in 1991 and was profitable through 1994. At the end of 1995, the company reported a pretax operating loss of $125,000 for both financial reporting and income taxes. Because the tax rate was increased to 40% in 1995 and the company expects future taxable income, it elects to forgo any carryback of the operating loss. In 1996, the company reported pretax operating income of $150,000.

**Required**

1. Prepare the income tax journal entry of the Baxter Company at the end of 1995.
2. Prepare the income tax journal entry of the Baxter Company at the end of 1996.
3. Prepare the lower portion of Baxter's 1995 income statement.
4. Prepare the lower portion of Baxter's 1996 income statement.

**E17-12    *Intraperiod Tax Allocation***    The Wright Company reports the following information for the year ended December 31, 1995:

| | |
|---|---|
| Pretax income from continuing operations | $160,000[a] |
| Pretax gain from sale of investment (extraordinary item) | 30,000 |
| Pretax income from operations of discontinued Segment M | 27,000 |
| Pretax loss on disposal of Segment M | (45,000) |
| Pretax cumulative effect of change in accounting principle | 12,000 |
| Pretax error in understating depreciation in 1994 | (8,000) |
| Retained earnings, January 1, 1995 | 410,000 |
| Cash dividends during 1995 | 48,000 |
| Total income tax | 39,000[b] |

a. Of this amount, revenues are $400,000 and expenses are $240,000.
b. Of this amount: $7,500 relates to the extraordinary item; $6,750 relates to the pretax income from the operations of discontinued Segment M; the pretax loss on the disposal of Segment M resulted in an income tax savings of $11,250; $3,000 relates to the pretax cumulative effect of the change in accounting principle; and the pretax depreciation error resulted in an income tax savings of $2,000.

**Required**

1. Prepare the year-end journal entry necessary to record the 1995 intraperiod income tax allocation in regard to the preceding information.
2. Prepare Wright's 1995 income statement and statement of retained earnings.

**E17-13** *Calculating Intraperiod Income Taxes*  The Mahoney Corporation reports the following *pretax* accounting (and taxable) income items during 1995:

| | |
|---|---|
| Income from continuing operations | $100,000[a] |
| Loss from operations of a discontinued segment | (10,000) |
| Gain from the disposal of the discontinued segment | 25,000 |
| Extraordinary gain from the early extinguishment of debt | 20,000 |
| Cumulative effect of change in accounting principle | (9,000) |

a.  Of this amount, revenues are $330,000 and expenses are $230,000.

**Required**

1.  Prepare the journal entry necessary to record the 1995 intraperiod income tax allocation in regard to the preceding information. Assume a tax rate of 15% on the first $40,000 of income and a rate of 30% on income in excess of $40,000.
2.  Prepare Mahoney's 1995 income statement.

**E17-14** *Disclosure of Intraperiod Tax Allocation*  The Lester Corporation reports $125,000 of both *pretax* accounting "income" and taxable income in 1995. In addition to income from continuing operations (of which revenues are $500,000), included in this income is a $25,000 extraordinary loss from a fire, a $17,000 loss from operations of discontinued Segment W, a $15,000 gain on the disposal of Segment W, a $6,000 gain from changing from double-declining balance to straight-line depreciation, and a $14,000 correction of an error due to the understatement of bad debt expense in 1994. The company is subject to a 20% tax rate on the first $50,000 of income and a rate of 25% on income in excess of $50,000.

**Required**

1.  Show how this information is disclosed on Lester's 1995 income statement.
2.  Prepare Lester's 1995 statement of retained earnings. (Assume a beginning retained earnings balance of $191,000 and cash dividends during 1995 amounting to $65,000.)

**E17-15** *Balance Sheet Presentation*  The Thiel Company reports the following deferred tax items at the end of 1995:

| Deferred Tax Item # | Account Balance | Related Asset or Liability |
|---|---|---|
| 1 | $ 7,200 credit | Current asset |
| 2 | 6,700 debit | Current liability |
| 3 | 15,500 credit | Noncurrent asset |
| 4 | 10,600 debit | Noncurrent liability |

**Required**

Show how the preceding deferred tax items are reported on the Thiel Company's December 31, 1995 balance sheet.

**E17-16** *Change in Tax Rates*  At the end of 1995, Rowet Company reported a deferred tax liability of $6,360 based on an income tax rate of 30%. On June 1, 1996, Congress changed the income tax rate to 35%.

**Required**

1.  Calculate the amount of the adjustment to Rowet Company's 1995 year-end deferred tax liability.
2.  Prepare the journal entry to correct Rowet Company's deferred tax liability.

## PROBLEMS

*P17-1    Temporary and Permanent Differences*  In the current year, you are calculating a diversified company's deferred taxes. Based on an analysis of the company's current taxable income and pretax financial income, you have identified the following items that create differences between the two amounts and that may result in differences between the company's future taxable income and its future pretax financial income:

_____   1. Percentage depletion deducted for taxes in excess of cost depletion for financial reporting
_____   2. Warranty costs to be deducted for taxes that were deducted as warranty expense for financial reporting
_____   3. Gross profit to be recognized for taxes under the percentage-of-completion capitalized cost method that was recognized for financial reporting under the percentage-of-completion method
_____   4. Goodwill amortization expense deducted for financial reporting
_____   5. Rent revenue to be recognized for financial reporting that was reported for taxes when collected in advance
_____   6. Loss from writedown of inventory that was recognized for financial reporting but that will be deducted for taxes when the inventory is sold
_____   7. Interest revenue on municipal bonds recognized for financial reporting
_____   8. Loss that was deducted due to contingent liability for financial reporting that will be deducted for taxes when the liability is actually paid
_____   9. Gross profit to be recognized under installment method for tax purposes that was recognized on accrual basis for financial reporting
_____  10. Depreciation to be recognized for financial reporting in excess of MACRS depreciation to be deducted for tax purposes
_____  11. Investment income that has been recognized under the equity method for financial reporting that will be recognized as fully taxable for tax purposes when dividends are collected

**Required**
For each difference, indicate whether it is a temporary difference (*T*) or a permanent difference (*P*) by placing the appropriate letter on the line provided. If the difference is a temporary difference, also indicate for the current year whether it will result in a future taxable amount (*T*) or a future deductible amount (*D*).

*P17-2    Definitions*  The FASB has defined several terms in regard to accounting for income taxes. Below are various code letters (for terms) followed by definitions.

| Code Letter | Term | Code Letter | Term |
|---|---|---|---|
| A | Deductible temporary difference | H | Deferred tax consequences |
| B | Income tax obligation (or refund) | I | Taxable temporary difference |
| C | Operating loss carryback | J | Deferred tax liability |
| D | Valuation allowance | K | Temporary difference |
| E | Deferred tax asset | L | Income tax expense (or benefit) |
| F | Operating loss carryforward | M | Deferred tax expense (or benefit) |
| G | Taxable income | | |

_____   1. The deferred tax consequences attributable to deductible temporary differences and operating loss carryforwards
_____   2. A difference between the tax basis of an asset or liability and its reported amount in the financial statements that will result in taxable or deductible amounts in future years when the reported amount of the asset or liability is recovered or settled, respectively
_____   3. Temporary difference that results in taxable amounts in future years when the related asset or liability is recovered or settled, respectively
_____   4. The future effects on income taxes as measured by the applicable enacted tax rate and provisions of the enacted tax law resulting from temporary differences and operating loss carryforwards at the end of the current year

_____ 5. The change during the year in a corporation's deferred tax liabilities and assets

_____ 6. The deferred tax consequences attributable to taxable temporary differences

_____ 7. The portion of a deferred tax asset for which it is more likely than not that a tax benefit will not be realized

_____ 8. Temporary difference that results in deductible amounts in future years when the related asset or liability is recovered or settled, respectively

_____ 9. The sum of income tax obligation and deferred tax expense (or benefit)

_____ 10. The amount of income taxes paid or payable (or refundable) for the current year

_____ 11. An excess of tax deductible expenses over taxable revenues in a year that may be carried forward to reduce taxable income in a future year

_____ 12. The excess of taxable revenues over tax deductible expenses and exemptions for the year

_____ 13. An excess of tax deductible expenses over taxable revenues in a year that may be carried back to reduce taxable income in a prior year

**Required**

Indicate which terms belongs with each definition by inserting the corresponding code letter on the line preceding the definition.

P17-3 *Multiple Temporary Differences*  Wilcox Company has prepared the following reconciliation of its pretax financial income with its taxable income for 1995:

| | |
|---|---:|
| Pretax financial income | $3,700 |
| Add: Estimated expense on one-year warranties recognized for financial reporting in excess of actual warranty costs deducted for income taxes | 100 |
| Less: Accelerated depreciation deducted for income taxes in excess of depreciation recognized for financial reporting | (250) |
| Taxable income | 3,550 |

At the beginning of 1995, Wilcox Company had a deferred tax liability of $495. The current tax rate is 30% and no change in the tax rate has been enacted for future years. At the end of 1995, the company anticipates that actual warranty costs will exceed estimated warranty expense by $100 and that financial depreciation will exceed tax depreciation by $1,900 in future years. The company has earned income in all past years and expects to earn income in the future.

**Required**

1. Prepare the income tax journal entry of the Wilcox Company at the end of 1995.
2. Prepare the lower portion of Wilcox's 1995 income statement.
3. Show how the income tax items are reported on Wilcox's December 31, 1995 balance sheet.

P17-4 *Interperiod Tax Allocation*  Klerk Company had four temporary differences between its pretax financial income and its taxable income during 1995, as follows:

| Number | Temporary Difference |
|:---:|---|
| 1 | Gross profit on certain installment sales is recognized under the accrual method for financial reporting and under the installment method for income taxes. |
| 2 | MACRS depreciation is used for income taxes; a different depreciation method is used for financial reporting. |
| 3 | Rent receipts are included in taxable income when collected in advance; rent revenue is recognized under the accrual method for financial reporting. |
| 4 | Warranty expense is estimated for financial reporting; warranty costs are deducted as incurred for income taxes. |

At the beginning of 1995, the company had a deferred tax liability of $84,300 related to temporary difference #2 and a deferred tax asset of $21,090 related to temporary difference #4. Based on its tax records, the company earned taxable income of $270,000 for 1995. The company's accountant has prepared the following schedule showing the total future taxable and deductible amounts at the end of 1995 for its four temporary differences:

| Taxable Amounts | | Deductible Amounts | |
|---|---|---|---|
| #1 | #2 | #3 | #4 |
| $77,900 | $241,000 | $20,000 | $55,300 |

The company has a history of earning income and expects to be profitable in the future. The income tax rate for 1995 is 40%, but in 1994 Congress enacted a 30% tax rate for 1996 and future years.

During 1995, for financial accounting purposes, the company reported revenues of $750,000 and expenses of $447,100. The deferred tax related to temporary differences #1, #2, and #4 are considered to be noncurrent by the company; the deferred tax related to temporary difference #3 is considered to be current.

**Required**

1. Prepare the income tax journal entry of the Klerk Company for 1995.
2. Prepare a condensed 1995 income statement for the Klerk Company.
3. Show how the income tax items are reported on Klerk Company's December 31, 1995 balance sheet.

P17-5    *Interperiod Tax Allocation*    Peterson Company has computed its pretax financial income to be $71,000 in 1995 *after* including the effects of the relevant items from the following information:

| | |
|---|---|
| 1. Depreciation taken for tax purposes | $40,000 |
| 2. Goodwill amortization expense recorded on accounting records | 15,000 |
| 3. Interest revenue on investment in municipal bonds recorded on accounting records | 25,000 |
| 4. Percentage depletion taken for tax purposes in excess of cost depletion taken for financial reporting purposes | 10,000 |
| 5. Depreciation taken for financial reporting purposes | 48,000 |
| 6. Actual product warranty costs deducted for tax purposes | 20,000 |
| 7. Gross profit on installment sales recognized for tax purposes | 80,000 |
| 8. Estimated product warranty expense recorded on accounting records | 27,000 |
| 9. Gross profit on installment sales recognized for financial reporting purposes | 91,000 |

The company's accountant has prepared the following schedule showing the future taxable and deductible amounts at the end of 1995 for its three temporary differences:

| | Totals |
|---|---|
| *Future Taxable Amounts* | |
| Depreciation difference | $33,800 |
| Installment sales: gross profit difference | 26,700 |
| *Future Deductible Amounts* | |
| Warranty difference | 56,500 |

At the beginning of 1995, the company had a deferred tax liability of $12,540 related to the depreciation difference and $4,710 related to the installment sales difference. In addition, it had a deferred tax asset of $14,850 related to the warranty difference. The current tax rate is 30% and no change in the tax rate has been enacted for future years.

**Required**

1. Compute the Peterson Company's taxable income for 1995.
2. Prepare the income tax journal entry of the Peterson Company for 1995 (assume no valuation allowance is necessary).

P17-6    *Interperiod Tax Allocation*    Quick Company reports the following revenues and expenses in its pretax financial income for the year ended December 31, 1995:

| | |
|---|---|
| Revenues | $230,900 |
| Expenses | (160,100) |
| Pretax financial income | $ 70,800 |

The revenues included in pretax financial income are the same amount as the revenues included in the company's taxable income. A reconciliation of the expenses reported for pretax financial income to the expenses reported for taxable income, however, reveals four differences:

1. Depreciation deducted for financial reporting exceeded depreciation deducted for income taxes by $11,000.
2. Percentage depletion deducted for income taxes exceeded cost depletion deducted for financial reporting by $15,600.
3. Warranty costs deducted for income taxes exceeded warranty expense deducted for financial reporting by $8,900.
4. Legal expense of $10,200 was deducted for financial reporting; it will be deducted for income taxes when paid in a future year.

The company expects its percentage depletion to exceed its cost depletion in each of the next 5 years by the same amount as in 1995. At the end of 1995, the other three expenses are expected to result in total future taxable or deductible amounts as follows:

| | Totals |
|---|---|
| *Future Taxable Amounts* | |
| Depreciation expense difference | $63,000 |
| *Future Deductible Amounts* | |
| Warranty expense difference | 48,400 |
| Legal expense difference | 10,200 |

At the beginning of 1995, the company had a deferred tax liability of $22,200 related to the depreciation difference and a deferred tax asset of $17,190 related to the warranty difference. The income tax rate for 1995 is 35%, but in 1994 Congress enacted a 30% rate for 1996 and future years.

**Required**

1. Compute the Quick Company's taxable income for 1995.
2. Prepare the income tax journal entry of the Quick Company for 1995. Assume no valuation allowance is necessary.
3. Prepare a condensed 1995 income statement for the Quick Company.

P17-7 **Deferred Tax Liability: Depreciation**   At the beginning of 1995, its first year of operations, Cooke Company purchased an asset for $100,000. This asset has an 8-year economic life with no residual value, and it is being depreciated by the straight-line method for financial reporting purposes. For tax purposes, however, the asset is being depreciated using the MACRS (200%, 5-year life) method.

During 1995, the company reported pretax financial income of $51,500 and taxable income of $44,000. The depreciation temporary difference caused the difference between the two income amounts. The current tax rate in 1995 was 30% and no change in the tax rate had been enacted for future years.

**Required**

1. Prepare a schedule that shows for each year, 1995 through 2002, (a) MACRS depreciation, (b) straight-line depreciation, (c) the annual depreciation temporary difference, and (d) the accumulated temporary difference at the end of each year.
2. Prepare a schedule that computes for each year, 1995 through 2002, (a) the ending deferred tax liability, and (b) the change in the deferred tax liability.
3. Prepare the income tax journal entry at the end of 1995.
4. Explain what happens to the balance of the deferred tax liability at the end of 1995 through 2002.

P17-8 **Deferred Tax Liability: Depreciation**   Gire Company began operations at the beginning of 1995, at which time it purchased a depreciable asset for $60,000. For 1995 through 1998, the asset was depreciated on the straight-line basis over a 4-year life (no residual value) for financial reporting. For income tax purposes, the asset was depreciated using MACRS (200%, 3-year life).

For 1995 through 1998, the company reported pretax financial income and taxable income of the following amounts (the differences are due solely to the depreciation temporary differences):

| Year | Pretax Financial Income | Taxable Income |
|------|------|------|
| 1995 | $24,998 | $20,000 |
| 1996 | 38,670 | 27,000 |
| 1997 | 27,886 | 34,000 |
| 1998 | 29,446 | 40,000 |

Over the entire 4-year period, the company was subject to an income tax of 30% and no change in the tax rate had been enacted for future years.

**Required**

1. Prepare a schedule that shows for each year, 1995 through 1998, the (a) MACRS depreciation, (b) straight-line depreciation, (c) annual depreciation temporary difference, and (d) accumulated temporary difference at the end of each year.
2. Prepare the income tax journal entry at the end of (a) 1995, (b) 1996, (c) 1997, and (d) 1998. (Round to the nearest dollar.)
3. Prepare the lower portion of the income statement for (a) 1995, (b) 1996, (c) 1997, and (d) 1998.

P17-9     *Deferred Taxes: Multiple Rates*     Wicks Corporation began operations on January 1, 1995. At the end of 1995, the company reported pretax financial income of $62,000 and taxable income of $57,700, due to two temporary differences. The income tax rate is 30% for 1995, but Congress has enacted a tax rate of 35% for 1998 and beyond. To determine its deferred taxes, the company prepared the following schedule of expected future taxable and deductible amounts for the two temporary differences:

| | 1996 | 1997 | 1998 | 1999 |
|------|------|------|------|------|
| Taxable amounts | $4,900 | $4,200 | $ 4,600 | $4,100 |
| Deductible amount | | | (13,500) | |

**Required**

1. Prepare the income tax journal entry of the Wicks Corporation at the end of 1995. Assume a valuation allowance is not required.
2. Prepare the lower portion of the 1995 income statement for the Wicks Corporation.

P17-10     *Operating Loss*     Burg Company has been in business for several years, during which time it has been profitable. For each of those years, the company reported (and paid taxes on) taxable income in the same amount as pretax financial income based on the following revenues and expenses:

| | Revenues | Expenses |
|------|------|------|
| 1991 | $182,000 | $150,000 |
| 1992 | 220,000 | 170,000 |
| 1993 | 253,000 | 180,000 |
| 1994 | 241,000 | 196,000 |

The company was subject to the following income tax rates during this period: 1991, 20%; 1992, 25%; 1993, 30%; and 1994, 25%. During 1995, the company experienced a severe decrease in the demand for its products. The company tried to offset this decrease with an expensive marketing campaign, but was unsuccessful. Consequently, at the end of 1995, the company determined that its revenues were $60,000 and its expenses were $240,000 during 1995 for both income taxes and financial reporting.

The company decided to carry back its 1995 operating loss because it was not confident it could earn taxable income in the future carryforward period. The income tax rate was 30% in 1995 and no change in the tax rate had been enacted for future years.

In 1996, the company developed and introduced a new product that proved to be in high demand. On June 1, 1996, the company received a refund check from the government based on the tax information it filed at the end of 1995. For 1996, the company reported revenues of $184,000 and expenses of $155,000 for both income taxes and financial reporting. The applicable income tax rate was 30%.

**Required**

1. Prepare the income tax journal entries of the Burg Company at the end of 1995.
2. Prepare the 1995 income statement. Include a note for any operating loss carryforward.
3. Prepare the journal entry to record the receipt of the refund check on June 1, 1996.
4. Prepare the income tax journal entry at the end of 1996.
5. Prepare the 1996 income statement.

P17-11 *Operating Loss*   Refer to the information in P17-10 and modify it as follows. The company decided to first carry back its 1995 operating loss. Furthermore, since the company had already begun to develop the new product at the end of 1995 and had contracts for its sale in 1996, the company was confident at the end of 1995 that it would earn sufficient taxable income in the future carryforward period.

**Required**

1. Prepare the income tax journal entries of the Burg Company at the end of 1995.
2. Prepare the 1995 income statement. Include a note for any operating loss carryforward recognition.
3. Prepare the journal entry to record the receipt of the refund check on June 1, 1996.
4. Prepare the income tax journal entry at the end of 1996.
5. Prepare the 1996 income statement.

P17-12 *Balance Sheet Reporting and Tax Rate Change*   At the end of 1995, Dolf Company prepared the following schedule of its deferred tax items (based on the currently enacted tax rate of 30%):

| Deferred Tax Item # | Account Balance | Related Asset or Liability |
|---|---|---|
| 1 | $ 9,300 debit | Current asset |
| 2 | 10,200 debit | Noncurrent asset |
| 3 | 5,700 credit | Current liability |
| 4 | 17,700 credit | Noncurrent liability |

On April 30, 1996, Congress changed the income tax rate to 40% for 1996 and future years. At the end of 1996, the company reported taxable income of $62,500 for 1996. At that time, the company determined that its deferred tax items should have balances as follows at the end of 1996 (based on the 40% tax rate): #1, $10,700 debit; #2, $15,000 debit; #3, $7,000 credit; #4, $25,900 credit.

**Required**

1. Show how the deferred tax items are reported on the Dolf Company's December 31, 1995 balance sheet.
2. Prepare the April 30, 1996 journal entry to correct Dolf Company's deferred tax items.
3. Prepare the income tax journal entry of the Dolf Company at the end of 1996.
4. Show how the current and deferred tax items are reported on the Dolf Company's December 31, 1996 balance sheet.
5. Calculate the total income tax expense for 1996.

P17-13 *Comprehensive*   Snellen Company reports *pretax* financial "income" of $155,000 in 1995. In addition to pretax income from continuing operations (of which revenues are $300,000), the following items are included in this pretax "income":

| | |
|---|---|
| Extraordinary gain | $30,000 |
| Loss from disposal of Segment B | (10,000) |
| Income from operations of discontinued Segment B | 16,000 |
| Cumulative effect of change in accounting principle | 7,000 |
| Prior period adjustment | (8,000) |

The taxable income of the company totals $135,000 in 1995. The difference between the pretax financial income and the taxable income is due to the excess of tax depreciation over financial depreciation on assets used in continuing operations.

At the beginning of 1995, the company had a retained earnings balance of $310,000 and a deferred tax liability of $8,100. During 1995, the company declared and paid dividends of $48,000. It is subject to tax rates of 15% on the first $50,000 of income and 30% on income in excess of $50,000. Based upon proper interperiod tax allocation procedures, the company has determined that its 1995 ending deferred tax liability is $14,100.

### Required

1. Prepare a schedule for the Snellen Company to allocate the total 1995 income tax expense to the various components of pretax income.
2. Prepare the income tax journal entry of the Snellen Company at the end of 1995.
3. Prepare Snellen Company's 1995 income statement.
4. Prepare Snellen Company's 1995 statement of retained earnings.
5. Show the related income tax disclosures on the Snellen Company's December 31, 1995 balance sheet.

P17-14 *Comprehensive* At the beginning of 1995, Norris Company had a deferred tax liability of $6,300, due to the use of MACRS depreciation for income tax purposes and units-of-production depreciation for financial reporting. The company is subject to an income tax rate of 30% and no change in the tax rate has been enacted for future years.

The accounting records of the Norris Company show the following *pretax* items of financial income for 1995: income from continuing operations, $125,000 (revenues of $357,000 and expenses of $232,000); gain on disposal of Segment F, $23,000; extraordinary loss, $18,000; loss from operations of discontinued Segment F, $10,000; and prior period adjustment, $15,000, due to an error that understated revenue in 1994. All of these items are taxable; however, financial depreciation for 1995 on assets related to continuing operations exceeds tax depreciation by $5,000. The company had a retained earnings balance of $161,000 on January 1, 1995 and declared and paid cash dividends of $32,000 during 1995.

### Required

1. Prepare the income tax journal entry of the Norris Company at the end of 1995.
2. Prepare Norris Company's 1995 income statement.
3. Prepare Norris Company's 1995 statement of retained earnings.
4. Show the related income tax disclosures on the Norris Company's December 31, 1995 balance sheet.

P17-15 *Comprehensive* Jayryan Company sells products in a volatile market. The company began operating in 1992 and reported (and paid taxes on) taxable income in 1992 through 1995. It has one taxable temporary difference, and reconciled its taxable income to its pretax financial income for 1992 through 1994 as follows:

|  | 1992 | 1993 | 1994 |
|---|---|---|---|
| Taxable income | $25,000 | $22,000 | $31,000 |
| Temporary difference | 2,500 | 1,800 | 3,000 |
| Pretax financial income | $27,500 | $23,800 | $34,000 |

In 1995, because of a downturn in the market, the company reported a taxable loss of $90,000 and it was uncertain as to future profits. A temporary difference of $2,700 resulted in an $87,300 pretax operating loss for financial reporting. In 1996 and 1997, the company was again profitable and reported the following items:

|  | 1996 | 1997 |
|---|---|---|
| Taxable income | $7,000 | $19,000 |
| Temporary difference | 2,300 | 2,800 |
| Pretax financial income | $9,300 | $21,800 |

The income tax rate has been 30% since 1991, and no change in the tax rate has been enacted for future years.

### Required

1. Prepare a schedule that shows the Jayryan Company's income taxes payable (or receivable) for each year, 1992 through 1997.
2. Prepare a schedule that shows the deferred tax information (change in temporary difference and operating loss carryforward) for each year, 1992 through 1997.
3. Prepare a schedule that shows the deferred taxes for each year, 1992 through 1997.
4. Based on the schedule prepared in Requirement 3, prepare the income tax journal entry at the end of 1995.
5. Prepare a partial income statement for 1995. Include a note for any operating loss carryforward.

# ACCOUNTING FOR POSTEMPLOYMENT BENEFITS

The average life expectancy of the U.S. population has increased to over 76 years. Consequently, an ever-increasing number of people are living long enough to retire from the work force and to become dependent on other sources of income. Both the government and companies have expressed concern about providing income to these individuals, in response to which Congress passed the *Federal Insurance Contribution Act* (commonly called Social Security) in 1935. This Act requires most employers and employees to contribute to a federal retirement program. To supplement Social Security, many companies also have adopted private retirement plans. Recently, it was estimated that more than $2.3 trillion was invested in company pension funds.[1] Because of the importance of these pension plans, Congress passed legislation affecting their operation. This legislation, the *Employee Retirement Income Security Act of 1974* (ERISA), often is referred to as the *Pension Reform Act of 1974*.

Accounting for the cost of Social Security taxes was discussed in Chapter 11. In this chapter, we focus on the recording, reporting, and disclosure procedures applicable to company pension plans under generally accepted accounting principles and the provisions of the *Pension Reform Act of 1974*. In addition to pensions, many employers provide other postemployment benefits to their employees, and accounting for these benefits is discussed at the end of the chapter.

---

1. *Deloitte Haskins and Sells Review*, August 14, 1989, p. 5.

## CHARACTERISTICS OF PENSION PLANS

A pension plan is an agreement between a company and its employee group whereby the company promises to provide income to its retired employees in return for the services that were provided by the employees during their employment. This retirement income, normally paid monthly, usually is determined on the basis of the employee's income and length of service with the company. For instance, under the retirement plan of one major company, employees who retire at age 65 have received annual retirement income according to the following formula: Average of last 5 years' salary × number of years of service × 0.0257. Thus, an individual who worked for this company for 30 years and had an average salary of $70,000 for the last five years of service would receive annual pension benefits of $53,970 ($70,000 × 30 × 0.0257). A pension plan of this type is a **defined benefit plan** because the plan specifically states either the *benefits* to be received by employees after retirement or the method of determining such benefits. In contrast, a pension plan is a **defined contribution plan** when the employer's *contribution* is determined based on a specified formula, and any future benefits are limited to those that can be provided by the contributions and the returns earned on the investment of those contributions. The two types of plans involve different risks to the company and the employees. With a defined benefit plan, most of the risks lie with the company because the payments to the retired employees have been defined and the company has the responsibility of ensuring that those amounts are paid. In contrast, with a defined contribution plan, most of the risks lie with the employees because the company's responsibilities essentially end once the required contribution for the period has been made by the company. Defined benefit plans raise many complex accounting issues, and those issues are the primary focus of this chapter. Defined contribution plans are briefly discussed later in the chapter.

Pension plans may be either **funded** or **unfunded**. Under a funded plan, the company typically makes periodic payments to a *funding agency* that assumes the responsibility for both safeguarding and investing the pension assets to earn a return on the investments for the pension plan, and for making payments to the recipients of benefits. An unfunded plan, on the other hand, is one in which no periodic payments are made to an external agency; instead, the pension payments to retired employees are made from current company resources. (Although the *Pension Reform Act of 1974* has eliminated unfunded plans for companies, some plans are underfunded. Also, many governmental plans are unfunded.) The amounts needed to fund a pension plan are determined (estimated) by **actuaries**, individuals trained in actuarial science who use compound interest techniques, projections of future events, and *actuarial funding methods* to calculate current contributions by the company.

Pension plans are either **contributory** or **noncontributory**. Under a contributory plan, employees bear part of the cost of the plan and make contributions from their salaries into the pension fund. With noncontributory plans, the entire pension cost is borne by the employer. We are concerned with noncontributory plans in this chapter.

In addition, most companies design their pension plans to meet the Internal Revenue Code qualifications, which allow:

1. Employer contributions to be deductible for income tax purposes

2. Pension fund earnings not to be subject to income taxes

3. Employer contributions to the pension fund not to be taxable to the employees until pension benefits are actually received

4. Employee contributions to the pension fund not to be taxable until pension benefits are actually received

**EXHIBIT 18-1**

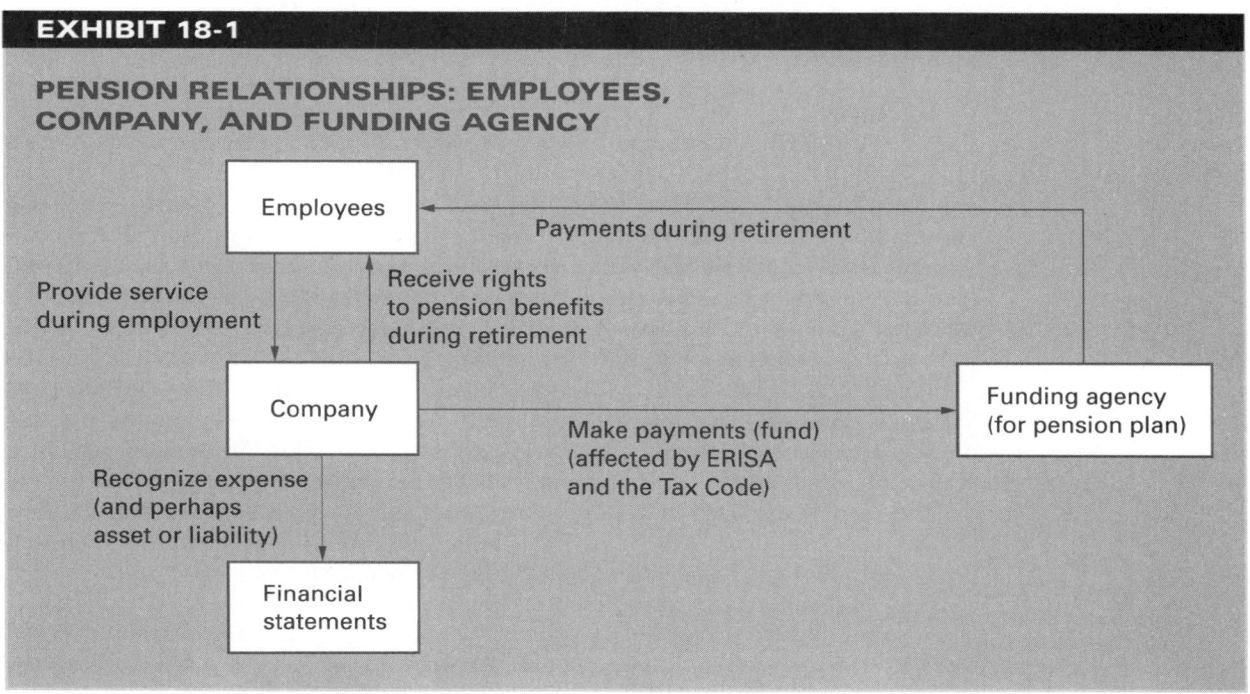

PENSION RELATIONSHIPS: EMPLOYEES, COMPANY, AND FUNDING AGENCY

The relationships among the employees, the company, and the funding agency for a noncontributory defined benefit pension plan are summarized in Exhibit 18-1.

## HISTORICAL PERSPECTIVE OF PENSION PLANS

Pension plans come in many and various forms, characterized by differences in eligibility requirements, retirement ages, amounts of retirement benefits, extent of actual funding, and the amount of employee contributions to the pension fund. These differences resulted in a long-term evolution of generally accepted accounting principles related to pension plans.

Accounting for the cost of pension plans has been analyzed for many years. The first authoritative statement on the subject was published by the Committee on Accounting Procedure as **Accounting Research Bulletin No. 47,** which recommended the recognition of pension cost on the accrual basis instead of the cash basis. That is, it recommended that pension expense be recorded during the periods of employment as benefits are earned by employees, and *not* delayed until the periods when retirement benefits are actually paid. The pension expense is based on the present value of the future benefits earned by employees during the current accounting period. Present value techniques (explained in Appendix D) are used in this chapter for the computation of amounts related to pension plans.

Since the pronouncements of the Committee on Accounting Procedure were not mandatory, most companies continued to use the cash basis of accounting for pension plans after the issuance of *ARB No. 47.* The use of the cash basis, however, violated the accrual concept and resulted in a lack of comparability among companies in reporting pension expense, sometimes causing wide year-to-year fluctuations in the pension expense for a single company. Such fluctuations were largely attributable to (1) gains and losses (discussed later), (2) the funding policies adopted by individual companies, and (3) provisions of some pension plans that limited the legal liability of the company to the amount funded. In an effort to solve such problems, the APB authorized **Accounting Research Study No. 8,** which ultimately resulted in the release of **APB Opinion No. 8,** "Accounting for the Cost of Pension Plans." This *Opinion* required the use of the accrual method for the recognition of the pension expense. However, considerable latitude was allowed in determining the amount of the pension expense through the use of various actuarial methods. Criticism soon arose over the fact that companies with plans for which the obligation to pay benefits greatly exceeded the plan assets available did not record a liability. As a result, in 1974, the FASB added pension accounting to its agenda, and in 1980, **FASB Statement No. 35,** "Accounting and Reporting by Defined Benefit Pension Plans," was issued. This *Statement* defined the principles to be used, and the disclosures required by, the funding agency administering a company's pension plan. This information, which is briefly discussed later in the chapter, is primarily for the benefit of the participants in the plan, but is also used by the sponsoring company for its accounting calculations and disclosures. In the same year, **FASB Statement No. 36,** "Disclosure of Pension Benefit Information," was issued. This *Statement* required certain disclosures by the company and has since been superseded. The FASB issued a Discussion Memorandum in 1975 and numerous Exposure Drafts in subsequent years, and in December 1985, **FASB Statement No. 87,** "Employers' Accounting for Pensions," was issued. The discussion in this chapter primarily focuses on the provisions of this *Statement.* Also in December 1985, the FASB issued **FASB Statement No. 88,** "Employers' Accounting for Settlements and Curtailments of Defined Benefit Pension Plans and for Termination Benefits," which is briefly discussed later in this chapter.

## ACCOUNTING PRINCIPLES FOR DEFINED BENEFIT PENSION PLANS

The generally accepted accounting principles to be used by an employer in accounting for its defined benefit pension plans are determined by *FASB Statement No. 87.* These principles are very complex and, thus, only the basic elements are included in the following discussion, i.e., the computation of periodic pension expense, liabilities and assets, measurement methods, and disclosures. It should be noted that these items are defined by generally accepted accounting principles, whereas the minimum amount funded by the employer is defined by ERISA (discussed later).

*The conceptual issues related to pensions are discussed later in the chapter.*

### Key Terms Related to Pension Plans

Before discussing the accounting principles for pension plans, an understanding of the terms in Exhibit 18-2 is important.[2] These terms should be reviewed now and carefully examined as each is introduced in the chapter. In addition, several other terms are introduced later in the chapter as they relate to specific issues. Note that actuaries often use the term *accrue* to refer to amounts associated with the pension plan, in contrast to the more specific meaning used by accountants.

---

2.   "Employers' Accounting for Pensions," *FASB Statement of Financial Accounting Standards No. 87* (Stamford, Conn.: FASB, 1985), Appendix D and par. 44.

## EXHIBIT 18-2

## KEY TERMS RELATED TO PENSION PLANS

**Accumulated Benefit Obligation.** The actuarial present value of all the benefits attributed by the pension benefit formula to employee service rendered before a specified date. The amount is based on current and past compensation levels of employees and, therefore, includes no assumptions about future pay increases.

**Actual Return on Plan Assets.** The difference between the fair value of the plan assets at the end of the period and the fair value at the beginning of the period, adjusted for contributions and payments of benefits during the period.

**Actuarial Funding Method.** Any of several techniques that actuaries use in determining the amounts and timing of employer contributions to provide for pension benefits.

**Actuarial Present Value.** The value, on a specified date, of an amount or series of amounts payable or receivable in the future. The present value is determined by discounting the future amount or amounts at a predetermined discount rate. The future amounts are adjusted for the probability of payment (affected by factors such as death, disability, or withdrawal from the plan).

**Assumptions.** Estimates of the occurrence of future events affecting pension costs, such as mortality, withdrawal, disablement and retirement, changes in compensation and national pension benefits, and discount rates. Sometimes called *actuarial* assumptions.

**Expected Return on Plan Assets.** An amount calculated by applying the expected long-term rate of return on plan assets to the fair market value of the plan assets at the beginning of the period.

**Discount Rate.** The rate at which the pension benefits can be effectively settled, e.g., the rate implicit in current prices of annuity contracts that could be used to settle the pension obligation. The discount rate is used in the computation of the service cost, the projected benefit obligation, and the accumulated benefit obligation.

**Gain or Loss.** A change in the value of either the projected benefit obligation (or the plan assets) resulting from experience different from that assumed or from a change in an actuarial assumption. Sometimes called *actuarial* or *experience* gain or loss.

**Pension Benefit Formula.** The basis for determining payments to which employees will be entitled during retirement.

**Prior Service Cost.** The cost of retroactive benefits granted in a plan amendment or at the initial adoption of the plan. The cost is the present value of the additional benefits attributed by the pension benefit formula.

**Projected Benefit Obligation.** The actuarial present value, at a specified date, of all the benefits attributed by the pension benefit formula to employee service rendered prior to that date. The amount includes future increases in compensation that the company projects it will pay to employees during the remainder of their employment, provided the pension benefit formula is based on those future compensation levels. The projected benefit obligation differs from the accumulated benefit obligation in that it includes anticipated future pay increases.

**Service Cost.** The actuarial present value of benefits attributed by the pension benefit formula to services rendered by employees during the current period. If the pension benefit formula is based on future compensation levels (e.g., average of last 5 years' salary), the service cost is based on those future compensation levels.

**Vested Benefits.** Benefits for which the employee's right to receive a present or future pension benefit is no longer contingent on remaining in the service of the employer.

### Pension Expense

In defining the annual pension cost, *FASB Statement No. 87* uses the term *net periodic pension cost* because some of the annual pension cost may be capitalized as part of the cost of an asset, such as inventory. For simplicity, we will use the term *pension expense* and assume that none of the pension costs are capitalized. The net periodic pension expense recognized by a company includes five components: service cost, interest cost, actual return on plan assets, amortization of unrecognized prior service cost, and gain or loss.[3]

1.  **Service cost. The service cost is the actuarial present value of the benefits attributed by the pension benefit formula to services rendered by the employees during the current period.** This amount is the present value of the deferred compensation to be paid to employees during their retirement in return for their current services. The measurement of the benefits attributed to the period and the discount rate are discussed later. Note also that the service cost is a function of the discount rate selected by the company. If the discount rate increases (decreases), the present value decreases (increases). Since the discount rate is defined as a settlement rate, it will vary as economic conditions change. The discount rate also is used in the computation of the projected benefit obligation and the accumulated benefit obligation; therefore, these amounts will be affected similarly by a change in the discount rate.

2.  **Interest cost. The interest cost is the increase in the projected benefit obligation due to the passage of time.** The projected benefit obligation is the present value of the deferred compensation earned by the employees to date (based on their expected future compensation levels). The interest cost is the projected benefit obligation at the beginning of the period multiplied by the discount rate used by the company. Since the pension plan is a deferred compensation agreement in which future payments are discounted to their present values, interest accrues due to the passage of time. The interest cost is added in the computation of pension expense.

3.  **Actual return on plan assets. The actual return on plan assets is the difference between the fair value of the plan assets at the end of the period and the fair value at the beginning of the period, adjusted for contributions by the company and payments of benefits to retired employees during the period.** Plan assets are held by the funding agency and consist of investments such as stocks, bonds, and real estate. If the plan assets earn a positive (negative) return, this amount is subtracted (added) in the computation of pension expense. The return on plan assets is subtracted because the earnings "compensate" for the interest on the projected benefit obligation.

4.  **Amortization of unrecognized prior service cost.** Amendments to the pension plan often include provisions that grant increased retroactive benefits to employees based on services they rendered in prior periods, thereby increasing the projected benefit obligation. Similar retroactive benefits may also be granted

---

3.  A sixth component is the amortization of any unrecognized liability or asset that existed at the initial application of *FASB Statement No. 87*. This item is a result of the transition from the requirements of *APB Opinion No. 8* and is briefly discussed later.

at the initial adoption of a plan. An actuary determines the amount of the cost associated with these retroactive benefits, known as the **prior service cost.** The prior service cost is not recognized in the financial statements (i.e., not recorded in the accounts) in total in the period granted. **The unrecognized prior service cost is amortized by assigning an equal amount to each future period of service of each active employee who, at the date of the amendment, is expected to receive future benefits under the plan.** Alternatively, straight-line amortization over the average remaining service life of active employees may be used for simplicity. Note that employees hired after the date of the amendment or the plan adoption are not included in either calculation. In the usual case, the plan amendment increases the projected benefit obligation and, therefore, the amortization is added in the computation of pension expense. However, there have been several instances in recent years where companies in financial difficulty or under pressure from competition have amended their pension plans to reduce the projected benefit obligation, in which case, the amortization is subtracted in the computation.

Note that the amount of the prior service cost is *not* included as a liability or asset. Therefore, this amount is referred to as the *unrecognized* prior service cost. It is important to understand that the prior service cost is unrecognized because it is not included in the balance sheet but, of course, it has been "recognized" by the actuaries as a relevant cost and in the computation of pension expense. Note, however, that the existence of an unrecognized prior service cost makes it more likely that an additional pension liability will be recognized, as discussed later.

5. **Gain or loss.** The gain or loss includes two elements: (a) **the difference between the actual return on plan assets and the expected return,** and (b) **the amortization of any unrecognized net gain or loss from previous periods.**

To understand the first element (the difference between the actual and expected return on plan assets for the current period), recall that pension expense explicitly includes a deduction of the actual return on plan assets, as discussed earlier.[4] The inclusion of this second element of the net gain or loss means that the total pension expense implicitly involves a deduction of the *expected* return. That is, since the actual return is deducted from pension expense and the difference between the actual and expected return is also included in pension expense as part of the net gain or loss, the net result is a deduction of the expected return. The reason for this procedure is to require that a company report the actual return on plan assets while reducing the volatility of the amount of pension expense. The volatility is reduced because the pension expense is based on a deduction of the expected return (e.g., an assumption of a 10% return each period) that will fluctuate less than the actual return.

To understand the second element of the gain or loss, recall that actuaries make assumptions about many of the items included in the computation of pension costs and benefits, including future compensation levels, the interest

---

4. The element of the net gain or loss that includes the differences between the actual and expected return on plan assets is different than the element that includes changes in plan assets resulting from experience different from that assumed. The latter element can occur because of the use of the market-related value of the plan assets, as explained in footnote 6. Further discussion of this subject is beyond the scope of the book.

(discount) rate, employee turnover, retirement rates, and mortality rates. Actual experience will not be the same as these assumptions. As a result, the actual projected benefit obligation at year-end will not be equal to the expected projected benefit obligation. Therefore, gains and losses result from (a) changes in the amount of the projected benefit obligation resulting from experience different from that assumed, and (b) changes in the assumptions.[5] Gains result when actual experience is more favorable than that assumed (e.g., the future compensation levels are lower than expected because of lower inflation), and losses result when the actual experience is unfavorable. It is important to distinguish between the impact on the company as compared to the impact on the employees. For example, a lower-than-expected mortality rate is obviously favorable to the employees, but it creates a loss to the company because it will have to make more pension payments than expected.

The second component of the gain and loss is not recognized in the period in which it occurs because it may reflect changes in estimates as well as real changes in economic values, and because gains in one period may be offset by losses in another period and vice versa. Furthermore, immediate recognition in full would tend to create fluctuations in the computation of pension expense. Therefore, the amount of any unrecognized net gain or loss is amortized over *future* periods. **Amortization of any unrecognized net gain or loss is included in the pension expense of a given year if, at the beginning of the year, the cumulative unrecognized net gain or loss from previous periods exceeds 10% of the greater of the actual projected benefit obligation or the fair value of the plan assets.**[6] If amortization is required, the minimum amortization is the amount of the excess at the beginning of the year divided by the average remaining service period of the active employees expected to receive benefits under the plan. The amortization of an unrecognized net gain is subtracted in the computation of pension expense, and the amortization of an unrecognized net loss is added.[7]

To summarize, the gain or loss component of pension expense generally consists of two of the following four items:

1. Actual return on plan assets in excess of expected return for the current period (added to pension expense), or
2. Expected return on plan assets in excess of actual return for the current period (deducted from pension expense), and
3. Amortization of any unrecognized net loss from previous periods (added to pension expense), or
4. Amortization of any unrecognized net gain from previous periods (deducted from pension expense).

---

5. Although these gains and losses frequently are referred to as *experience* gains and losses or *actuarial* gains and losses, the FASB avoided using these terms.
6. In *FASB Statement No. 87*, the term **market-related value** is used. The market-related value of plan assets is either the fair value or a calculated value that recognizes changes in fair value in a systematic and rational manner over not more than five years. The use of the market-related value is allowed in order to reduce the volatility of the pension expense amount. For simplicity, we will always use the fair value of the plan assets as the market-related value.
7. Alternatively, any systematic method of amortization may be used instead of the minimum just described, as long as it results in greater amortization. We will use the minimum amount each period.

Gains and losses that arise from a single occurrence not directly related to the pension plan are recognized in the period in which they occur. For example, a gain or loss that is directly related to the disposal of a segment is included in the "gain or loss on disposal" and reported in accordance with the requirements of *APB Opinion No. 30.*

### Components of Pension Expense

In summary, the net periodic pension expense reported on a company's income statement generally consists of the following components: service cost, plus interest cost, minus actual return on plan assets, plus amortization of any unrecognized prior service cost, minus (or plus) gain or loss (to the extent recognized). It should be noted that in unusual cases, a negative actual return on plan assets would be added and the amortization of a reduction in unrecognized prior service cost would be deducted in the pension expense calculation.

## Pension Liabilities and Assets

The amount of the pension expense may be different from the assets contributed by the company to the pension plan (the amount funded) because they are defined by different sets of rules. The expense is defined by *FASB Statement No. 87,* whereas the funding must be consistent with the rules of ERISA, as discussed later. Therefore, a liability is recognized and reported on the company's balance sheet if the net periodic pension expense recognized to date is greater than the amount funded to date. Alternatively, an asset is recognized and reported on the company's balance sheet if the net periodic pension expense recognized to date is less than the amount funded to date. This asset or liability is similar to the numerous assets and liabilities that arise from the use of the accrual basis of accounting. Since either an asset or a liability can occur (but not both at the same time), we will use a single title for the account, **prepaid/accrued pension costs**. If the account has a debit balance at the end of the year, it is reported as an asset (prepaid pension cost) on the balance sheet; if it has a credit balance at the end of the year, it is reported as a liability (accrued pension cost). Typically, it will be classified as noncurrent. The minimum pension liability that a company must recognize is the **unfunded accumulated benefit obligation**, which is the excess of the *accumulated* benefit obligation over the fair value of the plan assets at the end of the period. Therefore, an Additional Pension Liability may have to be reported on a company's balance sheet, calculated as follows:

| Additional Pension Liability | = | Accumulated Benefit Obligation | − | Fair Value of Plan Assets | − | Prepaid/Accrued Pension Cost (credit balance) | or + | Prepaid/Accrued Pension Cost (debit balance) |
|---|---|---|---|---|---|---|---|---|

The total pension-related net liability recognized, including any prepaid/accrued pension cost, is at least equal to the unfunded accumulated benefit obligation. The accumulated benefit obligation in excess of the fair value of the plan assets is a measure of the obligation of the company based on the legal concept of a liability. That is, it is based on historical events such as the actual service of the employees and their current pay levels. Therefore, the unfunded accumulated benefit obligation provides information about the liability a company would have if its pension plan were discontinued. Alternatively, if the plan is continued, the unfunded accumulated benefit obligation provides a minimum measure of the additional funds that a company will have to contribute in future periods.

Generally, an additional liability is recognized only in situations where a company either (1) has a large unrecognized prior service cost, or (2) has experienced substantial losses in the investment of its plan assets. If this additional liability is recognized because there is an unrecognized prior service cost, an intangible asset, **deferred pension cost,** of an equal amount also is recognized and reported on the company's balance sheet. The reason for recognizing an intangible asset is that the prior service cost has created an expectation of enhanced future performance by employees from such factors as reduced turnover and higher productivity. The amount of the intangible asset, however, must not exceed the amount of any unrecognized prior service cost (plus any unrecognized transition liability or asset, as noted in footnote 3). In the case where the additional liability exceeds the unrecognized prior service cost, the excess (debit) is reported as a reduction of stockholders' equity because it is assumed that it results from poor returns on plan assets. Whenever a subsequent balance sheet is prepared, the amount of the additional liability is recomputed and the related intangible asset or separate component of stockholders' equity is adjusted or eliminated as necessary.

In summary, the pension assets, liabilities, and stockholders' equity items that may be reported, depending on the circumstances, on a company's balance sheet include:

| *Assets* | *Liabilities* |
|---|---|
| 1. Prepaid/accrued pension cost (debit balance) | 1. Prepaid/accrued pension cost (credit balance) |
| 2. Deferred pension cost (intangible asset) | 2. Additional pension liability |

*Stockholders' Equity*

1. Excess of additional pension liability over unrecognized prior service cost (negative element)

### Measurement Methods

The calculation of the service cost typically uses the benefit/years-of-service method, in which a constant amount of the total estimated pension benefit based on an estimate of final salary is **attributed** to each period. The **benefit/years-of-service** approach is used if the pension benefit formula is based on future compensation levels and defines benefits similarly for all years of service.[8] For example, the illustration of the pension benefit formula given at the beginning of the chapter is based on the average salary for the employee's last 5 years of service and the number of years of service. Therefore, the formula is based on future compensation levels (salaries to be earned in future periods rather than salary earned in the current period) and defines benefits similarly for all years of service (equal benefits each period rather than, for example, a step-rate plan that would provide higher benefits for years of service longer than some minimum period).

In computing the projected benefit obligation, the company uses a **discount rate that reflects the rates at which the pension benefits could be effectively settled.** For example, if the company could settle its obligation by purchasing an annuity from an insurance company for each employee, the rate on that annuity would be used as the appropriate discount rate. The rate of return on high quality fixed-income investments

8.  *FASB Statement No. 87, op. cit.,* par. 17 and 40. Plans with more complex pension benefit formulas are beyond the scope of this book.

currently available and expected to be available in the future could also be used. However determined, this same discount rate is used to compute the interest cost component of pension expense.

On the other hand, the expected (assumed) long-term rate of return on plan assets used to compute the expected return on assets (for the computation of the net gain or loss) is based on the average rate of earnings expected on the funds invested (or to be invested). Actual experience is considered along with the rates of return expected to be available in the future.

## Disclosures

To provide users with additional relevant information, *FASB Statement No. 87* requires a company with a defined benefit pension plan to make the following disclosures:

1. A description of the plan, including employee groups covered, type of benefit formula, funding policy, and types of assets held.

2. The amount of the pension expense showing separately the service cost component, the interest cost component, the actual return on assets for the period, and the net total of other components.

3. A schedule reconciling the funded status of the plan with amounts reported in the company's balance sheet, showing separately: (a) the fair value of plan assets, (b) the projected benefit obligation identifying the accumulated benefit obligation and the vested benefit obligation, (c) the amount of unrecognized prior service cost, (d) the amount of unrecognized gain or loss, (e) the amount of any remaining unrecognized net obligation or net asset existing at the transition from *APB Opinion No. 8* to *FASB Statement No. 87*, (f) the amount of any additional liability recognized, and (g) the amount of net pension asset or liability recognized in the balance sheet (the net of the previous six items).

4. The weighted average discount rate and rate of compensation increase used to measure the projected benefit obligation and the weighted average expected long-term rate of return on plan assets.

5. The amounts and types of securities included in plan assets.

This additional information generally is disclosed in a note accompanying the company's financial statements.

## EXAMPLES OF ACCOUNTING FOR PENSIONS

As noted earlier, many of the amounts used in pension accounting are computed by actuaries and are based on actuarial assumptions. For simplicity, various situations related to accounting for defined benefit pension plans are illustrated in this section using assumed amounts. In the Appendix to the chapter, an illustration of the present value calculations for pension plans is provided. In this example, the amounts of the service cost, the projected benefit obligation, and the prior service cost, as well as the computation of pension expense, are calculated from basic information about a company's pension plan.

### Example 1: Pension Expense Equal to Pension Funding

Assume the following facts for the Carlisle Company:

1. The company adopts a pension plan on January 1, 1995. No retroactive benefits were granted to employees.

2. The service cost each year is: 1995, $400,000; 1996, $420,000; and 1997, $432,000.

3. The projected benefit obligation at the beginning of each year is: 1996, $400,000; and 1997, $840,000.

4. The discount rate is 10%.

5. The actual rate of return on plan assets is 10%.

6. The expected rate of return on plan assets is 10%.

7. The company adopts a policy of funding an amount equal to the pension expense and makes the payment to the funding agency at the end of each year.[9]

8. Plan assets are based on the amounts contributed each year, plus a return of 10% per year, less an assumed payment of $20,000 at the end of each year to retired employees (beginning in 1996).

Based on the preceding information, the only component of the pension expense in 1995 is the $400,000 service cost. This situation occurs because there is (1) no interest cost since there is no projected benefit obligation at the beginning of the year, (2) no actual return on plan assets since the expense recognition and funding were made at the end of the first year, (3) no prior service cost, and (4) no gain or loss because the actual and expected rates of return are equal. Since the company funds an amount equal to the pension expense, the following journal entry is made on December 31, 1995:

| | | |
|---|---|---|
| **Pension Expense** | 400,000 | |
| Cash | | 400,000 |

The calculation of the pension expense for 1996 is more complex because it now has three components: service cost, interest cost, and actual return on plan assets. The service cost is assumed to be $420,000. Since the projected benefit obligation at January 1, 1996 is assumed to be $400,000 (the service cost for 1995), the interest cost is $40,000 (the projected benefit obligation of $400,000 multiplied by the discount rate of 10%). The actual return on the plan assets is the $400,000 invested by the funding agency for the pension fund at the end of 1995 multiplied by the 10% actual rate of return. Therefore, the pension expense for 1996 is computed as follows:

| | |
|---|---|
| Service cost (assumed) | $420,000 |
| Interest cost ($400,000 × 10%) | 40,000 |
| Actual return on plan assets ($400,000 × 10%) | (40,000) |
| Pension expense | $420,000 |

---

9. Companies are required by law to make payments to funding agencies on a quarterly basis. For simplicity, in all examples and homework, we assume a single annual payment is made at the end of each year.

Since the company funds an amount equal to the expense, the following journal entry is made on December 31, 1996:

| | | |
|---|---|---|
| **Pension Expense** | 420,000 | |
| Cash | | 420,000 |

For 1997, the service cost is assumed to be $432,000. The projected benefit obligation at the beginning of 1997 is assumed to be $840,000. The assets at the beginning of 1997 are $840,000 ($400,000 invested at the end of 1995 + $40,000 actual return in 1996 − $20,000 payment to retired employees at the end of 1996 + $420,000 invested at the end of 1996). Therefore, the pension expense for 1997 is computed as follows:

| | |
|---|---|
| Service cost (assumed) | $432,000 |
| Interest cost ($840,000 × 10%) | 84,000 |
| Actual return on plan assets ($840,000 × 10%) | (84,000) |
| Pension expense | $432,000 |

Since the company funds an amount equal to the expense, the following journal entry is made on December 31, 1997:

| | | |
|---|---|---|
| **Pension Expense** | 432,000 | |
| Cash | | 432,000 |

Note that the interest cost and the return on the plan assets offset each other in this example. This situation occurs because the discount rate and the actual rate of return on plan assets are both 10%, and because the company funds an amount equal to the expense.

## Example 2: Pension Expense Greater Than Pension Funding

Assume the same facts for the Carlisle Company as in Example 1, except that instead of funding an amount equal to the pension expense, the company funds $385,000 in 1995, $400,000 in 1996, and $415,000 in 1997.[10] Since the company provides *fewer* assets to the pension fund, the return on those assets each period is less and, therefore, the pension expense must be larger to compensate for the lower actual return. The company's pension expense in 1995 is the $400,000 service cost, so the journal entry on December 31, 1995 is:

| | | |
|---|---|---|
| **Pension Expense** | 400,000 | |
| Cash | | 385,000 |
| **Prepaid/Accrued Pension Cost** | | 15,000 |

Since the company funds only $385,000 in 1995 when the expense is $400,000, a liability, Prepaid/Accrued Pension Cost, of $15,000 is recognized.

In 1996, the only difference from the previous example in the computation of the pension expense is the reduced return on the plan assets. Since only $385,000 was

---

10. For illustrative purposes, the amount funded is less than the service cost. In some circumstances, this procedure might be a violation of the minimum funding requirements of ERISA. However, the amount funded may be less than the *total* pension expense.

contributed by the company on December 31, 1995, a return of only $38,500 was earned in 1996. The pension expense for 1996 is computed as follows:

| | |
|---|---:|
| Service cost | $420,000 |
| Interest cost ($400,000 × 10%) | 40,000 |
| Actual return on plan assets ($385,000 × 10%) | (38,500) |
| Pension expense | $421,500 |

Since the company funds $400,000 in 1996, the following journal entry is made on December 31, 1996:

| | | |
|---|---:|---:|
| **Pension Expense** | 421,500 | |
| **Cash** | | 400,000 |
| **Prepaid/Accrued Pension Cost** | | 21,500 |

The balance in the liability account at the end of 1996 is $36,500 ($15,000 + $21,500).

In 1997, the computation of the pension expense is again affected by the reduced return on the plan assets. Since only $400,000 was contributed by the company, the assets of the pension fund on January 1, 1997 are $803,500 ($385,000 invested at the end of 1995 + $38,500 actual return in 1996 − $20,000 payment to retired employees at the end of 1996 + $400,000 invested at the end of 1996), and a return of $80,350 on those assets is earned during 1997. Therefore, the pension expense for 1997 is computed as follows:

| | |
|---|---:|
| Service cost | $432,000 |
| Interest cost ($840,000 × 10%) | 84,000 |
| Actual return on plan assets ($803,500 × 10%) | (80,350) |
| Pension expense | $435,650 |

Since the company funds $415,000 in 1997, the following journal entry is made on December 31, 1997:

| | | |
|---|---:|---:|
| **Pension Expense** | 435,650 | |
| **Cash** | | 415,000 |
| **Prepaid/Accrued Pension Cost** | | 20,650 |

The balance in the liability account at the end of 1997 is $57,150 ($36,500 + $20,650).

### Example 3: Pension Expense Less Than Pension Funding, and Actual Return on Plan Assets Different From Discount Rate

Assume the same facts for the Carlisle Company as in Example 1, except that (a) instead of funding an amount equal to the pension expense, the company funds $415,000 in 1995, $425,000 in 1996, and $440,000 in 1997, and (b) the actual (and expected) return is 11%. Since the company provides *more* assets to the pension fund and earns a higher return on those assets, the pension expense must be less to compensate for the higher return. The company's pension expense in 1995 is the $400,000 service cost and the journal entry on December 31, 1995 is:

| | | |
|---|---:|---:|
| **Pension Expense** | 400,000 | |
| **Prepaid/Accrued Pension Cost** | 15,000 | |
| **Cash** | | 415,000 |

Since the company funds $415,000 in 1995 when the expense is $400,000, an asset, Prepaid/Accrued Pension Cost, of $15,000 is recognized.

In 1996, the only difference in the computation of the pension expense from Example 1 is the increased return on the plan assets. Since $415,000 was contributed by the company on December 31, 1995, a return of $45,650 was earned in 1996. The pension expense for 1996 is computed as follows:

| | |
|---|---:|
| Service cost | $420,000 |
| Interest cost ($400,000 × 10%) | 40,000 |
| Actual return on plan assets ($415,000 × 11%) | (45,650) |
| Pension expense | $414,350 |

Since the company funds $425,000 in 1996, the following journal entry is made on December 31, 1996:

| | | |
|---|---:|---:|
| **Pension Expense** | 414,350 | |
| **Prepaid/Accrued Pension Cost** | 10,650 | |
| **Cash** | | 425,000 |

The balance in the asset account at the end of 1996 is $25,650 ($15,000 + $10,650).

In 1997, the computation of the pension expense is again affected by the increased return on the plan assets. Since $425,000 was contributed by the company, the assets of the pension fund on January 1, 1997 are $865,650 ($415,000 invested at the end of 1995 + $45,650 actual return in 1996 − $20,000 payment to retired employees in 1996 + $425,000 invested at the end of 1996), and a return of $95,222 (rounded) on those assets is earned during 1997. Therefore, the pension expense for 1997 is computed as follows:

| | |
|---|---:|
| Service cost | $432,000 |
| Interest cost ($840,000 × 10%) | 84,000 |
| Actual return on plan assets ($865,650 × 11%) | (95,222) |
| Pension expense | $420,778 |

Since the company funds $440,000 in 1997, the following journal entry is made on December 31, 1997:

| | | |
|---|---:|---:|
| **Pension Expense** | 420,778 | |
| **Prepaid/Accrued Pension Cost** | 19,222 | |
| **Cash** | | 440,000 |

The balance in the asset account at the end of 1997 is $44,872 ($25,650 + $19,222).

### Example 4: Pension Expense Including Amortization of Unrecognized Prior Service Cost

The previous three examples illustrated relatively simple computations of pension expense and the related pension liability or asset. The remaining examples deal with more complex issues. Recall that an amendment to a pension plan frequently includes provisions that grant increased retroactive benefits based on services performed by employees in prior periods. The cost of providing these benefits is called a prior service cost. A prior service cost also may arise when a plan is adopted. A prior service cost causes an increase in the projected benefit obligation. However, it is not recognized in the balance sheet, but is amortized as a component of pension expense.

To illustrate this amortization, assume the same facts for the Carlisle Company as in Example 2, except that the company awarded retroactive benefits to the employees when it adopted the pension plan on January 1, 1995. The unrecognized prior service cost was computed by the company's actuary to be $2 million and, therefore, created a projected benefit obligation of that amount on January 1, 1995. To fund this projected benefit obligation, the company decided to increase its contribution by $290,000 per year. For simplicity, it is also assumed that the unrecognized prior service cost is amortized by the straight-line method over the remaining 20-year service life of the company's active employees. Thus, the amount of the amortization is $100,000 ($2,000,000 ÷ 20) per year.

The company's pension expense in 1995 now has three components. In addition to the service cost of $400,000, both the interest cost on the $2 million projected benefit obligation and the $100,000 amortization of the unrecognized prior service cost are recognized. Therefore, the pension expense for 1995 is computed as follows:

| | |
|---|---:|
| Service cost | $400,000 |
| Interest cost ($2,000,000 × 10%) | 200,000 |
| Amortization of unrecognized prior service cost | 100,000 |
| Pension expense | $700,000 |

Since the company funds $675,000 ($385,000 + $290,000) in 1995, the following journal entry is made on December 31, 1995:

| | | |
|---|---:|---:|
| **Pension Expense** | 700,000 | |
| **Cash** | | 675,000 |
| **Prepaid/Accrued Pension Cost** | | 25,000 |

Note that the unrecognized prior service cost of $2 million is *not* included in the company's balance sheet, but is included in the disclosures discussed earlier.[11]

On January 1, 1996, the projected benefit obligation is assumed to be $2,600,000. Therefore, the pension expense for 1996 is computed as follows:

| | |
|---|---:|
| Service cost | $420,000 |
| Interest cost ($2,600,000 × 10%) | 260,000 |
| Actual return on plan assets ($675,000 × 10%) | (67,500) |
| Amortization of unrecognized prior service cost | 100,000 |
| Pension expense | $712,500 |

Since the company funds $690,000 ($400,000 + $290,000) in 1996, the following journal entry is made on December 31, 1996:

| | | |
|---|---:|---:|
| **Pension Expense** | 712,500 | |
| **Cash** | | 690,000 |
| **Prepaid/Accrued Pension Cost** | | 22,500 |

On January 1, 1997, the projected benefit obligation is assumed to be $3,260,000, the plan assets are $1,412,500 ($675,000 + $67,500 + $690,000 − $20,000 paid to retired employees), and the pension expense for 1997 is computed as follows:

| | |
|---|---:|
| Service cost | $432,000 |
| Interest cost ($3,260,000 × 10%) | 326,000 |
| Actual return on plan assets ($1,412,500 × 10%) | (141,250) |
| Amortization of unrecognized prior service cost | 100,000 |
| Pension expense | $716,750 |

---

11. It is possible that an additional pension liability would have to be included in the company's year-end balance sheet. This topic is discussed in Example 7.

Since the company funds $705,000 ($415,000 + $290,000) in 1997, the following journal entry is made on December 31, 1997:

| | | |
|---|---|---|
| Pension Expense | 716,750 | |
|     Cash | | 705,000 |
|     Prepaid/Accrued Pension Cost | | 11,750 |

## Example 5: Calculation of Amortization of Unrecognized Prior Service Cost

In Example 4, the calculation of pension expense included the amortization of unrecognized prior service cost. In that example, the amount of the amortization was assumed. Two methods of calculating the amount of the amortization are explained in this example. The preferred method assigns an equal amount to each future period of service for each active participating employee at the date of the amendment who is expected to receive future benefits under the plan. Since the FASB did not give this method a title, we will refer to it as the "years-of-future-service" method. Alternatively, straight-line amortization over the average remaining service life of employees may be used for simplicity.

The preferred years-of-future-service method of amortization is illustrated in Exhibits 18-3 and 18-4. It is assumed that, at the beginning of 1995, the Watts Company has nine employees participating in its pension plan who are expected to receive benefits. One employee (A) is expected to retire after 3 years, one (B) after 4, two (C and D) after 5, two (E and F) after 6, and three (G, H, and I) after 7 years. In Exhibit 18-3, the amortization fraction is computed. First, the number of service years rendered by the nine employees in each calendar year is computed. Thus, in 1995, there are 9 service years rendered, while in 1999, there are only 7 service years rendered because employees A and B have retired. The total number of these service years is 50. Finally, the amortization fraction for each year is computed by dividing the total service years in each calendar year by the total of 50. Thus, in 1995, 9/50 is the amortization fraction, whereas in 1999, 7/50 is the fraction.

If it is assumed that the company's actuary computed the total unrecognized prior service cost at the beginning of 1995 to be $400,000, the amount of the amortization

---

### EXHIBIT 18-3

#### COMPUTATION OF AMORTIZATION FRACTION

| Employees | Expected Years of Future Service | Number of Service Years Rendered in Each Year | | | | | | | |
|---|---|---|---|---|---|---|---|---|---|
| | | 1995 | 1996 | 1997 | 1998 | 1999 | 2000 | 2001 | |
| A | 3 | 1 | 1 | 1 | | | | | |
| B | 4 | 1 | 1 | 1 | 1 | | | | |
| C, D | 5 | 2 | 2 | 2 | 2 | 2 | | | |
| E, F | 6 | 2 | 2 | 2 | 2 | 2 | 2 | | |
| G, H, I | 7 | 3 | 3 | 3 | 3 | 3 | 3 | 3 | |
| Total | | 9 | 9 | 9 | 8 | 7 | 5 | 3 | = 50 |
| Amortization Fraction | | 9/50 | 9/50 | 9/50 | 8/50 | 7/50 | 5/50 | 3/50 | |

### EXHIBIT 18-4

### AMORTIZATION OF UNRECOGNIZED PRIOR SERVICE COST: YEARS-OF-FUTURE-SERVICE METHOD

| Year | Total Unrecognized Prior Service Cost[a] | Amortization Fraction[b] | Amortization to Increase Pension Expense[c] | Remaining Unrecognized Prior Service Cost[d] |
|------|------|------|------|------|
| 1995 | $400,000 | 9/50 | $72,000 | $328,000 |
| 1996 | 400,000 | 9/50 | 72,000 | 256,000 |
| 1997 | 400,000 | 9/50 | 72,000 | 184,000 |
| 1998 | 400,000 | 8/50 | 64,000 | 120,000 |
| 1999 | 400,000 | 7/50 | 56,000 | 64,000 |
| 2000 | 400,000 | 5/50 | 40,000 | 24,000 |
| 2001 | 400,000 | 3/50 | 24,000 | — |

a. Computed by actuary.
b. From Exhibit 18-3.
c. $400,000 × amortization fraction.
d. Balance from end of previous year (or initial balance) − amortization for the current year.

each year is calculated as shown in Exhibit 18-4. For instance, $72,000 ($400,000 × 9/50) is amortized in 1995, while $56,000 ($400,000 × 7/50) is amortized in 1999.[12] This amount is included in the total pension expense on the income statement for each year. The remaining unrecognized prior service cost is the balance at the end of the previous year less the amount amortized for the year. Remember that this amount is *not* included in the company's balance sheet; that is why it is referred to as the remaining *unrecognized* prior service cost. However, the remaining unrecognized prior service cost *is* included in the required pension plan disclosures, as discussed earlier.

To compute the alternative straight-line amortization, the average remaining service life of the participating employees is calculated. This method is illustrated using the same employee group as assumed earlier. The total number of service years rendered (50) is computed by adding the years of service for all employees [i.e., 3(A) + 4(B) + 5(C) + 5(D) + 6(E) + 6(F) + 7(G) + 7(H) + 7(I)] and dividing by the number of employees (9) to give an average service life of 5.56 years. The computation of the straight-line amortization is illustrated in Exhibit 18-5. Under this method, $71,942 is amortized each year from 1995 through 1999 to increase the pension expense. In 2000, the amortization is only $40,290, the amount needed to reduce the remaining unrecognized prior service cost to zero. This straight-line method is also used for the amortization of the unrecognized net gain or loss discussed in the next example. It should be noted that if an amendment caused a decrease in future benefits, the resulting "negative" prior service cost would be amortized in the same manner to *decrease* pension expense each period.

---

12. In *FASB Statement No. 87* (par. 85 and 86), a similar schedule and an amortization table are illustrated, but an assumption that an equal number of employees retire each year is made. This assumption provides a "pure" sum-of-the-years'-digits set of fractions that yield a constantly decreasing amortization amount each period. Since this may not be a realistic assumption, we assume a varying number of employees retiring each period, which results in a modified sum-of-the-years'-digits set of fractions.

**EXHIBIT 18-5**

## AMORTIZATION OF UNRECOGNIZED PRIOR SERVICE COST: STRAIGHT-LINE METHOD

| Year | Total Unrecognized Prior Service Cost[a] | Amortization to Increase Pension Expense[b] | Remaining Unrecognized Prior Service Cost[c] |
|------|------|------|------|
| 1995 | $400,000 | $71,942 | $328,058 |
| 1996 | 400,000 | 71,942 | 256,116 |
| 1997 | 400,000 | 71,942 | 184,174 |
| 1998 | 400,000 | 71,942 | 112,232 |
| 1999 | 400,000 | 71,942 | 40,290 |
| 2000 | 400,000 | 40,290[d] | — |

a. Computed by actuary.
b. $400,000 total unrecognized prior service cost ÷ 5.56 (50 total service years ÷ 9 employees) average remaining service life.
c. Balance from end of previous year (or initial balance) − amortization for the year.
d. To reduce the remaining unrecognized prior service cost to zero.

### Example 6: Pension Expense Including Net Gain or Loss (to Extent Recognized)

Recall that the net gain or loss included in the pension expense has two elements. The first element is the difference between the actual return on plan assets and the expected return. If the actual return *exceeds* the expected return, the difference is *added* to pension expense as part of the gain or loss calculation. Since the intent of *FASB Statement No. 87* is to include the *expected* return as a reduction of pension expense, the difference is *added* because the higher *actual* return has already been *subtracted* (as the third component of the expense). For example, if the actual return on plan assets for a year was $50,000, whereas the expected return was $40,000, the $50,000 would be subtracted as the third component of the pension expense, and the difference of $10,000 would be added to pension expense as part of the net gain or loss. Therefore, the expected return of $40,000 would be the net amount deducted from pension expense. Similarly, if the actual return is *less* than the expected return, the difference is *subtracted* from pension expense as part of the gain or loss calculation.

The second element is the amortization of the unrecognized net gain or loss from previous periods. An unrecognized gain or loss arises from (a) changes in the amount of the projected benefit obligation resulting from experience different from that assumed, and (b) changes in actuarial assumptions. The excess of this unrecognized gain or loss over a "corridor" amount (discussed later) is amortized over the remaining service life of active employees expected to receive benefits under the plan. Any amortization of an unrecognized net loss is *added* to pension expense and any amortization of an unrecognized net gain is *subtracted* from pension expense as part of the net gain or loss.

The computation of the net gain or loss to be included in pension expense for the years 1995 through 1998 is shown in Exhibit 18-6. This example is for the Bliss Company, which has had a defined benefit pension plan for its employees for several years. The amounts of the cumulative unrecognized net loss (gain), the projected

## EXHIBIT 18-6

## COMPUTATION OF NET GAIN OR LOSS

| Year | Cumulative Unrecognized Net Loss (Gain)[a] | Projected Benefit Obligation: Actual[a] | Fair Value of Plan Assets[a] | Corridor[b] | Excess Unrecognized Net Loss (Gain)[c] | Amortization[d] | Difference in Return on Plan Assets[e] | Total Net Loss (Gain)[f] |
|---|---|---|---|---|---|---|---|---|
| 1995 | $13,000 | $110,000 | $100,000 | $11,000 | $2,000 | $200 | $(3,000) | $(2,800) |
| 1996 | (2,300) | 135,000 | 130,000 | 13,500 | — | — | 2,000 | 2,000 |
| 1997 | 18,700 | 168,000 | 170,000 | 17,000 | 1,700 | 170 | (4,000) | (3,830) |
| 1998 | 27,500 | 230,000 | 215,000 | 23,000 | 4,500 | 450 | 1,000 | 1,450 |

a. At the beginning of the year.
b. 10% of the greater of the actual projected benefit obligation or the fair value of the plan assets at the beginning of the year.
c. Absolute value of the cumulative unrecognized net loss (gain) − corridor.
d. Excess unrecognized net loss (gain) ÷ average remaining service life (10 years).
e. Actual return on plan assets − expected return on plan assets; if the actual return exceeds (is less than) the expected return, the difference is added to (subtracted from) pension expense.
f. Amortization of excess unrecognized net loss (gain) + difference in return on plan assets.

benefit obligation (actual), and the fair value of the plan assets are assumed to be based on information provided by the company's actuary and funding agency. The first six columns (after the Year column) of Exhibit 18-6 include amounts involved in computing the second element of the net gain or loss, which is the amortization of any unrecognized net gain or loss from prior periods. The next column reflects the first element of the net gain or loss, which is the difference between the actual and expected return on plan assets. The final column is the net gain or loss to be included as a component of pension expense.

To compute the amortization, the initial step is to determine the cumulative unrecognized net gain or loss at the beginning of the year. This amount reflects prior differences between the actual and expected projected benefit obligation and the related prior amortization. As noted earlier, these differences may be due to experience different from that assumed or from changes in actuarial assumptions. Although the calculations to determine the cumulative unrecognized net gain or loss are too complex to make here, a brief discussion is helpful to illustrate the computational process. For instance, in a given year, the expected projected benefit obligation at year-end is computed by adjusting the beginning actual projected benefit obligation for the expected current service cost, interest cost, and benefits paid. The actual projected benefit obligation at year-end is computed by the company's actuary based on current information. Any difference between the expected and actual projected benefit obligation is the unrecognized gain or loss for the year. This, in turn, is combined with any previously unamortized cumulative unrecognized net gain or loss to determine the cumulative unrecognized net gain or loss subject to potential amortization over future periods.

The amounts in the Cumulative Unrecognized Net Loss (Gain) column of Exhibit 18-6 are calculated at the beginning of the year, based on previous periods. Thus, for instance, the $13,000 amount of cumulative unrecognized net loss at the beginning of 1995 is a result of experience different from that assumed and changes in actuarial assumptions in periods prior to 1995. Note in this example that we have assumed a high volatility to better explain the calculations. Also note that a cumulative unrecognized net *loss* is shown without parentheses because the related amortization is *added* to pension expense, whereas a gain is shown in parentheses because the amortization is deducted.

The amounts in the Projected Benefit Obligation and the Fair Value of Plan Assets columns are also calculated at the beginning of the year. For instance, the $110,000 projected benefit obligation and the $100,000 fair value of the plan assets in 1995 were calculated at the beginning of 1995 based on information provided by the company's actuary and funding agency. These amounts are necessary in order to determine the **corridor** amount. **The corridor is 10% of the greater of the actual projected benefit obligation or the fair value of the plan assets at the beginning of the period.** The amortization of any cumulative unrecognized net gain or loss occurs in a given year only if, at the beginning of the year, the (absolute value of the) cumulative unrecognized net gain or loss exceeds the corridor. This 10% threshold (the corridor) is intended to reduce fluctuations in pension expense. That is, by establishing the corridor amount, a company with, for example, a large cumulative unrecognized net gain at the beginning of a given year would reduce its pension expense only by the amortization of the cumulative unrecognized net gain in excess of the corridor amount. It is unlikely that the company would have a cumulative unrecognized net loss at the beginning of the next year in excess of the corridor amount. Even in such an extreme situation, the pension expense would be increased only by the amount of the amortization of the cumulative unrecognized net loss in excess of the corridor amount.

In Exhibit 18-6, the amount in the Corridor column for a given year is 10% of the higher of the actual projected benefit obligation or the fair value of the plan assets at the beginning of that year. Thus, in 1995, the $11,000 corridor is computed as 10% of the $110,000 actual projected benefit obligation because it is the higher of the two amounts. In 1997, however, the $17,000 corridor is computed as 10% of the $170,000 fair value of the plan assets.

The amount in the Excess Unrecognized Net Loss (Gain) column for a given year is simply the excess of the (absolute value of the) cumulative unrecognized net loss (gain) over the corridor at the beginning of that year. Thus, in 1995, the $2,000 excess unrecognized net loss is the difference between the $13,000 cumulative unrecognized net loss and the $11,000 corridor. In 1996, however, the corridor exceeds the cumulative unrecognized net gain, so there is no excess.

The amount in the Amortization column for a given year is the adjustment to pension expense for the first element of the net loss (gain). Each amortization amount is computed by dividing the excess unrecognized net loss (gain) for that year by the average remaining service life of the active employees expected to receive benefits under the plan. In this example, a 10-year average service life is assumed for all years. In reality, the average service life may have to be recomputed each year to reflect changes in the employee work force. In 1995, the $200 amortization to be *added* to pension expense is determined by dividing the $2,000 excess unrecognized net loss by the 10-year average service life.

As discussed earlier, the first element of the net gain or loss is the difference between the actual return on plan assets and the expected return. An excess of the actual return over the expected return is added in the computation of pension expense, while an excess of the expected return over the actual return is *subtracted*. The difference between the actual return and expected return on plan assets for the Bliss Company in each year is shown in the second column from the right in Exhibit 18-6. These amounts are computed based on information provided by the company's actuary and funding agency. Thus, for instance, in 1995 the expected return on plan assets exceeded the actual return by $3,000, and this amount is shown in parentheses to indicate that it is deducted in the computation of pension expense. In 1996, however, the actual return on plan assets exceeded the expected return by $2,000, and this amount is added in the computation of pension expense.

The Total Net Loss (Gain) column contains, for each year, the net amount to be included as a component of pension expense in that year. The amount in each year is determined by combining the amount of the amortization of the excess unrecognized net loss (gain) with the amount of the difference in the return on plan assets. For instance, in 1995 the $200 amortization of the excess unrecognized net loss increases pension expense, while the $3,000 excess of the expected return on plan assets over the actual return reduces pension expense. These amounts are combined and the result is a $2,800 ($3,000 − $200) net gain component that is treated as a *reduction* in pension expense. In 1998, however, the $450 amortization of the excess unrecognized net loss is added to the $1,000 excess of the actual return on plan assets over the expected return to determine the $1,450 net loss component, which is treated as an *increase* in pension expense.

### Example 7: Recognition of Additional Pension Liability

The previous examples focused on the computation of pension expense and the related pension liability or asset. This example deals with the recognition of an additional pension liability, which may arise when the accumulated benefit obligation (see the definition in Exhibit 18-2) is greater than the fair value of the plan assets. To illustrate the recognition of the additional liability, assume the following facts for the Devon Company at the end of 1995:

| | |
|---|---|
| Projected benefit obligation | $2,000,000 |
| Accumulated benefit obligation | 1,200,000 |
| Plan assets (fair value) | 1,000,000 |
| Prepaid/accrued pension cost (liability) | 50,000 |

Remember that the difference between the two benefit obligations is that the *projected* benefit obligation includes assumed future pay increases, whereas the *accumulated* benefit obligation is based on current pay levels. The unfunded *accumulated* benefit obligation is computed as the difference between the accumulated benefit obligation and the fair value of the plan assets as follows:

| | |
|---|---|
| Accumulated benefit obligation | $1,200,000 |
| Plan assets (fair value) | (1,000,000) |
| Unfunded accumulated benefit obligation | $ 200,000 |

This unfunded accumulated benefit obligation of $200,000 is the minimum liability that the company must recognize. Since the company already has recorded a liability (prepaid/accrued pension cost) of $50,000, the *additional* liability of $150,000 recognized at the end of 1995 is calculated as follows:

| | |
|---|---|
| Unfunded accumulated benefit obligation | $200,000 |
| Prepaid/accrued pension cost (liability) | (50,000) |
| Additional pension liability | $150,000 |

Besides recognizing the additional liability, the company also recognizes an intangible asset of an equal amount. Since no title is suggested by the FASB, we will call it Deferred Pension Cost. Thus, the journal entry on December 31, 1995 to record the intangible asset and to increase the pension liability from $50,000 to $200,000 is as follows:

| | | |
|---|---|---|
| **Deferred Pension Cost** | 150,000 | |
|    **Additional Pension Liability** | | 150,000 |

On the 1995 year-end balance sheet, the Devon Company reports the Deferred Pension Cost account balance of $150,000 as an intangible asset. The balances of the Additional Pension Liability and Prepaid/Accrued Pension Cost are combined to report a total pension liability of $200,000 on the balance sheet. Also, the additional liability ($150,000) is included in the pension plan disclosures.

A different journal entry is made if the preceding facts remained the same except that the company had a prepaid/accrued pension cost *asset* of $40,000 instead of the liability of $50,000. In this case, the minimum liability must still be $200,000, but a $40,000 asset exists. Consequently, it is necessary to record a liability and an intangible asset of $240,000 (the unfunded accumulated benefit obligation of $200,000 + the prepaid/accrued pension cost asset of $40,000). The journal entry is as follows:

| | | |
|---|---|---|
| **Deferred Pension Cost** | 240,000 | |
|    **Additional Pension Liability** | | 240,000 |

The balances of the Additional Pension Liability and Prepaid/Accrued Pension Cost are combined ("netted") to report a net pension liability of $200,000 on the balance sheet. Also, the additional liability is included in the pension plan disclosures.

The previous situations have assumed that the additional liability does not exceed the unrecognized prior service cost. In other words, it is likely that the need for the recognition of the additional liability arose because of amendments to the plan that created prior service costs and increased the accumulated benefit obligation, but have not yet been funded by the company.

Another complexity in the recognition of the additional liability occurs if it exceeds the unrecognized prior service cost. Typically, this situation arises because there have been negative returns on the plan assets. Since it would be inappropriate to record such declines in value of the plan assets as an intangible asset of the company, stockholders' equity is reduced instead. To illustrate this situation, assume the same facts as originally given for the Devon Company, but, in addition, the company has an unrecognized prior service cost of $120,000. The same additional liability of $150,000 is recognized, but the intangible asset cannot exceed the unrecognized prior service cost of $120,000. Therefore, the $30,000 difference is subtracted from stockholders' equity. The journal entry by the Devon Company is as follows:

| | | |
|---|---|---|
| **Deferred Pension Cost** | 120,000 | |
| **Excess of Additional Pension Liability over** | | |
|     **Unrecognized Prior Service Cost** | 30,000 | |
|    **Additional Pension Liability** | | 150,000 |

In this case, on the year-end balance sheet of the Devon Company, the $120,000 balance in Deferred Pension Cost is reported as an intangible asset, the Prepaid/Accrued Pension Cost liability of $50,000 and the Additional Pension Liability of $150,000 are combined in a single amount, and the $30,000 excess is reported in the stockholders' equity section as follows (other amounts assumed):

### Stockholders' Equity

| | |
|---|---|
| Common stock | $600,000 |
| Additional paid-in capital | 230,000 |
| Retained earnings | 170,000 |
| Excess of additional pension liability over unrecognized prior service cost | (30,000) |
| Total stockholders' equity | $970,000 |

It should be noted that the additional liability, the intangible asset, and the reduction in stockholders' equity are *not* amortized. The appropriate amounts are computed each year and included in the balance sheet for that year. For example, refer back to the original facts for the Devon Company. In that situation, the additional liability was recorded at $150,000 at the end of 1995. Now suppose that at the end of 1996, the following information was available:

| | |
|---|---|
| Accumulated benefit obligation | $1,300,000 |
| Plan assets (fair value) | 1,220,000 |
| Prepaid/accrued pension cost (liability) | 60,000 |

The unfunded accumulated benefit obligation is $80,000 ($1,300,000 − $1,220,000) and the required additional liability at the end of 1996 is $20,000 ($80,000 − $60,000). The journal entry on December 31, 1996 to adjust the additional liability is as follows:

| | | |
|---|---|---|
| **Additional Pension Liability** | 130,000 | |
| **Deferred Pension Cost** | | 130,000 |

This entry reduces the existing account balances of $150,000 by $130,000 to $20,000. Thus, the changes in the account balances have no effect on the income statement.

### Example 8: Disclosures

To improve the usefulness of a company's disclosures about its pension plan, we noted earlier that the company must report certain information in the notes to the financial statements, in addition to the amounts contained in the financial statements. An illustration of these disclosures is presented for Amoco in Exhibit 18-7.

---

**EXHIBIT 18-7**
**Illustration of Pension Disclosures**

**AMOCO**

*Note 18. Retirement Plans*
The corporation and its subsidiaries have a number of defined benefit pension plans covering most employees. Plan benefits are generally based on employees' years of service and average final compensation. Essentially all of the cost of these plans is borne by the corporation. The corporation makes contributions to the plans in amounts that are intended to provide for the cost of pension benefits over the service lives of employees. The status of the funded plans as of December 31 for 1992 and 1991 is presented in the following:

## EXHIBIT 18-7, Continued
## Illustration of Pension Disclosures

| | Plans for which | |
|---|---|---|
| millions of dollars | Assets Exceed Benefits | Benefits Exceed Assets |
| **1992** | | |
| Fair value of plan assets, principally equity and fixed-income securities | $2,364 | $ 189 |
| Actuarial present value of benefit obligations: | | |
| Accumulated benefit obligation* | 1,833 | 287 |
| Additional benefits based on estimated future salary levels | 476 | 79 |
| Projected benefit obligation (PBO) | 2,309 | 366 |
| Plan assets over (under) PBO | 55 | (177) |
| Unrecognized net gains at transition | (63) | (1) |
| Other unrecognized net losses | 13 | 40 |
| Unrecognized prior service cost | 85 | 41 |
| Net pension cost prepaid (accrued) | $ 90 | $ (97) |
| **1991** | | |
| Fair value of plan assets, principally equity and fixed-income securities | $2,711 | $ 130 |
| Actuarial present value of benefit obligations: | | |
| Accumulated benefit obligation* | 2,033 | 218 |
| Additional benefits based on estimated future salary levels | 523 | 113 |
| Projected benefit obligation (PBO) | 2,556 | 331 |
| Plan assets over (under) PBO | 155 | (201) |
| Unrecognized net gains at transition | (78) | (2) |
| Other unrecognized net losses/(gains) | (89) | 78 |
| Unrecognized prior service cost | 103 | 29 |
| Net pension cost prepaid (accrued) | $ 91 | $ (96) |

* Accumulated benefits totaling $28 million and $24 million were non-vested at December 31, 1992 and 1991, respectively.

The assumptions used for the corporation's principal pension plans for 1992 and 1991 were as follows:

| | 1992 | 1991 |
|---|---|---|
| Discount rate for service and interest cost | 7.5% | 8.0% |
| Discount rate for the projected benefit obligation | 7.5% | 7.5% |
| Rate of increase in compensation levels | 6.0% | 6.0% |
| Long-term rate of return on assets | 10.0% | 9.5% |

The components of net pension cost for the past three years were as follows:

| millions of dollars | 1992 | 1991 | 1990 |
|---|---|---|---|
| Service cost—benefits earned during the period | $ 114 | $ 106 | $ 82 |
| Interest cost on projected benefit obligation | 221 | 213 | 202 |
| Actual (return) loss on assets | (141) | (597) | 103 |
| Less—unrecognized gain (loss) | (124) | 355 | (340) |
| | (265) | (242) | (237) |
| Curtailment gain | (51) | — | — |
| Amortization of unrecognized amounts | 11 | 4 | 9 |
| Net pension cost | $ 30 | $ 81 | $ 56 |

### Summary of Issues Related to Pensions

In Exhibit 18-8, the major issues related to accounting for defined benefit pension plans are summarized in T-account form. While each "entry" balances, it is important to note that four of the "accounts" (plan assets, projected benefit obligation, unrecognized loss or gain, and unrecognized prior service cost) are *not* included in the company's financial statements. The other two accounts (pension expense and cash) are included in the financial statements. All amounts are assumed, and the company funds an amount equal to the pension expense. Each entry is discussed in the following sections.

---

**EXHIBIT 18-8**

## SUMMARY OF ISSUES RELATED TO DEFINED BENEFIT PENSION PLANS

*Not included in the company's financial statements:*

### Plan Assets

| | | | |
|---|---|---|---|
| Beginning balance | 100* | (g) Payments to retirees | 14 |
| (c) Actual return on plan assets | 9 | | |
| (h) Funding | 21 | | |
| Ending balance | 116 | | |

### Projected Benefit Obligation (Liability)

| | | | |
|---|---|---|---|
| (g) Payments to retirees | 14 | Beginning balance | 90 |
| | | (a) Service cost | 15 |
| | | (b) Interest | 12 |
| | | (d) Prior service cost | 40 |
| | | Ending balance | 143 |

### Unrecognized Loss/Gain

| | | |
|---|---|---|
| | (f) Actual − expected return on plan assets | 1 |

### Unrecognized Prior Service Cost

| | | | |
|---|---|---|---|
| (d) Prior service cost | 40 | (e) Amortization | 2 |

*Included in the company's financial statements:*

### Pension Expense

| | | | |
|---|---|---|---|
| (a) Service cost | 15 | (c) Actual return on plan assets | 9 |
| (b) Interest | 12 | | |
| (e) Amortization of prior service cost | 2 | | |
| (f) Actual − expected return on plan assets | 1 | | |
| Total expense | 21 | | |

### Cash

| | | | |
|---|---|---|---|
| | | (h) Funding | 21 |

---

\* All amounts in thousands of dollars.

### Beginning Balances

It is assumed that the company has an ongoing defined benefit pension plan. At the beginning of 1995, the plan assets are $100,000, and the projected benefit obligation (liability) is $90,000.

(a) **Service Cost.** The service cost for 1995 of $15,000 is a component of the pension expense and increases the projected benefit obligation.

(b) **Interest Cost.** The interest cost for 1995 of $12,000 is a component of the pension expense and increases the projected benefit obligation.

(c) **Actual Return on Plan Assets.** The actual return on plan assets for 1995 of $9,000 increases the plan assets and reduces the pension expense.

(d) **Unrecognized Prior Service Cost.** During 1995, the company provides retroactive benefits with a present value of $40,000. This increases the unrecognized prior service cost and the projected benefit obligation.

(e) **Amortization of the Unrecognized Prior Service Cost.** During 1995, the company amortizes the unrecognized prior service cost by $2,000. This increases the pension expense and decreases the unrecognized prior service cost.

(f) **Difference Between the Actual and Expected Return on Plan Assets.** The actual return on plan assets is $9,000 and the expected return is $8,000. The $1,000 by which the actual return exceeds the expected return increases the pension expense and the unrecognized gain.

(g) **Payments to Retired Employees.** Payments of $14,000 by the funding agency to retired employees in 1995 decrease the plan assets and the projected benefit obligation.

(h) **Funding by the Company.** The payment by the company to the funding agency of $21,000 increases the plan assets and decreases cash.

## CONCEPTUAL ISSUES RELATED TO DEFINED BENEFIT PENSION PLANS

In their analyses of pension accounting, the APB and the FASB have considered several conceptual issues related to pension expense, pension liabilities, pension assets, and disclosures. Each of these conceptual issues is briefly discussed in the sections that follow.[13]

### Pension Expense

The first conceptual issue in accounting for pension plans involves the proper amount of pension cost to recognize and when to report that amount as pension expense on the employer-company's income statement. *Expenses* are defined as "outflows or other using up of assets or incurrences of liabilities . . . (during a period) from delivering or producing goods, rendering services, or carrying out other activities that constitute an entity's ongoing major or central operations."[14] Recall also that once revenues have been assigned to a particular accounting period, expenses are matched against the revenues by association of cause and effect, systematic and rational allocation, or immediate recognition.

---

13. This discussion is a summary of that presented in "Employers' Accounting for Pensions and Other Postemployment Benefits," *FASB Discussion Memorandum* (Stamford, Conn.: FASB, 1981).

14. "Elements of Financial Statements," *FASB Statement of Financial Accounting Concepts No. 6* (Stamford, Conn.: FASB, 1985), par. 80.

*Components*

Pension cost may consist of several components, which include:

1. *Deferred Compensation.* The primary component of pension cost is the deferred compensation (service cost) to be paid to employees in the future in return for their current services.

2. *Interest Cost.* Since employees' compensation is deferred until retirement, the employees are, in effect, providing a "loan" to the employer. The interest on that loan may be a component of pension cost.

3. *Return on Assets.* An employer generally invests its pension contributions into a pension fund with the intent to earn a return on these assets. A possible *negative* component of pension cost is the return earned on the pension fund assets.

4. *Prior Service Cost.* When an employer begins a pension plan or makes modifications in its existing plan, additional benefits generally are due to employees as a result of services they performed in previous years. Part or all of the cost of these previously earned benefits may be a component of pension cost.

5. *Gains and Losses.* Unforeseen events related to a pension plan may result in (a) deviations in the current period between actual experience and the assumptions used, and (b) changes in the assumptions about the future. The resulting gains and losses may be a component of pension cost.

Pension expense computed under *FASB Statement No. 87* includes all these components, although some are in a modified form.

*Measurement*

**Attribution is the process of assigning pension benefits or cost to periods of employee service.** Thus, a basic issue in accounting for pension plans is the proper amount of pension cost to be attributed (recognized) as pension expense on the employer's income statement during each accounting period. Three different viewpoints on this issue have been identified:

1. *The amount of pension expense should be the same as the increase in the pension liability.* If this view is accepted, the amount must be an appropriate measure of both the expense and the liability. Possibilities include the *change* during the period in the amount attributed to employee service to date, the amount of contributions to date based on an actuarial funding method, the amount owed to employees if the plan were terminated, the amount of vested benefits, or the amount currently payable to retirees. These alternatives are more fully discussed under the pension liabilities section.

2. *The amount of pension expense should be attributable to employee service during the period.* This expense recognition would be applicable even if the pension liability is recognized on another basis. The argument for this alternative is that the portion of pension cost attributed to employee services used to produce revenues should be recognized along with those revenues. Under this viewpoint, pensions are a form of supplemental benefit to the *current* employee group. Therefore, the amount of pension expense is established by determining the costs of providing the benefits that were earned during the current period and are expected to become payable to specific employees in the future. This is the approach adopted by *FASB Statement No. 87.*

3. *The amount of pension expense should be the contribution to the plan for the period as determined by an actuarial method.* The argument for this alternative is that the pension agreement involves a promise to make contributions to the plan rather than a promise to provide specified benefits. According to this view, pensions are a means of promoting efficiency by (1) providing for the systematic retirement of older employees, and (2) fulfilling a social obligation that is expected of a company. Consequently, the amount of pension expense is determined by the amount that must be contributed to keep the plan in existence indefinitely.

A corollary issue, particularly in regard to viewpoint 2, involves how pension cost should be attributed to the years of service. Two methods involving five **attribution approaches** have been identified. The first method includes three approaches [accumulated benefits, benefits/years-of-service (required by *FASB Statement No. 87*), and benefit/compensation] that assign an amount of pension benefit to each year of service and then compute the cost of the assigned benefits. The second method includes two approaches (cost/years-of-service and cost/compensation) that calculate the total estimated pension benefits and then assign a portion of the cost to each year. Further discussion of these methods is beyond the scope of this book, but an issue for debate is whether the same approach should be used by every company for computing pension expense. On the one hand, it is argued that if only one approach is used, comparability across different companies would be enhanced. On the other hand, the use of a single approach might lead to a false appearance of comparability.

### Complexities

The issue of pension expense becomes more complex when the pension plan is modified, when deviations exist between actual experience and the assumptions used, and when the assumptions change.

Pension plan modifications are changes in the terms of a pension plan. Most changes result in *increases* in the amounts of future benefits. Changes may include the inception of a new plan that gives retroactive credit to employees for past service, an increase in benefits related to past service for active employees, or an increase in benefits for retired former employees. A question arises as to how to account for the prior service cost that arises from these pension plan modifications.

Four alternative methods have been suggested to account for this cost. The first would be to account for it prospectively, which is the approach adopted by *FASB Statement No. 87*. This method requires that the cost be expensed in the current and future periods, and that no liability be recorded when the cost arises. It is often argued that this method violates the matching concept because all the services to be performed by the employees have been completed in previous periods. Also, it is often suggested that the lack of recognition of a pension obligation is a violation of the concept of a liability.

The second alternative would be to recognize the total amount as an expense in the period in which it arises (i.e., the current period) and record a liability. This procedure also violates the matching concept because the services were performed by the employees in previous periods and not in the current period. It might also tend to dissuade companies from adopting, or changing, pension plans because of the related effect (i.e., decrease) on net income of the current period.

The third alternative would be to debit retained earnings (as a prior period adjustment) and record a liability. This procedure would violate the all-inclusive income concept because the total amounts would never be included in the income statement. Also, many companies would resist the recording of a liability because of the effect it would have on their debt-to-equity ratios and on similar measures of financial performance.

The fourth alternative would be to record an intangible asset and liability of equal amounts. Although it is difficult to see how an asset is created by the recognition of pension benefits earned by employees in previous periods, the argument is that an employer's decision to improve a pension plan is forward-looking and rational. That is, the employer would take on an increased obligation only if future benefits of at least an equal amount were expected to result. In this sense, the future economic benefits (intangible asset) should be recognized along with the liability and should be expensed over some future period.

Gains and losses are the effects of (1) deviations in the current period between actual experience and the assumptions used, and (2) changes in the assumptions regarding future periods. These gains and losses are inevitable because only by coincidence will actual experience conform to assumptions regarding such items as mortality, turnover, early retirement, and pay increases. If actual experience differs significantly from the assumptions, then the assumptions should be changed. The proper accounting treatment of gains and losses is also an important issue in regard to pension plans. (Although the terms *gains* and *losses* are commonly used in pension accounting, they are not necessarily synonymous with *gains* and *losses* as defined in the *FASB Conceptual Framework*.) The alternatives are similar to those discussed earlier in regard to prior service cost. That is, gains and losses could be accounted for prospectively, currently, as a prior period adjustment, or as a deferred item.

### Pension Liabilities

A second conceptual issue regarding accounting for pension plans involves the identification and recording of pension plan liabilities. *Liabilities* are probable future sacrifices of economic benefits arising from present obligations of a company to transfer assets or provide services to other entities in the future as a result of past transactions or events.[15] Furthermore, once a liability is identified, it must be measurable to be reported on a company's balance sheet.

Generally, it is agreed that a pension is a form of deferred compensation. The pension obligation is viewed by some as an obligation to make contributions to the plan, while it is viewed by others as an obligation to employees for pensions promised. However viewed, the exact amount of the pension obligation for each employee cannot be known until the employee (or related beneficiary) dies. Before that time, actuaries can estimate the amount of the obligation using assumptions about employee turnover, life expectancy, and other variables.

Due to the complex nature of pension plans, there is uncertainty concerning what part, if any, of an employer-company's pension obligation meets the definition of a liability, and whether the liability is sufficiently measurable to be reported as a pension liability on the company's balance sheet. Five alternatives for meeting the recognition-measurement criteria have been identified. Each alternative describes a method of determining the extent of a company's pension plan liability and is briefly summarized as follows:

1. *Amount Attributed to Employee Service to Date.* This alternative is based on the concept that the employer's pension obligation arises as the employees work and that the event or transaction resulting in the obligation is the em-

---

15. *Ibid.,* par. 35.

ployees' service. The pension transaction is viewed here as an exchange whereby employees render service in return for pension benefits (deferred wages) in addition to current compensation. The amount of pension obligation resulting from employees' service would be measured by one of the attribution approaches discussed in regard to pension expense. The resulting obligation for deferred wages (the projected benefit obligation) would be recorded in a manner similar to current compensation.

2. *Contributions Based on an Actuarial Funding Method.* Under this alternative, it is argued that the employer has an obligation to make contributions to the plan rather than directly to employees. In this situation, the employer's liability could be based on the actuarial funding method used for funding the plan, in which case, the only recorded pension liability would be for contributions due but not yet paid. This is the approach adopted by *FASB Statement No. 87.*

3. *Termination Liability.* This alternative is based on the argument that the employer's obligation should be limited to the amount that would be payable on termination of the plan. Those disagreeing believe that a company is a going concern and that an assumption of plan termination is inappropriate unless there is clear evidence to the contrary.

4. *Amount of Vested Benefits.* Under this alternative, the employer's obligation is based on the vested benefits earned by the employees. Nonvested benefits are contingent on and result from future services and, therefore, create a liability only as they become vested in future periods. Those disagreeing believe that vesting is a legal transaction, and that a portion of the nonvested benefits will become vested and, therefore, meet the definition of a liability.

5. *Amount Payable to Retirees.* This alternative is a form of "pay-as-you-go" accounting whereby a liability arises only during the period in which the employees will be paid their pension benefits. Under this alternative, the liability is readily measurable. Those disagreeing believe that this approach is a violation of the accrual concept of accounting.

If one of these alternatives meets the definition of a liability, the amount of the liability must be measurable in order to be recorded and reported on a company's balance sheet. Most of the amounts would be estimates. If uncertainty is considered to be so great that a reasonable estimate cannot be made because of the long-term nature of pension plans, then a liability cannot be recorded (although disclosure may be required).

## Balance Sheet Presentation of Pension Plan Assets

A third conceptual issue involves the disclosure of assets used in the pension plan. *Assets* are probable future economic benefits obtained or controlled by a company as a result of past transactions or events.[16] As indicated earlier, a company having a pension plan typically makes periodic payments to a funding agency. This agency, then, assumes the responsibility for safeguarding and investing the pension assets (to

---

16. *Ibid.,* par. 25.

earn a return on the assets) held in trust, and for making benefit payments to retired employees. There are two alternative views in regard to the proper accounting by the employer-company for these pension assets.

The first view holds that funding is a discharge of the pension liability and that the assets of the pension plan held by the funding agency are not assets of the employer. The principal reasons are that: (1) the funding agency is a separate legal entity (e.g., a trust) with legal title to the plan assets; (2) the assets can be used only for the benefit of the employees and retirees, and ordinarily cannot be returned to the employer; (3) the employer's obligation is to make contributions to the funding agency, and the agency pays the actual pension benefits; and (4) the employer's obligation may be limited by termination of the plan. Accountants holding this view would exclude plan assets from the employer's balance sheet. This is the approach adopted by *FASB Statement No. 87.*

A second view is that the pension liability is not discharged until the retiree receives the pension payment, and that the pension plan assets are assets of the employer. Accountants holding this view argue that the employer remains obligated to provide benefits defined by the plan, and the trust is a legal device controlled by the employer for funding the pension obligation. Although the funding agency holds legal title to the assets, the employer is at risk with regard to the assets and ultimately reaps the rewards of economic ownership of them. If the assets grow, the employer's future contributions will be reduced. If the assets do not grow, or if losses are sustained, future contributions will be increased. These accountants would include plan assets on the employer's balance sheet. In doing so, however, it would still need to be decided whether the plan assets should be shown separately on the asset side of the balance sheet or deducted from the pension liability.

Similar questions apply to any intangible asset recorded in regard to accounting for prior service costs and for gains and losses, as discussed earlier in the pension expense section. That is, it must be resolved whether these items meet the conceptual definition of an asset and, if so, how they should be reported on the employer's balance sheet.

### Disclosures

The final conceptual issue involves what additional disclosures beyond those reported on the employer-company's income statement, balance sheet, and statement of cash flows should be made for pension plans. An objective of financial reporting is to help external users assess the amounts, timing, and uncertainty of cash flows. Additional information about pension plans might be helpful in understanding the effect of the pension agreement on the employer's operating performance, liquidity, and financial flexibility.

The additional information that might be disclosed includes: (1) the pension obligation (e.g., vested benefits); (2) the pension cost (e.g., description of attribution approach used); (3) assets in the pension plan trust (e.g., types, market value); (4) funding in past periods and changes in funding policy; (5) estimates of future funding (e.g., forecasts of assets, benefits, and contributions); (6) the actuarial methods and assumptions used (e.g., retirement ages); (7) employees (e.g., number and average age); (8) actuary (e.g., professional qualifications); and (9) unusual or infrequent events or transactions (e.g., plant closings). In evaluating this potential additional information, consideration should be given to *whether* it should be made (i.e., does it pass a cost/benefit test) and *where* it should be reported (i.e., parenthetically supplementally, or in the notes to the financial statements).

## ADDITIONAL ASPECTS OF PENSION ACCOUNTING

Several other issues have an impact on some aspects of pension accounting. These include the transition requirements from *APB Opinion No. 8* to *FASB Statement No. 87*, vested benefits, accounting for defined contribution plans, disclosures by funding agencies, the Employee Retirement Income Security Act of 1974, pension settlements and curtailments, termination benefits paid to employees, and multi-employer plans. Each of these topics, along with international accounting differences, is briefly discussed in the following sections.

### Transition Requirements

Although *FASB Statement No. 87* was issued in 1985, adoption was not required until 1987 because of the complexities of the requirements and a need to allow companies time to adjust their accounting systems. Furthermore, recognition of the minimum liability was not required until 1989, although early application of the entire *Statement* was encouraged.

In the period in which the *Statement* was adopted, an unrecognized net obligation or an unrecognized net asset may have existed. To make this determination, at the beginning of the year of transition, the projected benefit obligation was computed and compared with the fair value of the plan assets plus (minus) any recognized prepaid/ accrued pension cost liability (asset). If the projected benefit obligation was larger (smaller), an unrecognized obligation (asset) existed.

This obligation or asset is amortized on a straight-line basis over the remaining service life of employees expected to receive benefits under the plan. The amount of this amortization is included as the sixth component of pension expense by adding it if an obligation exists and subtracting it if an asset exists. However, if the average remaining service period is less than 15 years, a company may use a 15-year amortization period. The purpose of this exception is to lessen the impact of the transition on companies with short average remaining service lives.

### Vested Benefits

**Vested benefits** are pension benefits earned by employees that are not contingent on future service with the company. That is, the employees will receive retirement benefits based on service to date, even if they terminate employment. ERISA specifies the minimum vesting requirements that companies must follow. A company with a defined benefit plan discloses the vested portion of the accumulated benefit obligation. Also, the vesting provisions affect calculations made by the company's actuary because it is necessary to estimate the number of employees who will leave before vesting of their pension benefits occurs.

### Accounting for Defined Contribution Plans

As explained earlier, some pension plans are **defined contribution plans** because the employer's contribution is determined based on a specified formula, and any future benefits paid to retired employees are limited to those that can be provided by the contributions and the earnings on those contributions. Accounting for defined contribution plans is very straightforward and is specified in *FASB Statement No. 87*.

The pension expense recorded by a company is equal to the contribution that the company is required to make in that period. Thus, the journal entry is a debit to Pension Expense and a credit to Cash for the annual contribution. A liability is recognized only in the rare situation that the contribution for a given year has not been paid.

The company also is required to disclose the following two items:

1. A description of the plan, including employee groups covered, the basis for determining contributions, and the nature and effect of significant matters affecting the comparability of the information for all periods presented.

2. The amount of the pension expense recognized during the period.[17]

## Disclosures by Funding Agencies

A company typically makes its periodic pension plan payments to a funding agency that administers the plan. A funding agency may be a specific corporate or individual trustee or an insurance company. These agencies issue financial statements that summarize the financial aspects of a company's pension plan, aimed primarily toward providing financial information about the pension plan's ability to pay benefits when due. **FASB Statement No. 35** requires the annual financial statements issued by a funding agency for a company's pension plan to include: (1) a financial statement (on an accrual accounting basis) presenting information about the net assets (at fair value) available for benefits at the end of the plan year, (2) a financial statement presenting information about the changes during the year in the net assets available for benefits, (3) information regarding the actuarial present value of accumulated plan benefits as of either the beginning or end of the plan year, and (4) information regarding the significant effects of factors affecting the year-to-year change in the actuarial present value of accumulated plan benefits.[18] Although these funding agency financial statements are beyond the scope of this book, certain of this information is disclosed in the notes to the financial statements of the *company* sponsoring the pension plan, as discussed earlier.

## Employee Retirement Income Security Act of 1974

The **Employee Retirement Income Security Act of 1974** (ERISA), alternatively known as the *Pension Reform Act of 1974* (mentioned earlier in this chapter), is based upon recommendations made by various individuals and organizations. Its primary aim is to create standards for the operation and maintenance of pension funds in an effort to correct reported abuses in the handling of these funds. Also, it attempts to increase the protection given to employees covered by such plans. For example, at the Congressional Hearings, it was revealed that some companies routinely followed a policy of terminating employees at ages 60 to 62, even though service until the age of 65 was a requirement for pension eligibility. This practice greatly minimized the company's pension liabilities and deprived these employees of pension income on their retirement.

The *Pension Reform Act of 1974* provides guidelines for employee participation in pension plans, vesting provisions, minimum funding requirements, financial statement disclosure, and the administration of the plan. In addition, the administrators of pension plans are required to file annual reports with the Department of Labor that include a description of the plan and copies of the relevant financial statements.

---

17. *FASB Statement No. 87, op. cit.,* par. 65.
18. "Accounting and Reporting by Defined Benefit Pension Plans," *FASB Statement of Financial Accounting Standards No. 35* (Stamford, Conn.: FASB, 1980), par. 5 and 6.

The Act also created the Pension Benefit Guaranty Corporation (PBGC), an organization that provides benefits to employees covered by plans that have been terminated (usually because of the bankruptcy of the sponsoring company). The PBGC receives an annual fee for every employee covered by a pension plan that is subject to the PBGC. The PBGC can also impose a lien against 30% of the net assets of the company. This lien has the status of a tax lien and, therefore, ranks above the claims of most other creditors. Since the company may be bankrupt, however, this lien may not result in many assets being received by the PBGC.

## Pension Plan Settlements and Curtailments

In recent years, many companies have either settled (terminated) or curtailed their defined benefit pension plans. Some have settled their defined benefit pension plans and substituted defined contribution plans. Others have reduced (curtailed) the benefits to be paid to employees, while continuing the defined benefit pension plans. In each situation, the company is likely to "recapture" the excess plan assets. For example, a company may decide to terminate its pension plan and buy from an insurance company an annuity for each of its employees that provides the same expected benefits during retirement. If the plan assets exceed the costs of the annuities, the excess assets revert to the general use of the company.

**FASB Statement No. 88,** "Employers' Accounting for Settlements and Curtailments of Defined Benefit Pension Plans and for Termination Benefits," requires that the net gain or loss from a settlement or curtailment be included in the net income of the period. When a plan is *settled,* the net gain or loss is the unrecognized net gain or loss that has not been recognized as part of pension expense, as discussed earlier, plus any remaining unrecognized net asset existing when *FASB Statement No. 87* was initially applied. When a plan is *curtailed,* the portion of the unrecognized prior service cost associated with the estimated reduced future benefits is a loss. This amount is combined with any gain or loss from a change in the projected benefit obligation due to the curtailment in order to determine the net gain or loss.[19]

## Termination Benefits Paid to Employees

When a company wishes to reduce the size of its work force without firing employees, it may provide special benefits for a period of time in the hope of encouraging some employees to terminate voluntarily. These benefits may include lump-sum cash payments, payments over future periods, or similar inducements. *FASB Statement No. 88* requires that a company record a loss and a liability for these *termination benefits* when the following two conditions are met:

1.  The employee accepts the offer, and

2.  The amount can be reasonably estimated.[20]

The amount of the loss includes the amount of any lump-sum payments and the present value of any expected future benefits.

---

19. "Employers' Accounting for Settlements and Curtailments of Defined Benefit Pension Plans and for Termination Benefits," *FASB Statement of Financial Accounting Standards No. 88* (Stamford, Conn.: FASB, 1985), par. 9–14.
20. *Ibid.,* par. 15.

### Multi-Employer Plans

The discussion in this chapter has assumed that the pension plan is a single-employer plan. That is, the plan is maintained by one company for its employees. In contrast, **a multi-employer plan involves two or more unrelated companies in which assets contributed by each company are available to pay benefits to the employees of all the involved companies.** Generally, these plans result from collective-bargaining agreements with unions. Each company recognizes as pension expense the required contribution for the period. In other words, cash basis accounting is used for these plans. This difference in accounting principles results from the difference in the nature of the obligation of the company and the difficulty of obtaining *reliable* information for each separate company.

### International Accounting Differences

There are major differences around the world in the accounting rules for defined benefit pension plans. One type of difference occurs because it is common for foreign governments to provide significantly higher benefits to retirees. Therefore, pension benefits provided by foreign companies usually are not as significant, and there has been less need to develop detailed accounting principles. For example, Italian and Swiss accounting standards do not address defined benefit pension plans. In such situations, the amount funded would be expensed.

A second type of difference occurs in the actual principles. Most countries base pension expense only on the amount funded. When more detailed rules exist, these still differ from the U.S. standards, which are more restrictive and specific. For example, the U.S. is the only country that has a "corridor" provision or uses a discount rate based on current market conditions. The annual reevaluation of the discount rate is likely to make the pension expense more volatile in the U.S. Also, U.S. standards require annual actuarial valuations and the use of the projected unit credit method, whereas most foreign countries require less frequent valuations (every five years in Japan and every three years in Australia, Canada, and France) and more flexibility in the actuarial method used. Amortization of prior service costs also varies, with some countries not specifying the method to be used and others requiring immediate recognition (e.g., Germany). Foreign disclosure requirements are also less detailed. For example, the disclosure of the components of pension expense is generally not required.[21] These differences impair the comparability of financial statements prepared in different countries.

## OTHER POSTEMPLOYMENT BENEFITS

In addition to providing pensions to their employees, many companies also offer two types of additional benefits. *Postemployment* benefits are provided to former employees after employment but *before* retirement. Under **FASB Statement No. 112,**[22] the cost of these benefits is accrued during employment and recognized as an expense and a liability if the four criteria for the recognition of compensated absences defined in *FASB Statement No. 43* are met. If any one of the criteria is not met, the company

*Criteria for recognition of compensated absences are discussed in Chapter 11.*

---

21. For an additional discussion, see Arthur Andersen and Co., et. al., *Survey of International Accounting Practices* (New York: AICPA, 1991).
22. "Employers' Accounting for Postemployment Benefits," *FASB Statement No. 112* (Norwalk, Conn.: FASB, 1992).

would record the expense and liability when the liability is probable and the amount can be reasonably estimated, in accordance with the provision of *FASB Statement No. 5.*

The rest of this section discusses *postretirement* benefits, which include all forms of benefits provided to former employees *after* their retirement, other than pensions. For convenience, we will use the widely-used acronym, OPEB, for these benefits.

Healthcare benefits typically are the most significant of these OPEBs, but some companies also provide dental benefits, eye care, tuition assistance, life insurance, legal services, and financial advisory services. Our discussion focuses on accounting for healthcare benefits because they usually comprise the largest dollar amount, present the greatest measurement difficulties, and are the most controversial.

When Medicare was first created in the 1960s, many companies decided to offer an additional benefit by agreeing to pay for the medical costs of those retirees who were not covered by the federal plan. At that time, healthcare costs and the retiree population were relatively small, so management believed that it was providing a valuable benefit to employees at a low cost. Companies accounted for OPEBs by recording the costs as they were paid. This cash basis of accounting was accepted because the liability was thought to be immaterial and because the benefits were considered to be revocable. However, the costs of the plans have increased significantly in recent years because

1. Inflation in healthcare costs has significantly exceeded general inflation,

2. Medicare reimbursements have been decreasing, leaving a larger portion to be covered by companies,

3. The number of retired employees has increased both absolutely and relative to the number of current employees as companies have matured and life expectancies have increased, and

4. Many companies have encouraged early retirement and their healthcare programs cover the entire healthcare costs of the retired employees until age 65, when Medicare is available.

In reaction to these changes, in 1990 the FASB issued **FASB Statement No. 106** on employers' accounting for OPEBs, "Employers' Accounting for Postretirement Benefits Other Than Pensions."[23] The objectives of this *Statement* are:

1. To enhance the relevance of reported income by recognizing the cost of OPEBs over the period they are earned by employees.

2. To enhance the relevance of the balance sheet by including a measure of the obligation to provide OPEBs.

3. To enhance the ability of users to understand the extent and effects of an employer's promise to provide OPEBs.

4. To improve the understandability and comparability of amounts reported by mandating a single method for measuring the cost and obligation.

---

23. "Employers' Accounting for Postretirement Benefits Other Than Pensions," *FASB Statement of Financial Accounting Standards No. 106* (Norwalk, Conn.: FASB, 1990).

The *Statement* requires that companies accrue the cost of OPEBs during the periods in which the employees earn the benefits. That is, accounting principles require the use of the accrual basis rather than the cash basis and are similar to those for pensions. (The principles are discussed later.) This accounting has had a dramatic impact on the financial statements of many companies, as discussed later.

Many companies have provided OPEBs without computing the long-term costs involved. It is interesting, for example, that companies have generally refused to index *pension* benefits because of the inflation risk involved. However, *healthcare* benefits are essentially indexed because companies have committed to benefits in terms of *services* rather than in terms of a specific dollar amount of those services. Also, healthcare benefits are more egalitarian, because they are usually *not* based on length of service or salary, but rather on some minimum length of service after which the same benefits are provided equally to every employee.

Since pensions and OPEBs are both postemployment benefits, it is helpful to understand their similarities and differences in considering GAAP for OPEBs.

## Similarities to and Differences from Pensions

The basic argument that accounting for OPEBs should be similar to the principles used for pensions involves the concept of a liability. Recall that a liability is a probable future sacrifice of economic benefits arising from present obligations of a company to transfer assets or provide services to other entities in the future as a result of past transactions or events. The term "obligations" not only includes legal duties defined in a contract, but also equitable and constructive obligations based on promises or moral responsibility.

Those who agree with the concepts underlying the accounting principles argue that a company offering OPEBs is essentially providing deferred compensation to employees because the benefits received during retirement were earned during the period of employment. Therefore, the company incurs an obligation as its employees provide services. *FASB Statement No. 106* follows this viewpoint.

Those who disagree with the concepts argue that many OPEBs do not have the same explicit legal contract as a pension agreement, and the obligation of the company to continue to provide benefits is not as clear. In other words, they argue that there is no liability because the company has the right to withdraw the benefits. That is, a company has no obligation for OPEBs until its employees retire, since they must retire to obtain the benefit. However, recent court decisions have not allowed companies to withdraw rights from retired employees, and there are indications that it may be difficult to withdraw rights already earned by current employees. Therefore, the concept of a liability appears to have been satisfied.

Also, if a liability does exist prior to the employees' retirement, it can be argued that it arises only when employees become eligible for the benefits. OPEB plans typically specify a minimum number of years of active service before the employees are eligible for the benefits. Vesting for these plans is "cliff" vesting because vesting occurs when the requirements are met. A liability would be recorded then and not gradually over a period of years.

The major differences between OPEBs and pensions are summarized in Exhibit 18-9, which focuses on healthcare benefits. While the beneficiary of a pension plan is generally the retired employee, OPEBs are usually provided to the retired employee, spouse, and dependents up to, say, age 21. The pension benefit is defined as a fixed dollar amount that is paid monthly. The OPEB, however, usually is not limited in amount because benefits are paid no matter how long or serious the illness, benefits are paid as used, and the amount of benefits varies geographically. Also, the amount is difficult to predict because of the incidence of new illnesses, such as AIDS, and the use of new treatments. Finally, pension plans are funded because of ERISA requirements, and the contributions are tax deductible. OPEBs, on the other hand, are generally not funded because there are no legal requirements and the contributions are *not* tax deductible.

---

**EXHIBIT 18-9**

**MAJOR DIFFERENCES BETWEEN POSTRETIREMENT HEALTHCARE BENEFITS AND PENSIONS**

| Item | Pensions | Healthcare |
|------|----------|------------|
| Beneficiary | Retired employee (some residual benefit to surviving spouse) | Retired employee, spouse, and dependents |
| Benefit | Defined, fixed dollar amount, paid monthly | Not limited, paid as used, varies geographically |
| Funding | Funding legally required and tax deductible | Usually not funded because not legally required and not tax deductible |

---

## Accounting Principles

*FASB Statement No. 106* requires that companies follow accounting principles for OPEBs that closely parallel those for pensions. (It is assumed that the reader has studied the discussion of accounting for pensions so that the explanation in this section may be simplified. Also, it may be helpful to review those principles as the OPEB principles are discussed.)

Two concepts also need to be understood. The **expected postretirement benefit obligation** (*EPBO*) is the actuarial present value on a particular date of the benefits expected to be paid under the terms of the postretirement benefit plan. The amount is measured based on the benefits that employees will receive after their expected retirement dates. In contrast, the **accumulated postretirement benefit obligation** (*APBO*) is the actuarial present value of the benefits attributed to employee service rendered to a specific date. Prior to an employee's full eligibility date, the APBO is the portion of the EPBO attributed to that employee's service rendered to that date; on or after the full eligibility date, the APBO and EPBO for an employee are the same. Thus, the difference between the EPBO and APBO is that the accumulated amount is based on benefits earned to date, whereas the expected amount is based on all benefits expected to be paid to employees. (In comparison, the difference between the projected and accumulated benefit obligation for pensions is the inclusion of expected salary increases in the projected amount.)

## OPEB Expense

The net postretirement benefit expense[24] includes the following components:

1.  **Service cost. The service cost is the actuarial present value of the expected postretirement benefit obligation attributed to services rendered by the employees during the current period.** Typically, OPEB benefits are provided on an all-or-nothing basis; that is, benefits are generally not defined in terms of years of service. Therefore, an equal amount of the expected benefits is attributed to each year of the attribution period (discussed later). The discount (interest) rate used to calculate the service cost is the rate of return on high-quality, fixed-income investments currently available, whose maturities match the expected timing of benefit payments.

2.  **Interest cost. The interest cost is the increase in the accumulated postretirement benefit obligation due to the passage of time.** Since the OPEB is a deferred compensation plan in which future payments are discounted to their present values, interest accrues due to the passage of time. Thus, the interest cost is the accumulated postretirement benefit obligation at the beginning of the period multiplied by the discount rate. The interest rate used to calculate the accumulated postretirement benefit obligation is the same rate as used for the service cost. The interest cost is added in the computation of the postretirement benefit expense.

3.  **Actual return on plan assets. The actual return on plan assets is the difference between the fair value of the plan assets at the end of the period and the fair value at the beginning of the period, adjusted for contributions by the company and payments of benefits to retired employees during the period.** If the plan assets earn a positive (negative) return, this amount is subtracted (added) in the computation of pension expense. Since OPEBs usually have *not* been funded, this component is not discussed further.

4.  **Amortization of unrecognized prior service cost.** The prior service cost is the increase (decrease) in the accumulated postretirement benefit obligation that results from plan amendments (and at the initiation of the plan) and that is not recognized in total in the period granted. **The unrecognized prior service cost is amortized by assigning an equal amount to each remaining year of service until full eligibility for benefits is reached for each plan participant active at the date of amendment.** If all or almost all of a plan's participants are fully eligible for benefits, the prior service cost is amortized based, instead, on the remaining life expectancy of those plan participants. Straight-line amortization over the average remaining years of service to full eligibility is also allowed for simplicity. The amortization amount is added (subtracted) in the computation of the postretirement benefit expense if the benefits are increased (decreased).

5.  **Gain or loss. The gain or loss includes two elements: (a) the difference between the actual return on plan assets and the expected return on plan assets, and (b) the net gain or loss recognized.** In our discussion, the first element of

---

24. The FASB prefers this term to the more commonly used term, OPEB, because other benefits such as layoff benefits may be paid after employment but before retirement.

the gain or loss is assumed to be zero because the plan is not funded. For the second element, gains and losses are changes in the amount of either the accumulated postretirement benefit obligation resulting from experience different from that assumed or from changes in assumptions. Gains and losses may be recognized in the periods in which they occur, or recognition may be delayed. If the company chooses to delay recognition, the amortization of any unrecognized net gain or loss is included in the postretirement benefit expense of a given year if, at the beginning of the year, the unrecognized net gain or loss exceeds 10% of the greater of the accumulated postretirement benefit obligation or the fair value of the plan assets. If amortization is required, the minimum amortization is the excess divided by the average remaining service period of active plan participants (or if most of the plan participants are retired, over their average remaining life expectancy). The total amount of any gain (loss) recognized is deducted (added) in the computation of the postretirement benefit expense.

6. **Recognition of the obligation or asset existing at the date of the initial adoption of the *Statement*.** The obligation is known as the **transition obligation.** The transition obligation is equal to the accumulated postretirement benefit obligation less the fair value of the plan assets. (Since the fair value of the plan assets is assumed to be zero, there would *not* be a transition *asset*.) The transition obligation is either recognized in full in the year in which the *Statement* is adopted as a cumulative effect adjustment due to a change in accounting principle, or recognition is delayed and the unrecognized transition obligation is amortized on a straight-line basis over the average remaining service life of active plan participants or 20 years, whichever is greater. The amount of the transition obligation recognized in any year is added in the computation of the postretirement benefit expense. (The amount of the transition obligation recognized may also be affected by certain complexities that are beyond the scope of the book.)

*Changes in accounting principles are discussed in Chapter 22.*

## OPEB Liability or Asset

The *Statement* also addresses the calculation of the OPEB liability or asset because the amount of the net postretirement benefit expense to date may be different than the amount funded to date. Since the plan is usually not funded, a liability, **prepaid/accrued postretirement benefit cost,** is increased each period by an amount equal to the expense. It is decreased by payments made to retired employees. However, in contrast to accounting for pensions, there is *no* provision for recognizing an **additional liability**.

## Transition

Adoption of the *Statement* was required for fiscal years beginning after December 15, 1992. Implementation may be delayed until fiscal years beginning after December 15, 1994 for non-public companies with 500 or fewer participants, and for plans that cover employees working outside the U.S.

## Disclosures

The *Statement* requires disclosures in the notes to the financial statements that are very similar to those for pensions. Two differences are discussed later.

## Settlements and Curtailments

The *Statement* deals with the accounting for settlements and curtailments of post-retirement benefit plans in substantially the same way as *FASB Statement No. 88.*

## Differences from Accounting for Pensions

It can be seen from the preceding discussion that the *Statement* requires accounting principles that closely parallel the accounting for pensions. The major differences are:

1. Although the attribution period is defined in the same way, the effect is different because the benefit formulas for most pension plans link benefits to years of service and salary levels. The result is that, for pension plans, the expected retirement date and date of full eligibility are the *same*. For many OPEBs, however, the benefit formula causes the two dates to be *different*. The attribution period for OPEBs generally begins with the date of hire (or the date on which credited service begins) and ends on the date the employee attains eligibility for full benefits. For example, for a plan which provides OPEBs to employees who render 15 years of service after age 35, the attribution (recognition) period is from 35 to 50 and, therefore, ceases prior to the retirement dates of the employees.

2. There is no provision for recognizing a minimum liability and the related intangible asset or reduction in stockholders' equity for OPEBs.

3. The interest component of the net postretirement benefit expense is based on the accumulated postretirement benefit obligation, whereas the interest component of the pension expense is based on the projected benefit obligation.

4. The *Statement* requires two disclosures not required for pensions: (a) the amortization (if any) of the transition obligation, and (b) the effect of a 1% increase in the healthcare cost trend rate on the measurement of the accumulated postretirement benefit obligation and on the combined service and interest cost components of the postretirement benefit expense.

## ILLUSTRATION OF ACCOUNTING FOR OPEBs

To illustrate the basic principles for OPEBs, the following simplified example is used. Assume that the Livingston Company adopts a healthcare plan for retired employees on January 1, 1995. At that time, the company has two employees and one retired employee, as shown in Exhibit 18-10. To determine eligibility for benefits, the company retroactively gives credit to the date of hire for each employee. Based on the information in the exhibit, the company makes the following two journal entries to record the OPEB items at December 31, 1995:

| | | |
|---|---|---|
| Postretirement Benefit Expense | 31,100 | |
| Accrued Postretirement Benefit Cost | | 31,100 |

The first entry records the expense for the year and, since the plan is not funded, the accompanying liability.

| | | |
|---|---|---|
| Accrued Postretirement Benefit Cost | 1,500 | |
| Cash | | 1,500 |

The second entry records the payment of retirement benefits.

## EXHIBIT 18-10

### LIVINGSTON COMPANY

**Accrual of Postretirement Healthcare Benefits**

*Basic Information*

The plan is not funded.
The discount rate is 10%.
All employees were hired at age 25.
All employees become eligible for full benefits at age 55.
Employee C was paid $1,500 postretirement healthcare benefits in 1995.
The company elects to use straight-line amortization for any unrecognized prior service cost.
Additional information on January 1, 1995:

| Employee | Status | Age | Expected Retirement Age | Expected Postretirement Benefit Obligation[a] | Accumulated Postretirement Benefit Obligation |
|---|---|---|---|---|---|
| A | Employee | 40 | 65 | $ 30,000 | $ 15,000[a] |
| B | Employee | 60 | 65 | 60,000 | 60,000[b] |
| C | Retired | 70 | — | 25,000 | 25,000[b] |
| | | | | $115,000 | $100,000[c] |

a. Actuarially determined at January 1, 1995.
b. Expected and accumulated postretirement benefit obligations are equal because employees are past the date for full eligibility, which occurred at age 55.
c. This amount is the unrecognized prior service cost.

*Computation of Postretirement Benefit Expense for 1995*

| | |
|---|---|
| 1. Service cost | $ 1,100[a] |
| 2. Interest cost | 10,000[b] |
| 3. Actual return on plan assets | 0 |
| 4. Amortization of unrecognized prior service cost | 20,000[c] |
| 5. Gain or loss | 0 |
| 6. Amortization of transition obligation | 0 |
| | $31,100 |

a. Actuarially determined. Note that there is no service cost for B and C because they have passed the date for full eligibility.
b. Accumulated postretirement benefit obligation at January 1, 1995 × Discount rate, or $100,000 × 10%.
c. $100,000 ÷ 5, or $20,000. Employees A, B, and C have 15, 0, and 0 years of remaining service to the full eligibility date (age 55), respectively. Therefore, the average remaining service period is 15 ÷ 3 = 5 years.
*Note:* If the company was changing from the cash to the accrual method, the accumulated postretirement benefit obligation of $100,000 would be the transition amount. The company could choose to recognize the amount immediately, or amortize it over 20 years.

## ACCOUNTING FOR OPEBs: AN EVALUATION

Since *FASB Statement No. 106* is based on accrual accounting, it might be expected that it would not be controversial. Instead, several aspects have been questioned by critics.

### Relevance and Reliability

It can easily be argued that accrual accounting is more *relevant* than cash basis accounting because costs are matched as expenses against revenues in the period in which the benefits are earned. For OPEBs, the benefits are earned while the employee is working, not when he or she is retired. Therefore, the *relevance* of the income statement is enhanced by inclusion of the OPEB expense. There is relatively little dispute about the nature of the obligation because of the similarity between the provisions of the *Statement* and the accounting for pensions.

Opposition did arise from corporations that must implement the requirements of the *Statement*. In particular, the measurement problems created considerable controversy. The biggest argument is that OPEB costs cannot be measured with sufficient *reliability* to offset the increased relevance because of the numerous assumptions about future events that are required. The measurement of the various amounts used in accounting for OPEBs is even more difficult than for pensions. For example, healthcare plans agree to pay for some or all of a service, the amount and cost of which are unknown, whereas pension payments are tied to more predictable variables of length of service and pay levels. Also, healthcare plans require an estimate of such items as the medical cost trend rate and marital and dependency status during retirement. Furthermore, because of the totally new information that is required, concern was expressed that the costs of implementation will be fairly high and may well exceed the benefits obtained. As a result of these concerns, the FASB included in the *Statement,* for the first time, an extensive discussion of the costs and benefits.

Those who favor the new principles argue that knowledge of these costs is essential for rational decision making by management and that accounting includes many estimates. Also, they argue that this OPEB cost information is useful for lending and investment decisions and that such decisions are never based on certainty. Therefore, it can be argued that it is better to record the information based on the best estimates and provide disclosures of the subjectivity of the amounts rather than to report only cash payments.

### Differences in Funding

As can be seen from the discussion, there are few differences between pension and OPEB accounting. However, there will be some differences in the practical impacts because the OPEB plans are generally not funded. Suppose, for example, that one company has an *unfunded* OPEB plan that is expected to provide exactly the same cash payments to retired employees as a *funded* pension plan of another company. The expense for the OPEB would be higher because the actual return on plan assets is not subtracted. This difference is appropriate because the company with the unfunded OPEB will have to pay more assets in the future, whereas the company with the pension plan has already paid the assets into a fund which is earning a return on those assets.

## Transition Liability

As discussed earlier, the transition liability may be recognized either immediately or prospectively over 20 years (or the average remaining service period of active plan participants, if greater). Some accountants argued that a period longer than 20 years should be used in order to reduce the impact on company income statements.

The *Statement* allows the use of a cumulative effect adjustment so that future earnings are not "penalized" because of the past use of cash basis accounting, which was the accounting principle at that time. In this case, the FASB decided that companies that could recognize the transition obligation immediately should be allowed to do so and should not be penalized because others cannot. Recognizing the benefit obligation as soon as possible and eliminating the impact on future income may be considered desirable by companies that have "strong" balance sheets. These transition rules are inconsistent with the usual FASB policy of requiring retroactive adjustment when a new accounting principle has been mandated, as discussed in Chapter 22. Also, they are inconsistent with the transition rules for pensions, which only allowed amortization, as discussed earlier in this chapter. However, *FASB Statement No. 87* required the adoption of a new accrual method instead of the existing accrual method, whereas *FASB Statement No. 106* requires the adoption of a new accrual method instead of the cash method.

Many accountants and users of financial statements have criticized the FASB's decision to allow two alternative transition methods. Very simply, the choice means that there will be a lack of comparability for 20 years between companies that adopt different alternatives.

## Attribution Period

**Attribution is the process of assigning the cost of postretirement benefits to periods of employee service.** The attribution period begins with the date of hire or the date that credit for service begins, and ends on the date that the employee is eligible for full benefits, as illustrated in Exhibit 18-11. Thus, the expected postretirement benefit obligation is attributed to the periods of employee service until the full eligibility date. However, the measurement of the accumulated postretirement benefit obligation at the full eligibility date is based on the benefits an employee is expected to receive and the expected retirement date (the expected postretirement benefit obligation). Thus, the attribution period (recognition) and the measurement period are different. Specifically, the period over which the service cost is recognized is based only on the period to full eligibility, whereas measurement of the service cost is based on the period beyond that date to the expected retirement date.

The decision that the attribution period ends on the date the employee attains full eligibility was adopted by the FASB because it more closely follows the implicit contract between the company and the employee. Since the employee service after the date of eligibility does not earn additional OPEB benefits, the FASB reasoned that the expenses should be fully recognized by then. However, it can be argued that this alternative follows legal form rather than economic substance because employers expect employees to render services up to the date of expected retirement rather than only up to the date of full eligibility for the benefits.

Others argue that the attribution period should end at the expected retirement date because the OPEB cost should be recognized over the entire employment period rather than recognizing only the interest cost after the date of eligibility.

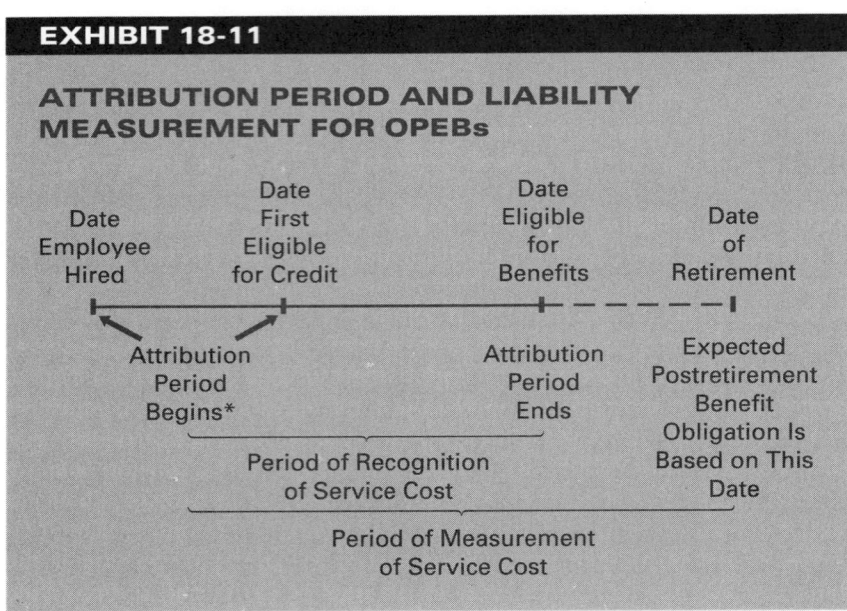

**EXHIBIT 18-11**

**ATTRIBUTION PERIOD AND LIABILITY MEASUREMENT FOR OPEBs**

\* Begins on either date depending on terms of agreement.

This argument is consistent with the fundamental exchange of retirement benefits for employee service. It follows that the use of this period is more consistent with the measurement of the expected postretirement benefit obligation, which is based on the expected retirement date. This alternative would also lower the annual expense and liability accrued, thereby reducing the impact on the financial statements.

Some accountants suggest that the prior service costs also should be amortized over the period to the expected retirement date just like attribution.

### Interaction with Deferred Income Taxes

As discussed in Chapter 17, recognizing a postretirement benefit expense for financial reporting without a related deduction for income tax reporting creates a temporary deductible difference. Indeed, OPEBs will be one of the primary causes of companies reporting deferred tax assets. The change in the deferred tax rules from *FASB Statement No. 96* to *FASB Statement No. 109,* which made it easier to recognize deferred tax assets, enables companies to recognize the full benefit of an asset (assuming realization is more likely than not).

### Minimum Liability

As discussed earlier, in contrast to the accounting for pensions, there is no requirement to recognize a minimum liability for OPEBs. The FASB decided that a minimum liability is not required because users can obtain sufficient information from disclosures in the notes to the financial statements. Also, it may be argued that the only liability is the difference between the expense and the funding if the company has no legal obligation to pay postretirement benefits. Therefore, recognition of the minimum liability would be inappropriate. Also, the corresponding intangible asset is conceptually questionable and may not be understood by users. However, it may also be argued that the difference between accounting for pensions and OPEBs is undesirable because the same concept is accounted for in the financial statements for pensions and by disclosure in the notes to the financial statements for OPEBs.

The requirement to recognize the minimum liability for pensions was based on the belief that most pension plans were adequately funded. The purpose of the minimum liability provision is to identify those relatively rare situations in which the plan is significantly underfunded. In contrast, virtually all OPEB plans are significantly underfunded, and recognition of a minimum liability would not serve to identify exceptions. Instead, information about the funded status is provided in the notes to the financial statements.

## Impacts of the Adoption of *FASB Statement No. 106*

Adoption of the *Statement* has had two basic effects. One is on the financial statements of companies, and the second *may* be on the retirement benefits offered by companies. As an indication of the effect on the financial statements of companies, IBM adopted the new principles in 1991 and reported a cost of $2.26 billion on its income statement and balance sheet. The loss reduced earnings per share by about $4 per share, and IBM recorded its first-ever quarterly loss. Note that there is no impact on cash flows. The cash flow statement includes only the cash payments to retired employees (unless funding of the plan occurs). The General Accounting Office has estimated that the total liabilities of all companies to their current and retired employees for retiree health benefits is $402 billion.

Although the accounting issues and their impacts on the financial statements are important, the effects of the *Statement* on benefit plans raise some difficult social issues. These effects are more difficult to evaluate since they involve management decisions that may be affected by the financial reporting. According to a recent study, about 65% of companies already have cut back on their coverage of retirees' healthcare benefits.[25] About 47% are increasing premium payments and 40% are making retirees bear more of their medical bills. For example, retirees of Texas Instruments will lose free coverage and Chrysler requires retirees to pay $100 or more yearly.

It may appear to be undesirable for companies to reduce benefits. However, it must be remembered that the *Statement* does not change the benefits promised to the retirees or the cost of the healthcare involved. Most people would argue that it is desirable to force companies realistically to face the costs of their promises and how much they can afford and, if necessary, to reduce the benefits now rather than face financial difficulty in the future because of an inability to pay costs that have not been recognized. However, any cost reductions by companies will raise the costs incurred by other entities, whether it be the individual retirees or the public through state and federal taxation.

It is also likely that companies will exert pressure on Congress to allow the funding of OPEB plans to be tax deductible, but they will probably not be successful in view of the current federal budget deficits. Some people may also argue that the principles will place U.S. companies at a competitive disadvantage with foreign companies.

A qualitative characteristic of accounting information is *neutrality*. Accounting information is not intended to either encourage or discourage particular decisions such as the offering of OPEBs, their funding, their tax deductibility, or their impacts on foreign trade. Instead, its purpose is to provide useful information for those types

---

25. *Business Week*, August 24, 1992, p. 39.

of decisions. Accrual accounting does not change the nature, extent, or cost, of the OPEB promise. However, it does require companies to report the effects of their commitments on the financial statements, and helps users understand the nature of the OPEB commitments and the ability of companies to fulfill their obligations.

There is a cost of implementing the accounting principles for OPEBs. Whether the benefits exceed the costs will, of course, never be known with certainty. However, the FASB, many accountants, many users of financial statements, and many company executives believe that they do.

## APPENDIX: ILLUSTRATION OF PRESENT VALUE CALCULATIONS FOR DEFINED BENEFIT PENSION PLANS

In the chapter, various situations related to defined benefit pension plans were illustrated in examples using assumed amounts. This illustration is provided to explain *how* the amounts of several key elements are computed. The example involves the application of *FASB Statement No. 87* for the Lonetree Company, which adopted a defined benefit pension plan on January 1, 1995. The following are the relevant facts:

| | |
|---|---|
| 1. Number of employees | 100 |
| 2. Years to retirement at December 31, 1995 | 30 |
| 3. Years of life expectancy after retirement | 18 |
| 4. Discount rate | 10% |
| 5. Benefit formula | Average of last 5 years' salary × Number of years of service × 0.02 |
| 6. Average of last 5 years' salary (based on expected salary levels) | $90,000 per employee |
| 7. Annual pension benefit earned each year of service by each employee | $90,000 × 0.02 = $1,800 |
| 8. Actual (and expected) rate of return on plan assets | 8% |
| 9. Amount funded each year | Equal to the annual service cost |
| 10. Date of computation of pension expense and pension funding | December 31 each year |

Note that, for simplicity of computations and explanations, it is assumed all employees are the same age, retire at the same time, and have the same life expectancy after retirement. Furthermore, it is assumed that there are no changes in actuarial assumptions and there are no differences between the expected and actual return on plan assets or between the expected and actual projected benefit obligation. The expected return on plan assets of 8% is less than the discount rate of 10% in order to create a liability at the time the pension expense is recorded and the contribution is made. The computations of the components of pension expense for the Lonetree Company are shown in Exhibit 18-12 (there is no gain or loss component). Each component of the expense is discussed in the following sections.

### Service Cost

The service cost per employee each year is the present value of the future pension benefits earned *that* year by each employee. Under *FASB Statement No. 87,* this cost

**EXHIBIT 18-12**

## LONETREE COMPANY

Computation of Pension Expense

| Date | Service Cost[a] | Projected Benefit Obligation[b] | Interest Cost[c] | Cash Payment[d] | Plan Assets[e] | Return on Plan Assets[f] | Amortization of Prior Service Cost[g] | Pension Expense[h] |
|---|---|---|---|---|---|---|---|---|
| 12/31/95 | $ 84,603 | $ 84,603 |  | $ 84,603 | $ 84,603 |  |  | $ 84,603 |
| 12/31/96 | 93,062 | 186,123 | $ 8,460 | 93,062 | 184,433 | $ 6,768 |  | 94,754 |
| 12/31/97 | 102,368 | 307,104 | 18,612 | 102,368 | 301,556 | 14,755 |  | 106,225 |
| 12/31/98 | 118,236 | 472,944 | 32,246 | 118,236 | 443,916 | 24,124 | $548 | 126,906 |
| 12/31/99 | 130,058 | 650,292 | 47,294 | 130,058 | 609,487 | 35,513 | 548 | 142,387 |

a. For current year. Annual benefits earned × present value of annuity for period of retirement × present value of $1 for remaining period of employment. In 1995, $180,000 × present value of annuity for 18 years at 10% × present value of $1 for 30 years at 10%. In each subsequent year, the present value of $1 factor is reduced by 1 year. In 1998, the annual benefits earned are increased to $189,000.

b. At end of year. Total benefits earned to date × present value of annuity for period of retirement × present value of $1 for remaining period of employment. In 1995, $180,000 × present value of annuity for 18 years at 10% × present value of $1 for 30 years at 10%. In each subsequent year, the benefits are increased by the service cost for that year and the present value of $1 factor is reduced by 1 year. In 1995, the benefits earned to date are increased by the prior service cost.

c. Projected benefit obligation at end of previous year × discount rate, or 10%. In 1995, beginning projected benefit obligation is $307,104 + $15,355 adjustment due to amendment providing increased benefits to date.

d. Assumed equal to the service cost.

e. Balance at end of previous year + return on plan assets + contributions − payments ($0 in this example).

f. Plan assets at the end of previous year × rate of return (8%), rounded.

g. Prior service cost ÷ average remaining service life of employees; $15,355 ÷ 28 years, rounded.

h. Service cost + interest cost − return on plan assets + amortization of prior service cost.

is computed using the benefit/years-of-service method. The computation of the service cost for the current year may be diagrammed as follows:

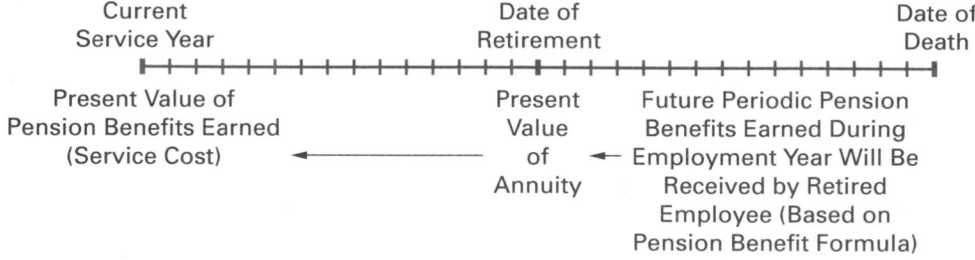

This diagram reads from right to left. Initially, the present value of the future periodic pension benefits earned during the current year is computed as of the date of the retirement, based on the pension benefit formula, the discount rate, and the retirement period (from the date of retirement to the date of death).[26] Then, this present value, as of the retirement date, is discounted back to the current year (based on the discount rate and the remaining years to the date of retirement) to determine the present value of the future pension benefits earned that year. This amount is the service cost for the current year. The equation for the calculation of the service cost is as follows:

$$\text{Service Cost} = \begin{array}{c}\textbf{Present Value of Future Pension Benefits}\\ \textbf{Earned by Employees in the Current Period}\end{array}$$

$$= \begin{array}{c}\textbf{Annual}\\ \textbf{Benefits}\\ \textbf{Earned}\end{array} \times \begin{array}{c}\textbf{Present Value of}\\ \textbf{Annuity for Period}\\ \textbf{of Retirement}\end{array} \times \begin{array}{c}\textbf{Present Value of \$1}\\ \textbf{for Remaining Period}\\ \textbf{of Employment}\end{array}$$

In our example, the future pension benefits earned for each year of service by each employee of the Lonetree Company under the benefit formula is \$1,800 (\$90,000 × 0.02), as calculated earlier. These benefits are earned by each of the 100 employees and therefore the company's service cost is based on the \$180,000 (\$1,800 × 100) of future pension benefits earned each year by the employees. These amounts are expected to be received each year by each employee during the 18 years of retirement.

At the end of 1995, the remaining period of employment is assumed to be 30 years. Therefore, the service cost in 1995 for the Lonetree Company is calculated based on the 10% discount rate, as follows:

$$1995 \text{ Service Cost} = \begin{array}{c}\textbf{Annual}\\ \textbf{Benefits}\\ \textbf{Earned}\end{array} \times \begin{array}{c}\textbf{Present Value of}\\ \textbf{Annuity for}\\ \textbf{18 Years at 10\%}\end{array} \times \begin{array}{c}\textbf{Present Value of \$1}\\ \textbf{for 30 Years at 10\%}\end{array}$$

$$= \$180,000 \times 8.201412 \times 0.057309$$

$$= \$84,603 \text{ (rounded)}$$

Each year, a similar calculation is made, but the remaining period of employment decreases. In 1996, the present value of \$1 factor for 29 years is used, and in 1997, for 28 years, and so on.[27] The amount of the service cost for each year resulting from this calculation process is summarized in the second column of Exhibit 18-12. Note that the progression in amounts arises because it has been assumed for simplicity that there is no turnover in the employees of the Lonetree Company. A typical company would have employees retiring each year and would be hiring new, younger employees, and the service cost might increase or decrease depending on the characteristics of the particular employees. Note that if the Lonetree Company had selected a discount rate of 8%, the service cost in 1995 would be \$167,643 (\$180,000 × 9.371887 × 0.099377).

### Interest on Projected Benefit Obligation

The projected benefit obligation is the actuarial present value, at a specified date, of all the benefits attributed by the pension benefit formula to employee service

---

26. The present value calculations in this Appendix use factors from the tables in Appendix D.
27. As discussed later, however, note that a change in the pension benefit formula in 1998 increases the annual benefits earned from \$180,000 to \$189,000. This change causes a corresponding increase (on a present value basis) in the service cost for 1998 and 1999.

rendered prior to that date. The computation of the projected benefit obligation at a particular date may be diagrammed as follows:

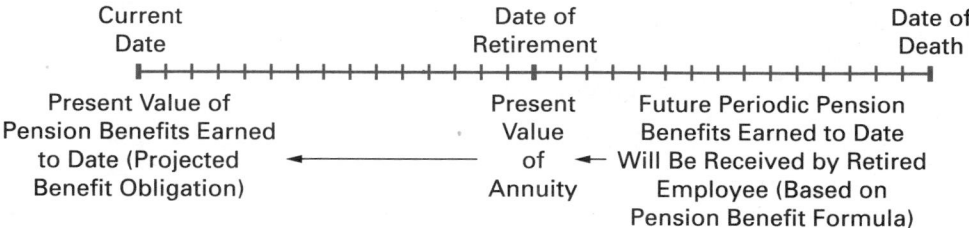

This diagram also reads from right to left. The present value of the future periodic pension benefits earned to date is computed as of the date of the retirement, based on the pension benefit formula, the discount rate, and the retirement period. Then, this present value, as of the retirement date, is discounted back to the current date (based on the discount rate and the remaining years to the date of retirement) to determine the present value of the future pension benefits earned to date. This amount is the projected benefit obligation on the current date. Note that this diagram is similar to the one illustrated for the service cost, except that it focuses on the projected pension benefits earned *to date*, while the service cost focuses on the future pension benefits earned *in a particular year*. There is a logical relationship between the two amounts, however, because the projected benefit obligation is the sum of the service costs to date (giving consideration to interest due to the passage of time and assuming there are no prior service costs and no employees have retired). The equation for the calculation of the projected benefit obligation is as follows:

$$\begin{matrix}\text{Projected Benefit} \\ \text{Obligation}\end{matrix} = \begin{matrix}\text{Present Value of Future Pension Benefits Earned by} \\ \text{Employees to Date (based on expected salary levels)}\end{matrix}$$

$$= \begin{matrix}\text{Total} \\ \text{Benefits} \\ \text{Earned}\end{matrix} \times \begin{matrix}\text{Present Value of} \\ \text{Annuity for Period} \\ \text{of Retirement}\end{matrix} \times \begin{matrix}\text{Present Value of \$1} \\ \text{for Remaining Period} \\ \text{of Employment}\end{matrix}$$

In our example, at December 31, 1995, the employees have earned pension benefits for *one* year ($90,000 × 1 × 0.02 × 100 employees, or $180,000) and, therefore, the projected benefit obligation is calculated as follows:

$$\begin{matrix}\text{12/31/95} \\ \text{Projected Benefit} \\ \text{Obligation}\end{matrix} = \begin{matrix}\text{Total} \\ \text{Benefits} \\ \text{Earned}\end{matrix} \times \begin{matrix}\text{Present Value of} \\ \text{Annuity for Period} \\ \text{of Retirement}\end{matrix} \times \begin{matrix}\text{Present Value of \$1} \\ \text{for Remaining Period} \\ \text{of Employment}\end{matrix}$$

$$= \begin{matrix}\text{Total} \\ \text{Benefits} \\ \text{Earned}\end{matrix} \times \begin{matrix}\text{Present Value of} \\ \text{Annuity for} \\ \text{18 Years at 10\%}\end{matrix} \times \begin{matrix}\text{Present Value of \$1} \\ \text{for 30 Years at 10\%}\end{matrix}$$

$$= \$180,000 \times 8.201412 \times 0.057309$$

$$= \$84,603 \text{ (rounded)}$$

At December 31, 1996, the employees have earned pension benefits for *two* years ($90,000 × 2 × 0.02 × 100 employees, or $360,000) and, therefore, the projected benefit obligation is:

$$
\begin{array}{l}
\text{12/31/96} \\
\text{Projected Benefit} \\
\text{Obligation}
\end{array}
= \$360,000 \times
\begin{array}{c}
\text{Present Value of} \\
\text{Annuity for 18} \\
\text{Years at 10\%}
\end{array}
\times
\begin{array}{c}
\text{Present Value of \$1} \\
\text{for 29 Years at 10\%}
\end{array}
$$

$$= \$360,000 \times 8.201412 \times 0.063039$$

$$= \$186,123 \text{ (rounded)}$$

The amount of the projected benefit obligation at the end of each year is shown in the third column of Exhibit 18-12. To determine its pension expense for each year, the Lonetree Company must include the interest cost on the projected benefit obligation. This interest cost is computed by multiplying the projected benefit obligation at the *beginning* of the year by the 10% discount rate, as illustrated in the fourth column of Exhibit 18-12. Thus, in 1995, there is no interest cost included in pension expense because there was no projected benefit obligation at the beginning of the year. In 1996, the interest cost is $8,460 ($84,603 × 0.10), and this amount is included in pension expense.[28] Note that if any retired employees had died unexpectedly during the year, the projected benefit obligation would be decreased by the total remaining benefits that were lost by each deceased employee.

### Actual Return on Plan Assets

The funding of a pension plan must be within the guidelines of ERISA. Since those rules are beyond the scope of the book, in this example, we assume that the company funds an amount each year that is equal to the service cost. We also assume that the annual contribution is made on December 31 of each year. Therefore, the company makes its first payment of $84,603 to the plan on December 31, 1995, and this amount is invested in plan assets, such as bonds, stocks, and real estate. The annual contribution is shown in the fifth column of Exhibit 18-12.

To determine its pension expense for each year, the Lonetree Company must *subtract* the actual return on its plan assets for that year. In 1995, no return was earned on the plan assets because the contribution was not made until the end of the year. In 1996, the company earns an actual return based on the plan assets available at the beginning of the year and held during the year. Thus, if we assume that the plan assets earn 8% per year, the return earned in 1996 is $6,768 ($84,603 × 0.08, rounded). This amount *increases* the plan assets and *decreases* the 1996 pension expense. Therefore, on December 31, 1996 (before the contribution for 1996), the total assets are $91,371 ($84,603 + $6,768). The contribution of $93,062 on that date increases the plan assets to $184,433. During 1997, the assets earn $14,755 ($184,433 × 0.08), which is added to the plan assets and deducted from the 1997 pension expense. As a result, the total plan assets on December 31, 1997, after the contribution for 1997, are $301,556 ($184,433 + $14,755 + contribution for 1997 of $102,368). The plan assets and return on plan assets for each year are shown in the sixth and seventh columns, respectively, of Exhibit 18-12. Note that if any

---

28. As discussed later, however, note that an amendment to the pension benefit formula in 1998 causes an increase in the projected benefit obligation. This change causes a corresponding increase in interest cost.

employees had retired, the plan assets would be reduced each year by the payments made to the retired employees.

## Amortization of Unrecognized Prior Service Cost

Prior service cost is the cost of retroactive additional benefits granted in a plan amendment or at the initial adoption of the plan. The cost causes an increase in the projected benefit obligation, and the unrecognized prior service cost is amortized as a component of pension expense in subsequent years. To illustrate the computation of the prior service cost, assume that on January 1, 1998, the Lonetree Company changes the factor in the benefit formula from 0.02 to 0.021, retroactive to the adoption of the plan. This action creates additional pension benefits for each employee that are calculated as follows:

$$\begin{array}{l} \text{Additional Benefits} \\ \text{per Employee} \end{array} = \begin{array}{l} \text{Average of Last} \\ \text{5 Years' Salary} \end{array} \times \begin{array}{l} \text{Number of Years} \\ \text{of Service to Date} \end{array} \times \begin{array}{l} \text{Change in} \\ \text{Formula} \end{array}$$

$$= \$90,000 \times 3 \times 0.001$$

$$= \$270$$

Since the Lonetree Company has 100 employees, the total additional benefits assigned to the employees is $27,000 ($270 × 100 employees). The prior service cost is the present value of those additional benefits, calculated as follows:

$$\text{Prior Service Cost} = \begin{array}{l} \text{Present Value of Additional Pension} \\ \text{Benefits Granted by Plan Amendment} \end{array}$$

$$= \begin{array}{l} \text{Additional} \\ \text{Benefits} \end{array} \times \begin{array}{l} \text{Present Value of} \\ \text{Annuity for Period} \\ \text{of Retirement} \end{array} \times \begin{array}{l} \text{Present Value of \$1} \\ \text{for Remaining Period} \\ \text{of Employment} \end{array}$$

Recall that the life expectancy during retirement is assumed to be 18 years and, at the *beginning* of 1998, the remaining period of employment is 28 years. Therefore, the prior service cost for the Lonetree Company is calculated as follows:

$$\text{Prior Service Cost} = \begin{array}{l} \text{Additional} \\ \text{Benefits} \end{array} \times \begin{array}{l} \text{Present Value of} \\ \text{Annuity for} \\ \text{18 Years at 10\%} \end{array} \times \begin{array}{l} \text{Present Value of \$1} \\ \text{for 28 Years at 10\%} \end{array}$$

$$= \$27,000 \times 8.201412 \times 0.069343$$

$$= \$15,355 \text{ (rounded)}$$

The $15,355 unrecognized prior service cost is amortized as an element of pension expense in the current and future years. The Lonetree Company amortizes its unrecognized prior service cost over the average remaining service life of its employees. Thus, the amortization in each year is $548 ($15,355 ÷ 28, rounded). This amount for each year is shown in the eighth column of Exhibit 18-12.

### Adjustments of Service Cost and Projected Benefit Obligation

The amendment of the pension benefit formula at the beginning of 1998 causes not only an unrecognized prior service cost, but also an increase in the projected benefit obligation and the service cost of the current and future years. The increase in the service cost causes an increase in pension expense. The increase in the projected benefit obligation also causes an increase in pension expense due to the additional interest cost. Since the company continues to fund an amount equal to the annual service cost, there is no change in the plan assets at the beginning of 1998.

The service cost in 1998 and 1999 shown in Exhibit 18-12 is based on annual benefits earned of $189,000 ($90,000 × 0.021 × 100 employees), instead of $180,000. Thus, the 1998 service cost is computed as follows:

$$\text{1998 Service Cost} = \begin{array}{c}\text{Annual}\\\text{Benefits}\\\text{Earned}\end{array} \times \begin{array}{c}\text{Present Value of}\\\text{Annuity for}\\\text{18 Years at 10\%}\end{array} \times \begin{array}{c}\text{Present Value of \$1}\\\text{for 27 Years at 10\%}\end{array}$$

$$= \$189,000 \times 8.201412 \times 0.076278$$

$$= \$118,236 \text{ (rounded)}$$

A similar calculation is made in 1999 to determine the $130,058 service cost.

The present value of the additional benefits granted must also be included in the projected benefit obligation. Since the amendment occurred on January 1, 1998, the $307,104 projected benefit obligation on December 31, 1997 in Exhibit 18-12 has not been adjusted because it is based upon the benefit formula at that time. The 1998 interest cost calculation, however, is based on the adjusted January 1, 1998 projected benefit obligation, which amounts to $322,459 ($307,104 + $15,355 prior service cost). Thus, the 1998 interest cost is $32,246 ($322,459 × 0.10).

The December 31, 1998 projected benefit obligation is based on the total benefits earned to date (after the amendment) and is calculated as follows:

$$\begin{array}{c}\text{Total}\\\text{Benefits}\\\text{Earned}\end{array} = \$90,000 \times \begin{array}{c}\text{Number of Years}\\\text{of Service}\end{array} \times 0.021 \times 100 \text{ Employees}$$

$$= \$90,000 \times 4 \times 0.021 \times 100$$

$$= \$756,000$$

$$\begin{array}{c}\text{Projected}\\\text{Benefit}\\\text{Obligation}\end{array} = \begin{array}{c}\text{Total}\\\text{Benefits}\\\text{Earned}\end{array} \times \begin{array}{c}\text{Present Value of}\\\text{Annuity for Period}\\\text{of Retirement}\end{array} \times \begin{array}{c}\text{Present Value of \$1}\\\text{for Remaining Period}\\\text{of Employment}\end{array}$$

$$= \$756,000 \times \begin{array}{c}\text{Present Value of Annuity}\\\text{for 18 Years at 10\%}\end{array} \times \begin{array}{c}\text{Present Value of \$1}\\\text{for 27 Years at 10\%}\end{array}$$

$$= \$756,000 \times 8.201412 \times 0.076278$$

$$= \$472,944 \text{ (rounded)}$$

A similar calculation is made the next year to determine the projected benefit obligation on December 31, 1999 of $650,292.

## Pension Expense and Liability

The pension expense each year for the Lonetree Company is the service cost, plus the interest on the projected benefit obligation, minus the actual return on plan assets, plus the amortization of the unrecognized prior service cost. (The gain or loss component does not arise in this example.) Any difference between the amount of the pension expense and the amount funded is recorded as a prepaid/accrued pension cost liability or asset. The pension expense and amounts funded for the Lonetree Company are shown in the ninth and fifth columns, respectively, of Exhibit 18-12. The journal entry to record the pension expense on December 31, 1995 is as follows:

| | | |
|---|---|---|
| Pension Expense | 84,603 | |
| Cash | | 84,603 |

The journal entry to record the pension expense on December 31, 1996 is as follows:

| | | |
|---|---|---|
| Pension Expense | 94,754 | |
| Cash | | 93,062 |
| Prepaid/Accrued Pension Cost | | 1,692 |

A similar journal entry is made at the end of each succeeding year, and each year the debit to Pension Expense is greater than the credit to Cash. As a result, the pension liability account balance at the end of each year increases as follows:

**Prepaid/Accrued Pension Cost (Liability)**

| | |
|---|---|
| 12/31/95 | $ 0 ($84,603 − $84,603) |
| 12/31/96 | 1,692 ($0 + $94,754 − $93,062) |
| 12/31/97 | 5,549 ($1,692 + $106,225 − $102,368) |
| 12/31/98 | 14,219 ($5,549 + $126,906 − $118,236) |
| 12/31/99 | 26,548 ($14,219 + $142,387 − $130,058) |

In addition to the Prepaid/Accrued Pension Cost, the Lonetree Company must determine whether an additional liability needs to be recorded at the end of each year. This depends on whether an unfunded accumulated benefit obligation exists. Recall that an unfunded accumulated benefit obligation exists when the *accumulated* benefit obligation is greater than the fair value of the plan assets at the end of each year. An additional liability is recognized when this unfunded accumulated benefit obligation exceeds the Prepaid/Accrued Pension Cost liability to date.

To determine if the Lonetree Company must recognize an additional liability in each year, it is necessary first to compute the accumulated benefit obligation at the end of the year. This calculation is made in exactly the same manner as the projected benefit obligation except that future pay increases are *not* included. Instead, the accumulated benefit obligation is based on the *current* salary level. None of the annual calculations are shown here because the accumulated benefit obligation at the end of each year based on current salary levels is assumed not to be greater than the fair value of the plan assets. Thus, an unfunded accumulated benefit obligation does not exist, and there is no additional liability in this example. Generally, an additional liability is recognized only in situations where a company has a large unrecognized prior service cost or has experienced substantial losses in the investment of its plan assets.

## QUESTIONS

*Q18-1* What is a pension plan? Explain how yearly income of retired employees is determined under a defined benefit pension plan.

*Q18-2* Distinguish between a defined benefit pension plan and a defined contribution pension plan.

*Q18-3* Distinguish between funded and unfunded pension plans; between contributory and noncontributory pension plans.

*Q18-4* What is service cost? How does this differ from prior service cost?

*Q18-5* Define *projected benefit obligation*. How does this differ from an accumulated benefit obligation?

*Q18-6* In regard to pension plans, define *assumptions*. What is the relationship between a gain or loss and an assumption?

*Q18-7* List and briefly define the five components of pension expense according to *FASB Statement No. 87*.

*Q18-8* What is an accrued pension cost liability and when does it arise? What is a prepaid pension cost asset and when does it arise?

*Q18-9* When is an additional pension liability recorded for a pension plan?

*Q18-10* List the additional disclosures a company must make for its defined benefit pension plan in accordance with *FASB Statement No. 87*.

*Q18-11* List the conceptual issues of importance in regard to pension expense.

*Q18-12* List the conceptual issues of importance in regard to pension liabilities and pension assets.

*Q18-13* List and define the potential components of pension expense.

*Q18-14* What are the three different viewpoints for attributing pension expense in an accounting period?

*Q18-15* Briefly explain the two groups of attribution approaches to allocate pension cost to years of service. List the approaches included in each group.

*Q18-16* Conceptually, what are the four possible alternative methods for accounting for the prior service cost that arises from pension plan modifications?

*Q18-17* What are the five possible alternative methods of determining the extent of a company's pension plan liability?

*Q18-18* What is a defined contribution pension plan and what are the related accounting principles?

*Q18-19* What must be included in the annual financial statements issued by a funding agency?

*Q18-20* What is a pension plan settlement? Curtailment? How should the net gain or loss from a settlement or curtailment be accounted for by a company according to *FASB Statement No. 88*?

*Q18-21* What are other postemployment benefits? How are they distinguished from postretirement benefits?

*Q18-22* List and briefly define the six components of OPEB expense according to *FASB Statement No. 106*.

# CASES

## C18-1 Financial Reporting for a Defined Benefit Pension Plan

The Fink Company is considering establishing a defined benefit pension plan for its employees. The president of Fink Company is slightly familiar with *FASB Statement No. 87* and understands that accounting for a defined benefit pension plan may result in certain items being included in the financial statements of the sponsoring company. The president has come to you for help in better understanding these items.

### Required
List each item, summarize how it is calculated, and briefly explain its meaning.

## C18-2 Additional Pension Liability

The development of *FASB Statement No. 87* took many years and included compromises among competing arguments. One of the areas of compromise was the additional pension liability.

### Required
Explain how the additional pension liability is calculated and describe any aspects that might be considered to be the result of compromises.

## C18-3 Income Smoothing

Generally, accounting principles do not support the concept of income smoothing (the avoidance of year-to-year fluctuations in the amount of income). A friend of yours, however, after studying *FASB Statement No. 87*, claims, "Pension accounting includes income smoothing."

### Required
Describe the methods by which *FASB Statement No. 87* avoids year-to-year fluctuations in the amount of pension expense.

## C18-4 Pension Cost Components

Carson Company sponsors a single-employer defined benefit pension plan. The plan provides that pension benefits are determined by age, years of service, and compensation. Among the components that should be included in the net pension cost recognized for a period are service cost, interest cost, and actual return on plan assets.

### Required
1. What two accounting issues result from the nature of the defined benefit pension plan? Why do these issues arise?
2. How should Carson determine the service cost component of the net pension cost?
3. How should Carson determine the interest cost component of the net pension cost?
4. How should Carson determine the actual return on plan assets component of the net pension cost? (*AICPA adapted*)

## C18-5 Pension and Future Vacation Costs

Essex Company has a single-employer defined benefit pension plan, and a compensation plan for future vacations for its employees.

**Required**

1. Define the interest cost component of net pension cost for a period. How should Essex determine its interest cost component of net pension cost for a period?
2. Define prior service cost. How should Essex account for prior service cost? Why?
3. What conditions must be met for Essex to accrue compensation for future vacations? What is the theoretical rationale for accruing compensation for future vacations? (*AICPA adapted*)

## C18-6 *Conceptual Issues*

In the chapter, the conceptual issues related to pension expense, pension liabilities, and pension plan assets are discussed.

**Required**

Explain how each of these three conceptual issues is resolved by *FASB Statement No. 87*.

## C18-7 *Other Postemployment Benefits*

Companies often provide their employees with postemployment benefits other than pensions. These benefits may include health insurance, life insurance, and disability benefits.

**Required**

How is the accounting for these other postemployment benefits similar or dissimilar to accounting for pensions?

## C18-8 *Pension Issues*

The MacAdams Company had engaged in large amounts of R&D to develop a new product that would put the company ahead of the Japanese competition. As a result, the company's profits were severely reduced and the president was concerned about the possibility of a takeover by a European competitor. The president was discussing the situation with the controller and said, "Your accounting principles make me so mad. Here we are working hard to develop a product to beat the rest of the world and you won't let me treat any of those costs as an asset."

The controller replied, "I understand your frustration. And please remember they are not 'my' principles."

"I know," responded the president. "Do you have any suggestions?"

"Well," the controller replied, "one easy way to increase our profits would be for the Board of Directors to vote to increase the discount rate used for computing the present values and to increase the expected rate of return on plan assets. Both of those would have the effect of reducing the pension expense."

"Great idea. I will have to remember that when it is time for the year-end bonuses."

**Required**

Evaluate the controller's suggestion.

## C18-9 *OPEB Issues*

"Will it cost your company your company? Ready for one of the most difficult challenges ever to confront corporate America? One that is estimated to cost up to $400 billion. New FASB regulations will force companies to measure and post as a debit their health expense obligation to current and *future* retirees.... we'll help you minimize the financial impact of these regulations and still enable you to remain responsive to the benefit needs of employees." (Excerpts from an advertisement by CIGNA, a large insurance company.)

"Forget about retiring with all-expenses-paid health care from your employer. About 65% of U.S. companies have reduced benefits. Some have asked retirees to pay more of the costs, while others have eliminated the plans altogether. Blame soaring medical expenses and a new accounting rule that requires companies to post long-term retiree medical benefits as liabilities on their balance sheets." (Adapted from *Business Week*, August 24, 1992, p. 39.)

**Required**

1. Critically evaluate the content of the advertisement.
2. Explain why companies may reduce benefits when they adopt *FASB Statement No. 106*.

## C18-10 *OPEBs and Deferred Income Taxes*

The following information is for the Dermer Company's OPEB plan, which was adopted on January 1, 1995:

| | |
|---|---|
| Service cost, 1995 | $100,000 |
| Interest cost, 1995 | 20,000 |
| Unrecognized prior service cost, 1/1/95 | 300,000 |
| Benefits paid to employees, 1995 | 18,000 |
| Pretax accounting income and taxable income for 1995 before any deductions for OPEB costs | 500,000 |
| Average remaining service period | 12 years |
| Enacted tax rate for 1995 | 30% |
| Enacted tax rate for 1996 and beyond | 35% |
| Any deferred tax assets are more likely than not to be realized | |

**Required**

1. a. Prepare the journal entries to record the OPEB expense and payments for 1995.
   b. Prepare the income tax journal entry for 1995.
2. a. Assume instead that the $300,000 was the accumulated postretirement benefit obligation at the date of adoption of *FASB Statement No. 106*, instead of the unrecognized prior service cost. Prepare the journal entries to record the OPEB expense and payments for 1995 if the company uses the maximum period for the amortization of the transition liability and adopted the *Statement* on January 1, 1993.
   b. Prepare the income tax journal entry for 1995.

c. What is the balance of the deferred tax asset at December 31, 1995 if it is assumed that in each year since 1993, pretax accounting income and taxable income before any deductions for OPEB costs have been $500,000? Also assume that each year, the OPEB expense and payments were the same as in 1995.

3. a. Assume instead that the $300,000 accumulated postretirement benefit obligation was recognized as a cumulative effect. Prepare the journal entries to record the activities related to the OPEB for 1995 if the *Statement* was adopted on January 1, 1993.

   b. Prepare the income tax journal entry for 1995.

   c. What is the balance of the deferred tax asset at December 31, 1995 if it is assumed that in each year since 1993, pretax accounting income and taxable income before any deductions for OPEB costs have been $500,000? Also assume that each year the OPEB expense (before including the cumulative effect adjustment) and payments were the same as in 1995.

## MULTIPLE CHOICE

*Select the best answer for each of the following.*

M18-1   The actuarial present value of all the benefits attributed by the pension benefit formula to employee service rendered before a specified date based on expected future compensation levels is the
   a. Projected benefit obligation
   b. Prior service cost
   c. Service cost
   d. Accumulated benefit obligation

Items 2, 3, and 4 are based on the following information:

Spath Company adopted a noncontributory defined benefit pension plan on January 1, 1995. Spath Company uses the benefit/years-of-service method, which results in the following information:

|  | 1995 | 1996 |
|---|---|---|
| Service cost | $300,000 | $450,000 |
| Amount funded | 240,000 | 390,000 |
| Discount rate | 10% | 10% |
| Actual rate of return | 10% | 10% |

The fair value of the plan assets at the end of each year exceeded the accumulated benefit obligation.

M18-2   What is the balance of the accrued pension cost as of December 31?

|  | 1995 | 1996 |
|---|---|---|
| a. | $    0 | $ 60,000 |
| b. | $60,000 | $ 60,000 |
| c. | $60,000 | $ 66,000 |
| d. | $60,000 | $126,000 |

M18-3   What is the pension expense for the year ended December 31, 1996?
   a. $390,000
   b. $426,000
   c. $456,000
   d. $480,000

M18-4   As of December 31, 1996, what is the balance in the pension plan asset fund?
   a. $456,000
   b. $630,000
   c. $654,000
   d. $840,000

M18-5   Which of the following is not a component of pension expense?
   a. Amount funded
   b. Service cost
   c. Actual return on plan assets
   d. Interest cost

**M18-6** Davison Company has a noncontributory defined benefit pension plan for its employees. During 1995, the pension plan has a discount rate of 8%, service cost of $98,000, plan assets as of 1/1/95 of $432,000, and an actual return on plan assets of $34,560. On December 31, 1995, the company contributed $90,000 to the pension plan, resulting in a credit to Prepaid/Accrued Pension Cost of $6,300. What is the amount of the projected benefit obligation on January 1, 1995?

a. $332,000      c. $410,750
b. $345,600      d. $432,000

**M18-7** On January 1, 1995, the Soloman Company changes the factor in the benefit formula from 0.02 to 0.022, retroactive to the adoption of the plan. The amendment will result in a(an)

a. Decrease in projected benefit obligation      c. Decrease in pension expense
b. Increase in service cost      d. Increase in plan assets

**M18-8** The McCollum Company amended its noncontributory defined benefit pension plan at the beginning of 1995. The unrecognized prior service cost related to this amendment amounts to $240,000. Information regarding the four participating employees is as follows:

| Employee | Expected to Retire After |
|----------|--------------------------|
| A | Year 1 |
| B | Year 2 |
| C | Year 4 |
| D | Year 5 |

Using the straight-line method, what is the amount of unrecognized prior service cost to be amortized in 1998?

a. $0      c. $60,000
b. $40,000      d. $80,000

**M18-9** *FASB Statement No. 88* requires that a company record a loss and a liability for termination benefits to paid employees when

a. The employee accepts the offer
b. The amount can be reasonably estimated
c. The employee accepts the offer or the amount can be reasonably estimated
d. The employee accepts the offer and the amount can be reasonably estimated

**M18-10** *FASB Statement No. 87* requires a company with a defined benefit pension plan to make all of the following disclosures except

a. The amount of the pension expense showing each of the components separately
b. The estimates of future contributions
c. A schedule reconciling the funded status of the plan
d. A description of the plan

## EXERCISES

**E18-1** *Pension Expense* The Bailey Company has had a defined benefit pension plan for several years. At the end of 1995, the company's actuary provided the following information for 1995 regarding the pension plan: (1) service cost, $115,000; (2) actual return on plan assets, $14,000; (3) amortization of unrecognized net loss, $2,000; (4) interest cost on projected benefit obligation, $16,000; and (5) amortization of unrecognized prior service cost, $4,000. The company decides to fund an amount at the end of 1995 equal to its pension expense.

**Required**
Compute the amount of Bailey Company's pension expense for 1995 and prepare the related journal entry.

*E18-2    Pension Expense*   On December 31, 1995 the Robey Company accumulated the following information for 1995 in regard to its defined benefit pension plan:

| | |
|---|---|
| Service cost | $100,000 |
| Interest cost on projected benefit obligation | 12,000 |
| Actual return on plan assets | 11,000 |
| Amortization of unrecognized prior service cost | 3,000 |
| Amortization of unrecognized net gain | 1,000 |

On its December 31, 1994 balance sheet, the company had reported a prepaid/accrued pension cost liability of $14,000.

**Required**

1. Compute the amount of Robey Company's pension expense for 1995.
2. Prepare the journal entry to record Robey's 1995 pension expense if it funds the pension plan in the amount of: (a) $103,000, (b) $100,000, and (c) $108,000.

*E18-3    Interest Cost and Return on Assets*   On December 31, 1995 the Palmer Company determined that the 1995 service cost on its defined benefit pension plan was $120,000. At the beginning of 1995, Palmer Company had pension plan assets of $520,000 and a projected benefit obligation of $600,000. Its discount rate (and actual rate of return on plan assets) for 1995 was 10%. There are no other components of Palmer Company's pension expense; the company had a prepaid/accrued pension cost liability at the end of 1994.

**Required**

1. Compute the amount of Palmer Company's pension expense for 1995.
2. Prepare the journal entry to record Palmer's 1995 pension expense if it funds the pension plan in the amount of: (a) $128,000, and (b) $120,000.

*E18-4    Pension Expense Different Than Funding: One Year*   The Verna Company has had a defined benefit pension plan for several years. At the end of 1995, the company accumulated the following information: (1) service cost for 1995, $127,000; (2) projected benefit obligation, 1/1/1995, $634,000; (3) discount rate, 9%; (4) plan assets, 1/1/1995, $589,000; and (5) actual rate of return on plan assets, 9%. There are no other components of Verna Company's pension expense; the company had a prepaid/accrued pension cost liability at the end of 1994. The company contributed $128,000 to the pension plan at the end of 1995.

**Required**

Compute the amount of Verna Company's pension expense for 1995 and prepare the related journal entry.

*E18-5    Pension Expense Different Than Funding: Multiple Years*   Baron Company adopted a defined benefit pension plan on January 1, 1994. The following information pertains to the pension plan for 1995 and 1996:

| | **1995** | **1996** |
|---|---|---|
| Service cost | $150,000 | $172,000 |
| Projected benefit obligation (1/1) | 120,000 | 279,600 |
| Plan assets (1/1) | 120,000 | 269,600 |
| Company contribution (funded 12/31) | 140,000 | 160,000 |
| Discount rate | 8% | 8% |
| Actual rate of return on plan assets | 8% | 8% |

There are no other components of Baron Company's pension expense.

**Required**

1. Compute the amount of Baron Company's pension expense for 1995 and 1996.
2. Prepare the journal entries to record the pension expense for 1995 and 1996.

*E18-6    Determination of Projected Benefit Obligation*   Several years ago, the Hazelrigg Company established a defined benefit pension plan for its employees. The following information is available for 1995 in regard to its pension plan: (1) discount rate, 10%; (2) service cost, $142,000; (3) plan assets (1/1), $659,000; and (4) actual return on plan assets, $65,900. There is no amortization of unrecognized prior service cost and there is no gain or loss. On December 31, 1995, the company contributed $140,000 to the pension plan, resulting in a credit to Prepaid/Accrued Pension Cost of $8,200.

**Required**

Compute the amount of Hazelrigg Company's projected benefit obligation on January 1, 1995.

**E18-7** *Pension Expense Different Than Funding: Multiple Years* Carli Company adopted a defined benefit pension plan on January 1, 1994, and funded the entire amount of its 1994 pension expense. The following information pertains to the pension plan for 1995 and 1996:

|  | 1995 | 1996 |
|---|---|---|
| Service cost | $200,000 | $215,000 |
| Projected benefit obligation (1/1) | 180,000 | 396,200 |
| Plan assets (1/1) | 180,000 | 406,400 |
| Company contribution (funded 12/31) | 212,000 | 220,000 |
| Discount rate | 9% | 9% |
| Actual (and expected) rate of return on plan assets | 8% | 8% |

There are no other components of Carli Company's pension expense.

**Required**

1. Compute the amount of Carli Company's pension expense for 1995 and 1996.
2. Prepare the journal entries to record the pension expense for 1995 and 1996.

**E18-8** *Unrecognized Prior Service Cost* On January 1, 1995, the Smith Company adopted a defined benefit pension plan. At that time, the company awarded retroactive benefits to its employees, resulting in an unrecognized prior service cost that created a projected benefit obligation of $1,250,000 on that date. The company decided to amortize the unrecognized prior service cost by the straight-line method over the 25-year average remaining service life of its active participating employees. The company's actuary has also provided the following additional information for 1995 and 1996: (1) Service cost: 1995, $147,000; 1996, $153,000; (2) actual return on plan assets: 1996, $34,000; and (3) projected benefit obligation: 1/1/1996, $1,522,000. The discount rate was 10% in both 1995 and 1996. The company contributed $340,000 and $350,000 to the pension fund at the end of 1995 and 1996, respectively. There are no other components of Smith Company's pension expense; disregard any additional pension liability.

**Required**

1. Compute the amount of Smith Company's pension expense for 1995 and 1996.
2. Prepare the journal entries to record the pension expense for 1995 and 1996.

**E18-9** *Straight-Line Amortization* At the beginning of 1995, the Brent Company amended its defined benefit pension plan. The amendment entitled five active participating employees to receive increased future benefits based on their prior service. The company's actuary determined that the unrecognized prior service cost for this amendment amounts to $300,000. Employee A is expected to retire after 1 year, employee B after 2, employee C after 3, employee D after 4, and employee E after 5 years.

**Required**

Using the straight-line method, (1) compute the average remaining service life, and (2) prepare a schedule to amortize the unrecognized prior service cost.

**E18-10** *Years-of-Future-Service Amortization* Refer to the information provided in E18-9.

**Required**

Using the years-of-future-service method, prepare a set of schedules to determine (1) the amortization fraction for each year, and (2) the amortization of the unrecognized prior service cost.

**E18-11** *Methods to Amortize Unrecognized Prior Service Cost* Wolz Company, a small business, has had a defined benefit pension plan for its employees for several years. At the beginning of 1995, the company amended the pension plan; this amendment provides for increased benefits based on services rendered by certain employees in prior periods. The company's actuary has determined that the related unrecognized prior service cost amounts to $140,000. The company has four participating employees who are expected to receive the increased benefits. The following is a schedule identifying the employees and their expected years of future service:

| Employee Numbers | Expected Years of Future Service |
|---|---|
| 1 | 2 |
| 2 | 3 |
| 3 | 4 |
| 4 | 5 |

**Required**
1. Using the straight-line method, (a) compute the average remaining service life, and (b) prepare a schedule to amortize the unrecognized prior service cost.
2. Using the years-of-future-service method instead, prepare a set of schedules to determine (a) the amortization fraction for each year, and (b) the amortization of the unrecognized prior service cost.

*E18-12   Net Gain or Loss: Single Component*   Lee Company has a defined benefit pension plan. During 1994, for the first time, the company experienced a difference between its expected and actual projected benefit obligation. At the beginning of 1995, the company's actuary accumulated the following information:

| | |
|---|---|
| Unrecognized net loss (1/1/1995) | $ 44,000 |
| Actual projected benefit obligation (1/1/1995) | 228,000 |
| Fair value of plan assets (1/1/1995) | 260,000 |

On December 31, 1995, the company is in the process of computing the net gain or loss to include in its pension expense for 1995. The company has determined that the average remaining service life of its employees is 9 years. There was no difference between the company's expected and actual return on plan assets in 1995.

**Required**
Compute the amount of the net gain or loss to include in the pension expense for 1995. Indicate whether it is an addition to or a subtraction from pension expense.

*E18-13   Net Gain or Loss: Multiple Components*   The actuary of the Hudson Company has provided the following information concerning the company's defined benefit pension plan at the end of 1995:

| | |
|---|---|
| Fair value of plan assets (1/1/1995) | $350,000 |
| Actual projected benefit obligation (1/1/1995) | 360,000 |
| Expected projected benefit obligation (1/1/1995) | 424,000 |
| Actual return on plan assets for 1995 | 28,000 |
| Expected return on plan assets for 1995 | 24,000 |
| Average remaining service life of employees | 10 years |

The difference between the actual and expected projected benefit obligation first occurred in 1994.

**Required**
1. Compute the amount of the unrecognized gain or loss for the Hudson Company's pension plan at the beginning of 1995.
2. Compute the amount of the net gain or loss to include in the Hudson Company's pension expense for 1995. Indicate whether it is an addition to or a subtraction from pension expense.

E18-14 *Additional Pension Liability* Derosa Company has a defined benefit pension plan for its employees. Prior to 1995, the company has not had an additional pension liability. At the end of 1995, the company's actuary developed the following information regarding its pension plan:

| | |
|---|---|
| Projected benefit obligation | $1,429,000 |
| Accumulated benefit obligation | 987,000 |
| Plan assets (fair value) | 852,000 |
| Unrecognized prior service cost | 200,000 |

**Required**

1. Calculate the additional pension liability required at the end of 1995 and prepare the appropriate journal entry, assuming that the company had a prepaid/accrued pension cost (liability) of $73,000 before considering the preceding information.
2. Repeat Requirement 1 assuming, instead, that the company had a prepaid/accrued pension cost (asset) of $46,000.
3. Indicate how the liability and asset in Requirement 2 would be disclosed on the 1995 ending balance sheet.

E18-15 *Accounting for an OPEB Plan* On January 1, 1995, Flash and Dash Company adopted a healthcare plan for its retired employees. To determine eligibility for benefits, the company retroactively gives credit to the date of hire for each employee. The following information is available about the plan:

| | |
|---|---|
| Service cost | $ 30,000 |
| Accumulated postretirement benefit obligation (1/1/95) | 100,000 |
| Accumulated postretirement benefit obligation for employees fully eligible to receive benefits (12/31/95) | 40,000 |
| Actual return on plan assets | 0 |
| Unrecognized prior service cost | 12,000 |
| Payments to retired employees during 1995 | 5,000 |
| Interest rate | 10% |
| Average remaining service period of active plan participants (1/1/95) | 20 years |

**Required**

1. Compute the OPEB expense for 1995.
2. Prepare all the required journal entries for 1995 if the plan is not funded.

E18-16 *Appendix: Pension Plan Present Value Calculations* The Ark Company adopted a defined benefit pension plan for its employees on January 1, 1995. All its employees are the same age, retire at the same time, and have the same life expectancy after retirement. The company decided to compute its pension expense on December 31 of each year; it also decided to fund an amount on that date equal to the year's service cost. The following is a listing of other relevant facts:

| | |
|---|---|
| Annual pension benefits earned by all employees for each year of service | $100,000 |
| Years to retirement (at end of 1995) | 20 |
| Years of life expectancy after date of retirement | 15 |
| Discount rate | 9% |
| Actual rate of return on plan assets | 8% |

For the years 1995 through 1997, the company experienced no net gain or loss and did not have an additional pension liability in regard to the pension plan.

**Required**

1. Prepare a schedule to compute the Ark Company's pension expense for 1995 through 1997. Round to the nearest dollar.
2. Prepare the year-end journal entries to record the company's pension expense for 1995 through 1997.

## PROBLEMS

P18-1     *Components of Pension Expense*   The Nelson Company has a defined benefit pension plan for its employees. At the end of 1995 and 1996, the following information is available in regard to this pension plan:

|                                                    | 1995      | 1996      |
|----------------------------------------------------|-----------|-----------|
| Actual return on plan assets                       | $ 28,000  | $ 29,000  |
| Amortization of unrecognized net gain              | 3,000     | —         |
| Amortization of unrecognized net loss              | —         | 4,000     |
| Amortization of unrecognized prior service cost    | 7,000     | 6,000     |
| Company contribution (funded 12/31)                | 200,000   | 240,000   |
| Interest cost on projected benefit obligation      | 32,000    | 35,000    |
| Service cost                                       | 211,000   | 217,000   |

There are no other components of Nelson Company's pension expense in either year; the fair value of the plan assets at the end of each year exceeded the accumulated benefit obligation.

**Required**

1. Compute the amount of Nelson Company's pension expense in 1995 and 1996.
2. Prepare the December 31 journal entry to record the pension expense in 1995 and 1996.
3. What is the total prepaid/accrued pension cost at the end of 1995, assuming no prepaid/accrued pension cost existed prior to 1995? Is it an asset or a liability?

P18-2     *Pension Expense Different Than Funding*   On January 1, 1995, the Parkway Company adopted a defined benefit pension plan. At that time, the company awarded retroactive benefits to its employees, resulting in an unrecognized prior service cost of $2,180,000 on that date. The company decided to amortize these costs by the straight-line method over the 16-year average remaining service life of its active participating employees. The company's actuary and funding agency have also provided the following additional information for 1995 and 1996:

|                                                    | 1995         | 1996         |
|----------------------------------------------------|--------------|--------------|
| Service cost                                       | $  340,000   | $  348,000   |
| Projected benefit obligation (1/1)                 | 2,180,000*   | 2,738,000    |
| Plan assets (1/1)                                  | -0-          | 670,000      |
| Discount rate                                      | 10%          | 10%          |
| Actual (and expected) rate of return on plan assets| —            | 9%           |

\* Due to the unrecognized prior service cost

The company contributed $670,000 and $700,000 to the pension fund at the end of 1995 and 1996, respectively. There are no other components of Parkway Company's pension expense; the fair value of the plan assets at the end of each year exceeded the accumulated benefit obligation.

**Required**

1. Compute the amount of Parkway Company's pension expense for 1995 and 1996.
2. Prepare the December 31 journal entry to record the pension expense for 1995 and 1996.
3. What is the total prepaid/accrued pension cost at the end of 1996? Is it an asset or a liability?

P18-3     *Pension Expense Different Than Funding*   When Turner Company adopted its defined benefit pension plan on January 1, 1995, it awarded retroactive benefits to its employees. These retroactive benefits resulted in an unrecognized prior service cost of $980,000 that created a projected benefit obligation of the same amount on that date. The company decided to amortize the unrecognized prior service cost using the years-of-future-service method. The company's actuary and funding agency have also provided the following additional information for 1995 and 1996: (1) service cost: 1995, $187,000; 1996, $189,000; (2) plan assets: 1/1/1995, $0; 1/1/1996, $342,000; (3) actual (and expected) rate of return on plan assets: 1996, 7%; (4) projected benefit obligation: 1/1/1996, $1,225,400; (5) discount rate for both 1995 and 1996: 8%; and (6) amortization fraction for unrecognized prior service cost: 1995, 80/980; 1996, 79/980. The company contributed $342,000 and $336,000 to the pension fund at the end of 1995 and 1996, respectively. There are no other components of Turner Company's pension expense; the fair value of the plan assets at the end of each year exceeded the accumulated benefit obligation. The company rounds its calculations to the nearest dollar.

#### Required

1. Compute the amount of Turner Company's pension expense for 1995 and 1996.
2. Prepare the journal entry to record the pension expense at the end of 1995 and 1996.
3. Calculate the total prepaid/accrued pension cost at the end of 1996. Indicate whether it is an asset or liability.
4. Calculate the remaining unrecognized prior service cost at the end of 1996.

P18-4  *Pension Expense Different Than Funding*  The Lane Company was incorporated in 1986. Because it had become successful, the company established a defined benefit pension plan for its employees on January 1, 1995. Due to the loyalty of its employees, the company granted retroactive benefits to them. These retroactive benefits resulted in $1,240,000 of unrecognized prior service cost on that date. The company decided to amortize these costs using the years-of-future-service method. The company's actuary and funding agency have provided the following additional information for 1995 and 1996:

|  | 1995 | 1996 |
| --- | --- | --- |
| Actual rate of return on plan assets | — | 9% |
| Amortization fraction for unrecognized prior service cost | 48/620 | 46/620 |
| Discount rate | 9% | 9% |
| Plan assets (1/1) | $  -0- | $ 690,000 |
| Projected benefit obligation (1/1) | 1,240,000* | 1,786,600 |
| Service cost | 465,000 | 470,000 |

* Due to the unrecognized prior service cost

The company contributed $690,000 and $650,000 to the pension fund at the end of 1995 and 1996, respectively. There are no other components of Lane Company's pension expense; the accumulated benefit obligation at the end of each year was less than the fair value of the plan assets. The company rounds its calculations to the nearest dollar.

#### Required

1. Compute the amount of Lane Company's pension expense for 1995 and 1996.
2. Prepare the December 31 journal entry to record the pension expense for 1995 and 1996.
3. What is the total prepaid/accrued pension cost at the end of 1996? Is it an asset or a liability?

P18-5  *Pension Expense Different Than Funding*  The Carpenter Company adopted a defined benefit pension plan for its employees on January 1, 1995. At the time of adoption, the pension contract provided for retroactive benefits for the company's active participating employees. These retroactive benefits resulted in an unrecognized prior service cost of $1,860,000 that created a projected benefit obligation of the same amount on that date. The company decided to amortize the unrecognized prior service cost by the straight-line method over the 20-year average remaining service life of the employees. The following additional information is also available for 1995 and 1996: (1) discount rate for both 1995 and 1996: 10%; (2) company contribution (funded 12/31): 1995, $550,000; 1996, $510,000; (3) actual (and expected) rate of return on plan assets: 1996: 9%; (4) projected benefit obligation: 1/1/1996, $2,303,000; (5) service cost: 1995, $257,000; 1996, $264,000; and (6) plan assets: 1/1/1995, $0; 1/1/1996, $550,000. There are no other components of Carpenter Company's pension expense; the accumulated benefit obligation at the end of each year is less than the fair value of the plan assets.

#### Required

1. Compute the amount of Carpenter Company's pension expense for 1995 and 1996.
2. Prepare the journal entry to record the pension expense at the end of 1995 and 1996.
3. Calculate the total prepaid/accrued pension cost at the end of 1996. Indicate whether it is an asset or liability.
4. Calculate the remaining unrecognized prior service cost at the end of 1996.

P18-6   *Amortization of Unrecognized Prior Service Cost*   On January 1, 1995, the Baznik Company adopted a defined benefit pension plan. At that time, the company awarded retroactive benefits to certain employees. These retroactive benefits resulted in an unrecognized prior service cost of $1,200,000 on that date. The company has six participating employees who are expected to receive the retroactive benefits. Following is a schedule that identifies the participating employees and their expected years of future service as of January 1, 1995:

| Employee | Expected Years of Future Service |
|---|---|
| A | 1 |
| B | 3 |
| C | 4 |
| D | 5 |
| E | 5 |
| F | 6 |

The company decided to amortize the unrecognized prior service cost to pension expense using the years-of-future-service method. The following are the amounts of the components of Baznik Company's pension expense, in addition to the amortization of the unrecognized prior service cost for 1995 and 1996:

|  | 1995 | 1996 |
|---|---|---|
| Service cost | $469,000 | $507,000 |
| Interest cost on projected benefit obligation | 108,000 | 153,000 |
| Actual return on plan assets | — | 70,000 |
| Amortization of net loss | — | 5,000 |

The company contributed $850,000 and $830,000 to the pension fund at the end of 1995 and 1996, respectively. The fair value of the plan assets at the end of each year exceeded the accumulated benefit obligation.

**Required**
1. Prepare a set of schedules for the Baznik Company to determine (a) the amortization fraction for each year, and (b) the amortization of the unrecognized prior service cost.
2. Prepare the journal entries to record the pension expense for 1995 and 1996.

P18-7   *Net Gain or Loss*   For several years, Kent Company has had a defined benefit contribution plan for its employees. During those years, the company experienced differences between its expected and actual projected benefit obligation. These differences resulted in a cumulative net gain or loss at the beginning of each subsequent year. In addition, the company's actual return on plan assets has been different from its expected return in each year. The following schedule summarizes the amounts related to the preceding information for the years 1995 through 1997:

| Year | Cumulative Unrecognized Net Loss (Gain)[a] | Actual Return on Plan Assets[b] | Expected Return on Plan Assets[b] |
|---|---|---|---|
| 1995 | $25,000 | $20,000 | $18,000 |
| 1996 | 26,000 | 24,500 | 27,000 |
| 1997 | 36,500 | 30,000 | 30,900 |

a. At beginning of year
b. For the current year

The company's actuary and funding agency have also provided the following information about the company's actual projected benefit obligation and fair value of plan assets at the beginning of each year:

| Year | Projected Benefit Obligation | Plan Assets |
|---|---|---|
| 1995 | $220,000 | $200,000 |
| 1996 | 275,000 | 270,000 |
| 1997 | 320,000 | 325,000 |

The company amortizes any excess unrecognized gain or loss by the straight-line method over the average remaining service life of its active participating employees. Because of a consistent pattern of employee hirings and retirements, this average service life has remained at 20 years for 1995 through 1997.

**Required**

Prepare a schedule to compute the amount of the net gain or loss to include in the Kent Company's pension expense for 1995 through 1997. Indicate whether the gain or loss is added to or subtracted from the pension expense.

P18-8   *Additional Pension Liability*   In the Fisk Company's negotiations with its employees' union on January 1, 1995, the company agreed to an amendment which substantially increased the employee benefits based on services rendered in prior periods. This resulted in an $80,000 unrecognized prior service cost that increased both the projected benefit obligation and the accumulated benefit obligation of the company. Due to financial constraints, the company decided not to fund the total increase in its pension obligation at that time.

Prior to 1995, it had been the company's policy to fund enough of its pension expense each year so that the fair value of the plan assets at the end of the year was greater than the year-end accumulated benefit obligation. As a result, the company reported a prepaid/accrued pension cost liability of $40,000 on its December 31, 1994 balance sheet.

The company has appropriately amortized the unrecognized prior service cost as a component of pension expense in 1995 and 1996. The resulting pension and other information for 1995 and 1996 are as follows:

| Year | Pension Expense | Company Contribution[a] | Accumulated Benefit Obligation[b] | Fair Value of Plan Assets[b] |
|------|-----------------|--------------------------|-----------------------------------|------------------------------|
| 1995 | $137,000 | $125,000 | $562,000 | $500,000 |
| 1996 | 145,000 | 160,000 | 682,000 | 637,000 |

a. Funded December 31
b. At year-end

**Required**

1. Prepare the December 31, 1995 journal entries related to the Fisk Company's pension plan.
2. List the amounts of any assets and liabilities to be reported on the company's December 31, 1995 balance sheet.
3. Prepare the December 31, 1996 journal entries related to the Fisk Company's pension plan.
4. List the amounts of any assets and liabilities to be reported on the company's December 31, 1996 balance sheet.

P18-9   *Determination of Pension Plan Amounts*   Various pension plan information of the Kerem Company for 1995 and 1996 is as follows:

| | 1995 | 1996 |
|---|---|---|
| Service cost | $100,000 | (j) |
| Interest cost on projected benefit obligation | 54,000 | (g) |
| Accumulated benefit obligation, 12/31 | (f) | (l) |
| Discount rate | 9% | 9% |
| Amortization of unrecognized prior service cost | 4,000 | 4,000 |
| Plan assets (fair value), 1/1* | 500,000 | 615,000 |
| Projected benefit obligation, 1/1 | (a) | 720,000 |
| Deferred pension cost, 12/31 | 3,000 | (k) |
| Actual rate of return on plan assets | (b) | 11% |
| Amortization of unrecognized net loss | (d) | 700 |
| Additional pension liability, 12/31 | 3,000 | 5,000 |
| Accrued pension cost (liability), 12/31 | 17,000 | 26,000 |
| Average service life of employees | 10 years | 10 years |
| Pension expense | (e) | 110,850 |
| Cumulative unrecognized net loss, 1/1 | 68,000 | (i) |
| Actual return on plan assets | 50,000 | (h) |
| Corridor | (c) | 72,000 |

* 1/1/1997: $740,000

**Required**

Fill in the blanks lettered (a) through (l). All the necessary information is listed. It is not necessary to calculate your answers in alphabetical order.

P18-10 *Comprehensive*   The Jay Company has had a defined benefit pension plan for several years. At the beginning of 1995, the company amended the plan; this amendment provided for increased benefits to employees based on services rendered in prior periods. The unrecognized prior service cost related to this amendment totaled $77,000; as a result, both the projected and accumulated benefit obligation increased.

The company decided not to fund the increased obligation at the time of the amendment, but rather to increase its periodic year-end contributions to the pension plan. In the past, the company has not always funded as much as its annual pension expense; thus, it had an unfunded accrued pension liability on December 31, 1994. The company, however, had contributed a sufficient amount each year so that it has never had an additional pension liability at year-end.

The following information for 1995 has been provided by the company's actuary and funding agency, and obtained from a review of its accounting records:

| | |
|---|---|
| Accumulated benefit obligation (12/31) | $750,000 |
| Service cost | 183,000 |
| Discount rate | 9% |
| Cumulative unrecognized net loss (1/1) | 64,500 |
| Actual return on plan assets | 46,300 |
| Company contribution to pension plan (12/31) | 200,000 |
| Projected benefit obligation (1/1)* | 513,000 |
| Plan assets, fair value (12/31) | 726,300 |
| Accrued pension cost (liability) (1/1) | 22,000 |
| Expected return on plan assets | 48,000 |
| Plan assets, fair value (1/1) | 480,000 |

* Before the increase of $77,000 due to the unrecognized prior service cost from the amendment.

The company decided to amortize the unrecognized prior service cost and any excess cumulative unrecognized net loss by the straight-line method over the average remaining service life of the participating employees. It has developed the following schedule concerning these 50 employees:

| Employee Numbers | Expected Years of Future Service* | Employee Numbers | Expected Years of Future Service* |
|---|---|---|---|
| 1–5 | 2 | 26–30 | 12 |
| 6–10 | 4 | 31–35 | 14 |
| 11–15 | 6 | 36–40 | 16 |
| 16–20 | 8 | 41–45 | 18 |
| 21–25 | 10 | 46–50 | 20 |

* Per employee

**Required**

1. Compute the average remaining service life and prepare a schedule to determine the amortization of the unrecognized prior service cost of the Jay Company for 1995.
2. Prepare a schedule to compute the net gain or loss component of pension expense for 1995.
3. Prepare a schedule to compute the pension expense for 1995.
4. Prepare a schedule to determine the additional pension liability (if any) at the end of 1995.
5. Prepare all the December 31, 1995 journal entries related to the pension plan.

P18-11 *Comprehensive*   The TAN Company has a defined benefit pension plan for its employees. The plan has been in existence for several years. During 1994, for the first time, the company experienced a difference between its expected and actual projected benefit obligation. This resulted in a cumulative unrecognized loss of $29,000 at the beginning of 1995. The company also experienced a similar difference in 1995 that resulted in a cumulative unrecognized loss of $81,650 at the beginning of 1996. The company amortizes any excess unrecognized loss by the straight-line method over the average remaining service life of its active participating employees. It has developed the following schedule concerning these 40 employees:

| Employee Numbers | Expected Years of Future Service* | Employee Numbers | Expected Years of Future Service* |
|---|---|---|---|
| 1–5 | 3 | 21–25 | 15 |
| 6–10 | 6 | 26–30 | 18 |
| 11–15 | 9 | 31–35 | 21 |
| 16–20 | 12 | 36–40 | 24 |

* Per employee

The company makes its contribution to the pension plan at the end of each year. However, it has not always funded the entire pension expense in a given year. As a result, it had a prepaid/accrued pension cost liability of $36,000 on December 31, 1994. Furthermore, the company's accumulated benefit obligation exceeded the fair value of the plan assets at the end of 1994 so that the company also had an additional pension liability (and deferred pension cost asset) of $8,300 on December 31, 1994.

In addition to the preceding information, the following set of facts for 1995 and 1996 has been assembled based on information provided by the company's actuary and funding agency, and obtained from its accounting records:

| | 1995 | 1996 |
|---|---|---|
| Plan assets, fair value (12/31) | $559,500 | $785,476 |
| Cumulative unrecognized net loss (1/1) | 29,000 | 81,650 |
| Expected return on plan assets | 35,000 | 50,355 |
| Company contribution to pension plan (12/31) | 175,000 | 173,000 |
| Projected benefit obligation (1/1) | 470,000 | 737,000 |
| Discount rate | 10% | 9% |
| Accumulated benefit obligation (12/31) | 623,000 | 836,750 |
| Actual return on plan assets | 34,500 | 52,976 |
| Service cost | 169,000 | 163,000 |
| Plan assets, fair value (1/1) | 350,000 | 559,500 |

**Required**

1. Calculate the average remaining service life of the TAN Company's employees. Compute to one decimal place.
2. Prepare a schedule to compute the net gain or loss component of pension expense for 1995 and 1996. For simplicity, assume the average remaining life calculated in Requirement 1 is applicable to both years.
3. Prepare a schedule to compute the pension expense for 1995 and 1996.
4. Prepare a schedule to determine the adjustment (if any) to additional pension liability required at the end of 1995 and 1996.
5. Prepare all the December 31, 1995 and December 31, 1996 journal entries related to the pension plan.

**P18-12** *Accounting for an OPEB Plan* On January 1, 1995, the Vasby Software Company adopted a healthcare plan for its retired employees. To determine eligibility for benefits, the company retroactively gives credit to the date of hire for each employee. The service cost for 1995 is $8,000. The plan is not funded, and the discount rate is 10%. All employees were hired at age 28 and become eligible for full benefits at age 58. Employee C was paid $7,000 postretirement healthcare benefits in 1995. On December 31, 1995, the accumulated postretirement benefit obligation for Employees B and C were $77,000 and $41,500, respectively. Additional information on January 1, 1995 is as follows:

| Employee Status | Age | Expected Retirement Age | Expected Postretirement Benefit Obligation | Accumulated Postretirement Benefit Obligation |
|---|---|---|---|---|
| A Employee | 38 | 65 | $ 42,000 | $ 14,000 |
| B Employee | 62 | 65 | 70,000 | 70,000 |
| C Retired | 67 | — | 45,000 | 45,000 |
| | | | $157,000 | $129,000 |

**Required**

1. Compute the OPEB expense for 1995 if the company uses the maximum amortization period for the transition obligation.
2. Prepare all the required journal entries for 1995 if the plan is not funded.

P18-13    *Appendix: Pension Plan Present Value Computations*   On January 1, 1995, the Cromwell Company adopted a defined benefit plan for its employees. All the employees are the same age, retire at the same time, and have the same life expectancy after retirement. The following are the relevant facts concerning the pension plan factors and the employee characteristics:

**Pension Plan Factors**

| Benefit formula | Average of last 4 years' salary × Number of years of service × 0.025 |
| --- | --- |
| Expected average of last 4 years' salary | $80,000 per employee |
| Annual pension benefit earned each year of service by each employee | $80,000 × 0.025 = $2,000 |
| Date of computation of pension expense and pension funding | December 31 |
| Amount funded each year | Equal to annual service cost |
| Discount rate | 10% |
| Actual rate of return on plan assets | 9% |

**Employee Characteristics**

| Number of employees | 60 |
| --- | --- |
| Age of employees | 35 |
| Years to retirement (at end of 1995) | 25 |
| Years of life expectancy after date of retirement | 14 |

For the years 1995 through 1999, the company experienced no net gain or loss in regard to the pension plan. On January 1, 1998, however, the company agreed to an amendment of the pension plan. This amendment changed the factor in the pension benefit formula from 0.025 to 0.03. This amendment was made retroactive to the adoption of the plan. At the end of years 1995 through 1999, the company did not have an additional pension liability.

**Required**

1. Prepare a schedule to compute the Cromwell Company's pension expense for 1995 through 1999. Round to the nearest dollar.
2. Prepare the year-end journal entries to record the company's pension expense for 1995 through 1999.
3. Determine the balance in the Prepaid/Accrued Pension Cost account on December 31, 1999. Indicate whether it is an asset or liability.

# ACCOUNTING FOR LEASES

Many companies choose to lease an asset, rather than to purchase it. *In FASB Statement No. 13 as Amended and Interpreted through January 1990, a lease is defined "as an agreement conveying the right to use property, plant, or equipment (land or depreciable assets or both) usually for a stated period of time."[1] A lease involves a lessee and a lessor. A lessee acquires the right to use the property, plant, and equipment; a lessor gives up the right.*

There are many kinds of leases: short-term, long-term, personal property, real property, cancelable, noncancelable, two-party, three-party, and others. Since it is a contractual agreement, the parties can incorporate in the lease contract any provision that they desire. Today, all kinds of assets can be leased. Among the most popular are photocopiers, computers, airplanes, railroad boxcars, and warehouses.

This chapter emphasizes the long-term noncancelable leases involving depreciable personal property such as equipment, machinery, trucks, and other movable assets. The lease of real property (land, buildings, and other items firmly attached to the land) and certain other specialized lease issues are discussed in the Appendix to this chapter.

---

1. "Accounting for Leases," *FASB Statement No. 13 as Amended and Interpreted through January 1990* (Norwalk, Conn.: FASB, 1990), sec. L10.101.

## ADVANTAGES OF LEASING AND AN HISTORICAL PERSPECTIVE

The lease arrangement does have certain shortcomings—it is, for example, usually more expensive in the long run to lease than to buy. However, judging by its tremendous growth in popularity, the advantages of leasing for many companies must outweigh the disadvantages.

### Advantages of Leasing from Lessee's Viewpoint

From the lessee's point of view, the commonly discussed advantages are:

1. Financing benefits:
   a. The lease provides 100% financing so that the lessee acquires the asset without having to make a down payment. Because cash flow is critical to the survival and growth of a company, its management is very important.
   b. The lease contract may contain fewer restrictive provisions and be more flexible than other debt agreements.
   c. The leasing arrangement creates a claim that is against only the leased equipment and not against all assets.

2. Risk benefit: Under some circumstances, the leasing arrangement may reduce the risk of obsolescence and inadequacy; in these cases, the risk is borne by the lessor.

3. Tax benefit: By deducting lease payments, the lessee can write off the full cost of the asset, including the part that relates to land. The tax deduction may be accelerated since it is often spread over the period of the lease rather than the actual economic life of the property.

4. Financial reporting benefit: In certain cases (for operating leases), the lease does not add a liability to the balance sheet, and does not affect certain financial ratios, such as the rate of return on total investment. The resulting higher rate of return and other ratios (particularly the current ratio and ratio of debt to stockholders' equity) that tend to be inflated because of the omission of the leased asset and liability from the balance sheet may add to the borrowing capacity of the lessee.

5. Billing benefit: For certain contract-type work, leasing may permit higher charges because the interest element contained in the rental payments is allowed as a contract charge, whereas interest on borrowed money to purchase assets usually is not.

*Capital leases will be defined more fully later.*

Advantage number 4 is critical to some companies. In essence, certain leases (called "capital leases") are legal devices enabling lessees to acquire substantially all the risks and benefits associated with asset ownership. If a company can in substance acquire an asset but record neither it nor the liability in its accounts, those key ratios mentioned previously can be improved substantially. The company would be practicing "off balance sheet financing."

### Historical Perspective of Leasing

In the early 1960s, before the issuance of any authoritative pronouncements concerning leasing, most lessees that leased personal property for a long period by the use of a noncancelable lease (capital lease) had the option of reporting the lease information in the notes to the financial statements or, in certain cases, disclosing nothing in regard to these leases. From an accounting point of view, the major issue concerned the reporting and accounting for such leases. The accounting for the alternative types of leases (called "operating leases") that do not convey ownership rights and privileges has presented fewer significant accounting issues.

*Operating leases are defined more fully later.*

A simple illustration will help to place some of the issues into historical perspective. Assume that in 1993, two identical companies, A and B, have the following financial data prior to any new acquisitions:

| | |
|---|---|
| Current assets | $2,100,000 |
| Noncurrent assets | 2,900,000 |
| Current liabilities | 1,000,000 |
| Noncurrent liabilities | 1,600,000 |
| Stockholders' equity | 2,400,000 |

On December 31, 1995, A Company purchases equipment with a 10-year life costing $2,825,112 by signing a 10-year, 12% note requiring $500,000 to be paid at the end of each year starting December 31, 1996. The payments include interest at 12% on the beginning-of-year principal balance, and the remainder of each annual payment reduces principal. Since this transaction represents a purchase by the issuance of a debt instrument, A records the asset purchased and the note payable (part of which is a current liability). A's financial data show these changes: noncurrent assets increase to $5,725,112 ($2,900,000 + $2,825,112); current liabilities increase to $1,446,429 ($1,000,000 + the present value of $500,000 discounted for one year at 12%); and noncurrent liabilities increase to $3,978,683 ($1,600,000 + $2,825,112 less current amount of $446,429). The remaining items do not change. Considering these changes, note the effect on two balance sheet ratios of A Company:

| | Before Acquisition | After Acquisition |
|---|:---:|:---:|
| Current ratio (ratio of current assets to current liabilities) | 2.10 | 1.45[a] |
| Ratio of debt to stockholders' equity | 1.08 | 2.26[b] |

a. Current assets of $2,100,000 divided by current liabilities of $1,446,429 ($1,000,000 + $446,429)
b. Debt of $5,425,112 ($1,446,429 + $3,978,683) divided by stockholders' equity of $2,400,000

The current ratio falls significantly, thus perhaps affecting the willingness of a bank to make a short-term loan. The ratio of debt to stockholders' equity more than doubles, thereby affecting the perceptions of long-term creditors or stockholders as to the stability of the corporation. These adverse changes, coupled with the impact that the purchase has on the rate of return on investment in 1996, might have impaired A's borrowing capacity or its ability to sell stock.

Next assume that in 1995, B Company leases identical equipment by the use of a lease and agrees to pay $500,000 rent each year for the next 10 years (assume that the property has a 10-year life). If the interest rate is 12%, then the present value of 10 payments of $500,000 discounted at 12% is $2,825,112 ($500,000 × 5.650223).[2]

---

2. The present value calculations in this chapter use factors from the tables in Appendix D.

If the lease is classified as a capital lease, B records an asset and a liability and the effects on its balance sheet are the same as the effects of the purchase on A's balance sheet. However, if the lease is classified as an operating lease, B does not record an asset or a liability. The current ratio after the lease remains at 2.10-to-1 and the ratio of debt to stockholders' equity, 1.08-to-1. Also, the rate of return on investment in 1996 (assuming that plant expansion was profitable) is significantly higher than for A, even though B acquires equipment identical to that of A. In summary, two virtually identical economic events are reported very differently in the financial statements. Today, many companies lease certain assets, but some object to capitalizing the lease payments (where required by *FASB Statement No. 13 as Amended*) because of the impact that reporting the asset and liability on the balance sheet has on the key ratios discussed.

The preceding discussion is based on the lessee's point of view. The opposite effect occurs in regard to the lessor. Thus, for an operating lease, the asset remains on the lessor's books, and rent revenue is recognized periodically, usually at an amount equal to the amount of the rent receipts. These alternatives affect significant ratios of the lessor.

### Advantages of Leasing from Lessor's Viewpoint

From the lessor's point of view, the chief advantages are that leasing provides (1) a way of indirectly making a sale and (2) an alternative means of obtaining a profit opportunity by engaging in a transaction that enables the lessor company to transfer an asset by the lease agreement. This financial-type transfer permits the lessor to earn a normal rate of return in the form of interest on the cost of the asset acquired and leased.

## KEY TERMS RELATED TO LEASING

**FASB Statement No. 13 as Amended and Interpreted through January 1990** defines a number of terms that are used in leasing arrangements. These terms are listed in Exhibit 19-1 because they are necessary for an understanding of accounting for leases.[3] The terms should be reviewed now and carefully examined as each is introduced in the chapter.

---

**EXHIBIT 19-1**

**KEY TERMS RELATED TO LEASING**

**Bargain purchase option.** A provision allowing the lessee to purchase the leased property at the end of the life of the lease at a price so favorable that the exercise of the option appears, at the inception of the lease, to be reasonably assured.

**Bargain renewal option.** A provision allowing the lessee to renew the lease for a rental that is so favorable that the exercise of the option by the lessee appears, at the inception of the lease, to be reasonably assured.

**Estimated economic life of leased property.** Regardless of the lease term, the estimated remaining period during which the property is expected to be usable for the purpose that was intended at the inception of the lease, with normal repairs and maintenance.

**Estimated residual value of leased property.** The estimated fair value of the leased property at the end of the lease term. (Note that this value is a different concept from the estimated residual value at the end of the *economic* life of the property.)

---

3.    Adapted from *FASB Statement No. 13 as Amended and Interpreted through January 1990, op. cit.,* sec. L10.401–.424.

## EXHIBIT 19-1, Continued

**Executory costs.** Ownership-type costs, such as insurance, maintenance, and property taxes. These costs may be paid by either the lessor or the lessee. Normally, it is expected that the cost should be borne by the party to the contract who controls the asset essentially in the manner of an owner.

**Fair value of leased property.** The price for which the property could be sold in an arm's length transaction between unrelated parties. If the lessor is a manufacturer or dealer, the fair value of the property at the inception of the lease is normally the selling price adjusted for any unusual market conditions and less any trade discounts that may be applicable. If the lessor is not a manufacturer or dealer, the fair value is ordinarily the cost of the asset to the lessor.

**Guaranteed residual value.** The portion of the estimated residual value of the leased property that is guaranteed by the lessee or by a third party unrelated to the lessor.

**Inception of the lease.** The date of the lease agreement or written commitment, if earlier; or, if the leased property is being constructed or acquired in the future, the date that title passes to the lessor.

**Initial direct costs.** Costs incurred by the lessor to originate a lease that (1) result directly from and are essential to acquiring that lease and (2) would not have been incurred had that leasing transaction not occurred. These costs also include certain costs directly related to specified activities performed by the lessor for that lease, such as evaluating the lessee's financial condition, negotiating lease terms, preparing and processing lease documents, and closing the transaction.

**Interest rate implicit in the lease.** The interest (discount) rate that, when applied on a present value basis to the sum of the minimum lease payments and any unguaranteed residual value accruing to the lessor, causes the resulting aggregate present value to be equal to the fair value of the leased property to the lessor.*

**Lease term.** The duration of the lease, which may be from a brief period to the full economic life of the leased property. More precisely, the lease term is the fixed noncancelable term of the lease plus (1) any periods covered by bargain renewal options, (2) any periods for which failure to renew the lease imposes a significant penalty on the lessee, (3) any periods covered by ordinary renewal options during which a guarantee by the lessee of the lessor's debt related to the leased property is expected to be in effect, or a loan from the lessee to the lessor directly or indirectly related to the leased property is expected to be outstanding, (4) any periods covered by ordinary renewal options preceding the exercise date of a bargain purchase option, and (5) any periods during which the lessor has the option to renew or to extend the lease. The lease term, however, in no case extends beyond the date a bargain purchase option becomes exercisable.

**Lessee's incremental borrowing rate.** The rate that, at the inception of the lease, the lessee would have incurred to borrow, over a similar term, the funds necessary to purchase the leased property.

**Manufacturer's or dealer's profit or loss.** This profit or loss is the difference between the following two items: (1) the fair value of the property at the inception of the lease and (2) the cost or carrying amount of the leased asset.

**Minimum lease payments.** These are the payments that are required or that may be required to be paid by the lessee to the lessor over the life of the lease. Specifically, for a lease that contains a *bargain purchase option*, the minimum lease payments include (1) the minimum periodic payments required by the lease over the lease term and (2) the payment required by the bargain purchase option. Otherwise, the minimum lease payments include (1) the minimum periodic payments plus (2) any guaranteed residual value, and (3) any payments on failure to renew or extend the lease. Executory costs are *not* included in minimum lease payments.

**Minimum lease payments receivable.** The sum of (1) the undiscounted *minimum lease payments* plus (2) any unguaranteed residual value accruing to the benefit of the lessor at the end of the lease. Sometimes called *gross investment in the lease*.

**Unguaranteed residual value.** That portion of the estimated residual value of the leased property that is not guaranteed by the lessee or by a third party unrelated to the lessor.

**Unreimbursable cost.** These costs may include commitments by the lessor to guarantee performance of the leased property in a manner more extensive than the typical product warranty, or to effectively protect the lessee from obsolescence of the leased property. However, the necessity of estimating executory costs such as insurance, maintenance, and taxes to be paid by the lessor does not by itself constitute an important uncertainty.

---

* *FASB Statement No. 13 as Amended and Interpreted through January 1990* requires that the fair value of the leased property be reduced by any investment tax credit retained by the lessor. Since the Tax Reform Act of 1986 repealed the investment tax credit, it is not considered further in this chapter.

## CLASSIFICATION OF PERSONAL PROPERTY LEASES

The classification and accounting for leasing of personal property (mostly that of equipment) is discussed here; the variations involving real property (land, buildings, and other property attached to the land) are summarized in the Appendix to this chapter.

The basic premise of *FASB Statement No. 13 as Amended* is that **a lease that transfers substantially all the risks and benefits of ownership represents in substance a purchase by the lessee and a sale by the lessor.** Using the concept of economic substance over legal form (as discussed in Chapters 4 and 16), such a transaction should be viewed by the lessee as an asset acquisition and a liability incurrence, and by the lessor as either a sale of an asset and the creation of a financing instrument (a sales-type lease) or just the creation of a financing instrument (a direct financing lease). The *Statement* provides criteria for determining the classification of leases by both the lessee and the lessor that are intended to prevent the distortions described earlier. The criteria used to determine the classification of a lease are shown in Exhibit 19-2. The criteria that relate to the transfer of the risks and benefits of ownership are listed in Column A, whereas the criteria in Column B relate to revenue recognition.

By using the criteria shown in Exhibit 19-2, a **lessee** classifies a lease as one of two types: (1) capital lease, or (2) operating lease. A lease that meets any *one* of the four criteria listed in Column A of Exhibit 19-2 is a *capital lease* for the lessee. Since the transfer of substantially all the risks and benefits of ownership is considered to have occurred, the lessee treats the lease as, in substance, a purchase of an asset and the creation of an accompanying liability. Only if the lease meets *none* of the four criteria is a transfer of the risks and benefits considered not to have occurred, and the lease is an *operating lease*. In this case, neither an asset nor a liability is recognized by the lessee.

By using the criteria listed in Exhibit 19-2, a **lessor** classifies a lease as one of three types: (1) sales-type lease, (2) direct financing lease, or (3) operating lease.

A lease that meets any *one* of the four criteria listed in Column A and *both* criteria in Column B of Exhibit 19-2 is either a sales-type or a direct financing lease for the lessor. The lease is a *sales-type lease* if it involves a manufacturer's or dealer's profit (or loss); otherwise, it is a *direct financing lease*. Since the transfer of substantially all the risks and benefits of ownership is considered to have occurred and the revenue recognition criteria have been met, the lessor treats the lease as, in substance, a sale of an asset and the creation of an accompanying receivable. Only if the lease meets *none* of the four criteria *or* fails *one* of the revenue recognition criteria is the lease an *operating lease*. In this case, neither a sale nor a receivable is recognized by the lessor, and the leased asset remains on its books along with the related depreciation. The criteria and alternative classifications are summarized in Exhibit 19-3 using a flow chart. A summary of the accounting principles used by the lessee and lessor is included in Exhibit 19-22.

## ACCOUNTING AND REPORTING BY LESSEES

Examples of accounting for leases by the lessee are included in this section, while accounting for leases by the lessor is discussed later in the chapter.

## EXHIBIT 19-2

## CLASSIFICATION OF LEASES INVOLVING PERSONAL PROPERTY

I.  General criteria for classifying leases

| Column A<br>Criteria Applicable to Both Lessee and Lessor | Column B<br>Criteria Applicable to Lessor Only |
|---|---|
| A. The lease transfers ownership of the property to the lessee by the end of the lease term. | A. The collectibility of the minimum lease payments is reasonably assured (i.e., predictable). |
| B. The lease contains a bargain purchase option. | B. No important uncertainties surround the amount of unreimbursable costs yet to be incurred by the lessor under the lease. |
| C. The lease term is equal to 75% or more of the estimated economic life of the leased property.[a] | |
| D. The present value of the minimum lease payments is equal to 90% or more of the fair value of the leased property to the lessor.[ab] | |

II. Classification by the lessee
   A. *Capital lease.* Lease that meets *one or more* of the criteria in Column A (Part I).
   B. *Operating lease.* Lease that does *not* meet any of the criteria in Column A (Part I). In other words, all leases other than capital leases are called operating leases.

III. Classification by the lessor[c]
   A. *Sales-type lease.* Lease that meets these three criteria:
      1. *One or more* of the four criteria listed in Column A (Part I), *and*
      2. *Both* of the criteria listed in Column B (Part I), *and*
      3. It must involve a transaction giving rise to a manufacturer's or dealer's profit (or loss) to the lessor. A profit exists when the fair value of the leased property at the inception of the lease is greater than its cost or carrying value.
   B. *Direct financing lease.* Lease that meets these three criteria:
      1. *One or more* of the four criteria listed in Column A (Part I), *and*
      2. *Both* of the criteria listed in Column B (Part I), *and*
      3. It must *not* involve a transaction giving rise to a manufacturer's or dealer's profit (or loss) to the lessor.
   C. *Operating lease.* Lease that meets none of the criteria in Column A (Part I) or that does *not* meet both of the criteria in Column B. In other words, all leases other than sales-type or direct financing leases are called operating leases.

a. Items C and D do not apply if the beginning of the lease term falls within the last 25% of the total estimated economic life. This qualification was added by the FASB to prevent the possible manipulation of the kinds of leases that may result from renewal options. For example, without this qualification, for a tank car having an estimated useful life of 25 years and placed under five, successive, 5-year leases, the first four leases would be classified as operating leases and the last lease would be classified as a capital lease.
b. The fair value is reduced by an investment tax credit accruing to the lessor. (However, see footnote in Exhibit 19-1.)
c. A fourth type of lease, from the lessor's viewpoint, is the leveraged lease. This type of lease is a special three-party lease and is discussed in the Appendix to this chapter.

**EXHIBIT 19-3**

## LEASE CRITERIA AND CLASSIFICATIONS

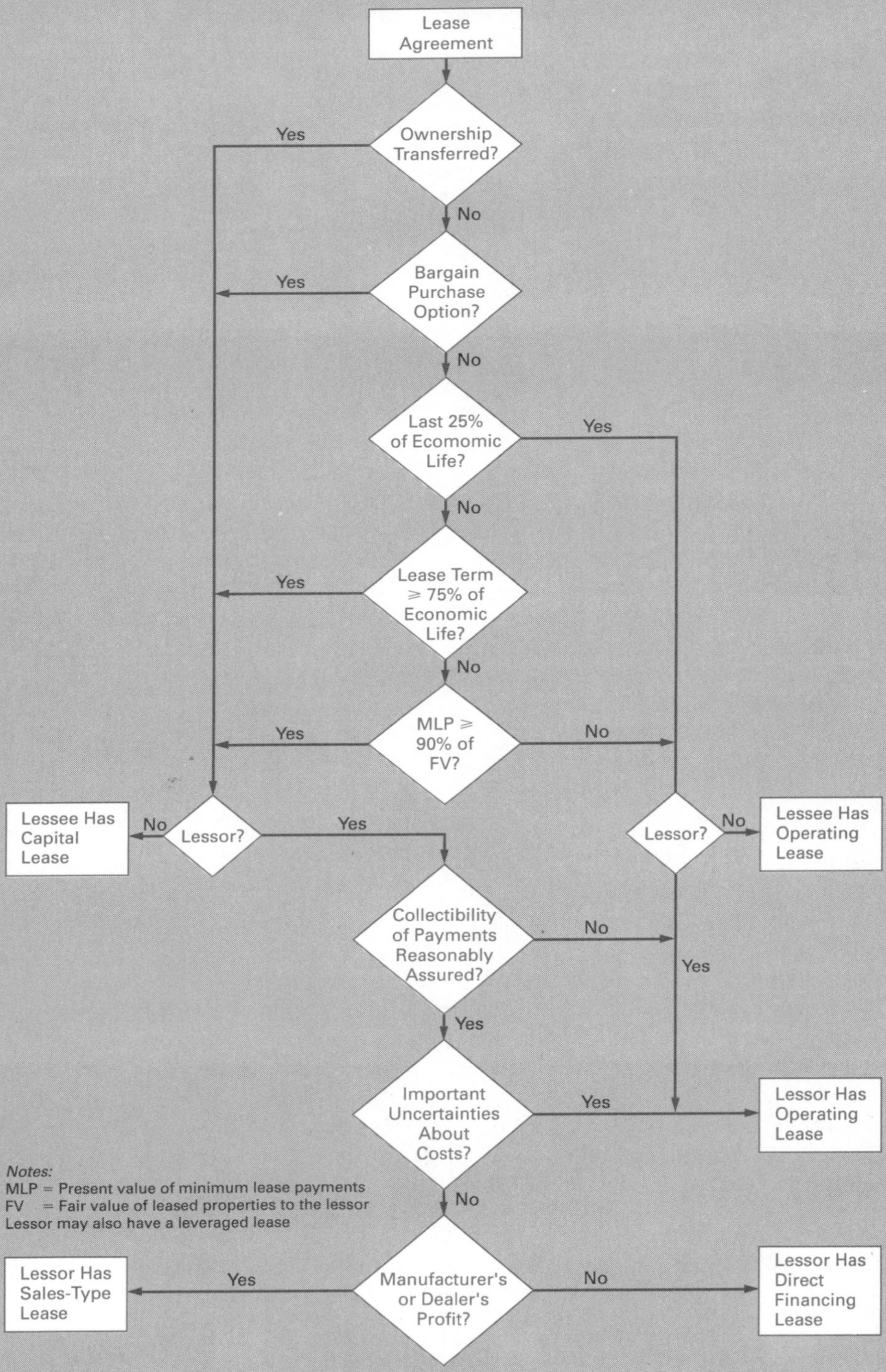

Notes:
MLP = Present value of minimum lease payments
FV = Fair value of leased properties to the lessor
Lessor may also have a leveraged lease

*Source:* Adapted from "Accounting for Leases: Decisions Flowcharts Supplement," *FASB Statement No. 13 as Amended and Interpreted through January 1990* (Norwalk, Conn.: FASB, 1990), pp. 5 and 15.

## Operating Lease (Lessee)

An operating lease is the simplest type. To illustrate, assume that a lease agreement is signed between the Tenant Company and the Landlord Company that contains the terms and provisions listed in Exhibit 19-4. In this illustration, the lease does not transfer ownership or provide a bargain purchase option, and the lease term is 50% of the economic life. In addition, the present value of the minimum lease payments is $201,867, as shown in Exhibit 19-4, which is only 67% of the fair market value of the property. Therefore, this lease is an operating lease for the lessee because it meets none of the four criteria, as summarized in Exhibit 19-5.

---

### EXHIBIT 19-4

**TERMS AND PROVISIONS OF LEASE AGREEMENT BETWEEN LANDLORD COMPANY (LESSOR) AND TENANT COMPANY (LESSEE) DATED JANUARY 1, 1995**

1. The lease term is 5 years. The lease is noncancelable and requires equal rental payments of $50,000 at the beginning of each year.
2. The cost, and also fair value, of the equipment to the Landlord Company at the inception of the lease is $300,000. The equipment has an estimated economic life of 10 years and has a zero estimated residual value at the end of this time.
3. There is no guarantee of the residual value by the Tenant Company.
4. The Landlord Company agrees to pay all executory costs.
5. The equipment reverts to the Landlord Company at the end of the 5 years; that is, the lease contains no bargain purchase option and no agreement to transfer ownership at the end of the lease.
6. The Tenant Company's incremental borrowing rate is 12.5% per year.
7. For the Landlord Company, the interest rate implicit in the lease is 12%.
8. The present value of an annuity due (in advance) of 5 payments of $50,000 each at 12% is $201,867, calculated as follows:
   4.037349 × $50,000 = $201,867.45

---

### EXHIBIT 19-5

**APPLICATION OF CRITERIA FOR DETERMINATION OF LEASE CLASSIFICATION BY TENANT (LESSEE)**

| Classification Criteria | Criteria Met? | Remarks |
|---|---|---|
| 1. Transfer of ownership at end of lease | No | |
| 2. Bargain purchase option | No | |
| 3. Lease term is 75% of economic life | No | It is 50% |
| 4. Present value of lease payments is 90% of fair value | No | The present value is $201,867.45, or 67% of fair value |

*Decision:* A capital lease must meet one or more of the classification criteria; otherwise the lease is an operating lease.
*Conclusion:* The lease is an operating lease. It meets none of the criteria.

The only journal entry recorded by the Tenant Company is the following, which is made each year on January 1, 1995 through 1999.

| | | |
|---|---|---|
| Rent Expense | 50,000 | |
| Cash | | 50,000 |

If monthly or quarterly interim statements are prepared, the unexpired portion of the expense is reported as an asset, Prepaid Rent. The rented equipment is not reported in the lessee's balance sheet; however, future minimum rental payments and other information are disclosed in the notes to the financial statements, as discussed at the end of this section.

### Capital Lease (Lessee)

When equipment is leased under a capital lease, **the lessee records an asset and a liability equal to the sum of the present value, at the beginning of the lease term, of the minimum lease payments during the lease term.**[4] In accounting for the asset and liability, consideration must be given to executory costs, the discount rate, amortization of the leased asset, and reduction of the lease obligation.

*Executory Costs*
Costs such as insurance, maintenance, and property taxes, called **executory costs,** may be *paid* by either the lessee or the lessor, depending on how the lease contract is written. However, since the risks and benefits of ownership have been transferred in a capital lease, the *lessee* is usually responsible for these costs. Therefore, if these *ownership-type* costs are paid by the *lessor,* a portion of each lease payment that represents these executory costs is *excluded* in computing the present value of the minimum lease payments. The reason is that part of the lease payments represents a reimbursement by the lessee of the executory costs paid by the lessor. The remainder of the payment represents the interest cost and the reduction of the lease liability. That is, **the lease payment minus the executory costs paid by the lessor equals the minimum lease payment.** If the executory costs are not specifically stated in the lease contract, then before computing the present value, the lessee would estimate the amount of the executory costs contained in each lease payment in order to determine the amount to subtract from each lease payment.

Many capital leases provide for the *lessee* to pay the executory costs directly. In such cases, the executory costs are expensed as incurred. Therefore, the values of the asset and liability are determined by discounting the minimum lease payments without an adjustment for executory costs. Each lease payment represents the interest cost and the reduction of the lease liability.

*Discount Rate*
The lessee computes the present value of the minimum lease payments by using the *lower* of the following:

1. *The lessee's incremental borrowing rate,* or

2. *The lessor's interest rate implicit in the lease,* if known by the lessee (or if it is practicable for the lessee to learn[5]).

---

4.   *Ibid.,* sec. L10.106. Note also that the asset cannot be recorded at an amount that exceeds its fair market value.
5.   *Ibid.,* sec. L10.103.

Since the lessee is acquiring an asset, the rate used to borrow money to acquire an asset (the incremental borrowing rate) is the preferred rate. Alternatively, if the rate in the contract (the implicit rate) is known and lower, it is a more relevant rate to use. The lessor typically will disclose its implicit rate. If it does not and there is a guaranteed residual value, or a bargain purchase option, or the lessor's estimate of the unguaranteed residual value is known, the lessee can compute the implicit rate. If none of these amounts are known, the lessee does not have sufficient information to compute the implicit rate. If the lessor does not disclose the implicit rate and the lessee cannot compute it, the lessee would have to use its incremental borrowing rate.

### Amortization of Leased Asset

Since the lessee records an asset, amortization has to be computed. The FASB uses the term **amortization** more frequently than it does **depreciation** because the leased asset technically is an intangible asset, although it usually is shown in the property, plant, and equipment section of the lessee's balance sheet. Either term could be appropriately applied to the name of the expense. If the asset is written off over the estimated economic life of the property, the usual term that is applied is **depreciation.** If the asset is written off over a shorter period of time (the term of the lease), the process is more often referred to as **amortization.**

Regardless of which term is used, if the capital lease agreement (1) transfers ownership of the asset to the lessee or (2) contains a bargain purchase option, the asset is depreciated (or amortized) over the estimated *economic* life of the property to the estimated residual value at the end of the economic life. The estimated economic life is used because the lessee is expected to acquire ownership of the asset. If the capital lease does not transfer ownership of the asset to the lessee, or if it does not contain a bargain purchase option, the leased asset is amortized over the lease life because the rights to the use of the asset cease at the end of the lease. The leased asset is amortized down to its guaranteed residual value to the lessee at the end of the lease term.[6] The lessee uses an amortization (depreciation) method that is consistent with its normal depreciation policy for similar, owned assets. The depreciation of leased property by the lessee (or the lessor if there is an operating lease) is summarized in Exhibit 19-6, using a flow chart.

*The principles involved in the selection of an appropriate depreciation method are discussed in Chapter 9.*

### Reduction of the Lease Obligation

Since the lessee records a liability, interest expense and the reduction of the principal have to be computed for each lease payment. The effective interest method (also called the interest method) is used to compute these amounts. This method produces a constant rate of interest on the balance of the lease obligation outstanding at the beginning of each period. *FASB Statement No. 13 as Amended* permits the use of other methods, provided the results obtained are not materially different from those that result from the use of the effective interest method. In this chapter, only the effective interest method is used.

## Illustration of Lessee's Capital Lease Method

### Example 1: Equipment Is Leased Under an Agreement Without a Purchase or Bargain Purchase Option

The Martin Company, the lessee, and the Gardner Company, the lessor, sign a lease agreement dated January 1, 1995 that provides for the Martin Company to lease a piece of equipment from the Gardner Company beginning January 1, 1995. The lease contains the terms and provisions shown in Exhibit 19-7.

---

6. *Ibid.*, sec. L10.107.

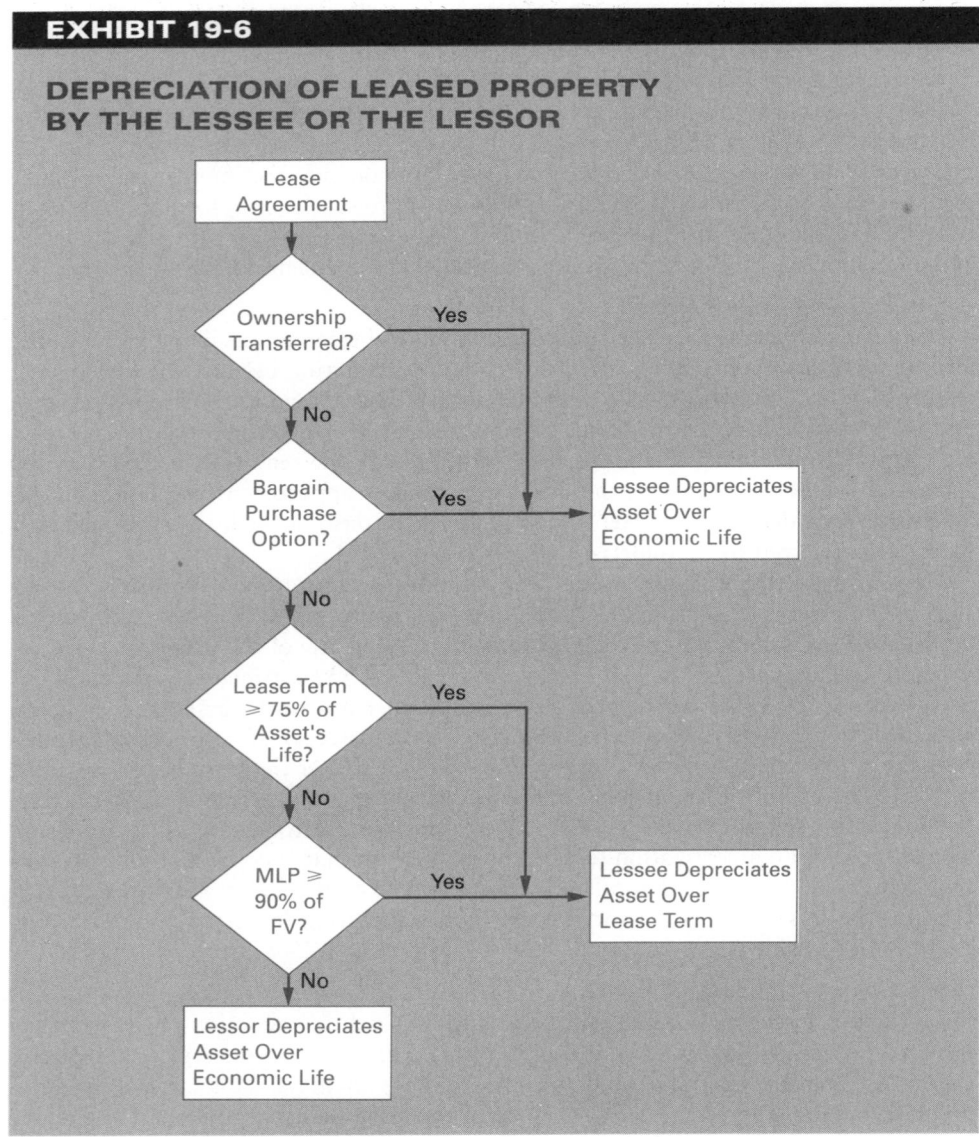

**EXHIBIT 19-6**

**DEPRECIATION OF LEASED PROPERTY BY THE LESSEE OR THE LESSOR**

First, it must be determined whether the lease is a capital lease. The test shown Exhibit 19-8 reveals that it is. Since it is a capital lease, the lessee records the leased asset at the present value of the minimum lease payments (executory costs are paid by the lessee), and this amount does not exceed the fair market value. The discount rate is 12%, the interest rate implicit in the lease, since it is assumed that this rate is known and is lower than the lessee's incremental borrowing rate of 12.5%.

The journal entries to record the acquisition of the leased asset, the amortization (depreciation), and the minimum lease payments for 2 years by the Martin Company are as follows:

1. *Initial Recording of Capital Lease on January 1, 1995*

| | | |
|---|---|---|
| Leased Equipment Under Capital Leases | 100,000.00 | |
|     Obligation Under Capital Leases | | 100,000.00 |

---

**EXHIBIT 19-7**

**TERMS AND PROVISIONS OF LEASE AGREEMENT
BETWEEN GARDNER COMPANY (LESSOR) AND
MARTIN COMPANY (LESSEE) DATED JANUARY 1, 1995**

1. The lease term is 4 years. The lease is noncancelable and requires equal payments of $32,923.45 at the end of each year.
2. The cost, and also fair value, of the equipment to the Gardner Company at the inception of the lease is $100,000. The equipment has an estimated economic life of 4 years and has a zero estimated residual value at the end of this time.
3. There is no guarantee of the residual value by the Martin Company.
4. The Martin Company agrees to pay all executory costs.
5. The equipment reverts to the Gardner Company at the end of the 4 years; that is, the lease contains no purchase provisions.
6. The Martin Company's incremental borrowing rate is 12.5% per year.
7. The Martin Company uses the straight-line method to record depreciation on similar equipment.
8. For the Gardner Company, the interest rate implicit in the lease is 12%. The Martin Company knows this rate.
9. The present value of an ordinary annuity of 4 payments of $32,923.45 each at 12% is $100,000, calculated as follows: $3.037349 \times \$32,923.45 = \$100,000$. (This is the only present value calculation necessary, since there is no guaranteed residual value or bargain purchase option.)

---

**EXHIBIT 19-8**

**APPLICATION OF CRITERIA FOR DETERMINATION OF LEASE
CLASSIFICATION BY MARTIN COMPANY (LESSEE)**

| Classification Criteria | Criteria Met? | Remarks |
|---|---|---|
| 1. Transfer of ownership at end of lease | No | Title reverts to lessor |
| 2. Bargain purchase option | No | |
| 3. Lease term is 75% of economic life | Yes | 100% of estimated life |
| 4. Present value of lease payments is 90% of fair value | Yes | The present value is $100,000, or 100% of fair value |

*Decision:* A capital lease must meet one or more of the classification criteria; otherwise, the lease is an operating lease.
*Conclusion:* The lease is a capital lease. It meets two of the four criteria.

---

The accounting methods and account titles used in the example are those recommended by *FASB Statement No. 13 as Amended*. The *Statement* requires the use of the $100,000 "net" present value for both the asset and the liability rather than the "gross" value of $131,693.80 ($4 \times \$32,923.45$). It is acceptable, however, to record the liability at this gross amount with an accompanying debit to an account that is a contra-liability, Discount on Lease Obligation, for $31,693.80. This alternative procedure may be useful in the preparation of the required disclosures that are discussed later.

2. *First Annual Payment and Recognition of Interest Expense on Capital Lease on December 31, 1995*

| | | |
|---|---|---|
| Interest Expense | 12,000.00 | |
| Obligation Under Capital Leases | 20,923.45 | |
|    Cash | | 32,923.45 |

The annual payment is $32,923.45. This amount represents (1) a payment of interest of $12,000 (12% $\times$ $100,000) and (2) a reduction of the lease obligation liability of $20,923.45 ($32,923.45 − $12,000). Note that this lease requires the payment to be made at the end of the year; thus, the annuity is an ordinary annuity. If the payments are required to be made at the beginning of the year, the annuity is an annuity due (illustrated later in this chapter).

3. *Recognition of Annual Depreciation of Leased Equipment on December 31, 1995*

| | | |
|---|---|---|
| Depreciation Expense: Leased Equipment | 25,000.00 | |
|    Accumulated Depreciation: | | |
|       Leased Equipment | | 25,000.00 |

The asset is amortized (depreciated) over the lease term because the lease does not include a transfer of ownership or a bargain purchase option. The straight-line method is used by the lessee, and the annual depreciation is $25,000 ($100,000 ÷ 4). The credit is made to an Accumulated Depreciation account. It is acceptable (but less desirable) accounting to make the credit directly to the asset, Leased Equipment Under Capital Leases.

On the balance sheet prepared as of December 31, 1995, the Leased Equipment under Capital Leases less the Accumulated Depreciation (amortization) is included in the property, plant, and equipment section of the assets, and the Obligation Under Capital Leases is divided between current liabilities and long-term liabilities, as discussed in the next section. The appropriate journal entries for 1996 are as follows:

4. *Second Annual Payment and Recognition of Interest Expense on December 31, 1996*

| | | |
|---|---|---|
| Interest Expense | 9,489.19 | |
| Obligation Under Capital Leases | 23,434.26 | |
|    Cash | | 32,923.45 |

The amount of the second payment is the same as that for 1995, but the payment for interest is only $9,489.19 (12% $\times$ $79,076.55); that is, the effective rate of 12% multiplied by the balance of the lease obligation at the beginning of 1996. The remainder of the annual payment represents a reduction of the principal of $23,434.26 ($32,923.45 − $9,489.19). The interest expense and the reduction of the liability over the life of the lease are shown in Exhibit 19-9.

5. *Recognition of Annual Depreciation on December 31, 1996*

| | | |
|---|---|---|
| Depreciation Expense: Leased Equipment | 25,000.00 | |
|    Accumulated Depreciation: | | |
|       Leased Equipment | | 25,000.00 |

Under the straight-line method, the amortization (depreciation) entry for 1996 is the same as that for 1995.

---

**EXHIBIT 19-9**

## SUMMARY OF LEASE PAYMENTS AND INTEREST EXPENSE OF MARTIN COMPANY (LESSEE)

Payments at End of Year

| (1) Date | (2) Annual Lease Payment | (3) Interest at 12% on Unpaid Obligation[a] | (4) Reduction of Lease Obligation[b] | (5) Balance of Lease Obligation Liability[c] |
|---|---|---|---|---|
| January 1, 1995 | — | — | — | $100,000.00 |
| December 31, 1995 | $32,923.45 | $12,000.00 | $20,923.45 | 79,076.55 |
| December 31, 1996 | 32,923.45 | 9,489.19 | 23,434.26 | 55,642.29 |
| December 31, 1997 | 32,923.45 | 6,677.07 | 26,246.38 | 29,395.91 |
| December 31, 1998 | 32,923.45 | 3,527.54[d] | 29,395.91 | — |

a. Column 5 at beginning of year × 12%.
b. Column 2 − Column 3.
c. Column 5 at beginning of year − Column 4.
d. Adjusted for rounding error of $0.03.

The journal entries through 1998 would follow a pattern similar to those presented for 1995 and 1996. Omitted from the preceding entries are those to record the payment by the Martin Company of executory costs such as insurance, maintenance, and property taxes. These are recorded in regular operating expense accounts of the lessee. For example, if the Martin Company paid $3,000 for repairs on the leased equipment during 1995, it would record the payment as a debit to Repair Expense.

### Classification of Obligation Under Capital Leases

In classifying the lease obligation in the balance sheet, *FASB Statement No. 13 as Amended* requires that the obligation is separately identified in the balance sheet as an obligation under capital leases and is subject to the same considerations as other obligations in classifying them with current and noncurrent liabilities in classified balance sheets.[7] Since no guidelines were provided to measure the respective amounts, accounting theory and practice differ as to the measurement of the amount of the current liability portion. Two approaches are used: (1) the present value of next year's payments and (2) the change in the present value.[8]

### Present Value of Next Year's Payments

Under the present value of next year's payments approach, the amount of the current liability is the payment(s) to be made in the next year discounted to the balance sheet date. For the Martin Company, the current liability each year is $29,395.93 (0.892857 × $32,923.45). The remaining portion of the obligation is classified as a noncurrent liability. This approach, which produces the same current liability each

---

7. *Ibid.*, sec. L10.112.
8. R. J. Swieringa, "When Current Is Noncurrent and Vice Versa!", *The Accounting Review* (January 1984), pp. 123–130.

year for a given lease, is conceptually sound and consistent with the theoretical measurement of liabilities in general. In this chapter, the present value of next year's payments approach is used to determine the current liability portion of the lease obligation.

### Change in the Present Value

The change in present value approach often is used in practice to measure the amount of the current liability. In this approach, the current liability is the amount by which the total balance of the lease liability will decrease in the next year. For the Martin Company, the current portion of the liability on December 31, 1995 is \$23,434.26 (\$79,076.55 − \$55,642.29); on December 31, 1996, \$26,246.38 (\$55,642.29 − \$29,395.91). Note that the current liability on December 31, 1997 (the balance sheet preceding the last year's lease payment) is the same for each approach (with minor differences for rounding).

### Example 2: Lease Payments Are Required to Be Made at the Beginning of the Year

Suppose that all the lease provisions described in Exhibit 19-7 are the same *except* that the lease payments are required to be made in advance on January 1 of each year and that the *cost* (and also fair value) of the equipment is \$112,000. The annuity calculation is now the present value of an *annuity due* rather than that of an ordinary annuity. The value of the asset and the liability is different, as shown by the following calculation:

$$\text{Present Value of Four Rents of } \$32{,}923.45 \text{ in Advance at } 12\% = \$32{,}923.45 \times 3.401831$$

$$= \$112{,}000 \text{ (rounded)}$$

The information for the interest expense and the reduction of the lease obligation liability for each period is shown in Exhibit 19-10. The journal entries through January 1, 1996 are as follows:

1. *Initial Recording of Capital Lease on January 1, 1995*

| | | |
|---|---|---|
| **Leased Equipment Under Capital Leases** | 112,000.00 | |
| **Obligation Under Capital Leases** | | 112,000.00 |

Both the asset and the obligation are recorded at the present value computed earlier.

2. *First Annual Payment in Advance on January 1, 1995*

| | | |
|---|---|---|
| **Obligation Under Capital Leases** | 32,923.45 | |
| **Cash** | | 32,923.45 |

The first payment is entirely a reduction of principal, since no interest has accrued. (The preceding two journal entries could be made as one compound entry.)

3. *Recognition of Annual Depreciation of Leased Equipment on December 31, 1995*

| | | |
|---|---|---|
| **Depreciation Expense: Leased Equipment** | 28,000.00 | |
| **Accumulated Depreciation: Leased Equipment** | | 28,000.00 |

The straight-line amortization (depreciation) is \$112,000 ÷ 4 years, or \$28,000.

4. *Recognition of Interest Expense on Capital Lease on December 31, 1995*

| | |
|---|---|
| Interest Expense | 9,489.19 |
|     Accrued Interest on Obligation Under | |
|         Capital Leases[9] | 9,489.19 |

Even though the next payment will not be made until January 1, 1996, the accrual concept requires that the interest expense be recognized in the year that it is incurred. In 1995, the amount is $9,489.19, or 12% of $79,076.55 ($112,000 − $32,923.45), as shown in Exhibit 19-10. It should be recognized that the Obligation Under Capital Leases must be divided into its current and noncurrent portions in the year-end balance sheet. In the December 31, 1995 balance sheet, $32,923.45 is shown as a current liability and the remaining part, $55,642.29, is disclosed as a long-term liability.

5. *Second Annual Payment in Advance on January 1, 1996*

| | | |
|---|---|---|
| Accrued Interest on Obligation Under | | |
|     Capital Leases | 9,489.19 | |
| Obligation Under Capital Leases | 23,434.26 | |
|     Cash | | 32,923.45 |

The interest applicable to 1996 is $9,489.19, as shown in Exhibit 19-10. The remaining entries would follow the pattern of those for 1996.

## EXHIBIT 19-10

### SUMMARY OF LEASE PAYMENTS AND INTEREST EXPENSE OF MARTIN COMPANY (LESSEE)

**Payments in Advance**

| (1) Date | (2) Annual Lease Payment | (3) Interest at 12% on Unpaid Obligation[a] | (4) Balance of Lease Obligation Liability[b] |
|---|---|---|---|
| January 1, 1995 | Before the initial lease payment | | $112,000.00 |
| January 1, 1995 | $32,923.45 | | 79,076.55 |
| December 31, 1995 | | $9,489.19 | 88,565.74[d] |
| January 1, 1996 | 32,923.45[c] | | 55,642.29 |
| December 31, 1996 | | 6,677.07 | 62,319.36[d] |
| January 1, 1997 | 32,923.45 | | 29,395.91 |
| December 31, 1997 | | 3,527.54[e] | 32,923.45[d] |
| January 1, 1998 | 32,923.45 | | 0 |

a. Column 4 at beginning of year × 12%.
b. Column 4 at beginning of year − Column 2 + Column 3.
c. Each lease payment, after the initial payment, includes the accrued interest for the previous year.
d. $32,923.45 of this amount is a current liability; it will be paid January 1 of the next year. The remaining amount is a noncurrent liability.
e. Adjusted for $0.03 rounding error.

---

9. If not material, this amount may be credited to the liability account, Obligation Under Capital Leases.

## Other Lessee Capitalization Issues

Two other capitalization issues regarding the asset and liability of the lessee for capital leases require additional consideration: (1) the impact of a bargain purchase option and (2) the impact of a guaranteed residual value.

### Impact of Bargain Purchase Option

To illustrate the impact of a bargain purchase option, assume that Redd Company leases equipment for 4 years and agrees to a payment of $40,000 at the end of each year. The lease also includes an option to pay $2,000 at the end of the fourth year to purchase the asset. This amount is so much lower than the expected fair value at the end of the fourth year that exercise of the option is reasonably assured. Therefore, it is a bargain purchase option. The incremental borrowing rate is 10%; this is lower than the lessor's implicit interest rate. The cost and fair market value of the equipment is $128,160.63. This lease qualifies as a capital lease because there is a bargain purchase option. The lessee records the leased equipment at the present value of the minimum lease payments (which includes the bargain purchase option), calculated as follows:

| | |
|---|---:|
| Present value of the annual payments discounted at 10% ($40,000 × 3.169865) | $126,794.60 |
| Add: Present value of the single sum of $2,000 (the bargain purchase option) discounted at 10% ($2,000 × 0.683013) | 1,366.03 |
| Present value of the minimum lease payments | $128,160.63 |

The lessee records the leased asset as follows:

| | | |
|---|---:|---:|
| Leased Equipment Under Capital Leases | 128,160.63 | |
|    Obligation Under Capital Leases | | 128,160.63 |

The subsequent accounting for the lessee follows the same principles as in the previous capital lease examples except that the Leased Equipment Under Capital Leases asset amount of $128,160.63 is depreciated over the estimated *economic life* of the asset (not over the term of the lease) to its estimated residual value (*not* the bargain purchase option of $2,000). The liability account, Obligation Under Capital Leases, is reduced as previously illustrated by the effective interest method, but at the end of the fourth year, it will have a balance of $2,000. When the lessee exercises the bargain purchase option, it will debit Obligation Under Capital Leases and credit Cash for, $2,000.

### Impact of Guaranteed Residual Value

The lessee may agree to guarantee part or all of the residual value; that is, it guarantees that the value of the leased asset at the end of the lease term will be the stated amount of the guarantee. If the asset is not worth this guaranteed value, the lessee must pay the lessor any difference between this smaller value and the guaranteed value. The guaranteed residual value is included in the minimum lease payments and, therefore, the lessee capitalizes the present value of the amount guaranteed. To illustrate, assume that Karpas Company leases equipment for 4 years that cost the lessor $147,284.99 (its fair market value) and agrees to pay an annual rent of $40,000 at the end of each year. The equipment has an estimated residual value of $30,000 at the end of the fourth year. The Karpas Company agrees to guarantee the entire amount of this residual value (and there is no transfer of ownership or bargain purchase option). Again, assume an appropriate interest rate of 10%. This lease is a capital lease because the present value of the minimum lease payments ($147,284.99), as shown in the following calculation, is equal to 90% or more of the fair value of the leased property ($147,284.99).

| | |
|---|---|
| Present value of the annual lease payments discounted at 10% ($40,000 × 3.169865) | $126,794.60 |
| Add: Present value of the single sum of $30,000 (the guaranteed residual value) discounted at 10% ($30,000 × 0.683013) | 20,490.39 |
| Present value of minimum lease payments | $147,284.99 |

The lessee records the leased equipment at the present value of the minimum lease payments (which includes the guaranteed residual value) as follows:

| | | |
|---|---|---|
| Leased Equipment Under Capital Leases | 147,284.99 | |
| Obligation Under Capital Leases | | 147,284.99 |

The subsequent accounting for the lease follows the same principles as in the previous capital lease examples. The asset account is amortized by an appropriate method over the *lease term* down to the guaranteed residual value. The liability is reduced by the use of the effective interest method, and at the end of the fourth year it would have a balance of $30,000. The elimination of this balance depends on the condition of the leased asset at the end of the lease term and the terms of the lease agreement.

*Illustration of Disposal Where Lease Has a Guaranteed Residual Value*
Based on the previous information, at the beginning of the fifth year the records of the Karpas Company would contain the following accounts with balances as indicated:

| Account | Balance |
|---|---|
| Leased Equipment Under Capital Leases | $147,284.99 (debit) |
| Accumulated Depreciation: Leased Equipment | 117,284.99 (credit) |
| Obligation Under Capital Leases | 30,000.00 (credit) |

If the fair market value of the leased asset is less than $30,000, part of the liability may be paid by returning the asset to the lessor. The remaining part then is paid in cash and recognized as a loss on disposal of the asset. To illustrate this situation, assume that the Karpas Company returns the leased equipment to the lessor. Both the Karpas Company and the lessor agree that, because of damage to the equipment, it is worth only $20,000. The Karpas Company pays the lessor $10,000 in cash. This information is recorded by Karpas as follows:

| | | |
|---|---|---|
| Accumulated Depreciation: Leased Equipment | 117,284.99 | |
| Obligation Under Capital Leases | 30,000.00 | |
| Loss on Disposal of Leased Equipment | 10,000.00 | |
| Leased Equipment Under Capital Leases | | 147,284.99 |
| Cash | | 10,000.00 |

If the fair market value is greater than $30,000, the liability is paid in full by the return of the asset to the lessor. In this case, no gain or loss is recognized by the lessee. Note that any *unguaranteed* residual value is ignored by the lessee.

Leases may be written with various provisions. Often, for example, the lessee will be required to pay the lessor the full guaranteed residual value (in this case, $30,000) in cash. The lessee then may choose to sell the asset or keep it for continued use in its operating activities.

### Disclosure Requirements of the Lessee

*FASB Statement No. 13 as Amended* requires certain disclosures by the lessee for both operating and capital leases. The information presented in Exhibit 19-11 is disclosed in the lessee's balance sheet or in notes[10] to the financial statements. Wal-Mart Stores discloses its lease information in Note 7 of its 1992 financial statements, as illustrated in Exhibit 19-12.

---

**EXHIBIT 19-11**

## DISCLOSURE REQUIREMENTS FOR LESSEE: OPERATING AND CAPITAL LEASES

A. For operating leases having initial or remaining noncancelable lease terms in excess of one year:
  1. Future minimum rental payments required as of the date of the latest balance sheet presented, in the aggregate and for each of the 5 succeeding fiscal years.
  2. The total of minimum rentals to be received in the future under noncancelable subleases as of the date of the latest balance sheet presented.
B. For all operating leases, rental expense for each period, with separate amounts for minimum rentals, contingent rentals, and sublease rentals. Rental payments under leases with terms of a month or less that were not renewed need not be included.
C. For capital leases:
  1. The gross amount of assets recorded under capital leases as of the date of each balance sheet presented by major classes according to nature or function. This information may be combined with comparable information for owned assets.
  2. Future minimum lease payments as of the date of the latest balance sheet presented, in the aggregate and for each of the 5 succeeding fiscal years, with separate deductions from the total (1) for the amount representing executory costs, including any profit, included in the minimum lease payments, and (2) for the amount of the imputed interest necessary to reduce the net minimum lease payments to present value.
  3. The total of minimum sublease rentals to be received in the future under noncancelable subleases as of the date of the latest balance sheet presented.
  4. Total contingent rentals incurred for each period.
  5. Assets, accumulated amortization, amortization expense, and liabilities.
D. For all leases, a general description of the lessee's leasing arrangements including, but not limited to, the following:
  1. The basis on which contingent rental payments are determined.
  2. The existence and term of renewal or purchase options and escalation clauses.
  3. Restrictions imposed by lease agreements, such as those concerning dividends, additional debt, and further leasing.

---

10. *FASB Statement No. 13 as Amended and Interpreted through January 1990, op. cit.,* sec. L10.112.

**EXHIBIT 19-12**

## WAL-MART STORE

## LONG-TERM LEASE OBLIGATIONS

*Note 7*
The Company and certain of its subsidiaries have long-term leases for stores and equipment. Rentals (including, for certain, leases amounts applicable to taxes, insurance, maintenance, other operating expenses, and contingent rentals) under all operating leases were $313,346,000 in 1993, $285,856,000 in 1992, and $267,455,000 in 1991. Aggregate minimum annual rentals at January 31, 1993, under non-cancelable leases are as follows:

| Fiscal Years | Operating Leases | Capital Leases |
|---|---|---|
| 1994 | $ 250,513,000 | $ 235,534,000 |
| 1995 | 241,113,000 | 234,914,000 |
| 1996 | 234,948,000 | 234,833,000 |
| 1997 | 240,302,000 | 234,575,000 |
| 1998 | 230,250,000 | 233,782,000 |
| Thereafter | 2,341,094,000 | 2,984,596,000 |
| Total minimum rentals | $3,538,220,000 | 4,158,234,000 |
| Less estimated executory costs | | 65,283,000 |
| Net minimum lease payments | | 4,092,951,000 |
| Less imputed interest at rates ranging from 8.0% to 14.0% | | 2,275,246,000 |
| Present value of net minimum lease payments | | $1,817,705,000 |

Certain of the leases provide for contingent additional rentals based on percentage of sales. Such additional rentals amounted to $29,746,000 in 1993, $25,774,000 in 1992, and $23,204,000 in 1991. Substantially all of the store leases have renewal options for additional terms from five to 25 years at the same or lower minimum rentals.

The Company has entered into lease commitments for land and buildings for 61 future locations. These lease commitments with real estate developers or through sale/leaseback arrangements provide for minimum rentals for 15 to 25 years, excluding renewal options, which if consummated based on current cost estimates will approximate $48,433,000 annually over the lease terms.

## ACCOUNTING AND REPORTING BY LESSORS

Recall that leases are classified by the lessor as follows:

1. **Operating lease.** A lease that meets none of the criteria in Column A or does not meet both of the criteria in Column B of Exhibit 19-2.

2. **Sales-type lease.** A sales-type lease involves the recognition of a manufacturer's or dealer's profit (or loss) and meets one or more of the criteria in Column A and both the criteria in Column B of Exhibit 19-2.

3. **Direct financing lease.** A direct financing lease involves no manufacturer's or dealer's profit (or loss) and meets one or more of the criteria in Column A and both the criteria in Column B of Exhibit 19-2.

4. **Leveraged lease.** A leveraged lease is a special three-party lease that is always considered to be a direct financing lease. These leases are discussed briefly in the Appendix to this chapter.

The accounting method for each of the first three leases is discussed in the following sections.

## Operating Lease (Lessor)

**Under an operating lease, a lessor company leasing an asset to a lessee retains substantially all the risks and benefits of ownership.** The lessor includes the leased asset, say equipment, on its balance sheet in a subsection of property, plant, and equipment entitled Plant and Equipment Leased to Others, and records depreciation on it. The lessor usually pays executory costs and records the rental receipts as revenue when they become receivable. If these rental receipts vary from a uniform straight-line basis, the revenue still is recognized on a straight-line basis unless another systematic and rational basis is more representative of the time pattern in which the benefits from the leased property are earned.[11]

For an illustration of an operating lease, assume that the Landlord Company leases a piece of equipment to Tenant Company for 5 years under the terms described in Exhibit 19-4. Tenant Company agrees to pay $50,000 at the beginning of each year. In addition, the equipment was purchased by Landlord Company at a cost of $300,000; it has an estimated life of 10 years. Landlord Company uses the straight-line method of depreciation. On January 10, 1995, the lessor pays the annual insurance premium of $2,000 and on December 15, 1995, pays for repairs of $1,500. Assume that there are no initial direct costs involved in this lease. The preceding information is recorded in the following journal entries:

1. *Purchase of Equipment to Be Leased on January 1, 1995*

| | | |
|---|---|---|
| **Equipment Leased to Others** | 300,000 | |
| Cash (or Accounts Payable) | | 300,000 |

The acquisition of the equipment is shown to reinforce understanding of its classification. If the equipment was already owned by the company, the credit in the preceding entry would be to the Equipment account, and Accumulated Depreciation would also be reclassified.

2. *Collection of Annual Payment on Operating Lease on January 1, 1995*

| | | |
|---|---|---|
| **Cash** | 50,000 | |
| Rental Revenue | | 50,000 |

The annual rental payments are collected at the beginning of each year and are recorded as revenue. If receivable at this date but not yet collected, a Rent Receivable account would be debited. If monthly or quarterly interim statements are prepared, the unearned portion of the preceding revenue is reported as a liability, Unearned Rent.

---

11. *Ibid.*, sec. L10.111.

3. *Payment of Annual Insurance Premium on January 10, 1995*

| | | |
|---|---|---|
| **Insurance Expense** | 2,000 | |
| Cash | | 2,000 |

Under operating leases, executory costs such as insurance are normally paid by the lessor; they are recorded as operating expenses and matched against the gross rental revenue. An adjustment to Prepaid Insurance is made for the monthly or quarterly interim statements.

4. *Payment of Repairs on December 15, 1995*

| | | |
|---|---|---|
| **Repair Expense** | 1,500 | |
| Cash | | 1,500 |

The repair expense is another example of an executory cost paid by the lessor.

5. *Recognition of Annual Depreciation Expense on December 31, 1995*

| | | |
|---|---|---|
| **Depreciation Expense: Equipment Leased to Others** | 30,000 | |
| **Accumulated Depreciation: Equipment Leased to Others** | | 30,000 |

The lessor records depreciation on the leased equipment over its 10-year economic life and reports the equipment with the accompanying accumulated depreciation on the balance sheet.

### Initial Direct Costs Involved in an Operating Lease

In the preceding lease illustration, it was assumed that there were no initial direct costs. **Initial direct costs are costs that result directly from acquiring a lease and would not have been incurred had that leasing transaction not occurred.** For an operating lease, these costs are recorded as a prepaid asset and are allocated to an operating expense in proportion to the rental receipts over the term of the operating lease. This procedure results in an appropriate matching of the initial direct costs as an expense against the rental revenue. If the rental receipts are of an equal amount, the amortization of the prepaid asset is by the straight-line method.

## Direct Financing Leases (Lessor)

Under a direct financing lease, the lessor "sells" the asset at a fair market value equal to its cost or carrying value and records an accompanying receivable. Since no manufacturer's or dealer's profit (or loss) arises out of a direct financing lease, **the net amount at which the lessor's receivable is recorded must equal the cost or carrying value of the property.** The *net* receivable is equal to the present value of the future lease payments to be received. There are, however, two components of the net receivable (net investment), the *gross receivable* (the total undiscounted cash flows) and the *unearned interest* (the interest to be earned over the life of the lease). The gross receivable of the lessor includes the sum of[12]

1. The *undiscounted* minimum lease payments to be received by the lessor (net of executory costs paid by the lessor) plus

2. The unguaranteed residual value accruing to the benefit of the lessor.

---

12. *Ibid.*, sec. L10.114.

Note that the gross receivable includes the residual value, whether guaranteed or unguaranteed. If the residual value is guaranteed, it is included in the minimum lease payments. If it is unguaranteed, it is explicitly included as the second item. The difference between the gross receivable, the Minimum Lease Payments Receivable[13] account, and the cost or carrying value of the leased property is recorded as unearned revenue, with a title such as Unearned Interest: Leases. This account is a contra account and is deducted from the Minimum Lease Payments Receivable account to determine the net investment of the lessor in the direct financing lease. This net investment is reported on the balance sheet of the lessor and is divided between the current and noncurrent asset sections. The current asset portion is determined by the present value of next year's payments approach or by the change in present value approach, as explained earlier for the lessee's accounting. Note that the lessor's accounting according to *FASB Statement No. 13 as Amended* follows the "gross" method whereas, as discussed earlier, the lessee's follows the "net" method. It is acceptable, however, for the lessor to record the asset at the "net" amount, provided the appropriate disclosures are made, as illustrated later. However, the main advantage of recording the receivable at the gross (undiscounted) amounts is that this accounting provides the information for the required disclosures, as discussed later.

The interest revenue each period is determined so as to produce a constant periodic rate of return on the net investment of the lease; that is, by the effective interest method. At the inception of the lease, the net investment is equal to the original cost of the asset, if it is new, or the carrying value, if it has been owned in previous periods. **The interest rate implicit in the lease is the rate that, when applied to the gross receivable, will discount that amount to a present value that is equal to the net receivable.** Thus, there are three variables: the present value (the net receivable), the implicit rate, and the future cash flows (the gross receivable). If two of these three variables are known, the third one can be calculated. Three examples of accounting for a direct financing lease are illustrated in the following sections.

*Example 1: Direct Financing Lease with No Unguaranteed*
*Residual Value and Payments Made at End of Year*
For the first example, consider the mirror-image of the Gardner Company leasing equipment to the Martin Company outlined in Exhibit 19-7. In addition to the items contained in this exhibit, assume that:

1. The collectibility of the rentals is reasonably assured, and there are no uncertainties involved in the lease.

2. There are no initial direct costs of negotiating and closing the lease transaction.

The cost, and fair value, of the equipment is $100,000. The interest rate implicit in the lease is 12% on the net investment. Though given in the data for the lessee, the annual rental payments charged the lessee by the lessor are calculated as follows:

$$\text{Annual Payments} = \frac{\text{Known Present Value Equal to the Cost of Equipment}}{\text{Present Value of an Annuity for 4 Periods at 12\%}}$$
$$= \frac{\$100,000}{3.037349}$$
$$= \$32,923.45$$

13. The title "Minimum Lease Payments Receivable" is appropriate when there is a *guaranteed* residual value. The title "Gross Investment in the Lease" is most appropriate when there is an *unguaranteed* residual value because of the lower probability of collection of the residual value, thereby making the use of the term *Receivable* undesirable. For simplicity, we use the title "Minimum Lease Payments Receivable."

As indicated by the test shown in Exhibit 19-13, the lease is a direct financing rather than a sales-type lease because the fair (present) value of the property is equal to its cost.

The Minimum Lease Payments Receivable of the lessor is recorded at the sum of the undiscounted annual payments to be collected from the lessee (less any executory costs paid by the lessor) plus the undiscounted unguaranteed residual value accruing to the benefit of the lessor at the end of the lease term. In the Gardner Company example, since there are no executory costs or unguaranteed residual value, this asset is recorded at

$$[4 \times (\$32,923.45 - \$0)] + \$0 = \$131,693.80$$

The beginning balance of the account, Unearned Interest: Leases, is the difference between the Minimum Lease Payments Receivable account and the cost or carrying value of the leased asset. For the Gardner Company lease, this difference is $31,693.80 ($131,693.80 − $100,000). The journal entries on the Gardner Company books for 1995 and 1996 are as follows:

1. *Initial Recording of the Lease on January 1, 1995*

| | | |
|---|---|---|
| Minimum Lease Payments Receivable | 131,693.80 | |
| Equipment | | 100,000.00 |
| Unearned Interest: Leases | | 31,693.80 |

---

## EXHIBIT 19-13

### APPLICATION OF CRITERIA FOR DETERMINATION OF LEASE CLASSIFICATION BY GARDNER COMPANY (LESSOR)

| Classification Criteria | Criteria Met? | Remarks |
|---|---|---|
| *Group I* | | |
| 1. Transfer of ownership | No | |
| 2. Bargain purchase option | No | |
| 3. Lease term is 75% of economic life | Yes | 100% of economic life |
| 4. Present value of lease payments is 90% of fair value | Yes | The present value is $100,000, or 100% of fair value |
| *Group II* | | |
| 1. Collectibility reasonably assured | Yes | |
| 2. No uncertainties | Yes | |

*Decision:* If the lease meets one or more of the Group I criteria and both of Group II criteria, it is either a direct financing or a sales-type lease. In addition, if there is a manufacturer's or dealer's profit or loss, it is a sales-type lease. If it meets the criteria and does not contain a profit or loss element, it is a direct financing lease.

*Conclusion:* The lease is a direct financing lease, since appropriate criteria are met and there is no manufacturer's or dealer's profit or loss indicated. The present (fair) value of the lease payments equals the cost of the property.

The effect of this transaction is to replace the equipment asset with a financial asset of equal amount. Again, observe that the receivable is recorded at the amount of the gross (undiscounted) rentals plus the estimated unguaranteed residual value of the leased asset (zero in this case). The Equipment account is credited for the cost of the item, because the transaction is interpreted from an *economic-substance-over-legal-form* point of view as the disposal of an asset, even though legal transfer of ownership has not occurred. The Unearned Interest: Leases account is recorded as the difference between the cost of the equipment and the receivable; it is a contra account to the Minimum Lease Payments Receivable account.

2. *Collection of Annual Payment at End of First Year on December 31, 1995*

| | | |
|---|---|---|
| **Cash** | **32,923.45** | |
|     **Minimum Lease Payments Receivable** | | **32,923.45** |

The agreed-upon payment of $32,923.45 is collected and recorded.

3. *Recognition of Interest Revenue for First Year on December 31, 1995*

| | | |
|---|---|---|
| **Unearned Interest: Leases** | **12,000.00** | |
|     **Interest Revenue: Leases** | | **12,000.00** |

The Unearned Interest account is amortized by the use of the effective interest method; that is, the amount of interest revenue recognized in this case is 12% of the net investment at the beginning of the period (the January 1, 1995 balance of the Minimum Lease Payments Receivable less the January 1, 1995 balance of the Unearned Interest: Leases) or $12,000.00 [12% × $100,000 (that is, $131,693.80 − $31,693.80)].

The receivable is divided into current and noncurrent portions for proper balance sheet disclosure. The current and noncurrent amounts of the Net Investment reported on the lessor's December 31, 1995 balance sheet are calculated as follows:

| | Current | Noncurrent |
|---|---|---|
| Minimum lease payments receivable | $32,923.45 | $65,846.90[a] |
| Unearned interest: leases | (3,527.52) | (16,166.27)[b] |
| Net investment | $29,395.93 | $49,680.63 |

a. 2 × $32,923.45
b. [$32,923.45 − ($32,923.45 × 0.797194)] + [$32,923.45 − ($32,923.45 × 0.711780)]

Note that the $29,395.93 current portion plus the $49,680.63 noncurrent portion sum to the $79,076.55 (with a $0.01 rounding error) total Net Investment on December 31, 1995 listed in Exhibit 19-14.

The appropriate journal entries for 1996 are:

4. *Collection of Annual Payment for Second Year on December 31, 1996*

| | | |
|---|---|---|
| **Cash** | **32,923.45** | |
|     **Minimum Lease Payments Receivable** | | **32,923.45** |

The receipt of the payment for the second period is recorded in the same manner as during the first period.

5. *Recognition of Interest Revenue for Second Year on December 31, 1996*

| | | |
|---|---|---|
| **Unearned Interest: Leases** | 9,489.19 | |
| **Interest Revenue: Leases** | | 9,489.19 |

The calculation of the 1996 interest revenue by the effective interest method follows the same procedure as that of 1995. The only difference is that the net investment as of January 1, 1996 is less than that of January 1, 1995. The calculation for 1996 is 12% of the January 1, 1996 balance of the Minimum Lease Payments Receivable less the January 1, 1996 balance of the Unearned Interest: Leases. In this year, the interest revenue is $9,489.19 [12% × $79,076.55 (that is, $100,000 − $20,923.45)].

The interest revenue and the reductions in the receivable and the unearned interest over the life of the lease are shown in Exhibit 19-14. The company would use the information as shown in Exhibit 19-14 to record the journal entries for the remaining years of the lease. At the end of 1998, the net investment is zero.

### Example 2: Direct Financing Lease with No Unguaranteed Residual Value and Payments Received in Advance

To illustrate a direct financing lease with a different timing of the rent receipts, assume that on January 1, 1995 the Watkins Company leases equipment to the Hutton Company, with the terms and provisions of the lease as indicated in Exhibit 19-15. This lease is a direct financing lease because the provisions of the lease agreement outlined in Exhibit 19-15 meet one or more of the Group I and both of the Group II classification criteria, do not include any manufacturer's or dealer's profit, and the fair (present) value of the property is equal to its cost.

### EXHIBIT 19-14

### SUMMARY OF LEASE PAYMENTS RECEIVED AND INTEREST REVENUE EARNED BY GARDNER COMPANY (LESSOR)

Receipts at End of Year

| (1)<br>Date | (2)<br>Annual Lease<br>Payment<br>Received | (3)<br>Interest<br>Revenue at<br>12% on Net<br>Investment[a] | (4)<br>Amount<br>of Net<br>Investment<br>Recovered[b] | (5)<br>Minimum<br>Lease<br>Payments<br>Receivable[c] | (6)<br>Unearned<br>Interest<br>Leases[d] | (7)<br>Net Investment[e] |
|---|---|---|---|---|---|---|
| January 1, 1995 | | | | $131,693.80 | $31,693.80 | $100,000.00 |
| December 31, 1995 | $32,923.45 | $12,000.00 | $20,923.45 | 98,770.35 | 19,693.80 | 79,076.55 |
| December 31, 1996 | 32,923.45 | 9,489.19 | 23,434.26 | 65,846.90 | 10,204.61 | 55,642.29 |
| December 31, 1997 | 32,923.45 | 6,677.07 | 26,246.38 | 32,923.45 | 3,527.54 | 29,395.91 |
| December 31, 1998 | 32,923.45 | 3,527.54[f] | 29,395.91 | 0 | 0 | 0 |

a. Column 7 at beginning of year × 12%.
b. Column 2 − Column 3.
c. Annual lease payment × Number of years remaining on lease, or Previous balance − Column 2.
d. Previous balance − Column 3.
e. Column 5 − Column 6.
f. Adjusted for $0.03 rounding error.

**EXHIBIT 19-15**

**TERMS AND PROVISIONS OF LEASE AGREEMENT
BETWEEN WATKINS COMPANY (LESSOR) AND
HUTTON COMPANY (LESSEE) DATED JANUARY 1, 1995**

1. The cost, and fair value, of the equipment is $391,371.20.
2. The initial direct costs incurred by Watkins Company are assumed to be zero.
3. The term of the lease is 5 years, with annual payments of $100,000 received in advance at the beginning of each year.
4. The economic useful life of the equipment is 5 years, there is no estimated unguaranteed residual value and the lessee is not required to guarantee any estimated residual value.
5. The lease receipts are determined at an amount that will yield to the Watkins Company a 14% annual rate of return on net investment.
6. The Hutton Company pays all the executory costs.
7. The equipment reverts to the Watkins Company at the end of the fifth year; the lease contains no bargain purchase option.
8. The present value of the minimum lease payments receivable for the lessor is $391,371.20, calculated as follows:

Present value of 5 rents of
$100,000 in advance at 14% $= 3.913712 \times \$100,000$

$= \$391,371.20$

9. The collectibility of the payments is reasonably assured, and there are no uncertainties involved in the lease.

The Watkins Company records the information for this lease in 1995 as follows. The amounts used are obtained from Exhibit 19-16, which summarizes the lease payments received and interest revenue earned by the Watkins Company for the 5 years of the lease.

1. *Initial Recording of Lease on January 1, 1995*

| | | |
|---|---|---|
| **Minimum Lease Payments Receivable** | 500,000.00 | |
| Equipment | | 391,371.20 |
| Unearned Interest: Leases | | 108,628.80 |

The Minimum Lease Payments Receivable is recorded at the undiscounted 5 annual rental payments totaling $500,000 (5 × $100,000) plus the unguaranteed residual value ($0 in this case). The Unearned Interest is recorded at $108,628.80, so that the net receivable is recorded at the cost of the equipment of $391,371.20. Because the transaction is considered a disposal of an asset, the Equipment amount is removed from the books.

2. *Collection of Annual Payment for First Year on January 1, 1995*

| | | |
|---|---|---|
| **Cash** | 100,000.00 | |
| Minimum Lease Payments Receivable | | 100,000.00 |

The payments are collectible in advance. The first payment collected consists entirely of principal since no interest has accrued. (The two preceding journal entries could be made as one compound entry.)

3. *Recognition of Interest Revenue for First Year on December 31, 1995*

| | | |
|---|---|---|
| Unearned Interest: Leases | 40,791.97 | |
|     Interest Revenue: Leases | | 40,791.97 |

As shown in Exhibit 19-16, the interest earned in 1995 is $40,791.97 (14% × $291,371.20). This interest revenue is recognized by the adjusting entry. The company would use the information as shown in Exhibit 19-16 to record the journal entries for the remaining years of the lease. At the end of the lease term, there will be a zero balance in both the Minimum Lease Payments Receivable and Unearned Interest: Leases accounts.

*Example 3: Direct Financing Lease with an Unguaranteed Residual Value at the End of the Lease and Payments Made in Advance*

To illustrate a direct financing lease with additional complications, assume that on January 1, 1995 the Carlson Company leases equipment to the Johnson Company, with the terms and provisions of the lease as indicated in Exhibit 19-17.

Since the provisions of the lease agreement in Exhibit 19-17 meet one or more of the Group I and both of the Group II lease classification criteria, and do not include any manufacturer's or dealer's profit, this lease is a direct financing lease.

### EXHIBIT 19-16

### SUMMARY OF LEASE PAYMENTS RECEIVED AND INTEREST REVENUE EARNED BY WATKINS COMPANY (LESSOR)

Receipts in Advance

| (1)<br>Date | (2)<br>Annual Lease<br>Payment<br>Received | (3)<br>Interest<br>Revenue at<br>14% on Net<br>Investment[a] | (4)<br>Minimum Lease<br>Payments<br>Receivable[b] | (5)<br>Unearned<br>Interest:<br>Leases[c] | (6)<br>Net Investment[d] |
|---|---|---|---|---|---|
| January 1, 1995 | | | $500,000 | $108,628.80 | $391,371.20 |
| January 1, 1995 | $100,000 | | 400,000 | | 291,371.20 |
| December 31, 1995 | | $40,791.97 | | 67,836.83 | 332,163.17[e] |
| January 1, 1996 | 100,000 | | 300,000 | | 232,163.17 |
| December 31, 1996 | | 32,502.84 | | 35,333.99 | 264,666.01[e] |
| January 1, 1997 | 100,000 | | 200,000 | | 164,666.01 |
| December 31, 1997 | | 23,053.24 | | 12,280.75 | 187,719.25[e] |
| January 1, 1998 | 100,000 | | 100,000 | | 87,719.25 |
| December 31, 1998 | | 12,280.75[f] | | 0 | 100,000.00[e] |
| January 1, 1998 | 100,000 | | 0 | | 0 |

a. Column 6 at beginning of year × 14%.
b. Annual lease payment × Number of years remaining on lease, or Previous balance − Column 2.
c. Previous balance − Column 3.
d. Column 4 − Column 5.
e. $100,000 of this amount is a current asset; it will be received on January 1 of the next year. The remaining amount is a noncurrent asset.
f. Adjusted for $0.05 rounding error.

**EXHIBIT 19-17**

**TERMS AND PROVISIONS OF LEASE AGREEMENT BETWEEN CARLSON COMPANY (LESSOR) AND JOHNSON COMPANY (LESSEE) DATED JANUARY 1, 1995**

1. The cost, and fair value, of the equipment is $11,149.06.
2. The initial direct costs incurred by Carlson Company are assumed to be zero.
3. The term of the lease is 4 years, with annual payments of $3,000 received at the beginning of each year. The Johnson Company does not guarantee any of the estimated residual value.
4. The estimated economic life of the equipment is 6 years, the lease is for only 4 years, there is an estimated unguaranteed residual value of $2,000 at the end of the lease, and it accrues to the benefit of the Carlson Company.
5. The lease payments are determined at an amount that will yield to the Carlson Company a 14% annual rate of return on its net investment.
6. The Johnson Company pays all the executory costs.
7. The equipment reverts to the Carlson Company at the end of the sixth year. The lease contains no renewal or bargain purchase options.
8. The present value of the minimum lease payments receivable for the lessor, plus the unguaranteed residual value, is $11,149.06, calculated as follows:

Present value of 4 rents of $3,000 in advance at 14% (3.321632 × $3,000) = $ 9,964.90

Add: Present value of a single sum of $2,000 (the unguaranteed residual value) at 14% for 4 periods (0.592080 × $2,000) = 1,184.16

Total present value = $11,149.06

9. The collectibility of the payments is reasonably assured, and there are no uncertainties involved in the lease.

The Carlson Company records the information relevant to this lease for the year 1995 as follows. The amounts used are obtained from Exhibit 19-18, which is a summary of the lease payments received and interest revenue earned by the Carlson Company for the 4-year life of the lease.

1. *Initial Recording of Lease on January 1, 1995*

| | | |
|---|---|---|
| Minimum Lease Payments Receivable | 14,000.00 | |
| Equipment | | 11,149.06 |
| Unearned Interest: Leases | | 2,850.94 |

The Minimum Lease Payments Receivable is recorded at $14,000 (the undiscounted 4 annual rental payments totaling $12,000 plus the $2,000 unguaranteed residual value). Note that the discounted amount of the $2,000 unguaranteed residual value included in the receivable for purposes of determining the net investment must earn a return (14% in this case), as well as the remaining part of the net investment. The Unearned Interest is recorded at

$2,850.94, so that the net receivable is recorded at the cost of the equipment of $11,149.06. Because the transaction is considered a disposal of an asset, the Equipment amount is removed from the books.

2. *Collection of Annual Payment for First Year on January 1, 1995*

| Cash | 3,000.00 | |
| Minimum Lease Payments Receivable | | 3,000.00 |

The payments are collectible in advance. This journal entry reduces the net investment that will earn interest.

3. *Recognition of Interest Revenue for First Year on December 31, 1995*

| Unearned Interest: Leases | 1,140.87 | |
| Interest Revenue: Leases | | 1,140.87 |

As shown in Exhibit 19-18, the interest that is earned during 1995 is $1,140.87. This interest revenue is recognized by the adjusting entry.

The pattern is now set. The company would use the information as shown in Exhibit 19-18 to record the entries for the remaining years. At the end of the lease, there will be $2,000 left in the Minimum Lease Payments Receivable account. When the asset is received by the lessor, it is recorded at the lowest of the cost, carrying value, or fair market value. At that time, a loss may arise if the recorded amount is less than $2,000.

## EXHIBIT 19-18

### SUMMARY OF LEASE PAYMENTS RECEIVED AND INTEREST REVENUE EARNED BY CARLSON COMPANY (LESSOR)

Rents Payable in Advance

| (1) Date | (2) Annual Lease Payment Received | (3) Interest Revenue at 14% on Net Investment[a] | (4) Minimum Lease Payments Receivable[b] | (5) Unearned Interest: Leases[c] | (6) Net Investment[d] |
|---|---|---|---|---|---|
| January 1, 1995 | | | $14,000 | $2,850.94 | $11,149.06 |
| January 1, 1995 | $3,000 | | 11,000 | | 8,149.06[e] |
| December 31, 1995 | | $1,140.87 | | 1,710.07 | 9,289.93 |
| January 1, 1996 | 3,000 | | 8,000 | | 6,289.93 |
| December 31, 1996 | | 880.59 | | 829.48 | 7,170.52[e] |
| January 1, 1997 | 3,000 | | 5,000 | | 4,170.52 |
| December 31, 1997 | | 583.87 | | 245.61 | 4,754.39[e] |
| January 1, 1998 | 3,000 | | 2,000[f] | | 1,754.39 |
| December 31, 1998 | | 245.61 | | 0 | 2,000.00[f] |

a. Column 6 at beginning of year × 14%.
b. Annual lease payment × Number of years remaining on lease + $2,000 residual value, or Previous balance − Column 2.
c. Previous balance − Column 3.
d. Column 4 − Column 5.
e. $3,000 of each of these December 31 balances is a current asset; the remaining amount is a noncurrent asset.
f. The estimated unguaranteed residual value.

## Initial Direct Costs Involved in a Direct Financing Lease

The accounting for initial direct costs incurred by the lessor is different for each of the main types of leases. Recall that for an operating lease, these initial direct costs are recorded as a prepaid asset, allocated as an operating expense over the term of the operating lease, and matched against the rental revenue. For a direct financing lease, the original requirements of *FASB Statement No. 13* have been replaced by those of **FASB Statement No. 91.**[14] According to this *Statement*, the *initial direct costs* of a completed lease transaction include incremental direct costs and certain other direct costs. *Incremental direct costs* include those costs that result directly from and are essential to the leasing transaction and would not have been incurred by the lessor if the transaction had not occurred. The *other direct costs* that may be included are those related to evaluating the lessee's financial condition, negotiating terms, preparing and processing lease documents, and closing the transaction. The costs directly related to these activities may include only the portion of the employee's compensation and fringe benefits directly associated with the time spent performing those activities and other costs that would have not been incurred but for that lease.

Since there is no revenue recognized at the time of signing a direct financing lease, the initial direct costs are *not* expensed at that time and, therefore, there is no effect on net income at the time the direct financing lease is recorded. Instead, the initial direct costs are deferred. This accounting procedure requires that the lessor determine a *new* (lower) implicit rate that will discount the remaining future minimum lease payments to the net investment as of the inception of the lease.[15] All other lease-related costs, such as the costs of advertising, servicing existing leases, unsuccessful lease originations, supervision, and administration, are expensed as incurred.

To illustrate, if a lessor incurs initial direct costs of $5,000 on a direct financing lease, it records the costs as follows:

| | | |
|---|---|---|
| **Unearned Interest: Leases** | 5,000 | |
|    Cash, etc. | | 5,000 |

This entry facilitates appropriate matching because the initial direct costs are deferred and recognized over the lease term. The reduction in the Unearned Interest: Leases account increases the net investment, while the future cash flows have remained unchanged, thereby lowering the implicit rate. The lower rate results in less interest revenue being recognized each period, thereby achieving the goal of deferring the initial direct costs and including them as a reduction of income over the life of the lease.

The calculation of the new implicit rate requires the use of compound interest techniques, as discussed in Appendix D, and is not presented here with an illustration. In the related problems at the end of the chapter, a new implicit rate will be assumed and listed.

---

14. "Accounting for Nonrefundable Fees and Costs Associated with Originating or Acquiring Loans and Initial Direct Costs of Leases," *FASB Statement No. 91* (Stamford, Conn.: FASB, 1987), par. 5–7. This *Statement* was clarified by *FASB Statement No. 98*.
15. *FASB Statement No. 13 as Amended and Interpreted through January 1990*, op. cit., sec. L10.114.

### Sales-Type Leases (Lessor)

In a sales-type lease, like a direct financing lease, the lessor "sells" the asset and records an accompanying receivable.[16] In contrast, however, in a sales-type lease, the fair market value of the asset that is "sold" is greater (or less) than its cost or carrying value. Thus, **in distinguishing between a sales-type lease and a direct financing lease, the major differences are the presence of a manufacturer's or dealer's profit or loss in a sales-type lease and the accounting for initial direct costs.** The manufacturer's or dealer's profit or loss is measured as the difference between the following two items: (1) the present value of the minimum lease payments (net of executory costs) computed at the interest rate implicit in the lease (i.e., the sales price) and (2) the cost or carrying value of the asset plus any initial direct costs less the present value of the unguaranteed residual value accruing to the benefit of the lessor.[17]

To illustrate a sales-type lease, assume that on January 1, 1995, the York Company leases a piece of specialty equipment to the Lake Company with the terms and provisions of the lease as indicated in Exhibit 19-19. The test in Exhibit 19-20 shows that this lease qualifies as a sales-type lease.

---

**EXHIBIT 19-19**

**TERMS AND PROVISIONS OF LEASE AGREEMENT BETWEEN YORK COMPANY (LESSOR) AND LAKE COMPANY (LESSEE) DATED JANUARY 1, 1995**

1. The cost of the equipment is $120,000. The fair market value is $190,008.49
2. No initial direct costs are incurred by the York Company.
3. The term of the lease is 10 years, with annual payments of $30,000 received at the beginning of each year. The estimated economic life of the equipment is also 10 years.
4. The Lake Company agrees to absorb all executory costs.
5. The Lake Company is given an option to buy the equipment for $500 at the end of the lease term, December 31, 2004. This is a bargain purchase option.
6. The interest rate implicit in the lease is 12%.
7. The present value of 10 payments of $30,000 at 12% on an annuity-due basis plus the present value of the bargain purchase option is $190,008.49, calculated as follows:

Present value of 10 rents in advance at 12% (6.328250 × $30,000) = $189,847.50

Plus: Present value of $500 discounted at 12% (0.321973 × $500) = 160.99

Total present value = $190,008.49

8. The collectibility of the payments is reasonably assured, and there are no uncertainties involved in the lease.

---

16. A lease involving real estate may not be classified as a sales-type lease unless the lease agreement provides for the transfer of title to the lessee at or shortly after the end of the lease term.
17. *FASB Statement No. 13 as Amended and Interpreted through January 1990, op. cit.,* sec. L10.113.

**EXHIBIT 19-20**

## APPLICATION OF CRITERIA FOR DETERMINATION OF LEASE CLASSIFICATION BY YORK COMPANY (LESSOR)

| Classification Criteria | Criteria Met? | Remarks |
|---|---|---|
| *Group I* | | |
| 1. Transfer of ownership | No | |
| 2. Bargain purchase option | Yes | |
| 3. Lease term is 75% of economic life | Yes | 100% of life |
| 4. Present value of lease payments is 90% of fair value | Yes | The present value is $190,008.49, or 100% of estimated fair value |
| *Group II* | | |
| 1. Collectibility reasonably assured | Yes | |
| 2. No uncertainties | Yes | |

*Decision:* If the lease meets one or more of the Group I criteria and both of Group II criteria, it is either a direct financing or a sales-type lease. In addition, if there is a manufacturer's or dealer's profit or loss, it is a sales-type lease. If it meets the criteria and does not contain a profit or loss element, it is a direct financing lease.

*Conclusion:* The lease is a sales-type lease, since appropriate criteria are met and there is a manufacturer's or dealer's profit, because the amount used as the selling price ($190,008.49) exceeds the cost ($120,000); that is, the present (fair) value of the lease payments is greater than the cost of the property.

Assuming that the York Company uses the perpetual inventory system and is a manufacturer or dealer in the specialty equipment being leased, it records the information relevant to the lease for 1995 as follows:

1. *Initial Recording of the Sales-Type Lease on January 1, 1995*

| | | |
|---|---|---|
| Minimum Lease Payments Receivable | 300,500.00 | |
| Cost of Goods Sold | 120,000.00 | |
|     Sales Revenue | | 190,008.49 |
|     Merchandise Inventory (or Equipment | | |
|         Held for Lease) | | 120,000.00 |
|     Unearned Interest: Leases | | 110,491.51 |

Because this lease contains a bargain purchase option, the minimum lease payments receivable is recorded at the sum of the undiscounted annual rental payments ($300,000) plus the amount of the bargain purchase option. Cost of goods sold is recorded at the assigned inventory cost because the unguaranteed residual value does *not* accrue to the lessor. The $190,008.49 sales revenue is recorded at the present value of the minimum lease payments, which is the present value of the annual payments of $189,847.50 plus the present value of the bargain purchase option of $160.99. The accounting treatment of the bargain purchase option is the same as that for a guaranteed residual value since each is included in the minimum lease payments. Thus, the present value of the bargain purchase option (or a guaranteed residual value) is included as a part of the sales price of the equipment. The Unearned Interest: Leases amount of $110,491.51 is the difference between the receivable of $300,500 (the gross investment) and the sales revenue of $190,008.49. In general, however, the Unearned Interest: Leases amount is the difference between the gross investment in the lease and the sum of the present value of the two components of the gross investment, i.e., the present value of the minimum lease payments and the present value of the unguaranteed residual value accruing to the lessor (none in this example because of the bargain purchase option).

2. *Collection of Annual Payment for First Year on January 1, 1995*

| | | |
|---|---|---|
| **Cash** | **30,000.00** | |
| **Minimum Lease Payments Receivable** | | 30,000.00 |

The lease provisions require that the collection of the payments be made in advance at the beginning of each year. Also, keep in mind that this collection reduces the net investment by $30,000 (the amount on which interest revenue is calculated).

3. *Recognition of Interest Revenue for First Year on December 31, 1995*

| | | |
|---|---|---|
| **Unearned Interest: Leases** | **19,201.02** | |
| **Interest Revenue: Leases** | | 19,201.02 |

The Unearned Interest: Leases account is amortized by use of the effective interest method. The amount of interest that is recognized is 12% of the net investment *after* the collection of the first rent, or $19,201.02, calculated as follows:

$$12\% \times [(\$300,500 - \$30,000) - \$110,491.51] = \$19,201.02$$

As indicated in the direct financing lease case, a schedule of the lease amortization may be prepared. It is not presented here, but would be similar to that shown in Exhibit 19-18.

The journal entries on the lessor's books for the following 9 years will show a pattern similar to the preceding ones. After the entries for the tenth year are made, the net investment on December 31, 2004 will be $500, the amount of the bargain purchase option. Also, as with a direct financing lease, since a sale is deemed to have taken place, the lessor does not record any depreciation on the leased asset. The lessee typically would pay and record the executory costs. Other entries on the books of the lessee are not affected by the lessor's classification of the lease as sales-type or direct financing.

### Initial Direct Costs Involved in a Sales-Type Lease

As indicated previously, the accounting for the lessor's initial direct costs is different for each of the three main types of leases. In the preceding sales-type lease, it is assumed that there are no initial direct costs. For this type of lease, if initial direct costs are incurred, they are expensed in the same period.[18] This could be accomplished by including them in cost of goods sold, but since the initial direct costs contain a large element of selling expense, it is appropriate to report them as a selling expense entitled Initial Direct Sales-Type Lease Expense. This procedure results in an appropriate matching of the costs against the revenue recognized.

### Unguaranteed and Guaranteed Residual Values

As discussed in the introduction to sales-type leases, the present value of any *unguaranteed* residual value is deducted from the cost or carrying value of the asset when the expenses associated with the signing of the lease are recognized. Note that it is *not* included in Sales Revenue because it represents an item that is *not* sold.

The present value of any *guaranteed* residual value, on the other hand, is *not* subtracted from the expense measurement and is included in Sales. Since both the expense and the revenue items contain the present value of the guaranteed residual value, the gross margin element would be the same as for an unguaranteed residual value of the same amount. The sales and expenses for a sales-type lease with an unguaranteed residual value would both be less by the present value of the unguaranteed residual value. This method of accounting for the guaranteed residual value contained in a sales-type lease indicates that there has been a transfer of risks and benefits to the lessee usually associated with ownership of an asset. Since the unguaranteed residual value accrues to the lessor, there has been a transfer of fewer ownership risks and benefits. Note, however, as indicated earlier, this distinction does not prohibit a lease containing an unguaranteed residual value from qualifying as a sales-type lease.

### Disclosure Requirements for the Lessor

Certain disclosures in the financial statements or the related notes are required by *FASB Statement No. 13 as Amended* for lessors whose leasing activities represent a significant part of their business activities in terms of revenue, net income, or assets. For these lessors, the disclosures for operating, direct financing, and sales-type leases are shown in Exhibit 19-21.[19]

## SUMMARY OF ACCOUNTING BY LESSEE AND LESSOR

The accounting issues involved in the various types of leases are numerous and sometimes complex. To assist in identifying the key issues involved, a summary of the accounting by the lessee and lessor is included in Exhibit 19-22.

---

18. *Ibid.*
19. *Ibid.*, sec. L10.119.

---

**EXHIBIT 19-21**

**DISCLOSURE REQUIREMENTS FOR LESSOR: OPERATING, DIRECT FINANCING, AND SALES-TYPE LEASES**

A. For operating leases:
1. As of the date of the latest balance sheet presented, the cost and carrying amount, if different, of property on lease or held for leasing by major classes of property according to nature or function, and the amount of the total accumulated depreciation.
2. Minimum future rentals on noncancelable leases as of the date of the latest balance sheet presented, in the aggregate and for each of the 5 succeeding fiscal years.
3. Total contingent rentals included in income for each period for which an income statement is presented.
B. For direct financing and sales-type leases:
1. The components of the net investment in direct financing and sales-type leases as of the date of each balance sheet presented:
   a. The future minimum lease payments to be received, with separate deductions for amounts representing executory costs, including any profit thereon, included in the minimum lease payments, and the accumulated allowance for uncollectible minimum lease payments receivable.
   b. The unguaranteed residual values accruing to the benefit of the lessor.
   c. For direct financing leases only, initial direct costs.
   d. Unearned income.
2. Future minimum lease payments to be received for each of the 5 succeeding fiscal years as of the date of the latest balance sheet presented.
3. Total contingent rentals included in revenue for each period for which an income statement is presented.
C. A general description of the lessor's leasing arrangements.

## ADDITIONAL LEASE ISSUES

Some aspects of lease accounting are controversial. In addition, international differences in accounting for leases exist.

### Evaluation of Accounting for Leases

The four criteria used to determine if there is a capital lease are reasonable measures of whether the risks and benefits of ownership are transferred. However, the criteria are fairly easy to avoid. For example, consider a lease that does not transfer ownership or contain a bargain purchase option. The economic life may be "estimated" as a time period that causes the lease life to be less than 75% of that period. Also, third party guarantees of the residual value have been fairly widely used, thereby ensuring that the present value of the minimum lease payments is less than 90% of the fair value, while providing the lessor with an effective guarantee of the residual value.

### EXHIBIT 19-22

## SUMMARY OF ACCOUNTING FOR LEASES BY THE LESSEE AND THE LESSOR

### Lessee

*Operating Lease*

Rent Expense is recognized each period.

*Capital Lease*

Leased Property is recorded at the present value of the minimum lease payments.
Lease Obligation is recorded at the present value of the minimum lease payments.
   The minimum lease payments are discounted at the lessee's incremental borrowing
      rate unless the lessor's implicit rate is both known and lower.
   The Leased Property cannot be recorded at an amount that exceeds its fair market
      value.
Amortization (depreciation) of the leased property
   Over the economic life if the lease is capitalized under either of the following
      criteria:
         · the lease transfers ownership of the property to the lessee by the end of
           the lease term
         · the lease contains a bargain purchase option
   Over the lease life if the lease is capitalized but does not meet either of the
      preceding criteria
   Use the normal amortization (depreciation) policy
Interest Expense is recognized by use of the effective interest method.

### Lessor

*Operating Lease*

Rent Revenue is recognized each period.
The Property Leased to Others is depreciated using the normal depreciation policy.

*Direct Financing Lease*

Minimum Lease Payments Receivable (or Gross Investment in the Lease) is recorded at
   the sum of the minimum lease payments plus the unguaranteed residual value (not
   discounted).
Unearned Interest is recorded at an amount equal to the gross investment in the lease
   minus the cost or carrying value of the leased property.
Initial Direct Costs are deferred and amortized over the life of the lease.
Interest Revenue is recognized by use of the effective interest method.

*Sales-Type Lease*

Minimum Lease Payments Receivable (or Gross Investment in the Lease) is recorded at
   the sum of the minimum lease payments plus the unguaranteed residual value (not
   discounted).
Unearned Interest is recorded at an amount equal to the gross investment in the lease
   minus the sum of the present value of the two components of the gross investment.
Sales Revenue is recorded at the present value of the minimum lease payments.
Expenses that are recognized include the cost or carrying amount of the leased property
   plus the initial direct costs minus the present value of the unguaranteed residual
   value.
Interest Revenue is recognized by use of the effective interest method.

These examples raise the issue of why the lessee and lessor want to avoid a capital lease. The motivation usually comes from the lessee who wants to avoid reporting the liability on its balance sheet. Such lessees apparently believe that a "stronger" balance sheet allows them to either borrow more money or to borrow money at lower interest rates. However, the required disclosure in the notes to the financial statements of the future cash flows each year for the next five years and all years thereafter allows the user to perform a present value calculation that determines the approximate amount of the balance sheet liability (and asset) that the lessee has avoided. Therefore, it appears that the lessee must assume that users do not read (or understand) the notes.

Many users believe that both the relevance and reliability of lease accounting would be enhanced by having a simple rule that requires capitalization of all leases with, say, a life of more than one year. However, companies lobbied not to have such a rule included in *FASB Statement No. 13*. Instead, the FASB opted for the four capitalization criteria. However, the *Statement* also has been criticized for being very "mechanical." That is, the criteria used for capitalization are "absolutes" and are either met or not, thereby leaving no room for professional judgment.

### International Accounting Differences

U.S. lease accounting standards are generally more comprehensive (and detailed) than those in other countries. For example, Australia, Canada, and the United Kingdom require capitalization by the lessee when the risks and rewards of ownership are transferred. This is consistent with the principle underlying U.S. accounting, but allows more flexibility because of the absence of detailed criteria. This flexibility results in more operating leases abroad than in the U.S. In other countries, including Japan and Italy, no leases are capitalized. Principles in other countries are affected by the tax laws. For example, German accounting principles provide a disincentive for capitalization because depreciation tax deductions generally remain with the lessor.

International Accounting Standards also require capitalization when substantially all the risks and rewards of ownership are transferred, as measured by four criteria. While the first two criteria are very similar to those in the U.S. standards, the third criterion is less precise because it states that "the lease term is for a major part of the asset's useful life," as compared to the 75% used in the U.S. The fourth criterion is different because it states that "the present value of the lease payments is equal to or greater than the fair value of the asset," as compared to the 90% used in the U.S.[20] These differences impair the comparability of financial statements prepared in different countries.

### APPENDIX: SPECIALIZED LEASE ISSUES AND CHANGES IN LEASE PROVISIONS

Some companies engage in specialized leases. Three specialized lease issues are discussed briefly in this Appendix: (1) real estate leases, (2) sales-leaseback transactions, and (3) leveraged leases. Other companies may be involved in lease agreements whose provisions are modified. Changes in lease provisions are discussed briefly in this Appendix.

---

20. For an additional discussion, see Arthur Andersen & Co., et al., *Survey of International Accounting Practices* (New York, AICPA, 1991).

## LEASE ISSUES RELATED TO REAL ESTATE

In the main portion of this chapter, we considered only the leasing of personal property (the example used was equipment). Special issues are involved in the classification of leases that include land, either alone or in combination with buildings or equipment.[21] The differences in the classification of leases involving real estate are indicated in Exhibit 19-23.

### Lease of Land Only

If land is the sole item of property leased, the lessee accounts for the lease as a capital lease only if the lease meets either criterion 1 of Column A (Part I) of Exhibit 19-23, the transfer of ownership at the end of the lease, or criterion 2, a bargain purchase

---

**EXHIBIT 19-23**

## CLASSIFICATION OF LEASES INVOLVING REAL PROPERTY

I.  General Criteria for Classifying Leases
    (Brief titles are given in this exhibit—see Exhibit 19-2 for fuller titles)

| Column A | Column B |
|---|---|
| Criteria Applicable to Both Lessees and Lessors | Criteria Applicable to Lessors Only |
| 1. Transfer of ownership | 1. Collectibility reasonably assured |
| 2. Contains bargain purchase option | 2. No uncertainties |
| 3. Lease term is 75% of economic life | |
| 4. Present value of lease payments is 90% of fair value | |

II.  Lease of Land Only

A.  Lessee
    1.  Capital lease. Lease must meet either criterion 1 or 2 in Column A (Part I). (Criteria 3 and 4 are *not* applicable.)
    2.  Operating lease. Lease must not meet either criterion 1 or 2 in Column A (Part I).

B.  Lessor
    1.  Sales-type lease. Lease must
        a.  Meet either criterion 1 or 2 in Column A (Part I), *and*
        b.  Meet both criteria in Column B (Part I), *and*
        c.  Give rise to a profit or loss.
    2.  Direct financing lease. Lease must meet
        a.  Either criterion 1 or 2 in Column A (Part I), *and*
        b.  Both criteria in Column B (Part I).
    3.  Operating lease. Lease that does *not* qualify as a sales-type or direct financing lease.

---

21. *FASB Statement No. 13 as Amended and Interpreted through January 1990, op. cit.,* sec. L10.120–.124.

**EXHIBIT 19-23, Continued**

III. Lease of Both Land and Buildings
    A. Lease of both land and buildings that transfers ownership or contains a bargain purchase option

| 1. Lessee | 2. Lessor |
|---|---|
| a. Capital lease. The lease is a capital lease since one or more of the criteria of Column A (Part I) are met. Land and buildings are separately capitalized. | a. Sales-type lease. The two assets, land and buildings, are considered as a single unit and the lease must<br>(1) Meet either criterion 1 or 2 in 2 in Column A (Part I), *and*<br>(2) Meet both criteria in Column B (Part I), *and*<br>(3) Give rise to a profit or loss.<br>b. Direct financing lease. The lease of the two assets combined must meet<br>(1) Either criterion 1 or 2 in Column A (Part I), *and*<br>(2) Both criteria in Column B (Part I). |

    B. If lease meets neither criterion 1 nor 2 stated in Column A (Part I) and if fair value of land is less than 25% of fair value of both land and buildings. (The land portion is ignored and the classification is determined using the characteristics of building.)

| 1. Lessee | 2. Lessor |
|---|---|
| a. Capital lease. Lease must meet either criterion 3 or 4 in Column A (Part I).<br>b. Operating lease. Lease meets none of the criteria in Column A (Part I). | a. Sales-type lease. Lease must<br>(1) Meet either criterion 3 or 4 in Column A (Part I), *and*<br>(2) Meet both criteria in Column B (Part I), *and*<br>(3) Give rise to a profit or loss.<br>b. Direct financing lease. Lease must meet<br>(1) Either criterion 3 or 4 in Column A (Part I), *and*<br>(2) Both criteria in Column B (Part I).<br>c. Operating Lease. Lease that does *not* qualify as a sales-type or direct financing lease. |

    C. If lease meets neither criterion 1 nor 2 stated in Column A (Part I) and if fair value of land is more than 25% of fair value of both land and buildings. (The lease is separated into land and building portions.)

| 1. Lessee | 2. Lessor |
|---|---|
| a. Land portion. Always an operating lease.<br>b. Building portion. Classified by remaining criteria of Column A (Part I). | a. Land portion. Always an operating lease.<br>b. Building portion. Classified by remaining criteria of Columns A and B (Part I). |

option. Otherwise, the lease is accounted for as an operating lease. Criterion 3 (dealing with the 75% of the estimated economic life) and criterion 4 (dealing with the 90% of the fair value of the leased property) do *not* apply because the asset would have to be depreciated over the lease life. Such a situation would be inappropriate for land. The lessee does *not* amortize the asset, Leased Land Under Capital Leases, because title to the land is expected to be transferred, and land as such is not subject to amortization. The lessor accounts for the lease of land as a sales-type lease if (1) the lease transfers ownership or contains a bargain purchase option, (2) the lease meets both the collectibility and uncertainty criteria of Column B (Part I) of Exhibit 19-23, and (3) there is a dealer's profit or loss. If the criteria for a sales-type lease are met with the exception that there is no dealer's profit or loss, then the lease qualifies as a direct financing one. Otherwise, it is an operating lease.

### Lease of Both Land and Buildings That Transfers Title or Contains a Bargain Purchase Option

When both land and buildings are leased, a new issue arises as to the classification of the lease because one portion involves a depreciable asset with an estimated economic life and the other involves a nondepreciable asset. The accounting treatment is considered in two parts: (1) a lease of both land and buildings that meets criteria 1 and 2 of Column A (Part I) of Exhibit 19-23 and (2) a lease of both land and buildings that does *not* meet either criterion 1 or 2.

*Lessee's Accounting*
For a capital lease of land and buildings that transfers ownership or that contains a bargain purchase option, the present value of the minimum lease payments (net of executory costs) is allocated between the two leased assets in proportion to their fair values at the inception of the lease (Exhibit 19-23, IIIA). The amount assigned to Leased Buildings Under Capital Leases is amortized over the estimated economic life of the buildings, and the amount assigned to Leased Land Under Capital Leases is *not* amortized.

*Lessor's Accounting*
The lessor accounts for the lease as a single unit, either as a direct financing, a sales-type, or an operating lease. The term **single unit** means that for a sales-type or direct financing lease, the lessor uses one Minimum Lease Payments Receivable account to record the appropriate values for the lease of both land and buildings. In the original lease entry, however, the lessor credits both the land and the buildings accounts.

### Lease of Land and Buildings That Does Not Transfer Title or Contain a Bargain Purchase Option

*Value of Land Is Less Than 25%*
If a lease of land and buildings does not transfer ownership or contain a bargain purchase option, it still may be a capital lease if it meets one of the other two criteria. If the fair value of the land is less than 25% of the total fair value of the leased property at the inception of the lease, the land is considered to be immaterial. Therefore, *both* the lessee and the lessor consider the land and buildings as a single unit. Note that for the purpose of applying criterion 3 of Column A (Part I) of Exhibit 19-23, the estimated economic life of the building is considered as the economic life of the unit.

1. *Lessee's Accounting.* If either criterion 3 or 4 of Column A (Part I) of Exhibit 19-23 is met, the lessee classifies the lease as a capital lease, recognizes the

leased land and buildings as a single asset, and amortizes the total amount over the term of the lease, even though it is implicitly depreciating the land portion of the asset. If the lease does not meet any of the criteria in Column A (Part I), it is an operating lease.

2. *Lessor's Accounting.* If the lease meets either criterion 3 or 4 of Column A (Part I) of Exhibit 19-23 and both of the criteria of Column B (Part I), the lessor accounts for the lease as a single unit, as either a direct financing or a sales-type lease as appropriate; otherwise, the lease is an operating lease.

### Value of Land Is More than 25%

On the other hand, if, at the inception of the lease, the land represents 25% or more of the fair value of the leased property, the amount of the land is considered to be a material amount. Then, both the lessee and the lessor must consider the land and the buildings separately for purposes of applying the criteria listed in Exhibit 19-23. In this case, the lessee and lessor separate the minimum lease payments (net of executory costs paid by lessor) into amounts applicable to land and to buildings. Since the lease of the land as indicated here results in an operating lease, the recommended way to make the preceding calculation is to determine the fair value of land, and then use the appropriate interest rate to determine the periodic minimum lease payments applicable to the land portion, as follows:

$$\text{Incremental Borrowing Rate} \times \text{Fair Market Value of Land} = \text{Periodic Minimum Lease Payment Applicable to Land}$$

The periodic minimum lease payments applicable to both land and buildings less the amount calculated is the amount attributed to the buildings.

1. *Lessee's Accounting.* Once the amount assigned to the buildings is determined, if the lease of this portion meets either criterion 3 or 4 of Column A (Part I) of Exhibit 19-23, it is accounted for as a capital lease. The present value amount assigned to the asset, Leased Buildings Under Capital Leases, is amortized over the life of the lease. The land portion of the lease is accounted for separately as an operating lease. Therefore, if the buildings portion of the lease meets neither criterion 3 nor 4 of Column A (Part I) of Exhibit 19-23, both the buildings and the land are accounted for as a single operating lease.

2. *Lessor's Accounting.* If the buildings portion of the lease meets either criterion 3 or 4 of Column A (Part I) and both criteria of Column B of Exhibit 19-23, it is accounted for as a direct financing or sales-type lease, depending on whether a manufacturer's or dealer's profit or loss arises out of the transaction. The land portion of the lease is accounted for separately as an operating lease. If the buildings portion of the lease does not meet the relevant criteria, both the buildings and land are accounted for as a single operating lease.

## Lease Involving Equipment as Well as Real Estate

If a lease involves both equipment and real estate, the portion of the minimum lease payments applicable to the equipment portion of the lease is estimated by whatever means are appropriate under the circumstances. The equipment then is considered separately for the purposes of applying the criteria listed in Exhibit 19-23 and is accounted for separately according to its classification by both lessees and lessors. The accounting for the remaining real estate portion follows the accounting standards described in the preceding section.

## SALE-LEASEBACK ISSUES

If a company has limited cash resources, it may sell an asset (often land and buildings, but not real property exclusively) and then immediately lease it back from the buyer. This kind of transaction may be advantageous to both the lessee and lessor: the lessee receives cash from the sale that is needed for the activities of the company, and may derive a tax advantage; the lessor acquires a financial asset.

The sale of the asset and the leaseback are considered to be a single transaction that essentially is like a secured loan, with the creditor obtaining legal title to the asset. The sales price of the asset, any profit earned thereon, and the minimum lease payments must be considered together. If the lease meets one of the criteria for treatment as a capital lease (see Exhibit 19-2), the seller-lessee accounts for the lease as a capital lease[22]; otherwise, it accounts for the lease as an operating lease. Any profit on the sale is deferred and amortized in proportion to the amortization of the leased asset, if a capital lease, or in proportion to rental payments over the period of time the asset is expected to be used, if an operating lease. However, when the fair value of the property at the time of the transaction is less than its undepreciated cost, a *loss is recognized immediately* up to the amount of the difference between the undepreciated cost and fair value.[23]

### Lessor's Accounting Issues

The purchaser-lessor follows the principles developed in the preceding sections in accounting for the purchase of the asset and the immediate leasing of it back to the seller. From the lessor's point of view, no new issues are involved, so its accounting entries are not illustrated here.

### Lessee's Accounting Issues

If the lease meets at least one of the four criteria in Column A of Exhibit 19-2, the seller-lessee accounts for the lease as a capital lease. Otherwise, if none of the criteria are satisfied, the seller-lessee accounts for the lease as an operating lease. The accounting for the main provisions of the lease follows those procedures already illustrated. The primary new issue from the lessees viewpoint is the accounting for the profit or loss on the sale of the property by the seller-lessee. To illustrate, assume that on January 1, 1995, the High Point Railroad built 10 boxcars, Rolling Stock, costing $400,000. Because of a cash flow problem resulting from this new acquisition, High Point decided to sell these boxcars immediately to Landlord Company for $600,000, then lease them back under the conditions shown in Exhibit 19-24.

Typical journal entries to record the information related to the preceding sales-leaseback for High Point Railroad (the seller-lessee) for 1995 are as follows:

1. *Sale of the Boxcars to Landlord Company on January 1, 1995*

| | | |
|---|---|---|
| Cash | 600,000.00 | |
| Rolling Stock | | 400,000.00 |
| Unearned Profit on Sale-Leaseback | | 200,000.00 |

22. A sale-leaseback transaction involving real estate must qualify as a sale under the provisions of *FASB Statement No. 66,* "Accounting for Sales of Real Estate."
23. *FASB Statement No. 13 as Amended and Interpreted through January 1990, op. cit.,* sec. L10.129.

**EXHIBIT 19-24**

**TERMS AND PROVISIONS OF LEASE AGREEMENT BETWEEN LANDLORD COMPANY AND HIGH POINT RAILROAD DATED JANUARY 1, 1995**

1. The cost of the boxcars to High Point Railroad (the seller-lessee) is $400,000. The selling price to Landlord Company (the purchaser-lessor) is $600,000; thus, this amount becomes the new cost of the equipment to the seller-lessee.
2. The term of the lease is 15 years, with annual payments of $92,771.13 in advance at the beginning of each year. The estimated economic life of the equipment is 20 years, with no expected residual value at the end of this time. (The residual value at the end of 15 years is not considered because title passes at that time.)
3. The High Point Railroad agrees to pay all executory costs.
4. Title to the boxcars will be transferred to the seller-lessee at the end of lease term.
5. The interest rate implicit on the lease is 16%. High Point Railroad knows this rate, and the rate equals its incremental borrowing rate.
6. The present value of 15 payments of $92,771.13 at 16% on an annuity-due basis is $600,000, calculated as follows:

   Present value of 15 rents in advance at 16% = 6.467529 × $92,771.13
   = $600,000 (rounded)
7. The lease qualifies as a capital lease to High Point Railroad, since it meets the criteria stated in Exhibit 19-2.

2. *Initial Recording of the Leaseback as a Capital Lease on January 1, 1995*

| | | |
|---|---|---|
| Leased Rolling Stock Under Capital Leases | 600,000.00 | |
| Obligation Under Capital Leases | | 600,000.00 |

3. *Annual Payment on January 1, 1995*

| | | |
|---|---|---|
| Obligation Under Capital Leases | 92,771.13 | |
| Cash | | 92,771.13 |

4. *Payment of Executory Costs on Various Dates in 1995 (amounts assumed)*

| | | |
|---|---|---|
| Insurance Expense | 2,600.00 | |
| Repairs and Maintenance Expense | 2,300.00 | |
| Property Tax Expense | 9,700.00 | |
| Cash | | 14,600.00 |

5. *Recording Depreciation of Rolling Stock on December 31, 1995*

| | | |
|---|---|---|
| Depreciation Expense: Leased Rolling Stock | 30,000.00 | |
| Accumulated Depreciation: Leased Rolling Stock | | 30,000.00 |

The company uses the straight-line method and a life of 20 years because ownership is transferred at the end of the lease. Depreciation for 1995 is $30,000 ($600,000 ÷ 20).

6. *Amortization of Unearned Profit on Sale-Leaseback on December 31, 1995*

| | | |
|---|---|---|
| **Unearned Profit on Sale-Leaseback** | 10,000.00 | |
| **Realized Profit on Sale-Leaseback (or Depreciation Expense: Leased Rolling Stock)** | | 10,000.00 |

The amortization is $10,000 ($200,000 ÷ 20). Note that the Unearned Profit on Sale-Leaseback is amortized and profit is recognized over a 20-year period. *FASB Statement No. 13 as Amended* requires that, for a capital lease, realized profit is recognized by use of the same rate that the Leased Rolling Stock Under Capital Leases is depreciated. By implication, therefore, it is acceptable to make the preceding credit directly to Depreciation Expense. For an operating lease, such profit (or loss) is deferred and amortized in proportion to the lease payments over the period the leased assets are expected to be used by the seller-lessee. A loss could be sustained by the seller-lessee if the book value or carrying amount were larger than the fair value of the asset. The entire amount of this loss is recognized in the year of the sale-leaseback.

7. *Recognition of Interest Expense on December 31, 1995*

| | | |
|---|---|---|
| **Interest Expense** | 81,156.62 | |
| **Obligation Under Capital Leases** | | 81,156.62 |

This year-end adjusting entry is the same as that made for any capital lease for which the payment is made in advance. The amount is calculated as $81,156.62 [16% × ($600,000 − $92,771.13)].

## LEVERAGED LEASES

A leveraged lease is a special arrangement involving three different participants to the agreement: (1) the equity participant, the owner-lessor; (2) the asset user, the lessee; and (3) the debt participant, the long-term creditor who provides nonrecourse financing for the leasing transaction between the lessee and lessor. The interrelated activities of the three parties to a leveraged lease are shown in Exhibit 19-25. If the owner-lessor buys the equipment from a manufacturer, a fourth party to the transaction would be present.

Currently, over $5 billion worth of capital equipment—such as aircraft, ships, and heavy machinery—is financed annually through the use of leveraged leases. This kind of leasing arrangement began in the late 1960s and has grown rapidly since then. The lease is designed to provide income tax benefits to the three parties involved in the transaction. The lessor may be able to retain various tax credits, and also has the right to the immediate recognition of all the cost of the asset as an income tax deduction. The lessee receives the right to income tax deductions for the rent of land, buildings, and other personal property. The creditor receives the tax protection provided for the leveraged lease contract.

From the standpoint of the lessee, no new accounting issues arise. The leveraged leases are classified and accounted for in the same way as nonleveraged leases. *FASB Statement No. 13 as Amended* requires that the lessor classify leveraged leases as

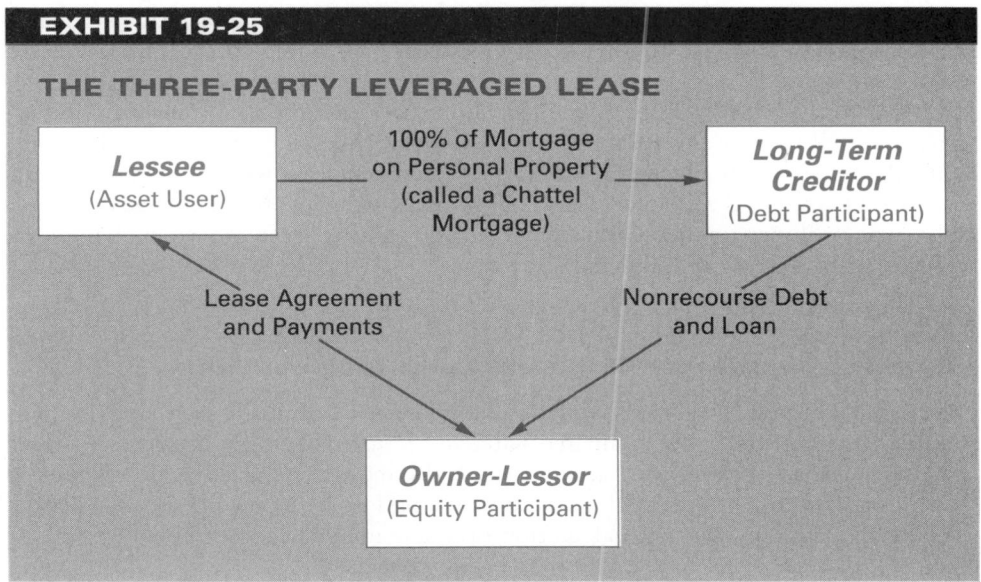

**EXHIBIT 19-25**

**THE THREE-PARTY LEVERAGED LEASE**

direct financing leases, since no manufacturer's or dealer's profit can arise from the transaction and therefore it cannot be classified as a sales-type lease.[24]

The lessor records its investment in a leveraged lease net of the nonrecourse debt, which usually consists of:

1. Rental receivables, net of that portion applicable to the nonrecourse debt.

2. Amount of any tax credits to be realized on the transaction.

3. Estimated residual value of the leased asset.

4. Reduction for the unearned revenue items.

Since leveraged leases are complex financial arrangements that vary in structure, the lessor's accounting for them is also complex and is beyond the scope of the book.[25]

## CHANGES IN LEASE PROVISIONS

As discussed earlier, lease contracts are written with many provisions, including renewal, extension, or purchase options, and penalties. Lessees and lessors may opt to change certain provisions that, in effect, change the classification of the lease. If, at any time, the lessee and lessor change the provisions of a lease (other than by renewing or extending its term) in such a way that the lease would have been classified differently *had the changed terms been in effect at the beginning of the lease term,* the

---

24. *Ibid.,* sec. L10.144.
25. See Appendix E of *FASB Statement No. 13 as Amended and Interpreted through January 1990,* sec. L10.161, for an illustration of the accounting and financial statement presentation of leveraged leases.

revised agreement is considered a new agreement. The new agreement is reclassified as operating, direct financing, or sales-type, according to the criteria in Exhibit 19-2.

*FASB Statement No. 13 as Amended* also addresses the issue of renewals and extensions. A change in an operating lease to a direct financing or sales-type lease presents the fewest issues, since the accounting for the new lease would be similar to that described earlier in the chapter. The most complex issue involves a change in either a sales-type or direct financing lease. Some of the possible lease provision changes are considered briefly in the following sections.

### Review of Estimated Unguaranteed Residual Value

The estimated unguaranteed residual value is reviewed annually by the lessor. Any upward adjustments in the estimated value *are ignored,* but any downward adjustments require a revision in the accounting. A decline is recognized as a reduction in the lessor's net investment, with an accompanying loss being recorded in the period. This recognition involves the calculation of a new implicit interest rate.

### Impact of Renewal of Lease on Guarantee of Residual Value

Suppose, for example, a lessee records a lease as a capital lease while the lessor records it as a direct financing lease, and the lease contains a guarantee of the residual value of the leased property. If at the end of the lease term the lessee elects to renew the lease, this election would cancel the guarantee of residual value. The renewal, however, is *not* treated as a new agreement, because there is no change in the lease classification. The lessee company adjusts the remaining balances of the asset and obligation from the original lease by an amount equal to the difference between the present value of the future minimum lease payments under the new renewal agreement and the existing present balance of the obligation.

### Changes to Sales-Type or Direct Financing Lease Prior to Lease Term Expiration That Result in an Operating Lease

If changes are made in either sales-type or direct financing lease provisions prior to the expiration of the lease term, and if these changes would have created a new agreement at inception classified as an operating lease, the net investment remaining on the lessor's books is removed from the accounts. The Minimum Lease Payments Receivable is replaced on the lessor's books by an asset at its original cost, fair value, or carrying amount, whichever is lowest, and any net adjustment is reported as a loss to operations in the period of change. The new lease then is accounted for as any other operating lease.

An exception occurs when a guarantee or penalty is rendered inoperative as provided for in *FASB Statement No. 13 as Amended.* In this case, if the renewal or extension results in an operating lease, the existing lease continues to be accounted for on the books of the lessor as either a sales-type or direct financing lease (depending on the original classification) to the end of its original term, and then the renewal or extension is accounted for as any other operating lease. The accounting by the lessee follows a similar pattern.

### Renewal or Extension of Sales-Type or Direct Financing Lease Resulting in a New Lease That Qualifies as a Sales-Type Lease

The accounting for a renewal or extension of sales-type and direct financing leases that results in a lease that qualifies as a new sales-type lease has been debated by the FASB since it originally issued *FASB Statement No. 13* in 1976. The original *FASB Statement No. 13* clearly indicated that a renewal or extension of an existing sales-type or direct financing lease *cannot* be classified as a sales-type lease even though it may otherwise meet the necessary criteria. This renewal lease would have to be treated as a direct financing lease. *FASB Statement No. 13 as Amended* qualifies this previous position. If the renewal or extension takes place *during the term* of the lease, the position of the original *FASB Statement No. 13* will be followed. If the renewal or extension takes place *at the end* of the lease (or during the last few months of the existing lease), the lease change can qualify as a sales-type lease. These two renewal situations are discussed briefly.

#### Renewal or Extension Occurring During Lease Term

The FASB concluded that if a renewal or extension of a sales-type or direct financing lease is treated as a sales-type lease at the time of an interim renewal, a "second sale" would result in recognition of revenue before its realization. For this reason, the FASB reiterates, in *FASB Statement No. 13 as Amended,* that a renewal or extension of an existing sales-type or direct financing lease that *otherwise qualifies as a sales-type lease* is classified as a direct financing lease if the lease change occurs *during the term* of the lease.

#### Renewal or Extension Occurring at End of Lease Term

The FASB then altered its position regarding this type of lease change. It concluded that if the renewal or extension occurs at the end of the lease term, and if the new agreement qualifies as a sales-type lease (according to criteria stated in Exhibit 19-2), the renewal or extension is accounted for as a sales-type lease at the end of the original term of the existing lease.

Many other changes may be made in lease terms. These often involve complex changes in accounting and, thus, require careful consideration. The preceding discussion indicates the scope of the issues. The accountant faced with new changes should study carefully all current pronouncements before taking action on a particular change.

## QUESTIONS

*Q19-1* What does *FASB Statement No. 13 as Amended* provide in reference to the measuring and reporting of leases?

*Q19-2* List seven advantages to the lessee of leasing, as compared with purchasing, an asset.

*Q19-3* Assume that a lessee leases equipment and insists on terms that qualify it as an operating lease, barely escaping the qualification as a capital lease. Discuss the impact that such an operating lease has on financial statements and related financial information as compared to the effect that a capital lease would have.

*Q19-4* Define the following terms: (a) *lease*, (b) *sales-type lease*, (c) *direct financing lease*, (d) *sale-leaseback transaction*, (e) *operating lease*, (f) *leveraged lease*.

*Q19-5* Define the following terms used in *FASB Statement No. 13 as Amended*: (a) *inception of lease*, (b) *bargain purchase option*, (c) *unguaranteed residual value*, (d) *implicit interest rate*, (e) *initial direct costs*.

*Q19-6* What components make up the minimum lease payments of a typical capital lease?

*Q19-7* List the four criteria used to determine if a lease is classified as a capital lease by the lessee.

*Q19-8* Describe briefly the accounting procedures followed by the lessor and by the lessee for an operating lease.

*Q19-9* Describe briefly the procedures followed by the lessee to account for a capital lease.

*Q19-10* From the standpoint of the lessor, a sales-type lease must meet one or more of the criteria of a capital lease as well as two additional criteria. Name these two additional criteria.

*Q19-11* What is the basic difference between the lessor's accounting procedures used for a sales-type lease and those used for a direct financing lease?

*Q19-12* Why are compound interest concepts appropriate and applicable in accounting for a direct financing lease?

*Q19-13* The Owens Company leased equipment for 4 years at $50,000 a month, with an option to renew the lease for 6 years at $2,000 per month or to purchase the equipment for $25,000 (a price considerably less than the expected fair market value) after the initial lease term of 4 years. How is this transaction recorded by the Owens Company?

*Q19-14* McFarland Corporation leased equipment under a lease calling for the payment of $50,000 a year in rent. At the end of the current year, when the capital lease had a remaining term of 20 years, McFarland Company subleased the asset for a rental of $75,000 a year for 20 years. The new lease is acceptable to the lessor, who agrees that McFarland Company has completed its primary obligation. When will the gain from this transaction be reported by McFarland Company? Explain.

*Q19-15* a. What disclosures are required for leases in the financial statements of lessees?
b. What disclosures are required in the financial statements of lessors for various types of leases?

*Q19-16* (Appendix). From the point of view of the seller-lessee, what is the primary accounting issue involved in accounting for a sales-leaseback transaction as compared to other lessee transactions? Discuss.

*Q19-17* (Appendix). What distinguishes a leveraged lease from other leases? What, if any, is the major difference in the accounting of the lessee for a leveraged lease?

## CASES

*C19-1   Capitalized and Operating Leases*
On January 1, Borman Company, a lessee, entered into three noncancelable leases for brand new equipment, Lease J, Lease K, and Lease L. None of the three leases transfer ownership of the equipment to Borman at the end of the lease term. For each of the three leases, the present value at the beginning of the lease term of the minimum lease payments, excluding that portion of the payments representing executory costs such as insurance, maintenance, and taxes to be paid by the lessor, including any profit thereon, is 75% of the fair value of the equipment to the lessor at the inception of the lease.

The following information is peculiar to each lease:

(a) Lease J does not contain a bargain purchase option. The lease term is equal to 80% of the estimated economic life of the equipment.
(b) Lease K contains a bargain purchase option. The lease term is equal to 50% of the estimated economic life of the equipment.
(c) Lease L does not contain a bargain purchase option. The lease term is equal to 50% of the estimated economic life of the equipment.

**Required**
1. How should Borman Company classify each of the preceding three leases, and why? Discuss the rationale for your answer.

2. What amount, if any, should Borman record as a liability at the inception of the lease for each of the preceding three leases?
3. Assuming that the minimum lease payments are made on a straight-line basis, how should Borman record each minimum lease payment for each of the preceding three leases? (*AICPA adapted*)

*C19-2   Disclosure of Leases and Related Issues*
United Manufacturing Company manufactures and leases computers to its customers. During 1995, the following lease transactions take place:

1. On January 1, a computer is leased to Superior Microelectronics Industries and is guaranteed by United against obsolescence. The present value of the lease payments is greater than 90% of the fair market value of the computer to both United and Superior.
2. Also on January 1, a computer is leased to Pitt Steel Company. Because of Pitt's unstable financial condition, its incremental borrowing rate is substantially greater than United's rate implicit in the lease (which Pitt did not know and could not estimate).

**Required**
1. On whose financial statements is the computer leased in the first transaction shown? Discuss.

2. Under what conditions in the second transaction could the computer fail to be shown on either United or Pitt Steel's balance sheets at December 31, 1995? Discuss.

### C19-3 *Initial Direct Costs*
The Efland Company leases equipment to Orange Company. Efland pays $3,000 initial direct costs in negotiating the lease.

**Required**
1. Specifically, what are initial direct costs?
2. Indicate precisely how Efland should account for initial direct costs if this lease is (a) an operating lease, (b) a sales-type lease, (c) a direct financing lease.
3. For a sales-type lease, *FASB Statement No. 13 as Amended* requires that: "The cost or carrying amount, if different, of the leased property, plus any initial direct costs..., less the present value of the unguaranteed residual value accruing to the benefit of the lessor, computed at the interest rate implicit in the lease, shall be charged against income in the same period." Does this provision require that initial direct costs for sales-type leases be charged to cost of goods sold? Discuss the reasons for or against this accounting treatment.

### C19-4 *Sales-Type Lease Issues*
Jordan Industries manufactures and leases to its customers 5-ton construction dump trucks. The lease arrangements are usually as follows:
1. Payments on the lease are due for 5 years after its inception, but their present value is not greater than 90% of the fair value of the trucks at the time of sale.
2. The trucks revert to Jordan at the end of the lease. Estimated economic life of the trucks is 10 years.
3. No substantial uncertainties exist as to future payments Jordan must make, and potential customers are thoroughly checked for creditworthiness before the trucks are leased to them.
4. Jordan's accountant has informed the company that there are advantages from a reporting standpoint in treating the leases as sales-type instead of operating leases.

**Required**
1. Discuss the reasons why Jordan would want to treat the leases as sales-type instead of operating leases.
2. What should Jordan do, under the requirements of *FASB Statement No. 13 as Amended,* to treat the leases properly as sales-type leases?

### C19-5 *Types of Leases and Related Issues*
Circuit Village Company entered into a lease arrangement with Thomas Leasing Company for a certain machine. Thomas's primary business is leasing, and it is not a manufacturer or dealer. Circuit Village will lease the machine for a period of 4 years, which is 50% of the machine's economic life. Thomas will take possession of the machine at the end of the initial 4-year lease and lease it to another smaller company that does not need the most current version of the machine. Circuit Village does not guarantee any residual value for the machine and will not purchase the machine at the end of the lease term. Circuit Village's incremental borrowing rate is 16% and the implicit rate on the lease is 14%. Circuit Village has no way of knowing or estimating the implicit rate used by Thomas. Using either rate, the present value of the minimum lease payments is between 90% and 100% of the fair value of the machine at the lease agreement. Circuit Village has agreed to pay all executory costs directly, and no allowance for these costs is included in the lease payments. Thomas is reasonably certain that Circuit Village will pay all lease payments, and, because it has agreed to pay all executory costs, there are no important uncertainties regarding costs to be incurred by Thomas.

**Required**
1. With respect to Circuit Village (the lessee), answer the following:
   a. What type of lease has been entered into? Explain the reason for your answer.
   b. How should Circuit Village compute the appropriate amount to be recorded for the lease or asset acquired?
   c. What accounts will be created or affected by this transaction, and how will the lease or asset or other cost be matched with earnings?
2. With respect to Thomas (the lessor), answer the following:
   a. What type of leasing arrangement has been entered into? Explain the reason for your answer.
   b. How should this lease be recorded by Thomas, and how are the appropriate amounts determined?
   c. How should Thomas determine the appropriate amount of earnings to be recognized from each lease payment? (*AICPA adapted*)

### C19-6 *Classification of Leases*
*Part a.* Capital leases and operating leases are the two classifications of leases described in FASB pronouncements, from the standpoint of the lessee.

**Required**
1. Describe how a capital lease is accounted for by the lessee both at the inception of the lease and during the first year of the lease, assuming the lease transfers ownership of the property to the lessee by the end of the lease.
2. Describe how an operating lease is accounted for by the lessee both at the inception of the lease and during the first year of the lease, assuming equal monthly payments are made by the lessee at the beginning of each month of the lease. Describe the change in accounting, if any, when rental payments are not made on a straight-line basis.

Do not discuss the criteria for distinguishing between capital leases and operating leases.

*Part b.* Sales-type leases and direct financing leases are two of the classifications of leases described in FASB pronouncements, from the standpoint of the lessor.

**Required**
Compare and contrast a sales-type lease with a direct financing lease as follows:
1. Gross investment in the lease.
2. Amortization of unearned interest income.
3. Manufacturer's or dealer's profit.

Do not discuss the criteria for distinguishing between the leases described above and operating leases. (*AICPA adapted*)

### C19-7   Capital Lease Issues
On January 1, 1995, Lani Company entered into a noncancelable lease for a machine to be used in its manufacturing operations. The lease transfers ownership of the machine to Lani by the end of the lease term. The term of the lease is 8 years. The minimum lease payment made by Lani on January 1, 1995 was one of eight equal annual payments. At the inception of the lease, the criteria established for classification as a capital lease by the lessee were met.

**Required**
1. What is the theoretical basis for the accounting standard that requires certain long-term leases to be capitalized by the lessee? Do not discuss the specific lease as a capital lease.
2. How should Lani account for this lease at its inception and determine the amount to be recorded?
3. What expenses related to this lease will Lani incur during the first year of the lease, and how will they be determined?
4. How should Lani report the lease transaction on its December 31, 1995 balance sheet? (*AICPA adapted*)

### C19-8   Miscellaneous Lease Issues
On January 1, 1995, Von Company entered into two noncancelable leases for new machines to be used in its manufacturing operations. The first lease does not contain a bargain purchase option. The lease term is equal to 80% of the estimated economic life of the machine. The second lease contains a bargain purchase option. The lease term is equal to 50% of the estimated economic life of the machine.

**Required**
1. What is the theoretical basis for requiring lessees to capitalize certain long-term leases? Do not discuss the specific criteria for classifying a lease as a capital lease.

2. How should a lessee account for a capital lease at its inception?
3. How should a lessee record each minimum lease payment for a capital lease?
4. How should Von classify each of the two leases? Why? (*AICPA adapted*)

### C19-9   Sale-Leaseback
On January 1, 1995, Metcalf Company sold equipment for cash and leased it back. As seller-lessee, Metcalf retained the right to substantially all of the remaining use of the equipment.

The term of the lease is 8 years. There is a gain on the sale portion of the transaction. The lease portion of the transaction is classified appropriately as a capital lease.

**Required**
1. What is the theoretical basis for requiring lessees to capitalize certain long-term leases? Do **not** discuss the specific criteria for classifying a lease as a capital lease.
2. a. How should Metcalf account for the sale portion of the sale-leaseback transaction at January 1, 1995?
   b. How should Metcalf account for the leaseback portion of the sale-leaseback transaction at January 1, 1995?
3. How should Metcalf account for the gain on the sale portion of the sale-leaseback transaction during the first year of the lease? Why? (*AICPA adapted*)

### C19-10   Sale-Leaseback
On December 31, 1994, Port Co. sold 6-month-old equipment at fair value and leased it back. There was a loss on the sale. Port pays all insurance, maintenance, and taxes on the equipment. The lease provides for 8 equal annual payments, beginning December 31, 1995, with a present value equal to 85% of the equipment's fair value and sales price. The lease's term is equal to 80% of the equipment's useful life. There is no provision for Port to reacquire ownership of the equipment at the end of the lease term.

**Required**
1. a. Why is it important to compare an equipment's fair value to its lease payments' present value and its useful life to the lease term?
   b. Evaluate Port's leaseback of the equipment in terms of each of the four criteria for determination of a capital lease.
2. How should Port account for the sale portion of the sale-leaseback transaction at December 31, 1994?
3. How should Port report the leaseback portion of the sale-leaseback transaction on its December 31, 1995 balance sheet? (*AICPA adapted*)

*C19-11  Capital Lease Issues*   ⬭

The Cliborn Retail Company negotiated a lease for a retail store in a new shopping center that included 30 stores. The accountant for Cliborn, Gail Naugle, was given the lease agreement to analyze. She looked into whether the lease was a capital lease. The lease did not include a transfer of ownership or an option to purchase. The lease term was for 20 years and the present value of the minimum lease payments was $100,000. Unsure of the fair market value of the property or its life, she called the lessor's controller.

"That is easy," he replied. "There is no fair market value because we would never sell a single store in a shopping center. And, let's see, 20 years divided by 75% is about 27 years, so the life of the property must be at least that much. Or do you want a capital lease?"

**Required**

Assuming that you are Gail Naugle, research the generally accepted accounting principles and prepare a short memo to the controller of Cliborn that summarizes how to classify the lease. Cite your reference and applicable paragraph numbers.

*C19-12  Capital Lease Issues*   ⬭

The Stirbis Company was negotiating a lease for a new building that would be used for a warehouse. Its accountant, Shannon Fenimore, had been invited to join Jim Stirbis (the president) in a meeting where the lease

agreement was settled. The president of the company owning the building said, "I assume that you want an operating lease."

"That is correct," replied Jim Stirbis.

The president responded, "So we will not include a transfer of ownership or an option to purchase. Anyway, I am sure you do not want to get into the real estate business."

"No, of course not."

"And we agree that the lease term is 30 years."

"Yes, but that seems to present some problems. We would have to argue that the life of the building is more than 40 years."

"You should not have any trouble persuading your auditors to agree to that."

"Maybe not. But the present value of the $53,040 annual lease payment is $500,000, which is the fair market value of the building."

"That is a problem. But I think I have a solution. We will adjust the annual payments to $45,000 so their present value is only 85% of the fair market value. Then we will add a clause that you also pay 1% of your total sales up to a maximum of $8,040 each year."

**Required**

Assuming that you are Shannon Fenimore, research the generally accepted accounting principles and prepare a short memo to the controller of Stirbis that summarizes how to classify the lease. Cite your reference and applicable paragraph numbers.

## MULTIPLE CHOICE

*Select the best answer for each of the following.*

*M19-1*  The present value of the minimum lease payments should be used by the lessee in the determination of a(an)

|    | Capital lease liability | Operating lease liability |
|----|-------------------------|---------------------------|
| a. | Yes | No |
| b. | Yes | Yes |
| c. | No | Yes |
| d. | No | No |

*M19-2*  East Company leased a new machine from North Company on May 1, 1995 under a lease with the following information:

| | |
|---|---|
| Lease term | 10 years |
| Annual rental payable at beginning of each lease year | $40,000 |
| Useful life of machine | 12 years |
| Implicit interest rate | 14% |
| Present value factor for an annuity of 1 in advance for 10 periods at 14% | 5.95 |
| Present value factor for 1 for 10 periods at 14% | 0.27 |

East has the option to purchase the machine on May 1, 2005 by paying $50,000, which approximates the expected fair value of the machine on the option exercise date. On May 1, 1995, East should record a capitalized lease asset of

a. $251,500
b. $238,000
c. $224,500
d. $198,000

M19-3    For a lease that transfers ownership of the property to the lessee by the end of the lease term, the lessee should
   a. Record the minimum lease payment as an expense
   b. Amortize the capitalizable cost of the property using the interest method
   c. Amortize the capitalizable cost of the property in a manner consistent with the lessee's normal depreciation policy for owned assets, except that the period of amortization should be the lease term
   d. Amortize the capitalizable cost of the property in a manner consistent with the lessee's normal depreciation policy for owned assets

*Items 4 and 5 are based on the following information:*

Fox Company, a dealer in machinery and equipment, leased equipment to Tiger, Inc. on July 1, 1995. The lease is appropriately accounted for as a sale by Fox and as a purchase by Tiger. The lease is for a 10-year period (the useful life of the asset) expiring June 30, 2005. The first of 10 equal annual payments of $500,000 was made on July 1, 1995. Fox had purchased the equipment for $2,675,000 on January 1, 1995 and established a list selling price of $3,375,000 on the equipment. Assume that the present value at July 1, 1995 of the rent payments over the lease term discounted at 12% (the appropriate interest rate) was $3,165,000.

M19-4    What is the amount of profit on the sale and the amount of interest income that Fox should record for the year ended December 31, 1995?
   a. $0 and $159,900
   b. $490,000 and $159,900
   c. $490,000 and $189,900
   d. $700,000 and $189,900

M19-5    Assuming that Tiger uses straight-line depreciation, what is the amount of depreciation and interest expense that Tiger should record for the year ended December 31, 1995?
   a. $158,250 and $159,900
   b. $158,250 and $189,900
   c. $168,750 and $159,900
   d. $168,750 and $189,900

M19-6    Rent received in advance by the lessor for an operating lease should be recognized as revenue
   a. When received
   b. At the lease's inception
   c. In the period specified by the lease
   d. At the lease's expiration

M19-7    For a 6-year capital lease, the portion of the minimum lease payment in the third year applicable to the reduction of the obligation should be
   a. Less than in the second year
   b. More than in the second year
   c. The same as in the fourth year
   d. More than in the fourth year

M19-8    On January 2, 1995, Lafayette Machine Shops, Inc. signed a 10-year noncancelable lease for a heavy-duty drill press, stipulating annual payments of $15,000 starting at the end of the first year, with title passing to Lafayette at the expiration of the lease. Lafayette treated this transaction as a capital lease. The drill press has an estimated useful life of 15 years, with no salvage value. Lafayette uses straight-line depreciation for all of its fixed assets. Aggregate lease payments were determined to have a present value of $92,170, based on implicit interest of 10%. For 1995, Lafayette should record

|    | Interest expense | Depreciation expense |
|----|------------------|----------------------|
| a. | $0               | $0                   |
| b. | $7,717           | $6,145               |
| c. | $9,217           | $6,145               |
| d. | $9,217           | $9,217               |

M19-9 On August 1, 1995, Kern Company leased a machine to Day Company for a 6-year period requiring payments of $10,000 at the beginning of each year. The machine cost $48,000, which is the fair value at the lease date, and has a useful life of 8 years with no residual value. Kern's implicit interest rate is 10% and present value factors are as follows:

Present value for an annuity due of $1 at 10% for 6 periods     4.791
Present value for an annuity due of $1 at 10% for 8 periods     5.868

Kern appropriately recorded the lease as a direct financing lease. At the inception of the lease, the gross lease receivables account balance should be

  a. $60,000            c. $48,000
  b. $58,680            d. $47,910

M19-10 At its inception, the lease term of Lease G is 65% of the estimated remaining economic life of the leased property. This lease contains a bargain purchase option. The lessee should record Lease G as

  a. Neither an asset nor a liability       c. An expense
  b. An asset but not a liability         d. An asset and a liability

*(AICPA adapted)*

## EXERCISES

E19-1 *Determining Type of Lease and Subsequent Accounting*   On January 1, 1995, the Caswell Company signs a 10-year cancelable (at the option of either party) agreement to lease a storage building from the Wake Company. The following information pertains to this lease agreement:

1. The agreement requires rental payments of $90,000 at the end of each year.
2. The cost and fair value of the building on January 1, 1995 is $2 million.
3. The building has an estimated economic life of 50 years, with no residual value. The Caswell Company depreciates similar buildings according to the straight-line method.
4. The lease does not contain a renewable option clause. At the termination of the lease, the building reverts to the lessor.
5. Caswell's incremental borrowing rate is 14% per year. The Wake Company set the annual rental to ensure a 16% rate of return (the loss in service value anticipated for the term of the lease).
6. Executory costs of $10,000 annually related to taxes on the property are paid by Wake Company.

### Required

1. Determine what type of lease this is for the lessee.
2. Prepare appropriate journal entries on the lessee's books to reflect the signing of the lease agreement and to record the payments and expenses related to this lease for the years 1995 and 1996.

E19-2 *Lessee Accounting Issues*   The Sax Company signs a lease agreement dated January 1, 1995 that provides for it to lease computers from the Appleton Company beginning January 1, 1995. The lease terms, provisions, and related events are as follows:

1. The lease term is 5 years. The lease is noncancelable and requires equal rental payments to be made at the end of each year.
2. The computers have an estimated life of 5 years and have a zero estimated residual value at the end of this time.
3. Sax Company agrees to pay all executory costs.
4. The lease contains no renewal or bargain purchase option.
5. The annual rental is set by Appleton at $83,222.92 to earn a rate of return of 12% on its net investment. The Sax Company is aware of this rate, which is equal to its borrowing rate.
6. Sax Company uses the straight-line method to record depreciation on similar equipment.

**Required**

1. Determine what type of lease this is for Sax Company.
2. Calculate the amount of the asset and liability of the Sax Company at the inception of the lease (round to the nearest dollar).
3. Prepare a table summarizing the lease payments and interest expense.
4. Prepare journal entries on the books of Sax Company for the years 1995 and 1996.

E19-3     *Lessee Accounting with Payments Made at Beginning of Year*     The Adden Company signs a lease agreement dated January 1, 1995 that provides for it to lease heavy equipment from the Scott Rental Company beginning January 1, 1995. The lease terms, provisions, and related events are as follows:

1. The lease term is 4 years. The lease is noncancelable and requires annual rental payments of $20,000 each to be paid in advance at the beginning of each year.
2. The cost, and also fair value, of the heavy equipment to Scott at the inception of the lease is $68,036.62. The equipment has an estimated life of 4 years and has a zero estimated residual value at the end of this time.
3. Adden Company agrees to pay all executory costs.
4. The lease contains no renewal or bargain purchase option.
5. Scott's interest rate implicit in the lease is 12%. Adden Company is aware of this rate, which is equal to its borrowing rate.
6. Adden Company uses the straight-line method to record depreciation on similar equipment.
7. Executory costs paid at the end of the year by Adden Company are:

| 1995 | 1996 |
|---|---|
| Insurance, $1,500 | Insurance, $1,300 |
| Property taxes, $6,000 | Property taxes, $5,500 |

**Required**

1. Determine what type of lease this is for Adden Company.
2. Prepare a table summarizing the lease payments and interest expense for Adden Company.
3. Prepare journal entries on the books of Adden Company for the years 1995 and 1996.

E19-4     *Lessor Accounting Issues*     The Rexon Company leases equipment to Ten-Care Company beginning January 1, 1995. The lease terms, provisions, and related events are as follows:

1. The lease term is 8 years. The lease is noncancelable and requires equal rental payments to be made at the end of each year.
2. The cost, and also fair value, of the equipment is $500,000. The equipment has an estimated life of 8 years and has a zero estimated value at the end of that time.
3. Ten-Care Company agrees to pay all executory costs.
4. The lease contains no renewal or bargain purchase option.
5. The interest rate implicit in the lease is 14%.
6. The initial direct costs are insignificant and assumed to be zero.
7. The collectibility of the rentals is reasonably assured, and there are no important uncertainties surrounding the amount of unreimbursable costs yet to be incurred by the lessor.

**Required**

1. Assuming that the lease is a direct financing lease from Rexon's point of view, calculate the amount of the equal rental receipts.
2. Prepare a table summarizing the lease receipts and interest revenue earned by Rexon.
3. Prepare journal entries on the books of Rexon for the years 1995 and 1996.

E19-5     *Lessor Accounting Issues*     Ramallah Company leases heavy equipment to Terrell, Inc. on January 2, 1995 on the following terms:

1. Forty-eight lease rentals of $1,200 at the end of each month are to be paid by Terrell, Inc., and the lease is noncancelable.

2. The cost of the heavy equipment to Ramallah Company was $45,569.
3. Ramallah Company will account for this lease using the direct financing method. The difference between total rental receipts ($1,200 × 48 = $57,600) and the cost of the equipment ($45,569) was computed to yield a return of 1% per month over the lease term.

**Required**

Prepare journal entries in the accounts of Ramallah Company (the lessor) to record the lease contract and the receipt of the first lease rental on January 31, 1995. Record the part of the $12,031 Unearned Interest that was earned during the first month and carry calculations to the nearest dollar.

**E19-6** *Lessee and Lessor Accounting Issues*  Lessor Leasing Company agrees to provide Lessee Company with equipment under a noncancelable lease for 5 years. The equipment has a 5-year life, cost Lessor Company $30,000, and will have no residual value when the lease term ends. Lessee Company agrees to pay all executory costs ($500 per year) throughout the lease period. On January 1, 1995, the equipment is delivered. Lessor expects a 14% return. The five equal annual rents are payable in advance starting January 1, 1995.

**Required**

1. Assuming this is a direct financing lease for the lessor and a capital lease for the lessee, prepare a table summarizing the lease and interest payments suitable for use by either party.
2. On the assumption that both companies adjust and close books each December 31, prepare journal entries relating to the lease for both companies through December 31, 1995 based on data derived in the table. Assume that Lessee Company depreciates similar equipment by the straight-line method.

**E19-7** *Lessor Accounting with Receipts at End of Year*  The Berne Company, the lessor, enters into a lease with Fox Company to lease equipment to Fox beginning January 1, 1995. The lease terms, provisions, and related events are as follows:

1. The lease term is 4 years. The lease is noncancelable and requires annual rental payments of $60,000 to be made at the end of each year.
2. The cost of the equipment is $155,000. The equipment has an estimated life of 4 years and an estimated residual value at the end of the lease term of zero.
3. Fox agrees to pay all executory costs.
4. The interest rate implicit in the lease is 12%.
5. The initial direct costs are insignificant and assumed to be zero.
6. The collectibility of the rentals is reasonably assured, and there are no important uncertainties surrounding the amount of unreimbursable costs yet to be incurred by the lessor.

**Required**

1. Assuming that the lease is a sales-type lease from Berne's point of view, calculate the selling price and assume that this is also the fair value.
2. Prepare a table summarizing the lease receipts and interest revenue earned by the lessor.
3. Prepare journal entries on the books of Berne Company, the lessor, for the years 1995 and 1996.

**E19-8** *Lessor Accounting with Receipts at Beginning of Year*  The Edom Company, the lessor, enters into a lease with Jebusite Company to lease equipment to Jebusite beginning January 1, 1995. The lease terms, provisions, and related events are as follows:

1. The lease term is 5 years. The lease is noncancelable and requires annual rental receipts of $100,000 to be made in advance at the beginning of each year.
2. The cost of the equipment is $313,000. The equipment has an estimated life of 6 years and, at the end of the lease term, has an unguaranteed residual value of $20,000 accruing to the benefit of Edom.
3. Jebusite agrees to pay all executory costs.
4. The interest rate implicit in the lease is 14%.
5. The initial direct costs are insignificant and assumed to be zero.
6. The collectibility of the rentals is reasonably assured, and there are no important uncertainties surrounding the amount of unreimbursable costs yet to be incurred by the lessor.

**Required**

1. Assuming that the lease is a sales-type lease from Edom's point of view, calculate the selling price and assume that this is also the fair value.
2. Prepare a table summarizing the lease receipts and interest revenue earned by the lessor.
3. Prepare journal entries on the books of Edom Company, the lessor, for the years 1995 and 1996.

E19-9    *Lessee and Lessor Accounting Issues*    The following information is available for a noncancelable lease of equipment that is classified as a sales-type lease by the lessor and as a capital lease by the lessee. Assume that the lease payments are made at the beginning of each month, interest and straight-line depreciation are recognized at the end of each month, and the residual value of the leased asset is zero at the end of a 3-year life.

| | |
|---|---:|
| Cost of equipment to lessor (Anson Company) | $50,000 |
| Initial payment by lessee (Bullard Company) at inception of lease | 2,000 |
| Present value of remaining 35 payments of $2,000 each discounted at 1% per month | 58,817 |

**Required**

1. Record the lease (including the initial receipt of $2,000) and the receipt of the second and third installments of $2,000 in the accounts of the Anson Company. Carry computations to the nearest dollar.
2. Record the lease (including the initial payment of $2,000), the payment of the second and third installments of $2,000, and monthly depreciation in the accounts of the Bullard Company. The lessee records the lease obligation at net present value. Carry computations to the nearest dollar.

E19-10    *Comparisons of Operating and Sales-Type Leases*    On January 1, 1995, Nelson Company leases certain property to Queens Company at an annual rental of $60,000 payable in advance at the beginning of each year for 10 years. The first payment is received immediately. The leased property, which is new, cost $300,000 and has an estimated economic life of 10 years and no residual value. The interest rate implicit in the lease is 12% and the lease is noncancelable. Nelson Company had no other costs associated with this lease. It should have accounted for this lease as a sales-type lease, but mistakenly treated it as an operating lease.

**Required**

Compute the effect on income before income taxes during the first year of the lease as a result of Nelson Company's classification of this lease as an operating rather than a sales-type lease.

E19-11    *Lease Income and Expense*    Reuben Company retires a machine from active use on January 2, 1995 for the express purpose of leasing it. The machine had a carrying value of $800,000 after 12 years of use and is expected to have 10 more years of economic life. The machine is depreciated on a straight-line basis. On March 2, 1995, Reuben Company leases the machine to Owens Company for $150,000 a year for a 5-year period ending February 28, 2000. Under the provisions of the lease, Reuben Company incurs total maintenance and other related costs of $20,000 relating to the year ended December 31, 1995. Owens Company pays $150,000 to Reuben Company on March 2, 1995. The lease was properly classified as an operating lease.

**Required**

1. Compute the income before income taxes derived by Reuben Company from this lease for the calendar year ended December 31, 1995.
2. Compute the amount of rent expense incurred by Owens Company from this lease for the calendar year ended December 31, 1995.

E19-12    *Determining Type of Lease and Subsequent Accounting*    The Ravis Rent-A-Car Company leases a car to Ira Reem, an employee, on January 1, 1995. The term of the noncancelable lease is 4 years. The following information about the lease is provided:

1. Title to the car passes to Ira Reem on the termination of the lease with no additional payment required by the lessee.
2. The cost and fair value of the car to the Ravis Rent-A-Car Company is $8,400. The car has an economic life of 5 years.
3. The lease payments are determined at an amount that will yield Ravis Rent-A-Car Company a rate of return of 10% on its net investment.
4. Collectibility of the lease payments is reasonably assured.

5. There are no important uncertainties surrounding the amount of unreimbursable costs yet to be incurred by the lessor.
6. Equal annual lease payments are due at the end of each year.

**Required**

1. What type of lease is this to Ravis Rent-A-Car Company? Why?
2. Prepare a table summarizing the lease receipts and interest revenue earned by the Ravis Rent-A-Car Company for the 4-year lease term.
3. Prepare the journal entries for 1995 and 1996 to record the lease agreement, the lease receipts, and the recognition of income on the books of Ravis Rent-A-Car Company.

**E19-13** *Appendix: Sales-Leaseback* On January 1, 1995, the Stimpson Company sells land to Barker Company for $2.5 million, then immediately leases it back. The relevant information is as follows:

1. The land was carried on Stimpson's books at a value of $2 million.
2. The term of the noncancelable lease is 25 years.
3. The lease agreement requires equal rental payments of $357,007 at the end of each year.
4. The incremental borrowing rate of Stimpson Company is 15%. Stimpson is aware that Barker Company set the annual rental to ensure a rate of return of 14%.
5. The land has a fair value of $2.5 million on January 1, 1995.
6. Stimpson Company has the option of purchasing the land for $150 at the end of 25 years.
7. Stimpson Company pays all executory costs. These costs consist of insurance and property taxes amounting to $12,000 per year.
8. There are no important uncertainties surrounding the amount of unreimbursable costs yet to be incurred by the lessor, and the collectibility of the rentals is reasonably assured.

**Required**

1. Prepare the journal entries for the seller-lessee, Stimpson, for 1995 to reflect the sale and leaseback agreement. In calculating the present value of the lease payments, ignore the $150 bargain purchase option as immaterial.
2. Describe briefly the accounting treatment of the gain by the seller-lessee.

## PROBLEMS

**P19-1** *Determining Type of Lease and Subsequent Accounting* On January 1, 1995, the Alice Company leases electronic equipment for 5 years, agreeing to pay $80,000 annually at the beginning of each year under the noncancelable lease. The Superior Electronics Company, the lessor, agrees to pay all executory costs, estimated to be $4,550 per year. The cost and also fair value of the equipment is $500,000. Its estimated life is 10 years. The estimated residual value at the end of 5 years is $200,000. At the end of 10 years, it is $5,000. There is no bargain purchase option in the lease nor any agreement to transfer ownership at the end of the lease to the lessee. The lessee's incremental borrowing rate is 12%. During 1995, Superior Electronics pays property taxes of $750, maintenance costs of $2,600, and insurance of $1,200. There are no important uncertainties surrounding the amount of unreimbursable costs yet to be incurred by the lessor. Straight-line depreciation is considered the appropriate method by either company.

**Required**

1. Identify the type of lease involved for Alice Company and Superior Electronics Company and give reasons for your classifications.
2. Prepare appropriate journal entries for 1995 on the books of the lessee and lessor.

**P19-2** *Determining Type of Lease and Subsequent Accounting* On January 1, 1995, the Ballieu Company leases specialty equipment with an economic life of 8 years to the Anderson Company. The lease contains the following terms and provisions:

The lease is noncancelable and has a term of 8 years. The annual rentals are $35,000, payable at the beginning of each year. The interest rate implicit in the lease is 14%. The Anderson Company agrees to pay all executory costs and is given an option to buy the equipment for $1 at the end of the lease term, December 31, 2002.

The cost of the equipment to the lessor is $150,000 and the fair retail market value is approximately $185,100. The lessor incurs no material initial direct costs. The collectibility of the rentals is reasonably assured, and there are no important uncertainties surrounding the amount of unreimbursable costs yet to be incurred by the lessor. The lessor estimates that the fair market value is expected to be significantly greater than $1 at the end of the lease term.

The lessor calculates that the present value on January 1, 1995 of 8 annual payments in advance of $35,000 discounted at 14% is $185,090.68 (the $1 purchase option is ignored as immaterial).

**Required**
1. Identify the classification of the lease transaction from the point of view of Ballieu Company. Give the reasons for your classification.
2. Prepare all the journal entries on the books of Ballieu Company relevant to the lease for the years 1995 and 1996.
3. Discuss the disclosure requirements for the lease transaction for the Ballieu Company.

P19-3   *Lessee Accounting Issues*   The Timmer Company signs a lease agreement dated January 1, 1995 that provides for it to lease equipment from Landau Company beginning January 1, 1995. The lease terms, provisions, and related events are as follows:

The lease is noncancelable and has a term of 5 years. The annual rentals are $94,319.31, payable at the end of each year, and provide Landau with a 12% annual rate of return on its net investment. The Timmer Company agrees to pay all executory costs at the end of each year. In 1995, these were: insurance $3,760; property taxes, $5,440. In 1996: insurance, $3,100; property taxes, $5,330. There is no renewal or bargain purchase option.

Timmer estimates that the equipment has an economic life of 5 years and a zero residual value. Timmer's incremental borrowing rate is 16%, it knows the rate implicit in the lease, and it uses the straight-line method to record depreciation on similar equipment.

**Required**
1. Calculate the amount of the asset and liability of the Timmer Company at the inception of the lease. (Round to the nearest dollar.)
2. Prepare a table summarizing the lease payments and interest expense.
3. Prepare journal entries on the books of Timmer for 1995 and 1996.
4. Prepare a partial balance sheet in regard to the lease for Timmer for December 31, 1995.

P19-4   *Direct Financing Lease*   The Calder Company, the lessor, enters into a lease with Darwin Company, the lessee, to provide heavy equipment beginning January 1, 1995. The lease terms, provisions, and related events are as follows:

The lease is noncancelable, has a term of 8 years, and has no renewal or bargain purchase option. The annual rentals are $65,000, payable at the end of each year. The interest rate implicit in the lease is 15%. The Darwin Company agrees to pay all executory costs.

The cost and fair value of the equipment to the lessor is $308,021.30. The lessor incurs no material initial direct costs. The collectibility of the rentals is reasonably assured, and there are no important uncertainties surrounding the amount of unreimbursable costs yet to be incurred by the lessor. The lessor estimates that the fair market value at the end of the lease term will be $50,000 and that the economic life of the equipment is 9 years.

The following present value factors are relevant:

$$PV_{n=8, i=15\%} = 4.487322; \quad PV_{n=8, i=15\%} = 0.326902; \quad PV_{n=1, i=15\%} = 0.869565$$

**Required**
1. Prepare a table summarizing the lease receipts and interest revenue earned by the lessor for this direct financing lease.
2. State why the lease is a direct financing lease.
3. Prepare journal entries on the books of Calder Company for the years 1995, 1996, and 1997.
4. Prepare partial balance sheets for December 31, 1995 and December 31, 1996, showing how the accounts should be disclosed.

**P19-5** *Comprehensive* Landlord Company and Tenant Company enter into a noncancelable direct financing lease on January 1, 1995 for new heavy equipment that cost the Landlord Company $300,000 (useful life is 6 years with no residual value). The fair value is also $300,000. Landlord Company expects a 14% return over the 6-year period of the lease. Lease provisions require 6 equal annual amounts payable each January 1, beginning with January 1, 1995. The Tenant Company pays all executory costs. The heavy equipment reverts to the lessor at the termination of the lease. Assume that there are no initial direct costs. The collectibility of the rentals is reasonably assured and there are no important uncertainties surrounding the amount of unreimbursable costs yet to be incurred by the lessor.

**Required**

1. Show how the Landlord Company should compute the annual rental amounts. Discuss how the Tenant Company should compute the present value of the lease rights. What additional information would be required to make this computation?
2. Prepare a table summarizing the lease and interest receipts that would be suitable for the Landlord Company. Under what conditions would this table be suitable for the Tenant Company?
3. Assuming that the table prepared in Requirement 2 is suitable for both the lessee and the lessor, prepare the journal entries for both firms for the years 1995 and 1996. Use the straight-line depreciation method for the leased equipment. The executory costs paid by the lessee are: 1995—insurance, $700; property taxes, $800; and 1996—insurance, $600; property taxes, $750.
4. Show the items and amounts that would be reported on the comparative 1995 and 1996 income statements and ending balance sheets for both the lessor and the lessee. Include appropriate notes to the financial statements.

**P19-6** *Direct Financing Lease with Unguaranteed Residual Value* Lessor Company and Lessee Company enter into a 5-year noncancelable direct financing lease on January 1, 1995 for a new computer that cost the Lessor Company $400,000 (useful life is 5 years). The fair value is also $400,000. Lessor Company expects a 12% return over the 5-year period of the lease. The computer will have an estimated unguaranteed residual value at the end of the fifth year of the lease of $20,000. The lease provisions require 5 equal annual amounts payable each January 1, beginning with January 1, 1995. The Lessee Company pays all executory costs. The computer reverts to the lessor at the termination of the lease. Assume that there are no initial direct costs, no important uncertainties surrounding the amount of unreimbursable costs yet to be incurred by the lessor, and that the collectibility of rentals is reasonably assured.

**Required**

1. Show how the Lessor Company should compute the annual rental amounts.
2. Prepare a table summarizing the lease and interest receipts that would be suitable for the Lessor Company.
3. Prepare the journal entries for Lessor Company for the years 1995, 1996, and 1997.

**P19-7** *Sales-Type Lease with Receipts at End of Year* The Lamplighter Company, the lessor, agrees to lease equipment to Tilson Company, the lessee, beginning January 1, 1995. The lease terms, provisions, and related events are as follows:

The lease is noncancelable and has a term of 8 years. The annual rentals are $32,000, payable at the end of each year. The Tilson Company agrees to pay all executory costs. The interest rate implicit in the lease is 14%.

The cost of the equipment to the lessor is $110,000. The lessor incurs no material initial direct costs. The collectibility of the rentals is reasonably assured, and there are no important uncertainties surrounding the amount of unreimbursable costs yet to be incurred by the lessor. The lessor estimates that the fair market value at the end of the lease term will be $20,000 and that the economic life of the equipment is 9 years.

**Required**

1. Calculate the selling price implied by the lease and prepare a table summarizing the lease receipts and interest revenue earned by the lessor for this sales-type lease.
2. State why this is a sales-type lease.
3. Prepare journal entries on the books of Lamplighter Company for the years 1995, 1996, and 1998.
4. Prepare partial balance sheets for Lamplighter Company for December 31, 1995 and December 31, 1996, showing how the accounts should be disclosed.

*P19-8    Various Lease Issues for Lessor and Lessee*   Lessee Company leases heavy equipment on January 1, 1995 under a capital lease from Lessor Company with the following lease provisions:

The lease is noncancelable and has a term of 10 years. The lease does not contain a renewal or bargain purchase option. The annual rentals are $23,703.24, payable at the beginning of each year. The Lessee Company agrees to pay all executory costs. The interest rate implicit in the lease is 12%, which is known by Lessee Company. The residual value of the property at the end of 10 years is estimated to be zero.

The cost and fair value of the equipment to the lessor is $175,000. The lessor incurs no material initial direct costs. The collectibility of the rentals is reasonably assured, and there are no important uncertainties surrounding the amount of unreimbursable costs yet to be incurred by the lessor.

Lessee's incremental borrowing rate is 15% and it uses the straight-line method to record depreciation on similar equipment. In 1995, the lessee pays insurance of $1,900, property taxes of $1,300, and maintenance of $600; and in 1996, the lessee pays insurance of $1,800, property taxes of $1,200, and maintenance of $500.

**Required**

1. Identify the type of lease involved for the lessee and the lessor, and give reasons for your classifications.
2. Prepare all the journal entries related to the lease contract on both the lessee's and the lessor's books for 1995 and 1996.

*P19-9    Various Lease Issues for Lessor and Lessee*   Benjamin Company has rented new equipment to Murrell Builders that cost $50,000. This equipment has a life of 4 years and no residual value at the end of that time. The lease is noncancelable and is signed on January 1, 1995. Murrell Builders assumes all normal risks and executory costs of ownership. The title to the property is transferred to Murrell Builders at the end of the 4 years. The Benjamin Company computes the rents on the basis of a 14% return. The lessee's incremental borrowing rate is also 14%. The collectibility of rentals is reasonably assured and there are no important uncertainties surrounding the amount of unreimbursable costs yet to be incurred by the lessor.

**Required**

1. Assuming the annual rentals are payable at the end of each year, complete the following:
   a. Lessor computation of periodic rental receipts.
   b. Lessee computation of the present value of the special property rights under the lease.
   c. A table summarizing lease and interest payments that would be suitable for both lessor and lessee.
2. Assuming the annual rentals are payable at the start of each year, compute the same three items listed in Requirement 1.
3. Prepare the journal entries for the lessor and lessee for Requirement 2 throughout 1995. Use the straight-line depreciation method.
4. Indicate the asset and liability amounts that would be reported on the balance sheets at December 31, 1995 under Requirement 2 by the lessor and lessee.

*P19-10    Initial Direct Costs and Related Issues*   On January 1, 1995, the Amity Company leases a crane to Baltimore Company. The lease contains the following terms and provisions:

The lease is noncancelable and has a term of 10 years. The lease does not contain a renewal or bargain purchase option. The annual rentals are $4,000, payable at the beginning of each year. The Baltimore Company agrees to pay all executory costs.

The cost and fair value of the equipment to the lessor is $24,913.94. The lessor incurs initial direct costs of $1,364.98. The interest rate implicit in the lease is 12.5%. After including the initial direct costs, the implicit rate is 12%. The collectibility of the rentals is reasonably assured, and there are no important uncertainties surrounding the amount of unreimbursable costs yet to be incurred by the lessor. The lessor estimates that the fair market value at the end of the lease term will be $3,000 and that the economic life of the crane is 12 years.

**Required**

1. What are initial direct costs? Discuss the accounting treatment of these costs. Are they treated in the same manner for: (a) an operating lease, (b) a sales-type lease, and (c) a direct financing lease?
2. From the lessor's viewpoint, is the preceding lease a sales-type or direct financing lease? Give reasons to support your conclusion.
3. Prepare the journal entries that should appear on the books of Amity Company relevant to the lease for 1995.

**P19-11**  *Various Lease Issues*  Farrington Company leases a computer from the Wilson Company. The lease includes the following provisions:

The lease is noncancelable and has a term of 8 years. The annual rentals are $60,000, payable at the end of each year. The Farrington Company agrees to pay all executory costs and has an option to purchase the computer for $1,000 at the end of the life of the lease. The interest rate implicit in the lease is 10%, which is known to Farrington.

Farrington estimates that the computer has an economic life of 12 years and a value of $70,000 at the end of 8 years. Farrington's incremental borrowing rate is 16% and it uses the straight-line method to record depreciation on similar equipment.

The computer cost Wilson $200,000 to manufacture. The lessor incurs initial direct costs of $10,000. The collectibility of the rentals is reasonably assured, and there are no important uncertainties surrounding the amount of unreimbursable costs yet to be incurred by the lessor.

**Required**

1.  What is the correct classification of the lease for the lessee and lessor? Explain whether the lease meets *each* of the required criteria.
2.  Assuming that the lease is signed on January 1, 1995, prepare all journal entries for 1995 for the lessor only.
3.  After 6 years, because of changes in the technology, the lessee and lessor independently conclude that the expected residual value of the computer at the end of the life of the lease is only $10,000. Discuss how the lessor should account for the change.

**P19-12**  *Accounting for Leases by Lessee and Lessor*  Scuppermong Farms, the lessee, and Tyrrell Equipment, the lessor, sign a lease agreement on January 1, 1995 that provides for Scuppermong Farms to lease a tobacco cultivator from Tyrrell Equipment. The lease terms, provisions, and other related events are as follows:

The lease is noncancelable and has a term of 6 years. The annual rentals are $50,550, payable at the beginning of each year. Tyrrell Equipment agrees to pay all executory costs, which are expected to be $550 annually, including property taxes of $300, insurance of $150, and maintenance of $100. Scuppermong Farms guarantees a residual value of $60,000 at the end of 6 years. The interest rate implicit in the lease is 14%, which is known by Scuppermong.

Scuppermong Farms' incremental borrowing rate is 15% and it uses the sum-of-the-years'-digits method to record depreciation on similar equipment.

The cost and fair value of the cultivator to Tyrrell Equipment is $248,989.27. The lessor incurs no material initial direct costs. The collectibility of the rentals is reasonably assured, and there are no important uncertainties surrounding the amount of unreimbursable costs yet to be incurred by the lessor.

**Required**

1.  Identify the type of lease involved for both Scuppermong Farms and Tyrrell Equipment, and give reasons for your classifications.
2.  Prepare the journal entries for both Scuppermong Farms and Tyrrell Equipment for 1995. (*Hint*: Scuppermong Farms should expense executory costs when annual payments are made to Tyrrell.)

**P19-13**  *Lessor's Income Statement*  The Dahlia Company has two divisions, the Astor Division which started operating in 1993, and the Tulip Division which started operating in 1994. The Astor Division leases medical equipment to hospitals. All of its leases are appropriately recorded as operating leases for accounting purposes except for a major lease entered into on January 1, 1995, which is appropriately recorded as a sale-type lease for accounting purposes.

Under long-term contracts, Tulip constructs waste water treatment plants for small communities throughout the United States. All of its long-term contracts are appropriately recorded for accounting purposes under the percentage-of-completion method except for two contracts, which are appropriately recorded for accounting purposes under the completed-contract method because of a lack of dependable estimates at the time of entering into these contracts.

For the year ended December 31, 1995 the following information is available:

Astor Division:

*Operating Leases.* Revenues from operating leases were $800,000. The cost of the related leased equipment is $3,700,000, which is being depreciated on a straight-line basis over a 5-year period. The estimated residual value of the leased equipment at the end of the 5-year period is $200,000. No leased equipment was acquired or constructed in 1995. Maintenance and other related costs and the costs of any other services rendered under the provisions of the leases were $70,000 in 1995.

*Lease Recorded as a Sale.* The January 1, 1995 lease recorded as a sale is for a 6-year period expiring December 31, 2000. The cost of this leased equipment is $3,500,000. This leased equipment is estimated to have no residual value at the end of the lease. Maintenance and other related costs, and the costs of any other services rendered under the provisions of this lease, all of which were paid by the lessee, were $120,000 in 1995. Equal annual payments under the lease are $750,000 and are due on January 1. The first payment was made on January 1, 1995. The present value for an annuity of $1 in advance at 10% is as follows:

| Number of Periods | Present Value |
|:-----------------:|:-------------:|
| 5 | 4.170 |
| 6 | 4.791 |
| 7 | 5.355 |

## Tulip Division:

*Long-Term Contracts: Percentage-of-Completion Method.* Long-term contracts recorded under the percentage-of-completion method aggregate $6,000,000. Costs incurred on these contracts were $1,500,000 in 1994 and $3,000,000 in 1995. Estimated additional costs of $1,000,000 are required to complete these contracts. Revenues of $1,740,000 were recognized in 1994 and a total of $4,800,000 has been billed of which $4,600,000 has been collected. No long-term contracts recorded under the percentage-of-completion method were completed in 1995.

*Long-Term Contracts: Completed-Contract Method.* The two long-term contracts recorded under the completed-contract method were started in 1994. One is a $5,000,000 contract. Costs incurred were $1,400,000 in 1994 and $1,600,000 in 1995. A total of $3,100,000 has been billed and $2,800,000 collected. Although it is difficult to estimate the additional costs required to complete this contract, indications are that this contract will prove to be profitable.

The second contract is for $4,000,000. Costs incurred were $1,200,000 in 1994 and $2,600,000 in 1995. A total of $3,300,000 has been billed and $2,900,000 collected. Although it is difficult to estimate the additional costs required to complete this contract, indications are that there will be a loss of approximately $550,000.

## Dahlia Company:

Selling, general, and administrative expenses exclusive of amounts specified earlier were $600,000 in 1995. Other income exclusive of amounts specified earlier was $50,000 in 1995.

## Required

Prepare an income statement of the Dahlia Company for the year ended December 31, 1995, stopping at income (loss) before income taxes. Show supporting schedules and computations in good form. *Ignore income tax and deferred tax considerations.* Notes are *not* required. (*AICPA adapted*)

*P19-14  Appendix: Determining Types of Leases*  Rigdon Company leases 50 acres of land to Christmas Tree International on January 1, 1995. The provisions of the lease are as follows:

The lease is noncancelable and has a term of 25 years. The annual rentals are $10,000, payable at the end of each year. The lease contains no bargain purchase option and the land reverts to Rigdon at the end of the lease. The incremental borrowing rate of Christmas Tree International is 12%.

The cost of the land to Rigdon Company is $60,000. The fair market value is $78,431.39. The lessor incurs no material initial direct costs. The collectibility of the rentals is reasonably assured, and there are no important uncertainties surrounding the amount of unreimbursable costs yet to be incurred by the lessor.

**Required**

1. Determine the classification of this lease from the standpoint of both the lessor and the lessee.
2. Why are the final two criteria (lease term 75% of economic life and present value of lease payments 90% of fair value) not applicable when classifying a lease of land?

P19-15  *Appendix: Sales-Leaseback*   On January 1, 1995, the Orr Company sells heavy equipment to Foible Company for $3 million, then immediately leases it back. The relevant information is as follows:

The lease is noncancelable and has a term of 8 years. The annual rentals are $603,908.50, payable at the end of each year. The seller-lessee agrees to pay all executory costs. The interest rate implicit in the lease is 12%.

The cost of the heavy equipment to Orr Company is $2,100,000. The purchaser-lessor incurs no material initial direct costs. The collectibility of the rentals is reasonably assured, and there are no important uncertainties surrounding the amount of unreimbursable costs yet to be incurred by the lessor.

Orr's incremental borrowing rate is 12% and the company estimates that the economic life of the equipment is 8 years. The present value on January 1, 1995 of 8 payments of $603,908.50 discounted at 12% is $3 million ($603,908.50 × 4.967640). The executory costs for 1995 are:

| | |
|---|---|
| Repairs and maintenance | $10,200 |
| Property taxes | 20,500 |
| Insurance | 18,000 |

**Required**

1. What type of lease is this to the seller-lessee? Discuss.
2. Prepare the journal entries for both the seller-lessee and the purchaser-lessor for 1995 to reflect the sale and leaseback agreement. Assume that the straight-line depreciation method is appropriate.

# 20

# THE STATEMENT OF CASH FLOWS

Users are interested in the operating, investing, and financing activities of companies. For a particular company, they pose such questions as: (1) What is the relationship between net income and cash provided by operations? (2) Why are dividends not larger, especially in light of rising income? (3) What expansion activities took place and how were those financed? (4) Why did cash decrease even though a net income was reported? and (5) What happened to the proceeds received from the issuance of capital stock? Each of these questions relates, either directly or indirectly, to the cash flows of the company. The FASB recognized the importance of providing answers to these questions by stating that financial reporting should provide information about how a company obtains and spends cash, about its borrowing and repayment of borrowing, about its capital transactions, including cash dividends and other distributions of its resources to owners, and about other factors that may affect its liquidity or solvency.[1]

To satisfy these objectives, the FASB issued *FASB Statement No. 95*, "Statement of Cash Flows," which requires that a company present a *statement of cash flows* for the accounting period along with its income statement and balance sheet.[2] The cash flow statement evolved over the years. Traditionally, it has been called a *funds statement,* where funds usually were defined as either cash or working capital (current assets less current liabilities). Initially, the statement was a simple "where got—where gone" schedule. This developed into the statement of sources and applications of funds, then into the statement of changes in financial position (required by *APB Opinion No. 19* before it was superseded by *FASB Statement No. 95*), and eventually into the statement of cash flows that is an integral part of the financial statements and is the subject of this chapter.

---

1.  "Objectives of Financial Reporting by Business Enterprises," *FASB Statement of Financial Accounting Concepts No. 1* (Stamford, Conn.: FASB, 1978), par. 49.
2.  "Statement of Cash Flows," *FASB Statement of Financial Accounting Standards No. 95* (Stamford, Conn.: FASB, 1987), par. 3.

## CONCEPTUAL OVERVIEW AND REPORTING GUIDELINES

In Chapter 2, we noted that one of the specific objectives of financial reporting is to provide information about a company's funds (cash) flows. Consequently, the FASB is concerned that a company's financial statements include information useful to external users about its cash inflows and outflows, borrowings and repayments, and capital transactions (including dividends). A company's receivables, payables, and inventory (i.e., items of working capital) are the links between its operations and its cash inflows and outflows, and information about these relationships may be useful in understanding the operations of the company.

Information about a company's liquidity, financial flexibility, operating capability, and risk is related to the objectives as well. The *liquidity* indicates the company's ability to meet its obligations as they come due. *Financial flexibility* is the company's ability to take effective actions to change the amounts and timings of its cash flows to adapt to unexpected needs and opportunities. Financial flexibility arises primarily from a company's ability to modify operations to increase net operating cash inflows. It also comes from the ability to raise cash from the issuance of new debt or equity securities or to obtain cash by disposing of assets. *Operating capability* is the company's ability to maintain a given physical level of operations, measured in terms of either the quantity of goods (inventory) produced and sold or the physical capacity of the company's property, plant, and equipment. *Risk* is the uncertainty or unpredictability of the future results of a company. The wider the range within which future results are likely to fall, the greater the risk associated with an investment in or extension of credit to the company.

**The primary purpose of a statement of cash flows is to provide relevant information about a company's cash receipts and cash payments during an accounting period** that is useful in evaluating the preceding items. In this regard, the FASB states that the information in a statement of cash flows, if used with information in the other financial statements, helps external users to assess (1) a company's ability to generate positive future net cash flows, (2) a company's ability to meet its obligations and pay dividends, (3) a company's need for external financing, (4) the reasons for differences between a company's net income and associated cash receipts and payments, and (5) both the cash and noncash aspects of a company's financing and investing transactions during the accounting period.[3]

### Reporting Guidelines and Practices

In order to understand how to use and to prepare a statement of cash flows, it is important to have a precise definition of the statement and guidelines as to the form and content of the statement. **A statement of cash flows is a financial statement that shows the cash inflows, cash outflows, and net change in cash from the operating, investing, and financing activities of a company during an accounting period, in a manner that reconciles the beginning and ending cash balances.**

#### Operating Activities

Operating activities include all transactions and other events that are not investing and financing activities. These include transactions involving acquiring, selling, and delivering goods for sale, as well as providing services. Cash inflows from operating activities include cash receipts from the sale of goods or services and collections of accounts receivable, as well as returns on loans (i.e., collections of interest) and on

---

3. *Ibid.*, par. 5.

investments in equity securities (i.e., receipts of dividends). Cash outflows for operating activities include cash payments to suppliers for inventory and on account, to employees, for taxes, to lenders for interest (unless capitalized), and to other suppliers for various expenses.

### Investing Activities

Investing activities include transactions involving lending money and collecting on the loans, acquiring and selling investments (both current and noncurrent), and acquiring and selling property, plant, and equipment. Cash inflows from investing activities include cash receipts from principal repayments of loans by borrowers (i.e., collections of notes receivable), from sales of loans (i.e., discounting of notes receivable), from sales of investments in other companies (e.g., stocks and bonds), and from sales of property, plant, and equipment. Cash outflows for investing activities include cash payments for loans made to borrowers, for purchases of loans, for investments, and for acquisitions of property, plant, and equipment. The classification of certain items depends on the company's operations. For instance, if a company regularly factors its accounts receivable, then the cash receipts are treated as cash inflows from operating activities. Similarly, if a company requires its customers to sign notes for credit sales, then the cash receipts from collections are treated as cash inflows from operating activities.

### Financing Activities

Financing activities include transactions involving obtaining resources from owners and providing them with a return on, and of, their investment, as well as obtaining money and other resources from creditors and repaying the amounts borrowed. Cash inflows from financing activities include cash receipts from the issuance of equity securities (i.e., common stock and preferred stock), from bonds, from mortgages, from notes, and from other short- or long-term borrowings. Cash outflows for financing activities include payments for dividends, for repurchase of the company's equity securities, and for repayments of amounts borrowed. Most borrowings and repayments of borrowings are financing activities. However, as noted, the settlement of liabilities such as accounts payable incurred to acquire inventory and salaries payable are operating activities.

### Format

From a conceptual standpoint, **analysis by external users to predict the amounts, timing, and uncertainty of future cash flows requires financial information to be segregated into reasonably homogeneous groups.**[4] To implement these guidelines and for consistent reporting, the statement of cash flows for the accounting period must clearly show: (1) the cash provided by or used in the company's operating activities, (2) the cash provided by or used in the company's investing activities, (3) the cash provided by or used in the company's financing activities, (4) the net increase or decrease in cash, and (5) a reconciliation of the beginning cash balance to the ending cash balance reported on the company's year-end balance sheet.

As we will see, most financing and investing activities affect cash; however, some transactions (such as the acquisition of land by the issuance of common stock) are "simultaneous" investing and financing activities that do not affect cash. Because

---

4.  "Recognition and Measurement in Financial Statements of Business Enterprises," *FASB Statement of Financial Accounting Concepts No. 5* (Stamford, Conn.: FASB, 1984), par. 20.

of their importance in providing an overall picture of a company's investing and financing activities, these items are reported either in a separate schedule or narrative explanation (in this chapter, we will always use a schedule) that accompanies the statement of cash flows. Furthermore, if a company uses the indirect method (discussed later) of reporting operating cash flows, the amounts of interest paid and income taxes paid during the accounting period are also disclosed. (For simplicity, this disclosure is discussed only briefly later in this chapter.)

### Cash and Cash Equivalents

As discussed in Chapter 5, as part of its cash management procedures, a company may invest its cash in short-term, highly liquid investments, such as treasury bills, commercial paper, and money market funds. These investments are called *cash equivalents*. Then, instead of reporting "Cash" as a current asset on its balance sheet, the company reports "Cash and Cash Equivalents." In this case, the purpose of the statement of cash flows is to explain the change during the accounting period in *cash and cash equivalents*. In this chapter, however, for simplicity we will focus only on changes in *cash*.

## Illustration

The 1992 statement of cash flows for The Coca-Cola Company is shown in Appendix A. A typical statement of cash flows is illustrated in Exhibit 20-1 for the Ryan Corporation and discussed here. Note that the statement of cash flows is divided into three sections entitled (1) Net Cash Flow From Operating Activities, (2) Cash Flows From Investing Activities, and (3) Cash Flows From Financing Activities. These are the titles generally used in a statement of cash flows. Note also the schedule of investing and financing activities not affecting cash.

### Content

The net cash provided by or used in a company's operating activities is shown in the first section of a statement of cash flows. It is likely that a company will be successful only if it is able to obtain most of its cash from its operations. This situation occurs when the cash received from selling goods or services exceeds the cash paid to provide the goods or services. Generating cash from operations generally is considered to be the most important cash flow activity of a company. The Ryan Corporation provided a net cash inflow of $16,400 from its operating activities during 1995, as shown in Exhibit 20-1. This $16,400 amount was determined by adjusting the $14,000 net income for several differences between the income flows and cash flows from operating activities; this procedure is called the "indirect method" and is explained later in the chapter. External users can compare the company's net cash flow from operating activities with the same information from previous years in order to detect favorable or unfavorable *trends* in the company's liquidity, financial flexibility, operating capability, and risk. This information can be compared with the same information from other companies for the same purposes.

The cash inflows and outflows from a company's investing activities are reported in the second section of the statement of cash flows. Each investing cash inflow and outflow is listed and the amounts are subtotaled to determine the net cash used for (or provided by) investing activities. During 1995, the Ryan Corporation had a cash outflow of $28,000 to purchase a building and a cash outflow of $4,000 to purchase equipment. It received a cash inflow of $10,000 from the sale of land, at cost. The net result was that $22,000 of cash was used for its investing activities.

**EXHIBIT 20-1**

**RYAN CORPORATION**

Statement of Cash Flows
For Year Ended December 31, 1995

| | | |
|---|---:|---:|
| **Net Cash Flow From Operating Activities** | | |
| Net income | $ 14,000 | |
| Adjustments for differences between income flows and cash flows from operating activities: | | |
| Add: Depreciation expense | 8,000 | |
| Decrease in accounts receivable | 2,600 | |
| Increase in salaries payable | 800 | |
| Less: Increase in inventory | (2,000) | |
| Decrease in accounts payable | (7,000) | |
| Net cash provided by operating activities | | $16,400 |
| **Cash Flows From Investing Activities** | | |
| Payment for purchase of building | $(28,000) | |
| Payment for purchase of equipment | (4,000) | |
| Proceeds from sale of land, at cost | 10,000 | |
| Net cash used for investing activities | | (22,000) |
| **Cash Flows From Financing Activities** | | |
| Proceeds from issuance of common stock | $ 18,000 | |
| Proceeds from issuance of bonds | 12,000 | |
| Payment of dividends | (9,000) | |
| Payment of note payable | (13,000) | |
| Net cash provided by financing activities | | 8,000 |
| Net Increase in Cash (see Schedule 1) | | $ 2,400 |
| Cash, January 1, 1995 | | 10,900 |
| Cash, December 31, 1995 | | $13,300 |
| | | |
| **Schedule 1: Investing and Financing Activities Not Affecting Cash** | | |
| Investing Activities | | |
| Acquisition of land by issuance of common stock | | $ (6,000) |
| Financing Activities | | |
| Issuance of common stock for land | | 6,000 |

The cash inflows and outflows from a company's financing activities are reported in the third section of the statement of cash flows. Each financing cash inflow and outflow is listed and the amounts are subtotaled to determine the net cash provided by (or used for) financing activities. During 1995, the Ryan Corporation had cash inflows of $18,000 and $12,000 from the issuance of common stock and bonds, respectively. It had a cash outflow of $9,000 for the payment of dividends, and a $13,000 cash outflow for the payment of a note. The net result was that $8,000 of cash was provided by its financing activities.

The net increase or decrease in cash is determined by adding the amounts of the net cash flow from operating activities, the net cash flow from investing activities, and the net cash flow from financing activities. The $16,400 net cash provided by operating activities combined with the $22,000 net cash used for investing activities and the $8,000 net cash provided by financing activities resulted in a $2,400 net increase in cash for the Ryan Corporation in 1995. This $2,400 net increase in cash reconciles the $10,900 beginning cash balance to the $13,300 ending cash balance.

The investing and financing activities not affecting cash are reported in a separate schedule accompanying the statement of cash flows. Each investing and/or financing activity is listed and the related amounts are offset against each other. During 1995, the Ryan Corporation engaged in a simultaneous investing and financing transaction, the acquisition of land costing $6,000 by the issuance of common stock. The investing portion of the transaction was the acquisition of the land, while the financing portion was the issuance of common stock. The investing activity is shown on Schedule 1 as a $6,000 "outflow" and is offset by the $6,000 "inflow" from the financing activity. Although no cash was exchanged, both items are listed to show all of the Ryan Corporation's investing and financing activities during 1995.

*Usefulness*

By reviewing the three sections of the statement of cash flows, external users can see how a company obtained and used its cash. From the accompanying schedule, they can determine the types of investing and financing activities of the company that did not affect cash. They can examine the items in each section to see if important changes have occurred. For instance, the investing activities involving the acquisition of the building and equipment by the Ryan Corporation in 1995 may indicate an increase in its operating capability. In addition, the financing activities involving the issuance of both bonds and common stock by the Ryan Corporation in 1995 reveal a change in its capital structure and may indicate a change in its financial flexibility and risk. A comparison with other companies can also reveal, for instance, whether the company is obtaining or using a greater proportion of its cash from financing or investing activities rather than operations. This may be important in assessing the relative risk of investing in the company. External users can evaluate the likelihood of future cash dividends as well as the need for additional cash to finance existing operations or the expansion of operations. They also can evaluate the ability of the company to pay current obligations, make periodic interest payments, and pay off long-term debt when the debt reaches its maturity date. Thus, the statement of cash flows provides external users with information about a company's liquidity, financial flexibility, operating capability, and risk. In so doing, the statement enhances the predictive value and feedback value and, therefore, the *decision usefulness,* of a company's financial statements to help fulfill the objectives of financial reporting.

## CASH INFLOWS AND OUTFLOWS

To classify a company's cash flows, the relationships between the changes in balance sheet accounts and the company's cash flows must be analyzed. Inflows of cash are caused by decreases in assets (other than cash) and by increases in liabilities and in stockholders' equity during an accounting period. Outflows of cash are caused by increases in assets (other than cash) and by decreases in liabilities and in stockholders' equity during the accounting period. The difference between the inflows and outflows is the change in cash during the accounting period. This relationship is further illustrated by the equations shown in Exhibit 20-2, starting with the basic accounting equation. Each equation is a modification of the previous equation to eventually show the increases and decreases in cash. With this background in mind, we can refine the relationships shown in the last two equations of Exhibit 20-2.

## EXHIBIT 20-2

### EQUATIONS FOR CHANGE IN CASH

$$\text{Assets} = \text{Liabilities} + \text{Stockholders' Equity}$$

$$\text{Changes in Assets} = \text{Changes in Liabilities} + \text{Changes in Stockholders' Equity}$$

$$\text{Changes in Cash} + \text{Changes in Assets Other Than Cash} = \text{Changes in Liabilities} + \text{Changes in Stockholders' Equity}$$

$$\text{Changes in Cash} = \text{Changes in Liabilities} + \text{Changes in Stockholders' Equity} - \text{Changes in Assets Other Than Cash}$$

*Where:*

$$\text{Increases in Cash} = \text{Increases in Liabilities} + \text{Increases in Stockholders' Equity} + \text{Decreases in Assets Other Than Cash}$$

*And:*

$$\text{Decreases in Cash} = \text{Decreases in Liabilities} + \text{Decreases in Stockholders' Equity} + \text{Increases in Assets Other Than Cash}$$

### Inflows of Cash

There are three categories of inflows (increases) of cash:

1. *Decreases in Assets Other Than Cash.* The sale or other disposal of assets (other than cash) causes an inflow (increase) of cash because cash is received in exchange for the assets.

2. *Increases in Liabilities.* The issuance or other incurrence of liabilities causes an inflow (increase) of cash because cash is received in exchange for the liabilities.[5]

3. *Increases in Stockholders' Equity.* Stockholders' equity increases mainly because of net income and additional investments by owners. Additional investments cause an inflow (increase) of cash because cash is received in exchange for the stock issued. Net income is slightly more complicated because the inflows and outflows of cash for operations are different than the revenues and expenses included in net income (this topic is discussed later).

### Outflows of Cash

There are also three categories of outflows (decreases) of cash:

1. *Increases in Assets Other Than Cash.* The acquisition of assets (other than cash) causes an outflow (decrease) of cash because cash is paid in exchange for the assets.[6]

2. *Decreases in Liabilities.* The payment of liabilities causes an outflow (decrease) of cash because cash is paid to satisfy the liabilities.

---

5. Alternatively, as discussed later, the increase in a liability such as accounts payable results, in effect, in a "savings" (i.e., increase) in cash because of a smaller cash outflow.
6. Alternatively, as discussed later, the increase in an asset such as accounts receivable results, in effect, in a decrease in cash because of a smaller cash inflow.

3. *Decreases in Stockholders' Equity.* Stockholders' equity may decrease as a result of several transactions. Two common transactions are the payment of dividends and the acquisition of treasury stock. In each case, a decrease in stockholders' equity is accompanied by an outflow (decrease) of cash.

## Classifications of Cash Flows

The categories of inflows and outflows of cash discussed in the previous section can now be further classified as relating to operating, investing, and financing activities.

1. *Operating Cash Flows*
   A. *Inflows:* Increases in stockholders' equity (i.e., retained earnings) due to certain revenues, adjusted for changes in certain current assets (related to operating cycle) and for changes in certain current liabilities (related to operating cycle).
   B. *Outflows:* Decreases in stockholders' equity (i.e., retained earnings) due to certain expenses, adjusted for changes in certain current assets (related to operating cycle) and for changes in certain current liabilities (related to operating cycle).

2. *Investing Cash Flows*
   A. *Inflows:* Decreases in noncurrent assets and certain current assets (e.g., notes receivable, temporary investments).
   B. *Outflows:* Increases in noncurrent assets and certain current assets (e.g., notes receivable, temporary investments).

3. *Financing Cash Flows*
   A. *Inflows:* Increases in noncurrent liabilities, stockholders' equity, and certain current liabilities (e.g., notes payable).
   B. *Outflows:* Decreases in noncurrent liabilities, stockholders' equity, and certain current liabilities (e.g., notes payable).

Changes in assets (other than cash), liabilities, and stockholders' equity may be the result of investing and financing activities *not* affecting cash. Examples of these transactions include acquisitions of assets by issuing equity securities (noncash investing and financing activities), acquisitions of assets by assuming liabilities such as capital lease obligations (noncash investing and financing activities), exchanges of debt securities for equity securities (noncash financing activities), exchanges of assets for assets (noncash investing activities), and exchanges of liabilities for liabilities (noncash financing activities). Although these transactions are relatively rare, they do involve "simultaneous" investing activities and/or financing activities not affecting cash and are reported in a schedule (or narrative explanation) that accompanies the statement of cash flows, as discussed earlier.

The operating cash flows involve several adjustments for items relating to the operating cycle. The net cash flow from operating activities is further explained in the next section.

## NET CASH FLOW FROM OPERATING ACTIVITIES

The calculation of the net cash flow from operating activities is usually the most complex part of the statement of cash flows. To prepare this section, it is useful to understand the relationship between sales revenues, expenses, and cash flows within a company's operating cycle.

*Operating cycles are discussed and illustrated in Chapter 3.*

Recall that a company's operating cycle is the average time taken to spend cash for inventory, process and sell the inventory, and collect the accounts receivable, converting them back into cash. To begin a company's operating cycle, the company initially purchases inventory for cash or on account. To make cash or credit sales, it incurs cost of goods sold and selling expenses, and reduces inventory, pays cash, incurs current liabilities, or reduces prepaid items. In its operations, the company incurs general and administrative expenses and either pays cash, incurs current liabilities, or reduces prepaid items. Finally, the company collects its accounts receivable and converts them back into cash. This step completes the operating cycle.

Each phase of the operating cycle has an impact on both net income and the net cash flow from operating activities. The impact is not the same for both items, however, because of differences in the recording of revenues and expenses and the timing of cash flows. For instance, when inventory is purchased for cash an outflow of cash occurs but no expense is recorded. A purchase of inventory on credit increases accounts payable (a current liability) but involves no immediate expense or cash outflow. Later, when the accounts payable is paid, no expense is recorded but a cash outflow occurs. The expense is recorded (as cost of goods sold) when the inventory is sold even though no cash outflow occurs at that time. When a cash sale is made, revenue is recorded and there is a cash inflow. However, cash inflows may occur and be recorded as a current liability in the accounting period before the revenue is recognized (e.g., deferred revenues). When a credit sale is made, both revenue and accounts receivable (a current asset) are increased but no inflow of cash occurs. Later, when the accounts receivable is collected, no revenue is recorded but a cash inflow occurs. Some accounts receivable are not collected so an expense (bad debts) is incurred even though no cash outflow occurs. In addition, throughout the accounting period, when selling expenses and general and administrative expenses are paid in cash, expenses are recorded and cash outflows occur. However, when these expenses are accrued at the end of the period, both the expenses and current payables are recorded but no cash outflows occur. The cash outflows are made in the next accounting period when the payables are paid. Furthermore cash outflows for some of these expenses may occur and be recorded as a current asset in the accounting period before the expenses are recorded (e.g., prepaid insurance).

Exhibit 20-3 illustrates the basic differences between revenues and cash inflows from operating activities, and between expenses and cash outflows for operating activities that are discussed in this section. For example, assume for simplicity that the Smith Company made cash sales of $30,000 and credit sales of $42,000 during its first year of operations and collected $37,000 of the related accounts receivable. At the end of the year, the Sales Revenue account has a credit balance of $72,000 and the Accounts Receivable account has a debit balance of $5,000. As shown in Exhibit 20-4, an analysis of the related T-accounts shows an increase of $67,000 in the cash inflows from operating activities. (This $67,000 is equal to the cash sales of $30,000 plus the collections on accounts receivable of $37,000.)

Similarly, assume that Smith Company paid salaries of $13,000 and recorded salaries payable of $1,000 during its first year of operations. At the end of the year, the Salaries Expense account has a debit balance of $14,000 and the Salaries Payable account has a credit balance of $1,000. As shown in Exhibit 20-4, an analysis of the related T-account shows an increase of $13,000 in the cash outflows for operating activities. There are additional changes in other current asset and current liability accounts that may affect the net cash flow from operating activities, and each of these changes is analyzed to determine the impact on operating cash inflows and outflows.

## EXHIBIT 20-3

### DIFFERENCES BETWEEN REVENUES, EXPENSES, AND CASH FLOWS FROM OPERATING ACTIVITIES

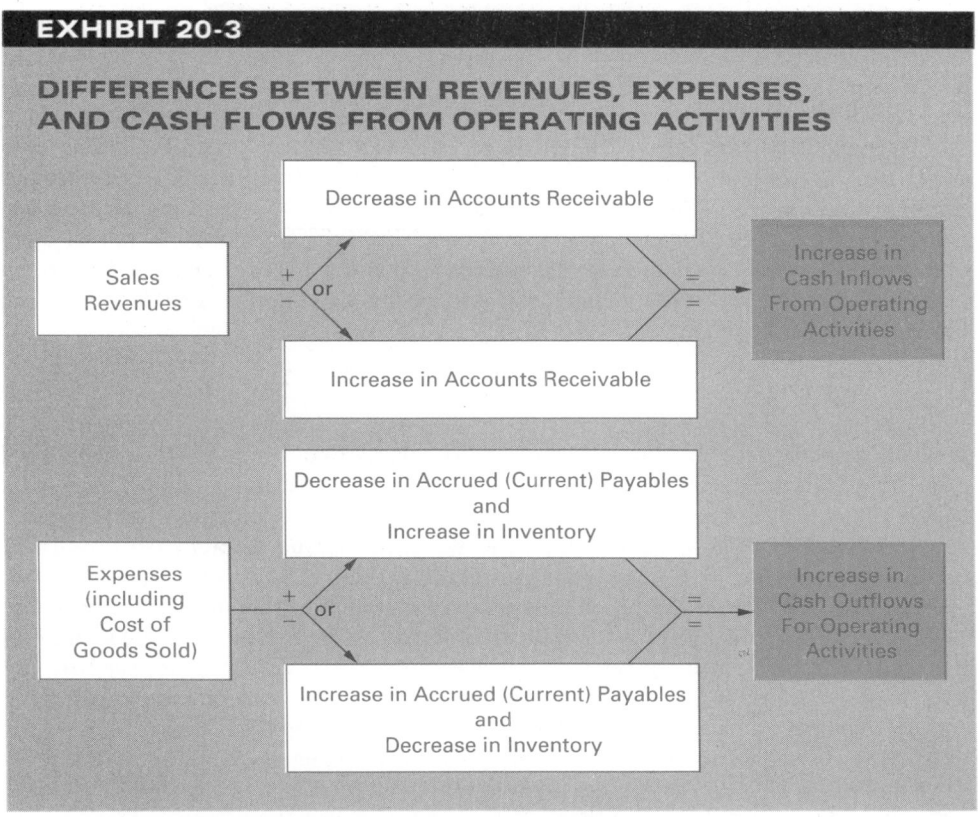

## EXHIBIT 20-4

### CALCULATION OF CASH FLOWS FROM OPERATING ACTIVITIES

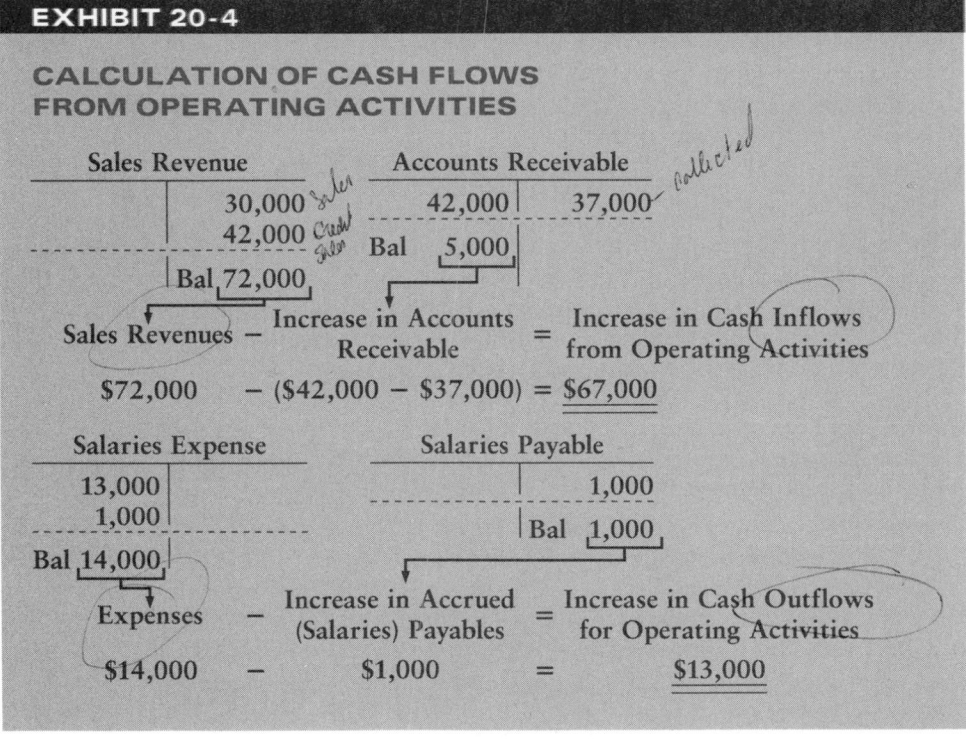

There are also changes in certain noncurrent asset accounts that affect net income but do not result in a cash inflow or outflow for operating activities. For instance, when depreciation is recorded, the journal entry involves a debit to Depreciation Expense (a reduction of net income) and a credit to Accumulated Depreciation (a reduction of noncurrent assets). Although depreciation expense reduces net income (and noncurrent assets), there is no cash outflow for operating activities. The recording of amortization expense and depletion expense for intangible assets (such as a patent) and natural resource assets (such as a coal mine) have the same effect. That is, there is a reduction in net income (and noncurrent assets) but no operating cash outflow. Each of the changes in these noncurrent asset accounts is analyzed to determine the effect on the net cash flow from operating activities.

## Direct Method

*FASB Statement No. 95* allows two ways to calculate and report a company's net cash flow from operating activities on its statement of cash flows. The first way is called the *direct* method. **Under the direct method, the operating cash outflows are deducted from the operating cash inflows to determine the net cash flow from operating activities.** Under this method, the cash inflows from operating activities are computed first, based on an analysis like that shown in the upper portion of Exhibit 20-4. The cash outflows for operating activities are computed next, similar to the analysis shown in the lower portion of Exhibit 20-4. To illustrate, suppose the Ryan Corporation presents the following income statement information for the year ended December 31, 1995:

| | | |
|---|---:|---:|
| Sales revenue (cash and accounts receivable) | | $70,000 |
| Less: | | |
| Cost of goods sold (cash and accounts payable) | $29,000 | |
| Salaries expense (cash and salaries payable) | 13,000 | |
| Depreciation expense | 8,000 | (50,000) |
| Income before income taxes | | $20,000 |
| Income tax expense (cash) | | (6,000) |
| Net income | | $14,000 |

A further analysis reveals the following changes in current asset and current liability accounts for 1995: accounts receivable decreased by $2,600, inventory increased by $2,000, accounts payable decreased by $7,000, and salaries payable increased by $800. Under the direct method, the cash flows from operating activities section of the statement of cash flows is reported as follows:

| | | |
|---|---:|---:|
| Cash Flows From Operating Activities | | |
| Cash Inflows: | | |
| Cash received from customers | $72,600 | |
| Cash inflows from operating activities | | $72,600 |
| Cash Outflows: | | |
| Cash paid to suppliers | $38,000 | |
| Cash paid to employees | 12,200 | |
| Cash paid for income taxes | 6,000 | |
| Cash outflows for operating activities | | (56,200) |
| Net cash provided by operating activities | | $16,400 |

The $72,600 cash received from customers is computed by adding the decrease in accounts receivable ($2,600) to the sales revenue ($70,000). This is the only cash receipt, so that cash inflows from operating activities are $72,600. The $38,000 cash paid to suppliers is computed by adding the increase in inventory ($2,000) and the decrease in accounts payable ($7,000) to the cost of goods sold ($29,000). The $12,200 cash paid to employees is computed by deducting the increase in salaries payable ($800) from the salaries expense ($13,000). The entire amount of income tax expense ($6,000) was paid in cash. These cash outflows for operating activities total $56,200, so that the net cash provided by operating activities is $16,400. It should be noted that the depreciation expense is *not* included in the net cash flows from operating activities because it did not result in an outflow of cash.

The direct method has the advantage of reporting operating cash inflows separately from operating cash outflows, which may be useful in estimating future cash flows. However, the direct method is criticized because it does not "tie" the net income reported on a company's income statement to the net cash provided by operating activities reported on the company's statement of cash flows. Furthermore, the direct method does not show how the changes in the elements (i.e., current assets and current liabilities) of a company's operating cycle affected its operating cash flows.

### Indirect Method

Use of the *indirect* method to report a company's net cash flow from operating activities on its statement of cash flows resolves the two criticisms of the direct method. Under the indirect method, net income is adjusted to the net cash flow from operating activities on the statement of cash flows. To do so, net income is listed first and then adjustments (additions or subtractions) are made to net income (1) to eliminate certain amounts (such as depreciation expense) that are included in net income but did not involve a cash inflow or cash outflow for operating activities and (2) to include any changes in the current assets (other than cash) and current liabilities involved in the company's operating cycle that affected cash flows differently than net income. In other words, under the indirect method, income flows are converted from an *accrual* basis to a *cash flow* basis. In this manner, the indirect method shows the "quality" of income by providing information about intervals of leads and lags between income flows and operating cash flows.

To illustrate, refer back to the Ryan Corporation's income statement and additional information presented earlier. Under the indirect method, the net cash flow from the operating activities section of the statement of cash flows is reported as follows:

Net Cash Flow From Operating Activities

| | | |
|---|---|---|
| Net income | $14,000 | |
| Adjustments for differences between income flows and cash flows for operating activities: | | |
| Add: Depreciation expense | 8,000 | |
| Decrease in accounts receivable | 2,600 | |
| Increase in salaries payable | 800 | |
| Less: Increase in inventory | (2,000) | |
| Decrease in accounts payable | (7,000) | |
| Net cash provided by operating activities | | $16,400 |

It is important to understand the nature of each adjustment to convert net income to the net cash provided by operating activities. First, the $8,000 depreciation expense is *added* to the $14,000 net income because it had been deducted to determine net income but did not involve an outflow of cash. The $2,600 decrease in the current asset, accounts receivable, is added to net income because it resulted in an additional inflow of cash from operations. The $800 increase in the current liability, salaries payable, resulted in an increase in expenses and a decrease in net income. It is added to net income because there was a reduced cash outflow for operations. The $2,000 increase in the current asset, inventory, and the $7,000 decrease in the current liability, accounts payable, are both deducted from net income because they resulted in additional operating cash outflows. Note that by using either the direct method or the indirect method, net cash provided by operating activities is the same amount ($16,400). The indirect method is the method used by the Ryan Corporation in Exhibit 20-1 at the beginning of the chapter.

Prior to *FASB Statement No. 95*, nearly all companies reported the results of their operating activities using the indirect method on their statements of changes in financial position. *FASB Statement No. 95* allows the use of either the direct method or the indirect method. However, if a company uses the direct method on its statement of cash flows, it must also include a separate schedule that reconciles its net income to its net cash flow provided by (or used in) operating activities (i.e., the indirect method). Because of the previous use of the indirect method and the extra schedule required under the direct method, most companies have continued to use the indirect method. In a recent survey, 585 of 600 companies used the indirect method.[7] It is likely, however, that as more companies become familiar with the direct method, its use will increase. Therefore, we focus on the indirect method in the main part of the chapter, but fully discuss the direct method in the Appendix at the end of the chapter. (**You should use the *indirect method* for *all homework,* unless otherwise indicated.**)

In the previous example, under the indirect method only a few simple adjustments were made to convert net income to the net cash flow from operating activities. Furthermore, the adjustments for changes in current assets and current liabilities involved only increases in these items. In reality, there may be many adjustments involving both increases and decreases in current assets and current liabilities, as well as other noncurrent accounts. Exhibit 20-5 lists the major adjustments needed to convert net income to the net cash flow from operating activities. These adjustments are explained in the examples that follow.

## PROCEDURES FOR PREPARATION OF STATEMENT

When preparing the statement of cash flows, information for the accounting period from the following financial statements is required: (1) beginning and ending balance sheets, (2) income statement, and (3) retained earnings statement. In addition, other information is needed that explains the changes in the balance sheet accounts (other than cash). This additional information is obtained from the company's accounting records.

### Visual Inspection Method of Analysis

There are two methods of analysis that may be used to prepare the statement of cash flows, the **visual inspection method** and the worksheet method.[8] Under the visual in-

---

7. *Accounting Trends and Techniques* (New York: AICPA, 1992), p. 392.
8. A third method involving T-accounts is sometimes used to analyze and develop the information for the statement of cash flows. The T-account method, however, results in cumbersome working papers when the analysis becomes complex. Because the worksheet method uses the same general technique as the T-account method, but in a more efficient worksheet format, only the worksheet method is discussed in this chapter.

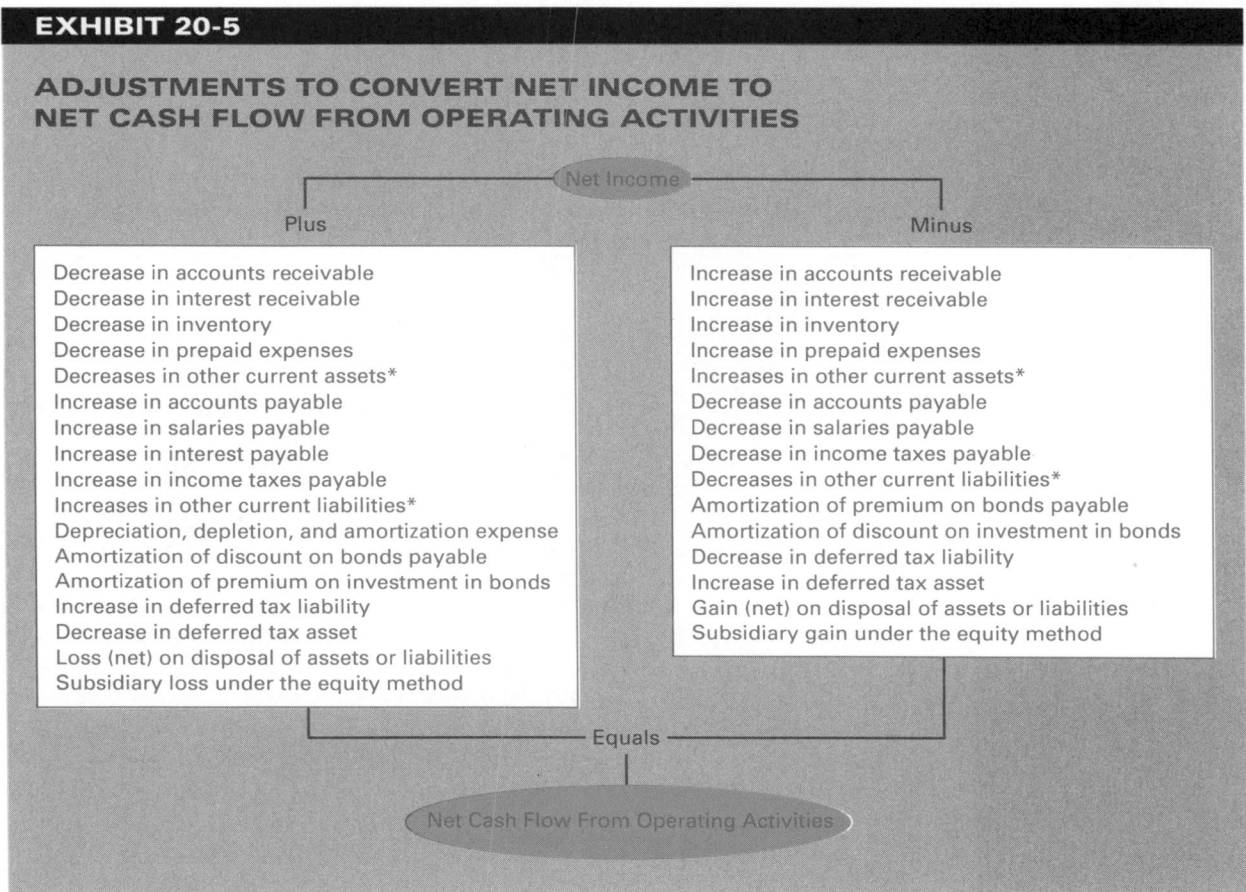

**EXHIBIT 20-5**

**ADJUSTMENTS TO CONVERT NET INCOME TO NET CASH FLOW FROM OPERATING ACTIVITIES**

Net Income

**Plus**

Decrease in accounts receivable
Decrease in interest receivable
Decrease in inventory
Decrease in prepaid expenses
Decreases in other current assets*
Increase in accounts payable
Increase in salaries payable
Increase in interest payable
Increase in income taxes payable
Increases in other current liabilities*
Depreciation, depletion, and amortization expense
Amortization of discount on bonds payable
Amortization of premium on investment in bonds
Increase in deferred tax liability
Decrease in deferred tax asset
Loss (net) on disposal of assets or liabilities
Subsidiary loss under the equity method

**Minus**

Increase in accounts receivable
Increase in interest receivable
Increase in inventory
Increase in prepaid expenses
Increases in other current assets*
Decrease in accounts payable
Decrease in salaries payable
Decrease in income taxes payable
Decreases in other current liabilities*
Amortization of premium on bonds payable
Amortization of discount on investment in bonds
Decrease in deferred tax liability
Increase in deferred tax asset
Gain (net) on disposal of assets or liabilities
Subsidiary gain under the equity method

Equals

Net Cash Flow From Operating Activities

* Related to operating activities.

spection method, the financial statements are visually reviewed and the statement of cash flows is prepared without the use of a worksheet. This method may be used when the financial statements are not complex and when the relationships between changes in account balances can be easily observed and analyzed. There are seven steps in the visual inspection method, as shown in Exhibit 20-6.

Steps 5 and 6 do not have to be completed in sequential order; what is important is a complete analysis of the relevant information.[9] The visual inspection method is rarely used in practice because of the lack of supporting documentation for the statement of cash flows.

### Simple Example (Visual Inspection Method)

Knowledge of the visual inspection method is helpful in understanding the more complex worksheet method. To illustrate the visual inspection method, review the condensed financial information of the Leyton Company for 1995, shown in Exhibit 20-7. The statement of cash flows prepared from that information is shown in Exhibit 20-8.

---

9. If the company engaged in any investing and financing transactions not affecting cash, the heading for a schedule of Investing and Financing Activities Not Affecting Cash is also prepared in Step 1 of Exhibit 20-6.

---

**EXHIBIT 20-6**

### STEPS IN VISUAL INSPECTION METHOD

1. Prepare the heading for the statement of cash flows and list the three major sections: (a) Net Cash Flow from Operating Activities, (b) Cash Flows From Investing Activities, and (c) Cash Flows From Financing Activities.
2. Calculate the net change in cash that occurred during the accounting period. This amount is a major subtotal, or "target figure," on the statement of cash flows.
3. Determine the company's net income and list this amount as the first item in the net cash flow from operating activities section.
4. Calculate the increase or decrease that occurred during the accounting period in each balance sheet account (except cash).
5. Determine whether the increase or decrease in each balance sheet account (except cash) caused an inflow or outflow of cash and, if so, whether the cash flow was related to an operating, investing, or financing activity.
6. If no cash flow occurred in Step 5, determine whether the increase or decrease in each balance sheet account (except cash) was the result of a non-cash income statement item or a simultaneous investing and/or financing transaction. If the former, then determine the adjustment (addition or subtraction) to help convert net income to the net cash flow from operating activities. If the latter, then identify the components of the simultaneous investing and/or financing activity.
7. Complete the various sections of the statement of cash flows (based on the analysis in Steps 5 and 6), being certain to check that the subtotals of the sections sum to the net change (increase or decrease) in cash (from Step 2), and that the sum of the net change in cash and the beginning cash balance is equal to the ending cash balance reported on the balance sheet.

---

After preparing the heading and listing the three sections of the statement, the $2,600 net increase in cash was determined. This increase was computed by comparing the $4,000 cash balance on the beginning balance sheet to the $6,600 cash balance on the ending balance sheet. Then, the $7,000 net income was obtained from the income statement and listed as the first item in the net cash flow from operating activities section. The following discussion explains the remaining steps in the visual inspection method by reviewing the items in each section of the statement.

*Net Cash Flow From Operating Activities*
In this section, there are three adjustments to convert net income to the net cash flow from operating activities. The first adjustment involves the $2,300 depreciation expense. This amount was obtained from the income statement in Exhibit 20-7. It is also the $2,300 increase (from $12,500 to $14,800) in the accumulated depreciation account on the balance sheets during the year. Because depreciation was deducted in the computation of net income but did not cause a cash outflow, the $2,300 depreciation expense is added to net income. The second adjustment involves the $1,500 increase (from $7,500 to $9,000 in Exhibit 20-7) in accounts payable. Accounts payable increased because other operating expenses recorded during the year exceeded the cash payments for these items. Therefore, the expenses deducted to compute net

## EXHIBIT 20-7

### LEYTON COMPANY

Condensed Financial Information

#### Income Statement Information for 1995

| | | |
|---|---|---|
| Sales revenue | | $31,800 |
| Operating expenses | | |
| Depreciation expense | $ 2,300 | |
| Interest expense | 1,400 | |
| Other expenses | 18,100 | (21,800) |
| Income before income taxes | | $10,000 |
| Income tax expense | | (3,000) |
| Net Income | | $ 7,000 |

#### Retained Earnings Information for 1995

| | |
|---|---|
| Beginning retained earnings | $11,300 |
| Add: Net income | 7,000 |
| | $18,300 |
| Less: Dividends | (3,500) |
| Ending retained earnings | $14,800 |

#### Balance Sheet Information

| | Balances | |
|---|---|---|
| Accounts | 01/01/95 | 12/31/95 |
| Cash | $ 4,000 | $ 6,600 |
| Accounts receivable | 6,300 | 9,000 |
| Land | 9,000 | 6,000 |
| Buildings and equipment | 48,000 | 60,000 |
| Accumulated depreciation | (12,500) | (14,800) |
| Total Assets | $54,800 | $66,800 |
| | | |
| Accounts payable | $ 7,500 | $ 9,000 |
| Bonds payable, 10% | 14,000 | 21,000 |
| Common stock, $10 par | 22,000 | 22,000 |
| Retained earnings | 11,300 | 14,800 |
| Total Liabilities and Stockholders' Equity | $54,800 | $66,800 |

#### Supplemental Information for 1995

(a) A building was purchased for cash during the year.
(b) Land was sold (at cost) for cash during the year.
(c) No buildings or equipment were sold during the year.
(d) Bonds payable were issued at the end of the year.

income were greater than the related cash outflows. Consequently, the $1,500 increase in accounts payable is added to net income. The third adjustment involves the $2,700 increase (from $6,300 to $9,000) in accounts receivable. Accounts receivable increased during the year because sales on account exceeded the cash collections on account. Therefore, sales revenue and net income were greater than the related cash inflows. Consequently, the $2,700 increase in accounts receivable is deducted from net income.

As a result of the preceding adjustments, the net cash flow from operating activities was $8,100 for the Leyton Company in 1995, as shown in Exhibit 20-8. Note that, with the exception of depreciation, the adjustments to net income involve changes in current assets (except cash) and current liabilities.

### Cash Flows From Investing Activities

There are only two cash flows from investing activities, one cash outflow and one cash inflow. During 1995, the buildings and equipment account increased by $12,000, from $48,000 to $60,000, as shown on the balance sheets in Exhibit 20-7. This increase was the result of the purchase of a building, an investing activity, which required a cash outflow of $12,000. This cash outflow is listed as the first item in this section. During 1995, the land account decreased by $3,000, from $9,000 to $6,000. This was the result of the sale of land, an investing activity.

## EXHIBIT 20-8

**LEYTON COMPANY**

Statement of Cash Flows
For Year Ended December 31, 1995

| | | |
|---|---:|---:|
| **Net Cash Flow From Operating Activities** | | |
| Net income | $ 7,000 | |
| Adjustments for differences between income flows and cash flows from operating activities: | | |
| Add: Depreciation expense | 2,300 | |
| Increase in accounts payable | 1,500 | |
| Less: Increase in accounts receivable | (2,700) | |
| Net cash provided by operating activities | | $8,100 |
| **Cash Flows From Investing Activities** | | |
| Payment for purchase of building | $(12,000) | |
| Proceeds from sale of land, at cost | 3,000 | |
| Net cash used for investing activities | | (9,000) |
| **Cash Flows From Financing Activities** | | |
| Proceeds from issuance of bonds | $ 7,000 | |
| Payment of dividends | (3,500) | |
| Net cash provided by financing activities | | 3,500 |
| Net Increase in Cash | | $2,600 |
| Cash, January 1, 1995 | | 4,000 |
| Cash, December 31, 1995 | | $6,600 |

Because the land was sold at cost, there was no gain or loss.[10] The $3,000 cash inflow is listed as the second item in this section. As a result of these two cash flows, net cash of $9,000 was used for investing activities by the Leyton Company in 1995, as shown in Exhibit 20-8.

### Cash Flows From Financing Activities

There are also two cash flows from financing activities, one cash inflow and one cash outflow. During 1995, the bonds payable account increased by $7,000, from $14,000 to $21,000, as shown in Exhibit 20-7. This increase was the result of the issuance of bonds, a financing activity, which provided a cash inflow of $7,000. This cash inflow is listed as the first item in this section. There was no change in the common stock account during the year, so there was no cash inflow or outflow related to common stock. During 1995, the company declared and paid dividends of $3,500. The amount of the dividends was obtained from the retained earnings statement in Exhibit 20-7. [Note also that the $7,000 net income, offset by the $3,500 dividends, accounts for the $3,500 increase (from $11,300 to $14,800) in the retained

10. The reporting of the sale of noncurrent assets at a gain or loss is discussed in a later example.

earnings account shown on the balance sheets.] The payment of dividends, a financing activity, caused a cash outflow of $3,500. This cash outflow is listed as the second item in this section. As a result of these two cash flows, net cash of $3,500 was provided by the financing activities of the Leyton Company during 1995.

*Summary*

Note that in the preparation of the three sections, we accounted for all the changes in the assets (except cash), liabilities, and stockholders' equity accounts during 1995, as shown in Exhibit 20-7. Note also that, with the exception of depreciation, the adjustments to net income in the net cash flow from operating activities section involve changes in current asset (except cash) and current liability accounts. On the other hand, all of the cash inflows and outflows listed in the cash flows from investing activities section and the cash flows from financing activities section involve changes in noncurrent asset, noncurrent liability, and stockholders' equity accounts. The statement of cash flows shown in Exhibit 20-8 is now complete. The $8,100 net cash provided by operating activities, less the $9,000 net cash used for investing activities, plus the $3,500 net cash provided by financing activities equals the $2,600 net increase in cash. And, the $2,600 net increase in cash added to the $4,000 beginning cash balance is equal to the $6,600 ending cash balance (as reported on the company's December 31, 1995 balance sheet). With this background in mind, we now turn to the worksheet method of analysis.

## Worksheet Method of Analysis

The **worksheet method** is commonly used in practice. Under this method, the cash flow effects of operating, investing, and financing activities during the accounting period are entered on the worksheet to: (1) record the cash inflows and outflows according to the three sections of the statement of cash flows, (2) record the investing and financing activities not affecting cash, and (3) account for the change in each asset, liability, and stockholders' equity account. This method is most often used in practice because the analysis of a complex set of financial statements may be documented in a concise working paper. Because the worksheet method is used in more complex situations, it is helpful to follow a series of steps.

## Steps in Preparation (Worksheet Method)

After gathering information from the financial statements and supplemental information from the accounting records, several steps are completed to prepare the worksheet and the statement of cash flows. These steps are listed in Exhibit 20-9, followed by two examples that explain each step.

There are three issues related to the steps listed in Exhibit 20-9. First, other than usually starting with net income, there is no particular order in which the worksheet entries are reconstructed. You should develop a method so that you can account for all the changes in the noncash accounts in an orderly way. Second, you may have to make more than one worksheet entry to reconcile the change in an account. For instance, the change in the Land account may be the result of both a sale and purchase of land. In such cases, both the cash inflow and cash outflow are accounted for separately. Finally, remember that these worksheet entries are *not* posted to any accounts. They are recorded on the worksheet only to help in preparing the statement of cash flows.

## EXHIBIT 20-9

### STEPS IN WORKSHEET METHOD

**Step 1.** Prepare the column headings on a worksheet (see Exhibit 20-11). Then enter the account title Cash on the first line of the account titles column and list the beginning balance, ending balance, and change in cash in the respective columns.

**Step 2.** Enter the titles of all the remaining accounts from the balance sheets on the worksheet and list each beginning and ending account balance, and the change in the account balance directly below the cash information. (To simplify the worksheet, only the change in each account balance could be entered.) The accounts with debit balances are listed first, followed by the accounts with credit balances. Total the amount columns to verify that the debit totals equal the credit totals.

**Step 3.** Directly below these accounts, add the following headings:

A. Net Cash Flow From Operating Activities

B. Cash Flows From Investing Activities

C. Cash Flows From Financing Activities

D. Investing and Financing Activities Not Affecting Cash

Leave sufficient room below each heading so that each type of cash flow may be listed.

**Step 4.** Account for all the changes in the noncash accounts that occurred during the current period. *Reconstruct* the journal entries that caused the changes in the noncash accounts directly on the worksheet, making certain modifications to show the cash inflows and outflows for operating, investing, and financing activities. Remember that you are preparing this worksheet at the *end* of the accounting period. The actual journal entries that caused the changes have already been made and posted to the accounts. In this step, you are reconstructing the journal entries on the worksheet to prepare the statement of cash flows. Use the following general rules:

A. *Start with net income.* The net income is a summary of all the journal entries from operating activities affecting current assets or current liabilities and retained earnings. The net income is adjusted on the worksheet to change it to the net cash flow from operating activities. Therefore, the entry on the worksheet to list net income and to explain the impact on retained earnings is a debit to the caption Net Income under the heading Net Cash Flow From Operating Activities and a credit to Retained Earnings.[a]

B. *Account for the changes in the current asset (except cash) and current liability accounts.* Because nearly all of the changes in the current assets and current liabilities are part of the company's *operating cycle*, the impacts of these changes on cash are listed as *adjustments* (*additions* or *deductions*) to *net income* in the Net Cash Flow From Operating Activities section of the worksheet.[b] Review each current asset (except cash) and current liability account. Make an entry on the worksheet to record the change (debit or credit) in that account and the adjustment [credit (deduction) or debit (addition)] to net income.

## EXHIBIT 20-9, Continued

C. *Account for the changes in the noncurrent accounts.* Review each noncurrent account and determine the journal entry responsible for its change. Identify whether the transaction involves an operating, investing, or financing activity. If the transaction involved an investing or financing activity, make the entry on the worksheet with the following changes:

1. If the entry affects cash, replace a debit to cash with either an investing or financing cash inflow caption, and list the item as a debit (inflow) under the proper heading. Replace a credit to cash with a proper cash outflow caption, and list the item as a credit (outflow) under the proper heading.

2. If the entry involves an operating activity and affects a noncash income statement item (e.g., depreciation, gain, or loss), replace the debit or credit to this noncash item with an adjustment to net income under the Net Cash Flow From Operating Activities heading.

3. If the entry does not affect an operating activity or cash, it is a simultaneous financing and/or investing transaction. For this type of transaction, create expanded entries to record both the financing and/or investing activities.

**Step 5.** Make a final worksheet entry to record the net change in cash. The worksheet entries must account for all the changes in the noncash accounts recorded in Step 2. The difference between the total cash inflows and outflows must be equal to the change in the Cash account. The final worksheet entry to record a net increase in cash is a debit to Cash and a credit to Net Increase in Cash.[c] Total the debit and credit worksheet entries in the upper and lower portions to verify that the respective totals are equal.

**Step 6.** Prepare the statement of cash flows and accompanying schedule. Use the information developed in the lower portion of the worksheet (and the beginning and ending cash balances). Under the major sections of the statement, list the various cash inflows and outflows. Subtotal the items under each major section and add or subtract the subtotals to determine the net change in cash. Add the net change in cash to the beginning cash balance to determine the ending cash balance. In an accompanying schedule, list the various investing and financing activities not affecting cash.

a. The entry to show a net loss involves a debit to Retained Earnings and a credit to Net Loss. Any adjustments for noncash items included in net income such as in Step 4C(2) are made as usual.
b. The major exceptions to this adjustment are changes in short-term notes receivable and notes payable, changes in temporary investments (i.e., marketable securities), and changes in dividends payable. These changes are the results of investing or financing activities and are handled like the changes in the noncurrent accounts discussed in Step 4(C), except that changes in temporary investments may require additional analysis as discussed in a later section.
c. For a net decrease in cash, an opposite entry (a debit to Net Decrease in Cash and a credit to Cash) is made.

## Basic Example (Worksheet Method)

It is easier to understand the process of preparing a worksheet and statement of cash flows by studying a basic example, as shown next. The example includes a detailed discussion of each step presented in Exhibit 20-9. As you study this example, it will be helpful to reread these steps. The condensed financial information of the Prawn Company for 1995 shown in Exhibit 20-10 is used in the example.

*Steps 1, 2, and 3: Setting Up the Worksheet*
Steps 1 and 2 involve setting up the worksheet, entering the account titles, their beginning and ending balances, and changes in the appropriate columns of the worksheet, and totaling the columns to check your work. In Step 3, the major headings, Net Cash Flow From Operating Activities, Cash Flows From Investing Activities, Cash Flows From Financing Activities, and Investing and Financing Activities Not Affecting Cash, are then listed on the worksheet. Enough space is left under each heading so that the cash flows may be listed accordingly. These accounts and headings are shown in Exhibit 20-11 for the Prawn Company.

### EXHIBIT 20-10

## PRAWN COMPANY

Condensed Financial Information

*Income Statement Information for 1995*

| | | |
|---|---|---|
| Sales revenue | | $80,000 |
| Cost of goods sold | | (48,600) |
| Gross profit | | $31,400 |
| Operating expenses | | |
| Depreciation expense | $ 3,400 | |
| Other expenses | 15,900 | (19,300) |
| Operating income | | $12,100 |
| Other items: | | |
| Gain on sale of equipment | $ 600 | |
| Interest expenses | (700) | (100) |
| Income before income taxes | | $12,000 |
| Income tax expense | | (3,600) |
| Net Income | | $ 8,400 |

*Retained Earnings Information for 1995*

| | |
|---|---|
| Beginning retained earnings | $13,300 |
| Add: Net income | 8,400 |
| | $21,700 |
| Less: Dividends | (1,800) |
| Ending retained earnings | $19,900 |

*Balance Sheet Information*

| | Balances | |
|---|---|---|
| Accounts | 01/01/95 | 12/31/95 |
| Cash | $ 3,500 | $ 5,500 |
| Accounts receivable | 4,400 | 3,600 |
| Inventory | 5,000 | 6,600 |
| Land | 8,200 | 12,200 |
| Buildings and equipment | 35,700 | 48,700 |
| Accumulated depreciation | (6,000) | (8,700) |
| Total Assets | $50,800 | $67,900 |
| | | |
| Accounts payable | $ 5,100 | $ 3,200 |
| Salaries payable | 1,400 | 1,800 |
| Bonds payable, 10% | 7,000 | 15,000 |
| Common stock, $10 par | 8,000 | 9,000 |
| Additional paid-in capital | 16,000 | 19,000 |
| Retained earnings | 13,300 | 19,900 |
| Total Liabilities and Stockholders' Equity | $50,800 | $67,900 |

*Supplemental Information for 1995*

(a) Equipment was purchased for cash at a cost of $15,200.
(b) Ten-year bonds payable with a face value of $8,000 were issued for $8,000 at the end of the year.
(c) Land was acquired through the issuance of 100 shares of $10 par common stock when the stock was selling at a market price of $40 per share.
(d) Equipment with a cost of $2,200 and a book value of $1,500 was sold for $2,100 cash.

## EXHIBIT 20-11

### PRAWN COMPANY

Worksheet for Statement of Cash Flows
For Year Ended December 31, 1995

| Account Titles | Balances 01/01/95 | Balances 12/31/95 | Change | Worksheet Entries Debit | | Worksheet Entries Credit | |
|---|---|---|---|---|---|---|---|
| *Debits* | | | | | | | |
| Cash | 3,500 | 5,500 | 2,000 | (l) | 2,000 | | |
| *Noncash Accounts:* | | | | | | | |
| Accounts receivable | 4,400 | 3,600 | (800) | | | (c) | 800 |
| Inventory | 5,000 | 6,600 | 1,600 | (d) | 1,600 | | |
| Land | 8,200 | 12,200 | 4,000 | (i-2) | 4,000 | | |
| Buildings and equipment | 35,700 | 48,700 | 13,000 | (g) | 15,200 | (k) | 2,200 |
| Totals | 56,800 | 76,600 | 19,800 | | | | |
| *Credits* | | | | | | | |
| Accumulated depreciation | 6,000 | 8,700 | 2,700 | (k) | 700 | (b) | 3,400 |
| Accounts payable | 5,100 | 3,200 | (1,900) | (e) | 1,900 | | |
| Salaries payable | 1,400 | 1,800 | 400 | | | (f) | 400 |
| Bonds payable | 7,000 | 15,000 | 8,000 | | | (h) | 8,000 |
| Common stock, $10 par | 8,000 | 9,000 | 1,000 | | | (i-1) | 1,000 |
| Additional paid-in capital | 16,000 | 19,000 | 3,000 | | | (i-1) | 3,000 |
| Retained earnings | 13,300 | 19,900 | 6,600 | (j) | 1,800 | (a) | 8,400 |
| Totals | 56,800 | 76,600 | 19,800 | | 27,200 | | 27,200 |
| Net Cash Flow From Operating Activities | | | | | | | |
| Net Income | | | | (a) | 8,400 | | |
| Add: Depreciation expense | | | | (b) | 3,400 | | |
| Decrease in accounts receivable | | | | (c) | 800 | | |
| Increase in salaries payable | | | | (f) | 400 | | |
| Less: Increase in inventory | | | | | | (d) | 1,600 |
| Decrease in accounts payable | | | | | | (e) | 1,900 |
| Gain on sale of equipment | | | | | | (k) | 600 |
| Cash Flows From Investing Activities | | | | | | | |
| Payment for purchase of equipment | | | | | | (g) | 15,200 |
| Proceeds from sale of equipment | | | | (k) | 2,100 | | |
| Cash Flows From Financing Activities | | | | | | | |
| Proceeds from issuance of bonds | | | | (h) | 8,000 | | |
| Payment of dividends | | | | | | (j) | 1,800 |
| Investing and Financing Activities Not Affecting Cash | | | | | | | |
| Issuance of common stock for land | | | | (i-1) | 4,000 | | |
| Acquisition of land by issuance of common stock | | | | | | (i-2) | 4,000 |
| Net Increase in Cash | | | | | | (l) | 2,000 |
| Totals | | | | | 27,100 | | 27,100 |

*Step 4: Completion of the Worksheet*

The worksheet entries to account for all the changes in the noncash accounts are entered directly on the worksheet in Step 4, as shown in Exhibit 20-11. To explain them better, however, each of the entries is also presented in journal entry *form* here. The following entries are listed (a) through (l) to correspond to the entries on the worksheet. You should review the financial information in Exhibit 20-10, analyze each entry and explanation in the text, and then trace the entry back to the corresponding entry on the worksheet in Exhibit 20-11.

The usual procedure is to start with the net income figure because it is a summary amount including the results of both cash and noncash operating activities. Net income caused an increase in retained earnings. To list net income and to record the impact on retained earnings, the following entry[11] is made on the worksheet:

**(a) Net Cash Flow From Operating Activities:**

| | | |
|---|---|---|
| Net Income | 8,400 | |
| Retained Earnings | | 8,400 |

To adjust net income to the net cash flow from operating activities requires adjustments for depreciation and for the changes in the current assets (except cash) and current liabilities. Depreciation is usually treated first. During the year, Depreciation Expense was increased (debited) for $3,400, and this amount was shown as a deduction on the income statement to determine net income. The noncurrent account, Accumulated Depreciation, was also increased (credited) for $3,400. Although the depreciation expense reduced net income, there was no outflow of cash for operating activities. Therefore, this depreciation deduction is *added* back to net income to help adjust it to show the net cash flow from operating activities. To do this, as well as to show the increase in the Accumulated Depreciation account, the following worksheet entry is made:

**(b) Net Cash Flow From Operating Activities:**

| | | |
|---|---|---|
| Depreciation Expense | 3,400 | |
| Accumulated Depreciation | | 3,400 |

It is important to understand that depreciation is *not* a cash inflow from operating activities! It is added back to net income because at the time depreciation was originally deducted in computing the amount of net income, there was no corresponding outflow of cash. It is also important to note that entry (b) does not account for the change ($2,600 increase) in Accumulated Depreciation, because another transaction (k) also affected the Accumulated Depreciation account, as discussed later.

The next adjustments all deal with the changes in the current assets (except cash) and current liabilities. The Accounts Receivable decreased $800 during the year because cash collections exceeded credit sales by this amount (see Exhibit 20-4). To adjust for the additional cash inflow from operating activities, the following worksheet entry is made:

**(c) Net Cash Flow From Operating Activities:**

| | | |
|---|---|---|
| Decrease in Accounts Receivable | 800 | |
| Accounts Receivable | | 800 |

---

11. For illustrative purposes, in our entries we always first list the heading of the worksheet and then indicate the caption to write under the heading. Thus, in this case the caption, Net Income, is written under the heading, Net Cash Flow From Operating Activities, on the worksheet.

Inventory increased by $1,600 during the year, indicating that purchases exceeded the cost of goods sold. To show the additional operating cash outflow due to the purchase of inventory, the net cash flow from operating activities is decreased. The following worksheet entry is made:

| | | |
|---|---|---|
| **(d) Inventory** | **1,600** | |
| **Net Cash Flow From Operating Activities:** | | |
| **Increase in Inventory** | | **1,600** |

Accounts Payable decreased by $1,900 during the year, indicating that cash payments for operating activities exceeded expenses. This additional cash outflow is shown as a decrease in the net cash flow from operating activities as follows:

| | | |
|---|---|---|
| **(e) Accounts Payable** | **1,900** | |
| **Net Cash Flow From Operating Activities:** | | |
| **Decrease in Accounts Payable** | | **1,900** |

Salaries Payable increased by $400 during the year, indicating that less cash was paid than that shown as salaries expense for the year. To adjust net income to show a higher net cash flow from operating activities, the following worksheet entry is made:

| | | |
|---|---|---|
| **(f) Net Cash Flow From Operating Activities:** | | |
| **Increase in Salaries Payable** | **400** | |
| **Salaries Payable** | | **400** |

At this point, all of the changes in the current assets (except cash) and current liabilities have been accounted for. We now turn to the noncurrent accounts; the investing and financing transactions affecting these accounts are summarized in the supplemental information of Exhibit 20-10.

During the year, the company purchased equipment at a cost of $15,200. The purchase was an investing activity and required a cash outflow (i.e., a debit to Buildings and Equipment and a credit to Cash). The worksheet entry to record the purchase is as follows (note that the original credit to Cash is replaced with the caption Payment for Purchase of Equipment under the heading Cash Flows From Investing Activities):

| | | |
|---|---|---|
| **(g) Buildings and Equipment** | **15,200** | |
| **Cash Flows From Investing Activities:** | | |
| **Payment for Purchase of Equipment** | | **15,200** |

Note that entry (g) does not account for the change (increase of $13,000) in the Buildings and Equipment account. This is because another transaction (k) also affected the account.

The issuance of the long-term bonds was a financing activity that caused an increase in Bonds Payable and an inflow of cash (e.g., debit to Cash and credit to Bonds Payable). The worksheet entry to record the issuance is as follows (the debit to the current asset Cash is replaced by the caption Proceeds from Issuance of Bonds under the heading Cash Flows From Financing Activities):

| | | |
|---|---|---|
| **(h) Cash Flows From Financing Activities:** | | |
| **Proceeds From Issuance of Bonds** | **8,000** | |
| **Bonds Payable** | | **8,000** |

When the company issued shares of its common stock in exchange for land, the exchange was recorded at the market price of the 100 shares of stock. At that time, the Land account was increased (debited) by $4,000, the Common Stock, $10 par account was increased (credited) for the par value of $1,000, and the Additional Paid-in Capital account was increased (credited) for the excess of the market value over par value, $3,000. Although this transaction did not affect cash, it did involve a simultaneous financing and investing activity. The company invested in land and financed it by issuing common stock. Both the financing and the investing activities information are disclosed on a schedule accompanying the statement of cash flows. To do so, the original transaction is "expanded" into two transactions, a financing transaction and an investing transaction, which are recorded on the worksheet as follows:

| | | |
|---|---|---|
| (i-1) Investing and Financing Activities Not Affecting | | |
| Cash: Issuance of Common Stock for Land | 4,000 | |
| Common Stock, $10 par | | 1,000 |
| Additional Paid-in Capital | | 3,000 |
| | | |
| (i-2) Land | 4,000 | |
| Investing and Financing Activities Not | | |
| Affecting Cash: Acquisition of | | |
| Land by Issuance of Common Stock | | 4,000 |

The recording of these expanded entries on the worksheet accounts for the changes in the Land, Common Stock, and Additional Paid-in Capital accounts and shows both the investing and financing segments of the original transaction.

Retained earnings and cash were reduced by the declaration and payment of cash dividends (i.e., a debit to Retained Earnings and a credit to Cash). This is a financing activity. The worksheet entry to record the decrease in retained earnings as well as the cash outflow for dividends is as follows (note that the original credit to the current asset Cash is replaced with the caption Payment of Dividends under the heading Cash Flows From Financing Activities):

| | | |
|---|---|---|
| (j) Retained Earnings | 1,800 | |
| Cash Flows From Financing Activities: | | |
| Payment of Dividends | | 1,800 |

The increase in Retained Earnings of $8,400 resulting from net income, reduced by the decrease of $1,800 because of dividends, accounts for the $6,600 change in Retained Earnings.

During the year, the company sold equipment. At that time, it recorded an increase (debit) in Cash of $2,100, a decrease (debit) in Accumulated Depreciation for $700, and a decrease (credit) in Buildings and Equipment for $2,200. The proceeds are a cash inflow from an *investing* activity. Because the $2,100 proceeds were more than the $1,500 ($2,200 − $700) book value, the company also recorded (credited) a Gain on Sale of Equipment of $600. As shown on the income statement in Exhibit 20-10, this gain caused net income to increase even though there was no cash inflow from *operating* activities. In preparing the worksheet entry for this transaction, two modifications are made: (1) instead of debiting Cash, the caption Proceeds From Sale of Equipment under the heading Cash Flows From Investing Activities is debited for the $2,100 proceeds, and (2) the caption Gain on Sale of Equipment is *credited* under the heading Net Cash Flow From Operating Activities to *deduct* the gain from net income in order to avoid double counting and to correctly show the cash provided by operating activities.[12] The entry is:

| (k) Cash Flows From Investing Activities: | | |
|---|---|---|
|     Proceeds from Sale of Equipment | 2,100 | |
|   Accumulated Depreciation | 700 | |
|     Net Cash Flow From Operating Activities: | | |
|       Gain on Sale of Equipment | | 600 |
|   Buildings and Equipment | | 2,200 |

After recording this worksheet entry and combining the results with those from entry (b), it may be seen that the change ($2,700 increase) in Accumulated Depreciation is now accounted for. In addition, combining the results of this worksheet entry with those from entry (g) accounts for the change ($13,000 increase) in the Buildings and Equipment account. It is often necessary to record the results of two (or more) unrelated transactions in accounting for the change in an account.

## Step 5: Final Worksheet Entry

In Step 5, a check of the debit and credit entries on the worksheet shows that all changes in the noncash accounts on the balance sheet have been accounted for. A final worksheet entry is made to record the increase in cash and to bring the debit and credit columns into balance, as follows:

| (l) Cash | 2,000 | |
|---|---|---|
|   Net Increase in Cash | | 2,000 |

The debit and credit columns in the upper and lower portions of the worksheet are now totaled. As shown in Exhibit 20-11, the columns in the upper portion total $27,200, and the columns in the lower portion total $27,100. The worksheet is now complete.

## Step 6: Preparation of Statement

After completing the worksheet, the statement of cash flows and accompanying schedule of investing and financing activities not affecting cash are prepared (Step 6). The statement of cash flows for the Prawn Company and accompanying schedule are shown in Exhibit 20-12. The information developed in the lower portion of the worksheet (Exhibit 20-11), along with the beginning and ending cash balances, is used to list the items in each section of the statement of cash flows and in the schedule. The $8,900 net cash provided by operating activities, less the $13,100 net cash used in investing activities, plus the $6,200 net cash provided by financing activities equals the $2,000 net increase in cash. The $2,000 net increase in cash added to the $3,500 beginning cash balance equals the $5,500 ending cash balance. In the accompanying schedule, the amount of the investing activity not affecting cash (acquisition of land by issuance of common stock) is offset by the amount of the financing activity not affecting cash (issuance of common stock for land), to report on all the company's investing and financing activities.

After studying the six steps and the completed worksheet of the basic example, you should understand the procedures for preparing the statement of cash flows. Not all the possible operating, investing, and financing transactions were included in this example. Additional transactions are shown in the comprehensive example.

---

12. If the equipment had been sold at a loss, the loss would have decreased net income even though there was no outflow of cash for operating activities. In this case, the worksheet entry would be modified as discussed, except that the caption Loss on Sale of Equipment is *debited* under the heading Net Cash Flow From Operating Activities to *add back* the loss to net income in a manner similar to depreciation expense.

---

**EXHIBIT 20-12**

## PRAWN CORPORATION

**Statement of Cash Flows**
**For Year Ended December 31, 1995**

| | | |
|---|---:|---:|
| Net Cash Flow From Operating Activities | | |
| Net income | $ 8,400 | |
| Adjustments for differences between income flows | | |
| and cash flows from operating activities: | | |
| Add: Depreciation expense | 3,400 | |
| Decrease in accounts receivable | 800 | |
| Increase in salaries payable | 400 | |
| Less: Increase in inventory | (1,600) | |
| Decrease in accounts payable | (1,900) | |
| Gain on sale of equipment | (600) | |
| Net cash provided by operating activities | | $ 8,900 |
| | | |
| Cash Flows From Investing Activities | | |
| Payment for purchase of equipment | $(15,200) | |
| Proceeds from sale of equipment | 2,100 | |
| Net cash used for investing activities | | (13,100) |
| | | |
| Cash Flows From Financing Activities | | |
| Proceeds from issuance of bonds | $ 8,000 | |
| Payment of dividends | (1,800) | |
| Net cash provided by financing activities | | 6,200 |
| Net Increase in Cash (see Schedule 1) | | $ 2,000 |
| Cash, January 1, 1995 | | 3,500 |
| Cash, December 31, 1995 | | $ 5,500 |
| | | |
| Schedule 1: Investing and Financing Activities Not Affecting Cash | | |
| Investing Activities | | |
| Acquisition of land by issuance of common stock | | $ (4,000) |
| Financing Activities | | |
| Issuance of common stock for land | | 4,000 |

## COMPREHENSIVE EXAMPLE

Many companies enter into operating, investing, and financing transactions of greater complexity than those illustrated in the preceding example. Consequently, the development of the statement of cash flows requires substantial analysis and a more complex worksheet. The condensed information for the Jones Company for 1995 shown in Exhibit 20-13 is used for a comprehensive example. This comprehensive example illustrates the development of the worksheet and statement of cash flows for a company engaging in a number of typical complex transactions. They include: (1) an extraordinary loss, (2) conversion of bonds payable to common stock, (3) issuance of long-term bonds at a discount, (4) declaration and issuance of a stock dividend, (5) lease of equipment under a capital lease, (6) amortization of bond discount, (7) amortization of patents, and (8) recording of deferred taxes. This list is not intended to be all-inclusive but rather to provide a basis from which to develop a logical approach to analyzing similar operating, investing, and financing transactions.

## EXHIBIT 20-13

### JONES COMPANY

Condensed Financial Information

**Income Statement Information for 1995**

| | | |
|---|---|---|
| Sales | | $ 88,020 |
| Less: Cost of goods | $(52,200) | |
| Other operating expenses | (15,800) | |
| Depreciation expense: equipment | (2,820) | |
| Depreciation expense: building | (5,100) | |
| Patent amortization expense | (600) | |
| Bond interest expense | (1,100) | |
| Income tax expense | (3,630) | |
| Plus: Gain on sale of equipment | 1,700 | (79,550) |
| Income before extraordinary items | | $ 8,470 |
| Extraordinary loss (net of income taxes) | | (2,100) |
| Net Income | | $ 6,370 |

**Balance Sheet Information**

| | Balances | |
|---|---|---|
| Accounts | 01/01/95 | 12/31/95 |
| Cash | $ 3,200 | $ 5,900 |
| Accounts receivable | 5,600 | 7,600 |
| Inventories | 7,300 | 7,000 |
| Prepaid expenses | 1,200 | 1,400 |
| Land | 10,000 | 18,200 |
| Equipment | 35,000 | 35,000 |
| Accumulated depreciation: equipment | (12,000) | (14,820) |
| Buildings | 144,000 | 149,000 |
| Accumulated depreciation: buildings | (39,300) | (39,600) |
| Leased equipment | 0 | 5,300 |
| Patents (net) | 5,000 | 4,400 |
| Total Assets | $160,000 | $179,380 |
| Accounts payable | $ 8,600 | $ 7,300 |
| Income taxes payable | 1,500 | 2,130 |
| Interest payable | 0 | 500 |
| Note payable | 0 | 2,600 |
| Obligation under capital lease | 0 | 5,300 |
| Bonds payable, 10% | 0 | 10,000 |
| Discount on bonds payable | 0 | (900) |
| Convertible bonds payable | 7,000 | 0 |
| Deferred taxes payable | 1,920 | 2,100 |
| Common stock, $10 par | 34,000 | 37,400 |
| Premium on common stock | 67,000 | 73,700 |
| Retained earnings | 39,980 | 39,250 |
| Total Liabilities and Stockholders' Equity | $160,000 | $179,380 |

**Retained Earnings Information for 1995**

| | | |
|---|---|---|
| Beginning retained earnings | | $39,980 |
| Add: Net income | | 6,370 |
| | | $46,350 |
| Less: Stock dividends | $3,100 | |
| Cash dividends | 4,000 | (7,100) |
| Ending retained earnings | | $39,250 |

**Supplemental Information for 1995**

(a) On December 31, 1995 the company borrowed $2,600 from a bank by issuing a 12%, 90-day note payable.

(b) During the year, additional land was acquired at a cost of $10,400.

(c) During the year, land that cost $2,200 was sold for $3,900, resulting in a $1,700 gain.

(d) During the year, a new building was acquired at a purchase price of $15,000.

(e) During the year, an earthquake completely destroyed a building that cost $10,000 and had a book value of $5,200. Settlement with the insurance company, combined with the tax credit, resulted in after-tax cash proceeds of $3,100 and an extraordinary loss (net of income taxes) of $2,100.

(f) On December 31, 1995 the company leased equipment under a long-term capital lease, recording the lease at $5,300.

(g) On January 1, 1995 the company issued $10,000 of long-term bonds at 90. The bonds pay interest semiannually on July 1 and January 1 at a 10% annual rate and mature in 10 years on January 1, 2005. The company uses straight-line amortization for the bond discount; consequently, bond discount amortization was $100 for the year.

(h) On January 1, 1995 convertible bonds with a face value and book value of $7,000 were converted into 240 shares of common stock. The book value method was used to record the conversion.

(i) Taxable income was less than pretax accounting income for the year, resulting in an increase in deferred taxes payable of $180.

(j) During the year, a small stock dividend was declared and issued. Involved were 100 shares of $10 par common stock. The market value of the stock on the declaration date was $31 per share.

**EXHIBIT 20-14**

## JONES COMPANY

Worksheet for Statement of Cash Flows
For Year Ended December 31, 1995

| Account Titles | Balances 01/01/95 | Balances 12/31/95 | Change Increase (Decrease) | Worksheet Entries Debit | | Worksheet Entries Credit | |
|---|---|---|---|---|---|---|---|
| *Debits* | | | | | | | |
| Cash | 3,200 | 5,900 | 2,700 | (w) | 2,700 | | |
| *Noncash Accounts:* | | | | | | | |
| Accounts receivable (net) | 5,600 | 7,600 | 2,000 | (e) | 2,000 | | |
| Inventories | 7,300 | 7,000 | (300) | | | (f) | 300 |
| Prepaid expenses | 1,200 | 1,400 | 200 | (g) | 200 | | |
| Land | 10,000 | 18,200 | 8,200 | (l) | 10,400 | (m) | 2,200 |
| Equipment | 35,000 | 35,000 | 0 | | | | |
| Buildings | 144,000 | 149,000 | 5,000 | (n) | 15,000 | (o) | 10,000 |
| Leased equipment | 0 | 5,300 | 5,300 | (p-2) | 5,300 | | |
| Patents (net) | 5,000 | 4,400 | (600) | | | (d) | 600 |
| Discount on bonds payable | 0 | 900 | 900 | (q) | 1,000 | (r) | 100 |
| Totals | 211,300 | 234,700 | 23,400 | | | | |
| *Credits* | | | | | | | |
| Accumulated depreciation: equipment | 12,000 | 14,820 | 2,820 | | | (b) | 2,820 |
| Accumulated depreciation: buildings | 39,300 | 39,600 | 300 | (o) | 4,800 | (c) | 5,100 |
| Accounts payable | 8,600 | 7,300 | (1,300) | (h) | 1,300 | | |
| Income taxes payable | 1,500 | 2,130 | 630 | | | (i) | 630 |
| Interest payable | 0 | 500 | 500 | | | (j) | 500 |
| Note payable | 0 | 2,600 | 2,600 | | | (k) | 2,600 |
| Obligation under capital lease | 0 | 5,300 | 5,300 | | | (p-1) | 5,300 |
| Bonds payable, 10% | 0 | 10,000 | 10,000 | | | (q) | 10,000 |
| Convertible bonds payable | 7,000 | 0 | (7,000) | (s-2) | 7,000 | | |
| Deferred taxes payable | 1,920 | 2,100 | 180 | | | (t) | 180 |
| Common stock, $10 par | 34,000 | 37,400 | 3,400 | | | (s-1) | 2,400 |
| | | | | | | (u) | 1,000 |
| Premium on common stock | 67,000 | 73,700 | 6,700 | | | (s-1) | 4,600 |
| | | | | | | (u) | 2,100 |
| Retained earnings | 39,980 | 39,250 | (730) | (u) | 3,100 | (a) | 6,370 |
| | | | | (v) | 4,000 | | |
| Totals | 211,300 | 234,700 | 23,400 | | 56,800 | | 56,800 |

(Lower portion continued on next page.)

The worksheet for the statement of cash flows of the Jones Company is shown in Exhibit 20-14. (Because the exhibit is so long, the lower portion is shown on the facing page.) The following discussion explains each entry. Entries (a) through (j) generally affect current assets and current liabilities and relate to operating activities. Entries (k) through (w) generally affect noncurrent assets, noncurrent liabilities, and stockholders' equity items and relate to investing and financing activities.

**EXHIBIT 20-14, Continued**

| Account Titles | Balances 01/01/95 | Balances 12/31/95 | Change Increase (Decrease) | Worksheet Entries Debit | Worksheet Entries Credit |
|---|---|---|---|---|---|
| **Net Cash Flow From Operating Activities** | | | | | |
| Net Income | | | | (a) 6,370 | |
| Add: Depreciation expense: equipment | | | | (b) 2,820 | |
| Depreciation expense: buildings | | | | (c) 5,100 | |
| Patent amortization expense | | | | (d) 600 | |
| Decrease in inventories | | | | (f) 300 | |
| Increase in income taxes payable | | | | (i) 630 | |
| Increase in interest payable | | | | (j) 500 | |
| Extraordinary loss | | | | (o) 2,100 | |
| Bond discount amortization | | | | (r) 100 | |
| Increase in deferred taxes payable | | | | (t) 180 | |
| Less: Increase in accounts receivable | | | | | (e) 2,000 |
| Increase in prepaid expenses | | | | | (g) 200 |
| Decrease in accounts payable | | | | | (h) 1,300 |
| Gain on sale of land | | | | | (m) 1,700 |
| **Cash Flows From Investing Activities** | | | | | |
| Payment for purchase of land | | | | | (l) 10,400 |
| Proceeds from sale of land | | | | (m) 3,900 | |
| Payment for purchase of building | | | | | (n) 15,000 |
| Proceeds from building destroyed by earthquake | | | | (o) 3,100 | |
| **Cash Flows From Financing Activities** | | | | | |
| Proceeds from issuance of short-term note payable | | | | (k) 2,600 | |
| Proceeds from issuance of bonds | | | | (q) 9,000 | |
| Payment of dividends | | | | | (v) 4,000 |
| **Investing and Financing Activities Not Affecting Cash** | | | | | |
| Incurrence of capital lease obligation for equipment | | | | (p-1) 5,300 | |
| Acquisition of equipment under capital lease | | | | | (p-2) 5,300 |
| Issuance of common stock to convert bonds | | | | (s-1) 7,000 | |
| Conversion of bonds to common stock | | | | | (s-2) 7,000 |
| **Net Increase in Cash** | | | | | (w) 2,700 |
| Totals | | | | 49,600 | 49,600 |

## Worksheet Entries for Operating Activities

Entry (a) records the net income as the first item on the worksheet under the heading Net Cash Flow From Operating Activities. A review of the expenses on the income statement in Exhibit 20-13 reveals three "noncash" expenses, depreciation expense on equipment, depreciation expense on buildings, and patent amortization expense.

Each of these is added back to net income to help reconcile it to the net cash flow from operating activities, as shown in entries (b), (c), and (d). Note that entries (b) and (d) account for the changes in Accumulated Depreciation: Equipment and Patents (net), respectively. Entry (o), discussed later, is also recorded to account for the change in the Accumulated Depreciation: Buildings account.

A review of the changes in the current assets (except cash) and the current liabilities reveals several additional adjustments that are made to help reconcile net income to the net cash flow from operating activities. Accounts receivable increased by $2,000 during the year because cash collections were less than credit sales. To adjust net income for the lower operating cash inflow, entry (e) is made. Note that, for simplicity, we ignore bad debts here. If accounts receivable (net) are affected by a provision for bad debts, both the change due to the recognition of bad debts expense and the change due to cash collections in excess of (or less than) sales are treated as adjustments of net income.

In regard to the other current assets, inventories decreased by $300 during the year, indicating that less inventory was purchased than recorded as cost of goods sold. To adjust net income for the lower operating cash outflow, entry (f) is made. Prepaid expenses increased by $200 during the year, indicating the cash paid for these items was greater than the amount of expense included in other operating expenses. To adjust net income for the higher operating cash outflow, entry (g) is made.

Turning to the current liabilities, accounts payable decreased by $1,300 during the year, indicating that cash payments for operating activities exceeded expenses. To adjust net income for the higher cash outflow, entry (h) is made. Both income taxes payable and interest payable increased during the year, indicating that less cash was paid than reported as the respective expenses. To adjust net income for the lower cash outflows, entries (i) and (j) are made. A few entries recorded later will also affect the net cash flow from operating activities.

### Worksheet Entries for Investing and Financing Activities

Note that no adjustment is made to the net cash flow from operating activities for the $2,600 increase in the current liability, notes payable. This is because the increase was due to a *financing* activity, summarized in the supplemental information of Exhibit 20-13. To record the cash inflow from this financing activity, entry (k) is made.

At this point, all the changes in the current assets (except cash) and current liabilities have been accounted for. Turning to the noncurrent items, a review of the supplemental information is needed to identify the various investing and financing activities. During the year, land was both purchased and sold; each is an investing activity. The acquisition of land resulted in a $10,400 cash outflow for an investing activity which is recorded in entry (l). Land was sold for $3,900, which resulted in a $1,700 gain (not extraordinary) that increased net income. Because the entire $3,900 proceeds is reported as a cash inflow from an investing activity, the gain is excluded (*deducted*) from net income to avoid double counting. To do so, entry (m) is made. Note that entries (l) and (m) account for the $8,200 increase in the Land account. The acquisition of a new building during the year resulted in a $15,000 cash outflow for an investing activity, which is recorded in entry (n).

*FASB Statement No. 95* requires that the cash flows from extraordinary items be reported as investing or financing activities and not be included in net cash flows from operating activities.[13] During the year, an earthquake (extraordinary event) oc-

---

13. *FASB Statement No. 95, op. cit.*, par. 28.

curred that destroyed a building with a cost of $10,000 and a book value of $5,200. Because the company received after-tax cash proceeds of $3,100 from its insurance company, it incurred an extraordinary loss (net of taxes) of $2,100, which is included in (and reduced) net income. The proceeds received is a cash inflow *from an investing activity*. To record the cash inflow, eliminate the book value, and exclude (i.e., *add back*) the extraordinary loss from net income, entry (o) is made. Note that entries (n) and (o) account for the $5,000 increase in the Building account and that entries (c) and (o) account for the $300 increase in the Accumulated Depreciation account. Note also that the Extraordinary Loss is shown on the worksheet as an addition to net income in the usual manner along with the other added items.

At the end of the year, the company leased equipment under a capital lease, recording the asset and liability at $5,300. Although not affecting cash, this is a simultaneous investing and financing transaction, and both activities are reported in a schedule accompanying the statement of cash flows. Entries (p-1) and (p-2) record these events.

On January 1, the company issued $10,000 face value bonds payable at a discount, receiving proceeds of $9,000. This is a financing activity and is recorded in entry (q). Note that the $1,000 debit to Discount on Bonds Payable does not equal the net change ($900) in the account. This is because of the amortization of the discount during the year. On the income statement in Exhibit 20-13, note that the bond interest expense is $1,100; however, the cash paid or owed on the bonds is 10% of $10,000, or $1,000. The additional $100 of interest expense is due to the amortization of the discount. This amortization increased interest expense and reduced net income but did not involve a cash outflow. To adjust for the lower operating cash outflow, entry (r) is made. The $900 increase in Discount on Bonds Payable is now accounted for. The adjustment for the amortization of a premium on bonds payable would be handled in a similar but opposite manner. Bond premium amortization reduces interest expense to an amount *less* than the operating cash outflow. Therefore, the worksheet entry would involve a debit to Premium on Bonds Payable and a credit to Net Cash Flow From Operating Activities: Bond Premium Amortization for the amount of the amortization.

During the year, $7,000 of convertible bonds payable were converted to 240 shares of $10 par common stock; the transaction was accounted for by the book value method. Although not affecting cash, two simultaneous financing activities were involved that are disclosed in a schedule accompanying the statement of cash flows. Entries (s-1) and (s-2) record these events. Note that entry (s-1) did not account for the changes in the Common Stock and Premium on Common Stock accounts. Entry (u) also affects these accounts.

Deferred taxes payable increased by $180 because income tax expense was higher than the actual income taxes paid or owed (because of a temporary difference between pretax financial income and taxable income). To adjust net income for the lower operating cash outflow, entry (t) is made. A small stock dividend was declared and issued during the year; the transaction was recorded at the market price of the stock. Recall that stock dividends affect only stockholders' equity accounts and do not involve the transfer of assets to stockholders. Consequently, the issuance of stock dividends is *not* considered to be a financing activity and is *not* reported on the statement of cash flows. However, in order to account for the $3,100 effect on the stockholders' equity accounts, entry (u) is made in the *upper* portion of the worksheet. The $730 net decrease in retained earnings during the year has not yet been accounted for. Entry (a) increased retained earnings for the net income of $6,370, while entry (u) decreased it for the stock dividend of $3,100. The remaining decrease in retained earnings was due to the declaration and payment of $4,000 cash dividends. This is a financing activity and is recorded in entry (v).

*Temporary differences are discussed in Chapter 17.*

In Step 5, a check of the debit and credit entries in the upper portion of the worksheet reveals that all the changes in the noncash accounts have been accounted for. A final worksheet entry is made to record the increase in cash and to bring the debit and credit column totals into balance. This is entry (w). The debit and credit totals in the upper portion of Exhibit 20-14 are $56,800 and in the lower portion are $49,600. The worksheet for the Jones Company is now complete.

### Preparation of Statement

The statement of cash flows and the accompanying schedule of investing and financing activities not affecting cash for the Jones Company are shown in Exhibit 20-15. They were prepared from the *lower* portion of the worksheet in Exhibit 20-14, along with the beginning and ending cash balances. Observe that in the Cash Flows From Investing Activities section, the payment for the purchase of land is reported separately from the proceeds from the sale of land. Likewise, the payment for the purchase of the building is reported separately from the proceeds from the building destroyed by the earthquake. *FASB Statement No. 95* requires that the cash inflows and cash outflows for related investing activities as well as related financing activities be shown separately and *not* "netted" against each other.[14] Note also that the reconciliation of the beginning and ending cash balances at the bottom of the statement of cash flows enables a user to trace the change in cash to related amounts on successive balance sheets. Finally, note the schedule of investing and financing activities not affecting cash discloses the one noncash transaction that had both an investing and financing element, and the other that involved two financing elements.

## SPECIAL TOPICS

The previous discussion and examples were designed to illustrate the common issues involved in the preparation of the worksheet and statement of cash flows. For simplicity, several topics were omitted. These topics are discussed briefly in the following sections.

### Interest Paid and Income Taxes Paid

*FASB Statement No. 95* requires that companies using the indirect method of reporting operating cash flows also disclose their interest *paid* and income taxes *paid*. These disclosures may be made in a separate schedule or narrative description. Interest *expense* is affected by the cash paid, accruals, and any premium or discount amortizations on bonds (or notes) payable. Income tax *expense* is affected by the cash paid, accruals, and changes in deferred income taxes. To convert interest expense to

---

14. *Ibid.*, par. 31 and 75.

**EXHIBIT 20-15**

## JONES COMPANY

Statement of Cash Flows
For Year Ended December 31, 1995

**Net Cash Flow From Operating Activities**

| | | |
|---|---:|---:|
| Net income | $ 6,370 | |
| Adjustments for differences between income | | |
| flows and cash flows from operating activities: | | |
| Add: Depreciation expense: equipment | 2,820 | |
| Depreciation expense: buildings | 5,100 | |
| Patent amortization expense | 600 | |
| Decrease in inventories | 300 | |
| Increase in income taxes payable | 630 | |
| Increase in interest payable | 500 | |
| Extraordinary loss (net) from earthquake | 2,100 | |
| Increase in deferred taxes payable | 180 | |
| Bond discount amortization | 100 | |
| Less: Increase in accounts receivable | (2,000) | |
| Increase in prepaid expenses | (200) | |
| Decrease in accounts payable | (1,300) | |
| Gain on sale of land | (1,700) | |
| Net cash provided by operating activities | | $13,500 |

**Cash Flows From Investing Activities**

| | | |
|---|---:|---:|
| Payment for purchase of land | $(10,400) | |
| Proceeds from sale of land | 3,900 | |
| Payment for purchase of building | (15,000) | |
| Proceeds from building destroyed by earthquake | 3,100 | |
| Net cash used for investing activities | | (18,400) |

**Cash Flows From Financing Activities**

| | | |
|---|---:|---:|
| Proceeds from issuance of short-term note payable | $ 2,600 | |
| Proceeds from issuance of bonds | 9,000 | |
| Payment of dividends | (4,000) | |
| Net cash provided by financing activities | | 7,600 |
| Net Increase in Cash (see Schedule 1) | | $ 2,700 |
| Cash, January 1, 1995 | | 3,200 |
| Cash, December 31, 1995 | | $ 5,900 |

**Schedule 1: Investing and Financing Activities Not Affecting Cash**

| | |
|---|---:|
| Investing Activities | |
| Acquisition of equipment under capital lease | $ (5,300) |
| Financing Activities | |
| Issuance of capital lease obligation for equipment | 5,300 |
| Conversion of bonds to common stock | (7,000) |
| Issuance of common stock to convert bonds | 7,000 |

interest paid, and to convert income tax expense to income taxes paid, the following adjustments[15] are necessary:

| Interest | Income Taxes |
|---|---|
| Interest *expense* | Income tax *expense* |
| + Decrease in interest payable | + Decrease in income taxes payable |
| *or* | *or* |
| − Increase in interest payable | − Increase in income taxes payable |
| + Amortization of premium on bonds payable | + Decrease in deferred tax liability |
| *or* | *or* |
| − Amortization of discount on bonds payable | − Increase in deferred tax liability |
| = Interest *paid* | + Increase in deferred tax asset |
| | *or* |
| | − Decrease in deferred tax asset |
| | = Income taxes *paid* |

To illustrate, refer back to the Jones Company information shown in Exhibits 20-13 and 20-14. To determine its interest paid and income taxes paid for 1995, the Jones Company prepares the following schedules:

| | | | |
|---|---|---|---|
| Bond interest expense | $1,100 | Income tax expense | $3,630 |
| − Increase in interest payable | (500) | − Increase in income taxes payable | (630) |
| − Bond discount amortization | (100) | − Increase in deferred taxes payable | (180) |
| Interest paid | $ 500 | Income taxes paid | $2,820 |

Based on these computations, Jones Company reports interest paid of $500 and income taxes paid of $2,820 in conjunction with its 1995 statement of cash flows shown in Exhibit 20-15. **Unless directed otherwise, you are *not* required to make these disclosures in the chapter homework.**

### Flexibility in Reporting

*FASB Statement No. 95* permits flexibility of reporting a company's net cash flow from operating activities under the indirect method. That is, the company may show the reconciliation of net income to the net cash provided by (or used in) operating activities in a separate schedule accompanying its statement of cash flows. Thus, for instance, if the Jones Company used this approach, the first section of Exhibit 20-15 would appear as follows:

Net Cash Flow From Operating Activities
    Net cash provided by operating activities (Schedule 1)    $13,500

---

15. A company may have a valuation allowance related to its deferred tax asset. Since the valuation allowance is a contra account, any changes in the account are handled in a manner opposite to that of the deferred tax asset.

Then the reconciliation of the $6,370 net income to the $13,500 net cash provided by operating activities would be reported in Schedule 1. The rest of the statement of cash flows would remain the same. (The schedule to report the investing and financing activities not affecting cash would be numbered as Schedule 2.) The advantage of reporting the reconciliation in a separate schedule is that it reduces the amount of detail shown on the statement of cash flows. The disadvantage is that it removes from the statement a key factor in assessing the quality of net income and its relationship to cash flows. By relegating the reconciliation to a separate schedule, this analysis may be overlooked by external users. For this reason, the authors advocate including the reconciliation directly on the statement of cash flows.

## Partial Cash Investing and Financing Activities

Throughout the previous examples and discussion, we have assumed that no cash was exchanged in any transactions involving investing and financing activities not affecting cash. In some transactions, a small amount of cash may be exchanged even though the majority of the transaction involves a noncash exchange. In other transactions, a large amount of cash may be exchanged even though some of the transaction is a noncash exchange. In these cases, there are alternative ways of disclosing the simultaneous investing and financing activities involving an amount of cash. For instance, suppose a company acquired land costing $10,000 by paying $1,000 down and signing a $9,000 note payable to the seller. One method of disclosing the effects of this transaction is to report the cash payment on the statement of cash flows and the noncash element on the accompanying schedule of investing and financing activities not affecting cash as follows:

*Statement of Cash Flows*:
  Cash Flows From Investing Activities
    Payment for purchase of land                              $(1,000)

*Schedule: Investing and Financing Activities Not Affecting Cash*
  Investing Activities
    Purchase of land for $10,000 by issuance of note          $(9,000)
  Financing Activities
    Issuance of note to acquire land                            9,000

The advantage of this approach is that it keeps the significant noncash elements of the transaction separate from the cash elements. The disadvantage is that the external user cannot identify the relationships between the items.

When the amount of cash is large in such an exchange, then it may be more appropriate to report the items in a cash flow section. Several alternative disclosure formats are acceptable. For instance, if land costing $18,000 was acquired by paying $15,000 down and signing a $3,000 note payable to the seller, the effects might be reported on the statement of cash flows as:

Cash Flows From Investing Activities
  Purchase of land by issuance of note and cash      $(18,000)
  Less: Issuance of note                                 3,000
  Cash payment for purchase of land                  $(15,000)

The advantage of this approach is that the related items are shown in close proximity. The disadvantage is that a financing element (issuance of note) is disclosed in an investing section. Each of the alternative disclosures has its advantages and disadvantages; good judgment must be used to determine the most informative disclosure for the given circumstances.

## Temporary and Long-Term Investments

As discussed in Chapter 13, investments (whether temporary or long-term) in debt and equity securities "available for sale" are reported as assets at their fair value (by use of an allowance account) on a company's year-end balance sheet, and any resulting unrealized increase or decrease in value is reported as an element of stockholders' equity. When this type of temporary or long-term investment is sold, the fair value (cost and allowance accounts) of the security as well as any related unrealized increase or decrease in value is eliminated from the accounting records, and a realized gain or loss on the sale is recorded. The realized gain or loss is computed by comparing the proceeds to the *cost* of the security.

Because of the use of an allowance account as well as an unrealized increase or decrease account in valuing the investment in securities available for sale, any changes in these accounts must be carefully analyzed to determine the impact (if any) on the statement of cash flows. An increase in the investment account due to the purchase of securities is reported on the statement of cash flows as a cash outflow for an investing activity, and the entry on the worksheet to prepare the statement is also made in the usual manner. Any change in the allowance and unrealized increase or decrease accounts resulting from a revaluation to fair value at year-end is *not* reported on the statement of cash flows, but must be accounted for on the worksheet. A decrease in the investment account due to the sale of securities is reported on the statement of cash flows as a cash inflow from an investing activity in the usual manner, but the worksheet entry must reconcile the changes in the investment, allowance, unrealized increase/decrease, and realized gain (or loss) accounts.

To illustrate, assume that on November 28, 1994, the Dougherty Company purchased 1,000 shares of Bear Company common stock for $40,000 as a temporary investment in securities available for sale. On December 31, 1994, the fair value of the stock has risen to $42 per share so that the temporary investment is reported as a current asset of $42,000 ($40,000 cost + $2,000 allowance), and a $2,000 unrealized increase in value of securities available for sale is reported in stockholders' equity on its December 31, 1994 balance sheet. For cash flow analysis, the worksheet entries at the end of 1994 to reconcile the $42,000 change in the carrying value of the temporary investment are as follows:

| | | |
|---|---|---|
| **Temporary Investment in Securities Available for Sale** | 40,000 | |
|    **Cash Flows From Investing Activities:** | | |
|       **Payment for Purchase of Temporary Investments** | | 40,000 |
| **Allowance for Change in Value of Investment** | 2,000 | |
|    **Unrealized Increase in Value of Securities Available** | | |
|       **for Sale** | | 2,000 |

The debit portion of the first entry is listed in the upper portion of the worksheet and helps reconcile the change in the temporary investment account. The credit portion of the first entry is listed in the lower portion of the worksheet and accounts for the cash outflow for the purchase of the temporary investment, which is reported on the 1994 statement of cash flows. Both the debit and credit portions of the second entry are listed in the upper portion of the worksheet and complete the reconciliation of the changes in the allowance and unrealized increase accounts. This portion of the increase in the carrying value of the temporary investment is *not* listed on the 1994 statement of cash flows because there was no cash outflow.

Now suppose that the Dougherty Company sold its investment in Bear Company stock for $45,000 on January 16, 1995. The worksheet entry at the end of 1995 to reconcile the changes in the various accounts is as follows:

| | | |
|---|---|---|
| Cash Flows From Investing Activities: Proceeds | | |
|     from Sale of Temporary Investment | 45,000 | |
| Unrealized Increase in Value of Securities | | |
|     Available for Sale | 2,000 | |
|     Temporary Investment in Securities Available for Sale | | 40,000 |
|     Allowance for Change in Value of Investment | | 2,000 |
|     Net Cash Flow From Operating Activities: | | |
|         Gain on Sale of Temporary Investment | | 5,000 |

This entry (1) reconciles the changes in the temporary investment, allowance, and unrealized increase accounts, (2) records the $45,000 investing cash inflow from the sale of the securities, and (3) treats the $5,000 gain on the sale as a deduction from net income to convert it from an accrual to a cash flow basis. The latter two items are reported on the 1995 statement of cash flows in the usual manner.

A company may also make a long-term investment in debt securities (e.g., bonds) that it expects to hold to maturity. Any premium or discount is amortized each year as an adjustment to interest revenue, and the investment is reported at its book value on the year-end balance sheet. For cash flow reporting purposes, the amortization of a premium on this type of investment is added back to net income in the operating activities section of the statement of cash flows because it reduced interest revenue to an amount lower than the cash received. The amortization of a discount is subtracted from net income because it increased interest revenue to an amount higher than the cash received. Each of these adjustments helps convert net income from an accrual to a cash basis. Although rare, if a company sells such an investment before maturity, any gain or loss is computed by comparing the proceeds to the unamortized cost. The proceeds are reported as a cash inflow from investing activities and the gain is deducted from net income in the usual manner on the statement of cash flows.

## Cash Dividends Declared

In the previous examples, whenever we discussed cash dividends, it was assumed that the dividends were declared *and* paid in the current year. The declaration and payment of cash dividends causes a decrease in both Retained Earnings and Cash and is disclosed as a cash outflow from financing activities.

In some instances, a company will declare a cash dividend in the *current* year and pay the cash dividend in the *next* year. In this situation, the cash dividend is handled differently in preparing the worksheet for the statement of cash flows. The declaration of the cash dividend is recorded on the worksheet as a decrease (debit) in Retained Earnings and an increase (credit) in Dividends Payable. Because no cash outflow occurs in the current year, no dividends are reported on the statement of cash flows. In the next year, the payment of the cash dividends is recorded on the worksheet as a decrease (debit) in Dividends Payable and a decrease (credit) in Cash. The outflow is then reported in the cash flows from financing activities section of the statement of cash flows.

When a company follows a policy of declaring a dividend in one year and paying the dividend in the next year, the Dividends Payable account balance will change during each year. A comparison of the change in the account balance to the dividends reported on the retained earnings statement will determine the worksheet entry necessary to account for the cash dividends.

### Financial Institutions

When the FASB was deliberating on the requirements of *FASB Statement No. 95,* one issue that created controversy was the proper reporting of interest collected and interest paid, and collections and payments of notes receivable and notes payable. For most companies, dealing in notes receivable and notes payable is not a primary part of their operating activities. On the other hand, it is a major aspect of the operating activities of banks and other financial institutions. Banks frequently buy and sell notes, mortgages, and similar securities. The question arose as to whether the related cash inflows and outflows (i.e., interest and principal) should be reported as operating activities or as investing and financing activities. As discussed in the chapter, after much deliberation, the FASB finally concluded that interest collected and interest paid are reported as cash flows relating to operating activities to provide consistency with the reporting of the related interest revenue and interest expense on the income statement. However, collections and payments of the principal of notes receivable and notes payable are reported as cash flows relating to investing and financing activities, respectively.

In *FASB Statement No. 102,* the FASB reversed parts of its original requirements. For banks, brokers and dealers in securities, and other similar companies holding loans for resale on a short-term basis or carrying securities in a "trading account," other requirements now apply. (A trading account includes securities that are acquired specifically for resale and are turned over very quickly.) In these situations, the cash flows from the purchases or sales of these trading securities are reported in the operating activities section of the statement of cash flows.[16] In coming to this conclusion, the FASB reasoned that these types of assets for financial institutions are similar to inventory for other businesses and, as such, are part of the operating cycle.

Furthermore, in *FASB Statement No. 115,* the FASB required that trading securities be reported at fair value and that any resulting unrealized holding gain or loss be reported in net income. Consequently, for reporting its operating cash flows under the indirect method, a financial institution adds (deducts) an unrealized holding loss (gain) on trading securities to net income to help adjust net income from an accrual to a cash flow basis.

As discussed earlier in the chapter, in most situations, *FASB Statement No. 95* does *not* allow "netting" of cash outflows against cash inflows for reporting the results of related investing or financing activities. An exception is made for certain activities of banks and other financial institutions. These institutions are allowed to report the net cash flows for (1) deposits and withdrawals with other financial institutions, (2) time deposits accepted and repaid, and (3) loans made to customers and principal collections of these loans.[17] This exception is allowed because showing

16. "Statement of Cash Flows—Exemption of Certain Enterprises and Classification of Cash Flows from Certain Securities Acquired for Resale," *FASB Statement of Financial Accounting Standards No. 102* (Norwalk, Conn.: FASB, 1989), par. 8 and 9.
17. "Statement of Cash Flows—Net Reporting of Certain Cash Receipts and Cash Payments and Classification of Cash Flows from Hedging Transactions," *FASB Statement of Financial Accounting Standards No. 104* (Norwalk, Conn.: FASB, 1989), par. 7.

these items on a "gross" basis provides information that is costly to accumulate and of limited value to external users.

## Effects of Exchange Rates

Many companies have operations in foreign countries. When a company with foreign operations prepares a statement of cash flows, the statement must disclose the "reporting currency equivalent" of the "foreign currency" cash flows using the exchange rates in effect at the time of the cash flows. A weighted average exchange rate for the period may be used if it yields similar results. On the statement, then, the effect of exchange rate changes on cash balances held in foreign currencies is reported as a separate part of the reconciliation of the change in cash during the period.[18]

## Cash Flow Per Share

In accordance with *APB Opinion No. 15,* a company must report the earnings per share on the face of its income statement. Although the cash flow information presented in a company's statement of cash flows is useful in evaluating the performance of the company, the FASB believes that cash flow (or any component) is not an alternative to income as an indicator of a company's performance. Consequently, in accordance with *FASB Statement No. 95,* a cash flow per share amount is *not* reported in a company's financial statements.[19]

## APPENDIX: DIRECT METHOD FOR REPORTING OPERATING CASH FLOWS

Throughout the main part of the chapter, the *indirect* method was used to report the net cash flow from operating activities on the statement of cash flows. This is the method used by most companies. Under this method, we started with net income and adjusted (reconciled) it for any noncash items and for changes in current assets (except cash) and current liabilities to convert net income to net cash provided by (or used in) operating activities. This approach has the advantage of providing information about intervals of leads and lags between income and operating cash flows.

*FASB Statement No. 95* allows use of either the indirect method or the direct method, but encourages the use of the *direct method* to report the cash flows from operating activities on the statement of cash flows. As briefly discussed earlier in the chapter, **under the direct method, the operating cash outflows are deducted from the operating cash inflows to determine the net cash provided by (or used in) operating activities.** This approach has the advantage of separating operating cash receipts from operating cash payments, which may be useful in estimating future cash flows. Because of the FASB's support for the direct method, use of this method is likely to increase. Consequently, application of the direct method is explained in this Appendix.

Under the direct method, the cash flows from *investing* activities and the cash flows from *financing* activities are *reported* on the statement of cash flows in exactly the same manner as under the indirect method. Therefore, the focus in this Appendix is on determining and reporting the cash flows from *operating* activities of a company. However, because there are some slight differences in *preparing* the information concerning the investing and financing activities, this analysis is discussed as well.

---

18. *FASB Statement No. 95, op. cit.,* par. 25.
19. *Ibid.,* par. 33.

## OPERATING CASH FLOWS

According to *FASB Statement No. 95,* under the direct method, a company reports its operating cash inflows separately from its operating cash outflows. Each of these classifications is discussed in the following sections.

### Operating Cash Inflows

Under the direct method, a company reports its cash inflows from operating activities in three categories: (1) collections from customers, (2) interest and dividends collected, and (3) other operating receipts, if any. Generally, these cash inflows from operating activities are calculated by an analysis of income statement and balance sheet items as follows:

1. *Collections from Customers:* Sales revenue, plus decrease in accounts receivable or minus increase in accounts receivable.

2. *Interest and Dividends Collected.* Interest revenue and dividend revenue, plus decrease in interest/dividends receivable or minus increase in interest/dividends receivable, and plus amortization of premium on investment in bonds or minus amortization of discount on investment in bonds.

3. *Other Operating Receipts.* Other revenues, plus increase in deferred revenues or minus decrease in deferred revenues, minus gains on disposals of assets and liabilities, and minus investment income recognized under the equity method.

Most of the adjustments relate to the company's operating cycle. One adjustment was illustrated earlier in Exhibit 20-5. These adjustments are further discussed and illustrated later in the Appendix.

### Operating Cash Outflows

A company reports its cash outflows from operating activities in five categories: (1) payments to suppliers,[20] (2) payments to employees, (3) payments of interest, (4) other operating payments (if any), and (5) payments of income taxes. Generally, these cash outflows for operating activities are calculated by an analysis of income statement and balance sheet items as follows:

1. *Payments to Suppliers.* Cost of goods sold, plus increase in inventory or minus decrease in inventory, plus decrease in accounts payable or minus increase in accounts payable.

---

20. *FASB Statement No. 95* (par. 27) combines payments to suppliers and payments to employees into one category. However, it encourages companies to provide further breakdowns of operating cash receipts and operating cash payments, when useful. The authors believe that separating payments to suppliers from payments to employees may be useful to different external users, and do so throughout the Appendix. In a manufacturing company, a separation of payments to suppliers and payments to employees may not be practical. This is because various manufacturing costs, including direct and indirect materials as well as direct and indirect labor, may be recorded directly in the goods in process inventory and not shown as separate expenses. In such a case, it would be difficult to separate the related cash flows, so that reporting the combined payments to suppliers and employees may be the only practical disclosure.

2. *Payments to Employees.* Salaries expense, plus decrease in salaries payable or minus increase in salaries payable.

3. *Payments of Interest.* Interest expense, plus decrease in interest payable or minus increase in interest payable, plus amortization of premium on bonds payable or minus amortization of discount on bonds payable.

4. *Other Operating Payments.* Other expenses, plus increase in prepaid items or minus decrease in prepaid items; minus depreciation, depletion, and amortization expense; minus losses on disposals of assets and liabilities; minus investment loss recognized under the equity method.

5. *Payments of Income Taxes.* Income tax expense, plus decrease in income taxes payable or minus increase in income taxes payable, plus decrease in deferred tax liability or minus increase in deferred tax liability.[21]

Most of the adjustments relate to the company's operating cycle. One adjustment was illustrated earlier in Exhibit 20-5. These adjustments are further discussed and illustrated later in the Appendix.

### Diagram of Operating Cash Flows

To summarize the discussion in the preceding sections, under the *direct* method, the cash inflows from operating activities for the statement of cash flows may be computed by adjusting the various revenue accounts for changes in certain asset accounts (primarily current assets involved in the operating cycle) and to eliminate certain "noncash" revenues (gains). The cash outflows for operating activities may be computed by adjusting the various expense accounts for changes in certain liability (and asset) accounts (primarily current liabilities and current assets in the operating cycle) and to eliminate certain "noncash" expenses (losses). These adjustments are shown in Exhibit 20-16. It should be noted that these adjustments may have to be modified depending on the manner in which a company reports and classifies the related items in its financial statements. For instance, an increase in deferred revenue may be due to a collection of sales in advance. In this case, the adjustment would be to sales revenue instead of other revenues. Under the direct method, then, net cash provided by (or used in) operating activities is the difference between the cash inflows from operating activities and the cash outflows for operating activities, as computed according to Exhibit 20-16.

If a company uses the direct method of reporting its operating cash flows, *FASB Statement No. 95* requires the company to reconcile its net income to the net cash provided by (or used) in operating activities in a separate schedule accompanying the statement of cash flows. This reconciliation is intended to link the information on the income statement, prepared on an accrual basis, with the operating activities information on the statement of cash flows, prepared on a cash basis. This reconciliation is, in effect, prepared under the *indirect* method. Because the indirect method of reconciling net income to operating cash flows is fully discussed in the main part of the chapter, the discussion is not repeated here.

---

21. For a company that has a deferred tax asset, an increase in the deferred tax asset is added to income tax expense or a decrease is subtracted. A change in a related valuation allowance (contra account) is handled in an opposite manner.

**EXHIBIT 20-16**

## MAJOR ADJUSTMENTS TO CONVERT INCOME STATEMENT AMOUNTS TO OPERATING CASH FLOWS

| Income Statement Amounts | Adjustments | Cash Flows From Operating Activities | Net Operating Cash Flows |
|---|---|---|---|
| Sales revenue | +Decrease in accounts receivable<br>or<br>−Increase in accounts receivable | = Collections from customers | Cash Inflows From Operating Activities |
| Interest revenue and dividend revenue | +Decrease in interest receivable<br>or<br>−Increase in interest receivable<br>+Amortization of premium on investment in bonds<br>or<br>−Amortization of discount on investment in bonds | = Interest and dividends collected | |
| Other revenues | +Increase in deferred revenues<br>or<br>−Decrease in deferred revenues<br>−Gains on disposals of assets and liabilities[a]<br>−Investment income (equity method)[a] | = Other operating receipts | |
| Cost of goods sold | +Increase in inventory<br>or<br>−Decrease in inventory<br>+Decrease in accounts payable<br>or<br>−Increase in accounts payable | = Payments to suppliers | Cash Outflows For Operating Activities |
| Salaries expense | +Decrease in salaries payable<br>or<br>−Increase in salaries payable | = Payments to employees | |
| Interest expense | +Decrease in interest payable<br>or<br>−Increase in interest payable<br>+Amortization of premium on bonds payable<br>or<br>−Amortization of discount on bonds payable | = Payments of interest | |
| Other expenses | +Increase in prepaid items<br>or<br>−Decrease in prepaid items<br>−Depreciation, depletion, and amortization expense[a]<br>−Losses on disposals of assets and liabilities[a]<br>−Investment loss (equity methods)[a] | = Other operating payments | |
| Income tax expense | +Decrease in income taxes payable<br>or<br>−Increase in income taxes payable<br>+Decrease in deferred tax liability[b]<br>or<br>−Increase in deferred tax liability | = Payments of income taxes | |

a. Unless listed as separate items on income statement
b. A change in a deferred tax asset is handled in an opposite manner.

# PROCEDURES FOR STATEMENT PREPARATION

When using the direct method to prepare the information for the statement of cash flows, either the visual inspection method or the worksheet method may be used depending on the complexity of the accounting information. The information may be obtained, however, in a slightly different manner. Normally, under the direct method, the information for the statement of cash flows is obtained from the following working papers:

1. **Post-closing trial balance (or balance sheet) from *previous* period:** Recall that a post-closing trial balance contains the debit and credit balances of all the *permanent* accounts in a company's general ledger. In other words, a post-closing trial balance of the previous period contains the same information as the *ending balance sheet* of the previous period.

2. **Adjusted trial balance of *current* period:** Recall that an adjusted trial balance contains the debit and credit balances (after adjustments but before closing) of all the temporary and permanent accounts in a company's general ledger. In other words, an adjusted trial balance of the current period contains the *balance sheet, income statement,* and *retained earnings statement* information for the current period.

In addition, other information is needed that explains the changes in the balance sheet (permanent) accounts (other than cash). This information is obtained from the accounting records. In complex situations, use of the post-closing trial balance of the prior period and the adjusted trial balance of the current period is the most efficient way to prepare the statement of cash flows. In more simple situations, however, the statement may be developed based on the information contained in the beginning and ending balance sheets, the income statement, and the retained earnings statement of the current year.

## Visual Inspection Method

Under the visual inspection approach, the steps to complete the statement of cash flows using the direct method are virtually the same as for the indirect method, except that the information for the cash flows from operating activities section is computed as follows:

> Make adjustments to the applicable revenues for the period (e.g., to sales revenue for change in account receivable) to determine the amounts of collections from customers, interest and dividend receipts, and other operating receipts, if any. Make adjustments to the applicable expenses for the period (e.g., to cost of goods sold for change in accounts payable) to determine the amounts of payments to suppliers, payments to employees, payments of interest, other operating payments, if any, and payments of income taxes. Use of Exhibit 20-16 is helpful for these adjustments.

Once the operating activities section is completed, the investing activities section and the financing activities section are completed by analyzing the changes in the other balance sheet accounts in a manner identical to the indirect method.

To illustrate preparation of the operating activities section, assume the following income statement items were taken from the adjusted trial balance of the Betha Company at the end of 1995:

|  | Debit | Credit |
|---|---|---|
| Sales |  | $94,000 |
| Interest revenue |  | 5,400 |
| Cost of goods sold | $43,000 |  |
| Salaries expense | 18,500 |  |
| Depreciation expense | 11,000 |  |
| Interest expense | 9,200 |  |
| Other expenses | 4,700 |  |
| Income tax expense | 3,900 |  |

Also assume that a comparison of the post-closing trial balance for 1994 with the adjusted trial balance for 1995 shows the following *changes* in selected balance sheet accounts:

| Accounts receivable | $ 8,200 credit |
|---|---|
| Interest receivable | 1,200 debit |
| Inventory | 6,300 debit |
| Prepaid expenses | 600 debit |
| Accumulated depreciation | 11,000 credit |
| Accounts payable | 4,800 credit |
| Salaries payable | 500 debit |
| Income taxes payable | 300 credit |
| Discount on bonds payable | 200 credit |

Based on the preceding information, Exhibit 20-17 is prepared to determine each of the operating cash inflows and outflows. The $94,000 of sales revenue is increased by the $8,200 decrease (credit) in accounts receivable to determine the $102,200 collections from customers. This is because cash collections exceeded sales during the year. The $5,400 interest revenue is decreased by the $1,200 increase (debit) in inter-

**EXHIBIT 20-17**

**SCHEDULE TO COMPUTE OPERATING CASH FLOWS: BETHA COMPANY**

| Income Statement Amounts |  | Adjustments |  | | Operating Cash Flows |
|---|---|---|---|---|---|
| Sales | $ 94,000 | + Decrease in accounts receivable of | $8,200 | = $102,200 | Collections from customers |
| Interest revenue | 5,400 | − Increase in interest receivable of | 1,200 | = 4,200 | Interest collected |
|  |  |  |  | $106,400 | Operating cash inflows |
| Cost of goods sold | $(43,000) | + Increase in inventory of / − Increase in accounts payable of | 6,300 / 4,800 | = $ (44,500) | Payments to suppliers |
| Salaries expense | (18,500) | + Decrease in salaries payable of | 500 | = (19,000) | Payments to employees |
| Interest expense | (9,200) | − Decrease in discount on bonds payable (amortization) of | 200 | = (9,000) | Payments of interest |
| Other expenses | (4,700) | + Increase in prepaid expenses of | 600 | = (5,300) | Other operating payments |
| Income tax expense | (3,900) | − Increase in income taxes payable of | 300 | = (3,600) | Payments of income taxes |
|  |  |  |  | $ (81,400) | Operating cash outflows |
|  |  |  |  | $ 25,000 | Net cash provided by operating activities |

est receivable to determine the $4,200 interest collected because less cash was received than recorded as interest revenue. The total operating cash inflows were $106,400 in 1995.

The $43,000 cost of goods sold is adjusted for two items. It is increased for the $6,300 increase (debit) in inventory because purchases exceeded cost of goods sold by that amount. It is decreased by the $4,800 increase (credit) in accounts payable because cash payments were less than purchases. Thus, payments to suppliers totaled $44,500 in 1995. The $18,500 of salaries expense is increased by the $500 decrease (debit) in salaries payable to determine the $19,000 paid to employees, because salaries paid exceeded salaries expense. The discount on bonds payable account decreased (credit) because of the amortization of the discount. Recall that the amortization of discount on bonds payable increases interest expense to an amount greater than the cash paid for interest. Therefore, the $200 decrease (credit) to discount on bonds payable is subtracted from the $9,200 interest expense to determine the $9,000 interest paid. The $4,700 other expenses are increased by the $600 increase (debit) in prepaid expenses to determine the $5,300 other operating payments because cash payments for prepaid items exceeded expenses. Note that the $11,000 depreciation expense (debit) is the same as the $11,000 credit to accumulated depreciation. Because this is a "noncash" income statement item and is listed separately from other operating expenses, no adjustment is made for operating cash flows. The $3,900 income tax expense is decreased by the $300 increase (credit) to income taxes payable to determine the $3,600 payments of income taxes, because less taxes were paid than recorded as expense. The total operating cash outflows were $81,400 in 1995, so that $25,000 net cash was provided by operating activities during 1995.

The cash flows from operating activities section of the Betha Company's statement of cash flows, under the direct method, is shown in Exhibit 20-18. The cash flows from investing activities and the cash flows from financing activities are included in the usual manner to complete the statement of cash flows.

---

**EXHIBIT 20-18**

**BETHA COMPANY**

Statement of Cash Flows (Partial)
For Year Ended December 31, 1995

| | | |
|---|---:|---:|
| Cash Flows From Operating Activities | | |
| Cash Inflows: | | |
| Collections from customers | $102,200 | |
| Interest collected | 4,200 | |
| Cash inflows from operating activities | | $106,400 |
| Cash Outflows: | | |
| Payments to suppliers | $ (44,500) | |
| Payments to employees | (19,000) | |
| Payments of interest | (9,000) | |
| Other operating payments | (5,300) | |
| Payments of income taxes | (3,600) | |
| Cash outflows for operating activities | | (81,400) |
| Net cash provided by operating activities | | $ 25,000 |

## Worksheet Method

Under the worksheet approach, the steps completed using the direct method are very similar to those of the indirect method. There are enough slight differences, however, that all of the steps using the direct method are listed in Exhibit 20-19, after which an example is presented.

---

### EXHIBIT 20-19

#### STEPS IN WORKSHEET APPROACH FOR DIRECT METHOD

**Step 1.** Prepare the column headings on a worksheet (see Exhibit 20-20). Then enter the account titles and debit and credit amounts of the post-closing trial balance from the previous year and the adjusted trial balance for the current year in the respective columns. Total the amount columns to check the equality.

**Step 2.** Compare each account balance in the post-closing trial balance and adjusted trial balance, and record the debit or credit difference in the change column. Note that each revenue and expense account listed on the adjusted trial balance will not have a beginning balance, so that the ending balance is the change in the amount. (To simplify the worksheet, sometimes the debit and credit amounts of the accounts in the trial balances are omitted, and only the changes in the accounts are listed.) Total the amount columns to check the equality.

**Step 3.** Directly below the account titles, add the following headings:

A. Cash Flows From Operating Activities
B. Cash Flows From Investing Activities
C. Cash Flows From Financing Activities
D. Investing and Financing Activities Not Affecting Cash

Under the heading Cash Flows From Operating Activities, list the eight possible inflow and outflow captions (e.g., collections from customers). Leave sufficient room below each of the subheadings so that each cash flow may be listed where appropriate.

**Step 4.** Account for all the changes in the noncash accounts that occurred during the current period. *Reconstruct* the journal entries that caused the changes in the noncash accounts directly on the worksheet, making the necessary modifications to show the cash inflows and outflows related to operating, investing, and financing activities. Use the following general rules for the worksheet entries:

A. *Start with the routine, ongoing revenue and expense accounts.* The changes in these accounts during the year represent potential operating cash inflows or outflows. Therefore, the entry on the worksheet is to debit or credit the related operating cash inflow or outflow caption and to credit or debit the revenue or expense account. Observe that these changes represent potential cash flows. They may have to be adjusted later for changes in certain current assets (e.g., accounts receivable) and current liabilities (e.g., accounts payable) as well as other accounts to reflect the actual cash flows.

Note that there are two exceptions to the previous procedures. First, the worksheet entries for any noncash revenues and expenses (e.g., depreciation expense) are made in the usual manner, without any modifications.

Second, worksheet entries are *not* prepared at this time to account for gains or losses (either ordinary or extraordinary). The changes in these accounts will be accounted for later when dealing with the investing or financing transactions to which they relate (e.g., retirement of bonds at a gain).

**EXHIBIT 20-19, Continued**

B. *Account for the changes in the current asset (except cash) and current liability accounts.* Because nearly all of the changes in the current assets and current liabilities are part of the *operating cycle*, the impacts of these changes on cash are listed as adjustments to the related operating cash inflow or outflow. There are several exceptions to this procedure. These exceptions involve changes in short-term notes receivable and notes payable, changes in temporary investments (i.e., marketable securities), and changes in dividends payable. These changes are the results of investing or financing activities and are handled like the changes in the noncurrent accounts discussed in Step 4(C).

C. *Account for the changes in the remaining current assets (except cash) and current liabilities, as well as the changes in noncurrent accounts.* Review each account and determine the journal entry responsible for its change. Identify whether the transaction involves an operating,\* investing, or financing activity. If the transaction involved an investing or financing activity, make the entry on the worksheet with the following changes:

1. If the entry affects cash, replace a debit to cash with either an investing or financing cash inflow caption, and list the item as a debit (inflow) under the proper heading of the worksheet. Replace a credit to cash with a proper cash outflow caption, and list the item as a credit (outflow) under the proper heading of the worksheet. In the case of a transaction involving a gain or loss, record the gain or loss portion of the worksheet entry in the usual manner.

2. If the entry does not affect an operating activity or cash, it is a "simultaneous" financing and/or investing transaction. For this type of transaction, create "expanded" entries on the worksheet to record both the financing and/or investing activities. The first entry shows the financing aspect of the exchange, while the second entry shows the investing aspect. These types of transactions are disclosed on a schedule accompanying the statement of cash flows.

**Step 5.** Make a final worksheet entry to record the net change in cash. The worksheet entries must account for all the changes in the noncash accounts recorded in Step 2. The difference between the total cash inflows and outflows must be equal to the change in the Cash account. Total the debit and credit worksheet entries in the upper and lower portions of the worksheet to verify that the respective totals are equal.

**Step 6.** Prepare the statement of cash flows and accompanying schedule. Use the information developed in the *lower* portion of the worksheet, along with the beginning and ending cash balances.

---

\* The primary examples of changes in noncurrent accounts that affect operating activities are the amortization of premiums or discounts on bonds payable or investments in bonds, and changes in deferred taxes. In these cases, the related income statement item (interest expense or interest revenue, and income tax expense) has already been treated as an adjustment to an operating cash flow (payment of interest or receipt of interest, and payment of income taxes) in Step 4A. Therefore, the worksheet entry involves a direct adjustment to the operating cash flow. For instance, a change (credit) in discount on bonds payable due to amortization is accounted for as a debit to Cash Flows From Operating Activities: Payments of Interest and a credit to Discount on Bonds Payable to adjust for the lesser cash outflow.

## EXAMPLE: WORKSHEET AND DIRECT METHOD

To illustrate the use of a worksheet under the direct method, consider Exhibit 20-20. Assume that the post-closing trial balance and adjusted trial balance were obtained from the Copeland Company's accounting records. In addition, the following information was extracted from the accounting records for 1995:

1. Investments in nonmarketable securities costing $2,000 were sold for $2,800.

2. Equipment was purchased at a cost of $24,700.

3. Common stock was issued for $10,000.

4. Dividends of $3,500 were declared and paid.

After entering the accounts and amounts of the trial balances, the changes in the accounts are entered in the appropriate change column of the worksheet. Then, based on the preceding information, entries (a) through (r) are entered on the worksheet to complete it. Each of the worksheet entries is briefly explained next.

Entries (a) and (b) account for the sales and interest revenue and record the potential collections from customers and receipts of interest. (There are no other operating receipts.) Entries (c), (d), (e), (f), and (g) account for the cost of goods sold, salaries expense, interest expense, other expenses, and income tax expense, and record the potential payments to suppliers, payments to employees, payments of interest, other operating payments, and payments of income taxes. Entry (h) accounts for the depreciation expense and increase in accumulated depreciation. Note that it is made in the normal manner in the upper portion of the worksheet and, therefore, has no impact on the operating cash flows. The entry is necessary, however, to help account for the changes in all the income statement and balance sheet accounts.

Entries (i) through (m) account for the effect of the changes in the current assets and current liabilities on the "potential" operating cash flows recorded earlier. Entry (i) reduces the collections from customers because of the increase in accounts receivable. Entries (j) and (k) reduce the payments to suppliers because of the decrease in inventory and the increase in accounts payable. Entry (l) increases the payments to employees because of the decrease in salaries payable. Finally, entry (m) reduces the interest payments because of the increase in interest payable. There are no adjustments to the other operating payments or to the payments of income taxes in this example.

Entries (n) through (q) record the investing and financing cash flows. Entry (n) records the $2,800 investing cash inflow from the sale of investments costing $2,000. Note that the $800 gain is recorded in the usual manner and accounts for that respective income statement item. Entry (o) records the investing cash outflow for the purchase of equipment. Entry (p) records the financing cash inflow from the sale of common stock. Entry (q) records the financing cash outflow for the payment of dividends.

Entry (r) is the final entry and records the increase in cash. The debit and credit columns in the upper and lower portions are totaled to check for equality and the worksheet is complete. The statement of cash flows of the Copeland Company, prepared from the worksheet in Exhibit 20-20, is shown in Exhibit 20-21. Note that the only difference between this statement prepared under the direct method and a statement of cash flows prepared under the indirect method is in the presentation of the cash flows from operating activities. (Remember, however, that a separate schedule

## EXHIBIT 20-20

## COPELAND COMPANY

### Worksheet for Statement of Cash Flows
### For Year Ended December 31, 1995

| Accounts | 12/31/94 Post-Closing Trial Balance Debit | Credit | 12/31/95 Adjusted Trial Balance Debit | Credit | Change Debit | Credit | Worksheet Entries Debit | | Credit | |
|---|---|---|---|---|---|---|---|---|---|---|
| Cash | 5,300 | | 9,800 | | 4,500 | | (r) | 4,500 | | |
| Accounts receivable | 9,600 | | 10,900 | | 1,300 | | (i) | 1,300 | | |
| Inventory | 12,500 | | 11,000 | | | 1,500 | | | (j) | 1,500 |
| Investments | 22,000 | | 20,000 | | | 2,000 | | | (n) | 2,000 |
| Property and equipment | 82,600 | | 107,300 | | 24,700 | | (o) | 24,700 | | |
| Accumulated depreciation | | 32,800 | | 41,900 | | 9,100 | | | (h) | 9,100 |
| Accounts payable | | 10,300 | | 12,100 | | 1,800 | | | (k) | 1,800 |
| Salaries payable | | 1,100 | | 800 | 300 | | (l) | 300 | | |
| Interest payable | | 300 | | 500 | | 200 | | | (m) | 200 |
| Notes payable | | 34,000 | | 34,000 | | 0 | | | | |
| Common stock, no par | | 30,000 | | 40,000 | | 10,000 | | | (p) | 10,000 |
| Retained earnings | | 23,500 | | 20,000 | 3,500 | | (q) | 3,500 | | |
| Sales | | | | 98,700 | | 98,700 | | | (a) | 98,700 |
| Interest revenue | | | | 2,500 | | 2,500 | | | (b) | 2,500 |
| Gain on sale of investments | | | | 800 | | 800 | | | (n) | 800 |
| Cost of goods sold | | | 51,000 | | 51,000 | | (c) | 51,000 | | |
| Salaries expense | | | 23,000 | | 23,000 | | (d) | 23,000 | | |
| Depreciation expense | | | 9,100 | | 9,100 | | (h) | 9,100 | | |
| Interest expense | | | 4,000 | | 4,000 | | (e) | 4,000 | | |
| Other expenses | | | 1,900 | | 1,900 | | (f) | 1,900 | | |
| Income tax expense | | | 3,300 | | 3,300 | | (g) | 3,300 | | |
| **Totals** | 132,000 | 132,000 | 251,300 | 251,300 | 126,600 | 126,600 | | 126,600 | | 126,600 |

| | | | |
|---|---|---|---|
| **Cash Flows From Operating Activities** | | | |
| Collections from customers | (a) | 98,700 | (i) 1,300 |
| Interest and dividends collected | (b) | 2,500 | |
| Other operating receipts | | | |
| Payments to suppliers | (j) | 1,500 | (c) 51,000 |
| | (k) | 1,800 | |
| Payments to employees | | | (d) 23,000 |
| | | | (l) 300 |
| Payments of interest | (m) | 200 | (e) 4,000 |
| Other operating payments | | | (f) 1,900 |
| Payments of income taxes | | | (g) 3,300 |
| **Cash Flows From Investing Activities** | | | |
| Proceeds from sale of investments | (n) | 2,800 | |
| Payment for purchase of equipment | | | (o) 24,700 |
| **Cash Flows From Financing Activities** | | | |
| Proceeds from issuance of common stock | (p) | 10,000 | |
| Payment of dividends | | | (q) 3,500 |
| Net Increase in Cash | | | (r) 4,500 |
| **Totals** | | 117,500 | 117,500 |

reconciling net income to the net cash provided by operating activities would accompany the statement of cash flows under the direct method; the schedule is not illustrated here.) The presentations of the cash flows from investing and financing activities are identical under both methods. Although most companies will continue to use the indirect method, with the encouragement of the FASB, more companies are likely to begin using the direct method.

---

### EXHIBIT 20-21

**COPELAND COMPANY**

Statement of Cash Flows
For Year Ended December 31, 1995

| | | |
|---|---:|---:|
| **Cash Flows From Operating Activities** | | |
| Cash Inflows: | | |
| Collections from customers | $ 97,400 | |
| Interest and dividends collected | 2,500 | |
| Cash inflows from operating activities | | $99,900 |
| Cash Outflows: | | |
| Payments to suppliers | $(47,700) | |
| Payments to employees | (23,300) | |
| Payments of interest | (3,800) | |
| Other operating payments | (1,900) | |
| Payments of income taxes | (3,300) | |
| Cash outflows for operating activities | | (80,000) |
| Net cash provided by operating activities | | $19,900 |
| | | |
| **Cash Flows From Investing Activities** | | |
| Proceeds from sale of investments | $  2,800 | |
| Payment for purchase of equipment | (24,700) | |
| Net cash used for investing activities | | (21,900) |
| | | |
| **Cash Flows From Financing Activities** | | |
| Proceeds from issuance of common stock | $ 10,000 | |
| Payment of dividends | (3,500) | |
| Net cash provided by financing activities | | 6,500 |
| Net Increase in Cash | | $ 4,500 |
| Cash, January 1, 1995 | | 5,300 |
| Cash, December 31, 1995 | | $ 9,800 |

---

## QUESTIONS

**Q20-1**   What is a *statement of cash flows*?

**Q20-2**   Briefly describe the three types of activities reported in a statement of cash flows.

**Q20-3**   What does the information in a statement of cash flows help external users to assess?

**Q20-4**   Name the five items a statement of cash flows must clearly show. What items are reported in a separate schedule accompanying the statement?

**Q20-5**   What are "cash equivalents"? How does a company's reporting on its cash and cash equivalents affect the statement of cash flows?

**Q20-6** What are the three categories of inflows of cash? What are the three categories of outflows of cash?

**Q20-7** Starting with the basic accounting equation, derive a set of equations that illustrate the relationship between increases (decreases) in cash and increases (decreases) in assets other than cash, liabilities, and stockholders' equity.

**Q20-8** Briefly describe a company's operating cycle and the relationship of its various stages to cash inflows and outflows.

**Q20-9** What are the two ways to calculate and report a company's net cash flow from operating activities? Briefly describe each method.

**Q20-10** Briefly describe the *indirect method* for reporting a company's net cash flow from operating activities. List several adjustments to net income and indicate whether they are additions or subtractions.

**Q20-11** Give two examples of (a) cash inflows from investing activities and (b) cash outflows for investing activities.

**Q20-12** Give two examples of (a) cash inflows from financing activities and (b) cash outflows for financing activities.

**Q20-13** Give two examples of investing and financing activities not affecting cash.

**Q20-14** What is the *visual inspection method*? List the steps in this method.

**Q20-15** Briefly describe the *worksheet method* of analyzing the information for the statement of cash flows. (Do *not* list the steps in preparation.)

**Q20-16** Indicate how a company would compute the amount of interest and income taxes that it paid during the year.

**Q20-17** What two alternatives are allowed for *where* the net cash flow from operating activities prepared under the indirect method may be disclosed in regard to the statement of cash flows?

**Q20-18** A company purchases equipment costing $12,500 by paying $5,000 down and signing a $7,500 note payable. Illustrate two ways of disclosing the effects of this transaction in regard to the statement of cash flows.

**Q20-19** (*Appendix*). Define the *direct* method of reporting the cash flows from operating activities.

**Q20-20** (*Appendix*). List the three operating cash inflows reported under the direct method.

**Q20-21** (*Appendix*). List the five operating cash outflows reported under the direct method.

**Q20-22** (*Appendix*). Briefly describe how to determine each of the operating cash inflows and operating cash outflows under the direct method.

## CASES

### C20-1  Financial Statement Interrelationships
Prepare an outline of the general format of the statement of cash flows (indirect method). Include examples of cash inflows and outflows that would be reported under each major section. Finally, discuss the information that is disclosed on the income statement, balance sheet, and statement of cash flows, respectively, that is not disclosed on the other statements.

### C20-2  Statement of Cash Flows
A friend of yours is taking an elementary accounting course. He says, "I understand the income statement and balance sheet, but I am confused by the statement of cash flows (and accompanying schedule). What is this statement, what is it useful for, what are its major sections, and what items are reported in each section and the accompanying schedule? I need to understand this statement better so I can do well in my class."

**Required**
Prepare a written response to your friend's questions.

### C20-3  Cash Flow Activities
A statement of cash flows shows the cash inflows, cash outflows, and net change in cash from the operating, investing, and financing activities of a company during an accounting period.

**Required**
Define operating, investing, and financing activities, and identify the cash inflows and cash outflows related to each activity.

### C20-4  Worksheet Method
The worksheet method is commonly used to analyze the information for preparing the statement of cash flows. This method involves the completion of several steps.

**Required**
Describe the worksheet method and list and briefly discuss the steps in this method.

## C20-5   Operating Cash Flows

There are two methods to calculate and report a company's net cash provided by (or used in) operating activities.

### Required

Identify the two methods and discuss the calculations necessary for each method.

## C20-6   Financing and Investing Activities Not Involving Cash

The statement of cash flows is normally a required basic financial statement for each period for which an earnings statement is presented. The statement should include a separate schedule listing the financing and investing activities not involving cash.

### Required

1. What are financing and investing activities not involving cash?
2. What are two types of financing and investing activities not involving cash?
3. What effect, if any, would each of the following seven items have on the statement of cash flows?
   a. Accounts receivable.
   b. Inventory.
   c. Depreciation.
   d. Deferred tax liability.
   e. Issuance of long-term debt in payment for a building.
   f. Payoff of current portion of debt.
   g. Sale of a fixed asset resulting in a loss. (*AICPA adapted*)

## C20-7   Inflows and Outflows

Alfred Engineering Company is a young and growing producer of electronic measuring instruments and technical equipment. You have been retained by Alfred to advise it in the preparation of a statement of cash flows. For the fiscal year ended October 31, 1995, you have obtained the following information concerning certain events and transactions of Alfred:

1. The amount of reported earnings for the fiscal year was $800,000.
2. Depreciation expense of $240,000 was included in the earnings statement.
3. Uncollectible accounts receivable of $30,000 were written off against the allowance for uncollectible accounts. Also, $37,000 of bad debts expense was included in determining earnings for the fiscal year, and the same amount was added to the allowance for uncollectible accounts.
4. A gain of $4,700 was realized on the sale of a machine; it originally cost $75,000, of which $25,000 was undepreciated on the date of sale.

5. On July 3, 1995, building and land were purchased for $600,000; Alfred gave in payment $100,000 cash, $200,000 market value of its unissued common stock, and a $300,000 mortgage.
6. On August 3, 1995, $700,000 face value of Alfred's 6% convertible debentures were converted into $140,000 par value of its common stock. The bonds were originally issued at face value.
7. The board of directors declared a $320,000 cash dividend on October 20, 1995, payable on November 16, 1995 to stockholders of record on November 6, 1995.

### Required

For each of the seven items, explain whether each is an inflow or outflow of cash and explain how it should be disclosed in Alfred's statement of cash flows (indirect method) for the fiscal year ended October 31, 1995. If any item is neither an inflow nor outflow of cash, explain why it is not and indicate the disclosure, if any, that should be made of the item in Alfred's statement of cash flows for the fiscal year ended October 31, 1995. (*AICPA adapted*)

## C20-8 Researching GAAP   ⓪

You are the new accountant for 12th National Bank and are preparing its 1995 statement of cash flows. The bank reports net income of $75,800 on its 1995 income statement. Included in this net income are the following items: $6,700 gain on sale of trading securities, $1,200 unrealized holding gain on trading securities, and $5,100 loss on sale of securities available for sale. Among its 1995 transactions, the bank sold trading securities with a carrying value of $22,900 for $29,600, and purchased trading securities for $65,200. The bank sold securities available for sale with a cost (and carrying value) of $58,700 for $53,600, and purchased securities available for sale for $39,400. It also made routine 90-day loans of $47,500 to customers and collected $20,000 principal on these types of customer loans. As a result of the preceding information, the bank's trading securities account increased by $43,500, the securities available for sale account decreased by $19,300, and the loans receivable account increased by $27,500. The bank uses the indirect approach to report operating cash flows on its statement of cash flows.

### Required

Research the applicable generally accepted accounting principles and prepare a written memo to the 12th National Bank's auditors that explains how you plan to report the preceding items on the bank's 1995 statement of cash flows. Cite your reference and applicable paragraph numbers.

## MULTIPLE CHOICE

*Select the best answer for each of the following.*

M20-1  If a company issues a balance sheet and an income statement with comparative figures from last year, a statement of cash flows

    a.  Is no longer necessary; but may be issued at the company's option

    b.  Should not be issued

    c.  Should be issued for each period for which an income statement is presented

    d.  Should be issued for the current year only

M20-2  Selected information from Brook Corporation's accounting records and financial statements for 1995 is as follows:

| | |
|---|---|
| Net cash provided by operating activities | $1,500,000 |
| Mortgage payable issued to acquire land and building | 1,800,000 |
| Common stock issued to retire preferred stock | 500,000 |
| Proceeds from sale of equipment | 400,000 |
| Cost of office equipment purchased | 200,000 |

On the statement of cash flows for the year ended December 31, 1995, Brook should disclose a net increase in cash in the amount of

    a.  $1,700,000

    b.  $2,400,000

    c.  $3,700,000

    d.  $4,200,000

M20-3  In a statement of cash flows (indirect method), the amortization of goodwill of a company with substantial operating profits should be presented as a (an)

    a.  Cash flow from investing activities

    b.  Cash flow from financing activities

    c.  Deduction from net income

    d.  Addition to net income

M20-4  The net cash provided by operating activities in Seat's statement of cash flows for 1995 was $8,000,000. For 1995, depreciation on fixed assets was $3,800,000, amortization of goodwill was $100,000, and dividends on common stock were $2,000,000. Based on the preceding information, Seat's net income for 1995 was

    a.  $2,100,000

    b.  $4,100,000

    c.  $8,000,000

    d.  $11,900,000

M20-5  The retirement of long-term debt by the issuance of common stock should be presented in a statement of cash flows as a

| | Cash Flow From Financing Activities | Cash Flow From Investing Activities |
|---|---|---|
| a. | No | No |
| b. | No | Yes |
| c. | Yes | No |
| d. | Yes | Yes |

M20-6  The net income for Mountain Corporation was $4,000,000 for the year ended December 31, 1995. Additional information is as follows:

| | |
|---|---|
| Depreciation on fixed assets | $2,000,000 |
| Proceeds from sale of land | 200,000 |
| Increase in accounts payable | 300,000 |
| Dividends on preferred stock | 400,000 |

The net cash provided by operating activities in the statement of cash flows for the year ended December 31, 1995 should be

a.  $6,000,000                        c.  $6,300,000
b.  $6,100,000                        d.  $6,500,000

M20-7  Which of the following need not be disclosed in a schedule accompanying the statement of cash flows as an investing and financing activity not affecting cash?

a.  Acquisition of fixed assets in exchange for capital stock
b.  Dividend paid in capital stock of the company (stock dividend)
c.  Retirement of a bond issue through the issuance of another bond issue
d.  Conversion of convertible debt to capital stock

M20-8  The following information on selected transactions for 1995 has been provided by the Smith Company:

| | |
|---|---:|
| Net income | $20,000,000 |
| Proceeds from short-term borrowings | 1,200,000 |
| Proceeds from long-term borrowings | 4,000,000 |
| Purchases of fixed assets | 3,200,000 |
| Decrease in inventories | 8,000,000 |
| Proceeds from sale of Smith's common stock | 2,000,000 |
| Depreciation expense | 500,000 |

What is the net increase in cash for the year ended December 31, 1995 as a result of the preceding information?

a.  $32,500,000                        c.  $16,500,000
b.  $25,700,000                        d.  $12,500,000

M20-9  The following information was taken from the accounting records of Oregon Corporation for 1995:

| | |
|---|---:|
| Proceeds from issuance of preferred stock | $4,000,000 |
| Dividends paid on preferred stock | 400,000 |
| Bonds payable converted to common stock | 2,000,000 |
| Payment for purchase of machinery | 500,000 |
| Proceeds from sale of plant building | 1,200,000 |
| 2% stock dividend on common stock | 300,000 |
| Gain on sale of plant building | 200,000 |

Oregon's statement of cash flows for the year ended December 31, 1995 should show the following amounts for investing and financing activities, based on the preceding information:

| | Net Cash Flows From Investing Activities | Net Cash Flows From Financing Activities |
|---|---|---|
| a. | $700,000 | $3,600,000 |
| b. | $700,000 | $3,900,000 |
| c. | $900,000 | $3,900,000 |
| d. | $900,000 | $5,600,000 |

M20-10  (*Appendix*). A company reports sales of $200,000 and interest revenue of $17,000 for the current year. During the year, accounts receivable increased by $21,000 and interest receivable decreased by $3,000. Under the direct method, the company would report cash inflows from operating activities of

a.  $235,000                        c.  $241,000
b.  $193,000                        d.  $199,000

## EXERCISES

E20-1     *Classification of Cash Flows*    The following are several transactions and events that might be disclosed on a company's statement of cash flows:

1. Issuance of common stock
2. Purchase of building
3. Net income
4. Increase in accounts receivable
5. Depreciation expense
6. Sale of land at cost
7. Conversion of bonds to common stock
8. Increase in accounts payable
9. Payment of cash dividends
10. Issuance of a stock dividend

**Required**

Identify in which section (if any) of the statement of cash flows each of the preceding items would appear and indicate whether it would be an inflow (addition) or outflow (subtraction).

E20-2     *Net Cash Flow From Operating Activities*    The following is accounting information taken from the Hyde Company's records for 1995:

1. Amortization of premium on bonds payable, $600
2. Purchase of equipment, $6,000
3. Depreciation expense, $7,400
4. Decrease in accounts receivable, $800
5. Decrease in accounts payable, $2,800
6. Issuance of long-term note for cash, $4,200
7. Increase in inventories, $7,500
8. Gain on sale of land, $8,000
9. Increase in prepaid assets, $500
10. Declaration and payment of cash dividends, $1,800
11. Increase in wages payable, $300
12. Patent amortization expense, $1,000
13. Net income, $11,000

**Required**

Prepare the net cash flow from operating activities section of the 1995 statement of cash flows for the Hyde Company.

E20-3     *Statement of Cash Flows*    The following is a list of the items to be included in the 1995 statement of cash flows of the Roering Company:

1. Depreciation expense, $4,200
2. Proceeds from sale of land, $5,600
3. Payment of dividends, $5,000
4. Net income, $7,900
5. Conversion of bonds to common stock, $7,000
6. Increase in accounts payable, $3,100
7. Proceeds from issuance of note, $6,200
8. Gain on sale of land, $1,800
9. Payment for purchase of building, $13,000
10. Increase in accounts receivable, $2,700
11. Ending cash balance, $13,900

**Required**

Prepare the statement of cash flows.

E20-4     *Statement of Cash Flows*    The following is a list of items to be included in the 1995 statement of cash flows of the Witts Company:

1. Proceeds from sale of equipment, $2,700
2. Increase in inventory, $3,900
3. Net income, $14,100
4. Payment for purchase of building, $29,000
5. Depreciation expense, $8,700
6. Proceeds from issuance of bonds, $8,000
7. Increase in prepaid expenses, $800
8. Loss on sale of equipment, $2,200
9. Payment of dividends, $5,200
10. Decrease in accounts receivable, $1,700
11. Issuance of common stock for land, $6,900
12. Decrease in accounts payable, $1,500
13. Beginning cash balance, $12,200

**Required**

Prepare the statement of cash flows.

E20-5   *Direct and Indirect Methods*   The Dean Company reported the following condensed income statement for 1995:

| | | |
|---|---|---|
| Sales | | $100,000 |
| Cost of goods sold | | (58,000) |
| Gross profit | | $ 42,000 |
| Operating expenses: | | |
| Depreciation expense | $ 8,000 | |
| Salaries expense | 12,000 | (20,000) |
| Income before income taxes | | $ 22,000 |
| Income tax expense | | (6,600) |
| Net income | | $ 15,400 |

During 1995, the following changes occurred in the company's current assets and current liabilities:

| | Increase (Decrease) |
|---|---|
| Cash | $3,700 |
| Accounts receivable | (5,500) |
| Inventories | 8,900 |
| Accounts payable (purchases) | (4,600) |
| Salaries payable | 2,800 |

**Required**
1. By visual inspection, prepare the net cash flow from operating activities section of the Dean Company's 1995 statement of cash flows using the indirect method.
2. By visual inspection, prepare the net cash flow from operating activities section of the Dean Company's 1995 statement of cash flows using the direct method.

E20-6   *Fixed Asset Transactions*   The following is an Equipment account and its associated Accumulated Depreciation account:

| Equipment | | | |
|---|---|---|---|
| Beginning | | | |
| balance | $49,000 | Machine A | 8,100 |
| Machine C | 25,000 | Machine B | 5,200 |
| Ending | | | |
| balance | $60,700 | | |

| Accumulated Depreciation | | | |
|---|---|---|---|
| Related to | | Beginning | |
| Machine A | 6,300 | balance | $29,000 |
| Related to | | Depreciation | |
| Machine B | 4,600 | expense | 12,000 |
| | | Ending | |
| | | balance | $30,100 |

Additional data:
1. Machine A was sold at a gain of $900.
2. Machine B was sold for its scrap value of $200.
3. Machine C was acquired during the year.

**Required**
Analyze the two accounts shown and illustrate, in journal entry form, the entries that would be made in preparation of the statement of cash flows to reflect all of the changes listed in the accounts.

E20-7   *Visual Inspection*   The following changes in account balances and other information for 1995 were taken from the accounting records of the Gordon Company:

| | Net Changes for 1995 | |
|---|---|---|
| | Debit | Credit |
| Cash | $ 1,000 | |
| Accounts receivable | | $ 1,100 |
| Inventory | 2,000 | |
| Buildings and equipment | 8,800 | |
| Accumulated depreciation | | 2,900 |
| Accounts payable | 900 | |
| Common stock, no par | | 5,500 |
| Retained earnings | | 3,200 |
| | $12,700 | $12,700 |

Other information: Net income totaled $6,200. Dividends were declared and paid. Equipment was purchased for $8,800. No buildings and equipment were sold during the year. One hundred shares of common stock were sold for $55 per share. The ending cash balance was $3,900.

**Required**

Using visual inspection, prepare a 1995 statement of cash flows for the Gordon Company.

E20-8 *Visual Inspection* The following changes in account balances and other information for 1995 were taken from the accounting records of the Sampson Company:

| | Net Changes for 1995 | |
|---|---|---|
| | Debit | Credit |
| Cash | | $ 2,000 |
| Accounts receivable | $ 1,900 | |
| Inventory | | 2,400 |
| Land | | 1,700 |
| Buildings and equipment | 23,000 | |
| Accumulated depreciation | | 4,500 |
| Accounts payable | | 1,600 |
| Salaries payable | 600 | |
| Bonds payable | | 5,000 |
| Common stock, no par | | 3,000 |
| Retained earnings | | 5,300 |
| | $25,500 | $25,500 |

Other information: Net income was $9,900. Dividends were declared and paid. Land was sold for $1,700; a building was purchased for $23,000. No land was purchased and no buildings and equipment were sold. Bonds payable were issued at the end of the year. Two hundred shares of stock were issued for $15 per share. The beginning cash balance was $4,800.

**Required**

Using visual inspection, prepare a 1995 statement of cash flows for the Sampson Company.

E20-9 *Balance Sheet* The following beginning balance sheet and statement of cash flows for 1995 are available for Braun Company:

| Balance Sheet January 1, 1995 | | | | |
|---|---|---|---|---|
| Cash | | $ 900 | Accounts payable | $ 1,600 |
| Accounts receivable | | 2,300 | Notes payable | 3,900 |
| Land | | 4,900 | Common stock, $5 par | 4,500 |
| Equipment | $20,000 | | Additional paid-in capital | 1,800 |
| Less: Accumulated depreciation | (9,100) | 10,900 | Retained earnings | 7,200 |
| Total assets | | $19,000 | Total liabilities and stockholders' equity | $19,000 |

### Statement of Cash Flows
### For Year Ended December 31, 1995

| | | |
|---|---:|---:|
| Net Cash Flow From Operating Activities | | |
| Net income | | $3,900 |
| Adjustments for differences between income flows | | |
| and cash flows from operating activities: | | |
| Add: Depreciation expense | | 900 |
| Increase in accounts payable | | 100 |
| Less: Increase in accounts receivable | | (700) |
| Gain on sale of land | | (200) |
| Net cash provided by operating activities | | $4,000 |
| Cash Flows From Investing Activities | | |
| Payment for purchase of equipment | $(5,000) | |
| Proceeds from sale of land | 1,200 | |
| Net cash used for investing activities | | (3,800) |
| Cash Flows From Financing Activities | | |
| Proceeds from issuance of common stock (200 shares) | $ 2,600 | |
| Payment of long-term note | (900) | |
| Payment of dividends | (1,300) | |
| Net cash provided by financing activities | | 400 |
| Net Increase in Cash | | $ 600 |
| Cash, January 1, 1995 | | 900 |
| Cash, December 31, 1995 | | $1,500 |

**Required**

On the basis of this information, prepare a balance sheet for the Braun Company as of December 31, 1995.

**E20-10  Erroneous Statement of Cash Flows**  The 1995 statement of cash flows for the Andell Company, as developed by its bookkeeper, is shown here:

### Cash Flows Statement
### December 31, 1995

| | | |
|---|---:|---:|
| *Inflows of Cash* | | |
| Operating Activities | | |
| Net income | | $11,300 |
| Add: Proceeds from sale of equipment | | 3,800 |
| Proceeds from issuance of stock | | 4,300 |
| Less: Payment for investment in bonds | | (6,000) |
| Payment of long-term note | | (5,000) |
| Net cash inflows from operations | | $ 8,400 |
| Other Inflows | | |
| Decrease in accounts receivable | $ 2,100 | |
| Depreciation expense | 4,800 | |
| Total other inflows of cash | | 6,900 |
| Total inflows of cash | | $15,300 |
| *Outflows of Cash* | | |
| Payment for purchase of land | $(5,200) | |
| Decrease in accounts payable | (2,800) | |
| Payment of dividends | (3,000) | |
| Gain on sale of equipment | (700) | |
| Total outflows of cash | | (11,700) |
| Net Increase in Cash | | $ 3,600 |
| Cash, December 31, 1995 | | 12,300 |
| Cash, January 1, 1995 | | $ 8,700 |

You determine that the *amounts* of the items listed on the statement are correct, but in certain circumstances, incorrectly classified.

**Required**

Prepare a corrected 1995 statement of cash flows for the Andell Company.

E20-11 *Partially Completed Worksheet*  The Ellis Company has prepared the following changes in account balances for the worksheet to support its 1995 statement of cash flows:

| Account Title | Increase (Decrease) | Worksheet Entries Debit | Credit | Account Title | Increase (Decrease) | Worksheet Entries Debit | Credit |
|---|---|---|---|---|---|---|---|
| | *Debits* | | | | *Credits* | | |
| Cash | $ 830 | | | Accumulated depreciation | $ 350 | | |
| *Noncash Accounts:* | | | | Accounts payable | 120 | | |
| Accounts receivable | (290) | | | Bonds payable | 2,000 | | |
| Inventory | 1,280 | | | Premium on bonds payable | 300 | | |
| Investments | 1,550 | | | Common stock, $2 par | 480 | | |
| Land | (700) | | | Premium on common stock | 1,120 | | |
| Equipment | 2,300 | | | Retained earnings | 500 | | |
| Patents (net) | (100) | | | Total | $4,870 | | |
| Total | $4,870 | | | | | | |

Additional information: The net income was $1,300. Depreciation expense was $350 and patent amortization expense was $100. Cash dividends declared and paid totaled $600. Forty shares of common stock were issued as a "small" stock dividend, the relevant market price being $5 per share. At the end of 1995, long-term investments were purchased at a cost of $1,550. Land that cost $700 was sold for $900. Two hundred shares of common stock were issued at $7 per share. On December 30, 1995, bonds payable with a face value of $2,000 were issued for equipment valued at $2,300.

**Required**

On the basis of the preceding information, align the accounts with credit changes below the accounts with debit changes and complete the worksheet.

E20-12 *Worksheet*  The following 1995 information is available for the Payne Company:

| | Comparative Balance Sheets | |
|---|---|---|
| | January 1, 1995 | December 31, 1995 |
| Cash | $ 400 | $ 700 |
| Accounts receivable | 220 | 200 |
| Inventory | 370 | 610 |
| Land | 250 | 410 |
| Equipment | 2,070 | 2,200 |
| Less: Accumulated depreciation | (310) | (400) |
| Total assets | $3,000 | $3,720 |
| Accounts payable | $ 800 | $ 500 |
| Notes payable (long-term) | 900 | 720 |
| Common stock, no par | 600 | 1,000 |
| Retained earnings | 700 | 1,500 |
| Total liabilities and stockholders' equity | $3,000 | $3,720 |

Partial additional information: The net income for 1995 totaled $1,500. During 1995, the company sold for $390 equipment that cost $390 and had a book value of $300. The company sold land for $200, resulting in a loss of $40. The remaining change in the Land account resulted from the purchase of land through the issuance of common stock.

**Required**

Making whatever additional assumptions that are necessary, prepare a worksheet to support the 1995 statement of cash flows for the Payne Company.

**E20-13** *Worksheet and Statement*    The following 1995 information is available for the Harris Company:

| Condensed Income Statement for 1995 | |
|---|---|
| Sales | $9,000 |
| Cost of goods sold | (6,000) |
| Other expenses | (2,000) |
| Loss on sale of equipment | (260) |
| Gain on sale of land | 400 |
| Net income | $1,140 |

| | Comparative Balance Sheets | |
|---|---|---|
| | January 1, 1995 | December 31, 1995 |
| Cash | $ 700 | $1,130 |
| Accounts receivable | 450 | 310 |
| Inventory | 350 | 400 |
| Land | 300 | 500 |
| Equipment | 1,600 | 1,800 |
| Less: Accumulated depreciation | (200) | (150) |
| Total assets | $3,200 | $3,990 |
| Accounts payable | $ 600 | $ 750 |
| Bonds payable (due 1/1/2000) | 1,000 | 1,000 |
| Common stock, $10 par | 900 | 1,400 |
| Retained earnings | 700 | 840 |
| Total liabilities and stockholders' equity | $3,200 | $3,990 |

Partial additional information:
1. The equipment that was sold for cash had cost $400 and had a book value of $300.
2. Land that was sold brought a cash price of $530.
3. Fifty shares of stock were issued at par.

**Required**
Making whatever additional assumptions that are necessary:
1. Prepare a worksheet to support a statement of cash flows for the Harris Company for 1995.
2. Prepare the statement of cash flows.

**E20-14** *Interest and Income Taxes*    The Staggs Company has prepared its 1995 statement of cash flows. In conjunction with this statement, it plans to disclose the interest and income taxes it paid during 1995. The following information is available from its 1995 income statement and beginning and ending balance sheet:

| Income Statement | |
|---|---|
| Interest expense | $11,600 |
| Income tax expense | 35,200 |

| | Balance Sheet | |
|---|---|---|
| | Cr. Bal. 01/01/95 | Cr. Bal. 12/31/95 |
| Interest payable | $ 600 | $ 2,300 |
| Income taxes payable | 5,000 | 3,000 |
| Bonds payable | 80,000 | 80,000 |
| Premium on bonds payable | 9,000 | 8,100 |
| Deferred taxes payable | 3,300 | 4,400 |

**Required**

Compute the amounts of interest paid and income taxes paid by the Staggs Company for 1995.

E20-15 *Investments*   On October 6, 1994, Collins Company purchased 100 shares of Steph Company common stock for $64 per share as a temporary investment in securities available for sale. On December 31, 1994, the stock had a fair value of $63 per share, and on February 8, 1995, Collins sold the stock for $67 per share.

**Required**

In journal entry form, prepare the worksheet entries to record these transactions for the 1994 and 1995 statement of cash flows.

E20-16 *Appendix: Operating Cash Flows*   Use the information in E20-13.

**Required**

Based only on the information presented, using the direct method, prepare the cash flows from operating activities section of the 1995 statement of cash flows for the Harris Company.

E20-17 *Appendix: Operating Cash Flows*   The following is accounting information taken from the adjusted trial balance of the Woodrail Company for 1995:

|  | Debit | Credit |
|---|---|---|
| Sales |  | $72,000 |
| Interest revenue |  | 4,300 |
| Cost of goods sold | $37,500 |  |
| Salaries expense | 13,600 |  |
| Interest expense | 5,400 |  |
| Income tax expense | 3,000 |  |

In addition, the following changes occurred in selected accounts during 1995:

| | |
|---|---|
| Accounts receivable | $6,100 credit |
| Inventory | 9,800 debit |
| Accounts payable | 7,000 credit |
| Salaries payable | 900 debit |
| Interest payable | 400 credit |

**Required**

Using the direct method, prepare the cash flows from operating activities section of the 1995 statement of cash flows for the Woodrail Company.

E20-18 *Appendix: Statement of Cash Flows*   The following is a list of items to be included in the 1995 statement of cash flows of the Thomas Company:

1. Payments to suppliers, $31,500
2. Other operating receipts, $1,200
3. Payments of dividends, $4,000
4. Payments of income taxes, $5,000
5. Collections from customers, $68,400
6. Payment for purchase of equipment, $18,500
7. Payments to employees, $19,300
8. Interest and dividends collected, $7,100
9. Other operating payments, $900
10. Proceeds from issuance of bonds, $11,300
11. Payments of interest, $8,400
12. Proceeds from sale of investments, $6,000
13. Beginning cash balance, $28,400

**Required**

Prepare the statement of cash flows, using the direct method for operating cash flows.

**E20-19** *Appendix: Visual Inspection*   The following changes in account balances were taken from the adjusted trial balance of the Walson Company at the end of 1995:

| | Net Changes for 1995 | |
| --- | --- | --- |
| | Debit | Credit |
| Cash | $ 1,800 | |
| Accounts receivable | 9,000 | |
| Inventory | | $ 2,500 |
| Land | | 1,900 |
| Buildings and equipment | 10,400 | |
| Accumulated depreciation | | 6,800 |
| Accounts payable | 4,500 | |
| Salaries payable | | 800 |
| Income taxes payable | | 1,000 |
| Common stock, no par | | 9,000 |
| Retained earnings | 4,000 | |
| Sales | | 75,000 |
| Cost of goods sold | 40,000 | |
| Salaries expense | 17,200 | |
| Depreciation expense | 6,800 | |
| Income tax expense | 3,300 | |
| Totals | $97,000 | $97,000 |

In addition, the following information was obtained from the company's records:

1. Land was sold, at cost, for $1,900.
2. Dividends of $4,000 were declared and paid.
3. Equipment was purchased for $10,400.
4. Common stock was issued for $9,000.
5. Beginning cash balance was $17,000.

**Required**

Using visual inspection and the direct method, prepare a 1995 statement of cash flows for the Walson Company. (A separate schedule reconciling net income to cash provided by operating activities is not necessary.)

# PROBLEMS

**P20-1**   *Classifications of Cash Flows*   A company's statement of cash flows or accompanying schedule of investing and financing activities not affecting cash may contain the following major sections:

A. Net Cash Flow From Operating Activities
B. Cash Flows From Investing Activities
C. Cash Flows From Financing Activities
D. Investing and Financing Activities Not Affecting Cash

The following is a list of items that might appear on a company's statement of cash flows or accompanying schedule.

1. Decrease in accounts payable
2. Payment of dividends
3. Increase in income taxes payable
4. Proceeds from issuance of note
5. Payment for purchase of temporary investments available for sale
6. Amortization of premium on investment in bonds
7. Increase in prepaid expenses
8. Payment of note
9. Gain on sale of equipment
10. Proceeds from sale of land
11. Net income
12. Payment for acquisition of building

13. Depreciation expense
14. Issuance of common stock for land
15. Proceeds (principal) from collection of note
16. Amortization of discount on bonds payable
17. Decrease in deferred taxes payable
18. Proceeds from issuance of bonds
19. Issuance of stock dividend
20. Payment for purchase of treasury stock
21. Depletion expense
22. Increase in inventory
23. Conversion of bonds payable to common stock
24. Proceeds from issuance of stock
25. Lease of equipment under capital lease
26. Proceeds from sale of patent

**Required**

In the space provided, using the letters A through D, indicate in which section of the statement of cash flows (or accompanying schedule) the preceding items would most likely be classified. After each letter, indicate with a plus (+) or a minus (−) whether the items would be reported as an increase (inflow) or decrease (outflow). If an item would not be reported in the statement (or accompanying schedule), indicate with an X.

**P20-2** *Net Cash Flow From Operating Activities* The following is accounting information taken from the Verna Company's records for 1995:

1. Decrease in accounts payable, $4,600
2. Loss on sale of land, $1,900
3. Increase in inventory, $7,800
4. Increase in income taxes payable, $2,700
5. Net income, $64,400
6. Patent amortization expense, $1,600
7. Extraordinary loss (net) from flood, $6,200
8. Decrease in deferred taxes payable, $2,500
9. Amortization of discount on bonds payable, $1,300
10. Payment of cash dividends, $24,000

11. Depletion expense, $5,000
12. Decrease in salaries payable, $1,400
13. Decrease in accounts receivable, $3,500
14. Gain on sale of equipment, $6,100
15. Proceeds from issuance of stock, $57,000
16. Extraordinary gain (net) from debt retirement, $3,700
17. Depreciation expense, $10,000
18. Amortization of discount on investment in bonds, $1,500

**Required**

Prepare the net cash flow from operating activities section of the 1995 statement of cash flows for the Verna Company.

**P20-3** *Statement of Cash Flows* The following is a list of the items to be included in the preparation of the 1995 statement of cash flows for the Orange Company:

1. Net income, $59,200
2. Payment for purchase of building, $98,000
3. Increase in accounts receivable, $7,400
4. Proceeds from issuance of common stock, $37,100
5. Increase in accounts payable, $4,500
6. Proceeds from sale of land, $7,000
7. Depreciation expense, $12,600
8. Payment of dividends, $36,000
9. Gain on sale of land, $5,300

10. Decrease in inventory, $3,700
11. Payment for purchase of long-term investments, $9,600
12. Amortization of discount on bonds payable, $1,900
13. Proceeds from issuance of note, $18,000
14. Increase in deferred taxes payable, $5,000
15. Equipment acquired by capital lease, $19,500
16. Decrease in salaries payable, $2,300
17. Beginning cash balance, $20,300

**Required**

Prepare the statement of cash flows.

**P20-4** *Statement of Cash Flows* The following is a list of the items to be included in the preparation of the 1995 statement of cash flows for the Trone Company:

1. Extraordinary gain (net) on retirement of bonds, $9,200
2. Proceeds from issuance of note, $25,000
3. Decrease in accounts receivable, $5,000
4. Payment for purchase of patent, $19,800
5. Increase in inventory, $6,700
6. Payment of dividends, $30,000
7. Decrease in accounts payable, $4,000
8. Proceeds from sale of investments, $8,500
9. Amortization of premium on bonds payable, $2,100

10. Net income, $55,400
11. Common stock exchanged for land, $14,000
12. Payment for purchase of equipment, $39,400
13. Loss on sale of investments, $4,800
14. Decrease in deferred taxes payable, $3,600
15. Proceeds from issuance of preferred stock, $52,800
16. Payment to retire bonds, $37,800
17. Depreciation expense, $10,700
18. Ending cash balance, $27,800

**Required**

Prepare the statement of cash flows.

**P20-5**  *Infrequent Transactions*  The following transactions were recorded on the books of the Baxter Company during 1995. The company:

1. Issued a "small" common stock dividend of 400 shares. The par value is $10 per share and the relevant market price was $20 per share.
2. Exchanged equipment with a cost of $10,000 and a book value of $3,800 for land valued at $12,000, paying an additional $8,500. The transaction was properly considered a dissimilar asset exchange.
3. Traded in equipment with a cost of $14,000 and a book value of $8,000 on a similar machine, paying an additional $1,000. The transaction was properly considered a similar asset exchange; the new asset was recorded at a cost of $9,000.
4. Created an Appropriation of Retained Earnings for Contingencies in the amount of $5,000 as a result of a debit to Retained Earnings.
5. Converted bonds payable with a face value of $20,000 and a book value of $18,700 to 1,500 shares of its $10 par common stock. The book value method was used to account for the conversion.
6. Recorded an extraordinary loss (net of income taxes) of $4,200 as a result of retiring bonds payable with a face value of $30,000 and a related premium of $5,000 by paying $39,200.
7. Recorded an extraordinary gain (net of income taxes) of $6,000 as a result of a tornado that destroyed a building costing $100,000 and having an associated book value of $70,000. The insurance proceeds (net of income taxes) totaled $76,000.
8. Acquired equipment by entering into a capital lease. The lease required lease payments of $5,000 in advance; the present value of the lease payments (before the initial payment) was $34,000.

**Required**

For each of the preceding items, discuss *if* and illustrate *how* the transaction would be recorded on the worksheet to support the statement of cash flows. Use a journal entry format for your illustrations.

**P20-6**  *Partially Completed Worksheet*  The following partially completed worksheet has been prepared for the 1995 statement of cash flows of the Perrin Company:

| Account Titles | Balances 01/01/95 | Balances 12/31/95 | Change Increase (Decrease) | Worksheet Entries Debit | Worksheet Entries Credit |
|---|---|---|---|---|---|
| *Debits* | | | | | |
| Cash | $ 800 | $ 1,670 | 870 | | |
| *Noncash Accounts:* | | | | | |
| Accounts receivable | 1,500 | 2,050 | | | |
| Inventory | 3,100 | 6,055 | | | |
| Investments in stock | — | 2,800 | | | |
| Land | 6,000 | 9,200 | | | |
| Buildings | 20,000 | 20,000 | | | |
| Office equipment | 4,000 | 6,100 | | | |
| Delivery equipment | 3,000 | 5,900 | | | |
| Treasury stock | — | 2,000 | | | |
| Totals | $38,400 | $55,775 | $ ? | | |
| *Credits* | | | | | |
| Accumulated depreciation | $ 7,000 | $ 8,500 | | | |
| Accounts payable | 3,300 | 3,695 | | | |
| Wages payable | 600 | 500 | | | |
| Bonds payable | — | 5,000 | | | |
| Premium on bonds payable | — | 240 | | | |
| Common stock, $10 par | 6,000 | 8,200 | | | |
| Additional paid-in capital | 9,000 | 13,640 | | | |
| Retained earnings | 12,500 | 16,000 | $3,500 | | |
| Totals | $38,400 | $55,775 | $ ? | | |

Problems

Other relevant information:

(a)
| | | |
|---|---|---|
| Beginning retained earnings | | $12,500 |
| Plus: Net income | | 7,000 |
| | | $19,500 |
| Less: Stock dividends | $ 840 | |
| Cash dividends | 2,660 | (3,500) |
| Ending retained earnings | | $16,000 |

(b) Accumulated depreciation is a contra account for all the depreciable assets. Depreciation on these assets totaled $2,200 for the year.

(c) On January 1, 1995, the company issued 10% bonds with a face value of $5,000 at 106. Interest was paid semiannually on June 30 and December 31. The bonds mature on January 1, 2000. Straight-line amortization is used for bond discount or premium. Bond interest expense was $440.

(d) Land was purchased for $3,200 during the year.

(e) Two hundred shares of common stock were issued for delivery equipment valued at $2,900 and office equipment valued at $3,100.

(f) Twenty shares of stock were issued as a stock dividend. The market price per share was $42.

(g) Office equipment with a cost of $1,000 and a book value of $300 was sold for $50.

(h) Fifty shares of its own common stock were reacquired by the company as treasury stock. The company purchased the shares for $40 per share.

(i) One hundred shares of Doe Company stock were purchased for $28 per share at year-end.

**Required**

Complete the worksheet.

P20-7   *Worksheet and Statement of Cash Flows*   The following accounts were taken from the balance sheets of the Hawkins Company:

| | Account Balances | |
|---|---|---|
| | January 1, 1995 | December 31, 1995 |
| *Debits* | | |
| Cash | $ 1,400 | $ 2,400 |
| Accounts receivable (net) | 2,800 | 2,690 |
| Marketable securities (at cost) | 1,700 | 3,000 |
| Allowance for change in value | 500 | 800 |
| Inventories | 8,100 | 7,910 |
| Prepaid items | 1,300 | 1,710 |
| Investments (long-term) | 7,000 | 5,400 |
| Land | 15,000 | 15,000 |
| Buildings and equipment | 32,000 | 46,200 |
| Discount on bonds payable | — | 290 |
| | $69,800 | $85,400 |
| *Credits* | | |
| Accumulated depreciation | $16,000 | $16,400 |
| Accounts payable | 3,800 | 4,150 |
| Income taxes payable | 2,400 | 2,504 |
| Wages payable | 1,100 | 650 |
| Interest payable | — | 400 |
| 10% convertible bonds | 9,000 | — |
| Note payable (long-term) | 3,500 | — |
| 12% bonds payable | — | 10,000 |
| Deferred taxes payable | 800 | 1,196 |
| Common stock, $10 par | 14,000 | 21,500 |
| Additional paid-in capital | 8,700 | 13,700 |
| Unrealized increase in value of marketable securities | 500 | 800 |
| Retained earnings | 10,000 | 14,100 |
| | $69,800 | $85,400 |

Additional information for the year:

(a)
| Sales | $39,930 |
|---|---|
| Cost of goods sold | (19,890) |
| Depreciation expense | (2,100) |
| Wages expense | (11,000) |
| Other operating expenses | (1,000) |
| Bond interest expense | (410) |
| Dividend revenue | 820 |
| Gain on sale of investments | 700 |
| Loss on sale of equipment | (200) |
| Income tax expense | (2,050) |
| Net income | $ 4,800 |

(b) Dividends declared and paid totaled $700.

(c) On January 1, 1995 the 10% convertible bonds that had originally been issued at their face value were converted into 500 shares of common stock. The book value method was used to account for the conversion.

(d) Long-term nonmarketable investments that cost $1,600 were sold for $2,300.

(e) The long-term note payable was paid by issuing 250 shares of common stock at the beginning of the year.

(f) Equipment with a cost of $2,000 and a book value of $300 was sold for $100. The company uses one Accumulated Depreciation account for all depreciable assets.

(g) Equipment was purchased at a cost of $16,200.

(h) The 12% bonds payable were issued on September 1, 1995 at 97. They mature on September 1, 2005. The company uses the straight-line method to amortize the discount.

(i) Taxable income was less than pretax accounting income, resulting in a $396 increase in deferred taxes payable.

(j) Short-term marketable securities were purchased at a cost of $1,300. The portfolio was increased by $300 to a $3,800 fair value at year-end by adjustment of the related allowance account.

**Required**

1. Prepare a worksheet to support the statement of cash flows for 1995.

2. Prepare the statement of cash flows.

*P20-8    Worksheet and Statement of Cash Flows*    The following information is available for the Bott Company:

| | Account Balances | |
|---|---|---|
| | January 1, 1995 | December 31, 1995 |
| *Debits* | | |
| Cash | $ 1,800 | $ 2,200 |
| Accounts receivable | 4,600 | 4,720 |
| Notes receivable (short-term) | 0 | 1,000 |
| Inventories | 12,000 | 9,700 |
| Prepaid items | 1,700 | 1,380 |
| Land | 11,000 | 17,100 |
| Buildings and equipment | 78,000 | 110,000 |
| Goodwill | 4,400 | 4,000 |
| Treasury stock (common, at cost, $25 per share) | 2,500 | 1,000 |
| Totals | $116,000 | $151,100 |

| | Account Balances | |
|---|---|---|
| | January 1, 1995 | December 31, 1995 |
| *Credits* | | |
| Accumulated depreciation | $ 24,000 | $ 31,800 |
| Accounts payable | 6,000 | 8,210 |
| Salaries payable | 2,600 | 3,500 |
| Miscellaneous current payables | 1,400 | 1,200 |
| Interest payable | 0 | 140 |
| 12% bonds payable | 0 | 7,000 |
| Premium on bonds payable | 0 | 650 |
| Convertible preferred stock, $50 par | 9,000 | 6,500 |
| Premium on preferred stock | 3,000 | 2,500 |
| Common stock, $10 par | 18,000 | 23,500 |
| Premium on common stock | 28,800 | 40,850 |
| Retained earnings | 23,200 | 25,250 |
| Totals | $116,000 | $151,100 |

Additional information for the year:

| | | |
|---|---|---|
| (a) Beginning retained earnings, unadjusted | | $23,200 |
|     Less: Prior period adjustment—correction of understatement of depreciation (net of income taxes) | | (1,300) |
|     Adjusted beginning retained earnings | | $21,900 |
|     Add: Net income | | 12,000 |
| | | $33,900 |
|     Less: Cash dividends | $(4,000) | |
|          Stock dividends (150 shares at $31 per share) | (4,650) | (8,650) |
|     Ending retained earnings | | $25,250 |

(b) Last year, depreciation expense was inadvertently understated in the amount of $1,800. The correction was made this year to Accumulated Depreciation and to Retained Earnings as a prior period adjustment. The company also received a related income tax refund of $500.

(c) Sixty shares of treasury stock (common) were reissued at $30 per share.

(d) Bonds payable with a face amount of $7,000 were issued for $7,750 on May 1, 1995. The bonds mature on May 1, 2000, and pay interest semiannually. The straight-line method is used to amortize the bond premium. Interest expense totaled $460 for 1995.

(e) Fifty shares of preferred stock (originally issued at $60 per share) were converted into 100 shares of common stock.

(f) Land costing $2,900 was sold for $3,800.

(g) Three hundred shares of common stock were sold for $32 per share.

(h) Equipment costing $32,000 was purchased during the year.

(i) Land was acquired at a cost of $9,000 during the year.

(j) Depreciation expense was $6,000.

(k) Goodwill amortization was $400.

(l) The company loaned money to one of its executives and received a $1,000 short-term note receivable on December 31, 1995. The note matures 90 days from the date of issuance.

### Required

1. Prepare a worksheet to support a statement of cash flows for 1995.
2. Prepare the 1995 statement of cash flows for the Bott Company. Show the reconciliation of the net income to the net cash provided by operating activities in a separate schedule accompanying the statement.

*P20-9*   *Worksheet from Trial Balance*   The post-closing trial balance as of December 31, 1994 and the adjusted trial balance as of December 31, 1995 are shown here for the Heinz Company:

| | December 31, 1994 Post-closing Trial Balance | | December 31, 1995 Adjusted Trial Balance | |
|---|---|---|---|---|
| Cash | $ 2,700 | | $ 3,820 | |
| Accounts receivable | 5,900 | | 6,215 | |
| Inventories | 15,300 | | 15,530 | |
| Prepaid items | 1,400 | | 1,000 | |
| Investments in bonds (long-term) | 8,300 | | 7,300 | |
| Land | 16,300 | | 19,000 | |
| Buildings | 68,700 | | 60,700 | |
| Accumulated depreciation: buildings | | $ 35,000 | | $ 34,500 |
| Equipment | 29,600 | | 25,600 | |
| Accumulated depreciation: equipment | | 14,200 | | 14,700 |
| Patents (net) | 8,700 | | 9,185 | |
| Accounts payable | | 8,900 | | 9,195 |
| Interest payable | | 630 | | 300 |
| Wages payable | | 2,500 | | 2,600 |
| Bonds payable | | 23,000 | | 17,000 |
| Discount on bonds payable | 0 | | 715 | |
| Common stock, $10 par | | 22,000 | | 22,650 |
| Additional paid-in capital | | 15,320 | | 15,970 |
| Retained earnings | | 35,350 | | 35,350 |
| | $156,900 | $156,900 | | |
| | | | | |
| Sales (net) | | | | 50,000 |
| Cost of goods sold | | | 23,800 | |
| Wages expense | | | 16,510 | |
| Other operating expenses | | | 1,100 | |
| Depreciation expense: buildings | | | 2,700 | |
| Depreciation expense: equipment | | | 3,100 | |
| Patent amortization | | | 815 | |
| Interest expense | | | 1,715 | |
| Loss (ordinary) on sale of investments | | | 200 | |
| Interest revenue | | | | 790 |
| Gain (ordinary) on exchange of dissimilar assets | | | | 1,300 |
| Income tax expense | | | 650 | |
| Extraordinary loss (net of income taxes) | | | 2,600 | |
| Dividends declared | | | 2,100 | |
| Totals | | | $204,355 | $204,355 |

A review of the accounting records reveals the following additional information:

(a) Bonds payable with a face value, book value, and market value of $14,000 were retired on June 30, 1995.

(b) Bonds payable with a face value of $8,000 were issued at 90.25 on August 1, 1995. They mature on August 1, 2000. The company uses the straight-line method to amortize bond discount.

(c) A tornado completely destroyed a small building that had an original cost of $8,000 and book value of $4,800. Settlement with the insurance company resulted in after-tax proceeds of $2,200 and an extraordinary loss (net of income taxes) of $2,600.

(d) Equipment with a cost of $4,000 and a book value of $1,400 was exchanged for an acre of land valued at $2,700. No cash was exchanged. The transaction was properly considered to be a dissimilar asset exchange.

(e) Long-term investments in bonds being held to maturity with a cost of $1,000 were sold for $800.

(f) Sixty-five shares of common stock were exchanged for a patent. The common stock was selling for $20 per share at the time of the exchange.

**Required**

Prepare a worksheet to support a statement of cash flows for 1995.

**P20-10** *Prepare Ending Balance Sheet*  On December 31, 1995, a fire destroyed a significant portion of the Elder Company accounting records. Only the January 1, 1995 balance sheet, the statement of cash flows for 1995, and several additional documents were saved as follows:

**Balance Sheet**
**January 1, 1995**

| | | | |
|---|---:|---:|---:|
| *Assets* | | | |
| Current assets: | | | |
|   Cash | | | $ 1,900 |
|   Accounts receivable | | | 5,100 |
|   Inventories | | | 13,900 |
|   Prepaid items | | | 1,300 |
|     Total current assets | | | $22,200 |
| Property, plant, and equipment: | | | |
|   Land | | | $12,000 |
|   Buildings | $60,000 | | |
|   Equipment | 20,000 | $80,000 | |
|     Less: Accumulated depreciation | | (29,000) | 51,000 |
|     Total fixed assets | | | $63,000 |
| Patents (net) | | | 7,100 |
|     Total assets | | | $92,300 |
| | | | |
| *Liabilities* | | | |
| Current liabilities: | | | |
|   Accounts payable | | | $ 5,500 |
|   Income taxes payable | | | 4,100 |
|   Miscellaneous payables | | | 1,200 |
|     Total current liabilities | | | $10,800 |
| Long-term liabilities: | | | |
|   10% bonds payable (due 12/31/2004) | | $15,000 | |
|     Less: Discount on bonds payable | | (1,000) | 14,000 |
|     Total liabilities | | | $24,800 |
| *Stockholders' Equity* | | | |
| Preferred stock, $100 par | | $17,000 | |
| Premium on preferred stock | | 1,500 | $18,500 |
| Common stock, $10 par | | $14,000 | |
| Premium on common stock | | 11,200 | 25,200 |
| Retained earnings | | | 23,800 |
|     Total stockholders' equity | | | $67,500 |
|     Total liabilities and stockholders' equity | | | $92,300 |

**Statement of Cash Flows**
**For Year Ended December 31, 1995**

| | | |
|---|---:|---:|
| Net Cash Flow From Operating Activities | | |
|   Net income | $ 10,000 | |
|   Adjustments for differences between income flows and | | |
|     cash flows from operating activities: | | |
|   Add:  Depreciation expense | 5,100 | |
|         Patent amortization expense | 600 | |
|         Loss on sale of land | 400 | |
|         Decrease in accounts receivable (net) | 1,100 | |
|         Decrease in inventories | 3,010 | |
|         Increase in income taxes payable | 190 | |
|         Increase in miscellaneous payables | 200 | |
|         Bond discount amortization | 100 | |
|   Less:  Gain on sale of equipment | (180) | |
|         Gain on sale of patent | (1,100) | |
|         Increase in prepaid items | (120) | |
|         Decrease in accounts payable | (400) | |
|   Net cash provided by operating activities | | $18,900 |
| Cash Flows From Investing Activities | | |
|   Purchase of building by issuance of mortgage and cash | $(43,000) | |
|   Less:  Issuance of mortgage | 20,000 | |
|   Payment for purchase of building | $(23,000) | |
|   Proceeds from sale of land | 2,800 | |
|   Proceeds from sale of equipment | 500 | |
|   Proceeds from sale of patent | 2,100 | |
|   Net cash used for investing activities | | (17,600) |
| Cash Flows From Financing Activities | | |
|   Proceeds from issuance of common stock (150 shares) | $ 3,000 | |
|   Payment of dividends | (5,000) | |
|   Net cash used for financing activities | | (2,000) |
| Net Decrease in Cash (see Schedule 1) | | $ (700) |
| Cash, January 1, 1995 | | 1,900 |
| Cash, December 31, 1995 | | $ 1,200 |

**Schedule 1: Investing and Financing Activities Not Affecting Cash**

| | |
|---|---:|
| Investing Activities | |
|   Acquisition of land by issuance of preferred stock (40 shares) | $(4,800) |
| Financing Activities | |
|   Issuance of preferred stock to acquire land | 4,800 |

The remaining financial documents reveal the following additional data:

1. The new building was acquired on December 31, 1995. The related mortgage requires equal annual re-payments of the principal over a 5-year period beginning December 31, 1999.
2. The company issued a stock dividend of 200 shares of common stock on December 15, 1995. At the date of declaration, the stock was selling for $18 per share.
3. The equipment that was sold had an original cost of $1,900.

**Required**
Prepare a December 31, 1995 balance sheet for Elder Company. Include supporting calculations.

P20-11 *Erroneous Statement of Cash Flows* The bookkeeper of the Ryan Company prepared the following 1995 statement of cash flows:

**Flows of Cash Statement**
**December 31, 1995**

| | | |
|---|---:|---:|
| *Sources (Inflows) of Cash* | | |
| Net Source from Operations | | |
|    Net income | $ 48,300 | |
|    Add: Cash receipt from sale of land | 6,500 | |
|       Inflow from issuing 10% bonds payable | 25,000 | |
|       Depreciation expense | 13,200 | |
|       Reduction in inventory | 1,900 | |
|    Less: Outflow to buy equipment | (18,400) | |
|       Increase in prepaid expenses | (700) | |
|       Cash (principal) paid on long-term note | (9,500) | |
|       Extraordinary gain (net) on bond retirement | (2,000) | |
|    Total source from operations | | $ 64,300 |
| Other Sources (Inflows) of Cash | | |
|    Loss on sale of land | $ 2,300 | |
|    Increase in accounts payable | 1,000 | |
|    Cash from issuing preferred stock | 37,800 | |
|    Patent amortization expense | 1,100 | |
|    Total other sources of cash | | 42,200 |
| Sources (Financing) Not Affecting Cash | | |
|    Issuance of common stock for patent | | 11,000 |
|    Total inflows of cash | | $117,500 |
| *Uses (Outflows) of Cash* | | |
|    To purchase building | $(62,000) | |
|    Increase in accounts receivable | (7,800) | |
|    For acquiring marketable securities | (7,100) | |
|    Decrease in income taxes payable | (1,400) | |
|    Total uses of cash | | (78,300) |
| Uses (Investing) Not Affecting Cash | | |
|    Acquisition of patent by issuing common stock | | (11,000) |
|    Net inflow before dividends | | $ 28,200 |
|    Less: Cash dividends | | (24,000) |
| Net Increase in Cash | | $ 4,200 |
| Cash, January 1, 1995 | | 15,300 |
| Cash, December 31, 1995 | | $ 19,500 |

After a thorough investigation, you have determined that the *amounts* of the items listed on the statement are correct. However, you notice several items that are incorrectly classified and reported.

**Required**

Prepare a corrected 1995 statement of cash flows for the Ryan Company.

P20-12 *Comprehensive* Angel Company has prepared its financial statements for the year ended December 31, 1994 and for the three months ended March 31, 1995. You have been asked to prepare a statement of cash flows for the three months ended March 31, 1995. The company's balance sheet data at December 31, 1994 and March

31, 1995, and its income statement data for the three months ended March 31, 1995, follow. You have previously satisfied yourself as to the correctness of the amounts presented.

|  | Balance Sheet | |
|  | December 31, 1994 | March 31, 1995 |
| --- | --- | --- |
| Cash | $ 25,300 | $ 79,400 |
| Marketable investments (at cost) | 17,500 | 8,300 |
| Allowance for decrease in value | (1,000) | (900) |
| Accounts receivable | 24,320 | 49,320 |
| Inventory | 31,090 | 48,590 |
| Total current assets | $ 97,210 | $184,710 |
| Land | 40,000 | 18,700 |
| Building | 250,000 | 250,000 |
| Equipment | — | 81,500 |
| Accumulated depreciation | (15,000) | (16,250) |
| Investment in 30% owned company | 61,220 | 67,100 |
| Other assets | 15,100 | 15,100 |
| Total | $448,530 | $600,860 |
|  |  |  |
| Accounts payable | $ 21,220 | $ 38,081 |
| Income taxes payable | — | 13,865 |
| Total current liabilities | $ 21,220 | $ 51,946 |
| Other liabilities | 187,000 | 187,000 |
| Bonds payable | 50,000 | 115,000 |
| Discount on bonds payable | (2,300) | (2,150) |
| Deferred taxes payable | 510 | 846 |
| Preferred stock | 30,000 | — |
| Common stock | 80,000 | 110,000 |
| Unrealized decrease in value of marketable investments | (1,000) | (900) |
| Dividends declared | — | (8,000) |
| Retained earnings | 83,100 | 147,118 |
| Total | $448,530 | $600,860 |

|  | Income Statement Data For the Three Months Ended March 31, 1995 |
| --- | --- |
| Sales | $242,807 |
| Gain on sale of marketable investments | 2,400 |
| Equity in earnings of 30% owned company | 5,880 |
| Extraordinary gain on condemnation of land (net of tax) | 8,560 |
| Total revenues | $259,647 |
|  |  |
| Cost of sales | $157,354 |
| General and administrative expenses | 22,010 |
| Depreciation | 1,250 |
| Interest expense | 1,150 |
| Income taxes | 13,865 |
| Total expenses | $195,629 |
| Net income | $ 64,018 |

Your discussion with the company's controller and a review of the financial records have revealed the following information:

(a) On January 9, 1995, the company sold marketable securities for cash. These securities had cost $9,200, and had a fair value of $8,600 at December 31, 1994. The remaining marketable securities were adjusted to their $7,400 fair value on March 31, 1995 by adjustment of the related allowance account. The dividend and interest revenue on these marketable securities is not material.

(b) The company's preferred stock was converted into common stock at a rate of 1 share of preferred for 2 shares of common. The preferred stock and common stock have par values of $2 and $1, respectively.

(c) On January 17, 1995, 3 acres of land were condemned. An award of $32,000 in cash was received on March 23, 1995. Purchase of additional land as a replacement is not contemplated by the company.

(d) On March 25, 1995, the company purchased equipment for cash.

(e) On March 27, 1995, bonds payable were issued by the company at par for cash.

(f) The investment in 30% owned company included an amount attributable to goodwill of $9,600 at December 31, 1994. Goodwill is being amortized at a quarterly rate of $480.

**Required**

1. Prepare a worksheet to support the statement of cash flows for Angel Company for the 3 months ended March 31, 1995.
2. Prepare the statement of cash flows. (*AICPA adapted*)

P20-13 *Comprehensive*   The following are the balance sheets of Farrell Corporation as of December 31, 1995 and 1994, and the statement of income and retained earnings for the year ended December 31, 1995:

|  | Balance Sheets | | |
|---|---|---|---|
|  | December 31 | | Increase |
|  | 1995 | 1994 | (Decrease) |
| *Assets* | | | |
| Cash | $ 275,000 | $ 180,000 | $ 95,000 |
| Accounts receivable, net | 295,000 | 305,000 | (10,000) |
| Inventories | 549,000 | 431,000 | 118,000 |
| Investment in Hall, Inc., at equity | 73,000 | 60,000 | 13,000 |
| Land | 350,000 | 200,000 | 150,000 |
| Plant and equipment | 624,000 | 606,000 | 18,000 |
| Less: Accumulated depreciation | (139,000) | (107,000) | (32,000) |
| Goodwill | 16,000 | 20,000 | (4,000) |
| Total assets | $2,043,000 | $1,695,000 | $348,000 |
| | | | |
| *Liabilities and Stockholders' Equity* | | | |
| Accounts payable and accrued expenses | $ 604,000 | $ 563,000 | $ 41,000 |
| Note payable, long-term | 150,000 | — | 150,000 |
| Bonds payable | 160,000 | 210,000 | (50,000) |
| Deferred taxes payable | 41,000 | 30,000 | 11,000 |
| Common stock, $10 par | 430,000 | 400,000 | 30,000 |
| Additional paid-in capital | 226,000 | 175,000 | 51,000 |
| Retained earnings | 432,000 | 334,000 | 98,000 |
| Treasury stock, at cost | — | (17,000) | 17,000 |
| Total liabilities and stockholders' equity | $2,043,000 | $1,695,000 | $348,000 |

### Statement of Income and Retained Earnings
### For the Year Ended December 31, 1995

| | |
|---|---:|
| Net sales | $1,950,000 |
| Operating expenses: | |
| Cost of sales | 1,150,000 |
| Selling and administrative expenses | 505,000 |
| Depreciation | 53,000 |
| | 1,708,000 |
| Operating income | 242,000 |
| Other (income) expense: | |
| Interest expense | 15,000 |
| Equity in net income of Hall, Inc. | (13,000) |
| Loss on sale of equipment | 5,000 |
| Amortization of goodwill | 4,000 |
| | 11,000 |
| Income before income taxes | 231,000 |
| Income taxes: | |
| Current | 79,000 |
| Deferred | 11,000 |
| Provision for income taxes | 90,000 |
| Net income | $  141,000 |
| Retained earnings, January 1, 1995 | 334,000 |
| | 475,000 |
| Cash dividends, paid August 14, 1995 | 43,000 |
| Retained earnings, December 31, 1995 | $  432,000 |

Additional information:

1. On January 2, 1995, Farrell sold equipment costing $45,000, with a book value of $24,000, for $19,000 cash.
2. On April 3, 1995, Farrell issued 1,000 shares of common stock for $23,000 cash.
3. On May 15, 1995, Farrell sold all of its treasury stock for $25,000 cash.
4. On June 1, 1995, individuals holding $50,000 face value of Farrell's bonds exercised their conversion privilege. Each of the 50 bonds was converted into 40 shares of Farrell's common stock.
5. On July 3, 1995, Farrell purchased equipment for $63,000 cash.
6. On December 31, 1995, land with a fair market value of $150,000 was purchased through the issuance of a long-term note in the amount of $150,000. The note bears interest at the rate of 15% and is due on December 31, 2000.
7. Deferred taxes payable represent temporary differences relating to the use of accelerated depreciation methods for income tax reporting and the straight-line method for financial statement reporting.

**Required**

1. Prepare a worksheet to support a statement of cash flows for the Farrell Corporation for the year ended December 31, 1995, based on the preceding information.
2. Prepare the statement of cash flows. (*AICPA adapted*)

**P20-14** *Appendix: Operating Cash Flows*   Use the information presented in P20-7.

**Required**

1. Using the direct method, prepare the cash flows from operating activities section of the 1995 statement of cash flows for the Hawkins Company.
2. *(Optional).* If you completed P20-7 earlier, prepare the remaining portion of the statement of cash flows. (A separate schedule reconciling net income to cash provided by operating activities is not necessary.)

P20-15 *Appendix: Statement of Cash Flows* The following is a list of the items to be included in the preparation of the 1995 statement of cash flows for the Yellow Company:

1. Proceeds from sale of land, $2,100
2. Payments of interest, $5,000
3. Equipment acquired by capital lease, $7,200
4. Proceeds from issuance of preferred stock, $11,000
5. Other operating payments, $1,300
6. Interest and dividends collected, $4,700
7. Payments to employees, $19,800
8. Payment for purchase of investments, $13,300
9. Collections from customers, $55,300
10. Payments of income taxes, $2,900
11. Payment of dividends, $5,200
12. Other operating receipts, $1,600
13. Payments to suppliers, $29,500
14. Beginning cash balance, $33,100

**Required**
Prepare the statement of cash flows, using the direct method for operating cash flows.

P20-16 *Appendix: Worksheet and Statement* Use the information presented in P20-13 for the Farrell Corporation.

**Required**
1. Using the direct method for operating cash flows, prepare a worksheet to support a statement of cash flows. (*Hint*: Combine the income statement and December 31, 1995 balance sheet items for the adjusted trial balance. Use a retained earnings balance of $291,000 in this adjusted trial balance.)
2. Prepare the statement of cash flows. (A separate schedule reconciling net income to cash provided by operating activities is not necessary.)

P20-17 *Appendix: Comprehensive* The following are the December 31, 1994 post-closing trial balance and the December 31, 1995 adjusted trial balance of the Adair Company:

| Accounts | 12/31/94 Post-Closing Trial Balance | | 12/31/95 Adjusted Trial Balance | |
|---|---|---|---|---|
| | Debit | Credit | Debit | Credit |
| Cash | 2,700 | | 3,300 | |
| Accounts receivable | 7,300 | | 6,200 | |
| Inventory | 8,100 | | 9,900 | |
| Investments in bonds | 10,000 | | 18,600 | |
| Property and equipment | 105,300 | | 133,300 | |
| Accumulated depreciation | | 42,400 | | 49,200 |
| Accounts payable | | 8,100 | | 8,500 |
| Salaries payable | | 1,300 | | 700 |
| Interest payable | | 0 | | 300 |
| Notes payable | | 0 | | 9,000 |
| Common stock, no par | | 43,600 | | 58,100 |
| Retained earnings | | 38,000 | | 31,500 |
| Sales | | | | 89,000 |
| Cost of goods sold | | | 48,800 | |
| Depreciation expense | | | 6,800 | |
| Salaries expense | | | 12,000 | |
| Other operating expenses | | | 1,700 | |
| Interest revenue | | | | 1,200 |
| Interest expense | | | 900 | |
| Income tax expense | | | 6,000 | |
| Totals | 133,400 | 133,400 | 247,500 | 247,500 |

A review of the accounting records reveals the following additional information for 1995:

(a) Investments in bonds to be held to maturity were purchased at year-end for $8,600.
(b) A building was purchased for $28,000.
(c) A note payable was issued for $9,000.
(d) Common stock was issued for $14,500.
(e) Dividends of $6,500 were declared and paid.

### Required

1. Using the direct method for operating cash flows, prepare a worksheet to support the 1995 statement of cash flows for the Adair Company.
2. Prepare the statement of cash flows. (A separate schedule reconciling net income to cash provided by operating activities is not necessary.)

**P20-18** *Appendix: Complex Worksheet*   Use the information presented in P20-9 for the Heinz Company.

### Required

Using the direct method for operating cash flows, prepare a worksheet to support a statement of cash flows.

# 21

# EARNINGS PER SHARE

Corporations have been disclosing earnings per share data for many years. The guidelines for the computation and reporting of this data evolved over the years, following the issuance of several accounting documents. *Accounting Research Bulletin No. 49* (1958) first addressed the issue by suggesting general guidelines to be used in computing and presenting earnings per share. However, no position was taken concerning required disclosures. *APB Opinion No. 9* (1966) considered several additional complexities in the computation of earnings per share. Although at that time the APB did not require disclosure, it did "strongly recommend that earnings per share be disclosed in the statement of income." Because of the increasing significance being placed upon the earnings per share data by investors and other user groups, *APB Opinion No. 15* was issued in 1969. It *requires* the disclosure of such data on the face of the income statement. Finally, *APB Opinion No. 30* clarified the disclosure of several earnings per share items, and *FASB Statements No. 55* and *85* modified one of the calculations.[1]

The objective of these pronouncements was to *establish* consistency *in the computations of earnings per share in order to promote* comparability *of accounting information.* A further goal was to *reflect the economic substance rather than the legal form of the securities in a complex corporate capital structure*, although the convention of *conservatism* is evident in these pronouncements. Not only does *APB Opinion No. 15* require the disclosure of earnings per share data, but it also addresses many of its complexities. The lengthy *Opinion* itself is such a complex document that, shortly after its issuance, the AICPA published a 189-page document[2] containing accounting interpretations for computing earnings per share. The major issues concerning the computation of earnings per share are the topics of this chapter.

## Chapter Topics

*Simple Capital Structure*

*Earnings Per Common Share Outstanding*

*Complex Capital Structure*

*Primary Earnings Per Share*

*Fully Diluted Earnings Per Share*

*Earnings Per Share Disclosures*

1.  "Earnings Per Share," *Accounting Research Bulletin No. 49* (New York: AICPA, 1958), "Reporting the Results of Operations," *APB Opinion No. 9* (New York: AICPA, 1966), "Earnings Per Share," *APB Opinion No. 15* (New York: AICPA, 1969), "Reporting the Results of Operations," *APB Opinion No. 30* (New York: AICPA, 1973), "Determining Whether a Convertible Security Is a Common Stock Equivalent," *FASB Statement of Financial Accounting Standards No. 55* (Stamford, Conn.: FASB, 1982), and "Yield Test for Determining Whether a Convertible Security Is a Common Stock Equivalent," *FASB Statement of Financial Accounting Standards No. 85* (Stamford, Conn.: FASB, 1985).
2.  J. T. Ball, "Computing Earnings Per Share," *Unofficial Accounting Interpretations of APB Opinion No. 15* (New York: AICPA, 1970).

## USES OF EARNINGS PER SHARE INFORMATION

All the information included in the financial statements and the related notes should be useful to external decision makers. Most users, however, focus on selected items that they consider to be of greatest relevance. Earnings per share is one measure that is considered to be very important by most users. It often is considered to be the single measure that best summarizes the performance of a company, particularly for common shareholders.

The amount of earnings per share, the change in earnings per share from the previous period, and the trend in earnings per share are all important indicators of the success, or failure, of the company. Many investors also are interested in the cash flow per share of the company. Although companies are prohibited from reporting cash flow per share, as discussed in Chapter 20 and later in this chapter, the earnings per share may be considered to be a long-run indicator of cash flow per share.

*The price/earnings ratio is discussed in Chapter 23.*

Earnings per share may be divided into the price per share of the common stock to compute the price/earnings ratio. For example, at the time of writing this book, Wal-Mart and Kmart had price/earnings ratios of 29 and 11, respectively. Wal-Mart's price/earnings ratio indicates that the stock is selling for a price of 29 times the most recent year's earnings per share. Compared to the Kmart's lower price/earnings ratio, investors are more optimistic about the future of Wal-Mart and expect that it will experience a higher growth in earnings per share.

Investors often are interested in predicting earnings per share for future periods. While accountants generally do not provide information about the future, two earnings per share computations are intended to indicate the potential impacts of possible future events. When a company has issued common stock options (discussed in Chapter 15), convertible debt (discussed in Chapter 12), or convertible preferred stock (discussed in Chapter 14), additional common shares will be issued when the options are exercised or the securities converted, thereby affecting earnings per share. Primary and fully diluted earnings per share (defined later) include the potential effects of such conversions. A company with these types of securities is said to have a complex capital structure; we begin by discussing earnings per share for a company with a simple capital structure.

## SIMPLE CAPITAL STRUCTURE

For purposes of computing earnings per share, there are two types of corporate capital structures—simple and complex. **A simple capital structure is one that consists of only common stock or includes no potentially dilutive convertible securities, options, warrants, or other rights that upon conversion or exercise could in the aggregate dilute earnings per share by more than 3%.**[3] When a simple capital structure exists, the **simple earnings per share** computation is as follows:

$$\text{Earnings Per Common Share Outstanding} = \frac{\text{Net Income} - \text{Preferred Dividend}}{\text{Weighted Average Number of Common Shares Outstanding}}$$

The resulting earnings per common share (or in the case of a net loss, the loss per share) is disclosed on the face of the income statement, directly below net income. It also is disclosed for each comparative income statement presented.[4]

---

3.  *APB Opinion No. 15, op. cit.*, par. 14.
4.  If prior period adjustments have been made, the earnings per share data for the prior period is restated.

Even in this relatively simple calculation, several complexities arise. Although these complexities are discussed within the simple capital structure framework, they are also applicable to corporations with complex capital structures (discussed in a later section).

## Numerator Adjustments

Only the amount of *earnings available to common stockholders* is used in the numerator of the earnings per share computation. If a corporation has outstanding *noncumulative* preferred stock, the dividends declared during the current period are deducted from the net income to determine the earnings available to common stockholders. If *cumulative* preferred stock is outstanding, the dividends for the *current* period, *whether declared or not,* are deducted. The amount of the deduction is disclosed in the notes to the financial statements.

## Weighted Average

Since a corporation earns its net income over the entire year, the earnings are related to the common shares outstanding during the year. Thus, the denominator of the equation is the weighted average number of common shares outstanding. This number is disclosed in the notes to the financial statements. If a corporation has not issued any shares during the year, the number of common shares outstanding at the end of the accounting period is equal to the weighted average. If common shares have been issued (or reacquired) during the period, the denominator is based on the weighted average number of common shares outstanding during the period.

The weighted average is calculated by starting with the actual common shares outstanding at the beginning of the period and multiplying this "layer" of shares by the fraction of the year it is outstanding until another block of common stock is issued (or shares are reacquired). These new shares are added to (or subtracted from) the actual beginning outstanding shares, and the new layer is multiplied by the fraction of the year it is outstanding. This process is continued for all the issuances of common stock during the year. The resulting "equivalent whole units" of stock for all the layers are summed to determine the weighted average number of common shares. To illustrate, assume a corporation had 12,000 shares of common stock outstanding at the beginning of the year. On March 2, it issued 2,700 shares; on July 3, it issued another 3,300 shares; and on December 1, it reacquired 480 shares as treasury stock. The weighted average number of common shares to be used in computing earnings per share is 15,860 shares, as computed in Exhibit 21-1. Note that for simplicity, the nearest whole month was used to determine the fraction of the year each layer of shares was outstanding.

### EXHIBIT 21-1

#### WEIGHTED AVERAGE SHARES

| Months Shares Are Outstanding | Shares Outstanding | × Fraction of Year Outstanding = | Equivalent Whole Units |
|---|---|---|---|
| January–February | 12,000 | 2/12 | 2,000 |
| March–June | 14,700 | 4/12 | 4,900 |
| July–November | 18,000 | 5/12 | 7,500 |
| December | 17,520 | 1/12 | 1,460 |
| | Total weighted average common shares | | 15,860 |

## Stock Dividends or Splits

When the common shares outstanding increase as a result of a stock dividend or stock split, *retroactive* recognition is given to these events for all comparative income statements presented.[5] This retroactive adjustment results in comparable earnings per share amounts for all periods expressed in terms of the most recent capital structure.

The simplest way of giving effect to this retroactive recognition is to assume (for earnings per share computations) that the stock dividend or split occurred at the *beginning* of the earliest comparative period and that all stock transactions between this beginning date and the *actual* date of the stock dividend or split included the additional shares resulting from the assumed dividend or split.

Assume, for example, that a corporation begins operations in January 1994, and issues 5,000 shares of common stock that are outstanding during all of 1994. On December 31, 1994, it issues a two-for-one stock split. At the end of 1994, the weighted average number of shares to be used in the earnings per share computation for 1994 is 10,000 (5,000 × 200% × 12/12) because the two-for-one stock split is *assumed* to have occurred on January 1, 1994. On May 29, 1995, the company issues 5,000 shares of common stock; on August 3, 1995, it issues a 20% stock dividend; and on October 5, 1995, it issues 2,000 shares of stock. At the end of 1995, when presenting comparative earnings per share for 1994 and 1995, the weighted average numbers of shares to be used in the computation are 12,000 shares for 1994 and 16,000 shares for 1995, as shown in Exhibit 21-2.

---

### EXHIBIT 21-2

### COMPARATIVE WEIGHTED AVERAGE SHARES

Retroactive Recognition of Stock Split and Stock Dividend

| Months Shares Are Outstanding | Actual Shares Outstanding | Assumed Shares Outstanding | × Fraction of Year Outstanding | = Equivalent Whole Units |
|---|---|---|---|---|
| *1994* | | | | |
| January–December | 5,000 | 12,000 (5,000 × 200% × 120%) | 12/12 | 12,000 |
| | | | | |
| *1995* | | | | |
| January–May | 10,000 | 12,000 (10,000 × 120%) | 5/12 | 5,000 |
| June–July | 15,000 | 18,000 (15,000 × 120%) | 2/12 | 3,000 |
| August–September | 18,000 | 18,000 (15,000 × 120%) | 2/12 | 3,000 |
| October–December | 20,000 | 20,000 (15,000 × 120% + 2,000) | 3/12 | 5,000 |
| | | | | 16,000 |

---

5. This is the case even if the stock dividend or split occurs after the end of the accounting period but before the financial statements are issued.

For comparative purposes at the end of 1995, the two-for-one stock split actually issued on December 31 *and* the 20% stock dividend actually issued on August 3, 1995 are both *assumed* to have been issued on January 1, 1994. Under this assumption, 12,000 shares of stock would have been outstanding during all of 1994. Similarly, during 1995, 12,000 shares initially would have been outstanding. The 5,000 shares issued on May 29 would have increased by 20% to 6,000 shares, resulting in 18,000 shares outstanding until October 5, 1995. The 2,000 shares issued on October 5, 1995 would *not* have increased because this issuance occurred *after* the actual stock dividend. The resulting weighted average number of shares is 16,000 at the end of 1995. Remember that the assumptions discussed earlier, although not reflecting the actual timing of the transactions, are necessary to compute comparable earnings per share amounts for all income statements presented.

### Earnings Per Share Subtotals

Net income is the final earnings figure on the income statement. If any results from discontinued operations, extraordinary items, or the cumulative effects of changes in accounting principles are included in this figure, separate earnings per share amounts are presented for *both* income from continuing operations and net income. Corporations also include separate earnings per share amounts for the results from discontinued operations, extraordinary items, and the cumulative effects of changes in accounting principles. Each of these earnings per share is based upon the same weighted average number of shares, and the components usually are summed to disclose the total earnings per share. The intent is to show the contribution of each income statement component to the total earnings per share. When preferred dividends have been deducted in computing total earnings per share, these dividends also are deducted from the income related to continuing operations in order to reconcile the earnings per share amounts. Exhibit 21-3 illustrates the disclosure of the earnings per common share outstanding.

---

**EXHIBIT 21-3**

**NORCAT CORPORATION**

Earnings Per Share Disclosure

Earnings per common share outstanding:

| | |
|---|---|
| Income before extraordinary items | $2.03 |
| Extraordinary loss | (0.27) |
| Net income | $1.76 |

---

### Example of Simple Earnings Per Share

Exhibit 21-4 shows the computation and disclosure of the earnings per common share outstanding (often referred to as *simple* earnings per share) for the Roberts Corporation, a corporation with a simple capital structure.

---

**EXHIBIT 21-4**

## ROBERTS CORPORATION

Computation and Disclosure of Simple Earnings Per Share
(Simple Capital Structure)

1. Income statement information:
   a. Net income for 1995 is $14,000.
   b. An extraordinary gain (net of income taxes) of $3,600 is included in net income.
2. Stockholders' equity information (end of 1995):
   a. 8% Preferred stock, $100 par     $30,000
   b. Common stock, $10 par        $60,000
3. Additional information:
   a. No preferred stock was issued or reacquired during 1995.
   b. Preferred dividends were declared during 1995 at the stated rate.
   c. A review of the common stock account shows that on January 1, 1995, 2,000 shares of common stock were outstanding. On April 3, 500 shares of common stock were issued for cash. On June 1, a two-for-one stock split occurred, resulting in 5,000 total common shares. On November 2, 1,000 shares of common stock were issued for cash.
4. Earnings per share computations for 1995:

| Explanation | Earnings (Adjustments) | ÷ | Shares (Adjustments) | = | Earnings Per Share |
|---|---|---|---|---|---|
| Net income | $14,000 | | | | |
| Preferred dividends[a] | (2,400) | | | | |
| Common shares[b] | | | 4,917 | | |
| Earnings and shares | $11,600 | ÷ | 4,917 | = | $2.36 |

    a. Preferred dividends:     $30,000 × 0.08 = $2,400
    b. Weighted average shares:
      4,000 (2,000 × 200% stock split) × 3/12 = 1,000
      5,000 (2,500 × 200%)        × 7/12 = 2,917
      6,000 (2,500 × 200% + 1,000)   × 2/12 = 1,000
      Weighted average common shares       4,917

5. Condensed income statement presentation for 1995:

| | |
|---|---|
| Income before extraordinary items | $10,400 |
| Extraordinary gain (net of income taxes) | 3,600 |
| Net income | $14,000 |
| | |
| Earnings per common share outstanding (see Note A): | |
|    Income before extraordinary items | $1.63 |
|    Extraordinary gain | 0.73 |
|    Net income | $2.36 |

6. Note A to financial statements: Preferred dividends of $2,400 are deducted from income before extraordinary items and net income to determine earnings available to common stock. The resulting amounts of $8,000 and $11,600 divided by the 4,917 weighted average common shares yield $1.63 and $2.36 earnings per share, respectively.

## COMPLEX CAPITAL STRUCTURE

Many corporations have a more complex capital structure, including items such as convertible preferred stock and convertible bonds, stock options and warrants, participating securities and two-class stocks, and contingent shares. Each of these is potentially a common stock equivalent (to be specifically defined later). Since conversion of these items into common stock would affect earnings per share, they are considered in computing earnings per share.

Instead of a single, simple earnings per share disclosure, **corporations with complex capital structures generally are required to make two presentations on the face of the income statement.** The two amounts are known as primary earnings per share and fully diluted earnings per share. **Primary earnings per share** is based on the outstanding common shares and the common stock equivalents that would reduce earnings per share. **Fully diluted earnings per share** reflects the dilution of earnings per share after including *all* contingent issuances of common stock that would reduce earnings per share.[6] The computations and disclosures of primary and fully diluted earnings per share are considered in the following sections.

## PRIMARY EARNINGS PER SHARE

**In computing primary earnings per share for a complex capital structure, the potential impact of common stock equivalents is considered** in addition to the weighted average common shares calculation, stock dividends and split assumptions, and earnings presentations discussed earlier. Only the more common types of potential common stock equivalents—stock options and warrants, and convertible preferred stock and bonds—are included in this section.

**A common stock equivalent is a security that is not a common stock, but that contains a provision enabling its holder to acquire common stock under terms which, at issuance, make it in substance equivalent to a common stock.** The determination (discussed later) of whether a security is a common stock equivalent is made when the security is *issued* and is not changed as long as it remains outstanding. However, **to be included in the primary earnings per share calculation, the common stock equivalent must have a *dilutive* effect on (that is, decrease) earnings per share.** Thus, a common stock equivalent may be included in the primary earnings per share computation in one accounting period and not in another.[7] Consequently, an accountant must be familiar with the types of common stock equivalents, the tests to determine the common stock equivalency and dilution of each security, and the primary earnings per share computations.

To evaluate the dilutive effect of each security, it is necessary to include common stock equivalents in the primary earnings per share (PEPS) calculations in a certain order. Therefore, the following sequence of steps should be followed:

Step 1. Compute the simple earnings per share.
Step 2. Include dilutive stock options and warrants and compute a tentative PEPS.
Step 3. Determine the common stock equivalency status of all convertible preferred stock and convertible bonds.
Step 4. Develop a ranking of the impact of each common stock equivalent (other than stock options and warrants) on PEPS.
Step 5. Include each common stock equivalent in PEPS in a sequential order based on the ranking and compute a new tentative PEPS.
Step 6. Select as the primary earnings per share the lowest computed tentative PEPS.

---

6. *APB Opinion No. 15, op. cit.,* par. 15.
7. *Ibid.,* par. 25, 28, and 30.

Since we already have discussed the computation of simple earnings per share, the following discussion begins with stock options and proceeds through the steps necessary to compute primary earnings per share. A flowchart summarizing these steps is shown in Exhibit 21-8 on page 1098.

### Stock Options and Warrants

**Stock options, warrants, and similar arrangements are always considered to be common stock equivalents.** However, they are included in primary earnings per share only if they are *dilutive*. Since the exercise of stock options or warrants normally does not affect net income, the focus is on the earnings per share denominator. **The treasury stock method is used to determine the change in the number of shares.** In this method, the impact upon common shares is computed under the assumption (for earnings per share computations) that the options were exercised at the beginning of the period (or at the time of the issuance of the options if later) and that the assumed proceeds obtained from the exercise were used by the corporation to reacquire common stock at the average market price during the period. The intent is to approximate the impact upon the corporate capital structure if all stock options had been exercised. **Under the treasury stock method, the number of shares added to the earnings per share denominator is the difference between the assumed shares issued and the assumed shares reacquired.** This relationship is illustrated by the following diagram:

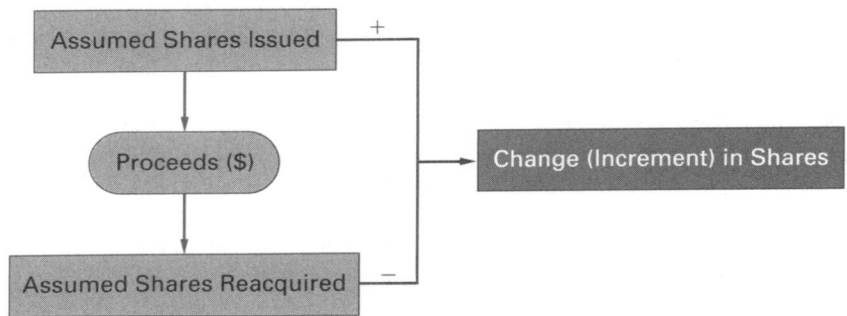

Whenever shares issued exceed shares reacquired, the effect is a dilution of earnings per share. **Dilution occurs whenever the average market price is greater than the option price.** In this case, it is assumed that fewer shares are reacquired than are issued via the exercise of the option. As a practical matter, the assumed exercise is not reflected in earnings per share until the average market price has exceeded the exercise price for the last 3 months of the accounting period.[8] If the average market price is less than the option price, the assumed exercise would be antidilutive (i.e., would *increase* earnings per share) and the options are *excluded* from the primary earnings per share computation. The normal steps to implement the treasury stock method are as follows:

Step 1. Determine the average market price of common shares during the period (if less than the option price, there is no need to continue; the assumed exercise of the options and warrants would be antidilutive).

---

8. *Ibid*, par 36.

Step 2. Compute the shares issued from the assumed exercise of all options and warrants.

Step 3. Compute the proceeds received from the assumed exercise by multiplying the shares issued by the option price.

Step 4. Compute the assumed shares reacquired by dividing the proceeds (Step 3) by the average market price (Step 1).

Step 5. Compute the incremental common shares (the results of Step 2 minus Step 4).

To illustrate, assume a corporation has 10,000 common shares and options to purchase 1,000 common shares at $20 per share outstanding the entire year, and that the average market price for the common stock during the year was $25 per share. The net increase in the denominator would be 200 shares, which would have a dilutive effect on earnings per share. The share calculation is as follows:

Shares assumed issued per assumed exercise          1,000

Shares assumed reacquired:

$$\frac{\text{Proceeds}}{\text{Average Market Price Per Share}} = \frac{1,000 \times \$20}{\$25} = \frac{\$20,000}{\$25} = \underline{(800)}$$

Assumed increment in common shares for computing primary earnings per share        <u>200</u>

Once the number of incremental shares resulting from the assumed exercise of the options or warrants is computed, the increase is added to the denominator of the simple earnings per share. The original numerator is then divided by the new denominator to determine the tentative primary earnings per share. If no other common stock equivalents are outstanding, this tentative figure is the final primary earnings per share.

### Application of 20% Rule

The treasury stock method is modified whenever the number of common shares issued via the assumed exercise of options and warrants exceeds 20% of the number of actual common shares *outstanding at the end of the period*. In this case, the average market price may not be a realistic approximation of the price the corporation would have to pay to reacquire shares. Accordingly, *APB Opinion No. 15* established the following guidelines: If the shares issued in the assumed exercise exceed 20%, the assumed aggregate proceeds obtained from the exercise are applied in two steps: (1) the proceeds are first used to reacquire common shares at the average market price (the treasury stock method discussed earlier) but not to exceed 20% of the actual shares outstanding at year-end; and (2) if any proceeds remain, the balance is used first to retire short-term or long-term debt, and any proceeds still remaining are invested in government securities. When Step 2 is implemented, the *numerator* of the simple earnings per share calculation is affected because either a reduction in interest expense (net of income taxes) due to the assumed retirement of debt or an increase in interest revenue (net of income taxes) from the assumed investments will cause earnings to increase. To be included in primary earnings per share, the net effect must be dilutive. Because both the numerator and denominator are affected, simple earnings per share must be computed initially in order to test for dilution. Exhibit 21-5 illustrates the computation of primary earnings per share for Harmon Corporation assuming (1) a large number of stock options are outstanding, and (2) no other common stock equivalents are outstanding.

**EXHIBIT 21-5**

## HARMON CORPORATION

Computation of Primary Earnings Per Share
(20% Rule, Only Stock Options Outstanding)

1. Income statement information:
   a. Net income for 1995 is $14,000.
   b. The income tax rate is 30%.
2. Balance sheet information:
   a. 5,000 common shares were outstanding the entire year. The stock sold at an average price of $52 per share during the year.
   b. Options to purchase 1,500 common shares at $40 per share were outstanding the entire year.
   c. 400 shares of nonconvertible preferred stock were outstanding the entire year. Dividends totaling $2,000 were declared on this stock in 1995.
   d. 12.5%, $20,000 mortgage payable was outstanding the entire year.
3. Primary earnings per share computations for 1995:

| Explanation | Earnings (Adjustments) | ÷ | Shares (Adjustments) | = | Earnings Per Share |
|---|---|---|---|---|---|
| Simple earnings and shares | $12,000$^b$ | ÷ | 5,000$^a$ | | = $2.40 Simple |
| Savings in interest expense | 700$^c$ | | | | |
| Increment in shares (options) | | | 500$^c$ | | |
| Primary earnings and shares | $12,700 | ÷ | 5,500 | | = $2.31 Primary |

a. Weighted average shares: 5,000 × 12/12 = 5,000

b. Simple earnings: $14,000  Net income
   $\underline{(2,000)}$  Preferred dividends
   $\underline{\$12,000}$

c. Adjustments for stock options:

   (1) Shares issued via assumed exercise                                    1,500
       Shares assumed reacquired (limited to 20% × 5,000*)              (1,000)
       Incremental shares                                                            500

   (2) Proceeds: 1,500 shares issued × $40                              $60,000
       Proceeds applied: 1,000 shares retired × $52                    (52,000)
       Balance of proceeds                                                      $ 8,000

   (3) Balance assumed applied to reduce mortgage payable, thereby decreasing interest expense by $1,000 ($8,000 × 0.125) but increasing net income by only $700 (due to a $300 increase in income taxes).

       *Shares outstanding at end of year

4. Evaluation of dilutive effect:
   a. $2.31 is less than $2.40; therefore, the common stock equivalent (stock options) is dilutive.
   b. Primary earnings per share is $2.31, since the stock options are the only common stock equivalents.

Because the stock options are the only common stock equivalents outstanding in Exhibit 21-5, the primary earnings per share computed by including the stock options is the primary earnings per share disclosed on the income statement. If common stock equivalents in the form of convertible bonds or convertible preferred stock also were outstanding, the primary earnings per share figure, which included the options and warrants, would be "tentative"; it would be subject to the possible inclusion of the convertible securities in primary earnings per share.

## Convertible Securities

Convertible bonds and convertible preferred stock may contain provisions that, at the time of issuance, make them essentially equivalent to common stock. To make this evaluation consistently and objectively, the FASB established an "effective yield test."

*Effective Yield Test*
Recall that in Chapter 12, we discussed how convertible securities are issued at a lower interest rate and/or at a higher selling price than nonconvertible securities, and the difference is due to the value of the conversion feature. Thus, the greater the difference, the more valuable the conversion feature and the more likely it will be exercised. To evaluate the likelihood of conversion, the effective yield test was developed. **A convertible security is considered a common stock equivalent if, at the time of issuance, it has an effective yield of less than $66\frac{2}{3}$ percent of the then current average Aa corporate bond yield.**[9] The effective yield test (or simply **yield test**) may be formulated as follows:

$$\text{If:} \quad \begin{array}{c}\text{Effective Yield at Issuance}\\ \text{of Convertible Security}\end{array} < \left(66\tfrac{2}{3}\% \times \begin{array}{c}\text{Average Aa Corporate}\\ \text{Bond Yield at Issuance}\end{array}\right)$$

**Then: The security is a common stock equivalent**

Once a convertible security is determined to be a common stock equivalent at the date of issuance, it is *always* considered a common stock equivalent. Conversely, if a convertible security is determined *not* to be a common stock equivalent at its issuance date, it is *never* considered to be a common stock equivalent.

The designation *Aa* refers to the rating given to the quality of bonds by financial institutions and investor information services such as *Moody's* or *Standard & Poor's*. Aa corporate bond ratings have varied over the years as economic conditions have changed. Therefore, it is important to remember that it is the Aa corporate bond rating at the time of *issuance* of a convertible security that is used in the effective yield test. The *average* Aa corporate bond yield is based on bond yields for a brief period of time, say, one week including or immediately preceding the security issuance date.

The effective yield is based on the convertible security's stated annual interest or dividend payments, stated maturity date, and any original issuance premium or discount. Generally, semiannual compounding of interest is assumed. The calculation of

---

9. *FASB Statement No. 85, op. cit.,* par. 3, and *FASB Statement No. 55, op. cit.,* par. 7, amending *APB Opinion No. 15,* par. 33. Prior to *FASB Statement No. 85,* a "cash yield" (computed by dividing the annual cash interest or dividend for the convertible security by the market price at issuance) was compared to $66\frac{2}{3}\%$ of the average Aa bond yield at the time of issuance. This cash yield comparison is still in effect for securities issued from March 1, 1982 through March 31, 1985. Furthermore, prior to *FASB Statement No. 55,* the cash yield was compared to $66\frac{2}{3}\%$ of the *bank prime rate* at the time of issuance. Thus, this version of the cash yield comparison is still in effect for convertible securities issued before March 1, 1982. In either case, however, retroactive application of *FASB Statement No. 85* is permitted.

the effective yield for debt securities is illustrated in Chapter 12; however, in this chapter, the effective yield of a convertible bond at the time of its issuance will always be given. In the case of a convertible security (such as convertible preferred stock) that does *not* have a stated maturity date, the effective yield is computed by dividing the annual cash interest or dividend by the market price at the time of issuance.

To illustrate, assume a corporation issues convertible bonds at a price that results in an effective yield of 8.5% when the average Aa corporate bond yield is 12%. Since $66\frac{2}{3}$% of the 12% Aa corporate bond yield is 8%, the convertible bonds are *never* a common stock equivalent. At a later date, it also issues 8%, $100 par convertible preferred stock for $120 per share when the average Aa corporate bond yielded is 11%. The effective yield at issuance of the preferred stock is 6.67% [(0.08 × $100) ÷ $120)]. Since $66\frac{2}{3}$% of the 11% Aa corporate bond yield is 7.33%, the convertible preferred stock are *always* a common stock equivalent. Each of these effective yield tests is shown as follows:

*Convertible bonds:*

$8.5\% > (66\frac{2}{3}\% \times 12\%)$;      Not a common stock equivalent

*Convertible preferred stock:*

$\dfrac{\$8}{\$120} < (66\frac{2}{3}\% \times 12\%)$;      Common stock equivalent

In this illustration, the convertible bonds are excluded from the primary earnings per share computation. The convertible preferred stock are included, but *only* if it has a dilutive effect upon earnings per share.

*Conceptual Issues*

Although the effective yield test is an objective way of evaluating common stock equivalents, many accountants are critical of this test for several reasons. First, the use of $66\frac{2}{3}$% is arbitrary and has no direct correlation to the economic value of a conversion feature. Second, each corporation's bond yield (and bond market price) is established based upon its perceived risk, so that a comparison to the average Aa corporate bond yield is often inappropriate. Third, a comparison of a convertible preferred stock effective yield to the average Aa corporate bond yield is also inappropriate. Finally, use of the effective yield test may lead to the unrealistic inclusion (or exclusion) of certain securities in earnings per share. That is, due to changed financial conditions, the conversion option of a convertible security that initially satisfied the effective yield test may not be currently perceived as valuable by investors, and so ultimate conversion is unlikely. Likewise, the conversion feature of a security initially not classified as a common stock equivalent may become more valuable because of changed conditions, so that conversion is likely. Nonetheless, once a security is classified by the effective yield test on the date of issuance as either a common stock equivalent or not a common stock equivalent, that classification is never changed for earnings per share calculations, regardless of future events.

*Ranking of Common Stock Equivalents That Are Convertible*

As discussed earlier, stock options and warrants always are considered to be common stock equivalents and are the first to be included (assuming they are dilutive) in primary earnings per share. Other common stock equivalents also are included in primary earnings per share after stock options and warrants, but only if their inclusion also has a dilutive impact upon the earnings per share. Care must be taken to include the individual common stock equivalents, one at a time, in the proper sequence, because a mistake in that sequence may lead to the inclusion of an antidilutive security in primary earnings per share. That is, **a security that may appear to be individually dilutive may, in fact, be antidilutive in combination with other common stock equivalents.**

To determine the sequence in which to include common stock equivalents in primary earnings per share, the securities are ranked. This ranking is determined by comparing the individual impacts on primary earnings per share that result from the assumed conversion of each common stock equivalent into common shares. To compute this impact, the *if-converted* method is used. Here, **each common stock equivalent is *assumed* (for computing primary earnings per share) to have been converted into common stock at the beginning of the earliest period reported** (or at the date of issuance of the security, if later). This assumed conversion causes two changes in the earnings per share calculation: an increase in the denominator and an increase in the numerator. The denominator increases by the number of shares applicable to the assumed conversion. If bonds are assumed to be converted into common stock, the numerator increases because the net income would be larger, since the interest expense (net of income taxes) for the converted bonds would not have been incurred.[10] If preferred stock is assumed to be converted into common stock, the preferred dividends would not have been declared and the earnings available to common stockholders is increased.

The numerical value impact on primary earnings per share for each common stock equivalent is computed by dividing the change in the numerator by the change in the denominator,[11] as shown in the following equation:

$$\text{Impact on PEPS} = \frac{\text{Change in Earnings Per Share Numerator}}{\text{Change in Earnings Per Share Denominator}}$$

Once the impact on primary earnings per share has been computed for each common stock equivalent, the ranking is established. The common stock equivalent having the *lowest* impact on primary earnings per share is listed at the *top* of the ranking, and the other common stock equivalents are ranked in sequential order so that the security with the *highest* impact is listed at the *bottom* of the ranking. Beginning with the common stock equivalent listed at the top of the ranking, the securities are sequentially entered into the primary earnings per share computations.

It is important to understand that the common stock equivalent with the lowest numerical value impact on primary earnings per share causes the least increase in the numerator relative to the increase in the denominator from the assumed conversion. Consequently, **that security with the *lowest impact causes the greatest decrease* in primary earnings per share, is the most dilutive common stock equivalent, and is the first (after options and warrants) to be included in primary earnings per share.** The ranking enables the common stock equivalents to be sequentially included in primary earnings per share in the descending order of their dilutive effect on earnings per share.

Exhibit 21-6 illustrates the calculation of the impact of each common stock equivalent on primary earnings per share and the development of the ranking, assuming that Poston Corporation has four common stock equivalents outstanding the entire year.

---

10. The pretax savings in interest expense includes the interest paid or accrued plus any bond discount amortization or less any bond premium amortization. The net of tax interest expense savings is computed by multiplying the pretax interest expense savings times one minus the effective income tax rate.

11. This and the subsequent discussion dealing with the computation of tentative primary earnings per share is modified from that presented by S. Davidson and R. Weil in "A Shortcut in Computing Earnings Per Share," *Journal of Accountancy* (December, 1975), pp. 45–47.

---

**EXHIBIT 21-6**

## POSTON CORPORATION

Computation of Impact of Common Stock
Equivalents on Primary Earnings Per Share

### A. Summary of Common Stock Equivalents

| Security | Description |
|---|---|
| A | 9% convertible preferred stock. Dividends of $5,400 were declared during the year. The preferred shares are convertible into 3,000 shares of common stock. |
| B | 10% convertible bonds. Interest expense (net of income taxes) of $4,800 was recorded during the year. The bonds are convertible into 1,920 shares of common stock. |
| C | 8% convertible preferred stock. Dividends of $8,000 were declared during the year. The preferred shares are convertible into 5,000 shares of common stock. |
| D | 7% convertible bonds. Interest expense (net of income taxes) of $6,300 was recorded during the year. The bonds are convertible into 3,150 shares of common stock. |

### B. Computations and Rankings

| Security | Impact | Order in Ranking |
|---|---|---|
| A | $\dfrac{\$5,400}{3,000} = \$1.80$ | 2 |
| B | $\dfrac{\$4,800}{1,920} = \$2.50$ | 4 |
| C | $\dfrac{\$8,000}{5,000} = \$1.60$ | 1 |
| D | $\dfrac{\$6,300}{3,150} = \$2.00$ | 3 |

---

As may be seen, security C has the lowest impact on primary earnings per share and is the most dilutive common stock equivalent. It is the first common stock equivalent (after options and warrants) to be included in primary earnings per share.

*Computation of Tentative and Final Primary Earnings Per Share*
As indicated earlier, the computation of primary earnings per share begins with determining the increment in shares from the assumed exercise of stock options and warrants. This increment is added to the denominator from the simple earnings per share and an initial tentative primary earnings per share is calculated. Next, the remaining common stock equivalents are included in primary earnings per share in sequential order according to the ranking discussed earlier. The common stock equivalent listed at the top of the ranking is included first. This involves computing a new numerator and denominator by adding the changes in the numerator and denominator resulting

from the assumed conversion to the amounts used to compute the initial tentative primary earnings per share. A second tentative primary earnings per share is computed based on the revised numerator and denominator. If this second computation is less than the initial tentative primary earnings per share, the security is dilutive and the iterative process continues.[12] The change in the numerator and denominator from the next common stock equivalent in the ranking is added to the revised numerator and denominator and a third tentative earnings per share is computed. This procedure is repeated for each security in the ranking until the tentative primary earnings per share is *less* than the impact of the next common stock equivalent in the ranking (or the ranking is exhausted). The remaining securities in the ranking are antidilutive and are excluded from primary earnings per share. The final primary earnings per share is the last tentative figure and contains all the dilutive common stock equivalents included in the tentative primary earnings per share computations.

Exhibit 21-7 illustrates the computation of primary earnings per share for the Sokolich Corporation, assuming (1) stock options are outstanding, (2) both convertible bonds and convertible preferred stock are outstanding, and (3) each is a common stock equivalent, but (4) the convertible bonds are dilutive whereas the convertible preferred stock is antidilutive. The computations result in primary earnings per share of $1.95. Note that if no ranking had been prepared, and if both the convertible preferred stock and bonds had been included in primary earnings per share, an erroneous $1.96 [($2,000 + $800 + $210) ÷ (985 + 400 + 150)] primary earnings per share would have resulted.

## FULLY DILUTED EARNINGS PER SHARE

**The purpose of disclosing fully diluted earnings per share is to show the *maximum* potential dilution of current earnings per share that would have occurred if *all* dilutive contingent issuances had taken place.** This is an example of the application of the conservatism convention. Essentially, there are two differences between computing primary earnings per share and fully diluted earnings per share: (1) how convertible securities are included in the ranking for determining dilution, and (2) what market price is used under the treasury stock method for stock options and warrants. That is, it is possible for a convertible security designated as a common stock equivalent to be dilutive when included in primary earnings per share but antidilutive if included in fully diluted earnings per share. Furthermore, stock options and warrants may have a more dilutive impact than that assumed in primary earnings per share. Thus, a new set of computations must be made for fully diluted earnings per share. However, the sequence of steps is very similar to that for primary earnings per share.

The fully diluted earnings per share computations begin with the *simple* earnings per share numerator and denominator. Next, the incremental shares from the assumed exercise of stock options and warrants are added to the denominator. If the average market price during the period is the same as or higher than the ending market price, the incremental shares for fully diluted earnings per share are the *same* as those used in computing primary earnings per share. However, **if the ending market**

---

12. If no stock options or warrants are outstanding, the changes in the numerator and denominator resulting from the assumed conversion of the top-ranked common stock equivalent are added to the numerator and denominator used to compute simple earnings per share. The resulting primary earnings per share is then compared with simple earnings per share to test for dilution.

**EXHIBIT 21-7**

## SOKOLICH CORPORATION

Computation of Primary Earnings Per Share
(Options, Convertible Bonds, and Convertible Preferred Stock Are Outstanding)

1. Income statement information:
   a. Net income for 1995 is $2,800.
   b. The income tax rate is 30%.
2. Balance sheet information:
   a. 900 shares of common stock were outstanding the entire year.
   b. Options were outstanding the entire year. The assumed exercise of these options results in an increment of 85 shares of common stock.
   c. 100 shares of 8%, $100 par (and issuance price) convertible preferred stock were outstanding the entire year. $800 dividends were declared on this stock in 1995. The average Aa corporate bond yield was 14% at time of issuance. The preferred stock is a common stock equivalent [$8/$100 < $(66\frac{2}{3}\% \times 14\%)$]. Each share of preferred stock is convertible into 4 shares of common stock.
   d. 6% convertible bonds, $5,000 face value were outstanding the entire year. $300 interest was paid on the bonds in 1995. These bonds were issued to yield 6% at a time when the average Aa corporate bond yield was 10%. The bonds are common stock equivalents [6% < $(66\frac{2}{3}\% \times 10\%)$]. Each $1,000 bond is convertible into 30 shares of common stock.
3. Impact on primary earnings per share and resulting ranking:

| Security | Impact | Ranking |
|---|---|---|
| Preferred | $\frac{\$800}{100 \times 4} = \$2.00$ | 2 |
| Bonds | $\frac{\$300 \times (1 - 0.3)}{5 \times 30} = \$1.40$ | 1 |

4. Primary earnings per share computations for 1995:

| Explanation | Earnings (Adjustments) | ÷ | Shares (Adjustments) | = | Earnings Per Share |
|---|---|---|---|---|---|
| Simple earnings per share | $2,000[a] | ÷ | 900 | | = $2.22 Simple |
| Increment in shares (options) | | | 85 | | |
| PEPS₁ earnings and shares | $2,000 | ÷ | 985 | | = $2.03 PEPS₁ |
| Savings in interest expense (bonds) | 210[b] | | | | |
| Increment in shares (bonds) | | | 150[c] | | |
| Primary earnings and shares | $2,210 | ÷ | 1,135 | | = $1.95 Primary |

a. $2,000 = $2,800 net income − $800 preferred dividends
b. $210 = $300 pretax interest expense savings × (1 − 0.3). Note: The bonds were issued at their face value so there is no discount or premium amortization.
c. 150 = 5 bonds × 30 common shares

5. Evaluation of dilutive effect:
   a. $1.40 is less than $2.03; therefore, the convertible bonds' common stock equivalents are dilutive and are included in primary earnings per share.
   b. The $2.00 impact on primary earnings per share of the convertible preferred stock is more than $1.95; therefore, inclusion of the preferred stock in primary earnings per share would be antidilutive.
   c. Primary earnings per share is $1.95.

price of the common stock is *higher* than the average market price during the period, this *ending* market price is used in the *treasury stock method* to determine the assumed number of common shares reacquired with the proceeds from the assumed option exercise. To illustrate, assume a corporation has outstanding 8,000 common shares and options to purchase 900 common shares at a price of $20 per share. The average and ending market prices per share of the stock are $25 and $30, respectively. Under the treasury stock method, the incremental shares for computing *primary* earnings per share are 180 (900 issued at $20 per share option price for proceeds of $18,000, less 720 reacquired at an *average* price of $25 per share), but the incremental shares are 300 for computing *fully diluted* earnings per share because of the higher ending market price. This latter calculation is as follows:

Shares issued per assumed exercise                                                   900

Shares assumed reacquired:

$$\frac{\text{Proceeds}}{\text{Ending Market Price per Share}} = \frac{900 \times \$20}{\$30} = \frac{\$18,000}{\$30} = \underline{(600)}$$

Assumed increment in common shares for computing
fully diluted earnings per share                                        $\underline{\underline{300}}$

*Instead of* the 180 shares, these 300 shares are included in the denominator for computing an initial tentative fully diluted earnings per share. If the 20% limitation is in effect, the same steps are completed as for primary earnings per share. However, when the higher ending market price is being used to reacquire common stock, fewer proceeds will remain to retire short-or long-term debt.

Next, the impact on fully diluted earnings per share of the assumed conversion of each convertible security is calculated (as illustrated for primary earnings per share). A new ranking is made, with the convertible security having the lowest impact on fully diluted earnings per share listed at the top. The remaining convertible securities are included in sequential order, so that the security having the highest impact on fully diluted earnings per share is listed at the bottom of the ranking. **The only difference between this ranking and the one prepared for primary earnings per share is that this ranking includes *all* convertible securities, whereas the primary ranking included only common stock equivalents.**[13] This difference may be significant. It is possible for a common stock equivalent to be highly ranked in the primary ranking and included in primary earnings per share because of its individual dilution. However, the same security may be ranked lower in the fully diluted ranking in relation to other more dilutive convertible securities and be *excluded* from the fully diluted earnings per share computations because it is antidilutive.

Finally, each convertible security is included in fully diluted earnings per share in sequential order based on the fully diluted ranking. This procedure is identical to that described for primary earnings per share. Beginning with the convertible security listed at the top of the ranking (that is, the one with the lowest numerical value impact), a new numerator and denominator are computed by adding the changes resulting from the assumed conversion to the numerator and denominator used to compute the initial tentative fully diluted earnings per share (including the options and

---

13. Both the impacts on primary earnings per share and on fully diluted earnings per share, as well as the rankings, are usually prepared at the same time, directly after testing for the common stock equivalency status of each convertible security.

warrants). The iterative process is continued until the tentative fully diluted earnings per share is less than the impact of the next convertible security in the ranking. The remaining securities in the ranking are antidilutive and are not included in fully diluted earnings per share. The last tentative figure is the fully diluted earnings per share. It contains all the dilutive convertible securities included in the tentative calculations.[14]

The computation of fully diluted earnings per share is shown in the comprehensive illustration in Exhibit 21-10 presented later in the chapter.

## ADDITIONAL CONSIDERATIONS

Several other issues are relevant to simple, primary, and fully diluted earnings per share. These issues involve the 3% rule, conversion ratios, contingent issuances, and disclosures on the income statement and in the notes to the financial statements.

### The 3% Rule

To provide "relief" from the complex analysis involved in computing primary and fully diluted earnings per share, any reduction in earnings per share due to dilutive options and convertible securities is ignored if it is less than 3% in the aggregate. Unfortunately, this evaluation is made *after* all the complex calculations have been completed. This materiality criterion may be expressed as follows: If the aggregate dilution from all the dilutive options and convertible securities is less than 3% of the simple earnings per common share outstanding, it is not necessary to disclose primary or fully diluted earnings per share.[15] Thus, **if fully diluted earnings per share is more than 97% of simple earnings per common share outstanding,** *only* **simple earnings per common share outstanding is disclosed.** On the other hand, **if fully diluted earnings per share is less than or equal to 97% of simple earnings per share, then** *both* **primary and fully diluted earnings per share are disclosed** (and simple earnings per common share outstanding is *not* disclosed).

### Conversion Ratios

At the time of issuance, convertible preferred stock and convertible bonds are convertible into a specified number of common shares based upon the conversion contract. Similarly, the number of common shares that may be acquired under a stock option generally is established when the option is granted. If a convertible security or stock option is not immediately convertible or exercisable, the earliest effective conversion rate or exercise price during the succeeding 5 years is used for primary earnings per share. For fully diluted earnings per share, the most advantageous (from the standpoint of the security holder) conversion or exercise rights that become effective within 10 years of the end of the current period is used in the computations.

After the issuance of convertible securities or stock options, a corporation may declare a stock dividend or stock split. Typically, the "conversion ratio" for convertible securities and stock options is proportionally adjusted for the stock dividend or split. For instance, assume a share of preferred stock is convertible into 4 shares of com-

---

14. For a detailed flowchart to compute both primary and fully diluted earnings per share, see S. Matulich, L. Nikolai, and S. Olson, "Earnings Per Share: A Flowchart Approach to Teaching Concepts and Procedures," *The Accounting Review,* (January, 1977), pp. 233–247, and W. Stephens, "Earnings Per Share: A Flow Chart Approach to Teaching Concepts and Procedures: A Comment," *The Accounting Review,* (January, 1978), pp. 260–262.

15. *APB Opinion No. 15, op. cit.,* fn. 2, and Ball, *op. cit.,* p. 22.

mon stock before a two-for-one stock split on the common stock. *After* the stock split, the preferred stock is convertible into 8 shares of common stock. The *current* conversion ratio for convertible securities and stock options is used in any earnings per share computations.

## Contingent Issuances

Common shares may be "earmarked" for future issuance. Such stock is referred to as contingently issuable common stock. When no further conditions must be met before issuance, these shares are considered outstanding for earnings per share purposes. Some contingent issuances depend on the satisfaction of certain conditions, such as attaining or maintaining a certain level of earnings. These shares are considered outstanding for both primary and fully diluted earnings per share if the conditions have been met. Even if the conditions have not been met, if dilutive, the shares are included in fully diluted earnings per share based on the assumed conditions.

## Income Statement Disclosures

Assuming that there is material dilution from the inclusion of convertible securities in the earnings per share of a corporation with a complex capital structure, presentation of both primary and fully diluted earnings per share is required on the face of the income statement. Furthermore, if any results from discontinued operations, extraordinary items, or cumulative effects of changes in accounting principles are included in net income, both the primary and fully diluted earnings per share are separated into the components relating to each of these items as well as income from continuing operations.[16] These components are summed to disclose the total primary and fully diluted earnings per share, respectively. The primary earnings per share related to income from continuing operations is calculated by adding the results from discontinued operations, extraordinary items, and the cumulative effects of changes in accounting principles to (or deducting them from) the earnings used in the total primary earnings per share computation, and dividing the result by the number of shares used in the total primary earnings per share computation. A similar technique is used to calculate fully diluted earnings per share related to income from continuing operations. Exhibit 21-10 illustrates the recommended disclosure format.

## Other Disclosures

When primary and fully diluted earnings per share are disclosed on the face of the income statement, additional disclosures are made in the notes to the financial statements. These include a description of the rights and privileges of the various securities outstanding and a schedule or note explaining the bases on which both primary and fully diluted earnings per share are calculated. The schedule or note includes information that:

1. Identifies any securities regarded as common stock equivalents.
2. Identifies the other securities included in the fully diluted earnings per share computation.
3. Describes all assumptions and adjustments made.
4. Discloses the number of shares issued on conversion, exercise, or satisfaction of required conditions.

---

16. *APB Opinion No. 30, op. cit.,* par. 9 and 12.

**EXHIBIT 21-8**

**FLOWCHART OF EPS COMPUTATIONS**

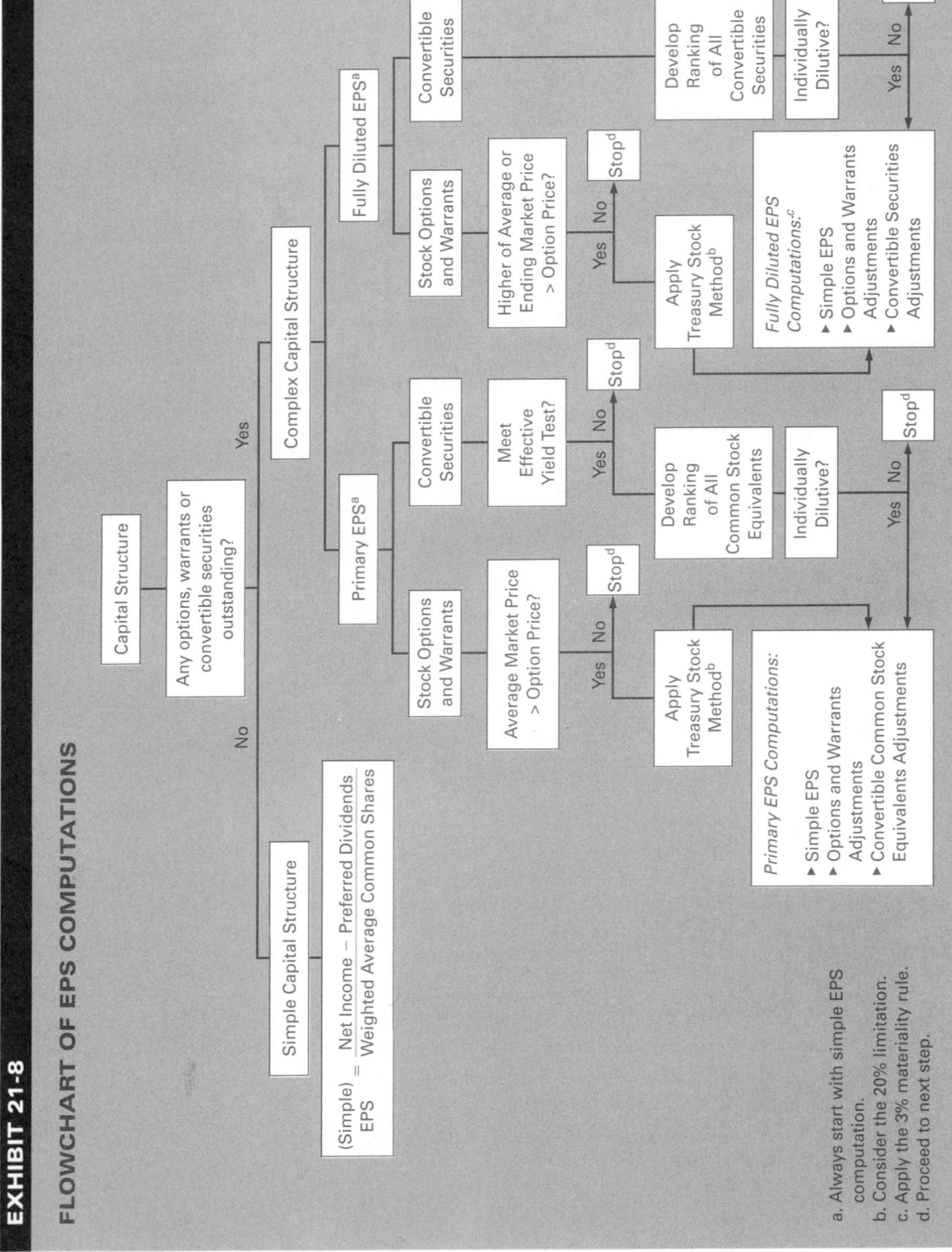

a. Always start with simple EPS computation.
b. Consider the 20% limitation.
c. Apply the 3% materiality rule.
d. Proceed to next step.

5. Describes the impact on earnings per share of subsequent conversions after the close of the accounting period but before the issuance of the financial report.[17]

## Earnings Per Share Flowchart

Exhibit 21-8 summarizes the major steps in the computation of earnings per common share outstanding for a simple capital structure and primary and fully diluted earnings per share for a complex capital structure. For the details involved in each step, refer back to the related previous sections.

## Disclosure Illustration

An illustration of the earnings per share disclosures of General Mills and the related note in its 1992 annual report is shown in Exhibit 21-9. Note that General Mills discloses its average number of common shares used in computing its earnings per share directly on the income statement.

## COMPREHENSIVE EARNINGS PER SHARE ILLUSTRATION

Exhibit 21-10 illustrates the computation and disclosure of primary and fully diluted earnings per share for the Watts Corporation that has (1) stock options outstanding, (2) three other common stock equivalents outstanding, and (3) one convertible bond issue outstanding that is not a common stock equivalent.

---

### EXHIBIT 21-9
### Earnings Per Share Disclosures

**GENERAL MILLS**

**Net Earnings and Earnings Per Share (in part)**

|  | Fiscal Year Ended | | |
| --- | --- | --- | --- |
| Amounts in Millions, Except Per Share Data | May 31, 1992 | May 26, 1991 | May 27, 1990 |
| Earnings from Continuing Operations | $505.6 | $464.2 | $373.7 |
| Discontinued Operations after Taxes | (10.0) | 8.5 | 7.7 |
| Net Earnings | $495.6 | $472.7 | $381.4 |
| Earnings per Share: | | | |
|   Continuing operations | $ 3.05 | $ 2.82 | $ 2.27 |
|   Discontinued operations | (.06) | .05 | .05 |
| Net Earnings per Share | $ 2.99 | $ 2.87 | $ 2.32 |
| Average Number of Common Shares | 165.7 | 164.5 | 164.4 |

**Notes to Consolidated Financial Statements (in part)**

*Note One: Summary of Significant Accounting Policies (in part)*

*G. Earnings per Share*

Earnings per share has been determined by dividing the appropriate earnings by the weighted average number of common shares outstanding during the year. Common share equivalents were not material.

---

17. *APB Opinion No. 15, op. cit.*, par. 20.

## EXHIBIT 21-10

## WATTS CORPORATION

Computation of Primary and Fully Diluted Earnings Per Share (Comprehensive Illustration)

1. Income statement information (1995):
   a. Income before extraordinary items        $17,400
      Extraordinary loss (net of income taxes)   (1,500)
      Net income                                $15,900
   b. The effective income tax rate is 30%.
2. Balance sheet information:
   a. 6,000 shares of common stock were outstanding the entire year. The stock sold at an average price of $25 per share during the year, but the year-end market price is $30 per share.
   b. Options to purchase 800 shares of common stock at $20 per share were outstanding the entire year.
   c. 7.5%, $100 par convertible preferred stock, $16,000 par value (and issuance price), were outstanding the entire year. $1,200 dividends were declared on the stock in 1995. The average Aa corporate bond yield was 12% at time of issuance. The 7.5% preferred stock is a common stock equivalent [$7.50/$100 < ($66\frac{2}{3}\% \times 12\%$)]. Each preferred stock is convertible into 5 shares of common stock.
   d. 9%, 100 par convertible preferred stock, $10,000 par value (issued at 112), were outstanding the entire year. $900 dividends were declared on the stock in 1995. The average Aa corporate bond yield was 13% at time of issuance. The 9% preferred stock is a common stock equivalent [$9/$112 = 8.04\% < ($66\frac{2}{3}\% \times 13\%$)]. Each preferred stock is convertible into 4 shares of common stock.
   e. 6% convertible bonds, $30,000 face value, were outstanding the entire year. The bonds were issued for $32,000, a price that yielded 5.4% when the average Aa corporate bond yield was 9%. The 6% bonds are common stock equivalents [$5.4\% < ($66\frac{2}{3}\% \times 9\%$)]. Bond interest expense of $1,720 was recorded in 1995; the total premium is being amortized at the rate of $80 per year. Each $1,000 bond is convertible into 19 shares of common stock.
   f. 9.2% convertible bonds, $25,000 face value, were outstanding the entire year. The bonds were issued at $23,750, a price that yielded 9.7% when the average Aa corporate bond yield was 14%. The 9.2% bonds are not common stock equivalents [$9.7\% > ($66\frac{2}{3}\% \times 14\%$)]. Bond interest expense of $2,350 was recorded in 1995; the total discount is being amortized at the rate of $50 per year. Each $1,000 bond is convertible into 45 shares of common stock.
3. Impact on earnings per share and resulting rankings:

| Security | Impact on EPS | Primary Ranking | Fully Diluted Ranking |
|---|---|---|---|
| 7.5% Preferred | $\dfrac{0.075 \times \$16,000}{160 \times 5} = \$1.50$ | 1 | 2 |
| 9% Preferred | $\dfrac{0.09 \times \$10,000}{100 \times 4} = \$2.25$ | 3 | 4 |
| 6% Bonds | $\dfrac{[(\$30,000 \times 0.06) - \$80] \times (1 - 0.3)}{30 \times 19} = \$2.11$ | 2 | 3 |
| 9.2% Bonds | $\dfrac{(\$25,000 \times 0.092) + \$50] \times (1 - 0.3)}{25 \times 45} = \$1.46$ | — | 1 |

4. Primary earnings per share computations for 1995:

| Explanation | Earnings (Adjustments) | ÷ | Shares (Adjustments) | = Earnings Per Share |
|---|---|---|---|---|
| Simple earnings and shares | $13,800[a] | ÷ | 6,000 | = $2.30 Simple |
| Increment in shares (options) | | | 160[b] | |
| PEPS$_1$ earnings and shares | $13,800 | ÷ | 6,160 | = $2.24 PEPS$_1$ |
| Savings in 7.5% preferred dividends | 1,200[c] | | | |
| Increment in shares | | | 800[d] | |
| PEPS$_2$ earnings and shares | $15,000 | ÷ | 6,960 | = $2.16 PEPS$_2$ |
| Savings in 6% bond interest expense | 1,204[e] | | | |
| Increment in shares | | | 570[f] | |
| Primary earnings and shares | $16,204[g] | ÷ | 7,530 | = $2.15[h] Primary |

a. $13,800 = $15,900 − $1,200 preferred dividends − $900 preferred dividends

b. $160 = 800 - \dfrac{800 \times \$20}{\$25}$

c. $1,200 = 0.075 × $16,000

## EXHIBIT 21-10, Continued

    d. $800 = 160$ preferred shares $\times$ 5 common shares

    e. $\$1,204 = [(\$30,000 \times 0.06) - \$80 \text{ premium amortization}] \times (1 - 0.3)$

    f. $570 = 30$ bonds $\times$ 19 common shares

    g. The 9% convertible preferred stocks, although common stock equivalents, are *not* included in primary earnings per share because their impact ($2.25) is greater than $2.15 and these securities are antidilutive.

    h. Primary earnings per share related to income before extraordinary items equals $2.35 [($16,204 + $1,500 extraordinary loss) $\div$ 7,530 shares].

5. Fully diluted earnings per share computations for 1995:

| Explanation | Earnings (Adjustments) | $\div$ | Shares (Adjustments) | = Earnings Per Share |
|---|---|---|---|---|
| Simple earnings and shares | $13,800[a] | $\div$ | 6,000 | = $2.30 Simple |
| Increment in shares (options) | | | 267[b] | |
| FDEPS$_1$ earnings and shares | $13,800 | $\div$ | 6,267 | = $2.20 FDEPS$_1$ |
| Savings in 9.2% bond interest expense | 1,645[c] | | | |
| Increment in shares | | | 1,125[d] | |
| FDEPS$_2$ earnings and shares | $15,445 | $\div$ | 7,392 | = $2.09 FDEPS$_2$ |
| Savings in 7.5% preferred dividends | 1,200[e] | | | |
| Increment in shares | | | 800[f] | |
| Fully diluted earnings and shares | $16,645[g] | $\div$ | 8,192[h] | = $2.03[i] Fully diluted |

    a. $\$13,800 = \$15,900 - \$1,200 - \$900$

    b. $267 = 800 - \dfrac{800 \times \$20}{\$30}$

    c. $\$1,645 = [(\$25,000 \times 0.092) + \$50] \times (1 - 0.3)$

    d. $1,125 = 25$ bonds $\times$ 45 common shares

    e. $\$1,200 = 0.075 \times \$16,000$

    f. $800 = 160$ preferred shares $\times$ 5 common shares

    g. The 6% convertible bonds and the 9% convertible preferred stocks are *not* included in fully diluted earnings per share because their impacts ($2.11 and $2.25, respectively) are greater than $2.03 and each security is antidilutive.

    h. Fully diluted earnings per share related to income before extraordinary items equals $2.21 [($16,645 + $1,500 extraordinary loss) $\div$ 8,192 shares].

    i. $2.03 < 97%$ of $2.30; therefore, both primary and fully diluted earnings per share are disclosed on the income statement.

6. Condensed income statement presentation for 1995:

| | |
|---|---|
| Income before extraordinary items | $17,400 |
| Extraordinary loss (net of income taxes) | (1,500) |
| Net income | $15,900 |
| | |
| Primary earnings per share (see Note A) | |
| Income before extraordinary items | $2.35 |
| Extraordinary loss | (.20) |
| Net income | $2.15 |
| | |
| Fully diluted earnings per share (see Note A) | |
| Income before extraordinary items | $2.21 |
| Extraordinary loss | (.18) |
| Net income | $2.03 |

7. Note A to financial statements: Primary earnings per share is based on 6,000 average shares outstanding plus 1,530 incremental shares from giving effect to the assumed exercise or conversion of dilutive common stock equivalents. Earnings available to common stockholders were adjusted for any savings in interest (net of income taxes) and dividends as a result of the assumed conversions. Securities considered to be common stock equivalents include stock options, 7.5% convertible preferred stock, 6% convertible bonds, and 9% convertible preferred stock. The last security is not included in primary earnings per share because it is antidilutive.

    Fully diluted earnings per share is based on 6,000 average shares outstanding plus 2,192 incremental shares from giving effect to the assumed exercise of stock options and the conversion of two dilutive convertible securities, 9.2% convertible bonds and the 7.5% convertible preferred stock. Earnings available to common stockholders were adjusted accordingly. The remaining convertible securities are antidilutive and are not included in fully diluted earnings per share.

## QUESTIONS

**Q21-1**   What is a *simple capital structure*?

**Q21-2**   How is "earnings per common share outstanding" computed for a corporation with a simple capital structure?

**Q21-3**   What is the "weighted average" number of shares for computing earnings per share and how is it calculated?

**Q21-4**   On what date are stock dividends and splits considered to be issued for computing earnings per share?

**Q21-5**   Identify several securities that might be found in the complex capital structure of a corporation.

**Q21-6**   What two earnings per share figures generally are reported for a corporation with a complex capital structure? Besides common shares outstanding, what additional securities are included in each earnings per share calculation?

**Q21-7**   What is a *common stock equivalent*? When is it included in earnings per share?

**Q21-8**   What is the *treasury stock method*? How is the increase in the earnings per share denominator determined under the treasury stock method?

**Q21-9**   How is the increase in the number of common shares determined in regard to stock options (assume options are outstanding to acquire less than 20% of the actual common stock) for computing (a) primary and (b) fully diluted earnings per share?

**Q21-10**   For primary earnings per share calculations, what modifications must be made in the treasury stock method when the number of shares obtainable in stock options is greater than 20% of the actual common shares outstanding at year-end?

**Q21-11**   What is the "yield test" and how is it applied?

**Q21-12**   Discuss how to develop a ranking for determining in which order to include common stock equivalents in the primary earnings per share calculations. How does this ranking differ from the one developed for fully diluted earnings per share?

**Q21-13**   What is the purpose of disclosing fully diluted earnings per share?

**Q21-14**   Explain the 3% rule.

**Q21-15**   What additional disclosures are made concerning the primary and fully diluted earnings per share figures shown on the income statement?

## CASES

*C21-1   Earnings Per Share*
"Earnings per share" (EPS) is the most featured single financial statistic about modern corporations. Daily published quotations of stock prices also include a "times earnings" figure for many securities that is based on EPS. Often, the focus of analysts' discussions will be on the EPS of the corporations receiving their attention.

**Required**
1. Explain how dividends or dividend requirements on any class of preferred stock that may be outstanding affect the computation of EPS.
2. One of the technical procedures applicable in EPS computations is the "treasury stock method."
   a. Briefly describe the circumstances under which it might be appropriate to apply the treasury stock method.
   b. There is a limit to the extent to which the treasury stock method is applicable. Indicate what this limit is and give a succinct indication of the procedures that should be followed beyond the treasury stock limits.

3. Under some circumstances, convertible bonds would be considered "common stock equivalents," while under other circumstances, they would not.
   a. When is it proper to treat convertible bonds as common stock equivalents? What is the effect on computation of EPS in such cases?
   b. In case convertible bonds are not considered as common stock equivalents, explain how they are handled for purposes of EPS computations. (*AICPA adapted*)

*C21-2   Complex Capital Structure*
The earnings per share data required of a company depend on the nature of its capital structure. A corporation may have a simple capital structure and only compute "earnings per common share" or may have a complex capital structure and have to compute "primary earnings per share" and "fully diluted earnings per share."

**Required**
1. Define the term *common stock equivalent* and describe what securities would be considered common

stock equivalents in the computation of earnings per share.

2. Define the term *complex capital structure* and discuss the disclosures (both financial and explanatory) necessary for earnings per share when a corporation has a complex capital structure. (*AICPA adapted*)

### C21-3 Common Stock Equivalents

Public enterprises are required to present earnings per share data on the face of the income statement.

**Required**

Compare and contrast primary earnings per share with fully diluted earnings per share for each of the following:

1. The effect of common stock equivalents on the number of shares used in the computation of earnings per share data.
2. The effect of convertible securities that are *not* common stock equivalents on the number of shares used in the computation of earnings per share data.
3. The effect of antidilutive securities. (*AICPA adapted*)

### C21-4 Stock Options and EPS

Jones Company has adopted a traditional stock option plan for its officers and other employees. This plan is properly considered a compensatory plan.

**Required**

Discuss how accounting for this plan will affect net earnings and earnings per share. *Ignore income tax considerations and accounting for income tax benefits.* (*AICPA adapted*)

### C21-5 Researching GAAP  ⟳

You are the accountant for Monnig Company. On January 2, 1995, the company issued a "package" of securities for $65,000, when the average Aa corporate bond yield was 9.6%. The package consisted of 600 shares of $5 par common stock, 200 shares of 8%, $100 par convertible preferred stock, and thirty 9%, $1,000 face value nonconvertible bonds. At the time of issuance, the common stock had a market value of $24 per share, the preferred stock had a market value of $126 per share, and the bonds had a market value of $980 per bond. It is the end of 1995 and you are in the process of computing Monnig Company's 1995 primary earnings per share.

**Required**

Research the related generally accepted accounting principles and prepare a written memo to the Monnig Company's auditors that explains whether or not the shares of convertible preferred stock are included in the computation of the 1995 primary earnings per share. Cite your reference and applicable paragraph numbers.

### C21-6 Researching GAAP  ⟳

In 1994, its first year of operations, Tara Corporation appropriately reported simple earnings per share of $1.05 on its income statement. During 1995, the company instituted a stock option plan and is required to report both primary and fully diluted earnings per share of $1.12 and $0.98, respectively, on its 1995 income statement. In its 1995 annual report, Tara Company presents comparative income statements for 1994 and 1995.

**Required**

Research the related generally accepted accounting principles and prepare a short memo to the Tara Corporation's president that explains how to report the 1994 and 1995 comparative earnings per share in its 1995 annual report. Cite your reference and applicable paragraph numbers.

## MULTIPLE CHOICE

*Select the best answer for each of the following.*

Items 1 and 2 are based on the following data:

At December 31, 1995 and 1996, Gravin Corporation had 90,000 shares of common stock and 20,000 shares of convertible preferred stock outstanding, in addition to 9% convertible bonds payable in the face amount of $2,000,000. During 1995, Gravin paid dividends of $2.50 per share on the preferred stock. The preferred stock is convertible into 20,000 shares of common stock, and is considered a common stock equivalent. The 9% convertible bonds are convertible into 30,000 shares of common stock, but are not considered common stock equivalents. Net income for 1995 was $970,000. Assume an income tax rate of 30%.

*M21-1* How much is the primary earnings per share for the year ended December 31, 1995?

| | |
|---|---|
| a. $7.70 | c. $8.82 |
| b. $8.36 | d. $10.78 |

*M21-2* How much is the fully diluted earnings per share for the year ended December 31, 1995?

| | |
|---|---|
| a. $7.83 | c. $9.35 |
| b. $8.21 | d. $10.22 |

M21-3    In determining earnings per share, interest expense (net of applicable income taxes) on convertible debt that is both a common stock equivalent and dilutive should be

a.  Added back to net income for primary earnings per share and ignored for fully diluted earnings per share
b.  Added back to net income for both primary earnings per share and fully diluted earnings per share
c.  Deducted from net income for primary earnings per share and ignored for fully diluted earnings per share
d.  Deducted from net income for both primary earnings per share and fully diluted earnings per share

M21-4    Appling Company had 300,000 shares of common stock issued and outstanding at December 31, 1994. No common stock was issued during 1995. On January 1, 1995, Appling issued 200,000 shares of nonconvertible preferred stock. During 1995, Appling declared and paid $150,000 cash dividends on the common stock and $120,000 on the preferred stock. Net income for the year ended December 31, 1995 was $660,000. What should be Appling's 1995 earnings per common share?

a.  $1.30                                            c.  $1.80
b.  $1.70                                            d.  $2.20

M21-5    In determining primary earnings per share, dividends on nonconvertible cumulative preferred stock should be

a.  Deducted from net income whether declared or not
b.  Deducted from net income only if declared
c.  Added back to net income whether declared or not
d.  Disregarded

M21-6    When computing fully diluted earnings per share, convertible securities that are *not* common stock equivalents are

a.  Recognized whether they are dilutive or antidilutive
b.  Recognized only if they are dilutive
c.  Recognized only if they are antidilutive
d.  Ignored

M21-7    Redford Corporation's capital structure at December 31, 1994 was as follows:

|  | **Shares issued and outstanding** |
| --- | --- |
| Common stock | 100,000 |
| Nonconvertible preferred stock | 20,000 |

On July 3, 1995, Redford issued a 10% stock dividend on its common stock, and paid a cash dividend of $2.00 per share on its preferred stock. Net income for the year ended December 31, 1995 was $780,000. What should be Redford's 1995 earnings per common share?

a.  $7.80                                            c.  $7.05
b.  $7.09                                            d.  $6.73

M21-8    In applying the treasury stock method of computing the dilutive effect of outstanding options or warrants, for fully diluted earnings per share, when is it appropriate to use the ending market price of common stock as the assumed repurchase price?

a.  Always
b.  Never
c.  When the ending market price is lower than the average market price and higher than the exercise price
d.  When the ending market price is higher than the average market price and the exercise price

M21-9    Faucet Company has 2,500,000 shares of common stock outstanding on December 31, 1994. An additional 500,000 shares of common stock were issued on April 3, 1995, and 250,000 more on July 3, 1995. On October 2, 1995, Faucet issued 5,000, $1,000 face value, 7% convertible bonds. Each bond is convertible into 40 shares of common stock. The bonds were *not* considered common stock equivalents at the time of their issuance, and *no* bonds were converted into common stock in 1995. What is the number of shares to be used in computing primary earnings per share and fully diluted earnings per share, respectively, for the year ended December 31, 1995?

a.  2,875,000 and 2,975,000                          c.  3,000,000 and 3,050,000
b.  2,875,000 and 3,075,000                          d.  3,000,000 and 3,200,000

**M21-10** For purposes of computing the weighted average number of shares outstanding during the year, a midyear event that must be treated as occurring at the beginning of the year is the

a. Issuance of stock warrants

b. Purchase of treasury stock

c. Sale of additional common stock

d. Declaration and payment of stock dividend

*(AICPA adapted)*

## EXERCISES

**E21-1** *Weighted Average Shares* At the beginning of the current year, Heath Company had 20,000 shares of $10 par common stock outstanding. During the year, it engaged in the following transactions related to its common stock, so that at year-end it had 63,800 shares outstanding:

| | | |
|---|---|---|
| Apr. | 2 | Issued 5,000 shares of stock |
| June | 4 | Issued 4,000 shares of stock |
| July | 1 | Issued a 10% stock dividend |
| Sept. | 28 | Issued a two-for-one stock split, reducing the par value to $5 per share |
| Oct. | 3 | Reacquired 1,000 shares as treasury stock |
| Nov. | 27 | Reissued the 1,000 shares of treasury stock |

**Required**

Determine the weighted average number of shares outstanding for computing the current earnings per share.

**E21-2** *Comparative Earnings Per Share* Ryan Company reports net income of $5,125 for the year ended December 31, 1994, its first year of operations. On January 2, 1994, the company issued 9,000 shares of common stock. On August 2, 1994, it issued an additional 3,000 shares of stock, resulting in 12,000 shares outstanding at year-end.

During 1995, Ryan Company earned net income of $16,400. It issued 2,000 additional shares of stock on March 3, 1995 and declared and issued a two-for-one stock split on November 2, 1995, resulting in 28,000 shares outstanding at year-end.

During 1996, Ryan Company earned net income of $23,520. The only common stock transaction during 1996 was a 20% stock dividend issued on July 3, 1996.

**Required**

1. Compute the earnings per common share outstanding that would be disclosed in the 1994 annual report.
2. Compute the 1994 and 1995 comparative earnings per common share outstanding that would be disclosed in the 1995 annual report.
3. Compute the 1994, 1995, and 1996 comparative earnings per common share outstanding that would be disclosed in the 1996 annual report.

**E21-3** *Simple Earnings Per Share* Sardel Company reported net income of $28,275 for 1995. During all of 1995, the company had 1,000 shares of 10%, $100 par nonconvertible preferred stock outstanding, on which the year's dividends had been paid. At the beginning of 1995, the company had 7,000 shares of common stock outstanding. On April 3, 1995, the company issued another 2,000 shares of common stock so that 9,000 common shares were outstanding at the end of 1995. Common dividends of $17,000 had been paid during 1995.

**Required**

Compute the earnings per common share outstanding of Sardel Company.

**E21-4** *Simple Earnings Per Share* Burke Company shows the following condensed income statement information for the year ended December 31, 1995:

| | |
|---|---|
| Income before extraordinary items | $28,712 |
| Less: Extraordinary loss (net of income tax credit) | (2,312) |
| Net income | $26,400 |

The company declared dividends of $6,000 on preferred stock and $17,280 on common stock. At the beginning of 1995, 10,000 shares of common stock were outstanding. On May 4, 1995 the company issued 2,000 additional common shares, and on October 19, 1995 it issued a 20% stock dividend on its common stock. The preferred stock is not convertible.

**Required**

1. Compute the earnings per common share outstanding.
2. Show the income statement disclosure of earnings per share.
3. Draft a related note to accompany the financial statements.

E21-5    *Primary EPS: Ranking Common Stock Equivalents*    Paulette Company has a complex capital structure and reported net income of $35,000 for 1995. It had 10,000 shares of common stock outstanding for all of 1995. Paulette has three common stock equivalents (all convertible bonds) in its capital structure. In applying the "if converted" method for computing its primary earnings per share, the company prepared the following schedule for these three common stock equivalents (CSE):

| Security | Change in EPS Numerator | ÷ Change in EPS Denominator | = Impact on PEPS |
|---|---|---|---|
| $CSE_1$ | $7,000 | 2,100 | $3.33 |
| $CSE_2$ | $5,000 | 2,500 | $2.00 |
| $CSE_3$ | $6,000 | 2,000 | $3.00 |

**Required**

1. Prepare a ranking of the order in which the common stock equivalents of Paulette Company should be included in primary earnings per share.
2. Prepare a schedule to compute the primary earnings of the Paulette Company for 1995.

E21-6    *Impact on EPS and Rankings*    Matthews Company had five convertible securities outstanding during all of 1995. It paid the appropriate interest (and amortized any related premium or discount using the straight-line method) and dividends on each security during 1995. Each convertible security is described in the following table. The corporate income tax rate is 30%.

| Security | Description |
|---|---|
| 9.5% Preferred stock | $200,000 par value. Issued at 112. Common stock equivalent. Each $100 par preferred stock is convertible into 4.2 shares of common stock. |
| 11.0% Bonds | $220,000 face value. Issued at par. Common stock equivalent. Each $1,000 bond is convertible into 44 shares of common stock. |
| 8.0% Preferred stock | $150,000 par value. Issued at par. Not a common stock equivalent. Each $100 par preferred stock is convertible into 3.8 shares of common stock. |
| 10.0% Bonds | $100,000 face value. Issued at 94. Discount being amortized over 20-year life. Not a common stock equivalent. Each $1,000 bond is convertible into 55 shares of common stock. |
| 9.0% Bonds | $200,000 face value. Issued at 108. Premium being amortized over 25-year life. Common stock equivalent. Each $1,000 bond is convertible into 48 shares of common stock. |

**Required**

1. Prepare a schedule that lists the impact of the assumed conversion of each convertible security on earnings per share.
2. Prepare a ranking of the order in which the securities would be included in (a) primary earnings per share computations and (b) fully diluted earnings per share computations.

E21-7    *Stock Options, EPS*    Butler Company has 30,000 shares of common stock outstanding during all of 1995. This common stock has been selling at an average market price of $45 per share. The ending market price is $50 per share. The company also has outstanding a $15,000 note payable upon which it is paying interest at a 12% annual rate. During 1995, Butler Company earned income of $36,000 after income taxes of 30%.

**Required**

1. Assuming that stock options to purchase 4,000 shares of common stock at $35 per share are outstanding the entire year, compute the primary and fully diluted earnings per share.
2. Repeat your analysis, assuming instead that the stock options allowed the purchase of 8,000 shares.

**E21-8** *Convertible Preferred Stock and EPS* Jamieson Company earned net income of $43,800 during 1995. At the beginning of 1995, it had 10,000 shares of common stock outstanding; an additional 4,000 shares were issued on July 3. During 1995, 600 shares of 8%, $100 par convertible preferred stock were outstanding the entire year. These shares were issued in 1993 for $128 per share when the average Aa corporate bond yield was 10%; each share is convertible into 5 shares of common stock. The corporate income tax rate is 30%.

**Required**

Compute primary and fully diluted earnings per share.

**E21-9** *Convertible Bonds and EPS* Clark Company's capital structure consists of common stock and convertible bonds. At the beginning of 1995, the company had 15,000 shares of common stock outstanding; an additional 4,500 shares were issued on May 4. The 7% convertible bonds have a face value of $80,000 and were issued in 1992 at par to yield 7% when the Aa corporate bond yield was 9%. Each $1,000 bond is convertible into 25 shares of common stock; to date, none of the bonds has been converted. During 1995, the company earned net income of $79,200 and was subject to an income tax rate of 30%.

**Required**

Compute primary and fully diluted earnings per share.

**E21-10** *Stock Splits, Convertibles, EPS* On January 1, 1995, Early Company had 10,000 shares of $10 par common stock and 1,000 shares of 9.7%, $100 par cumulative convertible preferred stock outstanding. On that date, each share of preferred stock was convertible into 2.5 shares of common stock. These convertible preferred shares are common stock equivalents. On August 3, 1995, the company issued a two-for-one stock split on the common stock, reducing the par value to $5 per share. This resulted in 20,000 shares of common stock outstanding at the end of 1995. During 1995, the company earned net income of $89,700.

**Required**

Compute the primary and fully diluted earnings per share.

**E21-11** *Convertible Securities and Earnings Per Share* Walker Company has 15,000 shares of common stock outstanding during all of 1995. It also has two convertible securities outstanding at the end of 1995. These are:

1. Convertible preferred stock: 1,000 shares of 9%, $100 par preferred stock were issued in 1994 for $140 per share. The average Aa corporate bond yield at the date of issuance was 10%. Each share of preferred stock is convertible into 3.5 shares of common stock. The current dividends have been paid. To date, no preferred stock has been converted.
2. Convertible bonds: Bonds with a face value of $100,000 and an interest rate of 10% were issued at par to yield 10% on July 5, 1995. The average Aa corporate bond yield at that time was 11%. Each $1,000 bond is convertible into 35 shares of common stock. To date, no bonds have been converted.

The company earned net income of $54,000 during 1995. Its income tax rate is 30%.

**Required**

Compute primary earnings per share and fully diluted earnings per share. Check for individual and aggregate dilution. What amount(s) would be disclosed on the income statement?

**E21-12** *Convertible Securities and Earnings Per Share* Caldwell Company has 20,000 shares of common stock outstanding during all of 1995. It also has two convertible securities outstanding at the end of 1995. These are:

1. Convertible preferred stock: 2,000 shares of 9.5%, $50 par preferred stock were issued on January 2, 1995 for $60 per share. The average Aa corporate bond yield at the date of issuance was 10%. Each share of preferred stock is convertible into 3 shares of common stock. Current dividends have been declared. To date, no preferred stock has been converted.
2. Convertible bonds: Bonds with a face value of $200,000 and an interest rate of 5.7% were issued at par to yield 5.7% in 1994. The average Aa corporate bond yield at that time was 9%. Each $1,000 bond is convertible into 22 shares of common stock. To date, no bonds have been converted.

The company earned net income of $61,500 during 1995. Its income tax rate is 30%.

**Required**
Compute primary earnings per share and fully diluted earnings per share. Check for individual and aggregate dilution. What amount(s) would be disclosed on the income statement?

## PROBLEMS

P21-1    *Income Statement and Simple EPS*    Pyle Company listed the following selected pretax items in its December 31, 1995 adjusted trial balance:

|  | Debit | Credit |
|---|---|---|
| Nonconvertible, 8% preferred stock, $100 par |  | $ 60,000 |
| Common stock, $5 par |  | 90,000 |
| Sales |  | 221,000 |
| Cost of goods sold | $131,000 |  |
| Gain on disposal of discontinued Segment B |  | 8,000 |
| Extraordinary gain from bond retirement |  | 15,000 |
| Operating expenses | 19,200 |  |
| Loss from operations of discontinued Segment B | 20,000 |  |

Additional information:

The preferred shares had been outstanding the entire year; annual dividends were declared and paid in 1995. During 1995, 2,000 common shares were issued on July 3 and 6,000 common shares were issued on November 2. Common dividends of $12,500 were declared and paid in 1995. The company is subject to a 30% income tax rate; there are no deferred taxes.

**Required**
Prepare the Pyle Company's 1995 income statement (multiple-step) and the related note.

P21-2    *Comparative Income Statements and Simple EPS*    Cody Company reported the following selected items in the stockholders' equity section of its balance sheet on December 31, 1994 and 1995:

|  | December 31, | |
|---|---|---|
|  | 1994 | 1995 |
| 7% preferred stock (nonconvertible), $100 par | $50,000 | $50,000 |
| Common stock, $10 par | 70,000 | 84,000 |

In addition, it listed the following selected pretax items in its December 31, 1994 and 1995 adjusted trial balances:

|  | December 31, 1994 | | December 31, 1995 | |
|---|---|---|---|---|
|  | Debit | Credit | Debit | Credit |
| Sales |  | $124,300 |  | $140,000 |
| Extraordinary gain |  | 6,000 |  | — |
| Cost of goods sold | $75,000 |  | $80,000 |  |
| Operating expenses | 18,000 |  | 20,000 |  |
| Extraordinary loss | — |  | 9,000 |  |

The preferred shares were outstanding during all of 1994 and 1995; annual dividends were declared and paid in each year. During 1994, 2,000 common shares were sold for cash on October 3. During 1995, a 20% stock dividend was declared and issued in early May. The company is subject to a 30% income tax rate; there are no deferred taxes.

**Required**

Prepare the comparative 1994 and 1995 income statements (multiple-step), and the related note that would appear in the Cody Company's 1995 annual report.

P21-3   *Earnings Per Share*  Wheeler Company began 1995 with 10,000 shares of $10 par common stock and 2,000 shares of 9.4%, $100 par convertible preferred stock outstanding. On April 3 and June 2, the company issued 2,000 and 6,000 additional shares of common stock, respectively. On November 18, the company declared a two-for-one stock split. Stock options that currently allow the purchase of 2,000 shares of common stock at $18 per share were outstanding during 1995. To date, none of these options have been exercised. The preferred stock was issued in 1994 at $138 per share when the average Aa corporate bond yield was 10%. Each share of preferred stock is currently convertible into 4 shares of common stock. To date, no preferred stock has been converted. Current dividends have been paid on both preferred and common stock. Net income for 1995 totaled $109,800. This amount included an extraordinary gain (net of income taxes) of $20,000. The company is subject to a 30% income tax rate. The common stock sold at an average market price of $20 per share during 1995, and the ending market price was $24 per share.

**Required**

1. Prepare supporting calculations and compute:
    a. Primary earnings per share
    b. Fully diluted earnings per share
2. Show how earnings per share would be disclosed on the income statement and draft an accompanying note to the financial statements.

P21-4   *Impact on EPS, Rankings, and Computations*  Madsen Company had five convertible securities outstanding during all of 1995. It paid the appropriate interest (and amortized any related premium or discount using the straight-line method) and dividends on each security during 1995. Each of the convertible securities is described in the following table:

| Security | Description |
|---|---|
| 10.2% Bonds | $200,000 face value. Issued at par. Determined to be a common stock equivalent. Each $1,000 bond is convertible into 28 shares of common stock. |
| 12.0% Bonds | $160,000 face value. Issued at 110. Premium being amortized over 20-year life. Not a common stock equivalent. Each $1,000 bond is convertible into 47 shares of common stock. |
| 9.0% Bonds | $200,000 face value. Issued at 95. Discount being amortized over 10-year life. Determined to be a common stock equivalent. Each $1,000 bond is convertible into 44 shares of common stock. |
| 8.3% Preferred stock | $120,000 par value. Issued at 108. Determined to be a common stock equivalent. Each $100 par preferred stock is convertible into 3.9 shares of common stock. |
| 7.5% Preferred stock | $180,000 par value. Issued at par. Not a common stock equivalent. Each $100 par preferred stock is convertible into 6 shares of common stock. |

Additional data:

Net income for 1995 totaled $119,460. The weighted average number of common shares outstanding during 1995 was 40,000 shares. No stock options or warrants are outstanding. The effective corporate income tax rate is 30%.

**Required**

1. Prepare a schedule that lists the impact of the assumed conversion of each convertible security on earnings per share.
2. Prepare a ranking of the order in which the common stock equivalents should be included in primary earnings per share.
3. Prepare a ranking of the order in which each of the convertible securities should be included in fully diluted earnings per share.
4. Compute primary earnings per share.
5. Compute fully diluted earnings per share.
6. Indicate the amount(s) of the earnings per share to be disclosed on the income statement.

*P21-5*   *Missing Amounts and EPS*   During 1995, the Olson Company earned net income and was subject to a 30% income tax rate. At the beginning of 1995, it had 42,000 common shares outstanding. On July 7, several thousand common shares were issued for cash. The 1995 ending market price of the common stock was $62.50 per share. The company has a stock option plan for its key executives. Under this plan, the executives may purchase 5,000 shares of common stock at a specified option price per share. To date, none of these options have been exercised.

    The company has three convertible securities in its capital structure. These securities have been outstanding for several years and include: (a) 7.8% preferred stock, $100 par value, issued at $113 per share, common stock equivalent, each share is convertible into 2.6 shares of common stock, current dividends have been paid, no preferred shares have been converted to date; (b) 8.5% bonds, $500,000 face value, issued at a discount when the average Aa corporate bond rating was 12.9%, not a common stock equivalent, each $1,000 bond is convertible into 20 shares of common stock, no bonds have been converted to date; and (c) 8% bonds, $800,000 face value, issued at face value, common stock equivalent, no bonds have been converted to date.

    To determine if each convertible security should be included in its earnings per share calculations, the company prepared the following schedule:

| Security | Impact on EPS |
|---|---|
| 7.8% preferred | $3.00 |
| 8.5% bonds | $3.15 |
| 8% bonds | $3.50 |

Using the preceding (and other) information, the company prepared the following schedules to compute its 1995 primary and fully diluted earnings per share:

| Explanation | Earnings $\div$ Shares $=$ | Earnings Per Share |
|---|---|---|
| Simple earnings and shares | $181,700 $\div$ 46,000 $=$ | $3.95 Simple |
| Stock option share increment | 700 | |
| Tentative PEPS$_1$ amounts | $181,700 $\div$ 46,700 $=$ | $3.89 PEPS$_1$ |
| 7.8% preferred dividend savings | 46,800 | |
| Increment in shares | 15,600 | |
| Tentative PEPS$_2$ | $228,500 $\div$ 62,300 $=$ | $3.67 PEPS$_2$ |
| 8% bond interest expense savings | 44,800 | |
| Increment in shares | 12,800 | |
| Primary earnings and shares | $273,300 $\div$ 75,100 $=$ | $3.64 Primary |

| Explanation | Earnings $\div$ Shares $=$ | Earnings Per Share |
|---|---|---|
| Simple earnings and shares | $181,700 $\div$ 46,000 $=$ | $3.95 Simple |
| Stock option share increment | 1,000 | |
| Tentative FDEPS$_1$ amounts | $181,700 $\div$ 47,000 $=$ | $3.87 FDEPS$_1$ |
| 7.8% preferred dividend savings | 46,800 | |
| Increment in shares | 15,600 | |
| Tentative FDEPS$_2$ amounts | $228,500 $\div$ 62,600 $=$ | $3.65 FDEPS$_2$ |
| 8.5% bond interest expense savings | 31,500 | |
| Increment in shares | 10,000 | |
| Fully diluted earnings and shares | $260,000 $\div$ 72,600 $=$ | $3.58 Fully diluted |

### Required

Based on the preceding information, answer the following questions (show supporting calculations):

1. What was the net income in 1995?
2. What was the yield rate on the 8% bonds when they were issued?
3. What is the option price per share on the stock options?
4. What is the conversion ratio on each $1,000, 8% bond?

5. What is the total par value of the 7.8% preferred stock?
6. What was the 1995 average market price per share of common stock?
7. What was the minimum percent that the effective yield could have been on the 8.5% bonds when they were issued?
8. What was the effective yield on the preferred stock when it was issued?
9. What was the minimum percent that the average Aa corporate bond yield could have been when the 8% bonds were issued?
10. What was the amount of the straight-line discount amortization on the 8.5% bonds for 1995?

P21-6 *Missing Amounts and EPS*  Broughton Company is subject to a 30% income tax rate and prepared the following schedules to compute its primary and fully diluted earnings per share for 1995:

| Explanation | Earnings ÷ | Shares = | Earnings Per Share |
|---|---|---|---|
| Simple earnings and shares | $100,800 ÷ | 21,000 = | $4.80 Simple |
| Stock option share increment | | 300 | |
| Tentative PEPS₁ amounts | $100,800 ÷ | 21,300 = | $4.73 PEPS₁ |
| 8% bond interest expense savings | 15,960 | | |
| Increment in shares | | 4,050 | |
| Tentative PEPS₂ amounts | $116,760 ÷ | 25,350 = | $4.61 PEPS₂ |
| 9% bond interest expense savings | 28,350 | | |
| Increment in shares | | 6,300 | |
| Primary earnings and shares | $145,110 ÷ | 31,650 = | $4.58 Primary |

| Explanation | Earnings ÷ | Shares = | Earnings Per Share |
|---|---|---|---|
| Simple earnings and shares | $100,800 | 21,000 = | $4.80 Simple |
| Stock option share increment | | 404 | |
| Tentative FDEPS₁ amounts | $100,800 ÷ | 21,404 = | $4.71 FDEPS₁ |
| 8.2% preferred dividend savings | 16,400 | | |
| Increment in shares | | 4,400 | |
| Tentative FDEPS₂ amounts | $117,200 ÷ | 25,804 = | $4.54 FDEPS₂ |
| 8% bond interest expense savings | 15,960 | | |
| Increment in shares | | 4,050 | |
| Fully diluted earnings and shares | $133,160 ÷ | 29,854 = | $4.46 Fully diluted |

In preparing these schedules, the company used the following (and other) information:
1. *Common shares:* At the end of 1995, 24,000 shares were outstanding. On October 5, several thousand shares had been issued for cash, the only stock transaction during 1995.
2. *Convertible securities:* There are three convertible securities that have been outstanding for several years: (a) 8% bonds, $300,000 face value, issued at a premium, common stock equivalent, each $1,000 bond is convertible into 13.5 shares of common stock, no bonds have been converted to date; (b) 9% bonds, $450,000 face value, issued at face value, common stock equivalent, no bonds have been converted to date; and (c) 8.2% preferred stock, $100 par, 2,000 shares, issued at an effective yield of 7.5%, not a common stock equivalent, current dividends have been paid, no preferred stock has been converted to date.
3. *Stock options:* Key executives may purchase 3,000 common shares at an option price of $45 per share. To date, no options have been exercised.
4. *Impact on EPS:* To determine whether to include each convertible security in the earnings per share calculations, the company had computed the following:

| Security | Impact on EPS |
|---|---|
| 8% bonds | $3.94 |
| 9% bonds | $4.50 |
| 8.2% preferred | $3.73 |

**Required**

Based on the preceding information, answer the following questions (show supporting calculations):

1. What was the net income in 1995?
2. What was the 1995 average market price per share of common stock?
3. What is the conversion ratio on each $1,000, 9% bond?
4. What was the effective yield on the 9% bonds when they were issued?
5. At what price were the 8.2% preferred shares originally issued?
6. How many shares of common stock were issued on October 5?
7. What was the minimum percent that the average Aa corporate bond yield could have been when the 9% bonds were issued?
8. What is the conversion ratio on each 8.2% preferred stock?
9. What was the 1995 ending market price per share of common stock?
10. What was the amount of the straight-line premium amortization on the 8% bonds for 1995?

P21-7  *Comprehensive*  Newton Company is preparing its annual earnings per share amounts to be disclosed on its 1995 income statement. It has collected the following information at the end of 1995:

1. Net income, $120,400. Included in the net income is an extraordinary loss (net of income taxes) of $10,000. Corporate income tax rate, 30%. Average Aa corporate bond yield at the end of 1995 is 10.6%.
2. Common stock outstanding on January 1, 1995: 20,000 shares.
3. Common stock issuances during 1995: July 6, 4,000 shares; August 24, 3,000 shares.
4. Stock dividend: On October 19, 1995, the company declared a 10% stock dividend that resulted in 2,700 additional outstanding shares of common stock.
5. Common stock prices: 1995 average market price, $26.50 per share; 1995 ending market price, $30 per share.
6. 7% preferred stock outstanding on January 1, 1995: 1,000 shares. Terms: $100 par, nonconvertible. Current dividends have been paid. No preferred stock issued during 1995.
7. 8% convertible preferred stock outstanding on January 1, 1995: 800 shares. The stock was issued at 130 when the average Aa corporate bond yield was 9%. Each $100 par preferred stock is currently convertible into 1.8 shares of common stock. Current dividends have been paid. To date, no preferred stock has been converted.
8. Bonds payable outstanding on January 1, 1995: $100,000 face value. These bonds were issued several years ago at 97 to yield 10.1%, and pay annual interest of 9.6%. The discount is being amortized in the amount of $300 per year. The average Aa corporate bond yield on the issuance date was 12.9%. Each $1,000 bond is currently convertible into 22 shares of common stock. To date, no bonds have been converted.
9. Stock options outstanding: Key executives may currently acquire 3,000 shares of common stock at $24 per share. The options were granted in 1994. To date, none have been exercised.

**Required**

1. Compute the primary earnings per share. Show supporting calculations.
2. Compute the fully diluted earnings per share. Show supporting calculations.
3. Indicate how these per share figures would be disclosed on the income statement. Include an explanatory note.

P21-8  *Comprehensive*  The Frost Company has accumulated the following information relevant to its 1995 earnings per share.

1. Net income for 1995, $150,500.
2. Bonds payable: On January 1, 1995, the company had issued 10%, $200,000 bonds at 110 to yield 8.9%. The premium is being amortized in the amount of $1,000 per year. Each $1,000 bond is currently convertible into 22 shares of common stock. To date, no bonds have been converted.
3. Bonds payable: On December 31, 1993, the company had issued 5.8%, $540,000 bonds at par to yield 5.8%. Each $1,000 bond is currently convertible into 11.6 shares of common stock. To date, no bonds have been converted.
4. Preferred stock: On July 1, 1994, the company had issued 3,800 shares of 7.5%, $100 par preferred stock at $108 per share. Each share of preferred stock is currently convertible into 2.45 shares of common stock. To date, no preferred stock has been converted and no additional shares of preferred stock have been issued. The current dividends have been paid.
5. Common stock: At the beginning of 1995, 25,000 shares were outstanding. On August 4, 7,000 additional shares were issued. During September, a 20% stock dividend was declared and issued. On November 30, 2,000 shares were reacquired as treasury stock.

6. Stock options: Options to acquire common stock at a price of $38 per share were outstanding during all of 1995. Currently, 4,000 shares may be acquired. To date, no options have been exercised.
7. Miscellaneous: Average Aa corporate bond yields were 9% on 12/31/93, 10% on 7/1/94, 13.6% on 12/31/94, and 12.4% on 12/31/95. Stock market prices on common stock averaged $40 per share during 1995, and the 1995 ending stock market price was $41 per share. The corporate income tax rate is 30%.

**Required**

1. Compute the primary earnings per share. Show supporting calculations.
2. Compute the fully diluted earnings per share. Show supporting calculations.
3. Indicate which earnings per share figure(s) would be disclosed on the income statement.

P21-9 *Earnings Per Share*   The following schedule sets forth the short-term debt, long-term debt, and stockholders' equity of Darren Company as of December 31, 1995. The president of Darren has requested that you assist the controller in preparing figures for earnings per share computations.

| | |
|---|---:|
| Short-term debt: | |
|    Notes payable—banks | $ 4,000,000 |
|    Current portion of long-term debt | 10,000,000 |
|    Total short-term debt | $ 14,000,000 |
| Long-term debt: | |
|    4% convertible debentures due April 15, 2007 | $ 30,000,000 |
|    Other long-term debt less current portions | 20,000,000 |
|    Total long-term debt | $ 50,000,000 |
| Stockholders' equity: | |
|    $4 cumulative, convertible preferred stock; par value, $20 per share; authorized, 2,000,000 shares; issued and outstanding, 1,200,000 shares; liquidation preference, $30 per share aggregating $36,000,000 | $ 24,000,000 |
|    Common stock; par value, $1 per share; authorized, 20,000,000 shares; issued, 7,500,000 shares, including 600,000 shares held in treasury | 7,500,000 |
|    Additional paid-in capital | 4,200,000 |
|    Retained earnings | 76,500,000 |
|    Total | $112,200,000 |
|    Less cost of 600,000 shares of common stock held in treasury (acquired prior to 1995) | (900,000) |
|    Total stockholders' equity | $111,300,000 |
|    Total long-term debt and stockholders' equity | $161,300,000 |

**Explanation of Short-Term Debt, Long-Term Debt, and Stockholders' Equity Including Transactions During the Year Ended December 31, 1995**

- The "Other long-term debt" and the related amounts due within one year are amounts due on unsecured promissory notes which require payments each year to maturity. The interest rates on these borrowings range from 6% to 7%. At the time that these monies were borrowed, the average Aa corporate bond yield was 7%.
- The 4% convertible debentures were issued at their face value of $30,000,000 in 1977 when the bank prime interest rate was 5%. The debentures are due in 2007 and until then are convertible into the common stock of Darren at the rate of 25 shares for each $1,000 debenture.
- The $4 cumulative, convertible preferred stock was issued in 1994. The stock had a market value of $75 at the time of issuance when the average Aa corporate bond yield was 9%. On July 3, 1995 and on October 2, 1995, holders of the preferred stock converted 80,000 and 20,000 preferred shares, respectively, into common stock. Each share of preferred stock is convertible into 1.2 shares of common stock.
- On April 4, 1995, Darren acquired the assets and business of Brett Industries by the issuance of 800,000 shares of Darren common stock in a transaction appropriately accounted for as a purchase.
- On October 3, 1994, the company granted options to its officers and selected employees to purchase 100,000 shares of Darren's common stock at a price of $33 per share. The options are not exercisable until 1997.

Additional information:

The average and ending market prices during 1995 of Darren common stock were as follows:

| | Average Market Price | Ending Market Price |
|---|---|---|
| First quarter | $31 | $29 |
| Second quarter | 33 | 32 |
| Third quarter | 35 | 33 |
| Fourth quarter | 37 | 34 |
| Average for the year | 34 | — |
| December 31, 1995 | — | 34 |

Dividends on the preferred stock have been paid through December 31, 1995. Dividends paid on the common stock were $0.50 per share for each quarter.

The net income of Darren Company for the year ended December 31, 1995 was $8,600,000. There were no extraordinary items. The provision for income taxes was computed at a rate of 30%.

**Required**

1. Prepare a schedule that shows the adjusted number of shares for 1995 to compute:
   a. Primary earnings per share
   b. Fully diluted earnings per share
2. Prepare a schedule that shows the adjusted net income for 1995 to compute:
   a. Primary earnings per share
   b. Fully diluted earnings per share (do not compute earnings per share) (*AICPA adapted*)

*P21-10  Earnings Per Share*   The controller of Lafayette Corporation has requested assistance in determining income, primary earnings per share, and fully diluted earnings per share for presentation in the Company's income statement for the year ended September 30, 1995. As currently calculated, the Company's net income is $540,000 for fiscal year 1994–1995.

Your working papers disclose the following opening balances and transactions in the Company's capital stock accounts during the year:

1. Common stock (at October 1, 1994, stated value $10, authorized 300,000 shares; effective December 1, 1994, stated value $5, authorized 600,000 shares):
   Balance, October 1, 1994—issued and outstanding 60,000 shares.
   December 1, 1994—60,000 shares issued in a 2-for-1 stock split.
   December 1, 1994—280,000 shares (stated value $5) issued at $39 per share.
2. Treasury stock—common:
   March 2, 1995—purchased 40,000 shares at $38 per share.
   April 1, 1995—sold 40,000 shares at $40 per share.
3. Stock purchase warrants, Series A (initially, each warrant was exchangeable with $60 for one common share; effective December 1, 1994, each warrant became exchangeable for two common shares at $30 per share):
   October 1, 1994—25,000 warrants issued at $6 each.
4. Stock purchase warrants, Series B (each warrant is exchangeable with $40 for one common share):
   April 1, 1995—20,000 warrants authorized and issued at $10 each.
5. First mortgage bonds, 5 1/2%, due 2010 (nonconvertible; priced to yield 5% when issued):
   Balance October 1, 1994—authorized, issued, and outstanding—the face value of $1,400,000.
6. Convertible debentures, 7%, due 2014 (initially, each $1,000 bond was convertible at any time until maturity into 20 common shares; effective December 1, 1994, the conversion rate became 40 shares for each bond):
   October 1, 1994—authorized and issued at their face value (no premium or discount) of $2,400,000.

The following table shows market prices for the company's securities and the assumed average Aa corporate bond yield during 1994–1995:

| | Price (or Rate) at | | | Average for Year Ended September 30, 1995 |
|---|---|---|---|---|
| | October 1, 1994 | April 1, 1995 | September 30, 1995 | |
| Common stock | 66 | 40 | 36 ¼ | 37 ½* |
| First mortgage bonds | 88 ½ | 87 | 86 | 87 |
| Convertible debentures | 100 | 120 | 119 | 115 |
| Series A Warrants | 6 | 22 | 19 ½ | 15 |
| Series B Warrants | — | 10 | 9 | 9 ½ |
| Average Aa corporate bond yield, % | 8 | 7 ¾ | 7 ½ | 7 ¾ |

*Adjusted for stock split.

### Required

Prepare a schedule computing:

1. The primary earnings per share and
2. The fully diluted earnings per share that should be presented in the Company's income statement for the year ended September 30, 1995.

A supporting schedule computing the numbers of shares to be used in these computations should also be prepared. (Because of the relative stability of the market price for its common shares, the annual average market price may be used where appropriate in your calculations. Assume an income tax rate of 30%.) (*AICPA adapted*)

**P21-11** *Earnings Per Share*  Mason Corporation's capital structure is as follows:

| | December 31 | |
|---|---|---|
| | 1995 | 1994 |
| Outstanding shares of: | | |
|   Common stock | 336,000 | 300,000 |
|   Nonconvertible preferred stock | 10,000 | 10,000 |
| 8% convertible bonds | $1,000,000 | $1,000,000 |

The following additional information is available:

On September 1, 1995, Mason sold 36,000 additional shares of common stock.

Net income for the year ended December 31, 1995 was $750,000.

During 1995, Mason paid dividends of $3 per share on its nonconvertible preferred stock.

The 8% convertible bonds are convertible into 40 shares of common stock for each $1,000 bond and were not considered common stock equivalents at the date of issuance.

Unexercised stock options to purchase 30,000 shares of common stock at $22.50 per share were outstanding at the beginning and end of 1995. The average market price of Mason's common stock was $36 per share during 1995. The market price was $33 per share at December 31, 1995.

Warrants to purchase 20,000 shares of common stock at $38 per share were attached to the preferred stock at the time of issuance. The warrants, which expire on December 31, 2000, were outstanding at December 31, 1995.

Mason's effective income tax rate was 30% for 1994 and 1995.

### Required

(Show supporting computations in good form, and round earnings per share to the nearest penny.)

1. Compute the number of shares that should be used for the computation of primary earnings per common share for the year ended December 31, 1995.
2. Compute the primary earnings per common share for the year ended December 31, 1995.
3. Compute the number of shares that should be used for the computation of fully diluted earnings per common share for the year ended December 31, 1995.
4. Compute the fully diluted earnings per common share for the year ended December 31, 1995. (*AICPA adapted*)

# 22

## ACCOUNTING CHANGES AND ERRORS

### Chapter Topics

*Changes in Accounting Principles*

*Changes in Accounting Estimates*

*Changes in Accounting Entities*

*Prior Period (Retroactive) Adjustments*

*Cumulative Effect Adjustments*

*Prospective Adjustments*

*Accounting Errors*

One of the qualitative characteristics of accounting is consistency (discussed in Chapter 2)—a conformity of accounting principles, policies, and procedures from period to period. However, in some instances, a company may improve its reporting by changing its accounting to adopt preferable or newly mandated generally accepted accounting principles, or to reflect changing economic conditions. When accounting principles are changed, the consistency of financial statements is impaired; therefore, it is important to report the effects of the changes in the financial statements. Accounting for the effects of changes in accounting principles is the primary topic of this chapter. Accounting for errors is discussed also.

## TYPES OF ACCOUNTING CHANGES

The generally accepted accounting principles to be used when accounting changes are made were established by **APB Opinion No. 20,** which defines three types of changes as follows:

1. *Change in an Accounting Principle.* This type of change occurs when a company adopts a generally accepted accounting principle different from the one used previously for reporting purposes, such as changing from the FIFO to the LIFO inventory cost flow assumption or changing from straight-line to accelerated depreciation.

2. *Change in an Accounting Estimate.* This type of change is a result of the periodic presentation of financial statements. Preparing financial statements requires estimation of the effects of future events, and such estimates sometimes must be changed as new events occur, as more experience is acquired, or as additional information is obtained. For example, the estimated life of a depreciable asset may be changed to reflect newly available information.

3. *Change in a Reporting Entity.* This type of change is caused by a change in the entity being reported. For example, a change in the subsidiaries included in the consolidated financial statements is a change in a reporting entity.

In addition to the preceding changes, *APB Opinion No. 20* also specifies the accounting principles to be followed when errors are discovered in published financial statements. *Errors* are not considered to be accounting changes, but are the results of mathematical mistakes or mistakes in the application of accounting principles.

## METHODS OF DISCLOSING AN ACCOUNTING CHANGE

There are three possible methods of disclosing an accounting change in the financial statements: (1) by **retroactively adjusting past financial statements** (restating financial statements of prior periods), (2) by including the **cumulative effect** of the change in the income of the current period, or (3) by adjusting for the change **prospectively.** The APB established rules stipulating one particular method to be used for each of the preceding changes and errors. To introduce the three alternative methods, the following example of a change in depreciation is presented. It should be understood clearly that *these methods are **not** alternatives* that may be used to account for a change in a depreciation method under generally accepted accounting principles, but are presented to illustrate the differences between the methods. A summary of the impacts of the various rules on the financial statements is presented in Exhibit 22-8, and it may be helpful to use that exhibit with the following discussion. For this example, assume that at the beginning of year 1, the Dowson Company purchased an asset for $20,000, which had an estimated life of 4 years and a zero residual value. The company has been depreciating the asset by the sum-of-the-years'-digits method and decides to switch to the straight-line method at the beginning of year 3. Straight-line and sum-of-the-years'-digits methods produce the annual depreciation amounts shown in Exhibit 22-1. In this example, the effects of income taxes are ignored.

## EXHIBIT 22-1

### DOWSON COMPANY

Alternative Depreciation Methods

| Year | Method Sum-of-the-Years'-Digits | Straight-Line | Reduced Depreciation Under Straight-Line Method |
|------|------|------|------|
| 1 | $ 8,000 | $ 5,000 | $3,000 |
| 2 | 6,000 | 5,000 | 1,000 |
| 3 | 4,000 | 5,000 | (1,000) |
| 4 | 2,000 | 5,000 | (3,000) |
|  | $20,000 | $20,000 | $    0 |

Assume that the Dowson Company presents comparative financial statements for years 1 and 2 in its annual report for year 3. If the change in depreciation method is disclosed by *retroactive adjustment* of the financial statements, the prior statements are changed to what they *would have been* if the new method had been used since the asset was first acquired. Therefore, $5,000 of depreciation expense (computed under the straight-line method) is included each year in the restated comparative income statements of year 1 and year 2 *instead* of the amounts (computed under the sum-of-the-years'-digits method) originally reported of $8,000 and $6,000, respectively. This change increases the reported income of the two years by $3,000 and $1,000 (ignoring income taxes). The reduced depreciation expense in both years also results in corresponding decreases in accumulated depreciation and increases in the carrying value of the asset of $3,000 and $4,000 ($3,000 + $1,000) on the ending comparative balance sheets of year 1 and year 2, respectively. Similarly, since income is closed to retained earnings, the ending retained earnings balances are increased by the same amounts. For the beginning balance sheet of the year of the change (year 3), the asset is reported at its increased carrying value, and the balance of retained earnings also is higher by $4,000. The depreciation expense in year 3 is $5,000.

Alternatively, if the change is reported as a *cumulative effect change*, the $4,000 difference between the two depreciation methods for years 1 and 2 is included in the income on the income statement of the current period (i.e., year 3). No adjustments are made to the comparative financial statements of prior periods (i.e., years 1 and 2) for a cumulative effect change. Therefore, the carrying value of the asset at the beginning of year 3 is increased by $4,000 in conjunction with the inclusion of the $4,000 of additional income in the period of the change in accounting principle (year 3). The depreciation expense in year 3 is $5,000.

Finally, if the change is accounted for *prospectively*, the unadjusted carrying value of the asset at the beginning of year 3 is written off over the remaining life of the asset. In this case, under the sum-of-the-years'-digits method, the asset has a carrying value at the beginning of year 3 of $6,000 ($20,000 − $8,000 − $6,000). This amount is written off by the straight-line method through a depreciation expense of $3,000 per year over the remaining life of 2 years. Thus, if the change is reported prospectively, the only effect in the year of the change (year 3) is a depreciation expense of $3,000 instead of the $4,000 that would have been reported under the sum-of-the-years'-digits method. No change is made in the financial statements for years

1 and 2. Once again, note that the three methods are **not** allowable alternatives to account for a change in depreciation, but are presented for illustrative purposes.

The retroactive, cumulative, and prospective methods are all required under particular circumstances, according to the provisions of *APB Opinion No. 20*. The basic principles are that generally:

- A *change in an accounting principle* is accounted for by the *cumulative* effect method.

- A *change in an accounting estimate* is accounted for *prospectively*.

- A *change in a reporting entity* is accounted for by prior period restatement (*retroactively*).

- An *error* is accounted for by prior period restatement (*retroactively*).

Each of these methods and rules is discussed in greater detail in the following sections of the chapter, along with the exceptions to the rules. Summaries are provided in Exhibits 22-7 and 22-8. It should be noted that accounting changes are reported in the financial statements only if they are material.

## ACCOUNTING FOR A CHANGE IN ACCOUNTING PRINCIPLE

*APB Opinion No. 20* states that a change in accounting principle results from the adoption of a generally accepted accounting principle that is different from the one used previously for reporting purposes, and includes both principles and practices as well as the methods of applying them. However, a change in an accounting principle does *not* include the initial adoption of a generally accepted accounting principle in recognition of events or transactions occurring for the first time, nor the adoption or modification of an accounting principle for transactions or events that are clearly different in substance from those previously occurring.[1] Also, a change to a generally accepted accounting principle from one that is *not* generally accepted is a correction of an error and *not* a change in accounting principle.

### Cumulative Effect Method

**Most changes in accounting principles are accounted for as a *cumulative effect change* as follows:**

1. The financial statements for prior periods included for comparative purposes are presented as previously reported.

2. The cumulative effect of changing to the new accounting principle (net of applicable income taxes) on the amount of retained earnings at the *beginning* of the period in which the change is made is reported immediately before the caption "net income" on the income statement of the period of the change.

---

1. "Accounting Changes," *APB Opinion No. 20* (New York: AICPA, 1971), par. 7 and 8.

3. Income before extraordinary items and net income computed on a **pro forma** basis (that is, *as if* the new principle had been in effect for all past periods) are shown on the face of the income statements (below earnings per share) for *all* periods presented.

4. A description of the change and the reason for it, as well as the effect of the change on income before extraordinary items and on net income (and on related earnings per share amounts) of the period of the change are disclosed in the notes to the financial statements.[2]

To illustrate the cumulative effect method of accounting for a change in accounting principle, suppose that the Goddard Company has assets on which it has been using straight-line depreciation for its financial reporting, and Modified Accelerated Cost Recovery System (MACRS) depreciation for its income tax reporting. At the beginning of 1995, it adopts an accelerated depreciation method for its financial reporting instead of the straight-line method previously used. This change results in additional depreciation of $40,000 ($140,000 instead of $100,000) for the year 1995. The company has calculated the information in Exhibit 22-2, which pertains to the change (assuming a 30% income tax rate). The cumulative effect reported on the income statement of the year of the change (1995) is determined by computing the difference between (1) the amount of the retained earnings at the *beginning* of the year of the change and (2) the amount of retained earnings that *would have been reported* at that date if the new accounting principle (accelerated depreciation) had been applied retroactively for all affected prior periods. For the Goddard Company, the difference in the depreciation amounts at the beginning of 1995 is $90,000 ($430,000 − $340,000) before income taxes. The after-tax difference of $63,000 is the effect on retained earnings at the beginning of 1995 and is included as a *reduction* in income for 1995 because the change *to* an accelerated depreciation method results in additional depreciation expense for all affected prior periods.

The disclosure of the change in accounting principle is illustrated in Exhibit 22-3, assuming the company presents both the current year's (1995) and the previous year's (1994) income statements for comparative purposes. The top portion of Exhibit 22-3

---

## EXHIBIT 22-2

### GODDARD COMPANY

Effects of Different Depreciation Methods

| Year | Straight-Line Depreciation | Accelerated Depreciation | Difference | Difference Net of Tax |
|------|---------------------------|-------------------------|------------|----------------------|
| Prior to 1994 | $240,000 | $300,000 | $60,000 | $42,000 |
| 1994 | 100,000 | 130,000 | 30,000 | 21,000 |
| Total at beginning of 1995 | $340,000 | $430,000 | $90,000 | $63,000 |
| 1995 | $100,000 | $140,000 | $40,000 | $28,000 |

---

2. *Ibid.*, par. 19.

**EXHIBIT 22-3**

## GODDARD COMPANY

Reporting the Cumulative Effect of a Change in Accounting Principle

*Condensed Comparative Income Statements*

|  | 1995 | 1994 |
|---|---|---|
| Revenues (amounts assumed) | $3,000,000 | $2,600,000 |
| Expenses (amounts assumed) | (1,800,000)* | (1,600,000)* |
| Income before income tax | $1,200,000 | $1,000,000 |
| Income tax expense (30%) | (360,000) | (300,000) |
| Income before cumulative effect of a change in accounting principle | $ 840,000 | $ 700,000 |
| Cumulative effect on prior years (to December 31, 1994) of changing to a different depreciation method (net of $27,000 income taxes) | (63,000) | |
| Net income | $ 777,000 | $ 700,000 |
| | | |
| Earnings per common share (assuming 100,000 shares outstanding and a simple capital structure): | | |
| Income before cumulative effect of a change in accounting principle | $8.40 | $7.00 |
| Cumulative effect on prior years (to December 31, 1994) of changing to a different depreciation method | (0.63) | |
| Earnings per common share | $7.77 | $7.00 |
| | | |
| Pro forma amounts assuming the new depreciation method is applied retroactively: | | |
| Net income | $ 840,000 | $ 679,000 |
| Earnings per common share | $8.40 | $6.79 |

*Note:* Depreciation of plant equipment has been computed by the double-declining-balance method in 1995. Depreciation of plant equipment in prior years was computed by the straight-line method. The new method of depreciation was adopted to recognize . . . (state justification for change of depreciation method) . . . and has been applied retroactively to equipment acquisitions of prior years. The effect of the change in 1995 was to decrease income by $28,000 ($0.28 per share). The retroactive adjustment of $63,000 (after reduction for income taxes of $27,000) to apply the new method is included in income of 1995. The pro forma amounts shown on the income statement have been adjusted for the effect of retroactive application on depreciation, and related income taxes.

*Includes depreciation of $140,000 (accelerated depreciation) in 1995 and $100,000 (straight-line depreciation) in 1994.

is condensed and only includes total revenues and total expenses for each year. The revenues and expenses are not restated, but the expenses for 1995 include depreciation of $140,000 based on the newly adopted accelerated method, while the expenses for 1994 include depreciation of $100,000 based on the straight-line method used at that time. The $63,000 after-tax cumulative effect is reported on the 1995 income statement (the $27,000 related income taxes are shown parenthetically) in a special category between "extraordinary items" and "net income",[3] as discussed in Chapter 4. Additionally, the effect of this change on the earnings per share amounts is disclosed on the face of the income statement. The third section of Exhibit 22-3 shows the pro forma amounts for 1994 and 1995. These are the amounts that would have been reported *if* the newly adopted depreciation method had been applied in past periods. There is no difference between the pro forma income for 1995 and the income *before* the cumulative effect of a change in accounting principle in 1995 because the new depreciation method is used in computing that income for the year. However, the pro forma income for 1994 is reduced by $21,000. This amount represents the after-tax effect of the increased depreciation (from $100,000 to $130,000) for 1994, *assuming* that the accelerated method had been used (see Exhibit 22-3). The note to the Goddard Company's financial statements illustrates the required disclosure describing the change, the reasons for the change, and the effect of the change upon the current year's net income and earnings per share.

In addition to the $63,000 after-tax reduction in income due to the cumulative effect change, the accumulated depreciation is increased so that the carrying value of the assets at the beginning of 1995 is decreased by $90,000. The difference between these amounts is a $27,000 adjustment of the company's deferred income tax liability. The journal entry to record the cumulative effect change is as follows:

| | | |
|---|---|---|
| **Loss on Cumulative Effect of a Change in Depreciation Method** | 63,000 | |
| **Deferred Tax Liability** | 27,000 | |
|     **Accumulated Depreciation** | | 90,000 |

Since MACRS depreciation has been used for income tax purposes in previous years, the use of the straight-line method in the financial statements has created a deferred tax liability, as discussed in Chapters 4 and 17. The change to the accelerated method for financial reporting has reduced the difference between the tax and financial statement depreciation. Therefore, the liability is reduced because part of the past temporary difference is reversed in this period. In other situations, however, there may be an effect on income taxes payable or receivable. Generally, if a company also adopts the new accounting principle for income tax reporting, it must file for permission with the Internal Revenue Service. Upon approval, the company either will have to repay prior income taxes saved (such as with a change from LIFO), in which case it would record income taxes payable, or will receive a tax refund, in which case income taxes receivable would be recorded. Knowledge of the income tax regulations affecting the income taxes applicable to a change in accounting principle is essential to properly account for the change for financial reporting purposes.

---

3. Conceptually, the FASB has discussed the possibility of including the cumulative effect in "comprehensive income" but not in net income. See "Elements of Financial Statements," *FASB Statement of Financial Accounting Concepts No. 6* (Stamford, Conn.: FASB, 1985), fn. 1 and the related discussion in Chapter 4.

## Direct and Indirect Effects

In the Goddard Company example, we assumed that the change in depreciation method was the only item affecting the previous year's income. In more complex situations, a change in accounting principle might have an "interactive" effect on other items affecting prior years' income. For instance, a company might have such items as bonus arrangements with management, profit sharing with employees, or payments of royalties, all of which are based on the company's income. In these cases, a change in an accounting principle has both a "direct" and "indirect" effect on the company's income of prior years. The *direct effect* is the amount by which the prior years' income is increased or decreased specifically as a result of the change in accounting principle. The *indirect effect* is the amount by which the company's income of prior years is affected by the impact of the change in principle upon other elements of income. For instance, suppose the Goddard Company also has a bonus arrangement with management based upon net income. If the company had been using accelerated depreciation in prior years instead of straight-line, the direct effect is a decrease in income due to higher depreciation expense. However, this decrease in income would have been partially offset by the indirect effect on the bonus arrangement. That is, because income was reduced due to higher depreciation, the bonus expense would have been lower, which, in turn, would have offset some of the income reduction.

In situations in which a change in accounting principle has both a direct and indirect effect on prior years' income, *APB Opinion No. 20* states that **only the *direct effect* (net of applicable income taxes) is recognized in determining the amount of the cumulative effect change included in net income. However, the combined result of both the direct effect and the indirect effect (net of taxes) is included in the pro forma amounts shown on the income statement.**[4] This difference in reporting the direct and indirect effects is appropriate because the direct effect is based on events of past periods. For example, a bonus of a prior period that has already been paid would not be changed because of a change in an accounting principle applicable to the current and future periods. The pro forma amounts are prepared to assist users in comparing past information with that of current and future periods in which the bonus is paid based on income computed under the new accounting principle. Therefore, the pro forma amount for prior periods is also computed using the new principle and the *assumption* that a bonus was paid based on that income, making the amounts more *comparable* and enhancing their *predictive ability*.

Returning to the Goddard Company example, suppose that the example remains the same except that management receives a bonus of 10% of income before taxes and the bonus. In this case, the cumulative effect change would remain at $63,000 on the income statement. However, the pro forma amount of net income for 1994 would be different. The change in depreciation method reduced 1994 income before taxes by $30,000 (see Exhibit 22-2); therefore, the bonus expense is reduced by $3,000 (10% × $30,000). In this case, the net effect is a reduction in the pro forma net income for 1994 of $18,900 [0.70 after-tax rate × ($30,000 − $3,000)] to $681,100 ($700,000 − $18,900), which would be shown in Exhibit 22-3 instead of $679,000. Similarly, pro forma earnings per share would be shown as $6.81 instead of $6.79.

---

4. *APB Opinion No. 20, op. cit.*, par. 19, 22, and fn. 6.

## Exceptions to the General Rule

The previous example illustrates the general rule for reporting a change in an accounting principle. **There are four exceptions to this rule:**[5]

1. **Adoption of New Principle for Future Events.** If a company adopts a new accounting principle for use in the future but does not change the method currently used, a cumulative effect change is *not* made. For example, a new depreciation method might be applied to newly acquired assets, but the old method continues to be used for currently owned assets. In this situation, a description of the nature of the change and its effect on income before extraordinary items and net income of the period of the change, together with the earnings per share amounts, are disclosed in the notes to the financial statements.

2. **Cumulative Effect Not Determinable.** In some situations, the cumulative effect is not determinable because the accounting system does not include sufficient information. The principal example of this type of change is a change *to* the LIFO cost flow method because records of the costs of the additions to and reductions in the LIFO layers that would have occurred in the past if LIFO had been used are probably not available. In these situations, the effect of the change on the results of operations of the period of change (including earnings per share data) and the reason for omitting the cumulative effect, as well as the pro forma amounts for prior years, are disclosed in the notes to the financial statements.

3. **Initial Public Sale of Common Stock.** If accounting changes are made when a company makes an initial public distribution (the first sale of common stock made available to the general public), the financial statements for all prior periods presented are restated retroactively. This exemption from the normal rules is available only once for changes made at the time a company's financial statements are first used to (1) obtain additional equity capital from investors, (2) effect a business combination, or (3) register securities. This exemption is logical because the financial statements have never before been available to the public and therefore there is no danger of confusion as a result of changes being made to the statements.

4. **Prior Period Restatement (Retroactive Adjustment) More Useful.** With regard to certain changes in accounting principles, the APB considered the advantages of retroactive restatement of prior periods to outweigh its disadvantages. Therefore, **prior period restatement (retroactive adjustment) is required instead of a cumulative effect adjustment for the following changes in accounting principles: (1) a change *from* the LIFO inventory cost flow method to another method; (2) a change in the method of accounting for long-term construction-type contracts; (3) a change to or from the "full cost" method of accounting that is used in the extractive industries; (4) a change from retirement-replacement-betterment accounting to depreciation accounting for railroad track structures; and (5) a change from the fair value method to the equity method for investments in common stock.** The reason for these excep-

5. *Ibid.*, par. 24, 26, and 27; "Reporting a Change in Accounting for Railroad Track Structures," *FASB Statement of Financial Accounting Standards No. 73* (Stamford, Conn.: FASB, 1983); and "The Equity Method of Accounting for Investments in Common Stock," *APB Opinion No. 18* (New York: AICPA, 1971), par. 19(m).

tions to the general rule is that the size of the cumulative effect change may be so much greater than operating income that including it in the income statement might appear to reduce the significance of the income from operations.

Accounting for a change in accounting principle by prior period restatement involves the following steps:

1. The revenues and expenses (including applicable income taxes) affected by the change are restated in the income statements of previous years included for comparative purposes.

2. The aggregate change in income (net of applicable income taxes) at the beginning of each year is added to (or subtracted from) retained earnings, as a prior period adjustment, on the comparative statements of retained earnings.

3. The related assets and liabilities, including applicable income taxes, are restated in the comparative balance sheets of previous years.

4. A description of the change and the reason for it, as well as the effect of the change on income before extraordinary items and on net income (and on related earnings per amounts) for all periods, are disclosed in the notes to the financial statements.

### Illustration of Prior Period Restatement

As previously noted, the prior period restatement method is used for exceptions to the general rule for a change in accounting principle, for a change in entity, and for the correction of errors. This method is discussed more thoroughly in this section as it applies to a change in accounting principle. Recall that prior period restatement requires changing the prior financial statements to what they would have been if the new method had been used in previous periods. Exhibits 22-4 and 22-5 illustrate a prior period restatement. In this example, the Werner Company changes *from* the LIFO to the FIFO inventory method at the beginning of 1995.

---

**EXHIBIT 22-4**

**WERNER COMPANY**

Change in Accounting for Inventory

| | Pretax Income Under | | | |
| | LIFO Inventory Method | FIFO Inventory Method | | |
| Year | | | Difference | Difference Net of Tax |
|---|---|---|---|---|
| Prior to 1994 | $ 550,000 | $ 850,000 | $300,000 | $210,000 |
| 1994 | 650,000 | 600,000 | (50,000) | (35,000) |
| Total at beginning of 1995 | $1,200,000 | $1,450,000 | $250,000 | $175,000 |
| 1995 | 500,000 | 700,000 | 200,000 | 140,000 |
| Total | $1,700,000 | $2,150,000 | $450,000 | $315,000 |

## EXHIBIT 22-5

### WERNER COMPANY

Reporting a Change in Accounting Principle by Prior Period Restatement

*Condensed Comparative Income Statements*

|  | 1995 | 1994 |
|---|---|---|
| Revenues (amounts assumed) | $3,000,000 | $2,800,000 |
| Expenses (amounts assumed) | (2,300,000)* | (2,200,000)* |
| Income before income taxes | $ 700,000 | $ 600,000 |
| Income tax expense (30%) | (210,000) | (180,000) |
| Net income | $ 490,000 | $ 420,000 |
| Earnings per share (assuming 100,000 shares) | $4.90 | $4.20 |

*Comparative Statements of Retained Earnings*

|  | 1995 | 1994 |
|---|---|---|
| Balance at beginning of year, as previously reported (assumed) | $2,455,000 | $2,000,000 |
| Add adjustment for the cumulative effect on prior years of applying retroactively the new method of accounting for inventory (net of $75,000 income taxes in 1995 and $90,000 income taxes in 1994) | 175,000 | 210,000 |
| Balance at beginning of year, as adjusted | $2,630,000 | $2,210,000 |
| Net income | 490,000 | 420,000 |
| Balance at end of year | $3,120,000 | $2,630,000 |

*Note*: The company has accounted for inventory and cost of goods sold under the FIFO cost flow assumption in 1995, whereas in all prior years, inventory and cost of goods sold were determined under the LIFO cost flow assumption. The new method of accounting for inventory was adopted to recognize...(state justification for change in accounting principle)...and financial statements of prior years have been restated to apply the new method retroactively. For income tax purposes, FIFO has also been adopted. The effect of the accounting change on income of 1995 and in income as previously reported in 1994 is:

|  | Increase | |
|---|---|---|
|  | 1995 | 1994 |
| Net income | $140,000 | $(35,000) |
| Earnings per share | $1.40 | $(0.35) |

The balance of retained earnings for 1994 and 1995 has been adjusted for the effect (net of income taxes) of applying retroactively the new method of accounting.

* Includes cost of goods sold under the FIFO method.

It presents comparative financial statements for 1995 and 1994. Exhibit 22-4 includes information for the Werner Company under the two methods. In addition, assume the income tax rate is 30% and the retained earnings balance at the beginning of 1994 (before adjustment) is $2 million. For simplicity, Exhibit 22-5 shows condensed comparative income statements and complete retained earnings statements for 1995 and 1994. In actual practice, the cost of goods sold on the income statements is reported at the proper amount, assuming use of FIFO. Likewise, the comparative balance sheets include the correct amounts as if FIFO had always been used. Therefore, the balances of the inventory, income taxes payable, and retained earnings accounts are adjusted to their proper amounts in the respective 1995 and 1994 balance sheets. It is assumed that the company also changes the inventory method used for income tax reporting purposes because of the LIFO conformity rule.

In Exhibit 22-5, the net income of the Werner Company is reported in 1995 for both 1994 and 1995 on the basis of the FIFO method as $490,000 and $420,000. Note that when the 1994 income was reported in 1994, it was based on the LIFO method and was $455,000 [70% (the after-tax rate) × $650,000]. The cumulative effect to date is adjusted to the retained earnings balance for each year reported. The adjustment of $210,000 in 1994 is the difference in income, net of tax, for the two methods for all years prior to 1994. Therefore, the balance in retained earnings at the beginning of 1994 would have been $2,210,000 if FIFO had been used in all previous years. The 1994 net income of $420,000 is based on FIFO and so the retained earnings balance at the beginning of 1995 (the end of 1994) would have been $2,630,000. However, it was only $2,455,000 under LIFO. The adjustment of $175,000 in 1995 changes the beginning retained earnings balance to the $2,630,000, which is the correct amount for FIFO. Of course, the $175,000 adjustment is also the difference, net of tax, between the two methods at the beginning of 1995, as shown in Exhibit 22-4. A description of the change and the reasons for it are disclosed in the note to the financial statements. In addition to this information, the effect of the change on income before extraordinary items, net income, and the related earnings per share amounts is also disclosed for each year reported.

The journal entry at the beginning of 1995 to record the retroactive adjustment is:

| | | |
|---|---|---|
| **Inventory** | 250,000 | |
| **Retained Earnings** | | 175,000 |
| **Income Taxes Payable** | | 75,000 |

The $250,000 difference in the inventory amounts at the beginning of 1995 is added to the inventory account. The $175,000 credit to retained earnings was explained earlier. The adoption of FIFO means that LIFO may no longer be used for income tax reporting and the company is obligated under the Internal Revenue Code to repay the taxes saved by the use of LIFO.[6] Therefore, $75,000 (0.30 × $250,000) is recorded as income taxes payable.

## Transition Methods Required by the FASB

As discussed earlier, *APB Opinion No. 20* specifies the general rules to be applied for a change in an accounting principle. However, when issuing *Statements,* the FASB has specified transition rules if appropriate. **Transition rules** define the accounting method to be used when an accounting principle is changed to conform to a principle required by the issuance of a *Statement.* In these situations, the accounting principle being used is no longer acceptable and a new principle is required. In the *Statements* where a method is specified, these transition rules usually require retroactive (prior period) restatement.[7] However, each *Statement* should be carefully examined so that the specific transition rules are followed.

---

6. The repayment is required to be made over a maximum of 6 years.
7. An exception was *FASB Statement of Financial Accounting Standards No. 5,* "Accounting for Contingencies," which required a cumulative effect adjustment. However, this was amended by *FASB Statement of Financial Accounting Standards No. 11,* "Accounting for Contingencies—Transition Method," which requires that prior period restatement be used.

**FASB Interpretation No. 20** specifies the transition method required for an accounting change made according to the provisions of an *AICPA Statement of Position.* The company conforms to the method required by the *Statement,* if specified, or to the provisions of *APB Opinion No. 20* if no transition method is specified.

In summary, the cumulative effect adjustment required by *APB Opinion No. 20* applies to a *voluntary* change by a company from one generally accepted accounting principle to another. The *mandatory* adoption of a new accounting principle as a result of an FASB *Statement* usually requires prior period restatement. These conflicting requirements may tend to confuse the reporting of a change in an accounting principle, and it might be more desirable if one method were used in all situations.

## ACCOUNTING FOR A CHANGE IN AN ESTIMATE

Generally accepted accounting principles require frequent use of estimates for such items as uncollectible accounts receivable, inventory obsolescence, service lives, residual values, recoverable mineral reserves, warranty costs, pension costs, and the periods that are expected to be benefited by a deferred cost. Since estimation of future events is an inherently uncertain process, changes in those estimates are inevitable as new events occur, as more experience is acquired, or as additional information is obtained.

*APB Opinion No. 20* requires that **a change in an accounting estimate is accounted for in the period of the change if the change affects that period only, or the period of the change and future periods if the change affects both.**[8] In other words, a change in an accounting estimate does *not* result in a cumulative change or a prior period restatement, but is accounted for *prospectively.*

For example, if the estimated service life of an asset is changed, a revised periodic depreciation expense is calculated based on the current book value, the estimated residual value, and the new estimated service life. Suppose that an asset had an original cost of $100,000, an estimated life of 20 years, an estimated residual value of zero, and that straight-line depreciation is being used. The company has been recording depreciation of $5,000 each year, so that the book value at the end of 8 years is $60,000 [$100,000 − (8 × $5,000)]. Now suppose that at the beginning of the ninth year of the asset's life, the company changes the estimate of its life to a total of 23 years, so that 15 years now remain in the asset's life. The remaining book value is depreciated over the remaining service life so that the depreciation expense of current and subsequent years is $4,000 ($60,000 ÷ 15) per year.

In addition to including this new amount of depreciation in the financial statements, the effect of the change on income and the related earnings per share amounts of the current period is disclosed in the notes to the financial statements. (Such disclosure is not required for estimates made each period in the ordinary course of accounting for items such as uncollectible accounts or inventory obsolescence, unless the change is material.) To continue the preceding example, assume that the income tax rate is 30% and there are 10,000 shares outstanding. Then the after-tax effect of the change is an increase in net income (due to lower depreciation expense) of $700 [($5,000 − $4,000) × 0.70] and the effect on earnings per share is an increase of $0.07 per share ($700 ÷ 10,000), and these amounts are disclosed in the notes to the financial statements. Another example of a change in estimate was presented in Chapter 9.

---

8.  *APB Opinion No. 20, op. cit.,* par. 31.

# CONCEPTUAL EVALUATION OF ACCOUNTING FOR A CHANGE IN ACCOUNTING PRINCIPLE AND A CHANGE IN ESTIMATE

As discussed earlier, there are three possible alternatives that might be used to account for a change in an accounting principle or in an accounting estimate. These alternatives are prior period (retroactive) restatement, cumulative effect adjustment, and prospective adjustment. Their advantages and disadvantages and selected additional items are discussed in the following sections.

## Prior Period Restatement

The major argument in favor of prior period (retroactive) restatement is that if this method is used, all financial statements presented at a given date are prepared on the basis of *consistent* accounting principles. Thus, when a user of the financial statements evaluates the current period's financial results, it is possible to make a comparison with the previous year's financial statements that also are presented without encountering a change in accounting principle. Prior period restatement is the usual method required for a change in accounting principle mandated by the FASB because it does not penalize (or increase) current year's earnings for an event that is beyond the control of management.

On the other hand, several disadvantages are associated with the prior period restatement method. First, financial statements issued in previous years are changed under this method. This creates the possibility that users may be confused by the change in the reported results, and that confidence in the accounting profession may be reduced because "they change the numbers." Second, the method is not consistent with the all-inclusive income concept, which has become the basis of generally accepted accounting principles as discussed in Chapter 4. Third, there may be an impact on contractual arrangements (such as bonus agreements, borrowing indentures, royalties, or profit sharing) when the previously reported income is changed. Fourth, prior period restatement lends itself to income manipulation by management because items are excluded from the current year's income statement. Use of prior period restatement means that a decrease in retained earnings can occur without being included as a reduction in the current year's income. Thus, the sum of the net incomes reported over the years would be more than the increase in retained earnings (excluding consideration of dividends). Conversely, a prior period restatement that increases the balance in retained earnings does so without being added to the current year's net income.

## Cumulative Effect Adjustment

In contrast to prior period restatement, the use of the cumulative effect adjustment method *is* consistent with the all-inclusive income concept. The emphasis placed on the income statement by users of financial statements makes it desirable that changes in stockholders' equity (excluding capital contributions and dividends) be included in net income rather than directly in retained earnings. In addition, an event that occurs during the period of the change in accounting principle is reported in the financial statements of that period, and past financial statements are not adjusted. Cumulative effect adjustment is the basic method required for a voluntary change in accounting principle because the company reports the results of current decisions by its management in current year's earnings.

The major argument against the cumulative effect adjustment method is that comparative financial statements are not being prepared on the basis of the consistent application of accounting principles. Thus, past financial statements are prepared on the basis of the old principle, the current financial statements include the cumulative effect of the change, and both current and future financial statements utilize the new principle. Users of financial statements may be confused by the lack of consistency between the years, and an analysis of trends may be disrupted. However, the potential confusion may be mitigated by two factors. First, the auditor's report included with the financial statements is modified to indicate that there has been a change in accounting principle. This draws the reader's attention to the change. Second, the requirement to report *pro forma* information is intended to enable the user of the financial statements to understand the impact of the change in accounting principle on the financial statements that are still being presented on the basis of the previously used principle.

### Prospective Adjustment

Accounting estimates used for periodic reporting inevitably change over time. New accounting principles also are adopted from time to time. It may be argued that it is better to account for such changes by considering their effect on the future and to make no attempt to change what has already been reported.

Since an estimate is made with the best information available at that time, and is changed only to reflect new information, accounting for a change in an estimate with a prospective adjustment is especially appropriate. In addition, the alternative of reporting the effect of a change of estimate cumulatively or retroactively might cause considerable confusion among users of financial statements because of the frequency of such changes.

In the case of a change in an accounting principle, the same arguments can be made about the desirability of not changing what has already been reported (that is, confusion and the all-inclusive income concept). Moreover, it may be argued that a change in an accounting principle, although it occurs in the current period, has little or no relationship to the current period's economic events, or to the income generated from providing goods and services to customers. Therefore, it should be accounted for prospectively. Conversely, it can be argued that a change in an accounting principle is an event of the current period. Therefore, the change should not be accounted for prospectively, but by a cumulative effect adjustment.

### A Change in Principle Distinguished from a Change in an Estimate

Sometimes, it is difficult to distinguish between a change in an accounting principle and a change in an estimate. For example, a company may change from capitalizing and amortizing a cost to recording it as an expense when incurred because future benefits associated with the cost have become doubtful. The new accounting method is adopted in recognition of the change in estimated benefits and therefore is *inseparable* from the change in estimate. *APB Opinion No. 20* specifies that a change in accounting estimate that is recognized in whole or in part by a change in accounting principle is reported as a change in an estimate because the cumulative effect attributable to the change in accounting principle cannot be separated from the current or future effects of the change in estimate.[9]

---

9. *Ibid.*, par. 32.

An additional complexity arises with respect to the amortization (including depreciation and depletion) of the cost of an asset over its useful life. It can be argued that a change in the method of amortization is in fact a change in estimate. That is, the criteria used to select a method of amortization are that it is systematic and rational, and results in an appropriate matching of costs and benefits. Therefore, if the estimate of the pattern of future benefits is changed, for example, from declining benefits to constant benefits, a change in the depreciation method is appropriate. Thus, a change in an accounting method (depreciation) results from a change in an estimate. Nevertheless, a change in the amortization or depreciation method is considered a change in an accounting principle under the provisions of *APB Opinion No. 20*, which specifies that the effect of a change in a method of amortization can be separated from the effect of a change in (an) estimate. A change in method of amortization for previously recorded assets is treated as a change in accounting principle, whereas a change in the estimated period of benefit or residual value is treated as a change in accounting estimate.[10]

## Preferability of the New Accounting Principle

When a company changes an accounting principle, management must justify the change on the grounds that the new principle is preferable to the old. The issuance of an FASB *Statement* is sufficient support for a change in accounting principle and does not require special justification; that is, the newly mandated principle is automatically considered to be preferable.[11] When the change is from one acceptable principle to another, the justification is usually included in a note to the financial statements in which the effect of the change is discussed. For example, two changes to LIFO were justified by stating that:

1. The change reflects earnings more realistically by matching current costs with current revenues (Ford Motor Company).

2. The change was implemented in order to match current costs with current revenues, and to partially offset the effect of inflation on earnings (General Motors Corporation).

Neither of these typical disclosures is extensive, and it is interesting to note that they are both technically incorrect, since LIFO does not match current costs with current revenues, but only the most recently incurred historical costs.

The SEC requires that when a company that files with it makes an accounting change, the auditor must submit a letter indicating whether or not the change is to an alternative principle that, in the auditor's judgment, is preferable under the circumstances. "Preferable" is defined to mean that the new method represents an improved method of measuring business operations in the particular circumstances. Some accountants object to the SEC's requirement because it relates only to companies making a change in an accounting principle. There is no requirement that the auditor make a statement about the preferability of the accounting principles currently being used.

---

10. *Ibid.*
11. "The Meaning of 'Present Fairly in Conformity With Generally Accepted Accounting Principles' in the Independent Auditor's Report," *Statement on Auditing Standards No. 69* (New York: AICPA, 1992), specifies that companies must adopt principles specified in pronouncements included in Categories A through D, as discussed in Chapter 1.

## Accounting Changes in Interim Financial Statements

The principles to be followed when accounting changes are reported in interim financial statements are established by **FASB Statement No. 3.**[12] If a cumulative effect accounting change is made during the *first* interim period of the fiscal year, the cumulative effect of the change on retained earnings at the beginning of the year is included in the net income of the first interim period. However, if a cumulative-type change is made in *other than the first interim period,* no cumulative effect change is included in the net income of the period of the change. Instead, the prior interim periods are restated by applying the newly adopted accounting principle to those prechange interim periods. The cumulative effect of the change on retained earnings at the beginning of the fiscal year is included in the restated net income of the first interim period. In summary, **a cumulative effect change is accounted for in the first interim period, regardless of the interim period in which it occurs.**

For the special situations in which sufficient information is not available for determining the amount of the cumulative effect adjustment, an alternative procedure is followed. (These types of changes were discussed earlier and primarily consist of a change to LIFO.) If the change occurs in the *first* interim period, disclosure of the change is necessary, but no adjustments are required. However, if the change is made in *other than the first interim period,* the financial statements of the prechange interim periods are restated by applying the newly adopted accounting principle to those periods. Again, the effect is to account for the change in the first interim period, no matter in which interim period the change is made.

# ACCOUNTING FOR A CHANGE IN A REPORTING ENTITY

The third type of change defined by *APB Opinion No. 20* is a change in a reporting entity. As noted earlier, **a change in reporting entity is reported by prior period restatement (retroactively) so that all financial statements presented are for the same entity.**[13] This procedure improves consistency.

A change in an accounting entity occurs mainly when (1) consolidated or combined statements are presented in place of the statements of individual companies, (2) there is a change in the specific subsidiaries that make up the group of companies for which consolidated financial statements are presented, and (3) the companies included in combined financial statements change.

When a change in an accounting entity occurs, the notes to the financial statements of the period in which it is made include a description of the change as well as the reason for it, and the effect of the change on income before extraordinary items, net income, and related earnings per share amounts for all periods presented. However, financial statements of subsequent periods need not repeat the disclosures. Accounting for a change in an accounting entity is not discussed here, but is included in advanced accounting books.

# ACCOUNTING FOR A CORRECTION OF AN ERROR

The correction of an error is *not* an accounting change under the requirements of *APB Opinion No. 20.* However, after the issuance of the *Opinion,* it was still unclear whether accounting for the results of a litigation settlement should be consid-

---

12. "Reporting Accounting Changes in Interim Statements," *FASB Statement of Financial Accounting Standards No. 3* (Stamford, Conn.: FASB, 1974).
13. *APB Opinion No. 20, op. cit.,* par. 34.

ered a prior period adjustment. It could be argued that such a settlement is a prior period adjustment because it relates to either the period in which the event causing the litigation occurred or the period in which the litigation was filed. Alternatively, it could be argued that the litigation settlement is an event of the period of settlement and should be included in the current period's income. This issue was resolved by **FASB Statement No. 16,** which specifies that corrections of errors are reported as prior period adjustments.[14] **Material errors of past periods that are discovered in the current period are accounted for as prior period adjustments (restatements)** and therefore are excluded from the determination of net income for the period. On the current period financial statements, an error of a past period (net of related income tax effects) is reported as an adjustment to the beginning balance of retained earnings. As illustrated in Exhibit 22-5, when comparative statements are presented, corresponding adjustments are made to the affected items on the income statements and to the retained earnings balances, as well as the affected items on the balance sheets for *all* periods reported. In addition, the nature of the error in previously issued financial statements and the effect of its correction on income before extraordinary items, net income, and the related earnings per share amounts are disclosed in the notes to the financial statements for each year reported. The journal entries required to correct errors are discussed later in the chapter.

Examples of errors include:

1. The use of an accounting principle that is *not* generally accepted.

2. The use of an estimate that was *not* made in good faith.

3. Mathematical miscalculations, such as the incorrect computation of the inventory, or logical errors, such as the omission of residual value in the calculation of straight-line depreciation.

4. The omission of a deferral or accrual, such as the failure to accrue warranty costs.

## Error Analysis

Because errors, by their very nature, happen in unpredictable and often illogical ways, it is difficult to generalize about the kinds of errors that may occur and the journal entries that may be required to correct them. Many errors are discovered automatically through proper use of the double-entry system; others are found by internal or external auditors before being included in the financial statements. In this section, we are concerned about errors that escaped detection until after they were included in the published financial statements. They may be categorized according to the effect they have on the financial statements.

### Errors Affecting Only the Balance Sheet

Some errors affect only balance sheet accounts. For example, a long-term note receivable may be included as a current note receivable. Reclassification of the note affects only the balance sheet. Therefore, if the error occurred in a prior period, no correcting journal entry is required, but if comparative financial statements are shown in the current year, the financial statements of the prior period are corrected by reclassifying the item.

---

14. "Prior Period Adjustments," *FASB Statement of Financial Accounting Standards No. 16* (Stamford, Conn.: FASB, 1977).

*Errors Affecting Only the Income Statement*

Errors that affect only income statement accounts usually result from the misclassification of items. For example, interest revenue may be included with sales revenue. Errors of this kind require reclassification but do not affect net income. Therefore, if the error occurred in a prior period, no correcting journal entry is required, but if comparative financial statements are shown in the current year, the financial statements of the prior period are corrected by reclassifying the item.

*Errors Affecting Both the Income Statement and Balance Sheet*

Errors may affect both an income statement account and a balance sheet account. An error of this type is the failure to accrue a liability at the end of the period. For example, if accrued interest is omitted, interest expense is understated on the current income statement and interest payable is omitted from the ending balance sheet.

Errors that affect both the income statement and the balance sheet can be classified as counterbalancing or noncounterbalancing. **Counterbalancing** errors are those that are automatically corrected in the next accounting period, even if they are not discovered. Consider the effect of unrecorded interest in the previous paragraph, and assume that the amount of the interest is $2,000 and the income tax rate 30%. The effects of the error on the financial statements of the period in which the error is made are as follows:

1. Interest expense is understated by $2,000.

2. Income before income taxes is overstated by $2,000.

3. Income tax expense is overstated by $600.

4. Net income is overstated by $1,400.

5. Retained earnings is overstated by $1,400.

6. Interest payable is understated by $2,000.

7. Income taxes payable is overstated by $600.

In the next period, when the interest is paid and the entire payment is considered as an expense, the following additional errors occur:

1. Interest expense is overstated by $2,000.

2. Income before income taxes is understated by $2,000.

3. Income tax expense is understated by $600.

4. Net income is understated by $1,400.

Since the amount of the interest expense overstatement in the second period is equal to the understatement of the previous period, the net income understatement in the second period offsets the overstatement in the first period. Therefore, no balance sheet accounts are in error at the end of the second period. That is, the total liabilities are no longer understated, and the retained earnings balance is now correct. The errors have automatically counterbalanced. Note also that even though the errors counterbalance, the necessity for a correcting journal entry and for correction of the financial statements depends upon *when* the error is discovered. If the error is discovered *during* the second year, a journal entry is necessary so that the interest expense and net income for the second year are reported correctly. If the error is discovered *after* the second year, no correcting journal entry is necessary. However, the financial statements for the two years are in error, so a correction (restatement) of the statements is required unless sufficient time has passed so that they are *not* being presented for comparative purposes.

**Noncounterbalancing** errors are those that are not offset in the next accounting period. For example, suppose that the purchase of an asset at a cost of $10,000 is erroneously recorded as supplies expense in the year of purchase, but it should have been capitalized and depreciated by the straight-line method over 10 years with no residual value for both financial reporting and income tax purposes. Furthermore, the company records a full year's depreciation in the year of acquisition, the income tax rate is 30% and the MACRS depreciation is assumed to be $1,400. The effects of the error on the financial statements of the period in which the error is made are as follows:

1. Supplies expense is overstated by $10,000.

2. The asset is understated by $10,000.

3. Depreciation expense is understated by $1,000 ($10,000 ÷ 10)

4. Accumulated depreciation is understated by $1,000.

5. Income before income taxes is understated by $9,000 ($10,000 − $1,000).

6. Income tax expense is understated by $2,700 ($9,000 × 0.30).

7. Net income is understated by $6,300 ($9,000 − $2,700).

8. Retained earnings is understated by $6,300.

9. Deferred tax liability is understated by $120 [($1,400 − $1,000) × 30%]

10. Income taxes payable are understated by $2,580 ($2,700 − $120).

The understatement of the asset and the depreciation expense continues until the end of the asset's life, at which point the balance sheet accounts (asset, accumulated depreciation, income taxes payable, and retained earnings) are correct for the first time since the error was made. Consequently, if the error is discovered before the end of the life of the asset, a correcting journal entry is required.

## Error Correction

The approach to correcting an error is difficult to generalize because of the variety of errors that may occur. Each error must be examined carefully to determine how the transaction *was* recorded and how it *should have been* recorded. The correction can then be made by (1) a single comprehensive entry (which is the preferred method in practice) or (2) a reversal of the original entry and a recording of the original transaction or event as it should have been recorded initially. For example, consider a building improvement costing $20,000 that was recorded as Repair Expense when it should have been capitalized. A single comprehensive journal entry to correct the error when it is discovered *in the next period* is:

| | | |
|---|---|---|
| **Building** | 20,000 | |
|     **Retained Earnings** | | 20,000 |

Note that in this entry, we are ignoring income taxes and depreciation, which will be discussed later. Note also that the correction is not made by a credit to Repair Expense because the error is discovered in the period following the one in which it was made. At this point, revenue and expense accounts for the previous period have been closed, so the correction of the previous year's income is made to Retained Earnings (or to an account, Correction of Prior Years' Income Due to Error in Recording Building Improvement, which is closed to Retained Earnings). If comparative financial statements are presented, they are corrected as discussed earlier.

If the second approach is used, two separate journal entries are required. First, the original entry is reversed (but the credit is again to Retained Earnings because the Repair Expense account has been closed), and then the entry that should have been made is recorded, as follows:

| | | |
|---|---|---|
| Cash | 20,000 | |
| Retained Earnings | | 20,000 |
| Building | 20,000 | |
| Cash | | 20,000 |

In this simple situation, the second approach may seem unnecessary, but it can prove useful in more complex circumstances.

In the previous example, it also is necessary to correct the recorded amount of depreciation. Since the error was discovered in the next period, Retained Earnings (for the previous period's depreciation understatement and income overstatement) and Accumulated Depreciation are corrected by the following journal entry (assuming a 10-year life, no residual value, straight-line depreciation, and that a full year's depreciation is recorded in the year of acquisition):

| | | |
|---|---|---|
| Retained Earnings | 2,000 | |
| Accumulated Depreciation | | 2,000 |

The depreciation expense for the second year is recorded in the normal way (because it is assumed that the error is discovered during the second year).

A logical sequence of steps for the analysis and correction of an error is indicated by the preceding discussion:

Step 1. Analyze the original erroneous journal entry and determine all the debits and credits that were recorded.

Step 2. Determine the correct journal entry and the appropriate debits and credits.

Step 3. Evaluate whether the error has caused additional errors in other accounts.

Step 4. Prepare the correcting entry(ies), remembering to record any corrections of the revenues and expenses for prior years as adjustments to retained earnings.

Additional examples of some errors that can be expected to occur more frequently are illustrated in the following sections for the Huggins Company. For simplicity, these corrections ignore the potential impact on taxable income, income tax expense, and deferred income taxes, although in reality, correcting entries for these items may be required. Assume all errors are material.

### Omission of Unearned Revenue

In December 1994, the Huggins Company received $10,000 as a prepayment for renting a building to another company for all of 1995. This transaction was recorded by a debit to Cash and a credit to Rent Revenue. The revenue should be reported in 1995, but was erroneously included in 1994 income. If this error is discovered in 1995, income for 1994 has been overstated by the inclusion of rent revenue and therefore Retained Earnings has to be decreased. The rent revenue has to be recorded in 1995, and so the correcting entry is:

| | | |
|---|---|---|
| **Retained Earnings** | 10,000 | |
| **Rent Revenue** | | 10,000 |

If the error is not discovered until 1996, no entry is required because the error has been counterbalanced. However, if the 1994 and 1995 financial statements are presented for comparative purposes, they are corrected (restated) as discussed earlier.

### Failure to Accrue Revenue

On December 31, 1994, the Huggins Company failed to accrue interest revenue of $500 that had been earned on an outstanding note receivable but not received. If the error is discovered in 1995, income for 1994 has been understated by the omission of interest revenue and therefore Retained Earnings has to be increased. If it is assumed that any cash received in 1995 is credited to Interest Revenue, the revenue account is overstated in 1995, and so the correcting entry is:

| | | |
|---|---|---|
| **Interest Revenue** | 500 | |
| **Retained Earnings** | | 500 |

If the error is discovered in 1996, no entry is required because the error has been counterbalanced. However, if the 1994 and 1995 financial statements are presented for comparative purposes, they are corrected.

### Omission of Prepaid Expense

In December 1994, the Huggins Company paid $1,000 for insurance coverage for the year 1995. The original entry was recorded by a debit to Insurance Expense and a credit to Cash, and no year-end adjustment was recorded. If this error is discovered at the end of 1995, income for 1994 is understated by the overstatement of insurance expense and therefore Retained Earnings has to be increased. Since no prepaid insurance was recorded in 1994, Insurance Expense for 1995 is understated and so the correcting entry is:

| | | |
|---|---|---|
| **Insurance Expense** | 1,000 | |
| **Retained Earnings** | | 1,000 |

Alternatively, if the payment of $1,000 in 1994 was for a 2-year insurance policy, the correcting entry at the end of 1995 is:

| | | |
|---|---|---|
| **Insurance Expense** | 500 | |
| **Prepaid Insurance** | 500 | |
| **Retained Earnings** | | 1,000 |

If this error is not discovered until 1996 and the payment in 1994 was for 1 year's insurance, no correcting entry is required because the error has been counterbalanced. If the error is discovered in 1996 and the payment was for 2 years' insurance, the correcting entry is:

| | | |
|---|---|---|
| **Insurance Expense** | 500 | |
| **Retained Earnings** | | 500 |

In this situation, $500 of the error has been counterbalanced, leaving only $500 to be corrected. Once again, the 1994 and 1995 financial statements are corrected if they are presented for comparative purposes.

*Error in Ending Inventory*

At December 31, 1994, the ending inventory of the Huggins Company was recorded at $50,000. During 1995, it is discovered that the correct inventory value should have been $55,000 because there was an error in the inventory count. Since the ending inventory for 1994 was understated, cost of goods sold for 1994 was overstated, income was understated and therefore Retained Earnings has to be increased. Since the beginning inventory is understated in 1995, it has to be increased, and so the correcting entry is:

| | | |
|---|---|---|
| Inventory | 5,000 | |
|     Retained Earnings | | 5,000 |

If the error is not discovered until 1996, no correcting entry is required because the error has been counterbalanced, but the 1994 and 1995 financial statements are corrected because the error in the inventory affects cost of goods sold in both years.

*Error in Purchases*

During December 1994, the Huggins Company made a purchase on credit that had not been paid at year's end. This transaction was incorrectly recorded at $17,000 when the invoice price of the inventory was $27,000. Since the purchases and accounts payable were understated, cost of goods sold in 1994 was understated (assuming the ending inventory was correctly recorded) and income was overstated and therefore Retained Earnings has to be decreased. The Accounts Payable in 1995 is understated, and so the correcting entry is:

| | | |
|---|---|---|
| Retained Earnings | 10,000 | |
|     Accounts Payable | | 10,000 |

Because of the creditor's demand for payment, it is difficult to conceive of such an error remaining undetected until 1996, but if that did happen, the correcting entry is as shown. Since the ending inventory was correct, the error was not counterbalanced and income for 1994 and retained earnings are overstated until the correction is made. Further examples of the effects of errors in inventory and purchases are given in Chapter 6.

*Failure to Accrue Estimated Bad Debts*

The Huggins Company failed to accrue an allowance for doubtful accounts of $7,000 in the 1994 financial statements. The result of this error was the understatement of bad debt expense and therefore Retained Earnings has to be decreased. The discovery of the error in 1995 indicates that Accounts Receivable (net) is overstated, and so the correcting entry is:

| | | |
|---|---|---|
| Retained Earnings | 7,000 | |
|     Allowance for Doubtful Accounts | | 7,000 |

Alternatively, if the error is discovered after the estimate of doubtful accounts is made and recorded by the aging method at the end of 1995, the bad debt expense is overstated because part of the charge relates to the 1994 error. Therefore, this correcting entry is required:

| | | |
|---|---|---|
| Retained Earnings | 7,000 | |
|     Bad Debt Expense | | 7,000 |

It is obviously not possible to give examples of every possible error. In each situation, the facts must be carefully examined, with particular consideration given to the time periods involved and the possibility of additional errors resulting from the initial error. For example, the effect of errors on the company's prior and current income tax expense and deferred income taxes must be assessed. Adjustments to retained earnings may need to be made for changes in income tax expense of prior periods. Furthermore, if taxable income is incorrect for prior periods, amended tax returns may be necessary.

A schedule which summarizes the effects of the multiple errors on the income before income taxes of the years affected by the errors for the Huggins Company is shown in Exhibit 22-6. Each of the errors is included in the schedule. Note that the omission of the prepaid expense assumes the situation of a 2-year insurance policy (and not the illustration of a 1-year insurance policy). The net effect of the errors is to reduce pretax income for 1994 by $20,500, increase pretax income for 1995 by $4,000, and reduce assets by $6,500 and increase liabilities by $10,000 on the 1995 balance sheet. If the income tax rate is 30% and the correction of each of these errors affects taxable income, the 1994 errors enable the company to obtain a tax refund of $6,150 (30% × $20,500), and the following journal entry is also made:

| | | |
|---|---|---|
| Income Tax Refund Receivable | 6,150 | |
|     Retained Earnings | | 6,150 |

The 1995 corrections do not need a separate correction for income taxes because, in this example, it is assumed that the books have not been closed for 1995.

## International Accounting Differences

Considerable flexibility is allowed by International Accounting Standards in regard to accounting changes. Correction of an error may be accounted for by a prior period restatement or in the current period. A change in accounting principle may be accounted for by a prior period restatement, a cumulative effect adjustment, or in the current and future periods. Accounting for a change in estimate is the same as U.S. GAAP.

---

### EXHIBIT 22-6

#### HUGGINS COMPANY

Summary of Corrections of Errors Discovered in 1995

| Error | Effect of Correction on Income 1994 | 1995 | Increases on Balance Sheet December 31, 1995 |
|---|---|---|---|
| Omission of unearned revenue | $(10,000) | $10,000 | |
| Failure to accrue interest revenue | 500 | (500) | |
| Omission of prepaid expense (2-year insurance policy) | 1,000 | (500) | Prepaid insurance $500 |
| Error in ending inventory | 5,000 | (5,000) | |
| Error in purchases | (10,000) | | Accounts payable $10,000 |
| Failure to accrue estimated bad debts | (7,000) | | Allowance for doubtful accounts $7,000 |
| Total pretax effect | $(20,500) | $ 4,000 | |
| Less: Income tax effect | 6,150 | | |
| After-tax effect | $(14,350) | | |

There are also considerable variations in how accounting changes are reported in particular countries. For example, in Canada, New Zealand, and the United Kingdom, all changes in accounting principles are treated as prior period restatements. In Mexico, Sweden, and Switzerland, they are accounted for by a cumulative effect change. There is much more consistency for changes in accounting estimates and corrections of errors. Changes in estimates are generally accounted for in the current period, although some countries require disclosure of the effect on income of prior periods. Corrections of errors are generally accounted for as prior period restatements.[15]

## SUMMARY OF METHODS FOR ACCOUNTING CHANGES AND ERRORS

A summary of the methods to be used in the various situations discussed in the chapter is presented in Exhibit 22-7. The impacts of these methods on the financial statements are presented in Exhibit 22-8.

---

### EXHIBIT 22-7

#### SUMMARY OF METHODS TO BE USED FOR CHANGES IN ACCOUNTING PRINCIPLES AND CORRECTIONS OF ERRORS

| | |
|---|---|
| 1. Change in Accounting Principle | Cumulative effect adjustment |
| *Exceptions to this rule:* | |
| Cumulative effect not determinable | Disclose effects of change |
| Change *from* LIFO to another inventory cost flow method | Retroactive (prior period) restatement |
| Change *to* LIFO from another inventory cost flow method (if cumulative effect not determinable) | Prospective adjustment |
| Change for long-term construction-type contracts | Retroactive (prior period) restatement |
| Change to or from the full cost method for extractive industries | Retroactive (prior period) restatement |
| Change from retirement-replacement-betterment accounting to depreciation accounting | Retroactive (prior period) restatement |
| Change from fair value to equity method for investments | Retroactive (prior period) restatement |
| Change mandated by the FASB | Retroactive (prior period) restatement (usually) |
| 2. Change in Accounting Estimate | Prospective adjustment |
| 3. Change in Entity | Retroactive (prior period) restatement |
| 4. Correction of Error | Retroactive (prior period) restatement |

---

15. For additional discussion, see Coopers & Lybrand, *1991 International Accounting Summaries: A Guide for Interpretation and Comparison* (New York: John Wiley and Son, Inc., 1991).

---

**EXHIBIT 22-8**

## SUMMARY OF IMPACTS ON FINANCIAL STATEMENTS OF METHODS USED FOR ACCOUNTING CHANGES AND ERRORS

### Retroactive (Prior Period) Restatement

| Previous Years | Current Year |
|---|---|
| *Income Statement* | *Income Statement* |
| Change revenue or expense amounts to reflect new accounting principle, correct information, or new accounting entity. | Compute revenue or expense amounts using new accounting principle, corrected information, or new accounting entity. |
| *Ending Balance Sheet* | *Ending Balance Sheet* |
| Change asset, liability, and stockholders' equity account balances to reflect amounts that would have been computed if the principle had always been used, the error had not been made, or the new entity had always existed. | No additional changes. Asset, liability, and stockholders' equity account balances are amounts that would have been computed if the new principle had always been used, the error had not been made, or the new entity had always existed. |

### Cumulative Effect Adjustment

| Previous Years | Current Year |
|---|---|
| *Income Statement* | *Income Statement* |
| No change | Include the cumulative effect of differences in revenues or expenses of previous years (net of tax) in net income. |
| *Ending Balance Sheet* | *Ending Balance Sheet* |
| No change | Change the asset, liability, and stockholders' equity account balances to amounts that would have been computed if the new principle had always been used. |

### Prospective Adjustment

| Previous Years | Current Year |
|---|---|
| *Income Statement* | *Income Statement* |
| No change | Compute revenue and expense amounts using the new estimate or the newly adopted accounting principle for new events. |
| *Ending Balance Sheet* | *Ending Balance Sheet* |
| No change | Asset, liability, and stockholders' equity account balances include amounts based on the use of the old estimate or principle in past years and the new estimate or newly adopted principle for new events in the current (and future) year(s). |

## QUESTIONS

*Q22-1*   Describe the three types of accounting changes.

*Q22-2*   Describe the three possible methods that could be used to report the effect of accounting changes. Give one reason in favor of, and one against, each alternative.

*Q22-3*   Describe two situations in which a change in an accounting principle would be justified.

*Q22-4*   Distinguish a change in an accounting principle from a change in an estimate. How should each be accounted for?

*Q22-5*   What are the four exceptions to the normal method used to account for a change in an accounting principle?

*Q22-6*   In which situations is it likely that the cumulative effect may not be determinable? What is the correct accounting in such cases?

*Q22-7*   Which changes in accounting principles should be accounted for retroactively? Why?

*Q22-8*   What is a *pro forma statement?* In which situations is it required that a pro forma statement be reported?

*Q22-9*   How is a change in an accounting principle reported in interim financial statements?

*Q22-10*   Give three examples of a change in an estimate. How are such changes accounted for?

*Q22-11*   Describe a change in a reporting entity. How is such a change accounted for?

*Q22-12*   How is an error of a prior period that is discovered in the current period reported?

*Q22-13*   Describe two errors that affect only the balance sheet.

*Q22-14*   Describe two errors that affect only the income statement.

*Q22-15*   Describe two errors that are counterbalanced in the following period.

*Q22-16*   Describe two errors that are not counterbalanced in the following period.

*Q22-17*   Why are errors corrected even after they have been counterbalanced?

## CASES

*C22-1   Accounting Changes*
There are three types of accounting changes: changes in accounting principles, changes in accounting estimates, and changes in reporting entities.

**Required**
Explain the differences and similarities between each of these types of changes, and explain the correct accounting for each. Include a discussion of the advantages and disadvantages of the required accounting method.

*C22-2   Accounting Changes*
There are four types of exceptions to the general rule that a change in accounting principle should be accounted for by a cumulative effect change.

**Required**
Explain each of the exceptions, and why cumulative effect accounting is not appropriate.

*C22-3   Transition Methods for a
        Change in Accounting Principle*
*FASB Statement No. 5*, "Accounting for Contingencies," requires that a cumulative effect adjustment be made at the adoption of the *Statement* by a company. Paragraph 104 states that the adoption of the prior period adjust-

ment method was opposed because of "...significant difficulties involved in determining the degree of probability and estimability that had existed in prior periods."

*FASB Statement No. 11*, "Accounting for Contingencies—Transition Method," requires prior period adjustments instead of the previously required cumulative effect adjustment. Paragraph 6 states, "It is preferable for an enterprise adopting *FASB Statement No. 5* to restate its financial statements for as many immediately preceding periods as is practicable."

**Required**
1. Evaluate the reasonableness of the FASB change.
2. Why do you think that the FASB has generally required the use of prior period restatement rather than cumulative effect adjustments when the newly required accounting principle is adopted?

*C22-4   Accounting Changes*
Sometimes a business entity may change its method of accounting for certain items. The change may be classified as a change in accounting principle, a change in accounting estimate, or a change in reporting entity.

The following are three independent, unrelated sets of facts relating to accounting changes.

### Situation I

A company determined that the depreciable lives of its fixed assets are presently too long to fairly match the cost of the fixed assets with the revenue produced. The company decided at the beginning of the current year to reduce the depreciable lives of all of its existing fixed assets by 5 years.

### Situation II

On December 31, 1995, Hyde Company owned 51% of Patten Company, at which time Hyde reported its investment using the cost method owing to political uncertainties in the country in which Patten was located. On January 2, 1996, the management of Hyde Company was satisfied that the political uncertainties were resolved and the assets of the company were in no danger of nationalization. Accordingly, Hyde will prepare consolidated financial statements for Hyde and Patten for the year ended December 31, 1996.

### Situation III

A company decides in January 1996 to adopt the straight-line method of depreciation for plant equipment. The straight-line method will be used for new acquisitions as well as for previously acquired plant equipment for which depreciation had been provided on an accelerated basis.

#### Required

For each of the preceding situations, provide the following information indicated. Complete your discussion of each situation before going on to the next situation.

1. Type of accounting change.
2. Manner of reporting the change under current generally accepted accounting principles, including a discussion, where applicable, of how amounts are computed.
3. Effect of the change on the statement of financial position and earnings statement.
4. Note disclosures that would be necessary. (*AICPA adapted*)

#### C22-5 *Accounting Changes*

It is important in accounting theory to be able to distinguish the types of accounting changes.

#### Required

1. If a public company desires to change from the sum-of-the-years'-digits depreciation method to the straight-line method for its fixed assets, what type of accounting change would this be? Discuss the permissibility of this change.
2. When pro forma disclosure is required for an accounting change, how are these pro forma amounts determined?

3. If a public company obtained additional information about the service lives of some of its fixed assets that showed that the service lives previously used should be shortened, what type of accounting change would this be? Include in your discussion how the change is reported in the income statement of the year of the change, and what disclosures are made in the financial statements or notes.
4. Changing specific subsidiaries comprising the group of companies for which consolidated financial statements are presented is an example of what type of accounting change, and what effect does it have on the consolidated income statements? (*AICPA adapted*)

#### C22-6 *Accounting Changes*

The various types of accounting changes may significantly affect the presentation of both financial position and results of operations for an accounting period and the trends shown in comparative financial statements and historical summaries.

#### Required

1. Describe a change in accounting principle and how it is reported in the income statement of the period of the change.
2. Describe a change in accounting estimate and how it is reported in the income statement of the period of the change.
3. Describe a change in reporting entity and how it is reported. Give an appropriate example of a change in reporting entity. (*AICPA adapted*)

#### C22-7 *Accounting Changes*

Berkeley Company, a manufacturer of many different products, changed its depreciation method for its production machinery from the double-declining-balance method to the straight-line method effective January 1, 1995. The straight-line method was determined to be preferable.

In addition, Berkeley changed the salvage values used in computing depreciation for its office equipment. This change was made on January 1, 1995 because additional information was obtained.

On December 31, 1995, Berkeley changed the specific subsidiaries comprising the group of companies for which consolidated financial statements are presented.

#### Required

1. What kind of accounting change is each of the preceding three situations? For each situation, indicate whether or not each should show:
   a. The cumulative effect of a change in accounting principle in net income of the period of change.
   b. Pro forma effects of retroactive application.
   c. Restatement of the financial statements of all prior periods.
2. Why does a change in accounting principle have to be disclosed by the company? (*AICPA adapted*)

## MULTIPLE CHOICE

*Select the best answer for each of the following.*

M22-1   During 1995, White Company determined that machinery previously depreciated over a 7-year life had a total estimated useful life of only 5 years. An accounting change was made in 1995 to reflect the change in estimate. If the change had been made in 1994, accumulated depreciation at December 31, 1994 would have been $1,600,000 instead of $1,200,000. As a result of this change, the 1995 depreciation expense was $100,000 greater. The income tax rate was 30% in both years. What should be reported in White's income statement for the year ended December 31, 1995 as the cumulative effect on prior years of changing the estimated useful life of the machinery?

    a.   $0                        c.   $300,000
    b.   $280,000                d.   $400,000

Items 2 and 3 are based on the following information:

The Shannon Corporation began operations on January 1, 1995. Financial statements for the years ended December 31, 1995 and 1996 contained the following errors:

|  | December 31 | |
|---|---|---|
|  | **1995** | **1996** |
| Ending inventory | $16,000 understated | $15,000 overstated |
| Depreciation expense | $ 6,000 understated | — |
| Insurance expense | $10,000 overstated | $10,000 understated |
| Prepaid insurance | $10,000 understated | — |

In addition, on December 31, 1996, fully depreciated machinery was sold for $10,800 cash, but the sale was not recorded until 1997. There were no other errors during 1995 or 1996 and no corrections have been made for any of the errors.

M22-2   Ignoring income taxes, what is the total effect of the errors on 1996 net income?

    a.   Net income understated by $1,800      c.   Net income overstated by $11,000
    b.   Net income overstated by $5,800       d.   Net income overstated by $30,200

M22-3   Ignoring income taxes, what is the total effect of the errors on the amount of working capital at December 31, 1996?

    a.   Working capital overstated by $4,200     c.   Working capital understated by $6,000
    b.   Working capital understated by $5,800   d.   Working capital understated by $9,800

M22-4   A change in the expected service life of an asset arising because additional information has been obtained is

    a.   An accounting change that should be reported by restating the financial statements of all prior periods represented
    b.   An accounting change that should be reported in the period of change and future periods if the change affects both
    c.   A correction of an error
    d.   Not an accounting change

M22-5   The cumulative effect of an accounting change, on the amount of retained earnings at the beginning of the period in which the change is made, should generally be included in net income for the period of the change for a

|  | Change in accounting principle | Change in accounting entity |
|---|---|---|
| a. | Yes | Yes |
| b. | No | Yes |
| c. | Yes | No |
| d. | No | No |

M22-6  On January 1, 1996, Belmont Company changed its inventory cost flow method to the FIFO cost method from the LIFO cost method. Belmont can justify the change, which was made for both financial statement and income tax reporting purposes. Belmont's inventories aggregated $4,000,000 on the LIFO basis at December 31, 1995. Supplementary records maintained by Belmont showed that the inventories would have totaled $4,800,000 at December 31, 1995 on the FIFO basis. Ignoring income taxes, the adjustment for the effect of changing to the FIFO method from the LIFO method should be reported by Belmont in the 1996
  a.  Income statement as an $800,000 debit
  b.  Retained earnings statement as an $800,000 debit adjustment to the beginning balance
  c.  Income statement as an $800,000 credit
  d.  Retained earnings statement as an $800,000 credit adjustment to the beginning balance

M22-7  When a cumulative effect type change in accounting principle is made during the year, the cumulative effect on retained earnings is determined
  a.  During the year using the weighted average method
  b.  As of the date of the change
  c.  As of the beginning of the year in which the change is made
  d.  As of the end of the year in which the change is made

M22-8  How should a change in accounting estimate that is recognized by a change in accounting principle be reported?

|  | Change in accounting estimate | Change in accounting principle |
|---|---|---|
| a. | No | No |
| b. | Yes | Yes |
| c. | No | Yes |
| d. | Yes | No |

M22-9  On January 2, 1995, Garr Company acquired machinery at a cost of $320,000. This machinery was being depreciated by the double-declining-balance method over an estimated useful life of 8 years, with no residual value. At the beginning of 1997, it was decided to change to the straight-line method of depreciation. Ignoring income tax considerations, the cumulative effect of this accounting change is
  a.  $0                       c.  $65,000
  b.  $60,000                  d.  $140,000

M22-10 A company has included in its consolidated financial statements this year a subsidiary acquired several years ago that was appropriately excluded from consolidation last year. This results in
  a.  An accounting change that should be reported prospectively
  b.  An accounting change that should be reported by restating the financial statements of all prior periods presented
  c.  Neither an accounting change nor a correction of an error
  d.  A correction of an error

*(AICPA adapted)*

## EXERCISES

E22-1  *Identification and Effects of Changes and Errors*  The following are several independent events:
  1.  Change from the LIFO to the FIFO inventory cost flow assumption.
  2.  Reduction in remaining service life of machinery from 10 to 8 years.
  3.  A change from an accelerated method to the straight-line method of depreciating assets.
  4.  Write-down of inventories due to obsolescence.
  5.  Receipt of damages won in a court suit instigated 5 years ago.
  6.  Recording as an asset, costs that were erroneously expensed in a previous period.
  7.  Write-down of property, plant, and equipment because of closure of inefficient plants.
  8.  A change from successful efforts to full cost accounting for oil exploration costs.

**Required**
Indicate how the preceding items are reported (specify whether increases or decreases can generally be expected) in the financial statements of the current year.

E22-2 *Identification and Effects of Changes and Errors* The following are several independent events:
1. Change from the FIFO to the LIFO inventory cost flow assumption.
2. Write-off of patent due to the introduction of a competing product.
3. Payment to the Internal Revenue Service in settlement of a dispute over previous year's taxes.
4. Increase in allowance for uncollectible accounts from 2% to 4% of credit sales.
5. Change from straight-line to double-declining-balance method.
6. Write-down of an asset to reflect probable future losses.
7. A change from full cost to successful efforts accounting for oil exploration costs.

**Required**
Indicate how the preceding items are reported (specify whether increases or decreases can generally be expected) in the financial statements of the current year.

E22-3 *Identification and Accounting for Changes and Errors* The following are several independent events:
1. A partnership is preparing to become a corporation and sell stock to the public. At this time, it is decided to switch from accelerated to straight-line depreciation.
2. A company has been debiting half its advertising costs to an intangible asset account and amortizing these costs over 3 years.
3. A company has been using accelerated depreciation. It now estimates that the pattern of benefits to be received in the future will be equal each period, so it decides to change to the straight-line depreciation method.
4. A company has been using straight-line depreciation in its property, plant, and equipment. It is now buying a new type of machine and elects to use accelerated depreciation on the new machines.
5. A company has been expensing all its manufacturing cost variances. It decides to allocate them between cost of goods sold and inventory in the future.

**Required**
Describe the correct accounting treatment for the changes (if any) related to the preceding events.

E22-4 *Change in Depreciation Method* At the beginning of 1996, the Ardo Company decides to change from the double-declining-balance method to the straight-line depreciation method for all its assets. The following data are available for the Ardo Company:

| Year | Reported Income Before Income Taxes | Excess of Double-Declining Over Straight-Line Depreciation |
|---|---|---|
| Prior to 1994 | $800,000 | $50,000 |
| 1994 | 500,000 | 70,000 |
| 1995 | 200,000 | 80,000 |
| 1996 | 400,000 | 60,000 |

The tax rate is 30%. The MACRS method has been, and will continue to be, used for tax purposes. Assume that the company has a simple capital structure with 100,000 shares of common stock outstanding. Ardo's 1995 and 1996 total revenues were $500,000 and $1,000,000, respectively.

**Required**
1. Prepare the journal entry for 1996 to reflect the change.
2. At the end of 1996, prepare comparative income statements for 1996 and 1995.

E22-5 *Change in Depreciation Method* The McCallum Company purchased a machine on January 2, 1991 for $154,000. It is being depreciated by the straight-line method over an 8-year life to a residual value of $10,000. At the beginning of 1995, the pattern of benefits generated by the asset indicated that a change to the sum-of-the-years'-digits method is appropriate. In 1995 and 1994, the company reported revenues of $250,000 and

$220,000 and expenses (other than depreciation and income tax) of $120,000 and $100,000, respectively. The tax rate is 30%. The MACRS method is used for tax purposes. The company has a simple capital structure with 20,000 shares of common stock outstanding during 1994 and 1995.

**Required**

1. Prepare the journal entry to reflect the change.
2. At the end of 1995, prepare the comparative income statements for 1995 and 1994.

E22-6 *Change in Inventory Cost Flow Assumption* At the beginning of 1996, the Brett Company decided to change from the FIFO to the average cost inventory cost flow assumption for financial reporting purposes. The following data are available in regard to reported pretax operating income and cost of goods sold:

| Year | Reported Income Before Income Taxes | Excess of Average Cost of Goods Sold Over FIFO Cost of Goods Sold |
|---|---|---|
| Prior to 1994 | $900,000 | $85,000 |
| 1994 | 500,000 | 50,000 |
| 1995 | 600,000 | 45,000 |
| 1996 | 700,000 | 70,000 |

The tax rate is 30%, and the company received permission from the IRS to also make the change for income tax purposes. The company has a simple capital structure with 100,000 shares of common stock outstanding. Assume that the reported income before income taxes of the Brett Company in 1996 was computed using the newly adopted inventory cost flow method. Brett's 1995 and 1996 revenues were $1,500,000 and $1,750,000, respectively.

**Required**

1. Prepare the journal entry for 1996 to reflect the change.
2. At the end of 1996, prepare comparative income statements for 1996 and 1995.

E22-7 *Change in Inventory Cost Flow Assumption* The Berg Company began operations on January 1, 1995 and uses the FIFO method in costing its raw material inventory. During 1996, management is contemplating a change to the LIFO method and is interested in determining what effect such a change will have on net income. Accordingly, the following information has been developed:

| | 1995 | 1996 |
|---|---|---|
| FIFO—Ending inventory | $240,000 | $270,000 |
| LIFO—Ending inventory | 200,000 | 210,000 |
| Income before income taxes (computed under the FIFO method) | 120,000 | 170,000 |

**Required**

What is the effect on income before income taxes in 1996 of a change to the LIFO method? (*AICPA adapted*)

E22-8 *Change in Inventory Method* The Fava Company began operations in 1994. It had been using the LIFO inventory method for both financial reporting and income taxes. At the beginning of 1995, the anticipated cost trends in the industry had changed so that the FIFO method was adopted for both financial reporting and income taxes. The company reported revenues of $300,000 and $270,000 in 1995 and 1994, respectively. The company incurred expenses (excluding income tax expense) of $125,000 and $120,000 in 1995 and 1994, including cost of goods sold of $55,000 and $45,000, respectively. An analysis indicates that FIFO cost of goods sold would have been lower by $6,000 in 1994. The tax rate is 30%. The company has a simple capital structure with 15,000 shares of common stock outstanding during 1994 and 1995. No dividends were paid in either year.

**Required**

1. Prepare the journal entry to reflect the change.
2. At the end of 1995, prepare the comparative income statements for 1995 and 1994.
3. At the end of 1995, prepare the comparative retained earnings statements for 1995 and 1994.

**E22-9**   *Change in Accounting Principle*   The Delta Company has been using the completed-contract method of accounting for long-term construction contracts. The company had started business in 1993 and had prepared the following income statements:

|                              | 1993      | 1994       |
|------------------------------|-----------|------------|
| Construction revenue         | $100,000  | $300,000   |
| Construction expense         | (40,000)  | (130,000)  |
| Other expenses               | (50,000)  | (70,000)   |
| Income before income taxes   | $ 10,000  | $100,000   |
| Income tax expense (30%)     | (3,000)   | (30,000)   |
| Net income                   | $   7,000 | $ 70,000   |

The company changes to the percentage-of-completion method at the beginning of 1995. It determines the construction revenue and expense amounts under the percentage-of-completion method to be as follows:

|                       | 1993      | 1994      | 1995      |
|-----------------------|-----------|-----------|-----------|
| Construction revenue  | $200,000  | $420,000  | $900,000  |
| Construction expense  | 80,000    | 182,000   | 420,000   |

The other expenses remain unchanged for 1993 and 1994, and are $80,000 in 1995. No dividends have been paid on the 10,000 common shares outstanding. With the 1995 financial statements, the company issues comparative statements for the previous two years. Under the completed-contract method, construction revenue and construction expense would have been $600,000 and $280,000, respectively, in 1995. The company uses the percentage-of-completion method for income tax purposes.

**Required**
Prepare the income statements and the statements of retained earnings that would be issued in 1995.

**E22-10** *Journal Entries to Correct Errors*   The following are several independent errors:
1. Goods in transit, purchased on account and shipped FOB destination, $10,000, were included in purchases but not in the ending inventory.
2. A purchase of a machine for $2,000 was expensed. The machine has a 5-year life, no residual value, and straight-line depreciation is used.
3. Wages payable of $2,000 were not accrued.
4. Payment of next year's rent, $4,000, was recorded as rent expense.
5. Allowance for doubtful accounts of $5,000 was not recorded. The company normally uses the aging method.
6. Equipment with a book value of $70,000 and a fair value of $100,000 was sold at the beginning of the year. A 2-year non-interest-bearing note for $121,000 was received and recorded at its face value. No interest revenue was recorded and 10% is a fair rate of interest.

**Required**
Prepare the correcting journal entry or entries for each of the preceding errors, assuming the error is discovered in the year after it was made. (Ignore income taxes.)

**E22-11** *Journal Entries to Correct Errors*   Use the information in E22-10.

**Required**
Prepare the correcting journal entries if each error is discovered 2 years after it is made and the books have been closed for the second year. (Ignore income taxes.)

**E22-12** *Effects of Errors*   The following are several independent errors:
1. Ending inventory is overstated.
2. Failure to record a purchase of inventory although the items are correctly recorded in the physical inventory.
3. Expensing the purchase of a machine.
4. Failure to accrue wages.

5. Failure to record an allowance for uncollectibles.
6. Including collections in advance as revenue.
7. Including payments in advance as expenses.
8. Failure to accrue warranty costs.
9. Discount on a note payable issued for purchase of a machine is ignored.
10. Failure to record depreciation expense on assets purchased during the year.

### Required

Indicate the effect of each of the preceding errors on (1) assets, (2) liabilities, (3) owners' equity, and (4) net income in the year in which the error occurs. State whether the error causes an overstatement ( + ), an understatement ( − ), or no effect (NE).

E22-13 *Correcting Journal Entries for Errors*   The following are several independent errors:

1. In January 1995, repair costs of $7,000 were debited to the Machinery account. At the beginning of 1995, the book value of the machinery was $90,000. No residual value is expected, the remaining estimated life is 10 years, and straight-line depreciation is used.
2. All purchases of materials for construction contracts still in progress have been immediately expensed. It is discovered that the use of such materials was $10,000 during 1994 and $12,000 during 1995.
3. Depreciation on manufacturing equipment has been excluded from manufacturing costs and treated as a period expense. During 1995, $40,000 of depreciation was accounted for in that manner. Production was 12,000 units during 1995, of which 3,000 remained in inventory at the end of the year. Assume there was no inventory at the beginning of 1995.

### Required

Prepare journal entries for the preceding errors discovered during 1996. (Ignore income taxes.)

E22-14 *Omission of Accruals and Prepayments*   The Dudley Company failed to recognize the following accruals. It also recorded the prepaid expenses and unearned revenues as expenses and revenues, respectively, in the year of payment or collection.

|  | 1994 | 1995 | 1996 |
|---|---|---|---|
| Prepaid expenses | $500 | $ 900 | $1,100 |
| Accrued expenses | 800 | 700 | 950 |
| Revenue received in advance | 300 | 400 | 1,300 |
| Revenue earned but not received | 600 | 1,000 | 1,200 |

The reported net income was $20,000 in 1994, $25,000 in 1995, and $23,000 in 1996.

### Required

1. Compute the correct net income for 1994, 1995, and 1996.
2. Prepare the journal entries necessary in 1996 if the errors are discovered at the end of that year.
3. Prepare the journal entries necessary in 1997 if the errors are discovered at the end of that year.

## PROBLEMS

P22-1   *Changes in Inventory Cost Flow Assumption*   At the beginning of 1996, the Flynne Company decided to change from the average cost to the FIFO inventory cost flow assumption. The following data are available:

| Year | Reported Income Before Income Taxes | Excess of Average Cost of Goods Sold Over FIFO Cost of Goods Sold |
|---|---|---|
| Prior to 1994 | $200,000 | $30,000 |
| 1994 | 40,000 | 12,000 |
| 1995 | 90,000 | 18,000 |
| 1996 | 80,000 | 6,000 |

The tax rate is 30%. The company has a simple capital structure and 10,000 shares of common stock outstanding. Assume that the balance in Retained Earnings is the sum of the company's reported income amounts (net of tax) and that the reported income before income taxes in 1996 uses the newly adopted method. Flynne's revenues for 1995 and 1996 were $225,000 and $200,000, respectively.

**Required**

1. At the end of 1996, prepare comparative income statements for 1996 and 1995.
2. If the change had been from LIFO to FIFO, prepare the comparative income statements and retained earnings statements that would be required. Indicate what items (if any) would be restated on the 1995 beginning and ending balance sheets. *Note:* In Requirements 2 and 3, assume that the "excess" figures represent the amount by which LIFO cost of goods sold exceeds FIFO cost of goods sold.
3. If the change had been from FIFO to LIFO, what disclosures would be required (assuming that only the excess cost of goods sold for 1996 was determinable)?
4. How would your answer to Requirement 1 change if the employees received a bonus of 10% of income before deducting the bonus and taxes?

P22-2    *Change from FIFO to Average Cost*    Koopmann Company began operations on January 1, 1994. It had been using the FIFO inventory method for financial reporting and the average cost inventory method for income taxes. At the beginning of 1996, the company decided to switch to the average cost inventory method for financial reporting. The company had previously reported the following financial statements for 1995:

**Income Statement**

|                           | 1995       |
|---------------------------|------------|
| Revenues                  | $100,000   |
| Cost of goods sold        | (60,000)   |
| Gross profit              | $ 40,000   |
| Operating expenses        | (25,000)   |
| Income before income taxes| $ 15,000   |
| Income tax expense        | (4,500)    |
| Net income                | $ 10,500   |
| Earnings per share        | $1.05      |

**Retained Earnings Statement**

|                              | 1995      |
|------------------------------|-----------|
| Beginning retained earnings  | $15,000   |
| Add: Net income              | 10,500    |
|                              | $25,500   |
| Less: Dividends              | (6,000)   |
| Ending retained earnings     | $19,500   |

**Balance Sheet (12/31/95)**

| Cash         | $ 9,000  | Accounts payable      | $ 3,000  |
|--------------|----------|-----------------------|----------|
| Inventory    | 38,000   | Income taxes payable  | 4,500    |
| Other assets | 66,800   | Deferred tax liability| 4,800    |
|              |          | Common stock, no par  | 82,000   |
|              |          | Retained earnings     | 19,500   |
|              | $113,800 |                       | $113,800 |

An analysis of the accounting records discloses the following cost of goods sold under the FIFO and average cost inventory methods:

|      | FIFO Cost of Goods Sold | Average Cost of Goods Sold |
|------|-------------------------|----------------------------|
| 1994 | $50,000                 | $57,000                    |
| 1995 | 60,000                  | 69,000                     |
| 1996 | 70,000                  | 80,000                     |

There are no indirect effects of the change in inventory method. Revenues for 1996 total $130,000; operating expenses for 1996 total $30,000. The company is subject to a 30% income tax rate in all years; income taxes payable of a current year are paid in the first quarter of the next year. The company had 10,000 shares of common stock outstanding during all years; dividends of $1 per share were paid in 1996. At the end of 1996, the company had cash of $10,000, inventory of $24,000, and other assets of $82,000. The company desires to show financial statements for the current year and previous year in its 1996 annual report.

### Required

1. Prepare the journal entry to reflect the change in methods at the beginning of 1996. Show supporting calculations.
2. Prepare the 1996 annual report. Notes to the financial statements are not necessary. Show supporting calculations.

P22-3    *Change from LIFO to Average Cost*   Schmidt Company began operations on January 1, 1994. It had been using the LIFO inventory method for both financial reporting and income taxes, but at the beginning of 1996 decided to switch to the average cost inventory method for financial and income tax reporting. The company had previously reported the following financial statements for 1995:

### Income Statement

| | 1995 |
|---|---|
| Revenues | $128,000 |
| Cost of goods sold | (78,000) |
| Gross profit | $ 50,000 |
| Operating expenses | (25,000) |
| Income before income taxes | $ 25,000 |
| Income tax expense | (7,500) |
| Net income | $ 17,500 |
| Earnings per share | $1.75 |

### Retained Earnings Statement

| | 1995 |
|---|---|
| Beginning retained earnings | $27,000 |
| Add: Net income | 17,500 |
| | $44,500 |
| Less: Dividends | (6,000) |
| Ending retained earnings | $38,500 |

### Balance Sheet (12/31/95)

| | | | |
|---|---|---|---|
| Cash | $ 8,000 | Accounts payable | $ 4,000 |
| Inventory | 42,000 | Income taxes payable | 7,500 |
| Other assets | 60,000 | Common stock, no par | 60,000 |
| | | Retained earnings | 38,500 |
| | $110,000 | | $110,000 |

An analysis of the accounting records discloses the following cost of goods sold under the LIFO and average cost inventory methods:

| | LIFO Cost of Goods Sold | Average Cost of Goods Sold |
|---|---|---|
| 1994 | $62,000 | $56,000 |
| 1995 | 78,000 | 69,000 |
| 1996 | 90,000 | 80,000 |

There are no indirect effects of the change in inventory method. Revenues for 1996 total $130,000; operating expenses for 1996 total $30,000. The company is subject to a 30% income tax rate in all years; all income taxes payable are paid in the next quarter. The company had 10,000 shares of common stock outstanding during all years; dividends of $1 per share were paid in 1996. At the end of 1996, the company had cash of $12,000, inventory of $34,000, other assets of $76,000, income taxes payable of $6,000, and accounts payable of ?. The company desires to show financial statements for the current year and previous year in its 1996 annual report.

**Required**

1. Prepare the journal entry to reflect the change in method at the beginning of 1996. Show supporting calculations.
2. Prepare the 1996 annual report. Notes to the financial statements are not necessary. Show supporting calculations.

P22-4  *Change in Depreciation Method*  At the beginning of 1995, the Clarke Company decided to change from the straight-line method to the double-declining-balance method of depreciation because of a perceived change in the pattern of benefits. The following information is available:

| Year | Income Before Income Taxes | Excess of Double-Declining over Straight-Line Depreciation |
|------|------|------|
| Prior to 1993 | $400,000 | $40,000 |
| 1993 | 200,000 | 60,000 |
| 1994 | 80,000 | 50,000 |
| 1995 | 160,000 | 70,000 |

The company's 1995 and 1994 revenues were $950,000 and $900,000, respectively. The company has been using MACRS depreciation for income taxes, and the income tax rate is 30%. Assume a simple capital structure with 100,000 shares of common stock outstanding during 1994 and 1995.

**Required**

1. Prepare the journal entry to reflect the change.
2. At the end of 1995, prepare the comparative income statements for 1995 and 1994.
3. If the company paid a bonus to employees of 10% of pretax income, how would your answers to Requirements 1 and 2 change?
4. At the end of 1995, prepare the comparative retained earnings statements if the change was accounted for as a prior period adjustment. Assume the retained earnings balance at the beginning of 1994 was $500,000 and that no dividends were paid in 1994 or 1995.

P22-5  *Change in Method of Accounting for Long-Term Construction Contracts*  Since the Goode Construction Company was formed in 1994, it has used the completed-contract method for financial reporting, but at the beginning of 1996 it changes to the percentage-of-completion method. The company had previously reported the following pretax income:

| | 1994 | 1995 |
|------|------|------|
| Sales of completed contracts | $300,000 | $800,000 |
| Less: Cost of completed contracts | (200,000) | (550,000) |
| Gross profit | $100,000 | $250,000 |

Analysis of the accounting records discloses that the following gross profit was earned on each of the company's projects based on the percentage-of-completion method:

| | 1994 | 1995 | 1996 |
|------|------|------|------|
| Project A | $100,000 | — | — |
| Project B | 120,000 | $125,000 | — |
| Project C | — | 75,000 | $400,000 |

In 1996, the company would have reported sales and cost of completed contracts of $820,000 and $350,000, respectively, under the completed-contract method. The tax rate is 30%. The company has a simple capital structure with 100,000 shares of common stock outstanding. No dividends were paid. Ignore other expenses (i.e., gross profit is income before income taxes). The company uses the percentage-of-completion method for income taxes.

**Required**

1. Prepare the journal entry to reflect the change in method at the beginning of 1996.
2. If the company also presents the 1994 and 1995 financial statements for comparative purposes, prepare the income statement disclosures (starting with income before income taxes) and retained earnings disclosures that are required in 1996. What items (if any) would be restated on the financial statements?

P22-6 *Changes Related to Machinery* At the beginning of 1996, the Freeman Company revised its estimate of the expected life of machinery. The machinery had been purchased on January 1, 1986 for $50,000, at which time it was estimated that the residual value would be $5,000 and the economic life 20 years. The revised estimate was that the total economic life was only 13 years. Straight-line depreciation is used for financial accounting purposes, and sum-of-the-years'-digits depreciation is used for income tax purposes.

**Required**

1. Prepare the journal entry to record the depreciation on December 31, 1996.
2. Ignore the change in the estimated life. Assume, instead, that the estimated residual value was revised to zero at the beginning of 1996. Prepare the journal entry to record the depreciation on December 31, 1996.
3. Ignore the change in the estimated life and the change in the estimated residual value. At the beginning of 1996, the company decided to change to sum-of-the-years'-digits depreciation for financial accounting purposes. Prepare the necessary journal entries assuming a tax rate of 30%. By how much would the pro forma net income for 1995 be different from the reported 1995 net income?

P22-7 *Change in Accounting for Inventory* The Kraft Manufacturing Company manufactures two products: Mult and Tran. At December 31, 1995, Kraft used the first-in, first out (FIFO) inventory method. Effective January 1, 1996, Kraft changed to the last-in, first out (LIFO) inventory method. The cumulative effect of this change is not determinable and, as a result, the ending inventory of 1995, for which the FIFO method was used, is also the beginning inventory for 1996 for the LIFO method. Any layers added during 1996 should be costed by reference to the first acquisitions of 1996, and any layers liquidated during 1996 should be considered a permanent liquidation.

The following information was available from Kraft's inventory records for the two most recent years:

|  | Mult | | Tran | |
|---|---|---|---|---|
|  | Units | Unit Cost | Units | Unit Cost |
| 1995 purchases: |  |  |  |  |
| January 7 | 5,000 | $4.00 | 22,000 | $2.00 |
| April 17 | 12,000 | 4.50 |  |  |
| November 9 | 17,000 | 5.00 | 18,500 | 2.50 |
| December 14 | 10,000 | 6.00 |  |  |
| 1996 purchases: |  |  |  |  |
| February 12 | 3,000 | 7.00 | 23,000 | 3.00 |
| May 21 | 8,000 | 7.50 |  |  |
| October 15 | 20,000 | 8.00 |  |  |
| December 24 |  |  | 15,500 | 3.50 |
| Units on hand: |  |  |  |  |
| December 31, 1995 | 15,000 |  | 14,500 |  |
| December 31, 1996 | 16,000 |  | 13,000 |  |

**Required**

Compute the effect on income before income taxes for the year ended December 31, 1996, resulting from the change from the FIFO to the LIFO inventory method. (*AICPA adapted*)

P22-8 *Change in Accounting Principle and Estimate* Mitchell Corporation has decided that in the preparation of its 1996 financial statements, two changes will be made from the methods used in prior years:

1. *Depreciation.* Mitchell has always used the Modified Accelerated Cost Recovery System (MACRS) for tax and financial reporting purposes. This method was considered acceptable for financial reporting because the differences in the depreciation amounts were considered to be immaterial. The company has decided to change

during 1996 to the straight-line method for financial reporting only, and to account for the change as a change in accounting principle. The effect of this change is shown as follows:

|  | **Excess of MACRS Over Straight-Line Depreciation** |
|---|---|
| Prior to 1995 | $1,300,000 |
| 1995 | 101,000 |
| 1996 | 99,000 |
|  | $1,500,000 |

Depreciation is charged to cost of sales and to selling, general, and administrative expenses on the basis of 75% and 25%, respectively.

   2. *Bad debt expense.* In the past, Mitchell has recognized bad debt expense equal to 1.5% of net sales. After careful review, it has been decided that a rate of 2% is more appropriate for 1996. Bad debt expense is charged to selling, general, and administrative expenses.

   The following information is taken from the Mitchell Corporation's preliminary financial statements, prepared before giving effect to the two changes:

**Condensed Comparative Balance Sheets**

|  | December 31 | |
|---|---|---|
|  | **1996** | **1995** |
| *Assets* | | |
| Current assets | $43,561,000 | $43,900,000 |
| Fixed assets, at cost | 45,792,000 | 43,974,000 |
| Less accumulated depreciation | (23,761,000) | (22,946,000) |
|  | $65,592,000 | $64,928,000 |
| *Liabilities and Stockholders' Equity* | | |
| Current liabilities | $19,091,620 | $22,505,920 |
| Long-term debt | 15,154,000 | 14,097,000 |
| Capital stock | 11,620,000 | 11,620,000 |
| Retained earnings | 19,726,380 | 16,705,080 |
|  | $65,592,000 | $64,928,000 |

**Comparative Income Statements**

|  | For the Year Ended December 31 | |
|---|---|---|
|  | **1996** | **1995** |
| Net sales | $80,520,000 | $78,920,000 |
| Cost of sales | (54,847,000) | (53,074,000) |
|  | $25,673,000 | $25,846,000 |
| Selling, general, and administrative expenses | (19,540,000) | (18,411,000) |
|  | $ 6,133,000 | $ 7,435,000 |
| Other income (expenses) net | (1,198,000) | (1,079,000) |
| Income before federal income taxes | $ 4,935,000 | $ 6,356,000 |
| Federal income taxes | (1,480,500) | (1,906,800) |
| Net income | $ 3,454,500 | $ 4,449,200 |

There have been no temporary differences between any book and tax items prior to the preceding changes. The effective rate is 30%.

**Required**

Based on *APB Opinion No. 20*, "Accounting Changes," compute for the following 7 items the amounts that would appear on the comparative (1996 and 1995) financial statements of Mitchell Corporation after adjustment for the two accounting changes. Show amounts for both 1996 and 1995 and prepare supporting schedules as necessary.

1. Accumulated depreciation.
2. Deferred tax liability.
3. Selling, general, and administrative expenses.
4. Current portion of federal income tax expense.
5. Deferred portion of federal income tax expense.
6. Retained earnings.
7. Pro forma net income. (*AICPA adapted*)

P22-9   *First Issuance of Financial Statements*   The Jackson Company has decided to issue common stock to the public in 1995. This will be the first public sale and therefore the company will issue its first publicly available financial statements since it was formed in 1992. The financial statements that it has prepared for its own use follow:

**Income Statements**

| | For Years Ended December 31, | | |
|---|---|---|---|
| | **1992** | **1993** | **1994** |
| Sales | $100,000 | $130,000 | $180,000 |
| Cost of goods sold | (35,000) | (45,000) | (65,000) |
| Gross profit | $ 65,000 | $ 85,000 | $115,000 |
| Other expenses | (62,500) | (75,000) | (83,200) |
| Income before income taxes | $  2,500 | $ 10,000 | $ 31,800 |
| Income tax expense | (750) | (3,000) | (9,540) |
| Net income | $  1,750 | $  7,000 | $ 22,260 |

**Balance Sheets**

| | December 31 | | |
|---|---|---|---|
| | **1992** | **1993** | **1994** |
| Cash | $  5,500 | $ 12,500 | $  9,960 |
| Accounts receivable | 30,000 | 50,000 | 63,000 |
| Inventory | 40,000 | 60,000 | 65,000 |
| Equipment | 100,000 | 100,000 | 140,000 |
| Less: Accumulated depreciation | (20,000) | (52,000) | (79,200) |
| | $155,500 | $170,500 | $198,760 |
| Current liabilities | $ 19,250 | $ 27,250 | $ 33,250 |
| Notes payable | 50,000 | 50,000 | 50,000 |
| Common stock | 84,500 | 84,500 | 84,500 |
| Retained earnings | 1,750 | 8,750 | 31,010 |
| | $155,500 | $170,500 | $198,760 |

These financial statements are audited for the first time at the beginning of 1995, and the following facts are discovered:

1. The company has not made any allowance for noncollection of accounts receivable. An allowance of 1% of total sales is considered appropriate. Uncollectible accounts of $630 should have been written off in 1994.
2. The notes payable are to officers of the company and have an interest rate of 12%. They were issued on January 1, 1992. No interest has been accrued or paid. (Assume simple interest and no compounding.)

3. The company has been using the Modified Accelerated Cost Recovery System over a 5-year life for both financial reporting and income tax purposes. It has been decided that the straight-line method should have been used for financial reporting based on an economic life of 10 years and a zero residual value, with a full year's depreciation being recorded in the year of acquisition. No disposals of property, plant, and equipment have occurred.
4. After adjustments, with the exception of depreciation, expenses deducted for financial accounting purposes are the same as those deducted for income tax purposes.
5. The company is subject to a 30% income tax rate and pays its taxes at the end of each year.

**Required**

1. Prepare the financial statements for 1992, 1993, and 1994 that would be issued at the beginning of 1995.
2. Describe what method would be used to account for each item if the financial statements for all 3 years had previously been publicly issued.

**P22-10**   *Error Correction*   At the end of 1996, while auditing the books of the Sandlin Company, *before* the books have been closed, you find the following items:

a. A building with a 30-year life (no residual value, straight-line depreciation) was purchased on January 1, 1996, by issuing a $60,000 non-interest-bearing, 4-year note. The entry made to record the purchase was a debit to Building and a credit to Notes Payable for $60,000; 10% is a fair rate of interest on the note.
b. The inventory at the end of 1996 was found to be overstated by $15,000. At the same time, it was discovered that the inventory at the end of 1995 had been overstated by $40,000. The company uses the perpetual inventory system.
c. For the last 3 years, the company has failed to accrue salaries and wages. The correct amounts at the end of each year were: 1994—$12,000; 1995—$18,000; 1996—$10,000.

**Required**

1. Prepare journal entries to correct the errors (ignore income taxes).
2. Assume, instead, the errors are discovered *after* the books have been closed. Prepare journal entries to correct the errors (ignore income taxes).

**P22-11**   *Error Correction*   At the beginning of 1996, Tanham Company discovered the following errors made in the preceding 2 years:

|  | 1994 | 1995 |
|---|---|---|
| Overstatement of ending inventory | $5,000 | $2,000 |
| Omission of wages payable | 700 | 800 |
| Omission of allowance for doubtful accounts | 1,300 | 1,700 |
| Prepayment of insurance recorded as expense | 500 | 200 |

Reported net income was $27,000 in 1994 and $35,000 in 1995. The allowance for doubtful accounts had a zero balance at the beginning of 1994. No accounts were written off during 1994 or 1995. Ignore income taxes.

**Required**

1. What is the correct net income for 1994 and 1995?
2. Prepare the adjusting journal entry in 1996 to correct the errors.

**P22-12**   *Error Correction*   A review of the books of the Anderson Corporation indicates that the errors and omissions pertaining to the balance sheet accounts shown as follows had not been corrected during the applicable years:
    The net income per the books is: 1993—$10,000; 1994—$12,000; 1995—$15,000; and 1996—$20,000. No dividends were declared during these years and no adjustments were made to retained earnings. The Retained Earnings balance on December 31, 1996, is $50,000.

| December 31 | Ending Inventory Overvalued | Ending Inventory Undervalued | Omissions | | | |
|---|---|---|---|---|---|---|
|  |  |  | Prepaid Expense | Unearned Revenues | Accrued Expense | Accrued Revenues |
| 1993 | $ — | $4,000 | $600 | $ — | $300 | $ — |
| 1994 | 3,000 | — | — | 500 | — | 700 |
| 1995 | 2,000 | — | 400 | — | 100 | — |
| 1996 | — | 1,000 | 900 | 200 | 350 | 800 |

**Required**

Prepare a worksheet to determine the correct net income for the years 1993, 1994, 1995, and 1996 and the adjusted balance sheet accounts as of December 31, 1996. (Ignore possible income tax effects.)

P22-13 *Error Correction* The bookkeeper of the Cask Company, who has maintained its accounting records since the company's formation in January 1993, has prepared the unaudited financial statements. In your examination of these statements at the end of 1995, you discover the following items:

1. Sales taxes collected from customers have been included in the sales account. The Sales Tax Expense account is debited when the sales taxes are remitted to the state in the month following the sale. All sales are subject to a 6% sales tax. Total sales (excluding sales tax) for the three years 1993 through 1995 were $200,000, $300,000, and $500,000, respectively. The Sales Tax Expense account balance for the three years was $10,000, $15,000, and $26,000, respectively.

2. An account payable of $15,000 for merchandise purchased in December 1993 was recorded in January 1994. The merchandise was not included in inventory at December 31, 1993.

3. Merchandise with a cost of $4,000 was included twice in the December 31, 1994 inventory.

4. The company has used the direct write-off method of accounting for bad debts. Accounts written off in the three years 1993 through 1995 were $2,000, $4,500, and $6,500, respectively. The appropriate balances of Allowance for Doubtful Accounts at the end of 1993 through 1995 are $5,000, $6,000, and $8,200, respectively.

5. On January 1, 1994, 12% 10-year bonds with a face value of $600,000 were issued at 102. The premium was credited to Additional Paid-in Capital. The bonds pay interest on June 30 and December 31, and use of the straight-line amortization method is appropriate.

6. Travel advances to the sales personnel of $18,000 were included as selling expenses for 1994. The travel occurred in 1995.

7. Salaries payable at the end of each year have not been accrued. Appropriate amounts at the end of 1993 through 1995 are $10,000, $11,000, and $7,000, respectively.

8. Installation, freight, and testing costs of $25,000 on a machine purchased in January 1993 were expensed at that time. The machine has a life of 5 years and a residual value of $10,000.

**Required**

Analyze the effects of the errors on income for 1993, 1994, and 1995, and the 1995 ending balance sheet (ignore income taxes), according to the following format:

| Explanation | Income 1993 | | Income 1994 | | Income 1995 | | Balance Sheet December 31, 1995 | | |
|---|---|---|---|---|---|---|---|---|---|
| | | | | | | | Amount | | |
| | Debit | Credit | Debit | Credit | Debit | Credit | Debit | Credit | Account |

P22-14 *Comprehensive* The financial statements of the Gray Company showed income before income taxes of $4,030,000 for the year ended December 31, 1996, and $3,330,000 for the year ended December 31, 1995. Additional information is as follows:

1. Capital expenditures were $2,800,000 in 1996 and $4,000,000 in 1995. Included in the 1996 capital expenditures is equipment purchased for $1,000,000 on January 1, 1996, with no salvage value. Gray used straight-line depreciation based on a 10-year estimated life in its financial statements. As a result of additional information now available, it is estimated that this equipment should have only an 8-year life.

2. Gray made an error in its financial statements that should be regarded as material. A payment of $180,000 was made in January 1996 and charged to expense in 1996 for insurance premiums applicable to policies commencing and expiring in 1995. No liability had been recorded for this item at December 31, 1995.

3. The allowance for doubtful accounts reflected in Gray's financial statements was $7,000 at December 31, 1996, and $97,000 at December 31, 1995. During 1996, $90,000 of uncollectible receivables were written off against the allowance for doubtful accounts. In 1995, the provision for doubtful accounts was based on a percentage of net sales. The 1996 provision has not yet been recorded. Net sales were $58,500,000 for the year ended December 31, 1996, and $49,230,000 for the year ended December 31, 1995. Based on the latest available facts, the 1996 provision for doubtful accounts is estimated to be 0.2% of net sales.

4. A review of the estimated warranty liability at December 31, 1996, which is included in "other liabilities" in Gray's financial statements, has disclosed that this estimated liability should be increased $170,000.

5. Gray has two large blast furnaces that it uses in its manufacturing process. These furnaces must be periodically relined. Furnace A was relined in January, 1990 at a cost of $230,000 and in January, 1995 at a cost of $280,000. Furnace B was relined for the first time in January, 1996 at a cost of $300,000. In Gray's financial statements, these costs were expensed as incurred.

Since a relining will last for 5 years, a more appropriate matching of revenues and costs would result if the cost of the relining were capitalized and depreciated over the productive life of the relining. Gray has decided to make a change in accounting principle from expensing relining costs as incurred to capitalizing them and depreciating them over their productive life on a straight-line basis with a full year's depreciation in the year of relining. This change meets the requirements for a change in accounting principle under *APB Opinion No. 20,* "Accounting Changes."

**Required**

1. For the years ended December 31, 1996 and 1995, prepare a worksheet reconciling income before income taxes as given previously with income before income taxes and cumulative effect of a change in accounting principle as adjusted for the preceding additional information. Show supporting computations in good form. Ignore income taxes and deferred tax considerations in your answer. The worksheet should have the following format:

|  | Year Ended December 31 | |
| --- | --- | --- |
|  | 1996 | 1995 |
| Income before income taxes, before adjustments | $4,030,000 | $3,330,000 |
| Adjustments: | | |
| Net adjustments | | |
| Income before income taxes and cumulative effect of a change in accounting principle, after adjustments | $ | $ |

2. For the year ended December 31, 1996 compute the cumulative effect before income taxes of the change in accounting principle from expensing to capitalizing relining costs. Ignore income taxes and deferred tax considerations in your answer. (*AICPA adapted*)

P22-15 *Comprehensive*   The Ingalls Corporation is in the process of negotiating a loan for expansion purposes. The books and records have never been audited, and the bank has requested that an audit be performed. Ingalls has prepared the following comparative financial statements for the years ended December 31, 1996 and 1995:

**Balance Sheet**

|  | As of December 31, | |
| --- | --- | --- |
|  | 1996 | 1995 |
| *Assets* | | |
| Current assets | | |
| Cash | $163,000 | $ 82,000 |
| Accounts receivable | 392,000 | 296,000 |
| Allowance for uncollectible accounts | (37,000) | (18,000) |
| Securities available for sale | 78,000 | 78,000 |
| Merchandise inventory | 207,000 | 202,000 |
| Total current assets | 803,000 | 640,000 |
| Fixed assets | | |
| Property, plant, and equipment | 167,000 | 169,500 |
| Accumulated depreciation | (121,600) | (106,400) |
| Total fixed assets | 45,400 | 63,100 |
| Total assets | $848,400 | $703,100 |

**Balance Sheet**

| | As of December 31, | |
| :--- | ---: | ---: |
| | 1996 | 1995 |
| *Liabilities and Stockholders' Equity* | | |
| Liabilities | | |
| Accounts payable | $121,400 | $196,100 |
| Stockholders' equity | | |
| Common stock, par value $10, authorized 50,000 shares, issued and outstanding 20,000 shares | 260,000 | 260,000 |
| Retained earnings | 467,000 | 247,000 |
| Total stockholders' equity | 727,000 | 507,000 |
| Total liabilities and stockholders' equity | $848,400 | $703,100 |

**Statement of Income**

| | For the Years Ended December 31, | |
| :--- | ---: | ---: |
| | 1996 | 1995 |
| Sales | $1,000,000 | $900,000 |
| Cost of sales | (430,000) | (395,000) |
| Gross profit | 570,000 | 505,000 |
| Operating expenses | 210,000 | 205,000 |
| Administrative expenses | 140,000 | 105,000 |
| | (350,000) | (310,000) |
| Net income | $ 220,000 | $195,000 |

During the course of the audit, the following additional facts were determined:

1. An analysis of collections and losses on accounts receivable during the past 2 years indicates a drop in anticipated losses due to bad debts. After consultation with management, it was agreed that the loss experience rate on sales should be reduced from the recorded 2% to 1%, beginning with the year ended December 31, 1996.
2. An analysis of the securities available for sale revealed that this portfolio consisted entirely of short-term investments in marketable equity securities that were acquired in 1995. The total market valuation for these investments as of the end of each year was as follows: December 31, 1995—$81,000; December 31, 1996—$62,000.
3. The merchandise inventory at December 31, 1995 was overstated by $4,000 and the merchandise inventory at December 31, 1996 was overstated by $6,100.
4. On January 2, 1995, equipment costing $12,000 (estimated useful life of 10 years and residual value of $1,000) was incorrectly charged to Operating Expenses. Ingalls records depreciation via the straight-line method. In 1996, fully depreciated equipment (with no residual value) that originally cost $17,500 was sold as scrap for $2,500. Noble credited the proceeds of $2,500 to Property and Equipment.
5. An analysis of 1995 operating expenses revealed that Ingalls charged to expense a 3-year insurance premium of $2,700 on January 15, 1995.

**Required**

1. Prepare the journal entries to correct the books at December 31, 1996. The books for 1996 have not been closed. Ignore income taxes.
2. Prepare a schedule showing the computation of corrected net income for the years ended December 31, 1996 and 1995, assuming that any adjustments are to be reported on comparative statements for the 2 years. The first items on your schedule should be the net income for each year. Ignore income taxes. (Do not prepare financial statements.) (*AICPA adapted*)

# 23

## ADDITIONAL ASPECTS OF FINANCIAL REPORTING AND FINANCIAL ANALYSIS

A company's financial statements summarize its various financial activities and operations. The information contained in the statements is examined, synthesized, and related to other information by external users for a variety of reasons. Current stockholders, for example, are concerned about their investment income, as well as about the company's overall profitability, stability, and sound capital structure needed for continued successful operations. Some potential investors are interested in "safe" companies, ones whose financial statements indicate stable earnings and dividends with limited or moderate growth. Others prefer companies whose financial statements indicate a trend for financial flexibility, rapid growth, and diversification into different lines of business. Short-term creditors are interested in a company's short-run liquidity, its ability to pay current obligations as they mature. Long-term creditors are concerned about the long-term security of their interest income and the company's ability to maintain successful earnings and cash flows to meet continuing financial commitments. These are just a few of the users and uses of financial statements.

This book is designed for *preparers* of *general purpose* financial statements—statements that serve the needs of a diverse set of external users. The information contained in these statements should be comprehensible to those users who have a reasonable understanding of business and economic activities and who are willing to examine the information with reasonable diligence.[1] These general purpose financial statements covering a fiscal year are published in a corporation's *annual report* to its stockholders. In addition to the specific financial statements and accompanying notes, an annual report includes a variety of items. Those items directly or indirectly related to the financial statements include the auditor's report, the report of management, and management's discussion and analysis. Companies also prepare *interim reports* which include all or parts of general purpose financial statements for accounting periods of less than a year. Accountants must be familiar with these additional aspects of financial reporting.

---

1.  "Objectives of Financial Reporting by Business Enterprises," *FASB Statement of Financial Accounting Concepts No. 1* (Stamford, Conn.: FASB, 1978), par. 34.

Accountants, in the role of *preparers of financial statements,* do not themselves use the statements in investment and credit decisions. However, a better understanding of how external decision makers examine and analyze the data contained in the financial statements can lead to insights on how to improve that information. In some cases, companies may be required or may choose to present certain reports and analyses in conjunction with their annual reports as an aid to external users, and accountants must know how to prepare these items. Finally, accountants often are called on by management, lending institutions, and other groups to provide additional analyses of the financial statements.

Included in this chapter is a discussion of (1) market efficiency, (2) the auditor's report, (3) the report of management, (4) management's discussion and analysis, (5) segment reports, (6) interim reports, and (7) SEC reports. Also covered is a discussion of various aspects of financial analysis, including in an Appendix an explanation of financial analysis comparisons, as well as a discussion of (1) horizontal analysis, (2) vertical analysis, and (3) ratio analysis.

## MARKET EFFICIENCY

Over the past two decades, researchers have conducted studies based on an **efficient markets** hypothesis. Evidence from this research tends to show that (1) the prices of securities traded in the capital markets fully reflect all *publicly* available information, and (2) these prices are adjusted based on new information almost *immediately* in an *unbiased* manner. That is, as soon as a new item of information becomes publicly available, it is interpreted, analyzed, and incorporated into the market prices. Information about companies becomes publicly available through a variety of ways, including news releases reported in such newspapers as *The Wall Street Journal,* management forecasts, interim financial statements, and annual reports. The market prices adjust in an unbiased and immediate manner because of the communication system in the marketplace and sophisticated investors (those professionals such as security analysts and stockbrokers) who continuously gather, interpret, analyze, and process information.

An efficient capital market means that an individual investor cannot use published information to earn an "abnormal" return on a security investment with a given amount of risk. That is, all securities with a similar amount of risk will yield approximately the same rate of return; only through the use of "insider information" can abnormal returns be obtained. If the efficient markets hypothesis is valid, how does the related research affect financial reporting and financial analysis, the topics of this chapter?

Since the market efficiently processes many types of public information, **full disclosure** of financial information is important for two reasons. First, full disclosure (so that the information becomes "public") helps to prevent the use of insider information by unscrupulous investors to earn abnormal returns. Second, full disclosure (at a reasonable cost) in the financial statements, the accompanying notes, or by other means that complement the information in the financial statements helps the market to operate efficiently and in a cost-effective fashion.

The efficiency of the capital markets does not detract from the use of various financial analysis techniques. In fact, one of the reasons why the markets tend to be efficient is because professional analysts interpret and analyze the information. Furthermore, financial analysis techniques are useful in situations where an investor is considering the investment potential of a company whose securities are *not* traded in an organized capital market, where a financial institution is considering a lending arrangement with a company, or where a company must be monitored to make certain that it is adhering to any financial restrictions imposed by various lending agreements. Finally, not all investors believe in the efficient market hypothesis; some continue to use financial analysis techniques to improve their investment decisions.[2]

## AUDITOR'S REPORT (OPINION)

Many investment and credit decisions are based on the information presented in a company's financial statements, which are prepared by and are the responsibility of its management. To provide an external perspective, most published financial statements are audited by an *independent* certified public accountant. In an **audit**, the certified public accountant conducts an examination of the accounting system, records, and financial statements in accordance with generally accepted auditing standards. Based on the examination, **the auditor expresses an opinion concerning the fairness of the financial statements in conformity with generally accepted accounting principles.** An auditor's standard report (opinion) includes the following statements:

1.  The auditor is independent.

2.  An audit was performed on specified financial statements.

3.  The financial statements are the responsibility of the company's management; the opinion is the responsibility of the auditors.

4.  The audit was conducted according to generally accepted auditing standards.

5.  The audit was planned and performed to obtain reasonable assurance about whether the financial statements are free of material misstatement.

6.  The audit included examination, assessment, and evaluation stages.

7.  The audit provides a reasonable basis for an opinion.

8.  An opinion is expressed concerning the fair presentation.[3]

The report is also signed and dated by the auditing firm.

An audit report is *not* part of the financial statements because it is a report by the independent auditor. Nonetheless, it is considered an important item of information because external users place reliance on the report as to the fairness of the financial statements. The "standard" form of an auditor's report on *comparative* financial statements (often referred to as an *unqualified* opinion) is shown in Exhibit 23-1. (The audit report for Eli Lilly and Company is shown in Exhibit 3-11 of Chapter 3. The audit report of The Coca-Cola Company is shown in Appendix A at the end of this book.)

An unqualified opinion contains three paragraphs. The first paragraph, known as the *introductory* paragraph, lists the financial statements that were audited, declares that management is responsible for those statements, and asserts that the auditor is responsible for expressing an opinion on them.

---

2.  For a more complete discussion of efficient capital markets research and its implications, see R. L. Watts and J. L. Zimmerman, "Positive Accounting Theory: A Ten Year Perspective," *The Accounting Review* (January, 1990), pp. 131–156, and T. R. Dyckman and D. Morse, *Efficient Capital Markets and Accounting: A Critical Analysis*, 2nd ed. (Englewood Cliffs, N.J.: Prentice-Hall, 1986).

3.  *Codification of Statements of Auditing Standards* (New York: AICPA, 1992), sec. 508.05.

## EXHIBIT 23-1

### UNQUALIFIED AUDIT REPORT

INDEPENDENT AUDITOR'S REPORT

We have audited the accompanying balance sheets of X Company as of December 31, 19X5 and 19X4, and the related statements of income, retained earnings, and cash flows for the years then ended. These financial statements are the responsibility of the Company's management. Our responsibility is to express an opinion on these financial statements based on our audits.

We conducted our audits in accordance with generally accepted auditing standards. Those standards require that we plan and perform the audit to obtain reasonable assurance about whether the financial statements are free of material misstatement. An audit includes examining, on a test basis, evidence supporting the amounts and disclosures in the financial statements. An audit also includes assessing the accounting principles used and significant estimates made by management, as well as evaluating the overall financial statement presentation. We believe that our audits provide a reasonable basis for our opinion.

In our opinion, the financial statements referred to above present fairly, in all material respects, the financial position of X Company as of [at] December 31, 19X5 and 19X4, and the results of its operations and its cash flows for the years then ended in conformity with generally accepted accounting principles.

[*Signature*]

[*Date*]

The second paragraph, known as the *scope* paragraph, describes what the auditor has done. Specifically, it states that the auditor has examined the financial statements in accordance with generally accepted auditing standards and has performed appropriate tests. The auditor does *not* examine *all* of the information used to generate the financial statements, but performs tests to evaluate the reasonableness of the information. The auditor exercises skill and judgment in deciding what evidence to examine, when to examine it, and how much to examine. As we have seen throughout this book, financial statements include many estimates made by management. An auditor also designs tests to evaluate the reasonableness of the assumptions and other factors used in the estimates. Because estimates are inherently imprecise, the auditor's involvement supports their reasonableness but does not guarantee their accuracy.

The third paragraph, known as the *opinion* paragraph, gives the auditor's opinion. Like a doctor or lawyer, an auditor's opinion is based on professional judgment, not absolute certainty. When the opinion is unqualified, the auditor states that the financial statements present *fairly* in accordance with *generally accepted accounting principles* (GAAP). Thus the emphasis is not on presenting "fairly" in some general sense of the word but on presenting in accordance with GAAP. In other words, GAAP are defined as being fair. Therefore, the user of the financial statements must understand GAAP to be able to understand and interpret the statements. (In exceptional cases, the management of the company and the auditor may agree that a method other than GAAP provides more useful and "fairer" information about a transaction or event. In such a case, the non-GAAP method would be fully disclosed.) The opinion also emphasizes that the statements comply with GAAP in all *material* respects; that is, the financial statements are free of material misstatements rather than absolutely accurate. An audit enhances the confidence of users because the auditor is an objective, independent expert who is knowledgeable about the company's business and financial reporting requirements.

Note that there are three things that the audit report does *not* say. First, an unqualified opinion is not a "clean bill of health." The report does not, for example, endorse a company's policy decisions, its use of resources, or even the adequacy of its internal control. Second, an unqualified opinion provides no assurance of the future success of the company. Generally accepted auditing standards include procedures to be followed to examine the financial viability of the company. However, a company may suffer financial difficulty, or even failure, within a relatively short time of receiving an unqualified opinion, a situation that does not necessarily indicate that the audit was negligent. In other words, there is a difference between a business failure and an audit failure. Third, an audit report does not provide an assurance that fraud has not been committed by a member, or members, of the company unless such fraud would cause a material misstatement in the financial statements. An audit is planned and performed with professional skepticism. The auditor assesses the risk of material misstatement and designs the audit to provide reasonable assurance of detection of significant errors or fraud. However, fraud that is concealed through forgery and collusion among the personnel of the company, especially management, may escape detection by the auditor. For large companies, such fraud would have to involve millions of dollars to be material.

In certain circumstances, a modified report may be issued or a qualified opinion, adverse opinion, or disclaimer of opinion may be expressed by the independent auditor. A *modified* report includes a fourth explanatory paragraph. The two most common types of modified reports are caused by material uncertainties and changes in accounting principles. A *qualified* opinion states that except for the effects of the qualified item, the financial statements present fairly the information in conformity with GAAP. An *adverse* opinion states that the financial statements do not present fairly the information in conformity with GAAP. A *disclaimer* of opinion states that the auditor does not express an opinion. These types of reports and opinions are discussed more fully in standard auditing books.

## AUDIT COMMITTEE AND MANAGEMENT'S REPORT

Audit committees have existed in some companies for many years. Both the AICPA and the SEC have encouraged companies to establish audit committees; the New York Stock Exchange requires companies whose shares are traded on the Exchange to have such a committee. As a result, the number of companies using audit committees is increasing. An **audit committee is a group that has oversight over the financial reporting process of a company.** Since an auditor must keep close communication with a company's management, the possibility exists that the auditor will not maintain independence from this management. A lack of independence would reduce the reliability that external users place on the company's financial statements. Consequently, a primary responsibility of an audit committee is to help maintain auditor independence, and usually most audit committee members are "outside directors" (not officers or employees of the company). The audit committee acts as the liaison between the auditor and management. Although the duties of an audit committee vary among companies, generally an audit committee of a company: (1) oversees the internal control structure, (2) helps in the selection of accounting policies, (3) helps select the auditor, (4) reviews the audit plan, (5) reviews suggestions by auditors concerning weaknesses in internal control, and (6) reviews the financial statements and audit report. Use of an audit committee enhances the credibility of a company's financial statements.

As we noted earlier, **the preparation and presentation of a company's financial statements are the responsibility of its management.** In the past, many external users have had the mistaken impression that because auditors reviewed the financial statements, the financial statements were the responsibility of the auditor. Then, if a company experienced financial difficulties resulting in a "business failure," they erroneously thought this was an "audit failure." Consequently, the officers of companies have been encouraged to acknowledge their responsibilities regarding financial statements. Although not part of the financial statements, many companies are including a **"Management Report"** section in their annual report. In this report, management acknowledges that it is responsible for preparing and presenting the financial statements. Furthermore, since sound internal control plays a vital role in these activities, this section frequently includes a discussion of internal control. Because the audit committee has oversight over internal control, reference to the audit committee's responsibilities often is made in this section. Finally, the report may identify the independent auditor's responsibilities. An example of the management report section of Westinghouse is shown in Exhibit 23-2. Note the references to management's responsibility, the auditor's responsibility, internal control, and the company's audit committee.

## EXHIBIT 23-2
## Management Responsibility Report

### WESTINGHOUSE

REPORT OF MANAGEMENT

The Corporation has prepared the consolidated financial statements and related financial information included in this Annual Report. Management has the primary responsibility for the financial statements and other financial information and for ascertaining that the data fairly reflect the financial position, results of operations and cash flows of the Corporation. The financial statements were prepared in accordance with generally accepted accounting principles appropriate in the circumstances, and necessarily include amounts that are based on best estimates and judgments with appropriate consideration given to materiality. Financial information included elsewhere in this Annual Report is presented on a basis consistent with the financial statements.

The Corporation maintains a system of internal accounting controls, supported by adequate documentation, to provide reasonable assurance that assets are safeguarded and that the books and records reflect the authorized transactions of the Corporation. Limitations exist in any system of internal accounting controls based upon the recognition that the cost of the system should not exceed the benefits derived. Westinghouse believes its system of internal accounting controls, augmented by its corporate auditing function, appropriately balances the cost/benefit relationship.

The independent accountants provide an objective assessment of the degree to which management meets its responsibility for fair financial reporting. They regularly evaluate the system of internal accounting controls and perform such tests and procedures they deem necessary to express an opinion on the fairness of the financial statements.

The Board of Directors pursues its responsibility for the Corporation's financial statements through its Audit Review Committee composed of directors who are not officers or employees of the Corporation. The Audit Review Committee meets regularly with the independent accountants, management and the corporate auditors. The independent accountants and the corporate auditors have direct access to the Audit Review Committee, with and without the presence of management representatives, to discuss the scope and results of their audit work and their comments on the adequacy of internal accounting controls and the quality of financial reporting.

We believe that the Corporation's policies and procedures, including its system of internal accounting controls, provide reasonable assurance that the financial statements are prepared in accordance with the applicable securities laws and with a corresponding standard of business conduct.

## MANAGEMENT'S DISCUSSION AND ANALYSIS

As discussed later in this chapter, the Securities and Exchange Commission (SEC) requires certain information to be included in the *Form 10-K* annual report filed with it. One of these SEC reporting requirements involves a discussion and analysis *by management* of the company's financial condition, changes in financial condition, and results of operations. This discussion is called "management's discussion and analysis" or simply MD&A. The intent is to give investors the opportunity to look at the company "through the eyes of management" by providing both a short-term and a long-term analysis of the company's business. One focus of the MD&A is on "forward-looking" information. Thus, the MD&A provides a narrative explanation of the financial statements so that investors can judge the "quality" of earnings and the likelihood that past performance is indicative of future performance in regard to cash flows from operations and from outside sources. Although most companies are not under the jurisdiction of the SEC, its disclosure requirements have influenced accounting practice so that many companies include the MD&A in their annual report.

In its MD&A, a company must provide information regarding liquidity, capital resources, and the results of operations, as well as other information necessary to understand its financial condition and changes in financial condition. This disclosure includes descriptions and amounts of items that would have an impact on future operations but that did not affect past operations, as well as amounts of items that affected past operations but are not expected to have an impact on future operations. Furthermore, where knowledge of segment information is useful to understanding a company's business, the discussion is to focus on each relevant, reportable segment, as well as on the whole company.

*Regulation S-K* of the SEC provides instructions for preparing the nonfinancial statement information required in *Form 10-K*. It includes specific instructions concerning appropriate MD&A disclosures as well as general instructions about overall MD&A disclosures. *Financial Reporting Release No. 36* provides additional guidance for MD&A disclosures, particularly those dealing with prospective information. The following is a brief discussion of the major disclosure issues that may involve intracompany and intercompany comparisons, and may include horizontal, vertical, and ratio analyses (discussed in the chapter Appendix). The discussion assumes that any items included in a company's MD&A are material.

1. **Liquidity.** A company is to identify any known trends or demands, commitments, events, or uncertainties that are likely to result in an increase or decrease in its short-term and long-term liquidity. If a significant deficiency in liquidity is identified, the company is to indicate the actions it expects to take to remedy the situation. The company also must identify and separately describe its internal and external sources of liquidity, and discuss any major unused sources of liquid assets.

2. **Capital Resources.** A company is to describe its commitments for capital expenditures at the end of the current period, as well as indicate the purpose of these commitments and the anticipated sources of funds needed to fulfill the commitments. In this regard, the company must describe any known favorable or unfavorable trends in its capital resources. This description is to include a discussion of any expected significant changes in the mix of its capital resources and the relative cost. The discussion also must explain any changes between debt and equity financing, and off-balance sheet financing arrangements.

3. **Results of Operations.** A number of disclosures relate to income from continuing operations. First, a company is to describe any significant unusual or infrequent events or transactions and their effect on income from continuing operations. This description must include the impact on the various affected revenues and expenses. Second, a description of any known trends or uncertainties that are likely to favorably or unfavorably affect income from continuing operations must be included. Third, if a significant change in the relationship between costs and revenues is expected to occur, the change is to be described. Fourth, if there is a significant increase in net sales revenues, a discussion must be included to explain whether the increase was due to increased selling prices, increased volume, or the introduction of new products or services. Finally, a discussion must be included of the impact of inflation and changing prices on net sales revenues and income from continuing operations.[4]

4. **General Instructions.** Lengthy general instructions for the presentation of a company's MD&A are included in *Regulation S-X* and various *Financial Reporting Releases*. Of particular concern to the SEC is distinguishing between the "required" disclosures (that were briefly discussed earlier) and "voluntary" disclosures that are encouraged but not required in regard to prospective information. That is, *required* disclosures involve *currently known* trends, events, and uncertainties that are *reasonably* expected to have significant effects on a company. In contrast, *voluntary* (optional) forward-looking disclosures involve *anticipated future* trends or events, or a less predictable impact of a known trend, event, or uncertainty.[5] This distinction is somewhat similar to that made for the accrual versus narrative disclosures of contingencies, discussed in Chapter 11.

The Coca-Cola Company's financial review, incorporating its management discussion and analysis, is shown in Appendix A at the end of this book.

## SEGMENT REPORTING

The financial statements of multidivisional companies are prepared on a "consolidated" basis; that is, the accounting results of various legal segments are *aggregated* into a set of financial statements encompassing the entire economic entity (briefly discussed in Chapter 13). Although investors and creditors recognize the importance of consolidated statements in evaluating overall company performance, the *disaggregation* of total financial data also can be important in their financial analysis.

The evaluations of risk and return are significant factors in investment and credit decisions. Risk results from, among others, (1) the nature and current status of the industries in which the company operates, (2) the changing conditions in the geographic areas within which the company operates, (3) the characteristics of its major customers, and (4) the national and international economic and political factors that may affect its operations. The profitability, or return, offered by a company also is affected by its types of industrial segments, the relationships between the revenues and expenses of its industrial segments, its major customers, and national and international factors.

---

4. "Codification of Financial Reporting Policies," *SEC Accounting Rules* (Chicago: Commerce Clearing House, June 1989), sec. 229.303.
5. *Ibid.*, sec. 501.02.

Financial analysis information on risk and return is improved through the presentation of disaggregated segment financial information. In light of the need for such data, **FASB Statement No. 14** requires that a company's financial statements include information about its operations in different industries, its foreign operations and export sales, and its major customers.[6] The intent of this disaggregation also is to improve the *predictive value* and *feedback value* of financial statement information.

## Reporting on Industry Operations

**An industry segment is a component of a company that provides a product or service, or a *group* of related products and services, primarily to unaffiliated customers, for a profit.** To apply *FASB Statement No. 14*, a company first determines its industry segments. To do so, a company may use the Standard Industrial Classification (a federal system for classifying businesses according to the type of economic activity in which they are engaged), look internally at its "profit centers," or consider (1) the nature of the product, (2) the nature of the production process, and (3) its markets and marketing methods.

*Reportable Segments*
A company need not provide financial information about all these segments, however. Materiality determines whether or not a segment is a **reportable segment**—one whose operations are significant enough that its financial activities must be reported. **An industry segment is considered significant and is defined as a reportable segment if it satisfies at least *one* of the three following tests:**

1. **Revenue Test.** Its revenues (*including* intersegment sales or transfers) are 10% or more of the combined revenues of all the company's industry segments.

2. **Operating Profit Test.** The absolute amount of its operating profit (loss) is 10% or more of the combined operating profits of all industry segments that did not incur an operating loss.[7]

3. **Asset Test.** Its identifiable assets are 10% or more of the combined identifiable assets of all industry segments.

The terms "revenues," "operating profits and losses," and "identifiable assets" as applied in this *Statement* are defined in the next section.

In addition to these tests, an overall materiality test states that the reportable segments must be a substantial portion of the company's total operations. That is, enough reportable segments must be disclosed so that their combined revenues (*excluding* intersegment sales) are at least 75% of the entire company revenues (*excluding* intersegment sales). If a company operates predominantly or exclusively in a single industry, it need not apply the disclosure requirements except that it must identify the industry. This occurs when a single dominant segment's revenues, operating

---

6. "Financial Reporting for Segments of a Business Enterprise," *FASB Statement of Financial Accounting Standards No. 14* (Stamford, Conn.: FASB, 1976), par. 1. Nonpublic companies, those whose securities are not traded publicly or who are not required to file financial statements with the SEC, are not required to report segment information. "Suspension of the Reporting of Earnings per Share and Segment Information by Nonpublic Enterprises," *FASB Statement of Financial Accounting Standards No. 21* (Stamford, Conn.: FASB, 1978), par. 12.

7. If the combined operating losses of all industry segments that incurred an operating loss exceed the combined operating profits as calculated earlier, the combined operating loss amount would be used for this 10% test.

profit (or loss), and identifiable assets each are more than 90% of the combined totals for all industry segments.

## Information Reported

The following financial information is reported separately for each reportable segment:

1. **Revenues.** The revenues of a reportable industry segment include those from sales to unaffiliated customers and from intersegment sales or transfers. Intersegment sales or transfers are those between one segment and another segment within the company. *Excluded* from revenues are revenues earned at the corporate level (e.g., interest revenue on corporate investments) and the equity in income or loss from unconsolidated subsidiaries.

2. **Operating Profit or Loss.** The operating profit or loss of a reportable industry segment is its revenues (defined earlier) minus all operating expenses. Operating expenses include (a) traceable expenses that relate to revenues from sales (external and intersegment) and (b) those operating expenses incurred by a company that are allocable on a reasonable basis among those industry segments for whose benefit the expenses were incurred. *Excluded* from operating expenses are such items as general corporate expenses (e.g., certain administrative expenses), interest expense, income taxes, results from discontinued operations, extraordinary items, and the cumulative effects of changes in accounting principles.

3. **Identifiable Assets.** The identifiable assets of a reportable industry segment are the tangible and intangible assets that are used by the segment, including (a) those used exclusively by that segment and (b) a reasonably allocated portion of assets used jointly by two or more segments. *Excluded* from identifiable assets are those maintained for general corporate purposes, intersegment loans and advances, and investments in unconsolidated subsidiaries.

4. **Other Related Disclosures.** Several other disclosures are made in regard to each reportable industry segment. The primary ones include: (a) the aggregate amount of depreciation, depletion, and amortization expense included in the computation of operating profit; (b) its capital expenditures for property, plant, and equipment; (c) the types of products and services from which its revenue is derived; and (d) the accounting policies relevant to the segment's data.[8]

This same information also is reported for the rest of the company's insignificant industry segments. That is, the remaining insignificant industry segments are *combined*, and their combined revenues, operating profits (or losses), and identifiable assets are reported.

## Issues in Measurement

The *Statement* only briefly discusses the issues involved in measuring a segment's operating profit, which are the same issues as those involved in developing an internal managerial performance evaluation system. They primarily involve transfer pricing methods related to intersegment sales and operating expense allocations.

---

8. *FASB Statement No. 14, op. cit.,* par. 10 and 27.

A transfer price is the charge made to a segment of a company that "purchases" a good or service from another company segment. Several transfer pricing methods are in use, including charging the purchasing segment on the basis of market (external selling) prices, the "full" costs of the producing segment, the variable cost, or a negotiated price. Any transfer price method may be used in the determination of intersegment sales included in segment revenues, as long as the method is the same as that used for internal accounting purposes. Whenever a significant amount of intersegment sales occur, the lack of specificity regarding transfer pricing may lead to a *lack of comparability* of segment information between companies. For instance, two similar companies, one using a transfer price based on the market price and the other using a transfer price based on variable cost, would report different revenues and operating profits simply because of the different transfer prices.

Another issue exists regarding the allocation of operating expenses. Only those that are allocable to the benefiting segments on a "reasonable" basis are included in the computation of operating profits. General corporate expenses are excluded. The identification of allocable operating expenses and the selection of an allocation method can have a significant effect on the comparability of operating income across companies as well as among segments of the same company. What one company considers an allocable operating expense, another may consider a general corporate expense. To some extent, this classification depends on the sophistication of each company's management information system. Differences in classifications of expenses among similar companies will lead to differences in and noncomparability of results.

The allocation of operating expenses to segments may be made on various bases, including sales, contribution margins, assets or investments, numbers of employees, and physical measures such as square footages. Again, the basis or bases for allocation will depend on a company's management information system. Selection from several alternative bases for allocation of operating expenses may lead to different operating results across segments as well as noncomparable operating results for similar segments in different companies. Issues of this type also exist regarding the exclusion from and allocation of identifiable assets to industry segments.

### Methods of Presentation

The financial information about the reportable industry segments of a company may be disclosed (1) within the body of the financial statements, with supporting notes; (2) entirely in the notes to the financial statements; or (3) in a separate schedule that is an integral part of the financial statements. Most companies use a separate schedule to disclose their segment information. This information is presented in dollars, although percentage relationships also may be shown. A **reconciliation** also is included. The revenues listed for the reportable industry segments and the other aggregated industry segments are reconciled to the total revenue reported in the company's income statement, the operating profits or losses of the segments are reconciled to the pretax income from continuing operations, and the identifiable assets of the segments are reconciled to the company's total assets. Any unallocated revenues, expenses, and assets are separately identified in the reconciliation. When developing the supplemental schedule, a working paper is generally prepared. In it, the revenues, cost of goods sold, selling, general, and administrative expenses, and identifiable assets are allocated to each *industry* segment. Based on the resulting allocations, the revenue, operating profit, and identifiable asset tests are made to determine the *reportable* segments. The results of the reportable segments are then shown separately and the results of the insignificant industry segments are combined for reporting purposes.

*Illustration*

To illustrate the presentation of reportable industry segment financial information, assume the X Company presents the income statement[9] shown in Exhibit 23-3. In addition, the X Company reports total assets of $19,000 on its December 31, 1995 balance sheet.

## EXHIBIT 23-3

### X COMPANY

Income Statement
For Year Ended December 31, 1995

| | | |
|---|---:|---:|
| Sales | | $3,800 |
| Cost of goods sold | $2,470 | |
| General and administrative expenses | 620 | |
| Operating expenses | | (3,090) |
| Pretax operating profit | | $ 710 |
| Other items: | | |
|    Interest expense | $ (80) | |
|    Equity in net income of Y Company (25% owned) | 200 | 120 |
| Pretax income from continuing operations | | $ 830 |
| Income taxes | | (250) |
| Income from continuing operations | | $ 580 |
| Results of discontinued operations: | | |
|    Loss from operations of discontinued West Coast | | |
|      division (net of income tax effect of $35) | $ 80 | |
|    Loss on disposal of West Coast division (net of | | |
|      income tax effect of $55) | 130 | (210) |
| Income before extraordinary items | | $ 370 |
| Extraordinary gain (net of income tax effect of $40) | | 90 |
| Net income | | $ 460 |

(Earnings per share are not shown.)

X Company discloses its reportable segment information in a supplemental schedule. In developing the information to be included in this schedule, X Company prepared the working paper shown in Exhibit 23-4. It identified five industry segments and allocated the revenues, operating expenses (which include depreciation), and identifiable assets to each segment as shown. Next, the company applied the reporting principles established in *FASB Statement No. 14* to determine which industry segments were reportable. The revenue test was applied first. Segment B met the 10% test, but the others did not. After deducting operating expenses from revenues, it was

---

9. This example is modified from that shown in *FASB Statement No. 14*, Exhibits A and B of Appendix F. Since intersegment sales are a concern of "consolidation" accounting, generally discussed in an advanced accounting book, they are not further considered in this chapter.

---

**EXHIBIT 23-4**

**X COMPANY**

Working Paper for Segment Reporting
For Year Ended December 31, 1995

| | All Industry Segments | | | | | Segment Totals | Unallocated | Totals |
|---|---|---|---|---|---|---|---|---|
| | A | B | C | D | E | | | |
| Total revenues (sales) | $ 300 | $2,530ᵃ | $ 370 | $ 280 | $ 320 | $ 3,800 | $    0 | $ 3,800 |
| Operating expenses: | | | | | | | | |
|   Cost of goods sold | $ 190 | $1,685 | $ 210 | $ 185 | $ 200 | $ 2,470 | $    0 | $ 2,470 |
|   General and administrative | 40 | 350 | 55 | 30 | 45 | 520 | 100 | 620 |
|   Total operating expenses | $ 230 | $2,035 | $ 265 | $ 215 | $ 245 | $ 2,990 | $ 100 | $ 3,090 |
| Operating profit | $  70 | $ 495 | $ 105ᵇ | $  65 | $  75 | $   810 | $ (100) | $   710 |
| Identifiable assets | $1,800ᶜ | $9,400 | $2,000 | $1,300ᵈ | $1,500ᵈ | $16,000 | $3,000 | $19,000 |

a. Segment B meets the revenue test.
b. Segment C meets the operating profit test. (Segment B also meets this test.)
c. Segment A meets the asset test. (Segments B and C also meet this test.)
d. Segments D and E meet none of the tests and are combined for reporting purposes.

determined that Segment C's $105 operating profit (and also Segment B's) was at least 10% of the $810 total operating profit of all the segments. Finally, Segment A has $1,800 of identifiable assets that are more than 10% of the $16,000 combined identifiable assets of all the industry segments. (The identifiable assets of Segments B and C also meet this test.) Thus, Segments A, B, and C all qualify as reportable segments, whereas Segments D and E are combined for reporting purposes. Note that the $3,200 ($300 + $2,530 + $370) revenues from Segments A, B, and C exceed 75% of the $3,800 total revenues from all the operating segments so that enough reportable segments are included.

Exhibit 23-5 shows the schedule that X Company includes in its annual report. Note that the revenues and operating profits of the industry segments are reconciled to the appropriate totals on the income statement. Segment revenues are reconciled to total sales. The segment operating profits are reconciled to the pretax income from continuing operations by adding the income from the unconsolidated Y Company subsidiary and deducting the general corporate expenses and interest expense. Similarly, the industry segment identifiable assets are reconciled to the total corporate assets.

## Reporting on Foreign Operations and Export Sales

The financial statements of a company must report on significant foreign operations. Foreign operations are defined as those revenue-producing operations that are located outside the United States and that are generating revenue either from sales to unaffiliated customers or to other intracompany segments.[10] Revenue and asset tests are used to define significant foreign operations. That is, if either (1) revenue generated by the

---

10. The FASB recognizes that the distinction between foreign operations and export sales may sometimes be difficult to make. It provides several examples to help distinguish between the two (see *FASB Statement No. 14, op. cit.*, par. 31 and fn. 12), which are not discussed here.

---

**EXHIBIT 23-5**

## X COMPANY

Industry Segment Financial Results
For Year Ended December 31, 1995

| | Reportable Industry Segments | | | Other Industry Segments | Total Results |
|---|---|---|---|---|---|
| | A | B | C | | |
| Total revenues (sales) | $ 300 | $2,530 | $ 370 | $ 600 | $ 3,800 |
| Operating profit | $ 70 | $ 495 | $ 105 | $ 140 | $ 810 |
| General corporate expenses | | | | | (100) |
| Equity in net income of Y Company | | | | | 200 |
| Interest expense | | | | | (80) |
| Pretax income from continuing operations | | | | | $ 830 |
| Identifiable assets at December 31, 1995 | $1,800 | $9,400 | $2,000 | $2,800 | $16,000 |
| Investment in net assets of Y Company | | | | | 800 |
| Corporate assets | | | | | 2,200 |
| Total assets at December 31, 1995 | | | | | $19,000 |

*Note:* The company operates principally in three industries, A, B, and C. Operations in Industry A involve production and sales of (describe types of products and services). Operations in Industry B involve production and sales of (describe types of products and services). Operations in Industry C involve production and sales of (describe types of products and services). Total revenue by industry includes sales to unaffiliated customers. The company makes no intersegment sales.

Operating profit is total revenue less operating expenses. In computing operating profit, none of the following items have been added or deducted: general corporate expenses, interest expense, income taxes, equity in income from unconsolidated investee, loss from discontinued operations of the West Coast division (which was a part of the company's operations in Industry B), or extraordinary gain (relating to the company's operations in Industry C).

Depreciation for Industries A, B, and C was $20, $300, and $40, respectively. Capital expenditures for the three industries were $100, $400, and $200, respectively. Identifiable assets by industry are those assets that are used in the company's operations in each industry. Corporate assets are principally cash and investments in marketable securities.

The company has a 25% interest in Y Company, whose operations are in the United States and are vertically integrated with the company's operations in Industry A. Equity in net income of Y Company was $200; investment in net assets of Y Company was $800.

Contracts with a U.S. government agency account for $600 of the sale to unaffiliated customers of Industry B.

---

company's foreign operations from sales to unaffiliated customers is at least 10% of total company revenues or (2) identifiable assets of the company's foreign operations are at least 10% of total company assets, then certain foreign and domestic financial information (as discussed later) are disclosed. Furthermore, activities in significant foreign geographic areas are important. If, in a particular foreign geographic area, a company's revenues from sales to unaffiliated customers or its identifiable assets are 10% or more of *total* company revenues or assets, respectively, it is considered a "significant" geographic area and additional geographic financial information is disclosed.

### Information Reported

The financial information reported concerning foreign operations is similar to the disclosure requirements for industry segments. That is, for both domestic and foreign operations (1) revenues, (2) operating profits or loss (or net income or some measure of profitability between operating profits or loss and net income), and (3) identifiable assets (as defined earlier) are disclosed separately. In addition, if the foreign operations include one or more significant geographic areas, the foreign revenues, operating profits or losses, and identifiable assets of these geographic areas are separately disclosed. Finally, if the *domestic* operations make 10% or more of their sales to unaffiliated customers in foreign countries, that amount of *export* sales are separately reported in the aggregate and by geographic areas when these area sales are significant. All the preceding information is presented in U.S. dollar amounts, although percentages may be shown as well. Geographic areas are identified and revenues, operating profits or loss, and identifiable assets are reconciled to totals reported on the company's financial statements.[11]

### Illustration

To illustrate the presentation of the foreign and domestic financial information, the X Company example is continued in Exhibit 23-6. The working paper used to identify

---

### EXHIBIT 23-6

## X COMPANY

**Foreign Geographic Operating Results**
**For Year Ended December 31, 1995**

|  | United States | Foreign Geographic Area A | Foreign Geographic Area B | Total Results |
|---|---|---|---|---|
| Total revenues (sales) | $ 2,430 | $ 750 | $ 620 | $ 3,800 |
| Operating profit | $ 500 | $ 180 | $ 130 | $ 810 |
| General corporate expenses |  |  |  | (100) |
| Equity in net income of Y Company |  |  |  | 200 |
| Interest expense |  |  |  | (80) |
| Pretax income from continuing operations |  |  |  | $ 830 |
| Identifiable assets at December 31, 1995 | $11,300 | $2,600 | $2,100 | $16,000 |
| Investment in net assets of Y Company |  |  |  | 800 |
| Corporate assets |  |  |  | 2,200 |
| Total assets of December 31, 1995 |  |  |  | $19,000 |

*Note*: Operating profit is total revenues less operating expenses. In computing operating profit, none of the following items have been added or deducted: general corporate expenses, interest expense, income taxes, equity in income from unconsolidated investee, loss from discontinued operations of West Coast division (which was part of the company's U.S. operations), or extraordinary gain (which relates to the company's operations in Geographic Area B). The company makes no intersegment sales.

Identifiable assets are those assets of the company that are identified with the operations in each geographic area. Corporate assets are principally cash and investments in marketable securities.

Of the $2,430 U.S. sales, $470 were export sales, principally to Geographic Area A.

---

11. *FASB Statement No. 14, op. cit.*, par. 31–36.

the information disclosed in Exhibit 23-6 is not presented here but would be similar to that shown in Exhibit 23-4. In Exhibit 23-6, the income statement information from Exhibit 23-3 is disaggregated to report on X Company's foreign activities.[12]

The foreign financial information is separated into Geographic Areas A and B, since revenues in each area are more than 10% of total company revenues. The revenues, operating profit, and identifiable assets are reconciled with the related amounts in the company's financial statements. The note includes the amount of export sales made by its domestic operations. Observe that since X Company has reportable industry segments as well as significant foreign operations, Exhibit 23-6 is *not* a substitute for Exhibit 23-5. Instead, *both* schedules are shown as supporting information in X Company's financial statements.

## Information About Major Customers

If at least 10% of a company's revenue is derived from sales to a single customer, the amount of revenue from each such customer is disclosed, together with the identity of the industry segment or segments making the sales. A single customer is defined as a group of entities under common control, the federal government, a state government, a local government, or a foreign government.[13] This disclosure is made in the notes to Exhibit 23-5.

## INTERIM FINANCIAL REPORTS

External users often want more frequent accounting information than that provided in the annual report. **Interim financial statements are reports for periods of less than a year.** Their purpose is to improve the *timeliness* of accounting information. These *interim reports* are issued by all companies whose stock is being traded on the New York or American Stock Exchange and by most companies filing with the SEC. One issue involving interim reports is the difficulty inherent in determining meaningful operating results for intervals of less than a year. Revenues of some businesses are seasonal and fluctuate widely across interim periods. Some companies incur heavy fixed costs in one interim period that benefit the operating activities in other periods. Other companies must estimate costs that will not be paid until subsequent interim periods but that benefit the current one. Estimates also must be made of such items as inventories and income taxes if the interim reports are to be relevant and reliable.

The APB studied these issues and established guidelines in **APB Opinion No. 28** for the presentation of interim financial information. The intent of this *Opinion* is to indicate which generally accepted accounting principles apply to interim financial statements and to specify the disclosures that are necessary to present meaningful information for an interim period of less than a year. Of particular concern to the Board was the reconciliation of two different views concerning interim periods. One view is that each interim period is a basic accounting period and the results of operations should be determined in essentially the same way as if the interim period were an annual accounting period. The other view is that each interim period is an integral period of the annual accounting period. Thus, deferrals, accruals, and estimates made at the end of each interim period should consider the impact on the results of

12. This example is also modified from that shown in *FASB Statement No. 14*, Exhibit C of Appendix F.
13. "Disclosure of Information About Major Customers," *FASB Statement of Financial Accounting Standards No. 30* (Stamford, Conn.: FASB, 1979), par. 6

operations for the rest of the annual period. The Board concurred with the second view and concluded that **each interim period is viewed primarily as an integral part of an annual period** and that a company must continue to use the generally accepted accounting principles that were used in the preparation of its latest annual report. However, certain principles are modified for interim reporting purposes so that the results will be more informative and articulate better with the annual report results. The FASB has issued two *Statements* (Nos. 3 and 18) and an *Interpretation* (No. 18) to clarify various aspects of *APB Opinion No. 28*. The current generally accepted accounting principles established in *APB Opinion No. 28* focus primarily on the income statement items and are summarized briefly in the following sections.

## Revenues

Revenues from products or services are recognized during an interim period in the same manner (when earned and realized) as during the annual accounting period. For example, when the percentage-of-completion method is used to recognize long-term construction contracts, revenues are recognized on the basis of the percent completed during that interim period. In cases where revenues are subject to seasonal variations, the company must disclose the seasonal nature of its activities and consider presenting supplemental information regarding revenues for previous periods.

## Expenses

The expenses that are associated directly with product sales or the provision of services are matched against interim revenues in the period the revenues are recognized. These include such items as inventory costs, wages, and warranties. With regard to inventories, companies generally must use the same inventory pricing methods (for example, LIFO, FIFO, average) and make provisions for write-downs to market for interim reporting in the same way as they do for annual reporting, with the following exceptions:

1.  Companies that utilize a periodic inventory system and use estimated gross profit rates (or other estimation methods) to determine the cost of goods sold during interim periods must disclose the method used and any significant adjustments that result from reconciliation with the annual physical inventory.

2.  If a company using the LIFO method encounters a temporary partial liquidation of its base-period inventory that is expected to be replaced by year-end, cost of goods sold must include the expected cost to replace the liquidated inventory, and the inventory at the interim reporting date must *not* take the liquidation into account. Assuming rising prices, this requirement avoids the possibility of showing abnormally high interim period income due to LIFO "liquidation profits."

3.  Permanent losses due to inventory market declines must be recognized in accordance with the lower of cost or market procedures, discussed in Chapter 7, in the interim period during which the decline occurred. Any recovery of such losses in subsequent interim periods within the same year must be recognized as gains (not to exceed the previously recognized losses) in those later periods. Temporary market declines need not be recognized in interim periods.

4.  The accounting for all variances for companies using standard cost accounting systems must follow routine annual procedures. Any significant unplanned or unanticipated purchase price or volume variances must be disclosed in the interim period.

Expenses that are not directly associated with product sales (or services) are matched against revenues using a variety of bases. Expenses that can be identified as affecting the operating activities of more than one interim period are allocated among the interim periods based on an estimate of (a) time expired, (b) benefit received, or (c) activity associated with the periods. Such allocation procedures must be consistent with those used for annual reporting purposes. For example, accrued or deferred property taxes, advertising costs, depreciation charges, and uncollectible accounts (bad debts) expense are allocated among the interim periods. Expenses that cannot be identified with activities other than those of the current interim period are allocated to that period. No arbitrary allocations are allowed. Disclosure of the nature and amount of such costs must be made. For example, office utilities, rent expense, and interest costs are expensed as incurred in the interim period. Gains and losses that occur in an interim period and that would not be deferred at year-end are recognized in the interim period of occurrence. For example, a gain on the sale of land or a loss on the disposal of equipment is recognized in the interim period.[14]

## Income Taxes

To present fairly the results of operations, at the end of *each* interim period a company must make its best estimate of the effective income tax rate expected to be applicable for the *entire* year. The effective rate includes the appropriate tax rate on *annual* income from continuing operations, after consideration of such items as foreign tax rates, percentage depletion, and other available tax planning techniques. In determining the rate, no consideration is given to the income tax related to any items (such as extraordinary items) that are reported separately, net of income taxes. Consequently, each quarter the company estimates its annual income from continuing operations and, based on this annual income, estimates its annual income taxes to derive an effective annual income tax rate. The effective rate is then used to provide for income taxes related to income from continuing operations on a year-to-date basis. The amount of income taxes applicable to the current interim period is the difference between the income tax computed on year-to-date income from continuing operations and the related income taxes reported on previous interim reports of the accounting period.[15] This procedure must be completed for each of the four interim periods; it follows the general principle of intraperiod tax allocation.

To illustrate, assume a corporation reported pretax income from continuing operations of $20,000 at the end of the first quarter and estimated its income tax on this income to be $5,220. (This estimate was derived at the end of the first quarter, using the technique discussed previously.) For simplicity, this example ignores temporary differences and tax credits. The corporation now is preparing an interim income statement at the end of the second quarter for that quarter and the first 6 months. It determines that its pretax income from continuing operations for the second quarter is $26,000 and anticipates it will earn $25,000 and $29,000 in each of the next two quarters, respectively. The corporate income tax rates are 15% on the first $20,000 of earnings and 30% on earnings in excess of $20,000. As shown in Exhibit 23-7, based on an estimated effective income tax rate of 27%, the corporation lists income tax expense of $12,420 for the first 6 months and $7,200 for the second quarter of operations.

---

14. "Interim Financial Statements," *APB Opinion No. 28* (New York: AICPA, 1973), par. 11–15.
15. "Accounting for Income Taxes in Interim Periods," *FASB Interpretation No. 18* (Stamford, Conn.: FASB, 1977), par. 9.

### EXHIBIT 23-7

## COMPUTATION OF INTERIM INCOME TAXES

1. Estimation of Annual Income:

| | | |
|---|---|---|
| First quarter: | $ 20,000 | actual income |
| Second quarter: | 26,000 | actual income |
| Third quarter: | 25,000 | estimated income |
| Fourth quarter: | 29,000 | estimated income |
| | $100,000 | estimated annual income |

2. Estimated Effective Income Tax Rate:

$$15\% \times \$20,000 = \$ 3,000$$
$$30\% \times (\$100,000 - \$20,000) = 24,000$$
$$\text{Estimated total tax} = \$27,000$$

$$27\% \text{ Effective Income Tax Rate} = \frac{\$27,000 \text{ Estimated Income Tax}}{\$100,000 \text{ Estimated Income}}$$

3. Estimated Income Tax for First 6 Months:

$46,000 \times 27\% = \underline{\$12,420}$ estimated income tax on first 6 months' income

4. Estimated Income Tax for Second Quarter:

| | |
|---|---|
| $12,420 | estimated income tax on first 6 months of income |
| (5,220) | estimated income tax on first-quarter income |
| $ 7,200 | estimated income tax on second-quarter income |

In the case of an *established* pattern of seasonal revenues resulting in an earlier interim period operating loss that is offset by income in later periods, the income tax effects (that is, the income tax credit) of the earlier loss are recognized in that interim period and offset against the income taxes incurred on the income of the later interim periods.

### Extraordinary Items, Discontinued Operations, and Cumulative Effects

Material extraordinary items and results of discontinued operations are disclosed (net of income taxes) in the usual manner in the interim period during which the events occurred. The cumulative effect of a change in accounting principle (net of income taxes) is disclosed in the first interim period, regardless of the interim period in which it occurs. None of these items is prorated over the entire annual accounting period. Materiality, however, is determined on the basis of a relationship of the item to the estimated income for the entire *year* and not to the interim period results.

### Earnings Per Share

Earnings per share is computed for each interim period presented, in accordance with **APB Opinion No. 15.** That is, for computing a weighted average number of common shares outstanding as well as for other earnings per share issues, the quarter (or year-to-date, for longer periods) is considered the accounting "period." The resulting simple or primary and fully diluted earnings per share is disclosed on the face of the interim income statement. A breakdown of earnings per share related to income from continuing operations, results of discontinued operations, extraordinary items, and the cumulative effect of a change in accounting principle is also disclosed.

Care should be taken in disclosing comparative interim earnings per share because of differences arising as a result of the short time periods. Shares issued in the second quarter result in a different number of outstanding shares than in the first quarter, making it difficult for the user to predict an annual earnings per share. Similarly, an extraordinary loss occurring in the fourth quarter affects earnings per share for that quarter and the year but does not affect the earnings per share listed in the first three quarters.

### Preparation and Disclosure of Summarized Interim Financial Data

The accounting procedures involved in the preparation of interim reports are similar to those for annual reports. Typically, a trial balance of the year-to-date account balances is taken. The trial balance is entered on a worksheet or other working paper. Year-to-date adjusting entries are prepared on the working paper, after which the year-to-date financial statements are prepared. However, the interim accounting procedures differ in several respects from those completed at year-end.

First, for those companies using a periodic inventory system, the determination of the ending inventory for the interim reports is usually based on an estimation technique rather than on a physical inventory. Thus, the gross profit method, retail inventory method, or some other estimation technique is used to derive the ending interim inventory to be recorded on the working paper and in the financial statements. Second, the adjusting entries required at the end of the interim period to bring the accounts up to date usually are prepared only on the working paper and are not entered into the accounts. When this approach is used, only at the end of the year are the annual adjusting entries journalized and posted to the accounts.

Third, the accounts are not closed at the end of each interim period. Consequently, in an interim period subsequent to the first period, care must be taken not to include amounts applicable to previous interim periods in the revenue and expense accounts. To avoid this problem, as mentioned previously, companies typically prepare the interim income statement on a year-to-date basis and then eliminate the income statement results from any previous interim periods. For example, at the end of 6 months, a company would prepare a half-year income statement and then "back out" (subtract) the first-quarter income statement results to determine the second-quarter income statement. Finally, interim reports typically are not audited because of the time and cost involved. However, auditing procedures have been developed for cases where an accountant is engaged to make a review of the interim financial information.

The APB recognized the advantages of presenting more timely information through the issuance of interim reports, but it also recognized that this advantage may be partially offset by the reduction in detail in the interim reports and provided guidelines regarding *minimum* disclosure. When publicly-traded companies report interim summaries of financial information, the following data must be reported at a minimum: (1) sales or gross revenues, income taxes, extraordinary items (net of tax), the cumulative effect of a change in accounting principle, and net income; (2) primary and fully diluted (or simple) earnings per share for each period presented; (3) seasonal revenues, costs, and expenses; (4) significant changes in estimates of income taxes; (5) results of discontinued operations and material unusual or infrequent items; (6) contingent items; (7) changes in accounting principles[16] or estimates; and (8) significant changes in financial position (i.e., cash flows).

When the preceding information is presented on a quarterly basis, current year-to-date information, along with comparable data from the previous year, is provided as well. Companies are encouraged to provide condensed balance sheet and cash flow data for the interim periods to assist security holders in their financial analysis related to *financial flexibility* and *liquidity*. When this information is not presented, significant changes since the last reporting date in liquid assets, working capital, long-term liabilities, and stockholders' equity are reported. Segment information is not required to be disclosed in interim reports,[17] but if it is, the disclosure must be made in accordance with the requirements of *FASB Statement No. 14*. The SEC requires more extensive interim disclosures, as discussed later in the chapter. Although interim financial statements are too lengthy to illustrate here, The Coca-Cola Company includes quarterly data at the end of its annual report, as shown in Appendix A.

## SEC REPORTS

The Securities and Exchange Commission (SEC) was created to administer various securities acts under powers provided by Congress in the Securities Act of 1933 and the Securities Exchange Act of 1934. The intent of Congress was to regulate the disclosure of all significant financial information provided by companies issuing publicly-traded securities (e.g., stocks and bonds). The SEC has the legal authority to prescribe accounting principles and reporting practices for these regulated companies.

The SEC is a large organization with its headquarters in Washington, D.C. Among the administrative offices, the **Office of the Chief Accountant** is of particular interest to accountants because it is responsible for providing the SEC with advice concerning accounting and auditing. The *Chief Accountant* helps in the establishment of administrative policies regarding accounting matters, is directly responsible for *Regulation S-X* (which establishes the form and content of financial statements filed with the SEC), and is primarily responsible for the *Financial Reporting Releases* (which prescribe accounting principles for regulated companies). Among the divi-

---

16. *APB Opinion No. 28* established certain guidelines for reporting accounting changes in interim reports. These guidelines were similar to those established in *APB Opinion No. 20* and are not discussed in this chapter. As a result of difficulties in interpretation, *FASB Statement of Financial Accounting Standards No. 3*, "Reporting Accounting Changes in Interim Financial Statements" (Stamford, Conn.: FASB, 1974), was issued to clarify the reporting of such changes. The reader is directed to Chapter 22 and to this *Statement* for more technical discussion.

17. "Financial Reporting for Segments of a Business Enterprise—Interim Financial Statements," *FASB Statement of Financial Accounting Standards No. 18* (Stamford, Conn.: FASB, 1977), par. 7.

sions, the **Division of Corporation Finance** is also of primary importance to accountants. This division is responsible for assisting in the establishment of reporting standards (except those directly related to financial statements, which are the responsibility of the Chief Accountant) and the requirements for adherence to these standards by regulated companies. The division is also responsible for reviewing the financial reports submitted to the SEC by these companies. Since all these reports generally must be certified by certified public accountants, an understanding of its activities is useful to accountants responsible for filing these reports.[18]

Numerous forms are required to be filed with the SEC by regulated companies. Of primary concern to accountants are:

- *Form 10-K*. An annual report.

- *Form 10-Q*. A quarterly report of operations.

**Form 10-K is the most common SEC annual report form** and is required to be filed with the SEC within 90 days of a company's fiscal year-end. The current Form 10-K consists of four major parts, as summarized in Exhibit 23-8. Prior to 1980, Form 10-K required the inclusion of considerably more and different information than that presented in a company's published annual report. In 1980, however, the SEC adopted several amendments intended to minimize the differences between documents filed with it and those sent to stockholders. As a result, the SEC now separates its required financial information into two types: (1) information that must be reported in *both* annual reports filed with the SEC and annual reports issued to stockholders and (2) information required to be filed only with the SEC.

Information of the first type is included in Part II of Exhibit 23-8. This information, as well as any or all of the Part I information, can be included in the Form 10-K by *reference* to the company's annual report issued to stockholders. Note, however, that all the information in Part II *must* be included in the annual report. Thus, for instance, many companies are including a management discussion and analysis, as well as 3 years of comparative financial statements, in their stockholders' annual reports. The second type of information (required to be filed with the SEC only) is considered to be important primarily to a limited and sophisticated group of users (e.g., security analysts). This type includes the information contained in Parts I, III, and IV of Exhibit 23-8.

**Form 10-Q is used to report a company's quarterly financial information to the SEC** and is required to be filed within 45 days of the end of each of the company's first three fiscal quarters. It contains similar disclosures to that of Form 10-K, but includes only quarterly and year-to-date information. The accounting principles established in *APB Opinion No. 28,* "Interim Financial Reporting," discussed earlier in the chapter, are used to prepare the Form 10-Q financial statement disclosures, so that this financial information is very similar to that provided in a company's quarterly report to stockholders. However, it may be more extensive because the SEC *requires* the presentation of comparative interim financial statements.

---

18. For a more extensive discussion of the history and administrative responsibilities of the various segments of the SEC, see K. F. Skousen, *An Introduction to the SEC*, Fifth Edition (Cincinnati, Ohio: South-Western Publishing Company, 1991).

## EXHIBIT 23-8

### SEC FORM 10-K REQUIRED DISCLOSURES

| Part | Item | Heading | Summary of Contents |
|---|---|---|---|
| I | 1 | Business | Description of business. History. Recent developments. Industry segments. Principal products and services. |
| | 2 | Properties | Location and general character of plants and other physical properties. Industry segments using properties. |
| | 3 | Legal proceedings | Description of pending legal proceedings, including principal parties, dates, allegations, and relief sought. |
| | 4 | Voting matters | Listing and description of matters submitted to a vote of security holders. |
| II | 5 | Market for common stock | Identification of market(s) where corporation's common stock is traded. Number of shares, frequency, and amount of dividends. |
| | 6 | Selected financial data | Five-year summary of net sales, income (loss) from continuing operations (and EPS), total assets, long-term obligations, and cash dividends, including adjustments for changing prices. |
| | 7 | Management's discussion and analysis | Discussion of information regarding liquidity, capital resources, results of operations, and impact of inflation, necessary to understand the corporation's financial condition, changes in financial condition, and operating results. |
| | 8 | Financial statements and supplementary data | Consolidated financial statements, including balance sheet (2 years), income statement and statement of cash flows (3 years). Statement of changes in stockholders' equity (3 years), selected quarterly information. Auditor's opinion. |
| | 9 | Disagreements on accounting and disclosures | If accountants were changed due to disagreement on accounting principles, description of disagreement and summary of effect of accounting change on financial statements. |
| III | 10 | Directors and officers | Listing of names, ages, and positions of directors and executive officers. |
| | 11 | Executive compensation | Listing of names, positions, salaries, stock options, and other benefits. |
| | 12 | Security ownership | Listing of beneficial owners and management owners of corporation's securities. |
| | 13 | Certain relationships | Description of certain business relationships and transactions with management and other related parties. |
| IV | 14 | Exhibits, schedules, and reports | Detailed supporting schedules, such as marketable securities, property, plant, and equipment (and related depreciation), and short-term borrowings. Listing of subsidiaries. Computation of ratios. |
| | | Signatures | Signatures of chief executive, financial, and accounting officers, and majority of board of directors. |

## APPENDIX: FINANCIAL ANALYSIS COMPARISONS

This Appendix deals with various tools of financial analysis. Before discussing the preparation of the additional financial analyses, it is helpful to point out how this information is used. The decision process employed by external users may be summarized as follows: (1) The external users examine the various data of importance to them in financial reports. (2) They look for criteria to assist them in analyzing the results and making decisions; usually, although not exclusively, they make comparisons with a particular company's past results as well as with similar companies within the same or related industries. (3) They make their decision. (4) They evaluate their decision based on feedback. Of importance to the present discussion are the comparisons made in the financial analysis.

## INTRACOMPANY COMPARISONS

One method of evaluating a company's current financial performance and condition is to compare them with the company's past results. This is referred to as **intracompany comparison**. An important factor in such comparisons is the evidence of **trends**—indications that a company's performance is stable, is improving, or is deteriorating, not only in the short run but also in the longer run. Most companies now present at least 2 years of comparable data in their financial statements, and many also include 5-, 10-, or 15-year summaries of key financial data.

A critical point to remember when preparing financial analysis information for use in such comparisons is the aspect of **consistency** over time. Whether business segment information, interim data, percentage analyses, ratios, or SEC reports are prepared, each year's information should be presented in a consistent fashion in terms of arrangement and content so that valid comparisons and reliable trend indications may be obtained.

## INTERCOMPANY COMPARISONS

A second method of evaluation is to compare a company's performance with that of competitors, with the industry as a whole, or with the results in related industries. This is known as **intercompany comparison** and may be made for a single period or for several past periods. A competitor's financial information may be drawn from its respective financial statements. Information on the performance of the industry as a whole or of related industries may be based on compilations of financial information by such financial analysis companies as Moody's Investors Service, Standard and Poor's, Dun and Bradstreet, and Robert Morris and Associates. These companies not only provide information from annual reports but also publish periodic updates and supplements. Other organizations and trade associations supply similar information on a more selective basis.

A user preparing financial analysis information for intercompany comparisons is concerned not only with consistency over time, but also with comparability of data across companies. A preparer of a company's financial information may not be able to exercise much control over the consistency of data across other companies. Nevertheless, the preparation of this data should take into consideration such factors as the use of comparable numbers in the numerator and denominator of financial ratios, the use of common industry classifications in the development of business segment results, and the impact of different generally acceptable accounting practices (for example, LIFO versus FIFO for inventory costing or accelerated versus straight-line depreciation) on the results. When preparing financial analysis data, an accountant should be aware that this information may be used in both intracompany and intercompany comparisons.

## PERCENTAGE ANALYSES

The interpretation of current results and the comparison of a company's operating results and financial position across several periods or with other companies may be enhanced by converting the monetary relationships in the financial statements to percentage relationships. The three types of analyses that use percentage relationships are referred to as horizontal analysis, vertical analysis, and ratio analysis. The first two are discussed in this section; ratio analysis is discussed in the following section.

### Horizontal Analysis

In horizontal analysis, changes in a company's operating results and financial position *over time* are expressed in terms of percentages as well as in dollars. If this method is employed, it usually is performed in conjunction with the income statement. Horizontal analysis also is used for balance sheet comparisons. It is used less frequently in the analysis of the statement of cash flows because of the lack of consistency with which items recur on this statement.

When only 2 years of comparative data are disclosed in percentages, the earlier year is used as the base year and the amount of change in each item is expressed as a percentage of that item's base-year amount. When data are shown for more than 2 years, two alternative approaches may be used. In the first approach, the preceding year is used as the base year for each later year, and the percentage change from year to year is shown. This "year-to-year" approach is illustrated for the Cooper Company in column (1) of Exhibit 23-9. Although this approach has the advantage of identifying and highlighting year-to-year changes, it does not allow for an easy analysis of the relative changes over an extended period. Because different years are used as bases, it is not possible to add the changes from year to year to derive the total cumulative change. When such an analysis is desired, a second approach may be used where the *initial* year is used as the base year, and the cumulative results from later years are compared with the initial year to determine the cumulative percentage changes. This "base-year-to-date" approach is illustrated for the Cooper Company in column (2) of Exhibit 23-9. With this approach, selection of a weak initial year can make the cumulative percentage changes appear stronger than may be warranted.

Whenever horizontal analysis is used, care must be taken in computing and interpreting percentage changes. If a base figure is zero or negative, although an *amount* of the change may be shown, *no percentage* change may be validly expressed. Furthermore, in cases where changes are expressed as percentages, no vertical addition or subtraction of the percentages (as discussed in the next section) can be made because the percentage changes result from the use of different bases. Finally, for items of small base amounts, a relatively small dollar change may result in a very high percentage change, thus potentially attaching more significance to the item than may be warranted.

### Vertical Analysis

In vertical analysis, the focus is on expressing the monetary relationships between items on the financial statements of a company for a particular period in terms of

**EXHIBIT 23-9**

## COOPER COMPANY

Comparative Income Statements
(Horizontal Analysis)

| | For Years Ended December 31, | | | (1) Year-to-Year Increase (Decrease) | | | | (2) Base-Year-to-Date Increase (Decrease) | |
| --- | --- | --- | --- | --- | --- | --- | --- | --- | --- |
| | | | | 1994 to 1995 | | 1993 to 1994 | | 1993 to 1995 | |
| | 1995 | 1994 | 1993 | Amount | Percent | Amount | Percent | Amount | Percent |
| Sales | $138,000 | $130,000 | $109,500 | $ 8,000 | 6.2 | $20,500 | 18.7 | $28,500 | 26.0 |
| Sales returns | (8,000) | (10,000) | (9,500) | (2,000) | (20.0) | 500 | 5.3 | (1,500) | (15.8) |
| Sales (net) | $130,000 | $120,000 | $100,000 | $10,000 | 8.3 | $20,000 | 20.0 | $30,000 | 30.0 |
| Cost of goods sold | (74,100) | (67,200) | (58,000) | 6,900 | 10.3 | 9,200 | 15.8 | 16,100 | 27.8 |
| Gross profit | $ 55,900 | $ 52,800 | $ 42,000 | $ 3,100 | 5.9 | $10,800 | 25.7 | $13,900 | 33.1 |
| Selling expenses | (14,900) | (14,300) | (10,800) | 600 | 4.2 | 3,500 | 32.4 | 4,100 | 38.0 |
| General expenses | (22,300) | (22,240) | (17,350) | 60 | 0.3 | 4,890 | 28.1 | 4,950 | 28.5 |
| Interest expense | (3,000) | (2,400) | (2,400) | 600 | 25.0 | 0 | 0.0 | 600 | 25.0 |
| Total expenses | $ (40,200) | $ (38,940) | $ (30,550) | $ 1,260 | 3.2 | $ 8,390 | 27.5 | $ 9,650 | 31.6 |
| Pretax continuing income | $ 15,700 | $ 13,860 | $ 11,450 | $ 1,840 | 13.3 | $ 2,410 | 21.0 | $ 4,250 | 37.1 |
| Income tax expense | (4,700) | (4,160) | (3,450) | 540 | 13.0 | 710 | 20.6 | 1,250 | 36.2 |
| Net income | $ 11,000 | $ 9,700 | $ 8,000 | $ 1,300 | 13.4 | $ 1,700 | 21.3 | $ 3,000 | 37.5 |
| Number of common shares | 5,400 | 4,800 | 4,000 | 600 | 12.5 | 800 | 20.0 | 1,400 | 35.0 |
| Earnings per share* | $1.81 | $1.77 | $1.70 | $.04 | 2.3 | $.07 | 4.1 | $.11 | 6.5 |

* Earnings Per Share = $\dfrac{\text{Net Income} - \text{Preferred Dividends (\$1,200)}}{\text{Average Common Shares Outstanding}}$

**percentages as well as dollars.** When vertical analysis is used for comparisons of financial statements from several periods, trends or changes in the relationships between items are more easily identified. Financial statements expressed in percentages only are referred to as **common-size statements.**

Vertical analysis may be used in conjunction with the income statement, retained earnings statement, balance sheet, or the statement of cash flows. In the case of the income statement, net sales usually are expressed as 100% and all other components are expressed accordingly. On the balance sheet, total assets represent 100%; on the retained earnings statement, beginning retained earnings is 100%; and in the case of the statement of cash flows, the increase in cash is usually expressed as 100%. Vertical analyses for the Cooper Company are illustrated in Exhibits 23-10 and 23-11.

## EXHIBIT 23-10

### COOPER COMPANY

Comparative Income Statements (Vertical Analysis)
For Years Ended December 31, 1994 and 1995

|  | 1995 Amount | 1995 Percent | 1994 Amount | 1994 Percent |
|---|---|---|---|---|
| Sales | $138,000 | 106.2 | $130,000 | 108.3 |
| Sales returns | (8,000) | (6.2) | (10,000) | (8.3) |
| Sales, net (70% on credit) | $130,000 | 100.0 | $120,000 | 100.0 |
| Cost of goods sold | (74,100) | (57.0) | (67,200) | (56.0) |
| Gross profit | $ 55,900 | 43.0 | $ 52,800 | 44.0 |
| Selling expenses | (14,900) | (11.5) | (14,300) | (11.9) |
| General expenses | (22,300) | (17.1)* | (22,240) | (18.5) |
| Interest expense | (3,000) | (2.3) | (2,400) | (2.0) |
| Total expenses | $ (40,200) | (30.9) | $ (38,940) | (32.4) |
| Pretax continuing income | $ 15,700 | 12.1 | $ 13,860 | 11.6 |
| Income tax expense | (4,700) | (3.6) | (4,160) | (3.5) |
| Net income | $ 11,000 | 8.5 | $ 9,700 | 8.1 |
| Number of common shares | 5,400 |  | 4,800 |  |
| Earnings per share | $1.81 |  | $1.77 |  |

Comparative Retained Earnings Statements (Vertical Analysis)
For Years Ended December 31, 1994 and 1995

|  | 1995 Amount | 1995 Percent | 1994 Amount | 1994 Percent |
|---|---|---|---|---|
| Beginning retained earnings | $32,000 | 100.0 | $28,300 | 100.0 |
| Net income | 11,000 | 34.4 | 9,700 | 34.3 |
|  | $43,000 | 134.4 | $38,000 | 134.3 |
| Preferred dividends, $8/share | (1,200) | (3.7) | (1,200) | (4.2) |
| Common dividends, $1/share | (5,400) | (16.9) | (4,800) | (17.0) |
| Ending retained earnings | $36,400 | 113.8 | $32,000 | 113.1 |

* Rounded to balance.

**EXHIBIT 23-11**

## COOPER COMPANY

Comparative Condensed Balance Sheets (Vertical Analysis)
December 31, 1994 and 1995

|  | 1995 Amount | 1995 Percent | 1994 Amount | 1994 Percent |
|---|---|---|---|---|
| Cash | $ 3,900 | 3.0 | $ 4,800 | 4.3 |
| Receivables (net) | 7,600 | 5.9 | 8,600 | 7.7 |
| Inventories | 8,900 | 6.9 | 10,100 | 9.0 |
| Prepaid items | 1,000 | .8 | 1,200 | 1.1 |
| Total current assets | $ 21,400 | 16.6 | $ 24,700 | 22.1 |
| Noncurrent assets (net) | 107,800 | 83.4 | 87,300 | 77.9 |
| Total assets | $129,200 | 100.0 | $112,000 | 100.0 |
| | | | | |
| Accounts payable | $ 5,000 | 3.9 | $ 6,600 | 5.9 |
| Other current liabilities | 6,200 | 4.8 | 6,400 | 5.7 |
| Total current liabilities | $ 11,200 | 8.7 | $ 13,000 | 11.6 |
| Long-term liabilities (12%) | 25,000 | 19.3 | 20,000 | 17.9 |
| Total liabilities | $ 36,200 | 28.0 | $ 33,000 | 29.5 |
| Preferred stock, 8%, $100 par[a] | $ 15,000 | 11.6 | $ 15,000 | 13.4 |
| Common stock, $5 par[b] | 27,000 | 20.9 | 24,000 | 21.4 |
| Additional paid-in capital | 14,600 | 11.3 | 8,000 | 7.1 |
| Retained earnings | 36,400 | 28.2 | 32,000 | 28.6 |
| Total stockholders' equity | $ 93,000 | 72.0 | $ 79,000 | 70.5 |
| Total liabilities and stockholders' equity | $129,200 | 100.0 | $112,000 | 100.0 |

a. The 150 shares of preferred stock are noncumulative and have a liquidation value of $140 per share.
b. December 31, 1995 market price is $14.25 per share.

Both vertical and horizontal analysis may be used in conjunction with interim reports and reports of the results of business segments. Vertical and horizontal analyses also are used in conjunction with ratio analysis.

## RATIO ANALYSIS

Another form of percentage analysis involves the use of ratios. Ratios, which entail the division of one or more items on the financial statements by another related item or items, are frequently used to evaluate the financial aspects (i.e., return, risk, financial flexibility, liquidity, and operating capability) of a particular company. Many ratios have become standardized; they have been recognized as useful indicators of financial performance and are computed routinely and published on a company and industry basis by financial analysis companies. These ratios become "benchmarks" against which to compare a company's results to evaluate its effectiveness. The ratios are used by different external users in intracompany and intercompany comparisons for a variety of economic decisions. Other ratios are developed by individual users or user groups for their own specific needs.

More than 30 different ratios or variations of ratios have been discussed in the financial analysis literature. However, we focus on the primary standard ratios. These may be classified into five groups: (1) stockholder profitability ratios, (2) company profitability ratios, (3) liquidity ratios, (4) activity ratios, and (5) stability ratios. The intended use of each ratio and its proper computation are discussed briefly in the following sections. The 1995 data for the computation of these ratios can be obtained from Exhibits 23-10 and 23-11 for the Cooper Company. Since the numerical calculations of these ratios are not discussed in the text, reference should be made to these exhibits to identify the proper information inputs for each ratio.

## Stockholder Profitability Ratios

Stockholder profitability ratios serve as indicators of how effective a company has been in meeting the profit (i.e., return) objectives of its owners. Several stockholder profitability ratios are shown in Exhibit 23-12, along with the calculations for the Cooper Company. Each of these ratios is discussed in the following sections.

*Earnings Per Share*
The earnings per share information is probably the most frequently cited ratio in a financial analysis. It is considered important enough to be a required disclosure on the face of the income statement. As its name indicates, it shows the amount of earnings attributable to each share of common stock held by stockholders. Corporations with complex capital structures are required to disclose both primary and fully diluted earnings per share amounts. As discussed in Chapter 21, earnings per share computations can be very complex.

*Price/Earnings*
Although not precisely a stockholder profitability ratio, the price/earnings ratio is used by actual and potential stockholders to evaluate the attractiveness of an investment in a particular stock. A higher price/earnings ratio compared to other similar companies may indicate that investors perceive expansion potential for the company. Care must be taken, however, that the comparison is made to other "similar" companies. The price/earnings ratios for companies in certain "growth" industries, such as the electronics industry, are likely to be higher than for, say, companies in the automobile or steel industries. Interpretation of the ratio also is affected by investors' perceptions of the company's quality and trend of earnings, relative risk, use of alternative

---

**EXHIBIT 23-12**

**STOCKHOLDER PROFITABILITY RATIOS**

| Ratio | Formula | Calculations (1995) |
|---|---|---|
| 1. Earnings Per Share | $\dfrac{\text{Net Income-Preferred Dividends}}{\text{Average Common Shares Outstanding}}$ | $\dfrac{\$11,000 - \$1,200}{5,400} = \$1.81$ |
| 2. Price/Earnings | $\dfrac{\text{Market Price Per Common Share}}{\text{Earnings Per Share}}$ | $\dfrac{\$14.25}{\$1.81} = 7.9$ times |
| 3. Dividend Yield | $\dfrac{\text{Dividends Per Common Share}}{\text{Market Price Per Common Share}}$ | $\dfrac{\$1.00}{\$14.25} = 7.0\%$ |

accounting methods, and other factors. Primary (or simple) earnings per share based on income from continuing operations usually is used as the denominator.

### Dividend Yield

The market value of the stock represents the value a stockholder must forgo in order to continue holding the security. Stockholders are interested in their individual rates of return based on the actual dividends received as compared with the ending market price (or market price on another particular date) of the stock. The dividend yield provides this information. The dividend yield, combined with the percentage change in the market price of the stock held during the period, often is considered the total annual return on the stockholders' investment.

## Company Profitability Ratios

Company profitability ratios are used as indicators of how effective a company has been in meeting its overall profit (return) objectives, particularly in relation to the resources invested. Several overall company profitability ratios are shown in Exhibit 23-13, along with the calculations for the Cooper Company. Each is discussed in the following sections.

### Profit Margin

The relationship of net income to net sales commonly is used to evaluate a company's efficiency in controlling costs and expenses in relation to sales. That is, the lower a company's expenses relative to sales, the higher the sales dollars remaining for other activities. If a company has nonrecurring items of income, income from continuing operations typically is used in the numerator. The reporting of industry and foreign segment information permits a variation of this ratio to be computed for the major segments of a company. For each segment, the profit margin *before* income taxes can be computed by dividing the segment's operating profits by its revenues. A weakness of the ratio is that it does not consider the investment (the total assets or stockholders' equity) necessary to generate the sales and income. A "return on investment" (either total assets or stockholders' equity) overcomes this weakness.

---

### EXHIBIT 23-13

#### COMPANY PROFITABILITY RATIOS

| Ratio | Formula | Calculations (1995) |
|---|---|---|
| 1. Profit Margin | $\dfrac{\text{Net Income}}{\text{Net Sales}}$ | $\dfrac{\$11,000}{\$130,000} = 8.5\%$ |
| 2. Return on Total Assets | $\dfrac{\text{Net Income} + \text{Interest Expense (net of tax)}}{\text{Average Total Assets}}$ | $\dfrac{\$11,000 + (\$3,000 \times 0.7)}{\dfrac{\$129,200 + \$112,000}{2}} = 10.9\%$ |
| 3. Return on Stockholders' Equity | $\dfrac{\text{Net Income}}{\text{Average Stockholders' Equity}}$ | $\dfrac{\$11,000}{\dfrac{\$93,000 + \$79,000}{2}} = 12.8\%$ |

### Return on Total Assets

The amount of net income earned in relation to total assets is an indicator of a company's efficiency in the use of its economic resources. When a comparison is made of the return on total assets of one company to the return of another company, consideration should be given to the age of the assets of each company. That is, the return on a company's assets will get higher as the assets become older because the denominator will decrease each year due to the increase in accumulated depreciation. Furthermore, since prices tend to increase due to inflation, a company that uses recently purchased assets will tend to show a relatively lower return on these assets. Typically, extraordinary items, results of discontinued operations, and the effects of changes in accounting principles are excluded from the numerator because they are the result of infrequent events not directly related to the ongoing economic resources used in a company's operations. Interest expense (after income taxes)[19] is added back to net income because it is a financial cost paid to creditors to acquire the assets as opposed to a cost of generating sales. Since net income is earned over the entire period, the *average* total assets (beginning plus ending assets divided by two) for the period are used as the denominator. Reporting the results of industry and foreign segments permits the computation of a variation of this ratio for the major segments of a company. For each segment, the *pretax* return on identifiable assets can be computed by dividing the segment's operating profit by its identifiable assets.

### Return on Stockholders' Equity

Net income may be divided by stockholders' equity to reflect the residual return on the owners' equity. When this return is higher than the return on total assets, the company has favorable financial leverage (that is, it is trading on the equity, discussed later). A weakness of the return on stockholders' equity ratio (as well as the return on total assets ratio), however, is that it does not consider the current value of the capital invested, since financial statements are based primarily on historical cost dollar amounts. Extraordinary items and other nonrecurring items usually are excluded from the numerator, and *average* stockholders' equity typically is used for the denominator. Some companies deduct preferred dividends from net income and use only common stockholders' equity in this ratio; they argue that preferred stock is more similar in nature to long-term liabilities than it is to common stock.

## Liquidity Ratios

Liquidity ratios are used to evaluate a company's ability to meet its currently maturing financial obligations. These ratios generally involve all or most of the components of a company's working capital, its current assets less its current liabilities. Current assets include cash, temporary investments, receivables, inventories, and prepaid items. Among current liabilities are such items as accounts payable incurred in the normal acquisition of goods or services, accruals for wages, taxes, and interest payable, short-term notes payable, advance collections of unearned revenues, and the current maturing portion of long-term debt. The common liquidity ratios are shown in Exhibit 23-14, along with the calculations for the Cooper Company. Each is discussed in the following sections.

---

19. After-tax interest expense is usually computed by multiplying the pretax interest expense by 1 minus the effective income tax rate. In the case of the Cooper Company, the effective tax rate approximates 30% ($4,700 ÷ $15,700), so that the $3,000 pretax interest expense is multiplied by 70% (1 − 0.30) to determine the after-tax results.

---

**EXHIBIT 23-14**

**LIQUIDITY RATIOS**

| Ratio | Formula | Calculations (1995) |
|---|---|---|
| 1. Current Ratio | $\dfrac{\text{Current Assets}}{\text{Current Liabilities}}$ | $\dfrac{\$21,400}{\$11,200} = 1.91$ times |
| 2. Acid-Test Ratio | $\dfrac{\text{Quick Assets}}{\text{Current Liabilities}}$ | $\dfrac{\$11,500}{\$11,200} = 1.03$ times |

---

*Current Ratio*

The current ratio probably is the most commonly used indicator of a company's short-run liquidity. Sometimes it is referred to as the *working capital* ratio. It is considered to be a better indicator of a company's current debt-paying ability than simply working capital. This is because working capital shows only the absolute difference between a company's current assets and its current liabilities. By computing the current ratio, the relative relationship between the current assets and current liabilities is known, so that comparisons of different sized companies can be made. In the past, as a "rule of thumb," a 2.0 current ratio was considered satisfactory. Today, however, more attention is given to (1) industry practices, (2) the length of a company's operating cycle, and (3) the mix of the current assets. Too *high* a current ratio relative to similar companies within the same industry may indicate inefficient management of current assets. The shorter a company's operating cycle, the less likely that it will need a substantial amount of working capital, or as high a current ratio, to operate efficiently. A company's operating cycle position is evaluated through the use of activity ratios, discussed in the next section. The proportion of different items that make up the total current assets is referred to as the "mix" of the current assets. This mix has an effect upon how quickly the current assets can be converted into cash. As an extreme, a high proportion of prepaid items within current assets may indicate a weak liquidity position, since prepaid assets are consumed within the operating cycle rather than converted back into cash. The mix of a company's current assets and the impact on its liquidity are considered in the acid-test ratio.

*Acid-Test Ratio*

The acid-test or *quick* ratio is a more severe test of a company's short-term debt-paying abilities. In this ratio, only the current assets that may be readily converted into cash are used in the calculation. These items, referred to as **quick assets**, generally consist of cash, temporary investments, accounts receivable, and short-term notes receivable. Inventories are excluded because their salability is uncertain and they frequently are sold on credit; thus they may not be quickly converted into cash. Prepaid items are excluded because they are not convertible into cash. The acid-test ratio highlights potential liquidity problems attributable to an inadequate mix of current assets. For instance, the use of this ratio usually reveals the lower liquidity of a company having a significant investment in inventories that would not be revealed in the current ratio. However, care must be taken to consider which assets to include. Even though inventories usually are excluded from the acid-test ratio, sometimes these are, in fact, more liquid than certain receivables. A quick ratio of 1.0 used to be a general rule of thumb. Today, as with the current ratio, greater consideration is given to such factors as industry practices and the company's typical operations.

## Activity Ratios

Activity ratios are used to provide a general idea regarding the length of various segments of a company's operating cycle in order to evaluate the liquidity of certain current assets. The ratios are indicators of the efficiency with which the company uses its short-term economic resources. The three common activity ratios are shown in Exhibit 23-15, along with the calculations for the Cooper Company. Each is discussed in the following sections.

### Inventory Turnover

Inventories are acquired, sold, and replenished in the normal course of a company's operations during its accounting period. The company's operating cycle is the length of time it takes to invest in inventory, make credit sales, and convert the receivables into cash. Dividing a company's cost of goods sold for the period by its average inventory indicates the number of times the inventory is "turned over" or sold during that period. As a general rule, the higher the inventory turnover, (1) the more effective the company is in its operations, (2) the lesser the amount of investment that must be tied up in inventories, and (3) the shorter the operating cycle necessary to replenish cash. A company with a higher inventory turnover is usually more efficient. It is also minimizing the chance of having obsolete inventory. The lesser amount needed for investment in inventory means the company either needs less capital or can invest its capital in other earnings activities. However, *too* high an inventory turnover may indicate lost sales as a result of insufficient inventory on hand.

Often the inventory turnover is divided into the number of operating days in a "business" year (365, 300, or 250, depending on the industry) so that the inventory segment of the operating cycle may be expressed in days. Care should be taken in developing the average inventory; seasonal factors can affect this average substantially. Furthermore, when a comparison is made of one company to another, both companies should be using similar inventory costing methods. In periods of rising prices, no valid comparison of inventory turnovers can be made when one company is using FIFO and another company is using LIFO. This is because the company using LIFO

---

**EXHIBIT 23-15**

## ACTIVITY RATIOS

| Ratio | Formula | Calculations (1995) |
|---|---|---|
| 1. Inventory Turnover | $\dfrac{\text{Cost of Goods Sold}}{\text{Average Inventory}}$ | $\dfrac{\$74,100}{\dfrac{\$8,900 + \$10,100}{2}} = 7.8$ times or 47 days* |
| 2. Receivables Turnover | $\dfrac{\text{Net Credit Sales}}{\text{Average Net Receivables}}$ | $\dfrac{\$130,000 \times 0.70}{\dfrac{\$7,600 + \$8,600}{2}} = 11.2$ times or 33 days* |
| 3. Payables Turnover | $\dfrac{\text{Cost of Goods Sold}}{\text{Average Accounts Payable}}$ | $\dfrac{\$74,100}{\dfrac{\$5,000 + \$6,600}{2}} = 12.8$ times or 29 days* |

\* 365-day business year.

will show a higher cost of goods sold and lower inventory than the FIFO company, even though their operations are similar.

## Receivables Turnover

Once inventories have been sold on credit, the company collects the receivables to complete its operating cycle. Dividing net credit sales by average net trade receivables indicates how many times receivables are "turned over" or collected each period. The receivables turnover is an indicator of the efficiency with which the company collects its receivables and converts them back into cash. As a general rule, the higher the turnover the better, because the company has fewer resources tied up in receivables, collects these resources at a faster pace, and usually has fewer uncollectible accounts. When net credit sales information is not readily available, net sales are used in the calculations. Care should be taken to consider seasonal factors and to exclude non-trade receivables in developing the average receivables.

The receivables turnover often is divided into the number of days in the business year to show the average collection period in days. A comparison of a company's average collection period to the days in its typical credit terms gives an indication of how aggressively the company's credit department collects overdue accounts.

## Payables Turnover

The payables turnover ratio measures the number of times accounts payable turn over during the year. The higher the turnover, the shorter the time between the purchase of inventory and the cash payment. However, too high a turnover may indicate that the company is making payments too quickly and losing the "free" credit provided by accounts payable. Alternatively, if a company's payables turn over slower than the average for its industry, it may indicate that the company is having financial difficulty. It may be preferable to compute the ratio by using purchases as the numerator, in which case purchases can be computed by adding the ending inventory to the cost of goods sold and subtracting the beginning inventory. The payables turnover ratio also may be divided into the number of days in the business year to show the average payment period in days.

The three turnover ratios may be analyzed together to assess the total number of days in the company's operating cycle from the payment of cash to purchase inventory to the collection of cash from sales. This period may be computed by adding the number of days in the receivables turnover to the number of days in the inventory turnover and subtracting the number of days in the payables turnover. For example, in Exhibit 23-15, the Cooper Company's operating cycle is 51 (47 + 33 − 29) days.

## Stability Ratios

Stability ratios are used as indicators of the long-run solvency and stability of the company. They provide evidence of the safety (risk) of the investments in the company by long-term bondholders, preferred stockholders, and common stockholders. Several stability ratios are shown in Exhibit 23-16, along with the calculations for the Cooper Company. Each is discussed in the following sections.

## Debt Ratio

The debt ratio indicates the percentage of total assets contributed by creditors. Subtraction of this ratio from 100% yields the percentage of total assets (or *equity* ratio) contributed by stockholders.[20] Sometimes, when a company has issued a significant

---

20. Sometimes total liabilities are divided by total stockholders' equity to determine the *debt/equity* ratio.

**EXHIBIT 23-16**

**STABILITY RATIOS**

| Ratio | Formula | Calculations (1995) |
|---|---|---|
| 1. Debt Ratio | $\dfrac{\text{Total Liabilities}}{\text{Total Assets}}$ | $\dfrac{\$36,200}{\$129,200} = 28\%$ |
| 2. Times Interest Earned | $\dfrac{\text{Pretax Operating Income}}{\text{Interest Expense}}$ | $\dfrac{\$15,700 + \$3,000}{\$3,000} = 6.2 \text{ times}$ |
| 3. Book Value per Common Share | $\dfrac{\text{Common Stockholders' Equity}}{\text{Outstanding Common Shares}}$ | $\dfrac{\$93,000 - (\$140 \times 150)}{5,400} = \dfrac{\$13.33 \text{ per}}{\text{common share}}$ |

amount of preferred stock (which has some characteristics of both debt and common stock), the equity ratio is further divided into a preferred equity ratio and a common equity ratio. The appropriate relationship (or "mix") between the debt and equity ratios depends on the industry. In general, creditors prefer to see a lower debt ratio because, in the event of business decline, their interests are better protected and there is less risk. Up to a point, stockholders prefer a higher debt ratio, particularly when the company is favorably "trading on the equity," or applying favorable "financial leverage." This occurs when the company borrows money from creditors at an interest rate (net of income taxes) that is lower than the return the company can earn in its operations. However, an extremely high debt ratio is likely to be a disadvantage when a company wishes to attract additional external capital. Investors in both long-term bonds and stocks usually consider a highly leveraged company a relatively unstable and more risky investment.

*Times Interest Earned*

The times interest earned ratio (sometimes called the *interest coverage* ratio) is used as an indicator of the ability of a company to cover its interest obligations through its annual earnings. As such, it is a measure of the safety of creditors' (particularly long-term) investments in the company. As a general rule, the higher the ratio the better able the company is to meet its interest obligations. While interest obligations are legal commitments, it is also true that continued interest payments are endangered by low earnings over an extended period of time. Because both earnings and interest expense are based on accrual accounting, the times interest earned ratio is slightly inaccurate, since it should include only cash outflows for interest and cash inflows from earnings. Such refinements are rarely made to this ratio, however.

The numerator of the times interest earned ratio usually is a form of pretax *operating* income—that is, pretax continuing income to which interest expense is added back. If a company has preferred stock outstanding, a similar calculation may be made to evaluate the safety of preferred dividends. The *preferred dividends coverage ratio* is computed by dividing net income by the annual preferred dividends.

*Book Value*

The book value per common share reflects the net assets per share of stock. It is sometimes erroneously referred to as the liquidation value per share. Although the book value per common share frequently is computed, for several reasons, it is not very useful as an indicator of a company's financial stability. First, most companies are going concerns and a related liquidation value is of no consequence. Second, even if a liquidation value were of importance, the book value per share is based on assets recorded primarily in terms of historical costs and thus has no relation to the liquidation value per share. Third, the market value per share of a company's common stock is important in evaluating its stability. Since book value is based on historical costs, it also has no direct relation to this market value. However, if the market price of a company's common stock falls below its book value per common share, some investors attach unfavorable significance to this event.

When the book value per share is computed and the company has both preferred and common stock outstanding, the equity relating to the common stock is determined first. To do so, stockholders' equity is separated into its preferred and common stock components on the basis of the legal claims of each class upon liquidation. Typically, preferred stock is allocated its par value unless the stock's characteristics include a liquidation value, in which case the latter value is used. When preferred dividends are cumulative and in arrears, an appropriate portion of retained earnings is also assigned as preferred stockholders' equity. The residual amount of stockholders' equity then is assigned as common stockholders' equity. The book value per common share is computed by dividing this residual stockholders' equity by the number of common shares outstanding. A book value per share of preferred stock also may be computed on the basis of the preferred stockholders' equity and the number of preferred shares outstanding.

## QUESTIONS

*Q23-1* In a standard auditor's report, what statements are included?

*Q23-2* What is an *audit committee*? What is a *management report* and what is generally included in this report?

*Q23-3* What is *management's discussion and analysis*? Why is it included in a company's annual report?

*Q23-4* Why do investors and creditors desire financial information concerning the operating segments of a company?

*Q23-5* Briefly describe the three alternative tests used to determine a "reportable segment."

*Q23-6* Briefly describe the three major items of information that are reported for each reportable industry segment.

*Q23-7* What financial information is reported regarding a company's (a) foreign operations, (b) export sales, and (c) major customers?

*Q23-8* What are *interim financial statements* and why are they issued?

*Q23-9* What specific principles must be applied to the reporting of inventories in interim financial reports?

*Q23-10* What principles are applied to the accounting for expenses not directly associated with product sales during an interim period?

*Q23-11* Briefly explain how the accounting procedures for preparing interim reports are (a) similar and (b) dissimilar to those used in preparing annual reports.

*Q23-12* List the minimum disclosures that must be made by a publicly-traded company in its interim financial report.

*Q23-13* List the responsibilities of the Chief Accountant and the Division of Corporation Finance of the SEC.

*Q23-14* List the items and headings of the contents of SEC Form 10-K.

*Q23-15* (*Appendix*). What two types of comparisons may external users make in their financial decision making? Why is knowledge of these comparisons important to accountants?

*Q23-16* (*Appendix*). What is *horizontal analysis* and how is it prepared?

*Q23-17* (*Appendix*). What is *vertical analysis* and how does it differ from horizontal analysis?

*Q23-18* (*Appendix*). What is *ratio analysis* and how is it used?

*Q23-19* (*Appendix*). Briefly describe how each of the stockholder profitability ratios is computed.

*Q23-20 (Appendix).* Briefly describe how each of the company profitability ratios is computed.

*Q23-21 (Appendix).* Which financial ratios may be used to evaluate the effectiveness and efficiency of a company's reportable industry segments?

*Q23-22 (Appendix).* Briefly describe how each of the liquidity ratios is computed.

*Q23-23 (Appendix).* Briefly describe how each of the activity ratios is computed.

*Q23-24 (Appendix).* Briefly describe how each of the stability ratios is computed.

# CASES

### C23-1   Auditor's Report
Meyer Company is considering being audited for the first time. Mary Thomas, its president, has asked your advice. She says: "I understand that after an audit the accountant expresses an opinion, and that one type of opinion is 'unqualified.' What exactly is involved in an audit and what is included in an unqualified opinion?"

**Required**
Prepare a written response to the president of Meyer Company.

### C23-2   Management's Report
The subject of management reports has been prominent the past few years. A *management report* is a fairly new item included in the annual report to shareholders. This report should not be confused with management's discussion and analysis of operations and financial condition that also is relatively new to the annual report.

The management report is now being included in the annual report to shareholders as a result of the urging of a number of groups and organizations. Consequently, the form and content of the annual report to shareholders continues to evolve as management attempts to present additional information that will be useful to the readers.

**Required**
1. What are the general purposes of the management report?
2. Identify five subject areas or topics which have been recommended for inclusion in the management report.
3. Under what circumstances does the content of the management report influence the activities of the external auditor during the audit engagement? Explain your answer. (*CMA adapted*)

### C23-3   Securities and Exchange Commission
The U.S. Securities and Exchange Commission (SEC) was created in 1934 and consists of five commissioners and a staff of approximately 1,900. The SEC professional staff is organized into four divisions and several principal offices. The primary objectives of the SEC are to support fair securities markets and to foster enlightened shareholder participation in major corporate decisions. The SEC has a significant presence in financial markets and corporation-shareholder relations and has the authority to exert significant influence on entities whose actions lie within the scope of its authority. The SEC chairman has identified enforcement cases and full disclosure filings as major activities of the SEC.

**Required**
1. The SEC must have some "license" to exercise power. Explain where the SEC receives its authority.
2. Discuss in general terms the major ways in which the SEC:
    a. supports fair securities markets.
    b. fosters enlightened shareholder participation in major corporate decisions.
3. The major responsibilities of the SEC's Division of Corporation Finance include full disclosure filings. Describe the means by which the SEC attempts to assure the material accuracy and completeness of registrants' financial disclosure filings. (*CMA adapted*)

### C23-4   Segment Reporting
Many accountants and financial analysts contend that companies should report financial data for segments of the enterprise.

**Required**
1. What does financial reporting for segments of a business enterprise involve?
2. Identify the reasons for requiring financial data to be reported by segments.
3. Identify the possible disadvantages of requiring financial data to be reported by segments.
4. Identify the accounting difficulties inherent in segment reporting. (*AICPA adapted*)

### C23-5   Segment Reporting
In order to properly understand current generally accepted accounting principles with respect to accounting for and reporting on segments of a business enterprise, as stated by the Financial Accounting Standards Board in its *Statement No. 14*, it is necessary to be familiar with certain unique terminology. Furthermore, a central issue in reporting on industry segments of a business enterprise is the determination of which segments are reportable.

#### Required

1. With respect to segments of a business enterprise, explain the following terms:
   a. Industry segment
   b. Revenue
   c. Operating profit or loss
   d. Identifiable assets
2. What are the tests to determine whether or not an industry segment is reportable?
3. What is the test to determine if enough industry segments have been separately reported on, and what is the guideline on the maximum number of industry segments to be shown? (*AICPA adapted*)

#### C23-6 Interim Reporting

The unaudited quarterly statements of income issued by many corporations to their stockholders are usually prepared on the same basis as annual statements, the statement for each quarter reflecting the transactions of that quarter.

#### Required

1. Why do problems arise in using such quarterly statements to predict the income (before extraordinary items) for the year? Explain.
2. Discuss the ways in which quarterly income can be affected by the behavior of the costs recorded in a Repairs and Maintenance of Factory Machinery account.
3. Do such quarterly statements give management opportunities to manipulate the results of operations for a quarter? If so, explain or give an example. (*AICPA adapted*)

#### C23-7 Interim Reporting

Interim financial reporting has become an important topic in accounting. There has been considerable discussion as to the proper method of reflecting results of operations at interim dates. Accordingly, the Accounting Principles Board issued an opinion clarifying some aspects of interim financial reporting.

#### Required

1. Discuss generally how revenue should be recognized at interim dates and specifically how revenue should be recognized for industries subject to large seasonal fluctuations in revenue and for long-term contracts using the percentage-of-completion method at annual reporting dates.
2. Discuss generally how product and period costs should be recognized at interim dates. Also discuss how inventory and cost of goods sold may be afforded special accounting treatment at interim dates.
3. Discuss how the provision for income taxes is computed and reflected in interim financial statements. (*AICPA adapted*)

#### C23-8 Management's Discussion and Analysis

Many companies must now include a management's discussion and analysis (MD&A) as a component part of their annual reports. The Coca-Cola Company includes an MD&A in the financial section of its annual report, as shown in Appendix A.

#### Required

1. Explain the purpose of an MD&A and describe what it includes.
2. Review The Coca-Cola Company's MD&A and answer the following questions:
   a. In what two lines of business does the company operate? Briefly describe each sector.
   b. By how much, and why, did revenues in the Soft Drinks line of business increase in 1992?
   c. What were selling expenses in 1992, and why did they increase over 1991?
   d. What is the company's "free cash flow," and for what is it used?
   e. What was the cash used in investment activities for 1992, and why did it increase?

## MULTIPLE CHOICE

*Select the best answer for each of the following.*

M23-1 The computation of a company's third quarter provision for income taxes should be based on earnings
   a. For the quarter at an expected annual effective income tax rate
   b. For the quarter at the statutory rate
   c. To date at an expected annual effective income tax rate less prior quarters' provisions
   d. To date at the statutory rate less prior quarters' provisions

M23-2 Which of the following ratios measures short-term solvency?
   a. Current ratio
   b. Age of receivables
   c. Creditors' equity to total assets
   d. Return on investment

M23-3   Kaycee Corporation's revenues for the year ended December 31, 1995 were as follows:

| | |
|---|---|
| Consolidated revenue per income statement | $1,200,000 |
| Intersegment sales | 180,000 |
| Intersegment transfers | 60,000 |
| Combined revenues of all industry segments | $1,440,000 |

Kaycee has a reportable segment if that segment's revenues exceed

a.  $6,000          c.  $120,000
b.  $24,000         d.  $144,000

M23-4   An inventory loss from a market decline occurred in the first quarter that was not expected to be restored in the fiscal year. For interim financial reporting purposes, how would the dollar amount of inventory in the balance sheet be affected in the first and fourth quarters?

| | First quarter | Fourth quarter |
|---|---|---|
| a. | Decrease | No effect |
| b. | Decrease | Increase |
| c. | No effect | Decrease |
| d. | No effect | No effect |

M23-5   Barr Corporation's capital stock at December 31, 1995 consisted of the following:

Common stock, $2 par value; 100,000 shares authorized, issued, and outstanding
10% noncumulative, nonconvertible preferred stock, $100 par value; 1,000 shares authorized, issued,
    and outstanding

Barr's common stock, which is listed on a major stock exchange, was quoted at $4 per share on December 31, 1995. Barr's net income for the year ended December 31, 1995 was $50,000. The 1995 preferred dividend was declared. No capital stock transactions occurred during 1995. What was the price/earnings ratio on Barr's common stock at December 31, 1995?

a.  8 to 1           c.  16 to 1
b.  10 to 1          d.  20 to 1

M23-6   In August 1995, Ella Company spent $150,000 on an advertising campaign for subscriptions to the magazine it sells on getting ready for the skiing season. There are only two issues: one in October and one in November. The magazine is only sold on a subscription basis and the subscriptions started in October 1995. Assuming Ella's fiscal year ends on March 31, 1996, what amount of expense should be included in Ella's quarterly income statement for the three months ended December 31, 1995 as a result of this expenditure?

a.  $37,500          c.  $75,000
b.  $50,000          d.  $150,000

M23-7   In financial reporting for segments of a business enterprise, the operating profit or loss of a segment should include

| | Reasonably allocated common operating costs | Traceable operating costs |
|---|---|---|
| a. | No | No |
| b. | No | Yes |
| c. | Yes | No |
| d. | Yes | Yes |

M23-8 Utica Company's net accounts receivable were $250,000 at December 31, 1994 and $300,000 at December 31, 1995. Net cash sales for 1995 were $100,000. The accounts receivable turnover for 1995 was 5.0. What were Utica's total net sales for 1995?

a. $1,475,000
b. $1,500,000
c. $1,600,000
d. $2,750,000

M23-9 During 1995, Red, Incorporated purchased $2,000,000 of inventory. The cost of goods sold for 1995 was $2,200,000, and the ending inventory at December 31, 1995 was $400,000. What was the inventory turnover for 1995?

a. 4.0
b. 4.4
c. 5.5
d. 11.0

M23-10 In financial reporting for segments of a business enterprise, which of the following assets should be included as an identifiable asset of industry segment A?

a. An advance from nonfinancial industry segment A to another industry segment
b. An allocation of a tangible asset used for general corporate purposes and not used in the operations of any particular industry segment
c. An intangible asset used by industry segment A
d. An allocation of a tangible asset used by another industry segment which transfers products to industry segment A

(*AICPA adapted*)

# EXERCISES

E23-1 *Segment Reporting*  The Wilson Diversified Company has total assets of $130,000 at the end of 1995 and the following condensed income statement for 1995:

| | |
|---|---|
| Sales | $90,000 |
| Operating expenses | (66,600) |
| Income before income taxes | $23,400 |
| Income tax expense | (7,020) |
| Net income | $16,380 |

The company has two reportable industry segments and has developed the following related information:

| | Segments | | | |
|---|---|---|---|---|
| | 1 | 2 | Other | Totals |
| Sales | $51,420 | $24,400 | $14,180 | $ 90,000 |
| Operating expenses | 36,780 | 15,400 | 10,420 | 66,600[a] |
| Identifiable assets | 70,300 | 28,740 | 21,960 | 130,000[b] |

a. Of the $66,600 total operating expenses, $4,000 are general corporate expenses.
b. Of the $130,000 total assets, $9,000 are general corporate assets.

### Required
Prepare a schedule that reports on the revenues, operating profits, and identifiable assets of Segments 1 and 2 and the other segments of the Wilson Diversified Company for 1995. Be sure to include the appropriate reconciliations.

**E23-2** *Segment Reporting* Parks Conglomerate Company does business in several different industries. The following is a 1995 condensed income statement for the entire company:

| | | |
|---|---|---|
| Sales | | $300,000 |
| Less: | | |
| Cost of goods sold | $140,000 | |
| Depreciation expense | 30,000 | |
| Other operating expenses | 60,000 | |
| Total expenses | | (230,000) |
| Pretax income | | $ 70,000 |
| Income tax expense | | (21,000) |
| Net income | | $ 49,000 |
| | | |
| Earnings per share (20,000 shares) | | $2.45 |

Parks has two major segments, A and B. No other segment contributes 10% or more of the company's activities. Segments A and B make no sales to each other or to the other segments of the company. An analysis reveals that $2,000 of the total depreciation expense and $6,000 of the total other operating expenses are related to general corporate activities. The *remaining* expenses and total revenues are directly allocable to segment activities according to the following percentages:

| | Segment A | Segment B | Other Segments |
|---|---|---|---|
| | **Percent Identified With** | | |
| Sales | 40% | 46% | 14% |
| Cost of goods sold | 35 | 50 | 15 |
| Depreciation expense | 40 | 45 | 15 |
| Other operating expenses | 42 | 40 | 18 |

**Required**

Prepare a schedule that reports on the revenues and operating profits of Segments A and B and the other segments of the Parks Conglomerate Company for 1995. Be sure to reconcile these amounts with the related totals on the preceding income statement. Include notes summarizing the depreciation related to each segment and the computation of operating profits.

**E23-3** *Determination of Reportable Segments* Straub Diversified Company has five different industry segments. None of these segments makes sales to the other segments. The company has total assets of $155,000 at the end of 1995 and lists the following condensed income statement for 1995:

| | |
|---|---|
| Sales | $100,000 |
| Operating expenses | (72,000) |
| Pretax income | $ 28,000 |
| Income taxes | (8,400) |
| Net income | $ 19,600 |

In preparing its segmental reporting schedule, it has developed the following information for each of its five segments:

| | 1 | 2 | 3 | 4 | 5 |
|---|---|---|---|---|---|
| | **Segment** | | | | |
| Sales | $ 9,200 | $ 8,800 | $ 9,000 | $63,900 | $ 9,100 |
| Operating profit | 3,300 | 3,200 | 3,400 | 21,500 | 3,600 |
| Identifiable assets | 15,100 | 13,900 | 14,300 | 87,900 | 13,800 |

**Required**

On the basis of the preceding information:

1. Determine which segments are reportable industry segments (justify your conclusions).
2. Prepare a schedule that reports on the revenues, operating profits, and identifiable assets of the reportable industry segments and the remaining segments for 1995. Reconcile these amounts to the related totals on the income statement and to total assets. Notes to the schedule are not necessary.

**E23-4** *Foreign Segments*   Evans Company has several U.S. and foreign-based divisions. The foreign divisions operate in several geographic areas. The U.S. divisions make no export sales, and no intersegment sales are made by any division (foreign or U.S.). The following is the 1995 Evans Company condensed income statement:

| | |
|---|---|
| Sales | $80,000 |
| Cost of goods sold | (50,000) |
| Gross profit | $30,000 |
| Operating expenses | (22,000) |
| Pretax operating income | $ 8,000 |
| Income taxes | (2,400) |
| Net income | $ 5,600 |
| Earnings per share (2,000 shares) | $2.80 |

The company has total assets of $110,000 on December 31, 1995. It has determined, for segment reporting purposes, that $2,000 of the operating expenses are general corporate expenses and $10,000 of the total assets are general corporate assets. The *remaining* expenses, assets and total revenues are allocable to U.S. divisions and foreign geographic areas according to the following percentages:

| | United States | Foreign Geographic Areas | | | |
|---|---|---|---|---|---|
| | | 1 | 2 | 3 | 4 |
| Sales | 68% | 9% | 7% | 2% | 14% |
| Cost of goods sold | 70 | 10 | 7 | 2 | 11 |
| Operating expenses | 71 | 8 | 8 | 2 | 11 |
| Identifiable assets | 67 | 11 | 6 | 3 | 13 |

**Required**

Prepare a schedule that discloses the U.S. and foreign revenues, operating profits, and assets for 1995. Include a breakdown of results in the significant foreign geographic areas. Notes to the schedule are not necessary.

**E23-5** *Interim Reporting*   Jersey Company is in the process of developing its first-quarter interim report. It has developed the following condensed trial balance as of March 31, 1995:

| | Debit | Credit |
|---|---|---|
| Cash | $ 900 | |
| Accounts receivable (net) | 4,000 | |
| Inventory (1/1/95) | 5,000 | |
| Prepaid insurance | 4,800 | |
| Note receivable | 6,000 | |
| Land | 3,000 | |
| Buildings and equipment (net) | 36,000 | |
| Accounts payable | | $ 9,100 |
| Common stock, $1 par | | 6,600 |
| Premium on common stock | | 12,400 |
| Retained earnings (1/1/95) | | 22,480 |
| Sales (net) | | 50,000 |
| Purchases (net) | 30,000 | |
| Selling expenses | 6,500 | |
| General and administrative expenses | 4,380 | |
| | $100,580 | $100,580 |

Additional information:

1.  The company makes formal adjusting entries at year-end and enters the amounts in the appropriate accounts at that time.
2.  The company uses control accounts for selling expenses and for general and administrative expenses.
3.  The gross profit method is used to determine the interim inventory. Historical gross profit has averaged 45% of net sales.
4.  Uncollectible accounts typically average 1% of net sales.
5.  On January 1, 1995, buildings and equipment (net) have an average remaining life of 10 years. One-third of the account balance consists of assets related to selling activities. The company uses straight-line depreciation with no residual value.
6.  The note receivable is dated January 1, 1995, matures on January 1, 1997, and carries an annual interest rate of 12% (interest will not be collected until the maturity date).
7.  On January 1, 1995, the company had purchased a 3-year insurance policy, debiting Prepaid Insurance for the $4,800 payment.
8.  The company expects its annual effective income tax rate to be 30%. Income taxes for 1995 will be paid at the beginning of 1996.
9.  No common stock has been issued or retired in 1995.

**Required**
On the basis of the preceding information, prepare the Jersey Company income statement for the first quarter of 1995 and a March 31, 1995 balance sheet. A worksheet is not required, but you should be prepared to document any adjustments you make to the preceding accounts.

**E23-6**     *Interim Reporting*    The Howard Corporation presented the following trial balance for the quarter ended March 31, 1995:

|                                          | Debit       | Credit      |
| ---------------------------------------- | ----------- | ----------- |
| Cash                                     | $   9,800   |             |
| Accounts receivable                      | 13,000      |             |
| Inventory (1/1/95)                       | 10,000      |             |
| Prepaid insurance                        | 9,600       |             |
| Land                                     | 16,000      |             |
| Buildings and equipment                  | 108,000     |             |
| Accumulated depreciation                 |             | $  36,000   |
| Accounts payable                         |             | 28,200      |
| Common stock, $1 par                     |             | 13,200      |
| Additional paid-in capital               |             | 24,800      |
| Retained earnings (1/1/95)               |             | 44,900      |
| Sales (net)                              |             | 100,000     |
| Purchases (net)                          | 59,000      |             |
| Selling expenses                         | 12,000      |             |
| General and administrative expenses      | 9,700       |             |
| Totals                                   | $247,100    | $247,100    |

Additional information:

1.  The company uses control accounts for selling expenses and for general and administrative expenses.
2.  The company makes formal adjusting entries at year-end and enters the amounts in the appropriate accounts at that time.
3.  The company uses the gross profit method to determine interim inventory. Historical gross profit has averaged 43% of net sales.
4.  On January 1, 1995, the company purchased a 4-year insurance policy for $9,600.
5.  No common stock has been issued or retired in 1995.
6.  The buildings and equipment have an estimated life of 15 years with no residual value. The company uses straight-line depreciation; it records one-fourth of the depreciation as a selling expense and the remainder as a general and administrative expense.

7. The company expects its annual effective income tax rate to be 30%; income taxes will be paid at the beginning of the next year.

**Required**

On the basis of the preceding information, prepare the Howard Corporation income statement for the first quarter of 1995 and a March 31, 1995 balance sheet. A worksheet is not required, but you should be prepared to substantiate any adjustments you make to the preceding accounts.

E23-7 **Interim Reporting**  The Hill Company prepares quarterly and year-to-date interim reports. The following is its interim income statement for the quarter ended March 31, 1995:

| | | |
|---|---:|---:|
| Sales (net) | | $150,000 |
| Cost of goods sold | | (90,000) |
| Gross profit | | $ 60,000 |
| Operating expenses | | |
|     Selling expenses | $18,000 | |
|     General expenses | 10,600 | |
|     Depreciation expense | 8,000 | (36,600) |
| Pretax operating income | | $ 23,400 |
| Other items | | |
|     Dividend revenue | $ 600 | |
|     Interest expense | (1,000) | (400) |
| Income before income taxes | | $ 23,000 |
| Income tax expense | | (7,000) |
| Net income | | $ 16,000 |
| Earnings per share (20,000 shares) | | $.80 |

On June 30, 1995, the company accountant completed a worksheet in preparation for developing the year-to-date interim income statement. The following are the accounts and amounts listed in the income statement debit and credit columns of this worksheet:

| | Debit | Credit |
|---|---:|---:|
| Sales (net) | | $340,000 |
| Interest revenue | | 500 |
| Dividend revenue | | 1,000 |
| Cost of goods sold | $190,000 | |
| Selling expenses | 50,000 | |
| General expenses | 20,000 | |
| Depreciation expense | 18,000 | |
| Interest expense | 2,100 | |
| Income tax expense | 18,400 | |

**Required**

Based on the given information, and assuming 20,000 shares of common stock have been outstanding for the entire 6 months, prepare:

1. A year-to-date interim income statement for the first 6 months of 1995.
2. An interim income statement for the second quarter of 1995.

E23-8 **Interim Taxes**  Farris Company is subject to income taxes at a rate of 20% on its first $50,000 of income and 35% on any income in excess of $50,000. In the process of preparing its interim reports, each quarter Farris Company uses an estimated effective income tax rate based on its estimated annual income. The following is a schedule that shows the company's actual year-to-date pretax income and the estimate of the annual pretax income made at the end of each quarter. The company neither anticipates nor incurs any extraordinary items, and its pretax accounting income is the same as its taxable income.

| | Pretax Income Amounts at End of | | | |
| --- | --- | --- | --- | --- |
| | First Quarter | Second Quarter | Third Quarter | Fourth Quarter |
| Actual income (year-to-date) | $20,000 | $42,000 | $60,000 | $82,000 |
| Estimated remaining income | 60,000 | 44,000 | 21,000 | — |
| Estimated annual pretax income | $80,000 | $86,000 | $81,000 | $82,000 |

### Required

Based on the preceding information, prepare a schedule to compute the income tax expense that would be listed on *each* quarterly income statement. (Carry your effective income tax rate computation to three decimal places.)

**E23-9    *Appendix: Horizontal Analyses***  Slusher Company presents the following condensed comparative income statements for 1994, 1995, and 1996:

| | For Years Ended December 31, | | |
| --- | --- | --- | --- |
| | 1996 | 1995 | 1994 |
| Sales (net) | $120,000 | $100,000 | $85,000 |
| Cost of goods sold | (72,000) | (55,000) | (45,000) |
| Gross profit | $ 48,000 | $ 45,000 | $40,000 |
| Operating expenses | (22,000) | (20,000) | (18,000) |
| Operating income | $ 26,000 | $ 25,000 | $22,000 |
| Other items | | | |
| Dividend revenue | 400 | 500 | 200 |
| Interest expense | (1,200) | (1,000) | (500) |
| Income before income taxes | $ 25,200 | $ 24,500 | $21,700 |
| Income tax expense | (8,200) | (8,000) | (6,000) |
| Net income | $ 17,000 | $ 16,500 | $15,700 |
| Number of common shares | 6,000 | 6,000 | 5,000 |
| Earnings per share | $2.83 | $2.75 | $3.14 |

### Required

Based on the preceding information, prepare horizontal analyses for the years 1994, 1995, and 1996 using (1) a year-to-year approach and (2) a base-year-to-date approach. Do your analyses reveal any favorable or unfavorable trends?

**E23-10    *Appendix: Vertical Analyses***  The Samuels Company presents the following condensed income statement and balance sheet information for 1995 and 1996.

***Income Statements***

| | For Years Ended December 31, | |
| --- | --- | --- |
| | 1996 | 1995 |
| Sales (net) | $100,000 | $ 90,000 |
| Cost of goods sold | (59,000) | (51,000) |
| Gross profit | $ 41,000 | $ 39,000 |
| Operating expenses | (21,300) | (21,900) |
| Interest revenue | 1,500 | 1,400 |
| Interest expense | (3,700) | (2,500) |
| Income before income taxes | $ 17,500 | $ 16,000 |
| Income tax expense | (5,200) | (5,000) |
| Net income | $ 12,300 | $ 11,000 |
| Earnings per share | $2.05 | $1.90 |

**Balance Sheets**

|  | December 31, | |
|---|---|---|
|  | **1996** | **1995** |
| Cash | $ 3,000 | $ 2,000 |
| Receivables (net) | 7,000 | 8,000 |
| Inventories | 11,000 | 12,000 |
| Long-term investments (bonds) | 20,000 | 15,000 |
| Property and equipment (net) | 79,000 | 63,000 |
| Total assets | $120,000 | $100,000 |
| Current liabilities | $ 10,000 | $ 11,400 |
| Bonds payable, 10% | 37,000 | 25,000 |
| Common stock, $2 par | 12,000 | 11,600 |
| Premium on common stock | 21,000 | 19,500 |
| Retained earnings | 40,000 | 32,500 |
| Total liabilities and stockholders' equity | $120,000 | $100,000 |

**Required**

Based on the preceding information, prepare vertical analyses of the income statements and balance sheets for the 2 years. Do your analyses reveal any trends in the company's operations and financial position?

**E23-11** *Appendix: Ratios*  The following are a condensed income statement for 1995 and a December 31, 1995 balance sheet for the Allen Company:

| **Income Statement** | |
|---|---|
| Sales (net) | $304,400 |
| Cost of goods sold | (183,600) |
| Gross profit | $120,800 |
| Operating expenses | (82,000) |
| Interest expense | (7,000) |
| Income before income taxes | $ 31,800 |
| Income taxes | (10,000) |
| Net income | $ 21,800 |

| **Balance Sheet** | | | |
|---|---|---|---|
| Cash | $ 8,200 | Accounts payable | $ 18,000 |
| Receivables (net) | 14,700 | Other current liabilities | 6,800 |
| Inventory | 19,300 | Bonds payable, 10% | 70,000 |
| Property, plant, and equipment (net) | 195,800 | Common stock, $10 par | 80,500 |
|  |  | Premium on common stock | 24,000 |
|  |  | Retained earnings | 38,700 |
| Total assets | $238,000 | Total liabilities and stockholders' equity | $238,000 |

Additional information: The corporate common stock was outstanding the entire year and is selling for $16 per share at year-end. On January 1, 1995, the inventory was $21,500, the total assets were $224,000, the accounts payable were $18,800, and the total stockholders' equity was $130,800. The company operates on a 300-day business year.

**Required**

For the Allen Company, compute the following ratios:

1. Price/earnings
2. Profit margin
3. Return on total assets
4. Return on stockholders' equity
5. Current
6. Inventory turnover (in days)
7. Payables turnover (in days)
8. Debt

Is the company favorably "trading on its equity"? Explain.

**E23-12** *Appendix: Ratios*   The Byers Company presents the following condensed income statement for 1995 and condensed December 31, 1995 balance sheet:

### Income Statement

| | | |
|---|---|---|
| Sales (net) | | $267,000 |
| Less: Cost of goods sold | $160,000 | |
| Operating expenses | 62,000 | |
| Interest expense | 11,000 | |
| Income taxes | 10,000 | |
| Total expenses | | (243,000) |
| Net income | | $ 24,000 |

### Balance Sheet

| | | | |
|---|---|---|---|
| Cash | $ 10,000 | Current liabilities | $ 40,000 |
| Receivables (net) | 22,000 | Bonds payable, 10% | 110,000 |
| Inventory | 56,000 | Preferred stock, $100 par | 50,000 |
| Long-term investments | 30,000 | Common stock, $10 par | 100,000 |
| Property and equipment (net) | 282,000 | Additional paid-in capital | 45,000 |
| | | Retained earnings | 55,000 |
| Total assets | $400,000 | Total liabilities and stockholders' equity | $400,000 |

Additional information:

1. The company's common stock and preferred stock were outstanding the entire year.
2. Dividends of $1.70 per share on the common stock and $8 per share on the preferred stock were declared in 1995.
3. On December 31, 1995, the common stock is selling for $20 per share.
4. The preferred stock has a liquidation value of $110 per share.
5. On January 1, 1995, the accounts receivable (net) balance was $24,000 and the total stockholders' equity was $230,000.
6. Of the company's net sales, 75% are on credit.
7. The company operates on a 365-day business year.

**Required**

On the basis of the preceding information, compute the following ratios for the Byers Company:

1. Earnings per share
2. Dividend yield
3. Return on stockholders' equity
4. Current
5. Acid-test
6. Receivables turnover (in days)
7. Times interest earned
8. Book value per common share

On the basis of applicable "rules of thumb," what information is revealed by the acid-test ratio that is not disclosed by the current ratio?

## PROBLEMS

**P23-1** *Income Statement and Segment Reporting*   Frahm Corporation presents the following account balances, after adjustments, on December 31, 1995:

| | | | |
|---|---|---|---|
| Administrative and office salaries | $ 43,000 | Sales salaries and commissions | $ 59,000 |
| Interest expense | 8,800 | Property taxes | 7,000 |
| Bad debts expense | 6,000 | Depreciation expense: buildings, | |
| Sales (net) | 600,000 | sales equipment, and office equipment | 31,000 |
| Loss due to tornado (pretax) | 10,000 | Cost of goods sold | 323,700 |
| Advertising expense | 40,000 | Delivery expense | 25,000 |
| Miscellaneous office expenses | 2,300 | Interest revenue | 3,000 |

The following information is also available:

1. The income tax rate on all items is 30%.
2. 10,000 shares of common stock have been outstanding the entire year.
3. Frahm Corporation operates several divisions, two of which, Divisions B and C, are considered reportable industry segments.
4. Sales (net) are made as follows: Division B, 60%; Division C, 25%; other divisions, 15% of the total. No intersegment sales are made.
5. The cost of goods sold as a *percentage of net sales* in each division is as follows: Division B, 55%; Division C, 52%; other divisions, 53%.
6. Operating expenses are traceable to divisions as follows:
   a. Sales salaries directly traceable to Division B total $27,000; Division C, $12,000; other divisions, $8,000.
   b. Sales commissions in each division are 2% of net sales.
   c. Bad debts average 1% of net sales in each division.
   d. Of the total delivery expense, 64% was spent in Division B, 20% was spent in Division C, and 16% was spent in the other divisions.
   e. Of the total advertising expense, $5,000 was spent on general advertising. Of the remainder, 52% was spent in Division B, 28% in Division C, and 20% in the other divisions.
   f. Administrative and office salaries are considered general corporate expenses, except for $15,000 allocated for the management of Division B, $10,000 for the management of Division C, and $14,000 for the management of the other divisions.
   g. Property taxes paid are $4,000 in Division B, $2,000 in Division C, and $1,000 in other divisions.
   h. Miscellaneous office expenses are not directly traced to divisions.
7. The depreciation expense is listed as a separate component on the corporate income statement. Of the total listed, $6,000 is due to depreciation on the corporate headquarters building and is not allocated. Of the remainder, $15,000 is traceable to Division B, $6,000 is traceable to Division C, and $4,000 is traceable to the other divisions.
8. Interest expense is for corporate bonds used to finance overall operating activities. Interest revenue is from corporate investments in marketable securities.
9. An infrequent and unusual tornado caused a warehouse used in Division B to be severely damaged, resulting in the material $10,000 pretax loss shown earlier.
10. Of the $1,600,000 total company assets at year-end, $890,000 are identifiable with Division B, $370,000 with Division C, $210,000 with the remaining divisions, and $130,000 with corporate headquarters.
11. Capital expenditures of Divisions B and C amounted to $50,000 and $27,000, respectively, in 1995 and are included in the total company assets at year-end.

**Required**

1. Prepare a single-step 1995 income statement for the Frahm Corporation.
2. Prepare a working paper that allocates the revenues, expenses, and assets to the industry segments.
3. Prepare a separate schedule that shows the revenues, operating profits, and identifiable assets of Divisions B and C and the remaining divisions.
4. Prepare appropriate segment notes relating to depreciation, operating profits, and capital expenditures.

P23-2 *Income Statement and Segment Reporting* The following accounts are taken from the December 31, 1995 adjusted trial balance of the Reed Company:

| | | | |
|---|---|---|---|
| Cost of goods sold | $121,120 | Loss due to flood (pretax) | $ 5,000 |
| Interest expense | 4,880 | Sales (net) | 200,000 |
| Depreciation expense | 7,000 | Administrative expenses | 16,000 |
| Selling expenses | 26,000 | Interest revenue | 1,000 |

Additional information:

1. The company had 5,000 shares of common stock outstanding the entire year.
2. The income tax rate is 30% on all items.
3. The Reed Company operates several divisions, two of which, Divisions 1 and 2, are reportable segments.
4. No intersegment sales are made by any division. Of the total sales (net), Division 1 made 49%; Division 2, 30%; and the remaining segments, 21%.

5. Cost of goods sold as a *percentage of net sales* in each division was: Division 1, 62%; Division 2, 60%; other segments, 58%.
6. Selling expenses consist of sales salaries, sales commissions, delivery costs, advertising, and miscellaneous expenses. These are traceable to the segments as follows:
   a. Sales salaries ($6,000): $3,000 to Division 1, $2,000 to Division 2, and $1,000 to the remaining segments.
   b. Sales commissions ($4,000): 2% of net sales in all segments.
   c. Delivery costs ($5,000): 60% to Division 1, 30% to Division 2, and 10% to the remaining segments.
   d. Advertising ($10,500): Of the total, $1,200 was spent on general advertising. The remainder was spent as follows: $4,600 in Division 1, $3,200 in Division 2, and $1,500 in the other segments.
   e. The miscellaneous selling expenses of $500 are considered common costs and are not allocated to any segments.
7. Administrative expenses consist of bad debts, administrative salaries, property taxes, and miscellaneous expenses. These are allocable to the segments as follows:
   a. Bad debts ($2,000): 1% of net sales in all segments.
   b. Administrative salaries ($10,000): Of the total, $2,100 are considered general corporate salaries. The remainder is allocated $4,000 to Division 1, $2,300 to Division 2, and $1,600 to the other segments.
   c. Property taxes ($3,000): Of the total, $1,600 are general corporate expenses. Of the remainder, 40% is allocable to Division 1, 35% to Division 2, and 25% to the remaining segments.
   d. The miscellaneous administrative expenses of $1,000 are considered common costs and are not allocated to any segments.
8. Depreciation expense is listed as a separate item on the income statement. Of the total, $1,400 is a general corporate expense. Of the remainder, 40% is allocable to Division 1, and 30% to Division 2, and 30% to the remaining segments.
9. Interest revenue is from corporate investments in marketable securities. Interest expense is related to corporate bonds used to finance general operating activities.
10. An unusual and infrequent flood causing the material pretax loss occurred in Division 1.
11. Of the $300,000 total assets on December 31, 1995, 46% are identifiable with Division 1, 28% with Division 2, 18% with the remaining segments, and 8% with corporate headquarters.
12. Capital expenditures amounted to $25,000 in Division 1 and $6,000 in Division 2 during 1995 and are included in the total assets on December 31, 1995.

**Required**

1. Prepare a multiple-step income statement for 1995.
2. Prepare a working paper that allocates the revenues, expenses, and assets to the industry segments.
3. Prepare a separate schedule that discloses the revenues, operating profits, and identifiable assets of Divisions 1 and 2, and the remaining segments.
4. Prepare appropriate segment notes related to depreciation, operating profits, and capital expenditures.

P23-3  *Reportable Industry and Foreign Segments*  Stel Company operates segments in the United States and several foreign countries. The following is the Stel Company 1995 condensed income statement for its entire operations:

| | | |
|---|---:|---:|
| Sales | | $53,000 |
| Interest revenue | | 300 |
| Total revenues | | $53,300 |
| Less: Cost of goods sold | $32,000 | |
| Selling expenses | 10,100 | |
| Administrative expenses | 7,700 | |
| Interest expense | 200 | |
| Income taxes | 1,000 | (51,000) |
| Net income (earnings per share $2.30) | | $ 2,300 |

Total assets of the company are $62,000 on December 31, 1995. No segments make any intersegment sales. Interest expense and interest revenue are related to general corporate activities. To identify reportable industry segments, the company has determined that $1,000 of the selling expenses and $600 of the administrative expenses are general corporate expenses, and $4,000 of the total assets are general corporate assets. The *remaining* revenues, expenses, and assets are allocable as follows:

| | Segment 1 | Segment 2 | Segment 3 | Segment 4 | Segment 5 |
|---|---|---|---|---|---|
| Sales | $4,500 | $4,700 | $4,600 | $4,800 | $34,400 |
| Cost of goods sold | 2,710 | 2,800 | 2,760 | 2,910 | 20,820 |
| Selling expenses | 760 | 800 | 790 | 820 | 5,930 |
| Administrative expenses | 600 | 610 | 610 | 620 | 4,660 |
| Identifiable assets | 5,600 | 5,500 | 5,900 | 5,700 | 35,300 |

Part of the company's operations are located outside the United States. The U.S. operations make no export sales. The company has also developed the following allocation schedule of revenues, expenses, and assets (*excluding* common corporate revenues, expenses, and assets):

| | United States | Foreign Geographic Areas | | | |
|---|---|---|---|---|---|
| | | A | B | C | D |
| Sales | $36,000 | $5,100 | $5,000 | $5,300 | $1,600 |
| Cost of goods sold | 22,000 | 3,000 | 2,900 | 3,100 | 1,000 |
| Selling expenses | 6,100 | 900 | 880 | 940 | 280 |
| Administrative expenses | 4,700 | 720 | 710 | 740 | 230 |
| Identifiable assets | 39,000 | 5,500 | 6,200 | 5,400 | 1,900 |

### Required

Based on the preceding information for the Stel Company:

1. Prepare a working paper that allocates the revenues, expenses, and assets to each segment and identifies the reportable industry segments.
2. Prepare a schedule that discloses the revenues, operating profits, and assets of the reportable industry segments and remaining segments. Notes to the schedule are not required.
3. Prepare a working paper that identifies the significant foreign geographic areas.
4. Prepare a schedule that discloses the U.S. and foreign revenues, operating profits, and assets (include a breakdown according to significant foreign geographic areas). Notes to the schedule are not required.

**P23-4** *Interim Reporting* The Schultz Company prepares interim financial statements at the end of each quarter. The income statement presented at the end of the first quarter of 1995 is as follows:

| | | |
|---|---|---|
| Sales (net) | | $40,000 |
| Cost of goods sold: | | |
| Beginning inventory | $18,000 | |
| Purchases (net) | 27,000 | |
| Cost of goods available for sale | $45,000 | |
| Ending inventory | (22,000) | (23,000) |
| Gross profit | | $17,000 |
| Operating expenses: | | |
| Selling expenses | $ 8,800 | |
| Administrative expenses | 4,210 | |
| Total operating expenses | | (13,010) |
| Pretax operating income | | $ 3,990 |
| Other items: | | |
| Interest revenue | $   40 | |
| Rent revenue | 300 | |
| Interest expense | (330) | 10 |
| Income before income taxes | | $ 4,000 |
| Income tax expense | | (700) |
| Net income | | $ 3,300 |
| Earnings per share (8,000 shares) | | $.41 |

Shown next is the Schultz Company trial balance as of June 30, 1995:

|  | Debit | Credit |
|---|---|---|
| Cash | $ 7,200 | |
| Accounts receivable (net) | 10,300 | |
| Note receivable (due 9/1/95) | 4,000 | |
| Inventory (1/1/95) | 18,000 | |
| Prepaid insurance | 960 | |
| Property and equipment | 80,000 | |
| Accumulated depreciation | | $ 20,000 |
| Accounts payable | | 8,000 |
| Dividends payable | | 3,200 |
| Unearned rent | | 1,800 |
| Bonds payable, 10% (due 1/1/2000) | | 12,000 |
| Discount on bonds payable | 600 | |
| Common stock, $1 par | | 8,000 |
| Premium on common stock | | 34,580 |
| Retained earnings | | 26,400 |
| Sales (net) | | 90,000 |
| Purchases (net) | 55,000 | |
| Selling expenses | 19,750 | |
| Administrative expenses | 8,170 | |
|  | $203,980 | $203,980 |

Additional information:

1. The company uses control accounts for selling and administrative expenses.
2. The company journalizes and posts its adjusting entries to its accounts *only at year-end.*
3. The gross profit method is used to estimate the interim inventory. Historical gross profit has averaged 45% of net sales.
4. Uncollectible accounts average 0.5% of net sales.
5. The $4,000 note receivable was received on March 1, 1995. The 6-month note carries an annual interest rate of 12%, the interest to be collected at the maturity date.
6. The balance in the Prepaid Insurance account represents payment made on January 1, 1995 for a one-year comprehensive insurance policy.
7. The Property and Equipment account consists of land, $5,000; buildings, $55,000; and equipment, $20,000. The buildings are being depreciated over a 25-year life; the equipment over an 8-year life. Straight-line depreciation is used; residual value is disregarded. No acquisitions have been made in 1995. The depreciation on the buildings is treated as an administrative expense; depreciation on the equipment as a selling expense.
8. On February 1, 1995, the company rented some floor space to another company, receiving one year's rent of $1,800 in advance.
9. The bonds pay interest semiannually on January 1 and July 1. Straight-line amortization of the discount is recorded at the end of each year.
10. The company estimates that its pretax income for the second half of 1995 will total $12,450. All items in income are subject to the same income tax rate schedule. The income tax rate schedule is 15% on the first $20,000 of taxable income and 30% on the excess. There is no difference between the company's pretax financial income and taxable income, and no tax credits are available. The company rounds its estimated effective income tax rate to the nearest tenth of a percent. Income taxes will be paid during the first quarter of 1996.
11. On June 29, 1995, the company had declared and recorded (directly in Retained Earnings) a semiannual dividend of 40¢ per share, payable on August 1, 1995.
12. The 8,000 shares of common stock have been outstanding the entire 6 months of 1995.

**Required**

1. Prepare a 10-column worksheet to develop the Schultz Company financial statements for the first 6 months of 1995 (refer to Appendix C a for worksheet illustration, if necessary).
2. Prepare the income statement for (a) the first 6 months of 1995 and (b) the second quarter of 1995.
3. Prepare a retained earnings statement for the first 6 months of 1995.
4. Prepare the June 30, 1995 balance sheet.

P23-5  *Interim Reporting*  The Taft Company prepares quarterly and year-to-date financial statements at the end of each quarter. The income statement presented at the end of the first quarter of 1995 is:

| | | |
|---|---:|---:|
| Sales (net) | | $62,000 |
| Cost of goods sold: | | |
| Inventory, January 1, 1995 | $23,000 | |
| Purchases (net) | 38,200 | |
| Cost of goods available for sale | $61,200 | |
| Inventory, March 31, 1995 | (24,000) | |
| Cost of goods sold | | (37,200) |
| Gross profit | | $24,800 |
| Operating expenses | | (14,074) |
| Pretax operating income | | $10,726 |
| Other items | | |
| Interest expense (bonds) | | (726) |
| Income before income taxes | | $10,000 |
| Income tax expense | | (2,000) |
| Net income | | $ 8,000 |
| Earnings per share (8,000 shares) | | $1.00 |

The following is the Taft Company trial balance as of June 30, 1995:

| | Debit | Credit |
|---|---:|---:|
| Cash | $ 10,200 | |
| Accounts receivable | 14,700 | |
| Allowance for doubtful accounts | | $ 400 |
| Note receivable (due April 2, 1996) | 5,000 | |
| Inventory (January 1, 1995) | 23,000 | |
| Prepaid rent (warehouse) | 2,400 | |
| Land | 12,000 | |
| Buildings | 80,000 | |
| Equipment | 18,000 | |
| Accumulated depreciation: buildings and equipment | | 23,000 |
| Accounts payable | | 9,100 |
| Dividends payable | | 3,000 |
| Note payable (due October 1, 1995) | | 6,000 |
| Bonds payable, 12% (due January 1, 2005) | | 25,000 |
| Premium on bonds payable | | 960 |
| Common stock, $0.50 par | | 5,000 |
| Additional paid-in capital | | 52,000 |
| Retained earnings | | 22,968 |
| Sales (net) | | 120,000 |
| Purchases (net) | 77,920 | |
| Operating expenses | 24,208 | |
| | $267,428 | $267,428 |

Additional information:

1. The company journalizes and posts adjusting entries only at *the end of the year.*
2. The company uses a control account for operating expenses.
3. Bad debts average 0.5% of net sales.
4. The retail inventory method (average cost) is used to estimate the ending inventory at the end of each quarter. The ending inventories at cost and retail for each quarter are then used as the beginning inventories for the subsequent quarter, and the retail inventory method is applied based on the relevant information for *that quarter.* For the second quarter, the following information is available: 4/1/1995—inventory at retail, $40,000; sales (net), $58,000; purchases (net) at cost, $39,720, and at retail, $65,900; markups (net), $2,100; no markdowns.
5. On March 1, 1995, the company rented a small warehouse, paying a year's rent of $2,400 in advance.
6. The note receivable was received from a customer on April 1, 1995. The customer will pay the note plus interest of 14% on April 1, 1996.
7. The buildings are being depreciated over a 25-year life, the equipment over a 10-year life. No acquisitions have been made in 1995. The company uses straight-line depreciation. Residual value is expected to be nominal and is not considered for depreciation.
8. The note payable was issued on April 1, 1995. It carries an annual interest rate of 13%; interest is payable on the maturity date.
9. The bonds pay interest semiannually on January 1 and July 1. Straight-line amortization of the premium is recorded at the end of each year.
10. At the end of the second quarter, it estimated that the pretax income for the remaining 6 months would total $20,000. The income tax rate schedule is 15% on the first $20,000 of taxable income and 30% on the excess. The company rounds its estimated effective income tax rate to the nearest tenth of a percent. There is no difference between the company's pretax financial income and taxable income. Income taxes will be paid during the first quarter of 1996.
11. The company declared and recorded (directly in Retained Earnings) a 30¢ per share semiannual dividend (on 10,000 shares) on June 30, 1995, payable on July 31, 1995.
12. A total of 8,000 shares of common stock had been outstanding during all of the first quarter of 1995. On April 3, 1995, the company issued another 2,000 common shares so that on June 30, 1995, 10,000 shares of common stock were outstanding.

**Required**

1. Prepare a 10-column worksheet to develop the Taft Company financial statements for the first 6 months of 1995 (refer to Appendix C for a worksheet illustration, if necessary).
2. Prepare the income statement for (a) the first 6 months of 1995 and (b) the second quarter of 1995.
3. Prepare a retained earnings statement for the first 6 months of 1995.
4. Prepare the June 30, 1995 balance sheet.

**P23-6**     *Interim Reporting*     The Anderson Manufacturing Company, a California corporation listed on the Pacific Coast Stock Exchange, budgeted activities for 1995 as follows:

|  | Amount | Units |
|---|---|---|
| Net sales | $6,000,000 | 1,000,000 |
| Cost of goods sold | (3,600,000) | 1,000,000 |
| Gross margin | $2,400,000 | |
| Selling, general, and administrative expenses | (1,400,000) | |
| Operating earnings | $1,000,000 | |
| Nonoperating revenues and expenses | 0 | |
| Earnings before income taxes | $1,000,000 | |
| Estimated income taxes (current and deferred) | (350,000) | |
| Net earnings | $ 650,000 | |
| Earnings per share of common stock | $6.50 | |

Anderson has operated profitably for many years and has experienced a seasonal pattern of sales volume and production similar to the following forecasted for 1995. Sales volume is expected to follow a quarterly pattern of 10%, 20%, 35%, 35%, respectively, because of the seasonality of the industry. Also, due to production and storage capacity limitations, it is expected that production will follow a pattern of 20%, 25%, 30%, 25%, respectively.

At the conclusion of the first quarter of 1995, the controller of Anderson has prepared and issued the following interim report for public release:

|  | Amount | Units |
|---|---|---|
| Net sales | $ 600,000 | 100,000 |
| Cost of goods sold | (360,000) | 100,000 |
| Gross margin | $ 240,000 | |
| Selling, general, and administrative expenses | (275,000) | |
| Operating loss | $ (35,000) | |
| Loss from warehouse fire | (175,000) | |
| Loss before income taxes | $ (210,000) | |
| Estimated income taxes | 0 | |
| Net loss | $ (210,000) | |
| Loss per share of common stock | $(2.10) | |

The following additional information is available for the first quarter just completed, but was not included in the public information released:

1. The company uses a standard cost system in which standards are set at currently attainable levels on an annual basis. At the end of the first quarter, there was underapplied fixed factory overhead (volume variance) of $50,000 that was treated as an asset at the end of the quarter. Production during the quarter was 200,000 units, of which 100,000 were sold.
2. The selling, general, and administrative expenses were budgeted on a basis of $900,000 fixed expenses for the year plus $0.50 variable expenses per unit of sales.
3. Assume that the warehouse fire loss met the conditions of an extraordinary loss. The warehouse had an undepreciated cost of $320,000; $145,000 was recovered from insurance on the warehouse. No other gains or losses are anticipated this year from similar events or transactions, nor has Anderson had any similar losses in preceding years; thus, the full loss will be deductible as an ordinary loss for income tax purposes.
4. The effective income tax rate, for federal and state taxes combined, is expected to average 35% of earnings before income taxes during 1995. There are no permanent differences between pretax financial income and taxable income.
5. Earnings per share were computed on the basis of 100,000 shares of capital stock outstanding. Anderson has only one class of stock issued, no long-term debt outstanding, and no stock option plan.

### Required

1. Without reference to the specific situation described previously, what are the standards of disclosure for interim financial data (published interim financial reports) for publicly-traded companies? Explain.
2. Identify the weaknesses in form and content of Anderson's interim report without reference to the additional information.
3. For each of the five items of additional information, indicate the preferable treatment for each item for interim-reporting purposes and explain why that treatment is preferable. (*AICPA adapted*)

*P23-7     Financial Statement Presentation and Ratios*     The Horizon Company is listed on the New York Stock Exchange. The market value of its common stock was quoted at $18 per share at both December 31, 1996 and December 31, 1995. Horizon's balance sheets at December 31, 1996 and December 31, 1995, and statements of income and retained earnings for the years then ended are as follows:

### Balance Sheets

| | December 31, 1996 | December 31, 1995 |
|---|---|---|
| **Assets** | | |
| Current assets: | | |
| Cash | $ 3,500 | $ 3,600 |
| Marketable securities, at market | 13,000 | 11,000 |
| Accounts receivable, net of allowance for doubtful accounts | 105,000 | 95,000 |
| Inventories at lower of cost or market | 126,000 | 154,000 |
| Prepaid expenses | 2,500 | 2,400 |
| Total current assets | $250,000 | $266,000 |
| Property, plant and equipment, net of accumulated depreciation | 311,000 | 308,000 |
| Other assets | 29,000 | 34,000 |
| Total assets | $590,000 | $608,000 |
| **Liabilities** | | |
| Current liabilities: | | |
| Notes payable | $ 5,000 | $ 15,000 |
| Accounts payable and accrued expenses | 62,500 | 74,500 |
| Income taxes payable | 1,000 | 1,000 |
| Payments due within one year on long-term debt | 6,500 | 7,500 |
| Total current liabilities | $ 75,000 | $ 98,000 |
| Long-term debt | 169,000 | 180,000 |
| Deferred income taxes | 74,000 | 67,000 |
| Other liabilities | 9,000 | 8,000 |
| **Stockholders' Equity** | | |
| Common stock, par value $1.00 per share; authorized 20,000 shares; issued and outstanding 10,000 shares | 10,000 | 10,000 |
| Additional paid-in capital | 110,000 | 110,000 |
| Unrealized increase in value of marketable securities | 1,000 | 1,000 |
| Retained earnings | 142,000 | 134,000 |
| Total stockholders' equity | 263,000 | 255,000 |
| Total liabilities and stockholders' equity | $590,000 | $608,000 |

*Statement of Income and Retained Earnings*

| | Year Ended December 31, | |
| --- | --- | --- |
| | 1996 | 1995 |
| Net sales | $600,000 | $500,000 |
| Costs and expenses: | | |
| Cost of goods sold | 480,000 | 400,000 |
| Selling, general and administrative expenses | 74,200 | 68,000 |
| Other, net | 17,000 | 6,000 |
| Total costs and expenses | 571,200 | 474,000 |
| Income before income taxes | $ 28,800 | $ 26,000 |
| Income taxes | 8,600 | 7,800 |
| Net income | $ 20,200 | $ 18,200 |
| Retained earnings at beginning of period, as previously reported | 141,000 | 132,000 |
| Adjustment required for correction of an error | (7,000) | (6,000) |
| Retained earnings at beginning of period, as restated | $134,000 | $126,000 |
| Dividends on common stock | 12,200 | 10,200 |
| Retained earnings at end of period | $142,000 | $134,000 |

Additional facts are as follows:

(a) "Selling, general and administrative expenses" for 1996 included a usual but infrequently occurring charge of $9,000.
(b) "Other, net" for 1996 included an extraordinary item (charge) of $10,000. If the extraordinary item (charge) had not occurred, income taxes for 1996 would have been $11,600, instead of $8,600.
(c) "Adjustment required for correction of an error" was a result of a change from an accounting principle that is not generally accepted to one that is generally accepted.
(d) Horizon Company has a simple capital structure and has disclosed earnings per common share for net income in the Notes to the Financial Statements.

**Required**
1. Determine from the preceding additional facts whether or not the presentation of those facts in the Horizon Company statements of income and retained earnings is appropriate. If the presentation is appropriate, discuss the theoretical rationale for the presentation. If the presentation is not appropriate, describe the appropriate presentation and discuss its theoretical rationale. Do not discuss disclosure requirements for the notes to the financial statements.
2. Describe the general significance of the following financial analysis tools:
   (a) Quick (acid-test) ratio
   (b) Inventory turnover
   (c) Return on stockholders' equity
3. Based on the Horizon Company balance sheets, statements of income and retained earnings, and additional facts, describe how to determine each of the above financial analysis tools (for the year 1996 only). (*AICPA adapted*).

*P23-8*  *Disclosures and Ratios*  Selected information from the financial statements of the Pace Company follows:

**Current Assets Section of Balance Sheets**

| | December 31, | |
| | 1995 | 1994 |
|---|---|---|
| (in thousands) | | |
| Cash | $    7,000 | $    7,200 |
| Marketable securities, at market | 26,000 | 22,000 |
| Accounts receivable, net of allowance for doubtful accounts | 210,000 | 190,000 |
| Inventories | 252,000 | 308,000 |
| Prepaid expenses | 5,000 | 4,800 |
| Total current assets | $  500,000 | $  532,000 |

**Statements of Income**

| | Year Ended December 31, | |
| | 1995 | 1994 |
|---|---|---|
| (in thousands) | | |
| Net sales | $1,200,000 | $1,000,000 |
| Costs and expenses: | | |
| Cost of goods sold | 960,000 | 800,000 |
| Selling, general and administrative expenses | 147,000 | 120,000 |
| Other, net | 24,000 | 18,300 |
| Total costs and expenses | 1,131,000 | 938,300 |
| Income from continuing operations before income taxes | 69,000 | 61,700 |
| Income taxes | 26,900 | 25,300 |
| Income from continuing operations | 42,100 | 36,400 |
| Cumulative effect of change in estimates of salvage values of property, plant, and equipment, less applicable income taxes of $1,500,000 | — | 3,000 |
| Net income | $    42,100 | $    33,400 |
| Earnings per share of common stock: | | |
| Income from continuing operations | $      4.21 | $      3.64 |
| Cumulative effect of change in estimates of salvage values of property, plant, and equipment, less applicable income taxes | — | .30 |
| Net income | $      4.21 | $      3.34 |

Selected information from the notes to the financial statements of the Pace Company is as follows:

[*From Summary of Significant Accounting Policies*]:

*Inventories*—Inventories are stated at the lower of cost (first-in, first-out) or market.

*Deferred Income Taxes*—Deferred income taxes arise from temporary differences when profits or expenses are included in taxable income on the income tax return later or earlier than they are included in the statement of income. Such temporary differences principally relate to depreciation.

A provision for deferred income taxes of $6,700,000 in 1995 and $6,300,000 in 1994 is included in the statements of income in "other, net."

[*From Notes to Financial Statements*]:

*Inventories*—Inventories are composed of the following:

|                   | December 31, | |
|                   | 1995 | 1994 |
| --- | --- | --- |
| (in thousands) | | |
| Finished goods | $176,000 | $215,000 |
| Goods in process | 13,000 | 14,000 |
| Raw materials | 63,000 | 79,000 |
| | $252,000 | $308,000 |

Inventories at December 31, 1995 were reduced from a cost of $292,000,000 to a market value of $252,000,000 using the direct inventory reduction method. The cost of inventories at December 31, 1994 approximated their market value.

*Accounting Change*—During the third quarter of 1994, Pace Company revised earlier estimates of salvage values for its property, plant, and equipment. This change in accounting reduced the 1994 net income by $3,000,000 ($0.30 per share).

**Required**

1. Are inventories and the related cost of goods sold presented appropriately? Explain why or why not. If the presentation is not appropriate, specify the appropriate presentation and explain why.
2. a. What are the components of the quick (acid-test) ratio?
   b. How should the quick (acid-test) ratio be used?
3. Is the provision for deferred income taxes presented appropriately? Explain why or why not. If the presentation is not appropriate, specify the appropriate presentation and explain why.
4. Is the accounting change presented appropriately? Explain why or why not. If the presentation is not appropriate, specify the appropriate presentation and explain why. Assume that the accounting change did not involve deferred income taxes. (*AICPA adapted*)

P23-9 *Multiple-Step Income Statement* Before closing the books for the year ended December 31, 1995, Pitt Corp. prepared the following condensed trial balance:

|                                       | Debit | Credit |
| --- | --- | --- |
| Total assets | $ 7,082,500 | |
| Total liabilities | | $ 1,700,000 |
| Common stock | | 1,250,000 |
| Additional paid-in capital | | 2,097,500 |
| Donated capital | | 90,000 |
| Retained earnings, 1/1/95 | | 1,650,000 |
| Net sales | | 6,250,000 |
| Cost of sales | 3,750,000 | |
| Selling and administrative expenses | 1,212,500 | |
| Interest expense | 122,500 | |
| Gain on sale of long-term investments | | 130,000 |
| Income tax expense | 300,000 | |
| Loss on disposition of plant assets | 225,000 | |
| Loss due to earthquake damage | 475,000 | |
| | $13,167,500 | $13,167,500 |

Other financial data for the year ended December 31, 1995:

*Federal income tax*

| | |
|---|---:|
| Estimated tax payments | $200,000 |
| Accrued | 100,000 |
| Total charged to income tax expense (Does not properly reflect current or deferred income tax expense or interperiod income tax allocation for income statement purposes.) | $300,000 |

Pitt applied the provisions of FASB Statement No. 109, *Accounting for Income Taxes*, in its financial statements for the year ended December 31, 1995. The enacted tax rate on all types of taxable income for the current and future years is 30%. The alternative minimum tax is less than the regular income tax.

*Temporary difference*

| | |
|---|---:|
| Excess of book basis over tax basis in depreciable assets (arising from equipment donated as a capital contribution on December 31, 1995 and expected to be depreciated over five years beginning in 1996). There were no temporary differences prior to 1995. | $ 90,000 |

*Nondeductible expenditure*

| | |
|---|---:|
| Officers' life insurance expense | $ 70,000 |

*Earthquake damage*
This damage is considered unusual and infrequent.

*Capital structure*
Common stock, par value $5 per share, traded on a national exchange:
Number of shares:

| | |
|---|---:|
| Outstanding at 1/1/95 | 200,000 |
| Issued on 3/30/95 as a 10% stock dividend | 20,000 |
| Sold for $25 per share on 6/30/95 | 30,000 |
| Outstanding at 12/31/95 | 250,000 |

**Required**
1. Using the multiple-step format, prepare a formal income statement for Pitt for the year ended December 31, 1995.
2. Prepare a schedule to reconcile net income to taxable income reportable on Pitt's tax return for 1995. (*AICPA adapted*)

**P23-10   *The Coca-Cola Company Disclosures***   Review the financial statements and related notes of The Coca-Cola Company in Appendix A.

**Required**
Answer the following questions. (*Note*: All information is given in the financial report.) Indicate on what page of the financial report you located the answer.
1. What was the gross profit for 1992?
2. What were the (a) income before change in accounting principle, (b) "transition effect" of change in accounting principle, and (c) net income for 1992? What were the related earnings per share amounts?
3. What was the reason for the "transition effect," and why was it included in net income for 1992?
4. What were the total assets on December 31, 1992? How much of this total were current assets?
5. What was the total shareholders' equity on December 31, 1992? How much was deducted from this shareholders' equity for treasury stock? What method does the company use to account for its treasury stock?
6. What was the net decrease in cash and cash equivalents in 1992? How much of this was from net cash provided by operating activities?
7. Where does the company summarize its accounting policies? How are inventories valued and, generally, what costing methods are used? On what basis are goodwill and other intangible assets stated and how are they being amortized? How are property, plant, and equipment being depreciated?

8. What is the total of the lines of credit and other short-term credit facilities contractually available, and how much was outstanding on December 31, 1992?
9. What was the percentage of total debt to total capital in 1992? How does this compare to 1990?
10. What was the return on capital in 1992? How does this compare to 1987?
11. What was the net cash used in financing activities in 1992? What was the net cash used in investing activities in 1992?
12. How many stock options were outstanding at December 31, 1992? What was the range of option prices per share for exercised stock options in 1992?
13. What was the net periodic pension cost for U.S. plans in 1992? What was the fair value of the U.S. pension plan assets on December 31, 1992?
14. What happened on April 15, 1992 in regard to the common stock?
15. For the fourth quarter of 1992, what were the (a) net operating revenues, (b) gross profit, and (c) net income available to common share owners? What were the related earnings per share for (c)?
16. What was the largest major line of business of the company in 1992? What was its total operating income for 1992?
17. What were the net operating revenues in the European Community for 1992? What were the identifiable operating assets held in Latin America at December 31, 1992?
18. Who are the auditors of the company? On what date was the audit report issued?
19. How is the internal accounting control system augmented to provide reasonable assurance that assets are safeguarded and that transactions are authorized, recorded, and reported properly?
20. Outside the U.S., by what percent did (a) unit case volume and (b) gallon shipments increase in 1992? 1991? Why was the percent lower in 1992 than 1991?
21. How much were administrative and general expenses in 1992? What was the primary reason for the increase from 1991?

**P23-11** *Appendix: Horizontal Analysis and Ratios* The following are comparative financial statements of the Cohen Company for 1994, 1995, and 1996:

*Comparative Income Statements*

| | For Years Ended December 31, | | |
| --- | --- | --- | --- |
| | **1996** | **1995** | **1994** |
| Sales (net) | $102,200 | $ 91,500 | $ 81,700 |
| Cost of goods sold | (61,100) | (52,800) | (47,150) |
| Gross profit | $ 41,100 | $ 38,700 | $ 34,550 |
| Selling expenses | (11,400) | (10,000) | (8,900) |
| Administrative expenses | (8,700) | (7,843) | (6,950) |
| Interest expense | (3,000) | (4,000) | (4,000) |
| Total expenses | (23,100) | (21,843) | (19,850) |
| Income before income taxes | $ 18,000 | $ 16,857 | $ 14,700 |
| Income tax expense | (5,400) | (5,057) | (4,410) |
| Net income | $ 12,600 | $ 11,800 | $ 10,290 |
| Earnings per share | ? | ? | ? |

*Comparative Retained Earnings Statements*

| | For Years Ended December 31, | | |
| --- | --- | --- | --- |
| | **1996** | **1995** | **1994** |
| Beginning retained earnings | $ 28,800 | $ 20,800 | $ 14,310 |
| Add: Net income | 12,600 | 11,800 | 10,290 |
| | $ 41,400 | $ 32,600 | $ 24,600 |
| Less: Dividends distributed | (4,410) | (3,800) | (3,800) |
| Ending retained earnings | $ 36,990 | $ 28,800 | $ 20,800 |

### Comparative Balance Sheets

| | December 31, | | |
|---|---|---|---|
| | **1996** | **1995** | **1994** |
| Cash | $  4,200 | $  4,000 | $  4,100 |
| Receivables (net) | 7,600 | 7,000 | 6,200 |
| Inventories | 9,800 | 9,000 | 8,600 |
| Noncurrent assets | 119,390 | 112,000 | 107,100 |
| Total assets | $140,990 | $132,000 | $126,000 |
| Current liabilities | $ 12,000 | $ 10,000 | $ 12,000 |
| Bonds payable, 10% | 30,000 | 40,000 | 40,000 |
| Common stock, $2 par | 8,400 | 7,600 | 7,600 |
| Premium on common stock | 53,600 | 45,600 | 45,600 |
| Retained earnings | 36,990 | 28,800 | 20,800 |
| Total liabilities and stockholders' equity | $140,990 | $132,000 | $126,000 |

Additional information: Credit sales were 65% of net sales in 1995 and 60% in 1996. At the beginning of 1996, 400 shares of common stock were issued, the first sale of stock in several years.

The Cohen Company is concerned. Although it increased the dividends paid per share by 5% in 1996 and its 1996 net income is higher than 1995 net income, the market price of its common stock dropped from $22 per share at the beginning of 1996 to $21 per share at year-end.

**Required**

1. For 1994, 1995, and 1996, prepare horizontal analyses using a year-to-year approach.
2. For 1995 and 1996, compute the following ratios:

   a. Current
   b. Acid-test
   c. Inventory turnover
   d. Receivables turnover
   e. Earnings per share
   f. Dividend yield
   g. Return on total assets
   h. Return on stockholders' equity
   i. Debt

3. Based on your results, discuss the possible reasons for the decrease in the market price per share in 1996.

**P23-12** *Appendix: Vertical Analysis, Ratios*   The Goodman Company operates a high-volume retail outlet. The following are comparative financial statements for the company:

### Comparative Income Statements

| | For Years Ended December 31, | |
|---|---|---|
| | **1996** | **1995** |
| Sales (net) | $180,000 | $150,000 |
| Cost of goods sold | (108,000) | (85,500) |
| Gross profit | $ 72,000 | $ 64,500 |
| Selling expenses | (21,600) | (15,000) |
| Administrative expenses | (23,770) | (23,410) |
| Interest expense | (3,200) | (2,800) |
| Income before taxes | $ 23,430 | $ 23,290 |
| Income tax expense | (7,030) | (6,990) |
| Net income | $ 16,400 | $ 16,300 |
| Earnings per share (6,000 shares) | $2.73 | $2.72 |

## Comparative Balance Sheets

| | December 31, | | | December 31, | |
| --- | --- | --- | --- | --- | --- |
| | **1996** | **1995** | | **1996** | **1995** |
| Cash | $ 4,200 | $ 3,000 | Accounts payable | $ 12,000 | $ 10,000 |
| Investments (short-term) | 2,000 | 2,100 | Other current liabilities | 1,000 | 2,400 |
| Receivables (net) | 8,600 | 6,400 | Bonds payable | 40,000 | 35,000 |
| Inventory | 11,300 | 9,700 | Common stock, $3 par | 18,000 | 18,000 |
| Noncurrent assets (net) | 129,900 | 118,800 | Additional paid-in capital | 30,000 | 30,000 |
| Total assets | $156,000 | $140,000 | Unrealized capital | 900 | 1,000 |
| | | | Retained earnings | 54,100 | 43,600 |
| | | | Total liabilities and stockholders' equity | $156,000 | $140,000 |

Additional data: The company has not issued any common stock for several years and the price of its common stock has remained relatively constant over that time. At the beginning of 1995, it had outstanding accounts receivable (net) of $7,600, an inventory of $11,000, accounts payable of $7,400, total liabilities of $44,600, and stockholders' equity of $85,400. The company typically makes 50% of its sales on credit.

Goodman Company management has become concerned. Although it feels that progress has been made in "tightening up" the company's operating cycle, this has caused only a modest increase in profits and no increase in the company's stock market price. Management has asked for your assistance in identifying problem areas as well as strong points.

### Required

1. Prepare a vertical analysis for the 1995 and 1996 financial statements.
2. Compute the following ratios for 1995 and 1996:

   a. Current              f. Return on total assets

   b. Acid-test          g. Return on stockholders' equity

   c. Inventory turnover    h. Debt

   d. Receivables turnover    i. Times interest earned

   e. Payables turnover
3. Briefly discuss any findings that your analyses reveal.

**P23-13** *Appendix: Horizontal and Vertical Analyses* The following are comparative financial statements of the Perez Company for 1994, 1995, and 1996:

## Comparative Income Statements

| | For Years Ended December 31, | | |
| --- | --- | --- | --- |
| | **1996** | **1995** | **1994** |
| Sales | $ 407,000 | $ 361,500 | $ 332,000 |
| Sales returns | (7,000) | (11,500) | (12,000) |
| Net sales | $ 400,000 | $ 350,000 | $ 320,000 |
| Cost of goods sold | (244,000) | (222,000) | (205,000) |
| Gross profit | $ 156,000 | $ 128,000 | $ 115,000 |
| Selling expenses | (45,825) | (39,550) | (35,690) |
| Administrative expenses | (60,232) | (46,664) | (44,213) |
| Interest expense | (4,150) | (4,200) | (3,580) |
| Total expense | $(110,207) | $ (90,414) | $ (83,483) |
| Income before income taxes | $ 45,793 | $ 37,586 | $ 31,517 |
| Income tax expense | (13,738) | (11,276) | (9,455) |
| Net income | $ 32,055 | $ 26,310 | $ 22,062 |
| Number of common shares | 10,000 | 9,000 | 8,000 |
| Earnings per share | $3.21 | $2.92 | $2.76 |

*Comparative Balance Sheets*

| | December 31, | | |
| --- | --- | --- | --- |
| | **1996** | **1995** | **1994** |
| Cash | $ 15,500 | $ 12,650 | $ 9,300 |
| Receivables (net) | 11,000 | 9,350 | 6,600 |
| Inventories | 38,000 | 30,000 | 22,250 |
| Noncurrent assets | 286,500 | 250,000 | 220,350 |
| Total assets | $ 351,000 | $ 302,000 | $ 258,500 |
| Accounts payable | $ 11,800 | $ 9,500 | $ 9,300 |
| Notes payable | 16,200 | 13,500 | 11,700 |
| Bonds payable | 38,000 | 39,000 | 36,500 |
| Common stock, $5 par | 50,000 | 45,000 | 40,000 |
| Premium on common stock | 90,000 | 72,000 | 56,000 |
| Retained earnings | 145,000 | 123,000 | 105,000 |
| Total liabilities and stockholders' equity | $ 351,000 | $ 302,000 | $ 258,500 |

**Required**

On the basis of the given information:

1. Prepare horizontal analyses using a base-year-to-date approach for 1994 through 1995, and 1994 through 1996.
2. Prepare vertical analyses for the 1995 and 1996 financial statements.

*P23-14 Appendix: Ratio Analysis*   Comparative financial statements of the Boeckman Company for 1995 and 1996 are as follows:

*Comparative Balance Sheets*

| | December 31, | |
| --- | --- | --- |
| | **1996** | **1995** |
| *Assets* | | |
| Current assets | | |
| Cash | $ 7,940 | $ 5,760 |
| Temporary investments (at market) | 10,060 | 4,240 |
| Accounts receivable | 18,000 | 19,500 |
| Inventories | 32,000 | 27,000 |
| Prepaid insurance | 15,000 | 14,000 |
| Total current assets | $ 83,000 | $ 70,500 |
| Property and plant (net) | 64,000 | 46,000 |
| Investments | 36,000 | 32,000 |
| Long-term receivables | 38,600 | 31,000 |
| Patents, net | 13,000 | 9,000 |
| Other assets | 30,000 | 27,500 |
| Total assets | $ 264,600 | $ 216,000 |
| *Liabilities* | | |
| Current liabilities | | |
| Accounts payable | $ 17,800 | $ 16,500 |
| Income taxes payable | 7,500 | 6,800 |
| Accrued payables | 1,500 | 1,400 |
| Current portion of long-term debt | 3,200 | 3,200 |
| Total current liabilities | $ 30,000 | $ 27,900 |
| Long-term debt | $ 56,300 | $ 48,000 |
| Deferred income taxes | 12,500 | 11,800 |
| Total other liabilities | 7,200 | 8,300 |
| Total liabilities | $ 106,000 | $ 96,000 |

*Comparative Balance Sheets (continued)*

| | December 31, | |
|---|---|---|
| | 1996 | 1995 |
| *Stockholders' Equity* | | |
| Common stock, $5 par | $ 35,000 | $ 30,000 |
| Premium on common stock | 36,000 | 24,600 |
| Unrealized capital | 1,000 | 600 |
| Retained earnings | 86,600 | 64,800 |
| Total stockholders' equity | $ 158,600 | $ 120,000 |
| Total liabilities and stockholders' equity | $ 264,600 | $ 216,000 |

*Comparative Income Statements*

| | For Years Ended December 31, | |
|---|---|---|
| | 1996 | 1995 |
| Sales | $ 278,000 | $ 256,000 |
| Sales returns | (8,000) | (6,000) |
| Net sales (68% on credit) | $ 270,000 | $ 250,000 |
| Cost of goods sold | (175,500) | (170,000) |
| Gross profit | $ 94,500 | $ 80,000 |
| Selling expenses | (21,500) | (18,200) |
| General expenses | (27,560) | (23,550) |
| Interest expense | (4,300) | (3,100) |
| Total expenses | $ (53,360) | $ (44,850) |
| Income before income taxes | $ 41,140 | $ 35,150 |
| Income tax expense | (12,340) | (10,550) |
| Net income | $ 28,800 | $ 24,600 |
| Beginning retained earnings | 64,800 | 43,200 |
| Common stock dividends | (7,000) | (3,000) |
| Ending retained earnings | $ 86,600 | $ 64,800 |

Additional information: The Boeckman Company is listed on the New York Stock Exchange. It issued 1,000 additional shares of common stock at the beginning of 1996. The market value of its common stock was quoted at $17 per share at December 31, 1996. The company uses a 365-day business year in its ratio analysis.

**Required**

1. Based on the preceding information, compute (for the year 1996 only) the following ratios:
   a. Dividend yield
   b. Price/earnings
   c. Profit margin
   d. Return on total assets
   e. Return on stockholders' equity
   f. Current
   g. Acid-test
   h. Inventory turnover (in days)
   i. Receivables turnover (in days)
   j. Payables turnover (in days)
   k. Average operating cycle (in days)
   l. Debt
   m. Times interest earned
   n. Book value per common share
2. Briefly discuss what a potential investor might do to evaluate the results of these ratios.

**P23-15**  *Appendix: Ratio Analysis*  The Printing Company is listed on the New York Stock Exchange. The market value of its common stock was quoted at $10 per share at December 31, 1996 and 1995. Printing's balance sheet at December 31, 1996 and 1995, and statement of income and retained earnings for the years then ended are as follows:

**Balance Sheet**

|  | December 31, | |
|---|---|---|
|  | **1996** | **1995** |
| *Assets* | | |
| Current Assets: | | |
|   Cash | $ 3,500,000 | $ 3,600,000 |
|   Marketable securities, at market | 13,000,000 | 11,000,000 |
|   Accounts receivable (net) | 105,000,000 | 95,000,000 |
|   Inventories, lower of cost or market | 126,000,000 | 154,000,000 |
|   Prepaid expenses | 2,500,000 | 2,400,000 |
|     Total current assets | $ 250,000,000 | $ 266,000,000 |
| Property and plant (net) | 311,000,000 | 308,000,000 |
| Investments, at equity | 2,000,000 | 3,000,000 |
| Long-term receivables | 14,000,000 | 16,000,000 |
| Goodwill and patents (net) | 6,000,000 | 6,500,000 |
| Other assets | 6,000,000 | 7,600,000 |
|     Total assets | $ 589,000,000 | $ 607,100,000 |
| | | |
| *Liabilities* | | |
| Current Liabilities: | | |
|   Notes payable | $ 5,000,000 | $ 15,000,000 |
|   Accounts payable | 38,000,000 | 48,000,000 |
|   Accrued expenses | 24,500,000 | 27,000,000 |
|   Income taxes payable | 1,000,000 | 1,000,000 |
|   Current portion of long-term debt | 6,500,000 | 7,000,000 |
|     Total current liabilities | 75,000,000 | 98,000,000 |
| Long-term debt | 169,000,000 | 180,000,000 |
| Deferred income taxes | 74,000,000 | 67,000,000 |
| Other liabilities | 9,000,000 | 8,000,000 |
| | | |
| *Stockholders' Equity* | | |
| Common stock, $1 par value | 10,000,000 | 10,000,000 |
| 5% cumulative preferred stock, $100 par value; $100 liquidating value | 4,000,000 | 4,000,000 |
| Additional paid-in capital | 107,000,000 | 107,000,000 |
| Unrealized decrease in value of marketable securities | (1,000,000) | (900,000) |
| Retained earnings | 142,000,000 | 134,000,000 |
|   Total stockholders' equity | 262,000,000 | 254,100,000 |
|   Total liabilities and stockholders' equity | $ 589,000,000 | $ 607,100,000 |

### Statement of Income and Retained Earnings

|  | Year Ended December 31, | |
|---|---|---|
|  | **1996** | **1995** |
| Net sales | $ 600,000,000 | $ 500,000,000 |
| Costs and expenses: | | |
|    Cost of goods sold | $ 490,000,000 | $ 400,000,000 |
|    Selling and general expenses | 71,900,000 | 66,000,000 |
|    Other, net | 7,000,000 | 6,000,000 |
|       Total costs and expenses | 568,900,000 | 472,000,000 |
| Income before taxes | $ 31,100,000 | $ 28,000,000 |
| Income tax expense | 10,900,000 | 9,800,000 |
| Net income | $ 20,200,000 | $ 18,200,000 |
| Beginning retained earnings | 134,000,000 | 126,000,000 |
| Dividends on common stock | 12,000,000 | 10,000,000 |
| Dividends on preferred stock | 200,000 | 200,000 |
| Ending retained earnings | $ 142,000,000 | $ 134,000,000 |

### Required

Based on the preceding information, compute (for the year 1996 only) the following:

1. Current (working capital) ratio
2. Quick (acid-test) ratio
3. Number of days' sales in average receivables, assuming a business year consists of 300 days and all sales are on account
4. Inventory turnover
5. Book value per share of common stock
6. Earnings per share on common stock
7. Price/earnings ratio on common stock
8. Dividend yield ratio on common stock (*AICPA adapted*)

# 24

# ACCOUNTING FOR CHANGES IN PRICES

## Chapter Topics

*General Price-Level Adjusted Historical Cost Financial Statements (Historical Cost/Constant Purchasing Power)*

*Current Value Financial Statements (Current Cost/Nominal Dollar)*

*General Price-Level Adjusted Current Value Financial Statements (Current Cost/Constant Purchasing Power)*

*Exit Value Financial Statements*

*Comprehensive Adjustments*

*FASB Statement No. 89 Voluntary Disclosures*

The primary purpose of financial statements is to provide useful information to external users, such as investors and creditors. For example, different methods of asset valuation provide different information to users if the prices of individual assets owned by companies change with time. Suppose a parcel of land is purchased for $100,000. A year later the value of the land is $120,000, but there has been inflation of 5%. Theoretically the land could be valued in the balance sheet either at its current value of $120,000 or at $105,000—the historical cost of $100,000 adjusted for the 5% inflation. However, under generally accepted accounting principles, the land is valued in the balance sheet at $100,000. In other words, the change in the value of the land is ignored, as is the change in the value of the dollar due to inflation.

Furthermore, under historical cost accounting the effect of a change in value is recognized only when a transaction takes place, such as when the land is sold. Suppose that the land is sold for $120,000. At this time, a gain of $20,000 (the $120,000 selling price less the $100,000 original cost) is recognized. However, should a gain of zero (the $120,000 less the $120,000 current value) or of $15,000 ($120,000 less the $105,000 historical cost adjusted for the 5% inflation rate) be recognized instead? Which information is more useful to users of financial statements?

This chapter explains the logic underlying the alternative methods (including entry and exit values) of accounting for changing prices. It also illustrates the comprehensive constant purchasing power adjustment process and the comprehensive current cost adjustment process. *FASB Statement No. 33 required* selected supplementary disclosures about changing prices, but it was rescinded by *FASB Statement No. 89*. The *voluntary* supplementary disclosures encouraged by this later *Statement* are also briefly discussed in the chapter.

# CURRENT VALUE AND THE GENERAL PRICE LEVEL

For accounting purposes, two types of price changes are of concern, as can be seen from the previous example. First, the price of an individual asset or liability such as inventory, buildings, or bonds payable changes in response to the dynamics of the market for that particular item. This is known as a **specific price change** or a **current value change.** Second, there may be a change in the value, or purchasing power, of the dollar. Such a change is caused by the overall change in the prices of all goods and services in the economy, and is known as a **general price-level change.** Changes in the general purchasing power of money are known as inflation or deflation. During inflation, the general purchasing power of money declines as the general level of prices of goods and services rises. During deflation, the general purchasing power of money increases as the general level of prices falls. The general purchasing power of money and the general price level are reciprocals.

For a company's specific assets and liabilities, the price changes may be very different from the change in the general price level. For example, while the general price level rises, the specific price of an inventory item (its current value) may increase faster or slower, or even decline as compared with the general price level.

The two types of price changes thus are related, but it is very important to recognize that accounting for the current value of assets and accounting for changes in the general price level are *not* alternatives or substitutes for each other. Each method represents the implementation of a different concept and, therefore, has a different purpose. Although neither method is required to be used in the financial statements under generally accepted accounting principles (except for fair values of certain investments as discussed in Chapter 13), selected current cost and general price-level adjusted *supplementary* disclosures are encouraged (but not required) under *FASB Statement No. 89,* as discussed later in the chapter.

## Current Value

**Current value adjustments account for the changes in the values of individual assets and liabilities and *not* for the change in the value of the dollar.** As the specific current values change, they are recognized in the financial statements by recording assets and liabilities in the balance sheet at their current values. In the income statement, expenses are matched against revenues at the current value of the assets used up or the liabilities created. Therefore, this method significantly changes the basic concepts of asset valuation and income measurement. Current value is a general concept and may be measured in several ways, including an *exit value* such as net realizable value (the net amount that can be realized from sale), the present value of future cash flows, and an *input value* such as current cost. Our discussion concentrates on **current cost** as the measure of current value because this method is the basis for the current value disclosures encouraged by *FASB Statement No. 89.* **Current cost is the cost in the current period of replacing (i.e., acquiring or producing) the items concerned,** as discussed later.

## General Price Level

**General price-level adjustments account for the change in the value of the *dollar* and *not* for changes in the value of individual assets and liabilities.** As the general price level increases, the goods and services that can be purchased with a given number of dollars decreases. Therefore, financial statements that include dollars measured at different times are potentially misleading because the dollars vary in purchasing power. The adjustments for changes in the general price level convert these dollars of different purchasing power into dollars of constant purchasing power. In essence, the adjustments account for changes in the size of the measuring unit used in accounting. In contrast to a physical measuring unit such as a foot or a meter, which remains constant, the dollar is not a constant measure because its purchasing power changes. Just as no one advocates adding and subtracting U.S. and Canadian dollars, for example, it can be argued that it is equally inappropriate to add and subtract dollars of different purchasing power, even though they are always called U.S. dollars.

## Four Alternative Concepts

Just as with historical costs, current costs may be measured in different time periods. Since the general price-level adjustments account only for the change in the value of the dollar over time, these adjustments are equally applicable to historical cost and current cost financial statements. In both cases, amounts are included in the adjusted financial statements (or selected supplemental disclosures) that are measured in dollars of different dates, and so of different values. Thus, there are four alternative accounting methods to be considered (the common terminology used to differentiate the alternatives is given in parentheses):

1. Historical cost

2. Historical cost adjusted for changes in the general price level (historical cost/ constant purchasing power)

3. Current value (current cost)

4. Current value adjusted for changes in the general price level (current cost/ constant purchasing power)

Constant purchasing power amounts also are known as **constant dollar** amounts. The historical cost concept, which is the basis of generally accepted accounting principles, is covered in the other chapters of this book. Remember that generally accepted accounting principles do allow occasional uses of current value, such as when there is a decline in the price of inventory and the lower of cost or market rule is invoked, and for certain investments. The other three alternatives are discussed in the following section.

## THREE ALTERNATIVES TO HISTORICAL COST

To introduce the differences between constant purchasing power and current cost financial statements, consider the following sequence of events for the Hallas Company:

1. The company begins operations with $3,000 cash from issuing capital stock.

2. One unit of inventory is purchased for $1,000 cash.

3. The current (replacement) cost of the inventory increases to $1,250 and the general price-level index increases from 100 to 110, an increase of 10%.

4. The inventory is sold for $2,000 cash.

5. Another unit of inventory is purchased for $1,250.

The events are reflected in the historical cost financial statements in Exhibit 24-1 (ignoring operating expenses and income taxes). A set of financial statements is prepared after each event, labeled Steps 1 through 5. Income is recognized only in Step 4 when the inventory is sold; consequently the only increase in asset values is recognized at the same time.

---

### EXHIBIT 24-1

**HALLAS COMPANY**

Historical Cost Financial Statements

| | Step | | | | |
|---|---|---|---|---|---|
| | 1 | 2 | 3 | 4 | 5 |
| *Income Statements* | | | | | |
| Revenue | — | — | — | $2,000 | — |
| Cost of goods sold | — | — | — | (1,000) | — |
| Net income | — | — | — | $1,000 | — |
| *Balance Sheets* | | | | | |
| Cash | $3,000 | $2,000 | $2,000 | $4,000 | $2,750 |
| Inventory | — | 1,000 | 1,000 | — | 1,250 |
| Total Assets | $3,000 | $3,000 | $3,000 | $4,000 | $4,000 |
| Capital | $3,000 | $3,000 | $3,000 | $4,000 | $4,000 |

---

### Current Cost Financial Statements

The current cost financial statements for the Hallas Company are shown in Exhibit 24-2. The financial statements at Steps 1 and 2 are the same as the historical cost statements because no changes in current costs have occurred. However, in Step 3, when the current cost of the inventory rises to $1,250, the $250 increase is recognized. Since this gain results from holding the asset and is not realized through a sale, it is known as an **unrealized holding gain**. In Step 4, when the inventory is sold for $2,000, the cost of goods sold is recognized at the current cost of the inventory, or $1,250. Therefore, operating income is $750 as compared with the historical cost income of $1,000. The unrealized holding gain is now realized through a sale, so a **realized holding gain** is recognized, and the unrealized holding gain removed.

The basic argument in favor of current cost financial statements can be seen by comparing the balance sheets in Steps 2 and 5. At both steps, the company has only two assets—cash and one unit of inventory. Since the inventory is identical at both steps in terms of its physical characteristics, the company is better off at Step 5 by the increase in its cash balance, or $750. The current cost financial statements recognize an *operating income* of only $750. Therefore, this measure of income is consistent with the increase in the wealth of the company (the amount the company can distribute to the owners and remain as well off). In contrast, the historical cost financial statements recognize an operating income of $1,000. However, this income

---

**EXHIBIT 24-2**

## HALLAS COMPANY

Current Cost Financial Statements

| | Step | | | | |
|---|---|---|---|---|---|
| | 1 | 2 | 3 | 4 | 5 |
| *Income Statements* | | | | | |
| Revenue | — | — | — | $2,000 | — |
| Cost of goods sold | — | — | — | (1,250) | — |
| Operating income | — | — | — | $ 750 | — |
| Unrealized holding gain | — | — | $ 250 | (250) | — |
| Realized holding gain | — | — | — | 250 | — |
| Net income | — | — | $ 250 | $ 750 | — |
| *Balance Sheets* | | | | | |
| Cash | $3,000 | $2,000 | $2,000 | $4,000 | $2,750 |
| Inventory | — | 1,000 | 1,250 | — | 1,250 |
| Total Assets | $3,000 | $3,000 | $3,250 | $4,000 | $4,000 |
| Capital | $3,000 | $3,000 | $3,250 | $4,000 | $4,000 |

includes $250 that is not really income, because the company is required to replace the inventory to remain in business. For example, suppose that after Step 4 the company decides to distribute the historical cost income of $1,000 as dividends. This would leave the company with $3,000 cash. After purchasing a unit of inventory of $1,250, the company would have $1,750 cash left, and thus would have suffered a decrease in wealth of $250 since Step 2, when it held $2,000 cash and one unit of inventory.

Note that the unrealized and realized holding gains are included in income in this example. Many accountants, however, argue that these gains are not really income, as illustrated in the previous discussion. Therefore, they argue, the gains should be excluded from the income statement and credited directly to stockholders' equity. Whichever way the gains (or losses) are reported in the financial statements, it is very important to understand the nature of these gains in contrast to income that represents real profit obtained through a sale.

### Historical Cost/Constant Purchasing Power Financial Statements

The historical cost/constant purchasing power financial statements of the Hallas Company are shown in Exhibit 24-3. Remember that this adjustment process is completely separate from the current cost financial statements just discussed. The only change in the general price level is in Step 3, when the price-level index rises from 100 to 110, an increase of 10%. When the financial statements for Steps 1 and 2 were prepared *originally*, they were identical to the historical cost financial statements in

Exhibit 24-1 because no change in the general price level had occurred. However, *all* the financial statements in Exhibit 24-3 are presented in terms of the value of the dollar *after* the 10% increase in the price level (that is, in Step 3 prices). Therefore, the cash and capital in Step 1 and the cash, inventory, and capital in Step 2 are all increased by 10% to reflect the increase in the general price level that has occurred since these amounts were measured originally. For example, the $3,000 in the historical cost balance sheet in Step 1 of Exhibit 24-1 is measured in dollars *before* the rise in the general price level. This amount has a purchasing power that is equivalent to $3,300 after the price rise (an increase of 10%). The $3,000 measured in dollars before the price rise is adjusted to $3,300 measured in dollars after the price rise, so that the statements in Steps 1 and 3 reflect dollars of the same purchasing power.

In Step 3, the rise in the general price level takes place. Thus the $2,000 cash in the historical cost balance sheet is measured in dollars after the price-level increase. As a result, the company has lost $200 ($2,200 − $2,000) of purchasing power because it held the cash while the price level rose. This $200 loss is included in income, and it also reduces the purchasing power of the capital to $3,100. The inventory is measured at the historical cost of $1,000 adjusted for the 10% increase in the general price level. The $1,100 is the current purchasing-power equivalent of the original $1,000. No purchasing-power gain or loss results from holding a nonmonetary asset such as inventory, as discussed later in the chapter. In Step 4, the inventory is sold for $2,000. The cost of goods sold is recorded at the constant purchasing power of the inventory, $1,100, and therefore the net income is $900.

The major argument in favor of historical cost/constant purchasing power financial statements can be illustrated by considering the income statement in Step 4 and the balance sheets in Steps 1 and 4. In the historical cost income statement in Exhibit 24-1,

---

### EXHIBIT 24-3

### HALLAS COMPANY

**Historical Cost/Constant Purchasing Power Financial Statements**

|  | Step | | | | |
| --- | --- | --- | --- | --- | --- |
|  | 1 | 2 | 3 | 4 | 5 |
| *Income Statements* | | | | | |
| Revenue | — | — | — | $2,000 | — |
| Cost of goods sold | — | — | — | (1,100) | — |
| Purchasing power loss | — | — | $ (200) | — | — |
| Net income | — | — | $ (200) | $ 900 | — |
| *Balance Sheets* | | | | | |
| Cash | $3,300 | $2,200 | $2,000 | $4,000 | $2,750 |
| Inventory | — | 1,100 | 1,100 | — | 1,250 |
| Total Assets | $3,300 | $3,300 | $3,100 | $4,000 | $4,000 |
| Capital | $3,300 | $3,300 | $3,100 | $4,000 | $4,000 |

General price-level index: Step 1, 100; Step 2, 100; Step 3, 110; Step 4, 110; and Step 5, 110.

dollars of one price level (the cost of goods sold) are subtracted from dollars of another price level (the revenue). Since these dollars do not have the same purchasing power, subtracting one from the other may not be very relevant. In contrast, the constant purchasing power income is measured by comparing two amounts measured in dollars of the same purchasing power.

Comparing Steps 1 and 4 in the historical cost balance sheets in Exhibit 24-1 raises similar issues. The capital in Step 4 includes $3,000 original capital (and $1,000 retained earnings). However, Step 1 also shows original capital of $3,000. Does this reflect reality? If it is agreed that the purpose of dollars is to purchase goods and services, then to show the contributed capital as $3,000 in both balance sheets may be misleading. The owners of the company contributed $3,000 of purchasing power in Step 1, when the company was formed. However, in Step 4 an appropriate measure of the capital contributed is in terms of the dollars existing at the time the financial statements are prepared. In these terms, the owners have contributed $3,300 of purchasing power. The same argument may be applied to inventory. Although the inventory cost $1,000, that $1,000 is equivalent to $1,100 of purchasing power after the price-level increase. Thus, the historical cost/constant purchasing power financial statements do not reflect current value. They simply adjust the historical costs for changes in the purchasing power, or value, of the dollar that have occurred since the historical cost was recorded.

### Current Cost/Constant Purchasing Power Financial Statements

The arguments in favor of current cost financial statements and of historical cost/constant purchasing power statements are entirely separate. Current cost financial statements do *not* reflect the changing value of the dollar, and historical cost/constant purchasing power statements do *not* recognize the current cost of assets. However, the two concepts may be combined so that financial statements prepared on the current cost basis are adjusted for changes in the general price level. Financial statements prepared on this basis are illustrated in Exhibit 24-4.

The financial statements in Steps 1 and 2 are prepared on a current cost/constant purchasing power basis in terms of the price level existing *after* the rise in the general price level. That is, they are adjusted to reflect the 10% rise in the price level in the same manner as the historical cost/constant purchasing power statements in Exhibit 24-3. In Step 3, the rise in the general price level is recognized through the purchasing-power loss from holding cash. In addition, the unrealized holding gain on the inventory is recognized, but in this situation it is $150. This is the difference between the current cost of the inventory ($1,250) and the constant purchasing power cost of the inventory ($1,100). In Step 4, the inventory is sold and the cost of goods sold is recorded at the current cost of $1,250.

The advantages of this method may be understood by considering the income statement in Step 4 and by comparing the balance sheets in Steps 2 and 5. The $750 operating income recognized in Step 4 is the real increase in value for the company for exactly the same reasons as discussed earlier for the unadjusted current cost financial statements in Exhibit 24-2. A comparison of the balance sheets in Steps 2 and 5 shows an increase in value of $550 since the cash has increased by $550 and one unit of inventory is held in each case. The $550 increase is the operating income of $750 in Step 4 less the purchasing power loss of $200 in Step 3. The relationship between the increase in wealth and the income statement is clearer if the holding

---

**EXHIBIT 24-4**

## HALLAS COMPANY

Current Cost/Constant Purchasing Power Financial Statements

| | Step | | | | |
|---|---|---|---|---|---|
| | 1 | 2 | 3 | 4 | 5 |
| *Income Statements* | | | | | |
| Revenue | — | — | — | $2,000 | — |
| Cost of goods sold | — | — | — | (1,250) | — |
| Operating income | — | — | — | $ 750 | — |
| Unrealized holding gain | — | — | $ 150 | (150) | — |
| Realized holding gain | — | — | — | 150 | — |
| Purchasing power loss | — | — | (200) | — | — |
| Net income | — | — | $ (50) | $ 750 | — |
| *Balance Sheets* | | | | | |
| Cash | $3,300 | $2,200 | $2,000 | $4,000 | $2,750 |
| Inventory | — | 1,100 | 1,250 | — | 1,250 |
| Total Assets | $3,300 | $3,300 | $3,250 | $4,000 | $4,000 |
| Capital | $3,300 | $3,300 | $3,250 | $4,000 | $4,000 |

gains are omitted from the income statement, which lends support to those accountants who advocate such exclusion.

## ADDITIONAL MEASUREMENT ISSUES

The previous section dealt with a simple example involving current cost and constant purchasing power financial statements. Several additional issues related to measuring constant purchasing power amounts and current costs are discussed in this section.

### Constant Purchasing Power Adjustments

As emphasized previously, the purpose of constant purchasing power adjustments is to account for changes in the size of the measuring unit used in financial statements—that is, the dollar. This section discusses some general characteristics of the constant purchasing power adjustment process in terms of the historical cost financial statements, rather than in terms of the current cost financial statements.

#### General Price-Level Indexes

When constant purchasing power financial statements (or selected disclosures) are prepared, the unadjusted amounts are adjusted by using a general price-level index. A **general price-level index** is a measure of the relationship between money and its ability to purchase a wide variety of goods and services. For example, if it takes $100 to purchase a particular combination of goods and services one year and $120 to purchase the identical goods and services in the next year, the price level has risen by 20% and the purchasing power of the dollar has fallen. This rise in the price level may be expressed as an index. If the year in which it took $100 to make the purchases is used as the *base* year and assigned an index value of 100, the next year's index is 120. But suppose that a year in which it took only $80 to purchase the same goods and services had been used as the base and assigned an index value of 100. The index for the two years when it took $100 and $120 to purchase the same goods and services then would be 125 (100 ÷ 80 = 1.25) and 150 (120 ÷ 80 = 1.50). Note that the increase between the second two years is still 20%, since 20% of 125 is 25 and 125 plus 25 equals 150.

The computation of a general price-level index is a very complex problem. What goods and services should be included? How are the prices measured to give a national average? How are changes in taste included? How are technological changes included? Numerous general price-level indexes are available that answer these questions in different ways. Until *FASB Statement No. 33*, there was a consensus that the most appropriate measure of changing prices for use in general price-level financial statements was the GNP Implicit Price Deflator. *Accounting Research Study No. 6,* the APB, and the earlier FASB deliberations all considered it the most appropriate index. However, *FASB Statement No. 89* requires the use of the Consumer Price Index for All Urban Consumers (CPI-U) because it is more readily available than the GNP Implicit Price Deflator, it is prepared on a monthly basis, and it is considered by the FASB to be a better indicator of the effects of inflation for financial statement users who normally are concerned with the consumption of end products. Exhibit 24-5 shows the recent history of the Consumer Price Index for All Urban Consumers and its measurement of inflation.

*Adjustment of Historical Dollars*

The conversion of historical dollars to the purchasing power of the current period by means of a price-level index is a simple mathematical procedure. Dividing the index of the current period by the index of the period in which the historical dollar was

---

**EXHIBIT 24-5**

## CONSUMER PRICE INDEX AND THE MEASUREMENT OF INFLATION (1982-4 = 100)

| Year | Consumer Price Index for All Urban Consumers | Annual Inflation Rate | Year | Consumer Price Index for All Urban Consumers | Annual Inflation Rate |
|------|------|------|------|------|------|
| 1970 | 38.8 | 5.7% | 1981 | 90.9 | 10.3% |
| 1971 | 40.5 | 4.4% | 1982 | 96.5 | 6.2% |
| 1972 | 41.8 | 3.2% | 1983 | 99.6 | 3.2% |
| 1973 | 44.4 | 6.2% | 1984 | 103.9 | 4.3% |
| 1974 | 49.3 | 11.0% | 1985 | 107.6 | 3.6% |
| 1975 | 53.8 | 9.1% | 1986 | 109.6 | 1.9% |
| 1976 | 56.9 | 5.8% | 1987 | 113.6 | 3.6% |
| 1977 | 60.6 | 6.5% | 1988 | 118.3 | 4.1% |
| 1978 | 65.2 | 7.6% | 1989 | 124.0 | 4.8% |
| 1979 | 72.6 | 11.3% | 1990 | 130.7 | 5.4% |
| 1980 | 82.4 | 13.5% | 1991 | 136.2 | 4.2% |

originally recorded provides a measure of the relative price change. Multiplying the historical dollar amount by this relative price change gives the constant purchasing power dollar amount. This computation can be stated as follows:

$$\text{Constant Purchasing Power Dollars} = \text{Historical Dollars} \times \frac{\text{Current Period Price-Level Index}}{\text{Historical Price-Level Index}}$$

For example, suppose land was purchased for $24,000 when the price index was 120 and that the index is now 150. The cost of the land in constant purchasing power dollars is $30,000 [$24,000 × (150 ÷ 120)].

The computation of the adjusted amounts is made slightly more complex by considering the exact time in each year that the historical transaction took place. Since price indexes are not published daily, exact adjustment is not possible. However, since the CPI-U is published monthly, the historical index used in the preparation of constant purchasing power information is the index for the month in which the historical dollars originally were measured. The current index depends on the financial statement. The use of the average index for the year is most appropriate for the income statement and the cash flow statement, which measure flows over a period of time. The use of the index at the end of the year is most appropriate for the balance sheet, which measures amounts at the end of the year. The average index is used for the disclosures encouraged by *FASB Statement No. 89.*

### Purchasing-Power Gain or Loss on Net Monetary Items

Holding cash during periods of *inflation* results in a purchasing-power *loss*. If $100 can buy a certain quantity of goods and services, and prices later rise, the $100 can then buy fewer goods and services and purchasing power has been lost. The same principle applies to all **monetary assets**. A monetary asset is defined as "money or a claim to receive a sum of money, the amount of which is fixed or determinable without reference to future prices of specific goods or services."[1] In addition to cash, principal monetary assets are accounts receivable and notes receivable.

The reverse effect occurs with **monetary liabilities**. Since an obligation exists to *repay* a fixed amount of dollars in the future, inflation reduces the purchasing power of the dollars necessary to repay these liabilities, thus resulting in a purchasing-power *gain*. Principal monetary liabilities include accounts payable, notes payable, and bonds payable.

Suppose Peter Cameron borrows $1,000 from a bank when the price index is 120. He has a monetary liability of $1,000 and the bank has a monetary asset of $1,000. Disregarding interest, if the money is repaid when the price index is 150, Peter Cameron has a general purchasing-power gain. The equivalent purchasing power of the $1,000 when it is repaid is $1,250 [$1,000 × (150 ÷ 120)] and since he only has to repay the $1,000, he has a gain of $250. Conversely, the bank has a general purchasing-power loss because it has received $1,000 in full payment of a historical debt that now has a current purchasing-power equivalent of $1,250.

Monetary assets and liabilities are combined to derive **net monetary items** on which gains or losses from inflation are computed. The FASB calls these gains and losses purchasing-power gains and losses. (They are also known as *monetary gains and losses,* or *general price-level gains and losses.*) **Purchasing-power gains result**

---

1. "Financial Reporting and Changing Prices," *FASB Statement of Financial Accounting Standards No. 89* (Stamford, Conn.: FASB, 1986), par. 44.

from holding negative net monetary items (liabilities exceed assets) and **purchasing-power losses result from holding positive net monetary items** (assets exceed liabilities) **during periods of rising general prices.** Therefore, it is critical to the calculation of the purchasing-power gain or loss that the monetary assets and liabilities be correctly identified. Exhibit 24-6 lists selected items found in the balance sheet and their classification as monetary or nonmonetary.

In contrast to monetary items, holders of **nonmonetary assets and liabilities**

do not gain or lose general purchasing power simply as a result of general price-level changes. If the price of a nonmonetary item changes at the same rate as the general price level no gain or loss of general purchasing power results. Holders of nonmonetary assets and liabilities gain or lose general purchasing power if the specific price of the item owned or owed rises or falls faster or slower than the change in the general price level.[2]

Historical cost financial statements usually report gains and losses on nonmonetary items only when the items are *sold*. Gains and losses from *holding* nonmonetary items are recognized in the period of the sale by inclusion in the profit or loss from the sale.[3]

## EXHIBIT 24-6

### CLASSIFICATION OF ITEMS AS MONETARY OR NONMONETARY

|  | Monetary | Nonmonetary |
|---|:---:|:---:|
| Cash on hand and in banks | X |  |
| Foreign currency on hand and claims to foreign currency | X |  |
| Receivables | X |  |
| Allowance for doubtful accounts | X |  |
| Inventories |  | X |
| Inventories produced under fixed price contracts | X |  |
| Prepaid expenses that are claims to future services |  | X |
| Prepaid interest | X |  |
| Investments in common stocks (at fair value) |  | X |
| Investments in bonds (at fair value) |  | X |
| Investments in bonds (at amortized cost) | X |  |
| Property, plant, and equipment |  | X |
| Accumulated depreciation |  | X |
| Cash surrender value of life insurance | X |  |
| Deferred income taxes | X |  |
| Intangibles |  | X |
| Payables and accrued expenses | X |  |
| Bonds payable and other long-term debt | X |  |
| Unamortized premium or discount on debt | X |  |

*Source: FASB Statement No. 89, par. 96, as modified.*

---

2.  "Financial Statements Restated for General Price-Level Changes," *APB Statement No. 3* (New York: AICPA, 1969), par. 19.

3.  Current cost financial statements report (holding) gains and losses on nonmonetary items in the period in which the gain or loss occurs. When current cost financial statements are adjusted for general price-level changes, the holding gain or loss is adjusted for the purchasing-power gain or loss from holding the nonmonetary items. For example, in Exhibit 24-4, the unrealized holding gain on the inventory in Step 3 is $150. This is the increase in the current cost of $250, less the increase that results from inflation of $100 (10% × $1,000).

## MEASUREMENT OF CURRENT COST

The two most significant current cost adjustments are usually made to inventory and property, plant, and equipment. The FASB defines the current cost of *inventory* as the current cost of purchasing or producing the goods concerned, and the current cost of *property, plant,* or *equipment* as the current cost of acquiring the same service potential (indicated by operating costs and physical output capacity) provided by the asset owned.[4] The current cost of property, plant, and equipment may be determined by either (1) the current cost of a used asset of the same age and in the same condition as the asset owned, (2) the current cost of a new asset with the same service potential as the used asset had when new, less a deduction for depreciation, or (3) the current cost of a new asset with a different service potential, less a deduction for depreciation, and adjusted for the cost of the difference in service potential due to differences in life, output capacity, and nature of service, including any operating cost savings.

Three alternative methods of measuring the current costs of inventory and property, plant, and equipment have been suggested:

1. *Direct pricing:* Current invoice prices, vendors' price lists, other quotations or estimates (e.g., appraisals), or standard manufacturing costs.

2. *Functional or unit pricing:* The estimation of construction (or acquisition) costs per unit (such as per square foot of building space) and multiplication by the number of units in the asset being measured.

3. *Revision of historical acquisition cost (indexation):* Using (a) externally (independently) generated specific price indexes for the class of goods or services being measured, or (b) internally generated indexes of cost changes for the class of goods or services being measured.

A company might choose any one of the methods for any asset or liability. Generally direct pricing is used for inventory and readily available property, plant, and equipment such as office equipment. Functional, or unit, pricing is used to estimate the current cost of a complete productive asset such as a building or a chemical plant. A specific price index could be used for any asset, and often it is the simplest to use because once the index for the asset is selected, the adjustment process is arithmetically simple. Exhibit 24-7 lists the principal techniques used by a sample of companies to measure the current cost of fixed assets while *FASB Statement No. 33* was in effect.[5]

## THE CONSTANT PURCHASING POWER ADJUSTMENT PROCESS

Now that we have examined the basic principles of constant purchasing power and current cost adjustments, along with the related measurement issues, our discussion moves to comprehensive adjustments. This section discusses the *comprehensive* process of adjusting the 1995 historical cost financial statements of the Foley Company shown in Exhibit 24-8 (the financial statements for 1996 are discussed later) to constant purchasing power. The next section discusses the comprehensive current cost adjustment process.

---

4. *FASB Statement No. 89, op. cit.,* par. 17 and 18.
5. Functional pricing was included in *FASB Statement No. 33* as a method of calculating current cost, but is excluded from *FASB Statement No. 89.*

**EXHIBIT 24-7**

## PRINCIPAL TECHNIQUES USED TO MEASURE THE CURRENT COST OF FIXED ASSETS

| Asset Classification | Indexation | | | Analytical Techniques | | | | | | |
| --- | --- | --- | --- | --- | --- | --- | --- | --- | --- | --- |
| | Specific Price Indexes | CPI | Total Indexation | Direct Pricing | Functional Pricing | Unit Pricing | Appraisals | Assessed Valuations For Tax Purposes | Other[a] | Total Analytical |
| Land | 22% | 27% | 49% | 6% | 0% | 2% | 24% | 14% | 5% | 51% |
| Buildings | 73 | 2 | 75 | 1 | 1 | 14 | 4 | 0 | 5 | 25 |
| Machinery and equipment | 84 | 1 | 85 | 4 | 4 | 1 | 1 | 0 | 5 | 15 |
| Vehicles | 76 | 5 | 81 | 13 | 1 | 1 | 1 | 0 | 3 | 19 |
| Furniture and fixtures | 84 | 7 | 91 | 3 | 0 | 2 | 0 | 0 | 4 | 9 |
| Other fixed assets[b] | 30 | 3 | 33 | 33 | 5 | 12 | 5 | 0 | 12 | 67 |

a. Includes indexation of prior-year current cost amount determined using an analytical method.
b. Includes fixed assets such as airplanes, marine vessels, and assets leased to others.

*Source:* "Financial Reporting and Changing Prices—A Survey of Preparers' Views and Practices," *Arthur Young and Company* (New York: Arthur Young and Company, 1981).

---

**EXHIBIT 24-8**

**FOLEY COMPANY**

Historical Cost Financial Statements for 1995 and 1996

### Comparative Income Statements

| | For Year Ended December 31 | | | |
|---|---|---|---|---|
| | 1995 | | 1996 | |
| Sales | | $100,000 | | $110,000 |
| Cost of goods sold | | | | |
| Beginning inventory | $15,000 | | $25,000 | |
| Purchases | 50,000 | | 70,000 | |
| Cost of goods available | $65,000 | | $95,000 | |
| Ending inventory | (25,000) | | (35,000) | |
| Cost of goods sold | | (40,000) | | (60,000) |
| Gross profit | | $ 60,000 | | $ 50,000 |
| Operating expenses | | | | |
| Wages and salaries | $20,000 | | $25,000 | |
| Depreciation | 10,000 | | 10,000 | |
| Interest expense | 4,000 | | 4,000 | |
| Total expenses | | (34,000) | | (39,000) |
| Income before income taxes | | $ 26,000 | | $ 11,000 |
| Income tax expense | | (7,800) | | (3,300) |
| Net Income | | $ 18,200 | | $ 7,700 |

### Comparative Balance Sheets

| | December 31 | | |
|---|---|---|---|
| | 1994 | 1995 | 1996 |
| **Assets** | | | |
| Cash | $ 35,000 | $ 48,200 | $ 45,900 |
| Accounts receivable | — | 10,000 | 20,000 |
| Inventory | 15,000 | 25,000 | 35,000 |
| Building and equipment | 50,000 | 50,000 | 50,000 |
| Less: Accumulated depreciation | — | (10,000) | (20,000) |
| Total Assets | $100,000 | $123,200 | $130,900 |
| **Liabilities and Stockholders' Equity** | | | |
| Accounts payable | $ 10,000 | $ 20,000 | $ 25,000 |
| Bonds payable | 40,000 | 40,000 | 40,000 |
| Capital stock | 50,000 | 50,000 | 50,000 |
| Retained earnings | — | 13,200 | 15,900 |
| Total Liabilities and Stockholders' Equity | $100,000 | $123,200 | $130,900 |

General Price-Level Index: December 1994, 120; September 1995, 132; December 1995, 136; average for 1995, 128; September 1996, 148; December 1996, 152; average for 1996, 144.

The Foley Company was formed on December 31, 1994. It operated successfully during 1995 and decided to prepare historical cost/constant purchasing power financial statements at the end of 1995, as shown in Exhibit 24-9. Dividends of $5,000 were paid on December 31. The income statement and the balance sheets are all adjusted to the average price level for 1995 when the index is 128 (the average price level is used because companies preparing the disclosures under *FASB Statement No. 89* use the average price level). Following the discussion of the adjustments for 1995, the adjustment of the financial statements for 1996 and the presentation of the 1995 financial statements in 1996 for comparative purposes are discussed. It should be noted that this is an illustration of constant purchasing power adjustments to historical cost financial statements. Adjustment of current cost financial statements for changes in the general price level utilizes the same principles. As discussed earlier in the chapter, constant purchasing power adjustments are based on the equation:

$$\frac{\text{Constant Purchasing}}{\text{Power Dollars}} = \text{Historical Dollars} \times \frac{\text{Current Period Price-Level Index}}{\text{Historical Price-Level Index}}$$

## Income Statement Adjustments (First Year)

The adjustments to the 1995 income statement items (shown in parentheses in Exhibit 24-9) are discussed in the following sections.

*Sales*
Sales are made throughout the year. Ideally, the adjustment process would utilize the price level at the time each sale was made, but such detailed information generally is not available. Therefore, a simplifying assumption usually is made that sales occur evenly throughout the year and that the average price level for the year may be used. An alternative for a company that has a seasonal business is to adjust the sales of each period by the price level of that period. In our example, the sales do not need adjustment because it is assumed that they occur evenly throughout the year. The calculation of the constant purchasing power amount may be stated as follows:

Sales     [$100,000 × (128 ÷ 128)] = $100,000

*Cost of Goods Sold*
It is assumed that the Foley Company is using the FIFO inventory cost flow assumption. Since the beginning inventory for 1995 was purchased when the company was formed, it is adjusted for the 120 price level of December 1994. The purchases are assumed to be made throughout the year, and so were made at the average index for the year. The ending inventory is adjusted based on the date it was purchased. It is assumed in this example that the purchases included in the ending inventory were purchased in September 1995, when the index was 132.

| | | |
|---|---|---|
| Beginning Inventory | $15,000 × (128 ÷ 120) = | $ 16,000 |
| Purchases | 50,000 × (128 ÷ 128) = | 50,000 |
| Cost of Goods Available | | $ 66,000 |
| Ending Inventory | 25,000 × (128 ÷ 132) = | (24,242) |
| Cost of Goods Sold | | = $ 41,758 |

It should be recognized that these adjustments depend on the assumptions made about the timing of the purchases and the inventory costing method used, and that

**EXHIBIT 24-9**

## FOLEY COMPANY

Historical Cost/Constant Purchasing Power Financial Statements for 1995 (Avg. CPI-U = 128)

*Income Statement*
*For Year Ended December 31, 1995*

| | | | |
|---|---|---|---|
| Sales | [$100,000 × (128 ÷ 128)] | | $100,000 |
| Cost of goods sold | | | |
| Beginning inventory | [$ 15,000 × (128 ÷ 120)] | $16,000 | |
| Purchases | [$ 50,000 × (128 ÷ 128)] | 50,000 | |
| Cost of goods available | | $66,000 | |
| Ending inventory | [$ 25,000 × (128 ÷ 132)] | (24,242) | |
| Cost of goods sold | | | (41,758) |
| Gross profit | | | $ 58,242 |
| Operating expenses | | | |
| Wages and salaries | [$ 20,000 × (128 ÷ 128)] | $20,000 | |
| Depreciation | [$ 10,000 × (128 ÷ 120)] | 10,667 | |
| Interest expense | [$  4,000 × (128 ÷ 128)] | 4,000 | |
| Total expenses | | | (34,667) |
| Income before income taxes | | | $ 23,575 |
| Income tax expense | [$  7,800 × (128 ÷ 128)] | | (7,800) |
| Income from continuing operations | | | $ 15,775 |
| Purchasing power gain | | | 812 |
| Net Income | | | $ 16,587 |

*Statement of Retained Earnings*
*For Year Ended December 31, 1995*

| | | |
|---|---|---|
| Retained earnings, January 1, 1995 | $    0 | |
| Plus: Net income | 16,587 | |
| | $16,587 | |
| Less: Dividends [$5,000 × (128 ÷ 136)] | (4,706) | |
| Retained earnings, December 31, 1995 | $11,881 | |

*Comparative Balance Sheets*
December 31

| | 1994 | | 1995 | |
|---|---|---|---|---|
| **Assets** | | | | |
| Cash | [$35,000 × (128 ÷ 120)] | $ 37,334* | [$48,200 × (128 ÷ 136)] | $ 45,365 |
| Accounts receivable | — | | [$10,000 × (128 ÷ 136)] | 9,412 |
| Inventory | [$15,000 × (128 ÷ 120)] | 16,000 | [$25,000 × (128 ÷ 132)] | 24,242 |
| Building and equipment | [$50,000 × (128 ÷ 120)] | 53,333 | [$50,000 × (128 ÷ 120)] | 53,333 |
| Less: Accumulated depreciation | — | | [$10,000 × (128 ÷ 120)] | (10,667) |
| Total Assets | | $106,667 | | $121,685 |
| **Liabilities and Stockholders' Equity** | | | | |
| Accounts payable | [$10,000 × (128 ÷ 120)] | $ 10,667 | [$20,000 × (128 ÷ 136)] | $ 18,824 |
| Bonds payable | [$40,000 × (128 ÷ 120)] | 42,667 | [$40,000 × (128 ÷ 136)] | 37,647 |
| Capital stock | [$50,000 × (128 ÷ 120)] | 53,333 | [$50,000 × (128 ÷ 120)] | 53,333 |
| Retained earnings | — | | | 11,881 |
| Total Liabilities and Stockholders' Equity | | $106,667 | | $121,685 |

* Adjusted for a $1 rounding error.

the numerical answers would change as those assumptions are changed. For example, if the Foley Company were using the LIFO inventory cost flow assumption, the following adjustments would be necessary to compute cost of goods sold:

| | | |
|---|---|---|
| Beginning Inventory | $15,000 × (128 ÷ 120) = | $ 16,000 |
| Purchases | 50,000 × (128 ÷ 128) = | 50,000 |
| Cost of Goods Available | | $ 66,000 |
| Ending Inventory   $25,000 $\left\{ \begin{array}{l} \$15,000 \times (128 \div 120) \\ \$10,000 \times (128 \div 128) \end{array} \right\}$ | | (26,000) |
| Cost of Goods Sold | | $ 40,000 |

The procedure under the LIFO method is more complex because the LIFO inventory layers must be accounted for at the price level appropriate to the time of acquisition. It is assumed in this example that the increases in the layers are made at the average price level for the year.

*Wages and Salaries*
The wages and salaries are assumed to be paid evenly throughout the year and so the average index is used.

Wages and Salaries     $20,000 × (128 ÷ 128) = $20,000

If bonuses or commissions were paid once a year, that portion of the expense would be adjusted by the index appropriate for that time of year.

*Depreciation*
Since depreciation is the allocation of the historical cost of the asset, the price-level index for the date of *purchase* of the asset is used and *not* the current period average index.

Depreciation     $10,000 × (128 ÷ 120) = $10,667

When companies have assets purchased at different times, the price-level adjusted depreciation expense for each asset is based on the price-level index for the period when the asset was purchased. In such situations, "layers" of price-level adjusted depreciation for the individual assets are computed using the process previously described and summed to determine the total price-level adjusted depreciation.

*Interest Expense and Income Tax Expense*
The interest and income taxes are assumed to be paid throughout the year; therefore, no adjustment is necessary, although the calculation may be stated as follows:

| | |
|---|---|
| Interest | $4,000 × (128 ÷ 128) = $4,000 |
| Income Tax | $7,800 × (128 ÷ 128) = $7,800 |

*Purchasing-Power Gain or Loss*
Purchasing-power gains and losses were discussed earlier in the chapter. The calculation of the gain or loss for the Foley Company's comprehensively adjusted financial statements is considerably more complex since it requires consideration of the monetary assets and liabilities held throughout the year, and also the changes in these assets and liabilities. The schedule to compute the purchasing-power gain or loss is shown in Exhibit 24-10. Effectively, a statement of the change in *net* monetary items

(monetary assets less monetary liabilities) is required in which transactions that increased and decreased net monetary items are added to and subtracted from beginning net monetary items. The beginning net monetary items are determined from the beginning monetary assets (cash and accounts receivable) of $35,000 less the beginning monetary liabilities (accounts payable and bonds payable) of $50,000. The liabilities exceed the assets so that the company has *negative* beginning net monetary items (that is, net monetary liabilities) of $15,000. To this beginning balance are added the transactions that caused an increase (inflow) in net monetary items. Sales are the only transactions of this type for the Foley Company, but in more complex situations other increases in net monetary items are included, such as the sale of used property, plant, and equipment or of investments, and the issuance of common stock. Transactions that caused a decrease (outflow) in net monetary items are then subtracted. For the Foley Company, these include purchases, wages and salaries, interest, income tax, and dividends. In more complex situations, other outflows of net monetary items might include the purchase of property, plant, and equipment, or of investments in stock. As a check, the unadjusted ending net monetary items ($1,800) obtained from the beginning net monetary items plus the increases less the decreases must equal the net monetary items computed from the unadjusted ending balance sheet.

To gain a better understanding of the relationship between the beginning and ending net monetary items and the changes in these items on a historical cost basis, refer to the income statement in Exhibit 24-8. For example, all sales, whether for cash or on credit, increase monetary items because both cash and accounts receivable are monetary assets. Similarly, all purchases decrease net monetary items, whether acquired for cash or on credit.

---

### EXHIBIT 24-10

**FOLEY COMPANY**

Purchasing-Power Gain or Loss
For Year Ended December 31, 1995

|  | Historical Cost | Adjustment | Constant Purchasing Power |
|---|---|---|---|
| Beginning net monetary items | $ (15,000) | × (128 ÷ 120) = | $ (16,000) |
| Sales | 100,000 | × (128 ÷ 128) = | 100,000 |
| Purchases | (50,000) | × (128 ÷ 128) = | (50,000) |
| Wages and salaries | (20,000) | × (128 ÷ 128) = | (20,000) |
| Interest | (4,000) | × (128 ÷ 128) = | (4,000) |
| Income tax | (7,800) | × (128 ÷ 128) = | (7,800) |
| Dividends | (5,000) | × (128 ÷ 136) = | (4,706) |
| Ending net monetary items unadjusted | $ (1,800) | | |
| Constant purchasing power ending balance (at average price level) | | | $ (2,506) |
| Historical ending balance adjusted to average price level [$(1,800) × (128 ÷ 136)] | | | (1,694) |
| Purchasing-power gain (at average price level) | | | $ (812) |

To determine the purchasing-power gain or loss shown in Exhibit 24-10, the beginning unadjusted net monetary items as well as changes in unadjusted net monetary items are adjusted to constant purchasing power by using the appropriate indexes. That is, as noted earlier the numerator of the fraction is the average price-level index for the year and the denominator is the historical index for the time when the measurement of the historical dollar amount occurred. This enables the ending net monetary items in terms of adjusted (average) dollars to be calculated.

In Exhibit 24-10, the historical ending net negative monetary items of $1,800 are measured in year-end purchasing power (CPI-U = 136), whereas the constant purchasing power ending negative balance of $2,506 is measured in average purchasing power (CPI-U = 128). To complete the computation of the purchasing-power gain, the historical ending negative balance of $1,800 is adjusted to the average purchasing power of the period ($1,694) by multiplying times (128 ÷ 136). The purchasing-power gain of $812 (measured in terms of the average purchasing power of the period) is computed by comparing the constant purchasing power ending balance to the adjusted historical ending balance.

The purchasing-power gain completes the adjusted income statement in Exhibit 24-9, which shows a net income of $16,587. If the Foley Company had held positive net monetary items (i.e., monetary assets greater than monetary liabilities) during the period as prices increased, it would have had a purchasing-power loss.

## Comparative Balance Sheets (First Year)

The company was formed at the end of 1994, and so all amounts in the December 31, 1994 balance sheet are stated in dollars at that time. When this balance sheet is presented at the end of 1995, each item has to be "rolled forward" to the average price level for 1995. The historical cost balance sheet for December 31, 1995 contains amounts in terms of varying dollar values, depending on when the underlying transaction occurred. Each of these amounts also has to be adjusted to the average price level for 1995. The adjustment of each item in the two balance sheets is discussed in the following section and shown in parentheses in Exhibit 24-9.

*Cash and Accounts Receivable*
Cash and accounts receivable are the two *monetary* assets of the Foley Company. The 1995 historical cost ending balances are in terms of the price level at the end of 1995. Therefore, they have to be adjusted to the average price level of 1995. Also the historical cost balances in the beginning balance sheet are stated in terms of the price level at the end of 1994 and have to be adjusted to the average price level of 1995.

*December 31, 1994*
  Cash                  $35,000 × (128 ÷ 120) = $37,334*

*December 31, 1995*
  Cash                  $48,200 × (128 ÷ 136) = $45,365
  Accounts receivable   $10,000 × (128 ÷ 136) = $ 9,412

* Adjusted for a $1 rounding error.

*Inventory*
The adjustment of the inventory was discussed as part of the adjustment of cost of goods sold (based on a FIFO cost flow assumption).

December 31, 1994    $15,000 × (128 ÷ 120) = $16,000
December 31, 1995    $25,000 × (128 ÷ 132) = $24,242

If it is assumed that a LIFO cost flow assumption is used, the ending inventory would be computed as illustrated for the calculation of cost of goods sold under LIFO.

## Building and Equipment

The building and equipment were purchased when the company was formed on December 31, 1994. Therefore, the building and equipment on the beginning balance sheet, and the building and equipment and accumulated depreciation on the ending balance sheet are adjusted from the December 1994 price level to the average price level for 1995.

Building and equipment $\quad\quad\quad\quad$ $\$50,000 \times (128 \div 120) = \$53,333$
Accumulated depreciation, 12/31/95 $\quad$ $\$10,000 \times (128 \div 120) = \$10,667$

Note that the 1995 depreciation expense calculated earlier as $\$10,667$ also can be computed as one-fifth of the adjusted cost of the asset of $\$53,333$.

## Accounts Payable and Bonds Payable

Accounts payable and bonds payable are the two *monetary* liabilities of the Foley Company. The 1995 historical cost ending balances are in terms of the price level at the end of 1995. Therefore, they have to be adjusted to the average price level of 1995. Also the historical cost balances in the beginning balance sheet are stated in terms of the price level at the end of 1994 and have to be adjusted to the average price level of 1995 in the same manner as shown for cash and accounts receivable.

*December 31, 1994*
$\quad$ Accounts payable $\quad$ $\$10,000 \times (128 \div 120) = \$10,667$
$\quad$ Bonds payable $\quad\quad$ $\$40,000 \times (128 \div 120) = \$42,667$

*December 31, 1995*
$\quad$ Accounts payable $\quad$ $\$20,000 \times (128 \div 136) = \$18,824$
$\quad$ Bonds payable $\quad\quad$ $\$40,000 \times (128 \div 136) = \$37,647$

## Capital Stock

The capital stock of the Foley Company was issued when the company was formed on December 31, 1994, and thus is adjusted to the 1995 price level in both the beginning and ending balance sheet.

Capital Stock $\quad\quad$ $\$50,000 \times (128 \div 120) = \$53,333$

Additional paid-in capital and preferred stock accounts would be adjusted in the same manner. Treasury stock would have to be adjusted according to the date it was acquired.

## Retained Earnings

The ending retained earnings is computed in the same manner as for historical cost statements. That is, the net income of $\$16,587$, on an adjusted basis, is added to the previous balance of retained earnings on an adjusted basis ($\$0$ in this case). From the $\$16,587$ subtotal, the dividends are deducted. The dividends of $\$5,000$ were paid at the end of the year and therefore are measured in end-of-the-year dollars. They have to be adjusted to the average price level of the year, and the adjusted amount ($\$4,706$) is subtracted to give the ending retained earnings balance for 1995 of $\$11,881$.

It should be noted that the ending retained earnings balance can be computed in this manner because the complete information for adjustments since the formation of the company is available. When the adjustment process is started after the company has been in business for some time, sufficient information about past periods may not be available to permit the adjustment of the retained earnings balance in the first year in which price-level adjusted statements are prepared. In that case, retained earnings is computed as a "balancing amount"—the amount necessary to make the balance sheet balance. However, in later years, the ending retained earnings balance can be computed as the beginning balance plus the net income less the dividends (all on an adjusted basis). It should also be noted that if the company had a retained earnings balance other than $0, this amount would have been rolled forward by multiplying it by a factor of 128/120 on both the beginning balance sheet and the retained earnings statement.

## Financial Statement Adjustments (Second Year)

Exhibits 24-8 and 24-11 show, respectively, the historical cost and historical cost/constant purchasing power financial statements for 1996. The constant purchasing power financial statements in Exhibit 24-11 are presented in terms of the average general price-level index for 1996, which is 144. Dividends of $5,000 were paid on December 31, 1996. The calculations are shown in parentheses in Exhibit 24-11. The process that is followed in preparing Exhibit 24-11 is the same as for the 1995 financial statements, but special attention should be paid to the following items.

### December 31, 1995 Balance Sheet

For comparative purposes, all items on the December 31, 1995 balance sheet are rolled forward to the average price level for 1996. Since the balance sheet already has been adjusted to 1995 average dollars, the adjustment is accomplished by multiplying each of the *adjusted* amounts in the December 31, 1995 balance sheet (from Exhibit 24-9) by the factor:

$$\frac{\text{1996 Average Index}}{\text{1995 Average Index}} \quad \text{or} \quad \frac{144}{128}$$

The following discussion relates to particular items included in the income statement for 1996 and the 1996 *ending* balance sheet.

### Cost of Goods Sold

The beginning inventory was purchased in September 1995 and thus has to be raised from the price level of 132 to 144. Again it is assumed that purchases were made at the average price level for 1996 and that the ending inventory was purchased in September 1996, or at an index of 148.

### Building and Equipment, Accumulated Depreciation, and Depreciation Expense

Since the building and equipment were purchased on December 31, 1994 the price-level index for that time continues to be used for the adjustment of the cost and the accumulated depreciation. Similarly, depreciation expense is measured in those same historical dollars and is adjusted to the current index in the same way.

### Capital Stock

Capital stock is measured in terms of historical costs at December 31, 1994 and therefore has to be adjusted from the index at that time, 120, to the current index of 144.

**EXHIBIT 24-11**

## FOLEY COMPANY

### Historical Cost/Constant Purchasing Power Financial Statements for 1996 (Avg. CPI-U = 144)

*Income Statement*
*For Year Ended December 31, 1996*

| | | | |
|---|---|---:|---:|
| Sales | $110,000 × (144 ÷ 144) | | $110,000 |
| Cost of goods sold | | | |
|   Beginning inventory | $ 25,000 × (144 ÷ 132) | $27,273 | |
|   Purchases | $ 70,000 × (144 ÷ 144) | 70,000 | |
|   Cost of goods available | | $97,273 | |
|   Ending inventory | $ 35,000 × (144 ÷ 148) | (34,054) | |
|   Cost of goods sold | | | (63,219) |
| Gross profit | | | $ 46,781 |
| Operating expenses | | | |
|   Wages and salaries | $ 25,000 × (144 ÷ 144) | $25,000 | |
|   Depreciation | $ 10,000 × (144 ÷ 120) | 12,000 | |
|   Interest expense | $  4,000 × (144 ÷ 144) | 4,000 | |
|   Total expenses | | | (41,000) |
| Income before income taxes | | | $  5,781 |
| Income tax expense | $  3,300 × (144 ÷ 144) | | (3,300) |
| Income from continuing operations | | | $  2,481 |
| Purchasing-power loss | | | (204) |
| Net income | | | $  2,277 |

*Statement of Retained Earnings*
*For Year Ended December 31, 1996*

| | | |
|---|---|---:|
| Retained earnings, December 31, 1995 | $11,881 × (144 ÷ 128) | $13,366 |
| Plus: Net income | | 2,277 |
| | | $15,643 |
| Less: Dividends | $ 5,000 × (144 ÷ 152) | (4,737) |
| Retained earnings, December 31, 1996 | | $10,906 |

*Comparative Balance Sheets*

| | | December 31 | | |
|---|---|---|---|---|
| | **1995** | | **1996** | |
| Assets | | | | |
|   Cash | $45,365 × (144 ÷ 128) | $ 51,036 | $45,900 × (144 ÷ 152) | $ 43,484 |
|   Accounts receivable | $ 9,412 × (144 ÷ 128) | 10,588 | $20,000 × (144 ÷ 152) | 18,947 |
|   Inventory | $24,242 × (144 ÷ 128) | 27,272 | $35,000 × (144 ÷ 148) | 34,054 |
|   Building and equipment | $53,333 × (144 ÷ 128) | 60,000 | $50,000 × (144 ÷ 120) | 60,000 |
|     Less: Accumulated depreciation | $10,667 × (144 ÷ 128) | (12,000) | $20,000 × (144 ÷ 120) | (24,000) |
|   Total Assets | | $136,896 | | $132,485 |
| Liabilities and Stockholders' Equity | | | | |
|   Accounts payable | $18,824 × (144 ÷ 128) | $ 21,177 | $25,000 × (144 ÷ 152) | $ 23,684 |
|   Bonds payable | $37,647 × (144 ÷ 128) | 42,353 | $40,000 × (144 ÷ 152) | 37,895 |
|   Capital stock | $53,333 × (144 ÷ 128) | 60,000 | $50,000 × (144 ÷ 120) | 60,000 |
|   Retained earnings | $11,881 × (144 ÷ 128) | 13,366 | | 10,906 |
|   Total Liabilities and Stockholders' Equity | | $136,896 | | $132,485 |

*Purchasing-Power Gain or Loss*

The purchasing-power gain is computed in Exhibit 24-12. Note that the company has negative beginning but positive ending monetary items. Therefore, the company has a purchasing-power loss in 1996.

*Retained Earnings*

The 1996 beginning balance of retained earnings is measured in terms of the average price-level index for 1995. This balance has to be rolled forward to the average index for 1996, and then the adjusted net income is added and adjusted dividends are subtracted to determine the ending balance included in the December 31, 1996 balance sheet as shown in Exhibit 24-11.

## Comparative Financial Statements (Second Year)

When the adjusted income statement for 1996 is published, the 1995 income statement should be presented for comparative purposes, as has been shown for the beginning and ending balance sheets. Since the adjusted income statement for 1995 is already in terms of the average price level for 1995, the only adjustment needed is to roll forward each value in this income statement by the following factor:

$$\frac{1996 \text{ Average Index}}{1995 \text{ Average Index}} \quad \text{or} \quad \frac{144}{128}$$

The roll forward of the 1995 income statement is shown in Exhibit 24-13. This process was illustrated for the balance sheet in Exhibit 24-11. Note that the roll-forward process results in certain items being the same on both the beginning and ending balance sheets. For example, in Exhibit 24-11 the buildings and equipment and capital stock are recorded at $60,000 in both, although these numbers were calculated by

---

**EXHIBIT 24-12**

**FOLEY COMPANY**

Purchasing-Power Gain or Loss
For Year Ended December 31, 1996

| | Historical Cost | Adjustment | Constant Purchasing Power |
|---|---|---|---|
| Beginning net monetary items | $ (1,800) | × (144 ÷ 136) = | $ (1,906) |
| Sales | 110,000 | × (144 ÷ 144) = | 110,000 |
| Purchases | (70,000) | × (144 ÷ 144) = | (70,000) |
| Wages and salaries | (25,000) | × (144 ÷ 144) = | (25,000) |
| Interest | (4,000) | × (144 ÷ 144) = | (4,000) |
| Income tax | (3,300) | × (144 ÷ 144) = | (3,300) |
| Dividends | (5,000) | × (144 ÷ 152) = | (4,737) |
| Ending net monetary items unadjusted | $ 900 | | |
| Constant purchasing power ending balance (at average price level) | | | $ 1,057 |
| Historical ending balance adjusted to average price level [$900 × (144 ÷ 152)] | | | 853 |
| Purchasing-power loss (at average price level) | | | $ 204 |

**EXHIBIT 24-13**

## FOLEY COMPANY

1995 Historical Cost/Constant Purchasing Power Income Statement
Presented in Terms of the 1996 Price Level

|  | 1995 Adjusted Amount × Adjustment Factor | | 1995 Amount in 1996 Dollars |
| --- | --- | --- | --- |
| Sales | $100,000 × (144 ÷ 128) | | $112,500 |
| Cost of goods sold | | | |
|   Beginning inventory | $ 16,000 × (144 ÷ 128) | $18,000 | |
|   Purchases | $ 50,000 × (144 ÷ 128) | 56,250 | |
|   Cost of goods available | $ 66,000 | $74,250 | |
|   Ending inventory | $ 24,242 × (144 ÷ 128) | (27,272) | |
|   Cost of goods sold | | | (46,978) |
| Gross profit | | | $ 65,522 |
| Operating expenses: | | | |
|   Wages and salaries | $ 20,000 × (144 ÷ 128) | $22,500 | |
|   Depreciation | $ 10,667 × (144 ÷ 128) | 12,000 | |
|   Interest expense | $ 4,000 × (144 ÷ 128) | 4,500 | |
|   Total expenses | | | (39,000) |
| Income before income taxes | | | $ 26,522 |
| Income tax expense | $ 7,800 × (144 ÷ 128) | | (8,775) |
| Income from continuing operations | | | $ 17,747 |
| Purchasing-power gain | $ 812 × (144 ÷ 128) | | 914 |
| Net Income | | | $ 18,661 |

slightly different processes. On the beginning balance sheet, it is the adjusted value of $53,333 from the previous year rolled forward; on the ending balance sheet, it is the original dollar amount of $50,000 adjusted to the current index. Both processes resulted in the same amount, because they are two alternative methods of measuring the original dollar amounts in terms of the value of the dollar in the current period.

## THE CURRENT COST ADJUSTMENT PROCESS

The comprehensive current cost adjustment process is illustrated in this section and the resulting financial statements are shown in Exhibit 24-14, using the same historical cost data for the Foley Company shown in Exhibit 24-8. In addition, the following *current cost* information is available:

| | |
| --- | --- |
| Cost of goods sold, 1995 (at average current cost) | $44,000 |
| Cost of goods sold, 1996 (at average current cost) | 63,000 |
| Inventory, December 1994 | 15,000 |
| Inventory, December 1995 | 26,000 |
| Inventory, December 1996 | 37,000 |
| Building and equipment, December 1994 | 50,000 |
| Building and equipment, December 1995 | 55,000 |
| Building and equipment, December 1996 | 58,000 |

**EXHIBIT 24-14**

## FOLEY COMPANY

Current Cost Financial Statements for 1995 and 1996

### Comparative Income Statements

| | For Years Ended December 31 | | | |
|---|---|---|---|---|
| | | 1995 | | 1996 |
| Sales | | $100,000 | | $110,000 |
| Cost of goods sold | | (44,000) | | (63,000) |
| Gross profit | | $ 56,000 | | $ 47,000 |
| Operating expenses | | | | |
| Wages and salaries | $20,000 | | $25,000 | |
| Depreciation | 10,500 | | 11,300 | |
| Interest expense | 4,000 | | 4,000 | |
| Total expenses | | (34,500) | | (40,300) |
| Income before income taxes | | $ 21,500 | | $ 6,700 |
| Income tax expense | | (7,800) | | (3,300) |
| Income from continuing operations | | $ 13,700 | | $ 3,400 |
| Realized holding gain: inventory | | 4,000 | | 3,000 |
| Realized holding gain: building and equipment | | 500 | | 1,300 |
| Unrealized holding gain: inventory | | 1,000 | | 2,000 |
| Unrealized holding gain: building and equipment | | 4,000 | | 4,800 |
| Less: Unrealized holding gains recognized previously | | | | |
| Inventory | | | | (1,000) |
| Building and equipment | | | | (4,000) |
| Net Income | | $ 23,200 | | $ 9,500 |

### Comparative Balance Sheets

| | December 31 | | |
|---|---|---|---|
| | 1994 | 1995 | 1996 |
| **Assets** | | | |
| Cash | $ 35,000 | $ 48,200 | $ 45,900 |
| Accounts receivable | — | 10,000 | 20,000 |
| Inventory | 15,000 | 26,000 | 37,000 |
| Building and equipment | 50,000 | 55,000 | 58,000 |
| Less: Accumulated depreciation | — | (11,000) | (23,200) |
| Total Assets | $100,000 | $128,200 | $137,700 |
| **Liabilities and Stockholders' Equity** | | | |
| Accounts payable | $ 10,000 | $ 20,000 | $ 25,000 |
| Bonds payable | 40,000 | 40,000 | 40,000 |
| Capital stock | 50,000 | 50,000 | 50,000 |
| Retained earnings | — | 18,200 | 22,700 |
| Total Liabilities and Stockholders' Equity | $100,000 | $128,200 | $137,700 |

Recall that the current cost is the cost to reproduce (purchase or produce) the item. The methods by which these current costs may be determined were discussed earlier in the chapter. The comprehensive adjustments to the financial statements in Exhibit 24-14 are discussed in the following sections.

## Inventory and Cost of Goods Sold

The inventory is valued on the balance sheet at its current cost at the end of the period (i.e., units on hand × ending current cost per unit), and the cost of goods sold is valued on the income statement at the average current cost during the period. That is, since cost of goods sold is accumulated throughout the period and since current costs rise throughout this period, the cost of goods sold is based on the average current cost of the units sold during the period (i.e., units sold × [(beginning current cost per unit + ending current cost per unit) ÷ 2]). If sales fluctuated over the year, a weighted-average current cost could be used. The values included in the current cost financial statements in Exhibit 24-14 are taken directly from the current cost information given earlier.

## Building and Equipment and Depreciation

The building and equipment are valued on the balance sheet at their current costs at the end of the period. A 5-year life is used to compute the depreciation expense for the Foley Company. Current cost depreciation expense on the income statement is based on the average current cost of the asset for the year. An average is used because sales are made at prices current throughout the period, and it is appropriate to match the average cost of the assets used during the period against those sales. In 1995, the average current cost is $52,500 [($50,000 + $55,000) ÷ 2] and the depreciation expense is $10,500 ($52,500 ÷ 5 years). In 1996, the average current cost is $56,500 [($55,000 + $58,000) ÷ 2] and the depreciation expense is $11,300 ($56,500 ÷ 5 years). The accumulated depreciation on the balance sheet is based on the current cost and the age of the asset. At the end of 1995, the asset is 1 year old and the accumulated depreciation ($11,000) is one-fifth of the current cost ($55,000) on that date. At the end of 1996, the asset is 2 years old and the accumulated depreciation ($23,200) is two-fifths of the current cost ($58,000) on that date. Note that the accumulated depreciation at the end of 1996 ($23,200) is *not* the sum of the current cost depreciation expense for the 2 years ($10,500 + $11,300). The accumulated depreciation is based on the current cost of the asset at the *end* of the particular year and the length of time the asset has been owned, whereas the depreciation expense each year is based on the *average* current cost for that year.

## Other Income Statement Items

The other income statement items, sales, wages and salaries, interest, and income taxes, do not need adjustment because they already represent the current values of the period.

## Holding Gains and Losses

Since assets are recorded initially at their acquisition costs, and then adjusted to their current costs, the difference in these values is recorded as a gain or loss. Because these gains or losses result from holding the assets over time as their prices change, they are known as holding gains or losses. Holding gains and losses are separated into their realized and unrealized components. **A realized holding gain or loss is the difference between the current cost and historical cost values included in income.** For the Foley Company, the realized holding gain on the inventory is $4,000 in 1995, which is the cost of goods sold on the current cost basis ($44,000) minus the cost of goods sold on a historical cost basis ($40,000), and $3,000 in 1996 ($63,000 − $60,000). On the building and equipment, the realized holding gain is $500 in 1995 (the current cost depreciation of $10,500 minus the historical cost depreciation of $10,000), and $1,300 in 1996 ($11,300 − $10,000).

   **An unrealized holding gain or loss is *in total* the difference between the current cost and historical cost of the book value of the asset (or liability) on the balance sheet.** However, that value is the unrealized holding gain for the life of the asset, so that the unrealized holding gain *for the year* is that value less the previously recognized unrealized holding gains. The total unrealized holding gain on the inventory is $1,000 in 1995 (the current cost of the ending inventory of $26,000 minus the historical cost of the ending inventory of $25,000), and $2,000 by the end of 1996 ($37,000 − $35,000). Since $1,000 has been recognized to date, only $1,000 remains to be recognized in 1996 ($2,000 − $1,000). The total unrealized holding gain on the building and equipment is $4,000 in 1995 (the current cost book value of $44,000 minus the historical cost book value of $40,000), and by the end of 1996 it is $4,800 ($34,800 − $30,000). Since $4,000 has been recognized to date, $800 remains to be recognized in 1996 ($4,800 − $4,000).

### Other Balance Sheet Items

The other balance sheet items (cash, accounts receivable, and the liabilities) are not adjusted because it is assumed that they already represent the current values at the end of the period. Capital stock is not adjusted because it represents the value of the assets originally contributed by the stockholders of the company. Retained earnings is determined in the normal manner. That is, it represents the sum of the net income earned by the company over its life (on a current cost basis) less dividends of $5,000 each year.

### Alternative Reporting in Current Cost Financial Statements

On the current cost financial statements of the Foley Company presented in Exhibit 24-14, the realized and unrealized holding gains are included in income. However, there is some disagreement among accountants about whether such gains (and losses) should be treated as income or credited directly to stockholders' equity, as discussed earlier in the chapter. Whichever method is followed, it is important to recognize the nature of such gains and their distinction from operating income. In the case of the Foley Company, the current cost net income is higher than historical cost net income because of the inclusion of holding gains in income. Only the operating income represents an increase in wealth of the company, and if the total net income were distributed to stockholders, they would be receiving a return *of* capital as well as a return *on* capital.

   It should also be noted that this is an example of a fairly simple current cost adjustment process. For example, the bonds payable have not been adjusted for a change in the interest rate because it is assumed that the yield has not changed, and expenses other than cost of goods sold and depreciation have not been adjusted. Furthermore, the preparation of current cost/constant purchasing power financial statements would apply the principles of the general price-level adjustment process to the current cost financial statements.

# CONCEPTUAL ISSUES RELATING TO ALTERNATIVES TO HISTORICAL COST

The examples of the current cost, historical cost/constant purchasing power, and current cost/constant purchasing power concepts discussed earlier in this chapter focus on the logic underlying the adjustment processes, and deliberately avoid the introduction of the many complexities that would be involved in preparing comprehensive financial statements for a company.[6] On the other hand, sufficient detail has been included to enable the reader to understand the nature of the adjustment processes and the general principles involved. In this section, the three methods are evaluated in greater detail with respect to selected criteria and are compared with historical cost financial statements. Also, the concept of using an exit value as a measure of current value is discussed. It should be noted that although current generally accepted accounting principles primarily include measurements based *only* on historical costs, they also include selected current value measurements—for example, for certain investments or when the lower of cost or market rule is used for inventories.

## Capital Maintenance Concept (Income Statement)

One of the major purposes of financial accounting is to measure a company's income. But what is income? A common definition is that corporate income for a year is

> **the amount the corporation can distribute to the owners of equity in the corporation and be as well off at the end of the year as at the beginning.**[7]

This is a useful definition of income, but it does raise the question of what is meant by being "as well off." In other words, what is the capital that is to be maintained during the year so that income may be measured as the excess above the capital maintained? Another way of looking at this issue is to consider the distinction between the maintenance of capital and the return on capital. During each period, a company first should earn enough to maintain the capital invested in the business. Any excess, or return on capital, then is considered income.

The capital maintenance concepts underlying each type of financial statement illustrated in Exhibits 24-1 through 24-4 are as follows:

| Financial Statements | Capital Maintenance Concept |
|---|---|
| Historical cost | Historical dollars of capital at the beginning of the year |
| Historical cost/constant purchasing power | Purchasing power of the capital at the beginning of the year |
| Current cost | Operating capacity (the ability to provide goods and services) at the beginning of the year measured in dollars |
| Current cost/constant purchasing power | Operating capacity (the ability to provide goods and services) measured in units of constant purchasing power |

---

6. See *APB Statement No. 3, op. cit.,* Appendix C, for an example of general price-level adjustments, and the "Conceptual Framework for Financial Accounting and Reporting: Elements of Financial Statements and Their Measurement," *FASB Discussion Memorandum* (Stamford, Conn.: FASB, 1976), Appendix B, for examples of general price-level, replacement cost, and general price-level adjusted replacement cost financial statements.

7. Sydney S. Alexander, "Income Measurement in a Dynamic Economy," *Five Monographs on Business Income* (New York: Study Group on Business Income, AICPA, 1950), p. 15.

Although it is not reasonable to make a categorical statement that one of the alternative capital maintenance concepts is the best, it should be clear that they are different, and that each has advantages and disadvantages. The historical cost concept has the advantage of being the most *verifiable* and widely understood of the different methods, but it may not be the most relevant to the needs of the user of financial statements. The user has no assurance that the purchasing power of a company's capital is being maintained, or that the company can continue to operate at the same level. In other words, income may be overstated since it is likely to include a return *of* some of the capital as well as a return *on* the capital.

To ensure that the company maintains the purchasing power of its capital probably would be considered desirable by most stockholders. They did contribute a certain number of dollars to the company, but they are more concerned about the purchasing power of those dollars than about the number of their dollars originally contributed. Surely the stockholders would not be satisfied to get back the same number of dollars as they contributed when these dollars represent less purchasing power. Therefore, the stockholders are likely to be interested in knowing that the purchasing power represented by the capital of the company is maintained before income is reported as a return on capital. Historical cost/constant purchasing power income statements disclose this information.

A company needs specific assets to conduct its operations, and it is possible that the company could be maintaining the general purchasing power of its capital but not its ability to replace these assets. Use of the current cost concept ensures that the operating capability of the company is maintained before earnings are reported as a return on capital. However, when these results are reported in unadjusted dollars, a flexible measuring unit is being used. For example, cost of goods sold at its current cost is subtracted from sales. Both measures are in terms of current dollars, so no problem exists. But any holding gain or loss is computed as the difference between the current cost and the historical cost of the inventory, and these two values are measured in terms of different dollar values. Consequently, it is difficult to evaluate the meaning of the holding gain, and also to compare the holding gain with operating income; in each case, the two amounts being compared are measured in different dollar values. Use of current cost/constant purchasing power income statements resolves these difficulties.

In summary, the historical dollar/constant purchasing power income statements resolve one issue with the historical dollar measurement concept, and current cost income statements resolve a different issue. Only current cost/constant purchasing power income statements resolve both issues and ensure that income is the excess after the capital is maintained in terms of operating capacity measured in units of constant purchasing power.

## Balance Sheet

The values attached to items on the balance sheet are closely related to the capital maintenance concept and the resulting rules of valuation and income realization. However, the balance sheet values are worth considering separately.

Historical cost balance sheets disclose items at the historical dollars exchanged. The difficulty of interpreting these statements arises because the dollar figures represent different purchasing powers, and adding and subtracting them is as inappropriate as relating U.S. and Canadian dollars, as discussed earlier. Use of historical cost/constant purchasing power amounts does ensure that all the values on the balance sheet represent equivalent purchasing power.

Current cost balance sheets present assets and liabilities at their current replacement cost or, in other words, at a measure of their current value at the balance sheet date. It is difficult to compare them over time (for example, on the balance sheets for 2 years), however, because of the changing value of the dollar. Only current cost/constant purchasing power balance sheets value the assets at their current cost and also enhance comparability over time by measuring those current costs in dollars of constant purchasing power.

## Reliability

Historical cost financial statements clearly are the most reliable, and adjusting historical dollars for changes in the general price level affects that reliability very little, if at all. The historical dollars are adjusted by an index published by the federal government, and all companies would use the same index and follow established procedures.

Current cost financial statements are considerably less reliable than historical cost financial statements. Several general approaches (discussed earlier in the chapter) to the determination of current cost are allowed. Although each approach is more suitable for certain types of assets, there are no requirements that a particular method be used in any given situation. For example, Shell Oil Company tested four indexes for estimating the current cost of refineries and found that the current cost varied by 25%.

## Understandability

An argument frequently made in favor of historical cost financial statements is that they are more understandable than financial statements prepared under other concepts. This is difficult to disagree with, because historical costs have been used for so many years. This argument suggests, however, that no change should ever take place, because initially users would be less familiar with the new method than with the old.

There also is a trend toward giving greater consideration to the needs of sophisticated users of financial statements, who presumably have, or would soon develop, the ability to understand financial statements prepared on a different basis. Many supporters of the use of a changed concept have argued that the historical cost financial statements should be continued and the new data supplied in supplementary form. This would enable users to gain experience with the new methods and concepts and limit the potential for misunderstandings from the adoption of alternative concepts. This was the approach used by the FASB, as discussed later.

## Costs and Benefits

The implementation of each of the different concepts discussed in this chapter would involve additional costs for the company in preparing the data, and for audit fees if the financial statements are to be audited. For example, in a survey of companies, 62% of the respondents estimated that up to 800 hours of employee time would be necessary to compute the supplementary disclosure requirements of *FASB Statement No. 33*.[8] Although it may be expected that such costs would decline as experience increased, it was still a significant cost, and the FASB requirements did not involve complete implementation of current costs.

---

8. K. Evans and R. Freeman, "Statement 33 Disclosures Confirm Profit Illusion in Primary Statements," *FASB Viewpoints* (Stamford, Conn.: June 24, 1983), p. 13.

Historical cost/constant purchasing power financial statements would also involve additional costs, but these would be much less than with current cost financial statements. Since the adjustment process involves the use of generally accepted accounting principles and a publicly available price-level index, the costs mainly result from increased computational work.

## Alternative Concepts of Current Cost

The current cost of an asset can be measured in several different ways, as discussed earlier. However, there are also alternative concepts of what the current cost is measuring. The **reproduction cost** is the current cost of acquiring assets identical to those currently owned (the concept used by *FASB Statement No. 89*). **Replacement cost** is the current cost of acquiring the best asset available to undertake the function of the asset owned. A significant difference between the reproduction cost and replacement cost measures of current cost may arise, as indicated by a company that estimated the replacement cost of a chemical plant at $350 million, which was approximately half the estimated reproduction cost.[9] The difference arises because of the technologically superior, and more energy-efficient, manufacturing process that would be incorporated in the new plant. Current cost also could be measured as the cost of acquiring an asset that could produce the same volume of goods and services, thereby giving consideration to changes in technology (the approach used by the SEC under its rescinded requirements, as discussed later). It could refer to the cost of replacing the asset with one that could produce the same value of goods and services, thereby giving consideration to changes in technology and prices.

## Current Cost and Operating Savings

Current cost net income includes depreciation expense based on the current cost of the property, plant, and equipment. If the current cost is based on the current productive capacity of the assets, and thus incorporates technological changes, it is argued that the *savings* that would result from those technological changes should be included as well as the higher depreciation charges. For example, suppose a company owns a fleet of automobiles. The current cost depreciation expense would be based on the higher purchase price of automobiles. But if new automobiles get better gas mileage and have lower repair and maintenance costs, other operating expenses would be lower. Since the new automobiles have not been acquired, the operating savings have not been realized but would have to be estimated. Complete implementation of this current cost framework would require that these lower costs be reflected in the income statement as well as the higher depreciation. However, it is difficult to estimate operating savings objectively. The SEC's rescinded requirements (discussed later) allowed estimation of such operating savings. Bethlehem Steel reported that its estimated cost savings were 167% of the excess of current cost depreciation over historical cost depreciation. Sears reported savings of 86% and the Ford Motor Company savings of 72%. It should also be noted that the operating savings might be offset to some extent by the increased interest costs on the money that would have to be borrowed to finance the acquisition of the new property, plant, and equipment.

The FASB avoided this issue by requiring that current cost be measured in terms of the reproduction cost of currently owned assets, thereby ignoring any changes in

---

9. "Financial Reporting and Changing Prices—A Survey of Preparers' Views and Practices," *Arthur Young and Company* (New York: Arthur Young and Company, 1981), p. 18.

technology and the operating savings that might result. This advantage is offset by the fact that the current cost is measuring replacements that the company may not make.

## Current Cost Versus Partial Adjustments

Generally accepted accounting principles allow two current cost methods that tend to modify the historical dollar concept, so that historical cost financial statements achieve some of the objectives of current cost accounting. The LIFO inventory costing method matches approximately the current cost of the inventory (or a value close to the current cost) as cost of goods sold against revenue. Accelerated depreciation methods expense a high percentage of the historical cost of the asset against revenue early in the life of the asset, thus partially offsetting the effects of price changes on those assets. However, the extra amount of the expense may not be related in any rational way to the change in the asset's current cost. Also, the total depreciation expense over the life of the asset is limited by the historical dollars paid for it. Furthermore, neither LIFO nor accelerated depreciation methods reflect current costs in the balance sheet. The use of LIFO and accelerated depreciation do reduce income, so that it is likely to be closer numerically to current cost income, but they should not be considered rational substitutes for current cost financial statements.

## Current Exit Values

The three alternative measurement methods that have been discussed use *entry*, or input, values. An historical cost is, of course, the cost measured at the time of the acquisition of the item. A constant purchasing power amount is an adjusted historical cost amount. A current cost is the amount that would have to be paid to purchase an item. In contrast, some users of financial statements argue that it would be more appropriate to use exit values. **A current exit value is the net cash amount that a company would receive if it sold the item.** An exit value often is referred to as the *net realizable value* because it is the net amount to be received from the sale after deducting any costs associated with the sale, such as transportation costs and sales commissions. The basic argument in favor of the use of exit values in a company's financial statements is that the company will have to dispose of each item at some point in the future, and therefore the current measure of the cash to be received from such sales is relevant to users of financial statements. It is argued that exit values provide a better measure of the return on investment, liquidity, and financial flexibility.

The use of exit values is illustrated in Exhibit 24-15 using the facts for the Hallas Company earlier in the chapter. In addition, it is assumed that at Steps 2 and 5, the exit values of the inventory are $1,800 and $2,200, respectively. There are two components of income. The first is the **purchasing margin,** which is the difference between the exit value and the acquisition cost of the assets on the date of acquisition. The second is the **holding gain or loss,** which is the change in the exit values of the assets. In the Hallas Company example, at Step 2, inventory is acquired for $1,000 when its exit value is $1,800, so that a purchasing margin of $800 is recognized and included in net income. At Step 4, when the inventory is sold, the exit value is $2,000 and the holding gain of $200 (the increase in the exit value from $1,800) is recognized. At Step 5, inventory is acquired for $1,250 when its exit value is $2,200, so that a purchasing margin of $950 is recognized and included in net income. At all times, the exit value of the inventory is included in the balance sheet.

Generally accepted accounting principles require the use of exit values in the financial statements of a company for reporting certain investments (as discussed in Chapter 13) because the securities are readily saleable. Many people argue that the

**EXHIBIT 24-15**

## HALLAS COMPANY

Exit Value Financial Statements

| | Step | | | | |
|---|---|---|---|---|---|
| | 1 | 2 | 3 | 4 | 5 |
| *Income Statements* | | | | | |
| Purchasing margin | — | $ 800 | — | — | $ 950 |
| Holding gain | — | — | — | $ 200 | — |
| Net Income | — | $ 800 | — | $ 200 | $ 950 |
| *Balance Sheets* | | | | | |
| Cash | $3,000 | $2,000 | $2,000 | $4,000 | $2,750 |
| Inventory | — | 1,800 | 1,800 | — | 2,200 |
| | $3,000 | $3,800 | $3,800 | $4,000 | $4,950 |
| Capital | $3,000 | $3,800 | $3,800 | $4,000 | $4,950 |

use of exit values for other items would not provide relevant information, however. Consider two examples. If a company used an exit value for its inventory, it would record that inventory at its selling price (less costs of disposal) before any sale transaction occurred and therefore would recognize income simply by acquiring inventory. Second, suppose that a company acquired a specialized machine for use in its activities. If the machine has no value to another company, its value would immediately be recorded as zero and its entire purchase price expensed in the period of acquisition even though the company intends to use the machine for several years.

Alternatively, it can be argued that in certain situations (in addition to certain investments) exit values have more relevance than input values. For example, if a company is to be liquidated, then exit values are more relevant. Of course, in this case the going concern (continuity) assumption is no longer valid. Furthermore, when a company is being sold in its entirety, many purchasers are interested in exit values because they may intend to sell some of the assets. Regardless of their position on the relevance of exit values, few accountants argue that exit values should be the basis of the accounting principles for financial statements used in most investment and lending decisions.

## DISCLOSURES CONSIDERED BY THE APB, FASB, AND SEC

In 1969, the APB issued **APB Statement No. 3,** which stated that general price-level adjusted historical cost financial statements present useful information not available from historical cost financial statements but concluded that:

> General price-level information is not required at this time for fair presentation of financial position and results of operations in conformity with generally accepted accounting principles in the United States.[10]

---

10. *APB Statement No. 3, op. cit.,* par. 25.

The APB also stated that:

> General price-level information may be presented in addition to the basic historical dollar financial statements but general price-level financial statements should not be presented as the basic statements.[11]

In 1974, the FASB issued an *Exposure Draft* that would have required that financial statements "include certain information that is stated in terms of units of general purchasing power of the U.S. dollar."[12] However, after the *Exposure Draft* had been field tested and discussed, it was withdrawn because the FASB concluded that general price-level adjusted information was not sufficiently understood by preparers and users. In addition, the Board was not convinced that the benefits to be derived from the information justified the cost of implementation that would be incurred by the preparers of financial statements.

In 1977, the Securities and Exchange Commission adopted a requirement for supplementary disclosure on the annual 10-K report of the current replacement cost of the inventories, cost of goods sold, net productive assets, and depreciation for companies with inventories and gross property, plant, and equipment of more than $100 million that represented more than 10% of their total assets. These requirements were rescinded when *FASB Statement No. 33* was issued.

In 1979, the FASB issued **FASB Statement No. 33,** "Financial Reporting and Changing Prices," which required disclosure of the effects of changing prices as a supplement to the basic historical cost financial statements.[13] Public companies having $1 billion of assets (after deducting accumulated depreciation) or $125 million of inventories and property, plant, and equipment (before deducting accumulated depreciation) were required to make such disclosures, although all companies were encouraged to do so. The FASB also issued additional *Statements* that covered the reporting of the effects of changing prices in specialized industries and **FASB Statement No. 82,** which amended certain disclosure requirements.[14] This *Statement* eliminated many of the constant purchasing power disclosures that were previously required. Then in 1986, **FASB Statement No. 89** was issued, which rescinded the *requirement* that qualifying companies disclose the information specified in *FASB Statement No. 33* as amended.[15] However, *FASB Statement No. 89* encourages the continued disclosure of information about the effects of changing prices and includes guidelines for measurement and disclosure. The reasons for making the disclosures voluntary are

---

11. *Ibid.*
12. "Financial Reporting in Units of General Purchasing Power," *FASB Proposed Statement of Financial Accounting Standards* (Stamford, Conn.: FASB, 1974), par. 31.
13. "Financial Reporting and Changing Prices," *FASB Statement of Financial Accounting Standards No. 33* (Stamford, Conn.: FASB, 1979).
14. "Financial Reporting and Changing Prices: Specialized Assets—Mining and Oil and Gas," *FASB Statement of Financial Accounting Standards No. 39* (Stamford, Conn.: FASB, 1980); "Financial Reporting and Changing Prices: Specialized Assets—Timberlands and Growing Timber," *FASB Statement of Financial Accounting Standards No. 40* (Stamford, Conn.: FASB, 1980); "Financial Reporting and Changing Prices: Specialized Assets—Income Producing Real Estate," *FASB Statement of Financial Accounting Standards No. 41* (Stamford, Conn.: FASB, 1980); "Financial Reporting and Changing Prices: Motion Picture Films," *FASB Statement of Financial Accounting Standards No. 46* (Stamford, Conn.: FASB, 1981); "Financial Reporting and Changing Prices: Investment Companies," *FASB Statement of Financial Accounting Standards No. 54* (Stamford, Conn.: FASB, 1982); "Financial Reporting and Changing Prices: Foreign Currency Translation," *FASB Statement of Financial Accounting Standards No. 70* (Stamford, Conn.: FASB, 1982); and "Financial Reporting and Changing Prices: Elimination of Certain Disclosures," *FASB Statement of Financial Accounting Standards No. 82* (Stamford, Conn.: FASB, 1984).
15. *FASB Statement No. 89* also rescinded the remaining *Statements* listed in footnote 14.

discussed later in the chapter. Since the *FASB Statement No. 89* selected disclosures are encouraged on a voluntary basis, they are discussed in the next section. (Comprehensive financial statements were discussed earlier in the chapter.)

## FASB DISCLOSURE GUIDELINES

If a company decides to voluntarily report supplementary information on the effects of changing prices, the FASB disclosure guidelines for the current year and for a 5-year summary are as follows:

**The selected disclosures for the current year are:**[16]

1. Income from continuing operations under the current cost basis, including disclosure of the current cost amounts of cost of goods sold and depreciation, depletion, and amortization expense.

2. Purchasing power gain or loss on net monetary items (excluded from income from continuing operations).

3. Current cost (or lower recoverable) amount of inventory and of property, plant, and equipment at the end of the current year.

4. Increase or decrease in the current cost (or lower recoverable) amount of inventory and of property, plant, and equipment, before and after eliminating the effects of inflation (excluded from income from continuing operations).

5. Aggregate foreign currency translation adjustment on a current cost basis, if applicable.

**The selected disclosures included in a 5-year summary, adjusted to average-for-the-year, end-of-year, or base-period constant purchasing power are:**[17]

1. Net sales and other operating revenues.

2. Income from continuing operations (and related earnings per share) under the current cost basis.

3. Purchasing power gain or loss on net monetary items.

4. Increase or decrease in the current cost (or lower recoverable) amount of inventory and of property, plant, and equipment, net of inflation.

5. Aggregate foreign currency translation adjustment on a current cost basis, if applicable.

6. Net assets at year-end on a current cost basis.

7. Cash dividends declared per common share.

8. Market price per common share at year-end.

---

16. *FASB Statement No. 89, op. cit.,* par 11–13.
17. *FASB Statement No .89, op. cit.,* par. 7 and 8.

**Additional disclosures include:**

1.  The principal types of information used to calculate the current costs.

2.  Differences between the depreciation methods, estimates of useful lives, and residual values used for calculations of current cost depreciation and the methods and estimates used in the primary financial statements (there is a presumption that the methods and estimates should be the same).

A company may substitute historical cost/constant purchasing power income from continuing operations for income from continuing operations on a current cost basis in the current year and in the 5-year summary if there is no material difference in these amounts.[18] As indicated previously, assets and the related expenses are recorded at their recoverable amount, if materially and permanently lower than the adjusted amount. Recoverable amount is the "current worth of the net amount of cash expected to be recoverable from the use or sale of an asset"[19] and may be measured by either the current market value or the value in use. The reduction is included in income from continuing operations in the supplementary disclosures. However, situations in which the recoverable amount is less than the adjusted amount should be infrequent and are not discussed further in this chapter.

The FASB states that the objective of the calculations is "to obtain a *reasonable degree* of accuracy" and that "preparers are encouraged to devise short-cut methods."[20]

**The *Statement* requires that the constant purchasing power adjustments use the average Consumer Price Index for All Urban Consumers (CPI-U) for the year,** as used in the comprehensive examples. However, particular aspects of *FASB Statement No. 89* as they relate to the selected disclosures are different from the simple and comprehensive illustrations presented earlier.

When a 5-year summary of selected financial data (as discussed earlier) is presented according to *FASB Statement No. 89*, the information may be presented either in current purchasing power (year-end or average-for-the-year) or in the purchasing power of the base period of the Consumer Price Index. Either method can cause confusion among users of the financial statements. When current year-end or average-for-the-year purchasing power is used, prior-year information in the 5-year summary has to be restated each year, so that these dollar amounts change each year. However, when using base-period purchasing power, the amounts shown in the current year's supplementary information and in the 5-year summary for the current year are different, which also may be confusing. Illustration of the calculations involved in these supplementary disclosures are not included in this book because companies rarely make these disclosures.

## Impacts of FASB Statement No. 33

The purpose of the required disclosures of *FASB Statement No. 33* (and the voluntary disclosures of *FASB Statement No. 89*) was to improve financial reporting, specifically by separating the effects of price changes from measures of operating performance. As indicated by the list of recommended disclosures, the adjustments have many effects on financial statements. One commonly used measure of performance is the return on investment (ROI), or the ratio of operating income to common

---

18. *Ibid.,* par. 20.
19. *Ibid.,* par. 44.
20. *Ibid.,* par. 48.

stockholders' equity (i.e., net assets), as discussed in Chapter 23. While *FASB Statement No. 33* was still in effect, a study of the reporting by over 500 nonfinancial companies developed the following results:

### Return on Investment

|  | 1981 | 1980 |
| --- | --- | --- |
| Current cost operating income | 2.5% | 2.7% |
| Constant purchasing power operating income | 2.9% | 1.9% |
| Historical cost operating income | 14.3% | 14.8% |

These results indicate that the historical cost ROI was five and eight times higher than the alternative constant purchasing power and current cost measures, respectively. When prices are rising, the numerators of both the current cost and constant purchasing power ROI ratio fall because higher adjusted expenses are subtracted in the computation of operating income (constant purchasing power and current cost measures of operating income were about 40% of the historical cost amounts in 1981). In addition, the denominator increases because higher adjusted values for net assets are used (in 1981 constant purchasing power net assets were almost 90% larger than the historical cost amounts, and current cost net assets were another 10% larger than the constant purchasing power amounts).

Despite the fact that the years 1980 and 1981 were a period of severe recession in the United States, the historical cost financial statements reported increasing income during the period. The study also stated that, under both the current cost and constant purchasing power measures, the supplementary disclosures required by *FASB Statement No. 33* reported that corporate profits dropped in 1980 and there was widespread capital disinvestment in both 1980 and 1981. The study concluded that the "supplementary disclosures are more consistent with the underlying economic conditions than are conventional statements."[21]

## Evaluation of the Elimination of the Disclosures on the Effects of Changing Prices

When *FASB Statement No. 33* was adopted in 1979, it was intended that its provisions would be reviewed after a period of not more than 5 years. Consequently, the FASB sponsored and monitored research to help assess the usefulness of information about the effects of changing prices. In 1983, the FASB issued an *Invitation to Comment* on the need for disclosures of information on the effects of changing prices and the best way to meet that need. In 1984, the FASB responded to the related comments and research results by issuing *FASB Statement No. 82* (discussed earlier), which eliminated certain disclosure requirements. Then in 1986, *FASB Statement No. 89* eliminated the requirement for the remaining disclosures. This *Statement* was adopted by a 4-to-3 majority, whereas a 5-to-2 vote is now required for adoption.

There were several arguments in favor of eliminating the required disclosures. First, there was evidence that the disclosures were not widely used. Among the rea-

---

21. K. Evans and R. Freeman, *op. cit.*

sons for the lack of use were concerns that the information was not *relevant*. It was argued that the concept of current cost (the cost of replacing existing service potential) was not relevant because many companies intended to replace their assets with others that had a different service potential. It was also argued that applying a specific price index to the historical cost did not provide a relevant value because technological change may not be appropriately reflected in the index. The lack of use also resulted from concerns about the *reliability* of the information. For example, the determination of the current cost when an asset with equivalent service potential was not available required considerable judgment and therefore could be viewed as unreliable. Also, the determination of the recoverable amount required substantial judgment. Furthermore, since the disclosures were labeled "unaudited" and "supplementary," they were considered to lack reliability.

Second, responses to the *Invitation to Comment* expressed the concern that the *costs of providing the information exceeded the benefits*. Although both the costs and the benefits could not be accurately measured, it is appropriate for the FASB to suspend disclosure requirements if preparers and users perceive an unfavorable cost/benefit relationship. Third, it was argued that the disclosures lacked *comparability*. This situation resulted from the degree of flexibility in methods of application, from differences in the quality of the raw data used to prepare the disclosures, and from failure to disclose the assumptions used. Fourth, concern was expressed that the disclosures lacked *understandability* because they were overly complex. Also, it was argued that the disclosures were difficult to understand because they were not adequately explained and did not include comprehensive financial statements. Fifth, many users of financial statements indicated that they used information about changing prices in their decisions but had developed their own methods for making the adjustments. Therefore, additional disclosures might not be useful because users had information that was better or different from that required by *FASB Statement No. 33*.

The final argument against continuing the required disclosures was that the significance of the disclosures had decreased because prices were changing much less than in previous years. Therefore, other concerns were more important to users, such as the ability of the company to finance replacements of productive capacity or the effects of changing interest rates on monetary assets and liabilities.

There were several arguments in favor of continuing the required disclosures. First, it was argued that the basic concept underlying *FASB Statement No. 33* (inflation causes historical cost financial statements to show illusory profits and to mask the erosion of capital) is virtually undisputed. Second, although there was evidence of limited use of the disclosures, 5 years is an insufficient time to assess the usefulness of the information. Therefore, an effort should be made to improve any shortcomings of the information. Third, suspension of the required disclosures will encourage companies to remove the systems used to develop the information. Therefore, information will no longer be available for research on the relevance and reliability of the information.

The final argument against the elimination of the required disclosures was that when inflation rates increase at some time in the future, the FASB will again be asked to require supplementary disclosures of the effects of changing prices. The effort required at that time will be as difficult, time-consuming, and costly as the implementation of *FASB Statement No. 33* disclosures. The due process (e.g., open hearings and a 5-to-2 super majority vote) required for adoption of a new *Statement* in the future may delay its adoption until a lack of credibility arises for both the FASB and financial reporting.

### International Accounting Differences

Except for countries with hyperinflationary economies (defined later), supplementary disclosures of the effects of changing prices are voluntary under International Accounting Standards and in many countries such as Australia, Canada, France, and the United Kingdom. Countries that have no optional disclosures include Denmark, Germany, and Italy. Most of these countries have experienced low inflation in recent years. However, inflation rates vary widely around the world. Some countries, particularly in Central and South America, have experienced hyperinflation, which is defined by *FASB Statement No. 52* as cumulative inflation of approximately 100% or more over a 3-year period.

Accounting for changing prices is much more important in those countries. For example, in Brazil and Mexico, the primary financial statements are adjusted for changes in purchasing power.[22] Also, International Accounting Standards require that companies in hyperinflationary economies compute the purchasing power gain or loss on net monetary items and that it be included in net income.

## QUESTIONS

**Q24-1**  Distinguish between a *general price-level change* and a *specific price change*. What, if any, is the relationship between them?

**Q24-2**  What is the meaning of the term *inflation*? How does it relate to the purchasing power of the dollar?

**Q24-3**  List the four alternative accounting methods discussed in the chapter. What is the appropriate capital maintenance concept for each?

**Q24-4**  What causes a purchasing-power gain or loss?

**Q24-5**  Distinguish between *monetary* and *nonmonetary* items.

**Q24-6**  Indicate which of the following items are classified as monetary and whether holding them during a period of inflation would result in a purchasing-power gain or loss: (a) cash in a checking account; (b) investment in common stock; (c) allowance for doubtful accounts; (d) land; (e) goodwill; (f) bonds payable.

**Q24-7**  Consider the major items included in the income statement. Which are most nearly measured on a current cost basis on historical cost financial statements? Which are least?

**Q24-8**  What is the major argument in favor of historical cost/constant purchasing power financial statements? Of current cost financial statements?

**Q24-9**  How may historical cost net income include a return of capital in income?

**Q24-10**  Explain the meaning of the following alternative measures of current value: (a) *replacement cost*; (b) *reproduction cost*; (c) *current cost*.

**Q24-11**  Are current values allowed in the primary financial statements under generally accepted accounting principles? If so, in what situations?

**Q24-12**  What is an *exit value*? What are the two components of income when exit value financial statements are prepared?

**Q24-13**  What is a *realized holding gain*? How is it measured? Where should it appear in current cost financial statements?

**Q24-14**  What is an *unrealized holding gain* for an accounting period? How is it measured? Where should it appear in current cost financial statements?

**Q24-15**  Are historical cost constant/purchasing power financial statements allowed under generally accepted accounting principles? Explain.

**Q24-16**  What general price-level index is required by *FASB Statement No. 89* for the supplementary disclosures to the historical cost financial statements?

**Q24-17**  What information about the effects of changing prices are reported under the supplementary disclosures encouraged by the FASB?

**Q24-18**  How does the FASB define *current cost*? Describe the alternative methods of measuring current cost. Name two assets suitable for measurement by each approach.

---

22. For additional discussion, see Coopers & Lybrand, *1991 International Accounting Summaries: A Guide for Interpretation and Comparison* (New York: John Wiley and Son, Inc., 1991).

# CASES

## C24-1  Four Alternative Accounting Methods

*Part a.* Advocates of current value accounting propose several methods for determining the valuation of assets to approximate current values. Two of the methods proposed are replacement cost and present value of future cash flows.

**Required**

Describe each of the two previously cited methods and discuss the pros and cons of the various procedures used to arrive at the valuation for each method.

*Part b.* The financial statements of a business entity could be prepared by using historical cost or current value as a basis. In addition, the basis could be stated in terms of unadjusted dollars or dollars restated for changes in purchasing power. The various permutations of these two separate and distinct areas are shown in the following matrix:

|  | Unadjusted Dollars | Dollars Restated for Changes in Purchasing Power |
|---|---|---|
| Historical cost | 1 | 2 |
| Current value | 3 | 4 |

Block number 1 of the matrix represents the traditional method of accounting for transactions in accounting today, wherein the absolute (unadjusted) amount of dollars given up or received is recorded for the asset or liability obtained (relationship between resources). Amounts recorded in the method described in block 1 reflect the original cost of the asset or liability and do not give effect to any change in value of the unit of measure (standard of comparison). This method assumes the validity of the accounting concepts of going concern and stable monetary unit. Any gain or loss (including holding and purchasing power gains or losses) resulting from the sale or satisfaction of amounts recorded under this method is deferred in its entirety until sale or satisfaction.

**Required**

For each of the remaining matrix blocks (2, 3, and 4), respond to the following questions. Limit your discussion to nonmonetary assets only.

1. How will this method of recording assets affect the relationship between resources and the standard of comparison?
2. What is the conceptual justification for using each method?
3. How will each method of asset valuation affect the recognition of gain or loss during the life of the asset and ultimately from the sale or abandonment of the asset? Your response should include a discussion of the timing and magnitude of the gain or loss and conceptual reasons for any difference from the gain or loss computed using the traditional method. (*AICPA adapted*)

## C24-2  Constant Purchasing Power Adjustments

*Part a.* Price-level adjusted financial statements are prepared in an effort to eliminate the effects of inflation or deflation. An integral part of determining restated amounts and applicable gain or loss from restatement is the segregation of all assets and liabilities into monetary and nonmonetary classifications. One reason for this classification is that price-level gains and losses for monetary items are currently matched against earnings.

**Required**

What are the factors that determine whether an asset or liability is classified as monetary or nonmonetary? Include in your response the justification for recognizing gains and losses from monetary items and not for nonmonetary items.

*Part b.* Proponents of price-level restatement of financial statements state that a basic weakness of financial statements not adjusted for price-level changes is that they are made up of "mixed dollars."

**Required**

1. What is meant by the term *mixed dollars* and why is this a weakness of unadjusted financial statements?
2. Explain how financial statements restated for price-level changes eliminate this weakness. Use property, plant, and equipment as your example in this discussion. (*AICPA adapted*)

## C24-3  Current Value and Fair Presentation of Financial Statements

The total assets of the Sunset Land Company were $2½ million on December 31, 1995, including land of $150,000. Net income was negligible because no land sales took place and none were planned.

The land consisted of 50,000 acres valued at its acquisition cost in the early part of the century of $3 per acre. The market value of the land is now believed to exceed $15 million.

The auditor's opinion attached to the financial statements states, in part, "The financial statements present fairly the financial position of the Sunset Land Company...in conformity with generally accepted accounting principles."

**Required**

Does the use of generally accepted accounting principles enable the financial position of the Sunset Land Company to be presented fairly?

## C24-4  Constant Purchasing Power Adjustments

Barden Corp., a manufacturer with large investments in plant and equipment, began operations in 1941. The company's history has been one of expansion in sales, production, and physical facilities. Recently, some concern has been expressed that the conventional financial statements do not provide sufficient information for decisions by investors. After consideration of proposals for various types of supplementary financial statements to be included in the 1995 annual report, management has decided to present a balance sheet as of December 31, 1995 and a statement of income and retained earnings for 1995, both restated for changes in the general price level.

**Required**

1. On what basis can it be contended that Barden's conventional statements should be restated for changes in the general price level?
2. Distinguish between historical cost/constant purchasing power financial statements and current value financial statements.
3. Distinguish between monetary and nonmonetary assets and liabilities, as the terms are used in general price-level accounting. Give examples of each.
4. Outline the procedures the Barden Corp. should follow in preparing the proposed supplementary statements.
5. Indicate the major similarities and differences between the proposed supplementary statements and the corresponding conventional statements.
6. Assuming that in the future Barden will want to present comparative supplementary statements, can the 1995 supplementary statements be presented in 1996 without adjustment? Explain. (*AICPA adapted*)

### C24-5 *Current Costs*

The controller of the Robinson Company is discussing a comment you made in the course of presenting your audit report.

". . . and frankly," Mr. Fisher continued, "I agree that we, too, are responsible for finding ways to produce more relevant financial statements which are as reliable as the ones we now produce."

"For example, suppose the company acquired a finished item for inventory for $40 when the general price-level index was 110. And, later, the item was sold for $75 when the general price-level index was 121 and the current replacement cost was $54. We could calculate a 'holding gain.'"

**Required**

1. Explain to what extent and how current replacement costs already are used within generally accepted accounting principles to value inventories.
2. Calculate in good form the amount of the holding gain in Fisher's example.
3. Why is the use of current replacement cost for both inventories and cost of goods sold preferred by some accounting authorities to the generally accepted use of FIFO or LIFO? (*AICPA adapted*)

### C24-6 *Constant Purchasing Power Adjustments*

Published financial statements of United States companies are currently prepared on a stable dollar assumption, even

though the general purchasing power of the dollar has declined because of inflation in recent years. To account for this changing value of the dollar, many accountants suggest that financial statements should be adjusted for general price-level changes. Three independent, unrelated statements regarding constant purchasing power financial statements follow. Each statement contains some fallacious reasoning.

**Statement I**

The accounting profession has not seriously considered constant purchasing power financial statements before, because the rate of inflation usually has been so small from year to year that the adjustments would have been immaterial in amount. Constant purchasing power financial statements represent a departure from the historical cost basis of accounting. Financial statements should be prepared from facts, not estimates.

**Statement II**

If financial statements were adjusted for general price-level changes, depreciation charges in the earnings statement would permit the recovery of dollars of current purchasing power and, thereby, equal the cost of new assets to replace the old ones. General price-level adjusted data would yield statement-of-financial-position amounts closely approximating current values. Furthermore, management can make better decisions if constant purchasing power financial statements are published.

**Statement III**

When adjusting financial data for general price-level changes, a distinction must be made between monetary and nonmonetary assets and liabilities, which, under the historical cost basis of accounting, have been identified as "current" and "noncurrent." When using the historical cost basis of accounting, no purchasing power gain or loss is recognized in the accounting process, but when financial statements are adjusted for general price-level changes, a purchasing-power gain or loss will be recognized on monetary and nonmonetary items.

**Required**

Evaluate each of the independent statements and identify the areas of fallacious reasoning in each and explain why the reasoning is incorrect. Complete your discussion of each statement before proceeding to the next statement. (*AICPA adapted*)

### C24-7 *Constant Dollar and Current Cost*

Financial reporting should provide information to help investors, creditors, and other users of financial statements. *Statement of Financial Accounting Standards No. 89* encourages companies to disclose certain supplementary information.

**Required**

1. Describe the historical cost/constant purchasing power method of accounting. Include in your discussion how historical cost amounts are used to make historical cost/constant purchasing power measurements.

2. Describe the principal advantage of the historical cost/constant purchasing power method of accounting over the historical cost method of accounting.

3. Describe the current cost method of accounting.

4. Why would depreciation expense for a given year differ using the current cost method of accounting instead of the historical cost method of accounting? Include in your discussion whether depreciation expense is likely to be higher or lower using the current cost method of accounting instead of the historical cost method of accounting in a period of rising prices, and why. (*AICPA adapted*)

## MULTIPLE CHOICE

*Select the best answer for each of the following.*

**M24-1** Financial statements that are expressed assuming a stable monetary unit are

    a. General price-level financial statements

    b. Historical-cost financial statements

    c. Current-value financial statements

    d. Fair-value financial statements

**M24-2** Victor Company purchased a machine on December 31, 1993 for $100,000. The machine is being depreciated on the straight-line basis with no salvage value and a 5-year life. Assume that there was a rise in current (replacement) cost of the machine of 10% during 1994, and of 10% during 1995 (based on the December 31, 1994 current cost). In a supplementary current cost statement at December 31, 1995, Victor would report accumulated depreciation for the machine of

    a. $42,000

    b. $44,000

    c. $46,200

    d. $48,400

**M24-3** Cartwright Corporation prepared the following data needed to compute the purchasing power gain or loss on net monetary items for inclusion in its supplementary information for the year ended December 31, 1995:

| | Amount in Historical Dollars | |
|---|---|---|
| | December 31, 1994 | December 31, 1995 |
| Monetary assets | $ 600,000 | $1,000,000 |
| Monetary liabilities | $1,566,000 | $2,449,000 |
| Net monetary liabilities | $ 966,000 | $1,449,000 |

Assumed Consumer Price Index numbers: At December 31, 1994, 105; at December 31, 1995, 115; and average for 1995, 110.

Cartwright's purchasing-power gain or loss (expressed in average 1995 constant dollars) on net monetary items for the year ended December 31, 1995 should be

    a. $109,000 gain

    b. $109,000 loss

    c. $111,000 gain

    d. $111,000 loss

**M24-4** When computing information on a historical cost/constant purchasing power basis, which of the following is classified as monetary?

    a. Investments in common stock

    b. Inventories

    c. Unamortized discount on bonds payable

    d. Accumulated depreciation

M24-5  Dart Company was formed on January 1, 1994. Selected balances from the historical cost balance sheet at December 31, 1995 were as follows:

| | |
|---|---|
| Land (purchased January 1, 1994) | $90,000 |
| Investment in securities, nonconvertible bonds (purchased July 1, 1994, and expected to be held to maturity) | 50,000 |
| Long-term debt | 70,000 |

The average Consumer Price Index was 100 for 1994, and 110 for 1995. In a supplementary constant dollar balance sheet (adjusted for changing prices) at December 31, 1995, these selected account balances should be shown at

| | Land | Investment in securities | Long-term debt |
|---|---|---|---|
| a. | $90,000 | $50,000 | $70,000 |
| b. | $90,000 | $55,000 | $77,000 |
| c. | $99,000 | $50,000 | $70,000 |
| d. | $99,000 | $55,000 | $77,000 |

M24-6  A method of accounting based on measures of current cost or lower recoverable amount, without restatement into units having the same general purchasing power, is

a.  Historical cost/constant purchasing power accounting
b.  Historical cost accounting
c.  Current cost/constant purchasing power accounting
d.  Current cost accounting

M24-7  The following schedule lists the average consumer price index (all urban consumers) of the indicated year:

| | |
|---|---|
| 1993 | 100 |
| 1994 | 125 |
| 1995 | 150 |

Carl Corporation's plant and equipment at December 31, 1995 are as follows:

| Date acquired | Percent depreciated | Historical cost |
|---|---|---|
| 1993 | 30 | $30,000 |
| 1994 | 20 | 20,000 |
| 1995 | 10 | 10,000 |
| | | $60,000 |

Depreciation is calculated at 10% per annum, straight-line. A full year's depreciation is recorded in the year of acquisition. There were no disposals in 1995.

What amount of depreciation expense would be included in the 1995 income statement adjusted for general inflation (historical cost/constant purchasing power accounting)?

a.  $6,000                          c.  $7,900
b.  $7,200                          d.  $9,000

M24-8  When computing information on a historical cost/constant purchasing power basis, which of the following is classified as nonmonetary?

a.  Allowance for doubtful accounts
b.  Accumulated depreciation of equipment
c.  Unamortized premium on bonds payable
d.  Deferred income taxes

**M24-9** Details of Monmouth Corporation's fixed assets at December 31, 1995 are as follows:

| Year acquired | Percent depreciated | Historical cost | Estimated current cost |
|---|---|---|---|
| 1993 | 30 | $50,000 | $70,000 |
| 1994 | 20 | 15,000 | 19,000 |
| 1995 | 10 | 20,000 | 22,000 |

Monmouth calculates depreciation at 10% per annum, using the straight-line method. A full year's depreciation is recorded in the year of acquisition. There were no disposals of fixed assets. Monmouth prepares supplementary information for inclusion in its 1995 annual report as recommended by the Financial Accounting Standards Board. In Monmouth's supplementary information restated into current cost, the net current cost (after accumulated depreciation) of the fixed assets should be stated as

a. $91,000
b. $84,000

c. $65,000
d. $58,000

**M24-10** *FASB Statement No. 89* recommends that the current cost for inventories be measured as the

a. Recoverable amount regardless of the current cost
b. Current cost regardless of the recoverable amount
c. Higher of current cost or recoverable amount
d. Lower of current cost or recoverable amount

*(AICPA adapted)*

## EXERCISES

**E24-1** *Four Alternative Accounting Methods*  A company purchased inventory for $10,000 at the beginning of the year when the CPI-U was 100. The inventory was sold in the middle of the year for $16,000 when the index was 110 and the current cost was $13,000.

**Required**

Compute the gross profit on the sale of the inventory under each of the following methods (compute the constant purchasing power amounts in terms of the average CPI-U of 110): (1) historical cost, (2) historical cost/constant purchasing power, (3) current cost, and (4) current cost/constant purchasing power.

**E24-2** *Constant Purchasing Power Adjustment*  Land was purchased for $50,000 on January 1, 1989, when the CPI-U was 100. The ending and average CPI-U for 1995 were 154 and 150, respectively.

**Required**

1. What is the constant purchasing power cost of the land included in the adjusted December 31, 1995 balance sheet in terms of the average CPI-U for 1995?
2. How would your answer to Requirement 1 change if the index on the date of purchase was 75?

**E24-3** *Constant Purchasing Power Adjustments to Balance Sheet Items*  The Desmond Company is preparing a constant purchasing power balance sheet at the average CPI-U for the year of 150. The CPI-U at the end of the year is 155. The following are the amounts in selected accounts and the index when the amount was recorded:

| | Amount | Index |
|---|---|---|
| Accounts receivable (net) | $10,000 | 155 |
| Machinery | 50,000 | 130 |
| Accumulated depreciation on machinery | 10,000 | 130 |
| Patent (net) | 5,000 | 125 |
| Accounts payable | 20,000 | 155 |
| Bonds payable | 50,000 | 120 |
| Common stock | 40,000 | 80 |

**Required**

Compute the amounts that would appear in the constant purchasing power year-end balance sheet.

E24-4     *Constant Purchasing Power Adjustments to Income Statement Items*     The Fishburn Company is preparing a constant purchasing power income statement for the year at the average CPI-U of 150. The following are the amounts in selected accounts and the index when the amount was recorded:

|  | Amount | Index |
|---|---|---|
| Sales revenue | $150,000 | 150 |
| Cost of goods sold | 60,000 | 145 |
| Depreciation expense | 20,000 | — |
| Wages expense | 30,000 | 150 |
| Interest expense | 10,000 | — |

The depreciation expense was for assets purchased when the index was 130 and the interest expense is on bonds issued (at par) when the index was 120. The tax rate is 30%. Taxes and interest are paid evenly throughout the year.

**Required**

1.  Prepare an historical cost income statement.
2.  Prepare a constant purchasing power income statement.

E24-5     *Purchasing-Power Gain or Loss*     The Gray Company had the following monetary assets and liabilities:

|  | January 1, 1995 | December 31, 1995 |
|---|---|---|
| Cash | $ 20,000 | $ 30,000 |
| Accounts receivable (net) | 40,000 | 50,000 |
| Total monetary assets | $ 60,000 | $ 80,000 |
| Accounts payable | $ 20,000 | $ 35,000 |
| Bonds payable | 80,000 | 75,000 |
| Total monetary liabilities | $100,000 | $110,000 |

Sales, purchases, and wages and salaries were $150,000, $80,000, and $60,000, respectively, and occurred evenly during the year. The CPI-U was 140 and 150 at the beginning and end of the year, respectively. Depreciation of $20,000 was recorded on assets purchased when the CPI-U was 120.

**Required**

Compute the purchasing-power gain or loss for the year of 1995 at the average index of 145.

E24-6     *Purchasing Power Gain or Loss*     The Herman Company, which has been selling stuffed animals for the past seven years, began the current year with a negative beginning net monetary items balance of $25,000. Uniformly throughout the year, the company earned and collected $90,000 in sales revenues, paid $36,000 in wages to its employees, and purchased and paid for $50,000 of stuffing and materials. The company also paid interest and income taxes of $6,000 and $9,000, respectively, at the end of the year.

**Required**

If the CPI-U was 128 at the beginning of the year, 136 at the end of the year, and averaged 132 for the whole year, compute Herman Company's purchasing-power gain or loss.

E24-7     *Purchasing-Power Gain or Loss*     Level, Inc. was formed in December 1994, when common stock of $200,000 was issued for cash of $50,000 and land valued at $150,000. Level did not begin operations until 1996, and no transactions occurred in 1995.

**Required**

If the CPI-U was 100 in December 1994 and 110 in December 1995, what would the purchasing-power gain or loss be in Level's 1995 constant purchasing power income statement adjusted to the average index? (*AICPA adapted*)

**E24-8** *Constant Purchasing Power Adjustments to Property, Plant, and Equipment*  The Grembar Company purchased a building on January 1, 1995 for $100,000 when the CPI-U was 125. The building has an expected residual value of zero and a life of 10 years, and straight-line depreciation is used. The December 1995 price index is 150 and the December 1996 index is 160, and it rose evenly during the year.

**Required**

1. What is the depreciation expense for 1995 and 1996 if a constant purchasing power income statement is prepared adjusted to the average index for each year?
2. What is the carrying value of the asset at December 31, 1995 and December 31, 1996, if a constant purchasing power balance sheet is prepared each year at the average index for the year?
3. How will the amounts in the 1995 constant purchasing power financial statements be adjusted when those statements are published in 1996 for comparison with the constant purchasing power financial statements of 1996?

**E24-9** *Constant Purchasing Power Adjustments and Cost of Goods Sold*  The Herder Company started operations on January 1, 1994 and is preparing constant purchasing power financial statements. The following are the historical cost inventory transactions that occurred in the next 2 years and the CPI-U at the time:

|  | Units | Cost/Unit | Index |
|---|---|---|---|
| Inventory, January 1, 1994 | 100 | $10 | 100 |
| Purchases, 1994 | 500 | $11 | 105 |
| Sales, 1994 | 400 | — | — |
| December 31, 1994 |  |  | 110 |
| Purchases, 1995 | 800 | $12 | 115 |
| Sales, 1995 | 600 | — | — |
| December 31, 1995 |  |  | 120 |

**Required**

Prepare the constant purchasing power ending inventory and cost of goods sold for each year at the average CPI-U for each year of 105 and 115, respectively, for the (1) FIFO cost flow assumption, and (2) LIFO cost flow assumption.

**E24-10** *Constant Purchasing Power Adjustments and the Sale of an Asset*  The Hinkins Company purchased land in January 1994 for $20,000 when the CPI-U was 90. The CPI-U in December 1994 and December 1995 was 99 and 108, respectively. The company sold the land for $45,000 in September 1996 when the index was 117. The index in December 1996 was 120 and it rose evenly during the year.

**Required**

If constant purchasing power financial statements, adjusted to the average index, are prepared each year:

1. What is the carrying value of the land at December 31, 1994 and December 31, 1995?
2. What is the gain on the sale of the land in 1996?
3. Is a purchasing-power gain recognized on the land at any time?

**E24-11** *Current Costs: Inventory*  The following is the cost of goods sold section of the 1995 income statement for the Higgins Company:

| | |
|---|---|
| Inventory, 12/31/1994 | $ 39,000 |
| Purchases | 138,000 |
| Cost of goods available for sale | $177,000 |
| Less: Inventory, 12/31/1995 | (60,000) |
| Cost of goods sold | $117,000 |

Additional information:

1. The December 31, 1994 inventory consisted of 10,000 units purchased in August 1994.
2. The December 31, 1995 inventory consisted of 12,000 units purchased in October 1995.
3. Purchases of 30,000 units were made during the year.
4. The current cost of the inventory was $4.10 per unit in December 1994 and $5.10 per unit in December 1995.

**Required**

Prepare the following 1995 disclosures for the Higgins Company:

1. Cost of goods sold on a current cost basis.
2. Current cost of ending inventory.

**E24-12** *Current Costs: Inventory* The Tangard Company shows the following cost of goods sold section on its 1995 income statement:

| | |
|---|---|
| Inventory, December 31, 1994 | $16,000 |
| Purchases | 70,000 |
| Cost of goods available for sale | $86,000 |
| Less: Inventory, December 31, 1995 | (10,950) |
| Cost of goods sold | $75,050 |

The December 31, 1994 inventory consisted of 5,000 units purchased in September 1994. Purchases of 20,000 units were made during 1995. The December 31, 1995 inventory consisted of 3,000 units purchased in November 1995. The current cost of the inventory was $3.30 per unit in December 1994 and $3.70 per unit in December 1995.

**Required**

Prepare the following 1995 disclosures for the Tangard Company:

1. Cost of goods sold on a current cost basis.
2. Current cost of ending inventory.

**E24-13** *Current Costs: Property and Plant* The Turner Company has the following fixed assets at the end of 1995:

Land: Purchased for $15,000 in January, 1989
Current cost, December, 1994: $25,000
Current cost, December, 1995: $30,000
Building: Purchased for $100,000 in January 1989
Estimated life: 25 years
Depreciation method: Straight-line (no residual value)
Current cost, December 1994: $180,000
Current cost, December 1995: $200,000

No land or buildings were acquired or sold in 1995.

**Required**

Prepare the following 1995 disclosures for the Turner Company:

1. Depreciation expense on a current cost basis.
2. Current cost (net) of property and plant.

**E24-14** *Current Cost and Property, Plant, and Equipment* The Lalli Company purchased three machines at various times as shown in the table. Each machine has an expected residual value of zero and a life of 10 years, and straight-line depreciation is used. The current cost of the assets is determined by using a specific price-level index appropriate for those assets. Accumulated depreciation is based on the current cost and the age of the assets. The value of the index in December 1995 and December 1996 is 110 and 120, respectively, and the value of the index when each machine was purchased is as shown:

| Machine | Cost | Date Acquired | Index at Acquisition |
|---|---|---|---|
| A | $20,000 | January 1, 1990 | 80 |
| B | 32,000 | January 1, 1993 | 100 |
| C | 33,000 | January 1, 1996 | 110 |

**Required**

1. Compute the current cost (net) of the assets at December 31, 1996.
2. Compute the current cost depreciation expense for 1996.

**E24-15** *Measuring Current Cost*   The Norbeck Company purchased a building in January 1991 that had a residual value of zero and an estimated life of 25 years. The building cost $1 million and included 20,000 square feet. The cost of constructing a similar building in December 1994 and December 1995 was $70 and $80 per square foot, respectively. The specific price-level index for buildings has risen from 112 in January 1991 to 168 in December 1994 and 189 in December 1995.

**Required**

1. If the company estimates current costs by functional pricing, compute the 1995 current cost depreciation expense and ending current cost (net) of the building.
2. Repeat Requirement 1, except assume the company uses a specific price-level index to estimate current costs.

**E24-16** *Current Cost and Cost of Goods Sold*   Refer to the information given in Exercise 24-9. In addition, the current cost of the inventory in December 1994 and December 1995 is $11.50 and $13 per unit, respectively. Assume the FIFO method is used for the historical cost financial statements.

**Required**

1. Compute the cost of goods sold and inventory that would appear in the current cost financial statements for 1994 and 1995.
2. What is the realized holding gain on the inventory for 1994 and 1995 if current cost financial statements are prepared?
3. What is the unrealized holding gain for the year on the inventory at the end of 1994 and 1995 if current cost financial statements are prepared?

**E24-17** *Current Cost*   The Jaeger Company is preparing a comprehensively adjusted current cost balance sheet. The following are the amounts in selected accounts:

| | |
|---|---|
| Inventory (materials) | $30,000 |
| Debt securities held to maturity | 21,000 |
| Machinery | 50,000 |
| Accumulated depreciation on machinery | 10,000 |
| Patent (net) | 5,000 |

The following additional information is available:

1. The average cost inventory method is used. The acquisition cost of the units in inventory rose from $1.40 to $1.60 per unit during the year. The weighted average current cost is $1.55 per unit.
2. Debt securities held to maturity:

| Security | Cost | Market Value |
|---|---|---|
| Company A | $10,000 | $12,000 |
| Company B | 8,000 | 6,000 |
| Company C | 3,000 | 2,000 |

3. The machinery was purchased at the beginning of the year. Double-declining-balance depreciation is being used. The current cost of the machinery fell by 10% during the year.
4. The patent was purchased 5 years ago for $10,000. It is estimated that an equivalent patent would cost $25,000 now.

**Required**

1. At what amount should each item be included in the current cost balance sheet?
2. Cost of goods sold on the historical cost basis is $100,000. This includes wages of $30,000, the depreciation on the machinery, and cost of materials. What is the cost of goods sold on a current cost basis?

*E24-18   Current Cost and Sale of an Asset*   The Marino Company purchased some land for $100,000 on January 1, 1994. In December 1994 and December 1995, the current cost of the land was $110,000 and $130,000, respectively. The land was sold on January 5, 1996 for $140,000.

**Required**

If current cost financial statements are prepared:

1. What is the realized holding gain on the land in 1994 and 1995?
2. What is the unrealized holding gain on the land in 1994 and 1995?
3. What is the gain on the sale of the land in 1996?

## PROBLEMS

*P24-1   Inventory and the Four Alternative Accounting Methods*   The Turner Company, a retail company, began operations on January 1, 1995 and engaged in the following transactions:

| | |
|---|---|
| January 1, 1995 | Purchased 100 units of inventory for $200 per unit. The general price-level index was 110. |
| First quarter, 1995 | Sold 50 units for $400 per unit. The average replacement cost of the inventory was $220 per unit and the general price-level index was 115. |
| Second quarter, 1995 | Purchased 200 units for $250 per unit. The general price-level index was 118. |
| Third quarter, 1995 | Sold 100 units for $450 per unit. The average replacement cost of the inventory was $260 per unit and the general price-level index was 120. |
| Fourth quarter, 1995 | No purchases or sales were made. The average replacement cost of the inventory was $275 per unit and the general price-level index was 120. |

**Required**

If the company uses a FIFO inventory flow assumption, compute the value of the inventory at December 31, 1995, the gross profit, and the holding gains for 1995 under each of four alternatives:

1. Historical cost
2. Constant purchasing power (at the average index of 115)
3. Current cost
4. Constant purchasing power adjusted current cost (at the average index of 115)

*P24-2   Land and the Four Alternative Accounting Methods*   Several transactions concerning one asset (land) of a company are summarized as follows:

| | |
|---|---|
| 1994 | Purchased land for $40,000 cash on December 31. |
| 1995 | Held the land all year; replacement cost at year-end was $52,000. |
| 1996 | Sold the land for $68,000 on December 31. |

General price-level index (CPI-U):

| | | | |
|---|---|---|---|
| December 1993 | 90 | December 1995 | 110 |
| December 1994 | 100 | December 1996 | 120 |

**Required**

Compute the value of the land on the ending balance sheets and the gain recognized (including holding gains) on the income statements for 1994, 1995, and 1996 under each of the following alternatives:

1. Historical cost
2. Constant purchasing power (at the average index for each year)
3. Current cost
4. Constant purchasing power adjusted current cost (at the average index for each year)

P24-3 *Purchasing Power Gain or Loss* At the beginning of 1995, the Molly Company's beginning monetary liabilities exceeded its monetary assets by $20,000. During the year, the following events occurred which affected Molly's net monetary items balance:

1. Earned and collected revenue of $120,000 evenly throughout the year.
2. Paid wages and salaries of $60,000 evenly throughout the year.
3. Sold investment in Dan Corporation stock for $35,000 at the end of June.
4. Issued 1,000 shares of common stock at $20 per share at the end of September.
5. Purchased building for $90,000 cash, paid income taxes of $15,000, and paid dividends of $4,000 at the end of the year.

The CPI-U for 1995 was as follows:

| | | | |
|---|---|---|---|
| Beginning of year | 120 | End of 3rd quarter | 130 |
| End of 1st quarter | 121 | End of 4th quarter | 137 |
| End of 2nd quarter | 125 | Average for year | 128 |

**Required**
Compute Molly's purchasing-power gain or loss for 1995.

P24-4 *Constant Purchasing Power Financial Statements* The Stegman Company prepared the following historical cost financial statements for 1995:

### Income Statement
#### For Year Ended December 31, 1995

| | | |
|---|---:|---:|
| Sales | | $400,000 |
| Cost of goods sold | | |
| Inventory, December 31, 1994 | $ 60,000 | |
| Purchases | 200,000 | |
| Cost of goods available | $260,000 | |
| Inventory, December 31, 1995 | (70,000) | |
| Cost of goods sold | | (190,000) |
| Gross profit | | $210,000 |
| Operating expenses | | |
| Depreciation | $ 19,000 | |
| Wages and salaries | 51,000 | |
| Interest | 5,000 | |
| Total operating expenses | | (75,000) |
| Income before income tax | | $135,000 |
| Income tax expense | | (40,500) |
| Net Income | | $ 94,500 |

### Retained Earnings Statement
#### For Year Ended December 31, 1995

| | |
|---|---:|
| Retained earnings, December 31, 1994 | $120,000 |
| Plus: Net income | 94,500 |
| | $214,500 |
| Less: Dividends | (10,000) |
| Retained earnings, December 31, 1995 | $204,500 |

### Balance Sheets

|                              | December 31, 1994 | December 31, 1995 |
|------------------------------|-------------------|-------------------|
| Cash                         | $ 40,000          | $110,000          |
| Accounts receivable (net)    | 50,000            | 80,000            |
| Inventory                    | 60,000            | 70,000            |
| Building and equipment (net) | 160,000           | 141,000           |
| Total Assets                 | $310,000          | $401,000          |
| Accounts payable             | $ 40,000          | $ 46,500          |
| Bonds payable                | 50,000            | 50,000            |
| Capital stock                | 100,000           | 100,000           |
| Retained earnings            | 120,000           | 204,500           |
| Total Liabilities and Stockholders' Equity | $310,000 | $401,000     |

The following information is available:

1. The CPI-U was as follows: December 1994—180; December 1995—200; average, 1995—190.
2. Sales and expenses occurred evenly throughout the year.
3. The inventory was valued on a FIFO cost flow assumption. The ending inventory of each year was purchased in December of the year.
4. The depreciation related to the following assets:

| Asset     | Cost      | Index at Acquisition    | Depreciation Rate |
|-----------|-----------|-------------------------|-------------------|
| Building  | $ 80,000  | 90 (January 1, 1985)    | 5%                |
| Equipment | 150,000   | 150 (January 1, 1993)   | 10%               |

5. Dividends of $5,000 were paid on June 30 and on December 31.
6. The company was formed on January 1, 1985.

**Required**

Prepare constant purchasing power financial statements for 1995 using the average index. Include a December 31, 1994 balance sheet for comparative purposes. (*Note:* The retained earnings for the December 31, 1994 balance sheet is a balancing amount because there is not sufficient information since the formation of the company to adjust retained earnings.)

**P24-5** *Constant Purchasing Power Financial Statements and Current Cost Adjustments* The 1995 financial statements of the Ryan Corporation are as follows (the company was formed on December 31, 1994):

### Balance Sheets

|                              | December 31, 1994 | December 31, 1995 |
|------------------------------|-------------------|-------------------|
| Cash                         | $ 40,000          | $ 36,000          |
| Inventory                    | —                 | 70,000            |
| Equipment                    | 40,000            | 40,000            |
| Less: Accumulated depreciation | —               | (10,000)          |
| Total Assets                 | $ 80,000          | $136,000          |
| Bonds payable                | $ 50,000          | $ 50,000          |
| Capital stock                | 30,000            | 30,000            |
| Retained earnings            | —                 | 56,000            |
| Total Liabilities and Stockholders' Equity | $ 80,000 | $136,000     |

### Income Statement
#### For Year Ended December 31, 1995

| | | |
|---|---:|---:|
| Sales | | $300,000 |
| Cost of goods sold | | |
|   Inventory, December 31, 1994 | — | |
|   Purchases | $240,000 | |
|   Inventory, December 31, 1995 | (70,000) | |
|     Cost of goods sold | | (170,000) |
| Gross profit | | $130,000 |
| Operating expenses | | |
|   Depreciation expense | $ 10,000 | |
|   Administrative expenses | 40,000 | |
|     Total operating expenses | | (50,000) |
| Income before income taxes | | $ 80,000 |
| Income tax expense | | (24,000) |
| Net Income | | $ 56,000 |

The CPI-U was 100 in December 1994 and 120 in December 1995, and it rose evenly during the year. The purchases were made in four equal installments on January 1, April 1, July 1, and October 1, 1995. The FIFO inventory system is used. Sales and expenses occurred evenly during the year. The tax rate is 30% and taxes are paid evenly throughout the year.

**Required**

1. Prepare constant purchasing power financial statements for 1995 using the average index of 110.
2. If the specific price level of the inventory had risen by 40% during the year, and the specific price level of the equipment by 20% during the year, prepare a current cost income statement (ignore holding gains) for 1995.
3. How much is the realized holding gain for 1995?

P24-6 *Comprehensively Adjusted Financial Statements* The historical cost financial statements of the Burke Company are as follows:

### Income Statement
#### For Year Ended December 31, 1995

| | | |
|---|---:|---:|
| Sales | | $150,000 |
| Cost of goods sold | | |
|   Inventory, December 31, 1994 | $ 30,000 | |
|   Purchases | 74,000 | |
|   Cost of goods available | $104,000 | |
|   Less: Inventory, December 31, 1995 | (40,000) | |
|     Cost of goods sold | | (64,000) |
| Gross profit | | $ 86,000 |
| Operating expenses | | |
|   Depreciation expense | $ 10,000 | |
|   Other operating expenses | 26,000 | |
|     Total operating expenses | | (36,000) |
| Income before income taxes | | $ 50,000 |
| Income tax expense | | (15,000) |
| Net Income | | $ 35,000 |

### Comparative Balance Sheets

|                                   | December 31, 1994 | December 31, 1995 |
|-----------------------------------|-------------------|-------------------|
| Cash                              | $   5,000         | $  10,000         |
| Accounts receivable               | 10,000            | 15,000            |
| Inventory                         | 30,000            | 40,000            |
| Property and equipment            | 90,000            | 90,000            |
| Less: Accumulated depreciation    | (20,000)          | (30,000)          |
| Total Assets                      | $115,000          | $125,000          |
| Accounts payable                  | $  30,000         | $    5,000        |
| Bonds payable                     | 25,000            | 25,000            |
| Common stock, no par              | 20,000            | 20,000            |
| Retained earnings                 | 40,000            | 75,000            |
| Total Liabilities and Stockholders' Equity | $115,000 | $125,000          |

The following additional information is available:

1. Sales and other operating expenses occurred evenly throughout 1995.
2. The income tax rate is 30% and taxes are paid evenly during the year.
3. The December 31, 1994 inventory consisted of 10,000 units purchased at $3 each in September 1994. The December 31, 1995 inventory consisted of 10,000 units purchased at $4 each in September 1995. Purchases of 20,000 units were made evenly during 1995.

   The current cost per unit of the inventory was as follows:

   | December 1994 | $3.30 |
   |---------------|-------|
   | Average 1995  | 3.70  |
   | December 1995 | 4.10  |

4. The property and equipment included the following items:

| Item     | Cost    | Date of Purchase | Current Cost of Equivalent New Assets | | Depreciation Life | Depreciation Method |
|----------|---------|------------------|-----------|-----------|-------------------|---------------------|
|          |         |                  | Dec. 1994 | Dec. 1995 |                   |                     |
| Land     | $10,000 | 1/1/1989         | $40,000   | $44,000   | —                 | —                   |
| Building | 80,000  | 1/1/1993         | 90,000    | 96,000    | 8 years           | Straight-line (no residual value) |

5. The bonds payable were issued in January 1993.
6. The common stock was sold when the company was formed on January 1, 1989.
7. The CPI-U index was as follows: January 1989, 110; January 1993, 240; September 1994, 254; December 1994, 260; average 1995, 275; September 1995, 282; and December 1995, 290.

### Required

1. Prepare a constant purchasing power income statement for 1995 and the beginning and ending balance sheets in terms of the average index for 1995. Include a purchasing power gain or loss schedule. (*Hint:* Use the retained earnings as a balancing amount in the beginning balance sheet.)
2. Prepare a current cost income statement for 1995 in terms of the average current cost for the year (exclude holding gains and losses).
3. Prepare current cost balance sheets at the beginning and end of 1995 in terms of the current cost at that time. (*Hint:* Use the retained earnings as a balancing amount in the beginning balance sheet.)

P24-7   *Current Cost Disclosures*   The following information pertains to the Cricket Company for 1995:

Inventory: Beginning inventory: 2,000 units purchased in January 1989 at $10 each
                                                    2,000 units purchased in January 1994 at $20 each
             Purchases: 2,500 units at $23 each in March 1995
                          2,500 units at $25 each in September 1995
             Ending Inventory: 4,500 units
             Current cost, December 1994: $22 per unit
             Current cost, December 1995: $26 per unit

Property, Plant, and Equipment:
             Land:        Purchased for $50,000 in January 1989
                           Current cost, December 1994: $110,000
                           Current cost, December 1995: $120,000
                           Purchased for $60,000 in December 1995
             Equipment: Purchased for $72,000 in January 1994
                           Estimated life: 8 years
                           Residual value: Zero
                           Depreciation method: Sum-of-the-years'-digits
                           Current cost, December 1994: $75,000
                           Current cost, December 1995: $85,000
             Building:    Purchased for $120,000 in January 1989
                           Estimated life: 30 years
                           Residual value: Zero
                           Depreciation method: Straight-line
                           Current cost, December 1994: $250,000
                           Current cost, December 1995: $280,000

**Required**
1. Compute the current cost of goods sold and ending inventory for 1995.
2. Compute the current cost of property, plant and equipment and the depreciation expense for 1995.

P24-8   *Current Cost Disclosures*   The following information pertains to the Mello Company for 1995:
1. Inventory:

   December 31, 1994: 10,000 units purchased in October 1994 for $3 each
   December 31, 1995: 12,000 units purchased in August 1995 for $3.70 each
   Purchases:        30,000 units
   Current cost:     December 1994: $3.10 per unit
                       December 1995: $3.50 per unit

2. Property, plant, and equipment:

   Building purchased for $150,000 in January 1991. Straight-line depreciation is used over a life of 10 years with a zero residual value.
   Current cost:       December 1994: $180,000
                         December 1995: $190,000

   Machinery purchased for $30,000 in January 1994. Straight-line depreciation is used over a life of 5 years with a zero residual value.
   Current cost:       December 1994: $32,000
                         December 1995: $40,000

**Required**
1. Calculate the current cost of goods sold and ending inventory for 1995.
2. Calculate the current cost of property, plant, and equipment and the depreciation expense for 1995.

P24-9  *Current Cost Balance Sheet*   The Wiese Company's historical cost balance sheet at December 31, 1995 is as follows:

| | |
|---|---:|
| Cash | $ 30,000 |
| Accounts receivable (net) | 70,000 |
| Inventory | 80,000 |
| Debt securities held to maturity | 40,000 |
| Property, plant, and equipment (net) | 151,000 |
| Total Assets | $371,000 |
| Accounts payable | $ 50,000 |
| Bonds payable | 100,000 |
| Capital stock | 70,000 |
| Retained earnings | 151,000 |
| Total Liabilities and Stockholders' Equity | $371,000 |

The following additional information is available:

1.  The accounts receivable consists of $77,000 of accounts less $7,000 for estimated uncollectibles. An aging of the accounts discloses the following:

| Age | Amount | Percentage Uncollectible |
|---|---|---|
| Less than 30 days | $40,000 | 1% |
| 30 to 60 days | 25,000 | 4% |
| Over 60 days | 12,000 | 10% |
| | $77,000 | |

2.  A LIFO cost flow assumption is used. The specific price index at the end of 1995 is 140. The LIFO layers of inventory are as follows:

| Amount | Year Added | Specific Price Index |
|---|---|---|
| $50,000 | 1987 | 90 |
| 25,000 | 1992 | 120 |
| 5,000 | 1994 | 135 |

3.  The debt securities held to maturity consist of the following items:

| Securities | Cost | Market Value December 31, 1995 |
|---|---|---|
| A | $25,000 | $30,000 |
| B | 10,000 | 8,000 |
| C | 5,000 | 12,000 |

4.  The property, plant, and equipment consists of the following:

| Asset | Cost | Purchased | Depreciation Rate |
|---|---|---|---|
| Land | $ 50,000 | January 1, 1989 | — |
| Building | 80,000 | January 1, 1989 | 5% |
| Machinery | 70,000 | January 1, 1993 | 10% |
| | $200,000 | | |

Additional information:

a. The land, 100 acres, was appraised at $90,000.
b. Similar land in the area has been selling for $1,000 per acre.
c. The building covers 6,000 square feet. The company has estimated that current building costs are $20 per square foot.
d. The specific price index for buildings has risen by 40% since the beginning of 1989.
e. Machinery to produce the same products made by the company would currently cost $110,000.

5. The bonds payable:
a. pay interest semiannually,
b. were issued at par for 8%, and
c. mature on December 31, 2005.
The current yield on similar bonds is 10%.

**Required**

Prepare a current cost balance sheet for December 31, 1995. (*Hint*: Retained earnings is a balancing amount. Accumulated depreciation is based on the current cost, depreciation rate, and age of the assets.)

P24-10 *Current Cost Financial Statements* The following are the historical cost financial statements of the Swedberg Company for 1995:

### Income Statement
### For Year Ended December 31, 1995

| | | |
|---|---|---|
| Sales | | $250,000 |
| Cost of goods sold | | (80,000) |
| Gross profit | | $170,000 |
| Operating expenses | | |
| Depreciation expense | $ 20,000 | |
| Other expenses | 50,000 | (70,000) |
| Income before income taxes | | $100,000 |
| Income tax expense | | (30,000) |
| Net Income | | $ 70,000 |

### Balance Sheets

| | December 31, 1994 | December 31, 1995 |
|---|---|---|
| Cash | $ 30,000 | $ 68,000 |
| Accounts receivable (net) | 20,000 | 40,000 |
| Inventory | 60,000 | 80,000 |
| Building and equipment (net) | 80,000 | 60,000 |
| Total Assets | $190,000 | $248,000 |
| Accounts payable | $ 20,000 | $ 30,000 |
| Bonds payable | 40,000 | 40,000 |
| Capital stock | 70,000 | 70,000 |
| Retained earnings | 60,000 | 108,000 |
| Total Liabilities and Stockholders' Equity | $190,000 | $248,000 |

The following additional information is available:

1. A FIFO inventory cost flow assumption is used for the historical cost financial statements. The average current cost during the period was 5% higher than the FIFO cost of the units sold. The current costs at the beginning and end of the period were 4% and 7% higher, respectively, than the historical cost of the units in inventory.

2.  The building and equipment were purchased at the same time (July 1, 1991) and consist of the following:

| Asset | Cost | Replacement Costs of Equivalent New Assets | | Depreciation Rate |
| | | December 1994 | December 1995 | |
|---|---|---|---|---|
| Building | $ 50,000 | $80,000 | $85,000 | 5% |
| Equipment | 100,000 | 60,000 | 58,000 | $17\frac{1}{2}\%$ |

**Required**

Prepare current cost financial statements for 1995, ignoring all holding gains. (*Hint*: Retained earnings is a *balancing amount*. Accumulated depreciation is based on the current cost, depreciation rate, and age of the assets.)

P24-11   *Current Cost Financial Statements*   The historical cost financial statements of the Golosow Company for 1995 and additional information are as follows:

*Income Statement*
*For Year Ended December 31, 1995*

| | | |
|---|---:|---:|
| Sales | | $150,000 |
| Cost of goods sold | | (40,000) |
| Gross profit | | $110,000 |
| Operating expenses | | |
|   Depreciation | $ 8,000 | |
|   Other expenses | 42,000 | (50,000) |
| Income before income taxes | | $ 60,000 |
| Income tax expense | | (18,000) |
| Net Income | | $ 42,000 |

*Balance Sheets*

| | December 31, 1994 | | December 31, 1995 | |
|---|---:|---:|---:|---:|
| Cash | | $ 16,000 | | $ 29,000 |
| Inventory | | 50,000 | | 65,000 |
| Building and equipment | $80,000 | | $80,000 | |
| Less: Accumulated depreciation | (16,000) | 64,000 | (24,000) | 56,000 |
| Land | | 20,000 | | 20,000 |
|   Total Assets | | $150,000 | | $170,000 |
| Accounts payable | | $ 10,000 | | $ 20,000 |
| Capital stock | | 100,000 | | 100,000 |
| Retained earnings | | 40,000 | | 50,000 |
|   Total Liabilities and Stockholders' Equity | | $150,000 | | $170,000 |

Additional information:

1.  A LIFO cost flow assumption is used. The current cost of the units in inventory on December 31, 1994 is twice the original purchase price. The average current cost of the units in inventory rose 10% during the year.
2.  The building and equipment were purchased at the beginning of 1993. They are being depreciated on the straight-line basis with a 10-year life and no residual value. The current cost has risen by 5% each year since the purchase.
3.  Land is appraised at $25,000 and $28,000 at the end of 1994 and 1995, respectively.

**Required**

Prepare current cost financial statements for 1995 ignoring all holding gains. (*Hint*: Retained earnings is a balancing amount. Accumulated depreciation is based on the current cost, depreciation rate, and age of the assets.)

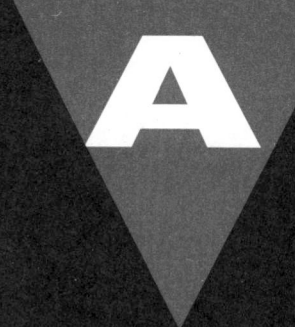

# THE COCA-COLA COMPANY 1992 ANNUAL REPORT: FINANCIAL SECTION

Reproduced with permission of The Coca-Cola Company.

*Financial Review Incorporating*
*Management's Discussion and Analysis*

Management's primary objective is to maximize share-owner value over time. To accomplish this objective, The Coca-Cola Company and subsidiaries (the Company) have developed a comprehensive business strategy that emphasizes maximizing long-term cash flows. This strategy focuses on continuing aggressive investment in the high-return soft drink business, increasing returns on existing investments and optimizing the cost of capital through appropriate financial policies. The success of this strategy is evidenced by the growth in the Company's cash flows and earnings, its increased returns on total capital and equity and the total return to its share owners over time.

### Investments

The Company has a global business system which distributes its products in more than 195 countries. In 1992, the Coca-Cola system continued to aggressively expand its production and distribution infrastructure in emerging markets such as eastern Germany, Poland and Romania. With its pervasive global business system in place, the Company is well positioned to capitalize on investment opportunities as they arise.

Management seeks investments that strategically enhance existing operations and offer cash returns that exceed the Company's long-term after-tax weighted average cost of capital, estimated by management to be approximately 12 percent. The Company's soft drink business provides an attractive area for investment due to its inherent high returns. Most soft drink markets are relatively undeveloped compared to the U.S. market. International per capita consumption of Company products is still only 14 percent of the U.S. level. As a result, attractive investment opportunities exist for the Company and its bottlers to expand the production, distribution and

marketing systems in international markets. Additional strategic investments are also required in the relatively more developed markets to increase product availability, enhance marketing focus and improve overall efficiency. The Company has already benefited from the continued consolidation of production and distribution networks, plus investment in the latest technology and information systems.

Over the last decade, bottling investments have represented a significant portion of the Company's capital investments. The principal objective of these investments is to ensure strong and efficient production, distribution and marketing systems in order to maximize long-term growth in volume, cash flows and share-owner value of the bottler and the Company.

When considered appropriate, the Company makes equity investments in bottling companies (typically between 20 percent and 50 percent). Through these investments, the Company is able to help focus and improve sales and marketing programs, assist in the development of effective business and information systems and help establish capital structures appropriate for these respective operations.

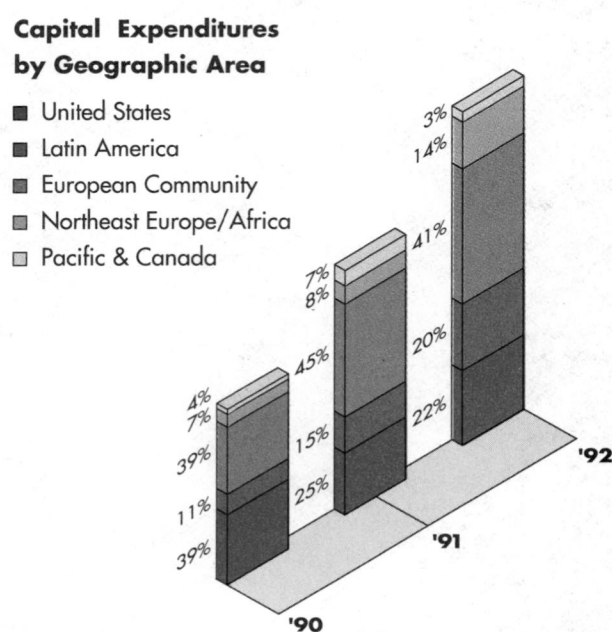

### Capital Expenditures by Geographic Area

- United States
- Latin America
- European Community
- Northeast Europe/Africa
- Pacific & Canada

*Financial Review Incorporating
Management's Discussion and Analysis*

In certain situations, management believes it is advantageous to own a controlling interest in bottling operations. For example, in eastern Germany, the Company's objective is to establish a modern soft drink business quickly. Due to limited local resources for a timely undertaking, this is being accomplished through a wholly-owned bottling subsidiary.

The Company's consolidated bottling, canning and fountain/post-mix operations produced and distributed approximately 15 percent of worldwide unit case volume. Equity investee bottlers produced and distributed an additional 30 percent of worldwide unit case volume.

In restructuring the bottling system, the Company periodically participates in bottler ownership changes or takes temporary ownership positions in bottlers. The length of ownership is influenced by various factors, including operational changes, management changes and the process of identifying appropriate new investors.

At December 31, 1992, the Company owned approximately 52 percent of Coca-Cola Amatil Limited, an Australian-based bottler of Company products. The Company expects to reduce its ownership interest to below 50 percent within the next 2 years. Accordingly, the investment has been accounted for by the equity method of accounting. If valued at the December 31, 1992, quoted closing price of the publicly traded Coca-Cola Amatil common shares, the calculated value of the Company's investment in Coca-Cola Amatil exceeded its carrying value by approximately $74 million.

At December 31, 1992, the Company had an additional $397 million of investments that represented majority interests in companies that were not consolidated. These investments were accounted for by the cost or equity methods, depending on the circumstances. These investments relate primarily to temporary majority interests which management expects to reduce to below 50 percent. The Company owns a temporary majority interest in The Coca-Cola Bottling Company of New York, Inc. which management expects to reduce to below 50 percent within the next year. Based on management's estimates, the market values of these majority-owned investments exceeded their carrying values at December 31, 1992.

**Increasing Returns**

The Company manages its concentrate and bottling operations so as to optimize profit margins, while at the same time increasing volume and its share of soft drink sales. The Company also provides expertise and resources to equity investees to build their businesses and to build long-term volume, cash flows and share-owner value.

Through cost control, strategic price increases and efficient allocation of marketing resources, the Company has generally been able to maintain or improve margins in 1992 despite difficult economic climates in many markets.

Growth in volume and the Company's share of sales depend on continuous reinvestment in the form of advertising. Advertising enhances the Company's products as industry leaders. Advertising expenditures increased to $1.1 billion in 1992, compared to $988 million in 1991 and $932 million in 1990.

Volume and profits have benefited from the Company's ownership of and investments in bottling operations. While the bottling business has relatively lower margins on revenue compared to the concentrate business, aggressive investment in soft drink infrastructure has resulted in growth in share of sales and unit case volume at the bottler level, which in turn generates gallon shipment gains for the concentrate business.

Equity income, which primarily represents returns from the Company's unconsolidated bottling investments, was $65 million in 1992. The Company's joint ventures and investments in bottling entities include Coca-Cola Enterprises Inc., Coca-Cola Amatil and Coca-Cola & Schweppes Beverages Ltd. (CC&SB).

*Financial Review Incorporating
Management's Discussion and Analysis*

**Financial Policies**

Maximizing returns on invested capital necessitates optimizing the Company's cost of capital through appropriate financial policies.

*Debt Financing:* The Company maintains debt levels considered prudent based on the Company's cash flows and the percentage of debt to the Company's total capital. The Company's overall cost of capital is lowered by the use of debt financing, resulting in increased return to share owners.

The Company's capital structure and financial policies have resulted in long-term credit ratings of "AA" from Standard & Poor's and "Aa3" from Moody's, as well as the highest credit ratings available for its commercial paper programs. The Company's strong financial position and cash flows allow it opportunistic access to financing in financial markets around the world.

*Foreign Currency Management:* With approximately 81 percent of operating income in 1992 generated by operations outside the United States, foreign currency management is another key element of the Company's financial policies. The Company closely monitors its exposure to fluctuations in currencies and adopts strategies to reduce the impact of these fluctuations on the Company's financial performance where cost-justified. The Company benefits from operating in a number of different currencies, because weakness in any particular currency is often offset by strengths in other currencies. The Company also engages in various hedging activities to enhance income and cash flows denominated in foreign currencies. Furthermore, the Company uses foreign currency borrowings when appropriate to finance investments outside the United States.

*Share Repurchases:* In July 1992, the Board of Directors authorized a plan to repurchase up to 100 million additional shares of the Company's common stock through the year 2000.

No shares were repurchased under this plan until February 1993. In 1992, the Company repurchased 29.7 million shares approved under the 1989 share repurchase plan at a total cost of approximately $1.2 billion. The Company completed the 1989 share repurchase plan in January 1993. From the inception of share repurchase programs in 1984 to December 31, 1992, the Company has repurchased 414.8 million shares at a total cost of approximately $5.3 billion. This represents over 25 percent of the Company's common shares that were outstanding at the beginning of 1984. The value of these shares, based on the quoted closing price of the Company's common stock traded on December 31, 1992 on the New York Stock Exchange, was approximately $17.4 billion.

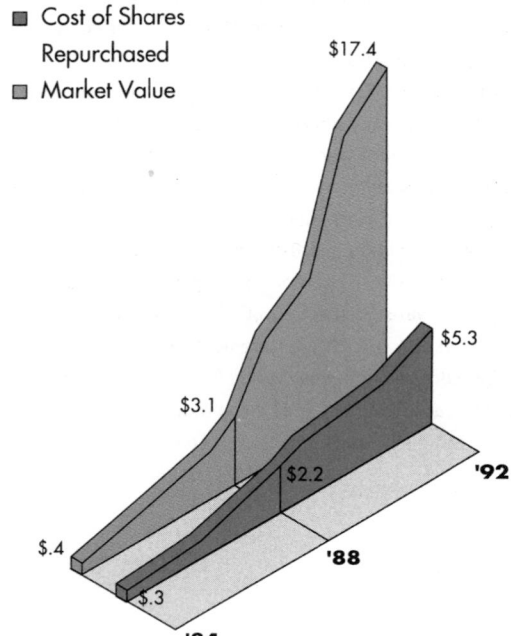

**Stock Repurchase Programs
Shares Purchased vs.
Market Value**

(In billions)

■ Cost of Shares Repurchased
■ Market Value

$17.4

$5.3

$3.1

$2.2

'92

$.4

$.3

'88

'84

*Financial Review Incorporating
Management's Discussion and Analysis*

*Dividend Policy:* Strong earnings growth has enabled the Company to increase the cash dividend per common share by an average annual compounded growth rate of 10.3 percent since December 31, 1982. The annual common stock dividend was $.56 per share, $.48 per share and $.40 per share in 1992, 1991 and 1990, respectively, adjusted for stock splits. At its February 1993 meeting, the Board of Directors increased the quarterly dividend per common share to $.17, equivalent to a full-year common dividend of $.68 in 1993. This is the 31st consecutive year in which the Board of Directors has approved common stock dividend increases.

With approval from the Board of Directors, management plans to maintain a common stock dividend payout ratio of approximately 40 percent of net income available to common share owners. The 1992 dividend payout ratio was 45.6 percent based on 1991 results and 44.3 percent based on 1992 results.

**Measuring Performance**
A significant portion of the increase in the rate of growth of the Company's earnings, returns and cash flows can be attributed to the Company taking actions to increase its investments in the high-margin, high-return soft drink business; increase share and volume growth for its products; and manage its existing asset base effectively and efficiently.

Economic Profit and Economic Value Added provide management a framework to measure the impact of these value-oriented actions. Economic Profit is defined as net operating profit after taxes in excess of a computed capital charge for average operating capital employed. Economic Value Added represents the growth in Economic Profit from year to year.

Over the last five years, Economic Profit has increased at an average annual compounded rate of 27 percent, resulting in Economic Value Added to the Company of $952 million. Over the same period, the Company's stock price has increased at an average rate of 34 percent. Management believes that, over the long term, growth in Economic Profit, or Economic Value Added, will have a positive impact on the growth in share-owner value.

**Total Return to Share Owners**
During the past decade, share owners of the Company have enjoyed an excellent return on their investment. A $100 investment in the Company's common stock at December 31, 1982, together with reinvested dividends, would be worth approximately $1,286 at December 31, 1992—an average annual compounded return of 29 percent.

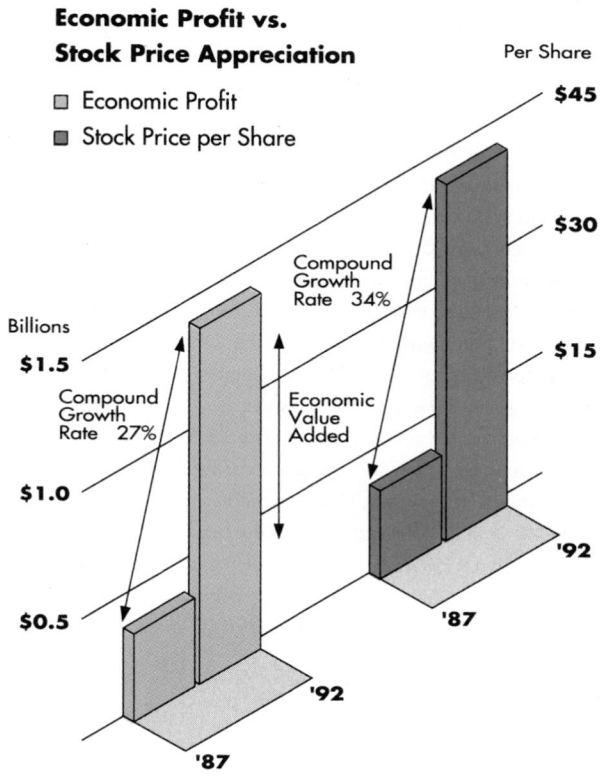

**Economic Profit vs.
Stock Price Appreciation**

Per Share

☐ Economic Profit
■ Stock Price per Share

$45

$30

Compound
Growth
Rate   34%

$15

Billions
$1.5

Compound
Growth
Rate   27%

Economic
Value
Added

$1.0

'92

'87

$0.5

'92

'87

*Financial Review Incorporating
Management's Discussion and Analysis*

## Management's Discussion and Analysis

### Lines of Business

*Soft Drinks:* The Company is the largest manufacturer, marketer and distributor of soft drink concentrates and syrups in the world. It manufactures soft drink concentrates and syrups, which it sells to bottling and canning operations, and manufactures fountain/post-mix soft drink syrups, which it sells to authorized fountain wholesalers and some fountain retailers. The Company has substantial equity investments in numerous soft drink bottling and canning operations, and it owns and operates certain bottling and canning operations outside the United States.

*Foods:* The foods business sector's principal business is processing and marketing citrus and other juice and juice-drink products, primarily orange juice. It is the world's largest marketer of packaged citrus products.

### Operations

*Volume:* The Company measures soft drink volume in two ways: gallon shipments of concentrates and syrups and equivalent unit cases of finished product. Gallon shipments represent the primary business of the Company since they measure concentrates and syrups sold by the Company to its bottling partners. Most of the Company's revenues are based on this measure of "wholesale" activity. The Company also monitors unit case volume, a measure of finished product sold by bottling partners to retail customers who make sales to consumers. Management believes unit case volume more accurately measures the underlying strength of the global business system because it measures trends at the retail level and is less impacted by inventory management practices at the wholesale level. Fountain/post-mix syrups sold by the Company directly to customers are included in both measures.

Worldwide soft drink volume increased in 1992, with unit case volume and gallon shipments increasing 3 percent. In 1991, both unit cases and gallon shipments increased 5 percent. In the United States, continued slow economic recovery impacted volume in 1992. Unit case volume and gallon shipments increased 2 percent in 1992, compared to growth of 2½ percent and 2 percent, respectively, in 1991. The increase in

1991 was due in part to full-year results from significant fountain customers added in 1990.

Outside the United States, unit case volume increased 4 percent in 1992, while gallon shipments increased 3 percent, reflecting the difficult economic environments in a number of markets, particularly Brazil. Approximately 69 percent of soft drink gallon shipments were made outside the United States in 1992, compared to 68 percent in 1991. In 1991, both unit case volume and gallon shipments outside the United States increased 6 percent.

In the European Community, unit cases increased 5 percent in 1992, including gains of 10 percent in the Benelux and Denmark Division and 6 percent in France and Germany. Gallon shipments increased 3 percent in 1992, compared to 6 percent in 1991.

In Northeast Europe/Africa, unit cases increased 14 percent in 1992, while gallon shipments increased 15 percent. Unit case growth was driven by expansion into new markets in East Central Europe and continued expansion of the Company's infrastructure in many existing markets. In 1991, gallon shipments increased 3 percent in Northeast Europe/Africa.

Unit case volume in the Pacific grew 3 percent in 1992. Gallon shipments grew 2 percent, compared to 4 percent in 1991. Unit cases increased 2 percent in Japan and 12 percent in the China Division, offsetting a 1 percent decrease in the Philippines, where natural disasters hampered distribution.

Unit case volume and gallon shipments in Latin America were even with the prior year, primarily because of an 18 percent decrease in unit cases and a 19 percent decrease in gallon shipments in Brazil, where severe economic conditions eroded consumer purchasing power. The decline in Brazil was offset by unit case volume growth of 3 percent in Mexico and 30 percent in Argentina. Gallon shipments in Latin America increased 8 percent in 1991.

In the foods business sector, 1992 unit volume for juice and juice-drink products was unchanged following the strong performance in 1991, when volume increased 12 percent. Frozen orange juice volume decreased 8 percent in 1992, following an increase of 29 percent in 1991. The 1992 decline in frozen orange juice volume was offset by a 4 percent increase in chilled product volume and an 8 percent increase in volume for shelf stable products.

*Financial Review Incorporating
Management's Discussion and Analysis*

*Net Operating Revenues and Gross Margin:* For the Company's soft drink business, revenues grew 15 percent in 1992, primarily due to gallon shipment increases, favorable exchange movement, price increases and continued expansion of bottling and canning operations. Revenues for the foods business sector in 1992 increased 2 percent due to price increases.

In 1991, revenues for the Company's soft drink business increased 15 percent, primarily due to gallon shipment growth, price increases and continued expansion of bottling and canning operations. In the foods business sector, 1991 revenues increased 2 percent primarily due to volume increases, partially offset by price decreases.

On a consolidated basis, the Company's worldwide revenues grew 13 percent in 1992 while gross profit grew 16 percent, expanding the Company's gross margin from 60 percent in 1991 to 61 percent in 1992. Gross profits grew 15 percent in 1991 on consolidated revenue growth of 13 percent. Gross margins improved in both years due to price increases and lower raw material costs.

*Selling, Administrative and General Expenses:* Selling expenses were $4.0 billion in 1992, $3.5 billion in 1991 and $3.2 billion in 1990. The increases in 1992 and 1991 were due primarily to higher marketing investments in line with expansion of the business.

## Margin Analysis

☐ Net Operating Revenues (In billions)
◩ Gross Margin
■ Operating Margin

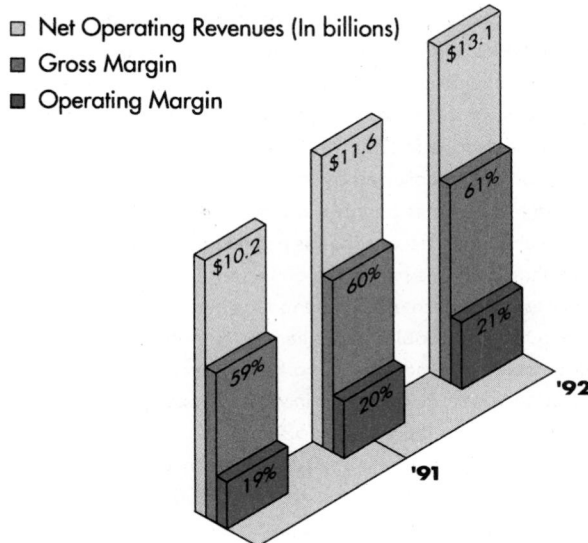

Administrative and general expenses were $1.2 billion in 1992, $1.1 billion in 1991 and $859 million in 1990. The 1992 increase was due primarily to expansion of the business, particularly newly formed, Company-owned bottling operations. The 1991 increase was due to the growth of the business and stock-related employee benefits. Administrative and general expenses, as a percentage of net operating revenues, were approximately 10 percent in 1992, 9 percent in 1991 and 8 percent in 1990.

*Operating Income and Operating Margin:* Operating income increased 19 percent in 1992 and 1991, and operating margins grew from 20 percent in 1991 to 21 percent in 1992. The expansion in operating margins resulted from gross margin expansion and a reduction in the costs of stock-related employee benefits.

*Interest Income and Interest Expense:* Interest expense declined in 1992 and 1991 due primarily to lower interest rates. Interest income in 1992 declined primarily due to lower interest rates. Interest income in 1991 was consistent with 1990 levels.

*Equity Income:* Equity income increased 63 percent, to $65 million, in 1992 due primarily to one-time charges recorded by Coca-Cola Enterprises in 1991, partially offset by increased start-up costs of Coca-Cola Nestle Refreshments Company in 1992.

Equity income decreased $70 million in 1991 due primarily to a decrease in earnings of Coca-Cola Enterprises. Coca-Cola Enterprises' 1991 results were less than 1990 earnings due to pretax restructuring charges of $152 million and a pretax charge of $15 million to increase insurance reserves in 1991 and a nonrecurring gain that was recorded by Coca-Cola Enterprises in 1990. The decrease in equity income from Coca-Cola Enterprises was partially offset by improved results of CC&SB, which successfully implemented a cost reduction program during 1991.

*Other Income (Deductions)–Net:* Other income (deductions)–net in 1992 was lower than 1991 due to nonrecurring gains recorded in 1991.

The $28 million favorable change in other income–net in 1991 resulted from a pretax gain of $69 million on the sale of property no longer required as a result of a consolidation of concentrate operations in Japan and a pretax gain of $27 million on the sale of the Company's 22 percent ownership interest in Johnston Coca-Cola Bottling Group, Inc. to Coca-Cola Enterprises. This favorable change was partially

*Financial Review Incorporating
Management's Discussion and Analysis*

offset by an increase in net foreign exchange costs (including certain hedging costs) and a nonrecurring gain that was recorded in 1990.

*Income Taxes:* The Company's effective tax rate was 31.4 percent in 1992, 32.1 percent in 1991 and 31.4 percent in 1990.

*Transition Effect of Change in.Accounting Principle:* As of January 1, 1992, the Company recognized a one-time, noncash after-tax charge of $219 million resulting from the adoption of Statement of Financial Accounting Standards No. 106, "Employers' Accounting for Postretirement Benefits Other Than Pensions" (SFAS 106). The cumulative charge consists of postretirement health care and life insurance benefit obligations to employees of the Company and the Company's portion of postretirement benefit obligations of its equity investees. The Company elected to absorb this charge immediately rather than amortizing the obligation over a period of up to twenty years.

*Income Per Common Share:* Accelerated by the Company's share repurchase program, income per common share before change in accounting principle grew 18 percent and 19 percent

in 1992 and 1991, respectively. Net income per common share grew 4 percent in 1992, reflecting the $.17 per share impact of the adoption of SFAS 106 in 1992.

**Liquidity and Capital Resources**

One of the Company's financial strengths is its ability to generate cash from operations in excess of requirements for capital reinvestment and dividends.

*"Free Cash Flow":* Free Cash Flow is the cash from operations remaining after the Company has satisfied its business reinvestment opportunities. Management focuses on growing Free Cash Flow to achieve management's primary objective, maximizing share-owner value. The Company uses Free Cash Flow, along with borrowings, to make share repurchases and dividend payments. The consolidated statements of cash flows are summarized as follows (in millions):

| Year Ended December 31, | 1992 | 1991 | 1990 |
|---|---|---|---|
| Cash flows provided by (used in): | | | |
| Operations | $2,232 | $2,084 | $1,284 |
| Investment activities | (1,359) | (1,124) | (440) |
| "Free Cash Flow" | 873 | 960 | 844 |
| Cash flows provided by (used in): | | | |
| Financing | (917) | (1,331) | (544) |
| Exchange | (59) | — | 33 |
| Increase (decrease) in cash | $ (103) | $ (371) | $ 333 |

Cash provided by operations continued to grow in 1992, reaching $2.2 billion, resulting from growth in net income before the noncash charges for depreciation, amortization and the change in accounting principle. Cash used in investment activities increased in 1992 due primarily to purchases of property, plant and equipment, investments and acquisitions of bottling operations, offset by the collection of certain finance subsidiary receivables added in 1991.

The payments collected by the finance subsidiary were used to reduce notes payable in 1992. The noncash charge for the change in accounting for postretirement benefits other than pensions resulted in an increase in other long-term liabilities and a decrease in deferred tax benefits. The increase in long-term receivables and other assets in 1992 is primarily attributable to an increase in marketable securities held in accordance with.a negotiated income tax exemption grant.

Cash from operations grew 62 percent in 1991, resulting from growth in net income and a reduction in tax payments. Tax payments in 1990 reflect approximately $300 million related to the 1989 gain on the sale of Columbia Pictures Entertainment,

## Cash Provided by Operations
(In billions)

■ Reinvestment
□ Free Cash Flow

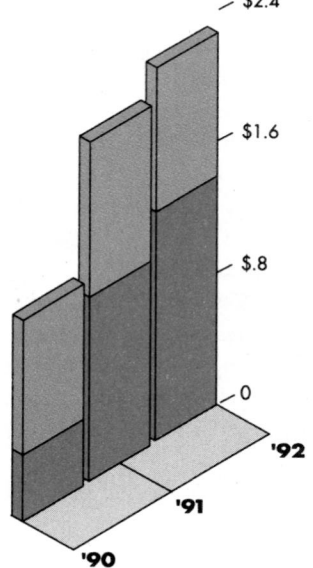

*Financial Review Incorporating*
*Management's Discussion and Analysis*

Inc. stock. In 1991, cash used in investment activities increased due to purchases of property, plant and equipment, additions to finance subsidiary receivables and the impact of a disposal of a temporary investment in 1990.

*Financing:* Financing activities primarily represent the Company's net borrowing activities, dividend payments and share repurchases. Cash used in financing activities totaled $917 million in 1992, $1.3 billion in 1991 and $544 million in 1990. The change between years was due primarily to net borrowings in 1992 and 1990 compared to net reductions of debt in 1991. Cash used to fund the share repurchase program increased to $1.2 billion in 1992, from $397 million in 1991.

The Company aggressively manages its mix of short-term versus long-term debt to lower its overall cost of borrowing. This process, coupled with the share repurchase program and investment activity, resulted in an increase in loans and notes payable and current liabilities exceeding current assets at December 31, 1992.

The Company manages its debt levels based on the Company's cash flows relative to fixed charges and debt and the percentage of debt to the Company's total capital. The Company's ratio of earnings to fixed charges was 14.1 in 1992, 11.6 in 1991 and 8.5 in 1990. Debt levels are measured excluding the debt of the Company's finance subsidiary, and are net of cash, cash equivalents and marketable securities in excess of operating requirements and temporary bottling investments. At December 31, 1992 and 1991, the Company's net debt totaled $1.8 billion and $1.0 billion. Net debt represented 31.9 percent of net capital at December 31, 1992, compared with 19.2 percent at December 31, 1991. The ratio of Free Cash Flow to the Company's net debt was 48 percent at December 31, 1992, compared to 95 percent at December 31, 1991.

At December 31, 1992, the Company had $1.6 billion in lines of credit and other short-term credit facilities contractually available, under which $171 million was outstanding. Included were $1.3 billion in lines designated to support commercial paper and other borrowings, under which no amounts were outstanding at December 31, 1992.

*Exchange:* International operations are subject to certain opportunities and risks, including currency fluctuations and government actions. The Company closely monitors its methods of operating in each country and adopts strategies responsive to changing economic and political environments.

The Company uses approximately 42 functional currencies. For the Company, the weighted average annual exchange rates of foreign hard currencies, compared to the U.S. dollar, strengthened approximately $3\frac{1}{2}$ percent in 1992 and weakened slightly during 1991. In 1992, 1991 and 1990, weighted average exchange rates for certain key foreign currencies strengthened (weakened) against the U.S. dollar as follows:

| Year Ended December 31, | 1992 | 1991 | 1990 |
|---|---|---|---|
| Australian dollar | (5)% | 1 % | 0 % |
| British pound | 1 % | (1)% | 10 % |
| Canadian dollar | (4)% | 1 % | 2 % |
| German mark | 8 % | (3)% | 17 % |
| Japanese yen | 6 % | 8 % | (5)% |

The foreign currency translation adjustment decreased in 1992 due primarily to the weakening of certain European currencies against the U.S. dollar in the fourth quarter of 1992. Exchange effects include costs of hedging certain balance sheet, translation and transaction exposures, net gains or losses on foreign currency transactions and the remeasurement of certain currencies into functional currencies. Exchange losses recorded in other income (deductions)—net amounted to $25 million in 1992, $22 million in 1991 and $.5 million in 1990.

**Impact of Inflation and Changing Prices**
Inflation is a factor in many markets around the world and consequently impacts the way the Company operates. In general, management believes that the Company is able to adjust prices to counteract the effects of increasing costs and generate sufficient cash flows to maintain its productive capability.

In highly inflationary countries, the Company has benefited from its net monetary liability position. This position is viewed as a hedge against the effects of high inflation, since net liabilities will ultimately be paid with devalued currency.

**Additional Information**
For additional information concerning the Company's operations, cash flows, liquidity and capital resources, this analysis should be read in conjunction with the information on pages 48 through 66 of this Annual Report. Additional information concerning operations in different lines of business and geographic areas is presented on pages 63 and 64.

## Selected Financial Data

| Year Ended December 31, | 1992 [3][4] | 1991 [4] | 1990 [4] | 1989 [4] |
|---|---|---|---|---|
| (In millions except per share data and ratios) | | (Restated) | (Restated) | (Restated) |
| **Summary of Operations** | | | | |
| Net operating revenues | $13,074 | $11,572 | $10,236 | $8,622 |
| Cost of goods sold | 5,055 | 4,649 | 4,208 | 3,548 |
| Gross profit | 8,019 | 6,923 | 6,028 | 5,074 |
| Selling, administrative and general expenses | 5,249 | 4,604 | 4,076 | 3,348 |
| Provisions for restructured operations and disinvestment | — | — | — | — |
| Operating income | 2,770 | 2,319 | 1,952 | 1,726 |
| Interest income | 164 | 175 | 170 | 205 |
| Interest expense | 171 | 192 | 231 | 308 |
| Equity income | 65 | 40[5] | 110 | 75 |
| Other income (deductions)—net | (82) | 41 | 13 | 66 |
| Income from continuing operations before income taxes and changes in accounting principles | 2,746 | 2,383 | 2,014 | 1,764 |
| Income taxes | 862 | 765 | 632 | 553 |
| Income from continuing operations before changes in accounting principles | $ 1,884 | $ 1,618 | $ 1,382 | $1,211 |
| Net income | $ 1,664 | $ 1,618 | $ 1,382 | $1,537 |
| Preferred stock dividends | — | 1 | 18 | 21 |
| Net income available to common share owners | $ 1,664 | $ 1,617 | $ 1,364 | $1,516[6] |
| Average common shares outstanding [1] | 1,317 | 1,333 | 1,337 | 1,384 |
| **Per Common Share Data** [1] | | | | |
| Income from continuing operations before changes in accounting principles | $ 1.43 | $ 1.21 | $ 1.02 | $ .86 |
| Net income | 1.26 | 1.21 | 1.02 | 1.10[6] |
| Cash dividends | .56 | .48 | .40 | .34 |
| Market price at December 31 | 41.88 | 40.13 | 23.25 | 19.31 |
| **Balance Sheet Data** | | | | |
| Cash, cash equivalents and current marketable securities | $ 1,063 | $ 1,117 | $ 1,492 | $1,182 |
| Property, plant and equipment—net | 3,526 | 2,890 | 2,386 | 2,021 |
| Depreciation | 310 | 254 | 236 | 181 |
| Capital expenditures | 1,083 | 792 | 593 | 462 |
| Total assets | 11,052 | 10,189 | 9,245 | 8,249 |
| Long-term debt | 1,120 | 985 | 536 | 549 |
| Total debt | 3,208 | 2,288 | 2,537 | 1,980 |
| Share-owners' equity | 3,888 | 4,239 | 3,662 | 3,299 |
| Total capital [2] | 7,096 | 6,527 | 6,199 | 5,279 |
| **Other Key Financial Measures** [2] | | | | |
| Total-debt-to-total-capital | 45.2% | 35.1% | 40.9% | 37.5% |
| Net-debt-to-net-capital | 31.9% | 19.2% | 23.7% | 14.7% |
| Return on common equity | 46.4% | 41.3% | 41.4% | 39.4% |
| Return on capital | 29.4% | 27.5% | 26.8% | 26.5% |
| Economic profit | $ 1,369 | $ 1,046 | $ 878 | $ 821 |
| Dividend payout ratio | 44.3% | 39.5% | 39.2% | 31.0%[6] |

[1] Adjusted for a two-for-one stock split in 1992, a two-for-one stock split in 1990 and a three-for-one stock split in 1986.
[2] See Glossary on page 70.
[3] In 1992, the Company adopted SFAS No. 106, "Employers' Accounting for Postretirement Benefits Other Than Pensions."
[4] The Company adopted SFAS No. 109, "Accounting for Income Taxes," in 1992 by restating financial statements beginning in 1989.

| | 1988 | 1987 | 1986 | 1985 | 1984 | 1983 | 1982 |
|---|---|---|---|---|---|---|---|
| | $8,065 | $7,658 | $6,977 | $5,879 | $5,442 | $5,056 | $4,760 |
| | 3,429 | 3,633 | 3,454 | 2,909 | 2,738 | 2,580 | 2,472 |
| | 4,636 | 4,025 | 3,523 | 2,970 | 2,704 | 2,476 | 2,288 |
| | 3,038 | 2,665 | 2,446 | 2,163 | 1,855 | 1,648 | 1,515 |
| | — | 36 | 180 | — | — | — | — |
| | 1,598 | 1,324 | 897 | 807 | 849 | 828 | 773 |
| | 199 | 232 | 154 | 151 | 133 | 90 | 119 |
| | 230 | 297 | 208 | 196 | 128 | 77 | 76 |
| | 92 | 64 | 45 | 52 | 42 | 35 | 25 |
| | (33) | 40 | 410 | 69 | 13 | 2 | 11 |
| | 1,626 | 1,363 | 1,298 | 883 | 909 | 878 | 852 |
| | 537 | 496 | 471 | 314 | 360 | 374 | 379 |
| | $1,089 | $ 867 | $ 827 | $ 569 | $ 549 | $ 504 | $ 473 |
| | $1,045 | $ 916 | $ 934 | $ 722 | $ 629 | $ 559 | $ 512 |
| | 7 | — | — | — | — | — | — |
| | $1,038 | $ 916 | $ 934 | $ 722 | $ 629 | $ 559 | $ 512 |
| | 1,458 | 1,509 | 1,547 | 1,573 | 1,587 | 1,635 | 1,558 |
| | $ .74 | $ .57 | $ .53 | $ .36 | $ .35 | $ .31 | $ .30 |
| | .71 | .61 | .60 | .46 | .40 | .34 | .33 |
| | .30 | .28 | .26 | .25 | .23 | .22 | .21 |
| | 11.16 | 9.53 | 9.44 | 7.04 | 5.20 | 4.46 | 4.33 |
| | $1,231 | $1,489 | $ 895 | $ 843 | $ 768 | $ 559 | $ 254 |
| | 1,759 | 1,602 | 1,538 | 1,483 | 1,284 | 1,247 | 1,233 |
| | 167 | 152 | 151 | 130 | 119 | 111 | 104 |
| | 387 | 304 | 346 | 412 | 300 | 324 | 273 |
| | 7,451 | 8,606 | 7,675 | 6,341 | 5,241 | 4,540 | 4,212 |
| | 761 | 909 | 996 | 801 | 631 | 428 | 423 |
| | 2,124 | 2,995 | 1,848 | 1,280 | 1,310 | 520 | 493 |
| | 3,345 | 3,187 | 3,479 | 2,948 | 2,751 | 2,912 | 2,779 |
| | 5,469 | 6,182 | 5,327 | 4,228 | 4,061 | 3,432 | 3,272 |
| | 38.8% | 48.4% | 34.7% | 30.3% | 32.3% | 15.2% | 15.1% |
| | 18.9% | 15.4% | 10.9% | 15.6% | 19.7% | 5.6% | 13.6% |
| | 34.7% | 26.0% | 25.7% | 20.0% | 19.4% | 17.7% | 18.7% |
| | 21.3% | 18.3% | 20.1% | 16.8% | 16.7% | 16.4% | 17.9% |
| | $ 7.48 | $ 417 | $ 311 | $ 269 | $ 268 | $ 138 | $ 61 |
| | 42.1% | 46.0% | 43.1% | 53.8% | 57.9% | 65.3% | 62.8% |

[5] *Equity income in 1991 includes a reduction of $44 million related to restructuring charges recorded by Coca-Cola Enterprises Inc.*

[6] *Net income available to common share owners in 1989 includes after-tax gains of $604 million ($.44 per common share) from the sale of the Company's equity interest in Columbia Pictures Entertainment, Inc. and the Company's bottled water business and the transition effect of $265 million related to the change in accounting for income taxes. Excluding these nonrecurring items, the dividend payout ratio in 1989 was 39.9 percent.*

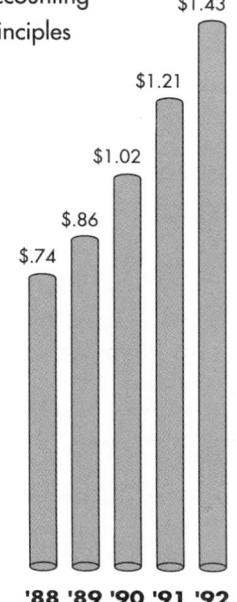

**Earnings Per Share**
From Continuing Operations Before Changes in Accounting Principles

$.74  $.86  $1.02  $1.21  $1.43
'88  '89  '90  '91  '92

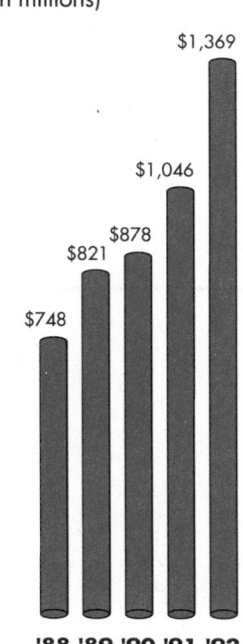

**Economic Profit**
(In millions)

$748  $821  $878  $1,046  $1,369
'88  '89  '90  '91  '92

*Consolidated Balance Sheets*

| December 31,<br>(In thousands except share data) | 1992 | 1991<br>(Restated) |
|---|---:|---:|
| **Assets** | | |
| | | |
| **Current** | | |
| Cash and cash equivalents | $ 955,608 | $ 1,058,250 |
| Marketable securities, at cost | 107,380 | 58,946 |
| | 1,062,988 | 1,117,196 |
| | | |
| Trade accounts receivable, less allowances of $32,512 | | |
| in 1992 and $34,567 in 1991 | 1,055,170 | 933,448 |
| Finance subsidiary receivables | 30,466 | 36,172 |
| Inventories | 1,018,621 | 987,764 |
| Prepaid expenses and other assets | 1,080,432 | 1,069,664 |
| **Total Current Assets** | 4,247,677 | 4,144,244 |
| | | |
| **Investments and Other Assets** | | |
| Investments | | |
|   Coca-Cola Enterprises Inc. | 518,312 | 592,561 |
|   Coca-Cola Amatil Limited | 548,077 | 570,774 |
|   Other, principally bottling companies | 1,096,705 | 957,467 |
| Finance subsidiary receivables | 94,916 | 288,471 |
| Long-term receivables and other assets | 636,682 | 442,135 |
| | 2,894,692 | 2,851,408 |
| | | |
| **Property, Plant and Equipment** | | |
| Land | 203,247 | 172,781 |
| Buildings and improvements | 1,528,722 | 1,200,672 |
| Machinery and equipment | 3,137,121 | 2,680,446 |
| Containers | 373,785 | 390,737 |
| | 5,242,875 | 4,444,636 |
| Less allowances for depreciation | 1,716,614 | 1,554,754 |
| | 3,526,261 | 2,889,882 |
| | | |
| **Goodwill and Other Intangible Assets** | 383,304 | 303,681 |
| | $11,051,934 | $10,189,215 |

| *December 31,* | **1992** | 1991 |
|---|---|---|
| | | (Restated) |

**Liabilities and Share-Owners' Equity**

**Current**

| | | |
|---|---|---|
| Accounts payable and accrued expenses | **$ 2,252,975** | $ 1,914,379 |
| Loans and notes payable | **1,967,540** | 845,823 |
| Finance subsidiary notes payable | **104,950** | 346,767 |
| Current maturities of long-term debt | **14,794** | 109,707 |
| Accrued taxes | **962,963** | 1,038,497 |
| **Total Current Liabilities** | **5,303,222** | 4,255,173 |

| | | |
|---|---|---|
| **Long-Term Debt** | **1,120,064** | 985,258 |

| | | |
|---|---|---|
| **Other Liabilities** | **658,631** | 493,765 |

| | | |
|---|---|---|
| **Deferred Income Taxes** | **81,629** | 216,072 |

**Share-Owners' Equity**

| | | |
|---|---|---|
| Common stock, $.25 par value— | | |
| Authorized: 2,800,000,000 shares; Issued: 1,696,202,840 shares in 1992, | | |
| 1,687,351,094 shares in 1991 | **424,051** | 421,838 |
| Capital surplus | **871,349** | 639,990 |
| Reinvested earnings | **8,165,024** | 7,238,643 |
| Unearned compensation related to outstanding restricted stock | **(99,631)** | (114,909) |
| Foreign currency translation adjustment | **(271,211)** | (4,909) |
| | **9,089,582** | 8,180,653 |

| | | |
|---|---|---|
| Less treasury stock, at cost (389,431,622 common shares in 1992; | | |
| 358,390,928 common shares in 1991) | **5,201,194** | 3,941,706 |
| | **3,888,388** | 4,238,947 |
| | **$11,051,934** | $10,189,215 |

*See Notes to Consolidated Financial Statements.*

## Consolidated Statements of Income

| Year Ended December 31,<br>(In thousands except per share data) | 1992 | 1991 | 1990 |
|---|---|---|---|
| **Net Operating Revenues** | **$13,073,860** | $11,571,614 | $10,236,350 |
| Cost of goods sold | **5,054,377** | 4,648,385 | 4,208,850 |
| **Gross Profit** | **8,019,483** | 6,923,229 | 6,027,500 |
| Selling, administrative and general expenses | **5,249,392** | 4,604,184 | 4,075,936 |
| **Operating Income** | **2,770,091** | 2,319,045 | 1,951,564 |
| Interest income | **163,784** | 175,406 | 169,985 |
| Interest expense | **171,351** | 192,515 | 230,979 |
| Equity income | **65,111** | 39,975 | 110,139 |
| Other income (deductions)–net | **(81,547)** | 41,368 | 13,727 |
| **Income before Income Taxes and**<br>    **Change in Accounting Principle** | **2,746,088** | 2,383,279 | 2,014,436 |
| Income taxes | **862,273** | 765,277 | 632,532 |
| **Income before Change in Accounting Principle** | **1,883,815** | 1,618,002 | 1,381,904 |
| Transition effect of change in accounting for<br>    postretirement benefits other than pensions | | | |
|     Consolidated operations | **(146,364)** | — | — |
|     Equity investments | **(73,069)** | — | — |
| **Net Income** | **1,664,382** | 1,618,002 | 1,381,904 |
| Preferred stock dividends | **—** | 521 | 18,158 |
| **Net Income Available to Common Share Owners** | **$ 1,664,382** | $ 1,617,481 | $ 1,363,746 |
| **Income per Common Share** | | | |
| Before change in accounting principle | **$      1.43** | $      1.21 | $      1.02 |
| Transition effect of change in accounting for<br>    postretirement benefits other than pensions | | | |
|     Consolidated operations | **(.11)** | — | — |
|     Equity investments | **(.06)** | — | — |
| **Net Income per Common Share** | **$      1.26** | $      1.21 | $      1.02 |
| **Average Common Shares Outstanding** | **1,316,758** | 1,332,944 | 1,337,140 |

*See Notes to Consolidated Financial Statements.*

*Consolidated Statements of Cash Flows*

| Year Ended December 31,<br>(In thousands) | 1992 | 1991<br>(Restated) | 1990<br>(Restated) |
|---|---|---|---|
| **Operating Activities** | | | |
| Net income | $ 1,664,382 | $ 1,618,002 | $1,381,904 |
| Transition effect of change in accounting for postretirement benefits | 219,433 | — | — |
| Depreciation and amortization | 321,922 | 261,427 | 243,888 |
| Deferred income taxes | (26,608) | (94,313) | (74,755) |
| Equity income, net of dividends | (30,249) | (16,013) | (93,816) |
| Foreign currency adjustments | 23,611 | 65,534 | (77,068) |
| Gain on sale of investments | — | (34,577) | (60,277) |
| Other noncash items | 103,009 | 33,338 | 97,752 |
| Net change in operating assets and liabilities | (43,130) | 251,003 | (133,701) |
| Net cash provided by operating activities | 2,232,370 | 2,084,401 | 1,283,927 |
| **Investing Activities** | | | |
| Additions to finance subsidiary receivables | (53,984) | (210,267) | (31,551) |
| Collections of finance subsidiary receivables | 254,280 | 51,942 | 58,243 |
| Acquisitions and investments | (717,487) | (399,183) | (301,010) |
| Proceeds from disposals of investments and other assets | 247,052 | 180,058 | 391,180 |
| Decrease (increase) in marketable securities | (52,191) | 2,735 | 16,733 |
| Purchases of property, plant and equipment | (1,083,270) | (791,677) | (592,971) |
| Proceeds from disposals of property, plant and equipment | 47,078 | 43,958 | 19,208 |
| All other investing activities | (1,004) | (2,246) | 504 |
| Net cash used in investing activities | (1,359,526) | (1,124,680) | (439,664) |
| Net cash provided by operations after reinvestment | 872,844 | 959,721 | 844,263 |
| **Financing Activities** | | | |
| Issuances of debt | 1,381,227 | 989,926 | 592,417 |
| Payments of debt | (432,380) | (1,246,664) | (81,594) |
| Preferred stock redeemed | — | (75,000) | (225,000) |
| Common stock issued | 131,264 | 39,394 | 29,904 |
| Purchases of common stock for treasury | (1,259,488) | (399,076) | (306,667) |
| Dividends (common and preferred) | (738,001) | (640,064) | (552,640) |
| Net cash used in financing activities | (917,378) | (1,331,484) | (543,580) |
| **Effect of Exchange Rate Changes on Cash<br>and Cash Equivalents** | (58,108) | 458 | 32,852 |
| **Cash and Cash Equivalents** | | | |
| Net increase (decrease) during the year | (102,642) | (371,305) | 333,535 |
| Balance at beginning of year | 1,058,250 | 1,429,555 | 1,096,020 |
| Balance at end of year | $   955,608 | $ 1,058,250 | $1,429,555 |

*See Notes to Consolidated Financial Statements.*

## Consolidated Statements of Share-Owners' Equity

| Three Years Ended December 31, 1992 | Preferred Stock | Common Stock | Capital Surplus | Reinvested Earnings | Outstanding Restricted Stock | Foreign Currency Translation | Treasury Stock |
|---|---|---|---|---|---|---|---|
| *(In thousands except per share data)* | | | | | | | |
| **Balance December 31, 1989** | $ 300,000 | $418,910 | $437,324 | $5,618,312 | $ (45,892) | $ (7,206) | $(3,235,963) |
| Restatement for change in accounting principle for income taxes | — | — | — | (186,871) | — | — | — |
| **Balance December 31, 1989 as restated** | 300,000 | 418,910 | 437,324 | 5,431,441 | (45,892) | (7,206) | (3,235,963) |
| Sales of stock to employees exercising stock options | — | 905 | 28,999 | — | — | — | (2,762) |
| Tax benefit from employees' stock option and restricted stock plans | — | — | 13,286 | — | — | — | — |
| Translation adjustments (net of income taxes of $573) | — | — | — | — | — | 11,237 | — |
| Stock issued under restricted stock plans, less amortization of $11,655 | — | 429 | 33,094 | — | (21,868) | — | — |
| Purchases of common stock for treasury | — | — | — | — | — | — | (303,905) |
| Redemption of preferred stock | (225,000) | — | — | — | — | — | — |
| Net income | — | — | — | 1,381,904 | — | — | — |
| Dividends | | | | | | | |
| Preferred | — | — | — | (18,158) | — | — | — |
| Common (per share—$.40) | — | — | — | (534,482) | — | — | — |
| **Balance December 31, 1990 as restated** | 75,000 | 420,244 | 512,703 | 6,260,705 | (67,760) | 4,031 | (3,542,630) |
| Sales of stock to employees exercising stock options | — | 972 | 38,422 | — | — | — | (2,421) |
| Tax benefit from employees' stock option and restricted stock plans | — | — | 20,015 | — | — | — | — |
| Translation adjustments (net of income taxes of $958) | — | — | — | — | — | (8,940) | — |
| Stock issued under restricted stock plans, less amortization of $22,323 | — | 622 | 68,850 | — | (47,149) | — | — |
| Purchases of common stock for treasury | — | — | — | — | — | — | (396,655) |
| Redemption of preferred stock | (75,000) | — | — | — | — | — | — |
| Net income | — | — | — | 1,618,002 | — | — | — |
| Dividends | | | | | | | |
| Preferred | — | — | — | (521) | — | — | — |
| Common (per share—$.48) | — | — | — | (639,543) | — | — | — |
| **Balance December 31, 1991 as restated** | — | 421,838 | 639,990 | 7,238,643 | (114,909) | (4,909) | (3,941,706) |
| Sales of stock to employees exercising stock options | — | 2,155 | 129,109 | — | — | — | (34,552) |
| Tax benefit from employees' stock option and restricted stock plans | — | — | 92,758 | — | — | — | — |
| Translation adjustments (net of income taxes of $67) | — | — | — | — | — | (266,302) | — |
| Stock issued under restricted stock plans, less amortization of $24,828 | — | 58 | 9,492 | — | 15,278 | — | — |
| Purchases of common stock for treasury | — | — | — | — | — | — | (1,224,936) |
| Net income | — | — | — | 1,664,382 | — | — | — |
| Common dividends (per share—$.56) | — | — | — | (738,001) | — | — | — |
| **Balance December 31, 1992** | $ — | $424,051 | $871,349 | $8,165,024 | $ (99,631) | $(271,211) | $(5,201,194) |

*See Notes to Consolidated Financial Statements.*

*Notes to Consolidated Financial Statements*

## Note 1  Accounting Policies

The significant accounting policies and practices followed by The Coca-Cola Company and subsidiaries (the Company) are as follows:

### Consolidation

The consolidated financial statements include the accounts of the Company and all subsidiaries except where control is temporary or does not rest with the Company. The Company's investments in companies in which it has the ability to exercise significant influence over operating and financial policies, including certain investments where there is a temporary majority interest, are accounted for by the equity method. Accordingly, the Company's share of the net earnings of these companies is included in consolidated net income. The Company's investments in other companies are carried at cost. All significant intercompany accounts and transactions are eliminated.

Certain amounts in the prior years' financial statements have been reclassified to conform to the current year presentation.

### Net Income per Common Share

Net income per common share is computed by dividing net income less dividends on preferred stock by the weighted average number of common shares outstanding.

### Cash Equivalents

Marketable securities that are highly liquid and have maturities of three months or less at the date of purchase are classified as cash equivalents.

### Inventories

Inventories are valued at the lower of cost or market. In general, inventories are valued on the basis of average cost or first-in, first-out methods. However, certain inventories are valued on the last-in, first-out (LIFO) method. The excess of current costs over LIFO stated values amounted to approximately $24 million and $27 million at December 31, 1992 and 1991, respectively.

### Property, Plant and Equipment

Property, plant and equipment are stated at cost, less allowances for depreciation. Property, plant and equipment are depreciated principally by the straight-line method over the estimated useful lives of the assets.

### Goodwill and Other Intangible Assets

Goodwill and other intangible assets are stated on the basis of cost and are being amortized, principally on a straight-line basis, over the estimated future periods to be benefited (not exceeding 40 years). Accumulated amortization was approximately $26 million and $16 million at December 31, 1992 and 1991, respectively.

### Changes in Accounting Principles

Statement of Financial Accounting Standards No. 106, "Employers' Accounting for Postretirement Benefits Other Than Pensions" (SFAS 106), was adopted as of January 1, 1992, as discussed in Note 13. Statement of Financial Accounting Standards No. 109, "Accounting for Income Taxes" (SFAS 109), was adopted in 1992 by restating financial statements beginning in 1989. The impact of adopting SFAS 109 is discussed in Note 14.

In 1992, the Financial Accounting Standards Board (FASB) issued Statement of Financial Accounting Standards No. 112, "Employers' Accounting for Postemployment Benefits" (SFAS 112). SFAS 112 requires employers to accrue the cost of benefits to former or inactive employees after employment but before retirement. The Company's required adoption date is January 1, 1994. The impact of adoption on the Company's results of operations and financial position has not yet been determined.

## Note 2  Inventories

Inventories consist of the following (in thousands):

| December 31, | 1992 | 1991 |
|---|---|---|
| Raw materials and supplies | $  619,411 | $615,459 |
| Work in process | 22,971 | 23,475 |
| Finished goods | 376,239 | 348,830 |
| | $1,018,621 | $987,764 |

## Note 3  Bottling Investments

The Company invests in bottling companies to ensure the strongest and most efficient production, distribution and marketing systems possible, in order to maximize long-term growth in volume, cash flows and share-owner value of the bottler and the Company.

*Notes to Consolidated Financial Statements*

**Coca-Cola Enterprises Inc.**

Coca-Cola Enterprises is the largest bottler of Company products in the United States. The Company owns approximately 44 percent of the outstanding common stock of Coca-Cola Enterprises and, accordingly, accounts for its investment by the equity method of accounting. A summary of financial information for Coca-Cola Enterprises is as follows (in thousands):

| December 31, | 1992 | 1991 |
|---|---|---|
| Current assets | $ 700,994 | $ 706,298 |
| Noncurrent assets | 7,384,400 | 5,970,297 |
| Total assets | $8,085,394 | $6,676,595 |
| Current liabilities | $1,304,364 | $1,385,445 |
| Noncurrent liabilities | 5,526,710 | 3,848,519 |
| Total liabilities | $6,831,074 | $5,233,964 |
| Share-owners' equity | $1,254,320 | $1,442,631 |
| Company equity investment | $ 518,312 | $ 592,561 |

| Year Ended | December 31, 1992 | December 31, 1991 | December 28, 1990 |
|---|---|---|---|
| Net operating revenues | $5,127,257 | $3,914,905 | $3,933,343 |
| Cost of goods sold | 3,219,189 | 2,420,158 | 2,399,667 |
| Gross profit | $1,908,068 | $1,494,747 | $1,533,676 |
| Operating income | $ 306,437 | $ 120,178 | $ 325,548 |
| Operating cash flow [1] | $ 695,499 | $ 538,422 | $ 592,391 |
| Income (loss) before changes in accounting principles | $ (14,672) | $ (91,675) | $ 77,148 |
| Net income (loss) available to common share owners | $ (186,259) | $ (91,675) | $ 77,148 |
| Company equity income (loss) | $ (6,422) | $ (39,732) | $ 34,429 |

[1] *Excludes nonrecurring charges.*

The above 1992 results of Coca-Cola Enterprises include $172 million of noncash after-tax adjustments resulting from the adoption of SFAS 106 and SFAS 109 as of January 1, 1992. The Company's financial statements reflect the adoption of SFAS 109 by Coca-Cola Enterprises as if it occurred on January 1, 1989. The change in accounting did not have a material effect on equity income (loss) from Coca-Cola Enterprises for the years ended December 31, 1991 and 1990, and accordingly, equity income (loss) has not been restated.

The 1991 results of Coca-Cola Enterprises include pretax restructuring charges of $152 million and a pretax charge of $15 million to increase insurance reserves.

In a 1991 merger, Coca-Cola Enterprises acquired Johnston Coca-Cola Bottling Group, Inc. (Johnston) for approximately $196 million in cash and 13 million shares of Coca-Cola

Enterprises common stock. The Company exchanged its 22 percent ownership interest in Johnston for approximately $81 million in cash and 50,000 shares of Coca-Cola Enterprises common stock, resulting in a pretax gain of $27 million to the Company. The Company's ownership interest in Coca-Cola Enterprises was reduced from 49 percent to 44 percent as a result of this transaction.

If the Johnston acquisition had been completed on January 1, 1990, Coca-Cola Enterprises' 1991 and 1990 pro forma net income (loss) available to common share owners would have been approximately ($137) million and $20 million, respectively. Summarized financial information and net concentrate/syrup sales related to Johnston prior to its acquisition by Coca-Cola Enterprises has been combined with other equity investments below.

Net concentrate/syrup sales to Coca-Cola Enterprises were $889 million in 1992, $626 million in 1991 and $602 million in 1990. Coca-Cola Enterprises purchases sweeteners through the Company under a pass-through arrangement, and, accordingly, related collections from Coca-Cola Enterprises and payments to suppliers are not included in the Company's consolidated statements of income. These transactions amounted to $225 million in 1992 and $185 million in 1991 and 1990. The Company also provides certain administrative and other services to Coca-Cola Enterprises under negotiated fee arrangements.

The Company engages in a wide range of marketing programs, media advertising and other similar arrangements to promote the sale of Company products in territories in which Coca-Cola Enterprises operates. The Company's direct support for certain Coca-Cola Enterprises marketing activities and participation with Coca-Cola Enterprises in cooperative advertising and other marketing programs amounted to approximately $253 million, $199 million and $181 million in 1992, 1991 and 1990, respectively.

In 1992, the Company sold 100 percent of the common stock of the Erie, Pennsylvania Coca-Cola bottler to Coca-Cola Enterprises for approximately $11 million, which approximated the Company's original investment plus carrying costs. In 1990, the Company sold a temporary investment, Coca-Cola Holdings (Arkansas) Inc., to Coca-Cola Enterprises for approximately $241 million and assumed indebtedness, which approximated the Company's original 1989 investment, plus carrying costs.

In 1990, Coca-Cola Enterprises recorded a pretax gain of approximately $56 million from the sale of two of its bottling subsidiaries. The purchaser of these former Coca-Cola Enterprises bottling subsidiaries was Johnston, which, at the time of the sale, was 22 percent owned by the Company.

*Notes to Consolidated Financial Statements*

During 1990, the Company sold 4 million shares of Coca-Cola Enterprises common stock to Coca-Cola Enterprises for $60 million under a share repurchase program.

If valued at the December 31, 1992, quoted closing price of the publicly traded Coca-Cola Enterprises shares, the calculated value of the Company's investment in Coca-Cola Enterprises common stock would have exceeded the Company's carrying value by approximately $172 million.

**Other Equity Investments**

The Company owns approximately 52 percent of Coca-Cola Amatil, an Australian-based bottler of Company products. In separate transactions during 1990, Coca-Cola Amatil acquired an independent Australian bottler and the Company's 50 percent interest in a New Zealand bottling joint venture in exchange for consideration that included previously unissued common stock of Coca-Cola Amatil, resulting in a net reduction of the Company's ownership interest from 59.5 percent to 51 percent. The Company's participation in Coca-Cola Amatil's Dividend Reinvestment Plan has increased the Company's ownership interest to its present level. The Company intends to reduce its ownership interest in Coca-Cola Amatil to below 50 percent. Accordingly, the investment has been accounted for by the equity method of accounting.

At December 31, 1992, the excess of the Company's investment over its equity in the underlying net assets of Coca-Cola Amatil was approximately $259 million, which is being amortized over 40 years. The Company recorded equity income from Coca-Cola Amatil of $28 million, $15 million and $17 million in 1992, 1991 and 1990, respectively. These amounts are net of the amortization charges discussed above.

In January 1993, Coca-Cola Amatil sold its snack food segment for approximately $299 million, and recognized a gain of $169 million. The Company's ownership interest in the sale proceeds received by Coca-Cola Amatil approximated the carrying value of the Company's investment in the snack food segment.

Operating results include the Company's proportionate share of income from equity investments since the respective dates of investment. A summary of financial information for the Company's equity investments, other than Coca-Cola Enterprises, is as follows (in thousands):

| December 31, | 1992 | 1991 |
|---|---|---|
| Current assets | $1,944,907 | $1,797,396 |
| Noncurrent assets | 4,172,347 | 3,794,114 |
| Total assets | $6,117,254 | $5,591,510 |
| Current liabilities | $2,219,033 | $1,947,025 |
| Noncurrent liabilities | 1,720,290 | 1,594,696 |
| Total liabilities | $3,939,323 | $3,541,721 |
| Share-owners' equity | $2,177,931 | $2,049,789 |
| Company equity investments | $1,386,587 | $1,433,962 |

| Year Ended December 31, | 1992 | 1991 | 1990 |
|---|---|---|---|
| Net operating revenues | $7,027,431 | $7,876,737 | $7,312,904 |
| Cost of goods sold | 4,740,891 | 5,243,943 | 4,609,004 |
| Gross profit | $2,286,540 | $2,632,794 | $2,703,900 |
| Operating income | $ 364,146 | $ 559,885 | $ 574,712 |
| Operating cash flow | $ 923,487 | $ 979,232 | $ 940,244 |
| Income before changes in accounting principles | $ 199,366 | $ 214,144 | $ 205,436 |
| Net income | $ 74,291 | $ 214,144 | $ 205,436 |
| Company equity income | $ 71,533 | $ 79,707 | $ 75,710 |

*Equity investments include certain non-bottling investees.*

Net sales to equity investees, other than Coca-Cola Enterprises, were $1.3 billion in 1992 and 1991 and $1.2 billion in 1990. The Company participates in various marketing, promotional and other activities with these investees, the majority of which are located outside the United States.

If valued at the December 31, 1992, quoted closing prices of shares actively traded on stock markets, the net calculated value of the Company's investment in publicly traded bottlers, other than Coca-Cola Enterprises, would have exceeded the Company's carrying value by approximately $31 million.

The consolidated balance sheet caption "Other, principally bottling companies" also includes various investments that are accounted for by the cost method.

*Notes to Consolidated Financial Statements*

Note 4 **Finance Subsidiary**

Coca-Cola Financial Corporation (CCFC) provides loans and other forms of financing to Coca-Cola bottlers and customers for the acquisition of sales-related equipment and for other business purposes. The approximate contractual maturities of finance receivables for the five years succeeding December 31, 1992, are as follows (in thousands):

| | |
|---|---|
| 1993 | $30,466 |
| 1994 | 21,753 |
| 1995 | 20,731 |
| 1996 | 31,288 |
| 1997 | 9,904 |

These amounts do not reflect possible prepayments or renewals.

In connection with the 1991 acquisition of Sunbelt Coca-Cola Bottling Company, Inc. by Coca-Cola Bottling Co. Consolidated (Consolidated), CCFC purchased 25,000 shares of Consolidated preferred stock for $50 million, provided to Consolidated a $153 million bridge loan and issued a $77 million letter of credit on Consolidated's behalf. Consolidated redeemed the 25,000 shares of preferred stock for $50 million plus accrued dividends in 1992. Consolidated also repaid all amounts due under the bridge loan in 1992. The Company beneficially owns a 30 percent economic interest and a 23 percent voting interest in Consolidated.

Finance receivables at December 31, 1991, also include $68 million due from Coca-Cola Enterprises (substantially all of which were assumed by Coca-Cola Enterprises upon its acquisition of Johnston). In 1992, substantially all of these notes were repaid by Coca-Cola Enterprises.

Note 5 **Short-Term Borrowings and Credit Arrangements**

Loans and notes payable consist primarily of commercial paper issued in the United States. At December 31, 1992, the Company had $1.6 billion in lines of credit and other short-term credit facilities contractually available, under which $171 million was outstanding. Included were $1.3 billion in lines designated to support commercial paper and other borrowings, under which no amounts were outstanding at December 31, 1992. These facilities are subject to normal banking terms and conditions. Some of the financial arrangements require compensating balances, none of which are presently significant to the Company.

Note 6 **Accrued Taxes**

Accrued taxes consist of the following (in thousands):

| December 31, | 1992 | 1991 |
|---|---|---|
| Income taxes | **$819,833** | $ 927,245 |
| Sales, payroll and miscellaneous taxes | **143,130** | 111,252 |
| | **$962,963** | $1,038,497 |

Note 7 **Long-Term Debt**

Long-term debt consists of the following (in thousands):

| December 31, | 1992 | 1991 |
|---|---|---|
| 7¾% U.S. dollar notes due 1996 | **$ 250,000** | $ 250,000 |
| 5¾% Japanese yen notes due 1996[1] | **241,250** | 239,987 |
| 5¾% German mark notes due 1998[1] | **155,380** | 165,206 |
| 7⅞% U.S. dollar notes due 1998 | **249,367** | 249,262 |
| 6⅝% U.S. dollar notes due 2002 | **149,009** | — |
| 9⅞% U.S. dollar notes due 1992 | **—** | 89,565 |
| Other, due 1993 to 2013[2] | **89,852** | 100,945 |
| | **1,134,858** | 1,094,965 |
| Less current portion | **14,794** | 109,707 |
| | **$1,120,064** | $ 985,258 |

[1] Portions of these notes have been swapped for liabilities denominated in other currencies.
[2] The weighted average interest rate is approximately 10.4 percent.

Maturities of long-term debt for the five years succeeding December 31, 1992, are as follows (in thousands):

| | |
|---|---|
| 1993 | $ 14,794 |
| 1994 | 22,033 |
| 1995 | 38,136 |
| 1996 | 496,833 |
| 1997 | 4,216 |

The above notes include various restrictions, none of which are presently significant to the Company.

Interest paid was approximately $174 million, $160 million and $233 million in 1992, 1991 and 1990, respectively.

Note 8 **Financial Instruments**

Financial instruments at December 31, 1992, consist of the following (in thousands):

| | Carrying Value | Fair Value |
|---|---|---|
| Current marketable securities | $ 107,380 | $ 124,914 |
| Finance subsidiary receivables | 125,382 | 135,271 |
| Long-term receivables and other assets | 636,682 | 635,816 |
| Long-term debt | 1,134,858 | 1,155,646 |
| Foreign currency hedging instruments | 102,091 | 98,747 |

*Notes to Consolidated Financial Statements*

**Cash and cash equivalents**

The carrying amount reflected in the balance sheet approximates the fair value for cash and cash equivalents.

**Marketable securities, long-term receivables and other assets**

The fair values for marketable debt and equity securities, long-term receivables, investments and other assets are based primarily on quoted market prices for those or similar instruments.

**Loans, notes payable and long-term debt**

The carrying amounts of the Company's loans and notes payable approximate their fair values. The fair values of the Company's long-term debt are based primarily on quoted market prices.

**Foreign currency hedging transactions**

The Company has entered into foreign currency hedging transactions to reduce its exposure to adverse fluctuations in foreign exchange rates. While the hedging instruments are subject to the risk of loss from changes in exchange rates, these losses would generally be offset by gains on the exposures being hedged. Realized and unrealized gains and losses on those hedging instruments that are designated and effective as hedges of probable anticipated and firmly committed foreign currency transactions are deferred and recognized in income in the same period as the hedged transaction. The fair values of the Company's foreign currency hedging instruments are based on quoted market prices of these or similar instruments, adjusted for maturity differences.

At December 31, 1992 and 1991, the Company had forward exchange contracts, options and other financial market instruments, principally to exchange foreign currencies for U.S. dollars, of $4.9 billion and $2.6 billion, respectively. The Company has entered into foreign currency option contracts to hedge probable anticipated transactions over the succeeding year. The pretax net gain deferred on those contracts was $8 million at December 31, 1992. No amounts were deferred at December 31, 1991.

**Guarantees**

At December 31, 1992, the Company is contingently liable for guarantees of indebtedness owed by third parties of $124 million, of which $43 million is related to independent bottling licensees. The fair value of these contingent liabilities is immaterial to the Company's consolidated financial statements. In the opinion of management, it is not probable that the Company will be required to satisfy these guarantees.

**Note 9   Preferred Stock**

In 1991, the Company redeemed the remaining $75 million of its Cumulative Money Market Preferred Stock (MMP). There were 750 shares outstanding at December 31, 1990. Of the 100 million shares of $1 par value MMP which are authorized, 3,000 shares have been issued and subsequently redeemed. The weighted average dividend rate (per annum) for the MMP was approximately 6 percent during 1991, prior to the redemption, and 1990.

**Note 10   Common Stock**

On April 15, 1992, the Company's share owners approved an increase in the authorized common stock of the Company from 1.4 billion shares to 2.8 billion shares, a two-for-one stock split, and a change in the par value of common stock from $.50 per share to $.25 per share. Accordingly, all share data have been restated for periods prior to the stock split. Common shares outstanding and related changes for the three years ended December 31, 1992, are as follows (in thousands):

| | **1992** | 1991 | 1990 |
|---|---|---|---|
| Outstanding at January 1, | **1,328,960** | 1,336,478 | 1,348,059 |
| Issued to employees exercising stock options | **8,619** | 3,887 | 3,620 |
| Issued under restricted stock plans | **233** | 2,489 | 1,716 |
| Purchased for treasury | **(31,041)** | (13,894) | (16,917) |
| Outstanding at December 31, | **1,306,771** | 1,328,960 | 1,336,478 |

**Note 11   Restricted Stock, Stock Options and Other Stock Plans**

The Company sponsors restricted stock award plans, stock option plans, Incentive Unit Agreements and Performance Unit Agreements.

Under the amended 1989 Restricted Stock Award Plan and the amended 1983 Restricted Stock Award Plan (the Restricted Stock Plans), 20 million and 12 million shares of restricted common stock, respectively, may be granted to certain officers and key employees of the Company.

*Notes to Consolidated Financial Statements*

In 1992, 1991 and 1990, 233,000 shares, 2,489,500 shares and 1,716,000 shares, respectively, were granted under the Restricted Stock Plans. At December 31, 1992, 17.2 million shares were available for grant under the Restricted Stock Plans. The participant is entitled to vote and receive dividends on the shares, and, under the 1983 Restricted Stock Award Plan, the participant is reimbursed by the Company for income taxes imposed on the award, but not for taxes generated by the reimbursement payment. The shares are subject to certain transfer restrictions and may be forfeited if the participant leaves the Company for reasons other than retirement, disability or death, absent a change in control of the Company. On July 18, 1991, the Restricted Stock Plans were amended to specify age 62 as the minimum retirement age. In addition, the 1983 Restricted Stock Award Plan was further amended to conform to the terms of the 1989 Restricted Stock Award Plan by requiring a minimum of five years of service prior to retirement. The amendments affect shares granted subsequent to July 18, 1991.

Under the Company's 1991 Stock Option Plan (the Option Plan), a maximum of 60 million shares of the Company's common stock may be issued or transferred to certain officers and employees pursuant to stock options and stock appreciation rights granted under the Option Plan. The stock appreciation rights permit the holder, upon surrendering all or part of the related stock option, to receive cash, common stock or a combination thereof, in an amount up to 100 percent of the difference between the market price and the option price. No stock appreciation rights have been granted since 1990, and the Company presently does not intend to grant additional stock appreciation rights in the future. Options outstanding at December 31, 1992, also include various options granted under previous plans. Further information relating to options is as follows (in thousands, except per share amounts):

|  | **1992** | 1991 | 1990 |
|---|---|---|---|
| Outstanding at January 1, | **36,383** | 33,065 | 27,008 |
| Granted | **3,823** | 7,993 | 10,392 |
| Exercised | **(8,619)** | (3,887) | (3,620) |
| Canceled | **(463)** | (788) | (715) |
| Outstanding at December 31, | **31,124** | 36,383 | 33,065 |
| Exercisable at December 31, | **23,220** | 24,052 | 19,138 |
| Shares available at December 31, for options that may be granted | **51,411** | 55,378 | 3,117 |
| Prices per share |  |  |  |
| Exercised | **$4-$28** | $3-$28 | $3-$20 |
| Unexercised at December 31, | **$4-$41** | $4-$30 | $3-$24 |

In 1988, the Company entered into Incentive Unit Agreements, whereby, subject to certain conditions, certain officers will receive cash awards based on the market value of 1.2 million shares of the Company's common stock at the measurement dates. The Incentive Unit Agreements provide for a cash payment for income taxes when the value of the units is paid.

In 1985, the Company entered into Performance Unit Agreements, whereby certain officers will receive cash awards based on the difference in the market value of approximately 2.2 million shares of the Company's common stock at the measurement dates and the base price of $5.16, the market value as of January 2, 1985.

Note 12 **Pension Benefits**
The Company sponsors and/or contributes to pension plans covering substantially all U.S. employees and certain employees in international locations. The benefits are primarily based on years of service and the employees' compensation for certain periods during the last years of employment. Pension costs are generally funded currently, subject to regulatory funding limitations. The Company also sponsors nonqualified, unfunded defined benefit plans for certain officers and other employees. In addition, the Company and its subsidiaries have various pension plans and other forms of postretirement arrangements outside the United States.

*Notes to Consolidated Financial Statements*

Total pension expense for all benefit plans, including defined benefit plans, amounted to approximately $49 million in 1992, $42 million in 1991 and $30 million in 1990. Net periodic pension cost for the Company's defined benefit plans in 1992, 1991 and 1990 consists of the following (in thousands):

| Year Ended December 31, | U.S. Plans | | | International Plans | | |
|---|---|---|---|---|---|---|
| | **1992** | 1991 | 1990 | **1992** | 1991 | 1990 |
| Service cost—benefits earned during the period | **$ 14,459** | $ 12,475 | $ 10,684 | **$ 17,636** | $ 15,894 | $ 12,902 |
| Interest cost on projected benefit obligation | **50,009** | 45,860 | 41,786 | **20,238** | 18,523 | 14,720 |
| Actual return on plan assets | **(35,720)** | (112,530) | (9,121) | **(19,136)** | (17,498) | (3,811) |
| Net amortization and deferral | **(8,873)** | 71,090 | (31,168) | **3,283** | 555 | (11,273) |
| Net periodic pension cost | **$ 19,875** | $ 16,895 | $ 12,181 | **$ 22,021** | $ 17,474 | $ 12,538 |

The following table sets forth the funded status for the Company's defined benefit plans at December 31, 1992 and 1991 (in thousands):

| December 31, | U.S. Plans | | | | International Plans | | | |
|---|---|---|---|---|---|---|---|---|
| | Assets Exceed Accumulated Benefits | | Accumulated Benefits Exceed Assets | | Assets Exceed Accumulated Benefits | | Accumulated Benefits Exceed Assets | |
| | **1992** | 1991 | **1992** | 1991 | **1992** | 1991 | **1992** | 1991 |
| Actuarial present value of benefit obligations | | | | | | | | |
| Vested benefit obligation | **$400,925** | $ 359,857 | **$ 81,545** | $ 66,907 | **$119,325** | $ 96,074 | **$ 90,173** | $ 81,609 |
| Accumulated benefit obligation | **$431,314** | $ 383,972 | **$ 88,751** | $ 72,610 | **$126,585** | $106,286 | **$100,146** | $ 91,208 |
| Projected benefit obligation | **$520,164** | $ 455,357 | **$100,829** | $ 82,251 | **$167,327** | $145,435 | **$147,759** | $144,245 |
| Plan assets at fair value[1] | **586,913** | 583,819 | **1,269** | — | **188,160** | 175,392 | **73,259** | 74,640 |
| Plan assets in excess of (less than) projected benefit obligation | **66,749** | 128,462 | **(99,560)**[2] | (82,251)[2] | **20,833** | 29,957 | **(74,500)** | (69,605) |
| Unrecognized net (asset) liability at transition | **(37,070)** | (40,764) | **19,161** | 21,292 | **(6,064)** | (29,229) | **32,666** | 40,908 |
| Unrecognized prior service cost | **22,942** | 25,756 | **2,873** | 2,795 | **(186)** | 105 | **8,349** | 5,243 |
| Unrecognized net (gain) loss | **(60,554)** | (114,934) | **23,876** | 14,506 | **1,983** | 10,265 | **(3,300)** | (1,672) |
| Adjustment required to recognize minimum liability | **—** | — | **(33,832)** | (28,952) | **—** | — | **(2,718)** | (453) |
| Accrued pension asset (liability) included in the consolidated balance sheet | **$ (7,933)** | $ (1,480) | **$ (87,482)** | $(72,610) | **$ 16,566** | $. 11,098 | **$ (39,503)** | $ (25,579) |

[1] Primarily listed stocks, bonds and government securities.
[2] Substantially all of this amount relates to nonqualified, unfunded defined benefit plans.

The assumptions used in computing the above information are as follows:

| | U.S. Plans | | | International Plans (weighted average rates) | | |
|---|---|---|---|---|---|---|
| | **1992** | 1991 | 1990 | **1992** | 1991 | 1990 |
| Discount rates | **8 1/2%** | 9% | 9% | **7%** | 7 1/2% | 8% |
| Rates of increase in compensation levels | **6%** | 6% | 6% | **5 1/2%** | 6% | 6% |
| Expected long-term rates of return on assets | **9 1/2%** | 9 1/2% | 9 1/2% | **7%** | 7 1/2% | 8% |

*Notes to Consolidated Financial Statements*

### Note 13  **Other Postretirement Benefits**

The Company has plans that provide postretirement health care and life insurance benefits to substantially all U.S. employees and certain employees in international locations who retire with a minimum of five years of service. SFAS 106 requires companies to accrue the cost of postretirement health care and life insurance benefits within the employees' active service periods. As discussed in Note 1, the Company adopted SFAS 106 for all U.S. and international plans as of January 1, 1992. The Company elected to immediately recognize the accumulated postretirement benefit obligation upon adoption of SFAS 106. For consolidated operations, the Company recorded an accumulated obligation of $146 million, which is net of $92 million in deferred tax benefits. The Company also recorded an additional charge of $73 million, net of $13 million of deferred tax benefits, representing the Company's proportionate share of accumulated postretirement benefit obligations recognized by bottling investees accounted for by the equity method.

Annual pretax postretirement benefits expense for 1992 increased $20 million due to the implementation of SFAS 106. Equity income in 1992 decreased $10 million due to additional postretirement benefit expense of the Company's equity investees.

The net periodic cost for postretirement health care and life insurance benefits during 1992 includes the following (in thousands):

| Year Ended December 31, | 1992 |
| --- | --- |
| Service cost | $  8,727 |
| Interest cost | 20,718 |
| Other | (267) |
| | $29,178 |

The Company has begun contributing to a Voluntary Employees' Beneficiary Association trust that will be used to partially fund health care benefits for future retirees. The Company is funding benefits to the extent contributions are tax-deductible, which under current legislation is limited. In general, retiree health benefits are paid as covered expenses are incurred. The following table sets forth the funded status for the Company's postretirement health care and life insurance plans (in thousands):

| December 31, | 1992 |
| --- | --- |
| Accumulated postretirement benefit obligations: | |
| Retirees | $110,527 |
| Fully eligible active plan participants | 34,179 |
| Other active plan participants | 113,178 |
| Total obligation | 257,884 |
| Plan assets at fair value[1] | 23,667 |
| Accrued postretirement benefit liability included in the consolidated balance sheet | $234,217 |

[1] Consists of money market investments

The assumed discount rate and the assumed rate of increase in compensation levels are 8.5 percent and 6 percent, respectively. The rate of increase in the per capita costs of covered health care benefits is assumed to be 13 percent in 1993, decreasing gradually to 7 percent by the year 2005. Increasing the assumed health care cost trend rate by 1 percentage point would increase the accumulated postretirement benefit obligation as of December 31, 1992, by approximately $32 million and increase net periodic postretirement benefit cost by approximately $5 million in 1992.

### Note 14  **Income Taxes**

As discussed in Note 1, the Company adopted SFAS 109 in 1992 and has applied the provisions of SFAS 109 retroactively to January 1, 1989. SFAS 109 requires the recognition of deferred tax assets and liabilities for the future tax consequences attributable to differences between the financial statement carrying amounts of existing assets and liabilities and their respective tax bases. In addition, the new accounting standard requires the recognition of future tax benefits, such as net operating loss carryforwards, to the extent that realization of such benefits is more likely than not. The adoption of SFAS 109 resulted in a cumulative effect charge of $265 million, or $.19 per common share, at January 1, 1989. Excluding the cumulative effect charge, the application of SFAS 109 increased net income by $78 million in 1989, which primarily relates to the sale of the Company's equity interest in Columbia Pictures Entertainment, Inc. The change in accounting for income taxes did not have a material effect on the consolidated statements of income for the years ended December 31, 1991 and 1990. Accordingly, these statements have not been restated and the immaterial effect related to 1991 and 1990 has been included in 1992 results.

*Notes to Consolidated Financial Statements*

The components of income before income taxes and change in accounting principle consist of the following (in thousands):

| Year Ended December 31, | 1992 | 1991 | 1990 |
|---|---|---|---|
| United States | $ 761,911 | $ 648,471 | $ 494,544 |
| International | 1,984,177 | 1,734,808 | 1,519,892 |
| | $2,746,088 | $2,383,279 | $2,014,436 |

Income tax expense (benefit) consists of the following (in thousands):

| Year Ended December 31, | United States | State & Local | International | Total |
|---|---|---|---|---|
| **1992** | | | | |
| **Current** | **$277,543** | **$36,145** | **$575,193** | **$888,881** |
| **Deferred**[1] | **(60,086)** | **(667)** | **34,145** | **(26,608)** |
| 1991 | | | | |
| Current | $ 232,947 | $ 30,981 | $ 595,662 | $ 859,590 |
| Deferred | (89,395) | (5,267) | 349 | (94,313) |
| 1990 | | | | |
| Current | $ 179,474 | $ 26,515 | $ 501,298 | $ 707,287 |
| Deferred | (93,888) | (2,596) | 21,729 | (74,755) |

[1]An additional deferred tax benefit of $105 million has been included in the SFAS 106 transition effect charge.

The Company made income tax payments of approximately $856 million, $672 million and $803 million in 1992, 1991 and 1990, respectively.

A reconciliation of the statutory U.S. federal rate and effective rates is as follows:

| Year Ended December 31, | 1992 | 1991 | 1990 |
|---|---|---|---|
| Statutory U.S. federal rate | **34.0%** | 34.0% | 34.0% |
| State income taxes—net of federal benefit | **1.0** | 1.0 | 1.0 |
| Earnings in jurisdictions taxed at rates different from the statutory U.S. federal rate | **(3.8)** | (3.1) | (2.6) |
| Equity income | **(1.0)** | (.6) | (1.8) |
| Other—net | **1.2** | .8 | .8 |
| | **31.4%** | 32.1% | 31.4% |

The Company has manufacturing facilities in Puerto Rico that operate under a negotiated exemption grant that expires December 31, 2009.

Appropriate U.S. and international taxes have been provided for earnings of subsidiary companies that are expected to be remitted to the parent company. The cumulative amount of unremitted earnings of international subsidiaries that are expected to be required for use in the international operations, exclusive of amounts that, if remitted, would result in little or no tax, and the taxes which would be paid upon remittance of

these earnings were approximately $83 million and $28 million, respectively, at December 31, 1992.

The tax effects of temporary differences and carryforwards that give rise to significant portions of deferred tax assets and liabilities consist of the following (in thousands):

| December 31, | 1992 | 1991 |
|---|---|---|
| Deferred tax assets: | | |
| Benefit plans | **$297,429** | $175,540 |
| Liabilities and reserve~ | **119,295** | 113,309 |
| Net operating loss carryforwards | **100,966** | 80,452 |
| Other | **83,756** | 70,003 |
| Gross deferred tax assets | **601,446** | 439,304 |
| Valuation allowance | **(63,251)** | (76,104) |
| Total | **$538,195** | $363,200 |
| Deferred tax liabilities: | | |
| Depreciation | **$311,761** | $260,017 |
| Equity investments | **197,108** | 238,629 |
| Amortization | **68,113** | 36,013 |
| Other | **42,842** | 44,613 |
| Total | **$619,824** | $579,272 |
| Net deferred tax liability | **$ 81,629** | $216,072 |

At December 31, 1992, the Company had $285 million of operating loss carryforwards available to reduce future taxable income of certain international subsidiaries. These loss carryforwards must be utilized within the carryforward periods of certain international jurisdictions, which are primarily four years. A valuation allowance has been provided for a portion of the deferred tax assets related to these loss carryforwards.

Note 15 **Net Change in Operating Assets and Liabilities**
The changes in operating assets and liabilities, net of effects of acquisitions and divestitures of businesses and unrealized exchange gains/losses, are as follows (in thousands):

| Year Ended December 31, | 1992 | 1991 | 1990 |
|---|---|---|---|
| Increase in trade accounts receivable | **$(146,718)** | $ (31,826) | $ (87,749) |
| Increase in inventories | **(138,126)** | (3,020) | (169,442) |
| Increase in prepaid expenses and other assets | **(112,350)** | (325,595) | (65,758) |
| Increase in accounts payable and accrued expenses | **404,734** | 266,684 | 198,631 |
| Increase (decrease) in accrued taxes | **57,438** | 244,043 | (66,513) |
| Increase (decrease) in other liabilities | **(108,108)** | 100,717 | 57,130 |
| | **$ (43,130)** | $ 251,003 | $(133,701) |

*Notes to Consolidated Financial Statements*

The net change in operating assets and liabilities in 1990 reflects estimated tax payments of approximately $300 million related to the 1989 gain on the sale of Columbia Pictures Entertainment, Inc. stock.

Note 16 **Acquisitions and Investments**
During 1992, the Company's acquisition and investment activity, which includes investments in bottling operations in the Netherlands, the United States and Brazil, totaled $717 million. During 1991 and 1990, the Company's acquisition and investment activity totaled $399 million and $301 million, respectively. None of the acquisitions were individually significant.

The acquisitions have been accounted for by the purchase method of accounting and, accordingly, their results have been included in the consolidated financial statements from their respective dates of acquisition. Had the results of these businesses been included commencing with operations in 1990, the reported results would not have been materially affected.

Note 17 **Other Nonrecurring Items**
"Other income (deductions)—net" in 1991 includes a $69 million pretax gain on the sale of property no longer required as a result of consolidating concentrate operations in Japan and a $27 million pretax gain on the sale of the Company's 22 percent ownership interest in Johnston to Coca-Cola Enterprises. "Selling, administrative and general expenses" and "Interest expense" include 1991 pretax charges of $13 million and $8 million, respectively, for potential future costs related to bottler litigation. In addition, 1991 equity income has been reduced by $44 million related to restructuring charges recorded by Coca-Cola Enterprises.

"Other income (deductions)—net" in 1990 includes a pretax gain of $52 million on the Company's investment in BCI Securities L.P. (BCI) resulting from BCI's sale of Beatrice Company stock. "Selling, administrative and general expenses" in 1990 include nonrecurring pretax charges of $49 million related to the Company's U.S. soft drink business. These charges reflect accelerated amortization of certain software costs due to management plans to upgrade and standardize information systems and adjustments to the carrying value of certain fountain equipment and marketing-related items to amounts estimated to be recoverable in future periods.

## Net Operating Revenues by Line of Business

■ Soft Drinks–United States
■ Soft Drinks–International
☐ Foods

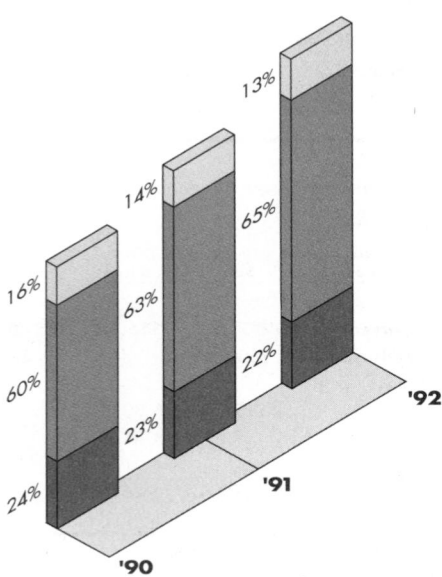

## Operating Income by Line of Business

■ Soft Drinks–United States
■ Soft Drinks–International
☐ Foods

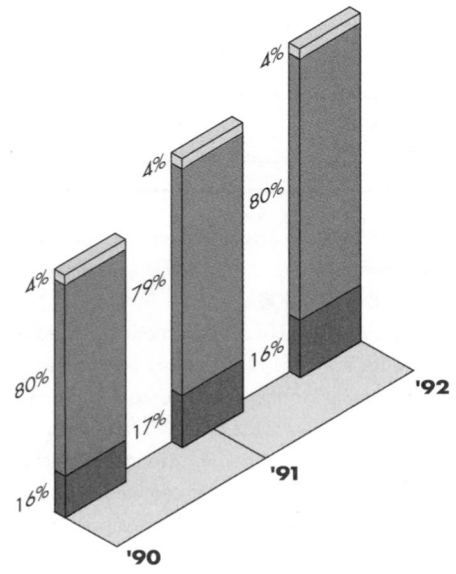

*Notes to Consolidated Financial Statements*

Note 18  **Lines of Business**

The Company operates in two major lines of business: soft drinks and foods (principally juice and juice-drink products). Information concerning operations in these businesses at December 31, 1992, 1991 and 1990, and for the years then ended, is presented below (in millions):

| **1992** | Soft Drinks | | Foods | Corporate | Consolidated |
|---|---|---|---|---|---|
| | United States | International | | | |
| Net operating revenues | $2,813.1 | $8,550.5 | $1,675.0 | $   35.3 | $13,073.9 |
| Operating income | 510.1 | 2,520.4 | 112.4 | (372.8) | 2,770.1 |
| Identifiable operating assets | 1,811.8 | 5,250.6 | 791.2 | 1,035.2[3] | 8,888.8 |
| Equity income | | | | 65.1 | 65.1 |
| Investments (principally bottling companies) | | | | 2,163.1 | 2,163.1 |
| Capital expenditures | 168.8 | 736.1 | 38.4 | 140.0 | 1,083.3 |
| Depreciation and amortization | 87.2 | 157.0 | 34.9 | 42.8 | 321.9 |

| 1991 (Restated) | Soft Drinks | | Foods | Corporate | Consolidated |
|---|---|---|---|---|---|
| | United States | International | | | |
| Net operating revenues | $2,645.2 | $7,244.8 | $1,635.7 | $   45.9 | $11,571.6 |
| Operating income | 468.7 | 2,141.1 | 103.7 | (394.5) | 2,319.0 |
| Identifiable operating assets | 1,447.0 | 4,742.3 | 755.0 | 1,124.1[3] | 8,068.4 |
| Equity income | | | | 40.0[1] | 40.0 |
| Investments (principally bottling companies) | | | | 2,120.8 | 2,120.8 |
| Capital expenditures | 131.1 | 546.3 | 57.1 | 57.2 | 791.7 |
| Depreciation and amortization | 81.9 | 111.9 | 30.8 | 36.8 | 261.4 |

| 1990 (Restated) | Soft Drinks | | Foods | Corporate | Consolidated |
|---|---|---|---|---|---|
| | United States | International | | | |
| Net operating revenues | $2,461.3 | $6,125.4 | $1,604.9 | $   44.8 | $10,236.4 |
| Operating income | 358.1[2] | 1,801.4 | 93.5 | (301.4) | 1,951.6 |
| Identifiable operating assets | 1,691.0 | 3,672.2 | 759.2 | 1,131.2[3] | 7,253.6 |
| Equity income | | | | 110.1 | 110.1 |
| Investments (principally bottling companies) | | | | 1,991.4 | 1,991.4 |
| Capital expenditures | 138.4 | 321.4 | 68.2 | 65.0 | 593.0 |
| Depreciation and amortization | 88.5 | 94.4 | 28.3 | 32.7 | 243.9 |

*Intercompany transfers between sectors are not material.*

[1] *Reduced by $44 million related to restructuring charges recorded by Coca-Cola Enterprises.*
[2] *Includes nonrecurring charges of $49 million.*
[3] *Corporate identifiable operating assets are composed principally of marketable securities and fixed assets.*

*Notes to Consolidated Financial Statements*

Note 19 **Operations in Geographic Areas**

Information about the Company's operations in different geographic areas at December 31, 1992, 1991 and 1990, and for the years then ended, is presented below (in millions):

| 1992 | United States | Latin America | European Community | Northeast Europe/ Africa | Pacific & Canada | Corporate | Consolidated |
|---|---|---|---|---|---|---|---|
| Net operating revenues | $4,339.2 | $1,383.0 | $3,983.6 | $788.4 | $2,544.4 | $ 35.3 | $13,073.9 |
| Operating income | 608.3 | 502.2 | 888.8 | 236.8 | 906.8 | (372.8) | 2,770.1 |
| Identifiable operating assets | 2,563.5 | 1,184.7 | 2,586.5 | 574.2 | 944.7 | 1,035.2[3] | 8,888.8 |
| Equity income | | | | | | 65.1 | 65.1 |
| Investments (principally bottling companies) | | | | | | 2,163.1 | 2,163.1 |
| Capital expenditures | 204.6 | 187.9 | 385.7 | 131.9 | 33.2 | 140.0 | 1,083.3 |
| Depreciation and amortization | 120.6 | 27.3 | 98.6 | 17.3 | 15.3 | 42.8 | 321.9 |

| 1991 (Restated) | United States | Latin America | European Community | Northeast Europe/ Africa | Pacific & Canada | Corporate | Consolidated |
|---|---|---|---|---|---|---|---|
| Net operating revenues | $4,124.8 | $1,103.2 | $3,338.3 | $613.6 | $2,345.8 | $ 45.9 | $11,571.6 |
| Operating income | 560.2 | 404.6 | 767.3 | 204.1 | 777.3 | (394.5) | 2,319.0 |
| Identifiable operating assets | 2,160.9 | 814.6 | 2,558.0 | 423.5 | 987.3 | 1,124.1[3] | 8,068.4 |
| Equity income | | | | | | 40.0[1] | 40.0 |
| Investments (principally bottling companies) | | | | | | 2,120.8 | 2,120.8 |
| Capital expenditures | 184.8 | 105.5 | 330.6 | 61.3 | 52.3 | 57.2 | 791.7 |
| Depreciation and amortization | 111.3 | 23.3 | 65.8 | 9.7 | 14.5 | 36.8 | 261.4 |

| 1990 (Restated) | United States | Latin America | European Community | Northeast Europe/ Africa | Pacific & Canada | Corporate | Consolidated |
|---|---|---|---|---|---|---|---|
| Net operating revenues | $3,931.0 | $ 813.0 | $2,804.8 | $562.8 | $2,080.0 | $ 44.8 | $10,236.4 |
| Operating income | 440.4[2] | 300.2 | 666.5 | 174.2 | 671.7 | (301.4) | 1,951.6 |
| Identifiable operating assets | 2,414.2 | 640.3 | 1,818.8 | 400.1 | 849.0 | 1,131.2[3] | 7,253.6 |
| Equity income | | | | | | 110.1 | 110.1 |
| Investments (principally bottling companies) | | | | | | 1,991.4 | 1,991.4 |
| Capital expenditures | 204.0 | 59.7 | 203.5 | 38.8 | 22.0 | 65.0 | 593.0 |
| Depreciation and amortization | 115.6 | 18.0 | 54.5 | 7.6 | 15.5 | 32.7 | 243.9 |

Intercompany transfers between geographic areas are not material.
Identifiable liabilities of operations outside the United States amounted to approximately $1.9 billion, $1.8 billion and $1.5 billion at December 31, 1992, 1991 and 1990, respectively.

[1] Reduced by $44 million related to restructuring charges recorded by Coca-Cola Enterprises.
[2] Includes nonrecurring charges of $49 million.
[3] Corporate identifiable operating assets are composed principally of marketable securities and fixed assets.

## Net Operating Revenues by Geographic Area

- ■ United States
- ■ Latin America
- ■ European Community
- ■ Northeast Europe/Africa
- □ Pacific & Canada

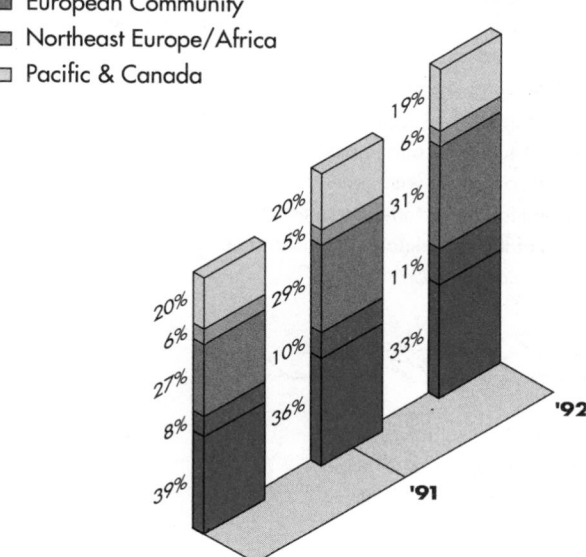

## Operating Income by Geographic Area

- ■ United States
- ■ Latin America
- ■ European Community
- ■ Northeast Europe/Africa
- □ Pacific & Canada

*Report of Independent Auditors*

**Board of Directors and Share Owners
The Coca-Cola Company**

We have audited the accompanying consolidated balance sheets of The Coca-Cola Company and subsidiaries as of December 31, 1992 and 1991, and the related consolidated statements of income, share-owners' equity and cash flows for each of the three years in the period ended December 31, 1992. These financial statements are the responsibility of the Company's management. Our responsibility is to express an opinion on these financial statements based on our audits.

We conducted our audits in accordance with generally accepted auditing standards. Those standards require that we plan and perform the audit to obtain reasonable assurance about whether the financial statements are free of material misstatement. An audit includes examining, on a test basis, evidence supporting the amounts and disclosures in the financial statements. An audit also includes assessing the accounting principles used and significant estimates made by management, as well as evaluating the overall financial statement presentation. We believe that our audits provide a reasonable basis for our opinion.

In our opinion, the financial statements referred to above present fairly, in all material respects, the consolidated financial position of The Coca-Cola Company and subsidiaries at December 31, 1992 and 1991, and the consolidated results of their operations and their cash flows for each of the three years in the period ended December 31, 1992, in conformity with generally accepted accounting principles.

As discussed in Note 1 to the consolidated financial statements, in 1992 the Company changed its methods of accounting for income taxes and postretirement benefits other than pensions.

*Ernst + Young*

Atlanta, Georgia
January 26, 1993

## Report of Management

Management is responsible for the preparation and integrity of the consolidated financial statements appearing in this Annual Report. The financial statements were prepared in conformity with generally accepted accounting principles appropriate in the circumstances and, accordingly, include some amounts based on management's best judgments and estimates. Financial information in this Annual Report is consistent with that in the financial statements.

Management is responsible for maintaining a system of internal accounting controls and procedures to provide reasonable assurance, at an appropriate cost/benefit relationship, that assets are safeguarded and that transactions are authorized, recorded and reported properly. The internal accounting control system is augmented by a program of internal audits and appropriate reviews by management, written policies and guidelines, careful selection and training of qualified personnel and a written Code of Business Conduct adopted by the Board of Directors, applicable to all employees of the Company and its subsidiaries. Management believes that the Company's internal accounting controls provide reasonable assurance that assets are safeguarded against material loss from unauthorized use or disposition and that the financial records are reliable for preparing financial statements and other data and for maintaining accountability of assets.

The Audit Committee of the Board of Directors, composed solely of Directors who are not officers of the Company, meets with the independent auditors, management and internal auditors periodically to discuss internal accounting controls and auditing and financial reporting matters. The Committee reviews with the independent auditors the scope and results of the audit effort. The Committee also meets with the independent auditors and the chief internal auditor without management present to ensure that the independent auditors and the chief internal auditor have free access to the Committee.

The independent auditors, Ernst & Young, are recommended by the Audit Committee of the Board of Directors, selected by the Board of Directors and ratified by the share owners. Ernst & Young is engaged to audit the consolidated financial statements of The Coca-Cola Company and subsidiaries and conduct such tests and related procedures as it deems necessary in conformity with generally accepted auditing standards. The opinion of the independent auditors, based upon their audits of the consolidated financial statements, is contained in this Annual Report.

Roberto C. Goizueta
Chairman, Board of Directors,
and Chief Executive Officer

Jack L. Stahl
Senior Vice President
and Chief Financial Officer

Patrick M. Worsham
Vice President
and Controller

January 26, 1993

*Quarterly Data* (Unaudited)

For the years ended December 31, 1992 and 1991
(In millions except per share data)

| 1992 | First Quarter | Second Quarter | Third Quarter | Fourth Quarter | Full Year |
|---|---|---|---|---|---|
| Net operating revenues | $2,771.9 | $3,550.4 | $3,507.5 | $3,244.1 | $13,073.9 |
| Gross profit | 1,740.4 | 2,176.8 | 2,122.2 | 1,980.1 | 8,019.5 |
| Income before change in accounting principle | 386.2 | 565.4 | 539.7 | 392.5 | 1,883.8 |
| Net income available to common share owners | 166.8 | 565.4 | 539.7 | 392.5 | 1,664.4 |
| Income per common share before change in accounting principle | .29 | .43 | .41 | .30 | 1.43 |
| Net income per common share | .13 | .43 | .41 | .30 | 1.26 |

| 1991 | First Quarter | Second Quarter | Third Quarter | Fourth Quarter | Full Year |
|---|---|---|---|---|---|
| Net operating revenues | $2,481.0 | $3,039.5 | $3,172.1 | $2,879.0 | $11,571.6 |
| Gross profit | 1,516.9 | 1,853.8 | 1,864.9 | 1,687.6 | 6,923.2 |
| Net income | 320.9 | 482.4 | 456.3 | 358.4 | 1,618.0 |
| Net income available to common share owners | 320.4 | 482.4 | 456.3 | 358.4 | 1,617.5 |
| Net income per common share | .24 | .36 | .34 | .27 | 1.21 |

All per share data has been adjusted for a two-for-one stock split in 1992.

The Company filed a Form 8-K with the Securities and Exchange Commission in February 1993 restating the 1992 quarterly reports for the adoption of SFAS 106 and 109. The impact of the restatement on the first quarter of 1992 includes the after-tax transition charge of $219 million related to the change in accounting for postretirement benefits other than pensions. This charge decreased net income per common share by $.16 for the quarter and $.17 for the year. The restatement reduced first quarter net income by $216 million ($.16 per common share), reduced second quarter net income by $16 million ($.01 per common share) and reduced third quarter net income by $1 million (no change in net income per common share). The sum of net income per common share for the four quarters was $.01 higher than the reported full year amount due to rounding.

The second quarter of 1991 includes a nonrecurring pretax charge of $21 million ($.01 per common share after income taxes) for potential future costs, including interest, related to bottler litigation.

The fourth quarter of 1991 includes a $69 million pretax gain ($.03 per common share after income taxes) on the sale of property in Japan, a $27 million pretax gain ($.01 per common share after income taxes) on the sale of a bottling investment to Coca-Cola Enterprises Inc. and a reduction to equity income of $44 million ($.03 per common share after income taxes) related to restructuring charges recorded by Coca-Cola Enterprises.

*Stock Prices*

Below are the New York Stock Exchange high, low and closing prices of The Coca-Cola Company stock for each quarter of 1992 and 1991, adjusted for a 2-for-1 stock split in May 1992.

| 1992 | First Quarter | Second Quarter | Third Quarter | Fourth Quarter |
|---|---|---|---|---|
| High | $41.69 | $45.13 | $45.38 | $44.50 |
| Low | 35.56 | 38.88 | 39.75 | 36.50 |
| Close | 40.88 | 40.00 | 40.50 | 41.88 |

| 1991 | First Quarter | Second Quarter | Third Quarter | Fourth Quarter |
|---|---|---|---|---|
| High | $27.75 | $29.00 | $33.25 | $40.88 |
| Low | 21.31 | 25.69 | 27.25 | 31.19 |
| Close | 27.13 | 27.25 | 32.25 | 40.13 |

# LIST OF OFFICIAL PRONOUNCEMENTS OF THE AICPA AND FASB

Listed below are the major official pronouncements of the AICPA and the FASB which have established generally accepted accounting principles or which have had a significant impact upon the establishment of these principles.

| *Number* | *Title* | *Date of Issuance* |
|---|---|---|

### Accounting Terminology Bulletins, Committee on Terminology, AICPA

1  Review and Résumé (of eight original terminology bulletins)................................... August 1953
2  Proceeds, Revenue, Income, Profit, and Earnings........................................... March 1955
3  Book Value ................................................................................ August 1956
4  Cost, Expense, and Loss.................................................................... July 1957

### Accounting Principles Board (APB) Statements, AICPA

1  Statement by the Accounting Principles Board .............................................. April 1962
2  Disclosure of Supplemental Financial Information by Diversified Companies ................. September 1967
3  Financial Statements Restated for General Price-Level Changes............................. June 1969
4  Basic Concepts and Accounting Principles Underlying Financial
   Statements of Business Enterprises........................................................ October 1970

### Accounting Principles Board (APB) Opinions, AICPA

1  New Depreciation Guidelines and Rules..................................................... November 1962
2  Accounting for the "Investment Credit" .................................................... December 1962
3  The Statement of Source and Application of Funds .......................................... October 1963
4  Accounting for the "Investment Credit" (Amending No. 2).................................... March 1964
5  Reporting of Leases in Financial Statements of Lessee...................................... September 1964
6  Status of Accounting Research Bulletins ................................................... October 1965
7  Accounting for Leases in Financial Statements of Lessors................................... May 1966
8  Accounting for the Cost of Pension Plans .................................................. November 1966
9  Reporting the Results of Operations........................................................ December 1966
10  Omnibus Opinion—1966..................................................................... December 1966
11  Accounting for Income Taxes .............................................................. December 1967
12  Omnibus Opinion—1967..................................................................... December 1967
13  Amending Paragraph 6 of the *APB Opinion No. 9*, Application to Commercial Banks ......... March 1969
14  Accounting for Convertible Debt and Debt Issued with Stock Purchase Warrants............. March 1969
15  Earnings per Share ....................................................................... May 1969
16  Business Combinations .................................................................... August 1970
17  Intangible Assets ........................................................................ August 1970
18  The Equity Method of Accounting for Investments in Common Stock........................... March 1971
19  Reporting Changes in Financial Position .................................................. March 1971
20  Accounting Changes ....................................................................... July 1971
21  Interest on Receivables and Payables...................................................... August 1971
22  Disclosure of Accounting Policies ........................................................ April 1972
23  Accounting for Income Taxes—Special Areas................................................. April 1972
24  Accounting for Income Taxes—Investments in Common Stock Accounted
    for by the Equity Method................................................................. April 1972
25  Accounting for Stock Issued to Employees.................................................. October 1972
26  Early Extinguishment of Debt ............................................................. October 1972
27  Accounting for Lease Transactions by Manufacturer or Dealer Lessors...................... November 1972
28  Interim Financial Reporting............................................................... May 1973
29  Accounting for Nonmonetary Transactions................................................... May 1973
30  Reporting the Results of Operations—Reporting the Effects of Disposal of a Segment of a
    Business, and Extraordinary, Unusual and Infrequently Occurring Events and Transactions ... June 1973
31  Disclosure of Lease Commitments by Lessees................................................ June 1973

### Financial Accounting Standards Board (FASB) Statements of Financial Accounting Standards

1  Disclosure of Foreign Currency Translation Information .................................... December 1973
2  Accounting for Research and Development Costs............................................. October 1974

| Number | Title | Date of Issuance |
|---|---|---|

**Financial Accounting Standards Board (FASB) Statements of Financial Accounting Standards, Continued**

3 Reporting Accounting Changes in Interim Financial Statements
(an amendment of *APB Opinion No. 28*) .............................................. December 1974
4 Reporting Gains and Losses from Extinguishment of Debt
(an amendment of *APB Opinion No. 30*) .............................................. March 1975
5 Accounting for Contingencies........................................................... March 1975
6 Classification of Short-Term Obligations Expected to Be Refinanced
(an amendment of *ARB No. 43, Chapter 3A*)......................................... May 1975
7 Accounting and Reporting by Development Stage Enterprises ...................... June 1975
8 Accounting for the Translation of Foreign Currency Transactions and Foreign
Currency Financial Statements.......................................................... October 1975
9 Accounting for Income Taxes—Oil and Gas Producing Companies
(an amendment of *APB Opinion Nos. 11 and 23*).................................... October 1975
10 Extension of "Grandfather" Provisions for Business Combinations
(an amendment of *APB Opinion No. 16*) .............................................. October 1975
11 Accounting for Contingencies—Transition Method (an amendment of *FASB Statement No. 5*)....December 1975
12 Accounting for Certain Marketable Securities ........................................December 1975
13 Accounting for Leases .................................................................. November 1976
14 Financial Reporting for Segments of a Business Enterprise ......................... December 1976
15 Accounting by Debtors and Creditors for Troubled Debt Restructurings............ June 1977
16 Prior Period Adjustments .............................................................. June 1977
17 Accounting for Leases—Initial Direct Costs (an amendment of *FASB Statement No. 13*)........ November 1977
18 Financial Reporting for Segments of a Business Enterprise Interim Financial Statements
(an amendment of *FASB Statement No. 14*)........................................... November 1977
19 Financial Accounting and Reporting by Oil and Gas Producing Companies.................... December 1977
20 Accounting for Forward Exchange Contracts (an amendment of *FASB Statement No. 8*) ........ December 1977
21 Suspension of the Reporting of Earnings per Share and Segment Information by
Nonpublic Enterprises (an amendment of *APB Opinion No. 15* and *FASB Statement No. 14*)........April 1978
22 Accounting for Leases—Changes in the Provisions of Lease Agreements Resulting from
Refundings of Tax-Exempt Debt (an amendment of *FASB Statement No. 13*)...................... June 1978
23 Inception of the Lease (an amendment of *FASB Statement No. 13*) ............................August 1978
24 Reporting Segment Information in Financial Statements that Are Presented in Another
Enterprise's Financial Report (an amendment of *FASB Statement No. 14*)..................... December 1978
25 Suspension of Certain Accounting Requirements for Oil and Gas Companies
(an amendment of *FASB Statement No. 19*)............................................ February 1979
26 Profit Recognition on Sales-Type Leases of Real Estate
(an amendment of *FASB Statement No. 13*)............................................ April 1979
27 Classification of Renewals or Extensions of Existing Sales-Type or Direct Financing Leases
(an amendment of *FASB Statement No. 13*)............................................ May 1979
28 Accounting for Sales with Leasebacks (an amendment of *FASB Statement No. 13*) .................. May 1979
29 Determining Contingent Rentals (an amendment of *FASB Statement No. 13*) ...................... June 1979
30 Disclosure of Information About Major Customers (an amendment of *FASB Statement No. 14*)..... August 1979
31 Accounting for Tax Benefits Related to U.K. Tax Legislation Concerning Stock Relief .......... September 1979
32 Specialized Accounting and Reporting Principles and Practices in AICPA Statements of Position
and Guides on Accounting and Auditing Matters (an amendment of *APB Opinion No. 20*)...... September 1979
33 Financial Reporting and Changing Prices ................................................ September 1979
34 Capitalization of Interest Cost......................................................... October 1979
35 Accounting and Reporting by Defined Benefit Pension Plans................................. March 1980
36 Disclosure of Pension Information........................................................ May 1980
37 Balance Sheet Classification of Deferred Income Taxes (an amendment of *APB Opinion No. 11*) .......July 1980
38 Accounting for Preacquisition Contingencies of Purchased Enterprises
(an amendment of *APB Opinion No. 16*) ............................................... September 1980

| Number | Title | Date of Issuance |
|---|---|---|

**Financial Accounting Standards Board (FASB) Statements of Financial Accounting Standards, Continued**

39  Financial Reporting and Changing Prices: Specialized Assets—Mining and Oil and Gas (a supplement to *FASB Statement No. 33*) ................................................... October 1980

40  Financial Reporting and Changing Prices: Specialized Assets—Timberlands and Growing Timber (a supplement to *FASB Statement No. 33*) ........................................ November 1980

41  Financial Reporting and Changing Prices: Specialized Assets—Income-Producing Real Estate (a supplement to *FASB Statement No. 33*) ........................................ November 1980

42  Determining Materiality for Capitalization of Interest Cost (an amendment of *FASB Statement No. 34*) .................................................... November 1980

43  Accounting for Compensated Absences ............................................... November 1980

44  Accounting for Intangible Assets of Motor Carriers (an amendment of Chapter 5 of *ARB No. 43* and an interpretation of *APB Opinion Nos. 17* and *30*) ...................... December 1980

45  Accounting for Franchise Fee Revenue ................................................... March 1981

46  Financial Reporting and Changing Prices: Motion Picture Films .............................. March 1981

47  Disclosure of Long-Term Obligations ..................................................... March 1981

48  Revenue Recognition When Right of Return Exists........................................... June 1981

49  Accounting for Product Financing Arrangements ............................................ June 1981

50  Financial Reporting in the Record and Music Industry.................................... November 1981

51  Financial Reporting by Cable Television Companies ..................................... November 1981

52  Foreign Currency Translation............................................................December 1981

53  Financial Reporting by Producers and Distributors of Motion Picture Films ...............December 1981

54  Financial Reporting and Changing Prices: Investment Companies (an amendment of *FASB Statement No. 33*) ................................................... January 1982

55  Determining Whether a Convertible Security Is a Common Stock Equivalent (an amendment of *APB Opinion No. 15*) .............................................. February 1982

56  Designation of AICPA Guide and Statement of Position (SOP) 81-1 on Contractor Accounting and SOP 81-2 Concerning Hospital-Related Organizations as Preferable for Purposes of Applying *APB Opinion 20* (an amendment of *FASB Statement No. 32*) ................. February 1982

57  Related Party Disclosures ............................................................... March 1982

58  Capitalization of Interest Cost in Financial Statements That Include Investments Accounted for by the Equity Method ................................................................April 1982

59  Deferral of the Effective Date of Certain Accounting Requirements for Pension Plans of State and Local Governmental Units (an amendment of *FASB Statement No. 35*) ................April 1982

60  Accounting and Reporting by Insurance Enterprises ......................................... June 1982

61  Accounting for Title Plant .............................................................. June 1982

62  Capitalization of Interest Cost in Situations Involving Certain Tax-Exempt Borrowings and Certain Gifts and Grants ........................................................... June 1982

63  Financial Reporting by Broadcasters....................................................... June 1982

64  Extinguishments of Debt Made to Satisfy Sinking-Fund Requirements (an amendment of *FASB Statement No. 4*) ............................................. September 1982

65  Accounting for Certain Mortgage Banking Activities .................................... September 1982

66  Accounting for Sales of Real Estate....................................................October 1982

67  Accounting for Costs and Initial Rental Operations of Real Estate Projects ....................October 1982

68  Research and Development Arrangements ................................................October 1982

69  Disclosures About Oil- and Gas-Producing Activities ................................... November 1982

70  Financial Reporting and Changing Prices: Foreign Currency Translation (an amendment of *FASB Statement No. 33*)......................................... December 1982

71  Accounting for the Effects of Certain Types of Regulation ............................. December 1982

72  Accounting for Certain Acquisitions of Banking or Thrift Institutions (an amendment of *APB Opinion No. 17*, an interpretation of *APB Opinion Nos. 16* and *17*, and an amendment of *FASB Statement No. 9*) ................................................... February 1983

73  Reporting a Change in Accounting for Railroad Track Structures (an amendment of *APB Opinion No. 20*) ........................................... August 1983

| Number | Title | Date of Issuance |
|---|---|---|

**Financial Accounting Standards Board (FASB) Statements of Financial Accounting Standards, Continued**

74 Accounting for Special Termination Benefits Paid to Employees ................................. August 1983

75 Deferral of the Effective Date of Certain Accounting Requirements for Pension Plans of State and Local Governmental Units (an amendment of *FASB Statement No. 35*) .................. November 1983

76 Extinguishment of Debt (an amendment of *APB Opinion No. 26*)...................... November 1983

77 Reporting by Transferors for Transfers of Receivables with Recourse ....................... December 1983

78 Classification of Obligations That Are Callable by the Creditor (an amendment of *ARB No. 43*, Chapter 3A) ............................................... December 1983

79 Elimination of Certain Disclosures for Business Combinations by Nonpublic Enterprises (an amendment of *APB Opinion No. 16*) ................................................ February 1984

80 Accounting for Futures Contracts .................................................... August 1984

81 Disclosure of Postretirement Health Care and Life Insurance Benefits ....................... November 1984

82 Financial Reporting and Changing Prices: Elimination of Certain Disclosures (an amendment of *FASB Statement No. 33*)............................................ December 1984

83 Designation of AICPA Guides and Statement of Position on Accounting by Brokers and Dealers in Securities, by Employee Benefit Plans, and by Banks as Preferable for Purposes of Applying *APB Opinion No. 20* ............................................ March 1985

84 Induced Conversions of Convertible Debt (an amendment of *APB Opinion No. 26*).............. March 1985

85 Yield Test for Determining Whether a Convertible Security Is a Common Stock Equivalent (an amendment of *APB Opinion No. 15*) ............................................ March 1985

86 Accounting for the Costs of Computer Software to Be Sold, Leased, or Otherwise Marketed....... August 1985

87 Employers' Accounting for Pensions .................................................. December 1985

88 Employers' Accounting for Settlements and Curtailments of Defined Benefit Pension Plans and for Termination Benefits .......................................... December 1985

89 Financial Reporting and Changing Prices ............................................. December 1986

90 Regulated Enterprises—Accounting for Abandonments and Disallowances of Plant Costs (an amendment of *FASB Statement No. 71*)............................................ December 1986

91 Accounting for Nonrefundable Fees and Costs Associated with Originating or Acquiring Loans and Initial Direct Costs of Leases ............................................. December 1986

92 Regulated Enterprises—Accounting for Phase-in Plans (an amendment of *FASB Statement No. 71*) ............................................ August 1987

93 Recognition of Depreciation by Not-for-Profit Organizations............................... August 1987

94 Consolidation of All Majority-Owned Subsidiaries (an amendment of *ARB No. 51*, with related amendments of *APB Opinion No. 18* and *ARB No. 43*, Chapter 12).................... October 1987

95 Statement of Cash Flows ........................................... November 1987

96 Accounting for Income Taxes........................................ December 1987

97 Accounting and Reporting by Insurance Enterprises for Certain Long-Duration Contracts and for Realized Gains and Losses from the Sale of Investments .................... December 1987

98 Accounting for Leases: Sale-Leaseback Transactions Involving Real Estate, Sales-Type Leases of Real Estate, Definition of the Lease Term, and Initial Direct Costs of Direct Financing Leases (an amendment of *FASB Statement Nos. 13, 66,* and *91* and a rescission of *FASB Statement No. 26* and *Technical Bulletin No. 79-11*)..................................... May 1988

99 Deferral of the Effective Date of Recognition of Depreciation by Not-for-Profit Organizations (an amendment of *FASB Statement No. 93*)........................................ September 1988

100 Accounting for Income Taxes—Deferral of the Effective Date of *FASB Statement No. 96* (an amendment of *FASB Statement No. 96*)........................................ December 1988

101 Regulated Enterprises—Accounting for the Discontinuation of Application of *FASB Statement No. 71*.......................................... December 1988

102 Statement of Cash Flows—Exemption of Certain Enterprises and Classification of Cash Flows from Certain Securities Acquired for Resale (an amendment of *FASB Statement No. 95*) ............................................ February 1989

103 Accounting for Income Taxes—Deferral of the Effective Date of *FASB Statement No. 96* (an amendment of *FASB Statement No. 96*)......................................... December 1989

| Number | Title | Date of Issuance |
|---|---|---|

### Financial Accounting Standards Board (FASB) Statements of Financial Accounting Standards, Continued

104 Statement of Cash Flows—Net Reporting of Certain Cash Receipts and Cash Payments and Classification of Cash Flows from Hedging Transactions (an amendment of *FASB Statement No. 95*).............................December 1989

105 Disclosure of Information about Financial Instruments with Off-Balance-Sheet Risk and Financial Instruments with Concentrations of Credit Risk................................... March 1990

106 Employers' Accounting for Postretirement Benefits Other Than Pensions ..................... December 1990

107 Disclosure about Fair Value of Financial Instruments ..........................................December 1991

108 Accounting for Income Taxes—Deferral of the Effective Date of *FASB Statement No. 96* (an amendment of *FASB Statement No. 96*)..........................................December 1991

109 Accounting for Income Taxes........................................................ February 1992

110 Reporting by Defined Benefit Pension Plans of Investment Contracts (an amendment of *FASB Statement No. 35*).....................................................August 1992

111 Rescission of *FASB Statement No. 32* and Technical Corrections ......................... November 1992

112 Employers' Accounting for Postemployment Benefits (an amendment of *FASB Statement Nos. 5 and 43*)........................................................ November 1992

113 Accounting and Reporting for Reinsurance of Short-Term and Long-Term Contracts........... December 1992

114 Accounting by Creditors for Impairment of a Loan (an amendment of *FASB Statement Nos. 5 and 15*)........................................................ May 1993

115 Accounting for Certain Investments in Debt and Equity Securities............................... May 1993

### Financial Accounting Standards Board (FASB) Statements of Financial Accounting Concepts

1 Objectives of Financial Reporting by Business Enterprises ................................... November 1978

2 Qualitative Characteristics of Accounting Information............................................. May 1980

3 Elements of Financial Statements of Business Enterprises .................................... December 1980

4 Objectives of Financial Reporting by Nonbusiness Organizations................................ December 1980

5 Recognition and Measurement in Financial Statements of Business Enterprises ................. December 1984

6 Elements of Financial Statements (a replacement of *FASB Concepts Statement No. 3*, incorporating an amendment of *FASB Concepts Statement No. 2*) ............................December 1985

### Financial Accounting Standards Board (FASB) Interpretations

1 Accounting Changes Related to the Cost of Inventory (an interpretation of *APB Opinion No. 20*)....... June 1974

2 Imputing Interest on Debt Arrangements Made under the Federal Bankruptcy Act (an interpretation of *APB Opinion No. 21*)............................................ June 1974

3 Accounting for the Cost of Pension Plans Subject to the Employee Retirement Income Security Act of 1974 (an interpretation of *APB Opinion No. 8*)............................ December 1974

4 Applicability of *FASB Statement No. 2* to Business Combinations Accounted for by the Purchase Method............................................................. February 1975

5 Applicability of *FASB Statement No. 2* to Development Stage Enterprises ....................... February 1975

6 Applicability of *FASB Statement No. 2* to Computer Software................................ February 1975

7 Applying *FASB Statement No. 7* in Financial Statements of Established Operating Enterprises ..... October 1975

8 Classification of a Short-Term Obligation Repaid Prior to Being Replaced by a Long-Term Security (an interpretation of *FASB Statement No. 6*) ............................. January 1976

9 Applying *APB Opinion Nos. 16 and 17* When a Savings and Loan Association or a Similar Institution Is Acquired in a Business Combination Accounted for by the Purchase Method........ February 1976

10 Application of *FASB Statement No. 12* to Personal Financial Statements....................... September 1976

11 Changes in Market Value after the Balance Sheet Date (an interpretation of *FASB Statement No. 12*) ..................................................... September 1976

12 Accounting for Previously Established Allowance Accounts (an interpretation of *FASB Statement No. 12*)....................................................... September 1976

13 Consolidation of a Parent and Its Subsidiaries Having Different Balance Sheets Dates (an interpretation of *FASB Statement No. 12*)......................................... September 1976

| Number | Title | Date of Issuance |
|---|---|---|

### Financial Accounting Standards Board (FASB) Interpretations

14   Reasonable Estimation of the Amount of a Loss (an interpretation of
*FASB Statement No. 5*) ...................................................... September 1976

15   Translation of Unamortized Policy Acquisition Costs by a Stock Life Insurance Company
(an interpretation of *FASB Statement No. 8*) ................................ September 1976

16   Clarification of Definitions and Accounting for Marketable Equity Securities That Become
Nonmarketable (an interpretation of *FASB Statement No. 12*) .................... February 1977

17   Applying the Lower of Cost or Market Rule in Translated Financial Statements
(an interpretation of *FASB Statement No. 8*) .................................. February 1977

18   Accounting for Income Taxes in Interim Periods (an interpretation of *APB Opinion No. 28*) ........ March 1977

19   Lessee Guarantee of the Residual Value of Leased Property (an interpretation of
*FASB Statement No. 13*) ...................................................... October 1977

20   Reporting Accounting Changes under AICPA Statements of Position (an interpretation
of *APB Opinion No. 20*) ...................................................... November 1977

21   Accounting for Leases in a Business Combination (an interpretation of
*FASB Statement No. 13*) ...................................................... April 1978

22   Applicability of Indefinite Reversal Criteria to Timing Differences (an interpretation
of *APB Opinion Nos. 11 and 23*) .............................................. April 1978

23   Leases & Certain Property Owned by a Governmental Unit or Authority (an interpretation
of *FASB Statement No. 13*) ................................................... August 1978

24   Lease Involving Only Part of a Building (an interpretation of *FASB Statement No. 13*) ......... September 1978

25   Accounting for an Unused Investment Tax Credit (an interpretation of *APB Opinion
Nos. 2, 4, 11, and 16*) ....................................................... September 1978

26   Accounting for Purchase of a Leased Asset by the Lessee during the Term of the Lease
(an interpretation of *FASB Statement No. 13*) ................................. September 1978

27   Accounting for a Loss on a Sublease (an interpretation of *FASB Statement No. 13*) ............ November 1978

28   Accounting for Stock Appreciation Rights and Other Variable Stock Option or Award
Plans (an interpretation of *APB Opinion Nos. 15 and 25*) ...................... December 1978

29   Reporting Tax Benefits Realized on Disposition of Investments in Certain Subsidiaries
and Other Investees (an interpretation of *APB Opinion Nos. 23 and 24*) ........ February 1979

30   Accounting for Involuntary Conversions of Nonmonetary Assets to Monetary Assets
(an interpretation of *APB Opinion No. 29*) ................................... September 1979

31   Treatment of Stock Compensation Plans in EPS Computations (an interpretation
of *APB Opinion No. 15* and a modification of *FASB Interpretation No. 28*) ...... February 1980

32   Application of Percentage Limitations in Recognizing Investment Tax Credit
(an interpretation of *APB Opinion Nos. 2, 4, and 11*) ......................... March 1980

33   Applying *FASB Statement No. 34* to Oil and Gas Producing Operations Accounted for
by the Full Cost Method (an interpretation of *FASB Statement No. 34*) .......... August 1980

34   Disclosure of Indirect Guarantees of Indebtedness of Others (an interpretation of
*FASB Statement No. 5*) ....................................................... March 1981

35   Criteria for Applying the Equity Method of Accounting for Investments in Common Stock
(an interpretation of *APB Opinion No. 18*) ................................... May 1981

36   Accounting for Exploratory Wells in Progress at the End of a Period (an interpretation
of *FASB Statement No. 19*) ................................................... October 1981

37   Accounting for Translation Adjustments Upon Sale of Part of an Investment in a Foreign
Entity (an interpretation of *FASB Statement No. 52*) .......................... July 1983

38   Determining the Measurement Date for Stock Option, Purchase, and Award Plans Involving
Junior Stock (an interpretation of *APB Opinion No. 25*) ....................... August 1984

39   Offsetting of Amounts Related to Certain Contracts (an interpretation of *APB Opinion
No. 10* and *FASB Statement No. 105* ......................................... March 1992

40   Applicability of Generally Accepted Accounting Principles to Mutual Life Insurance and
Other Enterprises (an interpretation of *FASB Statement Nos. 12, 60, 97, and 113*) ......... April 1993

# C

# REVIEW OF THE ACCOUNTING PROCESS

A primary objective of financial reporting is to provide information that is useful to present and potential investors and creditors and other users in making rational investment, credit, and similar decisions.[1] Financial statements and the accompanying notes are summary reports used to provide this information. These statements are the result of a complex financial accounting process which is discussed throughout this book. To understand financial accounting, it is necessary to be familiar with the accounting system used to accumulate the information in these financial statements. This system is the topic of this Appendix.

**Appendix Topics**

*The Accounting Model and System*

*The Accounting Cycle*

*Reversing Entries*

*The Worksheet*

*Subsidiary Ledgers and Control Accounts*

*Special Journals*

*Computer Software*

---

1. "Objectives of Financial Reporting by Business Enterprises," *FASB Statement of Financial Accounting Concepts No. 1* (Stamford, Conn.: FASB, 1978), par. 34.

## THE ACCOUNTING SYSTEM

Although a major purpose of financial accounting is to provide information to external users, much accounting data is also useful to a company's managers in making operating decisions. Many transactions result in important financial and managerial accounting information. **An accounting system is a means by which the financial and managerial information of a company's transactions is recorded and stored so that it can be retrieved and reported in an accounting statement.** All companies have accounting systems, ranging from the very simple, such as a checkbook, to the very complex, involving the use of computers.

The intent in this Appendix is to present the basics of a *financial* accounting system that can be used in either a manual or a computer accounting process. For convenience, the discussion is primarily in terms of a manual system. The components of an accounting system include (1) the framework for operation of the system, (2) the input source documents, (3) the records used to store accounting information, and (4) the output reports. Each of these is discussed in subsequent sections.

### Accounting Equation

The financial accounting recording process for a company involves (1) identifying events occurring within its economic environment that are financial transactions, (2) gathering the documents related to these transactions, (3) analyzing the documents to determine the relevant financial information to be recorded, (4) recording the financial information, and (5) storing this information for future retrieval and use. A basic accounting model has been developed that provides a framework for the accounting system and that serves as the basis for recording transactions. This model for a corporation, called the **residual equity theory** model, is usually expressed in equation form as follows:

**Assets = Liabilities + Stockholders' Equity**

where **assets** are defined as the corporation's economic resources, **liabilities** are its obligations owed to creditors, and **stockholders' equity** is the owners' residual interest in its assets. This equation must remain in balance at all times because each side presents a different "picture" of the same information. That is, the left side summarizes the economic resources while the right side summarizes the sources of (or claims upon) the economic resources. Evolving from this basic equation are several other interrelated equations pertaining to information desired by external users. These are shown in Exhibit C-1.

**Contributed capital** includes the amounts of stockholder investments resulting from the sale of shares of stock by the corporation, while **retained earnings** is the lifetime amount of earnings reinvested in the corporation and not distributed to stockholders. **Dividends** (which are *not* expenses) are the amounts distributed to stockholders as a return on their investment. **Revenues** are charges to customers for goods or services provided and **expenses** are the costs incurred by the corporation to provide the goods or services.[2]

---

2.  In this Appendix, for simplicity, included in revenues are *gains*, or those revenues from other than the sale of goods or services; included in expenses are *losses*, or those costs incurred that provide no revenues. Throughout the book, gains and losses are discussed and classified separately from revenues and expenses.

**EXHIBIT C-1**

**INTERRELATED ACCOUNTING EQUATIONS**

Assets = Liabilities + Stockholders' Equity

Stockholders' Equity = Contributed Capital + Retained Earnings

Retained Earnings = Beginning Retained Earnings + Net Income − Dividends

Net Income = Revenues − Expenses

## Transactions, Events, and Supporting Documents

For financial accounting purposes, a change in the economic resources (assets), obligations (liabilities), or residual interest (stockholders' equity) of a company may be caused by a transaction or an event. A **transaction** involves the transfer of something valuable between the company and another party. An **event** is a happening of consequence to the company. The event may be *internal,* such as using equipment in operations, or *external,* such as a decline in price. The transactions and events affecting economic resources and obligations are recorded in the accounting system. The business documents, or **source documents**, relating to these transactions and events are used as initial input information for the recording process. These documents (such as sales invoices, checks, and freight bills) normally contain information about the monetary amount to be recorded, the parties involved, the terms of the transactions, and other relevant information. Once a transaction or event is recorded, the supporting source documents are stored as a means of verifying and substantiating the accounting records.

## Accounts

Within the accounting system, **accounts are used to store the recorded monetary information from the transactions and events.** A separate account is maintained for each asset, liability, revenue, expense, and other stockholders' equity items. Examples of these accounts include Cash, Accounts Receivable (amounts due from customers), Buildings, Accounts Payable (amounts owed to suppliers), Mortgage Payable, Sales Revenue, Salaries Expense, Purchases, Capital Stock, Retained Earnings, and Dividends Distributed. Each account is assigned a number from the company's **chart of accounts**, a numbering system designed to efficiently organize the accounts and to minimize errors in the recording process.

An account can be in several physical forms. It might be a location on a computer disk or a standardized business paper in a manual system. No matter which physical form is employed, a single logical format is used. The format for the accounts in a manual system is called a *T-account.* Each T-account has a left (or *debit*) and a right (or *credit*) side for storing monetary information. Since each account accumulates information about both increases and decreases resulting from various transactions or events, there is a "double-entry" rule that standardizes the method of recording these changes. **In the double-entry system, for each transaction or event recorded, the total dollar amount of the debits entered in all the related accounts must be equal to the total dollar amount of the credits.**

The framework of an accounting system includes the accounts in the basic accounting equation as well as the double-entry system. In an accounting system, all accounts on the left side of the equation (assets) are increased by debits (entries on the left side of the accounts) and decreased by credits, while accounts on the right side of the equation (liabilities and stockholders' equity) are increased by credits (entries on the right side of the accounts) and decreased by debits. This relationship is shown on the left side of Exhibit C-2.

To illustrate, suppose that stockholders invest $20,000 into a corporation by purchasing 2,000 shares of its no-par stock at $10 per share. The corporation records this transaction as a debit (increase) of $20,000 to an asset account, Cash, and as a $20,000 credit (increase) to a contributed capital account in stockholders' equity, Capital Stock. Note that the accounting equation remains in balance (both sides increase by $20,000) and that the total debits equal the total credits.

| Assets | = | Liabilities | + | Stockholders' Equity |
|---|---|---|---|---|
| **Cash** | | | | **Capital Stock** |
| (debit) | | | | (credit) |
| 20,000 | | | | 20,000 |

Accounts are classified as **permanent** (or real) accounts and **temporary** (or nominal) accounts. The permanent accounts are the asset, liability, and stockholders' equity accounts which have balances at the *end* of the accounting period that are carried forward into the next accounting period. The accounts on the far right of Exhibit C-2, namely the revenue, expense, and dividend accounts, are temporary accounts because they are "temporarily" used to determine the change in retained

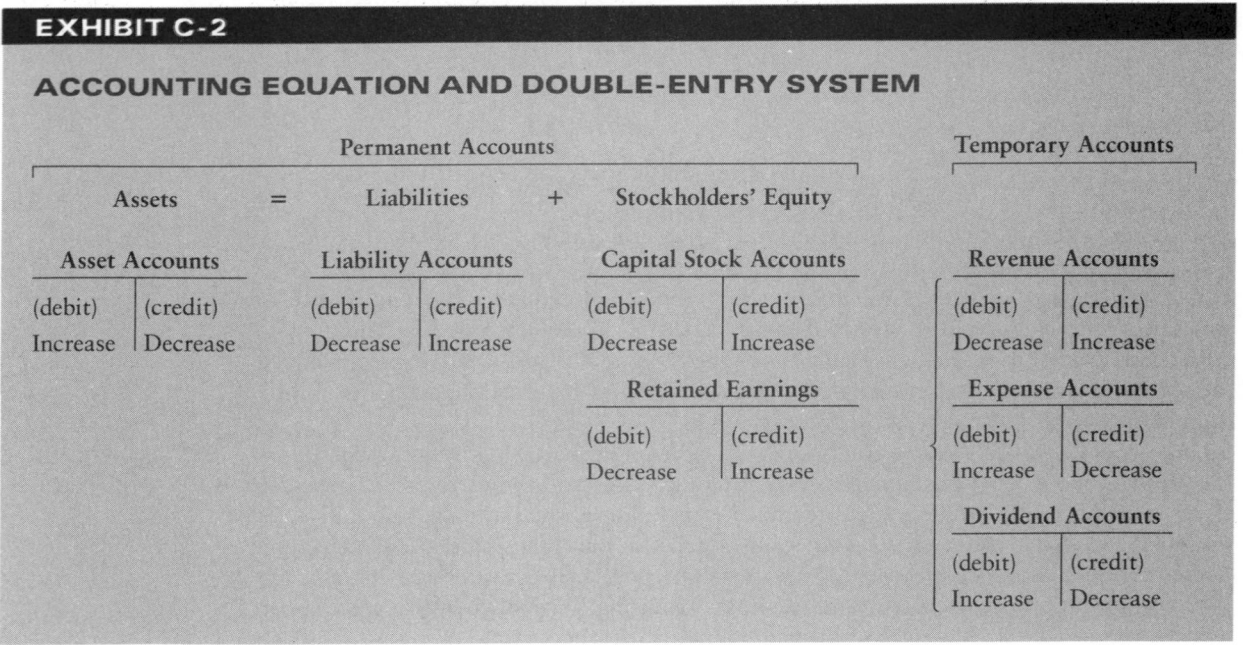

**EXHIBIT C-2**

**ACCOUNTING EQUATION AND DOUBLE-ENTRY SYSTEM**

earnings that occurred *during* the accounting period and, therefore, their account balances are *not* carried forward into the next period. The rules for recording transactions in temporary accounts are also shown in Exhibit C-2. Because an increase in revenues causes an increase in retained earnings, the rules for recording transactions in these accounts are the same as those for retained earnings. However, because an increase in several temporary accounts (such as expenses and dividends) causes a decrease in retained earnings, the rules for recording transactions in these accounts are the reverse of those for retained earnings.[3] For instance, since the payment of dividends reduces retained earnings, an increase in a Dividends account is recorded as a debit.

In certain instances a company will use a **contra** (or negative) account to emphasize a reduction in a related account. The rules for increasing or decreasing a contra account are also exactly the *reverse* of those for the related account. A contra account may be related to a permanent account or a temporary account. For instance, a Sales Discounts Taken account is used to accumulate the cash discounts taken by customers on Sales Revenues, while an Accumulated Depreciation account is used to accumulate the depreciation recorded for Buildings. Contra accounts are further illustrated in a later section.

**The balance of an account on a particular date is the difference between the total debits and credits recorded in that account.** These balances are used in the preparation of the company's financial statements.

## Financial Statements

A company's financial statements are output summary reports of the accounting system. These statements are derived from the interrelated equations presented earlier. The major financial statements include (1) the income statement, (2) the balance sheet (alternatively titled the statement of financial position), and (3) the statement of cash flows. Financial statements are prepared at the end of each year, called the **accounting period**. The annual set of financial statements and accompanying supporting schedules and notes, along with other data that are distributed to the various external users, is called the **annual report**. Financial statements are often prepared for a shorter time period such as three months; these are called **interim** (or quarterly) financial statements.

**The income statement is used to summarize the results of a company's income-producing activities for the accounting period.** In the income statement, the net income is determined by subtracting the total expenses from the total revenues. A supporting schedule (statement) is usually prepared to tie the income statement to the balance sheet. **The statement of retained earnings summarizes the amount of a company's net income retained in the business.** This procedure involves adding the current net income to the retained earnings balance at the beginning of the period and subtracting the dividends distributed to stockholders. **The balance sheet summarizes the amounts of the assets, liabilities, and stockholders' equity of a company on a particular date.** The stockholders' equity includes the ending retained earnings balance from the statement of retained earnings. Usually a balance sheet is presented for the end of the previous accounting period as well as the end of the current accounting period. The balance sheet is so named because it is an expansion of the basic accounting equation, which always remains in balance. Because of the "linkage"

---

3. Since *gains* are classified as revenues and *losses* are classified as expenses, the rules for increasing these accounts are the same as those for revenues and expenses, respectively.

between the income statement, statement of retained earnings, and balance sheet due to net income and retained earnings, these financial statements are said to be **articulated**. These statements are illustrated later as part of a comprehensive example in Exhibits C-8, C-9, and C-10. The third major statement, **the statement of cash flows, summarizes the cash receipts and cash payments of a company during the accounting period.** It is not illustrated here but is briefly discussed in Chapter 3 and more fully in Chapter 20. The statement of cash flows articulates with the balance sheet because it reconciles the beginning cash balance with the ending cash balance. Other supporting schedules, such as the schedule of changes in stockholders' equity and the schedule of investing and financing activities not involving cash receipts or cash payments, are also discussed in these chapters.

## THE ACCOUNTING CYCLE

A series of steps are completed during each accounting period to record, store, and report the accounting information contained in the recorded transactions. These steps are referred to as the **accounting cycle.** The *major* steps include: (1) recording daily transactions in a journal, (2) posting the journal entries to the accounts in the ledger, (3) preparing and posting adjusting entries, (4) preparing the financial statements, and (5) preparing and posting closing entries for the revenue, expense, and dividend accounts.

### Recording in the General Journal (Step 1)

**A journal is called a "document of original entry" because a company's transactions (and events) are initially recorded here.** All transactions *could* be recorded in a single journal, called the **general** journal. However, most companies have a number of different **special** journals, each designed for the recording of a particular type of transaction. These are briefly discussed in a later section of this Appendix.

The focus in this section is on the general journal. This journal consists of a date column, a column to list the accounts affected by each transaction, a column to list the account numbers (to save space, account numbers are *not* used in the subsequent comprehensive illustration), and a debit column and a credit column for listing the amounts to be recorded as a debit or credit to each account. Just below the listing of the accounts a written explanation of the transaction is presented. **The process of recording the transaction in the journal is called journalizing. The resulting entry is referred to as a journal entry.** An example of a general journal is shown in Exhibit C-4 later in this Appendix.

There are a number of advantages to using a general journal (and special journals). First, it helps to prevent errors. The accounts and debit and credit amounts for each transaction are initially recorded on a single journal page rather than directly in the numerous accounts. This makes it easier to verify the equality of the debits and credits. Second, all the transactional information (including the explanation) is recorded in one place, thereby providing a complete "picture" of the transaction. This is especially useful during the auditing process or if an error is discovered later in the accounting cycle, because the general journal can be reviewed to determine the nature of the transaction. Finally, since the transactions are recorded as they occur, the journal also provides a chronological record of the company's financial transactions.

To illustrate the entire accounting cycle, a comprehensive illustration is presented throughout this section. Dapple Corporation incorporates on January 1, 1995 as a wholesaler. It purchases one type of product from suppliers and resells this inventory to commercial customers. It opens for business on April 1, 1995. The company uses a

**periodic inventory system;** that is, it takes a physical inventory at the end of the accounting period. The company *derives* its **cost of goods sold** (a major operating expense) at the end of the period by computing the cost of goods available for sale (beginning inventory plus purchases of inventory during the period) and subtracting the amount of the ending inventory. Under this system neither the cost of inventory on hand nor the cost of goods sold is known until the end of the accounting period.[4] During 1995, the company engages in several transactions. These transactions and an analysis of the accounts and amounts to be debited and credited are listed in Exhibit C-3. Some of these transactions are partially condensed and overly simplified so that a variety of transactions may be illustrated.

## EXHIBIT C-3

### DAPPLE CORPORATION

1995 Transactions and Analyses

| Date | Transaction | Analysis |
|---|---|---|
| 01/01 | Various stockholders invest in Dapple by purchasing 2,000 shares of no-par stock at $10 per share. | Asset account Cash increased (debited) by $20,000; stockholder's equity account Capital Stock increased (credited) by $20,000. |
| 01/16 | Dapple purchases 2 acres of land as a building site, paying $1,500 an acre. | Asset account Land increased (debited) by $3,000; asset account Cash decreased (credited) by $3,000. |
| 03/30 | A building is built and equipment purchased for $15,320 and $2,120, respectively. Dapple pays $10,840 and signs a 12% mortgage (interest and principal to be paid after 2 years) for $6,600 balance. | Asset accounts Building and Equipment increased (debited) by $15,320 and $2,120, respectively; asset account Cash decreased (credited) by $10,840; liability account Mortgage Payable increased (credited) by $6,600. |
| 03/30 | Dapple purchases 1-year comprehensive insurance policy for $360. | Asset account Prepaid Insurance increased (debited) by $360; asset account Cash decreased (credited) by $360. |
| 03/31 | Dapple purchases $7,400 of inventory on account. Supplier (Bark Company) allows a $100 cash discount if paid within 10 days. | Cost of goods sold expense account* Purchases increased (debited) by $7,400; liability account Accounts Payable increased (credited) by $7,400. |
| 04/03 | Dapple sells inventory at total cash selling price of $8,000. | Asset account Cash increased (debited) by $8,000; revenue account Sales Revenue increased (credited) by $8,000. |
| 04/08 | Dapple pays $7,300 to Bark for inventory purchased on 03/31. | Liability account Accounts Payable decreased (debited) by $7,400; contra-purchases account Purchases Discounts Taken increased (credited) by $100; asset account Cash decreased (credited) by $7,300. |

---

4. Alternatively, a company could use a **perpetual inventory system**. Here the inventory records are continuously updated for the goods purchased and sold. Purchases of merchandise are recorded as increases in the Inventory account and sales of merchandise are recorded as decreases in the Inventory account and as increases in a Cost of Goods Sold expense *account*. This inventory system is more expensive to operate than the periodic system but enables a company to plan more accurately and to control the amounts of its inventory and cost of goods sold on a continuous basis. A complete discussion of inventories is presented in Chapter 6.

## EXHIBIT C-3, Continued

| Date | Transaction | Analysis |
|------|-------------|----------|
| 04/15 | A customer returns defective inventory items purchased on 02/02 and is given a $250 refund. | Contra-revenue account Sales Returns and Allowances increased (debited) by $250; asset account Cash decreased (credited) by $250. |
| 04/20 | Dapple returns defective inventory to its supplier and receives a $160 cash refund. | Asset account Cash increased (debited) by $160; contra-purchases account Purchases Returns and Allowances increased (credited) by $160. |
| 07/15 | Dapple makes $3,100 cash purchase of inventory and pays $200 of associated freight charges. | Cost of goods sold expense accounts* Purchases and Freight-in increased (debited) by $3,100 and $200, respectively; asset account Cash decreased (credited) by $3,300. |
| 09/01 | Dapple sells one acre of land (original cost $1,500) for $1,320. It accepts a 6-month, 15% promissory note from buyer. | Asset account Notes Receivable increased (debited) by $1,320; loss account Loss on Sale of Land increased (debited) by $180; asset account Land decreased (credited) by $1,500. |
| 10/02 | Dapple pays the first 6 months' salaries (April through September) totaling $1,800 to employees. | Expense account Salaries Expense increased (debited) by $1,800; asset account Cash decreased (credited) by $1,800. |
| 11/23 | Dapple makes sales on account of $5,000 to Frank Company and $4,000 to Knox Company. Terms of the sale are 2/10, n/60 (2% discount allowed if accounts paid within 10 days, total amount due in 60 days). | Asset account Accounts Receivable increased (debited) by $9,000; revenue account Sales Revenue increased (credited) by $9,000. |
| 12/01 | Dapple rents part of its building to Fritz Company, receiving 3 months' rent in advance at $150 per month. | Asset account Cash increased (debited) by $450; liability account Unearned Rent increased (credited) by $450. |
| 12/04 | Dapple collects $2,000 of accounts receivable from Frank Company. Frank takes a cash discount of $40, remitting remaining $1,960. | Asset account Cash increased (debited) by $1,960; contra-revenue account Sales Discounts Taken increased (debited) by $40; asset account Accounts Receivable decreased (credited) by $2,000. |
| 12/26 | Dapple purchases $1,900 of inventory on account from the Ajax Company. Supplier pays freight charges. | Cost of goods sold expense account* Purchases increased (debited) by $1,900; liability account Accounts Payable increased (credited) by $1,900. |
| 12/28 | Dapple pays $428 miscellaneous operating expenses. | Expense account Other Expenses increased (debited) by $428; asset account Cash decreased (credited) by $428. |
| 12/29 | Dapple distributes dividends of $500 ($0.25 per share for 2,000 shares) to stockholders. | Account Dividends Distributed increased (debited) by $500; asset account Cash decreased (credited) by $500. |

* Literally, the Purchases and Freight-in accounts include the cost of goods *available* for sale rather than the cost of goods *sold*. However, for convenience, the latter phrase is used to classify these accounts. The inclusion of the Purchases and Freight-in accounts in the computation of cost of goods sold is shown in Exhibit C-8.

Based upon the transactional analysis listed in Exhibit C-3, the general journal entries shown in Exhibit C-4 are prepared. Traditionally, all accounts to be debited are listed first. Accounts to be credited are listed next and indented. Finally, a brief explanation of the journal entry is made.

## EXHIBIT C-4

### DAPPLE CORPORATION

General Journal Entries

| Date | Account Titles and Explanations | Debit | Credit |
|---|---|---|---|
| *1995*<br>Jan. 1 | Cash<br>    Capital Stock<br>Issued 2,000 shares of no-par stock at $10 per share. | 20,000 | 20,000 |
| 16 | Land<br>    Cash<br>Purchased 2 acres of land at $1,500 per acre. | 3,000 | 3,000 |
| Mar. 30 | Building<br>Equipment<br>    Cash<br>    Mortgage Payable<br>Purchased a building and equipment. The mortgage bears annual interest of 12% and is due on March 30, 1997. | 15,320<br>2,120 | 10,840<br>6,600 |
| 30 | Prepaid Insurance<br>    Cash<br>Purchased a 1-year comprehensive insurance policy. | 360 | 360 |
| 31 | Purchases<br>    Accounts Payable<br>Purchased inventory for resale on account from Bark Company. Terms of sale include a $100 cash discount if paid within 10 days. | 7,400 | 7,400 |
| Apr. 3 | Cash<br>    Sales Revenue<br>To record cash sales. | 8,000 | 8,000 |
| 8 | Accounts Payable<br>    Purchases Discounts Taken<br>    Cash<br>Paid Bark Company for purchases made on account on March 31, less the cash discount. | 7,400 | 100<br>7,300 |
| 15 | Sales Returns and Allowances<br>    Cash<br>Customer returned defective inventory and cash refund was given. | 250 | 250 |
| 20 | Cash<br>    Purchases Returns and Allowances<br>Returned defective inventory to Bark Company and received a cash refund. | 160 | 160 |
| July 15 | Purchases<br>Freight-in<br>    Cash<br>Purchased inventory for resale and paid associated freight charges. | 3,100<br>200 | 3,300 |

## EXHIBIT C-4, Continued

| Date | Account Titles and Explanations | Debit | Credit |
|---|---|---|---|
| Sept. 1 | Notes Receivable<br>Loss on Sale of Land<br>   Land<br>Sold 1 acre of land at less than its cost, incurring a loss. Buyer issued a<br>note due in 6 months and bearing 15% annual interest. | 1,320<br>180 | 1,500 |
| Oct. 2 | Salaries Expense<br>   Cash<br>Paid 6 months of employees' salaries. | 1,800 | 1,800 |
| Nov. 23 | Accounts Receivable<br>   Sales Revenue<br>Made sales on account to Frank Company ($5,000) and Knox Company<br>($4,000). Terms of sale are 2/10, n/60. | 9,000 | 9,000 |
| Dec. 1 | Cash<br>   Unearned Rent<br>Received 3 months' rent in advance at $150 per month. Company owes use<br>of portion of building to Fritz Company for the 3-month period. | 450 | 450 |
| 4 | Cash<br>Sales Discounts Taken<br>   Accounts Receivable<br>Frank Company paid a portion of its accounts receivable less applicable<br>2% discount. | 1,960<br>40 | 2,000 |
| 26 | Purchases<br>   Accounts Payable<br>Purchased inventory on account from Ajax Company. | 1,900 | 1,900 |
| 28 | Other Expenses<br>   Cash<br>Paid miscellaneous operating expenses. | 428 | 428 |
| 29 | Dividends Distributed<br>   Cash<br>Distributed dividends of $0.25 per share to stockholders. | 500 | 500 |

## Posting to the Ledger (Step 2)

A general ledger is the entire group of accounts for a company. It might take several forms, such as a computer storage location on a disk, or in the case of our manual system, a loose-leaf binder with a page for each T-account. Once a company's transactions and events have been journalized in a general journal, each account in the general ledger is updated. This is accomplished through the process of **posting**. Posting involves transferring the date and debit and credit amounts from the journal entries in the general journal to the debit and credit sides of the accounts in the general ledger. Thus, **after posting, the general ledger accounts contain the same information as in the general journal, just in a different format.** Exhibit C-5 illustrates *all* the accounts in the general ledger of the Dapple Corporation. To conserve space, these accounts include the postings not only for the journal entries shown in Exhibit C-4, but also for the *adjusting* entries (*Adj* is shown in the account) and the *closing* entries (*Cl*) discussed later in Exhibits C-6 and C-11.

*Trial Balance* After the journal entries have been prepared and posted for the accounting period, the balance in each account is determined. Then a trial balance is

## EXHIBIT C-5

## DAPPLE CORPORATION

### General Ledger

**Cash**

| Debit | | Credit | |
|---|---|---|---|
| 01/01 | 20,000 | 01/16 | 3,000 |
| 04/03 | 8,000 | 03/30 | 10,840 |
| 04/20 | 160 | 03/30 | 360 |
| 12/01 | 450 | 04/08 | 7,300 |
| 12/04 | 1,960 | 04/15 | 250 |
| | | 07/15 | 3,300 |
| | | 10/02 | 1,800 |
| | | 12/28 | 428 |
| | | 12/29 | 500 |
| Balance | 2,792 | | |

**Accounts Receivable**

| Debit | | Credit | |
|---|---|---|---|
| 11/23 | 9,000 | 12/04 | 2,000 |
| Balance | 7,000 | | |

**Allowance for Doubtful Accounts**

| Debit | | Credit | |
|---|---|---|---|
| | | 12/31 Adj | 170 |

**Notes Receivable**

| Debit | | Credit | |
|---|---|---|---|
| 09/01 | 1,320 | | |

**Interest Receivable**

| Debit | | Credit | |
|---|---|---|---|
| 12/31 Adj | 66 | | |

**Inventory**

| Debit | | Credit | |
|---|---|---|---|
| 12/31 Cl | 2,140 | 12/31 Cl | 0 |
| Balance | 2,140 | | |

**Prepaid Insurance**

| Debit | | Credit | |
|---|---|---|---|
| 03/30 | 360 | 12/31 Adj | 270 |
| Balance | 90 | | |

**Land**

| Debit | | Credit | |
|---|---|---|---|
| 01/16 | 3,000 | 09/01 | 1,500 |
| Balance | 1,500 | | |

**Building**

| Debit | | Credit | |
|---|---|---|---|
| 03/30 | 15,320 | | |

**Accumulated Depreciation: Building**

| Debit | | Credit | |
|---|---|---|---|
| | | 12/31 Adj | 264 |

**Equipment**

| Debit | | Credit | |
|---|---|---|---|
| 03/30 | 2,120 | | |

**Accumulated Depreciation: Equipment**

| Debit | | Credit | |
|---|---|---|---|
| | | 12/31 Adj | 120 |

**Accounts Payable**

| Debit | | Credit | |
|---|---|---|---|
| 04/08 | 7,400 | 03/31 | 7,400 |
| | | 12/26 | 1,900 |
| | | Balance | 1,900 |

**Mortgage Payable**

| Debit | | Credit | |
|---|---|---|---|
| | | 03/30 | 6,600 |

**Salaries Payable**

| Debit | | Credit | |
|---|---|---|---|
| | | 12/31 Adj | 900 |

**Interest Payable**

| Debit | | Credit | |
|---|---|---|---|
| | | 12/31 Adj | 594 |

**Income Taxes Payable**

| Debit | | Credit | |
|---|---|---|---|
| | | 12/31 Adj | 600 |

**Unearned Rent**

| Debit | | Credit | |
|---|---|---|---|
| 12/31 Adj | 150 | 12/01 | 450 |
| | | Balance | 300 |

**Capital Stock**

| Debit | | Credit | |
|---|---|---|---|
| | | 01/01 | 20,000 |

**Retained Earnings**

| Debit | | Credit | |
|---|---|---|---|
| 12/31 Cl | 500 | 12/31 Cl | 1,400 |
| | | Balance | 900 |

**Dividends Distributed**

| Debit | | Credit | |
|---|---|---|---|
| 12/29 | 500 | 12/31 Cl | 500 |

**Sales Revenue**

| Debit | | Credit | |
|---|---|---|---|
| 12/31 Cl | 17,000 | 04/03 | 8,000 |
| | | 11/23 | 9,000 |

**Sales Returns and Allowances**

| Debit | | Credit | |
|---|---|---|---|
| 04/15 | 250 | 12/31 Cl | 250 |

**Sales Discounts Taken**

| Debit | | Credit | |
|---|---|---|---|
| 12/04 | 40 | 12/31 Cl | 40 |

**Interest Revenue**

| Debit | | Credit | |
|---|---|---|---|
| 12/31 Cl | 66 | 12/31 Adj | 66 |

**Rent Revenue**

| Debit | | Credit | |
|---|---|---|---|
| 12/31 Cl | 150 | 12/31 Adj | 150 |

**Purchases**

| Debit | | Credit | |
|---|---|---|---|
| 03/31 | 7,400 | 12/31 Cl | 12,400 |
| 07/15 | 3,100 | | |
| 12/26 | 1,900 | | |

**Purchases Returns and Allowances**

| Debit | | Credit | |
|---|---|---|---|
| 12/31 Cl | 160 | 04/20 | 160 |

**Purchases Discounts Taken**

| Debit | | Credit | |
|---|---|---|---|
| 12/31 Cl | 100 | 04/08 | 100 |

**Freight-in**

| Debit | | Credit | |
|---|---|---|---|
| 07/15 | 200 | 12/31 Cl | 200 |

**Salaries Expense**

| Debit | | Credit | |
|---|---|---|---|
| 10/02 | 1,800 | 12/31 Cl | 2,700 |
| 12/31 Adj | 900 | | |

**Other Expenses**

| Debit | | Credit | |
|---|---|---|---|
| 12/28 | 428 | 12/31 Cl | 428 |

**Loss on Sale of Land**

| Debit | | Credit | |
|---|---|---|---|
| 09/01 | 180 | 12/31 Cl | 180 |

**Depreciation Expense: Building**

| Debit | | Credit | |
|---|---|---|---|
| 12/31 Adj | 264 | 12/31 Cl | 264 |

**Depreciation Expense: Equipment**

| Debit | | Credit | |
|---|---|---|---|
| 12/31 Adj | 120 | 12/31 Cl | 120 |

**Bad Debts Expense**

| Debit | | Credit | |
|---|---|---|---|
| 12/31 Adj | 170 | 12/31 Cl | 170 |

**Insurance Expense**

| Debit | | Credit | |
|---|---|---|---|
| 12/31 Adj | 270 | 12/31 Cl | 270 |

**Interest Expense**

| Debit | | Credit | |
|---|---|---|---|
| 12/31 Adj | 594 | 12/31 Cl | 594 |

**Income Tax Expense**

| Debit | | Credit | |
|---|---|---|---|
| 12/31 Adj | 600 | 12/31 Cl | 600 |

**Income Summary**

| Debit | | Credit | |
|---|---|---|---|
| 12/31 Cl | 18,216 | 12/31 Cl | 19,616 |
| 12/31 Cl | 1,400 | | |

often prepared. **A trial balance is a working paper that lists all the general ledger accounts and their account balances.** These account balances are listed in either the debit or the credit column. The trial balance is used to verify that the total of the debit balances is equal to the total of the credit balances. This working paper is not illustrated here but is shown on the worksheet in Exhibit C-13.

If a trial balance does not balance, an error has been made. To find the error, the debit and credit columns of the trial balance should be added again. If the column totals do not agree, the amounts in the debit and credit columns should be checked to be sure that a debit or credit account balance was not mistakenly listed in the wrong column. If the error is still not found, the difference in the column totals should be computed and divided by 9. When the difference is evenly divisible by 9, there is a good chance that a *transposition* or a *slide* has occurred. A transposition occurs when two digits in a number are mistakenly reversed. For instance, if the $1,500 Land balance had been listed as $5,100 on the trial balance in Exhibit C-13, the debit column would have totaled $49,810 instead of $46,210. The difference, $3,600, is evenly divisible by 9. A slide occurs when the digits are listed in the correct order but are mistakenly moved one decimal place to the left or right. For instance, if the $1,900 Accounts Payable balance had been listed as $190 in Exhibit C-13, the credit column would have totaled $44,500 instead of $46,210. The $1,710 difference is evenly divisible by 9.

If a transposition or slide has occurred, the error may have been made when the account balances were transferred from the accounts to the trial balance or when the account balances were initially computed. Thus the account balances listed on the trial balance should be compared with the account balances listed in the ledger. Then the ledger account balances should be recomputed, and if no error is found, the postings should be double-checked. Finally, the journal entries should be reviewed for accuracy.

If the trial balance is in balance, it is likely that (1) equal debit entries and credit entries were recorded for each transaction; (2) the debit and credit entries were posted to the accounts; and (3) the account balances were correctly computed. The equality of the debit and credit totals, however, does not necessarily mean that the information in the accounting system is error-free. Several types of errors are not found by a trial balance. First, an entire transaction may not have been journalized. Second, an entire transaction may not have been posted to the accounts. Third, equal debits and credits, but of the wrong amount, may have been recorded for a transaction. Fourth, a transaction may have been journalized to a wrong account. Finally, a journal entry may have been posted to the wrong account.

## Preparation of Adjusting Entries (Step 3)

Because generally accepted accounting principles require use of the accrual method of accounting, most companies use this method. Under accrual accounting, revenues are recorded in the accounting period in which they are earned and realization has taken place, and expenses are recorded in the accounting period in which they are incurred, regardless of the inflow or outflow of cash. In many instances not all accounts are up to date at the end of the accounting period. Certain amounts must be *adjusted* so that all revenues and expenses are recorded and the balance sheet accounts have correct ending balances. **Adjusting entries are journal entries made at the end of the accounting period so that the financial statements include the correct amounts for the current period.**

An adjusting entry ordinarily affects both a permanent (balance sheet) and a temporary (income statement) account. Adjusting entries may be classified into three categories. These categories and the types of balance sheet accounts involved in the adjusting entries are:

1.  Apportionment of prepaid and deferred items
    a. Prepaid expenses
    b. Deferred revenues

2.  Recording of accrued items
    a. Accrued expenses
    b. Accrued revenues

3.  Recording estimated items

*Prepaid Expenses* A prepaid expense (sometimes called a prepaid asset) is an item of goods or services purchased by the company for its operations but not fully used by the end of the accounting period. When the goods or services are initially purchased, the *cost* is recorded as an acquisition of an asset (prepaid expense). At the end of the accounting period, some of these items have been used in the process of generating revenues. The costs must be systematically *matched,* as expenses, against the current revenues, while the unused cost remains as an asset on the balance sheet. Examples of prepaid expenses include prepaid rent, office supplies, and prepaid insurance.

In the Dapple Corporation example, a one-year comprehensive insurance policy was purchased on March 30, 1995. An asset, Prepaid Insurance, was recorded for $360. At the end of the year, 9 months of insurance coverage has expired while 3 months of coverage remains in force. The cost is apportioned as an expense on a straight-line basis (an equal amount each month). Consequently Insurance Expense is increased (debited) by $270 ($30 per month for 9 months) and Prepaid Insurance decreased (credited) by $270. The result is a $270 increase in expenses and a $90 remaining balance in the asset Prepaid Insurance. The adjusting entry is shown in Exhibit C-6 and is posted to the ledger accounts shown in Exhibit C-5. Since the December 31 date of the adjusting entries is the same as the December 31 date for the closing entries (discussed in Exhibit C-11), to clarify the postings each adjusting entry date is followed by the abbreviation *Adj.*

*Deferred Revenues* Deferred (or unearned) revenue is payment received by the company in advance for the future sale of inventory or performance of services. Initially a liability usually is recorded because the company has an obligation to provide the goods or services. When these have been provided to the customer, the liability is eliminated and the revenue is recorded in an adjusting entry. Although the adjusting entry might be made at the time the goods or services are provided, typically it is made at the end of the accounting period.

On December 1, Dapple Corporation received 3 months' rent of $450 in advance. It recorded the receipt as a liability, Unearned Rent. On December 31, an adjusting entry must be made because 1 month of rent has now been earned. The adjusting entry is a debit (decrease) of $150 to Unearned Rent and a credit (increase) of $150 to Rent Revenue. The result is a $150 increase in revenues and a $300 remaining balance in the liability Unearned Rent. The adjusting entry is shown in Exhibit C-6.

Some companies *initially* record the entire prepayment of a cost as an expense (instead of as an asset) or the entire receipt in advance as a revenue (instead of a liability). In this case adjusting entries are still necessary at the end of the accounting period, but they are different in form and amount. For example, Dapple Corporation *could* have recorded the March 30 payment as a $360 debit to Insurance Expense (instead of Prepaid Insurance) and it *could* have recorded the December 1 receipt as a

## EXHIBIT C-6

## DAPPLE CORPORATION

Adjusting Entries for 1995

| Date | Account Titles and Explanations | Debit | Credit |
|------|-------------------------------|-------|--------|
| | *Adjusting Entries* | | |
| Dec. 31 | Insurance Expense | 270 | |
| |    Prepaid Insurance | | 270 |
| | To record expiration of 9 months of insurance coverage purchased on March 30. | | |
| 31 | Unearned Rent | 150 | |
| |    Rent Revenue | | 150 |
| | To record earning of 1 month of rent revenue from receipt collected in advance on December 1. | | |
| 31 | Salaries Expense | 900 | |
| |    Salaries Payable | | 900 |
| | To record 3 months' salaries earned by employees but not yet paid. | | |
| 31 | Interest Expense | 594 | |
| |    Interest Payable | | 594 |
| | To record interest accumulated on the mortgage payable issued on March 30 and due March 30, 1997. | | |
| 31 | Interest Receivable | 66 | |
| |    Interest Revenue | | 66 |
| | To record interest accumulated on the note receivable accepted on September 1. | | |
| 31 | Depreciation Expense: Building | 264 | |
| |    Accumulated Depreciation: Building | | 264 |
| | To record 9 months' depreciation on building acquired March 30. | | |
| 31 | Depreciation Expense: Equipment | 120 | |
| |    Accumulated Depreciation: Equipment | | 120 |
| | To record 9 months' depreciation on equipment acquired March 30. | | |
| 31 | Bad Debts Expense | 170 | |
| |    Allowance for Doubtful Accounts | | 170 |
| | To record estimated uncollectible accounts receivable. | | |
| 31 | Income Tax Expense | 600 | |
| |    Income Taxes Payable | | 600 |
| | To record income taxes for the period. | | |

$450 credit to Rent Revenue (instead of Unearned Rent). In this case the adjusting entry procedure is to calculate the appropriate ending balances in the permanent accounts and adjust the accounts accordingly. For instance, Prepaid Insurance should have an ending balance of $90. The year-end adjusting entry must *reduce* the expense and *increase* the Prepaid Insurance account by this amount. The adjusting entry is a debit (increase) to Prepaid Insurance for $90 and a credit (decrease) to Insurance Expense for $90. Similarly, Unearned Rent should have an ending balance of $300. The year-end adjusting entry must *reduce* the revenue and *increase* the Unearned Rent account by this amount. The adjusting entry is a debit (decrease) to Rent Revenue for $300 and a credit (increase) to Unearned Rent for $300. The results of these adjusting entries are the *same* balances in the respective accounts as in the comprehensive illustration. Care must be taken to determine how advance payments and receipts were recorded before the adjusting entry is determined.

*Accrued Expenses* An accrued expense is an expense incurred during the accounting period that has been neither paid nor recorded. In order to match expenses against revenues and to reflect the proper liabilities at the end of the period, an adjusting entry must be made for each accrued expense.

Dapple Corporation has three accrued expenses it has not yet recorded: employees' salaries, interest, and income taxes. For simplicity assume the company pays employees' salaries every six months, the last $1,800 payment having been made on October 1. At the end of December, its employees have earned salaries for 3 months (October through December) although they have not been paid. The adjusting entry is a debit (increase) to Salaries Expense for $900 and a credit (increase) to Salaries Payable for $900. The result is a $900 increase in expenses and a $900 ending balance in the liability, Salaries Payable. The adjusting entry is shown in Exhibit C-6.

On March 30, Dapple Corporation issued a $6,600, 12% mortgage due at the end of 2 years. Although the mortgage and interest will not be *paid* until 1997, 9 months of interest expense has accumulated and is a liability at the end of 1995. The interest is computed using the equation: Interest = Principal × Rate × Time, where time is expressed as a fraction of a year. The adjusting entry involves a debit (increase) to Interest Expense for $594 ($6,600 × 0.12 × 9/12) and a credit (increase) to Interest Payable for $594, as shown in Exhibit C-6.

Corporations are subject to a federal (and often state) income tax on their income. Although income taxes may not be paid until the following period, they are an expense and year-end obligation of the period in which the income is earned. The adjusting entry for income taxes is prepared *after* all the other adjusting entries because the amount is computed by multiplying the income tax rate times the current income before income taxes. Based on its current income before income taxes and tax rate,[5] Dapple Corporation calculates that its 1995 income taxes are $600, the entire amount payable in 1996. The adjusting entry is a debit (increase) to Income Tax Expense for $600 and a credit (increase) to Income Taxes Payable for $600, and is shown as the last item in Exhibit C-6.

*Accrued Revenues* An accrued revenue is a revenue earned during the accounting period that has been neither received nor recorded. An adjusting entry is necessary to increase the assets and revenues at the end of the period.

On September 1, Dapple Corporation accepted a $1,320, 15% note as payment when it sold an acre of land. Although the note and interest will not be collected until 1996, the company has earned 4 months of interest in 1995. The $66 of interest ($1,320 × 0.15 × 4/12) is recorded as a debit (increase) to Interest Receivable and a credit (increase) to Interest Revenue. The result is a $66 increase in revenues and a $66 increase in the asset Interest Receivable. The adjusting entry is shown in Exhibit C-6.

*Estimated Items* Certain other adjusting entries are based on estimated amounts because they are a function, at least in part, of expected future events. Adjustments involving (1) the depreciation on assets such as buildings and equipment and (2) the uncollectibility of some accounts receivable are both based upon estimates.

---

5.  As may be seen in Exhibit C-8, the Dapple Corporation's income before income taxes totals $2,000. Multiplying an assumed tax rate of 30% times this amount yields income taxes of $600.

When an asset, such as a machine, sales fixture, or building, is acquired for use in a company's operations, its cost is recorded as an economic resource (asset). It is expected that after several periods of use the asset will be disposed of at a value significantly less than its original cost. The difference between the original cost and an estimate of this later value (alternatively called residual value, salvage value, scrap value, or trade-in value) is the asset's depreciable cost. This depreciable cost is systematically and rationally allocated as an expense to each accounting period in which the asset is used. This cost allocation process is referred to as **depreciation**. One systematic depreciation method is straight-line depreciation, which allocates a proportionate amount as an expense to each accounting period. Its computation is as follows:

$$\text{Annual Depreciation Expense} = \frac{\text{Cost} - \text{Estimated Residual Value}}{\text{Estimated Service Life}}$$

Depreciation is recorded at the end of the accounting period in an adjusting entry. The entry increases Depreciation Expense and decreases the remaining depreciable cost of the asset. However, this decrease is *not* recorded directly in the asset account. Instead a contra (negative) asset account, entitled Accumulated Depreciation, is *increased*. This contra account is subtracted from the asset account on the balance sheet. The resulting balance is referred to as the *book* value (or carrying value) of the asset.

Dapple Corporation has two depreciable assets, the building and equipment acquired on March 30, 1995. The company estimates that these assets will have lives of 35 years and 12 years, respectively. At the end of these lives, the building is estimated to have a residual value of $3,000 and the equipment to have a residual value of $200. Since the building and equipment were used for only 9 months during 1995, the depreciation expense is $264 ([($15,320 − $3,000) ÷ 35] × 9/12) on the building and $120 ([($2,120 − $200) ÷ 12] × 9/12) on the equipment. The adjusting entry for the building is a debit (increase) to Depreciation Expense: Building for $264 and a credit (increase) to the contra-asset Accumulated Depreciation: Building for $264. The adjusting entry for the equipment is a debit to Depreciation Expense: Equipment for $120 and a credit to the contra-asset Accumulated Depreciation: Equipment for $120. The result is an increase in expenses and a *decrease* in the book value shown on the balance sheet for the building and the equipment. These adjusting entries are shown in Exhibit C-6.

Many companies make a significant proportion of their sales on credit. Regardless of the collection effort expended, a company is likely to experience a certain amount of bad debts—customer accounts that will not be collected. Although a company may not determine that particular customers will not pay their accounts until an accounting period after the sale, the bad debt expense must be matched against the revenues in the *period of the sale*. Furthermore the assets must be reduced in order to report the projected collectibility of accounts receivable at the end of the period in which the sale occurred. The adjusting entry to record the increase in expenses and the decrease in assets requires the use of an estimate of future uncollectible accounts. However, since in the period of sale it is not known which specific customers will default on their accounts, Accounts Receivable is not directly reduced. Instead a contra-asset account, Allowance for Doubtful Accounts, is *increased*. This account is deducted from Accounts Receivable on the balance sheet to report the estimated collectible amount.

To illustrate, assume for simplicity that Dapple Corporation estimates its bad debts to be 1% of total sales. Since the balance in the Sales Revenue account totals

$17,000, the adjusting entry is a debit (increase) to Bad Debts Expense for $170 and a credit (increase) to the contra-asset Allowance for Doubtful Accounts for $170. The result is an increase in expenses and a *decrease* in the collectible accounts receivable shown on the balance sheet. The adjusting entry is shown in Exhibit C-6.

## Preparation of the Financial Statements (Step 4)

After the adjusting entries are prepared and posted to the general ledger accounts, the financial statements are prepared. This procedure involves several steps. First, the balance of each account in the ledger is recomputed if necessary. Next, an adjusted trial balance is frequently prepared; it is similar to a trial balance. **An adjusted trial balance lists all the accounts and the account balances *after* adjustments (but *before* closing) in either a debit or a credit column.** The adjusted trial balance is used to verify that the total of the debit balances is equal to the total of the credit balances. This working paper also helps in the preparation of the financial statements because all the accounts and amounts included in the financial statements are listed on the adjusted trial balance. Dapple Corporation's adjusted trial balance is shown in Exhibit C-7. Finally, the income statement, statement of retained earnings, and balance sheet are prepared in sequential order directly from the information in the adjusted trial balance.

*Income Statement* The Dapple Corporation's income statement is shown in Exhibit C-8. Net sales are computed first by subtracting sales returns and allowances and sales discounts taken from sales revenue. Because cost of goods sold is directly related to net sales, it is shown next. Since the Dapple Corporation uses a periodic inventory system, it computes[6] the cost of goods sold. Cost of goods available for sale is computed first by adding the purchases and freight-in to the beginning inventory, and deducting the purchases returns and allowances and purchases discounts taken. Because 1995 is the company's first year of operations, it did not have a beginning inventory and the cost of goods available for sale is $12,340. At the end of 1995, a physical count showed an ending inventory of $2,140. The ending inventory is deducted from cost of goods available for sale to determine the cost of goods sold of $10,200. The manner in which the ending inventory is recorded in the *accounts* is discussed in the subsequent section entitled *Closing Entries*. The Cost of Goods Sold is deducted to derive the Gross Profit on Sales. Operating Expenses (often classified into two groups, Selling Expenses and Administrative Expenses) are next deducted to determine the Income from Operations. The total of the Other Items section (for recurring items that are not directly related to ongoing operations) is deducted to determine the Income Before Income Taxes. Finally the Income Tax Expense is deducted to determine the Net Income of $1,400. The $0.70 Earnings Per Share is computed by dividing the $1,400 net income by the 2,000 shares owned by the stockholders.

*Retained Earnings Statement* The retained earnings statement for the Dapple Corporation is shown in Exhibit C-9. Because 1995 is the first year of operations, the company did not have a beginning retained earnings balance. It did, however, earn net income of $1,400 and distributed dividends of $500, resulting in ending Retained Earnings (the excess of total earnings over total dividends) of $900.

---

6. If the company used a perpetual inventory system, no such computation would be necessary because the Cost of Goods Sold expense *account* would contain the $10,200 amount.

## EXHIBIT C-7

## DAPPLE CORPORATION

Adjusted Trial Balance
December 31, 1995

|  | Debit | Credit |
|---|---|---|
| Cash | $ 2,792 | |
| Accounts receivable | 7,000 | |
| Allowance for doubtful accounts | | $ 170 |
| Notes receivable | 1,320 | |
| Interest receivable | 66 | |
| Inventory | 0 | |
| Prepaid insurance | 90 | |
| Land | 1,500 | |
| Building | 15,320 | |
| Accumulated depreciation: building | | 264 |
| Equipment | 2,120 | |
| Accumulated depreciation: equipment | | 120 |
| Accounts payable | | 1,900 |
| Mortgage payable | | 6,600 |
| Salaries payable | | 900 |
| Interest payable | | 594 |
| Income taxes payable | | 600 |
| Unearned rent | | 300 |
| Capital stock | | 20,000 |
| Retained earnings | | 0 |
| Dividends distributed | 500 | |
| Sales revenue | | 17,000 |
| Sales returns and allowances | 250 | |
| Sales discounts taken | 40 | |
| Interest revenue | | 66 |
| Rent revenue | | 150 |
| Purchases | 12,400 | |
| Purchases returns and allowances | | 160 |
| Purchases discounts taken | | 100 |
| Freight-in | 200 | |
| Salaries expense | 2,700 | |
| Other expenses | 428 | |
| Loss on sale of land | 180 | |
| Depreciation expense: building | 264 | |
| Depreciation expense: equipment | 120 | |
| Bad debts expense | 170 | |
| Insurance expense | 270 | |
| Interest expense | 594 | |
| Income tax expense | 600 | |
| Totals | $48,924 | $48,924 |

## EXHIBIT C-8

### DAPPLE CORPORATION

Income Statement
For Year Ended December 31, 1995

| | | |
|---|---:|---:|
| Sales revenue | | $17,000 |
| Less: Sales returns and allowances | $ 250 | |
| Sales discounts taken | 40 | (290) |
| Net sales | | $16,710 |
| Cost of goods sold | | |
| Inventory, 1/1/1995 | $ 0 | |
| Purchases | 12,400 | |
| Purchases returns and allowances | (160) | |
| Purchases discounts taken | (100) | |
| Freight-in | 200 | |
| Cost of goods available for sale | $12,340 | |
| Less: Inventory, 12/31/1995 | (2,140) | |
| Cost of goods sold | | (10,200) |
| Gross profit on sales | | $ 6,510 |
| Operating expenses | | |
| Salaries expense | $ 2,700 | |
| Other expenses | 428 | |
| Depreciation expense: building | 264 | |
| Depreciation expense: equipment | 120 | |
| Bad debts expense | 170 | |
| Insurance expense | 270 | |
| Total operating expenses | | (3,952) |
| Income from operations | | $ 2,558 |
| Other items | | |
| Loss on sale of land | $ (180) | |
| Interest revenue | 66 | |
| Rent revenue | 150 | |
| Interest expense | (594) | (558) |
| Income before income taxes | | $ 2,000 |
| Income tax expense | | (600) |
| Net Income | | $ 1,400 |
| Earnings per share (2,000 shares) | | $0.70 |

## EXHIBIT C-9

### DAPPLE CORPORATION

Statement of Retained Earnings
For Year Ended December 31, 1995

| | |
|---|---:|
| Retained earnings, January 1, 1995 | $ 0 |
| Add: Net income for 1995 | 1,400 |
| | $1,400 |
| Less: Dividends for 1995 | (500) |
| Retained earnings, December 31, 1995 | $ 900 |

*Balance Sheet* The Dapple Corporation's balance sheet is shown in Exhibit C-10. It includes three sections: assets, liabilities, and stockholders' equity. The assets are divided into current assets and property and equipment. The current assets are cash and those assets that are expected to be converted into cash or consumed within one year or the operating cycle, whichever is longer. They generally include cash, receivables, temporary investments in marketable securities, inventories, and prepaid items such as insurance and office supplies. Property and equipment contains the longer-lived operational assets of the company. This section includes both nondepreciable assets and depreciable assets listed at their book values. The liabilities are divided into current liabilities and long-term liabilities. The current liabilities are those obligations that will become due within one year or the operating cycle, whichever is longer, and are expected to be paid with current assets or the creation of other current liabilities. Long-term liabilities are obligations that do not meet the current liability criteria. Stockholders' equity includes contributed capital (capital stock) and retained earnings. Total assets amount to $31,794, and equal the total of liabilities plus stockholders' equity.

### Preparation of Closing Entries (Step 5)

The next step in the accounting process consists of preparing and posting closing entries. **Closing entries are journal entries made at the end of the accounting period to**

---

## EXHIBIT C-10

## DAPPLE CORPORATION

**Balance Sheet**
**December 31, 1995**

*Assets*

| Current Assets | | |
|---|---|---|
| Cash | | $ 2,792 |
| Accounts receivable | $ 7,000 | |
| Less: Allowance for doubtful accounts | (170) | 6,830 |
| Notes receivable (due March 1, 1996) | | 1,320 |
| Interest receivable | | 66 |
| Inventory | | 2,140 |
| Prepaid insurance | | 90 |
| Total current assets | | $13,238 |
| Property and Equipment | | |
| Land | | $ 1,500 |
| Building | $15,320 | |
| Less: Accumulated depreciation | (264) | 15,056 |
| Equipment | $ 2,120 | |
| Less: Accumulated depreciation | (120) | 2,000 |
| Total property and equipment | | $18,556 |
| | | |
| Total Assets | | $31,794 |

*Liabilities*

| Current Liabilities | | |
|---|---|---|
| Accounts payable | | $ 1,900 |
| Salaries payable | | 900 |
| Income taxes payable | | 600 |
| Unearned rent | | 300 |
| Total current liabilities | | $ 3,700 |
| Long-Term Liabilities | | |
| Mortgage payable (due March 30, 1997) | | $ 6,600 |
| Interest payable (due March 30, 1997) | | 594 |
| Total long-term liabilities | | $ 7,194 |
| Total Liabilities | | $10,894 |

*Stockholders' Equity*

| Contributed Capital | | |
|---|---|---|
| Capital stock, no par | | |
| (2,000 shares) | $20,000 | |
| Retained Earnings | 900 | |
| Total Stockholders' Equity | | $20,900 |
| Total Liabilities and Stockholders' Equity | | $31,794 |

**(1) reduce the balance in each temporary account to zero and (2) update the retained earnings and inventory accounts.**

The temporary accounts (namely, all the revenue, expense, and dividend accounts) are used during each accounting period to accumulate and summarize information pertaining to the net income and dividends *for that period*. After the period is over and the financial statements are prepared, the balances in these accounts are no longer needed. Furthermore, these accounts must begin the *next* accounting period with a zero balance in order to summarize the next period's net income and dividend information. Also, the company's permanent stockholders' equity account, Retained Earnings, must be updated for the net income and dividend information contained in the temporary accounts. Finally, if a company uses a periodic inventory system, its ending inventory must be updated because this inventory affects net income (as part of the cost of goods sold computation) and it is also the beginning inventory of the next accounting period.

The revenue and expense accounts (including beginning and ending inventories used to compute cost of goods sold in a periodic system), are closed to a temporary closing account called Income Summary. The resulting balance in this account is the net income (or loss) for the period. This balance is then transferred to Retained Earnings.

The closing process is straightforward. Each temporary income statement account is debited or credited for the amount that will result in a zero balance in that account. The total of the credits to these accounts is recorded as a debit to the Income Summary account; the total of the debits to the other temporary accounts is recorded as a credit to Income Summary. A resulting *credit* balance in the Income Summary account is the net income for the period and is the same amount as that shown on the income statement. This credit balance is closed to zero with a debit entry to Income Summary and a credit entry to Retained Earnings for the amount of the net income. On the other hand, a resulting *debit* balance in the Income Summary account is a net loss for the period. This debit balance is closed to zero with a debit entry to Retained Earnings and a credit entry to Income Summary for the amount of the net loss. Finally, the Dividends Distributed account is credited for the amount necessary to reduce its balance to zero; the corresponding debit to Retained Earnings reduces it for the amount of the dividends.

The closing entries for the Dapple Corporation are shown in Exhibit C-11 and are posted to the ledger accounts shown in Exhibit C-5. The abbreviation *Cl* is used to identify each December 31 closing entry. The temporary income statement accounts with a credit balance are closed first. These include all the revenue accounts and the contra-purchases accounts, Purchases Returns and Allowances and Purchases Discounts Taken.[7] The amount of the *ending* inventory (determined by the physical year-end count) is also recorded at this time. The total credit to Income Summary amounts to $19,616.

The temporary income statement accounts with a debit balance are closed next. These include all the expense accounts and the contra-sales accounts. The amount of the *beginning* inventory is also eliminated at this time. Although Dapple Corporation

---

7. Some companies use a Cost of Goods Sold closing account to initially close the beginning inventory, purchases, and purchases related accounts, and to record the ending inventory. The resulting cost of goods sold debit balance in this additional closing account would then be closed (credited) to the Income Summary account in the remaining closing entries. For simplicity a Cost of Goods Sold closing account is not used in this book.

## EXHIBIT C-11

## DAPPLE CORPORATION

Closing Entries for 1995

| Date | Account Titles and Explanations | Debit | Credit |
|------|--------------------------------|-------|--------|
| | *Closing Entries* | | |
| Dec. 31 | Sales Revenue | 17,000 | |
| | Interest Revenue | 66 | |
| | Rent Revenue | 150 | |
| | Purchases Returns and Allowances | 160 | |
| | Purchases Discounts Taken | 100 | |
| | Inventory (12/31/1995) | 2,140 | |
| |    Income Summary | | 19,616 |
| | To close the temporary accounts with credit balances and to record the ending inventory. | | |
| | | | |
| 31 | Income Summary | 18,216 | |
| |    Sales Returns and Allowances | | 250 |
| |    Sales Discounts Taken | | 40 |
| |    Purchases | | 12,400 |
| |    Freight-in | | 200 |
| |    Salaries Expense | | 2,700 |
| |    Other Expenses | | 428 |
| |    Loss on Sale of Land | | 180 |
| |    Depreciation Expense: Building | | 264 |
| |    Depreciation Expense: Equipment | | 120 |
| |    Bad Debts Expense | | 170 |
| |    Insurance Expense | | 270 |
| |    Interest Expense | | 594 |
| |    Income Tax Expense | | 600 |
| |    Inventory (1/1/1995) | | 0 |
| | To close the temporary accounts with debit balances and the beginning inventory. | | |
| 31 | Income Summary | 1,400 | |
| |    Retained Earnings | | 1,400 |
| | To close the income summary balance (net income) to retained earnings. | | |
| | | | |
| 31 | Retained Earnings | 500 | |
| |    Dividends Distributed | | 500 |
| | To close the dividends to retained earnings | | |

did not have a beginning inventory, the account is shown for illustrative purposes. The total debit to Income Summary is $18,216.

The Income Summary account now has a credit balance of $1,400 ($19,616 credit less the $18,216 debit). This amount is the net income as computed on the income statement (Exhibit C-8). It is transferred to Retained Earnings by a debit to Income Summary for $1,400 (which creates a zero balance in this account) and a credit to Retained Earnings for $1,400 (which increases this account for the amount of the net income). Finally, the Dividends Distributed account debit balance is reduced to zero by a debit to Retained Earnings for $500 and a credit to Dividends Distributed for $500.

The result of the closing entries is that (1) all revenue, expense, and dividend accounts are closed (have zero balances) and are ready to accumulate the next accounting period's net income and dividend information, (2) the ending balance in the Retained Earnings account is increased by $900 due to the excess of net income over dividends, (3) the ending inventory of $2,140 is the balance shown in the Inventory account, and (4) only the permanent balance sheet accounts are open (have nonzero account balances).

After the closing entries have been prepared and posted, many companies will prepare a post-closing trial balance. **A post-closing trial balance is prepared to verify that the total of the debit balances is equal to the total of the credit balances in all the permanent accounts.** This working paper is not illustrated here. The accounting cycle is now complete and a new cycle for the next accounting period may begin.

Additionally, if a company uses a perpetual inventory system, only its Cost of Goods Sold expense account is closed with a credit to that account because the Inventory account already contains the proper ending balance. Under this system no purchases or purchases-related accounts exist.

A relatively simple accounting system was used to illustrate the accounting cycle. Certain additional complexities are fairly common in companies today. These include the use of reversing entries, a worksheet, subsidiary ledgers, special journals, and voucher systems. Each of these is discussed in the sections that follow.

## REVERSING ENTRIES

After the accounts have been adjusted and closed for the current period, a new accounting cycle is begun for the next accounting period. Prior to journalizing the daily transactions of the new accounting period in the general journal, most companies prepare reversing entries. **A reversing entry is the exact reverse (accounts and amounts) of an adjusting entry.** Reversing entries usually are made at the same time as closing entries but are dated the first day of the *next* accounting period. They are *optional* and have one purpose: to simplify the recording of a later transaction related to the adjusting entry. Reversing entries enable the later transaction to be recorded in a routine fashion, without having to consider the possible impact of the prior adjusting entry.

As a general guideline, reversing entries *should* be made for any adjusting entry that establishes a new balance sheet account, as follows:

1. Adjusting entries that establish accrued revenues or expenses to be collected or paid in the next accounting period

2. Adjusting entries related to prepayments of costs initially recorded as expenses or receipts in advance initially recorded as revenues

Reversing entries *should not* be made for:

1. Adjusting entries related to prepayments of costs initially recorded as assets or receipts in advance initially recorded as liabilities

2. Adjusting entries related to estimated items such as depreciation or bad debts

These guidelines are just that, *guidelines*. They are no substitute for good accounting judgment.

Two of the adjusting entries recorded in Exhibit C-6 should be considered for reversal, namely, the entries to record accrued interest revenue and accrued salaries expense. Each of these is related to a transaction that will occur in the *next* account-ing period. The entry to record income taxes is generally not reversed because com-plexities in the tax laws require careful analysis for each journal entry. Although the adjusting entry for interest expense established an accrued expense, Interest Payable, this entry is reversed because the subsequent transaction will not occur until 1997. To illustrate reversing entries and how they simplify the recording of subsequent transactions, Exhibit C-12 is presented for Interest Revenue and Salaries Expense.

## EXHIBIT C-12

### DAPPLE CORPORATION

Reversing Entries

**Accrued Revenue**

*Adjusting Entry*

| | | | |
|---|---|---|---|
| 12/31/95 | Interest Receivable | 66 | |
| | Interest Revenue | | 66 |
| 12/31/95 | Revenues and expenses are CLOSED. | | |

| If reversing entry is not made: | If reversing entry is made: |
|---|---|
| *Reversing Entry* | *Reversing Entry* |
| 1/1/96  None | 1/1/96  Interest Revenue          66 |
| | Interest Receivable                    66 |
| | |
| *Subsequent Entry* | *Subsequent Entry* |
| 3/1/96  Cash                    1,419 | 3/1/96  Cash                    1,419 |
| Notes Receivable          1,320 | Notes Receivable          1,320 |
| Interest Receivable          66 | Interest Revenue                99 |
| Interest Revenue          33 | |
| *Analysis of Subsequent Entry* | *Analysis of Subsequent Entry* |
| Interest of $99 is collected, but $66 was recorded in Interest Receivable at end of last period. Consequently, Interest Receivable must be credited for $66 and Interest Revenue credited for $33. | Interest of $99 is collected and credited to Interest Revenue. Because reversing entry was made for $66, the net result in Interest Revenue is a $33 credit balance. |

**Accrued Expense**

*Adjusting Entry*

| | | | |
|---|---|---|---|
| 12/31/95 | Salaries Expense | 900 | |
| | Salaries Payable | | 900 |
| 12/31/95 | Revenues and expenses are CLOSED. | | |

| If reversing entry is not made: | If reversing entry is made: |
|---|---|
| *Reversing Entry* | *Reversing Entry* |
| 1/1/96  None | 1/1/96  Salaries Payable          900 |
| | Salaries Expense                    900 |
| | |
| *Subsequent Entry* | *Subsequent Entry* |
| 4/1/96  Salaries Expense      900 | 4/1/96  Salaries Expense    1,800 |
| Salaries Payable      900 | Cash                            1,800 |
| Cash                      1,800 | |
| *Analysis of Subsequent Entry* | *Analysis of Subsequent Entry* |
| Salaries of $1,800 for 6 months are paid, but $900 was recorded in Salaries Payable at end of last period. Consequently, Salaries Payable must be debited for $900 and Salaries Expense debited for $900. | Salaries of $1,800 for 6 months are paid and debited to Salaries Expense. Because reversing entry was made for $900, the net result in Salaries Expense is a $900 debit balance. |

Whether or not reversing entries are made, the Dapple Corporation will receive payment of $1,419 on March 1, 1996 for the 15%, 6-month note receivable accepted on September 1, 1995. The $1,419 consists of the $1,320 note and $99 of interest ($1,320 × 0.15 × 6/12). Without the use of a reversing entry, when this collection is recorded it is necessary to determine what portion of the interest relates to 1995 ($66 of Interest Receivable) and what portion represents Interest Revenue for 1996 ($33 for 2 months). Often this analysis is complex and impractical. The use of a reversing entry eliminates this analysis and promotes operational efficiency. The entire amount of the $99 received in excess of the face value of the note is credited to Interest Revenue. Since the reversing entry established a $66 *debit* balance in Interest Revenue, the $99 credit results in a $33 *credit* balance, the 2 months of interest for 1996, in the Interest Revenue account.

Similarly, on April 1, 1996, the Dapple Corporation will pay its employees another 6 months of salaries, or $1,800. If a reversing entry is not used, at the time the salaries are paid it is necessary to determine what portion of the salary payment relates to 1995 ($900 of Salaries Payable) and what portion is Salaries Expense for 1996 ($900 for 3 months). The use of a reversing entry eliminates this analysis. The entire $1,800 payment is debited to Salaries Expense. When combined with the $900 *credit* balance in Salaries Expense established by the reversing entry, the result is a $900 *debit* balance, the amount representing 3 months of salaries expense for 1993.

As indicated in the discussion of the adjusting entry for deferred revenues, some companies initially record the receipt of revenues in advance of being earned as a revenue instead of a liability. It was illustrated that Dapple Corporation *could* have recorded the December 1 receipt of 3 months' advance rent as a credit to Rent Revenue for $450. In this case the adjusting entry is a debit to Rent Revenue for $300 and a credit to Unearned Rent for $300. This adjusting entry establishes a balance sheet account and should be reversed. On January 1, 1996, a reversing entry should be made debiting Unearned Rent for $300 and crediting Rent Revenue for $300. This entry eliminates the Unearned Rent account balance and establishes a $300 balance in Rent Earned for the 2 months of 1996. No further adjusting entry is necessary in 1996.

## THE WORKSHEET

At the end of an accounting period, a company prepares adjusting entries, closing entries, and its financial statements. **A worksheet is often prepared in conjunction with these activities to minimize errors, simplify the journal recording of the adjusting and closing entries, and facilitate the preparation of the financial statements.** A worksheet is *not* a substitute for any accounting records or financial statements; it is merely a working paper designed for these purposes.

A worksheet in a manual system is a large columnar accounting paper. A ten-column worksheet for the Dapple Corporation illustration is shown in Exhibit C-13. It consists of a column for listing all the ledger accounts, and debit and credit columns for the trial balance, adjustments, income statement, retained earnings statement, and balance sheet. The process of completing the worksheet begins with the preparation of the trial balance. All the accounts and account balances (prior to adjustments) are listed and the debit and credit columns of the trial balance are totaled to verify the equality of the debits and credits. Note that since this is the first year of operations for the Dapple Corporation, the Inventory, Accumulated Depreciation: Building, Accumulated Depreciation: Equipment, and Retained Earnings accounts do not have balances (prior to adjustments). Normally these accounts *do* have balances and are included in the illustrated trial balance.

**EXHIBIT C-13**

## DAPPLE CORPORATION

Worksheet
For Year Ended December 31, 1995

| Account Titles | Trial Balance Debit | Trial Balance Credit | Adjustments Debit | Adjustments Credit | Income Statement Debit | Income Statement Credit | Retained Earnings Statement Debit | Retained Earnings Statement Credit | Balance Sheet Debit | Balance Sheet Credit |
|---|---|---|---|---|---|---|---|---|---|---|
| Cash | 2,792 | | | | | | | | 2,792 | |
| Accounts receivable | 7,000 | | | | | | | | 7,000 | |
| Notes receivable | 1,320 | | | | | | | | 1,320 | |
| Inventory (1/1/95) | 0 | | | | 0 | | | | | |
| Prepaid insurance | 360 | | | (a) 270 | | | | | 90 | |
| Land | 1,500 | | | | | | | | 1,500 | |
| Building | 15,320 | | | | | | | | 15,320 | |
| Accumulated depreciation: building | | 0 | | (f) 264 | | | | | | 264 |
| Equipment | 2,120 | 0 | | | | | | | 2,120 | |
| Accumulated depreciation: equipment | | 0 | | (g) 120 | | | | | | 120 |
| Accounts payable | | 1,900 | | | | | | | | 1,900 |
| Mortgage payable | | 6,600 | | | | | | | | 6,600 |
| Unearned rent | | 450 | (b) 150 | | | | | | | 300 |
| Capital stock | | 20,000 | | | | | | | | 20,000 |
| Retained earnings (1/1/95) | | 0 | | | | | | 0 | | |
| Dividends distributed | 500 | | | | | | 500 | | | |
| Sales revenue | | 17,000 | | | | 17,000 | | | | |
| Sales returns and allowances | 250 | | | | 250 | | | | | |
| Sales discounts taken | 40 | | | | 40 | | | | | |
| Purchases | 12,400 | | | | 12,400 | | | | | |

## EXHIBIT C-13, Continued

| Account Titles | Trial Balance Debit | Trial Balance Credit | Adjustments Debit | Adjustments Credit | Income Statement Debit | Income Statement Credit | Retained Earnings Statement Debit | Retained Earnings Statement Credit | Balance Sheet Debit | Balance Sheet Credit |
|---|---|---|---|---|---|---|---|---|---|---|
| Purchases returns and allowances | | 160 | | | | 160 | | | | |
| Purchases discounts taken | | 100 | | | | 100 | | | | |
| Freight-in | 200 | | | | 200 | | | | | |
| Salaries expense | 1,800 | | (c) 900 | | 2,700 | | | | | |
| Other expenses | 428 | | | | 428 | | | | | |
| Loss on sale of land | 180 | | | | 180 | | | | | |
| | 46,210 | 46,210 | | | | | | | | |
| Insurance expense | | | (a) 270 | | 270 | | | | | |
| Rent revenue | | | | (b) 150 | | 150 | | | | |
| Salaries payable | | | | (c) 900 | | | | | | 900 |
| Interest expense | | | (d) 594 | | 594 | | | | | |
| Interest payable | | | | (d) 594 | | | | | | 594 |
| Interest receivable | | | (e) 66 | | | | | | 66 | |
| Interest revenue | | | | (e) 66 | | 66 | | | | |
| Depreciation expense: building | | | (f) 264 | | 264 | | | | | |
| Depreciation expense: equipment | | | (g) 120 | | 120 | | | | | |
| Bad debts expense | | | (h) 170 | | 170 | | | | | |
| Allowance for doubtful accounts | | | | (h) 170 | | | | | | 170 |
| | | | 2,534 | 2,534 | | | | | | |
| Inventory 12/31/95 | | | | | | 2,140 | | | 2,140 | |
| | | | | | 17,616 | 19,616 | | | | |
| Income tax expense | | | (i) 600 | | 600 | | | | | |
| Income taxes payable | | | | (i) 600 | | | | | | 600 |
| | | | 3,134 | 3,134 | 18,216 | 19,616 | | | | |
| Net income | | | | | 1,400 | | | →1,400 | | |
| | | | | | 19,616 | 19,616 | 500 | 1,400 | | |
| Retained earnings, 12/31/95 | | | | | | | 900 | | | →900 |
| | | | | | | | 1,400 | 1,400 | 32,348 | 32,348 |

Second, the accounts are analyzed to determine the necessary adjustments. These adjustments are initially entered on the worksheet in the adjustments columns. If an adjustment involves an account that does not currently have a balance, the account title is entered on the first available line below the other account titles. Each of the adjusting journal entries shown in Exhibit C-6 initially is prepared as shown on the worksheet. Note that the adjusting entry for income taxes is not made until after the income before income taxes is computed. Note also that the accounts in each adjusting entry are *keyed* with the same letter of the alphabet to reduce the likelihood of error. Explanations keyed to these entries are also usually prepared at the bottom of the worksheet. They are not illustrated in this example. The adjustments columns are subtotaled to prove the equality of the debits and credits. At this point some companies prepare an adjusted trial balance in a next set of columns. In an adjusted trial balance the adjustment amounts are combined with the trial balance amounts to determine the new account balances. This step may be omitted as in the Dapple Corporation worksheet.

Third, the trial balance amount of each account is combined with the adjustments to that account and carried over to the proper column of the financial statement in which the account is located. For instance, the $360 debit balance in Prepaid Insurance is combined with the $270 credit adjustment, and the new balance of $90 is carried over to the debit column of the balance sheet. Of particular importance is the handling of the Inventory in a periodic system. The *beginning* inventory ($0 in this case) is transferred to the debit column of the income statement because it eventually is added to purchases (which has a debit balance) to determine the cost of goods available for sale. The *ending* inventory (December 31, 1995) is listed near the bottom of the worksheet, and its amount is entered in *two* columns. The $2,140 is entered in the income statement *credit* column because it is a deduction from the cost of goods available for sale. It is also entered in the *debit* column of the balance sheet because it is an asset.[8]

Fourth, the income statement debit and credit columns are subtotaled. Ordinarily the debit column total differs from the credit column total, the difference being the income (or loss) before income taxes. For the Dapple Corporation the $19,616 credit total exceeds the $17,616 debit total, indicating income before income taxes of $2,000. At this point the applicable tax rate (30% in this case) is multiplied times the income before income taxes to determine the income taxes ($600). The adjusting entry for income taxes is recorded, and the amounts are carried to the proper columns of the financial statements.

Finally, the financial statement debit and credit columns are totaled in sequential order. First the income statement columns are totaled. The difference between the debit and credit totals is the net income or loss for the period. For the Dapple Corporation the net income is $1,400. This amount is used to balance the income statement columns. It is also entered in the retained earnings statement credit column. The arrows in Exhibit C-13 are used for illustrative purposes; they are ordinarily not included on the worksheet. The beginning retained earnings balance ($0 in this case) is combined with the net income to determine the $1,400 credit total. The $500 debit total is the dividends distributed. The $900 difference is the ending retained earnings. It is used to balance the retained earnings statement columns and is also transferred

---

8.  There are other methods for eliminating the beginning inventory and establishing the ending inventory. One method includes the elimination and the establishment of the respective inventories in the adjustment columns by associated debits and credits to the Income Summary account.

to the balance sheet credit column. The balance sheet debit and credit columns are finally totaled. The $32,348 total of the debit and credit columns indicates that the system is in balance and the worksheet is complete.

The worksheet is prepared as a preliminary step, prior to the recording of the adjusting and closing entries in the general journal and the preparation of the financial statements. A brief review of the Dapple Corporation worksheet indicates how such a worksheet facilitates the accounting process. All the adjusting entries are developed and shown in their basic format. They now must be recorded in the general journal. The closing entries are also simplified. The $19,616 total of the income statement credit column is credited to Income Summary, while the individual accounts with credit balances are debited. Similarly, the $18,216 debit subtotal is debited to Income Summary, while the individual accounts with debit balances are credited. The remaining closing entries involve closing both net income and dividends to Retained Earnings. Finally the preparation of the actual financial statements is facilitated. The amounts from the worksheet columns for each financial statement are rearranged in the proper order on that financial statement. The worksheet is particularly useful in preparing *interim* (such as quarterly) financial statements when a company does not actually adjust or close its accounts. The adjusting entries necessary to update the financial statements may be made on the worksheet only, thereby enabling the company to maintain its accounts on an annual basis.

## SUBSIDIARY LEDGERS

Even in the relatively simple Dapple Corporation example, the general ledger contains numerous accounts. For a larger company selling to many customers and purchasing from many suppliers, its general ledger substantially increases in size because it incurs additional types of expenses and earns other types of revenues. It also must maintain adequate records of amounts owed by each of its customers and to each of its suppliers.

In order to (1) reduce the size of its general ledger, (2) minimize errors, (3) divide the accounting task, and (4) keep up-to-date records of its dealings with charge customers and suppliers, a company establishes subsidiary ledgers that are *not* part of the double-entry system. **A subsidiary ledger is a group of accounts, all of which pertain to one specific company activity.** Most companies have separate subsidiary ledgers for accounts receivable and accounts payable. These ledgers enable the company to better focus its attention on the collection and payment process of the receivables and payables. Many companies also use subsidiary ledgers for major categories of accounts such as property and equipment, selling expenses, and administrative expenses. The *accounts receivable* subsidiary ledger contains the individual accounts of all the company's charge customers. Since these individual customer accounts have debit balances, it follows that this subsidiary ledger has a *total* debit balance (computed by preparing a *schedule* of the individual customer account balances). When this subsidiary ledger is used, an Accounts Receivable account is still maintained in the general ledger. It is referred to as a **control account** because its debit balance must be equal to that of the subsidiary ledger on any balance sheet date. The postings to this control account are significantly reduced because only summary postings of customer account activities are necessary. Similarly, the *accounts payable* subsidiary ledger contains the individual accounts of all the company's charge suppliers. Since these accounts have credit balances, the credit total of this subsidiary ledger must agree with the credit total of the Accounts Payable control account in the general ledger on any balance sheet date. If the Dapple Corporation used a subsidiary ledger for the accounts receivable, the ledger and control account balances at the end of 1995 appear as shown in Exhibit C-14.

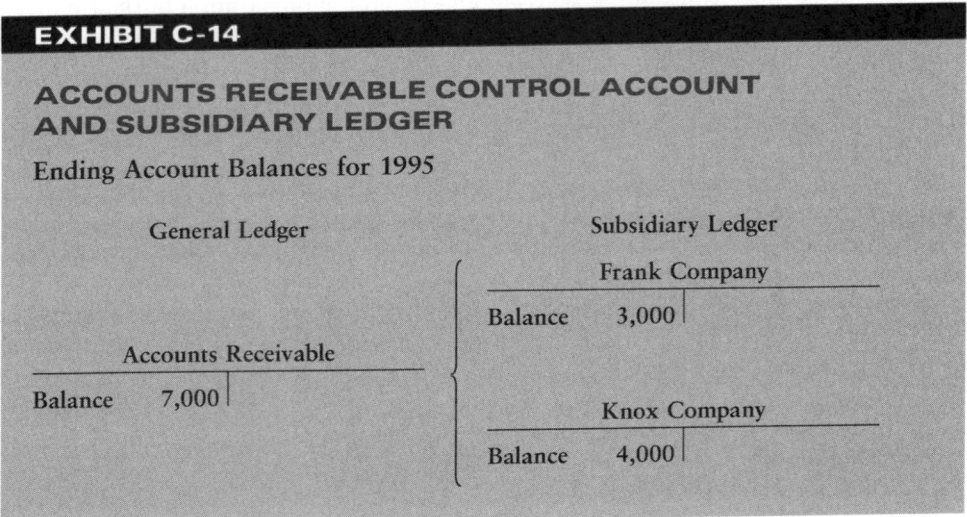

**EXHIBIT C-14**

## ACCOUNTS RECEIVABLE CONTROL ACCOUNT AND SUBSIDIARY LEDGER

Ending Account Balances for 1995

General Ledger

Accounts Receivable

Balance    7,000

Subsidiary Ledger

Frank Company

Balance    3,000

Knox Company

Balance    4,000

## SPECIAL JOURNALS

Just as a company's increasing size and complexity create the need for subsidiary ledgers, they also create the need for the efficient recording and summarizing of many daily transactions. Special journals are established for this purpose. **A special journal is a journal used to record business transactions with a similar characteristic.** Use of these journals (1) allows the accounting task to be divided, (2) reduces the time necessary to complete the various accounting activities, and (3) provides for a chronological listing of similar transactions. Because operating procedures and transactions vary across companies, each company organizes the special journals in a way best suited to its operations. However, four of the most common types of transactions are: (1) sales of merchandise on account, (2) purchases of merchandise on account, (3) cash receipts, and (4) cash payments. Special journals are usually established to record these transactions. A general journal is still needed to record various other transactions or events not repetitive enough to require the use of special journals.

The major journals and their uses are:

1. *Sales Journal.* Used to record all (and only) sales of merchandise on account.

2. *Purchases Journal.* Used to record all (and only) purchases of merchandise on account.

3. *Cash Receipts Journal.* Used to record all cash receipts.

4. *Cash Payments Journal.* Used to record all cash payments.

5. *General Journal.* Used to record adjusting, closing, and reversing entries and other transactions not recorded in the special journals.

Sometimes a company uses a voucher system, requiring modification of the special journals and the use of a different journal called a *voucher register*. This system is briefly discussed at the end of this section.

To illustrate the journalizing and posting activities involved with these special journals in a manual system, the Dapple Corporation transactions for 1995 listed in Exhibit C-3 are recorded in the special journals shown in Exhibit C-15 *instead of* the general journal. The adjusting and closing entries, which are made in the general journal, are the same as illustrated earlier and are not repeated here. These special journals are shown in abbreviated form. Actual journals could include columns for explanations, account numbers, terms of sale and purchase, and other information.

## Sales Journal

**The sales journal is used to record all sales on account** (cash sales are recorded in the cash receipts journal). Each transaction is recorded by listing the customer account and the amount of the sale. After the daily sales have been recorded, the amounts are posted as debits to the individual customer accounts in the accounts receivable subsidiary ledger. Use of this procedure ensures that these customer account balances are always current. At the end of the period (or perhaps more frequently, say weekly), the *total* of the sales journal is posted to two accounts: as a credit to the Sales Revenue account to record total sales on account and as a debit to the Accounts Receivable control account to bring its balance into agreement with the total of the accounts receivable subsidiary ledger.

## Purchases Journal

**The purchases journal is used to record all merchandise purchases on account.** (Cash purchases are recorded in the cash payments journal.) Each transaction is recorded by listing the supplier's account and the amount of the purchase. After the daily purchases have been recorded, the amounts are posted as credits to the individual supplier accounts in the accounts payable subsidiary ledger, thus maintaining current balances in these accounts. At the end of the period (or sooner) the *total* of the purchases journal is posted to two accounts, as a credit to the Accounts Payable control account to bring its balance into agreement with the subsidiary ledger total and as a debit to the Purchases account to record the total purchases on account.

## Cash Receipts Journal

**The cash receipts journal is used to record all transactions involving the receipt of cash.** A cash debit column is established for this purpose. Since a variety of transactions involve cash receipts, each company determines which of its accounts are frequently credited and establishes column headings for these accounts. A miscellaneous column is then used for recording the amounts of infrequent transactions. Many cash receipts are for cash sales and collections of accounts receivable (less the sales discounts taken), so column headings frequently are provided for these accounts.

To record a cash receipt transaction, it is necessary to list an account title only if the amount of the affected account is recorded in the miscellaneous column or if an individual customer account in the subsidiary ledger is involved. Account titles are *not* necessary for amounts listed in columns already identified as relating to a specific account in the general ledger. For instance, in Exhibit C-15 to record the April 3 cash sale it is necessary to enter the $8,000 only in the Cash debit and Sales Revenue

## EXHIBIT C-15

## DAPPLE CORPORATION

Special Journals

### Sales Journal

| Date | Customer Account | Amount |
|------|------------------|--------|
| 11/23 | Frank Company | 5,000 |
| 11/23 | Knox Company | 4,000 |
| | | 9,000 |

### Purchases Journal

| Date | Supplier Account | Amount |
|------|------------------|--------|
| 3/31 | Bark Company | 7,400 |
| 12/26 | Ajax Company | 1,900 |
| | | 9,300 |

### Cash Receipts Journal

| Date | Account Title | Cash Debit | Sales Discounts Taken Debit | Accounts Receivable Credit | Sales Revenue Credit | Miscellaneous Credit |
|------|---------------|------------|------------------------------|----------------------------|----------------------|----------------------|
| 1/1 | Capital Stock | 20,000 | | | | 20,000 |
| 4/3 | | 8,000 | | | 8,000 | |
| 4/20 | Purchases Returns and Allowances | 160 | | | | 160 |
| 12/1 | Unearned Rent | 450 | | | | 450 |
| 12/4 | Frank Company | 1,960 | 40 | 2,000 | | |
| | | 30,570 | 40 | 2,000 | 8,000 | 20,610 |

### Cash Payments Journal

| Date | Account Title | Cash Credit | Purchases Discounts Taken Credit | Miscellaneous Credit | Accounts Payable Debit | Purchases Debit | Miscellaneous Debit |
|------|---------------|-------------|----------------------------------|----------------------|------------------------|-----------------|---------------------|
| 1/16 | Land | 3,000 | | | | | 3,000 |
| 3/30 | Building | 10,840 | | | | | 15,320 |
| | Equipment | | | | | | 2,120 |
| | Mortgage Payable | | | 6,600 | | | |
| 3/30 | Prepaid Insurance | 360 | | | | | 360 |
| 4/8 | Bark Company | 7,300 | 100 | | 7,400 | | |
| 4/15 | Sales Returns and Allowances | 250 | | | | | 250 |
| 7/15 | Freight-in | 3,300 | | | | 3,100 | 200 |
| 10/2 | Salaries Expense | 1,800 | | | | | 1,800 |
| 12/28 | Other Expenses | 428 | | | | | 428 |
| 12/29 | Dividends Distributed | 500 | | | | | 500 |
| | | 27,778 | 100 | 6,600 | 7,400 | 3,100 | 23,978 |

### General Journal

| Date | Account Title | Debit | Credit |
|------|---------------|-------|--------|
| 9/1 | Notes Receivable | 1,320 | |
| | Loss on Sale of Land | 180 | |
| | Land | | 1,500 |

credit columns. However, to record the January 1 issuance of stock it is necessary to enter the $20,000 in the Cash debit and the Miscellaneous credit columns and to list the title of the account, Capital Stock, to be credited.

The cash receipts journal usually is posted on a daily and an end-of-period (or sooner) basis. The entries to all the miscellaneous accounts are posted daily, as are any entries to individual customer accounts. At the end of the period, all the columns are totaled, and the total of the debit columns is compared to the total of the credit columns to verify equality. The totals of the Cash and Sales Discounts Taken columns are posted as debits to each of these accounts, respectively. The credit total of the Accounts Receivable column is posted to the control account to bring it into agreement with the subsidiary ledger. Finally the credit total of the Sales Revenue column is posted to the Sales Revenue account to record the total cash sales. The total of the miscellaneous column is *not* posted because the miscellaneous accounts already have been posted.

## Cash Payments Journal

**The cash payments journal is used to record all transactions involving the payment of cash.** Its format and the journal entry and posting procedures are very similar to the cash receipts journal. A cash credit column is used to record each cash payment. Column headings are established for frequently debited accounts, and miscellaneous columns are used for recording amounts of infrequent transactions. Since cash payments frequently involve cash purchases and payments of accounts payable (less the purchases discounts taken), column headings are often provided for these accounts.

To record a cash payment transaction, an account title is listed only if its amount is recorded in the miscellaneous column or if it is an individual creditor account in the subsidiary ledger. Account titles are not necessary for entries in specific account columns. Posting usually is performed on a daily and an end-of-period basis. The miscellaneous accounts and the individual creditor subsidiary ledger accounts are posted daily. At the end of the period, the columns are totaled and the debit and credit equality is verified. The totals of the Cash and Purchases Discounts Taken columns are credited to these accounts, while the totals of the Accounts Payable and Purchases columns are debited to these accounts. The miscellaneous column totals are not posted.

## General Journal

The general journal is still needed even when special journals are used. It is used for recording adjusting, closing, and reversing entries as well as certain other transactions that occur relatively infrequently, such as purchases returns and sales returns on credit and the purchase or sale of assets (other than merchandise) on credit. The journalizing and posting process is the same as described earlier, with one exception. If subsidiary ledgers are used, any debit or credit to accounts receivable or accounts payable is posted *twice*, once to the individual subsidiary account that is *not* part of the double-entry system and once to the appropriate control account.

## Voucher System

To provide safeguards over the disbursement of cash, many companies establish a voucher system. The use of a **voucher system** requires that (1) a liability (Vouchers Payable, which replaces Accounts Payable) be established for each anticipated cash payment, (2) each cash payment be supported by a *voucher* (a written authorization) and substantiating documents to prove the validity of the payment, and (3) all payments be made by check.

When a voucher system is used, the purchases journal described earlier is expanded to include not only a column for purchases on account, but also a column for vouchers payable and columns for any other frequently used accounts as well as miscellaneous columns. This journal is referred to as a **voucher register**. Each expenditure initially is recorded in this voucher register as a liability by a credit to Vouchers Payable and a debit to the related asset or expense account (such as Salaries Expense, Purchases, Equipment). Each expenditure is assigned a voucher number in sequential order and each voucher contains a file of supporting evidence (for example, purchase order, sales invoice, freight receipt).

When payment is made, an authorization signature is required and a check is issued. The check number is entered in the voucher register beside the number of the paid voucher. In this manner all unpaid vouchers (which are liabilities) at the end of the period can be identified as those without an associated check number. Postings from the voucher register must be made daily and at the end of the period and are similar to those for the cash receipts and cash payments journals discussed earlier.

Because all expenditures are initially recorded in the voucher register, the *check register* (the cash payments journal in a nonvoucher system) is substantially reduced. An account title column is needed only for identifying individual supplier subsidiary accounts. Columns are needed only for debits to Vouchers Payable and Purchases Discounts Taken and credits to Cash. A column is also usually included to record the number of the paid voucher. After each payment is recorded, the daily and end-of-period postings are similar to those discussed earlier. Although the voucher system institutes greater control over the disbursement of cash, the related special journals involve relatively minor modifications from those discussed earlier. Consequently an example is not presented.

## COMPUTER SOFTWARE

In this Appendix (and throughout the book) we use a manual accounting system for convenience. In the business world, however, most companies use computers to process their accounting information. **Software** is the set of computer programs used to operate a computer. Software packages have been developed by software companies for the subsidiary ledgers and special journals discussed earlier, as well as other financial accounting functions relating to accounts receivable, accounts payable, inventory, payroll, and the general ledger. In addition, "spreadsheet" packages have been developed to serve a variety of accounting needs. Each of these software packages is briefly described next.

*Accounts Receivable* Because a company generates much of the cash needed for its operations from the collection of accounts receivable, the software program for accounts receivable is a very important aspect of a computer system. Accounts receivable software generally is designed to provide current balances in customers' accounts by immediately recording invoices and cash receipts from customers; print out monthly statements (bills) for customers; monitor sales returns and allowances as well as sales discounts taken by customers; generate a credit history of each customer to help avoid uncollectible accounts; and provide projections of future cash inflows.

*Accounts Payable* Accounts payable software is concerned with monitoring and controlling the cash paid to suppliers. In the case of a retailer or wholesaler, payments for purchases of inventory for resale is the primary activity. The software for accounts payable generally is designed to provide current balances in suppliers' accounts by immediately recording purchase orders and cash payments to suppliers; generate a verification listing of the quantity and unit price of an order when it is received from a supplier; monitor purchases returns and allowances and purchases discounts taken; write checks; and provide projections of future cash outflows.

*Inventory* Inventory is a very important asset for many companies. Most inventory software programs are linked to a company's accounts receivable and accounts payable software. Inventory software generally is designed to provide a current count of the number of units of each item of inventory by immediately recording all unit purchases and sales; highlight when a minimum or maximum stock level has been reached for each item of inventory; print price tags for newly acquired inventory; prepare reports on slow-moving or obsolete inventory items; and provide unit prices when a physical count of the inventory is taken.

*Payroll* Software for payroll was one of the first to be developed. Payroll software can be very complex because of the various federal, state, and local tax laws. Payroll software may be designed to compute the salaries earned by each employee based on pay rates and overtime; allocate the salaries across departments in the company; calculate federal, state, and local withholding taxes; compute other voluntary withholdings such as for investments in U.S. savings bonds; print payroll checks; generate comparisons of actual with projected salaries; and prepare various tax-withholding reports.

*General Ledger* A general ledger software package is broader than the name implies and includes many aspects of an accounting system. General ledger software usually includes all special journals and the general journal for recording transactions, a chart of accounts, and the ledger accounts on disks for storing the recorded information. Usually, the software is capable of preparing a trial balance and financial statements at any point in time. Frequently, supporting schedules (e.g., depreciation) and budgets also may be generated. The general ledger software of a company usually is linked to its accounts receivable, accounts payable, inventory, and payroll software.

*Spreadsheets* Spreadsheets are "electronic worksheets." They are laid out as a manual worksheet would appear on a large sheet of paper; the key difference is that they appear on a computer screen and the computer performs all the mathematical calculations defined by the user of the program. Spreadsheet software is "general purpose" because it is modified and programmed by a user for a particular purpose. Spreadsheets are, perhaps, more useful in managerial accounting. There they can be used, for example, to forecast sales, predict operating costs, and establish budgets for different levels of operations. Spreadsheet software is also used in financial accounting for preparing worksheets and financial statements, and for developing schedules involving such items as depreciation and interest computations.

## QUESTIONS

*QC-1* What is a primary objective of financial reporting?

*QC-2* What is an *accounting system*?

*QC-3* Illustrate how the basic accounting equation relates to the other equations pertaining to information useful to external investors.

*QC-4* Discuss the relationship between the accounting equation and the double-entry system of recording transactions.

*QC-5* What is the difference between a *permanent* and a *temporary* account? Give examples of each.

*QC-6* What are the major financial statements of a company and what information does each summarize?

QC-7    Define the following:
a. *Account*
b. *Contra account*
c. *Ledger*
d. *Journal*
e. *Posting*

QC-8    Why is it advantageous to initially record each transaction in a journal?

QC-9    Give examples of transactions that
a. Increase an asset and a liability.
b. Increase an asset and stockholders' equity.
c. Increase an asset and decrease an asset.
d. Decrease an asset and a liability.
e. Decrease an asset and stockholders' equity.

QC-10    Give examples of transactions that
a. Increase a cost of goods sold account and a liability.
b. Decrease a cost of goods sold account and a liability.
c. Increase a cost of goods sold account and decrease an asset.
d. Decrease a cost of goods sold account and increase an asset.

QC-11    What are the steps in the accounting cycle? Briefly discuss each step.

QC-12    Why are adjusting entries necessary?

QC-13    What are *prepaid expenses* and *deferred revenues*? Give an example of an adjusting entry to update each of these items at year-end.

QC-14    What are *accrued expenses* and *accrued revenues*? Give an example of an adjusting entry to record each of these items.

QC-15    Give two examples of adjusting entries to record estimated items. Include in one example a discussion of how depreciation is computed.

QC-16    What is the difference between a *trial balance* and an *adjusted trial balance*? Why is the latter a useful accounting working paper?

QC-17    What is the difference between a *periodic* and a *perpetual* inventory system? How is this difference reflected in the accounts and financial statements?

QC-18    How is cost of goods sold computed when a periodic inventory system is used?

QC-19    What are the objectives of closing entries?

QC-20    Illustrate, without amounts, the form of the closing entries for a retail store using a periodic inventory system.

QC-21    What are *reversing entries* and why are they used? Give an illustration of an adjusting entry and a reversing entry for salaries payable, and the later entry to pay the salaries.

QC-22    What is a *worksheet*? How does the use of a worksheet facilitate the completion of the accounting cycle?

QC-23    What are *subsidiary ledgers* and *control accounts*, and why are they used? Give an example of how they work.

QC-24    What are *special journals* and what advantages are achieved by using them?

QC-25    What are the major special journals? Give examples of transactions that would be recorded in each journal.

QC-26    Discuss the use of a voucher system.

QC-27    Identify the common software packages for the financial accounting functions.

## EXERCISES

EC-1    *Financial Statement Interrelationship*    Draw a diagram that shows the interrelationship between the beginning balance sheet, income statement, retained earnings statement, and ending balance sheet.

EC-2    *Journal Entries*    The Mead Company engaged in the following transactions during the month of May:

| Date | Transaction |
|---|---|
| May 1 | Made cash sales of $6,100. |
| 5 | Purchased $2,200 of merchandise on account, terms 2/10, n/30. |
| 9 | Made credit sales of $3,300. |
| 13 | Paid sales salaries of $900 and office salaries of $600. |
| 14 | Paid for the May 5 purchases less the applicable discount. |
| 18 | Purchased sales equipment costing $8,000; made a down payment of $2,000 and agreed to pay the balance in 60 days. |
| 21 | Purchased $600 of merchandise for cash and paid $20 for related freight. |
| 24 | Customer returned $400 of defective merchandise for credit to its account. |
| 27 | Sold land that had originally cost $1,900 for $2,600. |

**Required**

Record the preceding transactions in a general journal.

EC-3    *Journal Entries*  The following are selected accounts and account balances of the Sawyer Company on May 31:

|  | Debit (Credit) |
|---|---|
| Cash | $12,523 |
| Accounts receivable | 23,052 |
| Office equipment | 35,860 |
| Accumulated depreciation | (10,540) |
| Notes payable | (3,400) |
| Accounts payable | (3,500) |
| Sales revenue | (47,872) |
| Sales discounts taken | 240 |
| Gain on sale of office equipment | (400) |
| Purchases | 22,354 |
| Purchases discounts taken | (220) |
| Purchases returns and allowances | (420) |
| Utility expense | 1,124 |

The Sawyer Company entered into the following transactions during June:

| Date | Transaction |
|---|---|
| June 3 | Sold for $700 office equipment that had cost $2,000 and has associated accumulated depreciation of $1,500. |
| 7 | Made sales of $2,000 on account, terms 2/10, n/30. |
| 10 | Purchased $1,000 of merchandise for cash. |
| 15 | Purchased new office equipment costing $4,000, paying $1,500 and signing a 90-day note for the balance. |
| 16 | Received $1,960 check for June 7 credit sale less the discount. |
| 17 | Made cash sales of $4,200. |
| 20 | Purchased $2,600 of merchandise on account, terms 2/10, n/30. |
| 24 | Returned $200 of defective merchandise from the June 20 purchase for a credit to its account. |
| 29 | Paid for the June 20 purchase less the return and the discount. |
| 30 | Paid the monthly utility bill, $210. |

**Required**

1.  Record the preceding transactions in a general journal.
2.  Post to the accounts.

EC-4    *Partial Income Statement*  The following are selected account balances of the Rule Company:

| | Debit | Credit | | Debit | Credit |
|---|---|---|---|---|---|
| Cash | $3,900 | | Inventory, December 31, 1995 | $4,100 | |
| Sales returns and allowances | 600 | | Purchases | 9,500 | |
| Inventory, January 1, 1995 | 5,300 | | Delivery expense | 800 | |
| Purchases discounts taken | | $ 100 | Purchases returns and allowances | | $500 |
| Sales salaries expense | 1,200 | | Sales discounts taken | 200 | |
| Sales revenue | | 15,800 | Freight-in | 400 | |
| Accounts payable | | 6,000 | | | |

**Required**

Prepare a partial income statement through gross profit on sales.

EC-5    *Income Statement Calculations*   The following is partial information from the Ferdon Company income statements for 1995 and 1996:

|                     | 1995      |     | 1996      |     |
| ------------------- | --------- | --- | --------- | --- |
| Beginning inventory | $_____ | (2) | $_____ | (4) |
| Sales               | 220,000   |     | _____  | (6) |
| Purchases           | 118,000   |     | 140,000   |     |
| Purchases returns   | 2,000     |     | 3,000     |     |
| Ending inventory    | 48,000    |     | 74,000    |     |
| Sales returns       | 1,000     |     | 3,000     |     |
| Gross profit        | _____  | (1) | 77,000    |     |
| Cost of goods sold  | 106,000   |     | _____  | (5) |
| Expenses            | 65,000    |     | 62,000    |     |
| Net income          | _____  | (3) | 15,000    |     |

**Required**
Fill in the blanks numbered 1 through 6. (*Hint*: It probably is easiest to work through the blanks according to the sequential numbers.)

EC-6    *Financial Statements*   The Turtle Company has prepared the following adjusted trial balance for the year ended December 31, 1995:

|                              | Debit    | Credit   |
| ---------------------------- | -------- | -------- |
| Cash                         | $ 1,500  |          |
| Accounts receivable (net)    | 2,000    |          |
| Inventory, January 1, 1995   | 1,900    |          |
| Equipment                    | 5,400    |          |
| Accumulated depreciation     |          | $ 1,700  |
| Accounts payable             |          | 2,100    |
| Salaries payable             |          | 300      |
| Income taxes payable         |          | 330      |
| Capital stock (400 shares)   |          | 3,200    |
| Retained earnings            |          | 2,500    |
| Dividends distributed        | 200      |          |
| Sales revenue                |          | 8,000    |
| Purchases                    | 4,400    |          |
| Selling expenses             | 1,800    |          |
| Administrative expenses      | 600      |          |
| Income tax expense           | 330      |          |
| Totals                       | $18,130  | $18,130  |

In addition, the company has determined that its ending inventory on December 31, 1995 is $1,800.

**Required**
Prepare for 1995 in proper form: (1) an income statement, (2) a retained earnings statement, (3) an ending balance sheet, and (4) closing entries.

EC-7    *Adjusting Entries*   Your examination of the records of the Sullivan Company provides the following information for the December 31, 1995 year-end adjustments:
1. Bad debts are to be recognized at 2% of sales. Sales totaled $20,000 for the year.
2. Salaries at year-end that have accumulated but have not been paid total $1,300.
3. Annual straight-line depreciation for the company's equipment is based on a cost of $30,000, an estimated life of 8 years, and an estimated residual value of $1,600.
4. Prepaid insurance in the amount of $800 has expired.

5. Interest that has been earned but not collected totals $500.
6. Unearned rent in the amount of $1,000 has become earned.
7. Interest on a note payable that has accumulated but has not been paid totals $600.
8. The income tax rate is 30% on current income and is payable in the first quarter of 1996. The pretax income before the preceding adjusting entries is $6,800.

**Required**
Prepare the adjusting entries to record the preceding information.

EC-8    *Adjusting Entries*   The following are several transactions of the Pruitt Company that occurred during the current year and were recorded in *real* (that is, balance sheet) accounts unless indicated otherwise:

| Date | Transaction |
|---|---|
| Apr. 1 | Purchased a delivery van for $10,000, paying $1,000 down, and issuing a 1-year, 12% note payable for the $9,000 balance. It was estimated that the van would have a 4-year life and an $800 residual value; the company uses straight-line depreciation. The interest on the note will be paid on the maturity date. |
| May 15 | Purchased $830 of office supplies. |
| June 2 | Purchased a 2-year comprehensive insurance policy for $960. |
| Aug. 1 | Received 6 months' rent in advance at $260 per month and recorded the $1,560 receipt as Rent Earned. |
| Sept. 15 | Advanced $600 to sales personnel to cover their future travel costs. |
| Nov. 1 | Accepted a $6,000, 6-month, 12% (annual rate) note receivable from a customer, the interest to be collected when the note is collected. |

The following information also is available:

1. On January 1, the Office Supplies account had a $250 balance. On December 31, an inventory count showed $190 of office supplies on hand.
2. The weekly (5-day) payroll of Pruitt Company amounts to $2,000. All employees are paid at the close of business each Wednesday. A two-day accrual is required for the current year.
3. Sales personnel travel cost reports indicate that $490 of advances had been used to pay travel expenses.
4. The income tax rate is 30% on current income and is payable in the first quarter of next year. The pretax income before the adjusting entries is $8,655.

**Required**
On the basis of the above preceding information, prepare journal entries to record whatever *adjustments* are necessary to bring the accounts up to date on December 31. Each journal entry explanation should show any related computations.

EC-9    *Adjusting Entries*   The following partial list of accounts and account balances has been taken from the trial balance and the adjusted trial balance of the Barker Company:

| | Trial Balance Debit | Trial Balance Credit | Adjusted Trial Balance Debit | Adjusted Trial Balance Credit |
|---|---|---|---|---|
| Accumulated depreciation | | $5,500 | | $6,600 |
| Allowance for doubtful accounts | | 480 | | 650 |
| Income taxes payable | | 0 | | 2,250 |
| Interest payable | | 0 | | 380 |
| Prepaid insurance | $350 | | $90 | |
| Salaries payable | | 0 | | 720 |
| Unearned rent | | 900 | | 300 |

**Required**
Prepare the adjusting entry that caused the change in each account balance.

EC-10    *Closing Entries*   The Collins Corporation shows the following inventory, dividends, revenue, and expense account balances before closing:

| | | | | |
|---|---|---|---|---|
| Inventory (beginning) | $ 150 | | Purchases returns | $300 |
| Dividends distributed | 250 | | Salaries expense | $300 |
| Sales revenue | | $2,000 | Utilities expense | 130 |
| Sales discounts taken | 200 | | Miscellaneous expenses | 120 |
| Purchases | 1,200 | | Income tax expense | 180 |

At the end of the period, its ending inventory is $400.

**Required**
Prepare closing entries.

EC-11    *Reversing Entries*   On December 31, 1995, Adams Company made the following adjusting entries for its annual accounting period:

| | | |
|---|---|---|
| Depreciation Expense | 2,400 | |
|    Accumulated Depreciation | | 2,400 |
| To record depreciation on buildings. | | |
| | | |
| Interest Receivable | 300 | |
|    Interest Revenue | | 300 |
| To record interest on note receivable due January 28, 1996. | | |
| | | |
| Rent Expense | 400 | |
|    Prepaid Rent | | 400 |
| To record expired prepaid rent. | | |
| | | |
| Interest Expense | 510 | |
|    Interest Payable | | 510 |
| To record interest on note payable due March 15, 1996. | | |

**Required**
Prepare whatever reversing entries are appropriate.

EC-12    *Special Journals*   The following are several transactions of a company that uses special journals:

| Transaction | Journal | Accounts |
|---|---|---|
| 1. Purchase of merchandise for cash. | _____ | _____ |
| 2. Sale of merchandise on credit. | _____ | _____ |
| 3. Payment of sales salaries. | _____ | _____ |
| 4. Purchase of merchandise on credit. | _____ | _____ |
| 5. Sale of merchandise for cash. | _____ | _____ |
| 6. Purchase of land by issuing note payable. | _____ | _____ |
| 7. Collection of short-term note receivable and related interest. | _____ | _____ |
| 8. Return of defective merchandise to supplier for credit to account. | _____ | _____ |
| 9. Preparation of adjusting entries. | _____ | _____ |
| 10. Purchase of equipment for cash. | _____ | _____ |

**Required**
In the space provided:
1. Indicate in which journal the transaction would be recorded using the codes: *G* for general journal, *S* for sales journal, *P* for purchases journal, *CR* for cash receipts journal, and *CP* for cash payments journal.
2. Indicate the accounts that would be debited or credited in the journal for each transaction.

**EC-13  *Worksheet for Service Company***  The Grant Consulting Company has prepared a trial balance on the following partially completed worksheet for the year ended December 31, 1995:

| Accounts | Trial Balance Debit | Trial Balance Credit | Adjustments Debit | Adjustments Credit | Income Statement Debit | Income Statement Credit | Retained Earnings Statement Debit | Retained Earnings Statement Credit | Balance Sheet Debit | Balance Sheet Credit |
|---|---|---|---|---|---|---|---|---|---|---|
| Cash | 4,000 | | | | | | | | | |
| Prepaid rent | 2,400 | | | | | | | | | |
| Office equipment | 7,000 | | | | | | | | | |
| Accumulated depreciation | | 1,400 | | | | | | | | |
| Notes payable, due 7/1/96 | | 2,000 | | | | | | | | |
| Capital stock (200 shares) | | 4,000 | | | | | | | | |
| Retained earnings, 1/1/95 | | 3,200 | | | | | | | | |
| Dividends distributed | 200 | | | | | | | | | |
| Consulting revenues | | 6,300 | | | | | | | | |
| Salaries expense | 2,500 | | | | | | | | | |
| Miscellaneous expenses | 800 | | | | | | | | | |
| Totals | 16,900 | 16,900 | | | | | | | | |

Additional information: (a) On January 1, 1995, the company had paid 2 years' rent in advance at $100 a month on its office space; (b) the office equipment is being depreciated on a straight-line basis over a 10-year life, and no residual value is expected; (c) interest of $150 has accrued on the note payable but has not been paid; and (d) the income tax rate is 30% on current income and will be paid in the first quarter of 1996.

**Required**

1. Complete the worksheet.
2. Prepare financial statements for 1996.

**EC-14  *Worksheet, Including Inventory***  The Murphy Company prepared a trial balance on the following partially completed worksheet for the year ended December 31, 1995:

| Accounts | Trial Balance Debit | Trial Balance Credit | Adjustments Debit | Adjustments Credit | Income Statement Debit | Income Statement Credit | Retained Earnings Statement Debit | Retained Earnings Statement Credit | Balance Sheet Debit | Balance Sheet Credit |
|---|---|---|---|---|---|---|---|---|---|---|
| Cash | 2,500 | | | | | | | | | |
| Accounts receivable | 4,000 | | | | | | | | | |
| Allowance for doubtful accounts | | 300 | | | | | | | | |
| Inventory, 1/1/95 | 6,800 | | | | | | | | | |
| Prepaid rent | 3,600 | | | | | | | | | |
| Equipment | 30,000 | | | | | | | | | |
| Accumulated depreciation | | 12,000 | | | | | | | | |
| Accounts payable | | 3,700 | | | | | | | | |
| Notes payable, due 7/1/96 | | 5,000 | | | | | | | | |
| Capital stock (1,000 shares) | | 8,900 | | | | | | | | |
| Retained earnings, 1/1/95 | | 10,200 | | | | | | | | |
| Dividends distributed | 1,000 | | | | | | | | | |
| Sales revenues | | 45,000 | | | | | | | | |
| Purchases | 22,400 | | | | | | | | | |
| Salaries expense | 7,100 | | | | | | | | | |
| Utilities expense | 3,300 | | | | | | | | | |
| Advertising expense | 4,400 | | | | | | | | | |
| Totals | 85,100 | 85,100 | | | | | | | | |

Additional information: (a) The equipment is being depreciated on a straight-line basis over a 10-year life, with no residual value; (b) salaries accrued but not recorded total $500; (c) on January 1, 1995, the company had paid 3 years' rent in advance at $100 per month; (d) bad debts are expected to be 1% of total sales; (e) interest of $400 has accrued on the note payable; (f) the December 31, 1995 inventory is $8,200; and (g) the income tax rate is 40% on current income and will be paid in the first quarter of 1996.

**Required**

1. Complete the worksheet.
2. Prepare financial statements for 1995.
3. Prepare closing entries in the general journal.

## PROBLEMS

PC-1    *Journal Entries, Posting, and Trial Balance*    The account balances of the Antel Company on November 1, 1995 are as follows:

| | Debit | Credit | | Debit | Credit |
|---|---|---|---|---|---|
| Cash | $ 7,800 | | Common stock, no par | | $165,000 |
| Accounts receivable | 12,530 | | Retained earnings, January 1, | | |
| Allowance for doubtful | | | 1995 | | 24,958 |
| accounts | | $ 740 | Sales revenue | | 38,400 |
| Notes receivable | 6,000 | | Sales discounts taken | $ 725 | |
| Inventory, January 1, 1995 | 25,670 | | Sales returns and allowances | 842 | |
| Prepaid insurance | 840 | | Purchases | 32,000 | |
| Office supplies | 465 | | Purchases discounts taken | | 640 |
| Land | 74,350 | | Purchases returns and | | |
| Buildings | 66,580 | | allowances | | 1,042 |
| Accumulated depreciation: | | | Freight-in | 1,133 | |
| buildings | | 21,400 | Sales salaries expense | 6,200 | |
| Equipment | 37,620 | | Office salaries expense | 4,300 | |
| Accumulated depreciation: | | | Advertising expense | 1,250 | |
| equipment | | 11,480 | Utility expense | 1,845 | |
| Patents | 25,000 | | Interest revenue | | 550 |
| Accounts payable | | 38,750 | Interest expense | 210 | |
| Notes payable | | 2,400 | | | |

During the month of November, the following transactions took place:

| Date | Transaction |
|---|---|
| Nov.  2 | Made cash sales of $2,400. |
| 4 | Purchased $800 of merchandise for cash. |
| 6 | Sold an unused 1/2 acre of land for $4,000; the land had originally cost $3,650. |
| 7 | Purchased a 2-year comprehensive insurance policy for $528. |
| 9 | Returned $100 of defective merchandise for a cash refund. |
| 10 | Leased an unused portion of its building to Charles Company, collecting 6 months' rent in advance at $220 per month. |
| 13 | Made $2,300 of sales on account to Grant Company, terms 2/10, n/30. |
| 16 | Collected the $200 monthly payment plus $30 interest on a customer's note receivable. |
| 17 | Purchased $1,600 of merchandise on account from Mason Company, terms 1/10, n/30. Paid $60 of associated freight charges. |
| 18 | Grant Company returned $200 of defective merchandise (from the November 13 transaction) for credit to its account. |

| Date | Transaction |
|------|-------------|
| Nov. 21 | Purchased land for a future building site. Made a $2,000 down payment and signed a 12%, 90-day $6,000 note payable for the balance. |
| 23 | Collected the Grant Company account for the November 13 sale less the return and the cash discount. |
| 25 | Paid for the November 17 purchase of merchandise less the cash discount. |
| 27 | Paid the city newspaper $420 for advertising that had appeared during November. |
| 30 | Paid $520 of sales salaries and $390 of office salaries. |

**Required**

1. Prepare general journal entries to record the preceding transactions.
2. Post to the general ledger accounts.
3. Prepare a trial balance on November 30, 1995.

PC-2   *Financial Statements*   The Stern Company has prepared the following *adjusted trial balance* on December 31, 1995:

|  | Debit | Credit |
|---|---|---|
| Cash | $ 1,000 | |
| Accounts receivable | 2,700 | |
| Allowance for doubtful accounts | | $ 250 |
| Inventory, January 1, 1995 | 5,100 | |
| Prepaid insurance | 800 | |
| Land | 3,200 | |
| Buildings and equipment | 31,000 | |
| Accumulated depreciation | | 15,000 |
| Accounts payable | | 3,100 |
| Salaries payable | | 420 |
| Unearned rent | | 360 |
| Income taxes payable | | 1,725 |
| Note payable (due July 1, 1999) | | 5,000 |
| Interest payable (due July 1, 1999) | | 750 |
| Capital stock (1,500 shares) | | 9,000 |
| Retained earnings, January 1, 1995 | | 6,770 |
| Dividends distributed | 1,200 | |
| Sales revenue | | 30,000 |
| Sales returns | 2,100 | |
| Rent revenue | | 1,440 |
| Purchases | 15,900 | |
| Purchases returns | | 1,240 |
| Freight-in | 1,780 | |
| Selling expenses | 4,800 | |
| Administrative expenses | 3,000 | |
| Interest expense | 750 | |
| Income tax expense | 1,725 | |
| Totals | $75,055 | $75,055 |

In addition, the company took its annual physical inventory on December 31, 1995. It determined that its ending inventory is $6,500.

**Required**

Prepare in proper form for 1995: (1) the income statement, (2) the retained earnings statement, (3) the ending balance sheet, and (4) closing entries in the general journal.

PC-3    *Financial Statements*   The Action Company has prepared the following alphabetical adjusted trial balance on December 31, 1995:

| | Debit | Credit |
|---|---|---|
| Accounts payable | | $ 6,400 |
| Accounts receivable | $ 5,700 | |
| Accumulated depreciation: buildings | | 19,000 |
| Accumulated depreciation: equipment | | 11,000 |
| Additional paid-in capital | | 15,000 |
| Administrative expenses | 6,500 | |
| Allowance for doubtful accounts | | 600 |
| Buildings | 42,000 | |
| Capital stock, $1 par (4,000 shares) | | 4,000 |
| Cash | 5,000 | |
| Current income taxes payable | | 4,035 |
| Dividends distributed | 2,400 | |
| Equipment | 22,000 | |
| Freight-in | 3,500 | |
| Income tax expense | 4,035 | |
| Interest expense | 650 | |
| Interest payable (due July 1, 1996) | | 650 |
| Inventory, January 1, 1995 | 10,200 | |
| Land | 6,800 | |
| Notes payable (due July 1, 1999) | | 10,000 |
| Purchases | 27,000 | |
| Purchases discounts taken | | 900 |
| Purchases returns and allowances | | 1,600 |
| Rent revenue | | 2,800 |
| Retained earnings, January 1, 1995 | | 14,500 |
| Sales discounts taken | 1,200 | |
| Sales returns and allowances | 3,700 | |
| Sales revenue | | 59,800 |
| Selling expenses | 9,700 | |
| Unearned rent | | 700 |
| Unexpired insurance | 1,600 | |
| Wages payable | | 1,000 |
| | $151,985 | $151,985 |

Additional data: The December 31, 1995 ending inventory is $10,800.

**Required**

Prepare the following items in proper form for 1995: (1) the income statement, (2) the retained earnings statement, (3) the ending balance sheet, and (4) the closing entries in the general journal. (*Hint*: For the ending balance sheet, the Capital Stock, Additional Paid-in Capital, and Retained Earnings accounts are summed to determine the total stockholders' equity.)

PC-4    *Adjusting Entries*   The following 1995 information is available concerning the Drake Company, which adjusts and closes its accounts every December 31:

1. Salaries accrued but unpaid total $1,750 on December 31, 1995.
2. The $247 December utility bill arrived on December 31, 1995 and has not been paid or recorded.
3. Buildings with a cost of $78,000, 30-year life, and $9,000 residual value are to be depreciated; equipment with a cost of $44,000, 12-year life, and $2,000 residual value is also to be depreciated. The straight-line method is to be used.
4. A count of supplies indicates that the Store Supplies account should be reduced by $128 and the Office Supplies account reduced by $397 for supplies used during the year.

5. The company holds a $3,000, 12% (annual rate), 6-month note receivable dated September 30, 1995 from a customer. The interest is to be collected on the maturity date.
6. Bad debts expense is estimated to be 1% of annual sales. 1995 sales total $65,000.
7. An analysis of the company insurance policies indicates that the Prepaid Insurance account is to be reduced for the $528 of expired insurance.
8. A review of travel expense reports indicates that $310 advanced to sales personnel (and recorded as Travel Expenses) had not yet been used by these personnel.
9. The income tax rate is 30% on current income and will be paid in the first quarter of 1996. The pretax income of the company before adjustments is $11,270.

#### Required

Journalize the necessary adjusting entries at the end of 1995. Show supporting calculations in your journal entry explanations.

PC-5    *Adjusting Entries*   The Franklin Retail Company entered into the following transactions during 1995. [The transactions were properly recorded in *real* (balance sheet) accounts unless otherwise indicated.]

| Date | Transaction |
| --- | --- |
| Jan. 25 | Purchased $480 of office supplies. |
| Feb. 1 | Rented a warehouse from Tropple Company, paying 1 year's rent of $3,600 in advance. Recorded the $3,600 payment as rent expense. |
| Mar. 1 | Borrowed $10,000 from the bank, signing a 1-year note at an annual interest rate of 12%. The interest was collected in advance by the bank. The company recorded the transaction as a debit to Cash $8,800, debit to Interest Expense $1,200, and credit to Notes Payable $10,000. |
| May 1 | Purchased office equipment for $15,000, paying $3,000 down and signing a 2-year, 12% (annual rate) note payable for the balance. The office equipment is expected to have a useful life of 10 years and a residual value of $1,500. Straight-line depreciation is appropriate. |
| June 1 | Purchased a 3-year comprehensive insurance policy for $720. |
| Aug. 1 | Sold land for $9,000. The purchaser made a $2,000 down payment and signed a 1-year, 10% note for the balance. The interest and principal will be collected on the maturity date. |
| Sept. 30 | Rented a portion of the retail floor space to a florist for $120 per month, collecting 8 months' rent in advance. Recorded the $960 receipt as rent revenue. |
| Nov. 13 | Issued checks to sales personnel totaling $900. The checks are advances for expected travel costs during the remainder of the year. |

On December 31, 1995 the following additional information is available:

1. Property taxes for 1995 are due to be paid by April 1, 1996. The company has not paid or recorded its $2,300 property taxes for 1995.
2. The $302 December utility bill has not been recorded or paid.
3. Salaries accrued but not paid total $927.
4. Travel cost reports indicate that $787 of travel advances have been used to pay travel expenses.
5. The Office Supplies account had a balance of $129 on January 1, 1995. A physical count on December 31, 1995 showed $174 of office supplies on hand.
6. On January 1, 1995 the Buildings account and the Store Equipment account had balances of $100,000 and $65,000, respectively. The buildings are expected to have an $8,000 residual value, while the store equipment is expected to have a $2,000 residual value at the end of their respective lives. They are being depreciated using the straight-line method over 20- and 10-year lives, respectively.
7. The income tax rate is 30% on current income and is payable in the first quarter of 1996. The pretax income of the company before adjustments is $27,749.

#### Required

On the basis of the preceding information, prepare journal entries to adjust the company's books as of December 31, 1995. Each entry explanation should include supporting computations. (Round to the nearest dollar.)

PC-6    *Adjusting Entries*    At the end of 1995, the Ritter Company prepared a trial balance, recorded and posted its adjusting entries, and then prepared an adjusted trial balance. Selected accounts and account balances from the trial balance and adjusted trial balance are as follows:

|  | Partial Trial Balance | | Partial Adjusted Trial Balance | |
|---|---|---|---|---|
|  | Debit | Credit | Debit | Credit |
| Depreciation expense | $   0 |  | $4,250 |  |
| Interest payable (due May 14, 1997) |  | $   0 |  | $   760 |
| Bad debts expense | 0 |  | 410 |  |
| Utilities expense | 1,480 |  | 1,682 |  |
| Rental revenue |  | 1,650 |  | 2,635 |
| Income tax expense | 0 |  | 2,740 |  |
| Prepaid insurance | 1,742 |  | 1,380 |  |
| Office salaries payable |  | 0 |  | 540 |
| Rent expense | 0 |  | 800 |  |
| Accumulated depreciation |  | 14,820 |  | 19,070 |
| Interest receivable (due March 1, 1996) | 0 |  | 320 |  |
| Prepaid rent | 1,600 |  | 800 |  |
| Office salaries expense | 5,600 |  | 6,140 |  |
| Income taxes payable |  | 0 |  | 2,740 |
| Insurance expense | 300 |  | 662 |  |
| Allowance for doubtful accounts |  | 130 |  | 540 |
| Interest expense | 0 |  | 760 |  |
| Unearned rent |  | 600 |  | 0 |
| Utilities payable |  | 0 |  | 202 |
| Interest revenue |  | 620 |  | 940 |
| Sales salaries expense | 7,300 |  | 7,850 |  |
| Office supplies | 1,150 |  | 700 |  |
| Rent receivable | 0 |  | 385 |  |
| Advances to salespersons | 770 |  | 220 |  |
| Office supplies expense | 0 |  | 450 |  |

**Required**

1. By comparing the partial trial balance to the partial adjusted trial balance, determine the adjusting entries that were made on December 31, 1995. Prepare your answers in general journal form.
2. Assuming that the company uses reversing entries, indicate which adjusting entries should be reversed.

PC-7    *Adjusting Entries*    The trial balance of the Trishia Company on December 31, 1995 (the end of its *annual* accounting period) included the following account balances *before* adjustments:

| | | | |
|---|---|---|---|
| Notes receivable | $10,000 debit | Unearned rent | $4,320 credit |
| Insurance expense | 6,000 debit | Notes payable | 7,200 credit |
| Delivery equipment | 14,000 debit | Office supplies expense | 1,000 debit |
| Building | 60,000 debit | | |

Reviewing the company's recorded transactions and accounting records for 1995, you find the following data pertaining to the December 31, 1995 adjustments:

1. On July 1, 1995, the company had accepted an $8,000, 9-month, 10% (annual rate) note receivable from a customer. The interest is to be collected when the note is collected.
2. On August 1, 1995, the company had paid $6,000 for a 2-year insurance policy.
3. The building was acquired in 1983 and is being depreciated using the straight-line method over a 25-year life. It has an estimated residual value of $8,000.

4. The delivery equipment was purchased on April 1, 1995. It is to be depreciated using the straight-line method over a 10-year life with an estimated residual value of $2,000.
5. On September 1, 1995, the company had received 2 years' rent in advance ($4,320) for a portion of a building it is renting to Oscar Company.
6. On December 1, 1995, the company had issued a $7,200, 3-month, 12% (annual rate) note payable to a supplier. The interest is to be paid when the note is paid.
7. On January 2, 1995, the company purchased $1,000 of office supplies. A physical count on December 31, 1995 revealed that there are $200 of office supplies still on hand. No supplies were on hand at the beginning of the year.

### Required

Prepare the adjusting entries that are necessary to bring the Trishia Company accounts up to date on December 31, 1995. Each journal entry explanation should summarize your calculations.

**PC-8** *Reversing Entries*  During 1995, the Garson Company entered into two transactions involving promissory notes and properly recorded each transaction. These are listed next:

1. On November 1, 1995, it purchased land at a cost of $8,000. It made a $2,000 down payment and signed a note payable agreeing to pay the $6,000 balance in 6 months plus interest at an *annual* rate of 10%.
2. On December 1, 1995, it accepted a $4,200, 3-month, 12% (*annual* interest rate) note receivable from a customer for the sale of merchandise. On December 31, 1995, the Garson Company made the following related adjustments:

| | | |
|---|---|---|
| Interest Expense | 100 | |
|    Interest Payable | | 100 |
| | | |
| Interest Receivable | 42 | |
|    Interest Revenue | | 42 |

### Required

1. Assuming that the Garson Company uses reversing entries, prepare journal entries to record:
   a. The January 1, 1996 reversing entries
   b. The March 1, 1996 $4,326 collection of the note receivable
   c. The May 1, 1996 $6,300 payment of the note payable
2. Assuming instead that the Garson Company does *not* use reversing entries, prepare journal entries to record the collection of the note receivable and the payment of the note payable.

**PC-9** *Effects of Errors*  During the current accounting period Page Company makes the following errors. The company uses a periodic inventory system.

| Error | Net Income | Total Assets | Total Liabilities | Total Stockholders' Equity |
|---|---|---|---|---|
| *Example:* Failed to record a cash sale. | U | U | N | U |
| 1. The purchase of equipment for cash is recorded as a debit to Equipment and a credit to Accounts Payable. | | | | |
| 2. Failed to record the purchase of merchandise on account. | | | | |
| 3. Cash received from a customer as payment of its account is recorded as if the receipt were for a current period sale. | | | | |
| 4. Failed to record a credit sale. | | | | |
| 5. At the end of the year the receipt of money from a 60-day, 12% bank loan is recorded as a debit to Cash and a credit to Sales Revenue. | | | | |
| 6. Failed to record the depreciation at the end of the current period. | | | | |

**Required**

Indicate the effect of the errors on the net income, total assets, total liabilities, and total stockholders' equity at the end of the accounting period by using the following code: O = overstated, U = understated, N = no effect. Disregard income taxes.

PC-10   *Errors in Financial Statements*   At the end of the current year, the controller of the Jodi Corporation discovers the following items of information:

1. Salaries are paid every Friday for a 5-day work week. The normal weekly payroll is $40,000. The year-end falls on a Tuesday this year.
2. The company has a $20,000, 9-month, 12% (annual rate) note payable outstanding at the end of the year. The note was issued on October 1; the interest is to be paid when the note is paid.
3. Examining the rent expense account, the controller finds that it includes a $4,800 advance payment for 3 months' rent. The payment was made on November 1.
4. There are $500 of office supplies left in the storeroom. At the beginning of the year, there were no office supplies. During a year, the company purchased $3,500 of office supplies which were debited to the office supplies account.
5. The company received a large order in May with a $13,000 advance payment. The advance payment was credited to Unearned Revenue. In November, the last of the order was received by the customer.

**Required**

For each of the preceding items, indicate the effect on net income, assets, liabilities, and stockholders' equity in the financial statements of the company for the year if the controller fails to make an adjusting entry for the item (ignore income taxes). (*Contributed by Paula L. Koch*)

PC-11   *Reversing Entries*   On December 31, 1995, the Cochran Company made the proper year-end adjusting entries shown here:

| Dec. 31 | Bad Debts Expense | 530 | |
| | Allowance for Doubtful Accounts | | 530 |
| 31 | Salaries Expense | 880 | |
| | Salaries Payable | | 880 |
| 31 | Unearned Rent | 1,230 | |
| | Rent Revenue | | 1,230 |
| 31 | Interest Expense | 170 | |
| | Interest Payable (due July 1, 1996) | | 170 |
| 31 | Rent Receivable | 310 | |
| | Rent Revenue | | 310 |
| 31 | Depreciation Expense | 5,100 | |
| | Accumulated Depreciation | | 5,100 |
| 31 | Insurance Expense | 312 | |
| | Prepaid Insurance | | 312 |
| 31 | Interest Receivable (due February 1, 1997) | 225 | |
| | Interest Revenue | | 225 |
| 31 | Office Supplies | 100 | |
| | Office Supplies Expense | | 100 |
| 31 | Advances to Salespersons | 300 | |
| | Salaries Expense | | 300 |
| 31 | Income Tax Expense | 4,300 | |
| | Income Taxes Payable | | 4,300 |

**Required**

1. Prepare journal entries to record whatever reversing entries you think are appropriate.
2. Explain your reasoning for each reversing entry.

**PC-12** *Special Journals*  The Schnell Company uses a purchases, sales, cash receipts, cash payments, and general journal to record its transactions. The following are its transactions for May:

| Date | Transaction |
|------|-------------|
| May 1 | Made $5,500 sales on account to Gordon Company, terms 2/10, n/30. |
| 3 | Purchased office equipment from Myers Supply Company for $6,000, paying $2,000 down and agreeing to pay the remaining balance in 30 days. |
| 6 | Purchased merchandise from Ripley Company on account, $3,500. Terms 1/10, n/30. |
| 10 | Made cash sales of $3,000. |
| 11 | Collected the account receivable from May 1 less the discount. |
| 12 | Sold 1 acre of land for $4,500. The purchaser made a $600 down payment and signed a 90-day, 12% note for the balance. The land had originally cost $2,800. |
| 16 | Paid for the merchandise purchased on May 6 less the discount. |
| 24 | Made $6,300 sales on account to Altis Company, terms 2/10, n/30. |
| 26 | Purchased merchandise on account from Boon Company, $4,100. Terms 2/10, n/30. |
| 29 | Altis Company returned $1,000 of merchandise from the May 24 sale for credit to its account. |
| 31 | Paid the following expenses: salaries $500, utilities $220, advertising $325. |

**Required**

Record each of the preceding transactions in the appropriate special journal.

**PC-13** *Worksheet*  The Lehman Company has the following account balances on December 31, 1995 prior to any adjustments:

| | Debit | Credit | | Debit | Credit |
|---|---|---|---|---|---|
| Cash | $ 1,500 | | Mortgage payable (due | | |
| Accounts receivable | 4,700 | | January 1, 2002) | | $ 7,300 |
| Allowance for doubtful | | | Capital stock (2,000 shares) | | 10,000 |
| accounts | | $ 60 | Retained earnings, January 1, | | |
| Inventory, January 1, 1995 | 4,800 | | 1995 | | 18,075 |
| Prepaid insurance | 600 | | Dividends distributed | $ 1,300 | |
| Land | 4,100 | | Sales revenue | | 48,955 |
| Buildings | 38,000 | | Purchases | 31,105 | |
| Accumulated depreciation: | | | Purchases returns | | 1,300 |
| buildings | | 11,500 | Purchases discounts taken | | 760 |
| Equipment | 10,700 | | Freight-in | 2,040 | |
| Accumulated depreciation: | | | Salaries expense | 4,080 | |
| equipment | | 3,100 | Utilities expense | 2,000 | |
| Accounts payable | | 4,300 | Office supplies expense | 770 | |
| Note payable (due March 1, | | | Delivery expense | 1,275 | |
| 1996) | | 1,400 | Other expenses | 980 | |
| Unearned rent | | 1,200 | | | |

Additional adjustment and inventory information: (a) depreciation on buildings $1,100, on equipment $600; (b) bad debts expense $240; (c) interest accumulated but not paid: on note payable $50, on mortgage payable $530 (this interest is due during the next accounting period); (d) insurance expired $175; (e) salaries accrued but not paid $370; (f) rent that was collected in advance and is now earned at year-end $800; (g) office supplies on hand at year-end $230 (expensed when originally purchased earlier in the year); (h) the December 31, 1995 ending inventory is $8,700; and (i) the income tax rate is 30% on current income and is payable in the first quarter of 1996.

**Required**

1. Transfer the account balances to a ten-column worksheet and prepare a trial balance.
2. Complete the worksheet.
3. Prepare the income statement, retained earnings statement, and balance sheet.
4. Prepare (a) adjusting and (b) closing entries in the general journal.

**PC-14**  *Worksheet*  The Ebbe Company has prepared the following partially completed worksheet for the year ended December 31, 1995:

| Accounts | Trial Balance Debit | Trial Balance Credit | Adjustments Debit | Adjustments Credit | Income Statement Debit | Income Statement Credit | Retained Earnings Statement Debit | Retained Earnings Statement Credit | Balance Sheet Debit | Balance Sheet Credit |
|---|---|---|---|---|---|---|---|---|---|---|
| Cash | 1,000 | | | | | | | | | |
| Accounts receivable | 2,700 | | | | | | | | | |
| Allowance for doubtful accounts | | 30 | | | | | | | | |
| Note receivable (due 5/1/96) | 1,200 | | | | | | | | | |
| Inventory, 1/1/95 | 3,300 | | | | | | | | | |
| Land | 4,500 | | | | | | | | | |
| Buildings and equipment | 20,600 | | | | | | | | | |
| Accumulated depreciation | | 8,790 | | | | | | | | |
| Accounts payable | | 4,050 | | | | | | | | |
| Notes payable, due 4/1/98 | | 4,000 | | | | | | | | |
| Capital stock (2,000 shares) | | 5,000 | | | | | | | | |
| Retained earnings | | 6,120 | | | | | | | | |
| Dividends distributed | 600 | | | | | | | | | |
| Sales revenue | | 25,140 | | | | | | | | |
| Rent revenue | | 550 | | | | | | | | |
| Purchases | 15,950 | | | | | | | | | |
| Purchases returns | | 650 | | | | | | | | |
| Purchases discounts taken | | 350 | | | | | | | | |
| Salaries expense | 2,750 | | | | | | | | | |
| Delivery expense | 720 | | | | | | | | | |
| Heat and light expense | 820 | | | | | | | | | |
| Other expenses | 540 | | | | | | | | | |
| Totals | 54,680 | 54,680 | | | | | | | | |

The following additional information is available: (a) salaries accrued but unpaid total $250; (b) the $80 heat and light bill for December has not been recorded or paid; (c) depreciation expense totals $810 on the buildings and equipment; (d) interest accrued on the note payable totals $380 (this will be paid when the note is repaid); (e) the company leases a portion of its floor space to Brix Specialty Company for $50 per month, and Brix has not yet paid its December rent; (f) interest accrued on the note receivable totals $80; (g) bad debts expense is $70; (h) the December 31, 1995 ending inventory is $9,200; and (i) the income tax rate is 30% on current income and is payable in the first quarter of 1996.

**Required**

1. Complete the worksheet. (Round to the nearest dollar.)
2. Prepare financial statements.
3. Prepare (a) adjusting and (b) closing entries in the general journal.

**PC-15**  *Special Journals and Posting*  Refer to the transactions listed in PC-1.

**Required**

1. Journalize each of these transactions in the sales journal, purchases journal, cash receipts journal, cash payments journal, or general journal as illustrated in the chapter.
2. Post to the general ledger accounts and to the subsidiary (Grant Company and Mason Company) accounts.

*PC-16* *Comprehensive* On November 30, 1995, the Able Company had the following account balances:

| | Debit | Credit | | Debit | Credit |
|---|---|---|---|---|---|
| Cash | $ 3,200 | | Retained earnings (1/1/1995) | | $42,400 |
| Accounts receivable | 9,900 | | Dividends distributed | $ 2,000 | |
| Allowance for doubtful | | | Sales revenue | | 76,000 |
| accounts | | $ 100 | Sales returns and allowances | 6,300 | |
| Inventory (1/1/1995) | 12,600 | | Purchases | 41,000 | |
| Supplies | 1,400 | | Purchases returns and | | |
| Land | 9,000 | | allowances | | 3,400 |
| Building and equipment | 42,000 | | Freight-in | 4,300 | |
| Accumulated depreciation | | 4,200 | Salaries expense | 12,500 | |
| Accounts payable | | 10,700 | Advertising expense | 8,100 | |
| Capital stock, no-par | | | Other expenses | 4,500 | |
| (2,000 shares) | | 20,000 | | | |

During the month of December the Able Company entered into the following transactions:

| Date | Transaction |
|---|---|
| Dec. 4 | Made cash sales of $3,000. |
| 7 | Purchased $2,400 of merchandise on account. Paid $50 of related freight charges. |
| 11 | Customer returned $600 of defective merchandise for credit to its account. |
| 14 | Collected $900 of accounts receivable (no cash discount). |
| 18 | Sold land for $7,800; the land had originally cost $5,000. |
| 19 | Made credit sales of $4,000. |
| 21 | Returned $300 of defective merchandise to supplier for credit to the Able Company's account. |
| 26 | Purchased $1,250 of merchandise for cash. |
| 28 | Paid $1,100 of accounts payable (no cash discount). |
| 31 | Purchased land at a cost of $6,000; made a $1,000 down payment and signed a 12%, 2-year note for the balance. |

**Required**

1. Prepare general journal entries to record the preceding transactions.
2. Post to the general ledger accounts.
3. Prepare a year-end trial balance on a worksheet and complete the worksheet using the following information: (a) accrued salaries at year-end total $1,200; (b) for simplicity, the building and equipment are being depreciated using the straight-line method over an estimated life of 20 years with no residual value; (c) supplies on hand at the end of the year total $630; (d) bad debts expense for the year totals $830; (e) inventory on December 31, 1995 is $17,200; and (f) the income tax rate is 30%; income taxes are payable in the first quarter of 1996.
4. Prepare financial statements for 1995.
5. Prepare (a) adjusting and (b) closing entries in the general journal.

*PC-17* *Comprehensive* Tina Tunxis is the owner of Valley Sales, a distributor of horticulture supplies. The following is the balance sheet of the company as of December 31, 1994:

| | | | |
|---|---|---|---|
| Cash | $ 2,300 | Accounts payable | $ 6,400 |
| Accounts receivable | 10,400 | Salaries payable | 1,200 |
| Inventory | 12,500 | | |
| Equipment | 8,000 | | |
| Less: Accumulated depreciation | (6,500) | T. Tunxis, Capital | $19,100 |
| | $26,700 | | $26,700 |

Tina keeps very few records and has asked you to help her in the preparation of Valley Sales' 1995 financial statements. An analysis of the 1995 cash transactions recorded in the company's checkbook indicates deposits and checks as follows:

Total deposits:     $173,200; all were collections from customers except for a long-term $10,000 bank loan.

Checks written:     $169,800  summarized as follows:

| | | | |
|---|---|---|---|
| Merchandise | $123,100 | Note payments (including interest of $650) | $ 2,650 |
| Salaries | 4,250 | Office expense | 3,400 |
| Rent | 4,800 | Auto expense | 4,100 |
| Equipment | 4,000 | Withdrawals | 23,500 |

Other information about the company is as follows:

1. Accounts receivable at December 31, 1995, $9,200.
2. Accounts payable at December 31:

| | | | | | | |
|---|---|---|---|---|---|---|
| 1994: | Merchandise | $6,100 | 1995: | Merchandise | $8,500 | |
| | Office expense | 300 | | Auto expense | 200 | |
| | | $6,400 | | | $8,700 | |

3. Salaries payable at December 31, 1995, $1,800.
4. Equipment is depreciated by the straight-line method over a ten-year life. The equipment purchased in 1995 was acquired on July 1.
5. Interest payable at December 31, 1995, $140.
6. The company uses a periodic inventory system. Inventory at December 31, 1995, $16,300.

**Required**

1. Prepare a worksheet to summarize the transactions and adjustments of Valley Sales for 1995. (*Hint*: Include debit and credit columns for both transactions and adjustments.)
2. Prepare a 1995 income statement and a balance sheet as of December 31, 1995. (*Contributed by Walter A. Parker*)

**PC-18**  *Comprehensive*   Presented next is information pertaining to Ward Specialty Foods, a calendar-year sole proprietorship, maintaining its books on the cash basis during the year. At year-end, however, Mary Ward's accountant adjusts the books to the accrual basis only for sales, purchases, and cost of sales, and records depreciation to more clearly reflect the business income.

**Trial Balance**
**December 31, 1995**

| | Debit | Credit |
|---|---|---|
| Cash | $ 18,500 | |
| Accounts receivable, 12/31/94 | 4,500 | |
| Inventory, 12/31/94 | 20,000 | |
| Equipment | 35,000 | |
| Accumulated depreciation, 12/31/94 | | $ 9,000 |
| Accounts payable, 12/31/94 | | 4,800 |
| Payroll taxes withheld | | 850 |
| Mary Ward, withdrawals | 24,000 | |
| Mary Ward, capital, 12/31/94 | | 33,650 |
| Sales | | 187,000 |
| Purchases | 82,700 | |
| Salaries | 29,500 | |
| Payroll taxes | 2,900 | |
| Rent | 8,400 | |
| Miscellaneous expense | 3,900 | |
| Insurance | 2,400 | |
| Utilities | 3,500 | |
| | $235,300 | $235,300 |

During 1995, Ward signed a new 8-year lease for the store premises and is in the process of negotiating a loan for remodeling purposes. The bank requires Ward to present financial statements for 1995 prepared on the accrual basis. To do so, Ward's accountant obtained the following additional information:

1. Amounts due from customers totaled $7,900 at December 31, 1995.
2. A review of the receivables at December 31, 1995 disclosed that an allowance for doubtful accounts of $1,100 should be provided. Ward had no bad debt losses from the inception of the business through December 31, 1995.
3. The inventory amounted to $23,000 at December 31, 1995 based on a physical count of goods priced at cost. No reduction to market was required.
4. On signing the new lease on October 1, 1995, Ward paid $8,400 representing 1 year's rent in advance for the lease year ending October 1, 1996. The $7,500 annual rental under the old lease was paid on October 1, 1994 for the lease year ended October 1, 1995.
5. On April 1, 1995, Ward paid $2,400 to renew the comprehensive insurance coverage for one year. The premium was $2,160 on the old policy, which expired on April 1, 1995.
6. Depreciation on the equipment was computed at $5,800 for 1995.
7. Unpaid vendors' invoices for food purchases totaled $8,800 at December 31, 1995.
8. Accrued expenses at December 31, 1994 and December 31, 1995 were as follows:

|  | 12/31/94 | 12/31/95 |
|---|---|---|
| Payroll taxes | $250 | $400 |
| Salaries | 375 | 510 |
| Utilities | 275 | 450 |

After obtaining the preceding information, Ward's accountant prepared the following partially completed worksheet:

|  | Cash Basis | | Adjustments | | Accrual Basis | |
|---|---|---|---|---|---|---|
|  | Debit | Credit | Debit | Credit | Debit | Credit |
| Cash | $18,500 |  |  |  |  |  |
| Accounts receivable | 4,500 |  |  |  |  |  |
| Allow. for doubtful accts. | — | — |  |  |  |  |
| Inventory | 20,000 |  |  |  |  |  |
| Equipment | 35,000 |  |  |  |  |  |
| Accum. depreciation |  | $ 9,000 |  |  |  |  |
| Prepaid rent | — |  |  |  |  |  |
| Prepaid insurance | — | — |  |  |  |  |
| Accounts payable |  | 4,800 |  |  |  |  |
| Accrued expenses | — | — |  |  |  |  |
| Payroll taxes withheld |  | 850 |  |  |  |  |
| Ward, withdrawals | 24,000 |  |  |  |  |  |
| Ward, capital |  | 33,650 |  |  |  |  |
| Sales |  | 187,000 |  |  |  |  |
| Purchases | 82,700 |  |  |  |  |  |
| Income summary—inventory | — | — |  |  |  |  |
| Salaries | 29,500 |  |  |  |  |  |
| Payroll taxes | 2,900 |  |  |  |  |  |
| Rent | 8,400 |  |  |  |  |  |
| Miscellaneous expenses | 3,900 |  |  |  |  |  |
| Insurance | 2,400 |  |  |  |  |  |
| Utilities | 3,500 |  |  |  |  |  |
| Depreciation | — | — |  |  |  |  |
| Bad debts | — | — |  |  |  |  |
| Totals | $235,300 | $235,300 |  |  |  |  |

Required

1. Complete the preceding worksheet to convert the trial balance of Ward Specialty Foods to the accrual basis for the year ended December 31, 1995.
2. Prepare the statement of changes in Mary Ward, capital, for the year ended December 31, 1995. (*AICPA adapted*)

# COMPOUND INTEREST

### Appendix Topics

*Meaning of Time Value of Money*

*Distinction Between Simple Interest and Compound Interest*

*How to Determine the Future Value of a Single Sum and the Present Value of a Single Sum*

*How to Determine the Future Value of an Annuity and the Present Value of an Annuity*

Suppose someone asked you, "Would you rather have $1 today or $1 next year?" Your answer should be, "I'd rather have $1 today." This reply involves consideration of the *time value of money*. The difference in worth between the two amounts, the time value of money, is interest. *Interest is the cost of the use of money over time*. It is an expense to the borrower and revenue to the lender. Therefore, it is a very important element in decision making that involves the acquisition and disposal of many of the resources of a company.

Interest concepts are involved in the development of many values shown on financial statements. Also, managers need to understand the concept of interest when making decisions where cash paid or received *now* must be compared with amounts that will be received or paid in the *future*.

The cash flows at various dates, say some at 3 years from now, some at 2 years from now, and some at 1 year from now, cannot be added together to produce a relevant value. Future cash flows, before they can be added, must be converted to a common denominator by being restated to their present values as of a specific moment in time (often referred to as *time period zero*). The dollars to be received or paid 3 years from now have a *smaller* present value than those to be received or paid 2 years or 1 year from now. *The converting of these future value amounts to the present value common denominator is known as discounting* and involves the removal of the interest or discount—the time value of money—from those dollars that would be received or paid 3 years, 2 years, or 1 year from now.

Instead of restating some of the cash inflows and outflows to their present values as of time period zero, a common denominator is also achieved by stating them at a future value by adding the time value of money (interest) to these inflows and outflows. The future value of any series of inflows or outflows is the sum of these periodic amounts plus the compound interest calculated on the amounts.

Restatement for the present value or the future value is essential in many situations, such as (1) for measurement and reporting of some assets and liabilities, since many accounting pronouncements require the use of present value concepts in a number of measurement and reporting issues, and (2) when information inputs are accumulated for decision making involving, for example, property, plant, and equipment expenditures. These concepts are discussed in this Appendix and are applied in various chapters when we discuss the reporting of (1) long-term notes payable and notes receivable when the interest rate is not specified or differs from the market rate at the time of the transaction, (2) assets acquired by the issuance of long-term debt securities that carry either no stated rate of interest or a rate of interest that is different from the market rate at the time of the transaction, (3) bonds payable and investments in bonds and the amortization of bond premiums and discounts in each case, (4) long-term leases, and (5) various aspects of employees' post-employment benefits.

Various compound interest techniques are used in the measurement of the values (costs) of these and other types of transactions. Most compound interest applications can be calculated by a longhand arithmetic process. However, quicker approaches and shortcuts to the solutions of the problems are available. In this chapter the basic principles of compound interest are illustrated in a way that leads to the development of shortcuts to resolving issues introduced throughout this book.

## SIMPLE INTEREST AND COMPOUND INTEREST

Simple interest is interest on the original principal (amount originally received or paid) regardless of the number of time periods that have passed or the amount of interest that has been paid or accrued in the past. Interest rates are usually stated as an *annual* rate, which is adjusted for any other time period. Thus simple interest is calculated by the following equation:

   Interest = Principal × Rate × Time

where time is either a fraction of a year or a multiple of years. If the term of a note is stated in days, say 90 days, the denominator of the time fraction in the preceding equation is usually stated in terms of a commercial year of 360 days rather than a full year of 365 days. In this practice the year is assumed to be a period of 12 months of 30 days each. To illustrate, the simple interest on a $10,000, 90-day, 12% note given to a company by Allen Sanders is $300 ($10,000 × 0.12 × 90/360). However, if the term of this note is 15 months, the simple interest is $1,500 ($10,000 × 0.12 × 15/12). Observe that simple interest for more than 1 year is still calculated on only the principal amount (in this case $10,000).

Compound interest is the interest that accrues on both the principal and the past unpaid accrued interest. Simple interest for 15 months on the Allen Sanders note is $1,500. If, on the other hand, the 12% interest is *compounded quarterly* for 15 months (5 quarters), the total compound interest is $1,592.74, as shown in Exhibit D-1. Observe that in the compound interest computation the future accumulated amount at the end of each quarter becomes the principal sum for purposes of computing the interest for the following period.

## EXHIBIT D-1

### COMPUTATION OF QUARTERLY COMPOUNDED INTEREST

| Period | Value at Beginning of Quarter* × Rate × Time = | Compound Interest | Value at End of Quarter |
|---|---|---|---|
| 1st quarter | $10,000.00 × 0.12 × 1/4 | $ 300.00 | $10,300.00 |
| 2nd quarter | 10,300.00 × 0.12 × 1/4 | 309.00 | 10,609.00 |
| 3rd quarter | 10,609.00 × 0.12 × 1/4 | 318.27 | 10,927.27 |
| 4th quarter | 10,927.27 × 0.12 × 1/4 | 327.82 | 11,255.09 |
| 5th quarter | 11,255.09 × 0.12 × 1/4 | 337.65 | 11,592.74 |
| Compound interest on $10,000 at 12% compounded quarterly for 5 quarters | | $1,592.74 | |

\* This value is the amount on which interest is calculated.

To help solve the many business issues stated in the introductory section of this Appendix, accountants need to know the various types of compound interest computations. Although there are many variations, there are only four basic types:

1.  **Future value (amount) of a single sum** at compound interest

2.  **Present value of a single sum** due in the future

3.  **Future value (amount) of an annuity,** a series of receipts or payments

4.  **Present value of an annuity,** a series of receipts or payments

## FUTURE VALUE OF A SINGLE SUM AT COMPOUND INTEREST

As stated previously, the main objective of this Appendix is to explain shortcut methods of determining and applying the compound interest techniques. The following step-by-step procedure, introducing the entire topic, will be used *only* with the development of the future value of a single sum at compound interest:

1.  The idea or concept is diagrammatically stated.

2.  The computation is accomplished by a longhand calculation.

3.  The computation is accomplished by the use of formulas.

4.  The method of constructing and using tables is discussed.

5.  The use of the tables to solve a compound interest problem is illustrated.

### The Idea

The future value of a single sum at compound interest is the original sum plus the compound interest, stated as of a specific future date. It is also often referred to as

## EXHIBIT D-2

### DIAGRAM OF FUTURE VALUE OF A SINGLE SUM

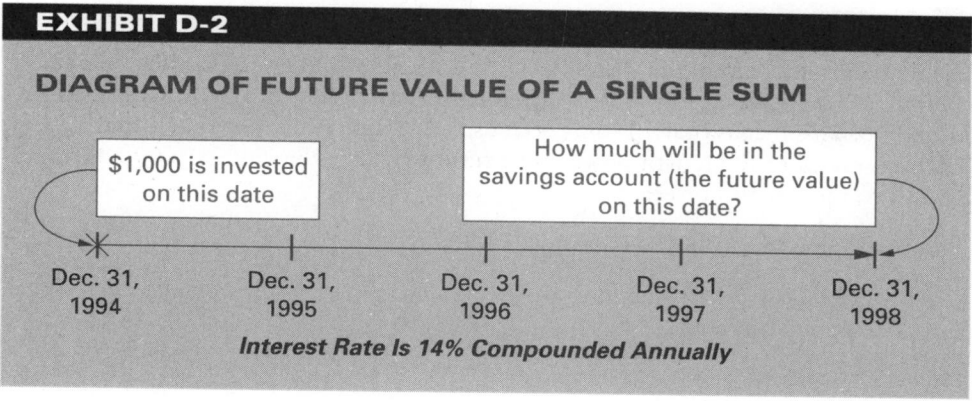

the **future amount** of a single sum. For example, suppose that a single amount of $1,000 is invested in a savings account on December 31, 1994. What will be the amount in the savings account on December 31, 1998 if interest at 14% is compounded annually each year? The issue is shown graphically in Exhibit D-2. Most compound interest calculations can be made by applying longhand arithmetic. This procedure is followed here only to clarify the various shortcut devices used.

The future value of $1,000 for 4 years at 14% a year can be calculated as shown in Exhibit D-3. The single sum of $1,000 invested on December 31, 1994 has grown to $1,688.96 by December 31, 1998. This is the **future value**. The total interest of $688.96 for the 4 years is referred to as **compound interest**.

## EXHIBIT D-3

### CALCULATION OF FUTURE VALUE OF SINGLE SUM AT COMPOUND INTEREST

| (1) Year | (2) Value at Beginning of Year | (3) Annual Compound Interest (Col. 2 × 0.14) | (4) Future Value at End of Year (Col. 2 + Col. 3) |
|---|---|---|---|
| 1995 | $1,000.00 | $140.00 | $1,140.00 |
| 1996 | 1,140.00 | 159.60 | 1,299.60 |
| 1997 | 1,299.60 | 181.94 | 1,481.54 |
| 1998 | 1,481.54 | 207.42 | 1,688.96 |

A slight variation of the longhand arithmetic approach is to determine what $1 invested on December 31, 1994 will amount to by December 31, 1998 if interest at 14% is compounded annually. Then this amount is multiplied by the principal sum to find the future value. In this case, $1 amounts to $1.68896 in 4 years. Knowing this fact, the value of 1,000 different $1 investments (or $1,000) at the end of 4 years can be calculated by multiplying the $1,000 by 1.68896 as follows: $1,000 × 1.68896 = $1,688.96. To avoid a significant rounding error in the final results, when solving this problem the intermediate figures must not be rounded to the nearest cent.

## Formula Approach

Each amount in column 4 of Exhibit D-3 is 1.14 times the corresponding amount in column 2. The final future value is therefore $\$1,000 \times 1.14 \times 1.14 \times 1.14 \times 1.14 = \$1,688.96$. This means that 1.14 has been used as a multiplier four times; that is, 1.14 has been raised to the fourth power. The future value is therefore $\$1,000$ multiplied by 1.14 to the fourth power:

**Future Value $= \$1,000(1.14)^4 = \$1,688.96$**

Thus the following formula can be used to compute the future value of a single sum at compound interest:

$$f = p(1 + i)^n$$

where $f$ = future value of a single sum at compound interest $i$ for $n$ periods
$\quad\quad p$ = principal sum (present value)
$\quad\quad i$ = interest rate for each of the stated time periods
$\quad\quad n$ = number of time periods

It is important to observe that the interest rate $i$ is the rate of interest applicable for the particular time period for which interest is compounded. For example, a stated annual rate of interest of 12% is

- 12% per year if interest is compounded annually

- 6% per one-half year if interest is compounded semiannually

- 3% per quarter if interest is compounded quarterly

- 1% per month if interest is compounded monthly

In general **an interest rate per period ($i$) is the annual stated rate (sometimes called the nominal rate) divided by the number of compounding time periods in the year, and $n$ is the number of time periods in the year multiplied by the number of years.**
The formula for the future value of 1 may be stated as follows:

$$f_{n,i} = (1 + i)^n$$

where $f_{n,i}$ is the future compound value of 1 ($\$1$ or 1 of any other monetary unit) at interest rate $i$ for $n$ periods.
Using the preceding formula for the future value of 1, a short formula can be stated for the future compound value of any single amount at compound interest as follows:

$$f = p(f_{n,i})$$

The example of the future value of $\$1,000$ invested at 14% with interest compounded annually can now be calculated in two steps:

**Step 1**     $f_{n=4,\, i=14\%} = (1.14)^4 = 1.688960$

**Step 2**     $f = \$1,000(1.688960) = \$1,688.96$

Recall that this is exactly the same as the *second* approach, which was used in the arithmetic method described previously.

## Table Approach

To develop additional shortcuts to the solution of the compound interest issue, tables for the future value of 1 have been constructed. These tables are simply a precalculation of the future values of 1 at different interest rates and for different time periods. They can be constructed by using the preceding formula with the desired interest rates and time periods. For example, suppose that we need tables of the future value of 1 at 2% and 14% for time periods 1 through 4 and for 40 years. The information for these can be calculated as follows:

$$f_{n=1, i=2\%} = (1.02)^1 = 1.020000 \qquad f_{n=1, i=14\%} = (1.14)^1 = 1.140000$$

$$f_{n=2, i=2\%} = (1.02)^2 = 1.040400 \qquad f_{n=2, i=14\%} = (1.14)^2 = 1.299600$$

$$f_{n=3, i=2\%} = (1.02)^3 = 1.061208 \qquad f_{n=3, i=14\%} = (1.14)^3 = 1.481544$$

$$f_{n=4, i=2\%} = (1.02)^4 = 1.082432 \qquad f_{n=4, i=14\%} = (1.14)^4 = 1.688960$$

$$f_{n=40, i=2\%} = (1.02)^{40} = 2.208040 \qquad f_{n=40, i=14\%} = (1.14)^{40} = 188.883514$$

This information can then be accumulated in a partial table as indicated in Exhibit D-4. In this kind of table the factors are shown without the use of the dollar sign. Each factor is an amount for a certain time period and rate. More complete tables are given at the end of this Appendix.

### EXHIBIT D-4

### FUTURE VALUE OF 1 TABLE $(1 + i)^n$

| Periods | 2% | 14% |
|---------|----------|------------|
| 1 | 1.020000 | 1.140000 |
| 2 | 1.040400 | 1.299600 |
| 3 | 1.061208 | 1.481544 |
| 4 | 1.082432 | 1.688960 |
| . | . | . |
| . | . | . |
| . | . | . |
| 40 | 2.208040 | 188.883514 |

Since the table factors in Exhibit D-4 and in Table 1 at the end of this Appendix are reflections of the formula $(1 + i)^n$, the table approach can be expressed in this manner:

$$f = p(\text{Table Factor for } f_{n, i})$$

To calculate the future value that $1,000 will accumulate to in 4 years at 14% compounded annually, it is necessary to look up the table factor for $f_{n=4, i=14\%}$, namely, 1.688960; then, to arrive at the answer of $1,688.96, the following calculation must be made: $f = \$1,000(1.688960) = \$1,688.96$.

## Summary and Illustration

In addition to the straightforward situation of calculating the future value of a single sum at compound interest, other issues can be solved with the "future value of 1" table. An example follows.

*Example: Finding an Unstated Interest Rate* If $1,000 is invested on December 31, 1994 to earn compound interest and if the future value on December 31, 2001 is $2,998.70, what is the quarterly interest rate on the investment?

The known facts are shown in Exhibit D-5. Using the table approach

$$f = p \text{ (Table Factor for } f_{n,i})$$

and substituting in the formula the amounts shown in Exhibit D-5, the problem can be solved as follows:

$$\$2,998.70 = \$1,000(\text{Table Factor for } f_{n=28,\, i=?})$$

$$\text{Table Factor for } f_{n=28,\, i=?} = \frac{\$2,998.70}{\$1,000.00} = 2.99870$$

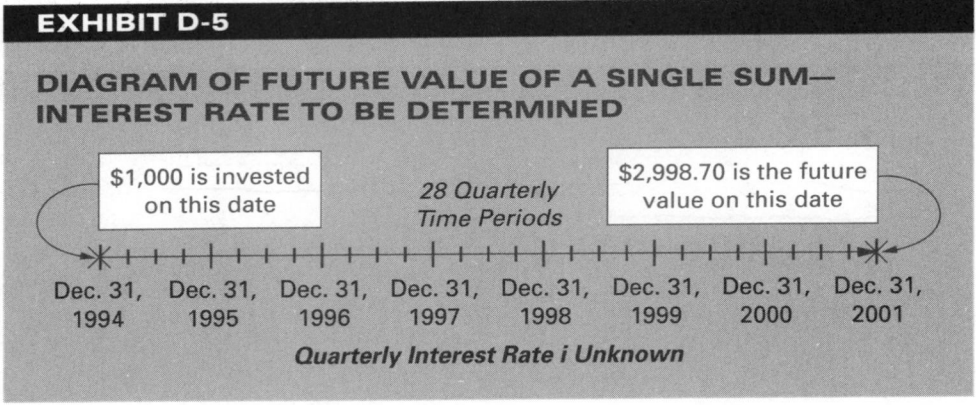

**EXHIBIT D-5**

**DIAGRAM OF FUTURE VALUE OF A SINGLE SUM—
INTEREST RATE TO BE DETERMINED**

$1,000 is invested on this date

*28 Quarterly Time Periods*

$2,998.70 is the future value on this date

Dec. 31, 1994   Dec. 31, 1995   Dec. 31, 1996   Dec. 31, 1997   Dec. 31, 1998   Dec. 31, 1999   Dec. 31, 2000   Dec. 31, 2001

*Quarterly Interest Rate i Unknown*

The table factor of 2.99870 is the future value of 1 for 28 time periods at an unknown interest rate. Using the future-value-of-1 table (Table 1) as shown at the end of this Appendix, we look down the periods ($n$) column until we get to 28. Then we move horizontally on the $n = 28$ line to the column table factor closest to 2.99870. If the value appears in the table, we can determine the interest rate (shown at the top of the column) that produces this value. In this case, 2.99870 is equal to 2.998703 (rounded) located in the 4% column; thus the quarterly interest rate is 4%. This is often referred to as being a stated annual rate of 16%; it should be understood, however, that a quarterly rate of 4% compounded four times yields an effective rate in excess of 16%. If the factor of 2.99870 does not appear in the table, an interpolation procedure is required to approximate the quarterly interest rate.[1] Calculators that compute the interest rate are widely available.

Other problems can be solved by the use of the future-amount-of-1 tables. Keep in mind, however, that most tables are incomplete. At times it will be necessary to construct tables for odd interest rates and time periods or to use a calculator.

## PRESENT VALUE OF A SINGLE SUM

For the remaining compound interest techniques, the discussion focuses on the short-cut approach. After the idea has been discussed, the formula is stated and table factors derived from the formula are used.

### The Idea

**The present value is the principal that must be invested at time period zero to produce the known future value. Also, discounting is the process of converting the future value to the present value.** For example, if $1,000 is worth $1,688.96 when it earns 14% compound interest per year for 4 years, then it follows that $1,688.96 to be received 4 years from now is worth $1,000 now at time period zero; that is, $1,000 is the present value of $1,688.96 discounted at 14% for 4 years. This information is presented graphically in Exhibit D-6.

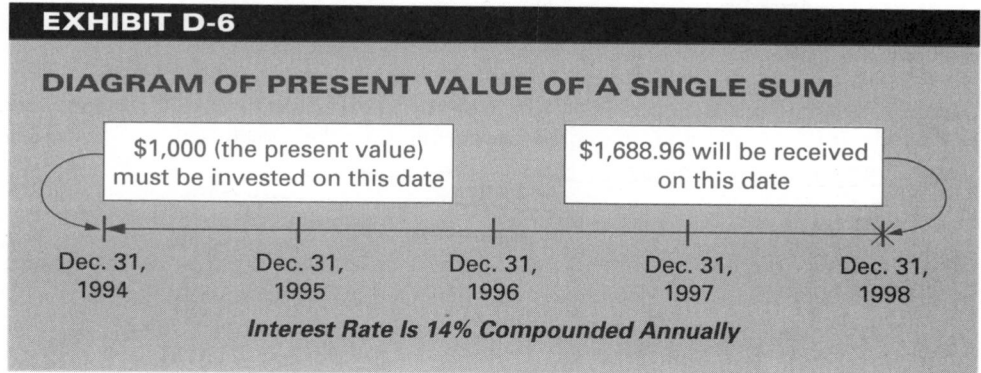

**EXHIBIT D-6**

**DIAGRAM OF PRESENT VALUE OF A SINGLE SUM**

$1,000 (the present value) must be invested on this date

$1,688.96 will be received on this date

| Dec. 31, 1994 | Dec. 31, 1995 | Dec. 31, 1996 | Dec. 31, 1997 | Dec. 31, 1998 |

*Interest Rate Is 14% Compounded Annually*

### Shortcut Approaches

While it is possible to calculate the present value of $1,688.96 to be received at the end of 4 years discounted at 14% by a longhand approach by reversing the process

---

1. The following six steps are used to determine an interest rate by linear interpolation. (1) Calculate the compound interest factor as shown in the preceding example. (2) Look up in compound interest tables the two interest rates that yield the next largest and the next smallest table factors from the calculated factor determined in step 1. (3) Determine (a) the difference between the two table factors in step 2 and (b) the difference between the calculated factor from step 1 and the table factor of the smaller interest rate from step 2. (4) Find the difference between the two interest rates found in step 2. (5) Apportion the difference in the interest rates in step 4 by multiplying it by a fraction: The numerator is the difference determined in step 3b and the denominator is the difference determined in step 3a. (6) The interest rate is then the lower rate found in step 2 *plus* the apportioned difference from step 5.

described in the calculation of the future value, this approach is not illustrated here. Instead we focus on the development of shortcut approaches to finding the present value of a single sum. First the formula is presented; then we consider how table factors are created and used.

*Formula Approach* Since the present value of a single future amount is the reciprocal value of the future value of a single sum, the formula for this calculation can be stated as follows:

$$p = f\frac{1}{(1 + i)^n}$$

where $p$ = present value of any given future value due in the future
$\quad\quad f$ = future value
$\quad\quad i$ = interest rate for each of the stated time periods
$\quad\quad n$ = number of time periods

In this example the present value of \$1,688.96 received at the end of 4 years discounted at 14% is \$1,000, calculated as follows:

$$p = \$1,688.96\frac{1}{(1.14)^4} = \$1,000$$

As with the future value, the formula for the present value of 1 may be stated as follows:

$$p_{n,i} = \frac{1}{(1 + i)^n}$$

where $p_{n,i}$ is the present value of 1 (\$1 or 1 of any monetary unit) at interest rate $i$ for $n$ periods. It is now possible to express the formula for the present value of any given future amount in this manner:

$$p = f(p_{n,i})$$

The example of the present value of \$1,688.96 to be received 4 years from now with interest of 14% compounded annually can be calculated in two steps:

**Step 1**    $p_{n=4,\,i=14\%} = \dfrac{1}{(1.14)^4} = 0.592080$

**Step 2**    $p = \$1,688.96(0.592080) = \$1,000$

*Table Approach* Using the formula for $p_{n,i}$, tables have been constructed for any interest rate and for any number of periods by simply substituting in the formula the selected various interest rates for the various time periods desired. The table factors for the present value of 1 ($p_{n,i}$) are presented in Table 3 at the end of this Appendix.

Since Table 3 reflects the precalculation of various $p_{n,i} = 1/(1 + i)^n$ values, the generalized table approach can be stated in the following manner:

$$p = f(\text{Table Factor for } p_{n,i})$$

To calculate the present value of \$1,688.96 to be received at the end of 4 years, discounted at 14%, it is necessary to look up the table factor for $p_{n=4,\,i=14\%}$ in Table 3; it is 0.592080. Then the future value of \$1,688.96 is multiplied by this present-value-of-1 table factor to obtain the present value amount of \$1,000, as follows: $p = \$1,688.96(0.592080) = \$1,000$.

## Summary and Illustration

In addition to calculating the present value of a single sum using compound interest, other kinds of problems can be solved by the use of the "present-value-of-1" table. An example follows.

*Example: Finding an Unstated Interest Rate* Assuming that the present value of $10,000 to be paid at the end of 10 years is $3,855.43, what interest rate compounded annually is used in the calculation of the present value?

The known facts are shown in Exhibit D-7. Since both the present value and the future amount are known, this problem can be solved in two different ways: (1) by using the method described in the future value section or (2) by using the present value approach described here. Since the future value approach was discussed earlier in this chapter, only the present value approach is used here to solve the problem. Using the table approach

$$p = f(\text{Table Factor for } p_{n,i})$$

and substituting in the formula the known amounts shown in Exhibit D-7, solve the equation as follows:

$$\$3,855.43 = \$10,000.00 \ (\text{Table Factor for } p_{n=10, i = ?})$$

$$\text{Table Factor for } p_{n=10, i=?} = \frac{\$3,855.43}{\$10,000.00} = 0.385543$$

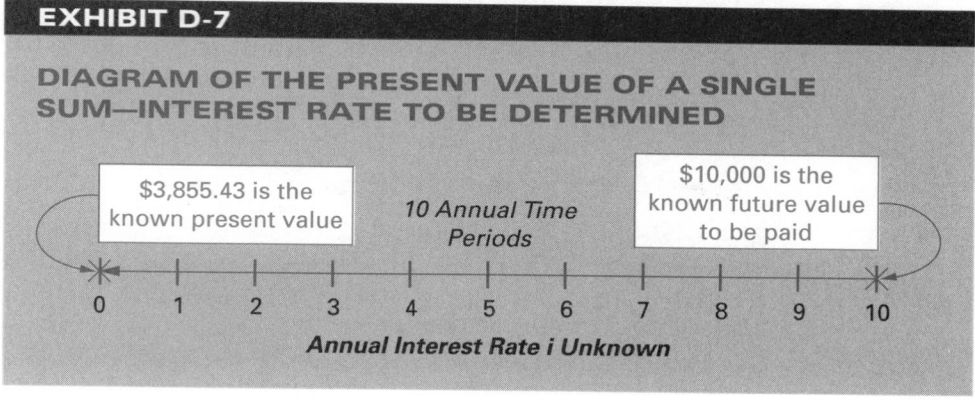

**EXHIBIT D-7**

**DIAGRAM OF THE PRESENT VALUE OF A SINGLE SUM—INTEREST RATE TO BE DETERMINED**

$3,855.43 is the known present value

*10 Annual Time Periods*

$10,000 is the known future value to be paid

0   1   2   3   4   5   6   7   8   9   10

*Annual Interest Rate i Unknown*

The table factor of 0.385543 is the present value of 1 for 10 periods at an unknown interest rate. Using the present-value-of-1 table (Table 3), we look down the periods ($n$) column until we get to 10. Then we move horizontally on the $n = 10$ line to the column table factor closest to 0.385543. If the amount appears in the table, we can determine the interest rate (shown at the top of the column) that produces this amount. In this case, 0.385543 is in the 10% column. Thus the annual rate is 10%. If the factor of 0.385543 does not appear in the table, an interpolation procedure is required to approximate the annual interest rate (see footnote 1).

## MEASUREMENTS INVOLVING AN ANNUITY

An annuity is a series of equal cash flows (deposits, receipts, payments, or withdrawals), often referred to as *rents,* made at regular intervals with interest compounded at a certain rate. The regular intervals between the cash flows may be any time period—for example, a year, a 6-month period, a month, or even 1 day. In solving most measurement problems involving the use of annuities, these four conditions must be present: (1) the periodic cash flows are equal in amount, (2) the time periods between the cash flows are the same length, (3) the interest rate is constant for each time period, and (4) the interest is compounded at the end of each time period.

## FUTURE VALUE OF AN ORDINARY ANNUITY

For the future value of an ordinary annuity, the idea is discussed first, followed by the shortcut approaches and an illustration.

### The Idea

**The future value of an ordinary annuity is determined *immediately* after the last cash flow (rent) in the series is made.** For the first example, assume that Debbi Whitten wants to calculate the future value of 4 rents of $1,000, each with interest compounded annually at 14%, where the first $1,000 cash flow occurs on December 31, 1994 and the last $1,000 occurs on December 31, 1997. This information is presented graphically in Exhibit D-8.

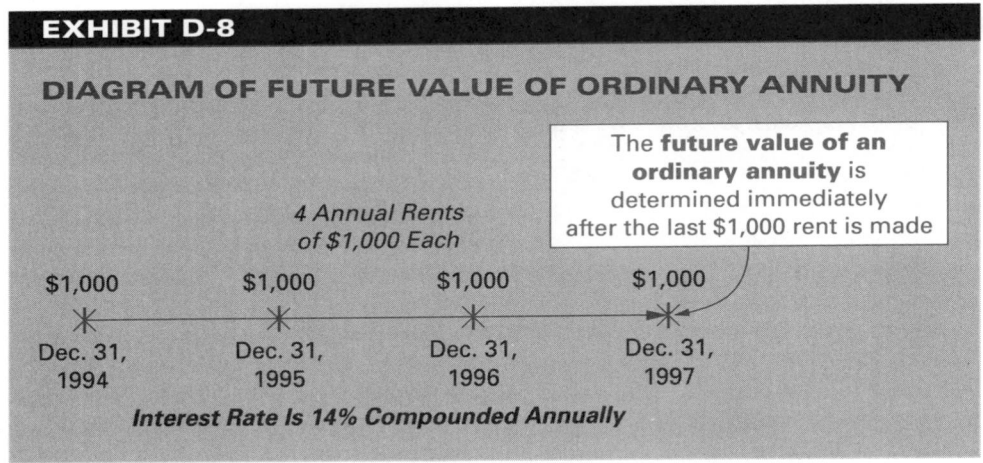

**EXHIBIT D-8**

**DIAGRAM OF FUTURE VALUE OF ORDINARY ANNUITY**

The **future value of an ordinary annuity** is determined immediately after the last $1,000 rent is made

*4 Annual Rents of $1,000 Each*

| $1,000 | $1,000 | $1,000 | $1,000 |
| Dec. 31, 1994 | Dec. 31, 1995 | Dec. 31, 1996 | Dec. 31, 1997 |

*Interest Rate Is 14% Compounded Annually*

In drawing a **time line** such as that in Exhibit D-8, some accountants prefer to add a beginning time segment to the left of the time when the first cash flow (rent) occurs. For example, they would draw the time line for the future amount of an ordinary annuity as shown in Exhibit D-9. This approach is acceptable if it is understood that the time from January 1, 1994 to December 31, 1994 (at that moment of time immediately *before* the first cash flow occurs) is not relevant to the solution of the future value of the ordinary annuity. It is similar to stating a decimal as .4 or 0.4. The zero in front of the decimal may help some individuals to better understand the issue but does not change it. In the case of the future value of an ordinary annuity, however, placing the broken line segment to the left of the first cash flow may lead the reader to think that the cash flows in an ordinary annuity *must occur* at the end of a given year. That statement is *not* true; the cash flows can occur, for example, on March 15 of each year, or November 5 of each year. For the calculation to be the future value of an *ordinary* annuity, the *future value* is determined *immediately after* the last cash flow in the series occurs. Because of the potential hazards of misinterpreting the information, we prefer not to use the broken line segment to the left of the first cash flow in the time lines describing the future value of an ordinary annuity.

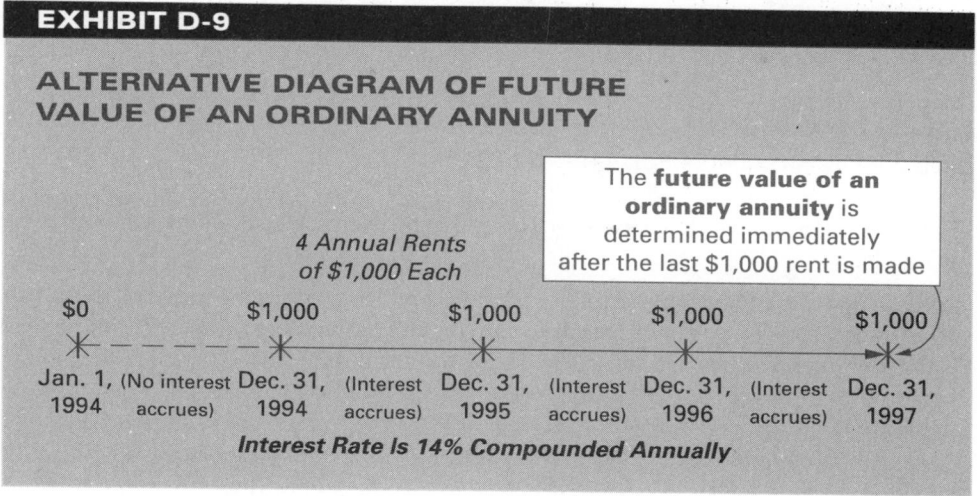

**EXHIBIT D-9**

**ALTERNATIVE DIAGRAM OF FUTURE VALUE OF AN ORDINARY ANNUITY**

The **future value of an ordinary annuity** is determined immediately after the last $1,000 rent is made

*4 Annual Rents of $1,000 Each*

| $0 | $1,000 | $1,000 | $1,000 | $1,000 |
|---|---|---|---|---|
| Jan. 1, (No interest 1994 accrues) | Dec. 31, (Interest 1994 accrues) | Dec. 31, (Interest 1995 accrues) | Dec. 31, (Interest 1996 accrues) | Dec. 31, 1997 |

*Interest Rate Is 14% Compounded Annually*

## Shortcut Approaches

*Formula Approach* The formula for the future value of an ordinary annuity of any amount is:

$$F_0 = R\left[\frac{(1 + i)^n - 1}{i}\right]$$

where $F_0$ = future value of an ordinary annuity of a series of rents of any amount
$R$ = amount of each rent (cash flow)
$n$ = number of rents (not the number of time periods)
$i$ = interest rate for each of the stated time periods

In the example the future value of an ordinary annuity of 4 rents of $1,000 each at 14% compounded annually can be calculated as follows:

$$F_0 = \$1,000\left[\frac{(1.14)^4 - 1}{0.14}\right] = \$4,921.14$$

The formula for the future value of an ordinary annuity with rents of 1 each may be stated as follows:

$$F_{0_{n,i}} = \frac{(1 + i)^n - 1}{i}$$

where $F_{0_{n,i}}$ is the future value of an *ordinary* annuity of $n$ rents of 1 each at interest rate $i$.[2]

---

2. $F_{0_n}$ is often expressed as $F_{0_{n,i}}$, read as "large $F$ sub-zero sub $n$ at $i$."

With the preceding formula for $F_{0_{n,i}}$ it is possible to express another formula for the future value of an ordinary annuity of rents of any size in this manner:

$$F_0 = R(F_{0_{n,i}})$$

In a two-step approach the future value of an ordinary annuity of 4 rents of $1,000 each at 14% compounded annually can be recalculated in the following two steps:

**Step 1**    $F_{0_{n=4,\,i=14\%}} = \dfrac{(1.14)^4 - 1}{0.14} = 4.921144$

**Step 2**    $F_0 = \$1,000(4.921144) = \$4,921.14$

This two-step approach is used to solve the problem when table factors are not available.

*Table Approach* The formula for $F_{0_{n,i}}$ can be used to construct a table of the future value of any series of rents of 1 each for any interest rate. Here the number of rents of 1 and the interest rates are substituted into the formula

$$\frac{(1 + i)^n - 1}{i}$$

The table factors for $F_{0_{n,i}}$ are shown in Table 2 at the end of this Appendix. Turning to Table 2, we may observe the following:

1. The numbers in the first column (*n*) represent the number of rents.

2. The future values are always equal to or larger than the number of rents of 1. For example, the future value of 4 rents of 1 each at 14% is 4.921144. This figure comprises two elements: (a) the number of rents of 1 each *without* any interest and (b) the compound interest on the rents with the exception of the compound interest on the last rent in the series, which in the case of an ordinary annuity *does not* earn any interest.

Since Table 2 reflects the precalculation of $F_{0_{n,i}}$ or

$$\frac{(1 + i)^n - 1}{i}$$

values, the generalized table approach can be stated as follows:

$$F_0 = R(\text{Table Factor for } F_{0_{n,i}})$$

To calculate the future value of an ordinary annuity of 4 rents of $1,000 each at 14%, the $F_{0_{n=4,\,i=14\%}}$ factor is found in the future value of an ordinary annuity of 1 table (Table 2); it is 4.921144. Then the amount of each rent, here $1,000, is multiplied by the Table 2 factor to obtain the future value of $4,921.14:

$$F_0 = \$1,000(4.921144) = \$4,921.14$$

## Summary and Illustration

Several kinds of problems can be solved by the use of the future value of an ordinary annuity of 1 table such as (1) the calculation of the future value when the rents and interest rate are known (the preceding problem); (2) the calculation of the value of each rent where the number of rents, interest rate, and future value are known; (3) the calculation of the number of rents when the amount of each rent, the interest rate, and the future value are known; and (4) the calculation of an unknown interest rate when the rents and the future value are known. To demonstrate the analysis that is used in the solution of all problems, item (2) is illustrated as follows.

*Example: Determining the Amount of Each Rent to Accumulate a Fund to Retire Debt* At the beginning of 1994 the Rexson Company issued 10-year bonds with a face value of $1,000,000 due on December 31, 2003. The company will accumulate a fund to retire these bonds at maturity. It will make annual deposits to the fund beginning on December 31, 1994. How much must the company deposit each year, assuming that the fund will earn 12% interest compounded annually?

The facts of the problem are shown in Exhibit D-10. The future value and the compound interest rate are known. The amount of each of the 10 rents is the unknown factor. Starting with the formula

$$F_0 = R(\text{Table Factor for } F_0)$$

and then shifting the elements and substituting the known amount and applicable table factor (from Table 2), the amount of each rent (the annual deposit) is determined to be $56,984.16:

$$R = \frac{F_0}{\text{Table Factor for } F_{0_{n,i}}}$$

$$= \frac{F_0}{\text{Table Factor for } F_{0_{n=10,\, i\, =\, 12\%}}}$$

$$= \frac{\$1,000,000}{17.548735}$$

$$= \$56,984.16$$

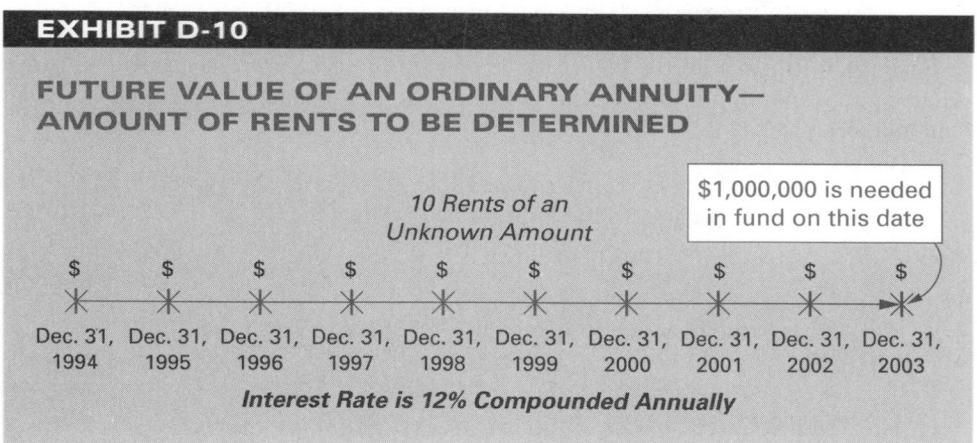

**EXHIBIT D-10**

**FUTURE VALUE OF AN ORDINARY ANNUITY—
AMOUNT OF RENTS TO BE DETERMINED**

10 Rents of an Unknown Amount

$1,000,000 is needed in fund on this date

$      $      $      $      $      $      $      $      $      $

Dec. 31, Dec. 31, Dec. 31, Dec. 31, Dec. 31, Dec. 31, Dec. 31, Dec. 31, Dec. 31, Dec. 31,
1994     1995     1996     1997     1998     1999     2000     2001     2002     2003

*Interest Rate is 12% Compounded Annually*

The 10 annual deposits of $56,984.16 plus the compound interest will accumulate to $1,000,000 by December 31, 2004.

# FUTURE VALUE OF AN ANNUITY DUE

For the future value of an annuity due, the idea is discussed first, followed by the solution approach.

### The Idea

**The future value of an annuity due ($F_d$) is determined 1 period after the last cash flow (rent) in the series.** For example, assume that Ronald Jacobson deposits in a fund 4 payments of $1,000 each beginning December 31, 1994, with the last deposit being made on December 31, 1997. How much will be in the fund on December 31, 1998, 1 year after the final payment has been made, if the fund earns interest at 14% compounded annually? The facts of this problem are presented in Exhibit D-11.

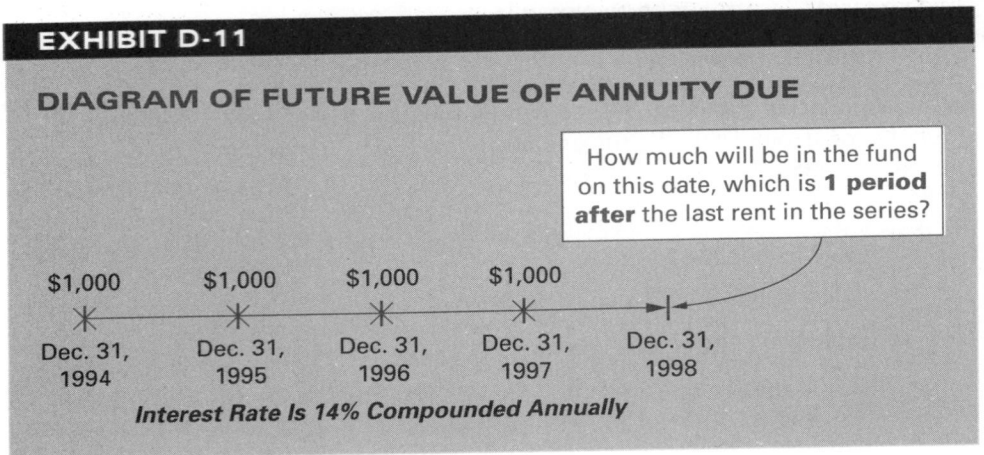

**EXHIBIT D-11**

**DIAGRAM OF FUTURE VALUE OF ANNUITY DUE**

How much will be in the fund on this date, which is **1 period after** the last rent in the series?

| $1,000 | $1,000 | $1,000 | $1,000 | |
| Dec. 31, 1994 | Dec. 31, 1995 | Dec. 31, 1996 | Dec. 31, 1997 | Dec. 31, 1998 |

*Interest Rate Is 14% Compounded Annually*

### Solution Approach

By observing the information contained in Exhibits D-11 and D-8, we can determine a quick way to compute the future value of an annuity due.[3] When only the future value of an *ordinary* annuity table is available, we can use the table factors by taking the following steps:

**Step 1.**   In the *ordinary* annuity table (Table 2), look up the value of $n + 1$ rents at 14% or the value of 5 rents at 14%.     6.610104

**Step 2.**   Then subtract 1 without interest from the value obtained in Step 1.     (1.000000)

This is the converted future value table factor for

$F_{d_{n=4, i = 14\%}}$     5.610104

**Step 3.**   Multiply the amount of each rent, here $1,000, by the converted table factor for $F_{d_{n=4, i=14\%}}$ determined in Step 2:

$F_d = \$1,000(5.610104) = \$5,610.10$

---

3. An alternative approach is to multiply the future value of an ordinary annuity factor by 1 plus the interest rate. Thus, the future value in this example would be computed as $1,000 × (4.921144 × 1.14) = $5,610.10.

Tables of the future value of an annuity due of rents of 1 each are available in some mathematics and finance books but not in this book. Hence these values must be calculated by the use of the tables of the future value of an *ordinary* annuity. As illustrated previously, **the general rule is to use the future value of an ordinary annuity factor for *n* + 1 rents and subtract 1 from the factor.** (Note that we do include in this Appendix a present value of an annuity due table, as discussed later.)

## PRESENT VALUE OF AN ANNUITY

**The present value of an annuity is the present value of a series of equal cash flows (rents) that occur in the future.** In other words, it is the amount that must be invested now and, if left to earn compound interest, will provide for a receipt or payment of a series of equal rents at regular intervals. Over time the present value balance is *increased* periodically for interest and is *decreased* periodically for each receipt or payment. Thus the last rent in the series exhausts the balance on deposit.

The present value of an annuity concept is frequently used in reporting many items in the financial statements as stated in the introduction to this Appendix. Because of the importance of the present value of an annuity, we will discuss the (1) present value of an ordinary annuity, (2) present value of an annuity due, and (3) present value of a deferred annuity.

## PRESENT VALUE OF AN ORDINARY ANNUITY

For the present value of an ordinary annuity, the idea is discussed first, followed by the shortcut approaches and an illustration.

### The Idea

**The present value of an ordinary annuity is determined 1 period before the first cash flow (rent) in the series is made.** For example, assume that Kyle Vasby wants to calculate the present value on January 1, 1995 of 4 future withdrawals of $1,000, with the first withdrawal being made on December 31, 1995, 1 year after the determination of the present value. The applicable interest rate is 14% compounded annually. This information is presented graphically in Exhibit D-12.

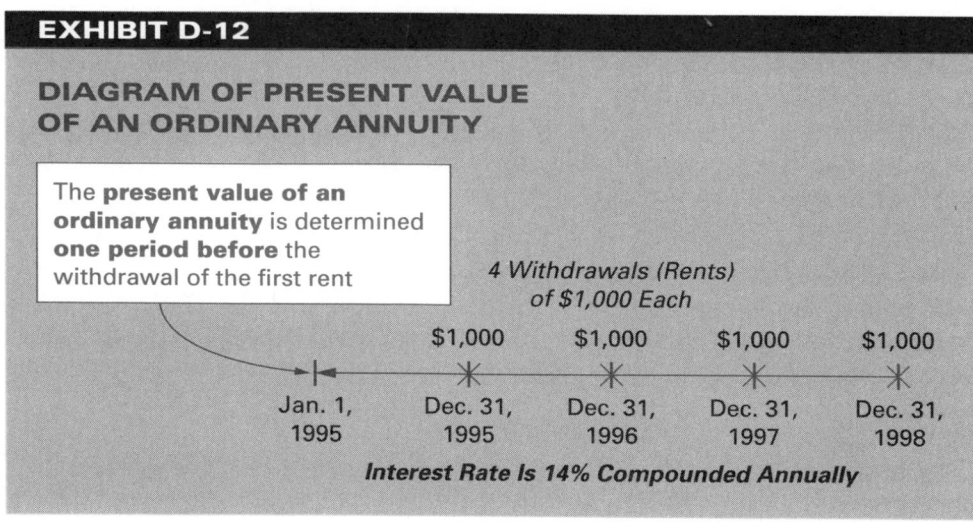

**EXHIBIT D-12**

**DIAGRAM OF PRESENT VALUE OF AN ORDINARY ANNUITY**

The **present value of an ordinary annuity** is determined **one period before** the withdrawal of the first rent

4 Withdrawals (Rents) of $1,000 Each

| | $1,000 | $1,000 | $1,000 | $1,000 |

Jan. 1, 1995   Dec. 31, 1995   Dec. 31, 1996   Dec. 31, 1997   Dec. 31, 1998

*Interest Rate Is 14% Compounded Annually*

## Solution by Determining the Present Value of a Series of Single Sums

The solution to this problem can be obtained by using information on the present value of a single sum. For instance, the answer can be calculated in the following two steps: (1) determine the present value of 4 individual rents of 1 each for 1, 2, 3, and 4 years, as shown in Exhibit D-13, and (2) then multiply the final results of the summation by $1,000.

**Step 1.**     The present value of 4 rents of 1 for 1, 2, 3, and 4 years discounted at 14% is determined in Exhibit D-13.

**Step 2.**     Now it is possible to determine the present value of the 4 rents of $1,000 each by multiplying the $1,000 by 2.913713:

$1,000 × 2.913713 = $2,913.71

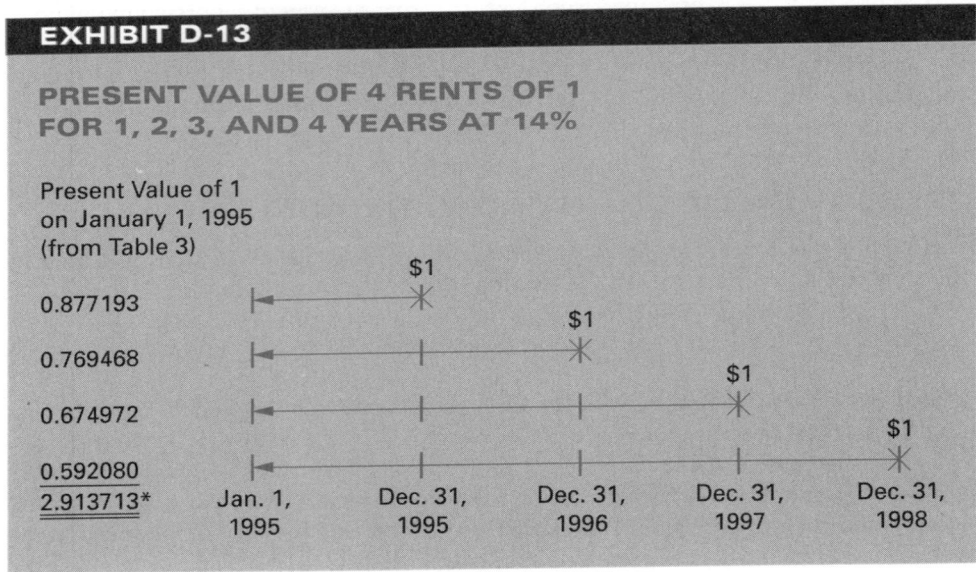

**EXHIBIT D-13**

**PRESENT VALUE OF 4 RENTS OF 1 FOR 1, 2, 3, AND 4 YEARS AT 14%**

Present Value of 1 on January 1, 1995 (from Table 3)

0.877193
0.769468
0.674972
0.592080
2.913713*

Jan. 1, 1995    Dec. 31, 1995    Dec. 31, 1996    Dec. 31, 1997    Dec. 31, 1998

\* The value of 2.913713 is slightly larger than the table factor for $P_{0_{n=4, \, i=14\%}}$ of 2.913712 in Table 4 discussed later in this section; this is the result of rounding each of the four table factors for $p_{n,i}$.

The present value on January 1, 1995 is $2,913.71; or it can be said that $2,913.71 must be invested on January 1, 1995 to provide for 4 withdrawals of $1,000 each starting on December 31, 1995, given an interest rate of 14%.

## Shortcut Approaches

*Formula Approach* Even though the preceding approach can be used, it is time-consuming for calculations involving a large number of rents. The formula for the present value of an ordinary annuity of any amount is:

$$P_0 = R \left[ \frac{1 - \dfrac{1}{(1 + i)^n}}{i} \right]$$

where $P_0$ = present value of an ordinary annuity of a series of rents of any amount
$R$ = amount of each rent (cash flow)
$n$ = number of rents (not the number of time periods)
$i$ = interest rate for each of the stated time periods

In the example the present value of an ordinary annuity of 4 rents of $1,000 each at 14% compounded annually can be calculated as follows:

$$P_0 = \$1,000 \left[ \frac{1 - \dfrac{1}{(1.14)^4}}{0.14} \right] = \$2,913.71$$

Several observations can be drawn from these calculations and formula:

1. The results are the same as those produced in the first approach, $2,913.71.

2. The formula is developed from the formulas for both the future value of $1(f)$ and the present value of $1(p)$:

$$(1 + i)^n = f$$

$$\frac{1}{(1 + i)^n} = p$$

3. Thus the formula can be restated as follows:

$$P_0 = R\left(\frac{1 - p}{i}\right)$$

The formula for the present value of an ordinary annuity can be converted to that for a series of rents of 1 each as follows:

$$P_{0_{n,i}} = \left[ \frac{1 - \dfrac{1}{(1 + i)^n}}{i} \right]$$

where $P_{0_{n,i}}$ is the present value of an ordinary annuity of $n$ rents of 1 each at interest rate $i$.[4] This formula can be expressed for the present value of an ordinary annuity of rents of *any size* in this manner:

$$P_0 = R(P_{0_{n,i}})$$

In a two-step approach the present value of 4 future withdrawals of $1,000 each discounted at 14% can be recalculated in the following two steps:

**Step 1** $\quad P_{0_{n=4, i=14\%}} = \left[ \dfrac{1 - \dfrac{1}{1.14^4}}{0.14} \right] = 2.913712$

**Step 2** $\quad P_0 = \$1,000(2.913712) = \$2,913.71$

This calculation is exactly the same as that of the first formula, except that the process is divided into two steps. The two-step approach is the one used when tables of the present value of an ordinary annuity of 1 are available.

---

4. $P_{0_{n,i}}$ is often stated as $P_{0_{n,i}}$, read as "large $P$ sub-zero sub $n$ at $i$."

*Table Approach* The formula for $P_{0_{n,i}}$ can be used to construct a table of the present value of any series of rents of 1 each for any interest rate. All that is necessary is to substitute in the formula the desired number of rents for the various required interest rates. These precalculations of the $P_{0_{n,i}}$ table factors for numerous rents and selected interest rates are presented in Table 4 at the end of the Appendix. Turning to Table 4, we may observe the following:

1. The numbers in the first column ($n$) represent the number of rents of 1 each. In this calculation the number of rents and time periods are equal.

2. The present value amounts are always smaller than the number of rents of 1. For example, the present value of 3 rents of 1 at 2% is 2.883883.

Since Table 4 reflects the precalculation of $P_{0_{n,i}}$ or

$$\frac{1 - \dfrac{1}{(1 + i)^n}}{i}$$

the generalized table approach can be stated as follows:

$$P_0 = R(\text{Table Factor for } P_{0_{n,i}})$$

Thus, to calculate the present value on January 1, 1995 of 4 future withdrawals of $1,000 discounted at 14% with the first rent being withdrawn on December 31, 1995, first we must look up the $P_{0_{n=4, i=14\%}}$ value in the present value of an ordinary annuity of 1 table (Table 4); it is 2.913712. This factor is then multiplied by $1,000 to determine the present value figure of $2,913.71:

$$P_0 = \$1,000(2.913712) = \$2,913.71$$

Over the 4 periods, the annuity yields interest each period as follows:

| Period | Beginning Balance | Interest | Rent | Ending Balance |
|--------|-------------------|----------|------|----------------|
| 1 | $2,913.71 | $407.92 | $(1,000) | $2,321.63 |
| 2 | 2,321.63 | 325.03 | (1,000) | 1,646.66 |
| 3 | 1,646.66 | 230.53 | (1,000) | 877.19 |
| 4 | 877.19 | 122.81 | (1,000) | 0 |

## Summary and Illustration

Several kinds of problems can be solved by the use of the present value of an ordinary annuity of 1 table. One additional example is presented: a problem involving the calculation of the periodic rents when the present value and interest rate are known.

*Example: Determining the Value of Periodic Rents When the Present Value Is Known* Suppose that on January 1, 1995 Rex Company borrows $100,000 to finance a plant expansion project. It plans to pay this amount back with interest at 12% in equal annual payments over a 10-year period, with the first payment being due on December 31, 1995. What is the amount of each payment?

The facts of the problem are shown in Exhibit D-14. The present value and the compound interest rate are known. The amount of each of the 10 rents is the unknown item and is determined to be $17,698.42:

$$R = \frac{P_0}{\text{Table Factor for } P_{0_{n,i}}}$$

$$= \frac{P_0}{\text{Table Factor for } P_{0_{n=10,\, i=12\%}}}$$

$$= \frac{\$100,000}{5.650223}$$

$$= \$17,698.42$$

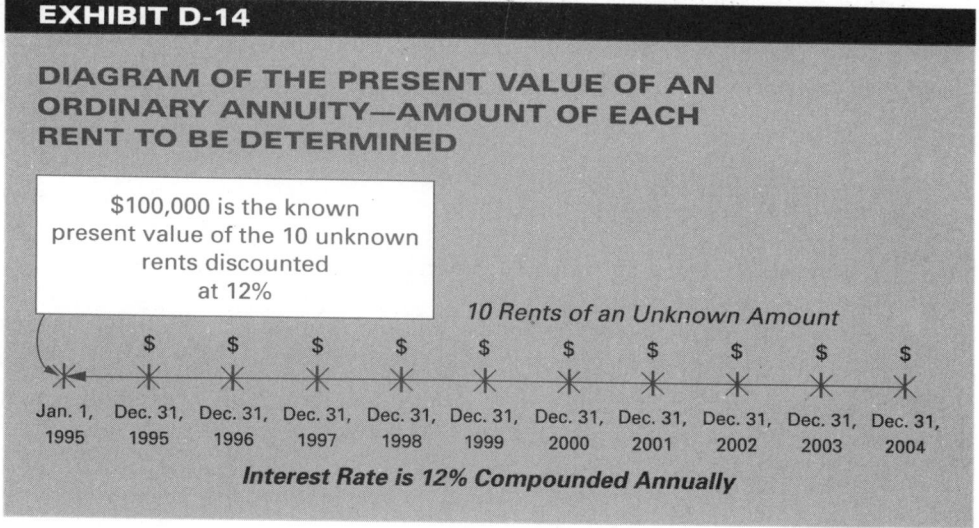

**EXHIBIT D-14**

**DIAGRAM OF THE PRESENT VALUE OF AN ORDINARY ANNUITY—AMOUNT OF EACH RENT TO BE DETERMINED**

$100,000 is the known present value of the 10 unknown rents discounted at 12%

*10 Rents of an Unknown Amount*

| $ | $ | $ | $ | $ | $ | $ | $ | $ | $ |

| Jan. 1, 1995 | Dec. 31, 1995 | Dec. 31, 1996 | Dec. 31, 1997 | Dec. 31, 1998 | Dec. 31, 1999 | Dec. 31, 2000 | Dec. 31, 2001 | Dec. 31, 2002 | Dec. 31, 2003 | Dec. 31, 2004 |

*Interest Rate is 12% Compounded Annually*

Remember that each of these payments of $17,698.42 includes (1) a payment of annual interest and (2) a retirement of debt principal. For example, the interest for 1995 is $12,000 (12% × $100,000). Thus the amount of the payment on principal is $5,698.42 ($17,698.42 − $12,000). For the year 1996 the interest is $11,316.19 [12% × ($100,000 − $5,698.42)], and the retirement of principal is $6,382.23 ($17,698.42 − $11,316.19). The *last* payment of $17,698.42, which will be made on December 31, 2004, will be sufficient to retire the remaining principal and to pay the interest for the tenth year.

## PRESENT VALUE OF AN ANNUITY DUE

**The present value of an annuity due ($P_d$) is determined on the date of the first cash flow (rent) in the series.** For example, assume that Barbara Livingston wants to calculate the present value of an annuity on December 31, 1994, which will permit 4 annual future receipts (rents) of $1,000 each, the first to be received on December 31, 1994. The interest rate is 14% compounded annually. The facts of this problem are presented in Exhibit D-15.

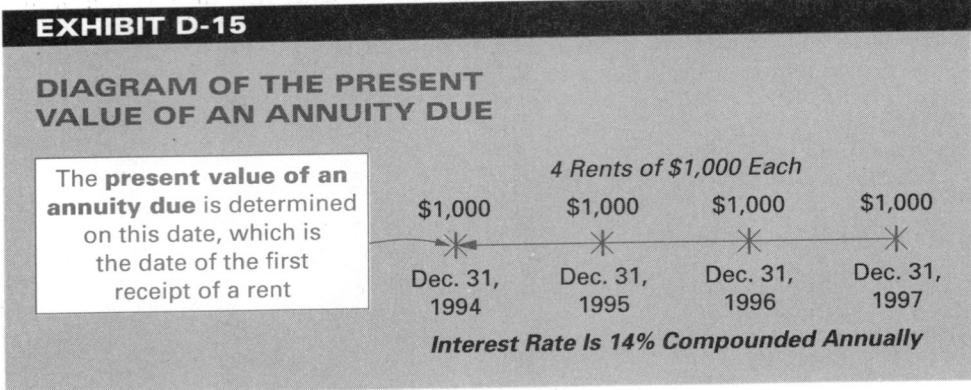

**EXHIBIT D-15**

**DIAGRAM OF THE PRESENT VALUE OF AN ANNUITY DUE**

The **present value of an annuity due** is determined on this date, which is the date of the first receipt of a rent

*4 Rents of $1,000 Each*

| $1,000 | $1,000 | $1,000 | $1,000 |
|--------|--------|--------|--------|
| Dec. 31, 1994 | Dec. 31, 1995 | Dec. 31, 1996 | Dec. 31, 1997 |

*Interest Rate Is 14% Compounded Annually*

## Shortcut Approaches

*Formula Approach* The formula for the present value of an annuity due of any amount is

$$P_d = R \left[ \frac{1 - \dfrac{1}{(1 + i)^{n-1}}}{i} + 1 \right]$$

where $P_d$ = present value of an ordinary annuity of a series of rents of any amount
$\quad\quad R$ = amount of each rent (cash flow)
$\quad\quad n$ = number of rents (not the number of time periods)
$\quad\quad i$ = interest rate for each of the stated time periods

In the example the present value of an annuity due of 4 rents of $1,000 each at 14% compounded annually can be calculated as follows:

$$P_d = \$1,000 \left[ \frac{1 - \dfrac{1}{1.14^3}}{0.14} + 1 \right] = \$3,321.63$$

The formula for the present value of an annuity due with rents of 1 each may be stated as follows:

$$P_{d_{n,i}} = \left[ \frac{1 - \dfrac{1}{(1 + i)^{n-1}}}{i} + 1 \right]$$

where $P_{d_{n,i}}$ is the present value of an annuity *due* of $n$ rents of 1 each at interest rate $i$.

With the preceding formula for $P_{d_{n,i}}$ it is possible to express another formula for the future value of an ordinary annuity of rents of any size in this manner:

$$P_d = R \left( P_{d_{n,i}} \right)$$

In a two-step approach the present value of an annuity due of 4 rents of $1,000 each at 14% compounded annually can be recalculated in the following two steps:

**Step 1** $\quad P_{d_{n=4,\, i=14\%}} = \left[ \dfrac{1 - \dfrac{1}{1.14^3}}{0.14} + 1 \right] = 3.321632$

**Step 2** $\quad P_d = \$1,000(3.321632) = \$3,321.63$

This two-step approach is used to solve the problem when table factors are not available.

*Table Approach* The formula for $P_{d_{n,i}}$ can be used to construct a table of the future value of any series of rents of 1 each for any interest rate. The table factors for $P_{d_{n,i}}$ are shown in Table 5 at the end of this Appendix. Since Table 5 reflects the precalculation of $P_{d_{n,i}}$ or

$$\frac{1 - \dfrac{1}{(1 + i)^{n-1}}}{i} + 1$$

values, the generalized table approach can be stated as follows:

$$P_d = R(\text{Table Factor for } P_{d_{n,i}})$$

To calculate the present value of an annuity due of 4 rents of $1,000 each at 14%, the $P_{d_{n=4, i=14\%}}$ factor is found in the present value of an annuity due table (Table 5); it is 3.321632. Then the amount of each rent, here $1,000, is multiplied by the Table 5 factor to obtain the present value of $3,321.63:

$$P_d = \$1,000(3.321632) = \$3,321.63$$

*Alternative Table Approach* By observing the information contained in Exhibits D-15 and D-12, we can determine another way to compute the present value of an annuity due.[5] When only the present value of an *ordinary* annuity table is available, we can use the table factors to determine the present value of an annuity due by taking the following steps:

| | | |
|---|---|---|
| **Step 1.** | In the ordinary annuity table (Table 4), look up the present value of $n - 1$ rents at 14% or the value of 3 rents at 14%. | 2.321632 |
| **Step 2.** | Then add 1 without interest to the value obtained in Step 1. | (1.000000) |
| | This is the converted present value table factor for $P_{d_{n=4, i=14\%}}$. | 3.321632 |
| **Step 3.** | Multiply the amount of each rent, here $1,000, by the converted table factor for $P_{d_{n=4, i=14\%}}$ determined in Step 2: | |

$$P_d = \$1,000(3.321632) = \$3,321.63$$

---

5. An alternative approach is to multiply the present value of an ordinary annuity factor by 1 plus the interest rate which is consistent with the formula:

$$\frac{1 - \dfrac{1}{(1 + i)^n}}{i} \times [1 + i]$$

Thus, the present value in this example would be computed as $1,000 × (2.913712 × 1.14) = $3,321.63.

Thus, if the present value of an annuity due is calculated by the use of tables of the present value of an *ordinary* annuity, **the general rule is to use present value of an ordinary annuity factor for *n*-1 rents and add 1 to the factor.**

## Another Application

Besides determining the present value of an annuity due where the amount of each rent is known, other types of problems can be solved by using the preceding approaches. Suppose, for example, that Katherine Spruill purchases on January 1, 1995 an item that costs $10,000. She is allowed to pay for this item in 10 equal annual installments with the first installment being made on January 1, 1995 as a down payment. The equal installments are to include interest at 16% on the unpaid balance at the beginning of each year. After the interest is deducted, the balance of each payment reduces the principal of the debt. This problem involves the present value of an annuity due. It requires the determination of the amount of each of 10 rents that have a present value of $10,000 when discounted at an annual rate of 16%. These facts are shown graphically in Exhibit D-16.

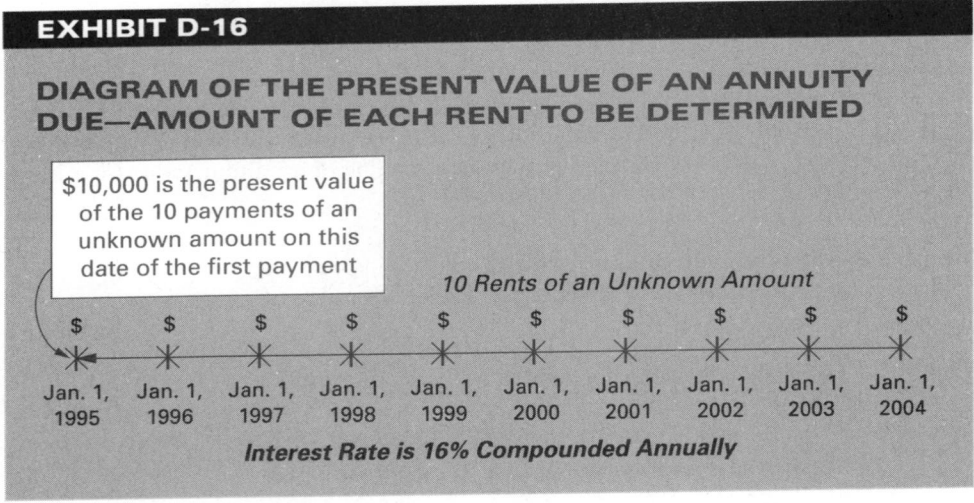

**EXHIBIT D-16**

**DIAGRAM OF THE PRESENT VALUE OF AN ANNUITY DUE—AMOUNT OF EACH RENT TO BE DETERMINED**

$10,000 is the present value of the 10 payments of an unknown amount on this date of the first payment

*10 Rents of an Unknown Amount*

$   $   $   $   $   $   $   $   $   $

Jan. 1, 1995   Jan. 1, 1996   Jan. 1, 1997   Jan. 1, 1998   Jan. 1, 1999   Jan. 1, 2000   Jan. 1, 2001   Jan. 1, 2002   Jan. 1, 2003   Jan. 1, 2004

*Interest Rate is 16% Compounded Annually*

The solution to this problem requires the rearrangement of the present value of an annuity due formula:

$$R = \frac{P_0}{\text{Table Factor for } P_{d_{n,i}}}$$

$$= \frac{\$10,000}{5.606544} = \$1,783.63$$

The down payment of $1,783.63 plus 9 more payments of this same amount will retire the principal in 9 years plus pay interest at 16% on the balance of the principal outstanding at the beginning of each year.

# PRESENT VALUE OF A DEFERRED ORDINARY ANNUITY

For the present value of a deferred ordinary annuity, the idea is discussed first, followed by illustrations.

## The Idea

The present value of a deferred ordinary annuity ($P_{deferred}$) is determined on a date 2 or more periods before the first cash flow (rent) in the series. Suppose, for example, that Helen Swain buys an annuity on January 1, 1995 that yields her 4 annual rents of $1,000 each, with the first rent to be received on January 1, 1999. The interest rate is 14% compounded annually. What is the cost of the annuity—that is, what is the present value on January 1, 1995 of the 4 rents of $1,000 each to be received on January 1, 1999, 2000, 2001, and 2002—discounted at 14%? The facts of this problem are shown diagrammatically in Exhibit D-17.

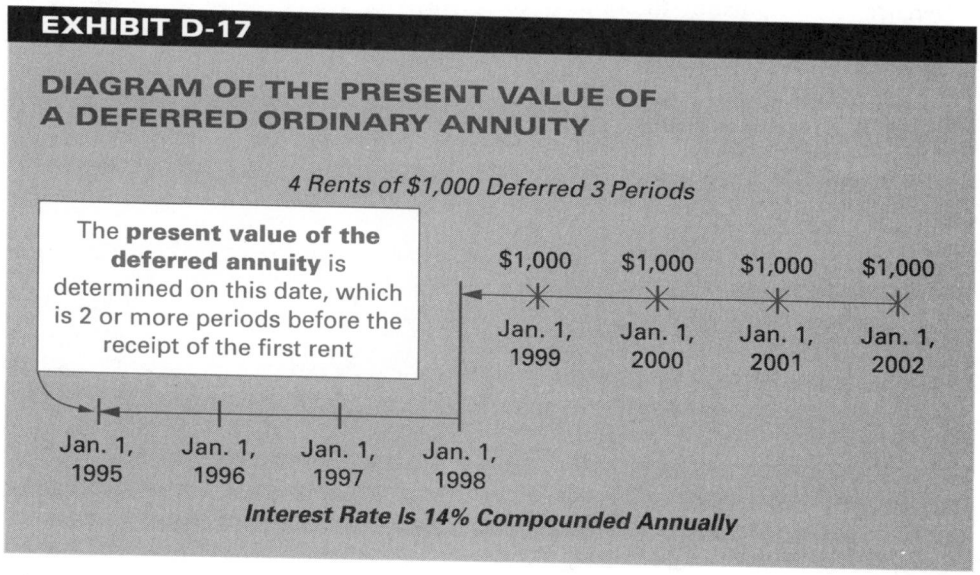

**EXHIBIT D-17**

**DIAGRAM OF THE PRESENT VALUE OF A DEFERRED ORDINARY ANNUITY**

*4 Rents of $1,000 Deferred 3 Periods*

The **present value of the deferred annuity** is determined on this date, which is 2 or more periods before the receipt of the first rent

$1,000   $1,000   $1,000   $1,000

Jan. 1, 1999   Jan. 1, 2000   Jan. 1, 2001   Jan. 1, 2002

Jan. 1, 1995   Jan. 1, 1996   Jan. 1, 1997   Jan. 1, 1998

*Interest Rate Is 14% Compounded Annually*

There are two possible ways to compute the present value of a deferred annuity. The first method involves a combination of the present value of an ordinary annuity ($P_0$) and the present value of a single sum due in the future ($p$). For the stated problem it is necessary to determine first the present value of an *ordinary* annuity of 4 rents of $1,000 each in order to find a single present value figure discounted to January 1, 1998. Note that, because the present value of an ordinary annuity table is used, the present value of the 4 rents is computed on January 1, 1998, *not* January 1, 1999. That single sum is discounted for 3 more periods at 14% to arrive at the present value on January 1, 1995. Using the table factors of $1 each, the present value can be stated as follows:

$$P_{deferred} = R[(P_{0_{n,i}})(p_{k,i})]$$

where $P_{0_{n,i}}$ = present value of the ordinary annuity of the $n$ rents of 1 at the given interest rate $i$

$p_{k,i}$ = present value of the single sum of 1 for $k$ periods of deferment

Substituting appropriate table factors from Tables 4 and 3, respectively, in this formula, the following solution is obtained:

$$P_{deferred} = R[(P_{0_{n=4, i=14\%}})(p_{k=3, i=14\%})]$$
$$= \$1,000[(2.913712)(0.674972)]$$
$$= \$1,966.67$$

An alternative approach involves a combination of two ordinary annuities. For example, it is possible to calculate the present value of an ordinary annuity of $n + k$ rents of 1. From this amount is subtracted the present value of the $k$ (the period of deferment, which is 3 in this example) rents of 1. This procedure removes the rents that were not available to be received; yet the discount factor for the 3 periods of deferments on the 4 rents that are to be received remains in the calculated factor. This difference is multiplied by the value of each rent to determine the final present value of the deferred annuity. Exhibit D-18 illustrates this approach.

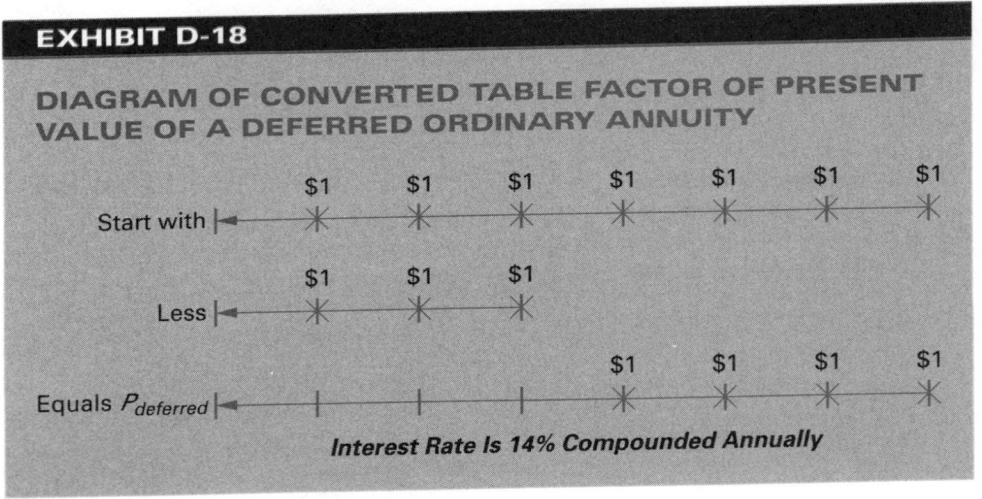

**EXHIBIT D-18**

**DIAGRAM OF CONVERTED TABLE FACTOR OF PRESENT VALUE OF A DEFERRED ORDINARY ANNUITY**

*Interest Rate Is 14% Compounded Annually*

In effect the present value of an ordinary annuity of $n + k$ rents minus the present value of an ordinary annuity of the $k$ rents becomes a converted table factor for the present value of a deferred annuity, as follows:

$$P_{deferred} = R(\text{Converted Table Factor for Present Value of Deferred Annuity of 1})$$

Using the table factors from Table 4, the converted table factor for the deferred ordinary annuity stated in the preceding problem is determined as follows:

$$P_{0_{n+k=7, i=14\%}}(4.288305) - P_{0_{k=3, i=14\%}}(2.321632) = 1.966673$$

The present value of the 4 rents of \$1,000 each deferred 3 periods is \$1,966.67, determined as follows:

$$P_{deferred} = \$1,000(1.966673) = \$1,966.67$$

Observe that the two methods produce the same present value figure. Also, observe that the period of deferment is *only* 3 periods and *not* 4 because the present value of an ordinary annuity table is used (see Exhibit D-18 in the second approach). This assumption *is* required if the problem is to be solved by the use of *ordinary* annuity factors rather than annuity due factors.

## Another Application

Besides determining the present value of a deferred annuity, other types of problems can be solved by using the approaches suggested previously. For example, suppose that David Jones wants to invest $50,000 on January 1, 1995 so that he may withdraw 10 annual rents of equal amounts beginning January 1, 2001. If the fund earns 12% annual interest over its life, what will be the amount of each of the 10 withdrawals?

The facts of this problem are identified in Exhibit D-19. A simpler method to solve this problem is a variation of the second suggested solution. Here the value of R can be determined from the following expression of the present value of a deferred annuity formula:

$$R = \frac{P_{deferred}}{\text{Converted Table Factor for Present Value of Deferred Annuity of 1}}$$

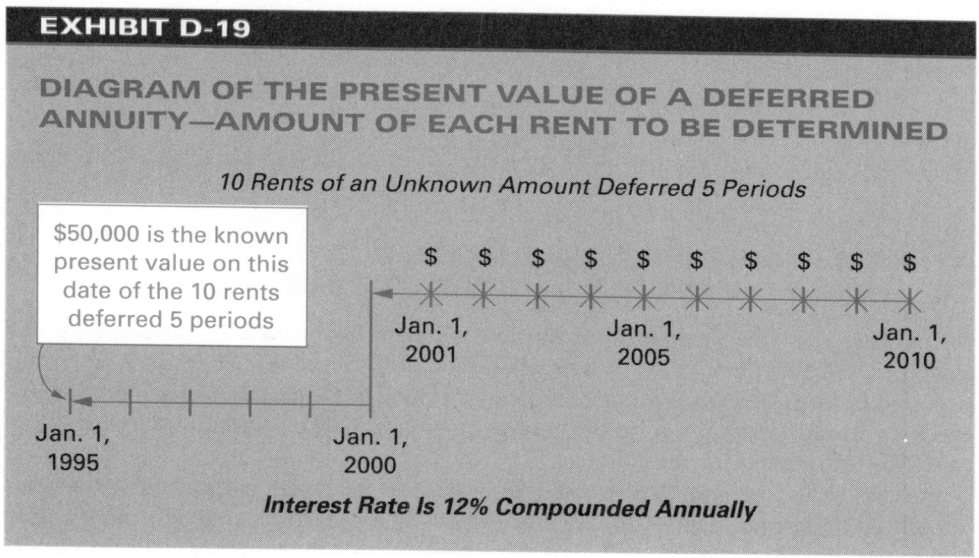

**EXHIBIT D-19**

**DIAGRAM OF THE PRESENT VALUE OF A DEFERRED ANNUITY—AMOUNT OF EACH RENT TO BE DETERMINED**

*10 Rents of an Unknown Amount Deferred 5 Periods*

$50,000 is the known present value on this date of the 10 rents deferred 5 periods

$ $ $ $ $ $ $ $ $ $

Jan. 1, 2001     Jan. 1, 2005     Jan. 1, 2010

Jan. 1, 1995     Jan. 1, 2000

**Interest Rate Is 12% Compounded Annually**

Using Table 4, the converted table factor for 10 rents of 1 each deferred 5 periods at 12% is as follows:

**Converted Table Factor** $= P_{0_{n+k=15,\, i=12\%}}(6.810864) - P_{0_{k=5,\, i=12\%}}(3.604776)$

$$= 3.206088$$

Then the amount of each rent is

$$R = \frac{\$50,000}{3.206088} = \$15,595.33$$

The accuracy of the answer produced by the second approach can be tested using the amount of each rent and the first solution approach suggested previously. The present value of 10 rents of $15,595.33 deferred 5 periods discounted at 12% must be $50,000 if the first solution is correct. The proof can be calculated as follows:

$$P_{deferred} = \$15,595.33[(5.650223)(0.567427)]$$

$$= \$50,000$$

A slight rounding-error difference may be present with this method, since the solution requires the multiplication of two factors, $P_{0_{n,i}}$ and $p_{k,i}$, which are in themselves also rounded.

## SUMMARY OF PRESENT AND FUTURE VALUE CALCULATIONS

The present and future value calculations discussed in this Appendix may be summarized by the following diagrams:

## AN ANALYSIS OF PRESENT VALUE TECHNIQUES IN FINANCIAL REPORTING

Accounting principles have evolved without a unifying objective or rationale for determining when present value techniques should and should not be used. Among the issues to be considered are the use of present value for the initial valuation of assets and liabilities, the amortization of those assets and liabilities, and any subsequent revaluation when interest rates change.

Present value techniques are used in generally accepted accounting principles for certain monetary items. A "monetary item" is money or a claim to money that is not affected by changes in the prices of specific goods or services. For example, a note payable is a monetary item whereas a warranty payable is a nonmonetary item. Those monetary items for which present value techniques are used in generally accepted accounting principles include bonds payable and bond investments, long-term notes payable and receivable, leases, and post-retirement benefits (e.g., pensions). Present value is not used for such items as deferred income taxes. Some accountants argue that present value should be used for nonmonetary items including property, plant, and equipment. However, accounting principles have not been extended to the use of present value for such nonmonetary items. Therefore, present value principles are not used for warranties, unearned revenue, compensated absences, and nonmonetary assets. Each of the previously mentioned topics is discussed in this book.

Most accountants would argue that the use of present value creates a *relevant* accounting measurement. For example, in the situations discussed earlier, the present value amounts are more relevant than, say, the total of the undiscounted cash flows because they represent the equivalent current cash amount. However, the use of present value may create measurements that are less *reliable* (especially if used for nonmonetary items) because the computation requires:

1. The estimation of the future cash flows, including the timing, amount, and risk of those cash flows.

2. The estimation of the interest rate. Interest rates that could be used include the historical rate, the current rate, the average expected rate, the weighted average cost of capital, or the incremental borrowing rate.[6]

3. The degree to which the cash flows from the individual assets may be added (and the liabilities subtracted) to give a measure of the value of the company.

In 1988 the FASB added the topic of "interest methods" to its agenda and in 1990 it issued a related *Discussion Memorandum*.[7] The three major issues being addressed by the FASB are:

1. Under what circumstances should an amount recognized in the financial statements be based on the present value of estimated cash flows?

2. Under what circumstances should accounting allocations over the life of an asset or liability be made using the interest method?

3. Under what circumstances should the interest element that results from the use of present value or an interest method of amortization be reported in the financial statements as an interest revenue or expense?[8]

The FASB has concluded that the objective of the initial measurement of a transaction or event is to represent the fair value of the asset acquired or the liability incurred. Transaction prices, market values, or current costs typically provide the most verifiable information about fair values, and thus are usually preferred. If they are not available, or are not representationally faithful, the present value of the estimated cash flows provides a better estimate of fair value than the undiscounted sum of those cash flows. In summary, present value is used in financial reporting but without a basic concept that determines its use or nonuse. In the next few years, there will be considerable discussion as the FASB proceeds with its deliberations.

---

6. R. Aggarwal and C. H. Gibson, *Discounting in Financial Accounting and Reporting* (Morristown, N.J.: Financial Executives Research Foundation, 1989), p. 45.
7. "Present Value-Based Measurements in Accounting," *FASB Discussion Memorandum* (Norwalk, Conn.: FASB, 1990).
8. *Status Report* (Norwalk, Conn.: FASB, July 9, 1992), p. 2.

## QUESTIONS

**QD-1** Define *interest*. How is the cost of interest similar to the price of any merchandise item? Discuss.

**QD-2** Discuss the following concepts of interest: *simple interest, compound interest, time value of money, discount*.

**QD-3** Distinguish between the *future value of 1* and the *future value of an ordinary annuity of 1*.

**QD-4** What is the interest rate per period and the frequency of compounding per year in each of the following?
a. 18% compounded semiannually
b. 16% compounded quarterly
c. 15% compounded monthly

**QD-5** Distinguish between the *future value of 1* and the *present value of 1* and between the *present value of 1* and the *present value of an ordinary annuity of 1*.

**QD-6** Distinguish between the *future value of an ordinary annuity* and the *future value of an annuity due*. Draw a time line of each.

**QD-7** Distinguish between the *present value of an annuity due* and the *present value of a deferred annuity*. Draw a time line of each.

**QD-8** Explain how each of the following would be solved without tables (in each case, use the quickest approach possible):
a. The present value of $10,000 for 4 years at 10% compounded annually
b. The present value of $5,000 for 5 years at 10% [start with information developed in (a)]
c. The future value of 5 rents of an ordinary annuity of $3,000 each at 10% compound interest.

**QD-9** Potter wishes to deposit a sum that at 12% interest compounded semiannually will permit two withdrawals:

$40,000 at the end of 4 years and $50,000 at the end of 10 years. Analyze the problem to determine the required deposit, stating the procedure to be followed and the tables to be used in developing the solution.

**QD-10** The following factors are taken from the compound interest tables for the same number of time periods and/or rents for the same interest rate:
a. 8.137249
b. 50.980352
c. 6.265060
d. 7.142168
e. 0.122892

Identify each of the five compound interest table factors without reference to the tables. Discuss briefly.

**QD-11** Explain how to determine the converted table factor for any deferred annuity by using the present value of an ordinary annuity table.

**QD-12** Samuel Ames owes $20,000 to a friend. He wants to know how much he would have to pay if the debt were to be paid in 3 annual installments payable at the end of each year which would include interest at 14%. Draw a time line for the problem. Indicate what table is used. Look up the table value and place in a brief formula, but do not solve.

**QD-13** Starting with the given value for $(1.16)^{10} = 4.411435$, describe the fastest way to solve each of the following:
a. $p_{n=10, i=16\%}$
b. $f_{n=20, i=16\%}$
c. $F_{0_{n=10, i=16\%}}$
d. $P_{0_{n=10, i=16\%}}$
e. $F_{0_{n=20, i=16\%}}$

## CASES

**CD-1**    *Cost of Insurance Plans*
The Johnson Company is considering three different time periods for an insurance policy on its main office building. The premiums on a fire insurance policy covering the building for the amount of $2,000,000 on a 1-year, 3-year, and 5-year basis are as follows:

| | |
|---|---|
| One year | $ 4,480 |
| Three years | 11,200 |
| Five years | 17,920 |

In each case the entire premium for the full term of the policy is payable at the beginning of the year in which the policy is purchased.

**Required**
Evaluate the annual cost of each insurance plan for the insured, assuming that money is worth 12% compounded annually. Which plan do you recommend? State the savings that would be made.

**CD-2**    *Acquisition of Equipment*
The manager of the Taylor Company has consulted you, the controller, as to which of the following plans you would recommend in acquiring the use of a piece of heavy equipment:

1. Purchase the equipment and pay immediately a cash price of $36,800. The service life of the heavy

equipment is estimated to be 5 years, with a resale value at the end of that time of $5,500.

2. Lease the equipment at the rate of $9,100 per year for 5 years, payable at the beginning of each year.

**Required**

Assuming that the time value of money is 12%, evaluate the two alternatives and indicate which plan you would recommend to the manager, stating the value of savings that would be made.

### CD-3 *Effective Interest in Various Situations*

On March 1, 1995 the White Company purchased $400,000 worth of inventory on credit with terms of 1/20, n/60. In the past, White has always followed the policy of making payment 1 month (30 days) after the goods are purchased.

A new member of White's staff has indicated that the company he previously worked for never passed up its cash discounts, and he wonders if this is not a sound policy. It was pointed out, however, that if White were to pay the bill on March 20 rather than on March 30, it would have to borrow the necessary funds for the 10 extra days. White's borrowing terms with a local bank were estimated to be at 14% (annual rate) with a 15% compensating balance (a requirement by the bank that White maintain an amount in its account equal to 15% of the loan) for the term of the loan. Most members of White's staff felt that it made little sense to take out a 14% loan with a compensating balance of 15% in order to save 1% on $400,000 by paying the account 10 days earlier than they had planned.

**Required**

1. In terms of simple effective annual interest cost, would it be to White's advantage to borrow the amount necessary to take the 1% discount by paying the bill 10 days early?

2. It has also been pointed out to White that if it does not take advantage of the cash discount, it should wait the entire 60-day period to pay the full bill rather than pay within 30 days. How would your answer to Requirement 1 change if White undertook this policy?

3. Your answer to Requirement 2 indicates that, in relation to Requirement 1, it has become either more desirable or less desirable to borrow in order to take advantage of the 1% cash discount.
   a. If you said *more desirable*, explain why.
   b. If you said *less desirable*, make a similar explanation.

### CD-4 *Future Value of Single Investment and Annuity*

Jane Dough was a teller in a large northeastern bank. She was single and approaching age 30, and she considered herself an honest and upright citizen. After considering what she might do to build a retirement plan for the future, she decided to embezzle $1,500,000. Subsequently she gave herself up to the authorities but did not return

the $1,500,000. She was tried, convicted, and sentenced to 20 years in prison. After completing her 20-year term, she returned the $1,500,000 that she had stolen. She then decided to take a world cruise. On board ship someone asked her how she had accumulated enough money to afford the trip. She replied, "Do you know how much *interest* $1,500,000 will earn in 20 years if invested at an annual rate of 16% compounded quarterly?"

**Required**

1. Determine the answer to Jane Dough's question. The table factor for $f_{n=40, i=4\%}$ is 4.801021.

2. Evaluate Jane's retirement decision, assuming that she could have earned $21,000 each year for each of the 20 years she was in prison. Assume that $11,000 is required each year to cover living expenses and that she could have invested the remaining $10,000 at the end of each year to earn interest at 16% compounded annually.

### CD-5 *Value of a Note*

You have just been promoted to manager at a national CPA firm. On your first job a new junior accountant approaches you with the following situation: He has discovered that the president of the client company has a brother who is both the major stockholder and the president of a local bank. Your client has a $300,000, 5-year note payable to the bank at 4% interest compounded annually. In light of the fact that the going interest rate is 16%, the junior accountant suggests that the note be recorded at its present value using this going rate. The president says that the effective liability is $300,000 and should be reported on the balance sheet at this figure. The note was issued on January 1, 1995 and is due on January 1, 2000.

**Required**

1. Who is correct and why?

2. At what amount should the note have been valued at January 1, 1995 assuming that the junior accountant's assessment is correct?

### CD-6 *Future Value and Present Value Issues*

Jean Perry has a $25,000 whole-life life insurance policy that she began many years ago. She is presently 55 years old. One of the benefits of the policy is that Perry can borrow up to a given amount at 12% interest (2% below the current rate), with the principal due 2 years after the loan is made. The policy states that should Perry default on the principal payment, it will simply be deducted from the amount given her beneficiary when she dies. However, the interest will continue to accrue as long as the note is not paid. Perry has just borrowed $5,000 on this policy to take a vacation in Hawaii.

**Required**

Assuming that a woman of Perry's health is expected to live to be 72, would it be financially advantageous for Perry to repay the principal on the loan in 2 years? Why or why not? (Calculations are not required.)

## MULTIPLE CHOICE

*Select the best answer for each of the following.*

Items 1 through 4 require use of present value tables. The following are the present value factors of $1.00 discounted at 8% for 1 to 5 periods. Each item is based on 8% interest compounded annually from day of deposit to day of withdrawal.

| Periods | Present value of $1 discounted at 8% per period |
|---------|---------------------------------------------------|
| 1 | 0.926 |
| 2 | 0.857 |
| 3 | 0.794 |
| 4 | 0.735 |
| 5 | 0.681 |

MD-1    What amount should be deposited in a bank today to grow to $1,000 three years from today?

a.  $\dfrac{\$1,000}{0.794}$

b.  $\$1,000 \times 0.926 \times 3$

c.  ($1,000 × 0.926) + ($1,000 × 0.857)  + ($1,000 × 0.794)

d.  $1,000 × 0.794

MD-2    What amount should an individual have in his bank account today before withdrawal if he needs $2,000 each year for 4 years with the first withdrawal to be made today and each subsequent withdrawal at 1-year intervals? (He is to have exactly a zero balance in his bank account after the fourth withdrawal.)

a.  $2,000 + ($2,000 × 0.926) + ($2,000 × 0.857) + ($2,000 × 0.794)

b.  $\dfrac{\$2,000}{0.735} \times 4$

c.  ($2,000 × 0.926) + ($2,000 × 0.857) + ($2,000 × 0.794) + ($2,000 × 0.735)

d.  $\dfrac{\$2,000}{0.926} \times 4$

MD-3    If an individual put $3,000 in a savings account today, what amount of cash would be available 2 years from today?

a.  $3,000 × 0.857

b.  $3,000 × 0.857 × 2

c.  $\dfrac{\$3,000}{0.857}$

d.  $\dfrac{\$3,000}{0.926} \times 2$

MD-4    What is the present value today of $4,000 to be received 6 years from today?

a.  $4,000 × 0.926 × 6

b.  $4,000 × 0.794 × 2

c.  $4,000 × 0.681 × 0.926

d.  Cannot be determined from the information given.

MD-5    On January 1, 1995, Kern Company sold a machine to Burns Company. Burns signed a non-interest-bearing note requiring payment of $30,000 annually for 7 years. The first payment was made on January 1, 1995. The prevailing rate of interest for this type of note at the date of issuance was 10%. Information on present value factors is as follows:

| Periods | Present Value of 1 at 10% | Present Value of Ordinary Annuity of 1 at 10% |
|---------|----------------------------|------------------------------------------------|
| 6 | 0.56 | 4.36 |
| 7 | 0.51 | 4.87 |

Kern should record the sale in January 1995 at

a.  $107,100

b.  $130,800

c.  $146,100

d.  $160,800

MD-6 On May 1, 1995, a company purchased a new machine that it does not have to pay for until May 1, 1997. The total payment on May 1, 1997 will include both principal and interest. Assuming interest at a 10% rate, the cost of the machine would be the total payment multiplied by what time value of money concept?
  a.  Future value of annuity of 1          c.  Present value of annuity of 1
  b.  Future value of 1                     d.  Present value of 1

MD-7 An office equipment representative has a machine for sale or lease. If you buy the machine, the cost is $7,596. If you lease the machine, you will have to sign a noncancellable lease and make 5 payments of $2,000 each. The first payment will be paid on the first day of the lease. At the time of the last payment you will receive title to the machine. The present value of an ordinary annuity of $1 is as follows:

| Present Value<br>Number<br>of Periods | 10% | 12% | 16% |
|---|---|---|---|
| 1 | 0.909 | 0.893 | 0.862 |
| 2 | 1.736 | 1.690 | 1.605 |
| 3 | 2.487 | 2.402 | 2.246 |
| 4 | 3.170 | 3.037 | 2.798 |
| 5 | 3.791 | 3.605 | 3.274 |

The interest rate implicit in this lease is approximately
  a.  10%                                   c.  Between 10% and 12%
  b.  12%                                   d.  16%

MD-8 An accountant wishes to find the present value of an annuity of $1 payable at the beginning of each period at 10% for 8 periods. He has only one present value table, which shows the present value of an annuity of $1 payable at the end of each period. To compute the present value factor he needs, the accountant would use the present value factor in the 10% column for
  a.  Seven periods                         c.  Eight periods
  b.  Seven periods and add 1               d.  Nine periods and subtract 1

MD-9 On July 1, 1995, James Rago signed an agreement to operate as a franchisee of Fast Foods, Inc., for an initial franchise fee of $60,000. Of this amount, $20,000 was paid when the agreement was signed and the balance is payable in 4 equal annual payments of $10,000 beginning July 1, 1996. The agreement provides that the down payment is not refundable and no future services are required of the franchisor. Rago's credit rating indicates that he can borrow money at 14% for a loan of this type. Information on present and future value factors is as follows:

Present value of $1 at 14% for 4 periods                        0.59
Future value of $1 at 14% for 4 periods                         1.69
Present value of an ordinary annuity of $1 at 14% for 4 periods    2.91

Rago should record the acquisition cost of the franchise on July 1, 1995 at
  a.  $43,600                               c.  $60,000
  b.  $49,100                               d.  $67,600

MD-10 For which of the following transactions would the use of the present value of an annuity due concept be appropriate in calculating the present value of the asset obtained or liability owed at the date of incurrence?
  a.  A capital lease is entered into with the initial lease payment due one month subsequent to the signing of the lease agreement
  b.  A capital lease is entered into with the initial lease payment due upon the signing of the lease agreement
  c.  A 10-year 8% bond is issued on January 2 with interest payable semiannually on July 1 and January 1 yielding 7%
  d.  A 10-year 8% bond is issued on January 2 with interest payable semiannually on July 1 and January 1 yielding 9%

*(AICPA adapted)*

# EXERCISES

**ED-1**    *Future Value of an Investment and Compound Interest*   Using the future value tables, solve the following:

**Required**
1. What is the value on January 1, 2002 of $40,000 deposited on January 1, 1995 which accumulates interest at 12% compounded annually?
2. What is the value on January 1, 2001 of $10,000 deposited on July 1, 1995 which accumulates interest at 16% compounded quarterly?
3. What is the compound interest on an investment of $6,000 left on deposit for 5 years at 10% compounded annually?

**ED-2**    *Future Value of an Investment*   Hugh Colson deposited $30,000 in a special savings account that provides for interest at the annual rate of 12% compounded semiannually if the deposit is maintained for 4 years.

**Required**
Calculate the balance of the savings account at the end of the 4-year period.

**ED-3**    *Present Value of a Sum and Compound Discount*   Using the present value tables, solve the following problems:

**Required**
1. What is the present value on January 1, 1995 of $40,000 due on January 1, 2000 and discounted at 12% compounded annually?
2. What is the present value on July 1, 1995 of $8,000 due January 1, 2000 and discounted at 16% compounded quarterly?
3. What is the compound discount on $9,000 due at the end of 5 years at 10% compounded annually?

**ED-4**    *Future Value of Annuity*   Using appropriate tables, solve the following future value of annuity problems:

**Required**
1. What is the future value on December 31, 2001 of 7 rents of $10,000 with the first rent being made on December 31, 1995 and interest at 12% being compounded annually?
2. What is the future value on December 31, 2002 of 7 rents of $10,000 with the first rent being made on December 31, 1995 and interest at 12% being compounded annually?

**ED-5**    *Present Value of an Annuity*   Samuel David wants to make 5 equal annual withdrawals of $8,000 from a fund that will earn interest at 10% compounded annually.

**Required**
How much would David have to invest on:
1. January 1, 1995 if the first withdrawal is made on January 1, 1996?
2. January 1, 1995 if the first withdrawal is made on January 1, 1995?

**ED-6**    *Amount of Each Rent*   Six equal annual contributions are made to a fund, with the first deposit on December 31, 1995.

**Required**
Using the future value tables, determine the equal contributions that, if invested at 12% compounded annually, will produce a fund of $30,000, assuming that this sum is desired on December 31, 2000.

**ED-7**    *Amount of an Annuity*   Beginning December 31, 1999, 5 equal annual withdrawals are to be made.

**Required**
Using the appropriate tables, determine the equal annual withdrawals if $25,000 is invested at an interest of 12% compounded annually on
1. December 31, 1998
2. December 31, 1999
3. December 31, 1995

*ED-8*  *Amount of Each Rent*  R. Lee Rouse borrows $10,000 that is to be repaid in 24 equal monthly installments payable at the end of each subsequent month with interest at the rate of 1½% a month.

**Required**

Using the appropriate table, calculate the equal installments.

*ED-9*  *Amount of Each Rent*  On January 1, 1995, Charles Jamison borrows $40,000 from his father to open a business. The son is the beneficiary of a trust created by his favorite aunt from which he will receive $20,000 on January 1, 2005. He signs an agreement to make this amount payable to his father and, further, to pay his father equal annual amounts from January 1, 1996 to January 1, 2004, inclusive, in retirement of the debt. Interest is to be charged at 12%.

**Required**

What are the annual payments?

*ED-10*  *Amount of an Annuity*  Beginning with January 1, 1995, 6 equal deposits are to be made in a fund.

**Required**

Using the appropriate tables, determine the equal deposits if interest at 10% is compounded annually and if $200,000 must be in the fund on

1.  January 1, 2000
2.  January 1, 2001

*ED-11*  *Series of Compound Interest Techniques*  The following are several situations involving compound interest.

**Required**

Using the appropriate table, solve each of the following:

1.  Hope Dearborn invests $40,000 on January 1, 1995 in a savings account that earns interest of 10% compounded semiannually. What will be the amount in the fund on December 31, 2000?
2.  Ben Johnson receives a bonus of $5,000 each year on December 31. He starts depositing his bonus on December 31, 1995 in a savings account that earns interest of 12% compounded annually. What will be the amount in the fund on December 31, 1999 after he deposits his bonus received on that date?
3.  Ron Sewert owes $30,000 on a non-interest-bearing note due January 1, 2005. He offers to pay the amount on January 1, 1995 provided that it is discounted at 10% on a compound annual discount basis. What would he have to pay on January 1, 1995 under this assumption?
4.  June Stickney purchased an annuity on January 1, 1995 which, at a 12% annual rate, would yield $5,000 each June 30 and December 31 for the next 6 years. What must have been the cost of the annuity to Stickney?
5.  Five equal annual contributions are to be made to a fund, the first deposit on December 31, 1995. Determine the equal contributions that, if invested at 10% compounded annually, will produce a fund of $30,000 on December 31, 2000.
6.  Beginning on December 31, 1996, 6 equal annual withdrawals are to be made. Determine the equal annual withdrawals if $12,000 is invested at 10% interest compounded annually on December 31, 1995.

*ED-12*  *Amount of an Annuity*  John Goodheart wishes to provide for 6 annual withdrawals of $3,000 each beginning January 1, 2005. He wishes to make 10 annual deposits beginning January 1, 1995, with the last deposit to be made on January 1, 2004.

**Required**

If the fund earns interest compounded annually at 10%, what is the amount of each of the 10 deposits?

*ED-13*  *Present Value of Leased Asset*  On January 1, 1995 Ashly Farms leased a hay baler from Agrico Tractor Company. Ashly was having cash flow problems, so Agrico drew up the lease to allow Ashly to reestablish itself. The lease requires Ashly to make $3,000 payments on January 1 of each year for 5 years beginning in 1995.

**Required**

Calculate the present value of the cost of the lease payments to Ashly on January 1, 1995. Assume a 12% interest rate.

ED-14   *Number of Rents*   On July 1, 1995 Boston Company purchased a machine at a cost of $80,000. It paid $56,046.06 in cash and signed a 10% note for the difference. This note is to be paid off in annual installments of $5,000 each, payable each July 1, beginning immediately. The $5,000 includes a payment of interest on the balance of the principal at the beginning of each period and a payment on the principal.

**Required**
Calculate the number of annual payments to be made by Boston Company.

## PROBLEMS

PD-1   *Future Value of an Investment*   Several questions involving the future value of a single investment are presented as follows:

**Required**
Using the appropriate tables, solve each of the following:
1. What is the future value on December 31, 1999 of a deposit of $30,000 made on December 31, 1995 assuming interest of 10% compounded annually?
2. What is the future value on December 31, 1999 of a deposit of $10,000 made on December 31, 1995 assuming interest of 16% compounded quarterly?
3. What is the future value on December 31, 1999 of a deposit of $20,000 made on December 31, 1995 assuming interest of 12% compounded semiannually?

PD-2   *Present Value Issues*   Several questions involving the present value of a single sum are presented next.

**Required**
Using the appropriate tables, solve each of the following:
1. What is the present value on January 1, 1995 of $30,000 due on January 1, 1999 and discounted at 10% compounded annually?
2. What is the present value on January 1, 1995 of $40,000 due on January 1, 1999 and discounted at 11% compounded semiannually?
3. What is the present value on January 1, 1995 of $50,000 due on January 1, 1999 and discounted at 16% compounded quarterly?

PD-3   *Future Value Issues*   Several questions involving future values are presented next.

**Required**
Using the appropriate tables, solve each of the following:
1. What is the future value on December 31, 2004 of 10 rents of $30,000 with the first rent being made on December 31, 1995 and interest at 10% being compounded annually?
2. What is the future value on June 30, 2005 of 20 rents of $15,000 with the first rent being made on December 31, 1995 and the annual interest rate of 10% being compounded semiannually?
3. What is the future value on December 31, 2005 of 20 rents of $15,000 with the first rent being made on December 31, 1995 and the annual interest rate of 10% being compounded semiannually?

PD-4   *Amount of Each Rent*   On December 31, 2002 Michael McDowell desires to have $60,000. He plans to make 6 deposits in a fund to provide this amount. Interest is compounded annually at 12%.

**Required**
Compute the equal annual amounts that McDowell must deposit assuming that the first deposit is made on
1. December 31, 1997
2. December 31, 1996

PD-5   *Value of an Annuity*   John Joshua wants to make 5 equal annual withdrawals of $20,000 from a fund that will earn interest at 10% compounded annually.

**Required**

How much would Joshua have to invest on January 1, 1995 if the first withdrawal is made on

1. January 1, 1996?
2. January 1, 1995?
3. January 1, 2000?

PD-6   *Value of an Annuity*   Ralph Benke wants to make 8 equal semiannual withdrawals of $8,000 from a fund that will earn interest at 11% compounded semiannually.

**Required**

How much would Benke have to invest on:

1. January 1, 1995 if the first withdrawal is made on July 1, 1995?
2. July 1, 1995 if the first withdrawal is made on July 1, 1995?
3. January 1, 1995 if the first withdrawal is made on January 1, 1998?

PD-7   *Various Compound Interest Issues*   You are given the following situations:

1. Thomas Petry owes a debt of $8,000 from the purchase of a boat. The debt bears interest of 12% payable annually. Petry desires to pay the debt and interest in 5 annual installments beginning one year hence. Calculate the equal annual installments that will pay off the debt and interest at 12% on the unpaid balance.
2. On January 1, 1995 John Cothran offers to buy Ruth House's used tractor and equipment for $4,000, payable in 10 equal semiannual installments, which are to include payment of 10% interest on the unpaid balance and payment of a portion of the principal, with the first installment to be made on January 1, 1995. Calculate the amount of each of these installments.
3. Nadine Love invests in a $60,000 annuity at 12% compounded annually on March 1, 1995. The first of 15 receipts from the annuity is payable to Love on March 1, 2005, 10 years after the annuity is purchased and on the date Love expects to retire. Calculate the amount of each of the 15 equal annual receipts.

**Required**

Using the appropriate tables, solve each of the preceding situations.

PD-8   *Value of an Annuity*   Several questions involving the value of an annuity are presented next.

**Required**

Using the appropriate tables, solve each of the following:

1. Beginning December 31, 1996, 5 equal withdrawals are to be made. Determine the equal annual withdrawals if $30,000 is invested at 10% interest compounded annually on December 31, 1995.
2. Ten payments of $3,000 are due at annual intervals beginning June 30, 1996. What amount will be accepted in cancellation of this series of payments on June 30, 1995 assuming a discount rate of 14% compounded annually?
3. Ten payments of $2,000 are due at annual intervals beginning December 31, 1995. What amount will be accepted in cancellation of this series of payments on January 1, 1995 assuming a discount rate of 12% compounded annually?

PD-9   *Amount of Each Rent*   On January 1, 1995 Philip Holding invests $40,000 in an annuity to provide 8 equal semiannual payments. Interest is 10%, compounded semiannually.

**Required**

Compute the equal semiannual amounts that Holding will receive, assuming that the first withdrawal is to be received on

1. July 1, 1995
2. January 1, 1995
3. July 1, 1998
4. January 1, 2000

**PD-10**   *Number of Rents*   The following are two independent situations.

1. Houser wishes to accumulate a fund of $40,000 for the purchase of a house and lot. He plans to deposit $4,000 semiannually at the end of each 6 months. Assuming interest at 14% a year compounded semiannually, how many deposits of $4,000 each will be required and what is the amount of the last deposit?
2. On January 1, 1995 Joan Campbell borrows $20,000 from Susan Rone and agrees to repay this amount in payments of $4,000 a year until the debt is paid in full. Payments are to be of an equal amount and are to include interest at 12% on the unpaid balance of principal at the beginning of each period. Assuming that the first payment is to be made on January 1, 1996, determine the number of payments of $4,000 each to be made and the amount of the final payment.

**Required**

Using the appropriate tables, solve each of the preceding situations.

**PD-11**   *Serial Installments; Amounts Applicable to Interest and Principal*   Ronald McDuffie purchases a new automobile at a cost of $12,600. He pays $2,500 down and issues an installment note payable by which he promises to pay the balance in 18 equal monthly installments, which include interest at an annual rate of 18% on the remaining unpaid balance at the beginning of each month, starting with the first month after the purchase.

**Required**

1. Compute the equal installment payments.
2. Compute the interest that will be paid for each of the first 2 periods. Indicate the amount of each payment that will be considered to be a reduction of principal.

**PD-12**   *Determining Loan Repayments*   Rockness needs $40,000 to pay off a loan due on December 31, 2004. His plans included the making of 10 annual deposits beginning on December 31, 1995 in accumulating a fund to pay off the loan. Without making a precise calculation, Rockness made 3 annual deposits of $4,000 each on December 31, 1995, 1996, and 1997, which have been earning interest at 10% compounded annually.

**Required**

What is the equal amount of each of the next 7 deposits for the period December 31, 1998 to December 31, 2004 to reach the fund objective, assuming that the fund will continue to earn interest at 10% compounded annually?

**PD-13**   *Purchase of Asset*   William Thomas intends to purchase a tractor on credit. Two local implement dealers have offered him the following payment plans for identical tractors:

1. Redd Truck & Tractor's plan calls for 5 annual payments of $10,350, with the first payment now and the remaining payments at the beginning of each of the next 4 years.
2. Greene Farm Implements requires semiannual payments of $5,750 at the end of each of the next 10 semiannual periods, with the first payment to be in 6 months.

**Required**

Determine which of the preceding plans offers Thomas the lower present value. The applicable annual interest rate is 12% for both alternatives.

**PD-14**   *Fund to Retire Bonds*   At the beginning of 1995 Shanklin Company issued 15-year bonds with a face value of $1,000,000 due on December 31, 2009. The company desires to accumulate a fund to retire these bonds at maturity by making annual deposits beginning on December 31, 1995.

**Required**

How much must the company deposit each year, assuming that the fund will earn 12% interest a year compounded annually?

**PD-15** *Asset Purchase Price*  BWP, Inc., is considering the purchase of an asset. BWP's required rate of return on new assets is 12%. The expected net cash inflows generated by the new asset are as follows:

| Years | Amount | Nature of the Cash Inflows |
|---|---|---|
| 1–4 | $3,000 | Net operating revenues |
| 5–9 | 2,500 | Net operating revenues |
| 10 | 2,000 | Net operating revenues |
| 10 | 1,000 | Sale of asset |

**Required**

Given that the net cash inflows can be realized, what is the maximum amount BWP should be willing to pay for the new asset? Assume that each cash inflow occurs at the end of the year. (*Contributed by Norma C. Powell*)

**PD-16** *Acquisition of Asset*  SuMar Company purchased a new piece of machinery by paying $2,000 down and agreeing to pay $1,000 at the end of each year for 5 years. The appropriate interest rate is 8%.

**Required**

1. What is the cost of the machinery?
2. Prepare the journal entry to record the purchase of the machinery.
3. Prepare a table that shows the interest and ending balance of the liability each year. (*Contributed by Norma C. Powell*)

**PD-17** *Present Value Issues*  Nello Construction Company has just purchased several major pieces of road-building construction equipment. Since the purchase price is so large, the equipment company is giving Nello an option of choosing one of four different payment plans:

1. $600,000 immediately in cash.
2. $200,000 down payment now; $65,000 per year for 12 years, beginning at the end of the current year.
3. $200,000 down payment now; $25,000 per year for 3 years beginning at the end of the current year; $75,000 per year for 11 years beginning at the end of the fourth year after the purchase.
4. $80,000 now and at the beginning of each of the next 13 years.

**Required**

You have been asked by the Nello Construction Company to decide which payment plan will provide the smallest present value. The expected effective interest rate during the future periods stated above is 12%.

**PD-18** *Comprehensive*  *Part a.* Reproduced in the following table are the first three lines from the 2% columns of each of several tables of mathematical values. For each of the following items, you are to select from among these fragmentary tables the one from which the amount required can be obtained *most directly* (assuming that the complete table was available in each instance):

| Periods | Table A | Table B | Table C | Table D | Table E | Table F |
|---|---|---|---|---|---|---|
| 0 | 1.0000 | | 1.0000 | | | |
| 1 | 0.9804 | 1.0200 | 1.0200 | 1.0000 | 0.9804 | 1.0200 |
| 2 | 0.9612 | 2.0604 | 1.0404 | 0.4950 | 1.9416 | 0.5150 |
| 3 | | 3.1216 | | 0.3268 | 2.8839 | 0.3468 |

1. The amount to which a single sum would accumulate at compound interest by the end of a specified period (interest compounded annually).
2. The amount that must be appropriated at the end of each of a specific number of years to provide for the accumulation, at annually compounded interest, of a certain sum.

3. The amount that must be deposited in a fund that will earn interest at a specified rate, compounded annually, in order to make possible the withdrawal of certain equal sums annually over a specified period starting 1 year from date of deposit.
4. The amount of interest that will accumulate on a single deposit by the end of a specified period (interest compounded semiannually).
5. The amount, net of compound discount, that if paid now would settle a debt of larger amount due at a specified future date.

*Part b.* The following tables of values at 10% interest may be used as needed in answering the questions in this part of the problem.

| Periods | Future Value of 1 at Compound Interest | Present Value of 1 at Compound Interest | Future Value of Annuity of 1 at End of Each Period | Present Value of Annuity of 1 at End of Each Period |
|---|---|---|---|---|
| 1 | 1.100 | 0.9091 | 1.0000 | 0.9091 |
| . | . | . | . | . |
| . | . | . | . | . |
| . | . | . | . | . |
| 6 | 1.7716 | 0.5645 | 7.7156 | 4.3553 |
| 7 | 1.9487 | 0.5132 | 9.4872 | 4.8684 |
| 8 | 2.1436 | 0.4665 | 11.4359 | 5.3349 |
| 9 | 2.3579 | 0.4241 | 13.5795 | 5.7590 |
| 10 | 2.5937 | 0.3855 | 15.9374 | 6.1446 |
| 11 | 2.8531 | 0.3505 | 18.5312 | 6.4951 |
| 12 | 3.1384 | 0.3186 | 21.3843 | 6.8137 |
| 13 | 3.4523 | 0.2897 | 24.5227 | 7.1034 |
| 14 | 3.7975 | 0.2633 | 27.9750 | 7.3667 |
| 15 | 4.1772 | 0.2394 | 31.7725 | 7.6061 |
| 16 | 4.5950 | 0.2176 | 35.9497 | 7.8237 |

1. Your client has made annual payments of $2,500 into a fund at the close of each year for the past 3 years. The fund balance immediately after the third payment totaled $8,275. He has asked you how many more $2,500 annual payments will be required to bring the fund to $22,500, assuming that the fund continues to earn interest at 10% compounded annually. Compute the number of full payments required and the amount of the final payment if it does not require the entire $2,500. Carefully label all computations supporting your answer.
2. Your client wishes to provide for the payment of an obligation of $200,000 due on July 1, 2002. He plans to deposit $20,000 in a special fund each July 1 for 7 years, starting July 1, 1996. He wishes to make an initial deposit on July 1, 1995 of an amount that, with its accumulated interest, will bring the fund up to $200,000 at the maturity of the obligation. He expects that the fund will earn interest at the rate of 10% compounded annually. Compute the amount to be deposited July 1, 1995. Carefully label all computations supporting your answer. (*AICPA adapted*)

PD-19   *Comprehensive*   The following are three independent situations:

1. M. Herman has decided to set up a scholarship fund for students. She is willing to deposit $5,000 in a trust fund at the end of each year for 10 years. She wants the trust fund to then pay annual scholarships at the end of each year for 30 years.
2. Charles Jordy is planning to save for his retirement. He has decided that he can save $3,000 at the end of each year for the next 10 years, $5,000 at the end of each year for years 11 through 20, and $10,000 at the end of each year for years 21 through 30.

3. Patricia Karpas has $200,000 in her savings on the day she retires. She intends to spend $2,000 per month traveling around the world for the next two years, during which her savings will earn 18%, compounded monthly. For the next 5 years, she intends to spend $6,000 every six months, during which her savings will earn 12%, compounded semiannually. For the rest of her life expectancy of 15 years, she wants an annuity to cover her living costs. During this period, her savings will earn 10%, compounded annually. Assume that all payments occur at the end of each period.

### Required

1. In situation 1, how much will the annual scholarships be if the fund can earn 6%? 10%?
2. In situation 2,
   (a) How much will Jordy have at the end of 30 years if his savings can earn 10%? 6%?
   (b) If Jordy expects to live for 20 years in retirement, how much can he spend each year, if his savings earn 10%? 6%?
   (c) How much would Jordy need to invest today to have the same amount available at the time he retires as calculated in 2(a) at 10%? 6%?
3. In situation 3, how much will Karpas's annuity be?

## COMPOUND INTEREST TABLES

**TABLE 1 Future Value of 1:** $f = (1 + i)^n$

**TABLE 2 Future Value of an Ordinary Annuity of 1:**

$$F_0 = \frac{(1 + i)^n - 1}{i}$$

**TABLE 3 Present Value of 1:** $p = \dfrac{1}{(1 + i)^n}$

**TABLE 4 Present Value of an Ordinary Annuity of 1:**

$$P_o = \frac{1 - \dfrac{1}{(1 + i)^n}}{i}$$

**TABLE 5 Present Value of Annuity Due:** $P_d = \dfrac{1 - \dfrac{1}{(1 + i)^{n-1}}}{i} + 1$

## Table 1 FUTURE VALUE OF 1: $f = (1 + i)^n$

| n | 1.5% | 4.0% | 4.5% | 5.0% | 5.5% | 6.0% | 7.0% |
|---|------|------|------|------|------|------|------|
| 1 | 1.015000 | 1.040000 | 1.045000 | 1.050000 | 1.055000 | 1.060000 | 1.070000 |
| 2 | 1.030225 | 1.081600 | 1.092025 | 1.102500 | 1.113025 | 1.123600 | 1.144900 |
| 3 | 1.045678 | 1.124864 | 1.141166 | 1.157625 | 1.174241 | 1.191016 | 1.225043 |
| 4 | 1.061364 | 1.169859 | 1.192519 | 1.215506 | 1.238825 | 1.262477 | 1.310796 |
| 5 | 1.077284 | 1.216653 | 1.246182 | 1.276282 | 1.306960 | 1.338226 | 1.402552 |
| 6 | 1.093443 | 1.265319 | 1.302260 | 1.340096 | 1.378843 | 1.418519 | 1.500730 |
| 7 | 1.109845 | 1.315932 | 1.360862 | 1.407100 | 1.454679 | 1.503630 | 1.605781 |
| 8 | 1.126493 | 1.368569 | 1.422101 | 1.477455 | 1.534687 | 1.593848 | 1.718186 |
| 9 | 1.143390 | 1.423312 | 1.486095 | 1.551328 | 1.619094 | 1.689479 | 1.838459 |
| 10 | 1.160541 | 1.480244 | 1.552969 | 1.628895 | 1.708144 | 1.790848 | 1.967151 |
| 11 | 1.177949 | 1.539454 | 1.622853 | 1.710339 | 1.802092 | 1.898299 | 2.104852 |
| 12 | 1.195618 | 1.601032 | 1.695881 | 1.795856 | 1.901207 | 2.012196 | 2.252192 |
| 13 | 1.213552 | 1.665074 | 1.772196 | 1.885649 | 2.005774 | 2.132928 | 2.409845 |
| 14 | 1.231756 | 1.731676 | 1.851945 | 1.979932 | 2.116091 | 2.260904 | 2.578534 |
| 15 | 1.250232 | 1.800944 | 1.935282 | 2.078928 | 2.232476 | 2.396558 | 2.759032 |
| 16 | 1.268986 | 1.872981 | 2.022370 | 2.182875 | 2.355263 | 2.540352 | 2.952164 |
| 17 | 1.288020 | 1.947900 | 2.113377 | 2.292018 | 2.484802 | 2.692773 | 3.158815 |
| 18 | 1.307341 | 2.025817 | 2.208479 | 2.406619 | 2.621466 | 2.854339 | 3.379932 |
| 19 | 1.326951 | 2.106849 | 2.307860 | 2.526950 | 2.765647 | 3.025600 | 3.616528 |
| 20 | 1.346855 | 2.191123 | 2.411714 | 2.653298 | 2.917757 | 3.207135 | 3.869684 |
| 21 | 1.367058 | 2.278768 | 2.520241 | 2.785963 | 3.078234 | 3.399564 | 4.140562 |
| 22 | 1.387564 | 2.369919 | 2.633652 | 2.925261 | 3.247537 | 3.603537 | 4.430402 |
| 23 | 1.408377 | 2.464716 | 2.752166 | 3.071524 | 3.426152 | 3.819750 | 4.740530 |
| 24 | 1.429503 | 2.563304 | 2.876014 | 3.225100 | 3.614590 | 4.048935 | 5.072367 |
| 25 | 1.450945 | 2.665836 | 3.005434 | 3.386355 | 3.813392 | 4.291871 | 5.427433 |
| 26 | 1.472710 | 2.772470 | 3.140679 | 3.555673 | 4.023129 | 4.549383 | 5.807353 |
| 27 | 1.494800 | 2.883369 | 3.282010 | 3.733456 | 4.244401 | 4.822346 | 6.213868 |
| 28 | 1.517222 | 2.998703 | 3.429700 | 3.920129 | 4.477843 | 5.111687 | 6.648838 |
| 29 | 1.539981 | 3.118651 | 3.584036 | 4.116136 | 4.724124 | 5.418388 | 7.114257 |
| 30 | 1.563080 | 3.243398 | 3.745318 | 4.321942 | 4.983951 | 5.743491 | 7.612255 |

| n | 8.0% | 9.0% | 10.0% | 12.0% | 14.0% | 16.0% | 18.0% |
|---|------|------|-------|-------|-------|-------|-------|
| 1 | 1.080000 | 1.090000 | 1.100000 | 1.120000 | 1.140000 | 1.160000 | 1.180000 |
| 2 | 1.166400 | 1.188100 | 1.210000 | 1.254400 | 1.299600 | 1.345600 | 1.392400 |
| 3 | 1.259712 | 1.295029 | 1.331000 | 1.404928 | 1.481544 | 1.560896 | 1.643032 |
| 4 | 1.360489 | 1.411582 | 1.464100 | 1.573519 | 1.688960 | 1.810639 | 1.938778 |
| 5 | 1.469328 | 1.538624 | 1.610510 | 1.762342 | 1.925415 | 2.100342 | 2.287758 |
| 6 | 1.586874 | 1.677100 | 1.771561 | 1.973823 | 2.194973 | 2.436396 | 2.699554 |
| 7 | 1.713824 | 1.828039 | 1.948717 | 2.210681 | 2.502269 | 2.826220 | 3.185474 |
| 8 | 1.850930 | 1.992563 | 2.143589 | 2.475963 | 2.852586 | 3.278415 | 3.758859 |
| 9 | 1.999005 | 2.171893 | 2.357948 | 2.773079 | 3.251949 | 3.802961 | 4.435454 |
| 10 | 2.158925 | 2.367364 | 2.593742 | 3.105848 | 3.707221 | 4.411435 | 5.233836 |
| 11 | 2.331639 | 2.580426 | 2.853117 | 3.478550 | 4.226232 | 5.117265 | 6.175926 |
| 12 | 2.518170 | 2.812665 | 3.138428 | 3.895976 | 4.817905 | 5.936027 | 7.287593 |
| 13 | 2.719624 | 3.065805 | 3.452271 | 4.363493 | 5.492411 | 6.885791 | 8.599359 |
| 14 | 2.937194 | 3.341727 | 3.797498 | 4.887112 | 6.261349 | 7.987518 | 10.147244 |
| 15 | 3.172169 | 3.642482 | 4.177248 | 5.473566 | 7.137938 | 9.265521 | 11.973748 |
| 16 | 3.425943 | 3.970306 | 4.594973 | 6.130394 | 8.137249 | 10.748004 | 14.129023 |
| 17 | 3.700018 | 4.327633 | 5.054470 | 6.866041 | 9.276464 | 12.467685 | 16.672247 |
| 18 | 3.996019 | 4.717120 | 5.559917 | 7.689966 | 10.575169 | 14.462514 | 19.673251 |
| 19 | 4.315701 | 5.141661 | 6.115909 | 8.612762 | 12.055693 | 16.776517 | 23.214436 |
| 20 | 4.660957 | 5.604411 | 6.727500 | 9.646293 | 13.743490 | 19.460759 | 27.393035 |
| 21 | 5.033834 | 6.108808 | 7.400250 | 10.803848 | 15.667578 | 22.574481 | 32.323781 |
| 22 | 5.436540 | 6.658600 | 8.140275 | 12.100310 | 17.861039 | 26.186398 | 38.142061 |
| 23 | 5.871464 | 7.257874 | 8.954302 | 13.552347 | 20.361585 | 30.376222 | 45.007632 |
| 24 | 6.341181 | 7.911083 | 9.849733 | 15.178629 | 23.212207 | 35.236417 | 53.109006 |
| 25 | 6.848475 | 8.623081 | 10.834706 | 17.000064 | 26.461916 | 40.874244 | 62.668627 |
| 26 | 7.396353 | 9.399158 | 11.918177 | 19.040072 | 30.166584 | 47.414123 | 73.948980 |
| 27 | 7.988061 | 10.245082 | 13.109994 | 21.324881 | 34.389906 | 55.000382 | 87.259797 |
| 28 | 8.627106 | 11.167140 | 14.420994 | 23.883866 | 39.204493 | 63.800444 | 102.966560 |
| 29 | 9.317275 | 12.172182 | 15.863093 | 26.749930 | 44.693122 | 74.008515 | 121.500541 |
| 30 | 10.062657 | 13.267678 | 17.449402 | 29.959922 | 50.950159 | 85.849877 | 143.370638 |

## Table 2 FUTURE VALUE OF AN ORDINARY ANNUITY OF 1: $F_0 = \dfrac{(1 + i)^n - 1}{i}$

| n | 1.5% | 4.0% | 4.5% | 5.0% | 5.5% | 6.0% | 7.0% |
|---|---|---|---|---|---|---|---|
| 1 | 1.000000 | 1.000000 | 1.000000 | 1.000000 | 1.000000 | 1.000000 | 1.000000 |
| 2 | 2.015000 | 2.040000 | 2.045000 | 2.050000 | 2.055000 | 2.060000 | 2.070000 |
| 3 | 3.045225 | 3.121600 | 3.137025 | 3.152500 | 3.168025 | 3.183600 | 3.214900 |
| 4 | 4.090903 | 4.246464 | 4.278191 | 4.310125 | 4.342266 | 4.374616 | 4.439943 |
| 5 | 5.152267 | 5.416323 | 5.470710 | 5.525631 | 5.581091 | 5.637093 | 5.750739 |
| 6 | 6.229551 | 6.632975 | 6.716892 | 6.801913 | 6.888051 | 6.975319 | 7.153291 |
| 7 | 7.322994 | 7.898294 | 8.019152 | 8.142008 | 8.266894 | 8.393838 | 8.654021 |
| 8 | 8.432839 | 9.214226 | 9.380014 | 9.549109 | 9.721573 | 9.897468 | 10.259803 |
| 9 | 9.559332 | 10.582795 | 10.802114 | 11.026564 | 11.256260 | 11.491316 | 11.977989 |
| 10 | 10.702722 | 12.006107 | 12.288209 | 12.577893 | 12.875354 | 13.180795 | 13.816448 |
| 11 | 11.863262 | 13.486351 | 13.841179 | 14.206787 | 14.583498 | 14.971643 | 15.783599 |
| 12 | 13.041211 | 15.025805 | 15.464032 | 15.917127 | 16.385591 | 16.869941 | 17.888451 |
| 13 | 14.236830 | 16.626838 | 17.159913 | 17.712983 | 18.286798 | 18.882138 | 20.140643 |
| 14 | 15.450382 | 18.291911 | 18.932109 | 19.598632 | 20.292572 | 21.015066 | 22.550488 |
| 15 | 16.682138 | 20.023588 | 20.784054 | 21.578564 | 22.408663 | 23.275970 | 25.129022 |
| 16 | 17.932370 | 21.824531 | 22.719337 | 23.657492 | 24.641140 | 25.672528 | 27.888054 |
| 17 | 19.201355 | 23.697512 | 24.741707 | 25.840366 | 26.996403 | 28.212880 | 30.840217 |
| 18 | 20.489376 | 25.645413 | 26.855084 | 28.132385 | 29.481205 | 30.905653 | 33.999033 |
| 19 | 21.796716 | 27.671229 | 29.063562 | 30.539004 | 32.102671 | 33.759992 | 37.378965 |
| 20 | 23.123667 | 29.778079 | 31.371423 | 33.065954 | 34.868318 | 36.785591 | 40.995492 |
| 21 | 24.470522 | 31.969202 | 33.783137 | 35.719252 | 37.786076 | 39.992727 | 44.865177 |
| 22 | 25.837580 | 34.247970 | 36.303378 | 38.505214 | 40.864310 | 43.392290 | 49.005739 |
| 23 | 27.225144 | 36.617889 | 38.937030 | 41.430475 | 44.111847 | 46.995828 | 53.436141 |
| 24 | 28.633521 | 39.082604 | 41.689196 | 44.501999 | 47.537998 | 50.815577 | 58.176671 |
| 25 | 30.063024 | 41.645908 | 44.565210 | 47.727099 | 51.152588 | 54.864512 | 63.249038 |
| 26 | 31.513969 | 44.311745 | 47.570645 | 51.113454 | 54.965981 | 59.156383 | 68.676470 |
| 27 | 32.986678 | 47.084214 | 50.711324 | 54.669126 | 58.989109 | 63.705766 | 74.483823 |
| 28 | 34.481479 | 49.967583 | 53.993333 | 58.402583 | 63.233510 | 68.528112 | 80.697691 |
| 29 | 35.998701 | 52.966286 | 57.423033 | 62.322712 | 67.711354 | 73.639798 | 87.346529 |
| 30 | 37.538681 | 56.084938 | 61.007070 | 66.438848 | 72.435478 | 79.058186 | 94.460786 |

| n | 8.0% | 9.0% | 10.0% | 12.0% | 14.0% | 16.0% | 18.0% |
|---|---|---|---|---|---|---|---|
| 1 | 1.000000 | 1.000000 | 1.000000 | 1.000000 | 1.000000 | 1.000000 | 1.000000 |
| 2 | 2.080000 | 2.090000 | 2.100000 | 2.120000 | 2.140000 | 2.160000 | 2.180000 |
| 3 | 3.246400 | 3.278100 | 3.310000 | 3.374400 | 3.439600 | 3.505600 | 3.572400 |
| 4 | 4.506112 | 4.573129 | 4.641000 | 4.779328 | 4.921144 | 5.066496 | 5.215432 |
| 5 | 5.866601 | 5.984711 | 6.105100 | 6.352847 | 6.610104 | 6.877135 | 7.154210 |
| 6 | 7.335929 | 7.523335 | 7.715610 | 8.115189 | 8.535519 | 8.977477 | 9.441968 |
| 7 | 8.922803 | 9.200435 | 9.487171 | 10.089012 | 10.730491 | 11.413873 | 12.141522 |
| 8 | 10.636628 | 11.028474 | 11.435888 | 12.299693 | 13.232760 | 14.240093 | 15.326996 |
| 9 | 12.487558 | 13.021036 | 13.579477 | 14.775656 | 16.085347 | 17.518508 | 19.085855 |
| 10 | 14.486562 | 15.192930 | 15.937425 | 17.548735 | 19.337295 | 21.321469 | 23.521309 |
| 11 | 16.645487 | 17.560293 | 18.531167 | 20.654583 | 23.044516 | 25.732904 | 28.755144 |
| 12 | 18.977126 | 20.140720 | 21.384284 | 24.133133 | 27.270749 | 30.850169 | 34.931070 |
| 13 | 21.495297 | 22.953385 | 24.522712 | 28.029109 | 32.088654 | 36.786196 | 42.218663 |
| 14 | 24.214920 | 26.019189 | 27.974983 | 32.392602 | 37.581065 | 43.671987 | 50.818022 |
| 15 | 27.152114 | 29.360916 | 31.772482 | 37.279715 | 43.842414 | 51.659505 | 60.965266 |
| 16 | 30.324283 | 33.003399 | 35.949730 | 42.753280 | 50.980352 | 60.925026 | 72.939014 |
| 17 | 33.750226 | 36.973705 | 40.544703 | 48.883674 | 59.117601 | 71.673030 | 87.068036 |
| 18 | 37.450244 | 41.301338 | 45.599173 | 55.749715 | 68.394066 | 84.140715 | 103.740283 |
| 19 | 41.446263 | 46.018458 | 51.159090 | 63.439681 | 78.969235 | 98.603230 | 123.413534 |
| 20 | 45.761964 | 51.160120 | 57.274999 | 72.052442 | 91.024928 | 115.379747 | 146.627970 |
| 21 | 50.422921 | 56.764530 | 64.002499 | 81.698736 | 104.768418 | 134.840506 | 174.021005 |
| 22 | 55.456755 | 62.873338 | 71.402749 | 92.502584 | 120.435996 | 157.414987 | 206.344785 |
| 23 | 60.893296 | 69.531939 | 79.543024 | 104.602894 | 138.297035 | 183.601385 | 244.486847 |
| 24 | 66.764759 | 76.789813 | 88.497327 | 118.155241 | 158.658620 | 213.977607 | 289.494479 |
| 25 | 73.105940 | 84.700896 | 98.347059 | 133.333870 | 181.870827 | 249.214024 | 342.603486 |
| 26 | 79.954415 | 93.323977 | 109.181765 | 150.333934 | 208.332743 | 290.088267 | 405.272113 |
| 27 | 87.350768 | 102.723135 | 121.099942 | 169.374007 | 238.499327 | 337.502390 | 479.221093 |
| 28 | 95.338830 | 112.968217 | 134.209936 | 190.698887 | 272.889233 | 392.502773 | 566.480890 |
| 29 | 103.965936 | 124.135356 | 148.630930 | 214.582754 | 312.093725 | 456.303216 | 669.447450 |
| 30 | 113.283211 | 136.307539 | 164.494023 | 241.332684 | 356.786847 | 530.311731 | 790.947991 |

## Table 3 PRESENT VALUE OF 1: $p = \dfrac{1}{(1 + i)^n}$

| n | 1.5% | 4.0% | 4.5% | 5.0% | 5.5% | 6.0% | 7.0% |
|---|------|------|------|------|------|------|------|
| 1 | 0.985222 | 0.961538 | 0.956938 | 0.952381 | 0.947867 | 0.943396 | 0.934579 |
| 2 | 0.970662 | 0.924556 | 0.915730 | 0.907029 | 0.898452 | 0.889996 | 0.873439 |
| 3 | 0.956317 | 0.888996 | 0.876297 | 0.863838 | 0.851614 | 0.839619 | 0.816298 |
| 4 | 0.942184 | 0.854804 | 0.838561 | 0.822702 | 0.807217 | 0.792094 | 0.762895 |
| 5 | 0.928260 | 0.821927 | 0.802451 | 0.783526 | 0.765134 | 0.747258 | 0.712986 |
| 6 | 0.914542 | 0.790315 | 0.767896 | 0.746215 | 0.725246 | 0.704961 | 0.666342 |
| 7 | 0.901027 | 0.759918 | 0.734828 | 0.710681 | 0.687437 | 0.665057 | 0.622750 |
| 8 | 0.887711 | 0.730690 | 0.703185 | 0.676839 | 0.651599 | 0.627412 | 0.582009 |
| 9 | 0.874592 | 0.702587 | 0.672904 | 0.644609 | 0.617629 | 0.591898 | 0.543934 |
| 10 | 0.861667 | 0.675564 | 0.643928 | 0.613913 | 0.585431 | 0.558395 | 0.508349 |
| 11 | 0.848933 | 0.649581 | 0.616199 | 0.584679 | 0.554911 | 0.526788 | 0.475093 |
| 12 | 0.836387 | 0.624597 | 0.589664 | 0.556837 | 0.525982 | 0.496969 | 0.444012 |
| 13 | 0.824027 | 0.600574 | 0.564272 | 0.530321 | 0.498561 | 0.468839 | 0.414964 |
| 14 | 0.811849 | 0.577475 | 0.539973 | 0.505068 | 0.472569 | 0.442301 | 0.387817 |
| 15 | 0.799852 | 0.555265 | 0.516720 | 0.481017 | 0.447933 | 0.417265 | 0.362446 |
| 16 | 0.788031 | 0.533908 | 0.494469 | 0.458112 | 0.424581 | 0.393646 | 0.338735 |
| 17 | 0.776385 | 0.513373 | 0.473176 | 0.436297 | 0.402447 | 0.371364 | 0.316574 |
| 18 | 0.764912 | 0.493628 | 0.452800 | 0.415521 | 0.381466 | 0.350344 | 0.295864 |
| 19 | 0.753607 | 0.474642 | 0.433302 | 0.395734 | 0.361579 | 0.330513 | 0.276508 |
| 20 | 0.742470 | 0.456387 | 0.414643 | 0.376889 | 0.342729 | 0.311805 | 0.258419 |
| 21 | 0.731498 | 0.438834 | 0.396787 | 0.358942 | 0.324862 | 0.294155 | 0.241513 |
| 22 | 0.720688 | 0.421955 | 0.379701 | 0.341850 | 0.307926 | 0.277505 | 0.225713 |
| 23 | 0.710037 | 0.405726 | 0.363350 | 0.325571 | 0.291873 | 0.261797 | 0.210947 |
| 24 | 0.699544 | 0.390121 | 0.347703 | 0.310068 | 0.276657 | 0.246979 | 0.197147 |
| 25 | 0.689206 | 0.375117 | 0.332731 | 0.295303 | 0.262234 | 0.232999 | 0.184249 |
| 26 | 0.679021 | 0.360689 | 0.318402 | 0.281241 | 0.248563 | 0.219810 | 0.172195 |
| 27 | 0.668986 | 0.346817 | 0.304691 | 0.267848 | 0.235605 | 0.207368 | 0.160930 |
| 28 | 0.659099 | 0.333477 | 0.291571 | 0.255094 | 0.223322 | 0.195630 | 0.150402 |
| 29 | 0.649359 | 0.320651 | 0.279015 | 0.242946 | 0.211679 | 0.184557 | 0.140563 |
| 30 | 0.639762 | 0.308319 | 0.267000 | 0.231377 | 0.200644 | 0.174110 | 0.131367 |

| n | 8.0% | 9.0% | 10.0% | 12.0% | 14.0% | 16.0% | 18.0% |
|---|------|------|-------|-------|-------|-------|-------|
| 1 | 0.925926 | 0.917431 | 0.909091 | 0.892857 | 0.877193 | 0.862069 | 0.847458 |
| 2 | 0.857339 | 0.841680 | 0.826446 | 0.797194 | 0.769468 | 0.743163 | 0.718184 |
| 3 | 0.793832 | 0.772183 | 0.751315 | 0.711780 | 0.674972 | 0.640658 | 0.608631 |
| 4 | 0.735030 | 0.708425 | 0.683013 | 0.635518 | 0.592080 | 0.552291 | 0.515789 |
| 5 | 0.680583 | 0.649931 | 0.620921 | 0.567427 | 0.519369 | 0.476113 | 0.437109 |
| 6 | 0.630170 | 0.596267 | 0.564474 | 0.506631 | 0.455587 | 0.410442 | 0.370432 |
| 7 | 0.583490 | 0.547034 | 0.513158 | 0.452349 | 0.399637 | 0.353830 | 0.313925 |
| 8 | 0.540269 | 0.501866 | 0.466507 | 0.403883 | 0.350559 | 0.305025 | 0.266038 |
| 9 | 0.500249 | 0.460428 | 0.424098 | 0.360610 | 0.307508 | 0.262953 | 0.225456 |
| 10 | 0.463193 | 0.422411 | 0.385543 | 0.321973 | 0.269744 | 0.226684 | 0.191064 |
| 11 | 0.428883 | 0.387533 | 0.350494 | 0.287476 | 0.236617 | 0.195417 | 0.161919 |
| 12 | 0.397114 | 0.355535 | 0.318631 | 0.256675 | 0.207559 | 0.168463 | 0.137220 |
| 13 | 0.367698 | 0.326179 | 0.289664 | 0.229174 | 0.182069 | 0.145227 | 0.116288 |
| 14 | 0.340461 | 0.299246 | 0.263331 | 0.204620 | 0.159710 | 0.125195 | 0.098549 |
| 15 | 0.315242 | 0.274538 | 0.239392 | 0.182696 | 0.140096 | 0.107927 | 0.083516 |
| 16 | 0.291890 | 0.251870 | 0.217629 | 0.163122 | 0.122892 | 0.093041 | 0.070776 |
| 17 | 0.270269 | 0.231073 | 0.197845 | 0.145644 | 0.107800 | 0.080207 | 0.059980 |
| 18 | 0.250249 | 0.211994 | 0.179859 | 0.130040 | 0.094561 | 0.069144 | 0.050830 |
| 19 | 0.231712 | 0.194490 | 0.163508 | 0.116107 | 0.082948 | 0.059607 | 0.043077 |
| 20 | 0.214548 | 0.178431 | 0.148644 | 0.103667 | 0.072762 | 0.051385 | 0.036506 |
| 21 | 0.198656 | 0.163698 | 0.135131 | 0.092560 | 0.063826 | 0.044298 | 0.030937 |
| 22 | 0.183941 | 0.150182 | 0.122846 | 0.082643 | 0.055988 | 0.038188 | 0.026218 |
| 23 | 0.170315 | 0.137781 | 0.111678 | 0.073788 | 0.049112 | 0.032920 | 0.022218 |
| 24 | 0.157699 | 0.126405 | 0.101526 | 0.065882 | 0.043081 | 0.028380 | 0.018829 |
| 25 | 0.146018 | 0.115968 | 0.092296 | 0.058823 | 0.037790 | 0.024465 | 0.015957 |
| 26 | 0.135202 | 0.106393 | 0.083905 | 0.052521 | 0.033149 | 0.021091 | 0.013523 |
| 27 | 0.125187 | 0.097608 | 0.076278 | 0.046894 | 0.029078 | 0.018182 | 0.011460 |
| 28 | 0.115914 | 0.089548 | 0.069343 | 0.041869 | 0.025507 | 0.015674 | 0.009712 |
| 29 | 0.107328 | 0.082155 | 0.063039 | 0.037383 | 0.022375 | 0.013512 | 0.008230 |
| 30 | 0.099377 | 0.075371 | 0.057309 | 0.033378 | 0.019627 | 0.011648 | 0.006975 |

*Table 4* PRESENT VALUE OF AN ORDINARY ANNUITY OF 1: $P_0 = \dfrac{1 - \dfrac{1}{(1+i)^n}}{i}$

| n | 1.5% | 4.0% | 4.5% | 5.0% | 5.5% | 6.0% | 7.0% |
|---|------|------|------|------|------|------|------|
| 1 | 0.985222 | 0.961538 | 0.956938 | 0.952381 | 0.947867 | 0.943396 | 0.934579 |
| 2 | 1.955883 | 1.886095 | 1.872668 | 1.859410 | 1.846320 | 1.833393 | 1.808018 |
| 3 | 2.912200 | 2.775091 | 2.748964 | 2.723248 | 2.697933 | 2.673012 | 2.624316 |
| 4 | 3.854385 | 3.629895 | 3.587526 | 3.545951 | 3.505150 | 3.465106 | 3.387211 |
| 5 | 4.782645 | 4.451822 | 4.389977 | 4.329477 | 4.270284 | 4.212364 | 4.100197 |
| 6 | 5.697187 | 5.242137 | 5.157872 | 5.075692 | 4.995530 | 4.917324 | 4.766540 |
| 7 | 6.598214 | 6.002055 | 5.892701 | 5.786373 | 5.682967 | 5.582381 | 5.389289 |
| 8 | 7.485925 | 6.732745 | 6.595886 | 6.463213 | 6.334566 | 6.209794 | 5.971299 |
| 9 | 8.360517 | 7.435332 | 7.268790 | 7.107822 | 6.952195 | 6.801692 | 6.515232 |
| 10 | 9.222185 | 8.110896 | 7.912718 | 7.721735 | 7.537626 | 7.360087 | 7.023582 |
| 11 | 10.071118 | 8.760477 | 8.528917 | 8.306414 | 8.092536 | 7.886875 | 7.498674 |
| 12 | 10.907505 | 9.385074 | 9.118581 | 8.863252 | 8.618518 | 8.383844 | 7.942686 |
| 13 | 11.731532 | 9.985648 | 9.682852 | 9.393573 | 9.117079 | 8.852683 | 8.357651 |
| 14 | 12.543382 | 10.563123 | 10.222825 | 9.898641 | 9.589648 | 9.294984 | 8.745468 |
| 15 | 13.343233 | 11.118387 | 10.739546 | 10.379658 | 10.037581 | 9.712249 | 9.107914 |
| 16 | 14.131264 | 11.652296 | 11.234015 | 10.837770 | 10.462162 | 10.105895 | 9.446649 |
| 17 | 14.907649 | 12.165669 | 11.707191 | 11.274066 | 10.864609 | 10.477260 | 9.763223 |
| 18 | 15.672561 | 12.659297 | 12.159992 | 11.689587 | 11.246074 | 10.827603 | 10.059087 |
| 19 | 16.426168 | 13.133939 | 12.593294 | 12.085321 | 11.607654 | 11.158116 | 10.335595 |
| 20 | 17.168639 | 13.590326 | 13.007936 | 12.462210 | 11.950382 | 11.469921 | 10.594014 |
| 21 | 17.900137 | 14.029160 | 13.404724 | 12.821153 | 12.275244 | 11.764077 | 10.835527 |
| 22 | 18.620824 | 14.451115 | 13.784425 | 13.163003 | 12.583170 | 12.041582 | 11.061240 |
| 23 | 19.330861 | 14.856842 | 14.147775 | 13.488574 | 12.875042 | 12.303379 | 11.272187 |
| 24 | 20.030405 | 15.246963 | 14.495478 | 13.798642 | 13.151699 | 12.550358 | 11.469334 |
| 25 | 20.719611 | 15.622080 | 14.828209 | 14.093945 | 13.413933 | 12.783356 | 11.653583 |
| 26 | 21.398632 | 15.982769 | 15.146611 | 14.375185 | 13.662495 | 13.003166 | 11.825779 |
| 27 | 22.067617 | 16.329586 | 15.451303 | 14.643034 | 13.898100 | 13.210534 | 11.986709 |
| 28 | 22.726717 | 16.663063 | 15.742874 | 14.898127 | 14.121422 | 13.406164 | 12.137111 |
| 29 | 23.376076 | 16.983715 | 16.021889 | 15.141074 | 14.333101 | 13.590721 | 12.277674 |
| 30 | 24.015838 | 17.292033 | 16.288889 | 15.372451 | 14.533745 | 13.764831 | 12.409041 |

| n | 8.0% | 9.0% | 10.0% | 12.0% | 14.0% | 16.0% | 18.0% |
|---|------|------|-------|-------|-------|-------|-------|
| 1 | 0.925926 | 0.917431 | 0.909091 | 0.892857 | 0.877193 | 0.862069 | 0.847458 |
| 2 | 1.783265 | 1.759111 | 1.735537 | 1.690051 | 1.646661 | 1.605232 | 1.565642 |
| 3 | 2.577097 | 2.531295 | 2.486852 | 2.401831 | 2.321632 | 2.245890 | 2.174273 |
| 4 | 3.312127 | 3.239720 | 3.169865 | 3.037349 | 2.913712 | 2.798181 | 2.690062 |
| 5 | 3.992710 | 3.889651 | 3.790787 | 3.604776 | 3.433081 | 3.274294 | 3.127171 |
| 6 | 4.622880 | 4.485919 | 4.355261 | 4.111407 | 3.888668 | 3.684736 | 3.497603 |
| 7 | 5.206370 | 5.032953 | 4.868419 | 4.563757 | 4.288305 | 4.038565 | 3.811528 |
| 8 | 5.746639 | 5.534819 | 5.334926 | 4.967640 | 4.638864 | 4.343591 | 4.077566 |
| 9 | 6.246888 | 5.995247 | 5.759024 | 5.328250 | 4.946372 | 4.606544 | 4.303022 |
| 10 | 6.710081 | 6.417658 | 6.144567 | 5.650223 | 5.216116 | 4.833227 | 4.494086 |
| 11 | 7.138964 | 6.805191 | 6.495061 | 5.937699 | 5.452733 | 5.028644 | 4.656005 |
| 12 | 7.536078 | 7.160725 | 6.813692 | 6.194374 | 5.660292 | 5.197107 | 4.793225 |
| 13 | 7.903776 | 7.486904 | 7.103356 | 6.423548 | 5.842362 | 5.342334 | 4.909513 |
| 14 | 8.244237 | 7.786150 | 7.366687 | 6.628168 | 6.002072 | 5.467529 | 5.008062 |
| 15 | 8.559479 | 8.060688 | 7.606080 | 6.810864 | 6.142168 | 5.575456 | 5.091578 |
| 16 | 8.851369 | 8.312558 | 7.823709 | 6.973986 | 6.265060 | 5.668497 | 5.162354 |
| 17 | 9.121638 | 8.543631 | 8.021553 | 7.119630 | 6.372859 | 5.748704 | 5.222334 |
| 18 | 9.371887 | 8.755625 | 8.201412 | 7.249670 | 6.467420 | 5.817848 | 5.273164 |
| 19 | 9.603599 | 8.950115 | 8.364920 | 7.365777 | 6.550369 | 5.877455 | 5.316241 |
| 20 | 9.818147 | 9.128546 | 8.513564 | 7.469444 | 6.623131 | 5.928841 | 5.352746 |
| 21 | 10.016803 | 9.292244 | 8.648694 | 7.562003 | 6.686957 | 5.973139 | 5.383683 |
| 22 | 10.200744 | 9.442425 | 8.771540 | 7.644646 | 6.742944 | 6.011326 | 5.409901 |
| 23 | 10.371059 | 9.580207 | 8.883218 | 7.718434 | 6.792056 | 6.044247 | 5.432120 |
| 24 | 10.528758 | 9.706612 | 8.984744 | 7.784316 | 6.835137 | 6.072627 | 5.450949 |
| 25 | 10.674776 | 9.822580 | 9.077040 | 7.843139 | 6.872927 | 6.097092 | 5.466906 |
| 26 | 10.809978 | 9.928972 | 9.160945 | 7.895660 | 6.906077 | 6.118183 | 5.480429 |
| 27 | 10.935165 | 10.026580 | 9.237223 | 7.942554 | 6.935155 | 6.136364 | 5.491889 |
| 28 | 11.051078 | 10.116128 | 9.306567 | 7.984423 | 6.960662 | 6.152038 | 5.501601 |
| 29 | 11.158406 | 10.198283 | 9.369606 | 8.021806 | 6.983037 | 6.165550 | 5.509831 |
| 30 | 11.257783 | 10.273654 | 9.426914 | 8.055184 | 7.002664 | 6.177198 | 5.516806 |

## Table 5 PRESENT VALUE OF ANNUITY DUE: $P_d = \dfrac{1 - \dfrac{1}{(1+i)^{n-1}}}{i} + 1$

| n | 1.5% | 4.0% | 4.5% | 5.0% | 5.5% | 6.0% | 7.0% |
|---|---|---|---|---|---|---|---|
| 1 | 1.000000 | 1.000000 | 1.000000 | 1.000000 | 1.000000 | 1.000000 | 1.000000 |
| 2 | 1.985222 | 1.961538 | 1.956938 | 1.952381 | 1.947867 | 1.943396 | 1.934579 |
| 3 | 2.955883 | 2.886095 | 2.872668 | 2.859410 | 2.846320 | 2.833393 | 2.808018 |
| 4 | 3.912200 | 3.775091 | 3.748964 | 3.723248 | 3.697933 | 3.673012 | 3.624316 |
| 5 | 4.854385 | 4.629895 | 4.587526 | 4.545951 | 4.505150 | 4.465106 | 4.387211 |
| 6 | 5.782645 | 5.451822 | 5.389977 | 5.329477 | 5.270284 | 5.212364 | 5.100197 |
| 7 | 6.697187 | 6.242137 | 6.157872 | 6.075692 | 5.995530 | 5.917324 | 5.766540 |
| 8 | 7.598214 | 7.002055 | 6.892701 | 6.786373 | 6.682967 | 6.582381 | 6.389289 |
| 9 | 8.485925 | 7.732745 | 7.595886 | 7.463213 | 7.334566 | 7.209794 | 6.971299 |
| 10 | 9.360517 | 8.435332 | 8.268790 | 8.107822 | 7.952195 | 7.801692 | 7.515232 |
| 11 | 10.222185 | 9.110896 | 8.912718 | 8.721735 | 8.537626 | 8.360087 | 8.023582 |
| 12 | 11.071118 | 9.760477 | 9.528917 | 9.306414 | 9.092536 | 8.886875 | 8.498674 |
| 13 | 11.907505 | 10.385074 | 10.118581 | 9.863252 | 9.618518 | 9.383844 | 8.942686 |
| 14 | 12.731532 | 10.985648 | 10.682852 | 10.393573 | 10.117079 | 9.852683 | 9.357651 |
| 15 | 13.543382 | 11.563123 | 11.222825 | 10.898641 | 10.589648 | 10.294984 | 9.745468 |
| 16 | 14.343233 | 12.118387 | 11.739546 | 11.379658 | 11.037581 | 10.712249 | 10.107914 |
| 17 | 15.131264 | 12.652296 | 12.234015 | 11.837770 | 11.462162 | 11.105895 | 10.446649 |
| 18 | 15.907649 | 13.165669 | 12.707191 | 12.274066 | 11.864609 | 11.477260 | 10.763223 |
| 19 | 16.672561 | 13.659297 | 13.159992 | 12.689587 | 12.246074 | 11.827603 | 11.059087 |
| 20 | 17.426168 | 14.133939 | 13.593294 | 13.085321 | 12.607654 | 12.158116 | 11.335595 |
| 21 | 18.168639 | 14.590326 | 14.007936 | 13.462210 | 12.950382 | 12.469921 | 11.594014 |
| 22 | 18.900137 | 15.029160 | 14.404724 | 13.821153 | 13.275244 | 12.764077 | 11.835527 |
| 23 | 19.620824 | 15.451115 | 14.784425 | 14.163003 | 13.583170 | 13.041582 | 12.061240 |
| 24 | 20.330861 | 15.856842 | 15.147775 | 14.488574 | 13.875042 | 13.303379 | 12.272187 |
| 25 | 21.030405 | 16.246963 | 15.495478 | 14.798642 | 14.151699 | 13.550358 | 12.469334 |
| 26 | 21.719611 | 16.622080 | 15.828209 | 15.093945 | 14.413933 | 13.783356 | 12.653583 |
| 27 | 22.398632 | 16.982769 | 16.146611 | 15.375185 | 14.662495 | 14.003166 | 12.825779 |
| 28 | 23.067617 | 17.329586 | 16.451303 | 15.643034 | 14.898100 | 14.210534 | 12.986709 |
| 29 | 23.726717 | 17.663063 | 16.742874 | 15.898127 | 15.121422 | 14.406164 | 13.137111 |
| 30 | 24.376076 | 17.983715 | 17.021889 | 16.141074 | 15.333101 | 14.590721 | 13.277674 |

| n | 8.0% | 9.0% | 10.0% | 12.0% | 14.0% | 16.0% | 18.0% |
|---|---|---|---|---|---|---|---|
| 1 | 1.000000 | 1.000000 | 1.000000 | 1.000000 | 1.000000 | 1.000000 | 1.000000 |
| 2 | 1.925926 | 1.917431 | 1.909091 | 1.892857 | 1.877193 | 1.862069 | 1.847458 |
| 3 | 2.783265 | 2.759111 | 2.735537 | 2.690051 | 2.646661 | 2.605232 | 2.565642 |
| 4 | 3.577097 | 3.531295 | 3.486852 | 3.401831 | 3.321632 | 3.245890 | 3.174273 |
| 5 | 4.312127 | 4.239720 | 4.169865 | 4.037349 | 3.913712 | 3.798181 | 3.690062 |
| 6 | 4.992710 | 4.889651 | 4.790787 | 4.604776 | 4.433081 | 4.274294 | 4.127171 |
| 7 | 5.622880 | 5.485919 | 5.355261 | 5.111407 | 4.888668 | 4.684736 | 4.497603 |
| 8 | 6.206370 | 6.032953 | 5.868419 | 5.563757 | 5.288305 | 5.038565 | 4.811528 |
| 9 | 6.746639 | 6.534819 | 6.334926 | 5.967640 | 5.638864 | 5.343591 | 5.077566 |
| 10 | 7.246888 | 6.995247 | 6.759024 | 6.328250 | 5.946372 | 5.606544 | 5.303022 |
| 11 | 7.710081 | 7.417658 | 7.144567 | 6.650223 | 6.216116 | 5.833227 | 5.494086 |
| 12 | 8.138964 | 7.805191 | 7.495061 | 6.937699 | 6.452733 | 6.028644 | 5.656005 |
| 13 | 8.536078 | 8.160725 | 7.813692 | 7.194374 | 6.660292 | 6.197107 | 5.793225 |
| 14 | 8.903776 | 8.486904 | 8.103356 | 7.423548 | 6.842362 | 6.342334 | 5.909513 |
| 15 | 9.244237 | 8.786150 | 8.366687 | 7.628168 | 7.002072 | 6.467529 | 6.008062 |
| 16 | 9.559479 | 9.060688 | 8.606080 | 7.810864 | 7.142168 | 6.575456 | 6.091578 |
| 17 | 9.851369 | 9.312558 | 8.823709 | 7.973986 | 7.265060 | 6.668497 | 6.162354 |
| 18 | 10.121638 | 9.543631 | 9.021553 | 8.119630 | 7.372859 | 6.748704 | 6.222334 |
| 19 | 10.371887 | 9.755625 | 9.201412 | 8.249670 | 7.467420 | 6.817848 | 6.273164 |
| 20 | 10.603599 | 9.950115 | 9.364920 | 8.365777 | 7.550369 | 6.877455 | 6.316241 |
| 21 | 10.818147 | 10.128546 | 9.513564 | 8.469444 | 7.623131 | 6.928841 | 6.352746 |
| 22 | 11.016803 | 10.292244 | 9.648694 | 8.562003 | 7.686957 | 6.973139 | 6.383683 |
| 23 | 11.200744 | 10.442425 | 9.771540 | 8.644646 | 7.742944 | 7.011326 | 6.409901 |
| 24 | 11.371059 | 10.580207 | 9.883218 | 8.718434 | 7.792056 | 7.044247 | 6.432120 |
| 25 | 11.528758 | 10.706612 | 9.984744 | 8.784316 | 7.835137 | 7.072627 | 6.450949 |
| 26 | 11.674776 | 10.822580 | 10.077040 | 8.843139 | 7.872927 | 7.097092 | 6.466906 |
| 27 | 11.809978 | 10.928972 | 10.160945 | 8.895660 | 7.906077 | 7.118183 | 6.480429 |
| 28 | 11.935165 | 11.026580 | 10.237223 | 8.942554 | 7.935155 | 7.136364 | 6.491889 |
| 29 | 12.051078 | 11.116128 | 10.306567 | 8.984423 | 7.960662 | 7.152038 | 6.501601 |
| 30 | 12.158406 | 11.198283 | 10.369606 | 9.021806 | 7.983037 | 7.165550 | 6.509831 |

# INDEX

Note: The letter *n* following a page number indicates a footnote. The abbreviation *illus.* indicates an exhibit; *def.*, a definition.

consolidated, *illus.*, 400; *def.*, 50, 60, C5; elements of the, 62–64; errors affecting only the, 1133; errors affecting the and income statement, 1134–1135; historical cost, 1254–1255; *illus.*, 70–71, 449, 670, 674, 726, C20; liabilities, 63–64; limitations of the, 67; liquidity, financial flexibility, and operating capability, 60–61; measurement of the elements of the, 64–67; other items (current costs), 1252; preparation of, C20; presentation of pension plan assets, 897–898; purposes of the, 60–62; recognition in the, 62; reporting classifications on the, 67–80; statement of changes in stockholders' equity and the, 58–106; statement format, 89; stockholders' equity, 64; valuation of today's, 66–67

Balance sheet approach, *def.*, 206
Bank overdrafts, 183
ank reconciliation, 186–193; causes of the difference, 187–188; *def.*, 186; *illus.*, 190; illustration of preparation, 189–191; procedures for preparing a, 188–189
Basic accounting equation, 60
Benefits, greater than costs (accounting information), 41
Benefit/years-of-service approach, measurement method (pension plans), 876
Bond certificate, *def.*, 524
Bond indenture, *def.*, 524
Bonds, accruing interest, 535–536; amortizing discounts and premiums, 528–537; amortization for acquired between interest dates, 601–602; characteristics of, 525; characteristics of, *illus.*, 525; convertible, 543–546, 618; *def.*, 524; interest expense and discount amortization schedules, *illus.*, 531, 534; interest expense and premium amortization schedules, *illus.*, 531, 535; investment interest revenue and discount amortization schedule, *illus.*, 600; investment interest revenue and premium amortization schedule, *illus.*, 599; issue costs, 534–535; issued between interest payment dates, 527–528; issued with detachable stock warrants, 542–543; payable, 524–527; recognition and amortization of premiums and discounts, 598; recording the issuance of, 527–528; retired at maturity, 537–538; retired prior to maturity, 538–539; sale of investment in before maturity, 602; selling prices, 526–527; serial, 566–569; with equity

characteristics, 541–546; zero coupon, 536
Bonds payable, 524–527
Bonuses, computation of bonus and income tax, *illus.*, 491; obligations, 490–491
Book value, *def.*, 527; per common share, 1194–1195
Book value per common share, 1194–1195
Boot, 351, 353
Buildings, determination of cost, 344–345
Business cycle, *illus.*, 44

## C

Callable preferred stock, 658; *def.*, 658
Capital, additional paid-in, 646; capital maintenance and, 61–62; capital stock and additional paid-in, 78–79; contributed, 78, 640–691; corporate structure, 643–646; *def.*, 61; financial, 61; legal, 78, 645; physical, 61; unrealized, 80; working, 73
Capital expenditure, *def.*, 362
Capital lease (lessee), 946–947; amortization of leased asset, 947; change in present value, 952; classification of obligation under, 951; discount rate, 946–947; executory costs, 946; illustration of lessee's method, 947–954; other capitalization issues, 954–956; present value of next year's payments, 951–952; reduction of the lease obligation, 947
Capital maintenance, concept, 109–110, 1253–1254; *def.*, 61
Capital markets, *illus.*, 3
Capital stock, additional paid-in capital and, 78–79; authorization, 647; authorized, *def.*, 644; basic terminology, 644; combined sales of stock, 650–651; *def.*, 644; issuance for cash, 647–648; issuance of, 647–653; issued, *def.*, 644; nonmonetary issuance of stock, 651–652; outstanding, *def.*, 644; reacquisition of (treasury stock), 662–669; stockholders' rights and, 644; stock rights to current stockholders, 653; stock splits, 652–653; subscription defaults, 649–650; stock issuance, 648; stock subscriptions, 648–649
Capital structure, complex, 1085; simple, 1080–1084
Carrybacks, operating loss, 826–833
Carryforwards, operating loss, 826–833
*CASB Standard 404*, 361n
Cash, 183–186; budget, 184; cash equivalents and, 183–184, 1005; compen-

sating balances, 194; *def.*, 68, 183; electronic funds transfer systems, 193; equations for change in, *illus.*, 1008; generating immediate from accounts receivable, 208–213; inflows and outflows, 1007–1009; inflows of, 1008; issuance (of capital stock) for, 647–648; management, 184–185; notes payable exchanged for rights or privileges, 548–549; notes payable issued for, 547–548; outflows of, 1008–1009; petty, 185–186; receivables and, 182–241; (sales) discounts, 198–200; special topics involving, 193–194
Cash budget, *def.*, 184
Cash control systems, 184
Cash dividends, 706–708; declared, 1039–1040; participating preferred stock, 707;
Cash equivalents, cash and, 183–184, 1005; *def.*, 68–69, 183
Cash flows, adjustments to convert net income to net cash flow from operating activities, *illus.*, 1015; calculations of from operating activities, *illus.*, 1011; classifications of, 1009; differences among revenues, expenses, and cash flows from operating activities, *illus.*, 1011; direct method for calculating from operating activities, 1012–1013; direct method for reporting operating, 1041–1052; income statement and the statement of, 108–179; indirect method for calculating net from operating activities, 1013–1014; information useful in assessing company, 32; net from financing activities, 1018–1019; net from investing activities, 1017–1018; net from operating activities, 1009–1014, 1016–1017; per share, 1041; statement of, 51, 144–150, 1002–1078; statement of, *def.*, C6; summary of GAAP for corporate earnings and, *illus.*, 149–150
Cash management, 184–185
Cash payments journal, *def.*, C33
Cash planning systems, 184
Cash receipts, information useful in assessing external users, 31–32
Cash receipts journal, *def.*, C31
Cash (sales) discounts, 198–200; *def.*, 198
Cash surrender value, of life insurance, 619
Casualty insurance, 369–370
Cause and effect, association of, 116
Ceiling, 296; floor and, conceptual evaluation of the, 298–300
Certificates of deposit (CDs), 183

*(Continued from inside front cover.)*

# VII. FINANCIAL STATEMENTS

A. **Balance Sheet:**
1. **Definition:** Summarizes a company's economic resources, economic obligations, and equity and their relationships on a particular date.
2. **Assets:** Probable future economic benefits obtained or controlled as a result of past transactions or events.
3. **Liabilities:** Probable future sacrifices of economic benefits arising from present obligations to transfer assets or provide services in the future as a result of past transactions or events.
4. **Equity:** Residual interest of owners in assets after deducting liabilities.
5. **Measurement Methods:** Alternative valuation methods of assets (and liabilities) include: (a) *Historical Cost:* Amount of cash (or equivalent) that would be paid to acquire asset, (b) *Current Cost:* Amount of cash (or equivalent) that would be paid currently to acquire same asset, (c) *Current Exit Value:* Amount of cash (or equivalent) that could be obtained currently by selling asset in orderly liquidation, (d) *Net Realizable Value:* Amount of cash (or equivalent) into which asset is expected to be converted in ordinary course of business, less direct conversion costs, and (e) *Present Value:* Present value of future net cash flows expected from conversion of asset in ordinary course of business.

B. **Income Statement:**
1. **Definition:** Summarizes the results of a company's income-producing operations for an accounting period.
2. **Revenues:** Inflows or other enhancements of assets or settlement of liabilities during a period from delivering or producing goods, rendering services, or other activities involving ongoing major operations.
3. **Expenses:** Outflows or other using-up of assets or incurrences of liabilities during a period from delivering or producing goods, rendering services, or other activities involving ongoing major operations.
4. **Gains (Losses):** Increases (decreases) in equity from peripheral or incidental transactions and from all other events and circumstances during a period except those resulting from revenues (expenses) or investments by (distributions to) owners.

C. **Statement of Cash Flows:**
1. **Definition:** Summarizes a company's cash inflows, cash outflows, and net change in cash from its operating, investing, and financing activities during an accounting period, in a manner that reconciles the beginning and ending cash balances.
2. **Operating Cash Flows:** Inflows and outflows of cash from acquiring, producing, selling, and delivering goods for sale, as well as providing services. Reported under either *indirect* or *direct method.*
3. **Investing Cash Flows:** Inflows and outflows of cash from lending money and collecting on loans, and acquiring and selling investments and property, plant, and equipment.
4. **Financing Cash Flows:** Inflows and outflows of cash from obtaining resources from owners and creditors, and providing a return on (and of) their investment as well as repaying amounts borrowed.

D. **Supporting Statements, Schedules, and Notes:** Supplement the primary financial statements. May include: (1) statement of retained earnings, which primarily reconciles retained earnings for the net income and the dividends of the accounting period, (2) statement of changes in stockholders' equity, which primarily itemizes the changes in the various components due to investments by and distributions to stockholders, (3) schedule of investing and financing activities not affecting cash, which summarizes the results of non-cash investing and/or financing activities, and (4) notes describing a company's required disclosures.

E. **Elements:** Items comprising a financial statement.